D1003770

Parapsychology, New Age and the Occult

A Source Encyclopedia

Cheryl Klein Lacoff - Editor

Reference Press International   Greenwich, Connecticut

Dedication

With heartfelt gratitude and love we dedicate this reference book to Bernard Klein, our mentor. Without his creativity, knowledge, generosity and love this book could not have been published. We want to thank him for putting aside his personal oath of E.M.F.H. and unselfishly offering his wisdom and experience so that this project could come to being. For this we thank him 300 times.

Parapsychology, New Age and the Occult - A Source Encyclopedia

Cheryl Klein Lacoff - Editor

Copyright © 1993 by Reference Press International. All rights reserved. Printed in the United States of America. Except as permitted under the United States Copyright Act of 1976, no part of this publication may be reproduced or distributed in any form or by any means, or stored in a data base or retrieval system, without the prior written permission of the publisher.

ISBN   1-879583-00-3 Trade Publication
ISBN   1-879583-01-1 Library Edition
ISSN   1065-3031

Reference Press International PO Box 4126, Greenwich, CT, 06830 USA 203-629-4900

Contents

Preface

There is an ever increasing amount of interest in the esoteric sciences known as Parapsychology, Metaphysics, New Age, the Occult and their many related fields. More and more individuals, once skeptical of these elusive subjects, are joining the ranks of the believers and devotees and are finding enlightenment and answers to often unanswerable questions. Through the study and pursuit of many of these topics such as holistic health, metaphysics and spirituality, people are finding self-help, peace and wellness of body, mind and spirit.

New Age, Metaphysics and their multitude of related fields encompass a vast amount of source material, much of which we have attempted to compile in this directory. We have gone to great lengths to bring you, the reader, thousands of current listings of major prominent sources as well as lesser known sources often impossible to find. Many of these listings are enhanced with annotations when provided by the listee through a questionnaire, however, if additional information is desired, the reader should contact the source directly using the address and phone number shown in the listing. We have also been able to assemble numerous mailing lists associated with these fields that are now available to the public.

This Source Encyclopedia is divided into 17 chapters each arranged alphabetically. A Topic Index comprised of 62 topics is also provided so that the reader may quickly look up information based on a particular subject and category. This Index is organized first by alphabetically arranged topics, then by chapter headings which are presented in the same order as they appear in the main section of the directory.

Topics are shown in each listing as they were provided to us by the source. Many are presented using broad terminology such as the topic Holistic Health. More specific terms such as Massage or Acupuncture are used whenever available. Some topics are not categorized by name at all, however, information and sources are available within other topics such as in the case of Theosophy where information can be found under Spirituality, Occult, Channeling, etc. Therefore it is recommended that all related topics be checked for additional sources of information.

Not all applicable topics could be shown in each listing, therefore, one topic is used to represent many other related topics. The following list shows some of those main topics and only a few of their related topics.

Acupuncture - Acupressure
Color Therapy - Color, Color Healing, Chromotherapy
Crystals - Crystal Therapy, Gemstones
Ghosts - Aberitions, Poltergeists
Health Food - Macrobiotics
Holistic Healing - Holistic Health
Holistic Health - Holistic Healing
Homeopathy - Flower Remedies, Essences, Oils, Aromatherapy
Meditation - Visualization, Affirmation
Paganism - Neo-Paganism

Past Life Regression - Past Life Therapy, Past Lives

Psychic Healing - Radionics

Psychology - Jungian, Gestalt, Transpersonal Transformational, Einsteinian, Psychosynthesis, Psychological Therapies

Spirituality - Zen, Buddhism, Eastern Philosophy, Western Philosophy, Religions, Goddesses, Anthroposophy, Theosophy

Tea Leaves - Tasseography

Vegetarianism - Fruitarianism, Veganism

Witchcraft - Witches, Wicca

Yoga - Kriya, Tantra, Acu-Yoga, Hatha, Integral, Raja, Kundalini, Japa, Jnana, Karma, Bhakti, Prana

Again we suggest that all related topics be checked for additional sources of information.

We would like to add three additional notes to ensure proper use of this reference sourcebook. In many cases throughout the book listings are repeated with different addresses and phone numbers which often represent branches of the same organization such as 3HO Foundation, School Of Metaphysics, etc. These listings may also appear multiple times in the Topic Index, however, they are not duplicate listings. In addition, there are also many sources of publications such as books, magazines, journals, etc. listed throughout the directory. Within these sources we use the term Editor interchangeably with the term Author. Finally, we recommend that the reader check other chapters for additional sources since many of the listings perform multiple functions such as Associations that are also Schools and Centers that are also Publishers.

Reference Press International does not endorse any information provided in this directory. Our information is current and has been thoroughly researched and compiled through questionnaires, however, because of our fast-paced world individuals as well as organizations, stores, publications, etc. do tend to relocate or terminate sometimes rather quickly. Even though information was verified just prior to printing, it is to be expected that data changes were taking place even while the book was on the press. If you would like to correct or add information to a current listing or to add a new listing to the next edition of Parapsychology, New Age and the Occult - A Source Encyclopedia, please contact us. With your help we will be able to continue to provide you with the most current and comprehensive up-to-date reference book in the field.

Throughout the centuries man has been searching for answers to the dark secrets of the Universe. New Age, Metaphysics and all their accompanying fields may hold the answers to some of those questions. We do know that although most of life's most perplexing questions will go unanswered for now, the New Age Movement, Parapsychology and Metaphysics are helping many people to look within themselves to find the answers. These cutting-edge sciences help people put their lives into perspective while bringing them comfort, spirituality, peace, balance and wellness. We hope that this reference sourcebook helps to guide them on their Journey to Enlightenment.

Cheryl Klein Lacoff
Editor

Introduction

Those who would control others depend upon apathy, ignorance and fear as agents of their domination. The obvious path to regaining and maintaining control of self is to take responsibility for being critically and broadly informed about what works not only for ourselves but for our living earth which is dependent upon our thoughtful decisions.

Parapsychology, New Age and the Occult - A Source Encyclopedia will help us acquire the knowledge necessary for enlightenment. It is a directory that is more than just informative and wide-ranging in subject-matter, it is an extraordinary view of our interests, concerns, fears and hopes. It is filled with abundant identified sources that are gateways to knowledge and action and it provides a basic map of where to start in helping us make those decisions that will improve our lives and our planet earth.

There are occurrences within the universe that can not be explained by conventional scientific methods and are often better addressed by subjects at the fringe or beyond the current boundaries of science. Clearly the box of science is too small, science as a process lacks adequate tools to gain entree into many ancient mysteries and most importantly the metaphysics of science is stunted and inadequate.

The field of UFO's can be used to illustrate this point. This is a complex situation and to discuss the science involved we must first identify and dispose of the roll that the U.S. government has been playing. The majority, if not consensus position of the best private researchers in the field, is that the government's policy is to cover up its knowledge about the existence of UFO's and extraterrestrial intelligence and to confuse and discredit researchers outside of government. Some day this policy will change and government will have the responsibility to explain it. When it does, it most certainly will involve a component currently excluded from the current scientific paradigm - dimensions beyond the current senses. Two hypotheses of the origin of UFO's are that they come from some part of the visible universe and/or that they are inter-dimensional. The hypotheses are not mutually exclusive. In fact, if some of them are from the visible universe, their physics (our future expanded science) undoubtedly allows travel at what we currently would call beyond the speed of light. While that may be upsetting to some physicists, it is not to all of them. In the later category are scientists who not only study quantum physics, but also have begun to integrate its reality and implications into their personal philosophy and lives.

A second example of the pall cast by the current scientific paradigm involves research into parapsychology. Discovery appears to be hung on the horns of our continued inability directly to measure phenomena, subtle and robust, when it happens. Thus the mechanisms remain unidentified even though attempts to apply the phenomena in practical situations are increasing in business and other sectors. Again it appears that too many of the field's researchers are unable to come to grips with a spiritual dimension that both coexists with and lies beyond the five senses of physical reality. The unseen universe certainly is larger and more comprehensive than the three dimensional one we worship. A fundamental characteristic of nonphysical reality must be its timelessness. Thus parapsychological issues of past, present and future that appear so novel and to some so threatening, are in

fact quite normal. We will get this knowledge and probably much more rapidly than most researchers anticipate. A few of those truly awake see a fundamental relationship between extraterrestrial intelligence and psychic phenomena. Perhaps the mysteries will be solved together.

The picture is not as discouraging as the above may suggest. Good work in science is being done. The best of it by men and women who personally are open to a multi-dimensional universe and eager to work with the element of spirituality that up to this point has been considered taboo. This is not a small issue and predictably there will be years of resistance ahead, but there are potentially earth ending pressures that demand a broader vision than that of current mainline science.

What are you to do in this scenario? What do you want to do? If you are a victim and slave to the old paradigm, grit your teeth and dig in your heels, but stand by for dramatic changes and soon. If you want to be involved, turn the page and start reading.

C.B. Scott Jones, Ph. D.
President, Human Potential Foundation
Past President, American Society For Psychical Research

Parapsychology, New Age and the Occult

A Source Encyclopedia

Associations & Organizations

Included in this chapter are alphabetical lists of associations and organizations involved in the New Age, Metaphysics and related subjects. These organizations offer a wealth of information in their specialized fields. Many conduct workshops and research, provide lectures and educational classes and publish books, newsletters, magazines, etc. Contact them for additional sources of information.

A Course In Miracles
50 Gungy Road
Lyme, CT 06731
TOPICS: Channeling

A Way Of Life
P.O. Box 1254
Studio City, CA 91604
TOPICS: Metaphysics

AA Thelemic Order Silver Star
P.O. Box 6411
Nashville, TN 37206
TOPICS: Witchcraft

Above The Clouds Trekking
Box 398
Worcester, MA 01602
(508)-799-4499 (800)-233-4499
TOPICS: New Age

Academy Of Religion And Psychical Research (ARPR)
P.O. Box 614
Bloomfield, CT 06002
(203)-242-4593
CONTACT: Boyce Batey, Exec. Sec. **TOPICS:** Parapsychology, Spirituality, PSI, ESP, Reincarnation, Meditation, Psychic Phenomena **FOUNDED:** 1972 **CONVENTIONS:** Annual Conferences **DESCRIPTION:** An affiliate of Spiritual Frontiers Fellowship. Formed to pursue dialogue & study the interrelationship between religion and psychical research. Offers a $250 award for the best paper on an announced related subject in their annual Robert H. Ashby Memorial Award Competition. **PUBLICATIONS:** *Journal Of Religion And Psychical Research* **EDITOR:** Mary Carmen Rose **TOPICS:** Parapsychology, Occult, Psychic Phenomena **TYPE:** Journal **DATE:** 1981 **FREQ:** quarterly **CIRC:** 301 **PRICE:** $8.00 **DESCRIPTION:** A scholarly approach to the interaction of religion & psychical research. **PUBLICATIONS:** *Proceedings* **TYPE:** Bulletin **FREQ:** annually **DESCRIPTION:** Annual publication reporting on the Academy's Annual Conference.

Acts 1:8 Outreach
P.O. Box 1300
Port Ewen, NY 12466
TOPICS: Skepticism, Counter-Cult **DESCRIPTION:** Cults, Satanism, Etc.

Acupuncture International Association (AIA)
2330 S. Brentwood Boulevard
St. Louis, MO 63144

(314)-961-2300
CONTACT: Dr. William F. White, V. Pres. **TOPICS:** New Age

Acupuncture Research Institute
313 West Andrix Street
Monterey Park, CA 91754
(213)-722-7353
TOPICS: Acupuncture **PUBLICATIONS:** *The Meridian* **EDITOR:** Louis Gasper, Ph.D. **TOPICS:** Acupuncture **TYPE:** Magazine

Addiction Research Foundation
33 Russell Street
Toronto, Ontario M5S 2S1
Canada
(416)-595-6059
TOPICS: Holistic Healing **PUBLICATIONS:** *Projection* **EDITOR:** R.J. Hall **TOPICS:** Holistic Healing **TYPE:** Newsletter

Advance Spiritual Church
4446 Ledge Avenue
North Hollywood, CA 91602
TOPICS: Metaphysics

Advances Awareness Research Organization
1111 West El Camino Real
Sunnyvale, CA 94087
TOPICS: Metaphysics

Adventures In Enlightenment, A Foundation
P.O. Box 528
Rochester, WA 98579
CONTACT: Terry Cole-Whittaker, Pres. **TOPICS:** Metaphysics, New Age **DESCRIPTION:** Promotes the teachings of Terry Cole-Whittaker through lectures & tapes. Offers techniques for people to live in harmony, respect, freedom & creativity. **PUBLICATIONS:** *How To Have More In A Have-Not World* **EDITOR:** Terry Cole-Whittaker **TOPICS:** New Age **TYPE:** Book **DATE:** 1983 **PUBLICATIONS:** *The Inner Path From Where You Are To Where You Want To Be* **EDITOR:** Terry Cole-Whittaker **TOPICS:** New Age, Metaphysics **TYPE:** Book **DATE:** 1986 **PUBLICATIONS:** *What You Think Of Me Is None Of My Business* **EDITOR:** Terry Cole-Whittaker **TOPICS:** New Age, Metaphysics **TYPE:** Book **DATE:** 1983

Adventures Into Time
P.O. Box 88
Independence, VA 24348
TOPICS: Metaphysics

Aerial Phenomenon Research

5108 South Findlay Street
Seattle, WA 98110
TOPICS: UFO's

Aesklepoen Of Light
5028 South 179th Place
Seattle, WA 98188
TOPICS: Metaphysics

Aetherius Society (AS)
6202 Afton Place
Los Angeles, CA 90028-8298
(213)-465-9652 (213)-467-4325
CONTACT: Archbishop Metropolitan, Pres. **TOPICS:** Psychic Phenomena, Parapsychology **PUBLICATIONS:** *Aetherius Society Books & Cassettes Catalogue* **TOPICS:** Parapsychology **TYPE:** Catalog **DATE:** 1980; 36 pgs. **PUBLICATIONS:** *Cosmic Voice* **TOPICS:** Psychic Phenomena **TYPE:** Newsletter **PUBLICATIONS:** *Spiritual Healing Bulletin* **EDITOR:** Dr. George King **TOPICS:** Psychic Phenomena **TYPE:** Bulletin

Ageless Expressions
P.O. Box 100
Troutdale, VA 24378
TOPICS: Metaphysics

Agency For Paranormal Tale
771 East 8 Mile Road, 125
Ferndale, MI 48220
TOPICS: Metaphysics

Aglaian Triad Of Wicca
P.O. Box 427
Midlothian, IL 60445
TOPICS: Witchcraft

Agni Yoga Society (AYS)
319 W. 107th Street
New York, NY 10025
(212)-864-7752
CONTACT: Edgar Lansbury, Pres. **TOPICS:** New Age

Airies Two LMI Church
P.O. Box 67
Bloomington, NJ 07403
TOPICS: Metaphysics

Akashic Organization
20110 Needles St.
Chatsworth, CA 91311
TOPICS: Metaphysics

Alchemical Medicine Research And Teaching Association (AMR'TA)
P.O. Box 14641

Portland, OR 97214
(503)-256-4530
TOPICS: Holistic Healing, Homeopathy, Astrology, Crystals, Color Therapy, Alchemy DESCRIPTION: A non-profit research & teaching membership association of individuals practicing the art of healing and the science of medicine. Offers education & research relating to the investigation, application & propagation of spiritual, metaphysical, magickal, esoteric, intuitional and energetic approaches to health & medicine. Involves the studies of natural medicine, astrology, homeopathy, crystal therapy, color therapy & alchemy. Offers IBIS, a computerized medical service.

Alert Ministry
P.O. Box 3406
San Luis Obispo, CA 93403
TOPICS: Skepticism, Counter-Cult DESCRIPTION: Mormonism, Cults, New Age, Satanism, Etc.

Alexandrian Temple Of Light And Institute
235 Berwick Drive
Atlanta, GA 30328
TOPICS: Channeling, Metaphysics

All In One Coven
P.O. Box 8170
Salem, MA 01971
TOPICS: Witchcraft

Alliance For Alternatives In Healthcare
P.O. Box 9178
Calabasas, CA 91372
(818)-509-5742 (800)-331-2713 FAX (818)-509-5743
TOPICS: Holistic Health, Body-Mind Connection, Herbalogy, Massage, Homeopathy, Vegetarianism, Acupuncture FOUNDED: 1983 MEM: 1,000 STAFF: 3 DESCRIPTION: Promotes greater credibility for alternative healthcare. Offers group insurance plans to members.

Aloha International
P.O. Box 665
Kiluea, HI 96754
TOPICS: Metaphysics

Alphan Society
11831 Ayres Avenue
Los Angeles, CA 90064
TOPICS: Metaphysics

Alternate Shadows
P.O. Box 507
Ithaca, NY 14851
TOPICS: Metaphysics

Alternative Communities Movement
18 Garth Road
Bangor,
North Wales
TOPICS: New Age

Alternative Medical Association (AMA)
7909 S.E. Stark Street
Portland, OR 97215
(503)-254-7555

CONTACT: F. Joseph Montagna, Exec. Dir.
TOPICS: New Age, Holistic Health

Amalgamated Flying Saucer Clubs Of America (AFSCA)
P.O. Box 39
Yucca Valley, CA 92286
(619)-365-1141
TOPICS: UFO's, New Age, Past Life Regression, Spirituality, Psychic Phenomena, Channeling FOUNDED: 1959 MEM: 5,600 GROUPS: U.S. and 23 countries DESCRIPTION: A non-profit organization founded by Gabriel Green in 1959. Dedicated to the physical, spiritual & economic emancipation of man. Studies UFO's, extraterrestrials, New Age economics & politics. PUBLICATIONS: AFSCA Information Sheets EDITOR: Gabriel Green TOPICS: UFO's TYPE: Newsletter; 10 pgs. FREQ: Irregular PUBLICATIONS: Flying Saucers International EDITOR: Gabriel Green TOPICS: UFO's TYPE: Journal DESCRIPTION: Reports on UFO's, alien encounters & the study of other planets & the universe.

American Acupuncture Association (AAA)
42-62 Kissena Boulevard
Flushing, NY 11355
(718)-886-4431
CONTACT: Dr. David P.J. Hung, Pres. TOPICS: New Age, Acupuncture, Holistic Health FOUNDED: 1972 MEM: 314 CONVENTIONS: Yearly meeting each December in New York City DESCRIPTION: Dedicated to promoting information & knowledge of Acupuncture & to work for legislation to keep the profession viable. Members are licensed acupuncturists, medical doctors, nurses, lay persons, dentists & herbalists. Last journal published in 1989.

American Apiotherapy Society (AAS)
252 Broad Street
Red Bank, NJ 07701-2012
(201)-842-5700
CONTACT: Dr. Christopher Kim, Pres. TOPICS: New Age

American Art Therapy Association
1202 Allanson Road
Mundelein, IL 60060
(312)-949-6064
TOPICS: New Age

American Association For Acupuncture And Oriental Medicine (AAAOM)
919 San Ramon Valley Boulevard, #155
Danville, CA 94526
(415)-449-4327
CONTACT: Dr. Mason Shen, Pres. TOPICS: New Age

American Association For Parapsychology (AAP)
23101 Sherman Place
Box 225
Canoga Park, CA 91305
(818)-883-0840
CONTACT: Ralph Merritt, Ph.D., Exec. Officer TOPICS: Parapsychology DESCRIPTION: Dedicated to the study of parapsychology, the spiritual aspect of man & the advancement of human understanding.

Membership includes the book A Complete Course In Parapsychology covering topics such as telepathy, clairvouyance, hypnosis, psychometry, auras , spiritual healing, the medium, psychokinesis, etc. Also the AAP Study Outline & Research Guide, consultation & advisory service, diploma & certificate of membership.

American Association Of Meta-Science (AAMS)
P.O. Box 1182
Huntsville, AL 35807
(205)-881-7165 (205)-922-7223
CONTACT: William F. Sowder, Pres. TOPICS: Psychic Phenomena, Metaphysics FOUNDED: 1977 MEM: 500 STAFF: 3 DESCRIPTION: Temporarily inactive. PUBLICATIONS: Specular Journal - inactive TOPICS: Psychic Phenomena TYPE: Journal

American Association Of Naturopathic Physicians (AANP)
P.O. Box 20386
Seattle, WA 98102
(206)-323-7610
TOPICS: Holistic Healing, Homeopathy, Nutrition, Health Food FOUNDED: 1985 DESCRIPTION: Promotes all aspects of naturopathy & the naturopathic medical profession. Supports the Council on Naturopathic Medical Education & the Naturopathic Physicians Licensing Examination. PUBLICATIONS: Journal Of Naturopathic Medicine TOPICS: Holistic Health, Homeopathy, Health Food, Nutrition TYPE: Journal FREQ: quarterly

American Association Of Professional Hypnotherapists
Box 731
McLean, VA 22101
(703)-448-9623
TOPICS: Hypnotism PUBLICATIONS: Hypnotherapy Today EDITOR: William Brink TOPICS: Hypnotism TYPE: Magazine

American Association-Electronic Voice Phenomena (AA-EVP)
726 Dill Road
Severna Park, MD 21146
(301)-647-8742
CONTACT: Sarah Estep, Pres. TOPICS: Metaphysics, Death, Parapsychology FOUNDED: 1982 MEM: 200 GROUPS: 34 states, 11 countries CONVENTIONS: 3 national conferences held in Baltimore area. DESCRIPTION: Established to provide objective evidence through electronic instruments, tape recorders, T.V, computers, that we survive death in an individual conscious state. Provides newsletter,research, tapes, counseling, referrals and cross-country list of members. Membership, open to all, is $20 per year. PUBLICATIONS: American Association-Electronic Voice Phenomena-Quarterly Newsletter EDITOR: Sarah Estep TOPICS: Metaphysics, Death, Parapsychology TYPE: Newsletter FREQ: quarterly CIRC: 230 DESCRIPTION: Newsletter included with membership. No advertising accepted.

American Bookdealers' Exchange
P.O. Box 606
Cottage Grove, OR 97424
(503)-942-7455

CONTACT: Al Galasso **TOPICS:** New Age, Metaphysics **FOUNDED:** 1980 **DESCRIPTION:** Marketing organization for publishers. Handles many New Age & Metaphysical publications. Offers exhibits, seminars, magazines & publications such as Publishers Review, Book Dealers World & National Press Release Bulletin.

American Botanical Council
P.O. Box 201660
Austin, TX 78720
(512)-331-8868 **FAX** (512)-331-1924
TOPICS: Herbalogy

American Celtic Order Of Wicca
P.O. Box 64383
St. Paul, MN 55164
TOPICS: Witchcraft

American Chiropractic Association
1701 Clarendon Boulevard
Arlington, VA 22209
(703)-276-8800
CONTACT: David Shingler, Director Of Communications **TOPICS:** Holistic Healing

American College Of Nurse-Midwives (ACNM)
1522 K Street, N.W., Ste. 1000
Washington, DC 20005
(202)-289-4379 (202)-289-0171 **FAX** (202)-289-4395
CONTACT: Sandra Hvidsten **TOPICS:** Birth

American College Of Orgonomy (ACO)
P.O. Box 490
Princeton, NJ 08542
(201)-821-1144
CONTACT: Linda Barrett, Exec. Dir. **TOPICS:** New Age

American Dental Institute
509 North Campbell, 9N
Tucson, AZ 85719
TOPICS: Holistic Health, New Age **DESCRIPTION:** A natural dental information center. Offers Dental Self Help: ($9.95 + .50 postage).

American Dietetic Association
216 West Jackson Boulevard
Suite 800
Chicago, IL 60606
(312)-899-0040
CONTACT: Jennifer Fairlamb **TOPICS:** Holistic Healing

American Family Foundation
P.O. Box 336
Weston, MA 02193
TOPICS: Skepticism, Counter-Cult **DESCRIPTION:** New Age, New & Unconventional Religions, Mysticism, Paganism

American Federation Of Astrologers
8306 Wilshire Boulevard, 537
Beverly Hills, CA 90211
TOPICS: Astrology

American Federation Of Astrologers, Inc. (AFA)
6535 S. Rural Road
P.O. Box 22040
Tempe, AZ 85285-2040
(602)-838-1751
CONTACT: Robert W. Cooper **TOPICS:** Astrology **FOUNDED:** 1938 **CONVENTIONS:** Biennial conventions **DESCRIPTION:** Purpose is to advance the cause of Astrological education & research. Membership open to everyone. **PUBLICATIONS:** *AFA Headquarters* **EDITOR:** Robert W. Cooper **TOPICS:** Astrology **TYPE:** Newsletter **PUBLICATIONS:** *American Federation Of Astrologers Bulletin* **EDITOR:** Robert W. Cooper **TOPICS:** Astrology **TYPE:** Bulletin **DATE:** 1938 **SIZE:** 6 x 9, 32 pgs. **FREQ:** Monthly **CIRC;** 5,000 **PRICE:** $20.00 **DESCRIPTION:** Purpose is to promote interest in the field of Astrology. Reports & conducts research, lecturing, teaching & practice on all aspects of the science. **PUBLICATIONS:** *Astro-Data II (formerly American Book Of Charts)* **EDITOR:** L. Rodden **TOPICS:** Astrology **TYPE:** Book **PRICE:** $27.95 **PUBLICATIONS:** *Essentials Of Medical Astrology* **EDITOR:** H. Darling **TOPICS:** Holistic Health, Astrology **TYPE:** Book **PRICE:** $14.00 **PUBLICATIONS:** *Health, Astrology And Spirituality* **EDITOR:** Miss Dee **TOPICS:** Holistic Health, Astrology **TYPE:** Book **PRICE:** $11.00 **PUBLICATIONS:** *How To Give An Astrological Health Reading* **EDITOR:** D. Cramer **TOPICS:** Holistic Health, Astrology **TYPE:** Book **PRICE:** $12.95 **PUBLICATIONS:** *Interpret Your Rays Through The Planets* **EDITOR:** M. Wilson-Ludlam **TOPICS:** Astrology **TYPE:** Book **PRICE:** $21.50 **PUBLICATIONS:** *Introduction To Holistic Medical Astrology* **EDITOR:** R. Jansky **TOPICS:** Holistic Health, Astrology **TYPE:** Book **PRICE:** $11.00 **PUBLICATIONS:** *Journal Of Research Of The American Federation of Astrologers* **EDITOR:** Richard Nolle **TOPICS:** Astrology **TYPE:** Journal

American Foundation For Alternative Healthcare Research And Development (AFAHCRD)
25 Landfield Avenue
Monticello, NY 12701
(914)-794-8181
CONTACT: Edwin M. Field, Exec. Dir. **TOPICS:** New Age

American Guild Of Hypnotherapists
7117 Fornam Street
Omaha, NE 68132
(402)-397-1500
TOPICS: Hypnotism **PUBLICATIONS:** *Journal Of Hypnotherapy* **EDITOR:** Reg Sheldrick **TOPICS:** Hypnotism **TYPE:** Journal

American Healing Association (AHA)
811 Ridge Drive
Glendale, CA 91206
CONTACT: Rev. Brian Zink, Exec. Officer **TOPICS:** New Age

American Herb Association
14648 Pear Tree Lane
Nevada City, CA 95959-2361
TOPICS: Holistic Healing

American Holistic Health Sciences Association
1766 Cumberland Green
Suite 208
St. Charles, IL 60174
(312)-377-1929
TOPICS: Holistic Healing **PUBLICATIONS:** *Herald Of Holistic Health* **EDITOR:** John M. Barry **TOPICS:** Holistic Healing **TYPE:** Magazine

American Holistic Medical Association (AHMA)
2727 Fairview Avenue, East
Seattle, WA 98102
(206)-322-6842
CONTACT: Marcia Meyer, Exec. Dir. **TOPICS:** Holistic Health **FOUNDED:** 1978 **CONVENTIONS:** Annual conference **DESCRIPTION:** Membership limited to holistic physicians & osteopaths. Created the American Holistic Medical Foundation. **PUBLICATIONS:** *American Holistic Medical Assocation-Directory Of Members* **EDITOR:** Tracey Weller **TOPICS:** Holistic Healing **TYPE:** Directory **PRICE:** $7.25 **PUBLICATIONS:** *Holistic Medicine* **EDITOR:** Marcia Meyer, Tracey Weller **TOPICS:** Holistic Healing **TYPE:** Newsletter **DATE:** 1980 **FREQ:** bi-monthly

American Holistic Medical Foundation (AHMA)
2727 Fairview Avenue, East
Seattle, WA 98102
(206)-322-6842
CONTACT: Marcia Meyer, Exec. Dir. **TOPICS:** Holistic Health **FOUNDED:** 1980 **CONVENTIONS:** Annual conference **DESCRIPTION:** Membership open to nonprofessionals interested in holistic health. Purpose is to promote education, research, growth & respect for the practice of holistic medicine.

American Holistic Veterinary Medical Assocation (AHVMA)
2214 Old Emmorton Road
Bel Air, MD 21014
(301)-838-7777
CONTACT: Dr. Carvel G. Tiekert, Pres. **TOPICS:** Holistic Healing

American Humanist Association
7 Harwood Drive
Box 146
Amherst, NY 14226
(716)-839-5080
TOPICS: New Age **PUBLICATIONS:** *Free Mind* **EDITOR:** Bette Chambers **TOPICS:** New Age **TYPE:** Magazine

American Institute For Preventive Medicine
24450 Evergreen Road
Southfield, MI 48075
(313)-352-7666 **TELEX** (313)-352-4005
CONTACT: Susan Jackson **TOPICS:** Holistic Healing

American Institute Of Homeopathy
1500 Massachusetts Avenue, NW
Washington, DC 20005
(800)-848-5477
TOPICS: Homeopathy **PUBLICATIONS:** *Journal Of The American Institute Of Homeopathy* **EDITOR:** Karl Robinson **TOPICS:** Homeopathy **TYPE:** Journal

American Kinesiotherapy Association (AKA)
259-08, 148 Road
Rosedale, NY 11422
(718)-276-0721

CONTACT: David Ser, Exec. Dir. TOPICS: New Age

American Massage Therapy Association
1130 West North Shore Avenue
Chicago, IL 60626
(312)-761-2682 FAX (815)-965-2329
TOPICS: Massage PUBLICATIONS: *Massage Therapy Journal* EDITOR: Rafael Tuburan
TOPICS: Massage TYPE: Journal

American Metaphysical Association
10502 Telephone Road, #332
Houston, TX 77075
(713)-649-7340
TOPICS: New Age, Metaphysics

American Naprapathic Association (ANA)
5913 W. Montrose Avenue
Chicago, IL 60634
(312)-685-6020
CONTACT: Roy P. Krueger, D.N., Corr. Sec.
TOPICS: New Age

American Natural Hygiene Society (ANHS)
11816 Race Track Road
P.O. Box 30630
Tampa, FL 33630
(813)-855-6607
CONTACT: James Michael Lennon, Exec. Dir.
TOPICS: Holistic Healing

American Oriental Bodywork Therapy Association (AOBTA)
50 Maple Place
Manhasset, NY 11030
(516)-365-5025
TOPICS: Holistic Healing

American Parapsychology Research Foundation
P.O. Box 225
Canoga Park, CA 91303
TOPICS: Metaphysics

American Parapsychology Research Foundaton
P.O. Box 8447
Calabasas, CA 91302
(818)-888-6570
TOPICS: Metaphysics, New Age, Channeling

American Poetry Association
3434 Janice Way
Palo Alto, CA 94303-4212
(408)-429-1122
CONTACT: Jennifer Manes TOPICS: New Age

American Rivers
801 Pennsylvania Avenue SE
Suite 303
Washington, DC 20003
(202)-547-6900
TOPICS: Holistic Healing

American Society For Psychical Research, Inc. (ASPR)
5 West 73rd Street
New York, NY 10023
(212)-799-5050
CONTACT: Donna L. McCormick, Dir. TOPICS: Parapsychology, Psychic Phenomena, ESP, Death, Dreams, Psychic Healing, Dowsing FOUNDED: 1885 DESCRIPTION: Seeks to promote & investigate all types of psychic phenomena. Provides programs in basic research, seminars, workshops & conferences. Some topics covered are ESP, Psychokinesis, Out-Of-Body & Near Death Experiences, Dreams, Apparitions, Psychic Healing, Dowsing, Poltergeists, Channelling & Reincarnation. Supports the efforts of laypersons & professionals to use the study of psychical research to expand & improve the full understanding of human nature & the broad scope of human abilities. See Schools. PUBLICATIONS: *Journal Of The American Society For Psychical Research* EDITOR: Rhea White TOPICS: Parapsychology TYPE: Journal DATE: 1885 SIZE: 6 x 9; 99 pgs. FREQ: Quarterly CIRC: 1,500 PRICE PER COPY: $6.25 DESCRIPTION: Scientific publication providing research reports, theoretical papers & book reviews. Available on film. PUBLICATIONS: *Newsletter Of The American Society For Psychical Research-ASPR Newsletter* EDITOR: Donna L. McCormick TOPICS: Parapsychology, Psychic Phenomena TYPE: Newsletter DATE: 1968 SIZE: 8 1/2 x 11, 10 pgs. FREQ: quarterly CIRC; 2,000 PRICE: $35.00 DESCRIPTION: Features articles & information about news, research & current developments in parapsychology. Discusses organizations, publications, educational opportunities and lectures about scientific parapsychology. PUBLICATIONS: *Proceedings Of The American Society For Psychical Research* EDITOR: Rhea White TOPICS: Parapsychology, Psychic Phenomena TYPE: Journal

American Society Of Clinical Hypnosis
2200 East Devon Avenue, #291
Des Plaines, IL 60018-4501
(404)-525-6158
TOPICS: Hypnotism PUBLICATIONS: *American Journal Of Clinical Hypnosis* EDITOR: Thurman Mott, Jr. TOPICS: Hypnotism TYPE: Journal PUBLICATIONS: *American Society Of Clinical Hypnosis Directory* EDITOR: William Hoffman TOPICS: Hypnotism TYPE: Directory

American Society Of Dowsers, Inc.
Brainerd Street
Box 24
Danville, VT 05828-0024
(802)-684-3417
CONTACT: Donna MacKay, Dir. TOPICS: Parapsychology, Dowsing PUBLICATIONS: *American Dowser* TOPICS: Parapsychology, Psychic Phenomena TYPE: Journal DATE: 1961 SIZE: 5.5 x 8.5; 56 pgs. FREQ: Quarterly CIRC: 3,500 PRICE: $20.00 PRICE PER COPY: $1.00 DESCRIPTION: Covers all aspects of dowsing. Presents information pertaining to study & evaluation such as theories, ideas, techniques & applications.

American Vegan Society
501 Old Harding Highway
Malaga, NJ 08328
(609)-694-2887
TOPICS: Health Food, Vegetarianism, Holistic Health FOUNDED: 1960 AFF ORG: North American Vegetarian Society, Vegetarian Union of North America CONVENTIONS: Annual educational convention DESCRIPTION: Advocates a diet & lifestyle excluding the use of animal products. Promotes vegetarianism for health. Offers cooking classes, lectures & discussions. Offers a mail-order book & literature service of books on veganism, vegetarianism, animal rights & health . PUBLICATIONS: *Ahimsa* TOPICS: Vegetarianism, Health Food, Holistic Health TYPE: Magazine FREQ: quarterly PRICE: $18.00 TERM: yearly DESCRIPTION: Teaches, encourages & supports people in the compassionate lifestyle free of the use of animal products. Features in depth articles on all aspects of veganism.

American Yoga Association (AYA)
3130 Mayfield Road, W-103
Cleveland Heights, OH 44118
(216)-371-0078
CONTACT: Catherine Ball TOPICS: New Age

American-International Reiki Association, Inc.
2210 Wilshire Boulevard, #831
Santa Monica, CA 90403
(214)-788-1821 (213)-394-6220
TOPICS: Holistic Healing, Reiki PUBLICATIONS: *Reiki Journal, The* TOPICS: Holistic Healing, Reiki TYPE: Journal

Americans For Safe Food/Center For Science In The Public Interest
1501 16th Street, N.W.
Washington, DC 20036
(202)-332-9110
TOPICS: Health Food PUBLICATIONS: *Organic Agriculture: What The States Are Doing* TOPICS: Health Food TYPE: Book

Americans For The Environment
1400 16th Street NW
Second Floor
Washington, DC 20036
(202)-797-6665
TOPICS: Holistic Healing

Ananda Marga (AM)
97-38 42nd Avenue, Suite 1F
Corona, NY 11368-2145
(718)-898-1603
CONTACT: James F. Kaeser, Pres. TOPICS: New Age

Ancient Astronaut Society (AAS)
1921 St. Johns Avenue
Highland Park, IL 60035
CONTACT: Gene M. Phillips TOPICS: UFO's

Ancient Hermitic Order Ascle
P.O. Box 95
Calumet City, IL 60409
TOPICS: Metaphysics

Ancient Mediterranean Research
1047 Gayley Avenue, 201
Los Angeles, CA 90024
TOPICS: UFO's

Ancient Spirits
P.O. Box 13072
Portland, OR 97213
TOPICS: Witchcraft

Ancient Wisdom Connection
P.O. Box 1204
North Myrtle Beach, SC 29598
TOPICS: Metaphysics

Angels Of Light
P.O. Box 629
New York, NY 10268
TOPICS: Metaphysics

Answer Books And Tapes
5166 Old Norcross Road
Norcross, GA 30071
TOPICS: Skepticism, Counter-Cult **DESCRIPTION:** Freemasonry, etc., Cults, Satanism.

Answers In Action
P.O. Box 2067
Costa Mesa, CA 92626
(714)-957-0249
CONTACT: Gretchen Passantino **TOPICS:** Skepticism, Counter-Cult **DESCRIPTION:** Religious organization discusses topics such as New Age, new and non-conforming religions, witchcraft, satan, the Occult, etc.

Antahkarana Circle, The
Star Route, Box 74
Oroville, WA 98844
TOPICS: Metaphysics

Anthroposophical Society In America
RD #1, Box 215
Ghent, NY 12075
(518)-672-4601
TOPICS: New Age, Spirituality

Anthroposophical Society In America
529 West Grant Place
Chicago, IL 60614
CONTACT: Clare Moore **TOPICS:** Metaphysics, Spirituality, New Age **DESCRIPTION:** Provides those interested in penetrating all aspects of human endeavor with the insights of spiritual science. Publishes the Journal For Anthroposophy which provides a window into the varied life of anthroposophy.

Apocalypse Society, The
P.O. Box 29
Jamaica, NY 11435
TOPICS: Metaphysics

Apologetic Research Coalition
P.O. Box 168
Trenton, MI 48183
TOPICS: Skepticism, Counter-Cult **DESCRIPTION:** New Age, New and Unconventional Religions, Cults, Satanism.

Apologetics Resource Center
9848 Business Park Drive
Sacramento, CA 95827
TOPICS: Skepticism, Counter-Cult **DESCRIPTION:** New Age, New and Unconventional Religions, etc.

Aquarian Age Network
3457 El Cajon Boulevard
San Diego, CA 92104
TOPICS: Metaphysics

Aquarian Church Universal
P.O. Box 1116

McMinnville, OR 97128
TOPICS: Metaphysics

Aquarian Crystal Connection
1497 Marine Drive, 300
W. Vancouver, BC, V7T1B8,
Canada
TOPICS: Metaphysics

Aquarian Education Foundation
30188 Mulholland Highway
Agoura, CA 91301
TOPICS: Metaphysics

Aquarian Education Group
P.O. Box 2264
Sedona, AZ 86336
TOPICS: Metaphysics

Aquarian Exchange
8101 Main Street
Ellicott City, MD 21043
TOPICS: Metaphysics

Aquarian Foundation
321 Northeast 20th Avenue
Portland, OR 97232
TOPICS: Metaphysics

Aquarian Foundation
315 15th Avenue
Seattle, WA 98112
TOPICS: Spirituality

Aquarian Minyan
P.O. Box 7224
Berkeley, CA 94707
TOPICS: Metaphysics

Aquarian Network
2685 West Broadway
Vancouver, BC, V6K2G2,
Canada
TOPICS: Metaphysics

Aquarian Research Foundation (A.R.F.)
5620 Morton Street
Philadelphia, PA 19144
(215)-849-3237
CONTACT: Art Rosenblum **TOPICS:** New Age **FOUNDED:** 1969 **DESCRIPTION:** Dedicated to research & social action to create world peace & harmony for the Age of Aquarius. **PUBLICATIONS:** *Aquarian Alternatives* **EDITOR:** Art Rosenblum **TOPICS:** New Age **TYPE:** Book

Aquarian Tabernacle Church
P.O. Box 85507
Seattle, WA 98145
(206)-793-1945
CONTACT: Rev. Peter Pathfinder **TOPICS:** Witchcraft, Occult, Paganism **FOUNDED:** 1979 **MEM:** 200 **DESCRIPTION:** A Wiccan Church which sponsors open public worship regularly & 2 annual festival gatherings, Spring Mysteries, over Easter weekend & Hecate's Sickle, in late Oct.

Aquarius Organization Of Astrologers
15 East 62nd Street
Kansas City, MO 64113

TOPICS: Astrology

Aquarius Ranch Communications
11020 Ventura Boulevard
Studio City, CA 91604
TOPICS: Channeling, Occult **PUBLICATIONS:** *Aquarius Ranch Communications* **TOPICS:** Channeling **TYPE:** Magazine

Aquarius Rising
775 River Road
Fair Haven, NJ 07704
(201)-842-3871
CONTACT: Flo Higgins **TOPICS:** Occult, Metaphysics

Arcana Workshops
P.O. Box 506
Manhattan Beach, CA 90266
(213)-379-9990 (213)-540-8689
TOPICS: Meditation, Metaphysics **PUBLICATIONS:** *Thoughtline* **EDITOR:** Marguerite Rompage **TOPICS:** Meditation **TYPE:** Book

Arcane Order (AO)
Studio of Contemplation
2904 Rosemary Lane
Falls Church, VA 22042
CONTACT: Leonard J. Mather, Ph.D. **TOPICS:** Psychic Phenomena

Archaeus Project (AP)
2402 University Avenue
St. Paul, MN 55114
(612)-641-0177 (612)-781-5012
CONTACT: Gail Duke, Managing Editor **TOPICS:** Parapsychology, New Age **PUBLICATIONS:** *Archaeus* **EDITOR:** Dennis Stillings, Gail Duke **TOPICS:** Parapsychology **TYPE:** Journal **DATE:** 1983; 200 pgs. **FREQ:** Annual **CIRC:** 500 **PRICE:** $20.00 **PRICE PER COPY:** $5.00 **DESCRIPTION:** Covers topics such as alternative medicine, body-mind connection, parapsychology & paranormal phenomena. **PUBLICATIONS:** *Artifex* **EDITOR:** Dennis Stillings, Gail Duke **TOPICS:** Parapsychology **TYPE:** Journal **DATE:** 1981 **SIZE:** 8.5 x 11, 26 pgs. **FREQ:** Bi-Monthly **CIRC;** 500 **PRICE:** $20.00 **DESCRIPTION:** Publishes papers on paranormal phenomena, the mind-body relationship & psi.

Archaeus Research Foundation, Inc.
P.O. Box 566
Valley Cottage, NY 10989
(914)-268-5144
TOPICS: Spirituality, New Age **DESCRIPTION:** Offers Life Energy Analysis, spiritual development, ethics, research & books.

Arcosanti Community
6433 Doubletree Road
Scottsdale, AZ 85253
TOPICS: Occult

Arian Enterprises
340 South Broadway, 203
Lexington, KY 40508
TOPICS: Metaphysics

Arizona Metaphysical Society
3639 East Clarendon Road
Phoenix, AZ 85018
(602)-956-1676

CONTACT: Frank Alper, Pres. TOPICS: Astrology, Channeling, Crystals, New Age, Metaphysics FOUNDED: 1974 DESCRIPTION: Dedicated to the study of Atlantis & crystals. Conducts channeling sessions with an entity from Atlantis. PUBLICATIONS: *Exploring Atlantis* EDITOR: Frank Alper TOPICS: Astrology, Metaphysics, Channeling, New Age, Crystals TYPE: Book; 82 pgs. PRICE: $9.95 DESCRIPTION: Three volume set.

Armageddon Time Base Ark
1500 North Texas
Weslco, TX 78596
TOPICS: UFO's

Asatru Free Assembly
P.O. Box 961
Payson, AZ 85547
TOPICS: Witchcraft

Assembly Of Light
P.O. Box 1470
Palm Springs, CA 92262
TOPICS: Metaphysics

Associa - Nanawasa
2509 North Campbell #355
Tucson, AZ 85719
TOPICS: New Age, Metaphysics

Associated Professional Massage Therapists
P.O. Box 1869
evergreen, CO 80439-1869
(303)-526-1740
TOPICS: Massage

Association For Consciousness Exploration
1643 Lee Road, #9G
Cleveland Heights, OH 44118
(216)-932-5421
CONTACT: Jeff Rosenbaum TOPICS: New Age, Metaphysics

Association For Cymmry Wicca
P.O. Box 49285
Atlanta, GA 30359
TOPICS: Witchcraft

Association For Holistic Health
Box 1122
Del Mar, CA 92014
(619)-275-2694
TOPICS: Holistic Healing PUBLICATIONS: *Holistic Health Focus* EDITOR: John Meyer TOPICS: Holistic Healing TYPE: Newsletter PUBLICATIONS: *National Directory Of Holistic Health Professionals* EDITOR: Margaret Marshik TOPICS: Holistic Healing TYPE: Directory

Association For Humanistic Education
P.O. Box 4054
University, WY 82071
TOPICS: New Age

Association For Humanistic Psychology (AHP)
1772 Vallejo Street, #3
San Francisco, CA 94123
(415)-346-7929

TOPICS: Holistic Health, Body-Mind Connection, New Age, Meditation FOUNDED: 1962 CONVENTIONS: Annual conference DESCRIPTION: Diverse group of therapists, teachers, consultants, body workers, healers, public servants, corporate managers, lawyers, social workers, activists, futurists and politicians dedicated to explore human potential and committed to global humanistic vision. PUBLICATIONS: *AHP Perspective* EDITOR: Deborah J. Breed, Edith Gladstone TOPICS: Holistic Health TYPE: Newsletter DATE: 1961 FREQ: monthly DESCRIPTION: Offers information & news about the Association For Humanistic Psychology such as meetings, conferences, board elections, members. Articles to explore and expand human potential and growth such as holistic health, psychotherapy, etc. Does book reviews. PUBLICATIONS: *Journal Of Humanistic Psychology* EDITOR: Thomas Greening, Ph. D. TOPICS: Holistic Health TYPE: Journal DATE: 1961 FREQ: quarterly PRICE: $34.00 TERM: yearly DESCRIPTION: Fosters a vision of human possibilites through articles on world peace, humanistic psychotherapy, holistic healing, personal growth and spiritual development which integrates theory, research and application.

Association For Love And Light
8585 Melrose Avenue
Los Angeles, CA 90069
TOPICS: Channeling

Association For Past-Life Research And Therapies, Inc. (A.P.R.T.)
P.O. Box 20151
Riverside, CA 92516-0151
(714)-784-1570
CONTACT: Chet B. Snow, Ph. D, Pres. TOPICS: Reincarnation, Past Life Regression, Hypnotism, Death, Parapsychology, Metaphysics, Meditation FOUNDED: 1980 MEM: 700 STAFF: 3 BUDGET: $100,00000 COMPUTER: yes CONVENTIONS: 2 conferences per year in Southern and Northern California; 2 training seminars per year in California; seminars held quarterly. DESCRIPTION: An internationally recognized non-profit organization which promotes the application of past-life therapy, research in the field, training of therapists and a network for the exchange of information and experience. Members travel to conferences, seminars and training workshops from all over the world. Offers referrals for Past Life Therapists, informative books, videos & cassette tapes. Founded by 7 therapists & practitioners of Past-Life work. PUBLICATIONS: *Association For Past-Life Research And Therapies Directory* TOPICS: Reincarnation, Past Life Regression, Hypnotism, Death, Parapsychology TYPE: Directory PRICE: $5.00 PUBLICATIONS: *Association For Past-Life Research And Therapies Journal* EDITOR: Russell Davis, Ph. D. TOPICS: Reincarnation, Past Life Regression, Hypnotism, Death, Parapsychology TYPE: Journal FREQ: bi-annually PRICE: $15.00 PUBLICATIONS: *Association For Past-Life Research And Therapy Newsletter* EDITOR: Terry Nash, M.A. TOPICS: Reincarnation, Past Life Regression, Hypnotism, Death, Parapsychology TYPE: Newsletter FREQ: quarterly PRICE: $10.00

Association For Research And Enlightenment, Inc. (A.R.E.)
215 67th Street & Atlantic Avenue

Box 595
Virginia Beach, VA 23451
(804)-428-3588 (800)-368-2727
CONTACT: Charles Thomas Cayce, Ph.D., Pres. TOPICS: Channeling, Holistic Health DESCRIPTION: Non-profit organization promotes holistic health through research & education. Based on the work of Edgar Cayce considered to be America's greatest mystic & psychic. PUBLICATIONS: *A.R.E. Meditation Course* EDITOR: Mark Thurston TOPICS: Meditation TYPE: Book PRICE: $39.95 PUBLICATIONS: *Creative Meditation: Inner Peace Is Practically Yours* EDITOR: Richard O. Peterson TOPICS: Channeling TYPE: Book PRICE: $9.95 PUBLICATIONS: *Edgar Cayce Handbook For Health Through Drugless Therapy* EDITOR: H. Reilly, R. Brod TOPICS: Channeling TYPE: Book PRICE: $12.95 PUBLICATIONS: *Edgar Cayce Predicts: Your Role In Creating A New Age* EDITOR: Mark Thurston TOPICS: New Age, Channeling TYPE: Book PRICE: $9.95 PUBLICATIONS: *Interpreting The Revelation With Edgar Cayce* EDITOR: J. Everett Irion TOPICS: Channeling, Metaphysics TYPE: Book PRICE: $19.95 PUBLICATIONS: *Lives Of The Master: The Rest Of The Jesus Story* EDITOR: G. Sanderfur TOPICS: Reincarnation TYPE: Book PRICE: $12.95 PUBLICATIONS: *Outer Limits Of Edgar Cayce's Power* EDITOR: Edgar Evans Cayce, Hugh Lynn Cayce TOPICS: Channeling TYPE: Book PRICE: $14.95 PUBLICATIONS: *Perspective On Consciousness & PSI Research* EDITOR: Scott Sparrow, Henry Reed TOPICS: Parapsychology TYPE: Newsletter DATE: 1979, 4 pgs. FREQ: Monthly CIRC; 70,000 PRICE: $10.00 PUBLICATIONS: *Revelation: A Commentary Based On The Study Of Twenty-Four Psychic Discourses By Edgar Cayce* EDITOR: Edgar Cayce TOPICS: Channeling TYPE: Book PRICE: $8.95 PUBLICATIONS: *Saving Your Skin* EDITOR: Eric Mein, M.D., Anne Hunt TOPICS: Homeopathy TYPE: Book, 64 pgs. PRICE: $4.95 PUBLICATIONS: *There Is A River: The Story Of Edgar Cayce* EDITOR: T. Sugrue TOPICS: Channeling TYPE: Book PRICE: $19.95 PUBLICATIONS: *Venture Inward* EDITOR: A. Robert Smith TOPICS: Holistic Health TYPE: Magazine DATE: 1984 FREQ: Bi-Monthly CIRC; 80,000 PUBLICATIONS: *Weight No More* EDITOR: Eric Mein, M.D., Anne Hunt TOPICS: Homeopathy TYPE: Book; 64 pgs. PRICE: $4.95 PUBLICATIONS: *Why Do We Dream?* EDITOR: J. Everett Irion TOPICS: Dreams, Channeling TYPE: Book PRICE: $15.95 PUBLICATIONS: *Winning The Cold War* EDITOR: Anne Hunt TOPICS: Homeopathy TYPE: Book, 64 pgs. PRICE: $4.95

Association For The Anthropological Study Of Consciousness
P.O. Box 4032
Irvine, CA 92716
(503)-257-0942
TOPICS: Metaphysics PUBLICATIONS: *AASC Newsletter* EDITOR: Jeffery MacDonald TOPICS: Metaphysics TYPE: Newsletter

Association For The Study Of Dreams
P.O. Box 1600
Vienna, VA 22183
CONTACT: Rita Dwyer, Pres.-Elect TOPICS: Dreams FOUNDED: 1983 MEM: 600

CONVENTIONS: Annual conference DESCRIPTION: Dedicated to the pure & applied investigation of dreams & dreaming. Purpose is to promote an awareness & appreciation of dreams in both professional & public arenas, to encourage research into the nature, function & significance of dreaming, to advance the application of the study of dreams & to provide a forum for the eclectic & interdisciplinary exchange of ideas & information. PUBLICATIONS: *ASD Journal Of Dreaming* TOPICS: Dreams TYPE: Journal FREQ: quarterly DESCRIPTION: New quarterly international journal of multidisciplinary scope. Features scholarly articles on every aspect of dreams & dreaming. PUBLICATIONS: *ASD Newsletter* TOPICS: Dreams TYPE: Newsletter FREQ: quarterly DESCRIPTION: Features articles, research reports, book reviews, interviews with noted dream authorities, letters to the editor, an open forum for discourse & dialogue on dreams & news of the association.

Association For The Study Of Karma (ASK)

23 South Knoxville Avenue
Tulsa, OK 74112-1116
(918)-835-5843

CONTACT: Ruth Davis, Pres. TOPICS: Psychic Phenomena, Metaphysics

Association For Theological Studies

P.O. Box 290168
Minneapolis, MN 55429

TOPICS: Skepticism, Counter-Cult DESCRIPTION: New Age, New and Unconventional Religions, etc.

Association For Transpersonal Anthropology

2906 Ocean Avenue
Venice, CA 90291

TOPICS: Ghosts

Association For Transpersonal Psychology

P.O. Box 3049
Stanford, CA 94305

TOPICS: Metaphysics

Association Of American Buddhists

301 West 45th Street
New York, NY 10036
(212)-489-1075

CONTACT: Dr. Kevin R. O'Neil TOPICS: Yoga, New Age, Spirituality, Metaphysics, Meditation PUBLICATIONS: *American Buddhist* EDITOR: Dr. Kevin O'Neil TOPICS: Yoga TYPE: Magazine

Association Of American Publishers

220 East 23th Street
New York, NY 10010-4686
(212)-689-8920

TOPICS: New Age

Association Of Crystal Healing Therapists

5, Sunnymeded Vale, Holcombe Brook
Bury, Lancashire BL0 9RR
England
020 488 3482

CONTACT: Gillian Collins TOPICS: Crystals DESCRIPTION: Promotes research & education & improves standards & acceptance of crystal therapy.

Association Of Cymmry Wicca

P.O. Box 674884
Marietta, GA 30067
(404)-423-9585

CONTACT: Rhuddlwm Gawr TOPICS: New Age, Occult, Witchcraft, Spirituality, Paganism FOUNDED: 1967 CONVENTIONS: 2 conventions yearly in Georgia DESCRIPTION: Welsh Witchcraft Association of Churches. Teaches witchcraft/wicca & ritual magick. Provides speakers nationwide. Offers courses. 1,623 member Churches nationwide. PUBLICATIONS: *Sword of Drynwyn* EDITOR: Vickie L. Wheeler TOPICS: New Age, Occult, Witchcraft, Spirituality, Metaphysics TYPE: Journal DATE: 1969; 30 pgs. FREQ: 8 x per year PRICE: $15.95 TERM: yearly DESCRIPTION: Journal of Welsh Witchcraft in America. Prints fiction, non-fiction, news, poetry, satire, reviews, and various forms of artwork.

Association Of New Age Societies Of Greece

4 Chiou
Psyhico
Athens, 152 31
Greece
67-25-485

CONTACT: Dr. Agis Sarakinos, Ph. D TOPICS: New Age, Vegetarianism DESCRIPTION: Offers free social meetings the first Wed. of each month.

Association Of Professional Massage Therapists

P.O. Box 1263
3575 South Fox
Englewood, CO 80150-1263
(303)-692-6571

TOPICS: Holistic Health, Massage DESCRIPTION: Membership open to bodyworkers. Offers liability insurance, product discounts & more.

Association Of Universal Understanding

P.O. Box 1745
Sun Valley, CA 91352

TOPICS: UFO's

Association Of Utah Christian Ministries

5680 South 1250 East
Salt Lake City, UT 84121

TOPICS: Skepticism, Counter-Cult DESCRIPTION: Mormonism and offshoots. Cults, New Age, Satanism, etc.

Association To Advance Ethical Hypnosis

4301 South Ocean Boulevard
Highland Beach, FL 33431
(305)-458-3039

TOPICS: Hypnotism

Astro-Psychology Institute (API)

2640 Greenwich, #403
San Francisco, CA 94123
(415)-921-1192

CONTACT: Milo Kovar, Dir. TOPICS: Astrology, Psychology FOUNDED: 1979 MEM: 400 STAFF: 2 AFF ORG: American Federation Of Astrologers; Foundation For Research Of Cycles CONVENTIONS: Every 2 years DESCRIPTION:

Organization dedicated to the pioneering work of researching the interconnection of astrology and psychology. Explains planetary cycles & its effects on mankind. PUBLICATIONS: *Astrology The Star Science From A To Z* TOPICS: Astrology TYPE: Book PUBLICATIONS: *Five Keys To Inner Wisdom* TOPICS: Astrology, Psychology TYPE: Book PUBLICATIONS: *New Age Astrology Annual Yearbook* TOPICS: Astrology TYPE: Yearbook FREQ: annually

Astrologers' Guild of America (AGA)

Rt. 116, R.R. 1
North Salem, NY 10560
(914)-279-4935

CONTACT: Joelle K.D. Mahoney, Pres. TOPICS: Astrology FOUNDED: 1924 MEM: 450 STAFF: 6 CONVENTIONS: Meetings quarterly. DESCRIPTION: Oldest professional organization for astrologers. International educational association dedicated to maintaining traditional & ethical standards in astrology. Teaches traditional & modern methods, does internal testing, & in-house certification. PUBLICATIONS: *Astrological Review* TOPICS: Astrology TYPE: Journal FREQ: quarterly CIRC: 450 PRICE: $35.00 TERM: year

Astrological Bureau

5 Old Quaker Hill Road
Monroe, NY 10950

TOPICS: Astrology

Astrological Methaphysical

784 Park Avenue
Cranston, RI 02801

TOPICS: Astrology

Astrological Society Of Connecticut

P.O. Box 9346
Wethersfield, CT 06109

TOPICS: Astrology

Astrology Guild For Educaton

448 Strawton Road
West Nyack, NY 10994

TOPICS: Astrology

Astrosophical Research

P.O. Box 6334
New York, NY 10150

TOPICS: Metaphysics

Astroview

P.O. Box 244
Wakefield, MA 01880

TOPICS: Astrology

Athanor Fellowship, The

P.O. Box 365
Medford, MA 02155

TOPICS: Witchcraft

AUM Temple Universal Truth

45837 Deva Lane
Newberry Springs, CA 92365

TOPICS: Metaphysics

Australian Institute Of Parapsychological Research

P.O. Box 445
Lane Cove, N.S.W. 2066
Australia
02-6607232

TOPICS: Paranormal Phenomena, Channeling, Ghosts, Psychic Phenomena, Dreams, Parapsychology, Spirituality **DESCRIPTION:** Non-profit scientific & community society that promotes research into psychic phenomena & related matters. Focuses on Australia & nearby countries. Advocates use of the scientific method. Scientific advisers support research. Members are both professionals & non-professionals. **PUBLICATIONS:** *A.I.P.R. News* **EDITOR:** Michael Hough **TOPICS:** Parapsychology, Occult **TYPE:** Newspaper **FREQ:** Bi-Monthly **CIRC:** 140 **DESCRIPTION:** Covers news & various aspects of parapsychology in Australia.

Australian Psychic's Association
P.O. Box C603
Clarence Street
Sydney, New South Wales 2001
Australia
00116123609424

CONTACT: Simon Turnbull, Pres. **TOPICS:** Psychic, Paranormal Phenomena **FOUNDED:** 1978 **MEM:** 2,800 **STAFF:** 3 **DESCRIPTION:** Purpose is to arrange lectures, classes, groups & other related activities including public & private functions in order to promote opportunities for individual investigation of psychic, paranormal & allied fields. Offers weekly Sat. psychic fairs, annual ESP fairs, referral services for professional psychics, evening lectures Mon. to Fri. & a bi-monthly newsletter.

Australian Society For Clinical & Experimental Hypnosis
P.O. Box 594
Chatswood, New South Wales 2067
Australia
(002)-419-2737

TOPICS: Hypnotism **PUBLICATIONS:** *Australian Journal Of Clinical And Experimental Hypnosis* **EDITOR:** Wendy-Louise Walker **TOPICS:** Hypnotism **TYPE:** Journal

Aware Parenting Institute/Shining Star Press
P.O. Box 206
Goleta, CA 93116
(805)-968-1868

CONTACT: Aletha Solter, Ph. D. **TOPICS:** New Age **FOUNDED:** 1983 **DESCRIPTION:** Purpose to disseminate information to parents about gentle & effective parenting skills, that use neither punishments nor rewards. Offers classes, workshops & consultations. **PUBLICATIONS:** *Helping Young Children Flourish* **EDITOR:** Aletha Solter, Ph. D. **TOPICS:** New Age **TYPE:** Book **PUBLICATIONS:** *The Aware Baby: A New Approach To Parenting* **EDITOR:** Aletha Solter, Ph. D. **TOPICS:** New Age **TYPE:** Book

Awareness Research Foundation (ARF)
DeSoto Square
35 Ritter Road, #29
Hayesville, NC 28904
(704)-389-8672

CONTACT: Helen I. Hoag, Exec. Dir. **TOPICS:** Astrology, Parapsychology, Channeling **PUBLICATIONS:** *Meet The Lords* **EDITOR:** Helen Hoag **TOPICS:** Astrology **TYPE:** Newsletter; 4 pgs. **FREQ:** Monthly **PRICE:** $15.00

Awareness Research Foundation
1518 Lee Street

Polk Street Station
Hollywood, FL 33020
(305)-920-3848
TOPICS: Channeling, Metaphysics

Aztec-Mayan Astrology
P.O. Box 39315
Fort Lauderdale, FL 33339
TOPICS: Astrology

Babst Magikal Supplies
2814 West El Caminito Drive
Phoenix, AZ 85051-4066
TOPICS: Occult

Baltimore Network Of Light
26 West Susquehanna Avenue
Towson, MD 21204
TOPICS: Metaphysics

Baltimore Vegetarians
P.O. Box 1463
Baltimore, MD 21203
(301)-752-8648

TOPICS: Health Food **PUBLICATIONS:** *Baltimore Vegetarians-Newsletter* **TOPICS:** Health Food **TYPE:** Newsletter **PUBLICATIONS:** *Vegetarianism For The Working Person* **EDITOR:** Charles Stahler, Debra Wassserman **TOPICS:** Health Food **TYPE:** Newsletter

Baras Foundation
P.O. Box 3189
San Diego, CA 92103
(619)-291-5252
TOPICS: Hypnotism, Metaphysics

Bawa Muhaiyaddeen Fellowship
5820 Overbrook Avenue
Philadelphia, PA 19131
(215)-879-6300

CONTACT: June Ridgeway **TOPICS:** New Age, Meditation, Spirituality, Metaphysics **FOUNDED:** 1971 **DESCRIPTION:** Purpose is to share the legacy & teachings of contemporary Sufi Bawa Muhaiyaddeen. Headquarters. Holds regular prayers daily & public meetings every evening. Operates Fellowship Press.

Bay Area Naturally
P.O. Box 27
Palo Alto, CA 94302
TOPICS: Occult

Bay Area Video Coalition
1111 17th Street
San Francisco, CA 94107
(415)-861-3280
TOPICS: New Age

Believers Guide
Rural Route 10, 8437 Bear Mountain Boulevard
Bakersfield, CA 93313
TOPICS: Metaphysics

Bell, Book and Candle
P.O. Box 5886
Rocky Point, NY 11778
TOPICS: Metaphysics

Belltree Grove
P.O. Box 335
Boston, MA 02215

TOPICS: Witchcraft

Berean Christian Ministries
14 Chiswick Drive
Churchville, NY 14428

TOPICS: Skepticism, Counter-Cult **DESCRIPTION:** Mormonism, Jehovah's Witnesses, Cults, Satanism, etc.

Berlin And Associates, Inc.
3333 Cavendish Boulevard, 425
Montreal, QU, H4B2M5,
Canada
TOPICS: Occult

Bethel Ministries
P.O. Box 3818
Manhattan Beach, CA 90266

TOPICS: Skepticism, Counter-Cult **DESCRIPTION:** Jehovah's Witnesses. Cults, New Age, Satanism, etc.

Beyond Belief Publishing Company
P.O. Box 1651
Kailua, HI 63734

TOPICS: Skepticism, Counter-Cult **DESCRIPTION:** Jehovah's Witnesses. Cults, New Age, Satanism, etc.

Biblical Evangelism
P.O. Box 940
Ingleside, TX 78362

TOPICS: Skepticism, Counter-Cult **DESCRIPTION:** Mormonism, New Age, New and Unconventional Religions, etc.

Biblical News Service
P.O. Box 10428
Costa Mesa, CA 92627

TOPICS: Skepticism, Counter-Cult **DESCRIPTION:** Miscellaneous New Age, Occult, Pagan, New Religions, etc.

Bio-Integral Resource Center (BIRC)
P.O. Box 7414
Berkeley, CA 94707
(415)-524-2567

TOPICS: Health Food **PUBLICATIONS:** *Common Sense Pest Control Quarterly* **TOPICS:** Health Food **TYPE:** Magazine

Blackwater Grove
P.O. Box 52062
Jacksonville, FL 32201
TOPICS: Witchcraft

Bloodroot Coven
P.O. Box 02031
Columbus, OH 43202
TOPICS: Witchcraft

Blue Light Astro Numerology
2847 Shattuck Avenue, D
Berkeley, CA 94705
TOPICS: Metaphysics

Blue Star Healing
P.O. Box 800
El Prado, NM 87529
TOPICS: Holistic Health

BMI
320 West 57th Street
New York, NY 10019
(212)-586-2000

TOPICS: New Age FOUNDED: 1940

Bob Larson Ministries
P.O. Box 36480
Denver, CO 80236
TOPICS: Skepticism, Counter-Cult DESCRIPTION:
New Age, Paganism, New and Unconventional
Religions, etc.

Body Balance Systems
1342 Lakeshore Avenue, #2
Oakland, CA 94606
(415)-763-8312
TOPICS: Acupuncture, Massage, Herbalogy,
Holistic Health DESCRIPTION: Offers holistic
therapy treatment using acupuncture, herbalogy &
massage.

Body-Mind-Spirit Metaphysics
7210 Vassar Avenue
Canoga Park, CA 91303
TOPICS: Metaphysics

Bones Of Our Ancestors
622 Shrader At Height
San Francisco, CA 94117
TOPICS: Metaphysics

Book Builders West
2880 Soquel Avenue, Suite 10
Santa Cruz, CA 95062
(408)-476-6990
CONTACT: Larry Lazopoulos TOPICS: New Age

Book Fellowship International
P.O. Box 164
North Syracuse, NY 13212
TOPICS: Skepticism, Counter-Cult DESCRIPTION:
Cults, Satanism, New and Unconventional Religions,
etc.

Borderland Science And Research Foundation (BSRF)
P.O. Box 429
Garberville, CA 95440-0429
(707)-986-7211
CONTACT: Thomas Joseph Brown, Dir. TOPICS:
Body-Mind Connection, Dowsing, Spirituality,
Color Therapy, Psychic Phenomena, Hypnotism,
UFO's FOUNDED: 1945 MEM: 1,100 STAFF: 3
CONVENTIONS: Occasional workshops and
conferences DESCRIPTION: A non-profit
organization of people who take an active interest in
observation of their physical, mental & spiritual
environment. Subjects studied are light & color,
radionics & radiesthesia, dowsing, ether physics, free
energy, orgone energy, living water, anomalies &
fortean phenomenon, hypnosis, photography of the
invisible & UFO's. Membership is $25/yr.
PUBLICATIONS: *Cosmic Pulse Of Life: The
Revoltionary Biological Power Behind Ufos*
EDITOR: Trevor J. Constable TOPICS: Metaphysics,
UFO's, Paranormal Phenomena TYPE: Book
PRICE: $24.95 PUBLICATIONS: *Gold Rush
Ghosts: Strange & Unexplained Phenomena In The
Mother Lode* EDITOR: Nancy Bradley, V. Gaddis
TOPICS: Occult TYPE: Book PRICE: $9.95
PUBLICATIONS: *Journal Of Borderland Research*
TOPICS: Metaphysics TYPE: Journal FREQ: 6xbi-
monthly DESCRIPTION: Catalog of books & video
tapes for sale on subjects such as homeopathy,
dowsing, energy fields, alchemy, hypnosis, UFO's &
fortean phenomena. Subscription free to members.

PUBLICATIONS: *Lakhovsky Multiple Wave
Oscillator Handbook* EDITOR: Thomas J. Brown
TOPICS: Holistic Health TYPE: Handbook PRICE:
$16.95 PUBLICATIONS: *My Search For Radionic
Truths: With Possibilities Of Acceptance By
Science & Medicine* EDITOR: R.M. Denning
TOPICS: Metaphysics, Holistic Health TYPE: Book
PRICE: $9.95

Boston Visionary Cell
36 Broomfield Street, Ste. 200
Boston, MA 02108
(617)-482-9044
CONTACT: Paul Laffoley, Pres. TOPICS:
Metaphysics, Occult, Spirituality FOUNDED: 1971
MEM: 58 STAFF: 5 DESCRIPTION: Non-profit
association of Neo-Platonic artists, supporters &
consultants whose purpose is to foster visionary art,
cosmic, cosmological, magical, mystical or occult
art, in the Boston & New England area. Members
believe in the mystical explanation for the Universe.
Spiritual mentor is the late Teilhard De Chardin.

Bothered About Dungeons and Dragons
P.O. Box 5513
Richmond, VA 23220
TOPICS: Skepticism, Counter-Cult DESCRIPTION:
Dungeons and Dragons fans, Cults, Satanism, etc.

Bridge To Spiritual Freedom
P.O. Box 333
Kings Point, NY 11754
TOPICS: Metaphysics

British Columbia Chiropractic Association
106-133 West 15th Street
North Vancouver, British Columbia V7M 1R8
Canada
(604)-980-4223
TOPICS: Holistic Healing

Brooke Medicine Eagle
829 Oeste Drive
Davis, CA 95616
TOPICS: Metaphysics

Brotherhood White Temple
General Delivery
Sedalia, CO 80135
TOPICS: Metaphysics

Buckminster Fuller Institute
1743 South LaCienega Boulevard
Los Angeles, CA 90035
(213)-837-7710
TOPICS: Metaphysics

Buddha Sasana Foundation
5459 Shafter Avenue
Oakland, CA 94618
(415)-658-6857
TOPICS: Metaphysics

Builders Of The Adytum (B.O.T.A.)
5101-05 North Figueroa Street
Los Angeles, CA 90042
TOPICS: Tarot, Spirituality, Kabbalah
DESCRIPTION: Founded by Dr. Paul Foster Case, a
noteable Spiritual Teacher & recognized as a world
authority on Tarot & Qabalah. Dedicated to the
study & advancement of spiritualism, enlightenment

& higher wisdom through the Tarot & Qabalah.
Purpose is to search for the answers to the Riddle of
the Universe & to develop advanced methods for
travelling the Path of Spiritual Return to the Most
High. PUBLICATIONS: *Book Of Tokens: Tarot
Meditations* EDITOR: P.F. Case TOPICS: Tarot
TYPE: Book PRICE: $13.00 PUBLICATIONS:
Tarot: Key To The Wisdom Of The Ages EDITOR:
P.F. Case TOPICS: Tarot TYPE: Book PRICE:
$14.50

C.A.F.H. Foundation
2061 Broadway at 71st Street
New York, NY 10023
(212)-783-4185
TOPICS: Metaphysics, New Age, Spirituality,
Holistic Health

C.I.R.C.E.S., International
P.O. Box 279
Plainfield, IN 46168
TOPICS: Metaphysics

C.O.P. Spiritual Foundation
P.O. Box 119
Victor, MT 59875
TOPICS: Metaphysics

Calendar Of Events
9527 Blake Lane Loop, 102
Fairfax, VA 22031
TOPICS: Metaphysics

California Astrology Association
P.O. Box 810
North Hollywood, CA 91603
(818)-340-9007
TOPICS: Astrology, Psychic, Witchcraft, Occult,
Voudoun, Psychic Healing, Psychic Phenomena
PUBLICATIONS: *Astrology* PUBLISHER: Skip Usen
TOPICS: Astrology TYPE: Newspaper DATE: 1970
SIZE: 11.5 x 15; 16 pgs. FREQ: Quarterly PRICE:
$6.00 PRICE PER COPY: $1.50 DESCRIPTION:
Offers descriptions & illustrations about news,
services & products pertaining to metaphysics.
PUBLICATIONS: *Astrology And Psychic News*
TOPICS: Astrology TYPE: Newspaper PRICE:
$20.00 PRICE PER COPY: $2.00 DESCRIPTION:
Provides articles and ads on Astrology, Witchcraft,
Wicca, Psychic Phenomena, Voodoo, Psychic
Healing, Divination, Past Life Regression, etc. The
newspaper's articles and ads are all offered on behalf
of the California Astrology Association.

California Astrology Association
130 Lyons Plain Road
Weston, CT 06883
(203)-227-6027
TOPICS: Astrology

California Holistic Veterinary Medical Association
c/o Beth Wildermann, D.V.M.
17333 Bear Creek Road
Boulder Creek, CA 95006
TOPICS: Holistic Healing

California Miracles Foundation
2269 Market Street
San Francisco, CA 94117
TOPICS: Metaphysics

California Parapsychology

P.O. Box 947
Lemon Grove, CA 92045
TOPICS: Metaphysics

California Society For Psychical Study
P.O. Box 844
Berkeley, CA 94705
TOPICS: Metaphysics

California Yoga Teachers Association
Goodfellow Publishers' Reps.
2054 University Avenue, #604
Berkeley, CA 94704
(415)-841-9200
TOPICS: Yoga, New Age, Meditation
PUBLICATIONS: *American Yoga Newsletter*
EDITOR: Linda Cogozzo TOPICS: Yoga TYPE:
Newsletter PUBLICATIONS: *Yoga Journal* EDITOR:
Michael Gliksohn, Stephan Bodian TOPICS: Yoga,
Meditation, New Age TYPE: Journal FREQ: bi-
monthly CIRC; 58,000 DESCRIPTION: Primarily
source for information on Yoga. Prints articles, ads
and reviews relating to meditation and yoga.

Canadian Independent Astrology
20 Draper Street
Toronto, ON, M5V2M4,
Canada
TOPICS: Astrology

Canadian Institute Of Cultural Affairs
577 Kingston Road
Toronto, Ontario M4E 1R3
Canada
(416)-691-2316 FAX (416)-691-2491
CONTACT: Bill Stapels TOPICS: New Age,
Metaphysics PUBLICATIONS: *Edges* EDITOR:
Brian Stanfield, Ronnie Seagren TOPICS: New Age,
Metaphysics TYPE: Magazine DATE: 1976; 48 pgs.
FREQ: quarterly CIRC: 3,500 DESCRIPTION:
Members of the Institute of Cultural Affairs, serves
an up-scale, educated Canadian & U.S. reader, who
seeks to break down the walls that separate people.
Prints non-fiction, news, reviews, interviews,
cartoons, and artwork. Accepts ads.

Canadian Psychic UFO Research
P.O. Box 455, Streetsville
Mississauga, ON, L5M2B9,
Canada
TOPICS: UFO's

Canadian UFO Research Network
P.O. Box 15, Station A
Willowdale, ON, M2N5S7,
Canada
TOPICS: UFO's

Cancer Support Community
401 Laurel Street
San Francisco, CA 94118
(415)-929-7400
TOPICS: Holistic Health, Holistic Healing

Carolina UFO Network
123 Moser Circle
Indian Trail, NC 28079
TOPICS: UFO's

Celebrate Life
939 West 19th Street

Costa Mesa, CA 92627
TOPICS: Metaphysics

Celestial Affirmations
P.O. Box 125
Anton, TX 79313
TOPICS: Metaphysics

Celestial Interpretor NAPP
552 Estate Road
Maple Shade, NJ 08052
TOPICS: UFO's

Celestial Vibrations
P.O. Box 694
Pinson, AL 35126
TOPICS: Metaphysics

Center For Studies Of The Person
1125 Torrey Pines Road
La Jolla, CA 92037
(619)-459-3861
TOPICS: New Age

Central PSI Research Institute (CPRI)
4800 North Milwaukee Avenue, # 210
Chicago, IL 60630
CONTACT: Ms. Terry Brennan TOPICS:
Parapsychology, Channeling

Chamber Of Holy Voodoo
P.O. Box 341
New York, NY 10021
TOPICS: Metaphysics

Chapel Of Healing Angeles
2 Vassar Court
Jackson, NJ 08527
TOPICS: Metaphysics

Charles Mason Remey Society
80-46 234th Street
Jamaica, NY 11427-2116
CONTACT: Dr. Francis Cajetan Sptaro TOPICS:
Spirituality FOUNDED: 1979 MEM: 750
CONVENTIONS: Meetings the last Sun. of each
month DESCRIPTION: Furthers the philosophy &
teachings of Charles Mason Remey & the Baha'i
Faith. PUBLICATIONS: *The Remey Journal* TYPE:
Journal PRICE: $3.50 PUBLICATIONS: *The Remey
Letter* TYPE: Booklet DESCRIPTION: Offered free.

Cheirological Society
Kongoryuji
29 London Road
East Dereham, Norfolk NR19 1AS
England
CONTACT: Mrs. U. Jaquin, Pres. TOPICS: Holistic
Health, Palmistry FOUNDED: 1889 DESCRIPTION:
Organization promoting the study of hand analysis,
the ancient art of interpreting character &
temperament from the shape & lineation of the hand.
Diploma courses offered on premises or by
correspondence. Maintains a record of approved
tutors & consultant practitioners. Publishes a journal,
text books & research notes. Offers teaching &
honorary diplomas. PUBLICATIONS: *Analysing
Palmar Quadrants* EDITOR: Shifu T. Dukes
TOPICS: Palmistry, Holistic Health TYPE: Book
DATE: 1985 PUBLICATIONS: *Chinese Hand
Analysis* EDITOR: Shifu T. Dukes TOPICS:
Palmistry, Holistic Health TYPE: Book DATE: 1987

PUBLICATIONS: *History Of Cheirology* EDITOR:
C.L. Jones TOPICS: Palmistry, Holistic Health
TYPE: Book DATE: 1990 PUBLICATIONS: *Medical
Cheirology* EDITOR: C.L. Jones TOPICS: Palmistry,
Holistic Health TYPE: Book DATE: 1991
PUBLICATIONS: *No Nonsense Hand Reading*
EDITOR: Shifu T. Dukes TOPICS: Palmistry,
Holistic Health TYPE: Book DATE: 1987
PUBLICATIONS: *Practical Cheirology* EDITOR:
Dr. R. Cigman TOPICS: Palmistry, Holistic Health
TYPE: Book DATE: 1983 PUBLICATIONS: *The
Cheirological Society Journal* TOPICS: Palmistry,
Holistic Health TYPE: Journal FREQ: quarterly
DESCRIPTION: Issued free to society members.

Chidvilas, Inc.
2840 Wilderness Place, Suite D
P.O. Box 17550
Boulder, CO 80301
(303)-449-7811 (303)-665-6611 (800)-777-7743
FAX (303)-449-7099
CONTACT: Parmita Pushman, Pres. TOPICS: New
Age, Meditation, Spirituality, Body-Mind
Connection, Metaphysics FOUNDED: 1981 MEM:
4,000 STAFF: 14 COMPUTER: no AFF ORG: none
DESCRIPTION: Distributor of books by the
contemporary mystic, Osho and audio/videos of New
Age and World Music. PUBLICATIONS: *Beyond
Words Newsletter* TOPICS: New Age, Meditation,
Spirituality, Body-Mind Connection TYPE:
Newsletter DATE: 1986; 8 pgs. DESCRIPTION:
Produces newsletter, prints cartoons, artwork and
reviews. PUBLICATIONS: *Don't Bite My Finger,
Look Where I Am Pointing* EDITOR: B. Rajneesh
TOPICS: New Age, Meditation, Spirituality, Body-
Mind Connection TYPE: Book PRICE: $14.95
PUBLICATIONS: *Meditation: First And Last
Freedom* EDITOR: Osho Rajneesh TOPICS:
Meditation, Body-Mind Connection, Spirituality
TYPE: Book PRICE: $14.95 PUBLICATIONS:
Rebellious Spirit EDITOR: B. Rajneesh TOPICS:
New Age, Meditation, Spirituality, Body-Mind
Connection TYPE: Book PRICE: $14.95
PUBLICATIONS: *Zen: The Quantum Leap From
Mind To No-Mind* EDITOR: B. Rajneesh TOPICS:
New Age, Meditation, Spirituality, Body-Mind
Connection TYPE: Book PRICE: $12.95

Children Of Earth Mother
P.O. Box 1652
Bethany, OK 73008
TOPICS: Witchcraft

Children Of Light
Star Route, Box 39
Dateland, AZ 85333
TOPICS: Metaphysics

Children's Campaign For A Positive Future (CCPF)
524 Sunset Way
Redwood City, CA 94062
(415)-365-3248
CONTACT: Artemas Yaffe, Exec. Officer TOPICS:
New Age

Chinmaya Mission
P.O. Box 397
Los Altos, CA 94023
TOPICS: Metaphysics

Christ Revealed, Incorporated
P.O. Box 15074

Del City, OK 73155
TOPICS: Skepticism, Counter-Cult DESCRIPTION: Mormonism, Jehovah's Witnesses, Cults, New Age, Satanism, etc.

Christian Apologetics
P.O. Box 1659
Milwaukee, WI 53201
TOPICS: Skepticism, Counter-Cult DESCRIPTION: Cults, New Age, Satanism, New And Unconventional Religions.

Christian Awareness Fellowship
P.O. Box 35335
Tucson, AZ 85740
TOPICS: Skepticism, Counter-Cult DESCRIPTION: Miscellaneous New Religions, New Age, Metaphysial Movements, etc.

Christian Counseling Center
1939 Lyntz Road, Southwest
Lordstown, OH 44481
TOPICS: Skepticism, Counter-Cult DESCRIPTION: Cults, New Age, Satanism, New And Unconventional Religions.

Christian Direction, Incorporated
455 St. Antoine Street, West
Montreal, Quebec, H2Z1J1,
Canada
TOPICS: Skepticism, Counter-Cult DESCRIPTION: New Age, New And Unconventional Religions. Secular Humanism.

Christian Education Previous Outreach
1802 Rutherford Street
Rahway, NJ 07065
TOPICS: Skepticism, Counter-Cult DESCRIPTION: New Age, New And Unconventional Religions, Cults, etc.

Christian Research Institute
P.O. Box 3216, Station B
Calgary, Alberta T2M4L7,
Canada
TOPICS: Skepticism, Counter-Cult DESCRIPTION: Cults, New Age, Satanism, New And Unconventional Religions.

Christian Research Institute
2075 South Unversity Boulevard, Ste. 111
Denver, CO 80210
TOPICS: Skepticism, Counter-Cult DESCRIPTION: Skeptical approach to cults, New Age, satanism, new and unconventional religions.

Christian Research Of Aerial Phenomena
1524 Ferndale Avenue
Johnstown, PA 15905
(814)-288-2314
TOPICS: UFO's PUBLICATIONS: *Christian Research Of Aerial Phonomena Newsletter* EDITOR: Art Leman TOPICS: UFO's TYPE: Newsletter DATE: 1968; 3 pgs. FREQ: Bi-Monthly

Christian Way International
P.O. Box 1675
Lancaster, CA 93539
TOPICS: Skepticism, Counter-Cult DESCRIPTION: New Age, Christian Science, Unity, etc.

Christian Witnesses
P.O. Box 690
Colton, CA 92324
TOPICS: Skepticism, Counter-Cult DESCRIPTION: Jehovah's Witnesses, Cults, New Age, Satanism, etc.

Christiananda
977 Asbury
San Jose, CA 95126
TOPICS: Metaphysics

Christians Address New Age
1310 South 75th Street
West Allis, WI 53214
TOPICS: Skepticism, Counter-Cult DESCRIPTION: New Age, New & Unconventional Religions, Occult, Paganism.

Church Cosmic Consciousness
10420 Palms Boulevard
Los Angeles, CA 90034
TOPICS: Metaphysics

Church Immortal Consciousness
916 East 7th Street
Mesa, AZ 85203
TOPICS: Metaphysics

Church Of All Worlds (CAW)
P.O. Box 1542
Ukiah, CA 95482
TOPICS: Witchcraft, Occult, Paganism

Church Of All Worlds
2140 Shattuck Avenue, 2093
Berkeley, CA 94704
TOPICS: Witchcraft

Church Of Crescent Moon
P.O. Box 1200
Camarillo, CA 93011
TOPICS: Witchcraft

Church Of Cryptotheology
1422 West Desert Cove
Phoenix, AZ 85029
TOPICS: Metaphysics

Church Of Divine Man
3314 Southwest 1st Avenue
Portland, OR 97201
TOPICS: Metaphysics

Church Of Humanity
507 West Holly Road
Virginia Beach, VA 23451
TOPICS: Metaphysics

Church Of Inner Light
1907 Benecia Avenue
Los Angeles, CA 90025
TOPICS: Metaphysics

Church Of Inner Light Wisdom
6635 Jonel Way
Bonita, CA 92002
TOPICS: Metaphysics

Church Of Mind Awareness
5114 Medina Road
Woodland Hills, CA 91364
TOPICS: Metaphysics

Church Of Religious Philosphy
6737 East Almeria
Scottsdale, AZ 85257
TOPICS: Metaphysics

Church Of Religious Research, Inc.
Box 208
Grand Island, FL 32735-0208
CONTACT: Rev. Isabel Pinkston, Director TOPICS: New Age, Past Life Regression, Death, Channeling FOUNDED: 1950 MEM: 250 STAFF: 5 DESCRIPTION: New Age ministry researching the soul through past-life recall. Offers a great volume of wisdom channeled through our high spirit guide, Dr. John Christopher Daniels gleaned from his long detailed study of the Akashic Records. Provides a research library containing books & audio & video cassettes. Also holds classes & discussions. Sells 18 self-researched & self-published books. PUBLICATIONS: *Religious Research Journal* EDITOR: Rev. Isabel Pinkston TOPICS: New Age, Death, Past Life Regression TYPE: Journal; 12 pgs. DESCRIPTION: Subscription included with a $45 membership contribution per year.

Church Of Satan
P.O. Box 896
Daly City, CA 94017
TOPICS: Occult

Church Of Satan, Inc.
P.O. Box 210082
San Francisco, CA 94121
(415)-752-3583
TOPICS: Occult PUBLICATIONS: *The Cloven Hoof* EDITOR: Anton Szandor La Vey TOPICS: Occult TYPE: Book

Church Of Scientology
1413 North Berendo Street
Los Angeles, CA 90027
TOPICS: Metaphysics

Church Of Scientology
696 Yonge Street
Toronto, ON, M4Y2A7,
Canada
TOPICS: Metaphysics

Church Of Spiritual Discovery (CSD)
166 West 72nd Street
New York, NY 10023
(212)-724-4081
CONTACT: Rev. Mary Blake, Dir. TOPICS: New Age, Metaphysics

Church Of Tamara
3002 East Fort Lowell Road
Tucson, AZ 85716
TOPICS: Metaphysics

Church Of The Cosmic Christ
711 Blacklidge Drive
Tucson, AZ 85719
TOPICS: Metaphysics

Church Of The Eternal Source
P.O. Box 7091
Burbank, CA 91505
TOPICS: Metaphysics

Church Of The Third Eye
P.O. Box 45220

Westlake, OH 44145
TOPICS: Witchcraft

Church Of The Tzaddi
11236 Dale Street
Garden Grove, CA 92641
TOPICS: Metaphysics

Church Of Tzaddi
Boulder, CO 80308-3729
CONTACT: Amy Merritt Kees TOPICS: Spirituality,
Psychic Healing, New Age, Psychology

Church Of Universal Brotherhood
111 West 72nd Street
New York, NY 10023
TOPICS: Metaphysics

Church Of Universal Love
8034 Lowd
El Paso, TX 79907
(915)-779-1259
TOPICS: Astrology, UFO's PUBLICATIONS: *Cosmic
Channelings* EDITOR: Linda Forman TOPICS:
Astrology TYPE: Newsletter; 10 pgs. FREQ: Bi-
Monthly PRICE: $6.00

Church Of Universal Love
P.O. Box 1620
Stanwood, WA 98292
TOPICS: Metaphysics

Church Of Y Twywyth Teg
P.O. Box 674884
Marietta, GA 30067
(404)-423-9585
CONTACT: Rhuddlwm Gawr TOPICS: Witchcraft,
Paganism, Spirituality, Occult, New Age MEM:
3,000 CONVENTIONS: Sponsors several gatherings
during the year. DESCRIPTION: Worships the Old
Gods of Nature referred to as Welsh Wicca, Nature
Religion founded in 1282. Promotes freedom of
religion, Paganism. Considered to be the old religion
for a New Age.

Church Universal And Triumphant (CUT)
Box A
Livingston, MT 59047
CONTACT: Elizabeth Clare Prophet TOPICS:
Metaphysics, Spirituality, New Age, Channeling

Churchill Livingstone
1560 Broadway, 7th Fl.
New York, NY 10036
(212)-819-5400
TOPICS: Holistic Healing PUBLICATIONS:
Midwifery TOPICS: Holistic Healing TYPE:
Magazine

Circle Cithaeron
P.O. Box 1701
College Park, MD 20740
TOPICS: Witchcraft

Circle In The Greenwood
P.O. Box 275
Niverville, NY 12130
TOPICS: Witchcraft

Circle Of Light
29 Queens Road
Rockaway, NJ 07866

TOPICS: Metaphysics

Circle Of Light
P.O. Box 41
Naperville, IL 60540
TOPICS: Metaphysics

Circle Of Light Coven
P.O. Box 68562
Virginia Beach, VA 23455
TOPICS: Witchcraft

Circle Of The Dance
P.O. Box 19021
Portland, OR 97219
TOPICS: Witchcraft

Circle Of The Whitefeather
P.O. Box 641
Helena, AR 72342
(501)-338-7966
CONTACT: Robert J. Titus TOPICS: New Age,
Psychic, Spirituality DESCRIPTION: The Ancient
Order Of The Whitefeather is a brotherhood of
Medicine Men & Women who formed the psychic,
philosophic, intellectural, spiritual & diplomatic core
of the great Hopewell Empire in Mid-America
between 500 B.C. & 1600 A.D. Offers books, stories
& personal communications. PUBLICATIONS: *Book
Of Shaman* EDITOR: Robert J. Titus TOPICS:
Spirituality TYPE: Book PRICE: $10.00

Circle Sanctuary/Church Of Circle Wicca
P.O. Box 219
Mount Horeb, WI 53572
(608)-924-2216
CONTACT: Dennis Carpenter TOPICS: New Age,
Metaphysics, Parapsychology, Spirituality,
Witchcraft, Paganism PUBLICATIONS: *Circle
Guide Of Wicca And Pagan Resources* EDITOR:
Selena Fox TOPICS: Occult, Metaphysics,
Witchcraft, Paganism TYPE: Directory DATE: 1979
PUBLICATIONS: *Circle Network News* EDITOR:
Dennis Carpenter TOPICS: New Age, Metaphysics,
Parapsychology, Spirituality, Occult, Paganism,
Witchcraft TYPE: Newspaper DESCRIPTION:
Newspaper explores nature, metaphysics and
spirituality through articles and book reviews.

Citizen's Clearinghouse For Hazardous Wastes
P.O. Box 926
Arlington, VA 22216
(703)-276-7070
TOPICS: Holistic Healing

Citizens Against UFO Secrecy (CAUS)
3518 Martha Custis Drive
Alexandria, VA 22302
(703)-931-3341
CONTACT: Larry W. Bryant, Admin. TOPICS:
UFO's

Citizens Alliance For Naturopathy
P.O. Box 277, Station A
Islington, ON, M9A4X3,
Canada
TOPICS: Metaphysics

City Of The Sun Foundation
Box 370

Columbus, NM 88029
(505)-531-2617
TOPICS: Astrology, Metaphysics PUBLICATIONS:
Golden Dawn TOPICS: Astrology TYPE:
Newsletter; 12 pgs. FREQ: Bi-Monthly

Civilian Aerial Phenomena Research Organization
13238 North 7th Drive
Phoenix, AZ 85029
(602)-942-7216
TOPICS: UFO's PUBLICATIONS: *Ground Saucer
Watch Newsletter* EDITOR: William Spaulding
TOPICS: UFO's TYPE: Newsletter; 20 pgs.

Clamshell Alliance
P.O. Box 734
Concord, NH 03301
(603)-224-4163
TOPICS: Holistic Healing

Clean Water Action Project
317 Pennsylvania Avenue SE
Washington, DC 20003
(202)-547-1196
TOPICS: Holistic Healing

Clear Light At Klara Simpla
10 Main Street
Wilmington, VT 05363
TOPICS: Channeling

Cleveland UFO Society
537 Juneway Drive
Bay Village, OH 44140
TOPICS: UFO's

Cleveland UFOlogy Project
7653 Normandie Boulevard C33
Cleveland, OH 44130
TOPICS: UFO's

Coalition For Alternatives In Nutrition And Healthcare
P.O. Box B-12
Richlandtown, PA 18955
(215)-346-8461
TOPICS: Holistic Healing

Collectors Of Unusual Data - International (COUD-I)
2312 Shields Avenue
St. Louis, MO 63136
(314)-388-0087
CONTACT: Raymond Nelke TOPICS: Psychic
Phenomena FOUNDED: 1970 MEM: 15 AFF ORG:
St. Louis UFO; St. Louis Skeptics DESCRIPTION:
Collects data for research on all types of unusual
phenomena such as Big Foot, UFO, Noah's Ark,
poltergeists, homeopathy, etc. Supplies information
to individuals, media, organizations etc.

Committee For Freedom Of Choice In Medicine (CFCM)
1180 Walnut Avenue
Chula Vista, CA 92011
(619)-429-8200
CONTACT: Mike Culbert TOPICS: New Age

Committee For The Scientific Investigation Of Claims Of The Paranormal
12000 NW 8th Street
Plantation, FL 33317
(305)-370-1128

CONTACT: James Randi **TOPICS:** Skepticism **MEM:** 5,000 **DESCRIPTION:** Organization founded by Randall James Hamilton Zwinge, known as James Randi - The Amazing Randi, investigates claims of paranormal phenomena and uncovers fraud. Offers $10,000 reward to anyone who can prove they have psychic or supernatural powers. Issac Asimov and Carl Sagan are also members.

Committee For The Scientific Investigations Of Claims Of The Paranormal (CSICOP)
P.O. Box 229
Central Park Station
Buffalo, NY 14215-0229
(716)-834-3222 (800)-634-1610 **FAX** (716)-834-0841

CONTACT: Barry Karr, Exec. Dir. **TOPICS:** Psychic Phenomena, Skepticism, Parapsychology, Occult, Counter-Cult **FOUNDED:** 1976 **STAFF:** 7 **CONVENTIONS:** Conferences approximately 2 times per year in various locations. 1991 in CA & Amsterdam, The Netherlands. **DESCRIPTION:** Investigates paranormal claims from a scientific point of view and disseminates factual information about the results of such inquiries to the scientific community and the public. Skeptical viewpoint debunkers. **PUBLICATIONS:** *The Skeptical Inquirer* **EDITOR:** Kendrick Frazier **TOPICS:** Psychic Phenomena, Skepticism, Parapsychology, Occult **TYPE:** Magazine **DATE:** 1976 **FREQ:** quarterly **CIRC:** 38,000 **PRICE:** $25.00 **TERM:** yearly **DESCRIPTION:** Offers scientific evidence to disprove claims of paranormal phenomena.

Common Boundary, Inc.
7005 Florida Street
Chevy Chase, MD 20815
(301)-652-9495

CONTACT: Charles H. Simpkinson, Ph.D. **TOPICS:** Spirituality, Dreams, Meditation, Holistic Health, Metaphysics, New Age **FOUNDED:** 1980 **STAFF:** 7 **GROUPS:** network groups **CONVENTIONS:** Annual conference. 2,000 attended in 1989. **DESCRIPTION:** A non-profit, educational organization for persons interested in the spiritual aspects of psychotherapy and the psychological dimensions of spiritual growth. Publishes a 50 page bi-monthly magazine, a directory of graduate degree programs in psychospiritual psychotherapy, and gives a $500 annual award to the outstanding psychospiritual thesis or dissertation. Kindred Spirit network groups meet across the country. **PUBLICATIONS:** *Common Boundary Magazine* **EDITOR:** Anne A. Simpkinson, Charles Simpkinson **TOPICS:** Spirituality, Dreams, Meditation, Holistic Health, Metaphysics, New Age **TYPE:** Magazine **FREQ:** bi-monthly **CIRC:** 18,000 **PRICE:** $19.00 **PRICE PER COPY:** $3.75 **DESCRIPTION:** Feature articles and reviews on topics such as Shamanism, expressive arts, meditation, contemplation, ecofeminism, co-dependency, bodywork and dreams. Accepts ads. **PUBLICATIONS:** *Directory Of Graduate Degree Programs In Psychospiritual Psychotherapy*

TOPICS: Spirituality, Dreams, Meditation, Holistic Health, Metaphysics **TYPE:** Directory

Communes Network
89 Ervington Road
Leicester,
England
TOPICS: New Age

Community Christian Ministries
1998 West Pullman Road
Moscow, ID 83843
TOPICS: Skepticism, Counter-Cult **DESCRIPTION:** Mormonism, Jehovah's Witnesses, New Age, etc.

Community Two
P.O. Box 82
Middletown, CA 95461
TOPICS: Metaphysics

Compassionate Friends
P.O. Box 3696
Oak Brook, IL 60522
(312)-990-0010
TOPICS: Death

Complete Spectrum, The
P.O. Box 8021
Ann Arbor, MI 48107
TOPICS: Metaphysics

Concepts Energy/Synergy (Lazarus)
302 South County Road, #109
Palm Beach, FL 33480
(407)-588-9599
CONTACT: Jach Pursel **TOPICS:** New Age, Metaphysics

Concern For Dying
250 West 57th Street
Room 831
New York, NY 10107
(212)-246-6962
TOPICS: Death

Concerned Christians
P.O. Box 22920
Denver, CO 80222
TOPICS: Skepticism, Counter-Cult **DESCRIPTION:** New Age, New And Unconventional Religions, etc.

Concerned Educators Allied For A Safe Environment
17 Gerry Street
Cambridge, MA 02138
(617)-864-0999
TOPICS: Holistic Healing

Conehead Coven
P.O. Box 691498
Tulsa, OK 74169
TOPICS: Witchcraft

Congregationalist Witchcraft Association (C.W.A.)
P.O. Box 86134
North Vancouver, BC V7L 4J5
Canada
CONTACT: Samuel Wagar **TOPICS:** Witchcraft, Occult, Paganism, Voudoun **FOUNDED:** 1991 **CONVENTIONS:** Annual Grand Council **DESCRIPTION:** An association of Witches' covens in Canada which have come together to achieve goals:

public presence for the religion, advanced training for the Priesthood, recognition as legal religious bodies, tax advantages, anti-discrimination, chaplaincy, etc. Based on the Wiccan religion.

Congress Of Astrological Organization
Box 75, Old Chelsea Station
New York, NY 10113
TOPICS: New Age **PUBLICATIONS:** *CAO Times* **EDITOR:** Al H. Morrison **TOPICS:** New Age **TYPE:** Magazine **CIRC:** 1,100 **DESCRIPTION:** Features articles, news & information on nature & natural events.

Conscious Breathing Association
P.O. Box 5320
Chico, CA 95927-5320
(916)-893-8643
CONTACT: Leonard Orr **TOPICS:** New Age, Holistic Health **PUBLICATIONS:** *International Rebirthers Directory* **EDITOR:** Leonard Orr, Jane Hartley **TOPICS:** Past Life Regression, Death **TYPE:** Directory; 50 pgs. **FREQ:** annual **PRICE:** $15.00 **DESCRIPTION:** Offers listing of professional Rebirthers.

Conscious Connections
P.O. Box 17310
Boulder, CO 80308
TOPICS: Metaphysics

Consciousness Research And Training Project, Inc. (CRTP)
Box 9G
315 E. 68th Street
New York, NY 10021
CONTACT: Joyce Goodrich, Ph.D., Project Dir. **TOPICS:** Holistic Healing, Meditation, Spirituality, Body-Mind Connection **FOUNDED:** 1970 **MEM:** 700 **STAFF:** 3 **DESCRIPTION:** Offers 5 day introductory seminars based on the work of Lawrence LeShan, Ph. D. Teaches meditation & healing based on LeShan's theoretical work. Conducts research in cooperation with the scientific community. Offers a newsletter, various research & educational materials, advanced work & a national network. See listing under Schools. **PUBLICATIONS:** *Consciousness Research And Training Project Newsletter* **TOPICS:** Holistic Healing, Meditation, Spirituality, Body-Mind Connection **TYPE:** Newsletter **DESCRIPTION:** Newsletter for persons who have studied with the organization.

Cooking For Survival Consciousness
P.O. Box 26762
Elkins Park, PA 19117
(215)-635-1022
TOPICS: Health Food

COSMEP, Inc.
P.O. Box 703
San Francisco, CA 94101
(415)-922-9490
CONTACT: Richard Morris **TOPICS:** New Age **FOUNDED:** 1968 **CONVENTIONS:** Annual conference. **DESCRIPTION:** Trade organization offering newsletter containing reviews of publications & publishing software. Also offers cooperative exhibits at ALA & ABA.

Cosmic Awareness Communications
P.O. Box 115

Olympia, WA 98507
TOPICS: Channeling, Spirituality, New Age, UFO's, Meditation, Metaphysics **PUBLICATIONS:** *Cosmic Awareness News* **TOPICS:** Channeling **TYPE:** Newspaper **PUBLICATIONS:** *Revelations Of Awareness* **EDITOR:** Avaton **TOPICS:** Channeling, Parapsychology **TYPE:** Newsletter **DATE:** 1972 **SIZE:** 8 1/2 x 11, 20 pgs. **FREQ:** Bi-Weekly **CIRC;** 5,000 **PRICE:** $52.00 **TERM:** yearly **PRICE PER COPY:** $3.00 **DESCRIPTION:** Information from the Universal Mind on all subjects such as religion, philosophy, mysteries, relationships, UFO's & the alien presence threat. Promotes spiritual, economic & humanitarian growth as influenced by the teachings of Edgar Cayce.

Cosmic Church
113 Second Street, Northeast
Washington, DC 20002
TOPICS: Metaphysics

Cosmic Contact Channel Reference/ Psychic Services
26 East 13th Street
New York, NY 10003
CONTACT: Mike Goodrich **TOPICS:** Channeling, Metaphysics, Psychic **DESCRIPTION:** Channeling Referral Service

Cosmic Council
212 North Parsons Avenue
Brandon, FL 33510
(813)-654-4386
CONTACT: William E. Woods **TOPICS:** New Age, Spirituality, Astrology, Holistic Healing **DESCRIPTION:** Associated with New Awareness, Inc. & its founder William E. Woods.

Cosmic Light Foundation
11716 221st Street, Southeast
Snomish, WA 98290
TOPICS: UFO's

Cosmic Lightbearers
P.O. Box 4112
Key West, FL 33041
TOPICS: Metaphysics

Cosmic Zee
2611 Kingsbridge
Dallas, TX 75252
TOPICS: Metaphysics

Cosmobiology Research
100 West Undercliff Street
Pittsburgh, PA 15223
TOPICS: Astrology

Cosmos
3225 South 8th Street
Long Beach, CA 90804
TOPICS: Metaphysics

Council For Responsible Nutrition
1300 19th Street, N.W.
Suite 310
Washington, DC 20036
(202)-872-1488 **FAX** (202)-872-9594
CONTACT: Mr. J.B. Cordaro **TOPICS:** Holistic Healing

Council On International Educational Exchange
205 East 42nd Street
New York, NY 10017
(212)-661-1414
TOPICS: New Age

Council On Mind Abust
P.O. Box 575, Station Z
Toronto, Ontario M5N2Z6,
Canada
TOPICS: Skepticism, Counter-Cult **DESCRIPTION:** New Age, New And Unconventional Religions, Occult, Paganism.

Count Dracula Fan Club
6000 Euper Lane
Fort Smith, AR 72903
CONTACT: Jeanne Youngson, Dir. **TOPICS:** Occult, Vampires **DESCRIPTION:** Focuses on both light-hearted & serious vampire lore. Offers lists on currently available occult & vampire books, societies & magazines. Newsletter published by Jeanne Younson Publishers.

Coven Circle Of Life
P.O. Box 621
Charleston, IL 61920
TOPICS: Witchcraft, Occult, Paganism

Coven Eldar
P.O. Box 28692
Columbus, OH 43228
TOPICS: Witchcraft, Occult, Paganism

Coven Garden Occult Supply
P.O. Box 1064
Boulder, CO 80302
TOPICS: Witchcraft, Occult, Paganism

Coven Of Astral Mysteries
P.O. Box 151
Berwyn, IL 60402
TOPICS: Witchcraft, Occult, Paganism

Coven Of Danu
P.O. Box 34686
Phoenix, AZ 85067
TOPICS: Witchcraft, Occult, Paganism

Coven Of Floating Spiral
P.O. Box 25
Kent, OH 44240
TOPICS: Witchcraft, Paganism, Occult **FOUNDED:** 1978 **DESCRIPTION:** Witchnage Tradition/Wiccan Coven. Offers Initiatory, Mystery School, Adept-Oriented Scholarship of Magickal Arts & World Religions. Lady Pythia is Elder High Priestess & legal clergy.

Coven Of Mother Mountain
P.O. Box 390
Van Nuys, CA 91408
TOPICS: Witchcraft, Occult, Paganism

Coven Of Our Lady Moon
4-333 Ritson Road, South
Oshawa, ON, L1H5J3,
Canada
TOPICS: Witchcraft, Occult, Paganism

Coven Of The Dawn
P.O. Box A
Thomaston, ME 04861
TOPICS: Witchcraft, Occult, Paganism

Coven Of The Dolphins
219 South Sparks Street, 22
State College, PA 16801
TOPICS: Witchcraft, Occult, Paganism

Coven Of The Dragon
P.O. Box 65
Mountain View, CA 94042
TOPICS: Witchcraft, Occult, Paganism

Coven Of The Fertile Earth
P.O. Box 64491
Virginia Beach, VA 23464
TOPICS: Witchcraft, Occult, Paganism

Coven Of The Pendragon
P.O. Box 2483
Des Moines, IA 50311
TOPICS: Witchcraft, Occult, Paganism

Coven Of The Spiral Castle
P.O. Box 531373
Miami Shores, FL 33153
TOPICS: Witchcraft, Occult, Paganism

Coven Of The Wyrd Sisters
22122 Trombly Street
Saint Clair Shores, MI 48080-3980
TOPICS: Witchcraft, Occult, Paganism

Coven Of White Familiar
P.O. Box 7482
Amarillo, TX 79109
TOPICS: Witchcraft, Occult, Paganism

Coven Starburst
P.O. Box 341383
Memphis, TN 38184
TOPICS: Witchcraft, Occult, Paganism

Covenant Of Gaea
P.O. Box 60151
Chicago, IL 60660
TOPICS: Witchcraft, Occult, Paganism

Covenant Of The Goddess (COG)
P.O. Box 1226
Berkeley, CA 94701
TOPICS: Witchcraft, Occult, Paganism **CONVENTIONS:** Annual national festival, Grand Council, held at a campground or resort. **DESCRIPTION:** Non-profit religious organization founded to increase coopertion among Witches & to secure for Witches & covens the legal protection enjoyed by other religions. A confederation of covens & solitaires of various traditions who share in the worship of the Goddess & the Old Gods & subscribe to a common code of ethics. **PUBLICATIONS:** *Covenant Of The Goddess News* **TOPICS:** Witchcraft, Occult, Paganism **TYPE:** Newsletter **DESCRIPTION:** Published at every Sabbat. Covers Craft & Pagan news, original articles, poetry, humor, rituals & announcements.

Covenstead, The
10364 Cooper Road
Deroche, BC, V0M1G0,
Canada
TOPICS: Witchcraft, Occult, Paganism

Craft Of The Wise
45 Grove Street
New York, NY 10014

TOPICS: Witchcraft

Creative Catalyst
6023 Majestic Avenue
Oakland, CA 94605
TOPICS: Metaphysics

Creative Energy Options
909 Sumneytown Pike
Box 603
Springhouse, PA 19477
(215)-643-4420
TOPICS: Holistic Healing, Channeling

Creative Path
2371 Delkus Crescent
Mississauga, ON, L5A1K8,
Canada
TOPICS: Metaphysics

Creative Resources Guild
P.O. Box 3397
Santa Monica, CA 90403
(213)-285-3495
CONTACT: John Tibayan TOPICS: New Age
FOUNDED: 1988

Crystal Chamber Healing
1 Northwes 102nd
Oklahoma City, OK 73114
TOPICS: Metaphysics

Crystal Cosmos Network
Box 2386
Winnipeg, Manitoba R3C 4A6
Canada
(204)-661-2551
TOPICS: New Age, Crystals, Metaphysics
PUBLICATIONS: *Crystal Cosmos Connections: A
Network Directory* EDITOR: Elizabeth Logan
TOPICS: Crystals TYPE: Directory DATE: 1988
SIZE: 8 1/2 x 11; 151 pgs. PRICE: $11.95
DESCRIPTION: Comprehensive directory dedicated
to all aspects of crystals. Covers activities, resources,
education, research, consultations, products, mining,
publications, arts, tapes, bookstores & centers. Has
more than 1,500 free listings & display ads.

Crystal Moon Coven
P.O. Box 536771
Orlando, FL 32853
TOPICS: Witchcraft

Crystal Sanctuary
P.O. Box 1036
Mission, KS 66222
TOPICS: Metaphysics

Crystal Stargate (CSG)
P.O. Box 1761
San Marcos, CA 92069
(619)-741-8148
CONTACT: Aline Gray, Mgr. TOPICS: Witchcraft,
Metaphysics

Crystal Therapeutics
P.O. Box 596
Bardonia, NY 10954
TOPICS: Holistic Health

Cult Awareness Ministry
P.O. Box 1671
Monrovia, CA 91016

TOPICS: Skepticism, Counter-Cult DESCRIPTION:
Cults, New Age, Satanism, etc.

Cult Awareness Network
2421 West Pratt Boulevard, 1173
Chicago, IL 60645
TOPICS: Skepticism, Counter-Cult DESCRIPTION:
Cults, New Age, Satanism, New And
Unconventional Religions.

Cult Exodus For Christ
P.O. Box 4033
Covina, CA 91723
TOPICS: Skepticism, Counter-Cult DESCRIPTION:
New Age, New And Unconventional Religions, etc.

Cult Project
3460 Stanley Street
Montreal, Que. H3A1R8,
Canada
TOPICS: Skepticism, Counter-Cult DESCRIPTION:
New Age, New And Unconventional Religions,
Occut, Paganism.

Cult Watch Of America
P.O. Box 515
Akron, OH 44309
TOPICS: Skepticism, Counter-Cult DESCRIPTION:
New Age, New And Unconventional Religions,
Occult, Paganism.

Cultural Integration Fellowship
2650 Fulton Street
San Francisco, CA 94118
TOPICS: Metaphysics

Cunningham/Copia Foundation
International Birth Project
P.O. Box 161113
Austin, TX 78716
(512)-327-8310
TOPICS: Birth

Cycles
2251 Berkeley Avenue
Schnectady, NY 12309
TOPICS: Occult

Dance Of The Deer Foundation
P.O. Box 699
Soquel, CA 95073
(408)-475-9560
TOPICS: New Age, Metaphysics

Daoist Sanctuary
P.O. Box 27806
Tempe, AZ 85282
TOPICS: Metaphysics

Dayspring Evangelism
P.O. Box 43331
Austin, TX 78745
TOPICS: Skepticism, Counter-Cult DESCRIPTION:
New Age, New And Unconventional Religions,
Cults, etc

Deepstar Coven
18 Gilman Lane
Willingboro, NJ 08046
TOPICS: Witchcraft

Defenders Of Wildlife
1244 19th Street NW
Washington, DC 20036

(202)-659-9510
TOPICS: Holistic Healing PUBLICATIONS:
Defenders TOPICS: Holistic Healing TYPE:
Magazine

Delval UFO, Inc.
948 Almshouse Road
Ivyland, PA 18974
TOPICS: UFO's

Dena Foundaton
4117 Northwest Willow Drive
Kansas City, MO 64116
TOPICS: Metaphysics

Denver Area Wiccan Network
P.O. Box 112
Englewood, CO 80151
TOPICS: Witchcraft

Denver Extraterrestrial Research
330 East 10th Avenue, 902
Denver, CO 80203
TOPICS: UFO's

Desert Community Psychic Research
388 Freeman
Long Beach, CA 90814
TOPICS: Metaphysics

Desert Henge Coven
P.O. Box 40451
Tucson, AZ 85717
TOPICS: Witchcraft, Occult, Paganism FOUNDED:
1982 DESCRIPTION: Wiccan Coven of Gardnerian
extraction following Traditional Wiccan values &
Thealogy. Members have lectured extensively on the
subject in public, print media, schools, Universities,
TV & Radio. The Coven has also assisted police
with occult investigations & with training police
personnel in dealing with the Pagan community.
Also teaches regular classes on Wicca.

Destiny Alterations
109 West Drive
Cottage Hills, IL 62018
TOPICS: Metaphysics

Deva Magic, Inc.
P.O. Box 280
Bearsville, NY 12409
TOPICS: Metaphysics

Diamond Shangita
2119 Kaloa Way
Honolulu, HI 96822
TOPICS: Metaphysics

Dimensions Music Club
2674 East Main Street, Suite C-124
Ventura, CA 93001
(805)-643-0965
CONTACT: R. Weinstock TOPICS: New Age
FOUNDED: 1990

Dinshah Health Society (DHS)
100 Dinshah Drive
Malaga, NJ 08328
(609)-692-4686
CONTACT: Darious Dinshah, Pres. TOPICS:
Holistic Healing, Color Therapy FOUNDED: 1976
MEM: 350 STAFF: 3 CONVENTIONS: Annually in
Malaga, NJ DESCRIPTION: Promotes lesser known

healing methods, primarily Dinshah's Color Therapy - Spectro Chrome, mainly by mail-order and phone. Unrestricted membership. **PUBLICATIONS:** *Dr. Baldwin Testifies* **EDITOR:** Dr. Kate W. Baldwin **TOPICS:** Holistic Healing, Color Therapy **TYPE:** Booklet; 26 pgs. **PUBLICATIONS:** *History Of Spectro-Chrome* **EDITOR:** Dinshah P. Ghadiali **TOPICS:** Holistic Healing, Color Therapy **TYPE:** Book, 6,000 pgs. **PRICE:** $220.00 **PUBLICATIONS:** *Let There Be Light* **EDITOR:** Darius Dinshah **TOPICS:** Holistic Healing, Color Therapy **TYPE:** Book, 164 pgs. **PRICE:** $15.00 **PUBLICATIONS:** *Therapeutic Value Of Light And Color* **EDITOR:** Dr. Kate W. Baldwin **TOPICS:** Holistic Healing, Color Therapy **TYPE:** Brochure **PUBLICATIONS:** *Woman's Hospital Trustees' Minutes* **EDITOR:** Dr. Kate W. Baldwin **TOPICS:** Holistic Healing, Color Therapy **TYPE:** Booklet

Discernment Ministry
P.O. Box 69
Highland Lakes, NJ 07422
TOPICS: Skepticism, Counter-Cult **DESCRIPTION:** Cults, New And Unconventional Religions, Satanism, etc.

Dispensable Church
P.O. Box 8444
Santa Fe, NM 87504
TOPICS: Metaphysics

Divine Science Federation
1819 East 14th Avenue
Denver, CO 80218
TOPICS: Metaphysics

Divine Science Of Light And Sound, The
2554 Lincoln Boulevard, Box 620
Marina del Rey, CA 90292
(213)-306-3322
TOPICS: Psychic Phenomena, Spirituality, Body-Mind Connection **DESCRIPTION:** Spiritual teaching with books and workshops on out-of-body exploration.

Dolphin Encounters
P.O. Box 37
Corindi Beach, NSW 2456,
Australia
066-49-2997
CONTACT: Taranath Andre **TOPICS:** Crystals **DESCRIPTION:** Devoted to the study of dolphins & whales. Uses crystals for channeling dolphin energy & consciousness.

Dolphin Net
1081 Alameda, 64
Belmont, CA 94002
TOPICS: Occult

Dolphin Perspective
428 Coronado Avenue, 7
Long Beach, CA 90814
TOPICS: UFO's, Channeling

Dr. Edward Bach Healing Society (DEBHS)
644 Merrick Road
Lynbrook, NY 11563
(516)-593-2206

CONTACT: Leslie J. Kaslof, Pres. **TOPICS:** Holistic Healing

Dracula And Company
P.O. Box 994
Metairie, LA 70004-0994
TOPICS: Occult

Dracula Unlimited
29 Washington Square, West
New York, NY 10011
(212)-533-5018
TOPICS: Metaphysics

Dragon Sidh
P.O. Box 182
DeWitt, NY 13214
TOPICS: Witchcraft

Druidiactos
P.O. Box 472143
Garland, TX 75047
TOPICS: Metaphysics

Druids Of California And Nevada
5851 Mission Street
San Francisco, CA 94112
TOPICS: Witchcraft

Dyer Meta Research
P.O. Box 545
Lovell, WY 82431
TOPICS: Metaphysics

E.P.I.C. Temple
P.O. Box 533
Anaheim, CA 92815
TOPICS: Metaphysics

Earth Alliance To Rescue The Humans
1505 Grandview Drive
Nashville, TN 37215
(615)-383-3773
TOPICS: New Age **DESCRIPTION:** Organization acts as a clearinghouse for New Age issues such as environmental concerns and alerts the public to take appropriate action.

Earth Base Project
P.O. Box 1328
Bloomington, IN 47402
TOPICS: Witchcraft

Earth Circle Association
235 C Street
San Rafael, CA 94901
TOPICS: Metaphysics

Earth First Collective
P.O. Box 170602
San Francisco, CA 94117
TOPICS: Witchcraft

Earth First!
P.O. Box 5871
Canton, NY 13617
(315)-379-9940
TOPICS: Holistic Healing **PUBLICATIONS:** *Earth First!* **TOPICS:** Holistic Healing, Occult **TYPE:** Magazine

Earth Odyssey And Shamanic Foundation
P.O. Box 2506, Station P
Thunder Bay, ON P7B 5E9
Canada
CONTACT: Dr. Ed Kenney **TOPICS:** New Age **DESCRIPTION:** Founded by Dr. Ed Kenney. Purpose is to help one another understand who we are by accessing our ancient knowledge from within so that we may live fuller lives of wisdom. The journey is one of kindness, compassion & Divine Love. Offers personal transitional counselling, workshops, private group sessions, retreats, public speaking, audio & video tapes, handcrafted native drums, articles & storytelling.

Earth Spirit Community (ESC)
P.O. Box 365
Medford, MA 02155
(617)-395-1023
CONTACT: Deirdre Pulgram Arthen, Dir. **TOPICS:** New Age, Witchcraft, Occult, Paganism **PUBLICATIONS:** *Earth Spirit Community Newsletter* **TOPICS:** Witchcraft, Occult, Paganism **TYPE:** Newsletter **PUBLICATIONS:** *Fire Heart* **EDITOR:** Myrriah Lavin, Ernest Walters **TOPICS:** New Age **TYPE:** Magazine **DATE:** 1988 **FREQ:** Semi-Annual **CIRC;** 500 **PRICE:** $12.00 **DESCRIPTION:** Deals with magic & spiritual growth & transformation in an atmosphere of undertanding and support.

Earth-Light Network, Inc.
8111 Lagos De Campo Boulevard
Ft. Lauderdale, FL 33321
(305)-721-8585
CONTACT: Beverly L. Brenner, M.S., Dir. **TOPICS:** New Age, Metaphysics, Spirituality **FOUNDED:** 1988 **DESCRIPTION:** Non-profit organization. Spiritually & metaphysically oriented. Focus is to raise the consciousness of people to the realization that we are all Citizens Of The Earth & that we need to have a Planetaryt Perspective. We all have a common purpose: To create a better world filled with peace, love & harmony. **PUBLICATIONS:** *Earth-Light Network Newsletter* **PUBLISHER:** Beverley L. Brenner, M.S. **TOPICS:** New Age, Metaphysics, Spirituality **TYPE:** Newsletter; 6 pgs. **DESCRIPTION:** Reports on the occurrences & philosophies of the Earth-Light Network organization. Offers a Calendar of Events, articles & commentaries on timely issues.

Earthsong
P.O. Box 39234
Phoenix, AZ 85069
TOPICS: Witchcraft

Earthstewards Network
Box 10697
Bainbridge Island, WA 98110
(206)-842-7986
CONTACT: Danaan Parry, Dir. **TOPICS:** New Age

Earthwatch
680 Mount Auburn Street
Watertown, MA 02272
(617)-926-8200
TOPICS: New Age

East West Academy Of Healing Arts (EWAHA)

P.O. Box 31211
San Francisco, CA 94131
(415)-285-9400
CONTACT: Dr. Effie Chow, Pres. TOPICS: New Age

Eastern Christian Outreach
5909 Elmhurst
Philadelphia, PA 19149
TOPICS: Skepticism, Counter-Cult DESCRIPTION: New Age, New And Unconventional Religions, Occult, Paganism.

Eastern Holistic Health Association
50 Maple Place
Manhasset, NY 11030
(516)-365-7590
TOPICS: Holistic Healing PUBLICATIONS: *Holistic Health Forum* EDITOR: Scott Wilson TOPICS: Holistic Healing TYPE: Newsletter

Ecclesia Gnostica Mysterious
3437 Alma Street, Ste. 23
Palo Alto, CA 94306
(415)-494-7412
TOPICS: Metaphysics

Echenian Church
P.O. Box 11893
Reno, NV 89510
TOPICS: Metaphysics

Eckankar
P.O. Box 27300
Minneapolis, MN 55427
(612)-544-3001
CONTACT: Diane Sorenson TOPICS: Spirituality, Parapsychology, Reincarnation, Past Life Regression AFF ORG: Illuminated Way Publishing DESCRIPTION: Religion that fosters beliefs in reincarnation, out-of-body experiences, soul travel, etc.

Eckankar
12 Birch Avenue
Toronto, ON, M4V1C8, Canada
TOPICS: Metaphysics

Eclipse
205 Neptune Avenue
Dorval, BC, H9S2L3, Canada
TOPICS: Witchcraft

Ecological Entrepreneurs Network, The
9100 Wilshire Boulevard, #211
Beverly Hills, CA 90212
(213)-275-1930
CONTACT: Carol Houst Or Marilyn Dunkel TOPICS: New Age

Ecosophical Research Association
P.O. Box 982
Ukiah, CA 95482
TOPICS: Metaphysics

Ecumenicon
404 East Melbourne
Silver Spring, MD 20901
TOPICS: Metaphysics

Emissary Foundation International (EFI)
4817 N. County Road 29
Loveland, CO 80537
(303)-679-4300
CONTACT: Diana Soto, Admin. TOPICS: New Age, Holistic Health, Spirituality

Emissary Foundation International
936 North 34th, Suite 204
Seattle, WA 98103
TOPICS: Metaphysics

End Of The World Enterprises
11684 Ventur Boulevard, 332
Studio City, CA 91604
TOPICS: Metaphysics

Environmental Action, Inc.
1525 New Hampshire Avenue, N.W.
Washington, DC 20036
(202)-745-4870
TOPICS: Holistic Healing PUBLICATIONS: *Environmental Action* TOPICS: Holistic Healing TYPE: Magazine PUBLICATIONS: *Powerline* TOPICS: Holistic Healing TYPE: Magazine PUBLICATIONS: *Wasteline* TOPICS: Holistic Healing TYPE: Magazine

Environmental Defense Fund
257 Park Avenue South
New York, NY 10010
(212)-505-2100
TOPICS: Holistic Healing

Environmental Policy Institute/Friends Of The Earth
218 D Street SE
Washington, DC 20003
(202)-544-2600
TOPICS: Holistic Healing

Equippers Countercult Ministries
4621 Soria Drive
San Diego, CA 92115
TOPICS: Skepticism, Counter-Cult DESCRIPTION: Mormonism, Jehovah's Witnesses, Cults, New Age, Satanism, etc.

Esotericon
P.O. Box 22775
Elizabeth, NJ 07101
TOPICS: Metaphysics

ESP Lab Of Texas
Box 216, 219 Southridge
Edgewood, TX 75117
TOPICS: Metaphysics

ESP Methods
P.O. Box 586
Loomis, CA 95650-0586
TOPICS: Metaphysics

Essene Teachings, Inc.
3427 Denson Place
Charlotte, NC 28215
TOPICS: Metaphysics, New Age, Channeling, Holistic Healing, Metaphysics

Esteves Productions
2675 West Highway 89-A

Sedona, AZ 86336
TOPICS: Metaphysics

Eureka Society (ES)
P.O. Box 1139
La Grange, TX 78945
(409)-968-3587
CONTACT: Bruce K. Avenell, Dir. TOPICS: New Age

Eurythemy Association Of North America
224 Hungry Hollow Road
Spring Valley, NY 10977
TOPICS: Occult

Evergreen Forest Coven
P.O. Box 61134
Raleigh, NC 27661
TOPICS: Witchcraft

Ex-Jehovah's Witnesses
P.O. Box 279
Fate, TX 75032
TOPICS: Skepticism, Counter-Cult DESCRIPTION: Cults, New Age, Satanism, etc.

Ex-Mormons And Christian All
P.O. Box 530
Orangedale, CA 95662
TOPICS: Skepticism, Counter-Cult DESCRIPTION: Mormonism. Cults, New Age, Satanism, etc.

Ex-Mormons For Jesus
P.O. Box 5194
Lakeland, FL 33807
TOPICS: Skepticism, Counter-Cult DESCRIPTION: Mormonism, New Age, Paganism, Freemasonr, New Religions.

Ex-Mormons For Jesus
P.O. Box 374
Orange, CA 92666
TOPICS: Skepticism, Counter-Cult DESCRIPTION: Mormonism. Cults, New Age, Satanism, etc.

Ex-Watchtower Slaves
P.O. Box 1162
Logansport, IN 46947
TOPICS: Skepticism, Counter-Cult DESCRIPTION: Jehovah's Witnesses. Cults, New Age, Satanism, etc.

Exceptional Cancer Patient (ECaP)
1302 Chapel Street
New Haven, CT 06511
(203)-865-8392
CONTACT: Bernie Siegel, M.D. TOPICS: Holistic Health

Exposing Satan's Power Ministry
P.O. Box 11029
St. Petersburg, FL 33733
TOPICS: Skepticism, Counter-Cult DESCRIPTION: New Age, New And Unconventional Religions, Occult, Paganism.

Extraterrestrial Earth Mission
4021 Southeast 46th Street
Oklahoma City, OK 73135
TOPICS: UFO's

Eyes Of Learning
P.O. Box 8007

Hicksville, NY 11802
TOPICS: Metaphysics

Fair-Witness Project, Inc. (FWP)
4219 West Olive Avenue, Ste. 247
Burbank, CA 91505
(213)-962-5687 (213)-463-0542
CONTACT: William L. Moore/Jaime H. Shandera
TOPICS: Psychic Phenomena, UFO's, Occult
FOUNDED: 1984 **MEM:** 600 **STAFF:** 3 **BUDGET:**
$25,00000 **CONVENTIONS:** Annually in Los
Angeles area. **DESCRIPTION:** Non-member
organization investigates and publishes information
about high-strangeness paranormal events, UFO's,
psychic/occult phenomena. Nine member board of
directors, plus advisory board. **PUBLICATIONS:**
Focus **EDITOR:** William L. Moore, Jimmy Ward
TOPICS: Psychic Phenomena, UFO's, Occult **TYPE:**
Journal **DATE:** 1985 **SIZE:** 8 1/2 x 11; 32 pgs.
FREQ: quarterly **CIRC:** 800 **PRICE:** $25.00 **TERM:**
yearly **PRICE PER COPY:** $6.00 **DESCRIPTION:**
Features in-depth, fact-filled articles that have been
thoroughly researched on paranormal phenomena &
UFOs. Reports on progress & results of
investigations & research projects undertaken by the
Fair-Witness Project. Heavily evidence oriented.
Avoids speculation, rumor & conjecture. Distributed
in 48 states & 20 foreign countries.

Fanscifiaroan Church Wicca
P.O. Box 145
Marion, CT 06444
CONTACT: Frank Hedgecock, Elder **TOPICS:**
Witchcraft, Spirituality, New Age, Herbalogy
FOUNDED: 1980 **DESCRIPTION:** Deals with
witchcraft, Native American traditions, herbalogy,
religions, mysticism, nature, psychic development &
the Spirit. Follows the laws of the Goddess & God.
Has Full Moon Rites & Sabbat celebrations. Offers
lectures, meetings & classes in Spells, herb lore,
animal & human rights, visualization, visionary
experiences, spiritual enlightenment & the
environment. Meets weekly & at Full Moon events.
PUBLICATIONS: *The Enchanting News* **EDITOR:**
Frank Hedgecock **TOPICS:** Spirituality, Witchcraft,
New Age **TYPE:** Booklet **DATE:** 1990 **SIZE:** 8 1/2 x
11; 70 pgs. **FREQ:** 6 x per year **PRICE:** $24.00
PRICE PER COPY: $6.00 **DESCRIPTION:** In search
of lost traditions. Deals with witchcraft, the love of
the earth, the unknown, philosophy & traditions of
the craft. Free to all who contribute articles or ads.

Farm Midwifery Center
The Farm
156 Drakes Lane
Summertown, TN 38483
(615)-964-3574
TOPICS: Birth

Farwander Fellowship
P.O. Box 1725
APO New York, NY 09130
TOPICS: Witchcraft

Federation Interplanetary Sightings
P.O. Box 627
Rochester, NH 03867
TOPICS: UFO's

Federation Of Astrologers
69 Center Avenue
Cheektowaga, NY 14277
TOPICS: Astrology

Federation Of Egalitarian Communities
Box 6B2, FS3
Tecumseh, MO 65760
(417)-679-4682
TOPICS: New Age

Federation Of Scientific Astrologers
2022 Ferrier Road
Eden, NY 14057
TOPICS: Astrology

Federation Of Spiritualist Church
1500 Portola Drive
San Francisco, CA 94127
TOPICS: Metaphysics

Fellow Seekers
P.O. Box 159
Prospect, KY 40059
TOPICS: Metaphysics

Fellowship For Spiritual Understanding (FSU)
P.O. Box 816
Palos Verdes Estates, CA 90274
(213)-373-2669
CONTACT: Marcus Bach, Ph.D., Dir. **TOPICS:** New
Age

Fellowship Foundation
P.O. Box 1300
Boyes Hot Springs, CA 95416
TOPICS: Metaphysics

Fellowship Of Pan
P.O. Box 58024
Houston, TX 77258
TOPICS: Witchcraft

Fellowship Spiral Path
P.O. Box 5521
Berkeley, CA 94705
TOPICS: Witchcraft

Fellowship Universal Guidance
1524 West Glen Oaks Boulevard
Glendale, CA 91201
TOPICS: Metaphysics

Financial Astrology Forecast
P.O. Box 8032
La Jolla, CA 92038
TOPICS: Astrology

Finding Our Own Ways (FOOW)
P.O. Box 1545
Lawrence, KS 66044
CONTACT: Toby, Editor & Coordinator **TOPICS:**
New Age

Fire Escape Ministry
233 Elgin
Forest Park, IL 60130
TOPICS: Skepticism, Counter-Cult **DESCRIPTION:**
New Age, New And Unconventional Religions, etc.

First American Spiritualist Assembly
2276 East Keys
Springfield, IL 62702
TOPICS: New Age

First Century Ministries
P.O. Box 37825
Phoenix, AZ 85069
TOPICS: Skepticism, Counter-Cult **DESCRIPTION:**
New Age, Miscellaneous New Religions, Eastern
Mysticism, etc.

First Christians' Essene Church
2536 Collier Avenue
San Diego, CA 92116
TOPICS: Spirituality, Holistic Health, New Age,
Vegetarianism

First Church Of Religious Science
12875 Fee Fee Road
St. Louis, MO 63134
TOPICS: Metaphysics

First Spiritualist Church
3777 42nd Street
San Diego, CA 92105
TOPICS: Metaphysics

Flat Earth Research Society International
P.O. Box 2533
Lancaster, CA 93539
(805)-727-1635
CONTACT: Charles K. Johnson, Pres. **TOPICS:** New
Age **DESCRIPTION:** Adheres to the philosophy that
it is a proven fact that the Earth is flat, that the Sun
& Moon move & that the Earth does not. Believes
that Science is a weird, occult, senseless theory &
that by discarding all scientific thoughts, the mind
becomes free. **PUBLICATIONS:** *Flat Earth News*
EDITOR: Charles K. Johnson **TOPICS.** New Age
TYPE: Newsletter **FREQ:** quarterly **PRICE:** $10.00
TERM: yearly **PRICE PER COPY:** $5.00
DESCRIPTION: Each issue contains further proof of
the fact- Earth is flat. Aim is to promote facts, logic,
reason & sanity.

Floating Healing Meditation Circle (F.H.M.C.)
P.O. Box 13
Uniondale, NY 11553
(516)-433-9118 (516)-483-7264
CONTACT: Brother Frank Revels-Bey **TOPICS:**
Meditation, Tai Chi, Spirituality, Parapsychology
FOUNDED: 1985 **STAFF:** 11 **GROUPS:** 2 **AFF ORG:**
Sylvan Society; Individuals Against Mediocrity
CONVENTIONS: New York area on continuous basis
DESCRIPTION: Unique circle devoted to aiding the
elevation of humanity through meditation & intuitive
arts, which also includes a new t'ai chi form called
I.S.A. Participants enhance skills through meditative
contact with nature & higher spiritual realms. Free
membership for all those who desire to live a more
positive life. Meeting place is within the individuals
inner most chamber of heart & mind.
PUBLICATIONS: *Inner Spiritual Attunement
Pamphlet* **TYPE:** Booklet

Florida UFO Study Group
205 North Brown Avenue
Orlando, FL 32801
TOPICS: UFO's

Flying Monkey Foundation
2618-B Hillsborough Road
Durham, NC 27705
TOPICS: Metaphysics

Flying Witch Farm
P.O. Box AB
Rielelsville, PA 18077
TOPICS: Witchcraft

FOCUS
2567 Columbus Avenue
Oceanside, NY 11572
TOPICS: Skepticism, Counter-Cult DESCRIPTION:
New Age, New And Unconventional Religions,
Occult, Paganism.

Focusing Institute
Fine Arts Building, Suite 212
410 South Michigan Avenue
Chicago, IL 60605
(312)-922-9277
TOPICS: Body-Mind Connection

Foreign Services Research Institute & Wheat Forders
Box 6317
Washington, DC 20015-0317
(202)-362-1588
CONTACT: John E. Whiteford Boyle, Pres. TOPICS:
New Age FOUNDED: 1974 STAFF: 3 BUDGET:
$100,00000 DESCRIPTION: Supervises American
cultural studies research. Publishes various research
projects & Primers for the Age of Inner Space.
Affiliated with the International Association For
Near-Death Studies.

Forever Forests
P.O. Box 312
Redwood Valley, CA 95470
TOPICS: Witchcraft

Fortean Research Center
P.O. Box 94627
Lincoln, NE 68509
(402)-483-7284
CONTACT: Scott II. Colborn, Dir. TOPICS: UFO's,
Paranormal Phenomena, Big Foot, Psychic
Phenomena FOUNDED: 1982 CONVENTIONS:
Holds meetings first Sunday of each month, four
dinners per year & one International Conference
each May. DESCRIPTION: Non-profit organization
staffed by volunteers. Purpose is to investigate all
aspects of unexplained phenomena including UFO's,
cryptozoological mysteries, animal sightings,
geological & archeological anomalies, psychic &
paranormal phenomena & all other areas of study
which may provide data useful to the resolution of
these perplexing mysteries. $15 per year
membership. Also offers, Exploring Unexplained
Phenomena, a weekly radio talk program on KZUM
89.3 FM, hosted by Scott Colborn & Dale Bacon.
PUBLICATIONS: *The Journal Of The Fortean
Research Center* EDITOR: Frank Dreier TOPICS:
Big Foot, Psychic Phenomena, Paranormal
Phenomena, UFO's TYPE: Journal DATE: 1982
FREQ: quarterly PRICE PER COPY: $3.50
DESCRIPTION: Reports on the work of the Fortean
Research Center & various aspects of paranormal
phenomena. Free with membership.

Forum, The (TF)
P.O. Box 5915
Santa Fe, NM 87502
(505)-983-3962
CONTACT: Carol Bell Knight, Dir. TOPICS: Body-
Mind Connection, Spirituality, Metaphysics
FOUNDED: 1969 STAFF: 4 BUDGET: $56,00000

AFF ORG: Mankind Research Foundation,
Maryland CONVENTIONS: Weekly inspirational
Sunday meetings. Classes, University Plaza, Santa
Fe, NM. DESCRIPTION: Offers seminars and classes
in consciousness transformation, world lecture tours,
published materials, and a New Alexandrian
Library. PUBLICATIONS: *And So It Is* TOPICS:
Body-Mind Connection, Spirituality, Metaphysics
TYPE: Newsletter PRICE: $12.00 TERM: yearly
PUBLICATIONS: *Passing The Torch, The Way Of
The Avatar* TOPICS: Body-Mind Connection,
Spirituality, Metaphysics TYPE: Book PRICE:
$8.00

Foundation Church Of Divine Truth
P.O. Box 66003
Washington, DC 20035-6003
CONTACT: Kathryn Stokes TOPICS: Metaphysics,
Channeling FOUNDED: 1985 DESCRIPTION: A by-
mail, non-profit Christian Spiritualist Church which
spreads the Truths of God's Divine Love as revealed
in this century by Jesus of Nazareth through the
channeled messages of James E. Padgett & Dr.
Daniel G. Samuels. A Ministerial ordination
program is offered to spread the Truths through
ministering, teaching, lecturing, healing, channeling
or spiritual counselling. Membership open to all who
spiritually & morally uphold the purpose of the
church. No fee. Sells publications & quarterly
newsletter.

Foundation For Advancement In Cancer Therapy
Box 1242
Old Chelsea Station
New York, NY 10113
(212)-741-2790
TOPICS: Holistic Healing

Foundation For Ancient Therapies
115 South Top Can Boulevard, 141
Topanga, CA 90290
TOPICS: Metaphysics

Foundation For Astrological Sciences
6600 York Road
Suite 105
Baltimore, MD 21212
CONTACT: Kelly Anderson, Dir. TOPICS:
Astrology

Foundation For Christian Psychic Research, Inc.
351 Main Street
Ridgefield, CT 06877
TOPICS: Parapsychology, Occult, Metaphysics
PUBLICATIONS: *Soul Searcher* TOPICS:
Parapsychology, Occult TYPE: Book DATE: 1977
PRICE: $0.00 TERM: Members PRICE PER COPY:
$6.00

Foundation For Homeopathic Education And Research
5916 Chabot Crest
Oakland, CA 94618
(415)-420-8791
TOPICS: Holistic Healing

Foundation For Inner Guidance
P.O. Box 335
Corte Madera, CA 94925
TOPICS: Metaphysics

Foundation For Inner Peace-Course In Miracles
P.O. Box 635
Tiburon, CA 94920
TOPICS: Metaphysics, Channeling

Foundation For Mind Research
P.O. Box 600
Pomona, NY 10970
CONTACT: Jean Houston, Dir. TOPICS:
Metaphysics, New Age, Psychology

Foundation For UFO Research
P.O. Box 182
Tucson, AZ 85702
TOPICS: UFO's

Foundation Of Human Understanding (FHU)
8780 Venice Boulevard
Los Angeles, CA 90034
(213)-559-3711
CONTACT: Roy Masters, Pres. TOPICS: New Age

Foundation Of Thanatology
630 West 168th Street
New York, NY 10032
TOPICS: Occult

Foundation Of Truth, Incorporated
P.O. Box 7133
Atlanta, GA 30309
TOPICS: Metaphysics

Fountain Of Eternal Youth
P.O. Box 9546
Phoenix, AZ 85068
TOPICS: Metaphysics

Fountain Of Light
7877 Jefferson Highway
Baton Rouge, LA 70809
TOPICS: Metaphysics, Channeling

Four Directions Foundation
632 Oak Street
San Francisco, CA 94117
TOPICS: Metaphysics, Channeling

Four Winds Foundation
P.O. Box 948
Sausalito, CA 94966
(415)-321-2106
TOPICS: New Age

Fox Valley UFO Group
1317 Green Valley Dr.
Neenah, WI 54956
TOPICS: UFO's

Fraternity For Canadian Astrologers
P.O. Box 4924 Station E
Ottawa, Ontario K1S 5J1
Canada
TOPICS: Astrology PUBLICATIONS: *Directions*
EDITOR: Marilyn F. Waram, Susan Kelly TOPICS:
Astrology TYPE: Newsletter

Fraternity Of Hidden Light
P.O. Box 5094
Covina, CA 91723
TOPICS: Metaphysics

Free Soul
P.O. Box 1762
Sedona, AZ 86336
CONTACT: Pete A. Sanders, Jr. **TOPICS:**
Metaphysics, Psychic **FOUNDED:** 1980
DESCRIPTION: Non-profit psychic educational
program dedicated to helping people pioneer their
inner technology. 200 instructors nationwide.

Free Spirit Alliance
P.O. Box 589
Bladensburg, MD 20710
TOPICS: Witchcraft

Free Templer Order
P.O. Box 1132
Fremont, CA 94538
(510)-796-9195
CONTACT: Nelson White **TOPICS:** Metaphysics,
Occult, Spirituality **DESCRIPTION:** An independent
Ancient Germanic Knightly Order seeking to
preserve & perpetuate the medieval lifestyle &
virtues of honor, truth & service. Headquarters in
Vienna, Austria. Members must speak or be studying
German. Membership expensive & all members must
travel to Austria.

Free The Masons Ministry
P.O. Box 1077
Issaquah, WA 98027
TOPICS: Skepticism, Counter-Cult **DESCRIPTION:**
Freemasonry in all forms.

Freemagicland
P.O. Box 94
Albuquerque, NM 87103
TOPICS: Metaphysics

Freewill Foundation, The
7210 Jordan Avenue D-23
Canoga Park, CA 91304
TOPICS: Metaphysics

Friends Of-I Am
P.O. Box 7525
Middletown, CA 95461
TOPICS: Metaphysics

Friends Vegetarian Society Of North America
P.O. Box 53168
Washington, DC 20009
TOPICS: Health Food

Fund For UFO Research, Inc. (FUFOR)
P.O. Box 277
Mt. Rainier, MD 20712
(703)-684-6032
CONTACT: Bruce S. Maccabee, Ph.D.,Chm.
TOPICS: UFO's **MEM:** 15 **DESCRIPTION:** Non-
profit scientific & educational corporation. Raises
money to support projects & grants dedicated to all
forms of UFO research including historical &
psychological. Information & brochures availabe
upon written request.

G-JO Institute
4950 S.W. 70th Avenue
Davie, FL 33314
(305)-791-1562

CONTACT: Michael Blate, Exec. Dir. **TOPICS:**
Holistic Health, Acupuncture, Reflexology
FOUNDED: 1976 **MEM:** 3,000 **DESCRIPTION:** A
non-profit natural health and spiritual educational
organization offering books, audio/video materials &
self-help programs for wellness. Sells wholesale,
retail, through distributors & mail-order.

Gaia Network
P.O. Box 49441
Colorado Springs, CO 80949
TOPICS: Witchcraft

Garden Of Sanjivani
P.O. Box 712
Santa Cruz, CA 95060
TOPICS: Metaphysics

Gather Of Affinity And Light
428 Coronado Avenue 7
Long Beach, CA 90814
TOPICS: Channeling

Gathering Together
11408 Audelia Road, 2474
Dallas, TX 75243
TOPICS: Skepticism, Counter-Cult **DESCRIPTION:**
Mormons, RLDS, New And Unconventional
Religions, New Age.

Gaudiya Vaishnava Society
1307 Church Street
San Francisco, CA 94114
(415)-372-6002 (415)-826-2115
CONTACT: Thomas Beaudry **TOPICS:** New Age,
Astrology, Holistic Health, Paranormal Phenomena
PUBLICATIONS: Clarion Call **EDITOR:** Thomas
Beaudry, Jack Hebner **TOPICS:** New Age, Holistic
Health, Astrology, Paranormal Phenomena **TYPE:**
Magazine **DATE:** 1988; 64 pgs. **FREQ:** quarterly
CIRC: 30,000 **PRICE:** $15.00 **TERM:** yearly
DESCRIPTION: Covers different topics in each issue
pertaining to New Age, health, Astrology,
paranormal occurences, lost civilizations, etc. Also
offers editorials, reviews & advertising. Publishes
book reviews and articles.

Gela Numerology
P.O. Box 265
Delanson, NY 12053
TOPICS: Metaphysics

Gene Aven Ministries
P.O. Box 1000
Bow, WA 98232
TOPICS: Skepticism, Counter-Cult **DESCRIPTION:**
New Age, New And Unconventional Religions,
Humanism, Occult.

General Assembly Of Spirituality
2107 Broadway
New York, NY 10023
TOPICS: New Age

Genesis II
11480 East 111th Street
Noblesville, IN 46060
(317)-845-9999
TOPICS: Channeling, New Age **DESCRIPTION:**
Meetings, workshops & channeling focused on
personal truth & responsibility.

Georgian Church, The

1908 Verde Street
Bakersfield, CA 93304
TOPICS: Witchcraft

Gerdjief Group
2036 16th Avenue
Forest Grove, OR 97116
TOPICS: Metaphysics

Ghost Research Society
P.O. Box 205
Oaklawn, IL 60454-0205
(708)-425-5163
CONTACT: Dale Kaczmarek, Pres. **TOPICS:** Ghosts,
Psychic Phenomena, Parapsychology, Reincarnation,
Past Life Regression, New Age **FOUNDED:** 1982
MEM: 148 **STAFF:** 4 **COMPUTER:** yes
CONVENTIONS: Annually in Chicago suburbs
DESCRIPTION: A membership organization devoted
to the study of ghosts, hauntings, poltergeists and
life-after-death. Various types of memberships
available includes Sustaining-opportunity to come
along with other members on field excursions and
Contributing-offers free newspaper clipping service.
Publishes Ghost Trackers Newletter.
PUBLICATIONS: Astrology Directory **EDITOR:**
Dale Kaczmarek **TOPICS:** Astrology **TYPE:**
Directory **PRICE:** $6.50 **DESCRIPTION:** Contains
names of individuals, groups, organizations,
magazines & newsletters on the topic.
PUBLICATIONS: Ghost Trackers Newsletter
EDITOR: Dale Kaczmarek **TOPICS:** Ghosts, Psychic
Phenomena, Parapsychology, Reincarnation, Past
Life Regression, New Age **TYPE:** Newsletter **DATE:**
1982, 24 pgs. **FREQ:** tri-annually **CIRC;** 200
PRICE: $10.00 **PRICE PER COPY:** $4.00
DESCRIPTION: Publishes articles, news, criticisms,
reviews, cartoons, photography, ads and illustrations
that deal with ghosts and life after death.
PUBLICATIONS: Glossary Of Occult Terms
EDITOR: Dale Kaczmarek **TOPICS:** Occult **TYPE:**
Directory **PRICE:** $6.50 **DESCRIPTION:** Lists the
most frequently used terms, references & words
pertaining to the Occult. **PUBLICATIONS:** Greater
Chicagoland Psychic Directory **EDITOR:** Dale
Kaczmarek **TOPICS:** Ghosts, Psychic Phenomena,
Parapsychology, Reincarnation, Past Life Regression
TYPE: Directory **PRICE:** $7.00 **PUBLICATIONS:**
International Directory of Psychic Sciences
EDITOR: Dale Kaczmarek **TOPICS:** Ghosts, Psychic
Phenomena, Parapsychology, Reincarnation, Past
Life Regression **TYPE:** Directory **PRICE:** $7.00
PUBLICATIONS: National Catalog Of Occult
Bookstores **EDITOR:** Dale Kaczmarek **TOPICS:**
Occult **TYPE:** Directory **PRICE:** $6.50
DESCRIPTION: Cross-country list of Occult
Bookstores, hours of operation & their specialties.
PUBLICATIONS: National Register Of Haunted
Locations **EDITOR:** Dale Kaczmarek **TOPICS:**
Ghosts, Parapsychology **TYPE:** Directory **PRICE:**
$6.50 **DESCRIPTION:** Lists haunted locations,
houses & landmarks in the U.S. Gives hours of
operations, tours & reference books.
PUBLICATIONS: Northwest Indiana Psychic
Directory **EDITOR:** Dale Kaczmarek **TOPICS:**
Ghosts, Psychic Phenomena, Parapsychology,
Reincarnation, Past Life Regression **TYPE:**
Directory **PRICE:** $7.00 **PUBLICATIONS:** Occult
Publications **EDITOR:** Dale Kaczmarek **TOPICS:**
Ghosts, Psychic Phenomena, Parapsychology,
Reincarnation, Past Life Regression, Metaphysics,
Holistic Health **TYPE:** Directory **PRICE:** $6.50
DESCRIPTION: Lists newsletters, tabloids,

directories, encyclopedias, etc. dealing with the occult. Includes Parapsychology, Metaphysics, Demonology, Holistic Health. **PUBLICATIONS:** *Special Interest Directory* **EDITOR:** Dale Kaczmarek **TOPICS:** Ghosts, Psychic Phenomena, Parapsychology, Reincarnation, Past Life Regression **TYPE:** Directory **PUBLICATIONS:** *UFOlogy Directory* **EDITOR:** Dale Kaczmarek **TOPICS:** Astrology **TYPE:** Directory **PRICE:** $6.50 **DESCRIPTION:** Contains names of individuals, groups, organizations, magazines & newsletters on the topic. **PUBLICATIONS:** *Witchcraft/Paganism Directory* **EDITOR:** Dale Kaczmarek **TOPICS:** Astrology **TYPE:** Directory **PRICE:** $6.50 **DESCRIPTION:** Contains names of individuals, groups, organizations, magazines & newsletters on the topic.

Global Tomorrow Coalition
1325 G Street NW
Suite 915
Washington, DC 20005
(202)-628-4016
TOPICS: Holistic Healing

Gnostic Association
42 Cummer Avenue
Willowdale, ON, M2M2E4,
Canada
TOPICS: Metaphysics

Gnostic Association, The
P.O. Box 291488
Los Angeles, CA 90029
TOPICS: Metaphysics

Gnostic Society
2229 Southeast Market Street
Portland, OR 97214
TOPICS: Metaphysics

Goddess Images
P.O. Box 15669
Long Beach, CA 90801
TOPICS: Witchcraft

Goddess Womyn Network
P.O. Box 17312
Phoenix, AZ 85011
TOPICS: Witchcraft

Golden Circlet Crown
P.O. Box 19903
Raleigh, NC 27612
TOPICS: Witchcraft

Golden Word
P.O. Box 1953
Sedona, AZ 86336
TOPICS: Metaphysics, Channeling

Good News Defenders
P.O. Box 8007
La Jolla, CA 92038
TOPICS: Skepticism, Counter-Cult **DESCRIPTION:** Jehovah's Witnesses. Cults, New Age, Satanism, etc.

Good News Stand, The
P.O. Box 2113
Gary, IN 46409
TOPICS: Skepticism, Counter-Cult **DESCRIPTION:** Mormonism, Jehovah's Witnesses, Catholicism, New Age, etc.

Grace And Truth Ministries
Box 1227
Fort Erie, Ont. L2A5Y2,
Canada
TOPICS: Skepticism, Counter-Cult **DESCRIPTION:** Jehovah's Witnesses, Mormonism, Cults, New Age, Satanism, etc.

Greater Washington, DC Association Of Professionals Practicing The Transcendental Meditation Program
1801 Quincy Street, N.W.
Washington, DC 20011
(301)-495-3111
CONTACT: A.J.Rachele, PR Dir. **TOPICS:** New Age

Green Alliance Network
P.O. Box 23
Bellingen, New South Wales 2454
Australia
TOPICS: New Age

Green Committees Of Correspondence
National Clearinghouse
P.O. Box 30208
Kansas City, MO 64112
(816)-931-9366
TOPICS: Holistic Healing

Greenleaf Fellowship
Rural Delivery 2, Box 305A
Williston, VT 05495
TOPICS: Skepticism, Counter-Cult **DESCRIPTION:** New Age, New And Unconventional Religions, Mysticism And Occult.

Greenpeace USA
1436 U Street NW
Washington, DC 20009
(202)-462-1177
TOPICS: New Age, Holistic Health

Greenville UFO Study Group
506 Central Avenue
Maudlin, SC 29662
TOPICS: UFO's

Greenwood Grove
P.O. Box 30908
Seattle, WA 98103
TOPICS: Witchcraft

Greeting Card Creative Network
1350 New York Avenue, North West, Suite 615
Washington, DC 20005
(202)-393-1780
TOPICS: New Age **FOUNDED:** 1988

Ground Saucer Watch (GSW)
13238 N. Seventh Drive
Phoenix, AZ 85029
CONTACT: William H. Spaulding, Dir. **TOPICS:** UFO's

Group Avatar
P.O. Box 41505
Tucson, AZ 85717
TOPICS: Metaphysics

Grove Of Lady Of Twilight
P.O. Box 14264

Madison, WI 53714
TOPICS: Witchcraft

Grove Of The Unicorn
P.O. Box 13384
Atlanta, GA 30324
TOPICS: Witchcraft

Guardian Action Publications
P.O. Box 27725
Salt Lake City, UT 84127
TOPICS: UFO's

Guild Communications II
2022 Taraval Street, 8513
San Francisco, CA 94116
TOPICS: Metaphysics

Habitat Institute For The Environment
10 Juniper Road
Box 136
Belmont, MA 02178
(617)-489-5050
TOPICS: New Age

Haelix Plus, Inc.
208 Bass Road
Box 304
Scotland, CT 06264
(203)-456-0646
TOPICS: Body-Mind Connection

Haitian Voodoo
P.O. Box 964
New York, NY 10150
TOPICS: Metaphysics

Hanuman Foundation (HF)
Box 478
Santa Fe, NM 87504
CONTACT: Jai Lakshman, Pres. **TOPICS:** New Age

Harmonial Philosophy Association
P.O. Box 277
Cassadaga, FL 32706
TOPICS: Metaphysics

Harmonic Connection With Jean
P.O. Box 4843
Stockton, CA 95204
TOPICS: Metaphysics

Harmony Grove Spiritualist
Rural Route 5, Box 179
Escondido, CA 92025
TOPICS: Metaphysics

Haunt Hunters (HH)
2188 Sycamore Hill Court
Chesterfield, MO 63017
(314)-831-1379
CONTACT: Gordon J. Hoener, Dir. **TOPICS:** Psychic Phenomena **FOUNDED:** 1965 **MEM:** 350 **DESCRIPTION:** Founded by Philip L. Goodwilling, Pres. Investigates & reports on psychic phenomena, especially ghosts & hauntings. Members in 17 countries.

Healers League Of The National Spiritualist Association Of Churches
8521 Worthington Boulevard
Westerville, OH 43081

(614)-895-0873
CONTACT: Rev. Neil Griffen, Pres. TOPICS: New Age

Healing Seminars
P.O. Box 327
New City, NY 10956
(914)-634-2450
TOPICS: Reiki

Healing Through Arts
28 Plain Road
Wayland, MA 01778
(207)-367-5076
TOPICS: Holistic Healing PUBLICATIONS: *Rose Window* EDITOR: Kay Gardner TOPICS: Holistic Healing TYPE: Book

Health Foundation
19, Peel Road Douglas
Isle Of Man,
United Kingdom
073-081-4154
CONTACT: Ivan U. Ghyssaert, Dr. Sc., Ph. D. TOPICS: Holistic Health, Crystals DESCRIPTION: Founded & directed by Dr. Ivan U. Ghyssaert. Developed a series of natural remedies to stimulate the Immune System. Good results obtained in the treatment of HIV positive & AIDS patients. Treatments are available at reasonable cost. Donations welcome. Works with gems, crystals, Radiesthesia, colors, trace elements, planetary energies.

Health Resource
209 Katherine Drive
Conway, AR 72032
(501)-329-5272
TOPICS: Holistic Healing

Healthy Back, Healthy Mind Institute
4150 Tivoli Avenue
Los Angeles, CA 90066
(213)-306-8845 FAX (213)-306-4632
TOPICS: Holistic Healing

Healthy Lifestyle
1 Penn Plaza, 100
New York, NY 10119
TOPICS: Holistic Health

Heartland Library
2237 Morse
Chicago, IL 60645
TOPICS: Metaphysics

Heartland Spiritual Alliance (HSA)
P.O. Box 3407
Kansas City, KS 66103
(816)-561-6111
CONTACT: Rhiannon Bennett, Pres. TOPICS: Paganism, New Age, Spirituality FOUNDED: 1988 MEM: 30 DESCRIPTION: Pagan organization sponsoring the Heartland Pagan Festival, Pagan Parenting Group & the Spirit Circle a class & networking group which meets once a month. Members local, in 16 States & in Canada. Also publishes the HSA News. PUBLICATIONS: *HSA News* TYPE: Newsletter FREQ: 8 x per year

Heartstone
P.O. Box 2283
Upper Darby, PA 19082
TOPICS: Witchcraft

Heartstone Circle
3301 Governors Drive
Huntsville, AL 35805
TOPICS: Witchcraft

Heartstone Connections
P.O. Box 115
Hawleyville, CT 06440
TOPICS: Witchcraft

Help Jesus Ministry, The
P.O. Box 2188, Square 1
Mississauga, Ont. L5B3C7,
Canada
TOPICS: Skepticism, Counter-Cult DESCRIPTION: Jehovah's Witnesses. Cults, Satanism, New Age, etc.

Hemlock Society
Box 11830
Eugene, OR 97440
TOPICS: Death DESCRIPTION: Helps ailing people die with dignity. Operating for more than a decade, it provides alternatives for those facing terminal illness.

Herb Research Foundation
Box 12006
Austin, TX 78711
(512)-331-4244
TOPICS: Herbalogy, Holistic Health PUBLICATIONS: *Herbalgram* EDITOR: Mark Blumenthal TOPICS: Herbalogy TYPE: Magazine

Herb Research Foundation
1007 Pearl Street, Ste. 200
Boulder, CO 80302
(303)-449-2265 (800)-748-2617 FAX (303)-449-7849
CONTACT: Ara Der Marderosian, Ph.D. TOPICS: Herbalogy, Holistic Health DESCRIPTION: Non-profit research & educational organization. Supplies botanical information for medicinal use of plants to members, scientists, doctors, the press & the public. Purpose is to increase professional & public knowledge about herbs especially in preventive medicine & cures for disease. PUBLICATIONS: *Herbal Gram* TOPICS: Herbalogy, Holistic Health TYPE: Journal; 50 pgs. FREQ: quarterly DESCRIPTION: Summaries of the most recent scientific research on herbs, news about government regulations of herbs, international botanicals market report & book reviews. Free to members.

HMA Foundation
P.O. Box 661
Strasburg, CO 80136
TOPICS: Metaphysics

Holistic Dental Association (HDA)
4801 Richmond Square
Oklahoma City, OK 73118
(405)-840-5600
CONTACT: Dr. Paul Plowman, Pres. TOPICS: New Age

Holistic Dental Association
974 North 21st Street
Newark, OH 43055
(614)-366-3309
TOPICS: Holistic Healing

Holistic Health Association Of The Princeton Area
360 Nassau Street
Princeton, NJ 08540
(609)-924-8580
CONTACT: Pat Hite TOPICS: Holistic Health, New Age PUBLICATIONS: *Holistic Health Resource Directory* EDITOR: Pat Hite TOPICS: Holistic Healing TYPE: Directory DESCRIPTION: Serves Central Jersey, Philadelphia and Bucks County areas with listings of practitioners and organizations. Published by the Holistic Health Association of Princeton Area, contains articles, reviews, ads & a calendar. PUBLICATIONS: *Holistic Living* EDITOR: Jackie Schilder-McLaughlin TOPICS: Holistic Healing TYPE: Magazine DESCRIPTION: Published by the Holistic Health Association of the Princeton Area, contains articles, reviews and a calendar.

Holistic Health Havens (HHH)
3419 Thom Boulevard
Las Vegas, NV 89106
(702)-873-4542
CONTACT: Dr. Joseph M Kadans, Pres. TOPICS: New Age

Holistic Health Works, Div. of Spiritual Awareness Dynamics
P.O. Box 327
New City, NY 10956
(914)-634-2450
TOPICS: Holistic Health, Channeling, Crystals PUBLICATIONS: *Advanced Crystal Therapeutics* EDITOR: O. Frank TOPICS: Crystals, Psychic Healing, Spirituality TYPE: Book PRICE: $18.95 PUBLICATIONS: *Crystal Therapeutics: Practitioner's Guide To Healing & Meditation W/Crystals & Gemstones* EDITOR: O. Frank TOPICS: Crystals, Meditation TYPE: Book PRICE: $15.95

Holistic Health/Academy
218 Avenue B
Redondo Beach, CA 90277
TOPICS: Holistic Healing PUBLICATIONS: *Holistic* TOPICS: Holistic Healing TYPE: Newsletter

Holistic Philosophy Consul
409 Marquette Drive
Louisville, KY 40222
TOPICS: Metaphysics

Holistic Resource Association
P.O. Box 563
Rye, NY 10580
TOPICS: Holistic Health PUBLICATIONS: *Holistic Resource Directory* EDITOR: Alan Green, Marc Grossman TOPICS: Holistic Health TYPE: Directory SIZE: 4 x 10 1/2; 40 pgs. PRICE: $0.00 PRICE PER COPY: $0.00 DESCRIPTION: Directory compiled by the Holistic Resource Association.Lists practitioners, health related services and products for Westchester, Fairfield County & the Hudson Valley area.

Holistic Resource Management
P.O. Box 7128
Albuquerque, NM 87194
(505)-242-9272
CONTACT: Susan Allison TOPICS: New Age

Holly And Oak Pagan Group
P.O. Box 5206, Station B

Victoria, BC, V8R6N4,
Canada
TOPICS: Witchcraft

Holy City Community
Rural Route 7, Box 390
Lake Charles, LA 70601
TOPICS: Metaphysics

Holy Grail Chapel
3 Burhans Place
Elsmere, NY 12054
TOPICS: Metaphysics

Holy Mountain Monastery
P.O. Box 1130
Groveland, CA 95321
TOPICS: Metaphysics

Holyearth Foundation (HF)
Box 10697
Bainbridge Island, WA 98110
(206)-842-7986
CONTACT: Danaan Parry, Dir. TOPICS: New Age

Hospice Care
300 East Bay Drive
Largo, FL 34640
(813)-586-4432
TOPICS: Death

House Of Maya
P.O. Box 9831
Fort Worth, TX 76107
TOPICS: Witchcraft

House Of Xaro Occult Supplies
P.O. Box 1933
New Port Richy, FL 34278
TOPICS: Witchcraft

Hubbard Dianetics Foundation
83 McAllister Street
San Francisco, CA 94102
TOPICS: Metaphysics

Hugh G. Carruthers Foundation
P.O. Box 460
Libertyville, IL 60048
TOPICS: Metaphysics

Humacom
P.O. Box 3009
Princeville, HI 96722
TOPICS: Metaphysics

Human Ecology Action League
Box 66637
Chicago, IL 60666
(404)-248-1898
TOPICS: New Age PUBLICATIONS: *Human
Ecologist* TOPICS: New Age TYPE: Newsletter

Huna International (OHI)
P.O. Box 665
Kilauea, HI 96754
(808)-826-9097
CONTACT: Serge King, Ph.D., Exec. Dir. TOPICS:
New Age

Huna Research, Inc. (HUNA)
126 Camellia Drive
Cape Girardeau, MO 63701

(314)-334-3478
CONTACT: Dr. E. Otha Wingo, Pres. TOPICS: New
Age

Huna Universal Ministries
P.O. Box 030397
Fort Lauderdale, FL 33303
TOPICS: Metaphysics

I Am Sanctuary
309 East Coronado
Phoenix, AZ 85004
TOPICS: Metaphysics

Illuminating Motorcycle Club
P.O. Box 9490
Tacoma, WA 98409
TOPICS: Occult

Illuminator, The
Rural Delivery 2, Box 246
Egg Harbor City, NJ 08215
TOPICS: Skepticism, Counter-Cult DESCRIPTION:
Jehovah's Witnesses, New Age, New And
Unconventional Religions.

Illumined Way, The
Clearlight Associates
4265 Round Top Drive
Honolulu, HI 96822
TOPICS: Metaphysics, Channeling

In His Grip Ministries
Route 1, Box 257-E
Crescent City, FL 32012
TOPICS: Skepticism, Counter-Cult DESCRIPTION:
New Age, Islam, Freemasonry, Mystical And
Occult, Paganism.

**Independent Association Of
Spiritualists**
7230 Forest Street, North, 2304
St. Petersburg, FL 33702
TOPICS: Metaphysics

Independent Spiritualist Association
2138 11th Street
Niles, MI 49120
TOPICS: New Age

**Informed Homebirth/Informed Birth
& Parenting**
P.O. Box 3675
Ann Arbor, MI 48106
(313)-662-6857 (313)-449-4181
CONTACT: Rahima Baldwin, Pres. TOPICS: Birth,
Holistic Health, New Age FOUNDED: 1977 MEM:
1,129 STAFF: 4 CONVENTIONS: Annual conference
on The Young Child DESCRIPTION: Provides
alternative birthing, parenting & education
information through written materials & workshops.
Offers training in childbirth education & midwifery
as well as referrals to childbirth educators &
midwives, quarterly newsletter for members, books
& videos, childbirth educators & birth assistant
training programs. PUBLICATIONS: *Special
Delivery* EDITOR: Rahima Baldwin TOPICS: Birth,
Holistic Health TYPE: Newsletter FREQ: quarterly
PRICE: $15.00 DESCRIPTION: Annual, Magical
Years, conference on the young child, April, Ann
Arbor, MI.

Inglewood Study Center

8105 North Pass Road
Everson, WA 98247
TOPICS: Skepticism, Counter-Cult DESCRIPTION:
Cults, New Age, Satanism, New And
Unconventional Religions.

Inn Of The Seventh Ray
128 Old Topanga Road
Topanga, CA 90290
TOPICS: Metaphysics

**Inner Circle Kethra E'Da
Foundation, Inc.**
San Diego, CA 92112-1722
TOPICS: Channeling, Yoga, Meditation, New Age
FOUNDED: 1945 DESCRIPTION: Members meet to
discuss & study the channeled material of Mark
Probert recorded on tape & through transcripts.

Inner Light Foundation
P.O. Box 750265
Petaluma, CA 94975
(707)-765-2200
CONTACT: Betty Bethards TOPICS: Holistic
Healing, Meditation, Spirituality, Psychology,
Psychic FOUNDED: 1969 DESCRIPTION: Non-
profit spiritual, educational, scientific & research
organization providing programs in the development
& understanding of human potential. Teaches basic
meditation techniques & offers lectures & psychic
readings. PUBLICATIONS: *Inner Light Foundation
Newsletter* EDITOR: Marynell Tipton, Betty
Bethards TOPICS: Holistic Healing TYPE:
Newsletter PUBLICATIONS: *The Dream Book*
TOPICS: Holistic Healing TYPE: Book

Inner Links
P.O. Box 16225
Seattle, WA 98116
(206)-937-0783
CONTACT: Kathy Tyler TOPICS: New Age,
Metaphysics

Inner Peace Movement
2326 6th Avenue, 238
Seattle, WA 98121
TOPICS: Metaphysics

Inner Space Interpreters
10633 1/3 Whipple
North Hollywood, CA 91607
TOPICS: Metaphysics

Institute For Astrological Studies
60 St. Clair Avenue, West 8
Toronto, ON, M4V1M7,
Canada
TOPICS: Astrology

Institute For Biogenetics And Gestalt
1307 University Avenue
Berkeley, CA 94702
(415)-849-0101
TOPICS: New Age

**Institute For Development Of Inner
Communications Alternatives**
10670 Barkley, Ste. 332
Overland Park, KS 66612
(913)-383-4632

CONTACT: Iris Tam Denham **TOPICS:** Psychology, Holistic Health, Occult **DESCRIPTION:** Offers counseling in growth, transformation & self-healing.

Institute For Individual And World Peace (IIWP)
2101 Wilshire Boulevard
Santa Monica, CA 90403
(213)-828-0535
CONTACT: Katherine Boussarie, Dir. **TOPICS:** New Age

Institute For Research In Hypnosis And Psychotherapy
1991 Broadway
Suite 18B
New York, NY 10023
(212)-799-2727
CONTACT: Dr. M.V. Kline **TOPICS:** Hypnotism

Institute For UFO Contactee Studies (IFUFOCS)
1425 Steele Street
Laramie, WY 82070
CONTACT: R. Leo Sprinkle, Ph. D. **TOPICS:** UFO's **FOUNDED:** 1980 **CONVENTIONS:** Annual conference last weekend each June **DESCRIPTION:** Small number of members who arrange an annual conference each year for UFO Contactees. Conference proceedings from 1980-1990 are available for $10 each from editor June Parnell, Ph. D.

Institute Of Behavioral Kinesiology
P.O. Drawer 37
Valley Cottage, NY 10989
(914)-268-5144
TOPICS: Holistic Health, New Age **DESCRIPTION:** Offers life energy analysis, music & art, books, tapes, counseling & consulting.

Institute Of Biblical Truth
1533 Mercer Way
Decatur, GA 30035
TOPICS: Skepticism, Counter-Cult **DESCRIPTION:** New Age, Freemasonry, Mormonism, New Religions, etc.

Institute Of Cultural Affairs (IIWP)
2101 Wilshire Boulevard
Santa Monica, CA 90403
(213)-828-0535
CONTACT: Katherine Boussarie, Dir. **TOPICS:** New Age

Institute Of Noetic Sciences
475 Gate Five Road, #300
P.O. Box 909
Sausalito, CA 94966-0909
(415)-331-5650
CONTACT: Edgar D. Mitchell **TOPICS:** Body-Mind Connection, Holistic Health, Spirituality, Past Life Regression, Death, Meditation, Hypnotism **CONVENTIONS:** Annual international conference **DESCRIPTION:** Founded by Apollo astronaut Edgar D. Mitchell,it uses the methods of scientific research to explore the nature and potential of the human mind. Tries to answer the questions: how does our innate mental abilities encourage good health, superior immune functioning, and even self-healing. Goals are to heal ourselves and heal the planet. Three levels of membership available. **PUBLICATIONS:** *Noetic Sciences Bulletin* **TOPICS:**

Body-Mind Connection, Holistic Health, Spirituality, Past Life Regression, Death, Meditation, Hypnotism **TYPE:** Bulletin **FREQ:** quarterly **DESCRIPTION:** Reports on Institute projects, member activites, and upcoming conferences and lectures. **PUBLICATIONS:** *Noetic Sciences Catalog* **TOPICS:** Body-Mind Connection, Holistic Health, Spirituality, Past Life Regression, Death, Meditation, Hypnotism **TYPE:** Catalog **DESCRIPTION:** Resource guide to books and audio and video tapes in related fields of study. **PUBLICATIONS:** *Noetic Sciences Review* **TOPICS:** Body-Mind Connection, Holistic Health, Spirituality, Past Life Regression, Death, Meditation, Hypnotism **TYPE:** Journal **FREQ:** quarterly **DESCRIPTION:** Offers discussion of emerging concepts in consciousness research, the mind-body connection and healing, and our changing global reality. Free to members. **PUBLICATIONS:** *Special Reports* **TOPICS:** Body-Mind Connection, Holistic Health, Spirituality, Past Life Regression, Death, Meditation, Hypnotism **TYPE:** Booklet **DESCRIPTION:** Offers in-depth reports of specific issues such as healing, remission and miracle cures, altered states of consciousness and the possibility of survival of bodily death.

Institute Of Psychic Development, The
2521 Dana Street
Berkeley, CA 94704
TOPICS: Channeling, Occult

Institute Of Relation Therapy
1255 5th Avenue
New York, NY 10029
(212)-410-7712
TOPICS: Spirituality

Institutes For The Enhancement Of Life Energy And Creativity (IELEC)
P.O. Drawer 37
Valley Cottage, NY 10989
(914)-268-5144
TOPICS: Spirituality, New Age **DESCRIPTION:** Offers spiritual development programs & Life Energy Analysis as well as books, tapes & music.

Integrity Electronics And Research
Lynn A. Surgalla
58 Breckenridge Street
Buffalo, NY 14222
TOPICS: Channeling

Inter-National Development, Improvement And Assistance
315 Fifth Avenue
New York, NY 10016
TOPICS: Channeling

Intercontinental UFO Network
35-40 75th Street, 4-G
Jackson Heights, NY 11372
TOPICS: UFO's

Interdimensional Temple Of Light
P.O. Box 1339
Los Alamos, NM 87544
TOPICS: Channeling **PUBLICATIONS:** *Crystal Connection Newsletter* **TOPICS:** Channeling **TYPE:** Newsletter

Interdisc Bible Research
P.O. Box 423

Hatfield, PA 19440
TOPICS: Skepticism, Counter-Cult **DESCRIPTION:** New Age, New And Unconventional Religions, Secular Humanism.

Interface
55 Wheeler Street
Cambridge, MA 02138-1125
TOPICS: Channeling

Internal Affairs Of Ex-Witnesses
P.O. Box 69
Worthville, KY 41098
TOPICS: Skepticism, Counter-Cult **DESCRIPTION:** Jehovah's Witnesses. Cults, Satanism, New Age, etc.

International Academy Holistic Health/Medicine
218 Avenue B
Redondo Beach, CA 90277
(213)-540-0564
TOPICS: Holistic Healing **PUBLICATIONS:** *Holistic & Preventive Update* **TOPICS:** Holistic Healing **TYPE:** Newsletter

International Association For Near Death Studies (IANDS)
c/o University Health Center
Dept. Of Psychiatry
Farmington, CT 06032
TOPICS: New Age

International Association For Near-Death Studies (IANDS)
P.O. Box 7767
Philadelphia, PA 19101-7767
(215)-947-4044
CONTACT: Elizabeth W. Fenske, Ph.D., Pres. **TOPICS:** Death **FOUNDED:** 1980 **MEM:** 800 **GROUPS:** 40 worldwide **CONVENTIONS:** Conducts numerous annual conferences in varied locations. **DESCRIPTION:** Founded by Dr. Kenneth Ring for professionals studying the Near Death Experience. Conducts research & provides written reports or lectures on related subjects, some of which are available on tape. **PUBLICATIONS:** *The Journal Of Near Death Studies* **TOPICS:** Death **TYPE:** Journal **FREQ:** quarterly **DESCRIPTION:** Scientific journal on the Near Death Experience. **PUBLICATIONS:** *Vital Signs* **TOPICS:** Death **TYPE:** Newsletter **FREQ:** quarterly **DESCRIPTION:** Provides information on related subjects such as new books, films or TV programs or research projects being conducted by individuals on the subject of Near Death Experiences.

International Association For New Science
755 Tyler Creek Road
Ashland, OR 97520-9408
(503)-488-8800
CONTACT: Brian O'Leary, Ph. D. **TOPICS:** Psychic Healing, Parapsychology, Reincarnation, Body-Mind Connection, UFO's, Spirituality, Metaphysics **DESCRIPTION:** New Science searches for answers to questions that have troubled & inspired humankind for hundreds of years. It explores the spiritual, psychic & metaphysical aspects of reality covering topics such as healing the self, near-death experience, out-of-body experience, extraterrestrial phenomena, reincarnation, psychokinesis, etc. Seminars &

workshops offered by Dr. Brian O'Leary on these & other related topics.

International Association Of Clinical Laser Acupuncturists (IACLA)
10704 Tesshire Drive
St. Louis, MO 63123
(314)-843-1677
CONTACT: Dr. John O. Edstrom, V. Pres. TOPICS: New Age

International Association of Holistic Health Practitioners (IAHHP)
3419 Thom Boulevard
Las Vegas, NV 89130
(702)-873-4542
CONTACT: Joseph M. Kadans, Exec. Dir. TOPICS: Holistic Healing

International Association Of Infant-Massage Instructors
2350 Bowen Road
Elma, NY 14059-9459
(503)-253-9977
TOPICS: Massage

International Association Of Professional Natural Hygienists (IAPNH)
204 Stambaugh Building
Youngstown, OH 44503
(216)-746-5000
CONTACT: Mark A. Huberman, Sec.-Treas. TOPICS: New Age

International Childbirth Education Association
P.O. Box 20048
Minneapolis, MN 55420
(612)-854-8660 (800)-624-4934
TOPICS: Birth PUBLICATIONS: *International Journal Of Childbirth Education* TOPICS: Birth TYPE: Journal

International Chiropractors Association
1110 North Glebe Road
Suite 1000
Arlington, VA 22201
(703)-528-5000
TOPICS: Holistic Healing PUBLICATIONS: *International Review Of Chiropractic* TOPICS: Holistic Healing TYPE: Newsletter PUBLICATIONS: *To Your Health* EDITOR: Heidi Freerks, Molly Rangnath TOPICS: Holistic Healing TYPE: Magazine

International Communes Network
Communidad
Box 15128
S-10465,
Sweden
TOPICS: New Age

International Count Dracular Fan Club
29 Washington Square West
New York, NY 10011
(212)-982-6754
TOPICS: Vampires MEM: 2,000 DESCRIPTION: Founded by current President Jeanne Keyes

Youngson, Ph. D. Prestigious society with 2,000 worldwide members.

International Federation Of Festival Organizations (IMOF)
4230 Stansbury Avenue, #105
Sherman Oaks, CA 91423
(818)-789-7596
CONTACT: Professor Armando Moreno TOPICS: New Age FOUNDED: 1967 MEM: 1,600 CONVENTIONS: Annual convention each January in Cannes, France. DESCRIPTION: Non-profit organization conducting New Age & cultural events worldwide. Publishes monthly Bulletins.

International Fortean Organization (INFO)
P.O. Box 367
Arlington, VA 22210-0367
(703)-522-9232
CONTACT: Raymond D. Manners, Pres. TOPICS: Psychic Phenomena FOUNDED: 1966 MEM: 800 STAFF: 12 BUDGET: $8,00000 CONVENTIONS: Annual FortFest is held in Washington, DC each fall. DESCRIPTION: Records, catalogs and researches anomalous events that are not explained by conventional scientific theories. Always intelligent, often humorous, findings are presented in the INFO Journal, a journal of Science and the Unknown. Membership is open to all. PUBLICATIONS: *INFO Journal* EDITOR: James Theisen TOPICS: Psychic Phenomena TYPE: Journal DATE: 1966; 40 pgs. FREQ: quarterly PRICE: $12.00 DESCRIPTION: Reports research results of unexplained events as conducted by the International Fortean Organization, which studies phenomena not explained by conventional scientific theories.

International Foundation For Homeopathy
4 Sherman Avenue
Fairfax, CA 94930
TOPICS: Holistic Healing

International Foundation For Homeopathy
2366 Eastlake Avenue East, Ste. 301
Seattle, WA 98102
(206)-324-8230
TOPICS: Holistic Health PUBLICATIONS: *Resonance* EDITOR: Dean Crothers TOPICS: Holistic Health TYPE: Magazine

International Foundation Of Oriental Medicine
P.O. Box 625
Oakland Gardens, NY 11364
(718)-465-0808 (718)-586-0030
CONTACT: Dr. David P.J. Hung, Pres. TOPICS: Holistic Health, Acupuncture, Herbalogy FOUNDED: 1989 DESCRIPTION: Non-profit group of designated Doctors & Associate Members interested in providing knowledge & quality Acupuncture, Oriental Medicine & Herbalogy. Offers discounts, seminars, lectures, speakers bureau, expert witness committee, referral service & research . Possible future scholarships.

International General Assembly Spiritualists
209 Newberry Court
Virginia Beach, VA 23462

TOPICS: Metaphysics

International Guild Of Hypnotists
410 South Michigan Avenue, 210
Chicago, IL 60605
TOPICS: Metaphysics

International Imports
236 West Manchester Avenue
Los Angeles, CA 90003
(213)-778-2233
CONTACT: Martin Mayer TOPICS: Witchcraft, New Age

International Imports Occult Supply
P.O. Box 2010
Toluca Lake, CA 91602
TOPICS: Metaphysics

International Institute Of Integral Human Sciences (IIIHS)
1974 de Maisonneuve West
Montreal, Quebec H3H 1K5
Canada
(514)-937-8359 FAX (514)-937-5380
TOPICS: New Age, Psychic, Spirituality FOUNDED: 1976 MEM: 10,000 GROUPS: 43 CONVENTIONS: Annual & biannual conferences in Canada, USA, India & Greece DESCRIPTION: Purpose is to provide a world-wide forum for the encouragement of studies which would help to reintegrate the inner spiritual & outer material life of human beings by restoring integral-human spiritual & psychic sciences to their proper place alongside of the natural, physical & social sciences. Offers seminars, lectures & special programs worldwide.

International Kirlian Research Foundation
2202 Quentin Road
Brooklyn, NY 11229
TOPICS: Metaphysics

International Medical And Dental Hypnotherapy Association
4110 Edgeland, #800
Royal Oak, MI 48073-2251
(313)-549-5594
CONTACT: Laurence L. Skolnik, Ph. D. TOPICS: Holistic Healing

International Mukti Mission
283 Homewood Avenue
Willowdale, Ont. M2R2N6,
Canada
TOPICS: Skepticism, Counter-Cult DESCRIPTION: Hinduism, Islam, Catholicism, New Age, Mysticism, Paganism.

International New Thought
7314 East Stetson Drive
Scottsdale, AZ 85251
TOPICS: Metaphysics

International Order Of Kabbalists (I.O.K.)
25 Circle Gardens
Merton Park
London, SW19 3JX
England
CONTACT: J. Sturzaker TOPICS: Parapsychology, Occult, Kabbalah FOUNDED: 1969 DESCRIPTION:

Purpose is to further the teachings of the Kabbalah & associated subjects such as occultism. Directors J. & D.L. Sturzaker. Send S.A.S.E. for publication list & information. PUBLICATIONS: *The Kabbalist* EDITOR: J. Sturzaker TOPICS: Parapsychology, Occult, Kabbalah TYPE: Magazine DATE: 1974; 22 pgs. FREQ: Quarterly CIRC: 3,000 DESCRIPTION: An Occult Magazine.

International Past Life Registry (IPLR)

P.O. Box 1616
Glendale, AZ 85311
(602)-939-6967
CONTACT: Dr. Leo Gagnon, Pres. TOPICS: Past Life Regression, Death, Hypnotism FOUNDED: 1990 MEM: 42 STAFF: 2 COMPUTER: yes CONVENTIONS: Annual conferences planned DESCRIPTION: Dedicated to the study of Past Life Regression. Trains & offers certification as a Professional Past Life Researcher. Maintains active Database & matches past life history of all members. Plans Registry Journal, Who's Who in Past Lives.

International Plant Conscious Society

5210 East 25th Street
Long Beach, CA 90815
TOPICS: Metaphysics

International Rolf Institute

P.O. Box 1868
Boulder, CO 80306
(303)-449-5903
TOPICS: Holistic Healing

International Society For Astrological Research (ISAR)

P.O. Box 38613
Los Angeles, CA 90038-0613
(213)-333-8702
CONTACT: Carol Tebbs, Sec. TOPICS: Astrology CONVENTIONS: Annual conferences DESCRIPTION: Offers tapes & a library. Provides research grants for the study & research of Astrology. Conducts monthly seminars in Los Angeles.

International Society Of Cryptozoology

P.O. Box 430070
Tucson, AZ 85733
TOPICS: Metaphysics

International Society Of Devine Love

809 Loma Prieta Drive
Aptos, CA 95003
TOPICS: Metaphysics

International Society Of Divine Love

234 West Upsal Street
Philadelphia, PA 19119
(215)-842-0300
TOPICS: Metaphysics, New Age

International Society Of Krishna Conscious

3764 Wateska Avenue
Los Angeles, CA 90034
TOPICS: Metaphysics

International Society Of Metaphysicians

9440 Lexington, Northeast, C
Albuquerque, NM 87112
TOPICS: Metaphysics

International Society Of Naturopath

1434 Fremont Avenue
Los Altos, CA 94022
TOPICS: Occult

International Theological Seminary

P.O. Box 5
Van Nuys, CA 94108
TOPICS: Metaphysics

International Veterinary Acupuncture Society

c/o Meredith Snader, V.M.D.
Rt. #401 RD4 Box 216
Chester Springs, PA 19425
(215)-827-7742
TOPICS: Holistic Healing

Interplanetary Cultural Exchange

P.O. Box 38132
Hollywood, CA 90038
TOPICS: UFO's

Intuitional Metaphysics

5017 New World Drive West
Glendale, AZ 85302
TOPICS: Metaphysics

Invisible Ministry

P.O. Box 4608
Salem, OR 97302-8608
TOPICS: Metaphysics

Inward Journey

P.O. Box 2592
Santa Barbara, CA 93120
TOPICS: Metaphysics

Isis Rasputin, Incorporated

38 North Main Street
Concord, NH 03301
TOPICS: Occult

Isis Rising

7001 North Glenwood
Chicago, IL 60626
TOPICS: Metaphysics

ISKCON (Hare Krishna)

5462 Southeast Marine Drive
Vancouver, BC, V5J3G8,
Canada
TOPICS: Metaphysics

Islands Holistic Association

1126A Dallas Road
Victoria, British Columbia V8W 1TS
Canada
(604)-389-1290
TOPICS: Holistic Healing

Istari Coven

275 Terhune Avenue
Passaic Park, NJ 07055
TOPICS: Witchcraft

Japanese Commune Movement

2083 Sakaecho
Imaichi-shi, Tochigi-ken 321-12
Japan
TOPICS: New Age

Jehovah's Christian Witness

P.O. Box 876
Colorado Springs, CO 80901
TOPICS: Skepticism, Counter-Cult DESCRIPTION: Jehovah's Witnesses, Cults, New Age, Satanism, etc.

Jersey Shore Pagan Way

P.O. Box 2015
Neptune City, NJ 07754
TOPICS: Witchcraft

Jersey Society Of Parapsychology, Inc.

P.O. Box 2071
Morristown, NJ 07960-2071
(201)-539-1466
TOPICS: Parapsychology, Metaphysics, New Age PUBLICATIONS: *Insights* EDITOR: Phyllis Kimec-Wilhelm, B.J. McKay TOPICS: Parapsychology TYPE: Newsletter DATE: 1969; 6 pgs. FREQ: Monthly CIRC: 700 PRICE: $10.00

Jesus Cares

P.O. Box 677
Easton, PA 18042
TOPICS: Skepticism, Counter-Cult DESCRIPTION: New Age, New And Unconventional Religions, Christian sects.

Jesus Cares Ministries

P.O. Box 377
Miamisburg, OH 45342
TOPICS: Skepticism, Counter-Cult DESCRIPTION: New Age, New And Unconventional Religions, Cults, Satanism.

Jesus Loves The Lost

P.O. Box 707
Easton, PA 18042
TOPICS: Skepticism, Counter-Cult DESCRIPTION: New Age, New And Unconventional Religions, etc.

Jesus People Information Center

4338 Third Avenue
Sacramento, CA 95817
TOPICS: Skepticism, Counter-Cult DESCRIPTION: New Age, New And Unconventional Religions, etc.

Jesus People, USA

4707 North Malden
Chicago, IL 60640
TOPICS: Skepticism, Counter-Cult DESCRIPTION: Denounces everything associated with the New Age movement including networking, new and unconventional religions, paganism, etc. PUBLICATIONS: *Directory Of Cult Research Organizations* EDITOR: Eric Pement TYPE: Directory

Jewel Tunnel Imports

P.O. Box 267
Arcadia, CA 91006
TOPICS: Occult

Jewish Meditation Network

P.O. Box 20615
Park West Station
New York, NY 10025-1515
(212)-518-4548

CONTACT: Devorah Devi TOPICS: Holistic Health, Meditation, Crystals, Spirituality, Past Life Regression, Color Therapy, Channeling FOUNDED: 1991 STAFF: 10 CONVENTIONS: Conferences in the U.S. & Israel. DESCRIPTION: Offers ongoing courses, networking, research into Jewish & Kabbalistic meditation & its applications in psychology & healing. Individual instruction & group workshops offered in various U.S. cities. Conducts Spiritual journeys to Israel each year. Produces books & tapes.

Jewish Vegetarians Of North America
P.O. Box 1463
Baltimore, MD 21203
(301)-366-8343
CONTACT: Rabbi Noach Valley TOPICS: Health Food, Vegetarianism FOUNDED: 1983 MEM: 400 CONVENTIONS: Annual weekend conference in New York State DESCRIPTION: Promotes the practice of vegetarianism within the Judaic tradition. Explores the relationship between Judaism, dietary laws, and vegetarianism. PUBLICATIONS: *Jewish Vegetarians Of North America Newsletter* TOPICS: Health Food, Vegetarianism TYPE: Newsletter FREQ: quarterly

Jin Shin Do Foundation
Box 1800
Idyllwild, CA 92349
(714)-659-5500
TOPICS: Massage, Acupuncture, Holistic Health, Body-Mind Connection PUBLICATIONS: *Jin Shin Do Foundation Newsletter* EDITOR: Iona Teeguarden TOPICS: Massage, Spirituality TYPE: Newsletter

Johrei Fellowship
818 Ramapo Valley Road
Oakland, NJ 07436
(201)-337-2031
TOPICS: Holistic Healing, Metaphysics DESCRIPTION: Creating a New Age of light through healing, agriculture and beauty.

Journeys Within
11711 Memorial Drive, #47
Houston, TX 77024
TOPICS: Metaphysics

Jude Three
P.O. Box 923
Staten Island, NY 10314
TOPICS: Skepticism, Counter-Cult DESCRIPTION: New Age, New And Unconventional Religions, Paganism, etc.

Jude Three Missions
P.O. Box 1901
Orange, CA 92668
TOPICS: Skepticism, Counter-Cult DESCRIPTION: Mormonism, Jehovah's Witnesses, Cults, New Age, Satanism, etc.

Jung Foundation
28 East 39th Street
New York, NY 10016
TOPICS: Metaphysics

Karin Kabalah
Rural Route 4, Box 118
Jasper, GA 30143
TOPICS: Metaphysics

Keepers Of Holy Chalice
Seelie Court
RR4, Box 511 G
Georgetown, DE 19947
CONTACT: Ivo Dominguez, Jr. TOPICS: Occult, Witchcraft, Astrology, Kabbalah FOUNDED: 1984 MEM: 21 DESCRIPTION: Wiccan group with strong leanings toward Celtica, Astrology & the Kaballah. The seed group of a new tradition known as The Assembly Of The Sacred Wheel. Celebrates holidays, fosters personal growth, perpetuates knowledge, sponsors community activities, encourages health in the local environment & encourages the formation of other groups. Its sign is a holly leaf, crescent moon & a sun.

Keepers Of The Cauldron
P.O. Box 1108
Glen Allen, VA 23060
TOPICS: Witchcraft

Keys To The Kingdom Ministries
P.O. Box 185
Selah, WA 98942
TOPICS: Skepticism, Counter-Cult DESCRIPTION: Mormonism, Jehovah's Witnesses, Cults, New Age, Satanism, etc.

Kibbutz-Federation International Communes Desk
P.O. Box 1777
Tel Aviv,
Israel
TOPICS: New Age

Kinsman Ministries
P.O. Box 636
Westfield, NJ 07091
TOPICS: Skepticism, Counter-Cult DESCRIPTION: Mormonism, Jehovah's Witnesses, Cults, Satanism, etc.

KIOMA, Incorporated
P.O. Box 791282
Dallas, TX 75379
TOPICS: Metaphysics

Kirpal Light Satsang
P.O. Box M
Beverly Hills, CA 90213
TOPICS: Metaphysics

Kirpal Light Satsang, Incorporated
Merwin Lake Road
Kinderhook, NY 12106
TOPICS: Metaphysics

Klark Kent, Super Science
P.O. Box 392
Dayton, OH 45409
TOPICS: UFO's

Knights Templar Aquarian
P.O. Box 31129
Phoenix, AZ 85046
TOPICS: Metaphysics

Knossos Coven
12 Fifth Avenue, 51
New York, NY 10011
TOPICS: Witchcraft

Krishnamurti Foundation Of America (KFA)
Box 1560
Ojai, CA 93023
(805)-646-2726
TOPICS: New Age PUBLICATIONS: *Krishnamurti Foundation Bulletin* TOPICS: New Age TYPE: Bulletin PUBLICATIONS: *Krishnamurti Foundation Of America Newsletter* EDITOR: R.E. Mark Lee TOPICS: New Age TYPE: Newsletter

Kriya Jyoti Tantra Society
633 Post Street, Ste. 647
San Francisco, CA 94109
CONTACT: Bodhi Avinasha TOPICS: Metaphysics, New Age, Yoga DESCRIPTION: Teaches courses on Tantric Kriya Yoga through books & audio & video tapes.

Kundalini Research Foundation, Ltd. (K.R.F.)
P.O. Box 2248
Darien, CT 06820
(203)-323-3437 FAX (203)-353-9363
CONTACT: Gene Kieffer, Dir. TOPICS: New Age, Spirituality FOUNDED: 1970 AFF ORG: F.I.N.D. of Canada & the Kundalini Research Network DESCRIPTION: Non-profit research & educational foundation organized for the purpose of investigating human potential, publicizing its findings & conducting full-scale scientific investigations of Kundalini. PUBLICATIONS: *Kundalini For The New Age* EDITOR: Gene Kieffer TOPICS: New Age, Spirituality TYPE: BookPUBLICATIONS: *Kundalini, The Evolutionary Energy In Man* EDITOR: Gopi Krishna TOPICS: New Age, Spirituality TYPE: Book DATE: 1970

Lake Champlain Phenomena Investigations
P.O. Box 2134
Wilton, NY 12866
TOPICS: UFO's

Lamb And Lion Ministries
P.O. Drawer K
McKinney, TX 75069
TOPICS: Skepticism, Counter-Cult DESCRIPTION: Cults, New Age, Satanism, New And Unconventional Religions.

Lambda Temple Of Olympus
P.O. Box 186
Wildwood, NJ 08260
TOPICS: Witchcraft

Lanark Hills Foundation
Rural Route 4
Perth, ON, K7H3C6,
Canada
TOPICS: Metaphysics

LAUFORG
P.O. Box 1421
Topanga, CA 90290
TOPICS: UFO's

Lectorium Rosicrucianum
P.O. Box 95421
Seattle, WA 98145
TOPICS: Metaphysics

Legacy International
Route 4
Box 265
Bedford, VA 24523
(703)-297-5982
TOPICS: New Age

Lemurian Fellowship
P.O. Box 397
Romona, CA 92065
TOPICS: UFO's

Licentiate Ministers And Certified Mediums Society (LMCMS)
2020 W. Turney Avenue
Phoenix, AZ 85015
CONTACT: Sandra Pfortsmiller, Sec. Treas. TOPICS: Spirituality FOUNDED: 1946 CONVENTIONS: In conjunction with the National Spiritualist Assoc. of Churches DESCRIPTION: Purpose is to train & to educate, to help & to promote the religion, to join together to solve & to resolve questions & to help & to enjoy one another. Member of the National Spiritualist Assoc. of Churches. Newsletter offered.

Life Spectrums/Rainbow Experience
P.O. Box 373
Harrisburg, PA 17108-0373
(717)-236-0080
CONTACT: Larry E. Arnold TOPICS: Metaphysics, New Age FOUNDED: 1979 DESCRIPTION: Non-profit educational & networking organization focused on Age Of Consciousness Themes. Sponsors & conducts annual week-long holistic conferences each July called the Rainbow Experience, dealing with New Age & Metaphysics topics. Offers exhibits & workshops pertaining to all levels of interest. $10 annual membership. PUBLICATIONS: *Rainbows* EDITOR: Charlotte Abell TOPICS: New Age TYPE: Newsletter; 16 pgs. FREQ: semi-annual PRICE: $5.00 TERM: annually DESCRIPTION: Prints articles and calendar.

Life Understanding Foundation
P.O. Box 30305
Santa Barbara, CA 93130
(805)-682-5151
CONTACT: William T. Cox, Pres. TOPICS: Dowsing FOUNDED: 1968 DESCRIPTION: Books, products, newsletter, audios & videos concerned with dowsing & pyramids.

Lifestudy Foundation
12 Randolph Court
Fairfield, OH 45014
TOPICS: Metaphysics

Lifestyles Travel (TLN)
2641 W. La Palma Avenue #A
Anaheim, CA 92801
(714)-520-4127
CONTACT: Robert L. McGinley, Ph.D., Pres. TOPICS: New Age

LIGHT
P.O. Box 644
Silver Spring, MD 20901
TOPICS: Metaphysics, Channeling

Light Ages Foundation
Box 278
Ashfield, MA 01330

TOPICS: New Age

Light Energy
1056 Northwest 179th Place
Seattle, WA 98177
TOPICS: Metaphysics

Light Of Divine Truth Foundation (LDTF)
304 Boulevard
Florence, NJ 08518
(609)-499-0542
CONTACT: Rev. Betty Latham TOPICS: Psychic Phenomena

Light Of The Universe (LOTU)
161 North Sandusky Road
Tiffin, OH 44883
CONTACT: Helen (Maryona) Spitler, Pres. TOPICS: Metaphysics, Channeling, Health Food, UFO's, Reincarnation, Meditation PUBLICATIONS: *Mini-Manual For Light-Bearers* EDITOR: Helen Spitler TOPICS: Channeling TYPE: Journal DATE: 1987 FREQ: quarterly PUBLICATIONS: *The Light Of The Universe* EDITOR: Helen Spitler TOPICS: Channeling TYPE: Book DATE: 1976 PUBLICATIONS: *The Lotus* EDITOR: Helen Spitler TOPICS: Channeling TYPE: Journal DATE: 1966 FREQ: quarterly

Light Transport Association
308 Nations Bank Building
Del Rio, TX 78840
TOPICS: UFO's

Light Wave Foundation
3151 Wilshire Boulevard
Los Angeles, CA 90010
TOPICS: Metaphysics

Lighthouse Universal
2119 Watbouse Avenue
Tampa, FL 33606
TOPICS: Metaphysics

Lindenself Foundation
P.O. Box 2321
Chapel Hill, NC 27514
TOPICS: Metaphysics

Ling Shen Temple
17102 Northeast 40th
Redmond, WA 98052
TOPICS: Metaphysics

Little Synagogue
27 East 20th Street
NY, NY 10003
(212)-475-7081
CONTACT: Joseph H. Gelberman, Rabbi, Pres. TOPICS: Spirituality, Kabbalah, Yoga, Metaphysics, New Age

Lodge Of The Silver Star
P.O. Box 505
Waukesha, WI 53187
TOPICS: Witchcraft

Logos Project, The
5 Druid Hills Drive
Lexington, NC 27292

TOPICS: Skepticism, Counter-Cult DESCRIPTION: Mormonism, New Age, New And Conventional Religions, etc.

Lost Horizon
301 West Broadway
Lewistown, MT 59457
TOPICS: Metaphysics

Lothlorien Fellowship
P.O. Box 1569
Harrison, AR 72601
TOPICS: Metaphysics

Louis Foundation On Orca Island
P.O. Box 210, Main Street
Eastsound, WA 98245
TOPICS: Metaphysics

Louisiana Society For Psychical Research
39376 Highway 929
Prairieville, LA 70769
CONTACT: Nell Smith, Director TOPICS: Channeling, Metaphysics

Love Project
P.O. Box 7601
San Diego, CA 92107-0601
(619)-225-0133
CONTACT: Arleen Lorrance, Exec. Dir. TOPICS: New Age FOUNDED: 1972 DESCRIPTION: Teaches people to create love in the world by loving each other. Offers beginning & advanced training. PUBLICATIONS: *The Seeker Newsletter* TOPICS: New Age TYPE: Newsletter

Loving Relationships Training, International (LRT)
P.O. Box 1465
Washington, CT 06793
TOPICS: Reincarnation, Metaphysics, New Age DESCRIPTION: An organization founded to promote peace relationships.

Lucidity Association
Dept. Of Psychology
University Of Northern Iowa
Cedar Falls, IA 50614
TOPICS: Parapsychology

Lucifer Society
P.O. Box 5276
Louisville, KY 40205
TOPICS: Metaphysics

Lupin Naturalist Club
P.O. Box 1274
Los Gatos, CA 95030
(408)-353-2250
TOPICS: New Age PUBLICATIONS: *California Naturalist* EDITOR: Mollie Moore-Sullivan TOPICS: New Age TYPE: Magazine

Lutheran General Health Care System (LGHCS)
1775 Dempster Street
Park Ridge, IL 60068
(312)-696-5113
CONTACT: George Caldwell, Pres. TOPICS: New Age

M.E.T.A.
12891 Gorda Circle West
Largo, FL 34643-1712
TOPICS: Metaphysics

M.S.H. Foundation
Rural Route 1, Box 192
Faber, VA 22938
(804)-361-2323 (800)-962-2033
TOPICS: Metaphysics

MacGregor Ministries
Box 1215
Delta BC, Y4M3T3,
Canada
TOPICS: Skepticism, Counter-Cult DESCRIPTION: Jehovah's Witnesses, Mormons, Cults, New Age, Satanism, etc.

MacGregor Ministries
Box 591
Point Roberts, WA 98281
TOPICS: Skepticism, Counter-Cult DESCRIPTION: Cults, New Age, Satanism, New And Unconventional Religions.

Madison Area Pagan Alliance
P.O. Box 294
Verona, WI 53593
TOPICS: Witchcraft

Magazine And Paperback Marketing Institute
1630 Newell Avenue, #205
Walnut Creek, CA 94596
(415)-938-0300
CONTACT: Mike Magee TOPICS: New Age

Magi Craftsmen
P.O. Box 100
McDonough, NY 13801-0100
TOPICS: Witchcraft

Magick Cauldron
11311 Katy Expressway
Houston, TX 77079
TOPICS: Witchcraft

Magick Garden
P.O. Box 9505
Charlotte, NC 28299
TOPICS: Holistic Health

Maharishi Ayurveda Association
Lake Shandelee Road
Livingston Manor, NY 12758
TOPICS: Metaphysics

Maharishi Ayurveda Association Of America
P.O. Box 282
Fairfield, IA 52556
(515)-472-8477
TOPICS: Holistic Healing

Mahavir
P.O. Box 4356
Taos, NM 87571
TOPICS: Metaphysics

Maindenhill Coven
P.O. Box 41101

Philadelphia, PA 19127
TOPICS: Witchcraft

Mandala Holistic Health Society (MHH)
P.O. Box 1233
Del Mar, CA 92014
(619)-481-7751
CONTACT: David J. Harris, Exec. Officer TOPICS: Holistic Healing, New Age DESCRIPTION: Non-profit organization offering conferences and seminars. Concerned with the future and evolution.

Mandella International
631 University Avenue
Minneapolis, MN 55413
TOPICS: Metaphysics

Mankind Research Foundation (MRF)
1315 Apple Avenue
Silver Spring, MD 20910
(301)-587-8686
CONTACT: Dr. Carl Schleicher, Pres. TOPICS: New Age

Mark-Age, Inc./Healing Haven/Centers Of Light/University Of Life/Meditations/Inform-Nations
P.O. Box 290368
Ft. Lauderdale, FL 33329
(305)-587-5555
CONTACT: Nada-Yolanda TOPICS: New Age, Holistic Health, Channeling, UFO's, New Age FOUNDED: 1960 DESCRIPTION: Non-profit spiritual-educational organization offering workshops & lectures given on such topics as holistic health, channeling, UFO's & extraterrestrial contacts. Primary channel is Nada-Yolanda. Publishes quarterly magazine, Main. Also sells audio & video cassettes, books & self-study courses dealing with metaphysics, UFO's, channeling, healing & angels. Operates Healing Haven, Centers Of Light, University Of Life, Mark-Age Meditations Network & Mark-Age Inform-Nations. PUBLICATIONS: *Main* EDITOR: Pauline Sharpe TOPICS: New Age, UFO's, Channeling, Holistic Healing, Metaphysics TYPE: Magazine DATE: 1960 FREQ: quarterly PRICE: $20.00 DESCRIPTION: Publishes news, information, education & guidelines for linking of lightworkers & groups as a preparation for the Second Coming & New Age Of Aquarius around the year 2000 A.D. PUBLICATIONS: *Visitors From Other Planets: A University Of Life Answer Book* EDITOR: Mark-Age TOPICS: Paranormal Phenomena, UFO's TYPE: Book PRICE: $14.00

Massachusetts State Spiritualist Association
RR 3145 Herring Pond Road
Buzzards Bay, MA 02532
TOPICS: New Age

Maternal And Child Health Center
2464 Massachusetts Avenue
Cambridge, MA 02140
(617)-864-9343
TOPICS: Birth

Maternity Center Association
48 East 92nd Street
New York, NY 10128

(212)-369-7300
TOPICS: Birth

Matri Satsang
P.O. Box 1796
Nevada City, CA 95939
TOPICS: Metaphysics

Mayan Order
P.O. Box 2710
San Antonio, TX 78206
TOPICS: Metaphysics

Mazdaznan Association
1701 Aryana Drive
Encinitas, CA 92024
TOPICS: Metaphysics

Mazdaznen Elector
1159 South Norton Avenue
Los Angeles, CA 90019
TOPICS: Metaphysics

Meher Baba Foundation
P.O. Box 1101
Berkeley, CA 94701
TOPICS: Metaphysics

Melia Foundation
1525 Shattuck Avenue
Berkeley, CA 94709
(415)-845-6966
TOPICS: Metaphysics, New Age

Mermade Magickal Arts
P.O. Box 33-402
Long Beach, CA 90803
TOPICS: Witchcraft

MERU Foundation
P.O. Box 1738
San Anselmo, CA 94960
TOPICS: Metaphysics

Messages From Michael
11 Sir Francis Drake Boulevard, Ste. 3C141
Greenboro, CA 94904
TOPICS: Channeling PUBLICATIONS: *Messages From Michael* TOPICS: Channeling TYPE: Magazine DESCRIPTION: The only Michael material authorized by Chelsa Quinn Yarbro.

Messages Of Light
P.O. Box 27063
Kansas City, MO 64110
TOPICS: Metaphysics

Messiah, The
P.O. Box 5
Weableau, MD 65774
TOPICS: Metaphysics

META
P.O. Box 6064
Long Island City, NY 11105
TOPICS: Metaphysics

Meta Network
20000 North 15th Street, 103
Arlington, VA 22201
TOPICS: Metaphysics

Metaphysical Church In America

P.O. Box 91986
Long Beach, CA 90809-1986
TOPICS: Metaphysics, Holistic Healing
DESCRIPTION: Offers Church charters, ordination & certification for healers and teachers.

Metaphysical Consultants
P.O. Box 64027
Tucson, AZ 85603
TOPICS: Metaphysics

Metaphysical Fellowship Church
10591 Flower Street
Stanton, CA 90680
TOPICS: Metaphysics, Parapsychology
PUBLICATIONS: *Metaphysical Fellowship Church Newsletter* **EDITOR:** Yvonne Goodale **TOPICS:** Metaphysics, Parapsychology **TYPE:** Newsletter; 6 pgs. **FREQ:** monthly

Metaphysical Research Society
4023 North Wall
Spokane, WA 99205
TOPICS: Channeling, Metaphysics

Metascience Foundation
Box 737
Franklin, NC 28734
(704)-524-5103
TOPICS: Holistic Healing, Channeling, Parapsychology, Psychic Phenomena **PUBLICATIONS:** *After We Die, What Then?* **EDITOR:** George W. Meek **TOPICS:** Death **TYPE:** Book **PRICE:** $8.95 **PUBLICATIONS:** *Unlimited Horizons* **EDITOR:** George Meek **TOPICS:** Holistic Healing **TYPE:** Newsletter

MetaScience Foundation
P.O. Box 32
Kingston, RI 02881
(401)-294-2414
CONTACT: Marc Siefer, Dir. **TOPICS:** Parapsychology, Psychic Phenomena, Occult, Channeling, Holistic Healing **PUBLICATIONS:** *Meta Science Annual* **PUBLISHER:** Marc J. Siefer **TOPICS:** Parapsychology, Occult **TYPE:** Journal **DATE:** 1976 **SIZE:** 4 x 8; 160 pgs. **FREQ:** Annual **CIRC:** 2,500 **PRICE:** $25.00 **DESCRIPTION:** Objectively explores & provides information on a wide variety of parapsychological topics such as telepathy, psychokinesis, precognition, synchronicity & UFO's. Also features articles about noted experts such as Wilhelm Reich, Gurdjieff, Uri Geller, The Delai Lama, Sigmund Freud & Carl Jung.

Mevlevi Order Of America
139 Mono Avenue
Fairfax, CA 94930
TOPICS: Metaphysics

Michael Educational Foundation
10 Muth Drive
Orinda, CA 94563
(510)-254-4730
CONTACT: JP Van Hulle, Pres. **TOPICS:** Channeling, Metaphysics **FOUNDED:** 1983 **DESCRIPTION:** Promotes the channeled Teachings of Michael. Provides the highest quality channeled information possible, to support Michael's students in their personal development, & to promote a sense of community within the Michael Teaching. Offers Michael Channeling , phone channeling, Repatterning Therapy, Prosperity Coaching,

Bodywork, Regression Guidance, classes & seminars.

Michigan Metaphysical Society
3018 12 Mile Road
Berkley, MI 48072
TOPICS: Metaphysics, Channeling

Michigan/Canadian Bigfoot Information Center (MCBIC)
152 W. Sherman
Caro, MI 48723
(517)-673-2715
CONTACT: Wayne W. King, Dir. **TOPICS:** Big Foot

Midwest Association Past Life Experiences
P.O. Box 308
Winfield, IL 60190
TOPICS: Metaphysics

Midwest Pagan Council
P.O. Box 160
Western Springs, IL 60558-0160
TOPICS: Witchcraft

Midwest Parentcraft Center
627 Beaver Road
Glenview, Il 60025
(312)-724-5488
TOPICS: Birth

Midwives Alliance Of North America
P.O. Box 1121
Bristol, VA 24203
TOPICS: Birth

Milton Erickson Foundation
3606 N. 24th Street
Phoenix, AZ 85016
(602)-956-6196
TOPICS: New Age

Mind Development And Control Association (MDCA)
9633 Cinnabar Drive
P.O. Box 29396
Sappington, MO 63126
(314)-849-3722
CONTACT: Raymond G. Jaegers, Vice Pres. **TOPICS:** Parapsychology, PSI, Holistic Healing, Dowsing, Psychic, Graphology, Channeling **FOUNDED:** 1974 **DESCRIPTION:** Offers studies in PSI, healing, dowsing, hand analysis, psychic detective work, Wall St. predictions. No formal membership required.

Mind Science Foundation
8301 Broadway, # 100
San Antonio, TX 78209
(512)-821-6094
CONTACT: Catherine Nixon Cooke, Exec. Director **TOPICS:** New Age, Parapsychology, Channeling, Psychic Phenomena **PUBLICATIONS:** *Mind Science Foundation News Bulletin* **TOPICS:** New Age, Parapsychology **TYPE:** Bulletin; 4 pgs. **FREQ:** quarterly

Miracle
109 Utica
Ithaca, NY 14850
TOPICS: Channeling

Miracles Media Project
20 Sunnyside Avenue, A112
Mill Valley, CA 94941
TOPICS: Metaphysics

Mission To Mormons
842 Round Lake Road
DeWitt, MI 48820
TOPICS: Skepticism, Counter-Cult **DESCRIPTION:** Cults, New Age, Satanism, etc.

Mobius Society
4801 Wilshire Boulevard
Suite 320
Los Angeles, CA 90010
TOPICS: New Age, Ghosts, Parapsychology, Psychic Phenomena

Monterey Transmission Med
P.O. Box 3076
Monterey, CA 93942
TOPICS: Metaphysics

Moon Dragon
P.O. Box 114
Wendell Depot, MA 01380
TOPICS: Witchcraft

Moonfire Coven
P.O. Box 395
Littleton, CO 80160
TOPICS: Witchcraft

Moonstone Path
P.O. Box 615
Vales Gate, NY 12584
TOPICS: Occult

Mormon Studies
P.O. Box 1091
Webster, NY 14580
TOPICS: Skepticism, Counter-Cult **DESCRIPTION:** Mormonism, Jehovah's Witnesses, Cults, Satanism, etc.

Mormonism Research Ministry
P.O. Box 20705
El Cajon, CA 92021
TOPICS: Skepticism, Counter-Cult **DESCRIPTION:** Mormonism, Cults, New Age, Satanism, etc.

Morning Wind
P.O. Box 961
Stevens Point, WI 54481
TOPICS: Witchcraft

Morphius, Inc.
223 Avenue B
New York, NY 10009
(212)-677-9585
CONTACT: Circe Karen Fraguadas, Pres. **TOPICS:** Paganism, Occult, Spirituality **DESCRIPTION:** Pagan-based organization dedicated to the pursuit of personal, religious & spiritual freedom. A political, spiritual support group devoted to the spiritual awareness & true freedom of the Human Race. Services offered: Occult Archives, Paranormal Investigations, Occult Theology & Consultations.

Morphius, Inc.
902 Strand
Manhattan Beach, CA 90266
(213)-374-9916

CONTACT: Morgana, Pres. **TOPICS:** Paganism, Occult, Spirituality **DESCRIPTION:** California chapter of the New York pagan-based organization dedicated to the pursuit of personal, religious & spiritual freedom.

Morris Pratt Institute Association (MPI)
11811 Watertown Plank Road
Milwaukee, WI 53226
(414)-774-2994
CONTACT: Joseph Sax, Sec. **TOPICS:** Psychic Phenomena, Metaphysics

Movement Inner Spiritual Awareness
P.O. Box 19458
Los Angeles, CA 90018
TOPICS: Metaphysics

Multi-Phasic Integration
P.O. Box 908
Mount Prospect, IL 60056
TOPICS: Metaphysics

Mutual UFO Network Of North Carolina, Inc. (MUFON-NC)
602 Battleground Road
Lincolnton, NC 28092
CONTACT: George D. Fawcett **TOPICS:** UFO's, Paranormal Phenomena **CONVENTIONS:** Quarterly meetings, 1st Sundays in Feb., May, Aug. & Nov. **DESCRIPTION:** Deals with all aspects of the phenomenon of UFOs & their occupants. Offers investigations, research & lectures. **PUBLICATIONS:** UFO Service **PUBLISHER:** George D. Fawcett **TOPICS:** UFO's, Paranormal Phenomena **TYPE:** Newsletter; 10 pgs. **DESCRIPTION:** Lists 162 Resources related to the worldwide phenomenon of UFO, their occupants & paranormal phenomena. Covers the U.S., England, Canada & Australia.

Mutual UFO Network, Inc. (MUFON)
103 Oldtowne Road
Seguin, TX 78155-4099
(512)-379-9216
CONTACT: Walter H. Andrus, Jr., Intl. Dir. **TOPICS:** UFO's **FOUNDED:** 1969 **MEM:** 3,300 **STAFF:** 6 **GROUPS:** 50 **COMPUTER:** no **AFF ORG:** none **CONVENTIONS:** Annual meetings **DESCRIPTION:** World's largest UFO investigative organization, dedicated to the scientific investigation and research of UFO phenomena. Various membership categories available depending upon education and experience. **PUBLICATIONS:** Mufon International UFO Symposium Proceedings **TOPICS:** UFO's **TYPE:** Magazine **FREQ:** annual **PRICE:** $16.50 **DESCRIPTION:** Speeches given at annual meeting. **PUBLICATIONS:** Mufon UFO Journal **TOPICS:** UFO's **TYPE:** Magazine, 24 pgs. **FREQ:** monthly **PRICE:** $25.00 **DESCRIPTION:** Conducts investigations, research & studies to uncover the facts & truth about UFO's.

Mystic Technologies
37 West 26th Street
New York, NY 10010
TOPICS: Metaphysics

Nada Productions
2216 Northwest 8th Terrace
Ft. Lauderdale, FL 33311
TOPICS: Holistic Health

NALTA Foundation, Inc.
P.O. Box 3578
Boulder, CO 80307
(303)-442-2551
CONTACT: Terry L. Dashiell, Dir. **TOPICS:** New Age, Holistic Healing **DESCRIPTION:** Scientific research in harmony with the Universal Forces. Offers books, tapes, inventions & new technologies. Investigates physics of the night side of nature that applies to the medical & space sciences, explores the scientific basis of the energy systems & related electrobiomagnetic phenomena relating to healing, & promotes the empowerment of the individual. Subsidiary companies: Institute For Advanced Studies In Photophysics & Electrobiomagnetics (IASPE) & NALTA Publishing. **PUBLICATIONS:** Harmonic Orb Information Packet (HIP) **TOPICS:** New Age, Holistic Healing **TYPE:** Booklet **PUBLICATIONS:** Manual Of The Harmonic Orb (MHO) **TOPICS:** New Age, Holistic Healing **TYPE:** Booklet **PUBLICATIONS:** NALTA Exchange **TOPICS:** New Age, Holistic Healing **TYPE:** Booklet **PUBLICATIONS:** The Harmonic Orb: Reflections Of The Heart **EDITOR:** Edward P. Gardner **TOPICS:** New Age, Holistic Healing **TYPE:** Book **DATE:** 1992, 288 pgs. **PRICE:** $12.95

Namaste Consciousness
Peacham Road, Box 578
Central Barnstead, NH 03225
TOPICS: Metaphysics

National Academy Of Astrology (NAA)
P.O. Box 6731
Washington, DC 20020
CONTACT: Martha Taub, Pres. **TOPICS:** Astrology

National Academy Of Songwriters
6381 Hollywood Boulevard, #780
Hollywood, CA 90028
(213)-463-7178
CONTACT: Steve Schalchlin **TOPICS:** New Age

National Alliance For Spiritual Growth (NASG)
P.O. Box 2683
Lafayette, LA 70502-2683
(318)-988-4584 (318)-237-0611
CONTACT: Dan or Missy Latour **TOPICS:** Metaphysics, Astrology, Numerology, Spirituality, Body-Mind Connection, Meditation, New Age **FOUNDED:** 1984 **DESCRIPTION:** Non-profit organization sponsoring New Age events & lecturers promoting spiritual growth. Publishes 2 bi-monthly publications, The Bulletin & a directory. **PUBLICATIONS:** Within & Beyond **EDITOR:** Dan Latour, Melissa Latour **TOPICS:** Metaphysics, Spirituality **TYPE:** Journal **DATE:** 1984 **SIZE:** 8 1/2 x 5; 14 pgs. **FREQ:** quarterly **CIRC:** 800 **PRICE:** $10.00 **TERM:** yearly **PRICE PER COPY:** $2.50 **DESCRIPTION:** Responsible guide to teachings, services & journal for transpersonal counselors. Purpose is to uplift consciousness by instilling spiritual principles in daily life. Offers articles, teachings, events, advertising, services, discounts, health, news, programs, etc.

National Association For Music Therapy
Box 1610
Lawrence, KS 66044
TOPICS: New Age **DESCRIPTION:** Organization dealing with the use of music for therapeutic purposes. Music used as a technique to attain holistic health - physical, mental & emotional. **PUBLICATIONS:** Journal Of Music Therapy **TYPE:** Journal **DESCRIPTION:** Concerned with music therapy.

National Association Of Childbearing Centers
RD 1
Box 1
Perkiomenville, PA 18074
(215)-234-8068
TOPICS: Birth

National Association Of Independent Publishers
P.O. Box 430
Highland City, FL 33846-0430
(813)-648-4420
CONTACT: Betsy Lampe **TOPICS:** New Age **FOUNDED:** 1985 **DESCRIPTION:** Provides support for the publishing community & a clearinghouse for information about publishing. Annual membership dues of $75 includes a subscription for the bi-monthly newsletter, Publisher's Report. Not specifically related to New Age. **PUBLICATIONS:** Publisher's Report **EDITOR:** Betty Wright, Betsy Lampe **TOPICS:** New Age **TYPE:** Newsletter **DATE:** 1985; 8 pgs. **FREQ:** bi-monthly **PRICE:** $75.00 **TERM:** annual **PRICE PER COPY:** $15.00 **DESCRIPTION:** Reports on the field of publishing. Subscription free with membership to organization. Annual dues $75.

National Association Of Parents & Professionals For Safe Alternatives In Childbirth (NAPSAC)
Rt. 1
Box 646
Marble Hill, MO 63764
(314)-238-2010
TOPICS: Holistic Health, Birth **PUBLICATIONS:** NAPSAC Directory Of Alternative Birth Services And Consumer Guide **TOPICS:** Holistic Healing, Birth **TYPE:** Directory

National Association Of Spiritual Churches Of Science & Revelation
5618 Wilson Boulevard
Arlington, VA 22205
TOPICS: New Age

National Astrological Society
205 Third Avenue, Ste. 2A
New York, NY 10003
(212)-673-1831
TOPICS: Astrology **PUBLICATIONS:** NASO International Astrological Directory **EDITOR:** Barbara Somerfield **TOPICS:** Astrology **TYPE:** Directory **DATE:** 1984; 78 pgs. **FREQ:** bi-annual **PRICE:** $6.00 **PUBLICATIONS:** NASO Journal **EDITOR:** Barbara Somerfield **TOPICS:** Astrology **TYPE:** Journal

National Campaign For Peace Tax Fund
2121 Decatur Place, N.W.
Washington, DC 20008
(202)-483-3751

TOPICS: New Age

National Center For Homeopathy
1500 Massachusetts Avenue, N.W.
Suite 41
Washington, DC 20005
(202)-223-6182
TOPICS: Holistic Healing PUBLICATIONS: *Homeopathy Today* EDITOR: Julian Winston
TOPICS: Holistic Healing TYPE: Magazine

National Commission For The Certification Of Acupuncturists (NCCA)
1424 16th Street, N.W., Suite 105
Washington, DC 20036
(202)-232-1404
CONTACT: Janet Smith, Exec. Dir. TOPICS: New Age

National Council For Geocosmic Research, Inc.
78 Hubbard Avenue
Stamford, CT 06905
(203)-357-7041
TOPICS: Astrology PUBLICATIONS: *Geocosmic News* PUBLISHER: Maria Simms EDITOR: Fran MacEvoy TOPICS: Astrology TYPE: Magazine DATE: 1972 SIZE: 8 1/2 x 11; 48 pgs. CIRC: 3,000 DESCRIPTION: Features geocosmic studies from a sociological & psychological viewpoint. PUBLICATIONS: *Journal Of Geocosmic Research* EDITOR: Marsha Kaplan TOPICS: Astrology TYPE: Journal SIZE: 6 x 9, 84 pgs. PUBLICATIONS: *National Council For Geocosmic Research Memberletter* PUBLISHER: Mary B. Downing EDITOR: Madalyn Hillis, Van Tuney TOPICS: Astrology TYPE: Newsletter DATE: 1984 SIZE: 8.5 x 11, 6 pgs. FREQ: Monthly CIRC; 3,000 DESCRIPTION: Reports on current news of association. PUBLICATIONS: *NCGR Membership Directory* EDITOR: Mary Downing TOPICS: Astrology TYPE: Directory DATE: 1984 SIZE: 5.5 x 8.5, 48 pgs. CIRC; 3,000

National Council Of Geocosmic Research (NCGR)
P.O. Box 34487
San Diego, CA 92163-4487
(619)-297-9203
TOPICS: Astrology PUBLICATIONS: *NCGR Journal* PUBLISHER: Maria Kay Simms EDITOR: Maritha Pottenger TOPICS: Astrology TYPE: Journal DATE: 1971

National Council Of Geocosmic Research
P.O. Box 14338
San Francisco, CA 94114
TOPICS: Astrology

National Federation Of Spiritual Healers Of America, Inc. (NFSHA)
P.O. Box 76476
Atlanta, GA 30358
TOPICS: Holistic Healing DESCRIPTION: Non-profit corporation operating as a support group for alternative healers. Its goal is to protect the public and give credibiity and visibility to reputable alternative health care healing practitioners who employ spiritual or holistic methods.

National Fringe Sciences Information
P.O. Box 17675
Fountain Hills, AZ 85268
TOPICS: UFO's

National Ghost Ranch Foundation (NGRF)
Ghost Ranch Conference Center
Abiquiu, NM 87510
(505)-685-4333
CONTACT: Bernie L. Epps, Admin. TOPICS: Psychic Phenomena

National Guild Of Hypnotists
P.O. Box 308
Merrimack, NH 03054
(603)-429-9438
TOPICS: Hypnotism

National Hemlock Society
P.O. Box 11830
Eugene, OR 97440
(503)-342-5748
TOPICS: Death

National Hospice Organization
1901 N. Moore Street
Suite 901
Arlington, VA 22209
(703)-243-5900
TOPICS: Death

National Institute Of Theology
6611 West Peoria Avenue
Glendale, AZ 85302
TOPICS: Mctaphysics

National Investigation Commission On Aerial Phenomena
5012 Del Ray Avenue
Washington, DC 20014
TOPICS: UFO's

National Investigation Committee On UFO's
22653 Pacific Cost Highway #330
Malibu, CA 90265-5000
TOPICS: UFO's

National Investigations Committee On Aerial Phenomena (NICAP)
Center for UFO Studies
2457 West Peterson Avenue
Chicago, IL 60659
(312)-271-3611
CONTACT: Mark Rodeghier, Pres. TOPICS: UFO's

National Investigations Committee On Unidentified Flying Objects (NICUFO)
14617 Victory Boulevard, Ste. 4
Van Nuys, CA 91411
(818)-989-5942
CONTACT: Dr. Frank E. Stranges TOPICS: UFO's DESCRIPTION: Formed to study & teach about the phenomena of UFO's. PUBLICATIONS: *Interspacelink Confidential Letter* EDITOR: Dr. Frank E. Stranges TOPICS: UFO's TYPE: Newsletter FREQ: monthly CIRC: 1,000 DESCRIPTION: Reports on all aspects of UFO phenomenon including advice & confidential information.

PUBLICATIONS: *UFO Journal* TOPICS: UFO's TYPE: Journal DESCRIPTION: Features photos, updates & information on UFO phenomena.

National Iridology Research Association
P.O. Box 179
Laguna Beach, CA 92652
(714)-499-6255
TOPICS: Holistic Healing

National Iridology Research Association
P.O. Box 5277
Santa Fe, NM 87502
(505)-983-6139
TOPICS: New Age, Holistic Health DESCRIPTION: Offers physical and psychological approaches, certification, eductional materials & a journal.

National Nutritional Foods Association
150 Paularino Avenue, Suite 285
Costa Mesa, CA 92626-3302
(714)-966-6632
TOPICS: Holistic Healing PUBLICATIONS: *National Nutritional Foods Association Monitor* TOPICS: Holistic Healing TYPE: Newsletter

National Psychic Science Association (NPSA)
17 Baird Place
Whippany, NJ 07981
CONTACT: Rev. Richard Breitbarth, Sec. TOPICS: Psychic Phenomena

National Research Institute
3095-D South Peoria
Aurora, CO 80014
TOPICS: Skepticism, Counter-Cult DESCRIPTION: New Age, New And Unconventional Religions, Paganism, etc.

National Society Of Hypnotherapists
2175 N.W. 86th Street, #6A
Des Moines, IA 50322
(515)-270-2280
CONTACT: Dr. Kathy Wolfe TOPICS: Hypnotism

National Spiritual Alliance Of The U.S.A. (NSA)
239 Washington Street
Keene, NH 03431
(603)-352-2008
CONTACT: Beth Armstrong, Sec. TOPICS: Psychic Phenomena

National Spiritualist Association Of Churches
1325 Stevens Street
P.O. Box 128
Cassadaga, FL 32706
(904)-228-2506
CONTACT: Joseph H. Merrill, Pres. TOPICS: Psychic Phenomena PUBLICATIONS: *National Spiritualist Association Of Churches-Yearbook* EDITOR: Rev. Elizabeth R. Edgar TOPICS: Psychic Phenomena TYPE: Yearbook

National Spiritualist Teachers
11 Fourth Street
Lily Dale, NY 14752

TOPICS: Metaphysics

National Spiritualist Teachers Club (NSTC)
2304 Hiddenmeadow
Manchester, MO 63021
(314)-225-0453
CONTACT: Rev. Dorothy Buss, Pres. TOPICS: Psychic Phenomena

Natural Food Association (NFA)
Hwy. 59 West
P.O. Box 210
Atlanta, TX 75551
(214)-796-3612
TOPICS: Health Food, Holistic Healing PUBLICATIONS: *Natural Food And Farming* EDITOR: Bill Francis TOPICS: Health Food TYPE: Magazine PUBLICATIONS: *Natural Food News* TOPICS: Health Food TYPE: Newspaper

Natural Hygiene, Inc.
P.O. Box 2132
Hungtington, CT 06484
CONTACT: Frank Sabatino, D.C., Ph.D. TOPICS: Holistic Health

Natural Marketing Association (NMA)
22704 Ventura Boulevard, Suite 506
Woodland Hills, CA 91364
(818)-702-0888
CONTACT: Steve Gorman, Pres. TOPICS: New Age

Nature Conservancy
1815 North Lynn Street
Arlington, VA 22209
(703)-841-5300
TOPICS: Holistic Healing

Near Death Experience Research Institute
702 North Fort Thomas Avenue
Fort Thomas, KY 41075
(800)-633-9673
TOPICS: New Age, Holistic Health

Near-Death Experience Project (NDE)
Box 76
Wichita State University
Wichita, KS 67208
(316)-689-3108
TOPICS: New Age

Neo-American Church
P.O. Box 3473
Austin, TX 78764
TOPICS: Metaphysics

Neoteric Pathway Systems
24 Colorado
Highland Park, MI 48203
TOPICS: Metaphysics

Network 2012
1404 Gale Lane
Nashville, TN 37212
(615)-298-9932
CONTACT: Anderson Hewitt TOPICS: New Age

New Age Ancient Ways

P.O. Box 9763
Ft. Lauderdale, FL 33310
TOPICS: Witchcraft

New Age Bible And Philosophy
1139 Lincoln Boulevard
Santa Monica, CA 90403
TOPICS: Metaphysics

New Age Christian Church
1763 Northwest 62nd Street
Seattle, WA 98107
TOPICS: Metaphysics

New Age Church Of Truth
Star Route 2
Box CLC
Deming, NM 88030
TOPICS: New Age, Metaphysics, Psychic

New Age Community Guidebook
P.O. Box 2672
Eugene, OR 97402
TOPICS: Metaphysics

New Age Education Exchange
551 Franklin Street
Framingham, MA 01701
TOPICS: Metaphysics

New Age Enterprises
2555 Junipero Street
Palm Springs, CA 92262
TOPICS: Metaphysics

New Age Foundation
P.O. Box 8044
Tacoma, WA 98408
TOPICS: Metaphysics

New Age Guild Of Connecticut
P.O. Box 1141
South Windsor, CT 06074
(203)-875-4101
CONTACT: Jon Roe, Secretary TOPICS: New Age, Metaphysics, Holistic Health FOUNDED: 1989 MEM: 150 CONVENTIONS: Monthly meetings at various CT locations alternating between members only & open to public. DESCRIPTION: A network of individuals & groups interested in associating with others who share similar holistic, metaphysical, New Age, or alternative interests. Share commitment to increased body-mind-spirit awareness. Bond is to share & support each other's pursuit. Each member signs a Code of Ethics. PUBLICATIONS: *Guild News* TYPE: Newsletter DATE: 1989 FREQ: monthly CIRC: 150 DESCRIPTION: Keeps members informed on Guild activities & other interesting topics & happenings. PUBLICATIONS: *Resource Directory* TYPE: Booklet DATE: 1989 DESCRIPTION: A booklet of members' areas of interest or profession for distribution to the public. Members may be included at their option. PUBLICATIONS: *The Door Opener* EDITOR: Jon Roe TOPICS: Holistic Health, Metaphysics, New Age TYPE: Magazine DATE: 1986 SIZE: 8 1/2 x11, 80 pgs. FREQ: quarterly CIRC; 2,000 PRICE: $8.00 TERM: yearly PRICE PER COPY: $2.50 DESCRIPTION: Holistic health & metaphysical networking magazine for Connecticut's New Age community. Keeps members informed on New Age classes, workshops, fairs & other events.

New Age Information Network
P.O. Box 566714
Atlanta, GA 30356
TOPICS: Metaphysics

New Age Link
P.O. Box 25097
Fort Wayne, IN 46825
(219)-637-5985
CONTACT: Randall Thorne TOPICS: New Age, Metaphysics FOUNDED: 1988 DESCRIPTION: Encourages the exchange of ideas, beliefs, books, services, tapes, etc. on New Age & Metaphysical topics. Publishes New Age Link newsletter 3 times per year. PUBLICATIONS: *New Age Link* EDITOR: Randall Thorne TOPICS: New Age TYPE: Newsletter DATE: 1988; 12 pgs. FREQ: 3 x per year CIRC: 500 PRICE: $9.00 PRICE PER COPY: $4.00 DESCRIPTION: Reports on activities, meetings, news, announcements, etc. related to the New Age Link Association.

New Age Priesthood
2940 16th Street, 308
San Francisco, CA 94103
TOPICS: Metaphysics

New Age Publishing and Retailing Alliance (NAPRA)
P.O. Box 9
Eastsound, WA 98245
(206)-376-2702
CONTACT: Marilyn McGuire, Exec. Dir. TOPICS: New Age, Metaphysics FOUNDED: 1987 MEM: 400 STAFF: 4 AFF ORG: Publishers Marketing Association; American Booksellers Association CONVENTIONS: Annual Meeting at the American Booksellers Association. DESCRIPTION: Serves & supports those in the publishing industry whose work supports positive individuals & social change. Members are publishers, retailers, authors, editors, musicians, designers, agents. Founded by Marilyn McGuire. PUBLICATIONS: *NAPRA Trade Journal* TOPICS: New Age TYPE: Journal DESCRIPTION: Distributed to bookstores, publishers, libraries and NAPRA members, this journal reports about and to the publishing and bookselling trade all aspects of New Age information which supports positive individual and social change.

New Age Study Of Humanity's Purpose
P.O. Box 41883
Tucson, AZ 85717
(602)-885-3258
TOPICS: Metaphysics, Channeling PUBLICATIONS: *Next Step...Re-Unification With The Presence Of God Within Our Hearts* EDITOR: Patricia Cota-Robles TOPICS: Spirituality TYPE: Book PRICE: $14.98

New Age World Religious & Scientific Research Foundation
62091 Valley View Circle
Joshua Tree, CA 92252
(619)-366-2833
CONTACT: Rev. Victoria E. Vandertuin, Pres. TOPICS: Occult, New Age, Spirituality, Metaphysics, Yoga, UFO's, Astrology DESCRIPTION: Dedicated to the study & research of the New Age & UFO's, both religious & scientific. Holds meetings every second Wed. Also offers

retreat facilities, Membership $30 per year. **PUBLICATIONS:** *My God - The Power & Wisdom Of The Universe* **PUBLISHER:** Victoria E. Vandertuin **TOPICS:** Parapsychology, New Age, Spirituality **TYPE:** Book **PUBLICATIONS:** *New Age World Polaris Newsletter* **PUBLISHER:** Victoria Vandertuin **EDITOR:** David K. Roy **TOPICS:** Parapsychology **TYPE:** Newsletter **DATE:** 1978 **SIZE:** 8 1/2 x 11, 25 pgs. **FREQ:** Annual **CIRC:** 500 **PRICE PER COPY:** $5.00 **DESCRIPTION:** Features non-fiction, fiction & poetry by new authors on topics such as the New Age Movement, occult and metaphysics.

New Awareness Network, Inc.
86 Dennis Street
Manhasset, NY 11030
(516)-365-1547

CONTACT: Rick Stack, Pres. **TOPICS:** Metaphysics, Channeling, Parapsychology **DESCRIPTION:** Offers workshops on Out Of Body Experiences, Dreams & The Seth Materials in New York, Boston, Chicago & Minneapolis. Publishes tapes & books on Out Of Body Experiences & Seth materials.

New Awareness, Inc.
212 North Parsons Avenue
Brandon, FL 33510-4516
(813)-654-4386 (800)-422-9273

CONTACT: William E. Woods **TOPICS:** New Age, Spirituality, Holistic Healing, Astrology **DESCRIPTION:** Spiritually directed & unifying the Lunatic Fringe, so its members are well regarded in society. Produces New Age books & the videotapes: Gateway To Eternity, Understanding Astrology. **PUBLICATIONS:** *Healing Rainbow* **EDITOR:** William E. Woods, J.L. Denchfield **TOPICS:** New Age, Holistic Healing, Occult, Crystals, Spirituality, Astrology **TYPE:** Book **PUBLICATIONS:** *New Awareness Magazine* **EDITOR:** William E. Woods, J.L. Denchfield **TOPICS:** New Age, Holistic Healing, Occult, Crystals, Spirituality, Astrology **TYPE:** Magazine **DATE:** 1987, 56 pgs. **FREQ:** monthly **PRICE:** $12.00 **DESCRIPTION:** New Age magazine featuring topics such as self-healing, occult, crystals. Also book reviews. Prints articles, reviews, columns, ads, resource guide and a local events' calendar. Deals primarily with Florida area.

New Directions Evangeline Association
P.O. Box 2347
Burlington, NC 27215
TOPICS: Skepticism, Counter-Cult **DESCRIPTION:** New Age, New And Unconventional Religions, etc.

New Earth Church
P.O. Box 5461
New Bern, NC 28561
TOPICS: Witchcraft

New England Network Of Light
c/o Sirius Community
P.O. Box 388
Amherst, MA 01004
(413)-259-1251
TOPICS: New Age

New England Sound Healers, Inc. (NESH)
42 Baker Street
Lexington, MA 02173
(617)-861-1625

CONTACT: Jonathan S. Goldman **TOPICS:** New Age, Body-Mind Connection, Holistic Healing, Spirituality, Meditation **DESCRIPTION:** Founded and directed by Jonathan S. Goldman who is also the founder and President of Sound Healers Association, Inc. in Boulder, CO. Conducts research and education of the uses of sound and music for health and wellness.

New England UFO Study Group
19 Longmeadow Road
Medfield, MA 02052
TOPICS: UFO's

New Life Research
1928 South Parkwood Drive
Olathe, KS 66052-2806
TOPICS: Metaphysics, Channeling

New Marketing Resources And Services Consortium
P.O. Box 2578
Sedona, AZ 86336
(602)-282-9574

CONTACT: Harry Turner **TOPICS:** New Age, Metaphysics, Holistic Health **FOUNDED:** 1990

New Mexico Network Of Light
222 Yale Boulevard, Southeast
Albuquerque, NM 87106
TOPICS: Metaphysics

New Seminary, The
7 West 96th Street, 19-B
New York, NY 10025
TOPICS: Metaphysics

New Wiccan Church
P.O. Box 162046
Sacramento, CA 95816
TOPICS: Witchcraft

New Wiccan Church Midwest
P.O. Box 64
Mt. Horeb, WI 53572
TOPICS: Witchcraft

New Wiccan Church Of Oregon
P.O. Box 35
Manning, OR 97125
TOPICS: Witchcraft

New Wiccan Church Of Washington
P.O. Box 30511
Seattle, WA 98103
TOPICS: Witchcraft

New York Fortean Society
P.O. Box 20024
New York, NY 10025
TOPICS: UFO's

New York Theosophical Society
240 East 53rd Street
New York, NY 10022
(212)-758-5521
TOPICS: Metaphysics, Spirituality **DESCRIPTION:** Offers lectures & workshops.

Nightflame Coven
P.O. Box 14056
Sarasota, FL 34278
TOPICS: Witchcraft

North American Vegetarian Society
P.O. Box 72
Dolgeville, NY 13329
(518)-568-7970

TOPICS: Health Food, New Age, Holistic Health, Vegetarianism **PUBLICATIONS:** *Jewish Vegetarians* **TOPICS:** Health Food **TYPE:** Book **PUBLICATIONS:** *Vegetarian Voice* **EDITOR:** Jennie Collura **TOPICS:** Health Food, New Age **TYPE:** Magazine **FREQ:** quarterly **DESCRIPTION:** Covers topics on New Age, nutrition, cooking, food and health.

North American Vegetarian Society
P.O. Box 854
Knoxville, TN 37901
TOPICS: Holistic Health, Vegetarianism, Health Food, New Age

North Coast Body Workers Association
798 South Spring Street
Ukiah, CA 95482-5345
(707)-462-3547

CONTACT: Darca Nicholson, Founder **TOPICS:** Holistic Healing, Homeopathy, Reiki, Hypnotism, Acupuncture, Massage, Spirituality

North Woodward Group
374 Pearson
Ferndale, MI 48220
TOPICS: Witchcraft

Northern Lights Alternatives (NLA)
2303 Bronson Hill Drive
Los Angeles, CA 90068
(213)-877-4846
TOPICS: Holistic Healing

Northern Ohio UFO Study Group
3403 West 119th Street
Cleveland, OH 44111
TOPICS: UFO's

Northwest Web
P.O. Box 393
Yachats, OR 97498
TOPICS: Witchcraft

Northwestern UFO Organization
P.O. Box 233
Tonawanda, NY 14120
TOPICS: UFO's

Nos Amis/Our Friends, Inc.
7519 Sausalito Avenue
Canoga Park, CA 91307
(818)-346-1465 (818)-703-1213

CONTACT: William Butler **TOPICS:** Holistic Healing, Psychology **DESCRIPTION:** Non-profit, metaphysical & spiritual organization dedicated to: the development of the whole person-mind, body & spirit; the growth of humanity through the realization of the brotherhood/sisterhood of humanity; the building of a new world based on cooperation, good will & love. Several divisions to achieve its work: Center For Self-Development, Church Of The Fellowship Of Light & Center For Child Development. **PUBLICATIONS:** *The Good News* **TOPICS:** New Age, Psychology, Metaphysics, Spirituality **TYPE:** Newsletter **FREQ:** bi-monthly

NRW Frontier Education Society
46 North Front Street, Side

Philadelphia, PA 19106
(215)-627-5683 **FAX** (215)-627-9945
CONTACT: Sw. Virato **TOPICS:** New Age, Holistic Health, Meditation, Yoga, Body-Mind Connection, Spirituality, Health Food **PUBLICATIONS:** *New Frontier Magazine* **EDITOR:** Swami Nostradamus Virato, Michael Diamond **TOPICS:** New Age, Metaphysics, Holistic Healing, Channeling **TYPE:** Magazine **DATE:** 1980 **SIZE:** 8 x 10; 84 pgs. **FREQ:** monthly **CIRC:** 60,000 **PRICE:** $18.00 **TERM:** yearly **PRICE PER COPY:** $1.95 **DESCRIPTION:** Subtitled: Magazine of Transformation. Deals with emerging concepts in holistic health, energy medicine, natural foods & New Age general subjects. Includes news items from around the world & columns by known leaders in the field of consciousness. Offers articles, ads, illustrations, photography & reviews on music, books, holistic health & the environment. Regional editions in Florida & Rocky Mountains.

NSAC Ministerial Association
4520 Southmore Drive
Orlando, FL 32812
(407)-857-1573
CONTACT: Rev. Pamela K. Ward **TOPICS:** Psychic Phenomena

Numerology Association
404 West Rowland Avenue
Santa Ana, CA 92707
TOPICS: Metaphysics

Numerology World
P.O. Box 108
Wantagh, NY 11793
TOPICS: Metaphysics

OAHSPE
P.O. Box 1028
Joshua Tree, CA 92252
TOPICS: Metaphysics

Occidental Society of Metempiric Analysis (OSMA)
32055 Highway 24 E
Box 308
Simia, CO 80835
(303)-541-2544
CONTACT: Robert J. Everhart, CEO **TOPICS:** Parapsychology, Psychic Phenomena **PUBLICATIONS:** *OSMA Beacon* **EDITOR:** Bob Rondell **TOPICS:** Parapsychology **TYPE:** Newsletter **SIZE:** 8 1/2 x 14; 8 pgs. **FREQ:** Bi-Monthly

Occult Research
P.O. Box 171
Roselle, IL 60172
TOPICS: Metaphysics

Office Of Paranormal Investigations (OPI)
P.O. Box 875
Orinda, CA 94563-0875
(415)-553-2588
TOPICS: Parapsychology, Psychic Phenomena, Ghosts **FOUNDED:** 1989 **STAFF:** 15 **AFF ORG:** Psionic Consultants, Ltd. **DESCRIPTION:** Conducts investigations of paranormal & psychic phenomena and experiences such as poltergeists, apparitions, hauntings, etc. Offers consulting services to media, legal & business communities and to others in the parapsychology community. Offers courses and seminars, publishes newsletter, provides referrals. **PUBLICATIONS:** *OPI Newsletter* **TOPICS:** Parapsychology, Psychic Phenomena, Ghosts **TYPE:** Newsletter **FREQ:** quarterly

Ohashi Institute (OI)
12 West 27th Street
New York, NY 10001
(212)-684-4190
CONTACT: Wataru Ohashi, Dir. **TOPICS:** New Age, Holistic Health, Body-Mind Connection

Ohio UFO Investigation League
5852 East River Road
Fairfield, OH 45014
TOPICS: UFO's

Omega Communications
P.O. Box 2051
Cheshire, CT 06410
TOPICS: UFO's

Omega-Letter
P.O. Box 744
North Bay, ON P1B 8J8
Canada
TOPICS: Skepticism, Counter-Cult **DESCRIPTION:** Cults, New Age, Satanism, New And Unconventional Religions.

Once Daily, Inc.
263 West End Avenue, #2A
New York, NY 10023
(212)-874-4212
TOPICS: Holistic Healing **PUBLICATIONS:** *Holistic Dental Digest* **EDITOR:** Jerry Mittelman, DDS **TOPICS:** Holistic Healing **TYPE:** Magazine

One Force
P.O. Box 1074
Alief, TX 77411
TOPICS: UFO's

One World Life Services
P.O. Box 161113
Austin, TX 78716
(512)-327-8310
TOPICS: Metaphysics

Open Channels
829 Lynhaven Parkway, Ste. 114-215
Virginia Beach, VA 23452
TOPICS: Metaphysics

Oracle, The
P.O. Box 1992
Shelby, NC 28150
TOPICS: Witchcraft

Order Eleusinian Mystery
15515 Ainsworth Street
Gardena, CA 90247
TOPICS: Metaphysics

Order Of Osiris
P.O. Box 4084
Roselle Park, NJ 07204
TOPICS: Witchcraft

Order Of Uriel, The
P.O. Box 1117, Station Q
Toronto, ON M4T 2P2

Canada
TOPICS: Metaphysics, New Age

Ordo Templi Baphemetis
P.O. Box 1219
Corpus Christi, TX 78403-1219
CONTACT: James M. Martin **TOPICS:** Metaphysics **FOUNDED:** 1985 **DESCRIPTION:** An occult oriented organization. Promotes Thelema. James M. Martin, Grand Master.

Ordo Templi Dianos
4700 Selberg Lane
Lake Worth, FL 33460
TOPICS: Metaphysics

Ordo Templi Orientis (O.T.O.)
JAF P.O. Box 7666
New York, NY 10116
CONTACT: Hymenaeus Beta, Frater Superior **TOPICS:** Metaphysics, New Age **FOUNDED:** 1897 **MEM:** 2,100 **GROUPS:** 119 worldwide **COMPUTER:** yes **CONVENTIONS:** Local group meetings & an annual convention of the governing bodies every March or April **DESCRIPTION:** Purpose is to study & preserve Western Mystery Tradition, as it relates to certain schools of Eastern thought & to advance the system of philosophy & religion called Thelema founded in 1904 by Aleister Crowley. Offers classes, study groups, formal celebration of the liturgy of the Gnostic Mass & participation in a structured system of ceremonial initiations. Maintains archives of Crowley's works. Publishes related materials. Membership by ceremonial initiation & sponsorship. **PUBLICATIONS:** *Equinox, The* **TOPICS:** Metaphysics, Spirituality **TYPE:** Newsletter **FREQ:** quarterly **DESCRIPTION:** Serial anthology of documents, essays, poetry & dramatic works of interest to current & prospective members of OTO, Thelemites in general & all others who follow Western mystical/magical paths. Available to the public. Limited advertising accepted. **PUBLICATIONS:** *Vegetarian Voice* **EDITOR:** Jennie Collura **TOPICS:** Health Food, New Age **TYPE:** Magazine **FREQ:** quarterly **DESCRIPTION:** Covers topics on New Age, nutrition, cooking, food and health.

Ordo Templi Orientis
P.O. Box 430
Fairfax, CA 94930
TOPICS: Metaphysics

Ordo Templi Orientis
P.O. Box 1075
Edmonton, AB T5J 2M1
Canada
TOPICS: Metaphysics

Ordo Templi Orientis/Grand
P.O. Box 2303
Berkeley, CA 94702
TOPICS: Metaphysics

Oregon Pagan Council
P.O. Box 1012
Oregon City, OR 97045
TOPICS: Witchcraft

Oregon Zen Priory
2539 Southeast Madison
Portland, OR 97214

TOPICS: Metaphysics

Organic Food Production Association Of North America
P.O. Box 31
Belchertown, MA 01007
(413)-323-6821
TOPICS: Health Food

Original Psychic Research Association
P.O. Box 60901
Midwest City, OK 73146
TOPICS: Metaphysics

Orion Foundation, The
P.O. Box 17
Warrenville, IL 60555
TOPICS: UFO's

OSIRIS UFO Research
P.O. Box 35364
Albuquerque, NM 87110
TOPICS: UFO's

OSIRIS UFO Research
2114 East 6805 South
Salt Lake City, UT 84121
TOPICS: UFO's

Overseas Development Network
2940 16th Street #110
San Francisco, CA 94103-3664
(415)-868-3002
TOPICS: New Age

Pacific Asian Evangelism
P.O. Box 1919
Honolulu, HI 96805
TOPICS: Skepticism, Counter-Cult DESCRIPTION: Cults, New Age, Satanism, New And Unconventional Religions.

Pagan Alliance Of Central Texas
P.O. Box 12041
Austin, TX 78711
TOPICS: Witchcraft

Pagan Aquarian Network
P.O. Box 66021
Roseville, MI 48066
TOPICS: Witchcraft

Pagan Arizona Network
P.O. Box 17933
Phoenix, AZ 85011
TOPICS: Witchcraft

Pagan Broadcasting Systems
P.O. Box 9513
North Hollywood, CA 91609
TOPICS: Witchcraft

Pagan Kith And Kin
P.O. Box 641
Lake Geneva, WI 53147
TOPICS: Witchcraft

Pagan/Occult/Witchcraft Special Interest Group (POWSIG)
P.O. Box 9336
San Jose, CA 95157
(415)-856-6911 (213)-719-9097

CONTACT: Valerie Voigt, Coordinator-IN-Chief TOPICS: Occult, Witchcraft, Paganism, Kabbalah, Alchemy, Voudoun FOUNDED: 1975 MEM: 400 STAFF: 16 BUDGET: $4,80000 CONVENTIONS: Irregular schedule for conferences. DESCRIPTION: Networking and educational organization affiliated with American Mensa. Conducts educational and social activities and consults to individuals, community organizations, law enforcement, and the media. PUBLICATIONS: *Pagana* TOPICS: Occult, Witchcraft, Paganism, Kabbalah, Alchemy, Voudoun TYPE: Newsletter FREQ: 6xyr. DESCRIPTION: Available to members only. Ads accepted. PUBLICATIONS: *POWSIG* TOPICS: Occult, Witchcraft, Paganism, Kabbalah, Alchemy, Voudoun TYPE: Brochure PUBLICATIONS: *What Are Paganism And Witchcraft?* TOPICS: Occult, Witchcraft, Paganism, Kabbalah, Alchemy, Voudoun TYPE: Booklet FREQ: every 3 yrs.

Pagans For Peace
P.O. Box 86134
North Vancouver, BC V7L 4J5
Canada
CONTACT: Samuel Wagar TOPICS: Witchcraft, Occult, Paganism, Voudoun FOUNDED: 1983 MEM: 300 DESCRIPTION: A network of politically active left-wing Pagans & Witches around the world, primarily active around peace & environmental issues. Operates Obscure Pagan Press. PUBLICATIONS: *Directory To Canadian Pagan Resources* EDITOR: Samuel Wagar, Maphis Wagar TOPICS: Paganism, Witchcraft, Occult, Voudoun TYPE: Directory DATE: 1988; 48 pgs. FREQ: annual PRICE: $4.00 TERM: yearly DESCRIPTION: Lists many resources in Witchcraft, Womanspirit/Dianic, Vodoun, Faerie, Druidic & other Pagan spiritual paths in Canada. Offers bookstores, supply stores, gatherings, festivals, groups & individuals. PUBLICATIONS: *Pagans For Peace Newsletter* EDITOR: Samuel Wagar TOPICS: Paganism, Witchcraft, Occult TYPE: Newsletter DATE: 1983 SIZE: 8 1/2 x 11, 10 pgs. FREQ: bi-monthly PRICE: $10.00 TERM: yearly DESCRIPTION: Purpose is the networking of politically active left-wing Pagans & Witches, their projects & reviews of various resources. Also offers thealogical discussion & exploration.

Pallas Society
P.O. Box 18211
Encino, CA 91316
TOPICS: Witchcraft, Metaphysics PUBLICATIONS: *Pallas Society News* TOPICS: Witchcraft, Occult, Paganism TYPE: Newspaper

Panpipes Magical Market Place
P.O. Box 1352
Hollywood, CA 90028
TOPICS: Occult

Pans Forest Herb Company
P.O. Box 218
Orient, WA 99160-0218
TOPICS: Holistic Health

Para Research
85 Eastern Avenue
Gloucester, MA 01930
(617)-283-3438
TOPICS: Parapsychology, Astrology
PUBLICATIONS: *World Of Books* EDITOR: Carol

Coles TOPICS: Parapsychology TYPE: Magazine DATE: 1984; 18 pgs. PRICE: $0.00

Paranormal Phenomena Research
P.O. Box 396
Skowhegan, MA 04976
CONTACT: Leslie Bugbee TOPICS: Psychic Phenomena

Parapsychological Association (PA)
Box 12236
Research Triangle Park, NC 27709
(919)-688-8241
CONTACT: Dr. Richard Broughton TOPICS: Parapsychology, Metaphysics, Psychic Phenomena PUBLICATIONS: *Research In Parapsychology* TOPICS: Parapsychology, Psychic Phenomena TYPE: Newsletter

Parapsychological Association
P.O. Box 7503
Alexandria, VA 22307
(919)-286-0714
TOPICS: Parapsychology, Metaphysics, Psychic Phenomena PUBLICATIONS: *Proceedings Of The Parapsychological Association* EDITOR: W. G. Roll TOPICS: Parapsychology TYPE: Newsletter DATE: 1957 SIZE: 5.5 x 8.5; 120 pgs. FREQ: Annual CIRC: 1,000 PRICE PER COPY: $3.50 DESCRIPTION: Provides research reports & information presented at the annual conventions of the Parapsychological Association. PUBLICATIONS: *PSI News* TOPICS: Parapsychology TYPE: Newsletter

Parapsychological Services Institute
1502 Maple Street
P.O. Box 217
Carrollton, GA 30117
(404)-834-1423
CONTACT: Joyce McKerahan, Sec. TOPICS: New Age

Parapsychology Association
3681 Beechwood Place
Riverside, CA 92506
TOPICS: Metaphysics

Parapsychology Foundation, Inc. (PF)
228 East 71st Street
New York, NY 10021
(212)-628-1550
CONTACT: Robert R. Coly, Adm. Sec. TOPICS: Parapsychology, Occult, Channeling, Psychic Phenomena PUBLICATIONS: *Parapsychological Monographs Of The Parapsychology Foundation* TOPICS: Parapsychology, Psychic Phenomena TYPE: Journal PUBLICATIONS: *Parapsychology Foundation, Proceedings Of International Conferences* TOPICS: Parapsychology, Occult TYPE: Magazine DATE: 1953 FREQ: Annual PUBLICATIONS: *Parapsychology Review* EDITOR: Betty Shapin TOPICS: Parapsychology TYPE: Magazine DATE: 1970 SIZE: 8 1/2 x 11, 16 pgs. FREQ: Bi-Monthly CIRC; 2,000 PRICE: $12.00 PRICE PER COPY: $2.00 DESCRIPTION: Offers information pertaining to current research & education in the field of parapsychology & psychic phenomena. Features articles, news & book reviews.

Parapsychology Institute Of America (PIA)
P.O. Box 252

Elmhurst, NY 11373
CONTACT: Dr. Stephen Kaplan, Exec. Dir. TOPICS:
Parapsychology, Vampires, Ghosts, Occult,
Channeling FOUNDED: 1971 MEM: 20 STAFF: 5
CONVENTIONS: Once a year in Los Angeles, San
Francisco or New York DESCRIPTION: Researchs
all aspects of Parapsychological Phenomena
especially ghosts and haunted houses. Gives lectures
on various aspects of the field. Acts as a consumers'
advocate in the field of Parapsychology. Dr. Stephen
Kaplan, exec. dir. & Max Toth, dir.

Parapsychology Sources Of Information Center-PSI Center (PSI)
Two Plane Tree Lane
Dix Hills, NY 11746
(516)-271-1243
CONTACT: Rhea A. White TOPICS:
Parapsychology FOUNDED: 1983 DESCRIPTION:
Dedicated to collecting and disseminating
information on parapsychology and psi research.
Produces a computerized database called PsiLine
covering the parapsychological literature from
earliest times to date. Publishes a semi-annual
journal Exceptional Human Experience, the
International Directory of Persons Granted Degrees
for Work in Parapsychology, PSI Center Fact Sheets,
Glossary of Parapsychological Terms & The Major
Membership Organizations of Parapsychology:
Historical Data. PUBLICATIONS: Exceptional
Human Experience EDITOR: Rhea A. White
TOPICS: Parapsychology TYPE: Journal
PUBLICATIONS: International Directory Of
Persons Granted Degrees For Work In
Parapsychology EDITOR: Rhea A. White TOPICS:
Parapsychology TYPE: Directory PUBLICATIONS:
Parapsychology Abstracts International TOPICS:
Parapsychology TYPE: Book

Parascience
P.O. Box 1362
Evanston, IL 60204
TOPICS: Metaphysics

Parascience International
1025 Miller Lane
Harrisburg, PA 17110-2899
(717)-236-0080
CONTACT: Larry E. Arnold, Dir. TOPICS:
Metaphysics, Psychic Phenomena FOUNDED: 1976
DESCRIPTION: Transnational network devoted to
collecting & disseminating information & research
about fortean events & anomalous phenomena,
spontaneous human combustion, anomaly triangle
zones & precognition of special interest. Operates the
Precognition Hotline.

Past Life Regression Therapy
P.O. Box 1551
San Anselmo, CA 94960
TOPICS: Metaphysics

Path Inner Resources
P.O. Box 60655
Palo Alto, CA 94306
TOPICS: Metaphysics

Path Of Roodmas, The
P.O. Box 486
New Hyde Park, NY 11040
TOPICS: Metaphysics

Path Of The Pentacle

P.O. Box 4773
Hollywood, FL 33083
TOPICS: Witchcraft

Pathways
Drawer 707-RPI
Derby, KS 67037-0707
(316)-788-4224
CONTACT: Pat Kirven Sawyer TOPICS: New Age,
Past Life Regression, Crystals, Metaphysics, Holistic
Healing, Channeling, Body-Mind Connection
FOUNDED: 1981 DESCRIPTION: A non-profit
organization devoted to helping others expand their
awareness and achieve their full potential in personal
development. Offers classes, booklets, tapes and
counseling in metaphysics to understand past lives and
develop present potentials through higher levels of
consciousness. Also offers a line of crystal products
& personal counselling. PUBLICATIONS: Footsteps
EDITOR: Patricia K. Sawyer TOPICS: New Age
TYPE: Newsletter PUBLICATIONS: Learning To
See And Interpret Auras EDITOR: Patricia K.
Sawyer TOPICS: Metaphysics, Spirituality TYPE:
Booklet PUBLICATIONS: Learning To Use A
Pendulum EDITOR: Patricia K. Sawyer TOPICS:
Metaphysics, Spirituality TYPE: Booklet
PUBLICATIONS: Pathways Profiles EDITOR:
Patricia K. Sawyer TOPICS: Metaphysics,
Spirituality TYPE: Bulletin PUBLICATIONS:
Recognizing, Confronting & Conquering Negative
Emotions EDITOR: Patricia K. Sawyer TOPICS:
Metaphysics, Spirituality TYPE: Booklet
PUBLICATIONS: Sedona: Are The Vortexes Real?
EDITOR: Patricia K. Sawyer TOPICS: Metaphysics,
Spirituality TYPE: Booklet

Pathways To Inner Peace
1834 Magnolia
Denver, CO 80220
TOPICS: Metaphysics

Peacevision
P.O. Box 271985
Houston, TX 77277
(713)-667-1413
TOPICS: New Age

Pearls Of Wisdom
3244 North High Street
Columbus, OH 43202
TOPICS: Metaphysics

Pegasus
1189 Branham Lane
San Jose, CA 95118
TOPICS: Occult

Pendragon
P.O. Box 381
Morganville, NJ 07751
TOPICS: Witchcraft

Pentacle Foundation, The
P.O. Box 11635
Omaha, NE 68111
TOPICS: Witchcraft

Personal Development Institue
P.O. Box 1056
Williamsburg, VA 23187
(804)-229-4873
TOPICS: Parapsychology, New Age, Metaphysics

Petals - Valley Of Roses
Rural Route 2, Box 208-16
Winston, OR 97496
TOPICS: UFO's

Phenomenon Of Man Project
515 South Olive Street, 1-102
Los Angeles, CA 90013
TOPICS: Metaphysics

Pheylonian Production Koh
Rural Route 1
Marlbank, ON, K0K2L0,
Canada
TOPICS: Metaphysics

Phillos Foundation
P.O. Box 6475
Anaheim, CA 92816
TOPICS: Metaphysics

Philosophers Stone
3814 24th Street
San Francisco, CA 94114
TOPICS: Occult

Philosophical Research Society, Inc.
3910 Los Feliz Boulevard
Los Angeles, CA 90027-2399
(213)-663-2167 FAX (213)-663-9443
CONTACT: Daniel Fritz, Managing Dir. TOPICS:
New Age, Tarot, Meditation, Kabbalah, Spirituality
FOUNDED: 1934 DESCRIPTION: Founded as a
center of practical idealism & dedicated to acquiring
knowledge in the fields of art, science, crafts,
philosophy, psychology & religion. Offers a research
library, auditorium, lecture room, book & gift shop,
museum, seminars & a university- level home-study
education program. Founder-Manly P. Hall, author
of Secret Teachings of All Ages & 3,500 other books
& publications. PUBLICATIONS: Alchemy And The
Alchemists EDITOR: E. Hitchcock TOPICS:
Alchemy TYPE: Book PRICE: $15.00
PUBLICATIONS: Collection Of Emblems, Ancient
And Moderne And Foundations Unearthed
EDITOR: George Wither, Marie B. Hall TOPICS:
Metaphysics, Psychic TYPE: Book PRICE: $22.50
PUBLICATIONS: Freemasonry Of The Ancient
Egyptians EDITOR: M.P. Hall TOPICS: New Age,
Paranormal Phenomena TYPE: Book PRICE:
$10.50 PUBLICATIONS: Isiac Tablet Or Bembine
Tablet Of Isis EDITOR: W. Wynn Westcott TOPICS:
Tarot TYPE: Book PRICE: $14.95 PUBLICATIONS:
Lectures On Ancient Philosophy EDITOR: M.P.
Hall TOPICS: Occult TYPE: Book PRICE: $12.50
PUBLICATIONS: Most Holy Trinosophia EDITOR:
M.P. Hall TOPICS: Spirituality TYPE: Book PRICE:
$15.00 PUBLICATIONS: Origin Of The Egyptians
EDITOR: A. LePlongeon TOPICS: New Age TYPE:
Book PRICE: $17.50 PUBLICATIONS: Phoenix
EDITOR: M.P. Hall TOPICS: New Age, Paranormal
Phenomena, Alchemy TYPE: Book PRICE: $19.95
PUBLICATIONS: PRS Journal EDITOR: M.P. Hall
TOPICS: Spirituality TYPE: Journal FREQ:
quarterly PUBLICATIONS: Pythagoras: His Life
And Teachings EDITOR: T. Stanley TOPICS:
Spirituality TYPE: Book PRICE: $16.95
PUBLICATIONS: Secret Teachings Of All Ages: An
Encyclopedic Outline Of Masonic, Hermetic,
Qabbalistic EDITOR: M.P. Hall TOPICS: Kabbalah
TYPE: Book PRICE: $35.00 PUBLICATIONS: Self-
Unfoldment By Disciples Of Realization EDITOR:

M.P. Hall TOPICS: Psychic TYPE: Book PRICE: $10.95

Phoenix Rising
P.O. Box 1192
Stockbridge, MA 01262
TOPICS: Metaphysics

Pittsburgh Pagan Alliance
P.O. Box 242
Monroeville, PA 15146
TOPICS: Witchcraft

Pleiades Foundation
1570 Nannette Drive
Reno, NV 89502
TOPICS: UFO's

Point Foundation
27 Gate Five Road
Sausalito, CA 94965
(415)-332-1716
CONTACT: Susan Rosberg TOPICS: New Age, Metaphysics PUBLICATIONS: *Whole Earth Review* EDITOR: David Burnor, Kevin Kelly TOPICS: New Age, Metaphysics TYPE: Magazine DATE: 1968 FREQ: bi-monthly CIRC: 50,000 DESCRIPTION: Features different themes such as the environment, self-help, health. Reviews books, videos, audio tapes and products.

Positive Action Center
P.O. Box 20997
Portland, OR 97220
TOPICS: Skepticism, Counter-Cult DESCRIPTION: Cults, New Age, Satanism, New And Unconventional Religions.

Poster Market Research
725 Pinon Drive
Santa Fe, NM 87501
(505)-989-8500
CONTACT: Bruce Poster, Pres. TOPICS: New Age, Tarot, Psychic FOUNDED: 1977 STAFF: 2 DESCRIPTION: Offers workshops to teach New Age practitioners of various field how to market their skills.

Practical Metaphysics
P.O. Box 366
Elkhorn, NE 68022
TOPICS: Metaphysics

Prakrti
P.O. Box 5041
Napa, CA 94559
TOPICS: Metaphysics

Private UFO Investigations
Route 1
Hazelton, IA 50641
TOPICS: UFO's

Probe Center Northwest
4750 18th Avenue, Northeast
Seattle, WA 98105
TOPICS: Skepticism, Counter-Cult DESCRIPTION: New Age, New And Unconventional Religions, Occult, Mysticism.

Probe Ministries
1900 Firman Drive, 100
Richardson, TX 75081

TOPICS: Skepticism, Counter-Cult DESCRIPTION: New Age, New And Unconventional Religions, etc.

Professional Psychics Unit
1839 South Elmwood
Berwyn, IL 60402
TOPICS: Metaphysics

Project Information Research
215 East Orangethorpe Dr.
Fullerton, CA 92632
TOPICS: UFO's

Project Mentifex
P.O. Box 31326
Seattle, WA 98103-1326
TOPICS: New Age FOUNDED: 1986 DESCRIPTION: Egalitarian organization promoting & studying machine intelligence. PUBLICATIONS: *Mentifex Communicat* TOPICS: New Age TYPE: Journal FREQ: Irregular DESCRIPTION: Archival journal. Free. PUBLICATIONS: *Mind* TOPICS: New Age TYPE: Book DATE: 1991 DESCRIPTION: AI design on CD-ROM for CDTV/Amiga Library Disk #411.

Project Starlight International (PSI)
P.O. Box 599
College Park, MD 20740
CONTACT: Ray Stanford, Dir. TOPICS: UFO's

Project Stigma
P.O. Box 1094
Paris, TX 75460
(214)-784-5922
TOPICS: Psychic Phenomena, UFO's PUBLICATIONS: *Crux Newsletter* TOPICS: Psychic Phenomena TYPE: Newsletter PUBLICATIONS: *Stigmata* EDITOR: Thomas R. Adams TOPICS: Psychic Phenomena TYPE: Magazine

Project Visit - Vehicle Internal Systems Investigative Team (VISIT)
P.O. Box 890327
Houston, TX 77289
(713)-488-2884
CONTACT: John F. Schuessler, Sec. TOPICS: UFO's

Promethian Network
P.O. Box 9094
San Rafael, CA 94912
TOPICS: Occult, New Age PUBLICATIONS: *Promethian Network* TOPICS: New Age, Occult TYPE: Magazine

Prosperity Coven
P.O. Box 4162
Pensacola, FL 32531
TOPICS: Witchcraft

PSI Associates
P.O. Box 2633
Hollywood, FL 33022
TOPICS: Metaphysics

PSI News
P.O. Box 7053
Alexandria, VA 22307
TOPICS: Channeling

PSI Research
484-B Washington Street, #317
Monterey, CA 93940-3090

(408)-655-1985
CONTACT: Larissa Vilenskaya, Dir. TOPICS: Parapsychology, PSI FOUNDED: 1982 DESCRIPTION: Focuses on Parapsychology in Russia, Eastern Europe & China. PUBLICATIONS: *Psi Research Journal* PUBLISHER: Larissa Vilenskaya TOPICS: Parapsychology TYPE: Journal DATE: 1982 SIZE: 5.5 x 8.5; 130 pgs. FREQ: Quarterly CIRC: 450 PRICE: $28.00 PRICE PER COPY: $8.00 DESCRIPTION: Articles & reports covering the field of parapsychology on an international level. Discusses research, findings, events from the USSR, China & Eastern Europe.

PSI Tech
P.O. Box 291
Wadsworth, IL 60083
TOPICS: Occult

Psychic Archeology Association
P.O. Box 191268
Dallas, TX 75219
TOPICS: Metaphysics

Psychic Connection International
13067 Calais Street
New Orleans, LA 70129
TOPICS: Psychic

Psychic Connections
484-B Washington Street, 317
P.O. Box 670022
Marietta, GA 30066
TOPICS: Metaphysics, Channeling PUBLICATIONS: *Psychic Connections* TOPICS: Metaphysics, Spirituality TYPE: Magazine

Psychic Foundation Of Knowledge, Inc.
P.O. Box 25504
Charlotte, NC 28229
TOPICS: Metaphysics, Channeling PUBLICATIONS: *Psychic Dimensions* TOPICS: Metaphysics, Spirituality TYPE: Book

Psychic Horizons
2240 Geary Boulevard
San Francisco, CA 94115
TOPICS: Metaphysics

Psychic Referral Bureau
P.O. Box 2195
Garden Grove, CA 92642
TOPICS: Metaphysics

Psychic Research Institute
1725 Little Orchard Street
San Jose, CA 95125
(408)-279-2291
CONTACT: Marcel Vogel, Ph.D. TOPICS: Parapsychology, Metaphysics, Channeling PUBLICATIONS: *Psychic Research Newsletter* PUBLISHER: Marcel Vogel EDITOR: Jennet Grover TOPICS: Parapsychology TYPE: Newsletter DATE: 1984; 16 pgs. FREQ: Bi-Monthly CIRC: 2,000 PRICE: $12.50 PRICE PER COPY: $4.00 DESCRIPTION: Non-profit corporation attempting to help people through scientific research & eduction.

Psychic Science International Special Interest Group
7514 Belleplaine Drive

Huber Heights, OH 45424
TOPICS: Metaphysics, Channeling

Psychic Spiritual Church
21729 Fenkell Avenue
Detroit, MI 48223
TOPICS: Metaphysics

Psychical Research Foundation
West Georgia College
Psychology Dept.
Carrollton, GA 30118
CONTACT: William G. Roll TOPICS: Parapsychology, Psychic Phenomena, Channeling, Psychic PUBLICATIONS: *Theta: The Journal Of The Psychical Research Foundation* EDITOR: Prof. William G. Roll TOPICS: Parapsychology, Psychic Phenomena, Channeling, Psychic TYPE: Journal

Psychics USA
137 Maddox Road, C
Milton, FL 32570
TOPICS: Metaphysics

Psychosynthesis Institute
5 Milligan Place
New York, NY 10011
TOPICS: Metaphysics

Psychosynthesis Institute
3352 Sacramento Street
San Francisco, CA 94118
TOPICS: Occult

Psyvestics Premonition Research
780 North Eculid, 205
Anaheim, CA 92801
TOPICS: Metaphysics

Publishers Marketing Association
2401 Pacific Coast Highway, #109
Hermosa Beach, CA 90254
(213)-372-2732
CONTACT: Jan Nathan TOPICS: New Age, Metaphysics FOUNDED: 1983

Pyntri Circle
P.O. Box 2834
Concord, NC 28025
TOPICS: Witchcraft

Pyramid Of One
251 Northwest Bailey
Hillsboro, OR 97133
TOPICS: Metaphysics

Quicksilver Coven
P.O. Box 3232
Louisville, KY 40201
TOPICS: Witchcraft

Radha Soami Society
7518 East 29th Street
Tucson, AZ 85364
TOPICS: Metaphysics

Radiance Technique Association International, Inc. (TRTAI)
P.O. Box 40570
St. Petersburg, FL 33743-0570
CONTACT: Fred W. Wright, Jr., Co-Exec. Dir. TOPICS: Reiki, Body-Mind Connection, Massage, New Age FOUNDED: 1980 GROUPS: groups

worldwide AFF ORG: The American-International Reiki Association, International Inc. CONVENTIONS: For members only in May, 1991. DESCRIPTION: Non-profit, membership organization for persons who have studied or are interested in The Radiance Technique, a stress reduction and energy balancing technique taught worldwide. Also called The Official Reiki Program, it promotes research & awareness of the technique which is the science of universal energy & the distribution of energy through the laying on of hands. Thousands of alumni worldwide. PUBLICATIONS: *Expanded Reference Manual Of The Radiance Technique* EDITOR: Dr. Barbara Ray TOPICS: Holistic Health, Reiki TYPE: Book PRICE: $22.00 PUBLICATIONS: *Official Handbook Of The Radiance Technique, The* EDITOR: Dr. Barbara Ray TOPICS: New Age TYPE: Handbook PRICE: $17.75 PUBLICATIONS: *Radiance Technique Journal, The* EDITOR: Marilyn Alvey, Fred Wright TOPICS: Reiki, Body-Mind Connection, Massage, Holistic Health TYPE: Journal DATE: 1980, 20 pgs. FREQ: quarterly CIRC; 5,000 PRICE: $20.00 PRICE PER COPY: $4.00 DESCRIPTION: Journal for members of the association. Includes a variety of features such as non-fiction, children's stories, poetry, reviews, ads, interviews, and more. Features current information & alumni sharing of the Radiance Technique. PUBLICATIONS: *Radiance Technique On The Job, The* EDITOR: Fred W. Wright, Jr. TOPICS: New Age TYPE: Book PRICE: $9.90 PUBLICATIONS: *Reiki Factor* EDITOR: Dr. Barbara Ray TOPICS: Reiki, Body-Mind Connection, Massage TYPE: Book PRICE: $15.00

Radiance Technique Association International, Inc.
4 Embarcadero Center
Suite 5124
San Francisco, CA 94111
TOPICS: Reiki

Radiant Love Foundation
741 Rosarita Lane
Santa Barbara, CA 93105
TOPICS: Metaphysics

Rainbow Connections
P.O. Box 264
Wilmington, VT 05363
TOPICS: Metaphysics, Channeling

Rainbow Family Of Living Light
Rural Route 1, Box 6
McCall, ID 83638
TOPICS: New Age DESCRIPTION: Organized group of individuals with common interests such as ecology & the use of drugs & sex for enlightenment. Sponsors an annual group meeting called gathering of the tribes which attracts 10,000-30,000 participants. PUBLICATIONS: *Rainbow Nation Cooperative Community Guide, The* TOPICS: New Age TYPE: Directory FREQ: Irregular DESCRIPTION: Lists several thousand members.

Rainbow Web Grove
P.O. Box 1296
Manassas, VA 22110
TOPICS: Witchcraft

Rainbow Web Grove
P.O. Box 10504
Towson, MD 21204

TOPICS: Witchcraft

Ramtha Dialogues
Church I AM
P.O. Box 1210
Yelm, WA 98597
TOPICS: Metaphysics, Channeling

Raven Of Odin
P.O. Box 545
Longmont, CO 80502
TOPICS: Metaphysics

Reclaiming Collective
P.O. Box 14404
San Francisco, CA 94114
(510)-237-6207
CONTACT: M. Macha NightMare TOPICS: Occult, Witchcraft FOUNDED: 1981 STAFF: 20 DESCRIPTION: Offers classes & workshops in witchcraft & magic in the San Francisco Bay Area. Produces public rituals at many of the eight Sabbats as well as a Halloween ritual called The Spiral Dance or a cycle of rituals called The Samhain Cycle. Also sponsors week-long, worldwide Witch Camps. Produces a 40-minute tape of ritual chants. PUBLICATIONS: *Reclaiming Newsletter* TOPICS: Occult, Witchcraft TYPE: Newsletter FREQ: quarterly PRICE PER COPY: $2.00 DESCRIPTION: Subscriptions available on a sliding fee basis.

Red Rose Gallerie
P.O. Box 1859
Burlingame, CA 94011
TOPICS: Metaphysics

Reflections Of Divinity
P.O. Box 30724
Santa Barbara, CA 93130
TOPICS: Metaphysics

Registry Of Sidereal Astrology
1317 Monterey
Monrovia, CA 91016
TOPICS: Astrology

Regulus Foundation
P.O. Box 532
Graton, CA 95444
TOPICS: Metaphysics

Reincarnation Research
P.O. Box 26563
Phoenix, AZ 85068
TOPICS: Metaphysics

Religion Analysis Service
2708 East Lake Street, 231
Minneapolis, MN 55406
TOPICS: Skepticism, Counter-Cult DESCRIPTION: New Age, New And Unconventional Religions, etc.

Religious Information Service
P.O. Box 8657
Long Beach, CA 90806
TOPICS: Skepticism, Counter-Cult DESCRIPTION: New Age, New And Unconventional Religions, Mysticism, etc.

Rescue Team Ministries
P.O. Box 1178
Fayetteville, GA 30214

TOPICS: Skepticism, Counter-Cult DESCRIPTION: New Age, New And Unconventional Religions, Cults, etc.

Research And Education Foundation
Rural Delivery 1, Box 637
Sherman's Dale, PA 17090
TOPICS: Skepticism, Counter-Cult DESCRIPTION: Cults, New And Unconventional Religions, Satanism, etc.

Research Division Spiritual Council
P.O. Box 108
Sharon, PA 16146
TOPICS: Skepticism, Counter-Cult DESCRIPTION: New Age, New And Unconventional Religions, Cults, etc.

Rhentonby, Limited
15 LaRose Avenue, Unit 908
Etobicoke, ON, M9P1A7,
Canada
TOPICS: Metaphysics

Rites Of Passage
144 Oak Avenue
Novato, CA 94947
TOPICS: Metaphysics

River Path Network
P.O. Box 114
Camp Hill, PA 17011
TOPICS: Witchcraft

Rockville Health Association
4808 Macon Road
Rockville, MD 20852
(301)-881-2406
TOPICS: Holistic Healing

Rocky Mountain Research Institute
1304 South College Avenue
Fort Collins, CO 80524
(303)-491-5753
CONTACT: Maurice L. Albertson, Ph. D. TOPICS: Holistic Healing, Psychology, Parapsychology, Crystals, Astrology, UFO's, Channeling CONVENTIONS: annual International Forum on New Science DESCRIPTION: The International Association For New Science is the unifying organization that helps initiates a shift in science & health care. New Science includes topics & phenomena which cannot be explained by traditional science & yet may have the potential for significant benefit to the health & conditions of humanity & Earth. Topics include alternative healing, new psychology, parapsychology, near-death experiences, ghosts, UFO's, channeling & out-of-body experiences.

Rocky Mountain Spiritual Emergence Network
935 Spruce Street
Boulder, CO 80302
TOPICS: Psychic

Rocky Mountian Book Publishers Association
755 Brook Road
Boulder, CO 80302
(303)-277-1623
CONTACT: Alan Star TOPICS: New Age FOUNDED: 1977

Rolf Institute For Structural Integration
Box 1868
Boulder, CO 80306
(303)-449-5903
TOPICS: Holistic Health, Massage DESCRIPTION: National training organization for teachers of the bodywork massage technique of Rolfing. Students must be college graduates & be members of the American Massage & Therapy Association or an equivalent organization. PUBLICATIONS: *Rolf Institute International Directory* EDITOR: Marcia Richardson TOPICS: New Age TYPE: Directory PUBLICATIONS: *Rolfing: The Integration Of Human Structures* EDITOR: Ida P. Rolf TOPICS: Massage, Holistic Health TYPE: Book DATE: 1977

Rosicrucian Fellowship
2222 Mission Avenue
P.O. Box 713
Oceanside, CA 92054
(619)-757-6600
TOPICS: Astrology, New Age, Metaphysics, Spirituality FOUNDED: 1907 DESCRIPTION: Dedicated to the study of Astrology. Supplies reference books & materials to professional astrologers. PUBLICATIONS: *Occult Principles Of Health And Healing* EDITOR: M. Heindel TOPICS: Spirituality, Psychic Healing, Occult TYPE: Book PRICE: $12.95 PUBLICATIONS: *Rays From The Rose Cross* TOPICS: Parapsychology, Occult TYPE: Magazine DATE: 1974 FREQ: Bi-Monthly PUBLICATIONS: *Rosicrucian Christianity Lectures* EDITOR: M. Heindel TOPICS: Spirituality, New Age, Astrology TYPE: Book PRICE: $16.95

Rothschild-Berlin Magical
2250 East Tropicana Avenue 19
Las Vegas, NV 89119
TOPICS: Occult

Rowanwood
P.O. Box 23686
Lexington, KY 40523
TOPICS: Witchcraft

Rudolf Steiner Library
10315 Wooley Avenue, 105
Granada Hills, CA 91344
TOPICS: Metaphysics

Rune-Gild, The
P.O. Box 7622
Austin, TX 78713
TOPICS: Witchcraft

S.T.A.R.
Rural Delivery 1, Studio House
Staatsburg, NY 12580
TOPICS: Astrology

S.Y.D.A. Foundation/Siddha Yoga Meditation Ashram
P.O. Box 600
South Fallsburg, NY 12779
(914)-434-2000
TOPICS: Meditation, Metaphysics PUBLICATIONS: *I Have Become Alive: Secrets Of The Inner Journey* EDITOR: Muktananda TOPICS: Spirituality TYPE: Book PRICE: $8.95 PUBLICATIONS: *In The Company Of A Siddha* EDITOR: Muktananda TOPICS: Spirituality TYPE:

Book PRICE: $8.95 PUBLICATIONS: *Meditate* TOPICS: Meditation TYPE: Magazine PUBLICATIONS: *Nectar Of Chanting* EDITOR: Muktananda TOPICS: Spirituality TYPE: Book PRICE: $9.95 PUBLICATIONS: *Play Of Consciousness: A Spiritual Autobiography* EDITOR: Muktananda TOPICS: Spirituality TYPE: Book PRICE: $9.95 PUBLICATIONS: *Secret Of The Siddhas* EDITOR: Muktananda TOPICS: Spirituality TYPE: Book PRICE: $9.95 PUBLICATIONS: *Where Are You Going? A Guide To The Spiritual Journey* EDITOR: Muktananda TOPICS: Spirituality TYPE: Book PRICE: $12.95

Sacred Earth Alliance
P.O. Box 545
Gambier, OH 43022
TOPICS: Metaphysics

Sacred Mysteries
15243 La Cruz, #1675
Pacific Palisades, CA 90272
TOPICS: Metaphysics

Sacred Order Golden Knights
P.O. Box 411
West Long Branch, NJ 07764
TOPICS: Metaphysics

Sacred Order Knights Rune
P.O. Box 2070
Decatur, GA 30031
TOPICS: Metaphysics

Sagittarius Rising
P.O. Box 252
Arlington, MA 02174
TOPICS: Astrology

Saints Alive In Jesus
P.O. Box 3813, Station B
Calgary, Alb. T2M4N6,
Canada
TOPICS: Skepticism, Counter-Cult DESCRIPTION: Mormonism, Jehovah's Witnesses, Cults, New Age, Satanism, etc.

Saints Alive In Jesus
P.O. Box 1143
Clovis, CA 93612
TOPICS: Skepticism, Counter-Cult DESCRIPTION: Mormonism, Cults, New Age, Satanism, etc.

Samadhi
Karme-Choling
Barnet, VT 05821
TOPICS: Metaphysics

Samaritan Order Of Many Affectations
526 Green Street
Cambridge, MA 02139
TOPICS: Metaphysics

Sanscrit Classics
P.O. Box 5368
San Diego, CA 92105
TOPICS: Metaphysics

Santana Dharma Information Committee
47 Clubhouse Avenue
Venice, CA 90291

TOPICS: Metaphysics

Santeria
P.O. Box 453336
Miami, FL 33245
TOPICS: Witchcraft

Saskatoon Citizens Against Mind Control
P.O. Box 74
Saskatoon, Sask. S7K3K1,
Canada
TOPICS: Skepticism, Counter-Cult DESCRIPTION: New Age, New And Unconventional Religions, Occult, Paganism.

Schismatic Druids Of North America
P.O. Box 9398
Berkeley, CA 94709
TOPICS: Witchcraft

Science Frontiers (SF)
2119 College Street
Cedar Falls, IA 50613
(319)-266-8669
CONTACT: Gerald Baker, Exec. Dir. TOPICS: Psychic Phenomena FOUNDED: 1984 MEM: 50 STAFF: 1 AFF ORG: Mensa DESCRIPTION: Dedicated to the research of anomalies such as the study of ghosts based on the work of William R. Corliss & the Sourcebook Project. PUBLICATIONS: *Science Quest* EDITOR: Gerald Baker TOPICS: Psychic Phenomena TYPE: Magazine FREQ: quarterly PRICE: $5.00

Science Of Identity Foundation
P.O. Box 27450
Honolulu, HI 96827
(808)-488-4798
TOPICS: Metaphysics PUBLICATIONS: *Reincarnation Explained* EDITOR: Chris Butler TOPICS: Reincarnation, Spirituality TYPE: Book PRICE: $12.95

Science Of Spirituality
115 Third Avenue
Napa, CA 94550
TOPICS: Metaphysics

Science Unlimited Research Foundation
311-D Spencer Lane
San Antonio, TX 78201
TOPICS: Parapsychology, Psychic Phenomena

Scientific Astrol Research
45 Sherman Bridge Road
Wayland, MA 01775
TOPICS: Astrology

Scientology
1404 North Catalina Street
Los Angeles, CA 90024
TOPICS: Metaphysics

Scribe Society
P.O. Box 1207
Albany, OR 97321
TOPICS: Witchcraft

Sea Shepherd Conservation Society
Box 7000-S
Redondo Beach, CA 90277

(213)-373-6979
TOPICS: Holistic Healing

Seax-Wica
Box 99324
San Diego, CA 92109
TOPICS: Witchcraft, Occult, Paganism MEM: 4,000 DESCRIPTION: Promotes the philosophy of Saxon Wicca which encourages each coven tofunction democratically & responsibly. Their educational center is Seax-Wica Seminary in Charlottesville, VA which offers correspondence instruction.

Seax-Wicca Earth Stone Grv
4405 Maple Avenue
Brookfield, IL 60513
TOPICS: Witchcraft

Secrets
RR 4, Box 156
Marshall, AR 72650
TOPICS: UFO's PUBLICATIONS: *Secrets* PUBLISHER: Norma Cox TOPICS: UFO's TYPE: Newsletter; 24 pgs. FREQ: Irregular DESCRIPTION: Reports on conspiracies regarding UFO's.

Sedona Institute
1645 East Missouri, #110, Ste. 115
Phoenix, AZ 85016
(602)-264-0123
TOPICS: Holistic Healing PUBLICATIONS: *Release* EDITOR: Virginia Lloyd, Janet Bechtel TOPICS: Holistic Healing TYPE: Book

Seekers After Truth
89 Kensington Road
Kensington, CA 94707
TOPICS: Metaphysics

Self-Awareness Association
8123 East 48th Street
Tulsa, OK 74145
(918)-665-7773
CONTACT: Walt Browne TOPICS: New Age, Metaphysics FOUNDED: 1989

Set Free Ministries
P.O. Box 955
Springfield, OR 97477
TOPICS: Skepticism, Counter-Cult DESCRIPTION: Cults, New Age, Satanism, New And Unconventional Religions.

Seva Foundation, The
108 Spring Lake Drive
Chelsea, MI 48118
TOPICS: New Age, Metaphysics

Seventh Sense Institute
754 Bradshaw
Drew, MS 38737
TOPICS: Metaphysics

Several Sources Foundation
P.O. Box 157
Ramsey, NJ 07446
TOPICS: Occult

Shadows Of Iga Society
P.O. Box 291947
Kettering, OH 45429
TOPICS: Metaphysics

Shamanic Drumming Circle
1070 Plymouth Drive
Sunnyvale, CA 94087
TOPICS: Metaphysics

Shambala Training
2288 Fulton Street
Berkeley, CA 94704
TOPICS: Metaphysics

Shanti Foundation
9060 Santa Monica Boulevard, 301
West Hollywood, CA 90069
TOPICS: Metaphysics

Share Foundation
1556 Halford Avenue, #288
Santa Clara, CA 95051
(408)-245-5457
CONTACT: Virginia Essene TOPICS: New Age, Spirituality DESCRIPTION: Non-profit foundation committed to planetary peace & the preservation of all life. Established the Spiritual Education Endeavors Publishing Company which publishes books, the Love Corps newsletter & offers personal tours to assist humanity's awakening to spiritual stewardship of the entire planet.

Shechinah Outreach Ministry
P.O. Box 58015
Fairbanks, AK 99711
TOPICS: Skepticism, Counter-Cult DESCRIPTION: General New Age, Cults, New Religions, etc.

Shepherdsfield Community
RR 4, Box 399
Fulton, MO 65251
(314)-642-1439
TOPICS: Metaphysics, New Age

Shield Of The Northwind
P.O. Box 1324
Knoxville, TN 37901
TOPICS: Witchcraft

Shri Maha Prabujl
P.O. Box 4762
Covina, CA 91722
TOPICS: Metaphysics

Siddhartha Foundation
91 Dobbins Street
Waltham, MA 02154
TOPICS: Metaphysics

Sierra Club
730 Polk Street
San Francisco, CA 94109
(415)-776-2211 FAX (415)-776-0350
TOPICS: Holistic Healing PUBLICATIONS: *Sierra* EDITOR: Michael L. Fischer, Jonathan F. King TOPICS: Holistic Healing TYPE: Newsletter

Sierra Two Community
P.O. Box 366
Sierraville, CA 96126
TOPICS: Metaphysics

Sight Of The Moon
P.O. Box 7517
Naples, FL 33941
TOPICS: Witchcraft

Signal Corps
89 Massachusetts Avenue, 184
Boston, MA 02115
TOPICS: Witchcraft

Sikh Study Circle
5575 Trowbridge Drive
Dunwoody, GA 30338
TOPICS: Witchcraft

Silva Method, The
P.O. Box 2158
Rancho Mirage, CA 92270
TOPICS: Metaphysics

Silva Supermind
5050 Calatrana
Woodland Hills, CA 91364
TOPICS: Occult

Silver Crescent
151 Haled Street, G
Winston-Salem, NC 27117
TOPICS: Witchcraft

Silver Elves
P.O. Box 2035
Guerneville, CA 95446
TOPICS: Witchcraft

Silver Mist Coven
P.O. Box 322
Trumbarsville, PA 18970
TOPICS: Witchcraft

Silverstar
P.O. Box 680
Clinton, MA 01510
TOPICS: Witchcraft

Silverwood Circle
P.O. Box 4418
Richmond, VA 23220
TOPICS: Witchcraft

Sirius 23
P.O. Box 884
Brookline, MA 02146
TOPICS: Metaphysics

Sister Spirit
P.O. Box 9246
Portland, OR 97207
TOPICS: Witchcraft

Sisterhood Of St. Clare
P.O. Box 293
Deming, WA 98244
CONTACT: Sister Julian Thomas TOPICS:
Spirituality, New Age FOUNDED: 1989 MEM: 30
DESCRIPTION: Founded by Sister Julian Thomas.
Informal organization giving aid & support to the
growth & development of the Hermit Monks of St.
Clare, a small group of unorthodox Hermits. Formed
for women who have the contemplative spirit, but
wish to be more active & involved with the holistic
learning & growth process. Goal is to develop a
permanent Center. Members must relate to Thomas
Merton's approach to Spirituality.

Sixth Sense
226 South 312th Street
Federal Way, WA 98003

TOPICS: Channeling

Skandinavisk UFO Information
Box 6
Gentofte, 2820
Denmark
TOPICS: UFO's FOUNDED: 1957 MEM: 1,000
DESCRIPTION: Conducts research of UFO's.
PUBLICATIONS: UFO Forskning EDITOR: Lars K.
Lassen TOPICS: UFO's TYPE: Newsletter DATE:
1983 FREQ: Irregular CIRC: 200 PUBLICATIONS:
UFO Vision EDITOR: Kim Moeller Hansen,
Flemming Rasmussen TOPICS: UFO's TYPE:
Magazine DATE: 1987 FREQ: Annual CIRC; 100
PUBLICATIONS: UFO-NYT EDITOR: Kim Moeller
Hansen TOPICS: UFO's TYPE: Magazine DATE:
1958, 24 pgs. FREQ: Quarterly CIRC; 2,000
DESCRIPTION: Deals with all aspects of UFO's.

SKY Foundation
601 St. Georges Road
Philadelphia, PA 19119
TOPICS: Metaphysics

Snapdragon
P.O. Box 4532
Seattle, WA 98104
TOPICS: Witchcraft

Society Creative Anachronisms
P.O. Box 360743
Milpitas, CA 95035
TOPICS: Occult

Society For Clinical & Experimental Hypnosis
111 North 49th Street
Philadelphia, PA 19139
(215)-472-1055
TOPICS: Hypnotism PUBLICATIONS: International
Journal Of Clinical And Experimental Hypnosis
EDITOR: Martin T. Orne TOPICS: Hypnotism
TYPE: Journal PUBLICATIONS: International
Society Of Hypnosis Newsletter TOPICS:
Hypnotism TYPE: Newsletter PUBLICATIONS:
Society For Clinical & Experimental Hypnosis
EDITOR: Marion Kenn TOPICS: Hypnotism TYPE:
Newsletter

Society For Clinical & Experimental Hypnosis
129-A Kings Park Drive
Liverpool, NY 13088
(315)-652-7299
TOPICS: Hypnotism PUBLICATIONS: International
Journal Of Clinical & Experimental Hypnosis
TOPICS: Hypnotism TYPE: Journal
PUBLICATIONS: SCEH Newsletter EDITOR:
Marion Kenn TOPICS: Hypnotism TYPE:
Newsletter

Society For Psychic Research
7761 Orangewood Avenue
Stanton, CA 90680
TOPICS: Metaphysics

Society For Psychical Research
1 Adam and Eve Mews
Kensington, London, W8 6UG
England
01-937-8984

TOPICS: Parapsychology, Occult PUBLICATIONS:
Journal Of The Society For Psychical Research
EDITOR: John Beloff TOPICS: Parapsychology,
Occult TYPE: Journal DATE: 1884 FREQ:
Quarterly CIRC: 1,000 PRICE: $36.00
DESCRIPTION: Scientifically explores man's psychic
abilities & attempts to explain the inexplicable.
PUBLICATIONS: Society For Psychical Research
Proceedings EDITOR: John Beloff TOPICS:
Parapsychology, Occult TYPE: Magazine DATE:
1882 FREQ: Irregular PUBLICATIONS: SPR
Newsletter EDITOR: Susan Balckmore TOPICS:
Parapsychology, Occult TYPE: Newsletter DATE:
1981 FREQ: Quarterly CIRC; 900

Society For Scientific Exploration (SSE)
University of Virginia, Department of Astronomy
P.O. Box 3818
Charlottesville, VA 22903
(804)-924-4905
CONTACT: Professor Laurence W. Fredrick
TOPICS: Psychic Phenomena, Parapsychology

Society For Scientific Exploration
Center For Space Science & Astrophysics
Stanford, CA 94305
CONTACT: Peter A. Sturrock TOPICS:
Parapsychology, Psychic Phenomena
PUBLICATIONS: Journal Of Scientifc Exploration
EDITOR: Peter Sturrock TOPICS: Parapsychology,
Psychic Phenomena TYPE: Journal

Society For The Application Of Free Energy (SAFE)
1315 Apple Avenue
Silver Spring, MD 20910
(301)-587-8686
CONTACT: C. Schleicher, Dir. TOPICS: Psychic
Phenomena, New Age

Society For The Investigation Of The Unexplained (SITU)
Box 265
Little Silver, NJ 07739
(201)-842-5229
CONTACT: Robert C. Warth, Pres. TOPICS:
Parapsychology, Occult, Psychic Phenomena
PUBLICATIONS: Pursuit - S.I.T.U. EDITOR: Robert
C. Warth TOPICS: Parapsychology, Occult,
Paranormal Phenomena TYPE: Magazine DATE:
1969 FREQ: Quarterly CIRC: 1,500 PRICE: $12.00

Society For The Right To Die, Inc.
250 West 57th Street
New York, NY 10107
(212)-246-6973
TOPICS: Death PUBLICATIONS: Society For The
Right To Die-Newsletter EDITOR: Shirley Neitlich
TOPICS: Death TYPE: Newsletter

Society Of Emissaries
Box 9
100 M1 House, BC, V0K2E0,
Canada
TOPICS: Metaphysics

Society Of Evening Star
P.O. Box 29182
Providence, RI 02909
TOPICS: Metaphysics

Society Of Inner Awareness
136 Whitney Place
Buffalo, NY 14201
TOPICS: Metaphysics

Society Of Mary Magdalen
P.O. Box 201
Cape Cottage, ME 04107
TOPICS: Metaphysics, Channeling

Society of Pragmatic Mysticism (SPM)
R.R.l, Box 800
Pawlett, VT 05761
(802)-325-3107
CONTACT: Leonebel Connaway, Dir. **TOPICS:** New Age, Metaphysics

Society Of Rosicrucianists
10 East Chestnut Street
Kingston, NY 12401
TOPICS: Metaphysics

Society Of The Magians
P.O. Box 46
Cathedral City, CA 92234
TOPICS: Metaphysics

SOL Association For Research - The Council Speaks
P.O. Box 2276
North Canton, OH 44720
CONTACT: William Allen LePar **TOPICS:** Channeling, Spirituality **CONVENTIONS:** Annual conferences in Canton, OH **DESCRIPTION:** Non-profit organization composed of members called Associates in search of true spiritual enlightenment & personal growth. Purpose is to record the word of the Council, 12 entities channeled by the psychic, William Allen LePar. Also offers lectures & workshops nationwide. Publishes books, tapes & a newsletter. Gives TV & radio interviews. **PUBLICATIONS:** *SOLAR (SOL Association For Research)* **TOPICS:** Channeling, Spirituality **TYPE:** Newsletter **FREQ:** quarterly

Solar Cross
P.O. Box 1129
Middletown, CA 95461
TOPICS: UFO's

Somatics Society (SS)
1516 Grant Avenue, Suite 220
Novato, CA 94945
(415)-897-0336
CONTACT: Thomas Hanna, Ph.D., Pres. **TOPICS:** New Age

Son-Zen Lotus Society
378 Markham Street, B-1
Toronto, ON, N6G2K9,
Canada
TOPICS: Metaphysics

Sonshine Ministries
P.O. Box 1024
Denniston, KY 40316
TOPICS: Skepticism, Counter-Cult **DESCRIPTION:** Mormonism, Jehovah's Witnesses, Cults, Satanism, New Age, etc.

Sound Healers Association, Inc. (SHA)
P.O. Box 2240
Boulder, CO 80306
(303)-443-8181
CONTACT: Jonathan S. Goldman **TOPICS:** Holistic Health, Holistic Healing, Body-Mind Connection, New Age, Spirituality, Meditation **DESCRIPTION:** Research & education of the uses of sound & music for health & wellness. Founder & President, Jonathan S. Goldman. Free articles & newsletter available upon request.

Southeast Paranormal Information
1539 Kenwood Avenue, Southwest
Winter Haven, FL 33880
TOPICS: Metaphysics

Southern California Society For Psychical Research
269 South Arden Boulevard
Los Angeles, CA 90004
TOPICS: Parapsychology, Metaphysics **PUBLICATIONS:** *Journal Of The Southern California Society For Psychical Research* **TOPICS:** Parapsychology **TYPE:** Journal **SIZE:** 6 x 8 1/2; 30 pgs. **FREQ:** Irregular

Southern California Society Of Clinical Hypnosis
14724 Ventura Boulevard, #604
Sherman Oaks, CA 91403
TOPICS: Hypnotism

Southern Cassadaga Spiritualist Camp Meeting Association
1112 Stevens Street
P.O. Box 319
Cassadaga, FL 32706
(904)-228-2880
CONTACT: Fran Ellison, Association Director **TOPICS:** Spirituality, Holistic Healing, Channeling, Psychic Phenomena, Psychic **FOUNDED:** 1894 **CONVENTIONS:** Weekly services: Sunday Church Services, Adult Sunday School, Childrens Lyceum, Free Message Services and Healing Services. **DESCRIPTION:** A non-profit, federally tax-exempt church organization that promotes spiritualism. Serves as an educational center for those seeking credentials in mediumship, healing and ministry. Provides guidance and counseling to those who come in search of enlightenment. **PUBLICATIONS:** *Southern Cassadaga Spiritualist Camp Meeting Handbook* **TOPICS:** Spirituality, Holistic Healing, Channeling, Psychic Phenomena, Psychic **TYPE:** Handbook; 40 pgs. **FREQ:** annual **PRICE:** $1.00 **DESCRIPTION:** 40 page annual informational booklet describing Cassadaga, principals of spiritualism, camp activities and the yearly calendar.

Southwestern Booksellers Association
P.O. Box 190831
Dallas, TX 75219
(214)-954-4469
CONTACT: Steve Davis **TOPICS:** New Age

Space Technology And Research Foundation, Inc. (S.T.A.R.)
448 Rabbit Skin Road
Waynesville, NC 28786
(704)-926-3440

TOPICS: New Age, UFO's **PUBLICATIONS:** *The Woodrew Update* **EDITOR:** Greta Woodrew, Richard Smolowe **TOPICS:** New Age **TYPE:** Newsletter

Spiral
P.O. Box 26414
Albuquerque, NM 87125
TOPICS: Metaphysics

Spirit Of The Warrior International
2 Crescent Road
Cape Elizabeth, ME 04107
(207)-767-2349
TOPICS: New Age, Metaphysics

Spirit Of Truth Ministry
223 South Magnolia
Fullerton, CA 92633
TOPICS: Skepticism, Counter-Cult **DESCRIPTION:** Unconventional and dissenting Religions, Cults, New Age, etc.

Spiritual Advisory Council (S.A.C.)
10345 SE 103rd Terrace
Summerfield, FL 32691
(407)-774-6151 (800)-245-1389
CONTACT: Dr. Paul V. Johnson, Pres. **TOPICS:** Parapsychology, Occult, Psychic, Channeling, Metaphysics, Spirituality **FOUNDED:** 1974 **MEM:** 1,000 **STAFF:** 2 **GROUPS:** 2 **COMPUTER:** yes **CONVENTIONS:** June-Annual Retreat-Lake Forest College, Lake Forest, IL; Feb.-Annual Conference-Las Palmas Inn, Orlando, FL. **DESCRIPTION:** Founded as an intermediary between religion, science & personal revelation of mystics, clairvoyants, etc. Purpose to update incorrect information about life after death, the meaning of life on earth, and bring occult sciences into proper perspective. Membership available. Conducts workshops, lectures & annual programs. Association & Church acting as a clearing house for metaphysical information & offering counselling services, book store & a program for ordination of ministers. **PUBLICATIONS:** *Spiritual Advisory Council Newsletter-Outreach* **EDITOR:** Rev. Paul V. Johnson **TOPICS:** Parapsychology, Occult, Psychic, Spirituality, Metaphysics **TYPE:** Newsletter **FREQ:** 10 x yearly **CIRC:** 1,000 **DESCRIPTION:** Newsletter included with membership.

Spiritual Awareness
11600 Washington Place, 102E
Los Angeles, CA 90066
TOPICS: Metaphysics

Spiritual Counterfeits Projects
P.O. Box 4308
Berkeley, CA 94704
TOPICS: Skepticism, Counter-Cult **DESCRIPTION:** New Age, New Religions, Non-conforming Christian groups.

Spiritual Frontiers Fellowship (SFF)
P.O. Box 7686
Philadelphia, PA 10101
(215)-222-8459
CONTACT: Frank C. Tribbe **TOPICS:** Psychic Phenomena, Spirituality, Reincarnation, Parapsychology, New Age **PUBLICATIONS:** *Spiritual Frontiers* **EDITOR:** Frank C. Tribbe **TOPICS:** Psychic Phenomena **TYPE:** Journal **FREQ:** quarterly **DESCRIPTION:** Contains articles on the

relationships between religion, psychical research & parapsychology as well as on spiritual growth, reincarnation, healing, psychic phenomena & the Spiritual Frontiers Fellowship. Offers book reviews & research reports.

Spiritual Frontiers Fellowship
390 West End Avenue, 9A
New York, NY 10024
TOPICS: Metaphysics, Channeling

Spiritual Network, The
P.O. 262
Evanston, IL 60204
TOPICS: Metaphysics

Spiritual Science Fellowship (S.S.F.)
P.O. Box 1445
Station H
Montreal, Quebec H3G 2N3
Canada
(514)-937-8359
TOPICS: Psychic, Spirituality, New Age FOUNDED: 1977 MEM: 8,000 GROUPS: 43 DESCRIPTION: Inter-faith fellowship providing spiritual services, educational programs & pastoral ministrations for persons who desire to understand experiences of psyche & spirit, & to dedicate themselves to personal spiritual growth & psychic development, in an atmosphere of informed free-thought & enquiry.

Spiritual Warfare Ministry
P.O. Box 396
Warrington, PA 18976
TOPICS: Skepticism, Counter-Cult DESCRIPTION: New Age, New And Unconventional Religions, Occult, Paganism.

Spiritualist Association Of America
19 Crofty Road
Lutchville, MD 21093
TOPICS: New Age

Spiritualist Healers League
8521 Worthington Boulevard
Westerville, OH 43081
TOPICS: Metaphysics

Spiritualist Medley
14482 Beach, F
Westminister, CA 92683
TOPICS: Metaphysics

SRI
333 Ravenswood Avenue
Menlo Park, CA 94025
TOPICS: Parapsychology, Psychic Phenomena

Star And Cross
P.O. Box 25541
Dallas, TX 75225
TOPICS: Metaphysics

Star Magic
4026-A 24th Street
San Francisco, CA 94114
TOPICS: Astrology

Star Of Isis Foundation
P.O. Box 4872
San Antonio, TX 78285
(512)-737-1733

CONTACT: Chrystine StarEagle TOPICS: Channeling, New Age DESCRIPTION: A mystery school established for the enlightenment of Human & Planetary consciousness through the alchemy of Divine Origin. Purpose is to help individuals achieve higher consciousness through a Doctrine Of Mysteries entitled Temple Doors & the Matrix program. Membership $25 per year. PUBLICATIONS: *Temple Doors* EDITOR: Christine Hayes TYPE: Magazine DATE: 1980 SIZE: 8 1/2 x 11; 25 pgs. FREQ: quarterly CIRC: 100 PRICE: $25.00 TERM: yearly PRICE PER COPY: $5.00 DESCRIPTION: Channelled insights into planetary transformation, inner earth tribes, meta-sciences, ancient cultures & angelic mandates.

Starbirth
12626 North Tatum Road
Phoenix, AZ 85032
TOPICS: UFO's

Starborn
P.O. Box 5801
Charlottesville, VA 22905
TOPICS: Astrology

Starbreeze Enterprises
5107 Lakewood Avenue
St. Louis, MO 63123
TOPICS: Metaphysics

Starline Connection
North Star Route 588
Corrales, NM 87048
TOPICS: UFO's

Starlink Seminary
7345 Healdsburg Avenue
Sebastopol, CA 95472
TOPICS: UFO's

Stealth UFOlogy Network
P.O. Box 821
Linden Hill, NY 11354
TOPICS: UFO's

Stellar Foundation
1704 Roosevelt Avenue
Ricmond, CA 94801-2812
TOPICS: Metaphysics

Stelle Group, The (TSG)
127 Sun Street
Stelle, IL 60919
(815)-256-2200
CONTACT: Tim Wilhelm, Exec. Dir. TOPICS: New Age

Still Waters Foundation (SWF)
615 Stafford Lane
Pensacola, FL 32506
(904)-455-9511
CONTACT: John and Carol Pepper TOPICS: New Age

Stillpoint Foundation
604 South 15th Street
San Jose, CA 95112
TOPICS: Occult

Street Meetings, Incorporated
P.O. Box 724
Dallas, TX 75221

TOPICS: Skepticism, Counter-Cult DESCRIPTION: New Age, New And Unconventional Religions, Occult, Paganism.

Sufi Order
P.O. Box 2113
Lake Oswego, OR 97035
TOPICS: Metaphysics

Sufi Order In The West
P.O. Box 574
Lebanon Springs, NY 12114
CONTACT: Pir Vilayat Inayat Khan TOPICS: New Age, Holistic Health, Spirituality DESCRIPTION: Dedicated to the holistic health movement, healing, spirituality & to bring Sufism to the West.

Sufi Order In The West
P.O. Box 30065
Seattle, WA 98103-2065
TOPICS: New Age, Holistic Health, Spirituality

Sufism Reoriented
1300 Boulevard Way
Walnut Creek, CA 94595
TOPICS: Metaphysics

Sun Foundation
1436 Chapala
Santa Barbara, CA 93101
TOPICS: Occult

Sun Spiritualist Camp Association
Star Route 2, Box 596
Tonopah, AZ 85354
TOPICS: New Age

Sundar
P.O. Box 9626
San Diego, CA 92109
TOPICS: UFO's

Sundoor-Foundation For Transpersonal Education
P.O. Box 669
Twain Harte, CA 95383
(209)-928-4800
CONTACT: Peggy Dylan TOPICS: New Age, Body-Mind Connection, Meditation, Spirituality, Firewalking FOUNDED: 1984 AFF ORG: F.I.R.E.-Firewalking, Institute of Research & Education DESCRIPTION: Facilitates personal transformation & empowerment through a variety of seminars: firewalking, relationships & vision quests which helps promote spiritual & emotional healing, positive thinking & body-mind interactions. Firewalking is a demonstration of what the mind is capable of doing & a way of overcoming all fears. After a 4 hour inspirational seminar people are able to walk unharmed on hot coals. Also offers spiritual adventures to places like Peru, India, Nepal, etc.

Sunrise New Age Community
Rural Route 1, Box 164-A
New Milton, WV 26411
TOPICS: Metaphysics

Sunrise: International Networking
P.O. Box 113
Warrenville, IL 60555
TOPICS: Metaphysics

Supreme Council Of The Independent Associated Spiritualists (SCIAS)
7230 Fourth Street, N., #2304
St. Petersburg, FL 33702
CONTACT: Rev. Marion Owens, Sec. TOPICS: Psychic Phenomena

Supreme Grand Lodge of AMORC, Inc. (AMORC)
Rosicrucian Order, Rosicrucian Park
1342 Nagle Avenue
San Jose, CA 95191
(408)-287-9171
CONTACT: Gary L. Stewart TOPICS: New Age, Parapsychology, Spirituality PUBLICATIONS: *Conscience Of Science And Other Essays* EDITOR: W. Albersheim TOPICS: Paranormal Phenomena, Spirituality TYPE: Book PRICE: $12.50 PUBLICATIONS: *El Rosacruz* EDITOR: Laura Torres TOPICS: Parapsychology TYPE: Magazine DATE: 1945 SIZE: 7.5 x 10.5, 24 pgs. FREQ: Bi-Monthly CIRC; 17,000 PRICE: $9.00 PRICE PER COPY: $1.50 DESCRIPTION: Covers topics such as philosophy, mysticism & science. Text in Spanish. PUBLICATIONS: *Glands: Mirror Of The Self* EDITOR: O. Wilson TOPICS: Parapsychology, Holistic Health TYPE: Book PRICE: $12.50 PUBLICATIONS: *Great Vision: Francis Bacon* EDITOR: P. Dalkins TOPICS: New Age TYPE: Book PRICE: $30.00 PUBLICATIONS: *Herbalism Through The Ages* EDITOR: R. Kerr TOPICS: Herbalogy, Spirituality, Alchemy TYPE: Book PRICE: $12.50 PUBLICATIONS: *Lemuria: Lost Continent Of The Pacific* EDITOR: W. Cerve TOPICS: New Age TYPE: Book PRICE: $12.50 PUBLICATIONS: *Mansions Of The Soul: Reincarnation, The Soul's Rebirth On Earth* EDITOR: H. Lewis TOPICS: Reincarnation, Spirituality TYPE: Book PRICE: $9.00 PUBLICATIONS: *Mysticism: The Ultimate Experience* EDITOR: C. Poole TOPICS: Paranormal Phenomena, Spirituality TYPE: Book PRICE: $12.50 PUBLICATIONS: *Rosicrucian Digest* EDITOR: Robin M. Thompson TOPICS: New Age TYPE: Magazine PUBLICATIONS: *Secret Symbols Of The Rosicrucians* EDITOR: Rosicrucian Order TOPICS: Spirituality TYPE: Book PRICE: $20.00 PUBLICATIONS: *Symbolic Prophcy Of The Great Pyramid* EDITOR: H. Lewis TOPICS: New Age TYPE: Book PRICE: $8.95

Survival Research Foundation
P.O. Box 8565
Pembroke Pines, FL 33024
TOPICS: Parapsychology, Psychic Phenomena

Susan B. Anthony Coven
P.O. Box 11363
Oakland, CA 94611
TOPICS: Witchcraft

Swami Buddananda
1440 Upas Street
San Diego, CA 92103
TOPICS: Metaphysics

Swedenborg Foundation, Inc.
139 East 23rd Street
New York, NY 10010
(212)-673-7310 (800)-366-7310

TOPICS: Spirituality, Psychology DESCRIPTION: Clearing house for information & books.

Swedenborgian Church
48 Sargent Street
Newton, MA 02158
TOPICS: Spirituality, Psychology DESCRIPTION: International movement primarily in U.S., Great Britain & Australia. Based on the spiritual/psychological findings of scientist & seer, Emanuel Swedenborg. Operates church centers, retreat & conference centers, publishing companies & educational institutions.

Sword Of Laban, The
1950 Grant Street
Concord, CA 94520
TOPICS: Skepticism, Counter-Cult DESCRIPTION: Mormonism. Cults, New Age, Satanism, etc.

Sword Of The Shepherd Ministry
P.O. Box 4707
Thousand Oaks, CA 91359
TOPICS: Skepticism, Counter-Cult DESCRIPTION: Mormonism, New And Unconventional Religions, New Age, etc.

Sylvan Society
52 Libby Avenue
Hicksville, NY 11801
(516)-433-9118
CONTACT: Maria D'Andrea TOPICS: New Age, Meditation, Spirituality FOUNDED: 1985 STAFF: 11 GROUPS: 2 COMPUTER: no AFF ORG: Floating Healing Meditation Circle; Individuals Against Mediocrity CONVENTIONS: New York area on continuous basis DESCRIPTION: Dedicated to the spiritual growth of the members of Sylvan & of the general populace as they become ready. Teaches students how to see reality from different points of views so that they may manipulate reality to their points of views. Concentrates on the areas of: finance, love, health, business, travel, re-location & unlimited positive horizons.

Take Heed Ministries
P.O. Box 350
Murrysville, PA 15668
TOPICS: Skepticism, Counter-Cult DESCRIPTION: New Age, New And Unconventional Religions, Cults, Masons, etc.

Taoist Sanctuary
3350 Rowena Avenue
Los Angeles, CA 90027
TOPICS: Metaphysics

Tapestry
P.O. Box 10
Stevenson, MD 21153
TOPICS: Witchcraft

Tara Canada
P.O. Box 15270
Vancouver, BC, V6B5B1,
Canada
TOPICS: Metaphysics

Task Outreach Ministry
13248 Roscoe Boulevard
Sun Valley, CA 91352

TOPICS: Skepticism, Counter-Cult DESCRIPTION: Cults, New Age, Satanism, New And Unconventional Religions.

Teaching Of The Inner Christ, Inc. (TIC)
3150 Main Street
Lemon Grove, CA 92045
(619)-697-3900
TOPICS: New Age, Channeling, Yoga, Spirituality PUBLICATIONS: *Vision* TOPICS: New Age TYPE: Magazine

Technical Research Institute
P.O. Box 2095
Arvada, CO 80001
TOPICS: Skepticism, Counter-Cult DESCRIPTION: New Age, Paganism, New And Unconventional Religions, etc.

Technicians Of The Sacred (T.O.T.S.)
1317 North San Fernando Boulevard, #310
Burbank, CA 91504
CONTACT: Courtney Willis, Pres. TOPICS: Voudoun, Occult, Metaphysics FOUNDED: 1983 GROUPS: 4 DESCRIPTION: Purpose is the preservation and practice of Voudoun and other Neo-African religious systems, its art, magic and culture. Affiliated organizations are Monastery Of The Seven Rays, La Couleuvre Noire, Ordo Templi Orientis Antiqua, International Religious And Magical Order Of Societe & the Neo-African Network. Offers Voodoo-Gnostic orientation, international membership, and personalized study programs. Supply catalog offers books, music, tapes & ritual supplies. PUBLICATIONS: *Societe Journal* EDITOR: Courtney Willis TOPICS: Voudoun TYPE: Journal FREQ: bi-annually PRICE: $10.00 DESCRIPTION: Promotes the preservation and practice of Voudoun and other Neo-African religious systems, its magic, art and culture. PUBLICATIONS: *The Voudoun Gnostic Workbook* EDITOR: Michael Bertiaux TOPICS: Voudoun TYPE: Book PRICE: $29.95

Telstar
P.O. Box 5187
Santa Fe, NM 87502
TOPICS: Metaphysics

Templar Circle
P.O. Box 1664342
Miami, FL 33116
TOPICS: Witchcraft

Temple Of Aton
7160 North 48th Avenue
Glendale, AZ 85301
TOPICS: Metaphysics

Temple Of Cosmic Religion
174 Santa Clara Avenue
Oakland, CA 94610
CONTACT: Satguru Sant Keshavadas TOPICS: Metaphysics

Temple Of Eldar
P.O. Box 1824
Indianapolis, IN 46206
TOPICS: Witchcraft

Temple Of Kriya Yoga
2414 N. Kedzie Avenue

Chicago, IL 60647
(312)-342-4600 (800)-248-0024
TOPICS: New Age, Metaphysics PUBLICATIONS: *Spiritual Science Of Kriya Yoga* Kriyananda TOPICS: Yoga, Holistic Health TYPE: Book PRICE: $16.95

Temple Of Man
1439 Cabrillo Avenue
Venice, CA 90291
TOPICS: Metaphysics

Temple Of Repthys
P.O. Box 4603
San Francisco, CA 94101
TOPICS: Witchcraft

Temple Of The Elder Gods
P.O. Box 4172
Sunland, CA 91040
TOPICS: Witchcraft

Temple Of The Masters
4731 Date Street
La Mesa, CA 92041
TOPICS: Metaphysics

Temple Of Thoth
P.O. Box 3684
Toledo, OH 43608
TOPICS: Witchcraft

Temple Of Wicca
P.O. Box 1302
Findlay, OH 45839
TOPICS: Parapsychology, Occult, Witchcraft PUBLICATIONS: *Magickal Unicorn Messenger* EDITOR: Samantha Pugh TOPICS: Parapsychology, Occult TYPE: Newspaper DATE: 1980 FREQ: Quarterly CIRC: 200 PRICE: $9.00 DESCRIPTION: Features news, events, articles & reviews concerning the practice of paganism & wicca.

Teramanto
10218 147th, Southeast
Renton, WA 98056
TOPICS: Metaphysics

Theosophical Movement
245 West 33rd Street
Los Angeles, CA 90027
TOPICS: Metaphysics

Theosophical Society
5612 14th Street, N.W.
Washington, DC 20011
TOPICS: Metaphysics

Theosophical Society
P.O. Bin C
Pasadena, CA 91109
(818)-798-3378
TOPICS: Metaphysics, Spirituality, New Age FOUNDED: 1886 DESCRIPTION: International headquarters. Operates the Theosophical University Press which has been publishing theosophical literature since 1886 & features the writings of H.P Blavatsky, W.Q. Judge & G. dePurucker.

Theosophical Society Of America
306 West Geneva Road
P.O. Box 270
Wheaton, IL 60189-0270

(312)-668-1571 FAX (312)-665-8791
TOPICS: Metaphysics, New Age

Thera
P.O. Box 747
Aurora, CO 80040
TOPICS: UFO's

Therapeutic Touch Network
123 Queen Street West
Brampton, Ontario L6Y 1M3
Canada
(416)-454-2688
CONTACT: Mary Simpson, R.N., C.A.C. TOPICS: Holistic Healing FOUNDED: 1986 DESCRIPTION: Devoted to the promotion of Therapeutic Touch (Krieger-Kunz Method). It connects patients with practitioners. Promotes educational opportunities in TT, encourages research & fosters consensus on professional guidelines for practice & conduct.

Thistledown
P.O. Box 227
Valhalla, NY 10595
TOPICS: Witchcraft

Tibetan Foundation
P.O. Box 27364
Santa Ana, CA 92799
TOPICS: Metaphysics

Tibetan Foundation
21 Spring Road
Orinda, CA 94563
TOPICS: Metaphysics

Tibetan Foundation, The
126 113th Avenue
Valley View Plaza, Ste. C19
Youngstown, AZ 85363
TOPICS: New Age, Spirituality

To Every Man An Answer
P.O. Box 493
Niles, OH 44446
TOPICS: Skepticism, Counter-Cult DESCRIPTION: Jehovah's Witnesses, New Age, New And Unconventional Religions

Tools For Change
Box 14141
San Francisco, CA 94114
(415)-861-6838
TOPICS: Holistic Healing

Tools Of Magic
1915 Page Street
San Francisco, CA 94117
TOPICS: Witchcraft

Touch For Health Foundation (THF)
1174 North Lake Avenue
Pasadena, CA 91104
(818)-794-1181
TOPICS: Holistic Healing PUBLICATIONS: *In Touch For Health* EDITOR: Barry Greenberg TOPICS: Holistic Healing TYPE: Book

Tract Ministry Crusades
P.O. Box 4404
Rocky Mount, NC 27803
TOPICS: Skepticism, Counter-Cult DESCRIPTION: New Age, New And Unconventional Religions, etc.

Traditional Acupuncture Foundation
American City Building
Suite 100
Columbia, MD 21044
(301)-997-4888
TOPICS: Acupuncture PUBLICATIONS: *Journal Of Traditional Acupuncture* EDITOR: Mary Ellen Zorbaugh TOPICS: Acupuncture TYPE: Journal

Transeekers
P.O. Box 185, Station Z
Toronto, ON, M5N2Z4,
Canada
TOPICS: Metaphysics

Transpersonal Astrology
1827 Haight Street, 10
San Francisco, CA 94117
TOPICS: Astrology

Tree Of Life Seminars
200 Spring Hill Road
Petaluma, CA 94952
(707)-778-6501
CONTACT: Gabriel Cousens, M.D. TOPICS: New Age, Holistic Health, Spirituality, Reiki, Nutrition DESCRIPTION: Offers seminars and lectures on New Age topics such as holistic health, nutrition, spirituality and Reiki. Gabriel Cousens, M.D. director. PUBLICATIONS: *Holistic Protocol For The Immune System: Aids/Arc/HIV, Candidiasis, Epstein-Barr, Herpes* EDITOR: Scott Gregory TOPICS: Acupuncture TYPE: Book PRICE: $14.95

Tri-County UFO Study Group
P.O. Box U
Sebring, OH 44672
TOPICS: UFO's

Triskellion Coven
P.O. Box 9654
Minneapolis, MN 55440
TOPICS: Witchcraft

True Light Ministry
P.O. Box 2295
Syracuse, NY 13220
TOPICS: Skepticism, Counter-Cult DESCRIPTION: Jehovah's Witnesses, Cults, Satanism, etc.

True Truth Ministries
6539 Shenandoah
Allen Park, MI 48101
TOPICS: Skepticism, Counter-Cult DESCRIPTION: Jehovah's Witnesses, New Age, Satanism, etc.

Truth Alliance Ministry
P.O. Box 21742, Liberty U
Lynchburg, VA 24506
TOPICS: Skepticism, Counter-Cult DESCRIPTION: New Age, New And Unconvential Religions, Occult And Paganism.

Truth Outreach
P.O. Box 3191
Fairfax, VA 22038
TOPICS: Skepticism, Counter-Cult DESCRIPTION: Mormonism, Cults, Satanism, New And Unconventional Religions.

Tucson Area Wiccan Network
P.O. Box 482
Tucson, AZ 85702

TOPICS: Witchcraft

Tutors For Christ
P.O. Box 54654
Lexington, KY 40555
TOPICS: Skepticism, Counter-Cult DESCRIPTION: Jehovah's Witnesses. Cults, New Age, Satanism, etc.

Twentieth Century UFO Bureau
756 Haddon Avenue
Collingswood, NJ 08108
TOPICS: UFO's

U.S.A. Legion Of Light
P.O. Box 107
Lytle Creek, CA 92358
TOPICS: UFO's

UFO Bureau
516 Colton Avenue
Thomasville, GA 31792
CONTACT: Billy J. Rachels, Director TOPICS: UFO's, Big Foot, Ghosts, Paranormal Phenomena FOUNDED: 1965 DESCRIPTION: Non-profit research organization, dedicated to keeping the publich better informed about UFO's, extraterrestrials, Bigfoot, ghosts, animal mutilations & paranormal phenomena. Offers a one page News Release 4 times a year. Can also contact Gordon H. Reeves , Field Director.

UFO Enterprises
P.O. Box 35
Versailles, IL 62378
TOPICS: UFO's

UFO Information Network
P.O. Box 5012
Rome, OH 44085
(216)-563-3412
TOPICS: UFO's PUBLICATIONS: *UFO Ohio Newsletter* EDITOR: Dennis Pilchis TOPICS: UFO's TYPE: Newsletter SIZE: 5 x 8; 20 pgs. FREQ: Bi-Monthly PRICE: $9.00

UFO Research
1025 West 14th Street
Pueblo, CO 81003-2014
(719)-543-3878
CONTACT: Burt Bolerjack TOPICS: UFO's

UFORM
P.O. Box 427, Station F
Toronto, ON, M4Y2L8,
Canada
TOPICS: UFO's

UFORUM
11020 Ventura Boulevard, 134CU
Studio City, CA 91604
TOPICS: UFO's

Unarius Academy Of Science & Education Foundation
145 South Magnolia Avenue
El Cajon, CA 92020-4522
(619)-447-4170 FAX (619)-447-6485
CONTACT: Charles Spaegel TOPICS: Reincarnation, New Age, UFO's PUBLICATIONS: *Biography Of An Archangel* EDITOR: Ruth Norman TOPICS: Reincarnation TYPE: Book; 365 pgs. PRICE: $24.95 PUBLICATIONS: *Interdimensional Physics: The Mind And The*

Universe EDITOR: Ruth Norman, Charles Spaegel TOPICS: Reincarnation TYPE: Book DATE: 1954, 342 pgs. PRICE: $24.95 PUBLICATIONS: *Man, The Regenerative Evolutionary Spirit* EDITOR: Ruth Norman, Charles Spaegel TOPICS: Reincarnation TYPE: Book, 347 pgs. PRICE: $12.95 PUBLICATIONS: *Return To Atlantis Vol I* EDITOR: Ruth Norman TOPICS: Reincarnation TYPE: Book, 340 pgs. PRICE: $11.95 PUBLICATIONS: *The Joining Of Science And Spirit* EDITOR: Ruth Norman, Charles Spaegel TOPICS: Reincarnation TYPE: Book DATE: 1954; 336 pgs. PRICE: $15.95 PUBLICATIONS: *Unarius Light* EDITOR: Ruth Norman, Crystal Hampton TOPICS: Reincarnation TYPE: Book

Unbound, Incorporated
P.O. Box 1963
Iowa City, IA 52244
TOPICS: Skepticism, Counter-Cult DESCRIPTION: Cults, New Age, Satanism, New And Unconventional Religions.

Understanding Cults...
P.O. Box 2508
Del Mar, CA 92014
TOPICS: Skepticism, Counter-Cult DESCRIPTION: New Age, New And Unconventional Religions, Yoga, Eckankar, etc.

Unicorn Coven
P.O. Box 219
Galveston, IN 46932
TOPICS: Witchcraft

Unification Church (Headquarters)
4 West 43rd Street
New York, NY 10036
TOPICS: Occult

Unitarian-Universal Pagans
P.O. Box 640
Cambridge, MA 02140
TOPICS: Witchcraft

United Lodge Of Theosophis
245 West 33rd Street
Los Angeles, CA 90007
TOPICS: Metaphysics

United New Age Network
6109 Broad Street
Bethesda, MD 20816
(301)-229-5575
TOPICS: New Age

United Sensitives Of America
P.O. Box 153
Tujunga, CA 91402
TOPICS: Metaphysics

United States Homeopathic Association
4600 West 12th Place
Chicago, IL 60650
TOPICS: Homeopathy PUBLICATIONS: *American Homeopathy* TOPICS: Homeopathy TYPE: Magazine

United States Of Awareness
3760 Wesson
Detroit, MI 48210
TOPICS: UFO's

United States Psychotronics Association (USPA)
2141 West Agatite
Chicago, IL 60625
(312)-275-7055
CONTACT: Bob Beutlich, Pres. TOPICS: Psychic Phenomena, Holistic Health, Homeopathy, Acupuncture, Crystals, Color Therapy, Herbalogy FOUNDED: 1975 MEM: 800 STAFF: 2 GROUPS: 17 COMPUTER: no CONVENTIONS: Annual convention, 3rd week in July at various colleges, universities, and retreats. DESCRIPTION: A non-profit, all volunteer organization that accepts as fact the existence of psychic phenomena but questions how and why from a technological viewpoint. Engaged in New Physics theories and instrumentation, they study alternative health methods, radionics, homeopathy, acupuncture, crystal and color healing. PUBLICATIONS: *Journal Of USPA* EDITOR: Robert Beutlich TOPICS: Psychic Phenomena, Holistic Health, Homeopathy, Acupuncture, Crystals, Color Therapy, Herbalogy TYPE: Journal DATE: 1975; 30 pgs. FREQ: 3xyr CIRC: 1,500 PRICE PER COPY: $5.00 DESCRIPTION: Features articles, news and reviews of music, videos and audio tapes. Sponsors conference. PUBLICATIONS: *USPA Newsletter Quarterly* EDITOR: Henry J. Nagorka TOPICS: Psychic Phenomena, Holistic Health, Homeopathy, Acupuncture, Crystals, Color Therapy, Herbalogy TYPE: Newsletter PUBLICATIONS: *Video and Audio Tapes From Annual Conferences* TOPICS: Psychic Phenomena, Holistic Health, Homeopathy, Acupuncture, Crystals, Color Therapy, Herbalogy TYPE: Video

Unity In Yoga
4150 Tivoli Avenue
Los Angeles, CA 90066
TOPICS: Holistic Health

Unity-And-Diversity World Organization
1010 South Flower Street, Ste. 500
Los Angeles, CA 90015
(213)-839-0758 (213)-742-6832
CONTACT: Leland Stewart TOPICS: New Age PUBLICATIONS: *Spectrum - Unity-And-Diversity World Directory Issue* EDITOR: Louis K. Acheson TOPICS: New Age TYPE: Directory

Universal Aquarian Church
1838 East Wardlow Road
Long Beach, CA 90807
(213)-494-1597 (213)-427-4418
TOPICS: New Age, Metaphysics, Spirituality DESCRIPTION: New Age Christian and Spiritualist Church.

Universal Awareness Research
252 Tunxis Road
West Hartford, CT 06107
TOPICS: Metaphysics

Universal Church Of Spirit Science
P.O. Box 188
Fern Park, FL 32730
TOPICS: Metaphysics

Universal Church Of The Master
P.O. Box 598
Glendora, CA 91740

TOPICS: Metaphysics

Universal Egyptian Arts
P.O. Box 90062
San Diego, CA 92109
TOPICS: Metaphysics

Universal Entity
2526 South 298
Federal Way, WA 98003
TOPICS: Metaphysics

Universal Faithists Of Kosmon, Inc.
1268 West 10775, South
South Jordan, UT 84065
(801)-254-6903
TOPICS: New Age, Channeling, Metaphysics
PUBLICATIONS: *Kosmon Voice* EDITOR: Erma
Jean Lee TOPICS: New Age, Metaphysics,
Channeling TYPE: Magazine

Universal Kingdom
P.O. Box 938
Roseburg, OR 97470
TOPICS: UFO's

Universal Life
P.O. Box 3549
New Haven, CT 06525
TOPICS: Channeling, Meditation, Psychic Healing
DESCRIPTION: American headquarters of Universal
Life-The Inner Religion in Germany. Also sponsors
a healing center which offers courses in meditation &
soul evolution. PUBLICATIONS: *World Wide
Messenger, The* TOPICS: Channeling TYPE:
Booklet DESCRIPTION: Contains information on the
channeled material of the Universal Life-The Inner
Religion

Universal Life Church
P.O. Box 161
New Port, MI 48166
TOPICS: Occult

Universal Life-The Inner Religion
Postfach 5643
Wurzburg, 8700
Germany
TOPICS: Channeling, Meditation, Psychic Healing
DESCRIPTION: Channeling group formed to study
the words of Jesus Christ & Brother Emmanuel as
channeled by Gabriele Wittek.

Universal Mind Adventures
P.O. Box 89191
San Diego, CA 92138
TOPICS: Metaphysics

Universal Mind Science
1618 North Las Palmas
Hollywood, CA 90028
TOPICS: Metaphysics

Universal Mind Science Church
3212 East 8th Street
Long Beach, CA 90804
TOPICS: Metaphysics

Universal Perspectives
P.O. Box 703
Medinah, IL 60157
TOPICS: Metaphysics

Universal Spiritualist Association
Maple Grove
5848 Pendleton Avenue
Anderson, IN 46011
TOPICS: New Age

Universe Society Church
P.O. Box 38132
Hollywood, CA 90028
TOPICS: UFO's

University Of Life
2837 North 21st Street
Phoenix, AZ 85006
TOPICS: Metaphysics

Unusual And Unique Esoteric
P.O. Box 1095
Folsom, CA 95630
TOPICS: Metaphysics

Update
P.O. Box 84116
San Deigo, CA 92138
TOPICS: Skepticism, Counter-Cult DESCRIPTION:
Newsletter debunking Religion, Cults, New Age, etc.

Urantia Foundation
533 Diversey Parkway
Chicago, IL 60614
(312)-525-3319
CONTACT: Vincent Myers TOPICS: New Age,
Metaphysics

US Aikido Federation
Central Headquarters
98 State Street
Northampton, MA 01060
(413)-586-7122
TOPICS: Aikido

Utah Christian Tract Society
P.O. Box 725
La Mesa, CA 92044
TOPICS: Skepticism, Counter-Cult DESCRIPTION:
Mormonism. Cults, New Age, Satanism, etc.

Utah Lighthouse Ministry
P.O. Box 1884
Salt Lake City, UT 84110
TOPICS: Skepticism, Counter-Cult DESCRIPTION:
Mormanism. Cults, New Age, Satanism, etc.

Utah Missions, Incorporated
P.O. Box 348
Marlow, OK 73055
TOPICS: Skepticism, Counter-Cult DESCRIPTION:
Mormanism. Cults, New Age, Satanism, etc.

Valaam Society Of America
P.O. Box 7
Platina, CA 96076
TOPICS: Metaphysics

Valiant For Truth
8714 Forest Hills
Dallas, TX 75218
TOPICS: Skepticism, Counter-Cult DESCRIPTION:
Mormanism. Cults, New Age, Satanism, etc.

Valley Of The Sun
2838 North 7th Street
Phoenix, AZ 85006

TOPICS: Metaphysics

Vampire
5116 Mill Race Circle
Richmond, VA 23234
(804)-271-6600
CONTACT: Mrs. Terry Cottrell TOPICS: Vampires

Vampire Information Exchange
Box 328
Brooklyn, NY 11229-0328
CONTACT: Eric S. Held TOPICS: Vampires
DESCRIPTION: Conducts research & offers
information on all aspects of vampirism.
PUBLICATIONS: *The Vampire Information
Exchange* EDITOR: Eric S. Held TOPICS: Vampires
TYPE: Newsletter DATE: 1978 FREQ: 6 x per year
PRICE PER COPY: $4.00 DESCRIPTION: Informs
paying members of association on all aspects of
vampirism, fact & fiction.

Vedanta Society Of Southern California
1946 Vedanta Place
Los Angeles, CA 90068-3996
(213)-465-7114
CONTACT: Bob Adjemian TOPICS: New Age,
Metaphysics

Vegetarian Awareness Network
P.O. Box 854
Knoxville, TN 37901
(800)-872-8343
TOPICS: Health Food

Vegetarian Awareness Network (Veganet)
P.O. Box 76390
Washington, DC 20013
(202)-347-8343 (800)-872-8343
CONTACT: Lige Weill TOPICS: Health Food

Vegetarian Gourmet Society
c/o Mark Scheinberg, M.D.
4101 NW 4th Street, Suite 309
Plantation, FL 33317
(305)-584-0855
TOPICS: Health Food

Vegetarian Information Service
P.O. Box 5888
Bethesda, MD 20014
(301)-530-5683
TOPICS: Health Food

Vegetarian Information Service Of Minnesota
5049 Thomas Avenue South
Minneapolis, MN 55410
(612)-920-6412
CONTACT: John Lowell Simcox TOPICS: Health
Food

Vegetarian Resource Group
P.O. Box 1463
Baltimore, MD 21203-3996
(301)-366-8343 (301)-752-8348
CONTACT: Debra Wasserman TOPICS: Health
Food, Holistic Health, Vegetarianism FOUNDED:
1982 MEM: 7,000 CONVENTIONS: Annual
weekend meeting, 1990 & 1991 on New Jersey
Shore; one day conference in Baltimore or New

York; and teenage meeting in MD or PA. **DESCRIPTION:** Educates public about various aspects of vegetarianism, no meat, fish, or fowl, and veganism, no dairy or eggs. Topics include health, nutrition, ethics, animal rights, environment, non-violence and world hunger issues. All nutrition articles are reviewed by a registered dietitian or medical doctor. Publishes books, posters, postcards, reprints, pamphlets and a journal. **PUBLICATIONS:** *Vegetarian Journal* **EDITOR:** Debra Wasserman **TOPICS:** Health Food, Holistic Health, Vegetarianism **TYPE:** Journal **DATE:** 1982; 36 pgs. **FREQ:** bi-monthly **PRICE:** $12.00 **PRICE PER COPY:** $1.50 **DESCRIPTION:** Promotes vegetarianism with book reviews and articles on holistic health, food-vegetarian cooking and animal rights. Does not accept advertising. Includes catalog.

Vegetarian Society
P.O. Box 34427
Los Angeles, CA 90034
(213)-281-1907

CONTACT: Vic Forsythe **TOPICS:** New Age, Health Food, Nutrition, Vegetarianism **FOUNDED:** 1948 **DESCRIPTION:** A support group for those wishing to explore the wide diversity of plant based foods in a social setting. Provides an extensive video library. Open to people of all faiths. **PUBLICATIONS:** *Jesus Was A Vegetarian* **TOPICS:** Health Food, Nutrition, Vegetarianism **TYPE:** Book **PUBLICATIONS:** *Vegetarian Living News* **TOPICS:** Health Food, Nutrition, Vegetarianism **TYPE:** Newspaper

Vegetarian Society Of San Francisco
1450 Broadway
San Francisco, CA 94109
(415)-775-6874

TOPICS: New Age, Vegetarianism, Nutrition, Holistic Health **DESCRIPTION:** Offers education & nutritional information on vegetarianism.

Vegetarian Society, Inc.
P.O. Box 126
Joshua Tree, CA 92252-0126
(619)-366-2478 **FAX** (619)-365-5449
CONTACT: Bianca Leonardo **TOPICS:** Health Food

Vegetarian Society, The
Parkdale Dunham Road
Altrincham, Cheshire WA14 4QG
England
(061)-928-0793

TOPICS: Health Food, Vegetarianism, Holistic Health **FOUNDED:** 1847 **MEM:** 22,000 **STAFF:** 25 **DESCRIPTION:** A charity which is the largest vegetarian organization in the world & the only national voice for Britain. Purpose is to raise public awareness, stop animal cruelty, save the environment, help the third world & promote health through vegetarianism. Operates youth & adult campaings, a cookery school, magazines, a vegetarian handbook & travel guide, a registered trademark & a research department. **PUBLICATIONS:** *Greenscene* **EDITOR:** Fiona McPhall, Bronwen Humphreys **TOPICS:** Health Food, Vegetarianism **TYPE:** Magazine **DESCRIPTION:** Covers all aspects of vegetarianism. Youth, under 18 years old, oriented. **PUBLICATIONS:** *The Vegetarian Handbook* **TOPICS:** Health Food, Vegetarianism **TYPE:** Handbook **FREQ:** annual **DESCRIPTION:** Contains information about the vegetarian diet, covers developing nations, factory farming & environmental

issues. New ideas for getting involved with the movement. **PUBLICATIONS:** *The Vegetarian Travel Guide* **TOPICS:** Health Food, Vegetarianism **TYPE:** Magazine **FREQ:** annual **DESCRIPTION:** Information on establishments which cater to vegetarian travelers, including hotels & guest houses, restaurants & cafes. Ideas for holidays & advice about travelling longer distances. **PUBLICATIONS:** *Vegetarian* **EDITOR:** Fiona McPhall, Bronwen Humphreys **TOPICS:** Health Food, Vegetarianism **TYPE:** Magazine **DESCRIPTION:** Covers all aspects of vegetarianism. Adult oriented.

Vegetarian Union Of North America
P.O. Box 9710
Washington, DC 20016
TOPICS: Health Food

Vestigia
56 Brookwood Road
Stanhope, NJ 07874
(201)-347-3638
CONTACT: Robert E. Jones, Pres. **TOPICS:** Psychic Phenomena

Vineyard Faith Research
P.O. Box 925
Picayune, MS 39466
TOPICS: Skepticism, Counter-Cult **DESCRIPTION:** New Age, New And Unconventional Religions, Paganism, etc.

Virginia Ki Society
Merrilee Drive
P.O. Box 2356
Merrifield, VA 22116
(703)-573-8843
TOPICS: Aikido

Vision Light
6569 South Keim Road
Evergreen, CO 80439
TOPICS: Channeling

Vision Weavers
P.O. Box 3653
Fairfax, VA 22038
TOPICS: Witchcraft

Visionary Arts Council
4843 50th Southwest
Seattle, WA 98116
(206)-935-9012
CONTACT: Astara **TOPICS:** New Age, Metaphysics **PUBLICATIONS:** *Visionary Arts Council* Astara **TOPICS:** New Age, Metaphysics **TYPE:** Directory **DATE:** 1988 **CIRC:** 4,000 **DESCRIPTION:** Serves Northwest, particularly Puget Sound, with listings that include art establishments, recording studios, radio/tv stations, designers and holistic practitioners.

Visionlink
P.O. Box 230
Green Isle, MN 55338
TOPICS: Metaphysics

VISUAL
50 Euclid Avenue
Ludlow, KY 41016
TOPICS: UFO's

Volunteers For Peace, Inc.
International Workcamps

43 Tiffany Road
Belmont, VT 05730
(802)-259-2759
TOPICS: New Age

Vortex Institute
P.O. Box 80849
Fairbanks, AK 99707
TOPICS: Occult

WANDS
P.O. Box 1761
San Marcos, CA 92069
TOPICS: Witchcraft

Washington Astrology Service
2055 36th Street SE
Washington, DC 20020
(202)-581-1303
CONTACT: Warren Kinsman **TOPICS:** Astrology, Metaphysics **DESCRIPTION:** Offers lectures and readings on Astrology.

Washington Works
707 Muskingum Avenue
Pacific Palisades, CA 90272
TOPICS: UFO's

Watchman Alert To Cult
P.O. Box 12638
El Paso, TX 79913
TOPICS: Skepticism, Counter-Cult **DESCRIPTION:** Paganism, New Age, New And Unconventional Religions, etc.

Watchman Fellowship, National Headquarters
P.O. Box 7681
Columbus, GA 31908
TOPICS: Skepticism, Counter-Cult **DESCRIPTION:** Mormonism, Jehovah's Witnesses, Cults, Satanism, etc.

Water Center, The
Route 3, Box 716
Eureka Springs, AR 72632
(501)-253-9431
CONTACT: Jacqueline Froelich **TOPICS:** New Age **DESCRIPTION:** Explores technical & metaphysical approaches to clean water. **PUBLICATIONS:** *Aqua Terra* **EDITOR:** Jacqueline Froelich **TOPICS:** New Age **TYPE:** Book **PRICE:** $5.95 **DESCRIPTION:** Water concepts for the Ecological Society. Richly illustrated pages. **PUBLICATIONS:** *Water Center News* **TOPICS:** Holistic Healing **TYPE:** Newspaper **PUBLICATIONS:** *We All Live Downstream* **TOPICS:** Holistic Healing **TYPE:** Guide **PRICE:** $9.95 **DESCRIPTION:** A guide to waste treatment.

Way Of Peaceful Warrior
P.O. Box 801
San Rafael, CA 94915
TOPICS: Metaphysics

We Care Ministries
3208 Highway 32
Chico, CA 95926
TOPICS: Skepticism, Counter-Cult **DESCRIPTION:** New Age, New And Non-Conforming Religions, etc.

Web Of Isis
P.O. Box 145
Woodstock, IL 60098

TOPICS: Witchcraft

Web Of OZ
P.O. Box 1517
Lawrence, KS 66044
TOPICS: Witchcraft

Western Research Institute
P.O. Box 6879
Thousand Oaks, CA 91359
TOPICS: Holistic Health

Western States Astrology
P.O. Box 1083
Newport Beach, CA 92663
TOPICS: Astrology

White Light Pentacles
P.O. Box 8163
Salem, MA 01971
TOPICS: Witchcraft

White Star
P.O. Box 307
Joshua Tree, CA 92252
TOPICS: UFO's

Whole Health, Inc.
HC 89, Box 409
Willow, AK 99688-9705
CONTACT: C.E. Studdert TOPICS: Holistic Health, Body-Mind Connection, Spirituality FOUNDED: 1980 MEM: 40 STAFF: 4 DESCRIPTION: Nonprofit. Purpose is to provide research & education in holistic, body/heart/mind/spirit, wellness & to develop & establish a healing center. Parent corporation of the Denali Center. Irregularly publishes a newsletter.

Wiccan Church Of Canada
109 Vaughan Road, 301-A
Toronto, ON M6C 2L9
Canada
TOPICS: Witchcraft PUBLICATIONS: *Wiccan Candle, The* TOPICS: Witchcraft, Occult, Paganism TYPE: Book

Wiccan Church Of Minnesota
P.O. Box 6715
Minneapolis, MN 55406
TOPICS: Witchcraft

Wiccan Church Of Vermont
Rural Route 1, Box 239
Bethel, VT 05032
TOPICS: Witchcraft

Wiccan Information Network
P.O. Box 2422, Main Post Office
Vancouver, BC V6B 3W7
Canada
CONTACT: Kerr Cuhulain, Exec. Dir. TOPICS: Witchcraft, Occult, Paganism FOUNDED: 1989 DESCRIPTION: Wiccan anti-defamation organization which supports the right of Wiccans to practice their faith as they see fit, works towards the return of Wiccan religion as a respected faith, provides accurate information on Wiccan religion, monitors anti-Wiccan activities, groups & individuals & researches occult & ritualistic crime while supplying the information to the Wiccan community. PUBLICATIONS: *WIN Intelligence Summary* TOPICS: Witchcraft, Occult, Paganism

TYPE: Newsletter FREQ: monthly PRICE: $20.00 TERM: yearly DESCRIPTION: Reports on anti-defamation topics of concern to Wiccans.

Wiccan/Druid Studies Outreach
1401 Williamston Street, 1
Madison, WI 53703
TOPICS: Witchcraft

Windstar Foundation
2317 Snowmass Creek Road
Box 286
Snowmass, CO 81654
(303)-927-4777
TOPICS: New Age FOUNDED: 1976 CONVENTIONS: Annual conference DESCRIPTION: Co-founded by John Denver & Thomas Crum. Located on 1,000 acres in the Rocky Mountains. Purpose is to advance positive environmental changes & create universal harmony. Offers courses concerned with global natural resources, food production, energy, land, individual & community growth, & world peace. Formed the Windstar Connection Program which allows members to network together, plan events to educate the public & further the teachings & philosophy of the organization. PUBLICATIONS: *Windstar Journal*, Thomas Crum TOPICS: New Age TYPE: Journal FREQ: quarterly DESCRIPTION: Concerned with positive environmental & planetary transformation. Contains articles & photographs to inspire, educate & raise consciousness. PUBLICATIONS: *Windstar Newsletter/Products Catalog* EDITOR: John Denver TOPICS: New Age TYPE: Newsletter

Winged Mercury Networking
P.O. Box 5010
Ashville, NC 28813
TOPICS: Metaphysics

Witches Anti-Discrimination Lobby
153 West 80th Street, 1-B
New York, NY 10024
TOPICS: Witchcraft

Witches League Public Awareness
P.O. Box 8736
Salem, MA 01971
TOPICS: Witchcraft

Witness, Incorporated
P.O. Box 597
Clayton, CA 94517
TOPICS: Skepticism, Counter-Cult DESCRIPTION: Jehovah's Witnesses. Cults, New Age, Satanism, etc.

Wolf Song
P.O. Box 293
River Falls, WI 54022
TOPICS: Witchcraft

Woman's Journal, A
P.O. Box 27655
Escondido, CA 92027
TOPICS: Witchcraft

Womangathering
Rural Route 5, Box 185
Franklinville, NJ 08322
TOPICS: Metaphysics

Women's Spirituality Forum (WSF)
P.O. Box 11363

Oakland, CA 94611
(415)-444-7724
CONTACT: Z. Budapest, Exec. Officer TOPICS: New Age

Words For Living Ministries
102 West Carlisle Street
Marion, KY 42064
TOPICS: Skepticism, Counter-Cult DESCRIPTION: Mormonism, New And Unconventional Religions, Freemasonry, etc.

World Association Vision Experiences
146 Oakvale Boulevard
Walnut Creek, CA 94596
TOPICS: Metaphysics

World Government Of The Age Of Enlightenment - U.S. (WGAE-US)
5000 14th Street, N.W.
Washington, DC 20011
(202)-723-9111
CONTACT: Thomas A. Headley, Pres. TOPICS: New Age

World Investigations Of Strange Phenomena
Rural Route 2, Box 159
Vina, AL 35592
TOPICS: Metaphysics

World Messianity
3068 San Marino
Los Angeles, CA 90006
TOPICS: Metaphysics

World Prophetic Ministry
P.O. Drawer 907
Colton, CA 92324
TOPICS: Metaphysics

World University Roundtable
Desert Sanctuary Campus
P.O. Box 2470
Benson, AZ 85602
(602)-586-2985
CONTACT: Dr. Howard John Zitko, Pres. TOPICS: Parapsychology, Metaphysics, New Age, Spirituality PUBLICATIONS: *Liftoff* EDITOR: Howard John Zitko TOPICS: Parapsychology TYPE: Newsletter DATE: 1947 SIZE: 8 1/2 x 11; 4 pgs. FREQ: bi-monthly CIRC: 1,000 PRICE: $25.00 TERM: yearly DESCRIPTION: International newsletter of current happenings in the World University development, now in 80 nations.

World Women For Animal Rights/Empowerment
616 Sixth Street
Brooklyn, NY 11215
(718)-788-1362
TOPICS: Health Food

Worldwide Curio House
P.O. Box 17095
Minneapolis, MN 55417
TOPICS: Occult

Wright/Gaby Nutrition Institute
P.O. Box 32188
Baltimore, MD 21208
(301)-486-9490 FAX (301)-486-1598

CONTACT: Fritz Perlberg **TOPICS:** Holistic Healing

Wynchwood
P.O. Box 3092
Decatur, AL 35602
TOPICS: Witchcraft

Y.C.C. Communities
2843 Keywest Court
Wichita, KS 67204
TOPICS: Metaphysics

Yoga Research Foundation (YRF)
6111 SW 74th Avenue
Miami, FL 33143
(305)-666-2006
CONTACT: Swami Jyotirmayananda **TOPICS:** Yoga, Spirituality **DESCRIPTION:** Directed by Founder & President Swami Jyotirmayananda. Publishes & produces books, cassettes & video tapes all pertaining to Yoga & Meditation. Also publishes the monthly magazine International Yoga Guide featuring articles on Integral Yoga, meditation, classic literature, exercise, & spiritual instruction. **PUBLICATIONS:** *International Yoga Guide* **EDITOR:** Swami Jyotirmayananda, Swami

Lalitananda **TOPICS:** Yoga **TYPE:** Magazine **SIZE:** 8 1/2 x 11; 120 pgs. **FREQ:** monthly **PRICE:** $15.00 **TERM:** yearly **DESCRIPTION:** Monthly magazine offering the finest in Yoga teachings. Features articles on meditation, classic literature, exercise & spiritual instructions.

Yogalayam/Prana Yoga Ashram
1717 Alcatraz Avenue
Berkeley, CA 94703
(415)-655-3664
CONTACT: Saraswathi Devi **TOPICS:** Yoga, Meditation, Holistic Health, Massage, Spirituality, Vegetarianism, Astrology **FOUNDED:** 1975 **MEM:** 200 **STAFF:** 7 **DESCRIPTION:** Purpose is for training in spiritual practices & Yoga.

Yoni Coven
P.O. Box 42
Fairfield, VT 05455
TOPICS: Witchcraft

Zanthyros Foundation
P.O. Box 91980
W. Vancouver, BC, V7V4S4,
Canada

TOPICS: Metaphysics

Zen Mission Society
P.O. Box 199
Mt. Shasta, CA 96067
TOPICS: Metaphysics

Zero Population Growth (ZPG)
1400 16th Street NW
Suite 320
Washington, DC 20036
(202)-332-2200 **FAX** (202)-332-2302
CONTACT: Dianne Sherman, Dir. of Communications. **TOPICS:** Birth, Holistic Health, New Age **FOUNDED:** 1968 **MEM:** 30,000 **STAFF:** 15 **BUDGET:** $1,306,78200 **GROUPS:** 10 Chapters **CONVENTIONS:** Biannual board meetings held in Washington, DC **DESCRIPTION:** National, non-profit, membership organization that works to achieve a sustainable balance among population, resources, & the environment both in the U.S. & worldwide. **PUBLICATIONS:** *Fact Sheets* **TYPE:** Newsletter **PUBLICATIONS:** *Planning The Ideal Family* **TYPE:** Book **PUBLICATIONS:** *ZPG Activist* **TYPE:** Newsletter **PUBLICATIONS:** *ZPG Reporter* **TYPE:** Newsletter

Centers, Spas, Retreats & Communities

Within this chapter you will find each listing labeled either Center, Spa or Retreat. Many can also be considered a Community although we did not label any as such. All of these terms are interchangeable since most of these organizations perform multi functions. Listed in this chapter are numerous 3HO Foundation Centers. 3HO stands for Health, Happy, Holy Organization and is the educational segment of the Sikh Dharma.

3HO Canadian Headquarters
346 Palmerston Boulevard
Toronto, Ontario M6G 2N6
Canada
(416)-530-4866
TOPICS: Metaphysics, New Age

3HO Center For Holistic Living
1704 Q Street N.W.
Washington, DC 20009
(202)-435-5599
TOPICS: Holistic Healing

3HO Foundation
4501 Bayview Drive
Anchorage, AK 99516
(907)-345-1339
TOPICS: New Age

3HO Foundation
308 5th Avenue
Fairbanks, AK 99701
(907)-456-2244
TOPICS: New Age

3HO Foundation
1172 16th Avenue South
Birmingham, AL 35205
(205)-322-7377
TOPICS: New Age

3HO Foundation
2302 North 9th Street
Phoenix, AZ 85006
(602)-271-4480 (602)-256-9731
TOPICS: New Age

3HO Foundation
1059 East New York Drive
Altadena, CA 91001
(818)-794-4148
TOPICS: New Age

3HO Foundation
Hargobind Sadan
2669 Le Conte
Berkeley, CA 94709
(415)-540-6332
TOPICS: New Age

3HO Foundation
419 West Commonwealth Avenue
Fullerton, CA 92632
(714)-738-9556
TOPICS: New Age

3HO Foundation
11075 Peach Street

Hesperia, CA 92345
(619)-244-0496
TOPICS: New Age

3HO Foundation
1620 Preuss Road
P.O. Box 351149
Los Angeles, CA 90035
(213)-552-3416
CONTACT: Shakti Parwha Kaur Khalsa, Exec. Sec.
TOPICS: New Age

3HO Foundation
P.O. Box 1088
Monterey, CA 93842-1088
(408)-899-3256
TOPICS: New Age

3HO Foundation
630 North G Street
San Bernardino, CA 92410
(714)-885-4781
TOPICS: New Age

3HO Foundation
1421 Myrtle Avenue
San Diego, CA 92103
(619)-299-4196
TOPICS: New Age

3HO Foundation
1390 Waller Street
San Francisco, CA 94117
(415)-864-9642
TOPICS: New Age

3HO Foundation
3460 Berkley Avenue
Boulder, CO 80303
(303)-494-4643
TOPICS: New Age

3HO Foundation
1040 Bookcliff Avenue
Grand Junction, CO 81501
(303)-243-5451
TOPICS: New Age

3HO Foundation
400 Center Street
Altamonte Springs, FL 32701
(305)-831-2201
TOPICS: New Age

3HO Foundation
15040 South River Drive
Miami, FL 33167
(305)-685-5515

TOPICS: New Age

3HO Foundation
112 Millbrook Circle
Roswell, GA 30075
(404)-993-6633
TOPICS: New Age

3HO Foundation
1510 Carrol Street
Boone, IA 50036
(515)-432-1924
TOPICS: New Age

3HO Foundation
7015 North Sheridan Road
Chicago, IL 60626
(312)-822-0624
TOPICS: New Age

3HO Foundation
3027 Monroe
New Orleans, LA 70118
(504)-482-5225
TOPICS: New Age

3HO Foundation
436 Long Plain Road
Leverett, MA 01054
(513)-549-6449
TOPICS: New Age

3HO Foundation
368 Village Street
Mills, MA 02054
(617)-376-2010
CENTER; TOPICS: New Age, Yoga, Meditation, Nutrition, Holistic Health DESCRIPTION: Philosophy is that human beings are perfectly created & that by using your body & mind through exercises, breath & meditaiton you can balance & revitalize the physical body, nervous & glandular systems & bring balance & peace to your life. Promotes the ancient science of Kundalini Yoga which offers lifestyle guidelines on nutrition & health, interpersonal relations, child rearing & human behavior.

3HO Foundation
484 Academy
Ferndale, MI 48220
(313)-541-4834
TOPICS: New Age

3HO Foundation
4350 Garfield Avenue South
Minneapolis, MN 55409
(612)-822-6704
TOPICS: New Age

3HO Foundation
3525 Walnut
Kansas City, MO 64111
(816)-561-5337
TOPICS: New Age

3HO Foundation
421 East Story Street
Bozeman, MT 59715
(406)-587-0050
TOPICS: New Age

3HO Foundation
P.O. Box 27
Princeton Junction, NJ 08550
(609)-799-9487
TOPICS: New Age

3HO Foundation
219 Amherst, Southeast
Albuquerque, NM 87106
(505)-266-6374
TOPICS: New Age

3HO Foundation
Route 1, Box 132D
Espanola, NM 87532
(505)-753-9438
TOPICS: New Age

3HO Foundation
1653 Westfield Avenue
Reno, NV 89509
(702)-362-6123
TOPICS: New Age

3HO Foundation
146 Bergen Street
Brooklyn, NY 11217
(818)-855-4856
TOPICS: New Age

3HO Foundation
487 Ashland Avenue
Buffalo, NY 14222
(716)-882-5955
TOPICS: New Age

3HO Foundation
1560 Warncke Road
Rural Delivery 2
Lyons, NY 14489
(315)-946-5523
TOPICS: New Age

3HO Foundation
225 East 5th Street
Apartment #4-D
New York, NY 10003
(212)-260-1677
TOPICS: New Age

3HO Foundation
23 Cove Circle
Penfield, NY 14526
(716)-671-3401
TOPICS: New Age

3HO Foundation
401 Dakin Street
Syracuse, NY 13224
(315)-476-3005 (315)-452-0952
TOPICS: New Age

3HO Foundation
92 East Northwood Avenue
Columbus, OH 43201
(614)-299-5687
TOPICS: New Age

3HO Foundation
830 East 37th Avenue
Eugene, OR 97405
(503)-686-0432 (503)-484-1093
TOPICS: New Age

3HO Foundation
2539 Southeast Madison
Portland, OR 97214
(503)-232-0895
TOPICS: New Age

3HO Foundation
3545 Bella Vista Court, South
Salem, OR 97302
(503)-364-2380
TOPICS: New Age

3HO Foundation
108 Harrison Drive
New Cumberland, PA 17070
(717)-774-2654
TOPICS: New Age

3HO Foundation
2621 Sorento Drive
Philadelphia, PA 19131
(215)-477-1483
TOPICS: New Age

3IIO Foundation
P.O. Box 21953, University Station
San Juan, PR 00931
(809)-763-6027
TOPICS: New Age

3HO Foundation
3507 Pecan Springs
Austin, TX 78723
(512)-928-4645
TOPICS: New Age

3HO Foundation
5702 Gaston Avenue
Dallas, TX 75214
(214)-827-2947
TOPICS: New Age

3HO Foundation
1117 Jackson Boulevard
Houston, TX 77006
(713)-524-2547 (713)-522-3235
TOPICS: New Age

3HO Foundation
4790 Cherry Street
Murray, UT 84123
(801)-262-4144
TOPICS: New Age

3HO Foundation
950 27th Street
Ogden, UT 84403
(801)-399-3614
TOPICS: New Age

3HO Foundation

1740 Whitewood Lane
Herndon, VA 22070
(703)-435-4411
TOPICS: New Age

3HO Foundation
10319 42nd Northeast
Seattle, WA 98125
(206)-524-5101
TOPICS: New Age

3HO Foundation
111 View Street
Anandale, NSW 2038
Australia
61-2-389-5556
TOPICS: New Age

3HO Foundation
633 Hawthorne Road
East Brighton, 3187
Australia
03-578-4615
TOPICS: New Age

3HO Foundation
P.O. Box 5422, Station A
Calgary, Alb. T2H1X8
Canada
(403)-262-4983
TOPICS: New Age

3HO Foundation
3204 West 13th Avcnuc
Vancouver, BC V6K 2V5
Canada
(604)-733-4575 (604)-733-5072
TOPICS: New Age

3HO Foundation
5489 Cote Street
Montrel, QUE. H4A 1R1
Canada
(514)-481-2551
TOPICS: New Age

3HO Foundation
246 Belsize Road
London,
England
011-44-1
TOPICS: New Age

3HO Foundation
Den Texstraat 46, 1017zc
Amsterdam,
The Netherlands
24-19-77
TOPICS: New Age

3HO Superhealth
2545 North Woodland Road
Tuscon, AZ 85749
(602)-749-0404
TOPICS: Holistic Healing

A Hero's Journey
619 Arapahoe Avenue
Boulder, CO 80302-5708
(303)-442-2088
TOPICS: Holistic Healing

A New Age Center

502 Emily Center
West Chester, PA 19382
CONTACT: Karen Lander Hughes TOPICS: Channeling

A Private Place
309 Lomisa Street
Key West, FL 33040
(305)-294-7709
TOPICS: Holistic Healing

A.R.E. Medical Clinic/Energy Medicine
4017 North 40th Street
Phoenix, AZ 85018
(602)-955-8409 (602)-955-7729
CENTER; CONTACT: Margaret Grady TOPICS: Crystals, Channeling, Holistic Healing DESCRIPTION: Offers classes, lectures, research & therapy on energy medicine involving the use of crystals. Sponsors the Annual Medical Symposium. PUBLICATIONS: Pathways To Health EDITOR: Ann Graham, Anna Blackstone TOPICS: Holistic Healing TYPE: Magazine

A.T.O.M. Center, The
216 East 53rd
Anchorage, AK 99518
TOPICS: Metaphysics, Channeling

Abode Of The Message
R.R. #1
P.O. Box 1030 D
New Lebanon, NY 12125
(518)-794-8090 (518)-794-9720
RETREAT; TOPICS: New Age, Meditation, Holistic Health, Yoga, Spirituality, Body-Mind Connection, Massage DESCRIPTION: Community of the Sufi Order of the West offering visitor accommodations, seminars & events conducted by branch called Aegis. Dedicated to the ideals of love, harmony and the beauty of life, attempts to raise spirituality in man. Presents the teachings of the Sufi Order, mystical path, eclectic philosophy, respect for all religions & respect for all life. Call or write for catalog.

Acharya Sushil Jain Ashram-Siddhachalam
RD #4
Box 374
Blairstown, NJ 07825
(201)-362-9793
SPA; CONTACT: Shri Janardan Ajapa TOPICS: New Age, Meditation, Holistic Health, Massage, Yoga, Body-Mind Connection, Spirituality DESCRIPTION: Spiritual community dedicated to raising the higher consciousness of man through spiritual education, practice & the study of Arhum Yoga. Offers seminars and camps for children and adults covering topics such as meditation, chakras, healing, yoga, color, & psychic studies.

ACIM Workshop
6052 Plunkett Street
Hollywood, FL 33021
(305)-961-2283
TOPICS: New Age

Actualism Wholistic Center
739 East Pennsylvania, #D
Escondido, CA 92026
(714)-741-7827
TOPICS: Holistic Healing

Actualizations
1412 Van Ness Avenue
San Francisco, CA 94109
(415)-776-9520
TOPICS: New Age

Acupressure Workshop
1533 Shattuck Avenue
Berkeley, CA 94709
(415)-845-1059
CENTER; TOPICS: Yoga, Massage, Nutrition, Holistic Health, Body-Mind Connection, Herbalogy, Meditation DESCRIPTION: Offers 150 to 1000 hour training program in acupressure massage, including Shiatsu, Jin Shin, Touch for Health, Do-In, Reflexology, Anatomy, Physiology and Oriental exercises. Courses lead to certification as Acupressure Massage Technician.

Acupuncture Center
10 Pleasant Street
Cambridge, MA 02139
(617)-864-0507
TOPICS: Holistic Healing PUBLICATIONS: Acupuncture Newsletter TOPICS: Holistic Healing TYPE: Newsletter

Advancement Of Natural Teachings
16757 Linsay
Detroit, MI 48235
(313)-837-8460
TOPICS: Holistic Healing

Aesculapia
1480 Dutcher Creek Road
Grants Pass, OR 97527
(503)-476-0492
TOPICS: Holistic Healing

Aiki Works
Box 7845
Aspen, CO 81612
(303)-925-7099 (800)-332-7736
TOPICS: Aikido

Ajapa Yoga Foundation
P.O. Box 1731
Placerville, CA 95667
(916)-626-1585
CENTER; CONTACT: Shri Janardan Ajapa TOPICS: Yoga, Body-Mind Connection, Meditation, Holistic Health DESCRIPTION: Learning center for the teachings of Guru Janardan Parmahansa; Teaches simple, practical, scientific breathing and meditation techniques.

Akahi Farm Retreat & Conference Center
915 Kaupakalua Road
Haiku, Maui, HI 96708
(808)-572-8795
RETREAT; TOPICS: New Age, Holistic Health, Yoga, Meditation DESCRIPTION: 55 acre Refuge From The Ordinary where the spirit of Aloha thrives. Dedicated to providing a nurturing, healing & conscious environment. Offers a meditation hall, Yoga, massage & intuitive counseling. Can accommodate up to 75 people.

Akala Point
Box 4
Site 28, R.R. 1
Tantallon, Nova Scotia B0J 3J0

Canada
(902)-823-2160
TOPICS: Holistic Healing

Akasha Metaphysical Center
1124 State Street
Bellingham, WA 98225
TOPICS: Metaphysics

Akashic Services Network/Center & Bookstore
1414 East Thousand Oaks Boulevard
Thousand Oaks, CA 91362
(805)-495-5824
TOPICS: Holistic Healing, Metaphysics

Albintra Wellness Center/Natural Medicine Works
438 N.E. 72nd
Seattle, WA 98115
(206)-522-9384
TOPICS: Holistic Healing

Alcyone
Box 225
Ashland, OR 97520
(503)-482-0552 (503)-482-0057
RETREAT; TOPICS: New Age, Spirituality, Meditation, Holistic Health MEMBERS: 6 DESCRIPTION: Located on 360 acres, offers new age education programs on topics such as spritualism and meditation.

Alcyone Light Centre
1965 Hilt Road
Hornbrook, CA 96044-9744
(916)-475-3310
CENTER; TOPICS: New Age, Spirituality, Holistic Health, Body-Mind Connection, Metaphysics OWNER: Lawrence Schechter, Sylvia Schechter DESCRIPTION: Educational/spiritual foundation. Purpose is an expression of awareness of a responsibility to explore, develop & disseminate the ageless, universal wisdoms. Offers retreats, seminars, conferences & intern programs regularly scheduled. PUBLICATIONS: Alcyone Journal EDITOR: Diane Rasmussen, Sylvia Schechter TOPICS: New Age TYPE: Journal

Aletheia Psycho-Physical Foundation & Center
1809 North Highway 99
Ashland, OR 97520
(503)-488-0709
CENTER; TOPICS: Holistic Health, Body-Mind Connection, New Age, Meditation, Spirituality OWNER: Jack Schwarz DESCRIPTION: Offers consulting, research & education about the interrelationship of body & mind functions. Educates in self-health & awareness, & brings together research on health & human energies. Conducts workshops, seminars, symposiums & lectures on holistics.

Alive Polarity At Murrieta Hot Springs
39648 Old Spring Road
Murrieta, CA 92362-5548
(714)-677-7451
TOPICS: New Age, Body-Mind Connection, Holistic Health, Vegetarianism, Spirituality

Aloe
Rt #1
Box 100
Cedar Grove, NC 10950
RETREAT; TOPICS: Holistic Health, Vegetarianism, New Age **MEMBERS:** 10 **DESCRIPTION:** Member of Federation of Egalitarian Communities. Produces income from tinnery crafts and promotes a vegetarian lifestyle.

Alpha Farm
Deadwood, OR 97430
(503)-964-5102
RETREAT; TOPICS: New Age, Holistic Health **MEMBERS:** 14 **DESCRIPTION:** Located on 280 acres. Cooperative farm producing its own food and fuel. Operates income bearing stores in town. All income and property owned jointly amongst all members.

American Anopson Institute
8530 Wilshire Blvd., #309
Beverly Hills, CA 90211
(213)-854-5071
TOPICS: New Age, Holistic Health, Nutrition, Body-Mind Connection, Health Food

Amiya Institute
8627 Lubao Avenue
Canoga Park, CA 91306
(818)-998-3702
TOPICS: Holistic Healing

Amron Metaphysical Center
2254 Van Ness Avenue
San Francisco, CA 94109
(415)-775-0027
CENTER; TOPICS: Crystals, Metaphysics, Holistic Healing **DESCRIPTION:** Sponsors Amron Mystery School offering a 3 year course in all aspects of Metaphysics. Dedicated to the art of crystal therapy & healing. Provides free Metaphysical lectures. Church of Amron conducts services 11:30 AM & 4 PM every Sunday.

Ananda Cooperative Village AT Ocean Song
Box 659
19999 Coleman Valley Road
Occidental, CA 95465
(707)-874-2475
TOPICS: New Age

Ananda Cooperative Village/Family Fellowship Of Inner Communion/Expanding Light
14618 Tyler Foote Road
Nevada City, CA 95959
(916)-265-5877 (916)-292-3494 (800)-346-5350
RETREAT; TOPICS: Spirituality, Meditation, Holistic Healing, New Age, Health Food, Nutrition, Body-Mind Connection **MEMBERS:** 100 **DESCRIPTION:** Located on 700 acres & inhabited by disciples of Paramahansa Yogananda. Offers yoga, meditation, seminars on healing, Yoga Teachers Training, spiritual school, visitor retreat cabins & self-published books & tapes. Earns income with organic gardens, dairy , health food store, restaurant, gift shop, construction company & the sale of oils & incense. **PUBLICATIONS:** *Clarity* **EDITOR:** Sonia Wiberg **TOPICS:** New Age **TYPE:** Newsletter **PUBLICATIONS:** *Expanding Light*

Program Guide **EDITOR:** Richard McCord **TOPICS:** New Age **TYPE:** Calendar **DATE:** 1981 **FREQ:** 3 x/yr. **CIRC;** 16,000 **PRICE:** $0.00 **DESCRIPTION:** Describes retreat programs promoting spiritual growth offered by the Fellowship.

Ananda Healing Arts Center
1151 Massachusetts Avenue
Cambridge, MA 02139
(617)-492-3359
TOPICS: Holistic Healing

Ananda Marga
854 Pearl Street
Denver, CO 80203
CONTACT: Sri Anandamurti **TOPICS:** New Age

Ananda Meditation Retreat
900 Allegheny Star Route
Nevada City, CA 95959
TOPICS: Metaphysics

Anglesey Alternative Healing Centre
White Lodge Pen Lon, Newborough
Anglesey,Gwynedd LL61 6RS,
Wales
Newborough 254
CENTER; CONTACT: Alexandra And Janet Holt **TOPICS:** Crystals **DESCRIPTION:** Dedicated to the art of crystal therapy & healing.

Ann Wigmore Foundation
Division Of Hippocrates Health Institute, Inc.
196 Commonwealth Avenue
Boston, MA 02116
(617)-267-9424
CENTER; TOPICS: Holistic Health, Health Food, Vegetarianism, Homeopathy **OWNER:** Ann Wigmore **DESCRIPTION:** Promotes holistic health through vegetarianism, polarity therapy, natural food & homeopathy.

Another Place
Route 123
Greenville, NH 03048
(603)-878-1510
TOPICS: Holistic Healing

Appletree
Box 5
Cottage Grove, OR 97424
(503)-942-4372
RETREAT; TOPICS: New Age, Holistic Health, Spirituality **MEMBERS:** 6 **DESCRIPTION:** A member of the Federation of Egalitarian Communities operated as a cooperative promoting non-sexist, non-ageist, non-racist & nonviolent beliefs. Members share money, community decisions & child rearing.

Aqua Retreat Center
214 Market Street
Brighton, MA 02135
(617)-787-3511
TOPICS: Holistic Healing

Aquarian Age Church
9575 Canterbury Avenue
Arleta, CA 91331
(213)-892-1832
TOPICS: New Age, Meditation, Spirituality

Aquarian Center

5600 Tamiami Trail, #14
Naples, FL 33963
(813)-597-3241
CENTER; TOPICS: Crystals **DESCRIPTION:** Dedicated to the art of crystal therapy & healing.

Aquarian Center, The
116 Montowese Street
Branford, CT 06405
TOPICS: Metaphysics, Channeling

Aquarian Fellowship Foundation
107 Main Street
P.O. Box 226
West Upton, MA 01587
(617)-529-4248
CENTER; TOPICS: Crystals, Metaphysics **DESCRIPTION:** Dedicated to the art of crystal therapy & healing.

Aquarian Institute
2939 Galindo Street
Oakland, CA 94601
(415)-534-1856
TOPICS: Holistic Healing

Aquarian Minyan
P.O. Box 7224
Berkeley, CA 94707
(415)-848-0965
TOPICS: New Age, Spirituality

Arcosanti
HC 74
Box 4136
Mayer, AZ 86333
(602)-632-7135 (602)-948-6145
CENTER; TOPICS: New Age **DESCRIPTION:** Created as a model city for 5,000 people by the architect Paulo Soleri. Combines architecture with ecology-named, arcology. Offers courses on construction work including solar greenhouse design & working with concrete. Income through the sale of self produced bronze bells. Provides a visitors center, crafts building, music center & conferences.

Arlin J. Brown Information Center (TABIC)
P.O. Box 251
Fort Belvoir, VA 22060
(703)-752-4324
CENTER; CONTACT: Arlin J. Brown, Director **TOPICS:** New Age, Holistic Health **BOOKSTORE; STAFF:** 2 **MEMBERS:** 215 **BUDGET:** $25,000.00 **DESCRIPTION:** Non-profit tax-exempt organization which disseminates information on constructive, safe methods of successfully preventing & treating cancer & other ailments. **REGIONAL, STATE, LOCAL GROUPS:** 1 **AFFILIATED ORGS:** Arizona Chapter **COMPUTER SERVICES:** no **PUBLICATIONS:** *Health Victory Bulletin*, Monthly Publication $20 per year; *March Of Truth On Cancer*, $10.95.

Arnel Chiropractic Center
100 Mamaroneck Avenue
White Plains, NY 10601
(914)-686-8989
CONTACT: Dr. Marc D. Arnel **TOPICS:** Chiropractic, Holistic Health

Artemisia Institute For Botanical, Medical and Preventive Health Care Education
Box 190
Jackson's Point, Ontario L0E 1L0
Canada
(416)-722-8604
TOPICS: Holistic Healing

Artists For Planetary Renewal - Martin Steinberg Center
15 E. 84 Street
New York, NY 10028
(212)-879-4500
TOPICS: New Age, Spirituality

Arunachala Ashrama
72-63 Yellowstone Boulevard
Forrest Hills, NY 11375
TOPICS: Metaphysics

Ashram Healthort
P.O. Box 8009
Calabasas, CA 91302
(818)-888-0232
TOPICS: Holistic Healing

Aslan House-Jacksonville Center For Attitudinal Healing
P.O. Box 52116
Jacksonville, FL 32201
(904)-353-4357
TOPICS: Holistic Healing

Association Of Holistic Health Practitioners
3419 Thom Boulevard
Las Vegas, NV 89106
(702)-873-4542
TOPICS: Holistic Healing

Association Of Metaphysical And Philosophical Societies
c/o Dr. Agis Sarakinos, 12th Floor
Chiou Str. 4, 15231, Chalandri
Athens,
Greece
6725485
TOPICS: New Age

Astara Foundation, Inc.
800 West Arrow Highway
P.O. Box 5003
Upland, CA 91786
(714)-981-4941 (714)-981-8033
CENTER; TOPICS: Metaphysics, Channeling OWNER: Ray Stanbro, Exec. Dir. DESCRIPTION: Retreat center with accommodations of 100 plus with complete restaurant facilities, vegetarian meals upon request. Also school for the Ancient Mysteries. Publishes 40 metaphysical & mysticism books. PUBLICATIONS: Astara Voice EDITOR: Annette Shape TOPICS: Metaphysics TYPE: Newsletter DATE: 1951 PUBLICATIONS: Beyond Tomorrow EDITOR: E. Chaney TOPICS: Metaphysics, Psychic TYPE: Book PRICE: $9.95 PUBLICATIONS: Initiation In The Great Pyramid EDITOR: E. Chaney TOPICS: Metaphysics, Spirituality TYPE: Book PRICE: $14.95 PUBLICATIONS: Kundalini And The Third Eye EDITOR: E. Chaney, W. Messick TOPICS: Spirituality TYPE: Book PRICE:

$12.95 PUBLICATIONS: Mysticism: Journey Within EDITOR: E. Chaney TOPICS: Metaphysics, Spirituality, Psychic TYPE: Book PRICE: $13.95 PUBLICATIONS: Revelations Of Things To Come EDITOR: E. Chaney TOPICS: Metaphysics, Psychic TYPE: Book PRICE: $13.95

Astrology And Spiritual Science Center
4535 Hohman Avenue
Hammond, IN 46327
(219)-931-8050
CENTER; CONTACT: Darlene M. Enber TOPICS: Crystals, Metaphysics, Astrology, New Age DESCRIPTION: Dedicated to the art of crystal therapy & healing.

Astrology Et Al Metaphysical Center
4728 University Way N.E.
Seattle, WA 98105
(206)-524-6365
CENTER; TOPICS: Metaphysics, Tarot, Astrology OWNER: Maggie Nalbandian BOOKSTORE; STAFF: 5 DESCRIPTION: Full spectrum metaphysical center: 3000 plus title bookstore, gifts, tarot cards, personal consultations in Astrology or Tarot & School of Metaphysics. Also sponsors the Northwest Astrological Conference (NORWAC) annually which is held in the Spring in Seattle, WA. A faculty of 15-17 nationally & internationally known astrologers meet for 3 days of intensive astrological study & sharing for the novice to the professional. COMPUTER SERVICES: Available CONVENTIONS: Meets annually each Spring in Seattle, WA. PUBLICATIONS: 6 yearly bulletins of events along with catalogs of books & services.

Atlanta Center For Attitudinal Awareness
P.O. Box 675015
Marietta, GA 30067
(404)-953-3136
TOPICS: Holistic Healing

Atlantis Rising Health Education
7915 S.E. Stark Street
Portland, OR 97215
(503)-253-4031
TOPICS: Holistic Healing

Atmaniketan Ashram
1291 Weber Street
Pomona, CA 91768
(714)-629-8255 (714)-629-0108
CENTER; TOPICS: New Age, Spirituality, Yoga DESCRIPTION: Provides residence facilites & vegetarian meals for the practice of Sri Aurobindo's Integral Yoga. Dedicated to the work-oriented Karma Yoga lifestyle & to the desire for a divine life upon earth. New Center in Northern California.

Attitudinal Healing Center
1145 Cambridge S.E.
Grand Rapids, MI 49506
(616)-245-3438
TOPICS: Holistic Healing

Attitudinal Healing Center Of San Diego
5736 Good Karma Lane
Bonita, CA 92002
(619)-565-7172

TOPICS: Holistic Healing

Attitudinal Healing Center Of Southern California
24432 Muirlands Boulevard
El Toro, CA 92630
(714)-556-8000 (714)-768-3343
TOPICS: Holistic Healing

Aurobindo Ashram
Pondicherry, 605002
India
RETREAT; TOPICS: New Age, Yoga, Meditation DESCRIPTION: Promotes the teachings of Sri Aurobindo & The Mother through the practice of Yoga & meditation.

Aurobindo Center
140 West 58th Street
New York, NY 10019
TOPICS: Yoga, Spirituality, Holistic Health, Meditation

Auroville
P.O. Box 1977
Boulder, CO 80306
(303)-499-3313
TOPICS: New Age, Spirituality

Auroville Association
212 Farley Drive
Aptos, CA 95003
TOPICS: Holistic Healing

Auroville Cooperative
Aspiration, Kottakuppam
Matrimandir Office Center
Auroville, Tamil Nadu 605101
India
RETREAT; TOPICS: New Age, Spirituality, Holistic Health MEMBERS: 500 DESCRIPTION: A spiritual community on 11,000 acres founded on the teachings of Sri Aurobindo and The Mother. Members from 24 countries with the purpose of creating a material environment that will advance the development of mankind. Conducts projects such as afforestation & building a spherical Matrimandir temple.

Austin Seth Center (ASC)
P.O. Box 7786
Austin, TX 78713-7786
(512)-479-8909
CENTER; CONTACT: Maude Cardwell, Ph.D. TOPICS: Channeling, Metaphysics, New Age BOOKSTORE; STAFF: 2 MEMBERS: 100 BUDGET: $20,000.00 DESCRIPTION: Non-profit educational organization which studies & teaches Seth Material. Purpose is to enhance human dignity by teaching a philosophy that empowers people everywhere to achieve positive life changes with love, fun & awareness. Networks readers of the Seth/Jane Roberts books. COMPUTER SERVICES: Mailing Lists PUBLICATIONS: Path To The Stars EDITOR: Maude Cardwell TOPICS: Channeling, New Age, Metaphysics TYPE: Catalog FREQ: Annual PUBLICATIONS: Reality Change EDITOR: Maude Cardwell, Ph. D. TOPICS: Channeling, New Age, Metaphysics TYPE: Magazine DATE: 1980, 68 pgs. FREQ: quarterly PRICE: $18.00 PRICE PER COPY: $5.95 DESCRIPTION: Purpose is to enhance human dignity by teaching a philosophy that empowers people to achieve positive life changes with love, fun

& awareness. Prints articles, both fiction & non-fiction, news & reviews, poetry, interviews and various art materials. Accepts ads.

Avadhut Ashram, The
P.O. Box 80804
Santa Cruz, CA 95061
(408)-338-3923 (408)-338-9493
TOPICS: Spirituality, Meditation, Metaphysics, New Age DESCRIPTION: An Eastern meditation group under the direct guidance of the Sage Nome.

Avanta Network
139 Forest Avenue
Palo Alto, CA 94301
(415)-327-1424
TOPICS: New Age, Holistic Health

Avatar Meher Baba Center
10808 Santa Monica Boulevard
Los Angeles, CA 90025
TOPICS: Metaphysics

Avery Ranch
Box 155
Vallecito, CA 95251
(209)-533-2851
TOPICS: Holistic Healing

Awareness Ashram
P.O. Box 892
Paia Maui, HI 96779
TOPICS: Metaphysics

Awosting Retreat
Box 367
Parksville, NY 12768
TOPICS: Holistic Healing

Ayurvedic Wellness Center And Institute
11311 Menaul N.E., Suite A
Albuquerque, NM 87112
(505)-291-9698
TOPICS: Holistic Healing, Metaphysics

Badarikashrama
15602 Maubert Avenue
San Leandro, CA 94578
(415)-278-2444
TOPICS: New Age, Yoga, Meditation

Baha'i Faith
112 Linden Street
Wilmette, IL 60091
(312)-869-9039
TOPICS: New Age

Bald Mountain Hot Springs
Box 426
Ketchum, ID 83340
(208)-726-9963
TOPICS: Holistic Healing

Baltimore Spiritual Science Center
3305 Essex Road
Baltimore, MD 21207
TOPICS: Metaphysics

Banff National Park
Banff Lake Louise Chamber Of Commerce
P.O. Box 1298
Banff, Alberta T0L 0C0
Canada
(403)-762-3777
TOPICS: Holistic Healing

Bay 'N Gulf Health Resort
18207 Gulf Boulevard
Redington Shores, FL 33708
(813)-392-4213
TOPICS: Holistic Healing

Beacon Hill Health Association
14 Beacon Street, #620
Boston, MA 02108
(617)-523-8017
TOPICS: Holistic Healing

Bear Tribe Medicine Society
P.O. Box 9167
Spokane, WA 99209
(509)-326-6561
RETREAT; TOPICS: Holistic Healing, New Age, Spirituality, Crystals MEMBERS: 10 DESCRIPTION: Located on 40 acres & founded on the teachings of the Cheppewa medicine man, Sun Bear. Residents try to live in harmony with The Earth Mother & The Great Spirit. Offers lectures, seminars & Medicine Wheel Gatherings. Conducts crystal mining tours to Lake Tahoe & Arkansas. Prints magazine through Bear Tribe Publications. PUBLICATIONS: *Wildfire Magazine: A Networking Magazine* TOPICS: Holistic Healing, New Age TYPE: Magazine CIRC: 39,000 PRICE PER COPY: $2.95 DESCRIPTION: The magazine of Bear Tribe Medicine Society Network. Prints fiction, non-fiction, news, poetry, ads, reviews and more.

Belknap Hot Springs
Box 1
McKenzie Bridge, OR 97401
(503)-822-3535
TOPICS: Holistic Healing

Berkeley Buddhist Priory
1358 Marin Avenue
Albany, CA 94706
(415)-528-2139
TOPICS: New Age, Meditation

Berkeley Massage Associates
1962 University Avenue
Berkeley, CA 94704
(415)-845-5998
TOPICS: Holistic Healing

Berkeley Psychic Institute-Church of Divine Man
2436 Haste Street
Berkeley, CA 94704
(415)-548-8020
TOPICS: Psychic, Spirituality, Holistic Health

Berkeley Springs State Park
Berkeley Springs, WV 25411
(304)-258-2711
TOPICS: Holistic Healing

Berkeley Women's Health Collective
2908 Ellsworth
Berkeley, CA 94705
(415)-843-6194
TOPICS: Holistic Healing

Berkshire Village, Incorporated

P.O. Box 245 (Jug End Road)
South Egremont, MA 01258
(413)-528-3103
TOPICS: New Age DESCRIPTION: A life sharing community with mentally handicapped adults. Dedicated to an anthroposophic philosophy.

Beth Or - A New Paradigm Jewish Community
P.O. Box 160081
Miami, FL 33116
(305)-596-4523
TOPICS: New Age, Psychology, Kabbalah

Biba Hot Springs
1422 E Burnside Road
Portland, OR 97214
TOPICS: Holistic Healing

Biofeedback & Family Therapy Institute
2236 Derby Street
Berkeley, CA 94705
(415)-841-7227
CENTER; CONTACT: Erik Peper, Ph. D., Co-Dir. TOPICS: Holistic Healing, Psychology DESCRIPTION: Behavioral medicine using an holistic approach through therapeutic & educational programs which enhance awareness & mobilize self-healing. Treatments include biofeedback, voluntary self-control, psychotherapy & family therapy. Tape series available - Breathing For Health.

Biofeedback Institute Of San Francisco (BISF)
3428 Sacramento Street
San Francisco, CA 94118
(415)-921-6500 (415)-921-5455
CENTER; TOPICS: Holistic Health OWNER: Dr. George Fuller von Bozzay DESCRIPTION: One of the oldest, most respected behavioral medicine clinics. Offers innovative application, research & publication in the areas of stress management, stress-related disorders, pain management & behavioral medicine. Provides biofeedback training for professionals, consults with organizations & conducts research on applications of biofeedback.

Bircher-Benner Clinic
Keltenstrasse 48
Zurich, CH-8044
Switzerland
TOPICS: Holistic Health, Vegetarianism, Homeopathy, Nutrition

Birchwood Hall
Storridge
Malvern, Worcestershire
England
(205)08864
RETREAT; TOPICS: New Age MEMBERS: 18 DESCRIPTION: Operates a shelter for battered women. Members share all tasks & responsibilities & practice a 10-minute meeting system to strenghten member unity. PUBLICATIONS: *Communes Network Newsletter*

Bluegrass Retreat
901 Galloway Road
Stamping Ground, KY 40379
(502)-535-6261

SPA; RETREAT; TOPICS: Holistic Healing, Tai Chi, Crystals, Yoga, Reflexology, Meditation OWNER: Nancy Rutherford BOOKSTORE; STAFF: 12 DESCRIPTION: A tranquil wholistic fitness retreat promoting the advancement of preventive medicine, holistic health & healing through yoga, Tai Chi, massage, reflexology, sports, exercise, recreation, relaxation, personal health & beauty regiments. Also provides meals low in fat, salt & sugar & high in fiber & complex carbohydrates. Publishes a quarterly newsletter.

BodiFerier
1200 East Putnam Avenue
Greenwich, CT 06878
(203)-698-1104
TOPICS: Holistic Health

Boulder Hot Springs
P.O. Box 457
Boulder, MT 59632
(406)-225-4273
TOPICS: Holistic Healing

Brahma Kumaris Center
401 Baker Street
San Francisco, CA 94117
TOPICS: Metaphysics

Brandlen Institute
6784 North Positano Way
Tucson, AZ 85741-3031
(602)-297-1207
TOPICS: Holistic Healing

Breathconnection
P.O. Box 54
South Lismore, N.S.W. 2480
Australia
(066)-21-3340
RETREAT; TOPICS: Meditation, Yoga, Reincarnation, Channeling, Spirituality DESCRIPTION: Dedicated to raising the consciousness of the planet by teaching rebirthing, meditation & Yoga. Intent is to establish communities where people strive to live in the free spirit abiding by the laws of the universe. Conventions & classes held in Rebirthing , Relationship Trainings, Transformation Trainings, Yoga Retreats, Light-Channeling & Aura Balancing. Diploma offered in Rebirthing & Transpersonal Psychodynamics. Also certificates offered in Spiritual Light Healing & Yoga. PUBLICATIONS: *Breathconnection* TOPICS: Meditation, Yoga, Reincarnation, Holistic Healing, Channeling TYPE: Newsletter FREQ: quarterly DESCRIPTION: Newsletter covering various New Age topic such as Yoga, meditation & rebirthing.

Breitenbush Hot Springs Retreat And Conference Center
P.O. Box 578
Detroit, OR 97342
(503)-854-3314 (503)-854-3501
SPA; TOPICS: Holistic Healing, Holistic Health, New Age, Meditation MEMBERS: 25 DESCRIPTION: Wholistic health resort offering hot springs & healing mineral waters. Conducts meditation & healing workshops at conference center.

Bright Farm
R.R. 1

Tripp Road
Ganges, British Columbia V0S 1E0
Canada
(604)-537-2378
TOPICS: Holistic Healing

Brockway Springs Resort
Box 276
King's Beach, CA 95719
(916)-546-4201
TOPICS: Holistic Healing

Bruderhof, The
P.O. Box 903
Rifton, NY 12471-0903
(914)-658-3141
RETREAT; TOPICS: New Age DESCRIPTION: 3 communities in U.S. founded by the Christian society of Hutterites. Income earned from the production of educational play equipment, Rifton Equipment for the Handicapped & Community Playthings.

Bryn Gweled Homesteads
1150 Woods Road
Southampton, PA 18966
(215)-357-3977
RETREAT; CONTACT: John Ewbank TOPICS: New Age DESCRIPTION: A neighborhood consisting of seventy-five homes built on approximately two acres each. Promoting honesty, family autonomy and cultural diversity.

Buena Vista Women's Center
2000 Van Ness Avenue
San Francisco, CA 94104
(415)-771-5000
TOPICS: Holistic Healing

Builders, The
P.O. Box 2278
Salt Lake City, UT 84110
(801)-364-7396
TOPICS: Metaphysics, New Age, Spirituality

By-The-Sea
218 43rd Street
Virginia Beach, VA 23451
(804)-428-1644
TOPICS: Holistic Healing

Calgary Esoteric Philosophy Centre
2127 Broadway N.W.
Calgary, Alberta
Canada
TOPICS: Holistic Healing

Camas Hot Springs
Hot Springs, MT 59845
(406)-741-2473
TOPICS: Holistic Healing

Cambridge Holistic Health Center
2557 Massachusetts Avenue
Cambridge, MA 02140
(617)-661-6225
TOPICS: Holistic Healing

Camp Lenox
Route 8
Lee, MA 01238
(413)-243-2223
TOPICS: New Age

Camp Lenox For Adults
345 Riverside Drive, #4C
New York, NY 10025
(212)-662-3182
TOPICS: Holistic Healing

Camp Sunburst
1415 3rd Street
San Rafael, CA 94901
(415)-459-1650
TOPICS: New Age, Holistic Healing

Campbell Hot Springs
P.O. Box 5320
Chico, CA 95927-5320
(916)-893-8643
TOPICS: Holistic Healing

Camphill Village
Kimberton Hills
Kimberton, PA 19442
RETREAT; TOPICS: New Age, Holistic Health, Health Food, Nutrition MEMBERS: 110 DESCRIPTION: Bio-dynamic farm located on 350 acres based on the teachings of Rudolf Steiner. Offers craft workshops to the mentally retarded. PUBLICATIONS: *The Kimberton Hills Agricultural Calendar*, published annually.

Canadian Attitudinal Healing Center
3589 Granville Street
Vancouver, British Columbia V6H 3K5
Canada
(604)-736-7112
TOPICS: Holistic Healing

Canyon Ranch Spa
8600 East Rockcliff Road
Tucson, AZ 85715
(602)-749-9000 (800)-742-9000
TOPICS: Holistic Healing

Canyon Ranch Spa
91 Kemble Street
Lenox, MA 01240
(413)-637-4100 (800)-326-7080
TOPICS: Holistic Healing

Casa de Marie Research Center And Bookstore
607 Southeast Everett Mall Way, #8
Everett, WA 98204
(206)-347-6833
CENTER; CONTACT: Maria de Rungs TOPICS: Crystals, Holistic Healing DESCRIPTION: Dedicated to the art of crystal therapy & healing.

Cedar Hill Retreat
6926 Willow Street N.W.
Washington, DC 20012
(202)-829-3289
TOPICS: Holistic Healing

Center For Alternate Realities
595 7th Avenue
Durango, CO 81301
TOPICS: Channeling, Psychic, New Age, Occult DESCRIPTION: New Age Center offering new & used books, supplies & seminars, psycic readings & channeling.

Center For American Archeology
Kampsville Archeology Center

Box 366
Kampsville, IL 62053
(618)-653-4395
TOPICS: New Age

Center For Arcane Wisdom
15446 East Chicory
Fountain Hills, AZ 85269
TOPICS: Metaphysics

Center For Attitudinal Healing
2803 Branaforte Drive
Santa Cruz, CA 95065
(408)-458-3675
TOPICS: Holistic Healing

Center For Attitudinal Healing
19 Main Street
Tiburon, CA 94920
(415)-435-5022
CENTER; TOPICS: Holistic Healing, Hypnotism
OWNER: Gerald Gersham Jampolsky, M.D.
DESCRIPTION: Developed techniques to promote
positive thinking & eliminate fears as a supplement
to standard medical treatment in severly ill people.
Strongly influenced by A Course In Miracles.

Center For Attitudinal Healing
4530 16th Street N.W.
Washington, DC 20016
(202)-797-5522
TOPICS: Holistic Healing

Center For Attitudinal Healing
P.O. Box 40162
Albuquerque, NM 87196
(505)-884-9127
TOPICS: Holistic Healing

Center For Attitudinal Healing
P.O. Box 111
Roslyn Heights, NY 11577
TOPICS: Holistic Healing

Center For Attitudinal Healing
2755 Bee Cave Road
Austin, TX 78746
(512)-327-1961
TOPICS: Holistic Healing

Center For Attitudinal Healing
1017 South Staples
Corpus Christi, TX 78404
(512)-882-4820
TOPICS: Holistic Healing

Center For Attitudinal Healing
911 Waterview Circle
Richardson, TX 75080
(214)-727-1818
TOPICS: Holistic Healing

Center For Attitudinal Healing
150 Willow Street
Sherwood Park, Alberta P8A 1PA
Canada
TOPICS: Holistic Healing

Center For Classical Homeopathy
26 West 9th Street, 3B
New York, NY 10011
(212)-789-2103
TOPICS: Occult, New Age, Homeopathy

Center For Conscious Living
2223 Main Street, #41
Huntington Beach, CA 92648
(714)-969-4202
RETREAT; TOPICS: Holistic Health, Yoga,
Spirituality, Psychology OWNER: Judith-Annette
Milburn DESCRIPTION: Psycho-Spiritual
Conference & Retreat Center offering workshops &
counselling for health & well-being. Conducts
workshops on anger, spiritual & self-exploration,
healing, relationships & Yoga. Psychological
counseling available with Psycho-Spiritual emphasis
by licensed psychologists & energy-work
practitioners.

Center for Creative Consciousness
P.O. Box 4432
Pagosa Springs, CO 81157-4432
TOPICS: Holistic Healing

Center For Creative Learning
6040 West Lisbon Avenue #200
Milwaukee, WI 53210
(414)-873-6040
CENTER; TOPICS: Holistic Healing OWNER:
Patricia Clason BOOKSTORE; STAFF: 1
DESCRIPTION: Personal & professional workshops
for wellness. PUBLICATIONS: Quarterly publication
accepting advertising with a circulation of 700.
Rates on request.

Center For Effective Living
450 West Hillsboro Boulevard
Deerfield Beach, FL 33441
(305)-427-6100
TOPICS: Holistic Healing

Center For Esoteric Studies
533 East Anapanu Street
Santa Barbara, CA 93103
TOPICS: Holistic Healing

Center For Feeling People
10170-4 Larwin Avenue
Chatsworth, CA 91311
(818)-882-7404
TOPICS: Holistic Healing

Center For Health And Well-Being
28892 Marguerite Parkway, #140
Mission Viejo, CA 92692
(714)-364-4434
TOPICS: Holistic Healing

Center For Health Promotion
2810 57th Avenue, #601
Brookdale Towers, MN 55430
(612)-574-7800
TOPICS: Holistic Healing

Center For Health Sciences
P.O. Box 111
Bat Yam, 59100
Israel
972-3-5077520
CENTER; CONTACT: Dr. Shoshana Margolin,
M.A., N.D., P.M.D. TOPICS: Crystals, Holistic
Health, Homeopathy OWNER: Dr. Shoshana
Margolin DESCRIPTION: Offers courses in
Homeopathy & Holistic Medicine. Dedicated to the
art of crystal therapy & healing.

Center For Holistic Healing

569 Selby Avenue
St. Paul, MN 55102
(612)-291-7637
TOPICS: Holistic Healing

Center For Holistic Health
42 Lincoln Street
Framingham, MA 01701
(508)-879-3002
TOPICS: Holistic Healing

Center For Holistic Medicine
1330 Southeast 39th Avenue
Portland, OR 97214-4322
(503)-287-7727
TOPICS: Holistic Healing

Center For Hope, Inc.
19 Old Kings Hwy. S.
Darien, CT 06820-4526
(203)-655-4693
TOPICS: Holistic Healing

Center For Non-Traditional Religion
P.O. Box 85507
Seattle, WA 98145
(206)-793-1945
CENTER; TOPICS: Witchcraft, Occult, Paganism
OWNER: Rev. Peter Pathfinder DESCRIPTION:
Neo-Pagan Center For Non-Traditional Religion
operates an anti-defamation center, outreach
programs for pagans, sponsors Pagan Church
Conference to promote professionalism of wiccan
clergy active in interfaith programs, prison ministry
& publishing. Provides media contacts, speakers,
publishes anti-defamation materials & maintains
media watch.

Center For Reiki Training
20782 Knobwoods Drive, Ste. 203
Southfield, MI 48076
(313)-948-8112
CENTER; TOPICS: Holistic Healing, Reiki,
Meditation, Spirituality OWNER: William L. Rand
DESCRIPTION: Offers 3 levels of Reiki Training
leading to holistic healing & personal development.
Heals by laying-on-hands. Spiritually directed life
force energy used to heal yourself & others, solve
problems, achieve goals, develop higher
consciousness & fulfull spiritual purpose. Non-profit
organization offering certificate programs.

Center For Release & Integration
1057 Steiner Street
San Francisco, CA 94115
(415)-929-0119
TOPICS: Holistic Healing

Center For Religious Experience
P.O. Box 4165
Overland Park, KS 66204
TOPICS: Metaphysics

Center For Scientific Anomalies
Research (CSAR)
P.O. Box 1052
Ann Arbor, MI 48106-1052
(313)-663-8823
CENTER; TOPICS: Ghosts, Parapsychology, Psychic
Phenomena OWNER: Prof. Marcello Truzzi
DESCRIPTION: Private center which brings together
scholars & researchers concerned with furthering
responsible scientific inquiry into & evaluation of

claims of anomalies & the paranormal. Wishes to promote open & fair-minded inquiry that will be constructively skeptical but places burden of proof on the claimant. **PUBLICATIONS:** *Anomalistics: The Csar Bulletin* **EDITOR:** Marcello Truzzi, Ph. D. **TOPICS:** Ghosts, Psychic Phenomena **TYPE:** Bulletin **PUBLICATIONS:** *Zetetic Scholar* **EDITOR:** Marcello Truzzi, Ph. D. **TOPICS:** Ghosts **TYPE:** Journal **SIZE:** 4 x 6, 100 pgs. **FREQ:** irregular **CIRC;** 600 **PRICE:** $15.00 **PRICE PER COPY:** $8.00 **DESCRIPTION:** Reports research & findings of CSAR which investigates & evaluates claims of anomalies & paranormal phenomena. While most people are looking for answers & certainties to these happenings, ZS seeks to ask the right questions. Looks for readers who've not yet made up their minds & who can tolerate uncertainty.

Center For Self Healing
1714-1718 Taraval Street
San Francisco, CA 94116
(415)-665-9574
TOPICS: Holistic Healing

Center For Shamanic Studies
P.O. Box 670, Belden Station
Norwalk, CT 06852
(203)-454-2827 (203)-454-2825
CENTER; TOPICS: Metaphysics, New Age **DESCRIPTION:** Produces New Age & Metaphysical audio tapes.

Center For Spiritual Awareness
Lake Rubun Road
P.O. Box 7
Lakemont, GA 30552
(404)-782-4723
TOPICS: Holistic Health, Metaphysics **PUBLICATIONS:** *Truth Journal* **EDITOR:** Roy E. Davis **TOPICS:** Holistic Health **TYPE:** Journal **DATE:** 1968 **FREQ:** 10 x/yr. **CIRC:** 7,500 **PRICE:** $6.00

Center For Taoist Arts
P.O. Box 1389
Alpharetta, GA 30239
(404)-664-6977
CENTER; TOPICS: Spirituality, Holistic Health, Acupuncture, Herbalogy **OWNER:** Master Ni **DESCRIPTION:** Committed to spreading the wealth of Tao through sharing the writings, lifestyle & practices of traditional Taoism. Offers classes, seminars & weekend programs on varied Taoist subjects. Publishes newsletter as a medium of communication for all students of Tao.

Center For The Behavioral Sciences
Harvard University, William James Hall
33 Kirland Street
Cambridge, MA 02138
TOPICS: New Age

Center For The Dances Of Universal Peace
114 Forrest Avenue
Fairfax, CA 94930
(415)-453-8159
TOPICS: New Age, Holistic Healing

Center For Transformation
P.O. Box 1491
Sanibel, FL 33957
(813)-472-5224

CONTACT: Arthur Cataldo **TOPICS:** Channeling, New Age **PUBLICATIONS:** *Channels* **EDITOR:** Anne Cataldo, Arthur Cataldo **TOPICS:** Channeling, New Age **TYPE:** Newsletter, 16 pgs. **DESCRIPTION:** Published by The Center of Transformation and includes articles, letters and a calendar. Accepts ads.

Center For Well Being, Inc.
70 Bond Street
Fitchburg, MA 01420
(508)-345-5964
CONTACT: Beatrice N. Niemi **TOPICS:** Holistic Healing, Reiki

Center For Well-Being
82644 Howe Lane
Creswell, OR 97426
(503)-895-2953
TOPICS: Holistic Healing

Center For Yoga
230 1/2 North Larchmont
Los Angeles, CA 90004
(213)-464-1276
CENTER; TOPICS: Yoga, Meditation **BOOKSTORE; STAFF:** 15 **DESCRIPTION:** L.A.'s oldest & largest institute of Yog located in a converted Masonic Lodge. Offers workshops, seminars & classes using a dynamic, non-dogmatic approach to Yoga.

Center For Zoroastrian Research
3270 East Robinson Road
Bloomington, IN 47401
TOPICS: Metaphysics

Center Of Artistic Counseling
6275 Harwood Avenue
Oakland, CA 94618-1341
(415)-654-4462
TOPICS: New Age

Center Of Divine Ishtar
P.O. Box 9494
San Jose, CA 95157
TOPICS: Witchcraft

Center Of Eagles
7701 East Pinchot
Scottsdale, AZ 85251
TOPICS: Metaphysics

Center Of Light
Box 22367
San Diego, CA 92122
(619)-560-4248
TOPICS: Holistic Healing

Center Of Light And Truth
3360 Fourth Street
Boulder, CO 80302
TOPICS: Metaphysics

Center Of Loving Light
P.O. Box 11334
Washington, DC 20008
(202)-362-4300
CENTER; TOPICS: Crystals **DESCRIPTION:** Dedicated to the art of crystal therapy & healing.

Center Of The Light
HCR 65
Box 140
Great Barrington, MA 01230

(413)-229-2396
CENTER; TOPICS: Holistic Healing, Channeling, New Age, Herbalogy, Nutrition **MEMBERS:** 12 **DESCRIPTION:** Operates an herbal salve business and offers training for healers in Graf's Body Systems, herbs and holistic techniques. Center located on 84 acres. **PUBLICATIONS:** *The Center Of The Light Newsletter* **EDITOR:** Eugene Graf, Eva Graf **TOPICS:** Holistic Healing **TYPE:** Newsletter

Centering Institute
6109 Broad Street
Bethesda, MD 20816
(301)-229-8890
TOPICS: Holistic Healing

Centre De Recherche Et De Compilation Cristal
919 Laurier Street East
Montreal, PQ, H2J 1G4
Canada
(514)-279-9312
CENTER; CONTACT: Jean St. Amand **TOPICS:** Crystals **DESCRIPTION:** Dedicated to the art of crystal therapy & healing.

Centre For Human Growth
1819 Quebec Street
Vancouver, British Columbia V5T 2Z3
Canada
(604)-876-0800
TOPICS: Holistic Healing

Centrepoint
P.O. Box 35
Albany, Auckland
New Zealand
4159-468
RETREAT; TOPICS: New Age, Spirituality, Body Mind Connection, Psychology **MEMBERS:** 100 **DESCRIPTION:** Located on thirty acres, a community believing in personal growth and finding God within in order to change society. Operates several businesses and workshops for the public to support their community.

Chabad House
2340 Piedmont Avenue
Berkeley, CA 94704
(415)-540-5824
TOPICS: New Age

Channeling Center
7400 Fourth Avenue
Melrose Park, PA 19047
TOPICS: Metaphysics, Channeling

Chapel Of Prayer, Inc.
101 Harwin, Ste. 103
Houston, TX 77036
(713)-776-8152
CENTER; TOPICS: ESP, Metaphysics **BOOKSTORE; DESCRIPTION:** Offers services, counseling & lectures.

Charan Springs Farm
Route 1
Box 521
Cambria, CA 93428
(805)-927-8289
TOPICS: Holistic Healing

Charles Motel & Bathhouse

701 Broadway
Truth Or Consequences, NM 87901
(505)-894-7154
TOPICS: Holistic Healing

Cheerhope, Inc.
29 Davis Branch Road
Bryson City, NC 28713
(704)-488-6920
TOPICS: Holistic Healing

Chinook Learning Center
Box 57
Clinton, WA 98236
(206)-321-1884
RETREAT; TOPICS: Holistic Healing, New Age, Spirituality **MEMBERS:** 25 **DESCRIPTION:** Offers New Age educational programs which fosters Christian beliefs & the appreciation of nature. Produces income from a spiritual bookstore. Located on 50 acres.

Choices International
Box 918
Williston, VT 05495-0918
(303)-442-0566
TOPICS: New Age

Christ Of The Hills Monastery - Orthodox Monks Of St. Benedict
P.O. Box 1049
Blanco, TX 78606
(512)-833-5363
TOPICS: New Age

Christiana
Christiana 1407
Copenhagen,
Denmark
(01)546748
RETREAT; TOPICS: New Age **MEMBERS:** 1,000 **DESCRIPTION:** A community founded in an abandoned area of Copenhagen. They have their own government & no taxes or police.

Chrysalis
P.O. Box 61
Helensburg, IN 47435
(812)-988-6446
RETREAT; TOPICS: New Age **DESCRIPTION:** Located on forty acres, a community designed after some of the Egalitarian Communities in the Federation. Offers conferences and workshops and derives income from a dairy goat business.

Chrysalis Center
1008 Milltown Road
Wilmington, DE 19808
(302)-994-0565
CENTER; TOPICS: Crystals, Holistic Healing **DESCRIPTION:** Dedicated to the art of crystal therapy & healing.

Church Of Light/Brotherhood Of Life, Inc.
P.O. Box 76862, Sanford Station
Los Angeles, CA 90076
(213)-226-0453
TOPICS: New Age, Metaphysics **PUBLICATIONS:** *Church Of Light Quarterly* **EDITOR:** Lea Riffle **TOPICS:** New Age **TYPE:** Newsletter **DATE:** 1925 **FREQ:** Quarterly **CIRC:** 1,000 **PRICE:** $8.00

Church Of Loving Hands, Inc.
111 Orchard Lane
Carlotta, CA 95528
(707)-768-3226 (707)-725-9627
RETREAT; CENTER; TOPICS: Holistic Healing, Spirituality, Massage, Acupuncture, Homeopathy, Nutrition, Metaphysics **BOOKSTORE; STAFF:** 5 **DESCRIPTION:** Spiritual Retreat located on the Van Dusen River. Traditional Medicine Camp offers camping, sweatlodge, massages, hot tub, hiking & classes approved by the CA Board of Registered Nursing Provider No. 9151 such as acupuncture, organic gardening, transforming stress, homeopathy, nutrition & whole foods. Purpose is to promote & practice spiritual expression in all daily activites of life. **PUBLICATIONS:** *Medicine Ways* **EDITOR:** Skyhawk **TOPICS:** Holistic Health, Spirituality **TYPE:** Newspaper **FREQ:** 2 x per year **PRICE:** $5.00 **TERM:** yearly **DESCRIPTION:** Journal of holistic health & natural healing arts. Deals with spiritual issues, massage techniques, homeopathy & numerous holistic health topics. Contains letters, editorials, classifed, display ads & a calendar of events.

Church Of Mercavah
P.O. Box 66703
Baton Rouge, LA 70896
(504)-665-7815
CENTER; CONTACT: Jeanne Re Montandor **TOPICS:** New Age, Spirituality, Metaphysics, Occult, Witchcraft **DESCRIPTION:** Interfaith fellowship & esoteric center offering free Ministerial training. Non-creedo denomination with structured liturgy. Provides mystical structure to a wide variety of Beliefs. Operates own magazine & publishing company. Also operates the International Witchcraft Archives.

Church Of New World Religion
2940 16th Street, #308
San Francisco, CA 94103
(415)-647-9665
TOPICS: New Age

Church Of The Golden Eagle
495A North Newport Boulevard
Newport Beach, CA 92663
(714)-631-4072
CENTER; TOPICS: Crystals **DESCRIPTION:** Dedicated to the art of crystal therapy & healing.

Church Of The Most High Goddess
Canyon Country, CA 91351
TOPICS: New Age

Church Of The Tree Of Life
P.O. Box 330155
San Francisco, CA 94133-0155
CENTER; TOPICS: New Age, Holistic Health **DESCRIPTION:** Offers publications, discount coupons, life extension techniques & vitamin therapy.

Claggett Retreat Center
P.O. Box 40
Buckeystown, MD 21717
(301)-874-5147
TOPICS: Holistic Healing

Clam Bay Farm
R.R. 1
North Pender Island, British Columbia V0N 2M0

Canada
(604)-629-6313
TOPICS: Holistic Healing

Clearlake Medical Center
Box 3370
Clearlake, CA 95422
(707)-994-9486
TOPICS: Holistic Healing

Cloud Mountain
373 Agren Road
Castle Rock, WA 98611
(206)-274-4859
TOPICS: Holistic Healing

Cloud Nine Flotation
Synergy Center
7925 North Oracle Road, #196
Tucson, AZ 85704
(602)-881-7171
TOPICS: Holistic Healing

Collegians International Church
P.O. Box 929
Fairbanks, AK 99707
(907)-452-2424
TOPICS: New Age

Colorado's Psychic Center
7352 North Washington
Denver, CO 80229
(303)-289-1117
TOPICS: Holistic Healing

Common Ground, Inc., And Inner City Hot Springs
2927 N.E. Everett Street
Portland, OR 97232
(503)-238-4010
TOPICS: Holistic Healing

Commonweal
Box 316
Bolinas, CA 94924
(415)-868-0970
TOPICS: Holistic Healing

Community for Creative Non-Violence
1345 Euclid Street NW
Washington, DC 20009
(202)-667-6407
CENTER; TOPICS: New Age, Spirituality **DESCRIPTION:** A Christian service community aiding the poor by sharing their resources and lives with them. Offers a drop-in center and soup kitchens.

Community Meditation Center
1041 South Elden Avenue
Los Angeles, CA 90006
(213)-384-7817
TOPICS: New Age, Meditation

Connecticut Homeopathic Research & Treatment Center
141 Sound Beach Avenue
Old Greenwich, CT 06870
(203)-637-8632
TOPICS: Homeopathy

Consciousness Village

P.O. Box 5320
Chico, CA 95927-5320
(916)-893-8643

CENTER; TOPICS: Holistic Healing **OWNER:** Leonard Orr **DESCRIPTION:** International Training Center for Rebirthing, Physical Immortality & Spiritual Purification. 5 day basic training every week of the year. **CONVENTIONS:** Annual month-long convention each July **PUBLICATIONS:** *Conscious Connection* **EDITOR:** Leonard Orr **TOPICS:** Holistic Healing **TYPE:** Newsletter **DESCRIPTION:** Produced by the Center. Deals with topics such as Rebirthing, Physical Immortality & Spiritual Purification.

Cooper Hill Inn
P.O. Box 146
East Dover, VT 05341
(802)-348-6333

RETREAT; TOPICS: Holistic Healing **OWNER:** Pat & Marilyn Hunt **STAFF:** 2 **DESCRIPTION:** Secluded setting offering workshops & tranquil surroundings for a retreat.

Coptic Fellowship International
1735 Pinnacle Southwest
Wyoming, MI 49509
(616)-531-1339

TOPICS: New Age

Cosmic Connections
84 South Street
Eatontown, NJ 07724-3406
(201)-747-7177

CENTER; TOPICS: Crystals **DESCRIPTION:** Dedicated to the art of crystal therapy & healing.

Cosmic Studies Center
7405 Masters Drive
Potomac, MD 20854
(301)-299-7158

TOPICS: UFO's, New Age

Cosmosis Radio
125 El Rancho Road North
Santa Fe, NM 87501
(505)-983-3059

TOPICS: Holistic Healing

Course In Mastery, Inc.
10 Locust Avenue
Southampton, NY 11968
(407)-487-8961

TOPICS: New Age

Coven Of Eternal Goddess
28-15 Utopia Parkway
Flushing, NY 11358

CENTER; TOPICS: Witchcraft, Occult, Paganism **OWNER:** Carl Truchel **DESCRIPTION:** Gardnerian/Alexandrian Wicca Study Group offering 1st, 2nd & 3rd degree teachings. Runs meetings every month as well as individual instruction.

Creative Aging, Inc.
700 West End Avenue, 11B
New York, NY 10025
(212)-864-1523

TOPICS: Holistic Healing

Creative Hypnosis Center
1721 East 3rd Street, Ste. 104

Duluth, MN 55812
(218)-728-6301

CENTER; TOPICS: Hypnotism **OWNER:** Leonard James Petersen **DESCRIPTION:** An educational service designed to further the positive use of hypnosis. Individual & group instruction.

Creative Innovations For New Age Growth
P.O. Box 1965
Carson City, NV 89702

CENTER; TOPICS: New Age, Metaphysics **DESCRIPTION:** Offers new approach to metaphysics through its many metaphysical publications.

Crystal Light Center
419 West Commonwealth
Fullerton, CA 92632
(714)-526-3239

TOPICS: Crystals

Crystal Light Center
P.O. Box 1946
Rockford, IL 61110

TOPICS: Metaphysics, Channeling

Crystal Vision Retreats
65 Metcalfe, 2
Toronto, ON, M4X1R9,
Canada

TOPICS: Metaphysics

Crystallyn Center, The
18 Baltimore Avenue
Rehobeth Beach, DE 19971
(302)-227-3621

CENTER; TOPICS: Crystals **DESCRIPTION:** Dedicated to the art of crystal therapy & healing.

D.O.M.E. Inner Guide Meditation Center
Box 46146
Los Angeles, CA 90046-2015
(213)-851-9333

CENTER; TOPICS: Metaphysics, Spirituality, Meditation, Astrology, Tarot **OWNER:** Edwin C. Steinbrecher **DESCRIPTION:** Staff teaches how to initiate into Inner Guide Meditation & Western Metaphysics. Offers initiator's Certificate of Qualification which corresponds to Minister/Priest/Priestess & independent study with a required reading list. Also has more than 100 audio tapes of teaching lectures on Inner Guide Meditation, Astrology, Tarot & Western Metaphysics. **PUBLICATIONS:** *White Sun Journal* **EDITOR:** Edwin C. Steinbrecher **TOPICS:** Metaphysics, Spirituality **TYPE:** Journal **DATE:** 1973, 32 pgs. **FREQ:** Quarterly **CIRC:** 5,000 **PRICE:** $15.00 **TERM:** annually

Dandelion
RR1
Enterprise, Ontario K0K 1Z0
Canada
(613)-358-2304

RETREAT; TOPICS: New Age **MEMBERS:** 12 **DESCRIPTION:** Located on fifty acres, a cooperative commununity sharing money & material items, believing in communal child raising and social change. Produces income from sales of handwoven rope hammocks, chairs & tinnery. Offers workshops and a mail-order book service.

Daybreak Star Center
P.O. Box 99100
Seattle, WA 98199
(206)-285-4425

TOPICS: Holistic Healing

Deirdre C. Beck Center
8338 W. Oakland Park Boulevard
Sunrise, FL 33351
(305)-731-2515

CENTER; TOPICS: Massage **OWNER:** Deirdre C. Beck, L.M.T. **DESCRIPTION:** Offers Swedish Massage to relieve sinus problems, headaches, T.M.J., accident victims, back pain, arthritis & relaxation.

DeLano Training Systems
Rt. 4
Box 60
Pittsboro, NC 27312
(919)-542-1332 (800)-451-2562

TOPICS: New Age

Denali Center For Holistic Health & Personal Growth
HC 89, Box 451
Willow, AK 99688-9705
(907)-495-6853

CONTACT: Wade Greyfox, Exec. Dir. **TOPICS:** Psychic, Tarot, Runes, Channeling, Spirituality **PUBLICATIONS:** *The Shaman Papers* **PUBLISHER:** Wade Greyfox **EDITOR:** Kathy Lynn Douglass **TOPICS:** Spirituality, Psychic, Tarot, Runes, Channeling **TYPE:** Newsletter **DATE:** 1989 **FREQ:** quarterly **PRICE:** $9.00 **TERM:** yearly **PRICE PER COPY:** $3.00 **DESCRIPTION:** Purpose is to spread Shamanic knowledge. Offers articles, humor & reviews.

Desert Inn Resort And Spa
10805 Palm Drive
Desert Hot Springs, CA 92240
(714)-329-6495

TOPICS: Holistic Healing

Dialogue House
80 East 11th Street
New York, NY 10003
(800)-221-5844

TOPICS: New Age **PUBLICATIONS:** *At A Journal Workshop: The Basic Text & Guide For Using The Intensive Journal Process* **EDITOR:** I. Progoff **TOPICS:** New Age, Psychology **TYPE:** Book **PRICE:** $15.95 **PUBLICATIONS:** *Dialogue House* **TOPICS:** New Age **TYPE:** Magazine **PUBLICATIONS:** *Practice Of Process Meditation: Intensive Journal Way To Spiritual Experience* **EDITOR:** I. Progoff **TOPICS:** Meditation, Spirituality **TYPE:** Book **PRICE:** $15.95

Discovery Center
168 Grand Street
White Plains, NY 10603
(914)-948-9286

TOPICS: Holistic Health

Dispensable Healing Center
403 Kingston Street
Victoria, British Columbia V8V 1V8
Canada
(604)-384-5560

TOPICS: Holistic Healing

Dolphin Holistic Center
3641 Diamond
Oakland, CA 94611
(415)-531-5509
TOPICS: Holistic Healing

Double D Ranch
Star Route
Box 14
Caliente, CA 93518
(213)-434-3453
TOPICS: Holistic Healing

Dr. Wilkinson's Hot Springs
1507 Lincoln Avenue
Calistoga, CA 94515
(707)-942-4102
SPA; TOPICS: Holistic Healing, Massage,
Acupuncture OWNER: Dr. John Wilkinson STAFF:
75 DESCRIPTION: Tranquil setting in the Napa
Valley region providing natural health through such
treatments as mineral & mud baths, hot & cold
mineral pools, natural mineral steam rooms, blanket
wraps, therapeutic massages, acupressure &
reflexology treatments & Cerfango Treatments using
volcanic ash, clay, herbs & paraffin.

Dream Center
P.O. Box 638
Fork Union, VA 23055
(804)-842-5555
CENTER; TOPICS: Dreams, Holistic Health,
Parapsychology, Holistic Healing, ESP OWNER:
Susanna Van de Castle DESCRIPTION: Promotes
health & happiness through the study of dreams.

Dream House
19 Elk Street
San Francisco, CA 94131
(415)-333-7326
CENTER; CONTACT: Fred Olsen, M.Div.,Director
TOPICS: Dreams, Body-Mind Connection STAFF: 1
DESCRIPTION: Purpose is to make a home for The
Dream. Offers ongoing dream groups, classes,
workshops, training, lecturing, research & advanced
dreamwork skills. Specializing in dream reentry
method & mind/body interaction. AFFILIATED
ORGS: Bay Area Professional Dream Workers;
Assoc. For The Study Of Dreams; Dream Network
Journal; Novato Center For Dreams
PUBLICATIONS: Dream Talk Audio Tapes Series,
$9 each

Dream Of The Forest
R.R. 1
Lone Butte, British Columbia V0K 1X0
Canada
(604)-593-4603
TOPICS: Holistic Healing

Durham Yoga & Meditation Center
1214 Broad Street, #2
Durham, NC 27705
(919)-342-0208
TOPICS: Holistic Healing

E. K. Learning Center
65 Coachwood Point
Lethrridge, AT, T1K6B1,
Canada
TOPICS: Metaphysics

Earth Rising, Inc.
P.O. Box 10442
Kansas City, MO 64111
RETREAT; TOPICS: Holistic Health, Spirituality
DESCRIPTION: Earth Rising, Inc. along with Tuatha
De Terre management team, establishes & maintains
conference & retreat centers such as Gala Retreat &
Conference Center. This center provides private
space for people of all life-affirming traditions &
particularly inter-faith sharing & networking. Brings
in speakers, musicians & teachers for spiritual
workshops & concerts.

Earthsong Institute
P.O. Box 20615
Park West Station
New York, NY 10025-1515
(212)-518-4548
CENTER; TOPICS: Holistic Health, Meditation,
Crystals, Spirituality, Past Life Regression, Color
Therapy, Channeling OWNER: Devorah Devi
DESCRIPTION: Promotes the study & practice of
consciousness, healing & recovery using channeling,
music, sound, voice, crystals, energy awareness,
intuitive & creative opening & feminine energy.
Provides tools, groups, practices & teachings to assist
in the transformation & enlightenment of people.
Offers classes, workshops, concerts therapy,
counseling & healing, practitioner & teacher
training. Certificate programs in Spiritual
Counseling & Healing. Independent study available.

EarthStar
P.O. Box 639
Camden, ME 04843-0639
(207)-236-6219
CENTER; TOPICS: Holistic Healing OWNER: Shell
Goldman DESCRIPTION: Offers personal growth
workshops, individual sessions, weekly classes with
the goal of creating a safe environment where one
can experience the inner-self with respect & support.

Earthwalk
227 Grove Street
Mt. Kisco, NY 10549
(914)-241-3506
CONTACT: Kenneth Leon Meyer, Ph.D. TOPICS:
New Age

East Bay Center For Attitudinal Healing
3534 Lakeshore
Oakland, CA 94609
(415)-893-5683
TOPICS: Holistic Healing

East Wind Community
RR 6
Box NY 188
Tecumseh, MO 65760
(417)-679-4682
RETREAT; TOPICS: New Age, Metaphysics
MEMBERS: 50 DESCRIPTION: A 160 acre
cooperative community with non-racist, equality,
non-sexist beliefs. All labor, resources and land
shared by members. Income derived through the sale
of rope sandals, nutbutter and casual furniture.
Politically & socialy progressive. Concerned with
equality & the environment.

El Reposo Spa
66334 West 5th Street
Desert Hot Springs, CA 92240
(619)-329-6632
TOPICS: Holistic Healing

Eldorado Springs Resort
Eldorado Springs, CO 80302
(303)-494-4940
TOPICS: Holistic Healing

Elisabeth Kubler-Ross Center/Shanti Nilaya
South Route 616
Headwaters, VA 24442
(703)-396-3441
TOPICS: Holistic Healing PUBLICATIONS: *The
Elisabeth Kubler-Ross Newsletter* TOPICS: Holistic
Healing TYPE: Newsletter

Ella's Hide-A-Way Hot Springs
Box 101
Tecopa, CA 92389
TOPICS: Holistic Healing

Emandel-A Farm On A River
16501 Hearst Road
Willits, CA 95490
(707)-459-5439
TOPICS: Holistic Healing

Emissaries Of Divine Light
5569 North County Road
Loveland, CO 80537
TOPICS: Holistic Healing

Emissaries Of Divine Light/Glen Ivy Community
25000 Glen Ivy Road
Corona, CA 91719
(714)-735-8701
TOPICS: Holistic Healing

Enrichment Center
27 Milburn Street
Bronxville, NY 10708
(914)-636-8937 (914)-337-3339
TOPICS: Body-Mind Connection

Esalen Institute
Pacific Coast Highway
Big Sur, CA 93920
(408)-667-2335 (408)-667-3000
SPA; TOPICS: New Age, Spirituality, Holistic
Healing, Psychic, Psychology, Body-Mind
Connection STAFF: 35 DESCRIPTION: Provides
programs to realize human potential on topics such
as therapy, body work, science & religion. Promotes
citizen exchanges of healers, scientists & psychics
between the USA & USSR. Offers mineral hot spring
baths & Gazebo School for children.

Esoteric Philosophy Center
10450 Stancliff
Suite 100
Houston, TX 77099
(713)-561-9556
TOPICS: Holistic Healing

Essence Light Center/Twelve Rays Of The Great Central Sun
3427 Denson Place
Charlotte, NC 28215
(704)-536-8159

TOPICS: Channeling, Holistic Healing, New Age, Metaphysics PUBLICATIONS: *Path Of Light* TOPICS: Channeling TYPE: Directory

Essex Retreat Center
Conomo Point Road
Essex, MA 01929
(617)-768-7374
TOPICS: Holistic Healing

Estar Human Awareness Center
P.O. Box 932
Soap Lake, WA 98851
TOPICS: Metaphysics

Eternal Spring Campground
611 Walker Street
Oliver Springs, TN 37840-1636
(615)-676-3703
TOPICS: Holistic Health

Evergreen Wellness Center
P.O. Box 994
Evergreen, CO 80439
TOPICS: Channeling

Evolutionary Education Foundation
Box 1613
Kapaa, HI 96746-7613
TOPICS: Holistic Healing

Experiences In Awareness
P.O. Box 296
Palm Springs, CA 92263
(619)-320-1517
CONTACT: Marcia Akal Kaur Wieting TOPICS: New Age, Holistic Health

Family Spiritual Camp
Camp NG
4545 Warwick Circle
Grand Blanc, MI 48439
(313)-695-0188
TOPICS: Yoga

Fannie Shaffer's Vegetarian Hotel
P.O. Box 457
Woodridge, NY 12789
(914)-434-4455
TOPICS: Holistic Healing

Farallones Institute Rural Centre
15290 Coleman Valley Road
Occidental, CA 95465
(707)-874-2441
RETREAT; TOPICS: New Age, Health Food, Holistic Health DESCRIPTION: Started by California State Architect as a non-profit establishment.Offers courses on topics such as edible landscaping, organic food production, solar and wind energy, composting toilets and permaculture. Has Integral Urban House model in Berkeley.

Fare-Thee-Well Center
Rt. 66
Huntington, MA 01050
(413)-238-5873 (413)-667-3027
RETREAT; TOPICS: New Age, Body-Mind Connection, Holistic Health, Spirituality DESCRIPTION: Ninety-two acres accommodating seven families in Worthington. Offersservices and classes to the public promoting inner self-healing.

Farm, The
P.O. Box 579
Sagle, ID 83860
TOPICS: Channeling

Farm, The
34 The Farm
Summertown, TN 38483
(615)-964-3574
RETREAT; TOPICS: Holistic Healing, New Age, Holistic Health, Vegetarianism, Spirituality, Health Food, Birth MEMBERS: 150 DESCRIPTION: A spiritual, pacifist and vegetarian community committed to saving the environment, animals, native & poor people. Founded the non-profit charitable organization, PLENTY, which aides the Third World. Produces income from a whole foods company, midwifery school & book publishing.

Feather Mountain Conference Center
P.O. Box 670
Paulden, AZ 86334
(602)-445-0911
TOPICS: Holistic Healing

Feathered Pipe Foundation (FPF)
P.O. Box 1682
Helena, MT 59624
(406)-442-8196
RETREAT; TOPICS: Yoga, Astrology, Holistic Health, Spirituality DESCRIPTION: Non-profit educational foundation offering seminars, tours & publications to promote health in body, mind & spirit. Purpose is to help individuals find new understanding, vision & direction. Emissary for peace on the planet, conducts tours all over the world to study ancient traditions & experience the transformative energies that emanate from places of pilgrimage. Also operates summer programs. PUBLICATIONS: *Circle* - a networking journal

Federation Of Christian Ministries
1011 Overlook Road
Berkeley, CA 94708
(415)-540-7696
TOPICS: New Age

Female Principle
456 Rich Street
Oakland, CA 94609
(415)-652-6798
TOPICS: Metaphysics

Findhorn Foundation & Press
The Park
Forres, Morayshire IV36 0TZ
Scotland
003-093-0582
CENTER; CONTACT: J. Wolcott TOPICS: New Age, Spirituality, Health Food, Metaphysics MEMBERS: 200 DESCRIPTION: Spiritually aware people from many countries and of all ages living and working together. Offers programs such as children's school, garden school, book publishing, performing arts and resource/networking center. PUBLICATIONS: *Circle Of Song: Chants, Dances & Ceremonies Of Love, Healing & Power* EDITOR: Katie Marks TOPICS: Occult TYPE: Book PRICE: $16.95 PUBLICATIONS: *Footprints On The Path* EDITOR: Eileen Caddy TOPICS: Spirituality TYPE: Book PUBLICATIONS: *God Spoke To Me* EDITOR: Eileen Caddy TOPICS: Spirituality, Paranormal Phenomena TYPE: Book PRICE: $10.95

PUBLICATIONS: *Holistic Herbal: An Herbal Celebrating The Wholeness Of Life* EDITOR: David Hoffman TOPICS: Holistic Health, Herbalogy TYPE: Book PRICE: $16.95 PUBLICATIONS: *One Earth* EDITOR: Andrew Murray, Eve Ward TOPICS: Metaphysics, New Age, Spirituality TYPE: Magazine DATE: 1976, 48 pgs. FREQ: quarterly PRICE: $20.00 TERM: annually PRICE PER COPY: $5.00 DESCRIPTION: Offers spiritual inspiration to help create social & ecological harmony. Promotes the unity of all life, the planet & the universe. Features articles, display ads pertaining to New Age topics. PUBLICATIONS: *Opening Doors Within* EDITOR: Eileen Caddy TOPICS: Spirituality TYPE: Book PRICE: $16.95 PUBLICATIONS: *The Findhorn Community* EDITOR: Carol Riddell TOPICS: Spirituality TYPE: Book DESCRIPTION: Traces the development of this 30 year old international spiritual community. PUBLICATIONS: *This New Age Business: Story Of The Ancient & Continuing Quest To Bring Down Heaven On Earth* EDITOR: P. Lemesurier TOPICS: New Age TYPE: Book PRICE: $13.95

Florida LRT
Box 2754
Delray Beach, FL 33447-2754
(305)-720-7112
TOPICS: Metaphysics

Flower Essence Society/Earth-Spirit, Inc.
P.O. Box 459
Nevada City, CA 95959
(916)-265-9163 (800)-548-0075 FAX (916)-265-6467
TOPICS: Holistic Healing PUBLICATIONS: *Flower Essence Society Newsletter* TOPICS: Holistic Healing TYPE: Newsletter

Fort Help Counseling Center
169 11th Street
San Francisco, CA 94103
(415)-864-4357
TOPICS: Holistic Healing

Foundation For A Course In Miracles Conference/Retreat Center
R.R. 2
Box 71
Roscoe, NY 12776
(607)-498-5611 (607)-498-4116 FAX (607)-498-5325
CENTER; CONTACT: Judith Beck TOPICS: Spirituality, Holistic Healing, Metaphysics, Channeling OWNER: Kenneth & Gloria Wapnick BOOKSTORE; STAFF: 25 DESCRIPTION: Educational-Spiritual Foundation located in a peaceful setting in the Catskill Mountains. Conducts workshops & seminars whose aim is to deepen intellectual understanding & application of the principles of A Course In Miracles, a spiritual-psychological thought system which teaches the attainment of peace through the process of forgiveness with the Holy Spirit. Also produces audio tapes, books & pamphlets. PUBLICATIONS: *Glossary Index For Course In Miracles* EDITOR: K. Wapnick TOPICS: Spirituality TYPE: Book PRICE: $16.00 PUBLICATIONS: *Love Does Not Condemn: The World, The Flesh & Devil According To Gnosticism & Acim* EDITOR: K. Wapnick TOPICS: Occult, New Age, Spirituality

TYPE: Book PRICE: $25.00 PUBLICATIONS: *Obstacles To Peace* EDITOR: K. Wapnick TOPICS: Spirituality TYPE: Book PRICE: $12.00

Foundation For Inner Peace
Box 1104
Glen Ellen, CA 95442-1104
TOPICS: Holistic Healing PUBLICATIONS: *Course In Miracles* EDITOR: J. Skutch TOPICS: Spirituality TYPE: Book PRICE: $40.00

Foundation For Life Action
902 S. Burnside Avenue
Los Angeles, CA 90036
(213)-933-5591
TOPICS: New Age

Foundation For Well-Being
P.O. Box 627
Plymouth Meeting, PA 19462
(215)-828-4674
CENTER; TOPICS: Holistic Healing, Psychology, Spirituality OWNER: Philip H. Friedman, Ph. D. BOOKSTORE; STAFF: 1 DESCRIPTION: Purpose to enhance the psychological, emotional, occupational, relational, physical & spiritual well-being of individuals, couples, families, groups & organizations. Offers seminars, workshops, support groups, psychotherapy & counseling. Produces 8 audio tapes on meditation, self-esteem, forgiveness, relaxation, etc. CONVENTIONS: Workshops & seminars every 3 months. PUBLICATIONS: *Creating Well-Being: The Healing Path To Love, Peace, Self-Esteem & Happiness* EDITOR: Philip H. Friedman, Ph. D. TOPICS: Holistic Health, Spirituality, Psychology TYPE: Book DATE: 1989 PRICE: $11.95

Foundation Of Light
399 Turkey Hill Road
Ithaca, NY 14850
TOPICS: Holistic Healing

Foundation Of Universal Unity
5569 North County Road 29
Loveland, CO 80537
(303)-667-4693
TOPICS: New Age, Metaphysics

Fountain Of Health
66705 East Sixth Street
Desert Hot Springs, CA 92240
(619)-329-6015
TOPICS: Holistic Healing

Fox Valley Gestalt Center
1-30 West State Street
Geneva, IL 60134
(312)-232-1223
TOPICS: Holistic Healing

Franciscan Renewal Center
5802 East Lincoln Drive
P.O. Box 220
Scottsdale, AZ 85252
(602)-948-7460
TOPICS: New Age

Free Enterprise Health Mine
Box 67
Boulder, MT 59632
(406)-225-3383
CONTACT: B. Lundsted TOPICS: Holistic Healing

French Lick Springs Golf & Tennis Resort
French Lick, IN 47432
(812)-935-9381 (800)-325-3535
TOPICS: Holistic Healing

Friends Of EKR
P.O. Box 80
Palmer, AK 99645
(907)-745-3751
TOPICS: Holistic Healing

Friends Of EKR
2909 Regent Street, #3
Berkeley, CA 94705
(415)-549-1561
TOPICS: Holistic Healing

Friends Of EKR
1917 Baxter Street
Los Angeles, CA 90039
(213)-661-9464
TOPICS: Holistic Healing

Friends Of EKR
1046 Leroy Street
San Diego, CA 92106
(619)-222-0104
TOPICS: Holistic Healing

Friends Of EKR
41 Carl Street, #C
San Francisco, CA 94117
(415)-564-1750
TOPICS: Holistic Healing

Friends Of EKR
3726 16th Street
San Francisco, CA 94114
(415)-861-2857
TOPICS: Holistic Healing

Friends Of EKR
336 8th Avenue
Santa Cruz, CA 95062
(408)-462-0585
TOPICS: Holistic Healing

Friends Of EKR
P.O. Box 6231
Santa Rosa, CA 95406
(707)-528-7046
TOPICS: Holistic Healing

Friends Of EKR
123B Wolcott Hill Road
Wethersfield, CT 06109
(203)-563-3035
TOPICS: Holistic Healing

Friends Of EKR
201 Merchant Street #2300
Honolulu, HI 96813-3934
(808)-526-4008
TOPICS: Holistic Healing

Friends Of EKR
561 Dogwood Trail
Elk Grove Village, IL 60007
(312)-437-4489
TOPICS: Holistic Healing

Friends Of EKR

P.O. Box 3696
Oakbrook, IL 60522
(312)-990-0010
TOPICS: Holistic Healing

Friends Of EKR
15 Parkinson Street
Needham, MA 02192
(617)-444-7977
TOPICS: Holistic Healing

Friends Of EKR
34 Clifford Street
Mechanic Falls, ME 04256
(207)-345-9873
TOPICS: Holistic Healing

Friends Of EKR
P.O. Box 5872
Helena, MT 59604
(406)-442-7811
TOPICS: Holistic Healing

Friends Of EKR
434 San Pasqual
Santa Fe, NM 87501
(505)-984-1872
CONTACT: Dr. Paula N. Bromberg TOPICS: Holistic Healing

Friends Of EKR
790 Lancaster Street
Albany, NY 12203
(518)-489-4431
TOPICS: Holistic Healing

Friends Of EKR
6 Russet Lane
Lake Grove, NY 11755
(516)-467-6582
TOPICS: Holistic Healing

Friends Of EKR
61 Hitchcock Lane
Old Westbury, NY 11568
(516)-997-9713
TOPICS: Holistic Healing

Friends Of EKR
2309 Kingsway Drive
League City, TX 77573
(713)-338-2439
TOPICS: Holistic Healing

Friends Of EKR
Route 2
Box 481
Marshall, VA 22115
(703)-364-3195
TOPICS: Holistic Healing

Friends Of EKR
17 Regis Circle
Sterling, VA 22170
(703)-450-6290
TOPICS: Holistic Healing

Friends Of EKR
1261 Colombia Street
Kamloops, British Columbia V2C 2W4
Canada
(604)-374-7239
TOPICS: Holistic Healing

Friends Of EKR
6190 Mac Donald Street
Vancouver, British Columbia V6N 1E6
Canada
(604)-261-6422
TOPICS: Holistic Healing

Friends Of EKR
225 Hill Street
Winnipeg, Manitoba R2H 2L7
Canada
(204)-233-2854
TOPICS: Holistic Healing

Gardom Lake International Earth Friendship Center
Twin Island Resort
P.O. Box 7
Salmon Arm, British Columbia V1E 4N2
Canada
(604)-838-7587
TOPICS: Holistic Healing PUBLICATIONS: *Gardom Lake International Earth Friendship Newsletter* EDITOR: Sarah Kipp TOPICS: Holistic Healing TYPE: Newsletter

Genesis, Spiritual Life Center
53 Mill Street
Westfield, MA 01085
TOPICS: Channeling, Metaphysics

Gerson Institute
Box 430
Bonita, CA 92002
(619)-267-1150
CENTER; CONTACT: Charlotte Gerson, Pres. TOPICS: Holistic Healing, Health Food DESCRIPTION: Uses the Gerson Therapy program which treats diseases such as Cancer with diet. PUBLICATIONS: *Healing Newsletter* EDITOR: Gar Hildenbrand TOPICS: Holistic Healing TYPE: Newsletter

Gila Hot Springs Vacation Center
Route 11
Silver City, NM 88061
(505)-534-9551
TOPICS: Holistic Healing

Gita-Nigari Community, Iskcon Farm
Rural Deliery 1, Box 163
Port Royal, PA 17082
(717)-527-4101
TOPICS: New Age

Glenwood Springs
Hot Springs Lodge And Pool
401 North River Road
Glenwood Springs, CO 81601
(303)-945-6571
TOPICS: Holistic Healing

God's Valley (Pandamarama)
R.R. 1, Box 478
Williams, IN 47470
(812)-388-5571
RETREAT; TOPICS: New Age, Spirituality MEMBERS: 200 DESCRIPTION: A non-denominational, spiritually oriented community on two thousand acres. Members have own housing with communal dining rooms. Produce income from sawmilling, log cabins, canning and craft shops.

Golden Door, The
777 Deer Springs Road
Escondido, CA 92925
(714)-744-5777
TOPICS: Holistic Healing

Golden Leaves Book Mart & Metaphysical Centre
211 Phlox Avenue
Metairie, LA 70001
TOPICS: Metaphysics

Golden Pathways Healing Center
17 Polaris Drive, North Star
Newark, DE 19711
(302)-239-4567
CENTER; TOPICS: Crystals DESCRIPTION: Dedicated to the art of crystal therapy & healing.

Golden Phoenix Healing And Light Center
P.O. Box 969
Rimrock, AZ 86335
(602)-567-4937
CENTER; CONTACT: Jane Blair, Asst. Director TOPICS: Holistic Health, Body-Mind Connection, Holistic Healing, Yoga, Meditation, Herbalogy, Nutrition OWNER: Rev. Mona F. Fore STAFF: 12 DESCRIPTION: Holistic retreat offering alternative healing methods for disease especially terminal diseases. Individualized programs by well trained staff specializing in therapies such as herbalogy, nutrition, massage, acupressure, yoga, meditation, physical therapy, emotional counseling & other wholistic disciplines. Healing is achieved through interaction of mind & body; through dedication, disciplin & devotion to treatment; balancing the body & strengthening the immune system. PUBLICATIONS: *Karmic Astrology Of Relationship* EDITOR: Jane Greven, Rev. Mona Fore TOPICS: Holistic Healing TYPE: Book PUBLICATIONS: *Personal Karmic Astrology Workbook* TOPICS: Holistic Healing TYPE: Book

Goodlife
2006 Vine Street
Berkeley, CA 94709
(415)-525-0251
RETREAT; TOPICS: New Age MEMBERS: 10 DESCRIPTION: Sexually open community promoting multi-relationships & striving to live well & attain happiness.

Graduate Theological Union Library New Religous Movements Research Collection
2400 Ridge Road
Berkeley, CA 94709
(415)-841-8222
TOPICS: New Age

Grand Hotel Des Thermes
100 Boulevard Herbert
St. Malo, Brittany
France
99-40-75-00
SPA; TOPICS: Holistic Health, Holistic Healing DESCRIPTION: Health resort offering thalassotherapy, hot sea-water therapy. Offers health cures through hot sea-water treatments.

GRD Health Clinic

301 East Palace
Santa Fe, NM 87501
(505)-984-0934
TOPICS: Holistic Healing

Green Pastures
Rt. 3
Box 80
Epping, NH 03042
(603)-679-8149
CENTER; TOPICS: New Age, Holistic Health, Spirituality MEMBERS: 80 DESCRIPTION: Produces income from wholistic health center and workshops in The Art of Living. Emissaries of Divine Light.

Greenbrie, The
White Sulphur Spring, WV 24986
(304)-536-1110
TOPICS: Holistic Healing

Group I Associates
Box 111
Wendell Depot, MA 01380
(302)-239-4567
CENTER; TOPICS: Crystals DESCRIPTION: Dedicated to the art of crystal therapy & healing.

Guadalupe River Ranch
Box 877
Boerne, TX 78006
(512)-537-4837
TOPICS: Holistic Healing

Gurdjieff Foundation Of California
P.O. Box 549
San Francisco, CA 94101
(415)-563-0399
TOPICS: New Age, Metaphysics

Guru Ram Das Ashram
1390 Waller St.
San Francisco, CA 94117
(415)-864-9642
CENTER; TOPICS: New Age, Yoga, Meditation, Spirituality DESCRIPTION: Yogi Bhajan instructs Kundalini Yoga.

Guru Ram Dass Ashram
5489 Cote St. Antoine
Montreal, QB, H4A1R1,
Canada
TOPICS: Metaphysics

Hahnemann Medical Clinic
1918 Bonita
Berkeley, CA 94704
(415)-849-1925
TOPICS: New Age, Holistic Health

Hailos Wholistic Living Society
Box 8
Lumby, British Columbia V0E 2G0
Canada
(604)-547-9680
TOPICS: Holistic Healing

Hakomi Therapy
P.O. Box 1873
Boulder, CO 80306
(303)-443-6209
TOPICS: Body-Mind Connection

Hale Akua
Star Route 1
Box 161
Haiku, Maui, HI 96708
(808)-572-9300
TOPICS: Holistic Healing

Harbin Hot Springs Retreat And Conference Center
P.O. Box 782
Middletown, CA 95461
(707)-987-2477 (800)-622-2477
SPA; TOPICS: Holistic Healing, Holistic Health, New Age, Massage, Health Food, Nutrition, Spirituality MEMBERS: 50 DESCRIPTION: Accommodates members with a wide variety of lifestyles and beliefs. Produces income from retreat businesses and workshops. Houses Harbinger Center New Age Work Study Program, East West Center for Macrobiotic Studies, Shiatsu Center and Niyama School of Massage. Located on 1,100 acres & offers services such as movies, a school & a community food store.

Hardscrabble Hill
Castine Road
Box 62A
Orland, ME 04472
(207)-469-7112
RETREAT; TOPICS: New Age, Psychology DESCRIPTION: A community of feminists providing workshops on self-sufficiency skills & personal growth.

Hartland Health Center
P.O. Box 1
Rapidan, VA 22733
(703)-672-3100
TOPICS: Holistic Healing

Hawaiian Fitness Holiday
P.O. Box 279
Kola, Kauai, HI 96756
(808)-332-9244 (800)-338-6977
RETREAT; TOPICS: Holistic Health, Astrology, Metaphysics, Numerology, Yoga, Massage, Reiki OWNER: Dr. Grady Deal & Roberleigh Deal STAFF: 6 DESCRIPTION: Astrological/Metaphysical retreat offering daily classes in astrology, numerology & yoga. Also outings to the energy vortexes, sacred sites & scenic spots. Discussions on various metaphysical topics, numerology readings, natural foods, massage, chiropractic therapy, reiki & aura balancing. Purpose is to help people establish a healthier way of life physically, mentally & spiritually. PUBLICATIONS: *Letters In Action*, 1976, Astro Press

Hay Institute
P.O. Box 2212
Santa Monica, CA 90406
(213)-394-7445
TOPICS: Holistic Healing

Healers' Resource Center, Inc.
90 Strawberry Hill Street
Dover, MA 02030
(617)-864-1989
TOPICS: Holistic Healing

Healing & Spiritual Center
Box 3162
Rancho Santa Fe, CA 92067

(619)-756-0641
TOPICS: Holistic Healing

Healing Arts Center
17280 Saticoy Street
Van Nuys, CA 91406
(818)-343-0339
TOPICS: Holistic Healing

Healing Arts Of Santa Fe
Box 1445
Santa Fe, NM 87501
(505)-988-4122
TOPICS: Holistic Healing

Healing Center of Arizona
25 Wilson Canyon Road
Sedona, AZ 86336
(602)-282-7710
CENTER; TOPICS: Holistic Healing, Vegetarianism, Meditation OWNER: John Paul Weber DESCRIPTION: Non-profit organization devoted to holistic health. Dedicated to serving the Divine through teaching people to heal themselves & the planet. Offering retreats, healing work, vegetarian meals, spa facilities, organic gardens, hiking, swimming, vortex tours & meditation room. Counselling available with professional therapists to promote personal growth & change or for group sessions or classes on healing.

Healing Center Of San Francisco
465 Brussels Street
San Francisco, CA 94134
(415)-468-4680
TOPICS: Holistic Healing

Healing Heart Center
189 George Street
New Brunswick, NJ 08901
(201)-247-3723
TOPICS: Holistic Healing

Healing Light Center
138 North Maryland
Glendale, CA 91206
(213)-244-8607
TOPICS: Holistic Healing

Healing Pines
P.O. Box 658
Pine, AZ 85544
(602)-476-3392
TOPICS: Holistic Healing

Healing Tao Center
P.O. Box 1194
Huntington, NY 11743
(516)-367-2701
TOPICS: Tai Chi PUBLICATIONS: *Bone Marrow Nei Kung: Taoist Ways To Improve Your Health By Rejuvenating Bone Marrow & Blood* EDITOR: M. Chia TOPICS: Tai Chi, Holistic Health TYPE: Book PRICE: $14.95 PUBLICATIONS: *Chi Self-Massage: Tao Of Rejuvenation* EDITOR: M. Chia TOPICS: Tai Chi TYPE: Book PRICE: $10.95 PUBLICATIONS: *Fusion Of The Five Elements I: Basic & Advanced Meditation For Transforming Negative Emotions* EDITOR: M. Chia TOPICS: Tai Chi, Holistic Health, Meditation TYPE: Book PRICE: $12.95 PUBLICATIONS: *Healing Love Through The Tao: Cultivating Female Sexuality* EDITOR: M. Chia, M. Chia

TOPICS: Holistic Healing, Spirituality TYPE: Book PRICE: $14.95 PUBLICATIONS: *Iron Shirt Chi Kung* EDITOR: M. Chia TOPICS: Tai Chi TYPE: Book PRICE: $14.95

Health Research Institute
2100 Bldg C Manchester Road #610
Wheaton, IL 60187
TOPICS: Holistic Healing

Health Training Group
3789 Hampton Avenue
Montreal, Quebec H4A 2K7
Canada
(514)-485-6373
TOPICS: Holistic Healing

Healthworks
2917 N.E. Everett Street
Portland, OR 97232
(503)-231-0090
TOPICS: Holistic Healing

Heart's Bend
P.O. Box 217
Newfane, VT 05345
(802)-365-7616
TOPICS: Holistic Healing

Heartspring Health Center
52 Hempstead Road
Jamaica Plain, MA 02130
(617)-738-4366
TOPICS: Holistic Healing

Heartwood Institute, Ltd.
220-Harmony Lane
Garberville, CA 95440
(707)-923-2021 (707)-923-3182
RETREAT; CONTACT: Nirmalo TOPICS: Holistic Healing, Massage, Hypnotism, Vegetarianism, Nutrition, Parapsychology OWNER: Bob Fasic & Roy Grieshaber BOOKSTORE; DESCRIPTION: A school, retreat & teaching community on 240 acres, providing resources for attaining physical, psychological & spiritual well-being. Acts as a catalyst for planetary healing through personal transformation & promotes living in balance with Mother Earth. retreat & school providing career training & certification in Massage Therapy, Transformational Therapy, Addictions Therapy & Hypnotherapy Training. Also courses in life exploration, personal growth & spiritual development. Independent study available.

Heathcote Center
21300 Heathcote Road
Freeland, MD 21053
(301)-343-1070
CENTER; TOPICS: New Age, Spirituality DESCRIPTION: Spiritually oriented community-retreat on 35 acres offering equality & freedom of self-expression.

Heaven, The
4605 Jefferson Avenue
Midland, MI 48640-3531
(616)-898-2360
TOPICS: Holistic Healing

Heavensong
P.O. Box 450
Kula, HI 96790-0811
(808)-878-6415

CONTACT: Michael **TOPICS:** Holistic Healing, New Age, Metaphysics

Heights Holistic Health Associates
100 Remsen Street
Brooklyn, NY 11201
(718)-625-4802
TOPICS: Holistic Healing

Herb-Pharm
Box 116
Williams, OR 97544
(503)-846-7178
TOPICS: New Age

Hidden Blessings
5933 West National Avenue
West Allis, WI 53214
(414)-259-1229
TOPICS: Holistic Healing

Hidden Valley Health Ranch
Route 1, Box 52
Escondido, CA 92025
(714)-749-2727
TOPICS: Holistic Healing

Hideaway Hot Springs Resort
1412 Fairway
Calistoga, CA 94515
(707)-942-4108
TOPICS: Holistic Healing

High Wind
RR 2
Plymouth, WI 53703
(414)-528-7212
RETREAT; TOPICS: New Age, Health Food, Nutrition, Holistic Health **MEMBERS:** 12 **DESCRIPTION:** A 46 acre farm providing a bio-shelter, a non-consuming micro-farm, greenhouses, solar showers & New Age workshops. Operates a bookstore.

Hill Of The Hawk
Box 48
Big Sur, CA 93920
(408)-667-2508
TOPICS: Holistic Healing

Himalayan Institute Of New York
At East West Books
78 Fifth Avenue
New York, NY 10011
(212)-243-5995
TOPICS: New Age

Himalayan International Institute Of Yoga Science and Philosophy
R.R. 1
Box 400
Honesdale, PA 18431
(717)-253-5551 (717)-253-3022 (800)-433-5472
RETREAT; CONTACT: Rudolph M. Ballentine, M.D.,Pres. **TOPICS:** New Age, Meditation, Holistic Health, Yoga, Spirituality, Nutrition, Psychology **DESCRIPTION:** Located on 442 acres. Instruction given in meditation, holistic health, nutrition, stress management, biofeedback & yoga. Income derived from publishing books. Also offers a program leading to an MSS degree. **PUBLICATIONS:** *Dawn Magazine* **TOPICS:** New Age, Meditation, Holistic Health, Yoga **TYPE:** Magazine **FREQ:** quarterly

DESCRIPTION: Published by the Himalayan Institute. Prints articles on philosophy and psychology of natural living. Accepts ads. **PUBLICATIONS:** *Freedom From Stress* **EDITOR:** P. Nuernberger **TOPICS:** Holistic Health **TYPE:** Book **PRICE:** $10.95 **PUBLICATIONS:** *Hatha Yoga Manual Vol. 1* **EDITOR:** Samskrti, Veda **TOPICS:** Yoga, Holistic Health **TYPE:** Book **PRICE:** $12.95 **PUBLICATIONS:** *Hatha Yoga Manual Vol. 2* **EDITOR:** S. Franks, J. Franks **TOPICS:** Yoga, Holistic Health **TYPE:** Book **PRICE:** $12.95 **PUBLICATIONS:** *Himalayan Institute Quarterly* **EDITOR:** Larry Clark **TOPICS:** New Age **TYPE:** Magazine **PUBLICATIONS:** *Living With The Himalayan Masters* **EDITOR:** S. Rama **TOPICS:** Spirituality, Yoga **TYPE:** Book **PRICE:** $15.95 **PUBLICATIONS:** *Perennial Psychology Of The Bhagavad Gita* **EDITOR:** S. Rama **TOPICS:** Spirituality **TYPE:** Book **PRICE:** $14.95 **PUBLICATIONS:** *Quiet Mind: Techniques For Transforming Stress* **EDITOR:** J. Harvey **TOPICS:** Holistic Health, New Age **TYPE:** Book **PRICE:** $12.95 **PUBLICATIONS:** *Research Bulletin* **TOPICS:** New Age **TYPE:** Bulletin **PUBLICATIONS:** *The Himalayan News* **EDITOR:** Katherine Avlonitis, Dale Colton **TOPICS:** New Age **TYPE:** Newspaper **PUBLICATIONS:** *Transition To Vegetarianism: An Evolutionary Step* **EDITOR:** R. Ballentine **TOPICS:** Vegetarianism, Health Food, Holistic Health **TYPE:** Book **PRICE:** $12.95 **PUBLICATIONS:** *Yoga And Psychotherapy* **EDITOR:** S. Rama **TOPICS:** Yoga, Holistic Health **TYPE:** Book **PRICE:** $12.95

Hippocrates Health Institute
1443 Palmdale Court
West Palm Beach, FL 33411
(407)-471-8876 (800)-842-2125
RETREAT; CONTACT: Brian R. Clement **TOPICS:** Holistic Health, Massage, Nutrition, Yoga, Vegetarianism, Body-Mind Connection **DESCRIPTION:** Known for its dietary & lifestyle program & its exploration into the interrelationship of body, mind & spirit. Offers treatments such as massage, yoga, vegetarian food, meditation, polarity & electromagnetic therapy. **PUBLICATIONS:** *Hippocrates Health Institute Newsletter* **EDITOR:** Alix Weill **TOPICS:** Holistic Healing **TYPE:** Newsletter **PUBLICATIONS:** *Hippocrates News* **PUBLISHER:** Brian Clement **EDITOR:** Alix Weill **TOPICS:** Holistic Health **TYPE:** Newsletter **DATE:** 1969 **SIZE:** 8 1/2 x 11, 8 pgs. **FREQ:** Semi-Annual **CIRC;** 17,000 **PRICE:** $25.00 **TERM:** yearly **DESCRIPTION:** Devoted to wellness & holistic health. Features media-covered health news. Promotes the benefits of a raw vegetarian diet as well as other health practices such as fasting, exercise, mind, body & aging.

Hippocrates Health Institute Of San Diego
6970 Central Avenue
Lemon Grove, CA 92045
(714)-464-3346
TOPICS: Holistic Healing **DESCRIPTION:** Western branch of the Hippocrates Institute of Boston known as Hippocrates West.

HLQ Associates
P.O. Box 86054
Pittsburgh, PA 15221
(412)-731-5533
CONTACT: Allen Goodman **TOPICS:** Holistic Health, New Age **PUBLICATIONS:** *Health, Holistic*

Health **TYPE:** Newsletter **PUBLICATIONS:** *Health and Learning Quarterly* **PUBLISHER:** Allen Goodman **EDITOR:** Margaret Laske, Steve Guidas **TOPICS:** Holistic Health **TYPE:** Directory, 16 pgs. **FREQ:** 4 x per year **PRICE PER COPY:** $3.50 **DESCRIPTION:** Serves Pittsburgh and surrounding areas with listings of products and services. **PUBLICATIONS:** *HLQ Wellness Calendar* **TOPICS:** Holistic Healing **TYPE:** Calendar **PUBLICATIONS:** *Wellness Directory For Three Rivers Area* **PUBLISHER:** Linda Klapak **EDITOR:** Allen Goodman, Dawn Richards **TOPICS:** Holistic Healing **TYPE:** Magazine **DATE:** 1980 **SIZE:** 8 1/2x 11, 56 pgs. **FREQ:** annually **CIRC;** 10,000 **PRICE PER COPY:** $3.50 **DESCRIPTION:** Primary focus is on alternative health care, global responsibility & self-sufficiency. Subscription included free with membership.

Holistic Health Center
2872 Folsom Street
San Francisco, CA 94110
(415)-285-2909
TOPICS: Holistic Healing

Holistic Health Centre
9 Red Hill
Stourbridge, West Middlesex DY8 1NA
England
0368 379 740
CENTER; TOPICS: Crystals, Holistic Healing, Spirituality **OWNER:** Dr. Helen Ford **DESCRIPTION:** Run by Dr. Helen Ford, Holistic Health Physician. Offers complimentary therapies, healing, Aura Diagnosis, spiritual causes of illness. Dedicated to the art of crystal therapy & healing. Purpose is to connect & integrate spiritual & physical health & well -being.

Hollyhock
Box 127
Manson's Landing
Cortes Island, British Columbia V0P 1K0
Canada
(604)-935-6465
TOPICS: Holistic Healing

Holy Spirit Retreat Center
4316 Lanai Road
Encino, CA 91436
(818)-784-4515
TOPICS: Holistic Healing

Homestead, The
Hot Springs, VA 24445
(703)-839-5500 (800)-336-5771
TOPICS: Holistic Healing

Hot Sulphur Springs Baths
Hot Sulphur Springs, CO 80451
(303)-395-2361
TOPICS: Holistic Healing

House Of The Dawn
2141 East Palm Lane
Phoenix, AZ 85006
(602)-267-1203
CENTER; TOPICS: Metaphysics **OWNER:** Calvin H. Vanness & Jack S. Stephens **DESCRIPTION:** A New Age all faiths church. Guides others into finding their own paths to enlightenment. Holds belief that all of creation is a part of the God-Essence. All is One.

Offers healing & counselling. **CONVENTIONS:** Meetings every Tues. night at 7 PM.

Human Relations Center
249 Lambert Road
Carpinteria, CA 93013-3019
(805)-967-4557
TOPICS: Holistic Healing

Hunter's Lodge
Box 950
Lakeview, OR 97630
(503)-947-2127
TOPICS: Holistic Healing

Hunuman Temple
Drawer W
Taos, NM 87571
TOPICS: Holistic Healing

I.C.S.A.
Nada-Brahmanda Ashram
2872 Folsom Street
San Francisco, CA 94110
(415)-285-5537
TOPICS: New Age

ICSA - Ananda Ashram
R.D. 3
P.O. Box 141
Monroe, NY 10950
(914)-782-5575
TOPICS: New Age **PUBLICATIONS:** *I Am News*
TOPICS: New Age **TYPE:** Newspaper
DESCRIPTION: Features news & articles on yoga methods & philosophy.

Image In Motion
1085 14th Street, #1175
Boulder, CO 80302
(303)-444-7926
TOPICS: Holistic Healing

Indian Valley Retreat
Route 2
Box 58
Willis, VA 24380
(703)-789-4295
TOPICS: Holistic Healing

Indianapolis Center For Attitudinal Healing
P.O. Box 55016
Indianapolis, IN 46205
(317)-251-5543
TOPICS: Holistic Healing

Inner Garden Activity Centre/ Reflexology Centre Of Vancouver
535 West 10th Avenue
Vancouver, British Columbia V5Z 1K9
Canada
(604)-875-8818
TOPICS: Holistic Healing

Inner Visions
2223 Main Street, #47-B
Huntington Beach, CA 92648
(714)-960-9995
TOPICS: Holistic Healing

Insight Meditation Center
Pleasant Street

Barre, MA 01005
(617)-355-4378
CENTER; TOPICS: New Age, Meditation, Body-Mind Connection **MEMBERS:** 14 **DESCRIPTION:** Retreat, located on 80 acres, established for the practice of Vipassana meditation. Offers Dharma talks.

Insight Seminars
2101 Wilshire Boulevard
Santa Monica, CA 90403
(213)-829-9816
TOPICS: New Age

Institut Fur Grenzgebiete Der Psychologie Und Psychohygiene
Eichhalde 12
D-7800 Freiburg Im Breisgau
Germany
(0761) 55035
CENTER; CONTACT: Eberhard Bauer, Research Associate **TOPICS:** Parapsychology, Psychology **STAFF:** 3 **DESCRIPTION:** Conducts investigations of spontaneous paranormal experiences such as field research, experiences of poltergeists & hauntings. Offers counseling services, a special library on parapsychology, lectures & workshops. **PUBLICATIONS:** *Zeitschrift Fuer Parapsychologie Und Grenzgebiete Der Psychologie*

Institute For Creative Solutions
947 Plumsock Road
Newtown Square, PA 19073-1112
(215)-356-1893 (215)-353-7383
CENTER; TOPICS: New Age, Holistic Health, Spirituality **OWNER:** Randy Rolfe **DESCRIPTION:** Research & education center promoting natural holistic & spiritual living. **PUBLICATIONS:** *You Can Postpone Anything But Love; Adult Children Raising Children; The Affirmations Book For Sharing*

Institute For Cultural Affairs
4750 N. Sheridan Road
Chicago, IL 60640
(312)-769-6363
CENTER; TOPICS: New Age, Spirituality **DESCRIPTION:** Christian society dedicated to aiding Third World Development. Members live communally in a house in the city & volunteer part of the year in Third World countries.

Institute For Human Development
Box 1616
Ojai, CA 93023
(805)-646-4359 (800)-443-0100
TOPICS: Parapsychology **PUBLICATIONS:** *Break-Through* **EDITOR:** Jonathan Parker **TOPICS:** Parapsychology **TYPE:** Newsletter **DATE:** 1985, 8 pgs. **PRICE:** $0.00 **PRICE PER COPY:** $0.00

Institute For Religious Development
7 Chardovoyne Road
RD2, Box 269
Warwick, NY 10990
(914)-258-4655
TOPICS: New Age, Holistic Health

Institute For The Development Of The Harmonious Human Being, Inc.
P.O. Box 370
Nevada City, CA 95959
(916)-477-1116

CONTACT: Nancy Christie, Pres. **TOPICS:** Parapsychology, New Age, Holistic Healing **PUBLICATIONS:** *Talk Of The Month* **PUBLISHER:** Nancy Christie **EDITOR:** Iven Lourie **TOPICS:** Parapsychology, Holistic Health **TYPE:** Journal **DATE:** 1983 **SIZE:** 8 1/2 x 11, 16 pgs. **FREQ:** Monthly **CIRC:** 150 **PRICE:** $120.00 **PRICE PER COPY:** $15.00 **DESCRIPTION:** Provides edited reports of recent metaphysical teachings. Explores metaphysical & transformational ideas.

Institute For The Study Of Natural Systems
P.O. Box 637
Mill Valley, CA 94942
(415)-383-5064
TOPICS: New Age

Institute Self Improvement
P.O. Box 6300
Beverly Hills, CA 90212-1300
(213)-933-6338
TOPICS: New Age

Integral Health Services
245 School Street
Putnam, CT 06260
(203)-928-7729
TOPICS: Holistic Healing

Integral Yoga Institute/Satchidananda Ashram
RR 1, Box 172
Buckingham, VA 23921
(804)-969-3121 (804)-969-4801 (800)-262-1008
RETREAT; TOPICS: Holistic Healing, Spirituality, Yoga, Meditation, Vegetarianism, New Age **MEMBERS:** 50 **DESCRIPTION:** Spiritual, celibate, vegetarian community located on 650 acres. Offers instruction in hatha yoga & meditation. Provides schools, gas station & air strip. Constructing non-denominational L.O.T.U.S. temple.

Integral Yoga International
227 West 13th Street
New York, NY 10011
CONTACT: Sri Swami Satchidananda **TOPICS:** New Age

Interface
55 Wheeler Street
Cambridge, MA 02120-1125
(617)-924-1100 **FAX** (617)-924-1163
CENTER; CONTACT: Susan Chiat **TOPICS:** Holistic Health, Spirituality, New Age, Holistic Healing, Meditation, Yoga, Body-Mind Connection **DESCRIPTION:** Education center that explores trends in health, personal growth, science and religion to encourage new ways of living, expand personal development & create a better world. Activities consist of lectures, courses & workshops presented by international faculty. Focus is on health for the whole person-body, mind & spirit. **PUBLICATIONS:** *Interface Catalog* **TYPE:** Catalog **FREQ:** 3 x per year **PRICE:** $8.00 **TERM:** yearly

Intergroup Committee
P.O. Box 5105
Beverly Hills, CA 90210
(213)-379-9990 (213)-540-8689
TOPICS: New Age, UFO's

International Center For Release And Integration (ICRI)
450 Hillside Avenue
Mill Valley, CA 94941
(415)-383-4017
TOPICS: New Age

International Church Of Ageless Wisdom Esoteric Seminary
P.O. Box 280
Wyalusing, PA 18853
(717)-746-1864
TOPICS: Parapsychology, Spirituality, Metaphysics, New Age PUBLICATIONS: *Lamp Of Learning Bookstore Books & Services Catalog* EDITOR: Roberta Herzog TOPICS: Parapsychology TYPE: Catalog DATE: 1985 PRICE PER COPY: $0.00

International Holistic Center
Box 15103
Phoenix, AZ 85060
(602)-957-2181
TOPICS: Holistic Healing

International Institute For The Study Of Death (IISD)
P.O. Box 630026
Miami, FL 33161-0026
TOPICS: Death, Parapsychology, Psychic Phenomena

IntiNet Resource Center
P.O. Box 150474-P
San Rafael, CA 94915
(415)-507-1739
CENTER; TOPICS: New Age OWNER: Dr. Deborah Anapol DESCRIPTION: Clearinghouse for information on ethical non-exclusive & alternative relationships. Also acts as network to link people & organizations & to promote health, happiness & well-being for families. Also provides an online computer conference service & technical assistance for local area support groups. Provides a quarterly report & networking letter with updates on resources for our members. Membership $30 per year. PUBLICATIONS: *Love Without Limits* EDITOR: Dr. Deborah Anapol TOPICS: New Age TYPE: Book DATE: 1992 PRICE: $16.00 PUBLICATIONS: *Resource Guide For The Responsible Non Monogamist* TOPICS: New Age TYPE: Book DATE: 1984 PRICE: $12.95

Intuitive Development Institute
17 El Cerrito Avenue
San Rafael, CA 94901
(415)-454-3477 (800)-882-8711
CENTER; TOPICS: Metaphysics, Psychic, Hypnotism, Past Life Regression, Channeling OWNER: Susan Stuart, Ph. D. DESCRIPTION: Purpose is to increase the awareness of intuition & psychic abilities. Offers psychic readings, intuitive counseling & hypnotherapy, Past Life Regressions, metaphysical healing, meditation workshops, psychic development classes & seminars.

Isis Educational Center
51-A West Fifth Avenue
Columbus, OH 43201
TOPICS: Metaphysics

Isis Oasis Lodge And Cultural Center
20889 Geyserville Avenue
Geyserville, CA 95441
(707)-857-3524
TOPICS: Holistic Healing

Isis-Osiris Temple, Order Of The Golden Dawn
P.O. Box 40094
Pasadena, CA 91104
TOPICS: New Age, Metaphysics

Iyengar Yoga In Ojai Valley/Ojai Yoga Center
203 North Signal Street
Ojai, CA 93023
(805)-640-0448
TOPICS: Holistic Healing

J. Allen Hynek Center For UFO Studies (CUFOS)
2457 West Peterson Avenue
Chicago, IL 60659
(312)-271-3611
CENTER; CONTACT: Mark Rodeghier, Scientific Dir. TOPICS: UFO's DESCRIPTION: Dedicated to the collection, investigation & analysis of UFO sighting reports. Trained & experienced volunteers examine qualified reports of UFO's. Center houses case files, maintains an extensive collection of UFO literature, periodicals & unpublished papers on the UFO phenomenon worldwide. The UFO Photo Exhibit Research Project & Public Relations Office address: Box 1621, Lima, OH 45802. PUBLICATIONS: *International UFO Reporter* PUBLISHER: Mark Rodeghier EDITOR: Jerome Clark TOPICS: UFO's TYPE: Magazine DATE: 1976 SIZE: 8 1/2 x 11, 20 pgs. FREQ: Bi-Monthly CIRC: 1,250 PRICE: $25.00 PRICE PER COPY: $4.00 DESCRIPTION: Features articles on UFO sitings & reports, book reviews, photos & correspondence. PUBLICATIONS: *Journal Of UFO Studies* EDITOR: Michael Swords TOPICS: UFO's TYPE: Journal DATE: 1979 SIZE: 6 x 9, 100 pgs. FREQ: Annually CIRC; 500 PRICE: $15.00 PRICE PER COPY: $15.00 DESCRIPTION: Reports on the UFO phenomenon by experts in the field.

Jean's Place
2407 Camino Capitan
Santa Fe, NM 87505
(505)-471-4053
CENTER; TOPICS: Crystals, Massage, Reiki OWNER: Jean D. Gosse DESCRIPTION: Center for healing & transformation offering crystal healing, hot tub, ascension chamber, therapy room, intuitive body work, bio-energetic therapy table & complete body alignment to reduce stress, improve health & open higher channels. Provides bed & breakfast accommodations.

Jemez Bodhi Mandala
P.O. Box 8
Jemez Springs, NM 87025
(505)-829-3854
TOPICS: New Age

Journeys Into The Known
P.O. Box 7422
San Diego, CA 92107
(619)-222-0904
TOPICS: Holistic Healing

Joy Lake Mountain Community
P.O. Box 1328
Reno, NV 89504
(702)-323-0378
SPA; CONTACT: Alan Morvay TOPICS: New Age, Holistic Health, Channeling DESCRIPTION: Offers seminars on holistic health incorporating all aspects of New Age including physical, psychological & spiritual.

Judith Jackson Aromatherapy
10 Serenity Lane
Cos Cob, CT 06807-1417
(203)-629-2240
CENTER; TOPICS: Holistic Health, Massage OWNER: Judith Jackson DESCRIPTION: Offers clients renewal of mind, body & spirit through aromatherapy treatments such as massage aromatherapy.

Julian Preventive Medicine Clinic
1654 Cahuenga
Hollywood, CA 90028
(213)-466-0126
TOPICS: Holistic Healing

K.C. & Company
386 LaGrange Street
West Roxbury, MA 02132
(617)-469-4700
TOPICS: Holistic Healing

Kai Mana
P.O. Box 612
Kilauea, HI 96754
CENTER; TOPICS: Holistic Healing, Spirituality OWNER: Shakti Gawain DESCRIPTION: Bed & Breakfast, personal healing retreat on the island of Kauai. Offers intensive workshops emphasizing emotional & spiritual growth.

Kalamazoo Attitudinal Healing Center
2601 Ricker
Richland, MI 49083
(616)-375-7222
TOPICS: Holistic Healing

Kalani Honua By The Sea International Conference And Retreat Center
R.R. 2
Box 4500 North
Kalapana Beach, HI 96778
(808)-965-7828 (800)-367-8047
RETREAT; TOPICS: Holistic Healing, Vegetarianism, Meditation, Tai Chi, Spirituality, Yoga OWNER: Richard Koob BOOKSTORE; STAFF: 30 DESCRIPTION: Located on 20 oceanside acres. Offers warm springs & natural steam baths, yoga, massage, personal growth & health classes, spirituality seminars, tai chi, meditation & workshops to enhance the harmony of body, mind & spirit. Meals are mainly vegetarian. PUBLICATIONS: *Hawaii events catalogue*, quarterly, $5.50 per year. PUBLICATIONS: *The Source* TYPE: Newspaper FREQ: quarterly PRICE: $5.50 PRICE PER COPY: $1.00 DESCRIPTION: Produced by & for Kalani Honua. Offering articles on topics such as addiction, astrology, psychology, world affairs & poetry. Provides a calendar of events, happenings & ads pertaining to the region.

Kathexis Coven
P.O. Box 4538
Sunnyside, NY 11104-4538
CENTER; TOPICS: Witchcraft **DESCRIPTION:** Kathexis Coven, Gardnerian Wicca Coven. Send S.A.S.E. for contact/networking information. **PUBLICATIONS:** *Moon Tides* **TOPICS:** Witchcraft, Occult, Paganism **TYPE:** Book

Kauai Attitudinal Healing Center
P.O. Box 1330
Koloa, HI 96756
(808)-245-1996
TOPICS: Holistic Healing

Kelvin Grove Healing Centre
259 Kelvin Grove Road
Brisbane, QLD,
Australia
(07) 856 4585
CENTER; CONTACT: Amanda Jones **TOPICS:** Crystals **DESCRIPTION:** Dedicated to the art of crystal therapy & healing.

Ken Keyes College
790 Commercial Avenue
Coos Bay, OR 97420
(503)-267-4232 (503)-267-6412
CENTER; TOPICS: Parapsychology, Holistic Healing, New Age, Psychology **MEMBERS:** 60 **DESCRIPTION:** A training center based on the Living Love Methods from the book Handbook to Higher Consciousness which teaches one to love & accept others. Offers Living Love & Healing Inner Child Workshops, weekends or up to 7 week residential personal growth workshops . Publishes quarterly catalog/newsletter, Love Line Books & Cornucopia Books. **PUBLICATIONS:** *Handbook To Higher Consciousness* **TOPICS:** New Age **TYPE:** Handbook **PUBLICATIONS:** *Ken Keyes College-Cornucopia* **PUBLISHER:** Ken Keyes, Jr. **TOPICS:** Parapsychology **TYPE:** Magazine **DATE:** 1975, 30 pgs. **FREQ:** Quarterly **CIRC;** 50,000 **DESCRIPTION:** Provides information about books, articles & training at Ken Keyes College.

Kerista Village
543 Frederick Street
San Francisco, CA 94117
(415)-566-6502 (415)-665-2988
RETREAT; TOPICS: New Age, Psychology **MEMBERS:** 24 **DESCRIPTION:** A cooperative, tribal-like community based on egalitarian beliefs. Sharing of money, parenting responsibilities & all aspects of daily life. Operates the University of Utopia/Storefront Classroom/Growth Co-op & publishes a quarterly periodical.

Keristan Islands Intentional Community
543 Frederick Street
San Francisco, CA 94117
(415)-753-1314
TOPICS: New Age

Kerr House
17777 Beaver Street
Grand Rapids, OH 43522
(419)-832-1733
TOPICS: Holistic Healing

Keshavashram International Spiritual Center
P.O. Box 260
Warrenton, VA 22186
(703)-347-9009
TOPICS: Metaphysics, Spirituality, New Age

Kinesionics Institute
1305 Northeast 45th, Suite 205
Seattle, WA 98105
(206)-634-3204
TOPICS: New Age

Kirpal Ashram
2 Canal Road, Vjay Nagar
Delhi,
India
110009
TOPICS: New Age

Koinonia Partners
Rt 2
Americus, GA 31709
RETREAT; TOPICS: New Age, Spirituality, Health Food **MEMBERS:** 27 **DESCRIPTION:** 600 acre farm founded on Christian beliefs such as peace, love, harmony & sharing of God's gifts.

Kontiki Spa
P.O. Box 63
3059 Bundy Road
Riverside, MI 49084
(616)-849-1400
TOPICS: Holistic Healing

Kotaka Center
354 High Street
Morgantown, WV 26505
(304)-292-8539
TOPICS: Holistic Healing

Kripalu Center For Yoga And Health
Rt. 183
P.O. Box 793
Lenox, MA 01240
(413)-637-3280 (413)-637-4747
CENTER; CONTACT: Barbara Nelson (Suniti) **TOPICS:** Holistic Healing, Holistic Health, Spirituality, Meditation, Massage, Tai Chi, Vegetarianism **DESCRIPTION:** Community of people seeking spiritual path as followers of Yogi Amrit Desai. Offers yoga, meditation, spiritual lectures, macrobiotic food, massage, acupressure, shiatsu, t'ai chi classes & prayer meetings. **PUBLICATIONS:** *Kripalu Experience* **EDITOR:** Lisa Sarasohn **TOPICS:** Holistic Healing **TYPE:** Newsletter

Kripalu Yoga Ashram
7 Waters Road
Box 250
Sumneytown, PA 18084
(215)-234-4568
TOPICS: Holistic Healing

Krotona Institute
P.O. Box 966
Ojai, CA 93023
(805)-646-1139
RETREAT; TOPICS: New Age, Spirituality **MEMBERS:** 40 **DESCRIPTION:** Based on Theosophy which is the philosophy of joining East & West science & religion. Separate homes located on 118 acres. Conducts classes, retreats. Operates bookstore, library & publishing facility.

Kushi Institute-East West Foundation
17 Station Street
P.O. Box 1100
Brookline Village, MA 02147
(617)-738-4334 (617)-738-0045
CENTER; TOPICS: Health Food, Holistic Health, Spirituality, Vegetarianism, Nutrition, Homeopathy, New Age **OWNER:** Michio Kushi **DESCRIPTION:** Purpose is to train leaders & teachers in macrobiotics. **PUBLICATIONS:** *Book Of Macrobiotics* **EDITOR:** Michio Kushi **TOPICS:** Health Food, Holistic Health, Vegetarianism, Nutrition, Spirituality **TYPE:** Book **DATE:** 1977 **PUBLICATIONS:** *Changing Seasons Macrobiotic Cookbook* **EDITOR:** Aveline Kushi **TOPICS:** Health Food, Holistic Health, Vegetarianism, Nutrition **TYPE:** Book **DATE:** 1984 **PUBLICATIONS:** *East West Journal* **EDITOR:** Michio Kushi **TOPICS:** Health Food, Holistic Health, Vegetarianism, New Age, Spirituality, Nutrition **TYPE:** Journal **DATE:** 1970 **DESCRIPTION:** Covers New Age information & macrobiotics. **PUBLICATIONS:** *Order Of The Universe* **EDITOR:** Michio Kushi **TOPICS:** Health Food, Holistic Health, Vegetarianism, Nutrition, Spirituality **TYPE:** Magazine **DATE:** 1968 **PUBLICATIONS:** *Worldwide Macrobiotic Directory* **EDITOR:** Elaine Altman **TOPICS:** Health Food, Holistic Health, Vegetarianism, Nutrition, Spirituality **TYPE:** Directory **DATE:** 1984, 42 pgs. **PRICE PER COPY:** $3.95

L.I.F.E. Project
209 Henry Street
Victoria, British Columbia V9A 3H8
Canada
(604)-384-2146
TOPICS: Holistic Healing

La Reginella
Laco Ameno, Ischia
Italy
994-300
SPA; TOPICS: Holistic Health, Holistic Healing **DESCRIPTION:** Health resort offering therapeutic treatments of mud baths & massage therapy.

La Sabranenque Centre International
217 High Park Boulevard
Buffalo, NY 14226
(716)-836-8698
TOPICS: New Age

Lama Foundation
P.O. Box 444
San Cristobol, NM 87564
(505)-586-1269
RETREAT; TOPICS: New Age, Metaphysics **MEMBERS:** 25 **DESCRIPTION:** Spiritual community influenced by Ram Dass. Run by democratic principles. Offers retreats, work camp, Summer & visitor's programs. Produces hand-made products for sale.

Lama Foundation
Brighton Star Rt.
Brighton, UT 84121
(505)-586-1269
TOPICS: Holistic Healing

Las Brisas Retreat Center

43500 Camino de las Brisas
Murrieta, CA 92362
(714)-499-5699
TOPICS: Holistic Healing

Last Resort
P.O. Box 6226
Cedar City, UT 84720
(801)-682-2289
TOPICS: Holistic Healing

Laurieston Hall
Castle Douglas
Kirkcudbrightshire,
Scotland
Laurieston 275
RETREAT; TOPICS: New Age MEMBERS: 30
DESCRIPTION: Large mansion on 123 acres. Shared
ownership of land, buildings, money. Democratically
run with philosophy of feminism, creativity &
cooperation. Income derived from crafts & summer
conferences.

Lava Hot Springs Foundation
Lava Hot Springs, ID 83246
(208)-776-5221
TOPICS: Holistic Healing

Learning For Health
1314 Westwood Boulevard, #107
Los Angeles, CA 90024
(213)-474-6929
TOPICS: Holistic Healing

Ledgehill Retreat And Study Centre
R.R. 1
Lawrencetown, Nova Scotia B0S 1M0
Canada
(902)-584-7124
TOPICS: Holistic Healing

Libbey Memorial Physical Medicine Center
Hot Springs National Park
501 Spring Street
Hot Springs, AR 71901
(800)-643-1570
TOPICS: Holistic Healing

Life And Light Center
P.O. Box 486
Northfield, VT 05663
CENTER; TOPICS: Holistic Healing, New Age,
Astrology, Psychic, Metaphysics OWNER: Judith
Hope Davis DESCRIPTION: Purpose is to assist the
individual to expand their awareness of their Divine
Nature through exploring past & present life
conditions & to live a more peaceful & productive
life experience using Psychic Readings, Healings &
Astrological Counselling.

Life Center
214 South Fielding Avenue
Tampa, FL 33606
(813)-251-0289
TOPICS: Holistic Healing

Life Center
P.O. Box 428
26 Bridge Street
Lambertville, NJ 08530
(609)-397-2541
TOPICS: New Age

Life Center For Attitudinal Healing
P.O. Box 8718
Santa Fe, NM 87504
(505)-983-5541
TOPICS: Holistic Healing

Life Integration Trainings
785 Centre Street
Newton, MA 02158
TOPICS: New Age

Life Purpose Institute
7801 Mission Center Court, #228
San Diego, CA 92108
(619)-296-5800
TOPICS: Holistic Healing

Life Space Holistic Center
1527 Davenport Road
Toronto, Ontario M6H 2H9
Canada
(416)-533-1903
TOPICS: Holistic Healing

Lifelong Learning Excellence
Box 380
Eugene, OR 97440
(503)-343-1202
TOPICS: Holistic Healing

Lifespan
Townhead
Dunford
Bridge, Near Sheffield
England
RETREAT; TOPICS: New Age MEMBERS: 15
DESCRIPTION: Operated on the principles of
democracy, harmony & equality. Income earned
from printing business.

Light Blew Inn
200 Sheldon Avenue, #6
Mount Shasta, CA 96067
(916)-926-5653
TOPICS: Holistic Healing

Light Of The Mountains
Big Sandy Mush Creek Road, Rt. 2
Box 166
Leicester, NC 28748
(704)-683-3930
RETREAT; TOPICS: Holistic Healing, New Age,
Spirituality, Meditation DESCRIPTION: Spiritual
Sufi community offering healing, prayer, meditation,
dance & Universal Worship Services. Teaching the
philosophy of Hazrat Inayat Khan.

Lily Dale Assembly
5 Melrose Park
Lily Dale, NY 14752
(716)-595-8721
TOPICS: Metaphysics

Linnaea Farm/Wilshire House
Mansons Landing
Cortes Island, British Columbia V0P 1K0
Canada
(604)-935-6424
RETREAT; TOPICS: New Age, Spirituality, Health
Food MEMBERS: 12 DESCRIPTION: Spiritual
community operating raw milk dairy. Rural branch
of Turtle Island Land Stewardship Society.

Little Stony Creek Haven
Route 1
Box 359-C
Edinburg, VA 22824
(703)-984-4462
TOPICS: Holistic Healing

Living Awareness Foundation
P.O. Box 343
Wallingford, PA 19086
(215)-565-5819
TOPICS: Holistic Healing, Metaphysics

Living Springs Retreat
Route 3
Box 357
Putnam Valley, NY 10579
(914)-526-2800
TOPICS: Holistic Healing

Logos Center And Bookstore
6333 East Thunderbird Road
Scottsdale, AZ 85254
(602)-483-8777
CENTER; TOPICS: Crystals BOOKSTORE;
DESCRIPTION: Church, Meditation & Learning
Center dedicated to the art of crystal therapy &
healing. Offers a university program, Edgar Cayce
Library, audio & video programs. Also bookstore
geared to self-help, religion & philosophy.

Looking Glass Foundation
19318 Ventura Boulevard, 206
Tarzana, CA 91356
(818)-884-6900
CENTER; TOPICS: Holistic Health, Nutrition,
Psychology OWNER: Dr. Medal DESCRIPTION:
Non-profit, tax exempt, community counseling
center offering a wholistic approach to family
therapy, diet, nutrition & exercise. Licensed
therapists offer help with eating disorders, abuse &
family violence, substance abuse, parenting skills,
divorce & legal information, child, youth, family,
couples & individual therapy.

Los Angeles Macrobiotic Learning Center
2651 Hodgson Circle Drive
Topanga, CA 90290
(213)-455-2367
TOPICS: Holistic Healing

Lost Horizon Health Awareness Center
Box 550
Oviedo, FL 32765
(407)-365-6681
TOPICS: Holistic Healing PUBLICATIONS: *Health
Consciousness* EDITOR: Roy Kupsinel, M.D., Carl
Thomason TOPICS: Holistic Healing TYPE:
Newsletter

Lotus Yoga Center
1131 University Boulevard West
Room 1012
Silver Spring, MD 20902
(301)-649-4581
TOPICS: Yoga

Lukats Resort
Route 1
Box 955
Safford, AZ 85546

(602)-428-2881
TOPICS: Holistic Healing

Ma Yoga Shakti International Mission (MYSIM)
114-23 Lefferts Boulevard
South Ozone Park, NY 11420
(718)-641-0402 (718)-322-5856
CENTER; TOPICS: New Age, Yoga, Holistic Health OWNER: Ma Yoga Shakti DESCRIPTION: Purpose is to teach all 4 aspects of Yoga & to promote the Yoga philosophy for health, happiness & wisdom. Offers Yoga retreats, classes, workshops, gatherings & East West festivals. PUBLICATIONS: *Hanuman Chalisa* PUBLISHER: Ma Yoga Shakti TOPICS: Yoga, Meditation, Spirituality TYPE: Book PUBLICATIONS: *Meditation* PUBLISHER: Ma Yoga Shakti TOPICS: Yoga, Meditation, Spirituality TYPE: Book PUBLICATIONS: *MYSIM Newsletter* PUBLISHER: Ma Yoga Shakti TOPICS: Yoga, Meditation, Spirituality TYPE: Newsletter PUBLICATIONS: *Psychic Lotus-Pictorial* PUBLISHER: Ma Yoga Shakti TOPICS: Yoga, Meditation, Spirituality TYPE: Book PUBLICATIONS: *Satya Narayan Kathaa* PUBLISHER: Ma Yoga Shakti TOPICS: Yoga, Meditation, Spirituality TYPE: Book PUBLICATIONS: *Spiritual Message* PUBLISHER: Ma Yoga Shakti TOPICS: Yoga, Meditation, Spirituality TYPE: Book PUBLICATIONS: *Yoga Syzygy* PUBLISHER: Ma Yoga Shakti TOPICS: Yoga, Meditation, Spirituality TYPE: Book PUBLICATIONS: *Yoga Vashishttha-Part I* PUBLISHER: Ma Yoga Shakti TOPICS: Yoga, Meditation, Spirituality TYPE: Book PUBLICATIONS: *Yoga Vashishttha-Part II* PUBLISHER: Ma Yoga Shakti TOPICS: Yoga, Meditation, Spirituality TYPE: Book

Macrobiotic Center Of Baltimore
c/o Murray Snyder
9 Highpasture Court
Owings Mills, MD 21117-1501
(301)-628-0880
TOPICS: Health Food PUBLICATIONS: *Changes* EDITOR: Murray Snyder TOPICS: Health Food TYPE: Magazine

Macrobiotics Canada
R.R. 3
Almonte, Ontario K0A 1A0
Canada
(613)-256-2665
CENTER; TOPICS: Holistic Healing, Health Food OWNER: Wayne Ciotte DESCRIPTION: Purpose is to promote the benefits of the macrobiotic diet. Offers educational consultations, cooking classes, seminars, lectures, Shiatzu Massage, counselling, Astrology & stress reduction, spiritual & meditation training & retreats, health & healing retreats. Also offers over 1,000 products: Macrobiotic & natural foods, books, kitchen utensils, water treatment systems, cleaning products & cookware. Mail-order catalog available. CONVENTIONS: Annual conference the first week of July.

Magi Center, Incorporated
P.O. Box 1166
Paradise, CA 95969
TOPICS: Metaphysics

Magic & Mystery Guide
P.O. Box 1227

Carmel, CA 93921
(408)-625-5792
TOPICS: Tarot

Magna and Walt Baptiste Center
405 Arguello Boulevard
1-9 Clement Street
San Francisco, CA 94118
(415)-387-6833
TOPICS: New Age

Maitreyans, The
Rural Route 1, Box 451
Ashby, MA 01431
(508)-386-7053
CENTER; TOPICS: Metaphysics, New Age, Yoga, Kabbalah, Astrology, Holistic Health, Parapsychology OWNER: Jerry C. Welch FRC (Khiron) DESCRIPTION: An Holistic Service Order. Maitreya is the long-awaited Buddha of the Future, experienced as the New Age Movement & cultivated through Yoga within the Kaballist tradition of Archangelic Invocation. Gatherings held at Solstices, Equinoxes & mid-season's points. Services provided through Maitreyan Network include Astrology, Holistic Health, Parapsychology & Esoteric Psychology for lifestyle development. Products offered are audio, video & software by mail-order. PUBLICATIONS: *Essays* EDITOR: Jerry C. Welch (Khiron) TOPICS: Astrology, Holistic Health, Parapsychology, New Age, Yoga, Kabbalah TYPE: Newsletter FREQ: monthly PRICE: $6.00 TERM: annually DESCRIPTION: Network newsletter.

Mana Kai-Maui Pritikin Better Health Program
2960 South Kihei Road
Maui, HI 96753
(808)-879-1561 (800)-525-2025
TOPICS: Holistic Healing

Mandala Centre
4318 Louisiana Street
San Diego, CA 92104
(619)-692-1497
CENTER; TOPICS: Crystals DESCRIPTION: Dedicated to the art of crystal therapy & healing.

Manhattan Plaza Health Club
482 West 43rd Street
NY, NY 10036
(212)-563-7001 FAX (212)-629-9539
CENTER; CONTACT: Lee Brunner, Dir. TOPICS: Holistic Health, New Age DESCRIPTION: Offers mind/body/spirit health workshops known as the Fully Alive Workshop Series which presents renowned authorities on stress reduction & personal health.

Manitou Springs
Manitou Springs Chamber Of Commerce
354 Manitou Avenue
Manitou Springs, CO 80829
(303)-685-5656
TOPICS: Holistic Healing

Mariposa Group Community
21450 Chagall Road
Topanga, CA 90290
(818)-340-1146
RETREAT; TOPICS: New Age MEMBERS: 6 DESCRIPTION: Community of 6 individuals creating an environment that supports human

development, successful relationships, financial & professional development & success. Purpose is to create a loving & nurturing place to raise children, & emphasize the importance of work, relationships & play all contained within the context of growth, spirituality & development of our fullest potential.

Mata Amritanandamayi Center
P.O. Box 613
San Ramon, CA 94583-0613
(415)-537-9417
TOPICS: Spirituality

Matagiri Sri Aurobindo Center (SAA)
P.O. Box 372
High Falls, NY 12440
(914)-667-9222 (914)-687-9222
CONTACT: Julian Lines TOPICS: Metaphysics, New Age, Spirituality

Matagiri Sri Aurobindo Center
Mt. Tremper, NY 12457
(914)-679-8322
CENTER; TOPICS: New Age, Yoga, Meditation, Spirituality DESCRIPTION: Offers information, products & teachings of Sri Aurobindo & Auroville. Gives readings & practice meditations & integral yoga as developed by Sri Aurobindo.

Matri Satsang
P.O. Box 1796
Nevada City, CA 95959
TOPICS: New Age

Maui Center For Attitudinal Healing
P.O. Box 134
Kahului, HI 96732
(808)-878-2945
TOPICS: Holistic Healing

Maui EcoPark/Center For Ecological Living
915 Kaupakalua Road
Haiku, Maui, HI 96708
(808)-572-5857
RETREAT; CENTER; TOPICS: New Age, Vegetarianism, Health Food, Holistic Health OWNER: Joe Pacal STAFF: 3 DESCRIPTION: Peaceful 55 acre retreat offering seminars dedicated to personal growth, wellness & transformation where people can experience the oneness of mind, body, nature & spirit. A holistic ecology laboratory providing hands-on experience of gentle & sensible approaches to agriculture, technology, economics, community & lifestyle. Has ongoing programs on organic gardening, ecological living & tropical home design & serves organically grown & vegetarian food. AFFILIATED ORGS: Akahi Farm CONVENTIONS: Ongoing educational programs & special events PUBLICATIONS: *Ecosense* TYPE: Newsletter FREQ: quarterly PRICE: $20.00 TERM: yearly DESCRIPTION: Devoted to applied ecology offering practical ideas for living into the 21st century. PUBLICATIONS: *Guidebook To Ecoconsciousness* TYPE: Book PRICE: $12.95 TERM: yearly DESCRIPTION: Five billion ways to create a paradise planet & harmonious human civilizations.

Mazdaznan Vegetarian Science Center In Hawaii
P.O. Box 1116
Pahoa, HI 96778

(808)-965-8643
TOPICS: Holistic Healing

Meadowlark Health And Growth Center
26126 Fairview Avenue
Hemet, CA 92344
(714)-927-1343
TOPICS: Holistic Healing

Medical Self-Care
P.O. Box 701
Providence, RI 02901-0701
TOPICS: Holistic Healing PUBLICATIONS: *Medical Self-Care* EDITOR: Carole Pisarczuk, Michael Castleman TOPICS: Holistic Healing TYPE: Magazine

Meditation Group For The New Age
P.O. Box 566
Ojai, CA 93023
(805)-646-6300
TOPICS: New Age, Metaphysics

Mele Mauka Center
P.O. Box 946
Captain Cook, HI 96704
(808)-328-2207
RETREAT; TOPICS: Holistic Healing, Yoga, New Age OWNER: Joni & Solomon Choo DESCRIPTION: Remote ocean-front retreat/center offering Yoga disciplines, dance & music training. Philosophy is to establish an international & universal connection on the paths of Yoga, dance & music. Rentals available.

Mendocino Institute
Box 1928
Mendocino, CA 95460
(707)-937-2622
TOPICS: Holistic Healing

Mendocino Sufi Camp
P.O. Box 1066
San Rafael, CA 94915
TOPICS: Metaphysics

Mendocino Woodlands Camp Association, Incorporated (MWCA)
P.O. Box 267
Mendocino, CA 95460
(707)-937-5755
TOPICS: Holistic Health DESCRIPTION: 720 acres offering 3 separate camp rental facilites for workshops, personal growth retreats, conferences, training seminars, etc. in a natural woodland setting. Cabins & facilities can accommodate 30 to 200 persons comfortably.

Mercy Hot Springs
Box 1363
Los Banos, CA 93635
TOPICS: Holistic Healing

Meridian Holistic Health Centre, Inc.
5575 West Saanich Road
R.R.5
Victoria, British Columbia V8X 4M6
Canada
(604)-727-3451
CENTER; CONTACT: Sally Lang TOPICS: Holistic Healing DESCRIPTION: Wellness education center. Multidisciplinary team using body/mind/spirit approach in outpatient & residential programs for chronic stress, pain, illness. Offers workshops & groups on self-healing techniques. PUBLICATIONS: *Meridian Newsletter* EDITOR: June Cable TOPICS: New Age TYPE: Newsletter DESCRIPTION: Features articles on health, calendar of events, new books & Meridian programs, workshops & classes.

Merriam Hill
102 Merriam Hill Road
Greenville, NH 03048
(603)-878-1818
CENTER; TOPICS: New Age DESCRIPTION: Educational center offering courses & visits to communities such as Findhorn, Auroville & Arcosanti.

Merry Widow Health Mine
P.O. Box 3444
Basin, MT 59631
(406)-225-3220
TOPICS: Holistic Healing

Meta Tantay
P.O. Box 707
Carlin, NV 89822
(702)-754-9928
RETREAT; TOPICS: New Age, Spirituality DESCRIPTION: Located on 262 acres. Practices self-sufficiency with the purpose of renewing & preserving Native American culture.

Metaphysical Center Of New Jersey
202 Oakwood Drive
North Haledon, NJ 07508
(201)-337-8835
CONTACT: Jean Perrotta, Treasurer TOPICS: Metaphysics

Metaphysical Center, The
3479 Sacramento Street
San Francisco, CA 94118
(415)-346-5844
CENTER; CONTACT: Rosemarie Danelle TOPICS: Crystals DESCRIPTION: Dedicated to the art of crystal therapy & healing.

Mettanokit
Another Place Conference Center
Route 123
Greenville, NH 03048
(603)-878-9883
CENTER; TOPICS: New Age DESCRIPTION: Founded by a Native American teacher & based on self-sufficiency, trust & independence. Income derived from the production of futons, cradleboards, baby carriers & a New Age conference center.

Min An Health Center
1144 Pacific Avenue
San Francisco, CA 94133
(415)-771-4040
TOPICS: Holistic Healing

Minnesota Center For Attitudinal Healing
22020 Juniper Street N.W.
Cedar, MN 55011
(612)-753-2490
TOPICS: Holistic Healing

Miracle Distribution Center
1141 East Ash Avenue
Fullerton, CA 92631
(714)-738-8380
TOPICS: Metaphysics, New Age

Mono Hot Springs
Mono Hot Springs, CA 93642
TOPICS: Holistic Healing

Monroe Institute
Rt. 1
Box 175
Faber, VA 22938
(804)-361-1252
RETREAT; TOPICS: New Age, Spirituality, Parapsychology DESCRIPTION: Spiritual community in search of an alliance with God. Members are housed in separate homes. PUBLICATIONS: *TMI Bulletin* PUBLISHER: Leslie Franch EDITOR: John Dumais TOPICS: Parapsychology TYPE: Bulletin, 2 pgs. FREQ: Quarterly CIRC: 2,000

Moonfire Retreat Center
Route 1
Box 171B
Durham, NC 27705
(919)-490-1849
TOPICS: Holistic Healing

Moonridge
4344 Aitchcson Road
Beltsville, MD 20705
(301)-470-3033
TOPICS: Holistic Healing

Moonspell
P.O. Box 2991
Santa Cruz, CA 95063
CENTER; TOPICS: Metaphysics, Spirituality, Tarot, Runes DESCRIPTION: Functions as the practical arm of the Goddess Ministry of Shekhinah Mountainwater, offering tapes, Runes, Tarot Readings, spells & charms, classes, workshops, personal appearances, concerts & rituals. Their path is woman-centered & eclectic. PUBLICATIONS: *Ariadne's Thread* published by The Crossing Press

Moors Health Spa
12673 Reposo Way
Desert Hot Springs, CA 92240
(712)-329-7121
TOPICS: Holistic Healing

Morning Glory Community
2700 Oaker
Arnold, MO 63010
(314)-296-7846
TOPICS: Holistic Healing

Motivation Development Center
Box 25643
Albuquerque, NM 87125
(505)-265-6557
TOPICS: Holistic Healing

Mount Madonna Center
445 Summit Road
Watsonville, CA 95076
(408)-722-7175
RETREAT; TOPICS: Holistic Healing, New Age, Yoga OWNER: Dr. Brajesh Friedberg MEMBERS: 100 DESCRIPTION: Conference, retreat, educational center located on 355 acres overlooking Monterey

Bay. Operated by a 100-member resident community of Yoga students taught & influenced by the teachings of Master Yogi Baba Hari Dass. Offering courses in Yoga, fine arts & healing.

Mount Princeton Hot Springs
Nathrop, CO 81236
(303)-395-2361
TOPICS: Holistic Healing

Mount Shasta Meditation Retreats
16742 Middlecoff Court
Lake Shastina Weed, CA 96094
(916)-938-3659
TOPICS: Meditation, Holistic Health
DESCRIPTION: Meditation retreats for groups & individuals in a homey setting.

Movement For A New Society-Philadelphia Life Center
4722 Baltimore Avenue
Philadelphia, PA 19143
(215)-724-1464
CENTER; TOPICS: New Age DESCRIPTION: Cooperative community where members use feminist, peaceful means to create a new society using democratic principles. Members consist of 18 families. Offers workshops & training programs.

Movement Of Spiritual Inner Awareness
P.O. Box 3935
Los Angeles, CA 90051
(213)-737-4055
TOPICS: New Age

Moving Center
P.O. Box 712, Cooper Station
New York, NY 10276
(212)-505-7928
TOPICS: New Age

Mt. Pleasant Chiropractic Center
1013 Highway 17 North
Mt. Pleasant, NC 29464
(803)-881-1242
CENTER; CONTACT: Richard P. Stamegma D.C.
TOPICS: Crystals DESCRIPTION: Dedicated to the art of crystal therapy & healing.

Munedowk Retreat
13111 Lax Chapel Road
Kiel, WI 53042
TOPICS: Metaphysics

Murrieta Hot Springs Resort, Spa And Conference Center
39405 Murrieta Hot Springs Road
Murrieta, CA 92362
(714)-677-7451 (800)-322-4542
TOPICS: Holistic Healing

Myers Institute For Creative Studies
3827 California Street
San Francisco, CA 94118
(415)-668-1555
TOPICS: New Age

Mystic Journey Retreat
P.O. Box 1021
Ganterville, AL 35976
TOPICS: Metaphysics

Mystic Life Center
2359 Bonifacio Street
Concord, CA 94520
TOPICS: Metaphysics

Mystical Path
Box 3055
Alexandria, VA 22302
(703)-978-1534
TOPICS: Holistic Healing

Nakee Healing Center
529 Old Santa Fe Trail
Santa Fe, NM 87501
(505)-986-0245
TOPICS: Holistic Healing

Nantahala Outdoor Center
US 19W, Box 41
Bryson City, NC 28713
(704)-488-2175
TOPICS: New Age

Narayanananda Universal Yoga Ashrama
Route 2, Box 24
Winter, WI 54896
(715)-266-4963
TOPICS: New Age

Narayanananda Universal Yoga Ashrama
S-31081
Langaryd,
Sweden
(046)371-48085
TOPICS: New Age

Narayanananda Universal Yoga Ashrama
D-7859
Blansingen,
West Germany
(049)7628-1999
TOPICS: New Age

Narayanananda Universal Yoga Center
2937 North Southport Avenue
Chicago, IL 60657
(312)-327-3650
TOPICS: New Age, Yoga

Narayanananda Universal Yoga Trust, Ashrama & Narayana Press
c/o Joergen Fog
Gylin
DK-8300 Odder,
Denmark
(045)6551700
TOPICS: Yoga, New Age PUBLICATIONS: Yoga EDITOR: Swami Sagunananda TOPICS: Yoga, Holistic Health TYPE: Magazine DATE: 1958 FREQ: Quarterly CIRC: 1,000 PRICE: $10.00 DESCRIPTION: Devoted to all aspects of Yoga which is considered to be the universal religion.

Natural Health Clinic
1455 Harvard Street N.W.
Washington, DC 20009
(202)-667-5162

TOPICS: Holistic Healing

Nechung Drayang Ling
Wood Valley Retreat Center
P.O. Box 250
Pahala, HI 96777
(808)-928-8539
TOPICS: New Age

Neve Shalom
D.N. Shimshon, 99760
Israel
RETREAT; TOPICS: New Age, Spirituality MEMBERS: 35 DESCRIPTION: Only cooperative community in Israel of Christians, Jews & Muslims.

New Age Center
One South Broadway
Nyack, NY 10960
(914)-353-2590
TOPICS: Holistic Healing

New Age Community Center
1962 West 4th Avenue
Vancouver, BC, V6J1M5,
Canada
TOPICS: Metaphysics

New Age Health Spa
Route 55
Neversink, NY 12765
(914)-985-7600 (800)-682-4348 FAX (914)-985-2467
SPA; CONTACT: Werner Mendel TOPICS: Holistic Health, New Age, Meditation, Massage, Vegetarianism, Yoga, Nutrition BOOKSTORE; STAFF: 65 DESCRIPTION: Serene mountain setting promoting a healthier mind, body & spirit. Offers aerobics, hiking, exotic massages, Dead Sead Mud Baths, Zen meditation, tai chi, reflexology, paraffin wraps, aromatherapy, colonics, seaweed wraps, energy balancing, homeopathy, astrology, herbalogy, hypnosis, nutrition counseling, tarot card readings & empowerment training. Vegetarian meals available.

New Age Learning Center
P.O. Box 207
Kemuela, HI 96743
TOPICS: Metaphysics

New Age Psychic Center
4328 N. Lincoln Avenue
Chicago, IL 60618-1712
(312)-478-2410
CENTER; TOPICS: Astrology, Spirituality, Holistic Health, Crystals, Numerology, Herbalogy OWNER: Michael J. Kurban DESCRIPTION: Center/store offers self-produced books & videos, crystals, herbs, natural cosmetics, hair products, oils, readings, lectures, charts, biorhythms, astrology & weekly psychic fairs. Classes in massage, foot reflexology, herbal wrap, anatomy & physiology, ESP, tarot, numerology & palmistry.

New Dawn Center
1230 North Poplar
Fresno, CA 93728
TOPICS: Metaphysics

New Directions
14 Jefferson Street
Waldoboro, ME 04572
(207)-832-6649

CENTER; TOPICS: Crystals DESCRIPTION: Dedicated to the art of crystal therapy & healing.

New Frontiers Center/Fellowship Farm
Fellowship Farm
RR 1
Oregon, WI 53575
(608)-835-3795

CENTER; CONTACT: Walter H. Uphoff TOPICS: Parapsychology, Holistic Health, Psychic Phenomena, Channeling, Meditation, Spirituality BOOKSTORE; DESCRIPTION: Non-Profit Foundation established for the exploration and dissemination of evidence related to the broader dimensions of holistic health, psychic phenomena and survival. Dedicated to the study & education of parapsychology and related subjects. Conducts research, counseling, referrals, conferences, meetings, lectures & workshops. Also produces publications, books & tapes. 400 members worldwide. Holds periodic educational meetings & conferences. CONVENTIONS: Annual meetings in May. Quarterly meetings for board of directors. PUBLICATIONS: New Frontiers EDITOR: Mary Jo Uphoff, Prof. Walter H. Uphoff TOPICS: Parapsychology, Holistic Health TYPE: Newsletter DATE: 1982 SIZE: 8 1/2 x 11, 24 pgs. FREQ: semi-annual CIRC: 1,100 PRICE: $5.00 DESCRIPTION: Supplies information, education & research on unusual events, alternative healing methods & psychic phenomena.

New Horizon Health And Tennis Spa
Major's Path
Southampton, NY 11968
(516)-283-5444

TOPICS: Holistic Healing

New Life Clinic
1301 Ashbury Road
Baltimore, MD 21209
(301)-435-9736

TOPICS: Holistic Healing

New Life Health Center
12 Harris Avenue
Jamaica Plain, MA 02130
(617)-524-9551

CENTER; TOPICS: Holistic Health, Yoga, Meditation, Nutrition, Homeopathy, Acupuncture, Herbalogy OWNER: Bo-In Lee, Pres. DESCRIPTION: Dedicated to helping people heal themselves. Guides people to a physical, emotional, psychological & spiritual health through proper diet, exercise, mental training, meditation & holistic therapies. Offers Yoga, herbal medicines, acupressure, acupuncture, meditation, diet, exercise & private consultations.

New Life Health Spa
Liftline Lodge
Box 144
Stratton Mountain, VT 05155
(802)-297-2534

TOPICS: Holistic Healing

New World Educational Center
812 south 6th Avenue
Phoenix, AZ 85003
(602)-934-9931

TOPICS: Holistic Healing

New York Center For Art And Awareness
440 Lafayette Street, 3rd Fl
New York, NY 10003
(212)-475-0212

CENTER; TOPICS: Yoga, Holistic Health, Meditation, Massage OWNER: Ravi Singh DESCRIPTION: Offers classes in Kundalini Yoga, meditation, deep bodywork such as shiatsu, swedish, polarity, reflexology & rolfing & personalized exercise programs.

New York Open Center, Inc.
83 Spring Street
New York, NY 10012
(212)-219-2527 (212)-219-3739

CENTER; CONTACT: Walter Beebe TOPICS: Metaphysics, Spirituality, Astrology, Numerology, New Age, Holistic Health, Spirituality BOOKSTORE; DESCRIPTION: Non-profit holistic learning center promoting health & wellness by offering lectures, courses, workshops, tours & therapy in wellness, healing, bodywork, spirituality, self-improvement, the arts, travel, astrology, numerology & A Course In Miracles.

Next Step, Inc.
16 Church Street
Keene, NH 03431
(603)-357-0744

TOPICS: Holistic Healing

Nityananda Institute
P.O. Box 1973
Cambridge, MA 02238
(617)-497-6263

RETREAT; TOPICS: Yoga, Spirituality, Meditation OWNER: Swami Chetanananda DESCRIPTION: A vital community of people practicing hatha yoga & meditation who are committed to bringing their spiritual understanding into everyday living.

Northern Pines Health Resort
RR 1
Box 279
Raymond, ME 04071
(207)-655-7624

SPA; TOPICS: Holistic Health, Holistic Healing, Meditation, Yoga, Nutrition, Massage OWNER: Marlee Turner BOOKSTORE; STAFF: 10 DESCRIPTION: Health resort offering meditation, yoga, massage therapy, nutrition & bowel management workshops, seaweed wraps & clay packs for the attainment of health & well-being. Also provides Conference Center. PUBLICATIONS: Northern Pioneer-bi monthly newsletter; Northern Pines Cookbook

Northwest Center For Holistic Medicine
4072 9th Avenue N.E.
Seattle, WA 98105
(206)-547-9665

TOPICS: Holistic Healing

Novato Center For Dreams
29 Truman Drive
Novato, CA 94947

TOPICS: Metaphysics

NW Center For Attitudinal Healing
11700 1st Avenue N.E.

Seattle, WA 98125
(206)-362-3897

TOPICS: Holistic Healing

Nyingma Institute
1815 Highland Place
Berkeley, CA 94709
(415)-843-6812

TOPICS: Holistic Healing, New Age

Oaks At Ojai
122 East Ojai Avenue
Ojai, CA 93023
(805)-646-5573

TOPICS: Holistic Healing

Oasis Center: New Horizons For Mind, Body, And Spirit
7463 North Sheridan Road
Chicago, IL 60626
(312)-274-6777

CENTER; TOPICS: Holistic Healing, Meditation, Hypnotism, Psychology, Massage, Spirituality DESCRIPTION: Non-profit, community-based organization that sponsors workshops, seminars & extended professional training programs in the area of human potential, personal growth, etc. The first Personal Growth Center in the Midwest, operating since 1968. Classes can be used for Continuing Education credits in: Professional Training in Art Therapy, Hypnotherapy, Massage Therapy, Psychodrama, Psychosynthesis, Gestalt, Meditation, Healing, Self-Empowerment & Communication Skills.

Ocamora Foundation
Box 43
Ocate, NM 87734
(505)-666-2389

TOPICS: Holistic Healing

Ojai Foundation
P.O. Box 1620
Ojai, CA 93023

RETREAT; TOPICS: New Age, Spirituality, Meditation MEMBERS: 15 DESCRIPTION: Spiritual community offering meditation & workshops with religious leaders.

Ojo Caliente Mineral Springs
P.O. Box 468
Highway 414
Ojo Caliente, NM 87549
(505)-583-2233

TOPICS: Holistic Healing

Olcott Library
1926 North Main Street
P.O. Box 270
Wheaton, IL 60189-0270
(312)-668-1571

TOPICS: Metaphysics, New Age

Olympic Center
P.O. Box 7534
Olympia, WA 98507
(206)-456-3078

TOPICS: Holistic Healing

Omega Energy System
224 20th Street
Manhattan Beach, CA 90266-4531
(714)-670-1705 (213)-202-4307 (800)-548-6694

TOPICS: Holistic Healing

Omega Institute For Holistic Studies
Lake Drive
RD 2, Box 377
Rhinebeck, NY 12572
(914)-338-6030 (414)-266-4301 (800)-862-8890
RETREAT; CONTACT: Sarah Priestman TOPICS: Holistic Health, Yoga, Psychology, Spirituality, Astrology, Tarot, Body-Mind Connection DESCRIPTION: Non-profit, nonsectarian holistic studies-vacation retreat. Offers workshops and conferences for holistic self-improvement, recreational activities, cottage & dormitory accomodations, vegetarian meals, stores, sauna & massage center & a meditation garden. Adult learning center. Offers over 35 winter & 250 summer retreats in health, ecology, social justice, fine arts & spiritual studies as well as educational journeys to destinations around the world. Call or write for catalog.

One Hundred Mile Lodge
Box 9
100 Mile House, British Columbia V0K 2E0
Canada
RETREAT; TOPICS: New Age, Spirituality DESCRIPTION: Spiritually conscious community associated with International Emissary Society. Offers Art Of Living workshops & publishes monthly, Integrity International.

Open Door New Age Center
P.O. Box 236
Otis, OR 97368-0236
(503)-994-2488
CENTER; TOPICS: Crystals DESCRIPTION: Dedicated to the art of crystal therapy & healing.

Open Door Spirit Center
814 Van Ness Avenue
Fresno, CA 93721
TOPICS: Metaphysics

Open Path, The
703 North 18th Street
Boise, ID 83702
(208)-342-0208
TOPICS: Holistic Healing

Option Institute & Fellowship- A Place For Miracles
RD #1, Box 174-A
Sheffield, MA 01257
(413)-229-2100
TOPICS: Holistic Health PUBLICATIONS: *A Miracle To Believe In* TOPICS: Holistic Healing TYPE: Book PUBLICATIONS: *Giant Steps* TOPICS: Holistic Healing TYPE: Book PUBLICATIONS: *Son Rise* EDITOR: Carol Wertz, Barry Neil Kaufman TOPICS: Holistic Healing TYPE: Book PUBLICATIONS: *To Love Is To Be Happy* TOPICS: Holistic Healing TYPE: Book

Ordo Templi Astartes
Church Of Hermetic Sciences, Inc.
P.O. Box 40094
Pasadena, CA 91106
TOPICS: New Age

Organization For A Workable Peace
1442A Walnut Street, #182
Berkeley, CA 94709

(415)-644-8200
TOPICS: New Age

Orion Center Of Kauai
4366 Kukui Grove, #207
Lihu, Kaui, HI 96766
(808)-245-4552
CENTER; TOPICS: Crystals DESCRIPTION: Dedicated to the art of crystal therapy & healing.

Orr Hot Springs
13201 Orr Springs Road
Ukiah, CA 95482
(707)-462-6277
TOPICS: Holistic Healing

Ortho-Bionomy
Tania Bedford
Box 766
Bolinas, CA 94924
(415)-868-2103
TOPICS: New Age, Holistic Health

Other Dimensions Services
P.O. Box 2269
40th Street, NW
Salmon Arm, BC V0E 2T0
Canada
(604)-832-8483
CONTACT: Andy Schneider TOPICS: Metaphysics, Spirituality, Holistic Healing, Metaphysics, Channeling, New Age DESCRIPTION: Offers esoteric studies & metaphysical holiday retreats. Video producers.

Our Lady & All Angels, The Liberal Catholic Church
4229 Hartford St.
St. Louis, MO 63116
(314)-776-5202
CENTER; TOPICS: New Age DESCRIPTION: Offers mystical influence in its teachings.

Ouray Swimming Pool
Ouray, CO 81427
(303)-325-4347
TOPICS: Holistic Healing

Outdoor Leadership Training Seminars
P.O. Box 20281
Denver, CO 80220
(303)-333-7831 (800)-331-7238
TOPICS: New Age

Outreach Institute
Kenmore Station
Box 368
Boston, MA 02215
TOPICS: Holistic Healing

Ovens Natural Park
P.O. Box 38
Riverport, Nova Scotia B0J 2W0
Canada
(902)-766-4621
TOPICS: Holistic Healing

P'Nai Or Religious Fellowship
7318 Germantown Avenue
Philadelphia, PA 19119-1793
(215)-242-4074

CENTER; CONTACT: Rabbi Julie Greenberg TOPICS: New Age, Meditation, Kabbalah OWNER: Rabbi Zalman Schachter-Shalomi DESCRIPTION: The Jewish Renewal Life Center is a progressive community offering one year immersion in Jewish renewal study, living, spiritual & social activism. Offers audio, videos, books & Judaica. Sponsors an international gathering known as Kallah every other year . PUBLICATIONS: *New Menorah* EDITOR: Arthur Waskow, Ph. D., Rabbi Shana Margolin TOPICS: Spirituality, Kabbalah TYPE: Journal, 20 pgs. FREQ: quarterly PRICE: $18.00 PUBLICATIONS: *Or Chadash* TOPICS: Spirituality TYPE: Book PRICE: $20.00 PUBLICATIONS: *Spiritual Intimacy* EDITOR: Zalmon Schachter-Shalomi TOPICS: Spirituality, Kabbalah TYPE: Book PRICE: $30.00 PUBLICATIONS: *The First Step: A Guide For The New Jewish Spirit* EDITOR: Zalmon Schachter-Shalomi, Donald Gropman TOPICS: Spirituality, Kabbalah TYPE: Book PRICE: $5.95

Pacific Process Institute
2295 Palou Avenue
San Francisco, CA 94124
(415)-546-6230
TOPICS: New Age

Parapsychology Education Center
2585 Dalmuir Court
San Jose, CA 95121
(408)-274-9036
CENTER; TOPICS: Parapsychology, Metaphysics, Crystals, PSI, Spirituality, Hypnotism, ESP OWNER: Korra Deaver, Ph. D. DESCRIPTION: Provides independent study in advanced metaphysics & soul growth. Offers personalized numerology reading & signature analysis-how your name affects your life. Offers certificate of completion. Sells Arkansas Crystals: Pendulums, Pendants & meditation balls. PUBLICATIONS: *Rock Crystal: The Magic Stone* EDITOR: Korra Deaver, Ph. D. TOPICS: Crystals, Meditation, Holistic Healing TYPE: Book PRICE: $5.00 DESCRIPTION: Deal with how to choose & care for your crystal, exercises in meditation, healing, crystal gazing, programming a crystal pendulum. PUBLICATIONS: *Where Will You Be At The Battle Of Armeggedon?* EDITOR: Korra Deaver, Ph. D. TOPICS: New Age TYPE: Book PRICE: $2.00 DESCRIPTION: New thoughts concerning the end of the Piscean Age.

Pawling Health Manor
P.O. Box 401
Hyde Park, NY 12538
(914)-889-4141
TOPICS: Holistic Healing

Peacehaven-Center For The Unity Of Man
P.O. Box 45
Deer, AR 72628
(501)-446-5793
TOPICS: New Age, Holistic Health

Pelly Health Farm
Box 273
Weslaco, TX 78596
(512)-968-5343
TOPICS: Holistic Healing

Penna Center For UFO Research
6 Oakhill Avenue

Greensburg, PA 15601
TOPICS: UFO's

Personal Healing Institute
1113 Spruce, #301
Boulder, CO 80302
(303)-449-0910
TOPICS: Holistic Healing

Philadelphia Institute, Inc.
401 Patterson Street
Sulphur Springs, AR 72768
(501)-298-3362
TOPICS: Holistic Healing

Philadelphia Well-Being Center
2475 South Napfle Street
Philadelphia, PA 19152
(215)-332-6996
TOPICS: Holistic Healing

Phoenicia Pathwork-Center For The Living Force
P.O. Box 66
Phoenicia, NY 12464
(914)-688-2211
CENTER; TOPICS: New Age, Spirituality, Channeling, Psychology MEMBERS: 40 DESCRIPTION: Located on 300 acres & founded on the channeled writings of Eva Pierrakos & the therapeutic process known as Core Energetics which teaches an integrated process of self-transformation & fosters the spiritual growth of the individual. Provides workshops & conferences. Members live in separate homes. Also has large & small group spaces, with double occupancy & dormitory accomodations & a large dining room.

Phoenix Rising
333 S.W. 5th Avenue, #404
Portland, OR 97204
(503)-223-8299
TOPICS: Holistic Healing

Piedmont Yoga Center
186 East Main Street
Pendleton, SC 29670
(803)-646-7002
TOPICS: Yoga

Pine Ridge Centre
P.O. Box 362
Pickering, ON L1V 2R6
Canada
(416)-683-3864
CENTER; TOPICS: Crystals DESCRIPTION: Dedicated to the art of crystal therapy & healing.

Planetary Citizens/Planetary Initiative For The World We Choose
P.O. Box 426
Menlo Park, CA 94026
(415)-325-2939
TOPICS: Astrology, New Age PUBLICATIONS: Initiator EDITOR: Mary Ann Klimek TOPICS: Astrology TYPE: Calendar SIZE: 11.5 x 16, 8 pgs.

Planetary Smile
P.O. Box 834
McMinnville, OR 97128
(503)-472-8815
TOPICS: Holistic Healing

Play Mountain Place
6063 Hargis Street
Los Angeles, CA 90034
(213)-870-4381
TOPICS: Holistic Healing

Plum Creek
Box 82A
Waitsfield, VT 05673
(802)-496-3262
TOPICS: Holistic Healing

Polarity Therapy Center Of San Francisco
409-A Lawton Street
San Francisco, CA 94122
(415)-753-1298
CENTER; CONTACT: Dr. Alan Siegel TOPICS: Holistic Health, New Age, Massage DESCRIPTION: Offers instructional video tapes in Polarity Therapy.

Polestar Retreat Center
604 Mt. Vernon Avenue
Charlotte, NC 28203
TOPICS: Holistic Healing

Ponderosa Village
Route 1, #17-81
Goldendale, WA 98620
(509)-773-3902
SPA; TOPICS: New Age DESCRIPTION: Self-sufficient cooperative community.

Port Centauri-Communities Of Light
P.O. Box 11919
Pueblo, CO 81001
(719)-546-3654
CENTER; TOPICS: UFO's DESCRIPTION: Cooperative, working farm community whose purpose is to activate & demonstrate the full potential of human consciousness during the present cycle of personal & planetary transformation. That pathway is open through the daily practice of unconditional love . PUBLICATIONS: Living Love TOPICS: New Age TYPE: Newsletter, 6 pgs. FREQ: quarterly DESCRIPTION: News articles written by the residents about their community.

Port Of Health
Apdo, 270
Chapala,Jalisco, 5-22-13
Mexico
TOPICS: Holistic Healing

Positive Alternatives Wellness Education Centre
123 Queen Street West
Brampton, Ontario L6Y 1M3
Canada
(416)-454-2688
CENTER; TOPICS: Holistic Healing OWNER: Mary Simpson, Dir. DESCRIPTION: Offers private consultations, counselling, education & workshops in holistic wellness, stress management, Imagery, Inner Child/Co-Dependency, addictions & Therapeutic Touch. Practitioner of Iridology, Homeopathy, Chinese Medicine, acupuncture, regressions therapy & Native Canadian teachings on premises. Also offers transformational feminist & dysfunctional families counselling, stop-smoking programs, coping skills for Cancer groups & Wellness in Recovery. By appointment only.

Potomac Massage Therapy Institute
421 Butternut Street N.W.
Washington, DC 20012
(202)-829-4201
TOPICS: Massage

Prana - Philadelphia Resource And Networking Association
Center For Holistic Education And Self-Development
638 South Street
Philadelphia, PA 19147
(215)-592-9035
TOPICS: Holistic Healing PUBLICATIONS: Connexions EDITOR: Ruth Hoskins TOPICS: Holistic Healing TYPE: Newsletter

Prana Yoga Ashram - Yogalayam
P.O. Box 1037
Berkeley, CA 94701
(415)-655-3664
CENTER; TOPICS: Yoga, Meditation, Holistic Health, Massage, Spirituality, Vegetarianism, Astrology OWNER: Swami Vignanananda BOOKSTORE; DESCRIPTION: Classes, workshops & private lessons in yoga exercise (body postures & movement), pranayama (breathing techniques) & meditation. Students who practice regularly learn to live a well-balanced life by gaining a healthy, fit body, a calm, clear mind & an awakened spiritual consciousness. Also gives instruction in massage, chakras & Astrology. Classes given at 1717 Alcatraz Avenue, Berkeley, CA 94703. PUBLICATIONS: Prana Yoga Leaves EDITOR: Saraswathi Devi, Yoganathan Devi TOPICS: Yoga TYPE: Newsletter PUBLICATIONS: Prana Yoga Life Magazine EDITOR: Saraswathi Devi, Yoganathan Devi TOPICS: Yoga TYPE: Magazine PUBLICATIONS: Yoga Vision PUBLISHER: Swami Vignanananda EDITOR: Saraswathi Devi, Ramesh Wallen TOPICS: Yoga TYPE: Newsletter DATE: 1975, 30 pgs. FREQ: irregular DESCRIPTION: Spiritual articles & Yoga news.

Preventative Health Center
3330 3rd Avenue, #400
San Diego, CA 92103
(619)-291-0261
TOPICS: Holistic Healing

Preventive Medicine Society
3743 West 10th Avenue
Vancouver, BC
Canada
(604)-224-1515
TOPICS: Holistic Healing

Pritikin Longevity Center
1910 Ocean Front Walk
Santa Monica, CA 90405
(213)-450-5433
TOPICS: Holistic Healing

Programs For Human Development
Western Greenwich Civic Center
449 Pemberwick Road
Greenwich, CT 06830
(203)-531-6650
CENTER; TOPICS: Metaphysics, Psychology, Astrology, Body-Mind Connection, New Age, Tarot, Parapsychology OWNER: Robert Stempson MEMBERS: 4,500 DESCRIPTION: Offers classes in

Metaphysics, Psychology & Education covering all aspects of Body, Mind & Spirit. Purpose is to inspire individuals to discover & express their highest potentials. Conducts Psychic Fairs in Fairfield County twice each month. Catalog available quarterly.

Project Rainbow Consulting Services
7529 3rd Avenue North
St. Petersburg, FL 33710
(813)-345-2698
TOPICS: Holistic Healing

Project: World Enlightenment Center For New Age Studies
Thompson's Point, Building 1A
Portland, ME 04102
(207)-775-7135
CENTER; TOPICS: Crystals DESCRIPTION: Dedicated to the art of crystal therapy & healing.

Proprioceptive Writing Center
39 Deering Street
P.O. Box 8333
Portland, ME 04104
(207)-772-1847
TOPICS: New Age

Prosper!
Box 134
Cambridge, MA 02140
(617)-497-8280
TOPICS: Holistic Healing

Providence Zen Center
528 Pound Road
RFD #5
Cumberland, RI 02864
(401)-769-6464
CENTER; TOPICS: New Age, Spirituality, Health Food, Meditation MEMBERS: 40 DESCRIPTION: Offers traditional Zen instruction led by Master Seung Sahn as well as programs in meditation, ecology, stone carving & organic gardening. Also offers retreats.

Psychic Awareness Library (P.A.L.)
P.O. Box 396
Skowhegan, ME 04976
(207)-277-4881 (207)-474-3176 FAX (207)-277-3040
CENTER; CONTACT: Leslie Bugbee, Director TOPICS: Parapsychology, Psychic Phenomena STAFF: 4 DESCRIPTION: P.A.L. exists to promote & conduct research, consultations, & instruction in a wide variety of psychic & paranormal activity. COMPUTER SERVICES: Biorhythmn/Database/Handwriting Analysis CONVENTIONS: Weekly meetings by appointment.

Psychic Institute Of Las Vegas
4800 South Maryland Parkway
Las Vegas, NV 89119
(702)-798-8448
CENTER; TOPICS: Crystals DESCRIPTION: Dedicated to the art of crystal therapy & healing.

Psychic Learning Center
P.O. Box 308
Rockport, MA 01966
TOPICS: Metaphysics

Psychosynthesis Center
311 West McGraw
Seattle, WA 98119
(206)-282-1171
TOPICS: Holistic Healing

Psychosynthesis Center Northwest
909 Northeast 43rd, Suite 308
Seattle, WA 98103
(206)-632-1328
TOPICS: New Age

Psychosynthesis Institute Of New York
500 West End Avenue 9C
New York, NY 10024
(212)-787-0600
TOPICS: New Age

Psynetics Foundation
1212 East Lincoln Avenue
Anaheim, CA 92805
(714)-533-2311
TOPICS: Holistic Healing

Pyramid Center For Bhakti Yoga
20395 Callon Drive
Topanga, CA 90290
(213)-455-1658
TOPICS: New Age, Yoga

Pyramid Foundation
P.O. Box 418
Cascade, CO 80809-0418
TOPICS: Holistic Healing

Quadrinity Center
2295 Palou Avenue
San Francisco, CA 94124
(415)-397-0466
TOPICS: Holistic Healing

Quest Institute, Inc.
P.O. Box 3265
Charlottesville, VA 22903
(804)-295-6923
TOPICS: Holistic Healing

Qumrah Desert Center
P.O. Box 41985
Tucson, AZ 85717
TOPICS: Metaphysics

Radiant Health Center Clinic
7310 Buckley Road
North Syracuse, NY 132121
(315)-458-3218
CENTER; CONTACT: Richard W. Werfelmann, D.D.S. TOPICS: Crystals DESCRIPTION: Dedicated to the art of crystal therapy & healing.

Radiant Life Center
123 Keen Street
Lismore 2480,
Australia
(066) 21-4350
CENTER; TOPICS: Crystals DESCRIPTION: Dedicated to the art of crystal therapy & healing.

Radium Hot Springs Spa
302 Soda Creek Road
Idaho Springs, CO 80452
(303)-567-2191
TOPICS: Holistic Healing

Rainbow Center For Attitudinal Healing
P.O. Box 2802
Toledo, OH 43606
(419)-478-0202
TOPICS: Holistic Healing

Rainbow Centre
559 Bloor Street, West
Toronto, ON M5S 1Y6
Canada
(416)-535-7204
CENTER; TOPICS: Crystals DESCRIPTION: Dedicated to the art of crystal therapy & healing.

Rainbow Connection For Attitudinal Healing And Learning
444 Piedmont Street, #309
Glendale, CA 91206
(818)-241-0691
TOPICS: Holistic Healing

Rainbow Place
525 Central Avenue, Northeast
Albuquerque, NM 87102
(505)-243-2444
CENTER; TOPICS: Crystals DESCRIPTION: Dedicated to the art of crystal therapy & healing.

Ramakrishna-Vivekananda Center Of New York
17 East 94th Street
New York, NY 10128
TOPICS: New Age, Metaphysics, Spirituality PUBLICATIONS: Gospel Of Sri Ramakrishna: Abridged Version EDITOR: S. Nikhilananda TOPICS: Spirituality TYPE: Book PRICE: $24.50 PUBLICATIONS: Vivekanada: The Yogas And Other Works EDITOR: S. Nikhilananda TOPICS: Yoga, Holistic Health TYPE: Book PRICE: $24.50

Ravenest
604 Mascontan Avenue
Belleville, IL 62220
(618)-234-1727
TOPICS: Holistic Healing

Re-Creation Center aka Hale Mauli Ola Hou
P.O. Box 1653
Pahoa, HI 96778
(808)-965-9880
TOPICS: Holistic Healing

Re-Vitalization Centers
Box 313
Upper Darby, PA 19082
(215)-352-7017
TOPICS: Holistic Healing

Red River Hot Springs
Elk City, ID 83525
TOPICS: Holistic Healing

Red Victorian Bed And Breakfast Inn/Global Family Networking Center
1665 Haight Street
San Francisco, CA 94117
(415)-864-1978
TOPICS: Holistic Healing

Reflexology Centre Of Vancouver
535 West 10th Avenue
Vancouver, British Columbia V5Z 1K9
Canada
(604)-875-8818
CENTER; TOPICS: Holistic Healing, Reflexology
OWNER: Christopher Shirley STAFF: 1
DESCRIPTION: Dedicated to the promotion &
development of reflexology. Offers certificate
courses, private sessions, books, charts, instruments,
sandals, a referecne library & public speakers.
AFFILIATED ORGS: Reflexology Assoc. of Canada;
Reflexology Assoc. of B.C PUBLICATIONS:
Reflexology Foot Charts

Regency Health Resort And Spa
2000 South Ocean Drive
Hallandale, FL 33009
(305)-454-2220
TOPICS: Holistic Healing

Renaissance
Box 281
Turners Falls, MA 01376
(413)-863-9711
RETREAT; TOPICS: New Age, Psychology
MEMBERS: 80 DESCRIPTION: Environmentally
conscious community on 80 acres in Gill, MA
featuring energy saving wind & solar designs.
Purpose is to raise self-awareness, increase creativity
& promote human development. Income derived
from recording studio, contracting work, &
production & sales of custom coaches.

Research Center Of Kaballah
200 Park Avenue, 303
New York, NY 10017
TOPICS: Metaphysics

Research Centre Of Kabbalah
85-03 114th Street
Richmond Hill, NY 11418
(718)-805-9122
CENTER; TOPICS: Spirituality, Kabbalah
DESCRIPTION: Non-profit organization offering
lectures on all aspects of Kabbalah. Also sells audio
& video cassettes on the teachings of Kabbalah.
PUBLICATIONS: *Heaven On Your Head: Esoteric
Stories From The Holy Land* EDITOR: S. Kahana
TOPICS: Paranormal Phenomena, Spirituality
TYPE: Book PRICE: $10.95 PUBLICATIONS:
*Wheels Of A Soul: Reincarnation, Your Life Today
And Tomorrow* EDITOR: P. Berg TOPICS:
Spirituality, Reincarnation TYPE: Book PRICE:
$10.95

Research Collection
2400 Ridge Road
Berkeley, CA 94709
(415)-841-8222
TOPICS: New Age

Resort Of The Mountains
1130 Morton Road
Morton, WA 98356
(206)-496-5885
TOPICS: Holistic Healing

Resource Center, The
3434 Central
Evanston, IL 60201
TOPICS: Channeling

Revivaria
P.O. Box 862
Clearlake Oaks, CA 95423
(707)-998-1366
TOPICS: Holistic Healing

Rim Institute
6835 Pepper Tree Lane
Scottsdale, AZ 85253
(602)-285-1048 (602)-263-0551
SPA; CONTACT: Joan Norris TOPICS: New Age,
Holistic Healing DESCRIPTION: Operates from
November to April each year in Scottsdale, AZ. Can
be reached from May to October at HCR Box 162D,
Payson, AZ 85541, phone number 602-478-4727.
PUBLICATIONS: *Rim Institute* TOPICS: New Age
TYPE: Magazine CIRC: 60,000 DESCRIPTION:
Publicizes events held at the Rim Institute.

Ritter Hot Springs
Box 16
Ritter, OR 97872
(503)-421-3846
TOPICS: Holistic Healing

Rivendell Holistic Retreat
3 Old Mill Road
Weston, CT 06883
(203)-227-3559
TOPICS: Holistic Healing

River Farm
Four Mile Point Road
RR 1, Box 371
Athens, NY 12015
(518)-731-8487
RETREAT; CONTACT: Zindel Elmer TOPICS: New
Age, Holistic Health STAFF: 2 BUDGET:
$26,000.00 DESCRIPTION: 7 acre farm on the
Hudson River, south of Albany, NY. Houses 4
guests & has apple orchard, organic garden & pond.
Offers vegetarian meals & accepts donations instead
of charging set fees. CONVENTIONS: bi-annually
PUBLICATIONS: Bi-monthly newsletter for the
Hygienic Community Network-a vegetarian
community movement dedicated to the principles of
natural hygiene. PUBLICATIONS: *Hygienic
Community Network News* EDITOR: Helen Jean
Story TOPICS: New Age TYPE: Newspaper

Rochester Center For The Healing Arts, Inc.
14 Cottage Row
Lily Dale, NY 14752
(716)-595-3452
CENTER; TOPICS: Spirituality OWNER: Shirley
Calkins Smith DESCRIPTION: Spiritual awareness
retreat/center provides a tranquil, lakeside setting for
spiritual growth & transformation. Offers workshops
in transformational breathwork, Reiki, spiritual
healing, counselling & readings. Provides low-cost
housing for get-away weekends.

Rocky Mountain Dharma Center
Red Feather Lakes, CO 80545
(303)-881-2530
TOPICS: Body-Mind Connection, Holistic Health

Rocky Mountain Institute
1919 14th Street, #711
Boulder, CO 80302
(303)-442-5373
TOPICS: Holistic Healing

Rocky Mountain Peace Center
P.O. Box 1156
Boulder, CO 80306
(303)-444-6981
TOPICS: New Age

Rocky Mountain Truth Center
P.O. Box 507
Castle Rock, CO 80104
TOPICS: Metaphysics

Rocky Mountain Wellness Spa And Institute
P.O. Box 777
Steamboat Springs, CO 80477
(303)-879-7772 (800)-345-7771
TOPICS: Holistic Healing

Roots And Wings
P.O. Box 426
Sea Cliff, NY 11579
(914)-679-5580
TOPICS: Holistic Healing

Rose Mountain Retreat Center
P.O. Box 355
Las Vegas, NM 87701
(505)-425-3144
TOPICS: Holistic Healing

Rotunda Center For Attitudinal Healing
15 Kitzbuhel
Parton, MD 21120
(301)-467-6333
TOPICS: Holistic Healing

Round Valley Indian Health Center
P.O. Box 247
Covelo, CA 95428
(707)-983-2981
TOPICS: Holistic Healing

Rowe Camp And Conference Center
Kings Highway Road
Rowe, MA 01367
(413)-339-4216 (413)-339-4954
RETREAT; CENTER; CONTACT: Doug Wilson,
Exec. Dir. TOPICS: Holistic Healing, Spirituality
OWNER: Unitarian Universalist Association STAFF:
7 DESCRIPTION: Retreat that revitalizes, located in
the beautiful Berkshires. Offers weekend retreats
with outstanding workshop leaders in personal
growth, psychology, spirituality, politics & health.
Runs summer camp for teenagers, families, single
people & women. PUBLICATIONS: Publishes 2
newspapers & 3 brochures per year with program
listings.

Ruh Inayat Sufi Center
3905 Southwest Alice
Portland, OR 97219
TOPICS: Metaphysics

Russell House Of Key West
611 Truman Avenue
Key West, FL 33040
(305)-294-8787
TOPICS: Holistic Healing

Safety Harbor Spa
Resort Hotel & Tennis Club

Safety Harbor, FL 33572
(800)-237-0155
TOPICS: Holistic Healing

Sakya TeGchen Choling Center
5042 18th Northeast
Seattle, WA 98105
TOPICS: Metaphysics

Salida Chamber Of Commerce
123 East Third Street
Salida, CO 81201
(303)-539-6738
TOPICS: Holistic Healing

Salt Spring Center-For The Creative And Healing Arts
Box 1133
Ganges, British Columbia V0S 1E0
Canada
TOPICS: Holistic Healing

Salt Springs Clinic
Box 4
Fulford Harbour, British Columbia V0S 1C0
Canada
(604)-653-4216
TOPICS: Holistic Healing

Sam's Family Spa
70875 Dillon Road
Desert Hot Springs, CA 92240
(619)-329-6457
TOPICS: Holistic Healing

Sambodhi Rajneesh Neo-Sannyas Commune
Conomo Point Road
Essex, MA 01929
(617)-768-7640
TOPICS: New Age, Metaphysics

Sancta Sophia Seminary
22 Summit Ridge Drive
Tahlequah, OK 74464
(918)-456-3421
CENTER; CONTACT: Carol E. Parrish-Harra
TOPICS: New Age, Spirituality, Meditation, Yoga, Health Food, Channeling **DESCRIPTION:** New Age intentional community & Ecumenical Church located on 332 acres & run by Pastor Carol Parrish-Harra. Offers programs in Agni Yoga, spiritual science & meditation. Property is partly used as nature sanctuary, partly agricultural production & partly developed for homes & schools located in the Northeast Oklahoma Ozarks. Examines East & West religions. Dedicated to spiritual discovery. Full moon rituals, prayer vigils, sacred music to reach inner potential. Earn minister degree, masters or doctorate.

Sandhill Farm
Route 1, Box 155
Rutledge, MO 63563
(816)-883-5543
RETREAT; TOPICS: New Age, Spirituality, Health Food, Metaphysics **MEMBERS:** 8 **DESCRIPTION:** Informally organized spiritual community on 63 acres & part of the Federation of Egalitarian Communities. Income derived from the production & sales of honey & sorghum molasses.

Santa Monica Healing Arts Center
1453 7th Street
Santa Monica, CA 90401
(213)-395-4667
TOPICS: Holistic Healing

Saratoga Spa State Park
Gideon Putnam Hotel
Saratoga Springs, NY 12866
(518)-584-3000
TOPICS: Holistic Healing

Sawan Kirpal Ruhani Mission
RR 1, Box 24
Bowling Green, VA 22427
(804)-633-9987
TOPICS: New Age, Spirituality

Science Of Mind Center
500 Marina Drive
Seal Beach, CA 90740
TOPICS: Metaphysics

Science Of Mind Church Counseling And Healing Center
Box 32236
Washington, DC 20007
(202)-333-6354
TOPICS: Holistic Healing, Metaphysics
PUBLICATIONS: *Alternative Health Therapies*
TOPICS: Holistic Healing **TYPE:** Magazine

Scott's Natural Health Institute
Box 8919
Cleveland, OH 44136
(216)-238-6930
TOPICS: Holistic Healing

Self-Actualization And Enlightenment Center
2717 East Central
Wichita, KS 67214
CENTER; TOPICS: Channeling, Metaphysics, New Age, Meditation, Reincarnation, Dreams **DESCRIPTION:** Non-profit educational organization offering classes & workshops on New Age topics such as meditation, self-awareness, metaphysics, reincarnation & dreams.

Self-Realization Fellowship (SRF)
3880 San Rafael Avenue
Los Angeles, CA 90065-9988
(213)-225-2471
CENTER; TOPICS: New Age **OWNER:** Daya Mata
DESCRIPTION: Teaches scientific methods of meditation & principles of living that balance the development of body, mind, & soul. By applying these principles you can find not only the keys to health, but the meaning of life itself.
PUBLICATIONS: *Self-Realization* **EDITOR:** Jane Brush **TOPICS:** New Age **TYPE:** Newsletter

Serenity Summit
600 Bolsa Chica
P.O. Box 367
Green Valley Lake, CA 92341
(714)-867-4109
TOPICS: Holistic Healing

Seven Oaks Pathwork Center
Route 1, Box 86
Madison, VA 22727
(703)-948-6544

CENTER; TOPICS: New Age, Spirituality, Body-Mind Connection, Psychology, Channeling, Holistic Health **MEMBERS:** 12 **DESCRIPTION:** 130 acre non-profit spiritual educational retreat promoting the philosophy of channeler Eva Pierrakos & the Core Energetics therapeutic process. Takes an holistic approach to spiritual enlightenment. Operates conference center & cottage industries.

Shalom Mountain Retreat And Study Center
Cattail Road
RD 2
Livingston Manor, NY 12758
(914)-482-5421
TOPICS: New Age

Shambhala Healing Centre
Coursing Batch, Glastonbury
Somerset, BA6 8BH
England
(0458)31797
RETREAT; TOPICS: Crystals, Holistic Health, Massage **OWNER:** Tara Livingstone **BOOKSTORE;**
DESCRIPTION: Healing retreat located on a sacred site on the slope of Glastonbury, offering guesthouse, jacuzzi, sauna, counseling, massage & Radionic therapy. New Age store, The Crystal Cave, selling books to inspire, crystals & music.

Shangri-La Natural Health Resort
Box 2328
Bonita Springs, FL 33959
(813)-992-3811
TOPICS: Holistic Healing

Shannon Farm
Route 2
Box 343
Afton, VA 22920
(804)-361-1180
RETREAT; TOPICS: New Age **MEMBERS:** 58
DESCRIPTION: Located on 500 commonly-owned acres. Community based on principles of democratic procedure, equality & feminism. Members own businesses & individual houses.

Shanti Anatam Ashram
3528 North Triunfo Canyon Road
Agouri Hills, CA 91301
TOPICS: Metaphysics

Shanti Yoga Institute
3 Union Street
Glassboro, NJ 08028
(609)-881-3357
TOPICS: New Age, Yoga

Shanti Yoga Institute
c/o Prassad Natural Foods
947 Asbury Avenue
Ocean City, NJ 08226
(609)-399-7974
TOPICS: Yoga

Shanti Yoga-Center For Harmony
4325 East West Highway
Bethesda, MD 20814-4405
(202)-362-2656
RETREAT; TOPICS: Holistic Healing, Yoga
OWNER: Victor Landa (Vyasa) **DESCRIPTION:** Purpose of retreat is for Yoga instruction. Offers tapes on Yoga including Hatha-Yoga, Meditation,

Relaxation & Visualization. **PUBLICATIONS:** *Shanti Yoga Newsletter* **PUBLISHER:** Victor Landa (Vyasa) **TOPICS:** Yoga **TYPE:** Newsletter **DESCRIPTION:** Covers various aspects of Yoga.

Shantivanam - Saccidananda Ashram
Tiruchirapalli
Tamil Nadu,
India

RETREAT; CONTACT: Father Bede Griffiths **TOPICS:** New Age, Spirituality, Meditation **DESCRIPTION:** Ashram founded by a Benedictine priest to merge East & West philosophy. Practices chanting & meditation of Christian, Hindu & Buddhist prayers.

Shastasong
16742 Middlecoff Court
Lake Shastina
Weed, CA 96094
(916)-938-3659
TOPICS: Holistic Healing

Shaw Health Center
5336 Fontain Avenue
Los Angeles, CA 90029
(213)-467-5200
TOPICS: Holistic Healing

Shenoa Retreat Center
P.O. Box 43
Philo, CA 95466
(707)-895-3156
TOPICS: Holistic Healing

Shepherd's Bush Centre
5416 Gaston Avenue
Dallas, TX 75214
(214)-823-0292
TOPICS: Holistic Healing

Shiatsu Institute Of Florida
9123 West Sunrise Boulevard
Fort Lauderdale, FL 33322-5273
(305)-476-2657
TOPICS: Massage

Shining Waters Ashram
Route 3
Box 560
Fredericktown, MO 63645
(314)-783-6715
TOPICS: Holistic Healing

Shirley MacLaine's Center-Higher Life Seminars
1900 Avenue Of The Stars
Los Angeles, CA 90067-4303
TOPICS: Holistic Healing, Metaphysics, Parapsychology

Shri Janardan Ajapa Ashram
P.O. Box 1731
Placerville, CA 95667
TOPICS: Metaphysics

Sibyl's Centre, The
P.O. Box 159
Nimbir, NSW 2480
Australia
(066) 891 642
CENTER; TOPICS: Crystals **OWNER:** Alanna Moore, Director **DESCRIPTION:** Called Sibyl's Centre of Dowsing Studies offers workshops in dowsing & earth mysteries. Alanna Moore, director & author of Dowsing Manual, also involved with permaculture design & teaching. Correspondence course-Dowsing For Harmony available.

Sierra Spirit Ranch
3000 Pinenut Road
Gardnerville, NV 89410
(702)-782-7011
TOPICS: Holistic Healing

Silent Meditation Retreat
Box 51BB
Shelburne Falls, MA 01370
(413)-625-9228
TOPICS: Holistic Healing

Sirius Community
P.O. Box 388
Amherst, MA 01004
(413)-259-1505 (413)-259-1251
RETREAT; TOPICS: Holistic Healing, New Age, Spirituality, Meditation, Health Food, Metaphysics **MEMBERS:** 25 **DESCRIPTION:** A democratically run cooperative spiritual community & alternative educational center on 86 acres. Offers meditation, programs in spiritual teachings & community living. Operates cooperative businesses & organic gardens. **PUBLICATIONS:** *New England Network Of Light Directory*, Directory Of 440 Communities **PUBLICATIONS:** *Builders Of The Dawn* **EDITOR:** Corrine McLaughlin, Gordon Davidson **TOPICS:** Holistic Healing **TYPE:** Book

Sivananda Ashram Vrindavan Yoga Farm
14651 Ballantree Lane
Grass Valley, CA 95949
(916)-272-9322
TOPICS: Yoga

Sivananda Ashram Yoga Retreat
P.O. Box N 7550
Paradise Island, Nassau
Bahamas
(809)-363-2902 **FAX** (809)-363-3783
RETREAT; CONTACT: Swami Shanmugananda, Director **TOPICS:** Yoga, Holistic Health, Spirituality, Vegetarianism, Meditation **OWNER:** International Sivananda Yoga Vedanta Ctr **BOOKSTORE; STAFF:** 20 **DESCRIPTION:** Purpose is to teach & provide a place to practice yoga, proper exercise, proper breathing, proper relaxation, proper diet & positive thinking & meditation. Offers a beach with an exercise deck, vegetarian meals served twice daily, 2 yoga exercise & breathing classes daily as well as morning & evening meditations. **PUBLICATIONS:** *Commentary On Ancient Hatha Yoga Pradipika* **EDITOR:** Swami Vishnu-Devananda **TYPE:** Book **PUBLICATIONS:** *Meditation And Mantras* **EDITOR:** Swami Vishnu-Devananda **TYPE:** Book **PUBLICATIONS:** *The Complete Illustrated Book Of Yoga* **EDITOR:** Swami Vishnu-Devananda **TYPE:** Book

Sivananda Yoga Vedanta Ashram
8th Avenue
Val Morin, Quebec J0T 2R0
Canada
(819)-322-3226
RETREAT; TOPICS: New Age, Spirituality, Yoga, Meditation, Holistic Healing **DESCRIPTION:** Spiritual community teaching Hatha Raja yoga, Yoga Teachers' Training course & meditation. Teachings inspired by Swami Vishnu-Devananda & Swami Sivananda.

Sivananda Yoga Vedanta Center
5178 St. Lawrence Boulevard
Montreal, QB, H2T1R8,
Canada
TOPICS: Metaphysics

Sivananda Yoga Vedanta Centers
243 West 24th Street
New York, NY 10011
(212)-255-4560 (800)-783-9642 **FAX** (212)-727-7392
CENTER; TOPICS: Yoga, Meditation, Vegetarianism, Spirituality **BOOKSTORE; STAFF:** 4 **MEMBERS:** 3,000 **DESCRIPTION:** Offers Yoga Asana classes, meditation, vegetarian cooking, residental programs, Yoga variations & retreat. Also provides Yoga teachers' training courses. Has 18 centers worldwide & 5 ashrams. **PUBLICATIONS:** *Meditation And Mantras* **TYPE:** Book **PUBLICATIONS:** *The Sivananda Companion To Yoga* **TYPE:** Book

Sky Foundation
527 South Street
Philadelphia, PA 19147
(215)-923-5946
TOPICS: New Age

Skynet
257 Sycamore Glen
Pasadena, CA 91105
CENTER; TOPICS: UFO's **OWNER:** Ann Druffel **DESCRIPTION:** A UFO filter center & tracking system covering Los Angeles Basin & surrounding areas. Receives reports from public. Most sightings identified as conventional. Strange object sightings investigated, documented & sent to UFO research journals worldwide.

Society For Cultural Advancement & World Brotherhood NOW!, Inc.
71 West Shore Street
Keansburg, NJ 07734
(201)-787-7777
TOPICS: New Age

Sol Duc Resort
Star Route 1
Box 2169
Port Angeles, WA 98362
TOPICS: Holistic Healing

Solar Light Retreat
7700 Avenue Of The Sun
White City, OR 97503
TOPICS: UFO's

Solstice Center For Transformational Medicine
116 West Avenue
Great Barrington, MA 01230
(413)-528-1386 (413)-528-3114
CENTER; TOPICS: Holistic Health, Psychology, Nutrition, Herbalogy, Homeopathy, Acupuncture, Massage **DESCRIPTION:** Dedicated to personal growth, development of the individual & holistic health. Based on Dr. Rudolf Steiner's philosophy of Anthroposophy. Therapy helps achieve a balance

between spiritual, mental, emotional, physical growth & healing as well as preventive medicine.

Source-Life Enrichment Center
2726 Ellendale
St. Louis, MO 63143
(314)-644-0641
CENTER; CONTACT: Rhonda K. Leifheit **TOPICS:** Holistic Healing **DESCRIPTION:** Offers classes in personal & spiritual growth, Imagery work, Readings for health, career, Past Life, Crossing of Paths, & prosperity consciousness. Readings help clients see cause & effect & offer suggestions for healing the body, mind, spirit or relationships. Clients need not be present for Readings.

Southern Dharma Retreat Center
Route 1
Box 34-H
Hot Springs, NC 28743
(704)-622-7112
TOPICS: Holistic Healing

Soyfoods Center
P.O. Box 234
Lafayette, CA 94549
(415)-283-2991
TOPICS: Health Food, New Age **PUBLICATIONS:** *The Book Of Kudzu* **TOPICS:** Health Food **TYPE:** Book **PUBLICATIONS:** *The Book Of Miso* **TOPICS:** Health Food **TYPE:** Book **PUBLICATIONS:** *The Book Of Tempeh* **TOPICS:** Health Food **TYPE:** Book **PUBLICATIONS:** *The Book Of Tofu* **TOPICS:** Health Food **TYPE:** Book

Sphinx Learning Center
1510 Piedmont Avenue
Atlanta, GA 30324
TOPICS: Channeling

Spirit Of Life At The Sharon Springs Health Spa
80 North Moore Street, #36F
New York, NY 10013-2737
(212)-962-2121 (518)-284-2885
SPA; TOPICS: Holistic Healing **DESCRIPTION:** Rejuvenates, regenerates, revitalizes natural beauty & health. Philosophy is life begets life. **PUBLICATIONS:** *Spa Times; Spa Spouts*

Spiritual Center
Box 2614
R.D. #2
Windsor, NY 13865
TOPICS: Holistic Health

Spiritual Frontiers/Northeast Retreat
Elizabethtown College
Elizabethtown, PA 18707
TOPICS: Channeling

Spiritual Healing Center
1739 Anza Street
San Francisco, CA 94118
(415)-221-4058
CENTER; TOPICS: Metaphysics, Holistic Healing **OWNER:** Rev. Joseph Martinez **DESCRIPTION:** Offers Healing performed by Spirit Psychic Surgeons. Psychic Surgery is a removal process which occurs beyond the range of the senses & can only be seen clairvoyantly. This spiritual method removes psychic blockages & energies invisibly although pulling & tugging are often felt. Seminars

offered such as Resurrection Of The Body as well as individual healing sessions.

Spiritual Life Institute
Nada Hermitage
Box 260
Crestone, CO 81131
(303)-256-4778
TOPICS: Metaphysics, New Age

Spiritual Life Institute
Nova Nada
Kemptville, NS B0W 1Y0
Canada
TOPICS: New Age

Spiritual Life Society And Yoga Center
1 East Main Street
Old Church On the Green
Hudson, OH 44236
(216)-650-1216
TOPICS: Holistic Healing

Spiritual Science Institute
P.O. Box 22714
Santa Barbara, CA 93121
TOPICS: Holistic Healing

Spiritual Studies Center (SSC)
P.O. Box 1104
Rockville, MD 20850
TOPICS: New Age, Metaphysics **PUBLICATIONS:** *SSC Booknews* **EDITOR:** Millard Nachtwey **TOPICS:** New Age, Metaphysics **TYPE:** Newsletter **DESCRIPTION:** Provides book review service for the Spiritual Studies Center.

Spiritual Unity Of Nations
1735 Pinnacle Southwest
Wyoming, MI 49509
(616)-531-1339
TOPICS: New Age

Spiritualist Center
6417 Lexington Avenue
Los Angeles, CA 90038
TOPICS: New Age

Spring Hill Of Ashby, Inc.
432 Columbia Street
Cambridge, MA 02141-1000
(617)-864-9181
TOPICS: Holistic Healing

Spring Valley
241 Hungry Hollow Road
Spring Valley, NY 10977
(914)-352-2295
RETREAT; TOPICS: New Age, Holistic Health, Health Food, Spirituality **MEMBERS:** 300 **DESCRIPTION:** New Age community founded on the teachings of Rudolph Steiner. Operates Eurythmy School for adults, nursing home for the elderly, Green Meadow Waldorf School for children, a natural health care products business, a publishing company & the Bio-Dynamic gardening program.

Sri Aurobindo Action Center
P.O. Box 1977
Boulder, CO 80306
TOPICS: Metaphysics

Sri Centre International
21 Olympia Plein
Amsterdam,
The Netherlands
0113120-731034
TOPICS: New Age

Sri Chinmoy Center
Box 32433
Jamaica, NY 11431
TOPICS: New Age, Metaphysics

St. Clare's Hermitage & Retreat
Hermit-Monks of St. Clare's
5984 Rutsatz Road
Deming, WA 98244
RETREAT; TOPICS: New Age, Spirituality **OWNER:** Father Michael Micari **DESCRIPTION:** Beautiful setting in the Cascade foothills. Non-traditional monastic setting established for former monastics who have a balanced view of Eastern & Western spirituality & interest in Thomas Merton's views & his search. Four Zen-type Tea Huts available for retreats. Open to single unattached individuals who cater to Meditation for Consciousness Raising within the realm of Christ. Cost by donation. Members must earn small living with arts or crafts.

Star Dance
1531 Fulton Street
San Francisco, CA 94121
(415)-929-0671
RETREAT; TOPICS: New Age **MEMBERS:** 8 **DESCRIPTION:** Democratically run cooperative household whose members share all responsibilities & resources. Operates a carpentry business.

Stelle
Box 12
Stelle, IL 60919
(815)-256-2200
CENTER; TOPICS: New Age, Holistic Health, Spirituality **MEMBERS:** 125 **DESCRIPTION:** Democratic, ecumenical center located on 240 acres. Comprised of a cooperative market, schools, a factory, greenhouses, an holistic health center & 42 homes. Offers classes on the human potential & workshops on wellness. **PUBLICATIONS:** *Communities Magazine*

Stevea Retreat Center
Box 1155
Arcata, CA 95521
(707)-433-8365
TOPICS: Holistic Healing

Stewart Mineral Springs
4617 Stewart Springs Road
Weed, CA 96094
(916)-938-2222
TOPICS: Holistic Healing

Stiles For Relaxation
4505 Northeast Tillamook
Portland, OR 97213
(503)-281-6789
CENTER; TOPICS: Crystals **DESCRIPTION:** Dedicated to the art of crystal therapy & healing.

Still Mountain Society
Route 1
Fernle, BC V0B 1M0

Canada
(604)-423-6406
TOPICS: New Age

Stillpoint School Of Massage And Center For The Healing Arts
P.O. Box 15
60 Main Street
Hatfield, MA 01038
TOPICS: Holistic Healing

Strong, Stretched And Centered Body/Mind Institute
P.O. Box 758
Paia, Maui, HI 96779
(808)-575-2178
CENTER; TOPICS: Holistic Healing, Body-Mind Connection, Yoga, Tai Chi OWNER: Gloria Keeling STAFF: 12 DESCRIPTION: Six-week body/mind program has a dual purpose. First to train participants as body/mind instructors & then to act as a personal wellness program. Held Spring, Summer & Fall. Students live in an Ocean-Front Condo & study Aerobics, Yoga, Tai Chi, Physiology , Anatomy, Weight Training & much more. PUBLICATIONS: Catalog available on request.

Studies Of Human Systems Center
8604 Jones Mill Road
Chevy Chase, MD 20015
(301)-657-8299
TOPICS: Holistic Healing

Stump Sprouts Lodge, X-Country Ski Center
West Hill Road
West Hawley, MA 01339
(413)-339-4265
RETREAT; TOPICS: Holistic Healing OWNER: Lloyd & Suzanne Crawford DESCRIPTION: Small retreat facility available for rental year round. Set amid breathtaking views of Western Mass. Large organic garden & hand-crafted architecture provide nurturing home-spun setting for cross-country ski vacations, ceremonies, retreats, workshops, etc.

Subud
1329 South Hope Street
Los Angeles, CA 90015
(213)-748-0688
TOPICS: New Age

Sufi Islamia Ruhaniat Society
Heartsong Farm
970 North Oakland Avenue
Fayetteville, AR 72701-1883
(501)-428-5503
TOPICS: New Age

Sufi Islamia Ruhaniat Society
Garden Of Bismillah
851 Regal Road
Berkeley, CA 94708
(415)-527-2569
TOPICS: New Age

Sufi Islamia Ruhaniat Society
Nur Mazil
122 Central Avenue
Capitola, CA 95010
(408)-462-1512
TOPICS: New Age

Sufi Islamia Ruhaniat Society
c/o Ford
P.O. Box 1872
Guerneville, CA 94556
(707)-869-9702
TOPICS: New Age

Sufi Islamia Ruhaniat Society
Garden Of Inayat
910 Railroad Avenue
Novato, CA 94947
(415)-897-5426
TOPICS: New Age

Sufi Islamia Ruhaniat Society
c/o Victoria Tackett
2730 Byron
Palo Alto, CA 94301
(415)-327-5391
TOPICS: New Age

Sufi Islamia Ruhaniat Society
c/o Mentorgarten
410 Precita Avenue
San Francisco, CA 94110
(415)-285-5208
CENTER; CONTACT: Ahmaddin as-Salik TOPICS: New Age, Spirituality OWNER: Samuel L. Lewis DESCRIPTION: Founded by Murshid Sufi Ahmed Murad Chisti (Samuel L. Lewis) a disciple of Pir-O-Murshid Hazrat Inayat Khan. Dedicated to the brotherhood work in uniting the worlds of genuine mysticism & modern philosophical thought. Provides training that leads to the Divine essence in each human being & a life of service to God & humanity. Developed the Dances of Universal Peace as a form of joyful meditation in movement & Sufi Islamia Prophecy Publications to publish the writings of its founder.

Sufi Islamia Ruhaniat Society
248 Laurel Place
San Rafael, CA 94901
(415)-459-4901
TOPICS: New Age

Sufi Islamia Ruhaniat Society
Psalmgarden
9195 Barnett Valley Road
Sebastopol, CA 95472
(707)-823-7106
TOPICS: New Age

Sufi Islamia Ruhaniat Society
200 East Kuiaha Street
Haiku, Maui, HI 96708
TOPICS: New Age

Sufi Islamia Ruhaniat Society
P.O. Box 3024
Taos, NM 87571
(505)-758-8793
CONTACT: c/o Tui Wilschinsky TOPICS: New Age

Sufi Islamia Ruhaniat Society
3100 Southeast 10th Avenue
Portland, OR 97202
(503)-245-0270
TOPICS: New Age

Sufi Islamia Ruhaniat Society
Aguas Callentes 1675 Venus Gardens
Rio Piedra, PR 00926

CONTACT: c/o Carlos Varona TOPICS: New Age

Sufi Islamia Ruhaniat Society
108 4th Street, Northeast
Charlottesville, VA 22901
(804)-293-8821
CONTACT: c/o DHO TOPICS: New Age

Sufi Islamia Ruhaniat Society
4003 1st Avenue, Northwest
Seattle, WA 98107
(206)-547-2374
TOPICS: New Age

Summit University
Box A
Corwin Springs, MT 59021
(406)-848-7441
RETREAT; CONTACT: Murray Steinman TOPICS: Spirituality, Meditation, Holistic Health, Nutrition, New Age OWNER: Elizabeth Clare Prophet DESCRIPTION: Self-sufficient New Age spiritual community & headquarters of Church Universal and Triumphant, The Summit Lighthouse, Montessori International, Henry Wadsworth Longfellow Academy & Summit University Press. Elizabeth Clare Prophet teaches people how to contact their Holy Christ Self & sustain contact with Jesus, Maitreya & the Ascended Masters. Offers seminars, meditaiton, organic farming & macrobiotic cooking on 28,000 acres on the Royal Teton Ranch in the Northern Rockies.

Sun, Man, Moon, Inc.
P.O. Box 5084
Huntington Beach, CA 92646
(714)-840-9192
CENTER; TOPICS: New Age, Dreams OWNER: Janice Baylis DESCRIPTION: Offers dream analysis.

Sun-Mt. Medicine Ways
35751 Oak Springs Drive
Tollhouse, CA 93667
(209)-855-3710
RETREAT; CONTACT: Elf, Coordinator TOPICS: Holistic Healing, Spirituality, Herbalogy OWNER: People, Food & Land Foundation BOOKSTORE; STAFF: 2 DESCRIPTION: Teaches modern tribal shamanic medicine. Seeks visions for the Monday mornings of our lives using drum, flower essences, voice, dance, play, bonding ritual, silence. These vibrational tools help us shut down our ordinary minds so we may journey into the vibrational realm of spirit which connects us all (vegetable, animal, mineral) outside of time & space. One-with-counseling precedes basic weekend training & then to monthly tribal gatherings & periodic mountain, desert pilgrimages. Vegetarian meals. PUBLICATIONS: Bi-monthly newspaper with calendar, articles on herbs, food, shamanic experiences. $25 per year. Sun MT. Recipes-over 200 recipes featuring regional crops, flowers, herbs & wild edibles. $15. PUBLICATIONS: Rainbow Elf TYPE: Book SIZE: 8 1/2 x 11, 100 pgs. PRICE: $15.00 DESCRIPTION: Shamanic visions for our Monday mornings.

Sunbow
14812 S.E. 368 Place
Auburn, WA 98002
(206)-939-8824
RETREAT; TOPICS: New Age, Spirituality MEMBERS: 12 DESCRIPTION: Located on 44 acres.

Comprised of spiritually oriented professional & business people interested in self-enlightenment, service to others & living in harmony & balance with the environment.

Sunflower Yoga Company
1305 Chalmers Road
Silver Spring, MD 20903
(301)-445-3882
TOPICS: Yoga

Sunray Meditation Society
P.O. Box 308
Bristol, VT 05443
(802)-453-4610
TOPICS: Holistic Healing

Sunrise Ranch
Loveland, CO 80537
(303)-667-4675
RETREAT; TOPICS: New Age DESCRIPTION: Headquarters of the organization Emissaries of Divine Light led by Lord Martin Cecil. Organization has 200 communities internationally. Offers workshops on leadership & the Art of Living.

SunRise Springs Resort
Route 14
Box 203
Santa Fe, La Cienega, NM 87505
(505)-471-3600 (800)-772-0500
TOPICS: Holistic Healing

Sunset Spiritualist Camp
P.O. Box 68
Wells, KS 67488
TOPICS: Metaphysics

Supercamp
P.O. Box 5000
Del Mar, CA 92014
(619)-755-7065
TOPICS: New Age

Swaha Meditation & Yoga Center
4210 Braganza Avenue
Coconut Grove, FL 33133
(305)-662-6625
TOPICS: New Age, Meditation, Yoga

Swan Center
23 Benedict Place
Greenwich, CT 06830
(203)-629-2620
CENTER; TOPICS: Holistic Health DESCRIPTION: Offers bodyworks & alternative therapies including Rolfing.

Sweetwater Gardens Hot Tub & Sauna Spa
Box 337
Mendocino, CA 95460
(707)-937-4140 (707)-937-3113
SPA; TOPICS: Holistic Healing, Massage OWNER: John Fliessbach DESCRIPTION: Purpose is to provide a healing center for the Mendocino Coast. A tranquil place with gardens, soothing saunas, hot tubs & a great massage staff. Also offers ocean view lodging. Located in historic Mendocino village.

Swiss Self Healing Retreat
HCR 1151
Payson, AZ 85541

(602)-474-6488
RETREAT; TOPICS: Holistic Health, Spirituality OWNER: Rene Haldimann DESCRIPTION: Non-profit commonwealth located in Gisela, AZ. Purpose is to awaken, heal, balance & integrate our physical, emotional, mental & spiritual aspects & to celebrate our sacred gift of consciousness. Motto: I Take Responsibility For My Self Well Being.

SYDA Foundation & Meditation Center
1107 Stanford Avenue
Oakland, CA 94611
(415)-655-8677
TOPICS: Holistic Healing, Metaphysics

Synergy
4321 Wisconsin Avenue N.W.
Washington, DC 20016
(202)-363-4664
TOPICS: Holistic Healing

Synerobics/Movement Expression
622 Las Lomas
Pacific Palisades, CA 90272
(213)-454-5335
TOPICS: New Age

Synthesis Center
P.O. Box 575
178A North Pleasant Street
Amherst, MA 01004
(413)-256-0772
CENTER; CONTACT: Thom Levy TOPICS: New Age, Body-Mind Connection, Holistic Health, Psychology OWNER: Dorothy Firman DESCRIPTION: Comprehensive approach to psychological health & well-being. Offers psychosynthesis counseling services. Provides holistic, psychospiritual weekend programs, presenting a path to right livelihood. Offers counselor training programs & Psychosynthesis Training.

T'ai Chi Chih Seminars: The Maximum CHI Program
732 Hamlin Way
San Leandro, CA 94578
(415)-895-8614
TOPICS: New Age, Tai Chi

T.A.R.O.T.
P.O. Box 720
Nevada City, CA 95959
(916)-265-3179
CENTER; TOPICS: Metaphysics, Tarot OWNER: Mary K. Greer & Ed Buryn DESCRIPTION: Tools And Rites Of Transformation New Age Learning Center. Presents lectures, classes, workshops relating to Tarot, Women's Mysteries, Menstrual Rites, Right Livlihood, writing & personal growth. Publishes books by owners & a newsletter. PUBLICATIONS: T.A.R.O.T. Newsletter PUBLISHER: Mary K. Greer EDITOR: Ed Buryn TOPICS: Tarot, Metaphysics TYPE: Newsletter

Taeria Spiritual Community Foundation
Box 782
Carrizozo, NM 88301
TOPICS: Holistic Healing

Tanana Sun Chiropractic Center
308 5th Avenue
Fairbanks, AK 99701
(907)-456-2244
CENTER; TOPICS: New Age, Chiropractic, Holistic Health DESCRIPTION: Natural holistic health programs.

Taoist Center, The
420 14th Street
Oakland, CA 94612
(415)-763-9352
TOPICS: New Age, Metaphysics

Taoist Institute
10630 Burbank Boulevard
North Hollywood, CA 91601
(818)-760-4219 (213)-271-9308
CENTER; TOPICS: New Age, Metaphysics OWNER: Rev. Carl Totton DESCRIPTION: Preserves the traditional applied Taoist arts. Courses offered in philosophy, Chinese medicine, Chi Kung, Chinese Yoga, Meditation & Chinese internal martial arts: Kung Fu, Tai Chi, Chuan, Hsing-I, Pa-Kua. Chinese physical & mental systems for health, personal growth & self defense. Certificates up to instructor level awarded in all arts.

Taorima
Krotona Hill
Ojai, CA 93023
(805)-646-5322
RETREAT; TOPICS: New Age, Spirituality MEMBERS: 100 DESCRIPTION: Organization of retired individuals conducting meetings & community activities. Connected with the Theosophical Society at Krotona.

Tara Center
P.O. Box 6001
North Hollywood, CA 91603
TOPICS: Metaphysics

Taurus Farm Bed 'n Breakfast
Box 1543
Ganges, British Columbia V0S 1E0
Canada
(604)-537-4076
TOPICS: Holistic Healing

Tav Center, The
36 Weston Road
Westport, CT 06880
TOPICS: Channeling

Tayu Center (TC)
P.O. Box 11554
Santa Rosa, CA 95406
(707)-829-9579
CENTER; CONTACT: Stuart Goodnick TOPICS: New Age, Metaphysics, Spirituality, Meditation DESCRIPTION: A Fourth Way spiritual school offering an ancient system of spiritual development, brought to the West by G.I. Gurdjieff. The primary Tayu practice is a special form of meditation called Self-observation, designed for those born in Western culture. Its focus is on the 3 major centers of the human organism-motor/instinctive, emotional & intellectual. It reveals the true nature & inner workings of the human organism & opens the way to full & continuous access to True Mind. PUBLICATIONS: The Way Fourth-A Journal Of The

Fourth Way TOPICS: Spirituality, Meditation TYPE: Journal

Tecopa Hot Springs Resort
Box 327
Tecopa, CA 92389
(619)-852-4373
TOPICS: Holistic Healing

Temenos
Box 84-A
Star Route
Shutesbury, MA 01072
RETREAT; TOPICS: New Age, Spirituality DESCRIPTION: Located on 18 acres. Yearround community merging Buddhist & Quaker philosophies of peace, ecology & feminism. Offers retreats & workshops.

Temple Of The Eternal Light
928 East 5th Street
Brooklyn, NY 11230-2104
(718)-438-4878
CENTER; TOPICS: Metaphysics, Yoga, Spirituality, Kabbalah, Witchcraft, Psychic Healing OWNER: Jerome Peartree, D. Th., Pastor DESCRIPTION: An omni-denominational spiritual fellowship devoted to creating awareness of member's divine essence, development & their higher self within through mutual encouragement, sharing knowledge & resources. Through proper meditation, ritual, study & dedication , one may align their consciousness with the divine light. Offers services in Mystical & Earth religion traditions, classes, home study programs, Kaballah, Yiddish Yoga, Magick, Wicca, robes, banners & altar cloths, psychic healing & marriage ceremonies.

Terra Nova Institute
Coast Highway 1
Box 69
Jenner, CA 95450
(707)-865-2377
TOPICS: Holistic Healing

Terre Nouvelle
BP 52-05300
Laragne,
France
RETREAT; TOPICS: New Age, Meditation, Health Food, Holistic Health MEMBERS: 11 DESCRIPTION: Restoration of old village in French Alps motivated by the teachings of the Findhorn Community. Offers meditations, New Age workshops & ceremonial dancing. Income derived from selling vegetables & cheese.

Thermopolis
Hot Springs State Park
State Park Building
Thermopolios, WY 82443
(307)-864-2636
TOPICS: Holistic Healing

Three Mountain Foundation
P.O. Box 1180
Lone Pine, CA 93545
(619)-876-4702
CONTACT: Victor Roberge TOPICS: New Age

Three Mountain Foundation
59 Commonwealth Avenue
Haverhill, MA 01830
(617)-372-5119

TOPICS: Holistic Healing

Tibet Society, The
University Of Indiana
Goodbody Hall 101
Bloomington, IN 47405
(812)-335-2233
TOPICS: New Age

Tibetan Buddhist Learning Center, Inc./Labsum Sherub Ling Monastery
RD 1, P.O. Box 306A
Washington, NJ 07882-9767
(908)-689-6080
CENTER; CONTACT: Joshua W.C. Cutler, Dir. TOPICS: Spirituality DESCRIPTION: Teaches Tibetan Buddhism & its relationship to one's daily life. PUBLICATIONS: *The Door Of Liberation*, 1973; *The Prince Who Became A Cuckoo: A Tale Of Liberation*, 1982; *The Jewelled Staircase*, 1987.

Toronto Healing Arts Centre
715 Bloor Street West
Toronto, Ontario M6G 1L5
Canada
(416)-535-8777
TOPICS: Holistic Healing

Toronto Health Education Centre
258 Dupont Street
Toronto, Ontario M5R 1V7
Canada
(416)-926-1788
TOPICS: Holistic Healing

Torralvoma Research Center
242 East 14th Street
New York, NY 10003
TOPICS: Metaphysics

Touchstone Center
12084 211th Street
Maple Ridge, British Columbia V2X 8K8
Canada
(604)-463-9879
TOPICS: Holistic Healing

Transcendental Meditation
17310 Sunset Boulevard
Pacific Palisades, CA 90272
TOPICS: New Age

Transformational Arts Institute
1380 Pacific Street
Redlands, CA 92373
(714)-793-0054
TOPICS: Holistic Healing

Transpersonal Institute
4933 Auburn Avenue
Bethesda, MD 20814
TOPICS: Holistic Healing

Traprock Peace Center-Woolman Hill
Keets Road
Deerfield, MA 01342
(413)-773-7427
RETREAT; TOPICS: New Age, Spirituality MEMBERS: 8 DESCRIPTION: Community based on Quaker philosophy. Offers conferences & workshops to educate & promote the principles of world peace.

Trusteeship Institute

Baker Road
Shutesbury, MA 01072
(413)-253-7500
TOPICS: Holistic Healing

Truth Center, The
640 East Grand Avenue
Englewood, CO 80110-6908
(303)-789-4979
TOPICS: Holistic Healing

Truth Of Life Center
14527 South Vermont Avenue
Gardena, CA 90247
TOPICS: Metaphysics

Truth Of Life Center
777 North 7th Street
San Jose, CA 95112
TOPICS: Metaphysics

Truth Of Life Center
305 East 16th Avenue
Vancouver, BC V5T 2T7
Canada
TOPICS: Metaphysics

Turning Point-Family Wellness Center
173 Mount Auburn Street
Watertown, MA 02172
(617)-923-4604
TOPICS: Holistic Healing

Turnwood Organic Gardens, Inc.
79 Quaker Hill Road
Monroe, NY 10950-1542
(914)-439-5702
TOPICS: Holistic Healing

Twin Oaks Community
R.R. 4G, Box 169
Louisa, VA 23093
(703)-894-5126
RETREAT; TOPICS: New Age, Health Food, Holistic Health MEMBERS: 60 DESCRIPTION: Ecology conscious, cooperative community located on 500 acres promoting peace, equality, unity & harmony. Practices the reversal of traditional roles for men & women. Economically self-sufficient from the production of a farm, garden & hammock business. PUBLICATIONS: *Leaves Of Twin Oaks* EDITOR: Kat Kinkade TOPICS: New Age TYPE: Magazine

Two Bunch Palms
67-425 Two Bunch Palms Trail
Desert Hot Springs, CA 92240
(714)-329-8791
TOPICS: Holistic Healing

Tzaddi Center
321 Ximeno Avenue
Long Beach, CA 90814
(213)-438-9706
TOPICS: Holistic Healing

UFO Contact Center International
1317 Green Valley Drive
Neenah, WI 94956-1920
TOPICS: UFO's

UFO Data Center

8033 Sunset Boulevard, 5117
Los Angeles, CA 90064
TOPICS: UFO's

UFO Educational Center
P.O. Box 55
Valley Central, CA 92092
TOPICS: UFO's

UFO Information Center
4256 Springboro Road
Lebanon, OH 45036
TOPICS: UFO's

UFO Information Retrieval Center (UFOIRC)
3131 West Cochise Drive, #158
Phoenix, AZ 85051
(602)-997-1523
CONTACT: Thomas M. Olsen, Pres. TOPICS: UFO's

United Federation Of Humankind
2505 Paris Avenue
Trevose, PA 19047
CENTER; TOPICS: Metaphysics BOOKSTORE; STAFF: 42 DESCRIPTION: Purpose is to achieve joyous wakefullness in all our members. The U.F.H. is going through reorganization & requires your input. The primary guides are Ouspensky's, The 4th Way; Millman's, Way Of The Peaceful Warrior; Heinlein's, Stranger In A Strange Land. AFFILIATED ORGS: Sylvan Society-Metaphysical Research Development & Education; Individuals Against Mediocrity Unlimited COMPUTER SERVICES: Bulletin Board on line on 92 CONVENTIONS: To begin in 1993 in NY, NC, PA, TN, KY, AZ, CA

United Research Light Center
2200 Highway 9, South
P.O. Box 1146
Black Mountain, NC 28711
(704)-669-6845
TOPICS: Holistic Healing

United World Prosperity Corporation
3275 Martin Road
Walled Lake, MI 48088
(313)-669-2620
TOPICS: Holistic Healing

Unity Center
871 Geary Road
Walnut Creek, CA 94596
(415)-937-2191
TOPICS: New Age

Unity Center For Growth And Healing
3500 Sharon View Road
Charlotte, NC 28211
(704)-553-0756
TOPICS: Holistic Healing

Unity Woods Yoga Center
4853 Cordell Avenue
Bethesda, MD 20814
(301)-656-8992
CENTER; CONTACT: Esther Geiger TOPICS: Yoga, Meditation, Spirituality OWNER: John Schumacher BOOKSTORE; STAFF: 9 MEMBERS: 450 DESCRIPTION: Offers Hatha Yoga classes for students of all ability levels, guest teachers, special workshops, teacher training & monthly discussion groups on yoga philosophy. Serves the Washington, D.C. metropolitan area. PUBLICATIONS: Quarterly newsletter

Universal Brotherhood Movement, Incorporated
1212 Southwest 15th Avenue
Ft. Lauderdale, FL 33312
(305)-763-4591
TOPICS: New Age

Universal Creative Center
177-F Riverside Avenue #2
Newport Beach, CA 92663
(714)-631-1668
CONTACT: Reverend Karlyn TOPICS: Psychic DESCRIPTION: Psychic teacher offering development classes, seasonal camping/retreats & parties.

Universal Great Brotherhood
Solarline
Box 9154
St. Louis, MO 63117
(314)-726-5133
CONTACT: Mark Shearman TOPICS: Holistic Healing, Metaphysics, Yoga, Meditation

Universal Great Brotherhood, Solar Line
Consejo Superior, Eugenia 1510
C.P. 03020
Mexico, 12 D.F.
Mexico
TOPICS: New Age

Universal Life Alliance
P.O. Box 46204
Seattle, AZ 98146-0204
(602)-894-6175
TOPICS: Holistic Healing

University Of Melchizedek
Route 1, Box 220
Castleton, VA 22716
(703)-937-5219
CENTER; CONTACT: Patricia Jepson Chase TOPICS: New Age, Spirituality, Metaphysics DESCRIPTION: Association of Sananda & Sanat Kumara. Spiritual, truth teachings from the Order of Melchizedek.

University Of The Trees
13151 Pine Street
P.O. Box 644
Boulder Creek, CA 95006
(408)-338-9362
CENTER; TOPICS: New Age, Meditation, Body-Mind Connection, Holistic Healing DESCRIPTION: Offers classes on self-healing, meditation, stress reduction. Operates cooperative companies such as University of the Trees Press & Lightforce-Spirulina Co. PUBLICATIONS: Ancient Egyptian Herbal EDITOR: Lise Manniche TOPICS: Herbalogy, Holistic Healing, Spirituality, Alchemy TYPE: Book PRICE: $19.95 PUBLICATIONS: Nuclear Evolution EDITOR: C. Hills TOPICS: New Age, Psychology TYPE: Book PRICE: $29.95 PUBLICATIONS: To The One I Love EDITOR: C. Hills TOPICS: Paranormal Phenomena, Spirituality TYPE: Book PRICE: $14.95

Unusual And Unique, The
1025 Fair Oaks Boulevard
Fair Oaks, CA 95628-7111
(916)-985-0271
CENTER; TOPICS: Crystals DESCRIPTION: Dedicated to the art of crystal therapy & healing.

Vail Athletic Club Hotel
352 East Meadow Drive
Vail, CO 81657
(303)-476-0700
TOPICS: Holistic Healing

Valley View Hot Springs
Box 175
Villa Grove, CO 81155
TOPICS: Holistic Healing

Vallombrosa Center
250 Oak Grove Avenue
Menlo Park, CA 94025
(415)-325-5614
TOPICS: Holistic Healing

Vampire Research Center
P.O. Box 252
Elmhurst, NY 11373
(718)-894-6564
CENTER; TOPICS: Vampires, Occult, Parapsychology DESCRIPTION: Conducts in-depth study of vampires. Created a new social science called Vampirology. Provides information services, conducts seminars & workshops, distributes publications & data compilations, & makes referrals to other sources of information.

Vancouver White Lodge
548 English Bluff Road
Delta, BC, V4M 2N3
Canada
(604)-943-6689
CENTER; TOPICS: Crystals DESCRIPTION: Dedicated to the art of crystal therapy & healing.

Vedanta Center - Anada Ashram
P.O. Box 8555
La Crescenta, CA 91214
(213)-248-1931
TOPICS: New Age

Vedanta Centre
130 Beechwood Street
Cohasset, MA 02025
(617)-383-0940
TOPICS: New Age, Metaphysics

Vedanta Society Of Northern California
2323 Vallejo Street
San Francisco, CA 94123
(415)-922-2323
TOPICS: Metaphysics, New Age

Vedic Research Center
P.O. Box 8357
Santa Fe, NM 87504
TOPICS: Metaphysics

Vega Study Center
1511 Robinson Street
Oroville, CA 95965
(916)-533-7702

CENTER; CONTACT: Carl Ferre TOPICS: Holistic Healing OWNER: Herman Aihara BOOKSTORE; STAFF: 18 DESCRIPTION: Offers 1 & 2 week workshops for new & advanced students on macrobiotic cooking, therapy, lifestyle & counselling. Students participate in hands-on cooking classes, lectures, chanting & natural exercise sessions.

Venkatesa Yoga And Healing Centre
P.O. Box 370
Reading RG4 0EW,
England

CENTER; CONTACT: Ambika Ife TOPICS: Crystals DESCRIPTION: Dedicated to the art of crystal therapy & healing.

Ventana Inn
Big Sur, CA 93920
(408)-628-6500

TOPICS: Holistic Healing

Vichy Springs Resort
2605 Vichy Springs Road
Ukiah, CA 95482
(707)-462-9515

TOPICS: Holistic Healing

Victoria Attunement Centre
Suite 1
2727 Quadra Street
Victoria, British Columbia V8T 4E5
Canada
(604)-383-1243

TOPICS: Holistic Healing

Vipassana Meditation Center
Box 24
Shelburne Falls, MA 01370

TOPICS: New Age

Vision Quest
3200 East Los Angeles Avenue
Simi Valley, CA 93063
(805)-527-7297

TOPICS: Holistic Healing

Visions And Dreams
1804 Newport Boulevard
Costa Mesa, CA 92627
(714)-650-6929

CENTER; TOPICS: Crystals DESCRIPTION: Dedicated to the art of crystal therapy & healing.

Vita-Dell Spa
13495 Palm Drive
Desert Hot Springs, CA 92240
(714)-329-6200

TOPICS: Holistic Healing

Vital Health Center
17200 Ventura Boulevard
Suite 305
Encino, CA 91316
(213)-986-0886

TOPICS: Holistic Healing

Vital-Life Training Institute
954 Capri Road
Encinitas, CA 92024
(619)-436-9642

TOPICS: Holistic Healing

Vortex CCM

8600 N.W. 24th Street
Sunrise, FL 33322
(305)-748-4848

TOPICS: New Age

Voyagers Of Light
462 South Golbert Road #787
Mesa, AZ 85204-2818
(602)-899-3338

TOPICS: Holistic Healing

Wainwright House-Center For Development Of Human Potential (WHCDHP)
260 Stuyvesant Avenue
Rye, NY 10580
(914)-967-6080

CENTER; CONTACT: Dr. Franklin E. Vilas, Jr., Exec. Officer TOPICS: New Age, Spirituality, Astrology, Numerology, Metaphysics, Holistic Health, Psychology BOOKSTORE; STAFF: 15 DESCRIPTION: Non-profit, non-sectarian education conference center offering lectures, courses & workshops in astrology, numerology, spirituality & A Course In Miracles, health, psychology, global issues, business leadership & the arts. Located in a stately stone mansion overlooking Long Island Sound, it seeks to bridge new frontiers of thought with the traditional. Publishes Catalogue of Programs 3 times a year.

Warm Mineral Springs
San Servando Avenue
Warm Mineral Springs, FL 33595
(813)-426-1231

TOPICS: Holistic Healing

Washington Center For Atitudinal Healing
P.O. Box 40901
Washington, DC 20016

TOPICS: Metaphysics

Washington Psychic Institute/Church Of Divine Man
1906 Southeast Ankeny
Portland, OR 97214
(503)-232-3443

CENTER; TOPICS: New Age DESCRIPTION: Offers psychic counseling & spiritual education.

Washington Psychic Institute/Church Of Divine Man
111 Central
Bellingham, WA 98225
(206)-671-4291

CENTER; TOPICS: New Age, Psychic Phenomena, Spirituality DESCRIPTION: Offers psychic counseling & spiritual education.

Washington Psychic Institute/Church Of Divine Man
2308 Lombard
Everett, WA 98201
(206)-258-1449

CENTER; TOPICS: New Age, Spirituality, Psychic Phenomena DESCRIPTION: Offers psychic counseling & spiritual education.

Washington Psychic Institute/Church Of Divine Man

2007 Northwest 61st
Seattle, WA 98207
(206)-782-3617

CENTER; TOPICS: New Age DESCRIPTION: Offers psychic counseling & spiritual education.

Washington Psychic Institute/Church Of Divine Man
2803 North Lincoln
Spokane, WA 99205
(509)-325-5771

CENTER; TOPICS: New Age DESCRIPTION: Offers psychic counseling & spiritual education.

Washington Psychic Institute/Church Of Divine Man
4604 North 38th
Tacoma, WA 98407
(206)-759-7460

CENTER; TOPICS: New Age DESCRIPTION: Offers psychic counseling & spiritual education.

Washington Psychic Institute/Church Of Divine Man
655 West 7th Avenue
Vancouver, BC V5Z 1B7
Canada
(604)-879-8707

CENTER; TOPICS: New Age, Metaphysics DESCRIPTION: Offers psychic counseling & spiritual education.

Waunita Hot Springs Ranch
Doyleville, CO 81225
(303)-641-1266

TOPICS: Holistic Healing

We Are One In The Spirit
Route 2, Box 535
Colville, WA 99114

SPA; TOPICS: New Age DESCRIPTION: Christ Maitreya service oriented community.

We Care Health Center
18000 Long Canyon Road
Dept. NAJ
Desert Hot Springs, CA 92240
(619)-251-2261

TOPICS: Holistic Healing

Well Being Center
100 Valley Road
Montclair, NJ 07042
(201)-746-5361 (201)-744-5667

CENTER; CONTACT: Martha Sachs TOPICS: Crystals, Holistic Health DESCRIPTION: Dedicated to the art of crystal therapy & varied forms of healing. Offers seminars & workshops such as The Human Aura, East Meets West Healing, Chinese Beliefs Of Energy & a Raw Foods Demonstration & Lecture.

Wellness Counseling Center And Holistic School Of Massage
173 Seminary Avenue
Box 1199
Ukiah, CA 95482
(707)-462-0609

TOPICS: Holistic Healing

Wellness Now
24432 Muirlands Boulevard, Ste. 111

El Toro, CA 92630
(714)-768-3343
TOPICS: Holistic Healing

Wellspring Renewal Center
Box 332
Philo, CA 95446
(707)-895-3893
TOPICS: Holistic Healing

Wellsprings Farm
5855 Yadlinville
Pfafftown, NC 27040
(919)-922-4082
TOPICS: Holistic Healing

West End Holistic Centre
12 Heintzman Street
Toronto, Ontario M6P 2J6
Canada
(416)-763-3211
TOPICS: Holistic Healing

Westchester Acupuncture Center
650 Main Street
Suite 4EE
New Rochelle, NY 10801
(914)-633-9550
CONTACT: Hui-Jun Song, C.M.D. TOPICS: Acupuncture

Westchester Kripalu Yoga Center
23 Merritt Avenue
White Plains, NY 10606
(914)-761-7491
TOPICS: Yoga

Whispering Pines
114 Pine Grove Raod
Scroggins, TX 75280
(214)-860-3326
TOPICS: Holistic Healing

White Dove Farm
P.O. Box 638
Fork Union, VA 23055
(804)-842-5555
SPA; TOPICS: Dreams, Holistic Health, Parapsychology, Holistic Healing, ESP OWNER: Susanna Van de Castle DESCRIPTION: Promotes health & happiness through the study of dreams, parapsychology, telepathy, ESP, holistic healing & health.

White Lotus Foundation
2500 San Marcos Pass
Santa Barbara, CA 93105
(805)-964-1944
RETREAT; CONTACT: Tracey Rich TOPICS: Yoga, Meditation BOOKSTORE; DESCRIPTION: Located on 40 acres in the mountains overlooking Santa Barbara & the Channel Islands. Offers hot tubs, stream & sandstone swimming holes, vegetarian food, world-class bodywork & accommodations in yurts-dome structures. PUBLICATIONS: *Flow Series Yoga Video*

White Sulphur Baths, Inc.
P.O. Box 328
Sharon Springs, NY 13459
(518)-284-2285
TOPICS: Holistic Healing

Whole Health Institute
4817 North County Road 29
Loveland, CO 80537
(303)-679-4306
TOPICS: Holistic Healing PUBLICATIONS: *Healing Currents* EDITOR: Larry Krantz, Janet Lang TOPICS: Holistic Healing TYPE: Magazine

Wholistic Center
10110 82nd Avenue
Edmonton, AT, T6E1Z4,
Canada
TOPICS: Holistic Health

Wholistic Health Center
1 Salt Creek Lane
Hinsdale, IL 60521-2936
(312)-323-1920
TOPICS: Holistic Healing

Wholistic Health Center
50 Maple Place
Manhasset, NY 11030
(516)-627-0309
TOPICS: Holistic Healing

Wholistic Health Center
4979 West 130th Street, Booth 24
Cleveland, OH 44135
(603)-363-4526
CENTER; TOPICS: Crystals DESCRIPTION: Dedicated to the art of crystal therapy & healing.

Wholistic Health Education Center
715 Monroe Avenue
Rochester, NY 14607
(716)-442-5480
TOPICS: Holistic Healing

Wholistic Resource Center
Box 5164
Eugene, OR 97405
(503)-683-1760
TOPICS: Astrology PUBLICATIONS: *Welcome To Planet Earth* EDITOR: Mark Lerner, Percy Franklin TOPICS: Astrology TYPE: Journal FREQ: monthly CIRC: 12,000 PRICE: $25.00 DESCRIPTION: Features articles, news & ads relating to astrology.

Wholistic Resource Center
838 Rivermont Avenue
Lynchburg, VA 24504
(804)-528-2816
TOPICS: Holistic Healing PUBLICATIONS: *Wholeperson Communications* EDITOR: Ellyn Cowels TOPICS: Holistic Healing TYPE: Newsletter

Wiesbaden Hot Springs And Lodgings
625 5th Avenue
P.O. Box 349
Ouray, CO 81427
(303)-325-4347
TOPICS: Holistic Healing

Wilbur Hot Springs Health Sanctuary
Star Route
Williams, CA 95987
(916)-473-2306
TOPICS: Holistic Healing

Wildwood Resort-Retreat
Box 78
Guerneville, CA 95446

(707)-632-5321
TOPICS: Holistic Healing

Willow Retreat
6517 Dry Creek Road
Napa, CA 94558
(707)-944-8173
RETREAT; TOPICS: Holistic Healing, Nutrition OWNER: Liz Luster DESCRIPTION: Secluded retreat facility in the hills between The Napa & Sonoma Valleys. Hot tub, sauna, tennis court, solar-healted pool, massage, hiking trails. Available to individuals & groups up to 85 persons.

Window Of The West
Star Route
Box 94
Carmel Valley, CA 93924
(408)-659-0433
TOPICS: Holistic Healing

Winged Heart Homestead
P.O. Box 552
Floyd, VA 24091
(703)-763-3728
TOPICS: Holistic Healing

Winning Edge, The
P.O. Box 5658
Somerset, NJ 08875
(201)-247-3685 (800)-462-3013
CENTER; CONTACT: Joan Fericy, Dir. TOPICS: Holistic Healing, Metaphysics, Spirituality BOOKSTORE; STAFF: 5 BUDGET: $40,000.00 DESCRIPTION: Provides metaphysical teachings & spiritual healing. Publishing house for 2 self-published books & 4 audio tapes. AFFILIATED ORGS: Holistic Health Association Of Princeton; National Spiritual Healers; World's Who Who Of Women; NJAWBO COMPUTER SERVICES: Phone modem PUBLICATIONS: *Choose To Love Yourself* EDITOR: Joan Fericy TYPE: Booklet DATE: 1987, 32 pgs. PRICE: $3.95 DESCRIPTION: Teaches one to love yourself which brings peaceful satisfaction & that self-esteem is your most important asset. PUBLICATIONS: *Let Go Of The Struggle* EDITOR: Joan Fericy TYPE: Booklet DATE: 1989, 42 pgs. PRICE: $3.95 DESCRIPTION: Inspirational messages that teach one to build on your own strengths & lead a happier life. Simplifed reminder of how to reclaim your peace of mind.

Winnipeg Center For Attitudinal Healing
P.O. Box 1
St. Norbert, Manitoba R3V 1L5
Canada
(204)-269-1502
TOPICS: Holistic Healing

Wise Woman Center
P.O. Box 64
Woodstock, NY 12498
(914)-246-8081
CENTER; TOPICS: Holistic Healing, Spirituality, Herbalogy, New Age BOOKSTORE; STAFF: 2 DESCRIPTION: A safe space for women to learn & heal. A place filled with fairies, green witches, goats & goddesses. Here we reweave the story cape of the ancient ones & resound the song lines. Focuses on women's health & spirituality. Courses offered: herbal medicine with Susun Weed, women's spirituality with Vicki Noble, Merlin Stone, etc.

Home study course for green witches available. **PUBLICATIONS:** *Wise Woman Calendar*, $1 per year.

Woman's Healing Ground
37010 S.E. Snuffin Road
Estacada, OR 97023
(503)-630-7848
TOPICS: Holistic Healing

Women In Spiritual Education (W.I.S.E.)
P.O. Box 697
Point Reyes Station, CA 94956
(415)-663-8280
TOPICS: New Age

Women's Massage Center
125-131 Main Street
Centre Parc, Suite 207
Mt. Kisco, NY 10549
(914)-242-9205
TOPICS: Massage

Women's Spiritual Center
P.O. Box 1831
Santa Fe, NM 87504
(505)-986-3499
TOPICS: Holistic Healing

Woodbury Yoga Center
122 West Side Road
Woodbury, CT 06798
(203)-263-2254
TOPICS: Yoga

Woolman Hill Conference Center
Keets Road
Deerfield, MA 01342
(413)-774-3431
RETREAT; CENTER; CONTACT: Douglas Bishop or Bonnie Deutsch, Directors **TOPICS:** Holistic Healing **STAFF:** 3 **DESCRIPTION:** Quaker center located on 110 tranquil acres offering clean but rustic accommodations for conferences & retreats. Topics discussed include peace & justic, personal growth & spiritual nurture. Provides opportunity for rest, renewal & reflection. **PUBLICATIONS:** *News From Woolman Hill Newsletter*, twice a year. A Conference Series Brochure, once a year.

World Council Unity-And-Diversity
1010 South Flower Street, #500
Los Angeles, CA 90015

(213)-742-6832
TOPICS: Holistic Healing

World Fellowship Center
Conway, NH 03818
(603)-447-2280
TOPICS: New Age

World Healing Center
725 Seabright Lane
Solana Beach, CA 92075
TOPICS: Holistic Healing

World Sideral Reserach Foundation
24 Colorado
Highland Park, MI 48203
(313)-883-1012
TOPICS: New Age

World Synergy Institute
P.O. Box 24242
Los Angeles, CA 90024
(213)-821-1302
TOPICS: Holistic Healing

Wy'East Healing Center
P.O. Box 1031
Sandy, OR 97005
(503)-668-7698
TOPICS: Holistic Healing

Wyebridge Centre, The
74 Madison Avenue
Toronto, Ontario M5R 2S4
Canada
(416)-924-9070
TOPICS: Holistic Healing

Yo San University Clinic
1314 Second Street
Santa Monica, CA 90401
(310)-207-3890
CENTER; TOPICS: Spirituality, Holistic Health, Acupuncture, Herbalogy **OWNER:** Master Ni **DESCRIPTION:** Affiliated teaching clinic of Yo San University. Offers medical care for a wide range of health conditions or preventive care for an enhanced quality of life. Services include treatments with acupuncture, herbs, moxibustion or massage. Also offers consultations on diet, exercise & lifestyle.

Yoga Anand Ashram, Incorporated
42 Merrick Road
Burdett, NY 11701

(516)-691-8475
TOPICS: New Age, Yoga

Yoga Shakti Mission
3895 Hield Road, N.W.
Palm Bay, FL 32907
(407)-725-4024
CENTER; CONTACT: Shyam Shakti **TOPICS:** Holistic Health, New Age, Yoga **OWNER:** Ma Yoga Shakti **DESCRIPTION:** Non-profit organization whose purpose is to teach all 4 aspects of Yoga & to promote the Yoga philosophy for health, happiness & wisdom. Offers Yoga retreats, Satsang, Yoga classes, workshops, gatherings & East-West functions.

Yoga Society Of San Francisco
2872 Folsom Street
San Francisco, CA 94110
(415)-285-5537
TOPICS: Yoga

Yoga Therapy Center
369 Tappan Street, Suite 1
Boston, MA 02146
(617)-232-3798
TOPICS: New Age, Yoga

Yoga Works
1426 Montana Avenue
Second Floor
Santa Monica, CA 90403
(213)-393-5150
TOPICS: Yoga

Zen Center Of Los Angeles, Incorporated
923 South Normandie Avenue
Los Angeles, CA 90006
(213)-387-2351
TOPICS: New Age

Zen Center San Francisco/Tassajara
300 Page Street
San Francisco, CA 94102
(415)-863-3136 (415)-626-3697
TOPICS: New Age

Zen Studies Society
223 East 67th Street
New York, NY 10021
(212)-861-3333
TOPICS: Body-Mind Connection, Metaphysics

Schools

This section provides listings of various types of schools and courses, accredited and unaccredited. It includes correspondence, unorthodox fields of study, independent study programs, etc. Also check Associations, Centers and Bookstores for additional schools and courses.

A-On'O Center Of Light
P.O. Box 484
Sedona, AZ 86336-0484
CONTACT: Rev. Cylvia Lowe TOPICS: Metaphysics, Meditation, Holistic Healing, Spirituality, Parapsychology DIRECTOR: Rev. Cylvia Lowe DESCRIPTION: Independent home study courses: healing techniques, guidelines to using the pendulum, meditation, concentration, observation, focusing, color values, detecting auras, psychic sciences, breathing exercises, parapsychology & metaphysics. Certificate upon completion of course.

Academy For Intuitive Arts
121 Melody Lane
Belton, MO 64012
(816)-322-3106
TOPICS: New Age, Metaphysics

Academy Of Astrologers
43 Jane Road
Hauppague, NY 11787
TOPICS: Astrology

Academy Of Astrology
1135 Clifton Avenue
Clifton, NJ 07013
TOPICS: Astrology

Academy Of Chinese Culture & Health Sciences
420 14th Street
Oakland, CA 94612
(415)-763-7787
TOPICS: Tai Chi, Yoga, Reincarnation, Holistic Healing, Acupuncture, Meditation

Academy Of New Church College And Theological School (General Church Of The New Jerusalem)
Bryn Athyn, PA 19009
TOPICS: Spirituality

Academy Of Psychic Arts And Science
3527 Oak Lawn, 233
Dallas, TX 75219
TOPICS: Metaphysics

Acadia University
Wolfville, NS BOP 1 XO
Canada
TOPICS: Parapsychology

Acupressure Institute
1533 Shattuck Avenue
Berkeley, CA 94709
(415)-845-1059
TOPICS: Holistic Healing, Acupuncture DEPT.: Emotional Balancing & Healing DEPT. HEAD: Candace Coar, Student Affairs COURSE: Basic Training In Oriental Bodywork INSTRUCTOR: 15 Acupressure Institute Instructors DESCRIPTION: A certified 150 hour training program, offered as a 3 week intensive, teaches 75 acupressure points, the 12 meridians, 5 element theory, pulse & face reading, Shiatsu, Jin Shin acupressure, oriental dietary therapy, breath work & acupressure techniques for all areas of the body. COURSE: Acupressure For Emotional Balancing INSTRUCTOR: Michael Reed Gach DESCRIPTION: Teaches how to care for sports injuries, increase athletic performance & relieve arthritic pains. Covers acupressure point formulas, body psychology & counseling skills for dealing with trauma, abuse & emotional release. DEGREES: 3 Certified Program Trainings BOOKSTORE; DESCRIPTION: Provides free color brochure to mail order special books, tapes & videos. Offers flexible course scheduling. Publications: Acupressure Workshop EDITOR: Michael Reed Gach TOPICS: Holistic Healing TYPE: Book

Acupressure-Acupuncture Institute
9835 Sunset Drive, Ste. 206
Miami, FL 33173
(305)-595-9500
TOPICS: Holistic Healing, Acupuncture, Herbalogy, Massage, Tai Chi, Homeopathy DEPT. HEAD: Nancy Browne COURSE: Acupuncture INSTRUCTOR: Richard Browne, C.A., Dr. of Acupuncture DESCRIPTION: Teaches you to discover your power to heal. 2 year course to become an Acupuncture Physician. Curriculum includes Chinese herbs, homeopathy, Tai Chi & Chi Kung. Oldest acupuncture school in Florida. Day or evening classes. COURSE: Massage INSTRUCTOR: Richard Browne, C.A., L.M.T. DESCRIPTION: 6 month training in Massage Therapy. Graduates eligible for State Exam. Emphasis on Shiatsu/Acupressure Therapy. DEGREES: Degrees in Acupuncture & Massage PUBLICATIONS: Newsletter published 3 times per year.

African Theological Archministry, Oyontunji African Yoruba Village
Box 51
Sheldon, SC 29941
TOPICS: Spirituality

Albert Grier School of Religious Studies (International Alliance of Churches of the Truth)
690 E. Orange Grove Boulevard
Pasadena, CA 91104
TOPICS: Spirituality

Alchemical Hypnotherapy Institute
2310 Warwick Drive
Santa Rosa, CA 95405-8614
(707)-579-4984 (800)-579-4984
TOPICS: Holistic Healing, Hypnotism DEPT.: Hypnotherapy DEPT. HEAD: David Quigley COURSE: Alchemical Hypnotherapy INSTRUCTOR: David Quigley DESCRIPTION: 100 hour professional Master Hypnotist Training certification course. Training in emotional clearing, regression, inner guide work, conference room, subpersonality work & conducting a professional practice. COURSE: 50 Hour Advanced Hypnotherapist Training DESCRIPTION: Specialized training in various applications of Alchemical Hypnotherapy such as weight loss, pain & disease control, etc. PUBLICATIONS: Alchemical Hypnotherapy Manual by David Quigley, 63 pages, $5.95. Alchemical Journal - free newsletter published annually since 1985.

Alexander Training Institute of San Francisco
450 Geary Street
San Francisco, CA 94114
TOPICS: Parapsychology

Alive & Well! Institute of Conscious Bodywork
100 Shaw Drive
San Anselmo, CA 94960
TOPICS: Holistic Healing, Body-Mind Connection, Nutrition

American Academy Of Shiatsu Therapy
602 Kailua Road
No. 205B
Kailua, HI 96734
TOPICS: Spirituality

American Buddhist Academy (Buddhist Churches of America)
331 Riverside Drive
New York, NY 10025
TOPICS: Spirituality

American Center For The Alexander Technique
129 W. 67th Street
New York, NY 10023
(212)-799-0468
TOPICS: Holistic Healing DEGREES: 3 year graduate Teacher's Certificate DESCRIPTION: Offers information, resources, a referral center, training & certificate programs in the Alexander Technique which is an educational process teaching improved use of the body and identifying & changing poor physical habits which may cause stress & fatigue . Founded 1964. Accepts a maximum of 6 students each Fall & Winter term. Application deadlines: July 1 & Oct. 1.

American College Of Nutripathy

6821 E. Thomas Road
Scottsdale, AZ 85251
(602)-946-5515
TOPICS: Holistic Healing, Nutrition

American College of Traditional Chinese Medicine
455 Arkansas Street
San Francisco, CA 94107
TOPICS: Holistic Healing, Yoga, Body-Mind Connection, Herbalogy

American Holistic College Of Nutrition
1704 11th Avenue S.
Birmingham, AL 35205
(800)-638-4590
TOPICS: Holistic Healing DESCRIPTION: Offers the B.S., M.S. & Ph. D. degrees in nutrition by correspondence. The graduate will have the knowledge & skills to operate a nutritional counseling practice. More than 1,000 students worldwide.

American Institute Of Hypnotherapy
1805 E. Garry Avenue, # 100
Santa Ana, CA 92705
(714)-261-6400
TOPICS: Hypnotism, Holistic Health

American School Of Astrology
21 Mellon Avenue
West Orange, NJ 07052
(201)-731-2255
CONTACT: Sylvia Sherman TOPICS: Astrology

American Society For Psychical Research, Inc. (ASPR)
5 West 73rd Street
New York, NY 10023
(212)-799-5050
CONTACT: Donna L. McCormick, Dir. TOPICS: Parapsychology, Psychic Phenomena, ESP, Death, Dreams, Psychic Healing, Dowsing COURSE: Historical & Modern Trends in Parapsychological Research INSTRUCTOR: Patrice Keane DESCRIPTION: Examines PSI research through experimentation & historical evaluation. Covers healing, psychokinesis & altered states of consciousness. DEGREES: non-credit

Ananda School
Ananda Community
14618 Tyler Foote
Nevada City, CA 95959
(916)-292-3777
TOPICS: Spirituality, Holistic Health DESCRIPTION: Based on Education For Life, a holistic system which invites personal & global transformation. Offers grade school program, K-9. Teacher training offered. Books & tapes available.

Anglo-American Institute of Drugless Therapy
30 Kinloch Road
Renfrew,
Scotland
TOPICS: Holistic Health, Herbalogy

Antioch University-SAEL
800 Livermore Street
Yellow Springs, OH 45387

(513)-767-6325
CONTACT: Lisa Hanes Netzley, Admissions Counselor TOPICS: Parapsychology DESCRIPTION: School for adult & experiential learning. Offers M.A. program.

Antioch/New England Graduate School
103 Roxbury Street
Keene, NH 03431
(603)-357-3120
TOPICS: New Age

Applied Creative Services
2075 Buffalo Creek Road
Lake Lure, NC 28746
(704)-625-9153
TOPICS: New Age

Aquilla School Of Astrology
P.O. Box 4662
Santa Rosa, CA 95403
TOPICS: Astrology

Arcane School
113 University Place, 11 Fl.
P.O. Box 722 Cooper Station
NY, NY 10276
TOPICS: Spirituality, Channeling

Arthur Ford Academy
P.O. Box 70
McCaysville, GA 30555
TOPICS: Metaphysics

Arthur Ford Academy Of Medium
P.O. Box 767121
Roswell, GA 30076
TOPICS: Metaphysics, Channeling

Arthur Morgan School
R. #5
Burnsville, NC 28714
(704)-675-4262
TOPICS: New Age

Aston-Patterning Training Center
P.O. Box 544
Mill Valley, CA 94941
TOPICS: Holistic Healing

Aston-Patterning Training Center
P.O. Box 3568
Incline Village, NV 87450
(415)-381-6683
TOPICS: Holistic Healing

Astral Physics School (Church of Revelation-Hawaii)
21475 Summit Road
Los Gatos, CA 95030
TOPICS: Spirituality

Astrology School
142 Curtis Street
South Attleboro, MA 02703
TOPICS: Astrology

Athabasca University
Box 10000
Athabasca, AB TOG 2RO
Canada

TOPICS: Parapsychology

Athens State College
Athens, AL 35611
(205)-232-1802
TOPICS: Parapsychology DEPT.: Psychology, Div. of Behavioral Sciences COURSE: Experimental Parapsychology (PS 401) INSTRUCTOR: Joseph H. Slate, Ph.D. DESCRIPTION: Explores parapsychological research, its procedures, methods, and applications. COURSE: Seminar In Parapsychology (PS 403) DESCRIPTION: Study of unexplained phenomena, ESP, psychokinesis, etc. INDEPENDENT STUDY

Atlanta Art Therapy Institute
925 Virginia Avenue
Atlanta, GA 30306
(404)-876-0633
TOPICS: New Age

Atlanta School Of Massage
2300 Peachwood Road, Suite 3200
Peachwood Park
Atlanta, GA 30338
(404)-454-7167
TOPICS: Massage

Atlantic Union College
South Lancaster, MA 01561
TOPICS: Parapsychology

AUM Esoteric Study Center (Savitria)
2405 Ruscombe
Baltimore, MD 21209
TOPICS: Spirituality

Austin School Of Massage Therapy
2525 Wallingwood Drive
Suite 900
Austin, TX 78746
(512)-328-3005
TOPICS: Massage

Backyard Scientist
c/o Jane Hoffman
P.O. Box 16966
Irvine, CA 92713
(714)-551-2392
TOPICS: New Age

Bastyr College
144 54th Street
Seattle, WA 98015
TOPICS: Holistic Health

Bemidji State University, Center for Extended Learning
Bemidji, MN 56601
TOPICS: Parapsychology, Spirituality

Berkshire Center for Psychosynthesis
Box 152
Monterey, MA 02145
(413)-528-4825
TOPICS: New Age DESCRIPTION: Offers monthly, summer & year long training for Professionals in Psychosynthesis Therapy.

Beshara School Of Esoteric Training
2448 Prospect
Berkeley, CA 94704
TOPICS: Metaphysics

Bhatkhande University
35001 Lilac Loop
Union City, CA 94587
TOPICS: Metaphysics

Bio Psiences Institute
P.O. Box 11026
Minneapolis, MN 55412
TOPICS: Metaphysics

Blazing Star Herbal School
P.O. Box 6
Shelburne Falls, MA 01370
(413)-625-6875
CONTACT: Gail Ulrich TOPICS: Metaphysics
DESCRIPTION: Offers workshops & apprenticeships
in herbal studies, plant identification, herbal
preparation, therapeutics & flower essences.
Certificate upon completion of 7 month
apprenticeship program.

Body Of Knowledge-Hellerwork
415 N. Mt. Shasta Boulevard, #4
Mt. Shasta, CA 96067
(916)-926-2639
TOPICS: Holistic Healing

Bongo Program
Fiorello H. LaGuardia Community College/CUNY
31-10 Thomson Avenue, Room S154
Long Island City, NY 11101
(718)-482-5440
CONTACT: Middle College High School TOPICS:
New Age

Bridgewater State College
Department of Psychology
Burrill Academic Bldg., Rm 330
Bridgewater, MA 02324
(617)-697-1200
TOPICS: Parapsychology DEPT.: Department of
Psychology COURSE: Parapsychology
INSTRUCTOR: Richard T. Colgan, Ph. D.
DESCRIPTION: Presentation of parapsychology &
psychical phenomena through research,
experimentation & discussions. INDEPENDENT
STUDY

Brigham Young University
327 HCEB
Provo, UT 84602
TOPICS: Parapsychology

Brooks Divinity School
1819 E. 14th Street
Denver, CO 80218
TOPICS: Spirituality

C.W. Post College
Philosophy Department
Greenvale, NY 11548
TOPICS: Parapsychology

California Coast University
700 N. Main Street
Santa Ana, CA 92131
TOPICS: Parapsychology DESCRIPTION: Offers
M.A. & Ph.D. programs.

California College Of Physical Arts
18582 Beach Boulevard
Suite 14
Huntington Beach, CA 92648

(714)-964-7744
TOPICS: Holistic Healing

California Institute For Integral Studies
765 Ashbury Street
San Francisco, CA 94117
(415)-753-6100
TOPICS: Parapsychology, Holistic Health, New Age
DESCRIPTION: Fully accredited M.A. & Ph. D.
programs

California Institute For Transpersonal Psychology
5905 Soquel Drive #650
Soquel, CA 95073-2850
(415)-327-2776
TOPICS: Parapsychology, Psychology

California Pacific University
10731 Treena Street
San Diego, CA 92131
TOPICS: Parapsychology DESCRIPTION: Offers
M.A. & Ph.D. programs.

California School Of Herbal Studies
P.O. Box 39
Forestville, CA 95436
(707)-887-7457
TOPICS: Holistic Healing, Herbalogy

California State University
1000 E. Victoria Street
Dominguez Hills, CA 90747
TOPICS: Parapsychology DESCRIPTION: Offers
M.A. program.

Cambridge Institute For Better Vision
538 Cherrier Street
Montreal, Quebec H2L 1H3
Canada
(800)-624-0020
TOPICS: Holistic Healing

Center For Teaching And Learning
Box 8158, University Station
Grand Forks, ND 58202
(701)-777-2674
TOPICS: New Age PUBLICATIONS: *Insights Into
Open Education* TOPICS: New Age TYPE: Book
PUBLICATIONS: *Teaching And Learning: The
Journal Of Natural Inquiry And Pathways* TOPICS:
New Age TYPE: Journal

Charles River Studio Workshop
103 Morse Street
Watertown, MA 02172
(617)-923-4520
TOPICS: New Age

Charter Oak College
340 Capitol Avenue
Hartford, CT 06106
TOPICS: Parapsychology

Chicago State University
University Without Walls
9500 S. King Drive
Chicago, IL 60628
TOPICS: Parapsychology

China Advocates
1635 Irving Street

San Francisco, CA 94122
(415)-665-4505 (800)-333-6474
TOPICS: Holistic Healing

Church & School Of Wicca
Box 1502
New Bern, NC 28560
TOPICS: Witchcraft, Occult, Paganism

Circle of Friends Community School
10364 Arapahoe
Lafayette, CO 80026
TOPICS: Parapsychology, Spirituality

City University
1661 Northup Way
Bellevue, WA 98008
TOPICS: Parapsychology DESCRIPTION: Offers
M.B.A. program.

Claymont School of Continuous Education (Gurdjieff Foundation)
Box 112
Charlestown, WV 25414
TOPICS: Spirituality

Clayton School Of Natural Healing
1704 11th Avenue, South
Birmingham, AL 35205
(800)-638-4590
TOPICS: Holistic Health, Homeopathy
DESCRIPTION: Offers the Doctor of Naturopathy
(N.D.) degree by correspondence. More than 2,500
students worldwide.

Clayton University
7710 Carondelet
St. Louis, MO 63105
TOPICS: Parapsychology DESCRIPTION: Offers
B.A., M.A., and Ph.D. programs.

College Of Buddhist Studies (International Buddhist Meditation Center)
928 S. New Hampshire
Los Angeles, CA 90006
TOPICS: Meditation, Spirituality

College Of Divine Metaphysics, Incorporated
P.O. Box 728
Glendora, CA 91740
(818)-963-2009
TOPICS: Metaphysics DESCRIPTION: Offers
courses, certificates & degrees.

College Of Egyptian Mysteries
P.O. Box 83
Tujunga, CA 91042
TOPICS: Metaphysics

College Of Life Science
6600 Burleson Road
Austin, TX 78744
TOPICS: Nutrition, Health Food, Herbalogy
DESCRIPTION: Offers Ph.D. in nutritional science.

College Of Metaphysical Studies
35905 16th Avenue, South
Federal Way, WA 98003
TOPICS: Metaphysics

College Of Oriental Medicine (Chapori-Ling Foundation Sangha)
766 8th Avenue
San Francisco, CA 94118
TOPICS: Spirituality, Holistic Healing, Yoga, Meditation, Acupuncture

College Of Seminarians (Federation Of St. Thomas Christian Churches)
Palo Alto, CA
TOPICS: Spirituality

College Of Staten Island
Department of Psychology
715 Ocean Terrace, Sunnyside Campus
Staten Island, NY 10301
(718)-390-7744
TOPICS: Parapsychology DEPT.: Department Of Psychology COURSE: Parapsychology INSTRUCTOR: Steven M. Rosen, Ph. D. DESCRIPTION: Basic survey of parapsychology, its history, research, definition, methodology, theory, etc. are discussed. DESCRIPTION: A parapsychology club is available on campus.

College Of William And Mary
Department Of Philosophy
Williamsburg, VA 23185
TOPICS: Parapsychology

Columbia Pacific University
1415 Third Street
San Rafael, CA 94901
(800)-227-0119
TOPICS: Parapsychology DESCRIPTION: Offers M.A. & Ph.D. programs.

Columbia Union College
7600 Flower Avenue
Takoma Park, MD 20912
TOPICS: Parapsychology

Connecticut School Of Massage
75 Kitts Lane
Newington, CT 06111
TOPICS: Massage

Consciousness Research And Training Project, Inc. (CRTP)
Box 9G
315 E. 68th Street
New York, NY 10021
CONTACT: Joyce Goodrich, Ph.D., Project Dir. TOPICS: Holistic Healing, Meditation, Spirituality, Body-Mind Connection COURSE: Seminar in LeShan Approach to Healing INSTRUCTOR: Joyce Goodrich, Ph. D. DESCRIPTION: Five day residential seminar developed by Dr. LeShan to train people as healers in this his experimental research project. DEGREES: non-credit

Consortium For Whole Brain Learning
3348 47th Avenue South
Minneapolis, MN 55406
TOPICS: New Age

Crystal Academy
P.O. Box 3208
Taos, NM 87571
TOPICS: Metaphysics

Dayspring Resources
Box 6503, GCPO
New York, NY 10163-6022
(212)-980-3146
CONTACT: Leonie Rosenstiel, Ph. D., T.R.M., Dir. TOPICS: Reiki, Holistic Health, Hypnotism DESCRIPTION: Offers courses leading to certification as a Reiki Practitioner & Hypnotherapy. Also distributes books on Reiki.

Desert Institute Of The Healing Arts
639 North 6th Avenue
Tucson, AZ 85705
(603)-882-0899
TOPICS: Holistic Health

Dharma Real Buddhist University, City of Ten Thousand Buddhas
Talmage, CA 95481-0217
TOPICS: Spirituality, Holistic Healing, Tai Chi

Dominion Herbal College
7527 Kingsway
Burnaby, BC V3N 3C1
Canada
TOPICS: Herbalogy, Health Food

DoveStar Alchemian Institute
50 Whitehall Road
Hooksett, NH 03106
(603)-669-9497 (207)-236-6219
TOPICS: Holistic Healing, Massage, Reiki, Hypnotism, Acupuncture DEGREES: Degree & Certificate Programs offered. INDEPENDENT STUDY; BOOKSTORE; DESCRIPTION: Purpose is to develop the natural practitioner in the individual & further the art of holistic health personal growth & professional advancement. Offers courses in Acupressure, Hypnotherapy, Kriya & Sports Massage, Alchemia Bodywork & Heart Breath, Reiki, Alchemical Synergy & Equine Massage. Offers degree & certificate programs: 2 year Alchemical Synergy-2nd degree 4 year Alchemical Synergy-3rd degree 8 year Alchemical Synergy-4th degree. Courses taught by numerous faculty, guest & associate instructors. PUBLICATIONS: Dovestar Newsletter TYPE: Newsletter FREQ: 3 x per year DESCRIPTION: Journal of articles, advertisements, news & course offerings for each trimester.

Dyke College
112 Prospect Avenue
Cleveland, OH 44115
TOPICS: Parapsychology

East Texas State University
Continuing Education
East Texas Station
Commerce, TX 75428
(214)-886-3067
TOPICS: Parapsychology COURSE: Beginning Parapsychology INSTRUCTOR: Betty Corbiere-Binder COURSE: Parapsychology & Reality INSTRUCTOR: Betty Corbiere-Binder

East-West College
812 Southwest 10th Street
Portland, OR 97205
TOPICS: Holistic Health

Eastern Illinois University
Charleston, IL 61920
TOPICS: Parapsychology

Eastern Michigan University
Department of Sociology
712 Pray-Harrold Bldg.
Ypsilanti, MI 48197
(616)-487-4246
TOPICS: Parapsychology DEPT.: Department Of Sociology COURSE: Sociology of Parapsychology INSTRUCTOR: Marcello Truzzi, Ph. D. DESCRIPTION: Investigation of psi claims & unexplained phenomena. INSTRUCTOR: Ron Westrum, Ph. D. INDEPENDENT STUDY

Eastern Montana University
Department Of Social Sciences
Billings, MT 59101
TOPICS: Parapsychology

Elizabethtown College
Elizabethtown, PA 17022
TOPICS: Parapsychology

Elysium Institute, Inc.
814 Robinson Road
Topanga, CA 90290
(213)-455-1000 FAX (213)-455-3404
CONTACT: Ed Lange TOPICS: New Age, Metaphysics

Emperor's College of Traditional Oriental Medicine
2515 Wilshire Boulevard
Santa Monica, CA 90403
TOPICS: Spirituality, Holistic Healing, Tai Chi

Empire State College
2 Union Avenue
Saratoga Springs, NY 12866
TOPICS: Parapsychology DESCRIPTION: Offers M.A. program.

Ernest Holmes College (United Church of Religious Science)
2205 Main Street
Huntington Beach, CA 92648
TOPICS: Spirituality

Essene School of Thought
831 W. Fir
San Diego, CA 92101
TOPICS: Spirituality

Ethical Hypnosis Training Center
60 Vose Avenue
South Orange, NJ 07079
(201)-762-3132
TOPICS: Hypnotism

Fair Lawn Community School
Continuing Education
P.O. Box 8
Fair Lawn, NJ 07410
(201)-791-7947
TOPICS: Parapsychology DEPT.: Continuing Education COURSE: ESP: New Frontier Of The Mind INSTRUCTOR: Douglas Dean, Ph. D. DESCRIPTION: History & research findings of ESP

Farm Alternative School
50 The Farm
Summertown, TN 38483
(615)-964-2325 (615)-964-3670

TOPICS: New Age **DEPT.:** Solar & Alternate Energy **DEPT. HEAD:** Mary Ellen Bowen **COURSE:** Solar Projects & Alternate Energy **INSTRUCTOR:** Frank Michaels, Mary Ellen Bowen **INDEPENDENT STUDY; DESCRIPTION:** The school is a part of The Farm Cooperative Community. Founded on principles of non-violence & respect for nature, its desire is to create innovations for education, produce quality academic achievement, competence in New Age technology, development of research techniques, foster artistic talents & creative expression & promote physical skills. Also operates a summer camp for inner city children called Kids To The Country & is a member of the National Coalition of Alternative Community Schools.

Ferris State University
Big Rapids, MI 49307
TOPICS: Parapsychology

Fielding Institute
2112 Santa Barbara Street
Santa Barbara, CA 93105
TOPICS: Parapsychology **DESCRIPTION:** Offers M.A. & Ph.D. programs.

Five Branches Institute, College of Traditional Chinese Medicine
200 Seventh Avenue
Santa Cruz, CA 95062
TOPICS: Holistic Healing, Acupuncture

Florida School Of Massage
6421 Southwest 13th Street
Gainesville, FL 32608-5419
(904)-378-7891
TOPICS: Holistic Healing

Fordham University
Department of Theology
Bronx, NY 10458
TOPICS: Parapsychology **DEPT.:** Department of Theology **COURSE:** Theology & Parapsychology **INSTRUCTOR:** John J. Heaney, STD **DESCRIPTION:** Study of the relationship between theology & parapsychology.

Foundation For Research On The Nature Of Man, Institute For Parapsychology (FRNM)
402 N. Buchanan Boulevard
Durham, NC 27701
(919)-688-8241 **FAX** (919)-683-4338
CONTACT: Dr. John Palmer **TOPICS:** Parapsychology, Psychic Phenomena **DEPT.:** Parapsychology **DEPT. HEAD:** Dr. K. Ramakrishna Rao, Director **COURSE:** Summer Study Program-Parapsychology **INSTRUCTOR:** John Palmer, Ph. D. **DESCRIPTION:** Examines history, theories, research, and procedures through lectures, workshops and experiments in parapsychology. **COURSE:** Advanced Program **INSTRUCTOR:** John Palmer, Ph. D. **DESCRIPTION:** Year-round residential program offering training in experimentation and original research projects. **DESCRIPTION:** Offers 1 graduate course in parapsychology. **DEGREES:** Certificates offered **INDEPENDENT STUDY; BOOKSTORE; DESCRIPTION:** Journal Of Parapsychology. Quarterly scientific journal. $30-individual, $40-institutional, $15-student. **PUBLICATIONS:** *Journal Of Parapsychology* **TOPICS:** Parapsychology **TYPE:** Journal **FREQ:** quarterly **PRICE:** $30.00

DESCRIPTION: Quarterly scientific journal covering all aspects of Parapsychology.

Four Winds Institute
P.O. Box 540
East Meadow, NY 11554
TOPICS: Metaphysics

Framingham State College
Framingham, MA 01701
TOPICS: Parapsychology

Franklin Pierce College
Campus Center
P.O. Box 825
Rindge, NH 03461
(603)-899-5111
TOPICS: Parapsychology, Occult **PUBLICATIONS:** *New England Journal Of Parapsychology* **EDITOR:** W. H. Jack **TOPICS:** Parapsychology, Occult **TYPE:** Journal **DATE:** 1977 **FREQ:** Quarterly

Galaxie School Of Astrology
4805 Sepulveda Boulevard, 7
Sherman Oaks, CA 91403
TOPICS: Astrology

Gateways Institute
P.O. Box 1778
Ojai, CA 93023
TOPICS: Metaphysics

Goddard College
Plainfield, VT 05667
TOPICS: Parapsychology

Golden State University
1727 Fifth Avenue
San Diego, CA 92101
TOPICS: Parapsychology **DESCRIPTION:** Offers B.A., M.A. and Ph.D. programs.

Governors State University
University Park, IL 60466
TOPICS: Parapsychology

Great School Of Natural Science
25355 Spanish Ranch Road
Los Gatos, CA 95030
(408)-353-4876 (408)-353-3646
TOPICS: Metaphysics, New Age, Body-Mind Connection

Great Western University, The Metaphysical University
545 Sutter Street
San Francisco, CA 94102
TOPICS: Metaphysics **DESCRIPTION:** Offers M.A. and Ph.D. programs.

Hahnemann College Of Homeopathy
1918 Bonita Avenue
Berkeley, CA 94704
TOPICS: Holistic Health

Harmony College of Applied Science
1434 Fremont Avenue
Los Altos, CA 94022
TOPICS: Parapsychology

Hayes School Inner Sense
P.O. Box 70

McCaysville, GA 30555
TOPICS: Metaphysics

Hendricks Institute
708 West Kiowa
Colorado Springs, CO 80904
TOPICS: Metaphysics

Her Voice, Our Voices
c/o Women's Alliance
P.O. Box 21454
Oakland, CA 94620-1454
(916)-477-1064
TOPICS: New Age

Heritage Institute Of Psychological Research
P.O. Box 174
Plainfield, WI 54966
TOPICS: Metaphysics

Hewitt Research Foundation
P.O. Box 9
Washougal, WA 98671
(206)-835-8708
TOPICS: New Age **PUBLICATIONS:** *The Parent Educator And Family Report* **TOPICS:** New Age **TYPE:** Book

Himalayan Institute
841 Delaware Avenue
Buffalo, NY 14209
TOPICS: Occult

Holistic Life University
1627 Tenth Avenue
San Francisco, CA 94122
TOPICS: Holistic Health, Spirituality, Meditation, Yoga

Holt Associates/Growing Without Schooling
2269 Massachusetts Avenue
Cambridge, MA 02140
(617)-864-3100
TOPICS: New Age **PUBLICATIONS:** *Growing Without Schooling* **TOPICS:** New Age **TYPE:** Book

Home Education Press
P.O. Box 1083
Tonasket, WA 98855
(509)-486-1351
CONTACT: Mark Or Helen Hegener **TOPICS:** New Age, Metaphysics **PUBLICATIONS:** *Alternatives In Education* **TOPICS:** New Age **TYPE:** Book **PUBLICATIONS:** *Home Education Magazine* **EDITOR:** Mark Hegener, Helen Hegener **TOPICS:** New Age, Metaphysics **TYPE:** Magazine **DATE:** 1983 **FREQ:** bi-monthly **PRICE:** $24.00 **DESCRIPTION:** Publishes non-fiction, news, reviews, interviews, satire, artwork, and photography pertaining to home schooling. **PUBLICATIONS:** *Home School Primer* **TOPICS:** New Age **TYPE:** Book **PUBLICATIONS:** *Home School Reader* **TOPICS:** New Age **TYPE:** Book

Hope Troxel School
P.O. Box 257
June Lake, CA 93529
TOPICS: UFO's

Humanistic Hypnosis Center

2609 Grant Street
Berkeley, CA 94703
TOPICS: Hypnotism

Hygeia Center OF Natural Hygiene
25530 Highway 281 North
San Antonio, TX 78260
(512)-497-3613
TOPICS: Holistic Healing

Hypnosis Clearing House
3704 Mt. Diablo Blvd., No. 300
Lafayette, CA 94549
TOPICS: Hypnotism

Hypnosis Motivation Institute
14640 Victory Boulevard, #210
Van Nuys, CA 91401
(818)-988-4690
TOPICS: Hypnotism

Hypnotherapy Training Institute
4640 Sonoma Highway
Santa Rosa, CA 95409
TOPICS: Hypnotism, Meditation, Spirituality

Hypnotism Training Institute Of Los Angeles
312 Riverdale Avenue
Glendale, CA 91204
(818)-242-1159
TOPICS: Hypnotism

Indiana University
620 Union Drive
Indianapolis, IN 46205
TOPICS: Parapsychology

Infinity Institute International, Inc.
4110 Edgeland, Dept. 800
Royal Oak, MI 48073-2251
(313)-549-5594
TOPICS: Hypnotism, Holistic Health, Meditation, Crystals, Massage, Body-Mind Connection, Yoga PUBLICATIONS: *Subconsciously Speaking* TOPICS: Hypnotism TYPE: Newsletter SIZE: 8 1/2x11, 12 pgs. FREQ: bi-monthly DESCRIPTION: Bi-monthly newsletter reporting on the activities of the International Medical and Dental Hypnotherapy Association as well as varied articles by numerous authors on hypnosis, meditation, visualization, healing and other mind/body relationships. Book reviews and ads printed.

Institute For Advanced Hypnosis
P.O. Box 271206
Concord, CA 74537-1206
(415)-381-9184
TOPICS: Body-Mind Connection

Institute For Advanced Study of Human Sexuality
1523 Franklin Street
San Francisco, CA 94109
CONTACT: Ted McIlvenna, Pres. TOPICS: Psychology, Parapsychology DIRECTOR: Ted McIlvenna, Pres. DESCRIPTION: Provides advanced degrees in sexology for health care professionals. Offers M.H.S., D.H.S, Ed.D and Ph.D. programs. Also offers adult continuing education courses & independent study programs.

Institute For Astrology And Metaphysics
2700 Lincoln
Merrick, NY 11566
TOPICS: Astrology

Institute For Effective Psychotherapy
626 Balboa Street
San Francisco, CA 94118
TOPICS: Parapsychology, Psychology

Institute For Graphological Science
3685 Ingleside
Dallas, TX 75229
TOPICS: Occult

Institute For Holistic Healing Studies
San Francisco State University, School Of Science
1600 Holloway Avenue
San Francisco, CA 94132
(415)-338-1210
CONTACT: Erik Peper, Ph. D., Dir. TOPICS: Holistic Healing, Body-Mind Connection, Meditation, Herbalogy COURSE: Holistic Health: Western Perspectives COURSE: Holistic Health & Human Nature COURSE: Chinese Body/Mind Energetics DEGREES: Minor Program in Holistic Health DESCRIPTION: Offers courses designed to provide students with new ways of viewing reality, including the concepts of health/illness, mind/body & consciousness. This holistic view coupled with practices derived from both Eastern & Western perspectives enables students to take more responsibility for self care, health maintenance & personal growth. Developing a certificate program via Extension Services on campus.

Institute for Metaphysics (Universal Church of Scientific Truth)
1250 Indiana Street
Birmingham, Al 35224
TOPICS: Metaphysics

Institute For Parapsychology-Duke University
Box 6847
College Station
Durham, NC 27708
TOPICS: Parapsychology, Psychic Phenomena

Institute For Social Ecology
P.O. Box 89
Plainfield, VT 05667
(802)-454-8493
TOPICS: New Age

Institute for Wholistic Education
Box 575
Amherst, MA 01002
TOPICS: Holistic Healing DESCRIPTION: Offers M.A. program.

Institute Of Astro-Psychology
2640 Greenwich Street, 403
San Francisco, CA 94123
TOPICS: Astrology

Institute Of Chinese Herbalogy
5459 Shafter Avenue
Oakland, CA 94618
(415)-658-6857
TOPICS: Holistic Healing, Herbalogy

Institute Of Diskenetics
P.O. Box 52191
Tulsa, OK 74152
TOPICS: Metaphysics

Institute of Graphological Research
610 Lochmoor Ct.
Danville, CA 94526
TOPICS: Graphology

Institute Of Health Sciences
975 Hornblend Street
Suite E
San Diego, CA 92109
(619)-581-9429
TOPICS: Holistic Healing

Institute Of Life
1002 East Market
New Albany, IN 47150
TOPICS: Metaphysics

Institute of Mentalphysics
P.O. Box 1000
Joshua Tree, CA 92252
TOPICS: Body-Mind Connection

Institute Of Mentalphysics
P.O. Box 640
Yucca Valley, CA 92286-0640
TOPICS: Metaphysics

Institute Of Metaphysics
5899 South Broadway
Los Angeles, CA 90003
TOPICS: Metaphysics

Institute Of Postural Restructuring
Box 840
St. Augustine, FL 32085
(505)-758-4503
TOPICS: Body-Mind Connection

Institute Of Psycho-Structural Balancing (IPSB)
4502 Cass Street
San Diego, CA 92109
(619)-272-4142
TOPICS: Massage

Institute Of Spiritual Sciences
P.O. Box 1944
Carmel, CA 93921
TOPICS: Metaphysics

Institute OF Transpersonal Psychology
250 Oak Grove Avenue
Menlo Park, CA 94025
(415)-326-1960
CONTACT: Arthur Hastings, Ph. D. TOPICS: Spirituality, Psychology, New Age DIRECTOR: Arthur Hastings, Ph.D. DEGREES: M.A., Ph. D. INDEPENDENT STUDY; DESCRIPTION: M.A. & Ph. D. degrees in transpersonal psychology & counselling. Courses address theory, emotional & clinical processes, body disciplines & therapy, spiritual studies, community & creative expression. Outstanding faculty in the transpersonal field. Residential & external programs. Founded 1975. Free information on programs available.

Institute Of Wholistic Education
33719 116th Street
Twin Lakes, WI 53181
(414)-877-9396
TOPICS: Holistic Healing

Institute/New Age
45 East 78th Street
New York, NY 10028
TOPICS: Astrology

Instituto de Estudios Parapsicologicos
Apartado 8000
Panama 7,
Panama
TOPICS: Parapsychology COURSE: Introduction To Experimental Parapsychology INSTRUCTOR: Roberto Mainieri DESCRIPTION: Five-day basic survey of parapsychology.

Integrative Studies Institute
P.O. Box 2349
Cambridge, MA 02238
TOPICS: Occult

International Association For Near-Death Studies
University Of Connecticut, Psychology #258
Box U-20
Storrs, CT 06268
(203)-486-4170
TOPICS: Death, Metaphysics, Parapsychology
PUBLICATIONS: Anabiosis TOPICS: Death TYPE: Book

International College
1019 Gayley Avenue
Los Angeles, CA 90024
TOPICS: Parapsychology DESCRIPTION: Offers M.A. and Ph.D. programs.

International College Of Astrology
P.O. Box 825
Capitola, CA 95010
TOPICS: Astrology

International College of Natural Health Sciences
Box 5181
Clearwater, FL 33518
TOPICS: Holistic Healing, Nutrition, Herbalogy
DESCRIPTION: Offers Ph.D. of Natural Health.

International Institute Of Chinese Medicine
P.O. Box 4991
Santa Fe, NM 87502
(505)-473-5233
TOPICS: Holistic Healing, Acupuncture, Herbalogy
DEPT.: Acupuncture & Chinese Herbalogy DEPT. HEAD: Michael Zeng COURSE: Chinese Medicine
DESCRIPTION: 1800 hours in acupuncture & herbalogy, including fundamental classes in Traditional Chinese Medicine Theory.
DESCRIPTION: Classes taught by more than 10 well-qualified faculty, including Drs. Nancy & Michael Zeng, Daniel Bruce, William Roberts, Clark Manning, Stewart Edwards & Maky Erdely.
DEGREES: Master Of Oriental Medicine
INDEPENDENT STUDY; BOOKSTORE

International Institute Of Hypnotherapy
4110 Edgeland, Suite 800
Royal Oak, MI 48073
(313)-549-5594
TOPICS: Hypnotism, Holistic Health
DESCRIPTION: State licensed school offering courses, books, tapes & newsletter.

International Montessori Society
912 Thayer Avenue
Silver Spring, MD 20910
(301)-589-1127
TOPICS: New Age COURSE: Montesssori Teacher Education INSTRUCTOR: Lee Havis DESCRIPTION: 22 lessons conducted entirely through correspondence. Subject areas are: Montessori Principles, Observation, Child Development, Materials. COURSE: Independent Study Course, Primary (2-6), Elem. (6-12) INSTRUCTOR: Lee Havis DEGREES: Montessori Teaching Credentials INDEPENDENT STUDY; BOOKSTORE; DESCRIPTION: A new approach to education - control the environment, not the child. Offers information, publications, teacher education, membership & conferences to support effective application of Montessori principles.
PUBLICATIONS: Montessori Observer Newsletter, quarterly publication PUBLICATIONS: Montessori News TOPICS: New Age TYPE: Newspaper
PUBLICATIONS: The Montessori Observer PUBLISHER: Lee Havis EDITOR: Elizabeth Hainstock TOPICS: New Age TYPE: Newsletter
DESCRIPTION: Free to members with $20 annual membership fee.

International School Of Massage Therapy
2872 Folsom Street
San Francisco, CA 94110
(415)-285-5040
TOPICS: New Age, Holistic Health, Massage

International School Of Shiatsu
P.O. Box 187
Buckingham, PA 18912
(215)-340-9918
CONTACT: Saul Goodman TOPICS: Body-Mind Connection, Acupuncture, Holistic Health DEPT.: Shiatsu Practitioner Training DEPT. HEAD: Saul Goodman COURSE: Introduction To The Art Of Shiatsu INSTRUCTOR: Saul Goodman, Edward Carlos DESCRIPTION: 12 hour introduction to Shiatsu held weekends 6 times per year. COURSE: 4 Level Shiatsu Practitioner Training INSTRUCTOR: Saul Goodman, Edward Carlos DESCRIPTION: 500 hour beginner to advanced & professional training. Certification offered at the completion of 3 levels. Diploma offered at completion of 4th level. American Oriental Bodywork Therapy Association approved. DEGREES: 500 Hour Certification DESCRIPTION: Specializes in the study of Shiatsu.
PUBLICATIONS: By Saul Goodman: The Book Of Shiatsu, 1986, $12.95; videos $69.95 each, 1986: The Art Of Shiatsu Massage; Shiatsu For Sexual & Reproductive Problems; The Art Of Structural Alignment

International Spiritualist University
809 N. 12th Street
Leavenworth, KS 66048

TOPICS: Spirituality DESCRIPTION: Offers B.A., M.A. and Ph.D. programs.

International University of Theology and Parapsychology/Church Of The Antiochean Rite
Box 8473
Tampa, FL 33674-8473
(813)-248-3091 FAX (813)-248-3091
CONTACT: Archbishop Dr. Sar Mar Roberto C. Toca, Pres. TOPICS: Parapsychology, Occult, Metaphysics, UFO's DESCRIPTION: Offers instruction in Metaphysics, Parapsychology, Gnosticism, Fourth Way, Magick, Occult & UFO's.

Jeshua Ben Josef School Of The Heart
P.O. Box 2097
Eugene, OR 97402
(503)-342-8069
TOPICS: New Age

Jin Shin Do Foundation For Bodymind Acupressure
Box 1097
Felton, CA 95018
TOPICS: Acupuncture, Body-Mind Connection, Holistic Health, Massage

Jin Shin Do Foundation For Bodymind Acupressure
366 California Avenue, # 16
Palo Alto, CA 94306
(415)-328-1811
CONTACT: Iona Teeguarden, Director TOPICS: Holistic Health, Acupuncture, Body-Mind Connection, Psychology, Massage DESCRIPTION: Offers the practice of Acupressure & Bodymind Therapy to attain holistic health. PUBLICATIONS: The Acupressure Way Of Health: Jin Shin Do, 1978

John Bastyr College
144 N.E. 54th Street, Ste. M
Seattle, WA 98105
(206)-523-9585
TOPICS: Holistic Healing, Metaphysics

John Fitzgerald Kennedy University
Graduate Parapsychology Program
12 Altarinda Road
Orinda, CA 94563
(415)-254-0200 (415)-228-6770
CONTACT: Mary Kay Wright-Malear, Dir. TOPICS: Parapsychology, Psychology, Holistic Health DIRECTOR: Susan Galvin DEPT.: Graduate School For The Study Of Human Consciousness DESCRIPTION: Offers some undergraduate course work but primarily 5000 level graduate courses in Interdisciplinary Consciousness Studies. Sample courses are: Topics In Consciousness Studies: Psychology Of Psychic Experience; Issues In Consciousness Studies: Altered States Of Consciousness. DEGREES: Masters Degree Program INDEPENDENT STUDY; BOOKSTORE; DESCRIPTION: Offers fully accredited M.A. programs dealing with New Age topics such as Interdisciplinary Consciousness Studies with a concentration in Parapsychology, Holistic Health Counselling Psychology, Transpersonal Counseling Psychology, Religious Studies & Arts and Consciousness.

Johnnie Coleman Institute (Universal Foundation for Better Living)
11901 Ashland Avenue
Chicago, IL 60643
TOPICS: New Age

Kahua Institute
P.O. Box 1747
Makawao, HI 96968
TOPICS: Metaphysics

Karoda Institute (Zen Center of Los Angeles)
923 S. Normandie Lane
Los Angeles, CA 90006
TOPICS: Spirituality

Kennedy-Western University
28310 Roadsid eDrive
Agoura Hills, CA 91301
TOPICS: Parapsychology DESCRIPTION: Offers B.A., M.A. and Ph.D. programs.

Kingsborough Community College
Behavioral Sciences & Human Services Department
2001 Oriental Boulevard
Brooklyn, NY 11235
(718)-934-5630
CONTACT: Dr. Philip Stander, Chairman TOPICS: Parapsychology DEPT.: Department of Behavioral Sciences COURSE: Principles of Parapsychology (PSY 12) INSTRUCTOR: Dr. Philip Stander, Ed. D., Chairman DESCRIPTION: Study of the many facets of parapsychology-telepathy, precognition, psychokinesis & clairvoyance-through theory & research.

Koh-E-Nor University (Church of the Movement of Spiritual Inner Awareness)
2101 Wilshire Boulevard
Santa Monica, CA 90403
TOPICS: Spirituality

Laurentian University
Environmental Psychology Laboratory
Sudbury, Ontario P3E 206
Canada
TOPICS: Parapsychology

Le Centre Du Silence Mime School
P.O. Box 1015 (ASE-92)
Boulder, CO 80306-1015
(303)-494-8729
CONTACT: Samuel Avital, Dir. TOPICS: Body-Mind Connection, Psychology, New Age DESCRIPTION: An independent school devoted to teaching the dynamics of personal creativity. Offers seminars & workshops that integrate thought with action by teaching the concepts of theatre & movement, how to learn to write your own script, play the lead role in your life story & awaken the creative child within you. Provides the honest tools of communication needed to integrate the conscious awareness of oneself to one's environment.

Lee College
1161 Parker Street, N.E.
Cleveland, TN 37311
TOPICS: Parapsychology

Lesley College Graduate School

29 Everett Street
Cambridge, MA 02238
TOPICS: Parapsychology, New Age DESCRIPTION: Offers M.A. program.

Life Forms Sculpture Program
The Waldorf Institute
260 Hungry Hollow Road
Spring Valley, NY 10977
(914)-425-0055
TOPICS: New Age

Life Research Institute
P.O. Box 73284
Puyallup, WA 98373
TOPICS: Astrology

Logos World University
6325 East Aster
Scottsdale, AZ 85254
TOPICS: Metaphysics

Lomi School
Box 318
Tomales, CA 94971
(707)-579-0465
TOPICS: Holistic Healing, Parapsychology

Loretto Heights College
3001 S. Federal Blvd.
Denver, CO 80236
TOPICS: Parapsychology

Lyndon State College
Philosophy & Religion Department
Lyndonville, VT 05851
TOPICS: Parapsychology COURSE: Parapsychology & Philosophy INSTRUCTOR: Kenneth D. Vos, Ph. D. DESCRIPTION: Examines research and experimentation of psi phenomena and the practical implications of parapsychology.

Maharishi International University
524 Schoolhouse Street
Coquitam, BC, V3J5N9,
Canada
TOPICS: Metaphysics

Mary Baldwin College
Staunton, VA 24401
TOPICS: Parapsychology

Medium Is Massage, The
6622 Tremont
Oakland, CA 94609
TOPICS: New Age, Massage, Holistic Health DESCRIPTION: Offers courses in bodywork.

Meiji College of Oriental Medicine
1426 Fillmore Street, Ste 301
San Francisco, CA 94115
(415)-771-1019 (415)-771-6266
TOPICS: Holistic Health, Acupuncture, Herbalogy, Massage, Tai Chi, Nutrition DEGREES: M.A. in Oriental Medicine DESCRIPTION: Offers courses in acupuncture, herbalogy, nutrition, massage & Tai Chi. Graduates are qualified to take the State of California Acupuncture Licensing Exam.

Mental Science Institute
3262 Edson Road
Rockford, IL 61109
TOPICS: Metaphysics

Meridian School Of Astrology
100 Nassau Street
Uniontown, PA 15401
TOPICS: Astrology

Metaphysical Theological Seminary
P.O. Box 91986
Long Beach, CA 90809-1986
(213)-494-1597 (213)-427-4418
TOPICS: Metaphysics DESCRIPTION: Self-directed study leading to Bachelor/Master/Doctorate of Divinity.

Metropolitan State University
7th & Robert Streets
St. Paul, MN 55101
TOPICS: Parapsychology

Millennium Institute
P.O. Box 935
Palo Alto, CA 94301
TOPICS: Holistic Health

Minnesota Institute For Shamanic Studies
P.O. Box 11341
Minneapolis, MN 55411
TOPICS: Metaphysics

Moore School Of Astrology
220 Swedesboro Road
Gibbstown, NJ 08027
TOPICS: Astrology

Mueller College Of Holistic Studies
4607 Park Boulevard
San Diego, CA 92116
(619)-291-9811
TOPICS: New Age, Massage, Acupuncture, Holistic Healing DESCRIPTION: Offers regular & intensive classes in American massage & acupressure.

Multidisciplinary Institute For Neuropsychological Development, Inc. (M.I.N.D.)
48 Garden Street
Cambridge, MA 02138
TOPICS: New Age DESCRIPTION: Diagnostic Learning Center specializing in education & research of handicaps & learning disabilities.

Naropa Institute (Vajradhatu)
1345 Spruce Street
Boulder, CO 80302
(303)-444-0202
TOPICS: Spirituality, Holistic Healing

Nassau Community College
Continuing Education
Garden City, NY 11530
(516)-222-7472
TOPICS: Parapsychology DEPT.: Continuing Education COURSE: Parapsychology 1 INSTRUCTOR: Shirley Wiedmer DESCRIPTION: Explores all aspects of parapsychology and its relationship with philosophy, literature, psychiatry, psychology and biology.

National Audubon Society Expedition Institute
Northeast Audubon Center
Sharon, CT 06069

(203)-364-0522
TOPICS: New Age

National Coalition Of Alternative Community Schools
58 Schoolhouse Road
Summertown, TN 38483
(615)-964-3670
TOPICS: New Age PUBLICATIONS: *National Directory Of Alternative Schools* TOPICS: New Age TYPE: Directory PUBLICATIONS: *Skole* TOPICS: New Age TYPE: Newsletter

National College Of Naturopathic Medicine
3100 McCormick Avenue
Wichita, KS 67213
TOPICS: Holistic Health

National College Of Naturopathic Medicine
11231 S.E. Market Street
Portland, OR 97216
(503)-255-4860
TOPICS: Holistic Healing

National Home School Association
P.O. Box 58746
Seattle, WA 98138
TOPICS: New Age

National Intensive Journal Program
Dialogue House
80 East 11th Street
New York, NY 10003
(212)-673-5880 (800)-221-5844
TOPICS: New Age

National Metaphysics Institute
11303 1/2 Moore Park
North Hollywood, CA 91604
TOPICS: Metaphysics

National Women's History Project
7738 Bell Road
Windsor, CA 95492
(707)-838-6000
TOPICS: New Age PUBLICATIONS: *Women's History Network News* TOPICS: New Age TYPE: Newspaper

Natural Gourmet Cookery School/Institute For Food And Health
48 West 21st Street
New York, NY 10010
(212)-645-5170
CONTACT: Pam Brooks TOPICS: Holistic Healing, Health Food, Nutrition, Vegetarianism DIRECTOR: Annemarie Colbin DEPT. HEAD: Lissa DeAngelis DESCRIPTION: Purpose is to empower people to use food as a support for their own healing process & to choose & prepare delicious food that contributes to or improves health. Offers cooking classes, lectures & workshops on Basics of Healthy Cooking, Kitchen Pharmacy, International Vegetarian & many other topics. Two-week summer intensive programs. Chef's Training Program in natural foods cooking: 600 hrs, full-time, part-time, externships, lifetime job referral. Apprenticeship Program in eves & weekends; catalog.

Navarro School Of Horary Astrology
112 Palmetto Drive
Edgewood, MO 21040
TOPICS: Astrology

Neotarian College of Philosophy
Box 8707
Kansas City, MO 64114
TOPICS: Parapsychology DESCRIPTION: Offers Ph.D. and D.D.

New Age School, The
1850 North DuBuque
Iowa City, IA 52240
TOPICS: Occult

New Canaan Academy
Canaan Street
Canaan, NH 03741
(603)-523-4385
TOPICS: Tai Chi, Meditation, Spirituality DESCRIPTION: Offers classes in T'ai Chi Chuan, daily Zazen meditation & philosophy as related to spiritual living.

New College of California
50 Fell Street
San Francisco, CA 94102
TOPICS: New Age, Parapsychology DESCRIPTION: Offers fully accredited B.A. & M.A. programs dealing with New Age topics.

New England Institute For Neuro-Linguistic Programming (NEINLP)
RFD 3, Pratt Corner Road
Amherst, MA 01002-9805
(413)-259-1248
CONTACT: Richard Clarke, Ph. D. TOPICS: New Age, Hypnotism, Holistic Health, Spirituality DESCRIPTION: Program that enables the individual to use the newest & most powerful available knowledge on the structure & function of the mind. Offers both introductions & comprehensive certification training in NLP, Ericksonian Hypnosis & Imperative Self. Conducts workshops in specialized topics, seminars, sales trainings & individually-customized executive mentoring programs. Recognized by the International Assoc. of NLP & the Imperative Self Analysis Assoc.

New Horizons For Learning
4649 Sunnyside North
Seattle, WA 98103
(206)-547-7936
TOPICS: New Age

New Jersey Institute Of Technology
Newark College Of Engineering
Newark, NJ 07102
TOPICS: Parapsychology

New Mexico Academy Of Massage And Advanced Healing Arts
Box 932
Santa Fe, NM 87504
(505)-982-6271 FAX (505)-988-2621
TOPICS: Massage, Holistic Health DEPT. HEAD: Lorin Parrish March, Director COURSE: Massage Therapy DESCRIPTION: Offers Massage Therapy Certification. Encompasses 1000-1200 hours of study & 10-18 months to complete. Full &/or part time programs available. DEGREES: Massage Therapy Certification INDEPENDENT STUDY; BOOKSTORE; DESCRIPTION: Non-profit

educational organization providing professional training in massage & other related healing arts. Supports the development of intuition, sensitivity, spiritual awareness & self-confidence.

New Mexico School Of Natural Therapeutics
117 Richmond, NE
Albuquerque, NM 87106
(505)-268-6870
TOPICS: Holistic Healing, Homeopathy

New School For Social Research
Social Science Division
66 West 12th Street
New York, NY 10011
(212)-741-5600
TOPICS: Parapsychology DEPT.: Social Science Division COURSE: Parapsychology INSTRUCTOR: Bob Brier, Ph. D. DESCRIPTION: Students design, research and conduct own experiments. COURSE: Parapsychology: 100 Years Of Research INSTRUCTOR: Michaeleen Maher, Ph. D. DESCRIPTION: Lectures & discussions on the various topics of parapsychology and its history.

New Seminary
7 W. 96th Street
New York, NY 10025
TOPICS: Spirituality

New York Institute Of Technology
Continuing Education
Carleton Avenue, Bldge 66, Rm 212
Central Islip, NY 11722
(516)-348-3325
TOPICS: Parapsychology DEPT.: Continuing Education COURSE: Parapsychology INSTRUCTOR: Shirley Wiedmer DESCRIPTION: Examines parapsychology and its relationship with biology, philosophy, psychology, psychiatry & literature.

New York School Of Astrology
545 Eighth Avenue, 10th FL.
New York, NY 10018-4307
(212)-947-3628
CONTACT: Henry Weingarten TOPICS: Astrology, Holistic Healing DEPT.: Astrology DEPT. HEAD: Henry Weingarten DESCRIPTION: Offers a 3 year professional training program INSTRUCTOR: Debra Burrell DESCRIPTION: Offers a 22 week Adult Education program DEGREES: Degree available in Astrology BOOKSTORE; DESCRIPTION: Non-profit independent college offering a 3 year traditional NYSA's certification programs for professional astrological training. Performance-based education providing both knowledge of Astrology & proficiency in its application. Provides financial aid & scholarships to undergraduates & graduate students. PUBLICATIONS: Catalog available. Send $3 postpaid.

Newman College Naturopathy School
Wichita, KS 67213
TOPICS: Homeopathy

Newport University
3720 Campus Drive
Newport Beach, CA 92660
TOPICS: Parapsychology DESCRIPTION: Offers B.A., Ph.D. and D.D.

Nine Gates Mystery School

437 Sausalito Street
Corte Madera, CA 94925
TOPICS: Metaphysics

Nine Gates, Inc.
220 Redwood Highway
Suite 61
Mill Valley, CA 94941
(415)-927-1677 FAX (415)-927-3418
CONTACT: Dr. Gay Luce TOPICS: Body-Mind Connection DESCRIPTION: Nine Gates Mystery School uses spiritual training to gain mastery in dealing with fear, stress, fatigue, and depression. Through breathing, movement, sound, sacred drama, and ritual students learn to detect and use the energies of 9 major chakras.

Niyama School And Shiatsu Center
Box 570-SB
Middletown, CA 95461
(415)-731-5652
TOPICS: New Age

NLP Comprehensive/Neuro-Linguistic Programming
2897 Valmont Road
Boulder, CO 80301
(303)-442-1102 (800)-233-1657 FAX (800)-845-9275
CONTACT: Steve Andreas, Dir. TOPICS: New Age DESCRIPTION: Offers training course in Neuro-Linguistic Programming which is a technique to help people get what they want in life, create their own future & have choices concerning their feelings. A state-of-the-art communication method for nurturing personal & professional growth. Offers Practitioner Certification, Master Pre-Training & Master Certification.

Northeastern Illinois University
5500 N. St. Louis Avenue
Chicago, Il 60625
TOPICS: Parapsychology

Northern Illinois University
Department Of Educational Psychology And Special Ed
Graham Hall
Dekalb, IL 60115
(815)-753-0657
TOPICS: New Age

Norwich University
Vermont College
Montpelier, VT 06502
TOPICS: Parapsychology DESCRIPTION: Offers M.A. & M.F.A. programs.

Nova University
3301 College Avenue
Fort Lauderdale, FL 33314
TOPICS: Parapsychology, UFO's DESCRIPTION: Offers M.A. & Ph.D. programs.

Nyigma Institute Of Arizona
4004 East McKellips Road
Mesa, AZ 85205
TOPICS: Metaphysics

Oak Grove School
Krishnamurti Foundation of America
220 W. Lomita
Ojai, CA 93023

TOPICS: Spirituality DESCRIPTION: Offers grade school program.

Oakland University
Department Of Philosophy
Rochester, MI 48063
TOPICS: Parapsychology

Ohio University
Scott Quadrangle
Athens, OH 45701
(614)-593-1155
TOPICS: Parapsychology

Oklahoma City University
N.W. 2501 Blackwelder
Oklahoma City, OK 73106
TOPICS: Parapsychology

Open Learning Institute
Box 94000
Richmond, BC Y6Y 2A2
Canada
TOPICS: Parapsychology, New Age

Our Lady Of Enchantment
Seminary Of Wicca, Church Of The Old Religion
Box 1366
Nashua, NH 03061
(603)-880-7237
CONTACT: Lady Sabrina TOPICS: Witchcraft, Spirituality DESCRIPTION: First public school of Witchcraft & the Occult in the U.S.A. offering courses & membership to more than 7,000 people in 28 different countries. Offers mail-order correspondence courses in Celtic Wicca & various other topics.

Our Lady Of The Lake University
Providence Building, Rm 2A
411 SW 24th Street
San Antonio, TX 78285
(512)-434-6711
TOPICS: Parapsychology COURSE: Parapsychology Today INSTRUCTOR: Marilyn Schlitz, M.A. DESCRIPTION: Basic survey of psi experimentation.

Pacific College Of Oriental Medicine
702 West Washington Street
San Diego, CA 92103
(619)-574-6909
TOPICS: Holistic Healing

Pacific Institute Of Aromatherapy
P.O. Box 903
San Rafael, CA 94915
TOPICS: Holistic Health

Pacific School Of Massage & Healing Arts
44000 Fish Rock Road
Gualala, CA 95445
(707)-884-3138
TOPICS: Holistic Healing, Massage

Pacific School Of Tai Chi
P.O. Box 962
Solana Beach, CA 92075-0962
TOPICS: Tai Chi

Pacific States University
1516 S. Western Avenue
Los Angeles, CA 90006

TOPICS: Parapsychology DESCRIPTION: Offers M.A. and Ph.D.

Palo Alto School Of Hypnotherapy
2443 Ash Street, Ste D
Palo Alto, CA 94306
TOPICS: Hypnotism, Meditation

Pansophic Institute
P.O. Box 2422
Reno, NV 89505
TOPICS: Body-Mind Connection, Holistic Health

Parents And Teachers For Social Responsibility
Box 517
Moretown, VT 05660
(802)-223-3409
TOPICS: New Age

Patricia Hayes School Of Inner Sense Development
P.O. Box 767121
Roswell, GA 30076
(919)-477-5349
CONTACT: Patricia Hayes TOPICS: Astrology, Psychic PUBLICATIONS: Inner Sense News EDITOR: Kelly Powers TOPICS: Astrology TYPE: Newsletter, 6 pgs. FREQ: Quarterly PRICE: Free

Platonic Academy
Box 409
Santa Cruz, CA 95061
(408)-423-7923
TOPICS: Holistic Healing

Plymouth State College
Plymouth, NH 03264
TOPICS: Parapsychology

Ponderosa School For Self-Reliant Living
195 Golden Pine
Goldendale, WA 98620
(509)-773-3902
TOPICS: New Age

Potomac Massage Training Institute
7826 Eastern Avenue NW
Suite LL-1
Washington, DC 20012
(202)-726-1150
TOPICS: Holistic Healing

Prana Theological Seminary and College of Philosophy
3500 West Adams Boulevard
Los Angeles, CA 90018
TOPICS: Spirituality

Prescott College
220 Grove Avenue
Prescott, AZ 86301
(602)-778-2090
TOPICS: New Age, Parapsychology

Princeton University
Human Information Processing Group
2-S-2 Green Hall
Princeton, NJ 08544
TOPICS: Psychic Phenomena DEPT.: Human Information Processing Group COURSE: Human

Information Processing Group **INSTRUCTOR:** Dean Radin, Ph. D. **DESCRIPTION:** Study & research in cognitive science, psychology, linguistics, philosophy & engineering.

Principia College (Church of Christ, Scientist)

Elsah, IL 62028
TOPICS: Spirituality

Questhaven Academy (Christward Ministry)

Route 5
Box 206
Escondido, CA 92025
TOPICS: Spirituality

Quimby Center

Box 453
Alamogordo, NM 88310
TOPICS: Parapsychology

Raj-Yoga Math

P.O. Box 547
Deming, WA 98244
CONTACT: Satchakrananda Bodhisattvaguru
TOPICS: New Age, Yoga, Spirituality
DESCRIPTION: Founded 1974 by Satchakranands Bodhisattvaguru. Primitive setting providing long & short-term learning/growth experiences for serious spiritual seekers who have a strong dharmic pull toward the Bodhisattva path & Liberation. Offers courses in Yogic & Buddhist Consciousness practices with strong emphasis on Transpersonal interactions under the direct tutelage of Divine Guidance. Prerequisite 5-10 years of Sadhna. Costs: $150 per month. No outside jobs allowed.

Reevis Mountain School Of Self-Reliance

HC 02, Box 1534
Roosevelt, AZ 85545
(602)-467-2536
TOPICS: New Age, Herbalogy, Holistic Healing, Meditation **INSTRUCTOR:** Peter Bigfoor & Angelique Zelle **DESCRIPTION:** Teaches outdoor survival skills, herbalogy, plant identification, natural healing, meditation, self-discovery & organic gardening. Work-exchange program available. Brochure available, send $1. **DEGREES:** Offers degree but not college credit. **BOOKSTORE;** **DESCRIPTION:** Offers retreats. **PUBLICATIONS:** *Book Of Natural Remedies Wild Crafted Herbal Tinctures*

Regents College

State University of New York
Cultural Education Center
Albany, NY 12230
TOPICS: Parapsychology

Rollins College

Department Of Philosophy
Winter Park, FL 32787
(305)-646-2178
TOPICS: Parapsychology **DEPT.:** Department of Philosophy **COURSE:** Introduction To Parapsychology **INSTRUCTOR:** Hoyt Edge, Ph. D. **DESCRIPTION:** Introduction to experimental parapsychology. **INDEPENDENT STUDY**

Rose Institute School Of Hypnosis

17 Rose Drive

Fort Lauderdale, FL 33316
(305)-522-7673
CONTACT: Richard P. Maulion, M.D. **TOPICS:** Hypnotism **DEPT. HEAD:** Richard P. Maulion, M.D., F.A.A.P., Dir. **DESCRIPTION:** Advanced Institute for Psychotherapy. Approved school for Clinical Psychologists, Social Workers, Mental Health Counselors, Nurses, Marriage & Family Therapists. Offers 50 CEU's credits.

Rose-Croix University (Ancient and Mystical Order of the Rosae Crucis)

Rosicrucian Order, Rosicrucian Park
1342 Nagle Avenue
San Jose, CA 95191
(408)-287-9171
TOPICS: Spirituality, New Age, Parapsychology

Royal University-School of Acupuncture and Oriental Medicine

3545 Wilshire Boulevard, #218
Los Angeles, CA 90010
(213)-385-4392
TOPICS: Acupuncture, Holistic Health **DESCRIPTION:** School of Oriental medicine and acupuncture.

Rubenfeld Synergy Association

The Rubenfeld Center
115 Waverly Place
New York, NY 10011
(212)-254-5100
TOPICS: Body-Mind Connection

Rudolf Steiner College-Waldorf Teacher Training

9200 Fair Oaks Bouleavrd
Fair Oaks, CA 95628
TOPICS: Parapsychology, Metaphysics

Rudolf Steiner Institute

2577 Newport Road
Ann Arbor, MI 48103
TOPICS: Metaphysics

Sage Femme Midwifery School

Box 183
Boulder Creek, CA 95006
TOPICS: Birth

SAGE: Earth Awareness & Herbs

Box 420
East Barre, VT 05649
(802)-479-9825
CONTACT: Rosemary Gladstar Slick **TOPICS:** Holistic Health, Herbalogy **DEPT.:** Herbs & Earth Ceremonies **COURSE:** All levels of herbalogy **INSTRUCTOR:** Rosemary Gladstar Slick & Karl Slick **DESCRIPTION:** Teaches all aspects of herbalogy. Offers a residential program & a correspondence course called The Science & Art Of Herbalogy. Also conducts travel tours to different locations around the world with the purpose of studying herbs & plants.

Samaritan College (Universal Fellowship of Metropolitan Community Churches)

5300 Santa Monica Boulevard, #304
Los Angeles, CA 90029
TOPICS: Spirituality

San Francisco College Of Acupuncture

P.O. Box 720974
San Jose, CA 95172-0974
(415)-863-3500
TOPICS: Acupuncture, Holistic Healing
DESCRIPTION: Ph. D. of Oriental Medicine

Sandeepany West (Chinmaya Mission West)

Box 9
Piercy, CA 95467
TOPICS: Spirituality

Sangetsu School Of Flower Arranging (World Messicunity)

3068 San Marino Avenue
Los Angeles, CA 90006
TOPICS: Spirituality

Santa Barbara College Of Oriental Medicine

1919 State Street
Suite 204
Santa Barbara, CA 93101
(805)-682-9594
TOPICS: Holistic Healing

Saybrook Institute

1550 Sutter Street
San Francisco, CA 94109
(415)-441-5034
TOPICS: Parapsychology **INSTRUCTOR:** Stanley Krippner, Ph.D. **DEGREES:** Ph.D. Program **INDEPENDENT STUDY; DESCRIPTION:** Ph.D. Program in psychology and humanistic sciences with concentration in parapsychology.

School For Esoteric Studies

40 East 49th Street, Ste. 1903
New York, NY 10017
(212)-755-3027
TOPICS: Body-Mind Connection, Spirituality, Metaphysics

School For Priestesses (Church Of Circle Wicca)

Box 219
Mt. Horeb, WI 53572
TOPICS: Spirituality, Witchcraft, Occult

School Of Ageless Wisdom

6005 Royal Oak Drive
Arlington, TX 76016
TOPICS: Metaphysics

School Of Creative Thought

P.O. Box 193
Franklin, NH 03235
TOPICS: Metaphysics

School Of Lost Borders

Box 55
Big Pine, CA 93513
TOPICS: Holistic Healing

School Of Metaphysics

1643 Galena
Beulah, CO 80010
TOPICS: Channeling

School Of Metaphysics
133 West Mill Street
Colorado Springs, CO 70903
TOPICS: Channeling

School Of Metaphysics
938 LaPorte Avenue
Fort Collins, CO 80521
(303)-484-4689
TOPICS: Metaphysics, Channeling

School Of Metaphysics
1462 Depew Street
Lakewood, CO 80214
(303)-238-1507
TOPICS: Metaphysics, Channeling

School Of Metaphysics
524 Emery Street
Longmont, CO 80501
(303)-678-0707
TOPICS: Metaphysics, Channeling

School Of Metaphysics
3715 University
Des Moines, IA 50311
(515)-255-5570
TOPICS: Channeling

School Of Metaphysics
219 North Third Street
Belleville, IL 62220
TOPICS: Channeling

School Of Metaphysics
2228 South Highland
Berwyn, IL 60402
(708)-788-0674
TOPICS: Metaphysics, Channeling

School Of Metaphysics
1281 West Early Avenue
Chicago, IL 60660
(312)-784-5377
TOPICS: Metaphysics, Channeling

School Of Metaphysics
222 West Wilson
Palatine, IL 60067
(708)-991-0140
TOPICS: Metaphysics, Channeling

School Of Metaphysics
7330 East 47th Street
Indianapolis, IN 46226
(317)-547-9800
TOPICS: Metaphysics, Channeling

School Of Metaphysics
1108 North 26th Street
Kansas City, KS 66102
(913)-621-2625
TOPICS: Metaphysics, Channeling

School Of Metaphysics
55 Kensington
Pleasant Ridge, MI 48069
(313)-398-6650
TOPICS: Metaphysics, Channeling

School Of Metaphysics
719 West Michigan
Ypsilanti, MI 48197

(313)-482-9600
TOPICS: Metaphysics, Channeling

School Of Metaphysics
210 Third Avenue
Columbia, MO 65201
(314)-449-8312
TOPICS: Metaphysics, Channeling

School Of Metaphysics
2009 North Douglas
Springfield, MO 65803
(417)-831-0955
TOPICS: Metaphysics, Channeling

School Of Metaphysics
9459 Roslan
St. John, MO 63114
(314)-429-0076
TOPICS: Metaphysics, Channeling

School Of Metaphysics
717 Marshall
Webster Groves, MO 63119
(314)-961-3321
TOPICS: Metaphysics, Channeling

School Of Metaphysics
1210 NW 36th Street
Oklahoma City, OK 73118
(405)-528-4310
TOPICS: Metaphysics, Channeling

School Of Metaphysics
1419 South Quincy
Tulsa, OK 74120
(918)-582-8836
TOPICS: Channeling

School Of Metaphysics
1937 East Washington
Madison, WI 53704
(608)-241-1953
TOPICS: Metaphysics, Channeling

School Of Metaphysics-National Headquarters
HCR 1
Box 15
Windyville, MO 65783
(417)-345-8411
CONTACT: Dr. Barbara O'Guinn TOPICS: New Age, Metaphysics, Past Life Regression, Holistic Health, Meditation, Psychic, Dreams INSTRUCTOR: Dr. Barbara O'Guinn, Chairman Of Board INSTRUCTOR: Dr. Daniel R. Condron, President INSTRUCTOR: Laurel J. Fuller, Vice-President DESCRIPTION: Non-profit educational & service institute offering workshops & lectures in Past Life Crossings, Health Analysis, Family & Business Analysis. Also sells audio/video tapes, t-shirts, sweatshirts & cards. Has 18 branch schools in 9 states all offering the same type of course work. Produces Thresholds Magazine through its publishing company S.O.M. Publishing & Production.

School Of Natural Medicine
P.O. Box 7369
Boulder, CO 80306-7369
(303)-443-8284 FAX (303)-449-8870
CONTACT: Farida Sharan TOPICS: Holistic Health, Herbalogy, Meditation, Color Therapy,

Homeopathy, Vegetarianism, Nutrition DIRECTOR: Farida Sharan DEGREES: Certificates & Diplomas BOOKSTORE; DESCRIPTION: On 3 acres in the foothills of the Rockies, classes are intensive 5 day seminars, advanced lectures & workshops in Iridology, Herbalogy & Naturopathy. Courses given in Bach flower remedies & counselling. Spa facilities. Correspondence courses available.

School Of Prophets (Sons Ahman Israel)
2/82 Banbury Road
Oxford, OX2 6JT
England
TOPICS: Spirituality

School Of Sacred Arts
133 West Fourth Street
New York, NY 10012
(212)-475-8048
TOPICS: New Age

School Of Spiritual Healing And Prophecy
7 Library Street
Lily Dale, NY 14752
(716)-595-3939 (800)-366-7094
TOPICS: Holistic Healing, Metaphysics

School Of T'ai Chi Chuan
47 West 13th Street
Fifth Floor
New York, NY 10011
(212)-929-1981
TOPICS: Tai Chi

School Of Universal Wisdom (Pansophic Institute-Tantric Buddhism)
Box 2422
Reno, NV 89505
TOPICS: Spirituality

Schumacher College
The Old Postern
Dartington
Totnes, Devon TQ9 8EA
England
TOPICS: Spirituality, New Age DESCRIPTION: Two-five week courses conducted by world renowned teachers in the field of ecology & spiritual values. A college for independent study. Teachers include: James Lovelock, Hazel Henderson, Rupert Sheldrake, Fritjof Capra & Vandana Shiva.

Seattle Midwifery School
2524 16th Avenue S., Room 300
Seattle, WA 98144
(206)-322-8834
TOPICS: Birth

Shasta Abbey (Order of Buddhist Contemplatives)
3612 Summit Drive
P.O. Box 199
Mt. Shasta, CA 96067-0199
TOPICS: Spirituality, Metaphysics DESCRIPTION: Teaches Buddhist philosophy & sells Buddhist supplies.

Shealy Institute For Comprehensive Pain And Health Care

1328 East Evergreen
Springfield, MO 65803
(417)-865-5940
TOPICS: Holistic Healing, Acupuncture, Occult

SHEN Therapy Institute
No. 20 FH Gate 6 Rd.
Sausalito, CA 94965
TOPICS: Spirituality

Sierra University
2900 Bristol D-207
Costa Mesa, CA 92626
TOPICS: Parapsychology DESCRIPTION: Offers
M.A. program.

Sirius School Of Spiritual Science
Baker Road
Shutesbury, MA 01072
(413)-259-1251 (413)-259-1505
TOPICS: Spirituality, Metaphysics, Meditation
DESCRIPTION: Offers courses in The Ageless
Wisdom & Meditation. Also based in Washington,
D.C., 301-320-6394.

Skidmore College
University Without Walls
Saratoga Springs, NY 12866
TOPICS: Parapsychology, Spirituality

Slippery Rock University
Department of Philosophy
Slippery Rock, PA 16057
(412)-794-7370
TOPICS: Psychic Phenomena DEPT.: Department Of
Philosophy COURSE: Mysticism And Psychical
Research INSTRUCTOR: Theodore L. Kneupper, Ph.
D. DESCRIPTION: Explores psi and psychical
research using philosophy as a basis. Psychic
Awareness Club on campus.

SM Seminary
Box 1407
San Francisco, CA 94101
TOPICS: Spirituality

Society For Scientific Exploration
Virginia Polytechnic Institute
College Of Arts And Sciences
Blacksburg, VA 24061
CONTACT: Dr. Henry Bauer TOPICS:
Parapsychology, Psychic Phenomena

Somerset University
Ilminster, Somerset TA19 OBQ
England
TOPICS: Parapsychology DESCRIPTION: Offers
B.A., M.A. and Ph.D.

Sonoma State University
Rohnert Park, CA 94928
TOPICS: Psychology DESCRIPTION: M.A. in
Psychology

Sophia Divinity School
P.O. Box 3616
Hartford, CT 06103
TOPICS: Metaphysics

Sophia Divinity School (Church of Antioch)
Box 1015
Mountain View, CA 94042

TOPICS: Spirituality

South African Society For Parapsychological Studies
University Of Witwatersrand
Johannesburg
South Africa
TOPICS: Parapsychology

Southern Illinois University
P.O. Box 3926
Department Of Psychiatry
Springfield, IL 62708
TOPICS: Parapsychology

Southwest Acupuncture College
712 West San Mateo
Santa Fe, NM 87501
(505)-988-3538
TOPICS: Holistic Healing, Acupuncture

Southwest School of the Healing Arts
1214 Mirarmar
Houston, TX 77006
TOPICS: Holistic Health

Southwestern College
900 Otay Lakes Road
Chula Vista, CA 92010
(619)-421-6700
TOPICS: Parapsychology DEPT.: Department Of
Math & Sciences COURSE: Parapsychology (PSY
103) INSTRUCTOR: Barbara K. Maze, Ph.D.
DESCRIPTION: A study of the many facets of
Parapsychology-clairvoyance, telepathy,
precognition, psychokinesis, out-of-body
experiences, etc. INDEPENDENT STUDY

Southwestern College
P.O. Box 4788
Santa Fe, NM 87502
(505)-471-5756
TOPICS: New Age

Spiritual Development Guild
P.O. Box 155
Tryon, NC 28782
(203)-457-9212
TOPICS: Body-Mind Connection

Spiritual Science Institute Of Philadelphia
2650 Meetinghouse Road
Jamison, PA 18929
(215)-343-2811
TOPICS: Channeling, Psychic Phenomena,
Spirituality DIRECTOR: George L. Mankin
DESCRIPTION: Offers courses & workshops in
esoteric studies

St. Bonaventure University
Department of Theology
St. Bonaventure, NY 14778
(716)-375-2000
TOPICS: Psychic Phenomena DEPT.: Department Of
Theology COURSE: Psychical Research & The
Nature Of Man INSTRUCTOR: Rev. Alphonsus
Trabold, D.F.M., M.A. DESCRIPTION: Explores
parapsychology, its research and relationship with
theology and religion.

St. John's University
Grand Central & Utopia Parkways

Psychology Laboratory SB15, Marillac Hall
Jamaica, NY 11439
(718)-990-6161
TOPICS: Parapsychology DEPT.: Department Of
Psychology COURSE: Altered States of
Consciousness & Parapsychological Events
INSTRUCTOR: Rex G. Stanford, Ph. D.
DESCRIPTION: Discusses various aspects of sleep &
dreams, hypnosis & suggestibility, the environment,
ESP & PK. INDEPENDENT STUDY

St. John's University-Congregational Church Of Practical Theology
31916 University Circle
Springfield, LA 70462
(504)-294-2129
TOPICS: Spirituality, New Age, Metaphysics,
Parapsychology DIRECTOR: Pamela Winkler, Ph.
D. DESCRIPTION: Accredited degree programs since
1969 by external or home-study. Associate,
Bachelor, Master or Ph. D. offered in 14
departments: Parapsychology, Metaphysics, Clinical
Hypnotherapy, Psychology, Counseling, Religion &
Social Services. Catalog available, $4 U.S. or $6
foreign. PUBLICATIONS: Attain TOPICS:
Spirituality, New Age TYPE: Magazine CIRC:
24,000 DESCRIPTION: Produced by the faculty of
St. John's University for its students, alumni and
friends. Publishes inspirational articles to help people
achieve holistic wellness for success & happiness.

St. Mary's College
Winona, MN 55987
TOPICS: Parapsychology DESCRIPTION: Offers
M.A. program.

St. Mary-of-the-Woods College
St. Mary-of-the-Woods, IN 47876
TOPICS: Parapsychology, Spirituality

Stanford University
Department Of Psychology
Jordan Hall, Building 420
Stanford, CA 94305
TOPICS: Parapsychology

State University College
Cooper Center
Brockport, NY 14420
TOPICS: Parapsychology

State University Of New York At Oswego
Psychology Department
Oswego, NY 13126
(315)-341-4013
CONTACT: Dr. Mahlon W. Wagner TOPICS:
Parapsychology, Psychology DEPT.: Psychology
Department COURSE: Current Topics:
Parapsychology (PSY 310) INSTRUCTOR: Mahlon
Wagner, Ph. D. DESCRIPTION: Explores research
and procedure in parapsychology and psychic
phenomena. COURSE: Experimental Psychology:
Parapsychology INSTRUCTOR: Mahlon Wagner, Ph.
D. DESCRIPTION: Study of advanced experimental
research and procedure of parapsychology.

State University Of New York At Stony Brook
Stony Brook, NY 11794
(516)-246-5126 (516)-246-2109

TOPICS: Parapsychology DESCRIPTION: Offers courses on parapsychology

State University Of New York-Geneseo
Psychology Department
Geneseo, NY 14454
TOPICS: Parapsychology DEPT.: Psychology Department COURSE: Parapsychology & Hypnosis (PSY 305) INSTRUCTOR: Lawrence Casler, Ph. D. DESCRIPTION: Critical investigation of the two fields and their interrelationship. INDEPENDENT STUDY

State University Of Utrecht
Parapsychology Laboratory
Sorobnnelaan 16
Utrecht, 3584 CA
The Netherlands
TOPICS: Parapsychology DEPT.: Parapsychology Laboratory INSTRUCTOR: Dr. Martin Johnson DEGREES: Doctorate Program DESCRIPTION: Weekly seminars on parapsychology

Stellar Research Institute
P.O. Box 74
Kempton, IL 60946
TOPICS: UFO's

Stephens College
Campus Box 2083
Columbia, Mo 65215
TOPICS: Parapsychology

Suncoast School Of Massage Therapy
4910 Cypress Street
Tampa, FL 33607
(813)-287-1099
TOPICS: Massage

Susan Wagner High School
Continuing Education Department
1200 Manor Road
Staten Island, NY 10314
(718)-761-0344
TOPICS: Psychic Phenomena DEPT.: Continuing Education Department COURSE: Psychic Phenomena: Myth & Reality INSTRUCTOR: Rosemarie Pilkington, Ph. D. DESCRIPTION: Explores the various aspects of psychical phenomena and its research.

Swedenborg School of Religion (General Convention of the New Jerusalem in the U.S.A.)
48 Sargent Street
Newton, MA 02158
TOPICS: Spirituality, Psychology DESCRIPTION: Offers educational opportunities ranging from correspondence courses to an accredited Masters Degree In Swedenborgian Studies which is based on the spiritual/psychological findings of scientist & seer, Emanuel Swedenborg.

Synanon College-The Synanon Church
50300 Highway 245
Box 42
Badger, CA 93603
TOPICS: Spirituality

Syracuse University
610 East Fayette Street
Syracuse, NY 13202
TOPICS: Parapsychology DESCRIPTION: Offers M.B.A., M.F.A., and M.S. programs.

Tai Hsuan Foundation Clinic, College of Acupuncture and Herbal Medicine
Box 11126
Honolulu, HI 96828
TOPICS: Acupuncture, Herbalogy

Tamalpa Institute
P.O. Box 794
Kentfield, CA 94914
TOPICS: Occult

Taoist Esoteric Yoga Center And Foundation:The Healing Tao
P.O. Box 1194
Huntington, NY 11743
(516)-549-9452
TOPICS: Holistic Healing

Theocentric Foundation
3341 E. Cambridge Avenue
Phoenix, AZ 85008
TOPICS: Spirituality

Thien-An Institute of Buddhist Studies (International Buddhist Meditation Centers)
928 S. New Hampshire
Los Angeles, CA 90006
TOPICS: Spirituality, Meditation

Thomas A. Edison State College
101 W. State Street
Trenton, NJ 08625
TOPICS: Parapsychology

Thought Therapy Institute
P.O. Box 875
Zephyr Cove, NV 89448-0875
TOPICS: Holistic Health

Trager Institute For Psychophysical Integration And Mentastics
10 Old Mill Street
Mill Valley, CA 94941-1891
(415)-388-2688
TOPICS: Holistic Healing, Body-Mind Connection, Psychology, New Age, Meditation DEPT. HEAD: Don Schwartz, Exec. Director COURSE: Beginning Trager Training DESCRIPTION: Teaches basics of Trager bodywork. 48 hours of instruction over 6 days. Taught by Gail Stewart, Deane Juhan, Gary Brownlee & Cathy Hammond. COURSE: Intermediate Trager Training DESCRIPTION: Course consists of 40 hours over 5 days, taught by Sheila Merle Johnson, Bill Scholl, Carol Campbell & Gwen Crowell. DEGREES: Certified Trager Bodywork Practitioner DESCRIPTION: The Trager Approach: A system of gentle, non-intrusive movements which facilitates deep relaxation, increased physical mobility & mental clarity. PUBLICATIONS: *Trager Newsletter; Trager Journal I & II*, $2 each; *Trager Mentastics* Video $30; *Trager Mentastics* (book) by Milton Trager, M.D. & Cathy Hammond, Ph.D. $14.95.

Trinity School Of Theology-Church Of The Trinity Invisible Ministry
P.O. Box 4608
Salem, OR 97302-8608
TOPICS: Spirituality

TSI-Yoga
105 East Fourth Street
Suite 1414B
Cincinnati, OH 45202
(513)-621-3733
TOPICS: Yoga

Turley Forge Blacksmithing School
Route 10, Box 88C
Santa Fe, NM 87501
CONTACT: Frank Turley TOPICS: New Age

Twin Lakes College Of The Healing Arts
1210 Brommer Street
Santa Cruz, CA 95062
TOPICS: Holistic Health, Homeopathy, Holistic Healing

Unification Theological Seminary
Barrytown, NY 12507
TOPICS: Spirituality

Union Graduate School
Box 85315
Cincinnati, OH 45201
TOPICS: Parapsychology DESCRIPTION: Offers Ph.D. program.

Unity School For Religious Studies (Unity School Of Christianity)
Unity Village, MO 64065
TOPICS: Spirituality

Universal Harmony Foundation Seminary
5903 Seminole Boulevard
Seminole, FL 33542
TOPICS: Spirituality, New Age

Universal Life University (Universal Life Church)
601 Third Street
Modesto, CA 95351
TOPICS: Spirituality

Universal Spiritualist University
5848 Pendleton Avenue
Anderson, IN 46013
TOPICS: Spirituality

Universidad del Salvador
Psychology Department
Sarandi 65-1081
Buenos Aires,
Argentina
TOPICS: Parapsychology DEPT.: Psychology Department COURSE: Curso de Parapsicologia-Dinanica del Inconsciente INSTRUCTOR: Enrique Novillo Pauli, M.A. INDEPENDENT STUDY

University Of Alabama
New College External Degree Program
University, AL 35496
TOPICS: Parapsychology, New Age

University Of Amsterdam
Department of Psychology
Weesperplein 8
Amsterdam, 1018 XA
The Netherlands
TOPICS: Parapsychology **DEPT.:** Department Of Psychology **COURSE:** Parapsychology **INSTRUCTOR:** Dick J. Bierman, Ph. D. **DESCRIPTION:** Basic introduction to parapsychology.

University Of California At Irvine
School Of Social Sciences
Irvine, CA 92717
TOPICS: Parapsychology

University Of Colorado
Boulder, CO 80309
(303)-492-6301
TOPICS: Parapsychology, Psychology **DESCRIPTION:** Offers courses on parapsychology

University Of Delaware
Department Of Philosophy
Newark, DE 19711
TOPICS: Parapsychology

University Of Edinburgh
Department of Psychology
7 George Square
Edinburgh, EH8 9JZ
Scotland
TOPICS: Parapsychology **DEPT.:** Department Of Psychology **INSTRUCTOR:** Robert L. Morris, Ph. D. **DEGREES:** Doctorate Program in Psychology **INDEPENDENT STUDY**

University Of Healing/God Unlimited
1101 Far Valley Road
Campo, CA 91906
(619)-478-5111
CONTACT: Dr. Ellen Jermini, Pres. **TOPICS:** Holistic Healing, Metaphysics **DESCRIPTION:** Founded 1975 by Dr. Herbert L. Beierle, Dean & Chairman. A metaphysical correspondence school teaching that the creative genius is within everyone & awaits to be claimed. It catalyzes each student to live a self fulfilled & self aware life. Offers books, tapes, lectures, seminars & workshops. Degrees offered: Bachelor of Philosophy; Practitioner; Minister-Ordination; Master of Healing Sciences, Doctor of Philosophy. Accredited by the Church Of God Unlimited. Non-profit. **PUBLICATIONS:** *GIST* **EDITOR:** Herbert Beierle Ingeborg Puchert **TOPICS:** Holistic Healing, Metaphysics **TYPE:** Magazine **FREQ:** monthly **PRICE:** $20.00 **TERM:** yearly **DESCRIPTION:** Discusses positive philosophy.

University Of Iceland
Department of Psychology
101 Reykjavik,
Iceland
TOPICS: Parapsychology **DEPT.:** Department Of Psychology **COURSE:** Parapsychology **INSTRUCTOR:** Erlendur Haraldsson, Ph. D.

University Of Idaho
Department Of Psychology
Moscow, ID 83843
(208)-885-7508
TOPICS: Parapsychology **DEPT.:** Department Of Psychology **COURSE:** Parapsychology (PSY 340) **INSTRUCTOR:** James E. Crandall, Ph. D.

DESCRIPTION: Examines the many aspects of parapsychology, its methods, procedures and research. **INDEPENDENT STUDY**

University Of Iowa
W400 Seashore Hall
Iowa City, IA 52242
TOPICS: Parapsychology

University Of London
Senate House
Male Street
London, WC1E 7HU
England
TOPICS: Parapsychology **DESCRIPTION:** Offers B.A., M.A., and Ph.D. programs.

University Of Loughborough
Extension Studies
Loughborough
Leicestershire, LE11 3TV
England
TOPICS: Parapsychology **DEPT.:** Extension Studies **COURSE:** The Paranormal **INSTRUCTOR:** Arthur J. Ellison, D. Sc. **DESCRIPTION:** Study of relationship of science and the paranormal.

University Of Maryland
Department of Philosophy
5401 Wilkens Avenue
Baltimore, MD 21228
(301)-455-2103
TOPICS: Parapsychology **DEPT.:** Department of Philosophy **COURSE:** Philosophy & Parapsychology **INSTRUCTOR:** Stephen Braude, Ph. D. **DEGREES:** Undergraduate & Graduate

University Of Miami
Department of Psychology
Coral Gables, FL 33129
(305)-284-2814
TOPICS: Parapsychology **DEPT.:** Department Of Psychology **COURSE:** Parapsychology (PSY 307) **INSTRUCTOR:** Jack A. Kapchan, Ph.D. **DESCRIPTION:** Explores all aspects of parapsychology, its history, credibility & methodology. **INDEPENDENT STUDY**

University Of Michigan Hospital
Department Of Psychiatry
Ann Arbor, MI 48109
TOPICS: Parapsychology

University Of Minnesota
201 Westbrook hall
Minneapolis, MN 55455
TOPICS: Parapsychology

University Of Missouri
Department of Psychology
5319 Holmes Street
Kansas City, MO 64110
(816)-276-1321
TOPICS: Parapsychology **DEPT.:** Department of Psychology **COURSE:** Parapsychology **INSTRUCTOR:** Lawrence Simkins **DESCRIPTION:** The study of parapsychology through research in ESP, PK & Theta phenomena, etc. **INDEPENDENT STUDY**

University Of New England
Department of Psychology
Armidale, New South Wales 2351

Australia
CONTACT: Harvey Jon Irwin **TOPICS:** Parapsychology **DEPT.:** Department Of Psychology **COURSE:** Parapsychology (PSY 220-1/320-1) **INSTRUCTOR:** Harvey Irwin, Ph. D. **DESCRIPTION:** Explores aspects of unexplained phenomena. **INDEPENDENT STUDY; DESCRIPTION:** Undergraduate course & Postgraduate Research Degrees in Parapsychology under Assoc. Prof. Harvey Irwin. Undergraduate: B.A., B. Soc. Sc., B. Sc.. Postgraduate: M.A., M. Soc. Sc., M. Litt., Ph. D.

University Of North Carolina
Department Of Psychology
Chapel Hill, NC 27514
TOPICS: Parapsychology **DEPT.:** Department Of Psychology **INSTRUCTOR:** David Price Rogers, Ph. D. **INDEPENDENT STUDY**

University Of Nottingham
Department Of Psychology
Nottingham NG7 2RD
England
TOPICS: Parapsychology

University Of Oklahoma
1700 Asp Avenue
Norman, OK 73037
TOPICS: Parapsychology **DESCRIPTION:** Offers M.L.S. program.

University Of Oriental Studies
939 S. New Hampshire Avenue
Los Angeles, CA 90006
TOPICS: Spirituality, Reincarnation **DESCRIPTION:** Offers Ph. D. of Dharma Degree.

University Of Regina
Psychology Department
Regina, Saskatchewan S4S 0A2
Canada
TOPICS: Parapsychology

University Of South Florida
4202 Fowler Avenue
Tampa, FL 33620
TOPICS: Parapsychology

University Of Southern Maine
Continuing Education
68 High Street
Portland, ME 04101
(207)-780-4045
TOPICS: Parapsychology **DEPT.:** Continuing Education **COURSE:** Introduction To Parapsychology (CPA 101A) **INSTRUCTOR:** Alex Tanous **DESCRIPTION:** Explores consciousness & energy through ESP, life after death, Kirlian photography, astral projection, reincarnation, time, space & mass.

University Of The Great Spirit (Confederate Nations Of Israel)
Box 151
Big Water, UT 84741
TOPICS: Spirituality

University Of Virginia, Division Of Parapsychology
Dept. of Behavioral Medicine & Psychiatry
Box 152, Medical Center
Charlottesville, VA 22908

CONTACT: Ian Stevenson, Dir. TOPICS: Parapsychology, Psychic Phenomena DIRECTOR: Ian Stevenson, M.D. DEPT.: Behavioral Medicine & Psychiatry INDEPENDENT STUDY; DESCRIPTION: Fellowships are offered for case research.

University Of Washington
RP10 Medical School
Department Of Psychiatry
Seattle, WA 98195
CONTACT: Director, Division Of Neuropsychiatry TOPICS: Parapsychology

University Of Waterloo
Waterloo, ON N2L 3G1
Canada
TOPICS: Parapsychology

University Of West Florida
Department of Psychology
Pensacola, FL 32514-5751
TOPICS: Parapsychology DEPT.: Department Of Psychology INSTRUCTOR: William L. Mikulas, Ph. D. DESCRIPTION: B.A. or M.A. degrees in psychology with a specialization in parapsychology.

University Of Wisconsin
Department of Psychology
2100 Main Street
Stevens Point, WI 54481
(715)-346-3953
TOPICS: Parapsychology DEPT.: Department Of Psychology COURSE: Parapsychology (PSY 285) INSTRUCTOR: Daniel Kortenkamp, Ph. D. DESCRIPTION: Basic survey of ESP, PK and Survival Research.

University Of Wyoming
Box 3708
University Station
Laramie, WY 82071
(307)-766-2187
TOPICS: Parapsychology DEPT.: Department Of Psychology COURSE: Literature Of Parapsychology INSTRUCTOR: R. Leo Sprinkle, Ph. D. DESCRIPTION: Basic survey of parapsychology and its literature with emphasis on the psychological aspects of psychic phenomena. INDEPENDENT STUDY

University Research Expedition Program
University Of California
Berkeley, CA 94720
(415)-642-6586
TOPICS: New Age

Urbana College (General Convention of the New Jerusalem in the United States of America)
Urbana, OH 43078
TOPICS: Spirituality

Virginia Commonwealth University
Department of Psychology
Richmond, VA 23284
TOPICS: Parapsychology DEPT.: Department Of Psychology COURSE: Parapsychology (PSY 307) INSTRUCTOR: Glenn R. Hawkes, Ph. D. DESCRIPTION: Study of ESP & PK as well as poltergeists, death, mediums, apparitions, healing,

dreams and unexplained phenomena. INDEPENDENT STUDY

Waldorf Institute
260 Hungry Hollow Road
Spring Valley, NY 10977
(914)-425-0055
TOPICS: New Age, Metaphysics

Waldorf Institute of Detroit
2555 Burns Street
Detroit, MI 48214
TOPICS: Parapsychology

West Coast Ministerial Directorate (Teaching of the Inner Christ)
San Diego, CA 92138
TOPICS: Spirituality

West Georgia College
Psychology Department
William James Laboratory for Psychical Research
Carrollton, GA 30118
(404)-834-1423
TOPICS: Parapsychology, Psychic Phenomena DEPT.: Department of Psychology COURSE: Developmental & Clinical Parapsychology INSTRUCTOR: William Roll. M. Litt. DESCRIPTION: Explores developmental & clinical parapsychology COURSE: Life After Death INSTRUCTOR: William Roll. M. Litt. DESCRIPTION: Examining the findings which suggest the continuation of existence after death. COURSE: Neuropsychology, System Theory & Psi INSTRUCTOR: William Roll. M. Litt. DESCRIPTION: The study of psi in relationship to parapsychology, psychology, biology and physical theories. DEGREES: Undergraduate & Graduate INDEPENDENT STUDY; DESCRIPTION: Parapsychological Services Institute, Inc.-A special interest group on campus.

West Side YMCA
Adult Education
5 West 63rd Street
New York, NY 10023
(212)-787-5302
TOPICS: Parapsychology COURSE: Parapsychology INSTRUCTOR: Nicole Lieberman DESCRIPTION: Workshop discussing aspects of psi: development, healing, out-of-body experiences, inductive states etc. Also experiments of ESP & PK.

Western Connecticut State University
Psychology Department
White Street
Danbury, CT 06801
(203)-797-4334
TOPICS: Parapsychology DEPT.: Psychology Department COURSE: Parapsychology (PSY 236) INSTRUCTOR: David Sheskin, Ph.D. DESCRIPTION: Lectures & experiments in parapsychology.

Western Illinois University
309 Sherman Hall
Macomb, IL 61455
TOPICS: Parapsychology

Western Institute For Social Research
3220 Sacramento Street
Berkeley, CA 94702

TOPICS: Parapsychology, Psychology DESCRIPTION: Offers M.A. and Ph.D. programs.

Western Michigan University
General Studies Science Department
338 Moore Hall
Kalamazoo, MI 49008
(616)-383-0460
TOPICS: Parapsychology DEPT.: General Studies Science Department COURSE: Science of Parascience (GSCI 432) INSTRUCTOR: Michael D. Swords, Ph. D. DESCRIPTION: Explores phenomena on the edge of science through individual research projects. INDEPENDENT STUDY

Whole Life University
409 Santa Monica Boulevard, #215
Santa Monica, CA 90401
TOPICS: Parapsychology

Wichita State University
Department of Religion
Box 76
Wichita, KS 67208
(316)-689-3108
TOPICS: Psychic Phenomena DEPT.: Department of Religion COURSE: Psychic Phenomena (Religion 2600) INSTRUCTOR: Howard A. Mickel, Ph. D. DESCRIPTION: Investigation of psychic phenomena using scientific methods. INDEPENDENT STUDY

Wild Rose College Of Natural Healing
302,1220 Kensington Road, N.W.
Calgary, Alberta T2N 3P5
Canada
(403)-270-0936
TOPICS: Holistic Healing, Parapsychology

William Lyon University
814 Moreno Boulevard
San Diego, CA 92110
TOPICS: Parapsychology DESCRIPTION: Offers Ph.D. program.

Winward Community College
Continuing Education
45-720 Keaahala Road
Kaneohe, HI 96744
(808)-235-0077
TOPICS: Parapsychology DEPT.: Continuing Education COURSE: Introduction Into Parapsychology INSTRUCTOR: Gharith A. Pendragon DESCRIPTION: Basic study of parapsychology, its history and research.

World College West
101 South San Antonio Road
Petaluma, CA 94952
(800)-821-2499
TOPICS: New Age

World Peace University
Box 10869
Eugene, OR 97440
(503)-741-1794
TOPICS: New Age

World University Of America-Ecumenical Ministry Of The Unity Of All Religions
107 N. Ventura Street
Ojai, CA 93023

(805)-646-1444

TOPICS: Spirituality, Metaphysics, New Age, Parapsychology **PUBLICATIONS:** *Conscious Dying: Psychology Of Death & Guidebook To Liberation* **EDITOR:** B. Reyes **TOPICS:** Death **TYPE:** Book **PRICE:** $12.95

Wright Institute Of Astrol Study
2136 East Sprague Road
Broadview Heights, OH 44147

TOPICS: Astrology

Yale University
Department Of Psychology
New Haven, CT 06520
TOPICS: Parapsychology

Yo San University Of Traditional Chinese Medicine
1314 Second Street

Santa Monica, CA 90401
(310)-207-1383
TOPICS: Spirituality, Holistic Health, Acupuncture, Herbalogy **DIRECTOR:** Master Ni **DESCRIPTION:** Promotes Taoist principles in training health care professionals in the disciplines of acupuncture, herbalogy & related arts. Offers 3 & 4 year Master's Degree programs, post-graduate & China internship programs.

Museums

The following is an alphabetical list of Museums related to the Topics of New Age, Spirituality, the Occult, Metaphysics and related fields. Many display artifacts and antiquities, conduct tours and offer educational materials.

American Museum Of Natural History
79th Street, Central Park West
New York, NY 10024
TOPICS: New Age DESCRIPTION: Contains ritual objects, masks, costumes & other spiritual artifacts.

Asian Art Museum Of San Francisco
The Avery Brundage Collection
Golden Gate Park
San Francisco, CA 94188
TOPICS: New Age, Spirituality

Cloisters, The
100 Margaret Corbin Drive
Ft. Tryon Park, NY 10040
(212)-923-3700
TOPICS: New Age DESCRIPTION: Contains parts of reassembled European monasteries & cloistered gardens with piped in Gregorian Chants for meditation.

Dracula Museum
Penthouse North
29 Washington Square, West
New York, NY 10011
(212)-533-5018
CONTACT: Dr. Jeanne Keyes Youngson, Curator TOPICS: Occult, Vampires DESCRIPTION: Founded by Dr. Jeanne Keyes Youngson. Contains a vast collection of items relating to Dracula, vampires & horror memorabilia. Admission limited to registered members of the International Count Dracula Fan Club.

Field Museum Of Natural History
Roosevelt Road At Lake Shore Drive
Chicago, IL 60614
(312)-975-9642

TOPICS: New Age DESCRIPTION: Various artifacts on display such as ancient Egyptian tombs & Native American shamanistic masks.

Jacques Marchais Center Of Tibetan Arts
338 Lighthouse Avenue
Staten Island, NY 10306
TOPICS: New Age DESCRIPTION: Contains ritual objects & thankas.

Metropolian Museum Of Art
Fifth Avenue At 82nd Street
New York, NY 10028
TOPICS: New Age DESCRIPTION: Contains an extensive Tibetan collection including costumes, jewelry, wall hangings, etc.

Museum Of Fine Arts
Huntington Avenue
Boston, MA 02115
TOPICS: New Age DESCRIPTION: Displays artifacts such as copper ritual objects & numerous thankas.

National UFO Museum
150 North Central Street, Ste. 223
Reno, NV 89501-1603
CONTACT: Jerry E. Smith, Exec. Dir. TOPICS: UFO's, Occult, New Age DESCRIPTION: Founded 1990. Offers major exhibits detailing each of the major theories of the nature & origin of UFO's, top UFO stories & a UFO Hall of Fame. Also unexplained mysteries & links to the Occult & New Age. Bookstore, catalog & publishes Journal of Ufology.

Nicholas Roerich Art Museum
319 West 107th Street
New York, NY 10026
(212)-864-7752

TOPICS: New Age DESCRIPTION: Part of the Agni Yoga Society containing numerous spiritual paintings.

Shaker Museum Foundations
95 Shaker Road
Old Chatham, NY 12136
TOPICS: New Age DESCRIPTION: Shows Shaker life as one of America's first spiritual communities.

Spiritual Museum
4328 N. Lincoln Avenue
Chicago, IL 60618-1712
(312)-478-2410
CONTACT: Michael J. Kurban, Dir. TOPICS: Astrology, Spirituality, Holistic Health, Crystals, Numerology, Herbalogy DESCRIPTION: Curators Rev. Michael Kurban & Dr. Loretta Hilsher-Kurban. Purpose is to educate people on spiritual history, gemology & minerals. Contains old occult books, antique spiritual voting box, voodoo dolls, phantom crystal, Spanish Tarot cards. Admission $3.

Westgate Gallery/Press
5219 Magazine Street #1
New Orleans, LA 70115-1358
(504)-899-3077
CONTACT: Leilah Wendell TOPICS: Death, Occult, New Age, Metaphysics DESCRIPTION: The only museum/gallery/publishing house in the world focusing on Necromantic Art & Literature. Specializes in the understanding of & encounters with the Angel of Death. PUBLICATIONS: *Westgate News* PUBLISHER: Leilah Wendell EDITOR: Lorraine Chandler, Daniel Kemp TOPICS: Parapsychology TYPE: Newsletter DATE: 1981 SIZE: 8 1/2 x 11, 10 pgs. FREQ: Irregular CIRC: 3,000 PRICE PER COPY: $2.50 DESCRIPTION: Deals with the interaction of metaphysics & spiritual entities such as THE ANGEL OF DEATH..

Events

Included in this section are individuals and companies that sponsor New Age events such as fairs and shows. Descriptions of these events are offered when available.

Ad-Com, Inc.
1259 Rt. 46, Bldg. 1
Parsippany, NJ 07054
(201)-256-5721 (201)-316-9511 (900)-820-8787
CONTACT: Vincent J. Tabatneck TOPICS: Parapsychology, Metaphysics FOUNDED: 1969 DESCRIPTION: Conducts psychic fairs, New Age festivals & health expos. Fairs every Sun. Offers workshops on Healing, Space, Astrology, Palmistry, Aliens. Offers Psychic Readings, 900-820-8787, ext. 100, by Psychic of your choice. $.65-1st min., $2.25 each min. after.

American And International Crafts
2 Park Avenue, Suite 1100
New York, NY 10016
(212)-686-6070
CONTACT: Carol Sturgeon TOPICS: New Age

American Booksellers Association
137 West 25 Street
New York, NY 10001
(800)-463-9353
TOPICS: New Age

American Federation Of Astrologers
Rural Route #2, Box 2292
Fredonia, PA 16124
(412)-475-3915
CONTACT: Rose Lineman TOPICS: New Age

Amigos De Las Americas
5618 Star Lane
Houston, TX 77057
(713)-782-5290 (800)-231-7796
TOPICS: New Age

Association For Humanistic Psychology
1301 Longfellow Street, North West, #302
Washington, DC 20011-3532
(202)-882-6515 FAX (202)-291-3347
CONTACT: Jim Stewart TOPICS: New Age

Brighter Side Promotions
P.O. Box 5273
Glendale, AZ 85312
(602)-938-9754
CONTACT: Linda Zubel TOPICS: New Age, Psychic FOUNDED: 1988 DESCRIPTION: Conducts New Age psychic fair which also offers lectures, seminars, workshops & trade exhibitors. Primarily in the West & Southwest.

Buddhism And Psychotherapy Conference
352 Meads Mountain Road
Woodstock, NY 12498
(914)-679-8079
CONTACT: Susan Pasternack TOPICS: New Age

Creative Resource Systems
1404 Gale Lane
Nashville, TN 37212

(615)-298-9932
CONTACT: Anderson Hewitt TOPICS: New Age, Metaphysics FOUNDED: 1984

Crystal Congress
P.O. Box 60575
Palo Alto, CA 94306
(415)-388-8355
CONTACT: Lawrence Stoller TOPICS: Crystals DESCRIPTION: The Quintessential Crystal Event dedicated to improve awareness & education about crystals.

Cycles Research Conferences & Seminars
P.O. Box 1460
Sebastopol, CA 95472
TOPICS: Astrology

Evolving Times Expo
904 Commons Drive
Sacramento, CA 95825-6647
(916)-863-1316
TOPICS: New Age

Exhibitor Show
150 Burlington Avenue
Clarendon Hills, IL 60514
(312)-752-6312
TOPICS: New Age FOUNDED: 1985

Fascinating Facets
60 Main Street
Atherton, QLD 4883,
Australia
(61) 70-912365
CONTACT: Rene Boissevain TOPICS: Crystals DESCRIPTION: Leading Mineral Exhibition specializing in all forms of crystals & gems. Also has a simulated underground Crystal Museum.

G.L.D.A., Incorporated
P.O. Box 2391
Tucson, AZ 85702
(602)-742-5455
TOPICS: New Age

Gem And Lapidary Wholesalers, Incorporated
P.O. Box 98
Flora, MS 39071-0098
(601)-879-8832
CONTACT: Tina Gray TOPICS: Crystals, New Age DESCRIPTION: Produces 25 gem & lapidary wholesale trade shows yearly in the U.S., conducts gem tours to Brazil each year & publishes Gem/Lapidary Quarterly.

Goodfellow Wholesale Craft Shows
2181 Greenwich Street
San Francisco, CA 94123
TOPICS: New Age

Health And Harmony Festival
P.O. Box 484
Graton, CA 95444
(707)-823-9355 FAX (707)-829-7681
CONTACT: Debra Guisti TOPICS: Holistic Health, New Age FOUNDED: 1978 DESCRIPTION: Annual New Age Expo offering outdoor music concerts & crafts fair held in June in Santa Rosa, CA.

Heartland Pagan Festival (HSA)
P.O. Box 3407
Kansas City, KS 66103
(816)-561-6111
CONTACT: Rhiannon Bennett, Pres. TOPICS: Paganism, New Age, Spirituality FOUNDED: 1986 DESCRIPTION: Sponsored & organized by the Heartland Spiritual Alliance. Provides sharing & networking for all pagan traditions. Held Memorial Day weekend each year. Over 500 participants.

Holistic Health Conference
Rosemont College
Rosemont, PA 19010
(215)-527-0189
TOPICS: New Age

Institute For Earth Education
P.O. Box 288
Warrenville, IL 60555
(312)-393-3096
CONTACT: Dave Wampler TOPICS: Holistic Healing, New Age FOUNDED: 1974 DESCRIPTION: Annual conference promoting education & information to environmentally conscious individuals. Offers lectures & workshops, a journal & educational information. PUBLICATIONS: The Institute For Earth Education TOPICS: Holistic Healing TYPE: Newsletter

Institute For Stellar Influence Studies
1565-A Fitzgerald Drive, Suite 143
Pinole, CA 94564
(415)-222-9436
TOPICS: New Age

Intercontinental Seth And Metaphysical Conference
409 Marquette Drive
Louisville, KY 40222
(502)-423-1188
TOPICS: New Age, Metaphysics

International Conference On Paranormal Research
P.O. Box 8447
Fort Collins, CO 80524
(303)-491-0633
TOPICS: New Age

International Gem And Jewelry Shows, Inc.
4601 North Park Avenue
Chevy Chase, MD 20815
(301)-656-9049

TOPICS: Crystals DESCRIPTION: Produces gem, mineral & jewelry shows throughout the U.S.

International Wholistic/Metaphysical Exposition
8388 Netherby Road, Rural Route 4
Welland, ON L3B 5N7
Canada
(416)-384-2481
CONTACT: Crossroads TOPICS: New Age

L.A. Weekend Health And Life Expo
P.O. Box 16790
Encino, CA 91416-6790
(818)-705-8865
CONTACT: Hank Krastman TOPICS: New Age

Life's Games
7149 West Berwyn Avenue
Chicago, IL 60656-0373
(312)-775-9301
CONTACT: Larry Garrett TOPICS: New Age

Magnificent You Expo
P.O. Box 566714
Atlanta, GA 30356-0373
(404)-255-1369
CONTACT: New Age Information Network
TOPICS: New Age, Metaphysics FOUNDED: 1985

Mind Body Spirit Festival
1st Floor, 18 Whistler Street
Manly 2095
Sydney, NSW
Australia
02/977-1200
TOPICS: New Age FOUNDED: 1989

Mount Ida Area Chamber Of Commerce
P.O. Box 6
Mount Ida, AR 71957
(501)-867-2723
CONTACT: Paul G. Griffith TOPICS: Crystals DESCRIPTION: Sponsors the annual Quartz Crystal Festival & World's Championship Quartz Crystal Dig.

National Gift Show
240 Peachtree Street, Suite 2200
Atlanta, GA 30043
(404)-220-2200
CONTACT: Donna Rossman TOPICS: New Age

National Whole Health Symposium And Expo
19913 Beach Boulevard, Suite 258
Huntington Beach, CA 92648
(714)-694-6826
CONTACT: Deborah Lally TOPICS: New Age

Natural Foods Expo
1301 Spruce Street
Boulder, CO 80302
(303)-939-8440
CONTACT: Pam Breen TOPICS: New Age

Natural Health Convention
P.O. Box 688
Monrovia, CA 91017
(818)-357-2181
CONTACT: Debra Barner TOPICS: New Age

Nature's Originals
749 East Ft. Union Boulevard
Midvale, UT 84047
(801)-255-9404
CONTACT: David J. Lewis TOPICS: New Age FOUNDED: 1950

New Age Expo V
P.O. Box 566822
Atlanta, GA 30356
(404)-552-1440
CONTACT: Rochel Haich Blehr TOPICS: New Age

New Age Renaissance Fair
3914 Leigh Avenue
San Jose, CA 95124
(408)-448-6726
CONTACT: Eric Meece, Organizer TOPICS: New Age FOUNDED: 1982 DESCRIPTION: Two day annual fair held at the San Jose Convention Center. Purpose is to present today's Renaissance in arts, health & spiritualism. Offers New Age products. Approximately 180-200 exhibitors, 3,000-5,000 attendees. Free lectures & concerts each day.

New Age Symposium
P.O. Box 81607
Cleveland, OH 81607
(216)-779-9509
CONTACT: Damon Foundation TOPICS: New Age FOUNDED: 1990

New Earth Expo
P.O. Box 758
Los Gatos, CA 95031-0758
(408)-356-4728
CONTACT: The Gentry TOPICS: New Age

Omega Arts Network
Box 1227
Jamaica Plains, MA 02130
(617)-522-8300
CONTACT: Saphira Linden, Director TOPICS: New Age

Pacific Crystal Guild
P.O. Box 1371
Sausalito, CA 94966-1371
(415)-641-1701 (415)-383-7837
CONTACT: Jerry Tomlinson, Pres. TOPICS: Crystals, New Age FOUNDED: 1986 DESCRIPTION: Conducts 5 crystal fairs each year in Northern California. Features metaphysical healing tools, crystals, minerals & jewelry. Usually 38 booths & 80 vendors. Also offers seminars, conferences, retail shops & produces The Crystal Merchant's Code of Ethics.

Planetwork
P.O. Box 804
Ketchum, ID 83340
(208)-726-4016
CONTACT: Jennifer And Ed Moffett TOPICS: New Age

Positive World
1662 South Geiger
Tacoma, WA 98465
(206)-565-3985
CONTACT: Laurie Brenner TOPICS: New Age

Psychic Expressions Fair
99 Gorski Street

Buffalo, NY 14206
(716)-826-2791
CONTACT: Carol Ruth TOPICS: New Age

Psychic Guild Of New Jersey And New York
P.O. Box 1236
Maywood, NJ 07607
(201)-778-3376
TOPICS: New Age

Rainbow Expressions
P.O. Box 436
Fairfield, CA 94533
(707)-422-4343
CONTACT: Reverend ShaRon TOPICS: New Age

Rainbow Family Of Living Light
Rural Route 1, Box 6
McCall, ID 83638
TOPICS: New Age FOUNDED: 1970 DESCRIPTION: Sponsors an annual meeting called gathering of the tribes which attracts 10,000 to 30,000 participants. Called the Woodstock of the New Age movement, meetings occur in Australia, New Zealand, Europe & the U.S.

Small Press Book Fair
20 West 44th Street
New York, NY 10036
(212)-764-7021
TOPICS: New Age

South Western Astrology Conference
24228-B Hawthorne Boulevard
Torrance, CA 90505
(213)-378-4192
TOPICS: New Age, Astrology DESCRIPTION: Annual Fall Astrology conference for novices & professionals in the field.

Spirit Of Christmas Crafts Faire
P.O. Box 484
Graton, CA 95444
(707)-823-9355
CONTACT: Debra Giusti TOPICS: New Age

Spiritual Awareness Expo
11737 Elkhead Range Road
Littleton, CO 80127
(303)-979-7797
CONTACT: Dawning Enterprises Organization TOPICS: New Age FOUNDED: 1988

Starfair - Visionary Arts Expo
P.O. Box 1748
Laguna Beach, CA 92652
(714)-472-7886
TOPICS: New Age

Total Life Expo
P.O. Box 13813
Salem, OR 97309-1813
TOPICS: New Age

Tradeshow Week
12233 West Olympic, #236
Los Angeles, CA 90064
TOPICS: New Age

Turning Point
299 Stratford Park Circle
Del Mar, CA 92014

(619)-755-6670

TOPICS: New Age, Metaphysics **FOUNDED:** 1985

U.S. Gems Expos

P.O. Box 8862
Tucson, AZ 85738
(602)-791-2210

CONTACT: George F. Topham **TOPICS:** Crystals, New Age **DESCRIPTION:** Conducts shows featuring gem, jewelry, fossil, mineral & lapidary suppliers. Produces the International Tucson Expo as well as the Denver Expo.

United Astrology Congress

78 Hubbard Avenue
Stamford, CT 06905
(203)-357-7041

CONTACT: Mary Downing **TOPICS:** New Age **FOUNDED:** 1986

Unity Christ Church

2690 Ocean Avenue
San Francisco, CA 94132
(415)-566-4122

CONTACT: Shay St. John **TOPICS:** New Age, Metaphysics, Holistic Health **FOUNDED:** 1945

Video Expo

701 Westchester Avenue
White Plains, NY 10604
(914)-328-9157

CONTACT: Knowledge Industry Publications **TOPICS:** New Age

Virginia Beach Holistic Health Expo

P.O. Box 595
Virginia Beach, VA 23451-0595
(804)-428-3588 (800)-333-4499

TOPICS: Holistic Health **FOUNDED:** 1991 **DESCRIPTION:** Annual holistic health expo featuring lectures & workshops by leading experts in the field. Also more than 40 exhibitors offering books, products & services in personal health care.

Visions 1990 - Sonship Productions

10008 Hogan Drive
Huntsville, AL 35803
(205)-883-6730

CONTACT: Frank Faulkner **TOPICS:** New Age

Visions And Business

P.O. Box 17248
Boulder, CO 80308
(303)-442-6543

CONTACT: Marianne Weidlein **TOPICS:** New Age

Whole Health Expo

100 King Street
Northampton, MA 01060-3225
(413)-586-4269 (800)-545-1534

CONTACT: Al Rapaport **TOPICS:** Holistic Health **FOUNDED:** 1985 **DESCRIPTION:** Largest wholistic expo in New England. Over 100 exhibitors, 150 workshops & 10,000 attendees. Operating 9 years in Northampton, MA & 8 years in Boston.

Whole Life Expo

Box 1317
Venice, CA 90291
(310)-396-7090

CONTACT: Alana Lee Or Kirk Feral **TOPICS:** New Age **DESCRIPTION:** Conducts annual exhibitions. Over 30,000 attendees. Offers workshops & booths. Also sponsors NY Whole Life Expo.

Whole Life Expo San Francisco

4961 Mission Street
San Francisco, CA 94112
(415)-333-4373

CONTACT: Cliff Dunning **TOPICS:** New Age, UFO's, Holistic Health **FOUNDED:** 1982 **DESCRIPTION:** 100 workshops, 180 seminars, lectures, 13 panel discussions, 400 booths offering products & services, performances of songs, dance & music all presented by experts in the fields of health, personal growth, the environment, UFO's & cutting edge technology.

Whole Self Festival

P.O. Box 513
Grants Pass, OR 97526-0043
(503)-474-7700

CONTACT: Michael Mirdad **TOPICS:** New Age

Wic-Can Festival

P.O. Box 125
Scarborough, ON, M1L1B1,
Canada

TOPICS: Witchcraft

World Congress

15300 Ventura Boulevard, Suite 405
Sherman Oaks, CA 91403

TOPICS: New Age

World Of Paid Speaking Seminar

18825 Hicrest Road
P.O. Box 1120
Glendora, CA 91740
(818)-335-8069

CONTACT: Dottie Walters **TOPICS:** New Age

117

Biographies

Included in this chapter are biographies of people often considered to be experts in their chosen fields. Most of these individuals are lecturers, many offer Readings and a large number of them have written books. We have only listed those individuals for whom we were able to obtain a current and verifiable address.

Aaloe, Annabelle
4681 W. 9th Avenue
Vancouver, British Columbia V6R 2E3
Canada
(604)-228-8910

TOPICS: Crystals

Abaddon, Brother
Society Of Mary Magdalen
Box 201
Cape Cottage, ME 04107

TOPICS: Channeling

Acers, Dr. Elva
Vita-Dell Spa
13495 Palm Drive
Desert Hot Springs, CA 92240
(714)-329-6200

TOPICS: Holistic Healing

Acheson, Louis K.
Unity-And-Diversity World Organization
1010 S. Flower Street, No. 500
Los Angeles, CA 90015
(213)-839-0758

TOPICS: New Age

Acker, Barbara
Southern Dharma Retreat Center
Route 1
Box 34-H
Hot Springs, NC 28743
(704)-622-7112

TOPICS: Holistic Healing

Ackerman, Marshall
Rodale Press, Inc.
33 East Minor Street
Emmaus, PA 18049
(215)-967-5171

TOPICS: Holistic Healing

Adams, Charles J., III
Exeter House Books
14 East 34th Street
Reading, PA 19606
(215)-779-8173

TOPICS: New Age OCCUPATION: Author, Lecturer, Investigator of the Supernatural DESCRIPTION: Investigator of supernatural phenomena, lecturer & author of several books about ghost stories, legends & folklore in the Mid-Atlantic region (PA, NJ, DE). Published by Exeter House Books.

Adams, Nancy, M.A.
Agape, Incorporated
9313 Rosstown Way
Houston, TX 77080
(713)-932-8951

TOPICS: Crystals, Channeling, Holistic Healing

Adams, Thomas R.
Project Stigma
P.O. Box 1094
Paris, TX 75460
(214)-784-5922

TOPICS: Psychic Phenomena

Afton, Anita
New Age Teachings
37 Maple Street
Brookfield, MA 01506
(617)-867-3754

TOPICS: New Age

Alashar, Waltz J.
Samadhi Dreams Press
1319 Dennis Court
Kalamazoo, MI 49007
(616)-381-7273

TOPICS: New Age

Albora-Goldman, Dianne
Crystal Adventure
938 Harding Street
Whitby, ON, L1N 1Y7
Canada
(416)-430-2390

TOPICS: Crystals

Alexander, Tom
New Moon Publishing, Inc.
P.O. Box 2046
Corvallis, OR 97339
(503)-757-2532

TOPICS: Holistic Healing

Allachaquora
Allachaguora Gem Tinctures
218 McKenzie Street
Santa Fe, NM 87501
(505)-988-9274

TOPICS: Crystals

Allen, Gerri
P.O. Box 1385
Westwood, CA 96137

TOPICS: Channeling

Allen, Gina
Sunhaven
c/o Bombay P.O.
South Auckland,
New Zealand

TOPICS: Crystals, Channeling, Holistic Healing, New Age, Homeopathy, Spirituality OCCUPATION: Teacher, Author, Healer, Lecturer DESCRIPTION: Channel, healer, events coordinator, naturopath, teacher in all New Age subjects. Network Facilitator, NZ crystal & gem essences, .

Allen, Gloria
P. O. Box 1066
Woodstock, NY 12498
(914)-679-2245

TOPICS: Astrology, Numerology DESCRIPTION: Typed astrology-numerology readings offering natal interpretations and predictions.

Allen, Michael R.
The Augury Press
P.O. Box 33054
Phoenix, AZ 85067-3054
(900)-454-1454 (602)-971-7478

TOPICS: Psychic, Occult, Astrology, Tarot, Metaphysics, Witchcraft, Tea Leaves DATE OF BIRTH: 03/27/67 PLACE OF BIRTH: Phoenix, AZ OCCUPATION: Astrologer, Occultist, Tarot Reader WORK EXPERIENCE: The Augury Press, Phoenix, AZ, Partner, Astrologer; Mystic Line, Phoenix, AZ, Tarot Reader PROFESSIONAL MEMBERSHIPS: Son Of A Witch Society; Defenders Of Wildlife

Allingham, Dorothy
Rocky Mountain Wellness Spa And Institute
P.O. Box 777
Steamboat Springs, CO 80477
(303)-879-7772

TOPICS: Holistic Healing

Allingham, Larry
Rocky Mountain Wellness Spa And Institute
P.O. Box 777
Steamboat Springs, CO 80477
(303)-879-7772

TOPICS: Holistic Healing

Allinson, Vicki
Visionary Crystals
P.O. Box C-164
El Toro, CA 92630
(714)-859-2127

TOPICS: Crystals

Allison, Kay
The Quest Institute, Inc.
P.O. Box 3265
Charlottesville, VA 22903
(804)-295-6923

TOPICS: Holistic Healing

Alper, Frank
Arizona Metaphysical Society
3639 East Clarendon Road
Phoenix, AZ 85018
(602)-956-1676

TOPICS: Astrology, Channeling, Crystals, New Age, Metaphysics DATE OF BIRTH: 01/22/30 PLACE OF

BIRTH: Brooklyn, NY **OCCUPATION:** Channeler, Author **WORK EXPERIENCE:** Arizona Metaphysical Society, Phoenix, AZ, Founder **DESCRIPTION:** Conducts channeling sessions for an entity from Atlantis. Developed the New Age attitude & information on Atlantis & crystals. **PUBLICATIONS:** *Exploring Atlantis*, 3 Vols., 1982

Alpine, Baha'Uddin
Common Ground
305 San Anselmo Avenue, #313
San Anselmo, CA 94960
(415)-459-4900

TOPICS: New Age

Altman, Nathaniel
169 Prospect Park West
Brooklyn, NY 11215
(718)-499-2384

TOPICS: Palmistry, Metaphysics, Holistic Health, Vegetarianism **DATE OF BIRTH:** 01/25/48 **PLACE OF BIRTH:** New York, NY **EDUCATION:** University of Wisconsin, Madison, WI **DEGREE:** B.A. **YEAR DEGREE:** 1971 **OCCUPATION:** Author, Palmist **PROFESSIONAL MEMBERSHIPS:** The Theosophical Society, member 1970-present; North American Vegetarian Society, member 1976-present **PUBLICATIONS:** *Discover Palmistry*, 1991 **PUBLISHER:** Aquarian Press **PUBLICATIONS:** *Living With Asthma*, 1991 **PUBLISHER:** Dell Books **PUBLICATIONS:** *Everybody's Guide To Chiropractic Health Care*, 1990 **PUBLISHER:** Jeremy P. Tarcher **PUBLICATIONS:** *Medical Palmistry*, 1989 **PUBLISHER:** Aquarian Press **PUBLICATIONS:** *Lovelight*, 1989 **PUBLISHER:** Pocket Books **PUBLICATIONS:** *Palmistry: Your Career In Your Hands*, 1988 **PUBLISHER:** Aquarian Press

Alvarado, Carlos
University Of Virginia
Division Of Parapsychology
Box 152, Medical Center
Charlottesville, VA 22908
TOPICS: Parapsychology

Amaya, Contessa Gypsy
P.O. Box 6011
Santurce, 00914
Puerto Rico
(809)-722-0902

TOPICS: Crystals, Psychic

Amdur, Shelley
4723 North Sacramento
Chicago, IL 60656
TOPICS: Channeling

Amelia
P.O. Box 6582
Moore, OK 73153
TOPICS: Channeling

Amorous, Lisa
Metamorphosis
P.O. Box 10581
Bainbridge Island, WA 98110
(206)-842-7788

TOPICS: Crystals

Anandamurti, Sri
Ananda Marga
854 Pearl Street

Denver, CO 80203
TOPICS: New Age

Anderson, Bill
Living Among Nature Daringly!
4466 Ike Mooney Road
Silverton, OR 97381
(503)-873-8829

TOPICS: New Age

Anderson, Bob
Runner's World Magazine Company
Box 366
Mountain View, CA 94042
(415)-965-8777

TOPICS: Holistic Healing

Anderson, Hilary, Ph. D.
P.O. Box 10261
Beverly Hills, CA 90213
TOPICS: Channeling

Andre, Taranath
Dolphin Encounters
P.O. Box 37
Corindi Beach, NSW 2456,
Australia
TOPICS: Crystals

Andrea, Miss
521 Queen Street
Westbury, NY 11590
(516)-997-9865

TOPICS: Psychic, Metaphysics **DATE OF BIRTH:** 01/19/70 **PLACE OF BIRTH:** Jamaica, West Indies **EDUCATION:** Hofstra University, Hempstead, NY **DEGREE:** B.A., English **OCCUPATION:** Metaphysician, Psychic, Writer **AWARDS:** Ms D **PROFESSIONAL MEMBERSHIPS:** Sylvan Society, FHM Circle

Andren, Michael G.
5670 Walnut Avenue
Long Beach, CA 90805-4871
(213)-423-2025

TOPICS: Crystals, Parapsychology **DESCRIPTION:** Member of the Crystal Skulls Society International & the Institute of Psychic & Hypnotic Sciences.

Anne, Georgia
c/o Clearlight Visions
110 Warren Street
New Rochelle, NY 10801
(212)-228-0900

TOPICS: Psychic, Tarot, Runes

Anthony, Carol K.
Anthony Publishing Company
206 Gleasondale Road
Stow, MA 01775
(508)-897-7191

TOPICS: Spirituality **DATE OF BIRTH:** 08/14/30 **PLACE OF BIRTH:** Cowen, W. VA. **EDUCATION:** Ward-Belmont Jr. College, Nashville, TN **DEGREE:** Certificate **YEAR DEGREE:** 1949 **EDUCATION:** W. VA. Wesleyan, Buckhannon, W. VA. **YEARS:** 1948 **EDUCATION:** University of Iowa, Iowa City, IA **DEGREE:** B.A. English **OCCUPATION:** Author, Lecturer, Publisher, Editor **WORK EXPERIENCE:** Anthony Publishing Company, Stow, MA., President 19 years **PROFESSIONAL MEMBERSHIPS:** Stow Historical Society, Prof. Member, Chief of

Publications **DESCRIPTION:** Fields of expertise includes I Ching, Insight Meditation, History. **PUBLICATIONS:** *History Of Stow*, 1960 **PUBLISHER:** Beacon Publications **PUBLICATIONS:** *A Guide To The I Ching*, 1980 **PUBLISHER:** Anthony Publishing Co. **PUBLICATIONS:** *Philosophy Of The I Ching*, 1981 **PUBLISHER:** Anthony Publishing Co. **PUBLICATIONS:** *The Other Way: A Book of Experiences in Meditation*, 1990 **PUBLISHER:** Anthony Publishing Co. **PUBLICATIONS:** *History Of Stow*, editor, 1984 **PUBLISHER:** Stow Historical Society Publishing Co. **PUBLICATIONS:** *Recollections Of Stow*, editor, 1990 **PUBLISHER:** Stow Historical Society Publishing Co.

Appel, Sage
Berkeley Massage Associates
1962 University Avenue
Berkeley, CA 94704
(415)-845-5998

TOPICS: Holistic Healing

Apsel, Charlain
Plenum Publishing Corporation
233 Spring Street
New York, NY 10013
(212)-620-8000

TOPICS: New Age

Arbe, Audrey
412 8th Avenue
New York, NY 10011
TOPICS: Channeling

Archer, Helen
P.O. Box 1118
Pompano Beach, FL 33061

TOPICS: Astrology **OCCUPATION:** Planetologist, Astrologer, Author, Psychic **DESCRIPTION:** Developed the Plantetology Individualized Computer Horoscope Program. Offers Egyptian ritual products, Planetology Booklet & a 900 daily telephone service.

Archer-Lowe, Cylvia, Rev.
Star-Lite Shadows Visitor Planning Service
P.O. Box 484
Sedona, AZ 86336-0484

TOPICS: Metaphysics, Meditation, Holistic Healing, Spirituality **DATE OF BIRTH:** 10/31/27 **PLACE OF BIRTH:** Hartford, CT **EDUCATION:** University of Healing, Campo,CA **DEGREE:** B.A., M.A., Ph.B Minister **EDUCATION:** New Hampshire College **YEARS:** 1985 **DEGREE:** Human Services **EDUCATION:** Hartford College For Women **YEARS:** 1989 **DEGREE:** Secretarial Skills **OCCUPATION:** Instructor & Lecturer of Metaphysics, Author, Counselor, Clairvoyant, Healer, Ordained Clergy **WORK EXPERIENCE:** Starlight Club Program, Sedona, AZ, Teacher, Lecturer 20 years **AWARDS:** Hartford Pronaos, Appreciation Award 1977; Spirit Of Christ Sanctum, Hartford, CT, 1984 Hon. Doctor Of Humanities; Who's Who Writers, Editors, Poets **PROFESSIONAL MEMBERSHIPS:** A-On'o Center Of Light, Inc., Founder 1972; White Eagle Lodge, TX; Spiritual Frontiers Fellowship, Hartford, Ct. **DESCRIPTION:** Offers teaching & lectures on meditation, holistic healing, metaphysics & spiritualism. **PUBLICATIONS:** *Wisdom Of Wisdom From The Masters*, 1978 **PUBLISHER:** The Book Department **PUBLICATIONS:** *Star Lighter Newsletter*

Ardron, Pete
Crystal Matrices, Pink Hampster Enterprises
44 Oakdale Road
London, SW 16 2HL
England
TOPICS: Crystals

Arenivar, Margie
Shining Waters Ashram
Route 3
Box 560
Fredericktown, MO 63645
(314)-783-6715

TOPICS: Holistic Healing

Arenz, Kenneth Charles
48 Byram Terrace Drive
Greenwich, CT 06831
(203)-532-0118

TOPICS: Astrology, Massage, Holistic Health, Meditation, Herbalogy, Body-Mind Connection DATE OF BIRTH: 07/05/48 PLACE OF BIRTH: Brooklyn, NY EDUCATION: Northeastern University, Boston, MA YEARS: 1966-68 EDUCATION: Ohashi Institute, NY, NY DEGREE: Certificate YEAR DEGREE: 1990 EDUCATION: Kushi Institute, Boston, MA DEGREE: Certificate YEAR DEGREE: 1986 OCCUPATION: Shiatsu Practitioner, Astrological Counselor PROFESSIONAL MEMBERSHIPS: National Council on Geocosmic Research

Arledge, Garnette
Crystal Journeys
Box 492
Delhi, NY 13753
(607)-538-1005

TOPICS: Crystals

Armstrong, Richard, MscD.
Crystal Talismans And Images
611 Larkspur
Corona Del Mar, CA 92628
(714)-760-6759

TOPICS: Crystals

Arnel, Dr. Marc D.
Arnel Chiropractic Center
100 Mamaroneck Avenue
White Plains, NY 10601
(914)-686-8989

TOPICS: Chiropractic, Holistic Health

Arnold, Wilma
Organization Of Psychic Research Associates
Box 60901
Oklahoma City, OK 73146
(405)-557-8048

TOPICS: Psychic Phenomena

Arnove, Ivan
Center For Feeling People
10170-4 Larwin Avenue
Chatsworth, CA 91311
(818)-882-7404

TOPICS: Holistic Healing

Aronson, Robert
High Times
211 East 43rd Street
New York, NY 10017
(212)-972-8484

TOPICS: New Age

Arrien, A.
P.O. Box 2077
Sausalito, CA 94966
(415)-331-5850 (707)-762-5138

TOPICS: Spirituality, New Age, Psychology, Tarot, Metaphysics EDUCATION: University of CA at Berkeley YEARS: 1967-69 DEGREE: M.A. Anthropology YEAR DEGREE: 1969 EDUCATION: CA Institute of Integral Studies, San Francisco,CA DEGREE: Honorary Ph.D. Philosophy YEAR DEGREE: 1988 OCCUPATION: Teacher, Lecturer, Consultant WORK EXPERIENCE: CA Institute of Integral Studies, San Francisco, CA, Asst. Prof. Division of Development, Faculty Consultant PROFESSIONAL MEMBERSHIPS: Association for Transpersonal Psychology, Palo Alto, CA, Board of Directors; The Child Care Center, President, Board of Directors PUBLICATIONS: *The Tarot Handbook*, 1989 PUBLISHER: Arcus Publishing Co.

Artemis, Zoe
Crystal Institute Of Los Angeles
1800 South Robertson Boulevard, #131
Los Angeles, CA 90035
(213)-655-5432

TOPICS: Crystals

Arum, Susan
10531-90th Street, #1116 South
Edmonton, AB, T5H 4E7
Canada
(403)-438-6962

TOPICS: Crystals

Ash, Jane
Crystal Care
1705 North Country Club
Tucson, AZ 85716
(602)-881-8032

TOPICS: Crystals

Ashfield, Nicholas
Toronto Healing Arts Centre
715 Bloor Street West
Toronto, On M6G 1L5
Canada
(416)-535-8777

TOPICS: Holistic Healing

Ashoff, Gibert
Vichy Springs Resort
2605 Vichy Springs Road
Ukiah, CA 95482
(707)-462-9515

TOPICS: Holistic Healing

Astounding Velma
Abracadabra Productions
310 East 46th Street
New York, NY 10017

TOPICS: Palmistry, ESP, Tarot, Tea Leaves, Occult, Psychic, Metaphysics DATE OF BIRTH: 10/26/43 PLACE OF BIRTH: New York, NY EDUCATION: New York University, New York, NY YEARS: 4 DEGREE: B.A. EDUCATION: Sorbonne, Paris, France YEARS: 2 OCCUPATION: Psychic, Palmist, ESP, Magician, Author, Lecturer WORK EXPERIENCE: Abracadabra Productions, New York, NY, President; Above And Beyond, New York, NY, Owner of Psychic Network AWARDS: International Brotherhood Of Magicians-Master of Magic Grand Trophy; Miss Hocus Pocus PROFESSIONAL MEMBERSHIPS: Society of American Magicians; International Brotherhood of Magicians DESCRIPTION: Called Queen of Illusion. Offers magic, palmistry, ESP, etc. for the purpose of entertainment &/or consultation. Lecture topics: How To Read Your Own Palm; Learn The Innermost Secrets Of Others; Excursion Into The Super Natural; Exploration Of The Occult. PUBLICATIONS: *Elements Of Contemporary Palmistry*, 1970

Atchity, Kennith
Plenum Publishing Corporation
233 Spring Street
New York, NY 10013
(212)-620-8000

TOPICS: New Age

Atwater, P.M.H.
P.O. Box 7691
Charlottesville, VA 22906
(804)-974-7945

TOPICS: Astrology, Death, Hypnotism, Numerology, Parapsychology, Runes, Psychic DATE OF BIRTH: 09/19/37 PLACE OF BIRTH: Twin Falls, ID EDUCATION: Boise State University, Boise, ID OCCUPATION: Author, Lecturer, Researcher, Teacher-Human Transformation Potential, Parapsychologist WORK EXPERIENCE: You Can Change Your Life, Charlottesville, VA, Founder, President AWARDS: Who's Who In American Women, World's Who's Who Of Women, Book Of Honor, Int'l Psychic Register, 2,000 Notable American Women, Personalities of America PROFESSIONAL MEMBERSHIPS: Idaho Writers League, Authors Guild of America, American Federation of Astrologer, U.S. Psychotronics, A.R.E., Inner Forum- Nonprofit Metaphysical Corp. DESCRIPTION: Since 1977 has been a pioneering researcher for near-death experience especially as relates to after-effects & the new sciences. Professional in hypnotic past-life regressions, dehaunting houses, auric massage, channeling, astrology, rune & numerology. PUBLICATIONS: *Coming Back To Life: The After-Effects Of The Near-Death Experience*,1989 PUBLISHER: Ballantine Books PUBLICATIONS: *The Magical Language Of Runes*, 1990 PUBLISHER: Bear & Co. PUBLICATIONS: *Future Memory: An Exploration Of Alternate Realities & the Illusion*

Aubrey, Patricia M.
P.O. Box 233
Cassadaga, FL 32706
(904)-228-0091

TOPICS: Psychic Healing, Psychic, Holistic Healing, Spirituality DATE OF BIRTH: 07/20/36 PLACE OF BIRTH: Boston, MA EDUCATION: Boston City Hospital, Boston, MA DEGREE: Bacteriologist YEAR DEGREE: 1957 OCCUPATION: Spiritual Counselor, Healer, Teacher AWARDS: Certified Healer 1990-present, Certified Medium 1988-present PROFESSIONAL MEMBERSHIPS: Southern Cassadaga Spiritualist Camp Meeting Association DESCRIPTION: Offers private counseling, healing, chakra balancing & self-development classes.

Aubrey, S.M.
rue Forel
1162 Saint-Prex,
Switzerland

TOPICS: Crystals

Audette, Rose
Environmental Action, Inc.
1525 New Hampshire Avenue, N.W
Washington, DC 20036
(202)-745-4870

TOPICS: Holistic Healing

Auerbach, Loyd
Office Of Paranormal Investigations
P.O. Box 875
Orinda, CA 94563-0875
(415)-553-2588

TOPICS: Parapsychology, Ghosts, Psychic Phenomena **DATE OF BIRTH:** 02/01/56 **PLACE OF BIRTH:** New Rochelle, NY **EDUCATION:** Northwestern University, Evanston, IL **YEARS:** 1974-1978 **DEGREE:** B.A. **YEAR DEGREE:** 1978 **EDUCATION:** John F. Kennedy University, Orinda, CA **YEARS:** 1979-1981 **DEGREE:** M.S. **YEAR DEGREE:** 1981 **OCCUPATION:** Parapsychological Consultant & Writer **WORK EXPERIENCE:** Office of Paranormal Investigations, Orinda, CA, Co-Dir., 1989-Pres.; John F. Kennedy University, Orinda, CA, Adjunct Prof., 1983-Pres.; American Society For Psychical Research, NY, NY,Consultant,1982-83 **PROFESSIONAL MEMBERSHIPS:** CA Society For Psychical Study, Pres., 1988-Pres.; American Society For Psychical Research; Parapsychological Assoc; Society of American Magicians **PUBLICATIONS:** *ESP, Hauntings And Poltergeists*, 1986 **PUBLISHER:** Warner **PUBLICATIONS:** *Psychic Dreaming*, 1991 **PUBLISHER:** Warner

Augustine, Marla
Nebraska State Department Of Health
301 Centennial Mall South
Box 95007
Lincoln, NE 68509
(403)-471-2101

TOPICS: Holistic Healing

Aurora, Barbara
The Radiance Technique Association International, Inc.
6860 Gulfport Boulevard #237
St. Petersburg, FL 33707
(813)-360-6564

TOPICS: Reiki

Austin, Phylis
Science/Health Abstracts
P.O. Box 319
Ft. Mitchell, AL 36856
(404)-288-5495

TOPICS: Holistic Healing

Avara, Rosalie
Rio Grande Press
P.O. Box 371371
El Paso, TX 79937
(915)-595-2625

TOPICS: Psychic Phenomena

Avital, Samuel
Le Centre Du Silence Mime School
P.O. Box 1015
Boulder, CO 80306
(303)-494-8729

TOPICS: Body-Mind Connection, Psychology, New Age **OCCUPATION:** Teacher, Author, Actor **WORK EXPERIENCE:** Boulder Mime Theatre, Boulder, CO, Founder, Director 1972-1982; International Summer Mime Workspace, Boulder, CO, 1975-present **DESCRIPTION:** Dedicated to the integration of the Arts & business through the study of the Avital Integrated Method which provokes one's creativity to discover unlimited possibilities beyond the creative edge, integrating body, mind & emotions through artistic expression **PUBLICATIONS:** *Mime Workbook*, 1971 **PUBLICATIONS:** *Mime & Beyond: The Silent Outcry*, 1985

Avlonitis, Katherine
Himalayan International Institute Of Yoga Science and P
R.R.1
Box 400
Honesdale, PA 18431
(717)-253-5551

TOPICS: New Age

Awtry-Smith, Marilyn
The Harmonial Philosophy Association
P.O. Box 284
Cassadega, FL 32706
(904)-228-3798

TOPICS: Metaphysics

Aze, Michael
Earthstar Foundation
2635 West First Avenue, #6
Vancouver, BC, V6K 1H1
Canada
(604)-733-5810

TOPICS: Crystals

Azzato, Jean
Raven Press
1185 Avenue Of The Americas
New York, NY 10036
(212)-930-9500

TOPICS: Dreams

Babbitt, Elwood
P.O. Box 25
Wendell Depot, MA 01380

TOPICS: Psychic

Babin, Laura
Biosocial Publications, International
Box 1174
Tacoma, WA 98401
(206)-272-0530

TOPICS: Holistic Healing

Badgley, Laurence
Health World, Inc.
1477 Rollins Road
Burlingame, CA 94010
(415)-343-1637

TOPICS: Holistic Healing

Baer, Randall Baer
Starcrest Academy
P.O. Box 6209
Hot Springs, AR 71902
(501)-525-2751

TOPICS: Crystals

Baer, Thomas
Starcrest Academy
P.O. Box 6209
Hot Springs, AR 71902
(501)-525-2751

TOPICS: Crystals

Baer, Vicki
Starcrest Academy
P.O. Box 6209
Hot Springs, AR 71902
(501)-525-2751

TOPICS: Crystals

Bailey, William
Center For Health & Safety Studies Indiana University
H P E R Building
Rm 116
Bloomington, IN 47405
(812)-335-7975

TOPICS: Holistic Healing

Baker, Dr. Robert A.
3495 Castleton Way North
Lexington, KY 40517
(606)-272-2561

TOPICS: New Age, Hypnotism, Body-Mind Connection **DATE OF BIRTH:** 06/27/21 **PLACE OF BIRTH:** Blackford, KY **EDUCATION:** University of Kentucky, Lexington, KY **DEGREE:** B.S., M.S. **YEAR DEGREE:** 1949 **EDUCATION:** Stanford University, Palo Alto, CA **YEARS:** 1949-1951 **DEGREE:** Ph. D. **YEAR DEGREE:** 1951 **OCCUPATION:** Psychologist-Industrial, Experimental, Clinical **WORK EXPERIENCE:** MIT, Cambridge, MA, Research Scientist 1951-53; Human Resources Research Office, Fort Knox, KY, Research Scientist; University of KY, Lexington, KY, Teacher, Researcher, Administration **AWARDS:** University of KY Alumni Assoc. Great Teacher Award 1985, CSICOP Fellow 1990 **PROFESSIONAL MEMBERSHIPS:** Kentucky Psychological Assoc., Pres. 1962-63 & 1970; Fellow, American Psychological Assoc. 1969 **PUBLICATIONS:** *They Call It Hypnosis*, 1990 **PUBLISHER:** Prometheus Books **PUBLICATIONS:** *Psychology In The Wry*, 1962 **PUBLISHER:** Van Nostrand **PUBLICATIONS:** *Stress Analysis Of Strapless Evening Gowns*, 1962 **PUBLISHER:** Doubleday

Baker, Rob
Parabola Books
656 Broadway
New York, NY 10012
(212)-505-6200

TOPICS: New Age

Baker, Sheryle R.
The Life Center
214 South Fielding Avenue
Tampa, FL 33606
(813)-251-0289

TOPICS: Holistic Healing

Baldwin, Rahima
Informed Homebirth
Box 3675
Ann Arbor, MI 48106
(313)-662-6857

TOPICS: Birth

Ballas, Joy, Certified Hypnotist
P.O. Box 9002, 375

Boulder, CO 80301
TOPICS: Channeling

Balzer, Pat
The Tibetan Foundation
P.O. Box 126
Richmond, ME 04357

TOPICS: Channeling DESCRIPTION: Certified Channeler by The Tibetan Foundation.

Banham, Dr. Katherine
Duke University
Box 6847
College Station
Durham, NC 27708

TOPICS: Parapsychology

Bannis, Myrtle
Plenum Publishing Corporation
233 Spring Street
New York, NY 10013
(212)-620-8000

TOPICS: New Age

Baras, Carol
Baras Foundation
P.O. Box 3189
San Diego, CA 92103
(619)-291-5252

TOPICS: Hypnotism

Baras, Vasilios Theophanis, Ph. D.
The Baras Foundation
P.O. Box 3189
San Diego, CA 92103
(619)-291-5252

TOPICS: Hypnotism

Barbor, Gerry
Akala Point
Box 4
Site 28, R.R. 1
Tantallon, No B0J 3J0
Canada
(902)-823-2160

TOPICS: Holistic Healing

Barklam, John W.B.
Foresight Magazine
44 Brockhurst Road
Hodge Hill, Birmingham B36 8JB
England
021-783-0587

TOPICS: Metaphysics DATE OF BIRTH: 07/08/55 PLACE OF BIRTH: England OCCUPATION: Author, Editor WORK EXPERIENCE: Foresight Magazine, Birmingham, England, Author, Editor PUBLICATIONS: *Masterplan*, 1986 PUBLISHER: United Writers, Ltd. PUBLICATIONS: *Foresight Magazine*

Barklam, Judy
Foresight Magazine
44 Brockhurst Road
Hodge Hill, Bi B36 8JB
England
(021)-783-0587

TOPICS: Metaphysics

Barlett, Kim
Animal Rights Network, Inc.
456 Monroe Turnpike

Monroe, CT 06468
(203)-452-0446

TOPICS: New Age

Barry, John M.
American Holistic Health Sciences Association
1766 Cumberland Green
Suite 208
St. Charles, IL 60174
(312)-377-1929

TOPICS: Holistic Healing

Bartlett, Deborah
Dancing Turtle Trading Co., c/o Eagle Nest Lodge
HCR 3, Box 592
Deer River, MN 56636
(218)-246-8701

TOPICS: Crystals

Bartley, Barbara
Box 434
Hartland, VT 05048

TOPICS: Channeling

Bartole, Reverend Barbara
1221 North Orange Street
La Habre, CA 90631
(213)-691-0131

TOPICS: New Age, Metaphysics, Channeling, Psychic, Spirituality DESCRIPTION: A practicing psychic, spiritual counselor, trance medium offering private & group readings, lectures & home demonstrations.

Barton, John
Biokinesiology Institute
5432 Highway 227
Trail, OR 97541
(503)-876-2080

TOPICS: Holistic Healing

Bassett, Anthony John
No. 1 Electronics
Arch 7, Stables Market
Camden Lock, Chalk Farm Road
London, NW1 8AH
071-284-3483

TOPICS: Crystals, Metaphysics, Parapsychology, Crystals, PSI, Holistic Healing OCCUPATION: Paranormal Researcher, Holistic Healer WORK EXPERIENCE: No. 1 Electronics, London, England, President DESCRIPTION: Producer & researcher of electronic equipment to demonstrate reality of paranormal abilities & to develop those abilites. Purpose is to promote healing & transcendental human potential.

Baxandall, Lee
Naturist Society, Inc.
P.O. Box 132
Oshkosh, WI 54902
(414)-231-9950

TOPICS: New Age

Bazinet, Rozanne, Ph.D.
P.O. Box 662005
Sacramento, CA 95866

TOPICS: Crystals

Beal-Ojala, Skyhawk,Rev.Rosalind
Church Of Loving Hands, Inc.
1100 Main, Ste. B

Fortuna, CA 95540
(707)-725-9627 (707)-768-3226

TOPICS: Holistic Healing, Spirituality, Massage DATE OF BIRTH: 11/12/45 PLACE OF BIRTH: Durham, NC EDUCATION: University of Arizona, Tucson, AZ YEARS: 1963-67 DEGREE: B.F.A. YEAR DEGREE: 1967 EDUCATION: Americana Leadership College, Osceola, IA YEARS: 1968-69 DEGREE: M.A. YEAR DEGREE: 1969 OCCUPATION: Educator, Author, Lecturer, Minister, Massage Therapist, Metis Pipe Carrier WORK EXPERIENCE: Church Of Loving Hands/Loving Hands Institute, Carlotta, CA, Founder & Director 1979-present AWARDS: Certified Massage Therapist, Cottonwood, AZ, 1974; Ministerial Credential, Mother Earth Church, 1976; Doctor of Divinity 1978; Metis Pipe Carrier 1982 PROFESSIONAL MEMBERSHIPS: International Clergy Assoc.; Associated Bodywork & Massage Professionals, Inc.; BPW International; Sierra Club; Pan American Indian Association DESCRIPTION: Teaches classes in Massage Therapy & the Healing Arts. PUBLICATIONS: *Medicine Ways* PUBLISHER: Church Of Loving Hands

Beamer, Alex
Breitenbush Hot Springs Retreat And Conference Center
P.O. Box 578
Detroit, OR 97342
(503)-854-3314

TOPICS: Holistic Healing

Bear, Vicki V.
P.O. Box 1339
Los Almos, NM 87544

TOPICS: Channeling

Beaulieu, Dr. J. David
Preventic, Inc.
P.O. Box 30327
Kansas City, MO 64112
(816)-444-4866

TOPICS: Holistic Health DESCRIPTION: Chiropractor, nutritional expert, radio talk show host and authority on preventive medicine.

Beavers, Betty
Whispering Pines
114 Pine Grove Raod
Scroggins, TX 75280
(214)-860-3326

TOPICS: Holistic Healing

Beavers, Gary
Whispering Pines
114 Pine Grove Raod
Scroggins, TX 75280
(214)-860-3326

TOPICS: Holistic Healing

Bechtel, Janet
Sedona Institute
1645 East Missouri, #110, Ste.
Phoenix, AZ 85016
(602)-264-0123

TOPICS: Holistic Healing

Beck, Deirdre C., L.M.T.
Deirdre C. Beck Center
2200 NW 47th Terrace
Lauderhill

Ft. Lauderdale, FL 33313
(305)-731-2515 (305)-731-2515

TOPICS: Massage OCCUPATION: Massage Therapist WORK EXPERIENCE: Deirdre, C. Beck Center, Sunrise, FL., Founder, Director DESCRIPTION: Licensed Massage Therapist offering Swedish Massage to relieve sinus problems, headaches, T.M.J., accident victims, back pain, arthritis, relaxation.

Bedford, Tania, MsT
Box 766
Bolinas, CA 94924
(415)-868-2103

TOPICS: New Age, Holistic Health DESCRIPTION: Practices alternative health methods such as Ortho-Bionomy, European Lymphatic Drainage, Bach remedies, & reflexology.

Bedi, Achal
Emissaries Of Divine Light/Glen Ivy Community
25000 Glen Ivy Road
Corona, CA 91719
(714)-735-8701

TOPICS: Holistic Healing

Beebe, Walter
New York Open Center, Inc.
83 Spring Street
New York, NY 10012
(212)-219-2527

TOPICS: Metaphysics

Beierle, Dr. Herbert L.
University Of Healing
1101 Far Valley Road
Campo, CA 91906
(619)-478-5111

TOPICS: Holistic Healing, Metaphysics

Beldon, Sanford
Practical Homeowner Publishing
27 Unquowa Road
Fairfield, CT 06430
(203)-259-9877

TOPICS: New Age

Bellos, Denise M.
235 Goldenrod Avenue
Bridgeport, CT 06606
(203)-374-8567

TOPICS: Holistic Healing

Beloff, Dr. John
University Of Edinburgh
Department Of Psychology
7 George Square
Edinburgh, Sc EH8 9JZ
United Kingdom

TOPICS: Parapsychology

Bender, Dr. Hans
Institut Fur Grenzgebiete
D-7800 Freiburg Im Breisgau
Eichhalde 12
West Germany

TOPICS: Parapsychology

Bensen, D.R.
Keats Publishing, Inc.
27 Pine Street
P.O. Box 876

New Canaan, CT 06840
(203)-966-8721

TOPICS: Holistic Healing

Benyo, Rich
Rodale Press, Inc.
33 East Minor Street
Emmaus, PA 18049
(215)-967-5171

TOPICS: Holistic Healing

Berger, Dr. Rick
Mind Science Foundation
8301 Broadway, Suite 100
San Antonio, TX 78209

TOPICS: Parapsychology

Berlitz, Charles
Avon Books
959 Eighth Avenue
New York, NY 10019
(212)-481-5600

TOPICS: New Age, Holistic Health

Bernards, Michelle
Point Hudson
Port Townsend, WA 98368

TOPICS: Channeling

Berres, Rosemarie H.
Hidden Blessings
5933 West National Avenue
West Allis, WI 53214
(414)-259-1229

TOPICS: Holistic Healing

Bertraud, Michael
Common Ground
P.O. Box 34090
Station D
Vancouver, BC V6J 4M1
Canada
(604)-733-2215

TOPICS: Homeopathy

Besant, Annie
Theosophical Society Of America
306 West Geneva Road
P.O. Box 270
Wheaton, IL 60189-0270
(312)-668-1571

TOPICS: Metaphysics

Besteman, K.
Alcohol And Drug Problems Association Of North America
444 North Capitol Street, NW
Washington, DC 20001
(202)-737-4340

TOPICS: Holistic Healing

Bethards, Betty
Inner Light Foundation
P.O. Box 761
Novato, CA 94948
(415)-382-1040

TOPICS: Holistic Healing

Betterton, Charles
Communities Publication Cooperative
105 Sun Street
Stelle, IL 60919

(815)-256-2252

TOPICS: New Age

Betts, Dee
11 First Street
Lily Dale, NY 14752

TOPICS: Channeling

Bezenar, Georgina
Holistic Animal News
c/o Georgina Bezenar
1245 S.W. Othello
Seattle, WA 98106
(206)-767-4374

TOPICS: Holistic Healing

Bibik, Su
Crystal Circle
3477 South Ninth Street
Kalamazoo, MI 49009
(616)-375-8047

TOPICS: Crystals

Biccum, Gerald E.
Box 4 Clarkson P.O.
Mississauga, Ontario L5J 3X9
Canada
(416)-855-3358

TOPICS: Palmistry, Metaphysics DATE OF BIRTH: 04/06/47 PLACE OF BIRTH: Cadomen Alta, Canada EDUCATION: Devry Technical College, Ontario, Canada OCCUPATION: Computer Analyst, Handologist, Author WORK EXPERIENCE: STM Systems Corp., Miss. Ontario, Canada, Computer Analyst 20 years DESCRIPTION: Created a new science called Handology. Methods of analyzing the hand & extracting unbiased data such as health, success, careers, relationships, personalities & life's obstacles. Way to discover yourself, identify strengths, weaknesses & aptitudes. PUBLICATIONS: *Handology: How To Unlock The Hidden Secrets Of Your Life*, 1989 PUBLISHER: Beyond Words

Billy, Allen T.
Moonstone Blue & Night Roses
P.O. Box 393
Prospect Heights, IL 60070
(312)-392-2435

TOPICS: New Age

Binder, Bettye B.
Reincarnation Books/Tapes
P.O. Box 7781
Culver City, CA 90233-7781
(310)-397-5757

TOPICS: New Age, Past Life Regression, Meditation, Astrology, Hypnotism OCCUPATION: Reincarnation Teacher, Counselor, Author WORK EXPERIENCE: Association For Past Life Research & Therapies, Riverside, CA, First Vice-Pres. DESCRIPTION: Professional reincarnation counselor. Conducted more than 3000 past life regressions & taught more than 11,000 people in classes & workshops since 1980. PUBLICATIONS: *Past Life Regression Guidebook*, 1992 PUBLISHER: Reincarnation Books/Tapes PUBLICATIONS: *Past Lives, Present Karma Workbook* PUBLISHER: Reincarnation Books/Tapes PUBLICATIONS: *Meditative & Past Life Journal* PUBLISHER: *Reincarnation Books/Tapes* PUBLICATIONS: *Finding Your Life's Purpose*

Through Astrology Workbook **PUBLISHER:** Reincarnation Books/Tapes

Birdzell, Dayna
1201 S.E. 2nd Street
Ft. Lauderdale, FL 33301
(305)-698-5072

TOPICS: Psychic

Birmingham, Bob
Chelo Publishing
350 5th Avenue, #6204
New York, NY 10118
(212)-947-4322

TOPICS: Holistic Healing

Blackstone, Anna
A.R.E. Clinic
4017 North 40th Street
Phoenix, AZ 85018
(602)-955-7729

TOPICS: Holistic Healing

Blanchard, Rick
Cosmoenergetics Publications
P.O. Box 86353
San Diego, CA 92138
(619)-295-1664

TOPICS: Metaphysics

Blanco, Humberto
Kalani Honua International Conference
R.R. 2
Box 4500 North
Kalapana Beach, HI 96778
(808)-965-7828

TOPICS: Holistic Healing

Blank, Bobbi-Van
B.V.I., Box 585B
New York, NY 10468
(212)-601-3025

TOPICS: New Age **DESCRIPTION:** Personal life consultant offering personal profiles-your personal link to the New Age.

Blank, Denise
P. O. Box 1659
Port Angeles, WA 98362
(206)-457-5918

TOPICS: Astrology, Tarot, Psychic **DESCRIPTION:** Psychic Consultant utilizing astrology and tarot to forecast events & analyze karma of relationships.

Blank, Mary of Carmel
c/o Mary's Gardens
Hinesburg, VT 05461
(802)-482-2294

TOPICS: Herbalogy, Holistic Health **DESCRIPTION:** Registered Medical Herbalist (MNIMH), specializing in Christian Mysticism.

Blank, Shyla Fern
Shyla's Magic Gems
16133 Ventura Boulevard
Encino, CA 91436
(818)-886-8816

TOPICS: Psychic, Crystals, Metaphysics **DESCRIPTION:** Psychic working with crystals offering readings by phone.

Blank, Sybil

2203 North Chelton Road
Colorado Springs, CO 80909

TOPICS: Psychic **DESCRIPTION:** Offers Readings to find understanding & self enlightenment.

Blank, Zana
12150 West Calle Senecca
Tucson, AZ 85743

TOPICS: New Age **DESCRIPTION:** Writer and artist widely published in feminist and lesbian press.

Blaylock, Debbie
Kelly Communications
410 East Water Street
Charlottesville, VA 22901
(804)-296-5676

TOPICS: Holistic Healing

Blodgett, Ralph
Review And Herald Publishing Association
55 West Oak Ridge Drive
Hagerstown, MD 21740
(301)-791-7000

TOPICS: Holistic Healing

Bloom, Alan
Crystal Palace, The
14201 Bodega Highway
Bodega, CA 94922
(707)-876-3314

TOPICS: Crystals, New Age

Blowey, Martin
1925 Joliet Street
Aurora, CO 80010
(303)-340-3676

TOPICS: Crystals

Blue, Jan
Blue Crystal Reflections
3032 Daisy Mae Road
Orlando, FL 32817
(305)-657-4375

TOPICS: Crystals

Blume, August G.
Augie Blume And Associates
P.O. Box 190
San Anselmo, CA 94960
(415)-457-0215

TOPICS: Crystals

Blumenthal, Mark
American Botanical Council
P.O. Box 201660
Austin, TX 78720
(512)-331-8868

TOPICS: Herbalogy, Holistic Health **DESCRIPTION:** Herbal Gram is a quarterly journal. **PUBLICATIONS:** *Herbal Gram*

Boddie, Caroline
Crystal Energy
65 Brighton Street
Rochester, NY 14607
(716)-461-2349

TOPICS: Crystals, Reiki, Metaphysics, Holistic Health **OCCUPATION:** Reiki Master, Teacher, Practitioner, Crystal Therapist, Tour Guide **DESCRIPTION:** Lectures & teaches crystal & Reiki classes. Crystal & Reiki practitioner. Also teaches Metaphysics. Conducts tours to Metaphysical sites.

Bodian, Stephan
California Yoga Teachers Association
Goodfellow Publishers' Reps.
2054 University Avenue, #604
Berkeley, CA 94704
(415)-841-9200

TOPICS: Yoga

Boissevain, Nelleke
Fascinating Facets
60 Main Street
Atherton, QLD 4883,
Australia

TOPICS: Crystals

Boissevain, Rene
Fascinating Facets
60 Main Street
Atherton, QLD 4883,
Australia

TOPICS: Crystals

Bonewitz, Ronald L.
c/o Element Books Limited
Longmead, Shafsbury
Dorset,
England

TOPICS: Crystals, Psychic

Boni, Miki
Interface
55 Wheeler Street
Cambridge, MA 02130-1125
(617)-924-1100

TOPICS: Holistic Healing

Borby, William
Holistic Life Magazine
1923 Crest Drive
Encinitas, CA 92024
(619)-298-4569

TOPICS: Holistic Healing

Borde, Evelyne
Alta Enterprises
5 Coburg Villas
Bath, BA1 5GH
England

TOPICS: Crystals

Borghi, Steve
Pyramis
20 Laurie Lane
Bridgewater, MA 023241
(716)-697-7504

TOPICS: Crystals

Botley, Beth
The Tibetan Foundation
110 West 96th Street, 5A
New York, NY 10025

TOPICS: Channeling **DESCRIPTION:** Certified Channel by The Tibetan Foundation.

Boudry, Frederic
La Marie Fee
Chemin de la Galante
Le Cannet des Maures, 83340
France

TOPICS: Crystals

Bourgault, Luc

Pedagogies Altrnatives, Eng.
315B Ste. Helene
Quebec City, PA, G1K 3L6
Canada
(418)-649-1938
TOPICS: Crystals

Bourque, Colleen
Denby Point Lodge
Star Route 1, Box 241
Mt. Ida, AR 71957
(501)-867-3651
TOPICS: Crystals

Bowcock, A. D.
Crystal Experience, The
P.O. Box 178
South Lismore N.S.W.2480,
Australia
TOPICS: Crystals

Bowcock, David J.
Crystal Experience, The
P.O. Box 178
South Lismore N.S.W.2480,
Australia
TOPICS: Crystals

Bower, Charles E.
Ledgehill Retreat And Study Centre
R.R. 1
Lawrencetown, No B0S 1M0
Canada
(902)-584-7124
TOPICS: Holistic Healing

Bowman, Gerry
Freewill Foundation, The
7210 Jordan Avenue D-23
Canoga Park, CA 91304
TOPICS: Channeling

Boyd, Sharon
Valley OF The Sun Publishing Co.
P.O. Box 38
Malibu, CA 90265
(818)-889-1575
TOPICS: Metaphysics, New Age

Boyko, Wally
National Fitness Association
Box 2378
Corona, CA 94043
(714)-371-0606
TOPICS: Holistic Healing

Boyne, Gil
Westwood Publishing Company
312 Riverdale Drive
Glendale, CA 91204
(818)-242-3497
TOPICS: Hypnotism, Psychology, Body-Mind
Connection

Brackett, Judy
4216 Beverly Boulevard, Suite 240
Los Angeles, CA 90004
TOPICS: Channeling

Brake, Barbara
Barbara Brake/Stan Pepe Enterprises
807 Esplanade Avenue #14

New Orleans, LA 70116
(504)-525-0591
TOPICS: Crystals

Brand, Stewart
Point Foundation
27 Gate Five Road
Sausalito, CA 94965
(415)-332-1716
TOPICS: New Age

Brandt, Colleen, N.D.
Brandt's Crystal Litehouse
Upstairs, Ulster Walk, Edward Street
Brisbane, QLD 4000,
Australia
TOPICS: Crystals

Brandt, Joss
Toronto Vegetarian Association
28 Walker Avenue
Toronto, On M4V 1G2
Canada
(416)-923-1933
TOPICS: Holistic Healing

Brandt, Rod, D.M. SM.AC
Brandt's Crystal Litehouse
Upstairs, Ulster Walk, Edward Street
Brisbane, QLD 4000,
Australia
TOPICS: Crystals

Branscomb, Anna
Cloud Mountain
373 Agren Road
Castle Rock, WA 98611
(206)-274-4859
TOPICS: Holistic Healing

Branscomb, David
Cloud Mountain
373 Agren Road
Castle Rock, WA 98611
(206)-274-4859
TOPICS: Holistic Healing

Braud, Dr. William
Mind Science Foundation
8301 Broadway, Suite 100
San Antonio, TX 78209
TOPICS: Parapsychology

Bravo, Brett
Bravo Designs
742 North Granados
Solana Beach, CA 92075
(619)-755-1530
TOPICS: Crystals

Breaux, Charles
P.O. Box 307
Port Townsend, WA 98368
TOPICS: Psychic, Spirituality, Meditation, Yoga,
Body-Mind Connection, Psychology DATE OF
BIRTH: 09/30/47 PLACE OF BIRTH: Sacromento,
CA EDUCATION: University of CA, Berkeley, CA
DEGREE: B.A. Humanities OCCUPATION:
Clairvoyant Consultant, Author, Lecturer, Past Life
Therapist, Workshop Leader PROFESSIONAL
MEMBERSHIPS: Berkeley Holistic Health Center,
Director, 1976-77; Health Enhancement Institute,

Santa Cruz, CA, Board of Directors, 1978-1980
DESCRIPTION: Offers Life Readings emphasizing
the origin & characteristics of the Soul, past lives &
core Karmic patterns. Receives guidance from spirit
guides. Readings by mail or phone. Send $75, photo,
questions & phone number. PUBLICATIONS:
*Journey Into Consciousness, The Chakras, Tantra,
Jungian Psychology,* 1989 PUBLISHER: Nicolas-
Hays PUBLICATIONS: *Life Lines, Weaving The
Web of Karma,* 1992 PUBLISHER: DoemanKnaur
PUBLICATIONS: *Healing The Heart,* 1978
PUBLISHER: Holistic Health Life Book
PUBLICATIONS: *Psychic Awareness & Health,*
1979 PUBLISHER: Holistic Health Life Book
PUBLICATIONS: *Inner Being Body Work,* 1978
PUBLISHER: Yoga Journal PUBLICATIONS: *The
Way Of Karma* PUBLISHER: Samuel Wieser

Breaux, Mimi
Attitudinal Healing Center Of San Diego
5736 Good Karma Lane
Bonita, CA 92002
(619)-565-7172
TOPICS: Holistic Healing

Brewer-Ortali, Barbara
870 Majela Lane
Hemet, CA 92343
(714)-652-0613
TOPICS: Crystals

Brier, Dr. Robert
C.W. Post College
Philosophy Department
Greenvale, NY 11548
TOPICS: Parapsychology

Brigham, Judith Truthstone
Box 313
Upper Darby, PA 19082
(215)-352-7017
TOPICS: Crystals

Brink, William
American Association Of Professional
Hypnotherapists
Box 731
McLean, VA 22101
(703)-448-9623
TOPICS: Hypnotism

Brodie, Renee
548 English Bluff Road
Delta BC, V4M 2N3
Canada
(604)-643-6689
TOPICS: Crystals

Bromberg, Dr. Paula N.
Friends Of EKR
23 Frasco Road
Santa Fe, NM 87505
(505)-984-1872
TOPICS: Holistic Healing, Death, Psychology,
Body-Mind Connection, Spirituality DATE OF
BIRTH: 04/29/42 PLACE OF BIRTH: Providence, RI
EDUCATION: Sierra University, Costa Mesa, CA
DEGREE: Ph.D. Clinical Psychology
OCCUPATION: Philosopher, Psychologist, Lecturer,
Author AWARDS: Elisabeth Kubler-Ross Program-
Life, Death, Transition; School Of Sacred
Psychology, Past Director PROFESSIONAL

MEMBERSHIPS: Gestalt Institute, Board of Directors; Association For Humanistic Psychology. **DESCRIPTION:** Private psychology practice for 26 years teaching & counseling in the fields of Sacred Psychology & Transformational Therapy. Teaches advanced psychology seminars at Northern NM Community College for the Elisabeth Kubler-Ross Hospice Training Institute. **PUBLICATIONS:** *Sacred Psychology: The Path Of The Heart, The Way Of The Lover* **PUBLICATIONS:** *Sacred Psychology: An Experience Of Transformation* **PUBLICATIONS:** *How To Create An Intimate Relationship With Yourself And Your Partner*

Brooks, Dr. Richard W.
Oakland University
Department Of Philosophy
Rochester, MI 48063
TOPICS: Parapsychology

Brooks, Svevo
Traditional Tours
P.O. Box 564
Creswell, OR 97426
(503)-895-2957

TOPICS: New Age, Holistic Health, Nutrition, Meditation, Massage, Body-Mind Connection, Herbalogy **EDUCATION:** University Of California, Berkeley, CA **DEGREE:** M.A. **YEAR DEGREE:** 1966 **OCCUPATION:** Author **WORK EXPERIENCE:** Optimal Health Institute, Eugene, OR, Director **PUBLICATIONS:** *Common Sense Diet And Health* **PUBLISHER:** Traditional Tours **PUBLICATIONS:** *The Art Of Good Living*, 1990 **PUBLISHER:** Houghton-Mifflin Co.

Broome, Michael
Ocamora Foundation
Box 43
Ocate, NM 87734
(505)-666-2389

TOPICS: Holistic Healing

Brouard, Regina V.
Energy Of A Different Persuasion
145 South Pinecrest Road
Bolingbrook, IL 60439
(312)-739-3084

TOPICS: Crystals

Broughton, Dr. Richard S.
Institute For Parapsychology
Box 6847 College Station
Durham, NC 27708
TOPICS: Parapsychology

Brown, Louise (Pat)
BroHuff Enterprises
Box 69067
Odessa, TX 76769
(915)-367-3637

TOPICS: Crystals, Metaphysics, Numerology, Hypnotism, New Age **DATE OF BIRTH:** 09/07/21 **PLACE OF BIRTH:** TX **OCCUPATION:** Teacher, Store Proprietor, Numerologist **WORK EXPERIENCE:** BroHuff Enterprises, Odessa, TX, Owner, Proprietor **DESCRIPTION:** Expertise in Metaphysics, various philosophies, Numerology Charts, Mind Research & Hypnosis. Sponsors Psychic Fairs & conducts seminars. Offers New Age & Metaphysical products & books.

Brown, Mary

American Chiropractic Association
8229 Maryland Avenue
St. Louis, MO 63105
(314)-862-7800
TOPICS: Holistic Healing

Brown, Stephan
Shenoa Retreat Center
P.O. Box 43
Philo, CA 95466
(707)-895-3156

TOPICS: Holistic Healing

Bruner, Randall
Rockbottom Minerals
2029 New Linden Road
Newport, KY 41071
(606)-491-7885

TOPICS: Crystals

Brunton, Paul
Larson Publications
TOPICS: Spirituality, Meditation, Holistic Healing, Birth **PLACE OF BIRTH:** London, England **EDUCATION:** Central Foundation School, London, England **DEGREE:** Ph. D. **OCCUPATION:** Author **DESCRIPTION:** Born 1898, Deceased 1981. Wrote numerous essays & books on topics such as Eastern philosophy, spiritualism, birth, healing, religion & human inner reflections. **PUBLICATIONS:** *Notebooks Of Paul Brunton, Vols. 1-16*, 1984-89 **PUBLISHER:** Larson Publications **PUBLICATIONS:** *A Search In Secret India* **PUBLICATIONS:** *The Secret Path* **PUBLICATIONS:** A Search In Secret Egypt **PUBLICATIONS:** *A Message From Arunachala* **PUBLICATIONS:** *A Hermit In The Himalayas*

Brush, Jane
Self-Realization Fellowship
3880 San Rafael Avenue
Los Angeles, CA 90065
(213)-225-2471

TOPICS: New Age

Bruyere, Rev. Rosalyn
Healing Light Center Church
204 East Wilson
Glendale, CA 91206
(818)-244-8607

TOPICS: Numerology

Bryant, Page
Sun
P.O. Box 4384
Albuquerque, NM 87196
TOPICS: Channeling

Buffet, Wendy
Min An Health Center
1144 Pacific Avenue
San Francisco, CA 94133
(415)-771-4040

TOPICS: Holistic Healing

Buhrman, Donna
Evolutionary Education Foundation
5039 Outlook
Mission, KS 66202
(913)-432-0622

TOPICS: Holistic Healing

Bunker, Dusty
Box 868
Exeter, NH 03833
TOPICS: Dreams, Numerology, Astrology, Tarot, Metaphysics **DATE OF BIRTH:** 11/05/37 **PLACE OF BIRTH:** Newport, RI **EDUCATION:** University of NH, Durham, NH **YEARS:** 1955-57 **OCCUPATION:** Author, Teacher, Lecturer, Consultant, Columnist **WORK EXPERIENCE:** Time-Life Books, Mysteries Of The Unknown-Visions & Prophecies, Consultant; Manchester Union Leader, Manchester, NH, Columnist for Dreams: Your Guiding Light; Seacoast Scene, Hampton, NH, Columnist for Metaphysical Muse; Hampton Union, Hampton, NH, Columnist for Shopping Column **PROFESSIONAL MEMBERSHIPS:** Seacoast Astrological Association, 1990-91 **PUBLICATIONS:** *Numerology And The Divine Triangle* **PUBLICATIONS:** *Numerology And Your Future* **PUBLICATIONS:** *Numerology, Astrology And Dreams* **PUBLICATIONS:** *Quintiles And Tredeciles: The Geometry Of The Goddess* **PUBLICATIONS:** *Broads And Narrows: A Thinking Wo/Man's Dictionary*

Buren, Jana Van
Health And Well Being Services
1550 West 11th Avenue
Eugene, OR 97402-3751
TOPICS: Crystals

Burghard, Shirley
Act-Action
710 Lodi Street
B-1104
Syracuse, NY 13203
(315)-471-4644
TOPICS: Holistic Healing

Burka, Christa Faye
585 Austin Avenue, #11
Coquitlam, BC, V3K 3N2
Canada
TOPICS: Crystals

Burmester, Helen S.
1320 Addison A 408
Berkeley, CA 94702
(415)-848-4271
TOPICS: New Age **DATE OF BIRTH:** 10/24/07 **PLACE OF BIRTH:** Seibranz/Leutkirch, Germany **EDUCATION:** State of Wuerttemberg **EDUCATION:** North Central College, Naperville, IL **DEGREE:** B.A. **YEAR DEGREE:** 1939 **EDUCATION:** New York University, New York, NY **DEGREE:** M.A. **YEAR DEGREE:** 1944 **OCCUPATION:** Teacher, Author, Editor **WORK EXPERIENCE:** San Bernardino High School, San Bernardino, CA, Teacher 14 years; American Home Magazine, New York, NY, Editor Arts & Crafts Dept. **AWARDS:** Walter Loewe Scholarship UCLA Germanic Dept. 1946-47 **PROFESSIONAL MEMBERSHIPS:** CTA **PUBLICATIONS:** *Seven Rays Made Visual* **PUBLISHER:** DeVorss & Company

Burnett, Ruth
P.O. Box 39
Fairfield, CT 06430
(203)-255-2502
TOPICS: Psychic, Metaphysics **DATE OF BIRTH:** 12/22/34 **PLACE OF BIRTH:** Vancouver, Canada **EDUCATION:** Hiram College, Hiram, Ohio **DEGREE:** B.A. **EDUCATION:** Yale University, New

Haven, CT. **DEGREE:** M.A. **OCCUPATION:** Psychic Reader **WORK EXPERIENCE:** The Psychic Advisory, President 5 years **DESCRIPTION:** Offers private psychic readings in Fairfield, CT. & in New York City. Lectures on How To Make The Most Of Your Own Psychic Resources & How To Use Your Own Psychic Awareness In Relationships. Readings also available by phone or mail.

Burrows, Dick
Taunton Press, Inc.
63 South Main Street
Box 355
Newtown, CT 06470
(203)-426-8171

TOPICS: New Age

Burrows, Robert J.L.
SCP Newsletter
P.O. Box 4308
Berkeley, CA 94704

TOPICS: Metaphysics

Burruss, Rhiannon Elizabeth
Keeper Of The Stone
611 12th Street, Northeast
Washington, DC 20002
(202)-399-4269

TOPICS: Crystals

Busby, Dr. Bill
Philadelphia Institute, Inc.
401 Patterson Street
Sulphur Springs, AR 72768
(501)-298-3362

TOPICS: Holistic Healing

Bushnell, A.C.
Executive Health Publications
Box 8880
Chapel Hill, NC 27515
(919)-929-7519

TOPICS: Holistic Healing

Buske, Terry
Llewellyn's Moon Sign Book And Daily Planetary Guide
Llewellyn Worldwide, Ltd.
P.O. Box 64383
St. Paul, MN 55164
(612)-291-1970

TOPICS: Astrology, Metaphysics **DATE OF BIRTH:** 11/16/52 **PLACE OF BIRTH:** Freeport, IL **EDUCATION:** Southern Illinois University, Carbondale, IL **YEARS:** 1970-1974 **DEGREE:** B.S. Education **YEAR DEGREE:** 1974 **EDUCATION:** Southern Illinois University, Carbondale, IL **YEARS:** 1978-1980 **DEGREE:** M.S. Media,Communications **YEAR DEGREE:** 1980 **OCCUPATION:** Art Director, Editor **WORK EXPERIENCE:** Llewellyn Publications, St. Paul, MN, Art Director, 9 years **PUBLICATIONS:** *Llewellyn's Moon Sign Book* (1981-1991) **PUBLISHER:** Llewellyn Publications **PUBLICATIONS:** *Llewellyn's Astrological Calendar* (1981-1991) **PUBLISHER:** Llewellyn Publications **PUBLICATIONS:** *Llewellyn's Daily Planetary Guide* (1981-1991) **PUBLISHER:** Llewellyn Publications **PUBLICATIONS:** *Llewellyn's Sun Sign Book* (1982-1990) **PUBLISHER:** Llewellyn Publications

Butler, Jim
New Age Press

P.O. Box 1373
Keala Kekua, HI 96750
(808)-328-8013

TOPICS: New Age

Butler, Kurt
59-215-F Ke Nui Road
Haleiwa, HI 96712
(808)-638-7338

TOPICS: Holistic Health, Nutrition **DATE OF BIRTH:** 08/16/44 **PLACE OF BIRTH:** Guadalajara, Mexico **EDUCATION:** University of CA at Berkeley **DEGREE:** B.S. Physiology **YEAR DEGREE:** 1975 **EDUCATION:** University of Hawaii **DEGREE:** M.S. Food & Nutrition **YEAR DEGREE:** 1976 **OCCUPATION:** Nutritional Consultant, Teacher, Author **DESCRIPTION:** Authored over 100 newspaper & magazine articles. Has special interest in health & nutrition quackery & other related frauds. **PUBLICATIONS:** *The New Handbook Of Health And Preventive Medicine*, 1990 **PUBLISHER:** Prometheus Books **PUBLICATIONS:** *The Best Medicine*, 1985 **PUBLISHER:** Harper & Row

Butler, William, M.A. M.Div.
Nos Amis/Our Friends, Inc.
7519 Sausalito Avenue
West Hills, CA 91307
(818)-703-1213

TOPICS: Psychology, Holistic Health, Metaphysics **OCCUPATION:** Psychotherapist, Teacher, Metaphysician **WORK EXPERIENCE:** Nos Amis/Our Friends, Inc., West Hill, CA, Pres. **PROFESSIONAL MEMBERSHIPS:** International Transactional Analysis Assoc., California Assoc. of Marriage & Family Therapists **DESCRIPTION:** Offers holistic therapy: self-esteem, anger, loving-child-within courses.

Button, Reverend Eleanor
Chapel Of Prayer, Incorporated
10161 Harwin Street, #103
Houston, TX 77036
(713)-776-8152

TOPICS: Crystals

Byes, Connie
Sweet Success
P.O. Box 66
Springhouse, PA 19477

TOPICS: Channeling, Astrology, Tarot, Runes, Numerology **DATE OF BIRTH:** 07/29/47 **PLACE OF BIRTH:** Wausau, WI **OCCUPATION:** Metaphysical Counselor **WORK EXPERIENCE:** Sweet Success, Springhouse, PA, Pres. **DESCRIPTION:** Offers metaphysical counselling using astrology, runes, tarot or chanelling. Also offers natal, numerology, new job, business, compatibility & romantic charts. Supplies dates for gambling & risk taking by astrology. Organizes tours to Tibet, etc.

Calderella, Leo
Vim & Vigor, Inc.
8805 North 23rd Avenue
Suite 11
Phoenix, AZ 85021
(602)-395-5850

TOPICS: Holistic Healing

Calia, Stephen Paulo
215 West 90th Street, #12D

New York, NY 10024

TOPICS: Astrology

Calkins-Smith, Shirley
Rochester Center For The Healing Arts, Inc.
14 Cottage Row
Lily Dale, NY 14752
(716)-595-3452

TOPICS: Spirituality

Callander-Travis, Meryn
Wellness Associates
P.O. Box 5433-G
Mill Valley, CA 94942
(415)-383-3806

TOPICS: Holistic Healing

Campbell, Denver, Jr.
10 Kyles Lanes, 2
Fort Thomas, KY 41075

TOPICS: Channeling

Campbell, Don
Sound Of Light
Box 835704
Richardson, TX 75083
(214)-644-2004

TOPICS: Crystals

Campbell, Stephanie
308 South Church
Bozeman, MT 59715
(406)-586-7343

TOPICS: Crystals

Campbell, Stu
Storey Communications
Pownal, VT 05261
(802)-823-5811

TOPICS: Health Food

Camps, Liz
Chakra
P.O. Box 8551
FDR Station
New York, NY 10022

TOPICS: Occult

Canby, Henry
46 Cross Street
Northampton, MA 01060
(413)-586-5424

TOPICS: Psychology, Body-Mind Connection, Holistic Healing **DESCRIPTION:** Offers psychophysical healing through a combination of bodywork & psychotherapy.

Capodieci, Gregor
Sage House 7C
4 Lexington Avenue
New York, NY 10010
(212)-473-2994

TOPICS: New Age, Tarot, Metaphysics **DATE OF BIRTH:** 03/14/47 **PLACE OF BIRTH:** Bronx, NY **OCCUPATION:** Tarot Reader **DESCRIPTION:** Tarot specialist. Studied under Frank Andrews in 1975. Available for private readings & consultations, parties, lectures, demonstrations & private & group instructions.

Carden, Cher
P.O. Box 1301

Princeton, NJ 08540
TOPICS: Channeling

Cardone, Pia
807 Franklin Avenue
Franklin Square, NY 11010
(718)-331-3429

TOPICS: Psychic

Cardwell, Maude
Austin Seth Center
P.O. Box 7786
Austin, TX 78713-7786
(512)-479-8909

TOPICS: Channeling, Metaphysics DATE OF
BIRTH: 12/05/27 PLACE OF BIRTH: Chicago, IL
EDUCATION: University of Texas, Austin, TX
DEGREE: Ph. D. YEAR DEGREE: 1964
OCCUPATION: Author, Teacher WORK
EXPERIENCE: Austin Seth Center, Austin, TX,
Director 12 years; University of British Columbia,
B.C., Canada, Instructor English 12 years
PUBLICATIONS: *Reality Change*, 1979-90
PUBLISHER: Austin Seth Center

Carl, Branda
4800 South Lake Park, Suite 707
Chicago, IL 60615
TOPICS: Channeling

Carl, Dr. Edward
Port Of Health
Apdo, 270
Chapala,Jalisco, 5-22-13
Mexico
TOPICS: Holistic Healing

Carlon, Barbara
1717 West Adair Drive
Knoxville, TN 37918
TOPICS: Channeling

Carmichael, Cliff
Box 3453
Courtenay, BC, V9N 5M5
Canada
(604)-338-1914

TOPICS: Crystals

Carnette, Count
1632 Broadway
Seattle, WA 98122
TOPICS: Channeling

Carol, Barry
Crystal Network, The
345 West 70th Street, #2D
New York, NY 10023
(212)-362-3527

TOPICS: Crystals

Carol, Elizabeth
Crystal Network, The
345 West 70th Street, #2D
New York, NY 10023
(212)-362-3527

TOPICS: Crystals

Carpenter, Dennis
Circle Sanctuary
Box 219
Mt. Horeb, WI 53572

(608)-924-2216
TOPICS: New Age

Carroll, Wilma
201 East 87th Street, Apt 10A
New York, NY 10128
(212)-757-6300 (212)-410-1299

TOPICS: Psychic, Palmistry, Astrology,
Numerology, Tarot, Psychic Phenomena,
Paranormal Phenomena PLACE OF BIRTH:
Salisbury, MD EDUCATION: Temple University,
Philadelphia, PA EDUCATION: University of
Madrid, Madrid, Spain OCCUPATION: Astrologer,
Numerologist, Tarot Card Reader, Palmist, Psychic,
Author, Lecturer, Counselor, Author, Teacher
WORK EXPERIENCE: Wilma Carroll Psychic
Productions, New York, NY, President
PROFESSIONAL MEMBERSHIPS: National Speakers
& Psychics Registry, Registered Psychic, National
Association For Campus Activities DESCRIPTION:
Offers lectures, party entertainment & private
readings in Astrology, Palmistry, Numerology &
Tarot through her company Wilma Carroll Psychic
Productions. Teaches classes on esoteric subjects.

Carter, Kathleen And Simon
2500 College Avenue
Baltimore, MD 21214
(301)-254-1172

TOPICS: Crystals

Carter, Marguerite
Box 807, Department 707
Indianapolis, IN 46206
TOPICS: Channeling

Carter, Marvelle
The Radiance Technique Association International,
Inc.
P.O. Box 86425
St. Petersburg, FL 33738
(813)-595-9772

TOPICS: Reiki

Case, Patricia J.
Source Net
Box 6767
Santa Barbara, CA 93160
TOPICS: Holistic Healing

Case, Randall L.
Vitality, Inc.
8080 North Central, LB 78
Dallas, TX 75206
(214)-691-1480

TOPICS: Holistic Healing

Cassandra
R.D. 1
Box 253
Manheim, PA 17545
(717)-898-3319

TOPICS: Psychic DESCRIPTION: Psychic
consultant.

Cataldo, Anne, M.A., M.Ed
Center For Transformation
P.O. Box 1491
Sanibel, FL 33957
(813)-472-5224

TOPICS: Channeling DESCRIPTION:
Psychotherapist who works with A Course In

Miracles and acts as a channel for Simon the Master
Teacher.

Cataldo, Arthur
Center For Transformation
P.O. Box 1491
Sanibel, FL 33957
(813)-472-5224

TOPICS: Channeling DESCRIPTION: Licensed
transformational psychotherapist, healer and past life
therapist.

Catchpole, Anne
5 Carters Leys
Bishop's Stortford
Hertfordshire, CM23 2RH,
England
TOPICS: Crystals

Cattes, Chris
9/2 Birraga Road
Bellevue Hill
Sydney, 2021,
Australia
TOPICS: Crystals

Caughlan, Craig
Orenda/Unity Press
Box 2215
Leucadia, CA 92024
(619)-753-9331

TOPICS: Massage

Caulder, Elizabeth
Daffodil Productions
13165 Deming Avenue
Downey, CA 90242
(213)-531-6159

TOPICS: New Age

Caulfield, D.J.
Communications Channels, Inc.
6255 Barfield Road
Atlanta, GA 30328
(404)-256-9800

TOPICS: Holistic Healing PUBLICATIONS: *Health
Foods Retailing*

Cavalletto, Pattie
Ocamora Foundation
Box 43
Ocate, NM 87734
(505)-666-2389

TOPICS: Holistic Healing

Cayce, Charles Thomas Taylor
Association For Research And Enlightenment
217 67th Street
Virginia Beach, VA 23451
(804)-428-3588

TOPICS: Channeling, New Age, Holistic Health,
Psychic, Dreams, Meditation DATE OF BIRTH:
10/07/42 PLACE OF BIRTH: Virginia Beach, VA
EDUCATION: Hampden-Sydney College DEGREE:
B.S. Psychology EDUCATION: University Of
Maryland DEGREE: Ph. D. Psychology YEAR
DEGREE: 1968 OCCUPATION: Psychologist,
Administrator WORK EXPERIENCE: A.R.E.,
Virginia Beach, VA, Pres.

Chabot, Roger
Super Magazine, Inc.

8050, boul, Metropolitain, est
Montreal, Qu H1K 1A1
Canada
(514)-353-7660

TOPICS: Astrology

Chagnon, Linda
P.O. Box 380
Greenville, RI 02828

TOPICS: Psychic Healing

Chambers, Bette
American Humanist Association
7 Harwood Drive
Box 146
Amherst, NY 14226
(716)-839-5080

TOPICS: New Age

Chambers, John
93 Jackson Avenue
Bridgeport, CT 06606
(203)-336-4994

TOPICS: Psychic

Chambers, Lauren
316 East 11th Street
New York, NY 10003

TOPICS: Channeling

Chaney, Dr. Robert
Astara, Inc.
800 West Arrow Highway
P.O. Box 5003
Upland, CA 91786
(714)-981-4941

TOPICS: Metaphysics

Chapman, Lee
Starlog Press, Inc.
475 Park Avenue, South
New York, NY 10016
(212)-689-2830

TOPICS: Astrology

Cheatham, John
Shangri-La Natural Health Resort
Box 2328
Bonita Springs, FL 33959
(813)-992-3811

TOPICS: Holistic Healing

Cheeseman, Daniel
Earth Nation
P.O. Box 158
Bloomington, IN 47402
(812)-988-6285

TOPICS: Crystals

Cherkes, Joseph K.
Nightshade Publications
P.O. Box 3342
Providence, RI 02906
(401)-781-9438

TOPICS: Psychic Phenomena

Chicovsky, Susan
Vision Light
6569 South Keim Road
Evergreen, CO 80439

TOPICS: Channeling

Child, Dr. Irvin L.
Yale University
Department Of Psychology
New Haven, CT 06520

TOPICS: Parapsychology

Childress, David Hatcher
303 Main Street
Kempton, IL 60946
(815)-253-6390

TOPICS: Spirituality, UFO's, New Age DATE OF BIRTH: 01/06/57 PLACE OF BIRTH: France EDUCATION: University of Montana, Missoula, MT YEARS: 1975-76 EDUCATION: Tibetan Educational Institute, Dharmsala, India YEARS: 1977-78 OCCUPATION: Archaeologist, Historian, Philosopher, Author, Lecturer WORK EXPERIENCE: Adventures Unlimited, Stelle, IL, President; World Explorers Club, Kempton, IL, Expedition Director AWARDS: Honorary Doctorate Degrees from World University, Tucson, AZ & Atlantic University, Virginia Beach, VA DESCRIPTION: Lectures on the topics of Ancient Science, History & Technology PUBLICATIONS: *Vimana Aircraft Of Ancient India & Atlantis*, 1991 PUBLISHER: Adventures Unlimited Press PUBLICATIONS: *Anti-Gravity & The Unified Field*, 1990 PUBLISHER: Adventures Unlimited Press PUBLICATIONS: *Lost Cities Of Africa & Arabia*, 1989 PUBLISHER: Adventures Unlimited Press PUBLICATIONS: *Lost Cities Of Ancient Lemuria & The Pacific*, 1988 PUBLISHER: Adventures Unlimited Press PUBLICATIONS: *Anti-Gravity & The Word Grid*, 1987 PUBLISHER: Adventures Unlimited Press PUBLICATIONS: *Lost Cities & Ancient Mysteries Of South America*, 1986 PUBLISHER: Adventures Unlimited Press

Chinmayananda, Swami
Family Spiritual Camp
Camp NG
4545 Warwick Circle
Grand Blanc, MI 48439
(313)-695-0188

TOPICS: Yoga

Chinmoy, Sri
Sri Chinmoy Center
Box 32433
Jamaica, NY 11431

TOPICS: New Age, Spirituality, Meditation, Yoga, Vegetarianism DATE OF BIRTH: 08/27/31 PLACE OF BIRTH: Chittagong, East Bengal, India OCCUPATION: Teacher, Author WORK EXPERIENCE: Sri Chinmoy Meditation Centres, Jamaica, NY, Founder DESCRIPTION: Promotes spiritual & physical & emotional wellbeing through meditation, vegetarianism, yoga & natural lifestyle. PUBLICATIONS: *Eastern Light For The Western Mind*, 1972 PUBLICATIONS: *Mother India's Light House: India's Spiritual Leaders*, 1973 PUBLICATIONS: *Death & Reincarnation: Eternity's Voyage*, 1974 PUBLICATIONS: *Meditation: Man-Perfection In God-Satisfaction*, 1978 PUBLICATIONS: *The Master And The Disciple*, 1985 PUBLICATIONS: *Canada Aspires, Canada Receives, Canada Achieves*, 1974

Choo, Joni
Mele Mauka Center
P.O. Box 946
Captain Cook, HI 96704

(808)-328-2207

TOPICS: Yoga, New Age, Holistic Health DATE OF BIRTH: 03/18/41 PLACE OF BIRTH: Bloomer, WI EDUCATION: University of Wisconsin, Madison, WI YEARS: 1959-63 DEGREE: B.S. YEAR DEGREE: 1963 EDUCATION: San Francisco State College YEARS: 1968-70 DEGREE: M.A. YEAR DEGREE: 1970 OCCUPATION: Teacher, Yoga Instructor WORK EXPERIENCE: Mele Mauka Waena, Milolii Maulca, HI, Dance Director, 1976-present; South Kona Education Association, 1989-91; Teacher Physical Education, High School & Grade School, 1963-75 AWARDS: Junior Leadership Award 1963 PROFESSIONAL MEMBERSHIPS: Buddhist Foundation 1983-present; AHPER; SKEA; 4-H, President, Secretary 1950-63

Christeaan, Aaron
Michael Educational Foundation
10 Muth Drive
Orinda, CA 94563
(510)-254-4730

TOPICS: Channeling, Metaphysics OCCUPATION: Channeler, Healer, Bodyworker WORK EXPERIENCE: Michael Educational Foundation, Orinda, CA, Co-Founder DESCRIPTION: Channeler of Michael since 1982. Healer & bodyworker who repatterns life's blocks with a combination of channeling, visualization & bodywork.

Christie, Nancy
Gateways Books And Tapes
P.O. Box 370
Nevada City, CA 95959

TOPICS: New Age

Chroman, Jerry
The Albintra Wellness Center/Natural Medicine Works
438 N.E. 72nd
Seattle, WA 98115
(206)-522-9384

TOPICS: Holistic Healing

Church, Dawson
Aslan Publishing
14795 West Park Avenue
Boulder Creek, CA 95006
(408)-338-7504

TOPICS: Spirituality, Holistic Healing, Birth, Body-Mind Connection DATE OF BIRTH: 11/15/56 PLACE OF BIRTH: South Africa EDUCATION: Baylor University, Waco, TX DEGREE: B.A. Mass Communications YEAR DEGREE: 1979 OCCUPATION: Publisher, Editor, Author WORK EXPERIENCE: Dawson Design, New York, NY, President 1979-86; Aslan Publishing, Boulder Creek, Vice-Pres., Publisher 1986-present AWARDS: Who's Who In The East, Earth Society Foundation, Planetary Initiative, Writers Intensive Workshop, Whole Life Expo, International Health Foundation PROFESSIONAL MEMBERSHIPS: Association For Responsible Communication, Santa Cruz Publishers Association, Publishers Marketing Association, Whole Health Institute PUBLICATIONS: *The Heart Of The Healer*, editor, 1989 PUBLISHER: New American Library PUBLICATIONS: *Gaia: The Human Journey From Chaos To Cosmos*, editor, 1989 PUBLISHER: Pocket Books PUBLICATIONS: *Intuition Workout*, editor, 1988 PUBLISHER: Aslan Publishing PUBLICATIONS: *Communing With The Spirit Of Your Unborn Child*, 1988 PUBLISHER:

Aslan Publishing **PUBLICATIONS:** *Empowerment*, editor, 1989 **PUBLISHER:** Dell Publishing **PUBLICATIONS:** *Finding The Great Creative You*, editor, 1989 **PUBLISHER:** Aslan Publishing

Ciancola, Dr. Anthony
6317 Wilshire Boulevard, Suite 602
Los Angeles, CA 90048
(213)-651-0733

TOPICS: Holistic Health **DESCRIPTION:** Chiropractic care integrating various body therapies and healing arts.

Clark, Carolyn Chambers
Wellness Institute
3451 Central Avenue
St. Petersburg, FL 33713
(813)-321-0641

TOPICS: Holistic Healing

Clark, F. Marvin
Mineral Research Company
P.O. Box 400
Perry, IA 50220
(515)-465-5010

TOPICS: Crystals

Clark, Jane
AMS Press, Inc.
56 East 13th Street
New York, NY 10003
(212)-777-4700

TOPICS: Holistic Healing

Clark, Larry
Himalayan International Institute Of Yoga Science and P
R.R.1
Box 400
Honesdale, PA 18431
(717)-253-5551

TOPICS: New Age

Clark, M.C.
The Michael Connection
P.O. Box 1873
Orinda, CA 94563
(415)-256-7639

TOPICS: Channeling

Clarke, Charlene
1683 South Ocean Drive #611
Hallandale, FL 33004-7641
(305)-564-8354

TOPICS: Psychic

Clausen, Henry C.
Supreme Council 33rd Degree A
1733 16th Street, N.W.
Washington, DC 20009
(202)-232-3579

TOPICS: New Age

Clay, Daniel
Box 100
Troutdale, VA 24378

TOPICS: Channeling

Cleveland, Ms. Grover
Crystals In Action
80 Austin Drive, #54
Burlington, VT 05401

(802)-863-7984

TOPICS: Crystals

Cloonan, John
The Tibetan Foundation
6912 Millbrook Lane
Fountain, CO 80303

TOPICS: Channeling **DESCRIPTION:** Certified Channel by The Tibetan Foundation.

Clow, B.
Bear & Company, Inc.
P.O. Box 2860
Santa Fe, NM 87504-2860
(505)-983-5968

TOPICS: New Age **DATE OF BIRTH:** 02/14/43 **PLACE OF BIRTH:** Saginaw, MI **EDUCATION:** Institute for Culture And Creation, Chicago, IL **DEGREE:** M.A. Art **OCCUPATION:** Editor, Publisher, Author **WORK EXPERIENCE:** Bear & Company, Santa Fe, NM, Vice-Pres., Editor, Author 8 years; Atlantic Little Brown, Boston, MA, Author 1976-82; Llewellyn Publications, Minneapolis, MN, Author 1986-present **AWARDS:** Massachusetts Woman of the Year 1975 **PUBLICATIONS:** *Heart Of The Christos: Starseeding From The Pleiades*, 1989 **PUBLISHER:** Bear & Company, Inc. **PUBLICATIONS:** *Eye Of The Centaur*, 1989 **PUBLISHER:** Llewellyn Publications **PUBLICATIONS:** *Chiron: Rainbow Bridge*, 1989 **PUBLISHER:** Llewellyn Publications

Cogozzo, Linda
California Yoga Teachers Association
Goodfellow Publishers' Reps.
2054 University Avenue, #604
Berkeley, CA 94704
(415)-841-9200

TOPICS: Yoga

Cohen, Adrienne
Crystal Essence
40 Railroad Street
Great Barrington, MA 01230
(413)-528-2595

TOPICS: Crystals

Cohen, Joseph
Crystal Journeys
9 Humewood Court #5
Toronto ON, M6C 1C9
Canada
(416)-658-0663

TOPICS: Crystals

Cohen, Lorraine
Dimensions
421 Village Walk
Exton, PA 19341
(215)-524-1045

TOPICS: Crystals

Cohen, Mark
Crystal Essence
40 Railroad Street
Great Barrington, MA 01230
(413)-528-2595

TOPICS: Crystals

Cohen, Michael
Davis Communications Company
13521 Cedar Road Up

Cleveland, OH 44118
(216)-662-6969

TOPICS: Holistic Healing

Cohen, William
Haworth Press, Inc.
12 West 32nd Street
New York, NY 10001

TOPICS: Holistic Healing

Coleman, Barbara
National Consumers League
815 15th Street NW
Suite 516
Washington, DC 20005
(202)-639-8140

TOPICS: Death

Coleman, Loren
University Of Southern Maine
96 Falmouth Street
Portland, ME 04103
(207)-780-4403

TOPICS: Big Foot, Psychic Phenomena, UFO's, Occult, Ghosts, Witchcraft, Loch Ness Monster **DATE OF BIRTH:** 07/12/47 **PLACE OF BIRTH:** Norfolk, VA **EDUCATION:** Southern Illinois University, Carbondale, Il **YEARS:** 1965-69 **DEGREE:** B.A. Anthropology **YEAR DEGREE:** 1976 **EDUCATION:** Simmons College School Of Social Work, Boston, MA **YEARS:** 1976-78 **DEGREE:** M.S.W. 1978 **OCCUPATION:** Research Associate, Adjunct Assoc. Professor, Human Services Research, Author **WORK EXPERIENCE:** U So. Maine, Portland, ME: Research Assoc. 1983-pres., Adj. Assoc. Prof. 1990-pres.,Instr.Cryptozoology 1990 **AWARDS:** Independent Television Producers Assoc., First Place Award For Videotape 1987 **PROFESSIONAL MEMBERSHIPS:** International Society Of Cryptozoology, Substaining Member; Society For The Investigation Of The Unexplained;Int'l Fortean Organization, Consulting Editor; Fortean Times, Special Correspondent; Strange Magazine, Consulting Editor **PUBLICATIONS:** *Tom Slick And The Search For The Yeti*, 1989 **PUBLISHER:** Faber & Faber **PUBLICATIONS:** *Curious Encounters*, 1985 **PUBLISHER:** Faber & Faber **PUBLICATIONS:** *Mysterious America*, 1983 **PUBLISHER:** Faber & Faber **PUBLICATIONS:** *Creatures Of The Goblin World*, 1984 **PUBLISHER:** Clark Publishing **PUBLICATIONS:** *The Unidentified*, 1975 **PUBLISHER:** Warner Books

Collins, Gillian
Association Of Crystal Healing Therapists
5, Sunnymeded Vale, Holcombe Brook
Bury, Lancashire, BL0 9RR,
England

TOPICS: Crystals

Collins, Stephanie
11A Winfrith Road Earlsfield
London SW18 3BE,
England

TOPICS: Crystals

Collura, Jennie
North American Vegetarian Society
P.O. Box 72
Dolgeville, NY 13329
(518)-568-7970

TOPICS: Health Food

Colton, Dale
Himalayan International Institute Of Yoga Science
and P
R.R.1
Box 400
Honesdale, PA 18431
(717)-253-5551

TOPICS: New Age

Condello, Ruth
509 Nathaniel Street
Winnipeg, Manitoba R3M 3E2
Canada
(204)-452-5678

TOPICS: Crystals

Constantino, Carolyn
820 S.E. 18th Street, apt.206
Ft. Lauderdale, FL 33316
(305)-763-5325

TOPICS: Psychic, Psychic Healing

Cooper, Robert W.
American Federation Of Astrologers
6535 S. Rural Road
P.O. Box 22040
Tempe, AZ 85285-2040
(602)-838-1751

TOPICS: Astrology

Cornelius, Fran
Fran's Place
14311 South Spangler Road
Oregon City, OR 97045

TOPICS: Herbalogy DESCRIPTION: Holistic health
through herbalogy.

Cosner, C.J.
Ann Wigmore Foundation
Division Of Hippocrates Health
196 Commonwealth Avenue
Boston, MA 02116
(617)-267-9424

TOPICS: Holistic Healing

Coughlan, Pat
Northern Pines
Route 85
P.O. Box 279
Raymond, ME 04071
(207)-655-7624

TOPICS: Holistic Healing

Cousens, Gabriel, M.D.
200 Spring Hill Road
Petaluma, CA 94952
(707)-778-6501 (707)-778-7244

TOPICS: Holistic Health, Nutrition, Spirituality,
Reiki, New Age, Crystals DATE OF BIRTH:
05/14/43 PLACE OF BIRTH: Chicago, IL
EDUCATION: Amherst College, Amherst, MA
YEARS: 1961-1965 DEGREE: B.A. YEAR
DEGREE: 65 EDUCATION: College of Physicians &
Surgeons, Columbia U., NY YEARS: 1965-1969
DEGREE: M.D. YEAR DEGREE: 1969
OCCUPATION: Wholistic Health Physician, Director
Tree of Life Seminars, Author WORK
EXPERIENCE: Private Practice Wholistic Health,
Petaluma, CA, 1972-Present; Tree of Life Seminars,
Petaluma, CA, Co-Director, 1987-Present; Sonoma

County Peace the 21st, Sonoma County, CA,
Director 1985-Pres. AWARDS: Who's Who In
California (1988) PROFESSIONAL MEMBERSHIPS:
Acad of Biological Medicine; CA Homeopathic
Medical Society; Bd of Dir, Society of Crystal
Skulls; National Center of Homeopathy; Bd of Dir,
Committee To Stop Food Irradiation DESCRIPTION:
Offers seminars & lectures through Tree of Life
Seminars on holistic health, nutrition, spirituality,
Reiki, etc. PUBLICATIONS: *Spiritual Nutrition &
The Rainbow Diet* (1986) PUBLISHER: Cassandra
Press PUBLICATIONS: *Seven Fold Peace* (1990)
PUBLISHER: H.J. Kramer, Inc.

Covey, Joy
Synergem
P.O. Box 39933
Phoenix, AZ 85069

TOPICS: Crystals

Cowan, Deborah Michele
New Age Concepts
1211 Smith Ridge Road
New Canaan, CT 06840
(203)-966-2608

TOPICS: Crystals DESCRIPTION: Certified Crystal
Healer practicing and teaching crystal therapy. Also
teaches and practices other healing arts such as foot
reflexology, hypnotherapy, body harmony,
rebirthing, polarity, mariel and reiki. Sells large
variety of crystals & jewelry.

Cowels, Ellyn
Wholistic Resource Center
838 Rivermont Avenue
Lynchburg, VA 24504
(804)-528-2816

TOPICS: Holistic Healing

Cox, Bill
Fine Media International
P.O. Box 1567
Stanwood, WA 93292-1567
(805)-682-5151

TOPICS: Crystals

Cox, Davina
Fine Media International
P.O. Box 1567
Stanwood, WA 98292-1567
(805)-682-5151

TOPICS: Crystals

Cox, W. Miles, Ph. D.
Society Of Psychologists In Addiction
Psychology Service
VA Medical Center
Indianapolis, IN 46202
(317)-635-7401

TOPICS: New Age

Craig, D.L.
Quest Enterprises Of Excelsior
464 2nd Street
Excelsior, MN 55331
(612)-474-5132

TOPICS: New Age

Craig, Linn
Eye Of The Fire
7131 Owensmouth, #22G
Canoga Park, CA 91303

(818)-348-4025

TOPICS: Crystals

Cramp, Mary E., R.N.
Crystal Corner, The
29318 Bonnie Drive
Warren, MI 48093
(313)-751-3054

TOPICS: Crystals

Crandall, Dr. James E.
University Of Idaho
Department Of Psychology
Moscow, ID 83843

TOPICS: Parapsychology

Crawford, Lloyd
Stump Sprouts Lodge, X-Country Ski Center
West Hill Road
West Hawley, MA 01339
(413)-339-4265

TOPICS: Holistic Healing

Crawford, Suzanne
Stump Sprouts Lodge, X-Country Ski Center
West Hill Road
West Hawley, MA 01339
(413)-339-4265

TOPICS: Holistic Healing

Croll-Young, Crystal
145 Strathhearn Road
Toronto, ON, M6C 1R7
Canada
(416)-656-0991

TOPICS: Crystals

Cromwell, Marlene
Cromwell-Sloan Publishing Company
63 Vine Road
Stamford, CT 06905
(203)-323-6839

TOPICS: Holistic Healing

Crothers, Dean
International Foundation For Homeopathy
2366 Eastlake Avenue East
Suite 301
Seattle, WA 98102
(206)-324-8230

TOPICS: Dowsing

Crum, James
International Association For Near-Death Studies
Psych #258
Box U-20
Storrs, CT 06268
(203)-486-4170

TOPICS: Death

Crum, Thomas
Windstar Foundation
2317 Snowmass Creek Road
Box 286
Snowmass, CO 81654
(303)-927-4777

TOPICS: New Age

Cunningham, Marci
Backwoods Books
McClellan Lane
P.O. Box 9

Gibbon Glade, PA 15440
(412)-329-4581

TOPICS: New Age

D'Andrea, Maria
Sylvan Society
52 Libby Avenue
Hicksville, NY 11801
(516)-433-9118

TOPICS: Psychic, Runes, Tarot, Metaphysics, Numerology, Hypnotism, Dowsing DATE OF BIRTH: 08/11/50 PLACE OF BIRTH: Budapest, Hungary EDUCATION: U.L.C DEGREE: D.D., D.R.H., Ms. D. YEAR DEGREE: 1988 EDUCATION: Long Island School of Applied Hypnosis DEGREE: Hypnotherapy YEAR DEGREE: 1987 EDUCATION: House Of Miracle, New York DEGREE: Ministry YEAR DEGREE: 1983 OCCUPATION: Psychic, Occultist, Parapsychologist, Certified Hypnotist, Teacher, Ordained Minister, Lecturer, Author WORK EXPERIENCE: Sylvan Society, Hicksville, NY, Founder; Inner Light Pubication, Assistant Editor AWARDS: Honorary Member of Tuscarora Tribe of Indians, Shaman; Listed in Crossroads: A Who's Who Of The Magical Community & in Where Are The Psychics? PROFESSIONAL MEMBERSHIPS: Authors Guild, Spiritual Frontiers Fellowship, Floating Healing Meditation Circle, A.R.E., Psychic Guild, Ghost Research Society, Long Island School Of Applied Hypnosis DESCRIPTION: Lectures on the topics of Metaphysics & Occult. Has appeared on radio & cable TV shows. Teaches Yoga, Meditation Principles & Techniques as well as Psychic & Spiritual Development. PUBLICATIONS: Psychic Vibrations Of Crystals, Gems & Stones, 1988 PUBLISHER: Inner Light Publications PUBLICATIONS: The New Age Formulary, 1990 PUBLISHER: Inner Light Publications PUBLICATIONS: The Quest For Meditation PUBLISHER: Psychic Fair Network News PUBLICATIONS: Journey To Another Plane PUBLISHER: Psychic Press PUBLICATIONS: The Concept Of Herbs Related To The Occult PUBLISHER: Psychic Fair Network News PUBLICATIONS: Children In The Path Of Light PUBLISHER: Inner Light Publications

da Silva, Arjuna
Hibiscus Enterprises
710 Northwest 14th Avenue
Gainesville, FL 32601-4017
(904)-332-2771

TOPICS: New Age

Dafoe, Steven
The Barbizon Foundation
Rural Route One
Lumby, Br V0E 2G0
Canada
(604)-547-6621

TOPICS: New Age

Dale, Theresa, Ph.D.
Society For Bio-Energetic Research
Box 6515
Malibu, CA 90264
(213)-457-4293

TOPICS: Crystals

Dalrymple, Chris
Texas Chiropractic Association

1704 Timberwood
Austin, TX 78741-5547
(512)-454-4551

TOPICS: Holistic Healing

Damiani, Anthony
Larson Publications

TOPICS: Metaphysics PLACE OF BIRTH: Brooklyn, NY OCCUPATION: Philosopher, Metaphysician, Teacher, Author, Advanced Meditator WORK EXPERIENCE: Wisdoms Goldenrod Center For Philosophic Studies, Valois, NY, Founder 1971-1984 DESCRIPTION: Born 1922, Deceased 1984. His manuscripts are currently being prepared for publication based on hundreds of hours of tapes. PUBLICATIONS: Looking Into Mind: How To Recognize Who You Are & How You Know, 1990 PUBLISHER: Larson Publications

Damron, Judy
HCR-l, Box 4A
Boiceville, NY 12412

TOPICS: Psychic

Daniels, Karil
Point Of View Productions
2477 Folsom Street
San Francisco, CA 94110
(415)-821-0435

TOPICS: Birth, Holistic Health, Homeopathy PLACE OF BIRTH: New York, NY EDUCATION: New York University, New York, NY DEGREE: B.A. Psychology OCCUPATION: Film/Video Producer, Director, Cinematographer, Author WORK EXPERIENCE: Point Of View Production, San Francisco, CA, President PROFESSIONAL MEMBERSHIPS: Association of Independent Video & Film Makers (AIVF), Film Arts Foundation (Founder), Women In Film & Television, Bay Area Video Coalition DESCRIPTION: The video, Water Baby: Experiences of Water Birth, has won 13 film & video festival awards. Has also authored many articles for various New Age & holistic health magazines and has lectured on the subject of Water Birth.

Daniels, Marcella
P.O. Box 1946
Rockford, IL 61110

TOPICS: Channeling

Das, Rama
P.O. Box 31131
San Francisco, CA 9431

TOPICS: Channeling

Dass, Hari
161 Robles Drive
Santa Cruz, CA 95060
(408)-426-8468

TOPICS: Yoga, Spirituality, New Age OCCUPATION: Monk, Author PUBLICATIONS: Fire Without Fuel: Aphorisms Of Baba Hari Dass PUBLISHER: Sri Rama Publishing PUBLICATIONS: Silence Speaks, 1976 PUBLISHER: Sri Rama Publishing PUBLICATIONS: Ashtanga Yoga Primer, 1981 PUBLISHER: Sri Rama Publishing PUBLICATIONS: A Childs Garden Of Yoga, 1980 PUBLISHER: Sri Rama Publishing

Davidson, Gordon
Sirius Community
Baker Road

Shutesbury, MA 01072
(413)-259-1251

TOPICS: Metaphysics, Spirituality, New Age, Meditation PUBLICATIONS: The Inner Side of World Events

Davidson, John
Wholistic Research Company
Bright Haven, Robin's Lane Lolworh
Cambridge, CB3 8HH,
England

TOPICS: Crystals

Davis, Beth
Bear Tribe Medicine Society
P.O. Box 9167
Spokane, WA 99209
(509)-326-6561

TOPICS: Holistic Healing

Davis, Courtney
36 Bodmin Road, Flat 2
St. Austen
Cornwall, PL25 5AE
England
0726 685 33

TOPICS: Tarot, Spirituality, Metaphysics DATE OF BIRTH: 10/31/46 PLACE OF BIRTH: South Wales EDUCATION: Barnsbury School For Boys, London OCCUPATION: Artist, Lecturer, Author PUBLICATIONS: Merlin The Immortal, 1984 PUBLISHER: Spirit Of Celtia PUBLICATIONS: Celtic Art Of Courtney Davis, 1985 PUBLISHER: Spirit Of Celtia PUBLICATIONS: Pathway Through The Labyrinth, 1988 PUBLISHER: Element Books PUBLICATIONS: Celtic Art Source Book, 1988 PUBLISHER: Blandford Press PUBLICATIONS: Celtic Transfer Book, 1989 PUBLISHER: Dover PUBLICATIONS: Celtic Tarot, 1990 PUBLISHER: Thorsons

Davis, Gail E.
Gail E. Davis
P.O. Box 773
North Little Rock, AR 72115

TOPICS: UFO's

Davis, Judith Hope
Life And Light Center
P.O. Box 486
Northfield, VT 05663

TOPICS: Channeling, Holistic Healing, Astrology, Psychic OCCUPATION: Psychic, Holistic Healer, Astrological Counsellor WORK EXPERIENCE: Life And Light Center, Northfield, VT, Founder, Director DESCRIPTION: Purpose is to assist individuals in attaining a peaceful & healthy life through healing, Psychic Readings & Astrological Counselling.

Davis, Lynda
Revivaria
P.O. Box 862
Clearlake Oaks, CA 95423
(707)-998-1366

TOPICS: Holistic Healing

Davison, Audy
Common Ground, Inc., And Inner City Hot Springs
2927 N.E. Everett Street
Portland, OR 97232
(503)-238-4010

TOPICS: Holistic Healing

Dawes, Philip
10 Crediton Hill
London NW6 1HP,
England
TOPICS: Crystals

Daze
5147 South Harvard, Suite 288
Tulsa, OK 74137
TOPICS: Channeling

Deal, Grady, Ph. D., D.C.
Hawaiian Fitness Holiday
P.O. Box 1147
Kapaa, Kauai, HI 96746
(800)-338-6977 (808)-332-9244

TOPICS: Holistic Health, Astrology, Metaphysics, Numerology, Yoga, Massage, Reflexology

Deal, Roberleigh C.
Hawaiian Fitness Holiday
P.O. Box 1147
Kapaa, Kauai, HI 96746
(800)-338-6977

TOPICS: Holistic Health, Astrology, Metaphysics, Numerology, Yoga, Massage, Reflexology DATE OF BIRTH: 05/23/30 PLACE OF BIRTH: Mineola, NY EDUCATION: First Temple of Astrology, Los Angeles, CA YEARS: 5 years DEGREE: Certificate YEAR DEGREE: 1969 OCCUPATION: Astrologer, Numerologer, Lecturer PROFESSIONAL MEMBERSHIPS: American Federation of Astrologers, 1984-85 DESCRIPTION: Offers astrology & numerology readings. Lectured at: American Federation of Astrology, Isabel Hickey's Astrology Conferences, Southwestern Astrological Conferences & the Quimby Center in NM. PUBLICATIONS: *Letters In Action*, 1976 PUBLISHER: Astro Press

Deaver, Korra, Ph. D.
2585 Dalmuir Court
San Jose, CA 95121
(408)-274-9036

TOPICS: Psychic, Metaphysics, Crystals, PSI, Spirituality, Hypnotism, ESP DATE OF BIRTH: 08/11/23 PLACE OF BIRTH: Warrenton, OR EDUCATION: St. John's University, Springfield, LA DEGREE: B.A. YEAR DEGREE: 1978 EDUCATION: St. John's University, Springfield, LA DEGREE: M.S. YEAR DEGREE: 1980 EDUCATION: St. John's University, Springfield, LA DEGREE: Ph. D.- Parapsychology YEAR DEGREE: 1984 OCCUPATION: Teacher, Lecturer, Ordained Minister, Author WORK EXPERIENCE: Parapsychology Education Center, Inc., Little Rock, AR, President, 1971-1983; Psychic Science Bookstore, Little Rock, AR, Manager, 1971-1983 DESCRIPTION: Teacher of Soul Development, ESP, Self-Hypnosis, and Advanced Metaphysics. Past life therapist. PUBLICATIONS: *Rock Crystal, The Magic Stone* (1985) PUBLISHER: Weiser Publishing PUBLICATIONS: *Psychic Power and Soul Consciousness* (1990) PUBLISHER: Hunter House PUBLICATIONS: *Where Will You Be At The Battle Of Armeggedon?* (1977) PUBLISHER: Institute of Psychic Science

DeBairalli Levy, Juliette
Traditional Tours
P.O. Box 564
Creswell, OR 97426

(503)-895-2957
TOPICS: New Age

Deering, Hallie
Elfinstones
2610 Jacks Canyon Road
Sedona, AZ 86336
(602)-284-1550

TOPICS: Crystals

Delawie, Billie C.
Journeys Into The Known
P.O. Box 7422
San Diego, CA 92107
(619)-222-0904

TOPICS: Holistic Healing

Dellinger, Jan
Strength & Health Publishing
Box 1707
York, PA 17405
(717)-767-6481

TOPICS: Holistic Healing

DeLong, Barbara
21 Atlantic Street
Stamford, CT 06901
(203)-327-2929

TOPICS: Psychic

Denver, John
Windstar Foundation
2317 Snowmass Creek Road
Box 286
Snowmass, CO 81654
(303)-927-4777

TOPICS: New Age DATE OF BIRTH: 12/31/43 PLACE OF BIRTH: Roswell, NM OCCUPATION: Singer, Actor, Composer, Environmentalist WORK EXPERIENCE: The Windstar Foundation, Snowmass, CO, Founder PROFESSIONAL MEMBERSHIPS: Presidential Commission on World Hunger, 1978; Chairman National UNICEF Day, 1984; National Space Institute; Save The Children; The Cousteau Society; Friends Of The Earth; The Human/Dolphin Foundation; European Space Agency DESCRIPTION: Born Henry John Deutschendorf, Jr. Advocate of environmental & planetary causes. Formed Windstar Foundation which promotes research & education for peace, ecology, alternative energy sources, raising public awareness, world hunger & macrobiotics.

Der Marderosian, Ara, Ph. D.
Herb Research Foundation
1007 Pearl Street, #200
Boulder, CO 80302
(800)-748-2617 (303)-449-2265

TOPICS: Herbalogy, Holistic Health

DeRonne, Dick
Sinai Hospital Of Detroit
6767 West Outer Drive
Detroit, MI 48235
(313)-493-5500

TOPICS: Holistic Healing

Devai, Christine E.
Artemisia Institute For Botanical, Medical and Preventi
Box 190
Jackson's Point, On L0E 1L0

Canada
(416)-722-8604
TOPICS: Holistic Healing

DeVault, George
Regenerative Agriculture Association
222 Main Street
Emmaus, PA 18098
(215)-967-5171

TOPICS: Health Food

Devi, Devorah
Earthsong Institute
P.O. Box 20615
New York, NY 10025-1515
(212)-518-4548

TOPICS: Crystals, Channeling PLACE OF BIRTH: Glen Cove, NY OCCUPATION: Psychic Counselor, Spiritual Teacher, Master Healer, Singer, Song Writer, Author WORK EXPERIENCE: Earthsong Institute, New York, NY, Founder, Director, 1979-Present; Jewish Meditation, New York, NY, Founder, Director, 1991-Present DESCRIPTION: Channels love & wisdom of the Divine Feminine presence. Offers Sound, Voice Music in Healing/Transformation; Chakra Psychology; Aura, Color & Crystal Therapeutics; Past Life Regression; Channeling; Flower Essence Healing, Women's Spirituality, Meditation.

Devi, Saraswathi
Prana Yoga Ashram
P.O. Box 1037
Berkeley, CA 94701
(415)-655-3664

TOPICS: Holistic Health, Meditation, Yoga, Spirituality, Nutrition, Massage, Vegetarianism DATE OF BIRTH: 06/04/46 PLACE OF BIRTH: San Francisco, CA EDUCATION: University of CA at Berkeley DEGREE: B.A. YEAR DEGREE: 1969 EDUCATION: Prana Yoga Ashram DEGREE: Teacher Certificate YEAR DEGREE: 1979 EDUCATION: University of CA at Berkeley DEGREE: Teacher Certificate YEAR DEGREE: 1989 OCCUPATION: Editor, Teacher of Yoga, Meditation, Nutrition, Natural Childbirth WORK EXPERIENCE: Prana Yoga Ashram, Berkeley, CA, Vice-President 1980-present, Yoga & Meditation Instructor 1976-present AWARDS: Peralta Colleges, Lifetime Credential, Early Childcare Certification PUBLICATIONS: *Prana Yoga Life Magazine*, 1976-present, editor PUBLISHER: Prana Yoga Ashram

Devi, Yoganathan
Prana Yoga Ashram
P.O. Box 1037
Berkeley, CA 94701
(415)-644-2544

TOPICS: Yoga

Devlin, Mary
2935 San Mateo #7
El Cerrito, CA 94530-3437
(415)-526-2392

TOPICS: Astrology, Metaphysics, Past Life Regression, Holistic Health, Vegetarianism, Psychology PLACE OF BIRTH: Great Lakes, IL EDUCATION: University of Nevada, Reno, NV YEARS: 1968-72 DEGREE: B.A. YEAR DEGREE: 1972 OCCUPATION: Author, Singer, Lecturer, Astrologer, Performer AWARDS: PMAFA-Professional Member of the American Federation of

Astrologers, 1975; Ananta Foundation Certificate Past Life Regression **PROFESSIONAL MEMBERSHIPS:** American Federation of Astrologers; San Francisco Early Music Society; San Francisco Film Arts Foundation **DESCRIPTION:** Specialist in Reincarnation, Astrology, Transpersonal Psychology & Medieval & New Age Music. **PUBLICATIONS:** *I Am Mary Shelley*, 1977 **PUBLISHER:** Condor **PUBLICATIONS:** *Astrology And Past Lives*, 1987 **PUBLISHER:** Whitford Press **PUBLICATIONS:** *Astrology & Relationships*, 1988 **PUBLISHER:** Whitford Press **PUBLICATIONS:** *Our Future Lives In The Age Of Aquarius, essay,* 1988 **PUBLISHER:** Whitford Press **PUBLICATIONS:** *On The Threshold Of Enlightenment*, essay, 1989 **PUBLISHER:** Center For The Healing Arts **PUBLICATIONS:** Your Future Lives

Dickinson, Bob
Chrysalis Gifts
3419 East Laurelhurst Drive, Northeast
Seattle, WA 98105
(206)-524-1710

TOPICS: Crystals

Dickson-Buchlater, Buck
Paradise Designs
P.O. Box 79
St. John, 00830
US Virgin Islands
(809)-776-7989

TOPICS: Crystals

Dickson-Buchlater, Suki
Paradise Designs
P.O. Box 79
St. John, 00830
US Virgin Islands
(809)-776-7989

TOPICS: Crystals

Dilley, Dr. Frank B..
University Of Delaware
Department Of Philosophy
Newark, DE 19711

TOPICS: Parapsychology

Dillon, James
Scranton Times
Box 59
Tunkhannock, PA 18657
(717)-836-2123

TOPICS: New Age

Dimon, Clint
Dimon, Inc.
3001 North San Fernando Boulev
P.O. Box 6489
Burbank, CA 91510
(818)-845-3748

TOPICS: Holistic Healing

Diotte, Wayne
Macrobiotics Canada
R.R. 3
Almonte, On K0A 1A0
Canada
(613)-256-2665

TOPICS: Holistic Healing

Disgonihi, Naniwea
Good Medicin' Way

77 Park Terrace East, D38
New York, NY 10034
(212)-304-9605

TOPICS: Crystals

Disney, Anthea
Conde Nast Publications, Inc.
350 Madison Avenue
New York, NY 10017
(212)-880-8800

TOPICS: Holistic Healing

Dixon, Jim
Guadalupe River Ranch
Box 877
Boerne, TX 78006
(512)-537-4837

TOPICS: Holistic Healing

Dodd, Gloria, D.V.M.
Naturo-Vet Services, Inc.
857 El Pintado Road
Danville, CA 94526
(415)-837-7759

TOPICS: Holistic Healing, Crystals

Dogoloff, Lee
American Council For Drug Education
204 Monroe Street, #110
Rockville, MD 20850
(301)-294-0600

TOPICS: Holistic Healing

Donais, MariJo
2221 East 30th Street
Vancouver, WA 98663

TOPICS: Channeling

Doney, Mike
10122 S.E. Hollywood
Milwaukie, OR 97222
(503)-659-0165

TOPICS: Dowsing

Donnelan, Stephen
Box 373, 1 Friar Road
Armadale Perth 6112,
Australia

TOPICS: Crystals

Donnelly, Gloria
Aspen Publishing, Inc.
7201 McKinney Circle
Frederick, MD 21701

TOPICS: Holistic Healing

Dorland, Frank N.
P.O. Box 6233
Los Osos, CA 03403

TOPICS: Crystals

Dorobiala, Dr. Jim
Sun Eagle Publishing
P.O. Box 33545
Granada Hills, CA 91394
(818)-360-2224

TOPICS: Holistic Health **DESCRIPTION:** He is Director Of Education and Research with the American Academy of Holistic Chiropractic and is an extension faculty member for the Los Angeles and Southern CA Colleges of Chiropractic.

PUBLICATIONS: *A Ten Minute Cure For The Common Cold*

Dotlo, Jill
National Council Of Geocosmic Research
425 Butternut Court
Orange, CT 06477

TOPICS: Metaphysics

Dougherty, Jude P.
Philosophy Education Society
Catholic University Of America
School Of Philosophy
Washington, DC 20064
(202)-635-8778

TOPICS: Metaphysics

Douglas, Apryl
7410 Vassar Avenue
Canoga Park, CA 91303
(818)-888-0487 (818)-998-5762

TOPICS: Psychic, Psychic Healing, Metaphysics, Meditation, Hypnotism **DATE OF BIRTH:** 05/12/53 **PLACE OF BIRTH:** Los Angeles, CA **EDUCATION:** Los Angeles Valley College, North Hollywood, CA **DEGREE:** A.A. **YEAR DEGREE:** 1974 **OCCUPATION:** Psychic, Healer, Behavior Therapist, Lecturer, Author **WORK EXPERIENCE:** Vision Quest Bookstores, Canoga Park, Simi Valley, Woodland Hills, CA, Owner 5 years **AWARDS:** Christian Travel Service, Manilla, Phillipines, Healing Certification, 1984; Behavioral Therapist-Hypnotherapist by Michael Consolo Ph. D., 1988 **PROFESSIONAL MEMBERSHIPS:** Profession Association For Healing Arts & Sciences; Universal Life Church, Minister 1981-present **DESCRIPTION:** Lecturer on the topics of Energy Balancing & Psychic Counseling **PUBLICATIONS:** *Developing Psychic Abilities* **PUBLISHER:** TEC Publications **PUBLICATIONS:** *Meditations Of The Heart* **PUBLISHER:** TEC Publications

Douglas, Leisha
Psychotherapist
Rural Delivery 2, Box 195 Amawalk Road
Katonah, NY 10536

TOPICS: Channeling

Douglass, Kathy Lynn
Denali Center For Holistic Health & Personal Growth
HC 89, Box 451
Willow, AK 99688-9705
(907)-495-6853

TOPICS: Psychic, Tarot, Runes, Channeling **DATE OF BIRTH:** 09/18/44 **PLACE OF BIRTH:** San Jose, CA **OCCUPATION:** Psychic Reader, Clinical Director, Editor, Nurse, Counselor **WORK EXPERIENCE:** Denali Center For Holistic Health & Personal Growth, Willow, AK, Clinical Director, Managing Editor **DESCRIPTION:** Offers psychic readings in tarot, runes & other old and new oracles by mail through the Denali Center. Fee is determined by the client after services are received. **PUBLICATIONS:** *The Shaman Papers*, 1989, Managing Editor **PUBLISHER:** Denali Center For Holistic Health & Personal Growth

Down, Michael
Earthstar Foundation
2635 West First Avenue, #6
Vancouver, BC, V6K 1H1
Canada

(604)-733-5810

TOPICS: Crystals

Dowson, Janice
Touchstone Center
12084 211th Street
Maple Ridge, Br V2X 8K8
Canada
(604)-463-9879

TOPICS: Holistic Healing

Dragon, Sidney J.
Baker Street Publications
P.O. Box 994
Metairie, LA 70004
(504)-733-9138

TOPICS: New Age

Drais, John
P.O. Box 421
Dulzura, CA 92017

TOPICS: New Age

Druffel, Ann
Skynet
257 Sycamore Glen
Pasadena, CA 91105

TOPICS: UFO's OCCUPATION: Investigator, Researcher, Lecturer, Author, UFO consultant WORK EXPERIENCE: Skynet, Pasadena, CA, Coordinator DESCRIPTION: UFO consultant, investigator, researcher, lecturer & author.

Drury, Nevill
P.O. Box 480
Roseville, NSW 2069
Australia
2-416 7342

TOPICS: Holistic Health, Occult, Spirituality, Body-Mind Connection DATE OF BIRTH: 10/01/47 PLACE OF BIRTH: Hastings, England EDUCATION: Macquarie University, Sydney, Australia DEGREE: M.A. Honours YEAR DEGREE: 1980 EDUCATION: Sydney University, Sydney, Australia DEGREE: B.A. YEAR DEGREE: 1968 OCCUPATION: Author, Publisher WORK EXPERIENCE: Harper & Row, Sydney, Australia, Managing Editor, 1976-80; Doubleday, Sydney, Australia, Managing Editor, 1980-82; Australian Broadcasting Corporation, Holistic Health Program, 1982-83; Nature & Health Journal, Sydney, Australia, Managing Editor, 1983-89; Craftsman House Art Publisher, Publishing Manager, 1989-present PUBLICATIONS: *The Occult Sourcebook*, 1978 PUBLISHER: Routledge PUBLICATIONS: *Inner Visions*, 1991 PUBLISHER: Arkana PUBLICATIONS: *Other Temples, Other Gods*, 1982 PUBLISHER: Hodder & Stoughton PUBLICATIONS: *The Healing Power*, 1981 PUBLISHER: Muller PUBLICATIONS: *Dictionary Of Mysticism & The Occult*, 1988 PUBLISHER: Droemer Knaur PUBLICATIONS: *The Occult Experience*, 1989 PUBLISHER: Avery

Duff, Kat
Cosmic Clockwatch
P.O. Box 1178
Taos, NM 87571
(505)-758-2203

TOPICS: Astrology PUBLICATIONS: *The Calendrix*

Dugan, Howard And Shane
Rural Route 1, Box 13A1

Fairfield, IA 52556
(515)-472-7009

TOPICS: Crystals

Dukes, Dr. T.
The Cheirological Society
Kongoryuji
London Road
East Dereham, NR19 1AS
England

TOPICS: Holistic Health, Palmistry PLACE OF BIRTH: London, England EDUCATION: A. Jackson University, Washington, D.C. DEGREE: Hon. Dean of Studies YEAR DEGREE: 1972 EDUCATION: Fellowship College, Washington State DEGREE: D.D. Theology YEAR DEGREE: 1974 OCCUPATION: Author, Lecturer WORK EXPERIENCE: Ryushinji Temple, Japan 1965-67; Hakurenji Temple, Japan 1974-77; Kongoruyji Temple, East Dereham, England 1977-present; Cambridge University, Lecturer Oriental Studies/Religion 1969-72 AWARDS: Temple Teaching Diplomas; International Black Belt Association, Greece 1971 PROFESSIONAL MEMBERSHIPS: Royal Institute of Philosophy, Japan Society, Tibet Society, Wakatake-Kai Guide Doge For The Blind, Chinese Yoga Foundation PUBLICATIONS: *Chinese Hand Analysis* PUBLISHER: Samuel Weiser PUBLICATIONS: *Source Book of Shinson Buddhism*, 1970 PUBLICATIONS: *Chinese Yoga Vol. I & II*, 1989 PUBLISHER: C.Y. Federation

Dunford, Mari
Crystals With Character
P.O. Box A
Mira Loma, CA 91752
(714)-681-0272

TOPICS: Crystals

Dunwich, Gerina
Golden Isis Magazine
P.O. Box 726
Salem, MA 01970

TOPICS: Metaphysics, Astrology, Occult, Witchcraft, Paganism, New Age DATE OF BIRTH: 12/27/59 PLACE OF BIRTH: Chicago, IL OCCUPATION: Author, Editor, Witch, Astrologer, Spiritualist Medium WORK EXPERIENCE: Golden Isis Magazine, West Hills, CA, Publisher, Editor 1980-Present PROFESSIONAL MEMBERSHIPS: Wiccan/Pagan Press Alliance, W.P.P.A., Mechanicsburg, PA PUBLICATIONS: *Golden Isis Magazine* PUBLISHER: Golden Isis Press PUBLICATIONS: *Candlelight Spells*, 1988 PUBLISHER: Citadel Press PUBLICATIONS: *The Magick Of Candleburning*, 1989 PUBLISHER: Citadel Press PUBLICATIONS: *The Concise Lexicon Of The Occult*, 1990 PUBLISHER: Citadel Press PUBLICATIONS: *Wicca Craft*, 1991 PUBLISHER: Citadel Press PUBLICATIONS: *Circle Of Shadows*, 1990 PUBLISHER: Golden Isis Press

Dyke, Rod B.
Lucius Farish
Rt. 1
Box 220
Plumerville, AR 72127
(501)-354-2558

TOPICS: UFO's

Dylan, Peggy

Sundoor Foundation For Transpersonal Education
P.O. Box 669
Twain Harte, CA 95383
(209)-928-4800

TOPICS: Psychology, Body-Mind Connection, Meditation, Spirituality, Firewalking DATE OF BIRTH: 03/14/53 PLACE OF BIRTH: Seattle, WA OCCUPATION: Transpersonal Psychologist, Author, Lecturer, Teacher WORK EXPERIENCE: Sundoor, Twain Harte, CA, President, Instructor, 1984-present DESCRIPTION: Acts as leader of Firewalk Instructor's Training, instructor of Firewalking Seminar, Rebirthing & Rebirther's Training. Also lectures on mind-body interaction & healing. Conducts young adult workshop, Roots & Wings. PUBLICATIONS: *Guiding Yourself Into A Spiritual Reality*, 1984 PUBLISHER: Reunion Press PUBLICATIONS: *Guiding Yourself*, 1985 PUBLISHER: Reunion Press

Dynan, Andrea
807 East 18th Street
Brooklyn, NY 11230

TOPICS: Channeling

Eageti, Richard
Gordon & Breach Science Publishers
Box 786
Cooper Station
New York, NY 10276
(212)-206-8900

TOPICS: New Age

Eagle, Brooke Medicine
P. O. Box 1682
Helena, MT 59624
(406)-442-8196

TOPICS: Spirituality, Holistic Healing DESCRIPTION: Contemporary Native teacher who carries the ancient voices. Offers tapes & classes.

Eagle, Jeanie
Aesculapia
1480 Dutcher Creek Road
Grants Pass, OR 97527
(503)-476-0492

TOPICS: Holistic Healing

Earley, Jay, Ph. D.
4 Carolyn Court
Syosset, NY 11791
(516)-921-7110

TOPICS: Spirituality, Holistic Healing, Body-Mind Connection, New Age, Psychology DATE OF BIRTH: 04/04/44 PLACE OF BIRTH: Philadelphia, PA EDUCATION: Carnegie-Mellon University, Pittsburgh, PA YEARS: 1966-68 DEGREE: Ph. D. YEAR DEGREE: 1968 EDUCATION: Saybrook Institute, San Francisco, CA YEARS: 1973-80 DEGREE: Ph. D. YEAR DEGREE: 1980 OCCUPATION: Psychotherapist, Workshop-Leader, Author, Lecturer, Social Theorist PUBLICATIONS: *Inner Journeys: A Guidebook To Personal And Social Transformation* , 1990 PUBLISHER: Samuel Weiser PUBLICATIONS: *A Course In Self-Esteem*

Edelson, Elihu
Free People Press
Route 6, Box 28
Tyler, TX 75704-9712
(214)-592-4263

TOPICS: New Age OCCUPATION: Editor WORK EXPERIENCE: Free People Press, Tyler, TX, Editor

Edgar, Rev. Elizabeth R.
National Spiritualist Association Of Churches
1325 Stevens Street
P.O. Box 128
Cassadaga, FL 32706
(904)-228-2506

TOPICS: Psychic Phenomena

Edge, Dr. Hoyt
Rollins College
Department Of Philosophy
Winter Park, FL 32787

TOPICS: Parapsychology

Edwards, Susan
844 19th Street
Boulder, CO 80302

TOPICS: Tarot

Edwords, Frederick
Creation/Evolution Journal
P.O. Box 146
7 Harwood Drive
Buffalo, NY 14226
(716)-839-5080

TOPICS: New Age

Einstein, Pat
765 Greenwich Street
New York, NY 10014

TOPICS: Psychic

Eisner, B.
P.O. Box 1035
Berkeley, CA 94701
(415)-540-6278

TOPICS: New Age, Psychology DATE OF BIRTH: 02/26/46 PLACE OF BIRTH: Brooklyn, NY EDUCATION: University of CA, Santa Barbara, CA YEARS: 1977-79 DEGREE: M.A. Psychology YEAR DEGREE: 1979 EDUCATION: Saybrook Institute, San Francisco, CA YEARS: 1982-87 DEGREE: Ph. D. candidate OCCUPATION: Author, Teacher, Psychologist WORK EXPERIENCE: University of CA, Santa Barbara, CA, Teaching Assistant Psychology AWARDS: Phi Eta Sigma Honor Society PUBLICATIONS: *Ecstasy: The MDMA Story*, 1989 PUBLISHER: Ronin Publishing, Inc.

Elliott, Susan
Women Healthsharing, Inc.
14 Skey Lane
Toronto, On M6J 3S4
Canada
(416)-532-0812

TOPICS: Holistic Healing

Ellis, N.
5000 Butte, #254
Boulder, CO 80301
(303)-444-9802

TOPICS: Spirituality, Death, Reincarnation DATE OF BIRTH: 09/24/53 PLACE OF BIRTH: Louisville, KY EDUCATION: University of Colorado, Boulder, CO YEARS: 1980-1981 DEGREE: M.A. YEAR DEGREE: 1981 EDUCATION: University of Kentucky, Lexington, KY YEARS: 1972-1976 DEGREE: B.A. YEAR DEGREE: 1976 OCCUPATION: Teacher, Author, Lecturer WORK

EXPERIENCE: Boulder Graduate School, Boulder, CO, Adjunct Faculty AWARDS: 1987 Bread Loaf Scholar PROFESSIONAL MEMBERSHIPS: Egyptian Study Society; Church of the Eternal Source DESCRIPTION: Teaches Feminine Mysteries, Ancient Texts, Hekau: Words of Power PUBLICATIONS: *Awakening Osiris* (1988) PUBLISHER: Phanes Press PUBLICATIONS: *Sorrowful Mysteries* (1991) PUBLISHER: Arrowood Books

Ellis, Trisha
Crystal Academy, The
Bidgeebah
Mt. Pleasant 5235, S.A.,
Australia

TOPICS: Crystals

Elzer, Don
The Barbizon Foundation
Rural Route One
Lumby, Br V0E 2G0
Canada
(604)-547-6621

TOPICS: New Age

Emery, Marcia Becker, Ph. D.
3512 McCoy Southeast
Grand Rapids, MI 49506
(616)-949-3574

TOPICS: Psychic, Psychology, Astrology, Parapsychology, Channeling DESCRIPTION: Practices as a consultant by mail & phone as an astrologer, psychic, psychotherapist & parapsychologist.

Emery, Sheldon
Foothills Crystal
P.O. Box 10432
Denver, CO 80210

TOPICS: Crystals

Epstein, Gerald, M.D.
Bantam Books
40 East 89th Street
New York, NY 10128
(212)-534-0155

TOPICS: Holistic Health DESCRIPTION: expet on the mind's power to heal physical and emotional disordersthru the use of mental imagery and visualizations. expert on dream work, meditation and hypnosis. PUBLICATIONS: *Healing Visualization:Creating Health Through Imagery*

Erickson, Steven E.
Vongrutnorv Og Press, Inc.
Randall Flat Road
P.O. Box 411
Troy, ID 83871-0411
(208)-835-4902 (208)-835-4902

TOPICS: Metaphysics, Holistic Health, New Age DATE OF BIRTH: 09/20/50 PLACE OF BIRTH: Moscow, ID EDUCATION: University of Idaho, Moscow, ID EDUCATION: Idaho State University, Pocatello, ID DEGREE: B.S., Pharmacy OCCUPATION: Author, Editor, Publisher WORK EXPERIENCE: Vongrutnorv Og Press, Inc., Troy, ID, President, 1977-Present PUBLICATIONS: *Teardrops and Silicon* (1978) PUBLISHER: Vongrutnorv Og Press, Inc. PUBLICATIONS: *The Emshock Letter* (1977-Present) PUBLISHER: Vongrutnorv Og Press, Inc.

Erlewine, Michael
Matrix Software
315 Marion Avenue
Big Rapids, MI 49307
(616)-796-2483 (616)-796-3437

TOPICS: Astrology, Metaphysics DATE OF BIRTH: 07/18/41 PLACE OF BIRTH: Lancaster, PA OCCUPATION: Astrologer, Computer Programmer, Editor, Counselor, Teacher, Lecturer WORK EXPERIENCE: Matrix Software, Big Rapids, MI, President, Editor AWARDS: Professional Astrologers, Inc. Award; Regulus Award-Enhancing Astrology's Image, 1989 PROFESSIONAL MEMBERSHIPS: NCGR, AFAN, AFA DESCRIPTION: Pioneer in computerizing Astrology for the beginner & the professional. PUBLICATIONS: *Manual of Computer Programming* PUBLISHER: Matrix Software PUBLICATIONS: *Astrophysical Directions* PUBLISHER: Matrix Software PUBLICATIONS: *Matrix Journal* PUBLISHER: Matrix Software PUBLICATIONS: *Astrotalk Bulletin* PUBLISHER: Matrix Software

Escalet, Marjorie J.
13 Fletcher Street
Kennebunk, ME 04043
(207)-985-7782

TOPICS: Psychic, Tarot DESCRIPTION: Psychic offering tarot readings by mail.

Estep, Sarah Wilson
American Association-Electronic Voice
726 Dill Road
Severna Park, MD 21146
(301)-647-8742 (301)-647-8742

TOPICS: Metaphysics, Death, Parapsychology, Channeling DATE OF BIRTH: 03/01/26 PLACE OF BIRTH: Altoona, PA EDUCATION: Mary Washington College, Fredericksburg, VA YEARS: 1945-1949 DEGREE: B.A. YEAR DEGREE: 1949 OCCUPATION: Author, Teacher, Counselor WORK EXPERIENCE: Blair County Children's Aid Society, Altoona, PA, Social Worker; American Association-Electronic Voice Phenomena, Severna Park, MD, Founder, Pres.; Board of Education, Ann Arundel County, Anapolis, MD, Teacher AWARDS: Who's Who In The East, 1991-92 PROFESSIONAL MEMBERSHIPS: American Association-Electronic Voice Phenomena PUBLICATIONS: *Voices Of Eternity* (1988) PUBLISHER: Fawcett

Evans Bush, Nancy
International Association For Near-Death Studies
Psych #258
Box U-20
Storrs, CT 06268
(203)-486-4170

TOPICS: Death

Exum, David
Exum Corporation, Publishing Division
5705 Cochiti Drive NW
Albuquerque, NM 87120
(505)-881-4413

TOPICS: New Age

Falsetto, Regina M., R.N.
6348 Conlon Avenue
El Cerrito, CA 94530
(415)-236-1430

TOPICS: Crystals

Farias, Helen
Juno's Peacock Press-Northwest Graphics
P.O. Box 8
Clear Lake, WA 98235
(206)-856-5494

TOPICS: New Age

Farish, Lucius
Lucius Farish
Rt. 1
Box 220
Plumerville, AR 72127
(501)-354-2558

TOPICS: UFO's

Farrar, Janet
Herne's Cottage
Ethelstown
Kells, Co. Meath
Ireland

TOPICS: Occult, Witchcraft, Spirituality, Voudoun, Paganism OCCUPATION: Author, Lecturer DESCRIPTION: Co-authored many books on the occult. Practicing witch. Founded own coven, with husband Stewart, on December 22, 1970. PUBLICATIONS: *Eight Sabbats For Witches*, 1988 PUBLISHER: Phoenix Publishing PUBLICATIONS: *The Witches' Way*, 1988 PUBLISHER: Phoenix Publishing PUBLICATIONS: *The Witches' Goddess*, 1988 PUBLISHER: Phoenix Publishing PUBLICATIONS: *Life And Times Of A Modern Witch*, 1988 PUBLISHER: Phoenix Publishing PUBLICATIONS: *The Witches' God: Lord Of The Dance*, 1989 PUBLISHER: Phoenix Publishing PUBLICATIONS: *Spells And How They Work*, 1991 PUBLISHER: Phoenix Publishing

Farrar, Stewart
Herne's Cottage
Ethelstown
Kells, Co. Meath
Ireland

TOPICS: Occult, Witchcraft, Spirituality, Voudoun, Paganism DATE OF BIRTH: 06/28/16 PLACE OF BIRTH: London, England EDUCATION: University of London, London, England DEGREE: Journalism YEAR DEGREE: 1937 OCCUPATION: Author, Journalist, Lecturer WORK EXPERIENCE: Reuters News Agency; Associated British-Pathe Ltd.; Reveille Magazine AWARDS: Writers' Guild Award, 1968; Award for Best British Television Series, 1965 PROFESSIONAL MEMBERSHIPS: National Union of Journalists; Association of Cinematograph, Television & Allied Technicians DESCRIPTION: Active in the occult, practicing witch. Founded own coven, with wife Janet, on December 22, 1970. PUBLICATIONS: *What Witches Do*, 1971 PUBLISHER: Phoenix Publishing PUBLICATIONS: *Eight Sabbats For Witches*, 1988 PUBLISHER: Phoenix Publishing PUBLICATIONS: *The Witches' Way*, 1988 PUBLISHER: Phoenix Publishing PUBLICATIONS: *The Witches' Goddess*, 1988 PUBLISHER: Phoenix Publishing PUBLICATIONS: *Life And Times Of A Modern Witch*, 1988 PUBLISHER: Phoenix Publishing PUBLICATIONS: *The Witches' God: Lord Of The Dance*, 1989 PUBLISHER: Phoenix Publishing

Fasic, Robert
Heartwood Institute, Ltd.
220 Harmony Lane
Garberville, CA 95440

(707)-923-3182

TOPICS: Holistic Healing

Fauna, Dean
Georgian Church
1908 Verde
Bakersfield, CA 93304
(805)-323-3309

TOPICS: Occult

Fauna, Lady
Georgian Church
1908 Verde
Bakersfield, CA 93304
(805)-323-3309

TOPICS: Occult

Fawcett, George D.
602 Battleground Road
Lincolnton, NC 28092

TOPICS: UFO's, Paranormal Phenomena DATE OF BIRTH: 07/21/29 PLACE OF BIRTH: Mount Airy, NC EDUCATION: Lynchburg College, Lynchburg, VA YEARS: 1950-1952 DEGREE: B.A. Psychology/Education YEAR DEGREE: 1952 OCCUPATION: Lecturer, UFO Investigator, Researcher, Teacher, Author, Consultant WORK EXPERIENCE: Mutual UFO Network of North Carolina, Inc., Lincolnton, NC, Founder PROFESSIONAL MEMBERSHIPS: Aerial Phenomena Research Organization, AZ; National Investigations Committee On Aerial Phenomena, Wash. D.C.; Scientific Bureau of Investigations, NY; J. Allen Hynek Center for UFO Studies, IL; Fund For UFO Research; MUFON, TX. DESCRIPTION: Studies & reports on all aspects of UFO phenomena & related paranormal occurrences. Investigated over 1,200 UFO sighting reports worldwide. Currently working on organizing a UFO Museum & research center. PUBLICATIONS: *Quarter Century Studies Of UFO's in Florida, North Carolina & Tennessee*

Fein, Ester
Common Ground Hawaii
47-155 Okana Road
Kaneohe, HI 96744
(808)-239-7190

TOPICS: New Age

Feirer, Mark
Taunton Press, Inc.
63 South Main Street
Box 355
Newtown, CT 06470
(203)-426-8171

TOPICS: New Age

Ferguson, Emma
Crystal People, The
6770 West Branche Drive, #4601
Houston, TX 77072
(713)-498-6183

TOPICS: Crystals

Ferguson, Marilyn
Brain/Mind Bulletin Newsletter
P.O. Box 42211
Los Angeles, CA 90042
(213)-223-2500 (213)-223-7665

TOPICS: New Age, Astrology, Metaphysics, Body-Mind Connection DATE OF BIRTH: 04/05/38 PLACE OF BIRTH: Grand Junction, CO

EDUCATION: University of CO, Denver, CO OCCUPATION: Author, Publisher WORK EXPERIENCE: The Brain/Mind Bulletin, Los Angeles, CA, President AWARDS: JFK University, Honorary Doctorate; University of CA at Los Angeles, Distinguished Service to Community Award DESCRIPTION: New Age speaker & writer stresses people's inner transformation & creative potentials as well as positive social changes. PUBLICATIONS: *The Brain Revolution*, 1975 PUBLISHER: Jeremy P. Tarcher PUBLICATIONS: *The Aquarian Conspiracy*, 1987 PUBLISHER: Jeremy P. Tarcher PUBLICATIONS: *Brain/ Mind Bulletin*, 1975, Periodical PUBLICATIONS: *The Leading Edge, Periodical*

Ferguson, Rick
Crystal People, The
6770 West Branche Drive, #4601
Houston, TX 77072
(713)-498-6183

TOPICS: Crystals

Fericy, Joan
The Winning Edge
P.O. Box 5658
Somerset, NJ 08875
(201)-247-3685

TOPICS: New Age OCCUPATION: Author, Editor, Publisher PUBLICATIONS: *Let Go Of The Struggle* PUBLISHER: The Winning Edge PUBLICATIONS: *Let Go Of The Struggle*, audio PUBLISHER: The Winning Edge PUBLICATIONS: *Choose To Love Yourself* PUBLISHER: The Winning Edge PUBLICATIONS: *Choose To Love Yourself*, audio PUBLISHER: The Winning Edge PUBLICATIONS: *The Strawberry Candle*, audio PUBLISHER: The Winning Edge PUBLICATIONS: *Choose To Love Yourself Workshop*, audio PUBLISHER: The Winning Edge

Ferre, Carl
George Ohsawa Macrobiotic Foundation
1511 Robinson Street
Oroville, CA 95965
(916)-533-7702

TOPICS: Holistic Healing

Ferrier, Dr. Loretta
24 Boulevard Terrace
Novato, CA 94947
(415)-898-2111

TOPICS: Spirituality, Psychology, Crystals DESCRIPTION: Ph. D & teacher of transcendant consciousness with energy, humor and compassion.

Feuerstein, Georg
Integral Publishing
P.O. Box 1030
Lower Lake, CA 95457
(707)-928-5751

TOPICS: Metaphysics

Fickow, Sid
Salt Spring Center-For The Creative And Healing Arts
Box 1133
Ganges, Br V0S 1E0
Canada

TOPICS: Holistic Healing

Field, Nancy

Leisure Publishers
3923 West 6th Street
Los Angeles, CA 90020
(213)-385-3926

TOPICS: Holistic Healing

Finster, Elaine Jay, R.N.
Color Magic
3826 South Yosemite
Denver, CO 80237
(303)-773-2268

TOPICS: Crystals, Holistic Healing OCCUPATION: Crystal Expert, Author DESCRIPTION: Specializes in rare, hard to find crystals, gems & stones & their use in health, healing & expanded awareness. Sells crystals mail-order. PUBLICATIONS: *ABC's Of Crystals* PUBLICATIONS: *Health, Wealth & Balance* PUBLICATIONS: *Crystals, Gems And Radionics*

Fischer, Michael L.
Sierra Club
730 Polk Street
San Francisco, CA 94109
(415)-776-2211

TOPICS: Holistic Healing

Fisher, Marjorie
Nutrition For Optimal Health Association
Box 380
Winnetka, IL 60093
(312)-835-5030

TOPICS: Holistic Healing

Fitzhugh, Elisabeth Y.
P.O. Box 5420
Takoma Park, MD 20912
(301)-231-3817

TOPICS: Crystals, Channeling

Fix, William
Mercury Media
P.O. Box 604
Whitestone, VA 22578
(804)-435-3612

TOPICS: Spirituality, Psychic Phenomena, Parapsychology, Psychic DATE OF BIRTH: 03/12/41 PLACE OF BIRTH: Madison, WI EDUCATION: U of Wisconscin, Madison WI YEARS: 1959-64 DEGREE: B.S. History YEAR DEGREE: 1964 EDUCATION: Simon Fraser U, Burnaby, BC, Canada YEARS: 1967-68 DEGREE: M.A. Education YEAR DEGREE: 1968 EDUCATION: Int'l Col of Spiritual & Psychic Sciences,Montreal YEARS: 1988-90 DEGREE: Ph. D. Humanities YEAR DEGREE: 1990 OCCUPATION: Author, Lecturer, Researcher, Editor, Seminar Presenter, Consultant PROFESSIONAL MEMBERSHIPS: International Institute of Integral Human Sciences; Fellowship Of Isis DESCRIPTION: Doctor of Humanities & Historian of Science & Religion. Primary field of interest: History of Science & Religion. Lectures widely on the theme that much of the content of the New Age is a renaissance of ancient knowledge. PUBLICATIONS: *Pyramid Odyssey*, 1984 PUBLISHER: Mercury Media PUBLICATIONS: *Star Maps*, 1979 PUBLISHER: Octopus PUBLICATIONS: *The Bone Peddlers*, 1984 PUBLISHER: Macmillan

Flanagan, Gael Crystal
22 South San Francisco Street, #219

Flagstaff, AZ 86001
TOPICS: Crystals

Flanigan, Jim And Judy
208 Busteed Drive-NAX
Midland Park, NJ 07432-1968
TOPICS: Crystals

Flannery, Judi
Iyengar Yoga In Ojai Valley/Ojai Yoga Center
203 North Signal Street
Ojai, CA 93023
(805)-640-0448

TOPICS: Holistic Healing

Fleming, Linda Frazer
LF Publishing
P.O. Box 3175
Falls Church, VA 22043
(703)-734-7927

TOPICS: Body-Mind Connection, Holistic Health DATE OF BIRTH: 11/21/51 PLACE OF BIRTH: Weisbaden, Germany EDUCATION: Bloomsburg University, Bloomsburg, PA YEARS: 1977-1978 DEGREE: M.S. YEAR DEGREE: 1978 EDUCATION: James Madison University, Harrisonburg, VA YEARS: 1973-1977 DEGREE: B.S. YEAR DEGREE: 1977 OCCUPATION: Author, Editor, Publisher WORK EXPERIENCE: LF Publishing, Falls Church, VA, President; Adult Education, Falls Church, VA, Teacher of Power To Choose. PUBLICATIONS: *The Dynamics of Relationships* (1987) PUBLISHER: Equal Partners PUBLICATIONS: *Releasing Arthritis* (1990) PUBLISHER: LF Publishing PUBLICATIONS: *Introduction To Communication* (1986) PUBLISHER: Gallaudet University

Fletcher, Edyth
P.O. Box 35, St. James
Winnipeg, MB, R3J 0II4
Canada
(204) 889 6586

TOPICS: Crystals

Fliessbach, John
Sweetwater Gardens Hot Tub & Sauna Spa
Box 337
Mendocino, CA 95460
(707)-937-4140

TOPICS: Holistic Healing, Massage

Floria, Barbara
Vitality, Inc.
8080 North Central, LB 78
Dallas, TX 75206
(214)-691-1480

TOPICS: Holistic Healing

Fluger, Lilly
Box 157
Fayetteville, WV 25840
TOPICS: Channeling

Foerster, L. William
Cloud On A Mountain
44 Main Street, P.O. Box 196
Chester, NJ 07930
(201)-819-6855

TOPICS: Crystals

Foley, Dr. Marcy

4100 180th Street North
East Moline, IL 61244
(309)-496-9490

TOPICS: Channeling, Homeopathy, Alchemy, New Age, Holistic Healing, Nutrition, Crystals PLACE OF BIRTH: Illinois OCCUPATION: Nutritionist, Chiropractor, Minister of Healing, Gemstone Therapist, Homeopathic Physician, Herbalist, Author WORK EXPERIENCE: New Age Resource Center, Founder, 1988-Present DESCRIPTION: Practices healing through the transformation in consciousness via alchemy, natural remedies & practices. Offers Psychometric Aura Readings, flower essences, gem elixirs, herbal & homeopathic remedies, & Vibrational Remedy Programs. PUBLICATIONS: *Psychometric Aura Reading* PUBLICATIONS: *Akanthos: A Book Of Channeled Insights* PUBLICATIONS: *Homeopathy: The Ancient Art Of Alchemy For Personal Transformation*

Fore, Rev. Mona
Golden Phoenix Healing And Light Center
P.O. Box 969
Rimrock, AZ 86335
(602)-567-4937

TOPICS: Holistic Healing

Forfreedom, Ann
The Wise Woman
2441 Cordova Street
Oakland, CA 94602
(415)-536-3174

TOPICS: New Age

Forrest, Reverend Sharon
Forrest Foundation For Effective Living, Incorporated
P.O. Box 4173, Succ. Westmount
Montreal PQ, H3Z 3B6
Canada
(514)-935-2448

TOPICS: Crystals

Forschmidt, Richard B.
30 Lotus Lane
Westbury, NY 11590
TOPICS: Channeling

Forster, Sarabess
The Sunflower Yoga Company
1305 Chalmers Road
Silver Spring, MD 20903
(301)-445-3882

TOPICS: Yoga

Fortmeyer, Elaine
Busch Publishing Company
5005 Rivera Court
Ft. Wayne, IN 46825
(219)-484-9600

TOPICS: Holistic Healing

Foster, Prof. Lewis A., Jr.
College Of William And Mary
Department Of Philosophy
Williamsburg, VA 23185

TOPICS: Parapsychology

Fox, Matthew
Friends Of Creation Spirituality
Box 19216

Oakland, CA 94619
(415)-253-1192

TOPICS: New Age DATE OF BIRTH: 12/21/40
PLACE OF BIRTH: Madison, WI OCCUPATION:
Author, Priest WORK EXPERIENCE: Institute In
Cultural & Creation Spirituality, Oakland, CA,
Founder, 1977 DESCRIPTION: Roman Catholic
Priest offering New Age philosophy rooted in
positive ecumenical theology based on the bible.
PUBLICATIONS: *The Coming Of The Cosmic
Christ*, 1988 PUBLICATIONS: *Is The Catholic
Church Today A Dysfunctional Family?*, 1988
PUBLICATIONS: *On Becoming A Musical, Mystical
Bear: Spirituality American Style*, 1972
PUBLICATIONS: *Original Blessing: A Primer In
Creation Spirituality*, 1983 PUBLICATIONS: *Whee!
We, Wee All The Way Home*, 1976

Fox, Norma
Plenum Publishing Corporation
233 Spring Street
New York, NY 10013
(212)-620-8000

TOPICS: New Age

Francina, Suza
Iyengar Yoga In Ojai Valley/Ojai Yoga Center
203 North Signal Street
Ojai, CA 93023
(805)-640-0448

TOPICS: Holistic Healing

Francis, Bill
Natural Food Association
Hwy. 59 West
Box 210
Atlanta, TX 75551
(214)-796-3612

TOPICS: Health Food

Francis, Michael
A.T.O.M. Center
216 East 53rd
Anchorage, Alaska 99518
TOPICS: Channeling

Frank, Rev. Ojela
Healing Seminars
Holistic Health Works
P.O. Box 327
New City, NY 10956
(914)-634-2450

TOPICS: Reiki, Channeling, Crystals

Franklin, Percy
Wholistic Resource Center
Box 5164
Eugene, OR 97405
(503)-683-1760

TOPICS: Astrology

Frazier, Kathleen
Healing Research, Inc.
257 Hyde Park Estates
Santa Fe, NM 87501
(505)-262-0541

TOPICS: Holistic Healing

Frazier, Kendrick
Committee For The Scientific Investigation Of
Claims Of
P.O. Box 229

Central Park Station
Buffalo, NY 14215
(716)-834-3222

TOPICS: Psychic Phenomena

Freerks, Heidi
International Chiropractors Association
1110 North Glebe Road
Suite 1000
Arlington, VA 22201
(703)-528-5000

TOPICS: Holistic Healing

French, John F.
Crystal Light Connection
1007 North Cass Street
Milwaukee, WI 53202
(414)-276-2101

TOPICS: Crystals

Friedberg, Dr. Brajesh
Mount Madonna Center
445 Summit Road
Watsonville, CA 95076
(408)-722-7175

TOPICS: Holistic Healing, Yoga

Friedman, Philip H., Ph. D.
Foundation For Well-Being
P.O. Box 627
Plymouth Meeting, PA 19462
(215)-828-4674

TOPICS: Holistic Healing

Friedman, Rodney
Health Letter Associates
University Of California
632 Broadway
New York, NY 10012
(212)-505-2255

TOPICS: Holistic Healing

Friend, Bente
Crystal Deva Designs
P.O. Box 1445
Santa Fe, NM 87504-1445
(505)-988-4122

TOPICS: Crystals

Fritchie, Robert G.
World Service Institute
13753 Berkeley Court
Fontana, CA 92336-3653
(714)-983-5240

TOPICS: Crystals

Fry, A.
Fry's Incredible Inquiry's
HC76, Box 2207
Garden Valley, ID 83622

TOPICS: Parapsychology, Psychic Phenomena,
Occult, Metaphysics, UFO's, ESP, Ghosts
OCCUPATION: Publisher WORK EXPERIENCE:
Fry's Incredible Inquiry's, Garden Valley, ID,
President DESCRIPTION: Publishes reports and
books dealing with the paranormal. PUBLICATIONS:
Incredible Inquiry PUBLISHER: Fry's Incredible
Inquiry's

Fry, Ellie
The Maui Center For Attitudinal Healing
P.O. Box 134

Kahului, HI 96732
(808)-878-2945

TOPICS: Holistic Healing

Fryer, Rita
United States Psychotronics Association
2141 West Agatite
Chicago, IL 60625
(312)-478-5374

TOPICS: Psychic Phenomena

Furchgott, Eve
Utopian Technology
547 Frederick Street
San Francisco, CA 94117
(415)-759-9508

TOPICS: New Age

Gabriell, Elisha
Crystal Light Center
419 West Commonwealth
Fullerton, CA 92632
(714)-526-3239

TOPICS: Crystals

Gach, Michael Reed
Acupressure Institute
1533 Shattuck Avenue
Berkeley, CA 94709
(415)-845-1059

TOPICS: Holistic Healing

Gackenbach, Dr. J.
Lucidity Association
Dept. Of Psychology
University Of Northern Iowa
Cedar Falls, IA 50614
TOPICS: Parapsychology

Gagnon, Leo, Ph.D.
P.O. Box 1616
Glendale, AZ 85311
(602)-939-6967 (602)-939-6967

TOPICS: Hypnotism, Reincarnation, Past Life
Regression, Death OCCUPATION: Specialist in Past
Life Regression DESCRIPTION: President of
International Past Life Registry, an organization
specializing in the study and Data Base matching of
Past Life Regression.

Gahn, Holly
Center For Health And Well-Being
28892 Marguerite Parkway, #140
Mission Viejo, CA 92692
(714)-364-4434

TOPICS: Holistic Healing

Gahn, Robert
Center For Health And Well-Being
28892 Marguerite Parkway, #140
Mission Viejo, CA 92692
(714)-364-4434

TOPICS: Holistic Healing

Gairdner, William
Fitness Institute
255 Yorkland Boulevard
Willowdale, On M2J 1S3
Canada
(416)-491-5830

TOPICS: Holistic Healing

Galanter, Marc
Manisses Communications Group, Inc.
3 Governor Street
Providence, RI 02906
(401)-831-6020

TOPICS: Holistic Healing

Gallagher, Paul
Deer Mountain Taoist Academy
R.D.3, Box 109A
Guilford, VT 05301

TOPICS: Psychic Healing

Galuppo, Jennie
Messenger Of Light
P.O. Box 1158
Agoura Hills, CA 91302

TOPICS: Channeling OCCUPATION: Channeler WORK EXPERIENCE: Messengers Of Light, Agoura Hills, CA, Channeler DESCRIPTION: Offers personal tapes channeled messages by mail or phone.

Ganley, W. Paul
W. Paul Ganley Publisher
P.O. Box 149
Amherst Branch
Buffalo, NY 14226
(716)-839-2415

TOPICS: Psychic Phenomena

Gardner, Joy
P.O. Box 3414
Santa Cruz, CA 95063
(408)-728-3757

TOPICS: Holistic Healing, Color Therapy, Crystals, Herbalogy, Meditation, New Age, Body-Mind Connection DATE OF BIRTH: 02/17/44 PLACE OF BIRTH: Chicago, IL OCCUPATION: Author, Master Herbalist, Wholistic Practitioner/Counselor DESCRIPTION: Studied with: Grandfather David (Hopi); Graham Ferrant, M.D.; Elisabeth Kubler Ross; Bethel Phaigh-Gestalt Therapist PUBLICATIONS: *Color & Crystals* PUBLISHER: The Crossing Press PUBLICATIONS: *New Healing Yourself* PUBLISHER: The Crossing Press PUBLICATIONS: *A Difficult Decision* PUBLISHER: The Crossing Press PUBLICATIONS: *Healing Yourself During Pregnancy* PUBLISHER: The Crossing Press PUBLICATIONS: *Book Of Guidance* PUBLICATIONS: *The Toning Workbook*

Gardner, Kay
Healing Through Arts
P.O. Box 411
Wayland, MA 01778

TOPICS: Holistic Healing

Gardner, Lynn
4146 N. Illinois Street
Indianapolis, IN 46208
(317)-283-7638

TOPICS: Psychic

Gardner, Richard
Resources
P.O. Box 1067
Harvard Square Station
Cambridge, MA 02138
(617)-876-2789

TOPICS: New Age

Gaskin, Ina

R & E Fund
42 The Farm
Summertown, TN 38483
(615)-964-2519

TOPICS: Holistic Healing

Gaskin, Stephen
The Farm
34 The Farm
Summertown, TN 38483
(615)-964-3574

TOPICS: Holistic Healing

Gasper, Louis, Ph. D.
Acupuncture Research Institute
313 West Andrix Street
Monterey Park, CA 91754
(213)-722-7353

TOPICS: Acupuncture

Gass, Judith
Spring Hill Of Ashby, Inc.
432 Columbia Street
Cambridge, MA 02141-1000
(617)-864-9181

TOPICS: Holistic Healing

Gass, Robert
Spring Hill Of Ashby, Inc.
432 Clumbia Street
Cambridge, MA 02141-1000
(617)-864-9181

TOPICS: Holistic Healing

Gauld, Dr. Alan
University Of Nottingham
Department Of Psychology
No NG7 2RD
England

TOPICS: Parapsychology

Gawain, Shakti
Kai Mana
P.O. Box 612
Kilauea, HI 96754

TOPICS: Holistic Healing, Spirituality OCCUPATION: Author, Healer, Teacher WORK EXPERIENCE: Kai Mana, Kilauea, HI, Founder DESCRIPTION: Healer offering workshops for emotional & spiritual growth. PUBLICATIONS: *Creative Visualization* PUBLISHER: New World Library PUBLICATIONS: *Living In The Light* PUBLISHER: New World Library PUBLICATIONS: *Return To The Garden* PUBLISHER: New World Library

Geiger, Esther
Unity Woods Yoga Center
4853 Cordell Avenue
Bethesda, MD 20814
(301)-656-8992

TOPICS: Yoga

Geller, Uri
P.O. Box 5175
New York, NY 10150

TOPICS: Psychic, Psychic Phenomena

Gere, Richard
c/o PMK
1 Lincoln Plaza
New York, NY 10023

TOPICS: New Age, Spirituality DATE OF BIRTH: 08/31/49 PLACE OF BIRTH: Philadelphia, PA OCCUPATION: Actor, Musician DESCRIPTION: Practicing Buddhist & follower of the Dalai Lama.

Gerking, Laura N.
Astrology Et Al Metaphysical Center
4728 University Way N.E.
Seattle, WA 98105
(206)-524-6365

TOPICS: Metaphysics, Tarot, Astrology WORK EXPERIENCE: Astrology Et Al Metaphysical Center, Seattle, WA, Director DESCRIPTION: Helps conduct the Northwest Astrological Conference (NORWAC) each Spring in Seattle, WA. Organized by the Astrology Et Al Metaphysical Center.

Ghyssaert, Ivan U., Ph. D.
The Health Foundation
Bottingdean Lodge
Bottingdean, Jr. Midhurst
West Sussex, GU 29 00N
England

TOPICS: Crystals, Holistic Health DATE OF BIRTH: 10/18/43 PLACE OF BIRTH: Kortryk, Belgium OCCUPATION: Dr. of Science, Ph. D. WORK EXPERIENCE: The Health Foundation, Isle Of Man, U.K., Founder AWARDS: White Cross first class, Grand Cross Of The Order Of The Holy Grave, Grand Cross Of The Order Of St. Andrew DESCRIPTION: Originator of 160 Gem Remedies, Colours, Trace Elements, Awareness Boosters & Planetary Energies. Developed Immune System boosting remedies, sleep remedies & breakthroughs in Sickle Cell & Malaria. Teaches seminars. PUBLICATIONS: *The Therapeutic Use Of Gem Remedies*

Gibbs, Elaine
P.O. Box 36190
Fort Worth, TX 76136
(817)-430-1861

TOPICS: Psychic

Gibson, Krysta
Silver Owl Publications, Inc.
P.O. Box 51186
Seattle, WA 98115
(206)-524-9071

TOPICS: New Age

Giesler, Patric
University Of Virginia
Division Of Parapsychology
Box 152, Medical Center
Charlottesville, VA 22908

TOPICS: Parapsychology

Gifford, Joseph
The Radiance Technique Association International, Inc.
27 Chestnut Street
Boston, MA 02108
(617)-723-6048

TOPICS: Reiki

Gill, Rachel
Alternatives Resource Center
5263 Bouldercrest Road
P.O. Box 429
Ellenwood, GA 30049
(404)-961-0102

TOPICS: New Age

Gillan, Judith

Organic Food Production Association Of North America
P.O. Box 31
Belchertown, MA 01007
(413)-323-6821

TOPICS: Health Food

Gillespie, Bruce

Metaphysical Review
G.P.O. Box 5195AA
Melbourne, Vic. 3001
Australia

TOPICS: Metaphysics

Gillette, Paul

Today's Chiropractic, Inc.
1269 Barclay Circle
Marietta, GA 30060
(404)-424-0554

TOPICS: Holistic Healing

Gilliam, Wendy

Crystal Grotto, The
P.O. Box 4743
Hilo, HI 96720
(809)-963-6195

TOPICS: Crystals

Gilman, Robert

In Context
Box 11470
Bainbridge Island, WA 98110
(206)-842-0216

TOPICS: New Age

Gips, Elizabeth

Changes
328-B Union Street
P.O. Box 7305
Santa Cruz, CA 95060
(408)-423-9687

TOPICS: New Age, Metaphysics OCCUPATION: Radio host WORK EXPERIENCE: Changes, Santa Cruz, CA, Radio host DESCRIPTION: Radio host of eclectic spiritual program called Changes on K.K.U.P. 91.5 FM, Tuesdays 2:00-6:00 PM. Features music, readings, interviews & talk. Covers spirituality in all its forms-leading edge of science, healing & love. Sells books & cassettes.

Givens, Phyllis

127 South Main Street
New Hope, PA 18938

TOPICS: Channeling

Glaskin, G.M.

10 Mosman Apartments
12 Murray Avenue
Mosman Park WA, 6012
Australia
09-3831313

TOPICS: Parapsychology, Body-Mind Connection, Spirituality, Psychic DATE OF BIRTH: 12/16/23 PLACE OF BIRTH: Perth, Western Australia EDUCATION: Perth Modern School, Subiaco, W.A. YEARS: 1938-9 DEGREE: Junior Certificate OCCUPATION: Author, Lecturer WORK EXPERIENCE: Lyall & Evatt, Singapore, Partner AWARDS: Commonwealth Literary Award, 1957;

UK Book Society Recommendation, 1959 PROFESSIONAL MEMBERSHIPS: Fellowship of Australian Writers, WA President 1968-69; Society of Authors, UK; P.E.N.; The Netherlands & Australia; Australian Writers Guild PUBLICATIONS: *Windows Of The Mind: Consciousness Beyond The Body* PUBLISHER: Avery Publishing Group, Inc. PUBLICATIONS: *Windows Of The Mind: The Christos Experiment*, 1974 PUBLISHER: Delacorte Press PUBLICATIONS: *Worlds Within: Probing The Christos Experience*, 1976 PUBLISHER: Wildwood House, UK PUBLICATIONS: *A Door To Eternity: Proving The Christos Experience*, 1989 PUBLISHER: Unity Press, Australia PUBLICATIONS: *A Door To Infinity*, 1989 PUBLISHER: Unity Press, Australia

Gliksohn, Michael

California Yoga Teachers Association
Goodfellow Publishers' Reps.
2054 University Avenue, #604
Berkeley, CA 94704
(415)-841-9200

TOPICS: Yoga

Gold, Andy

Rose Mountain Retreat Center
P.O. Box 355
Las Vegas, NM 87701
(505)-425-3144

TOPICS: Holistic Healing

Goldfarb, Reuven

Agada
2020 Essex Street
Berkeley, CA 94703
(415)-848-0965

TOPICS: New Age

Goldman, Jonathan S.

New England Sound Healers, Inc.
42 Baker Street
Lexington, MA 02173
(617)-861-1625

TOPICS: Crystals, Holistic Healing

Golowin, Sergius

Bergli-Hof
CH-3112
Allmendingen,
Switzerland
031-52-68-20

TOPICS: Tarot, Dreams, Metaphysics, Herbalogy, Crystals, Holistic Healing DATE OF BIRTH: 01/31/30 PLACE OF BIRTH: Prague EDUCATION: Stadt-U. Hochschulbibliothek, Bern, CH YEARS: 1950-58 DEGREE: Eidg. Diplom YEAR DEGREE: 1954 OCCUPATION: Lecturer, Translater, Author WORK EXPERIENCE: Stadtbibliothekar, Burgdorf, CH PROFESSIONAL MEMBERSHIPS: Swiss Association of Writers PUBLICATIONS: *World Of The Tarot*, 1988 PUBLISHER: Samuel Weiser PUBLICATIONS: *Das Reich des Schamanen*, 1989 PUBLISHER: Sphinx, Goldmann PUBLICATIONS: *Edelsteine - Kristallpforten*, 1986 PUBLISHER: Bauer Fbg PUBLICATIONS: *Die Weisen Frauen*, 1987 PUBLISHER: Sphinx, Goldmann PUBLICATIONS: *Gottin Katze*, 1989 PUBLISHER: Goldmann PUBLICATIONS: *The Gypsy Dream Book*, 1988 PUBLISHER: Samuel Weiser

Goodman, Allen

HLQ Associates
Box 86054
Pittsburgh, PA 15221
(412)-731-5533

TOPICS: Holistic Healing

Goodman, Hananya

Kabbalah: A Newsletter Of Current Research In Jewish My
41 Palyam Street
Jerusalem,
Israel

TOPICS: Psychic Phenomena

Goodman, Saul

22-28 South Main Street
Doylestown, PA 18901
(215)-340-9918

TOPICS: Massage, New Age DATE OF BIRTH: 06/24/50 PLACE OF BIRTH: Philadelphia, PA OCCUPATION: Author, Teacher WORK EXPERIENCE: International School of Shiatsu, Doylestown, PA, Director, Founder PROFESSIONAL MEMBERSHIPS: AOBTA-Certified Instructor & Practitioner PUBLICATIONS: *The Book Of Shiatsu*, 1986 PUBLISHER: Avery Publications PUBLICATIONS: *The Art Of Shiatsu*, video, 1986 PUBLISHER: International School of Shiatsu

Goodrich, Michael

Cosmic Contact Psychic Services
26 East 13th Street, 5C
New York, NY 10003

TOPICS: Psychic

Gordon, Kirpal

Heaven Bone Press
86 Whispering Hills Drive
P.O. Box 486
Chester, NY 10918
(914)-469-9018

TOPICS: New Age, Channeling, Psychic Phenomena, Crystals, Spirituality, Metaphysics

Gorman, Shotsie

Tattoo Advocate Journal
P.O. Box 8390
Haledon, NJ 07538
(201)-790-0429

TOPICS: New Age

Gosney, Michael

Slawsch Communications
165 Vallecitos de Oro
San Marcos, CA 92069
(619)-744-2299

TOPICS: Holistic Healing

Goss, John And Jill

Dieu Donne, Box 195
Franschhoek 7690,
South Africa

TOPICS: Crystals, Holistic Healing

Gosse, Jean D.

Jean's Place
2407 Camino Capitan
Santa Fe, NM 87505
(505)-471-4053

TOPICS: Crystals, Massage, Reiki OCCUPATION: Crystal Healer, Massage Therapist, Center director & instructor WORK EXPERIENCE: Jean's Place,

Santa Fe, NM, Founder, director, 1986-present **PROFESSIONAL MEMBERSHIPS:** Association of Crystal Healing Therapies in England **DESCRIPTION:** Founder & director of Jean's Place, a center for healing & transformation. Certified crystal energetics practitioner, massage therapist, reiki healer, aroma therapist & crystal healing instructor. Studied with Marcel Vogel & Katrina Raphaell.

Gotlib, Dr. Allan
Canadian Chiropractic Association
1396 Eglinton Avenue, West
Toronto, On M6C 2E4
Canada
(416)-781-7344

TOPICS: Holistic Healing

Gottlieb, Amy
Women Healthsharing, Inc.
14 Skey Lane
Toronto, On M6J 3S4
Canada
(416)-532-0812

TOPICS: Holistic Healing

Goulet, Paul-Henri
Super Magazine, Inc.
8050, boul, Metropolitain, est
Montreal, Qu H1K 1A1
Canada
(514)-353-7660

TOPICS: Astrology

Graf, Eugene
The Center Of The Light
HCR 65, Box 140
Great Barrington, MA 01230-8603
(413)-229-2396

TOPICS: Holistic Healing

Graf, Eva
The Center Of The Light
HCR 65, Box 140
Great Barrington, MA 01230-8603
(413)-229-2396

TOPICS: Holistic Healing

Graham, Ann
A.R.E. Clinic
4017 North 40th Street
Phoenix, AZ 85018
(602)-955-7729

TOPICS: Holistic Healing

Graham, David D.
David Graham Associates
309 East Main Street
Decorah, IA 52101-1943
(319)-382-5939

TOPICS: Psychic Phenomena

Grana, William
Year Book Medical Publishers, Inc.
200 North LaSalle Street
Chicago, IL 60601
(312)-726-9733

TOPICS: Holistic Healing

Grant, Linda
116-175 Greenway Crescent
Winnipeg MB, R2Y 2E6
Canada

(204)-837-5977

TOPICS: Crystals

Graves, Florence
Rising Star Associates
342 Western Avenue
Brighton, MA 02135
(617)-787-2005

TOPICS: New Age

Graves, Lary
Common Ground, Inc., And Inner City Hot Springs
2927 N.E. Everett Street
Portland, OR 97232
(503)-238-4010

TOPICS: Holistic Healing

Gredin, Lisa A.
For Your Health Association
15 Emerson Road
Wayland, MA 01778
(617)-655-5476

TOPICS: Crystals

Green, Gabriel
Amalgamated Flying Saucer Clubs Of America, Inc.
P.O. Box 39
Yucca Valley, CA 92286
(619)-365-1141

TOPICS: UFO's, Channeling, Psychic Phenomena, Spirituality, Past Life Regression, New Age **DATE OF BIRTH:** 11/11/24 **PLACE OF BIRTH:** Whittier, CA **EDUCATION:** Woodbury Business College, Los Angeles, CA **YEARS:** 1942 **EDUCATION:** Los Angeles City College, Los Angeles, CA **YEARS:** 1946-1948 **OCCUPATION:** Author, Lecturer, Flying Saucers, Extraterrestrial Economics, World Government **WORK EXPERIENCE:** Amalgamated Flying Saucer Clubs of America, Yucca Valley, CA, Founder, President, 1959-Present **DESCRIPTION:** Lecture topics are: Flying Saucers, Key to Earth's Destiny; Flying Saucers And Past Lives; Flying Saucers And Higher Self Contact; The Keys To The Kingdom, Universal Economics And The United World; Spiritual Power Politics And The Second Coming **PUBLICATIONS:** *Let's Face Facts About Flying Saucers* (1967) **PUBLISHER:** Popular Library **PUBLICATIONS:** *Flying Saucers International* (1957-69) **PUBLISHER:** Amalgamated Flying Saucer Clubs Of America

Green, Jerry
P. O. Box 5094
Mill Valley, CA 94942
(415)-383-6437

TOPICS: Holistic Health **DESCRIPTION:** Special mail order program offering seminars and private work in holistic health.

Green, Lorna
2260 Sparrow Ridge Drive
Marietta, GA 30066
(404)-928-2035

TOPICS: Psychic Healing

Green, Rev. Ruth
Hopkinson House, Ste 2916
Washington Square South
Philadelphia, PA 19106
(215)-922-1684

TOPICS: Spirituality, Psychic, Holistic Healing, Dreams, Channeling **PLACE OF BIRTH:** Philadelphia, PA **OCCUPATION:** Intuitive Counselor, Psychic, Lecturer, Teacher, Author **WORK EXPERIENCE:** New Seminary, New York, NY, Faculty Member **DESCRIPTION:** Ordained Interfaith Minister, clairvoyant, healer, dream analyst, & traditional eclectic therapeutic counselor conducts workshops, seminars & individual sessions in intuitive therapy. Teaches Creative Empowerment & How To Be Your Own Intuitive Guide.

Greenberg, Barry
Touch For Health Foundation
1174 North Lake Avenue
Pasadena, CA 91104
(818)-794-1181

TOPICS: Holistic Healing

Greenberg, Betty L.M.
2265 Westwood Boulevard, #740
Los Angeles, CA 90064

TOPICS: Crystals

Greer, Richard L.
Box 44, 2550 Shattuck Avenue
Berkeley, CA 94704

TOPICS: Channeling

Gregg, Susan
Summit Publishing Company
5401 N.W. Broken Sound Bouleva
Boca Raton, FL 33431
(407)-997-7733

TOPICS: Holistic Healing

Gregory, Dick
P.O. Box 3266, Tower Hill Farm
Plymouth, MA 02361

TOPICS: New Age, Holistic Health, Vegetarianism, Nutrition **OCCUPATION:** Lecturer, Author, Diet Specialist, Comedian **WORK EXPERIENCE:** Dick Gregory Health Enterprises, Inc., Founder, Pres. **DESCRIPTION:** Promotes vegetarianism & developed the Slim-Safe Bahamian Diet to advocate proper nutrition & a healthier lifestyle for people & to fight world hunger.

Greven, Jane
Golden Phoenix Healing And Light Center
P.O. Box 969
Rimrock, AZ 86335
(602)-567-4937

TOPICS: Holistic Healing

Greville, Dr. T.N.E.
University Of Virginia
Division Of Parapsychology
Box 152, Medical Center
Charlottesville, VA 22908

TOPICS: Parapsychology

Greyfox, Wade
Denali Center For Holistic Health & Personal Growth
HC 89, Box 451
Willow, AK 99688-9705
(907)-495-6853

TOPICS: Psychic, Spirituality **DATE OF BIRTH:** 10/12/47 **PLACE OF BIRTH:** Mechanicsburg, PA **EDUCATION:** Shippensburg University **DEGREE:** B.A. **OCCUPATION:** Shaman, Editor, Publisher

WORK EXPERIENCE: Denali Center For Holistic Health & Personal Growth, Willow, AK, Executive Director, Publisher **PROFESSIONAL MEMBERSHIPS:** Florida Tribe Of Eastern Creek Indians **DESCRIPTION:** Provides Shamanic services by mail through the Denali Center. **PUBLICATIONS:** *The Shaman Papers*, 1989, Publisher **PUBLISHER:** The Denali Center For Holistic Health & Personal Growth

Greyson, Bruce
Plenum Publishing Corporation
233 Spring Street
New York, NY 10013
(212)-620-8000

TOPICS: New Age

Grieshaber, Roy
Heartwood Institute, Ltd.
220 Harmony Lane
Garberville, CA 95440
(707)-923-3182

TOPICS: Holistic Healing

Griffith, Paul G.
Mount Ida Area Chamber Of Commerce
P.O. Box 6
Mount Ida, AR 71957
(501)-867-2723

TOPICS: Crystals

Griffith, William
Indianapolis Center For Attitudinal Healing
P.O. Box 55016
Indianapolis, IN 46205
(317)-251-5543

TOPICS: Holistic Healing

Griffiths, F.
Astrological Association
98 Hayes Road
Bromeley Kent, BR2 9AB
England

TOPICS: Astrology

Grishman, Ronnie
Dell Horoscope Magazines
245 Park Avenue
New York, NY 10167
(212)-984-7135

TOPICS: Astrology

Griswold, Bob
Effective Learning Systems
5221 Edina Industrial Boulevar
Edina, MN 55435
(612)-893-1680

TOPICS: New Age

Groce, Duane
Feather Mountain Conference Center
P.O. Box 670
Paulden, AZ 86334
(602)-445-0911

TOPICS: Holistic Healing

Gross, Dr. Robert
Pawling Health Manor
P.O. Box 401
Hyde Park, NY 12538
(914)-889-4141

TOPICS: Holistic Healing

Gross, H.
Regency Health Resort And Spa
2000 South Ocean Drive
Hallandale, FL 33009
(305)-454-2220

TOPICS: Holistic Healing

Gross, Joy
Pawling Health Manor
P.O. Box 401
Hyde Park, NY 12538
(914)-889-4141

TOPICS: Holistic Healing

Grossman, Dr. Michael
Wellness Now
24432 Muirlands Boulevard, Ste. 111
El Toro, CA 92630
(714)-768-3343

TOPICS: Holistic Healing

Grover, Jennet
c/o Psychic Research Institute
431 Pheasant Ridge Road
Del Rey Oaks, CA 93940-5719
(408)-279-2291

TOPICS: Crystals

Groves, Catherine
Christian New Age Quarterly
P.O. Box 276
Clifton, NJ 07011-0276

TOPICS: New Age, Spirituality **DATE OF BIRTH:** 11/21/52 **PLACE OF BIRTH:** New York, NY **EDUCATION:** Wagner College, Staten Island, NY **DEGREE:** B.A. Social Studies **YEAR DEGREE:** 1975 **OCCUPATION:** Editor, Publisher, Author **WORK EXPERIENCE:** Christian New Age Quarterly, Clifton, NJ, Editor, Publisher 3 years **DESCRIPTION:** Expertise in Christian Studies, Spiritualism and the New Age Movement. **PUBLICATIONS:** *Spirituality And Diapers*, 1989 **PUBLISHER:** The Church Herald **PUBLICATIONS:** *A Shoddy Form Of Silence*, 1989 **PUBLISHER:** Small Press Review **PUBLICATIONS:** *Owning Our Pain*, 1989 **PUBLISHER:** The New Times **PUBLICATIONS:** *We Of Like Mind*, 1989 **PUBLISHER:** The Emerald Path **PUBLICATIONS:** *The Tempering Trinity*, 1990 **PUBLISHER:** Transformation Times **PUBLICATIONS:** *Fundamentalists And New Agers: The Hidden Consensus*, 1990 **PUBLISHER:** Peacehaven Quarterly

Gruber, Elmar
Institut Fur Grenzgebiete
D-7800 Freiburg Im Breisgau
Eichhalde 12
West Germany

TOPICS: Parapsychology

Guenon, Rene
Larson Publications

TOPICS: Spirituality, Occult **PLACE OF BIRTH:** Blois, France **OCCUPATION:** Teacher, Author **WORK EXPERIENCE:** Etudes Traditionelles, France, Chief Editor of Journal **DESCRIPTION:** Born 1886, Deceased 1951. Sought to purify traditional East-West philosophic-spiritual symbolism from the occult trappings with which it had been contaminated in the West. Wrote numerous essays & 13 major books. **PUBLICATIONS:** *East And West*, 1941 **PUBLISHER:** Luzac **PUBLICATIONS:** *The Crisis Of The Modern World*, 1943 **PUBLISHER:** Luzac **PUBLICATIONS:** *Lord Of The World*, 1983 **PUBLISHER:** Coombe Springs Press **PUBLICATIONS:** *Symbolism Of The Cross*, 1958 **PUBLISHER:** Luzac **PUBLICATIONS:** *The Multiple States Of Being*, 1984 **PUBLISHER:** Larson Publications

Guidas, Steve
HLQ Associates
Box 86054
Pittsburgh, PA 15221
(412)-731-5533

TOPICS: Holistic Healing

Gursche, Siegfried
Alive
P.O. Box 67333
Vancouver, Br V5W 3T1
Canada
(604)-438-1919

TOPICS: Health Food

Gusic, Diane Brook, M.A.
241-20 Northern Boulevard
Douglaston, NY 11363

TOPICS: Astrology, Spirituality, Numerology, Metaphysics **DATE OF BIRTH:** 09/21/41 **PLACE OF BIRTH:** New York, NY **EDUCATION:** University of Michigan, Ann Arbor, MI **YEARS:** 1959-63 **DEGREE:** B.A. English **YEAR DEGREE:** 1963 **EDUCATION:** Hofstra University, Hempstead, NY **YEARS:** 1964-69 **DEGREE:** M.A. Humanities **YEAR DEGREE:** 1969 **OCCUPATION:** Lecturer, Astrologer, Numerologist **WORK EXPERIENCE:** New York Open Center, New York, NY, Lecturer of A Course In Miracles; Wainwright House, Rye, NY, Lecturer of A Course In Miracles **AWARDS:** New Seminary, Honorary Degree of Minister of Spiritual Counseling, 1990

Guthrie, Helen, Ph. D.
Williams & Wilkins
428 East Preston Street
Baltimore, MD 21202
(301)-528-4000

TOPICS: Holistic Healing

Guyer, Evelyn A., RN, BSN
S. 1140 Lyndale Lane
Elma, NY 14059
(716)-652-9789

TOPICS: Holistic Health, Massage **OCCUPATION:** Infant Massage Instructor **WORK EXPERIENCE:** State University College at Buffalo, Buffalo, NY, Director of BART Program **DESCRIPTION:** Project Director of the Bonding & Relaxation Techniques Program at the Research Foundation at SUNY Buffalo. Developed a stroking program for dual-sensory impaired children & young adults. Offers certification training in Infant Massage. **PUBLICATIONS:** *From The Hand To The Heart*

Haag, Dr. Gregory
Regency Health Resort And Spa
2000 South Ocean Drive
Hallandale, FL 33009
(305)-454-2220

TOPICS: Holistic Healing

Haddon, Genia Pauli, Ph. D.

Haelix Plus, Inc.
208 Bass Road
Box 304
Scotland, CT 06264
(203)-456-0646

TOPICS: Body-Mind Connection

Hager, Steve
High Times
211 East 43rd Street
New York, NY 10017
(212)-972-8484

TOPICS: New Age

Hall, R.J.
Addiction Research Foundation
33 Russell Street
Toronto, On M5S 2S1
Canada
(416)-595-6059

TOPICS: Holistic Healing

Halpern, Steven
Sound Rx
P.O. Box 2644
San Anselmo, CA 94960
(415)-453-9800

TOPICS: Psychic, Holistic Health OCCUPATION: Audio/Video Producer WORK EXPERIENCE: Sound Rx, San Anselmo, CA, Founder, Pres. DESCRIPTION: Composer & performer o tranquil, sensual music used for meditation & healing. Creator & producer of tapes & compact discs to enhance health, well being & psychic sensitivity. Free catalog of 44 titles available.

Halpin, Vince
Lindley Pharmacy And Clinic
17 Kupiano Drive
Bli Bli 4560, QLD,
Australia

TOPICS: Crystals

Hamilton, Barbara
Project Rainbow Consulting Services
7529 3rd Avenue North
St. Petersburg, FL 33710
(813)-345-2698

TOPICS: Holistic Healing

Hammond, Raylah
Amiya Institute
8627 Lubao Avenue
Canoga Park, CA 91306
(818)-998-3702

TOPICS: Holistic Healing

Hammond, Robert
Alcohol Research Information Service
1120 East Oakland Avenue
Lansing, MI 48906

TOPICS: Holistic Healing

Hampton, Crystal
Unarius Light
145 South Magnolia Avenue
El Cajon, CA 92020
(619)-447-4170

TOPICS: Reincarnation

Hand, Robert S.
Astrolabe, Inc.

Box 1750
Brewster, MA 02631
(508)-896-5081

TOPICS: Astrology, Numerology, Metaphysics DATE OF BIRTH: 12/05/42 PLACE OF BIRTH: Plainfield, NJ EDUCATION: Brandeis University, Waltham, MA DEGREE: A.B. YEAR DEGREE: 1965 EDUCATION: University of CA, Berkeley, CA EDUCATION: Princeton University, Princeton, NJ YEARS: 1967-68 OCCUPATION: Astrologer, Author, Computer Programmer, Lecturer WORK EXPERIENCE: Astrolabe, Inc., Brewster, MA, Founder & President 1979-present AWARDS: British Faculty of Astrological Studies, Honorary Patron 1986; United Astrological Conference, Regulus Award 1989 PROFESSIONAL MEMBERSHIPS: National Council For Geocosmic Research; Director 1974-present, President 1990-present PUBLICATIONS: *Planets In Transit*, 1976 PUBLISHER: Whitford Press PUBLICATIONS: *Planets In Composite*, 1975 PUBLISHER: Whitford Press PUBLICATIONS: *Planets In Youth*, 1977 PUBLISHER: Whitford Press PUBLICATIONS: *Horoscope Symbols*, 1980 PUBLISHER: Whitford Press PUBLICATIONS: *Essays On Astrology*, 1982 PUBLISHER: Whitford Press PUBLICATIONS: *World Ephemeris For The 20th Century*, 1983 PUBLISHER: Whitford Press

Hand, Sheila
Crystal Voyage, The
1712 Monroe Avenue
Rochester, NY 14618-1432
(716)-461-2137

TOPICS: Crystals

Hanrahan, Paula
The Next Step, Inc.
16 Church Street
Keene, NH 03431
(603)-357-0744

TOPICS: Holistic Healing

Hansen, Howard
Astrological Crystals
P.O. Box 11659
Marina Del Rey, CA 90295
(213)-207-6579

TOPICS: Crystals

Hansen, Michael
Center For Peace
Route 11
Box 369
Sevierville, TN 37862
(615)-428-3595

TOPICS: Holistic Healing

Hansen-Steiger, Sherry
Timewalker Productions
3104 East Camelback Road
Phoenix, AZ 85016
(602)-951-4466

TOPICS: Spirituality, UFO's, Holistic Health, Dreams, Psychic Phenomena, Hypnotism, New Age DATE OF BIRTH: 04/24/45 PLACE OF BIRTH: Dearborn, MI EDUCATION: Northern Illinois University School of Nursing YEARS: 1963-65 EDUCATION: Lutheran School of Theology, Chicago, IL EDUCATION: Ohio State Graduate School YEARS: 1966-70 OCCUPATION: Counselor, Author, Lecturer DESCRIPTION: Founder of one of

the first schools for holistic education. Also has interest & knowledge in the field of UFO's. Authored, co-authored & edited many books on various New Age & related topics. PUBLICATIONS: *Hollywood and the Supernatural*, co-author, 1989 PUBLISHER: St. Martin's Press PUBLICATIONS: *UFO Abductors*, editor, 1988 PUBLISHER: Berkeley PUBLICATIONS: *The Fellowship*, editor, 1987 PUBLISHER: Doubleday PUBLICATIONS: *Seasons of the Soul*, 1969 PUBLICATIONS: *Satan's Assasins*, co-author, 1991 PUBLISHER: Berkeley PUBLICATIONS: *The Philadelphia Experiment & Other UFO Conspiracies*, editor, 1990 PUBLISHER: Inner Light

Harbula, Patrick
Meditation Magazine
17211 Orozco Street
Granada Hills, CA 91344
(818)-366-5441 (818)-366-5441

TOPICS: Meditation, Spirituality, New Age, Metaphysics, Holistic Health, Body-Mind Connection DATE OF BIRTH: 10/11/56 PLACE OF BIRTH: Los Angeles, CA EDUCATION: Institute Of Spiritual Awareness, Woodland Hls, CA YEARS: 1981-1985 DEGREE: Ordination YEAR DEGREE: 1985 OCCUPATION: Executive Editor, Minister, President Board of Directors WORK EXPERIENCE: Meditation Magazine, Granada Hills, CA, Exec. Editor, 1985-Pres.; Intergroup For Planetary Oneness, Granada Hills, CA, Bd of Dir. Pres. 6 years PROFESSIONAL MEMBERSHIPS: Founder & Board of Directors Pres., Intergroup For Planetary Oneness PUBLICATIONS: *Meditation Magazine* (1985-Present) PUBLISHER: Intergroup For Planetary Oneness

Hardy, Douglas
East Meets West
753 North Kings Road, #205
Los Angeles, CA 90069
(213)-852-9600

TOPICS: Crystals

Hardy, Pat Esclavon
Energies, Trends, Cycles, Inc.
P.O. Box 76691
Atlanta, GA 30358
(404)-458-6776

TOPICS: Astrology OCCUPATION: Consultant in financial & business Astrology WORK EXPERIENCE: Energies, Trends, Cycles, Inc., Atlanta, GA, Financial & Business Astrology Consultant DESCRIPTION: Consultant in financial & business astrology & planetary cycle analysis. Named as one of the top five Wall Street Astrologers by the national stock brokers journal. Offers astrological trend & cycle forecasting for individuals & businesses. PUBLICATIONS: *Financial Astrology For The 1990's* PUBLICATIONS: *Planets And You*

Harkavy, Andrew
Girisho Institute For Meditation And Growth
5421 Rumsford Lane
Burke, VA 22015
(703)-425-0741

TOPICS: Crystals

Harms, Bill
International Graphoanalysis Society
111 North Canal Street, 10th F
Chicago, IL 60606
(312)-930-9446

TOPICS: New Age

Harper, Kath
Night Owl Publishers
Box 764
Shepparton, Vi 3630
Australia

TOPICS: Holistic Healing

Harris, Donna
Darkstar And The Crystal Courier
1820 Connors Road
Snohomish, WA 98290
(206)-334-7273

TOPICS: Crystals

Harris, Jay
Delphi Publications
P.O. Box 211
Rimrock, AZ 86335
(602)-634-2390

TOPICS: Parapsychology

Harris, Les
Darkstar And The Crystal Courier
1820 Connors Road
Snohomish, WA 98290
(206)-334-7273

TOPICS: Crystals

Harris, Marie, RN
3 West End Avenue
Old Greenwich, CT 06870
(203)-698-0796

TOPICS: Acupuncture

Harrison, Allen J., D.C.
Crystal Orchestrations
3665 Cherry Creek Drive North, #100
Denver, CO 80209
(303)-333-9613

TOPICS: Crystals

Harrison, Hossca
P.O. Box 1559
Boulder, CO 80302

TOPICS: Psychic

Hart, Mickey
Rykodisc USA
Pickering Wharf, Bldg. C-3G
Salem, MA 01970
(508)-744-7678

TOPICS: Birth

Hart, Roger
Fun Club
P.O. Box 428
Bellflower, CA 90706

TOPICS: New Age

Hartly, Harriette, Ph. D.
H And H Productions, Inc.
2006 Winewood
Lancaster, TX 76013
(817)-467-5980

TOPICS: Channeling, Psychic, Hypnotism, Astrology, Numerology EDUCATION: University of Texas, Arlington, TX EDUCATION: Texas Womans University DEGREE: M.A., Ph. D. OCCUPATION: Author, Teacher, Lecturer, Certified Hypnotherapist, Counselor, Psychic, Astrologer, Numerologer

AWARDS: National Speaker's Bureau, Nominee; Woman Of The Year DESCRIPTION: Offers astrology, numerology & compatibility charts. Conducts tours & holds seminars in Brazil & gives personal psychic consultations & channeling.

Hastings, Arthur, Ph. D.
Institute OF Transpersonal Psychology
250 Oak Grove Avenue
Menlo Park, CA 94025
(415)-326-1960

TOPICS: Spirituality, New Age, Psychology

Hathaway, Michael
Chiron Press
Route 2
Box 111
Saint John, KS 67576
(316)-549-3933

TOPICS: New Age

Haule, John R.
48 Chestnut Terrace
Newton Centre, MA 02159
(617)-964-7210 (617)-964-7210

TOPICS: Spirituality, New Age, Meditation, Hypnotism, Body-Mind Connection, Psychology DATE OF BIRTH: 02/26/42 PLACE OF BIRTH: Detroit, MI EDUCATION: Temple University, Philadelphia, PA YEARS: 1969-1973 DEGREE: Ph. D. YEAR DEGREE: 1973 EDUCATION: C.G. Jung Institute, Zurich, Switzerland YEARS: 1976-1980 DEGREE: IAAP YEAR DEGREE: 1980 OCCUPATION: Jungian Analyst, Author WORK EXPERIENCE: Northeastern University, Boston, MA, Asst. Professor Religion & Culture; Private Practice, Jungian Analysis, Newton, MA, 1980-Present PROFESSIONAL MEMBERSHIPS: Int'l Assoc. of Analytical Psychologists 1980-Pres., Exec. Committee Member 1989-92; New England Society of Jungian Analysts 1980-Pres., Pres.1983-88. PUBLICATIONS: *Divine Madness: Archetypes of Romantic Love*, 1990 PUBLISHER: Shambhala PUBLICATIONS: *Religion & Psychotherapy*, 1990 PUBLISHER: Abingdon PUBLICATIONS: *A Jungian Approach To Grandiosity: Empathy And A Big Stick*, 1989 PUBLISHER: Psychology Patient PUBLICATIONS: *The American Quest For Inner Experience*, 1988 PUBLISHER: Quadrant PUBLICATIONS: *Integrating Psychology And Theology With Bricolage*, 1986 PUBLISHER: Journal Of Psychology And Theology PUBLICATIONS: *Pierre Janet And Dissociation*, 1986 PUBLISHER: American Journal Of Clinical Hypnosis

Havern, J. Ronald, M. Div.
150 East 7th Street
New York, NY 10009

TOPICS: Tarot

Hawk, Kay
Three Of Cups
P.O. Box 508, 12 Tinker Street
Woodstock, NY 12498
(914)-679-2357

TOPICS: Crystals

Hawk, Susan
Technical Information Center Office On Smoking & Health
5600 Fishers Lane
Park Building, Rm. 116

Rockville, MD 20857
(301)-443-1690

TOPICS: Holistic Healing

Hay, Louise L.
Hay Institute
P.O. Box 2212
Santa Monica, CA 90406
(213)-394-7445

TOPICS: Holistic Healing

Hayes, Christine
Rainbow Earth Dwelling Society
P.O. Box 4782
San Antonio, TX 78285
(512)-737-1733 (512)-737-1733

TOPICS: Metaphysics, Crystals DATE OF BIRTH: 03/10/49 PLACE OF BIRTH: Caripito, Venezuela OCCUPATION: Author AWARDS: Texas Council of Teachers of English for Contributions in Communications in Texas, Feb. 23, 1974 PUBLICATIONS: *Red Tree* (1972) PUBLISHER: Naylor Publications PUBLICATIONS: *Magi I From The Blue Star* (1986) PUBLISHER: Burning Bush Publications PUBLICATIONS: *Source Edition Vol. I* PUBLISHER: Burning Bush Publications PUBLICATIONS: *Source Edition Vol. II* PUBLISHER: Burning Bush Publications PUBLICATIONS: *Runeweaving* PUBLISHER: Burning Bush Publications PUBLICATIONS: *Temple Doors* PUBLISHER: Burning Bush Publications

Hayes, Patricia
P.O. Box 767121
Roswell, GA 30076
(404)-887-5824

TOPICS: Psychic, Astrology WORK EXPERIENCE: Patricia Hayes School Of Inner Sense Development, Roswell, GA, Founder

Hayhow, Sally
Vegetarian Times
P.O. Box 570
Oak Park, IL 60303
(312)-848-8100

TOPICS: Health Food

Hazel, Robert H., Jr.
Williams & Wilkins
428 East Preston Street
Baltimore, MD 21202
(301)-528-4000

TOPICS: Holistic Healing

Heckler, Richard Strozzi
4101 Middle Two Rock Road
Petaluma, CA 94952
(707)-778-6505 (707)-778-6505

TOPICS: Aikido, Massage, Spirituality, Psychology DATE OF BIRTH: 08/29/44 PLACE OF BIRTH: Spokane, WA EDUCATION: Saybrook Institute, San Francisco, CA DEGREE: Ph. D. YEAR DEGREE: 1975 OCCUPATION: Psychologist, Author, Aikido Teacher WORK EXPERIENCE: Home School, Petaluma, CA, Founder, Director PUBLICATIONS: *In Search of the Warrior Spirit* (1990) PUBLISHER: North Atlantic Books PUBLICATIONS: *Aikido & The New Warrior* (1985) PUBLISHER: North Atlantic Books PUBLICATIONS: *The Anatomy of Change* (1984) PUBLISHER: Shambhala

Heeb, Dolores

Turning Point-Family Wellness Center
173 Mount Auburn Street
Watertown, MA 02172
(617)-923-4604

TOPICS: Holistic Healing

Helton, Jeanne
Harmonic Connections With Jeanne
P.O. Box 4843
Stockton, CA 95204
(209)-464-4059

TOPICS: Numerology, Psychic, Crystals
DESCRIPTION: Counseling through numerology to achieve harmonic link to self & others.

Hendrick, Ellen
13067 Calais Street
New Orleans, LA 70129

TOPICS: Psychic Healing

Henning, Hazel M., Ph. D.
Association For Past-Life Research And Therapies, Inc.
P.O. Box 20151
Riverside, CA 92516
(714)-784-1570

TOPICS: Reincarnation

Henry, Patricia
P.O. Box 753
Sebastopol, CA 95472
(707)-829-2007

TOPICS: New Age, Psychology DESCRIPTION: Psychotherapist offering private or group counseling. Provides hypnotherapy, spiritual development & ethics awareness.

Henry, Ronald D.
Personal Healing Institute
1113 Spruce, #301
Boulder, CO 80302
(303)-449-0910

TOPICS: Crystals

Herman, Edwin L.
3803 Clark's Lane
Baltimore, MD 21215
(301)-358-5258

TOPICS: Crystals

Herweg, Jim
Crystal Circle
3477 South Ninth Street
Kalamazoo, MI 49009
(616)-375-8047

TOPICS: Crystals

Hewitt, Stephen D.
3915 Prospect Avenue
Los Angeles, CA 90004

TOPICS: Channeling

Hickey, Janet
Gems Of Light
P.O. Box 299
Richmond, IA 52585
(319)-456-6816

TOPICS: Crystals

Hickey, Tom
Gems Of Light
P.O. Box 299

Richmond, IA 52585
(319)-456-6816

TOPICS: Crystals

Hieronymus, Dr. Sarah
Sarah And T. Galen Hieronymus
P.O. Box 109
Lakemont, GA 30552
(404)-782-5437

TOPICS: Metaphysics

Hildenbrand, Gar
Gerson Institute
Box 430
Bonita, CA 92002
(619)-267-1150

TOPICS: Holistic Healing

Hill, Linda, M.A.
46 Great Jones Street
New York, NY 10012

TOPICS: Astrology

Hill, Megan
SunRise Springs Resort
Route 14
Box 203
Santa Fe, La Cienega, NM 87505
(505)-471-3600

TOPICS: Holistic Healing

Hill, Melissa
Crystalove
116 West Houston Street
New York, NY 10012
(212)-473-6947

TOPICS: Crystals

Hilsher-Kurban, Dr. Loretta
Spiritual Museum
4328 North Lincoln Avenue
Chicago, IL 60618
(312)-478-2410

TOPICS: Astrology, Spirituality, Holistic Health, Crystals, Numerology, Herbalogy OCCUPATION: TV Host, Author, Consultant, Teacher, Reiki Certified, Nutritionist, Curator, Lecturer WORK EXPERIENCE: Spiritual Museum, Chicago, IL, Curator DESCRIPTION: Conducts workshops in stress control, health, spinal treatments, herbal wraps, facial classes, herbs, crystals & behavior solutions. PUBLICATIONS: *The Wholistic Diet Book* PUBLISHER: Libra Press PUBLICATIONS: *Women's Health* PUBLISHER: Libra Press PUBLICATIONS: *Learn To Massage To Music* PUBLISHER: Libra Press PUBLICATIONS: *Men's Health* PUBLISHER: Libra Press PUBLICATIONS: *Aids A Study* PUBLISHER: Libra Press

Hinda, Andrea
3312 Cripple Creek Trail
Boulder, CO 80303-7161

TOPICS: Psychic

Hinson, Paula
Aslan House-Jacksonville Center For Attitudinal Healing
P.O. Box 52116
Jacksonville, FL 32201
(904)-353-4357

TOPICS: Holistic Healing

Hirsch, Donna
Heaven Bone Press
86 Whispering Hills Drive
P.O. Box 486
Chester, NY 10918
(914)-469-9018

TOPICS: Channeling, Crystals, Psychic Phenomena, Spirituality, Metaphysics, New Age

Hirsch, Roger C.
P. O. Box 461100
Los Angeles, CA 90046
(213)-651-2361

TOPICS: Holistic Health, Acupuncture DESCRIPTION: Offers traditional medical practices & martial arts to attain balance & a higher awareness.

Hirsch, Steven
Heaven Bone Press
P.O. Box 486
Chester, NY 10918
(914)-469-9018

TOPICS: New Age, Crystals, Psychic Phenomena, Spirituality, Metaphysics, Channeling DATE OF BIRTH: 05/26/60 PLACE OF BIRTH: New York, NY EDUCATION: Sard College, Annandale-On-Hudson, NY DEGREE: B.A. YEAR DEGREE: 1985 EDUCATION: Naropa Institute, Boulder, CO DEGREE: A.A. YEAR DEGREE: 1981 OCCUPATION: Publisher, Editor, Computer Designer, Jeweler, Lecturer WORK EXPERIENCE: Heaven Bone Press, Chester, NY, Publisher AWARDS: The Yeats Club, Certificate of Distinction 1990 PROFESSIONAL MEMBERSHIPS: COSMEP; American Society of Gemcutters, Guildsman DESCRIPTION: Teaches & lectures on crystals & esoteric cosmology. PUBLICATIONS: *Heaven Bone Magazine*, editor, semi-annual PUBLISHER: Heaven Bone Press

Hirschfield, Jerry
15300 Ventura Boulevard, #520
Sherman Oaks, CA 91403
(818)-789-4118

TOPICS: Psychology DESCRIPTION: Author of My Ego, My Higher Power, and I.

Hisey, Lehmann
P.O. Box 1693
Sedona, AZ 86336

TOPICS: Crystals

Hite, Pat
Holistic Health Association Of The Princeton Area
360 Nassau Street
Princeton, NJ 08540
(609)-924-8580

TOPICS: Holistic Healing

Hoag, Gail Joy
Metaforms
P.O. Box 2262
Boulder, CO 80306
(303)-449-5918

TOPICS: Holistic Health, Crystals, Color Therapy OCCUPATION: Counselor, Healer WORK EXPERIENCE: Metaforms, Boulder, CO, Counselor, Healer DESCRIPTION: Performs healing & counselling with Metaforms.

Hoag, Gregory

Metaforms
P.O. Box 2262
Boulder, CO 80306
(303)-449-5918

TOPICS: Crystals, Holistic Health, Color Therapy **EDUCATION:** Kalamazoo College **DEGREE:** B.A., Art & Science **YEAR DEGREE:** 1970 **OCCUPATION:** Designer, Researcher, Artist, Scientist **WORK EXPERIENCE:** Metaforms, Boulder, CO, Researcher **DESCRIPTION:** Researcher & designer of Metaforms, energy tools for physical, mental & emotional health.

Hoehl, Helmut
P.O. Box 551
Edmondton, Alb. T6C4E9,
Canada
TOPICS: Channeling

Hoffman, Enid
Hawaiian Village
6403 Maui Drive
Bradenton, FL 34207
(813)-755-5023

TOPICS: Palmistry, Psychic, Metaphysics **DATE OF BIRTH:** 09/01/17 **PLACE OF BIRTH:** Oak Bluffs, MA **OCCUPATION:** Author, Lecturer **PROFESSIONAL MEMBERSHIPS:** IANDS, Life Member; ASD, Life Member **PUBLICATIONS:** *Hands: A Complete Guide To Palmistry* **PUBLISHER:** Whitford Press **PUBLICATIONS:** *Huna: A Guide For Beginners* **PUBLICATIONS:** *Develop Your Psychic Skills* **PUBLICATIONS:** *Expand Your Psychic Skills*

Hoffman, Maryanne
Star Visions
7537 Mentor Avenue
Mentor, OH 44060
(800)-678-4000

TOPICS: New Age, Metaphysics, Astrology **OCCUPATION:** Astrologer, Syndicated Columnist, Author, Artist **WORK EXPERIENCE:** Star Visions, Mentor, OH, President **DESCRIPTION:** Astrologer offering workshops, lectures & readings in Astrology, Rune Stones, Tea Leaf & Auras. **PUBLICATIONS:** *Rainbow In Your Life*

Hogg, Ian
Idad Press
1A Church Lane
Croft, Li PE24 4RR
United Kingdom
TOPICS: Occult

Holcomb, Henry C.
The American Association Of Nutritional Consultants
1641 East Sunset Road
B 117
Las Vegas, NV 89119
(702)-361-1132
TOPICS: Holistic Healing

Holcomb, Myra E.
The American Association Of Nutritional Consultants
1641 East Sunset Road
B 117
Las Vegas, NV 89119
(702)-361-1132
TOPICS: Holistic Healing

Holecek, Richard W.
52 Libby Avenue
Hicksville, NY 11801
(516)-433-9118

TOPICS: Tarot, Ghosts, Parapsychology, Psychic, Reincarnation, Metaphysics **DATE OF BIRTH:** 12/10/66 **PLACE OF BIRTH:** East Meadow, NY **EDUCATION:** State University of New York at Stony Brook **OCCUPATION:** Engineer, Psychic, Metaphysician **AWARDS:** Ms D, Ordained Minister **PROFESSIONAL MEMBERSHIPS:** Sylvan Society, Staff; F.H.M.C.; Individuals Against Mediocrity; Hungarian Literary Society; Honorary Member of Tuscarora Indian Tribe

Holman, Master Ho, DeDe
Hi-De-Ho Enterprises, DeDe's Crystals And Gifts
P.O. Box 1168-224
Studio City, CA 91604
(818)-761-0945

TOPICS: Crystals

Hopcroft, Ann-Victoria, J.D.
The Institute For The Development Of The Harmonious Hum
P.O. Box 370
Nevada City, CA 95959
(916)-477-1116

TOPICS: Holistic Healing

Hopman, Ellen Evert, M. Ed.
P.O. Box 219
Amherst, MA 01004

TOPICS: Herbalogy, Holistic Health, Homeopathy, Psychology, Paganism **OCCUPATION:** Master Herbalist, Author, Lecturer, Counselor **PROFESSIONAL MEMBERSHIPS:** Vice-Pres. Keltria, International Druid Order **DESCRIPTION:** Master Herbalist offering lectures & workshops on herbalism, flower essences, homeopathy, intergrated psychological wholeness, Druidism, tree magic, Druidic ritual practice & the re-emergence of the sacred landscape in our time. **PUBLICATIONS:** *Tree Medicine, Tree Magic*, 1991 **PUBLISHER:** Phoenix Press

Hopper-Butler, Deborah
Nos Amis/Our Friends, Inc.
7519 Sausalito Avenue
Canoga Park, CA 91307
(818)-346-1465

TOPICS: New Age, Holistic Health **DATE OF BIRTH:** 01/26/45 **OCCUPATION:** Teacher, Consultant, Holistic Counselor **WORK EXPERIENCE:** Center For Child Development, West Hills, CA, Founder, Dir., Teacher, Consultant; Nos Amis/Our Friends, Inc., West Hills, CA, Board Member **DESCRIPTION:** Teaches & consults parents & children & offers enrichment through creative expression groups, parent support groups & classes.

Hoskins, Ruth
Prana - Philadelphia Resource And Networking Associatio
Center For Holistic Education And Self-Development
638 South Street
Philadelphia, PA 19147
(215)-592-9035

TOPICS: Holistic Healing

Houston, Jean
Foundation For Mind Research
Box 600
Pomona, NY 10970
TOPICS: Metaphysics, New Age, Psychology **OCCUPATION:** Author, Lecturer **WORK EXPERIENCE:** Foundation For Mind Research, Pomona, NY, Director **DESCRIPTION:** Dedicated to the study & research of the human potential. Topics pursued include altered states of consciousness, drugs, & human creativity. Conducts worldwide lectures & seminars on the Possible Human & the development of the human brain. **PUBLICATIONS:** *The Possible Human*, 1982 **PUBLICATIONS:** *Listening To The Body*, 1979 **PUBLICATIONS:** *Lifeforce: The Psycho-Historical Recovery Of Self* 1980 **PUBLICATIONS:** *The Search For The Beloved*, 1987 **PUBLICATIONS:** *Mind Games*, 1972

Houston, Mark T.
Human Development Network
P.O. Box 24148
Omaha, NE 68124
(402)-399-9925

TOPICS: New Age **OCCUPATION:** New Age Financial Consultant **WORK EXPERIENCE:** Human Development Network, Omaha, NE, President **DESCRIPTION:** New Age Financial & Marketing Management Consultant to public & private businesses. Avid student of all types of New Age materials. Offers business management, event booking, networking, product marketing, publishing & career development.

Howard, H.
Sterlings Magazines
35 Wilbur Street
Lynbrook, NY 11563
(212)-391-1400

TOPICS: Astrology

Howatson, Marianne
Conde Nast Publications, Inc.
350 Madison Avenue
New York, NY 10017
(212)-880-8800

TOPICS: Holistic Healing

Howell, Beth
Portland Reflections
Box 13070
Portland, OR 97213
(503)-281-4486

TOPICS: Metaphysics

Howie, Heather
Trimel Publishing Group
5915 Airport Road
Suite 700
Mississauga, On L4V 1T1
Canada
(416)-673-2500

TOPICS: Holistic Healing

Hoyt, Venessa
A.R.E. Clinic
4017 North 40th Street
Phoenix, AZ 85018
(602)-955-7729

TOPICS: Holistic Healing

Huddlestone, Kathleen
Spiritual Venturers Association

Natural Healding Centre
72 Pasture Road, Goole, North Humberside DN14 6HE
England
TOPICS: Crystals

Huff, Bert
BroHuff Enterprises
Box 69067
Odessa, TX 79769-9067
(915)-367-3637

TOPICS: Crystals, Metaphysics, Numerology, Hypnotism, New Age

Huff, Viron
Ojo Caliente Mineral Springs
P.O. Box 468
Highway 414
Ojo Caliente, NM 87549
(505)-583-2233

TOPICS: Holistic Healing

Hughes, Karen Lander
A New Age Center
502 Emily Circle
West Chester, PA 19382
TOPICS: Channeling

Humphrey, James
AMS Press, Inc.
56 East 13th Street
New York, NY 10003
(212)-777-4700

TOPICS: Holistic Healing

Humphreys, Bronwen
Vegetarian Society Ltd.
Parkdale Dunham Road
Altrincham Cheshire, WA14 4QG
England
(061)-928-0793

TOPICS: Health Food

Hung, Dr. David P.J.
American Acupuncture Association
150 E. 56th Street, #1E
New York, NY 10022
TOPICS: Acupuncture, Holistic Health DATE OF BIRTH: 09/08/31 EDUCATION: Columbia Pacific University YEARS: 1978-80 DEGREE: Ph. D. YEAR DEGREE: 1980 EDUCATION: Butsugan Kosei School, Japan YEARS: 1966-69 EDUCATION: Tokyo Union Theological Seminary, Japan YEARS: 1959-61 DEGREE: M.A. Theology YEAR DEGREE: 1961 OCCUPATION: Licensed Acupuncture, Teacher WORK EXPERIENCE: Acupuncture Centers Of New York, Flushing, NY & Rochester, NY, Licensed Acupunturist, 1976-Present; Acupuncture International Center, Inc., Charleston, SC, Acupuncturist, 1974-76; National Acupuncture Center, Washington, D.C., Acupuncturist, 1973-74; Acupuncture Center Of New York, New York, NY, Acupuncturist, 1972; Hirose Therapeutic Clinic, Kyoto, Japan, Acupuncturist, 1961-72 PROFESSIONAL MEMBERSHIPS: American Acupuncture Assoc., Chairman, 1989-Present; Acupuncture Institute Of America, President, 1989-Present; International Foundation Of Oriental Medicine, President, 1989-Present DESCRIPTION: Licensed Acupuncturist in China, Japan, New York & California

Hurley, Bill

Crystal Reflections
P. O. Box 685
Carmel, CA 93921-0685
(916)-926-3755

TOPICS: Crystals

Hurley, Mark
Philosophy Education Society
Catholic University Of America
School Of Philosophy
Washington, DC 20064
(202)-635-8778

TOPICS: Metaphysics

Hurst, Brian
12418 LaMaida Street
North Hollywood, CA 91607
TOPICS: Psychic

Hurwich, Barbara
Center For Well-Being
82644 Howe Lane
Creswell, OR 97426
(503)-895-2953

TOPICS: Holistic Healing

Husch, Ann R.
518 East Polo Drive
St. Louis, MO 63105
(314)-725-0796

TOPICS: Holistic Health DESCRIPTION: Considered by many to be the mother of the Holistic Health movement in St. Louis. Yoga instructor for 20 years as well as a pain management therapist. Active in environmental protection.

Hussey, Susan
Aubrey Hampton Publishers
4419 North Manhattan Avenue
Tampa, FL 33614
(813)-876-4879

TOPICS: Holistic Healing

Hutner, Alan
Cosmosis Radio
125 El Rancho Road North
Santa Fe, NM 87501
(505)-983-3059

TOPICS: Holistic Healing

Hutner, Luann
Cosmosis Radio
125 El Rancho Road North
Santa Fe, NM 87501
(505)-983-3059

TOPICS: Holistic Healing

Iglehart, John K.
Project Hope
Carter Hall
Millwood, VA 22646
(703)-837-2100

TOPICS: Holistic Healing

Ingabetsen, Clarissa
P. O. Box 13079
Long Beach, CA 90803-3079
(213)-437-3450

TOPICS: Psychic, Tarot DESCRIPTION: Clairvoyant offering tarot readings & psychometry to locate

missing articles & people. Political activist for psychics.

Ingenito, Marcia Gervase
Highgate House Publishers
6 Surfside Drive
Ormond Beach, FL 32176-2325
TOPICS: Psychic Phenomena

Insel, Paul M.
The C.V. Mosby Co.
11830 Westline Industrial Driv
St. Louis, MO 63146
(314)-872-8370

TOPICS: Holistic Healing

Irving, Kenneth
Starlog Press, Inc.
475 Park Avenue, South
New York, NY 10016
(212)-689-2830

TOPICS: Astrology

Irwin, Chris
Sierra Spirit Ranch
3000 Pinenut Road
Gardnerville, NV 89410
(702)-782-7011

TOPICS: Holistic Healing

Irwin, Harvey Jon
University Of New England
Department Of Psychology
Armidale, NSW 2351
Australia
TOPICS: Parapsychology DATE OF BIRTH: 09/08/43 PLACE OF BIRTH: Sydney, Australia EDUCATION: University Of New England DEGREE: Ph. D. OCCUPATION: Teacher (Assoc. Prof.), Author, Editor AWARDS: M.S. Weiss Award from ASPR, 1979 PROFESSIONAL MEMBERSHIPS: Member, Parapsychological Assoc.; Fellow ASPR DESCRIPTION: Teaches & conducts research in Parapsychology & Thanatology. Writer for the Journal Of The American Society For Psychical Research & the Journal Of Parapsychology. Editor for the Australian Parapsychological Review. PUBLICATIONS: *Psi And The Mind*, 1979 PUBLICATIONS: *Flight Of Mind*, 1985 PUBLICATIONS: *An Introduction To Parapsychology,* 1989

Irwin, Robin
Sierra Spirit Ranch
3000 Pinenut Road
Gardnerville, NV 89410
(702)-782-7011

TOPICS: Holistic Healing

Isaacs, Dr. Julian
John F. Kennedy University
12 Altarinda Road
Orinda, CA 94563
(415)-254-0200

TOPICS: Parapsychology

Issac-Smith, Shawnee
Santa Monica Healing Arts Center
1453 7th Street
Santa Monica, CA 90401
(213)-395-4667

TOPICS: Holistic Healing

Ivy, John
Portland Reflections
Box 13070
Portland, OR 97213
(503)-281-4486

TOPICS: Metaphysics

Jackson, Bob
Jackson Mountain
Box 2652
Renton, WA 98056
(206)-255-6635

TOPICS: Crystals

Jackson, Judith
Judith Jackson Aromatherapy
96 Lewis Street
Greenwich, CT 06830
(203)-629-2240

TOPICS: Holistic Health, Massage DESCRIPTION: Offers clients renewal of mind, body & spirit through aromatherapy treatments at her renewal center.

Jacobs, Leonard
East West Journal
17 Station Street
Box 1200
Brookline Village, MA 02147
(617)-232-1000

TOPICS: Holistic Healing

Jacobsen, Christine
Little Stony Creek Haven
1286 Woodbridge Crossing Drive
Chesterfield, MO 63005-4608

TOPICS: Holistic Healing

Jacobsen, Lee
Little Stony Creek Haven
1286 Woodbridge Crossing Drive
Chesterfield, MO 63005-4608
(703)-984-4462

TOPICS: Holistic Healing

Jacobson, Vi
ACIM Workshop
6052 Plunkett Street
Hollywood, FL 33021
(305)-961-2283

TOPICS: New Age

Jaegers, Beverly C.
Aries Productions, Inc.
P.O. Box 29396
Sappington, MO 63126

TOPICS: Parapsychology, Dowsing, Ghosts, PSI, Graphology, Psychic, Holistic Healing DATE OF BIRTH: 01/09/35 PLACE OF BIRTH: St. Louis, MO EDUCATION: St. John's University DEGREE: B.A., M.A. OCCUPATION: Writer, Newspaper Columnist WORK EXPERIENCE: Aries Production Inc., Sappington, MO, President 1976-1984 PROFESSIONAL MEMBERSHIPS: RWA So. California Pen Collectors Club; St. Louis Pen Collectors, Pres. 1989-Present DESCRIPTION: Bevy Jaegers, along with husband Ray, authored and published many books on diverse topics like ghosts, crystals, auras, meditation, healing, ESP, and psychic development. PUBLICATIONS: Color, Light & Crystals PUBLICATIONS: Ghost Hunting PUBLICATIONS: The Human Aura PUBLICATIONS: Mind Power And Meditation PUBLICATIONS:

Practical ESP & Clairvoyance PUBLICATIONS: Predicting Tomorrow-Today!

James, Susan
Insight Northwest
Box 25450
Seattle, WA 98125
(206)-527-3324

TOPICS: Holistic Healing

Jamesson, Cheryl
815 Northeast 28 Street, #209
Fort Lauderdale, FL 33334
(305)-566-0089

TOPICS: New Age

Jampolsky, Gerald Gersham, M.D.
Center For Attitudinal Healing
19 Main Street
Tiburon, CA 94920
(415)-435-5022

TOPICS: Holistic Healing, Hypnotism DATE OF BIRTH: 02/11/25 PLACE OF BIRTH: Long Beach, CA EDUCATION: Stanford University DEGREE: B.A. YEAR DEGREE: 1947 DEGREE: M.D. YEAR DEGREE: 1950 OCCUPATION: Physician, Author, Lecturer WORK EXPERIENCE: Center For Attitudinal Healing, Tiburon, CA, Founder DESCRIPTION: Influenced strongly by A Course In Miracles, he incorporates many of its docturnes into his medical techniques. Uses hypnosis & visualization to eliminate patient's fears. PUBLICATIONS: Psychiatric Considerations In Reading Disabilites, 1965 PUBLICATIONS: Children As Teachers Of Peace, 1982 PUBLICATIONS: Love Is Letting Go Of Fear, 1979 PUBLICATIONS: Teach Only Love, 1983 PUBLICATIONS: There Is A Rainbow Behind Every Dark Cloud, 1978

Jannasch, Barbara
Akala Point
Box 4
Site 28, R.R. 1
Tantallon, No B0J 3J0
Canada
(902)-823-2160

TOPICS: Holistic Healing

Janney, Peter, Ed. D.
32 Hill Street
Lexington, MA 02173

TOPICS: Psychic

Jaskoviak, Paul A.
Busch Publishing Company
5005 Rivera Court
Ft. Wayne, IN 46825
(219)-484-9600

TOPICS: Holistic Healing

Jasper, Conny
The Rat Race Record
P.O. Box 1611
Union, NJ 07083

TOPICS: Holistic Healing

Jauchius, Suzanne
P.O. Box 256
Gresham, OR 97030
(503)-771-4874

TOPICS: Psychic

Javane, Faith
34 Pinecrest Lane
Dover, NH 03820

TOPICS: Numerology

Jayvanti
2 Brookside Drive
West Harriman, NY 10926
(914)-783-0467

TOPICS: Psychic Healing, Psychology, Holistic Healing, Crystals, Tarot DATE OF BIRTH: 11/12/49 PLACE OF BIRTH: Chicago, IL EDUCATION: Fordham University, New York, NY DEGREE: MSW YEAR DEGREE: 1983 EDUCATION: Crystal Therapeutics, New York, NY YEAR DEGREE: 1989 OCCUPATION: Psychotherapist, Psychic Healer, Crystal Healer AWARDS: Dept Of Social Sciences & Human Services Award, 1982, Ramapo College PROFESSIONAL MEMBERSHIPS: NASW DESCRIPTION: Private practice offering Psychotherapy, Pscyhic Healing & Crystal Therapeutics.

Jeanette
Cosmic Lightbearers
P. O. Box 4112
Key West, FL 33041

TOPICS: Channeling

Jeanne
3131-8th Avenue
Arcadia, CA 91006
(818)-447-7763

TOPICS: Crystals, Numerology, Astrology

Jensen, Bernard
Rt. 1, Box 52
Escondido, CA 92025
(714)-749-2727

TOPICS: Holistic Healing, Homeopathy, Health Food PLACE OF BIRTH: Stockton, CA EDUCATION: West Coast Chiropractic College DEGREE: Doctor of Chiropractic YEAR DEGREE: 1929 OCCUPATION: Chiropractor, Author, Lecturer WORK EXPERIENCE: Nature's Retreat, Redlands, CA, Founder; Hidden Valley Ranch, CA, Founder DESCRIPTION: Devoted to the attainment of universal good health. Researches, studies & promotes techniques for health such as naturopathy & iridoogy PUBLICATIONS: The Doctor-Patient Handbook, 1976 PUBLICATIONS: The Joy Of Health And How To Attain It, 1946 PUBLICATIONS: Nature Has A Remedy, 1978 PUBLICATIONS: The Science & Practice Of Iridology, 1952 PUBLICATIONS: Vital Foods For Total Health, 1950 PUBLICATIONS: You Can Master Disease, 1952

Jensen, Dr. Bernard
Hidden Valley Health Ranch
Route 1, Box 52
Escondido, CA 92025
(714)-749-2727

TOPICS: Holistic Healing PUBLICATIONS: Survive This Day: A Doctor's Guide To These Critical Times PUBLISHER: Bernard Jensen Publishing Co. PUBLICATIONS: Healing Mind Of Man: Arise & Shine PUBLISHER: Bernard Jensen Publishing Co.

Jermini, Dr. Ellen
University Of Healing
1101 Far Valley Road

Campo, CA 91906
(619)-478-5111

TOPICS: Holistic Healing, Metaphysics

Jerome, Lawrence
16495 Oleander Avenue
Los Gatos, CA 95032
(408)-356-1077 (408)-356-1077

TOPICS: Skepticism, Astrology, Crystals, Metaphysics, Psychic Phenomena, Occult DATE OF BIRTH: 01/15/44 PLACE OF BIRTH: Glen Cove, NY EDUCATION: Florida State University, Tallahassee, FL YEARS: 1961-1966 DEGREE: B.S., M.S. YEAR DEGREE: 1966 EDUCATION: Stanford University, Stanford, CA YEARS: 1966-1969 OCCUPATION: University Instructor, Consultant, Author WORK EXPERIENCE: University of San Francisco, San Francisco, CA, Instructor 1979-Pres.; MTA Consulting, San Jose, CA, Consultant; Publications & Communications, Inc., Western Correspondent,1986-Pres. PROFESSIONAL MEMBERSHIPS: Committee For Scientific Investigations of Claims of the Paranormal, Founding Fellow; Bay Area Skeptics, Board Member PUBLICATIONS: *Astrology Disproved*, 1977 PUBLISHER: Prometheus Books PUBLICATIONS: *Crystal Power: The Ultimate Placebo Effect*, 1989 PUBLISHER: Prometheus Books PUBLICATIONS: *Objections To Astrology*, 1975 PUBLISHER: Prometheus Books PUBLICATIONS: *Astrologie: en Bloff?*, 1979 PUBLISHER: Universitesforlage, Oslo

Johns, David
4129 Rabbit Run Drive
Cleveland, OH 44144

TOPICS: Channeling

Johnson, Bob
Free Enterprise Health Mine
Boulder Hot Springs
P.O. Box 1020
Boulder, MT 59632
(406)-225-4273 (406)-225-3383

TOPICS: Holistic Healing

Johnson, Daniel (Shahid)
Mystic Garden Press
Box 51
Crestone, CO 81131-0051
(719)-256-4137 (719)-256-4137

TOPICS: Psychic, Holistic Healing, Metaphysics DATE OF BIRTH: 02/05/54 PLACE OF BIRTH: Danbury, CT OCCUPATION: Psychic Healer, Medicine Man, Workshop Leader, Author WORK EXPERIENCE: Mystic Garden Press, Crestone, CO, Founder DESCRIPTION: Psychic Healer & Medicine Man conducting workshops for teens. Brings Metaphysical techniques & insights to modern problems. Radio & TV guest speaker. PUBLICATIONS: *Yhantishor, A Fantasy Based In Truth* PUBLISHER: Mystic Garden Press PUBLICATIONS: *Creative Rebellion, Positive Options For Teens In The 90's* PUBLISHER: Mystic Garden Press

Johnson, Deanna M.
Lotus Trading Company
P.O. Box 7724
Missoula, MT 59807
(406)-728-2175

TOPICS: Crystals

Johnson, Dr. Paul V.
Spiritual Advisory Council
10345 SE 103rd Terrace
Summerfield, FL 32691
(305)-898-2500

TOPICS: Spirituality, Metaphysics

Johnson, Judy, R.N.
Crystal Cluster, The
510 Kelley Avenue
Half Moon Bay, CA 94019
(415)-726-7644

TOPICS: Crystals

Johnson, Marie
6047 Talman
Chicago, IL 60629

TOPICS: Channeling

Johnson, Peggy
Free Enterprise Health Mine
Box 67
Boulder, MT 59632
(406)-225-3383

TOPICS: Holistic Healing

Johnson, Wista Jeanne
Wista Jeanne Johnson Publishers
P.O. Box 40-1232
Brooklyn, NY 11240-1232
(800)-649-4325 (718)-756-2245

TOPICS: Holistic Healing

Jones, C.B. Scott, Ph. D.
Human Potential Foundation
8000 Towers Crescent Drive, #600
Vienna, VA 22182
(703)-761-4281

TOPICS: New Age, Metaphysics, Psychology WORK EXPERIENCE: American Society For Psychical Research, NY, NY, Former Pres.; Human Potential Foundation, Vienna, VA, Pres.

Jones, Charles
Dream International Quarterly
121 North Ramona Street, #25
Ramona, CA 92065
(619)-789-3258

TOPICS: Dreams

Jones, D.
8326 Windwillow Drive
Houston, TX 77040

TOPICS: Channeling

Jones, Jim
Zero Hour
P.O. Box 766
Seattle, WA 98111
(206)-323-3648

TOPICS: Occult

Jones, Leslie H.
Dream International Quarterly
121 North Ramona Street, #25
Ramona, CA 92065
(619)-789-3258

TOPICS: Dreams

Joseph, Antonio
Ojo Caliente Mineral Springs

P.O. Box 468
Highway 414
Ojo Caliente, NM 87549
(505)-583-2233

TOPICS: Holistic Healing

Joy, Elizabeth
Elizabeth Joy Productions
P.O. Box 4507
Taos, NM 87571
(505)-758-1917

TOPICS: Crystals, Holistic Health, New Age, Spirituality OCCUPATION: Author, Lecturer, Publisher WORK EXPERIENCE: Elizabeth Joy Productions, Taos, NM, Publisher DESCRIPTION: Offers workshops, classes & seminars related to New Age, Metaphysics & health. Seminars held in Bali & the British Isles. PUBLICATIONS: Awakening Practical Spirituality PUBLICATIONS: *Living A Joyous Life*

Joy, Gloria
P. O. Box 6524
Orange, CA 92667

TOPICS: New Age DESCRIPTION: Designs greeting cards to the trade.

Joy, W. Brugh, M.D.
Feather Mountain Conference Center
P.O. Box 670
Paulden, AZ 86334
(602)-445-0911

TOPICS: Holistic Health, Dreams, Psychology OCCUPATION: Physician, Author, Lecturer WORK EXPERIENCE: Feather Mountain Conference Center, Prescott, AZ, Lecturer DESCRIPTION: Lectures on the unconscious, dreams & personalities & their affect on health & illness. PUBLICATIONS: *Joy's Way: A Map For The Transformational Journey* PUBLICATIONS: *Avalanche: Further Awakening Into Beinghood*

Joyce, Julian J.
P.O. Box 186
Paonia, CO 81428
(303)-527-3743

TOPICS: Metaphysics, Spirituality DATE OF BIRTH: 08/21/11 PLACE OF BIRTH: Fredonia, KA EDUCATION: Denver University, Denver, CO DEGREE: B.A. YEAR DEGREE: 1937 EDUCATION: U.S. Coast Guard Academy OCCUPATION: Economist, Metaphysics, Author, Lecturer AWARDS: National Musical Fraternity; National Psychological Fraternity; National Gymnastics Fraternity DESCRIPTION: Lecturer on the topics of metaphysics & religion. PUBLICATIONS: *Translation*, 1972 PUBLISHER: The John Press PUBLICATIONS: *The Spiritual Renaissance Of The New World*, 1982 PUBLISHER: Duverus Publishing Corp. PUBLICATIONS: *Cosmic Law*, 1986 PUBLISHER: The John Press PUBLICATIONS: *Thought*, 1987 PUBLISHER: Earth Star Publications PUBLICATIONS: *Lifted Up*, 1987 PUBLISHER: Earth Star Publications PUBLICATIONS: *Into The Shekinah*, 1988 PUBLISHER: Earth Star Publications

Jwing-Ming, Dr. Yang
Yang Martial Arts Assoc.
38 Hyde Park Avenue
Jamaica Plain, MA 02130
(617)-524-8892

TOPICS: Tai Chi, Holistic Health, Body-Mind Connection DATE OF BIRTH: 08/11/46 PLACE OF BIRTH: Taiwan EDUCATION: Perdue University, West Lafayette, IN DEGREE: Ph. D. Engineering OCCUPATION: Publisher, Author, Teacher of Martial Arts/Chi Kung/Tai Chi Chuan WORK EXPERIENCE: YMAA, Jamaica Plain, MA, President 1984-present DESCRIPTION: Promotes healing & well-being through Chinese martial arts. Publishes & produces books & tapes. PUBLICATIONS: *The Essence Of Tai Chi Chi Kung* PUBLISHER: YMAA PUBLICATIONS: *Hsing Yi Chuan* PUBLISHER: YMAA PUBLICATIONS: *The Root Of Chinese Chi Kung* PUBLISHER: YMAA PUBLICATIONS: *Chi Kung Health & Martial Arts* PUBLISHER: YMAA PUBLICATIONS: *The Eight Pieces Of Brocade* PUBLISHER: YMAA PUBLICATIONS: *Advanced Yang Style Tai Chi Chuan* PUBLISHER: YMAA

Jyotirmayananda, Swami
Yoga Research Foundation
5691 S.W. 102nd Avenue
Miami, FL 33143
(305)-666-2006 (305)-666-1718

TOPICS: Yoga, Spirituality DATE OF BIRTH: 02/03/31 PLACE OF BIRTH: Chapra-Bihar, India EDUCATION: Divine Life Society, Rishikesh, Himalayas, India YEARS: 9 years DEGREE: Sanyasa Order OCCUPATION: Professor, Author, Spiritual Guide WORK EXPERIENCE: Yoga Research Foundation, Miami, FL, President DESCRIPTION: Professor of Yoga & Vedante Philosophy as well as a Spiritual Guide. PUBLICATIONS: *International Yoga Guide* PUBLISHER: Yoga Research Foundation PUBLICATIONS: *Yoga Can Change Your Life* PUBLISHER: Yoga Research Foundation PUBLICATIONS: *Concentration And Meditation* PUBLISHER: Yoga Research Foundation PUBLICATIONS: *Yoga Guide* PUBLISHER: Yoga Research Foundation PUBLICATIONS: *Yoga Exercises For Health And Happiness* PUBLISHER: Yoga Research Foundation PUBLICATIONS: *Death And Reincarnation* PUBLISHER: Yoga Research Foundation

Ka Lange, Myrna
Sunstar Press
Box 1901
Prescott, AZ 86302
TOPICS: Channeling

Kabir-Bey, Alim Haakam
16 Beltane Drive
Dix Hills, NY 11746

TOPICS: Astrology, Meditation, Tai Chi DATE OF BIRTH: 10/09/64 PLACE OF BIRTH: Queens, NY EDUCATION: Howard University, Washington, D.C. YEARS: 1982-87 DEGREE: B.B.A. YEAR DEGREE: 1987 OCCUPATION: Astrologer, Teacher PROFESSIONAL MEMBERSHIPS: Floating Healing Meditation Circle; Sylvan Society DESCRIPTION: Professional Astrologer and teacher of I.S.A Meditation and Tai Chi.

Kabir-Bey, Brother Alim
P.O. Box 13
Uniondale, NY 11553
(516)-433-9118

TOPICS: Parapsychology

Kaczmarek, Dale
Ghost Research Society
P.O. Box 205
Oaklawn, IL 60454-0205
(708)-425-5163 (708)-425-5163

TOPICS: Ghosts, Reincarnation, Past Life Regression, Psychic Phenomena, Parapsychology DATE OF BIRTH: 12/19/52 PLACE OF BIRTH: Chicago, IL EDUCATION: Amos Alonzo Stagg HS, Palos Hills, IL YEARS: 1967-1971 OCCUPATION: Author, Lecturer, Ghost Hunter WORK EXPERIENCE: Ghost Research Society, Oak Lawn, IL, Pres.; Excursions Into The Unknown, Oak Lawn, IL, Pres., Dir. PROFESSIONAL MEMBERSHIPS: Society For The Investigation Of The Unexplained, International Fortean Organization, American Association-Electronic Voice Phenomena PUBLICATIONS: *True Tales Of The Unknown: The Uninvited*, 1989 PUBLISHER: Bantam PUBLICATIONS: *Ghost Trackers Newsletter* PUBLISHER: Ghost Research Society

Kahler, Harold
Wellness Councils Of America
1823 Harney Street, # 201
Omaha, NE 68102
(402)-444-1711

TOPICS: Holistic Healing

Kalina, Kathleen
Crystal Planet Gems
960 Victory Boulevard
Green Bay, WI 54304-3752
(603)-924-6098

TOPICS: Crystals

Kalson, Stan
Healing Pines
P.O. Box 658
Pine, AZ 85544
(602)-476-3392

TOPICS: Holistic Healing

Kaminski, Patricia
Flower Essence Society/Earth-Spirit, Inc.
P.O. Box 459
Nevada City, CA 95959
(916)-265-9163

TOPICS: Holistic Healing

Kane, Sally
P.O. Box 3335
7 Bluewater Hill South
Westport, CT 06880
(203)-222-7954

TOPICS: Holistic Healing DESCRIPTION: Teaches and practices holistic healing as a mariel healer, rebirther, certified reflexologist, massage therapist and certified teacher of technologies for creating. Distributes Sunrider products and Chinese herbal whole foods.

Kant, Michael
2527 Niles Street, 1
Bakersfield, CA 93306
TOPICS: Channeling

Kant, Michael
3689 Myrtle Avenue #15
North Highlands, CA 95660
TOPICS: Crystals, Holistic Healing

Kaplan, Dr. Stephen
Vampire Research Center
P.O. Box 252
Elmhurst, NY 11373
(718)-894-6564

TOPICS: Vampires, Occult, Parapsychology, Hypnotism DATE OF BIRTH: 09/19/40 PLACE OF BIRTH: Bronx, NY EDUCATION: City College of New York DEGREE: B.A., M.S. YEAR DEGREE: 1970 EDUCATION: State U of New York at Stony Brook DEGREE: M.A. EDUCATION: Pacific College DEGREE: Ph. D. YEAR DEGREE: 1977 OCCUPATION: Vampirologist, Author, Lecturer, Teacher WORK EXPERIENCE: Parapsychology Institute Of America, Elmhurst, NY, Founder, Director, Researcher 1971-present; Vampire Research Center, Elmhurst, NY, Founder, Director, Researcher 1971-present; S.U.N.Y at Stony Brook, Instructor of Parapsychology 1974; NY Board of Ed, Instr. Parapsychology and Occult Sciences 1974-pres.; F.B.I. Consultant of Parapsychology AWARDS: Montague Summers Memorial Award, 1977; Parapsychology Hall of Fame, 1982; Hypnosis Hall of Fame, 1987; Who's Who East; Who's Who World, 1991 PROFESSIONAL MEMBERSHIPS: American Cancer Society, NY; Laconia Presbyterian Church Community Center, Bronx, NY; Philthropic League For Handicap Children, NY DESCRIPTION: Conducts lectures, research & in-depth study of vampires. Created a new social science called vampirology. PUBLICATIONS: *True Tales Of The Unknown, Vols. I, II, III* PUBLISHER: Bantam Books PUBLICATIONS: *Hellzapoppin In Amityville*, 1991

Kaplan, Miriam
Crystal Heart, The
P.O. Box 508
Fallsburg, NY 12733
(914)-434-7923

TOPICS: Crystals

Kaplan, Stuart R.
U.S. Games Systems, Inc.
179 Ludlow Street
Stamford, CT 06902
(203)-353-8400

TOPICS: Tarot, Metaphysics DATE OF BIRTH: 04/01/32 PLACE OF BIRTH: New York, NY EDUCATION: Sorbonne University, Paris, France YEARS: 1950-51 DEGREE: Certificate YEAR DEGREE: 1951 EDUCATION: Wharton School, U. of PA, Philadelphia, PA YEARS: 1951-55 DEGREE: B.S. YEAR DEGREE: 1955 OCCUPATION: Publisher, Author WORK EXPERIENCE: U.S. Games Systems, Stamford, CT, President 1968-present DESCRIPTION: Produces & sells numerous varieties of tarot cards, playing cards & games. PUBLICATIONS: *The Encyclopedia Of Tarot, Vols I, II, III* PUBLISHER: U.S. Games Systems, Inc. PUBLICATIONS: *Tarot Classic*, 1972 PUBLISHER: U.S. Games Systems, Inc. PUBLICATIONS: *Tarot Cards For Fun & Fortune Telling*, 1970 PUBLISHER: U.S. Games Systems, Inc.

Kapuler, Alan M., Ph. D.
Peace Seeds
2385 S.E. Thompson Street
Corvallis, OR 97333
(503)-752-0421

TOPICS: Holistic Health, Health Food, New Age DATE OF BIRTH: 09/03/42 PLACE OF BIRTH: Brooklyn, NY EDUCATION: Yale University, New

Haven, CT **YEARS:** 1958-62 **DEGREE:** B.A. **YEAR DEGREE:** 1962 **EDUCATION:** Rockefeller University, New York, NY **YEARS:** 1962-68 **DEGREE:** Ph. D. **YEAR DEGREE:** 1968 **OCCUPATION:** Scientist-Biologist, Author **WORK EXPERIENCE:** Peace Seeds, A Planetary Gene Pool Resource & Service, Corvallis, OR, President 1975-present **PROFESSIONAL MEMBERSHIPS:** Oregon Tilth, Board Of Directors, 1987-89 **DESCRIPTION:** Works to develop a new system of gardening using coevolutionary gene pools to produce a superior species of plants. **PUBLICATIONS:** *Organics, The Gene Pool And Planetary Peace*, 1987 **PUBLICATIONS:** *The 1989 Catalog Of Seeds*, 1989 **PUBLICATIONS:** *A World Class Botanical Garden For The State Of Oregon*, 1987 **PUBLICATIONS:** *Analyses Of Free Amino Acids In The Juice Of 8 Distinctive Tomatoes*,1988 **PUBLICATIONS:** *The Fourth Peace Seeds Catalog And Research Journal*, 1988 **PUBLICATIONS:** *A Coevolutionary Structure For The Plant Kingdom*, 1988

Kardec, Alan
P.O. Box 6571
Syracuse, NY 13217
TOPICS: Channeling

Karen
Box 942
Bellflower, CA 90706
TOPICS: Channeling

Kargere, Audrey
116 Central Park South, Apt.3A
New York, NY 10019
(212)-262-0803
TOPICS: Holistic Health, Metaphysics, Color Therapy, Holistic Healing, New Age, Body-Mind Connection **DATE OF BIRTH:** 07/13/10 **PLACE OF BIRTH:** New York, NY **EDUCATION:** Sorbonne University, Paris, France **EDUCATION:** Psychological Institute, Zurich, Switzerland **EDUCATION:** University of Berlin, Berlin, Germany **OCCUPATION:** Author, Lecturer **DESCRIPTION:** Author & lecturer on the subjects of Color Therapy, Personality & Self-Healing. **PUBLICATIONS:** *Color & Personality* **PUBLISHER:** Samuel Weiser **PUBLICATIONS:** *The Miracle of Color & Self Healing*

Karou, Mariane Athey
Movement Expression
622 Las Lomas Avenue
Pacific Palisades, CA 90272
(213)-454-5335
TOPICS: Holistic Healing **OCCUPATION:** Teacher **WORK EXPERIENCE:** Movement Expression, Pacific Palisades, CA, Founder, teacher **DESCRIPTION:** Offers workshops, private sessions & teacher training in an holistic health & wellness program combining movement & Psychology or imagery.

Karr, Ms. Duane M.
Crystal Rainbow Company
P.O. Box 400
Milford, MI 48042
(313)-685-3628
TOPICS: Crystals

Kaufman, Barry Neil
The Option Institute & Fellowship- A Place For Miracles

RD #1
Box 174A
Sheffield, MA 01257
(413)-229-2100
TOPICS: Holistic Healing

Kaufman, Deborah
Mountain Home Publishing
Box 829
Ingram, TX 78025
(512)-367-4492
TOPICS: Holistic Healing

Kearns, Richard, D.V.M.
Keats Publishing, Inc.
27 Pine Street
P.O. Box 876
New Canaan, CT 06840
(203)-966-8721
TOPICS: Holistic Healing

Keats, Nathan
Keats Publishing, Inc.
27 Pine Street
P.O. Box 876
New Canaan, CT 06840
(203)-966-8721
TOPICS: Holistic Healing

Keeling, Gloria
Strong, Stretched And Centered Body/Mind Institute
P.O. Box 758
Paia, Maui, HI 96779
(808)-575-2178
TOPICS: Holistic Healing

Keith, Jim
Dharma Combat
P.O. Box 20593
Sun Valley, NV 89433
TOPICS: Metaphysics, UFO's **DATE OF BIRTH:** 09/21/49 **PLACE OF BIRTH:** Kansas City, MO **OCCUPATION:** Author, Editor **WORK EXPERIENCE:** Dharma Combat Magazine, Sun Valley, NV, Editor **PROFESSIONAL MEMBERSHIPS:** National UFO Museum, Chairman; Dharma Combat, Editor **DESCRIPTION:** Editor of Dharma Combat Magazine, Notes From The Hangar Magazine & has written approximately 150 works of fiction. **PUBLICATIONS:** *Dharma Combat*, (Quarterly) **PUBLISHER:** Drax Publishers **PUBLICATIONS:** *Notes From The Hangar Magazine*, (Quarterly) **PUBLISHER:** Nufom Publishers **PUBLICATIONS:** *The Gemstone File* **PUBLICATIONS:** *Secret And Suppressed* **PUBLICATIONS:** *Alternative 3: A Casebook*

Kelly, Corinne Dee
The Albintra Wellness Center/Natural Medicine Works
438 N.E. 72nd
Seattle, WA 98115
(206)-522-9384
TOPICS: Holistic Healing

Kelly, Joseph
Kelly Communications
410 East Water Street
Charlottesville, VA 22901
(804)-296-5676
TOPICS: Holistic Healing

Kelly, Kevin
Point Foundation
27 Gate Five Road
Sausalito, CA 94965
(415)-332-1716
TOPICS: New Age

Kelly, Susan
Fraternity For Canadian Astrologers
P.O. Box 4924 Station E
Ottawa, On K1S 5J1
Canada
TOPICS: Astrology

Kelman, Michael
Communications Channels, Inc.
6255 Barfield Road
Atlanta, GA 30328
(404)-256-9800
TOPICS: Holistic Healing **PUBLICATIONS:** *Better Nutrition*

Kelynda
P.O. Box 201
Clifton Heights, PA 19018
(215)-284-3118
TOPICS: Reincarnation, Psychic, Astrology, Tarot, Crystals, Metaphysics, Kabbalah **DATE OF BIRTH:** 08/07/59 **PLACE OF BIRTH:** Kingston, PA **EDUCATION:** Temple University, Philadelphia, PA **DEGREE:** B.A. English **YEAR DEGREE:** 1983 **OCCUPATION:** Psychic, Astrologer, Tarot & Crystal Reader, Lecturer, Author **PROFESSIONAL MEMBERSHIPS:** Astrological Council of Delaware Valley, Member **DESCRIPTION:** Psychic lecturer & author on many different aspects of metaphysicsincluding psychic development, divination, mythology, astrology, tarot, kabbalah & crystals. **PUBLICATIONS:** *The Eternal Quest*, 1988 **PUBLISHER:** Whitford Press **PUBLICATIONS:** *The Magnificent Quest: Practical Paths To The Inner Grail*, 1990 **PUBLISHER:** Whitford Press **PUBLICATIONS:** *Crystal Tree Book & Gemstones* **PUBLISHER:** Whitford Press

Kemery, W.E., Ph. D.
379 G Street
Chula Vista, CA 91910
(619)-427-6225 (619)-422-0402
TOPICS: Hypnotism, Psychology, Body-Mind Connection **DATE OF BIRTH:** 04/16/29 **PLACE OF BIRTH:** Portland, OR **EDUCATION:** Newport International University, Newport Beach,CA **DEGREE:** M.A., Ph. D. **YEAR DEGREE:** 1979 **OCCUPATION:** Psychotherapist, Hypnotherapist, Author, Teacher **WORK EXPERIENCE:** Kemery Institute, Chula Vista, CA, Director, Therapist, Teacher - 23 years; Academy Of Scientific Hypnotherapy, San Diego, CA, President - 13 years **AWARDS:** Fellow, Acad. of Scientific Hypnotherapy 1975; Acad. of Orthomolecular Psychiatry, Charter Member 1971; Int'l Assoc. of Clinical Hypnotherapy 1975 **PROFESSIONAL MEMBERSHIPS:** Assoc. Humanistic Psy.; American Health Counselors Assoc.; American Assoc. of Sex Educators, Counselors & Therapists; Int'l Assoc. of Spiritual Psy. **PUBLICATIONS:** *Hypnotherapy In Review* **PUBLISHER:** Academy of Scientific Hypnotherapy **PUBLICATIONS:** *Mental Mittens Of Repression*, 1971 **PUBLISHER:** Hypnosis Today **PUBLICATIONS:** *Neuro-Surgical Recovery With Hypnosis*, 1974 **PUBLISHER:** Journal of Suggestive

Theraputics **PUBLICATIONS**: *Dynamics Of Obesity & Weight Control*, 1977 **PUBLISHER**: Journal of Hypnotherapy

Kenn, Marion
Society For Clinical & Experimental Hypnosis
111 North 49th Street
Philadelphia, PA 19139
(215)-472-1055

TOPICS: Hypnotism

Kenn, Marion
Society For Clinical & Experimental Hypnosis
129-A Kings Park Drive
Liverpool, NY 13088
(315)-652-7299

TOPICS: Hypnotism

Kenny, Mary
1363 West 15th Street
North Vancouver
British Colombia V7P1N1,
Canada

TOPICS: Channeling

Kerr, Reverend Sharami
Box 17, Route 212
Bearsville, NY 12409
(914)-679-5439

TOPICS: Crystals

Keyes, Ken, Jr.
Ken Keyes Center
790 Commercial Avenue
Coos Bay, OR 97420
(503)-267-6412

TOPICS: Holistic Healing **DATE OF BIRTH**: 01/01/21 **PLACE OF BIRTH**: Atlanta, GA **OCCUPATION**: Teacher, Author **WORK EXPERIENCE**: Ken Keyes College, Coos Bay, OR, Founder **DESCRIPTION**: Dedicated to the study & understanding of the science of happiness, personal growth, attainment of higher consciousness, health, loving relationshhips & world harmony. Offers seminars based on his writings. **PUBLICATIONS**: *How To Develop Your Thinking Ability* **PUBLICATIONS**: *How To Live Longer-Stronger-Slimmer* **PUBLICATIONS**: *Handbook To Higher Consciousness* **PUBLICATIONS**: *Discovering The Secrets Of Happiness*, 1989 **PUBLICATIONS**: *The Hundredth Monkey*, 1982 **PUBLICATIONS**: *Loving Your Body*, 1974

Keyte, Geoffrey
Crystal Research Foundation
37 Bromley Road
St. Annes-On-Sea, Lancs FY8 1PQ
England

TOPICS: Crystals

Khalsa, Guru Atma K.
Deva Crystal
1121 Jackson Boulevard
Houston, TX 77006
(713)-521-2283

TOPICS: Crystals

Khalsa, Guruchander Singh
GRD Health Clinic
301 East Palace
Santa Fe, NM 87501
(505)-984-0934

TOPICS: Holistic Healing

Khalsa, Sat Kartar S.
Deva Crystal
1121 Jackson Boulevard
Houston, TX 77006
(713)-521-2283

TOPICS: Crystals

Khalsa, Siri Radha Kaur
Objects D'Art And Spirit
370-1/2 North La Cienega Boulevard
Los Angeles, CA 90048
(213)-935-5517

TOPICS: Crystals

Khan, Pir Vilayat Inayat
Sufi Order In The West
R.R. #1
P.O. Box 1030 D
New Lebanon, NY 12125
(518)-794-8090

TOPICS: New Age, Holistic Health, Spirituality **DESCRIPTION**: Founder of the Abode Of The Message in 1910. Presents teachings of the Sufi Order furthering respect for all religions & all life. Devoted to the holistic health movement & healing. **PUBLICATIONS**: *Toward The One*, 1974 **PUBLICATIONS**: *The Message In Our Time*, 1978 **PUBLICATIONS**: *New Age Meditations*, 1972 **PUBLICATIONS**: *Transformation*, 1980

Kibble, Charles
British Columbia Chiropractic Association
106-133 West 15th Street
North Vancouver, Br V7M 1R8
Canada
(604)-980-4223

TOPICS: Holistic Healing

Kiever, Linda
4982 Shoreline Loop North
Keizer, OR 97303
(503)-393-9653

TOPICS: Crystals

Kiewe, Howard
Health Training Group
3789 Hampton Avenue
Montreal, Qu H4A 2K7
Canada
(514)-485-6373

TOPICS: Holistic Healing

King, Dr. George
Aetherius Society
6202 Afton Place
Hollywood, CA 90028-8298
(213)-465-9652

TOPICS: Psychic Phenomena

King, Jonathan F.
Sierra Club
730 Polk Street
San Francisco, CA 94109
(415)-776-2211

TOPICS: Holistic Healing

King, Rey
Cosmic Circus Productions
411 28th Street
Oakland, CA 94609

(415)-451-5818

TOPICS: UFO's, Occult, Parapsychology, Witchcraft, Ghosts, Voudoun, Paganism **PLACE OF BIRTH**: Berkeley, CA **OCCUPATION**: Author, Publisher, Cartoonist, Occult Researcher **WORK EXPERIENCE**: Cosmic Circus Productions, Berkeley, CA, Publisher 1973 to present; Humanist Newsletter, Oakland, CA, Editor 1989-91 **AWARDS**: C.C.L.M. Grant Award 1979-80 **PROFESSIONAL MEMBERSHIPS**: Fellowship of Humanity, Vice-Pres. 1989-90; Artist Network, East Bay, Founder 1979 **PUBLICATIONS**: *The Last American Novel*, 1985 **PUBLISHER**: Cosmic Circus Productions **PUBLICATIONS**: *Cosmic Circus Magazine*, 1974-84 **PUBLICATIONS**: *The Universal Game*, 1991 **PUBLISHER**: Cosmic Circus Productions **PUBLICATIONS**: *Spirit Magazine*, 1990 **PUBLISHER**: Cosmic Circus Productions

Kinkade, Kat
Twin Oaks Community
Box 169
Route 4
Louisa, VA 23093
(703)-894-5126

TOPICS: New Age

Kinsman, Warren
Washington Astrology Service
P.O. Box 6731
Washington, D.C. 20020
(202)-581-1303 (202)-575-0098

TOPICS: Astrology, Metaphysics **DATE OF BIRTH**: 04/09/37 **PLACE OF BIRTH**: Springfield, MA **EDUCATION**: Syracuse University, Syracuse, NY **YEARS**: 1956-59 **DEGREE**: B.A. **YEAR DEGREE**: 1959 **OCCUPATION**: Astrologer, Author, Lecturer **WORK EXPERIENCE**: Washington Astrology Service, Washington, D.C., Director **PROFESSIONAL MEMBERSHIPS**: National Council for Geocosmic Research, Board Member, 1990 **PUBLICATIONS**: *Astrology & The Bible*, 1988 **PUBLISHER**: NCGR Journal

Kipnis, Hawk
Sweetwater Gardens Hot Tub & Sauna Spa
Box 337
Mendocino, CA 95460
(707)-937-4140

TOPICS: Holistic Healing, Massage

Kipp, Sarah
Gardom Lake International Earth Friendship Center
Twin Island Resort
P.O. Box 7
Salmon Arm, Br V1E 4N2
Canada
(604)-838-7587

TOPICS: Holistic Healing

Kirby, Lynda
Poster Market Research
725 Pinon Drive
Santa Fe, NM 87501
(505)-989-8500 (505)-473-4236

TOPICS: New Age, Tarot, Psychic **DATE OF BIRTH**: 09/05/61 **PLACE OF BIRTH**: Elyria, OH **EDUCATION**: Marshall University **YEARS**: 1979-81 **OCCUPATION**: Research Associate in Marketing **WORK EXPERIENCE**: Poster Market Research, Santa Fe, NM **PROFESSIONAL MEMBERSHIPS**: Chamber of Commerce, Santa Fe, NM

DESCRIPTION: Research Associate, Associate Director & Instructor for New Age Marketing Skills. Develops marketing strategies for New Age business.

Kirchheimer, Sid
Rodale Press, Inc.
33 East Minor Street
Emmaus, PA 18049
(215)-967-5171

TOPICS: Holistic Healing

Klausner, Warren
Crystal Consciousness
P.O. Box 714, Department C-2
Claremont, CA 91711

TOPICS: Crystals

Kleinknecht, C. Fred
Supreme Council 33rd Degree A
1733 16th Street, N.W.
Washington, DC 20009
(202)-232-3579

TOPICS: New Age

Kleinmann, Hank
Bertha v. Suttnerstr. 15
1037 L E Haarlem,
Holland

TOPICS: Crystals

Klimo, Jon
Jeremy P. Tarcher, Inc.
9110 Sunset Boulevard, Ste. 250
Los Angeles, CA 90069
(213)-273-3274

TOPICS: New Age

Klinger, Eric
Divison of Social Sciences-Psychology
University of Minnesota
Morris, MN 56267
(612)-589-6209 (612)-589-1023

TOPICS: Psychology, Dreams, New Age **DATE OF BIRTH:** 05/23/33 **PLACE OF BIRTH:** Vienna, Austria **EDUCATION:** Harvard University, Cambridge, MA **YEARS:** 1950-54 **DEGREE:** A.B. **YEAR DEGREE:** 1954 **EDUCATION:** University of Chicago, Chicago, IL **YEARS:** 1954-60 **DEGREE:** Ph. D. **YEAR DEGREE:** 1960 **OCCUPATION:** Professor of Psychology-Personality & Clinical **WORK EXPERIENCE:** University of Minnesota, Morris, MN, Professor 1962-present; University of Minnesota, Minneapolis, MN, Professosr 1978-present; University of Wisconsin, Madison, WI, Instructor 1960-62 **AWARDS:** Morse-Amoco Award 1972; MN Psychological Assoc. 1990 Outstanding Undergraduate Teacher of Psychology; Fulbright Senior Scholar 1975-75 **PROFESSIONAL MEMBERSHIPS:** Fellow, American Assoc, for the Advancement of Science; Fellow, American Psychological Assoc.; Fellow, American Psychological Society; American Assoc. for the Study of Mental Imagery, President 1981-82. **PUBLICATIONS:** *Daydreaming: Your Hidden Resource For Self-Knowledge & Creativity*, 1990 **PUBLISHER:** Jeremy P. Tarcher, Inc. **PUBLICATIONS:** *Meaning & Void:Inner Experience & the Incentives In People's Lives*, 1977 **PUBLISHER:** University of Minnesota Press **PUBLICATIONS:** *Structure & Function of Fantasy*, 1971 **PUBLISHER:** John Wiley & Sons

PUBLICATIONS: *Imagery (Vol.2): Concepts, Results & Applications*, 1981, editor **PUBLISHER:** Plenum

Knight, J.Z.
P.O. Box 1210
Yelm, WA 98597

TOPICS: Channeling, Psychic **DATE OF BIRTH:** 03/16/46 **PLACE OF BIRTH:** Dexter, NM **OCCUPATION:** Channel, Medium **DESCRIPTION:** Channel & medium of the entity Ramtha. Also founder of Sovereignty, Inc., a non-profit organization which publishes the Ramtha books, cassettes & videotapes & schedules appearances for Channel, Knight. **PUBLICATIONS:** *A State Of Mind*, 1987 **PUBLISHER:** Sovereignty, Inc. **PUBLICATIONS:** *Windwords...Ideas Foir Awakening Masters* **PUBLISHER:** Windworks

Knight, Vikki
Crystal Quest, The
7142 Glasgow Avenue
Los Angeles, CA 90045-2208
(213)-649-1419

TOPICS: Crystals

Knoche, Grace
Theosophical University Press
Bin C
Pasadena, CA 91109
(818)-798-3378

TOPICS: New Age

Knopf, Allison
Business Research Publications, Inc.
817 Broadway
New York, NY 10003
(212)-673-4700

TOPICS: Holistic Healing

Kok Sui, Choa
855 Pasay Road, Cor. Amorsolo Street
Makati 1200
Metro Manila,
Philippines
818-1568,1465

TOPICS: Holistic Health, New Age, Meditation, Spirituality, Holistic Healing, Psychology **OCCUPATION:** Master Pranic Healer **PUBLICATIONS:** *Pranic Healing* **PUBLISHER:** Samuel Weiser **PUBLICATIONS:** *The Ancient Science & Art of Pranic Healing*, 1987 **PUBLICATIONS:** *The Ancient Science & Art of Pranic Psychotherapy*, 1989

Koltuv, Barbara Black, Ph. D.
2 Fifth Avenue
New York, NY 10011
(212)-982-6707

TOPICS: Spirituality, Body-Mind Connection, Crystals, Psychology **PLACE OF BIRTH:** New York, NY **EDUCATION:** Columbia University, New York, NY **DEGREE:** Ph.D.-Clinical Psychology **YEAR DEGREE:** 1962 **EDUCATION:** N.Y.U., New York, NY **DEGREE:** Post Doct Psychoanalysis **YEAR DEGREE:** 1969 **EDUCATION:** C.G. Jung Institute, New York, NY **DEGREE:** Diplomate **YEAR DEGREE:** 1978 **OCCUPATION:** Clinical Psychologist, Jungian Analyst, Teacher, Lecturer, Author **WORK EXPERIENCE:** C.G. Jung Institute, New York, NY, Faculty Member, Training Analyst, Former Board Member **PROFESSIONAL**

MEMBERSHIPS: New York Association of Analytic Psychology; Analytic Psychology Club-Referring Analyst; American Psychological Association **DESCRIPTION:** Jungian analyst & lecturer in Feminine Psychology, Lilith, Solomon and Sheba, and Amulets, Talismans and Magical Jewelry. **PUBLICATIONS:** *Book of Lilith* (1986) **PUBLISHER:** Nicolas-Hays, Samuel Weiser **PUBLICATIONS:** *Weaving Woman* (1990) **PUBLISHER:** Nicolas - Hays, Samuel Weiser **PUBLICATIONS:** *Solomon and Sheba-The Hearts Journey: A Love Story* (1991) **PUBLISHER:** Nicolas-Hays, Samuel Weiser **PUBLICATIONS:** *Amulets, Talismans, and Magical Jewelry*

Komar, Anne C.
P.O. Box 31776
Omaha, NE 68132
(402)-558-4477

TOPICS: Crystals

Konicov, Barrie
Potentials Unlimited
3659 Cortez Road West #110
Bardenton, FL 34210-3106

TOPICS: New Age

Koob, Richard
R.R. 2
Box 4500
Kalapana Bcach, HI 96778
(808)-965-7828 (808)-965-8716

TOPICS: Holistic Healing, Vegetarianism, Meditation, Tai Chi, Spirituality, Yoga **DATE OF BIRTH:** 07/05/46 **PLACE OF BIRTH:** Iona, MN **EDUCATION:** Albrect Ludwig U., Freiburg, Germany **YEARS:** 1965-69 **DEGREE:** B.A. Math & Literature **YEAR DEGREE:** 1969 **EDUCATION:** University of Hawaii, Honolulu, HI **YEARS:** 1978-79 **DEGREE:** M.F.A. Dance & Drama **YEAR DEGREE:** 1979 **OCCUPATION:** Author, Administrator & Director, Lecturer **WORK EXPERIENCE:** Hawaii State Foundation On Culture And The Arts, Honolulu, HI, Arts Coordinator, 2 years; Kalani Honua Conference Center & Retreat, Pahoa, HI, Director & Founder, 10 years **PROFESSIONAL MEMBERSHIPS:** International Association of Conference Center Administrators **PUBLICATIONS:** *Modern Dance Pioneers*, 1980 **PUBLISHER:** Performing Arts Review

Koorbatoff, Robert
Emerald Enlightenment Services
3369 Flagstaff Place
Vancouver BC, V5S 4K9
Canada
(604)-433-0447

TOPICS: Crystals

Kossy, Donna
Out-Of-Kontrol Data Korporation
P.O. Box 953
Allston, MA 02134

TOPICS: Occult

Koury, George
1211 Smith Ridge Road
New Canaan, CT 06840
(203)-966-2608

TOPICS: Reiki **DESCRIPTION:** Traditional Reiki Master, psychotherapist and esoteric consultant teaching and practicing the reiki method of healing.

Kraig, Donald Michael
Llewellyn Publications
P.O. Box 64383
St. Paul, MN 55101-0856
(612)-291-1970

TOPICS: New Age, Occult, Kabbalah, Spirituality, Psychic, Paranormal Phenomena, Tarot DATE OF BIRTH: 03/28/51 PLACE OF BIRTH: Chicago, IL EDUCATION: U. of CA, Los Angeles, CA DEGREE: B.A. Philosophy YEAR DEGREE: 1974 OCCUPATION: Editor, Author, Lecturer WORK EXPERIENCE: Llewellyn Publications, St. Paul, MN, Editor 4 years; Fate Magazine, St. Paul, MN, Editor-in-Chief 1989-Pres.; New Times Magazine/Catalog, St. Paul, MN, Editor-in-Chief 1986-1988 PROFESSIONAL MEMBERSHIPS: Academy of Magical Arts and Sciences, 1975-present DESCRIPTION: Certified Tarot Master. Gives private Tarot Readings at psychic fairs. Taught classes on psychic development, mysticism, magick, Tarot, Kabalah, & Tantra. Hosts a radio program, The Fate Magazine Radio Hour & writes the column, I See By The Papers. PUBLICATIONS: *Modern Magick: Eleven Lessons In The High Magickal Art*, 1988 PUBLISHER: Llewellyn Publications PUBLICATIONS: *Fate Magazine*, editor, 1989-present PUBLISHER: Llewellyn Publications PUBLICATIONS: *New Times*, editor, 1986-89 PUBLISHER: Llewellyn Publications

Kramer, Carol
Body, Mind & Spirit Magazine
Box 701
Providence, RI 02901
(401)-351-4320 (401)-726-6943

TOPICS: New Age, Spirituality DATE OF BIRTH: 12/08/50 PLACE OF BIRTH: Putnam, CT EDUCATION: Rhode Island College, Providence, RI DEGREE: B.A. Anthropology YEAR DEGREE: 1987 OCCUPATION: Editor, Author WORK EXPERIENCE: Body, Mind & Spirit Magazine, Providence, RI, Editor AWARDS: National Junior Honor Society, Rhode Island Honor Society PUBLICATIONS: *The New Age Catalogue*, editor, 1988 PUBLISHER: Doubleday PUBLICATIONS: *The Magic Man*, 1990 PUBLISHER: Roaring Lion Publishing

Krantz, Larry
Whole Health Institute
4817 North County Road 29
Loveland, CO 80537
(303)-679-4306

TOPICS: Holistic Healing

Krastman, Dr. Hank, Ph. D.
Krastman Productions, Inc.
P.O. Box 16790
Encino, CA 91416
(818)-705-8865

TOPICS: Metaphysics, New Age

Krefft, Katherine, Ph. D.
Transpersonal Psychologis
2245 College Drive, Suite 80
Baton Rouge, LA 70808

TOPICS: Channeling

Krive, Taryn
P.O. Box 6026-425
Sherman Oaks, CA 91413
(818)-995-8081

TOPICS: Crystals, Channeling

Kronemeyer, Dr. Robert
New Horizon Health And Tennis Spa
Major's Path
Southampton, NY 11968
(516)-283-5444

TOPICS: Holistic Healing

Kronenthal, Myrna B.
319 East 24th Street
New York, NY 10010
(212)-679-9298

TOPICS: Parapsychology, Psychic, Psychic Healing, Spirituality, Channeling DATE OF BIRTH: 01/23/42 PLACE OF BIRTH: New York, NY EDUCATION: Brooklyn College, Brooklyn, NY YEARS: 2 years EDUCATION: City College of New York, NY YEARS: 3 years OCCUPATION: Spiritual Counselor, Healer WORK EXPERIENCE: Myrna Belle, New York, NY, Founder PROFESSIONAL MEMBERSHIPS: Association of Research & Enlightenment; Psychic Guild of N.J. & N.Y.

Krulick, Dianne
Kryolux, Incorporated
27 Hickory Street
Ellenville, NY 12428
(914)-647-8809

TOPICS: Crystals

Krulick, Steven
Kryolux, Incorporated
27 Hickory Street
Ellenville, NY 12428
(914)-647-8809

TOPICS: Crystals

Krysnal
1924 Beverly Hills
Norman, OK 73069

TOPICS: Channeling

Kubler-Ross, Elisabeth, M.D.
The Elisabeth Kubler-Ross Center/Shanti Nilaya
South Route 616
Headwaters, VA 24442
(703)-396-3441

TOPICS: Holistic Healing

Kulvinskas, Viktoras
21st Century Publications
P.O. Box 255
Wethersfield, CT 06109
(515)-472-5105

TOPICS: New Age, Health Food, Vegetarianism, Holistic Health, Nutrition, Herbalogy, Homeopathy DATE OF BIRTH: 02/26/39 PLACE OF BIRTH: Lithuania EDUCATION: University of Connecticut, Storrs, CT DEGREE: M.S. OCCUPATION: Lecturer, Author in Health Field PUBLICATIONS: *Survival Into The 21st Century* (1975) PUBLISHER: 21st Century Publications PUBLICATIONS: *Love Your Body* (1972) PUBLISHER: 21st Century Publications

Kunkin, Arthur
Elysium Institute, Inc.
814 Robinson Road
Topanga, CA 90290
(213)-455-1000

TOPICS: New Age

Kunz, Katharine
Chestnut Hill, Inc.
P.O. Box 454
R.R.1
Gormley, On L0H 1G0
Canada
(416)-888-1231

TOPICS: Holistic Healing

Kupelian, David
Foundation Of Human Understanding
P.O. Box 811
Grants Pass, OR 97526
(503)-479-0549

TOPICS: Holistic Healing

Kupsinel, Roy, M.D.
Lost Horizon Health Awareness Center
Box 550
Oviedo, FL 32765
(407)-365-6681

TOPICS: Holistic Healing

Kurban, Michael J.
New Age Psychic Center
4328 North Lincoln Avenue
Chicago, IL 60618-1712
(312)-478-2410

TOPICS: Astrology, Spirituality, Holistic Health, Crystals, Numerology, Herbalogy OCCUPATION: Numerologist, Author, Lecturer, Psychic, Past Life Reader, TV Host, Teacher, Counselor WORK EXPERIENCE: New Age Psychic Center, Chicago, IL, Dir.; Mike Kurban Psychic Show, Chicago, IL, Host; Libra Press, Chicago, IL, Author, Publisher; Spiritual Museum, Chicago, IL, Curator PUBLICATIONS: *Universal Secrets* PUBLISHER: Libra Press PUBLICATIONS: *Life After Death* PUBLISHER: Libra Press PUBLICATIONS: *Face & Body Language* PUBLISHER: Libra Press PUBLICATIONS: *Psychic Training* PUBLISHER: Libra Press

Kushi, Michio
Kushi Institute
62 Buckminster Road
Brookline, MA 02146
(617)-232-6876

TOPICS: Vegetarianism, Holistic Health, Nutrition, Spirituality, Health Food, New Age, Homeopathy DATE OF BIRTH: 05/17/26 PLACE OF BIRTH: Wakayama-Ken, Japan EDUCATION: Tokyo University, Tokyo, Japan DEGREE: M.A. Law EDUCATION: Columbia University, New York, NY DEGREE: M.A. Political Science OCCUPATION: Teacher, Author WORK EXPERIENCE: Kushi Institute, Becket, MA, Founder; Tokyo University, Tokyo, Japan, Faculty Member PROFESSIONAL MEMBERSHIPS: Windstar, Advisory Board; Earthsave, Advisory Board DESCRIPTION: Expert in macrobiotics. Also promote the use of acupuncture & acupressure. Founder of the East West Foundation, The East West Journal & The Order of the Universe magazine. PUBLICATIONS: *Other Dimenions: Exploring The Unexplained* PUBLISHER: Avery Publishing Group, Inc. PUBLICATIONS: *Macrobiotic Home Remedies*, 1985 PUBLISHER: Japan Publications, Inc. PUBLICATIONS: *Natural Healing Through Macrobiotics*, 1979 PUBLISHER: Japan Publications, Inc. PUBLICATIONS: *The Macrobiotic Way Of Healing*, 1978 PUBLISHER: The East West

Foundation **PUBLICATIONS:** *The Book Of DO-IN*, 1979 **PUBLISHER:** Japan Publication, Inc. **PUBLICATIONS:** *The Book Of Macrobiotics:The Universal Way Of Health And Happiness*, 1987 **PUBLISHER:** Japan Publications, Inc.

Kusta, Kathleen
International Graphoanalysis Society
111 North Canal Street, 10th F
Chicago, IL 60606
(312)-930-9446
TOPICS: New Age

La Vey, Anton Szandor
Church Of Satan, Inc.
P.O. Box 210082
San Francisco, CA 94121
(415)-752-3583
TOPICS: Occult

Lad, Dr. Vasant
The Ayurvedic Wellness Center And Institute
11311 Menaul N.E., Suite A
Albuquerque, NM 87112
(505)-291-9698
TOPICS: Holistic Healing

Lafair, Sylvia
Creative Energy Options
909 Sumneytown Pike
Box 603
Springhouse, PA 19477
(215)-643-4420
TOPICS: Holistic Healing

Laing, Betty
Cosmoenergetics Publications
P.O. Box 86353
San Diego, CA 92138
(619)-295-1664
TOPICS: Metaphysics

Lalitananda, Swami
Yoga Research Foundation
6111 SW 74th Avenue
Miami, FL 33143
(305)-595-5580
TOPICS: Yoga

Lamb, Laurie
135 Ocean Parkway
Brooklyn, NY 11218
TOPICS: Channeling

Lamkin, John Patrick
Paloma Blanca Press
P.O. Box 1751
Taos, NM 87571
(505)-751-2169
TOPICS: New Age **OCCUPATION:** Editor **WORK EXPERIENCE:** Paloma Blanca Press, Taos, NM, Editor **PUBLICATIONS:** *Self-Publishing In The New Age* **PUBLISHER:** Paloma Blanca Press

Lancaster, Dianne
American Institute Of Metaphysics
2000 L Street N.W.,
Suite 200
Washington, DC 20036
(202)-659-0689
TOPICS: Holistic Healing

Landsman, Dr. Sandra G.
Treehouse Enterprises
P.O. Box 7134
Jupiter, FL 33468-7134
(407)-575-0547 (407)-575-0547
TOPICS: New Age, Psychology **OCCUPATION:** Psychologist, Transactional Analyst, Teacher, Counsellor, Consultant, Author, Audio Producer, Lecturer **WORK EXPERIENCE:** Treehouse Enterprises, Jupiter, FL, Publisher **PROFESSIONAL MEMBERSHIPS:** Clinical Teaching Membership in International Transactional Analysis Assoc.; American Assoc. of Counseling Development; National Speakers Assoc.; Pre & Perinatal Psychology Assoc. of North America **DESCRIPTION:** Psychologist & Transactional Analyst specializing in the development of healing techniques to resolve disorders such as AquaGenesis & Prenatal Regressive Therapy. Conducts seminars & workshops such as Past Life; Flight Of The Spirit; Down To Earth. **PUBLICATIONS:** *I'm Special: An Experiential Workbook For The Child In Us All* **PUBLISHER:** Treehouse Enterprises **PUBLICATIONS:** *Found: A Place For Me* **PUBLISHER:** Treehouse Enterprises

Lang, Debra
Center For The Well-Being Of Health Professionals
5102 Chapel Hill Boulevard
Durham, NC 27707
(919)-489-9167
TOPICS: Holistic Healing

Lang, Fraser
Manisses Communications Group, Inc.
3 Governor Street
Providence, RI 02906
(401)-831-6020
TOPICS: Holistic Healing

Lang, Gayle
Health Training Group
3789 Hampton Avenue
Montreal, Qu H4A 2K7
Canada
(514)-485-6373
TOPICS: Holistic Healing

Lang, Janet
Whole Health Institute
4817 North County Road 29
Loveland, CO 80537
(303)-679-4306
TOPICS: Holistic Healing

Lang, Sally
Meridian Holistic Health Centre, Inc.
5575 West Saanich Road
R.R.5
Victoria, BC V8X 4M6
Canada
(604)-727-3451
TOPICS: Holistic Healing

Lang-Wescott, Martha
Treehouse Mountain
Reeds Bridge Road
Conway, MA 01341
(413)-369-4680
TOPICS: Astrology, Metaphysics **OCCUPATION:** Astrologer, Lecturer, Editor, Author **PROFESSIONAL MEMBERSHIPS:** NCGR, member

DESCRIPTION: Offers workshops, lectures & readings in Astrology with an emphasis on the 38 asteroids in natal & forecast charts. **PUBLICATIONS:** *The Mechanics Of Free Will*, 1988 **PUBLISHER:** Treehouse Mountain **PUBLICATIONS:** *Mechanics Of The Future: Asteroids*, 1989 **PUBLISHER:** Treehouse Mountain **PUBLICATIONS:** *Asteroid Mechanics, Vol I*, editor, 1990 **PUBLISHER:** Treehouse Mountain **PUBLICATIONS:** *Tools Of The Trade Newsletter*, editor, monthly

Lange, Ed
Elysium Institute, Inc.
814 Robinson Road
Topanga, CA 90290
(213)-455-1000
TOPICS: New Age

Langevin, Michael Peter
Magical Blend Magazine
P.O. Box 421130
San Francisco, CA 94142
(415)-673-1001 (415)-282-9776
TOPICS: Psychic Phenomena, Metaphysics, Witchcraft, Occult, Meditation, New Age **DATE OF BIRTH:** 12/30/52 **PLACE OF BIRTH:** Lawrence, MA **EDUCATION:** University of Massachusettes, Somerville, MA **DEGREE:** B.A. **YEAR DEGREE:** 1975 **OCCUPATION:** Publisher, Editor, Author, Lecturer **WORK EXPERIENCE:** Magical Blend Magazine, San Francisco, CA, Publisher, Editor **PUBLICATIONS:** *Magical Blend Magazine : A Transformative Journey* **PUBLISHER:** Magical Blend

Lanteri, Azarra
Global Vision TV & Radio Productions
1017 South Van Ness Avenue
San Francisco, CA 94110
(415)-647-6374
TOPICS: New Age **EDUCATION:** U. of PA. at West Chester, PA **DEGREE:** B.A. **EDUCATION:** N.Y.U. Film Institue, New York, NY **EDUCATION:** Lee Strasberg Actors' Studio, New York, NY **OCCUPATION:** TV Producer, TV Host **WORK EXPERIENCE:** Global Vision, San Francisco, CA, Producer, Host **DESCRIPTION:** Hosts & Produces: Global Vision, a weekly 1/2 hr. New Age program; World Service Forum, features groups who work to improve the world through understanding & good will; & Women Of The Americas, focuses on the impact of Latin American women in the U.S.

Larke, Kit
Sprouting Publications
Box 62
Ashland, OR 97520
(503)-488-2326
TOPICS: Holistic Healing

Larkin, Dr. Judith, Ph.D.
Gateway Community
7619 Romeria Street
Rancho La Costa, CA 92008
TOPICS: Crystals

Larkins, Caryl
Double D Ranch
Star Route
Box 14
Caliente, CA 93518
(213)-434-3453

TOPICS: Holistic Healing

Laske, Margaret
Holistic Learning Place
Box 86054
Pittsburgh, PA 15221
(412)-731-5533

TOPICS: Holistic Healing

Laskow, Leonard, M.D.
172 Lark Lane
Mill Valley, CA 94941
(415)-381-5000

TOPICS: Crystals

Latham, Rev. May Lou
4828 Abbott Avenue
Arlington, TX 76018
(817)-467-3426

TOPICS: Holistic Healing, Holistic Health **DESCRIPTION:** Spiritual healer/counselor, lecturer offering subtle energy & phone consultations.

Latour, Dan
National Alliance For Spiritual Growth
P.O. Box 2683
Lafayette, LA 70502
(318)-235-6535

TOPICS: Metaphysics, Astrology, Numerology, Spirituality, Body-Mind Connection, Meditation, New Age **DATE OF BIRTH:** 09/23/52 **PLACE OF BIRTH:** Lafayette, LA **EDUCATION:** Congregational Church Of Practical Theology, LA **DEGREE:** Ordained **YEAR DEGREE:** 1984 **EDUCATION:** National Alliance For Spiritual Growth, Lafayette **DEGREE:** Transpersonal Counselor **YEAR DEGREE:** 1986 **OCCUPATION:** Transpersonal Counselor, Minister, Hypnotherapist, Author **WORK EXPERIENCE:** National Alliance For Spiritual Growth, Lafayette, LA, Founder, Co-Dir, Transpersonal Counselor 1986-present; The Tower Group, Inc., Lafayette, LA, Counselor, Hypnotherapist **AWARDS:** St. John's U., Certified Hypnotherapist 1990 **PUBLICATIONS:** *Life, Love and Growth*, 1991 **PUBLISHER:** National Alliance For Spiritual Growth **PUBLICATIONS:** *Charting & Interpreting For Astrology & Numerology*, 1990 **PUBLISHER:** National Alliance For Spiritual Growth **PUBLICATIONS:** *Rays Of Light*, 1986 **PUBLISHER:** National Alliance For Spiritual Growth **PUBLICATIONS:** *Guide To Charting Astrology & Numerology*, 1990 **PUBLISHER:** National Alliance For Spiritual Growth

Latour, Missy
Within & Beyond
P.O. Box 2683
Lafayette, LA 70502
(318)-237-0611

TOPICS: Metaphysics

Lauck, M.
1036 Pine Avenue
San Jose, CA 95125
(408)-264-4970 (408)-264-4970

TOPICS: Spirituality, Dreams, Holistic Health **DATE OF BIRTH:** 02/13/50 **PLACE OF BIRTH:** Pittsburgh, PA **EDUCATION:** Pennsylvania State University, State College, PA **YEARS:** 1968-1971 **DEGREE:** B.A. **YEAR DEGREE:** 1971 **OCCUPATION:** Spiritual Director, Dream Analysis, Ceremonials **WORK EXPERIENCE:** Four Circles Foundation, San

Jose, CA, Director 1976-90, Lecturer on Dreamtime **PROFESSIONAL MEMBERSHIPS:** Association For The Study Of Dreams **PUBLICATIONS:** *At The Pool Of Wonder: Dreams & Visions Of An Awakening Humanity* (1989) **PUBLISHER:** Bear & Co., Inc.

Laughlin, Charles, Ph. D.
Dept. of Sociology-Anthropology
Carleton University
Ottawa K1S 5B6
Canada
(613)-788-2582 (819)-459-1121

TOPICS: New Age, Spirituality **DATE OF BIRTH:** 07/25/38 **PLACE OF BIRTH:** Swampscott, MA **EDUCATION:** San Francisco State College, San Francisco, CA **YEARS:** 1963-66 **DEGREE:** B.A. **YEAR DEGREE:** 1966 **EDUCATION:** University of Oregon, Eugene, OR **YEARS:** 1966-72 **DEGREE:** Ph. D. **YEAR DEGREE:** 1972 **OCCUPATION:** Neuroanthropologist, Professor, Author **WORK EXPERIENCE:** SUNY- Oswego, Oswego, NY, Assoc. Professor of Anthropology 1970-76; Carleton University, Ottawa, Canada, Professor of Anthropology 1976-present **AWARDS:** Senior Fellow, Institute of Neurological Sciences, U of PA, 1973-74 **PROFESSIONAL MEMBERSHIPS:** Buddhist Monk, Sakya Tradition, Tibetan Vajrayana 1978-85 **PUBLICATIONS:** *Brain, Symbol & Experience*, 1990 **PUBLISHER:** Shambhala Publications, Inc. **PUBLICATIONS:** *Spectrum Of Ritual*, 1979 **PUBLISHER:** Columbia University Press

Lauren, Phoebe
Center For Attitudinal Healing
19 Main Street
Tiburon, CA 94920
(415)-435-5022

TOPICS: Holistic Healing

Lawton, H. Cranston
Wellness Councils Of America
1823 Harney Street, # 201
Omaha, NE 68102
(402)-444-1711

TOPICS: Holistic Healing

Layne, Penny
Hollywood Crystal Connection
1400 Talmadge Street
Los Angeles, CA 49684
(213)-664-7788

TOPICS: Crystals

Lazarus, Pat
Keats Publishing, Inc.
27 Pine Street
P.O. Box 876
New Canaan, CT 06840
(203)-966-8721

TOPICS: Holistic Healing

Leachman, Cloris
10390 Santa Monica Boulevard, #310
Los Angeles, CA 90025

TOPICS: New Age, Vegetarianism, Holistic Health **DATE OF BIRTH:** 06/30/30 **PLACE OF BIRTH:** Des Moines, IA **OCCUPATION:** Actress, Health Advocate **DESCRIPTION:** Supporter of the New Age movement. Advocate of holistic health, vegetarianism & animal rights.

Learman, Rev. Kinzan

M.O.B.C.
P.O. Box 199
Mt. Shasta, CA 96067
(916)-926-4208

TOPICS: Meditation

Leavy, Hannelore R.
Spa-Finders
784 Broadway
New York, NY 10003
(212)-475-1000

TOPICS: Holistic Health, Massage, Meditation, Body-Mind Connection, New Age **DATE OF BIRTH:** 09/10/42 **PLACE OF BIRTH:** Vienna, Austria **OCCUPATION:** Author, Vice-Pres. of Sales & Marketing **WORK EXPERIENCE:** Spa-Finders, New York, NY, 4 years **DESCRIPTION:** Arranges travel plans for clients to health spas. **PUBLICATIONS:** *The Spa Finder* (1989) **PUBLISHER:** Jeffrey Joseph

Lee, Erma Jean
Universal Faithists Of Kosmon, Inc.
1268 West 10775, South
South Jordan, UT 84065
(801)-254-6903

TOPICS: New Age

Lee, Paul A., Ph. D.
Platonic Academy
Box 409
Santa Cruz, CA 95061
(408)-423-7923

TOPICS: Holistic Healing

Lee, R.E. Mark
Krishnamurti Foundation Of America
Box 1560
Ojai, CA 93023
(805)-646-2726

TOPICS: New Age

Lee, Romi
Miracles Unlimited
81 Central Avenue
Wailuku, Maui, HI 96793
(808)-242-7799

TOPICS: Crystals

Leiva, Margaux A.
Psychic Solutions
6964 West 29 Way
Hialeah Gardens, FL 33016
(305)-826-4781

TOPICS: Astrology, Psychic, Channeling **DATE OF BIRTH:** 08/12/52 **PLACE OF BIRTH:** New York, NY **EDUCATION:** Fashion Institute of Technology, New York, NY **DEGREE:** Retailing-Textiles **YEAR DEGREE:** 1974 **OCCUPATION:** Astrologer, Channeler, Psychic, Author **WORK EXPERIENCE:** Psychic Solutions, Hialeah Gardens, FL., Consultant **AWARDS:** Brian Weiss Workshop 5/90 **PROFESSIONAL MEMBERSHIPS:** Assoc. For Research & Enlightenment, Virginia Beach, VA.; Bureau Of Creativity, Tamarac, FL.

Lemanski, Darlene S.
29318 Bonnie Drive
Warren, MI 48093
(313)-751-3054

TOPICS: Crystals

LeMon, Kay

Sinai Hospital Of Detroit
6767 West Outer Drive
Detroit, MI 48235
(313)-493-5500

TOPICS: Holistic Healing

Lemons, Vanessa
Golden Rose Distributors
P.O. Box 10965
Hilo, HI 96721
(808)-959-3458

TOPICS: Crystals

Lenel, Katherine
The Radiance Technique Association International, Inc.
7 West 87th Street, #4B
New York, NY 10024
(212)-595-1634

TOPICS: Reiki

Leon, Shawn
148 Bismark Avenue
Valley Stream, NY 11581

TOPICS: Parapsychology

LePar, William Allen
SOL
P.O. Box 2276
North Canton, OH 44720

TOPICS: Channeling, Spirituality OCCUPATION: Lecturer, Author, Psychic, Channeler, Counselor WORK EXPERIENCE: SOL, North Canton, OH, Channeler DESCRIPTION: Psychic who channels the words of The Council, 12 entities, while in Deep Catatonic Trance. Conducts Deep Trance sessions privately while publicly doing psychometry, inspirational speaking & psychic counselling. Offers lectures & workshops through SOL. PUBLICATIONS: *Meditation: A Definitive Study* PUBLICATIONS: *Controlling The Creative Process: Androgyny* PUBLICATIONS: *Revelations On Life Everlasting,* co-author

Lerner, Mark
Wholistic Resource Center
Box 5164
Eugene, OR 97405
(503)-683-1760

TOPICS: Astrology

Lester, Joanna
Spectrum Chamber Productions
406 Belford Place
Takoma Park, MD 20912
(301)-891-2079

TOPICS: Crystals

Levic, Jack
P.O. Box 8527
University City, CA 91608-0527

TOPICS: Channeling

Levine, Sandra
House Of Zodiac
Shoppers World
Framingham, WA 02160
(617)-872-7321

TOPICS: Crystals

Levinson, Ann
20 Fifth Avenue

New York, NY 10011

TOPICS: Channeling

Levy, Joan, LCSW
Biofeedback & Family Therapy Institute
2236 Derby Street
Berkeley, CA 94705
(415)-841-7227

TOPICS: Holistic Healing, Psychology OCCUPATION: Psychotherapist, Biofeedback Therapist DESCRIPTION: Uses a biopsychosocial approach to promotes awareness, self-directed growth & improved health through Psychotherapy, stress management, Biofeedback training & Self-Regulation. Trained in Psychodynamic, Gestalt, Bioenergetic & Couples Therapy.

Levy, Rev. Elizabeth Ann, M.S.C., M.S.TH
175 West 13th Street, 4G
New York, NY 10011
(212)-886-9845 (212)-243-0579

TOPICS: Astrology, Tarot, Numerology, Psychic, Graphology, Spirituality, Holistic Health DATE OF BIRTH: 05/26/49 PLACE OF BIRTH: Trenton, NJ EDUCATION: The New Seminary, New York, NY DEGREE: M.S.C., M.S.TH YEAR DEGREE: 1988 EDUCATION: International Graphoanalysis Society, Chicago,IL DEGREE: CGA, MGA YEAR DEGREE: 1987 OCCUPATION: Interfaith Minister, Psychic Spiritual Counselor, Astrologer, Tarot, Handwriting Analyst, Lecturer WORK EXPERIENCE: Interfaith Inc., Interfaith Temple, New York, NY, Associate Interfaith Minister 1987-present; International Graphoanalysis Society, Chicago, IL, Associate Certified Master Graphoanalyst 1987-present AWARDS: Professional Psychics Of America, Certified, 1990; International Graphoanalysis Society, Certified Master Graphoanalyst, 1987-present PROFESSIONAL MEMBERSHIPS: Professional Psychics Of America; International Graphoanalysis Society; Association Of Interfaith Ministers; A.R.E. Member. DESCRIPTION: Conducts readings & counseling which helps individuals understand themselves and develop their own unique potentials in all areas of their lives. Offers guidance in relationships, career, finances, health & personal growth.

Lewis, Diane P., R.N.
Energy Therapeutics
713 Chilberg Avenue
La Conner, WA 98257-8905
(206)-826-3955

TOPICS: Crystals

Lewis, Jay
Manisses Communications Group, Inc.
3 Governor Street
Providence, RI 02906
(401)-831-6020

TOPICS: Holistic Healing

Lewis, John
Gordon & Breach Science Publishers
Box 786
Cooper Station
New York, NY 10276
(212)-206-8900

TOPICS: New Age

Light, Danielle

The Light Blew Inn
200 Sheldon Avenue, #6
Mount Shasta, CA 96067
(916)-926-5653

TOPICS: Holistic Healing

Light, Rick
The Tibetan Foundation
2571 36th Street
Los Alamos, NM 87544

TOPICS: Channeling DESCRIPTION: Certified Channel by The Tibetan Foundation.

Ligon, Linda
Interweave Press, Inc.
306 North Washington Avenue
Loveland, CO 80537
(303)-669-7672

TOPICS: Health Food

Lily, Kirk
Rainbow Path
1195 Wayne Street
Noblesville, IN 46060
(317)-773-5702

TOPICS: Crystals

Linden, Michael
Sprouting Publications
Box 62
Ashland, OR 97520
(503)-488-2326

TOPICS: Holistic Healing

Livingston, Rita
Livingston Tours And Seminars
P.O. Box 908
Black Mountain, NC 28711
(704)-669-9788

TOPICS: Crystals

Livngstone, Tara
Shambhala Healing Centre
Coursing Batch, Glastonbury
Somerset, BA6 8BH
England
0458-31797

TOPICS: Crystals, Holistic Health, Massage OCCUPATION: Massage & Radionic Practitioner, Counselor WORK EXPERIENCE: Shambhala Healing Centre, Somerset, England, Director

Lloyd, Virginia
Sedona Institute
1645 East Missouri, #110, Ste.
Phoenix, AZ 85016
(602)-264-0123

TOPICS: Holistic Healing

Logan, Daniel
Box 12
West Hurley, NY 12491

TOPICS: Channeling

Lombardi, Susana
We Care Health Center
18000 Long Canyon Road
Dept. NAJ
Desert Hot Springs, CA 92240
(619)-251-2261

TOPICS: Holistic Healing

London, Peter
Southeastern MA University
North Dartmouth, MA 02747
(508)-999-8550 (508)-993-0649

TOPICS: Body-Mind Connection, Psychology, New Age DATE OF BIRTH: 06/27/39 PLACE OF BIRTH: New York, NY EDUCATION: Queens College, New York, NY DEGREE: B.A. YEAR DEGREE: 1961 EDUCATION: Columbia University, New York, NY DEGREE: M.F.A. Painting YEAR DEGREE: 1962 EDUCATION: Columbia University Teachers College, New York, NY DEGREE: Ed. D. YEAR DEGREE: 1968 OCCUPATION: Professor, Author WORK EXPERIENCE: Southeastern MA University, N. Dartmouth, MA, Professor of Art Education & Art Therapy, 19 years PROFESSIONAL MEMBERSHIPS: National Art Education Assoc.; American Art Therapy Assoc.;International Assoc. of Education Through Art; Mass. Art Education Assoc. PUBLICATIONS: *Beyond Discipline Based Art Education*, editor, 1987

Long, Bernie
Walk The Rainbow
1281 Grubstake Circle
Billings, MT 59105
(406)-252-8108

TOPICS: Crystals, Channeling

Long, Gary
Rt. 3
Box 308
Hillsboro, OR 97124
(503)-647-5722

TOPICS: Reiki DESCRIPTION: Practices the Reiki Natural Healing Method to promote the healing of body, mind and spirit.

Long, George
Walk The Rainbow
1281 Grubstake Circle
Billings, MT 59105
(406)-252-8108

TOPICS: Crystals

Long, Joseph K., Ph. D.
Society For The Anthropology Of Consciousness
Social Science Dept., Anthropology
Plymouth State College
Plymouth, NH 03264
(603)-535-2424 (603)-726-4875

TOPICS: Parapsychology, Psychic Phenomena, Holistic Healing, New Age, PSI, Meditation, Spirituality DATE OF BIRTH: 03/31/37 PLACE OF BIRTH: Greenville, KY EDUCATION: University of NC, Chapel Hill, NC YEARS: 1968-70 DEGREE: Ph. D. YEAR DEGREE: 1973 EDUCATION: University of KY, Lexington, KY YEARS: 1962-64 DEGREE: M.S. YEAR DEGREE: 1963 EDUCATION: Southern Methodist University, Dallas, TX YEARS: 1956-59 DEGREE: B.A. YEAR DEGREE: 1959 OCCUPATION: Professor of Anthropology, Medical Authority on Parapsychology, Author WORK EXPERIENCE: Plymouth State College of NH, Plymouth, NH, Assoc. Prof. - Prof. 1974-present; University of CA at Irvine, Irvine, CA, Visiting Prof. 1979-80; Southern Methodist University, Dallas, TX, Asst. Prof 1971-74; University of Wisconsin, Green Bay, WI, Instructor 1966-68; St. Norbert College, Green Bay, WI, Instructor 1966-68 AWARDS: Encyclopedia Britannica Great Books Award 1961;

Who's Who in America 1976 & 1990. PROFESSIONAL MEMBERSHIPS: Pres. Society for the Anthro of Consciousness 1983-85; Editor SAC's Anthro of Consciousness 1990-pres; Pres. Assoc. Transpersonal Anthro 1980-82; Amer Anthro Assoc. Fellow 1966-pres.; Fellow Amer. Assoc./Advanc. of Science 1966-76 PUBLICATIONS: *Extrasensory Ecology: Anthropology & Parapsychology*, 1977 PUBLISHER: Scarecrow Press PUBLICATIONS: *Anthropology Films*, 1967 PUBLISHER: University of Wisconsin PUBLICATIONS: *Jamaican Medicine: Choices Between Folk Healing & Modern Medicine*, 1973 PUBLISHER: University Microfilms PUBLICATIONS: *Anthropology of Consciousness Quarterly*, editor, 1990-present PUBLISHER: Society for the Anthropology of Consciousness

Loomis, Jean
Aquarian Center
116 Montowese Street
Branford, CT 06405

TOPICS: Channeling

Lourie, Iven
Gateways Books And Tapes
P.O. Box 370
Nevada City, CA 95959

TOPICS: New Age

Luce, Gay, Ph.D.
Nine Gates, Inc.
220 Redwood Highway
Suite 61
Mill Valley, CA 94941
(415)-927-1677

TOPICS: Holistic Health DESCRIPTION: Director & master teacher of Nine Gates Mystery School. Teaches the transformative use of psycho-spiritual energies.

Lucia, Bob
New Jersey Chapter
Box 57
Passaic, NJ 07055
(201)-777-8372

TOPICS: Holistic Healing

Luckey, Mrs. Helen L.
Chiropractic News Publishing Company
29229 Six Mile Road
Livonia, MI 48152
(313)-427-5720

TOPICS: Holistic Healing

Ludsdin, Nanci
Blue Dolphin New Age Crystals
108 Rainsford Place
Toronto, ON, M4L 3N9
Canada
(416)-690-1840

TOPICS: Crystals

Lusher, Dr. Leah
2812 North Ocean Boulevard
Ft. Lauderdale, FL 33308
(305)-565-7535

TOPICS: Psychic, Parapsychology, Astrology, Vegetarianism DATE OF BIRTH: 09/30/28 PLACE OF BIRTH: Italy OCCUPATION: Psychic, Parapsychologist, Theosophist, Astropsychologist, Spiritual Counselor WORK EXPERIENCE: Center For Inner Awareness, Ft. Lauderdale, FL, Founder,

Pres. AWARDS: Two-time winner of National Enquirer World Psychic Contest, 1986 & 1991 PROFESSIONAL MEMBERSHIPS: European Academy Of Parapsychology DESCRIPTION: Psychic, Astrologer & Parapsychologist offering Readings in person or by phone. Theosophist who uses an holistic approach & is able to tell what's in a person by reading auras & voice vibrations. Opening another Center For Inner Awareness in NC.

Lynch, Debra A.
75 Bank Street, Ste. 6H
New York, NY 10014
(212)-243-6669

TOPICS: Psychic, Channeling EDUCATION: Fordham University, New York, NY DEGREE: M.A. OCCUPATION: Astrologer, Psychic, Lecturer, Teacher, Author, Consultant PROFESSIONAL MEMBERSHIPS: Founding Member-American Astrological Association DESCRIPTION: Astrologer-Psychic specializing in economic forecasts, money & business predictions. Known as the Wall St. Psychic. Advises prominent business persons, corporations & clients with personal problems. Offers consultations by telephone & a newsletter.

Lynn, Dr. Nina
Heart's Bend
P.O. Box 217
Newfane, VT 05345
(802)-365-7616

TOPICS: Holistic Healing

Lynne, Heather
Hugs Unlimited
Box 4041
Huntington Beach, CA 92605
(714)-530-9918

TOPICS: Holistic Healing

Macauley, Margaret
7 Kings Highway
Warwick, NY 10990

TOPICS: Channeling

MacClellan, Myron
3917 South Fox
Englewood, CO 80110

TOPICS: Channeling

MacDonald, Jeffery
Association For The Anthropological Study Of Consciousn
P.O. Box 4032
Irvine, CA 92716
(503)-257-0942

TOPICS: Metaphysics

MachStorm, Thadaeus A.
United Federation Of Humankind
2505 Paris Avenue
Trevose, PA 19047

TOPICS: Metaphysics EDUCATION: Starhaven Institute YEARS: 1981-1991 DEGREE: Metaphysics OCCUPATION: Reality Consultant in the Financial Clarity Dept. WORK EXPERIENCE: Individuals Against Mediocrity Unlimited, Yuma, AZ, Founder & President Pro Tem, 5 years AWARDS: Certified Professional Bastard, U.F. H., 1991 PROFESSIONAL MEMBERSHIPS: United Federation of Humankind, Pres. Pro Tem 1980-82; Tactical Advisor 1989-present; Sylvan Society, member PUBLICATIONS:

Reality Quest Newsletter, Quarterly **PUBLISHER:** Individuals Against Mediocrity Unlimited

MacLaine, Shirley
c/o Chasin
9255 Sunset Boulevard
Los Angeles, CA 90069
TOPICS: Holistic Healing, Metaphysics, Parapsychology **DATE OF BIRTH:** 04/24/34 **PLACE OF BIRTH:** Richmond, VA **OCCUPATION:** Actress, Singer, Dancer, Author, Lecturer **WORK EXPERIENCE:** Higher Life Seminars, Los Angeles, CA, Founder; Ariel Village, Crestone, CO, Founder **DESCRIPTION:** Actively involved in the New Age movement offering her psychic-spiritual messages to the general public through her books & films. Also offers classes & seminars through her string of New Age centers. **PUBLICATIONS:** *Out On A Limb*, 1983 **PUBLICATIONS:** *Dancing In The Light*, 1985 **PUBLICATIONS:** *It's All In The Playing*, 1987 **PUBLICATIONS:** *Don't Fall Off The Mountain*, 1970 **PUBLICATIONS:** *You Can Get There From Here*, 1975

MacRae, Janet, R.N., Ph. D.
834 Union Street
Brooklyn, NY 11215
TOPICS: Psychic Healing

Macy, Mark H.
M.H. Macy & Co.
845 West Linden Street
Louisville, CO 80027
(303)-666-8130
TOPICS: Holistic Health, Spirituality **DATE OF BIRTH:** 11/15/49 **PLACE OF BIRTH:** Greeley, CO **DEGREE:** B.A. Journalism **DEGREE:** B.S.E.E. **OCCUPATION:** Author, Editor, Researcher **PROFESSIONAL MEMBERSHIPS:** Institute of Noetic Science, International Association on New Science, International Foundation for Development Alternatives, World Future Society, U.N. Association/U.S.A. **DESCRIPTION:** 18 years experience in technical & nontechnical research & communication in the new sciences: frontier physics, new economics, spiritual realities, systems healing & holistic health. **PUBLICATIONS:** *Last Chance For Peace*, 1985 **PUBLICATIONS:** *Solutions For A Troubled World*, 1987 **PUBLICATIONS:** *Healing The World And Me*, 1991

Mainiero, Maureen
501 Lincoln Avenue
Sayville, NY 11782
(516)-563-9355
TOPICS: Psychic

Mamish, Mary Ester
P.O. Box 254
Boston, MA 02113
(617)-623-7984
TOPICS: Crystals

Mandel, Bob
Loving Relationships Training
145 West 87th Street
New York, NY 10024
(212)-799-7323
TOPICS: New Age

Mangravite, Ron
218 Columbia Avenue
Fort Lee, NJ 07024

(201)-224-3158
TOPICS: Psychic

Mann, Ernest
Little Free Press
Rt. 1, Box 102
Cushing, MN 56443
(218)-575-2007
TOPICS: New Age **DATE OF BIRTH:** 01/30/27 **PLACE OF BIRTH:** Chicago, IL **EDUCATION:** Minnesota School of Business, Minneapolis, MN **YEARS:** 1947-48 **OCCUPATION:** Publisher, Author **WORK EXPERIENCE:** Little Free Press, Cushing, MN, Founder, President 1970-present **DESCRIPTION:** Proposes a new world economic system that would have no motivators to start wars, pollute, steal or starve. Offers ideas on how to live better, cheaper, have more free time & be happier. **PUBLICATIONS:** *I Was Robot*, 1990 **PUBLISHER:** Little Free Press **PUBLICATIONS:** *Little Free Press Newsletter* **PUBLISHER:** Little Free Press

Manners, Sir Peter Guy, M.D.
Bretforton Hall Clinic
Bretforton, Evesham
Worcester, WR11 5JH
England
0386 830537
TOPICS: Crystals **OCCUPATION:** Physician **WORK EXPERIENCE:** Cymatic, Ltd., Worcester, England **DESCRIPTION:** Cymatic Medical Clinic Student Training Association in International University standards. Offers lectures, workshops, spa treatments, etc.

Manning, Clark
Pyramis
20 Laurie Lane
Bridgewater, MA 023241
(716)-697-7504
TOPICS: Crystals

Mansbach, Richard
The Tibetan Foundation
1705 Audubon Road
Chapel Hill, NC 27514
TOPICS: Channeling **DESCRIPTION:** Certified Channeler by The Tibetan Foundation.

Manz, Gilbert, Jr.
TOPS Club, Inc.
4575 South Fifth Street
P.O. Box 07360
Milwaukee, WI 53207
(414)-482-4620
TOPICS: Holistic Healing

March, Dr. Robert
New Mexico Academy Of Massage And Advanced Healing Arts
P.O. Box 932
Santa Fe, NM 87504
(505)-982-6271
TOPICS: Holistic Healing

Marchese, Nicky
59-1/2 Dundurn Street North
Hamilton, ON, L8R 3E2
Canada
TOPICS: Crystals

Margolin, Dr. Shoshana, M.A., N.D., P.M.D.
Center For Health Sciences
P.O. Box 111
Bat-Yam, 59100
Israel
972-3-5077520
TOPICS: Crystals, Holistic Health, Homeopathy **OCCUPATION:** Holistic Practitioner, Author **WORK EXPERIENCE:** Center For Health Sciences, Bat-Yam, Israel, Holistic Practitioner, Instructor **DESCRIPTION:** Discoverer of Holographic Testing, which uncovers causes of disease. Teaches courses in Homeopathy & Holistic Medicine. **PUBLICATIONS:** *Holistic Homeopathy-Medicine Of The Future* **PUBLICATIONS:** *Holistic Girth Control*

Maria, Diane
P.O. Box 12134
12162 East Mississippi Avenue
Aurora, CO 80012
TOPICS: Channeling

Mark, Barry R.
Dell Horoscope Magazines
245 Park Avenue
New York, NY 10167
(212)-984-7135
TOPICS: Astrology

Markota, Maya
Crystal Energy
10515 Ayres Avenue
Los Angeles, CA 90064
(213)-838-9857
TOPICS: Crystals

Marozsan, John
Aspen Publishing, Inc.
7201 McKinney Circle
Frederick, MD 21701
TOPICS: Holistic Healing

Marriott, Norman
Food & Nutrition Press Inc.
155 Post Road East
Westport, CT 06880
(203)-261-8587
TOPICS: Holistic Healing

Marshik, Margaret
Association For Holistic Health
Box 1122
Del Mar, CA 92014
(619)-275-2694
TOPICS: Holistic Healing

Martay, James
Hippocrates Inc.
475 Gate Five Road, #100
Sausalito, CA 94965
(212)-490-7806
TOPICS: Holistic Healing

Martello, Leo Louis
Hero Press
153 West 80th Street
Suite 1B
New York, NY 10024
TOPICS: Occult

Mass, Elizabeth, M.A.

215 Byrne Avenue
P.O. Box 1010
Staten Island, NY 10314
(212)-761-7249

TOPICS: New Age, Meditation, Spirituality, Holistic Health, Channeling DESCRIPTION: Offers meditation, guided imagery, mind power workshops, spiritual & touch therapy. Promotes higher awareness, self healing & stress release.

Massari, Thomas P.
Genesis Reflection
P. O. Box 4111
Simi Valley, CA 93063

TOPICS: Channeling

Masters, David
Foundation Of Human Understanding
P.O. Box 811
Grants Pass, OR 97526
(503)-479-0549

TOPICS: Holistic Healing

Masters, Roy
Robert Just
F.H.U., 8780 Venice Boulevard
Los Angeles, CA 90034
(213)-559-3711

TOPICS: Holistic Health DESCRIPTION: can also contact Phyllis Watkins at the above address. PUBLICATIONS: *How Your Mind Can Keep You Well* PUBLICATIONS: *Beyond The Known* PUBLICATIONS: *How To Conquer Suffering Without Doctors*

Matacia, Ginette A.
P.O. Box 11453
Alexandria, VA 22312
(703)-750-1877

TOPICS: Crystals

Matis, Shelbee
The Life Center For Attitudinal Healing
P.O. Box 8718
Santa Fe, NM 87504
(505)-983-5541

TOPICS: Holistic Healing

Matlock, James G.
799 Park Avenue
New York, NY 10021
(212)-772-4180 (718)-204-5154

TOPICS: Parapsychology, Past Life Regression, Reincarnation, Psychic Phenomena DATE OF BIRTH: 06/01/54 PLACE OF BIRTH: Hanover, NH EDUCATION: Emory University, Atlanta, GA YEARS: 1972-77 DEGREE: B.A. YEAR DEGREE: 1977 EDUCATION: University of Maryland, College Park, MD YEARS: 1984-86 DEGREE: M.L.S. YEAR DEGREE: 1986 EDUCATION: Hunter College, New York, NY YEARS: 1988-pres OCCUPATION: Parapsychologist, Anthropologist, Librarian, Author WORK EXPERIENCE: American Society For Psychical Research, New York, NY, Librarian & Archivist 1987-88; Institute For Parapsychology, Durham, NC, Library Consultant 1989; Duke University Library, Durham, NC, Assistant Librarian 1989 AWARDS: Arranged J.B. Rhine papers & Parapsychology Laboratory records collection at Duke University Manuscript Department 1989 PROFESSIONAL MEMBERSHIPS: Parapsychological Association; American Anthropological Association; Society For The Anthropology Of Consciousness, Treasurer, Secretary-Treasurer PUBLICATIONS: *Of Names And Signs: Reincarnation, Inheritance And Social Structure* PUBLISHER: Anthropology Of Consciousness PUBLICATIONS: *Past Life Memory Case Studies*, 1990 PUBLISHER: Advances In Parapsychological Research PUBLICATIONS: *Age And Stimulus In Past Life Memory Cases*, 1989 PUBLISHER: Journal Of The American Society For Psychical Research PUBLICATIONS: *Cat's Paw: Margery And The Rhines*, 1926, 1987 PUBLISHER: Journal Of Parapsychology PUBLICATIONS: *Archives And Psychical Research*, 1987 PUBLISHER: Journal Of The American Society For Psychical Research

Matthew, Sister Paula, C.S.J.
Spiritual Center
Box 2614
R.D. #2
Windsor, NY 13865

TOPICS: Holistic Health

Maurey, Eugene
4555 West 60th Street
Chicago, IL 60629
(312)-581-4555

TOPICS: Occult, Holistic Healing, Psychic Phenomena, Metaphysics, Spirituality, Dowsing DATE OF BIRTH: 10/07/16 PLACE OF BIRTH: Chicago, IL EDUCATION: Purdue University, Lafayette, IN DEGREE: B.S.M.E. EDUCATION: I.I.T., Chicago, IL DEGREE: M.S.I.E. OCCUPATION: Engineer, Lecturer, Teacher, Author WORK EXPERIENCE: Maurey Instrument Corporation, President PROFESSIONAL MEMBERSHIPS: World Federation Of Healing; American Society Of Dowsing; Theosophical Society; Rotary Chicago Southwest; 904th FA BN Association DESCRIPTION: Author, lecturer and teacher on exorcism, metaphysicsm, spiritual healing and dowsing. PUBLICATIONS: *Exorcism* (1988) PUBLISHER: Whitford Press PUBLICATIONS: *Power Of Thought* (1990) PUBLISHER: Midwest Books

Maxfield, Jennifer
Busch Publishing Company
5005 Rivera Court
Ft. Wayne, IN 46825
(219)-484-9600

TOPICS: Holistic Healing

Mayell, Mark
East West Journal
17 Station Street
Box 1200
Brookline Village, MA 02147
(617)-232-1000

TOPICS: Holistic Healing

Mayers, Rodney
3900 Kingshighway, Apt. 6L
Brooklyn, NY 11234

TOPICS: Parapsychology

Maynard, Barbara
Murrieta Hot Springs Resort, Spa And Conference Center
39405 Murrieta Hot Springs Roa
Murrieta, CA 92362
(714)-677-7451

TOPICS: Holistic Healing

Mays, Dr. Blaine C.
International New Thought Alliance
5003 East Broadway Road
Mesa, AZ 85206
(602)-945-0744

TOPICS: Metaphysics

Maywald, Sue
Channeled Bodywork
6615 Whitney Street
Oakland, CA 94559

TOPICS: Channeling

McAdams, Dr. Elizabeth
Southern California Society For Psychical Research
269 South Arden Boulevard
Los Angeles, CA 90004

TOPICS: Parapsychology

McBeath, Michael
Stanford University
Department Of Psychology
Jordan Hall, Building 420
Stanford, CA 94305

TOPICS: Parapsychology

McCarty, Patrick
International Macrobiotic Shiatsu Society
1122 M Street
Eureka, CA 95501
(707)-445-2290

TOPICS: Holistic Healing

McClure, Janet
Tibetan Foundation, The
12600 113th Avenue
Youngstown, AZ 85363

TOPICS: Channeling

McCombs, Lisa
P.O. Box 55971
Birmingham, Alabama 35205

TOPICS: Channeling

McCormick, Donna
American Society For Psychical Research
5 West 73rd Street
New York, NY 10023

TOPICS: Parapsychology

McCoy, Karen P.
P.O. Box 9966
Ft. Lauderdale, FL 33310
(305)-974-4408

TOPICS: Astrology, Tarot

McCoy, Robert W.
Minnesota Skeptics-Committee For The Scientific Investi
549 Turnpike Road
Golden Valley, MN 55416
(612)-545-1113

TOPICS: Psychic Phenomena

McCoy-Keyes, Viki
14 Harold Avenue, #4
Greenwich, CT 06830
(203)-622-1258

TOPICS: Psychic, Tarot, Metaphysics, Meditation, Past Life Regression, Spirituality, Occult DATE OF

BIRTH: 05/18/47 **PLACE OF BIRTH:** New York, NY **EDUCATION:** New York University, New York, NY **DEGREE:** B.A. **OCCUPATION:** Psychic Metaphysician **WORK EXPERIENCE:** Starlex Systems, Director of International Marketing, 1986; Quintile Center, Greenwich, Ct., Staff Psychic; Sunburst Crystal Center, Mt. Kisco, NY, Staff Psychic; Programs For Human Development, Greenwich, CT, Staff Psychic; Traprock Suite, LTD., Scarsdale, NY, Staff Psychic **AWARDS:** Stephens Minister, Valhalla Methodist Church 1987; New Careerist, NY Business & Professional Women's Organization 1986 **DESCRIPTION:** Offers Tarot readings for spiritualism, goal realization, career, family, romance & past lives. Gives lectures on the Tarot, past lives & personal relationships. Teaches meditation & classes on Tarot, Wicca, Earth Magic & the Western Mystery Tradition.

McCrary, Alfred
Total Health
6001 Topanga Canyon Boulevard
Suite 300
Woodland Hills, CA 91367
(818)-887-6484

TOPICS: Holistic Healing

McCready, Patricia
Heldref Publications, Inc.
4000 Albemarle Street, N.W.
Washington, DC 20016
(800)-365-9753 (202)-362-6445

TOPICS: Holistic Healing, Metaphysics, New Age, Holistic Health, Channeling

McCullagh, Ed-Chuck
Practical Homeowner Publishing
27 Unquowa Road
Fairfield, CT 06430
(203)-259-9877

TOPICS: New Age

McDonald, Dr. John
Biological Educational Products
P.O. Box 2677
Santa Rosa, CA 95405

TOPICS: Holistic Healing

McGann, Rev. Eve O'Neil
13221 S.W.7th Court
Davie, FL 33325
(305)-474-3432

TOPICS: Psychic

McGarey, Gladys Taylor, M.D.
A.R.E. Clinic
4017 North 40th Street
Phoenix, AZ 85018
(602)-955-7729

TOPICS: Holistic Health, Channeling, Acupuncture, Parapsychology **DATE OF BIRTH:** 10/30/20 **PLACE OF BIRTH:** Fategarh, India **EDUCATION:** Muskingum College, New Concord, OH **DEGREE:** B.S. **YEAR DEGREE:** 1941 **EDUCATION:** Medical College Of Pennsylvania **DEGREE:** M.D. **YEAR DEGREE:** 1946 **OCCUPATION:** Physician, Author, Authority on Edgar Cayce Materials **WORK EXPERIENCE:** A.R.E. Clinic, Phoenix, AZ, Co-Founder, 1970 **PROFESSIONAL MEMBERSHIPS:** Academy Of Parapsychology & Medicine; American Holistic Medical Association, Past Pres. **DESCRIPTION:** Leading advocate of holistic health.

Incorporates the teachings of Edgar Cayce into her medical practice. Specializes in holistic childbirth techniques. **PUBLICATIONS:** *Born To Live*, 1980 **PUBLISHER:** Gabriel Press **PUBLICATIONS:** *There Will Your Heart Be Also*, 1975 **PUBLISHER:** Prentice Hall

McGarey, William A., M.D.
A.R.E. Clinic
4017 North 40th Street
Phoenix, AZ 85018
(602)-955-7729

TOPICS: Holistic Health, Channeling, Acupuncture, Parapsychology **DATE OF BIRTH:** 10/31/19 **PLACE OF BIRTH:** Wellsville, OH **EDUCATION:** College Of The Ozarks **DEGREE:** B.S. **YEAR DEGREE:** 1944 **EDUCATION:** University Of Cincinnati, Cincinnati, OH **DEGREE:** M.D. **YEAR DEGREE:** 1947 **OCCUPATION:** Physician, Acupuncturist, Author, Authority on Edgar Cayce materials **WORK EXPERIENCE:** A.R.E. Clinic, Phoenix, AZ, Co-Founder, 1970 **PROFESSIONAL MEMBERSHIPS:** Academy Of Parapsychology And Medicine, Board Member; American Holistic Medical Association, Founder; Acupuncture Association Of Physicians & Surgeons, Pres. **DESCRIPTION:** Promoter of holistic health through the use of Edgar Cayce materials & acupuncture. Also served as director of medical research for the Edgar Cayce Foundation & as editor of the Medical Research Bulletin of the A.R.E. Clinic. **PUBLICATIONS:** *Acupuncture And Body Energies*, 1972 **PUBLICATIONS:** *Edgar Cayce And The Palma Christi*, 1970 **PUBLICATIONS:** *Edgar Cayce On Healing*, 1972 **PUBLICATIONS:** *Physician's Reference Notebook* **PUBLICATIONS:** *There Will Your Heart Be Also*

McGowan, Judith Page
206 North Cedar Avenue
Highland Springs, VA 23075
(804)-737-9209

TOPICS: Crystals

McKee, Char
Woman Of Power, Inc.
P.O. Box 2785
Orleans, MA 02653
(508)-240-7877

TOPICS: Occult

McKusick, Charmion
Biomagnetic Research
Route 1, Box 35-D
Globe, AZ 85501
(602)-425-5051

TOPICS: Crystals

McKusick, Robert T.
Biomagnetic Research
Route 1, Box 35-D
Globe, AZ 85501
(602)-425-5051

TOPICS: Crystals

McLaughlin, Corinne
Sirius Community
Sirius Community
Baker Road
Shutesbury, MA 01072
(413)-259-1251

TOPICS: Metaphysics, Spirituality, New Age, Meditation **PUBLICATIONS:** *The Inner Side of World Events*

McLaughlin, Corrine
Sirius Community
5904 Madawaska Road
Bethesda, MD 20816-2340

TOPICS: Holistic Healing

McLean, Donna B.
McLean Enterprises
Box 714
Philipsburg, MT 59858
(406)-859-3365

TOPICS: Ghosts

McMahan, Dr. Elizabeth
University Of North Carolina
Biology Department
Chapel Hill, NC 27514

TOPICS: Parapsychology

McMahon, John
Mothering Publishers, Inc.
515 Don Gaspar
P.O. Box 1690
Santa Fe, NM 87504
(505)-984-8116

TOPICS: Birth

McMahon, Peggy O'Mara
Mothering Publishers, Inc.
515 Don Gaspar
P.O. Box 1690
Santa Fe, NM 87504
(505)-984-8116

TOPICS: Birth

McMillan-El, Bobby
807 Ashford Street
Brooklyn, NY 11207

TOPICS: Parapsychology

McMurray, Preston V., Jr.
Vim & Vigor, Inc.
8805 North 23rd Avenue
Suite 11
Phoenix, AZ 85021
(602)-395-5850

TOPICS: Holistic Healing

McPhall, Fiona
Vegetarian Society Ltd.
Parkdale Dunham Road
Altrincham Cheshire, WA14 4QG
England
(061)-928-0793

TOPICS: Health Food

McWhorter, Margaret L.
3601 Main Street
Ramona, CA 92065
(619)-789-0620 (619)-789-2570

TOPICS: Psychic, Parapsychology, New Age, Herbalogy, PSI, Metaphysics, Tea Leaves **DATE OF BIRTH:** 09/05/22 **PLACE OF BIRTH:** Long Beach, CA **EDUCATION:** UCLA, Westwood, CA **YEARS:** 1940-44 **DEGREE:** B.A. **YEAR DEGREE:** 1944 **OCCUPATION:** Publisher, Author **WORK EXPERIENCE:** Ransom Hill Press, Ramona, CA, President, 1981-present **AWARDS:** Award for Self-

Publishing Workshop National University, Vista, CA, May, 1990 **PROFESSIONAL MEMBERSHIPS:** National Federation of Penwomen; National Press Women; S.D. Writers/Editors Guild; PMA Book Publicists of S.D.; National Writers' Club, COSMEP **PUBLICATIONS:** *The Outrageous Herb Lady*, 1990 **PUBLISHER:** Ransom Hill Press **PUBLICATIONS:** *The Herb Lady's Notebook*, 1984 **PUBLISHER:** Ransom Hill Press **PUBLICATIONS:** *San Diego Writers & Publishers Resource Guide*, 1989 **PUBLISHER:** Ransom Hill Press **PUBLICATIONS:** *Tea Cup Tales: Tales Of Tea And How To Read Tea Leaves* **PUBLISHER:** Ransom Hill Press

Medoff, Marc
Whole Life Enterprises, Inc.
P.O. Box 2058
Madison Square Station
New York, NY 10159
(212)-353-3395

TOPICS: Holistic Healing, New Age, Metaphysics

Meek, George
Metascience Foundation
Box 737
Franklin, NC 28734
(704)-524-5103

TOPICS: Holistic Healing

Meguid, Michael, M.D.
Dimon, Inc.
3001 North San Fernando Boulev
P.O. Box 6489
Burbank, CA 91510
(818)-845-3748

TOPICS: Holistic Healing

Mehler, Stephen S., M.A.
Chiron Productions
32 North 9th Street, #1
San Jose, CA 95112
(408)-294-0773

TOPICS: Crystals

Melton, Rev. J. Gordon
Gale Research Company
Religious Studies Dept.
University of Santa Barbara
Santa Barbara, CA 93190
(805)-893-3250

TOPICS: Spirituality, New Age **EDUCATION:** Northwestern University, Chicago, IL **DEGREE:** Ph. D., Religion **OCCUPATION:** Teacher, Author, Lecturer **WORK EXPERIENCE:** Institute For The Study Of American Religions, Director **PUBLICATIONS:** *New Age Almanac* (1990) **PUBLISHER:** Visible Ink Press **PUBLICATIONS:** *Encyclopedia Of American Religions* (1988) **PUBLISHER:** Gale Research

Mendel, Werner
New Age Health Spa
Route 55
Neversink, NY 12765
(914)-985-7600 (914)-985-2241

TOPICS: Holistic Health, New Age, Meditation, Massage, Vegetarianism, Yoga, Nutrition **DATE OF BIRTH:** 11/09/34 **PLACE OF BIRTH:** Mainz, Germany **EDUCATION:** Cornell University, Ithaca, NY **YEARS:** 1952-56 **DEGREE:** B.A. **YEAR DEGREE:** 1956 **OCCUPATION:** Minister, Healer, Director, Author **WORK EXPERIENCE:** American

Express, New York, NY, Senior V.P. 1975-85; New Age Health Spa, Neversink, NY, President & Owner 1968-present **AWARDS:** Lifespring Leadership Training, Sullivan County Hospice **PROFESSIONAL MEMBERSHIPS:** International Platform Association; Interfaith Ministers Association; National Speakers Association; New Seminary; Polarity Therapy Graduate **PUBLICATIONS:** *Asset Allocation & Strategy*, 1983-85 Monthly **PUBLISHER:** American Express

Mendelson, Lee Ames
4705 Satinwood Trail
Coconut Creek, FL 33066
(305)-977-9283

TOPICS: New Age

Meris, Linda
319 East 90th Street, Apt. 4D
New York, NY 10128
(212)-289-6413

TOPICS: Psychic **DATE OF BIRTH:** 05/18/49 **PLACE OF BIRTH:** Glen Cove, NY **OCCUPATION:** Clairvoyant, Psychic **PROFESSIONAL MEMBERSHIPS:** Professional Comedians Association, Treasurer

Mershon, Anne
58-128 Iwia Place
Sunset Beach, HI 96712
(808)-638-9025

TOPICS: Psychic

Metrick, S.B.
3200 Robinson Drive
Oakland, CA 94602
(415)-531-3346 (415)-482-5418

TOPICS: Psychology, Dreams, Hypnotism, Body-Mind Connection **DATE OF BIRTH:** 10/17/47 **PLACE OF BIRTH:** IL **EDUCATION:** Antioch University, San Francisco, CA **DEGREE:** B.A. **YEAR DEGREE:** 1981 **EDUCATION:** J.F.K. University, Orinda, CA **YEARS:** 1983-86 **DEGREE:** M.A. **YEAR DEGREE:** 1986 **OCCUPATION:** Transpersonal Psychologist, Author, Lecturer **WORK EXPERIENCE:** Aquarian Institute, Oakland, CA, Teacher, Counselor of Intuition Ritual 1979-present; Piedmont Adult School, Piedmont, CA, Teacher-Dreamwork 1989-present **AWARDS:** Institute For Education Therapy, Certified Clinical Hyponotherapist, 1991; American Expressive Therapy Assoc., Registered Expressive Therapist, 1990 **PROFESSIONAL MEMBERSHIPS:** National Writers Union, 1990-present; American Expressive Therapy Assoc. 1990-present; Artists Therapists of Northern CA, 1990-present **PUBLICATIONS:** *Art Of Ritual*, 1990 **PUBLISHER:** Celestial Arts Publishing Co.

Metzger, William
Theosophical Society Of America
306 West Geneva Road
P.O. Box 270
Wheaton, IL 60189-0270
(312)-668-1571

TOPICS: Metaphysics

Meyer, John
Association For Holistic Health
Box 1122
Del Mar, CA 92014
(619)-275-2694

TOPICS: Holistic Healing

Mickel, Prof. Howard
Near-Death Experience Project
Box 76
Wichita State University
Wichita, KS 67208
(316)-689-3108

TOPICS: New Age

Middleton, Riki
Lotus Yoga Center
1131 University Boulevard West
Room 1012
Silver Spring, MD 20902
(301)-649-4581

TOPICS: Yoga

Mihalasky, Prof. John
New Jersey Institute Of Technology
Newark College Of Engineering
Newark, NJ 07102

TOPICS: Parapsychology

Mikesell, Suzanne
Jalmar Press
45 Hitching Post Drive
Building 2
Rolling Hills Estate, CA 90274
(213)-547-1240

TOPICS: New Age

Miles, Tony
Summit Publishing Company
5401 N.W. Broken Sound Bouleva
Boca Raton, FL 33431
(407)-997-7733

TOPICS: Holistic Healing

Milewski, John, Ph.D.
Mystic Crystals, Inc.
1500 5th Street, #8
Santa Fe, NM 87504
(505)-984-1048

TOPICS: Crystals

Miller, A. Frank
1222 Laurel Lane
Schaumburg, IL 60172

TOPICS: Channeling

Miller, Dr. Richard
Wilbur Hot Springs Health Sanctuary
Star Route
Williams, CA 95987
(916)-473-2306

TOPICS: Holistic Healing

Miller, Larry
Natural Wonders
817 Ninth Street
Durham, NC 27705
(919)-286-4250

TOPICS: Crystals

Miller, Marjorie
The Life Center For Attitudinal Healing
P.O. Box 8718
Santa Fe, NM 87504
(505)-983-5541

TOPICS: Holistic Healing

Miller, Megg
Night Owl Publishers
Box 764
Shepparton, Vi 3630
Australia
TOPICS: Holistic Healing

Miller, Peter
Pergamon Press, Inc.
Maxwell House
Fairview Park
Elmsford, NY 10523
(914)-592-7700
TOPICS: Holistic Healing

Miller, Ron
Holistic Education Review
39 Pearl Street
Brandon, VT 05733-1007
TOPICS: Holistic Healing

Millstein, Dan
Attitudinal Healing Center Of Southern California
24432 Muirlands Boulevard
El Toro, CA 92630
(714)-556-8000
TOPICS: Holistic Healing

Milner, Dr. Martin
Center For Holistic Medicine
2104 N.E. 45th Avenue
Portland, OR 97213
(503)-287-7727
TOPICS: Holistic Healing

Miluck, Melva M.
1215 West Durston, 119
Bozeman, MT 59715
TOPICS: Channeling

Minister, Ruth
Foundation For Life Action
902 S. Burnside Avenue
Los Angeles, CA 90036
(213)-933-5591
TOPICS: New Age

Minney, Gloria
Dura Mater Body Works/La Gloria Matutina
Box 31143
El Paso, TX 79931
TOPICS: Crystals, Holistic Healing, Astrology, Tarot, Runes, Metaphysics, Massage EDUCATION: University of Oregon DEGREE: M.S. OCCUPATION: Teacher of Metaphysics, Massage Therapist, Author WORK EXPERIENCE: Dura Mater Body Works/Las Gloria Matutina, El Paso, TX, Founder, owner PROFESSIONAL MEMBERSHIPS: NEA, AAHPERD, AMTA, Rev. ULC, G.I.A. DESCRIPTION: Teacher & specialist in dance, wellness, crystals, gems, minerals, diet, exercise, nutrition, Massage Therapy, arts & crafts. Offers Readings in Astrology, I Ching, Tarot & Rune Stones.

Miracle
Possibilities
S. R. 173
Hana, Maui, HI 96713
(808)-248-8623
TOPICS: Crystals

Miranda, R.N.
Pergamon Press, Inc.
Maxwell House
Fairview Park
Elmsford, NY 10523
(914)-592-7700
TOPICS: Holistic Healing

Mitchell, Glenn
Spirit Speaks, Inc.
Box 84304
Los Angeles, CA 90073
(213)-826-9197
TOPICS: New Age

Mitchess, Edgar D.
Institute Of Noetic Sciences
475 Gate Five Road, #300
P.O. Box 909
Sausalito, CA 94966-0909
(415)-331-5650
TOPICS: Body-Mind Connection, Holistic Health, Spirituality, Past Life Regression, Death, Meditation, Hypnotism DATE OF BIRTH: 09/17/30 PLACE OF BIRTH: Hereford, TX OCCUPATION: Navy Pilot, Former Astronaut, Author WORK EXPERIENCE: Institute of Noetic Sciences, Sausalito, CA, Founder, 1973 AWARDS: Presidential Medal of Freedom; Distinguished Services Medal-Navy & NASA; Group Achievement Award-NASA DESCRIPTION: Dedicated to the exploration of consciousness & parapsychological phenomena. PUBLICATIONS: *Noetics: The Emerging Science Of Consciousness*, 1973

Mittelman, Jerry, D.D.S.
Once Daily, Inc.
263 West End Avenue, #2A
New York, NY 10023
(212)-874-4212
TOPICS: Holistic Healing

Mohini, Radha
Samadhi Dreams Press
1319 Dennis Court
Kalamazoo, MI 49007
(616)-381-7273
TOPICS: New Age

Monroe, Robert
Monroe Institute
Rt. 1
Box 175
Faber, VA 22938
(804)-361-1252
TOPICS: Parapsychology

Moonfeather, Tyshe
Three Of Cups
P.O. Box 508, 12 Tinker Street
Woodstock, NY 12498
(914)-679-2357
TOPICS: Crystals

Moore, Bernardine
Office Of Communications
5600 Fishers Lane
12C-15
Rockville, MD 20857
(301)-443-3783
TOPICS: Holistic Healing

Moore, Eleanor
210 Old Jaffrey Road
Peterborough, NH 03458
TOPICS: Channeling

Moore, Peter
Breitenbush Hot Springs Retreat And Conference Center
P.O. Box 578
Detroit, OR 97342
(503)-854-3314
TOPICS: Holistic Healing

Moore, William L.
Fair-Witness Project, Inc.
4219 West Olive Avenue, #247
Burbank, CA 91505
(818)-980-8758 (818)-506-4524
TOPICS: Psychic Phenomena, UFO's, Occult DATE OF BIRTH: 10/31/43 PLACE OF BIRTH: Pittsburgh, PA EDUCATION: Thiel College, Greenville, PA YEARS: 1961-1965 DEGREE: B.A. YEAR DEGREE: 1965 EDUCATION: Duquesne University, Pittsburgh, PA YEARS: 1972-1975 DEGREE: M.S. EDUCATION: Moorhead State University, Morrehead, MN YEARS: 1975-1978 DEGREE: M.S. OCCUPATION: Author, Journalist, Researcher WORK EXPERIENCE: Fair-Witness Project, Inc., Los Angeles, CA, Pres. 1984- Present; W.L. Moore Publishing & Research, Burbank, CA, 1979-Present; Ind. School District #264, Herman, MN, Teacher 1969-1979; Focus Journal, editor, 1984-Present; The Hollywood Gazette, columnist, 1988-Present AWARDS: Alpha Psi Omega National Dramatics Fraternity, 1964-Present PROFESSIONAL MEMBERSHIPS: Aerial Phenomena Research Organization, Dir., 1980-84; National UFO Conference, Dir., 1987-Present. DESCRIPTION: Co-owner of Peregrine Communications in North Hollywood, CA from 1990 to present. PUBLICATIONS: *The Philadelphia Experiment* (1980) PUBLISHER: Grosset & Dunlap/Fawcett PUBLICATIONS: *The Roswell Incident* (1988) PUBLISHER: Grosset & Dunlap/Berkeley PUBLICATIONS: *The M-J 12 Report* (1990) PUBLISHER: Fair-Witness Project, Inc. PUBLICATIONS: *Focus Journal* PUBLISHER: Fair-Witness Project, Inc.

Moore-Sullivan, Mollie
Lupin Naturalist Club
P.O. Box 1274
Los Gatos, CA 95030
(408)-353-2250
TOPICS: New Age

Morales, Barbara
Spiritual Growth Foundation
891 Haywood Road
Asheville, NC 28806
(704)-252-3408
TOPICS: Metaphysics

Moretti, Laura A.
Compassion For Animals Foundation, Inc.
3961 Landmark Street
Culver City, CA 90232
(213)-204-2929
TOPICS: New Age

Morgan, Ffiona
Magical Crystals

37155 Covelo Road
Wilits, CA 95490
(707)-459-2151

TOPICS: Crystals

Morgan, Mark
Gemini Gems
2704 Grand Avenue, P.O. Box 917
Bellmore, NY 11710
(516)-868-4853

TOPICS: Crystals

Morgan, Michael
Atlantean Antiquities Co.
230 West 76th Street
New York, NY 10023

TOPICS: Channeling, Psychic **OCCUPATION:** Psychic, Channeler **WORK EXPERIENCE:** Atlantean Antiquities Co., New York, NY, Founder, Pres. **DESCRIPTION:** Full-Trance Channel, Yokar, Atlantean Spirit Guide, offering workshops, lectures, tapes, private sessions & books. Expert in Ancient Pre-History, Body Readings & counselling for work & relationships. Leads mystical tours to Egypt, England, Mexico & Napal.

Moriarty, Tim
Feeling Great
45 West 34th Street
Room 407
New York, NY 10001
(212)-239-0855

TOPICS: Holistic Healing

Morlan, Barbara
Crystal Rainbow New Age Support Network
1939 Cadillac Avenue
Colorado Springs, CO 80909-2123

TOPICS: Crystals

Morningstar, Rose
Cheerhope, Inc.
29 Davis Branch Road
Bryson City, NC 28713
(704)-488-6920

TOPICS: Holistic Healing

Morris, Dr. Robert
University Of Edinburgh, Dept. Of Psychology
7 George Square
Edinburgh, Scotland EH8 9JZ
United Kingdom

TOPICS: Parapsychology

Morrison, Al H.
Congress Of Astrological Organization
Box 75
Old Chelsea Station
New York, NY 10113-0075

TOPICS: Astrology **DATE OF BIRTH:** 07/08/16 **EDUCATION:** University of Tennessee, Knoxville, TN **DEGREE:** B.A. **YEAR DEGREE:** 1938 **OCCUPATION:** Astrologer, Teacher, Publisher, Lecturer, Author **AWARDS:** Who's Who In The East, 1977; Guest of NASA for Apollo 13 launch to Moon. **PROFESSIONAL MEMBERSHIPS:** Am Fed of Astrologers Inc., Astrological Assoc of Great Britain, Irish Astrological Assoc., Pittsburgh Astrology Assoc., Astrological Council of Delaware Valley, Astrologers Guild of America, Keystone Guild of Astrologers **PUBLICATIONS:** *The Ephemeris Of The Void Of Course Moon* **PUBLISHER:** Al H. Morrison

PUBLICATIONS: *Contemporary Astrological Observation Times-CAO*

Morrison, Nannette
1310 Lester Drive
Charlottesville, VA 22901
(804)-293-7547

TOPICS: Crystals

Morvay, Alan
Joy Lake Mountain Seminar Center
P.O. Box 1328
Reno, NV 89504
(702)-323-1051

TOPICS: Crystals, Holistic Health

Morvay, Jacque
Joy Lake Mountain Seminar Center
P.O. Box 1328
Dept. T
Reno, NV 89504
(702)-323-0378

TOPICS: Holistic Healing

Morwyn
P.O. Box 403
Boulder, CO 80306

TOPICS: Occult, Witchcraft, Herbalogy, Tea Leaves, Ghosts, Metaphysics, Parapsychology **PLACE OF BIRTH:** Cleveland, OH **EDUCATION:** University of Colorado **DEGREE:** B.A., Latin Am. Studies **EDUCATION:** University of Colorado **DEGREE:** M.A., Spanish **EDUCATION:** University of Wisconsin **DEGREE:** Ph. D. **YEAR DEGREE:** 1977 **OCCUPATION:** Master Cross-Cultural Trainer, Brazilianist Translator, Author, Professor of Spanish & Portuguese **WORK EXPERIENCE:** Moran, Stahl & Boyer, Master Cross-Cultural Trainer 1981-present; University of Colorado, Assistant Professor, Portuguese, Spanish; University of Pittsburgh, Assistant Professor, Portuguese, Spanish; Brown University, Assistant Professor, Portuguese, Spanish **AWARDS:** Phi Beta Kappa, U. CO., 1969; Gulbenkian Fellow, WI., 1972; Fulbright Fellow- At Large, 1976-77; History Honorary, CO, 1969; NDEA Fellow, WI.,1971-73 **PROFESSIONAL MEMBERSHIPS:** Spanish Club Pres., CO, 1968-69; AATSP; CCFLT; High Priestess of Coven of Trer Dryw, 1979-present, initiated 1974 by Lady Sara Cunningham, Rock Mountain Writers' Guild, National Writers' Club **DESCRIPTION:** Author of numerous articles on Brazilian magic, witchcraft, ghosts, tea leaf reading, herbs, etc. Owner of Wild Wood Fragrances-metaphysical supplies. **PUBLICATIONS:** *Secrets Of A Witch's Coven*, 1988 **PUBLISHER:** Whitford Press **PUBLICATIONS:** *Pomba-Gira: Rituals To Invoke The Female Messenger Of The Gods*, 1991 **PUBLISHER:** The Technicians Of The Sacred **PUBLICATIONS:** *Web Of Light*, 1991 **PUBLISHER:** Llewellyn **PUBLICATIONS:** *Green Magic*, 1991 **PUBLISHER:** Llewellyn

Mosby, Robert D., Ph. D.
The Rim Institute
6835 Pepper Tree Lane
Scottsdale, AZ 85253
(602)-941-7121

TOPICS: Holistic Healing

Moss, Doug
Earth Action Network
28 Knight Street

Norwalk, CT 06851
(203)-226-9265

TOPICS: New Age

Moss, Richard
Camp Lenox For Adults
345 Riverside Drive, #4C
New York, NY 10025
(212)-662-3182

TOPICS: Holistic Healing

Moss, Richard, M.D.
Three Mountain Foundation
Box 1180
Lone Pine, CA 93545
(619)-876-4702

TOPICS: New Age

Mottor, Carol Neptune
Crystal Planet Gems
960 Victory Boulevard
Green Bay, WI 54304-3752

TOPICS: Crystals

Mounsey, Ed
Good Health
801 York Mills Road
Suite 201
Don Mills, On M3B 1X7
Canada
(416)-444-4952

TOPICS: Holistic Healing

Muhlendahl, Padma V.
Bismarckstr. 50
5 Cologne 1,
West Germany

TOPICS: Crystals

Mull, Carol S.
Mull Publications
P.O. Box 11133
Indianapolis, IN 46201
(317)-357-6855

TOPICS: Astrology

Munster, Bill
Footsteps Press
Box 75
Round Top, NY 12473

TOPICS: Psychic Phenomena

Murchie, Guy
333 Old Mill Road
Santa Barbara, CA 97110
(805)-964-0226

TOPICS: New Age, Spirituality, Metaphysics, Body-Mind Connection **DATE OF BIRTH:** 01/25/07 **PLACE OF BIRTH:** Boston, MA **EDUCATION:** Harvard University, Cambridge, MA **YEARS:** 1925-29 **DEGREE:** B.S. **YEAR DEGREE:** 1929 **OCCUPATION:** Author **AWARDS:** Phi Beta Kappa, 1969; Best Nature Book, 1955; Book of the Month, December, 1954 **PUBLICATIONS:** *Song Of The Sky*, 1954 **PUBLISHER:** Houghton Mifflin **PUBLICATIONS:** *Music Of The Spheres*, 1961 **PUBLISHER:** Houghton Mifflin **PUBLICATIONS:** *The Seven Mysteries Of Life*, 1978 **PUBLISHER:** Houghton Mifflin

Murphy, Michael
Esalen Institute

Pacific Coast Highway
Big Sur, CA 93920
(408)-667-2335 (408)-667-3000

TOPICS: Massage

Murray, Alexander
172 West 79th Street, 18C
New York, NY 10024

TOPICS: Channeling

Murray, Andrew
Findhorn Press
The Park
Forres
Mo IV36 OTZ
Scotland
(003)-093-0582

TOPICS: Metaphysics

Myers, Arthur
637 Washington Street
Wellesley, MA 02181
(617)-235-2501

TOPICS: Ghosts, Occult, Witchcraft DATE OF
BIRTH: 10/24/17 PLACE OF BIRTH: Buffalo, NY
EDUCATION: Hobart College, Geneva, NY YEARS:
1935-59 DEGREE: B.A. YEAR DEGREE: 1939
OCCUPATION: Author, Editor topic occult
AWARDS: The Associated Press Writing Awards;
Who's Who In America, 1966-present
PROFESSIONAL MEMBERSHIPS: National Writers
Union; PEN; Boston Authors Club; American
Society of Journalists and Authors DESCRIPTION:
Authored 13 books, 4 on occult as well as many
children & young adult books. Also published many
articles & short stories. Worked as newspaper &
magazine writer & editor. PUBLICATIONS: *The
Ghostly Register* PUBLISHER: Contemporary Books
PUBLICATIONS: *The Ghost Hunters*, 1980
PUBLISHER: Messner PUBLICATIONS: *The Ghostly
Gazetteer*, 1990 PUBLISHER: Contemporary Books
PUBLICATIONS: *Ghosts of the Rich & Famous*,
1988 PUBLISHER: Contemporary Books

Myersom, John
Center For Holistic Health
42 Lincoln Street
Framingham, MA 01701
(508)-879-3002

TOPICS: Holistic Healing

Nada-Yolanda
Mark-Age
P.O. Box 290368
Ft. Lauderdale, FL 33329
(305)-587-5555

TOPICS: Spirituality, UFO's, New Age, Channeling
DATE OF BIRTH: 09/01/25 PLACE OF BIRTH:
Brooklyn, NY OCCUPATION: Author, Channel
WORK EXPERIENCE: Mark-Age, Ft. Lauderdale,
FL, Exec. Director 30 years DESCRIPTION:
Company deals with New Age, Second Coming &
Channeling. Acts as the primary channel of Mark-
Age. PUBLICATIONS: *MAPP To Aquarius*, 1970,
1985 PUBLISHER: Mark-Age, Inc. PUBLICATIONS:
Evolution Of Man, 1971, 1988 PUBLISHER: Mark-
Age, Inc. PUBLICATIONS: *Angels And Man*, 1974
PUBLISHER: Mark-Age, Inc. PUBLICATIONS:
Visitors From Other Planets, 1974 PUBLISHER:
Mark-Age, Inc. PUBLICATIONS: *1000 Keys To The
Truth*, 1976 PUBLISHER: Mark-Age, Inc.

Nagorka, Henry J.
United States Psychotronics Association
2141 West Agatite
Chicago, IL 60625
(312)-478-5374

TOPICS: Psychic Phenomena

Nasatir, Dorothy
New Age Source
7538 Royer Avenue
Canoga Park, CA 91307
(213)-992-4526

TOPICS: New Age

Nash, Carroll B.
16493 Horado Court
San Diego, CA 92128

TOPICS: Parapsychology DATE OF BIRTH:
01/29/14 PLACE OF BIRTH: Louisville, KY
EDUCATION: George Washington University
DEGREE: B.S., M.S. YEAR DEGREE: 1937
EDUCATION: University of Maryland DEGREE: Ph.
D. YEAR DEGREE: 1939 OCCUPATION: Professor,
Author, Lecturer WORK EXPERIENCE: St. Joseph's
University, Philadelphia, PA, Professor of Biology,
Director of Parapsychology Lab. 1947-80;
Washington College, Chestertown, MD, Professor of
Biology 1944-47; American U., Washington, D.C.,
Assoc. Professor of Biology 1942-44 AWARDS:
William McDougall Award For Research in
Parapsychology 1961 PROFESSIONAL
MEMBERSHIPS: Parapsychology Association,
President 1963, Vice-Pres. 1962, Secretary 1981;
Sigma Xi; Beta Beta Beta PUBLICATIONS:
Parapsychology, 1986 PUBLISHER: Charles C.
Thomas PUBLICATIONS: *Science Of Psi*, 1978
PUBLISHER: Charles C. Thomas

Nassar, Autrey
Crystal Kingdom
P.O. Box 2280
Los Gatos, CA 95031
(408)-354-0870

TOPICS: Crystals

Navon, Robert
Selene Books
P.O. Box 220253
El Paso, TX 79913
(915)-584-3799

TOPICS: New Age, Spirituality DATE OF BIRTH:
05/18/54 PLACE OF BIRTH: New York, NY
EDUCATION: Lehman College, New York, NY
YEARS: 1971-75 DEGREE: B.A. History YEAR
DEGREE: 1975 EDUCATION: New School
University of Kansas YEARS: 1982-86 DEGREE:
Ph. D., A.B. D. YEAR DEGREE: 1986
OCCUPATION: Editor, Author, Lecturer,
Philosopher WORK EXPERIENCE: New York City
Board Of Education, New York, NY, Teacher,
English, 1983-86; Selene Books, El Paso, TX,
Editor 1985-90 AWARDS: Phi Beta Kappa, 1975;
National Merit Scholarship Award, 1971
PROFESSIONAL MEMBERSHIPS: American
Philosophical Association; Who's Who Of Writers,
Poets and Editors, 1987-90 DESCRIPTION: Lectures
all around the United States on the topics of Ancient
Thought and Cosmic Patterns. PUBLICATIONS:
Patterns Of The Universe, 1977 PUBLICATIONS:
Harmony Of The Spheres, 1991 PUBLICATIONS:
Autumn Songs, 1983 PUBLISHER: Selene Books

Nearing, Helen
Traditional Tours
P.O. Box 564
Creswell, OR 97426
(503)-895-2957

TOPICS: New Age

Nechodom, Mark
99 Sunset Drive
Watsonville, CA 95076
(408)-761-1854

TOPICS: Crystals

Nedrra
Beadwerks Plus
425 Dewey Street
San Diego, CA 92113
(619)-233-5024

TOPICS: Crystals, New Age

Neitlich, Shirley
Society For The Right To Die, Inc.
250 West 57th Street
New York, NY 10107
(212)-246-6973

TOPICS: Death

Nekritz, John A.
Crystal Integration Systems
165 Christopher Street
New York, NY 10014
(212)-929-7705

TOPICS: Crystals

Nelson, Pamela
American Alliance For Health, Physical Education,
Recre
1900 Association Drive
Reston, VA 22091
(703)-476-3400

TOPICS: Holistic Healing

Neppe, Dr. Vernon
University Of Washington
RP10 Medical School
Department Of Psychiatry
Seattle, WA 98195

TOPICS: Parapsychology

Neville, F.W.
P.O. Box 70
Keno, OR 07627
(503)-884-9781

TOPICS: Metaphysics, Tarot, Astrology DATE OF
BIRTH: 09/17/30 PLACE OF BIRTH: Los Angeles,
CA EDUCATION: California State-Sacramento
DEGREE: M.A. OCCUPATION: Government
Management-Materials Mgmt., Author WORK
EXPERIENCE: State Of California, Sacramento, CA,
25 years PROFESSIONAL MEMBERSHIPS: Dull
Men's Club of CA; Assoc. of Soft Drink Consumers;
Odinist Fellowship PUBLICATIONS: *Tarot For
Lovers*, 1987 PUBLISHER: Whitford Press
PUBLICATIONS: *Planets In Synastry*, 1990
PUBLISHER: Whitford Press

Ngandu, Kathleen
Foundation For Chiropractic Education And
Research
1701 Clarendon Boulevard
Arlington, VA 22209
(703)-276-7445

TOPICS: Holistic Healing

Nicholson, Darca
North Coast Body Workers Association
798 South Spring Street
Ukiah, CA 95482
(707)-462-3547

TOPICS: Holistic Healing, Homeopathy, Reiki, Hypnotism, Acupuncture, Massage, Spirituality OCCUPATION: Holistic Health Practitioner WORK EXPERIENCE: North Coast Body Workers Association, Ukiah, CA, Founder

Nickel, Kristine
477 Slater Avenue
Ottawa, ON, K1P 5H2
Canada
(613)-238-4920

TOPICS: Crystals

Nickell, Molli
Spirit Speaks Magazine, Inc.
P.O. Box 84304
Los Angeles, CA 90073
(800)-356-9104 (213)-826-9197

TOPICS: New Age, Channeling, Spirituality DATE OF BIRTH: 11/16/37 PLACE OF BIRTH: Kalamazoo, MI EDUCATION: USC - UCLA, Los Angeles, CA DEGREE: M.F.A YEAR DEGREE: 1982 OCCUPATION: Publisher, Author WORK EXPERIENCE: Spirit Speaks Magazine, Los Angeles, CA, Publisher 1985-present

Niehaus, Gloria
Astrology Express
1586 Spinnaker Lane
Half Moon Bay, CA 94019
(415)-726-6990

TOPICS: Crystals

Nielsen, Jocelyne M.
The Healing Center Of San Francisco
465 Brussels Street
San Francisco, CA 94134
(415)-468-4680

TOPICS: Holistic Healing

Niemi, Beatrice N.
Center For Well Being, Inc.
70 Bond Street
Fitchburg, MA 01420
(508)-345-5964

TOPICS: Holistic Healing, Reiki

Niendorff, John S.
Science Of Mind
3251 West 6th Street
Los Angeles, CA 90020
(213)-388-2181

TOPICS: New Age

Nisbit, Michael
Of Quartz!
P.O. Box 268
Crestone, CO 81131
(719)-256-4153

TOPICS: Crystals

Noble, J.W.
Naturopath Publishing Co.
3912 NE 44th Avenue
Vancouver, WA 98661

(206)-695-0213

TOPICS: Holistic Healing

Noble, Robert
Naturopath Publishing Co.
3912 NE 44th Avenue
Vancouver, WA 98661
(206)-695-0213

TOPICS: Holistic Healing

Nocerino, Frank R. 'Nick'
Crystal Skulls Society International
P.O. Box 302
Pinole, CA 94564
(415)-724-6603

TOPICS: Crystals

Nolle, Richard
Star Tech Services
P.O. Box 26599
Tempe, AZ 85285-6599
(602)-838-3245

TOPICS: Astrology DATE OF BIRTH: 03/13/50 PLACE OF BIRTH: Orland, FL EDUCATION: University of Florida YEARS: 1967-71 YEAR DEGREE: 1971 OCCUPATION: Astrologer, Author WORK EXPERIENCE: Star Tech Services, Tempe, AZ, Founder DESCRIPTION: Professional Astrologer since 1973. Author of numerous articles & books on Astrology. Provides charts & consultations by mail or appointment for over 2,500 clients. PUBLICATIONS: *Chiron* PUBLICATIONS: *Critical Astrology* PUBLICATIONS: *Interpreting Astrology*

Nordic, Rolla
121 West 72nd Street
New York, NY 10023

TOPICS: Tarot, Runes

Norins, Leslie
American Health Consultants, Inc.
67 Peachtree Park Drive, NE, #
Atlanta, GA 30309
(404)-351-4523

TOPICS: Holistic Healing

Norman, Ruth
Unarius Light
145 South Magnolia Avenue
El Cajon, CA 92020
(619)-447-4170

TOPICS: Reincarnation

Norris, Joan B.
The Rim Institute
6835 Pepper Tree Lane
Scottsdale, AZ 85253
(602)-941-7121

TOPICS: Holistic Healing

Novak, Linda
Creative Designs Crystal: Jewelry Collection
P.O. Box 5493
Santa Monica, CA 90405
(213)-392-6333

TOPICS: Crystals

November, Joseph
Aquarian Fellowship
1328 West Newport
Chicago, IL 60657

(312)-528-7254

TOPICS: New Age

Novoa, Kalika
Sri Chinmoy Centre
3502 Connecticut Avenue N.W.
Washington, DC 20008
(202)-363-4797

TOPICS: Holistic Healing

Null, Michael
Truths
155 North Michigan Avenue
Sixth Floor
Chicago, IL 60601
TOPICS: Metaphysics

O'Brien, Joan
62 Grove Street
Great Barrington, MA 01230
(413)-528-2671

TOPICS: Crystals

O'Connell, Patrick
207 Birch Street, S.E., Ste. 20
Topeka, KS 66609
(913)-862-0830

TOPICS: Metaphysics PUBLICATIONS: *Light-Net Prosperity Newsletter*

O'Donnell, Lily
Metaphysical Center Point Publications
1936 S.W. 63rd Terrace
Pompano, FL 33068
(305)-972-8951

TOPICS: Metaphysics, Psychic, Spirituality, ESP DATE OF BIRTH: 11/25/15 PLACE OF BIRTH: Budapest, Hungary EDUCATION: Wayne State University EDUCATION: Nova University OCCUPATION: Psychic, Minister, Lecturer, Teacher, Publisher, Editor, Author WORK EXPERIENCE: First Spiritualist Church, Brightmoor, MI, Pastor, 10 years; Church of Spiritual Love, Pompano, FL, Pastor, 3 years AWARDS: Independent Spiritualist Association Of America, Ordained 1976; Golden Poetry Award 1986, 87 & 89 PROFESSIONAL MEMBERSHIPS: Florida Freelance Writers Association, South Florida Poetry Institute,Adult Education Program Michigan DESCRIPTION: 30 years experience practicing as a professional psychic, lecturer, teacher, author & Pastor. Has also taught metaphysics for 3 years. PUBLICATIONS: *Confessions Of A Clairvoyant* PUBLISHER: National Summet Magazine PUBLICATIONS: *Manuel For Development & Understanding Of ESP*, 1979 PUBLISHER: Lily O'Donnell PUBLICATIONS: *The Messenger Magazine*, 1980 PUBLISHER: Lily O'Donnell

O'Leary, Brian
International Association For New Science
755 Tyler Creek Road
Ashland, OR 97520-9408
(503)-488-8800

TOPICS: Psychic Healing, Parapsychology, Reincarnation, Body-Mind Connection, UFO's, Spirituality, Metaphysics DATE OF BIRTH: 01/27/40 PLACE OF BIRTH: Boston, MA EDUCATION: Williams College, Williamstown, MA YEARS: 1957-61 DEGREE: B.A. YEAR DEGREE: 1961 EDUCATION: University of California, Berkeley, CA YEARS: 1964-67 DEGREE: Ph. D.,

Astronomy **YEAR DEGREE:** 1967 **OCCUPATION:** Scientist, Author, Lecturer, Astronomer, Astronaut **WORK EXPERIENCE:** Cornell University, Ithaca, NY, Faculty; University of CA at Berkeley, Faculty; Princeton University, Princeton, NJ, Faculty; California Institute of Technology, Faculty **AWARDS:** NASA Scientist-Astronaut 1967-68 **PROFESSIONAL MEMBERSHIPS:** International Association For New Science, Co-Founder, 1990 **DESCRIPTION:** Lecture topics: Healing the Self, Near-Death Experiences, Group Consciousness, Out-Of-Body Experiences, UFO's, Precognition, Mind-Over-Matter, Extraterrestrial Intelligence, The Gaia Hypothesis, Interconnectedness, Ancient Megaliths, Psychokinesis, etc. **PUBLICATIONS:** *Exploring Inner And Outer Space*, 1989 **PUBLISHER:** North Atlantic Books

O'Neil, Dr. Kevin
American Buddhist
301 West 45th Street
New York, NY 10036
(212)-489-1075

TOPICS: Yoga, Spirituality, New Age **EDUCATION:** Columbia University, New York, NY **DEGREE:** Ph. D. **YEAR DEGREE:** 1980 **OCCUPATION:** Author, Lecturer **WORK EXPERIENCE:** American Buddhist, New York, NY, President, Lecturer American Buddhism **AWARDS:** Buddhist of the Year 1986 Korea Choge Order **PROFESSIONAL MEMBERSHIPS:** American Buddhists Representative to the United Nations 1982-present **PUBLICATIONS:** *American Buddhist Directory*, 1986 **PUBLISHER:** American Buddhists **PUBLICATIONS:** *The American Buddhist Magazine*, 1980-present **PUBLISHER:** American Buddhists

O'Quinn, David
Evolutionary Education Foundation
5039 Outlook
Mission, KS 66202
(913)-432-0622

TOPICS: Holistic Healing

Obis, Paul
Vegetarian Times
P.O. Box 570
Oak Park, IL 60303
(312)-848-8100

TOPICS: Health Food

Ochaum, Shamaan
4111 Rosedale Avenue
Austin, TX 78756
(512)-452-2012

TOPICS: Crystals

Odent, Michel, M.D.
Pantheon Books/Random House
201 East 50th Street
New York, NY 10022
(212)-751-2600

TOPICS: Birth

Oelsner, Geoffrey
1329 Vandeventer
Fayetteville, AR 72703
(501)-521-2395

TOPICS: Crystals

Oh Shinnah

Four Directions Foundation
39-32 58th Street
Woodside, NY 11377
(718)-335-0702

TOPICS: Channeling, Crystals

Ohashi, Wataru
Ohashi Institute
12 West 27th Street
New York, NY 10001
(212)-684-4190

TOPICS: Body-Mind Connection, New Age, Holistic Health

Oldfield, Harry
School Of Electro-Crystal Therapy
117 Long Drive
South Ruislip, Middlesex HA4 OHL
England

TOPICS: Crystals

Oliver, John
SRI
Box 29
Earlysville, VA 22936

TOPICS: Channeling

Olivera, Angela
Girisho Institute For Meditation And Growth
5421 Rumsford Lane
Burke, VA 22015
(703)-425-0741

TOPICS: Crystals

Olsen, Fred C., M. Div.
The Dream House
19 Elk Street
San Francisco, CA 94131
(415)-333-7326

TOPICS: Dreams, Body-Mind Connection **DATE OF BIRTH:** 03/22/43 **PLACE OF BIRTH:** Spokane, WA **EDUCATION:** Seattle Pacific University, Seattle, WA **YEARS:** 1961-65 **DEGREE:** B.S. Math **YEAR DEGREE:** 1965 **EDUCATION:** Andover Newton Theological School, Newton, MA **YEARS:** 1976-79 **DEGREE:** M. Div. **YEAR DEGREE:** 1979 **OCCUPATION:** Consultant **WORK EXPERIENCE:** The Dream House, San Francisco, CA, Director, Dream Reentry Specialist, 4 years **PROFESSIONAL MEMBERSHIPS:** Association For The Study Of Dreams; Northern California Council For Meditation, Board of Directors 1985. **DESCRIPTION:** Dream Work consultant specializing in Dream Reentry Method.

Olson, Dale
Ice Flowers
P.O. Box 2092
Eugene, OR 97402
(503)-683-8418

TOPICS: Crystals

Oriniz, John
c/o A. Coyne
P.O. Box 1523
Ojai, CA 93023

TOPICS: Crystals, Psychic Healing

Orne, Martin T.
Society For Clinical & Experimental Hypnosis
111 North 49th Street
Philadelphia, PA 19139

(215)-472-1055

TOPICS: Hypnotism

Orr, Leonard
Consciousness Village
Box 234
Sierraville, CA 96126
(916)-994-3737 (916)-893-8643

TOPICS: Holistic Healing, Death, Reincarnation, Birth, Past Life Regression, Spirituality **PLACE OF BIRTH:** Walton, NY **EDUCATION:** Geneva College, Beaver Falls, PA **YEARS:** 3 **EDUCATION:** Los Angeles Pacific College, Los Angeles, CA **YEARS:** 3 **DEGREE:** B.A. **YEAR DEGREE:** 1962 **OCCUPATION:** Founder Rebirthing & Other Movements, Physical Immortality, Money, Politics **WORK EXPERIENCE:** Consciousness Village, Sierraville, CA, President, 14 years, topic-Breathing; Inspiration University, Chico, CA, Founder, 16 years, topic-Physical Immortality **AWARDS:** Rebirthing Movement, Founder, 1974; Money Seminar-Prosperity Consciousness, Founder; Who's Who of CA; Professor of Seminary-New Age Church of Being **PROFESSIONAL MEMBERSHIPS:** Conscious Breathers Association, Founder; Infinite Intelligence **PUBLICATIONS:** *Physical Immortality*, 1980, 1988 **PUBLISHER:** Inspiration University **PUBLICATIONS:** *Rebirthing In The New Age*, 1977 **PUBLISHER:** Celestial Arts **PUBLICATIONS:** *Breath Awareness*, 1985 **PUBLISHER:** Inspiration University

Orr, Tamra B.
P.O. Box 386
Leesburg, IN 46538

TOPICS: New Age **PUBLICATIONS:** *Priority Parenting*

Osborn, Nancy
1280 South Powerline Road, #721
Pompano Beach, FL 33069
(305)-979-1084

TOPICS: Psychic, Occult, Psychic Phenomena, Ghosts, Witchcraft **DATE OF BIRTH:** 08/26/39 **PLACE OF BIRTH:** East Chicago, Indiana **EDUCATION:** Indiana University **EDUCATION:** Nova University **YEARS:** 1972-73 **DEGREE:** Psychology **OCCUPATION:** Author, Lecturer, TV & Radio Interviews **WORK EXPERIENCE:** Bantam Books, New York, NY, In-House Author 1977-86 **PROFESSIONAL MEMBERSHIPS:** Authors Guild, New York, NY, member 1978-present **PUBLICATIONS:** *Haunted Houses, More Haunted Houses* **PUBLICATIONS:** *The Demon Syndrome*

Osgood, Sylvia K.
14291 East Warren Place
Aurora, CO 80014
(303)-752-1669

TOPICS: Crystals

Osis, Dr. Karlis
American Society Psychical Research
5 West 73rd Street
New York, NY 10023

TOPICS: Parapsychology

Ossana, Helen Roberta
Dream Network Journal
1337 Powerhouse Lane, Ste. 22
Moab, UT 84532-3031
(801)-259-5936

TOPICS: Dreams

Otten, Charlotte, Ph. D.
Calvin College
Grand Rapids, MI 49546
(616)-957-6468

TOPICS: Werewolves, Occult PLACE OF BIRTH: Chicago, IL EDUCATION: Michigan State University YEARS: 1969-71 DEGREE: Ph. D. YEAR DEGREE: 1971 EDUCATION: University of Michigan YEARS: 1967-69 DEGREE: M.A. YEAR DEGREE: 1969 OCCUPATION: Professor, Author WORK EXPERIENCE: Calvin College, Grand Rapids, MI, Professor English Literature 1977-present PROFESSIONAL MEMBERSHIPS: Modern Language Assoc.; Milton Society; Society For Textual Scholarship PUBLICATIONS: *Environ'd With Eternity*, 1985 PUBLISHER: Coronado PUBLICATIONS: *Buried Voices, Buried Lives*, 1991 PUBLISHER: University Presses of FL. PUBLICATIONS: *A Lycanthropy Reader Werewolves In Western Culture* PUBLISHER: Syracuse University Press

Otterpohl, Karen
43-09 54th Street, Apt. 3F
Woodside, NY 11377
TOPICS: Parapsychology

Otto, A. Stuart, Jr.
Dominion Press
P.O. Box 4608
Salem, OR 97302-8608
TOPICS: Metaphysics

Overlee, Vern
19 Scott Street
Post Falls, ID 83854
TOPICS: Channeling

Pacal, Joe
Maui EcoPark
P.O. Box 281
Makawao, HI 96768
(808)-572-5857

TOPICS: New Age, Vegetarianism, Health Food, Holistic Health DATE OF BIRTH: 10/05/52 PLACE OF BIRTH: Glendale, CA OCCUPATION: EcoFuturist, Gardener, Lecturer, Author, Teacher WORK EXPERIENCE: Center For Ecological Living, Haiku, HI, Director, 7 years AWARDS: Permaculture Design Certified PROFESSIONAL MEMBERSHIPS: International Brotherhood of Environmental Comedians 1976-present DESCRIPTION: Lectures on the Ecology of Human Spirit & Consciousness in Nature & the practical implications thereof. PUBLICATIONS: *Hatching Out*, 1988 PUBLISHER: Joe Pacal

Packer, Duane
LuminEssence
P. O. Box 19117
Oakland, CA 94619
TOPICS: Channeling

Painter, John
Internal Arts
Box 1777
Arlington, TX 76004
(817)-860-0129
TOPICS: New Age

Paladin, David

Box 11942
Albuquerque, NM 87192
TOPICS: Channeling

Palmer, Raenette
Natural Notes
Box 299
Flint, MI 48501
(313)-232-4632

TOPICS: Holistic Healing

Palmer, Sue
Essential Energies
16 Glebe Point Road
Glebe, N.S.W. 2037,
Australia
TOPICS: Crystals

Pardue, Leslie
Earth Action Network
28 Knight Street
Norwalk, CT 06851
(203)-226-9265

TOPICS: New Age

Parisi, Guido U.
Farind SAS, Corso Ciulio Cesare 155
10155 Torino,
Italy
TOPICS: Crystals

Parker, Alice Ann
59-075 Puula Road
Haleiwa, HI 96712
TOPICS: Channeling

Parrish-IIarra, Carol E.
Sparrow Hawk Press
22 Summit Ridge Drive
Tahlequah, OK 74464-9215
(918)-456-3421 (918)-456-3421

TOPICS: Meditation, Spirituality, Kabbalah, Yoga, Death, Psychic Healing, Reincarnation DATE OF BIRTH: 01/21/35 PLACE OF BIRTH: Nettleton, AR EDUCATION: Sancta Sophis Seminary, Tahlequah, OK DEGREE: Ph.D. YEAR DEGREE: 1990 OCCUPATION: Seminary Dean, Church Pastor, Author, Lecturer WORK EXPERIENCE: Light Of Christ Community Church, Tahlequah, OK, Pastor, President, 1981-91; Sparrowhawk Village, Tahlequah, OK, Founder AWARDS: D.D. National Christian University of Missouri PROFESSIONAL MEMBERSHIPS: International Council of Community Churches, Board Member; World Federation of Healing; U.S. Councillor 1988-91 DESCRIPTION: Lectures and writes on the topics of meditation, spiritual science, mystery teachings, Kabbalah, Esoteric Christianity, Agni Yoga, intuitive development, death & dying, spiritual healing, reincarnation & evolution. PUBLICATIONS: *Book Of Rituals*, 1990 PUBLISHER: IBS PUBLICATIONS: *Messengers Of Hope*, 1983 PUBLISHER: New Age Press PUBLICATIONS: *Aquarian Rosary*, 1988 PUBLISHER: Sparrow Hawk Press PUBLICATIONS: *New Age Handbook On Death & Dying*, 1989 PUBLISHER: IBS

Pasqua, Sandy
Academy of Scientific Hypnotherapy
Box 12041
San Diego, CA 92112
(619)-427-6225

TOPICS: Hypnotism

Pass, Bart
Spectrum Chamber Productions
406 Belford Place
Takoma Park, MD 20912
(301)-891-2079

TOPICS: Crystals

Pati, Kumar
Health World, Inc.
1477 Rollins Road
Burlingame, CA 94010
(415)-343-1637

TOPICS: Holistic Healing

Pattullo, Dr. E.L.
Center For The Behavioral Sciences
Harvard University, William Ja
33 Kirland Street
Cambridge, MA 02138
TOPICS: New Age

Paulson, Genevieve Lewis
Dimensions Of Evolvement, Inc.
Box 456
Melbourne, AR 72556
(501)-368-4468

TOPICS: Channeling, Holistic Health

Payne, Larry, Ph. D.
Healthy Back, Healthy Mind Institute
4150 Tivoli Avenue
Los Angeles, CA 90066
(213)-306-8845

TOPICS: Holistic Health DESCRIPTION: title above is a videotape. PUBLICATIONS: *Healthy Back, Healthy Mind*

Payne, Niravi B.
Heights Holistic Health Associates
100 Remsen Street
Brooklyn, NY 11201
(718)-625-4802

TOPICS: Holistic Healing

Pearcy, Gene
New Age Source
7538 Royer Avenue
Canoga Park, CA 91307
(213)-992-4526

TOPICS: New Age

Peck, Mary
Rural Route 1, Box 1335
Johnson, VT 05656
TOPICS: Channeling

Peck, Tom
Jeanne Youngson Publishers
29 Washington Square, West
New York, NY 10011
(212)-533-5018

TOPICS: Vampires

Peckman, Ann
969 Valleyvista Avenue
Pittsburgh, PA 18707
TOPICS: Channeling

Pelisson, Suzanne
Davis Communications Company

11426 Cedar Avenue #D-3
Cleveland, OH 44106-2611
(216)-662-6969

TOPICS: Holistic Healing

Pepe, Stan
Barbara Brake/Stan Pepe Enterprises
807 Esplanade Avenue #14
New Orleans, LA 70116
(504)-525-0591

TOPICS: Crystals

Peper, Erik
Biofeedback & Family Therapy Institute
2236 Derby Street
Berkeley, CA 94705
(415)-841-7227

TOPICS: Holistic Healing OCCUPATION: Author, Biofeedback Specialist, Teacher WORK EXPERIENCE: Biofeedback & Family Therapy Institute, Berkeley, CA, Co-Dir., 1973-Present; San Francisco State U., San Francisco, CA, Teacher; United States Rhythmic Gymnastic Team, Behavioral Scientist AWARDS: Award For Excellence, 1982, Nurse Healers Professional Associates. PROFESSIONAL MEMBERSHIPS: Biofeedback Society Of America, Past Pres.; Biofeedback Society Of California, Past Pres. DESCRIPTION: An international authority on Biofeedback. Has written numerous research articles & books on the subject.

Perasso, Joy
Michael Educational Foundation
10 Muth Drive
Orinda, CA 94563
(510)-254-4730

TOPICS: Past Life Regression, Metaphysics OCCUPATION: Past-Life Regression Therapist WORK EXPERIENCE: Michael Educational Foundation, Orinda, CA, Therapist PROFESSIONAL MEMBERSHIPS: American Association Of Past-Life Regression Therapists DESCRIPTION: Offers private sessions for past-life regression therapy. Also operates the Guided Crystal jewelry shops offering gems, minerals & jewelry.

Perelom, Renate
P.O. Box 4845
Key West, FL 33401

TOPICS: Channeling

Perlis, Michael
Rodale Press, Inc.
33 East Minor Street
Emmaus, PA 18049
(215)-967-5171

TOPICS: Holistic Healing

Perry, Lee
Meditation Magazine
17211 Orozco Street
Granada Hills, CA 91344-1132
(818)-343-4998

TOPICS: Meditation

Persinger, Michael A., Ph. D.
Neuroscience Laboratory
Laurentian University
Sudbury, Ontario P3E 2C6
Canada
(705)-675-1151 (705)-522-0203

TOPICS: Parapsychology DATE OF BIRTH: 06/26/45 PLACE OF BIRTH: Jacksonville, FL EDUCATION: University of Manitoba, Winnipeg, Canada DEGREE: Ph. D. YEAR DEGREE: 1971 EDUCATION: University of Tennessee, Knoxville, TN DEGREE: M.A. YEAR DEGREE: 1969 OCCUPATION: Professor, Author WORK EXPERIENCE: Laurentian University, Sudbury, Canada, Professor Neuroscience/Clinical Neuropsychology AWARDS: Laurentian University, Research Excellence Award, 1988 PUBLICATIONS: *Neuropsychological Bases Of God Beliefs*, 1987 PUBLISHER: Praeger PUBLICATIONS: *TM And Cultmania*, 1980 PUBLISHER: Christopher Publishing

Peterson, Jason
Metaphysial Consultants
P. O. Box 64027
Tucson, AZ 85603

TOPICS: Channeling

Petranker, Jack
Nyingma Institute
1815 Highland Place
Berkeley, CA 94709
(415)-843-6812

TOPICS: Holistic Healing

Petschek, Joyce
The Studio
10Λ Girdlers Road
London, W14 OPU
England
(071)-727-0882

TOPICS: Dreams, Spirituality, New Age, Psychic, PSI DATE OF BIRTH: 03/06/33 PLACE OF BIRTH: New York, NY EDUCATION: Vassar College DEGREE: B.A., Art/History YEAR DEGREE: 1955 EDUCATION: Radcliffe College DEGREE: M.A., Art History YEAR DEGREE: 1956 OCCUPATION: Dreams/ Visions, Author, Lecturer AWARDS: Vassar, 1955; Elinor Wardell Township Award PROFESSIONAL MEMBERSHIPS: The Society of Authors, London, England DESCRIPTION: Gives seminars, Dream Series. Explores the value & origin of dreams & visions through a slide collection of fairy tales, painting & sculpture & studies their practical application in daily life. Studies flying, lucid, precognitive & vision dreams. PUBLICATIONS: *Silver Dreams*, 1991 PUBLISHER: Celestial Arts PUBLICATIONS: *The Silver Bird*, 1981 PUBLISHER: Celestial Arts PUBLICATIONS: *Lucinda's Dreadful Dream*, 1992/93

Pettitt, Michael
Dispensable Healing Center
403 Kingston Street
Victoria, Br V8V 1V8
Canada
(604)-384-5560

TOPICS: Holistic Healing

Pettitt, Sabina
Dispensable Healing Center
403 Kingston Street
Victoria, Br V8V 1V8
Canada
(604)-384-5560

TOPICS: Holistic Healing

Pfarr, Don
Williams & Wilkins

428 East Preston Street
Baltimore, MD 21202
(301)-528-4000

TOPICS: Holistic Healing

Pfarr, Donald
Oxford University Press
200 Madison Avenue
New York, NY 10016
(212)-679-7300

TOPICS: Holistic Healing

Phillips, Elizabeth
Unity Center For Growth And Healing
3500 Sharon View Road
Charlotte, NC 28211
(704)-553-0756

TOPICS: Holistic Healing

Phillips, Jervais
Unity Center For Growth And Healing
3500 Sharon View Road
Charlotte, NC 28211
(704)-553-0756

TOPICS: Holistic Healing

Pievson, Janaki
Woodbury Yoga Center
122 West Side Road
Woodbury, CT 06798
(203)-263-2254

TOPICS: Yoga

Pike, Diane K.
LP Publications
P.O. Box 7601
San Diego, CA 92107-0601
(619)-225-0133

TOPICS: New Age

Pine, Mort
Regency Health Resort And Spa
2000 South Ocean Drive
Hallandale, FL 33009
(305)-454-2220

TOPICS: Holistic Healing

Pitts, Edward
Leisure Publishers
3923 West 6th Street
Los Angeles, CA 90020
(213)-385-3926

TOPICS: Holistic Healing

Pollack, Rachel
2150 Rt. 9-G
Rhinebeck, NY 12572
(914)-876-5797

TOPICS: Tarot, Metaphysics DATE OF BIRTH: 08/17/45 PLACE OF BIRTH: Brooklyn, NY EDUCATION: New York University, New York, NY YEARS: 1963-67 DEGREE: B.A. YEAR DEGREE: 1967 EDUCATION: Claremont Graduate School, Claremont, CA YEARS: 1967-68 DEGREE: M.A. YEAR DEGREE: 1968 OCCUPATION: Author AWARDS: Arthur C. Clark Award-Best Novel 1988 DESCRIPTION: Science Fiction Writers Of America PUBLICATIONS: *78 Degrees Of Wisdom, Part 1 & 2*, 1980, 1983 PUBLICATIONS: *Salvador Dali's Tarot*, 1985 PUBLICATIONS: *Teach Yourself Fortune Telling*, 1986 PUBLICATIONS: *The Open*

Labyrinth, 1986 PUBLICATIONS: *The New Tarot*, 1989 PUBLICATIONS: *The Haindl Tarot, Part 1 & 2*, 1990

Pollinger, Kenneth
New Age Center
One South Broadway
Nyack, NY 10960
(914)-353-2590

TOPICS: Holistic Healing

Pond, David
509 Orchard Lane
Port Angeles, WA 98362
(206)-452-3622 (206)-452-8211

TOPICS: Astrology, Metaphysics, Crystals DATE OF BIRTH: 12/04/48 PLACE OF BIRTH: Seattle, WA EDUCATION: Central Washington State U, Ellensburg, WA DEGREE: M.A. Metaphysics OCCUPATION: Astrologer, Author, Lecturer PUBLICATIONS: *Metaphysical Handbook*, 1984 PUBLISHER: Reflecting Pond Publications PUBLICATIONS: *Astrological Counseling*, 1991 PUBLISHER: Llewellyn

Popenoe, Cris
Yes Bookshop
1035 31st Street, NW
Washington, DC 20007
(202)-338-2727

TOPICS: New Age

Popenoe, Ollie
Yes! Educational Society
P.O. Box 5719
Tacoma Park, MD 20912
(202)-829-3289

TOPICS: Holistic Healing

Porter, Pat
Inner Dimensions, Incorporated
500 East Calaveras Avenue #210
Milpitas, CA 95035
(408)-263-4940

TOPICS: Crystals

Poster, Bruce
Poster Market Research
725 Pinon Drive
Santa Fe, NM 87501
(505)-989-8500

TOPICS: New Age, Tarot, Psychic DATE OF BIRTH: 02/17/46 PLACE OF BIRTH: Omaha, NE EDUCATION: University of Chicago, Chicago, Ill YEARS: 1964-68 DEGREE: B.A. YEAR DEGREE: 1968 EDUCATION: California State U at Fresno, Fresno, CA YEARS: 1970-72 DEGREE: MCRP YEAR DEGREE: 1972 OCCUPATION: President, Consultant & Owner of Marketing Skills Company for New Age businesses WORK EXPERIENCE: Poster Market Research, Santa Fe, NM, President 1977-present; Resource Planning Associates, Cambridge, MA, Senior Associate 1974-77 PROFESSIONAL MEMBERSHIPS: Santa Fe, NM, Chamber of Commerce DESCRIPTION: Owns & directs Marketing Skills Company that trains practitioners in the New Age field. Offers marketing workshops throughout the country.

Pottenger, Maritha
ACS Publications, Inc.
P.O. Box 34487

San Diego, CA 92163
(619)-297-9203

TOPICS: Astrology DATE OF BIRTH: 05/21/52 PLACE OF BIRTH: Tucson, AZ EDUCATION: University of California, Berkeley, CA YEARS: 1970-74 DEGREE: B.A. YEAR DEGREE: 1974 EDUCATION: California School of Professional Psychology YEARS: 1974-76 DEGREE: M.A. YEAR DEGREE: 1976 OCCUPATION: Editorial Directory, Author WORK EXPERIENCE: Astro Computing Services, Inc., San Diego, CA, Editorial Director of Astrology, 8 years PROFESSIONAL MEMBERSHIPS: International Society For Astrological Research; National Council For Geo Cosmic Research; American Federation Of Astrologers DESCRIPTION: Performs services as a private consultant & lecturer of Astrology. PUBLICATIONS: *Encounter Astrology*, 1978 PUBLISHER: TIA Publications PUBLICATIONS: *Healing With The Horoscope*, 1982 PUBLISHER: ACS Publications PUBLICATIONS: *Astro Essentials: Planets In Signs, Houses And Aspects* PUBLISHER: ACS Publications PUBLICATIONS: *Complete Horoscope Interpretation* PUBLISHER: ACS Publications

Prakashananda, Swami
Integral Yoga Magazine
Route 1
Box 172
Buckingham, VA 23921
(804)-969-4801

TOPICS: Holistic Healing

Precourt, Reverend Carolyn Lee
1930-82 Encinitas Road
San Marcos, CA 92069
(619)-727-2679

TOPICS: Crystals

Preston, Cliff
P.O. Box 35
Orangeville, Ont. L9W225,
Canada

TOPICS: Channeling

Price, Richard
Esalen Institute
Pacific Coast Highway
Big Sur, CA 93920
(408)-667-2335 (408)-667-3000

TOPICS: Massage

Price-Haberer, Sandra
P.O. Box 337
Clyde, NC 28721

TOPICS: Channeling

Priestman, Sarah
Omega Institute For Holistic Studies
Lake Drive
RD 2, Box 377
Rhinebeck, NY 12572
(914)-338-6030

TOPICS: Holistic Healing

Priya
Starseed Crystals
15 Montclair Court
Petaluma, CA 94952
(707)-778-8469

TOPICS: Crystals

Proes and Serena
3507 West Lakeside Drive
Birmingham, Alabama 35243

TOPICS: Channeling

Prophet, Elizabeth Clare
Summit University Press
Box A
Livingston, MT 59047
(406)-222-8300

TOPICS: Channeling, Spirituality, New Age, Metaphysics DATE OF BIRTH: 04/08/40 PLACE OF BIRTH: Red Bank, NJ EDUCATION: Antioch College EDUCATION: Boston U., Boston, MA DEGREE: B.A. Political Science OCCUPATION: Teacher, lecturer, author WORK EXPERIENCE: Church Universal & Triumphant, Royal Teton Ranch, Summit Lighthouse, Livingston, MT, Leader, Founder; Summit U., Montessori International, Summit U. Press, Livingston, MT, Leader, Founder; The Coming Revolution In Higher Consciousness, Host Cable TV Show DESCRIPTION: Author, teacher, lecturer, TV host on New Age spiritualism & the teachings of the Ascended Masters. PUBLICATIONS: *The Lost Years Of Jesus* PUBLISHER: Summit University Press PUBLICATIONS: *Saint Germain On Alchemy* PUBLISHER: Summit University Press PUBLICATIONS: *The Human Aura* PUBLISHER: Summit University Press PUBLICATIONS: *The Lost Teachings Of Jesus* PUBLISHER: Summit University Press PUBLICATIONS: *Climb The Highest Mountain* PUBLISHER: Summit University Press

Puchert, Ingeborg
University Of Healing
1101 Far Valley Road
Campo, CA 91906
(619)-478-5111

TOPICS: Holistic Healing, Metaphysics

Queenan, John T.
National Women's Health Report, Inc.
P.O. Box 25307
Georgetown Station
Washington, DC 20007

TOPICS: Holistic Healing

Quigley, David
2310 Warwick Drive
Santa Rosa, CA 95405
(707)-579-4984

TOPICS: Holistic Healing, Hypnotism DATE OF BIRTH: 10/01/50 PLACE OF BIRTH: China EDUCATION: Duke University, Durham, N.C. YEARS: 1968-72 DEGREE: B.A. YEAR DEGREE: 1972 EDUCATION: Applied Hypnosis Center, Santa Rosa, CA YEARS: 1981-82 DEGREE: C.H. OCCUPATION: Author, Director, Instructor WORK EXPERIENCE: Alchemical Hypnotherapy Institute, Santa Rosa, CA, Director, 1986-present PROFESSIONAL MEMBERSHIPS: American Council of Hypnotist Examiners, designated examiner & approved instructor. PUBLICATIONS: *Alchemical Hypnotherapy*, 1984 PUBLISHER: Lost Coast Press PUBLICATIONS: *Alchemical Journal*, 1985-90 PUBLISHER: Alchemical Hypnotherapy Institute

Quigley, Joan
1055 California Street
San Francisco, CA 94108

TOPICS: Astrology **OCCUPATION:** Astrologer, Author **PROFESSIONAL MEMBERSHIPS:** American Federation Of Astrologers **DESCRIPTION:** Offers Astrological Readings. Astrologer to Nancy Reagan. **PUBLICATIONS:** *What Does Joan Say - My Seven Years As White House Astrologer*

Raben, Norman
Raben Publishing Co.
711 Boylston Street
Boston, MA 02116
(617)-236-1885

TOPICS: Holistic Healing

Radhoff, Sandra J.
Universalia, Inc.
P.O. Box 6243
Denver, CO 80206
(303)-989-8727

TOPICS: Metaphysics, Channeling, New Age

Ragush, Sheila
Community Health Services Association
455 2nd Avenue, North
Saskatoon SK S7K 2,
Canada
(306)-664-4243

TOPICS: Holistic Healing

Raja
165 West 20th Street, Apt. 3J
New York, NY 10011
(212)-242-2635

TOPICS: Tarot, Numerology, Psychic, Past Life Regression, Crystals, Hypnotism, Metaphysics **PLACE OF BIRTH:** New York, NY **EDUCATION:** Bharatiya Kala Kendra, New Delhi, India **OCCUPATION:** Psychic, Teacher, Author, Lecturer **WORK EXPERIENCE:** Psychic Masters- New York Cable TV Show, Host **DESCRIPTION:** Specializes in Tarot, Hypnotherapy, Past Life Regression, Numerology & Crystal Therapy. Offers private or group readings.

Rak, Sheryl M.
SMR Consulting
4826 West Byron Street
Chicago, IL 60641
(312)-283-6957

TOPICS: Crystals

Rakela, Christine
166 West 75th Street
New York, NY 10023

TOPICS: Astrology

Ramakrishna, Rao Dr. K.
Institute For Parapsychology-Duke University
Box 6847
College Station
Durham, NC 27708
(919)-698-8241

TOPICS: Parapsychology

Raman, Dr. B.V.
Raman Publications
Sri Rajeswari
115/1, New Extension, Seshadripuram
Bangalore, 560 020
India
369-382

TOPICS: Astrology, Homeopathy, Spirituality **PLACE OF BIRTH:** Bangalore, India **EDUCATION:** Central College, Bangalore, India **DEGREE:** Homeopathy **OCCUPATION:** Author, Astrologer, Lecturer **WORK EXPERIENCE:** Astrological Magazine, Bangalore, India, President, Editor 1936-present **AWARDS:** Fellow, Royal Astronomical Society **PROFESSIONAL MEMBERSHIPS:** Royal Asiatic Society **DESCRIPTION:** Engaged in the study of relations between cosmic & terrestrial phenomena. Special fields of research are Hindu Astronomy, political forecasts, disease-diagnosis, astro-psychology, weather, Astrology, Philosophy & Indian Culture. **PUBLICATIONS:** *Planetary Influences On Human Affairs* **PUBLISHER:** Raman Associates **PUBLICATIONS:** *Notable Horoscopes* **PUBLISHER:** Raman Associates **PUBLICATIONS:** *B.V. Raman - The Man And His Mission* **PUBLISHER:** Raman Associates **PUBLICATIONS:** *Hindu Predictive Astrology* **PUBLISHER:** Raman Associates **PUBLICATIONS:** *Brihat Jataka* **PUBLISHER:** Raman Associates **PUBLICATIONS:** *Nirayana Tables Of Houses* **PUBLISHER:** Raman Associates

Ramanda, Azana
Reflections Of Divinity
P. O. Box 30724
Santa Barbara, CA 93130

TOPICS: Channeling

Ramirez, Rev. Jack
Metaphysical Fellowship
P.O. Box 13
Lebanon, OR 97355

TOPICS: Metaphysics, Channeling

Rand, William L.
Center For Reiki Training
20782 Knobwoods Drive, Ste. 203
Southfield, MI 48076
(313)-948-8112

TOPICS: Holistic Healing, Reiki, Meditation, Spirituality **OCCUPATION:** Reiki Master/Teacher, Hypnotherapist, Rosicrucian, Fire Walker, Rebirther, Astrologer, Tarot Reader **WORK EXPERIENCE:** Center For Reiki Training, Southfield, MI, Founder, Director **DESCRIPTION:** Reiki Master of the Usui lineage. Specializes in Metaphysics, Hypnotherapy, Past Life Regression Therapy, Spiritual Development, Fire Walking, Rebirthing, Astrology, Tarot & Neuro-Linguistic Programming. Teaches Reiki full time in the U.S. & Canada.

Randall, R.
Through Grace
234 East 58th Street, 22
New York, NY 10022

TOPICS: Channeling

Randi, James
Committee For The Scientific Investigation Of Claims
12000 NW 8th Street
Plantation, FL 33317
(305)-370-1128

TOPICS: Skepticism **PLACE OF BIRTH:** Toronto, Canada **OCCUPATION:** Magician, Skeptic and Debunker of Paranormal Phenomena **WORK EXPERIENCE:** Committee For The Scientific Investigation Of Claims Of The Paranormal **DESCRIPTION:** Magician and skeptic who exposes frauds and fraudulant claims in the field of paranormal phenomena.

Randolph, Betty Lee, Ph. D.
Success Education Insitute
Box 90608
San Diego, CA 92109

TOPICS: New Age

Rangnath, Molly
International Chiropractors Association
1110 North Glebe Road
Suite 1000
Arlington, VA 22201
(703)-528-5000

TOPICS: Holistic Healing

Ranjel, Robert
Sixth Sense
226 South 312 Street
Federal Way, WA 98003

TOPICS: Channeling

Rao, Dr. Dwarakanath
University Of Michigan Hospital
Department Of Psychiatry
Ann Arbor, MI 48109

TOPICS: Parapsychology

Raphael, Janice
521 Queens Street
Westbury, NY 11590

TOPICS: Parapsychology

Raphaell, Katrina
Crystal Academy Of Advanced Healing Arts
P.O. Box 3208
Taos, NM 87571
(505)-758-9333

TOPICS: Crystals

Rapkin, David, Ph. D.
3122 Santa Monica Boulevard P. H. West
Santa Monica, CA 90404

TOPICS: Channeling

Rasmussen, Diane
Alcyone Light Centre
1965 Hilt Road
Hornbrook, CA 96044-9744
(916)-475-3310

TOPICS: New Age

Rau, Pam
Astara, Inc.
800 West Arrow Highway
P.O. Box 5003
Upland, CA 91786
(714)-981-4941

TOPICS: Metaphysics

Rawls, Robert
Communications Channels, Inc.
390 Fifth Avenue
New York, NY 10018
(212)-613-9700

TOPICS: Holistic Healing

Ray, Dan
National Health Federation
212 West Foothill Boulevard
P.O. Box 688
Monrovia, CA 91016

(818)-357-2181

TOPICS: Holistic Healing

Ray, Eve Athey
Movement Expression
622 Las Lomas Avenue
Pacific Palisades, CA 90272
(213)-454-5335

TOPICS: Holistic Healing

Ray, Sondra
Loving Relationships Training
Founder Of Loving Relationships Training
P.O. Box 1465
Washington, CT 06793
(800)-468-5578 (206)-788-4920

TOPICS: Reincarnation DATE OF BIRTH: 08/24/41 EDUCATION: University of Florida College of Nursing YEARS: 1960-1963 DEGREE: Nursing YEAR DEGREE: 1963 EDUCATION: University of Arizona Graduate School YEAR DEGREE: 1969 OCCUPATION: Founder of Loving Relationships Training & Author WORK EXPERIENCE: Loving Relationships Training PROFESSIONAL MEMBERSHIPS: Rebirthing Society DESCRIPTION: Founder of peace organization called Loving Relationships Training, author of 11 books published by Celestial Arts Publishing, Rebirther, and international speaker on peace relationships, rejuvenation, rebirthing & healing. PUBLICATIONS: *I Deserve Love* PUBLICATIONS: *Loving Relationships* PUBLICATIONS: *Rebirthing In The New Age* PUBLICATIONS: *Idea Birth* PUBLICATIONS: *Birth And Relationships* PUBLICATIONS: *How To Be Chic, Fabulous, And Live Forever*

Ray, Sondra
Loving Relationships Training
Box 4
Palm Beach, FL 33480
(305)-720-7112 (212)-799-7323

TOPICS: New Age

Rea, Alayna
High Peak Crystal Company
1272 Bear Mountain Court
Boulder, CO 80303
(303)-494-5192

TOPICS: Crystals, Channeling

Rea, John
High Peak Crystal Company
1272 Bear Mountain Court
Boulder, CO 80303
(303)-494-5192

TOPICS: Crystals, Channeling

Redditt-Lyon, Elizabeth
Midwifery Today
Box 2672
Eugene, OR 97402
(503)-345-5536

TOPICS: Holistic Healing

Reed, Anderson
235 East Front Street
Media, PA 19063
(215)-565-6075

TOPICS: Crystals

Reed, Henry

Sundance Community Newsletter
503 Lake Drive
Virginia Beach, VA 23451
(804)-422-0371

TOPICS: Dreams

Reichenberg-Ullman, Dr. Judyth
The Northwest Center For Holistic Medicine
4072 9th Avenue N.E.
Seattle, WA 98105
(206)-547-9665

TOPICS: Holistic Healing

Reiss, Andrew
2314-6 Glendale Boulevard
Los Angeles, CA 90039

TOPICS: New Age, Psychic, Metaphysics, Channeling OCCUPATION: Author, Lecturer, Psychic, Counselor, Dr. of Metaphysics DESCRIPTION: Professional psychic & successful practitioner since 1954. Interviewed extensively on Radio & TV talk shows. Offers counselling, lectures, writings & world news proven predictions. Offers Whole-Life Speaker Workshops. Co-founder of UForum.

Reiss, Gary
Center For Well-Being
82644 Howe Lane
Creswell, OR 97426
(503)-895-2953

TOPICS: Holistic Healing

Renee, Deborah
Harmony Network
P.O. Box 976
Lake Oswego, OR 97034

TOPICS: New Age

Revels-Bey, Brother Frank
Floating Healing Meditation Circle
P.O. 13
Uniondale, NY 11553
(516)-483-7264 (516)-433-9118

TOPICS: Numerology, Tarot, Dreams, Psychic, Metaphysics, Tai Chi, New Age DATE OF BIRTH: 03/16/52 PLACE OF BIRTH: East Meadow, NY EDUCATION: Bard College, Annandale-On-The-Hudson, NY YEARS: 1970-74 DEGREE: B.A. Fine Arts YEAR DEGREE: 1974 EDUCATION: U.L.C., CA DEGREE: Ms. D. Metaphysician YEAR DEGREE: 1987 EDUCATION: U.L.C., CA DEGREE: Ministry YEAR DEGREE: 1987 OCCUPATION: Psychic, Occultist, Parapsychologist, Lecturer, Author WORK EXPERIENCE: Floating Healing Meditation Circle, Uniondale, NY, Founder 1985; Inner Spiritual Attunement, Hicksville, NY, Instructor 1990 AWARDS: Dean of Metaphysics 1984-85; New Life Institute Of Harlem PROFESSIONAL MEMBERSHIPS: Honorary Member of Martial Arts of China Society (Historical); Floating Healing Meditation Circle; AMORC DESCRIPTION: Lectures on Psychic and Metaphysical topics. Has appeared on numerous radio & cable TV programs. Participates in various psychic fairs & festivals. Teaches Inner Spiritual Attunement, ISA, to achieve balance through meditation & electromagnetic energy. PUBLICATIONS: *R.C.V. And The Light Within*, 1983 PUBLICATIONS: *Beyond The Veil, Into The Light, Crystal Horizon*, 1987

Reynolds, Dennis
Center For Holistic Health
42 Lincoln Street
Framingham, MA 01701
(508)-879-3002

TOPICS: Holistic Healing

Reynolds, Shiela
P.O. Box 155
Washington Crossing, PA 18977

TOPICS: Channeling

Rhea, Gerry
Indianapolis Center For Attitudinal Healing
P.O. Box 55016
Indianapolis, IN 46205
(317)-251-5543

TOPICS: Holistic Healing

Rice, John
American Institute Of Nutrition
9650 Rockville Pike
Bethesda, MD 20814
(301)-530-7100

TOPICS: Holistic Healing

Rich, Beatrice
14 Horatio Street
New York, NY 10014

TOPICS: Psychic

Rich, Tracey
White Lotus Foundation
2500 San Marcos Pass
Santa Barbara, CA 93105
(805)-964-1944

TOPICS: Yoga, Meditation, Holistic Health DATE OF BIRTH: 06/21/57 PLACE OF BIRTH: Nashville, TN EDUCATION: U. of Fl, Gainesville, FL YEARS: 2 years OCCUPATION: Yoga Master WORK EXPERIENCE: White Lotus Foundation, Santa Barbara, CA, Associate Director 8 years AWARDS: Yoga Acharya Degree, 1988 PUBLICATIONS: *Yoga: The Flow Series-A Workout Video*, 1990 PUBLISHER: White Lotus Foundation

Richard, Kathleen
Transpersonal Institute
Box 3049
Stanford, CA 94309
(415)-327-2066

TOPICS: New Age

Richards, Dawn
HLQ Associates
Box 86054
Pittsburgh, PA 15221
(412)-731-5533

TOPICS: Holistic Healing

Richards, Evan
P.O. Box 8464
Santa Cruz, CA 95061
(408)-462-6715

TOPICS: Holistic Health

Richardson, Gail
11709 Pawnee Drive, Southwest
Tacoma, WA 98499

TOPICS: Channeling

Richardson, Marcia
Rolf Institute
Box 1868
Boulder, CO 80306
(303)-449-5903

TOPICS: New Age

Richter, Cynthia
635 East 9th Street, #1
New York, NY 10009
(212)-674-7169

TOPICS: Channeling, Psychic, Astrology, Tarot, Numerology, Holistic Healing, Past Life Regression PLACE OF BIRTH: New York, NY EDUCATION: New York U., New York, NY DEGREE: B.A. EDUCATION: Long Island U., NY DEGREE: M.A. EDUCATION: United Nations DEGREE: Certificate of Completion OCCUPATION: Lecturer, Psychic, Healer, Consultant WORK EXPERIENCE: World Citizens' Assembly On Environmental Issues-United Nations, New York, NY; New Life Expo '91, New York, NY, Seminar & Workshop Leader DESCRIPTION: Psychic Channeler interested in Western & Chinese Astrology, Tarot, Numerology, Past Life Recall, Occult, Dreams, Astral Projection, Metaphysics & Healing via color, metals, music & gems. Offers seminars, workshops, consultations & healing cassettes.

Riendeau, Renee
Rainbow Connection For Attitudinal Healing And Learning
444 Piedmont Street, #309
Glendale, CA 91206
(818)-241-0691

TOPICS: Holistic Healing

Rifkin, Andrew
Nutrition Health Review
171 Madison Avenue
New York, NY 10016
(212)-679-3590

TOPICS: Holistic Healing

Rifkin, Frank R.
Nutrition Health Review
171 Madison Avenue
New York, NY 10016
(212)-679-3590

TOPICS: Holistic Healing

Riley, Betsy
American Health Consultants, Inc.
67 Peachtree Park Drive, NE, #
Atlanta, GA 30309
(404)-351-4523

TOPICS: Holistic Healing

Ring, Dr. Kenneth
University Of Connecticut
Department Of Psychology
Storrs, CT 06268
(203)-486-4170

TOPICS: Parapsychology

Rizzuto, Sharida
Baker Street Publications
P.O. Box 994
Metairie, LA 70004
(504)-733-9138

TOPICS: New Age

Roads, Michael J.
Serendipity
P.O. Box 778
Nambour, QLD 4560
Australia
074-421-995

TOPICS: Spirituality, New Age, Health Food DATE OF BIRTH: 04/14/37 PLACE OF BIRTH: Cambridge, England EDUCATION: Shrubbery School, Cambridge, England YEARS: 1942-52 OCCUPATION: Author, Lecturer PUBLICATIONS: *Journey Into Nature*, 1990 PUBLISHER: Kramer, Inc. PUBLICATIONS: *A Guide To Organic Gardening In Australia*, 1976 PUBLISHER: Mary Fisher Book Shop PUBLICATIONS: *A Guide To Organic Living In Australia*, 1977 PUBLISHER: Mary Fisher Book Shop PUBLICATIONS: *Communicating With Nature*, 1985 PUBLISHER: Night Owl PUBLICATIONS: *Talking With Nature*, 1987 PUBLISHER: Kramer, Inc. PUBLICATIONS: *Simple Is Powerful*, 1991 PUBLISHER: Kramer, Inc.

Robbins, Beth
The Gate
P.O. Box 43518
Richmond Heights, OH 44143

TOPICS: Occult

Roberts, Al
The Heaven
Route 1
Box 57
Walkerville, MI 49459
(616)-898-2360

TOPICS: Holistic Healing

Roberts, Bernadette
1901 1/2 Montana Avenue
Santa Monica, CA 90403
(213)-395-4895

TOPICS: Spirituality, Body-Mind Connection, Meditation DATE OF BIRTH: 05/20/32 PLACE OF BIRTH: Los Angeles, CA EDUCATION: University of Southern California, Los Angeles, CA DEGREE: B.A., M.A. YEAR DEGREE: 1972 OCCUPATION: Contemplative, Teacher, Author PUBLICATIONS: *Experience Of No-Self: A Contemplative Journey* PUBLISHER: Shambhala Publications, Inc. PUBLICATIONS: *What Is Self?*, 1989 PUBLISHER: Mary Goens PUBLICATIONS: *Path To No-Self*, 1985 PUBLISHER: Shambhala PUBLICATIONS: *Experience Of No Self*, 1982 PUBLISHER: Shambhala

Roberts, Beryl
26, Rollestone Road
Fawley, Southampton
Hampshire S04 1GB,
England

TOPICS: Crystals

Roberts, Joseph
Common Ground
P.O. Box 34090
Station D
Vancouver, BC V6J 4M1
Canada
(604)-733-2215

TOPICS: Homeopathy

Roberts, Sharyn
The Heaven

2096 Lakeshore Road
Applegate, MI 48401-9715
(616)-898-2360

TOPICS: Holistic Healing

Robertson, Bob
Crystal Adventure
P.O. Box 368
Evergreen, CO 80439
(303)-642-0910

TOPICS: Crystals

Robertson, Sally
Crystal Adventure
P.O. Box 368
Evergreen, CO 80439
(303)-642-0910

TOPICS: Crystals

Robinson, Karl
American Institute Of Homeopathy
1500 Massachusetts Avenue, NW
Washington, DC 20005

TOPICS: Homeopathy

Robinson, Perry
Center For Peace
Route 11
Box 369
Sevierville, TN 37862
(615)-428-3595

TOPICS: Holistic Healing

Robinsong, Shivon
Hollyhock
Box 127
Manson's Landing
Cortes Island, Br V0P 1K0
Canada
(604)-935-6465

TOPICS: Holistic Healing

Roche, John
Business Research Publications, Inc.
817 Broadway
New York, NY 10003
(212)-673-4700

TOPICS: Holistic Healing

Rockwell, Carole Jeanne
Mensa
2626 East 14th Street
Brooklyn, NY 11235

TOPICS: Psychic Phenomena

Rodale, Robert, C.E.O.
Rodale Press, Inc.
33 East Minor Street
Emmaus, PA 18049
(215)-967-5171

TOPICS: Holistic Healing, Health Food DATE OF BIRTH: 03/27/30 EDUCATION: Lehigh University YEARS: 1947-52 OCCUPATION: Editor, Publisher WORK EXPERIENCE: Rodale Press, Emmaus, PA, Publisher DESCRIPTION: Advocate of holistic health, organic food & natural lifestyle. PUBLICATIONS: *Prevention Magazine*, Publisher PUBLICATIONS: *Compost Science*, Publisher PUBLICATIONS: *Environmental Action Bulletin*, Publisher PUBLICATIONS: Executive Fitness Newsletter, Publisher PUBLICATIONS: *The Challenge Of Earthworm Research*, 1961

PUBLICATIONS: *The Basic Book Of Organic Gardening*, 1971

Rodegast, Pat
c/o Val Mylonas
37 Fairfield Place
Fairfield, CT 06430
TOPICS: Channeling

Rodgers, Bill
Re-Creation Center aka Hale Mauli Ola Hou
P.O. Box 1653
Pahoa, HI 96778
(808)-965-9880
TOPICS: Holistic Healing

Rodgers, Marilyn
Re-Creation Center aka Hale Mauli Ola Hou
P.O. Box 1653
Pahoa, HI 96778
(808)-965-9880
TOPICS: Holistic Healing

Rogalski, Leslie
220 Washington Avenue
Havertown, PA 19083
(215)-446-0616
TOPICS: New Age **DESCRIPTION:** Specializes in commercial illustration, book cover design, fiber arts, crafts & costumes.

Rogers, Dr. David Price
University Of North Carolina
Department Of Psychology
Chapel Hill, NC 27514
TOPICS: Parapsychology

Rolfe, Randy
Institute For Creative Solutions
947 Plumsock Road
Newtown Square, PA 19073-1112
(215)-353-7383
TOPICS: New Age, Holistic Health, Spirituality **OCCUPATION:** Lecturer, Counselor, Teacher **WORK EXPERIENCE:** Institute For Creative Solutions, Newtown Square, PA, Founder, director **DESCRIPTION:** Student, teacher, lecturer & counselor of natural holistic & spiritual living for 18 years. Topics include, family blueprint for health & communication for empowerment. Media guestspeaker on national TV & radio. **PUBLICATIONS:** *You Can Postpone Anything But Love* **PUBLICATIONS:** *Adult Children Raising Children* **PUBLICATIONS:** *The Affirmations Book For Sharing*

Roll, William G., Ph. D.
Parapsychological Services Institute
West Georgia College
Psychology Department
Carrollton, GA 30118
(404)-834-1423 (404)-834-1423
TOPICS: New Age, Parapsychology

Rollinson, Barbara, M.S.
279 Hookie
Kihei, HI 96753
TOPICS: Psychic

Roman, Sanaya
LuminEssence
P. O. Box 19117
Oakland, CA 94619

TOPICS: Channeling

Romero, Virginia
Wellness Counseling Center And Holistic School Of Massa
173 Seminary Avenue
Box 1199
Ukiah, CA 95482
(707)-462-0609
TOPICS: Holistic Healing

Rompage, Marguerite
Arcana Workshops
Box 506
Manhattan Beach, CA 90266
(213)-379-9990
TOPICS: Meditation

Ronner, John
107 South Second Avenue
Murfreesboro, TN 37130
TOPICS: Spirituality, Dreams, Psychic, Astrology, Meditation **DATE OF BIRTH:** 09/25/51 **PLACE OF BIRTH:** Long Island, NY **EDUCATION:** University of Alabama **DEGREE:** B.A. **YEAR DEGREE:** 1973 **EDUCATION:** Georgia State University **OCCUPATION:** Author, Journalist **DESCRIPTION:** Newspaper reporter for daily and weekly newspapers in GA, FL & Al, 1970-1990. Staffer for Associated Press news bureau, Atlanta, 1977-78. **PUBLICATIONS:** *Do You Have A Guardian Angel* (1985) **PUBLISHER:** Mamre Press **PUBLICATIONS:** *Seeing Your Future* (1990) **PUBLISHER:** Mamre Press

Rosen, Don
Professional Newsletter Program
524 5th Street
Box 632
Minneapolis, MN 55401
(612)-279-1255
TOPICS: Holistic Healing

Rosen, Dr. Steven M.
College Of Staten Island
Sunnyside Campus
715 Ocean Terrace
Staten Island, NY 10301
TOPICS: Parapsychology

Rosenberg, Dr. Irwin H.
International Life Sciences Institute-Nutrition Foundat
1126 16th Street, N.W.
Washington, DC 20036
(202)-659-0074
TOPICS: Holistic Healing

Rosenblum, Art
Aquarian Research Foundation
5620 Morton Street
Philadelphia, PA 19144
(215)-849-3237
TOPICS: New Age

Rosendahl, Richard D.
7800 W. Oakland Park Boulevard
Belle Terre Suite B-302
Sunrise, FL 33351
(305)-572-2846
TOPICS: Psychic Healing

Ross, Gary
Taroco Publishers
271 20th Avenue
San Francisco, CA 94121
(415)-387-6012
TOPICS: Tarot **DATE OF BIRTH:** 09/21/52 **PLACE OF BIRTH:** Chula Vista, CA **OCCUPATION:** Publisher, Editor, Speaker, Author **WORK EXPERIENCE:** Tarot Network News, San Francisco, CA, Publisher, Editor 1983-present **AWARDS:** San Francisco's International Tarot Symposium, presenter 1980, 82, 85; Host of Tarot Network News Video Magazine-60 minute home video cassette. **DESCRIPTION:** Worked with Tarot since 1968 & specializes in esoteric Tarot research. **PUBLICATIONS:** *Tarot Network News*, 1983-present **PUBLISHER:** Callisto Publishers **PUBLICATIONS:** *Tarot Network News Video Magazine* **PUBLISHER:** Callisto Pubishers

Ross, Linda Amori, R.Hy.
7 Benedict Place
Greenwich, CT 06830
(203)-622-4350
TOPICS: Hypnotism

Ross, Mary
Spiritual Center
90 Home Acres Avenue
Milford, CT 06460
(203)-874-7312
TOPICS: Holistic Health

Rossi, Ernest
C.G. Jung Institute Of Los Angeles
10349 West Pico Boulevard
Los Angeles, CA 90064
(213)-556-1193
TOPICS: New Age

Rossi, Joanne
51 Upland Avenue
Metuchen, NJ 08840
(201)-548-8579
TOPICS: Crystals

Rota, Eileen
829 Lynhaven Parkway, Suite 114-215
Virginia Beach, VA 23452
TOPICS: Channeling

Roth, Chipper
Lemur Tours
3641 Dimond Avenue
Oakland, CA 94602
(415)-530-0244
TOPICS: Crystals

Rothman, Sandy
George Ohsawa Macrobiotic Foundation
1511 Robinson Street
Oroville, CA 95965
(916)-533-7702
TOPICS: Holistic Healing

Roujansky, Carol
3354 Mount Carol Drive
San Diego, CA 92111-4631
TOPICS: Psychic

Rouse, Reverend Micki
P. O. Box 752

Mebane, NC 27302
(919)-563-4837

TOPICS: Spirituality, Psychic, Channeling
DESCRIPTION: Spiritualist, Minister and Counselor.

Rowat, Dr. R. Winona
Preventive Medicine
3743 West 10th Avenue
Vancouver, Br
Canada
(604)-228-1022

TOPICS: Holistic Healing

Rowe, Neville
7985 Santa Monica Boulevard, 109/223
West Hollywood, CA 90046
TOPICS: Channeling

Rowland, Edna Lewis
Astro News
5821 Cyrus Street
Baton Rouge, LA 70805
(504)-355-7282

TOPICS: Astrology

Royal, Lyssa
8585 Melrose Avenue
Los Angeles, CA 90069
TOPICS: Channeling

Rozman, Deborah
14780 West Park Avenue
Boulder Creek, CA 95006
(408)-338-2161 (408)-338-2605

TOPICS: New Age, Meditation, Psychology, Spirituality, Yoga **DATE OF BIRTH:** 11/08/49 **PLACE OF BIRTH:** Minneapolis, MN **EDUCATION:** University of CA, Santa Cruz, CA **DEGREE:** B.S. Psychology **YEAR DEGREE:** 1970 **EDUCATION:** University of the Trees, Santa Cruz, CA **YEARS:** 1974-78 **DEGREE:** M.A., Ph. D. Psychology **YEAR DEGREE:** 1978 **OCCUPATION:** Psychologist, Educational Consultant, Author, Lecturer **WORK EXPERIENCE:** Biogenics, Inc., Santa Cruz, CA, Exec. Vice-Pres. 1981-87; Light Force, Inc., Santa Cruz, CA, Exec. Vice-Pres. 1981-87; Evergreen School, Ben Lomond, CA, Founder, Director 1979-81; University of the Trees Press, Santa Cruz, CA, Editorial Director; Planetary Publications, General Partner **AWARDS:** Who's Who In California **PUBLICATIONS:** *Meditation For Children: Pathways To Happiness, Harmony, Creativity* **PUBLICATIONS:** *Fun For The Family* **PUBLICATIONS:** *Meditating With Children: The Art Of Concentration And Centering* **PUBLICATIONS:** *Exploring Inner Space: Awareness Games For All Ages* **PUBLICATIONS:** *The Crystal Lady* **PUBLICATIONS:** *Heart Magic*, audio

Rubel, C.W. Scott
Touch For Health Foundation
1174 North Lake Avenue
Pasadena, CA 91104
(818)-794-1181

TOPICS: Holistic Healing

Rudolph, Prof. Luther D.
Syracuse University
School Of Computer And Informa
Link Hall
Syracuse, NY 13210

TOPICS: Parapsychology

Rudow, Rev. Rita
6050 S.W.27th Street, #109
Miramar, FL 33023
(305)-963-4875

TOPICS: Psychic

Ruekberg, Laura
General Learning Corporation
60 Revere Drive
Northbrook, IL 60062
(708)-564-4070

TOPICS: Holistic Healing

Ruen, Sheldon
Plenum Publishing Corporation
233 Spring Street
New York, NY 10013
(212)-620-8000

TOPICS: New Age

Rugh, Maraiel
The Crystal Catalog
P.O. Box 1341
Nevada City, CA 95959
(916)-265-3159

TOPICS: Crystals

Ruhnau, Helena Elizabeth
Helena Elizabeth Ruhnau
P.O. Box 1198
Ava, MO 65608
TOPICS: Metaphysics

Russ, Raymond, Ph. D.
The Institute Of Mind And Behavior
P.O. Box 522
Village Station
New York, NY 10014
(212)-595-4853

TOPICS: Meditation

Russell, Marie
Mighty Natural Distributors
668 N.E. 128th Street
Miami, FL 33161
(305)-893-8829

TOPICS: Holistic Healing

Rutgers, Henry
Crystal Flute, The
P.O. Box 3340
Berkeley, CA 94703
(415)-655-1345

TOPICS: Crystals

Ryan, Allan, M.D.
Williams & Wilkins
428 East Preston Street
Baltimore, MD 21202
(301)-528-4000

TOPICS: Holistic Healing

Ryan, Frank
Crystals In Action
80 Austin Drive, #54
Burlington, VT 05401
(802)-863-7984

TOPICS: Crystals

Ryan, Mary

American Chiropractic Association
8229 Maryland Avenue
St. Louis, MO 63105
(314)-862-7800

TOPICS: Holistic Healing

Ryan, Tim
Source Net
Box 6767
Santa Barbara, CA 93160
TOPICS: Holistic Healing

Rychlenski, Ann
132-23 114th Street
Ozone Park, NY 11420
(516)-868-8277

TOPICS: Psychic

Ryerson, Kevin
3315 Sacramento Street, Suite 339
San Francisco, CA 94118
TOPICS: Channeling **OCCUPATION:** Channeler, Author, Lecturer **DESCRIPTION:** Channels the entity John. Channeling sessions recorded in Shirley MacLaine's books. Conducts private channeled readings & lectures.

Ryerson, Lynn Tate
3315 Sacramento Street
San Francisco, CA 94118
TOPICS: Channeling

Sabina, Jean
The Centre For Human Growth
1819 Quebec Street
Vancouver, Br V5T 2Z3
Canada
(604)-876-0800

TOPICS: Holistic Healing

Sabrina, Lady
Our Lady Of Enchantment
Box 1366
Nashua, NH 03061
(603)-880-7237

TOPICS: Witchcraft **OCCUPATION:** High Priestess of Wicca, Author, Minister, Lecturer **WORK EXPERIENCE:** Our Lady Of Enchantment, Nashua, NH, Founder **DESCRIPTION:** Minister & High Priestess of Wicca who founded Our Lady Of Enchantment. Authored 5 courses of study on witchcraft & the occult. Performs Wiccan marriage ceremonies, rites of passage, leads public rituals & conducts workshops to promote Wicca.

Sagendorph, Anne R.
48 Shattuck Square, #54
Berkeley, CA 94704
(415)-534-4551

TOPICS: Crystals

Sai, Sathya
1800 East Garvey Avenue
West Covina, CA 91791
TOPICS: New Age

Salaman, Maureen Kennedy
National Health Federation
212 West Foothill Boulevard
P.O. Box 688
Monrovia, CA 91016
(818)-357-2181

TOPICS: Holistic Healing

Sams, Jamie
55 Cordova Road, Suite 430
Santa Fe, NM 87501
TOPICS: Channeling

Sanborn, Carol
180 Isle Of Venice
Fort Lauderdale, FL 3301
(305)-522-8317
TOPICS: Psychic

Sanders, Pete A., Jr.
Free Soul
P.O. Box 1762
Sedona, AZ 86336
TOPICS: Psychic OCCUPATION: Psychic, Instructor, Audio/Video Producer WORK EXPERIENCE: Free Soul, Sedona, AZ, Founder DESCRIPTION: Producer of New Age related cassettes & books. PUBLICATIONS: *You Are A Psychic*

Sarantos, DeLacy
Oasis Center
7463 N. Sheridan Road
Chicago, IL 60626
(312)-274-6777
TOPICS: Spirituality, Psychology EDUCATION: Columbia University, New York, NY DEGREE: M.A. English Literature YEAR DEGREE: 1961 EDUCATION: Rosary College DEGREE: M.B.A. YEAR DEGREE: 1984 EDUCATION: University of Illinois, Champaign-Urbana, IL DEGREE: M.A. Continuing Education YEAR DEGREE: 1989 OCCUPATION: Director, Instructor WORK EXPERIENCE: Oasis Center, Chicago, IL, Certified Association Executive 1968-present PROFESSIONAL MEMBERSHIPS: Chicago Society of Association Executives DESCRIPTION: Director & instructor of Oasis Center courses promoting intellectual, spiritual & physical growth.

Satchindananda, Sri Swami
Integral Yoga International
227 West 13th Street
New York, NY 10011
TOPICS: New Age, Spirituality, Yoga, Meditation DATE OF BIRTH: 12/22/14 PLACE OF BIRTH: Coimbatore, India OCCUPATION: Author, Lecturer WORK EXPERIENCE: Integral Yoga International, NY, NY, Founder; Yoga East, Buckingham, VA, Founder DESCRIPTION: Spiritual guru teaches the benefits of yoga & meditation. Promotes the belief that all religions are one & that all lead to the one God which is truth. PUBLICATIONS: *Integral Yoga Hatha*, 1970

Satyam, Yogi Ananda
Moksha Journal
49 Forrest Place
Amityville, NY 11701
(516)-691-8475
TOPICS: Yoga

Saucer, Patrick
The Malkuthian Rite Temple Society
P.O. Box 3728
Augusta, GA 30914
TOPICS: Occult

Saunders, M.D.

Pyramid Research Center
P.O. Box 478
Odenton, MD 21113-0478
TOPICS: New Age

Savage, A. Paul
Trimel Publishing Group
5915 Airport Road
Suite 700
Mississauga, On L4V 1T1
Canada
(416)-673-2500
TOPICS: Holistic Healing

Sawyer, Patricia Kirven
Pathways
Drawer 707-RPI
Derby, KS 67037-0707
(316)-788-4224
TOPICS: New Age, Past Life Regression, Crystals, Metaphysics, Holistic Healing, Channeling, Body-Mind Connection DATE OF BIRTH: 06/26/32 PLACE OF BIRTH: Natchez, MS EDUCATION: Louisiana State University DEGREE: B.S. OCCUPATION: Teacher, Author, Lecturer, Counselor, Psychic, Astrologist, Numerologist WORK EXPERIENCE: Pathways, Derby, KS, Director PROFESSIONAL MEMBERSHIPS: Kansas Gas & Electric Company, Member Consumer Advisory Panel DESCRIPTION: Offers psychic counseling, Akashic Readings and therapy, crystal healing, past life therapy, numerology and astrology readings, dowsing, & expanded awareness classes covering Spiritual, Psychic and Personal development. Also tapes & booklets. PUBLICATIONS: *Footsteps Newsletter* PUBLISHER: Pathways PUBLICATIONS: *Sedona: Are The Vortexes Real?* PUBLISHER: Pathways PUBLICATIONS: *Recognizing, Confronting and Conquering Negative Emotions* PUBLISHER: Pathways PUBLICATIONS: *Learning To Use A Pendulum* PUBLISHER: Pathways PUBLICATIONS: *Learning To See And Interpret Auras* PUBLISHER: Pathways PUBLICATIONS: *Metaphysical Counselling: How To Get Your Money's Worth* PUBLISHER: Pathways

Saxmon, Susan
19 Parkside Road
Bedminster, NJ 07921
TOPICS: Psychic

Sayer, Zoe
Cloud On A Mountain
44 Main Street, P.O. Box 196
Chester, NJ 07930
(201)-819-6855
TOPICS: Crystals

Sayles, Clair
Healing Interiors
P.O. Box 121885
Nashville, TN 37212
(615)-889-4132
TOPICS: Crystals

Scharffenberg, R.S.
Acupuncture Index
11396 La Verne Drive
Riverside, CA 92505
(714)-688-8556
TOPICS: Holistic Healing

Schauss, Alexander
Biosocial Publications, International
Box 1174
Tacoma, WA 98401
(206)-272-0530
TOPICS: Holistic Healing

Schechter, Annie
Vital-Life Training Institute
954 Capri Road
Encinitas, CA 92024
(619)-436-9642
TOPICS: Holistic Healing

Schechter, Steve
Vital-Life Training Institute
954 Capri Road
Encinitas, CA 92024
(619)-436-9642
TOPICS: Holistic Healing

Schechter, Sylvia
Alcyone Light Centre
1965 Hilt Road
Horn Brook, CA 96044
(916)-475-3310
TOPICS: New Age, Spirituality, Holistic Health, Body-Mind Connection, Metaphysics DATE OF BIRTH: 11/09/29 PLACE OF BIRTH: England EDUCATION: Royal College of Music, England DEGREE: G.R.S.M. OCCUPATION: Professional Musician PROFESSIONAL MEMBERSHIPS: Alcyone Light Centre, Co-Founder PUBLICATIONS: *Letters Of Paul* (1989) PUBLISHER: Triad Publishers PUBLICATIONS: *Alcyone Journal* PUBLISHER: Alcyone Light Centre

Scheffler, Richard
JAI Press, Inc.
55 Old Post Road, #2
Greenwich, CT 06836
TOPICS: Holistic Healing

Schelz, J'aime, RN
Healing Crystals
8215 Southeast 13 Avenue
Portland, OR 97202
(503)-234-2224
TOPICS: Crystals

Schemberger, Gail
TOPS Club, Inc.
4575 South Fifth Street
P.O. Box 07360
Milwaukee, WI 53207
(414)-482-4620
TOPICS: Holistic Healing

Schenkman, Faye
Wholistic Health Center
50 Maple Place
Manhasset, NY 11030
(516)-627-0309
TOPICS: Holistic Healing

Schepper, Richard
Crystal Summit
185-01 Hillside Avenue
Jamaica, NY 11432
(718)-297-8944
TOPICS: Crystals

Schilder-McLaughlin, Jackie
Holistic Health Association Of The Princeton Area
360 Nassau Street
Princeton, NJ 08540
(609)-924-8580

TOPICS: Holistic Healing

Schlitz, Dr. Marilyn
Mind Science Foundation
8301 Broadway, Suite 100
San Antonio, TX 78209
(512)-821-6094

TOPICS: Parapsychology

Schmidt, Dr. Helmut
Mind Science Foundation
8301 Broadway, Suite 100
San Antonio, TX 78209
(512)-821-6094

TOPICS: Parapsychology

Schmidt, Margo A.
2678 Massachusetts Avenue
Lexington, MA 02173
(617)-863-1954

TOPICS: Psychic, Spirituality DATE OF BIRTH: 11/15/45 PLACE OF BIRTH: Juneau, AK EDUCATION: Boston University, Boston, MA YEARS: 1970-71 DEGREE: M. Ed. YEAR DEGREE: 1971 EDUCATION: Colby College, Waterville, ME DEGREE: B.A. OCCUPATION: Psychic Counselor DESCRIPTION: Works with individuals & groups offering training in spiritual & psychic development.

Schmidt, Stephen B.
Nutrition Action Health Letter
1501 16th Street N.W.
Washington, DC 20036
(202)-332-9110

TOPICS: Holistic Healing

Schneider, Andy
Other Dimensions Training Center
Box 2269
Salmon Arm, Br V1E 4R3
Canada
(604)-832-8483

TOPICS: Holistic Healing

Schneider, Bonnie
Other Dimensions Training Center
Box 2269
Salmon Arm, Br V1E 4R3
Canada
(604)-832-8483

TOPICS: Holistic Healing

Schneider, DeLores
Spirit Of Life At The Sharon Springs Health Spa
80 North Moore Street, 36F
New York, NY 10013
(212)-962-2121

TOPICS: Holistic Healing OCCUPATION: Health Director WORK EXPERIENCE: Spirit Of Life At The Sharon Springs Health Spa, New York, NY, Founder, Director DESCRIPTION: Founder & director of the Spa where she helps rejuvenate, regenerate & revitalize clients to natural beauty & health. Philosophy of life begets life.

Schneider, Michael

Feeling Great
45 West 34th Street
Room 407
New York, NY 10001
(212)-239-0855

TOPICS: Holistic Healing

Schneider, Philip
Williams & Wilkins
428 East Preston Street
Baltimore, MD 21202
(301)-528-4000

TOPICS: Holistic Healing

Schoonover, Gerald L.
1000 FM 1960 W. #210
Houston, TX 77090

TOPICS: Hypnotism OCCUPATION: Hypnosis Consultant DESCRIPTION: Offers a one hour VHS video that teaches a step-by-step modern method of hypnosis induction. Included are actual hypnosis demonstrations with full explanation & psychodynamics along with deepening techniques. Price $75.

Schrier, Eric
Hippocrates Inc.
475 Gate Five Road, #100
Sausalito, CA 94965
(212)-490-7806

TOPICS: Holistic Healing

Schukit, Mark
Vista Hill Foundation
3420 Camino del Rio North
San Diego, CA 92108
(619)-563-1770

TOPICS: Holistic Healing

Schumacher, John
Unity Woods Yoga Center
4853 Cordell Avenue
Bethesda, MD 20814
(301)-656-8992

TOPICS: Yoga

Schumann, Paul
1722 Avenida Alta Mira
Oceanside, CA 92056
(619)-726-4228

TOPICS: Psychic, Holistic Health, Past Life Regression, Massage, Herbalogy OCCUPATION: Psychic, Massage Therapist DESCRIPTION: Psychic counselor offering medical insight to problems doctors can't find through analysis of past life blockage & stress. Called The Total Body Experience, offers Psychic Readings, Massage Therapy, Chinese herbs & Mega Foods.

Schwarz, Jack
Aletheia Psycho-Physical Center
1809 N. Hwy. 99
Ashland, OR 97520

TOPICS: Holistic Health, Body-Mind Connection OCCUPATION: Instructor, lecturer, consultant, researcher WORK EXPERIENCE: Aletheia Foundation, Ashland, OR, Founder, President DESCRIPTION: Dedicated to educating others in self-health & awareness, & bringing together research on health & human energies. Work & teachings based on the interrelationship of body-mind functions. PUBLICATIONS: The Path Of

Action PUBLICATIONS: Voluntary Controls PUBLICATIONS: Human Energy Systems PUBLICATIONS: Its Not What You Eat, But What Eats You

Scolastico, Ron, Ph. D.
P.O. Box 1302
Pacific Palisades, CA 94118

TOPICS: Channeling

Scothorne, Roberta
The L.I.F.E. Project
209 Henry Street
Victoria, Br V9A 3H8
Canada
(604)-384-2146

TOPICS: Holistic Healing

Scott, Theodora
Theodora Scott & Associates
2269 Chestnut Street, Ste 136
San Francisco, CA 94123
(415)-362-1445

TOPICS: New Age, Occult, Metaphysics, Holistic Health PLACE OF BIRTH: Detroit, MI OCCUPATION: New Age Sales Representative, Author WORK EXPERIENCE: Theodora Scott & Associates, San Francisco, CA, President, Sales Rep, 3 years AWARDS: Healing Intensive Workshop with Genny Davis DESCRIPTION: Wholesaler's Rep for more than 25 quality & sometimes exclusive metaphysical, New Age & occult products such as herbs, oils, candles, potions, pendulums, incense, gems, crystals, lotions, creams, engraved stones, & velvet crystal & tarot card bags. PUBLICATIONS: Heart Of Healing, co-author

Seavey, William L.
Greener Pastures Institute/Relocation Research
P.O. Box 1122
Sierra Madre, CA 91025
(818)-355-1670

TOPICS: New Age

Sedillo, Sylvia
Women's Spiritual Center
P.O. Box 1831
Santa Fe, NM 87504
(505)-986-3499

TOPICS: Holistic Healing

Segal, Martin E.
New Age Publishing Company
P.O. Box 01-1549
Miami, FL 33101
(305)-534-8437

TOPICS: New Age

Seibold, David J.
Exeter House Books
14 East 34th Street
Reading, PA 19606
(215)-779-8173

TOPICS: New Age OCCUPATION: Author, researcher DESCRIPTION: Author & researcher of the supernatural in the Mid-Atlantic region. Co-authored several books on ghost stories with Charles J. Adams III. Published by Exeter House Books.

Seidler, Gary
U.S. Journal, Inc.
3201 SW 15th Street

Deerfield Beach, FL 33442
TOPICS: Holistic Healing

Seikus, Patti
Communications Channels, Inc.
390 Fifth Avenue
New York, NY 10018
(212)-613-9700

TOPICS: Holistic Healing

Semans, Maryann
3969 Cowan Road
Lafayette, CA 97549
(415)-283-3190

TOPICS: Crystals

Seraphine, Teddy
2899 Agoura Road, #172
Westlake Village, CA 91361
(818)-991-1988

TOPICS: Crystals

Serra, Irene
P.O. Box 670022
Marietta, GA 30066
(404)-973-5259

TOPICS: Metaphysics, Nutrition, Herbalogy, Holistic Health, Homeopathy, New Age DATE OF BIRTH: 06/15/35 PLACE OF BIRTH: Long Island, NY EDUCATION: Professional School of Business, Union, NJ YEARS: 2 DEGREE: Insurance & Real Estate YEAR DEGREE: 1965 OCCUPATION: Editor, Publisher, Consultant, Nutritionist, Herbalist WORK EXPERIENCE: Catalyst Magazine, Marietta, GA, Editor, Publisher; The Doctor's Answer, Marietta, GA, President, Nutritionist, Herbalist, Consultant

Setter, Mary
Executive Health Publications
Box 8880
Chapel Hill, NC 27515
(919)-929-7519

TOPICS: Holistic Healing

Shanklin, Beverly
Nakee Healing Center
529 Old Santa Fe Trail
Santa Fe, NM 87501
(505)-986-0245

TOPICS: Holistic Healing

Shanklin, Nancy
Nakee Healing Center
529 Old Santa Fe Trail
Santa Fe, NM 87501
(505)-986-0245

TOPICS: Holistic Healing

Shanks, Thomas
A.C.S Publications, Inc.
P.O. Box 16430
San Diego, CA 92116-0430
(619)-297-9203

TOPICS: Astrology, New Age DATE OF BIRTH: 04/09/42 PLACE OF BIRTH: Lima, OH EDUCATION: Ohio State University DEGREE: B.A. Math EDUCATION: University of Michigan DEGREE: M.A. Math OCCUPATION: Programmer, Researcher, Author WORK EXPERIENCE: Astro Computing Services, Inc., San Diego, CA, Research Director 1978-1990 AWARDS: Johndro Award,

1982; Cambridge Circle Prize, 1976 PROFESSIONAL MEMBERSHIPS: International Society For Astrological Research PUBLICATIONS: *American Atlas*, 1978 PUBLISHER: ACS Publications PUBLICATIONS: *International Atlas*, 1985 PUBLISHER: ACS Publications

Shape, Annette
Astara, Inc.
800 West Arrow Highway
P.O. Box 5003
Upland, CA 91786
(714)-981-4941

TOPICS: Metaphysics

Shapiro, Robert B.
Oasis Center: New Horizons For Mind, Body, And Spirit
7463 North Sheridan Road
Chicago, IL 60626
(312)-274-6777

TOPICS: Holistic Healing

Sharan, Farida
School Of Natural Medicine
1172 Dixon Road
Gold Hill, Salina Star Route
Boulder, CO 80302
(303)-449-8870

TOPICS: Holistic Health, Color Therapy, Herbalogy, Meditation, Homeopathy, Vegetarianism, Nutrition OCCUPATION: Naturopath, Master Herbalist, Iridologist, Lecturer, Teacher, Author WORK EXPERIENCE: British School Of Iridology, Cambridge, England, Founder, President; Herbs Of Grace, Cambridge, England, Founder, President AWARDS: Doctor of Medicine, Medicina Alternativa, Copenhagen, Denmark 1987; Gold Medal of Merit , Int'l Open U of Complementary Medicine 1988 PROFESSIONAL MEMBERSHIPS: American Herbalists Guild DESCRIPTION: Believes in health through natural healing attained through yoga, refexology, massage, shiatsu, herbs, natural childbirth, color therapy, Bach flower remedies, aromatherapy, iridology & naturopathy. PUBLICATIONS: *Iridology* PUBLISHER: Thorsons, England PUBLICATIONS: *Natural Fertility Awareness* PUBLISHER: C.W. Daniel, England

Sharpe, Pauline
Mark-Age, Inc./Healing Heaven
P.O. Box 290368
Ft. Lauderdale, FL 33329
(305)-587-5555

TOPICS: New Age

Shatzel, Rose
2 Third Street
Lily Dale, NY 14752
TOPICS: Channeling

Shea, Mary E.
14185 Day Farm Road
Glenelg, MD 21737
TOPICS: Holistic Health

Sheedy, Ally
P.O. Box 6327
Malibu, CA 90265

TOPICS: New Age, Yoga, Spirituality OCCUPATION: Actress DESCRIPTION: Advocate of

the New Age movement. Practitioner of yoga & participant of New Age spiritual retreats.

Sheldrick, Reg
American Guild Of Hypnotherapists
7117 Fornam Street
Omaha, NE 68132
(402)-397-1500

TOPICS: Hypnotism

Shelton, Abraham
Atlantia Crystal Technology
2265 Westwood Boulevard, #747
Los Angeles, CA 90064
(213)-451-3258

TOPICS: Crystals

Shenberg, Pat
4870 West Route 6
Morris, IL 60450

TOPICS: Channeling

Shepard, Bradley
Body Balance Systems
3927 Judah Street
San Francisco, CA 94122
(415)-664-9766 (415)-763-8312

TOPICS: Acupuncture, Massage, Herbalogy, Holistic Health DATE OF BIRTH: 05/29/58 PLACE OF BIRTH: Kerrville, TX EDUCATION: Academy Of Chinese Culture & Health Sciences, CA YEARS: 1985-90 DEGREE: M.A. OCCUPATION: Acupuncturist, Herbologist, Massage Therapist WORK EXPERIENCE: Body Balance Systems, Acupunturist, Herbologist, Massage Therapist AWARDS: Licensed Acupunturist PROFESSIONAL MEMBERSHIPS: A.A.C. Member

Shepard, Leslie A.
Gale Research Company
Book Tower
Detroit, MI 48226
(313)-961-2242

TOPICS: Psychic Phenomena

Sherbrook, Rev. Thomas A.
Hidden Blessings
5933 West National Avenue
West Allis, WI 53214
(414)-259-1229

TOPICS: Holistic Healing

Sheriff, Jemsa
Sunray Meditation Society
P.O. Box 308
Bristol, VT 05443
(802)-453-4610

TOPICS: Holistic Healing

Sherman, Mark
University Of Florida
Vegetable Crop Department
1255 HSPP Building
Gainesville, FL 32611
(904)-392-2134

TOPICS: Health Food

Sherwood, Nancy
The Ovens Natural Park
P.O. Box 38
Riverport, No B0J 2W0
Canada

(902)-766-4621

TOPICS: Holistic Healing

Shirley, Christopher
Inner Garden Activity Centre/ Reflexology
535 West 10th Avenue
Vancouver, British Columbia V5Z 1K9
Canada
(604)-875-8818

TOPICS: Holistic Healing, Reflexology

Short, Rev. Robert
Blue Rose Ministry
P.O. Box 332
Cornville, AZ 86325

TOPICS: UFO's, New Age OCCUPATION:
Publisher, Editor WORK EXPERIENCE: Blue Rose
Ministry, Cornville, AZ, Publisher, editor

Shuck, Carolyn
West Spring Leaf Lane
Lecanto, FL 32661

TOPICS: Channeling

Siegel, Bernie S., M.D.
Exceptional Cancer Patient
10 East 53rd Street
New York, NY 10022
(212)-207-7000

TOPICS: Holistic Health, Psychology, Body-Mind
Connection DATE OF BIRTH: 10/14/32
EDUCATION: Colgate University DEGREE: B.A.
YEAR DEGREE: 1953 EDUCATION: Cornell
University DEGREE: M.D. YEAR DEGREE: 1957
OCCUPATION: Physician, Author, Lecturer WORK
EXPERIENCE: Exceptional Cancer Patients, New
Haven, CT, Founder DESCRIPTION: Takes an
holistic approach to medicine & healing. Teaches
patients to use body/mind interaction, positive
thinking & self advocacy to combat illness.
PUBLICATIONS: *Love, Medicine, and Miracles*
PUBLICATIONS: *Peace, Love, and Healing*

Siegel, Cynthia
John F. Kennedy University
12 Altarinda Road
Orinda, CA 94563
(415)-254-0200

TOPICS: Parapsychology

Sieser, Laurie
Shelburne Center Road
Shelburne Falls, MA 01370

TOPICS: Channeling

Silva, David B.
Phantasm Press
14848 Misty Springs Lane
Oak Run, CA 96069
(916)-472-3540

TOPICS: New Age

Silver, Gail
Jeweler's Workbench
Mercer Mall
Lawrenceville, NJ 08648
(609)-452-0511

TOPICS: Crystals

Simcock, Mary
The Gitty, 7-9 North Square
Newport Pagnell

Bucks, MK16 8EP,
England

TOPICS: Crystals

Simkin, Penny
1100-23rd Avenue E.
Seattle, WA 98199
(206)-325-1419 (206)-325-5098

TOPICS: Birth, Holistic Health, New Age DATE OF
BIRTH: 05/31/38 PLACE OF BIRTH: Portland, ME
EDUCATION: Swarthmore College, Swarthmore, PA
YEARS: 1955-59 DEGREE: B.A. YEAR DEGREE:
1959 EDUCATION: University of PA, Philadelphia,
PA YEARS: 1959-61 DEGREE: M.A. Physical
Therapy YEAR DEGREE: 1961 OCCUPATION:
Author, Publisher & Teacher - Childbirth &
Parenting WORK EXPERIENCE: Childbirth
Education Association of Seattle, Childbirth
Preparation, 1968-present; Pennypress, Inc., Seattle,
WA, President, Treasurer, Editor, 1978-present
AWARDS: Annual Awards Midwives Association of
Washington State; Certified Childbirth Educator;
Board of Consultants- ICEA PROFESSIONAL
MEMBERSHIPS: Founding Member of Pacific
Association of Labor Support; ICEA; APTA; ASPO;
CEAS PUBLICATIONS: *The Birth Partner*, 1988
PUBLISHER: Harvard Common Press
PUBLICATIONS: *Pregnancy Childbirth & The
Newborn*, 1991 PUBLISHER: Meadowbrook

Simmons, J.L., Ph. D.
7336 Country Club Drive
St. Louis, MO 63121
(314)-382-3029

TOPICS: New Age, Psychology DATE OF BIRTH:
08/16/33 PLACE OF BIRTH: Sioux City, IA
EDUCATION: State University of Iowa DEGREE:
Ph. D. Social Psychology YEAR DEGREE: 1963
OCCUPATION: Author, Professor of Psychology,
Futurologist DESCRIPTION: Professor of
Psychology at U. Il, U. CA, U. MO, U. IA. Founded
2 couselling centers, worked as field researcher &
authored 9 books & 15 journal articles on New Age
& Psychology related topics. PUBLICATIONS: *The
Emerging New Age*, 1989 PUBLISHER: Bear &
Company PUBLICATIONS: *Future Lives: A
Fearless Guide To Our Transition Times*, 1990
PUBLISHER: Bear & Company

Simms, Clif
Wide Open Press
116 Lincoln Street
Santa Rosa, CA 95401
(707)-545-3821

TOPICS: New Age

Simms, Laura S.
Williams & Wilkins
428 East Preston Street
Baltimore, MD 21202
(301)-528-4000

TOPICS: Holistic Healing

Simms, Lynn L.
Wide Open Press
116 Lincoln Street
Santa Rosa, CA 95401
(707)-545-3821

TOPICS: New Age

Simon, Paul
Crystal Deva Designs

P.O. Box 1445
Santa Fe, NM 87504-1445
(505)-988-4122

TOPICS: Crystals

Simon, Sheila
The Next Step, Inc.
16 Church Street
Keene, NH 03431
(603)-357-0744

TOPICS: Holistic Healing

Simpkinson, Anne A.
Common Boundary, Inc.
7005 Florida Street
Chevy Chase, MD 20815
(301)-652-9495

TOPICS: Spirituality

Simpkinson, Charles, Ph. D.
Common Boundary, Inc.
7005 Florida Street
Chevy Chase, MD 20815
(301)-652-9495

TOPICS: Spirituality

Simpson, Mary
Positive Alternatives Wellness Education Centre
123 Queen Street West
Brampton, ON L6Y 1M3
Canada
(416)-454-2688

TOPICS: Holistic Healing

Sims, Barry
Community Careers Resource Center
1516 P Street, NW
Washington, DC 20005
(202)-667-0661

TOPICS: New Age

Simun, Francis
George Oshawa Macrobiotic Healing Center Of
Dallas
1507 North Garrett Avenue
Dallas, TX 75206
(214)-821-6769

TOPICS: Holistic Healing

Singer, Peter
Vegetarian Press
P.O. Box 61273
Denver, CO 80206
(303)-753-6964

TOPICS: Health Food

Singh, Ravi
New York Center For Art & Awareness
440 Lafayette Street, 3rd Fl
New York, NY 10003
(212)-475-0212

TOPICS: Yoga, Holistic Health, Meditation,
Massage DATE OF BIRTH: 09/21/53 PLACE OF
BIRTH: Chicago, IL EDUCATION: Northeastern IL
University, Chicago, IL YEARS: 1971-74 DEGREE:
B.A. Creative Writing YEAR DEGREE: 1974
OCCUPATION: Author, Teacher of Kundalini Yoga
WORK EXPERIENCE: New York Center For Art
And Awareness, New York, NY, Director 1986-
present AWARDS: Sri Chimnoy International Poetry
Awards, 1st Place 1985 DESCRIPTION: Teaches

yoga & meditation. Offers deep bodywork massage & personalized exercise programs. **PUBLICATIONS:** *Kundalini Yoga For Body, Mind And Beyond*, 1989 **PUBLISHER:** White Lion Press **PUBLICATIONS:** *Dong Song To The One I Love*, 1983 **PUBLISHER:** White Lion Press

Sinor, Barbara
300 Tamal Plaza, Ste 140
Corte Madera, CA 94925
(415)-924-4442

TOPICS: Psychology, Body-Mind Connection, New Age **DATE OF BIRTH:** 12/30/45 **PLACE OF BIRTH:** Upland, CA **EDUCATION:** John F. Kennedy University, Orinda, CA **DEGREE:** M.A. Human Consciousness **YEAR DEGREE:** 1987 **EDUCATION:** Pitzer College, Claremont, CA **DEGREE:** B.A. Sociology **YEAR DEGREE:** 1980 **OCCUPATION:** Transpersonal Therapist, Author **PROFESSIONAL MEMBERSHIPS:** Association For Transpersonal Psychology, Professional Member **PUBLICATIONS:** *Beyond Words: Terms For Transforming Consciousness*, 1990 **PUBLISHER:** Harbin Springs Publishing **PUBLICATIONS:** *Gifts From The Child Within*, 1991

Sipos, Alicia M.
Psychic Pathways
P.O. Box 418
Woodmere, NY 11598
(516)-561-7074

TOPICS: Crystals

Sirko, Ruth
American Chiropractic Association
8229 Maryland Avenue
St. Louis, MO 63105
(314)-862-7800

TOPICS: Holistic Healing

Skalski, Marian
ul.M., Buczka Ilm6
87-100 Torum 9,
Poland
TOPICS: Crystals

Skinner, Stephen
16 Ennismore Avenue
Chiswick
London, W4 1SF
England
071-994-1314

TOPICS: Astrology, Metaphysics, Occult **DATE OF BIRTH:** 03/22/48 **PLACE OF BIRTH:** Sydney, Australia **EDUCATION:** Sydney University, Sydney, Australia **DEGREE:** B.A. **YEAR DEGREE:** 1968 **OCCUPATION:** Publisher, Computer Programmer Analyst, Author **WORK EXPERIENCE:** ARP Publishing Ltd., Managing Director **PROFESSIONAL MEMBERSHIPS:** Authors Society; Mensa **PUBLICATIONS:** *Search For Abraxas* **PUBLICATIONS:** *Techniques Of High Magic* **PUBLICATIONS:** *The Living Earth Manual Of Feng Shui* **PUBLICATIONS:** *Terrestrial Astrology* **PUBLICATIONS:** *Crowley's Astrology* **PUBLICATIONS:** *Oracle Of Geomancy: Techniques Of Earth Divination*, 1986 **PUBLISHER:** Avery Publishing Group, Inc.

Slaten, Stephanie White
Delta Dimensions, Inc.
Box 9487

Rapid City, SD 57702
(605)-348-8061

TOPICS: Crystals

Slater, Herman
Magickal Childe, Inc.
35 West 19th Street
New York, NY 10011
(212)-242-7182

TOPICS: Witchcraft, Paganism, Occult **DATE OF BIRTH:** 02/06/38 **PLACE OF BIRTH:** Brooklyn, NY **EDUCATION:** Hunter College, New York, NY **EDUCATION:** N.Y.U., New York, NY **OCCUPATION:** Witch, Lecturer, Author **WORK EXPERIENCE:** Magickal Childe Bookstore, New York, NY, President, 20 years, Practicing Witchcraft **PUBLICATIONS:** *Pagan Ritual III* (1989) **PUBLISHER:** Magickal Childe **PUBLICATIONS:** *Magickal Formular I & II* (1981) **PUBLISHER:** Magickal Childe

Sloan, Paul
Cromwell-Sloan Publishing Company
63 Vine Road
Stamford, CT 06905
(203)-323-6839

TOPICS: Holistic Healing

Smalheiser, Marvin
Wayfarer Publications
Box 26156
Los Angeles, CA 90026
(213)-665-7773

TOPICS: Body-Mind Connection

Smith, Ellen
Bryan J. Smith
1645 South Quieto Court
Denver, CO 80223
(303)-934-8058

TOPICS: Holistic Healing

Smith, Emily
333 Crestview Drive
Palm Springs, CA 92262
(619)-327-9313

TOPICS: Channeling, Psychic, Spirituality **DESCRIPTION:** Spiritual medium and counselor offering Kirlian photos with readings.

Smith, Fred
Rainbow Collective
P.O. Box 675
Orinda, CA 94563
(510)-532-1890

TOPICS: Channeling, Metaphysics **OCCUPATION:** Lecturer, Teacher **WORK EXPERIENCE:** Rainbow Collective, Orinda, CA, Founder **DESCRIPTION:** Lectures & promotes the Teachings of Michael. Also retails & wholesales audio tapes, books, t-shirts & newsletters associated with Michael.

Smith, Jerry E.
National UFO Museum
150 North Central Street
Suite 223
Reno, NV 89501-1603

TOPICS: Spirituality, Psychology, Parapsychology, Metaphysics, New Age, UFO's, Occult **DATE OF BIRTH:** 04/08/50 **PLACE OF BIRTH:** Pomona, CA **EDUCATION:** Hubbard College **OCCUPATION:** Freelance writer, editor in CA, OR, NV 1968 to

present **WORK EXPERIENCE:** National UFO Museum, Reno, NV, Executive Director; Dharma Combat Magazine, Reno, NV, Production Editor 1988 to present; Notes From The Hangar-Journal of the National UFO Museum, Editor **PROFESSIONAL MEMBERSHIPS:** Valley Science Fiction Assoc., Secretary for two terms

Smith, Jim
Hay Institute
P.O. Box 2212
Santa Monica, CA 90406
(213)-394-7445

TOPICS: Holistic Healing

Smith, Kimber
Rainbow Collective
P.O. Box 675
Orinda, CA 94563
(510)-532-1890

TOPICS: Channeling, Metaphysics **OCCUPATION:** Channeler, Counselor **WORK EXPERIENCE:** Rainbow Collective, Orinda, CA, Counselor **DESCRIPTION:** Channeler & prosperity counselor serving the Michael community.

Smith, Marian
Esoteric Philosophy Center
10450 Stancliff
Suite 100
Houston, TX 77099
(713)-561-9556

TOPICS: Holistic Healing

Smith, Michael G.
MGS Communications
P.O. Box 26881
Lakewood, CO 80226
TOPICS: Crystals

Smith, Robert
Total Health
6001 Topanga Canyon Boulevard
Suite 300
Woodland Hills, CA 91367
(818)-887-6484

TOPICS: Holistic Healing

Smolowe, Richard
Space Technology And Research Foundation
448 Rabbit Skin Road
Waynesville, NC 28786
(704)-926-3440

TOPICS: New Age

Snow, Chet B., Ph.D.
54, rue Guy Moquet
75017 Paris,
France
TOPICS: Crystals

Snider, Jerry
Magical Blend
P.O. Box 421130
San Francisco, CA 94142
(415)-673-1001

TOPICS: Psychic Phenomena, Metaphysics, Witchcraft, Occult, New Age, Meditation **EDUCATION:** University Of MO **DEGREE:** B.A. **OCCUPATION:** Publisher, Editor, Lecturer, Author **WORK EXPERIENCE:** Magical Blend Magazine, San Francisco, CA, Publisher, Editor

PUBLICATIONS: *Magical Blend Magazine: A Transformative Journey* **PUBLISHER:** Magical Blend

Solfvin, Dr. Jerry
John F. Kennedy University
12 Altarinda Road
Orinda, CA 94563
(415)-254-0200

TOPICS: Parapsychology

Solomon, Raychel
Hippocrates Health Institute Of San Diego
6970 Central Avenue
Lemon Grove, CA 92045
(714)-464-3346

TOPICS: Holistic Healing

Sommers, Donna
Balance Center
359 Walden Green
Branford, CT 06405
(203)-481-6331

TOPICS: Holistic Healing

Song, Hui-Jun, C.M.D.
Westchester Acupuncture Center
650 Main Street, Suite 4EE
New Rochelle, NY 10801
(914)-633-9550

TOPICS: Acupuncture **DESCRIPTION:** Herbalist & licensed Acupuncturist.

Sosnoski, Karen
Rising Star Associates
342 Western Avenue
Brighton, MA 02135
(617)-787-2005

TOPICS: New Age

Soudanand, Swami
International Sivananda Yoga Vedanta Centers
8th Avenue
Val Morin, Qu V0T 2R0
Canada
(819)-322-3226

TOPICS: Yoga

Spangler, David
Lorian Association
Box 663
Issaquah, WA 98027
(206)-641-3846

TOPICS: New Age **DATE OF BIRTH:** 01/07/45 **PLACE OF BIRTH:** Columbus, OH **OCCUPATION:** Author, Channeler, Lecturer **WORK EXPERIENCE:** Lorian Association, Belmont, CA, Founder **DESCRIPTION:** Lectures, writes & theorizes about the New Age movement. Believes purpose of the New Age is for individuals to lead a more creative, empowering & compassionate life. **PUBLICATIONS:** *Revelation: The Birth Of A New Age*, 1976 **PUBLICATIONS:** *The Vision Of Findhorn Anthology*, 1976 **PUBLICATIONS:** *The Little Church*, 1976 **PUBLICATIONS:** *Relationship & Identity*, 1977 **PUBLICATIONS:** *Reflections On The Christ*, 1977 **PUBLICATIONS:** *Towards A Planetary Vision*, 1977

Springer, Joseph, C.A.
522 Washington Street
Hoboken, NJ 07030

(201)-795-0355

TOPICS: Acupuncture

Sprinkle, Dr. Leo
University Of Wyoming
Box 3708
Laramie, WY 82071

TOPICS: Parapsychology

St. Claire, Ginny
The Radiance Technique Association International, Inc.
1892 47th Avenue
San Francisco, CA 94122
(415)-664-5423

TOPICS: Reiki

St. Clare, Amber
Angel Island
1360 Pacific Highway, Turramurra
2074 Sydney,
Australia

TOPICS: Crystals

Stack, Rick
New Awareness Network, Inc.
86 Dennis Street
Manhasset, NY 11030
(516)-365-1547

TOPICS: Metaphysics, Channeling, Parapsychology **DATE OF BIRTH:** 10/07/50 **PLACE OF BIRTH:** New York, NY **EDUCATION:** Queens College, New York **DEGREE:** B.S. Education **YEAR DEGREE:** 1978 **EDUCATION:** City College, New York **DEGREE:** M.S. Education **YEAR DEGREE:** 1980 **OCCUPATION:** Author, Lecturer, Workshop Presenter, Publisher, Teacher **WORK EXPERIENCE:** New Awareness Network, Inc., New York, NY, President, Lecturer & Workshop Presenter, 15 years; Omega Institute, Rhinebeck, NY, Teacher; Interface, Boston, MA, Teacher **DESCRIPTION:** Major interests are the topics of astral projection (Out-Of-Body Experiences), the Seth Materials, and metaphysics. Student of the late Jane Roberts, author of the Seth Books. Teaches workshops on Out Of Body Experiences, Dreams & Seth Materials. **PUBLICATIONS:** *Out-Of-Body Adventures*, 1988 **PUBLISHER:** Contemporary Books, Inc. **PUBLICATIONS:** *The Seth Audio Collection*, 1990 **PUBLISHER:** New Awareness Network **PUBLICATIONS:** *Seth: The Voice And The Message*, 1990 **PUBLISHER:** Simon & Schuster **PUBLICATIONS:** *The Out-Of-Body Adventures* Audio Cassette, 1988 **PUBLISHER:** Audio Renaissance **PUBLICATIONS:** *The Out-Of -Body Induction Tapes*, 1989 **PUBLISHER:** New Awareness Network

Stafford, Gregory
Cross-Cultural Shaman's Network
Box 2636
Berkeley, CA 94702
(415)-525-5122

TOPICS: Holistic Healing

Stafford, Penny
Forgotten Aye
4634 Pillsbury Avenue South
Minneapolis, MN 55409
(612)-822-1840

TOPICS: Crystals

Stahler, Charles
Baltimore Vegetarians
P.O. Box 1463
Baltimore, MD 21203
(301)-752-8648

TOPICS: Health Food

Stanford, Dr. Rex
St. John's University
Marillac Hall
Psychology Laboratory SB15
Jamaica, NY 11439

TOPICS: Parapsychology

Stang, Ian
Fireside Books
Simon and Schuster, Inc.
1230 Avenue of the Americas
New York, NY 10020
(212)-373-8500

TOPICS: Psychic Phenomena

Stano, Marilyn, RN, BSN
Alternatives
1914 Charter Oak Drive
Rochester Hills, MI 48309-2702
(303)-773-6013

TOPICS: Crystals, Massage

Stara, Emerald
Crystal Emissary
P.O. Box 700233
San Jose, CA 95170-0233
(408)-973-0743

TOPICS: Crystals

Starr, Jo Ana
3959 North 26th Street
Arlington, VA 22207
(703)-528-8685

TOPICS: New Age

Stearns, Jim
Avery Ranch
Box 155
Vallecito, CA 95251
(209)-533-2851

TOPICS: Holistic Healing

Steen, David
Fitness Institute
255 Yorkland Boulevard
Willowdale, On M2J 1S3
Canada
(416)-491-5830

TOPICS: Holistic Healing

Stefany, Anne Marie
Biosis
2100 Arch Street
Philadelphia, PA 19103
(215)-587-4800

TOPICS: Holistic Healing

Steffan, Patricia
American Alliance For Health, Physical Education, Recre
1900 Association Drive
Reston, VA 22091
(703)-476-3400

TOPICS: Holistic Healing

Steiger, Brad
Timewalker Productions
3104 East Camelback Road
Phoenix, AZ 85016
(602)-951-4466

TOPICS: Dreams, Psychic Phenomena, Holistic Healing, UFO's, Occult, Hypnotism, Spirituality DATE OF BIRTH: 02/19/36 PLACE OF BIRTH: Ft. Dodge, IA EDUCATION: Luther College, Decorah, IA YEARS: 1953-57 DEGREE: B.A. YEAR DEGREE: 1957 EDUCATION: University of Iowa, Iowa City, IA YEARS: 1963 OCCUPATION: Author, lecturer AWARDS: Outstanding Young Men of America, Creative & Successful Personalities of the World, Two Thousand Men of Achievement, Dictionary of Int'l Biographies DESCRIPTION: A leading authority & respected author in the field of psychical research who has written more than 100 books, 2000 magazine articles and 200 short stories on various topics. Also had a syndicated newspaper column, The Strange World of Brad Steiger. PUBLICATIONS: Revelation: The Divine Fire PUBLICATIONS: The Healing Power of Love PUBLICATIONS: Gods of Aquarius PUBLICATIONS: Strangers From The Skies PUBLICATIONS: Project Bluebook PUBLICATIONS: The Shaman's Path to Inner Wisdom

Steiger, Francie Pascal
10445 Eastborne Avenue, Ste #204
Los Angeles, CA 90024
(213)-470-6516

TOPICS: Acupuncture, Homeopathy, Herbalogy, Psychology, Hypnotism, Meditation, Holistic Health DATE OF BIRTH: 01/20/38 PLACE OF BIRTH: Columbus, OH EDUCATION: Union College, Schenectady, NY EDUCATION: Ohio State University, Columbus, OH EDUCATION: Institute of Acupuncture/Homeopathy Sri Lanka DEGREE: Doctorate OCCUPATION: Dr. of Oriental Medicine, Psychotherapist/Hypnotist, Energy Transformer, Author AWARDS: Who's Who in the World, Who's Who in America/West, People's Almanac-named Leading Predictor in Science by Amy & Irving Wallace PROFESSIONAL MEMBERSHIPS: 135 organizations for Human, Animal & Earth Rights for 20 years PUBLICATIONS: Reflections From An Angel's Eye PUBLISHER: Berkeley PUBLICATIONS: Discover Your Own Past Lives PUBLISHER: Dell & Schiffer PUBLICATIONS: The Love Force PUBLISHER: Prentice Hall PUBLICATIONS: The Star People PUBLISHER: Berkeley

Stein, Art
Sat Sandesh: The Message Of The Masters
680 Curtis Corner Road
R.D. #3
Wakefield, RI 02879
(401)-783-0662

TOPICS: New Age

Stein, Diane
5119 17th Avenue S
Gulfport, FL 33707
(813)-327-6565

TOPICS: Holistic Healing, Spirituality, Psychic, Reiki, New Age DATE OF BIRTH: 09/22/48 PLACE OF BIRTH: Pittsburgh, PA EDUCATION: Duquesne University, Pittsburgh, PA YEARS: 1966-1970 DEGREE: B.S. Secondary Ed. YEAR DEGREE: 1970 EDUCATION: University of Pittsburgh, Pittsburgh, PA YEARS: 1970-1972 DEGREE: M.A.

English Literature YEAR DEGREE: 1972 OCCUPATION: Wholistic Healer, Author, Reiki Master, Teacher, Workshop Leader AWARDS: Reiki Master, 1990 DESCRIPTION: Author of 11 books on Women's Spirituality & Healing. PUBLICATIONS: Casting The Circle, A Woman's Book Of Rituals (1990) PUBLISHER: The Crossing Press PUBLICATIONS: All Women Are Healers (1989) PUBLISHER: The Crossing Press PUBLICATIONS: The Women's Spirituality Book (1987) PUBLISHER: Llewellyn Publications PUBLICATIONS: The Kwan Yin Book Of Changes (1985) PUBLISHER: Llewellyn Publications PUBLICATIONS: Stroking The Python: Women's Psychic Lives PUBLICATIONS: The Goddess Book Of Days

Stein, Gordon
Prometheus Books
700 E. Amherst Street
Buffalo, NY 14215
(716)-837-1475

TOPICS: Psychic Phenomena

Stein, Lin
Dead Of Night Magazine
916 Shaker Road, #143
Longmeadow, MA 01106

TOPICS: Vampires OCCUPATION: Publisher, Managing Editor WORK EXPERIENCE: Dead Of Night Publications, Longmeadow, MA, Publisher

Steinberg, Ellen
Metaphysically Speaking
1920 South Locust
Denver, CO 80302

TOPICS: Channeling

Steizner, Ione
Austin Area Holistic Health Association
Box 13281
Austin, TX 78711
(512)-472-9714

TOPICS: Holistic Healing

Stempson, Robert
Programs For Human Development
449 Pemberwick Road
Greenwich, CT 06830
(203)-531-6650

TOPICS: Spirituality, New Age DATE OF BIRTH: 03/04/45 EDUCATION: Harvard University, Cambridge, MA YEARS: 1964-68 DEGREE: B.A. YEAR DEGREE: 1968 EDUCATION: New School, New York, NY DEGREE: M.A. YEAR DEGREE: 1976 OCCUPATION: Spiritual Counselor, Interfaith Minister, Author WORK EXPERIENCE: Programs For Human Development, Greenwich, CT, Founder PUBLICATIONS: Sixth Sense, 1990 PUBLISHER: Prentice-Hall

Stephenson, John
MPI Medical Publishing, Inc.
14 Roman Avenue
Toronto, On M4N 2X9
Canada
(416)-481-6384

TOPICS: Holistic Healing

Stepro, Keith
Oxford Industries, Inc.
444 North Larchmont Boulevard

Box 74908
Los Angeles, CA 90004
(213)-469-3901

TOPICS: Holistic Healing

Stevens, Chi-Chi
7 Addison Avenue
London W11,
England

TOPICS: Crystals

Stevens, John
Tohoku Social Welfare University
Aoba-ku, Kunimi 1-8-1
Sendai, 981
Japan
022-233-3111

TOPICS: Spirituality, New Age, Body-Mind Connection, Aikido DATE OF BIRTH: 12/02/47 PLACE OF BIRTH: Chicago, IL OCCUPATION: Ordained Soto Zen priest, Aikido Senior Instructor, Author, Professor WORK EXPERIENCE: T.F.U. Aikido Club, Head Instructor; Tohoku Social Welfare University, Sendai, Japan, Professor of Buddhist Studies AWARDS: 5th Degree Black Belt PUBLICATIONS: One Robe, One Bowl: The Zen Poetry Of Ryokan, 1975 PUBLISHER: John Weatherhill PUBLICATIONS: Mountain Tasting: Zen Haiku by Santoka Taneda, 1980 PUBLISHER: John Weatherhill PUBLICATIONS: Sacred Calligraphy Of The East, 1988 PUBLISHER: Shambhala Publications PUBLICATIONS: Zen And The Art Of Calligraphy: The Essence Of Sho, 1983 PUBLISHER: Routledge & Kegan PUBLICATIONS: Aikido-The Way Of Harmony, 1984 PUBLISHER: Shambhala Publications PUBLICATIONS: Abundant Peace: The Life Of Morihei Ueshiba, The Founder Of Aikido, 1987 PUBLISHER: Shambhala Publications

Stevens, Suzi, H.H.P.
I Am Books And Things
4290 S. University Drive
Davie, FL 33328
(305)-370-2925

TOPICS: Psychic

Stevenson, Dr. Ian
University Of Virginia
Division Of Parapsychology
Box 152, Medical Center
Charlottesville, VA 22908

TOPICS: Parapsychology

Stewart, Leland P.
World Council Unity-And-Diversity
1010 South Flower Street, #500
Los Angeles, CA 90015
(213)-742-6832

TOPICS: Holistic Healing

Stiebing, William
U. of New Orleans, History Dept.
New Orleans, LA 70148
(504)-286-6892

TOPICS: UFO's, Spirituality DATE OF BIRTH: 12/21/40 PLACE OF BIRTH: New Orleans, LA EDUCATION: U of New Orleans, New Orleans, LA YEARS: 1958-62 DEGREE: B.A. YEAR DEGREE: 1962 EDUCATION: University of PA, Philadelphia, PA YEARS: 1962-70 DEGREE: Ph. D. YEAR DEGREE: 1970 OCCUPATION: Professor, Author,

Lecturer **WORK EXPERIENCE:** University of New Orleans, New Orleans, LA, Professor of Ancient History & Archaeology **AWARDS:** Who's Who In Biblical Studies and Archaeology, Washington D.C., Biblical Archaeology Society, 1987; L.S.U. Alumni Fed. Distinguished Faculty Award **PROFESSIONAL MEMBERSHIPS:** American Historical Association; Archaeological Institute Of America; Society Of Biblical Literature **PUBLICATIONS:** *Out Of The Desert?*, 1989 **PUBLISHER:** Prometheus Books **PUBLICATIONS:** *Ancient Astronauts, Cosmic Collisions and Other Popular Theories*, 1984 **PUBLISHER:** Prometheus Books **PUBLICATIONS:** *Velikovsky's Historical Revisions*, 1990 **PUBLISHER:** Paragon House **PUBLICATIONS:** *Comets And Cataclysmic Changes*, 1990 **PUBLISHER:** Paragon House **PUBLICATIONS:** *Comment On Bruce Maccabee*, 1990 **PUBLISHER:** Paragon House **PUBLICATIONS:** *The Nature And Dangers Of Cult Archaeology*, 1988 **PUBLISHER:** University of Iowa Press

Stiles, Tara
2526 27th Street
Sacramento, CA 95818
(916)-454-5526

TOPICS: New Age, Yoga, Tai Chi, Massage, Holistic Health **DESCRIPTION:** Offers instruction in massage, yoga & Tai Chi.

Stillings, Dennis
Archaeus Project
2402 University Avenue
St. Paul, MN 55114
(612)-641-0177 (612)-781-5012

TOPICS: Psychic Phenomena, Holistic Health, Parapsychology **DATE OF BIRTH:** 10/30/42 **PLACE OF BIRTH:** Valley City, ND **EDUCATION:** University of Minnesota, Minneapolis, MN **YEARS:** 1961-65 **DEGREE:** B.A. Math & Philosophy **YEAR DEGREE:** 1965 **EDUCATION:** University of Minnesota, Minneapolis, MN **YEARS:** 1966-70 **DEGREE:** M.A. Math & German **YEAR DEGREE:** 1970 **OCCUPATION:** Teacher, Researcher, Consultant, Librarian, Editor, Author **WORK EXPERIENCE:** Archaeus Project, St. Paul, MN, Founder & Director 1981-present; Medtronic, Inc., Minneapolis, MN, Research Librarian; Bakken Library of Electricity in Life, Minneapolis, MN, Director; Int'l Institute For The Study Of Death, Advisory Council Member **AWARDS:** Who's Who in Ufology **PROFESSIONAL MEMBERSHIPS:** Assoc. For The Scientific Study Of Anomalous Phenomena, U.S. Psychotronics Assoc., Bioelectromagnetics Society, CSAR, Int'l Society of Biometeorology, Society for Scientific Exploration, Int'l Psychosomatics Institute **DESCRIPTION:** Founder & director of Archaeus Project, a group of professional people interested in the investigation of unusual claims & anomalies for potential use in medicine & technology. Also is an authority on the work of Carl Gustav Jung. **PUBLICATIONS:** *Artifex*, editor **PUBLICATIONS:** *Archaeus Journal*, editor **PUBLICATIONS:** *Cyberbiological Studies*, editor, 1989 **PUBLISHER:** Archaeus Project **PUBLICATIONS:** *Theology Of Electricity*, editor, 1990 **PUBLISHER:** Pickwick

Stillwater, Maloah
Heavensong
P.O. Box 450-T
Kula, HI 96790
(808)-878-6415

TOPICS: Holistic Healing

Stillwater, Michael
Heavensong
P.O. Box 450-T
Kula, HI 96790
(808)-878-6415

TOPICS: Holistic Healing

Stimmel, Barry
Haworth Press, Inc.
12 West 32nd Street
New York, NY 10001

TOPICS: Holistic Healing

Stokes, Joseph, III, M.D.
Oxford University Press
200 Madison Avenue
New York, NY 10016
(212)-679-7300

TOPICS: Holistic Healing

Stoller, Lawrence
Crystal Congress, The
P.O.Box 60575
Palo Alto, CA 94306
(415)-388-8355

TOPICS: Crystals

Story, Helen Jean
Hygienic Community Network
Box 371
Route 1
Athens, NY 12015
(518)-731-8487

TOPICS: New Age

Stranges, Dr. Frank E.
National Investigations Committee On UFO's
14617 Victory Boulevard, Ste 4
Van Nuys, CA 91411
(818)-989-5942

TOPICS: UFO's, Spirituality, Psychology **DATE OF BIRTH:** 10/06/27 **PLACE OF BIRTH:** Brooklyn, NY **EDUCATION:** North Central Bible Seminary **YEAR DEGREE:** 1950 **EDUCATION:** Eastern Bible College, Greenlane, PA **YEAR DEGREE:** 1946 **OCCUPATION:** Minister, Psychologist, Researcher, Lecturer, Teacher, Author **WORK EXPERIENCE:** International Evangelism Crusades, Van Nuys, CA, President 42 years; National Investigations Committee On UFO's, Van Nuys, CA, President 22 years **AWARDS:** FBI Gold Medal Award **PROFESSIONAL MEMBERSHIPS:** United Science Federation; Planetary Society; Who's Who In The West; Who's Who In California; NICUFO. **DESCRIPTION:** Lectures on UFO's and Religion. **PUBLICATIONS:** *Interspace - Link* **PUBLISHER:** NICUFO

Streit, Fred
49B Brondesbury Villas, Kilburn
London NW6 6AJ,
England

TOPICS: Crystals

Stromberg, Simant
Forgotten Aye
4634 Pillsbury Avenue South
Minneapolis, MN 55409
(612)-822-1840

TOPICS: Crystals

Stuart-Patton, Susan, Ph. D.
Intuitive Development Institute
17 El Cerrito Avenue
San Rafael, CA 94901
(800)-882-8711 (415)-454-3477

TOPICS: Metaphysics, Past Life Regression, Hypnotism, Psychic, Channeling, Meditation

Stumm, Jim
Box 29-ND
Hiler Branch
Buffalo, NY 14223

TOPICS: New Age **PUBLICATIONS:** *Living Free*

Subramuniyaswami, Gurudeva Sivaya
Kadavul Hindu Temple Hall
Kapaa, Kauai, HI 96746
(808)-822-3012

TOPICS: Crystals

Sultana
Crystals Of Light
P.O. Box 341
New Lebanon, NY 12125
(518)-733-6717

TOPICS: Crystals

Summerscales, Joanne
49B Brondesbury Vilas, Kilburn
London NW6 6AJ,
England

TOPICS: Crystals

Supera, India
Feathered Pipe Foundation
P.O. Box 1682
Helena, MT 59624
(406)-442-8196

TOPICS: Yoga

Susann, Dr. Emily
P.O. Box 1910
Oakhurst, CA 93644
(209)-683-7998

TOPICS: New Age, Past Life Regression **DESCRIPTION:** Practices healing through past life regression therapy & balancing energy flows.

Sutphen, Dick
Valley OF The Sun Publishing Co.
P.O. Box 38
Malibu, CA 90265
(818)-889-1575

TOPICS: Metaphysics, Channeling, New Age, Hypnotism, Past Life Regression, Reincarnation **PLACE OF BIRTH:** Omaha, NE **OCCUPATION:** Hypnotherapist, Author, Lecturer **WORK EXPERIENCE:** Scottsdale Hypnosis Center, Scottsdale, AZ, Founder; Valley Of The Sun Publishing Company, Malibu, CA, Founder; Mystical Rose, Malibu, CA, Founder **DESCRIPTION:** Dedicated to the study & teachings of various aspects of the New Age movement such as hypnotherapy, past-life regression, psychic energy, reincarnation, etc. **PUBLICATIONS:** *Sedona: Psychic Energy Vortexes*, 1986 **PUBLICATIONS:** *Unseen Influences*, 1982 **PUBLICATIONS:** *You Were Born Again To Be Together*, 1976

Sutton, Dr. Robert P.
Center For Icarian Studies
Western Illinois University Center

University Libraries
Macomb, IL 61455
(309)-298-2411

TOPICS: New Age

Swan, James A.
The Institute For The Study Of Natural Systems
P.O. Box 637
Mill Valley, CA 94942
(415)-383-5064

TOPICS: New Age

Sweeney, Duane
Continuity Publishing
Box 224
Greenbank, WA 98253
(206)-678-7772

TOPICS: New Age

Swenson, Barbara Rose
Crystal Gazer, The
P.O. Box 1122
North Highlands, CA 95660
(415)-893-5440

TOPICS: Crystals

Swinney, Graywolf
Aesculapia
1480 Dutcher Creek Road
Grants Pass, OR 97527
(503)-476-0492

TOPICS: Holistic Healing

Tabatneck, Shirley Ann
Psychic Network Directory
1259 Rt. 46, Bldg. 1
Parsippany, NJ 07054
(201)-316-9511 (201)-335-8741

TOPICS: Psychic, Metaphysics, Astrology DATE OF BIRTH: 01/22/40 PLACE OF BIRTH: Hackensack, NJ EDUCATION: Fairleigh Dickinson University DEGREE: B.A. YEAR DEGREE: 1962 EDUCATION: Wichita State University, Wichita, KS YEARS: 1 year OCCUPATION: Teacher, Private Consultant, Author, Astrologer, Lecturer, Marketing & Communications Specialist WORK EXPERIENCE: Ad-Com, Inc., Parsippany, NJ, 22 years; Psychic Fair Network, Boonton, NJ, 15 years AWARDS: Who's Who Of American Women 1975-76; Humanitarianism Award & Work Above & Beyond the Call Of Duty Award, Rotary Club & North Jersey Ad Club PROFESSIONAL MEMBERSHIPS: American Federation Of Astrology; AMORC; SITU; NCGR PUBLICATIONS: *Effects Of Gamma Radiation*, 1970 PUBLICATIONS: *Obviousness Of Sun Sign Astrology*, 1972

Tabatneck, Vincent
Psychic Fair Network
152 D Twin Hills Drive
Boonton Township, NJ 07005
(201)-335-8741

TOPICS: Psychic, Metaphysics

Tadd, Maria
7 Dix Terrace
Winchester, MA 01890

TOPICS: Psychic Healing

Tanner, Wilda
215 Moonridge Road
Chapel Hill, NC 27516

(919)-932-1205

TOPICS: Dreams, Ghosts, Astrology, Metaphysics, Psychic, New Age DATE OF BIRTH: 07/31/25 PLACE OF BIRTH: Louisville, KY EDUCATION: University of Kentucky, Lexington, KY YEARS: 2 EDUCATION: Chesterfield School of Mediumship YEARS: 5 DEGREE: Ordained OCCUPATION: Author, Lecturer, Teacher-Metaphysics, Astrology, Dreams/Devas DESCRIPTION: Covers topics such as Dreams; Angels, Devas & You; How You Create Your Reality; & Psychic Development PUBLICATIONS: *The Mystical, Magical, Marvelous World Of Dreams*, 1988 PUBLISHER: Sparrow Hawk Press PUBLICATIONS: *Follow Your Dreamzz-z-z*, 1978 PUBLISHER: Queen City Press PUBLICATIONS: *Your Magic Wand*, 1991

Tanous, Alex
Box 3818
Portland, ME 04104
(207)-773-8328

TOPICS: Psychic

Tarila, Sophia, Ph. D.
First Editions
Box 2578
Sedona, AZ 86336
(602)-282-9574

TOPICS: New Age, Metaphysics

Tate, D.
46 Green Meadows Lane
Loudonville, NY 12211
(518)-489-8719

TOPICS: Holistic Health, Body-Mind Connection, Psychology DATE OF BIRTH: 08/19/41 PLACE OF BIRTH: Troy, NY EDUCATION: John F. Kennedy University, Orinda, CA DEGREE: M.A., Clinical Psychology YEAR DEGREE: 1980 EDUCATION: Albany Law School, Albany, NY DEGREE: L.L.B. YEAR DEGREE: 1967 OCCUPATION: Author, Lecturer AWARDS: NESCA, A Special Service Community Award; Northeast Subcontractor's Assoc., Albany, NY PROFESSIONAL MEMBERSHIPS: American Bar Assoc.; New York State Bar Assoc.; Assoc. for Transpersonal Psychology; Humanistic Psychology Assoc. DESCRIPTION: Lecturer on Health, Hope and Healing: A Patient's Perspective PUBLICATIONS: *Matter of Billy K* (1991) PUBLISHER: M. Evans & Co. PUBLICATIONS: *Health, Hope & Healing* (1990) PUBLISHER: M. Evans & Co.

Taylor, Kent Alen
Taylor's Herb Garden
1535 Lone Oak Road
Vista, CA 92084
(619)-727-3485

TOPICS: Herbalogy, Holistic Health DATE OF BIRTH: 07/24/44 PLACE OF BIRTH: Pasadena, CA OCCUPATION: Herbalist, Author WORK EXPERIENCE: Taylor's Herb Garden, Vista, CA, President DESCRIPTION: Mail-Order for organic herb gardeners.

Taylor, Mark
31 228th Street SE
Bothell, WA 98021

TOPICS: Parapsychology

Taylor, Terry Lynn
P.O. Box 481

Ojai, CA 93924
(805)-646-4573

TOPICS: Parapsychology PUBLICATIONS: *Messenger Of Light* PUBLISHER: H.J. Kramer

Tazewell, Nancy
Bluegrass Spa
901 Galloway Road
Stamping Ground, KY 40379
(502)-535-6261

TOPICS: Holistic Healing

Teabo, Shirley
Sixth Sense
226 South 312th Street
Federal Way, WA 98003

TOPICS: Channeling

Teague, Dr. Terri K., N.D., D.C.
4105 Terrace Street
Oakland, CA 94611
(415)-652-9801

TOPICS: New Age, Chiropractic, Nutrition, Holistic Health DESCRIPTION: Offers Chiropractic therapy & information on nutrition.

Tedesco, Joanne Henning
Logos Center
6333 East Thunderbird Road
Scottsdale, AZ 85254
(602)-483-8777

TOPICS: New Age

Teeguarden, Iona Marsag
Jin Shin Do Foundation For Bodymind Acupressure
366 California Avenue, Ste. 16
Palo Alto, CA 94306
(415)-328-1811

TOPICS: Acupuncture, Body-Mind Connection, Holistic Health, Psychology DATE OF BIRTH: 09/29/49 PLACE OF BIRTH: Rugby, ND EDUCATION: University of Michigan, Ann Arbor, MI YEARS: 1967-70 EDUCATION: Antioch University, Los Angeles, CA YEARS: 1979-80 DEGREE: M.A. Psychology YEAR DEGREE: 1980 OCCUPATION: Psychotherapist, Acupressurist WORK EXPERIENCE: Jin Shin Do Foundation For Bodymind Acupressure, Palo Alto, CA, Director of Bodymind Acupressure, 1987-pres.; Acupressure Workshop, Los Angeles, CA, Director of Acupressure, 1976-80 AWARDS: Associated Bodywork & Massage Professionals Award 1990 PROFESSIONAL MEMBERSHIPS: Associated Bodywork & Massage Professionals, Board of Advisors; American Oriental Bodywork Therapy Assoc., Modality Rep. PUBLICATIONS: *The Acupressure Way Of Health: Jin Shin Do*, 1978 PUBLISHER: Japan Publications PUBLICATIONS: *The Joy Of Feeling: Bodymind Acupressure*, 1987 PUBLISHER: Japan Publications

Temme, Thom
Well Being Community Calendar
6270 Carlotta Court
P.O. Box 819
Sebastopol, CA 95473
(707)-823-1489

TOPICS: Holistic Healing

Terkel, Lawrence
Spiritual Life Society And Yoga Center
1 East Main Street

Old Church On the Green
Hudson, OH 44236
(216)-650-1216

TOPICS: Holistic Healing

Terlingen, Hans, M.D.
Dream Of The Forest
R.R. 1
Lone Butte, Br V0K 1X0
Canada
(604)-593-4603

TOPICS: Holistic Healing

Terpak, John
Strength & Health Publishing
Box 1707
York, PA 17405
(717)-767-6481

TOPICS: Holistic Healing

Tersigni, Patrick
The Radiance Technique Association International,
Inc.
RD 1
Hammer Road
Wayland, NY 14572
(716)-728-5562

TOPICS: Reiki

Thackara, W.T.S.
Theosophical University Press
Bin C
Pasadena, CA 91109
(818)-798-3378

TOPICS: New Age

Thiel, M.E.
Quest Enterprises Of Excelsior
464 2nd Street
Excelsior, MN 55331
(612)-474-5132

TOPICS: New Age

Thomas, Kirk
Professional Newsletter Program
524 5th Street
Box 632
Minneapolis, MN 55401
(612)-279-1255

TOPICS: Holistic Healing

Thomas, Mark
Review And Herald Publishing Association
55 West Oak Ridge Drive
Hagerstown, MD 21740
(301)-791-7000

TOPICS: Holistic Healing

Thomas-Klausner, Carol
Crystal Consciousness
P.O. Box 714, Department C-2
Claremont, CA 91711

TOPICS: Crystals

Thomason, Carl
Lost Horizon Health Awareness Center
Box 550
Oviedo, FL 32765
(407)-365-6681

TOPICS: Holistic Healing

Thomberry, Milo

Alternatives Resource Center
5263 Bouldercrest Road
P.O. Box 429
Ellenwood, GA 30049
(404)-961-0102

TOPICS: New Age

Thompson, Carol
New Life Health Center
9 Oakdview Terrace #1
Boston, MA 02130-1036
(617)-524-9551

TOPICS: Holistic Healing

Thompson, Robin M.
Rosicrucian Order
Rosicrucian Park
1342 Nagle Avenue
San Jose, CA 95191
(408)-287-9171

TOPICS: New Age, Spirituality, Parapsychology

Thompson, Tom
Woodbury Yoga Center
122 West Side Road
Woodbury, CT 06798
(203)-263-2254

TOPICS: Yoga

Thorne, David
Rising Star Associates
342 Western Avenue
Brighton, MA 02135
(617)-787-2005

TOPICS: New Age

Tiers, Sophia
Spiritual Healing Center
1739 Anza Street
San Francisco, CA 94118
(415)-221-4058

TOPICS: Holistic Healing, Metaphysics

Tipton, Marynell
Inner Light Foundation
P.O. Box 761
Novato, CA 94948
(415)-382-1040

TOPICS: Holistic Healing

Toca, Archbishop Dr. Sar Mar R.
Catholic Church Of The Antiochean Rite
P.O. Box 8473
Tampa, FL 33674-8473
(813)-248-3091

TOPICS: Parapsychology, Occult, Metaphysics, UFO's OCCUPATION: Minister, Author, Radio & TV Producer WORK EXPERIENCE: International University Of Theology & Parapsychology, Tampa, FL, President; Catholic Church Of The Antiochean Rite, Tampa, FL, Archbishop Primate DESCRIPTION: The Archbishop Primate For Hispanic Jurisdiction in Spain, Latin America & U.S.A. Authors column & books on Parapsychology & Sociology of Religions. Produces a daily radio talk show & two weekly TV Cable shows dealing with Parapsychology & Public Affairs.

Todeschi, Kevin
Association For Research And Enlightenment, Inc.
215 67th Street & Atlantic Ave
P.O. Box 595

Virginia Beach, VA 23451
(804)-428-3588

TOPICS: Channeling

Tomlinson, Jerry
Pacific Crystal Guild
P.O. Box 1371
Sausalito, CA 94966-1371
(415)-641-1701

TOPICS: Crystals

Toms, Michael
New Dimensions Radio
P.O. Box 410510
Dept. JM
San Francisco, CA 94141
(415)-563-8899

TOPICS: New Age

Topham, George F.
U. S. Gems Expos
P.O. Box 8862
Tucson, AZ 85738L6
(602)-791-2210

TOPICS: Crystals

Torres, Penny
Mafu Seminars
P.O. Box 458
Eagle Point, OR 97524-0452

TOPICS: Channeling OCCUPATION: Channeler WORK EXPERIENCE: Mafu Seminars, Vacaville, CA, Pres. DESCRIPTION: Channels the entity Mafu.

Tosolt, Keith A.
Chiropractic News Publishing Company
29229 Six Mile Road
Livonia, MI 48152
(313)-427-5720

TOPICS: Holistic Healing

Travis, Dr. Terry A.
Southern Illinois University
P.O. Box 3926
Department Of Psychiatry
Springfield, IL 62708

TOPICS: Parapsychology

Travis, John W., M.D.
Wellness Associates
P.O. Box 5433-G
Mill Valley, CA 94942
(415)-383-3806

TOPICS: Holistic Healing

Trevino, Haven
Red Victorian Bed And Breakfast Inn/Global Family Netwo
1665 Haight Street
San Francisco, CA 94117
(415)-864-1978

TOPICS: Holistic Healing

Truner, Harry
First Editions
Box 1158
Sedona, AZ 86336
(602)-282-9574

TOPICS: New Age

Tuburan, Rafael
American Massage Therapy Association

1130 West North Shore Avenue
Chicago, IL 60626
(312)-761-2682

TOPICS: Massage

Turner, Marlee
Northern Pines Health Resort
RR 1
P.O. Box 279
Raymond, ME 04071
(207)-655-7624

TOPICS: Holistic Health, Yoga, Meditation, Nutrition, Massage

Ullman, Dana
Foundation For Homeopathic Education
5916 Chabot Crest
Oakland, CA 94618
(415)-649-8931

TOPICS: Homeopathy DESCRIPTION: Ullman is Pres. of Foundation For Homeopathic Education And Research. PUBLICATIONS: *Homeopathy: Medicine For The 21st Century*

Ullman, Dr. Robert
The Northwest Center For Holistic Medicine
4072 9th Avenue N.E.
Seattle, WA 98105
(206)-547-9665

TOPICS: Holistic Healing

Ulrich, Ann Carol
Earth Star Publication
P.O. Box 117
Paonia, CO 81428
(303)-527-3257

TOPICS: UFO's, Holistic Health, Crystals, Past Life Regression, Parapsychology DATE OF BIRTH: 07/17/52 PLACE OF BIRTH: Madison, WI EDUCATION: Michigan State University, East Lansing, MI YEARS: 1972-75 DEGREE: B.A. YEAR DEGREE: 1975 EDUCATION: Wisconsin State University, Whitewater, WI YEARS: 1970-71 OCCUPATION: Author, Editor, Publisher WORK EXPERIENCE: Earth Star Publications, Paonia, CO, Publisher 1987-present AWARDS: UFO Contact Center International, Seattle, WA, Assoc. Director Of The Year 1987; Institute of Children's Literature, Redding, CT; Graduate 1982 PROFESSIONAL MEMBERSHIPS: UFO Contact Center International, Delta County, CO, Assoc. Director 1986-present PUBLICATIONS: *Intimate Abduction*, 1988 PUBLISHER: Earth Star Publications PUBLICATIONS: *Birthday UFO*, 1989 PUBLISHER: The Star Beacon PUBLICATIONS: *Polarity And The Gift Of Healing*, 1989 PUBLISHER: The Star Beacon PUBLICATIONS: *Blue/Green Algae*, 1989 PUBLISHER: The Star Beacon PUBLICATIONS: *The Secret Power Of Crystals*, 1988 PUBLISHER: The Star Beacon PUBLICATIONS: *Needle Rock, An Enigma*, 1988 PUBLISHER: The Star Beacon

Uphoff, Prof. Walter H.
New Frontiers Center
Rt. 1
MM 2313
Oregon, WI 53575
(608)-835-3795

TOPICS: Parapsychology, Psychology DATE OF BIRTH: 02/28/13 PLACE OF BIRTH: Sheboygan County, WI EDUCATION: University of WI, Madison, WI YEARS: 1930-34 DEGREE: B.S. Biochemistry YEAR DEGREE: 1934 DEGREE: Ph. M. Sociology YEAR DEGREE: 1935 OCCUPATION: Professor, Lecturer, Author WORK EXPERIENCE: University of Wisconsin, Madison, WI, Instructor; University of Minnesota, Minneapolis, MN, Assoc. Professor, Industrial Relations Center, 1951-63; University of CO, Boulder,CO, Prof. Economics, Parapsychology 1963-76; New Frontiers Center, Oregon, WI, Pres. AWARDS: Alpha Zeta, Honorary Fraternity, U of WI, 1933; Senior Research Fulbright, U of Cologne, Germany, 1958-59; Honorary Doctorate, LHD, Montreal, 1989 PROFESSIONAL MEMBERSHIPS: NEA, AFT, IRRA, SPR, ASPR, SFF, SSF, MSF PUBLICATIONS: *New Psychic Frontiers: Your Key To New Worlds*, 1980 PUBLISHER: New Frontiers Center PUBLICATIONS: *Mind Over Matter*, 1980 PUBLISHER: New Frontiers Center PUBLICATIONS: *The Frontiers Newsletter* PUBLISHER: New Frontiers Center PUBLICATIONS: *The Kohler Strike: Its Socio-Economic Causes & Effects*, 1935 PUBLISHER: Charles Kerr PUBLICATIONS: *Kohler On Strike: 30 Years Of Conflict*, 1966 PUBLISHER: Beacon Press PUBLICATIONS: *Group Health - An American Success Story In Prepaid Health Care*, 1980 PUBLISHER: Dillon Press

Useldiaga, Ron
Fitness Motivation Institute Of America
36 Harold Street
San Jose, CA 95117
(408)-246-9191

TOPICS: Holistic Healing

Utne, Eric
Lens Publishing Company
1624 Harmon Place
Fawkes Bldg.
Minneapolis, MN 55403
(612)-338-5040

TOPICS: New Age

Vail, Valerie
Aquarius Rising
7001 West Center Street
Wauwatosa, WI 53210
(414)-258-0663

TOPICS: Crystals

Van Blaaderen, Dr. Maria
Eastern Montana University
Department Of Social Sciences
Billings, MT 59101

TOPICS: Parapsychology

Van de Castle, Robert L., Ph. D.
White Dove Farm
U. Of Virginia, Div. Of Parapsychology
Box 190, Medical Center
Charlottesville, VA 22908
(804)-842-5555

TOPICS: Dreams, Parapsychology, ESP, Holistic Healing, Holistic Health, Psychology DATE OF BIRTH: 11/16/27 PLACE OF BIRTH: Rochester, NY EDUCATION: University of Missouri, Columbia, MO YEARS: 1951-53 DEGREE: M.A. Psychology YEAR DEGREE: 1953 EDUCATION: University of North Carolina, Chapel Hill, NC YEARS: 1955-59 DEGREE: Ph. D. Psychology YEAR DEGREE: 1959 OCCUPATION: Clinical Psychologist, Lecturer, Author WORK EXPERIENCE: University of Virginia, Health Sciences Center, Charlottesville, VA, Director of Clinical Training; White Dove Farm, Fork Union, VA AWARDS: Diplomate Clinical Psychologist, ABPP, 1967; Licensed Clinical Psychologist, VA Board of Medicine, 1976 PROFESSIONAL MEMBERSHIPS: Assoc. for the Study of Dreams, President 1985; Parapsychology Assoc., President 1970 PUBLICATIONS: *The Content Analysis Of Dreams*, 1966 PUBLISHER: Appleton Century PUBLICATIONS: *The Psychology Of Dreaming*, 1971 PUBLISHER: General Learning Press

Van de Castle, Susanna
White Dove Farm
P.O. Box 638
Fork Union, VA 23055
(804)-842-5555

TOPICS: Parapsychology, Dreams, ESP, Holistic Health, Holistic Healing DATE OF BIRTH: 08/07/55 PLACE OF BIRTH: Fort Bragg, NC OCCUPATION: Director WORK EXPERIENCE: White Dove Farm, Fork Union, VA, Director; Dream Center, Fork Union, VA, Director

Van DeWalle, Dr. Michael
Texas Chiropractic Association
1704 Timberwood Dr.
Austin, TX 78741-5547
(512)-454-4551

TOPICS: Holistic Healing

Van Houten, Beckie
Vista Hill Foundation
3420 Camino del Rio North
San Diego, CA 92108
(619)-563-1770

TOPICS: Holistic Healing

Van Hulle, JP
Michael Educational Foundation
10 Muth Drive
Orinda, CA 94563
(510)-254-4730

TOPICS: Channeling, Metaphysics OCCUPATION: Channeler, Teacher WORK EXPERIENCE: Michael Educational Foundation, Orinda, CA, Founder DESCRIPTION: A Michael Channel & metaphysical teacher.

VanAtta, Marvin
Living Off The Land
Box 2131
Melbourne, FL 32902

TOPICS: Health Food

Vandenberg, Johanna
Creative Aging, Inc.
700 West End Avenue, 11B
New York, NY 10025
(212)-864-1523

TOPICS: Holistic Healing

Vandertuin, Rev. Victoria E.
New Age World Religious And Scientific Research Foundat
62091 Valley View Circle
Joshua Tree, CA 92252
(619)-366-2833

TOPICS: New Age, Spirituality, Body-Mind Connection, Occult, Metaphysics DATE OF BIRTH: 10/16/33 PLACE OF BIRTH: New Bedford, MA OCCUPATION: Author, Publisher,

Booksearcher/Literary Services **WORK EXPERIENCE:** New Age World Services & Books, Joshua Tree, CA, President **PROFESSIONAL MEMBERSHIPS:** Institute of Mentalphysics; NAPRA; Blue Rose Ministery **PUBLICATIONS:** *My God, The Power & Wisdom Of The Universe*, 1978 **PUBLISHER:** New Age World Religious And Scientific Research Found.

Veetgyan/Andaloro, Ross
Interdimensional Crystal Alchemy
34 Yammouth Road
Toronto, ON, M6G 1W8
Canada
(416)-530-4470

TOPICS: Crystals

Vegso, Peter
U.S. Journal, Inc.
3201 SW 15th Street
Deerfield Beach, FL 33442

TOPICS: Holistic Healing

Velazquez, Diana
75 Meade
Denver, CO 80219

TOPICS: Psychic Healing

Venaglia, Mark Victor
17 West 24th Street
New York, NY 10011

TOPICS: Channeling

Vich, Miles A.
Transpersonal Institute
Box 3049
Stanford, CA 94309
(415)-327-2066

TOPICS: New Age

Vignanananda, Swami
P.O. Box 1037
Berkeley, CA 94701
(415)-655-3664

TOPICS: Holistic Health, Meditation, Yoga, Spirituality, Nutrition, Massage, Vegetarianism **DATE OF BIRTH:** 06/14/32 **PLACE OF BIRTH:** Thinnanore, India **EDUCATION:** Divine Life Society, Rishikesh, Himalayas **OCCUPATION:** Swami-Master of Vedanta Philosophy, Meditation & Yoga, Author **WORK EXPERIENCE:** Prana Yoga Centres International, Founder, Director 1975-present **AWARDS:** Divine Life Society, Professor of Hatha Yoga; Peralta College District, Eminence Credential **DESCRIPTION:** Founded Prana Yoga Centres worldwide: California USA, PennsylvaniaUSA, India, Japan, Nicaragua, Burma, Malaysia, Singapore, Denmark, Germany, France, USSR, Bulgaria, Yugoslavia, & the United Arab Republic. **PUBLICATIONS:** *Wings Of Divine Wisdom* **PUBLICATIONS:** *Yoga Vision* **PUBLICATIONS:** *Heart Wisdom* **PUBLICATIONS:** *Song Of The Will* **PUBLICATIONS:** *Prana Yoga Life Magazine*

Vigne, Lora
Isis Oasis Lodge And Cultural Center
20889 Geyserville Avenue
Geyserville, CA 95441
(707)-857-3524

TOPICS: Holistic Healing

Viraj, Yogi Ananda

Moksha Journal
49 Forrest Place
Amityville, NY 11701
(516)-691-8475

TOPICS: Yoga

Virshop, Bernard
Center For The Well-Being Of Health Professionals
5102 Chapel Hill Boulevard
Durham, NC 27707
(919)-489-9167

TOPICS: Holistic Healing

Visek, Willard
American Institute Of Nutrition
9650 Rockville Pike
Bethesda, MD 20814
(301)-530-7100

TOPICS: Holistic Healing

Vodrey, T.K.
Oxford Industries, Inc.
444 North Larchmont Boulevard
Box 74908
Los Angeles, CA 90004
(213)-469-3901

TOPICS: Holistic Healing

Vogel, Marcel, Ph.D.
Psychic Research, Incorporated
819 Morse Street
San Jose, CA 95126-1715
(408)-279-2291

TOPICS: Crystals

Voigt, Valerie
Pagan/Occult/Witchcraft Special Interest Group
P.O. Box 9336
San Jose, CA 95157
(415)-856-6911

TOPICS: Occult, Voudoun, Witchcraft, Paganism, Kabbalah, Alchemy **DATE OF BIRTH:** 10/10/53 **PLACE OF BIRTH:** Selma, AL **EDUCATION:** University Of Kansas, Lawrence, KS **YEARS:** 1972-1977 **DEGREE:** B.A. Classical Languages **YEAR DEGREE:** 1977 **OCCUPATION:** Teacher, speaker, consultant & writer on Occult, Witchcraft, Paganism & various related topic. **WORK EXPERIENCE:** Fairy Tradition Training Circle, Founder & High Priestess, 1987-Pres.; San Francisco Police Department, Instructor & Investigator,1985-Pres.; Pastoral Counselor, 1982-Pres.; Centre of the Divine Ishtar, Founder & Chief Priestess, 1982-Pres.; Classes & Workshops Witchcraft & Related Topics, Teacher, 1981-Pres. **AWARDS:** Listed in Biographical Dictionary of American Religious Leaders; Nominated for Danforth & Marshall Fellowships; Graduate Fellowship to U. of Colorado. **PROFESSIONAL MEMBERSHIPS:** Arn Draiocht Fein; Bay Area Pagan Assemblies; Centre of the Divine Ishtar; Circle Network; Covenant of the Goddess; Fairy Training Circle. **PUBLICATIONS:** *Pagan/Occult/Witchcraft Special Interest Group Regional Guide* (1989) **PUBLICATIONS:** *What Are Paganism and Witchcraft?* (1981)

Volpe, Anthony
Del Val UFO
948 Almshouse Road
Ivyland, PA 18974
(215)-357-2909

TOPICS: UFO's

Volpe, Lynn
Del Val UFO
948 Almshouse Road
Ivyland, PA 18974
(215)-357-2909

TOPICS: UFO's

Von Erffa, Julie
Referral Service For Health Care Information
Rt. 10
Box 133
Santa Fe, NM 87501
(505)-473-7654

TOPICS: Holistic Healing

Wade, Carlson
Princeton Educational Publishers
117 Cuttermill Road
Great Neck, NY 11021
(516)-466-9300

TOPICS: Holistic Healing

Wager, Nancy
National Fitness Association
Box 2378
Corona, CA 94043
(714)-371-0606

TOPICS: Holistic Healing

Wagner, C.
P.O. Box 7292
Penndel, PA 19047
(215)-757-1911 (215)-295-1210

TOPICS: Nutrition, Meditation, Palmistry, Tai Chi, Herbalogy, Massage **DATE OF BIRTH:** 04/07/91 **PLACE OF BIRTH:** Hazleton, PA **EDUCATION:** Museum College Of Art **EDUCATION:** San Francisco State College **OCCUPATION:** Human Nature Specialist, Author, Lecturer, Herbalist **WORK EXPERIENCE:** Life Nourishment Center, Langhorne, PA, Counselor, Herbalist **AWARDS:** Gautama Institute For Oriental Medicine - Certificate in Traditional Chinese Pharmacology **PROFESSIONAL MEMBERSHIPS:** Masonic Blue Lodge; Oriental Healing Arts Institute, Assoc. Member **DESCRIPTION:** Works as lecturer, counselor, Chinese Herbalist & teacher of Tai Chi & Characterology which is face & palm analysis. **PUBLICATIONS:** *Characterology*, 1986 **PUBLISHER:** Samuel Weiser

Wagner, Lindsay J.
11500 West Olympic Boulevard, #300
Los Angeles, CA 90064

TOPICS: New Age, Meditation, Holistic Healing, Psychic Healing, Acupuncture, Body-Mind Connection **DATE OF BIRTH:** 06/22/49 **PLACE OF BIRTH:** Los Angeles, CA **OCCUPATION:** Actress, Author **DESCRIPTION:** Advocate of the New Age movement. Promotes the use of meditation, visualization, unorthodox healing techniques, spiritual mind treatment programs & acupressure. **PUBLICATIONS:** *Lindsay Wagner's New Beauty: The Acupressure Facelift*

Wagner, Prof. Dr. Mahlon W.
S.U.N.Y. Oswego
Psychology Dept.
S.U.N.Y - Oswego
Oswego, NY 13126
(315)-341-4013 (315)-652-5624

TOPICS: Parapsychology, Psychology, ESP DATE OF BIRTH: 08/23/35 PLACE OF BIRTH: Chaftee, NY EDUCATION: Bucknell U, Lewisburg, PA YEARS: 1953-57 DEGREE: B.S. Chemistry YEAR DEGREE: 1957 EDUCATION: U of Rochester, Rochester, NY YEARS: 1957-61 DEGREE: Ph. D. Psychology YEAR DEGREE: 1963 OCCUPATION: Professor of Psychology, Author, Lecturer WORK EXPERIENCE: University of MA, Amherst, MA, Instructor 1961-64; Valparaiso University, Valparaiso, IN, Associate Professor 1964-67; S.U.N.Y. Oswego, NY, Professor of Psychology 1967-present AWARDS: Fulbright Research Fellowship, University of Giessen, Germany 1989; Richard Merton Fellowship, University of Saarland, Germany, 1981 PROFESSIONAL MEMBERSHIPS: Parapsychological Assoc., A.S.P.R., Eastern Psychological Assoc., Sigma Xi, Psychonomic Society, Midwestern Psychological Assoc. DESCRIPTION: Conducts research on attitudes toward Parapsychology, border areas of Science as well as ESP. Also writes articles on cross cultural attitudes toward ESP.

Walker, Dr. Morton
484 High Ridge Road
Stamford, CT 06905-3095
(203)-322-1551

TOPICS: Holistic Health, Nutrition, Homeopathy, Birth, Color Therapy EDUCATION: Illinois College Of Podiatric Medicine, Chicago,IL YEARS: 1949-53 DEGREE: Dr. of Podiatric Medicine YEAR DEGREE: 1953 EDUCATION: New York University, New York, NY YEARS: 1947-49 OCCUPATION: Lecturer, Author-Medical Journalist WORK EXPERIENCE: Freelance Communications, Stamford, CT, Editorial Director 22 years AWARDS: Am Business Press, Jesse H. Neal Editorial Achievement Award; Am College of Advancement in Medicine, Humanitarian Award & 22 Awards Medical Journalism DESCRIPTION: Lecturer & award-winning author of 48 books & 1400 consumer magazine & clinical journal articles on topics such as orthomolecular nutrition, improved lifestyle, prolongevity, and safe, nontoxic alternatives for healing. PUBLICATIONS: *The Power Of Color*, 1991 PUBLISHER: Avery Publishing Group PUBLICATIONS: *The Chelation Way*, 1990 PUBLISHER: Avery Publishing Group PUBLICATIONS: *DMSO: The New Healing Power* PUBLICATIONS: *The Complete Book Of Birth* PUBLICATIONS: *Total Health* PUBLICATIONS: *Orthomolecular Nutrition*

Walker, Ralph H.
Loving Brotherhood, Inc.
P.O. Box 556
Sussex, NJ 07461
(201)-875-4710

TOPICS: New Age

Walker, Wendy-Louise
The Australian Society For Clinical & Experimental Hypn
P.O. Box 594
Chatswood, Ne 2067
Australia
(002)-419-2737

TOPICS: Hypnotism

Wallace, Robert
National Interagency Council On Smoking
7320 Greenville Avenue
Dallas, TX 75231

TOPICS: Holistic Healing

Wallace, Teri DeNeal
Gems And Minerals Of Dallas
6757 Arapaho, #719
Dallas, TX 75248
(214)-960-2380

TOPICS: Crystals

Walljasper, Jay
Lens Publishing Company
1624 Harmon Place
Fawkes Bldg.
Minneapolis, MN 55403
(612)-338-5040

TOPICS: New Age

Walsh, William B., M.D.
Project Hope
Carter Hall
Millwood, VA 22646
(703)-837-2100

TOPICS: Holistic Healing

Walters (Kriyananda), J. Donald
Crystal Clarity Publishers
14618 Tyler Foote Road
Nevada City, CA 95959
(916)-292-3485

TOPICS: Spirituality, Body-Mind Connection, Meditation DATE OF BIRTH: 05/19/26 PLACE OF BIRTH: Teleajen, Rumania OCCUPATION: Author, Teacher, Founder & Spiritual Director of Ananda World Brotherhood Village AWARDS: Keynote speaker: San Francisco Whole Life Expo, 4/89; NY Whole Life Expo, 10/89; Healing in the 90's Symposium with Louise Haye, 1/90. PUBLICATIONS: *The Path: A Spiritual Autobiography* (1976) PUBLISHER: Crystal Clarity Publishers PUBLICATIONS: *Your Sun Sign As A Spiritual Guide* (1991) PUBLISHER: Crystal Clarity Publishers PUBLICATIONS: *The Essence of Self-Realization:The Wisdom of Paramhansa Yogananda* (1990) PUBLISHER: Crystal Clarity Publishers

Wapnick, Gloria
Foundation For A Course In Miracles
Conference/Retreat
RD 2
Box 71
Roscoe, NY 12776
(607)-498-4116

TOPICS: Holistic Healing

Wapnick, Kenneth
Foundation For A Course In Miracles
Conference/Retreat
R.R. 2
Box 71
Roscoe, NY 12776
(607)-498-4116

TOPICS: Spirituality, Metaphysics, Channeling DATE OF BIRTH: 02/22/42 PLACE OF BIRTH: Brooklyn, NY EDUCATION: Lafayette College, Easton, PA YEARS: 1959-63 DEGREE: B.A. YEAR DEGREE: 1963 EDUCATION: Adelphi University, Garden City, NJ YEARS: 1963-68 DEGREE: Ph.D. Clinical Psychology YEAR DEGREE: 1968 OCCUPATION: Clinical Psychologist, Author, Lecturer, Teacher WORK EXPERIENCE: Foundation For A Course In Miracles, Roscoe, NY, President, 1983-present PROFESSIONAL MEMBERSHIPS: American Psychological Association; Association of Transpersonal Psychology; American Academy of Psychotherapists PUBLICATIONS: *Glossary-Index For A Course In Miracles*, 1989 PUBLISHER: Foundation For A Course In Miracles PUBLICATIONS: *Forgiveness And Jesus* PUBLISHER: Foundation For A Course In Miracles PUBLICATIONS: *The Fifty Miracle Principles Of A Course In Miracles* PUBLISHER: Foundation For A Course In Miracles PUBLICATIONS: *Christian Psychology In A Course In Miracles* PUBLISHER: Foundation For A Course In Miracles PUBLICATIONS: *A Talk Given On A Course In Miracles* PUBLISHER: Foundation For A Course In Miracles PUBLICATIONS: *Awaken From The Dream* PUBLISHER: Foundation For A Course In Miracles

Waram, Marilyn F.
Fraternity For Canadian Astrologers
P.O. Box 4924 Station E
Ottawa, On K1S 5J1
Canada

TOPICS: Astrology

Ward, Hilda
Alive
P.O. Box 67333
Vancouver, Br V5W 3T1
Canada
(604)-438-1919

TOPICS: Health Food

Ward, William
JAI Press, Inc.
55 Old Post Road, #2
Greenwich, CT 06836

TOPICS: Holistic Healing

Warren, Mary Alice
Planet Earth Book Center
1720 Colonial Boulevard
Ft. Myers, FL 33907
(813)-939-3969

TOPICS: Metaphysics

Wasserman, Howard I.
Howmark Publishing Corporation
567 Morris Avenue
Elizabeth, NJ 07208
(201)-353-7373

TOPICS: Health Food

Wassserman, Debra
Baltimore Vegetarians
P.O. Box 1463
Baltimore, MD 21203
(301)-366-8343

TOPICS: Health Food, Holistic Health, Vegetarianism EDUCATION: Georgetown University, Washington, D.C. DEGREE: Masters Int'l Relations OCCUPATION: Educator/Activist WORK EXPERIENCE: Vegetarian Resource Group, Baltimore, MD, for 8 years. PUBLICATIONS: *Meatless Meals For Working People* (1990) PUBLICATIONS: *I Love Animals & Broccoli Children's Activity Book* (1985) PUBLICATIONS: *No-Cholesterol Passover Recipes* (1986) PUBLICATIONS: *Simply Vegan* (1990)

PUBLICATIONS: *articles for Vegetarian Times & Vegetarian Journal*

Waterfield, Robin
97 Victor Road
Teddington, Middlesex TW11 8SS
England

TOPICS: Spirituality, Numerology, Metaphysics, New Age DATE OF BIRTH: 08/06/52 PLACE OF BIRTH: Banbury, England EDUCATION: University of Manchester, Manchester, England YEARS: 1971-1974 DEGREE: B.A. YEAR DEGREE: 1974 OCCUPATION: Author, Editor, Lecturer WORK EXPERIENCE: University of Newcastle Upon Tyne, England, Lecturer, 1978-9, Classics; University of St. Andrews, England, Lecturer, 1979-82, Ancient Greek; Penguin Books, London, England, Commissioning Editor, 1988-91, Arkana PUBLICATIONS: *Theology Of Arithmetic*, 1988 PUBLISHER: Phanes Press PUBLICATIONS: *Phantoms Of Fear*, 1987 PUBLISHER: Gallimard PUBLICATIONS: *Metaphysics*, 1987 PUBLICATIONS: *New Age Publishing Comes Of Age*, 1989

Watkins, Susan
Box 217
Dundee, NY 14837

TOPICS: Channeling

Watson, Shane
Orenda/Unity Press
Box 2215
Leucadia, CA 92024
(619)-753-9331

TOPICS: Massage

Watters, Pierce
Internal Arts
Box 1777
Arlington, TX 76004
(817)-860-0129

TOPICS: New Age

Weaver, Dennis
c/o Nashville International
116 17th Avenue South
Nashville, TN 37203

TOPICS: New Age DATE OF BIRTH: 06/04/24 PLACE OF BIRTH: Joplin, MO EDUCATION: University Of Oklahoma DEGREE: B.F.A. YEAR DEGREE: 1948 OCCUPATION: Actor DESCRIPTION: New Age advocate, environmentalist & crusader against world hunger. Follower of Swami Paramahansa Yogananda, a master of kriya yoga. Leader of the LIFE Project, Love Is Feeding Everyone, which collects & distributes food to the hungry in the LA area.

Weber, John Paul
The Healing Center of Arizona
25 Wilson Canyon Road
Sedona, AZ 86336
(602)-282-7710

TOPICS: Holistic Healing

Weber, Kate
The Healing Center of Arizona
25 Wilson Canyon Road
Sedona, AZ 86336
(602)-282-7710

TOPICS: Holistic Healing

Weber, Sylvia
Counseling And Mental Health Service
990 Main Street
East Greenwich, RI 02818
(401)-884-6880

TOPICS: Crystals

Weed, Susun
Wise Woman Center
P.O. Box 64
Woodstock, NY 12498
(914)-246-8081

TOPICS: Holistic Healing

Wegner, Sandra
Moonstone Blue & Night Roses
P.O. Box 393
Prospect Heights, IL 60070
(312)-392-2435

TOPICS: New Age

Weidemann, Sela
Rock-Medicine
628 Lake Street
Reno, NV 89501
(702)-329-1717

TOPICS: Crystals

Weider, Joe
The Weider Health & Fitness Group
21100 Erwin Street
Woodland Hills, CA 91367
(818)-884-6800

TOPICS: Holistic Healing

Weill, Alix
Hippocrates Health Institute
1443 Palmdale Court
West Palm Beach, FL 33411
(407)-471-8876

TOPICS: Holistic Healing

Weinberg, Armin
Slack, Inc.
6900 Grove Road
Thorofare, NJ 08086
(609)-848-1000

TOPICS: Holistic Healing

Weiner, Harry
American Chiropractic Association
8229 Maryland Avenue
St. Louis, MO 63105
(314)-862-7800

TOPICS: Holistic Healing

Weiser, Ann
Focusing Connection
5825 Telegraph Avenue, # 45
Oakland, CA 94609
(415)-654-4819

TOPICS: New Age

Wertz, Carol
The Option Institute & Fellowship- A Place For Miracles
RD #1
Box 174A
Sheffield, MA 01257
(413)-229-2100

TOPICS: Holistic Healing

West, Bruce
Natural Fitness Newsletter
Box 222797
Carmel, CA 93922
(408)-372-3370

TOPICS: Holistic Healing

West, Dennis
4, Bridgewater Road, Bleadon
Weston-Super-Mare, Avon,
England

TOPICS: Crystals

West, Sali Lou
546 Onate Place
Santa Fe, NM 87501

TOPICS: Channeling

Westen, Marilee
Crystal Radiance
606 Gilroy Drive
Capitola, CA 95010
(408)-479-9884

TOPICS: Crystals

Westen, Steve
Crystal Radiance
606 Gilroy Drive
Capitola, CA 95010
(408)-479-9884

TOPICS: Crystals

Weston, Jennifer
Route 5, Box 934
Ava, MO 65608

TOPICS: Paganism, Occult DESCRIPTION: Pagan graphic artist. Creator of ritual rattles and altar baskets.

Weyler, Rex
Hollyhock
Box 127
Manson's Landing
Cortes Island, Br V0P 1K0
Canada
(604)-935-6465

TOPICS: Holistic Healing

Whitaker, Terence
Contemporary Books, Inc.
180 North Michigan Avenue
Chicago, IL 60601
(312)-782-9181

TOPICS: Ghosts

White, April
Whitelights
2899 Agoura Road
Suite 193
Westlake Village, CA 91361
(805)-497-7496

TOPICS: Metaphysics, Channeling

White, Ganga
2500 San Marcos Pass
Santa Barbara, CA 93105
(805)-964-1944

TOPICS: Yoga, Meditation DATE OF BIRTH: 09/20/46 PLACE OF BIRTH: Detroit, MI EDUCATION: CAL State, Northridge, CA DEGREE: B.A. Science OCCUPATION: Yoga Master,

Meditator, Philosopher **WORK EXPERIENCE:** White Lotus Foundation, Santa Barbara, CA, Founder **AWARDS:** Yoga Acharya 1969-1970 & Yogi Raj 1979, Yoga Vedanta Forest University, India **PROFESSIONAL MEMBERSHIPS:** Unity In Yoga, Advisory Board **PUBLICATIONS:** *Double Yoga*, 1980 **PUBLISHER:** Viking-Penguin **PUBLICATIONS:** *Vinyasa-Flow Series Yoga Video*, 1990

White, John C.
P.O. Box 1166
Lily Dale, NY 14752
TOPICS: Channeling

White, Larry
Time Data Research
P.O. Box 717
Manchester, NH 03105
(603)-623-7733

TOPICS: Astrology, Metaphysics **OCCUPATION:** Astrologer, Columnist **PROFESSIONAL MEMBERSHIPS:** American Federation Of Astrologers; New England Astrological Association; Scientific Thought In Astrological Research **DESCRIPTION:** Does private astrological readings, miniscopes & professional charts. Writes a syndicated astrological column which is cartoon illustrated called Cosmic College. It appears in more than 100 weekly & monthly publications nationwide.

White, Rhea
Scarecrow Press, Inc.
52 Liberty Street
P.O. Box 656
Metuchen, NJ 08840
TOPICS: Parapsychology

White, Rhea A.
Parapsychology Sources Of Information Center
2 Plane Tree Lane
Dix Hills, NY 11746
(516)-794-2570 (516)-271-1243

TOPICS: Parapsychology **DATE OF BIRTH:** 05/06/31 **PLACE OF BIRTH:** Utica, NY **EDUCATION:** Pennsylvania State University, State College, PA **YEARS:** 1951-53 **DEGREE:** A.B. **YEAR DEGREE:** 1953 **EDUCATION:** Pratt Institute Library School, Brooklyn, NY **YEARS:** 1963-65 **DEGREE:** M.L.S. **YEAR DEGREE:** 1965 **OCCUPATION:** Parapsychologist, Librarian, Author, Editor **WORK EXPERIENCE:** American Society For Psychical Research, Editor of Journal 1959-62, 1983-present; East Meadow Public Library, East Meadow, NY, Reference Librarian 1965-present; Parapsychology Sources Of Information Center, Director 1982-present; Exceptional Human Experiences, Editor 1983-present **AWARDS:** American Society For Information Science, Hans Peter Luhn Award 1965; Honorary Fellow of College of Human Sciences **PROFESSIONAL MEMBERSHIPS:** Parapsychological Assoc. Pres. 1984; Society for Psychical Research; Academy of Religion & Psychical Research; Spiritual Frontiers Fellowship; Int'l Assoc for Near-Death Studies; Institute of Noetic Sciences **PUBLICATIONS:** *Psychic Experiences: A Bibliography*, 1990 **PUBLISHER:** PSI Center **PUBLICATIONS:** *Parapsychology: Sources On Applications & Implications*, 1989 **PUBLISHER:** PSI Center **PUBLICATIONS:** *On Being Psychic: A Reading Guide*, 1989 **PUBLISHER:** PSI Center **PUBLICATIONS:** *Parapsychology: A Reading And*

Buying Guide To The Best Books, 1987 **PUBLISHER:** PSI Center **PUBLICATIONS:** *Research In Parapsychology* 1984, 1985 **PUBLISHER:** Scarecrow Press **PUBLICATIONS:** *Research In Parapsychology* 1983, 1984 **PUBLISHER:** Scarecrow Press

White, Stephen
2899 Agoura Road, Suite 193
Westlake Village, CA 91361
TOPICS: Channeling, Metaphysics

White, Timothy
Cross-Cultural Shaman's Network
Box 2636
Berkeley, CA 94702
(415)-525-5122
TOPICS: Holistic Healing

Whitehead, Beverly
Radiant Light
P.O. Box 5409
Rockville, MD 20851
(301)-946-1079
TOPICS: Crystals

Whitesel, Betsy, R.N., N.P.
Dancing Hands
P.O. Box 41971
Tucson, AZ 85719
(602)-299-6374
TOPICS: Crystals

Wiberg, Sonia
Ananda-Family Fellowship Of Inner Communion
14618 Tyler Foote Road
Nevada City, CA 95959
(916)-292-3065
TOPICS: New Age

Wick, Michael
New Age Media Resource Network
Box 419
New York, NY 10002
(212)-777-4220
TOPICS: Holistic Healing

Wigmore, Ann
Ann Wigmore Foundation
Division Of Hippocrates Health Institute, Inc.
196 Commonwealth Avenue
Boston, MA 02116
(617)-267-9424

TOPICS: Holistic Health, Health Food, Vegetarianism, Homeopathy **PLACE OF BIRTH:** Cropos, Lithuania **OCCUPATION:** Author, Holistic Health Counselor **WORK EXPERIENCE:** Hippocrates Health Institute, Boston, MA, Founder **DESCRIPTION:** Dedicated to the study & teaching of holistic health practices through vegetarianism, polarity therapy, homeopathy & natural foods. **PUBLICATIONS:** *Why Suffer?*, 1964 **PUBLICATIONS:** *Naturama Living Textbook, You Are Your Own Healer*, 1979 **PUBLICATIONS:** *Be Your Own Doctor: Let Living Food Be Your Medicine*, 1983 **PUBLICATIONS:** *The Wheatgrass Book*, 1985

Wigmore, Dr. Ann
Hippocrates Health Institute Of San Diego
6970 Central Avenue
Lemon Grove, CA 92045

(714)-464-3346
TOPICS: Holistic Healing

Wilcox, Laird
Laird Wilcox Editorial Research Service
P.O. Box 2047
Olathe, KS 66061
(913)-829-0609

TOPICS: Psychic Phenomena, Occult, Witchcraft **DATE OF BIRTH:** 10/28/42 **PLACE OF BIRTH:** San Francisco, CA **OCCUPATION:** Editor, Publisher **WORK EXPERIENCE:** Editorial Research Service, San Francisco, CA, Editor, Dir.,1981-Pres. **PROFESSIONAL MEMBERSHIPS:** Mensa **PUBLICATIONS:** *Guide To The American Occult* (1989) **PUBLISHER:** Laird Wilcox, Editorial Research Service **PUBLICATIONS:** *Guide To The American Right* **PUBLISHER:** Laird Wilcox, Editorial Research Service **PUBLICATIONS:** *Guide To The American Right* **PUBLISHER:** Laird Wilcox, Editorial Research Service **PUBLICATIONS:** *Terrorism, Assassination, Espionage & Propaganda: A Master Bibliography* **PUBLISHER:** Laird Wilcox, Editorial Research Service **PUBLICATIONS:** *Selected Quotation For The Ideological Skeptic* **PUBLISHER:** Laird Wilcox, Editorial Research Service

Wilen, Joan
P.O. Box 416
Ansonia Station
New York, NY 10023
(212)-724-2930

TOPICS: Holistic Health **PUBLICATIONS:** *Chicken Soup & Other Folk Remedies* **PUBLICATIONS:** *More Chicken Soup & Other Folk Remedies*

Wilen, Lydia
P.O. Box 416
Ansonia Station
New York, NY 10023
(212)-724-2930

TOPICS: Holistic Health **PUBLICATIONS:** *Chicken Soup & Other Folk Remedies* **PUBLICATIONS:** *More Chicken Soup & Other Folk Remedies*

Wilkinson, Mark
Dr. Wilkinson's Hot Springs
1507 Lincoln Avenue
Calistoga, CA 94515
(707)-942-4102
TOPICS: Holistic Healing

Williams, David
Mountain Home Publishing
Box 829
Ingram, TX 78025
(512)-367-4492
TOPICS: Holistic Healing

Williams, Dayle
3405 South West Cedar Hill Boulevard
Beaverton Mall, OR 97005
(503)-641-4247
TOPICS: Crystals

Williams, Ise
Indian Valley Retreat
Route 2
Box 58
Willis, VA 24380
(703)-789-4295

TOPICS: Holistic Healing

Williams, Laurel, Reverend
Laurilee
2906 Sopris Avenue
Glenwood Springs, CO 81601
(303)-945-9621

TOPICS: Crystals

Williams, Leslie
Orr Hot Springs
13201 Orr Springs Road
Ukiah, CA 95482
(707)-462-6277

TOPICS: Holistic Healing

Williams, Reginald D.
919 West Maple Avenue
Sterling, VA 22170
(703)-444-2344

TOPICS: Crystals

Williams, Sid
Today's Chiropractic, Inc.
1269 Barclay Circle
Marietta, GA 30060
(404)-424-0554

TOPICS: Holistic Healing

Williams, Tom
Indian Valley Retreat
Route 2
Box 58
Willis, VA 24380
(703)-789-4295

TOPICS: Holistic Healing

Williamson, Cynthia
2926 North East Flanders
Portland, OR 97232
(503)-238-4010

TOPICS: Crystals

Williamson, Marianne
1550 North Hayworth
Los Angeles, CA 90046
(213)-883-1091

TOPICS: Spirituality, New Age **PLACE OF BIRTH:** Austin, TX **OCCUPATION:** Teacher, Lecturer **WORK EXPERIENCE:** Miracle Projects, Los Angeles, CA, Pres. **DESCRIPTION:** Presents lectures on A Course In Miracles.

Willis, Courtney
Technicians of the Sacred
1317 North San Fernando Boulevard, Suite 310
Burbank, CA 91504

TOPICS: Voudoun, Occult **DATE OF BIRTH:** 12/19/55 **PLACE OF BIRTH:** Buffalo, NY **EDUCATION:** St. Edwards University, TX **DEGREE:** B.S.W. **OCCUPATION:** Chemical Dependency Therapist/Social Worker **WORK EXPERIENCE:** Technicians of the Sacred, Burbank, CA **DESCRIPTION:** Founder of Technicians of the Sacred and The Societe Journal. Head of the largest and oldest Neo-African religious order. **PUBLICATIONS:** *Voodoo Primer* (1991) **PUBLISHER:** Technicians of the Sacred **PUBLICATIONS:** *Opening and Closing of the Gates* (1989) **PUBLISHER:** Technicians of the Sacred

Willoughby, Cossette

Willoughby Research Company
P.O. Box 317
Fairacres, NM 88033-0317
(505)-524-8777

TOPICS: Crystals

Willoughby, Ken
Willoughby Research Company
P.O. Box 317
Fairacres, NM 88033-0317
(505)-524-8777

TOPICS: Metaphysics, Astrology, Occult, Dowsing, Psychic Phenomena, UFO's, ESP **EDUCATION:** Nebraska Wesleyan U., Lincoln, NE **DEGREE:** B.A. Physics **YEAR DEGREE:** 1958 **DESCRIPTION:** Special interest in: PSI, Psychic, Occult, Theosophy, Astrology, Esoteric Wisdom, Mystic, Metaphysics, Dowsing, Clairvoyance, ESP, Crystals, White Magic, Rosicrucians, Esoteric Studies. Maintains extensive, current UFO library on computer disk.

Wills, Alma
Williams & Wilkins
428 East Preston Street
Baltimore, MD 21202
(301)-528-4000

TOPICS: Holistic Healing

Wills, Jerry
Crystal Dreams
8338 North 7th Street
Phoenix, AZ 85020
(602)-870-9764

TOPICS: Crystals

Wills, Sharon
Crystal Dreams
8338 North 7th Street
Phoenix, AZ 85020
(602)-870-9764

TOPICS: Crystals

Wilson, Scott
Eastern Holistic Health Association
50 Maple Place
Manhasset, NY 11030
(516)-365-7590

TOPICS: Holistic Healing

Wilson, Windy
Rainbow Path
1195 Wayne Street
Noblesville, IN 46060
(317)-773-5702

TOPICS: Crystals

Winch, Bradley L.
Jalmar Press
45 Hitching Post Drive
Building 2
Rolling Hills Estate, CA 90274
(213)-547-1240

TOPICS: New Age

Windsor, Dr. James C.
Personal Development Institute
P.O. Box 1056
Williamsburg, VA 23187
(804)-229-4873

TOPICS: Hypnotism

Windsor, Joan Ruth

Personal Development Institute
P.O. Box 1056
Williamsburg, VA 23187
(804)-229-4873

TOPICS: Dreams, Parapsychology **DESCRIPTION:** Writes Dreamlife, a bi-monthly column for Body, Mind and Spirit Magazine. **PUBLICATIONS:** *The Inner Eye* **PUBLICATIONS:** *Dreams And Healing* **PUBLICATIONS:** *Dreamwork*

Windsor, Roger G.
Spectrum
61 Dutile Road
Laconia, NH 03246
(603)-528-4710 (603)-528-4710

TOPICS: Holistic Health, Massage, New Age, Meditation, Body-Mind Connection, Yoga **DATE OF BIRTH:** 12/24/49 **PLACE OF BIRTH:** Baltimore, MD **EDUCATION:** Duke University, Durham, NC **YEARS:** 1967-1971 **DEGREE:** B.A. **YEAR DEGREE:** 1971 **EDUCATION:** Towson State University, Baltimore, MD **YEARS:** 1974-1976 **DEGREE:** M.A. **YEAR DEGREE:** 1976 **OCCUPATION:** Publisher, Editor **WORK EXPERIENCE:** North Star Foundation, Middletown, CA, Dir., Wholistic Health, 8 yrs.; Spectrum-Wholistic News Magazine, Laconia, NH, Publisher & Editor **AWARDS:** Associate Teacher & Counselor-Kushi Institute **PROFESSIONAL MEMBERSHIPS:** Harbin Hot Springs, Board of Directors, 1978 1985; North Star Foundation, Board of Directors, 1978-1985 **PUBLICATIONS:** *Spectrum-Wholistic News Magazine* **PUBLISHER:** Spectrum Publications

Windwalker, Wanita
5023 Durnham Drive
Pontiac, MI 48054
(313)-681-9758

TOPICS: Crystals

Winkelman, Michael
University Of California At Irvine
School Of Social Sciences
Irvine, CA 92717

TOPICS: Parapsychology

Winston, Julian
National Center For Homeopathy
1500 Massachusetts Avenue, N.W
Suite 41
Washington, DC 20005
(202)-223-6182

TOPICS: Holistic Healing

Winston, Reisa
Center For Feeling People
10170-4 Larwin Avenue
Chatsworth, CA 91311
(818)-882-7404

TOPICS: Holistic Healing

Winters, Jason
Vinton Publishing
P.O. Box 35
Mound, MN 55364
(800)-221-4331

TOPICS: Herbalogy **OCCUPATION:** Herbalist, Author **DESCRIPTION:** Herbalist producing herbal products for wholesale & retail sale. **PUBLICATIONS:** *Killing Cancer* **PUBLISHER:** Vinton Publishing **PUBLICATIONS:** *In Search Of The Perfect Cleanse* **PUBLISHER:** Vinton

Publishing PUBLICATIONS: *Breakthrough: An Australian Legend* PUBLISHER: Vinton Publishing PUBLICATIONS: *The Ultimate Combination* PUBLISHER: Vinton Publishing

Wishart, John A.
Jay's Minerals '77
3 Mark Street
Toronto, ON, M5A 1Z3
Canada
(416)-861-1964

TOPICS: Crystals

Wisman-Horther, Joe
Co-Op America
2100 M Street, N.W., Suite 310
Washington, DC 20063
(202)-872-5307

TOPICS: Psychic Phenomena

Withall, Virginia
Berkeley Massage Associates
1962 University Avenue
Berkeley, CA 94704
(415)-845-5998

TOPICS: Holistic Healing

Wolcott, Jerry
Crystal Energy Systems
P.O. Box 2141
Lake Oswego, OR 97035
(503)-635-4836

TOPICS: Crystals

Wolff, Tom
Foundation For Chiropractic Education And Research
1701 Clarendon Boulevard
Arlington, VA 22209
(703)-276-7445

TOPICS: Holistic Healing

Woman, Jade Wind
Heart Journey
677 East Palm Street
Altadena, CA 91001
(818)-791-8924

TOPICS: Crystals

Wood, Valerie
21 Streets Heath
West End, Woking
Surrey, GU24 9QY,
England

TOPICS: Crystals

Woodford, Julia
Ontario's Common Ground Magazine
320 Danforth Avenue
Suite 204
Toronto, On M4K 1P3
Canada
(416)-463-6677

TOPICS: Holistic Healing

Woodrew, Greta
Space Technology And Research Foundation
448 Rabbit Skin Road
Waynesville, NC 28786
(704)-926-3440

TOPICS: New Age

Woods, Craig
Raben Publishing Co.
711 Boylston Street
Boston, MA 02116
(617)-236-1885

TOPICS: Holistic Healing

Woodworth, Nancy
Wilbur Hot Springs Health Sanctuary
Star Route
Williams, CA 95987
(916)-473-2306

TOPICS: Holistic Healing

Woolf, Dr. Marsha, N.D.
Alternative Resources
54 Briarwood Plaza, New World Medical Ctr
Seekonk, MA 02771
(401)-941-3332

TOPICS: Crystals, Color Therapy

Woolsey, Raymond H.
Review And Herald Publishing Association
55 West Oak Ridge Drive
Hagerstown, MD 21740
(301)-791-7000

TOPICS: Holistic Healing

Wornom, Lonnie
American Institute Of Metaphysics
2000 L Street N.W.,
Suite 200
Washington, DC 20036
(202)-659-0689

TOPICS: Holistic Healing

Wright-Minter, Mary Linda
Wiesbaden Hot Springs And Lodgings
625 5th Avenue
P.O. Box 349
Ouray, CO 81427
(303)-325-4347

TOPICS: Holistic Healing

Wynn, Dr. William H.
University Of Regina
Psychology Department
Regina, Sa S4S 0A2
Canada

TOPICS: Parapsychology

Wynne, Patrice
The Womanspirit Catalogue Co.
1442-A Walnut Street, #184
Berkeley, CA 94709

TOPICS: New Age

Yamada, George
School Of Living
Box 1508AA
R.D. 1
Spring Grove, PA 17362
(717)-225-3745

TOPICS: New Age

Yogananda, Paramahansa
Self Realization Fellowship
3880 San Rafael Avenue
Los Angeles, CA 90065

TOPICS: New Age

Young-Sowers, Meredith Lady
Stillpoint Publishing
Box 640, Meetinghouse Road
Walpole, NH 03608
(603)-756-9281

TOPICS: Channeling OCCUPATION: Author, Channeler, Publisher WORK EXPERIENCE: Stillpoint Publishing, Walpole, NH, Publisher PUBLICATIONS: *Planetary Citizen* PUBLISHER: Stillpoint Publishing

Youngson, Jeanne Keyes, Ph. D.
The Count Dracula Fan Club
One Fifth Avenue, Ste 3H
New York, NY 10003

TOPICS: Vampires DATE OF BIRTH: 12/20/24 PLACE OF BIRTH: Syracuse, NY EDUCATION: Maryville College, Tennessee EDUCATION: The Sorbonne, Paris, France EDUCATION: New York University, New York, NY OCCUPATION: Animation Filmmaker, Author, Curator WORK EXPERIENCE: Museum of Modern Art, New York, NY, Public Relations, 1951-58; Music Corp. of America, New York, NY, Public Relations, 1958-60; The Dracula Museum, New York, NY, Curator AWARDS: ASIFA, International Animation Society Award for animated movie, The Horney Unicorn PROFESSIONAL MEMBERSHIPS: International Count Dracula Fan Club, Founder & Pres.; International Frankenstein Society, Founder; Bram Stoker Memorial Association, Founder PUBLICATIONS: *Dracula Made Easy*, 1979 PUBLISHER: Dracula Press PUBLICATIONS: *Count Dracula Chicken Cookbook*, 1979 PUBLISHER: Adams Press

Zahorian, S.N.
SMB Whole Health
Box 263
Little Falls, NJ 07424
(201)-256-4261

TOPICS: Holistic Healing

Zarathustra, Frater
Temple Of Truth
P.O. Box 1132
Fremont, CA 94538
(415)-796-9195

TOPICS: Occult, Witchcraft, Psychic Phenomena, Death, Kabbalah, Holistic Healing, Spirituality DATE OF BIRTH: 10/29/38 PLACE OF BIRTH: Baltimore, MD EDUCATION: University of Redlands, Redlands, CA YEARS: 1967-1968 DEGREE: B.A. YEAR DEGREE: 1968 EDUCATION: University of Redlands, Redlands, CA DEGREE: M.A.- Teaching YEAR DEGREE: 1969 OCCUPATION: Ceremonial Magick- Field of Occult, Author WORK EXPERIENCE: Temple of Truth, Founder & Grand Master, 1972-1990 Closed; The White Light-A Magazine of Ceremonial Magick, Editor & Publisher, 1973-1990 Ceased AWARDS: Knight, Free Templer Order, 1990, Vienna, Austria PROFESSIONAL MEMBERSHIPS: Who's Who In The West - Nelson H. White DESCRIPTION: Author & co-author of more than 100 books, 40 of which are on Magick, etc. PUBLICATIONS: *Magick & The Law (Vols. 1-5)* PUBLICATIONS: *The Complete Exorcist* PUBLICATIONS: *Spiritual Healing* PUBLICATIONS: *Magickal Qaballah* PUBLICATIONS: *Ye Olde Dream Book* PUBLICATIONS: *The Meaning Of Death*

Zaslow, Bob

Hunuman Temple
Drawer W
Taos, NM 87571
TOPICS: Holistic Healing

Zaslow, Bob
Hanuman Foundation Tape Library
524 San Anselmo Avenue, #203
San Anselmo, CA 94960-2614
(407)-272-9165
TOPICS: Holistic Healing, Spirituality, Yoga,
Metaphysics, New Age

Zelonka, June
The Wyebridge Centre
74 Madison Avenue
Toronto, On M5R 2S4
Canada
(416)-924-9070
TOPICS: Holistic Healing

Zeng, Dr. Michael
International Institute Of Chinese Medicine
Rt. 17
Box 52A
Santa Fe, NM 87505
(505)-473-5233 (505)-471-5258
TOPICS: Acupuncture, Herbalogy, Holistic Health
DATE OF BIRTH: 01/29/38 PLACE OF BIRTH:
Chengdn Sichuan, China EDUCATION: Western
China Medical University, China YEARS: 1956-61
EDUCATION: Chengdn College Of Traditional
Chinese Medicine YEARS: 1961-64 OCCUPATION:
Physician, Acupuncturist, Herbalist, Author WORK
EXPERIENCE: International Institute Of Chinese
Medicine, Santa Fe, NM, Director 1983-present;
Panda Acupuncture Clinic, Santa Fe, NM,
Acupuncturist & Herbalist PROFESSIONAL
MEMBERSHIPS: AAAOM, NMAOM
DESCRIPTION: Author of more than 10 Chinese
Medicine Articles published in China between 1970
& 1980.

Zerman, Patricia
The Atlanta Center For Attitudinal Awareness
P.O. Box 675015
Marietta, GA 30067
(404)-953-3136
TOPICS: Holistic Healing

Zeroth, Wendy
The Sunflower Yoga Company
1305 Chalmers Road
Silver Spring, MD 20903
(301)-445-3882
TOPICS: Yoga

Zion, Almitra
Crystal Journey, A
1549 Peace Lane
Bow, WA 98232
(800)-521-6333
TOPICS: Crystals

Zitko, Dr. Howard John
World University Roundtable
Desert Sanctuary Campus
P.O. Box 2470
Benson, AZ 85602
(602)-586-2985
TOPICS: Parapsychology, Metaphysics, New Age,
Spirituality DATE OF BIRTH: 10/26/11 PLACE OF
BIRTH: Milwaukee, WI EDUCATION: University of
Wisconscin, Milwaukee, WI EDUCATION:
University of California, Los Angeles, CA
EDUCATION: Golden State University, Los Angeles,
CA DEGREE: Doctor of Divinity OCCUPATION:
Minister, Author, Teacher, Lecturer, Educational
Administrator WORK EXPERIENCE: Lemurian
Fellowship, Los Angeles, CA, Senior Minister, Vice-
President 1981-present; World University
Roundtable, Tucson, AZ, President & CEO, 43
years; World University, Benson, AZ, President &
CEO, 23 years; Temple of the Jewelled Cross,
Hollywood, CA, Minister 1942-46; Church of the
Abundant Life, Huntington Park, CA, Minister
1955-59 AWARDS: Doctor of Letters, China
Academy, Taipei, Taiwan; Ordained Minister,
American Ministerial Assoc., Santa Monica, CA;
Gold Medal & Poet Laureate PROFESSIONAL
MEMBERSHIPS: International Assoc. of Educators
For World Peace, Arizona State Chancellor 1985-
present; International Order of the Knights of Justice,
Knight Commander 1987-present; American
Minsterial Assoc.; U.S. Assoc. of the United Nations
DESCRIPTION: Lectures & writes on New Age
parapsychological sciences such as telepathy,
intuition, pre-cognition, clairvoyance, past life recall
& other forms of altered states of consciousness as
well as yoga, meditation, the soul & the future of
man. PUBLICATIONS: *New Age Tantra Yoga*, 1974
PUBLISHER: World University Press
PUBLICATIONS: *World University Insights With
Your Future In Mind*, 1980 PUBLISHER: World
University Press PUBLICATIONS: *Streamers Of
Light From The New World*, 1947

Zorbaugh, Mary Ellen
Traditional Acupuncture Foundation
American City Building
Suite 100
Columbia, MD 21044
(301)-997-4888
TOPICS: Acupuncture

Zucker, Bennett
Rodale Press, Inc.
33 East Minor Street
Emmaus, PA 18049
(215)-967-5171
TOPICS: Holistic Healing

Zuckerman, Enid
Canyon Ranch Spa
8600 East Rockcliff Road
Tucson, AZ 85715
(602)-749-9000
TOPICS: Holistic Healing

Zuckerman, Mel
Canyon Ranch Spa
8600 East Rockcliff Road
Tucson, AZ 85715
(602)-749-9000
TOPICS: Holistic Healing

Zuromski, Paul
Body, Mind, & Spirit Magazine
Box 701
Providence, RI 02901
(401)-351-4320
TOPICS: Metaphysics, Holistic Health, Spirituality,
Herbalogy, Channeling, Yoga, Meditation DATE OF
BIRTH: 06/09/52 PLACE OF BIRTH: Pawtucket, RI
EDUCATION: Providence College, Providence, RI
DEGREE: B.A. OCCUPATION: Editor-In-Chief,
Publisher WORK EXPERIENCE: Island Publishing
Company, Body, Mind & Spirit Magazine,
Providence, RI, Pres., Editor-In-Chief, 1982-Pres.
PROFESSIONAL MEMBERSHIPS: NAPRA -
Director PUBLICATIONS: *New Age Catalogue*
(1988) PUBLISHER: Doubleday

Stores

Stores and bookstores often overlap in services and products offered. Although both may sell books and offer Readings, many stores specialize in the sale of a particular type of product. It is, therefore, advisable to check the Bookstore chapter for additional sources.

Alchemist Shop
2521 Woodson Road
Overland, MO 63114
TOPICS: Metaphysics

All The Best
8074 Lake City Way
Seattle, WA 98115
TOPICS: Holistic Healing

Amarit Ambrosia Essences
31 Clarkson Avenue
Brooklyn, NY 11226
(800)-262-7489
TOPICS: New Age DESCRIPTION: Offers Amber Essences and products.

Amazing Gifts By Grace
611 Walker Street
Oliver Springs, TN 37840-1636
(615)-676-3703
TOPICS: New Age

Aubrey Organic Products
4419 North Manhattan Avenue
Tampa, FL 33614
(813)-876-4879
TOPICS: New Age

Auro Trading Co.
Box 2525
Aptos, CA 95003
TOPICS: Holistic Healing

Avalon Metaphysical Center, Ltd.
62-560 Johnson Street
Victoria, BC V8W 3C6
Canada
FAX (604)-380-1721
TOPICS: Occult, Tarot, Astrology, Crystals, Runes, Herbalogy OFFERS: Books READINGS: Astrology, Rune, Tarot NON-BOOK ITEMS SOLD: incense, candles, Sweetgrass, jewelry, medicine pouches, crystals, wands, herbs, cards DESCRIPTION: Offers Astrology Readings, classes, video tapes & Rune Stones. Wholesale distributor offering retail sales & mail order catalog.

Berg's Rockhound's Paradise
1231 Pearl Street (North Of Highway 10)
Prescott, WI 54021
(715)-262-5841
TOPICS: Crystals, Holistic Health DESCRIPTION: Rock shop offering crystals, amethyst, agates and more!

Bodhi Tree Bookstore
8585 Melrose Avenue
Los Angeles, CA 90069
TOPICS: Metaphysics

Body, Mind And Spirit Book Shop
P.O. Box 701
Providence, RI 02901
(401)-351-4320 (800)-338-5216 FAX (401)-272-5767
TOPICS: Channeling, New Age

Boiron/Borneman
1208 Amosland Road
Norwood, PA 19074
(215)-532-2035 (800)-258-8823
TOPICS: Holistic Healing PUBLICATIONS: *Aspects Of Research In Homeopathy* EDITOR: J. Boiron, et.al. TOPICS: Homeopathy TYPE: Book PRICE: $18.95 PUBLICATIONS: *Essentials Of Homeopathic Therapeutics* EDITOR: Jacques Jounnay TOPICS: Homeopathy TYPE: Book PRICE: $49.95 PUBLICATIONS: *Family Guide To Homeopathy* EDITOR: A. Horvilleur TOPICS: Homeopathy TYPE: Guide PRICE: $14.95 PUBLICATIONS: *Homeopathic Practice In Childhood Disorders* EDITOR: M. Aubin, et.al TOPICS: Homeopathy TYPE: Book PRICE: $14.95 PUBLICATIONS: *How To Study Homeopathy* EDITOR: D. Demarque P. Joly TOPICS: Homeopathy TYPE: Book PRICE: $14.95

Breeders Equipment Company
Box 177
Flourtown, PA 19031
(215)-233-0799
TOPICS: Holistic Healing

BroHuff Enterprises
Box 69067
Odessa, TX 79769-9067
(915)-367-3637
OWNER: Louise (Pat) Brown TOPICS: Crystals, Metaphysics, Numerology, Hypnotism, New Age OFFERS: Books DESCRIPTION: Offers Numerology Charts, Psychic Fairs, seminars, books, jewelry, tapes, ceramic items, stones & pendulums. Sponsors speakers. Conducts research-mind/hypnosis. Open by appointment. Mail-order catalog available. Can drop-ship.

Calvert Group
4550 Montgomery Avenue
Bethesda, MD 20814
(301)-951-4864
TOPICS: New Age

Celebrations New Age Store
2209 West Colorado Avenue
Colorado Springs, CO 80904
(719)-634-1855
OWNER: Coreen & Shanti Toll TOPICS: Holistic Healing, New Age, Metaphysics, Occult, Astrology, Tarot, Channeling OFFERS: Workshops, Books READINGS: Astrology, Tarot NON-BOOK ITEMS SOLD: Occult tools, cotton clothes, crystal jewelry, New Age music, tapes DESCRIPTION: Offers Metaphysical, self-help, Occult books & tools.

Cotton clothes, crystal jewelry, New Age music, hypnosis tapes, video rental library, classes, workshops, Astrology & Tarot Readings, Trance Channeling & Shamanic healing. PUBLICATIONS: *Celebrations* TOPICS: Holistic Healing, New Age, Metaphysics TYPE: Newspaper DATE: 1980 FREQ: quarterly CIRC: 3,500 DESCRIPTION: A quarterly which serves the Pikes Peak area with news and events relating to New Age and wholistic subjects. Accepts ads.

Cell Tech, Inc.
1300 Main Street
Klamath Falls, OR 97601-5900
TOPICS: New Age

Cheese Junction
1 W. Ridgewood Avenue
Ridgewood, NJ 07450
(800) 631-0353
TOPICS: New Age

Cherry Tree
P.O. Box 361
Sonoma, CA 95476
(707)-938-3480
TOPICS: New Age

Chi Pants
Box 7400
Santa Cruz, CA 95061
(408)-425-4526
TOPICS: Tai Chi CONTACT: Lawrence Ostrow

Co-Op America
2100 M Street, N.W., Suite 310
Washington, DC 20063
(202)-872-5307 (800)-424-2667
TOPICS: Psychic Phenomena PUBLICATIONS: *Co-Op America - Organizational Membership Directory* EDITOR: Joe Wisman-Horther TOPICS: Psychic Phenomena TYPE: Directory

Coleman's Quartz Mine
Rt. 1
Box 160
Jessieville, AR 71949
TOPICS: Crystals

Conjurring Shop
P.O. Box 805
Lawrence, KS 66044
TOPICS: Metaphysics

Cornucopia Natural Pet Products
229 Wall Street
Huntington, NY 11743
(516)-427-7479
TOPICS: Holistic Healing

Cosmic Resources
3939 South Saratoga

P.O. Box 913
Langley, WA 98260
(206)-221-8574
TOPICS: Crystals CONTACT: Robert & Barbara
Matteson DESCRIPTION: Retailers and wholesalers
of crystals, gemstones, jewelry and books.

Crystal Blend
1689 Remsen Avenue
Brooklyn, NY 11236
(914)-693-2553 (718)-968-1005
TOPICS: Crystals DESCRIPTION: Offers
wholesale/retail sales of all gemstones on a custom-
order basis.

Crystal Cluster, The
510 Kelly Avenue
Half Moon Bay, CA 94019
(415)-726-7644
TOPICS: Crystals DESCRIPTION: Offers crystals,
jewelry, stones, crystal classes & crystal healing
sessions.

Crystal Mountain Rock Shop
Box 13
Royal, AR 71968
TOPICS: Crystals

Crystal Pyramid
Rt. 1
Box 136A
Mt. Ida, AR 71968
TOPICS: Crystals

Crystal Triad
3223 East Broadway Avenue
Long Beach, CA 90803
(213)-598-6406
TOPICS: Crystals DESCRIPTION: Offers specimen
quartz crystals, minerals, jewelry, books, tapes and
more.

**Crystals Above - San Francisco
Sunrise**
1001 Broadway
Sausalito, CA 94965
(415)-332-2683
TOPICS: Crystals DESCRIPTION: Carries a superior
collection of crystals. Has a mystical Angel
Chamber.

Deva
P.O. Box F83
Burkittsville, MD 21718
TOPICS: New Age

Dr. Goodpet Laboratories
P.O. Box 4489
Inglewood, CA 90309
(213)-672-3269 (800)-222-9932
TOPICS: Holistic Healing PUBLICATIONS: *Pet
Allergies: Remedies For An Epidemic* TOPICS:
Holistic Healing TYPE: Book

Earth Care Paper, Inc.
P.O. Box 3335
Madison, WI 53704
TOPICS: New Age

Earthrise Company
P.O. Box 7796
San Rafael, CA 94915
TOPICS: Holistic Healing

Earthstar
50 Whitehall Road
Hooksett, NH 03106
(603)-669-9497
TOPICS: Crystals DESCRIPTION: Offers crystal
therapy, classes, bodywork & counseling.

Ellon Bach USA, Inc.
644 Merrick Road
Lynbrook, NY 11563
(516)-593-2206 (800)-433-7523
TOPICS: Holistic Health OFFERS: Books NON-
BOOK ITEMS SOLD: Liquid & cream remedies
DESCRIPTION: Sells flower and herbal remedies to
relieve stress and attain holistic health.

Enchantments
16 McKown Street
Boothbay Harbor, ME 04538
(207)-633-4992
OWNER: William G. Kirby TOPICS: New Age,
Metaphysics, Occult, Tarot OFFERS: Books NON-
BOOK ITEMS SOLD: Incense, essential oils, crystals
& gems, jewelry, tapes, CD's, videos, candles
DESCRIPTION: Sells self-help, New Age &
Metaphysical books, magikal & ritual supplies & a
large selection of Tarot.

Enchantments, Inc.
341 East 9th Street
New York, NY 10003
(212)-228-4394
OWNER: Carol A. Bulzone TOPICS: New Age,
Metaphysics, Occult, Tarot, Astrology, Holistic
Healing OFFERS: Workshops, Lectures, Books
READINGS: Astrology, Tarot NON-BOOK ITEMS
SOLD: Herbs, incense, jewelry, crystals, essential
oils, candles, crystal balls, ritual tools.
DESCRIPTION: Free classes, workshops & lectures
on Goddess Worship, Wicca & Environmental
Healing. Tarot & Astrology Readings. Outdoor
temple-Enchanted Garden. 80 page mail-order
catalog, $3.00.

Erlander's Natural Products
P.O. Box 106
Altadena, CA 91001
TOPICS: New Age

Essential Alternatives
22 Center Street
Rutland, VT 05701
TOPICS: New Age

Everything Natural
P.O. Box 279
Forest Knolls, CA 94933
TOPICS: New Age

Excalibur Books
29-B Young Street East
Waterloo, ON N2J 2L4
Canada
(519)-746-4012
TOPICS: Metaphysics, New Age, Occult,
Reincarnation, Crystals, Runes, Tarot OFFERS:
Books DESCRIPTION: Specialists in New Age,
Wicca, Shamanism, Psychic Power, Reincarnation,
Religions, Crystals, Runes, Tarot Cards,
Numerology, Folklore, Personal Development,
Native Americans Studies, Cancer Healing,
Philosophy. New & used books.

Felix Company
3623 Fremont Avenue North
Seattle, WA 98103
(206)-547-0042
TOPICS: Holistic Healing

Friends Of The Earth Natural Foods
114 Reynoida Village
Winston-Salem, NC 27106
(919)-725-6781
TOPICS: New Age, Holistic Health, Health Food,
Nutrition

Gary's Gem Garden
128 Woodcrest Center
Cherry Hill, NJ 08003
(609)-795-5077
TOPICS: Crystals, New Age NON-BOOK ITEMS
SOLD: New Age stones & crystals DESCRIPTION: A
complete rock shop offering wholesale, retail &
mail-order catalog sales of New Age stone &
crystals.

Green Growcery
1510 A Walnut Street
Berkeley, CA 94709
(415)-845-6870
TOPICS: New Age

Hand Of Aries
620 South 4th Street
Philadelphia, PA 19147
OWNER: Ann Duckworth TOPICS: Occult,
Metaphysics OFFERS: Books NON-BOOK ITEMS
SOLD: Tarot cards, jewelry, Wiccan supplies
DESCRIPTION: Offers a full selection of Wiccan
Supplies, Goddess Jewelry, Occult Books & Tarot
Cards. Catalogue $2.00. Coffee house 1st & 3rd Wed.
of each month.

Heritage Store/Center
314 Laskin Road
P.O. Box 444
Virginia Beach, VA 23458
(804)-428-0100 (800)-862-2923
TOPICS: Channeling, Holistic Health, Massage, Tai
Chi, Yoga, Psychic, Crystals OFFERS: Workshops,
Lectures, Books READINGS: Psychic readings
available. NON-BOOK ITEMS SOLD: Health food &
organic produce, crystals, gems DESCRIPTION:
Specializing in Edgar Cayce materials. Offers hard
to find items related to & mentioned in the Cayce
readings. Also has holistic services, massage, Tai
Chi, Yoga, floatation, lectures, classes, workshops,
psychic fairs & Readings.

I Am Books And Things
4290 S. University Drive
Davie, FL 33328
(305)-370-2925
TOPICS: Metaphysics CONTACT: Suzi R. Stevens
and Kay Wandland

K-9 Kustom Mix
3018 79th Avenue NE
Everett, WA 98205
(206)-334-4843
TOPICS: Holistic Healing

Lotus Bakery
2201-D Bluebell Drive
Santa Rosa, CA 95401
(707)-526-1520

TOPICS: New Age, Health Food

Macrobiotic Book Shop
242 Washington Street
Brookline, MA 02146
(617)-277-4321
TOPICS: Holistic Healing PUBLICATIONS: *Mail Order Catalog* TOPICS: Holistic Healing TYPE: Catalog

Manifestations
816 N. Coolidge Street
Wichita, KS 67203-3114
(316)-265-2203
OWNER: Gary & Cindy Siebler TOPICS: Crystals, New Age OFFERS: Lectures NON-BOOK ITEMS SOLD: Jewelry, Minerals, Pouches & Bags, Clothing, Custom Rune Stones DESCRIPTION: Mines crystals which are used in original designs of Victorian, Egyptian & American Indian jewelry. Also uses lapidary, silversmithing & beadworking skills to produce such items as scarabs, rune stones & beaded healing wands.

McGregor & Watkins
Rt. 8
Box487
Hot Springs, AR 71913
TOPICS: Crystals

Mercantile Food Company
P.O. Box 1140
Georgetown, CT 06829
TOPICS: Holistic Healing

Metaphysical Motivation Institute (M.M.I.)
641 Soudderth Drive
P.O. Box 400
Ruidoso, NM 88345
TOPICS: Holistic Health, Metaphysics OFFERS: Books NON-BOOK ITEMS SOLD: Tapes DESCRIPTION: Store & Mail-order catalog offering metaphyscial books & tapes dealing with self-help & health. Motto: Helping others to help themselves.

Middle Earth Book Shop
2791 East 14 Mile Road
Sterling Heights, MI 48310
(313)-979-7340
OWNER: Paul B. Hudson TOPICS: New Age, Metaphysics, Occult, Astrology OFFERS: Workshops READINGS: Astrology DESCRIPTION: Specializes in out-of-print & rare Metaphysical books. Conducts rare book search service. Offers books & classes in Astrology, Philosophy & Metaphysics. Provides Astrology Readings. Catalog available.

Native Herb Company
Box 742
Capitola, CA 95010
TOPICS: Holistic Healing

Nature's Gate Herbal Cosmetics
9183-5 Kelvin Avenue
Chatsworth, CA 91311
TOPICS: New Age

Naturo-Vet Services
857 El Pintado Road
Danville, CA 94526
(415)-837-7759

TOPICS: Holistic Healing PUBLICATIONS: *Animal Emergency Handbook* EDITOR: Gloria Dodd, D.V.M. TOPICS: Holistic Healing TYPE: Handbook DESCRIPTION: Founder of the California Holistic Veterinary Medical Association.

New Age Books & Things, Inc.
4401 N. Federal Highway
Ft. Lauderdale, FL 33308
(305)-771-0026
OWNER: Corrina Dehn, Bobbie Springer TOPICS: New Age, Metaphysics, Occult OFFERS: Books READINGS: Astrology, Tarot, Readings available Monday to Saturday NON-BOOK ITEMS SOLD: Jewelry, statues, posters, crystals & stones, tapes, New Age music, calendars, cards DESCRIPTION: Offers metaphysical & occult books & items, self-help & meditation tapes, computer section on Astrology & products concerned with Wicca, Yoga, health & dreamwork.

New Age Concepts
1211 Smith Ridge Road
New Canaan, CT 06840
(203)-966-2608
TOPICS: Crystals CONTACT: Michele Cowan

New Age Creation
219 Carl Street
San Francisco, CA 94117
TOPICS: New Age

New York School Of Astrology
545 Eighth Avenue, 10th FL.
New York, NY 10018-4307
(212)-947-3628
TOPICS: Astrology, Holistic Healing CONTACT: Henry Weingarten OFFERS: Workshops, Books READINGS: Astrology DESCRIPTION: Offers books, charts, computers, classes, consultations, counseling & software.

Noah's Park
134 West 32nd Street #602
New York, NY 10001
(800)-842-6624
TOPICS: Holistic Healing

Northeast Metaphysics
33 High Road
Box 316
Cornish, ME 04020
(207)-625-7447
OWNER: Ernest Rose TOPICS: New Age, Metaphysics, Holistic Healing, Tarot, Crystals OFFERS: Workshops, Books READINGS: Tarot NON-BOOK ITEMS SOLD: Audio & visual tapes, Native American Ceremonial Tools, crystals, jewelry DESCRIPTION: Educational resource center for personal growth of spirit, mind & body. Offers workshops & classes. Performs Healing Circle Ceremony, Tarot Readings & Metaphysical Counselling by owner.

Nutrition Now
2527 North Haden Island Drive
Portland, OR 97217
(503)-285-2400
TOPICS: Holistic Healing

Occult Emporium, The
102 North 9th Street
Allentown, PA 18102
(215)-433-3610

OWNER: Jay Solomon TOPICS: Occult OFFERS: Books DESCRIPTION: All supplies for Occultists: herbs, candles, talismans, incense, oils, stones, occult jewelry, statuary, antiques, new & used books, altar implements & various occult weapons. Catalog $2.00.

Occultique
73 Kettering Road
Northampton, NN1 4AW
England
0604-27727
OWNER: M. John Lovett TOPICS: Parapsychology, Occult, Metaphysics, Witchcraft, Paganism OFFERS: Books NON-BOOK ITEMS SOLD: Ritual items, herbs, incense, essential oils, crystal balls, tarot cards, rune stones DESCRIPTION: Sells new & second-hand books.

Ocus Stanley & Son
Box 163
Mt. Ida, AR 71957
TOPICS: Crystals

Paul Penders D & P Products
P.O. Box 878
Old Canning Plant Road
Seffner, FL 33584
TOPICS: New Age

Pet Guard
P.O. Box 728
Orange Park, FL 32073
(904)-264-8500 (800)-874-3221
TOPICS: Holistic Healing

Pines International
P.O. Box 1107
Lawrence, KS 66044
TOPICS: Holistic Healing

Planet Earth Book Center
1720 Colonial Boulevard
Ft. Myers, FL 33907
(813)-939-3969
TOPICS: Metaphysics CONTACT: Mary Alice Warren

Portable Products
56 Plato Blvd E
St. Paul, MN 55107
TOPICS: New Age

Premier One Products, Inc.
7171 Mercy Road
Suite 135
Omaha, NE 68106
TOPICS: Holistic Healing

Purple Rose Trading Company
1079 Stevens Street
Cassadaga, FL 32706
(904)-228-3315
TOPICS: Metaphysics DESCRIPTION: Sells large variety of metaphysical items.

Pyramid Treasures
1015 E. Las Olas Boulevard
Ft. Lauderdale, FL 33301
(305)-525-4448
OWNER: Kandace Garand TOPICS: New Age, Metaphysics, Occult, Massage, Crystals, Hypnotism, Psychic OFFERS: Workshops, Books

DESCRIPTION: Largest store in So. Florida. Offers books, cassettes, videos, unusual gifts, jewelry, candles, incense, crystals, gemstones, Native American & Wicca supplies. Hypnotherapy, massage, synchroenergizer, classes & Psychic Readings.

Radon Environmental Safety Testing, Inc.

350 Route 46
Department N.A.
Rockaway, NJ 07866
(800)-545-7378
TOPICS: Holistic Healing

Rainbow Store/Earth Products Company

15368 Mowersville Road
Shippensburg, PA 17257
(717)-423-6701
OWNER: James & Theresa Berry **TOPICS:** Holistic Health, Meditation, Herbalogy, Crystals, Health Food **OFFERS:** Workshops, Books **NON-BOOK ITEMS SOLD:** crystals, music & videos tapes, natural foods, vitamins, herbal remedies, body care items **DESCRIPTION:** Offers Metaphysical & wellness books, natural body care products, supplements, environmental products, recycled paper, energy saving devices. Also holds meditation circle, women's groups, services, classes & workshops.

Rowan Tree

10833 Monroe Road
Box 4B, Ste. 40
Matthews, NC 28105
(704)-841-1113
TOPICS: Metaphysics, New Age **CONTACT:** Anne Neely **OFFERS:** Workshops, Books **NON-BOOK ITEMS SOLD:** Candles, incense, jewelry **DESCRIPTION:** Workshops held 1st Sat. of each month & free classes held Tues, Wed., & Thurs.

Siddha International/Blue Pearl

1801 Northeast 23rd Avenue
Gainesville, FL 32609
(904)-376-8173 (800)-826-4810
TOPICS: New Age, Metaphysics, Occult **DESCRIPTION:** Offers beautiful New Age items

such as crystals, jewelry, incense & tapes both wholesale and retail.

Standard Homeopathic Company

P.O. Box 61067
Los Angeles, CA 90061
(213)-321-4284 (800)-624-9659
TOPICS: Holistic Healing

Star Professional Pharmaceuticals

1500 New Horizons Boulevard
Amityville, NY 11701
TOPICS: Holistic Health, Nutrition, Health Food **NON-BOOK ITEMS SOLD:** Natural vitamins, health supplements, natural cosmetics, mail-order catalog available

Sun Chlorella, Inc.

4025 Spencer Street
Suite 103
Torrance, CA 90503
TOPICS: Holistic Healing

Tiffany Art Glass

121 East Main Street
Northville, MI 48167
(313)-349-2777
TOPICS: Crystals **DESCRIPTION:** Produces metaphysical stained glass designs using healing crystals.

Time To Live

P.O. Box 1866
Hillsboro, OR 97123
(503)-648-1794
TOPICS: Body-Mind Connection **DESCRIPTION:** Products to help achieve self-realization.

UMA Silbey / U-Music Inc.

655 DuBois Street, E
San Rafael, CA 94901
(415)-453-8845
TOPICS: Crystals, New Age **CONTACT:** Karin Solomon **DESCRIPTION:** Wholesale/retail sales of crystals, books, seminars and more.

Under The Stars

1760 N.W. 38th Avenue
Lauderhill, FL 33311
(305)-739-3537
TOPICS: Metaphysics

Unicorn Village

3565 Northeast 20th Street
Miami, FL 33180-3770
(305)-944-5595
TOPICS: New Age, Health Food, Nutrition **DESCRIPTION:** Offers natural foods restaurant, health foods store & bakery.

Vortex Crystal And Gem

218 East Washington Street
Iowa City, IA 52240
(319)-337-3434
TOPICS: Crystals **DESCRIPTION:** Offers designer jewelry, fine specimens, elixers, books, tapes & workshops.

Wegner Quartz Crystal Mine

Rt. 1
Box 528
Norman, AR 71960
TOPICS: Crystals

Weleda

P.O. Box 769
Spring Valley, NY 10977
TOPICS: New Age

Westgate, The

5219 Magazine Street
New Orleans, LA 70115
(504)-899-3077
TOPICS: Occult, Paganism **OFFERS:** Books **NON-BOOK ITEMS SOLD:** Art **DESCRIPTION:** A gallery of Necromantic art & literature.

Wild Wood Fragrances

P.O. Box 403
Boulder, CO 80306
OWNER: Morwyn **TOPICS:** Occult, Holistic Health, Witchcraft, Herbalogy, Metaphysics **DESCRIPTION:** Sells mail-order metaphysical products.

Wow-Bow Distributors

309 Burr Road
East Northport, NY 11731
(516)-499-8572
TOPICS: Holistic Healing

Bookstores

Many Stores offer services and products similar to those offered by Bookstores. We therefore suggest that the chapter, Stores, be examined for additional sources. Many of the Bookstores listed in this directory offer copies of Parapsychology, New Age and the Occult - A Source Encyclopedia.

A-Besto Book Store
7062 W Belmont
Chicago, IL 60634
(312)-777-4089
OWNER: James E. Bisconti **READINGS:** Runes

A. A. Michael Books
1541 S. Green River Road
Evansville, IN 47715
(812)-479-8979
OWNER: Elizabeth R. Yohe **EXPERTISE:** Metaphysics, Recovery **OFFERS:** Workshops, Lectures **NON-BOOK ITEMS SOLD:** Crystals, Jewelry, Native American Items, Pouches, Incense, Posters, Greeting Cards, New Age Music, Spoken Audio

Abyss Easthampton
34 Cottage Street
P.O. Box 1022
Easthampton, MA 01027
(413)-527-8765
OWNER: Adair **OFFERS:** Workshops **NON-BOOK ITEMS SOLD:** Herbs, Tarot, Jewelry, Magickal Items **DESCRIPTION:** Sells items on Witchcraft, Magick, UFO's, Egyptian & Celtic lore.

Academic Book Center, Inc.
5600 Ne Hassalo Street
Portland, OR 97213-3640
(503)-287-6657

Accelerated Learning Institute
Mankind Research Unlimited
1315 Apple Avenue
Silver Spring, MD 20910
(301)-587-8686
OFFERS: Workshops, Lectures

Acorn Potential Bookshop
2646 North 76th Avenue
Elmwood Park, IL 60635
(708)-452-6690
OWNER: Joseph Bruno

Afro-In Books N Things
5575 N.W. 7th Avenue
Miami, FL 33127
(305)-756-6107
OWNER: Eursla Wells

Agape Book Shoppe
4220 Brookside Drive
Rapid City, SD 57702
(605)-342-6998
OWNER: Suzanne Livermore **OFFERS:** Workshops, Lectures, Circles Of Life Integration, Crystal Healings, Reiki **READINGS:** Integrated Awareness Readings, Shusta Card Classes & Readings

Agartha Secret City

1618 Ponce de Leon Boulevard
Coral Gables, FL 33134
(305)-441-1618 (305)-443-5151
OFFERS: Workshops **DESCRIPTION:** Topics covered: Astrology, Kabbalah, Theosophy, Occult, Rosicrucians, Yoga, Dreams, Healing, Psychosynthesis, Gurdjieff, Tarot, Palmistry, I'Ching, Alchemy, Magic, Natal & Biorhythm Charts, Antroposophy, Metaphysics, Health, Diet.

Alchemist Shop, The
2521 Woodson Road
Overland, MO 63114
(314)-423-2711
OWNER: Albert J. Petschonek **ASSOCIATE:** Marge Walter **NON-BOOK ITEMS SOLD:** Herbs, Candles, Incense, Jewelry, Stones, Crystals

Alchemist, The
196 Washington Street
Hudson, MA 01749
(508)-562-2154
OWNER: Stephen Learnard **EXPERTISE:** Past Life Therapy **ASSOCIATE:** Basha Baldyga **OFFERS:** Workshops **READINGS:** Past Life **NON-BOOK ITEMS SOLD:** Health Foods

Alcove, The
17 Ohio River Plaza
Gallipolis, OH 45631
(614)-446-7653
OWNER: Gerald Vallee **ASSOCIATE:** Pat Ball Black **NON-BOOK ITEMS SOLD:** Tarot Cards, Rune Stones, Medicine Cards

Alexandria II Bookstore
567 So. Lake Avenue
Pasadena, CA 91101
(818)-792-7885
OWNER: Victoria Gevoian **OWNER:** Charles Gevoian **OWNER:** Ralph Chakalian **OFFERS:** Lectures **NON-BOOK ITEMS SOLD:** New Age Music & Lecture Tapes, Cards, Incense, Gifts

Alexandria II Bookstore
10944 Weyburn Avenue
Westwood, CA 90024
(213)-824-7575
OWNER: Charles Gevoian **OWNER:** Victoria Gevoian **OWNER:** Ralph Chakalian **OFFERS:** Lectures **NON-BOOK ITEMS SOLD:** New Age Music & Videos, Tarot Cards, Incense, Crystals, Jewelry, Greeting Cards

Allentown Bookstore/Enigma Books
RR 1
Box 85
Tremont, IL 61568
(312)-925-3907 **FAX** (309)-682-3101

OWNER: Dan Dexter **EXPERTISE:** Teacher, Lecturer **OFFERS:** Workshops, Lectures **NON-BOOK ITEMS SOLD:** Tapes

Alpha Book Center
New Age Community Church
1928 E. McDowell
Phoenix, AZ 85006
(602)-253-1223
ASSOCIATE: John Rodgers **EXPERTISE:** Religion, Metaphysics **NON-BOOK ITEMS SOLD:** Games, Cards, Posters, Tapes, Videos, Candles, Oils, Herbs

American School Of Astrology
21 Mellon Avenue
West Orange, NJ 07052
(201)-731-2255
OWNER: Sylvia Sherman **EXPERTISE:** Astrologer **READINGS:** Astrology, Palmistry, Numerology, Handwriting

Amron Esoteric Center
2254 Van Ness Avenue
San Francisco, CA 94109-2513
(415)-775-0227
OWNER: Jack Walder **ASSOCIATE:** James Roeser **OFFERS:** Workshops, Lectures **READINGS:** Astrology, Palmistry, Tarot, Aura, Numerology **NON-BOOK ITEMS SOLD:** Crystals, Tapes, Videos, Incense, Candles, Cards

Ananda Bookstore
3663 Canyon Crest Drive, #E
Riverside, CA 92507
(714)-686-3471
OWNER: Robert Moshier **READINGS:** Astrology, Runes, Tarot **NON-BOOK ITEMS SOLD:** Music, Incense, Gems, Minerals, Indian & Guatamalian Imports

Ananda-Church Of God-Realization
17544 Midvale Avenue N., #203
Seattle, WA 98133
(206)-542-8184
OFFERS: Workshops, Lectures, Spiritual Counseling, Meditation Techniques **READINGS:** Tea Leaves

Ancient Circles
P.O. Box 773
Laytonville, CA 95454
(707)-984-8033
OWNER: Ann Bogner **EXPERTISE:** Celtic History, Goddess Archetypes, Ancient Cultures **OWNER:** Orion **EXPERTISE:** Pagan Ritual, God Archetypes **READINGS:** Runes, Tarot **NON-BOOK ITEMS SOLD:** Mail-Order Jewelry

Aquarian Age Discovery
905 Dodds Avenue
Chattanooga, TN 37404

(615)-624-1798

OWNER: Wayne Schock **ASSOCIATE:** Mark Souders **ASSOCIATE:** Johnnie Lyons **OFFERS:** Workshops, Lectures, Readings performed with workshops **READINGS:** Tea Leaves **NON-BOOK ITEMS SOLD:** Crystals, Music, Jewelry, Art, Incense, Runes, Tarot Decks, Cards

Aquarian Bookshop, Inc., The
3519 Ellwood Avenue
Richmond, VA 23221
(804)-353-5575

OWNER: Jim Holzgrefe **OWNER:** Lacy Holzgrefe **OFFERS:** Workshops, Lectures **READINGS:** Astrology, Palmistry, Runes, Psychic **NON-BOOK ITEMS SOLD:** Crystals, Jewelry, Posters

Aquarian Center
116 Montowese Street
Branford, CT 06405
(203)-481-6091 (203)-481-5854

OWNER: Jean Loomis **EXPERTISE:** Psychic, Astrologer, Trance Medium **ASSOCIATE:** Jean Saunders **EXPERTISE:** Jungian Psychotherapy **ASSOCIATE:** Paul Gadebusch **EXPERTISE:** Rebirthing **OFFERS:** Workshops, Lectures, Channeled-Seth **READINGS:** Astrology, Palmistry, Runes, Tea Leaves

Aquarius
1614 King Street
Alexandria, VA 22314
(703)-836-0616

OWNER: Carroll Miles **OFFERS:** Workshops **READINGS:** Astrology, Tarot, I Ching, Past Life Readings **NON-BOOK ITEMS SOLD:** Crystals, Incense, New Age Music, Astrological Computer Printouts, Figurines

Arcturus Book Service
4431 Village Square Lane
P.O. Box 831383
Stone Mtn, GA 30083
(404)-297-4624

OWNER: Robert C. Girard **EXPERTISE:** UFOs **ASSOCIATE:** Monica A. Williams-Girard **EXPERTISE:** UFOs **NON-BOOK ITEMS SOLD:** Video & Audio Cassettes Dealing With UFOs

Aries Press, Inc.
Po Box 30081
Chicago, IL 60630
(312)-725-8300

OWNER: Ms. Del O'Connor **EXPERTISE:** Cycles Analyst **OFFERS:** Workshops, Lectures, Classes **READINGS:** Astrology **NON-BOOK ITEMS SOLD:** Cassette Taped Lectures, Classes, Workshops

Armchair Books
39 SW Dorion
Pendleton, OR 97801
(503)-276-7323

NON-BOOK ITEMS SOLD: Tarot Cards, I Ching Cards

Artist's Proof Bookstore
460 Magnolia Avenue
Larkspur, CA 94939
(415)-924-3801

OWNER: Zephyr Ceccih **MANAGER:** Maryjane Dunstan **OFFERS:** Workshops, Lectures **NON-BOOK ITEMS SOLD:** Tarot Cards, Sacred Path Cards-Native American

Aspects Pty Ltd.
P.O. Box 527
Clayton, VIC 3168
Australia
(003)-543-1570

OWNER: Claire Eadie **ASSOCIATE:** John Fitzsimons **EXPERTISE:** Psychic, Healer, Spiritualist, Past Life Regressionist **OFFERS:** Lectures, Psychic & Spiritual Counseling **NON-BOOK ITEMS SOLD:** Posters

Astro Gem Associates
Route 515
P.O. BOX 12
Makanda, IL 62958
(618)-457-0458

OWNER: Robert Presley, Jr. **EXPERTISE:** Marketing **OWNER:** Yolande Tullar **EXPERTISE:** Astrologer **READINGS:** Astrology **NON-BOOK ITEMS SOLD:** Crystals & Gem Stones, Astrological Gem Stone Prescriptions

Astrological Bureau Of Ideas
P.O. Box 251
Wethersfield, CT 06109
(203)-563-3146

OWNER: Capel McCutcheon, M.S., PMAFA **OFFERS:** Workshops, Lectures **READINGS:** Astrology, Tea Leaves **NON-BOOK ITEMS SOLD:** Computer Horoscopes, Interpretations

Atalanta's Records & Books
32 Main Street
P.O. Box 317
Bisbee, AZ 85603-0317
(602)-432-9976

OWNER: Joan Werner **DESCRIPTION:** Offers books, cassette tapes, CD's, incense, videos, magazines & calendars.

Atlantis Bookshop
Psychic Press
49A Museum Street
London, UK WCIAILY
England
(071)-405-2120

MANAGING DIRECTOR: Tony Ortzen **EXPERTISE:** Spiritualism, Paranormal **SECRETARY:** Karl Duncan **EXPERTISE:** Spiritualism, Paranormal **ASSOCIATE:** Nicholas Meczes **EXPERTISE:** Crowley, Magic

Atlantis Bookshop, The
Psychic Press Ltd.
49A Museum Street
London, WC1A ILY
England
071-405-2120

DESCRIPTION: Founded in 1922, the world's oldest occult bookshop. Enormous selection of books covering Spiritualism, Occult Sciences & related subjects too numerous to list. Also new, used & out-of-print books & New Age tapes.

Audubon Naturalist Bookshop
8940 Jones Mill Road
Chevy Chase, MD 20815
(301)-652-3606

Linda Hardman **DESCRIPTION:** Offers sources concerned with environmental education.

Auromere Books & Imports
1291 Weber Street

Pomona, CA 91768
(714)-629-8255 (800)-735-4691

ASSOCIATE: Dakshina Vanzetti **ASSOCIATE:** Michael Zucker **ASSOCIATE:** Vishnu Eschner **OFFERS:** Lectures, Sri Aurobindo's Yoga **READINGS:** Tea Leaves **NON-BOOK ITEMS SOLD:** Ayurvedic Health Products, Incense, Handicrafts From India

Austin Seth Center
P.O. Box 7786
Austin, TX 78713-7786
(512)-479-8909

DIRECTOR: Maude Cardwell, Ph.D. **EXPERTISE:** Metaphysics **NON-BOOK ITEMS SOLD:** Audiotapes

Avalon Book Center
375 Pharr Road
Atlanta, GA 30305
(404)-233-1611

OWNER: Albert Martin **EXPERTISE:** Metaphysics, Deming, Parapsychology **ASSOCIATE:** Don Burger **EXPERTISE:** Astrology, Tarot, Numerology, Psychic **ASSOCIATE:** Karl Welz **EXPERTISE:** Runes, Radionics, Metaphysics, Psionics **READINGS:** Astrology, Runes, Tarot, Psychic **NON-BOOK ITEMS SOLD:** Tarot Cards, Cassettes, Incense, Jewelry, Magazines, Egyptian & Indian Statuary, Games

Aware-House, Inc
Route 1
Box 325
Rabun Gap, GA 30568
(404)-746-2517

OWNER: Ruth McWilliams **EXPERTISE:** Minister, Hypnotherapist **OFFERS:** Workshops, Lectures

Awareness & Health Unlimited
3509 N. High Street
Columbus, OH 43214
(614)-262-7087 (800)-533-7087

OWNER: Phillip Wilson **ASSOCIATE:** Chris Linhart **OFFERS:** Lectures **READINGS:** Astrology, Runes **NON-BOOK ITEMS SOLD:** Massage Tools, Chinese Herbs, Gem Elixirs, Incense, Green Foods, Spirulina/Chlorella, Charts, Cards, Sandals, Cayce Materials

Baras Foundation
P.O. Box 3189
San Diego, CA 92163
(619)-297-4668 (619)-291-5252

OWNER: Carol Baras **EXPERTISE:** Hypnotherapist **MANAGER:** Kathy Preston **OFFERS:** Workshops, Lectures, Hypnotherapy **NON-BOOK ITEMS SOLD:** Audio Tapes

Be Here Now Book Center
1858 Broad Street
Cranston, RI 02905
(401)-461-5031

DESCRIPTION: Deals with psychology, philosophy, world religion, new thought, New Age, classes & videos.

Beauty And The Books
4213 University Way NE
Seattle, WA 98105
(206)-632-8510

OWNER: Richard Leffel

Best Seller Book Shop

130 N. San Fernando
Burbank, CA 91502
(818)-955-8243

ASSOCIATE: Kelly Goodside **EXPERTISE:** Out Of Print New Age Books **NON-BOOK ITEMS SOLD:** Books On Tape, Tarot Cards

Beyond Words Bookshop
150 Main Street
Northampton, MA 01060
(413)-586-6304

OWNER: Diana Krauth **OWNER:** Jeff Krauth **OFFERS:** Workshops, Lectures **NON-BOOK ITEMS SOLD:** Stationery, Meditation Supplies, Crystals, Gifts, Crafts

Blue Dragon Book Shop
283 East Main Street
Ashland, OR 97520
(503)-482-2142

OWNER: Bob Peterson **EXPERTISE:** Occult **NON-BOOK ITEMS SOLD:** Rare & Out Of Print Occult Books **DESCRIPTION:** Sells & buys used, out-of-print & rare Occult & Metaphysical books covering topics from Alchemy to Zen.

Blue Leaf Books
78 King Street West, 2nd Fl.
Kitchener, ON N2G 4G8
Canada
(519)-570-0950

OWNER: Kenneth Guse **NON-BOOK ITEMS SOLD:** Herbs, tapes, magazines, crystals, incense, essential oils, aromatherapy products. **DESCRIPTION:** Region's New Age & Occult bookstore offering Club Blue Leaf, meeting once a month, to discuss various related topics.

Blue Wolf Bookstore, The
118 1/2 West Wilshire (Rear)
Fullerton, CA 92632
(714)-526-3449

DESCRIPTION: Offers metaphysical books, tapes, crystals, readings, jewelry, art & healing stones.

Bodhi Tree Bookstore
8585 Melrose Avenue
Los Angeles, CA 90069
(213)-659-1733 (213)-659-2773

DESCRIPTION: Offers new and used books dealing with religions of the world, metaphysics & New Age music.

Body Balance System
3927 Judah
San Francisco, CA 94122
(415)-664-9766

Book And The Pendulum, Inc., The
304-37th St., S.E.
Charleston, WV 25304
(304)-925-7324

OWNER: Phyllis Margolis, R.N. **EXPERTISE:** Healer, Massage, Reiki, Rebirther **ASSOCIATE:** Debbie Rutherford **EXPERTISE:** Tarot **OFFERS:** Workshops, Lectures **READINGS:** Astrology, Runes, Tea Leaves **NON-BOOK ITEMS SOLD:** Crystals, Jewelry, Herbs, Tapes, Candles, Tarot Cards

Book Barn
Universal Force Dynamics, Inc.
410 Delaware
Leavenworth, KS 66048
(913)-682-6518

PUBLISHER, OWNER: Robert K. Spear

Book Bazaar
P.O. Box 42005
Las Vegas, NV 89116
(702)-384-4711

Book Bin, The
725 Arnold Avenue
Point Pleasant, NJ 08742
(908)-892-3456

OWNER: Gene Madeleine **EXPERTISE:** Yoga Teacher, Pyramid Energetics, Crystal Workshops, Numerology **OFFERS:** Workshops **READINGS:** Astrology, Runes, Tarot, Numerology **NON-BOOK ITEMS SOLD:** Crystals, Minerals, Jewelry, Tarot Decks

Book City
6627 Hollywood Boulevard
Los Angeles, CA 90028
(213)-466-2525 (213)-466-1049

ASSOCIATE: Joseph R. Johnson **EXPERTISE:** Metaphysics, Occult, Eastern Philosophy, Numerology **ASSOCIATE:** Michael Wilson **EXPERTISE:** Occult, Crowelyan Magick, Qabbalah **NON-BOOK ITEMS SOLD:** Tarot Cards, Rune Stones

Book Nook
2225 Cloverdale Plaza
Winston-Salem, NC 27103
(919)-725-3696

OWNER: Dan Hartigan

Book-Let, The
130 Balsam Street
Ridgecrest, CA 93555
(619)-375-1725

OWNER: Carol S. Rorex **ASSOCIATE:** Wallace Clary **NON-BOOK ITEMS SOLD:** Gift Items, Calendars

Bookland
102 North Palm Canyon Drive
CA 92262
(619)-325-1020 (619)-325-1026

OWNER: T.S. Lyons **ASSOCIATE:** John Crook **EXPERTISE:** Reincarnation, Astral Projection **NON-BOOK ITEMS SOLD:** Tarot Cards, New Age Music

Bookman, The
840 North Tustin Avenue
Orange, CA 92667
(714)-538-0166

David Hess

Books-By-Phone
Ronin Publishing, Inc.
Box 522
Berkeley, CA 94701
(800)-858-2665 (415)-268-0869

OWNER: Beverly Potter **MANAGER:** Sebastian **NON-BOOK ITEMS SOLD:** Controversial Occult & New Age Books.

Bookshelf
2456 Washington Boulevard
Ogden, UT 84401
(801)-621-4752

OWNER: Paatricio Ortega **EXPERTISE:** Western Philosophy **MANAGER:** Tim Chase **EXPERTISE:** Wicca, Western Tradition **ASSOCIATE:** Kirk

Dougherty **EXPERTISE:** Eastern Philosophy **NON-BOOK ITEMS SOLD:** Incense, Tarot Decks, Music, Runes

Booksville
2626 Honolulu Avenue
Montrose, CA 91020
(818)-248-9149

OWNER: Shirley McCormick **ASSOCIATE:** Dean K. McCormick

Booktown
606 Old Springville Road
Birmingham, AL 35215
(205)-854-2239

OWNER: Virginia Carlisle **ASSOCIATE:** Rebecca Liechty **NON-BOOK ITEMS SOLD:** Stones, Tarot Cards, Book Marks

Booktrader II
216 North 1st Avenue
Sandpoint, ID 83864
(208)-263-1041

OWNER: Richard Warren **EXPERTISE:** Metaphysics **OWNER:** Marie Warren **EXPERTISE:** Metaphysics **NON-BOOK ITEMS SOLD:** Calendar

Brigit Books
3434 4th Street North
St. Petersburg, FL 33704
(813)-522-5775

OWNER: Patty Callaghan **OFFERS:** Workshops **NON-BOOK ITEMS SOLD:** Jewelry, Runes, Tarot Cards, New Age Music, Goddess Statues, Greeting Cards, Magazines, Newspapers

BroHuff Enterprises
3136 N. Tom Green
Odessa, TX 79762
(915)-367-3637

ASSOCIATE: Louise E.(Pat) Brown **EXPERTISE:** Counseling, Cards, Candle Work **OWNER:** Bert Huff **EXPERTISE:** Casting, Custom Faceting & Designing Jewelry **OFFERS:** Craft & Pyschic Fairs **NON-BOOK ITEMS SOLD:** Crystals, Jewelry, Minerals, Ritual & Healing Stones

Byangee Book Shop
Shop 5
Settlement Arcade
Milton, NSW 2539
Australia

OWNER: Karen Tarlington **OWNER:** Suzy Greentree **NON-BOOK ITEMS SOLD:** Crystals, Ambient Music Tapes, Cards, Wilderness Posters

Candle, Incense & Herb Shop
Edward J. Kay Enterprises
3031 South Freeway
Ft. Worth, TX 76104
(817)-921-9580

OWNER: Edward J. Kay **EXPERTISE:** Advisor **ASSOCIATE:** Alberto Paba **EXPERTISE:** Tarot Card Reader **READINGS:** Tarot **NON-BOOK ITEMS SOLD:** Oils, Crystal Balls, New Age Jewelry, Incense, Candles, Catalog Sales

Cardinal Images
Pickett Center
50 S. Pickett Street
Alexandria, VA 22304
(703)-370-5228

ASSOCIATE: Barbara Curtis **OWNER:** June Reckert **OFFERS:** Lectures **READINGS:** Astrology, Palmistry, Runes **NON-BOOK ITEMS SOLD:** Gemstones, Crystals, Jewelry, Audio, Video, Greeting Cards, Gifts

Carol's Timeless Concepts
231 N. Chestnut Street
Palmyra, PA 17078
(717)-838-3897 (717)-838-3857

OWNER: Carol Strickler **EXPERTISE:** Yoga Instructor, Health Advisor **ASSOCIATE:** Lisa DiNunzio **EXPERTISE:** Health Advisor, Fashion Consultant **OFFERS:** Workshops, Lectures **READINGS:** Astrology, Runes **NON-BOOK ITEMS SOLD:** Cassette Tapes, Gourmet Foods, Cotton Clothing, Non-Animal Tested Beauty Products

Cassadaga Camp Bookstore
1112 Stevens Street
P.O. Box 319
Cassadaga, FL 32706
(904)-228-2880

MANAGER: Hazel Tomim-Phipps **ASSOCIATION DIRECTOR:** Fran Ellison **OFFERS:** Workshops, Lectures, Mediumship, Spiritual Counseling **NON-BOOK ITEMS SOLD:** Cassettes, CD's, Crystals, Stones, Smudge, Incense, Posters, Jewelry, Gift

Center Bookstore, The
Elm Street
Damariscotta, ME 04543
(207)-563-2123

Paul Gilman

Center For New Age Studies Bookstore
Thompsons Point Bldg 1A
Portland, ME 04102
(207)-775-7135

OWNER: Pat Balzer **EXPERTISE:** Metaphysics, Channeling **OFFERS:** Workshops, Lectures, Channeling With Ascended Masters **NON-BOOK ITEMS SOLD:** Crystals, Tapes, Jewelry, New Age Accessories, Native American Accessories

Center Of Loving Light
P.O. Box 11334
Washington, DC 20008

OWNER: The Lenardsons **EXPERTISE:** Counseling, Spiritual Guidance **ASSOCIATE:** Cassandra Spears **EXPERTISE:** Chakra Massage, Teacher **OFFERS:** Workshops, I Ching **READINGS:** Tarot **NON-BOOK ITEMS SOLD:** Massage Oils, Incense

Church Of Religious Science
P.O. Box 983
Portland, ME 04104
(207)-871-0032

OWNER: Carole B. Curran **EXPERTISE:** Counselor, Psychic, Healer, Clairvoyant **OFFERS:** Workshops, Lectures, Private Consultations Using Clairvoyance & Automatic Writing

Church Of Universal Forces
165 N. 20th Street
Columbus, OH 43203
(614)-252-2083

OWNER: Doris Bowers **EXPERTISE:** Psychic Advisor, Marriages **ASSOCIATE:** Lady Isis **EXPERTISE:** Hypnotist, Dreams, Psychic Phenomenon, Medium, Past Life **OFFERS:** Workshops, Lectures, Psychic Impressions

READINGS: Tea Leaves **NON-BOOK ITEMS SOLD:** Custom Made Ritual Supplies, Metaphysical Toys

City Book Store
1917 Creswell Avenue
Shreveport, LA 71101
(318)-425-5142

OWNER: B.L. Payton **OWNER:** Vida L. Payton **OFFERS:** Lectures

City Books Inc.
3609-1E Bradshaw Road
Sacramento, CA 95827
(916)-366-5643

OWNER: Darlene M. York **NON-BOOK ITEMS SOLD:** Tarot Cards, Book Marks, Maps

Collectors Market
113 Green Avenue
Taft, TX 78390
(512)-528-3353

OWNER: Ken Kruse **NON-BOOK ITEMS SOLD:** Jewelry, Records, Collectibles

Cosmic Crystal
309 East Main Street
Branford, CT 06405
(203)-488-4035

OWNER: V. Alice Worsham **EXPERTISE:** Healer, Crystals, Teacher, Lecturer, Rune Reader **ASSOCIATE:** Karen Nelson **EXPERTISE:** Healer, Crystals, Teacher, Lecturer, Rune Reader **OFFERS:** Workshops, Lectures **READINGS:** Runes, Tarot, Heart Cards

Coven Gardens
P.O. Box 1064
Boulder, CO 80306
(303)-444-4322

ASSOCIATE: Gwen Stevens **EXPERTISE:** Wiccan High Priestess, Herbalist, Healer, Teacher, Keeper **OFFERS:** Workshops, Lectures **READINGS:** Astrology, Palmistry, Runes, Tarot, Tea Leaves **NON-BOOK ITEMS SOLD:** Incense, Oils, Bath Products, Herbs

Crazy Wisdom Bookstore
206 N. 4th Avenue
Ann Arbor, MI 48104
(313)-665-2757

OWNER: Bill Zirinsky **ASSOCIATE:** Ruth Schekter **ASSOCIATE:** Debbie Szporluk **OFFERS:** Lectures **READINGS:** Astrology, Tarot **NON-BOOK ITEMS SOLD:** Buddhist Objects, Jewelry, Goddess Statuary, Cards, Video, Music & Audio Tapes, Incense, Crystals, Instruments

Crescent Rose, The
93 South Main
Eureka Springs, AR 72632
(501)-253-6759

OWNER: Nanshe Jean Baptiste **EXPERTISE:** Astrologer, Tarot, Clairvoyant **OFFERS:** Intuitive Resonance **READINGS:** Astrology, Palmistry, Runes, Tarot, Tea Leaves **NON-BOOK ITEMS SOLD:** Jewelry, Incense, Magical Items

Crystal Abbey
P.O. Box 293
Molalla, OR 97038
(503)-829-3477

ASSOCIATE: Philip C. Panepento **EXPERTISE:** Jeweler, Metaphysician **OFFERS:** Workshops,

Lectures **NON-BOOK ITEMS SOLD:** Crystals, Handcrafted Crystal Jewelry

Crystal Accents
7815 Maple Street
New Orleans, LA 70118
(504)-861-3303

OWNER: Ralph Pittman **EXPERTISE:** Minister, Yoga, Meditation, Instructor **ASSOCIATE:** Judith Faye **EXPERTISE:** Jungian-Astrologer **OFFERS:** Workshops, Lectures **READINGS:** Astrology, Palmistry, Runes, Tarot **NON-BOOK ITEMS SOLD:** Tapes, Gifts

Crystal Cave Bookstore
777 South Main Street, #2
Orange, CA 92668
(714)-543-0551

DESCRIPTION: Computerized services including reports on natal, transits, compatibility.

Crystal Chamber, The
1 Hawthorne Boulevard
Salem, MA 01970
(508)-745-9400

OWNER: Ed Amberman **ASSOCIATE:** Patti Cronin **ASSOCIATE:** Shawn Poirier **EXPERTISE:** Psychic **MANAGER:** Marilyn Millham **OFFERS:** Workshops, Lectures **READINGS:** Astrology, Palmistry, Runes, Tarot **NON-BOOK ITEMS SOLD:** Crystals, Jewelry, Musical Tapes

Crystal Expectations
854 Brock Avenue
New Bedford, MA 02744
(508)-990-7898

OWNER: Carole J. Moniz **ASSOCIATE:** Ronald Moniz **OFFERS:** Workshops, Lectures **READINGS:** Astrology, Palmistry, Runes

Crystal Fantasy
264 N Palm Canyon
CA 92262
(619)-322-7799

OWNER: Scott Meredith **EXPERTISE:** Crystals **OWNER:** Joy Meredith **EXPERTISE:** Crystals **ASSOCIATE:** Ann Tisher **EXPERTISE:** Shamanism, Native American Studies **OFFERS:** Lectures **NON-BOOK ITEMS SOLD:** Jewelry, Crystals, Music, Incense, Gifts $.25-$10,000

Crystal Forest
1801 NE 23rd Avenue
Gainesville, FL 32609
(904)-376-1201

OWNER: Michael Rage **EXPERTISE:** Fragrances **ASSOCIATE:** Susan Bacharach **EXPERTISE:** Imported Gifts **NON-BOOK ITEMS SOLD:** Crystals, Jewelry, Toys, Cards, Gifts

Crystal Gardens
21 Greenwich Avenue
New York, NY 10014
(212)-727-0692

OWNER: Joyce Kaessinger **EXPERTISE:** Crystals, Minerals, Bach Flower Remedies, Medicine Cards **OWNER:** Constance Barrett **EXPERTISE:** Crystals, Minerals, Bach Flower Remedies, Medicine Cards **OFFERS:** Workshops **NON-BOOK ITEMS SOLD:** Crystals

Crystal Oasis
13 Cedar Lane

Canaan, CT 06018
(203)-824-7840
OWNER: Marilyn J. Barney **EXPERTISE:** Reiki-2nd Degree **OFFERS:** Workshops, Healing Circles **READINGS:** Runes, Tarot **NON-BOOK ITEMS SOLD:** Crystals, Gemstones, Audio & Video, Holistic Health Products, Incense, Games

Crystal Rainbow
1939 Cadillac Avenue
Colorado Springs, CO 80909-2128
(719)-473-3533
OWNER: Barbara Morlan **EXPERTISE:** Empowerment Specialist, Networking **OFFERS:** Workshops, Lectures **READINGS:** Tea Leaves, Intuitive Empowerment Readings **NON-BOOK ITEMS SOLD:** Healing Stones, Jewelry, Healthy Lights

Crystal Store
7320 Ashcroft, Ste 303
Houston, TX 77081
(713)-774-3200
ASSOCIATE: Carol Wise **EXPERTISE:** Tibetan Bowls & Bells, Gems, Jewelry **ASSOCIATE:** Cedric Wise **EXPERTISE:** Quartz Crystal, Singing Bowls, Wicca **ASSOCIATE:** Marlyse Kusik **EXPERTISE:** Meditation Masters, Tapes, India **OFFERS:** Channeling, Meditations **READINGS:** Tea Leaves **NON-BOOK ITEMS SOLD:** Mind Machines, Jewelry, Geods, Juicers, Shiatsu Massage

Crystal Visions
P.O. Box 138117
Toledo, OH 43613
(419)-893-6155
OWNER: Nancy Suber **OFFERS:** Workshops, Lectures **NON-BOOK ITEMS SOLD:** Metaphysical Items, Crystals, Jewelry, Tapes, Tarot Cards

Crystal Wizard, The
19630-76th Avenue West
Lynnwood, WA 98036
(206)-778-4588
OWNER: Marti Brown **EXPERTISE:** Reiki Master, Tarot, Spiritualism **ASSOCIATE:** Ralph Fisher **EXPERTISE:** Spiritual Counselor, Healer **ASSOCIATE:** Janet Heckenlively **EXPERTISE:** Reiki Master, Inner Child Therapy **OFFERS:** Workshops, Channeling **READINGS:** Astrology, Tarot, Past Lives **NON-BOOK ITEMS SOLD:** Crystals, Minerals, Jewelry, Mystical Gifts, Music & Meditation Tapes, Candles, Oils, Incense, Herbs, Smudge Pots, Ceremonial Items

Crystal Works
170 Front Street
Bath, ME 04530
(207)-443-1065
OWNER: John Dougherty **OFFERS:** Workshops, Lectures **NON-BOOK ITEMS SOLD:** Minerals, Oils, Jewelry, Incense, Cards

Crystalarium
646 N Fuller Avenue
Los Angeles, CA 90036
(213)-932-1116 (213)-932-1114
OWNER: Robin Banchik **EXPERTISE:** Jeweler, Gemologist **READINGS:** Astrology **NON-BOOK ITEMS SOLD:** Crystals, Jewelry, Candles, Sculpture

Crystals Above - A Crystal Meadow
1001 Bridgeway

Sausalito, CA 94965
(415)-332-2683
OWNER: Marianne Alstrom **READINGS:** Astrology, Palmistry, Tarot, Medicine Cards, Pendulum Readings **NON-BOOK ITEMS SOLD:** Crystals, Crystal Products, Tarot Cards, Accessories, Candles, Boji Stones, Rain Sticks, Jewelry, Feathers

Curios And Candles
289 Divisadero Street
San Francisco, CA 94117
(415)-863-5669
OFFERS: Lectures **READINGS:** Tarot **NON-BOOK ITEMS SOLD:** Oils, Incense, Jewelry, Crystals, Herbs

D & F Seabury Bookstore
Episcopal Book & Resource Ctr.
815 Second Avenue
New York, NY 10017
(212)-661-4863
ASSOCIATE: Ana Hernandez **EXPERTISE:** Theology, Feminism, Eco-Spirituality **ASSOCIATE:** Bill Bailey **EXPERTISE:** Liturgy, Ritual, Mythology, Wicca **MANAGER:** Constancio De Jesus **EXPERTISE:** Theology, History **NON-BOOK ITEMS SOLD:** Jewelry, Cards, Tapes, CDs

Det Ukendtes Boghandel
Skindergade 19
Copenhagen, 1159
Denmark
(003)-313-3701
OWNER: Peter Juhl Svendsen **EXPERTISE:** Ancient Mysteries **ASSOCIATE:** Knud Mariboe **EXPERTISE:** UFO's **ASSOCIATE:** Pia Christensen **EXPERTISE:** New Age Music **ASSOCIATE:** Charlotte Ibsen **EXPERTISE:** Crystals **OFFERS:** Lectures **READINGS:** Astrology, Palmistry, Tarot, Numerology **NON-BOOK ITEMS SOLD:** Crystals, Music, Tarot Decks, Pendulums, Incense

Dick's Bookshelf
523 E N First Street
Seneca, SC 29678
(803)-882-3221
OWNER: Dick Lowdermilk **NON-BOOK ITEMS SOLD:** Mobil Bookstore

Doc Heben's Natural Foods
11841 Detroit Avenue
Lakewood, OH 44107
(216)-529-9170
OWNER: Ed Heben **MANAGER:** Sheira Genemaras **NON-BOOK ITEMS SOLD:** Incense, Alive Energy Supplements, Aromatherapy Oils, Bath Salts

Dragonfly Books
1701 Portland Avenue
Nashville, TN 37212
(615)-292-5699 (615)-242-1250
NON-BOOK ITEMS SOLD: Incense, Zafus, Tarot Decks, Essential Oils, Cassette Tapes, Videos

Dreams East
1 Tower Place
Box 295
Roslyn, NY 11576
(516)-484-5384
OWNER: Swami Satyam Vijay **EXPERTISE:** Meditation **ASSOCIATE:** George Gromaglia **ASSOCIATE:** Swami Adoshi **ASSOCIATE:** Bob George **EXPERTISE:** Masters **ASSOCIATE:** Ray

Pesonen **EXPERTISE:** Health, Aromatherapy, Tantra **OFFERS:** Workshops, Lectures **NON-BOOK ITEMS SOLD:** Futons, Music, Birkenstocks, Drums, Chimes, Instruments, Clothing, Crystals, Air & Water Filters, Gifts

Duncanville Bookstore
101-J W. Camp Wisdom
Duncanville, TX 75116
(214)-298-7546
OWNER: Jerry Hoffman **EXPERTISE:** Dolls, Gemstones, Native Americans **OWNER:** Pam Hoffman **EXPERTISE:** Dolls, Gemstones, Native Americans **ASSOCIATE:** Jeff Seward **EXPERTISE:** Tarot Readings, Crystal Wrapping, Gaming **READINGS:** Runes, Tarot **NON-BOOK ITEMS SOLD:** Jewelry, Dolls, Collectible Comics, Pewter, Crystals

Eagle's Nest Gifts & Books
Unity Of The Mountains Center
703 Merrimon Avenue
Asheville, NC 28804
(704)-253-5683
ASSOCIATE: Cynthia Nye **ASSOCIATE:** Carlos Burlar **ASSOCIATE:** Caroline Sandgren **OFFERS:** Workshops, Lectures, Clairvoyance, Dowsing **READINGS:** Astrology, Palmistry, Runes, Tarot

Earth Isle
116 E. Elkhorn Avenue
P.O. Box 2207
Estes Park, CO 80517-2207
(303)-586-3488
OWNER: John M. Grace **OWNER:** Janet Grace **OFFERS:** Massage, Hypnotherapy **NON-BOOK ITEMS SOLD:** Tapes, Jewelry, Craft Items, Environmental Items

East West Academy Of Healing
33 Ora Way
San Francisco, CA 94131
OFFERS: Workshops, Lectures **READINGS:** Astrology, Palmistry **NON-BOOK ITEMS SOLD:** Tapes

East West Bookshop
1170 El Camino Real
Menlo Park, CA 94025-4358
(415)-325-5709 (415)-325-0581
OWNER: Ananda Church Of God-Realization **ASSOCIATE, BOOKBUYER:** Norman Snitkin **CO-MANAGER:** Jacqueline Snitkin **OFFERS:** Lectures **READINGS:** Astrology, Tarot, Psychic **NON-BOOK ITEMS SOLD:** Shamanic gifts, cards, t-shirts, posters, crystals, jewelry, statues, New Age music/videos, incense, meditation supplies **DESCRIPTION:** Founded 1965. Largest Metaphysical/Spiritual bookstore in the country. Offers new & used Metaphysical/Spiritual books on Science, Psychology, Healing, Consciousness Expansion & World Religions. Sells incense & meditation supplies.

East West Bookshop Of Seattle
6417 Roosevelt Way NE
Seattle, WA 98115
(206)-523-3726
BOOK BUYER: Betsy Hay **MANAGER, BUYER:** Cathy Steensha **BUYER:** Susan McGinnis **OFFERS:** Lectures **READINGS:** Astrology, Runes, Tarot, Psychic **NON-BOOK ITEMS SOLD:** Cards, Tapes, Jewelry, Crystals, Incense, Gift Items

Elements Of Life, Ltd
977 State Street
New Haven, CT 06511
(203)-773-0084

OWNER: Nancy Doncaster **OWNER:** Anne Malone **EXPERTISE:** Massage Therapist **OFFERS:** Workshops, Lectures **READINGS:** Astrology, Runes, Tarot, Swedish Cards, Psychic, Aura **NON-BOOK ITEMS SOLD:** Music, Crystals, Jewelry, Massage Oils, Massage Tables, Essential Oils, Stained Glass, Pottery

Enchantments
16 Mckown Street
Boothbay Harbor, ME 04538
(207)-633-4992

OWNER: William G. Kirby **EXPERTISE:** Crystals, Tarot **ASSOCIATE:** Kim Snyder **EXPERTISE:** Metaphysics, Wicca, Native American Indians **OFFERS:** Workshops **NON-BOOK ITEMS SOLD:** Tarot, Crystal & Gem Jewelry, Crystal Specimens, Magical Tools, Fantasy Gifts

Enchantments, Inc.
341 E. 9th Street
New York, NY 10003
(212)-228-4394

OWNER: Carol A. Bulzone **OFFERS:** Workshops, Lectures **READINGS:** Astrology, Tarot **NON-BOOK ITEMS SOLD:** Jewelry, Native American Items, Tarot Cards, Candles, Ritual Tools, Essential Oils, Herbs, Occult Items, Incense, Crystals, Crystal Balls

Equinox Bay
314 E Court Avenue
Jeffersonville, IN 47130
(812)-284-1436

OWNER: Khryston Parush **EXPERTISE:** Clairvoyant, Prediction Astrology **OFFERS:** Workshops, Lectures **READINGS:** Astrology, Clairvoyant **NON-BOOK ITEMS SOLD:** Herbs, Candles, Goblets, Stones, Tarot, General Magical Supplies, Jewelry, Incense, Censors

Equinox Books
115 E. Maple Avenue
Langhorne, PA 19047
(215)-752-4332

Esoteric Bookshop
Glen Center Arcad
675 Glenferrie Road
Hawthorn
Melbourne, VICTORIA 3122
Australia
8181998

OWNER: Alison Loftus-Hills **ASSOCIATE:** Mary Weck **NON-BOOK ITEMS SOLD:** New Age Music, Jungian Books

Evenstar Bookstore
514 Cedar Avenue
Minneapolis, MN 55454
(612)-332-4739

ASSOCIATE: Loui Pieper **EXPERTISE:** Tarot **ASSOCIATE:** Zig Schuessler **EXPERTISE:** Reiki, Massage **OFFERS:** Workshops, Lectures, Dream Interpretations **READINGS:** Astrology, Palmistry, Tarot **NON-BOOK ITEMS SOLD:** Jewelry, Cards, Candles, Incense, T-Shirts, Statues, Animal Medicines

Eye Of Osiris

Starlight Technology
111 North Dunn
Bloomington, IN 47401
(812)-332-0048

OWNER, HIGH ELF ELDER: Nora (Arafel) Liell **EXPERTISE:** Tantra, Witch, Wise Woman **ASSOCIATE, HIGH ELF ELDER:** Terry (Tindome) White Feather **EXPERTISE:** Tantra, Witch, Herbalist **OFFERS:** Workshops, Lectures, Referrals to Readers **READINGS:** Astrology, Palmistry, Runes **NON-BOOK ITEMS SOLD:** Alternative Energy Technology, Herbs, Oils, Incense, Posters, Jewelry, Vintage Clothing, Tarot Cards

Eye Of The Cat Bookstore
3314 East Broadway
Long Beach, CA 90803
(213)-656-9373

DESCRIPTION: Offers herbs, crystals, candles, incense, oils, tarot cards, self-help tapes and books.

Florida Health Foods & Holistic Center
886 W. 11th Street
Panama City, FL 32402
(904)-785-3686

OWNER: Donna Adams **EXPERTISE:** Reiki **OWNER:** Darci Blakley **EXPERTISE:** Reiki Master **ASSOCIATE:** Marsha Johnson **ASSOCIATE:** Kim Brown **OFFERS:** Workshops, Lectures **READINGS:** Astrology, Runes, Tarot, Psychic **NON-BOOK ITEMS SOLD:** Health Items, Jewelry, Crystals, Tapes

Food For Thought Alternative Bookstore
116 12th St. S.
Moorhead, MN 56560
(218)-236-5434

OWNER: Gini Duval **EXPERTISE:** Shamanism **ASSOCIATE:** Margaret Hanson **EXPERTISE:** Codependency **ASSOCIATE:** Barb Chromy **EXPERTISE:** Herbs, Women's Spirituality **ASSOCIATE:** Jane Eitel **EXPERTISE:** Women's Music **READINGS:** Runes **NON-BOOK ITEMS SOLD:** Tapes, Incense, Oils, Gifts, Cards, Stones

Food For Thought Natural Foods
Ringwood Plaza
Skyline Drive
Ringwood, NJ 07456
(201)-962-6355

OWNER: Dona Garofano **EXPERTISE:** Vitamins, Herbs **ASSOCIATE:** Marilyn Cappelluti **EXPERTISE:** Vitamins, Body Building Supplements, Jewelry **CONSULTANT:** Gina Liberti **EXPERTISE:** Crystals, Gemstones, Jewelry **OFFERS:** Lectures **NON-BOOK ITEMS SOLD:** Crystals, New Age Jewelry, Health Foods

Footsteps Of Truth
8466 E Chaparral
Scottsdale, AZ 85253
(602)-990-1270 (602)-945-9476

OWNER: Margot E. Blake **EXPERTISE:** Metaphysics **OFFERS:** Workshops, Lectures, Metaphysics-Self Help, Regressions **READINGS:** Astrology **NON-BOOK ITEMS SOLD:** Astrological Charts

Forever After Books
1475 Haight Street
San Francisco, CA 94117

(415)-431-8299

OWNER: Pat Nathe **EXPERTISE:** Spirituality, Mysterious Occurrences **NON-BOOK ITEMS SOLD:** New Age Music Tapes

Fountain Of Light Bookstore
7877 Jefferson Highway
Baton Rouge, LA 70809
(504)-927-2385

OWNER: Henry Barksdale **MANAGER:** Michael O'Keefe **OFFERS:** Workshops, Lectures **READINGS:** Astrology, Runes **NON-BOOK ITEMS SOLD:** Jewelry, Crystals, Cards, Tapes

Four Elements
133 Rte 31
Lebanon, NJ 08833
(908)-735-9318

OWNER: Lucille Gunsett **OFFERS:** Workshops, Channeling **READINGS:** Astrology, Runes, Tarot **NON-BOOK ITEMS SOLD:** Jewelry, Tarot Cards, Giftware, Videos, Music Tapes

Four Winds Bookstore
47 Main Street
P.O. Box 2632
Orleans, MA 02653
(508)-255-7494

OWNER: Joy Johnson **NON-BOOK ITEMS SOLD:** Tapes, Crystals, Cards

Four Winds Village
P.O. Box 112
Tiger, GA 30576
(404)-782-6939

SECRETARY: Sandra McKey **ASSOCIATE:** Virginia Howard **OFFERS:** Workshops, Lectures, Consultations **NON-BOOK ITEMS SOLD:** Artifacts, Crafts, Jewelry, Gems

Free Spirit
160 Main Street
Flemington, NJ 08822
(201)-782-8168 (201)-788-0399

OWNER: Darilyn **OFFERS:** Workshops, Lectures **READINGS:** Astrology, Runes, Tarot **NON-BOOK ITEMS SOLD:** Incense, Tarot Cards, Rune Stones, Jewelry, Crystals

Fruit Of The Tree
P.O. Box 1129
Concord, NC 28026
(704)-786-7679

OWNER: Cora J. Harmon **EXPERTISE:** Channel For Archangel Michael **ASSOCIATE:** Johnathan Hatch **EXPERTISE:** Channel For Metatron **OFFERS:** Workshops, Lectures, Martial Arts Classes for Mind/Body/Soul Connection **READINGS:** Astrology, Runes, Tarot, Psychic Readings by Michael or Metatron **NON-BOOK ITEMS SOLD:** Crystals, Runes, Birthcharts, Tapes, Pleiadian Tapes, Indian Walking Sticks

Full Circle Books
2205 Silver, SE
Albuquerque, NM 87106
(505)-266-0022

OWNER: Anne Frost, Mary Morell **OFFERS:** Lectures **NON-BOOK ITEMS SOLD:** Runes, Sage, Incense, Tarot, Crystals, Goddess Images, Greeting Cards, Herbs

Futronics

P.O. Box 1400
Goleta, CA 93116
(805)-968-8720
OWNER: Joel Rosensweet NON-BOOK ITEMS SOLD: Bright Images Subliminal Audio Tapes, Dowsing Equipment

Future Pace, Inc.

P.O. Box 151175
San Rafael, CA 94915
(415)-485-1200
OWNER, SEMINAR PRESENTER: Metha Singleton EXPERTISE: NLP Self-Improvement OFFERS: Workshops NON-BOOK ITEMS SOLD: Video/Audio Tapes in NLP Self-Enrichment Areas

Garland Of Letters

527 South Street
Philadelphia, PA 19147
(215)-923-5946
OWNER: Candace L. Smith EXPERTISE: Yoga ASSOCIATE: Philip Davidoff EXPERTISE: Gemologist OFFERS: Workshops, Lectures, Yoga Classes READINGS: Tea Leaves NON-BOOK ITEMS SOLD: Music, Crystals, Gems, Tapes, Videos, Incense, Posters, Cards, Statues, Musical Instruments

Gary's Gem Garden

128 Woodcrest Center
Cherry Hill, NJ 08003
(609)-795-5077
OWNER: Gary Weinstein EXPERTISE: Mineralogist, Goldsmith, Silversmith, Lapidary, Gemologist MANAGER: Beth Weinstein EXPERTISE: Jeweler MANAGER OF WHOLESALE AND MAIL-ORDER: Estelle Weinstein NON-BOOK ITEMS SOLD: Minerals, Rocks, Gems, Jewelry, Carvings

Gautama Institute

Olde City Chiropractic
128 Chestnut Street
Philadelphia, PA 19106
(215)-627-3782
OWNER, DIRECTOR: Laila Wah, C.A. EXPERTISE: Oriental Medicine, Shiatsu, Chinese Herbalogy, Acupressure PRACTITIONER: Dr. Barry L. Silverman, D.C. EXPERTISE: Cranio-Sacral Work OFFERS: Workshops, Lectures, Healing Arts NON-BOOK ITEMS SOLD: Charts, Essences, Herbs, Healing Materials

Gemstone Collection

413 East Main Street
Charlottesville, VA 22901
(804)-293-4367
OWNER: Sara Watson EXPERTISE: Gemstones, Electromagnetic Healing OFFERS: Workshops, Lectures NON-BOOK ITEMS SOLD: Gems, Mineral Specimens, Pendulums, Jewelry

Genesis Books

188 Old Street
London, EC1V9BP
England
071-250-1868
OWNER: John Morley OWNER: Dorothy Morley MANAGER, BUYER: Winston Shields NON-BOOK ITEMS SOLD: Audio Cassettes, New Age Music Cassettes, Videos

Golden Leaves Book Mart

211 Phlox Avenue

Metairie, LA 70001
(504)-888-5208
OWNER: Donna M. France OFFERS: Workshops, Lectures, Bio-Rhythms, Channeling, Automatic Writing, Hypnotism READINGS: Astrology, Palmistry, Tarot, Astrology, Numerology NON-BOOK ITEMS SOLD: Cassettes, Videos, Crystals, Jewelry, Incense, Oils, Magazines, Tarot Cards, Psychic Games, Crystal Balls, Greeting Cards

Golden Leaves Book Store

308 Central Avenue
Hot Springs, AR 71901
(501)-623-7007
OWNER: Donna M. France MANAGER: Jean Williams NON-BOOK ITEMS SOLD: Cassettes, Videos, Crystals, Jewelry, Incense, Oils, Magazines

Golden Meadows Herbal Emporium

431 South St. Augustine
Dallas, TX 75217
(214)-398-3479
ASSOCIATE: Julie Thomas ASSOCIATE: Rusty Thomas OWNER: Jacque Owens OWNER: Jim Owens OFFERS: Lectures NON-BOOK ITEMS SOLD: Bulk Herbs, Oils, Vitamins

Golden Tree Books

2990 B Union Avenue
San Jose, CA 95124
(408)-559-0676
OWNER, ADMINISTRATOR: Edythe P. Willi OWNER, ADMINISTRATOR: Hatsuko Cho ASSOCIATE: Donette Mager OFFERS: Workshops, Lectures READINGS: Astrology, Tarot NON-BOOK ITEMS SOLD: Crystals, Gift Items, Emotional Remedies

Good Vibrations

Metaphysical Center & Giftshop
Rt 1, Hwy 87
Boiling Springs Lakes
Southport, NC 28461
(919)-845-2603
OWNER: Linda C. Finn EXPERTISE: Certified Reiki I & II ASSOCIATE: Suzanne Osborne, Ph. D. OFFERS: Workshops, Lectures READINGS: Astrology, Palmistry, Runes, Tarot, Tea Leaves, Psychometry NON-BOOK ITEMS SOLD: Incense, Hemi-Sync Dealer, Crystals, Tarot Cards, Tapes, Salt Baths

Govinda's Gallery

The Fisher Mansion
383 Lenox Avenue
Detroit, MI 48215
(313)-331-6740 (313)-824-5801
MANAGER: Paru Trivedi OFFERS: Workshops, Lectures READINGS: Astrology, Palmistry, Runes NON-BOOK ITEMS SOLD: Gift Items

Graceful Touch

46 Fairfield Street
Montclair, NJ 07042
(201)-509-7751
OWNER, BUYER: Talib Ilutzi EXPERTISE: Shiatsu Therapist STORE MANAGER: Lynda Lovell OFFERS: Workshops, Lectures, Acupressure, Shiatsu, Massage Therapy READINGS: Astrology, Tarot NON-BOOK ITEMS SOLD: Crystal & Gemstone Jewelry, Tapes, Natural Fiber Clothing, Windchimes

Gracraft Shop

140 W. Elkhorn Avenue
P.O. Box 2207
Estes Park, CO 80517
(303)-586-3488
OWNER: John M. Grace, CHT OWNER: Janet Z. Grace, MsT, NTS ASSOCIATE: Pat Russell ASSOCIATE: Susan McGinnis OFFERS: Massage, Hypnotherapy NON-BOOK ITEMS SOLD: Tapes, Jewelry, Craft Items, Environmental Items

Hand Of Aries

620 S. 4th Street
Philadelphia, PA 19147
(215)-923-5264
OWNER: H. Ann N. Duckworth EXPERTISE: Wiccan Priestess, Tarot Reader OFFERS: Workshops, Lectures READINGS: Tarot NON-BOOK ITEMS SOLD: Jewelry, Herbs, Candles, Incense

Hazel's Books

Ocean Plaza Mall
Ocean City, MD 21842
(301)-723-1983
OWNER, MANAGER, BUYER: Hazel Haney NON-BOOK ITEMS SOLD: Tarot Cards, Crystals, Massage Oils

Heartsong Crystals, Inc.

3115 Bay To Bay Boulevard
Tampa, FL 33629
(813)-832-3255
OWNER: Charlotte M. DeLuccia EXPERTISE: Crystals, Native American Spirituality ASSOCIATE: Geri Bommarito EXPERTISE: Psycho-Spiritual Counseling OFFERS: Workshops NON-BOOK ITEMS SOLD: Crystals, Jewelry, Minerals, Tapes, Native American Items

Helping You, Help Yourself

13405 Main Street
Grabill, IN 46741
(219)-627-3012
OWNER: Marjorie A. Coe OFFERS: Workshops, Lectures NON-BOOK ITEMS SOLD: Cards, Artwork, Videos, Tapes, CD's, Runes, Incense, Oils, Aromatherapy, Jewelry, Stones

Heritage Store, The

314 Laskin Road
Virginia Beach, VA 23451
(804)-428-0400
OWNER: Tom Johnson MANAGER: Jane McDonald HERITAGE CENTER DIRECTOR: Bob Clapp OFFERS: Workshops, Lectures, Channeling READINGS: Astrology, Palmistry, Tarot NON-BOOK ITEMS SOLD: Edgar Cayce Products, Health Foods, Gems, Stones, Jewelry, Greeting Cards, Incense, Meditation Supplies, International Gift Items, Art, Tarot Cards, Games, T-Shirts, Non-Animal Tested Body Care Products & Makeup

Higher Self Bookshelf

328 East Front Street
Traverse City, MI 49684
(616)-941-5805
DESCRIPTION: Offers books, music, crystals, jewelry, artwear & tapes.

Homeopathic Educational Services

2124 Kittredge Street
Berkeley, CA 94704
(415)-649-0294

OWNER: Dana Ullman, M.P.H. NON-BOOK ITEMS SOLD: Tapes, Medicines, Medicine Kits, Software

Horizons Plus-The Relaxation Center
7101 Country Club Road
Butler, PA 16001
(412)-865-2545
OWNER: John Bolger OWNER: Josephine Bolger ASSOCIATE: Brook Bolger EXPERTISE: Massage, Intuitive & Spiritual Counseling, Reiki, Touch Therapy ASSOCIATE: Marlene Bolger EXPERTISE: Massage, Intuitive & Spiritual Counseling, Reiki, Touch Therapy OFFERS: Workshops, Lectures NON-BOOK ITEMS SOLD: Crystals, Stones, Jewelry, Tapes, Oils

Horus Buchhandlung
Bismarckstr 19
Bonn, 5300
Germany
(022)-822-5946
OFFERS: Magic, Stones, Eastern Traditions, Reincarnation READINGS: Astrology, Palmistry, Runes, Tarot NON-BOOK ITEMS SOLD: Ouija Boards, Incense, Crystal Balls, Magic Mirrors

House Of Sagittarius Center
5244 West Irving Park
Chicago, IL 60641
(312)-545-0717
OWNER: Carol Ridgeway Franz EXPERTISE: Astrologer OFFERS: Workshops, Lectures READINGS: Astrology, Palmistry, Runes, Tarot, Past Lives NON-BOOK ITEMS SOLD: Crystals, Tarot Cards, Masks, Stationery, Tote Bags, Plaques, Gift Items, Jewelry

House Of The Dawn Church
2141 E. Palm Lane
Phoenix, AZ 85006
(602)-267-1203
OWNER: Calvin H. Vanness EXPERTISE: Hypnotism, Meditation, Self-Help, Yoga, ESP, Dowsing, Healing ASSOCIATE: Jack S. Stephens EXPERTISE: Channeling, Dreams, ESP, UFO's, Telepathy, Crystal Therapy OFFERS: Workshops, Lectures READINGS: Crystal Ball-Sight, Past Life, Channeled Readings NON-BOOK ITEMS SOLD: Self-Improvment Tapes

Humanspace Books, Inc.
1617 North 32nd Street, #5
Phoenix, AZ 85008
(602)-220-4419
DESCRIPTION: Bookstore & networking center for feminist, gay & New Age information.

I Am Books & Things
4290 S. University Drive
Davie, FL 33328
(305)-370-2925
OWNER: Kay Wandland OFFERS: Workshops, Lectures READINGS: Astrology, Palmistry, Runes, Tarot NON-BOOK ITEMS SOLD: Crystals, Jewelry, Tapes, Teas, Chimes

Ice Flowers
88004 Oak Hill Drive
Eugene, OR 97402
(503)-683-8418
OWNER: Dave W. Olson OFFERS: Workshops, Lectures, Transformational Therapy READINGS:

Tea Leaves NON-BOOK ITEMS SOLD: Crystals, Gemstones, Tools For The Intuition

Illuminarium Convergence
476 Storrs Road
Mansfield Center, CT 06250
(203)-456-1335
OWNER: Richaard M. Rudis OFFERS: Workshops, Lectures READINGS: Astrology, Tarot NON-BOOK ITEMS SOLD: Spiritual Artifacts, Tibetan Singing Bell Bowls

In Harmony-The Alternative-Bookstore
500 N. Calvert
Muncie, IN 47303
(317)-288-8806
OWNER: Michael King OWNER: Lu King OFFERS: Workshops, Lectures READINGS: Astrology, Runes NON-BOOK ITEMS SOLD: T-Shirts, Jewelry, Periodicals, Tea, Incense, Stones, Candles, Tarot Cards, UNICEF Materials

Incense Works, Inc., The
P.O. Box 427
Kula, HI 96790
(808)-878-2122
ASSOCIATE: David Baar EXPERTISE: Incense Production, Raw Materials, World Markets ASSOCIATE: Geri Aughton EXPERTISE: Direct Marketing, Incense NON-BOOK ITEMS SOLD: Stick Incenses, Resins & Woods, Charcoal Tablets, Aromatic Materials

Inner Light Foundation
959 Transport Way #A-2
P.O. Box 750265
Petaluma, CA 94975
(707)-765-2200
OWNER: Betty Bethards EXPERTISE: Psychic, Mystic, Author, Lecturer, Dream Expert, Healer PUBLIC RELATIONS: Jaclyn Catalfo OFFERS: Workshops, Lectures READINGS: Tea Leaves, Personal Psychic-Mystic Readings, Personal Life Readings NON-BOOK ITEMS SOLD: Tapes: Lectures, Trance, Meditation, Music

Inner Sound Metaphysical Bookstore
3110 Harborview Drive
P. O. Box 1581
Gig Harbor, WA 98335
(206)-851-8567
OWNER: Caroline Ketman OFFERS: Workshops READINGS: Tarot NON-BOOK ITEMS SOLD: Jewelry, Crystals, New Age Music

Inner Vision Bookstore
7852 Craft Road
Olive Branch, MS 38654
(901)-521-1478
DIRECTOR: Virginia Hornbuckle EXPERTISE: Holistic Healer, Parapsychologist, Counselor ASSOCIATE: Lou Denson EXPERTISE: Astrologer, Parapsychologist ASSOCIATE: Debbie Wright EXPERTISE: Parapsychologist, Psychic Reader ASSOCIATE: Mary Harris EXPERTISE: Parapsychologist, Palmistry OFFERS: Workshops, Lectures, Self-Awareness READINGS: Astrology, Palmistry, Runes, Tarot NON-BOOK ITEMS SOLD: Tarot Cards, Crystals, Jewelry, Astrology Charts, Code-A-Fortune Cards

Inner Visions Lifestyle Resource Center
3774 Fifth Avenue
San Diego, CA 92103
(619)-298-5575
OWNER, DIRECTOR: Paul Christopher Barkley EXPERTISE: Astrology, I Ching, Metaphysician, Runes ASSOCIATE: Donna Provancher EXPERTISE: Metaphysician, Tarot ASSOCIATE: Samuel Johnson EXPERTISE: Astrology OFFERS: Workshops, Lectures, I Ching READINGS: Astrology, Palmistry, Runes, Tarot NON-BOOK ITEMS SOLD: Cassette Tapes, Herbal Medicines, Crystals, Gems, Pyramids, Candles, Incense

Insight Metaphysical Bookstore
505 South First Street
Champaign, IL 61820
(217)-352-5683
OWNER: Jack Tuttle EXPERTISE: Music, Course In Miracles, Esoteric Teachings, Numerology OWNER: Mary Jane Tuttle EXPERTISE: Crystals, Tarot Native Americans Recovery OFFERS: Workshops, Lectures, Bodywork, Aromatherapy READINGS: Astrology, Runes, Tarot, Psychic, Channelings NON-BOOK ITEMS SOLD: Crystals, Jewelry, Native American Items, Tarot, Aromatherapy Oils, Incense, Cards DESCRIPTION: Psychic & Tarot Readings available by appointment.

Interlude Books
1427 Kalakaua Avenue
Honolulu, HI 96826
(808)-944-2665
OWNER: Tom Henderson OWNER: Lori Fletcher BUYER: Mauna Farias READINGS: Palmistry, Tarot NON-BOOK ITEMS SOLD: Crystals, Jewelry, Clothing, Incense, Metaphysical Tools

J A Majors Co Inc
1851 Diplomat
Dallas, TX 75234

Jewels Of The Earth
1200 Pearl Street, #250
Boulder, CO 80302-5529
(303)-444-3506
OWNER: Jacqueline Louise EXPERTISE: Astrologer OFFERS: Workshops, Lectures READINGS: Astrology, Tarot NON-BOOK ITEMS SOLD: Crystals, Jewelry

Journey Books
6851 W. Colfax
Lakewood, CO 80215
(303)-239-8773
OWNER: Valerie DuGay EXPERTISE: New Age, Meditation, Reincarnation, Dreams OFFERS: Workshops, Lectures READINGS: Tea Leaves, Past Life & Health Readings NON-BOOK ITEMS SOLD: Crystals, Jewelry, Environmental T-Shirts, Incense, New Age Music & Videos

Journey Books & Gifts
2717 East Central
Wichita, KS 67214
(316)-684-6951
OWNER: Valerie DuGay EXPERTISE: New Age, Meditation, Reincarnation, Dreams OFFERS: Workshops, Lectures READINGS: Tea Leaves, Past Life & Health Readings NON-BOOK ITEMS SOLD: Crystals, Jewelry, Environmental T-Shirts, Incense, New Age Music & Videos DESCRIPTION: Non-

profit Metaphysical & New Age retail store. Sells incense, tarot, music, crystals, jewelry, subliminals, Native American items, gifts, new & used books. Networks for environmental groups. 2 other stores: Lakewood & Denver, CO.

Jumping Off Place, The
P.O. Box 2147
164 West Main Street
Conway, NH 03818
(603)-447-5314

OWNER, TRADE BUYER: Ginger Blymyer **MANAGER:** Bette Roden **OFFERS:** Workshops, Lectures **READINGS:** Astrology, Tarot **NON-BOOK ITEMS SOLD:** Cards, Herbal Products, Music, Calendars, Gifts

Klara & Simpla Store
10 Main Street
Wilmington, VT 05363
(802)-464-5257

OWNER, MANAGER: Frances Hollander **EXPERTISE:** Health **ASSOCIATE:** Ann Andersson **EXPERTISE:** Herbs **ASSOCIATE:** Paula Fielding **EXPERTISE:** Books **OFFERS:** Workshops, Lectures **NON-BOOK ITEMS SOLD:** Birkenstock Footprint Shoes, Cards, Foods, Supplements, Toiletries, Natural Fiber Clothes, Utile Things, Homeopathic Remedies, Crystals

Krystal Kingdom
760 Marketplace
San Ramon, CA 94583
(415)-830-4050

OWNER: Kathy Fitzgerald **EXPERTISE:** Crystals **OFFERS:** Workshops, Lectures, Crystals **READINGS:** Astrology, Palmistry, Runes **NON-BOOK ITEMS SOLD:** New Age Items

L'Abysme Books & Gifts, Inc.
2401 NE Cornell Road
Hillsboro, OR 97124
(503)-648-0598

ASSOCIATE: Carry Smith **EXPERTISE:** Jeweler **ASSOCIATE:** Robert Smith **ASSOCIATE:** Joseph Smith **OFFERS:** Workshops **READINGS:** Astrology, Tarot, Tea Leaves **NON-BOOK ITEMS SOLD:** Jewelry, Tarot, Minerals, Games, Bags, Indian Fetishes, Drums, Cassettes, Videos, Oils, Incense, Candles

La Azteca
811 E. Elizabeth Street
Brownsville, TX 78520
(512)-542-2299

OWNER: Ruben Garcia **EXPERTISE:** Parapsychology, Metaphysics, Nutrition, Psychology, Mysticism **NON-BOOK ITEMS SOLD:** Crysal Balls

Lady Bountiful Shoppe
1513 Aviation Boulevard
Redondo Beach, CA 90278
(213)-376-5920

OWNER: Jacqueline Myers **EXPERTISE:** Wicca, High Priestess **ASSOCIATE:** Gary Alto **EXPERTISE:** Tarot Master **ASSOCIATE:** Martin Dement **EXPERTISE:** Artist **OFFERS:** Workshops **READINGS:** Astrology, Tarot **NON-BOOK ITEMS SOLD:** Herbs, Oils, Incense, Candles, Jewelry, Objects D'Art

Lakehouse Bookshop

Po Box 244
Colombo 2,
Sri Lanka
(000)-043-2104

MANAGER: Victor Walatara **ASSISTANT MANAGER:** Lyn Ockersz **READINGS:** Astrology, Palmistry **NON-BOOK ITEMS SOLD:** Audio Cassettes, Records, Stationary

Le Phenix
56 Rue Du Pot D'Or
Liege, 4000
Belgium

Leonard Dixon Bookstore
203 Veda Mae Drive
San Antonio, TX 78216-7136
(512)-342-8658

OWNER: Leonard Dixon **EXPERTISE:** Santo Master Astrologer, Mystic, Magi, Essene, Healer **ASSOCIATE:** Diane Star **EXPERTISE:** Teacher, Reader, Healer, Ontologist **ASSOCIATE:** Abar Santo **EXPERTISE:** Magi, Numerologist **OFFERS:** Workshops, Lectures, Channeling, Ontological Magic **READINGS:** Astrology, Palmistry, Runes, Tarot, Tea Leaves, Spiritual, Psychic, Mystic, Numerology

Leydet Oils
10100 Fair Oaks Blvd, Ste F
Fair Oaks, CA 95628
(916)-863-6121 (916)-965-7546

OWNER: Victoria Edwards **EXPERTISE:** Aromatherapist, Astrologer **ASSOCIATE:** Rodney Schwann **EXPERTISE:** Skin Care Make-up Artist **ASSOCIATE:** Ursula Stienke **EXPERTISE:** Iyengar Yoga Instructor **ASSOCIATE:** Phyllis Kriss **EXPERTISE:** Harpist, Sound Healer, Massage Therapist **OFFERS:** Workshops, Aromatherapy Consultations **READINGS:** Astrology, Runes **NON-BOOK ITEMS SOLD:** Essential Oils, Perfumes, Body & Skin Care Products, Natural Make-Up

Librairie Alexandrie Inc.
936 Rue St-Jean
Quebec, G1R 1R4
Canada
(418)-692-1378

OWNER: Adrien Brisson **OFFERS:** Lectures **READINGS:** Astrology, Runes, Tarot **NON-BOOK ITEMS SOLD:** New Age Music, Crystals, Incense, Audio/Video Tapes

Life-Renewal, Inc.
Hwy 18
Box 92
Garrison, MN 56450
(612)-692-4498

OWNER: Ron Holmquist **NON-BOOK ITEMS SOLD:** Herbs, Vitamins, Health Items

Magic Candle
30 Broadway
Massapequa, NY 11758
(516)-798-7772

OWNER: Donna R. Ciriello **EXPERTISE:** Witchcraft, Wicca **OFFERS:** Workshops **READINGS:** Astrology, Palmistry, Tarot **NON-BOOK ITEMS SOLD:** Quartz Crystals, New Age Items, Occult Supplies

Magical Forest, Inc.
5725 Hollywood Boulevard

Hollywood, FL 33021
(305)-987-3960

OWNER: Eileen Smith **OWNER:** Leona Levey **OFFERS:** Lectures **READINGS:** Astrology, Tarot **NON-BOOK ITEMS SOLD:** Jewelry, Gifts, Meditation Tapes, Oils, Candles, Herbs, Crystals **DESCRIPTION:** Offers Metaphysical books, gifts, jewelry, quartz crystals, videos, tarot cards, Astrological Charts, candles, herbs, meditation & subliminal tapes & incense.

Magical Rocks
12 Broad Street
P.O. Box 464
Red Bank, NJ 07701
(908)-741-1293

OWNER: Marcia J. Pokus **EXPERTISE:** Astrologer, Crystals, Lecturer **ASSOCIATE:** Ethel A. Melish **EXPERTISE:** Astrologer, Palmistry, Workshop Coordinator **OFFERS:** Workshops, Lectures **READINGS:** Runes, Tarot, Psychic **NON-BOOK ITEMS SOLD:** Crystals, Minerals, Jewelry, Incense, Oils, Pendulums, Candles, New Age Items

Magick Circle
956 N Lake Avenue
Pasadena, CA 91104
(818)-794-6013

OWNER: Rev. Anne White **EXPERTISE:** Ceremonial Magick, Theosophy **OWNER:** Mike Blankenhorn **EXPERTISE:** Ceremonial Magick, Theosophy **READINGS:** Tarot **NON-BOOK ITEMS SOLD:** Occult Supplies, Jewelry, Candles, Books

Magickal Childe, Inc.
35 W. 19th Street
New York, NY 10011
(212)-242-7182

OWNER: Herman Slater **EXPERTISE:** Witch, High Priest **READINGS:** Runes **NON-BOOK ITEMS SOLD:** Herbs, Incense, Oil, Crystals, Swords, Tarot, Jewelry

Maha Lakshmi Shop
Haidakhandi Universal Ashram
P.O. Box 9
Crestone, CO 81131
(719)-256-4108

NON-BOOK ITEMS SOLD: Incense, Sacred Statues, Babaji Photos & Books

Mayflower Bookshop
2645 W. 12 Mile Road
Berkley, MI 48072
(313)-547-8227

OWNER: Robert Thibodean **EXPERTISE:** Astrologer **ASSOCIATE:** Michael Martin **EXPERTISE:** Tarot **OFFERS:** Workshops, Lectures **READINGS:** Astrology, Runes **NON-BOOK ITEMS SOLD:** Jewelry, Drums, Crystals, Incense, Oils, Tapes

Merlin's Magic Crystal
6912 Village Parkway
Dublin, CA 94568
(415)-833-8009

OWNER: Deborah Hilson **EXPERTISE:** Crystals, Tarot **OFFERS:** Workshops, Lectures **READINGS:** Palmistry, Tarot **NON-BOOK ITEMS SOLD:** Crystals, Bach Flowers, Tapes, Incense, Jewelry

Metaphysical Book Store
9511 E. Colfax Avenue
Aurora, CO 80010
(303)-341-7562

OWNER: Cleta Williamson OFFERS: Workshops, Lectures, Spiritual Awareness READINGS: Astrology, Tarot NON-BOOK ITEMS SOLD: Tarot Cards, Crystals, Stones, Jewelry, Incense, Videos, Tapes, Greeting Cards

Metaphysical Center
440 Osborn Avenue
Bigfork, MT 59911
(406)-837-4683

OWNER: Nancy L. Watkins EXPERTISE: Astrologer OFFERS: Workshops, Channeling READINGS: Astrology, Palmistry, Tea Leaves NON-BOOK ITEMS SOLD: Tapes, Jewelry, Stones

Mi-World Supplies
9808 NW 80th Avenue, #10N
Hialeah Gardens, FL 33016
(305)-558-5021

OWNER: Stephen Poznanski EXPERTISE: Psychic, Witchcraft OFFERS: Psychic READINGS: Runes NON-BOOK ITEMS SOLD: Magical Supplies, Herbs, Incense, Oils

Michigan Metaphysical Society & Bookshop
3018 W. 12 Mile Road
Berkley, MI 48091
(313)-399-8299

OWNER: Elaine Lewis EXPERTISE: Numerologist, Teacher ASSOCIATE: Irene Rucinski EXPERTISE: Psychic, Teacher ASSOCIATE: Arthur Rucinski EXPERTISE: Healer, Teacher OFFERS: Workshops, Lectures READINGS: Runes, Psychic, Past Life NON-BOOK ITEMS SOLD: Tarot Cards, Cassette Tapes, Crystals, Stones, Candles, Oils, Incense, New Age Cards

Middle Earth Bookshop
2791 E. 14 Mile Road
Sterling Heights, MI 48310
(313)-979-7340

OWNER: Paul B. Hudson, Jr. EXPERTISE: Astrologer OFFERS: Workshops, Lectures READINGS: Astrology, Tarot NON-BOOK ITEMS SOLD: Rare & Out Of Print Occult Books, Jewelry, Crystals, Tarot, Catalogs

Mill City Music
3019 27th Avenue So.
Minneapolis, MN 55406
(612)-722-6649

OWNER: John Kolstad EXPERTISE: Music NON-BOOK ITEMS SOLD: New Age Music, Mood Music, Nature Sounds

Mind Center, The
2530 Crawford Avenue, #104
Evanston, IL 60201
(708)-676-4900

OWNER: Ruth Berger EXPERTISE: Clairvoyant, Author, Intuitive Training Consultant OFFERS: Workshops, Lectures, Intuitive Training READINGS: Clairvoyance

Mind Change
P.O. Box 8316
Durango, CO 81301
(303)-259-4445

OWNER: Dorothy Allen

Mind's Eye, The
3945 N. Sierra Way

San Bernardino, CA 92405
(714)-886-0014

OWNER: Gayle Shepard EXPERTISE: Archaeology, Egyptology ASSOCIATE: Mary Neese EXPERTISE: Psychology, Art Therapy OFFERS: Lectures READINGS: Palmistry NON-BOOK ITEMS SOLD: Egyptian Art, Jewelry, Music, Incense, Crystals

Miracles Recovery Books & Gifts
11269 Triangle Lane
Wheaton, MD 20902
(301)-929-2552

OWNER: Nancy Levine EXPERTISE: Recovery, Self-Help OWNER: Christy Gitlin EXPERTISE: Recovery, Self-Help NON-BOOK ITEMS SOLD: Cards, T-Shirts, Jewelry, Wall Plaques, God Boxes

Moneesh Ltd
Brickman Road
South Fallsburg, NY 12779
(914)-434-0732

OWNER: Santosh Bakshi ASSOCIATE: K. Bakshi ASSOCIATE: Moneesh Bakshi OFFERS: Yoga, Ayurveda READINGS: Astrology NON-BOOK ITEMS SOLD: New Age & Religious Items, Meditation Supplies

Monkeys Retreat
2400 N. High Street
Columbus, OH 43202
(614)-262-9511

OWNER: Stephen Mendelson EXPERTISE: Tai Chi, I Ching ASSOCIATE: Jeffrey Mendelson EXPERTISE: Tai Chi, I Ching OFFERS: Workshops, Tai Chi NON-BOOK ITEMS SOLD: Tarot Cards

Moon Beam
P.O. Box 41386
Chicago, IL 60639

OWNER: Robert Reger EXPERTISE: Astrology, Tarot, Computer Software READINGS: Astrology NON-BOOK ITEMS SOLD: Crystal Balls, Tarot Decks, Artwork, Tapes

Moonspire
6401 Cheri Lynne Drive
Dayton, OH 45449

Joel Charles Ashenbaum

Moonstar Psychic & Spirtual Center
38422 Lake Shore Boulevard
Willoughby, OH 44094
(216)-942-5652

OWNER: Marlo Ammon READINGS: Astrology, Runes, Tea Leaves, Psychic & Spiritual Readings NON-BOOK ITEMS SOLD: Tapes, Cards, Candles, Incense, Herbs, Oils, Jewelry DESCRIPTION: Offers a complete selection of books & supplies. Provides psychic & spiritual information & education. Mail-order catalog $2.00.

Mountaintop Bookstore
2587 Shiloh Springs Road
Dayton, OH 45426
(513)-854-2855

OWNER: Mary R. Bauer EXPERTISE: Astrologer ASSOCIATE: Bob Cooper EXPERTISE: Hypnotherapist OFFERS: Workshops, Lectures, Channeling READINGS: Astrology, Runes, Tarot, Numerology, Psychic NON-BOOK ITEMS SOLD: Music, Incense, Crystals, Stones, Gems, Jewelry, Cards

My Journey's Dawn Bookstore
5615 University Way N.E.
Seattle, WA 98105
(206)-527-8099

MANAGER: Jamini Young OFFERS: Workshops, Lectures, Meditation NON-BOOK ITEMS SOLD: Incense, Fine Art Giftwrap & Cards

Mystic Connection, The
Shop 26a, Centrepoint
54 Wood Street
Mackay, QLD 4740
Australia
(007)-951-4404

OWNER: Ann Williams-Fitzgerald EXPERTISE: Aromatherapist, Tarot Reader, Spiritual Healer, Clairvoyant OFFERS: Workshops, Lectures READINGS: Astrology, Runes NON-BOOK ITEMS SOLD: Crystals, Aromatherapy Oils, Pewter, Unusual Giftware, Silver Jewelry, Posters, Herbal Teas & Medications, New Age Music & Magazines, Tapes

Mystic Connection, The
North Town
Flinders Mall
Townsville, QLD 4800
Australia

OWNER: Ann Williams-Fitzgerald EXPERTISE: Aromatherapist, Tarot Reader, Spiritual Healer, Clairvoyant

Mystic Moon Metaphysical Bookstore
8818 Troy Street
Spring Valley, CA 92077
(619)-466-8064

OWNER: Judith Rhoads ASSOCIATE: Scot Rhoads OFFERS: Workshops, Lectures READINGS: Astrology, Runes, Tarot NON-BOOK ITEMS SOLD: Jewelry, Tarot, T-Shirts, Crystals, Incense, Candles

Mystical-Magical Wizards, Inc.
2570 N University Drive
Sunrise, FL 33322
(305)-572-3014

OWNER: Rev. Joy Hayward, MsD, DD EXPERTISE: Healer, Channeler, Meditation Therapist, Chakra Balancing,Author ASSOCIATE: Jason Schwartz EXPERTISE: Tarot ASSOCIATE: Dennis McCallson EXPERTISE: Channeler, Psychometrist, Healer, Chakra Balancing OFFERS: Workshops, Lectures, Psychometry, Channeling, Meditational Therapy, Classes READINGS: Astrology, Palmistry, Runes, Tarot, Numerology NON-BOOK ITEMS SOLD: Crystals, Stones, Tapes, Jewelry, Metaphysical Novalties, Cards, Gifts, Statuary, Objects D'Art

Mystique Books & Gifts
608A Junction Highway
Kerrville, TX 78028
(512)-257-6868

OWNER: Jean T. Clark EXPERTISE: Channeler, Teacher OFFERS: Workshops, Lectures READINGS: Astrology, Tarot, Psychic Readings NON-BOOK ITEMS SOLD: Stones, Jewelry, Candles, Incense, Gifts

Natural Choices
300 Elm Avenue, #217
Carlsbad, CA 92008
(619)-729-3792

OWNER: Patte Renner **NON-BOOK ITEMS SOLD:** Incense, Candles, Crystals, Buddhas, Kwan Yen, Meditation Supplies

Natural Harmony Book Store
1914 Maple Avenue
Palmyra, NY 14522
(315)-597-9290

OWNER: Ruth Drury **EXPERTISE:** Lectures & Workshops On Prosperity **OFFERS:** Workshops, Lectures, Consultations On Prosperity **NON-BOOK ITEMS SOLD:** Affirmation Cards, Boxes of Cards

Nature's Pantry Gourmet & Whole Foods Market
4928 Homberg Drive
Knoxville, TN 37919
(615)-584-4714

OWNER: Ann Yates **EXPERTISE:** Nutrition **ASSOCIATE:** Denny Loftus **ASSOCIATE:** Mary McCauley **OFFERS:** Workshops, Lectures **READINGS:** Astrology **NON-BOOK ITEMS SOLD:** Food Items, Supplements, Music, Gifts

New Age Books & Things, Inc.
4401 N Federal Highway
Ft. Lauderdale, FL 33308
(305)-771-0026 (305)-771-0027

OWNER: Corrina Dehn **OWNER:** Bobbie Springer **ASSOCIATE:** Rose **ASSOCIATE:** Krista **OFFERS:** Workshops, Lectures **READINGS:** Astrology, Tarot, Tea Leaves, Crystal Ball **NON-BOOK ITEMS SOLD:** Crystals, Stones, Jewelry, Self-Hypnosis Tapes

New Age Bookstore
582 Center Street, Rte 123
Brockton, MA 02402
(617)-826-5998 (508)-584-6573

OWNER: Beverly J. Briggs **OFFERS:** Workshops, Lectures **READINGS:** Runes, Psychic **NON-BOOK ITEMS SOLD:** Acusandals, Crystals, Oils, Incense, Tarot Cards, New Age Music, Calendars

New Age Resource Center
4100 180th Street No.
East Moline, IL 61244
(309)-496-9490

OWNER: Dr. Marcy Foley **EXPERTISE:** Chiropractor, Homeopath, Healer, Herbalist, Channeler, Gems **ASSOCIATE:** Michel Foley **EXPERTISE:** Inventor, Channeler **OFFERS:** Workshops, Lectures **READINGS:** Psychometric Aura Readings **NON-BOOK ITEMS SOLD:** Herbs, Crystals, Grids, Magnets

New Age World Services & Books
62091 Valley View Circle
Joshua Tree, CA 92252
(619)-366-2833

OWNER: Rev. Victoria E. Vandertuin **DESCRIPTION:** Sells new, used & out-of-print books. Topics include UFO's, Ancient Continents, Hermetic, Astrology, Yoga, Egyptian, Rosicrucian, New Thought, Crystals. Also offers stationary, jewelry & dolls.

New Pathways
103 Goldencrest Avenue
Waltham, MA 02154
(617)-890-0772

OWNER: Helen K. Hickey **EXPERTISE:** Physical Therapist, Counselor, Educator **OFFERS:**

Workshops, Lectures **NON-BOOK ITEMS SOLD:** Tapes

New Vision
Box 22
Johnstown, NY 12095
(518)-762-1191

OWNER: Lynn Lasher **EXPERTISE:** Tulsa Cards **OFFERS:** Workshops, Lectures **READINGS:** Tea Leaves, Tulsa Cards **NON-BOOK ITEMS SOLD:** Crystals, Jewelry, Incense, Oils, Fortune Telling Cards

New Visions Center
570 North Belvidere Avenue
York, PA 17404
(717)-843-8067

OWNER: William F. Trivett **EXPERTISE:** Astrology, Tarot, NLP **CO-OWNER, MANAGER:** Robert W. Hall **EXPERTISE:** Massage Therapist **OFFERS:** Workshops, Lectures, NLP Counseling, Psychic Fairs **READINGS:** Astrology, Tarot **NON-BOOK ITEMS SOLD:** Massage & Essential Oils, Meditation Supplies, Incense, Jewelry, Cards

New York Astrology Center
545 8th Avenue
New York, NY 10018
(212)-947-3603

OWNER: H. Weingarten **EXPERTISE:** Astrology **MANAGER:** Gerard Young **OFFERS:** Workshops, Lectures **READINGS:** Astrology **NON-BOOK ITEMS SOLD:** Computers, Programs

Nic Nac Nook
4280 Morrison Road
Denver, CO 80219
(303)-922-9063

OWNER: Candie Tsu **EXPERTISE:** Astrologer **ASSOCIATE:** Grace Isaacs **EXPERTISE:** Tarot **OFFERS:** Workshops, Lectures **READINGS:** Astrology, Palmistry, Runes, Tarot, Psychic **NON-BOOK ITEMS SOLD:** Jewelry, Crystals, Tarot Cards, Music, Cayce Products

Nine Muses Bookstore
411 Merchant Street
Ambridge, PA 15003
(412)-266-8939

OWNER: Paulette Capperis **EXPERTISE:** Shamanism, Psychic Consultations **OWNER:** Lance Capperis **EXPERTISE:** Shamanism, Psychic Consultations **READINGS:** Runes, Hopi Pima Readings **NON-BOOK ITEMS SOLD:** Incense, Crystals, Tarot, Jewelry, Runes, Pouches, Wands, Staffs

Ninth House Book Shop
8947 Brecksville Road
Brecksville, OH 44141
(216)-526-2210

DESCRIPTION: Offers metaphysical and astrological books & supplies. Accepts mail order and special orders.

Northeast Metaphysics
33 High Rd
Cornish, ME 04020
(207)-625-7447

OWNER: Ernest A. Rose **EXPERTISE:** Certified Counselor/Practitioner Of Metaphysics **OFFERS:** Workshops, Lectures, Metaphysical Counseling **READINGS:** Runes, Tea Leaves **NON-BOOK ITEMS**

SOLD: Minerals, Jewelry, Audio & Video Tapes, Crafts

Oasis
45 Central Square
Keene, NH 03431
(603)-352-5355

OWNER: Tom Herman **OWNER:** Jeremy Youst **OFFERS:** Workshops **NON-BOOK ITEMS SOLD:** Crystals, Clothes, Meditation & Yoga Supplies, Gifts

Oasis
22 Federal Street
Greenfield, MA 01301

OWNER: Tom Herman **OWNER:** Jeremy Youst **OFFERS:** Workshops **NON-BOOK ITEMS SOLD:** Crystals, Clothes, Meditation & Yoga Supplies, Gifts

Objets D'Art & Spirit
370 1/2 N. La Cienega Blvd.
Los Angeles, CA 90048
(213)-655-2088 (213)-935-5517

OWNER: Margaret Brown **EXPERTISE:** Crystal Reader, Psychic, Tarot **ASSOCIATE:** Kirpal Kaur **EXPERTISE:** Sensitive **ASSOCIATE:** Alexandra Courtney **EXPERTISE:** Ghostbuster Reader, Divination **ASSOCIATE:** Guru Dev Singh **EXPERTISE:** Yoga, Healer **READINGS:** Palmistry, Runes, Tea Leaves, Crystal Ball **NON-BOOK ITEMS SOLD:** Crystals, Sacred Art, Pewter, Religious & Mystic Antiques

Occult Bookstore
3230 N. Clark Street
Chicago, IL 60657
(312)-281-0599

OFFERS: Workshops, Lectures **READINGS:** Astrology, Palmistry, Runes, Psychometry **NON-BOOK ITEMS SOLD:** Tarot Cards, Magical Jewelry, Talismans, Crystals, Cassettes, Candles, Incense, Oils

Occult Emporium, The
102 N. 9th Street
Allentown, PA 18102
(215)-433-3610

OWNER: Jay Solomon **ASSOCIATE:** Alex MacGrew **ASSOCIATE:** Thomas Mack **OFFERS:** Workshops, Magic **NON-BOOK ITEMS SOLD:** Candles, Oils, Incense, Occult Items, Antiques

Opening Books
403 Pratt Avenue
Huntsville, AL 35801
(205)-536-5880

ASSOCIATE: Clere Englebert **EXPERTISE:** Buddhism **ASSOCIATE:** David Womack **EXPERTISE:** Anarchy **ASSOCIATE:** Rachel Rogers **EXPERTISE:** Lesbianism **OFFERS:** Lectures **NON-BOOK ITEMS SOLD:** Cards, Jewelry, T-Shirts, Bumperstickers

Oriental Bookstore
1713 E. Colorado Boulevard
Pasadena, CA 91106
(818)-577-2413

OWNER: Frank Mosher **EXPERTISE:** Asian Culture

Panpipes Magickal Marketplace
1641 N Cahuenga Blvd
Hollywood, CA 90028

(213)-462-7078

OWNER: Isis S. De Martin, O.M., H.P. **EXPERTISE:** Weddings, Rituals, Ceremonies **ASSOCIATE:** Nikiya-Apache Medicine Man **EXPERTISE:** Readings & Consultations **ASSOCIATE:** Rain **EXPERTISE:** Wiccan Reader, Spell Caster **OFFERS:** Workshops, Lectures **READINGS:** Runes **NON-BOOK ITEMS SOLD:** Robes, Jewelry, Herbs, Incense, Oils, Candles, Stones & Crystals, Occult Supplies

Passages
434 North College
Fayetteville, AR 72701
(501)-442-5845

OWNER: Barry Langford **EXPERTISE:** Massage Therapy, Jeweler **ASSOCIATE:** Derrick Sean Smith **OWNER:** Lorraine Langford **EXPERTISE:** Massage Therapy, Intuitive Consultant **OFFERS:** Workshops, Intuitive Consulting **READINGS:** Astrology, Tea Leaves, Intuitive Readings **NON-BOOK ITEMS SOLD:** Jewelry, Crystals, Stones, Cards, Incense, Gifts **DESCRIPTION:** Specializes in Massage Therapy & Intuitive Readings. Offers workshops, Astrology & Tea Leaf Readings, jewelry, incense, candles, stones, crystals, percussion instruments & gifts.

Pathway's Bookstore
Unity Church
929 Monroe
Quincy, IL 62301
(217)-222-1080

ASSOCIATE: Tricia Hine **EXPERTISE:** Theosophy, Astrology, Tarot **ASSOCIATE:** Claire Crotser **EXPERTISE:** Spiritual Development **OFFERS:** Workshops, Lectures **NON-BOOK ITEMS SOLD:** Incense, Oils, Jewelry, Tapes, Greeting Cards

Peaceful Living Publications
1040 Cameron Road
P.O. Box 300
Tauranga, B.O.P.
New Zealand
(007)-571-8105 **FAX** (007)-571-8513

OWNER, MANAGING DIRECTOR: Geoff W.Tibbotts **EXPERTISE:** New Age, Health, Metaphysics, Tarot **OFFERS:** Workshops, Lectures **READINGS:** Astrology, Palmistry, Runes, Tarot, Tea Leaves **NON-BOOK ITEMS SOLD:** Tarot Cards

Peacevision
10427 S. 46th Way
Phoenix, AZ 85044
(602)-893-0204

NON-BOOK ITEMS SOLD: Uplifting Peace Items

Pearls Of Widsom Bookstore
3224 North High Street
Columbus, OH 43202
(614)-262-0146

OWNER: Esther Matthews **ASSOCIATE:** Raymond Rosselot **ASSOCIATE:** James Matthews **ASSOCIATE:** Virginia Cassinelli **EXPERTISE:** Clairvoyant **OFFERS:** Health Related Lectures & Workshops **READINGS:** Astrology, Palmistry, Runes, Tea Leaves **NON-BOOK ITEMS SOLD:** Jewelry, Crystals, Calendars, Gift Items, Incense, Devotional Items

Pegasus Metaphysical Books & Gifts
341 Redondo Avenue
Long Beach, CA 90814
(213)-434-3869

OWNER: Sharon McWethy **OFFERS:** Workshops, Lectures **READINGS:** Astrology, Palmistry, Tarot, Psychic **NON-BOOK ITEMS SOLD:** Crystals, Tapes, Incense, Health Balls, Rain Sticks

Peking Book House
1520 Sherman Avenue
Evanston, IL 60201
(708)-491-0477

OWNER: C. C. Cheng **OFFERS:** Asian Literature & Culture **READINGS:** Astrology, Palmistry, Runes, Tarot **NON-BOOK ITEMS SOLD:** Gifts, Jewelry

Perceptions New Age Book Store
2654 Peach Street
Erie, PA 16508-1823
(814)-866-6715 (814)-454-7364

OWNER: Roseann Eimers **OFFERS:** Workshops, Lectures **READINGS:** Astrology, Palmistry, Tarot, Spirit, Psychic, Psychometry **NON-BOOK ITEMS SOLD:** Crystals, Jewelry, Incense, Cards, Audio & Video Tapes, Magazines, Used Books

Place In Time
7121 E. Sahuaro Drive So.
Scottsdale, AZ 85254
(602)-951-1056

OWNER: Joanne H. Tedesco **ASSOCIATE:** Robert Puryear **NON-BOOK ITEMS SOLD:** Taper, Crystals, Rocks, Videos, Incense, Jewelry

Poor Richard's Bookstore/Cinema/Food
324 North Tejon
Colorado Springs, CO 80903
(303)-572-0012 (303)-632-7721

DESCRIPTION: Offers New Age music, magazines, books, a restaurant, films, art gallery & live music.

Potentials Unlimited
2910 Camino Diablo, Ste. 100
Walnut Creek, CA 94596
(415)-935-8565

DIRECTOR: Bruce H. Stricker **ASSOCIATE:** Rosalind Stricker, R.N. **OFFERS:** Workshops, Lectures, Visualization Therapies

Present Moment Books And Herbs
3546 Grand Avenue S.
Minneapolis, MN 55408
(612)-824-3157

OWNER: Robert Gallagher **EXPERTISE:** Herbalist, Homeopath **ASSOCIATE:** Chris Hefner **EXPERTISE:** Herbalist, Homeopath **ASSOCIATE:** Victor Rangel **EXPERTISE:** Aromatherapist **ASSOCIATE:** Bebhyn Smegda **EXPERTISE:** Herbalist **ASSOCIATE:** Dr. Andrew Lucking **EXPERTISE:** NaturoPath **OFFERS:** Workshops, Lectures **READINGS:** Palmistry, Tarot **NON-BOOK ITEMS SOLD:** Herbs, Homeopathic Remedies, Flower Essences, Vitamins, Supplements, Cassettes, Videos

Prosperity Shop
1404 P Street NW
Washington, DC 20005
(202)-328-1740

OWNER: Rev. Hazel Cassell **EXPERTISE:** Psychic, ESP, Spiritual Healer **OFFERS:** Workshops, Lectures, Psychic Counseling, Healing, Spiritualism **NON-BOOK ITEMS SOLD:** Candles, Oils, Incense, Herbs, Crystals, Religious Supplies, Forever Living Products

Psychic Treasures
60 Genesee Street
New Hartford, NY 13413
(315)-735-5528 (315)-724-7337

OWNER: Louise A. Franchell **EXPERTISE:** Astrologer **OFFERS:** Workshops, Lectures **READINGS:** Astrology, Palmistry, Regular Card Readings **NON-BOOK ITEMS SOLD:** Incense, Crystal Jewelry, Herkimer Diamonds, Medicine Bags, Tapes, Videos

Pure Manifestations
1135 34th Avenue
Seattle, WA 98122
(206)-322-4822

OWNER: Monad Elohim **EXPERTISE:** Diet, Metaphysics, Spiritualism **ASSOCIATE:** Mary Fioravanti **NON-BOOK ITEMS SOLD:** Healthfood & Vegetarian Restaurant/Deli

Pyramid Treasures
920 East Las Olas Boulevard
Fort Lauderdale, FL 33301
(305)-525-4448

OWNER: Kandace Garand **EXPERTISE:** Astrologer, Psychic **CLAIRVOYANT:** Rev. Justin Boatwright **READINGS:** Astrology, Tarot **NON-BOOK ITEMS SOLD:** Crystals, Wands, Jewelry, New Age Music, Incense, Artworks, Wall Hangings, Tarot, Astro Charts, Gems, Herbs, Magical Implements, Cassettes, Videos

Quantum: The Metaphysical Bookshop
113 Melbourne Street
North Adelaide, South 5006
Australia
(008)-267-1579

OWNER: Noelle Rattray **EXPERTISE:** Astrologer **ASSOCIATE:** Chetan Rupa **EXPERTISE:** Women's Spirituality **ASSOCIATE:** Susan Vanderheipen **EXPERTISE:** Psychologist **READINGS:** Astrology **NON-BOOK ITEMS SOLD:** Tarot, Crystals, Tapes

Quest Bookshop
Theosophic Studies
7900 Emerson Avenue
P.O. Box 3727
Los Angeles, CA 90078
(213)-669-8536 (213)-466-5543

ASSOCIATE: Brett Forray **ASSOCIATE:** Doreen Domb **ASSOCIATE:** Steve Buscano **OFFERS:** Workshops, Lectures **NON-BOOK ITEMS SOLD:** Videos

Quest Bookshop
Theosophical Society
122 Bay State Road
Boston, MA 02215
(617)-266-0410

PRESIDENT: Duane Carpenter **PROGRAM COORDINATOR:** Bill Lampert **MANAGER:** Maria Range **OFFERS:** Workshops, Lectures, Healing & Study Groups **NON-BOOK ITEMS SOLD:** Tarot Cards, Crystals, Audio Tapes, Incense

Quest Bookshop
N.Y. Theosophical Society
240 East 53rd Street
New York, NY 10022
(212)-758-5521

ASSOCIATE: Ed Abdill OFFERS: Workshops, Lectures NON-BOOK ITEMS SOLD: Cassettes, Incense, Tarot Cards DESCRIPTION: Offers 5,000 titles.

Quest Bookshop Of Seattle
Theosophical Society
717 Broadway E.
Seattle, WA 98102
(206)-323-4281
MANAGER: Linda Shields NON-BOOK ITEMS SOLD: Crystals, Tapes, Buddhist Art

Quintile Books & Center
75 Mason Street
Greenwich, CT 06830
(203)-661-5770
OWNER: Frank M. Don EXPERTISE: Astrology, Color ASSOCIATE: Joyce McDonald OFFERS: Workshops, Lectures READINGS: Astrology, Tarot NON-BOOK ITEMS SOLD: Jewelry, Gifts, Health Remedies

Rainbow Books
2002 A 8th Street East
Po Box 7523
Saskatoon, SASKATCHEWAN S7K 4L4
Canada
(306)-477-1772
OWNER: Elsie P. Mah

Rainbow Moods
3532 E. Grant Road
Tucson, AZ 85716-2957
(602)-326-9643
OWNER: Karin L. Elliott CO-MANAGER: Stephanie Elliott CO-MANAGER: LaMaya OFFERS: Workshops, Lectures, Bodywork READINGS: Astrology, Palmistry, Runes, Tarot, Tea Leaves, Numerology NON-BOOK ITEMS SOLD: Crystals, Incense, Posters, Candles, Jewelry, Gifts, Smudge, Bookmarks, Pouches, New Age Music-Jazz, Guided Relaxation Tapes

Rainbow Store, The
15368 Mowersville Road
Shippensburg, PA 17257
(717)-423-6701
OWNER: James Berry OWNER: Theresa Berry NON-BOOK ITEMS SOLD: Organic Food, Natural Body Care, Crystals, Gemstone Jewelry, Incense, Tapes, Video Rentals, Recycled Stationery, Energy Saving & Environmental Products

Raven And The Rose, The
126-B South College
Fort Collins, CO 80524-0008
(303)-224-2434
OWNER: Diane Rose EXPERTISE: Counseling, Healing ASSOCIATE: Kim Pentecost EXPERTISE: Women's Spirituality, Healing OFFERS: Workshops, Clairvoyant NON-BOOK ITEMS SOLD: Incense, Music, Oils, Herbal Products, Art, Cards

Reading Corner
408 Main Street
Rockland, ME 04841
(207)-596-6651
OWNER: W. Bodine READINGS: Runes NON-BOOK ITEMS SOLD: Calendars, Rune Stones, Tarot Cards, Books-On-Cassette

Readmore Book World

2115 Fourth Ave
Rock Island, IL 61201
(309)-788-7517
OWNER: Amy Fields MANAGER: Tina Moran ASSISTANT MANAGER: Dawn Daxon NON-BOOK ITEMS SOLD: Tarot Cards

Red & Black Books Collective
432-15th Avenue E.
Seattle, WA 98112
(206)-322-7323
OUTREACH COORDINATOR: K. Phillips OFFERS: Workshops, Lectures, Women's Spirituality NON-BOOK ITEMS SOLD: Music, Cards, T-Shirts, Bumper Stickers, Buttons, Tarot & Medicine Cards, Periodicals, Rubber Stamps

Reincarnation Books/Tapes
P.O. Box 7781
Culver City, CA 90233
(213)-397-5757
OWNER: Bettye B. Binder EXPERTISE: Reincarnation Teacher, Author, Past Life Regression Counselor OFFERS: Workshops, Lectures, Past Life Regressions READINGS: Astrology, Tea Leaves NON-BOOK ITEMS SOLD: Spoken Audio Tapes Of Classes On Past Life Regressions

Reyna's Gallerias & American Indian Museum
106 3rd Street, Ste.1
P.O. Box 1022
San Juan Bautista, CA 95045
(408)-623-2379
OWNER: Sonne Reyna EXPERTISE: Native Spirituality OWNER: Elena Reyna EXPERTISE: Native Spirituality OFFERS: Workshops, Lectures, Native Spirituality NON-BOOK ITEMS SOLD: American Indian Art & Related Items

Rock Garden
981 State Street
New Haven, CT 06511
(203)-777-9997
OWNER: Marilyn Brand OWNER: Andy Sinclair-Day ASSOCIATE: Mary McDonnell EXPERTISE: Astrology NON-BOOK ITEMS SOLD: Beads, Findings, Crystals, Rocks, Minerals, Fossils, Pouches, Jewelry

Rowan Tree, The
10833 Monroe Road, Ste 40
Box 4B
Matthews, NC 28105
(704)-841-1113
ASSOCIATE: B. J. Creasman EXPERTISE: Wicca OWNER: Anne Neely EXPERTISE: Wicca OFFERS: Workshops, Lectures READINGS: Astrology, Palmistry, Runes, Tarot, I Ching NON-BOOK ITEMS SOLD: Tarot Decks, Tapes, Cards, Herbs, Robes, Essential Oils, Incense, Candles, Jewelry

Rubyfruit Books
666-4 W. Tennessee Street
Tallahassee, FL 32304
(904)-222-2627

Sage Spirit
Chrysalis Institute, Inc
195 Cottonwood Lane
Corrales, NM 87048
(505)-898-9172

David HeustonBrenda Heuston OFFERS: Workshops, Lectures NON-BOOK ITEMS SOLD: Incense, Native American Sacred Herbs & Ceremonials

Salamander
5 Spring Street
New Brunswick, NJ 08901
(908)-745-9293
OWNER: Conny Jasper EXPERTISE: Tarot Reader, Witch OFFERS: Workshops, Lectures READINGS: Tarot NON-BOOK ITEMS SOLD: Jewelry, Incense, Candles, Recorded Music, T-Shirts

Samadhi Metaphysical Literature
P.O. Box 170
Lakeview, AR 72642
(501)-431-8830
OWNER: Dennis Whelan EXPERTISE: Out-Of-Print Specialist

Sanctus Spiritus
P.O. Box 59
Western Springs, IL 60558
(312)-767-1113
OWNER: Stanley J.A. Modrzyk EXPERTISE: Occult, E.S.P., Witchcraft, Paganism ASSOCIATE: Dori Sholeen EXPERTISE: Tarot, Crystals, Wicca READINGS: Palmistry, Runes, Tea Leaves NON-BOOK ITEMS SOLD: Jewelry

Sands Of Time Bookshop & Psychic Center
2906 South 13th Street
Milwaukee, WI 53215
(414)-645-6968
OWNER: Anne Marie Janis EXPERTISE: Psychic Consultant ASSOCIATE: Marianne EXPERTISE: Psychic Consultant OFFERS: Workshops, Lectures, Healing Therapy READINGS: Astrology, Palmistry, Runes, Tarot, Tea Leaves, Psychometry, Past Life Regression, Numerology, Handwriting Analysis, Aura NON-BOOK ITEMS SOLD: Crystals, Candles, Incense, Jewelry

School Of Metaphysics
717 Marshall Avenue
Webster Groves, MO 63119
(314)-961-3321
DIRECTOR: Kateri Meyer EXPERTISE: Dream Interpretation ASSOCIATE: Antionette Patakas EXPERTISE: Dream Interpretation, Graphology OFFERS: Workshops, Lectures, Crossings, Health Consultations READINGS: Tea Leaves, Past Life

School Of Metaphysics
National Headquarters
Windyville, MO 65783
(417)-345-8411
CHAIRMAN OF BOARD: Dr. Barbara O'Guinn PRESIDENT: Dr. Daniel R. Condron VICE PRESIDENT: Laurel J. Fuller OFFERS: Workshops, Lectures, Past Life Crossing, Health Analysis, Family, Business Analysis READINGS: Past Life NON-BOOK ITEMS SOLD: Audio/Video Tapes, T-Shirts & Sweatshirts, Cards, Thresholds Magazine

School Of Metaphysics
719 W. Michigan Avenue
Ypsilanti, MI 48197
(313)-482-9600
DIRECTOR: Laura Rogers OFFERS: Workshops, Lectures READINGS: Life & Health Readings from

Akashic Records NON-BOOK ITEMS SOLD: T-Shirts, Sweatshirts, Tapes, Calendars

School Of Metaphysics Bookstore
School Of Metaphysics
222 W. Wilson
Palatine, IL 60067
(708)-991-0140

DIRECTOR: Bev Lauer OFFERS: Workshops, Lectures, Health, Family & Business Consultations READINGS: Tea Leaves, Past Life

School Of Metaphysics Bookstore
210 Third Avenue
Columbia, MO 65201
(314)-449-8312

DIRECTOR: Terryll L. Nemeth EXPERTISE: Teacher & Lecturer of Metaphysics OFFERS: Workshops, Lectures READINGS: Tea Leaves, Health, Business & Past Life Readings NON-BOOK ITEMS SOLD: Spirit Art Visionary Cards

School of Natural Medicine
P.O. Box 7369
Boulder, CO 80306
(303)-443-8284

Dr. Farida Sharan

Self-Awareness Association
8123 E. 48th Street
Tulsa, OK 74145-6906
(918)-665-7773

OWNER: Walt Browne EXPERTISE: Success Seminars ASSOCIATE: Ellen Browne EXPERTISE: Certified Public Accountant OFFERS: Workshops, Lectures NON-BOOK ITEMS SOLD: Tapes

Seven Stars
58 John F. Kennedy Street
Cambridge, MA 02138
(617)-547-1317

OWNER: Stuart Weinberg OWNER: Yvonne Paglia BUYER: James Heney OFFERS: Workshops, Lectures READINGS: Astrology, Palmistry, Tarot NON-BOOK ITEMS SOLD: Crystals, Incense, Tapes

Shining Two, Inc.
P.O. Box 91180
Lafayette, LA 70501
(318)-896-5209

OWNER: Mack Money EXPERTISE: Tarot, Spiritual Counselor ASSOCIATE: Steve LeBlanc EXPERTISE: Reiki, I Ching, Runes OFFERS: Workshops READINGS: Runes NON-BOOK ITEMS SOLD: Candles, Oils, Incense, Herbs, Charms, Mojo Bags

Sign Of Aquarius
815 Copeland Street
Pittsburg, PA 15232
(412)-681-3700

OWNER: Leonard Friedlander EXPERTISE: Psychology ASSOCIATE: Harriet Friedlander EXPERTISE: Astrology NON-BOOK ITEMS SOLD: Tarot Cards, New Age Cassettes, Crystals, Pyramids, Incense Burners, Lead Crystal Balls, Runes

Silent Light
234 Ellicott Street
Batavia, NY 14020
(716)-343-9256

OWNER: Rev. Ruthanne EXPERTISE: Psychic, Self-Awareness, Artist OFFERS: Workshops, Lectures READINGS: Runes, Tarot, Tea Leaves, Spiritual NON-BOOK ITEMS SOLD: Gemstones, Jewelry, Fantasy

Silent Partner Bookstore
P.O. Box 127
Gila, NM 88038
(505)-535-2855

OWNER: Marian Jones EXPERTISE: Teacher, Healer, Reader OFFERS: Lectures, I Ching, Spiritual Counseling READINGS: Palmistry, Tarot NON-BOOK ITEMS SOLD: Raw Crystals

Silver Chord Bookstore
615 Stafford Lane
Pensacola, FL 32506
(904)-453-6652

OWNER: Lillian H Schubert ASSOCIATE: Kelly Davis OFFERS: Workshops, Lectures READINGS: Astrology, Tarot, Psychic, Cartouche NON-BOOK ITEMS SOLD: Crystals, Music, Incense, Jewelry, Calendars, Herbs, Oils

Source Bookstore, The
329 East Fifth Avenue
Anchorage, AK 99501-2632
(907)-274-5850 (907)-279-2014

OWNER: Douglas R. Myers OWNER: Decma Myers OFFERS: Crystal Aura READINGS: Astrology, Palmistry, Runes, Tarot NON-BOOK ITEMS SOLD: Gifts, Candles, Ceremonial Incense DESCRIPTION: Metaphysical books & supplies. Over 10,000 titles, books & tapes.

Source Life Enrichment Center
2726 Ellendale Avenue
St. Louis, MO 63143
(314)-644-0641

OWNER: Rhonda Leifheit EXPERTISE: Personal & Spiritual Growth OFFERS: Workshops, Lectures READINGS: Tea Leaves, Past Life & Health Readings NON-BOOK ITEMS SOLD: Meditation & Regression Tapes

Sphinx Bookstore, The
1510-H Piedmont Avenue
Atlanta, GA 30324
(404)-875-2665

OWNER: T.E. Poole NON-BOOK ITEMS SOLD: Music, Incense, Cards

Spiritual Science Institute
2650 Meetinghouse Road
Jamison, PA 18929
(215)-343-2811

OWNER: George L. Mankin OFFERS: Workshops, Lectures, Healings READINGS: Astrology, Runes, Tarot, Tea Leaves

Sri Atman Bookstore
1308 Government Street
Victoria, British Columbia V8W 1Y8
Canada

BUYER: Elizabeth Connell

Star Gate Awareness Resources
1374 Willamette
Eugene, OR 97401
(503)-342-8348

OWNER, DISTRIBUTOR: Alan Stein EXPERTISE: New Age Networker OFFERS: Workshops, Lectures

READINGS: Astrology, Runes NON-BOOK ITEMS SOLD: Video/Audio, Gifts

Star Visions
7537 Mentor Avenue
Mentor, OH 44060
(800)-678-4000

OWNER: Maryanne Hoffman OFFERS: Workshops, Lectures READINGS: Astrology, Runes, Tea Leaves, Aura DESCRIPTION: Manufactures & sells their own greeting cards, clothing, posters, games, books & calendars. Specializes in Astrology & offers Astrology, Rune Stone, Tea Leaf & Aura Readings.

Stern's Book Service
2004 W. Roscoe Street
Chicago, IL 60618
(312)-883-5100

OWNER: Kathy Stern EXPERTISE: Psychology OFFERS: Workshops

Sunrise Books
6940 W. 130th Street
Middleburg Hts., OH 44130
(216)-884-2888

OWNER: Charlotte Scheiman EXPERTISE: Spirituality OFFERS: Workshops, Lectures, Spiritual/Mediumship, Spirit Portraits READINGS: Astrology, Runes NON-BOOK ITEMS SOLD: Incense, Oils, Greeting Cards, Candles

Survival Center
5555 Newton Falls Road
Box 707
Ravenna, OH 44266
(216)-678-4000

ASSOCIATE: Tim Gmvcs OFFERS: Workshops NON-BOOK ITEMS SOLD: Natural Foods

Swedenborg Book Store
Massachusetts New-Church Union
79 Newbury Street
Boston, MA 02116
(617)-262-5918

GENERAL SECRETARY: Rafael Guiu BOOK MANAGER: Michelle Joan OFFERS: Lectures NON-BOOK ITEMS SOLD: Music Cassette Tapes

T'ai-Chi-Ch'uan School
Artistic Video
87 Tyler Avenue
Sound Beach, NY 11789
(516)-744-0449

OWNER: Bob Klein EXPERTISE: Video Production, T'ai-Chi-Ch'uan Instructor OFFERS: Workshops, Massage Classes, Self Defense & T'ai-Chi Classes NON-BOOK ITEMS SOLD: Health, Exercise, Massage & Self Defense Videos

Three Of Cups
12 Tinker Street
Woodstock, NY 12498
(914)-679-2357

OWNER: Tyshe Moonfeather EXPERTISE: Crystal Counselor OWNER: Hawk EXPERTISE: Crystal Counselor OFFERS: Workshops, Lectures READINGS: Astrology, Palmistry, Runes, Tarot NON-BOOK ITEMS SOLD: Crystals, Stones, Psychic Tools

Threshold Books & Tapes
3409 So. Georgia, #10
Amarillo, TX 79109

(806)-359-9999
OWNER: Stacie McNulty White **OFFERS:** Workshops, Lectures **NON-BOOK ITEMS SOLD:** Music, Candles, Stones, Essential Oils

Time To Live
1791 N.E. 15th
P.O. Box 1866
Hillsboro, OR 97123
(503)-648-1794
OWNER: Colleen M. Curtis **OFFERS:** Meditations **NON-BOOK ITEMS SOLD:** Gemstone Jewelry

Todd Pratum
P.O. Box 1214
Glen Ellen, CA 95442
(707)-938-3145
OWNER: Todd Pratum **EXPERTISE:** Occult, Philosophy

Top Of The Mountain Publishing
11701 S. Belcher Road, #123
Largo, FL 34643
(813)-530-0110
OFFERS: Workshops, Lectures **NON-BOOK ITEMS SOLD:** Audio Cassettes, Energy Wheels

Total Health Network
170 Fulton Street
Farmingdale, NY 11735
(516)-694-1967
ASSOCIATE: Jim Deluca **EXPERTISE:** Crystals, Nutrition **OWNER:** Marty Meyer **EXPERTISE:** Yoga Instructor, Metaphysician **OFFERS:** Workshops, Lectures **READINGS:** Astrology, Palmistry, Runes **NON-BOOK ITEMS SOLD:** Vitamins, Herbs, Health Foods

Tree Of Knowledge
Box 16372
Seattle, WA 98116
(206)-937-0671
OWNER, BUSINESS MANAGER: Patty Mason **ASSOCIATE:** RainBow Dragon (Renee) **EXPERTISE:** Occult, Astrology **ASSOCIATE:** TieDye Dragon (David) **ACCOUNTANT:** Thoughtful Dragon (Mickie) **OFFERS:** Lectures **READINGS:** Astrology, Dragon's Wisdom **NON-BOOK ITEMS SOLD:** Gemstones, Occult & Dragon Items, Astrology & Numerology Charts

Tree Of Life Books/ A New Age Center
3437 Spring Street
Racine, WI 53405
(414)-637-3898
DESCRIPTION: Offers metaphysical books, gifts & tapes.

Tree Of Life Bookstore
Box E 99F
RD 001
Lewes, DE 19958
ASSOCIATE: Jean Keating **OFFERS:** Workshops, Lectures **READINGS:** Astrology **NON-BOOK ITEMS SOLD:** Medicines & Medical Items

Turning Wheel, The
8039-A Ritchie Highway
Pasadena, MD 21122
(301)-761-3130
OWNER: Peggy Booraem **EXPERTISE:** Wicca, Tarot, Astrology **OFFERS:** Workshops, Lectures

READINGS: Astrology, Palmistry, Runes, Tarot **NON-BOOK ITEMS SOLD:** Incense, Tapes, Stones, Jewelry, Sacred Native American Objects

Turtle Island Bookstore
318 E. 10th Avenue
Spokane, WA 99202
(509)-747-1189
OWNER: Saundra Rathweaver **OFFERS:** Workshops, Lectures, Medicine Wheel Consultations **READINGS:** Runes, Tea Leaves, Medicine Stone Readings **NON-BOOK ITEMS SOLD:** Jewelry, Ceremonial Items, Drums, T-Shirts, Pipes, Pottery

Twelfth House, The
Four Wizards, Inc.
1445 S. Pearl St
Denver, CO 80210
(303)-777-1112
MANAGER: Mark Husson **ASSOCIATE:** Roderick Mielo **ASSOCIATE:** John Bamburoski **OFFERS:** Workshops, Lectures **READINGS:** Astrology, Palmistry, Runes, Tarot, Tea Leaves **NON-BOOK ITEMS SOLD:** Music, Jewelry, Gift Items, Tarot, Candles, Essences

Unicorn Books
1210 Massachusetts Avenue
Arlington, MA 02174
(617)-646-3680
OWNER, GENERAL MANAGER, BUYER: Beth Bryant **OWNER:** Jan Brink **EXPERTISE:** Astrologer, Crystal Buyer **BOOKKEEPER:** Joanne Clancy **PROGRAM LIAISON:** Verna Barrie **OFFERS:** Workshops, Lectures **READINGS:** Astrology, Palmistry, Tarot **NON-BOOK ITEMS SOLD:** Music Tapes & CD's, Incense, Ritual Articles, Crystals, Chimes

Unique Books, Inc.
4230 Grove Avenue
Gurnee, IL 60031
(708)-623-9171 **FAX** (708)-623-7238
VICE-PRESIDENT: Jud Krick

Unity Church Bookstore
1000 S. 17th Avenue, Ste. 5
Hattiesburg, MS 39401
(601)-582-3954
COUNSELOR: Deborah Boleware **EXPERTISE:** Spiritual Leader **OFFERS:** Workshops, Lectures **NON-BOOK ITEMS SOLD:** Pamphlets, Brochures, Cassette Tapes

Unity Church Of Truth
300 West Seneca Turnpike
Syracuse, NY 13207
(315)-492-9548
OWNER: Rev. Daniel Douglas **EXPERTISE:** Metaphysics

Unity Metaphysical Bookstore
2409 N. 8th Street
Sheboygan, WI 53083
(414)-452-5447
OWNER: Dan Mueller **EXPERTISE:** Minister **MANAGER:** Judi Joba **OFFERS:** Workshops, Church Services **READINGS:** Tea Leaves **NON-BOOK ITEMS SOLD:** Tapes

Unity Woods Yoga Center
4853 Cordell Avenue, Ste PH9
Bethesda, MD 20814

(301)-656-8992
DIRECTOR: John Schumacher **ADMINISTRATIVE ASSISTANT:** Esther Geiger **OFFERS:** Workshops **NON-BOOK ITEMS SOLD:** Yoga Props, Clothing

Universal Centre Of Cassadaga
460 Cassadaga Road
Cassadaga, FL 32706
(904)-228-3190
OWNER: Ernest M. Sekunna **OFFERS:** Lectures, Psychics & Mediums **READINGS:** Astrology, Palmistry, Runes, Tarot **NON-BOOK ITEMS SOLD:** Jewelry, Gifts, Tapes, Stones, Herbs

Universal Mind Science Church Bookstore
Universal Mind Science Church
3212 East 8th Street
Long Beach, CA 90804
(213)-434-3453
VICE-PRES.: Beverly Baumann **OFFERS:** Workshops, Lectures **READINGS:** Astrology, Palmistry, Tarot, Tea Leaves, Psychometry, Numerology **NON-BOOK ITEMS SOLD:** New Age Music Cassette Tapes, Tarot Cards, Videos, Heart & Angel Cards, Vitamins, Candles

Unlimited Thought Foundation Bookstore
5525 Blanco Road, # 112
San Antonio, TX 78216
(512)-525-0693
PRESIDENT: Bill Utterback **VICE PRESIDENT:** Ann Utterback **OFFERS:** Workshops, Lectures **READINGS:** Astrology, Palmistry, Runes, Tarot, Channeled Readings, Intuitive Psychic Counseling **NON-BOOK ITEMS SOLD:** Posters, Oils, Incense, Jewelry, Crystals & Stones, Cards, Gifts, Music, Tapes, Herbs, T-Shirts **DESCRIPTION:** Also sells books & tapes in Spanish. Offers lectures & classes on Metaphysical & New Age topics.

Uprising
2826 Oak Ave.
Altoona, PA 16601
(814)-943-2195
OWNER: Carol Hepler

Uranian Agency And Books, The
27040 Cedar Road, #102
Beachwood, OH 44122
(216)-561-0970 (216)-765-0595
OWNER: Delores O'Bryant **EXPERTISE:** Metaphysician, Astrologer **OFFERS:** Workshops, Lectures **READINGS:** Astrology **NON-BOOK ITEMS SOLD:** Gemstones, Jewelry

Vattumannen Bookshop & Publishers
Drottninggatan 83
Stockholm, S-104 30
Sweden
08-109615
OWNER: Jan Seilitz **EXPERTISE:** Esoteric Philosophy **ASSOCIATE:** Mikael W. Gejel **EXPERTISE:** Western Occultism, Nordic Shamanism **ASSOCIATE:** Mikael Hedlund **EXPERTISE:** Western Occultism, Nordic Shamanism **ASSOCIATE:** Maria Seppanen **EXPERTISE:** Astrology, Numerology **READINGS:** Astrology, Runes **NON-BOOK ITEMS SOLD:** Crystals, Tarot Cards, Pendulums, Music

Vedanta Book Center

5423 S. Hyde Park Boulevard
Chicago, IL 60615
(312)-363-0027
ASSOCIATE: Swami Varadananda-Vedanta
ASSOCIATE: Bob Ringler-Vedanta **OFFERS:**
Lectures **NON-BOOK ITEMS SOLD:** Incense, Art
From India

Vedanta Press & Bookshop
Vedanta Society
1946 Vedanta Place
Hollywood, CA 90068
(213)-465-7114
NON-BOOK ITEMS SOLD: Incense, Cards, Statuary
From India, Nepal & Japan

Vision Quest Bookstore
3200 E. Los Angeles Avenue,#5
Simi Valley, CA 93065
(805)-527-7297
OWNER: Apryl Berlier **OWNER:** Rock Berlier
OFFERS: Workshops, Lectures, Metaphysical &
Psychic Counseling

Vision Quest Bookstore
7210 Vassar Avenue
Canoga Park, CA 91303
(818)-888-0487
OWNER: Apryl Douglas-Berlier **OWNER:** Rock
Berlier **OFFERS:** Workshops, Lectures,
Metaphysical Counseling, Psychic Fairs **NON-BOOK
ITEMS SOLD:** All Types of Metaphysical Products

Well Within
2517 El Camino del Norte #1
Encinitas, CA 92024-9798
(619)-632-1646
OWNER: Sheri Nakken,R.N., M.A. **EXPERTISE:**
Holistic Health, Metaphysics **OFFERS:** Workshops,
Lectures **READINGS:** Astrology, Runes, Tarot **NON-
BOOK ITEMS SOLD:** Crystals, Tapes, Jewelry

White Cloud
423 NW 10th Avenue
Gainesville, FL 32601
(906)-372-6724
OWNER: Bennett (Gyanarthi) Hoffman
EXPERTISE: Astrologer **READINGS:** Astrology,
Runes **NON-BOOK ITEMS SOLD:** Jewelry, Minerals,
Crystals

White Dolphin
218 F Street
Eureka, CA 95501
(707)-445-2094
OWNER: Elayne Lieberman **EXPERTISE:**
Nutritional Consultant, Tarot, Crystals, Intuitive
Awareness **OWNER:** Steve Schenck **EXPERTISE:**

Health, Metaphysical Information, Music
ASSOCIATE: Fran Mullin **EXPERTISE:**
Psychic/Spiritual Consultant, Crystals, Color
Therapy **OFFERS:** Workshops, Lectures **READINGS:**
Astrology, Tarot **NON-BOOK ITEMS SOLD:**
Crystals, Minerals, Music, Artwork, Visionary
Cards, Non-Toxic Items, Meditation Items,
Environmental Gifts, T-Shirts

White Rabbit Books
1833 Spring Garden Street
Greensboro, NC 27403
(919)-272-7604
NON-BOOK ITEMS SOLD: Tarot Cards, Crystal
Jewelry, Jewelry

Wikima
900 W Abram Street
Arlington, TX 76013
(214)-353-0092 (817)-261-4903
OWNER: Deanne Quarrie **EXPERTISE:** Wicca,
Native Americans **OFFERS:** Workshops, Lectures
READINGS: Tarot, Tea Leaves **NON-BOOK ITEMS
SOLD:** Tapes, Jewelry, Incense, Herbs, Oils,
Candles, Gemstones, Shamanic Items

Winged Disk, The
375 Rays Ford Circle
Earlysville, VA 22936
BUYER: Aileen Stone

Wings Of Change
115 2nd Avenue North
Nashville, TN 37201-1901
(615)-726-2550
OWNER: Gayle Walton **EXPERTISE:** Herbologist
OFFERS: Workshops **READINGS:** Astrology, Runes
NON-BOOK ITEMS SOLD: Music, Non-Animal
Tested Make-Up, Herb Remedies, Environmentally
Safe Products

Wings Of Light
9625 Bay Pines Boulevard
St. Petersburg, FL 33708
(813)-397-1221
OWNER: Donna McMullen **OWNER:** Lynda D'Urso
OFFERS: Workshops **READINGS:** Astrology,
Palmistry, Runes, Tarot, Tea Leaves, Psychometry,
Psychic **NON-BOOK ITEMS SOLD:** Jewelry, Crystals
& Stones, Music, Candles, Calendars

Wizard, The
565 Kings Highway East
Fairfield, CT 06430
(203)-367-6355
OWNER: John Binns **ASSOCIATE:** Brenda Kaplan
OFFERS: Workshops, Lectures **NON-BOOK ITEMS**

SOLD: Crystals, Healing Stones, Incense, Runes,
Tarot, Jewelry, Gifts

World Of Wisdom, Inc.
5142 Madison Avenue, #4
Indianapolis, IN 46227
(317)-787-3005
READINGS: Astrology, Palmistry, Runes, Tarot, Past
Life Regressions **NON-BOOK ITEMS SOLD:** Stones,
Jewelry, Tapes, Videos

World University Books
P.O. Box 2470
Benson, AZ 85602
(602)-586-2985
PRESIDENT, EXEC. MANAGER: Dr. H. John Zitko
NON-BOOK ITEMS SOLD: Sells Mail-Order

Written Words
6001 Johnson Drive
Mission, KS 66202
(913)-722-0486
OWNER: Billie Schupp **OFFERS:** Workshops,
Lectures **READINGS:** Astrology, Palmistry

Yankee Book Peddler Inc
Maple St
Contoocook, NH 03229
(603)-746-3102

Yoga Bookstore
Nekkersbergl. 39
9000 Gent,
Belgium
OWNER: Paul Meganck **OFFERS:** Workshops,
Lectures, Yoga, Meditation, Relaxation, Eastern
Philosophy **READINGS:** Astrology, Palmistry

Yoga Fitness, Inc.
321 Northlake Blvd., Ste 213
North Palm Beach, FL 33408
(407)-844-1434
OWNER: Alison A (Sue) Heil **EXPERTISE:** Licensed
Massage Therapist, Certified Yoga Instructor
OFFERS: Workshops, Lectures **NON-BOOK ITEMS
SOLD:** Yoga Supplies

Yoga Therapy Center
126 Harvard Street
Brookline, MA 02146
(617)-739-0717
OWNER: Tom Stiles **EXPERTISE:** Spiritual
Emergence, Personalized Practices, Teacher
ASSOCIATE: John Schlorholtz **EXPERTISE:**
Meditation **OFFERS:** Workshops, Lectures

Distributors/Wholesalers

Although some Distributors and Wholesalers have stores, most offer a wide range of products primarily through mail-order. Many offer catalogs and encourage inquiries. Contact them for additional information.

A.C.S. Publications-Astro Communications Services (ACS)
P.O. Box 34487
San Diego, CA 92163-4487
(619)-297-9203 (800)-888-9983 FAX (619)-297-9251

TOPICS: Astrology, New Age OWNER: Maria Kay Simms FOUNDED: 1973 TYPE OF BUSINESS: Astrological services DESCRIPTION: Publishers, wholesalers, distributors & retailers of astrological services & materials: astrological calculations, interpretations & books. Fills mail & phone orders to individuals, bookstores & major distributors. Catalog available.

Abyss Distribution
RR 1
Box 213
Chester, MA 01011-9735
(413)-623-2155

TOPICS: Occult, Witchcraft, Herbalogy, UFO's, Tarot TYPE OF BUSINESS: Mail order/Distributor DESCRIPTION: Distribution/mail-order company selling books & items on Witchcraft, Magick, herbs, UFO's, Tarot, Egyptian & Celtic lore.

Ageless Wisdom Distributors
1103 East Alameda Drive
Tempe, AZ 85282
(602)-829-0240

CONTACT: Niles S. Lipin TOPICS: New Age FOUNDED: 1990 TYPE OF BUSINESS: Book distributor DESCRIPTION: Wholesaler & distributor of New Age books.

American West Distributors
6992 El Caminio Real, Suite 104-335
Carlsbad, CA 92009
(619)-438-8884 FAX (619)-431-9003

CONTACT: Desiree Stevens TOPICS: New Age, Metaphysics, UFO's FOUNDED: 1986 TYPE OF BUSINESS: Book distributor DESCRIPTION: Wholesaler & distributor of New Age & UFO books.

Angelic Mercantile
Box 11556
Eugene, OR 97440
(503)-342-1624

CONTACT: Paul Finkel TOPICS: New Age, Metaphysics FOUNDED: 1987 TYPE OF BUSINESS: New Age products DESCRIPTION: Wholesaler & distributor of New Age & Metaphysical products related to crystals.

Aqua Aura
Box 2652
Renton, WA 98056
(206)-255-6635

CONTACT: Bob Jackson TOPICS: Crystals OWNER: Bob Jackson TYPE OF BUSINESS: Crystals DESCRIPTION: Wholesale distributors of Aqua Aura - gold coated quartz crystals. Catalog available. Mail-order only.

Aquarian Specialties
1069 Grouse Street
El Cajon, CA 92020
(619)-448-5715

TOPICS: New Age, Metaphysics, Occult OWNER: Tamiris Duke FOUNDED: 1979 TYPE OF BUSINESS: New Age products DESCRIPTION: Wholesale distributor catalog offering crystal & Egyptian jewelry, gifts, books, blown glass figures, gemstone runes, wands, magical oils, alter pieces, display materials, audio & video tapes, crystals, posters, etc. to stores & organizations.

Armadillo
928 California Avenue
Venice, CA 90291
(213)-821-1650

CONTACT: Edward Ferrera TOPICS: New Age

Askit Company
3517 Terhune
Ann Arbor, MI 48107
(313)-971-1034

TOPICS: New Age

Associations Book Distributors International, Incorporated
503 Thompson Park Drive
Mars, PA 16046
(412)-772-0070

CONTACT: Maureen P. Schwab TOPICS: New Age

Audio Publishers Group, Incorporated
237 North Michigan Street, Suite 609
South Bend, IN 46601
(219)-288-4950

CONTACT: Bruce Fingerhut TOPICS: New Age FOUNDED: 1987 DESCRIPTION: Distributor of New Age spoken audio tapes.

Auromere Books & Imports
1291 Weber Street
Pomona, CA 91768
(714)-629-8255 (800)-735-4691 FAX (714)-623-9877

CONTACT: Michael Zucker TOPICS: New Age, Metaphysics, Spirituality, Herbalogy FOUNDED: 1976 TYPE OF BUSINESS: New Age mail-order DESCRIPTION: New Age mail-order catalog offering Sri Aurobindo books, Ayurveda & spiritual texts, children's books from India, incense, herbs, teas, handicrafts, Ayurvedic herbal toothpaste, soap, oils, mud treatments, Chyavanprash Energy Supplements, jewelry & gifts. PUBLICATIONS: Garland Of Letters

Awareness And Health Unlimited
3509 North High Street
Columbus, OH 43214
(614)-262-7087

CONTACT: Phil TOPICS: New Age

Baker And Taylor (Eastern Division)
50 Kirby Avenue
Somerville, NJ 08876-0734
(201)-722-8000

CONTACT: Patricia Bostleman TOPICS: New Age TYPE OF BUSINESS: Book distributor DESCRIPTION: Leading distributor of books many being New Age, metaphysical, holistic health, etc..

Baker And Taylor (Midwest Division)
501 South Gladiolas Street
Momence, IL 60954-1799
(815)-472-2444

CONTACT: Donna Lippold TOPICS: New Age

Baker And Taylor (Southeastern Division)
Mount Olive Road
Commerce, GA 30599-0001
(404)-335-5000

CONTACT: Jill Bartholomew TOPICS: New Age

Baker And Taylor (Western Division)
380 Edison Way
Reno, NV 89564-2444
(702)-786-6700

CONTACT: Jackie Kelly TOPICS: New Age

Baker And Taylor New Book Division
P.O. Box 6920, 652 Main Street
Bridgewater, NJ 08807-0920
(201)-722-8000

CONTACT: Eleanor Fanicase TOPICS: New Age

Balanced Foods
2501 71st Street
North Bergen, NJ 07047
(201)-289-0363

CONTACT: Cheddy Pagan TOPICS: New Age DESCRIPTION: Distributor of health foods.

Ballantine Books, Inc.
201 East 50th Street
New York, NY 10022
(212)-572-2620 (800)-733-3000

CONTACT: Clair Ferraro TOPICS: New Age PUBLICATIONS: Avalanche: Heretical Reflections On The Dark And The Light, Predicting Your Future, Rainbow Oracle: The Divination Of Color, Exploring The World Of Lucid Dreaming

Bear Family Distributors
2954 North Campbell
Tucson, AZ 85719
(602)-881-0193

CONTACT: Bob Hitcke TOPICS: New Age, Metaphysics FOUNDED: 1976 TYPE OF BUSINESS: Magazine distributor DESCRIPTION: Wholesaler & distributor of New Age magazines.

Big State
4830 Lakawana #121
Dallas, TX 75427

(214)-631-1100
TOPICS: New Age TYPE OF BUSINESS: Audio/video distributor DESCRIPTION: Distributor of audio & video tapes.

Blackwell North America
1001 Fries Mill Road
Blackwood, NJ 08012
(609)-629-0070
TOPICS: New Age FOUNDED: 1975 TYPE OF BUSINESS: Book distributor DESCRIPTION: Distributes books primarily to libraries.

Book Tech Distributing, Incorporated
5961 East 39th Avenue
Denver, CO 80207-1231
(303)-761-2435
CONTACT: Tom Tarbert TOPICS: New Age, Metaphysics FOUNDED: 1980 TYPE OF BUSINESS: New Age distributor DESCRIPTION: Distributor of New Age magazines & computer materials.

Bookpeople
2929 Fifth Street
Berkeley, CA 94710
(415)-549-3030
CONTACT: Randy Beek TOPICS: New Age FOUNDED: 1968 DESCRIPTION: Wholesaler & distributor of New Age & Metaphysical products including books, magazines, cassettes & video tapes. Sells exclusively to bookstores.

Borgo Press
P.O. Box 2845
San Bernardino, CA 92406
(714)-884-5813
CONTACT: Mary Burgess TOPICS: New Age

Brotherhood Of Life
110 Dartmouth, S.E.
Albuquerque, NM 87106
(505)-873-2179
CONTACT: Richard Buhler TOPICS: Crystals, Metaphysics, Channeling FOUNDED: 1970 DESCRIPTION: Publisher & distributor of New Age books. PUBLICATIONS: *Other Tongues, Other Flesh*

Buckland Books & Tapes
P.O. Box 892
Wooster, OH 44691-0892
TOPICS: New Age TYPE OF BUSINESS: New Age Books & Tapes DESCRIPTION: Distributor of books, video & audio tapes of Raymond & Tara Buckland. Offers 16 page mail-order catalog for $2.00. Books autographed by the author.

Camenae Twins Unlimited
P.O. Box 728
Milton, WA 98354
(206)-952-4202 (206)-848-2052
CONTACT: Robert Draper, Pres. TOPICS: New Age, Spirituality OWNER: Robert Draper TYPE OF BUSINESS: New Age books DESCRIPTION: Publishes & distributes books on the teachings of Zanzoona including The Symphony Of Creation, Flight Of The Soul, The Book Of Love & Dove by MariJo Donais.

Carolina Cassette Distributors
P.O. Box 429, 2600 Oaks Road
New Bern, NC 28560
(919)-638-5583

CONTACT: Lief Eriksson TOPICS: New Age, Metaphysics FOUNDED: 1979 TYPE OF BUSINESS: Audio tape distributors DESCRIPTION: Distributor of New Age audio tapes.

Casa De Horus, S.A.
Jardin De S. Federico 15
Madrid,
Spain
(91) 402 9790
CONTACT: Sr. Sanchez TOPICS: New Age, Metaphysics FOUNDED: 1987 DESCRIPTION: Wholesaler & distributor of New Age & Metaphysical products including books, magazines, cassettes & video tapes.

Charles E. Tuttle Company, Inc.
P.O. Box 410
28 South Main Street
Rutland, VT 05701
(802)-773-8930
CONTACT: Barbara Brackett TOPICS: New Age, Metaphysics FOUNDED: 1832 PUBLICATIONS: *Aikido And The Dynamic Sphere, I Ching: Hexagrams Revealed, Tao Of I Ching: Way To Divination, Tao Of Meditation: Way To Enlightenment, Book Of Tea, Iron Flute: 100 Zen Koan With Commentary*

Children's Small Press
719 North 4th Avenue
Ann Arbor, MI 48104
(313)-668-8056
CONTACT: Kathleen Baxter TOPICS: New Age FOUNDED: 1985 TYPE OF BUSINESS: New Age distributor DESCRIPTION: Distributor of books, calendars & music & audio tapes for many publishers. Handles children's books & materials for parenting & family relationships.

Comstock Creations
190 Sawyer Drive
Durango, CO 81302
(303)-247-3836
CONTACT: Scott Browne TOPICS: New Age, Metaphysics FOUNDED: 1982 TYPE OF BUSINESS: Gift distributors DESCRIPTION: Distributor of New Age gifts, crystals & jewelry.

Consortium Book Sales And Distribution
237 East Sixth, Suite 365
St. Paul, MN 55101
(612)-221-9035
CONTACT: Bobbi Rix TOPICS: New Age TYPE OF BUSINESS: New Age products DESCRIPTION: Distributors of New Age books & audio/video tapes.

Consulting Psychologists Press, Incorporated
3803 East Bayshore Road
Palo Alto, CA 94303
(415)-857-1444
CONTACT: Maude Willner TOPICS: New Age TYPE OF BUSINESS: New Age books DESCRIPTION: Distributor of New Age books on psychology.

Contemplations, Inc.
P.O. Box 909
Durango, CO 81302
(303)-247-4621

CONTACT: Ed Heinemann TOPICS: New Age, Metaphysics FOUNDED: 1987 TYPE OF BUSINESS: New Age distributor DESCRIPTION: Wholesaler & distributor of New Age & Metaphysical products including books, magazines, cassettes & video tapes.

Coutts Library Service
736 Cayuga Street
Lewiston, NY 14092
TOPICS: New Age

Creative Source, The
20702 El Toro Road, #555
El Toro, CA 92630
(714)-458-7971
CONTACT: Joe Moriarity TOPICS: New Age, Metaphysics FOUNDED: 1970 TYPE OF BUSINESS: New Age products DESCRIPTION: Wholesaler & distributor of New Age & Metaphysical products including books, magazines, cassettes & video tapes.

Crystal Cave Enterprises
P.O. Box 1251
Rancho de Taos, NM 87557
(505)-758-7100
CONTACT: Lin Vernon TOPICS: New Age FOUNDED: 1985 DESCRIPTION: Wholesaler & distributor of New Age & Metaphysical products including books, magazines, cassettes & video tapes.

Deerhawk Enterprises
P.O. Box 3826
Spokane, WA 99220
(509)-326-5272
CONTACT: Richard V. Dalke TOPICS: New Age, Metaphysics FOUNDED: 1986 TYPE OF BUSINESS: New Age distributor DESCRIPTION: Wholesaler & mail-order distributor of New Age & Metaphysical products including books, magazines, cassettes & video tapes.

DeVorss & Company
Box 550
Marina Del Ray, CA 90294
(213)-870-7478 (800)-843-5743 FAX (213)-821-6290
CONTACT: Gary Peattie TOPICS: New Age, Metaphysics, Occult FOUNDED: 1929 PUBLICATIONS: *Universal Language Of Cabalah: The Master Key To The God Consciousness, Life And Teaching Of The Masters Of The Far East, Vols. 1-5, High Mysticism, Revelation For A New Age*

Discoveries
8055 Main Street
Ellicott City, MD 21043
(301)-461-9600
CONTACT: Carrie Bury TOPICS: New Age TYPE OF BUSINESS: Music distributor DESCRIPTION: Distributor of New Age music.

Disticor
155 Gordon Baker Road, #213
Toronto, Ontario,
Canada
(416)-496-8444
CONTACT: John Lafranier TOPICS: New Age FOUNDED: 1980 TYPE OF BUSINESS: Magazine distributor DESCRIPTION: Distributor of New Age & Metaphysical magazines.

Distributors, The

702 South Michigan
South Bend, IN 46618
(219)-232-8500
CONTACT: P. Walsh **TOPICS:** New Age, Metaphysics **FOUNDED:** 1971 **TYPE OF BUSINESS:** Publisher's Rep **DESCRIPTION:** Rep, wholesaler & distributor of New Age & Metaphysical books to the trade.

Don Olson Distribution

2645 16th Avenue, South
Minneapolis, MN 55407
(612)-724-2976
CONTACT: Don Olson **TOPICS:** New Age, Metaphysics **FOUNDED:** 1981 **TYPE OF BUSINESS:** New Age distributor **DESCRIPTION:** Wholesaler & distributor of New Age & Metaphysical products including books & magazines.

Earth Wisdom Music

314 East Liberty
Ann Arbor, MI 48104
(313)-769-0969
CONTACT: Minda Hart **TOPICS:** New Age **FOUNDED:** 1984 **TYPE OF BUSINESS:** New Age products **DESCRIPTION:** Wholesaler & distributor of New Age & Metaphysical products including books, magazines, cassettes & video tapes.

East West Books

807 Bloor Street, West
Toronto, Ontario M6G 1L8
Canada
(416)-530-1571
TOPICS: Witchcraft, New Age, Metaphysics **PUBLICATIONS:** *East West News*

Eastern News Distributors, Incorporated

250 West 55th Street
New York, NY 10019
(212)-649-4486
CONTACT: Margherita Tambini **TOPICS:** New Age **TYPE OF BUSINESS:** New Age magazines **DESCRIPTION:** Distributor of New Age & environmental magazines.

Encore Distribution

2219 Market Street
Denver, CO 80205
(303)-292-9333
CONTACT: Mark Noone, Buyer **TOPICS:** New Age **FOUNDED:** 1985 **DESCRIPTION:** Wholesaler & distributor of New Age music.

Entrepreneur Network Int.

2682 West Imperial Highway, Ste. 245
Inglewood, CA 90303
(213)-755-0453
CONTACT: Virgle Johnson **TOPICS:** New Age, Metaphysics **TYPE OF BUSINESS:** New Age products **DESCRIPTION:** Distributes New Age oriented how-to books & tapes.

Excelsior Incense Works, The

1413 Van Dyke Avenue
San Francisco, CA 94124
(415)-822-9124
CONTACT: Dipak Roy **TOPICS:** New Age, Metaphysics **FOUNDED:** 1965 **TYPE OF BUSINESS:** New Age products **DESCRIPTION:** Manufacturer, wholesaler & distributor of various forms of incense.

Exotic Minerals

P.O. Box 441
Felton, CA 95018
(408)-335-4036
CONTACT: Michael Sherer **TOPICS:** New Age

Falkynor Communications

4950 South West 70th Avenue
Davie, FL 33314-4201
(305)-791-1562
CONTACT: Gail C. Watson **TOPICS:** New Age **TYPE OF BUSINESS:** Publisher/Distributor **DESCRIPTION:** Publisher & distributor of New Age publications & tapes covering such topics as health-acupressure & reflexology, self-help & travel.

Feldenkrais Resources

P.O. Box 2067
Berkeley, CA 94702
(510)-525-1907
CONTACT: David Zemach Bersin **TOPICS:** New Age, Metaphysics **TYPE OF BUSINESS:** Producer tapes & books **DESCRIPTION:** Offers catalog of books & tapes of Feldenkrais materials & related books for those interested in Somatic Education. Advanced seminars.

Fine Print Distributors

6448 Highway 290E, Suite B104
Austin, TX 78723
(512)-452-8709
CONTACT: Ken Oakman **TOPICS:** New Age

G.T. International

1800 South Robertson Boulevard, #182
Los Angeles, CA 90035
(213)-551-0484 (213)-203-8598
CONTACT: Siri Ram Singh **TOPICS:** New Age, Holistic Health, Metaphysics, Herbalogy **OWNER:** Siri Ram Singh **TYPE OF BUSINESS:** New Age products **DESCRIPTION:** Offers health, metaphysical & New Age products such as herbs, vitamins, oils, perfumes, books, audio & video materials.

Gail Mayer Distribution

4987 Lake Bluff Road
West Bloomfield, MI 48033
(313)-683-0288
CONTACT: Gail Mayer **TOPICS:** New Age **OWNER:** Gail Mayer **TYPE OF BUSINESS:** New Age music **DESCRIPTION:** Distributes New Age music.

Genesis Reflections

P.O. Box 4111
Simi Valley, CA 93063
(805)-581-2241
CONTACT: Tom Massari **TOPICS:** New Age **FOUNDED:** 1986 **TYPE OF BUSINESS:** Tape distributor **DESCRIPTION:** Distributes a complete line of self-help tapes both wholesale & retail.

Global Peace Foundation

49 Summit Road
San Anselmo, CA 94960
(415)-258-9734
CONTACT: Raphael Ornstein, M.D. **TOPICS:** New Age, Metaphysics **FOUNDED:** 1986 **TYPE OF BUSINESS:** New Age distributor **DESCRIPTION:** Wholesaler & distributor of New Age & Metaphysical products including books, magazines, cassettes & video tapes. Sells mail-order.

Golden Lee Book Distributors

1000 Dean Street
Brooklyn, NY 11238
(718)-857-6333
CONTACT: Dennis Haritou, Buyer **TOPICS:** New Age, Metaphysics

Golden Spiral

Box 437
Boulder Creek, CA 95006
(408)-338-4488
CONTACT: Michael Moore, Pres. **TOPICS:** New Age, Metaphysics **OWNER:** Michael Moore **FOUNDED:** 1986 **TYPE OF BUSINESS:** New Age products **DESCRIPTION:** Offers tools that teach, inspire & delight. Products such as electronic & Earth oriented jewelry, toys that teach, etc. Works with Earth Save (John Robbins group) & Campaign For The Earth. Sells retail, wholesale & mail-order.

Goldenrod Distribution

5505 Delta River Drive
Lansing, MI 48906
(517)-323-4325
CONTACT: Terry Grant **TOPICS:** New Age, Metaphysics **FOUNDED:** 1973 **TYPE OF BUSINESS:** New Age music **DESCRIPTION:** Wholesaler & distributor of New Age music.

Gordon's Books

2323 Delgany Street
Denver, CO 80216
(303)-296-1830
CONTACT: Robbee Huseth **TOPICS:** New Age

Great Health

P.O. Box 1749
Brea, CA 92622
(714)-996-8600
CONTACT: Graham Bell **TOPICS:** New Age **TYPE OF BUSINESS:** Holistic Health products **DESCRIPTION:** Distributes books & products related to health.

Great Tradition, The

11270 Clayton Creek Road
Lower Lake, CA 95457
(707)-995-3906 (707)-492-9382 (800)-275-2606
CONTACT: Dawson Church **TOPICS:** New Age, Metaphysics, Spirituality, Holistic Health, Psychology **FOUNDED:** 1980 **TYPE OF BUSINESS:** Books & New Age products **DESCRIPTION:** Sells books around the world from numerous publishers on paranormal phenomena, spirituality, self-help, new age, religion, health, psychology & philosophy. Also New Age products such as incense, cards & calendars.

Happiness Unlimited

3274 Cabrillo Boulevard
Los Angeles, CA 90066
(213)-390-4589
CONTACT: Earle Reeves **TOPICS:** New Age, Metaphysics **FOUNDED:** 1984

Hare Krisna

711 East Blacklidge Drive
Tucson, AZ 85719
(602)-792-0630
CONTACT: Charles Cooksey **TOPICS:** New Age, Metaphysics **FOUNDED:** 1990 **TYPE OF BUSINESS:** New Age products **DESCRIPTION:** Wholesaler &

distributor of New Age & Metaphysical products including books, magazines, cassettes & video tapes.

Hazelden Educational Materials
Pleasant Valley Road
Box 176
Center City, MN 55012
(800)-257-0070 (800)-328-9000
CONTACT: Mark Crea TOPICS: New Age

Health Research
P.O. Box 70
Mokelumne Hill, CA 95245
TOPICS: Holistic Health, New Age, Metaphysics, Astrology, Occult, Parapsychology, Spirituality TYPE OF BUSINESS: New Age books DESCRIPTION: Distributors of rare, unusual, out-of-print & hard to find titles covering a wide range of New Age related subjects such as UFO's, health, metaphysics, etc.

Herbal Express
P.O. Box 181
Mound, MN 55364
(800)-435-4372 FAX (612)-472-1701
CONTACT: Alison Brown TOPICS: Herbalogy TYPE OF BUSINESS: Herbal products DESCRIPTION: Sells Jason Winter's herbal products retail & wholesale.

Home Health Products
1160 Millers Lane
Virginia Beach, VA 23451
(804)-491-2200 FAX (804)-491-8155
CONTACT: S.H. Knoll TOPICS: Holistic Health, Nutrition FOUNDED: 1981 TYPE OF BUSINESS: Health products DESCRIPTION: Distributes a quarterly catalog of natural health products for wellness & physical enhancement. Also offers health foods, crystals, tapes, books & oils.

Homeopathic Educational Services
2124 Kittredge Street
Berkeley, CA 94704
(415)-845-2206 (415)-653-9270
CONTACT: Dana Ullman TOPICS: Homeopathy FOUNDED: 1975 DESCRIPTION: Distributes sources & products related to homeopathy. PUBLICATIONS: *Homeopathic Educational Services*

Incense Sampler
P.O. Box 166186
Salt Lake City, UT 84116
(701)-363-3487
CONTACT: Apollo TOPICS: New Age FOUNDED: 1985 TYPE OF BUSINESS: New Age products DESCRIPTION: Distributor of incense.

Ingram Book Company
347 Redwood Drive
P.O. Box 17266
Nashville, TN 37217
(615)-793-5000 (800)-937-8100
CONTACT: Steven J. Mason, President TOPICS: New Age OWNER: Steven J. Mason FOUNDED: 1933 TYPE OF BUSINESS: New Age products DESCRIPTION: Wholesaler & distributor of New Age & Metaphysical products including books, magazines, cassettes & video tapes.

Inland Book Company
254 Bradley Street, P.O. Box 261

East Haven, CT 06512
(203)-467-4257
CONTACT: David Wilk, President TOPICS: New Age OWNER: David Wilk, Pres. FOUNDED: 1982 TYPE OF BUSINESS: New Age products DESCRIPTION: Wholesaler & distributor of New Age & Metaphysical products including books, magazines, cassettes & video tapes.

International Distributors
Shaker Street
North Sutton, NH 03260
(603)-927-4237
CONTACT: Georgia Blake TOPICS: New Age TYPE OF BUSINESS: Health products DESCRIPTION: Offers health related items including books, magazines & health products.

IPD International
674 Via de La Valle #204
Solana Beach, CA 92075-2462
(619)-481-5928
CONTACT: Luanne O'Loughlin TOPICS: New Age, Metaphysics FOUNDED: 1981 TYPE OF BUSINESS: New Age publications DESCRIPTION: Wholesaler & distributor of New Age magazines, cassettes & video tapes.

Irish World Imports
P.O. Box 98093
Lubbock, TX 79499
(800)-634-8554
CONTACT: Morgan O'Brien TOPICS: New Age OWNER: Morgan O'Brien TYPE OF BUSINESS: Mythology products DESCRIPTION: Offers New Age products related to mythology such as Acalla Greeting Cards & Legends of Ireland Posters.

Island Pacific NW
P.O. Box 999
Eastsound, WA 98245
(206)-376-5005
CONTACT: Diane Welty TOPICS: New Age TYPE OF BUSINESS: New Age products DESCRIPTION: New Age books & tapes. Publishes a catalog & a newspaper.

Jonathan Parker's Gateways Institute
P.O. Box 1778
Ojai, CA 93023
(805)-646-8148 FAX (805)-646-0980
CONTACT: Sylvia Thompson TOPICS: New Age, Metaphysics

Kable News Company, Incorporated
11 West 42nd Street, 28th Floor
New York, NY 10036
(800)-223-6640
CONTACT: Ed Skavkin TOPICS: New Age

Kampmann And Company, Incorporated
226 West 26th Street, 8th Floor
New York, NY 10001
(212)-727-0190
CONTACT: Eric Kampmann TOPICS: New Age

King Tut Trading
2123 Ridge Hollow
Houston, TX 77067
(713)-893-3062
CONTACT: Momtaz Louka TOPICS: New Age, Metaphysics OWNER: Momtaz Louka FOUNDED:

1988 TYPE OF BUSINESS: New Age products DESCRIPTION: Catalog & mail-order sales of Egyptian silver jewelry, greeting cards, book-marks, t-shirts & perfume oils.

Ladyslipper
P.O. Box 3124
Durham, NC 27715
(919)-683-1570 (800)-634-6044
CONTACT: Laurie Fuchs TOPICS: New Age, Metaphysics TYPE OF BUSINESS: Women's information DESCRIPTION: Offers written & audio materials concerning women. Produces New Age & women's spiritual music.

Levity
11116 Weddington Street
North Hollywood, CA 91601
(818)-506-7958
TOPICS: New Age, Metaphysics

Life Unlimited
8125 Sunset, #204
Fair Oaks, CA 95628
(916)-967-8442
TOPICS: New Age, Metaphysics OWNER: Tom Torian FOUNDED: 1973 TYPE OF BUSINESS: New Age products DESCRIPTION: Wholesaler & distributor of New Age & Metaphysical products including books, magazines, cassettes & video tapes.

Macoy Publishing Co.
P.O. Box 9759
Richmond, VA 23228
(804)-262-6551
CONTACT: H. Paul Scholte, IV TOPICS: Tarot, New Age PUBLICATIONS: *Builders: A Story And Study Of Freemasonry, Stonehenge: An Ancient Masonic Temple*

Meadowood Cottage
P.O. Box 86042
Portland, OR 97286
CONTACT: Virginia Winter TOPICS: Herbalogy, Holistic Health TYPE OF BUSINESS: Products of herbs & oils DESCRIPTION: Sells essential oils by vial or wholesale by the pound. Herbs for potpourri making, lotions for skin care, bulk wildflower seeds at $55 lb. & herb seeds at $ .50. Unlisted herbs, oils, lotions available on request. Send S.A.S.E.

Michael Ginsburg Distribution
1430 Tittsworth Road
Seymour, TN 37865
(615)-984-3803
CONTACT: Michael Ginsburg TOPICS: New Age

Mind & Miracles
16363 Cammi Lane
Ft. Lauderdale, FL 33326-1601
(305)-389-8076
CONTACT: Saul Steinberg TOPICS: New Age, Metaphysics, Parapsychology, Holistic Health OWNER: Saul Steinberg FOUNDED: 1984 TYPE OF BUSINESS: New Age books & videos DESCRIPTION: Produces New Age books & videos dealing with Parapsychology & Holistic Health. PUBLICATIONS: *We Want To Help*

Mountain Spirit
P.O. Box 368
Port Townsend, WA 98368
(206)-385-4491

TOPICS: New Age, Metaphysics, Holistic Health **FOUNDED:** 1987 **TYPE OF BUSINESS:** Holistic health products **DESCRIPTION:** Wholesaler & distributor of herbs & herbal items as well as New Age health related products.

Moving Books, Inc.
P.O. Box 20037
Seattle, WA 98102
(206)-762-1750 (800)-777-6683

CONTACT: Frank Kroger **TOPICS:** New Age, Metaphysics, Astrology, Witchcraft, Holistic Healing **OWNER:** Frank Kroger **FOUNDED:** 1979 **TYPE OF BUSINESS:** Book Wholesaler **DESCRIPTION:** Wholesaler & distributor of New Age, Metaphysical & health products including books, magazines, cassettes & video tapes.

Multi-Focus, Incorporated
1525 Franklin Street
San Francisco, CA 94109
(415)-673-5100

CONTACT: Renee Jones **TOPICS:** New Age, Metaphysics, Holistic Health **FOUNDED:** 1979 **TYPE OF BUSINESS:** Health products **DESCRIPTION:** Wholesaler & distributor of New Age educational health materials including video tapes.

Music New Hampshire
WGE - Forest Road
Hancock, NH 03449-0278
(603)-525-4423

CONTACT: Wayne Green **TOPICS:** New Age

Nagan Corporation
8011 North West 14th Street
Miami, FL 33126
(305)-477-3929 (800)-233-0766

TOPICS: New Age, Metaphysics **FOUNDED:** 1983 **TYPE OF BUSINESS:** New Age distributor **DESCRIPTION:** Wholesaler & distributor of New Age & Metaphysical products including books, magazines, cassettes & video tapes.

National Book Distributors
500 Kirst Boulevard
Troy, MI 48084
(313)-362-4400

TOPICS: New Age

National Council Of Natural Healing
42732 Blue Hills Drive
Lake Hughes, CA 93532
(805)-724-1814

CONTACT: Stuart White **TOPICS:** New Age

Native Scents
P.O. Box 5763
Taos, NM 87571
(505)-758-9656 (800)-748-2909 **FAX** (505)-758-9881

CONTACT: Alfred **TOPICS:** New Age

Naturegraph Publications, Inc.
3543 Indian Creek Road
P.O. Box 1075
Happy Camp, CA 96039
(916)-493-5353

CONTACT: Barbara Brown **TOPICS:** New Age, Metaphysics **FOUNDED:** 1946 **TYPE OF BUSINESS:** Book distributor **DESCRIPTION:** Distributor of

books concerned with Native American culture & nature. Sells through catalog.

Navarre Corporation
6750 West Broadway
Brooklyn Park, MN 55428
(612)-535-8333

CONTACT: Mike Gaffney **TOPICS:** New Age **FOUNDED:** 1983 **TYPE OF BUSINESS:** New Age music **DESCRIPTION:** Wholesaler & distributor of New Age music.

New Concepts Book, Tape And Video Distributors
P.O. Box 55068
9722 Pine Lake
Houston, TX 77055
(713)-465-7736

CONTACT: Jacqueline Ellis **TOPICS:** New Age, Metaphysics

New Leaf Distributing
5425 Tulane Drive, South West
Atlanta, GA 30336-2323
(404)-691-6996 (404)-601-6000 **FAX** (404)-699-7213

CONTACT: J. Hawkins (Books), A. Crutcher (Health) **TOPICS:** New Age, Metaphysics **FOUNDED:** 1975 **TYPE OF BUSINESS:** Book distributors **DESCRIPTION:** Distributes a large selection of New Age & Metaphysical books, magazines, music & related products to bookstores. Covers many varied New Age topics.

New Life Foundation
700 Wyoming Street
P.O. Box 684
Boulder City, NV 89005-0684
(702)-293-4444

CONTACT: Joan Phillips **TOPICS:** New Age **FOUNDED:** 1973 **TYPE OF BUSINESS:** New Age distributor **DESCRIPTION:** Wholesaler, distributor, publisher & retailer of New Age & Metaphysical products including books, magazines, cassettes & video tapes.

New Mind Productions
P.O. Box 5185
Jersey City, NJ 07305
(201)-434-1939

CONTACT: Armiya Nu'man **TOPICS:** New Age, Holistic Health

Northland Press
P.O. Box N
Flagstaff, AZ 86002
(602)-774-5251

CONTACT: Bruce Anderson **TOPICS:** New Age

Note-ably Yours
6865 Scarff Road
New Castle, OH 45344
(513)-845-8232

CONTACT: Ed And Judy Ireton **TOPICS:** New Age

Nutri-Books Corporation
P.O. Box 5793
Denver, CO 80217
(303)-778-8383

TOPICS: New Age, Holistic Health **DESCRIPTION:** Books & magazines related to the health field.

Omega Press

R.R. #1
P.O. Box 1030 D
New Lebanon, NY 12125
(518)-794-8181

CONTACT: Abi'l-Khayr **TOPICS:** New Age, Metaphysics

Omni Orion, Inc.
P.O. Box 232
Cassadaga, FL 32706
(904)-775-0454

CONTACT: Ernest M. Sekunna **TOPICS:** New Age, Metaphysics, Holistic Health **OWNER:** Ernest M. Sekunna **FOUNDED:** 1984 **TYPE OF BUSINESS:** Wholesale/Distributor **DESCRIPTION:** Wholesale/distributor of New Age books, tapes & gifts.

Os Brasileiros, Incorporated
140 West 69th Street, #51
New York, NY 10023
(212)-787-1787

CONTACT: Dennis Piunno **TOPICS:** New Age, Metaphysics **FOUNDED:** 1988 **TYPE OF BUSINESS:** Crystal & Jewelry **DESCRIPTION:** Wholesale distributors of crystals, minerals & New Age jewelry from Brazil. Carries a complete line of pyramids, obelisks, spheres & other worked items. Call for catalog, appointment or mail-order.

Pacific Pipeline, Incorporated
19215 66th Avenue South
Kent, WA 98032-1171
(206)-872-5523

CONTACT: Helen Ibach **TOPICS:** New Age, Metaphysics, Holistic Health **FOUNDED:** 1985 **TYPE OF BUSINESS:** Book distributors **DESCRIPTION:** Wholesaler & distributor of New Age & Metaphysical books as well as a magazine, cassettes & some video tapes.

Pacific Spirit Corp.
1334 Pacific Avenue
Forest Grove, OR 97116-2315
(503)-357-1566

CONTACT: Joseph Meyer **TOPICS:** New Age, Metaphysics, Spirituality, Holistic Health **OWNER:** Joseph Meyer **FOUNDED:** 1985 **TYPE OF BUSINESS:** Mail order catalog **DESCRIPTION:** Mail-order catalog featuring New Age, spiritual & alternative health items including imports from Tibet, Nepal, India & Baci. Also posters, books, statues, Ayurveda, herbs, cassettes & more.

Pacific Trade Group
94 - 527 Puahi Street
Waipahu, HI 96797
(808)-671-6735

CONTACT: Claudia Cannon **TOPICS:** New Age, Metaphysics, Spirituality **FOUNDED:** 1974 **TYPE OF BUSINESS:** New Age distributor **DESCRIPTION:** Wholesaler & distributor of New Age & Metaphysical items related to health, spirituality & Hawaii.

Pacifica Radio Archive
3729 Cahuenga Boulevard West
North Hollywood, CA 91604
(818)-506-1077

CONTACT: Bill Thomas **TOPICS:** New Age, Metaphysics **FOUNDED:** 1972 **TYPE OF BUSINESS:** Radio station **DESCRIPTION:** Operates 5 radio stations whose purpose is to promote peace. Also

distributes New Age & Metaphysical books & cassettes.

Paradigm Distribution
P.O. Box 16982
San Diego, CA 92116
(619)-563-1981
CONTACT: Karin Merry TOPICS: New Age, Metaphysics FOUNDED: 1984 TYPE OF BUSINESS: New Age distributor DESCRIPTION: Wholesaler & distributor of New Age & Metaphysical books, cassettes & video tapes.

Pathway Book Service
Lower Village
Gilsum, NH 03448
(603)-357-0236
CONTACT: F.N. Peter TOPICS: New Age, Metaphysics FOUNDED: 1979 TYPE OF BUSINESS: Book distributor DESCRIPTION: Wholesaler & distributor of New Age & Metaphysical books primarily to libraries.

Pegasus Products, Inc.
P.O. Box 228
Boulder, CO 80306
(303)-499-8434 (800)-527-6104
CONTACT: Fred Rubenfeld TOPICS: New Age, Holistic Health OWNER: Fred Rubenfeld TYPE OF BUSINESS: New Age products DESCRIPTION: Purpose is to create a greater harmony within the energetic parts of the body. Examines behavior patterns, beliefs & thoughts which will lead to diseases, emotional imbalance & spiritual disharmony. Sells gem & starlight elixirs, flower & gas essences. PUBLICATIONS: Catalog available for $1.00.

Portland News Company
270 Western Avenue
South Portland, ME 04106
(207)-774-2633
CONTACT: Leslie Carver TOPICS: New Age, Metaphysics FOUNDED: 1923 TYPE OF BUSINESS: New Age distributor DESCRIPTION: Wholesaler & distributor of New Age & Metaphysical products including books & magazines.

Prisma Products
Star Rt. 155
Wavecrest #C-109
Kaunakakai, HI 96748
(808)-558-8509
CONTACT: Alda Marian Jangl & James Jangl TOPICS: New Age, Metaphysics TYPE OF BUSINESS: New Age distributor DESCRIPTION: Sells New Age products wholesale & retail: Mood Jewelry pendants, keyrings & rings. Also authentic I Ching coins & New Age publications. PUBLICATIONS: *Ancient Legends Of Gems & Jewels, Birthstone Coloring Book*

Publishers Group West
4065 Hollis Street
P.O. Box 8843
Emeryville, CA 94608
(415)-658-3453
CONTACT: Charles Winton, President TOPICS: New Age

Pyramid Distributors
1577 Barry Avenue, Ste. 201
Los Angeles, CA 90025
(213)-207-2944

CONTACT: Michael Anderson, Pres. TOPICS: New Age OWNER: Michael Anderson TYPE OF BUSINESS: New Age products DESCRIPTION: Wholesale source for New Age music & pyramid energy products. Music division has tapes & CDs of high spirited & meditative music, self-help, guided meditation, environmental sounds, subliminals. Pyramid division has pyramids & energy related products.

Quality Books, Inc.
918 Sherwood Drive
Lake Bluff, IL 60044-2204
(312)-295-2010 (312)-295-2010
CONTACT: Tom Drewes, President TOPICS: New Age

Quartus Society
P.O. Box 1768
Boerne, TX 78006
(512)-537-4689
CONTACT: Dan Hutchinson TOPICS: New Age, Metaphysics TYPE OF BUSINESS: Distributor/Wholesaler DESCRIPTION: Distributor of New Age & Metaphysical books.

Quest Bookshops
306 West Geneva Road
P.O. Box 270
Wheaton, IL 60189-0270
(312)-665-0123
CONTACT: Von Braschler TOPICS: New Age, Metaphysics FOUNDED: 1927 TYPE OF BUSINESS: New Age products DESCRIPTION: Wholesaler & distributor of New Age & Metaphysical products including books, magazines, cassettes & video tapes. Publisher of books & the quarterly magazine Quest. Also produces a radio & TV program.

Rainbow Collective
P.O. Box 675
Orinda, CA 94563
(510)-532-1890 (510)-254-4730
CONTACT: Fred Smith, Pres. TOPICS: Channeling, Metaphysics OWNER: Fred Smith TYPE OF BUSINESS: Michael products DESCRIPTION: Retailer/wholesaler of Michael tapes & books.

Rainbow Innerprizes
2674 East Main Street, Suite C-273
Ventura, CA 93003-2899
(805)-652-0813
CONTACT: David Bitting TOPICS: New Age, Metaphysics FOUNDED: 1989 TYPE OF BUSINESS: New Age products DESCRIPTION: Wholesaler & distributor of New Age & Metaphysical products including books, magazines, cassettes & video tapes.

Rainbow Store/Earth Products Company
15368 Mowersville Road
Shippensburg, PA 17257
(717)-423-6701
CONTACT: James Berry TOPICS: Holistic Health, Meditation, Herbalogy, Crystals, Health Food OWNER: Theresa Berry TYPE OF BUSINESS: Natural Products DESCRIPTION: Offers Natural Products at wholesale: Organic Foods, Potpourri, Sachet, Oils, Soaps, Stationery, Pet Care Products, Hair Care Products, Smudge Sticks

Rare Treasures
4206 East Burnside

Portland, OR 97215
(503)-233-0133
CONTACT: Kathy Turner TOPICS: New Age FOUNDED: 1989 TYPE OF BUSINESS: New Age jewelry DESCRIPTION: Wholesaler & distributor of New Age & Metaphysical jewelry & crystals.

Redwing Book Company/Paradigm Publications
44 Linden Street
Brookline, MA 02146
(617)-738-4664
CONTACT: Martha Fielding TOPICS: New Age, Metaphysics, Holistic Health FOUNDED: 1986

Royal Publications
P.O. Box 5793
790 West Tennessee Avenue
Denver, CO 80223-2891
(303)-967-5171
CONTACT: Daniel Nidess TOPICS: New Age

Runeworks, The
P.O. Box 1320
Venice, CA 90294
(213)-399-3755
CONTACT: Bronwyn Jones TOPICS: Runes, Metaphysics TYPE OF BUSINESS: Metaphysical items DESCRIPTION: Sells wholesale & retail through their mail order catalog, The New Oracle. Offers audio cassettes, special sets of Runes, jewelry & books such as The Book Of Runes, The Book Of Rune Cards & Rune Play. PUBLICATIONS: *Book Of Rune: A Handbook For The Use Of An Ancient Oracle*

Salamander
P.O. Box 6031
Somerset, NJ 08873
TOPICS: Holistic Healing, Spirituality TYPE OF BUSINESS: New Age products DESCRIPTION: Sells books & supplies for healing & spiritual development. Free mail-order catalog.

Saul Borak, Incorporated
P.O. Box 21162
Woodhaven, NY 11421
(212)-969-0028
CONTACT: Saul Borak TOPICS: New Age, Metaphysics FOUNDED: 1976 TYPE OF BUSINESS: New Age crystal jewelry DESCRIPTION: Wholesaler & distributor of New Age & Metaphysical crystal jewelry.

SCB Distributors
501 Santa Monica Boulevard, Suite 601
Santa Monica, CA 90401
(213)-393-6422 FAX (213)-394-7986
CONTACT: Aaron Silverman TOPICS: New Age

Serendipity Couriers
470 Du Bois Street
San Rafael, CA 94901
(415)-459-4000
CONTACT: Richard Likins TOPICS: New Age, Metaphysics

Shabda
39110 Airport Road
Little River, CA 95456
(707)-937-3013
TOPICS: New Age, Metaphysics

Sheriar Press, Inc.
1414 Madison Street, So.
North Myrtle Beach, SC 29582
(803)-272-5333
TOPICS: New Age

Sigo Press
25 New Charoon Street, #8748
Boston, MA 02114
(617)-526-7064 (508)-281-4722 **FAX** (508)-283-6060
CONTACT: Kenneth H. Follette **TOPICS:** New Age,
Metaphysics, Holistic Health, Psychology **OWNER:**
Kenneth H. Follette **FOUNDED:** 1980 **TYPE OF
BUSINESS:** Book distributor **DESCRIPTION:**
Publishes & distributes own books & others on
Jungian Psychology & self-help. Also sells video
tapes. **PUBLICATIONS:** *C. G. Jung And The
Problem Of Evil: The Strange Trial Of Mr. Hyde,
Dream: Vision Of The Night, Meaning And
Significance Of Dreams, Black Madonna, Women
Dreaming-Into-Art, Grail Legend, Inward Journey*

Sirius Books And Crafts
2320 Young Street
Honolulu, HI 96826
(808)-947-4910
CONTACT: Larry Geller **TOPICS:** New Age,
Metaphysics

Small Changes
3443 12th Avenue West
Seattle, WA 98119-1608
(206)-282-3665
CONTACT: Shari Basom **TOPICS:** New Age,
Metaphysics, Holistic Health **FOUNDED:** 1977
TYPE OF BUSINESS: New Age products
DESCRIPTION: Wholesaler & distributor of New
Age & Metaphysical products including books,
magazines, cassettes & video tapes.

Small Press Distribution
1814 San Pablo Avenue
Berkeley, CA 94702-1624
(415)-549-3336
CONTACT: Lisa Domitrovich **TOPICS:** New Age

Software For Serenity
3038 North Mountain Avenue
Tucson, AZ 85719
(602)-881-1314 **FAX** (602)-744-7887
CONTACT: Rebecca Rizzo-Freedom **TOPICS:** New
Age, Metaphysics **OWNER:** Rebecca Rizzo-Freedom
FOUNDED: 1988 **TYPE OF BUSINESS:** New Age
products **DESCRIPTION:** Mail-order distributors of
educational materials helping people experience
inner peace. Offers Insight Cards, inspirational gifts
& stationery, Serenity God-Boxes, meditation &
hypnosis tapes, New Age music, computer software.
Wholesale & retail catalog.

St. Martin's Press, Inc.
175 Fifth Avenue
New York, NY 10010
(212)-674-5151 (800)-221-7945
TOPICS: Psychic **PUBLICATIONS:** *Mysticism And
Philosophy, Way Of Cartouche: An Oracle Of
Ancient Egyptian Magic, New Book Of Runes: A
Handbook For Use Of An Ancient Oracle, The
Enchanted Tarot*

Station Hill Press
Station Hill Road

Barrytown, NY 12507
(914)-758-5840
CONTACT: Cathy Lewis **TOPICS:** Holistic Healing,
Metaphysics **FOUNDED:** 1978 **PUBLICATIONS:**
*Rhythmic Integration: Wholeness & The Cycle Of
Change, Where Healing Waters Meet: Touching
The Mind & Emotions Through The Body,
Sportsmassage: Increasing Performance &
Endurance In 15 Popular Sports*

Sunstar Productions
P.O. Box 827
Kihei, HI 96753
(808)-879-6509
CONTACT: Michael Martin/Antoinette Pahia
TOPICS: New Age

Synektix
P.O. Box 64980-658
Dallas, TX 75206
(214)-692-6243
TOPICS: New Age, Metaphysics, Runes, Crystals
FOUNDED: 1989 **TYPE OF BUSINESS:**
Metaphysical gifts **DESCRIPTION:** Wholesaler of
New Age & Metaphysical gifts specializing in rune
stones, bags, crystals, jewelry & leather items. Also
sells mailing lists.

Talman Company
150 Fifth Avenue
New York, NY 10011
(212)-620-3182 **FAX** (212)-627-4682
CONTACT: Marilee Talman **TOPICS:** New Age
PUBLICATIONS: *Secret Of The Black
Chrysanthemum: Poetic Cosmology Of Charls
Olson & His Use Of C.G.Jung*

Tide-Mark Press, Limited
P.O. Box 280311
Hartford, CT 06128-0311
(203)-289-0363
CONTACT: Scott Kaeser **TOPICS:** New Age

Tree Frog Trucking Company
318 South West Taylor Street
Portland, OR 92704-2412
(503)-227-4760
CONTACT: Bill Kloster **TOPICS:** New Age

Triangle News Company, Incorporated
3498 Grand Avenue
Pittsburgh, PA 15225
(412)-771-4433
CONTACT: Andy Labisca **TOPICS:** New Age

Tucson Cooperative Warehouse
350 South Toole Avenue
Tucson, AZ 85701
TOPICS: New Age **TYPE OF BUSINESS:** New Age
products **DESCRIPTION:** New Age products related
to holistic health & homeopathy.

U.S. Games Systems, Inc.
179 Ludlow Street
Stamford, CT 06902
(203)-353-8400
CONTACT: Stuart Kaplan **TOPICS:** Tarot
PUBLICATIONS: *I Ching Cards, Encyclopedia Of
Tarot Vol. 1, Encyclopedia Of Tarot Vol. 2,
Encyclopedia Of Tarot Vol. 3*

Ubiquity Distributors

607 DeGraw Street
Brooklyn, NY 11217
(718)-875-5491 **FAX** (718)-875-8047
CONTACT: Joseph Massey **TOPICS:** New Age,
Metaphysics, Spirituality, Crystals, Herbalogy,
Holistic Health **OWNER:** John Massey **FOUNDED:**
1980 **TYPE OF BUSINESS:** Magazine distributor
DESCRIPTION: Wholesales nearly 800 magazines,
newspapers & journals in U.S. & Canada. Subjects:
politics, culture, New Age, health, feminism, fitness,
sports, spirituality, literature, travel, art, music, gay
lifestyle, gems, herbs, etc. Sells mail-order & to
stores.

Ultra Books, Inc.
P.O. Box 945
Oakland, NJ 07436
(201)-337-8787
CONTACT: Martin S. Ruback **TOPICS:** New Age
OWNER: Martin Ruback **TYPE OF BUSINESS:**
Wholesale to Bookstores **DESCRIPTION:** Wholesaler
of New Age, metaphysical, holistic & self-help books
& cassettes. Catalog & order form available.
Wholesale to stores & institutions only.

Union Of Tao And Man
1314 Second Street, #A
Santa Monica, CA 90401
(310)-576-1901
CONTACT: Master Ni **TOPICS:** Spirituality, Holistic
Health, Acupuncture, Herbalogy **OWNER:** Master
Ni **TYPE OF BUSINESS:** Distributor:books & tapes
DESCRIPTION: Distributor of books & tapes for The
Shrine Of The Eternal Breath Of Tao.
PUBLICATIONS: *Book Of Changes And The
Unchanging Truth, Gentle Path Of Spiritual
Progress, Attaining Unlimited Life: Teachings Of
Chuang Tzu, Way Of Integral Life*

Unique Books
4200 Grove Avenue
Gurnee, IL 60031
(312)-623-9171
CONTACT: Michael S. Isom **TOPICS:** New Age

Vision Works Distribution
P.O. Box 92, 16 Chapman Street
Greenfield, MA 01301
(413)-772-6569
CONTACT: Dick McLeester **TOPICS:** New Age,
Metaphysics **FOUNDED:** 1986 **TYPE OF BUSINESS:**
New Age products **DESCRIPTION:** Wholesaler &
distributor of New Age & Metaphysical products &
books.

Vitality Distributors
1010 North West 51st Place
Ft. Lauderdale, FL 33309
(305)-771-0445
CONTACT: Don Scarborough **TOPICS:** New Age
TYPE OF BUSINESS: New Age products
DESCRIPTION: New Age products & books, many
related to health. Sold primarily to health food stores.

Western Book Distributors
2970 San Pablo Avenue
Berkeley, CA 94702
(415)-849-2929
CONTACT: Tamara Austin **TOPICS:** New Age
TYPE OF BUSINESS: Health books **DESCRIPTION:**
Distributor of health related books.

White Dove International, Inc.

Box 1000
Taos, NM 87571
(505)-758-0500 FAX (505)-758-2265
CONTACT: Michael Vernon TOPICS: New Age
PUBLICATIONS: *Affirmations*

Whole Health Books

4735 Wunder Avenue
Trevose, PA 19047
(215)-322-2880
CONTACT: Mollie Kaufman TOPICS: New Age
TYPE OF BUSINESS: New Age products
DESCRIPTION: Distributor of New Age,
metaphysical & health related books & products.

Wishing Well Distributing

P.O. Box 529
Graton, CA 95444
(707)-823-9355 (800)-888-9355
CONTACT: Debra TOPICS: New Age, Metaphysics,
Occult FOUNDED: 1978

Womontyme Distribution Company

P.O. Box 50145

Long Beach, CA 90815-6145
(213)-429-4802 (800)-247-8903 FAX (213)-425-4258
CONTACT: Gwen Tucker TOPICS: New Age,
Spirituality, Holistic Healing OWNER: Janet Liss,
Gwenn Tucker FOUNDED: 1985 TYPE OF
BUSINESS: Wellness for women DESCRIPTION:
Offers Goddess spirituality, self-help & wellness
titles & audio tapes to bring healing to people
suffering from dysfunctional or traumatic
childhoods. Sells to stores through wholesale catalog
& to individuals through retail mail-order catalog.

Worldwide Media Service, Inc.

115 East 23rd Street
New York, NY 10010
(212)-420-0588
CONTACT: Ken Kaiman TOPICS: New Age,
Metaphysics TYPE OF BUSINESS: New Age rep
DESCRIPTION: Publisher's Rep offering many New
Age & metaphysical books.

Writers And Books

740 University Avenue

Rochester, NY 14607
(716)-473-2590
CONTACT: Todd Beers TOPICS: New Age
OWNER: Joel Flaherty TYPE OF BUSINESS: New
Age products DESCRIPTION: Literary organization
distributing numerous New Age books & tapes.

Z Tapes International

P.O. Box 728
Milton, WA 98354
(206)-952-4202 (206)-848-2052
CONTACT: Robert Draper, Pres. TOPICS: New Age,
Spirituality OWNER: Robert Draper TYPE OF
BUSINESS: New Age tapes DESCRIPTION:
Exclusive distributor for tapes on the teachings of
Zanzoona.

Zango Distributions

P.O. Box 6308
Albany, CA 94706
(415)-527-0187 FAX (415)-528-9342
CONTACT: Claudia Rosenthal TOPICS: New Age
TYPE OF BUSINESS: New Age products
DESCRIPTION: Distributes New Age books &
numerous types of music.

Products & Services

Listed in this section are individuals and companies offering New Age/Metaphysical related services and products. Many offer their product or service by mail-order or telephone. Catalogs are often available. Contact them for additional information.

2 M Communications Limited
121 West 27 Street #601
New York, NY 10001
(212)-741-1509
TOPICS: New Age, Metaphysics OWNER: Madeline Morel FOUNDED: 1982 TYPE OF BUSINESS: New Age services DESCRIPTION: Literary agents for New Age & Metaphysical books.

About Books
425 Cedar Street
Box 1500
Buena Vista, CO 81211
(719)-395-2459 FAX (719)-395-8374
TOPICS: New Age OWNER: Marilyn Ross TYPE OF BUSINESS: New Age services DESCRIPTION: Offers various services for the New Age industry such as marketing, publishing, etc.

Abracadabra Productions
310 East 46th Street
New York, NY 10017
CONTACT: Leslie Carr TOPICS: Palmistry, ESP, Tarot, Tea Leaves, Occult, Psychic, Metaphysics OWNER: Astounding Velma TYPE OF BUSINESS: Psychic Reading & lecture DESCRIPTION: Offers psychic readings, lectures & entertainment for parties or private consultations on topics such as How To Read Your Own Palm, Learn The Innermost Secrets Of Others, Excursion Into The Super Natural, & Exploration Of The Occult. Also magic, ESP, hypnosis, tarot, crystal ball, astrology, etc.

Abundant Life Seed Foundation
P.O. Box 772
Port Townsend, WA 98368
(206)-385-5660
TOPICS: Health Food

Accelerated Learning Institute
P.O. Box 8276
Silver Spring, MD 20910
(301)-587-8686
TOPICS: New Age TYPE OF BUSINESS: New Age products DESCRIPTION: Sells New Age products retail.

Adventures-Unlimited
P.O. Box 22
Stelle, IL 60919
(815)-253-6390 FAX (815)-256-2299
TOPICS: UFO's, Spirituality, New Age OWNER: David Hatcher Childress TYPE OF BUSINESS: Travel Expeditions DESCRIPTION: Offers travel expeditions, books & videos. Also operates Adventures Unlimited Press, publisher & distributors of unusual books on science, Archaeology, history & travel. Write for free catalog on anti-gravity, free energy devices, Lost Cities, Atlantis, Pyramid Power, Lemuria & secret societies.

Aeon Communications, Incorporated

P.O. Box 46155
Los Angeles, CA 90046
(213)-876-1729
TOPICS: New Age OWNER: Stefan Neilson FOUNDED: 1976 TYPE OF BUSINESS: New Age products DESCRIPTION: Personality Language & Winning Colors texts & workbooks for all ages. Offers books, videos, cassettes, posters, Christmas cards, communication cards & business manuals. Also Education Manuals for kindergarten to adult. Gives seminars & workshops entitled Winning Colors.

Aerial Phen Clipping Information
P.O. Box 9073
Cleveland, OH 44137
TOPICS: UFO's

Agroecology Program
University Of California
Santa Cruz, CA 95064
(408)-429-4140
TOPICS: Health Food

Alexander's Ink
81 North Katherine Drive
Ventura, CA 93003
(805)-643-9240
TOPICS: New Age OWNER: Nancy Alexander FOUNDED: 1983 TYPE OF BUSINESS: New Age art DESCRIPTION: Offers New Age art prints of mandalas.

All About Pyramids, Dowsing
P.O. Box 30305
Santa Barbara, CA 93105
TOPICS: New Age, Dowsing

All The Best Pet Care/ The Natural Pet Care Company
2713 East Madison
Seattle, WA 98112
(206)-329-8474 (800)-962-8266
TOPICS: Holistic Healing, New Age OWNER: Susan & Ira Moss TYPE OF BUSINESS: Mail Order Pet Supplies DESCRIPTION: Sells natural products for animals. Offers mail-order catalog, The Natural Pet Care Catalog. Workshops & products include natural foods & snacks, homeopathic & nutritional remedies, books & video tapes, enzyme supplements, toys, chews & grooming tools.

Allergy Filter Mfg.
57 Cooley Drive
Longmeadow, MA 01106-1397
(413)-567-0372
TOPICS: New Age, Holistic Health TYPE OF BUSINESS: Wholesalers of filters DESCRIPTION: Manufacturer & wholesaler of allergy filters for Bionaire, Bio-Medisphere & Boston Air Cleaners. Does not sell air purifiers. Write or call with model # of air purifier.

Alpha Omega Cassette Enterprises
516 South Oak Knoll, Suite 5
Pasadena, CA 91101
(818)-792-0220
TOPICS: New Age OWNER: Joe Brown FOUNDED: 1984 TYPE OF BUSINESS: New Age audio service DESCRIPTION: Offers recording, production, distribution & marketing services for New Age audio cassettes. Covers topics such as UFO's, channeling, etc.

Alpha-Bit
Box 465
Mapleton, OR 97453
(503)-268-4311
TOPICS: New Age DESCRIPTION: Health oriented restaurant.

Altara
P.O. Box 163841
Miami, FL 33116
(305)-279-7765
TOPICS: Crystals, Holistic Healing, Metaphysics, Channeling TYPE OF BUSINESS: Healing therapies DESCRIPTION: Offers private sessions, workshops & healing therapy using crystals. Also gives body, mind & spirit tune-ups through channeling & absent healing. Phone sessions available. Operates on a wholesale & retail basis.

Alternative Health Insurance Services
22704 Ventura Boulevard, Ste. 506
Woodland Hills, CA 91364
(818)-702-0888
TOPICS: New Age, Holistic Health OWNER: Sherry Gorman FOUNDED: 1984 TYPE OF BUSINESS: Insurance DESCRIPTION: Offers health insurance that covers holistic medicine as well as traditional medical services.

American Business Lists, Incorporated
5707 South 86th Circle
P.O. Box 27347
Omaha, NE 68127
(402)-331-7169
TOPICS: New Age

American Friends Service Committee
Summer Community Service In Mexico
1501 Cherry Street
Philadelphia, PA 19102
(215)-241-7104
TOPICS: New Age

American Hiking Society
1015 31st Street NW
Washington, DC 20007
(703)-385-3252
TOPICS: New Age

American Lists Council, Incorporated

88 Orchard Road, CN-5219
Princeton, NJ 08543
(201)-874-4300
TOPICS: New Age

American Marketing Resources
177-31 Edgerton Road
Jamaica, NY 11432
(718)-380-5826
TOPICS: New Age OWNER: Beverly Nadler TYPE OF BUSINESS: Marketing service DESCRIPTION: Offers New Age marketing resource services including consultations, training & networking.

American Pan-Indian Dance Workshops
Frank Turley
Route 10, Box 88C
Santa Fe, NM 87501
TOPICS: New Age

American Zionist Youth Foundation
Israel Program Center
515 Park Avenue
New York, NY 10022
(212)-751-6070
TOPICS: New Age

Analog Science Fiction/Science Fact
70 Riverdale Avenue
P.O. Box 4565
Greenwich, CT 06830
(203)-531-1091
TOPICS: New Age

Ananda Pilgrimages
14618 Tyler Foote Road
Nevada City, CA 95959
(800)-424-1055 FAX (916)-292-3488
TOPICS: Spirituality, Meditation, Yoga TYPE OF BUSINESS: Travel tours to India. DESCRIPTION: Conducts spiritual pilgrimages to India for meditation & contemplation on the life & teachings of Paramhansa Yogananda.

Angel Time with Suze Angel
P.O. Box 4693
Laguna Beach, CA 92652
(714)-494-4998 (714)-770-6002
TOPICS: Holistic Health DESCRIPTION: Mind/movement integration workshops and individual Feldenkrais lessons.

Arch-EEZ Institute For Back Health, Inc.
1011 East Ginter Road
Tucson, AZ 85706
(800)-326-2724
TOPICS: Holistic Health TYPE OF BUSINESS: Health products DESCRIPTION: Offers Archable-the body bridge used as a stretching & exercise device for meditation & stress release.

Archaeological Tours
30 East 42nd Street
Suite 1202
New York, NY 10017
(212)-986-3054
TOPICS: New Age

Arcturus Book Service
P.O. Box 831383
Stone Mountain, GA 30083

(404)-297-4624
TOPICS: UFO's TYPE OF BUSINESS: Books mail-order DESCRIPTION: Mail-order books on UFO's & related literature. Free catalog on request.

Ariel Press/Books Of Light
20 Doren Avenue
Hamden, CT 06517
(203)-287-9438
TOPICS: New Age

Aries Productions, Inc.
9633 Cinnabar Drive
P.O. Box 29396
Sappington, MO 63126
(314)-849-3722
TOPICS: Parapsychology, New Age, Metaphysics, Dowsing OWNER: Beverly C. Jaegers TYPE OF BUSINESS: New Age books & devices DESCRIPTION: Publishers of books & cassette tapes on numerous New Age topics. Also manufacturers of pendulums & dowsing aids. New Age subjects training aids & correspondence courses. ESP testing materials. Sells retail & wholesale only through mail-order. Catalog available. PUBLICATIONS: *Doorways To The Mind* TOPICS: Metaphysics, Spirituality TYPE: Book PUBLICATIONS: *Ultimate Energies* PUBLISHER: R. G. Jaegers EDITOR: Beverly Jaegers TOPICS: Parapsychology TYPE: Magazine DATE: 1973 SIZE: 8 1/2 x 11, 8 pgs. FREQ: Quarterly CIRC; 200 PRICE: $12.00 PRICE PER COPY: $3.00 DESCRIPTION: Covers topics such as ESP, PSI, dowsing, dreams, & mind development.

Art Community Project - Robin Lakes
P.O. Box 7077
Fullerton, CA 92634
TOPICS: New Age DESCRIPTION: Artist's community in Pahrump Valley, Nevada.

As-You-Like-It Library
915 East Pine, Ste. 401
Seattle, WA 98122
(206)-324-5177 (206)-329-1794
CONTACT: Philip Lipson TOPICS: Holistic Health, New Age, Metaphysics, Spirituality FOUNDED: 1961 TYPE OF BUSINESS: Lending Library DESCRIPTION: A co-operative lending library offering workshops & lectures on Astrology & Tarot. 12,000 books on Metaphysics, New Age, religion, ancient wisdom & topics relating to human potential. Membership $20 per year for mail-order members. Free book list. PUBLICATIONS: *As-You-Like-It Library* EDITOR: Phil Lipson TOPICS: Holistic Health, New Age, Metaphysics TYPE: Newsletter DATE: 1961 PRICE: $10.00 DESCRIPTION: New Age/Metaphysics newsletter devoted to book & video/audio tape reviews.

Asian Astrology Company
16617 S.E. 46th Street
Issaquah, WA 98027
TOPICS: Astrology OWNER: Elizabeth Selandia, Mike Munkasey TYPE OF BUSINESS: Astrology/computer data DESCRIPTION: Service computes individual's birthdata to give Astrology of I Ching reading. Also provides I Ching manual for individual to interpret own data. Send date, time & place of birth along with $37 for reading. 6 week processing time. Add $10 for day by day analysis from birthdate to birthdate, specify year.

Astro Intelligence U.S.A.
P.O. Box 40
Brewster, MA 02631
(508)-896-5081 (800)-544-4033 FAX (508)-896-5289
CONTACT: Liz Greene TOPICS: Astrology, Metaphysics, Psychology TYPE OF BUSINESS: Computerized Astrology DESCRIPTION: Offers astrological readings blended with Jungian psychology to produce computerized Psychological Horoscope Analysis. PUBLICATIONS: *Saturn, Relating, and The Outer Planets.*

Astrol-Items
6100 Westchester Park Drive, #803
P.O. Box 157
College Park, MD 20740
(301)-982-0518
TOPICS: Astrology OWNER: Jeanne A. Davis TYPE OF BUSINESS: Mail-order Astrology DESCRIPTION: Offers mail-order astrology items.

Astrolabe, Inc.
P.O. Box 1750
350 Underpass Road
Brewster, MA 02631
(508)-896-5081 (800)-843-6682 FAX (508)-896-5289
TOPICS: Astrology, Numerology, Metaphysics, New Age OWNER: Gary Christen TYPE OF BUSINESS: Astrology & Computers DESCRIPTION: Combines the practice of astrology with the technology of the computer. Offers 17 major software programs, books & astrological tools. Produces AstroAnalyst which studies astronomical cycles & Wall Street pricing. Object is to improve tools of Astrology. PUBLICATIONS: *Valliere's Natural Cycles Almanac*

Athene
6851 Bird Road
Miami, FL 33155
TOPICS: New Age DESCRIPTION: Sells New Age books & supplies.

Atlantean Antiquities Co.
230 W. 76th St., Ste. #2A
New York, NY 10023
TOPICS: New Age, Psychic OWNER: Michael Morgan FOUNDED: 1985 TYPE OF BUSINESS: New Age services DESCRIPTION: Offers workshops, lectures, tapes, private sessions & books covering topics such as Ancient Pre-History, Body Readings, Psychological & Emotional counselling for work, relationships, personal perspectives on life & the pursuit of happiness. Also conducts mystical tours to Egypt, England, Mexico & Napal. PUBLICATIONS: *Akhaden: The Atlantean News Journal* EDITOR: Michael Morgan TOPICS: Parapsychology, Occult TYPE: Journal DATE: 1987 FREQ: Monthly PRICE: $18.00

Atlantis Publications
P.O. Box 324
Carlsbad, CA 92018-0324
(619)-729-4133 FAX (619)-729-2326
TOPICS: New Age OWNER: Ed Krisher TYPE OF BUSINESS: New Age products DESCRIPTION: Offers New Age products such as affirmation cards.

Augury Press
P.O. Box 33054
Phoenix, AZ 85067-3054

(602)-971-7478

TOPICS: Psychic, Occult, Astrology, Tarot, Metaphysics, Witchcraft, Tea Leaves **OWNER:** Michael R. Allen **TYPE OF BUSINESS:** Mail-Ord. Occult Supplies **DESCRIPTION:** Sells Metaphysical & Occult books, supplies & services such as Astrology & Biorhythm readings. Also offers 900 line (1-900-454-1454) for 24 hour Tarot readings.

Aurora Book Companions
Box 5852
Denver, CO 80217

TOPICS: New Age, Homeopathy, Herbalogy, Vegetarianism, Nutrition **DESCRIPTION:** 2,000 books in the health field such as homeopathy, herbalogy, vegetarianism, nutrition & alternative therapies.

Authentic Marketing
25 West Fairview Avenue
Dover, NJ 07801
(201)-366-9326 (800)-777-4636

TOPICS: New Age, Metaphysics, Psychic **OWNER:** Dan Kassell **FOUNDED:** 1986 **TYPE OF BUSINESS:** Marketing services **DESCRIPTION:** Intuitive Right Livelihood Counseling, psychic business consulting. Offers marketing services & consulting in the New Age & Metaphysical fields. Counsels on job, career or business by telephone. Sliding scale fees.

Awake-in-Dream Creations
13863 Highland Drive
Grass Valley, CA 95945
(916)-272-1975

CONTACT: Daniel B. Holeman **TOPICS:** New Age **TYPE OF BUSINESS:** New Age products **DESCRIPTION:** Deals in visionary art, New Age mission, dolphin greeting cards, Member Brotherhood of Love.

Azomite Unlimited
3735 Malibu Country Drive
Malibu, CA 90265

TOPICS: New Age, Holistic Health **DESCRIPTION:** Natural mineral food product supplement from organic seabed.

B & B Publishing Service
P.O. Box 765
Middletown, CA 95461
(707)-987-0233

CONTACT: Tim And Libby Baltrusch **TOPICS:** New Age **FOUNDED:** 1988 **TYPE OF BUSINESS:** Publishing services **DESCRIPTION:** Offers various editorial & publishing services for the New Age field.

Beneficial Insectary
14751 Oak Run Road
Oak Run, CA 96069
(916)-472-3715

TOPICS: Health Food

Benson Promotions, Inc.
7762 East Gray Road, # 400
Scottsdale, AZ 85260

TOPICS: Holistic Health, Health Food, Nutrition **TYPE OF BUSINESS:** Weight loss program **DESCRIPTION:** Offers Pathway 30-day Nutritional Weight Management System, guaranteed to help the user lose weight & keep it off. Products are all natural, organically grown & high in fiber.

Biological Journeys
1696 Ocean Drive
McKinleyville, CA 95521
(707)-839-0179 (800)-548-7555

TOPICS: New Age

Biological Urban Gardening Services
P.O. Box 76
Citrus Heights, CA 95611
(916)-726-5377

TOPICS: Health Food **PUBLICATIONS:** *B.U.G.S. Flyer Newsletter* **TOPICS:** Health Food **TYPE:** Newsletter

Biotactics
7765 Lakeside Drive
Riverside, CA 92509
(714)-685-7681

TOPICS: Health Food

Bodoh Gems
Box 648, Highway 106
Edgerton, WI 53531

TOPICS: New Age, Crystals **DESCRIPTION:** Sells quartz crystal balls.

Body Tools
15829 Haynes Street
Van Nuys, CA 91406
(818)-908-9155 (800)-845-6202

CONTACT: Ken Kaufman **TOPICS:** New Age, Holistic Health **DESCRIPTION:** Sells portable massage tables & other health related New Age products.

Bodywork Emporium
602 Old Coast Highway 101
Leucadia, CA 92024
(619)-942-9565

TOPICS: New Age, Holistic Health **DESCRIPTION:** Offers holistic health classes, therapy & equipment.

Boji Stones
Box 156, West Side Station
Worcester, MA 01602
(617)-791-1666

TOPICS: Holistic Health **DESCRIPTION:** Boji Stones contain balanced energy. Available in smooth or multi-faceted & various sizes.

Book Barn, The
410 Delaware
Leavenworth, KS 66048
(913)-682-6578

CONTACT: Barbara Or Bob Spears **TOPICS:** New Age

Book Call
59 Elm Street
New Canaan, CT 06840
(800)-255-2665

CONTACT: Faye Dewitt **TOPICS:** New Age **TYPE OF BUSINESS:** Mail-order book service **DESCRIPTION:** Offers retail telemarketing mail-order book sales.

Book Marketing Group
1106 Main Street
Huntington Beach, CA 92648
(714)-960-7700

CONTACT: Peggy Glenn **TOPICS:** New Age

Book Of The Month Club

485 Lexington Avenue
New York, NY 10017
(212)-867-4300

TOPICS: New Age

Book Production Associates
Box 3289
Portland, OR 97208
(503)-281-4486

CONTACT: Dick Mort/Beth Howell **TOPICS:** New Age **TYPE OF BUSINESS:** Publishing services **DESCRIPTION:** Offers complete publishing services to the New Age field.

Bookmarket
4156 Elm Avenue
Brookfield, IL 60513
(708)-485-3800

CONTACT: Mark Habrel **TOPICS:** New Age **FOUNDED:** 1989 **TYPE OF BUSINESS:** Marketing services **DESCRIPTION:** Offers a full marketing service for New Age books.

Books Of Light
3854 Mason Road
P.O. Box 249
Canal Winchester, OH 43110
(614)-837-8263 (800)-336-7769

CONTACT: Leslie Swanson **TOPICS:** New Age, Occult **TYPE OF BUSINESS:** Book club

Bradley Communications
P.O. Box 299
Haverford, PA 19041
(215)-896-6146

CONTACT: Bill Harrison **TOPICS:** New Age **TYPE OF BUSINESS:** Media report services **DESCRIPTION:** Publishes & distributes monthly interview reports to radio & TV producers.

Brethern Volunteer Service
1451 Dundee Avenue
Elgin, IL 60120
(312)-742-5100

TOPICS: New Age

Bridge Of Beauty
2160 East Fry, #426
Sierra Vista, AZ 85635
(602)-378-0166

CONTACT: Bob Brock **TOPICS:** New Age, Metaphysics **FOUNDED:** 1987 **TYPE OF BUSINESS:** New Age art **DESCRIPTION:** New Age art company. Producers of occult & shamanic art reproductions.

Business Plans Plus
8663 Hollyhock Lane
Lafayette, CO 80026
(303)-494-1177

CONTACT: Faye Nelson **TOPICS:** New Age, Metaphysics **FOUNDED:** 1984 **TYPE OF BUSINESS:** Business information **DESCRIPTION:** Offers written information on how to start a New Age business.

Butterbrooke Farm
78 Barry Road
Oxford, CT 06483
(203)-888-2000

TOPICS: Health Food

CAMA
1710 Highway 35
Ocean, NJ 07712

(908)-531-7838

CONTACT: Richard Reinhart and Harriet Rosen TOPICS: New Age TYPE OF BUSINESS: Mailing list services DESCRIPTION: Offers mailing lists for the New Age field.

Cambridge Institute For Better Vision

65 Wenham Road
Topsfield, MA 01983
(800)-372-0020

TOPICS: Holistic Healing TYPE OF BUSINESS: Health techniques DESCRIPTION: Offers techniques for improving vision through simple relaxation & muscle-control exercises which only take minutes each day.

Camp Joy

131 Camp Joy Road
Boulder Creek, CA 95006
(408)-338-3651

TOPICS: Health Food

Canby's Camera

Box 4260
Sedona, AZ 86336
(602)-282-2069

CONTACT: Dick Canby TOPICS: New Age, Metaphysics FOUNDED: 1964 TYPE OF BUSINESS: Photographic services DESCRIPTION: Provides photographic services & thousands of in-stock photos with New Age related themes.

Canyon Explorations

Box 310
Flagstaff, AZ 86002
(602)-774-4559

TOPICS: New Age

Caracol Tours

P.O. Box 17
Erwinna, PA 18920
(215)-847-5719

TOPICS: New Age

Caryn M. Carangelo

70 Craigie Street
Somerville, MA 02143
(617)-776-8755

TOPICS: New Age, Metaphysics OWNER: Caryn M. Carangelo FOUNDED: 1989 TYPE OF BUSINESS: New Age representative DESCRIPTION: New Age Rep servicing retail stores. Reps numerous & varied types of New Age products.

Cascadian Farm

P.O. Box 568
Concrete, WA 98235
(206)-853-8175

TOPICS: Health Food

CDI Communications Group

860 Via de lla Paz, Suite B-2
Pacific Palisades, CA 90272
(213)-454-4406

CONTACT: John Raatz TOPICS: New Age TYPE OF BUSINESS: Communication services DESCRIPTION: Offers advertising & marketing services for New Age products & services.

Celebration Of Life

P.O. Box 152047
San Diego, CA 92115
(619)-465-5683

CONTACT: Barbara Dill TOPICS: New Age, Metaphysics FOUNDED: 1978

Celestial Dynamics

P.O. Box 17577
Asheville, NC 28816
(704)-254-5510 (800)-289-5510

TOPICS: Astrology TYPE OF BUSINESS: Astrological product DESCRIPTION: World time/space chart & day-by-day calendar of our planetary neighborhood.

Center For Global Education

Augsburg College
731 21st Avenue South
Minneapolis, MN 55454
(612)-330-1159

TOPICS: New Age

Center For Studies Of The Person

131 Camino Alto, Suite D
Mill Valley, CA 94941
(415)-381-0553

TOPICS: New Age

Center For Third World Organizing

3861 Martin Luther King, Jr., Way
Oakland, CA 94609
(415)-654-9601

TOPICS: New Age

Central Distribution Services

145 West Wisconsin Avenue
P.O. Box 368
Neenah, WI 54957-9976
(800)-558-5011

CONTACT: Wayne Nemecek TOPICS: New Age TYPE OF BUSINESS: Fulfillment services DESCRIPTION: Offers fulfillment services for publishers. Handles New Age books.

Ceremonies For Transformation

2801 Rodeo Road, Suite 623
Santa Fe, NM 87505
(505)-438-0468

CONTACT: Judith Polich TOPICS: New Age FOUNDED: 1988

Cerro Gordo Town Forum

Dorena Lake, Box 596
Cottage Grove, OR 97424

CONTACT: Chris Canfield, Fred Ure TOPICS: New Age, Metaphysics

Charles G. Possick

9967 57th Avenue North
St. Petersburg, FL 33708
(813)-392-3119

TOPICS: New Age, Metaphysics

Chelsea Forum

215 Park Avenue, South
New York, NY 10003
(212)-420-6000

TOPICS: New Age TYPE OF BUSINESS: Agency for lecturers DESCRIPTION: Agency representing New Age lecturers.

Christina Hopf-Lovette

1345 Edgewood Road
Redwood City, CA 94062
(415)-369-6286

TOPICS: New Age OWNER: Christina Hopf-Lovette TYPE OF BUSINESS: Consultant DESCRIPTION: Offers marketing consultations.

Church Of Religious Science

117 North Pomona
Fullerton, CA 92632
(714)-525-1126

CONTACT: Gail Frichen TOPICS: New Age, Metaphysics FOUNDED: 1962

Citizen Action

1300 Connecticut Avenue NW
Room 401
Washington, DC 20036
(202)-857-5153

TOPICS: New Age

Citizen Exchange Council

12 West 31st Street
New York, NY 10001
(212)-643-1985

TOPICS: New Age

CMG Information Services

50 Cross Street
Winchester, MA 01890-9971
(617)-729-7920

TOPICS: New Age

Community Referral Service (C.R.S.)

P.O. Box 2672
Eugene, OR 97402

TOPICS: New Age TYPE OF BUSINESS: Community Information DESCRIPTION: Provides information on alternative communities & contacts for forming new ones. PUBLICATIONS: *New Age Community Guidebook* TOPICS: New Age TYPE: Directory DATE: 1985 DESCRIPTION: Contains articles & resources on 210 communities in the U.S. & around the world.

Comp-Type, Incorporated

155 Cypress Street
Fort Bragg, CA 95437
(707)-964-9520

CONTACT: John Fremont TOPICS: New Age, Metaphysics FOUNDED: 1975 TYPE OF BUSINESS: Publishing services DESCRIPTION: Offers full scale publishing services covering every aspect of production.

CompCare Publishers

2415 Annapolis Lane
Minneapolis, MN 55441-3683
(800)-328-3330

TOPICS: New Age TYPE OF BUSINESS: Mail-order products DESCRIPTION: Sells mail-order.

Conference Book Service

80 Early Street
Alexandria, VA 22304

TOPICS: New Age TYPE OF BUSINESS: Sponsors conferences DESCRIPTION: Organizes conferences for the pubishing industry.

Connecting Link, The

827 Grant Street
Denver, CO 80203
(303)-831-6085

CONTACT: Judith Mahrer, M.A. TOPICS: New Age TYPE OF BUSINESS: Business services DESCRIPTION: Offers various business services for

New Age oriented companies such as marketing & sponsoring of workshops & events.

Connections, Incorporated
2552 East Ovid
Des Moines, IA 50317
(515)-265-0943
CONTACT: Scott A. Arnold TOPICS: New Age, Metaphysics FOUNDED: 1990

Conservatory Of American Letters
P.O. Box 88
Thomaston, ME 04861
(207)-354-6550
CONTACT: Robert W. Olmsted TOPICS: New Age

Cosma
44 University Heights, #B
Burlington, VT 05401
(802)-658-6782
TOPICS: New Age, Occult TYPE OF BUSINESS: New Age products DESCRIPTION: New Age tools such as stained glass pyramids, pendulums & crystal wands.

Council Oak Books
1428 South St. Louis
Tulsa, OK 74120
(918)-587-6454
CONTACT: Gretchen Collins TOPICS: New Age, Metaphysics FOUNDED: 1984

Country Life Natural Foods
Oak Haven
Pullman, MI 49450
(616)-236-5011
TOPICS: Health Food

Coyote Found Candles
P.O. Box 632
Port Townsend, WA 98363
(206)-385-4142
TOPICS: New Age DESCRIPTION: Specializing in fine handmade/manufactured candles for institutions & retailers.

Create Harmony Within
P.O. Box 162
Stanton, CA 90680
(714)-821-4894
TOPICS: Herbalogy, Holistic Health DESCRIPTION: Offering regenerative herbs, quality foods & quality living.

Creative Basics
Box 5041
Lincoln, NE 68510
(402)-488-4026
CONTACT: Shirley Maly TOPICS: New Age, Metaphysics FOUNDED: 1984 TYPE OF BUSINESS: New Age consultant DESCRIPTION: Marketing consultant for the New Age field.

Creative Change Consultants
3537 Old Conejo Road, Suite 13
Newbury Park, CA 91320
(805)-499-8511
CONTACT: Barbara Dobrin, Ph.D. TOPICS: New Age, Metaphysics FOUNDED: 1982 TYPE OF BUSINESS: New Age consultant DESCRIPTION: Business consultant for the New Age field.

Creative Connection
8114 Barbour Manor Drive

Louisville, KY 40241-1549
(502)-348-0958
CONTACT: Paul Sympson TOPICS: New Age FOUNDED: 1988

Creative Growth Unlimited
510 West Union Street
Newark, NY 14513
TOPICS: New Age, Holistic Health, Spirituality OWNER: Renee Vandermark TYPE OF BUSINESS: New Age conferences DESCRIPTION: Organizes & coordinates New Age conferences.

Creative Service Company
3136 Altura Avenue
La Crescenta, CA 91214
(818)-957-5580
CONTACT: Randall Davis TOPICS: New Age TYPE OF BUSINESS: New Age services DESCRIPTION: Public relations company specializing in New Age entertainment & music.

Cross Seed Company
HC-69
Box 2
Bunker Hill, KS 67626
(316)-483-6163
TOPICS: Health Food, Holistic Health OWNER: Marlin E. Cross FOUNDED: 1943 TYPE OF BUSINESS: Organic grains & cereals DESCRIPTION: Organically grown grains, cereals, sprouting seeds & beans.

Crystal Adventures
1417 15th Street
San Francisco, CA 94103
(415)-864-1050
TOPICS: Crystals DESCRIPTION: Offers tours to Brazil's Diamantina crystal mining region & conducts digs for crystals.

Crystal Awareness Group - Perth
Seekers Centre
44 Barker Road
Subiaco W.A.,
Australia
(09) 381 5164
TOPICS: Crystals, Holistic Healing DESCRIPTION: Group researching the healing aspects of crystals & gems.

Crystal Brokers Unlimited
2915 Kavanaugh Boulevard, #390
Little Rock, AR 72205
(501)-375-7862
TOPICS: Crystals DESCRIPTION: Offers crystal mining tours & services.

Crystal Congress, The
P.O. Box 5442
Mill Valley, CA 94942
(415)-388-8355
CONTACT: Sunni Kerwin TOPICS: New Age, Metaphysics FOUNDED: 1986

Crystal Connection
781 Bragg Street
Fond du Lac, WI
(414)-923-6603
CONTACT: Vicki Hillebrand TOPICS: New Age FOUNDED: 1988

Crystal Dreams

2048 Clairmont Terrace
Atlanta, GA 30359
(404)-633-4762
CONTACT: Nancy LaValley TOPICS: New Age FOUNDED: 1985

Crystal Journeys
9 Humewood Court #5
Toronto ON, M6C 1C9
Canada
(416)-658-0663
CONTACT: Joseph Cohen TOPICS: Crystals DESCRIPTION: Sponsors tours to energy sites around the world.

Crystal Magique
P.O. Box 29201
Oakland, CA 94604
(415)-891-9863
CONTACT: Lynda L. Luckey TOPICS: Crystals DESCRIPTION: Offers in-home crystal parties.

Crystal Miners Bed And Breakfast Inn
P.O. Box 65
Pencil Bluff, AR 71965
(501)-326-4678
TOPICS: Crystals DESCRIPTION: Offers tours & lodging to the Blue Phantom Mine in Arkansas.

Crystal Moon
P.O. Box 580
Belmont, CA 94002
(415)-595-4144
TOPICS: Crystals, Metaphysics DESCRIPTION: One-of-a-kind and custom crystal jewelry.

Crystalove
116 West Houston Street
New York, NY 10012
(212)-473-6947
CONTACT: Melissa Hill TOPICS: Crystals DESCRIPTION: Offers guided tours to Brazilian crystal mines & forming an alternative healing center in Brazil.

Daffodil Productions/Elizabeth Caulder & Associates
13165 Deming Avenue
Downey, CA 90242
(310)-531-6159
TOPICS: New Age OWNER: Elizabeth Caulder TYPE OF BUSINESS: Public Relations Company DESCRIPTION: Public Relations service specializing in the Human Potential Field. Provides individuals & companies with access to all types of media coverage such as talk shows on radio & T.V. locally & nationally. Active in the human potential movement for 20 years.

Datalang Associates
54 Atherton Street
Somerville, MA 02143
(617)-666-3260
CONTACT: George Langley TOPICS: New Age

David & Davidson, Inc.
42-62 Kissena Boulevard, #1A
Flushing, NY 11355
(718)-359-7788 FAX (718)-463-0808
TOPICS: Acupuncture, Holistic Health OWNER: David P.J. Hung, Pres. FOUNDED: 1991 TYPE OF BUSINESS: Acupuncturists DESCRIPTION:

Acupuncturists & members of the American Acupuncture Association. Sells 15 volume set of video tape specializing in the study of Traditional Chinese Acupuncture & Moxibustion known as China Zhenjiuology.

Deer Valley Farm
RD 1
Guilford, NY 13780
(607)-764-8556
TOPICS: Health Food

Deja Vu Shop
23 Enfield Street
Enfield, CT 06082
(203)-745-1823
CONTACT: Rachel Z. Salvas TOPICS: New Age
FOUNDED: 1988

Delphi Learning Systems
Box 6
Batesville, VA 22924
(703)-456-6544
TOPICS: New Age, Channeling, Spirituality
OWNER: Alan Mesher, Pres. FOUNDED: 1985
TYPE OF BUSINESS: Mail-order products
DESCRIPTION: Mail-order catalog offering channeled tapes, books & programs for personal & spiritual development. Tapes have high powered healing energy on them. Consultations available by phone.

Denby Point Lodge
Star Route 1, Box 241
Mt. Ida, AR 71957
(501)-867-3651
CONTACT: Colleen Bourque TOPICS: Crystals
DESCRIPTION: Resort in crystal mining area offering vegetarian meals, classes, gift shop & crystal digs for Denby Point crystals.

Dental-Info
2509 North Campbell
Tucson, AZ 85719
TOPICS: New Age, Holistic Health DESCRIPTION: Provides information on self-help dentistry.

Diamond K Enterprises
RR 1
Box 30A
St. Charles, MN 55972
(507)-932-4308
TOPICS: Health Food

Diane Loffmin Marketing
2896 Waterford Drive South
Deerfield Beach, FL 33442-5971
(407)-392-5278
TOPICS: New Age, Metaphysics OWNER: Diane Loffmin FOUNDED: 1989 TYPE OF BUSINESS: Marketing service DESCRIPTION: Full service marketing company specializing in New Age products.

Direct Mail List Rates And Data
3004 Glenview Road
Wilmette, IL 60091
(800)-323-4588
CONTACT: James Lilly TOPICS: New Age

Direct Marketing Club
1100 Park Central Boulevard, South
Pompano Beach, FL 33064-2213
(305)-974-7800

TOPICS: New Age

Directions Unlimited
P.O. Box 343-J
Wood-Ridge, NJ 07075-0343
(201)-939-2871
TOPICS: New Age OWNER: Joseph Abbott, Jr.
FOUNDED: 1986 TYPE OF BUSINESS: New Age mail-order DESCRIPTION: Mail-order company which markets New Age books, tapes & crystal balls. Promotes message: Life does not have to be a struggle if one knows how to contact the Self - the underlying reality of every personality.
PUBLICATIONS: *Absolute Power* EDITOR: Joseph Abbott, Jr. TOPICS: New Age TYPE: Book, 224 pgs. PRICE: $26.50 DESCRIPTION: Self-help program using a mind-expansion system called Feedback Amplification which teaches people how to use their dormant powers & unfold their latent abilities.

Discovery Center
2940 North Lincoln Avenue
Chicago, IL
(312)-348-8120
CONTACT: Bob Wagner TOPICS: New Age, Metaphysics FOUNDED: 1978

Discovery Center NYC, Incorporated
245 West 72nd Street #2
New York, NY 10023
(212)-877-0677
TOPICS: New Age TYPE OF BUSINESS: Educational courses DESCRIPTION: Offers adult education courses on many New Age related topics.

Drawing Room
1010 Damrosch Street
Largo, FL 33641
(000)-531-8523
CONTACT: Adele M. Sgro TOPICS: New Age TYPE OF BUSINESS: New Age art DESCRIPTION: Commercial & graphic art company serving the New Age field.

Dream Network
333 West 21st Street 2FW
New York, NY 10011
CONTACT: Wade Greyfox TOPICS: New Age

Dryad Graphics
2161 Hayes Street
San Francisco, CA 94117
(415)-668-0204
TOPICS: New Age OWNER: Scott Dryad TYPE OF BUSINESS: Computer graphics service DESCRIPTION: Computer graphics service specializing in images of goddesses.

Dutch Mill Cheese Shop
2001 North Date Road 1
Cambridge City, IN 47327
(317)-478-5847
TOPICS: Health Food

Earth Herbs Mail Order Catalog/Department A
3844 West Channel Islands Boulevard, 148
Oxnard, CA 93035
(805)-984-6656
TOPICS: Herbalogy, Holistic Health DESCRIPTION: Herbal health and body care products from around the world, $2.00.

Eartheart
P.O. Box 1443
Venice, CA 90294
CONTACT: Jim Berenholtz TOPICS: New Age, Metaphysics FOUNDED: 1988

Earthstar Foundation
2635 West First Avenue, #6
Vancouver, BC, V6K 1H1
Canada
(604)-733-5810
CONTACT: Michael Aze TOPICS: Crystals DESCRIPTION: Explores geomancy, works with quartz crystals & conducts tours to sacred sites.

Easy Does It Catering
13630 Ventura Boulevard
Sherman Oaks, CA 91423
(818)-986-9344
TOPICS: Health Food, Vegetarianism DESCRIPTION: Homemade catering offering vegetarian and non-vegetarian dishes.

Ecco Bella
6 Provost Square
Suite 602
Caldwell, NJ 07006
(201)-226-5799
TOPICS: Holistic Health TYPE OF BUSINESS: Mail-order products DESCRIPTION: Offers health related mail-order products.

Ecological Environments/Ecological Essentials
P.O. Box 854
Knoxville, TN 37901
(615)-588-7700
TOPICS: New Age DESCRIPTION: An natural ecological approach to interior design & furnishings.

Ecology Action
19550 Walker Road
Willits, CA 95490
TOPICS: Health Food PUBLICATIONS: *Bountiful Gardens Catalogue* TOPICS: Health Food TYPE: Catalog DESCRIPTION: Growing and Gathering Your Own Fertilizer, The Self-Sufficient Gardener, & Companion Plants and How To Use Them.

Ecopeace Media Network
P.O. Box 19592
Portland, OR 97219
(503)-745-5163
TOPICS: New Age, Metaphysics DESCRIPTION: Center for ecological issues, projects & information. Provides eco-action hotline.

Ed Sloan
224 73rd Street
Virginia Beach, VA 23451
(804)-428-1067
TOPICS: New Age, Metaphysics FOUNDED: 1980
TYPE OF BUSINESS: Business consultants DESCRIPTION: Marketing & business consultants helping companies raise their spiritual standards.

Elephant And Associates
c/o Aspen Travel
P.O. Box 2363
Aspen, CO 81611
(303)-923-3254
TOPICS: New Age

Ellen D. Steinberg
1920 South Locust
Denver, CO 80224
(303)-759-9403
TOPICS: New Age, Metaphysics **TYPE OF BUSINESS:** Consultant **DESCRIPTION:** New Age art marketing consultant.

Encinitas Imports
P.O. Box 419-A
Encinitas, CA 92024
(619)-436-9589
TOPICS: New Age **DESCRIPTION:** Offers East Indian musical instruments such as sitars, tablas, tanpuras & harmoniums.

Energies, Trends, Cycles, Inc.
P.O. Box 76691
Atlanta, GA 30358
(404)-458-6776
TOPICS: Astrology **OWNER:** Pat Esclavon Hardy **FOUNDED:** 1979 **TYPE OF BUSINESS:** Financial Astrology **DESCRIPTION:** Specializes in financial trend & cycle forecasting for individuals & companies using Astrology. Focus is to create opportunities for people to have access to information that enhance their perspective concerning personal & business issues.

Environmental Awareness Products
3600 Goodwin Road
Ionia, MI 48846
(517)-647-2535
TOPICS: New Age **TYPE OF BUSINESS:** Mail-order products **DESCRIPTION:** Offers mail-order products related to the benefit of the environment.

Esalen Institute
131 Camino Alto, Suite D
Mill Valley, CA 94941
(415)-381-0553
TOPICS: New Age

Esplanade Tours
581 Boylston Street
Boston, MA 02116
TOPICS: New Age

Ethnic Market
P.O. Box 3127
Morgantown, WV 26505
(304)-864-5646
TOPICS: New Age, Metaphysics **OWNER:** Jo & James Dixon **TYPE OF BUSINESS:** Metaphysical Supplies **DESCRIPTION:** Wholesalers & distributors of magickal, mystical & metaphysical supplies, including incense, aromatics, stones, herbs, tapes & books. Catalog available upon request. Send state resale tax number.

Evangelical Lutheran Church OF America Volunteer Services
8765 West Higgins Road
Chicago, IL 60631
(312)-380-2700 (312)-380-2650
CONTACT: Division For Global Mission **TOPICS:** New Age

Excalibur Dynamics
1963 Waltonia Drive, #6
Montrose, CA 91020
CONTACT: David Ginsberg **TOPICS:** New Age **TYPE OF BUSINESS:** Consultant **DESCRIPTION:** Computer & business consultant for the New Age field.

Excursions Into The Unknown
P.O. Box 205
Oaklawn, IL 60454-0205
(708)-425-5163
TOPICS: Ghosts, Psychic Phenomena, Parapsychology, Reincarnation, Past Life Regression **OWNER:** Dale Kaczmarek **TYPE OF BUSINESS:** Travel Tours **DESCRIPTION:** Provides legendary tours of haunted sites in the Chicago area.

Experience Zanzoona
P.O. Box 5589
Vancouver, WA 98668
CONTACT: Robert Draper, Pres. **TOPICS:** New Age, Spirituality

Expo Accessories, Inc.
47 Main Avenue, P.O. Box 938
Clifton, NJ 07017
(201)-661-9681
CONTACT: Martin Deeks **TOPICS:** New Age, Metaphysics **FOUNDED:** 1969

Extraordinary Expeditions
P.O. Box 1739
Hailey, ID 83333
(800)-234-1569
TOPICS: New Age

F.U.T.U.R.E.
P.O. Box 228
Butte, ND 58723
(701)-626-7360
TOPICS: New Age **OWNER:** Serena Dossenko **TYPE OF BUSINESS:** Organic Farming Products **DESCRIPTION:** Farmers Utilizing Techniques Ultimately Restoring Ecology are grain distributors & processors specializing in organic production & marketing. Services offered: OGBA Certified Processing Plant, commodities brokerage, seed procurement, organic & natural soil & plant input, consulting & Growers conference. **PUBLICATIONS:** *F.U.T.U.R.E. Newsletter-Calendar Of Events Section* **TOPICS:** New Age, Metaphysics **TYPE:** Newsletter **DATE:** 1984 **FREQ:** monthly **CIRC:** 125 **PRICE:** $15.00 **PRICE PER COPY:** $2.00 **DESCRIPTION:** Supports organic grain business with news, ads, articles and illustrations.

Fairfax Biological Laboratory, Inc.
P.O. Box 300
Clinton Corners, NY 12514
(914)-266-3705
TOPICS: Health Food, New Age **OWNER:** Howard & David Chittick **TYPE OF BUSINESS:** Natural Insect Control **DESCRIPTION:** Manufacture of Milky Disease Spore Powder for the control of the Japanese Beetle Larvae (a pest in turf in the Eastern U.S.). Trade mark is Doom & Japidemic & is sold in garden & hardware shops as well as mail order & some health food stores. **PUBLICATIONS:** Information brochures available.

Family Therapy Networker
131 Camino Alto, Suite D
Mill Valley, CA 94941
(415)-381-0553
TOPICS: New Age

Fantasy Enterprises

P.O. Box 1321
Arlington, MA 02174
(617)-641-2100
TOPICS: Metaphysics, Tarot **DESCRIPTION:** Metaphysical products & card readings.

Far Horizons
P.O. Box 1529
16 Fern Lane
San Anselmo, CA 94960
(415)-457-4575
TOPICS: New Age

Farm Verified Organic
P.O. Box 45
Redding, CT 06875
(203)-544-9896
TOPICS: Health Food

Fell Publishers, Inc.
2131 Hollywood Boulevard, #204
Hollywood, FL 33020
(305)-925-5242
CONTACT: Donald L. Lessne **TOPICS:** New Age, Metaphysics **TYPE OF BUSINESS:** Publisher & Mailing Lists **DESCRIPTION:** Publisher of New Age books also offering mailing lists of sale.

Fellowship Press
5820 Overbrook Avenue
Philadelphia, PA 19131
(215)-879-8604
TOPICS: New Age, Spirituality **OWNER:** Kelly Hayden **FOUNDED:** 1971 **TYPE OF BUSINESS:** New Age Books & Tapes **DESCRIPTION:** Publisher & producers of books, audio & video tapes of the Sufi teachings of M.R. Bawa Muhaiyaddeen. 25 books in print, hundreds of tapes.

Feminist Wicca Mail Order
249 North Brand Boulevard, Suite 674
Glendale, CA 91203
(818)-951-1908
TOPICS: Occult, Witchcraft, Tarot **DESCRIPTION:** Offers tools of the craft such as books, tarot, candles, oils & incense.

Figaro Cruises
P.O. Box 1336
Camden, ME 04843
(207)-236-8962 (800)-473-6169
TOPICS: New Age, Holistic Health, Yoga **OWNER:** Jen Martin & Barry King **TYPE OF BUSINESS:** New Age Cruises **DESCRIPTION:** Offers healthy, educational vacation alternatives through vegetarian sailing cruises. Theme cruises include yoga, natural history, photography & learn-to-sail weeks. Women's & men's cruises are also offered. Weekly cruises for health & relaxation.

Fine Median International
P.O. Box 30305
Santa Barbara, CA 93130
(805)-682-5151 (805)-569-0038 (800)-872-7245
TOPICS: Crystals, Dowsing, Holistic Healing, New Age **OWNER:** Bill Cox **FOUNDED:** 1969 **TYPE OF BUSINESS:** New Age & Dowsing Items **DESCRIPTION:** Offers a variety of books, tools & videos on dowsing both wholesale & retail. Imports Brazilian quartz crystals, publishes books on pyramids & conducts tours to Brazil for healing. **PUBLICATIONS:** *Cameron Aurameter In Action, The* **TOPICS:** Dowsing **TYPE:** Book

PUBLICATIONS: *Discover Dowsing* **TOPICS:** Dowsing **TYPE:** Video **DESCRIPTION:** 55 minute instructional videotape available in all worldwide formats. **PUBLICATIONS:** *Map Dowsing Handbook* **TOPICS:** Dowsing **TYPE:** Handbook **PUBLICATIONS:** *Psychology Of Treasure Dowsing* **TOPICS:** Dowsing **TYPE:** Book **PUBLICATIONS:** *Techniques Of Pendulum & Swing-Rod Dowsing* **TOPICS:** Dowsing **TYPE:** Book

Five Element Herb Company
1370 116th Avenue, N.E.
Suite 106
Bellevue, WA 98005
(206)-725-2020

TOPICS: Herbalogy **OWNER:** Stephen Morrissey **TYPE OF BUSINESS:** Mail-order products **DESCRIPTION:** Offers herbs & herbal items through mail-order.

FMA International, Incorporated
101 West Street
Hillsdale, NJ 07642
(201)-358-1212

CONTACT: Nat Batalion **TOPICS:** New Age, Metaphysics **FOUNDED:** 1988 **TYPE OF BUSINESS:** Business broker. **DESCRIPTION:** Business broker/agent for New Age oriented businesses.

Food First
Reality Tours Program
145 Ninth Street
San Francisco, CA 94103
(415)-864-8555

TOPICS: New Age

Foothill Agricultural Research
510 1/2 West Chase Drive
Corona, CA 91720
(714)-371-0120

TOPICS: Health Food

Foresight
4955 Lakeville Highway
Petaluma, CA 94952
(707)-762-7231

CONTACT: Carol Adrienne, M.A. **TOPICS:** Numerology, Metaphysics **TYPE OF BUSINESS:** Metaphysical services **DESCRIPTION:** Numerological service which analyzes names & birthdates to provide information & future predictions about the individual. Basic charts are $25, tapes $45 & extensive readings $75.

Forum Travel International
91 Gregory Lane
Suite 21
Pleasant Hill, CA 94523
(415)-671-2900

TOPICS: New Age

Foundation For Field Research
P.O. Box 2010
Alpine, CA 92001
(619)-445-9264

TOPICS: New Age

Fourth World Movement
7600 Willowhill Drive
Landover, MD 20785
(301)-336-9489

TOPICS: New Age

Free Spirit Communications
3039 East 2nd Street
Long Beach, CA 90803
(310)-433-3970

CONTACT: Diane Yankelevitz **TOPICS:** Astrology **FOUNDED:** 1988 **TYPE OF BUSINESS:** Astrology service **DESCRIPTION:** Astrological Chart Calculation Service offering Astrology classes & workshops. Purpose is to help people learn about themselves. Member of American Federation of Astrologers.

Freestone Innerprizes
70 North State Street
Joseph, UT 84754
(801)-527-3219 (801)-527-3738

CONTACT: Rico Or Jeannine **TOPICS:** New Age, Metaphysics **FOUNDED:** 1978

Friendship Force
575 South Tower
One CNN Center
Atlanta, GA 30303
(404)-522-9490

TOPICS: New Age

Future Source
P.O. Box 529
Graton, CA 95444
(707)-823-9355

CONTACT: Debra Guisti **TOPICS:** New Age, Metaphysics **FOUNDED:** 1985 **TYPE OF BUSINESS:** Marketing company **DESCRIPTION:** Full service marketing company for New Age products.

Future Studios
1223 Wilshire Boulevard, Suite 147
Santa Monica, CA 90403
(213)-281-8257

CONTACT: Michelle Goldberg **TOPICS:** New Age, Metaphysics **FOUNDED:** 1986

Garden Doctor
1684 Willow Street
Denver, CO 80220

TOPICS: Health Food

General Tours
770 Broadway
New York, NY 10003
(212)-598-1800

TOPICS: New Age

Gentle Beginning, Inc.
16 Darby Lane
Piscataway, NJ 08854
(908)-463-7384

TOPICS: New Age, Spirituality **OWNER:** Richard R. Erickson **TYPE OF BUSINESS:** Mail-Order products **DESCRIPTION:** Mail-order company of books & tapes specializing in spiritual materials, New Age & Psychic subjects. Sells mood & meditation aids such as incense, japas & crystals. Retail only. Free catalog. **PUBLICATIONS:** *Search For Meaning* **TOPICS:** New Age, Spirituality, Psychic **TYPE:** Book, 176 pgs. **PRICE:** $7.95 **DESCRIPTION:** Analyzes the great religions & shows a common core or message at the heart of their teachings.

Global Views
Route 3
Spring Green, WI 53588
(608)-583-5311

TOPICS: New Age

Gold Mine Natural Food Company
1947 30th Street
San Diego, CA 92102
(619)-234-9711 (800)-475-3663

TOPICS: Health Food, New Age, Holistic Health **OWNER:** Jean & Carlos Richardson **TYPE OF BUSINESS:** Health Foods & Supplies **DESCRIPTION:** Provides mail-order organic & macrobiotic foods & healthy lifestyle supplies. Distributors of Kyocera ceramic knives & other high-quality cookware, Seagull IV water purifiers, books & environmentally friendly household products. **PUBLICATIONS:** Free mail-order catalog available. Also news tabloid published twice a year,Oct. & Apr., with 10,000 circulation.

Grafic Health
737 Hymettus Avenue
Leucadia, CA 92024
(619)-944-0913

TOPICS: Astrology, Numerology **DESCRIPTION:** Astrology and numerology charts by computer offering low cost, precise predictions.

Granary Market
173 Central Avenue
Pacific Grove, CA 93950
(408)-372-2533

TOPICS: New Age, Metaphysics **FOUNDED:** 1971

Great Round, Inc.
P.O. Box 363
Bodega, CA 94922
(707)-874-2736

TOPICS: New Age, Spirituality **OWNER:** Sedonia Cahill & Bird Brother **FOUNDED:** 1986 **TYPE OF BUSINESS:** Spiritual quests **DESCRIPTION:** Escorts people into the California desert, about 8 times per year, for 10 day vision quests in search of spiritual peace & guidance. It is a time for asking questions & finding one's own answers. It connects one to the Earth & the Universe. **PUBLICATIONS:** Newsletter provided for vision quest participants. **PUBLICATIONS:** *Earth Circles News* **EDITOR:** Alexander Hart **TOPICS:** Spirituality, New Age **TYPE:** Magazine **DATE:** 1990, 16 pgs. **FREQ:** quarterly **PRICE:** $15.00 **TERM:** annually **DESCRIPTION:** Networks ceremonial circles.

Greater Horizons, Incorporated
P.O. Box 1156
Hillsboro, OR 97123-1156
(503)-648-9591

CONTACT: Carry Or Gail Smith **TOPICS:** New Age, Metaphysics **FOUNDED:** 1988

Greater Love Ministries
3437 Annandale Road
P.O. Box 2008
Falls Church, VA 22042

TOPICS: New Age, Skepticism, Counter-Cult, Parapsychology, Astrology, Spirituality, Occult **OWNER:** Phyl & Don Tobias **TYPE OF BUSINESS:** New Age articles **DESCRIPTION:** Offers articles on the New Age Movement, Parapsychology, Occult, Spiritualism, Astrology, Cults, Religions, Reincarnation, Meditation, Psychic Healing, Spirit World, Edgar Cayce ARE, Automatic Handwriting, Channeling, Clairvoyance, Speaking with the Dead, ESP,Magic, Materialism, Fortune Telling, Witchcraft.

Green Gulch Farm
Star Route
Sausalito, CA 94965
(415)-383-3134
TOPICS: New Age, Health Food

Green Tortoise Alternative Travel
P.O. Box 24459
San Francisco, CA 94124
(415)-821-0803 (800)-227-4766
TOPICS: New Age

Group One Communications
P.O. Box 1539
Jensen Beach, FL 34958
(305)-334-5205
TOPICS: New Age

Gurze Books
3420 Woodland Way
Carlsbad, CA 92008
(619)-434-7533
CONTACT: Leigh Cohn TOPICS: New Age

H And H Productions-Light Enhancers
P.O. Box 13737
Arlington, TX 76094-0737
(817)-461-5980
TOPICS: New Age, Metaphysics, Psychic, Astrology, Numerology, Hypnotism, Past Life Regression OWNER: Harriette Hartly FOUNDED: 1988 TYPE OF BUSINESS: New Age products DESCRIPTION: Lightenhancers is a retail catalog & store. H & H Productions produces, sells & distributes light enhancing products & services for the 90's such as audio tapes, books, candles & magic oils both wholesale & retail. Conducts workshops, lectures, rune stones, tea leaf & psychic readings.

Habitat For Humanity
Habitat And Church Streets
Americus, GA 31709
(912)-924-6935
TOPICS: New Age

Happy Ending, The
8021 South East Stark
Portland, OR 97215
(503)-256-5386
CONTACT: Yolanda TOPICS: New Age

Harbinger Of A New Age
9010 Lower Pack River Road
Sandpoint, ID 83864
(208)-263-7810
TOPICS: Holistic Health, Vegetarianism OWNER: James Peden TYPE OF BUSINESS: Vegetarian products DESCRIPTION: Promotes vegetarian diets for animals. Sells vegetarian food supplements for cats & dogs. Vet-approved supplements: Vegecat, Vegekit & Vegedog. PUBLICATIONS: Dogs And Cats Go Vegetarian TOPICS: Holistic Healing TYPE: Book

Harmony Farm Supply & Nursery
3244 Hwy. 116 No.
Sebastopol, CA 95472
(707)-823-9125 FAX (707)-823-1734
TOPICS: Health Food, New Age OWNER: Kate Burroughs & David Henry TYPE OF BUSINESS: Organic Farm Supplies DESCRIPTION: Purpose is to help farmers & gardeners be successful with organic methods & promote these methods. Offers drip & sprinkler irrigation system components, organic fertilizers, ecological pest controls, tools, plants for edible & drought tolerant landscaping PUBLICATIONS: Catalogs available: Spring, $2; Fall Seed Update, free; Winter Bareroot Edible Tree Crops, $2.

Harvest Health
1944 Eastern Avenue SE
Grand Rapids, MI 49507
(616)-245-6268
TOPICS: Health Food

Hawkwind Earth Renewal Cooperative
P.O. Box 11
Valley Head, AL 35989
(205)-635-6304
CONTACT: Charla Hermann TOPICS: New Age, Metaphysics FOUNDED: 1987

Healing Exchange Association
#507 620 View Street
Victoria, BC V8W 1J6
Canada
(604)-361-1875
TOPICS: New Age, Metaphysics FOUNDED: 1986

Healing Touch, The
1040 East Burnside
Portland, OR 97214
(503)-235-5658
CONTACT: Duane Fuller TOPICS: New Age, Massage, Chiropractic, Holistic Health

Health And Vitality Book Guild
Sylvan Avenue
Englewood Cliffs, NJ 07632
(201)-592-2477
CONTACT: Dwight Wardell TOPICS: New Age, Metaphysics

Health Food Industry Co-Op
P.O. Box 1858
Boulder, CO 80306
(303)-449-1515
TOPICS: New Age

Health Food Store List
4229 Birch Street
Newport Beach, CA 92660
TOPICS: New Age

Healthful Living
2034 Sparkman Rd.
Plant City, FL 33567
(401)-272-6910
TOPICS: Health Food

Heart And Soul Psychic Center
2695 West Broadway
Vancouver, BC V6K 2G2
Canada
(604)-736-7767
CONTACT: Dave Wilkinson TOPICS: New Age

Herb And Spice Collection
Box 118
Norway, IA 52318
(800)-365-4372
TOPICS: Health Food

Hi-De-Ho Enterprises
P.O. Box 1168-224
Studio City, CA 91604
(818)-761-0945
CONTACT: Master Ho/DeDe Holman TOPICS: New Age TYPE OF BUSINESS: Tour organizers DESCRIPTION: Organizes tours in Southern California.

Highams House Of Horrors
Box 180-204
Brooklyn, NY 11218
TOPICS: Occult, New Age OWNER: Mr. Higham TYPE OF BUSINESS: Occult Art DESCRIPTION: Creates realistic works of art for props, film, exhibit or the collector of bizarre necro-imagery.

Himalaya Trekking & Wilderness Expeditions
1900 8th Street
Berkeley, CA 94710-3015
(510)-540-8040 (800)-777-8735
TOPICS: New Age TYPE OF BUSINESS: Travel tours DESCRIPTION: Offers physical & cultural quests for spirited adventures to India, Nepal, Tibet, China, Pakistan & Siberia.

Holistic And Metaphysical Practitioner's Referral Service
P.O. Box 1076-RS
Columbia, MD 21044
(301)-995-1605
CONTACT: Kate Burton TOPICS: New Age TYPE OF BUSINESS: Referral Service DESCRIPTION: Full service referral company offering a directory, catalog, advertising, marketing assistance, etc.

Holistic Hypnosis
1772 Vallejo Street
San Francisco, CA 94109
(415)-885-4752
TOPICS: New Age, Hypnotism, Holistic Health

Holistic Life Seminars
P.O. Box 1682
Helena, MT 59624
TOPICS: Channeling

Hoover Herb House
1504 South Marengo Avenue
Pasadena, CA 91106
(818)-799-0467
TOPICS: New Age, Herbalogy

HSU's Ginseng Ent., Inc./Root To Health
P.O. Box 509
Wausau, WI 54402-0509
(800)-826-1577
CONTACT: Kim Kohlbeck TOPICS: Holistic Health, Nutrition, Homeopathy TYPE OF BUSINESS: Health food products DESCRIPTION: Offers American Ginseng which contains more ginsenosides, boosts the immune system & gives energy & vitality.

Human Development Network
Box 24148
Omaha, NE 68124
(402)-390-0342 (402)-399-9925
TOPICS: New Age OWNER: Mark T. Houston TYPE OF BUSINESS: New Age Consultant DESCRIPTION: New Age Financial & Marketing

Management Consulting Company for public & private businesses. Offers business management, event booking, networking, product marketing, publishing & career development.

Hyde Gem And Minerals
P.O. Box 2314
Irwindale, CA 91706
(818)-960-5778
TOPICS: Crystals, New Age DESCRIPTION: Wholesaler offering quartz, minerals, specimens & gems.

Hygieia
P.O. Box 398
Monroe, UT 84754
(801)-523-3219
CONTACT: Dr. Frederick Baker TOPICS: New Age, Metaphysics FOUNDED: 1978

Idaho Afloat
P.O. Box 542
Grangeville, ID 83530
(208)-983-2414
TOPICS: New Age

Image Tech
P.O. Box 229
30 Burnham Place
Cassadaga, NY 14718
(716)-595-2242
CONTACT: Holly Hewitt TOPICS: New Age, Metaphysics FOUNDED: 1988 TYPE OF BUSINESS: Business consultants DESCRIPTION: Full service business assistance including public relations, marketing, etc. for the New Age industry.

In Search Of The Super Self
1710 Highway 35
Ocean, NJ 07712
(908)-531-7838
CONTACT: George-Mann Associates, Inccorporated TOPICS: New Age

Indoculture Tours
6220 Canterbury Drive
Suite 100
Culver City, CA 90230-7917
(213)-649-0424
TOPICS: New Age

Inner Dimension Cruises
26 West Susquehanna Avenue
Baltimore, MD 21204
TOPICS: Channeling

Inner Light Metaphysical Center And Bookstore
1637 South Street Road 7
North Lauderdale, FL 33068
(305)-972-7931
CONTACT: Reverend M. L. Clarke Or Hildie Wheeler TOPICS: New Age FOUNDED: 1976

Inner Light Resources
P.O. Box 82542
Tampa, FL 33682
(813)-971-1244
TOPICS: Metaphysics, New Age, Holistic Health, Reflexology TYPE OF BUSINESS: New Age products DESCRIPTION: Produces the Rainbow Wallet Cards & Charts, a series of 12 different Self-Help/Health/New Thought cards & Reflexology

Charts. All fit in a clear acrylic counter-top display. Each card is a brightly colored reference guide to an entire field of information .

Inspiration University
P.O. Box 5320
Chico, CA 95927-5320
(916)-893-8643
TOPICS: New Age OWNER: Leonard Orr TYPE OF BUSINESS: Mail-order tapes/books DESCRIPTION: Mail-order sales of books & tapes dealing with various New Age, Health & Spiritual topics.

Institute For Noetic Sciences
131 Camino Alto, #D
Mill Valley, CA 94941
(415)-381-0553
TOPICS: New Age

Institute For The Advancement Of Human Behavior
131 Camino Alto, # D
Mill Valley, CA 94941
(415)-381-0553
TOPICS: New Age

Institute For The Study Of Human Knowledge
131 Camino Alto, # D
Mill Valley, CA 94941
(415)-381-0553
TOPICS: New Age

Institute Of Cultural Affairs
International Volunteer Program
4220 N. 25th Street
Pheonix, AZ 85016
(602)-955-4811
TOPICS: New Age

Institute Of Human Development
131 Camino Alto, # D
Mill Valley, CA 94941
(415)-381-0553
TOPICS: New Age

Intelligames
P.O. Box 156
Carlsbad, CA 92008
TOPICS: New Age

International Association Of Psychotronic Research
P.O. Box 8276
Silver Spring, MD 20910
(301)-587-8686
TOPICS: New Age

International Executive Service Corps
8 Stamford Forum
P.O. Box 10005
Stamford, CT 06904
(203)-967-6000
TOPICS: New Age

International Expeditions
1 Environs Park
Helena, AL 35080
(800)-633-4734
TOPICS: New Age

International Learning Institute
P.O. Box 60

Petaluma, CA 94953
(707)-763-1460
TOPICS: New Age, Metaphysics OWNER: Troy Rampy FOUNDED: 1983 TYPE OF BUSINESS: New Age producers DESCRIPTION: Producers of high quality learning & training programs in video, audio & print. Offers seminars & workshops on topics of social relevance. Accepts contract work.

International Voluntary Services
1424 16th Street NW
Suite 204
Washington, DC 20036
(202)-387-5533 FAX (202)-387-4234
TOPICS: New Age

Interns For Peace
270 West 89th Street
New York, NY 10024
(212)-580-0540
TOPICS: New Age

Intuitech
115 East 86th Street, #91
New York, NY 10128
CONTACT: D. Gayes TOPICS: New Age TYPE OF BUSINESS: Inspirational material DESCRIPTION: Offers inspirational materials such as tapes, lectures, workshops, etc.

ISHK Book Service
P.O. Box 1062
Cambridge, MA 02238
(800)-222-4745 FAX (800)-223-4200
TOPICS: Body-Mind Connection, Holistic Health, Psychology TYPE OF BUSINESS: Mail-Order Book Service DESCRIPTION: Promotes books that deal with the mind/body relationship & its effect on health & wellness. Deals with principles such as learning to live life as you like achieves better health & showing the direct effect of mood & mind on health. PUBLICATIONS: *The Evolution Of Consciousness, Healthy Pleasures, The Healing Brain*

Issac Asimov's Science Fiction Magazine
70 Riverdale Avenue
P.O. Box 4565
Greenwich, CT 06803
(203)-531-1091
TOPICS: New Age

ITV Productions
3812 Bagley
Culver City, CA 90232
(213)-559-7670
TOPICS: New Age

J & S Aquarian Networking
P.O. Box 1395
Pacifica, CA 94044
TOPICS: Metaphysics, UFO's, Crystals OWNER: Jeff Cohen & Richard Shapiro TYPE OF BUSINESS: Publishers & mailing list DESCRIPTION: Sells mailing lists to help network people with desired resources toward global harmony. Publishers of UFO & crystal-related books. PUBLICATIONS: *Mysteries Of The Crystal Skulls Revealed* EDITOR: S. Bowen TOPICS: Crystals, New Age, UFO's, Paranormal Phenomena TYPE: Book DATE: 1988 PRICE: $17.95 PUBLICATIONS: *UFO's, Space Brothers And The Aquarian Age* TOPICS: UFO's TYPE: Book DATE: 1985

J.D. Holmes Bookseller & Publishing Group
P.O. Box 623
Edmonds, WA 98020
(206)-771-2701
TOPICS: New Age, Metaphysics, Occult, Alchemy **OWNER:** J.D. Holmes **TYPE OF BUSINESS:** Antiquarian books **DESCRIPTION:** Sells Antiquarian Books in the Occult field, 16th to 20th century with special emphasis on Alchemy. Also publishes 150 titles on Alchemy, Gurdjieff, Crowley, Ancient Egypt, etc. Catalog available.

Jack Edmonston And Associates
21 Sylvan Way
Wayland, MA 01778-2414
(617)-444-4804
CONTACT: Jack Edmonston **TOPICS:** New Age **FOUNDED:** 1989 **TYPE OF BUSINESS:** Business services **DESCRIPTION:** Offers marketing & advertising services for New Age products.

Jackson Mountain
Box 2652
Renton, WA 98056
(206)-255-6635
TOPICS: Crystals **OWNER:** Bob Jackson **TYPE OF BUSINESS:** Crystal tours **DESCRIPTION:** Conducts crystal collecting trips & seminars. Retreat with mountaintop accomodations at large crystal deposit.

Jaffe Brothers
P.O. Box 636
Valley Center, CA 92082
(619)-749-1133
TOPICS: Health Food

James Henry River And Wilderness Journeys And Art Trek
P.O. Box 807-NA
Bolinas, CA 94924
(415)-868-1836
TOPICS: New Age

Jan's Work-The Future/Now Federation & New Intelligence
P.O. Box 1365
Stone Mountain, GA 30086
CONTACT: Jan Cox **TOPICS:** New Age **TYPE OF BUSINESS:** New Age books, videos,TV **DESCRIPTION:** Promotes the works of Jan Cox. Publishes his books, distributes his videos-wholesale & retail, produces his cable TV show & sponsors his live appearances.

Jeffrey Lant Associates, Incorporated
50 Follen Street, Suite 507
Cambridge, MA 02138
(617)-547-6372
TOPICS: New Age **OWNER:** Jeffrey Lant **TYPE OF BUSINESS:** Business service **DESCRIPTION:** Offers lectures & written materials on operating a successful business.

Jewel Tunnel Imports
222 Kruse Avenue (Just Off Myrtle Avenue)
Monrovia, CA 91016
(818)-357-6338 **FAX** (818)-358-0739 **TELEX** (510)-600-3710
TOPICS: Crystals **DESCRIPTION:** Largest wholesale only crystal sales in the southeast.

Joan Teresa Power Products
P.O. Box 442
Mars Hill, NC 28754
CONTACT: Joan Teresa **TOPICS:** Occult, Spirituality **TYPE OF BUSINESS:** New Age products **DESCRIPTION:** Free catalog offering complete spiritual & occult supplies: oils, incense, powders, books, minerals, jewelry, bath crystals & herbs. Sells retail & mail-order.

John McKenzie Associates
160 Adria Drive
Pleasant Hill, CA 94523
(415)-682-4959
TOPICS: New Age **OWNER:** John McKenzie **TYPE OF BUSINESS:** Conference organizer **DESCRIPTION:** Conference organizer for the New Age industry.

Journey Into Consciousness
P.O. Box 4241
Santa Fe Springs, CA 90670
(213)-692-6556
CONTACT: Dianne Morrissey **TOPICS:** Parapsychology, Counter-Cult, Metaphysics **DESCRIPTION:** Seminars on parapsychology & out-of-body experiences.

Journeys To The Earths Heart
P.O. Box 478
Fairfax, CA 94930
(415)-461-4636
CONTACT: Rachel Margolin **TOPICS:** New Age, Occult **TYPE OF BUSINESS:** Travel tours **DESCRIPTION:** Conducts transformational group tours to sacred sites worldwide.

Judy Schlosser
6331 Fairmount, Suite 367
El Cerrito, CA 94530
TOPICS: New Age **OWNER:** Judy Schlosser **FOUNDED:** 1983 **TYPE OF BUSINESS:** New Age Representative **DESCRIPTION:** Rep for New Age products to retail stores in the San Francisco & surrounding areas.

Juvenescent Research Corp.
807 Riverside Drive
New York, NY 10032
(212)-795-3749
CONTACT: Betty Elkan **TOPICS:** New Age, Holistic Health **OWNER:** Betty Yulin Ho **FOUNDED:** 1979 **TYPE OF BUSINESS:** Medical Research **DESCRIPTION:** Non-profit medical research organization. Publishes books by Betty Yulin Ho based on wellness & holistic health. **PUBLICATIONS:** *A Chinese & Western Daily Practical Health Guide* **EDITOR:** Betty Yulin Ho **TOPICS:** Holistic Health **TYPE:** Book **DATE:** 1982, 122 pgs. **PRICE:** $9.00 **DESCRIPTION:** Immediate suggestions with a holistic viewpoint to maintain health. **PUBLICATIONS:** *A Chinese & Western Guide To Better Health & Longer Life* **EDITOR:** Betty Yulin Ho **TOPICS:** Holistic Health **TYPE:** Book **DATE:** 1974, 50 pgs. **PRICE:** $5.00 **DESCRIPTION:** Ancient Chinese health principles related to best Western health principles to improve quality of life. **PUBLICATIONS:** *A Scientific Guide To Peaceful Living* **EDITOR:** Betty Yulin Ho **TOPICS:** Holistic Health **TYPE:** Book **DATE:** 1972, 170 pgs. **PRICE:** $15.00 **DESCRIPTION:** A view of the living body functioning as a whole. Covers exercise, foods & cooking, sicknesses, acupuncture. **PUBLICATIONS:** *How To Stay Healthy A Lifetime Without Medicines*

EDITOR: Betty Yulin Ho **TOPICS:** Holistic Health **TYPE:** Book **DATE:** 1979, 140 pgs. **PRICE:** $14.00 **DESCRIPTION:** Covers every facet of the living body to control life from first cell divison through adolescence, adulthood & delay death in terminal states. **PUBLICATIONS:** *Immediate Hints To Health Problems* **EDITOR:** Betty Yulin Ho **TOPICS:** Holistic Health **TYPE:** Book **DATE:** 1991, 264 pgs. **PRICE:** $25.00 **DESCRIPTION:** Immediate cures to multifarious health problems. **PUBLICATIONS:** *The Living Function Of Sleep, Life & Aging* **EDITOR:** Betty Yulin Ho **TOPICS:** Holistic Health **TYPE:** Book **DATE:** 1967, 56 pgs. **PRICE:** $6.00 **DESCRIPTION:** A development of 3 hypotheses on the physiology of sleep, life & aging. **PUBLICATIONS:** *The Origin Of Variation Of Races Of Mankind & The Cause Of Evolution* **EDITOR:** Betty Yulin Ho **TOPICS:** Holistic Health **TYPE:** Book **DATE:** 1969, 109 pgs. **PRICE:** $9.00 **DESCRIPTION:** A development of hypotheses on evolution. Principles derived for daily living. **PUBLICATIONS:** *To Be One's Own Physician* **EDITOR:** Betty Yulin Ho **TOPICS:** Holistic Health **TYPE:** Book **DATE:** 1991 **DESCRIPTION:** A holistic understanding of the living body.

Kathryn Hall
P.O. Box 2401
Mill Valley, CA 94942
(415)-381-2911
TOPICS: New Age, Metaphysics **OWNER:** Kathryn Hall **FOUNDED:** 1980 **TYPE OF BUSINESS:** Publicist **DESCRIPTION:** Public relations services for the New Age publishing field.

Kelsey Literary Agency
P.O. Box 457
Carlsbad, CA 92008
TOPICS: New Age, Metaphysics **OWNER:** Avonelle Kelsey **FOUNDED:** 1970 **TYPE OF BUSINESS:** Literary Agent **DESCRIPTION:** Literary Agent to the New Age author.

Kendall Enterprises
P.O. Box 2195
Garden Grove, CA 92642-2195
(714)-750-8066
TOPICS: Crystals, New Age, Metaphysics **DESCRIPTION:** Offers quartz and amethyst crystal gemstones, pendulums, jewelry and more.

Kindred Spirit
Foxhole, Dartington, Totnes
Devon, TQ9 6EB
England
(803) 866 686
CONTACT: Richard Beaumont **TOPICS:** New Age

Knobble Whole-Body Massage Tool
1187 Delaware Street
Berkeley, CA 94702
(415)-524-2788
TOPICS: Massage, Holistic Health **DESCRIPTION:** Equipment used and recommended by myotherapists, physical therapists & chiropractors.

Knoll Publishing Co., Inc.
P.O. Box 11956
Fort Wayne, IN 46862-1956
(219)-422-1926 (219)-422-7774
TOPICS: New Age, Metaphysics **OWNER:** Joseph Laiacona **FOUNDED:** 1986 **TYPE OF BUSINESS:** Mailing Lists, Book Pub. **DESCRIPTION:** Publishes

books on New Age & Metaphysical topics. Also rents mailing lists of individuals interested specifically in these topics. **PUBLICATIONS:** *Beyond Biofeedback* **EDITOR:** E. Green A. Green **TOPICS:** Parapsychology, Holistic Health **TYPE:** Book **PRICE:** $14.95

Krastman Productions, Inc.

P.O. Box 16790
Encino, CA 91416-6790
(818)-705-8865

CONTACT: Dr. Hank Krastman, Ph. D. **TOPICS:** New Age, Metaphysics **TYPE OF BUSINESS:** Magazine & tape publisher **DESCRIPTION:** Produces & distributes audio/video tapes. Publishes New Age magazine, The Unexplained. Also conducts New Age events & maintaines mailing list of 3,000 New Age exhibitors. Provides a list of 200 New Age lecturers. **PUBLICATIONS:** *The Unexplained Magazine* **EDITOR:** Dr. Hank Krastman, Ph. D. **TOPICS:** Metaphysics **TYPE:** Magazine **DATE:** 1961 **FREQ:** quarterly **PRICE:** $10.00 **PRICE PER COPY:** $2.00 **DESCRIPTION:** Official publication of Metaphysical Union. Includes feature articles, ads & video catalog supplement.

Krystal Haven

P.O. Box 331389
Fort Worth, TX 76163-9971
(817)-551-1205 (800)-232-1205

TOPICS: New Age, Metaphysics, Tarot, Runes **TYPE OF BUSINESS:** Mail-order products **DESCRIPTION:** Offers New Age & Metaphysical mail-order products such as crystals & gems, jewelry, tarot decks, pyramids, rune stones, candles, incense, books & tapes.

L & H Vitamins

37-10 Crescent Street
Long Island City, NY 11101

TOPICS: Holistic Health **TYPE OF BUSINESS:** Health products **DESCRIPTION:** Offers 10,000 natural health care products by mail-order. Products include homeopathic remedies, colon cleansing, herbs, vitamins, spirulina, aromatherapy products, Bach Flowr Remedies, Radiance, amino acids, etc.

Laser Digital

2490 Polk
Eugene, OR 97405
(503)-344-3935

CONTACT: Alan Minor **TOPICS:** New Age

Lawrence Blau And Associates

6 Sleater Drive
Ossining, NY 10562
(914)-941-5533

TOPICS: New Age **OWNER:** Lawrence Blau **TYPE OF BUSINESS:** Business services **DESCRIPTION:** Offers various business services to the New Age industry such as tax management, computers, etc.

Lemur Tours

3541 Dimond Avenue
Oakland, CA 94602
(415)-530-0244

CONTACT: Chipper Roth **TOPICS:** Crystals **DESCRIPTION:** Offers Great Crystal Hunt tours in Madagascar.

Liana R. Beckett, M.A.

3510 Park Boulevard
San Diego, CA 92103
(619)-543-0535

TOPICS: New Age **OWNER:** Liana R. Beckett **TYPE OF BUSINESS:** Editorial services **DESCRIPTION:** Offers editorial services & consulting to the publishing trade.

Library Corporation

Box 40035
Washington, DC 20016
(800)-624-0559

TOPICS: New Age **TYPE OF BUSINESS:** Computer services **DESCRIPTION:** Computer services for the publishing industry.

Lightworks

P.O. Box 1522
Skokie, IL 60076

TOPICS: New Age, Meditation, Holistic Healing **DESCRIPTION:** Promotes planetary healing through meditation & information.

Linda Bruce

P.O. Box 2938
Sedona, AZ 86336
(602)-282-3001

TOPICS: New Age, Metaphysics **OWNER:** Linda Bruce **TYPE OF BUSINESS:** New Age artist **DESCRIPTION:** Artist-illustrator using New Age themes.

Linda Jones Public Relations

16689 Rock Creek Road
Nevada City, CA 95959-8635
(916)-265-8095

TOPICS: Holistic Health, Metaphysics, Spirituality, New Age **TYPE OF BUSINESS:** Publicist **DESCRIPTION:** Public relations services & consulting for the media. Specializes in publicizing books and tapes on health, metaphysics, personal and spiritual growth & global issues.

Lindblad Travel

1 Sylvan Road North
P.O. Box 912
Westport, CT 06881
(800)-243-5657

TOPICS: New Age

List Counsellors, Inc.

1710 Highway 35
Ocean, NJ 07712
(908)-531-7838

TOPICS: New Age, Metaphysics **OWNER:** Rich Reinhart, Pres. **TYPE OF BUSINESS:** Mailing lists **DESCRIPTION:** A direct marketing firm specializing in mailing lists. Provides direct mail counselling particularly to smaller mailers. Offers free pre-planning counselling & post-mailing analysis. Clients include Mayan Order, Connecting White Dove, Mystic Trader, Astara, New Age Journal & Pyramid Link.

Literary Connection, The

6421 Congress Avenue
Boca Raton, FL 33487
(407)-997-7666

CONTACT: Iris Poland **TOPICS:** New Age, Metaphysics **FOUNDED:** 1989 **TYPE OF BUSINESS:** Literary Reps **DESCRIPTION:** Literary reps connecting authors & their works to agents, publishers, etc.

LIVE!

P.O. Box 262
Knoxville, TN 37901-0262

(615)-588-7700 (800)-548-3438

TOPICS: Health Food, Vegetarianism **DESCRIPTION:** Phone referral service for vegetarian information.

Living Farms

P.O. Box 50
Tracy, MN 56175
(507)-629-4431

TOPICS: Health Food

Livingston Tours & Seminars

P.O. Box 908
Black Mountain, NC 28711
(704)-669-9788

CONTACT: Rita Livingston **TOPICS:** Crystals **DESCRIPTION:** Conducts tours & seminars to Barbados for crystals & to tour the underground crystal caves.

Location/Identification Of Vegetarian Eateries (L.I.V.E.)

P.O. Box 854
Knoxville, TN 37901-0854
(615)-588-7700

TOPICS: New Age **DESCRIPTION:** Provides listings of vegetarian restaurants.

Lodestar Books

2020 B 11th Avenue South
Birmingham, AL 35205
(205)-939-3356

CONTACT: Sally **TOPICS:** New Age, Metaphysics, Channeling, Occult **FOUNDED:** 1984

Lois Newman Literary Services

6546 Hollywood Boulevard, Suie 201
Hollywood, CA 90028
(213)-464-8382

CONTACT: Lois Newman **TOPICS:** New Age **TYPE OF BUSINESS:** Consulting services **DESCRIPTION:** Offers full editorial, publishing, marketing, etc. services.

Longevity Pure Medicine

9595 Wilshire Boulevard
Suite 706
Beverly Hills, CA 90212
(213)-273-7423 (800)-327-5519

TOPICS: Holistic Health **TYPE OF BUSINESS:** Mail-order products **DESCRIPTION:** Offers health related products through mail-order.

Los Angeles World Affairs Council

Diplomatic Travel Program
900 Wilshire Boulevard, Suite 230
Los Angeles, CA 90017
(213)-628-2333

TOPICS: New Age

Lost World Adventures

1189 Autumn Ridge Drive
Marietta, GA 30066
(404)-971-8586 (800)-999-0558

TOPICS: New Age

Lou Gothard

10-3 Westerlea Avenue
Highstown, NJ 08520
(800)-338-3282

TOPICS: New Age **OWNER:** Lou Gothard **TYPE OF BUSINESS:** Tutoring service **DESCRIPTION:** Educational tutorial service.

Love/Harmony Corp.
Crystal Palace, The
14201 Bodega Highway
Bodega, CA 94922
(707)-876-3314
TOPICS: Crystals, New Age OWNER: Alan & Mark Bloom TYPE OF BUSINESS: Crystals & Minerals DESCRIPTION: Mining ventures offering crystal & mineral resources. Import, export, wearable stone art, magic wands, wholesale & mail-order list.

Luminous Dimensions
P.O. Box 3419
Hanalei, HI 96722
(808)-828-1120 (800)-828-8399
TOPICS: Holistic Health TYPE OF BUSINESS: Mail-order products DESCRIPTION: Offers mail-order health related products.

M And M Limited, Astrological Forecasts
130 Lyons Plains Road
Weston, CT 06883
(203)-277-6027
TOPICS: New Age

M.H. Beeman
P.O. Box 651
Georgetown, TX 78627
(512)-863-0521
TOPICS: New Age, Metaphysics OWNER: Martin Beeman FOUNDED: 1980 TYPE OF BUSINESS: Rep for New Age books. DESCRIPTION: New Age publisher's wholesale rep.

Mafu Seminars
Box 2094
Vacaville, CA 95696-2094
TOPICS: Channeling OWNER: Penny Torres FOUNDED: 1987 TYPE OF BUSINESS: Channeling Sessions DESCRIPTION: Produces & distributes books, videotapes & cassettes of channeling sessions of the entity Mafu as channeled through Penny Torres. PUBLICATIONS: *Reflections* TOPICS: Channeling TYPE: Journal FREQ: bi-monthly

Magic Marketing
9859 IH-10 West, Suite 157
San Antonio, TX 78230
(512)-340-0308
CONTACT: Christopher Dyal TOPICS: New Age, Metaphysics FOUNDED: 1980 TYPE OF BUSINESS: Marketing services DESCRIPTION: Consulting & marketing for New Age products.

Magick Marketing
Box 971
Redondo Beach, CA 90277
(213)-316-6772 FAX (213)-316-3169
CONTACT: Bill Stroup TOPICS: New Age, Metaphysics FOUNDED: 1968 TYPE OF BUSINESS: Marketing service DESCRIPTION: Wholesale marketing & rep service for New Age products.

Mailing List Catalog
99 West Sheffield Avenue
Englewood, NJ 07631
(201)-871-1100
CONTACT: Ed Burnett TOPICS: New Age

Maison de la Lune Noir
726 3rd Street
New Orleans, LA 70130

TOPICS: Occult, Paganism OWNER: Mishlen Linden & Louis Adams Martinie FOUNDED: 1991 TYPE OF BUSINESS: Bed & Breakfast Inn DESCRIPTION: Pagan Bed & Breakfast Inn.

Marah
P.O. Box 948
Madison, NJ 07940
TOPICS: Occult, Metaphysics, Runes, Tarot, Paganism, Herbalogy OWNER: Marah TYPE OF BUSINESS: New Age products DESCRIPTION: Sells bath salts, herbs, runestones, books, pagan calendars, scrying mirrors & the highest quality handmade ritual herbal incense & perfumes. Conducts Wicca, herb & Tarot courses by mail. Sells retail, wholesale & through mail-order catalog.

Marazul Tours
250 West 57th Street
Suite 1311
New York, NY 10107
(212)-582-9570 (800)-223-5334
TOPICS: New Age

Marjosa Star
P.O. Box 36044
3827 North 8th Avenue
Phoenix, AZ 85067
(602)-264-9471
TOPICS: New Age, Metaphysics OWNER: Marjosa Star TYPE OF BUSINESS: New Age artist DESCRIPTION: Artist/illustrator whose work is influenced by New Age themes.

Mark Sebastian Astrological Counseling
3809 Pacific Avenue
Long Beach, CA 90807
(213)-424-4998 (213)-424-6227
CONTACT: Mark Sebastian TOPICS: Astrology DESCRIPTION: Offers astrological counseling & consultations on cassette tapes.

Market And Media Analysis, Incorporated
4411 Bee Ridge Road, Suite 284
Sarasota, FL 34233
(813)-371-7960 FAX (813)-378-3768
CONTACT: Bob Aronson TOPICS: New Age FOUNDED: 1988

Marketing By Mail
2331 Fifth Street
Berkeley, CA 94710
(415)-548-2201
TOPICS: New Age TYPE OF BUSINESS: Marketing service DESCRIPTION: Offers direct marketing services to the New Age field.

Marketpoint
67 Mirabel Avenue
San Francisco, CA 94110
(415)-530-3896
CONTACT: Derrick Palmer TOPICS: New Age TYPE OF BUSINESS: Business services DESCRIPTION: Business marketing & management consultants.

Maryknoll Lay Missioners
Maryknoll, NY 10545
(914)-941-7590
TOPICS: New Age

Matrix Software
315 Marion Avenue
Big Rapids, MI 49307
(616)-796-2483 (616)-796-3437 (800)-752-6387
FAX (616)-796-3060
TOPICS: Astrology, Metaphysics OWNER: Michael Erlewine TYPE OF BUSINESS: Computerized Astrology DESCRIPTION: Astrological forecasting through the use of computers & various software. Home of the Heart Center Library, a non-profit astrological library containing an enormous collection of astrological books & periodicals. PUBLICATIONS: *Astro-Talk* EDITOR: Michael Erlewine TOPICS: Astrology TYPE: Bulletin PUBLICATIONS: *Astrophysical Directions* EDITOR: Michael Erlewine TOPICS: Astrology TYPE: Handbook PUBLICATIONS: *Manual Of Computer Programming* EDITOR: Michael Erlewine TOPICS: Astrology TYPE: Handbook PUBLICATIONS: *Matrix Journal* EDITOR: Michael Erlewine TOPICS: Astrology TYPE: Journal

Maya D, Incorporated
P.O. Box 333
Walton, NY 13856
(607)-865-5238
TOPICS: Metaphysics, Occult, Astrology DESCRIPTION: Computerized astrology and numerology reading. Also offers Metaphysical and occult supplies.

Maya Ventures
720 Worthshire
Houston, TX 77008
(800)-344-6292
TOPICS: New Age

McCaffrey Enterprises
15 Oakland Avenue
Harrison, NY 10528
(914)-835-0900
TOPICS: New Age OWNER: Neil McCaffrey FOUNDED: 1979 TYPE OF BUSINESS: Publishing services DESCRIPTION: Publishers fulfillment house catering to the New Age field.

Meadowcreek Project
Fox, AR 72051
(501)-363-4500
TOPICS: Health Food

Media Distribution Co-Op
1745 Louisiana Street
Lawrence, KS 66044
TOPICS: New Age

Media Placement Services
2142 Overland Lane
Mound, MN 55364
(612)-472-1701
TOPICS: New Age TYPE OF BUSINESS: Public Relations DESCRIPTION: Public Relations Firm specializing in placing New Age speakers on radio & TV talk programs nationwide.

Medicine Flower
P.O. Box 231011
Encinitas, CA 92023-1011
(800)-942-7188
TOPICS: New Age, Occult TYPE OF BUSINESS: Sells essential oils DESCRIPTION: Offers a complete selection of pure essential oils for use in Aromatherapy, perfumery & ritual arts either in bulk

or small quantites. Also seeks out rare oils for special orders. Sells wholesale, retail & mail order.

MegaMind
4013 Silver, Southeast
Albuquerque, NM 87108
(505)-268-0302
CONTACT: Phil Safier **TOPICS:** Holistic Health, New Age, Meditation

MetaBusiness Institute/ Conscious Books
316 California Ave., Ste. 210
Reno, NV 89509
(800)-322-9943
TOPICS: New Age **OWNER:** Greg Nielsen **FOUNDED:** 1991 **TYPE OF BUSINESS:** New Age Businesses **DESCRIPTION:** Purpose is to create a new global culture based on cooperative, creative & grateful business. A MetaBusiness thrives on creativity not competition & lets the creative forces flow freely. Offers quarterly seminars. **PUBLICATIONS:** *Beyond Pendulum Power: A Conscious Book* **EDITOR:** G. Nielsen **TOPICS:** Dowsing **TYPE:** Book **PRICE:** $9.95 **PUBLICATIONS:** *MetaBusiness Monthly Journal* **EDITOR:** Greg Nielsen **TOPICS:** New Age **TYPE:** Newsletter **FREQ:** monthly **PUBLICATIONS:** *MetaBusiness: Creating A New Global Culture* **EDITOR:** Greg Nielsen **TOPICS:** New Age **TYPE:** Book **PRICE:** $9.95

Metaforms
P.O. Box 2262
Boulder, CO 80306
(303)-449-5918 **FAX** (303)-442-4192
TOPICS: Holistic Health, Crystals, Color Therapy **OWNER:** Gregory Hoag **FOUNDED:** 1974 **TYPE OF BUSINESS:** Energy tools **DESCRIPTION:** Designs, manufactures & distributes energy tools for physical, mental, emotional health & soul connection. Works with form, color, magnets, inert gases & electromagnetic circuits. Also sculptures that assist in channeling. Offered through mail-order. Catalog available.

Metaphysical Booksellers
P.O. Box 606
Cottage Grove, OR 97424
(503)-942-7455
TOPICS: New Age, Metaphysics

Metaphysically Speaking
1920 South Locust
Denver, CO 80224
(303)-757-2778
CONTACT: Ellen Steinberg **TOPICS:** New Age, Metaphysics **FOUNDED:** 1981

Michael Wiese Film/Video
P.O. Box 406
Westport, CT 06811
(203)-226-6979
TOPICS: New Age **OWNER:** Michael Wiese **FOUNDED:** 1976 **TYPE OF BUSINESS:** Production Consultant **DESCRIPTION:** Video production consultant.

Mind's Eye, The
14124 1/2 San Antonio Drive
Norwalk, CA 90650
(213)-863-1714

CONTACT: Cheryl Galvan **TOPICS:** New Age, Metaphysics **FOUNDED:** 1970

Mirdad Center, The
429 Southeast 6th Street
Grants Pass, OR 97526
(503)-474-7711
TOPICS: New Age **OWNER:** Tatiana Gabriel **TYPE OF BUSINESS:** New Age products **DESCRIPTION:** Organizes events, publishes books & offers products all related to the New Age movement. **PUBLICATIONS:** *Whole Self* **TOPICS:** New Age **TYPE:** Magazine

Moon Stone Limited
521 East 81st Street, Ste. B
New York, NY 10028
(212)-734-8091
TOPICS: New Age, Metaphysics, Occult **OWNER:** Marguerite Elsbeth Chandler **FOUNDED:** 1987 **TYPE OF BUSINESS:** Book Advertising **DESCRIPTION:** Involved in advertising, marketing & distribution of books. Also sells rare books, jewelry, posters & New Age products.

Moonrose Occult Supplies
P.O. Box 5785
Denver, CO 80212
TOPICS: Occult

MoonSpire
3308 Ultimate Way
Dayton, OH 45449
(513)-433-8289
CONTACT: Joel **TOPICS:** New Age **FOUNDED:** 1988

Morgan Printing And Publishing
900 Old Koenig Lane, #135
Austin, TX 78756
(512)-459-5194
TOPICS: New Age

Morton Direct Mail Promotions, Incorporated
342 Madison Avenue
New York, NY 10017
CONTACT: Joseph Morton **TOPICS:** New Age

Mountain Ark Trading Company
120 South East Avenue
Fayetteville, AR 72701
(800)-643-8909
TOPICS: Health Food

Mountain Sunshine Books
P.O. Box 1052
Deerfield Beach, FL 33433
(305)-428-7738
CONTACT: Olympia Freeman **TOPICS:** New Age, Metaphysics **FOUNDED:** 1986

Mountain Travel
6420 Fairmount Avenue
El Cerrito, CA 94530
(800)-227-2384
TOPICS: New Age

Movement Expression
622 Las Lomas Avenue
Pacific Palisades, CA 90272
(213)-454-5335

TOPICS: Holistic Health **OWNER:** Mariane Karou & Eve Ray **FOUNDED:** 1976 **DESCRIPTION:** Series of unique exercises combining movement & guided imagery. Designed to give oneself higher quality of attention, breathe more fully & deeply, move more freely & easily, increase personal growth, tap one's energy & wisdom to stay centered. Offers workshops, private sessions & teacher training.

Music Book Pac
330 East 39th Street 34/C
New York, NY 10016
(212)-490-0546
CONTACT: Trent Hargrave **TOPICS:** New Age **TYPE OF BUSINESS:** Packaging design **DESCRIPTION:** Packaging design company for New Age music.

Music For Little People
P.O. Box 1460
Redway, CA 95560
(707)-923-3991
CONTACT: Stuart Schonfield **TOPICS:** New Age **FOUNDED:** 1985

Mysterium Corporation
P.O. Box 1836
2011 10th Street
Boulder, CO 80306
(303)-444-4650
CONTACT: Prem Purushottama **TOPICS:** New Age **FOUNDED:** 1986 **TYPE OF BUSINESS:** Marketing services **DESCRIPTION:** Marketing & rep services for New Age art & music.

Mystic Arts Book Society
120 Enterprise Avenue
Secaucus, NJ 07094
(201)-866-0490
CONTACT: Robert Salomon **TOPICS:** New Age, Metaphysics, Holistic Health

Mystic Crone
P.O. Box 489
Noel, MO 64854
(417)-436-2267
TOPICS: New Age, Metaphysics, Crystals **OWNER:** Jeri Lee **FOUNDED:** 1975 **TYPE OF BUSINESS:** New Age wholesaler **DESCRIPTION:** Manufacturer of symbolic jewelry, fantasy & mythological items, organic castings & crystals. Also produces a video on crystals, Flowers Of The Earth. Catalog $3.00, refundable.

Mystic Moon
8818 Troy Street
Spring Valley, CA 92077
(619)-466-8064
CONTACT: Judith Wise **TOPICS:** New Age, Metaphysics **FOUNDED:** 1988

Mystic Systems Books
P.O. Box 3554
Tallahassee, FL 32303
(904)-386-3429
TOPICS: Metaphysics **OWNER:** Janine Chapman, M.L.S. **TYPE OF BUSINESS:** Book search **DESCRIPTION:** Book search/find service for out-of-print occult books. $2.00 first title, $1.00 each additional title. Also sells limited number of titles. Specializes in Golden Dawn related literature, particularly Dion Fortune, Aleister Crowley,

Kenneth Grant & Austin Spare. Send for available listing of titles.

NAM-New Age Mailing Lists (NAM)
P.O. Box 970
Santa Cruz, NM 87567
(505)-753-5086
TOPICS: New Age, Metaphysics, Holistic Health **OWNER:** P.S. Khalsa **FOUNDED:** 1984 **TYPE OF BUSINESS:** New Age Mailing Lists **DESCRIPTION:** Mailing list broker & manager specializing in New Age, Metaphysical, Health, Environmental & Natural Lifestyle mailing lists for mail-order catalogs, publications seminars & fund raising. Also direct mail consultants.

Narada Productions, Inc.
1845 North Farwell Avenue
Milwaukee, WI 53202
(414)-272-6700 (800)-862-7232 **FAX** (414)-272-6131
TOPICS: New Age **TYPE OF BUSINESS:** Mail-order products **DESCRIPTION:** Sells New Age products by mail-order.

National Council Of The Churches Of Christ
Travel Seminar Office
475 Riverside Drive, Room 851
New York, NY 10115
(212)-870-2044
TOPICS: New Age

Natrol
20371 Prairie Street, #2
Chatsworth, CA 91311
(818)-701-9966
TOPICS: Holistic Health **TYPE OF BUSINESS:** Mail-order products **DESCRIPTION:** Offers health related items through mail-order.

Natural Food Institute
Box 185 WMB
Dudley, MA 01570
TOPICS: Health Food **PUBLICATIONS:** *Wonder Crops* **TOPICS:** Health Food **TYPE:** Book

Natural Gardener Research Center
P.O. Box 149
Sunman, IN 47041
(812)-623-3800
TOPICS: Health Food

Natural Pest Controls
8864 Little Creek Drive
Orangevale, CA 95662
(916)-726-0855
TOPICS: Health Food

Nature Expeditions International
474 Willamette Street
P.O. Box 11496
Eugene, OR 97440
(503)-484-6529
TOPICS: New Age

Necessary Trading Company
New Castle, VA 24127
(703)-864-5103
TOPICS: Health Food

Nedrra
Beadwerks Plus

425 Dewey Street
San Diego, CA 92113
(619)-233-5024
TOPICS: New Age, Crystals **TYPE OF BUSINESS:** Discount mail-order **DESCRIPTION:** Discount order service offering minerals, gem beads, jewelry, books, tapes, etc.

Nelson & Company
525 South Main, Ste. 308
Del Rio, TX 78840
TOPICS: New Age **TYPE OF BUSINESS:** Mail-order catalog **DESCRIPTION:** W & D mail-order catalog sales through Ancient Breath Catalogue. Offers unique findings such as jewelry of ancient Egyptian mummy beads, disciples of Buddha carved olive seed beads, unique hand-made items from different countries & do it yourself findings to create your own wearable art. Send S.A.S.E.

Neshaminy Valley Natural Foods Distributor
5 Louise Drive
Ivyland, PA 18974
(215)-443-5545
TOPICS: Health Food

Network Marketing
500 Ridge Road
Tiburon, CA 94920
(415)-435-0259
CONTACT: Geoff Workman **TOPICS:** New Age, Metaphysics **FOUNDED:** 1986 **TYPE OF BUSINESS:** New Age music **DESCRIPTION:** Marketing & distribution services for New Age music.

New Age Concepts/Color Magic
3826 South Yosemite
Denver, CO 80237
(303)-773-2268 (303)-620-7100
TOPICS: Crystals, Holistic Healing, New Age **OWNER:** Elaine Jay Finster, R.N. **TYPE OF BUSINESS:** Rare crystals **DESCRIPTION:** Offers rare, hard to find crystals, jewelry, gems & stones through mail-order. Sells wholesale & retail. Also operates a school teaching Chinese Feng Shui classes & field trips. Personal home or business inspection. Other address: P.O. Box 12, 8962 East Hampden Avenue, Denver, CO. 80231 **PUBLICATIONS:** *ABC's Of Crystals* **EDITOR:** Elaine Jay Finster **TOPICS:** New Age, Crystals, Holistic Healing **TYPE:** Book **DESCRIPTION:** Describes 160 different stones for healing & expanding awareness. **PUBLICATIONS:** *Crystals, Gems And Radionics* **EDITOR:** Elaine Jay Finster **TOPICS:** New Age, Crystals, Holistic Healing **TYPE:** Book **DESCRIPTION:** Discusses crystals & radionics & their healing abilities. **PUBLICATIONS:** *Health, Wealth & Balance Through Feng Shui* **EDITOR:** Elaine Jay Finster **TOPICS:** New Age, Crystals, Holistic Healing **TYPE:** Book **DESCRIPTION:** Addresses how to be in balance with your personal surroundings & with your work place.

New Age Marketing
P.O. Box 160 Nerang
Gold Coast, Qld
Australia 4211
(61) 7-2068869
CONTACT: Lesley Jean **TOPICS:** New Age, Metaphysics **TYPE OF BUSINESS:** New Age products **DESCRIPTION:** Distributes & markets numerous New Age products. Publishes books,

offers workshops & lecturers all related to the New Age field.

New Age Shop, The
#19 Habourtown SC Village
Gulf Breeze, FL 32561
(904)-932-1779
CONTACT: Jamie Williams **TOPICS:** New Age, Metaphysics **FOUNDED:** 1988

New Age Summer Seminars
611 Walker Street
Oliver Springs, TN 37840-1636
(615)-676-3703
TOPICS: New Age, Occult **DESCRIPTION:** Deals with all aspects of New Age & Amerindian subjects.

New Age World Services & Books (NAWSB)
62091 Valley View Circle
Joshua Tree, CA 92252
(619)-366-2833
TOPICS: New Age, Body-Mind Connection, Metaphysics, Occult, Spirituality **OWNER:** Rev. Victoria E. Vandertuin **TYPE OF BUSINESS:** New Age services **DESCRIPTION:** New Age & Occult specialists whose services include authors' & publishers' representatives, advertising & marketing, literary services & book searches.

New Dimensions Foundation
131 Camino Alto, Suite D
Mill Valley, CA 94941
(415)-381-0553
TOPICS: New Age

New Life Foundation
1710 Highway 35
Ocean, NJ 07712
(908)-531-7838
TOPICS: New Age

New Life Options
4520 Van Nuys Boulevard #547
Sherman Oaks, CA 91403
(818)-594-2305
CONTACT: Bo Lebeo **TOPICS:** New Age **FOUNDED:** 1980 **TYPE OF BUSINESS:** Marketing services **DESCRIPTION:** Offers marketing & rep services for New Age products including electronic media publishing.

New Oracle Catalog
P.O. Box 1320
Venice, CA 90294
TOPICS: Metaphysics

New York Zoological Society
Travel Department
185th Street and Southern Boulevard
Bronx, NY 10460
(212)-220-5085
TOPICS: New Age

Newday Group
P.O. Box 31367
Phoenix, AZ 85046
CONTACT: Bob Donley **TOPICS:** New Age **TYPE OF BUSINESS:** Agent for lecturers **DESCRIPTION:** Provides New Age & metaphysical lecturers.

News Times, The
P.O. Box 51186

Seattle, WA 98115-1186
(206)-524-9071
CONTACT: Krysta Gibson **TOPICS:** New Age

Nicaragua Network
2025 I Street NW
Suite 212
Washington, DC 20006
(202)-223-2328
TOPICS: New Age

Nichols Garden Nursery
1190 North Pacific Highway
Albany, OR 97321
(503)-928-9280
TOPICS: Health Food

No. 1 Electronics
Arch 7, Stables Market
Camden Lock, Chalk Farm Road
London, NW1 8AH
England
(071)-284-3483
TOPICS: Crystals, Metaphysics, Parapsychology, Crystals, PSI, Holistic Healing **OWNER:** Anthony John Bassett **FOUNDED:** 1973 **TYPE OF BUSINESS:** Electronic devices **DESCRIPTION:** A workshop engaged in fulltime research & production of equipment to demonstrate reality of paranormal abilities & to develop those abilities while working with electronic devices, crystals, orgone, magnetic & subtle energies, time travel, Radionics, PSI, brain machines, ultra-perception & learning devices.

North Country Organics
R.R. 1, Box 22321
Bradford, VT 05033
(802)-222-4277
TOPICS: Health Food

Northern Lights Expeditions
5220 N.E. 180th Street
Seattle, WA 98155
(206)-362-4506
TOPICS: New Age

Nova Dawn: New Age Service
2306 Madrona Drive
Lake Stevens, WA 98258
TOPICS: Metaphysics

Nu-World Amaranth
P.O. Box 2202
Naperville, IL 60567
(312)-369-6819
TOPICS: Health Food

Oceanview Wellness Center
11770 G. Warner Avenue, Suite 110
Fountain Valley, CA 92708
(714)-979-1700
CONTACT: Leslie Rosenthal **TOPICS:** New Age, Metaphysics **FOUNDED:** 1988

Off The Beaten Path
109 East Main Street
Bozeman, MT 59715
(406)-586-1311
TOPICS: New Age

Off The Deep End Travels
P.O. Box 7511-NW
Jackson, WY 83001

(307)-733-8707 (800)-233-6833
TOPICS: New Age

On Purpose
83 George Lane
Sausalito, CA 94965
CONTACT: Sandy Levey **TOPICS:** New Age **TYPE OF BUSINESS:** Marketing & consulting **DESCRIPTION:** Marketing & business consultant for the New Age field.

Open Door Management
15327 Sunset Boulevard, Suite 365
Pacific Palisades, CA 90272
(213)-459-2559
TOPICS: New Age **OWNER:** Bill Traut **FOUNDED:** 1987 **TYPE OF BUSINESS:** Business services **DESCRIPTION:** Offers business, management & marketing services for the music industry.

Open Door, The
1856 Colfax Street
Concord, CA 94520
(415)-676-3858
CONTACT: Judie Coop **TOPICS:** New Age, Metaphysics

Oracle Media
P.O. Box 15708
Phoenix, AZ 85060
(602)-840-7540
CONTACT: Sabine Hilten **TOPICS:** New Age **FOUNDED:** 1990 **TYPE OF BUSINESS:** New Age services **DESCRIPTION:** Provides New Age services such as marketing, distribution, advertising & mailing lists of individuals & organizations interested in the New Age movement.

Orchid Gallery
P.O. Box 1225
Mt. Shasta, CA 96067
(916)-926-2633
CONTACT: Jeff Palmer **TOPICS:** New Age

Other Publishers, The
P.O. Box 35
Barrytown, NY 12507
(914)-758-8163
CONTACT: Dick Higgins **TOPICS:** New Age **TYPE OF BUSINESS:** Marketing service **DESCRIPTION:** Publisher's marketing service.

Ozark Cooperative Warehouse
P.O. Box 1520A
Fayetteville, AR 72702
(501)-521-2667
TOPICS: Health Food

P.J. Birosik
760 Quail Tail Trail
Sedona, AZ 86336
(602)-282-4249
TOPICS: New Age, Metaphysics **OWNER:** P.J. Birosik **FOUNDED:** 1980 **TYPE OF BUSINESS:** Consultants **DESCRIPTION:** Consulting, marketing & publicity services.

Pacific Astrology Service
3228 Willow Street
Vancouver, BC, V5Z3P6,
Canada
TOPICS: Astrology

Pacifica
225 Mt. Ranier Place NW
Issaquah, WA 98027
(206)-391-7393
TOPICS: New Age

Paid Speakers Results Kit
P.O. Box 1120
Glendora, CA 91740
(818)-335-8069
TOPICS: New Age

Pamela J. Willits Photographic Services
P.O. Box 2923
Columbus, OH 43216
(614)-263-8754
TOPICS: New Age, Metaphysics **OWNER:** Pamela J. Willits **FOUNDED:** 1985 **TYPE OF BUSINESS:** Photographic services **DESCRIPTION:** Commercial photographic services influenced by & using many New Age themes.

Papa Jim Occult Supplies
P.O. Box 14128
San Antonio, TX 78214
TOPICS: Witchcraft

Paradise Boutique Records
4465 Katherine Avenue
Sherman Oaks, CA 91423
(818)-990-4935
CONTACT: Raymond Platt **TOPICS:** New Age **TYPE OF BUSINESS:** New Age music **DESCRIPTION:** Offers production, consulting & advertising services to the New Age music industry.

Parenting Press, Incorporated
P.O. Box 75267
Seattle, WA 98125-0267
(206)-527-2900
CONTACT: Karen Townsend **TOPICS:** New Age

Pathfinder Associates
P.O. Box 104
Cupertino, CA 95015
(408)-252-1438
TOPICS: New Age

Patricia Raskin
P.O. Box 58
Marion, CT 06444
(203)-250-9772
TOPICS: New Age **OWNER:** Patricia Raskin **TYPE OF BUSINESS:** New Age Consultant **DESCRIPTION:** Offers consulting, marketing, PR, lectures, classes, etc. to the New Age community.

Peace Seeds
2385 S.E. Thompson Street
Corvallis, OR 97333
(503)-752-0421
TOPICS: Health Food, New Age, Holistic Health **OWNER:** Alan M. Kapuler, Ph. D. **TYPE OF BUSINESS:** Organic Gardening **DESCRIPTION:** A Planetary Gene-Pool Service. A new system of gardening using coevolutionary gene pool gardening to produce superior species of plants. **PUBLICATIONS:** *Organics, The Gene Pool and Planetary Peace*, 1987; *The Effect of Sonic Bloom On The Germination Of 89 Kinds Of Flowering*

Plant Seed, 1987; *The Peace Seeds Odyssey*, 1984; *The 1989 Catalog Of Seeds*.

Peaceable Kingdom School
P.O. Box 313
Washington, TX 77880
(409)-878-2353
TOPICS: Health Food

Peaceful Valley Farm Supply
Box 2209
Grass Valley, CA 95945
(916)-272-4769
TOPICS: Health Food, New Age **OWNER:** Mark & Kathleen Fenton **FOUNDED:** 1976 **TYPE OF BUSINESS:** Farm & Garden Supplies **DESCRIPTION:** Committed to sustainable agriculture. Oldest, largest fully organic farm & garden supplier in the U.S. Complete selection of fertilizers, pest controls, bulk seeds, tools, agricultural equipment, season extenders, etc. Delivery via UPS, truck & U.S. Mail. **PUBLICATIONS:** 100 page catalog, $2 refundable with first purchase.

Perceptions/Attracting True Love
3610 West 6th Street, #964
Los Angeles, CA 90020-3097
(213)-382-0599
TOPICS: Psychic Phenomena, Hypnotism, Past Life Regression **DESCRIPTION:** Offers psychic readings, hypnosis & past-life regression therapy for the purpose of attracting love relationships.

Perchik's/The Judaic Book Service
345 South McDowell Boulevard, Suite 115-A
Petaluma, CA 94952
TOPICS: New Age, Kabbalah, Meditation **DESCRIPTION:** Offers books on Kabbalah, meditation & Jewish Mysticism.

Peruvian Whistling Vessels
Cundiyo RBN
Cundiyo, NM 87522
(505)-351-4500
CONTACT: Don Wright **TOPICS:** New Age **DESCRIPTION:** Transformative group experiences from blowing a set of seven vessels

Planetary Citizens
131 Camino Alto, Suite D
Mill Valley, CA 94941
(415)-381-0553
TOPICS: New Age

Planned Television Arts
25 West 43rd Street
New York, NY 10036
(212)-921-5111
TOPICS: New Age **OWNER:** M. Levine **TYPE OF BUSINESS:** Media organizers **DESCRIPTION:** Organizes media interviews & presentations for authors & the Publishing industry.

Power Places Tours
28802 Alta Laguna Boulevard
Laguna Beach, CA 92651
(714)-497-5138 (800)-234-8687 **FAX** (714)-494-7448
TOPICS: New Age, Spirituality, Holistic Healing **OWNER:** Dr. Toby Weiss, Director **TYPE OF BUSINESS:** Travel Tours **DESCRIPTION:** Conferences & guided travel tours are conducted to

sacred, spiritual & healing places in the world that have proven their power to energize, heal & transform the individual. Meet with local spiritual leaders & promote personal growth & spiritual insight. **PUBLICATIONS:** Brochure available.

PR Flash Database
51 North Fifth Street
P.O. Box 1102
Fairfield, IA 52556-3226
(515)-472-6617
CONTACT: John Kremer **TOPICS:** New Age, Metaphysics **FOUNDED:** 1983 **TYPE OF BUSINESS:** Marketing services **DESCRIPTION:** Marketing services with the use of computers.

Preventics, Inc.
6300 Main Street
P.O. Box 30327
Kansas City, MO 64112
(816)-444-4866 (800)-888-4866
TOPICS: Holistic Health **OWNER:** J. David Beaulieu, D.C. **TYPE OF BUSINESS:** Mail-order health items **DESCRIPTION:** Mail-order sales of vitamins & nutritional supplements. Owner is a Doctor of Chiropractic. **PUBLICATIONS:** *Vital Signs* **EDITOR:** Dr. J. David Beaulieu Lisa Beaulieu **TOPICS:** Holistic Health **TYPE:** Newsletter **PRICE:** $10.00 **DESCRIPTION:** Bi-monthly publication answering questions about health and nutrition. Promotes vitamin supplements sold by their company, Preventics. Free to their customers.

Prison Ashram Project
Route 1, Box 201-N
Durham, NC 27705
TOPICS: New Age

Pro Mark
4075 Yankee Drive
Augoura Hills, CA 91301
(818)-991-6458
CONTACT: Stephany Hamrell **TOPICS:** New Age, Metaphysics **FOUNDED:** 1981 **TYPE OF BUSINESS:** Business consultants **DESCRIPTION:** Offers business management & consulting services.

Professional Management Associates
1428 South Drexel Way
Lakewood, CO 80226
(303)-969-9260
CONTACT: Apryl Salz **TOPICS:** New Age, Metaphysics **FOUNDED:** 1985 **TYPE OF BUSINESS:** Business services **DESCRIPTION:** Business management service offering inspirational & transformational message.

Professional Metaphysical Services
P.O. Box 1401
Estes Park, CO 80517
(303)-586-5940
TOPICS: New Age, Metaphysics **DESCRIPTION:** Home-study course in metaphysics using meditation tapes, awareness, psychic readings & networking.

Professional Retail Services
22 West Mission Street, Suite B
Santa Barbara, CA 93101
(805)-687-1902
CONTACT: Tiffany M. Lach **TOPICS:** New Age, Metaphysics **FOUNDED:** 1987 **TYPE OF BUSINESS:** Consultants **DESCRIPTION:** Offers all aspects of consulting to New Age retail stores.

Project Concern International
AmDoc Option Agency
3550 Afton Road
San Diego, CA 92123
(619)-279-9690
TOPICS: New Age

Prometheus Books
700 East Amherst Street
Buffalo, NY 14215
(716)-837-1475 (716)-837-2475 (800)-421-0351
CONTACT: Lorraine Baranski **TOPICS:** Skepticism, Counter-Cult **TYPE OF BUSINESS:** Publisher of skeptics **DESCRIPTION:** Publisher of books debunking & investigating paranormal occurrences. All authors & titles are skeptics in the field of psychic & supernatural phenomena.

Promoting Enduring Peace, Inc./Peace Cruise
P.O. Box 5103
Woodmont, CT 06460
(203)-878-4769
TOPICS: New Age

Psychic And Astrological Cruise Club Of North America, The
P.O. Box 1184
Venice, FL 34282
TOPICS: New Age **DESCRIPTION:** Cruises

Psychic And Astrological Cruise, The
P.O. Box 1957, Station A
London, ON N6A 5J4
Canada
TOPICS: Channeling, Metaphysics, Psychic **DESCRIPTION:** Cruises

Psychic Fair Network
152 D Twin Hills Drive
Boonton, NJ 07005
(201)-316-9511 (201)-316-9611
TOPICS: Metaphysics, Psychic **OWNER:** Shirley & Vincent Tabatneck **FOUNDED:** 1976 **TYPE OF BUSINESS:** Conducts Psychic Fairs **DESCRIPTION:** Conducts Psychic Fairs in malls throughout the U.S., Canada & Puerto Rico. Offers books, readers & lecturers. Provides a 900 telephone number service to qualified psychics to upgrade their own businesses.

Psychic Solutions
6964 West 29th Way
Hialeah Gardens, FL 33016
(305)-826-4781
TOPICS: Astrology, Channeling, Psychic **OWNER:** Margaux A. Leiva **TYPE OF BUSINESS:** Psychic Readings **DESCRIPTION:** Offers psychic consultations, private readings & party planning.

Publishers Book & Audio Mailing Service
156 Petrus Avenue
P.O. Box 120159
Staten Island, NY 10312
(718)-317-8283
TOPICS: Metaphysics **TYPE OF BUSINESS:** Mail-order products **DESCRIPTION:** Offers metaphysical books & audio materials through mail-order.

Publishers Exchange Network
1605 Overlook Drive

Silver Spring, MD 20903
(304)-434-8432
CONTACT: Eric L. Carpenter TOPICS: New Age, Metaphysics FOUNDED: 1989

Pure Earth Products
255 Hope Street
Providence, RI 02906
(800)-926-1239
CONTACT: Diane Schlobahm TOPICS: New Age TYPE OF BUSINESS: Environmental Products DESCRIPTION: Catalog sales only. Environmentally friendly products including recycling aids, recycled products, pet care products, baby products, energy savers, crystals, t-shirts, gift items & toys, non-toxic household cleaners & recycled papers. Free catalog.

Purity Foods
2871 West Jolly Road
Okemos, MI 48864
(517)-351-9231
TOPICS: Health Food

Pyramid Books And The New-Age Collection
35 Congress Street
P.O. Box 4546
Salem, MA 01970-0902
(508)-744-6261
TOPICS: New Age, Metaphysics, Runes, Tarot, Crystals TYPE OF BUSINESS: Mail-order DESCRIPTION: Offers mail-order New Age products such as crystal jewelry, gems, books & audio tapes, Rune kits & Tarot decks. Also has retail stores in MA & RI.

Pyramid Products
P.O. Box 441
Union, MO 63084
TOPICS: Metaphysics

Quester Tours & Travel
Worldwide Nature Tours
257 Park Avenue South
New York, NY 10009
(212)-673-3120
TOPICS: New Age

R. H. Youngman Crystals
607 West Orangethorpe Avenue
Fullerton, CA 92632
(714)-526-6780
TOPICS: Crystals DESCRIPTION: Sells wholesale to trade only: quartz clusters shafts, tourmaline, amethyst, etc.

Radio Doctors
240 West Wells
Milwaukee, WI 53203
(414)-276-6422
CONTACT: Dan Smith TOPICS: New Age

Rainbow Blossom
106 Fairfax Avenue
Louisville, KY 40207
(502)-893-3627
CONTACT: Pumpkin Auerbach TOPICS: New Age, Metaphysics FOUNDED: 1977

Rainbow Bridge Group
23415 Ann Arbor Trail
Dearborn Heights, MI 48127
TOPICS: Channeling

Reed Literary Agency
12089 Lopez Canyon #201
Lakeview Terrace, CA 91342
(818)-896-1769
TOPICS: New Age, Metaphysics OWNER: Ellen Reed FOUNDED: 1989 TYPE OF BUSINESS: Literary Agent DESCRIPTION: Literary Agent for authors of New Age & related topics.

Renaissance Books
8101 Main Street
Ellicott City, MD 21043
(301)-465-0010
CONTACT: Charlotte Lawrence TOPICS: New Age, Metaphysics FOUNDED: 1986

Renaissance: A Catalogue For The New Age
2147 Oakland Drive
Kalamazoo, MI 49008
TOPICS: New Age DESCRIPTION: Offers a catalog of New Age products.

Responsible Tourism
2 Kensington Road
San Anselmo, CA 94960
(415)-258-6594
TOPICS: New Age

Retail Bookstores
P.O. Box 606
Cottage Grove, OR 97424
(503)-942-7455
TOPICS: New Age

Reviewer's Choice
P.O. Box 4232
Santa Barbara, CA 93140
(805)-968-7277
CONTACT: Dan Poynter TOPICS: New Age

RKM Tape and Book Club
P.O. Box 23042
Euclid, OH 44123-0208
(216)-261-2610
CONTACT: Stephanie TOPICS: New Age, Metaphysics, Astrology

Robert J. Adamich
781 Fourteenth Avenue
San Francisco, CA 94118
(415)-221-1612
TOPICS: New Age OWNER: Robert J. Adamich FOUNDED: 1986 TYPE OF BUSINESS: Consultant DESCRIPTION: Consultant offering information on all facets of production for the publishing industry.

Roc. Etc.
10330 Southeast 43 Court
Belleview, FL 32620
(904)-347-5100
CONTACT: Mary Ann TOPICS: New Age

Romney And Associates
23 South Last Chance Gulch Street
Helena, MT 59601-4132
(406)-443-7726
TOPICS: New Age OWNER: Bob Romney TYPE OF BUSINESS: Consultants DESCRIPTION: Editorial, art, computer & production consultants for the publishing industry.

Rondor Enterprises

8580 La Mesa Boulevard
La Mesa, CA 92041
(619)-465-2790
CONTACT: Ron Stadsklev TOPICS: New Age FOUNDED: 1976 TYPE OF BUSINESS: Publishing services DESCRIPTION: Offers publishing & publicity services to the author or publisher of New Age books.

Rosen Agency, The
345 7th Avenue
New York, NY 10001
(212)-465-9868
TOPICS: New Age, Metaphysics OWNER: Lucy Rosen FOUNDED: 1984 TYPE OF BUSINESS: Consulting services DESCRIPTION: Offers full range of services such as marketing, design, advertising, etc. for New Age companies.

Rowan Exchange, The
P.O. Box 63
Mt. Horeb, WI 53572
TOPICS: Witchcraft, Occult, Paganism OWNER: Kyril Oakwind TYPE OF BUSINESS: Pagan networking company DESCRIPTION: A pagan letter exchange & confidential contacts forwarding service. Networking organization for Wiccans. PUBLICATIONS: *The Rowan Exchange* EDITOR: Kyril Oakwind TOPICS: Occult, Witchcraft, Paganism TYPE: Booklet PRICE: $3.00 DESCRIPTION: Promotes networking between Wiccans. Offers personal profiles & interests of Wiccans.

Royal Publishing, Inc.
18825 Hicrest Road
Box 1120
Glendora, CA 91740
(818)-335-8069
CONTACT: Dottie Walters TOPICS: New Age, Metaphysics FOUNDED: 1980 TYPE OF BUSINESS: Lecturers service DESCRIPTION: Offers full range of services to would-be or experienced New Age lecturers including books, seminars, magazine, placement service, etc.

S.R. Reps And Company
Bridge Street
Box 246N
Roxbury, NY 12474
(607)-326-7906
TOPICS: New Age, Metaphysics OWNER: Steve Roth FOUNDED: 1985 TYPE OF BUSINESS: Reps & consultants DESCRIPTION: Reps & consultants for New Age health products.

Sacred Dance Jewelry--Huichol Earrings
Box 9055-N
Berkeley, CA 94709
(415)-537-8003
TOPICS: New Age DESCRIPTION: Offers luminous lacy beadwork & Mandalas by a spiritual people.

Sacred Earth News
1404 Gale Lane
Nashville, TN 37212
(615)-298-9932
CONTACT: Andy Hewitt TOPICS: New Age, Metaphysics FOUNDED: 1988

Sacred Earth Tours
Box 581

Graham, WA 98338
(206)-846-0496

TOPICS: Metaphysics **DESCRIPTION**: Spiritual & metaphysical tours that journey to sacred power places.

Saffron Naturalist
P.O. Box 85
Nokesville, VA 22123
(703)-594-2394

TOPICS: Holistic Health, Herbalogy, Homeopathy, Chiropractic **TYPE OF BUSINESS**: Saliva Analysis **DESCRIPTION**: Offers Saliva Crystallization Analysis home test kits. Test results provide an individual with a unique assessment of their Herbal profile. Widely used by Chiropractors, Homeopaths & Herbalists.

Saint Elmo's Books
2214 East Carson Street
Pittsburgh, PA 15203
(412)-431-9100

TOPICS: New Age, Metaphysics **FOUNDED**: 1987

Sales Call In An Envelope
1106 Main Street, Suite 402
Huntington Beach, CA 92648
(714)-536-4926

CONTACT: Peggy Glenn **TOPICS**: New Age

Sanctus Spiritus Supplies
2735 Chicago Road
South Chicago Heights, IL 60411

TOPICS: Occult

Sandra Watt
8033 Sunset Boulevard, Suite 4053
Hollywood, CA 91146
(213)-653-2339

TOPICS: New Age **OWNER**: Sandra Watt **TYPE OF BUSINESS**: Literary Agent **DESCRIPTION**: Literary Agent for authors of New Age books.

Science Fiction Book Club
Garden City, NY 11535-1104

TOPICS: New Age

Sedona Marketing Limited
58 Fore Street, Totnes
Devon, TQ9 4RU
England
(0803) 867788

CONTACT: Dean Holden, Pres. **TOPICS**: New Age, Metaphysics **OWNER**: Paul Scott **TYPE OF BUSINESS**: Marketing services **DESCRIPTION**: Offers marketing services for New Age products & music.

Service Civil International/USA
c/o Innisfree Village
Route 2, Box 506
Crozet, VA 22932
(804)-823-1826

TOPICS: New Age

Shabda/Tibetan Bells
P.O. Box 879
Mendocino, CA 95460
(707)-459-1508

TOPICS: New Age, Spirituality, Metaphysics **FOUNDED**: 1978 **DESCRIPTION**: Offers New Age products such as handbells, cymbals & singing bowls.

Shambala Publications
131 Camino Alto, #D
Mill Valley, CA 94941
(415)-381-0553

TOPICS: New Age **PUBLICATIONS**: *New Options Newsletter* **TOPICS**: New Age **TYPE**: Newsletter

Shyla's Mystic Gems
16133 Ventura Boulevard
Encino, CA 91436
(818)-886-8816

TOPICS: Metaphysics, Crystals

Signature Dynamics, Inc.
103 Washington Street, Suite 304
Morristown, NJ 07960

TOPICS: Graphology **OWNER**: Deborah Berk, M.A. **TYPE OF BUSINESS**: Handwriting Analysis **DESCRIPTION**: Handwriting analysis for personal and business needs. Provides all the tools to get to know & uplift yourself & others. Service performed by Deborah Berk, Master Handwriting Analyst & developer of The Four Corners Of The Page, helps to analyze what the writer is really saying.

Silva Mind Control Method
5150 East La Palma Avenue #208
Anaheim, CA 92807-2085
(714)-670-8622

TOPICS: Body-Mind Connection **DESCRIPTION**: Brain/mind/alpha/training.

Singer Media Corporation
3164 West Tyler Avenue
Anaheim, CA 92801
(714)-527-5650

TOPICS: New Age, Metaphysics **OWNER**: Kurt Singer **FOUNDED**: 1940 **DESCRIPTION**: Sells the reprint rights of copyrighted materials to other publishers.

Singh Seven Seas Publications
P.O. Box 22205
Lansing, MI 48909
(517)-332-0664 (517)-482-7094

TOPICS: Health Food, New Age **OWNER**: Swayam P. Singh **TYPE OF BUSINESS**: Publishers/Producers **DESCRIPTION**: Image developers, logo designers-resumes. Offers video biographies & cook books. Peace activists & founders of Unique Universal Gourmet Club whose purpose is to bring peace to the world.

Small Press
11 Ferry Lane West
Westport, CT 06880
(203)-226-6967

CONTACT: Brenda Mitchell-Powell **TOPICS**: New Age, Metaphysics **FOUNDED**: 1983

Small Press Library Service
796 South 980 East
Pleasant Grove, UT 84062
(801)-785-1578

TOPICS: New Age **TYPE OF BUSINESS**: Marketing services **DESCRIPTION**: Offers co-op direct market mailing services to libraries for publishers.

Sobek Expeditions
P.O. Box 1089
Angels Camp, CA 95222
(209)-736-4524

TOPICS: New Age

Society Expeditions
3131 Elliott Avenue
Suite 700
Seattle, WA 98121
(206)-285-9400 (800)-426-7794

TOPICS: New Age

Sohnen-Moe Associates
3906 West Ina Road #200-264
Tucson, AZ 85741-2295
(602)-744-0094 (602)-744-7887

TOPICS: New Age, Holistic Health **OWNER**: Cherie Sohnen-Moe **FOUNDED**: 1984 **TYPE OF BUSINESS**: New Age consultants **DESCRIPTION**: Business consultants & publishers. Purpose is to provide tools & techniques for empowering people in business. Associated with Practice Development Resources which publishes Newslogue. **PUBLICATIONS**: *Business Mastery: A Business Planning Guide For Creating A Fulfilling, Thriving Business and Keeping It Successful* **EDITOR**: Cherie Sohnen-Moe **TOPICS**: New Age **TYPE**: Book **DATE**: 1991 **SIZE**: 8 1/2 x 11, 256 pgs. **PRICE**: $19.95 **PUBLICATIONS**: *Newslogue* **EDITOR**: Cherie Sohnen-Moe **TOPICS**: New Age, Holistic Health **TYPE**: Newsletter **FREQ**: 3 x per year **DESCRIPTION**: A newsletter & catalogue geared to healing arts practitioners.

South American Craft Imports
6603 Whitney Street, Suite B
Oakland, CA 94609
(415)-428-1288

CONTACT: Fred Reyes **TOPICS**: New Age, Metaphysics

Southern Exposure Seed Exchange
Box 158
North Garden, VA 22959

TOPICS: New Age, Vegetarianism, Health Food **DESCRIPTION**: Organically produced, disease resistant vegetable seeds.

Southern Oregon Organics
1130 Tetherow Road
Dept. 30
Williams, OR 97544
(503)-846-7173

TOPICS: Health Food

Southern Traveller, The
P.O. Box 8337
Atlanta, GA 30306
(404)-872-7779

CONTACT: John Moss **TOPICS**: New Age, Metaphysics **FOUNDED**: 1978 **TYPE OF BUSINESS**: Publisher's Rep

Southwestern Mission Research Center
c/o Mrs. S. Franklin Gould
101 West River Road, #251
Tucson, AZ 85704
(602)-888-4037

TOPICS: New Age

Spa-Finders
784 Broadway
New York, NY 10003
(212)-475-1000 (800)-255-7727

TOPICS: Holistic Health, New Age, Massage, Meditation, Body-Mind Connection **OWNER**:

Jeffrey Joseph **TYPE OF BUSINESS**: Travel Agency **DESCRIPTION**: Supplies information and arranges travel plans to health spas. **PUBLICATIONS**: *The Spa Finder* (1989) **PUBLICATIONS**: *Spa Finder* **TOPICS**: Holistic Healing **TYPE**: Magazine

Special Libraries Association
1700 Eighteenth Street, Northwest
Washington, DC 20009
(202)-234-4700
CONTACT: Lori A. Keesee **TOPICS**: New Age

Specialty Grain
12202 Woodbine
Redford, MI 48239
(313)-535-9222
TOPICS: Health Food

Spiral Journeys
163 Water Street
Newburyport, MA 01950
(508)-462-1152
TOPICS: New Age

Spirit Company
2121 East Grand Avenue D-15
Escondido, CA 92027
(619)-743-8128
CONTACT: Nicki Monaco **TOPICS**: New Age **FOUNDED**: 1987 **TYPE OF BUSINESS**: Business services **DESCRIPTION**: Offers marketing, public relations & production services to the New Age industry.

Spiritual Emergence Network (SEN)
5905 Soquel Drive, Ste. 650
Soquel, CA 95073
(408)-464-8261
TOPICS: Holistic Healing, Channeling, Psychic Phenomena, Death, Spirituality **OWNER**: Stanislav Grof, M.D. & Christina Grof **FOUNDED**: 1980 **TYPE OF BUSINESS**: Information service **DESCRIPTION**: Information & referral service answering calls & letters worldwide concerning peoples' experiences with non-ordinary states of consciousness. Those include kundalini & psychic phenomena, shamanic journies, out-of-body & near-death experiences & possession . Offers educational training & materials. **PUBLICATIONS**: 2 newsletters & a journal **PUBLICATIONS**: *Spiritual Emergence Network Newsletter* **EDITOR**: Emma Bragdon, Ph. D. **TOPICS**: Holistic Healing, Psychic Phenomena, Death **TYPE**: Newsletter **FREQ**: bi-annual **DESCRIPTION**: Free with membership.

Sprout House
40 Railroad Street, #G-10
Great Barrington, MA 01230
(413)-528-5200
TOPICS: Health Food, Nutrition, Holistic Health **OWNER**: Steve Meyerowitz **TYPE OF BUSINESS**: Health products **DESCRIPTION**: Manufactures the Indoor Vegetable Kit & the Flaxseed Sprout Bag both designed to grow vegetables indoors. Sold in natural food stores nationwide & direct form the Sprout House mail-order. Also offers books & courses on cassette. **PUBLICATIONS**: *Dairy And Dairy Alternatives* **PUBLISHER**: Steve Meyerowitz **TOPICS**: Nutrition, Holistic Health, Health Food **TYPE**: Book **PUBLICATIONS**: *Food Combining And Digestion* **PUBLISHER**: Steve Meyerowitz **TOPICS**: Nutrition, Holistic Health, Health Food **TYPE**: Book **PUBLICATIONS**: *How To Grow*

Vegetables Indoors **PUBLISHER**: Steve Meyerowitz **TOPICS**: Nutrition, Holistic Health, Health Food **TYPE**: Book **PUBLICATIONS**: *Juice Fasting And Detoxification* **PUBLISHER**: Steve Meyerowitz **TOPICS**: Nutrition, Holistic Health, Health Food **TYPE**: Book **PUBLICATIONS**: *Making Sprout Bread* **PUBLISHER**: Steve Meyerowitz **TOPICS**: Nutrition, Holistic Health, Health Food **TYPE**: Book **PUBLICATIONS**: *Recipes From The Sproutman* **PUBLISHER**: Steve Meyerowitz **TOPICS**: Nutrition, Holistic Health, Health Food **TYPE**: Book **PUBLICATIONS**: *Sprout House Newsletter, The* **PUBLISHER**: Steve Meyerowitz **TOPICS**: Nutrition, Holistic Health, Health Food **TYPE**: Newsletter **FREQ**: quarterly **DESCRIPTION**: Provides information to the increasing number of home growers of sprouted vegetables. **PUBLICATIONS**: *Water Pollution And Purification* **PUBLISHER**: Steve Meyerowitz **TOPICS**: Nutrition, Holistic Health, Health Food **TYPE**: Book **PUBLICATIONS**: *Wheatgrass: Nature's Finest Medicine* **PUBLISHER**: Steve Meyerowitz **TOPICS**: Nutrition, Holistic Health, Health Food **TYPE**: Book

Star Crystals
6735 Broadmoor
Shawnee Mission, KS 66204
(913)-432-2340
TOPICS: New Age **DESCRIPTION**: Wholesale & retail sales of various New Age products such as crystals & gemstones. Also offers workshops.

Star Tech Services
Box 26599
Tempe, AZ 85285-6599
(602)-838-3245
TOPICS: Astrology **OWNER**: Richard Nolle **FOUNDED**: 1975 **TYPE OF BUSINESS**: Astrology services **DESCRIPTION**: Offers publications & Astrological services. **PUBLICATIONS**: *Star*Tech* **PUBLISHER**: Richard Nolle **TOPICS**: Astrology **TYPE**: Magazine **DATE**: 1987, 22 pgs. **FREQ**: Monthly **PRICE**: $16.50 **PRICE PER COPY**: $2.50 **DESCRIPTION**: Focuses on present-day ideas on astrology.

Star's Edge International
900 Markham Woods Road
Longwood, FL 32779
(407)-788-3090
CONTACT: Miken Ann Chappell **TOPICS**: Holistic Health, Psychology, New Age, Metaphysics **TYPE OF BUSINESS**: Consciousness courses **DESCRIPTION**: Offers Avatar courses nationwide which opens ones consciousness. Teaches the belief that one creates or attracts the situations & events which one then experiences. Explores ones belief system & teaches how to make positive changes. **PUBLICATIONS**: Avatar Journal; Creativism: The Art Of Living Deliberately by Harry Palmer **PUBLICATIONS**: *Avatar Journal, The* **TOPICS**: Metaphysics, Spirituality **TYPE**: Journal

Star-Lite Shadows Visitor Planning Service
P.O. Box 484
Sedona, AZ 86336-0484
TOPICS: Metaphysics, Meditation, Holistic Healing, Spirituality **OWNER**: Cylvia Lowe **FOUNDED**: 1989 **TYPE OF BUSINESS**: Tourist Information **DESCRIPTION**: Provides tourist attraction information: where to stay economically, what to see, choosing the right tour, healing arts & psychic

sciences. Intuitively selected information for visitors & Sedona profile & guidance for those planning to move to Sedona.

Starlight
615 Palmetto Avenue
Melbourne, FL 32901
(407)-724-4904
CONTACT: Cheri Nichols **TOPICS**: New Age, Metaphysics **FOUNDED**: 1984

State Of Jefferson Program, The
Shari Soza
P.O. Box 81
Yreka, CA 96097
TOPICS: New Age

Steven Lavaggi
10916 Peach Grove Street, #3
North Hollywood, CA 91601
(818)-760-7770
TOPICS: New Age **OWNER**: Steven Lavaggi **TYPE OF BUSINESS**: New Age artist **DESCRIPTION**: Artist, illustrator working with New Age themes.

Stress Management Services - Peggy Pratt
P.O. Box 13492
Arlington, TX 76094-0492
(817)-792-3218
TOPICS: Holistic Health **DESCRIPTION**: Offers counseling, rebirthing, rebirther training, seminars & vision quests.

Studio 31
27 West 20th Street, Room 1005
New York, NY 10011
(212)-463-0299
CONTACT: James Wasserman **TOPICS**: New Age **TYPE OF BUSINESS**: Book production **DESCRIPTION**: Full service book production company.

SUMMUM
707 Genesis Avenue
Salt Lake City, UT 84104
(801)-355-0137
TOPICS: Death **DESCRIPTION**: Specializes in mummification/transference: Mummi-fy body, guide soul to next destination.

Sun Spiritual Library
P.O. Box 5588
Santa Fe, NM 87502-5588
(505)-471-5177
TOPICS: New Age, Metaphysics, New Age, Spirituality **FOUNDED**: 1988 **TYPE OF BUSINESS**: Library **DESCRIPTION**: Library offering books on Metaphysics, New Age & Spiritualism.

Sunburst Crystals
237 East Main Street
Mt. Kisco, NY 10549
(914)-666-4135
CONTACT: Ginny Mackles **TOPICS**: New Age, Metaphysics **FOUNDED**: 1988

Synaptica
3855 Telluride Place
Boulder, CO 80303-7219
(303)-499-5860
CONTACT: Bartholemew Greenberg **TOPICS**: New Age, Metaphysics **FOUNDED**: 1980 **TYPE OF**

BUSINESS: Marketing services DESCRIPTION: Offers marketing & graphic design services.

T.H. Enterprises
1200 North Lake Avenue
Pasadena, CA 91104
(818)-798-7893
CONTACT: Ms. J. Manber TOPICS: Massage, New Age, Metaphysics

Target Marketing
6 Belmont Avenue
Belfast, ME 04915
(207)-338-3478
TOPICS: New Age

Tarot Interpreter Publications (TI)
P.O. Box 7786
Sugar Creek, MO 64054
TOPICS: Tarot OWNER: Judith L. Welpman FOUNDED: 1988 TYPE OF BUSINESS: New Age products DESCRIPTION: Mail-order business offering Tarot decks, New Age products & information booklets covering various aspects of Tarot & its use. PUBLICATIONS: *Tarot Interpreter* EDITOR: Judith L. Welpman TOPICS: Tarot TYPE: Magazine DATE: 1988, 24 pgs. FREQ: monthly PRICE: $18.00 TERM: 6 months DESCRIPTION: Devoted exclusively to the art of Tarot. Features interpretations, readings on issues affecting our lives today, interesting facts about Tarot, how-to features & information regarding Tarot decks & Tarot-related products.

Taylor's Herb Gardens
1535 Lone Oak Road
Vista, CA 92084
(619)-727-3485
TOPICS: Health Food, Herbalogy, Holistic Health OWNER: Kent Alen Taylor TYPE OF BUSINESS: Mail-Order Herbs DESCRIPTION: Mail-Order organic herb gardening supplies including herb plants of all varieties, bio-dynamic compost, cover crops, information on beneficial insects & planting by the moon.

TDS Badges
P.O. Box 1023
Garden Grove, CA 92642
(714)-775-2207
CONTACT: Milt Strong TOPICS: New Age TYPE OF BUSINESS: Manufacturers DESCRIPTION: Manufacturers of badges & related products for the New Age industry.

Teamwork Promotions
P.O. Box 1523
Topanga, CA 90290
(213)-455-0075
CONTACT: Brian Duggan TOPICS: New Age, Metaphysics FOUNDED: 1979 TYPE OF BUSINESS: Consultants DESCRIPTION: Marketing consultants to New Age companies.

Tenth Dimension Herbiotics
3001 South Winchester, #9
Campbell, CA 95008
(408)-370-7050 FAX (408)-370-2997
TOPICS: Herbalogy, Holistic Health TYPE OF BUSINESS: Herbal products DESCRIPTION: Offers various herbal products such as herbiotic baths, facial herbs, footbaths, soapless soap & herbiotic gifts.

Terrie Brill And Associates
770 El Caminio Real
Belmont, CA 94002
(415)-593-3068
CONTACT: Michael Brill TOPICS: New Age, Metaphysics FOUNDED: 1980

Theodora Scott & Association
2269 Chestnut Street, Ste. 136
San Francisco, CA 94123
(415)-362-1445
TOPICS: Metaphysics, New Age, Occult, Holistic Health OWNER: Theodora Scott TYPE OF BUSINESS: Wholesale Representative DESCRIPTION: Sales Rep for more than 25 Metaphysical, New Age & Occult sidelines, marketing wholesale to metaphysical stores. Some of the products are candles, incense, plants, gems & crystals, creams, potions, pendulums, tarot card bags, herbs & oils, tarot & angel cards, velvet bags, jewelry, Rune & Chakra Stones.

There's More Promotions
4864 Aster Drive
Nashville, TN 37211
(615)-832-8459
CONTACT: Debbie Runions TOPICS: New Age

Thought Technology, Limited
Rural Route 1, Route 9 North, #380
West Chazy, NY 12992
(514)-489-8251 (800)-361-3651
TOPICS: New Age, Holistic Health DESCRIPTION: Offers instruction in 5 types of biofeedback: control of stress, weight, sleep, smoking, sports.

Thunderbird Gems, Incorporated
P.O. Box 13227
El Paso, TX 79912
CONTACT: Charles Power TOPICS: New Age, Metaphysics FOUNDED: 1975

Time Data Research
P.O. Box 717
Manchester, NH 03105
(603)-623-7733
TOPICS: Astrology, Metaphysics OWNER: Larry White TYPE OF BUSINESS: Astrology Service/Column DESCRIPTION: Offers private astrological readings, miniscopes & professional charts. Produces a syndicated astrology column which is cartoon illustrated called Cosmic College. It appears in more than 100 weekly & monthly publications nationwide.

Tolodumare Bookstores
2440 Durant Avenue
Berkeley, CA 94704
(415)-843-3088
CONTACT: Ade. Y. Aro TOPICS: New Age, Metaphysics

Tom Peters Group
131 Camino Alto, Suite D
Mill Valley, CA 94941
(415)-381-0553
TOPICS: New Age

Total Mind Power Institute
1710 Highway 35
Ocean, NJ 07712
(908)-531-7838
TOPICS: New Age

Touchstone
1800 Robertson Boulevard, Suite 225
Los Angeles, CA 90035
(213)-273-3374
TOPICS: New Age TYPE OF BUSINESS: Business services DESCRIPTION: Offers various business services such as mailing lists, labels, business reports, etc..

Traditions Of Tao
1314 Second Street, #A
Santa Monica, CA 90401
(310)-576-1901
TOPICS: Spirituality, Holistic Health, Acupuncture, Herbalogy OWNER: Master Ni FOUNDED: 1990 TYPE OF BUSINESS: Herbal Foods DESCRIPTION: Offers natural herbs & herb foods to promote renewed health & recovery.

Travel Companion Exchange (TCE)
Box 833
Amityville, NY 11701
(516)-454-0880 FAX (516)-454-0170
TOPICS: New Age OWNER: Jens Jurgen, Pres. FOUNDED: 1982 TYPE OF BUSINESS: Singles' Travel Service DESCRIPTION: North America's largest Match-Up Service for travel-minded singles. More than 2000 active members of all age, nationwide in the U.S., Canada & some abroad. Locates compatible travel partners for all types of trips including New Age excursions. PUBLICATIONS: *Travel Companions* EDITOR: Jens Jurgen TYPE: Newsletter FREQ: bi-monthly PRICE PER COPY: $4.00 DESCRIPTION: Offers computerized listings of members travel plans attached to each newsletter. Subscription alone starts at $24 for 6 months. Membership starts at $36 for 6 months.

Travel Horizons
P.O. Box 4410
Laguna Beach, CA 92652-4410
(800)-531-5544
TOPICS: New Age

Triangle Training Center
Rt. 4, Box 60
Pittsboro, NC 27312
(919)-542-1332 (800)-451-2562
TOPICS: New Age TYPE OF BUSINESS: New Age camp DESCRIPTION: Offers vacations in the Florida Keys with Dolphins. Considered to be a transformational journey into self. Also offers audio tapes concerning dolphins.

Turtle River Rafting Company
P.O. Box 313
Mount Shasta, CA 96067-0313
(916)-926-3223
TOPICS: New Age DESCRIPTION: Offers unusual outdoor experiences.

Tyrad Company Occult Supplies
P.O. Box 17006
Minneapolis, MN 55417
TOPICS: Occult, Parapsychology, New Age OWNER: L. Wright TYPE OF BUSINESS: Mail-Order Books, etc. DESCRIPTION: Mail-order distributor of more than 7,000 Occult, Parapsychology & New Age items & books including novelties, gifts, curios & botanical supplies. Catalog, $2.00.

U.S. Business Directories
5707 South 86th Circle
P.O. Box 27347
Omaha, NE 68127
(402)-593-4600
TOPICS: New Age

U.S. Reps & Magick Marketing
P.O. Box 971
Redondo Beach, CA 90277
(310)-316-6772 (800)-888-2768 FAX (310)-316-3169
TOPICS: New Age, Tarot, Astrology, Metaphysics, Spirituality OWNER: Bill Stroup TYPE OF BUSINESS: Marketing Reps DESCRIPTION: Marketing reps & wholesale distributors of Astrology, Religious Science, New Thought & New Age products, Tarot Cards, Metaphysical books, tapes, audio & video. Also literary agents for New Thought, New Age, Metaphysical, Philosophy & Astrology books.

U.S. Servas
11 John Street
New York, NY 10038
(212)-267-0252
TOPICS: New Age

U.S. Small Business Administration
P.O. Box 15434
Fort Worth, TX 76119
(800)-368-5855
TOPICS: New Age TYPE OF BUSINESS: Business service DESCRIPTION: Offers information & assistance in operating a New Age business.

Unicorn
P.O. Box 2067
Littleton, CO 80161-2067
(303)-797-0364
TOPICS: Psychic, Holistic Healing, Channeling, Past Life Regression, Hypnotism OWNER: Norma Mitchell TYPE OF BUSINESS: Mail-Order Consultations DESCRIPTION: Offers mail-order consultations in healing, channeling, past life regressions, hypnosis & psychic readings. Also provides workshops, lectures, cards, tapes & gift items.

Unicorn Books
1210 Massachusetts Avenue
Arlington, MA 02174
(617)-646-3680
CONTACT: Beth Bryant TOPICS: New Age, Metaphysics FOUNDED: 1980

Unique Insect Control
5504 Sperry Drive
Citrus Heights, CA 95621
(916)-961-7945
TOPICS: Health Food

United Farm Workers
P.O. Box 62
La Paz
Keene, CA 93531
(805)-822-5571
TOPICS: New Age

Universe & Other Toys
P.O. Box 553
Huron, OH 44839
(419)-499-2310

TOPICS: Metaphysics OWNER: Mary Lee LaBay TYPE OF BUSINESS: Sponsors Fairs & Events DESCRIPTION: Sponsors metaphysical events in several cities in Ohio. Conducts metaphysical workshops & lectures. Offers readings in Astrology, Palmistry, Rune Stones, Tarot & Tea Leaves. Sells crystals, gifts, jewelry, tools, art, music & educational toys.

US/USSR Bridges For Peace
Box 710
Norwich, VT 05055
(802)-649-1000
TOPICS: New Age

Utah Christian Publications
P.O. Box 21052
Salt Lake City, UT 84121
TOPICS: Skepticism, Counter-Cult OWNER: Marvin Cowan TYPE OF BUSINESS: Literature Ministry DESCRIPTION: A literature ministry of the Conservative Baptist Home Mission Society. Conducts nationwide seminars dealing with topics such as Mormonism, cults, New Age, Satanism, etc. Offers counselling. Publishes a quarterly half page newsletter.

Venture Communications
114 East 32nd Street
New York, NY 10016
(212)-684-4800
CONTACT: Greg Greenberg TOPICS: New Age FOUNDED: 1983

Video Network
P.O. Box 529
Graton, CA 95444
(707)-823-9355
CONTACT: Debra Giusti TOPICS: New Age FOUNDED: 1985 TYPE OF BUSINESS: Video tape production DESCRIPTION: Nationwide video networking company for the production & distribution of video tapes.

VIDFX
9859 1H-10 West, Suite 157
San Antonio, TX 78230
(512)-340-0308
CONTACT: Christopher Dyal TOPICS: New Age FOUNDED: 1980 TYPE OF BUSINESS: New Age products DESCRIPTION: Produces, markets & distributes numerous New Age products such as music, books, crystals, jewelry, health items, etc.

Vision Works Distribution
P.O. Box 331
Amherst, MA 01004
(413)-665-7375
CONTACT: Dick McLeester TOPICS: New Age, Metaphysics FOUNDED: 1986 TYPE OF BUSINESS: New Age products DESCRIPTION: Reps & wholesale distributor of numerous New Age products such as cards, books, etc..

Visions Occult Supply House
923 Main Street
Velmar, NJ 07719
TOPICS: Occult

Visions Travel And Tours
2041 Business Center Drive
Irvine, CA 92715
TOPICS: Metaphysics

Visions Travel And Tours, Inc.
9841 Airport Boulevard, Ste. 520
Los Angeles, CA 90045
(213)-568-0138 (800)-888-5509 FAX (213)-568-0246
TOPICS: New Age OWNER: Abbas Nadim, Pres. & Noah Gale, V.P. TYPE OF BUSINESS: Travel Agency DESCRIPTION: Premier producers of transformational travel. The only full-service, bonded, travel agency specializing in custom designed deluxe tours to the sacred sites of the planet. All tours are led by nationally known speakers, teachers & authors. PUBLICATIONS: Publishes a quarterly listing of upcoming tours. Free brochures available.

Vita Florum Products
Box 85, Station A
Toronto, M5W 1A2
Canada
(416)-964-1126
TOPICS: Herbalogy, Holistic Health, Spirituality TYPE OF BUSINESS: Spiritual Energy products DESCRIPTION: A range of preparations-water, ointment, lotion, massage oil, talcum, tablets, superhealth & salve for animals, plus soil preparation & foliar spray for plants- whose active ingredient is Spiritual Energy. Encourages psychological/spiritual growth. Not medicine, but a harmonizing agent.

Warrior Information Network
3067 East Waterloo Road
Stockton, CA 95205
(209)-942-2436
CONTACT: Mindy Sassman TOPICS: New Age, Metaphysics FOUNDED: 1986 DESCRIPTION: Deals in various aspects of the New Age & martial arts. Also sells mailing lists concerning the martial arts. PUBLICATIONS: *Warrior Information Network* EDITOR: Mundy Sassman TOPICS: New Age, Metaphysics TYPE: Newspaper DATE: 1986 DESCRIPTION: Provides information about products, services and events relating to martial arts, holistic health and personal growth.

Way, The
114 East 32nd Street
New York, NY 10016
(212)-684-4800
TOPICS: New Age, Occult

Wellstone: Crystal Jewelry
11688 Polaris Drive
Grass Valley, CA 95945
TOPICS: New Age DESCRIPTION: Wholesale & retail sales of gold & silver natural quartz jewelry.

Wilderness Southeast
711-J Sandtown Road
Savannah, GA 31410
(912)-897-5108
TOPICS: New Age

Willow Tree
P.O. Box 151439
San Rafael, CA 94915
(415)-456-9335
CONTACT: Linda McKay TOPICS: New Age TYPE OF BUSINESS: Business services DESCRIPTION: Fulfillment house also offering various business services to writers, artists & musicians.

Wilson & Lake International
468 B Street, Ste. #3
Ashland, OR 97520
(503)-488-3350
TOPICS: New Age **OWNER:** Helen Lake **TYPE OF BUSINESS:** Travel Representatives **DESCRIPTION:** New Age tours to sacred sites in the British Isles. **PUBLICATIONS:** Brochures available.

Wish Garden Herbs
P.O. Box 1304
Boulder, CO 80306
TOPICS: New Age, Herbalogy, Holistic Health **DESCRIPTION:** Homeopathic formulas of oils & salves made on the new moons.

Womantrek
1411 East Olive Way
P.O. Box 20643
Seattle, WA 98102
(206)-325-4772
TOPICS: New Age

Wonderworks
51 Wolseley Street
Toronto, ON M5T 1A4
Canada
(416)-365-0809
CONTACT: Mary Anderson **TOPICS:** New Age **FOUNDED:** 1988

World Intra-Media Network, Incorporated
P.O. Box 3543
Chatsworth, CA 91313
(818)-341-8016
CONTACT: Shel Haims **TOPICS:** New Age **FOUNDED:** 1983 **TYPE OF BUSINESS:** Media licensing service **DESCRIPTION:** Media licensing service for Cable TV. Offers varied selections of programming.

Writers Publishing Service Company

1512 Western Avenue
Seattle, WA 98101
(206)-284-9954
CONTACT: William R. Griffin **TOPICS:** New Age, Metaphysics **FOUNDED:** 1976 **TYPE OF BUSINESS:** Publishing service **DESCRIPTION:** Offers a complete publishing service to authors who want to self-publish.

Wysong Medical Corporation
1880 North Eastman
Midland, MI 48640
(517)-631-0009
TOPICS: Holistic Healing, Nutrition, New Age **TYPE OF BUSINESS:** New Age products **DESCRIPTION:** Offers New Age products & activities in research, product development, environmental & nutritional health education. Produces several informative brochures & various literature.

Ye Olde Hawaiian Inn
P.O. Box 879
Big Island Kealakekua, HI 96750
(808)-322-9056
TOPICS: New Age

Yerba Prima
740 Jefferson Avenue
Ashland, OR 97520-3743
(503)-488-2228
TOPICS: Holistic Health **TYPE OF BUSINESS:** Health products **DESCRIPTION:** Manufacturer of Dietary Fiber & Internal Cleansing Products.

Yes! Inc.
P.O. Box 10726
Arlington, VA 22210
(703)-276-9550 **FAX** (202)-338-6969
CONTACT: Chris Popenoe **TOPICS:** New Age, Body-Mind Connection, Spirituality, Psychology, Occult **FOUNDED:** 1970 **DESCRIPTION:** Sells video

tapes & books.

Yoga In Bali
c/o Ann Barros
1540 Merrill Street
Santa Cruz, CA 95062-4064
(408)-475-8738
TOPICS: Yoga

Youth Ambassadors Of America
P.O. Box 5273
Bellingham, WA 98227
(206)-734-6132
TOPICS: New Age

Zeller And Letica, Incorporated
15 East 26th Street
New York, NY 10010
(800)-221-4112
TOPICS: New Age

Zumpfe Studio
4908 Martin Street
Lincoln, NE 68504-3068
(402)-476-6480
TOPICS: New Age, Metaphysics **OWNER:** Rosemary Zumpfe **FOUNDED:** 1988 **TYPE OF BUSINESS:** Commercial art **DESCRIPTION:** Commercial art company for New Age publishers, musicians, writers, etc.

Zygon International
1145 12th Avenue NW, #C-7
P.O. Box 7010
Issaquah, WA 98027
(206)-391-4595 (800)-869-7194
TOPICS: Body-Mind Connection, Holistic Health **OWNER:** Dane Spotts **TYPE OF BUSINESS:** Mail-order products **DESCRIPTION:** Offers New Age & holistic health mail-order items to expand the human mind & its potential: SuperMind Brainwave Syncronizer, Mind Development Library, SuperBrain Nutrient Program, Ultra Meditation, Super Brain Power Course.

Radio/Television

Following is an alphabetical list of Radio and Television stations offering New Age, Psychic and Metaphysical related programming. Shows feature talk, interviews, music, question and answer phone-ins, etc.

ABC Radio Network News
125 West End Avenue
New York, NY 10023
(212)-887-4159

RADIO PROGRAM; CONTACT: David Alpert, Producer **TOPICS:** New Age, Metaphysics **DESCRIPTION:** Daily program offering discussions on topics such as UFO's, crystals & the occult. Also offers news & music.

Aquarius Rising
P.O. Box 21251
Concord, CA 94521
(415)-827-9633

RADIO PROGRAM; CONTACT: Pamela Leigh **TOPICS:** New Age, Metaphysics, Astrology **FOUNDED:** 1988 **DESCRIPTION:** New Age radio show heard throughout Concord, San Francisco & Oakland areas.

Being There Now
P.O. Box 186, Station D
Scarborough, ONT M1R 5B5
Canada
(416)-482-0860

CONTACT: Anne Moore **TOPICS:** New Age, Dreams, Graphology, Psychic Phenomena, Meditation, Holistic Health, Channeling

CBS
524 West 57th Street
New York, NY 10019
(212)-975-3615

RADIO PROGRAM; TOPICS: New Age **DESCRIPTION:** Offers New Age music.

Celestial Dialogs
425 Butternut Court
Orange, CT 06477
(203)-795-5455

RADIO PROGRAM; CONTACT: Jill Dotlo **TOPICS:** New Age, Metaphysics, Occult, Paranormal Phenomena, UFO's, Holistic Health, Crystals **DESCRIPTION:** Interview & phone-in 1/2 hr. program for CT area. Covers numerous New Age, metaphysical, occult, etc. topics.

Changemakers
715 48th Avenue
San Francisco, CA 94121-3209
(415)-387-1771

RADIO PROGRAM; CONTACT: Gini Graham Scott **TOPICS:** New Age **FOUNDED:** 1968 **DESCRIPTION:** Weekly, 1/2 hour interview show on KUSF-FM in San Francisco. Host Gini Graham Scott. Deals with current social trends, changes in the field of consciousness & new discoveries. Books on shamanism, creativity, personal development & resolving conflict.

Changes
328-B Union Street
P.O. Box 7305

Santa Cruz, CA 95060
(408)-423-9687

RADIO PROGRAM; CONTACT: Elizabeth Gips **TOPICS:** New Age, Metaphysics **FOUNDED:** 1978 **DESCRIPTION:** Eclectic spiritual radio program featuring music, readings, interviews & talk. Broadcasted on K.K.U.P. 91.5 FM, Tuesdays 2:00-6:00 P.M. Host Elizabeth Gips.

Creative Catalyst
Box 10770
Oakland, CA 94610-0770
(415)-562-8617

CONTACT: James Thomas **TOPICS:** New Age

Cultural Media Services
11750 Lake Boulevard
Felton, CA 95018
(408)-335-2787

RADIO PROGRAM; CONTACT: Josh Wagner **TOPICS:** New Age, Metaphysics **FOUNDED:** 1985 **DESCRIPTION:** Non-profit organization, producing & syndicating educational radio programs in an interview format. Covers such topics as relationships, sexuality & recovery. Interviews authors, lecturers, workshop leaders & authorities in their respective fields.

EcoNews
P.O. Box 35473
Los Angeles, CA 90035
(310)-559-9160

TV PROGRAM; TOPICS: New Age **FOUNDED:** 1984 **DESCRIPTION:** The nation's only regular, weekly environmnetal series. Every ecological topic is explored in the field & in the studio. 200 half-hour shows available. Sponsored by Educational Communications.

Environmental Viewpoints
P.O. Box 351419
Los Angeles, CA 90035-0473
(310)-559-9160

RADIO PROGRAM; CONTACT: Nancy Pearlman **TOPICS:** New Age **FOUNDED:** 1977 **DESCRIPTION:** Weekly, half-hour magazine-style interview show in US & Canada. Hosted by Nancy Pearlman. Sponsored by Educational Communications & part of Environmental Directions radio series. Number one international environmental program offering news & information.

Eternity's Pillar, KTTV
5746 Sunset Boulevard
Hollywood, CA 90028

CONTACT: Alice Coltrane **TOPICS:** New Age

Focus Productions, Limited
P.O. Box 667
Lynden, WA 98264-0473
(206)-856-1536

RADIO PROGRAM; CONTACT: Bill Wilkinson **TOPICS:** New Age **FOUNDED:** 1979

Global Vision TV & Radio Productions
1017 South Van Ness Avenue
San Francisco, CA 94110
(415)-647-6374

TV PROGRAM; RADIO PROGRAM; CONTACT: Azarra Lanteri, Producer/Host **TOPICS:** New Age **FOUNDED:** 1988 **DESCRIPTION:** Focuses on positive approaches to peace. Emphasis is on social responsibility, environmental concerns, development of human potential, social & economic transformation, arts & entertainment. 1/2 hr. weekly on Viacom Cable 25; Marin 36 & Santa Rosa Cable.

Health Show, The
2249 South Josephine
Denver, CO 80210-4805
(303)-871-9191

CONTACT: Gretchen Pope **TOPICS:** New Age

Hearts Of Space
P.O. Box 1121
Larkspur, CA 94939
(415)-759-1130 **FAX** (415)-759-1166

RADIO PROGRAM; CONTACT: Leyla Rael Hill **TOPICS:** New Age, Metaphysics **FOUNDED:** 1972

Jack Gariss
KPFK 90.7 FM
3729 Cahuenga
North Hollywood, CA 91604
(818)-985-2711

CONTACT: Jack Gariss **TOPICS:** New Age

John Ankerberg Show, The
P.O. Box 8977
Chattanooga, TN 37411
(615)-892-7722

TV PROGRAM; CONTACT: John Weldon, Ph. D. **TOPICS:** Skepticism, Counter-Cult, Spirituality, New Age, UFO's, Holistic Health, Astrology **DESCRIPTION:** Weekly 1/2 hour TV show offering interviews between individuals whose religious views & truth claims differ. Informal debate format. Philosophy that Christianity is true & should be embraced & shared. Produces videos & books on New Age, UFO's & health.

KBOO 90.7 FM
20 Southeast 8th
Portland, OR 97214
(503)-231-8032

CONTACT: Linda Shirley **TOPICS:** New Age

KEST AM
1231 Market Street
San Francisco, CA 94103
(415)-626-5585

RADIO PROGRAM; CONTACT: LeBaron King **TOPICS:** New Age, Metaphysics **FOUNDED:** 1983

KFMU 103.9/105.5
2955 Village Drive, P.O. Box 772850

Steamboat Springs, CO 80477
(303)-879-5368
RADIO PROGRAM; CONTACT: Jonathan Christopher Renaud **TOPICS:** New Age **DESCRIPTION:** 5 hour program featuring mainly Jazz as well as New Age music. Serves the Vail-Steamboat Springs area.

KING 1090 AM

333 Dexter Avenue North
Seattle, WA 98109
(206)-455-3405
RADIO PROGRAM; CONTACT: Laura Lee **TOPICS:** New Age, Metaphysics, UFO's, Paranormal Phenomena, Holistic Health, Occult **DESCRIPTION:** Weekly live talk show with phone-ins every Sat. 11PM to 2 AM. Host Laura Lee. Covers numerous New Age, metaphysical, occult, etc. topics. Accepts ads.

KKUP-FM 91.5, Cupertino

P.O. Box 820
Cupertino, CA 95015
(408)-253-6000
RADIO PROGRAM; TOPICS: New Age, Psychic, Occult, Metaphysics, Paganism, Holistic Healing, Spirituality **DESCRIPTION:** Several regularly-scheduled shows dealing with New Age, Occult & numerous related topics. Heard throughout much of North-Central CA. Some shows: The Psychic Hour, Mystic Music & Musings, Neptune Currents, Jade Rain, Reality Check, Discovery, Changes, etc.

KLSK

2700 San Pedro Drive Northeast #104
Albuquerque, NM 87110-3333
(505)-983-5878
CONTACT: Alan & LuAnn Hutner, hosts **TOPICS:** New Age

KNPR 89.5

5151 Boulder Highway
Las Vegas, NV 89122
(702)-456-6695
CONTACT: Brian Sanders/John Stark **TOPICS:** New Age

KPFT

418 Lovett Boulevard
Houston, TX 77006
(713)-526-4000
TOPICS: New Age

KSTP-AM

2792 Maplewood Drive
St. Paul, MN 55109
(612)-481-9333
RADIO PROGRAM; CONTACT: Mike Coppock **TOPICS:** New Age, Metaphysics, Occult, UFO's **FOUNDED:** 1945

KUOM-AM

550 Rarig Center
330-21st Avenue, South
Minneapolis, MN 55455
(612)-625-3500
RADIO PROGRAM; CONTACT: Stuart Sanders **TOPICS:** New Age, Metaphysics **FOUNDED:** 1912

Les Productions Rubicon, Incorporated

B.P. 1370 Succ. Desjardins
Montreal, QC H5B 1H3

Canada
(514)-327-6172
CONTACT: Giles Bedard **TOPICS:** New Age

Lifeline: The Health Journal

825 Broughton Street
Victoria, BC V8W 1E5
Canada
(604)-386-1131
RADIO PROGRAM; CONTACT: Jerry Lucky **TOPICS:** New Age **FOUNDED:** 1989

Metaphysics Today/K-Video Production

14027 North 32nd Street
Phoenix, AZ 85032
(602)-971-9223
CONTACT: Dimension Cable Services **TOPICS:** New Age

Mike Kurban Variety Psychic Show

4328 North Lincoln Avenue
Chicago, IL 60618-1712
(312)-478-2410
TV PROGRAM; CONTACT: Michael Kurban **TOPICS:** New Age, Metaphysics, Occult, UFO's, Meditation, Crystals **DESCRIPTION:** One-half hour cable TV show aired twice a week on channel 19. Offers comedy, music & guests.

Musical Starstreams

P.O. Box 2004
Santa Fe, NM 87504
(505)-988-2004
RADIO PROGRAM; CONTACT: Frank Forest **TOPICS:** New Age, Metaphysics **FOUNDED:** 1981

New Age Cleveland

20800 Center Ridge #422
Rocky River, OH 44116
(216)-696-4444
CONTACT: John Rehac **TOPICS:** New Age

New Dimensions Radio

P.O. Box 410510
San Francisco, CA 94141
(415)-563-8899
RADIO PROGRAM; CONTACT: Justine Toms **TOPICS:** New Age, Metaphysics, Holistic Health, Spirituality **FOUNDED:** 1973 **DESCRIPTION:** Offers radio program & tapes covering New Age topics such as spirituality, health, the environment, social issues & mythology. Talk show interviews New Age experts & authors. Features New Age music.

New Era

P.O. Box 775
Bryn Mawr, PA 19010
TOPICS: New Age

News 2000

84 Main Street
Gloucester, MA 01930-1712
(508)-283-7310
CONTACT: Lewis Sandler **TOPICS:** New Age

Pacifica Radio Archive

3729 Cahuenga Boulevard West
North Hollywood, CA 91604
(818)-506-1077
RADIO PROGRAM; CONTACT: Bill Thomas **TOPICS:** New Age, Metaphysics **FOUNDED:** 1972 **DESCRIPTION:** Operates 5 radio stations whose

purpose is to promote peace. Also distributes New Age & Metaphysical books & cassettes.

Peaceworks

991 Terrace 49
Los Angeles, CA 90042
(213)-681-4292
CONTACT: Nancy Campeau **TOPICS:** New Age

Phoenix Phyre Show

704 North Highway 101
Leucadia, CA 92024
(619)-436-7740
CONTACT: Deborah Jordan **TOPICS:** New Age

Portraits In Sound

Box 2305
Livermore, CA 94550
TOPICS: New Age

Progressive Radio Network

170 Ludlow Avenue
Northvale, NJ 07647
CONTACT: James Wynbrandt, Editor **TOPICS:** New Age

Psychic Psychology

2146 D Alameda Avenue
Alameda, CA 94501-4340
(510)-523-1936
TV PROGRAM; CONTACT: Lance Thurston **TOPICS:** New Age, Metaphysics, Astrology, Tarot, Hypnotism, Past Life Regression, Crystals **FOUNDED:** 1988 **DESCRIPTION:** Live call-in interview talk show hosted by Lance Thurston. Alameda Cable Ch. 3, every Thurs. 7:30 PM. Replayed Marin Cable Ch. 36. Covers San Francisco/Sacramento areas. Topics include astrology, tarot, hypnosis, dowsing, auras, crystal, colors, health.

Radio Earth International, Incorporated

1724 Sherman Avenue
Evanston, IL 60201
(312)-492-9300
RADIO PROGRAM; CONTACT: Michael D. Poulos & Suzanne Poulos **TOPICS:** New Age **FOUNDED:** 1983

Sound Currents Of The Earth-Radio Series

12 Goodwin Street
Newport, ME 04953-1250
(207)-368-5866
RADIO PROGRAM; CONTACT: Jim Beam, Pres. **TOPICS:** New Age **FOUNDED:** 1986 **DESCRIPTION:** Radio series reviewing various forms of music including ancient, contemporary, spiritual vocal, environmental sounds & New Age. Promotes positive cultural understanding & peace through music. Heard worldwide on University For Peace & US FM stations.

Spiritual World Network

150 Hamakua Drive, #332
Kailua, HI 96734
(808)-944-1412
TV PROGRAM; RADIO PROGRAM; CONTACT: Don Smith **TOPICS:** New Age, Spirituality **FOUNDED:** 1986 **DESCRIPTION:** Produces programs reflecting the entire spiritual spectrum world-wide, non-denominational, unbiased &

impartial. Developing a worldwide TV/radio network for 24 hour programming. Advances love, peace & harmony by alerting people to their own spirituality.

Sun Fire Productions
10 Park Avenue
Basalt, CO 81621
(303)-927-9414
RADIO PROGRAM; CONTACT: Debra Nuzzi, M.H. TOPICS: New Age, Occult, Holistic Health, Herbalogy DESCRIPTION: Weekly radio show on KONK, 8-10 PM Mondays. Hosted by Debra Nuzzi, M.H. Conducts topical interviews on New Age & New World, the environment, music & transformation.

These Psychic Times
P.O. Box 641
Conifer, CO 80433-4805
(303)-794-7213
CONTACT: Jimmy Finns And Jennifer Sweete TOPICS: New Age

Thinking Allowed Productions
2560 Ninth Street, Ste. 123
Berkeley, CA 94710
(415)-548-4415

TV PROGRAM; CONTACT: Jeffrey Mishlove, Ph.D TOPICS: New Age, Spirituality, Holistic Health, Channeling, Parapsychology, Dreams, Psychology FOUNDED: 1987 DESCRIPTION: Conversations on the leading edge of knowledge & discovery with host Dr. Jeffrey Mishlove. Show based on select Thinking Allowed video programs. Shown on Public Television stations throughout the U.S.

Total Media Communications
11314 North East 26th Avenue
Vancouver, WA 98686
(206)-574-6618
TV PROGRAM; CONTACT: Sid Brown TOPICS: New Age, Metaphysics FOUNDED: 1980

Twilight Productions
1550 California Street
San Francisco, CA 94121
(415)-752-1453 FAX (415)-752-1453
CONTACT: David K. Waldman TOPICS: New Age

Visions Productions
P.O. Box 93155
Los Angeles, CA 90093
(213)-969-0247
TV PROGRAM; CONTACT: Villi Aman TOPICS: New Age, Metaphysics FOUNDED: 1984

Whole Life Radio Network
123 West Torrance Boulevard, #102
Redondo Beach, CA 90277
(213)-374-9796
CONTACT: Richard Greene And Dee Riggs TOPICS: New Age

WOMP-AM
P.O. Box 448
Bellaire, OH 43906
(614)-676-5661
CONTACT: Howard Monroe, News Director TOPICS: New Age, Occult, UFO's

WQBK
P.O. Box 1300
Albany, NY 12201
(518)-462-5555
RADIO PROGRAM; CONTACT: Alaina Zackery TOPICS: New Age, Metaphysics FOUNDED: 1989

WXPN 88.9
3095 Spruce Street
Philadelphia, PA 19104
(215)-898-6677
RADIO PROGRAM; CONTACT: Paradigm TOPICS: New Age, Metaphysics, Occult, UFO's, Meditation FOUNDED: 1974

Audio & Video Producers

Within this section is an alphabetical list of individuals and companies producing New Age, Metaphysical, etc. audio and video tapes featuring music, spoken audio, self-help, nature sounds, children's materials, CD's, etc. Many companies offer catalogs and sell mail-order. Contact them for further details. See the Music, Spoken Audio & Video Chapter for additional titles.

21st Century Publications
101 California Street, 35th Floor
San Francisco, CA 94111
(415)-954-1511
TOPICS: New Age

Access Video Productions
P.O. Box 5547
Berkeley, CA 94705
(415)-528-6044 (800)-843-3649
CONTACT: David Karp TOPICS: Metaphysics
TYPE OF BUSINESS: Video Production
DESCRIPTION: Produces and distributes video programs pertaining to healing, meditation, metaphysics and spirituality.

Achieve, Inc.
1801 North Georgia, #12
Little Rock, AR 72207
(501)-666-7304
VIDEO PRODUCER; TOPICS: Psychology, New Age
DESCRIPTION: Self-help educational videos & publications. Offering exclusive messaging & communication devices.

Acorn Music
323 Marine Street, #5
Santa Monica, CA 90405
(213)-392-6473
AUDIO PRODUCER; CONTACT: Jessie Marcus And Karma Viera TOPICS: New Age, Metaphysics
FOUNDED: 1983

Acoustic Medicine Productions
2462 Matilya Canyon
Ojai, CA 93023
(805)-646-9721
CONTACT: Eddie Guthmar TOPICS: New Age

Adventue Unlimited, Incorporated
101 Star Road
Livingston, MT 59047
(406)-222-1416
AUDIO PRODUCER; CONTACT: Robert J. Resetar
TOPICS: New Age FOUNDED: 1985

Alcazar
P.O. Box 429
Waterbury, VT 05676
(802)-244-8657 (800)-541-9904
AUDIO PRODUCER; CONTACT: Lori Morse
TOPICS: New Age TYPE OF BUSINESS: New Age music DESCRIPTION: Dedicated to the national promotion & sales of independent recording artists. 18,000 titles of New Age, World's Ethnic, classical, folk, Jazz & children's music. Annual catalog's available: New Age, Holiday, Children's.

Alpha J2 Services, Incorporated

9921 Carmel Mountain Road, Suite 183
San Diego, CA 92129
(619)-538-8484
TOPICS: New Age

Alpha Theta Omega Audio
1611 St. Dennis
Montreal, Quebec H2X 3K3
Canada
(514)-843-6943
TOPICS: New Age, Metaphysics

Anahata
Route 1, Box 952
Eastsound, WA 98245
(206)-376-4588
CONTACT: James Hardman TOPICS: New Age

Ancient Future
P.O. Box 264
Kentfield, CA 94914
(415)-459-1892
TOPICS: New Age

Aquarian Music Publishing, Inc.
4251 Kipling, Ste. 310
P.O. Box 0501
Wheat Ridge, CO 80034
(303)-238-9610
AUDIO PRODUCER; CONTACT: Fran Baxter
TOPICS: New Age TYPE OF BUSINESS: Music Publishers

Arche International
212 South Marion Street
Oak Park, IL 60302
(312)-848-9191
AUDIO PRODUCER; TOPICS: Metaphysics, New Age DESCRIPTION: Produces motivational, inspirational & self-help audio cassette tapes.

Ark Group, The
425 Alabama Street
San Francisco, CA 94110
(415)-863-3555
CONTACT: Alan Kessler TOPICS: New Age

Arsha Vidya Gurukulam
P.O. Box 1059
Saylorsburg, PA 18353
(717)-992-2399 (717)-992-2339
AUDIO PRODUCER; CONTACT: Irene Schleisher
TOPICS: New Age FOUNDED: 1982

Artifex Records
604 Overview Lane
Franklin, TN 37064
(615)-794-3349

AUDIO PRODUCER; CONTACT: Peter Miller
TOPICS: New Age FOUNDED: 1989

Artistic Video
87 Tyler Avenue
Sound Beach, NY 11789
(516)-744-0449
VIDEO PRODUCER; CONTACT: Bob Klein
TOPICS: New Age, Metaphysics FOUNDED: 1985

Astromusic
P.O. Box 118
New York, NY 10033
(212)-942-0004
AUDIO PRODUCER; TOPICS: Astrology, Metaphysics OWNER: Gerald Jay Markoe TYPE OF BUSINESS: New Age Music & Astrology FOUNDED: 1980 DESCRIPTION: Translates Astrological Charts into music.

Attunement
Box 32731
Phoenix, AZ 85064
(602)-225-8732
CONTACT: Lenore Culin TOPICS: New Age

Audio Forum
96 Broad Street
Department R
Guilford, CT 06437
(203)-453-9794
TOPICS: New Age

Audio Literature, Incorporated
P.O. Box 7327
Berkeley, CA 94707
(800)-841-2665
AUDIO PRODUCER; CONTACT: John Hunt
TOPICS: New Age, Metaphysics FOUNDED: 1987

Audio Renaissance Tapes, Inc.
9110 Sunset Boulevard
Suite 200
Los Angeles, CA 90069
(213)-273-9755
TOPICS: New Age

Automated Learning
336 Old Hook Road
Westwood, NJ 07675
(201)-664-8500
TOPICS: New Age

Awakening Heart Productions
2106 Sonoma Avenue
Santa Rosa, CA 95405
(707)-546-9744
AUDIO PRODUCER; CONTACT: Dean Tucker
TOPICS: New Age, Metaphysics FOUNDED: 1980

Backroads Distributors
417 Tamal Plaza
Corte Madera, CA 94925
(415)-924-4848 (800)-825-4848
CONTACT: Darlene Johnson TOPICS: New Age

Backroads Music
P.O. Box 1007
Larkspur, CA 94939
TOPICS: Holistic Health

Balance Productions, Incorporated
P.O. Box 425
Somerspoint, NJ 08244
(609)-653-0159
TOPICS: New Age

Bantam Audio Publishing
666 Fifth Avenue
New York, NY 10103
(212)-765-6500 (800)-223-6834
AUDIO PRODUCER; TOPICS: New Age

Beyond Science Fiction
414 South 41st Street
Richmond, CA 94804
(415)-451-5818
CONTACT: Rey King TOPICS: New Age

BHL
Box 6340ND
San Rafael, CA 94903
TOPICS: New Age

Blue Sky
655 Duboise #E
San Rafael, CA 94901
(415)-453-8845
TOPICS: New Age

Bokajo Enterprises
P.O. Box 1400
Wildomar, CA 92395
(714)-678-7078
CONTACT: Bob Rush TOPICS: New Age

Canyon Cinema
2325 3rd Street, #338
San Francisco, CA 94107
(415)-626-2255
TOPICS: New Age

Canyon Records And Indian Arts
4143 North 16th Street
Phoenix, AZ 85016
(602)-266-4823
AUDIO PRODUCER; CONTACT: Bob Nuss
TOPICS: New Age, Metaphysics, Occult FOUNDED:
1951

Celestial Harmonies
P.O. Box 30122
Tucson, AZ 85751
(602)-326-4400
AUDIO PRODUCER; CONTACT: Ethan Edgecombe
TOPICS: New Age, Metaphysics FOUNDED: 1979

Centerpoint Distributors, Inc.
434 South 1st Street
San Jose, CA 95113
(408)-993-9388
AUDIO & VIDEO PRODUCER; CONTACT: Michael
Cutler TOPICS: New Age, Metaphysics TYPE OF

BUSINESS: Producer, Distributor FOUNDED: 1986
DESCRIPTION: Producer & distributor of
audio/video tapes & books concerned with music &
holistic health. Offers Human Potential Series.

Chacra Alternative Music
35 Parklane Place, Department 3
Dollard-des-Ormeaux, QC H9G 1B8
Canada
(514)-624-0278
TOPICS: New Age

Chameleon Music Group
3355 West El Segundo Boulevard
Hawthorne, CA 90250
(213)-973-8282
AUDIO PRODUCER; CONTACT: Moose McMains
TOPICS: New Age FOUNDED: 1988

Chameleon Productions, Incorporated
5800 Arlington Avenue, Studio 3M
Bronx, NY 10471
(212)-548-2932
VIDEO PRODUCER; TOPICS: New Age OWNER:
Yvonne Chism-Peace TYPE OF BUSINESS:
Publisher/Producer DESCRIPTION: An arts media
company producing short films & books based on
modern creative personal mythology. Titles: I
Willa/Soil; I Willa/Scourge. Films: She; Sky.

Changeworks, The
P.O. Box 5909
Bend, OR 97708-5909
(503)-382-1894
TOPICS: Hypnotism

Cine Video, Incorporated
2800 Bellamah Drive
Santa Fe, NM 87505
(505)-473-4974
VIDEO PRODUCER; CONTACT: Richard Startzman
TOPICS: New Age, Metaphysics FOUNDED: 1981

Cinema Guild, Incorporated, The
1697 Broadway, Rm 802
New York, NY 10019
(212)-246-5522 FAX (212)-246-5525
VIDEO PRODUCER; CONTACT: Gary Crowdus
TOPICS: New Age, Metaphysics TYPE OF
BUSINESS: Film & videos producers FOUNDED:
1975 DESCRIPTION: Sales, rentals & distribution of
16mm films & videos. Catalog available upon
request.

Cinergy Entertainment
858 12th Street, #8
Santa Monica, CA 90403
TOPICS: Body-Mind Connection

Clarity Unlimited
P.O. Box 450
Templeton, CA 93465
(805)-434-1352
TOPICS: New Age

Clear Lake Productions
Box 3007
Santa Cruz, CA 95063
TOPICS: Yoga

Clear Productions, Inc.
1489 Coddington Road
Brooktondale, NY 14817

(607)-273-2974
AUDIO PRODUCER; CONTACT: Brian Earle
TOPICS: New Age, Metaphysics FOUNDED: 1988

**Conversations On The Leading Edge
Of Knowledge And Discovery**
315 Third Street
Suite 161
San Rafael, CA 94901
(415)-456-2532
TOPICS: New Age

Cooper Sound Waves
P.O. Box 5190
Santa Monica, CA 90405-0190
(213)-392-7784
AUDIO PRODUCER; CONTACT: Jessie Allen
Coooper TOPICS: New Age FOUNDED: 1983

Cosmic Temple Creations
90 Roca Roja Road
Sedona, AZ 86336
(602)-284-9473
AUDIO PRODUCER; TOPICS: New Age OWNER:
David Cosmo TYPE OF BUSINESS: New Age music
FOUNDED: 1986 DESCRIPTION: Offers New Age
East-West Music Fusion, relaxing & transcendental
music cassettes. Produces 11 titles by David Cosmo
including the Cosmic Voyage series, Sedona
Moonscapes & Joys of Nature.

Coyote Oldman Music
Rural Route 2, Box 857
Gerryville, AR 72616-9420
TOPICS: New Age

Creative Audio Services
1538 North Martel Avenue #104
Los Angeles, CA 90046-3600
AUDIO PRODUCER; CONTACT: Joe Martin
TOPICS: New Age, Metaphysics FOUNDED: 1987

Crystal Consciousness
P.O. Box 714, Department YP-1
Claremont, CA 91711
TOPICS: New Age DESCRIPTION: Offers large
selection of Marcel Vogel/W. Klausne audio/video
tapes.

Crystal Music Video
35 Aspen
Marble, CO 81623
(303)-963-3680
VIDEO PRODUCER; CONTACT: Barry TOPICS:
New Age, Metaphysics FOUNDED: 1987

DA Music
P.O. Box 3
Little Silver, NJ 07739
TOPICS: New Age

Dargason Music
P.O. Box 189
Burbank, CA 91503
(818)-846-4981
CONTACT: Jon Harvey TOPICS: New Age

David Hinz Productions
P.O. Box 45490
Seattle, WA 98145
(206)-523-5883
TOPICS: New Age

David Michael Productions
P.O. Box 694
Felton, CA 95018
(408)-479-1864
CONTACT: David Michael TOPICS: New Age

Daylight Music Productions
P.O. Box 284
Metuchen, NJ 08840
(201)-548-7918
AUDIO PRODUCER; CONTACT: Dennis Andrew
TOPICS: New Age, Holistic Health FOUNDED:
1984

Dean Aster Publishing Company
P.O. Box 10752
Merrillville, IN 46411-8810
(219)-980-6554
AUDIO PRODUCER; TOPICS: New Age, Holistic
Health OWNER: Anthony Phillip DESCRIPTION:
Publishers & producers of self-help & health related
audio tapes & books.

Deepspace Disc Productions
P.O. Box 911
Middletown, CA 95461
(707)-987-9467
AUDIO & VIDEO PRODUCER; TOPICS: New Age,
Spirituality OWNER: David Gibney TYPE OF
BUSINESS: Audio/video producers DESCRIPTION:
New Age record company & film producers. Titles:
Shaman Journey by David Gibney & Paul Horn;
Blissful Magic by David Gibney; Film Cue
Compilation by David Gibney.

Dharma Books
P.O. Box 724947
Atlanta, GA 30339
(404)-941-5634
AUDIO PRODUCER; TOPICS: New Age,
Metaphysics OWNER: Debra Cohen TYPE OF
BUSINESS: Producers & Publishers DESCRIPTION:
Publishers & producers of New Age & Metaphysical
books & audio tapes.

Dimi Press
3820 Oak Hollow Lane, Southeast
P.O. Box 3363
Salem, OR 97302
(503)-364-7698 FAX (503)-769-6207
AUDIO PRODUCER; CONTACT: Dick Lutz
TOPICS: New Age, Meditation TYPE OF BUSINESS:
New Age tapes & books FOUNDED: 1981
DESCRIPTION: Publishes & produces books & 12
tapes on Metaphysics & the New Age Movement.
PUBLICATIONS: *Feel Better! Live Longer! Relax*
EDITOR: Dick Lutz TOPICS: New Age, Meditation
TYPE: Book, 144 pgs. PRICE: $9.95

Dodona Music
P.O. Box 41
Claremont, CA 91711
(714)-595-6912
AUDIO PRODUCER; CONTACT: Daryl Fleming
TOPICS: New Age FOUNDED: 1986

Dogpleh
Box 4024
Hollywood, CA 90078
(213)-957-2286
AUDIO PRODUCER; CONTACT: Mauro Oliveria
TOPICS: New Age FOUNDED: 1989

Double Star Productions
P.O. Box 1864
Kahului, HI 96732
(808)-371-7737
TOPICS: New Age

Duvall Media, Incorporated
170 East 17th Street
Costa Mesa, CA 92627
(714)-631-3445
AUDIO PRODUCER; CONTACT: Neva Duyndam
TOPICS: New Age, Metaphysics FOUNDED: 1988

Dynamic Pathyways
P.O. Box 37106
Tucson, AZ 85740-7106
(602)-742-4384 FAX (602)-797-3557
AUDIO PRODUCER; TOPICS: New Age,
Metaphysics OWNER: Andrea Holly Gold TYPE OF
BUSINESS: New Age tapes FOUNDED: 1989
DESCRIPTION: Publishers & producers of New Age
books & audio tapes. Features Gold Stars Speakers
Bureau. Offers Successful Living Tapes, materials,
seminars, training for individuals & businesses.
Produces mail-order catalog: Resource Guide For
Successful Living. PUBLICATIONS: *Stress-Free
Living; Creative Dreaming: Transform Your Life;
Ending Co-Dependency Forever; God Of The 12
Steps; Energy Linking; All by Gary Yamamoto.
Music titles: Soaring; Peaceful Pond; Ocean
Dreams.*

Earth Mother Productions, Inc.
P.O. Box 43204
Tucson, AZ 85733
(602)-575-5114 (602)-885-9399
CONTACT: Tim Ballingham TOPICS: New Age

Earth View, Incorporated
6514 18th Avneue, Northeast
Seattle, WA 98115
(206)-527-3168
CONTACT: Bryan Brewer TOPICS: New Age

Earthsounds
2588 - D El Camino Real, #335
Carlsbad, CA 92008
CONTACT: Brian And Kara-Gail Meredith TOPICS:
New Age

Eastern Gate Publishing Company
P.O. Box 1485
Front Royal, VA 22630
(703)-636-3788
AUDIO PRODUCER; CONTACT: Alex Jones
TOPICS: New Age FOUNDED: 1980

Effective Learning Systems
5221 Edina Industrial Boulevard
Edina, MN 55435
(612)-893-1680
TOPICS: New Age

Elfin Music Company
P.O. Box 915
Camden, ME 04843
(207)-236-6339
AUDIO PRODUCER; CONTACT: Ed Van Fleet
TOPICS: New Age, Metaphysics FOUNDED: 1981

Emerald Green Sound Productions
P.O. Box 16144
Santa Fe, NM 87506

(505)-473-7383
AUDIO PRODUCER; TOPICS: New Age OWNER:
Margo Covington TYPE OF BUSINESS: New Age
Tapes FOUNDED: 1987 DESCRIPTION: Purpose is
to offer finest quality recordings available that
uplifts, engages the mind & spirit, invigorates
creativity & encourages the personal imperative in
all of us. Offers CDs, cassettes, soundtracks for
film/video, custom productions, music series.
PUBLICATIONS: By Crutcher: *Machu Picchu
Impression; Chaco Canyon; Amazon Song.* By
Crutcher & Oliver: *Love Dance.* By Martin: *Voyage
Of The Precious Child.* By *Momaday: Storyteller.*

Emerald Web
P.O. Box 3156
North Fort Myers, FL 33918
(813)-997-0323
CONTACT: Kat Epple TOPICS: New Age,
Metaphysics

Emerald Webb Music
P.O. Box 5503
Berkeley, CA 94705
(415)-548-9766
TOPICS: New Age, Occult DESCRIPTION: Offers
ethereal progressive music of flutes & synthesizers
on tapes, LPs & CDs.

Emmett Miller, MD Cassettes
945 Evelyn Street
Menlo Park, CA 94025
(415)-328-7171
AUDIO PRODUCER; TOPICS: New Age,
Metaphysics FOUNDED: 1982 DESCRIPTION:
Produces audio & video cassettes concerned with
meditation, visualization & deep relaxation. Also
publishes instructions books on the subject.

Empey Enterprises
810 Alexander
Greenville, MI 48838
(616)-754-7036
CONTACT: Maureen Burns TOPICS: New Age

Empty Bell Music
609 Jackson Street
Albany, CA 94706
(415)-528-8834
CONTACT: John Singer TOPICS: New Age

Epitapes
Box 458
Sunderland, MA 01375
AUDIO PRODUCER; TOPICS: Occult, New Age
OWNER: Michael Tetrault TYPE OF BUSINESS:
New Age music DESCRIPTION: A source for very
rare & unusual music such as Zero Kama whose
instruments are made from human skulls & bones.

Etherean Music
4685 Gordon Drive
Boulder, CO 80303
(303)-499-4484 (800)-456-5444
AUDIO PRODUCER; CONTACT: Richard Carey
TOPICS: New Age FOUNDED: 1989

Expansion Records
P.O. Box 996
Cardiff-By-The-Sea, CA 92007
(619)-944-3456
TOPICS: New Age

Explorers
964 Quivera Street
Laguna Beach, CA 92651-3822
(714)-962-8399
TOPICS: New Age

F.A.R.
277 Hudson Street
Cornwall-On-Hudson, NY 12520
(914)-534-8197
TOPICS: New Age

Firehusker Publishing Company
89 Massachusettss Avenue, Suite 438
Boston, MA 02115
(617)-247-4186
AUDIO PRODUCER; CONTACT: Rick Keuthe
TOPICS: New Age, Metaphysics FOUNDED: 1989

Firewalking Institute Of Research & Education
Box 1738
Twain Harte, CA 95383
(209)-928-4035
AUDIO PRODUCER; TOPICS: Firewalking TYPE OF BUSINESS: Firewalking Seminar DESCRIPTION: Offers audio cassette Firewalking Seminars by Tolly Burkan.

First Run Features
153 Waverly Place
New York, NY 10014
(212)-243-0600
TOPICS: New Age PUBLICATIONS: 28 Up TOPICS: New Age TYPE: Video

Flying Fish Records
1304 West Schubert
Chicago, IL 60614
(312)-528-5455
AUDIO PRODUCER; CONTACT: Jerry Seymour TOPICS: New Age FOUNDED: 1974

Focus On Animals
P.O. Box 150
Trumbull, CT 06611
(203)-377-1116
VIDEO PRODUCER; CONTACT: Esther Mechler TOPICS: New Age, Metaphysics FOUNDED: 1987

Forest Music
c/o John Niemi
1635-B Liholiho Street
Honolulu, HI 96822
(808)-536-1639
CONTACT: John Niemi TOPICS: New Age

Fortuna Records
P.O. Box 1116
Novato, CA 94947
TOPICS: New Age

Freshwater Records
P.O. Box 27713
Los Angeles, CA 90027-0713
(213)-660-5444
AUDIO PRODUCER; TOPICS: New Age FOUNDED: 1983

Funny Business
P.O. Box 3000-333
Santa Barbara, CA 93130
(800)-521-2315

AUDIO PRODUCER; TOPICS: New Age FOUNDED: 1983

GAIA Records
121 West 27th Street
New York, NY 10001
(212)-645-5252
TOPICS: New Age

GAIA Video Company
1122 South Roxbury Drive
Los Angeles, CA 90035
(213)-557-2112
CONTACT: Noelle Imparato TOPICS: New Age

Gateways Books And Tapes
P.O. Box 370
Nevada City, CA 95959
(916)-477-1116
AUDIO PRODUCER; CONTACT: Iven Lourie/Julia Glasse TOPICS: New Age, Metaphysics, Parapsychology, Occult, Holistic Healing FOUNDED: 1971 DESCRIPTION: Produces & publishes books & audio tapes. PUBLICATIONS: Inner Journeys EDITOR: Iven Lourie, Nancy Christie TOPICS: New Age TYPE: Audio PUBLICATIONS: Original American Book Of The Dead EDITOR: E.J. Gold TOPICS: Death TYPE: Book PRICE: $12.50 PUBLICATIONS: Practical Work On Self EDITOR: E.J. Gold TOPICS: Psychology TYPE: Book PRICE: $12.50 PUBLICATIONS: Visions In The Stone: Journey To The Source Of Hidden Knowledge EDITOR: E.J. Gold TOPICS: Tarot, Occult TYPE: Book PRICE: $14.50

Gateways Institute
P.O. Box 1778
Ojai, CA 93024
(805)-646-0267 (800)-477-8908
AUDIO PRODUCER; CONTACT: Leslie Brice, Pres. TOPICS: New Age, Psychology OWNER: Jonathan Parker, Ph. D. TYPE OF BUSINESS: Mail-order DESCRIPTION: Offers hundreds of self-help & transpersonal tape programs.

Genetic Music
6017 Bellingham Avenue
North Hollywood, CA 91606
(818)-763-3742
CONTACT: Richard Rosing TOPICS: New Age DESCRIPTION: Original New Age production of music & film scores with deluxe studio.

GLA Records
3055 Blackwell
Vista, CA 92084
(619)-758-2743
AUDIO PRODUCER; TOPICS: New Age OWNER: Richard Collins TYPE OF BUSINESS: New Age music DESCRIPTION: Produces soothing original New Age piano music. PUBLICATIONS: A Single Rose; Finding Your Heart

Global Pacific Records, Inc.
270 Perkins Street
P.O. Box 2001
Sonoma, CA 95476
(707)-996-2748 (800)-545-2001
AUDIO PRODUCER; CONTACT: Bette Timm TOPICS: New Age OWNER: Howard Sapper TYPE OF BUSINESS: Audio producers FOUNDED: 1979 DESCRIPTION: Founder & leader in New

Age/World music for over a decade & taking an instrumental role in its progress. Offers 43 titles of New Age, classical, jazz & world music such as Across A Rainbow Sea by Steve Kindler & Winter Classics by Georgia Kelly.

Golden Harp Enterprises
P.O. Box 335
Ben Lomond, CA 95005
(408)-336-8888
AUDIO PRODUCER; CONTACT: Joel Andrews/Karen TOPICS: New Age, Metaphysics FOUNDED: 1985

Grace And Goddess Unlimited
P.O. Box 4367
Boulder, CO 80306-4367
AUDIO PRODUCER; CONTACT: Cindee Grace TOPICS: New Age, Holistic Health, Hypnotism OWNER: Cindee Grace TYPE OF BUSINESS: Publisher/Audio Producers FOUNDED: 1983 DESCRIPTION: Offers audio tapes: Songs Of The Goddess (music) & Feminist Hypnosis Series. Also publishes New Age books. Distributed by New Leaf & Ladyslipper. Free catalog available upon request.

Gramavision
100 Seaview Drive
Secaucus, NJ 07094
(201)-863-6120
TOPICS: New Age

Great Northern Arts
114 Lexington Avenue
New York, NY 10016
(212)-532-1414
TOPICS: New Age

Green Linnet Records
70 Turner Hill Road
New Canaan, CT 06840
(203)-966-0864 FAX (203)-972-1338
AUDIO PRODUCER; CONTACT: Chris Teskey TOPICS: New Age FOUNDED: 1973

Grindle Audio
P.O. Box 5165
Scottsdale, AZ 85261-5165
(800)-624-5846
TOPICS: New Age

Hanuman Foundation Tape Library
524 San Anselmo Avenue, #201
San Anselmo, CA 94960-2614
AUDIO & VIDEO PRODUCER; CONTACT: Bob Zaslow TOPICS: New Age, Metaphysics, Holistic Healing, Spirituality TYPE OF BUSINESS: New Age tapes FOUNDED: 1973 DESCRIPTION: Produces New Age audio & video tapes related to spiritual education & concerned with the teachings of Stephen Levine, Ram Dass, Emmanuel & Soma Krishna. PUBLICATIONS: Death Is Not An Outrage; The Listening Heart; Kirtan

Harps Of Lorien
610 North Star Route
Questa, NM 87556
(505)-586-1307
AUDIO PRODUCER; CONTACT: Lorna Weisman TOPICS: New Age, Metaphysics FOUNDED: 1982

Hartley Film Foundation
Cat Rock Road

Cos Cob, CT 06807
(203)-869-1818 (800)-937-1819
VIDEO PRODUCER; TOPICS: New Age, Metaphysics, Parapsychology, Holistic Health, Psychic Phenomena, Spirituality, Meditation **OWNER:** Elda Hartley **TYPE OF BUSINESS:** New Age videos **FOUNDED:** 1969 **DESCRIPTION:** New Age film producers distributing to colleges, hospitals, libraries, churches & New Age centers. Covers numerous topics such as New Age, health, religion, parapsychology, death, meditation, etc. **PUBLICATIONS:** *Art Of Meditation* **TOPICS:** New Age, Meditation **TYPE:** Video **PUBLICATIONS:** *Taoism* **TOPICS:** New Age **TYPE:** Video **PUBLICATIONS:** *The Global Brain* **TOPICS:** New Age **TYPE:** Video **PUBLICATIONS:** *Therapeutic Touch* **TOPICS:** New Age **TYPE:** Video

Healing Arts Home Video
1229 Third Street
Santa Monica, CA 90401
(213)-458-9795
TOPICS: New Age

Healthy Alternatives, Incorporated
P.O. Box 3234
Reston, VA 22090
(703)-430-6650
TOPICS: New Age

Heart Consort Music - BMI
410 First Street West
Mt. Vernon, IA 52314
(319)-895-8557
AUDIO PRODUCER; CONTACT: James L. Kennedy/Catherine Lawson **TOPICS:** New Age, Metaphysics **FOUNDED:** 1980

Heartart Music
P.O. Box 811
Montrose, CA 91021-0811
(818)-957-1670
TOPICS: New Age

Hearts Of Space Records
P.O. Box 31321
San Francisco, CA 94131
(415)-759-1130
AUDIO PRODUCER; TOPICS: New Age **OWNER:** Stephen Hill **TYPE OF BUSINESS:** Audio producers **DESCRIPTION:** Producers of 32 audio titles including: Novus Magnificat by Constance Demey; Music To Disappear In Vol. I & II by Raphael; & Sirens by Mychael Danna.

Heavensong Recordings
P.O. Box 1087
Capitola, CA 95010-1087
(808)-878-6415
AUDIO PRODUCER; CONTACT: Michael **TOPICS:** New Age, Metaphysics, Holistic Healing **FOUNDED:** 1978

Heavensong Recordings
P.O. Box 450
Kula, HI 96790-0811
(808)-878-6415
TOPICS: New Age

Hermetic Records, Inc.
10653 Yankee Street
Miamisburg, OH 45342
(800)-446-7326

TOPICS: New Age

High Mesa Press
P.O. Box 2267
Taos, NM 87571
(505)-758-8769
AUDIO PRODUCER; CONTACT: Gi Mack **TOPICS:** New Age, Channeling **OWNER:** Joy Franklin **TYPE OF BUSINESS:** New Age tapes **DESCRIPTION:** Produces New Age tapes & books of Bartholomew channelings. Titles of tapes: We Call Can Read; Coming Of Wizard.

Higher Octave Music
8033 Sunset Boulevard, Ste. 41
Los Angeles, CA 90046
(213)-856-0039 **FAX** (213)-646-6490
AUDIO PRODUCER; TOPICS: New Age **OWNER:** Scott Bergstein **TYPE OF BUSINESS:** New Age music **DESCRIPTION:** Offers 50 titles of New Age/World music. Examples: Nouveau Flamenio by Ottmar Liebert; Apurimac by Cusco; Moon Water by Hime Kam. Sells wholesale & mail-order. Free catalog available.

Hummingbird Productions
Box 535
Rancho Santa Fe, CA 92067
(619)-966-0939
AUDIO PRODUCER; TOPICS: New Age **OWNER:** Joanne Peters **TYPE OF BUSINESS:** New Age music **DESCRIPTION:** Music publishing company & award winning radio producers featuring New Age & classical artists. Sells wholesale, retail & through distributors. **PUBLICATIONS:** *Titles: Healing Music; The Meditative Chopin Vol. I & II; Happy Birthday Chopin*

Iamco Subliminal Tape Service
P.O. Box 5146
Ormond Beach, FL 32175
(904)-672-2616
TOPICS: New Age

Idyllwild Music Company
P.O. Box 444
Idyllwild, CA 92349
(714)-659-4544
AUDIO PRODUCER; CONTACT: Joey Lattimer **TOPICS:** New Age, Metaphysics **FOUNDED:** 1988

Injoy Productions
1490 Riverside Avenue
Boulder, CO 80304-0839
(800)-326-2082
TOPICS: Birth **PUBLICATIONS:** *Special Delivery: Creating The Birth You Want For You And Your Baby* **EDITOR:** Charlie Stein, Ilana Gali-El **TOPICS:** Birth **TYPE:** Video

Inner Circle Of Enchantment, Inc. (I.C.E.)
P.O. Box 1046
Lodi, NJ 07644
(800)-288-5877
TOPICS: New Age, Metaphysics

Inner Harmonies
3 Crail View
Northleach, Gloucestershire GL54 3QH
England
TOPICS: New Age

Innergarden
P.O. Box 2113
Lake Oswego, OR 97035
TOPICS: New Age

InnerSong Records
500 Molino Street
Los Angeles, CA 90013
(213)-829-6711
AUDIO PRODUCER; TOPICS: New Age **FOUNDED:** 1988

Inside Track Productions
P.O. Box 1513
Glendora, CA 91740
(818)-339-5257
AUDIO PRODUCER; CONTACT: Tom Armbruster **TOPICS:** New Age **FOUNDED:** 1988

Insight Productions
P.O. Box 6571
Ashville, NC 28801
(704)-252-3626
TOPICS: New Age

Insight Publishing
P.O. Box 2070
Mill Valley, CA 94942
(415)-388-8225
TOPICS: New Age

Instar Communications
20 Sunnyside Avenue
Suite A199
Mill Valley, CA 94941
(415)-389-8841 (800)-544-7734
TOPICS: New Age

Institute For Creative Mastery
133 East De la Guerra Street, Suite G
Santa Barbara, CA 93101
(805)-969-9819
AUDIO PRODUCER; CONTACT: Diane Lee Cooper **TOPICS:** New Age, Metaphysics **FOUNDED:** 1978

Integral Yoga Distributors
Yogaville
RR 1, Box 172
Buckingham, VA 23921
(804)-969-3121 (804)-969-4801 (800)-262-1008
AUDIO PRODUCER; CONTACT: Marshall Mausaac **TOPICS:** New Age **FOUNDED:** 1968

Interarts
279 South Beverly Drive, Suite 1037
Beverley Hills, CA 90212
(213)-651-0277
VIDEO PRODUCER; CONTACT: Terry Dunn **TOPICS:** New Age, Metaphysics **FOUNDED:** 1985

International New Age Music Network, Inc.
648 North Fuller Avenue
Los Angeles, CA 90036
(213)-935-7774 (213)-934-2221
VIDEO PRODUCER; CONTACT: Suzanne Bell-Doucet **TOPICS:** New Age **FOUNDED:** 1983 **PUBLICATIONS:** *International New Age Music Magazine* **EDITOR:** Suzanee Doucet, James Bell **TOPICS:** New Age **TYPE:** Magazine **DATE:** 1989 **CIRC:** 1,000 **DESCRIPTION:** Includes interviews, news, articles, and listings of bestselling music titles.

Adopted by the International New Age Music Network as its official newsletter.

Invincible Recordings
P.O. Box 13045
Phoenix, AZ 85002
(602)-252-0077
AUDIO PRODUCER; CONTACT: Ravi Taj Singh **TOPICS:** New Age, Metaphysics **FOUNDED:** 1976

Invision Resources
P.O. Box 4039
St. Paul, MN 55104
(612)-642-5070
CONTACT: Pat Donworth **TOPICS:** New Age

Isaiahs Hills, Inc.-The Mary Project
P.O. Box 616
West Newbury, MA 01985
(508)-363-2453
AUDIO & VIDEO PRODUCER; TOPICS: New Age, Spirituality **OWNER:** Sara Street **TYPE OF BUSINESS:** Music videos **DESCRIPTION:** Produces & sells religious dance & music videos.

Islamic Productions International
739 East 6th Street
Tucson, AZ 85719
(602)-791-3989
AUDIO & VIDEO PRODUCER; CONTACT: Lisa Spray **TOPICS:** New Age **TYPE OF BUSINESS:** Producers/Publishers **FOUNDED:** 1968 **DESCRIPTION:** Producers of audio/video tapes & publishers of New Age & Metaphysical books.

Jean McClelland
P.O. Box 2281
New York, NY 10108
TOPICS: New Age

Jeremiah Films
Box 1710
Hemet, CA 92346
VIDEO PRODUCER; CONTACT: Pat Curtis, Pres. **TOPICS:** New Age, Metaphysics, Occult **OWNER:** Pat Curtis, Pres. **TYPE OF BUSINESS:** New Age videos **FOUNDED:** 1980 **DESCRIPTION:** Produces 30 informational documentary videos on New Age, AIDS, Satanism, Evolution, Prophecy. **PUBLICATIONS:** *Apocalypse Planet Earth; Halloween Tick Or Treat; Fear Is The Master*

Joe Hoffman Studios
P.O. Box 840
Occidental, CA 95465
AUDIO & VIDEO PRODUCER; TOPICS: New Age **OWNER:** Joe Hoffman **TYPE OF BUSINESS:** New Age products **DESCRIPTION:** Produces meditational audio & video tapes.

Journeys Within
2931 Bernadette
Houston, TX 77043
(713)-975-9504
TOPICS: New Age

Judalon's Sound And Light
7932 1/2 West 3rd Street
Los Angeles, CA 90048
(213)-655-3031
AUDIO PRODUCER; CONTACT: Judalon Smyth **TOPICS:** New Age **FOUNDED:** 1980

Karma Productions
701 Brush Street
Las Vegas, NV 89107
(702)-870-8749
AUDIO PRODUCER; CONTACT: Tony Wells **TOPICS:** New Age, Metaphysics **FOUNDED:** 1983

Kicking Mule Records, Incorporated
P.O. Box 158
Alderpoint, CA 95411
(707)-926-5312
TOPICS: New Age

Kodama Music
Rural Delivery 1, Box 52-A2
Munnsville, NY 13409
(315)-495-6597
AUDIO PRODUCER; CONTACT: Tim Emerson **TOPICS:** New Age, Metaphysics **FOUNDED:** 1987

Lawrence Museum Of Music
218 East Griffith Street
Galveston, IN 46932
TOPICS: Occult

Leonard Ellis Productions
P.O. Box 66002
Los Angeles, CA 90066
(213)-391-1664
AUDIO PRODUCER; TOPICS: New Age **OWNER:** Leonard Ellis **TYPE OF BUSINESS:** New Age music **FOUNDED:** 1984 **DESCRIPTION:** Composer & musician, publishes & distributes his own New Age instrumental music. Titles include: Starlight Sonata; Circle Of Dreams; The Bear Behind And Winter Waltz.

Li-Sem Enterprises, Inc.
1775 Old County Road, #10
Belmont, CA 94002
(415)-592-4901 (800)-331-4120
CONTACT: Carl Trodhjem **TOPICS:** New Age

Libertad Publishing Group
P.O. Box 557
Santa Fe, NM 87502
CONTACT: Caren Nielsen **TOPICS:** New Age

Life Energy Media
14755 Ventura Boulevard, Ste. 1908
Sherman Oaks, CA 91403
(213)-874-7100 **FAX** (818)-990-9383
VIDEO PRODUCER; CONTACT: Beverly Harpenan **TOPICS:** New Age, Metaphysics **FOUNDED:** 1978

Life Energy Productions
77 Bolton Street
Concord, MA 01742
(508)-369-3539
CONTACT: Robert Gerzon **TOPICS:** New Age

Lifedance Distribution
3479 N.W. Yoen
Portland, OR 97210
(503)-228-9430 (800)-456-8742
CONTACT: Lynn Hanrahan **TOPICS:** New Age, Metaphysics **DESCRIPTION:** Distributes instrumental background music to retail stores.

Light And Sound Research
6991 East Camelback Road C-151
Scottsdale, AZ 85251
(602)-941-4459 (800)-456-8742
AUDIO PRODUCER; CONTACT: Patrick Porter **TOPICS:** New Age **FOUNDED:** 1987

Light Unlimited Publishing
3785 Presidential Parkway, Ste. 120
Atlanta, GA 30340
(404)-936-0177
AUDIO PRODUCER; CONTACT: Jon Shore **TOPICS:** New Age, Metaphysics **FOUNDED:** 1979

LMH Productions/Linda Moulton Howe Productions
P.O. Box 538
Huntingdon Valley, PA 19006-0538
(215)-938-7869
VIDEO PRODUCER; TOPICS: Paranormal Phenomena, Psychic Phenomena, UFO's **OWNER:** Linda Moulton Howe **TYPE OF BUSINESS:** New Age videos **DESCRIPTION:** Produces videos, films & books on paranormal phenomena, aliens & UFO experiences. **PUBLICATIONS:** *A Strange Harvest* **EDITOR:** Linda Moulton Howe **TOPICS:** Paranormal Phenomena **TYPE:** Video **PRICE:** $30.00 **DESCRIPTION:** Investigations which link the worldwide animal mutilation & human abduction phenomena. **PUBLICATIONS:** *An Alien Harvest* **EDITOR:** Linda Moulton Howe **TOPICS:** Paranormal Phenomena **TYPE:** Video **PRICE:** $50.00 **DESCRIPTION:** Provides further evidence linking animal mutilations to alien life forms. **PUBLICATIONS:** *Cropcircle Communique* **EDITOR:** Linda Moulton Howe **TOPICS:** Paranormal Phenomena **TYPE:** Video **PRICE:** $35.00 **DESCRIPTION:** Discusses the mysterious worldwide crop formations. Features aerials & music, graphic animation, the investigators, their theories & scientific evidence that plant cells & soil have been altered. **PUBLICATIONS:** *Earth Mysteries* **EDITOR:** Linda Moulton Howe **TOPICS:** Paranormal Phenomena **TYPE:** Video

Lost Horizons Video
9007 Norma Place
Los Angeles, CA 90069
TOPICS: New Age

Lucis Productions
P.O. Box 722 - Cooper Station
New York, NY 10276
(212)-982-8770
AUDIO PRODUCER; CONTACT: Josette Allen **TOPICS:** New Age, Metaphysics **FOUNDED:** 1922

Macromedia
81 Elm Street
P.O. Box 279
Epping, NH 03042
(603)-679-5524
AUDIO & VIDEO PRODUCER; TOPICS: New Age, Channeling **OWNER:** Jeff Volk **TYPE OF BUSINESS:** New Age videos & tapes **DESCRIPTION:** Sells videos to inspire & enlighten & tapes channeling sessions. **PUBLICATIONS:** *Cymatics: The Healing Nature of Sound* **EDITOR:** Dr. Hans Jenny, Dr. Peter Guy Manners **TOPICS:** New Age, Holistic Healing **TYPE:** Video **DESCRIPTION:** Describes the application of audible sound to the body as a healing modality, & demonstrates the Cymatic Applicator developed for this purpose. **PUBLICATIONS:** *From Atom To Cosmos* **EDITOR:** Itzhak Bentov **TOPICS:** New Age **TYPE:** Video **DESCRIPTION:** Lecture presenting a clear & enlightening model of the workings of the universe,

from atom to cosmos, & of our own process of reunion with Universal Cause.

Maggie's Music
P.O. Box 4144
Annapolis, MD 21403
(301)-268-3394
TOPICS: New Age

Master Your Mind
881 Hawthorne Drive
Walnut Creek, CA 94956
(415)-945-0941
CONTACT: Mary Richards TOPICS: New Age

Media Catalog
Box 201000A
Austin, TX 78720
TOPICS: New Age

Media Exchange
80 Rising Trail Drive
Middletown, CT 06457
TOPICS: Metaphysics

Media Magic
P.O. Box 2069
Mill Valley, CA 94942
(415)-662-2426
AUDIO & VIDEO PRODUCER; TOPICS: New Age, Metaphysics OWNER: Michael Strasmieh TYPE OF BUSINESS: New Age audio/video DESCRIPTION: Distributor of more than 60 New Age video tapes & music. New Visions video catalog. Music videos dealing with nature, science, special effects.

Medicine Wind Productions
86 North West 55th Street
Gainesville, FL 32601
(906)-373-1837
TOPICS: New Age

Megalearning Institute
P.O. Box 9000
Carlsbad, CA 92009
(619)-438-9332
TOPICS: New Age

Merrill-West Publishing
P.O. Box 1227
Carmel, CA 93921
(408)-625-5792
TOPICS: New Age PUBLICATIONS: *Voyager Tarot: Way Of The Great Oracle* EDITOR: J. Wanless TOPICS: Tarot TYPE: Book PRICE: $14.95

Messengers Of Light
P.O. Box 1158
Agoura Hills, CA 91376
AUDIO PRODUCER; TOPICS: Metaphysics, Channeling OWNER: Jennie Galuppo TYPE OF BUSINESS: Channeled audio tapes DESCRIPTION: Produces channeled taped messages. Available by mail or phone.

Meta-Media
P.O. Box 250
Emmanus, PA 18049
VIDEO PRODUCER; TOPICS: New Age, Metaphysics FOUNDED: 1986

Midsummer Music Company, Incorporated
#270-1508 West 2nd Avenue
Vancouver, BC V5Y 1B8
Canada
(604)-737-2347
CONTACT: Graham Way TOPICS: New Age

Mindworks
Box 4809
Ketchum, ID 83340
(800)-635-4156
TOPICS: New Age

Mink
1783 Cable Street
San Diego, CA 92107
(619)-225-0900
TOPICS: New Age

Miracles Multiplied
2480-4 Briarcliff Road, North East
Suite 79
Atlanta, GA 30329
(404)-377-8218
TOPICS: New Age

Miramar Productions
200 Second Avenue West
Seattle, WA 98119-4204
(206)-284-4700 (800)-245-6472 FAX (206)-286-4433
VIDEO PRODUCER; CONTACT: Brendan Rorem TOPICS: New Age, Metaphysics OWNER: Brendan Rorem TYPE OF BUSINESS: New Age videos & music FOUNDED: 1984 DESCRIPTION: Produces New Age videos & music. 13 videos & 8 CD/cassettes. Titles: The Mind's Eye, A Computer Animated Odyssey by James Reynolds; Canyon Dreams by Tangerine Dream; Water Colors by Pete Bardens.

Mount Carmel
P.O. Box 243
Leavenworth, WA 98826
(509)-548-6472
TOPICS: New Age

Moving Hearts
P.O. Box 88
Montebello, CA 90640
(213)-723-1341
CONTACT: Lindee Brown TOPICS: New Age

Multiphase Records
P.O. Box 15176
St. Louis, MO 63176
AUDIO PRODUCER; CONTACT: Carl Weingarten TOPICS: New Age FOUNDED: 1980

Music Design
207 East Buffalo Street
Milwaukee, WI 53202
(414)-272-1199 (800)-862-7232 FAX (414)-272-6131
CONTACT: Wesley van Linda TOPICS: New Age

Music For A Better World
615 East 7th Avenue
Denver, CO 80203
(303)-830-7770 (800)-733-5193
CONTACT: Susie Kirk TOPICS: New Age

Music West
1000 4th Street, #800

San Rafael, CA 94901-3121
(415)-925-9800
AUDIO PRODUCER; CONTACT: Gary Chappell TOPICS: New Age, Metaphysics FOUNDED: 1986

Mystic Fire Video
P.O. Box 1092
New York, NY 10276-1092
(516)-668-1111
TOPICS: New Age

Mystic Fire Video
P.O. Box 9323, Department BF
South Burlington, VT 05407
(800)-727-8433
VIDEO PRODUCER; CONTACT: Nancy Riggins TOPICS: New Age, Metaphysics FOUNDED: 1985

Mystic Music
Route l, Box 400
Yukon Road
Taft, TN 38488
(615)-425-6420 (800)-542-8913
AUDIO PRODUCER; CONTACT: Kimberly Kerr TOPICS: New Age TYPE OF BUSINESS: Music production DESCRIPTION: Produces & sells contemporary instrumental music. Represents musical artist Chazz. Current releases: A Time To Dream, Make Happy, Refuge.

Narada Productions, Inc.
1845 North Farwell Avenue
Milwaukee, WI 53202
(414)-272-6700 (800)-862-7232 FAX (414)-272-6131
TOPICS: New Age

Nature Recordings
P.O. Box 2749
Friday Harbor, WA 98250
(206)-378-3979 FAX (206)-378-3977
AUDIO PRODUCER; CONTACT: Sharon Hooper TOPICS: New Age, Metaphysics FOUNDED: 1986

Nefilim Universal
2730 Pinehurst Road
P.O. Box 771
Muskegon, MI 49441
(616)-755-3411
AUDIO PRODUCER; TOPICS: New Age OWNER: Timothy William Hellem TYPE OF BUSINESS: New Age music FOUNDED: 1984 DESCRIPTION: New Age record label for composer Timothy William Hellem. Titles: Faeries; Cherubikon; Dark Angel. Catalog available.

Neo Video
Box 170158
San Francisco, CA 94117
(415)-495-3477
CONTACT: Michael Brand TOPICS: New Age, Massage

Neurosonics-The Sound/Mind Connection
P.O. Box 10241
Sedona, AZ 86336
(602)-282-0576
AUDIO PRODUCER; TOPICS: New Age, Meditation OWNER: R. Brian Caldwell, Dir. TYPE OF BUSINESS: Audio Production FOUNDED: 1987 DESCRIPTION: Cassettes & CDs enhancing alpha & theta brainwave activity. Evokes meditative states to

enhance learning, alleviate stress, bring forth spontaneous mental imagery & aid personal transformation. Adds Neurosonic Brainwave Enhancement to spoken messages. **PUBLICATIONS:** *Harmonic Brainwave Synergy*

New & Unique Videos
2336 Sumac Drive
San Diego, CA 92105
(619)-282-6126 **FAX** (619)-283-8264

VIDEO PRODUCER; CONTACT: Mark Schulze, Pres. **TOPICS:** New Age, Metaphysics **OWNER:** Patricia Mooney, Vice-Pres. **TYPE OF BUSINESS:** New Age videos **FOUNDED:** 1981 **DESCRIPTION:** Produces & distributes special interest video titles to educate & entertain. Titles include Massage For Relaxation with Cleo Mooney, Ultimate Mountain Biking with top pros & Lessons In Cycling with John Howard.

New Age Music
1238 Brandon Avenue
Akron, OH 44305

TOPICS: Holistic Health

New Life Institute
P.O. Box 1351
Santa Cruz, CA 95061
(408)-929-1701

CONTACT: David Cotter **TOPICS:** New Age

New Sound Paths To At-One-Ment
P.O. Box 20693
Houston, TX 77225-0693
(713)-661-8778

AUDIO PRODUCER; CONTACT: Rosemary Silversteen **TOPICS:** New Age **FOUNDED:** 1988

New World Cassettes
Freepost, Paradise Farm
Westhall
Halesworth, Suffolk 1P19 8BR
England
050-279-279

TOPICS: New Age

Newattitude
P.O. Box 56328
Sherman Oaks, CA 91413
(818)-376-8618

AUDIO PRODUCER; TOPICS: New Age, Spirituality **OWNER:** Chuck & Alexia Cirino **TYPE OF BUSINESS:** Self-Help Audio Tapes **DESCRIPTION:** Transformational self-help audio tapes covering topics such as Abundance, Spirituality, Well-Being, Relationships & Self-Esteem. Interactive musical/spoken-word tapes utilizing a new self-help process called Conscious Auditory Self-Healing.

Nightingale-Conant Corporation
7300 North Lehigh Avenue
Chicago, IL 60648
(312)-647-0300 (800)-525-9000

AUDIO PRODUCER; CONTACT: Kathy Jewett **TOPICS:** New Age, Spirituality, Psychology **OWNER:** Vic Conant, Pres. **TYPE OF BUSINESS:** Mail-order audio cassette **FOUNDED:** 1960 **DESCRIPTION:** Develop self-empowerment & spiritual serenity through Dr. Wayne Dyer's audiocassette program, The Awakened Life. The tape can help bring happiness, success, love, peace, serenity, relaxation through meditation, out-of-body experiences & self-fulfillment.

Norman Beerger Productions
3217 South Arville Street
Las Vegas, NV 89102
(702)-876-2328

VIDEO PRODUCER; CONTACT: Norman Beerger **TOPICS:** New Age, Metaphysics **FOUNDED:** 1983 **PUBLICATIONS:** *The Grand Canyon* **TOPICS:** New Age **TYPE:** Video

Ojas Music
P.O. Box 19691
Oklahoma City, OK 73144
(405)-682-9928

AUDIO PRODUCER; TOPICS: New Age **DESCRIPTION:** Provides electronic-acoustic music. Offers tapes, concerts, workshops & lectures.

Olivia Records
4400 Market Street
Oakland, CA 94608
(415)-655-0364

AUDIO PRODUCER; CONTACT: Janet Smith **TOPICS:** New Age **FOUNDED:** 1973

One To Grow On!/Trenna Productions
P.O. Box 2484
Malibu, CA 90265
(213)-457-2583

CONTACT: Rita **TOPICS:** Psychology, New Age **DESCRIPTION:** Cassette-tape adventure stories teaching self-esteem & values.

Order Of Uriel, The
P.O. Box 1117, STN. Q
Toronto, ON M4T 2P2
Canada

TOPICS: New Age, Metaphysics

Panoramic Sound
Box 58182
Houston, TX 77258
(713)-483-0819

AUDIO PRODUCER; TOPICS: New Age, Holistic Health, Spirituality, Meditation **OWNER:** J.C. High Eagle **TYPE OF BUSINESS:** New Age music **FOUNDED:** 1986 **DESCRIPTION:** 17 tapes offering American Indian flute music, relaxation & meditation. Owner J.C. High Eagle offers workshops & lectures on American Indian culture, basic spirituality & how to heal from a broken relationship. **PUBLICATIONS:** *Four Directions: Sacred Prayers & Meditations*

Parkside Publishing Corporation
205 West Touhy Avenue
Park Ridge, IL 60068
(708)-698-8550 (708)-698-4700 (800)-221-6364

AUDIO & VIDEO PRODUCER; TOPICS: New Age, Holistic Healing **OWNER:** John E. Small **TYPE OF BUSINESS:** New Age producers **DESCRIPTION:** Producers of audios, videos & books on Recovery, Wellness, Healing & New Age issues. Catalog available.

Pathways
1173 Hearst Avenue
Berkeley, CA 94702
(415)-848-5165

AUDIO PRODUCER; CONTACT: Robert **TOPICS:** New Age **FOUNDED:** 1985

Peace Dream Productions
P.O. Box 3852
South Pasadena, CA 91031
(818)-351-9595

AUDIO PRODUCER; CONTACT: Reavis Moore And Jeffrey Broneman **TOPICS:** New Age **FOUNDED:** 1987

Peace Films, Incorporated
1524 Yale Street
Santa Monica, CA 90404
(213)-828-2525

CONTACT: Cathy Zheutlin **TOPICS:** New Age

Peacemakers Television
P.O. Box 521
Los Angeles, CA 90053
(213)-485-8090

CONTACT: John Owen **TOPICS:** New Age

Pentamedia Associates, Incorporated
1200 Sacramento Street, Suite205
San Francisco, CA 94108
(415)-673-3581

CONTACT: Fred M. Watts **TOPICS:** New Age

Pinewood Studios Of Northern Arizona
P.O. Box 17007
Pinewood, AZ 86017
(602)-955-8034

VIDEO PRODUCER; CONTACT: Jessie Elders **TOPICS:** New Age, Metaphysics **FOUNDED:** 1989

Plumrose Music Unlimited
2015 Parker Street
Berkeley, CA 94704
(415)-548-2328

AUDIO PRODUCER; CONTACT: Rose Sergeant **TOPICS:** New Age **FOUNDED:** 1985

Point Of View Productions
2477 Folsom Street
San Francisco, CA 94110
(415)-821-0435

VIDEO PRODUCER; TOPICS: Birth, Holistic Health, Homeopathy **OWNER:** Karil Daniels **TYPE OF BUSINESS:** Educational videos **FOUNDED:** 1974 **DESCRIPTION:** Produces primarily documentary & educational films & videos. Projects focus on holistic healing, gentle childbirth, women's concerns, peace & anti-nuclear issues, Soviet/American relations, ecology & the arts. **PUBLICATIONS:** *Water Baby Information Book* **TOPICS:** Birth **TYPE:** Book **PUBLICATIONS:** *Water Baby: Experiences Of Water Birth* **EDITOR:** Karil Daniels **TOPICS:** Birth **TYPE:** Video **DESCRIPTION:** Water Baby: Experiences Of Water Birth, has won 13 film & video festival awards. **PUBLICATIONS:** *Well & Strong: A True Story* **TOPICS:** Birth **TYPE:** Video

Potentials Unlimited
3659 Cortez Road West #110
Bradenton, FL 34210-3106
(800)-426-3963

AUDIO PRODUCER; CONTACT: Barry Konicov **TOPICS:** New Age, Metaphysics **FOUNDED:** 1977 **PUBLICATIONS:** *Subliminal Persuasion Self Hypnosis Tapes* **TOPICS:** New Age **TYPE:** Video

Potentials Unlimited, Inc.
Box 891
Grand Rapids, MI 49518
(616)-698-7830

TOPICS: New Age

Private Music
220 East 23rd Street, Fl. 10
New York, NY 10070
(212)-684-2533
TOPICS: New Age

Production Renaud
P.O. Box 773911
Steamboat Springs, CO 80477-3911
(303)-736-2234
AUDIO PRODUCER; CONTACT: Jonathan Renaud
TOPICS: New Age FOUNDED: 1989

Psychodynamics Research Institute
Box 875
Zephyr Cove, NV 89448
(702)-588-7999
TOPICS: New Age

Public Media Video
5547 North Ravenswood Avenue
Chicago, IL 60640-1199
(312)-878-2600
CONTACT: John Hillsman TOPICS: New Age

Purelight, Inc.
P.O. Box 189
Sea Cliff, NJ 11579
(516)-759-5759
VIDEO PRODUCER; CONTACT: Eric Alan Braun
TOPICS: New Age, Metaphysics FOUNDED: 1989

Purnima Productions
P.O. Box 694
Felton, CA 95018
CONTACT: David Michael TOPICS: New Age

Randolph Success International, Incorporated
2108 Garnet Avenue
San Diego, CA 92109
(619)-276-9800
AUDIO PRODUCER; CONTACT: Betty Lee
Randolph TOPICS: New Age FOUNDED: 1978

RC Productions
3830 North 12th Street
Phoenix, AZ 85014
(602)-266-2306
VIDEO PRODUCER; CONTACT: John Ravert
TOPICS: New Age, Metaphysics FOUNDED: 1987

Real To Reel Distribution
1001 Bridgeway
Suite 440
Sausalito, CA 94965
(415)-331-8273
CONTACT: Rick Jeffrey TOPICS: New Age

Realidad Productions
P.O. Box 1644
Santa Fe, NM 87504
(505)-983-8956
TOPICS: New Age PUBLICATIONS: *Hoxsey: How Healing Becomes A Crime* TOPICS: New Age TYPE: Video

Redwood Records
P.O. Box 10408
Oakland, CA 94610-0408
(415)-428-9191 (800)-888-7664

AUDIO PRODUCER; CONTACT: Karen Hester
TOPICS: New Age, Metaphysics TYPE OF BUSINESS: Music Producers FOUNDED: 1973
DESCRIPTION: Also known as Redwood Cultural Works, produces & distributes audio tapes of music including vocals & instrumental arrangements. Also produces concerts.

Reflections
P.O. Box 1249
48 Los Ositos
Carmel Valley, CA 93924
(408)-659-0413 (800)-426-4733
TOPICS: New Age

Relaxercise
2421 Oregon Street
Berkeley, CA 94705
AUDIO PRODUCER; CONTACT: David Zemach-Bersin TOPICS: New Age, Metaphysics FOUNDED: 1980

Rhythms Productions
Box 34485
Los Angeles, CA 90034
(213)-836-4678
CONTACT: Ruth White TOPICS: New Age

RichHeart Music
P.O. Box 467
Woodstock, NY 12498
(914)-679-4183
AUDIO PRODUCER; TOPICS: New Age OWNER:
Richard Shulman TYPE OF BUSINESS: Music production FOUNDED: 1989 DESCRIPTION:
Dedicated to producing uplifting & heart opening music to awaken us to Spirit. Offered on tapes & CDs. 3 titles by artist Richard Shulman: Light From Assisi, A Higher Dimension, World Peace.

Right And Happy Productions
17 Ardor Drive
Orinda, CA 94563
TOPICS: Channeling DESCRIPTION: Audio/video production company taping channeling sessions.

Rose City Records
P.O. Box 13437
Portland, OR 97213
(503)-282-1675
TOPICS: New Age

Roundup Records
P.O. Box 154
North Cambridge, MA 02140
(617)-661-6308
TOPICS: New Age

Rudolf Steiner Research Foundation
1753 Appleton Street, Ste. D
Long Beach, CA 90802-3778
(213)-437-5438 (800)-776-5438
AUDIO PRODUCER; CONTACT: Donald C. Hosier
TOPICS: New Age, Metaphysics FOUNDED: 1958

Rudra Press
Box 1973
Cambridge, MA 02238
(617)-576-3394 (800)-876-7798
AUDIO & VIDEO PRODUCER; CONTACT: Sarah
Fahey TOPICS: New Age, Yoga, Metaphysics, Meditation, Holistic Health, Spirituality TYPE OF BUSINESS: New Age producers DESCRIPTION:
Publishes books, audio cassettes & videos on the subjects of Yoga, Meditation & Health.
PUBLICATIONS: *Breath Of God* EDITOR: Swami Chetanananda TOPICS: Spirituality TYPE: Book
PRICE: $14.95 PUBLICATIONS: *Dynamic Stillness Vol. 1: The Practice Of Trika Yoga* EDITOR:
Chetanananda TOPICS: New Age, Meditation, Yoga, Spirituality TYPE: Book PRICE: $17.95
PUBLICATIONS: *Energize With Yoga* EDITOR:
Lilias Folan TOPICS: Yoga, Holistic Health TYPE:
Video PUBLICATIONS: *Lilias! Alive With Yoga*
EDITOR: Lilias Folan TOPICS: Yoga, Holistic Health TYPE: Video PUBLICATIONS: *Lilias, Yoga And You* EDITOR: Lilias Folan TOPICS: Yoga, Holistic Health TYPE: Video PUBLICATIONS:
Meditation: An Invitation To Inner Growth
EDITOR: Swami Chetanananda TOPICS:
Meditation, Holistic Health TYPE: Audio

Rykodisc USA
Pickering Wharf, Bldg. C-3G
Salem, MA 01970
(508)-744-7678
TOPICS: Birth PUBLICATIONS: *Music To Be Born By* EDITOR: Mickey Hart TOPICS: Birth TYPE:
Audio

Sacred Spirit Music
P.O. Box 648
New Lebanon, NY 12125
(518)-794-7860
AUDIO PRODUCER; CONTACT: Mikhail Horowitz
TOPICS: New Age, Metaphysics FOUNDED: 1983

Sara Needham Galley
11 Broadway, Apartment 25
Kingston, NY 12401
(914)-339-7832
VIDEO PRODUCER; CONTACT: Sara Needham
TOPICS: New Age, Metaphysics FOUNDED: 1970

Scientific Sound Design
Rural Route 1, Box 52/A2
Munnsville, NY 13409
TOPICS: New Age

Scott Bruder Productions
P.O. Box 18222
Cleveland Heights, OH 44118
(216)-932-2172
TOPICS: New Age

Search For Serenity
180 West 25th Street
Upland, CA 91786-1113
(714)-981-2318
AUDIO PRODUCER; CONTACT: Joel Miller
TOPICS: New Age FOUNDED: 1985

Sequoia Records
Box 280
Topanga, CA 90290
(818)-343-0231 (818)-992-0880 (800)-824-4000
AUDIO PRODUCER; TOPICS: New Age OWNER:
David & Steve Gordon TYPE OF BUSINESS: New Age music DESCRIPTION: 14 releases of New Age music on cassette & CD. Some feature nature sounds. All recordings by David & Steve Gordon.
Titles: Misty Forest Morning; Garden Of Serenity; Oneness.

Serenity
180 West 25th Street

Upland, CA 91786
(714)-981-2318 (800)-869-1684
AUDIO PRODUCER; CONTACT: Jim Moeller
TOPICS: New Age, Meditation, Spirituality **TYPE OF BUSINESS:** New Age music **DESCRIPTION:** Offers music with styles ranging from New Age to Jazz. Also has cassettes on meditation, a Course In Miracles, guided imagery & relaxation.

Seven Arrows Music
P.O. Box 4904
Taos, NM 87571
TOPICS: Metaphysics

Shanachie Records Corp.
37 East Clinton Street
Newton, NJ 07860
(201)-579-6697 (201)-579-7763
AUDIO PRODUCER; TOPICS: New Age **OWNER:** Andrew Seidenfeld **TYPE OF BUSINESS:** New Age music **DESCRIPTION:** Sells 400 titles of various types of New Age music such as World, Celtic, Folk, New Acoustic, Cadysm, Black Mambazo-Classic, etc.

Shining Star Music
417 Tamal Plaza
Corte Madera, CA 94925
(415)-924-4848
TOPICS: New Age

Shining Star Productions
7820 East Evans #900
Scottsdale, AZ 85260
(602)-948-6856
AUDIO & VIDEO PRODUCER; CONTACT: Charles Wren **TOPICS:** New Age **TYPE OF BUSINESS:** Audio production **DESCRIPTION:** Offers complete audio & video production services for all occasions.

Shur-Sound And Sight, Incorporated
3350 Scott Boulevard, Building 5
Santa Clara, CA 95051
(408)-727-7620
AUDIO PRODUCER; TOPICS: New Age **TYPE OF BUSINESS:** Audio Producers **DESCRIPTION:** Offers complete audio services for the production of music & other audio tapes.

Silo Incorporated
P.O. Box 429
Waterbury, VT 05676
(802)-244-5178 (800)-342-0295
AUDIO & VIDEO PRODUCER; CONTACT: Dave Lovald **TOPICS:** New Age **TYPE OF BUSINESS:** New Age music **FOUNDED:** 1977 **DESCRIPTION:** Dedicated to the national promotion & distribution of independent recording artists. Large selection of recorded music & videos in multiple formats. 18,000 titles of classical, folk, jazz, blues, New Age, country, world & children's music. Free catalogs.

Silver Wave Records
P.O. Box 7943
Boulder, CO 80306
(303)-443-5617
CONTACT: Helen Broderick **TOPICS:** New Age

Sonic Atmospheres
14755 Ventura Boulevard, Suite 1776
Sherman Oaks, CA 91403
(818)-505-6003
TOPICS: New Age

Sound And Spirit
P.O. Box 461347
Los Angeles, CA 90046
(213)-876-5381
TOPICS: New Age

Sound Currents
334 Butterfield
San Anselmo, CA 94960
(415)-459-2041
AUDIO PRODUCER; CONTACT: Susan Weaver **TOPICS:** New Age **FOUNDED:** 1976

Sound Feelings Records
24266 Walnut Street, Ste. 310
Newhall, CA 91321
(805)-254-4938 (818)-344-3306
AUDIO PRODUCER; TOPICS: New Age **OWNER:** Howard Richman **TYPE OF BUSINESS:** New Age musical portraits **FOUNDED:** 1984 **DESCRIPTION:** Sound portraits. Original music composed for an individual to express their inner & outer qualities. By mail or private sittings. Party performances. Free brochure.

Sound Rx
P.O. Box 2644
San Anselmo, CA 94960
(415)-453-9800 (800)-726-3924
AUDIO PRODUCER; TOPICS: Holistic Health, Psychic **OWNER:** Steven Halpern **TYPE OF BUSINESS:** Audio producer **FOUNDED:** 1975 **DESCRIPTION:** Producers of tapes & compact discs to improve health, well-being & psychic sensitivity. Offers free catalog listing 44 titles including Spectrum Suite by Steven Halpern; Higher Ground (Alpha/Theta Entertainment); & Ancient Echoes (Past Life Recall Music).

Soundings Of The Planet Recordings
P.O. Box 43512
Tucson, AZ 85733
(602)-937-3223 (602)-883-1784 (800)-937-3223
CONTACT: Dean And Dudley **TOPICS:** New Age

Soundless Sound
Department C, P.O. Box 8005
Boulder, CO 80306-8005
TOPICS: New Age

Sounds True
735 Walnut Street
Boulder, CO 80302-5032
(303)-449-6229
AUDIO PRODUCER; CONTACT: Gilles Palmarini **TOPICS:** New Age **TYPE OF BUSINESS:** New Age tapes **DESCRIPTION:** Produces New Age tapes, both spoken & music, for self-enlightenment. Topics covered are the spiritual journey, psychology, self-discovery, myth & meaning, relationsips, healing & creativity. **PUBLICATIONS:** *Sounds True Catalog* **PUBLISHER:** Tami Simon **TOPICS:** New Age, Spirituality, Psychology, Holistic Healing **TYPE:** Catalog, 50 pgs. **DESCRIPTION:** Offers a selection of more than 150 enlightening tapes of words & music. Spoken tapes express the ideas of outstanding men & women, in their own words & voices, covering various New Age related fields of interest.

Source Cassette Learning System
P.O. Box W
Stanford, CA 94305
(415)-328-7171

TOPICS: New Age

Spectrum Video
18121 Napa Street
Northridge, CA 91325
TOPICS: Yoga

Spirit Music
P.O. Box 2240
Boulder, CO 80306
(303)-443-8181
AUDIO PRODUCER; TOPICS: New Age, Holistic Health, Holistic Healing, Spirituality, Meditation, Body-Mind Connection **OWNER:** Jonathan S. Goldman, Pres. **TYPE OF BUSINESS:** Music Production **DESCRIPTION:** Produces music for meditation, relaxation and well-being.

Spirit Music, Inc.
42 Baker Avenue
Lexington, MA 02173
(617)-861-1625
TOPICS: New Age

Spotted Fawn Music
P.O. Box 493
Bearsville, NY 12409
TOPICS: New Age

Spring Hill Music
P.O. Box 800
Boulder, CO 80306-0800
(303)-938-1188
CONTACT: D. P. Waldman **TOPICS:** New Age

Star Publishing
P.O. Box 161113
Austin, TX 78716
TOPICS: New Age

Star Sound Universal Production & Publishing
P.O. Box 931126
Los Angeles, CA 90093
(213)-469-8930
CONTACT: Jack R. Conrad **TOPICS:** New Age, Metaphysics

Starflight Music Productions
1175 South Lincoln
Denver, CO 80210
(303)-986-7166
TOPICS: New Age

Starseed Seminars
Star Route Box 70
Mountain View, MO 65548
TOPICS: Channeling

Steven Bergman Enterprises
220 De La Vina
Monterey, CA 93140
(408)-659-3259 (800)-626-2720
TOPICS: New Age

SubGenius Foundation, Inc.
Box 140306
Dallas, TX 75214
CONTACT: Ivan Stang **TOPICS:** New Age

Success Education Institute
Box 90608
San Diego, CA 92109

(619)-276-9800 (800)-248-2737
TOPICS: New Age

Sugar Hill Records
P.O. Box 4040
Duke Station
Durham, NC 27706
(919)-489-4349
TOPICS: New Age

Sun Fire Productions
10 Park Avenue
Basalt, CO 81621
(303)-927-9414
VIDEO PRODUCER; TOPICS: New Age, Occult,
Holistic Health, Herbalogy **OWNER:** Debra Nuzzi,
M.H. **TYPE OF BUSINESS:** New Age videos
DESCRIPTION: Video producers offering
information relevant to the healing of our planet &
its people. Topics include herbalogy, holistic healing
& the environment. Conducts a weekly radio show
offering interviews on the environment, music,
transformation & New Age.

Sun-Scape Records
P.O. Box 793, Station F
Toronto, Ontario M4Y 2N7
Canada
(416)-221-2461 **FAX** (416)-881-8119
CONTACT: Mrs. V. Webster **TOPICS:** New Age

Sunshine Communications
P.O. Box 1711
Tempe, AZ 85280
(602)-968-3217
AUDIO PRODUCER; CONTACT: David Belskis
TOPICS: New Age, Metaphysics **FOUNDED:** 1981

Superlearning, Inc.
450 Seventh Avenue, Ste. 500
New York, NY 10123
(212)-279-8450
AUDIO PRODUCER; CONTACT: Sheila Ostrander,
Chairwoman **TOPICS:** New Age **OWNER:** Lynn
Schroeder, Pres. **TYPE OF BUSINESS:** Audio tapes
DESCRIPTION: Produces more than 65 accelerated
learning books, cassettes & videos to improve
memory & learning. Offers instructional audio tapes
& mailing lists. Catalog available. **PUBLICATIONS:**
*Superlearning Music; Language Phrases For
Travelers; Relaxation And Imagery Exercises*

Sustainable Futures Audio/Video
Tipi Workshop, Box 84
Allenspark, CO 80510
(303)-278-7777
CONTACT: A. Das **TOPICS:** New Age

Sybervision
1 Sansome Street #1610
San Francisco, CA 94104-4431
(415)-846-3388 (800)-777-5885
TOPICS: New Age

Sylvia Woods Harp Center
P.O. Box 29521
Los Angeles, CA 90029
(818)-247-4177
TOPICS: New Age **DESCRIPTION:** Offers harp
music tapes, folk harps, lessons & concerts.

Synchronicity
M.S.H. Association

Route l, Box 192
Faber, VA 22938
(804)-361-2323 (800)-962-2033
TOPICS: New Age, Channeling

T.B.M. Productions
P.O. Box 3771
Hollywood, CA 90028
(213)-463-6000
VIDEO PRODUCER; CONTACT: Alan Ames
TOPICS: New Age **FOUNDED:** 1976

Tail Slate Productions
764 Old Topanga Canyon Road
Topanga, CA 90290
(213)-455-1770
VIDEO PRODUCER; CONTACT: Al Johnson
TOPICS: New Age, Metaphysics **FOUNDED:** 1986

Talking Taco Records
5402 Timber Trail
San Antonio, TX 78228
(512)-520-2622
TOPICS: New Age

Tapir Tapes
6171 Bernhard Avenue
Richmond, CA 94805
(415)-232-7310
TOPICS: New Age

Target Alpha Productions
716 West 33rd Street
San Pedro, CA 90731
TOPICS: New Age

Temple Of Living Prayer
P.O. Box 19352
Sacramento, CA 95819
(916)-455-8387
TOPICS: New Age, Metaphysics

Thinking Allowed Productions
2560 Ninth Street, Ste. 123
Berkeley, CA 94710
(415)-548-4415
VIDEO PRODUCER; TOPICS: New Age,
Spirituality, Holistic Health, Channeling,
Parapsychology, Dreams, Psychology **OWNER:**
Jeffrey Mishlove, Ph. D. **TYPE OF BUSINESS:** New
Age videos **DESCRIPTION:** InnerWork Video
Collection, a series of sixteen 90-minute video
intensives expanding & extending themes of personal
integration, healing & spiritual development.
Promotes awareness of new possibilities, new
potentials for personal growth & achievement.

Tiger's Nest Audio Publishing
3820 Benthaven Street
Ft. Collins, CO 80526
(303)-226-2804
AUDIO PRODUCER; CONTACT: Gayle **TOPICS:**
New Age **FOUNDED:** 1985

Timeless Productions
5050 Traverse Creek Road
Garden Valley, CA 95633
(916)-333-1335 (800)-729-1325
AUDIO PRODUCER; TOPICS: New Age **OWNER:**
David Blonski **TYPE OF BUSINESS:** New Age music
FOUNDED: 1986 **DESCRIPTION:** New Age
environmental recordings. Music of nature sounds.
Wholesales & distributes all self-works to retail

outlets through phone & mail order. Some titles:
Sierra Passage, Land Of The Midnight Sun, Dance
Of The Dolphin, Shoreline, Timeless Flight.
PUBLICATIONS: Other titles: *Elfin Sampler,
Thundering Skies, Point Reyes National Seashore,
Jonathan & The Glympsie.*

Touch Tapes
P.O. Box 412954
Kansas City, MO 64141-2954
(816)-474-7664
TOPICS: New Age

Trans Tech, Incorporated
P.O. Box 489
Woodstock, NY 12498-2954
(914)-679-7655
TOPICS: New Age

Treehouse Enterprises
P.O. Box 7134
Jupiter, FL 33468-7134
(407)-575-0547
AUDIO PRODUCER; TOPICS: New Age,
Psychology, Holistic Healing **OWNER:** Dr. Sandra
G. Landsman **TYPE OF BUSINESS:** Publishers &
Audio Prod. **DESCRIPTION:** Producers of audio
tapes: Crystal Cavern Of Enlightenment; Dance Of
The Elements; Star Shine; Wisdom Of Babies; Tree
Of Life; Path Of Forgiveness; Flight Of The Spirit;
The Circle. **PUBLICATIONS:** *Found: A Place For
Me* **PUBLISHER:** Dr. Sandra G. Landsman **TOPICS:**
New Age, Psychology, Holistic Health **TYPE:** Book
DESCRIPTION: Concerns the diagnosis & treatment
of Manic-Depressive illness. **PUBLICATIONS:** *I'm
Special: An Experiential Workbook For The Child
In Us All* **PUBLISHER:** Dr. Sandra G. Landsman
TOPICS: New Age, Psychology **TYPE:** Book

Two Wings Publications
204 North El Camino Real #E133
Encinitas, CA 92024-2867
(619)-471-1418
CONTACT: Jill Stevens **TOPICS:** New Age

U-Music, Incorporated
389 Marin Avenue
Mill Valley, CA 94941
(415)-381-8865
VIDEO PRODUCER; CONTACT: Paul Silbey
TOPICS: New Age, Metaphysics **FOUNDED:** 1986

Ultravision
8033 Sunset Boulevard, #3529
Los Angeles, CA 90046
(213)-878-6816
VIDEO PRODUCER; TOPICS: New Age **TYPE OF
BUSINESS:** TV & Video Producers **DESCRIPTION:**
Video & television production/distribution company.
Offers a complete support package to design,
produce & distribute videotapes for seminars,
workshops or businesses. Broadcast quality by
Hollywood trained professionals. Low prices. New
Age oriented.

Umbrella Media
11314 North East 26th Avenue
Vancouver, WA 98686
(206)-574-6618
VIDEO PRODUCER; CONTACT: Sid Brown
TOPICS: New Age, Metaphysics **FOUNDED:** 1976

Universal Guidance Press

P.O. Box 1145
Pacific Palisades, CA 90272
(213)-459-9345
AUDIO & VIDEO PRODUCER; CONTACT: Susan
Scolastico **TOPICS:** New Age **TYPE OF BUSINESS:**
Publisher/Producer **FOUNDED:** 1987
DESCRIPTION: Publishes & produces books, audio
& video tapes concerned with the New Age,
spiritualism & psychology.

Upstate Media Enterprises
P.O. Box 73
Woodstock, NY 12498
(914)-246-9995
CONTACT: Nathan Keonig **TOPICS:** New Age,
Metaphysics **PUBLICATIONS:** *An Evening With
Bernie Siegel, M.D.* **TOPICS:** New Age **TYPE:**
Video

Varied Directions
69 Elm Street
Camden, ME 04843
(207)-236-8506 (800)-888-5236
CONTACT: Curtiss MacDonald **TOPICS:** New Age

**Vegetarian Video - Healthy, Wealthy,
& Wise**
3764 Watseka
Los Angeles, CA 90034
VIDEO PRODUCER; TOPICS: New Age, Holistic
Health, Vegetarianism, Health Food, Nutrition
DESCRIPTION: Produces & distributes video on
vegetarianism.

Video Project, The
5332 College Avenue, Suite 101
Oakland, CA 94618
(415)-655-9050
CONTACT: Vivienne Verdonroe **TOPICS:** New Age

Video-Sig
1030 East Duane Avenue
Suite C
Sunnyvale, CA 94086
(408)-730-9291 (800)-222-2996

TOPICS: New Age

Vision Unlimited
P.O. Box 1034
Beltsville, MD 20705
(301)-572-9263
TOPICS: New Age **PUBLICATIONS:** *Meditation For
The Age Of Enlightenment* **TOPICS:** New Age
TYPE: Video

Visionary Video Production
P.O. Box 50865
Dallas, TX 75250
TOPICS: Metaphysics

Vital Body Marketing
Box 1067
Manhasset, NY 11303
(516)-759-5200
AUDIO PRODUCER; TOPICS: New Age **FOUNDED:**
1979

White Dove International, Inc.
Box 1000
Taos, NM 87571
(505)-758-0500 **FAX** (505)-758-2265
VIDEO PRODUCER; CONTACT: Michael Vernon
TOPICS: New Age **FOUNDED:** 1987
PUBLICATIONS: *Affirmations*

Wildflower Recordings
Box 1316
Arlington, MA 02174
TOPICS: New Age

Willow Mixed Media, Inc.
Lennox Avenue
P.O Box 194
Glenford, NY 12433
(914)-657-2914
VIDEO PRODUCER; CONTACT: Tobe Carey
TOPICS: New Age, Metaphysics **FOUNDED:** 1979

Windham Hill Productions
P.O. Box 9388
Stanford, CA 94305

(415)-329-0647 (800)-888-8544
TOPICS: New Age

Wisdom Films
361 Newbury Street, 4th Floor
Boston, MA 02115-2710
(617)-465-4000
TOPICS: New Age, Meditation

Woody Clark Productions
943 Howard Street, Suite 200
San Francisco, CA 94103
(415)-777-1668
VIDEO PRODUCER; CONTACT: Woody Clark
TOPICS: New Age **FOUNDED:** 1979

Words Ideas And Music
4564 Laurence Court
Bensalem, PA 19020
(215)-752-4517
AUDIO PRODUCER; CONTACT: Ray Monahan
TOPICS: New Age **FOUNDED:** 1979

Words Of Light Productions
P.O. Box 39597
Los Angeles, CA 90039
(213)-660-4580
AUDIO PRODUCER; CONTACT: Linda Atnip
TOPICS: New Age **FOUNDED:** 1990

Yansa Music
6925 5th Avenue, Suite E436
Scottsdale, AZ 85251
(602)-481-0696
CONTACT: Shayla **TOPICS:** New Age

Yes! Technologies
60 Biltmore Avenue
Asheville, NC 28801
(701)-258-0616
VIDEO PRODUCER; CONTACT: Gary Schwartz
TOPICS: New Age, Metaphysics **FOUNDED:** 1985

Music, Spoken Audio & Video

See the chapter Audio & Video Producers for additional sources and titles. Audio or video materials listed in this chapter can be ordered from your local New Age Bookstore, or by contacting Reference Press International, P.O. Box 4126, Greenwich, CT 06830, 203-629-4900.

A.R.E. Meditation Course
PUBLISHING COMPANY: A.R.E. Press ARTIST: M. Thurston TOPIC: Meditation, $39.95

Abundance: Sack Of Polished Emeralds
PUBLISHING COMPANY: White Dove Int'l., Inc. ARTIST: S. Wilde TOPIC: Hypnotism, $11.95

Abundance: You Can Have It All!
PUBLISHING COMPANY: White Dove Int'l., Inc. ARTIST: S. Wilde TOPIC: Hypnotism, $11.95

Accelerated Learning
PUBLISHING COMPANY: Steven Halpern ARTIST: S. Halpern TOPIC: Hypnotism, $10.98

Accept The Gift Of Abundance
PUBLISHING COMPANY: Light of Mind ARTIST: S. Gordon, D. Gordon TOPIC: Meditation, $14.95

Accepting More And More
PUBLISHING COMPANY: Reflections ARTIST: Star Sounds TOPIC: Hypnotism, $14.95

Achievement
PUBLISHING COMPANY: Channel Light Productions ARTIST: Marianne Williamson TOPIC: Spirituality, $10.95

Achieving Your Ideal Weight
PUBLISHING COMPANY: Soundwaves 2000 ARTIST: S. Halpern TOPIC: Hypnotism, $10.98

Acoustic Supported Learning
PUBLISHING COMPANY: Acoustic Brain Research ARTIST: Acoustic Brain Research TOPIC: Body-Mind Connection, $99.95

Active Methods Of Spiritual Growth
PUBLISHING COMPANY: Dialogue House ARTIST: I. Progoff TOPIC: Spirituality, $10.00

Acupuncture And Chinese Medicine
PUBLISHING COMPANY: Infinity Tapes - Blue Dolphin ARTIST: Stephen T. Chang TOPIC: Holistic Health, $10.00

Addiction Release: New World Subliminal
PUBLISHING COMPANY: New World Productions, Ltd. ARTIST: Y. Rhajan TOPIC: Hypnotism, $14.95

Admiring The Moon: Tranquil Recreations Of The Classics
PUBLISHING COMPANY: Vital Body Marketing Co., Inc. ARTIST: D. Kobialka TOPIC: New Age, $9.95

Adona! Eloheinu Adonai Ehad (Jewish Tradition)
PUBLISHING COMPANY: MSH * Association ARTIST: Brother Charles TOPIC: Spirituality, $25.00

Advanced Meditation Techniques
PUBLISHING COMPANY: Mayflower B/S ARTIST: Robert Thibodeau TOPIC: Meditation, $49.95

Adventure Of Self-Discovery
PUBLISHING COMPANY: Thinking Allowed Prod. ARTIST: S. Grof TOPIC: Psychology, $49.95

Aerial Boundaries
PUBLISHING COMPANY: Windham Hill Records ARTIST: M. Hedges TOPIC: Meditation, $11.98

Affirmations
PUBLISHING COMPANY: White Dove Int'l, Inc. ARTIST: S. Wilde TOPIC: Meditation, $21.95

After The Rain: Impressionistic Piano & Guitar
PUBLISHING COMPANY: Vital Body Marketing Co., Inc. ARTIST: Roderick Brown TOPIC: New Age, $9.95

Afternoon Of A Fawn
PUBLISHING COMPANY: Li-Sem Enterprises ARTIST: D. Kobialka TOPIC: Meditation, $15.98

Agartha Personal Life-Balancing Program
PUBLISHING COMPANY: Stillpoint Publishing ARTIST: Meredith Young TOPIC: Meditation, $59.95

Age Regression
PUBLISHING COMPANY: Dr. Bruce Goldberg ARTIST: Bruce Goldberg TOPIC: Meditation, $12.00

Aids And Anger
PUBLISHING COMPANY: Northern Lights Altern. ARTIST: S. Fisher TOPIC: Psychic Healing, $10.00

Aids, Life And Love: A Conversation With Elisabeth Kubler-Ross
PUBLISHING COMPANY: Elisabeth Kublier-Ross Center ARTIST: E. Kublier-Ross ARTIST: et.al. TOPIC: Holistic Healing, $29.95

Aids: A Positive Approach
PUBLISHING COMPANY: Hay House ARTIST: Louise Hay TOPIC: Psychic Healing, $10.00

Alchemical Journeys 1: Completing Communication/Child In The Garden
PUBLISHING COMPANY: Alchemy ARTIST: Alchemical Hypnotherapy Instit TOPIC: Meditation, $10.98

Alchemical Journeys 2: Meeting Your Inner Mate/Contacting An Inner Guide
PUBLISHING COMPANY: Alchemy ARTIST: Alchemical Hypnotherapy Instit TOPIC: Meditation, $10.98

Alchemical Journeys 3: Remembering Past Life Abilities/Journey Into The Body
PUBLISHING COMPANY: Alchemy ARTIST: Alchemical Hypnotherapy Instit TOPIC: Meditation, $10.98

Alchemical Journeys 4: Meeting The Money Deva/The Golden City
PUBLISHING COMPANY: Alchemy ARTIST: Alchemical Hypnotherapy Institute TOPIC: Hypnotism, $10.98

Alchemical Journeys 5: Meeting The Inner Healer/Hypnotic Symphony For The Immune System
PUBLISHING COMPANY: Alchemy ARTIST: Alchemical Hypnotherapy Institute TOPIC: Meditation, $10.98

Alchemical Journeys 6: Journey Into A Crystal/Crystal Meditation
PUBLISHING COMPANY: Alchemy ARTIST: Alchemical Hypnotherapy Instit TOPIC: Crystals, $10.98

Alchemist: Internalize The Transformation Of Problems Into Personal Power
PUBLISHING COMPANY: Valley of the Sun ARTIST: D. Sutphen TOPIC: Meditation, $8.98

Alcoholism And Nutrition
PUBLISHING COMPANY: New Dawn Nutrit.Services ARTIST: R. Gilday TOPIC: Nutrition, $9.95

Aleluia
PUBLISHING COMPANY: Spring Hill Music ARTIST: R. Gass ARTIST: On Wings of Song TOPIC: Spirituality, $10.00

Aligning To Your Nature Self
PUBLISHING COMPANY: White Dove Int'l., Inc. ARTIST: S. Wilde TOPIC: Hypnotism, $11.95

Aligning With Love: Support Tool For Recovery From Eating Disorders & Other Addictions
PUBLISHING COMPANY: Breeding, John ARTIST: John Breeding TOPIC: Meditation, $10.98

All You Can Do Is All You Can Do But All You Can Do Is Enough!
PUBLISHING COMPANY: Random House Audio ARTIST: A. L. Williams TOPIC: Meditation, $9.95

Alpharest: A Magical Journey To The Stars
PUBLISHING COMPANY: Sea Priestess Productions ARTIST: J. Serrie ARTIST: Narrated by Lady Isis Neal TOPIC: Meditation, $12.00

Amazon Song: A Sonic Trip To The Amazon Juncle
PUBLISHING COMPANY: Vital Body Marketing Co., Inc. ARTIST: R. Crutcher TOPIC: New Age, $9.95

Anatomy Of An Illness: A Guide To Healing & Regeneration
PUBLISHING COMPANY: Dove Books on Tape, Inc. ARTIST: N. Cousins ARTIST: Read by Jason Robards TOPIC: Holistic Healing, $14.95

Ancient Dreams
PUBLISHING COMPANY: Private Music ARTIST: P. O-Hearn TOPIC: Meditation, $10.98

Andromeda: Journey Through Inner Space
PUBLISHING COMPANY: Lorn Media Productions ARTIST: Anne Williams TOPIC: Psychology, $24.95

Angel Love
PUBLISHING COMPANY: Narada Productions ARTIST: Aeoliah TOPIC: Meditation, $18.50

Angelic Music
PUBLISHING COMPANY: Inter-Dimensional ARTIST: Iasos TOPIC: Meditation, $18.98

Anger Control
PUBLISHING COMPANY: Effective Learnings Systems, Inc. ARTIST: Love Tapes TOPIC: Hypnotism, $11.98

Answer To Cancer
PUBLISHING COMPANY: Source Cassettes ARTIST: E. Miller TOPIC: Meditation, $10.95

Anxiety-Free Living: Relaxed And In Control
PUBLISHING COMPANY: BFS Limited ARTIST: Bright Images TOPIC: Hypnotism, $11.95

Aquarian Conspiracy: Tools For Change - Personal & Social Transformation In Our Time
PUBLISHING COMPANY: Simon & Schuster Audio ARTIST: M. Ferguson TOPIC: Metaphysics, $9.95

Ariel
PUBLISHING COMPANY: Private Music ARTIST: Jerry Goodman TOPIC: Meditation, $11.98

Art Of Loving
PUBLISHING COMPANY: Caedmon ARTIST: E. Fromm ARTIST: Read by Jeff David TOPIC: Psychology, $15.95

Art Of Meditation
PUBLISHING COMPANY: Hartley Film Foundation ARTIST: Alan Watts TOPIC: Meditation, $39.95

Art Of Prescribing: Bach Flower Remedies
PUBLISHING COMPANY: Bach Educational Program ARTIST: N. Murray TOPIC: Herbalogy, $10.95

Arthritis Relief At Your Fingertips: Morning & Evening Routines
PUBLISHING COMPANY: Enhanced Audio Systems ARTIST: M. Gach TOPIC: Acupuncture, $9.95

As You Think
PUBLISHING COMPANY: New World Library ARTIST: James Allen, Marc Allen TOPIC: Body-Mind Connection, $10.95

Ascension
PUBLISHING COMPANY: Sona Gaia ARTIST: M. Genest TOPIC: Meditation, $16.98

Asia
PUBLISHING COMPANY: Geffen Records ARTIST: Kitaro TOPIC: Meditation, $20.98

Aspects
PUBLISHING COMPANY: Landscape Records ARTIST: T. Newman TOPIC: Meditation, $10.98

Aspects/Shaping Charts: Planetary Patterns
PUBLISHING COMPANY: Video Lecture Series ARTIST: R. Hand, C. Britton TOPIC: Astrology, $39.95

Assertiveness Training And How To Instantly Read People
PUBLISHING COMPANY: Valley of the Sun ARTIST: D. Stuphen TOPIC: Hypnotism, $24.95

Astral Projection
PUBLISHING COMPANY: Potentials Unlimited ARTIST: Potentials Unlimited TOPIC: New Age, $9.98

Astral Projection And Remote Viewing: Two Video Hypnosis Sessions
PUBLISHING COMPANY: Valley of the Sun ARTIST: D. Sutphen TOPIC: Psychic, $29.95

Astral Sounds
PUBLISHING COMPANY: Potentials Unlimited ARTIST: Potentials Unlimited TOPIC: New Age, $14.98

Astral Travel: A Spiritual Experience
PUBLISHING COMPANY: Centerpoint Distribution, Inc. ARTIST: E. Baron TOPIC: Astral Projection, $9.98

Astral Voyage
PUBLISHING COMPANY: Geffen Records ARTIST: Kitaro TOPIC: Meditation, $20.98

Astrology
PUBLISHING COMPANY: Audio Renaissance Tapes ARTIST: E. Cayce ARTIST: Read by Stanley Ralph TOPIC: Astrology, $9.95

Astrology Of Genius: A Study Of The Nobel Prize Winners
PUBLISHING COMPANY: Evolutionary Publications ARTIST: R. Tate TOPIC: Astrology, $4.95

Astrology Of Romance
PUBLISHING COMPANY: Visionary Video Productions ARTIST: L. Clarson TOPIC: Astrology, $39.95

Astronomy, 1 & 2
PUBLISHING COMPANY: Video Lecture Series ARTIST: R. Orr TOPIC: Astrology, $39.95

Ataraxia
PUBLISHING COMPANY: MSH Association ARTIST: NSA TOPIC: Meditation, $25.00

Atlantis, Crystal Chamber: Inner Harmony New Age Music
PUBLISHING COMPANY: Valley of the Sun ARTIST: R. Slap TOPIC: Meditation, $15.95

Attract Your Best Friend And Lover
PUBLISHING COMPANY: Happiness Unlimited Institute ARTIST: E. Kenyon ARTIST: Music by Steve Halpern TOPIC: Meditation, $10.95

Attracting More Love
PUBLISHING COMPANY: Effective Learnings Systems, Inc. ARTIST: Love Tapes TOPIC: Hypnotism, $11.98

Attracting The Right Love Relationship
PUBLISHING COMPANY: Valley of the Sun ARTIST: D. Sutphen TOPIC: Hypnotism, $18.98

Attunement: A Full Spectrum Experience For Personal & Planetary Transformation
PUBLISHING COMPANY: Attunement ARTIST: L. Culin, C. Pruess TOPIC: Spirituality, $39.95

Audio Companion To The Book Of Runes
PUBLISHING COMPANY: Audio Renaissance Tapes ARTIST: R. Blum TOPIC: Parapsychology, $14.95

Audio Exploration Of I Ching
PUBLISHING COMPANY: Audio Renaissance Tapes ARTIST: C. Ponce TOPIC: Parapsychology, $14.95

Audio Exploration Of Tarot
PUBLISHING COMPANY: Audio Renaissance Tapes ARTIST: M. Greer TOPIC: Parapsychology, $14.95

Aura/ESP: Sensing The World Around You
PUBLISHING COMPANY: Lorn Media Productions ARTIST: P. Murphy TOPIC: Psychic, $24.95

Aura: Its Color & Their Meanings (Plus Mysterious Powers Of Mind And Serpent Fire)
PUBLISHING COMPANY: Theosophical Pub. ARTIST: G. Hodson TOPIC: Body-Mind Connection, Parapsychology, $14.95

Auras
PUBLISHING COMPANY: A.R.E. Press ARTIST: E. Cayce TOPIC: Parapsychology, $8.95

Autoerotic Mysticism: A Lecture On Tantric Principles For Individual Use
PUBLISHING COMPANY: Llewellyn Worldwide, Ltd. ARTIST: Jonn Mumford TOPIC: Occult, $7.95

Autogenics And Meditation
PUBLISHING COMPANY: New Harbinger Publications ARTIST: M. McKay, P. Fanning TOPIC: Meditation, $10.95

Automatic Writing
PUBLISHING COMPANY: Valley of the Sun ARTIST: D. Sutphen TOPIC: Channeling, $29.95

Ave Maria Mater Dei (Christian Tradition)
PUBLISHING COMPANY: MSH * Association ARTIST: Brother Charles TOPIC: Spirituality, $25.00

Ave Maria Meditation
PUBLISHING COMPANY: Full Circle Music ARTIST: Joel Andrews TOPIC: Meditation, $10.98

Awake In The Cosmic Dream
PUBLISHING COMPANY: S.R.F. Publications ARTIST: Yogananda TOPIC: Spirituality, $11.50

Awaken Your Intuition
PUBLISHING COMPANY: Intuition Trainings ARTIST: J. Burr TOPIC: Psychology, $19.95

Awaken Your Psychic Powers: Edgar Cayce
PUBLISHING COMPANY: Audio Renaissance Tapes ARTIST: M. Thurston TOPIC: Psychic, $9.95

Awakening Bell: Thich Nhat Hanh And Cao Ngoc Phuong
PUBLISHING COMPANY: Parallax Press ARTIST: G. Coote TOPIC: Spirituality, $45.00

Awakening The Healer Within
PUBLISHING COMPANY: Mountain Spirit Tapes ARTIST: D. Keck TOPIC: Body-Mind Connection, $9.95

Awakening To Self Knowledge Pt. 4 Of Nothing Real Can Be Threatened Cim Video Workshop
PUBLISHING COMPANY: Life Action Press ARTIST: T. Singh TOPIC: Spirituality, $29.95

Awakening Your Body's Energies
PUBLISHING COMPANY: Thinking Allowed Prod. ARTIST: George Leonard TOPIC: Body-Mind Connection, $49.95

Awakening Your Psychic Powers: Audio Adaptation
PUBLISHING COMPANY: Harper & Row Publishers ARTIST: Henry Reed TOPIC: Channeling, $9.95

Ayurveda: Science Of Self-Healing
PUBLISHING COMPANY: Summit University Press ARTIST: V. Lad TOPIC: Holistic Healing, $29.95

Azuma
PUBLISHING COMPANY: Private Music ARTIST: Azuma TOPIC: Meditation, $11.98

Basic Baby Massage
PUBLISHING COMPANY: Visionary Video Productions ARTIST: B. Lustfield TOPIC: Massage, $39.95

Basic Handwriting Analysis

PUBLISHING COMPANY: Visionary Video Productions ARTIST: S. Burns TOPIC: Palmistry, $39.95

Basic Ideas Of Science Of Mind
PUBLISHING COMPANY: Science of Mind Publications ARTIST: E. Holmes TOPIC: Spirituality, $12.95

Basic Palmistry, Part 1
PUBLISHING COMPANY: Visionary Video Productions ARTIST: S. Burns TOPIC: Palmistry, $39.95

Basic Training In The Self-Healing State
PUBLISHING COMPANY: Wonder-Full Day Prod. ARTIST: L. Sereda TOPIC: Meditation, Holistic Healing, $10.95

Basics Of House Interpretation 1 & 2
PUBLISHING COMPANY: Video Lecture Series ARTIST: J. McEvers TOPIC: Astrology, $39.95

Bayou Moon
PUBLISHING COMPANY: Landscape Records ARTIST: T. Newman TOPIC: Meditation, $35.00

Be (Happy) Attitudes: Eight Positive Attitudes That Can Transform Your Life
PUBLISHING COMPANY: Nightingale Conant Corp. ARTIST: R. Schuller TOPIC: Body-Mind Connection, $14.95

Be Positive
PUBLISHING COMPANY: Potentials Unlimited ARTIST: Potentials Unlimited TOPIC: New Age, $9.98

Be Your Own Psychic
PUBLISHING COMPANY: A.R.E. Press ARTIST: A.R.E. TOPIC: Channeling, $59.95

Beauty, Pleasure, Sorrow And Love
PUBLISHING COMPANY: Harper & Row Publishers ARTIST: J. Krishnamurti TOPIC: Spirituality, $9.95

Becoming Happy
PUBLISHING COMPANY: Valley of the Sun ARTIST: D. Stuphen TOPIC: Hypnotism, $10.00

Behind The Gardens, Behind The Wall, Under The Tree
PUBLISHING COMPANY: CBS Records ARTIST: A. Vollenweider TOPIC: Meditation, $20.95

Behold Your Past Lives
PUBLISHING COMPANY: Light of Mind ARTIST: S. Gordon, D. Gordon TOPIC: Meditation, $14.95

Beholding The One In All
PUBLISHING COMPANY: S.R.F. Publications ARTIST: Yogananda TOPIC: Spirituality, $9.50

Being Born, Growing Up
PUBLISHING COMPANY: Blue Dolphin Publishing - 2 ARTIST: S. Ray, J. C. Pearce TOPIC: Spirituality, $10.00

Being Peace
PUBLISHING COMPANY: Parallax Press ARTIST: T. Hanh TOPIC: Spirituality, $12.00

Believe And Achieve

PUBLISHING COMPANY: Audio Renaissance Tapes ARTIST: W. C. Stone TOPIC: Body-Mind Connection, $15.95

Between Two Worlds
PUBLISHING COMPANY: Private Music ARTIST: P. O'Hearn TOPIC: Meditation, $11.98

Beyond Limits
PUBLISHING COMPANY: Reflections ARTIST: Star Sounds TOPIC: Hypnotism, $14.95

Beyond Positive Thinking: Live Life Fully
PUBLISHING COMPANY: BFS Limited ARTIST: Bright Images TOPIC: Hypnotism, $11.95

Beyond Science
PUBLISHING COMPANY: Blue Dolphin Publishing - 2 ARTIST: F. Capra, A. Young TOPIC: Occult, $10.00

Beyond The Brain I & II: Birth, Death & Transcendence
PUBLISHING COMPANY: Sounds True Records & Dupl. ARTIST: S. Grof TOPIC: Psychology, $15.95

Beyond The Rainbow
PUBLISHING COMPANY: Gaia Records ARTIST: J. Bello TOPIC: Meditation, $10.98

Beyond The Subconscious: The Ultimate Mind Game
PUBLISHING COMPANY: Imagination Store ARTIST: C. Francis TOPIC: Body-Mind Connection, $15.95

Beyond Your Wildest Dreams: Dream Clearing/Dream Recall
PUBLISHING COMPANY: Parker, Alice Anne ARTIST: Alice A. Parker TOPIC: Dreams, $9.98

Beyond Your Wildest Dreams: Dream Exploration/Dreamfree
PUBLISHING COMPANY: Parker, Alice Anne ARTIST: Alice A. Parker TOPIC: Dreams, $9.98

Beyond Your Wildest Dreams: Dream Guidance/Dream Healing
PUBLISHING COMPANY: Parker, Alice Anne ARTIST: Alice A. Parker TOPIC: Dreams, $9.98

Beyond Your Wildest Dreams: Dream Lover/The Dark Vessel
PUBLISHING COMPANY: Parker, Alice Anne ARTIST: Alice Anne Parker ARTIST: Music by Deuter TOPIC: Dreams, Meditation, $10.98

Beyond Your Wildest Dreams: Dreamsex/Corridor Of Dreams
PUBLISHING COMPANY: Parker, Alice Anne ARTIST: Alice Anne Parker ARTIST: Music by Deuter TOPIC: Meditation, $10.98

Bhagwan: The Way Of The Heart
PUBLISHING COMPANY: Chidvilas ARTIST: Chidvilas Foundation TOPIC: Spirituality, $39.95

Blossoming Rose: Evolve To A Higher Mind
PUBLISHING COMPANY: Valley of the Sun ARTIST: D. Sutphen TOPIC: Meditation, $8.98

Blue Dawn
PUBLISHING COMPANY: Chidvilas ARTIST: Spiritual Environments TOPIC: Meditation, $11.95

Body Alive/Deep Relaxation And Sleep
PUBLISHING COMPANY: Sutherland, Carolina ARTIST: Caroline Sutherland TOPIC: Dreams, $12.95

Body Beautiful: White Magic Techniques & Incantations
PUBLISHING COMPANY: Valley of the Sun ARTIST: D. Stuphen TOPIC: Occult, $12.50

Body Resonating
PUBLISHING COMPANY: Reflections ARTIST: Star Sounds TOPIC: Hypnotism, $14.95

Boundaries Of The Soul: Explorations In Jungian Analysis
PUBLISHING COMPANY: Thinking Allowed Prod. ARTIST: J. Singer TOPIC: Psychology, $49.95

Breaking Patterns
PUBLISHING COMPANY: Northern Lights Altern. ARTIST: S. Fisher TOPIC: Meditation, $10.00

Breaking The Chains Of Illusion
PUBLISHING COMPANY: Valley of the Sun ARTIST: D. Sutphen TOPIC: Metaphysics, $14.95

Breaking Through Illness: Igniting The Healing Power Within
PUBLISHING COMPANY: Stillpoint Publishing ARTIST: N. Shealy, C. Myss TOPIC: Holistic Healing, $29.95

Breath-Ercize: Work Out And Play With Full Breath
PUBLISHING COMPANY: Wonder-Full Day Prod. ARTIST: L. Sereda TOPIC: Meditation, $12.95

Breathe
PUBLISHING COMPANY: Vital Body Marketing Co., Inc. ARTIST: Marcus Allen, J. Bernoff TOPIC: New Age, $9.95

Brief History Of Time
PUBLISHING COMPANY: Dove Books On Tape, Inc. ARTIST: S. Hawking TOPIC: New Age, $24.95

Bringing A Course In Miracles Into Application
PUBLISHING COMPANY: Life Action Press ARTIST: T. Singh TOPIC: Spirituality, $21.95

Brother Sun, Sister Moon
PUBLISHING COMPANY: American Gramaphone ARTIST: J. Rutter ARTIST: Cambridge Singers TOPIC: Spirituality, $11.48

Buddhism: Path To Enlightenment
PUBLISHING COMPANY: Hartley Film Foundation ARTIST: Hartley Film Foundation TOPIC: Spirituality, $89.00

Building Self-Esteem
PUBLISHING COMPANY: A.R.E. Press ARTIST: A.R.E. TOPIC: Meditation, $9.95

Bushido: Personality Transformation
PUBLISHING COMPANY: Valley of the Sun ARTIST: D. Sutphen TOPIC: Hypnotism, $18.98

Calcium And Bone Disease
PUBLISHING COMPANY: New Dawn Nutrit.Services ARTIST: R. Gilday TOPIC: Nutrition, $9.95

Call Of The Unknown: Selected Pieces 1972-1986
PUBLISHING COMPANY: Celestial Harmonies ARTIST: Deuter TOPIC: Meditation, $18.98

Cancer, Your Diet And You
PUBLISHING COMPANY: Gentle World, Inc. ARTIST: M. Klaper TOPIC: Vegetarianism, $7.00

Cancer: Discovering Your Healing Power
PUBLISHING COMPANY: Hay House ARTIST: Louise Hay TOPIC: Psychic Healing, $10.00

Canyon Consort: The Paul Winter Consort In The Grand Canyon
PUBLISHING COMPANY: DUMM ARTIST: Paul Winter TOPIC: New Age, $39.95

Canyon Dreams
PUBLISHING COMPANY: Mira Mar Productions ARTIST: Tangerine Dream TOPIC: New Age, $29.95

Cauldron Journey For Healing
PUBLISHING COMPANY: Scully, Nicki ARTIST: N. Scully ARTIST: Music by Roland Barker with Jerry Garcia TOPIC: Meditation, $10.00

Cauldron Of Thoth
PUBLISHING COMPANY: Scully, Nicki ARTIST: J. Sergeant, N. Scully TOPIC: Meditation, $12.00

Cauldron Teachings: Journey With Eagle & Elephant
PUBLISHING COMPANY: Scully, Nicki ARTIST: N. Scully, R. Barker TOPIC: Meditation, $10.98

Caverna Magica
PUBLISHING COMPANY: CBS Records ARTIST: A. Vollenweider TOPIC: Meditation, $19.25

Celtic Harp: Secrets From The Stones
PUBLISHING COMPANY: Sona Gaia ARTIST: J. Pintar TOPIC: Meditation, $15.98

Celtic Magic And The Druids
PUBLISHING COMPANY: Thoth Publications ARTIST: M. Hope TOPIC: Occult, $9.95

Centering
PUBLISHING COMPANY: Fonix Musik ARTIST: F. Lorentzen TOPIC: Meditation, $10.95

Chakra Balance
PUBLISHING COMPANY: Valley of the Sun ARTIST: D. Stuphen TOPIC: Parapsychology, $10.00

Chakra Balancing/Song Of The Soul
PUBLISHING COMPANY: Astromusic ARTIST: S. Dean, G.J. Markoe TOPIC: Parapsychology, $9.98

Chakra Breathing: Meditations Of Bhagwan Shree Rajneesh
PUBLISHING COMPANY: Chidvilas ARTIST: B. Rajneesh TOPIC: Parapsychology, $9.95

Chakra Healing

Chakra Meditation
PUBLISHING COMPANY: Potentials Unlimited ARTIST: Potentials Unlimited TOPIC: New Age, $9.98

Chakra Sounds: Rajneesh Discourse
PUBLISHING COMPANY: Chidvilas ARTIST: B. Rajneesh TOPIC: Spirituality, Parapsychology, $9.95

Chakras And The Wings Of Life
PUBLISHING COMPANY: Omega Press ARTIST: Pir Vilayat Khan TOPIC: Parapsychology, $7.95

Chakras Of Enlightenment
PUBLISHING COMPANY: Mayflower B/S ARTIST: Robert Thibodeau TOPIC: Parapsychology, $49.95

Chakras: Motherpeace Cassette Vol. 5
PUBLISHING COMPANY: Wingbow Press ARTIST: V. Noble TOPIC: Parapsychology, $9.95

Channel For The Light: Meditation
PUBLISHING COMPANY: Valley of the Sun ARTIST: D. Sutphen TOPIC: Meditation, $19.95

Channeling
PUBLISHING COMPANY: Audio Renaissance Tapes ARTIST: Various Channels TOPIC: Channeling, $9.95

Channeling Your Higher Self
PUBLISHING COMPANY: Audio Renaissance Tapes ARTIST: E. Cayce TOPIC: Channeling, $9.95

Channeling: Gift From The Gods
PUBLISHING COMPANY: White Dove Int'l, Inc. ARTIST: S. Wilde TOPIC: Channeling, $39.95

Channeling: How To Reach Out To Your Spirit Guides
PUBLISHING COMPANY: Bantam Books ARTIST: K. Ridall TOPIC: Channeling, $8.95

Channels And Channeling
PUBLISHING COMPANY: Thinking Allowed Prod. ARTIST: K. Ryerson ARTIST: et.al. TOPIC: Channeling, $69.95

Chants And Mantras
PUBLISHING COMPANY: S.Y.D.A. Foundation ARTIST: Muktananda TOPIC: Spirituality, $10.00

Chaos: Making A New Science
PUBLISHING COMPANY: Dove Books On Tape, Inc. ARTIST: J. Gleick ARTIST: Read by Michael Jackson of KABC radio TOPIC: New Age, $14.95

Charisma: Drawing People To You
PUBLISHING COMPANY: Valley of the Sun ARTIST: D. Sutphen TOPIC: Hypnotism, $12.50

Charkra Meditation
PUBLISHING COMPANY: Potentials Unlimited ARTIST: Potentials Unlimited TOPIC: New Age, $9.98

Chi Kung Meditations: Taoist Inner Healing Exercises

PUBLISHING COMPANY: Sounds True Record & Dupl. ARTIST: K. Cohen ARTIST: Music by Beth Quist TOPIC: Holistic Health, $9.95

Chiaroscuro
PUBLISHING COMPANY: Windham Hill Records ARTIST: D. Anger, M. Marshall TOPIC: Meditation, $11.98

Christ Consciousness
PUBLISHING COMPANY: Inner Vision Publishing Co. ARTIST: J. Van Auken TOPIC: Channeling, $12.95

Christmas Collection 3-Pack (Celtic Xmas; Flute & Harp For Xmas; Xamas Classics/Guitar
PUBLISHING COMPANY: Vital Body Marketing Co., Inc. ARTIST: Various artists TOPIC: New Age, $19.95

Cicada
PUBLISHING COMPANY: Celestial Harmonies ARTIST: Deuter TOPIC: Meditation, $17.98

Circle The Earth With Song
PUBLISHING COMPANY: Susan Elizabeth Hale ARTIST: Susan Elizabeth Hale TOPIC: Spirituality, $10.00

Classic Art Of Sensual Massage
PUBLISHING COMPANY: Healing Arts Home Video ARTIST: G. Inkeles TOPIC: Massage, $19.95

Classic Fantasy
PUBLISHING COMPANY: Fonix Musik ARTIST: Anugama TOPIC: Meditation, $11.95

Cleansing The Chakras
PUBLISHING COMPANY: Omega Press ARTIST: Pir Vilayat Khan TOPIC: Parapsychology, $7.95

Clearing Your Channels Of Perception
PUBLISHING COMPANY: Marshall House, Inc. ARTIST: Jeanie Marshall, G. Smith TOPIC: Meditation, Crystals, $12.95

Cloud Of Unknowing
PUBLISHING COMPANY: Audio Literature, Inc. ARTIST: J. Walsh ARTIST: Read by Alan Jones TOPIC: Occult, $15.95

Cogitate Tape
PUBLISHING COMPANY: Gateways/IDHHB ARTIST: John Lilly, E. J. Gold TOPIC: Psychology, $9.98

Color Dynamics In Action
PUBLISHING COMPANY: Top of The Mountain Pub. ARTIST: Judith Powell TOPIC: Color Therapy, $19.95

Color Healing
PUBLISHING COMPANY: H. H. Productions ARTIST: H. Hartly TOPIC: Color Therapy, $9.98

Colour Therapy: Healing By Colours
PUBLISHING COMPANY: Centerpoint Distribution, Inc. ARTIST: E. Baron TOPIC: Color Therapy, Holistic Healing, $9.98

Comfort Affirmations Amd Meditations
PUBLISHING COMPANY: Butterfly Publishing Co. ARTIST: E. Rose TOPIC: Meditation, $9.95

Coming Of Age In The Milky Way
PUBLISHING COMPANY: Dove Books On Tape, Inc. ARTIST: Timothy Ferris TOPIC: New Age, $14.95

Commentaries On A Course In Miracles
PUBLISHING COMPANY: Life Action Press ARTIST: T. Singh TOPIC: Spirituality, $17.95

Commentaries On The Heart Sutra
PUBLISHING COMPANY: Parallax Press ARTIST: T. Hanh TOPIC: Spirituality, $15.00

Communicating With Your Own Soul
PUBLISHING COMPANY: Quest Northwest Pub. Co. ARTIST: D. Marshall, M. Kirkendoll TOPIC: Meditation, $29.95

Communication As Healing
PUBLISHING COMPANY: Thinking Allowed Prod. ARTIST: P. Sun TOPIC: Holistic Healing, $29.95

Communication: Get Your Points Across
PUBLISHING COMPANY: BFS Limited ARTIST: Bright Images TOPIC: Hypnotism, $11.95

Communing With The Spirit Of Your Unborn Child Combo
PUBLISHING COMPANY: Aslan Publishing ARTIST: D. Church TOPIC: Psychic, $15.95

Communion: A True Story
PUBLISHING COMPANY: Dove Books On Tape, Inc. ARTIST: W. Stieber TOPIC: Paranormal Phenomena, $14.95

Compassion In Action
PUBLISHING COMPANY: Thinking Allowed Prod. ARTIST: Ram Dass TOPIC: Spirituality, $49.95

Complete Financial Property - 3 Pack (Financial Freedom; Self Confidence; Do It Now?)
PUBLISHING COMPANY: Vital Body Marketing Co., Inc. ARTIST: D. Gordon, S. Gordon TOPIC: Hypnotism, $19.95

Complete Guide To Channeling
PUBLISHING COMPANY: Penny Price Productions ARTIST: B. Hubbard TOPIC: Channeling, $39.95

Complete Musical Massage
PUBLISHING COMPANY: Vital Body Marketing Co., Inc. ARTIST: Various Artists TOPIC: Meditation, $16.95

Complete Stop Smoking - 3 Pack (Kick Smoking Habit; Overcome Smoking...; Take Control..)
PUBLISHING COMPANY: Vital Body Marketing Co., Inc. ARTIST: D. Gordon, S. Gordon TOPIC: Hypnotism, $19.95

Complete Weight Loss - 3 Pack (Weight Loss; Self Esteem; Positive Body Image)
PUBLISHING COMPANY: Vital Body Marketing Co., Inc. ARTIST: D. Gordon, S. Gordon TOPIC: Hypnotism, $19.95

Computers And The Mind
PUBLISHING COMPANY: Thinking Allowed Prod. ARTIST: Theodore Rozak ARTIST: et.al TOPIC: New Age, $69.95

Concentration
PUBLISHING COMPANY: Potentials Unlimited ARTIST: Potentials Unlimited TOPIC: New Age, $9.98

Conditioning The Child Of Light
PUBLISHING COMPANY: Arizona Metaphysical Society ARTIST: F. Alper TOPIC: Spirituality, $10.00

Conferring With The Moon
PUBLISHING COMPANY: Windham Hill Records ARTIST: W. Ackerman TOPIC: Meditation, $11.98

Confluence
PUBLISHING COMPANY: Fonix Musik ARTIST: Kristian Borregaard TOPIC: Meditation, $10.95

Conscious Living/Conscious Dying
PUBLISHING COMPANY: Thinking Allow Prod. ARTIST: S. Levine TOPIC: Death, $49.95

Controlling Your Dreams
PUBLISHING COMPANY: Audio Renaissance Tapes ARTIST: S. LaBerge TOPIC: Dreams, $9.95

Conversations II
PUBLISHING COMPANY: Harper & Row Publishers ARTIST: J. Krishnamurti TOPIC: Spirituality, $9.95

Conversations On Living: Your Thoughts Create Your Life
PUBLISHING COMPANY: Hay House ARTIST: Louise Hay TOPIC: Meditation, $10.00

Conversations: A Remarkable Interview On Self-Discovery & Healing From Aids
PUBLISHING COMPANY: Brotherhood Press ARTIST: W. Garcia, G. Melton TOPIC: Psychic Healing, $10.00

Coping With Spiritual And Sexual Stress
PUBLISHING COMPANY: Arizona Metaphysical Society ARTIST: F. Alper TOPIC: Spirituality, $10.00

Cosmic Game
PUBLISHING COMPANY: Sounds True Records & Dupl. ARTIST: S. Grof TOPIC: Psychology, $9.95

Course In Miracles
PUBLISHING COMPANY: Blue Dolphin Publishing - 2 ARTIST: J. Skutch TOPIC: Spirituality, $10.00

Course In Miracles And The Destiny Of America
PUBLISHING COMPANY: Life Action Press ARTIST: T. Singh TOPIC: Spirituality, $29.95

Course In Miracles And The Limitation Of Learning
PUBLISHING COMPANY: Life Action Press ARTIST: T. Singh TOPIC: Spirituality, $34.95

Course In Miracles Explorations, Series I
PUBLISHING COMPANY: Life Action Press ARTIST: T. Singh TOPIC: Spirituality, $21.95

Course In Miracles Video
PUBLISHING COMPANY: Thinking Allowed Prod. ARTIST: J. Skutch-Whitson TOPIC: Spirituality, $29.95

Covert Modeling & Covert Reinforcement
PUBLISHING COMPANY: New Harbinger Publications ARTIST: M. David ARTIST: et.al. TOPIC: Psychology, $10.95

Create More Love In Your Life By Accepting Yourself
PUBLISHING COMPANY: Happiness Unlimited Institute ARTIST: E. Kenyon ARTIST: Music by Steve Halpern TOPIC: Meditation, $10.95

Create Wealth: Power Programming
PUBLISHING COMPANY: Valley of the Sun ARTIST: D. Sutphen TOPIC: Hypnotism, $10.98

Creating A World That Works
PUBLISHING COMPANY: Upstate Media Enterprises ARTIST: J. Houston TOPIC: Spirituality, $39.95

Creating Close Encounter And E.T. Situations
PUBLISHING COMPANY: Inner Light Publications ARTIST: B. Steiger TOPIC: Paranormal Phenomena, $8.95

Creating Harmonic Interiors
PUBLISHING COMPANY: Miles Design, Inc. ARTIST: Miles Design, Inc. TOPIC: Holistic Health, $14.95

Creating Miracles In Your Life
PUBLISHING COMPANY: Light of Mind ARTIST: S. Gordon, D. Gordon TOPIC: Meditation, $14.95

Creative Affirmations
PUBLISHING COMPANY: Audio Renaissance Tapes ARTIST: Jerry Gillies TOPIC: Meditation, $9.95

Creative Decision Making
PUBLISHING COMPANY: A. R. E. Press ARTIST: A.R.E. TOPIC: Meditation, $9.95

Creative Dreaming
PUBLISHING COMPANY: Light of Mind ARTIST: A. Alexander TOPIC: Dreams, $9.98

Creative Dreaming: Plan And Control Your Dreams
PUBLISHING COMPANY: Audio Renaissance Tapes ARTIST: P. Garfield TOPIC: Dreams, $9.95

Creative Inspiration
PUBLISHING COMPANY: Changeworks ARTIST: T. Condon TOPIC: Meditation, $12.95

Creative Mind And Success
PUBLISHING COMPANY: Science of Minds Publications ARTIST: E. Holmes TOPIC: Spirituality, $12.95

Creative Problem Solving
PUBLISHING COMPANY: Changeworks ARTIST: T. Condon TOPIC: Meditation, $12.95

Creative Self
PUBLISHING COMPANY: Light Institute Cassettes ARTIST: C. Griscom TOPIC: Spirituality, $10.75

Creative Thinking
PUBLISHING COMPANY: Potentials Unlimited ARTIST: Potentials Unlimited TOPIC: New Age, $9.98

Creative Visualization
PUBLISHING COMPANY: New World Library ARTIST: S. Gawain TOPIC: Meditation, $10.95

Creative Visualization And Beyond
PUBLISHING COMPANY: David Colliyer ARTIST: D. Collyer, D. Kobialka TOPIC: Meditation, $10.95

Creative Visualization Workshop
PUBLISHING COMPANY: New World Library ARTIST: S. Gawain TOPIC: Meditation, $39.95

Creativity
PUBLISHING COMPANY: White Dove Int'l., Inc. ARTIST: S. Wilde TOPIC: Hypnotism, $11.95

Crisis Tape
PUBLISHING COMPANY: Mellow Minds ARTIST: Janalea Hoffman TOPIC: Meditation, $10.95

Cristofori's Dream
PUBLISHING COMPANY: Narada Productions ARTIST: D. Lanz TOPIC: Meditation, $15.98

Critical Self-Awareness
PUBLISHING COMPANY: Thinking Allowed Prod. ARTIST: P. Sun ARTIST: et.al. TOPIC: Psychology, $69.95

Crystal Adventure
PUBLISHING COMPANY: Hopkins, Marge V./Ayamaya ARTIST: M. Hopkins TOPIC: Meditation, $11.95

Crystal Awareness And Techniques: A Complete Seminar Workshop
PUBLISHING COMPANY: Valley of the Sun ARTIST: R. Baer TOPIC: Crystals, $18.98

Crystal Chakras And Psychic Healing
PUBLISHING COMPANY: Mayflower B/S ARTIST: Robert Thibodeau TOPIC: Parapsychology, $49.95

Crystal Clear: Use The Earth's Magic Energy To Vitalize Your Mind, Body & Spirit
PUBLISHING COMPANY: Sound Editions ARTIST: C. Church TOPIC: Crystals, $14.95

Crystal Consciousness
PUBLISHING COMPANY: Light of Mind ARTIST: S. Gordon, D. Gordon TOPIC: Crystals, $14.95

Crystal Enchantment
PUBLISHING COMPANY: Valley of the Sun ARTIST: D. Sutphen TOPIC: Hypnotism, $18.98

Crystal Healing
PUBLISHING COMPANY: Kehr, Janie ARTIST: J. Kehr TOPIC: Crystals, $10.98

Crystal Hunting
PUBLISHING COMPANY: Glad Heart Productions ARTIST: R. McKinnon ARTIST: & Serenity TOPIC: Crystals, $29.95

Crystal Illumination: A Cosmic Journey Through The Inner Realms & Beyond
PUBLISHING COMPANY: Willow Tree ARTIST: Aeoliah TOPIC: Meditation, $18.00

Crystal Magick Vol. 1
PUBLISHING COMPANY: Crystal Seminars/Altara ARTIST: Altara TOPIC: Crystals, $39.95

Crystal Massage
PUBLISHING COMPANY: Coleman Crystal Co. ARTIST: J. Sato TOPIC: Massage, $24.95

Crystal Meditation
PUBLISHING COMPANY: Vital Body Marketing Co., Inc. ARTIST: Don G. Campbell TOPIC: New Age, $9.95

Crystal Meditations
PUBLISHING COMPANY: Arizona Metaphysical Society ARTIST: F. Alper TOPIC: Psychic Healing, $10.00

Crystal Path
PUBLISHING COMPANY: U-Read / U-Music ARTIST: Uma Silbey ARTIST: Ramana Das TOPIC: Crystals, $9.98

Crystal Star
PUBLISHING COMPANY: Vital Body Marketing Co., Inc. ARTIST: J. Oliver TOPIC: New Age, $9.95

Crystal Star: Visual Meditation Tape
PUBLISHING COMPANY: Colin Smythe, Ltd. ARTIST: J. Oliver TOPIC: New Age, $40.00

Crystal Suite
PUBLISHING COMPANY: Steven Halpern ARTIST: S. Halpern TOPIC: Meditation, $12.98

Crystal Understanding
PUBLISHING COMPANY: Kehr, Janie ARTIST: J. Kehr TOPIC: Crystals, $10.98

Crystal Vista
PUBLISHING COMPANY: Inter-Dimensional Music ARTIST: Iasos TOPIC: New Age, $50.00

Crystals For The New Age: The Complete Video
PUBLISHING COMPANY: Centerpoint Distribution Inc. TOPIC: Crystals, $29.95

Cultivating The Heart Of Compassion I & II
PUBLISHING COMPANY: Sounds True Record. & Dupl. ARTIST: Ram Dass TOPIC: Spirituality, $15.95

Cutting The Ties That Bind
PUBLISHING COMPANY: Janet Bock ARTIST: P. Krystal TOPIC: Meditation, $8.95

Cutting The Ties That Bind #2: Visualization Techniques
PUBLISHING COMPANY: Janet Bock ARTIST: P. Krystal TOPIC: Meditation, $8.95

Cycles Of Truth: Singing Awake The Dream
PUBLISHING COMPANY: Medicine Song Productions ARTIST: Rashani TOPIC: Spirituality, $11.00

Cymatics: The Healing Nature Of Sound
PUBLISHING COMPANY: Macro Media ARTIST: P. Manners TOPIC: Holistic Healing, $49.95

Daily Prayer Affirmations
PUBLISHING COMPANY: Joyful Light Foundation ARTIST: Fr. Gorayeb TOPIC: Meditation, $9.95

Dance For Me When I Die: Death As A Rite Of Passage
PUBLISHING COMPANY: Compcare Publications ARTIST: Alla Renee Bozarth TOPIC: Death, $9.95

Dance Of The Hi-Tech Shaman
PUBLISHING COMPANY: Gateways/IDHHB ARTIST: E. J. Gold TOPIC: Psychology, $9.98

Dances Of Relationship
PUBLISHING COMPANY: Light Institute Cassettes ARTIST: C. Griscom TOPIC: Spirituality, $10.75

Dances Of Universal Peace, Vol. 1
PUBLISHING COMPANY: Sufi Islamia/Prophecy Press ARTIST: Sufi Choir TOPIC: Spirituality, $9.95

Dances Of Universal Peace, Vol. 2
PUBLISHING COMPANY: Sufi Islamia/Prophecy Press ARTIST: Sufi Choir TOPIC: Spirituality, $9.95

Dances Of Universal Peace, Vol. 3
PUBLISHING COMPANY: Sufi Islamia/Prophecy Press ARTIST: Sufi Choir TOPIC: Spirituality, $15.95

Dancing Beyond The Shadow
PUBLISHING COMPANY: Upstate Media Enterprises ARTIST: J. Houston TOPIC: Spirituality, $39.95

Dancing With The Fire: Firewalking
PUBLISHING COMPANY: Macro Media ARTIST: M. Sky, J Volk TOPIC: Body-Mind Connection, $24.95

Dancing With The Lion
PUBLISHING COMPANY: Columbia Records ARTIST: A. Vollenweider TOPIC: Meditation, $20.98

Dancing Wu Li Masters: An Overview Of The New Physics
PUBLISHING COMPANY: Audio Renaissance Tapes ARTIST: G. (Jun) Zukav TOPIC: New Age, $15.95

Dawn Melodies
PUBLISHING COMPANY: Crystal Cave Enterprises ARTIST: Leonardo Rubinstein TOPIC: Meditation, $10.95

Dawning: Chants Of The Medicine Wheel
PUBLISHING COMPANY: Bear Tribe Medicine Society ARTIST: Bear Tribe TOPIC: Spirituality, $10.00

Death And Samadhi
PUBLISHING COMPANY: Light Institute Cassettes ARTIST: C. Griscom TOPIC: Death, $10.75

Deception Of Learning: Pt. 2 Of Nothing Real Can Be Threatened, Cim Video Workshop

PUBLISHING COMPANY: Life Action Press ARTIST: T. Singh TOPIC: Spirituality, $29.95

Deep Breakfast
PUBLISHING COMPANY: Music West Records ARTIST: R. Lynch TOPIC: Meditation, $17.50

Deep Daydreams
PUBLISHING COMPANY: Mellow Minds ARTIST: Janalea Hoffman TOPIC: Meditation, $11.95

Deep Relax
PUBLISHING COMPANY: Yes! Technologies ARTIST: Yes! Technologies TOPIC: Hypnotism, $11.95

Deep Relaxation
PUBLISHING COMPANY: Effective Learnings Systems, Inc. ARTIST: Love Tapes TOPIC: Hypnotism, $11.98

Deep Sleep
PUBLISHING COMPANY: White Dove Int'l., Inc. ARTIST: S. Wilde TOPIC: Hypnotism, $11.95

Deep Sleep And Sweet Dreams
PUBLISHING COMPANY: Changeworks ARTIST: C. Erickson, T. Condon TOPIC: Meditation, $12.95

Descendant And Your Alter Ego
PUBLISHING COMPANY: RKM Publishing ARTIST: R. Myers TOPIC: Astrology, $8.95

Describing The Thirty-Eight Healing Remedies
PUBLISHING COMPANY: Bach Educational Program ARTIST: N. Murray TOPIC: Herbalogy, $20.95

Desert Dance
PUBLISHING COMPANY: Celestial Harmonies ARTIST: R. C. Nakai TOPIC: Meditation, $18.98

Desert Vision
PUBLISHING COMPANY: Narada Productions ARTIST: D. Lanz, P. Speer TOPIC: Meditation, $16.98

Develop Enthusiasm
PUBLISHING COMPANY: Potentials Unlimited ARTIST: Potentials Unlimited TOPIC: New Age, $9.98

Develop Psychic Abilities
PUBLISHING COMPANY: Potentials Unlimited ARTIST: Potentials Unlimited TOPIC: New Age, $9.98

Develop Psychic Ability Now
PUBLISHING COMPANY: Valley of the Sun ARTIST: D. Sutphen TOPIC: Psychic, $19.95

Developing And Applying Psychic Abilities
PUBLISHING COMPANY: Thinking Allowed Prod. ARTIST: K. Ryerson TOPIC: Psychic, $29.95

Developing Intuition
PUBLISHING COMPANY: New World Library ARTIST: S. Gawain TOPIC: Meditation, $10.95

Developing Telepathy In Your Dreams: Dream Helper Approach
PUBLISHING COMPANY: Inner Vision Publishing Co. ARTIST: Henry Reed TOPIC: Dreams, $9.95

Developing The Sixth Sense
PUBLISHING COMPANY: White Dove Int'l., Inc. ARTIST: S. Wilde TOPIC: Psychic, $34.95

Diabetes And The Vegan Diet
PUBLISHING COMPANY: Gentle World, Inc. ARTIST: M. Klaper TOPIC: Vegetarianism, $7.00

Dick Sutphen Past-Life Hypnotic Regression Course Vol. 1
PUBLISHING COMPANY: Valley of the Sun ARTIST: D. Stuphen TOPIC: Hypnotism, $39.95

Dick Sutphen Past-Life Hypnotic Regression Course Vol. 2
PUBLISHING COMPANY: Valley of the Sun ARTIST: D. Stuphen TOPIC: Hypnotism, $39.95

Didjeridu For The Shamanic Journey
PUBLISHING COMPANY: FDN. Shamanic Studies ARTIST: M. Harner, S. McDonnell TOPIC: Meditation, $10.98

Diet For A New Planet
PUBLISHING COMPANY: Sounds True Record & Dupl. ARTIST: John Robbins TOPIC: Vegetarianism, $9.95

Different Drum: Community Making And Peace
PUBLISHING COMPANY: Simon & Schuster Audio ARTIST: M.Scott Peck TOPIC: Psychology, $14.95

Ding
PUBLISHING COMPANY: Fonix Musik ARTIST: Pushkar TOPIC: Meditation, $17.98

Discovering Your Life's Work
PUBLISHING COMPANY: Life Action Press ARTIST: T. Singh TOPIC: Spirituality, $17.95

Discovering Your Own Holiness
PUBLISHING COMPANY: Life Action Press ARTIST: T. Singh TOPIC: Spirituality, $17.95

Discovering Your Soul's Purpose
PUBLISHING COMPANY: A.R.E. Press ARTIST: M. Thurston TOPIC: Spirituality, $59.95

Discovering Your Spirit Teacher
PUBLISHING COMPANY: Inner Light Publications ARTIST: B. Steiger TOPIC: Channeling, $8.95

Discussions On A Course In Miracles
PUBLISHING COMPANY: Life Action Press ARTIST: T. Singh TOPIC: Spirituality, $21.95

Dissolving Barriers: Discover Your Subconscious Blocks To Love, Health & Self-Image
PUBLISHING COMPANY: Hay House ARTIST: Louise Hay TOPIC: Body-Mind Connection, Holistic Healing, $29.95

Divine Remembrance
PUBLISHING COMPANY: Heavensong Recordings ARTIST: M. Stillwater TOPIC: Meditation, $15.00

Divine Songs
PUBLISHING COMPANY: Avatar Book Distributors ARTIST: A. Coltrane, et.al. TOPIC: Spirituality, $11.00

Do Only That: A Course In Miracles & Working With Children
PUBLISHING COMPANY: Life Action Press ARTIST: T. Singh TOPIC: Spirituality, $29.95

Do-In Video
PUBLISHING COMPANY: Banker, Cindy ARTIST: C. Banker TOPIC: Holistic Healing, $49.00

Does Mind Matter
PUBLISHING COMPANY: Thinking Allowed Prod. ARTIST: U.G. Krishnamurti ARTIST: et.al. TOPIC: Spirituality, $69.95

Dolphin Dreams
PUBLISHING COMPANY: Spirit Music ARTIST: J. Goldman ARTIST: Spirit Sounds TOPIC: Meditation, $17.98

Doors Opening: A Positive Approach To Aids
PUBLISHING COMPANY: Hay House ARTIST: Louise Hay TOPIC: Holistic Healing, $35.00

Double Drumming For The Shamanic Journey
PUBLISHING COMPANY: FDN. Shamanic Studies ARTIST: M. Harner TOPIC: Meditation, $10.98

Down To The Moon
PUBLISHING COMPANY: CBS Records ARTIST: A. Vollenweider TOPIC: Meditation, $18.98

Dr. Fritz: Psychic Surgeon
PUBLISHING COMPANY: Postscript Productions, Inc. ARTIST: Postscript Productions TOPIC: Holistic Healing, $29.95

Dream Generator
PUBLISHING COMPANY: Private Music ARTIST: C. Alomar TOPIC: Meditation, $11.98

Dream Images
PUBLISHING COMPANY: Search For Serenity ARTIST: Shardad TOPIC: Meditation, $16.98

Dream Recall
PUBLISHING COMPANY: Mountain Spirit Tapes, Inc. ARTIST: D. Keck TOPIC: Dreams, $9.95

Dream Time
PUBLISHING COMPANY: Crystal Cave Enterprises ARTIST: Paul Fitzgerald, M. Flanagan TOPIC: Meditation, $10.95

Dreamer's Web: A Journey Through The Four Directions
PUBLISHING COMPANY: K. & T. Klein ARTIST: Kenny & Tzipora TOPIC: Witchcraft, $8.95

Dreamflight
PUBLISHING COMPANY: Mystic Visions, Inc. ARTIST: H. Paul TOPIC: Meditation, $17.95

Dreams Of Children
PUBLISHING COMPANY: Winham Hill Records ARTIST: Shadowfax Ensemble TOPIC: Meditation, $18.50

Dreamsounds: Synthesizer Improvisations For Listening, Massage & Relaxation
PUBLISHING COMPANY: Journey Tapes ARTIST: B. Kurnow TOPIC: Meditation, $10.98

Dreamtime Return
PUBLISHING COMPANY: Celestial Harmonies ARTIST: S. Roach TOPIC: Meditation, $18.98

Dreamwood
PUBLISHING COMPANY: Mystic Fire Video Co. ARTIST: J. Broughton TOPIC: Spirituality, $29.95

Drumming For The Shamanic Journey
PUBLISHING COMPANY: Fdn. Shamanic Studies ARTIST: M. Harner TOPIC: Meditation, $10.98

Dynamic Self Image: See Yourself As You Want To Be
PUBLISHING COMPANY: BFS Limited ARTIST: Bright Images TOPIC: Hypnotism, $11.95

Dynamic/Kundalini
PUBLISHING COMPANY: Chidvilas ARTIST: B. Rajneesh TOPIC: Spirituality, $9.95

Earth Dance
PUBLISHING COMPANY: Crystal Cave Enterprises ARTIST: Nick Ashron TOPIC: Meditation, $10.95

Earth Energy Meditations: How To Channel The Earth
PUBLISHING COMPANY: Sounds True Record & Dupl. ARTIST: A. Alli TOPIC: Channeling, $12.95

Earthlight: Guided Meditations For Self Transformation
PUBLISHING COMPANY: Earthlight, Inc. ARTIST: Samuel (Lea Schultz) TOPIC: Color Therapy, $10.00

Easing Into Sleep
PUBLISHING COMPANY: Source Cassettes ARTIST: E. Miller TOPIC: Dreams, $9.95

Eastern Opus
PUBLISHING COMPANY: Crystal Cave Enterprises ARTIST: Ron Magness TOPIC: Meditation, $10.95

Easy Enhanced Learning
PUBLISHING COMPANY: Changeworks ARTIST: C. Erickson, T. Condon TOPIC: Meditation, $12.95

Easy Yoga
PUBLISHING COMPANY: Phoenix Rising ARTIST: Michael Lee TOPIC: Yoga, $39.95

Eat To Succeed
PUBLISHING COMPANY: Sound Editions ARTIST: R. Haas TOPIC: Nutrition, $9.95

Eat, Drink And Think: Your Way To A New Life
PUBLISHING COMPANY: Centerpoint Distribution, Inc. ARTIST: E. Baron TOPIC: Holistic Healing, $9.98

Edgar Cayce
PUBLISHING COMPANY: Hartley Film Foundation ARTIST: Hartley Film Foundation TOPIC: Channeling, $39.95

Edgar Cayce's Pilgrimage In Dreams
PUBLISHING COMPANY: Inner Vision Publishing Co. ARTIST: H. Bro TOPIC: Dreams, $9.95

Edgar Cayce's Vision Of Building A New World
PUBLISHING COMPANY: Inner Vision Publishing Co. ARTIST: H. Bro TOPIC: Channeling, $9.95

Edgar Cayce: Revelations Of The Sleeping Prophet
PUBLISHING COMPANY: Audio Renaissance Tapes ARTIST: K. Todeschi ARTIST: Reader - Stanley R. Ross TOPIC: Channeling, $9.95

Edgar Cayce: The Sleeping Prophet
PUBLISHING COMPANY: A. R. E. Press ARTIST: Jess Stearn TOPIC: Channeling, $14.95

Effective Speaking
PUBLISHING COMPANY: Effective Learnings Systems, Inc. ARTIST: Love Tapes TOPIC: Hypnotism, $11.98

Effective Studying And Test Taking
PUBLISHING COMPANY: Effective Learnings Systems, Inc. ARTIST: Love Tapes TOPIC: Hypnotism, $11.98

Effortless Relaxation
PUBLISHING COMPANY: Soundwaves 2000 ARTIST: S. Halpern TOPIC: Hypnotism, $10.98

Eight Selves Within Us
PUBLISHING COMPANY: Gateways/IDHHB ARTIST: Robert Anton Wilson TOPIC: Occult, $16.98

Elemental Personalities: Motherpeace Cassette Vol. 4
PUBLISHING COMPANY: Wingbow Resources ARTIST: V. Noble TOPIC: Tarot, $9.95

Elementary Chart Synthesis 1 And 2
PUBLISHING COMPANY: Video Lecture Series ARTIST: J. Negus TOPIC: Astrology, $39.95

Elements, Modalities, Rulerships And Dignitaries
PUBLISHING COMPANY: Video Lecture Series ARTIST: M.E. Glass TOPIC: Astrology, $39.95

Emerald
PUBLISHING COMPANY: Narada Productions ARTIST: E. Tingstad ARTIST: et.al. TOPIC: Meditation, $16.98

Emergence Into The Light
PUBLISHING COMPANY: Valley of the Sun ARTIST: D. Sutphen TOPIC: Meditation, $8.98

Emotions In The Body
PUBLISHING COMPANY: Northern Lights Altern. ARTIST: S. Fisher TOPIC: Meditation, $10.00

Energy: I Am Power
PUBLISHING COMPANY: White Dove Int'l., Inc. ARTIST: S. Wilde TOPIC: Hypnotism, $11.95

Enhanced Self-Healing
PUBLISHING COMPANY: Soundwaves 2000 ARTIST: S. Halpern TOPIC: Hypnotism, $10.98

Enhancing Creativity
PUBLISHING COMPANY: Soundwaves 2000 ARTIST: S. Halpern TOPIC: Hypnotism, $10.98

Enhancing Massage
PUBLISHING COMPANY: Soundwaves 2000 ARTIST: S. Halpern TOPIC: Hypnotism, $10.98

Enhancing Peak Performance
PUBLISHING COMPANY: Soundwaves 2000 ARTIST: S. Halpern TOPIC: Hypnotism, $10.98

Enlightenment Affirmations
PUBLISHING COMPANY: Light of Mind ARTIST: D. Gordon, S. Gordon TOPIC: Meditation, $14.95

Enounter
PUBLISHING COMPANY: Hearts of Space ARTIST: M. Stearns TOPIC: Meditation, $18.95

Entity Attachment
PUBLISHING COMPANY: Valley of the Sun ARTIST: E. Fiore TOPIC: Metaphysics, $9.98

Entrance To The Tree Of Life Vol. 1
PUBLISHING COMPANY: Research Centre of Kabbalah ARTIST: P. Berg TOPIC: Kabbalah, $100.00

Entrance To The Tree Of Life Vol. 2
PUBLISHING COMPANY: Research Centre of Kabbalah ARTIST: P. Berg TOPIC: Kabbalah, $100.00

Environment Vol. 1
PUBLISHING COMPANY: Fonix Musik ARTIST: Anugama TOPIC: Meditation, $11.95

Environment Vol. 2
PUBLISHING COMPANY: Fonix Musik ARTIST: Anugama TOPIC: Meditation, $11.95

Enya
PUBLISHING COMPANY: Warner/Elektra/Atlant Corp. ARTIST: Enya TOPIC: Meditation, $11.98

Equilibrium
PUBLISHING COMPANY: MSH Association ARTIST: NSA TOPIC: Meditation, $25.00

Erasing Someone From Your Mind
PUBLISHING COMPANY: Valley of the Sun ARTIST: D. Sutphen TOPIC: Hypnotism, $18.98

Essence
PUBLISHING COMPANY: Full Circle Music ARTIST: Joel Andrews TOPIC: Meditation, $10.98

Essence Of Crystals: Science To Metaphysics
PUBLISHING COMPANY: John Baker Video ARTIST: John Baker TOPIC: Crystals, $19.95

Essene Gospel Of Peach
PUBLISHING COMPANY: Davidian, Bennett ARTIST: Bennctt Davidian ARTIST: Trs. by E. B. Szekely; music by Constance Demby TOPIC: Metaphysics, $11.98

Eternity
PUBLISHING COMPANY: Search For Serenity ARTIST: Shardad TOPIC: Meditation, $16.98

Etosha
PUBLISHING COMPANY: Private Music ARTIST: S. Ponder TOPIC: Meditation, $10.50

Evening With Dr. Bernie Siegal
PUBLISHING COMPANY: Upstate Media Enterprises ARTIST: Bernie Siegel TOPIC: Body-Mind Connection, $39.95

Evening With Ram Dass

PUBLISHING COMPANY: ARC A-V Enterprises ARTIST: Ram Dass TOPIC: Spirituality, $39.95

Evening With Windham Hill Live
PUBLISHING COMPANY: Windham Hill Records ARTIST: Windham Hill Artists TOPIC: Meditation, $18.50

Evolution Of A Yogi
PUBLISHING COMPANY: Hartley Film Foundation ARTIST: Ram Dass TOPIC: Spirituality, $39.95

Evolution Of The Magical Child 1
PUBLISHING COMPANY: Upstate Media Enterprises ARTIST: J.C. Pearce TOPIC: New Age, Psychology, $39.95

Evolution Of The Magical Child 2
PUBLISHING COMPANY: Upstate Media Enterprises ARTIST: J.C. Pearce TOPIC: New Age, Psychology, $39.95

Evolution Of The Magical Child 3
PUBLISHING COMPANY: Upstate Media Enterprises ARTIST: J.C. Pearce TOPIC: New Age, Psychology, $39.95

Evolutionary Astrology: A Comprehensive Course
PUBLISHING COMPANY: Mountain Astrologer ARTIST: T. Tarriktar TOPIC: Astrology, $98.95

Excursion
PUBLISHING COMPANY: Wishing Well Distributing ARTIST: M. Dolan, B. Synder TOPIC: Meditation, $39.95

Executive ESP: Access Your Intuition For Business Success
PUBLISHING COMPANY: Simon & Schuster Audtio ARTIST: G. Jackson TOPIC: Psychic, $9.95

Exercise Motivation
PUBLISHING COMPANY: Effective Learnings Systems, Inc. ARTIST: Love Tapes TOPIC: Hypnotism, $11.98

Expanding The Limits Of Consciousness
PUBLISHING COMPANY: Hartley Film Foundation ARTIST: Hartley Film Foundation TOPIC: Psychology, $89.00

Experience Yoga
PUBLISHING COMPANY: Hatha Yoga Center TOPIC: Yoga, $34.95

Experiences Of Awakening
PUBLISHING COMPANY: Infinity Tapes - Blue Dolphin ARTIST: C. Tart, J. Bolen TOPIC: Psychology, $10.00

Experimental Metaphysics Seminar
PUBLISHING COMPANY: Valley of the Sun ARTIST: D. Sutphen TOPIC: Metaphysics, $69.95

Exploring Parapsychology
PUBLISHING COMPANY: Thinking Allowed Prod. ARTIST: C. Tart ARTIST: et.al. TOPIC: Psychic, $69.95

Exploring The Heart Of Healing, Parts 1 & 2
PUBLISHING COMPANY: Access Group ARTIST: S. Levine, Ram Dass TOPIC: Death, $18.00

Exploring Your Past Lives
PUBLISHING COMPANY: Quest Northwest Pub. Co. ARTIST: D. Marshall, M. Kirkendoll TOPIC: Past Life Regression, $29.95

Extra Terrestrial Contact: Remembrance Of Beam Up Experiences/Reunion & Tour Of Starbase
PUBLISHING COMPANY: Deer Productions Unlimited ARTIST: L. Domnitz, P. Stenshoel TOPIC: Hypnotism, $10.00

Extra Terrestrial Perception: White Magic Techniques & Incantations
PUBLISHING COMPANY: Valley of the Sun ARTIST: D. Sutphen TOPIC: Hypnotism, $12.50

Extra-Temporal Perception: White Magic Techniques & Incantations
PUBLISHING COMPANY: Valley of the Sun ARTIST: D. Sutphen TOPIC: Psychic, $12.50

Faces Of Neptune
PUBLISHING COMPANY: Oliver Music ARTIST: J. Oliver TOPIC: Meditation, $11.98

Fairy Queen
PUBLISHING COMPANY: K. & T. Klein ARTIST: Kenny & Tzipora TOPIC: Witchcraft, $8.95

Family Harmony: Strengthen Your Famly Bond
PUBLISHING COMPANY: BFS Limited ARTIST: Bright Images TOPIC: Hypnotism, $11.95

Fasting Nature's Universal Cure
PUBLISHING COMPANY: Centerpoint Distribution, Inc. ARTIST: E. Baron TOPIC: Holistic Healing, $9.98

Fear Of Failure
PUBLISHING COMPANY: Potentials Unlimited ARTIST: Potentials Unlimited TOPIC: New Age, $9.98

Fear Of Success
PUBLISHING COMPANY: Potentials Unlimited ARTIST: Potentials Unlimited TOPIC: New Age, $9.98

Fearbusting Workshop
PUBLISHING COMPANY: Hay House ARTIST: Susan Jeffers TOPIC: Meditation, $25.00

Feed Your Kids Right
PUBLISHING COMPANY: NCC ARTIST: Lendon Smith TOPIC: Nutrition, $14.95

Feeding The Planet: The Politics Of Hunger
PUBLISHING COMPANY: Sounds True Record & Dupl. ARTIST: F. M. Lappe TOPIC: Vegetarianism, $9.95

Feel Fit To Your Core: Image Your Way To A Beautiful Body
PUBLISHING COMPANY: Wonder-Full Day Prod. ARTIST: L. Sereda TOPIC: Meditation, $12.95

Feeling Fine Affirmations (Subliminal)

PUBLISHING COMPANY: Hay House ARTIST: Louise Hay TOPIC: Meditation, $10.00

Feeling Good Through Massage The Edgar Cayce Way
PUBLISHING COMPANY: A.R.E. Press ARTIST: A. McGarey TOPIC: Massage, $39.95

Feminine Ancient Vision, Modern Wisdom
PUBLISHING COMPANY: Bear Tribe Medicine Society ARTIST: Wabun Wind TOPIC: Spirituality, $34.95

Feminine Spirituality
PUBLISHING COMPANY: White Dove Int'l., Inc. ARTIST: S. Wilde TOPIC: Hypnotism, $11.95

Femininity
PUBLISHING COMPANY: White Dove Int'l., Inc. ARTIST: S. Wilde TOPIC: Hypnotism, $11.95

Finding Peace Within
PUBLISHING COMPANY: Life Action Press ARTIST: T. Singh TOPIC: Spirituality, $17.95

Finding The Child Within
PUBLISHING COMPANY: Dr. Gloria Spitalny ARTIST: Gloria Spitalny TOPIC: Psychology, $11.98

Finding Your Inner Calling
PUBLISHING COMPANY: Life Action Press ARTIST: T. Singh TOPIC: Spirituality, $29.95

Fine Art Of Relaxation
PUBLISHING COMPANY: Earth View ARTIST: J. Levey TOPIC: Meditation, $17.98

Fire In The Rose
PUBLISHING COMPANY: Rising Sun Records ARTIST: S. Mazer, D. Smith TOPIC: Meditation, $16.98

Fit For Life
PUBLISHING COMPANY: Sound Editions ARTIST: H. Diamond, M. Diamond TOPIC: Nutrition, $9.95

Fitness/Exercise: Live The Difference
PUBLISHING COMPANY: BFS Limited ARTIST: Bright Images TOPIC: Hypnotism, $11.95

Five O'clock Refresher: Extra Energy After Work
PUBLISHING COMPANY: Simon & Schuster Audio TOPIC: Acupuncture, $9.95

Five Steps To Personal Freedom
PUBLISHING COMPANY: Creative Living Library ARTIST: C. O'Connell TOPIC: Spirituality, $10.00

Flirting From The Heart
PUBLISHING COMPANY: Hay House ARTIST: Susan Jeffers TOPIC: Meditation, $18.00

Flowing With The Tao
PUBLISHING COMPANY: Hartley Film Foundation ARTIST: Alan Watts ARTIST: Iasos TOPIC: Spirituality, $89.00

Flying Carpet
PUBLISHING COMPANY: Beyond ARTIST: K. Schaffner, L. Grimm TOPIC: Meditation, $12.98

Flying Dreams

PUBLISHING COMPANY: Fonix Musik ARTIST: S. Hyldgaard TOPIC: Meditation, $10.95

For My People
PUBLISHING COMPANY: Medicine Eagle/Harmony Net. ARTIST: Brooke Medicine Eagle TOPIC: Spirituality, $10.00

For Women Only: Techniques For Greater Beauty & Greater Vitality
PUBLISHING COMPANY: Simon & Schuster Audio ARTIST: M. Gach TOPIC: Acupuncture, $9.95

For Women Only: Techniques For Pms Relief & Greater Vitality
PUBLISHING COMPANY: Simon & Schuster Audio ARTIST: M. Gach TOPIC: Acupuncture, $9.95

For Women Only: Techniques For Weight Loss & Greater Vitality
PUBLISHING COMPANY: Simon & Schuster Audio ARTIST: M. Gach TOPIC: Acupuncture, $9.95

Forgotten Song: The Poetry Of A Course In Miracles
PUBLISHING COMPANY: Miracle Distribution Center ARTIST: S. Halpern, B. Hutchinson TOPIC: Spirituality, $10.00

Four Keys To Success: Self-Esteem & Motivation, Stress Reduction, Sense Of Purpose
PUBLISHING COMPANY: Starsong Publications ARTIST: D. Thornburg TOPIC: Holistic Health, $19.95

Freedom From Belief
PUBLISHING COMPANY: Life Action Press ARTIST: T. Singh TOPIC: Spirituality, $17.95

Freedom From Desk Job Stress And Computer Strain
PUBLISHING COMPANY: Tetrahedron ARTIST: L. Horowitz TOPIC: Holistic Health, $12.95

Freedom From Drugs
PUBLISHING COMPANY: Potentials Unlimited ARTIST: Potentials Unlimited TOPIC: New Age, $9.98

Freedom From Guilt
PUBLISHING COMPANY: Potentials Unlimited ARTIST: Potentials Unlimited TOPIC: New Age, $9.98

Freedome Chants From The Roof Of The World
PUBLISHING COMPANY: Rykodisc ARTIST: Gyuto Monks TOPIC: Spirituality, $10.98

Fresh Impressions
PUBLISHING COMPANY: Gothic Image Publications ARTIST: G. Kelly TOPIC: Meditation, $18.98

From Atom To Cosmos: Evolution Of Consciousness As A New Model Of The Universe
PUBLISHING COMPANY: Macro Media ARTIST: I. Bentov TOPIC: New Age, $49.95

From Heart To Crown

PUBLISHING COMPANY: Search For Serenity ARTIST: R. Whitesides-Woo TOPIC: Meditation, $16.98

From Here To Alternity: Adventures Of A Scientist
PUBLISHING COMPANY: Thinking Allowed Prod. ARTIST: John Lilly TOPIC: New Age, $49.95

From The Edgar Cayce Readings: Natural Remedies And Cures
PUBLISHING COMPANY: Summit University Press ARTIST: Jess Stearn, W. McGarey TOPIC: Homeopathy, $29.95

From The Silence: Piano Improvisations
PUBLISHING COMPANY: David Salminen Productions ARTIST: D. Salminen TOPIC: Meditation, $10.98

Frontiers Of Psychic Research
PUBLISHING COMPANY: Thinking Allowed Prod. ARTIST: R. Targ ARTIST: et.al. TOPIC: Psychic, $69.95

Full Moon Story
PUBLISHING COMPANY: Geffen Records ARTIST: Kitaro TOPIC: Meditation, $20.98

Function Of A Teacher Is To End Deception
PUBLISHING COMPANY: Life Action Press ARTIST: T. Singh TOPIC: Spirituality, $44.95

Further Along The Road Less Traveled: Going To Omaha -- Issue Of Death & Meaning
PUBLISHING COMPANY: Simon & Schuster Audio ARTIST: M. Scott Peck TOPIC: Death, $9.95

Fusion Of The Five Elements I
PUBLISHING COMPANY: Healing Tao Books ARTIST: M. Chia TOPIC: Holistic Health, $9.95

Fusion Of The Five Elements II
PUBLISHING COMPANY: Healing Tao Books ARTIST: M. Chia TOPIC: Holistic Health, $9.95

Fusion Of The Five Elements III
PUBLISHING COMPANY: Healing Tao Books ARTIST: M. Chia TOPIC: Holistic Health, $9.95

Future Of Mankind: The Branching Of The Road
PUBLISHING COMPANY: Life Action Press ARTIST: T. Singh ARTIST: Read by Charles Johnson TOPIC: Spirituality, $17.95

Galaxies
PUBLISHING COMPANY: Hearts of Space ARTIST: K. Braheny TOPIC: Meditation, $18.95

Gateway To The Astral World: Astral Projection Kit
PUBLISHING COMPANY: Llewellyn Worldwide, Ltd. ARTIST: M. Denning, O. Phillips TOPIC: Astral Projection, $19.95

Gensis: High-Tech Meditation
PUBLISHING COMPANY: MSH Association ARTIST: Brother Charles TOPIC: Meditation, $50.00

Genesis II: High-Tech Meditation
PUBLISHING COMPANY: MSH Association
ARTIST: Brother Charles TOPIC: Meditation,
$50.00

Gentle Healing: Flowing Music To Harmonize The Body, Mind & Spirit
PUBLISHING COMPANY: Sunray ARTIST: Paul
Temple, M.J. Walden TOPIC: Meditation, $11.00

Gentleness Within: Finding The Willingness To Accept Ourselves
PUBLISHING COMPANY: Riverrun Press ARTIST:
Stephen Schwartz TOPIC: Meditation, $16.00

Gerson Therapy: Regeneration For The Body's Immune System
PUBLISHING COMPANY: Summit University Press
ARTIST: C. Gerson TOPIC: Holistic Healing,
$12.95

Get More Joy Out Of Sex
PUBLISHING COMPANY: Potentials Unlimited
ARTIST: Potentials Unlimited TOPIC: New Age,
$9.98

Get More Joy Out Of Sex: Male
PUBLISHING COMPANY: Potentials Unlimited
ARTIST: Potentials Unlimited TOPIC: New Age,
$9.98

Getting By On Four Hours' Sleep
PUBLISHING COMPANY: Valley of the Sun
ARTIST: D. Sutphen TOPIC: Hypnotism, $18.98

Getting Into, Not Out Of
PUBLISHING COMPANY: Reflections ARTIST: Star
Sounds TOPIC: Hypnotism, $14.95

Getting Money Right: The Psychology Of Wealth
PUBLISHING COMPANY: ARC A-V Enterprises
ARTIST: Fredric Lehrman TOPIC: Body-Mind
Connection, $49.95

Gift Of Song
PUBLISHING COMPANY: Medicine Eagle/Harmony
Net. ARTIST: Brooke Medicine Eagle TOPIC:
Spirituality, $10.00

Gifts Of The Golden Sun/The Perfect Self
PUBLISHING COMPANY: Golden Rose Productions
ARTIST: A. Lowrie TOPIC: Hypnotism, $10.98

Gifts To Each Other: Native American Chants And Drum
PUBLISHING COMPANY: Milum, Lyn ARTIST: L.
Milum TOPIC: Spirituality, $10.50

Give Me Your Blessings, Holy Son Of God
PUBLISHING COMPANY: Life Action Press
ARTIST: T. Singh TOPIC: Spirituality, $39.95

Giving Permission
PUBLISHING COMPANY: Reflections ARTIST: Star
Sounds TOPIC: Hypnotism, $14.95

Global Brain
PUBLISHING COMPANY: Penny Price Productions
ARTIST: Peter Russell TOPIC: New Age, $49.95

Goal Achievement
PUBLISHING COMPANY: Valley of the Sun
ARTIST: D. Sutphen TOPIC: Hypnotism, $18.98

Goal Setting
PUBLISHING COMPANY: Potentials Unlimited
ARTIST: Potentials Unlimited TOPIC: New Age,
$9.98

God And Money
PUBLISHING COMPANY: Channel Light
Productions ARTIST: Marianne Williamson TOPIC:
Spirituality, $10.95

God Does Not Judge/Healing Relationships
PUBLISHING COMPANY: Life Action Press
ARTIST: T. Singh TOPIC: Spirituality, $29.95

Goddess In My Shoes: Seven Steps To Peace
PUBLISHING COMPANY: Humanics Limited
ARTIST: Rickie Moore TOPIC: Spirituality, $14.95

Going With The Flow
PUBLISHING COMPANY: Hartley Film Foundation
ARTIST: Alan Watts TOPIC: Spirituality, $89.00

Going Within: A Guide For Inner Transformation
PUBLISHING COMPANY: Bantam Audio ARTIST:
S. MacLaine TOPIC: Meditation, $14.95

Golden Dawn Tapes Series 1
PUBLISHING COMPANY: New Falcon Publications
ARTIST: I. Regardie TOPIC: Occult, $49.95

Golden Dawn Tapes Series 2
PUBLISHING COMPANY: New Falcon Publications
ARTIST: I. Regardie TOPIC: Occult, $39.95

Golden Dawn Tapes Series 3
PUBLISHING COMPANY: New Falcon Publications
ARTIST: I. Regardie TOPIC: Occult, $19.95

Golden Triad
PUBLISHING COMPANY: Arizona Metaphysical
Society ARTIST: F. Alper TOPIC: Spirituality,
$10.00

Golden Voyage 1
PUBLISHING COMPANY: Moss Music Group, Inc.
ARTIST: R. Dexter, R. Bearns TOPIC: Meditation,
$18.98

Good Health Through Color Therapy
PUBLISHING COMPANY: Inner Light Publications
ARTIST: B. Steiger TOPIC: Color Therapy, $8.95

Good Health: A Strong Immune System
PUBLISHING COMPANY: Valley of the Sun
ARTIST: D. Sutphen TOPIC: Holistic Healing,
$19.95

Good Night's Sleep
PUBLISHING COMPANY: Yes Technologies!
ARTIST: Yes Technologies! TOPIC: Hypnotism,
Dreams, $19.95

Grandmother Of Time
PUBLISHING COMPANY: Harper & Row Audio
ARTIST: Z. Budapest TOPIC: Witchcraft, $9.95

Greater Energy At Your Fingertips
PUBLISHING COMPANY: Enchanced Audio
Systems ARTIST: M. Gach TOPIC: Acupuncture,
$9.98

Greek Mysteries: Experiencing Your Male And Female Archetypes
PUBLISHING COMPANY: T. A. Helliwell
Publications ARTIST: T. Helliwell TOPIC:
Psychology, $9.95

Guide To Rational Living
PUBLISHING COMPANY: Thinking Allowed Prod.
ARTIST: Albert Ellis TOPIC: Psychology, $49.95

Guide To Walking Meditation
PUBLISHING COMPANY: Parallax Press ARTIST: T.
Hanh TOPIC: Spirituality, $35.00

Guided Imagery And Beyond
PUBLISHING COMPANY: David Collyer ARTIST:
D. Collyer TOPIC: Meditation, $10.95

Guided Imagery And Meditation
PUBLISHING COMPANY: Hay House ARTIST:
Bernie Siegel ARTIST: Music by Daniel Kobialka
TOPIC: Meditation, $10.00

Guided Meditations: Basic Techniques
PUBLISHING COMPANY: Integral Yoga
Publications ARTIST: Satchidananda TOPIC:
Spirituality, $10.95

Gyuto Monks
PUBLISHING COMPANY: Windham Hill Records
ARTIST: Gyuto Tantric Choir TOPIC: Spirituality,
$18.50

Haleakala
PUBLISHING COMPANY: Celestial Harmonies
ARTIST: Deuter TOPIC: Meditation, $10.98

Half Moon Bay
PUBLISHING COMPANY: Higher Octave Music
ARTIST: W. Aura TOPIC: Meditation, $16.98

Handbook To Higher Consciousness
PUBLISHING COMPANY: Audio Renaissance Tapes
ARTIST: Ken Keyes TOPIC: Psychology, $9.95

Hands
PUBLISHING COMPANY: Fonix Musik ARTIST: F.
Lorentzen TOPIC: Meditation, $10.95

Handwriting Analysis Professional Training Program
PUBLISHING COMPANY: Panorama Publishing Co.
ARTIST: J. Kappas TOPIC: Palmistry, $350.00

Happiness: Enhance The Joy Of Living
PUBLISHING COMPANY: BFS Limited ARTIST:
Bright Images TOPIC: Hypnotism, $11.95

Hara Hara
PUBLISHING COMPANY: Spring Hill Music
ARTIST: On Wings of Song TOPIC: Spirituality,
$10.00

Harmoney, Color And Music
PUBLISHING COMPANY: New Age
Study/Human.Purpose ARTIST: P. Cota-Robles
TOPIC: Color Therapy, $9.00

Harmonic Meetings
PUBLISHING COMPANY: Celestial Harmonies ARTIST: Harmonic Choir TOPIC: Meditation, $18.95

Hatha Yoga In Motion Vol. 1
PUBLISHING COMPANY: Rudra Press ARTIST: Nityananda Inst. Teaching Staff TOPIC: Yoga, $9.95

Hatha Yoga In Motion Vol. 2
PUBLISHING COMPANY: Rudra Press ARTIST: Nityananda Inst. Teaching Staff TOPIC: Yoga, $9.95

Hatha Yoga In Motion: Levels One And Two
PUBLISHING COMPANY: Rudra Press ARTIST: Nityananda Inst. Teaching Staff TOPIC: Yoga, $19.95

Hatha Yoga With Don Discenza
PUBLISHING COMPANY: Discenza, Don ARTIST: D. Discenza TOPIC: Yoga, $10.00

Hatha Yoga: The Hidden Language Of The Body--Your Personal Tool For Expanded Awareness
PUBLISHING COMPANY: Timeless Books ARTIST: S. Radha TOPIC: Yoga, $29.95

He: Understanding Masculine Psychology
PUBLISHING COMPANY: Audio Renaissance Tapes ARTIST: Robert A. Johnson TOPIC: Psychology, $9.95

Head First: The Biology Of Hope
PUBLISHING COMPANY: Nightingale Conant Corp. ARTIST: N. Cousins TOPIC: Body-Mind Connection, $14.95

Heal Thyself: Using Your Inner Power To Heal
PUBLISHING COMPANY: Steppingstones ARTIST: R. Jafolla, M. Jafolla TOPIC: Hypnotism, $12.95

Heal Your Body
PUBLISHING COMPANY: Hay House ARTIST: Louise Hay TOPIC: Meditation, $14.95

Heal Yourself
PUBLISHING COMPANY: Centerpoint Distribution, Inc. ARTIST: E. Baron TOPIC: Holistic Healing, $9.98

Healer Within: Healing Chronic Illness
PUBLISHING COMPANY: Light of Mind ARTIST: S. Bratman TOPIC: Meditation, $14.95

Healing
PUBLISHING COMPANY: Chidvilas ARTIST: Spiritual Environments TOPIC: Meditation, $11.95

Healing Acceleration
PUBLISHING COMPANY: Valley of the Sun ARTIST: D. Sutphen TOPIC: Hypnotism, $18.98

Healing And Pain Control
PUBLISHING COMPANY: Valley of the Sun ARTIST: D. Stuphen TOPIC: Hypnotism, $9.98

Healing And The Unconscious
PUBLISHING COMPANY: Thinking Allowed Prod. ARTIST: W. Brugh Joy TOPIC: Holistic Healing, $49.95

Healing And Theraputic Use Of Crystals
PUBLISHING COMPANY: Mayflowr B/S ARTIST: Robert Thibodeau TOPIC: Crystals, $49.95

Healing Brain Vol. 1: Health And Healing East West
PUBLISHING COMPANY: I.S.H.K. ARTIST: NSA TOPIC: Holistic Healing, $49.95

Healing Brain Vol. 2: Stress Management
PUBLISHING COMPANY: I.S.H.K. ARTIST: NSA TOPIC: Psychology, Holistic Health, $49.95

Healing Brain Vol. 3: How To Stay Healthy
PUBLISHING COMPANY: I.S.H.K. ARTIST: NSA TOPIC: Holistic Healing, $49.95

Healing Brain Vol. 4: Complete Healing Brain 1984 Workshop
PUBLISHING COMPANY: I.S.H.K. ARTIST: NSA TOPIC: Holistic Healing, $49.95

Healing Brain Vol. 5: Healing Brain Update 1984
PUBLISHING COMPANY: I.S.H.K. ARTIST: NSA TOPIC: Metaphysics, $29.95

Healing Force: Using Your Mind To Help Heal
PUBLISHING COMPANY: Valley of the Sun ARTIST: D. Stuphen TOPIC: Hypnotism, $9.95

Healing Hands
PUBLISHING COMPANY: Arizona Metaphysical Society ARTIST: F. Alper TOPIC: Psychic Healing, $10.00

Healing Heart: Antidotes To Panic & Helplessness
PUBLISHING COMPANY: Dove Books On Tape, Inc. ARTIST: N. Cousins ARTIST: Read by William Conrad TOPIC: Holistic Healing, Body-Mind Connection, $14.95

Healing Into Life And Death
PUBLISHING COMPANY: Sounds True Record. & Dupl. ARTIST: S. Levine TOPIC: Death, $9.95

Healing Journey
PUBLISHING COMPANY: Source Cassettes ARTIST: E. Miller TOPIC: Holistic Healing, $9.95

Healing Light
PUBLISHING COMPANY: Mountain Spirit Tapes, Inc. ARTIST: D. Keck TOPIC: Holistic Healing, $9.95

Healing Love Through The Tao
PUBLISHING COMPANY: Healing Tao Books ARTIST: M. Chia TOPIC: Holistic Health, $9.95

Healing Meditation
PUBLISHING COMPANY: Brotherhood Press ARTIST: W. Garcia, G. Melton TOPIC: Meditation, $10.00

Healing Meditations
PUBLISHING COMPANY: Hay House ARTIST: Bernie Siegel ARTIST: Music by Daniel Kobialka TOPIC: Meditation, $10.00

Healing Miracles: Using Your Body Energies--An Audio Adaption
PUBLISHING COMPANY: Harper & Row Publishers ARTIST: W. McGarey TOPIC: Channeling, $9.95

Healing Power Of Herbs: The European Tradition For Natural Health
PUBLISHING COMPANY: Summit University Press ARTIST: P. Theiss TOPIC: Herbalogy, $29.95

Healing Power Of The Breath
PUBLISHING COMPANY: Body Therapy Training Inst. ARTIST: M. Alpern TOPIC: Meditation, $12.50

Healing Spaces Vol. 1
PUBLISHING COMPANY: Yansa Music ARTIST: R. George TOPIC: Meditation, $10.98

Healing The Mother-Daughter Relationship
PUBLISHING COMPANY: Yes! Technologies ARTIST: Yes! Technologies TOPIC: Hypnotism, $11.95

Healing Through God's Pharmacy: Plants For Every Illness
PUBLISHING COMPANY: Summit University Press ARTIST: M. Treben TOPIC: Herbalogy, $29.95

Healing Through Ritual Action
PUBLISHING COMPANY: Medicine Eagle/Harmony N/W ARTIST: Brooke Medicine Eagle TOPIC: Psychic Healing, $10.00

Healing Waterfall
PUBLISHING COMPANY: ID ARTIST: M. Highstein TOPIC: Crystals, $9.98

Healing With Body Energy
PUBLISHING COMPANY: Audio Renaissance Tapes ARTIST: W. Brugh Joy TOPIC: Meditation, $15.95

Healing With Yoga, Visualization And Affirmation
PUBLISHING COMPANY: Shakti Press ARTIST: Satchidananda TOPIC: Body-Mind Connection, $24.95

Healing Your Perception Of The World
PUBLISHING COMPANY: Life Action Press ARTIST: T. Singh TOPIC: Spirituality, $17.95

Healing Yourself With Crystals
PUBLISHING COMPANY: New Visions ARTIST: J. Sotkin TOPIC: Holistic Healing, $9.98

Healing Yourself With Mental Imagery
PUBLISHING COMPANY: Thinking Allowed Prod. ARTIST: M. Rossman TOPIC: Holistic Healing, $49.95

Healing: Drawing On God's Strength
PUBLISHING COMPANY: Luramedia ARTIST: L.J. Geiger, A.M. Geiger TOPIC: Psychic Healing, $34.50

Health
PUBLISHING COMPANY: Effective Learnings Systems, Inc. ARTIST: Love Tapes TOPIC: Hypnotism, $11.98

Health And Wellness
PUBLISHING COMPANY: Source Cassettes ARTIST: E. Miller TOPIC: Holistic Healing, $9.95

Health Imagining: Maximize Your Immunity Against Disease
PUBLISHING COMPANY: OM Corporation ARTIST: O.M. Corporation TOPIC: Holistic Healing, $39.95

Health Through God's Pharmacy: A Plant For Every Illness
PUBLISHING COMPANY: Mountain Spirit Tapes, Inc. ARTIST: M. Treben ARTIST: Interviewed by Eliz Prophet TOPIC: Herbalogy, $7.95

Health, Healing And Aids
PUBLISHING COMPANY: Access Group ARTIST: A.S. Bhikkhu, A.A. Bhikkhu ARTIST: et.al. TOPIC: Psychic Healing, $18.00

Health, Healing And Aids (Practicing The Heart Of Healing Part 1)
PUBLISHING COMPANY: Access Group ARTIST: A.S. Bhikku, A.A. Bhikku TOPIC: Death, $18.00

Health, Yoga, Anatomy
PUBLISHING COMPANY: Shakti Press ARTIST: Amrita Sandra McLanahan TOPIC: Yoga, $29.95

Healthy Gums
PUBLISHING COMPANY: Valley of the Sun ARTIST: D. Stuphen TOPIC: Hypnotism, $12.50

Healthy Mind, Healthy Body: Positive Health With Positive Thinking
PUBLISHING COMPANY: BFS Limited ARTIST: Bright Images TOPIC: Hypnotism, $11.95

Heart Of Understanding: Commentaries On The Prajnaparamita Heart Sutra
PUBLISHING COMPANY: Parallax Press ARTIST: T. Hanh TOPIC: Spirituality, $15.00

Heartsounds
PUBLISHING COMPANY: Music Designs ARTIST: D. Lanz TOPIC: Meditation, $16.00

Heavensong Celebration Live!
PUBLISHING COMPANY: Heavensong Recordings ARTIST: M. Stillwater, M. Stillwater TOPIC: Spirituality, $10.00

Help Yourself Heal: 8 Steps To Health & Wholeness--Based On A Clinical Study
PUBLISHING COMPANY: Compcare Publications ARTIST: B. Little TOPIC: Holistic Healing, $9.95

Henry Reed's Dream Interpretation Workout: Make Your Dreams Work For You
PUBLISHING COMPANY: Video Home Companion ARTIST: Henry Reed TOPIC: Dreams, $49.95

Herb Magic
PUBLISHING COMPANY: Llewellyn Worldwide, Ltd. ARTIST: S. Cunningham TOPIC: Herbalogy, $19.95

Herbal Preparations And Natural Therapies
PUBLISHING COMPANY: Morningstar Publications ARTIST: Debra Nuzzi TOPIC: Herbalogy, $95.00

Herbs, Nutrition And Healing
PUBLISHING COMPANY: Hohm Press ARTIST: H. Santillo TOPIC: Holistic Healing, Nutrition, $40.00

Hergest Ridge
PUBLISHING COMPANY: JEM ARTIST: M. Oldfield TOPIC: Meditation, $10.98

Hero, The Wildman, And The Goddess: The Story Of Gilcamesh, Enkidu And Ishtar
PUBLISHING COMPANY: Four Trees Publications ARTIST: R. Metzner TOPIC: Spirituality, $10.50

Hidden Persuaders: Improve Performance & Increase Speed & Productivity
PUBLISHING COMPANY: Valley of the Sun ARTIST: D. Sutphen TOPIC: Hypnotism, $18.98

High And The Low
PUBLISHING COMPANY: Thinking Allowed Prod. ARTIST: Colin Wilson TOPIC: Psychology, $49.95

High Energy And Enthusiasm
PUBLISHING COMPANY: Valley of the Sun ARTIST: D. Sutphen TOPIC: Hypnotism, $18.98

High Performance
PUBLISHING COMPANY: Valley of the Sun ARTIST: D. Sutphen TOPIC: Hypnotism, $18.98

High Plateaux
PUBLISHING COMPANY: Windham Hill Records ARTIST: B. Rubaja, C. Hernandez TOPIC: Meditation, $11.98

Higher Self: Breakthrough To Illumination
PUBLISHING COMPANY: Light of Mind ARTIST: D. Gordon, S. Gordon TOPIC: Meditation, Hypnotism, Spirituality, $24.95

Higher-Self Wisdom And Guidance
PUBLISHING COMPANY: Light of Mind ARTIST: S. Gordon, D. Gordon TOPIC: Psychic, Meditation, $14.95

History Of My Heart
PUBLISHING COMPANY: Private Music ARTIST: S. Ciani TOPIC: Meditation, $11.98

Homage To Sol
PUBLISHING COMPANY: Acoustic Brain Research ARTIST: Acoustic Brain Research TOPIC: Meditation, $14.95

Homeopathy: Nontoxic Approach To Illness
PUBLISHING COMPANY: Summit University Press ARTIST: B. Gray TOPIC: Homeopathy, $29.95

Hope And A Prayer

PUBLISHING COMPANY: Hay House ARTIST: Bernie Siegel TOPIC: Body-Mind Connection, $24.95

Horizons: Improvisations For Harp And Flute
PUBLISHING COMPANY: Sri Rama Publishing ARTIST: H. Shakti ARTIST: Ambika TOPIC: Meditation, $12.95

House Of Sleeping Beauties
PUBLISHING COMPANY: Private Music ARTIST: L. Hwong TOPIC: Meditation, $11.98

How Miracles Happen
PUBLISHING COMPANY: Channel Light Productions ARTIST: Marianne Williamson TOPIC: Spirituality, $10.95

How Shall I Live? Transforming Surgery Or Health Crisis Into Greater Aliveness
PUBLISHING COMPANY: Three Mountain Fndt. ARTIST: Richard Moss TOPIC: Body-Mind Connection, $24.95

How Then Shall We Live #1: Opening To Grief/Purification By Fire
PUBLISHING COMPANY: Original Face Video ARTIST: S. Levine TOPIC: Spirituality, $49.95

How Then Shall We Live #2: From Tragedy To Grace-Stage In Process Of Dying/Meditation
PUBLISHING COMPANY: Original Face Video ARTIST: S. Levine TOPIC: Death, $49.95

How Then Shall We Live #3: Awakening Through Truthful Relationship/Work To Relieve Suffer
PUBLISHING COMPANY: Original Face Video ARTIST: Ram Dass TOPIC: Spirituality, $49.95

How Then Shall We Live #4: Finding A Path To An Open Heart/Wisdom Has No Fear Of Dying
PUBLISHING COMPANY: Original Face Video ARTIST: Ram Dass TOPIC: Death, Spirituality, $49.95

How Then Shall We Live #5: Caring For An Endangered Planet
PUBLISHING COMPANY: Original Face Video ARTIST: Helen Caldicott TOPIC: Spirituality, $49.95

How Then Shall We Live #6: America's Secret Nuclear Policy
PUBLISHING COMPANY: Original Face Video ARTIST: D. Ellsberg TOPIC: Spirituality, $49.95

How Then Shall We Live #7: Dialogue For Human Survival
PUBLISHING COMPANY: Parallax Press ARTIST: D. Ellsberg ARTIST: Ram Dass TOPIC: Spirituality, $49.95

How Then Shall We Live #8: No Other Generation

PUBLISHING COMPANY: Original Face Video ARTIST: D. Ellsberg ARTIST: Ram Dass, et.al. TOPIC: Spirituality, $49.95

How Then Shall We Live #9: Social Action & The Compassionate Heart
PUBLISHING COMPANY: Parallax Press ARTIST: Ram Dass TOPIC: Spirituality, $49.95

How To Attract Love
PUBLISHING COMPANY: Potentials Unlimited ARTIST: Potentials Unlimited TOPIC: New Age, $9.98

How To Attract Money
PUBLISHING COMPANY: Effective Learnings Systems, Inc. ARTIST: Love Tapes TOPIC: Hypnotism, $11.98

How To Be A Channel
PUBLISHING COMPANY: Crystal Clarity ARTIST: Donald Walters ARTIST: (Kriyananda) TOPIC: Channeling, $9.95

How To Be A True Student Of A Course In Miracles
PUBLISHING COMPANY: Life Action Press ARTIST: T. Singh TOPIC: Spirituality, $17.95

How To Be Positive
PUBLISHING COMPANY: Effective Learnings Systems, Inc. ARTIST: Love Tapes TOPIC: Hypnotism, $11.98

How To Be Your Own Nutritionist
PUBLISHING COMPANY: Dove Books on Tape, Inc. ARTIST: S. Berger ARTIST: Read by Betsy Palmer TOPIC: Nutrition, $14.95

How To Conduct A Dream Workshop: A Practical Introduction
PUBLISHING COMPANY: Thinking Allowed Prod. ARTIST: Jeremy Taylor TOPIC: Dreams, $49.95

How To Develop Your ESP Power
PUBLISHING COMPANY: Simon & Schuster ARTIST: Jane Roberts TOPIC: ESP, $8.95

How To Discover Your Past Lives
PUBLISHING COMPANY: A.R.E. Press ARTIST: L. Sparrow TOPIC: Past Life Regression, $59.95

How To Get Results Through Self-Hypnosis
PUBLISHING COMPANY: A. R. E. Press ARTIST: Henry Bolduc TOPIC: Hypnotism, $29.95

How To Learn From A Course In Miracles
PUBLISHING COMPANY: Life Action Press ARTIST: T. Singh ARTIST: Read by Charles Johnson TOPIC: Spirituality, $17.95

How To Pray And Meditate
PUBLISHING COMPANY: Richard Gordon Creat Prod. ARTIST: Richard Gordon TOPIC: Meditation, $29.95

How To Raise A Child Of God
PUBLISHING COMPANY: Life Action Press ARTIST: T. Singh ARTIST: Read by Charles Johnson TOPIC: Spirituality, $17.95

How To Rapidly Develop Psychic Ability
PUBLISHING COMPANY: Valley of the Sun ARTIST: D. Sutphen TOPIC: Hypnotism, $18.98

How To Read The Tarot Cards
PUBLISHING COMPANY: Richard Gordon Creat Prod ARTIST: Richard Gordon TOPIC: Tarot, $39.95

How To Use The Science Of Mind
PUBLISHING COMPANY: Science of Minds Publications ARTIST: E. Holmes TOPIC: Spirituality, $12.95

How To Use Your Psychic Talents
PUBLISHING COMPANY: Audio Renaissance Tapes ARTIST: C. Tart TOPIC: Psychic, $9.95

Human Computer
PUBLISHING COMPANY: Wishing Well Distributing ARTIST: N. Tauraso TOPIC: New Age, $89.00

Human Dilemma: Explorations Existential Psychotherapy
PUBLISHING COMPANY: Thinking Allowed Prod. ARTIST: Rollo May TOPIC: Psychology, $49.95

Human Journey
PUBLISHING COMPANY: Macro Media ARTIST: Mirtala TOPIC: New Age, $39.95

Humor Allies: 4 Humor Visualizations
PUBLISHING COMPANY: C. W. Metcalf & Co. ARTIST: C.W. Metcalf TOPIC: Meditation, $9.95

Humor, Risk And Change: Survival Skills For People Over 5 & Under Pressure
PUBLISHING COMPANY: C. W. Metcalf & Co. ARTIST: C. W. Metcalf TOPIC: Holistic Health, $49.95

Hypertension: The Mind/Body Connection
PUBLISHING COMPANY: Hartley Film Foundation ARTIST: Pat Norris, S. Fahrion TOPIC: Body-Mind Connection, $89.00

Hypno-Psychic Healing: A Powerful Aid To Any Given Health Problem
PUBLISHING COMPANY: Wonder-Full Day Prod. ARTIST: L. Sereda TOPIC: Meditation, $12.95

Hypnosis For Diabetes Self-Healing
PUBLISHING COMPANY: Translulions ARTIST: Transolutions TOPIC: Meditation, $10.95

Hypnosis For Improved Learning
PUBLISHING COMPANY: New Harbinger Publications ARTIST: J. Hadley, C. Staudcher TOPIC: Hypnotism, $10.95

Hypnosis For Motivating Change And Problem Solving
PUBLISHING COMPANY: New Harbinger Publications ARTIST: J. Hadley, C. Staudcher TOPIC: Hypnotism, $10.95

Hypnosis For Non-Smoking

PUBLISHING COMPANY: New Harbinger Publications ARTIST: J. Hadley, C. Staudacher TOPIC: Hypnotism, $10.95

Hypnosis For Self-Esteem
PUBLISHING COMPANY: New Harbinger Publications ARTIST: J. Hadley, C. Staudcher TOPIC: Hypnotism, $10.95

Hypnosis For Sleep
PUBLISHING COMPANY: New Harbinger Publications TOPIC: Hypnotism, $10.95

Hypnosis For Weight Control
PUBLISHING COMPANY: New Harbinger Publications ARTIST: J. Hadley, C. Staudcher TOPIC: Hypnotism, $10.95

Hypnosis To End Anxiety And Panic
PUBLISHING COMPANY: New Harbinger Publications ARTIST: M. McKay, P. Fanning TOPIC: Hypnotism, $10.95

Hypnotherapy And Regression
PUBLISHING COMPANY: Thoth Publications ARTIST: M. Hope TOPIC: Past Life Regression, $9.95

I Am A Monk
PUBLISHING COMPANY: Hartley Film Foundation ARTIST: T. Myrdahl TOPIC: Spirituality, $89.00

I Am Spirit
PUBLISHING COMPANY: Life Action Press ARTIST: T. Singh TOPIC: Spirituality, $17.95

I Can Do Anything
PUBLISHING COMPANY: White Dove Int'l., Inc. ARTIST: S. Wilde TOPIC: Hypnotism, $11.95

I Ching Video Workshop
PUBLISHING COMPANY: KGI Publications ARTIST: K. Lew TOPIC: Parapsychology, $39.95

I Dance To Be The Woman I Can Be
PUBLISHING COMPANY: Llewellyn Worldwide, Ltd. ARTIST: Antiga TOPIC: Witchcraft, $9.95

I Feel Great
PUBLISHING COMPANY: White Dove Int'l., Inc. ARTIST: S. Wilde TOPIC: Hypnotism, $11.95

I Forgive: Releasing Old Hurts Forever
PUBLISHING COMPANY: Steppingstones ARTIST: R. Jafolla TOPIC: Hypnotism, $12.95

I Have A Function God Would Have Me Fill
PUBLISHING COMPANY: Life Action Press ARTIST: T. Singh TOPIC: Spirituality, $29.95

I Love My Body: Female
PUBLISHING COMPANY: Potentials Unlimited ARTIST: Potentials Unlimited TOPIC: New Age, $9.98

I Love My Body: Male
PUBLISHING COMPANY: Potentials Unlimited ARTIST: Potentials Unlimited TOPIC: New Age, $9.98

Idea Tape: Develop Your Creativity
PUBLISHING COMPANY: BFS Limited ARTIST: Bright Images TOPIC: Hypnotism, $11.95

If I Defend Myself I Am Attacked
PUBLISHING COMPANY: Life Action Press ARTIST: T. Singh TOPIC: Spirituality, $34.95

Imagination's Door: Affirmations Of Health, Light And Love
PUBLISHING COMPANY: Eastern - Gate Publishing, Inc. ARTIST: Alex Jones, D. Cutler TOPIC: Meditation, $9.98

Imagineering: How To Profit From Your Creative Powers
PUBLISHING COMPANY: Simon & Schuster ARTIST: M. LeBoeuf TOPIC: Meditation, $8.95

Imaging
PUBLISHING COMPANY: Potentials Unlimited ARTIST: Potentials Unlimited TOPIC: New Age, $9.98

Improve Your Concentration
PUBLISHING COMPANY: Effective Learnings Systems, Inc. ARTIST: Love Tapes TOPIC: Hypnotism, $11.98

Improve Your Self-Image
PUBLISHING COMPANY: Effective Learnings Systems, Inc. ARTIST: Love Tapes TOPIC: Hypnotism, $11.98

Improving Relationships
PUBLISHING COMPANY: Effective Learnings Systems, Inc. ARTIST: Love Tapes TOPIC: Hypnotism, $11.98

In The Cosmic Flow
PUBLISHING COMPANY: Heart Music ARTIST: Akasha TOPIC: Spirituality, $10.00

In The Heart Of Relationship
PUBLISHING COMPANY: Access Group ARTIST: S. Levine, O. Levine TOPIC: Meditation, $18.00

Incantations: Raga Amrit Yarshni And Raga Jai Jai Vanti
PUBLISHING COMPANY: Chandi Productions ARTIST: G. S. Sachdev ARTIST: Popatkar TOPIC: Meditation, $13.00

Incarus
PUBLISHING COMPANY: Living Music Records, Inc. ARTIST: Paul Winter TOPIC: Meditation, $18.98

Incredible Self-Confidence
PUBLISHING COMPANY: Valley of the Sun ARTIST: D. Sutphen TOPIC: Hypnotism, $10.98

Indigo
PUBLISHING COMPANY: Crystal Cave Enterprises ARTIST: Ray Mitchell TOPIC: Meditation, $10.95

Initiation
PUBLISHING COMPANY: Search For Serenity ARTIST: Catherine Andrews TOPIC: Meditation, $16.98

Initiation Of Fire
PUBLISHING COMPANY: Arizona Metaphysical Society ARTIST: F. Alper TOPIC: Channeling, $10.00

Inner Blance/Outer Expression I

PUBLISHING COMPANY: Channel Light Productions ARTIST: K. Reynolds, L. Lief TOPIC: Spirituality, $10.95

Inner Blance/Outer Expression II
PUBLISHING COMPANY: Channel Light Productions ARTIST: Channel Light Productions TOPIC: Spirituality, $10.95

Inner Dance V.1: Inner Dance Talk
PUBLISHING COMPANY: Aquila Tapes ARTIST: D. Mariechild, S. Goodman TOPIC: Spirituality, $10.95

Inner Dance V.2: Healing The Hurt Child
PUBLISHING COMPANY: Aquila Tapes ARTIST: D. Mariechild, S. Goodman TOPIC: Spirituality, $10.95

Inner Dance V.3: Lovers And Warriors Talk
PUBLISHING COMPANY: Aquila Tapes ARTIST: D. Mariechild, S. Goodman TOPIC: Spirituality, $10.95

Inner Dance V.4: Body Movement Exercises
PUBLISHING COMPANY: Aquila Tapes ARTIST: D. Mariechild, S. Goodman ARTIST: Created by Bonnie Novakov-Lawlor TOPIC: Spirituality, $10.95

Inner Energy Workout
PUBLISHING COMPANY: Audio Renaissance Tapes ARTIST: George Leonard TOPIC: Holistic Health, $9.95

Inner Harvest
PUBLISHING COMPANY: Fonix Musik ARTIST: Pushkar TOPIC: Meditation, $10.98

Inner Palace I & II
PUBLISHING COMPANY: Medicine Song Productions ARTIST: Rashani TOPIC: Spirituality, $18.00

Inner Peace: Finding Security Within
PUBLISHING COMPANY: Luramedia ARTIST: L.J. Geiger, A.M. Geiger TOPIC: Meditation, $34.50

Inner Rhythms
PUBLISHING COMPANY: Music West Records ARTIST: S. Mazer, D. Smith TOPIC: Meditation, $17.50

Inner Smile
PUBLISHING COMPANY: Healing Tao Books ARTIST: M. Chia TOPIC: Holistic Health, $9.95

Inner Spaces
PUBLISHING COMPANY: Wishing Well Distributing ARTIST: C. Mitchell TOPIC: Psychic, $89.00

Inner Visions: Visualizing Superhealth
PUBLISHING COMPANY: Hartley Film Foundation ARTIST: Bernie Siegel TOPIC: Holistic Healing, $39.95

Inside The Crystal Cave: Creativity
PUBLISHING COMPANY: White Dove Int'l., Inc. ARTIST: S. Wilde TOPIC: Hypnotism, $11.95

Insight Meditation I: The Form Of Systematic Scanning
PUBLISHING COMPANY: Wonder-Full Day Prod. ARTIST: L. Sereda TOPIC: Holistic Healing, $12.95

Insight Meditation: Method Of More Spontaneous Witnessing
PUBLISHING COMPANY: Wonder-Full Day Prod. ARTIST: L. Sereda TOPIC: Holistic Healing, $12.95

Integral Yoga Hatha: Beginners 1
PUBLISHING COMPANY: Integral Yoga Publications ARTIST: Satchidananda TOPIC: Yoga, $10.95

Integral Yoga Hatha: Beginners II
PUBLISHING COMPANY: Integral Yoga Publications ARTIST: Integral Yoga Institute TOPIC: Yoga, $8.95

Integral Yoga: Youga Sutras Of Patanjali
PUBLISHING COMPANY: Integral Yoga Publications ARTIST: Satchidananda TOPIC: Spirituality, $9.95

Intensify Creative Ability
PUBLISHING COMPANY: Valley of the Sun ARTIST: D. Sutphen TOPIC: Hypnotism, $10.98

Interrupted Journey
PUBLISHING COMPANY: Cacdmon ARTIST: John G. Fuller ARTIST: Read by Whitney Steiber TOPIC: Paranormal Phenomena, $15.95

Intervals In Sunlight
PUBLISHING COMPANY: Gold Castle Records ARTIST: John Weider TOPIC: Meditation, $10.98

Introduction To A Course In Miracles
PUBLISHING COMPANY: Miracle Distribution Center ARTIST: Robert Perry ARTIST: Read by Beverly Hutchinson TOPIC: Spirituality, $14.95

Introduction To Acupuncture
PUBLISHING COMPANY: Hartley Film Foundation ARTIST: Hartley Film Foundation TOPIC: Acupuncture, $89.00

Introduction To Love-Centered Meditation
PUBLISHING COMPANY: Kit Wall Productions ARTIST: Louise Woods TOPIC: Meditation, $11.00

Introduction To The Change Process
PUBLISHING COMPANY: Reflections ARTIST: Star Sounds TOPIC: Hypnotism, $14.95

Introduction To Universal Principles
PUBLISHING COMPANY: Riverun Press ARTIST: Arnold Patent TOPIC: Metaphysics, $16.00

Introduction To Witchcraft
PUBLISHING COMPANY: Magickal Childe Inc ARTIST: H. Slater TOPIC: Witchcraft, $29.95

Invisible Partners: How The Male & Female In Each Of Us Affects Our Relationships
PUBLISHING COMPANY: Paulist Press ARTIST: John A. Sanford TOPIC: Psychology, $11.95

Inward Harmony: Music Of The Shpheres
PUBLISHING COMPANY: Kioma Inc. ARTIST: M. Hamm TOPIC: Meditation, $14.98

Iron Shirt Chi Kung
PUBLISHING COMPANY: Healing Tao Books ARTIST: M. Chia TOPIC: Holistic Health, $9.95

Is There Something Beyond Thought?
PUBLISHING COMPANY: Harper & Row Publishers ARTIST: J. Krishnamurti TOPIC: Spirituality, $9.95

Island
PUBLISHING COMPANY: Narada Productions ARTIST: D. Arkenstone, A. White TOPIC: Meditation, $16.98

It Means So Much To Know That Someone Cares
PUBLISHING COMPANY: Resolve Through Sharing ARTIST: Rana Limbou, Sara Wheeler TOPIC: Death, $29.95

Jai Shiva! Kirtan For Shivaratri
PUBLISHING COMPANY: Sri Rama Publishing ARTIST: NSA TOPIC: Spirituality, $10.95

Jambalaya: The Natural Woman's Book Of Personal Charms & Practical Rituals
PUBLISHING COMPANY: Harper & Row Audio ARTIST: L. Teish TOPIC: Metaphysics, Spirituality, $14.95

Jane Fonda's Stretch And Stress Reduction Program
PUBLISHING COMPANY: Warner/Elektra/Atlant Corp. ARTIST: J. Fonda TOPIC: Holistic Health, $11.98

Jane Roberts: The San Francisco Interview
PUBLISHING COMPANY: Kendall, Inc. ARTIST: Jane Roberts TOPIC: Channeling, $24.95

Japanese Shiatsu Massage: Advanced
PUBLISHING COMPANY: Artistic Video ARTIST: Jerry Luglio TOPIC: Holistic Healing, $39.95

Jay Jay Muktananda
PUBLISHING COMPANY: S.Y.D.A. Foundation ARTIST: Gurumayl Chidvilasananda TOPIC: Spirituality, $10.00

Jewel
PUBLISHING COMPANY: Sonic Atmospheres ARTIST: M. Stearns TOPIC: Meditation, $19.00

Jogging The Memory
PUBLISHING COMPANY: Windham Hill Records ARTIST: M. Dalglish TOPIC: Meditation, $11.98

Jonah's Journey
PUBLISHING COMPANY: Halpern Sounds ARTIST: S. Halpern TOPIC: Meditation, $10.98

Joshua: A Parable For Today
PUBLISHING COMPANY: Bantam Audio ARTIST: J. Girzone TOPIC: Channeling, $12.95

Journey Home
PUBLISHING COMPANY: Gothic Image Pubications ARTIST: G. Kelly TOPIC: Meditation, $18.98

Journey Into Dreamtime
PUBLISHING COMPANY: Channel Light Productions ARTIST: Lynn Andrews TOPIC: Spirituality, $10.95

Journey Into Manhood: Myths & Stories About Male Individuation
PUBLISHING COMPANY: Sounds True Record. & Dupl. ARTIST: Clarissa Pinkola Estes TOPIC: Psychology, $10.95

Journey Into New Dimensions
PUBLISHING COMPANY: Y.O.G.A. Productions ARTIST: Diana, Louise, et.al. TOPIC: Meditation, $10.98

Journey Into The Fourth Dimension: The 60-Day Non-Human Program
PUBLISHING COMPANY: Quartus Foundation ARTIST: John Pricc TOPIC: Spirituality, $29.95

Journey Into Time: Egypt
PUBLISHING COMPANY: Journey Into Time Videos TOPIC: Spirituality, $39.95

Journey Of Awakening: A Meditator's Guide
PUBLISHING COMPANY: Audio Reniassance Tapes ARTIST: Ram Dass TOPIC: Spirituality, $9.95

Journey Of Trust
PUBLISHING COMPANY: Morgan, Meg ARTIST: Meg Morgan TOPIC: Meditation, $13.95

Journeys Into Meditation And Music
PUBLISHING COMPANY: Theosophical Pub ARTIST: H. Lingerman TOPIC: Meditation, $14.95

Journeys Out Of The Body
PUBLISHING COMPANY: Audio Renaissance Tapes ARTIST: R. Monroe TOPIC: Astral Projection, $9.95

Joy! Joy! Joy!
PUBLISHING COMPANY: Vital Body Marketing Co., Inc. ARTIST: K. Robertson, S. Kujala TOPIC: New Age, $9.95

Joy: Falling In Love With Life
PUBLISHING COMPANY: White Dove Int'l., Inc. ARTIST: S. Wilde TOPIC: Hypnotism, $11.95

Jung: Interpreting Your Dreams
PUBLISHING COMPANY: Audio Renaissance Tapes TOPIC: Dreams, $9.95

Jungian Concepts And The Horoscope
PUBLISHING COMPANY: Llewellyn Worldwide, Ltd. ARTIST: I. Hickey TOPIC: Astrology, $7.95

Just Imagine
PUBLISHING COMPANY: Sound Editions ARTIST: W. Dyer TOPIC: Meditation, $9.95

Justin Stone Speaks On Tai Chi Chih
PUBLISHING COMPANY: Satori Resources ARTIST: Justin F. Stone TOPIC: Tai Chi, $9.95

Kabbalah For The Layman
PUBLISHING COMPANY: Research Centre of Kabbalah ARTIST: P. Berg TOPIC: Kabbalah, $100.00

Kali's Dream

PUBLISHING COMPANY: Eastern Gate Publishing, Inc. ARTIST: Alex Jones, D. Cutler TOPIC: Meditation, $16.98

Karma And Reincarnation
PUBLISHING COMPANY: Centerpoint Distribution, Inc. ARTIST: E. Baron TOPIC: Reincarnation, $9.98

Karma, Love And Detachment
PUBLISHING COMPANY: Arizona Metaphysical Society ARTIST: F. Alper TOPIC: Reincarnation, $10.00

Keepers Of The Mysteries
PUBLISHING COMPANY: Medicine Song Productions ARTIST: Rashani TOPIC: Spirituality, $10.00

Kitaro: In Person
PUBLISHING COMPANY: Kuckuck Records ARTIST: Kitaro TOPIC: Meditation, $18.98

Knowings
PUBLISHING COMPANY: Light Institute Cassettes ARTIST: C. Griscom TOPIC: Spirituality, $10.75

Knowledge Of Light
PUBLISHING COMPANY: Dawn Horse Press ARTIST: D. Free John TOPIC: Spirituality, $9.95

Kuan Yin's Crystal Rosary: Devotions To The Divine Mother East & West
PUBLISHING COMPANY: Summit University Press ARTIST: E. Prophet TOPIC: Spirituality, $14.95

Kundalini Yoga Workout
PUBLISHING COMPANY: Yoga Video Company ARTIST: R. Fenton, A. Khalsa ARTIST: narrated by Peter Khalsa TOPIC: Yoga, $29.95

Kyrie
PUBLISHING COMPANY: Spring Hill Music ARTIST: R. Gass ARTIST: On Wings of Song TOPIC: Spirituality, $10.00

La Illaha Il Allah (Islamic Tradition)
PUBLISHING COMPANY: MSH Association ARTIST: Brother Charles TOPIC: Spirituality, $25.00

Lake Of Time
PUBLISHING COMPANY: Hopkins, Marge V./Ayamaya ARTIST: M. Hopkins TOPIC: Meditation, $11.95

Land Of Enchantment
PUBLISHING COMPANY: Celestial Harmonies ARTIST: Deuter TOPIC: Meditation, $18.98

Landscape
PUBLISHING COMPANY: Coyote Oldham ARTIST: Coyote Oldman TOPIC: Meditation, $15.98

Launching Your Day: Energizing Affirmations For Peak Performance
PUBLISHING COMPANY: Source Cassettes ARTIST: E. Miller TOPIC: Meditation, $9.95

Lazy Man's Guide To Death And Dying
PUBLISHING COMPANY: Gateways/IDHHB ARTIST: E. J. Gold TOPIC: Death, $9.98

Learning To Channel

PUBLISHING COMPANY: Arizona Metaphysical Society ARTIST: F. Alper TOPIC: Channeling, $10.00

Learning To Channel: Creating Your Own Reality With Meredith Lady Young
PUBLISHING COMPANY: Hartley Film Foundation ARTIST: Meredith Young TOPIC: Channeling, $39.95

Learning To Love Yourself
PUBLISHING COMPANY: Light of Mind ARTIST: Susan Grace TOPIC: Meditation, $14.95

Left Brain Super Charge: An Exercise
PUBLISHING COMPANY: Reflections ARTIST: Star Sounds TOPIC: Hypnotism, $14.95

Left Brain Super Charge: An Explanation
PUBLISHING COMPANY: Reflections ARTIST: Star Sounds TOPIC: Hypnotism, $14.95

Left-Right Brain Super Charge: An Exercise
PUBLISHING COMPANY: Reflections ARTIST: Star Sounds TOPIC: Hypnotism, $14.95

Left-Right Brain Super Charge: An Explanation
PUBLISHING COMPANY: Reflections ARTIST: Star Sounds TOPIC: Hypnotism, $14.95

Letting Go Of Fear: Positive Affirmations And Music
PUBLISHING COMPANY: Fortuna Record & Tape ARTIST: J. Walter TOPIC: Meditation, $9.98

Letting Go Of Stress
PUBLISHING COMPANY: Halpern Sounds ARTIST: E. Miller, S. Halpern TOPIC: Holistic Health, $10.00

Letting Go Of The Past/Moving Forward
PUBLISHING COMPANY: Sutherland, Caroline ARTIST: Caroline Sutherland TOPIC: Meditation, $12.95

Letting Go With Love: The Grieving Process
PUBLISHING COMPANY: La Marirosa Press ARTIST: N. O'Connor TOPIC: Death, $15.95

Life After Death
PUBLISHING COMPANY: Hartley Film Foundation ARTIST: L. LeShan TOPIC: Death, $89.00

Life After Life
PUBLISHING COMPANY: Audio Renaissance Tapes ARTIST: R. A. Moody TOPIC: Death, $9.95

Life After Life: Understanding Near Death Experience
PUBLISHING COMPANY: Thinking Allow Prod. ARTIST: R.A. Moody TOPIC: Death, $49.95

Life And Teaching Of The Masters Of The Far East
PUBLISHING COMPANY: Devorss & Co. ARTIST: B. Spalding TOPIC: Occult, $18.95

Life In The Universe
PUBLISHING COMPANY: Thinking Allowed Prod. ARTIST: Jacques Valle ARTIST: et.al. TOPIC: New Age, $69.95

Life Is Goodbye, Life Is Hello: Gentle, Specific Help To Move Through/Stages Of Grief
PUBLISHING COMPANY: Compcare Publications ARTIST: A. Bozarth-Campbell TOPIC: Death, $9.95

Life Of Non-Compromise
PUBLISHING COMPANY: Life Action Press ARTIST: T. Singh TOPIC: Spirituality, $17.95

Lifesong
PUBLISHING COMPANY: Heart Music ARTIST: Akasha TOPIC: Spirituality, $10.00

Lifespring: Getting Yourself From Where You Are To Where You Want To Be
PUBLISHING COMPANY: Simon & Schuster ARTIST: J. Hanley TOPIC: Spirituality, $14.95

Lifestreams
PUBLISHING COMPANY: Soundings of the Planet ARTIST: D. Evenson TOPIC: New Age, $39.95

Light In The Darkness: Sensory Imagery & Meditations To Heal The Mind & Body
PUBLISHING COMPANY: Pacific-West Entertain.Grp. ARTIST: G. Koppel ARTIST: et.al. TOPIC: Holistic Healing, $29.95

Lighthouse: Achieve Mental Strength/Survival In Confusion & Indecision
PUBLISHING COMPANY: Valley of the Sun ARTIST: D. Sutphen TOPIC: Meditation, $8.98

Lillias Alive With Yoga
PUBLISHING COMPANY: Rudra Press ARTIST: L. Folan TOPIC: Yoga, $29.95

Lillias Alive With Yoga Vol. 2: Intermediate Yoga
PUBLISHING COMPANY: Rudra Press ARTIST: L. Folan TOPIC: Yoga, $29.95

Lillias Yoga For Beginning Students
PUBLISHING COMPANY: Audio Renaissance Tapes ARTIST: L. Folan TOPIC: Yoga, $9.95

Lillias Yoga For Experienced Students
PUBLISHING COMPANY: Audio Renaissance Tapes ARTIST: L. Folan TOPIC: Yoga, $15.95

Listening I: An Introduction
PUBLISHING COMPANY: Las Brisas Publishing Co. ARTIST: L. Colt TOPIC: Psychology, $10.95

Listening II: An Workshop
PUBLISHING COMPANY: Las Brisas Publishing Co. ARTIST: L. Colt TOPIC: Psychology, $10.95

Little Course In Dreams

PUBLISHING COMPANY: Shambhala Publications ARTIST: R. (May) Bosnak TOPIC: Dreams, $14.95

Living As A Peaceful Warrior
PUBLISHING COMPANY: Thinking Allowed Prod. ARTIST: D. Millman TOPIC: Spirituality, $49.95

Living Earth
PUBLISHING COMPANY: Search For Serenity ARTIST: A. Locke TOPIC: Meditation, $16.98

Living In The Light
PUBLISHING COMPANY: New World Library ARTIST: S. Gawain TOPIC: Psychology, $10.98

Living Philosophically
PUBLISHING COMPANY: Thinking Allowed Prod. ARTIST: J. Needleman ARTIST: et.al. TOPIC: Spirituality, $69.95

Living Traditions
PUBLISHING COMPANY: Thinking Allowed Prod. ARTIST: M. Harner ARTIST: et.al. TOPIC: Spirituality, $69.95

Living With An Open Heart: An Introduction To Universal Principles
PUBLISHING COMPANY: Sounds True Record & Dupl. ARTIST: Arnold Patent TOPIC: Metaphysics, $9.95

Locrian Invocation
PUBLISHING COMPANY: Full Circle Music ARTIST: Joel Andrews TOPIC: Meditation, $10.98

Logos: Through A Sideman
PUBLISHING COMPANY: Gold Castle Records ARTIST: David Hayes TOPIC: Meditation, $10.98

Looking Deeply
PUBLISHING COMPANY: Parallax Press ARTIST: T. Hanh TOPIC: Spirituality, $15.00

Lose Weight, Feel Great
PUBLISHING COMPANY: Audio Renaissance Tapes ARTIST: L. Glauberman TOPIC: Hypnotism, $15.95

Lost Years Of Jesus
PUBLISHING COMPANY: Janet Bock ARTIST: R. Bock TOPIC: Spirituality, $39.95

Love Is Unconditional Prepack
PUBLISHING COMPANY: New Age Books & Games ARTIST: Jay Bartlett TOPIC: Meditation, $119.95

Love Without An Agenda/Becoming Deep: Lectures Based On A Course In Miracles
PUBLISHING COMPANY: Miracle Projects ARTIST: Marianne Williamson TOPIC: Spirituality, $10.00

Love Your Body
PUBLISHING COMPANY: Hay House ARTIST: Louise Hay TOPIC: Meditation, $10.00

Love, Medicine And Miracles
PUBLISHING COMPANY: Caedmon ARTIST: Bernie Siegel TOPIC: Holistic Healing, $15.95

Love, Medicine And Miracles Gift Set (Bernie Siegel's Personal Reflections)

PUBLISHING COMPANY: Harper & Row Publishers **ARTIST:** Bernie Siegel **TOPIC:** Body-Mind Connection, $14.95

Love: New World Subliminals
PUBLISHING COMPANY: New World Products, Ltd. **ARTIST:** Y. Bhajan **TOPIC:** Hypnotism, $14.95

Lovely Day
PUBLISHING COMPANY: Aura Communications **ARTIST:** W. Aura **TOPIC:** Meditation, $11.98

Loving Self Meditations
PUBLISHING COMPANY: Dr. Gloria Spitalny **ARTIST:** Gloria Spitalny **TOPIC:** Meditation, $11.98

Loving Yourself
PUBLISHING COMPANY: Morgen, Meg **ARTIST:** Meg Morgan **TOPIC:** Meditation, $13.95

Lucid Dreaming
PUBLISHING COMPANY: Yes! Technologies **ARTIST:** Yes! Technologies **TOPIC:** Hypnotism, $19.95

Lullabies And Sweet Dreams
PUBLISHING COMPANY: Halpern Sounds **ARTIST:** S. Halpern **TOPIC:** Meditation, $11.98

Machu Picchu Impressions
PUBLISHING COMPANY: Emerald Green Sound Prod. **ARTIST:** R. Crutcher **TOPIC:** Meditation, $17.98

Magic Carpet
PUBLISHING COMPANY: Living Sound Productions **ARTIST:** Living Sound Productions **TOPIC:** Meditation, $14.98

Magic Of The Candle Flame
PUBLISHING COMPANY: Llewellyn Worldwide, Ltd. **ARTIST:** M. Leonesio **TOPIC:** Occult, $6.95

Magical Journey: Hallucinogens & Culture/Time & I Ching/Human Future
PUBLISHING COMPANY: Thinking Allowed Prod. **ARTIST:** T. McKenna **TOPIC:** Parapsychology, $49.95

Magical States Of Consciousness: 24th Path, Part 2
PUBLISHING COMPANY: Llewellyn Worldwide, Ltd. **ARTIST:** M. Denning, O. Phillips **TOPIC:** Occult, $9.95

Magical States Of Consciousness: 25th Path
PUBLISHING COMPANY: Llewellyn Worldwide, Ltd. **ARTIST:** M. Denning, O. Phillips **TOPIC:** Occult, $9.95

Magical States Of Consciousness: 26th & 24th Paths, Part 1
PUBLISHING COMPANY: Llewellyn Worldwide, Ltd. **ARTIST:** M. Denning, O. Phillips **TOPIC:** Occult, $9.95

Magical States Of Consciousness: 26th Path Part 2
PUBLISHING COMPANY: Llewellyn Worldwide, Ltd. **ARTIST:** M. Denning, O. Phillips **TOPIC:** Occult, $9.95

Magical States Of Consciousness: 27th Path
PUBLISHING COMPANY: Llewellyn Worldwide, Ltd. **ARTIST:** M. Denning, O. Phillips **TOPIC:** Occult, $9.95

Magical States Of Consciousness: 29th & 28th Paths
PUBLISHING COMPANY: Llewellyn Worldwide, Ltd. **ARTIST:** M. Denning, O. Phillips **TOPIC:** Occult, $9.95

Magical States Of Consciousness: 31th & 30th Paths
PUBLISHING COMPANY: Llewellyn Worldwide, Ltd. **ARTIST:** M. Denning, O. Phillips **TOPIC:** Occult, $9.95

Magical States Of Consciousness: The 32nd Path
PUBLISHING COMPANY: Llewellyn Worldwide, Ltd. **ARTIST:** M. Denning, O. Phillips **TOPIC:** Occult, $9.95

Magick Mirror Past Life Journey
PUBLISHING COMPANY: Circle Publications **ARTIST:** Dennis Carpenter **TOPIC:** Meditation, $12.00

Magickal Journeys
PUBLISHING COMPANY: Circle Publications **ARTIST:** Selene Fox **TOPIC:** Witchcraft, $10.00

Magnum Mysterium II
PUBLISHING COMPANY: Celestial Harmonies **ARTIST:** Various Artists **TOPIC:** Spirituality, $16.98

Majesty
PUBLISHING COMPANY: Willow Tree **ARTIST:** Aeoliah **TOPIC:** Meditation, $18.50

Major Arcana: Motherpeace Cassette Vol. 2
PUBLISHING COMPANY: Wingbow Resources **ARTIST:** V. Noble **TOPIC:** Tarot, $9.95

Making Relationships Holy
PUBLISHING COMPANY: Channel Light Productions **ARTIST:** Marianne Williamson **TOPIC:** Spirituality, $10.95

Making The Edgar Cayce Remedies At Home: An Edgar Cayce Video Presentation
PUBLISHING COMPANY: A.R.E. Press **ARTIST:** C.T. Cayce **TOPIC:** Homeopathy, $39.95

Male And Female Energies
PUBLISHING COMPANY: Arizona Metaphysical Society **ARTIST:** F. Alper **TOPIC:** Spirituality, $10.00

Male And Female Within
PUBLISHING COMPANY: New World Library **ARTIST:** S. Gawain **TOPIC:** Metaphysics, $9.95

Man And Nature
PUBLISHING COMPANY: Wishing Well Distributing **ARTIST:** Alan Watts **TOPIC:** Spirituality, $29.95

Managing Stress

PUBLISHING COMPANY: Effective Learnings Systems, Inc. **ARTIST:** Love Tapes **TOPIC:** Hypnotism, $11.98

Manchu Picchu Impressions: Recorded At The Ancient Incan City
PUBLISHING COMPANY: Vital Body Marketing Co., Inc. **ARTIST:** R. Crutcher **TOPIC:** New Age, $9.95

Mandalas: Visions Of Heaven And Earth
PUBLISHING COMPANY: Macro Media **ARTIST:** S. Halpern **ARTIST:** Mirtala **TOPIC:** New Age, $39.95

Manifesting Wealth
PUBLISHING COMPANY: Light of Mind **ARTIST:** M. Cohn **TOPIC:** Meditation, $14.95

Mansion Of Beauty: Drop Veils Of Cynicism & Negativity & Merge With Beauty
PUBLISHING COMPANY: Valley of the Sun **ARTIST:** D. Sutphen **TOPIC:** Meditation, $8.98

Massage For Health
PUBLISHING COMPANY: Healing Arts Home Video **ARTIST:** S. Belafonte-Harper **ARTIST:** et.al. **TOPIC:** Massage, $29.95

Massage For Relaxation
PUBLISHING COMPANY: New & Unique Videos **ARTIST:** M. Schulze, P. Mooney **TOPIC:** Massage, $29.95

Massage: Instructions For Beginners
PUBLISHING COMPANY: Bodymind Approach **ARTIST:** S. Abraham **TOPIC:** Massage, $39.95

Master Does Not Speak
PUBLISHING COMPANY: Arizona Metaphysical Society **ARTIST:** F. Alper **TOPIC:** Spirituality, $10.00

Master Meditation/The Sedona Vortex Story
PUBLISHING COMPANY: Valley of the Sun **ARTIST:** D. Stuphen **TOPIC:** Meditation, $12.50

Mastering Mental Imagining
PUBLISHING COMPANY: Audio Renaissance Tapes **ARTIST:** Jonathan Parker **TOPIC:** Meditation, $9.95

Mastering The Art Of Astral Projection
PUBLISHING COMPANY: Inner Light Publications **ARTIST:** B. Steiger **TOPIC:** Astral Projection, $8.95

Masters Of The Path
PUBLISHING COMPANY: Mayflower B/S **ARTIST:** Robert Thibodeau **TOPIC:** Spirituality, $49.95

Mastery Of Money
PUBLISHING COMPANY: White Dove Int'l. Inc. **ARTIST:** S. Wilde **TOPIC:** Body-Mind Connection, $39.95

Masturbation Magic
PUBLISHING COMPANY: Llewellyn Worldwide, Ltd. **ARTIST:** Jonn Mumford **TOPIC:** Occult, $7.95

Matriarchial History: Motherpeace Vol. 1

PUBLISHING COMPANY: Wingbow Resources **ARTIST:** V. Noble **TOPIC:** Tarot, $9.95

Medicine Woman
PUBLISHING COMPANY: Harper & Row **ARTIST:** Lynn Andrews **TOPIC:** Spirituality, $14.95

Meditation
PUBLISHING COMPANY: Audio Renaissance Tapes **ARTIST:** E. Cayce **ARTIST:** Read by Stanley Ross **TOPIC:** Channeling, $9.95

Meditation At Dawn
PUBLISHING COMPANY: White Dove Int'l., Inc. **ARTIST:** S. Wilde **TOPIC:** Hypnotism, $11.95

Meditation Is For Everyone
PUBLISHING COMPANY: H.H. Productions **ARTIST:** H. Hartley **TOPIC:** Meditation, $12.50

Meditation Made Easy
PUBLISHING COMPANY: A.R.E. Press **ARTIST:** L. Sparrow **TOPIC:** Meditation, $29.95

Meditation Methods And Practice
PUBLISHING COMPANY: Mayflower B/S **ARTIST:** Robert Thibodeau **TOPIC:** Meditation, $49.95

Meditation On The Goddess Within/Meditation On The Chakras: The Rainbow
PUBLISHING COMPANY: Llewellyn Worldwide, Ltd. **ARTIST:** D. Stein **TOPIC:** Parapsychology, $9.95

Meditation Sampler
PUBLISHING COMPANY: Fondix Musik **ARTIST:** Various Artists **TOPIC:** Meditation, $11.95

Meditation: An Invitation To Inner Growth
PUBLISHING COMPANY: Rudra Press **ARTIST:** Chetanananda **TOPIC:** Meditation, $15.95

Meditation: On The Edge
PUBLISHING COMPANY: White Dove Int'l., Inc. **ARTIST:** S. Wilde **TOPIC:** Meditation, $19.95

Meditations For Personal Harmony
PUBLISHING COMPANY: Nightingale Conant Corp. **ARTIST:** G. Jampolsky, D. Cirincione **TOPIC:** Meditation, $14.95

Meditations On The Tarot
PUBLISHING COMPANY: Luna Mix **ARTIST:** D. Wojton **ARTIST:** Laraaji **TOPIC:** Tarot, $9.95

Meditative Experience
PUBLISHING COMPANY: Thinking Allowed Prod. **ARTIST:** O. Nydahl **ARTIST:** et.al. **TOPIC:** Meditation, $69.95

Meetings
PUBLISHING COMPANY: Fondix Musik **ARTIST:** Tsumi **TOPIC:** Meditation, $10.98

Memories, Dreams, Reflectionsms
PUBLISHING COMPANY: Shambhala Publications **ARTIST:** C. Jung **TOPIC:** Psychology, $14.95

Memory Improvement
PUBLISHING COMPANY: Effective Learnings Systems, Inc. **ARTIST:** Love Tapes **TOPIC:** Hypnotism, $11.98

Memory Power: Sharpen Your Recall
PUBLISHING COMPANY: BFS Limited **ARTIST:** Bright Images **TOPIC:** Hypnotism, $11.95

Meta Fitness: Your Thoughts Taking Shape
PUBLISHING COMPANY: Hay House **ARTIST:** S. Prudden **TOPIC:** Body-Mind Connection, $24.95

Metaphysical Fitness: Complete 30-Day Plan For Your Mental/Spiritual & Emotional Health
PUBLISHING COMPANY: Mind's I Press **ARTIST:** David Harp, N. Feldman **TOPIC:** Metaphysics, $9.95

Metaphysical Hypnosis Course
PUBLISHING COMPANY: Light of Mind **ARTIST:** M. Cohn **TOPIC:** Hypnotism, $24.95

Metaphysical Secrets Of Manifesting Wealth
PUBLISHING COMPANY: Light of Mind **ARTIST:** M. Cohn **TOPIC:** Meditation, $14.95

Migraine Relief
PUBLISHING COMPANY: Potentials Unlimited **ARTIST:** Potentials Unlimited **TOPIC:** New Age, $9.98

Miles To Go: The Spiritual Quest Of Aging
PUBLISHING COMPANY: Harper & Row Audio **ARTIST:** Richard O. Peterson **TOPIC:** Channeling, $9.95

Mind Expansion/Cosmic Awareness
PUBLISHING COMPANY: Light of Mind **ARTIST:** A. Alexander **TOPIC:** Psychology, $9.98

Mind-Body Tempo
PUBLISHING COMPANY: Mellow Minds **ARTIST:** Janalea Hoffman **TOPIC:** Meditation, $11.95

Minor Arcana
PUBLISHING COMPANY: Visionary Video Productions **ARTIST:** L Clarson **TOPIC:** Tarot, $49.95

Minor Arcana: Motherpeace Vol. 3
PUBLISHING COMPANY: Wingbow Resources **ARTIST:** V. Noble **TOPIC:** Tarot, $9.95

Miracle Mountain Workshop Tapes
PUBLISHING COMPANY: Cohen, Allen **ARTIST:** A. Cohen **TOPIC:** Spirituality, $29.95

Miracles
PUBLISHING COMPANY: Search For Serenity **ARTIST:** R. Whitesides-Woo **TOPIC:** Meditation, $16.98

Miracles: The End Of Learning
PUBLISHING COMPANY: Life Action Press **ARTIST:** T. Singh **TOPIC:** Spirituality, $17.95

Mirror
PUBLISHING COMPANY: Beyond **ARTIST:** Pyramid **TOPIC:** Meditation, $12.98

Mission
PUBLISHING COMPANY: Virgin Records **ARTIST:** Motricone **TOPIC:** Meditation, $11.98

Misty Forest Morning
PUBLISHING COMPANY: Vital Body Marketing Co., Inc. **ARTIST:** D. Gordon, S. Gordon **TOPIC:** New Age, $9.95

Moment Of Truth: A Window On Life After Death
PUBLISHING COMPANY: Starpath Productions **ARTIST:** B. Hully, J. Smith **TOPIC:** Death, $34.95

Moments Of Flowers
PUBLISHING COMPANY: Chidvilas **ARTIST:** Spiritual Environments, Music by Gambheera **TOPIC:** Meditation, $11.95

Monuments Of Mars: Evidence Of A Lost City On Mars?
PUBLISHING COMPANY: Enhanced Audio Systems **ARTIST:** R. C. Hoagland **TOPIC:** Paranormal Phenomena, $10.95

Mood Of Zen
PUBLISHING COMPANY: Hartley Film Foundation **ARTIST:** Alan Watts **TOPIC:** Spirituality, $89.00

Moon Hooves In The Sand
PUBLISHING COMPANY: K. & T. Klein **ARTIST:** Kenny & Tzipora w/Blue Star **TOPIC:** Witchcraft, $8.95

Moon Lodge
PUBLISHING COMPANY: Medicine Eagle/Harmony N/W **ARTIST:** Brooke Medicine Eagle **TOPIC:** Spirituality, $10.00

Moon Time
PUBLISHING COMPANY: Medicine Eagle/Harmony N/W **ARTIST:** Brooke Medicine Eagle **TOPIC:** Spirituality, $10.00

Moonrise
PUBLISHING COMPANY: Invincible Recordings **ARTIST:** K. Robertson **TOPIC:** Meditation, $15.98

More Love
PUBLISHING COMPANY: White Dove Int'l., Inc. **ARTIST:** S. Wilde **TOPIC:** Hypnotism, $11.95

Morning And Evening Meditations
PUBLISHING COMPANY: Hay House **ARTIST:** Louise Hay **TOPIC:** Meditation, $10.00

Mother Earth's Lullaby
PUBLISHING COMPANY: Synchestra **ARTIST:** Synchestra **TOPIC:** Meditation, $17.98

Mother Wit: Friend Inside/Healing Stars Meditations
PUBLISHING COMPANY: Aquila Tapes **ARTIST:** D. Mariechild, S. Goodman **TOPIC:** Spirituality, $10.95

Mother Wit: Self-Healing Meditation/Inner Self Meditation
PUBLISHING COMPANY: Aquila Tapes **ARTIST:** D. Mariechild, S. Goodman **TOPIC:** Psychic Healing, $10.95

Mountains In The Sea
PUBLISHING COMPANY: Beyond **ARTIST:** K. Schaffner **TOPIC:** Meditation, $12.98

Movement With Brain Sync

PUBLISHING COMPANY: Acoustic Brain Research **ARTIST:** Acoustic Brain Research **TOPIC:** Meditation, $24.95

Moving Point Of Balance
PUBLISHING COMPANY: Yansa Music **ARTIST:** B.A. Swartz **TOPIC:** Meditation, $21.95

Murvin: Commander Of Jupiter
PUBLISHING COMPANY: Arizona Metaphysical Society **ARTIST:** F. Alper **TOPIC:** Paranormal Phenomena, $10.00

Music And Nature 3-Pack (Peaceful Evening; Misty Forest Morning; Radiant Sea)
PUBLISHING COMPANY: Vital Body Marketing Co., Inc. **ARTIST:** Various Artists **TOPIC:** New Age, $19.95

Music Box
PUBLISHING COMPANY: MCA Record Co. **ARTIST:** Philippe Sarde **TOPIC:** Meditation, $11.98

Music For Mellow Minds
PUBLISHING COMPANY: Mellow Minds **ARTIST:** Janalea Hoffman **TOPIC:** Meditation, $10.95

Music For Relaxation 3-Pack (Music For Relaxation; Paradise Island, Pachelbel Canon
PUBLISHING COMPANY: Vital Body Marketing Co., Inc. **ARTIST:** Various Artists **TOPIC:** Meditation, $19.95

Music From The Pleiades
PUBLISHING COMPANY: Astromusic **ARTIST:** G. J. Markoe **TOPIC:** Meditation, $17.95

Music Of Gurdjieff/De Hartmann
PUBLISHING COMPANY: Triangle Editions, Inc. **ARTIST:** G. Gurdjieff, T. De Hartmann **TOPIC:** Meditation, $62.50

Music To Disappear In
PUBLISHING COMPANY: Hearts of Space **ARTIST:** Raphael **TOPIC:** Meditation, $18.95

Musical Body: A Vitalizing Spiritua Exercise
PUBLISHING COMPANY: Willow Tree **ARTIST:** C. Tart **ARTIST:** & Geist **TOPIC:** Psychology, $10.00

Musical Sleep Induction
PUBLISHING COMPANY: Vital Body Marketing Co., Inc. **ARTIST:** Robert Sohn, Jim Oliver **TOPIC:** New Age, $9.95

Mysteries Of Atlantis Revised: An Audio Adaptation
PUBLISHING COMPANY: Harper & Row Publishers **ARTIST:** E. Cayce **ARTIST:** et.al. **TOPIC:** Channeling, $9.95

Mystical Marriage
PUBLISHING COMPANY: Oliver Music **ARTIST:** J. Oliver, R. Waterman **TOPIC:** Meditation, $11.99

Mystical Paths
PUBLISHING COMPANY: Thinking Allowed Prod. **ARTIST:** J.C. Pearce **ARTIST:** et.al. **TOPIC:** Spirituality, $69.95

Mysticism In The Modern World

PUBLISHING COMPANY: Thoth Publications **ARTIST:** M. Hope **TOPIC:** Occult, $9.95

Narada Sampler #1
PUBLISHING COMPANY: Narada Productions **ARTIST:** Narada Artists **TOPIC:** Meditation, $16.98

Narada Sampler #2
PUBLISHING COMPANY: Narada Productions **ARTIST:** Narada Artists **TOPIC:** Meditation, $16.98

Natural Healing
PUBLISHING COMPANY: Audio Renaissance Tapes **ARTIST:** E. Cayce **ARTIST:** Read by Stanley Ralph Ross **TOPIC:** Holistic Healing, $9.95

Natural Light
PUBLISHING COMPANY: Halpern Sounds **ARTIST:** S. Halpern **TOPIC:** Meditation, $10.98

Natural Response Weight Loss
PUBLISHING COMPANY: Light of Mind **ARTIST:** S. Gordon, D. Gordon **TOPIC:** Meditation, $24.95

Natural Self-Confidence
PUBLISHING COMPANY: Changeworks **ARTIST:** C. Erickson, T. Condon **TOPIC:** Meditation, Hypnotism, $12.95

Natural Sleep
PUBLISHING COMPANY: Living Sound Productions **ARTIST:** Living Sound Productions **TOPIC:** Meditation, $14.98

Natural States
PUBLISHING COMPANY: Narada Productions **ARTIST:** D. Lanz, P. Speer **TOPIC:** Meditation, $16.00

Natural Therapies For Colds, Flu And Allergies
PUBLISHING COMPANY: Pyramid Communications **ARTIST:** M. Tierra **ARTIST:** et.al. **TOPIC:** Homeopathy, $24.95

Nature And Power Of Dreams
PUBLISHING COMPANY: Thoth Publications **ARTIST:** M. Hope **TOPIC:** Dreams, $9.95

Nature Of Things
PUBLISHING COMPANY: Backroads Distributors **ARTIST:** B. BecVar **TOPIC:** Meditation, $21.95

Nature's Answer To Stress 3-Pack (Sea; Rainforest; Sailing
PUBLISHING COMPANY: Vital Body Marketing Co., Inc. **ARTIST:** NSA **TOPIC:** New Age, $19.95

Neverland
PUBLISHING COMPANY: Private Music **ARTIST:** S. Ciani **TOPIC:** Meditation, $11.98

New Christian Yoga: A Cowley Retreat Tape
PUBLISHING COMPANY: Cowley Publications **ARTIST:** Nancy Roth **TOPIC:** Yoga, $10.95

New Dawn Nutritional Tapes Pre-Pack
PUBLISHING COMPANY: New Dawn Nutrit.Services **ARTIST:** R. Gilday **TOPIC:** Nutrition, $132.00

New Friend

PUBLISHING COMPANY: Living Music Records, Inc. **ARTIST:** E. Friesen, P. Halley **TOPIC:** Meditation, $11.98

New Green Clear Blue
PUBLISHING COMPANY: Private Music **ARTIST:** D. Hartman **TOPIC:** Meditation, $11.98

New Man
PUBLISHING COMPANY: Chidvilas **ARTIST:** B. Rajneesh **TOPIC:** Spirituality, $39.95

Night Life I
PUBLISHING COMPANY: Reflections **ARTIST:** Star Sounds **TOPIC:** Hypnotism, $14.95

Night Life II
PUBLISHING COMPANY: Reflections **ARTIST:** Star Sounds **TOPIC:** Hypnotism, $14.95

Night Life III
PUBLISHING COMPANY: Reflections **ARTIST:** Star Sounds **TOPIC:** Hypnotism, $14.95

Night Life IV
PUBLISHING COMPANY: Reflections **ARTIST:** Star Sounds **TOPIC:** Hypnotism, $14.95

Nightfall
PUBLISHING COMPANY: Music Designs **ARTIST:** D. Lanz **TOPIC:** Meditation, $16.00

Nightingale Records Sampler V.1
PUBLISHING COMPANY: Fonix Musik **ARTIST:** Nightingale Artists **TOPIC:** Meditation, $11.95

Nightnoise
PUBLISHING COMPANY: Windham Hill Records **ARTIST:** B. Oskay, M. O'Domhnaill **TOPIC:** Meditation, $11.98

Nirvana Road
PUBLISHING COMPANY: Celestial Harmonies **ARTIST:** Deuter **TOPIC:** Meditation, $17.98

No Effort Weight Loss
PUBLISHING COMPANY: Valley of the Sun **ARTIST:** D. Sutphen **TOPIC:** Hypnotism, $18.98

No-Body Can Do Without Massage
PUBLISHING COMPANY: High-Energy **ARTIST:** High Energy **TOPIC:** Massage, $19.95

Nodes/Introduction To Interpretation: Twelve Letter Alphabet
PUBLISHING COMPANY: Video Lecture Series **ARTIST:** M. Lutin, M. Pottenger **TOPIC:** Astrology, $39.95

Non-Analytic Ways Of Growth
PUBLISHING COMPANY: Dialogue House **ARTIST:** I. Progoff **TOPIC:** Psychology, $10.00

Nothing Real Can Be Threatened
PUBLISHING COMPANY: Life Action Press **ARTIST:** T. Singh **TOPIC:** Spirituality, $100.00

Novus Magnificat: Through The Stargate
PUBLISHING COMPANY: Hearts of Space **ARTIST:** C. Demby **TOPIC:** Meditation, $18.95

Number, Form And Life

PUBLISHING COMPANY: Thinking Allowed Prod. ARTIST: R. Sheldrake ARTIST: et.al. TOPIC: New Age, $69.95

O'cean: Songs Of The Humpback Whale
PUBLISHING COMPANY: Sona Gaia ARTIST: Larkin TOPIC: Meditation, $16.00

Occult Healing: White Magic Techniques & Incantations
PUBLISHING COMPANY: Valley of the Sun ARTIST: D. Sutphen TOPIC: Occult, Psychic Healing, $12.50

Ocean Song
PUBLISHING COMPANY: White Heart Productions ARTIST: H. White TOPIC: Meditation, $10.98

Officium Tenebrarum: Gregorian Chants
PUBLISHING COMPANY: Celestial Harmonies ARTIST: Utrecht Stud. Gregorian Choir TOPIC: Spirituality, $18.98

Om Mani Padme Hum (Buddhist Tradition)
PUBLISHING COMPANY: MSH Association ARTIST: Brother Charles TOPIC: Spirituality, $25.00

Om Namaha Shivaya
PUBLISHING COMPANY: Spring Hill Music ARTIST: R. Gass ARTIST: On Wings of Song TOPIC: Spirituality, $10.00

Om Namaha Shivaya (Vedic Tradition)
PUBLISHING COMPANY: MSH Association ARTIST: Brother Charles TOPIC: Spirituality, $25.00

Om: Beside The Sea Of The Great Unmanifest
PUBLISHING COMPANY: Spirit Wings ARTIST: Joe F. Elliot TOPIC: Meditation, $11.95

Om: The Reverberation Of Source Universal
PUBLISHING COMPANY: MSH Association ARTIST: NSA TOPIC: Spirituality, $25.00

On The Future Of Aviation
PUBLISHING COMPANY: Private Music ARTIST: Jerry Goodman TOPIC: Meditation, $11.98

One Earth Songs
PUBLISHING COMPANY: Sunrise Publications ARTIST: R. Wardtop TOPIC: Spirituality, $10.00

Opening Doors To Creative Expression
PUBLISHING COMPANY: Hartley Film Foundation ARTIST: B. Taggart, B. Taggart TOPIC: New Age, $89.00

Opening For Learning: Death & Dying Process
PUBLISHING COMPANY: New Visions ARTIST: H. Cole TOPIC: Death, $9.98

Opening The Heart

PUBLISHING COMPANY: Blue Dolphin Publishing - 2 ARTIST: I. Tweedie, O. Nydahl TOPIC: Spirituality, $10.00

Opening To Intuition
PUBLISHING COMPANY: Thinking Allowed Prod. ARTIST: K. Ryerson ARTIST: et.al. TOPIC: Channeling, $69.95

Opening To Life, Opening To Death
PUBLISHING COMPANY: Blue Dolphin Publishing - 2 ARTIST: Sogyal Rinpoche, et.al. TOPIC: Death, $10.00

Opening Up To Intuition
PUBLISHING COMPANY: Changeworks ARTIST: T. Condon TOPIC: Meditation, $12.95

Opportunities: Pulling Opportunities, Like Plums From A Tree
PUBLISHING COMPANY: White Dove Int'l., Inc. ARTIST: S. Wilde TOPIC: Hypnotism, $11.95

Optimum Uses Of Inner Resources To Maintain Your Integrity
PUBLISHING COMPANY: Butterfly Publishing Co. ARTIST: E. Rose TOPIC: Holistic Healing, $9.95

Orientation To Brain Integration
PUBLISHING COMPANY: Reflections ARTIST: Star Sounds TOPIC: Hypnotism, $14.95

Orientation To Eyes Open Meditation
PUBLISHING COMPANY: Reflections ARTIST: Star Sounds TOPIC: Hypnotism, $14.95

Ossian: American Boy/Tibetan Monk
PUBLISHING COMPANY: Wishing Well Distributing ARTIST: TRA Film Productions TOPIC: Spirituality, $49.95

Other Lives, Other Selves: A Jungian Psychotherapist Discovers Past Lives
PUBLISHING COMPANY: Hartly Film Foundation ARTIST: R. Woolger TOPIC: Psychology, Past Life Regression, $39.95

Our Hearts And The Heart Of The Earth Are One: Native American Spiritual Wisdom
PUBLISHING COMPANY: Sunray ARTIST: D. Ywahoo TOPIC: Spirituality, $11.00

Out Of Body Adventures
PUBLISHING COMPANY: Audio Renaissance Tapes ARTIST: Rick Stack TOPIC: Astral Projection, $9.95

Out Of Body Experience
PUBLISHING COMPANY: Dr. Bruce Goldberg ARTIST: Bruce Goldberg TOPIC: Meditation, $12.00

Out Of Body Experiences
PUBLISHING COMPANY: Dr. Bruce Goldberg ARTIST: Bruce Goldberg TOPIC: Astral Projection, $12.00

Out Of Silence
PUBLISHING COMPANY: Private Music ARTIST: Yanni TOPIC: Meditation, $10.98

Outer Planets And Their Cycles: The Astrology Of The Collective

PUBLISHING COMPANY: C.R.C.S. Publications ARTIST: L. Greene TOPIC: Astrology, $7.95

Overcoming Proscratination
PUBLISHING COMPANY: Effective Learnings Systems, Inc. ARTIST: Love Tapes TOPIC: Hypnotism, $11.98

Overcoming Your Fear Of The Dentist: Self-Help Guide To Controlling Dental Fears
PUBLISHING COMPANY: Tetrahedron ARTIST: L. Horowitz TOPIC: Holistic Health, $19.95

Pachelbel Canon: The Meditative Classic With Ocean Waves
PUBLISHING COMPANY: Vital Body Marketing Co., Inc. ARTIST: G. Sill TOPIC: New Age, $9.95

Pain Control And Healing
PUBLISHING COMPANY: New Harbinger Publications ARTIST: M. Davis ARTIST: et.al. TOPIC: Holistic Healing, $10.95

Pain Relief
PUBLISHING COMPANY: Potentials Unlimited ARTIST: Potentials Unlimited TOPIC: New Age, $9.98

Pain Reliever
PUBLISHING COMPANY: Fourier, Aline ARTIST: A. Fourier TOPIC: Meditation, $10.95

Panel: Various Systems Of Astrology, 1 & 2
PUBLISHING COMPANY: Video Lecture Series ARTIST: R. Hand TOPIC: Astrology, $39.95

Parallel Lives, Separate Selves
PUBLISHING COMPANY: Potentials Unlimited ARTIST: Potentials Unlimited TOPIC: New Age, $9.98

Paranormal And The Spirit World
PUBLISHING COMPANY: Audio Renaissance Tapes TOPIC: Channeling, $9.95

Parent-Child Relations
PUBLISHING COMPANY: Light Institute Cassettes ARTIST: C. Griscom TOPIC: Reincarnation, $10.75

Passage
PUBLISHING COMPANY: Windham Hill Records ARTIST: W. Ackerman TOPIC: Meditation, $18.50

Passing Through
PUBLISHING COMPANY: Reflections ARTIST: Star Sounds TOPIC: Hypnotism, $14.95

Passion
PUBLISHING COMPANY: Geffen Records ARTIST: Peter Gabriel TOPIC: Meditation, $11.98

Past Life Journey
PUBLISHING COMPANY: Inner Journeys, Inc. ARTIST: K. Angeli TOPIC: Past Life Regression, $9.98

Past Life Regression
PUBLISHING COMPANY: Dr. Bruce Goldberg ARTIST: Bruce Goldberg TOPIC: Meditation, $12.00

Past Life Regression

PUBLISHING COMPANY: Potentials Unlimited **ARTIST:** Potentials Unlimited **TOPIC:** New Age, $9.98

Past Life Regression
PUBLISHING COMPANY: Inner Light Foundation **ARTIST:** B. Binder **TOPIC:** Meditation, $29.95

Past Life Regressions: Video Hypnosis
PUBLISHING COMPANY: Valley of the Sun **ARTIST:** D. Sutphen **TOPIC:** Past Life Regression, $19.95

Past Life Therapy Cause And Effect
PUBLISHING COMPANY: Potentials Unlimited **ARTIST:** Potentials Unlimited **TOPIC:** New Age, $9.98

Past Light
PUBLISHING COMPANY: Windham Hill Records **ARTIST:** W. Ackerman **TOPIC:** Meditation, $18.50

Past Lives, Present Problems
PUBLISHING COMPANY: Valley of the Sun **ARTIST:** E. Fiore **TOPIC:** Past Life Regression, $9.98

Past-Life Therapy Regression Album
PUBLISHING COMPANY: Valley of the Sun **ARTIST:** D. Sutphen **TOPIC:** Past Life Regression, $39.95

Pastel Shades
PUBLISHING COMPANY: Crystal Cave Enterprises **ARTIST:** Jacinta Wright **TOPIC:** Meditation, $10.95

Pastels
PUBLISHING COMPANY: Vital Body Marketing Co., Inc. **ARTIST:** G. Kelley **TOPIC:** New Age, $9.95

Path Of Compassion
PUBLISHING COMPANY: Theosophical University Press **ARTIST:** G. De Purucker **TOPIC:** Spirituality, $12.00

Path To Vibrant Health: The Power Of Positive Wholeness
PUBLISHING COMPANY: Summit University Press **ARTIST:** Bernard Jensen **TOPIC:** Holistic Healing, $12.95

Peace Album
PUBLISHING COMPANY: Kuckuck Records **ARTIST:** P. Horn **TOPIC:** Meditation, $10.98

Peace Of God: Poems By Helen Schucman With Music
PUBLISHING COMPANY: Riverrun Press **ARTIST:** H. Schucman **ARTIST:** Read by Michele R. Wamhouse **TOPIC:** Spirituality, $10.00

Peace Of God: Readings From A Course In Miracles
PUBLISHING COMPANY: Betty W. Sprague **ARTIST:** B. Sprague, D. Sherman **TOPIC:** Spirituality, $10.00

Peace Of Mind
PUBLISHING COMPANY: Valley of the Sun **ARTIST:** D. Stuphen **TOPIC:** Hypnotism, $9.98

Peace, Love And Healing: The Bodymind & The Path To Self-Healing -- An Exploration
PUBLISHING COMPANY: Caedmon **ARTIST:** Bernie Siegel **TOPIC:** Body-Mind Connection, Holistic Healing, $15.95

Peaceful Evening
PUBLISHING COMPANY: Vital Body Marketing Co., Inc. **ARTIST:** D. Gordon, S. Gordon **TOPIC:** New Age, $9.95

Peak Performance: Winner's Guide For Making That Quantum Leap To The Top
PUBLISHING COMPANY: NCC **ARTIST:** C. Garfield **TOPIC:** Body-Mind Connection, $14.95

Perfect Weight, Perfect Body
PUBLISHING COMPANY: Valley of the Sun **ARTIST:** D. Sutphen **TOPIC:** Hypnotism, $10.98

Permission To Grieve: Working Through Loss With Love, Patience & Compassion
PUBLISHING COMPANY: Sounds True Record. & Dupl. **ARTIST:** Claudia Helade **TOPIC:** Death, $9.95

Personal And Spiritual Development
PUBLISHING COMPANY: Thinking Allowed Prod. **ARTIST:** I. Tweedie **ARTIST:** et.al. **TOPIC:** Spirituality, $69.95

Personal Massage For Health And Relaxation
PUBLISHING COMPANY: Herbert Shapiro, Jr. Mst. **ARTIST:** H. Shapiro **TOPIC:** Massage, $29.95

Personal Power
PUBLISHING COMPANY: Valley of the Sun **ARTIST:** D. Sutphen **TOPIC:** Hypnotism, $18.98

Perspectives On Healing
PUBLISHING COMPANY: Thinking Allowed Prod. **ARTIST:** S. Krippner **ARTIST:** et.al. **TOPIC:** Holistic Healing, $69.95

Petals
PUBLISHING COMPANY: Rising Sun Records **ARTIST:** Marcus Allen, J. Bernoff **TOPIC:** Meditation, $16.98

Photographer
PUBLISHING COMPANY: CBS Records **ARTIST:** Phillip Glass **TOPIC:** Meditation, $10.98

Piano Means Soft
PUBLISHING COMPANY: Vital Body Marketing Co., Inc. **ARTIST:** C. Thweatt **TOPIC:** New Age, $9.95

Piano Meditation
PUBLISHING COMPANY: Vital Body Marketing Co., Inc. **ARTIST:** J. Oliver **TOPIC:** New Age, $9.95

Piano Reflections
PUBLISHING COMPANY: Channel Productions **ARTIST:** K. Yost **TOPIC:** Meditation, $15.98

Pianoscapes
PUBLISHING COMPANY: Narada Productions **ARTIST:** Michael Jones **TOPIC:** Meditation, $16.98

Planetary Energies
PUBLISHING COMPANY: Llewellyn Worldwide, Ltd. **ARTIST:** I. Hickey **TOPIC:** Astrology, $7.95

Planetary Unfolding
PUBLISHING COMPANY: Sonic Atmospheres **ARTIST:** M. Sterns **TOPIC:** Meditation, $20.00

Planets, 1 & 2
PUBLISHING COMPANY: Video Lecture Series **ARTIST:** Johanna Mitchell **TOPIC:** Astrology, $39.95

Playhouse On The Beach
PUBLISHING COMPANY: Living Sound Productions **ARTIST:** Living Sound Productions **TOPIC:** Meditation, $14.98

Positive Day Programming
PUBLISHING COMPANY: Valley of the Sun **ARTIST:** D. Sutphen **TOPIC:** Hypnotism, $10.00

Positive Thinking Programming
PUBLISHING COMPANY: Valley of the Sun **ARTIST:** D. Sutphen **TOPIC:** Body-Mind Connection, $19.95

Positively Yoga
PUBLISHING COMPANY: Hay House **ARTIST:** J. Gagner **TOPIC:** Meditation, $11.95

Power Affirmations For Unlimited Prosperity
PUBLISHING COMPANY: H. H. Productions **ARTIST:** H. Hartly **TOPIC:** Meditation, $9.98

Power Of Affirmations
PUBLISHING COMPANY: Mircles Publishing Co. **ARTIST:** J. Fankhauser **TOPIC:** Meditation, $10.00

Power Of Attention
PUBLISHING COMPANY: Life Action Press **ARTIST:** T. Singh **TOPIC:** Spirituality, $29.95

Power Of Positive Thinking Plus Believe And Succeed
PUBLISHING COMPANY: Simon & Schuster Audio **ARTIST:** N.V. Peale **TOPIC:** Body-Mind Connection, $59.95

Power Of The Mantra
PUBLISHING COMPANY: S.Y.D.A. Foundations **ARTIST:** Gurumayi Chidvilasananda **TOPIC:** Spirituality, $15.00

Power To Come To Decision
PUBLISHING COMPANY: Life Action Press **ARTIST:** T. Singh **TOPIC:** Spirituality, $17.95

Practical Wisdom I
PUBLISHING COMPANY: Channel Light Productions **ARTIST:** Lynn Andrews **TOPIC:** Spirituality, $10.95

Practical Wisdom II
PUBLISHING COMPANY: Channel Light Productions **ARTIST:** Lynn Andrews **TOPIC:** Spirituality, $10.95

Prayer And Forgiveness
PUBLISHING COMPANY: Life Action Press **ARTIST:** T. Singh **TOPIC:** Spirituality, $17.95

Predictions '89: Journey To Inspiration

PUBLISHING COMPANY: Video Lecture Series **ARTIST:** M. Lutin, G. Star **ARTIST:** et.al. **TOPIC:** Astrology, $24.95

Predictions '90: The Path Within
PUBLISHING COMPANY: Herb Hochman Prod. **ARTIST:** American Astrology **TOPIC:** Astrology, $29.95

Professional Hypnotism Training Program
PUBLISHING COMPANY: Panorama Publishing Co. **ARTIST:** J. Kappas **TOPIC:** Hypnotism, $295.00

Program For Better Vision
PUBLISHING COMPANY: Cambridge Inst. Better Vision **ARTIST:** M. Sussman **TOPIC:** Meditation, $49.00

Progression
PUBLISHING COMPANY: Dr. Bruce Goldberg **ARTIST:** Bruce Goldberg **TOPIC:** Meditation, $12.00

Progressive Relaxation
PUBLISHING COMPANY: I.S.H.K. **ARTIST:** E. Jacobson, F. J. McGuigan **TOPIC:** Holistic Health, $54.95

Progressive Relaxation And Breathing
PUBLISHING COMPANY: New Harbinger Publications **ARTIST:** M. McKay, P. Fanning **TOPIC:** Meditation, $10.95

Prosperity
PUBLISHING COMPANY: Steppingstones **ARTIST:** R. Jafolla, M. Jafolla **TOPIC:** Hypnotism, $12.95

Prosperity Is Yours
PUBLISHING COMPANY: A. R. E. Press **ARTIST:** A.R.E. **TOPIC:** Meditation, $9.95

Psychic And Spiritual Unfoldment
PUBLISHING COMPANY: Spiritual Science Fellowship **ARTIST:** M. Rossner **TOPIC:** Psychic, $9.95

Psychic Connection
PUBLISHING COMPANY: Postscript Productions **ARTIST:** Postscript Productions **TOPIC:** Psychic, $59.95

Psychic Discoveries Behind The Iron Curtain
PUBLISHING COMPANY: Audio Renaissance Tapes **ARTIST:** S. Ostrander, L. Schroeder **TOPIC:** ESP, $9.95

Psychic Dreaming: How To Prepare For, Send, Receive & Interpret Telepathic Dreams
PUBLISHING COMPANY: Audio Renaissance Tapes **ARTIST:** R. Van De Castle **TOPIC:** Dreams, $9.95

Psychic Factors Affecting Health With Clairvoyant Medical Diagnosis
PUBLISHING COMPANY: Theosophical Pub. **ARTIST:** G. Hodson, L. Bendit **TOPIC:** Psychic Healing, $14.95

Psychic Healing
PUBLISHING COMPANY: Potentials Unlimited **ARTIST:** Potentials Unlimited **TOPIC:** New Age, $9.98

Psychic Powers Programming
PUBLISHING COMPANY: Valley of the Sun **ARTIST:** D. Sutphen **TOPIC:** Hypnotism, $32.95

Psychic Protection
PUBLISHING COMPANY: Potentials Unlimited **ARTIST:** Potentials Unlimited **TOPIC:** New Age, $9.98

Psychics, Saints And Mystics
PUBLISHING COMPANY: Hartley Film Foundation **ARTIST:** Hartley Film Foundation **TOPIC:** Spirituality, $89.00

Psycho-Cybernetics
PUBLISHING COMPANY: Audio Renaissance Tapes **ARTIST:** M. Maltz **TOPIC:** Body-Mind Connection, $15.95

Psychodynamics Of Liberation
PUBLISHING COMPANY: Thinking Allowed Prod. **ARTIST:** K. Speeth **TOPIC:** Psychology, $49.95

Psychoimmunity
PUBLISHING COMPANY: Acoustic Brain Research **ARTIST:** Acoustic Brain Research **TOPIC:** Body-Mind Connection, $99.95

Psychological And Spiritual Blindspots
PUBLISHING COMPANY: Thinking Allowed Prod. **ARTIST:** P. Sun **TOPIC:** Psychology, $29.95

Pyramids And The Ark Of The Covenant
PUBLISHING COMPANY: Audio Renaissance Tapes **ARTIST:** T. Hudz **TOPIC:** New Age, $9.95

Question And The Holy Instant: Part 1 Of Nothing Real Can Be Threatened Cim Workshop
PUBLISHING COMPANY: Life Action Press **ARTIST:** T. Singh **TOPIC:** Spirituality, $29.95

Quick Thinking
PUBLISHING COMPANY: Valley of the Sun **ARTIST:** D. Sutphen **TOPIC:** Body-Mind Connection, $19.95

Quiet Heart
PUBLISHING COMPANY: Vital Body Marketing Co., Inc. **ARTIST:** R. Warner **TOPIC:** New Age, $9.95

Quiet Movements: Harp Improvisations For Listening, Massage & Relaxation
PUBLISHING COMPANY: Journey Tapes **ARTIST:** B. Kurnow **TOPIC:** Meditation, $10.98

Quiet Water
PUBLISHING COMPANY: Crystal Cave Enterprises **ARTIST:** Paul Fitzgerald, M. Flanagan **TOPIC:** Meditation, $10.95

Quit Smoking
PUBLISHING COMPANY: White Dove Int'l., Inc. **ARTIST:** S. Wilde **TOPIC:** Hypnotism, $11.95

Radiance: Love Songs Without Words
PUBLISHING COMPANY: Steven Halpern **ARTIST:** S. Halpern **TOPIC:** Meditation, $17.98

Radiant Health And A Strong Immune System
PUBLISHING COMPANY: Valley of the Sun **ARTIST:** D. Stuphen **TOPIC:** Hypnotism, $9.95

Rainbow Butterfly
PUBLISHING COMPANY: Heru Records **ARTIST:** E. Miller, G. Kelly **TOPIC:** Meditation, $10.98

Rainbow Path
PUBLISHING COMPANY: Vital Body Marketing Co., Inc. **ARTIST:** K. Gardner **TOPIC:** New Age, $9.95

Rainforest
PUBLISHING COMPANY: Hearts of Space **ARTIST:** R. Rich **TOPIC:** Meditation, $17.98

Rajneesh No-Mind Meditation: Being In The Presence Of A Living Buddha
PUBLISHING COMPANY: Chidvilas **ARTIST:** B. Rajneesh **TOPIC:** Spirituality, $9.95

Rapid Pain Control
PUBLISHING COMPANY: Changeworks **ARTIST:** C. Erickson, T. Condon **TOPIC:** Meditation, $12.95

Rapture Of Being
PUBLISHING COMPANY: Thinking Allowed Prod. **ARTIST:** Pir Vilayat Khan **TOPIC:** Meditation, $49.95

Reading The Horoscope
PUBLISHING COMPANY: Llewellyn Worldwide, Ltd. **ARTIST:** I. Hickey **TOPIC:** Astrology, $7.95

Real Environments, Real People
PUBLISHING COMPANY: Reflections **ARTIST:** Star Sounds **TOPIC:** Hypnotism, $14.95

Reawakening Ancestral Memory: Through The Veil Between The Worlds
PUBLISHING COMPANY: T. A. Helliwell Publications **ARTIST:** T. Helliwell **TOPIC:** Reincarnation, $9.95

Rebirth Of The Goddess
PUBLISHING COMPANY: Circle Publications **ARTIST:** Starhawk **TOPIC:** Witchcraft, Spirituality, $10.00

Reclaiming Our Past, Recreating Our Future: Reflections On The Chalice & The Blade
PUBLISHING COMPANY: Thinking Allowed Prod. **ARTIST:** R. Eisler **TOPIC:** Spirituality, $49.95

Reclaiming Your Feminine Authority I & II
PUBLISHING COMPANY: Sound True Record. & Dupl. **ARTIST:** Clara Barker **TOPIC:** Spirituality, $18.95

Reflecting Light Vol. 1
PUBLISHING COMPANY: Beyond **ARTIST:** S. Doucet **TOPIC:** Meditation, $12.98

Reflecting Light Vol. 2
PUBLISHING COMPANY: Beyond **ARTIST:** S. Doucet **TOPIC:** Meditation, $12.98

Reflections Experience: An Introduction
PUBLISHING COMPANY: Reflections ARTIST: Star Sounds TOPIC: Hypnotism, $14.95

Regressing Into The Past, Projecting Into The Future
PUBLISHING COMPANY: Blue Dolphin Publishing - 2 ARTIST: H. Wambach TOPIC: Past Life Regression, $10.00

Reincarnation (Includes Reincarnation In Christianity & Reincarnation Explored
PUBLISHING COMPANY: Theosophical Pub. ARTIST: G. MacGregor, J. Algeo TOPIC: Reincarnation, $14.95

Reincarnation And Past Lives
PUBLISHING COMPANY: Audio Renaissance Tapes ARTIST: E. Cayce ARTIST: Read by Stanley Ross TOPIC: Channeling, $9.95

Reincarnation And The Astrological Chart
PUBLISHING COMPANY: Llewellyn Worldwide, Ltd. ARTIST: I. Hickey TOPIC: Astrology, $7.95

Reincarnation, Karma And Heredity
PUBLISHING COMPANY: Thoth Publications ARTIST: M. Hope TOPIC: Reincarnation, $9.95

Reincarnation: Claiming Your Past, Creating Your Future Through Exploring Past Lives
PUBLISHING COMPANY: Harper & Row Publishers ARTIST: L. Sparrow TOPIC: Channeling, $9.95

Reincarnation: The Untrue Fact
PUBLISHING COMPANY: Theosophical Pub. ARTIST: J. Algeo TOPIC: Reincarnation, $21.95

Relax With Dennis Weaver
PUBLISHING COMPANY: Capstone Media ARTIST: Dennis Weaver TOPIC: Meditation, $29.95

Relax With Yoga During Pregnancy
PUBLISHING COMPANY: Rudra Press ARTIST: L. Goldstein TOPIC: Yoga, $11.95

Relaxation
PUBLISHING COMPANY: Potentials Unlimited ARTIST: Potentials Unlimited TOPIC: New Age, $9.98

Relaxation By The Sea
PUBLISHING COMPANY: Vital Body Marketing Co., Inc. ARTIST: Robert Sohn TOPIC: New Age, $9.95

Relaxation Training
PUBLISHING COMPANY: I.S.H.K. ARTIST: T. Budzynski TOPIC: Holistic Health, $39.95

Relaxation, Affirmations, Letting Go: Guided Meditations
PUBLISHING COMPANY: Ellie Janow ARTIST: E. Janow, Max Nass TOPIC: Meditation, $9.95

Relaxation/Affirmation Techniques
PUBLISHING COMPANY: Synergistic Systems ARTIST: N. Hopps TOPIC: Meditation, $11.00

Release Of Fears And Insecurities: New World Subliminal
PUBLISHING COMPANY: New World Products, Ltd. ARTIST: Y. Bhajan TOPIC: Hypnotism, $14.95

Release Your Breath: Expand Your Capacity To Celebrate Life
PUBLISHING COMPANY: Wonder-Full Day Prod. ARTIST: L. Sereda TOPIC: Meditation, $12.95

Releasing And Completing
PUBLISHING COMPANY: Reflections ARTIST: Star Sounds TOPIC: Hypnotism, $14.95

Relieve Stress And Anxiety
PUBLISHING COMPANY: Potentials Unlimited ARTIST: Potentials Unlimited TOPIC: New Age, $9.98

Remembering Egypt
PUBLISHING COMPANY: A.R.E. Press TOPIC: Past Life Regression, $39.95

Remembering--Your True Home And Present Mission
PUBLISHING COMPANY: Deer Productions Unlimited ARTIST: L. Domnitz TOPIC: Hypnotism, $10.00

Remembranza
PUBLISHING COMPANY: Windham Hill Records ARTIST: M. Lorimer TOPIC: Meditation, $11.98

Removing The Blocks To The Awareness Of Love's Presence
PUBLISHING COMPANY: Life Action Press ARTIST: T. Singh TOPIC: Spirituality, $17.95

Requiem For A Faith
PUBLISHING COMPANY: Hartley Film Foundation ARTIST: Huston Smith TOPIC: Spirituality, $89.00

Responsibility In A Chaotic World
PUBLISHING COMPANY: Harper & Row Publishers ARTIST: J. Krishnamurti TOPIC: Spirituality, $9.95

Rest, Relax, And Sleep
PUBLISHING COMPANY: Lillas Folan ARTIST: L. Folan TOPIC: Dreams, $11.98

Restful Revitalizing Sleep
PUBLISHING COMPANY: Effective Learnings Systems, Inc. ARTIST: Love Tapes TOPIC: Hypnotism, $11.98

Restive Woman/Universal Child
PUBLISHING COMPANY: Oliver Music ARTIST: J. Oliver TOPIC: Meditation, $11.98

Return Of The Goddess For The New Millenium
PUBLISHING COMPANY: U-Read/U-Music ARTIST: P. Silkey, J. Miller TOPIC: Spirituality, $29.95

Richard Hittleman's Yoga Video 1
PUBLISHING COMPANY: Clear Lake Productions ARTIST: R. Hittleman TOPIC: Yoga, $39.95

Richard Hittleman's Yoga Video 2
PUBLISHING COMPANY: Clear Lake Productions ARTIST: R. Hittleman TOPIC: Yoga, $39.95

Riches And Honor: White Magic Technqiues & Incantations
PUBLISHING COMPANY: Valley of the Sun ARTIST: D. Sutphen TOPIC: Occult, $12.50

Riddle Of The Sphinx
PUBLISHING COMPANY: Narada Productions ARTIST: M. Genest TOPIC: Meditation, $16.98

Right Brain Super Charge: An Explanation
PUBLISHING COMPANY: Reflections ARTIST: Star Sounds TOPIC: Hypnotism, $14.95

Right-Brain Experience
PUBLISHING COMPANY: Audio Renaissance Tapes ARTIST: M. Zdenek TOPIC: Body-Mind Connection, $15.95

Right-Brain Solutions: Programming To Find Creative Answers Within
PUBLISHING COMPANY: Valley of the Sun ARTIST: D. Stuphen TOPIC: Hypnotism, $10.98

Rivers Gonna Rise
PUBLISHING COMPANY: Private Music ARTIST: P. O'Hearn TOPIC: Meditation, $10.50

Rlike: Selected Poems
PUBLISHING COMPANY: Audio Literature, Inc. ARTIST: Stephen Mitchell ARTIST: Read by Stephen Mitchell TOPIC: Occult, $15.95

Road Less Traveled Tape Set
PUBLISHING COMPANY: Simon & Schuster Audio ARTIST: M.Scott Peck TOPIC: Psychology, $59.95

Royal Path Of Tarot
PUBLISHING COMPANY: Lorn Media Productions ARTIST: Jim Murphy TOPIC: Tarot, $24.95

Roots Of Consciousness
PUBLISHING COMPANY: Thinking Allowed Prod. ARTIST: J. Campbell ARTIST: et.al. TOPIC: Psychology, $69.95

Rose For You, The Buddha To Be: Songs Of Thich Nhat Hanh
PUBLISHING COMPANY: Medicine Song Productions ARTIST: Sister Phuong, Rashani, et.al. TOPIC: Spirituality, $10.00

Rosewood And Silver
PUBLISHING COMPANY: Vital Body Marketing Co., Inc. ARTIST: V. Koenig, W. Weisbach TOPIC: New Age, $9.95

Rush Hour Refresher
PUBLISHING COMPANY: Enchanced Audio Systems ARTIST: M. Gach TOPIC: Acupuncture, $9.98

Rythmetiques: How To Become All You Were Meant To Be
PUBLISHING COMPANY: Broadway Book Company ARTIST: M. C. Gallo TOPIC: Metaphysics, $16.95

S.H.A.R.E.: Self Healing Aids Related Experiment
PUBLISHING COMPANY: Brotherhood Press ARTIST: W. Garcia, G. Melton TOPIC: Psychic Healing, $10.00

Sacred Space Music
PUBLISHING COMPANY: Spirit Music ARTIST: C. Demby TOPIC: Meditation, $9.98

Sacred Trances In Bali And Java
PUBLISHING COMPANY: Hartley Film Foundation ARTIST: Hartley Film Foundation TOPIC: Spirituality, $89.00

Safety In Numbers
PUBLISHING COMPANY: Private Music ARTIST: D. Van Tieghem TOPIC: Meditation, $11.98

Sai Baba Birthday Party
PUBLISHING COMPANY: Janet Bock ARTIST: R. Bock TOPIC: Spirituality, $25.00

Sangoma
PUBLISHING COMPANY: Warner/Elektra/Atlant Corp. ARTIST: M. Maleba TOPIC: Spirituality, $10.98

Sathya Sai Baba: An Introduction
PUBLISHING COMPANY: Janet Bock ARTIST: R. Bock TOPIC: Spirituality, $25.00

Sathya Sai Baba: Aura Of Divinity
PUBLISHING COMPANY: Janet Bock ARTIST: R. Bock TOPIC: Spirituality, $35.00

Sathya Sai Baba: In The Light Of Prophecy
PUBLISHING COMPANY: Janet Bock ARTIST: R. Bock TOPIC: Spirituality, $35.00

Sathya Sai Baba: The Universal Teacher
PUBLISHING COMPANY: Janet Bock ARTIST: R. Bock TOPIC: Spirituality, $45.00

Saturn/Uranus Conjunction
PUBLISHING COMPANY: RKM Publishing ARTIST: R. Myers TOPIC: Astrology, $8.95

Say Goodbye To Back Pain
PUBLISHING COMPANY: Healing Arts Home Video ARTIST: A. Melleby TOPIC: Holistic Healing, $39.95

Science And Spiritual Tradition
PUBLISHING COMPANY: Thinking Allowed Prod. ARTIST: C. Tart TOPIC: New Age, $29.95

Science And The Spirit
PUBLISHING COMPANY: Thinking Allowed Prod. ARTIST: C. Tart ARTIST: ET.AL. TOPIC: New Age, $69.95

Science Of Happiness
PUBLISHING COMPANY: Ken Keyes College Bookroom ARTIST: Ken Keyes TOPIC: Spirituality, $17.00

Sea And Sky
PUBLISHING COMPANY: Celestial Harmonies ARTIST: S. Yamashta TOPIC: Meditation, $11.98

Seapeace
PUBLISHING COMPANY: Gothic Image Publications ARTIST: G. Kelly TOPIC: Meditation, $10.98

Seascapes
PUBLISHING COMPANY: Music Designs ARTIST: Micheal Jones TOPIC: Meditation, $16.00

Second Nature
PUBLISHING COMPANY: Vital Body Marketing Co., Inc. ARTIST: Allandin Mathieu TOPIC: New Age, $9.95

Secret Dreams
PUBLISHING COMPANY: Gold Castle Records ARTIST: Micheal Rubini TOPIC: Meditation, $10.98

Secret Luminescence
PUBLISHING COMPANY: Private Music ARTIST: L. Hwong TOPIC: Meditation, $11.98

Secrets Of The Tarot Vol. 1: Beginning
PUBLISHING COMPANY: Visionary Video Productions ARTIST: L Clarson TOPIC: Tarot, $39.95

Secrets Of The Tarot Vol. 2: Intermediate
PUBLISHING COMPANY: Visionary Video Productions ARTIST: L Clarson TOPIC: Tarot, $29.95

Secrets Of The Tarot Vol. 3: Advanced
PUBLISHING COMPANY: Visionary Video Productions ARTIST: L Clarson TOPIC: Tarot, $29.95

See Yourself Succeed: Top Performance Through Mental Imagery
PUBLISHING COMPANY: Nightingale Conant Corp. ARTIST: E. Miller TOPIC: Meditation, $8.95

Self Esteem: New World Subliminal
PUBLISHING COMPANY: New World Products, Ltd. ARTIST: Y. Bhajan TOPIC: Hypnotism, $14.95

Self Forgiveness: Healing Meditation
PUBLISHING COMPANY: Sacred Mysteries ARTIST: Rama TOPIC: Meditation, $11.50

Self Healing
PUBLISHING COMPANY: Hay House ARTIST: Louise Hay TOPIC: Psychic Healing, $10.00

Self Healing And Loving Yourself
PUBLISHING COMPANY: Hay House ARTIST: Louise Hay TOPIC: Meditation, $18.00

Self Hypnosis
PUBLISHING COMPANY: New Harbinger Publications ARTIST: M. McKay, P. Fanning TOPIC: Hypnotism, $10.00

Self Hypnosis For Reducing Your Stress
PUBLISHING COMPANY: Changeworks ARTIST: C. Erickson, T. Condon TOPIC: Hypnotism, $12.95

Self Love: Healing Tones Meditation
PUBLISHING COMPANY: Sacred Mysteries ARTIST: Rama TOPIC: Meditation, $11.50

Self Trust: Healing Tones Meditation
PUBLISHING COMPANY: Sacred Mysteries ARTIST: Rama TOPIC: Meditation, $11.50

Self-Confidence

PUBLISHING COMPANY: Potentials Unlimited ARTIST: Potentials Unlimited TOPIC: New Age, $9.98

Self-Creation Guided Meditations
PUBLISHING COMPANY: Valley of the Sun ARTIST: D. Stuphen TOPIC: Meditation, $18.98

Self-Healing
PUBLISHING COMPANY: Potentials Unlimited ARTIST: Potentials Unlimited TOPIC: New Age, $9.98

Self-Healing Affirmations
PUBLISHING COMPANY: Light of Mind ARTIST: S. Gordon, D. Gordon TOPIC: Meditation, $14.95

Self-Healing And Rejuvenation
PUBLISHING COMPANY: Audio Rennaisance Tapes ARTIST: Jonathan Parker TOPIC: Hypnotism, $9.95

Self-Hypnosis
PUBLISHING COMPANY: Potentials Unlimited ARTIST: Potentials Unlimited TOPIC: New Age, $9.98

Self-Hypnosis For Reducing Your Stress
PUBLISHING COMPANY: Changeworks ARTIST: C. Erickson, T. Condon TOPIC: Meditation, $12.95

Self-Hypnosis: Discover The Principles & Techniques Of Personal Change
PUBLISHING COMPANY: Audio Renaissance Tapes ARTIST: E. Cayce TOPIC: Channeling, $9.95

Self-Image: Claiming Your Power
PUBLISHING COMPANY: Luramedia ARTIST: L.J. Geiger, A.M. Geiger TOPIC: Meditation, $34.50

Self-Observation
PUBLISHING COMPANY: Thinking Allowed Prod. ARTIST: C. Hart TOPIC: Psychology, $29.95

Selling You! A Practical Guide To Achieving The Most By Becoming Your Best
PUBLISHING COMPANY: Audio Renaissance Tapes ARTIST: N. Hill TOPIC: Body-Mind Connection, $15.95

Sensual Massage For Couples
PUBLISHING COMPANY: Contemporary Image Media ARTIST: D. Greenwood TOPIC: Massage, $39.95

Serenity
PUBLISHING COMPANY: Hopkins, Marge V./Ayamaya ARTIST: Ayamaya Relaxation Series TOPIC: Meditation, $11.95

Set Free
PUBLISHING COMPANY: Hearts of Space ARTIST: C. Demby TOPIC: Meditation, $17.98

Seth Video
PUBLISHING COMPANY: Kendall, Inc. ARTIST: Jane Roberts TOPIC: Channeling, $54.95

Sexual Enchancement: Express Feelings And Enjoy

PUBLISHING COMPANY: BFS Limited ARTIST: Bright Images TOPIC: Hypnotism, $11.95

Shaka Zulu

PUBLISHING COMPANY: Warner/Elektra/Atlant Corp. ARTIST: L. Mambazo TOPIC: Spirituality, $10.98

Shamanic Dream

PUBLISHING COMPANY: Chidvilas ARTIST: Spiritual Environments - music by Anugama TOPIC: Meditation, $11.95

Shamans And Other Mystics

PUBLISHING COMPANY: Infinity Tapes - Blue Dolphin ARTIST: J. Halifax, G. Luce TOPIC: Occult, $10.00

Shambhala: The Sacred Path Of The Warrior

PUBLISHING COMPANY: Shambhala Publications ARTIST: C. Trungpa TOPIC: Spirituality, $14.95

Shanta Channels Restaban On Fear And Self Love

PUBLISHING COMPANY: Storywiz Records & Services ARTIST: Shanta TOPIC: Channeling, $10.00

Sharpen Your Learning Skills: Comprehend And Retain Information

PUBLISHING COMPANY: BFS Limited ARTIST: Bright Images TOPIC: Hypnotism, $11.95

She: Understanding Feminine Psychology

PUBLISHING COMPANY: Audio Renaissance Tapes ARTIST: Robert A. Johnson TOPIC: Psychology, $9.95

Showing Love: Loving, Giving And Caring

PUBLISHING COMPANY: BFS Limited ARTIST: Bright Images TOPIC: Hypnotism, $11.95

Sights And Sounds Of A New Age

PUBLISHING COMPANY: Bobkat Productions ARTIST: Emerald Web TOPIC: New Age, $29.98

Silence Is A Wondrous Thing

PUBLISHING COMPANY: Life Action Press ARTIST: T. Singh TOPIC: Spirituality, $17.95

Silence Is The Answer

PUBLISHING COMPANY: Celestial Harmonies ARTIST: Deuter TOPIC: Meditation, $15.98

Silent Joy

PUBLISHING COMPANY: Chidvilas ARTIST: Anugama TOPIC: Meditation, $11.95

Silent Motivators: Helping You Do Your Best Work

PUBLISHING COMPANY: Light of Mind ARTIST: D. Gordon, S. Gordon TOPIC: Hypnotism, $14.95

Sililoquy

PUBLISHING COMPANY: Windham Hill Records ARTIST: D. Qualey TOPIC: Meditation, $11.98

Silver Tree

PUBLISHING COMPANY: Fonix Musik ARTIST: Christian TOPIC: Meditation, $10.98

Singing Journey For Shamanic Voyaging

PUBLISHING COMPANY: Fdn. Shamanic Studies ARTIST: M. Harner TOPIC: Meditation, $10.98

Singing Joy To The Earth

PUBLISHING COMPANY: Medicine Eagle/Harmony N/W ARTIST: Brooke Medicine Eagle TOPIC: Spirituality, $10.00

Six Healing Sounds

PUBLISHING COMPANY: Healing Tao Books ARTIST: M. Chia TOPIC: Holistic Health, $9.95

Sixty Minutes To Unlocking Your Intuition

PUBLISHING COMPANY: Audio Renaissance Tapes ARTIST: P. Goldberg TOPIC: Psychic, $9.95

Sky Dance

PUBLISHING COMPANY: Earthsong Productions ARTIST: Anne Williams TOPIC: Meditation, $10.98

Sky Of Mind

PUBLISHING COMPANY: Music West Records ARTIST: R. Lynch TOPIC: Meditation, $17.50

Skys Beyond

PUBLISHING COMPANY: Chidvilas ARTIST: Karunesh TOPIC: Meditation, $11.95

Skywings

PUBLISHING COMPANY: Heart Music ARTIST: Akasha TOPIC: Spirituality, $10.00

Sleep Soundly

PUBLISHING COMPANY: Soundwaves 2000 ARTIST: S. Halpern TOPIC: Hypnotism, $10.98

Sleeping Easy

PUBLISHING COMPANY: Nightingale Conant Corp. ARTIST: E. Miller TOPIC: Dreams, $8.95

Slow Circle

PUBLISHING COMPANY: Windham Hill Records ARTIST: A. DeGrassi TOPIC: Meditation, $11.98

Slumberland

PUBLISHING COMPANY: Vital Body Marketing Co., Inc. ARTIST: S. Bergman TOPIC: New Age, $9.95

Smart Way To Relax

PUBLISHING COMPANY: Rudra Press ARTIST: Arlin Brown TOPIC: Holistic Health, $15.95

Smoke No More

PUBLISHING COMPANY: Source Cassettes ARTIST: E. Miller TOPIC: Hypnotism, $15.95

Solid Colors

PUBLISHING COMPANY: Windham Hill Records ARTIST: L. Story TOPIC: Meditation, $11.98

Solitudes, Episode I: Loon Country By Canoe

PUBLISHING COMPANY: Moss Music Group, Inc. ARTIST: Dan Gibson TOPIC: New Age, $25.98

Solitudes, Episode II: Wave Watching

PUBLISHING COMPANY: Moss Music Group, Inc. ARTIST: Dan Gibson, G. Gibson TOPIC: New Age, $25.98

Solomon: Universal Consciousness

PUBLISHING COMPANY: Arizona Metaphysical Society ARTIST: F. Alper TOPIC: Spirituality, $10.00

Solstice

PUBLISHING COMPANY: Narada Productions ARTIST: D. Lanz, M. Jones TOPIC: Meditation, $16.98

Songs Of Affirmation: Chants & Meditations

PUBLISHING COMPANY: Hay House ARTIST: Louise Hay, J. Leeds TOPIC: Spirituality, $10.00

Songs Of Affirmation Vol. 2: Chants & Meditations

PUBLISHING COMPANY: Hay House ARTIST: Louise Hay, J. Leeds TOPIC: Meditation, $10.00

Songs Of Goddess

PUBLISHING COMPANY: Grace & Goddess Unlimited ARTIST: C. Grace, L. Glenn TOPIC: Spirituality, $10.00

Songs Of Pagan Folk

PUBLISHING COMPANY: Circle Publications ARTIST: J. Alan, S. Fox ARTIST: Et.Al. TOPIC: Spirituality, $10.00

Soothing Lullabies

PUBLISHING COMPANY: Gothic Image Publications ARTIST: S. Bergman TOPIC: Meditation, $29.98

Sorcery And White Magic: Discover The Power Of Charms Spells & Talismans

PUBLISHING COMPANY: Audio Renaissance Tapes ARTIST: T. Hudz TOPIC: Occult, $9.95

Soul Journeys II: Guided Meditations

PUBLISHING COMPANY: Four Trees Publications ARTIST: R. Metzner TOPIC: Meditation, $10.50

Soul-Purpose: Discovering & Fulfilling Your Destiny

PUBLISHING COMPANY: Harper & Row Audio ARTIST: M. Thurston TOPIC: Channeling, $9.95

Soulmates

PUBLISHING COMPANY: Valley of the Sun ARTIST: D. Stuphen TOPIC: Hypnotism, $18.98

Sound And Crystal Workshop

PUBLISHING COMPANY: Crystal Network Fndt. ARTIST: R. Wyrsch ARTIST: Laraji & Vina TOPIC: Crystals, $13.00

Sound Of Rippling Water: Constructive Living Through Morita & Naikan Therapies

PUBLISHING COMPANY: Music & Sound Prod. Svcs. ARTIST: David K. Reynolds TOPIC: Psychology, $15.00

Sound Of Spirit

PUBLISHING COMPANY: Heru Records ARTIST: G. Kelly TOPIC: Meditation, $10.98

Sparkle Strings

PUBLISHING COMPANY: Vital Body Marketing Co., Inc. ARTIST: B. Desmond TOPIC: New Age, $9.95

Spectrum Color Consciousness
PUBLISHING COMPANY: Golden Rose Productions
ARTIST: A. Lowrie TOPIC: Color Therapy, $10.98

Spectrum Suite
PUBLISHING COMPANY: Steven Halpern ARTIST:
S. Halpern TOPIC: Meditation, $12.98

Spiral Dance: A Rebirth Of The Ancient Religion Of The Great Godess
PUBLISHING COMPANY: Harper & Row Audio
ARTIST: Starhawk TOPIC: Witchcraft, $9.95

Spirit Am I
PUBLISHING COMPANY: Hay House ARTIST: J.
Inae, B. Rogosich TOPIC: Spirituality, $10.00

Spirit Guides: Communicating With Your Unseen Friends
PUBLISHING COMPANY: Silver Forest Publishing
ARTIST: V. Young TOPIC: Channeling, $18.95

Spirit Of Love: A Bouquet Of Inspiriing Songs
PUBLISHING COMPANY: Awakening Heart Prod.
ARTIST: Various Artists TOPIC: Spirituality, $10.00

Spiritual Astrology
PUBLISHING COMPANY: Crystal Clarity ARTIST:
Kriyananda (Swami) TOPIC: Astrology, $8.95

Spiritual Channeling
PUBLISHING COMPANY: Mayflower B/S ARTIST:
Robert Thibodeau TOPIC: Channeling, $49.95

Spiritual Empowerment
PUBLISHING COMPANY: Light of Mind ARTIST: S.
Gordon, D. Gordon TOPIC: Meditation, $14.95

Spiritual Fitness
PUBLISHING COMPANY: Stillpoint Publishing
ARTIST: Meredith Young TOPIC: Spirituality, $89.95

Spiritual Healing
PUBLISHING COMPANY: Blue Dolphin Publishing -
2 ARTIST: B. Rubik, G. Luce TOPIC: Psychic Healing, $10.00

Spiritual Healing: Healing Ray From A Higher Power
PUBLISHING COMPANY: White Dove Int'l., Inc.
ARTIST: S. Wilde TOPIC: Hypnotism, $11.95

Spiritual Psychology
PUBLISHING COMPANY: Thinking Allowed Prod.
ARTIST: Frances Vaughan ARTIST: et.al. TOPIC:
Psychology, $69.95

Spiritual Renewal: Tapping Inner Resources
PUBLISHING COMPANY: Luramedia ARTIST: L.J.
Geiger, A.M. Geiger TOPIC: Meditation, $34.50

Spirituality: Teachings From A World Beyond
PUBLISHING COMPANY: Ferguson, Bill ARTIST:
B. Ferguson TOPIC: Spirituality, $18.00

Stairways To The Mayan Gods

PUBLISHING COMPANY: Hartley Film Foundation
ARTIST: J. Campbell TOPIC: Spirituality, $89.00

Standing Stones Of Callanish
PUBLISHING COMPANY: Kuckuck Records
ARTIST: J. Mark TOPIC: Meditation, $10.98

Star/Cross: An Entrance Meditation
PUBLISHING COMPANY: Dialogue House ARTIST:
I. Progoff TOPIC: Meditation, $12.00

Starbirth Odyssey
PUBLISHING COMPANY: Inner Light Publications
ARTIST: B. Steiger TOPIC: Paranormal Phenomena, $13.95

Starflight 1
PUBLISHING COMPANY: Hearts of Space ARTIST:
Various Artists TOPIC: Meditation, $10.98

Starlight Journey #1: Garden Of Thought
PUBLISHING COMPANY: Starlight Journey
ARTIST: M. Markham, J. Cusack TOPIC:
Meditation, $10.95

Starlight Journey #4: Magical Star Journey
PUBLISHING COMPANY: Starlight Journey
ARTIST: M. Markham, J. Cusack TOPIC:
Meditation, $10.95

Starlight Journey #5: Journey In Spiritual Awareness
PUBLISHING COMPANY: Starlight Journey
ARTIST: M. Markham, J. Cusack TOPIC:
Meditation, $10.95

Starlight Journey #6: Loving Relationships
PUBLISHING COMPANY: Starlight Journey
ARTIST: M. Markham, J. Cusack TOPIC:
Meditation, $10.95

Starlight Journey #9: The Forest/Genesis - A New Beginning
PUBLISHING COMPANY: Starlight Journey
ARTIST: M. Markham TOPIC: Meditation, $10.95

Starlight Journey #13: Keyboard Canyon/Bells Of Silence
PUBLISHING COMPANY: Starlight Journey
ARTIST: M. Markham TOPIC: Meditation, $10.95

Starsong
PUBLISHING COMPANY: Vital Body Marketing
Co., Inc. ARTIST: Rick Miller TOPIC: New Age, $9.95

Starting The Day
PUBLISHING COMPANY: Soundwaves 2000
ARTIST: S. Halpern TOPIC: Hypnotism, $10.98

Staying Happy And Calm
PUBLISHING COMPANY: A. R. E. Press ARTIST:
A.R.E. TOPIC: Meditation, $9.95

Stella Maris
PUBLISHING COMPANY: Grace Communications
ARTIST: R. Rhea TOPIC: Meditation, $10.95

Step From Illusion To Truth
PUBLISHING COMPANY: Life Action Press
ARTIST: T. Singh TOPIC: Spirituality, $29.95

Stepping Beyond: Workshop Introducing Concepts Of A Course In Miracles
PUBLISHING COMPANY: Coleman Publishing
ARTIST: M. Rynce TOPIC: Spirituality, $40.00

Stop Drinking
PUBLISHING COMPANY: Valley of the Sun
ARTIST: D. Stuphen TOPIC: Hypnotism, $10.00

Stop Procrastination: Reaching Your Goals Now
PUBLISHING COMPANY: Yes! Technologies
ARTIST: Yes! Technologies TOPIC: Hypnotism, $11.95

Stop Proscratination
PUBLISHING COMPANY: EII ARTIST: Bright
Images TOPIC: Hypnotism, $11.95

Stop Smoking
PUBLISHING COMPANY: Valley of the Sun
ARTIST: D. Stuphen TOPIC: Hypnotism, $18.98

Stop Smoking: Break The Heart
PUBLISHING COMPANY: BFS Limited ARTIST:
Bright Images TOPIC: Hypnotism, $11.95

Stress And Nutrition
PUBLISHING COMPANY: New Dawn
Nutrit.Services ARTIST: R. Gilday TOPIC:
Nutrition, $9.95

Stress Control
PUBLISHING COMPANY: Valley of the Sun
ARTIST: D. Stuphen TOPIC: Hypnotism, $9.98

Stress Control: Creating An Inner Calm
PUBLISHING COMPANY: BFS Limited ARTIST:
Bright Images TOPIC: Hypnotism, $11.95

Stress Inoculation
PUBLISHING COMPANY: New Harbinger
Publications ARTIST: M. Davis TOPIC: Holistic
Health, $10.95

Stress Management
PUBLISHING COMPANY: Full Circle Music
ARTIST: Gateways TOPIC: Holistic Health, $10.00

Stress Mastery: The Neuropsychology Of Relaxation
PUBLISHING COMPANY: MSH Association
ARTIST: Brother Charles TOPIC: Meditation, $50.00

Stress Reduction
PUBLISHING COMPANY: White Dove Int'l., Inc.
ARTIST: S. Wilde TOPIC: Hypnotism, $11.95

Stress Reduction And Creative Meditation
PUBLISHING COMPANY: New World Library
ARTIST: Marcus Allen TOPIC: Meditation, Holistic
Health, $10.95

Stress Release: New World Subliminal
PUBLISHING COMPANY: New World Products, Ltd.
ARTIST: Y. Bhajan TOPIC: Hypnotism, $14.95

Stress, Diet And Your Heart

PUBLISHING COMPANY: NCC ARTIST: D. Ornish TOPIC: Holistic Health, $14.95

Stretch For Life
PUBLISHING COMPANY: A.R.E. Press TOPIC: Meditation, $39.95

Strong Immune System
PUBLISHING COMPANY: Valley of the Sun ARTIST: D. Stuphen TOPIC: Hypnotism, $10.00

Structures From Silence
PUBLISHING COMPANY: Celestial Harmonies ARTIST: S. Roach TOPIC: Meditation, $18.98

Study Made Easy: Study And Win
PUBLISHING COMPANY: BFS Limited ARTIST: Bright Images TOPIC: Hypnotism, $11.95

Subconscious Sales Power
PUBLISHING COMPANY: Potentials Unlimited ARTIST: Potentials Unlimited TOPIC: New Age, $9.98

Success Is Not An Accident
PUBLISHING COMPANY: Panorama Publishing Co. ARTIST: J. Kappas TOPIC: Body-Mind Connection, $295.00

Success Motivation: Strengthen Your Drive
PUBLISHING COMPANY: BFS Limited ARTIST: Bright Images TOPIC: Hypnotism, $11.95

Success: New World Subliminal
PUBLISHING COMPANY: New World Products, Ltd. ARTIST: Y. Bhajan TOPIC: Hypnotism, $14.95

Sufi Way
PUBLISHING COMPANY: Wishing Well Distributing ARTIST: Huston Smith TOPIC: Spirituality, $59.95

Summer Wind
PUBLISHING COMPANY: Sound Rx ARTIST: S. Halpern TOPIC: New Age, $29.98

Sunbathing In Leningrad
PUBLISHING COMPANY: Gold Castle Records ARTIST: David Hayes TOPIC: Meditation, $10.98

Sundance Season
PUBLISHING COMPANY: Celestial Harmonies ARTIST: R. C. Nakai TOPIC: Meditation, $18.98

Sungsongs: Chants And Visions For The Peacekeeper
PUBLISHING COMPANY: Sunray ARTIST: D. Ywahoo TOPIC: Spirituality, $11.00

Sunscapes
PUBLISHING COMPANY: Narada Productions ARTIST: Michael Jones TOPIC: Meditation, $16.98

Super Joy: In Love With Living
PUBLISHING COMPANY: Simon & Schuster Audio ARTIST: P. Pearsall TOPIC: Body-Mind Connection, $10.95

Super Relationships: Here's How
PUBLISHING COMPANY: H.H. Productions ARTIST: H. Hartley TOPIC: Hypnotism, $18.98

Supercharging Your Immune System To Insure Optimum Health & Vitality

PUBLISHING COMPANY: Wonder-Full Day Prod. ARTIST: L. Sereda TOPIC: Meditation, $12.95

Superconscious Mind
PUBLISHING COMPANY: Dr. Bruce Goldberg ARTIST: Bruce Goldberg TOPIC: Meditation, $12.00

Superimmunity: Master Your Emotions & Improve Your Health
PUBLISHING COMPANY: Audio Renaissance Tapes ARTIST: P. Pearsall TOPIC: Body-Mind Connection, $15.95

Symphodysse
PUBLISHING COMPANY: Fonix Musik ARTIST: K. Schonning TOPIC: Meditation, $11.95

Systematic Desensitization And Visualizing Goals
PUBLISHING COMPANY: New Harbinger Publications ARTIST: M. Davis ARTIST: et.al. TOPIC: Meditation, $10.95

Tai Chi Chi Kung
PUBLISHING COMPANY: Healing Tao Books ARTIST: M. Chia TOPIC: Holistic Health, $9.95

Tai Chi Chih! Joy Through Movement
PUBLISHING COMPANY: Janet Bock ARTIST: Justin F. Stone TOPIC: Tai Chi, $39.95

Tai Chi-Chuan Kung-Fu: Moving Meditation, Stress Reduction
PUBLISHING COMPANY: Artistic Video ARTIST: Bob Klein TOPIC: Tai Chi, $24.95

Take It To Heart
PUBLISHING COMPANY: Backroads Distributors ARTIST: B. BecVar TOPIC: Meditation, $21.95

Taking Charge Of Your Life
PUBLISHING COMPANY: Effective Learnings Systems, Inc. ARTIST: Love Tapes TOPIC: Hypnotism, $11.98

Talents And Abilities From Past Life
PUBLISHING COMPANY: Potentials Unlimited ARTIST: Potentials Unlimited TOPIC: New Age, $9.98

Taming The Beast: Driving Without Stress
PUBLISHING COMPANY: Mind Resource Tech, Inc. ARTIST: P. Nuernberger TOPIC: Holistic Health, $18.95

Tantra
PUBLISHING COMPANY: Chidvilas ARTIST: Spiritual Environments - music by Anugama TOPIC: Meditation, $11.95

Tantric Harmonies
PUBLISHING COMPANY: Spirit Music ARTIST: Tibetan Monks of Guyume TOPIC: Spirituality, $11.00

Taoism
PUBLISHING COMPANY: Hartley Film Foundation ARTIST: J. Blofeld TOPIC: Spirituality, $89.00

Tapering Off Smoking

PUBLISHING COMPANY: Potentials Unlimited ARTIST: Potentials Unlimited TOPIC: New Age, $9.98

Tara Singh Tapes Pre-Pack Display
PUBLISHING COMPANY: Life Action Press ARTIST: T. Singh TOPIC: Spirituality, $115.70

Tear Of Moon
PUBLISHING COMPANY: Coyote Oldham ARTIST: Coyote Oldham TOPIC: Meditation, $15.98

Tender Ritual
PUBLISHING COMPANY: Music West Records ARTIST: J. Chappell TOPIC: Meditation, $17.50

Tender Touch: A Guide To Infant Massage
PUBLISHING COMPANY: Healthy Alternatives ARTIST: S. Truxell TOPIC: Massage, $39.95

Tension: Slowing Down Your Life
PUBLISHING COMPANY: Luramedia ARTIST: L. J. Geiger, A. M. Geiger TOPIC: Holistic Health, $34.50

Teotihuacan: Reincarnation Of The 25,000--A Metaphysical Exploration
PUBLISHING COMPANY: Valley of the Sun ARTIST: D. Sutphen TOPIC: Reincarnation, $18.98

Therapeutic Alternatives
PUBLISHING COMPANY: Thinking Allowed Prod. ARTIST: G. Bozzay ARTIST: et.al. TOPIC: Holistic Healing, $69.95

Therapeutic Touch
PUBLISHING COMPANY: Hartley Film Foundation ARTIST: D. Krieger TOPIC: Holistic Healing, $89.00

There Must Be Another Way: Exploring A Course In Miracles
PUBLISHING COMPANY: Life Action Press ARTIST: T. Singh TOPIC: Spirituality, $24.95

Think & Get Well
PUBLISHING COMPANY: Audio Renaissance Tapes ARTIST: A. Weil TOPIC: Body-Mind Connection, Holistic Healing, $9.95

Think And Grow Rich
PUBLISHING COMPANY: Audio Renaissance Tapes ARTIST: N. Hill, J. Slattery TOPIC: Body-Mind Connection, $15.95

Thirty-Three Steps Beyond The Earth Plane
PUBLISHING COMPANY: White Dove Int'l., Inc. ARTIST: S. Wilde TOPIC: Psychology, $99.95

Thoughs Of Thoreau
PUBLISHING COMPANY: Relax & Remember, Inc. ARTIST: P. Greaver ARTIST: et.al. TOPIC: Meditation, $29.95

Thousand Names Of God As Mother: Esctasy Of Peace
PUBLISHING COMPANY: MSH Association ARTIST: Brother Charles TOPIC: Spirituality, $40.00

Tibetan Bowl Sounds For The Shamanic Journey

PUBLISHING COMPANY: Fdn. Shamanic Studies
ARTIST: M. Harner TOPIC: Meditation, $10.98

Tibetan Medicine: A Buddhist Approach To Healing
PUBLISHING COMPANY: Mystic Fire Video Co.
ARTIST: A. Dolma TOPIC: Holistic Healing, $29.95

Tibetan Transformation Trilogy
PUBLISHING COMPANY: Mirror Image ARTIST: A. Domo TOPIC: Meditation, $28.95

Tideline
PUBLISHING COMPANY: Windham Hill Records
ARTIST: D. Anger ARTIST: Higbie Quintet TOPIC: Meditation, $11.98

Timeless Motion
PUBLISHING COMPANY: Li-Sem Enterprises
ARTIST: D. Kobialka TOPIC: Meditation, $15.98

To Body And Soul With Love
PUBLISHING COMPANY: Love Circle Music
ARTIST: K. Shelstad, K. LaSalvia TOPIC: Yoga, $9.98

To Heal Again
PUBLISHING COMPANY: Royal Priest Research
ARTIST: R. Berkus TOPIC: Death, $10.95

To Know Truth Beyond Words
PUBLISHING COMPANY: Life Action Press
ARTIST: T. Singh TOPIC: Spirituality, $17.95

To My Guru
PUBLISHING COMPANY: S.Y.D.A. Foundation
ARTIST: Gurumayi Chidvilasananda TOPIC: Spirituality, $15.00

Too Far To Whisper
PUBLISHING COMPANY: Windham Hill Records
ARTIST: Shadowfax Ensemble TOPIC: Meditation, $11.98

Total Relaxation: Set Aside All Worries
PUBLISHING COMPANY: BFS Limited ARTIST: Bright Images TOPIC: Hypnotism, $11.95

Total Self
PUBLISHING COMPANY: Thinking Allowed Prod.
ARTIST: H. Stone TOPIC: Psychology, $49.95

Touching The Heart Of Healing, Part 1: Opening To Acceptance
PUBLISHING COMPANY: Access Group ARTIST: J. Kornfield, R. Hall TOPIC: Psychic Healing, $18.00

Touching The Heart Of Healing, Part 2: Path Of The Mindful Heart
PUBLISHING COMPANY: Access Group ARTIST: J. Kornfield, R. Hall TOPIC: Meditation, $18.00

Trance States: Theta Brain Waves
PUBLISHING COMPANY: White Dove Int'l., Inc.
ARTIST: S. Wilde TOPIC: Hypnotism, $21.95

Transcending Body Sense: Pt. 3 Of Nothing Real Can Be Threatened:, Cim Video Workshop
PUBLISHING COMPANY: Life Action Press
ARTIST: T. Singh TOPIC: Spirituality, $29.95

Transcending Personality
PUBLISHING COMPANY: Blue Dolphin Publishing - 2 ARTIST: H. Palmer TOPIC: Spirituality, $10.00

Transformation And The Body
PUBLISHING COMPANY: Thinking Allowed Prod.
ARTIST: George Leonard, Michael Murphy, Stanley Keleman, et.al. TOPIC: Body-Mind Connection, $69.95

Transformation Now
PUBLISHING COMPANY: Acoustic Brain Research
ARTIST: Acoustic Brain Research TOPIC: Meditation, $24.95

Transformation Process
PUBLISHING COMPANY: Creative Living Library
ARTIST: C. O'Connell TOPIC: Spirituality, $15.00

Transformation: The Breakthrough
PUBLISHING COMPANY: Dove Books On Tape, Inc. ARTIST: W. Stieber ARTIST: Read by Roddy McDowall TOPIC: Paranormal Phenomena, $14.95

Transforming Awareness
PUBLISHING COMPANY: Thinking Allowed Prod.
ARTIST: V. Satir ARTIST: et.al. TOPIC: Psychology, $69.95

Transition: Nuturing Yourself For Change
PUBLISHING COMPANY: Luramedia ARTIST: L.J. Geiger, A.M. Geiger TOPIC: Meditation, $34.50

Transitions Vol 2: Music To Help Baby Sleep
PUBLISHING COMPANY: Placenta Music, Inc.
ARTIST: B. Wolff TOPIC: Meditation, $14.95

Transitions: Soothing Music For Mother & Child - Womb Sounds With Natural Harmonies
PUBLISHING COMPANY: Placenta Music, Inc.
ARTIST: B. Wolff, J. Wolff TOPIC: Meditation, $14.95

Transits As Triggers Of Meaning
PUBLISHING COMPANY: RKM Publishing ARTIST: M. Lutin TOPIC: Astrology, $8.95

Transmission
PUBLISHING COMPANY: Beyond ARTIST: C. Buhner, S. Doucet TOPIC: Meditation, $10.98

Transpersonal Psychology I & II
PUBLISHING COMPANY: Sounds True Records & Dupl. ARTIST: S. Grof TOPIC: Psychology, $15.95

Traveler's Refresher: Extra Energy On The Move
PUBLISHING COMPANY: Simon & Schuster Audio
TOPIC: Acupuncture, $9.95

Tread Lightly Upon The Earth
PUBLISHING COMPANY: Mountain Spirit Tapes, Inc. ARTIST: D. Keck TOPIC: Occult, $9.95

True Optimism: Confidence, Self-Worth And Inner Strength
PUBLISHING COMPANY: EII ARTIST: Bright Images TOPIC: Hypnotism, $11.95

Trust Versus Belief

PUBLISHING COMPANY: Life Action Press
ARTIST: T. Singh TOPIC: Spirituality, $17.95

Truth
PUBLISHING COMPANY: CBS Records ARTIST: T Square TOPIC: Meditation, $11.98

Truth And Responsiblity
PUBLISHING COMPANY: Arizona Metaphysical Society ARTIST: F. Alper TOPIC: Spirituality, $10.00

Truth Is A Pathless Land
PUBLISHING COMPANY: Theosophical Pub.
ARTIST: Ingram Smith TOPIC: Spirituality, $21.95

Truthfinding: Past Lives, Karma & Beyond--Teachings Of Bartholomew
PUBLISHING COMPANY: Cine Video, Inc. ARTIST: Bartholonew TOPIC: Reincarnation, Past Life Regression, $29.95

Tuning The Mind, Tuning The Body
PUBLISHING COMPANY: Infinity Tapes - Blue Dolphin ARTIST: M. Gach, J. Kirsh TOPIC: Acupuncture, Yoga, $10.00

Turiya Sings
PUBLISHING COMPANY: Avatar Book Institute
ARTIST: A. Coltrane TOPIC: Spirituality, $11.00

Turn Off Tension
PUBLISHING COMPANY: Audio Renaissance Tapes
ARTIST: L. Glauberman TOPIC: Hypnotism, $15.95

Turning, Turning Back
PUBLISHING COMPANY: Windham Hill Records
ARTIST: A. DeGrassi TOPIC: Meditation, $11.98

Turtle's Navel
PUBLISHING COMPANY: Windham Hill Records
ARTIST: W. Ackerman TOPIC: Meditation, $11.98

Twelve Initiations
PUBLISHING COMPANY: Arizona Metaphysical Society ARTIST: F. Alper TOPIC: Spirituality, $18.00

Twist Of Destiny
PUBLISHING COMPANY: Crystal Cave Enterprises
ARTIST: Jeffrey Wood TOPIC: Meditation, $10.95

Two Intuitive Arts
PUBLISHING COMPANY: Infinity Tapes - Blue Dolphin ARTIST: J. Ivory, R. Unger TOPIC: Numerology, $10.00

UFO's And Ancient Astronauts
PUBLISHING COMPANY: Audio Renaissance Tapes
TOPIC: Paranormal Phenomena, $9.95

Ultimate Library
PUBLISHING COMPANY: Changeworks ARTIST: T. Condon TOPIC: Meditation, $12.95

Ultimate Relaxation
PUBLISHING COMPANY: Valley of the Sun
ARTIST: D. Stuphen TOPIC: Hypnotism, $9.95

Ultimate You: The Best You Can Be
PUBLISHING COMPANY: BFS Limited ARTIST: Bright Images TOPIC: Hypnotism, $11.95

Ultra-Monetary Success

PUBLISHING COMPANY: Valley of the Sun
ARTIST: D. Stuphen TOPIC: Hypnotism, $18.98

Un-Stress Ultra-Relaxation Programming To Be At Peace
PUBLISHING COMPANY: Valley of the Sun
ARTIST: D. Sutphen TOPIC: Meditation, $19.95

Understanding Your Dreams
PUBLISHING COMPANY: Inner Vision Publishing Co. ARTIST: R. Van De Castle TOPIC: Dreams, $14.95

Universal Harmony Vol 1: Inner Awareness
PUBLISHING COMPANY: Artistic Studios ARTIST: A. Lawes TOPIC: Metaphysics, $9.98

Universal Harmony Vol 2: Verities Of Truth
PUBLISHING COMPANY: Artistic Studios ARTIST: A. Lawes TOPIC: Metaphysics, $9.98

Universal Harmony Vol 3: Mentation And Meditation
PUBLISHING COMPANY: Artistic Studios ARTIST: A. Lawes TOPIC: Metaphysics, $9.98

Universal Law
PUBLISHING COMPANY: Arizona Metaphysical Society ARTIST: F. Alper TOPIC: Metaphysics, $18.00

Unlimited Possibilities/Finding Fault Vs. Find Love: Lectures Based On Acim
PUBLISHING COMPANY: Miracle Projects ARTIST: Marianne Williamson TOPIC: Spirituality, $10.00

Unlocking Your Body: Regaining Youth Through Somatic Awareness
PUBLISHING COMPANY: Thinking Allowed Prod. ARTIST: T. Hanna TOPIC: Body-Mind Connection, $49.95

Unquiet Dead: An Introduction To Spirit Depossession Therapy
PUBLISHING COMPANY: Thinking Allowed Prod. ARTIST: E. Fiore TOPIC: Psychology, $49.95

Unstress: Ultra-Relaxation Programming To Be At Peace
PUBLISHING COMPANY: Valley of the Sun
ARTIST: D. Sutphen TOPIC: Meditation, $19.95

Unstroken
PUBLISHING COMPANY: Fonix Musik ARTIST: F. Lentz TOPIC: Meditation, $10.98

Up From Depression
PUBLISHING COMPANY: Potentials Unlimited ARTIST: Potentials Unlimited TOPIC: New Age, $9.98

Updated Pritikin Program
PUBLISHING COMPANY: Dove Books on Tape, Inc. ARTIST: N. Pritikin ARTIST: Read by Carl Reiner TOPIC: Nutrition, $14.95

Uplift
PUBLISHING COMPANY: Vital Body Marketing Co., Inc. ARTIST: L. Leeder TOPIC: New Age, $9.95

Upper Hand: Quick Thinking And Fast Action
PUBLISHING COMPANY: Valley of the Sun
ARTIST: D. Stuphen TOPIC: Hypnotism, $10.98

Valley In The Clouds
PUBLISHING COMPANY: Narada Productions
ARTIST: D. Arkenstone TOPIC: Meditation, $16.98

Vapor Drawings
PUBLISHING COMPANY: Windham Hill Records
ARTIST: M. Isham TOPIC: Meditation, $18.50

Velocity Of Love
PUBLISHING COMPANY: RCA Records ARTIST: S. Ciani TOPIC: Meditation, $21.00

Vibrations Workshop: For Those Wishing To Improve The Quality Of Their Lives
PUBLISHING COMPANY: Coleman Publishing
ARTIST: H. Ring TOPIC: Occult, $20.00

Viewing Past Lives: The Ascension Technique
PUBLISHING COMPANY: Valley of the Sun
ARTIST: D. Sutphen TOPIC: Past Life Regression, $18.98

Vipassana Meditation
PUBLISHING COMPANY: Chidvilas ARTIST: NSA TOPIC: Spirituality, $9.95

Vision Improvement
PUBLISHING COMPANY: Valley of the Sun
ARTIST: D. Stuphen TOPIC: Hypnotism, $9.98

Vision Seeker
PUBLISHING COMPANY: Yansa Music ARTIST: Shayla TOPIC: Meditation, $18.98

Visioning
PUBLISHING COMPANY: Medicine Eagle/Harmony N/W ARTIST: Brooke Medicine Eagle TOPIC: Spirituality, $20.00

Visualization/Aura Reading
PUBLISHING COMPANY: Potentials Unlimited
ARTIST: Potentials Unlimited TOPIC: New Age, $9.98

Visualizations For Physical Healing
PUBLISHING COMPANY: Butterfly Publishing Co.
ARTIST: E. Rose TOPIC: Holistic Healing, $9.95

Visualize Yourself To Success: The Success You Desire
PUBLISHING COMPANY: BFS Limited ARTIST: Bright Images TOPIC: Hypnotism, $11.95

Voice That Precedes Thought
PUBLISHING COMPANY: Life Action Press
ARTIST: T. Singh ARTIST: Read by Charles Johnson TOPIC: Spirituality, $17.95

Voodoo Connections
PUBLISHING COMPANY: Postscript Productions
ARTIST: Postscription Productions TOPIC: Spirituality, $59.95

Voyage Beyond
PUBLISHING COMPANY: Beyond ARTIST: Various Artists TOPIC: Meditation, $10.98

Wake-Up Refresher: Techniques For Extra Energy To The Start Of The Day
PUBLISHING COMPANY: Simon & Schuster Audio
ARTIST: M. Gach TOPIC: Acupuncture, $9.95

Waking Dream And Living Myth In The Creative Work Of Ingmar Bergman
PUBLISHING COMPANY: Dialogue House ARTIST: I. Progoff TOPIC: Psychology, $12.00

Waking Up
PUBLISHING COMPANY: Thinking Allowed Prod.
ARTIST: C. Hart TOPIC: Psychology, $29.95

Walking The Life Journey
PUBLISHING COMPANY: Upstate Media Enterprises
ARTIST: J. Houston TOPIC: Spirituality, $39.95

Watching My Life Go By
PUBLISHING COMPANY: Windham Hill Records
ARTIST: M. Hedges TOPIC: Meditation, $11.98

Watermark
PUBLISHING COMPANY: Warner/Elektra/Atlant Corp. ARTIST: Enya TOPIC: Meditation, $11.98

Wave Form
PUBLISHING COMPANY: Acoustic Brain Research
ARTIST: Acoustric Brain Research TOPIC: Meditation, $24.95

Waving Goodbye
PUBLISHING COMPANY: White Dove Int'l., Inc.
ARTIST: S. Wilde TOPIC: Hypnotism, $11.95

Way Home
PUBLISHING COMPANY: Hearts of Space ARTIST: K. Braheny TOPIC: Meditation, $18.95

Way Of Herbs
PUBLISHING COMPANY: Tierra, Michael ARTIST: M. Tierra TOPIC: Herbalogy, $29.95

Way Of Tai Chi Ch'uan: Gentle Exercise For Health & Inner Peace
PUBLISHING COMPANY: Tai Productions ARTIST: Lana Spraker TOPIC: Tai Chi, $39.95

Way Of The Dream
PUBLISHING COMPANY: Infinity Tapes - Blue Dolphin ARTIST: G. Delaney, F. Boa TOPIC: Dreams, $10.00

We All Come From The Goddess
PUBLISHING COMPANY: Medicine Song Productions ARTIST: Rashani, et.al. TOPIC: Spirituality, $11.00

We Are All Sangha
PUBLISHING COMPANY: Medicine Song Productions ARTIST: Rashani TOPIC: Spirituality, $10.00

Weight Control: Slim Image II
PUBLISHING COMPANY: Effective Learnings Systems, Inc. ARTIST: Love Tapes TOPIC: Hypnotism, $11.98

Weight Loss
PUBLISHING COMPANY: Steppingstones ARTIST: R. Jafolla, M. Jafolla TOPIC: Hypnotism, $12.95

Weight Loss: I Feel Thin
PUBLISHING COMPANY: White Dove Int'l., Inc.
ARTIST: S. Wilde TOPIC: Hypnotism, $11.95

Weight Loss: Lose Weight Permanently
PUBLISHING COMPANY: BFS Limited ARTIST: Bright Images TOPIC: Hypnotism, $11.95

Weight Reduction
PUBLISHING COMPANY: Light of Mind ARTIST: Threshold Response TOPIC: Hypnotism, $9.95

Weight Reduction Metaphysical Hypnosis
PUBLISHING COMPANY: Valley of the Sun ARTIST: D. Stuphen TOPIC: Hypnotism, $12.50

Welcome To My World
PUBLISHING COMPANY: MSH Association ARTIST: Brother Charles TOPIC: Meditation, $25.00

Well And The Cathedral: An Entrance Meditation
PUBLISHING COMPANY: Dialogue House ARTIST: I. Progoff TOPIC: Meditation, $12.00

What Are You Going To Give This World?
PUBLISHING COMPANY: Life Action Press ARTIST: T. Singh TOPIC: Spirituality, $17.95

What Astrology Can And Cannot Do/Signs Of The Zodiac
PUBLISHING COMPANY: Video Lecture Series ARTIST: N. Tyl, G. Star TOPIC: Astrology, $39.95

What I Believe And Morning And Evening Meditations
PUBLISHING COMPANY: Hay House ARTIST: Louise Hay TOPIC: Meditation, $18.00

What I Believe/Deep Relaxation
PUBLISHING COMPANY: Hay House ARTIST: Louise Hay TOPIC: Meditation, $10.00

What Is A Religious Mind?
PUBLISHING COMPANY: Harper & Row Publishers ARTIST: J. Krishnamurti TOPIC: Spirituality, $9.95

What Is Channeling
PUBLISHING COMPANY: Thinking Allowed Prod. ARTIST: A. Hastings TOPIC: Channeling, $29.95

What Is The Christ?
PUBLISHING COMPANY: Life Action Press ARTIST: T. Singh TOPIC: Spirituality, $39.95

What Your Doctor Didn't Learn In Medical School...And What You Can Do About It!
PUBLISHING COMPANY: Dove Books on Tape, Inc. ARTIST: S. Berger TOPIC: Holistic Healing, $14.95

Wheels Of Life
PUBLISHING COMPANY: Llewellyn Worldwide, Ltd. ARTIST: A. Judith TOPIC: Parapsychology, $9.95

Whisper Me
PUBLISHING COMPANY: Windham Hill Records ARTIST: W. Mertens TOPIC: Meditation, $11.98

Whisperings
PUBLISHING COMPANY: Crystal Cave Enterprises ARTIST: Leonardo Rubinstein TOPIC: Meditation, $10.95

White Winds
PUBLISHING COMPANY: CBS Records ARTIST: A. Vollenweider TOPIC: Meditation, $20.95

Why And How Of Spiritual Education
PUBLISHING COMPANY: Crystal Clarity ARTIST: Kriyananda TOPIC: Spirituality, $12.95

Why Ideals Fail
PUBLISHING COMPANY: Life Action Press ARTIST: T. Singh TOPIC: Spirituality, $17.95

Why Is This Happening To Me...Again?
PUBLISHING COMPANY: New Visions ARTIST: M. Ryce TOPIC: Body-Mind Connection, $40.00

Wild Iris: Spontaneous, Joyous Celtic Harp & Flute
PUBLISHING COMPANY: Vital Body Marketing Co., Inc. ARTIST: K. Robertson, S. Kujala TOPIC: New Age, $9.95

Will Power
PUBLISHING COMPANY: Potentials Unlimited ARTIST: Potentials Unlimited TOPIC: New Age, $9.98

Willow
PUBLISHING COMPANY: Winham Hill Records ARTIST: D. Hecht TOPIC: Meditation, $11.98

Wind And Whispers
PUBLISHING COMPANY: Sona Gaia ARTIST: Michael Jones TOPIC: Meditation, $16.98

Wind Dance
PUBLISHING COMPANY: Windham Hill Records ARTIST: S. Cossu TOPIC: Meditation, $11.98

Wind In The Heather
PUBLISHING COMPANY: Windham Hill Records ARTIST: G. Cromarty TOPIC: Meditation, $11.98

Wind Shadows
PUBLISHING COMPANY: Vital Body Marketing Co., Inc. ARTIST: K. Robertson TOPIC: New Age, $9.95

Windham Hill: Autumn Portrait
PUBLISHING COMPANY: Paramount Home Video ARTIST: Windham Hill Artists TOPIC: New Age, $29.95

Windham Hill: China
PUBLISHING COMPANY: Paramount Home Video ARTIST: Windham Hill Artists TOPIC: New Age, $29.95

Windham Hill: In Concert
PUBLISHING COMPANY: Paramount Home Video ARTIST: Windham Hill Artists TOPIC: New Age, $29.95

Winds Of Chance
PUBLISHING COMPANY: Crystal Cave Enterprises ARTIST: Matt Lester TOPIC: Meditation, $10.95

Winds Of Space

PUBLISHING COMPANY: Higher Octace Music ARTIST: P. Davison TOPIC: Meditation, $16.98

Wine Dark Sea
PUBLISHING COMPANY: JEM ARTIST: S. Caudel TOPIC: Meditation, $10.98

Wings Of Prayer
PUBLISHING COMPANY: Heavensong Recordings ARTIST: M. Stillwater TOPIC: Spirituality, $10.00

Wings Of The Spirit: Music For Meditation
PUBLISHING COMPANY: Theosophical Pub. ARTIST: Horatio Costa TOPIC: Meditation, $16.95

Winning Edge: Being A Winner
PUBLISHING COMPANY: BFS Limited ARTIST: Bright Images TOPIC: Hypnotism, $11.95

Winter Into Spring
PUBLISHING COMPANY: Windham Hill Records ARTIST: G. Winston TOPIC: Meditation, $18.50

Winter's Solstice
PUBLISHING COMPANY: Windham Hill Records ARTIST: Windham Hill Artists TOPIC: Meditation, $18.50

Winter's Solstice II
PUBLISHING COMPANY: Windham Hill Records ARTIST: Windham Hill Artists TOPIC: Meditation, $18.50

Wisdom Begins With Self-Knowing
PUBLISHING COMPANY: Life Action Press ARTIST: T. Singh TOPIC: Spirituality, $17.95

Witchcraft Yesterday And Today
PUBLISHING COMPANY: Llewellyn Worldwide, Ltd. ARTIST: R. Buckland TOPIC: Witchcraft, $29.95

Witches And Halloween
PUBLISHING COMPANY: Circle Publications ARTIST: Lady Cybele TOPIC: Witchcraft, $10.00

Women Making A Difference
PUBLISHING COMPANY: Hartley Film Foundation ARTIST: C. Russell TOPIC: Spirituality, $39.95

Women Who Run With The Wolves I & II: Myths & Stores About The Wild Woman Archetype
PUBLISHING COMPANY: Sounds True Record. & Dupl. ARTIST: Clarissa Pinkola Estes TOPIC: Psychology, $18.95

Words Of Gandhi
PUBLISHING COMPANY: Caedmon ARTIST: M. Gandhi ARTIST: Read by Ben Kingsley TOPIC: Spirituality, $12.95

Working On Oneself
PUBLISHING COMPANY: Thinking Allowed Prod. ARTIST: K. Speeth ARTIST: et.al. TOPIC: Spirituality, $69.95

Working With Creative Imagery
PUBLISHING COMPANY: Thinking Allowed Prod. ARTIST: S. Gawain TOPIC: Body-Mind Connection, $29.95

Working With Crystals: Visual Excerpts From The Complete Crystal Guidebook
PUBLISHING COMPANY: U-Read/U-Music **ARTIST:** Uma Silbey **ARTIST:** Ramana Das **TOPIC:** Crystals, $29.95

Working With The Unconscious
PUBLISHING COMPANY: Thinking Allowed Prod. **ARTIST:** S. Gawain **ARTIST:** et.al. **TOPIC:** Body-Mind Connection, $69.95

Workout Program: Body Toning Through Visualization
PUBLISHING COMPANY: EII **ARTIST:** Bright Images **TOPIC:** Hypnotism, $11.95

Workshop: Practical Synthesis With Examples 1 & 2
PUBLISHING COMPANY: Video Lecture Series **ARTIST:** G. Ceaglio, R. Merriman **TOPIC:** Astrology, $39.95

Yamantaka
PUBLISHING COMPANY: Celestial Harmonies **ARTIST:** Micky Hart **TOPIC:** Meditation, $10.98

Yearning And Harmony
PUBLISHING COMPANY: Fortuna Record & Tape **ARTIST:** T. Atma, K. Netzle **TOPIC:** Meditation, $19.98

Yoga For Beginners
PUBLISHING COMPANY: Healing Arts Home Video **ARTIST:** Patricia Walden **TOPIC:** Yoga, $29.95

Yoga For Children
PUBLISHING COMPANY: Shakti Press **ARTIST:** Satchidananda **TOPIC:** Yoga, $30.95

Yoga For Senior Citizens
PUBLISHING COMPANY: Quantum Leap Enterprises, Inc. **ARTIST:** Mark Demeter **TOPIC:** Yoga, $29.95

Yoga Of Love
PUBLISHING COMPANY: Houbrick, Saraswati Ulrike **ARTIST:** S. Houbrick **TOPIC:** Yoga, $10.00

Yoga Postures For Self Awareness
PUBLISHING COMPANY: Crystal Clarity **ARTIST:** Kriyananda **TOPIC:** Yoga, $9.95

Yoga With Rita 1 & 2
PUBLISHING COMPANY: Kane, Rita Nelson **ARTIST:** R. Kane **TOPIC:** Yoga, $19.00

Yoga, Meditation And Self Realization
PUBLISHING COMPANY: Body Therapy Training Inst. **ARTIST:** M. Alpern **TOPIC:** Yoga, $10.00

Yogaworks: Complete Hatha Yoga Workout
PUBLISHING COMPANY: Yogaworks **ARTIST:** Janet Smith **TOPIC:** Yoga, $14.95

Yogic Relaxation And Guided Meditation
PUBLISHING COMPANY: Cosmic Temple Creations **ARTIST:** David Cosmo **TOPIC:** Holistic Health, $9.98

You Are The Altar Of God
PUBLISHING COMPANY: Life Action Press **ARTIST:** T. Singh **TOPIC:** Spirituality, $17.95

You Are The Healer: A Journey To Your Heart
PUBLISHING COMPANY: Small Kindness **ARTIST:** Judith Sherven **TOPIC:** Holistic Healing, $9.95

You Are The Ocean
PUBLISHING COMPANY: Vital Body Marketing Co., Inc. **ARTIST:** S. Roth **TOPIC:** New Age, $9.95

You Are The Ocean Vol. 2
PUBLISHING COMPANY: Vital Body Marketing Co., Inc. **ARTIST:** S. Roth **TOPIC:** New Age, $9.95

You Can Contact UFO's
PUBLISHING COMPANY: Quest Northwest Pub. Co. **ARTIST:** D. Marshall, M. Kirkendoll **TOPIC:** Paranormal Phenomena, $29.95

You Can Heal Your Life
PUBLISHING COMPANY: Hay House **ARTIST:** Louise Hay **TOPIC:** Meditation, $25.00

You Can Heal Your Life Study Course
PUBLISHING COMPANY: Hay House **ARTIST:** Louise Hay **TOPIC:** Meditation, $18.00

You Can't Afford The Luxury Of A Negative Thought
PUBLISHING COMPANY: Prelude Press **ARTIST:** P. McWilliams **ARTIST:** John-Roger **TOPIC:** Body-Mind Connection, $39.95

You'll See It When You Believe It
PUBLISHING COMPANY: Nightingale Conant Corp. **ARTIST:** W. Dyer **TOPIC:** Body-Mind Connection, $14.95

Your Favorite Place: Path Of Life
PUBLISHING COMPANY: T. A. Helliwell Publications **ARTIST:** T. Helliwell **TOPIC:** Holistic Health, $9.95

Your Healing Hands And Beyond: Discovering Your Untapped Energy, Course In Life Force
PUBLISHING COMPANY: Wingbow Press **ARTIST:** Richard Gordon **TOPIC:** Holistic Healing, $16.95

Your Healing Path
PUBLISHING COMPANY: Master Your Mind **ARTIST:** Mary Richards **TOPIC:** Hypnotism, $12.95

Your Intuitive Guide
PUBLISHING COMPANY: Changeworks **ARTIST:** T. Condon **TOPIC:** Hypnotism, Meditation, $12.95

Your Last Cigarette: No Exceptions!
PUBLISHING COMPANY: Valley of the Sun **ARTIST:** D. Stuphen **TOPIC:** Hypnotism, $10.98

Your World Is A Direct Result Of Your Thoughts
PUBLISHING COMPANY: Connecting Link **ARTIST:** Barbara Marciniak **TOPIC:** Body-Mind Connection, $14.98

Z (Zee)
PUBLISHING COMPANY: Marcy, Inc. **ARTIST:** M. Hamm **TOPIC:** Meditation, $12.98

Zen And Now
PUBLISHING COMPANY: Hartley Film Foundation **ARTIST:** Alan Watts **TOPIC:** Spirituality, $89.00

Zen Basics
PUBLISHING COMPANY: Gateways/IDHHB **ARTIST:** E. J. Gold **TOPIC:** Meditation, $24.95

Zen Rise
PUBLISHING COMPANY: Chidvilas **ARTIST:** Bindhu **TOPIC:** Meditation, $10.95

Additional Audio/Video

28 Up
PUBLISHING COMPANY: First Run Features **TOPICS:** New Age **TYPE:** Video

A Strange Harvest
PUBLISHING COMPANY: LMH Productions/Linda Moulton Howe Productions **EDITOR:** Linda Moulton Howe **TOPICS:** Paranormal Phenomena **TYPE:** Video **PRICE:** $30.00 **DESCRIPTION:** Investigations which link the worldwide animal mutilation & human abduction phenomena.

An Alien Harvest
PUBLISHING COMPANY: LMH Productions/Linda Moulton Howe Productions **EDITOR:** Linda Moulton Howe **TOPICS:** Paranormal Phenomena **TYPE:** Video **PRICE:** $50.00 **DESCRIPTION:** Provides further evidence linking animal mutilations to alien life forms.

An Evening With Bernie Siegel, M.D.
PUBLISHING COMPANY: Upstate Media Enterprises **TOPICS:** New Age **TYPE:** Video

Art Of Meditation
PUBLISHING COMPANY: Hartley Film Foundation **TOPICS:** New Age, Meditation **TYPE:** Video

Boost Your Brainpower
PUBLISHING COMPANY: Rodale Press, Inc. **TOPICS:** Holistic Healing **TYPE:** Audio **DESCRIPTION:** Part of Prevention's Mind/Body Healing tape series.

Communicate With Creativity
PUBLISHING COMPANY: Poco Press **EDITOR:** Marilyn Miller **TOPICS:** New Age, Spirituality, Meditation **TYPE:** Audio **PRICE:** $69.99 **DESCRIPTION:** Helps listener resolve differences by listening & asking for what they want. Set of 6 tapes & workbook.

Cropcircle Communique
PUBLISHING COMPANY: LMH Productions/Linda Moulton Howe Productions **EDITOR:** Linda Moulton Howe **TOPICS:** Paranormal Phenomena **TYPE:** Video **PRICE:** $35.00 **DESCRIPTION:** Discusses the mysterious worldwide crop formations. Features aerials & music, graphic animation, the investigators, their theories & scientific evidence that plant cells & soil have been altered.

Cymatics: The Healing Nature Of Sound

PUBLISHING COMPANY: Macromedia **EDITOR:** Dr. Hans Jenny, Dr. Peter Guy Manners **TOPICS:** New Age, Holistic Healing **TYPE:** Video **DESCRIPTION:** Describes the application of audible sound to the body as a healing modality, & demonstrates the Cymatic Applicator developed for this purpose.

Discover Dowsing
PUBLISHING COMPANY: Fine Median International **TOPICS:** Dowsing **TYPE:** Video **DESCRIPTION:** 55 minute instructional videotape available in all worldwide formats.

Earth Mysteries
PUBLISHING COMPANY: LMH Productions/Linda Moulton Howe Productions **EDITOR:** Linda Moulton Howe **TOPICS:** Paranormal Phenomena **TYPE:** Video

Energize With Yoga
PUBLISHING COMPANY: Rudra Press **EDITOR:** Lilias Folan **TOPICS:** Yoga, Holistic Health **TYPE:** Video

Fatigue Free
PUBLISHING COMPANY: Rodale Press, Inc. **TOPICS:** Holistic Healing **TYPE:** Audio **DESCRIPTION:** Part of Prevention's Mind/Body Healing tape series.

Fatigue Free
PUBLISHING COMPANY: Rodale Press, Inc. **TOPICS:** Holistic Healing **TYPE:** Audio **DESCRIPTION:** Part of Prevention's Mind/Body Healing tape series.

From Atom To Cosmos
PUBLISHING COMPANY: Macromedia **EDITOR:** Itzhak Bentov **TOPICS:** New Age **TYPE:** Video **DESCRIPTION:** Lecture presenting a clear & enlightening model of the workings of the universe, from atom to cosmos, & of our own process of reunion with Universal Cause.

Get A Good Night's Sleep
PUBLISHING COMPANY: Rodale Press, Inc. **TOPICS:** Holistic Healing **TYPE:** Audio **DESCRIPTION:** Part of Prevention's Mind/Body Healing tape series.

Hoxsey: How Healing Becomes A Crime
PUBLISHING COMPANY: Realidad Productions **TOPICS:** New Age **TYPE:** Video

Immune Power
PUBLISHING COMPANY: Rodale Press, Inc. **TOPICS:** Holistic Healing **TYPE:** Audio **DESCRIPTION:** Part of Prevention's Mind/Body Healing tape series.

Immune Power
PUBLISHING COMPANY: Rodale Press, Inc. **TOPICS:** Holistic Healing **TYPE:** Audio **DESCRIPTION:** Part of Prevention's Mind/Body Healing tape series.

Inner Journeys
PUBLISHING COMPANY: Gateways Books And Tapes **EDITOR:** Iven Lourie, Nancy Christie **TOPICS:** New Age **TYPE:** Audio

Life Begins Again
PUBLISHING COMPANY: Poco Press **EDITOR:** Marilyn Miller **TOPICS:** New Age, Spirituality, Meditation **TYPE:** Audio **PRICE:** $39.99 **DESCRIPTION:** 7 daily action meditations for any life transition. Set of 4 tapes.

Life, Death & Reincarnation, The Soul's Choices
PUBLISHING COMPANY: Reincarnation Books & Tapes **EDITOR:** Bette B. Binder **TOPICS:** Past Life Regression, Reincarnation, Death **TYPE:** Audio **PRICE:** $13.00

Lilias! Alive With Yoga
PUBLISHING COMPANY: Rudra Press **EDITOR:** Lilias Folan **TOPICS:** Yoga, Holistic Health **TYPE:** Video

Lilias, Yoga And You
PUBLISHING COMPANY: Rudra Press **EDITOR:** Lilias Folan **TOPICS:** Yoga, Holistic Health **TYPE:** Video

Lose Weight The Natural Way
PUBLISHING COMPANY: Rodale Press, Inc. **TOPICS:** Holistic Healing **TYPE:** Audio **DESCRIPTION:** Part of Prevention's Mind/Body Healing tape series.

Meditation For The Age Of Enlightenment
PUBLISHING COMPANY: Vision Unlimited **TOPICS:** New Age **TYPE:** Video

Meditation: An Invitation To Inner Growth
PUBLISHING COMPANY: Rudra Press **EDITOR:** Swami Chetanananda **TOPICS:** Meditation, Holistic Health **TYPE:** Audio

Music To Be Born By
PUBLISHING COMPANY: Rykodisc USA **EDITOR:** Mickey Hart **TOPICS:** Birth **TYPE:** Audio

New Body
PUBLISHING COMPANY: Poco Press **EDITOR:** Juliann Connell **TOPICS:** New Age, Spirituality, Meditation **TYPE:** Audio **PRICE:** $15.00 **DESCRIPTION:** Meditation & inspiration tape.

New Dimensions Tapes
PUBLISHING COMPANY: New Dimensions Radio **EDITOR:** Michael Toms **TOPICS:** New Age **TYPE:** Audio

Psychic Phenomena Of Reincarnation
PUBLISHING COMPANY: Reincarnation Books & Tapes **EDITOR:** Bette B. Binder **TOPICS:** Past Life Regression, Reincarnation **TYPE:** Audio **PRICE:** $13.00

Soothing Sound Therapy
PUBLISHING COMPANY: Rodale Press, Inc. **TOPICS:** Holistic Healing **TYPE:** Audio **DESCRIPTION:** Part of Prevention's Mind/Body Healing tape series.

Special Delivery: Creating The Birth You Want For You And Your Baby
PUBLISHING COMPANY: Injoy Productions **EDITOR:** Charlie Stein, Ilana Gali-El **TOPICS:** Birth **TYPE:** Video

Stop Procrastination
PUBLISHING COMPANY: Rodale Press, Inc. **TOPICS:** Holistic Healing **TYPE:** Audio **DESCRIPTION:** Part of Prevention's Mind/Body Healing tape series.

Subliminal Persuasion Self Hypnosis Tapes
PUBLISHING COMPANY: Potentials Unlimited **TOPICS:** New Age **TYPE:** Video

Success Without Distress
PUBLISHING COMPANY: Poco Press **EDITOR:** Marilyn Miller **TOPICS:** New Age, Spirituality, Meditation **TYPE:** Audio **PRICE:** $49.99 **DESCRIPTION:** Offers life planning, goal setting & stress reduction. 4 tapes & workbook.

Super Memory
PUBLISHING COMPANY: Rodale Press, Inc. **TOPICS:** Holistic Healing **TYPE:** Audio **DESCRIPTION:** Part of Prevention's Mind/Body Healing tape series.

Tantra Love
PUBLISHING COMPANY: Peak Skill Publishing **TOPICS:** New Age **TYPE:** Video **DESCRIPTION:** Eastern secrets of intimacy & ecstasy for western lovers.

Tantra-Bliss Of Reality
PUBLISHING COMPANY: Peak Skill Publishing **TOPICS:** New Age **TYPE:** Audio

Taoism
PUBLISHING COMPANY: Hartley Film Foundation **TOPICS:** New Age **TYPE:** Video

The Global Brain
PUBLISHING COMPANY: Hartley Film Foundation **TOPICS:** New Age **TYPE:** Video

The Grand Canyon
PUBLISHING COMPANY: Norman Beerger Productions **TOPICS:** New Age **TYPE:** Video

Therapeutic Touch
PUBLISHING COMPANY: Hartley Film Foundation **TOPICS:** New Age **TYPE:** Video

Video and Audio Tapes From Annual Conferences
PUBLISHING COMPANY: United States Psychotronics Association **TOPICS:** Psychic Phenomena, Holistic Health, Homeopathy, Acupuncture, Crystals, Color Therapy, Herbalogy **TYPE:** Video

Walking For Health And Happiness
PUBLISHING COMPANY: Rodale Press, Inc. **TOPICS:** Holistic Healing **TYPE:** Audio **DESCRIPTION:** Part of Prevention's Mind/Body Healing tape series.

Water Baby: Experiences Of Water Birth
PUBLISHING COMPANY: Point Of View Productions **EDITOR:** Karil Daniels **TOPICS:** Birth

TYPE: Video **DESCRIPTION:** Water Baby: Experiences Of Water Birth, has won 13 film & video festival awards.

Well & Strong: A True Story

PUBLISHING COMPANY: Point Of View

Productions **TOPICS:** Birth **TYPE:** Video

Your Relationship, Your Mirror

PUBLISHING COMPANY: Peak Skill Publishing **TOPICS:** New Age **TYPE:** Audio

Zen Sex I

PUBLISHING COMPANY: Peak Skill Publishing **TOPICS:** New Age **TYPE:** Audio

Zen Sex II

PUBLISHING COMPANY: Peak Skill Publishing **TOPICS:** New Age **TYPE:** Audio

Bibliograpy

This chapter lists Books, Directories, Handbooks, Booklets, Yearbooks and Guides. The terms Editor and Author are used interchangeably. Any publication listed in this chapter can be ordered from the individual publisher listed in the Publishers Index, your local New Age Bookstore or by contacting Reference Press International, P.O. Box 4126, Greenwich, CT 06830, 203-629-4900.

A Chinese & Western Daily Practical Health Guide
PUBLISHING COMPANY: Juvenescent Research Corp. EDITOR: Betty Yulin Ho TOPICS: Holistic Health TYPE: Book DATE: 1982; 122 pgs. PRICE: $9.00 DESCRIPTION: Immediate suggestions with a holistic viewpoint to maintain health.

A Chinese & Western Guide To Better Health & Longer Life
PUBLISHING COMPANY: Juvenescent Research Corp. EDITOR: Betty Yulin Ho TOPICS: Holistic Health TYPE: Book DATE: 1974; 50 pgs. PRICE: $5.00 DESCRIPTION: Ancient Chinese health principles related to best Western health principles to improve quality of life.

A Coming Of Wizards
PUBLISHING COMPANY: High Mesa Press Reynolds TOPICS: New Age, Channeling TYPE: Book PRICE: $12.95

A Consumer Guide To Hospice Care
PUBLISHING COMPANY: National Consumers League EDITOR: Barbara Coleman TOPICS: Death TYPE: Guide

A Glimpse Of Your Future
PUBLISHING COMPANY: Life Tapestry Press EDITOR: Brenda Hoffman TYPE: Book DATE: 1989 SIZE: 8 1/2x 6; 372 pgs. PRICE: $12.95 DESCRIPTION: Combines couseling & prophecy in a series of short, easy-to-understand essays. Describes numerous institutions including the corporate & medical worlds, even the family will evolve when we claim our personal power. Provides an understanding of how & why the changes are occurring as well as pictures of the year 2000 & beyond.

A Guide To Channeling And Channeled Material
PUBLISHING COMPANY: Cassandra Press EDITOR: Lily Andrews TOPICS: Channeling TYPE: Book DATE: 1990; 136 pgs. PRICE: $9.95

A Lycanthropy Reader - Werewolves In Western Culture
PUBLISHING COMPANY: Syracuse University Press EDITOR: Charlotte Otten TOPICS: Werewolves TYPE: Book; 344 pgs. PRICE: $15.95 DESCRIPTION: Illustrated & indexed.

A Miracle To Believe In
PUBLISHING COMPANY: Option Institute & Fellowship- A Place For Miracles TOPICS: Holistic Healing TYPE: Book

A Scientific Guide To Peaceful Living
PUBLISHING COMPANY: Juvenescent Research Corp. EDITOR: Betty Yulin Ho TOPICS: Holistic Health TYPE: Book DATE: 1972; 170 pgs. PRICE: $15.00 DESCRIPTION: A view of the living body functioning as a whole. Covers exercise, foods & cooking, sicknesses, acupuncture.

A State Of Mind
PUBLISHING COMPANY: Sovereignty, Inc. EDITOR: J.Z. Knight TOPICS: Channeling, Psychic TYPE: Book

A Tibetan On Tibet
PUBLISHING COMPANY: Snow Lion Graphics TOPICS: New Age TYPE: Book PRICE: $12.95

A Vegetarian Sourcebook: The Nutrition, Ecology, And Ethics Of A Natural Foods Diet
PUBLISHING COMPANY: Vegetarian Press EDITOR: Peter Singer TOPICS: Health Food TYPE: Book

A.E. Waite: Magician Of Many Parts
PUBLISHING COMPANY: Crucible Books, Inner Traditions International, Ltd. EDITOR: R. Gilbert TOPICS: Occult TYPE: Book PRICE: $19.95

A.E. Waite: Selected Masonic Papers
PUBLISHING COMPANY: Aquarian Press EDITOR: E. Dunning TOPICS: Spirituality TYPE: Book PRICE: $14.95

A.R.E. Meditation Course
PUBLISHING COMPANY: Association For Research And Enlightenment, Inc. EDITOR: Mark Thurston TOPICS: Meditation TYPE: Book PRICE: $39.95

AAPB Membership Directory
PUBLISHING COMPANY: Association For Applied Psychophysiology & Biofeedback TOPICS: Holistic Healing TYPE: Directory

ABC's Of Crystals
PUBLISHING COMPANY: New Age Concepts/Color Magic EDITOR: Elaine Jay Finster TOPICS: New Age, Crystals, Holistic Healing TYPE: Book DESCRIPTION: Describes 160 different stones for healing & expanding awareness.

ABC's Of Handwriting Analysis
PUBLISHING COMPANY: Paragon House EDITOR: Claude Santoy TOPICS: Graphology TYPE: Book PRICE: $12.95

ABNOSTICORUAF
PUBLISHING COMPANY: ABNOSTICORUAF TOPICS: Channeling TYPE: Directory

Above Top Secret
PUBLISHING COMPANY: William Morrow & Co. EDITOR: T. Good TOPICS: UFO's, Paranormal Phenomena TYPE: Book PRICE: $12.95

Absolute Power
PUBLISHING COMPANY: Directions Unlimited EDITOR: Joseph Abbott, Jr. TOPICS: New Age TYPE: Book; 224 pgs. PRICE: $26.50 DESCRIPTION: Self-help program using a mind-expansion system called Feedback Amplification which teaches people how to use their dormant powers & unfold their latent abilities.

Abundant Peace: Biography Of Morihei Ueshiba, Founder Of Aikido
PUBLISHING COMPANY: Shambhala Publications, Inc. EDITOR: John Stevens TOPICS: Aikido TYPE: Book PRICE: $12.95

Acrobats Of The Gods: Dance And Transformation
PUBLISHING COMPANY: Inner City Books EDITOR: Joan D. Blackmer TOPICS: New Age TYPE: Book PRICE: $13.00

Across The Unknown
PUBLISHING COMPANY: Ariel Press EDITOR: E. Stewart TOPICS: Psychic TYPE: Book PRICE: $9.95

Active Imagination: Encounters With The Soul-Active Imagination As Developed By C.G. Jung
PUBLISHING COMPANY: Sigo Press EDITOR: B. Hannah TOPICS: Psychology TYPE: Book PRICE: $15.95

Active Meditation: The Western Tradition
PUBLISHING COMPANY: Ariel Press EDITOR: R. Leichtman, C. Japikse TOPICS: Meditation TYPE: Book PRICE: $24.50

Acu-Yoga: The Acupressure Stress Management Book
PUBLISHING COMPANY: Japan Publications, Inc. EDITOR: M. Gach, C. Marco TOPICS: Acupuncture TYPE: Book PRICE: $14.95

Acumoxa Therapy: Comprehensive Reference & Study

PUBLISHING COMPANY: Paradigm Publications **EDITOR:** Paul Zmlewski **TOPICS:** Acupuncture **TYPE:** Book **PRICE:** $19.95

Acupressure Way Of Health: Jin Shin Do

PUBLISHING COMPANY: Japan Publications, Inc. **EDITOR:** I. Teeguarden **TOPICS:** Acupuncture **TYPE:** Book **PRICE:** $12.95

Acupressure Workshop

PUBLISHING COMPANY: Acupressure Institute **EDITOR:** Michael Reed Gach **TOPICS:** Holistic Healing **TYPE:** Book

Acupressure Yoga And You

PUBLISHING COMPANY: Japan Publications, Inc. **EDITOR:** L. Taylor, B. Bryant **TOPICS:** Yoga, Acupuncture **TYPE:** Book **PRICE:** $11.95

Acupressure's Potent Points: A Guide To Self-Care For Common Ailments

PUBLISHING COMPANY: Bantam Books **EDITOR:** M. Gach **TOPICS:** Acupuncture **TYPE:** Guide **PRICE:** $14.95

Acupuncture Directory: Yellow Pages

PUBLISHING COMPANY: Center For Chinese Medicine **TOPICS:** Holistic Healing **TYPE:** Directory

Acupuncture Imaging

PUBLISHING COMPANY: Inner Traditions International, Ltd. **EDITOR:** Richard D. Wright **TOPICS:** Dowsing **TYPE:** Book **PRICE:** $9.95

Acupuncture In Gynecology And Obstetrics: An Essential Guide For Practitioners & Students

PUBLISHING COMPANY: Collins, Div. of William Collins **EDITOR:** Royston Low **TOPICS:** Acupuncture **TYPE:** Guide **PRICE:** $14.95

Acupuncture Medicine

PUBLISHING COMPANY: Japan Publications, Inc. **EDITOR:** Y. Omura **TOPICS:** Acupuncture **TYPE:** Book **PRICE:** $27.50

Acupuncture Treament Of Musculoskeletal Conditions: Practical Handbook For Practitioner

PUBLISHING COMPANY: Thorsens Publishing House **EDITOR:** Royston Low **TOPICS:** Acupuncture **TYPE:** Handbook **PRICE:** $16.95

Acupuncture Treatment Of Internal Disease

PUBLISHING COMPANY: Thorsens Publishing House **EDITOR:** G. Lewith **TOPICS:** Acupuncture **TYPE:** Book **PRICE:** $12.95

Acupuncture Treatment Of Pain

PUBLISHING COMPANY: Inner Traditions International, Ltd. **EDITOR:** Leon Chaitow, D.O., N.D. **TOPICS:** Acupuncture **TYPE:** Book **PRICE:** $16.95

Adepts

PUBLISHING COMPANY: Word Foundation, Inc., The **TOPICS:** Metaphysics **TYPE:** Book

Advanced Crystal Therapeutics

PUBLISHING COMPANY: Holistic Health Works, Div. of Spiritual Awareness Dynamics **EDITOR:** O. Frank **TOPICS:** Crystals, Psychic Healing, Spirituality **TYPE:** Book **PRICE:** $18.95

Advanced Yang Style Tai Chi Chuan Vol. 1

PUBLISHING COMPANY: Yang Martial Arts Assoc. **EDITOR:** Y. Jwing-Ming **TOPICS:** Tai Chi **TYPE:** Book **PRICE:** $18.95

Advanced Yang Style Tai Chi Chuan Vol. 2

PUBLISHING COMPANY: Yang Martial Arts Assoc. **EDITOR:** Y. Jwing-Ming **TOPICS:** Tai Chi **TYPE:** Book **PRICE:** $18.95

Affirmations

PUBLISHING COMPANY: White Dove International, Inc. **EDITOR:** S. Wilde **TOPICS:** New Age, Psychology **TYPE:** Book **PRICE:** $9.95

Affordable Spas & Fitness Resorts

PUBLISHING COMPANY: Ventana Press **EDITOR:** Ryan Vollmer **TOPICS:** New Age, Holistic Health **TYPE:** Book

After Death - What?

PUBLISHING COMPANY: Aquarian Press **EDITOR:** C. Lombroso **TOPICS:** Psychic, Spirituality, Death, Channeling **TYPE:** Book **PRICE:** $16.95

After Death Experience: Physics Of The Non-Physical World

PUBLISHING COMPANY: William Morrow & Co. **EDITOR:** Ian Wilson **TOPICS:** Occult **TYPE:** Book **PRICE:** $16.95

After We Die, What Then?

PUBLISHING COMPANY: Metascience Foundation **EDITOR:** George W. Meek **TOPICS:** Death **TYPE:** Book **PRICE:** $8.95

Afterlife: An Investigation

PUBLISHING COMPANY: Doubleday & Co.,Inc. **EDITOR:** Colin Wilson **TOPICS:** Death, Spirituality, Reincarnation **TYPE:** Book **PRICE:** $9.95

Ageless Wisdom

PUBLISHING COMPANY: T.S.G. Publishing Foundation, Inc. **EDITOR:** T. Saraydarian **TOPICS:** Spirituality **TYPE:** Book **PRICE:** $16.00

Aikido

PUBLISHING COMPANY: Japan Publications, Inc. **EDITOR:** K. Uyeshiba **TOPICS:** Aikido **TYPE:** Book **PRICE:** $24.95

Aikido And The Dynamic Sphere

PUBLISHING COMPANY: Charles E. Tuttle Company, Inc. **EDITOR:** A. Westbrook, O. Ratti **TOPICS:** Aikido **TYPE:** Book **PRICE:** $29.50

Aikido And The New Warrior

PUBLISHING COMPANY: North Atlantic Books **EDITOR:** R. Heckler **TOPICS:** Aikido **TYPE:** Book **PRICE:** $12.95

Aikido As A Clairsentient Practice

PUBLISHING COMPANY: North Atlantic Books **EDITOR:** Wendy Palmer **TOPICS:** Aikido **TYPE:** Book **PRICE:** $12.95

Aikido Complete

PUBLISHING COMPANY: Citadel Press **EDITOR:** Y. Yamada **TOPICS:** Aikido **TYPE:** Book **PRICE:** $8.95

Aikido For Life

PUBLISHING COMPANY: North Atlantic Books **EDITOR:** Gaku Homma **TOPICS:** Aikido **TYPE:** Book **PRICE:** $9.95

Aikido: The Way Of Harmony

PUBLISHING COMPANY: Random House, Inc. **EDITOR:** John Stevens, R. Shirata **TOPICS:** Aikido **TYPE:** Book **PRICE:** $19.95

Akashic Record Player

PUBLISHING COMPANY: Astrologik/Vigilantero Press **EDITOR:** Antero Alli **TOPICS:** New Age **TYPE:** Book

Alchemical Mandala: A Survey Of The Mandala In The Western Esoteric Traditions

PUBLISHING COMPANY: Phanes Press **EDITOR:** A. McLean **TOPICS:** Meditation **TYPE:** Book **PRICE:** $12.95

Alchemical Studies

PUBLISHING COMPANY: Princeton University Press **EDITOR:** C. Jung **TOPICS:** Psychology, Alchemy **TYPE:** Book **PRICE:** $16.95

Alchemy And The Alchemists

PUBLISHING COMPANY: Philosophical Research Society, Inc. **EDITOR:** E. Hitchcock **TOPICS:** Alchemy **TYPE:** Book **PRICE:** $15.00

Alchemy: An Introduction To The Symbolism And The Psychology

PUBLISHING COMPANY: Inner City Books **EDITOR:** M.L. Von Franz **TOPICS:** Psychology, Alchemy **TYPE:** Book **PRICE:** $18.00

All In The Name Of Love

PUBLISHING COMPANY: Alivening Publications **EDITOR:** B. Smyly, G. Smyly **TOPICS:** Spirituality **TYPE:** Book **PRICE:** $17.95

All Rites Reversed

PUBLISHING COMPANY: Astrologik/Vigilantero Press **EDITOR:** Antero Alli **TOPICS:** New Age **TYPE:** Book

All Women Are Healers: A Comprehensive Guide To Natural Healing

PUBLISHING COMPANY: Crossing Press **EDITOR:** D. Stein **TOPICS:** Psychic Healing, Holistic Healing, Spirituality, Homeopathy **TYPE:** Book **PRICE:** $12.95

Alphabet Of Creation: An Ancient Legend From The Zohar

PUBLISHING COMPANY: Random House, Inc. **EDITOR:** B. Shahn **TOPICS:** Channeling, Kabbalah **TYPE:** Book **PRICE:** $16.95

Altered States Of Consciousness
PUBLISHING COMPANY: Harper & Row Publishers, Inc. EDITOR: C. Tart TOPICS: Psychology TYPE: Book PRICE: $16.95

Alternative America
PUBLISHING COMPANY: Resources EDITOR: Richard Gardner TOPICS: New Age TYPE: Directory DESCRIPTION: Resource guide listing almost 2,000 publishers & 500 bookstores. Some considered radical & alternative.

Alternative Directory Of Holistic Health
PUBLISHING COMPANY: Hercules Press EDITOR: Michael Hercules TOPICS: Holistic Health TYPE: Directory DATE: 1980; 82 pgs.

Alternative Press: Children's Books
PUBLISHING COMPANY: Alternative Press: Children's Books TOPICS: New Age TYPE: Directory DESCRIPTION: Source directory produced by Cooperative Children's Book Center.

Alternatives In Education
PUBLISHING COMPANY: Home Education Press TOPICS: New Age TYPE: Book

American Atlas
PUBLISHING COMPANY: A.C.S. Publications, Inc./Astro Computing Services EDITOR: N. Michelsen TOPICS: Astrology TYPE: Book PRICE: $29.95

American Book Of Nutrition And Medical Astrology
PUBLISHING COMPANY: A.C.S. Publications, Inc./Astro Computing Services EDITOR: E. Nauman TOPICS: Holistic Health, Astrology TYPE: Book PRICE: $17.95

American Ephemeris '31-'80 (Midnight-includes American Table Of Houses & Calculations)
PUBLISHING COMPANY: A.C.S. Publications, Inc./Astro Computing Services EDITOR: N. Michelsen TOPICS: Astrology TYPE: Book PRICE: $29.95

American Heliocentric Ephemeris For 1901-2000
PUBLISHING COMPANY: A.C.S. Publications, Inc./Astro Computing Services EDITOR: N. Michelsen TOPICS: Astrology TYPE: Book PRICE: $25.00

American Holistic Medical Assocation-Directory Of Members
PUBLISHING COMPANY: American Holistic Medical Association EDITOR: Tracey Weller TOPICS: Holistic Healing TYPE: Directory PRICE: $7.25

American Medicinal Plants
PUBLISHING COMPANY: Dover Publications, Inc. EDITOR: C. Millspaugh TOPICS: Holistic Health, Herbalogy TYPE: Book PRICE: $15.95

American Sidereal Ephemeris 1976-2000
PUBLISHING COMPANY: A.C.S. Publications, Inc./Astro Computing Services EDITOR: N. Michelsen TOPICS: Astrology TYPE: Book PRICE: $19.50

American Society Of Clinical Hypnosis Directory
PUBLISHING COMPANY: American Society Of Clinical Hypnosis EDITOR: William Hoffman TOPICS: Hypnotism TYPE: Directory

American Yoga Association Beginner's Manual
PUBLISHING COMPANY: Simon & Schuster, Inc. EDITOR: A. Christensen TOPICS: Yoga, Holistic Health TYPE: Handbook PRICE: $12.95

Amulets And Superstitions
PUBLISHING COMPANY: Dover Publications, Inc. EDITOR: W. Budge TOPICS: Occult, Witchcraft TYPE: Book PRICE: $9.95

Anabiosis
PUBLISHING COMPANY: International Association For Near-Death Studies TOPICS: Death TYPE: Book

Analysing Palmar Quadrants
PUBLISHING COMPANY: Cheirological Society EDITOR: Shifu T. Dukes TOPICS: Palmistry, Holistic Health TYPE: Book DATE: 1985

Anatomy Of An Illness
PUBLISHING COMPANY: Bantam New Age Books EDITOR: Norman Cousins TYPE: Book

Anatomy Of Change: East-West Approaches To Body-Mind Therapy
PUBLISHING COMPANY: Shambhala Publications, Inc. EDITOR: R. Strozzi-Heckler TOPICS: Aikido TYPE: Book PRICE: $11.95

Anatomy Of The Psyche: Alchemical Symbolism In Psychotherapy
PUBLISHING COMPANY: Open Court Publishing Co. EDITOR: E. Edinger TOPICS: Spirituality TYPE: Book PRICE: $16.95

Ancient Astronauts, Cosmic Collisions And Other Popular Theories About Man's Past
PUBLISHING COMPANY: Prometheus Books EDITOR: William Stiebing TOPICS: Skepticism, Paranormal Phenomena, UFO's TYPE: Book PRICE: $13.95

Ancient Atlantic
PUBLISHING COMPANY: Palmer Publications/Amherst Press, Inc. EDITOR: L.T. Hansen TOPICS: New Age TYPE: Book PRICE: $17.00

Ancient Egyptian
PUBLISHING COMPANY: William Morrow & Co. EDITOR: B. Brier TOPICS: Occult TYPE: Book PRICE: $10.95

Ancient Egyptian Herbal
PUBLISHING COMPANY: University Of The Trees EDITOR: Lise Manniche TOPICS: Herbalogy, Holistic Healing, Spirituality, Alchemy TYPE: Book PRICE: $19.95

Ancient Hindu Astrology For The Modern Western Astrologer
PUBLISHING COMPANY: Hermetician Press EDITOR: J. Braha TOPICS: Astrology TYPE: Book PRICE: $24.95

Ancient Legends Of Gems & Jewels
PUBLISHING COMPANY: Prisma Products TOPICS: New Age TYPE: Book

Ancient Magicks For A New Age
PUBLISHING COMPANY: Llewellyn Publications EDITOR: A. Richardson, G. Hughes TOPICS: Occult TYPE: Book PRICE: $12.95

Ancient Mysteries
PUBLISHING COMPANY: Institute Of Geomantic Research TOPICS: New Age TYPE: Book

Ancient Mystic Rites
PUBLISHING COMPANY: Theosophical University Press EDITOR: C. Leadbeater TOPICS: Paranormal Phenomena TYPE: Book PRICE: $9.75

Angel Tech: A Modern Shaman's Guide To Reality Selection
PUBLISHING COMPANY: Astrologik/Vigilantero Press EDITOR: Antero Alli TOPICS: New Age, Psychic Phenomena TYPE: Book PRICE: $10.95

Animal Emergency Handbook
PUBLISHING COMPANY: Naturo-Vet Services EDITOR: Gloria Dodd, D.V.M. TOPICS: Holistic Healing TYPE: Handbook DESCRIPTION: Founder of the California Holistic Veterinary Medical Association.

Anthropic Cosmological Principle
PUBLISHING COMPANY: Oxford University Press, Inc. EDITOR: J. Barrow, F. Tipler TOPICS: New Age TYPE: Book PRICE: $15.95

Anti-Gravity Handbook
PUBLISHING COMPANY: Adventures-Unlimited Press EDITOR: D. Childress TOPICS: UFO's, Paranormal Phenomena TYPE: Book PRICE: $12.95

Apocalypse Now: The Coming Of A New Age
PUBLISHING COMPANY: Llewellyn Publications EDITOR: P. De Coppens TOPICS: New Age TYPE: Book PRICE: $9.95

Apostle Of Peace: Biography Of Sri Swami Satchidananda
PUBLISHING COMPANY: Integral Yoga Publications EDITOR: Sita Bordow TOPICS: Holistic Healing, Spirituality TYPE: Book PRICE: $14.95

Applied Magic/Aspects Of Occultism
PUBLISHING COMPANY: Samuel Weiser, Inc. EDITOR: D. Fortune TOPICS: Occult TYPE: Book PRICE: $11.95

Apprenticed To Magic And Magic And The Qabalah

PUBLISHING COMPANY: Aquarian Press **EDITOR:** W.E. Butler **TOPICS:** Occult, Kabbalah **TYPE:** Book **PRICE:** $12.95

Apprentices Of Wonder: Reinventing The Mind

PUBLISHING COMPANY: Bantam New Age Books **EDITOR:** W. Allman **TOPICS:** Body-Mind Connection, Psychology **TYPE:** Book **PRICE:** $19.95

Aqua Terra

PUBLISHING COMPANY: Water Center, The **EDITOR:** Jacqueline Froelich **TOPICS:** New Age **TYPE:** Book **PRICE:** $5.95 **DESCRIPTION:** Water concepts for the Ecological Society. Richly illustrated pages.

Aquarian Alternatives

PUBLISHING COMPANY: Aquarian Research Foundation **EDITOR:** Art Rosenblum **TOPICS:** New Age **TYPE:** Book

Aquarian Book Of Fortune Telling

PUBLISHING COMPANY: Aquarian Press **EDITOR:** S. Fenton **TOPICS:** Psychic, Occult **TYPE:** Book **PRICE:** $9.95

Aquarian Conspiracy: Personal And Social Transformation In Our Time

PUBLISHING COMPANY: Jeremy P. Tarcher, Inc. **EDITOR:** M. Ferguson **TOPICS:** New Age **TYPE:** Book **PRICE:** $10.95

Aquarian Guide To The New Age

PUBLISHING COMPANY: Aquarian Press **EDITOR:** Eileen Campbell, J. Brennan **TOPICS:** Psychic, New Age **TYPE:** Book **PRICE:** $9.95

Aquarian Rune Pack

PUBLISHING COMPANY: Aquarian Press **EDITOR:** Anthony Clark **TOPICS:** Runes **TYPE:** Book **PRICE:** $17.95

Aradia Or The Gospel Of The Witches

PUBLISHING COMPANY: Technology Group, The **PUBLISHER:** C.G. Leland **EDITOR:** Nelson White, Anne White **TYPE:** Book; 100 pgs.

Arcana Mundi: Magic & The Occult In The Greek & Roman World

PUBLISHING COMPANY: Crucible Books, Inner Traditions International, Ltd. **EDITOR:** G. Luck **TOPICS:** Occult **TYPE:** Book **PRICE:** $16.25

Archetypes And The Collective Consciousness

PUBLISHING COMPANY: Princeton University Press **EDITOR:** C. Jung **TOPICS:** Spirituality **TYPE:** Book **PRICE:** $15.95

Are You Really Too Sensitive?

PUBLISHING COMPANY: Blue Dolphin Publishing, Inc. **EDITOR:** Marcy Calhoun **TOPICS:** New Age **TYPE:** Book **PRICE:** $12.95

Arithmancy

PUBLISHING COMPANY: Technology Group, The **EDITOR:** Nelson White, Anne White **TYPE:** Book **PRICE:** $7.00

Aromatherapy To Heal And Tend The Body

PUBLISHING COMPANY: Lotus Light Publications **EDITOR:** Robert B. Tisserand **TOPICS:** Holistic Health **TYPE:** Book **PRICE:** $9.95

Art And Practice Of Astral Projection

PUBLISHING COMPANY: Samuel Weiser, Inc. Ophiel **TOPICS:** Astral Projection **TYPE:** Book **PRICE:** $9.95

Art And Practice Of Talismanic Magic

PUBLISHING COMPANY: Samuel Weiser, Inc. Ophiel **TOPICS:** Occult, Witchcraft **TYPE:** Book **PRICE:** $6.95

Art Is Healing

PUBLISHING COMPANY: Samuel Weiser, Inc. **EDITOR:** E. Adamson **TOPICS:** Spirituality, Psychic Healing **TYPE:** Book **PRICE:** $15.95

Art Of Aromatherapy: Healing And Beautifying Properties Of Oils, Flowers & Herbs

PUBLISHING COMPANY: Inner Traditions **EDITOR:** Robert B. Tisserand **TOPICS:** Holistic Health **TYPE:** Book **PRICE:** $10.95

Art Of Meditation

PUBLISHING COMPANY: Harper & Row Publishers, Inc. **EDITOR:** Joel Goldsmith **TOPICS:** Meditation **TYPE:** Book **PRICE:** $14.95

Art Of Ritual: A Guide To Creating & Performing Personalized Rituals For Growth & Change

PUBLISHING COMPANY: Celestial Arts Publishing Co./Sub. of Ten Speed Press **EDITOR:** R. Beck, S.B. Metrick **TOPICS:** Paganism, Spirituality **TYPE:** Book **PRICE:** $12.95

Art Of Spiritual Healing

PUBLISHING COMPANY: Harper & Row Publishers, Inc. **EDITOR:** Joel Goldsmith **TOPICS:** Spirituality, Psychic Healing **TYPE:** Book **PRICE:** $14.95

Artist As Channel

PUBLISHING COMPANY: Crystal Clarity Publishers **EDITOR:** Donald Walters **TOPICS:** Channeling **TYPE:** Book **PRICE:** $9.95

ArtNetwork

PUBLISHING COMPANY: Directors Guild Publishers **TOPICS:** New Age **TYPE:** Book; 80 pgs. **DESCRIPTION:** Erotic art by living artists.

Ashby Guidebook For Study Of The Paranormal

PUBLISHING COMPANY: Samuel Weiser, Inc. **EDITOR:** R. Ashby **TOPICS:** ESP, Psychic Phenomena **TYPE:** Book **PRICE:** $10.95

Aspects Of Research In Homeopathy

PUBLISHING COMPANY: Boiron/Borneman **EDITOR:** J. Boiron, et.al. **TOPICS:** Homeopathy **TYPE:** Book **PRICE:** $18.95

Association For Past-Life Research And Therapies Directory

PUBLISHING COMPANY: Association For Past-Life Research And Therapies, Inc. **TOPICS:** Reincarnation, Past Life Regression, Hypnotism, Death, Parapsychology **TYPE:** Directory **PRICE:** $5.00

Asteroid Goddesses: Ceres, Pallas, Juno & Vesta

PUBLISHING COMPANY: A.C.S. Publications, Inc./Astro Computing Services **EDITOR:** D. George **TOPICS:** Spirituality **TYPE:** Book **PRICE:** $14.95

Astral Plane

PUBLISHING COMPANY: Theosophical University Press **EDITOR:** C. Leadbeater **TOPICS:** Death **TYPE:** Book **PRICE:** $6.95

Astral Projection

PUBLISHING COMPANY: Whitford Press/Schiffer Publishing Limited **EDITOR:** Brad Steiger **TOPICS:** Astral Projection **TYPE:** Book **PRICE:** $12.95

Astral Projection Workbook: How To Achieve Out-Of-Body Experiences

PUBLISHING COMPANY: Aquarian Press **EDITOR:** J. Brennan **TOPICS:** Astral Projection **TYPE:** Book **PRICE:** $10.95

Astral Projection: Llewellyn's Practical Guide

PUBLISHING COMPANY: Llewellyn Publications **EDITOR:** M.. Denning, O. Phillips **TOPICS:** Astral Projection **TYPE:** Book **PRICE:** $7.95

Astro Essentials: Planets In Signs, Houses And Aspects

PUBLISHING COMPANY: A.C.S. Publications, Inc./Astro Computing Services **EDITOR:** Maritha Pottenger **TOPICS:** Astrology **TYPE:** Book **PRICE:** $19.95

Astro-Data II (formerly American Book Of Charts)

PUBLISHING COMPANY: American Federation Of Astrologers, Inc. **EDITOR:** L. Rodden **TOPICS:** Astrology **TYPE:** Book **PRICE:** $27.95

Astrological Healing: The History & Practice Of Astromedicine

PUBLISHING COMPANY: Samuel Weiser, Inc. **EDITOR:** R. Ebertin **TOPICS:** Holistic Health, Astrology **TYPE:** Book **PRICE:** $19.95

Astrologik: The Interpretive Art Of Astrology

PUBLISHING COMPANY: Astrologik/Vigilantero Press **EDITOR:** Antero Alli **TOPICS:** Astrology **TYPE:** Book **DESCRIPTION:** Redefines the language of Astrology by renaming the planets as Forces, the Houses as States & the Signs as Styles towards effective chart interpretation that is both imaginative & analytical.

Astrology Alive: Experiential Astrology, Astrodrama & The Healing Arts

PUBLISHING COMPANY: Aquarian Press **EDITOR:** Barbara Schermer **TOPICS:** Holistic Health, Astrology **TYPE:** Book **PRICE:** $9.95

Astrology And Past Lives

PUBLISHING COMPANY: Whitford Press/Schiffer Publishing Limited EDITOR: M. Devlin TOPICS: Past Life Regression, Astrology TYPE: Book PRICE: $18.95

Astrology And Past Lives: Explore Past Reincarnations Through Saturn's Placement

PUBLISHING COMPANY: Simon & Schuster, Inc. EDITOR: J. Avery TOPICS: Past Life Regression TYPE: Book PRICE: $9.95

Astrology And Spiritual Development

PUBLISHING COMPANY: Cassandra Press EDITOR: Donna Cunningham TOPICS: Astrology TYPE: Book; 144 pgs. PRICE: $9.95

Astrology And The Spiritual Path

PUBLISHING COMPANY: Samuel Weiser, Inc. EDITOR: Bruno Huber TOPICS: Astrology TYPE: Book PRICE: $12.95

Astrology And The Stock Market

PUBLISHING COMPANY: ASI Publishers, Inc. EDITOR: Louise McWhirter TOPICS: Astrology TYPE: Book PRICE: $30.00

Astrology And Vibrational Healing

PUBLISHING COMPANY: Cassandra Press EDITOR: Donna Cunningham TOPICS: Holistic Health, Astrology TYPE: Book; 168 pgs. PRICE: $9.95

Astrology Directory

PUBLISHING COMPANY: Ghost Research Society EDITOR: Dale Kaczmarek TOPICS: Astrology TYPE: Directory PRICE: $6.50 DESCRIPTION: Contains names of individuals, groups, organizations, magazines & newsletters on the topic.

Astrology Guide

PUBLISHING COMPANY: Sterlings Magazines, Inc. TOPICS: Astrology TYPE: Guide FREQ: bi-monthly

Astrology Inside Out

PUBLISHING COMPANY: Whitford Press/Schiffer Publishing Limited EDITOR: B. Nevin TOPICS: Astrology TYPE: Book PRICE: $18.95

Astrology Kit (2 books, note-pad & zodiac chart; consultant-Liz Greene)

PUBLISHING COMPANY: St. Martin's Press, Inc. EDITOR: G. Lewi TOPICS: Astrology TYPE: Book PRICE: $24.95

Astrology Of The Four Horsemen

PUBLISHING COMPANY: Summit University Press EDITOR: Elizabeth Clare Prophet TOPICS: Astrology TYPE: Book PRICE: $5.95

Astrology Plus

PUBLISHING COMPANY: Marcus Books Hilarion TOPICS: Astrology TYPE: Book PRICE: $8.95

Astrology The Star Science From A To Z

PUBLISHING COMPANY: Astro-Psychology Institute TOPICS: Astrology TYPE: Book

Astrology, Nutrition And Health

PUBLISHING COMPANY: Whitford Press/Schiffer Publishing Limited EDITOR: R. Jansky TOPICS: Holistic Health, Astrology TYPE: Book PRICE: $12.95

Astrology: Do The Heavens Rule Our Destiny?

PUBLISHING COMPANY: John Ankerberg Show, The EDITOR: John Ankerberg, John Weldon TOPICS: Astrology, New Age TYPE: Book DATE: 1989

Astrology: Key To Holistic Health

PUBLISHING COMPANY: Seek-It Publications EDITOR: M. Starck TOPICS: Holistic Health, Astrology TYPE: Book PRICE: $9.95

Astrophysical Directions

PUBLISHING COMPANY: Matrix Software EDITOR: Michael Erlewine TOPICS: Astrology TYPE: Handbook

At A Journal Workshop: The Basic Text & Guide For Using The Intensive Journal Process

PUBLISHING COMPANY: Dialogue House EDITOR: I. Progoff TOPICS: New Age, Psychology TYPE: Book PRICE: $15.95

At The Edge Of History And Passages About Earth

PUBLISHING COMPANY: Lindisfarne Press EDITOR: William Irwin Thompson TOPICS: New Age TYPE: Book PRICE: $15.95

At The Pool Of Wonder: Dreams & Visions Of An Awakening Humanity

PUBLISHING COMPANY: Bear & Company, Inc. EDITOR: M. Lauck, D. Koff-Chapin TOPICS: Dreams TYPE: Book PRICE: $16.95

Atlas Of The Supernatural

PUBLISHING COMPANY: Prentice-Hall, Inc. EDITOR: Derek Parker, Julia Parker TOPICS: ESP, Psychic Phenomena TYPE: Book PRICE: $24.95

Attaining Unlimited Life: Teachings Of Chuang Tzu

PUBLISHING COMPANY: Union Of Tao And Man EDITOR: M. Ni TOPICS: Spirituality, New Age TYPE: Book PRICE: $18.00

Attainment Through Magic

PUBLISHING COMPANY: Llewellyn Publications EDITOR: William G. Gray TOPICS: Occult, Witchcraft TYPE: Book PRICE: $9.95

Audubon Field Guide To Rocks And Minerals

PUBLISHING COMPANY: Random House, Inc. EDITOR: C. Chesterman TOPICS: Crystals TYPE: Book PRICE: $15.95

Authentic I Ching: A New Translation

PUBLISHING COMPANY: Newcastle Publishing Co., Inc. EDITOR: H. Wei TOPICS: Holistic Health TYPE: Book PRICE: $12.95

Autohypnosis Diet: Lose Weight And Keep It Off Naturally With The First Ever Mind Diet

PUBLISHING COMPANY: Sterling Publishing Company, Inc. EDITOR: M. Oechsli TOPICS: Hypnotism TYPE: Book PRICE: $12.95

Avalanche: Heretical Reflections On The Dark And The Light

PUBLISHING COMPANY: Ballantine Books, Inc. EDITOR: W. Brugh Joy TOPICS: Occult TYPE: Book PRICE: $19.95

Aveline Kushi's Introducing Macrobiotic Cooking

PUBLISHING COMPANY: Japan Publications, Inc. EDITOR: Wendy Esko TOPICS: Holistic Health, Vegetarianism, Health Food TYPE: Book PRICE: $14.95

Aveline: Life And Dream Of The Woman Behind Macrobiotics Today

PUBLISHING COMPANY: Japan Publications, Inc. EDITOR: A. Kushi, A. Jack TOPICS: Holistic Health, Vegetarianism, Health Food TYPE: Book PRICE: $19.95

Awaken Healing Energy Through The Tao

PUBLISHING COMPANY: Aurora Press, Inc. EDITOR: M. Chia TOPICS: Holistic Health TYPE: Book PRICE: $10.95

Awakening A Child From Within

PUBLISHING COMPANY: Life Action Press, Div. of Foundation for Life Action EDITOR: T. Singh TOPICS: Spirituality TYPE: Book PRICE: $12.95

Awakening Of Intelligence

PUBLISHING COMPANY: Harper & Row Publishers, Inc. EDITOR: S. Bhaktipada TOPICS: Spirituality TYPE: Book PRICE: $13.95

Awakening Osiris: The Egyptian Book Of The Dead

PUBLISHING COMPANY: Phanes Press EDITOR: N. Ellis TOPICS: Death TYPE: Book PRICE: $11.95

Awakening To The Animal Kingdom

PUBLISHING COMPANY: Cassandra Press EDITOR: Robert Shapiro, Julie Rapkin TOPICS: Channeling TYPE: Book; 96 pgs. PRICE: $8.95

Awakening: A Dream Journal

PUBLISHING COMPANY: Stewart, Tabori & Chang, Inc. EDITOR: E. Foreman TOPICS: Dreams TYPE: Book PRICE: $18.90

Awareness Through Movement

PUBLISHING COMPANY: Harper & Row Publishers, Inc. EDITOR: Moshe Feldenkrais TOPICS: Psychology TYPE: Book PRICE: $16.95

Awareness: A De Mello Spirituality Conference In His Own Words

PUBLISHING COMPANY: Doubleday & Co.,Inc. EDITOR: A. DeMello TOPICS: Spirituality TYPE: Book PRICE: $16.95

Ayurveda Cookbook

PUBLISHING COMPANY: Lotus Light Publications
EDITOR: Amadea Morningstar, U. Desai TOPICS:
Holistic Health TYPE: Book PRICE: $16.95

Ayurveda For Health And Long Life

PUBLISHING COMPANY: B. Jain Publishers, Ltd.
EDITOR: R. Garde TOPICS: Holistic Health TYPE:
Book PRICE: $12.00

Babaji: Meeting With Truth At The Haidakhan Vishwa Mahadham (Center Of The Universe)

PUBLISHING COMPANY: Coleman Publishing
EDITOR: S.S. Goodman TOPICS: Spirituality
TYPE: Book PRICE: $15.00

Baby Massage

PUBLISHING COMPANY: Sigo Press EDITOR: T.
Heinl TOPICS: Massage TYPE: Book PRICE:
$15.95

Bach Flower Therapy

PUBLISHING COMPANY: Thorsens Publishing
House EDITOR: M. Scheffer TOPICS: Homeopathy,
Holistic Health TYPE: Book PRICE: $9.95

Back To Eden

PUBLISHING COMPANY: Back To Eden Books
EDITOR: J. Kloss TOPICS: Homeopathy,
Herbalogy, Holistic Healing TYPE: Book PRICE:
$15.95

Baltimore Resources

PUBLISHING COMPANY: Baltimore Resources
EDITOR: Dan Rose-Redwood, Bonnie Raindrop
TOPICS: Holistic Health TYPE: Directory FREQ: bi-
monthly DESCRIPTION: A resource guide covering
topics on health, environment and spirituality for the
Baltimore area. Baltimore area guide, publishes
resources and reviews focusing on health and
environment.

Banished Knowledge

PUBLISHING COMPANY: Doubleday & Co.,Inc.
EDITOR: Dr. Alice Miller TOPICS: Holistic Health
TYPE: Book; 224 pgs. PRICE: $19.95

Barefoot Doctor's Manual: American Translation Of The Official Chinese Paramedical Manual

PUBLISHING COMPANY: Running Press EDITOR:
Rev. Hlth. Council Hunan Prov. TOPICS: Holistic
Health TYPE: Book PRICE: $12.95

Barefoot Shiatsu: Whole-Body Approach To Health

PUBLISHING COMPANY: Japan Publications, Inc.
EDITOR: S. Yamamoto TOPICS: Acupuncture
TYPE: Book PRICE: $12.95

Basic Dharma

PUBLISHING COMPANY: Blue Dolphin Publishing,
Inc. TOPICS: New Age TYPE: Book PRICE: $5.00

Basic Macrobiotics

PUBLISHING COMPANY: Harper & Row Publishers,
Inc. EDITOR: H. Aihara TOPICS: Holistic Health,
Vegetarianism, Health Food TYPE: Book PRICE:
$12.95

Basic Principles Of Ayurveda

PUBLISHING COMPANY: B. Jain Publishers, Ltd.
EDITOR: B. Dash, L. Kashyap TOPICS: Holistic
Health TYPE: Book PRICE: $39.00

Be As You Are: Teachings Of Sri Ramana Maharshi

PUBLISHING COMPANY: Routledge, Chapman &
Hall, Inc. EDITOR: D. Godman TOPICS:
Spirituality TYPE: Book PRICE: $9.95

Beacon Light

PUBLISHING COMPANY: Concord Grove Press,
Subs. of Institute of World Culture EDITOR: H.
Blavatsky TOPICS: Occult, Spirituality TYPE: Book
PRICE: $8.75

Beckett And Zen

PUBLISHING COMPANY: Wisdom Publications
EDITOR: Paul Foster TOPICS: New Age TYPE:
Book PRICE: $14.95

Beelzebub's Tales To His Grandson

PUBLISHING COMPANY: E.P. Dutton, Inc.
EDITOR: G. Gurdjieff TOPICS: Spirituality TYPE:
Book PRICE: $30.00

Behind Numerology: Complete Details On The Hidden Meaning Of Letters & Numbers

PUBLISHING COMPANY: Newcastle Publishing Co.,
Inc. EDITOR: S. Lawrence TOPICS: Numerology
TYPE: Book PRICE: $12.95

Being Human: The Art Of Feeling Alive

PUBLISHING COMPANY: Gardner Press, Inc.
EDITOR: Haskell Bernstein TOPICS: New Age,
Psychology TYPE: Book PRICE: $14.95

Beliefs: Pathways To Health And Well-Being

PUBLISHING COMPANY: Metamorphous Press
EDITOR: Robert Dilts TOPICS: Holistic Health,
Psychology, Body-Mind Connection TYPE: Book
PRICE: $12.95

Benham Book Of Palmistry: A Practical Treatise On The Laws Of Scientific Hand Reading

PUBLISHING COMPANY: Newcastle Publishing Co.,
Inc. EDITOR: W. Benham TOPICS: Palmistry
TYPE: Book PRICE: $14.95

Between Good And Evil: Polarities Of Power

PUBLISHING COMPANY: Llewellyn Publications
EDITOR: William G. Gray TOPICS: Occult,
Witchcraft TYPE: Book PRICE: $9.95

Between Time And Eternity

PUBLISHING COMPANY: Shambhala Publications,
Inc. EDITOR: I. Prigogine TOPICS: New Age TYPE:
Book PRICE: $22.50

Beyond Basic Health: Advanced Thinking For The Healing Arts

PUBLISHING COMPANY: Avery Publishing Group,
Inc. EDITOR: Bernard Jensen TOPICS: Holistic
Healing TYPE: Book PRICE: $11.95

Beyond Biofeedback

PUBLISHING COMPANY: Knoll Publishing Co., Inc.
EDITOR: E. Green, A. Green TOPICS:
Parapsychology, Holistic Health TYPE: Book
PRICE: $14.95

Beyond Death: The Gates Of Consciousness

PUBLISHING COMPANY: Thames & Hudson
EDITOR: S. Grof, C. Grof TOPICS: Death TYPE:
Book PRICE: $11.95

Beyond Death: The Undiscovered Country

PUBLISHING COMPANY: Theosophical University
Press EDITOR: H. Murphet TOPICS: Death TYPE:
Book PRICE: $9.95

Beyond Illness: Discovering The Experience Of Health

PUBLISHING COMPANY: Shambhala Publications,
Inc. EDITOR: Larry Dossey TOPICS: Holistic
Healing, Body-Mind Connection TYPE: Book
PRICE: $15.95

Beyond Pendulum Power: A Conscious Book

PUBLISHING COMPANY: MetaBusiness Institute/
Conscious Books EDITOR: G. Nielsen TOPICS:
Dowsing TYPE: Book PRICE: $9.95

Beyond Reality: The Role Unseen Dimensions Play In Our Lives

PUBLISHING COMPANY: Aquarian Press EDITOR:
D. Scott Rogo TOPICS: Psychic Phenomena, Occult,
Paranormal Phenomena, UFO's TYPE: Book
PRICE: $12.95

Beyond The Body

PUBLISHING COMPANY: Routledge, Chapman &
Hall, Inc. EDITOR: Benjamin Walker TOPICS: ESP,
Psychic Phenomena TYPE: Book PRICE: $12.95

Beyond The Body: An Investigation Of Out-Of-Body Experiences

PUBLISHING COMPANY: Academy Chicago
Publishers, Ltd. EDITOR: S. Blackmore TOPICS:
Astral Projection TYPE: Book PRICE: $8.95

Beyond The Mirror: Reflections On Death & Dying

PUBLISHING COMPANY: Continuum Publishing
Co. EDITOR: H. Nouwen TOPICS: Death TYPE:
Book PRICE: $10.95

Beyond The Occult: A Twenty Year Investigation Into The Paranormal

PUBLISHING COMPANY: Carroll & Graf Publishers
EDITOR: Colin Wilson TOPICS: ESP, Psychic
Phenomena, Paranormal Phenomena, Occult TYPE:
Book PRICE: $21.95

Beyond Tomorrow

PUBLISHING COMPANY: Astara Foundation, Inc.
EDITOR: E. Chaney TOPICS: Metaphysics, Psychic
TYPE: Book PRICE: $9.95

Beyond Within: A Philosophy For Inner Life

PUBLISHING COMPANY: AUM Publications EDITOR: S. Chinmoy TOPICS: Spirituality TYPE: Book PRICE: $10.95

Beyond Words: Terms For Transforming Consciousness

PUBLISHING COMPANY: Harbin Springs Publishing EDITOR: Paula Slater, Barbara Sinor TOPICS: New Age TYPE: Book PRICE: $14.95

Bhagavad Gita With Uttara Gita

PUBLISHING COMPANY: Concord Grove Press, Subs. of Institute of World Culture EDITOR: R. Iyer TOPICS: Spirituality TYPE: Book PRICE: $19.95

Bikram's Beginning Yoga Class

PUBLISHING COMPANY: Jeremy P. Tarcher, Inc. EDITOR: B. Choudhary TOPICS: Yoga, Holistic Health TYPE: Book PRICE: $12.95

Biocircuits: Amazing New Tools For Energy Health

PUBLISHING COMPANY: H.J. Kramer, Inc. EDITOR: L. Patten, T. Patten TOPICS: Holistic Health TYPE: Book PRICE: $10.95

Bioenergetic Medicines East And West: Acupuncture & Homeopathy

PUBLISHING COMPANY: North Atlantic Books EDITOR: C. Manning, L. Vanrenen TOPICS: Holistic Healing, Homeopathy TYPE: Book PRICE: $12.95

Biography Of An Archangel

PUBLISHING COMPANY: Unarius Academy Of Science & Education Foundation EDITOR: Ruth Norman TOPICS: Reincarnation TYPE: Book; 365 pgs. PRICE: $24.95

Birth Of A Modern Shaman

PUBLISHING COMPANY: Llewellyn Publications EDITOR: C. Bend, T. Wiger TOPICS: Psychic TYPE: Book PRICE: $9.95

Birth Reborn

PUBLISHING COMPANY: Pantheon Books/Random House EDITOR: Michel Odent, M.D. TOPICS: Birth TYPE: Book

Birthday Numerology

PUBLISHING COMPANY: Whitford Press/Schiffer Publishing Limited EDITOR: D. Bunker, V. Knowles TOPICS: Numerology TYPE: Book PRICE: $13.95

Birthstone Coloring Book

PUBLISHING COMPANY: Prisma Products TOPICS: New Age TYPE: Book

Black Madonna

PUBLISHING COMPANY: Sigo Press EDITOR: Fred Gustafson TOPICS: Spirituality TYPE: Book PRICE: $15.95

Blatant Raw Foodist Propaganda!

PUBLISHING COMPANY: Blue Dolphin Publishing, Inc. EDITOR: Joe Alexander TOPICS: Holistic Health, Health Food, Vegetarianism TYPE: Book PRICE: $9.95

Body Metaphors: Releasing The God-Feminine In Us All

PUBLISHING COMPANY: Continuum Publishing Co. EDITOR: G.P. Haddon TOPICS: Spirituality TYPE: Book PRICE: $19.95

Body Mind Directory

PUBLISHING COMPANY: Body Mind Directory PUBLISHER: Joy Ackerman TOPICS: Holistic Health TYPE: Directory FREQ: quarterly CIRC: 20,000 DESCRIPTION: A resource directory produced by the Holistic Institute, Inc.

Body Of Light

PUBLISHING COMPANY: Globe Press Books EDITOR: John Mann, Lar Short TOPICS: Channeling TYPE: Book PRICE: $14.95

Body Reading: The Complete Guide

PUBLISHING COMPANY: Aquarian Press EDITOR: S. Fenton TOPICS: Parapsychology TYPE: Book PRICE: $9.95

Body, Self And Soul: Sustaining Integration

PUBLISHING COMPANY: Humanics New Age, Ltd. EDITOR: J. Rosenberg TOPICS: Body-Mind Connection TYPE: Book PRICE: $14.95

Body-Centered Psychotherapy: The Hakomi Method

PUBLISHING COMPANY: LifeRhythm EDITOR: R. Kurtz TOPICS: Body-Mind Connection TYPE: Book PRICE: $15.95

Bodymind Energetics: Toward A Dynamic Model Of Health

PUBLISHING COMPANY: Thorsens Publishing House EDITOR: Mark Seem, Joan Kaplan TOPICS: Body-Mind Connection, Holistic Healing TYPE: Book PRICE: $14.95

Bodywork Directory of North America

PUBLISHING COMPANY: Bodywork Directory of North America PUBLISHER: L. Marc Haberman TOPICS: New Age, Metaphysics TYPE: Directory DATE: 1981 DESCRIPTION: Small directory of bodywork listings for all major cities.

Boenninghausen's Repertory

PUBLISHING COMPANY: B. Jain Publishers, Ltd. EDITOR: C. Boger TOPICS: Homeopathy TYPE: Book PRICE: $35.00

Bone Marrow Nei Kung: Taoist Ways To Improve Your Health By Rejuvenating Bone Marrow & Blood

PUBLISHING COMPANY: Healing Tao Center EDITOR: M. Chia TOPICS: Tai Chi, Holistic Health TYPE: Book PRICE: $14.95

Book Of Angelus Silesius

PUBLISHING COMPANY: Bear & Company, Inc. EDITOR: Frederick Franck TOPICS: Paranormal Phenomena TYPE: Book PRICE: $12.95

Book Of Changes And The Unchanging Truth

PUBLISHING COMPANY: Union Of Tao And Man EDITOR: H. Ni TOPICS: Parapsychology, Psychic TYPE: Book PRICE: $35.00

Book Of Do-In: Exercises For Physical And Spiritual Development

PUBLISHING COMPANY: Japan Publications, Inc. EDITOR: M. Kushi TOPICS: Tai Chi TYPE: Book PRICE: $14.95

Book Of Druidry

PUBLISHING COMPANY: Aquarian Press EDITOR: R. Phillip TOPICS: Occult TYPE: Book PRICE: $16.95

Book Of Goddesses And Heroines

PUBLISHING COMPANY: Llewellyn Publications EDITOR: Patricia Monaghan TOPICS: Spirituality TYPE: Book PRICE: $17.95

Book Of Ki: Co-Ordinating Mind And Body In Daily Life

PUBLISHING COMPANY: Japan Publications, Inc. EDITOR: K. Tohei TOPICS: Aikido TYPE: Book PRICE: $8.95

Book Of Light

PUBLISHING COMPANY: Magickal Childe Occult Supplies, Inc. Lady Sara TOPICS: Witchcraft, Occult TYPE: Book PRICE: $12.95

Book Of Macrobiotics

PUBLISHING COMPANY: Japan Publications, Inc. EDITOR: M. Kushi TOPICS: Holistic Health, Vegetarianism, Health Food TYPE: Book PRICE: $15.95

Book Of Macrobiotics

PUBLISHING COMPANY: Kushi Institute-East West Foundation EDITOR: Michio Kushi TOPICS: Health Food, Holistic Health, Vegetarianism, Nutrition, Spirituality TYPE: Book DATE: 1977

Book Of Massage

PUBLISHING COMPANY: Simon & Schuster, Inc. EDITOR: L. Lidell TOPICS: Massage TYPE: Book PRICE: $12.95

Book Of Pagan Rituals

PUBLISHING COMPANY: Samuel Weiser, Inc. EDITOR: H. Slater Frnds Craft TOPICS: Paganism, Spirituality TYPE: Book PRICE: $10.95

Book Of Rituals: Keys To Personal & Planetary Transformation

PUBLISHING COMPANY: IBS Press EDITOR: C. Parrish-Harra TOPICS: Occult TYPE: Book PRICE: $14.95

Book Of Rune: A Handbook For The Use Of An Ancient Oracle

PUBLISHING COMPANY: Runeworks, The EDITOR: R. Blum TOPICS: Runes, Metaphysics TYPE: Book PRICE: $14.95

Book Of Sacred Stones: Fact And Fallacy In The Crystal World

PUBLISHING COMPANY: Harper & Row Publishers, Inc. EDITOR: Barbara Walker TOPICS: Crystals TYPE: Book PRICE: $15.95

Book Of Serenity
PUBLISHING COMPANY: Lindisfarne Press EDITOR: T. Cleary TOPICS: Spirituality TYPE: Book PRICE: $14.95

Book Of Shaman
PUBLISHING COMPANY: Circle Of The Whitefeather EDITOR: Robert J. Titus TOPICS: Spirituality TYPE: Book PRICE: $10.00

Book Of Shiatsu: The Healing Art Of Finger Pressure
PUBLISHING COMPANY: Avery Publishing Group, Inc. EDITOR: Saul Goodman TOPICS: Acupuncture TYPE: Book PRICE: $12.95

Book Of Stress Survival: Identifying & Reducing The Stress In Your Life
PUBLISHING COMPANY: Simon & Schuster, Inc. EDITOR: A. Kirsta TOPICS: Holistic Health, New Age TYPE: Book PRICE: $11.95

Book Of Surrender: A Journey To Self-Awareness Through The Words Of Emmanuel
PUBLISHING COMPANY: Prentice-Hall, Inc. Emmanuel, Wingate Paine TOPICS: Channeling TYPE: Book PRICE: $8.95

Book Of Talismans, Amulets And Zodiacal Gems
PUBLISHING COMPANY: Wilshire Book Company EDITOR: W. Pavitt TOPICS: Occult, Witchcraft TYPE: Book PRICE: $7.00

Book Of Tea
PUBLISHING COMPANY: Charles E. Tuttle Company, Inc. EDITOR: O. Kakuzo TOPICS: Spirituality TYPE: Book PRICE: $12.95

Book Of The Dead
PUBLISHING COMPANY: Citadel Press EDITOR: W. Budge TOPICS: Death TYPE: Book PRICE: $14.95

Book Of Tokens: Tarot Meditations
PUBLISHING COMPANY: Builders Of The Adytum EDITOR: P.F. Case TOPICS: Tarot TYPE: Book PRICE: $13.00

Book On Mediums: Guide For Mediums & Invocators
PUBLISHING COMPANY: Samuel Weiser, Inc. EDITOR: A. Kardec TOPICS: ESP, Channeling, Psychic Phenomena, Psychic TYPE: Book PRICE: $12.95

Born Again And Again
PUBLISHING COMPANY: Inner Vision Publishing Co. EDITOR: J. Van Auken TOPICS: Reincarnation TYPE: Book PRICE: $9.95

Born In Blood: The Lost Secrets Of Freemasonry
PUBLISHING COMPANY: M. Evans & Co., Inc. EDITOR: John Robinson TOPICS: Spirituality TYPE: Book PRICE: $18.95

Bowl Of Saki Commentary: The Sutra On The Three Hundred Sixty-Six Aphorisms
PUBLISHING COMPANY: Sufi Islamia/Prophecy Press EDITOR: H.I. Khan, Samuel Lewis TOPICS: Spirituality TYPE: Book PRICE: $18.00

Boy Lama
PUBLISHING COMPANY: Harper & Row Publishers, Inc. EDITOR: V. Mackenzie TOPICS: Reincarnation TYPE: Book PRICE: $9.95

Brad Steiger Predicts The Future
PUBLISHING COMPANY: Whitford Press/Schiffer Publishing Limited EDITOR: Brad Steiger TOPICS: Metaphysics, Psychic TYPE: Book PRICE: $9.95

Brain Building: Exercising Yourself Smarter
PUBLISHING COMPANY: Bantam New Age Books EDITOR: Marilyn V. Savant TOPICS: Body-Mind Connection, Holistic Health, Psychology TYPE: Book PRICE: $18.95

Brain Power: A Neurosurgeon's Program To Maintain & Enhance Brain Fitness Throughout Life
PUBLISHING COMPANY: Houghton Mifflin Company EDITOR: V. Mark, J. Mark TOPICS: Holistic Health TYPE: Book PRICE: $18.95

Brain, Symbol And Experience: Toward A Neurophenomenology Of Human Consciousness
PUBLISHING COMPANY: Shambhala Publications, Inc. EDITOR: Charles Laughlin TOPICS: Body-Mind Connection, Psychology TYPE: Book PRICE: $19.95

Breaking The Mind Barrier: The Artscience Of Neurocosmology
PUBLISHING COMPANY: Simon & Schuster, Inc. EDITOR: Todd Siler TOPICS: Body-Mind Connection, Psychology TYPE: Book PRICE: $22.95

Breakthrough To Higher Psychism
PUBLISHING COMPANY: T.S.G. Publishing Foundation, Inc. EDITOR: T. Saraydarian TOPICS: Psychic TYPE: Book PRICE: $10.95

Breakthrough: Meister Eckhart's Creation Spirituality In New Translation
PUBLISHING COMPANY: Doubleday & Co.,Inc. EDITOR: Matthew Fox TOPICS: Spirituality TYPE: Book PRICE: $12.95

Breath Of God
PUBLISHING COMPANY: Rudra Press EDITOR: Swami Chetanananda TOPICS: Spirituality TYPE: Book PRICE: $14.95

Bridge Of Dreams: The Story Of Paramananda And His Community
PUBLISHING COMPANY: Inner Traditions International, Ltd. EDITOR: S. Levensky TOPICS: Spirituality TYPE: Book PRICE: $12.95

Bridge To The Other Side
PUBLISHING COMPANY: Authors Unlimited EDITOR: Vikee Vaughn TOPICS: Reincarnation, Spirituality TYPE: Book PRICE: $10.95

Buckland's Complete Witchcraft Workbook
PUBLISHING COMPANY: Llewellyn Publications EDITOR: R. Buckland TOPICS: Occult, Witchcraft TYPE: Book PRICE: $12.95

Buddhism Of Tibet
PUBLISHING COMPANY: Snow Lion Publications, Inc. EDITOR: J. Hopkins TOPICS: Spirituality TYPE: Book PRICE: $12.95

Buddhist I-Ching
PUBLISHING COMPANY: Shambhala Publications, Inc. EDITOR: T. Cleary TOPICS: Holistic Health TYPE: Book PRICE: $13.95

Builders Of The Dawn
PUBLISHING COMPANY: Sirius Community EDITOR: Corrine McLaughlin, Gordon Davidson TOPICS: Holistic Healing TYPE: Book

Builders: A Story And Study Of Freemasonry
PUBLISHING COMPANY: Macoy Publishing Co. EDITOR: Joseph Newton TOPICS: Spirituality TYPE: Book PRICE: $13.95

Business Mastery: A Business Planning Guide For Creating A Fulfilling, Thriving Business and Keeping It Successful
PUBLISHING COMPANY: Sohnen-Moe Associates EDITOR: Cherie Sohnen-Moe TOPICS: New Age TYPE: Book DATE: 1991 SIZE: 8 1/2 x 11; 256 pgs. PRICE: $19.95

Butterfly Rises
PUBLISHING COMPANY: Blue Dolphin Publishing, Inc. TOPICS: New Age TYPE: Book PRICE: $12.95

By Standing Stone And Elder Tree
PUBLISHING COMPANY: Llewellyn Publications EDITOR: William G. Gray TOPICS: Paganism, Spirituality TYPE: Book PRICE: $9.95

C. G. Jung And The Problem Of Evil: The Strange Trial If Mr. Hyde
PUBLISHING COMPANY: Sigo Press EDITOR: John A. Sanford TOPICS: Occult TYPE: Book PRICE: $12.95

Camelot
PUBLISHING COMPANY: Camelot Press Limited TOPICS: Witchcraft, Occult, Paganism TYPE: Book

Cameron Aurameter In Action, The
PUBLISHING COMPANY: Fine Median International TOPICS: Dowsing TYPE: Book

Campus-Free College Degrees
PUBLISHING COMPANY: Thorson Guides TOPICS: New Age TYPE: Book DATE: 1992 SIZE: 8 1/2 x 11; 155 pgs. PRICE: $16.95 DESCRIPTION: Thorson's Guide to accredited off-campus college degree programs for adults.

Can You Trust Your Doctor? The Complete Guide To New Age Medicine And Its Threat To Your Family
PUBLISHING COMPANY: John Ankerberg Show, The EDITOR: John Ankerberg, John Weldon TOPICS: Holistic Health, New Age TYPE: Book DATE: 1991

Career, Success And Self-Fulfillment: How Scientifc Hand Analysis Can Change Your Life
PUBLISHING COMPANY: Aquarian Press EDITOR: Nathaniel Altman TOPICS: Palmistry TYPE: Book PRICE: $10.95

Casting The Circle: A Women's Book Of Ritual
PUBLISHING COMPANY: Crossing Press EDITOR: D. Stein TOPICS: Occult, Witchcraft TYPE: Book PRICE: $12.95

Catalyst
PUBLISHING COMPANY: Irene Serra Publishing EDITOR: Irene Serra TOPICS: Metaphysics, Parapsychology, Occult TYPE: Directory DATE: 1985 SIZE: 8 1/2x 11; 10 pgs. FREQ: quarterly CIRC: 4,000 PRICE: $20.00 DESCRIPTION: New Age directory offering extensive & unique resources in the field of New Age/Metaphysics. Offers networking newsletters, publications, book reports & products, large personal section & natural health information.

Celebration Of Discipline: The Paths To Spiritual Growth
PUBLISHING COMPANY: Harper & Row Publishers, Inc. EDITOR: Richard J. Foster TOPICS: Spirituality TYPE: Book PRICE: $15.95

Celtic Crystal Magick Vol.2: Rituals & Magickal Workings
PUBLISHING COMPANY: Camelot Press Limited EDITOR: R. Gawr TOPICS: Occult TYPE: Book PRICE: $10.95

Cerebral Symphony: Seashore Reflections On The Structure Of Consciousness
PUBLISHING COMPANY: Bantam New Age Books EDITOR: William H. Calvin TOPICS: Body-Mind Connection, Psychology TYPE: Book PRICE: $19.95

Chaco Journey: Remembrance And Awakening
PUBLISHING COMPANY: Timewindow Publications, Subs. of Charles Bensinger Co. EDITOR: C. Bensinger TOPICS: Spirituality TYPE: Book PRICE: $14.50

Chakras And The Human Energy Fields
PUBLISHING COMPANY: Theosophical University Press EDITOR: S. Karagulla TOPICS: Holistic Health TYPE: Book PRICE: $12.95

Chakras: Energy Centers Of Transformation
PUBLISHING COMPANY: Inner Traditions International, Ltd. EDITOR: H. Johari TOPICS: Holistic Health TYPE: Book PRICE: $12.95

Chakras: Roots Of Power
PUBLISHING COMPANY: Samuel Weiser, Inc. EDITOR: Werner Bohm TOPICS: New Age, Holistic Health TYPE: Book PRICE: $12.95

Challenge Of Fate: The Esoteric Exploration Of Personal Destiny
PUBLISHING COMPANY: Sigo Press EDITOR: T. Dethlefsen TOPICS: Spirituality TYPE: Book PRICE: $14.95

Challenges: A Young Man's Journal For Self-Awareness & Peronal Planning
PUBLISHING COMPANY: Advocacy Press, Div. of Girls Club of Santa Barbara EDITOR: M. Bingham TOPICS: New Age, Psychology TYPE: Book PRICE: $14.95

Changing Seasons Macrobiotic Cookbook
PUBLISHING COMPANY: Kushi Institute-East West Foundation EDITOR: Aveline Kushi TOPICS: Health Food, Holistic Health, Vegetarianism, Nutrition TYPE: Book DATE: 1984

Changing Your Destiny: Dynamic New Astrological & Visualization Tools To Shape Your Future
PUBLISHING COMPANY: Harper & Row Publishers, Inc. EDITOR: M. Orser, R. Zarro TOPICS: Meditation, Psychology TYPE: Book PRICE: $9.95

Channelers: A New Age Directory
PUBLISHING COMPANY: Putnam Publishing Group EDITOR: Robin Westen TOPICS: Channeling TYPE: Book DATE: 1988 PRICE: $9.95 DESCRIPTION: Offers sclect biographies of the most prominent channelers in the field. Also offers information about the history of channeling & a directory listing addresses of chanelers, channeling services & organizations, video & audio tapes, magazines, newsletters , seminars & specialty bookstores.

Channeling: Investigations On Receiving Information From Paranormal Sources
PUBLISHING COMPANY: Jeremy P. Tarcher, Inc. EDITOR: Jon Klimo TOPICS: New Age, Channeling, Paranormal Phenomena TYPE: Book PRICE: $10.95

Channeling: The Intuitive Connection
PUBLISHING COMPANY: Harper & Row Publishers, Inc. EDITOR: W. Kautz, M. Branon TOPICS: Channeling TYPE: Book PRICE: $14.95

Character And Health: The Relationship Of Acupuncture And Psychology
PUBLISHING COMPANY: Paradigm Publications EDITOR: Y. Requena TOPICS: Holistic Health, Acupuncture, Psychology TYPE: Book PRICE: $16.95

Characterology

PUBLISHING COMPANY: Samuel Weiser, Inc. EDITOR: C. Wagner TOPICS: Parapsychology TYPE: Book PRICE: $12.95

Cheng Tzu's Thirteen Treatises On T'ai Ch'uan
PUBLISHING COMPANY: North Atlantic Books EDITOR: B. Lo, M Inn TOPICS: Tai Chi TYPE: Book PRICE: $16.95

Chi Self-Massage: Tao Of Rejuvenation
PUBLISHING COMPANY: Healing Tao Center EDITOR: M. Chia TOPICS: Tai Chi TYPE: Book PRICE: $10.95

Chicago & MW Psychic Guide
PUBLISHING COMPANY: Chicago & MW Psychic Guide TOPICS: Metaphysics, Spirituality TYPE: Guide

Chicago's New Spirit
PUBLISHING COMPANY: Chicago's Inner Quest TOPICS: Holistic Healing, New Age TYPE: Directory

Child's Changing Consciousness And Waldorf Education
PUBLISHING COMPANY: Anthroposophic Press, Inc. EDITOR: R. Steiner TOPICS: Spirituality TYPE: Book PRICE: $15.00

Chinese Acupuncture Points And Meridian Theory
PUBLISHING COMPANY: China Books & Periodicals, Inc. EDITOR: L. Ding TOPICS: Holistic Health, Acupuncture TYPE: Book PRICE: $34.95

Chinese Hand Analysis
PUBLISHING COMPANY: Samuel Weiser, Inc. EDITOR: T. Dukes TOPICS: Palmistry TYPE: Book PRICE: $29.95

Chinese Hand Analysis
PUBLISHING COMPANY: Cheirological Society EDITOR: Shifu T. Dukes TOPICS: Palmistry, Holistic Health TYPE: Book DATE: 1987

Chinese Medical As A Scientific System: Its History, Philosophy & Practice
PUBLISHING COMPANY: Henry Holt & Co. EDITOR: M. Porkert, C. Ullmann TOPICS: Holistic Health TYPE: Book PRICE: $12.95

Choices: A Teen Woman's Journal For Self-Awareness & Personal Planning
PUBLISHING COMPANY: Advocacy Press, Div. of Girls Club of Santa Barbara EDITOR: M. Bingham TOPICS: New Age, Psychology TYPE: Book PRICE: $14.95

Choose Once Again
PUBLISHING COMPANY: Poco Press EDITOR: Julius J. Finegold, William N. Thetford TOPICS: New Age, Spirituality TYPE: Book PRICE: $6.95

Choose To Love Yourself

PUBLISHING COMPANY: Winning Edge, The **EDITOR:** Joan Fericy **TYPE:** Booklet **DATE:** 1987; 32 pgs. **PRICE:** $3.95 **DESCRIPTION:** Teaches one to love yourself which brings peaceful satisfaction & that self-esteem is your most important asset.

Chronic Disease (2 Vols).

PUBLISHING COMPANY: B. Jain Publishers, Ltd. **EDITOR:** S. Hahnemann **TOPICS:** Homeopathy **TYPE:** Book **PRICE:** $25.00

Circle Guide Of Wicca And Pagan Resources

PUBLISHING COMPANY: Circle Sanctuary/Church Of Circle Wicca **EDITOR:** Selena Fox **TOPICS:** Occult, Metaphysics, Witchcraft, Paganism **TYPE:** Directory **DATE:** 1979

Circle Of Shadows

PUBLISHING COMPANY: Golden Isis Press **EDITOR:** Gerina Dunwich **TOPICS:** Metaphysics **TYPE:** Book **PRICE PER COPY:** $3.00

Circle Of Song: Chants, Dances & Ceremonies Of Love, Healing & Power

PUBLISHING COMPANY: Findhorn Foundation & Press **EDITOR:** Katie Marks **TOPICS:** Occult **TYPE:** Book **PRICE:** $16.95

Circular Evidence: An Investigation Of The Flattened Swirled Crops Phenomenon

PUBLISHING COMPANY: Phanes Press **EDITOR:** Pat Delgado, Colin Andrews **TOPICS:** New Age, Paranormal Phenomena **TYPE:** Book **DATE:** 1991; 190 pgs. **PRICE:** $16.95

Cities Of Light: A Plan For A New Age

PUBLISHING COMPANY: Crystal Clarity Publishers **EDITOR:** Donald Walters **TOPICS:** New Age **TYPE:** Book **PRICE:** $9.95

Clairvoyance And Occult Powers

PUBLISHING COMPANY: Yoga Publications Society **EDITOR:** S. Panchadasi **TOPICS:** Psychic, Parapsychology **TYPE:** Book **PRICE:** $8.00

Clairvoyant Investigations

PUBLISHING COMPANY: Theosophical University Press **EDITOR:** G. Hodson **TOPICS:** Psychic, Parapsychology **TYPE:** Book **PRICE:** $9.25

Classic Tarot Spreads

PUBLISHING COMPANY: Whitford Press/Schiffer Publishing Limited **EDITOR:** S. Konrad **TOPICS:** Tarot **TYPE:** Book **PRICE:** $12.95

Classics Of Indian Spirituality

PUBLISHING COMPANY: Nilgiri Press **EDITOR:** E. Easwaran **TOPICS:** Spirituality **TYPE:** Book **PRICE:** $24.00

Clean Yield Publications

PUBLISHING COMPANY: Clean Yield Publications **EDITOR:** Ryan Freed **TOPICS:** New Age **TYPE:** Directory **DESCRIPTION:** List of Stock Market Newsletters sent to socially responsible investors.

Clinical Acupuncture: A Practical Japanese Approach

PUBLISHING COMPANY: Japan Publications, Inc. **EDITOR:** K. Serizawa, M. Kusumi **TOPICS:** Holistic Health, Acupuncture **TYPE:** Book **PRICE:** $14.95

Clinical Materia Medica

PUBLISHING COMPANY: B. Jain Publishers, Ltd. **EDITOR:** E. Farrington **TOPICS:** Homeopathy **TYPE:** Book **PRICE:** $14.00

Closer To The Light: Learning From The Near-Death Experiences Of Children

PUBLISHING COMPANY: Villard Books, Random House, Inc. **EDITOR:** Melvin Morse, Paul Perry **TOPICS:** Death, Spirituality **TYPE:** Book **PRICE:** $17.95

Co-Op America - Organizational Membership Directory

PUBLISHING COMPANY: Co-Op America **EDITOR:** Joe Wisman-Horther **TOPICS:** Psychic Phenomena **TYPE:** Directory

Collected Rituals

PUBLISHING COMPANY: Technology Group, The **EDITOR:** Nelson White, Anne White **TYPE:** Book **SIZE:** 8 1/2 x 11

Collection Of Emblems, Ancient And Moderne And Foundations Unearthed

PUBLISHING COMPANY: Philosophical Research Society, Inc. **EDITOR:** George Wither, Marie B. Hall **TOPICS:** Metaphysics, Psychic **TYPE:** Book **PRICE:** $22.50

Color And Crystals: A Journey Through The Chakras

PUBLISHING COMPANY: Crossing Press **EDITOR:** Joy Gardner **TOPICS:** Holistic Health **TYPE:** Book **PRICE:** $10.95

Color And Personality

PUBLISHING COMPANY: Samuel Weiser, Inc. **EDITOR:** A. Kargere **TOPICS:** Holistic Health **TYPE:** Book **PRICE:** $7.95

Color Psychology And Color Therapy

PUBLISHING COMPANY: Citadel Press **EDITOR:** F. Birren **TOPICS:** Color Therapy **TYPE:** Book **PRICE:** $9.95

Color Synergy: How To Use The Power Of Color, Affirmations & Creative Visualizations

PUBLISHING COMPANY: Simon & Schuster, Inc. **EDITOR:** P. George, D. Lovett **TOPICS:** New Age, Color Therapy **TYPE:** Book **PRICE:** $9.95

Color Therapy

PUBLISHING COMPANY: Aurora Press, Inc. **EDITOR:** R. Amber **TOPICS:** Color Therapy, Holistic Healing **TYPE:** Book **PRICE:** $10.95

Color Your Life

PUBLISHING COMPANY: Strawberry Hill Press **EDITOR:** E. Ryan **TOPICS:** Color Therapy **TYPE:** Book **PRICE:** $9.95

Coming Into The Light

PUBLISHING COMPANY: Llewellyn Publications **EDITOR:** G. Schueler **TOPICS:** Occult, Witchcraft **TYPE:** Book **PRICE:** $14.95

Coming Of The Cosmic Christ

PUBLISHING COMPANY: Harper & Row Publishers, Inc. **EDITOR:** Matthew Fox **TOPICS:** Paranormal Phenomena **TYPE:** Book **PRICE:** $14.95

Coming To Life

PUBLISHING COMPANY: Blue Dolphin Publishing, Inc. **TOPICS:** New Age **TYPE:** Book **PRICE:** $9.95

Coming To Life: Traveling The Spiritual Path In Everyday Life

PUBLISHING COMPANY: Harper & Row Publishers, Inc. **EDITOR:** P. Berends **TOPICS:** Spirituality **TYPE:** Book **PRICE:** $16.95

Commentaries On A Course In Miracles

PUBLISHING COMPANY: Life Action Press, Div. of Foundation for Life Action **EDITOR:** T. Singh **TOPICS:** Spirituality **TYPE:** Book **PRICE:** $12.95

Commentary On Ancient Hatha Yoga Pradipika

PUBLISHING COMPANY: Sivananda Ashram Yoga Retreat **EDITOR:** Swami Vishnu-Devananda **TYPE:** Book

Commentary On Psychic Energy

PUBLISHING COMPANY: T.S.G. Publishing Foundation, Inc. **EDITOR:** T. Saraydarian **TOPICS:** Psychic Phenomena, Tai Chi **TYPE:** Book **PRICE:** $14.00

Common Ground: Resources For Personal Transformation

PUBLISHING COMPANY: Common Ground **EDITOR:** Baha'Uddin Alpine **TOPICS:** New Age **TYPE:** Directory **FREQ:** quarterly **CIRC:** 80,000 **DESCRIPTION:** A directory of resources for personal growth including almost 500 locations.

Common Sense Diet And Health

PUBLISHING COMPANY: Traditional Tours **EDITOR:** Svevo Brooks **TOPICS:** New Age **TYPE:** Book

Communing With The Spirit Of Your Unborn Child Combo

PUBLISHING COMPANY: Aslan Publishing **EDITOR:** Dawson Church **TOPICS:** Psychic, New Age, Birth **TYPE:** Book **PRICE:** $15.95 **DESCRIPTION:** A practical guide to intimate communication with your unborn or infant child. Also available as a 90 minute audio tape.

Companion To Senya

PUBLISHING COMPANY: Mar Crafts **PUBLISHER:** Marty Campbell **EDITOR:** Senya Darklight **TOPICS:** Spirituality **TYPE:** Book; 200 pgs. **PRICE:** $9.00 **DESCRIPTION:** Spiritual poetry. Senya's complete work.

Companions On The Inner Way: The Art Of Spiritual Guidance

PUBLISHING COMPANY: Continuum Publishing Co. EDITOR: M. Kelsey TOPICS: Spirituality TYPE: Book PRICE: $11.95

Complete Book Of Acupuncture

PUBLISHING COMPANY: Celestial Arts Publishing Co./Sub. of Ten Speed Press EDITOR: Stephen T. Chang TOPICS: Holistic Health, Acupuncture TYPE: Book PRICE: $11.95

Complete Book Of Amulets And Talismans

PUBLISHING COMPANY: Llewellyn Publications EDITOR: M. Gonzalez-Wippler TOPICS: Occult, Witchcraft TYPE: Book PRICE: $12.95

Complete Book Of Incense, Oils And Brews

PUBLISHING COMPANY: Llewellyn Publications EDITOR: S. Cunningham TOPICS: Occult TYPE: Book PRICE: $12.95

Complete Book Of Massage

PUBLISHING COMPANY: Random House, Inc. EDITOR: C. Maxwell-Hudson TOPICS: Massage TYPE: Book PRICE: $12.95

Complete Book Of Shiatsu Therapy

PUBLISHING COMPANY: Japan Publications, Inc. EDITOR: T. Namikoshi TOPICS: Acupuncture TYPE: Book PRICE: $14.95

Complete Book Of Spells, Ceremonies And Magic

PUBLISHING COMPANY: Llewellyn Publications EDITOR: M. Gonzalez-Wippler TOPICS: Occult, Witchcraft TYPE: Book PRICE: $12.95

Complete Book Of Vitamins And Minerals For Health

PUBLISHING COMPANY: Rodale Press, Inc. EDITOR: Editors of Prevention Magazine TOPICS: Holistic Health TYPE: Book PRICE: $27.95

Complete Books Of Charles Fort

PUBLISHING COMPANY: Dover Publications, Inc. EDITOR: C. Fort TOPICS: Paranormal Phenomena, ESP, Psychic Phenomena TYPE: Book PRICE: $29.95

Complete Guide To Oriental Manual Therapy

PUBLISHING COMPANY: Japan Publications, Inc. EDITOR: R. Teeguarden TOPICS: Acupuncture TYPE: Guide PRICE: $16.95

Complete Guide To Your Emotions And Your Health: New Dimensions In Mind-Body Healing

PUBLISHING COMPANY: Rodale Press, Inc. EDITOR: E. Padus TOPICS: Body-Mind Connection, Holistic Health TYPE: Guide PRICE: $24.95

Complete Horoscope Interpretation: Putting Together Your Planetary Profile

PUBLISHING COMPANY: A.C.S. Publications, Inc./Astro Computing Services EDITOR: Maritha Pottenger TOPICS: Astrology TYPE: Book PRICE: $19.95

Complete Illustrated Book Of Yoga

PUBLISHING COMPANY: Crown Publishers, Inc. EDITOR: S. Vishnudevananda TOPICS: Yoga, Holistic Health TYPE: Book PRICE: $14.95

Complete Meditation

PUBLISHING COMPANY: Whitford Press/Schiffer Publishing Limited EDITOR: S. Kravette TOPICS: Meditation, Spirituality TYPE: Book PRICE: $12.95

Complete Natural-Health Consultant: A Self-Help Guide To Drug-Free, Surgery-Free Remedies

PUBLISHING COMPANY: Prentice-Hall, Inc. EDITOR: M. Van Straten TOPICS: Homeopathy, Holistic Health TYPE: Guide PRICE: $12.95

Complete Palmist

PUBLISHING COMPANY: Newcastle Publishing Co., Inc. Niblo TOPICS: Palmistry TYPE: Book PRICE: $9.95

Complete Phrophecies Of Nostradamus

PUBLISHING COMPANY: Crown Publishers, Inc. EDITOR: C. Henry TOPICS: Psychic, Spirituality TYPE: Book PRICE: $12.95

Complete Relaxation

PUBLISHING COMPANY: Whitford Press/Schiffer Publishing Limited EDITOR: S. Kravette TOPICS: Holistic Health, New Age TYPE: Book PRICE: $12.95

Complete Yoga Book

PUBLISHING COMPANY: Schocken Books EDITOR: James Hewitt TOPICS: Yoga, Holistic Health TYPE: Book PRICE: $14.95

Comte De Saint Germain

PUBLISHING COMPANY: Theosophical University Press EDITOR: I. Cooper-Oakley TOPICS: Spirituality, Alchemy TYPE: Book PRICE: $17.95

Concepts Of Qabalah

PUBLISHING COMPANY: Samuel Weiser, Inc. EDITOR: William G. Gray TOPICS: Occult, Kabbalah TYPE: Book PRICE: $9.95

Concordance To The Gospel Of Sri Ramakrishna

PUBLISHING COMPANY: Vedanta Press, Div. of Vedanta Society EDITOR: Katherine Whitmarsh TOPICS: Spirituality TYPE: Book PRICE: $24.95

Concordance To The Science Of Mind

PUBLISHING COMPANY: Science of Mind Publications, Div. of United Church of Religious Science EDITOR: Martha Stewart, Albert Lowe TOPICS: Spirituality, Psychology TYPE: Book PRICE: $18.95

Confrontations: A Scientist's Search For Alien Contact

PUBLISHING COMPANY: Ballantine Books, Inc. EDITOR: Jacques Vallee TOPICS: UFO's, Paranormal Phenomena TYPE: Book PRICE: $19.95

Connecticut Naturally

PUBLISHING COMPANY: City Spirit Publications PUBLISHER: Jerome Rubin TOPICS: Holistic Health, New Age TYPE: Directory SIZE: 5 x 8; 194 pgs. PRICE: $5.95 DESCRIPTION: New Age/holistic health yellow-pages, resource directory offering 1200 listings, services & products from the Connecticut, New York & New Jersey area.

Connecting Arizona

PUBLISHING COMPANY: Connecting Arizona EDITOR: Sara Riely TOPICS: New Age TYPE: Directory DATE: 1989 FREQ: annual CIRC: 40,000 DESCRIPTION: A resource guide- A Natural Yellow Pages, published annually for Arizonians.

Connolly Book Of Numbers Vol 1: A New Path To Ancient Wisdom - The Fundamentals

PUBLISHING COMPANY: Newcastle Publishing Co., Inc. EDITOR: E. Connolly TOPICS: Numerology TYPE: Book PRICE: $12.95

Connolly Book Of Numbers Vol 2: The Consultants Manual

PUBLISHING COMPANY: Newcastle Publishing Co., Inc. EDITOR: E. Connolly TOPICS: Numerology TYPE: Book PRICE: $12.95

Conquest Of Mind

PUBLISHING COMPANY: Nilgiri Press EDITOR: E. Easwaran TOPICS: Meditation TYPE: Book PRICE: $12.00

Conscience Of Science And Other Essays

PUBLISHING COMPANY: Supreme Grand Lodge of AMORC, Inc. EDITOR: W. Albersheim TOPICS: Paranormal Phenomena, Spirituality TYPE: Book PRICE: $12.50

Conscious Dying: Psychology Of Death & Guidebook To Liberation

PUBLISHING COMPANY: World University Of America-Ecumenical Ministry Of The Unity Of All Religions EDITOR: B. Reyes TOPICS: Death TYPE: Book PRICE: $12.95

Converting Nine To Five: Bringing Spirituality To Your Daily Work

PUBLISHING COMPANY: Continuum Publishing Co. EDITOR: J. Haughey TOPICS: Spirituality TYPE: Book PRICE: $17.95

Core Energetics: Developing The Capacity To Love And Heal

PUBLISHING COMPANY: LifeRhythm EDITOR: J. Pierrakos TOPICS: Spirituality, Psychic Healing, Holistic Healing TYPE: Book PRICE: $18.95

Cosmetic Aromatherapy

PUBLISHING COMPANY: North Atlantic Books EDITOR: Jeanne Rose, Avery A. Rose TOPICS: Holistic Health TYPE: Book PRICE: $12.95

Cosmic Consciousness

PUBLISHING COMPANY: New American Library EDITOR: M. Bucke TOPICS: Paranormal Phenomena, Spirituality TYPE: Book PRICE: $10.95

Cosmic Consciousness Degrees

PUBLISHING COMPANY: Gibbs Publishing Co. PUBLISHER: James Calvin Gibbs TOPICS: Parapsychology TYPE: Book DESCRIPTION: Offers 6 quality lessons. Diploma Silva Mind Control.

Cosmic Cuisine: The Astrological Cookbook

PUBLISHING COMPANY: Harper & Row Publishers, Inc. EDITOR: T. Jaine TOPICS: Astrology, Holistic Health, Health Food, Nutrition TYPE: Book PRICE: $19.95

Cosmic Octave: Path To Universal Harmony

PUBLISHING COMPANY: LifeRhythm Cousto TOPICS: Numerology TYPE: Book PRICE: $12.95

Cosmic Pulse Of Life: The Revoltionary Biological Power Behind Ufos

PUBLISHING COMPANY: Borderland Science And Research Foundation EDITOR: Trevor J. Constable TOPICS: Metaphysics, UFO's, Paranormal Phenomena TYPE: Book PRICE: $24.95

Cosmic Revelation

PUBLISHING COMPANY: Spiritual Education Endeavours EDITOR: Virginia Essene, Ann Valentin TOPICS: New Age, Spirituality TYPE: Book

Cosmic Shocks

PUBLISHING COMPANY: T.S.G. Publishing Foundation, Inc. EDITOR: T. Saraydarian TOPICS: New Age, Psychology TYPE: Book PRICE: $18.00

Cosmo-Biological Birth Control

PUBLISHING COMPANY: Lotus Light Publications EDITOR: S. Sharamon, J. Christ TOPICS: Holistic Health, Astrology TYPE: Book PRICE: $14.95

Cosmos In Man

PUBLISHING COMPANY: T.S.G. Publishing Foundation, Inc. EDITOR: T. Saraydarian TOPICS: New Age, Psychology TYPE: Book PRICE: $13.00

Courage To Be Myself: Living The Fullness Of The Present With Acceptance & Knowledge

PUBLISHING COMPANY: Doubleday & Co.,Inc. EDITOR: C. Valles TOPICS: Spirituality TYPE: Book PRICE: $14.95

Course In Miracles

PUBLISHING COMPANY: Foundation For Inner Peace EDITOR: J. Skutch TOPICS: Spirituality TYPE: Book PRICE: $40.00

Course In Miracles Explorations, Series 1 (3 Cass.+ How To Learn From A Course In Miracles)

PUBLISHING COMPANY: Life Action Press, Div. of Foundation for Life Action EDITOR: T. Singh TOPICS: Spirituality TYPE: Book PRICE: $21.95

Create Your Own Happiness: A Seth Workbook

PUBLISHING COMPANY: Prentice-Hall, Inc. EDITOR: N. Ashley TOPICS: Channeling TYPE: Book PRICE: $9.95

Creating Well-Being: The Healing Path To Love, Peace, Self-Esteem & Happiness

PUBLISHING COMPANY: Foundation For Well-Being EDITOR: Philip H. Friedman, Ph. D. TOPICS: Holistic Health, Spirituality, Psychology TYPE: Book DATE: 1989 PRICE: $11.95

Creation Of Health: Merger Of Traditional Medical Diagnosis With Clairvoyant

PUBLISHING COMPANY: New American Library EDITOR: N. Shealy TOPICS: Spirituality, Psychic Healing TYPE: Book PRICE: $19.95

Creation-The Evolution Controversy

PUBLISHING COMPANY: Inquiry Press EDITOR: R.L. Wysong TOPICS: New Age, Holistic Health, Nutrition TYPE: Book DATE: 1976; 445 pgs.

Creative Imagery: How To Visualize In All Five Senses

PUBLISHING COMPANY: Simon & Schuster, Inc. EDITOR: W. Fezler TOPICS: New Age, Meditation, Psychology TYPE: Book PRICE: $9.95

Creative Meditation And Multi-Dimensional Consciousness

PUBLISHING COMPANY: Theosophical University Press EDITOR: A. Govinda TOPICS: Meditation TYPE: Book PRICE: $12.95

Creative Meditation: Inner Peace Is Practically Yours

PUBLISHING COMPANY: Association For Research And Enlightenment, Inc. EDITOR: Richard O. Peterson TOPICS: Channeling TYPE: Book PRICE: $9.95

Creative Mind And Success

PUBLISHING COMPANY: Putnam Publishing Group EDITOR: E. Holmes TOPICS: Spirituality, Psychology TYPE: Book PRICE: $12.95

Creative Power Of Mind

PUBLISHING COMPANY: Science of Mind Publications, Div. of United Church of Religious Science EDITOR: W. Kinnear TOPICS: Spirituality, Psychology TYPE: Book PRICE: $10.95

Creative Senility

PUBLISHING COMPANY: Blue Dolphin Publishing, Inc. TOPICS: New Age TYPE: Book PRICE: $9.95

Creative Visualization Workbook

PUBLISHING COMPANY: New World Library Publishing Co. EDITOR: S. Gawain TOPICS: Meditation, Psychology TYPE: Book PRICE: $9.95

Crime And Diet: The Macrobiotic Approach

PUBLISHING COMPANY: Japan Publications, Inc. EDITOR: M. Kushi & Associates TOPICS: Holistic Health, Vegetarianism, Health Food TYPE: Book PRICE: $17.95

Crisis In Modern Thought: Solutions To The Problem Of Meaninglessness

PUBLISHING COMPANY: Crystal Clarity Publishers EDITOR: Donald Walters TOPICS: New Age TYPE: Book PRICE: $11.95

Cross Currents: The Promise Of Electromedicine, The Perils Of Electropollution

PUBLISHING COMPANY: Jeremy P. Tarcher, Inc. EDITOR: R. O. Becker TOPICS: Holistic Health TYPE: Book PRICE: $19.95

Crystal Clear: Use The Earth's Magic Energy To Vitalize Your Mind, Body & Spirit

PUBLISHING COMPANY: Sound Editions EDITOR: C. Church TOPICS: Metaphysics, Spirituality, New Age, Crystals TYPE: Book PRICE: $14.95

Crystal Connections: A Guidebook For Personal And Planetary Ascension

PUBLISHING COMPANY: Harper & Row Publishers, Inc. EDITOR: R. Baer, V. Baer TOPICS: Crystals TYPE: Book PRICE: $17.95

Crystal Cosmos Connections: A Network Directory

PUBLISHING COMPANY: Crystal Cosmos Network EDITOR: Elizabeth Logan TOPICS: Crystals TYPE: Directory DATE: 1988 SIZE: 8 1/2 x 11; 151 pgs. PRICE: $11.95 DESCRIPTION: Comprehensive directory dedicated to all aspects of crystals. Covers activities, resources, education, research, consultations, products, mining, publications, arts, tapes, bookstores & centers. Has more than 1,500 free listings & display ads.

Crystal Healing: The Therapeutic Applications Of Crystals And Gem Stones Vol.2

PUBLISHING COMPANY: Aurora Press, Inc. EDITOR: K. Raphaell TOPICS: Crystals, Spirituality, Psychic Healing TYPE: Book PRICE: $14.95

Crystal Kit: What They Are And How To Grow Them

PUBLISHING COMPANY: Running Press EDITOR: Marlene Robinson TOPICS: Crystals TYPE: Book PRICE: $12.95

Crystal Legends

PUBLISHING COMPANY: Aquarian Press EDITOR: M. Coldecott TOPICS: Crystals TYPE: Book PRICE: $12.95

Crystal Power: The Ultimate Placebo Effect

PUBLISHING COMPANY: Prometheus Books EDITOR: Lawrence Jerome TOPICS: Skepticism, Crystals TYPE: Book PRICE: $12.95

Crystal Therapeutics: Practitioner's Guide To Healing & Meditation W/Crystals & Gemstones

PUBLISHING COMPANY: Holistic Health Works, Div. of Spiritual Awareness Dynamics EDITOR: O. Frank TOPICS: Crystals, Meditation TYPE: Book PRICE: $15.95

Crystal Tree
PUBLISHING COMPANY: Whitford Press/Schiffer Publishing Limited Kelynda TOPICS: New Age, Crystals, Kabbalah TYPE: Book PRICE: $24.95

Crystal Vision Through Crystal Gazing
PUBLISHING COMPANY: Yoga Publications Society EDITOR: F. Achad TOPICS: Metaphysics TYPE: Book PRICE: $7.00

Crystal Workbook: A Complete Guide To Working With Crystals
PUBLISHING COMPANY: Aquarian Press EDITOR: U. Markham TOPICS: Crystals TYPE: Book PRICE: $10.95

Crystalline Transmission: A Synthesis Of Light, Vol. 3
PUBLISHING COMPANY: Aurora Press, Inc. EDITOR: K. Raphaell TOPICS: Crystals TYPE: Book PRICE: $14.00

Crystals And Gemstones: Windows Of The Self
PUBLISHING COMPANY: Cassandra Press EDITOR: Miriam Kaplan TOPICS: Crystals TYPE: Book; 88 pgs. PRICE: $7.95

Crystals, Gems And Radionics
PUBLISHING COMPANY: New Age Concepts/Color Magic EDITOR: Elaine Jay Finster TOPICS: New Age, Crystals, Holistic Healing TYPE: Book DESCRIPTION: Discusses crystals & radionics & their healing abilities.

Cuchama And Sacred Mountains
PUBLISHING COMPANY: Swallow Press/Ohio U Press EDITOR: W. Evans-Wentz TOPICS: Metaphysics, Psychic TYPE: Book PRICE: $14.95

Culpeper's Color Herbal
PUBLISHING COMPANY: Sterling Publishing Company, Inc. EDITOR: N. Culpeper TOPICS: Holistic Health, Herbalogy TYPE: Book PRICE: $14.95

Cultwatch: What You Need To Know About Spiritual Deception
PUBLISHING COMPANY: John Ankerberg Show, The EDITOR: John Ankerberg, John Weldon TOPICS: Spirituality, New Age TYPE: Book DATE: 1991

Cunningham's Encyclopedia Of Crystal, Gem And Metal Magic
PUBLISHING COMPANY: Llewellyn Publications EDITOR: S. Cunningham TOPICS: Crystals, Witchcraft, Occult TYPE: Book PRICE: $12.95

Cunningham's Encyclopedia Of Magical Herbs
PUBLISHING COMPANY: Llewellyn Publications EDITOR: S. Cunningham TOPICS: Occult, Witchcraft, Herbalogy TYPE: Book PRICE: $12.95

Curious Encounters: Phantom Trains, Spooky Sports & Other Mysterious Wonders
PUBLISHING COMPANY: Faber & Faber, Affil. of Faber & Faber, Ltd., London EDITOR: L. Coleman TOPICS: Paranormal Phenomena TYPE: Book PRICE: $11.95

Cutting Through Spiritual Materialism
PUBLISHING COMPANY: Random House, Inc. EDITOR: C. Trungpa TOPICS: Channeling, Spirituality TYPE: Book PRICE: $12.95

Cycles Of Time
PUBLISHING COMPANY: Manifest Press EDITOR: Jacqueline C. Whyte TOPICS: New Age TYPE: Book

Daily Planetary Guide
PUBLISHING COMPANY: Llewellyn Publications EDITOR: Terry Buske TOPICS: Astrology TYPE: Guide DATE: 1978 FREQ: Annual CIRC: 12,000 PRICE: $6.95 DESCRIPTION: A notebook/calendar offering practical astrological applications.

Dairy And Dairy Alternatives
PUBLISHING COMPANY: Sprout House PUBLISHER: Steve Meyerowitz TOPICS: Nutrition, Holistic Health, Health Food TYPE: Book

Dalai Lama At Harvard: Lectures On The Buddhist Path To Peace
PUBLISHING COMPANY: Snow Lion Publications, Inc. EDITOR: Lama Dalai TOPICS: Spirituality TYPE: Book PRICE: $12.95

Dancing With The Fire
PUBLISHING COMPANY: Bear & Company, Inc. EDITOR: Michael Sky TOPICS: Body-Mind Connection, Firewalking TYPE: Book DATE: 1989 PRICE: $9.95 DESCRIPTION: Explores the scientific, artistic, psychological, historical & spiritual teachings of fire. Firewalking proves that one can transform any fear into positive evolutionary energy, any crisis into an opportunity for growth & any confrontation into a cause for celebration. Proves the immense power of our attitudes & beliefs & of the body-mind interrelationship. Documentation & vivid representation of a typical Firewalk, one of the earth's oldest rituals.

Dark Asteroids
PUBLISHING COMPANY: Arthur Publications, Inc. EDITOR: Debra Sapp TOPICS: Astrology TYPE: Book DATE: 1978

Dark Eros: The Sadeian Imagination
PUBLISHING COMPANY: Spring Publications, Inc. EDITOR: Thomas Moore TOPICS: Occult TYPE: Book PRICE: $14.50

Dark Wood To White Rose: Journey & Transformation In Dante's Divine Comedy
PUBLISHING COMPANY: Parabola Books EDITOR: Helen Luke TOPICS: Spirituality TYPE: Book PRICE: $19.95

Daughter Of Fire
PUBLISHING COMPANY: Blue Dolphin Publishing, Inc. EDITOR: I. Tweedle TOPICS: Spirituality TYPE: Book PRICE: $19.95

Daydreaming: Your Hidden Resource For Self-Knowledge & Creativity
PUBLISHING COMPANY: Jeremy P. Tarcher, Inc. EDITOR: Eric Klinger TOPICS: New Age, Psychology TYPE: Book PRICE: $17.95

Death And Immortality In The Religions Of The World
PUBLISHING COMPANY: Paragon House EDITOR: P. Badham, L. Badham TOPICS: Death TYPE: Book PRICE: $12.95

Death And Immortality: Change & Continuity
PUBLISHING COMPANY: Concord Grove Press, Subs. of Institute of World Culture EDITOR: R. Iyer TOPICS: Death TYPE: Book PRICE: $8.75

Death-Bed Visions
PUBLISHING COMPANY: Aquarian Press EDITOR: Sir William Barrett TOPICS: Psychic, ESP, Psychic Phenomena TYPE: Book PRICE: $12.95

Deity Yoga: In Action And Performance Tantras
PUBLISHING COMPANY: Snow Lion Publications, Inc. EDITOR: J. Hopkins TOPICS: Spirituality TYPE: Book PRICE: $14.95

Dell Horoscope Purse Book
PUBLISHING COMPANY: Dell Horoscope Magazines TOPICS: Astrology TYPE: Book FREQ: Annual

Democracy Is Self-Government
PUBLISHING COMPANY: Word Foundation, Inc., The TOPICS: Metaphysics TYPE: Book

Demons Of The Inner World: Understanding Our Hidden Complexes
PUBLISHING COMPANY: Shambhala Publications, Inc. EDITOR: Alfred Ribi TOPICS: Occult TYPE: Book PRICE: $12.95

Descent Of The Dove
PUBLISHING COMPANY: Spiritual Education Endeavours EDITOR: Virginia Essene, Ann Valentin TOPICS: New Age, Spirituality TYPE: Book

Destruction Of Atlantis: Ragnarok - The Age Of Fire And Gravel
PUBLISHING COMPANY: Steinerbooks, Garber Communications, Inc. EDITOR: L. Donnelly TOPICS: New Age TYPE: Book PRICE: $17.00

Develop Your Psychic Powers: Basic Tools Of Parapsychology
PUBLISHING COMPANY: Newcastle Publishing Co., Inc. EDITOR: E. Connolly TOPICS: Parapsychology, Psychic TYPE: Book PRICE: $12.95

Develop Your Psychic Skills
PUBLISHING COMPANY: Whitford Press/Schiffer Publishing Limited EDITOR: Enid Hoffman TOPICS: Psychic, Parapsychology TYPE: Book PRICE: $9.95

Developing Psychic Ability

PUBLISHING COMPANY: TEC Publications EDITOR: Apryl Douglas TOPICS: Psychic TYPE: Book PRICE: $9.95

Devotees' Collection: 3 Books By Yogananda

PUBLISHING COMPANY: Amrita Foundation Yogananda TOPICS: Yoga, Spirituality TYPE: Book PRICE: $40.00

Devotional Poems Of Mirabai

PUBLISHING COMPANY: South Asia Books EDITOR: A.J. Alston TOPICS: Spirituality TYPE: Book PRICE: $9.00

Diagnoses And Treatment In Ayurveda, 3 Vols.

PUBLISHING COMPANY: B. Jain Publishers, Ltd. EDITOR: B. Dash, L. Kashyap TOPICS: Holistic Health TYPE: Book PRICE: $70.00

Dialogues On A Course In Miracles

PUBLISHING COMPANY: Life Action Press, Div. of Foundation for Life Action EDITOR: T. Singh TOPICS: Spirituality TYPE: Book PRICE: $14.95

Dictionary Of Acupuncture And Moxibustion: A Practical Guide To Chinese Medicine

PUBLISHING COMPANY: Collins, Div. of William Collins EDITOR: N. Hiep TOPICS: Holistic Health, Acupuncture TYPE: Guide PRICE: $14.95

Dictionary Of Angels

PUBLISHING COMPANY: Macmillan Publishing Co., Inc. EDITOR: G. Davidson TOPICS: Kabbalah TYPE: Book PRICE: $19.95

Dictionary Of Astrology

PUBLISHING COMPANY: Routledge, Chapman & Hall, Inc. EDITOR: F. Gettings TOPICS: Astrology TYPE: Book PRICE: $19.95

Dictionary Of Practical Materia Medica

PUBLISHING COMPANY: B. Jain Publishers, Ltd. EDITOR: John H. Clarke TOPICS: Homeopathy TYPE: Book PRICE: $100.00

Dictionary Of Religion And Philosophy

PUBLISHING COMPANY: Paragon House EDITOR: G. MacGregor TOPICS: Yoga, Spirituality TYPE: Book PRICE: $35.00

Dictionary Of The Occult, Hermetic And Alchemical Sigils

PUBLISHING COMPANY: Routledge, Chapman & Hall, Inc. EDITOR: F. Gettings TOPICS: Alchemy TYPE: Book PRICE: $55.00

Diet For A New America: How Your Food Choices Affect Health, Happiness & The Future Of Life

PUBLISHING COMPANY: Stillpoint Publishing EDITOR: John Robbins TOPICS: Vegetarianism, Health Food, Holistic Health TYPE: Book PRICE: $13.95

Diet For A Small Planet

PUBLISHING COMPANY: Ballantine Books, Inc. EDITOR: F. M. Lappe TOPICS: Vegetarianism, Health Food, Holistic Health TYPE: Book PRICE: $12.95

Diet For Natural Beauty: Aveline Kushi's Anti-Aging Formula For Natural Skin & Hair Care

PUBLISHING COMPANY: Japan Publications, Inc. EDITOR: M. Kushi, W. Esko & Maya TOPICS: Holistic Health, Vegetarianism, Health Food TYPE: Book PRICE: $15.95

Dimensions Of Paradise: Proportions Of Symbolic Numbers Of Ancient Cosmology

PUBLISHING COMPANY: Harper & Row Publishers, Inc. EDITOR: J. Mitchell TOPICS: New Age TYPE: Book PRICE: $19.95

Directory Canadian Pagan Research

PUBLISHING COMPANY: Directory Canadian Pagan Research TOPICS: Witchcraft, Occult, Paganism TYPE: Directory

Directory Of Cult Research Organizations

PUBLISHING COMPANY: Jesus People, USA EDITOR: Eric Pement TYPE: Directory

Directory Of Graduate Degree Programs In Psychospiritual Psychotherapy

PUBLISHING COMPANY: Common Boundary, Inc. TOPICS: Spirituality, Dreams, Meditation, Holistic Health, Metaphysics TYPE: Directory

Directory Of Healing Practitioners

PUBLISHING COMPANY: Referral Service For Health Care Information EDITOR: Julie Von Erffa TOPICS: Holistic Healing TYPE: Directory DATE: 1984 SIZE: 8 1/2 x 11; 160 pgs. FREQ: annual CIRC: 4,000 PRICE PER COPY: $10.00 DESCRIPTION: Describes alternative healing methods & the healing practitioners. Includes planetary healing. Covers many catagories of metaphysical subjects. Listings focus mainly on the Santa Fe area.

Directory of Holistic Health Practitioners

PUBLISHING COMPANY: Directory of Holistic Health Practitioners EDITOR: Debbie Eagle TOPICS: Holistic Health TYPE: Directory DESCRIPTION: Serves Charlottesville, VA area.

Directory Of Holistic Medicine And Alternative Health Care Services In The U.S.

PUBLISHING COMPANY: Health Plus Publishers EDITOR: Shirley Linde, Donald J. Carrow TOPICS: Holistic Health TYPE: Directory PRICE: $6.95

Directory Of Holistic Practitioners

PUBLISHING COMPANY: Directory Of Holistic Practitioners TOPICS: Holistic Health TYPE: Directory

Directory Of Intentional Communities

PUBLISHING COMPANY: Fellowship For Intentional Community TOPICS: New Age TYPE: Book; 328 pgs. PRICE: $18.00 DESCRIPTION: Lists 375 North American communities, plus 55 on other continents. Offers 40 feature articles, 200 alternative resources & extensive cross-reference charts, maps & a full index. Published every 2-3 years. Next edition due Spring, 1993.

Directory Of New England Astrologers

PUBLISHING COMPANY: Sagittarius Rising EDITOR: Tracy Marks TOPICS: Astrology TYPE: Directory DATE: 1978 SIZE: 8 1/2 x 11; 135 pgs. PRICE: $6.00 DESCRIPTION: Offers detailed information on practicing astrologers in the New England region. Also give additional information about the study of astrology such as how to choose an astrologer, astrological keywords, organizations, bookstores, services, natal charts, computer calculation services, the nature & uses of astrology, magazines, resources & a bibliography.

Directory Of UFO Organizations For The 1990's

PUBLISHING COMPANY: S,S And S Publications EDITOR: Gene Duplantier TOPICS: UFO's TYPE: Directory PRICE: $9.95 DESCRIPTION: Lists over 1,000 names & addresses, including publications.

Directory To Canadian Pagan Resources

PUBLISHING COMPANY: Pagans For Peace EDITOR: Samuel Wagar, Maphis Wagar TOPICS: Paganism, Witchcraft, Occult, Voudoun TYPE: Directory DATE: 1988; 48 pgs. FREQ: annual PRICE: $4.00 TERM: yearly DESCRIPTION: Lists many resources in Witchcraft, Womanspirit/Dianic, Vodoun, Faerie, Druidic & other Pagan spiritual paths in Canada. Offers bookstores, supply stores, gatherings, festivals, groups & individuals.

Discover Your Past Lives

PUBLISHING COMPANY: Whitford Press/Schiffer Publishing Limited EDITOR: Brad Steiger, F. Steiger TOPICS: Past Life Regression TYPE: Book PRICE: $15.95

Discovering The Lost Pyramid

PUBLISHING COMPANY: Inner Light Publications EDITOR: G.C. Shellhorn TOPICS: New Age, Metaphysics TYPE: Book PRICE: $8.95

Discovering Your Past Lives: Spiritual Growth Through A Knowledge Of Past Lifetimes

PUBLISHING COMPANY: Aquarian Press EDITOR: G. Williston, J. Johnstone TOPICS: Past Life Regression TYPE: Book PRICE: $12.95

Disease And Diagnosis For The Acupuncturist: An Advanced Guide

PUBLISHING COMPANY: Thorsens Publishing House EDITOR: G. Dip TOPICS: Holistic Health, Acupuncture TYPE: Guide PRICE: $14.95

Disputers Of The Tao: Philosophical Argument In Ancient China

PUBLISHING COMPANY: Open Court Publishing Co. EDITOR: A.C. Graham TOPICS: Spirituality TYPE: Book PRICE: $16.95

Divided Legacy: The Conflict Between Homeopathy And The American Medical Association 1800-1914
PUBLISHING COMPANY: North Atlantic Books EDITOR: H. Coulter TOPICS: Homeopathy TYPE: Book PRICE: $14.95

Divination: The Search For Meaning
PUBLISHING COMPANY: Dryad Press EDITOR: Cherry Gilchrist TOPICS: Psychic, Metaphysics TYPE: Book PRICE: $12.95

Divine Horsemen: Living Gods Of Haiti
PUBLISHING COMPANY: McPherson & Company EDITOR: M. Deren TOPICS: Voudoun TYPE: Book PRICE: $12.00

Divine Invasions: A Life Of Philip K. Dick
PUBLISHING COMPANY: Crown Publishers, Inc. EDITOR: Lawrence Sutin TOPICS: Spirituality TYPE: Book PRICE: $25.95

Divine Madness: Archetypes Of Romantic Love
PUBLISHING COMPANY: Shambhala Publications, Inc. EDITOR: John Haule TOPICS: Spirituality TYPE: Book PRICE: $21.95

Divine Memories Of Sathya Sai Baba
PUBLISHING COMPANY: Birth Day Publishing Company EDITOR: Diana Baskin TOPICS: Spirituality TYPE: Book PRICE: $9.00

Divine Partnership-Truth For The New Age
PUBLISHING COMPANY: Teamup EDITOR: Jean K. Foster TOPICS: New Age TYPE: Book

Divining Hand
PUBLISHING COMPANY: New Age Press, Inc. EDITOR: C. Bird TOPICS: Palmistry TYPE: Book PRICE: $15.00

Divining Mind: A Systematic Approach To Becoming An Expert Dowser
PUBLISHING COMPANY: Destiny Books, Inner Traditions International, Ltd. EDITOR: Terry Ross, Richard Wright TOPICS: Dowsing TYPE: Book PRICE: $9.95

Do Less & Be Loved More
PUBLISHING COMPANY: Blue Dolphin Publishing, Inc. TOPICS: New Age TYPE: Book PRICE: $8.95

Do You Have A Guardian Angel?
PUBLISHING COMPANY: Mamre Press, Inc. EDITOR: John Ronner TOPICS: Metaphysics, Psychic TYPE: Book; 194 pgs. PRICE: $10.95

Doctor's Book Of Home Remedies: 1000s Of Tips & Techniques Anyone Can Use To Heal
PUBLISHING COMPANY: Rodale Press, Inc. EDITOR: Editors of Prevention Magazine TOPICS: Homeopathy, Holistic Health TYPE: Book PRICE: $26.95

Doctor's Vitamin And Mineral Encyclopedia
PUBLISHING COMPANY: Simon & Schuster, Inc. EDITOR: S. Hendler TOPICS: Holistic Health TYPE: Book PRICE: $24.95

Doctors Look At Macrobiotics
PUBLISHING COMPANY: Japan Publications, Inc. EDITOR: E. Esko TOPICS: Holistic Health, Vegetarianism, Health Food TYPE: Book PRICE: $14.95

Dogen Kigen: Mystical Realist
PUBLISHING COMPANY: University Of Arizona Press EDITOR: Hee-Jin Kim TOPICS: Spirituality TYPE: Book PRICE: $18.95

Dogs And Cats Go Vegetarian
PUBLISHING COMPANY: Harbinger Of A New Age TOPICS: Holistic Healing TYPE: Book

Don't Bite My Finger, Look Where I Am Pointing
PUBLISHING COMPANY: Chidvilas, Inc. EDITOR: B. Rajneesh TOPICS: New Age, Meditation, Spirituality, Body-Mind Connection TYPE: Book PRICE: $14.95

Don't You Want Somebody To Love
PUBLISHING COMPANY: Snow Lion Graphics TOPICS: New Age TYPE: Book PRICE: $15.95

Donning International Encyclopedic Psychic Dictionary
PUBLISHING COMPANY: Donning Company Publishers EDITOR: J. G. Bletzer TOPICS: Psychic TYPE: Book PRICE: $29.95

Doorways To The Mind
PUBLISHING COMPANY: Aries Productions, Inc. TOPICS: Metaphysics, Spirituality TYPE: Book

Dowser's Workbook: Understanding And Using The Power Of Dowsing
PUBLISHING COMPANY: Sterling Publishing Company, Inc. EDITOR: Tom Graves TOPICS: Dowsing TYPE: Book PRICE: $10.95

Dowsing For Everyone
PUBLISHING COMPANY: Stephen Greene Press, Div. of Viking Penguin, Inc. EDITOR: G. Howells TOPICS: Dowsing TYPE: Book PRICE: $7.95

Dowsing For Health: The Applications & Methods For Holistic Healing
PUBLISHING COMPANY: W. Foulsham & Co., Ltd. EDITOR: Arthur Bailey TOPICS: Dowsing TYPE: Book PRICE: $16.95

Dr. Baldwin Testifies
PUBLISHING COMPANY: Dinshah Health Society EDITOR: Dr. Kate W. Baldwin TOPICS: Holistic Healing, Color Therapy TYPE: Booklet; 26 pgs.

Dr. Deal's Delicious Detox Diet & Wellness Lifestyle
PUBLISHING COMPANY: Living Wellness, Inc. EDITOR: Dr. Grady Deal, Ph. D., D.C. TOPICS: Holistic Health, Nutrition, Health Food TYPE: Book DATE: 1991; 240 pgs. PRICE: $15.00 DESCRIPTION: Holistic health book with healing affirmations, natural therapies, detox diet & recipes. Explains which foods cause the most neck & back stiffness, pain & other health problems.

Dragon Rises, Red Bird Flies: Psychology & Chinese Medicine
PUBLISHING COMPANY: Station Hill Press EDITOR: L. Hammer TOPICS: Psychology, Holistic Health TYPE: Book PRICE: $28.95

Dragontime
PUBLISHING COMPANY: Ash Tree Publishing EDITOR: Sasha Daucus, Luisa Francia TOPICS: Spirituality, Herbalogy, Holistic Health TYPE: Book; 156 pgs. PRICE: $9.95 DESCRIPTION: Magic & mystery of Menstruation.

Drawing Down The Moon
PUBLISHING COMPANY: Beacon Press, Inc. EDITOR: M. Adler TOPICS: Paganism, Spirituality, Witchcraft, Occult TYPE: Book PRICE: $15.95

Drawing The Light From Within: Keys To Awakening Your Creative Power
PUBLISHING COMPANY: Prentice-Hall, Inc. EDITOR: J. Cornell TOPICS: New Age TYPE: Book PRICE: $14.95

Dream Journal
PUBLISHING COMPANY: Running Press NSA TOPICS: Dreams TYPE: Book PRICE: $14.95

Dream Lover: Transforming Relationships Through Dreams
PUBLISHING COMPANY: W. Foulsham & Co., Ltd. EDITOR: Les Peto TOPICS: Dreams TYPE: Book PRICE: $16.95

Dream Story
PUBLISHING COMPANY: Inner City Books EDITOR: Donald Broadribb TOPICS: New Age, Dreams, Psychology TYPE: Book PRICE: $18.00

Dream Work: Techniques For Discovering The Creative Power In Dreams
PUBLISHING COMPANY: Paulist Press EDITOR: Jeremy Taylor TOPICS: Dreams TYPE: Book PRICE: $10.95

Dream: Vision Of The Night
PUBLISHING COMPANY: Sigo Press EDITOR: M. Zeller TOPICS: Dreams TYPE: Book PRICE: $13.95

Dreambody Toolkit: Intro To The Philosophy, Goals & Practice Of Process-Oriented Psychotherapy
PUBLISHING COMPANY: Penguin Books EDITOR: J. Goodbread TOPICS: Body-Mind Connection TYPE: Book PRICE: $12.95

Dreambody: The Body's Role In Revealing The Self

PUBLISHING COMPANY: Sigo Press EDITOR: A. Mindell TOPICS: Body-Mind Connection TYPE: Book PRICE: $16.95

Dreamer's Workbook: A Complete Guide To Interpreting & Understanding Dreams

PUBLISHING COMPANY: Aquarian Press EDITOR: N. Dee TOPICS: Dreams TYPE: Book PRICE: $12.95

Dreaming: Remembering/Interpreting/Benefiting

PUBLISHING COMPANY: Prentice-Hall, Inc. EDITOR: Derek Parker, Julia Parker TOPICS: Dreams TYPE: Book PRICE: $14.95

Dreams Are Wiser Than Men

PUBLISHING COMPANY: North Atlantic Books EDITOR: R. Russo TOPICS: Dreams TYPE: Book PRICE: $14.95

Dreams Evolution And Value Fulfillment Vol.1

PUBLISHING COMPANY: Prentice-Hall, Inc. EDITOR: Jane Roberts TOPICS: Channeling TYPE: Book PRICE: $9.95

Dreams Evolution And Value Fulfillment Vol.2

PUBLISHING COMPANY: Prentice-Hall, Inc. EDITOR: Jane Roberts TOPICS: Channeling TYPE: Book PRICE: $9.95

Dreams In Analysis

PUBLISHING COMPANY: Chiron Publications EDITOR: N. Schwartz-Salant TOPICS: Dreams TYPE: Book PRICE: $15.95

Dreams: A Portal To The Source - A Guide To Dream Interpretation

PUBLISHING COMPANY: Routledge, Chapman & Hall, Inc. EDITOR: E. Whitmont, S. Perera TOPICS: Dreams, Psychology TYPE: Book PRICE: $19.95

Drinking The Divine

PUBLISHING COMPANY: Celestial Arts Publishing Co./Sub. of Ten Speed Press EDITOR: S. Ray TOPICS: Birth, Reincarnation TYPE: Book PRICE: $9.95

Dynamic Stillness Vol. 1: The Practice Of Trika Yoga

PUBLISHING COMPANY: Rudra Press Chetanananda TOPICS: New Age, Meditation, Yoga, Spirituality TYPE: Book PRICE: $17.95

Dzog Chen & Zen

PUBLISHING COMPANY: Blue Dolphin Publishing, Inc. TOPICS: New Age TYPE: Book PRICE: $5.00

Ear, Gateway To Balancing The Body: A Modern Guide To Ear Acupuncture

PUBLISHING COMPANY: Aurora Press, Inc. EDITOR: M. Wexu TOPICS: Holistic Health, Acupuncture TYPE: Guide PRICE: $14.00

Early Fathers From The Philokalia

PUBLISHING COMPANY: Faber & Faber, Affil. of Faber & Faber, Ltd., London EDITOR: G.E. Palmer TOPICS: Spirituality TYPE: Book PRICE: $18.95

Early Writings Of Alan Watts

PUBLISHING COMPANY: Celestial Arts Publishing Co./Sub. of Ten Speed Press EDITOR: John Snelling TOPICS: New Age TYPE: Book PRICE: $14.95

Earth Changes Survivial Handbook

PUBLISHING COMPANY: Sun Publishing Company EDITOR: P. Bryant TOPICS: Metaphysics, Psychic TYPE: Book PRICE: $20.00

Earth Energy: A Dowser's Investigation Of Ley Lines

PUBLISHING COMPANY: Aquarian Press EDITOR: J. Fidler TOPICS: Dowsing TYPE: Book PRICE: $12.95

Earth Mother Astrology: Ancient Healing Wisdom

PUBLISHING COMPANY: Llewellyn Publications EDITOR: M. Starck TOPICS: Spirituality, Psychic Healing TYPE: Book PRICE: $12.95

Earthly Knowledge And Heavenly Wisdom

PUBLISHING COMPANY: Anthroposophic Press, Inc. EDITOR: R. Steiner TOPICS: Spirituality TYPE: Book PRICE: $14.95

Earthway: A Native American Visionary's Path To Total Mind, Body & Spirit Health

PUBLISHING COMPANY: Pocket Books EDITOR: M. Rain TOPICS: New Age TYPE: Book PRICE: $19.95

Eastern Light For The Western Mind: University Talks By Sri Chinmoy

PUBLISHING COMPANY: AUM Publications EDITOR: S. Chinmoy TOPICS: Spirituality TYPE: Book PRICE: $5.95

Easy Does It Yoga: Yoga For People Over 60

PUBLISHING COMPANY: Harper & Row Publishers, Inc. EDITOR: A. Christensen, D. Rankin TOPICS: Yoga, Holistic Health TYPE: Book PRICE: $12.95

Easy Tao: Chinese Exercises For Health & Relaxation

PUBLISHING COMPANY: China Books & Periodicals, Inc. EDITOR: Simon Chang, F. Pokorny TOPICS: Spirituality, Tai Chi, Holistic Health TYPE: Book PRICE: $12.95

Easy Tarot Guide

PUBLISHING COMPANY: A.C.S. Publications, Inc./Astro Computing Services EDITOR: M. Masino TOPICS: Tarot TYPE: Book PRICE: $16.95

Echoes From Eternity: Voices From Spiritual Dimensions & How To Record Them

PUBLISHING COMPANY: Inner Light Publications EDITOR: J. Vilencia TOPICS: Occult TYPE: Book PRICE: $9.95

Eclipse Of The Sun

PUBLISHING COMPANY: Gothic Image Publications EDITOR: Janet McCrickard TOPICS: Spirituality TYPE: Book PRICE: $15.95

Ecstasy: In Secular And Religious Experiences

PUBLISHING COMPANY: Jeremy P. Tarcher, Inc. EDITOR: Marganita Laski TOPICS: Paranormal Phenomena, Spirituality TYPE: Book PRICE: $14.95

Ecstasy: The MDMA Story

PUBLISHING COMPANY: Ronin Publishing, Inc., Affil. of And/Or Pr., Inc. EDITOR: B. Eisner TOPICS: Body-Mind Connection, Psychology TYPE: Book PRICE: $17.95

Edgar Cayce Collection: 4 Vols. In 1 (On Dreams, Healing, Diet & Health and ESP)

PUBLISHING COMPANY: Outlet Book Co., Affil. of Crowns Pubs., Inc. EDITOR: Edgar Cayce TOPICS: Channeling TYPE: Book PRICE: $9.98

Edgar Cayce Handbook For Health Through Drugless Therapy

PUBLISHING COMPANY: Association For Research And Enlightenment, Inc. EDITOR: H. Reilly, R. Brod TOPICS: Channeling TYPE: Book PRICE: $12.95

Edgar Cayce Predicts: Your Role In Creating A New Age

PUBLISHING COMPANY: Association For Research And Enlightenment, Inc. EDITOR: Mark Thurston TOPICS: New Age, Channeling TYPE: Book PRICE: $9.95

Edgar Cayce's Massage, Hydrotherapy And Healing Oils

PUBLISHING COMPANY: Inner Vision Publishing Co. EDITOR: J. Duggan TOPICS: Channeling, Massage, Holistic Health TYPE: Book PRICE: $12.95

Edgar Cayce's Secrets Of Beauty Through Health

PUBLISHING COMPANY: Donning Company Publishers EDITOR: L. Steinhart TOPICS: Channeling TYPE: Book PRICE: $8.95

Edgar Cayce's Story Of The Soul

PUBLISHING COMPANY: Inner Vision Publishing Co. EDITOR: W.H. Church TOPICS: Reincarnation, Channeling TYPE: Book PRICE: $12.95

Edinburgh And Dore Lectures On Mental Science

PUBLISHING COMPANY: DeVorss & Company EDITOR: T. Troward TOPICS: New Age, Spirituality TYPE: Book PRICE: $10.95

Education For Peace

PUBLISHING COMPANY: Atrium Society TYPE: Book DESCRIPTION: Award winning children's book.

Effective Tsubo Therapy
PUBLISHING COMPANY: Harper & Row Publishers, Inc. EDITOR: K. Serizawa TOPICS: Acupuncture TYPE: Book PRICE: $14.95

Egyptian Miracle: The Wisdom Of The Temple
PUBLISHING COMPANY: Inner Traditions International, Ltd. EDITOR: R.A. Schwaller de Lubicz TOPICS: New Age, Metaphysics TYPE: Book PRICE: $14.95

Egyptian Mysteries: Account Of An Initiation
PUBLISHING COMPANY: Samuel Weiser, Inc. Iamblichus TOPICS: New Age, Paranormal Phenomena TYPE: Book PRICE: $9.95

Egyptian Mysteries: New Light On Ancient Knowledge
PUBLISHING COMPANY: W. W. Norton & Co., Inc. EDITOR: L. Lamy TOPICS: Paranormal Phenomena TYPE: Book PRICE: $11.95

Eleusinian And Bacchic Mysteries
PUBLISHING COMPANY: Wizards Bookshelf EDITOR: Thomas Taylor TOPICS: Paranormal Phenomena TYPE: Book PRICE: $12.00

Emanuel Swedenborg: Esstential Readings
PUBLISHING COMPANY: Crucible Books, Inner Traditions International, Ltd. EDITOR: M. Stanly TOPICS: Paranormal Phenomena TYPE: Book PRICE: $14.95

Emerging New Age
PUBLISHING COMPANY: Bear & Company, Inc. EDITOR: J.L. Simmons TOPICS: New Age TYPE: Book PRICE: $9.95

Emmanuel's Book II: Cassette
PUBLISHING COMPANY: Bantam New Age Books EDITOR: P. Rodegast, J. Stanton TOPICS: Channeling TYPE: Book PRICE: $8.95

Emmanuel's Book II: The Choice For Love
PUBLISHING COMPANY: Bantam New Age Books EDITOR: P. Rodegast TOPICS: Channeling TYPE: Book PRICE: $9.95

Emmanuel's Book: A Manual For Living Comfortably In The Cosmos
PUBLISHING COMPANY: Bantam New Age Books EDITOR: P. Rodegast TOPICS: Channeling TYPE: Book PRICE: $9.95

Empowerment Through Reiki: The Path To Personal And Global Transformation - A Handbook
PUBLISHING COMPANY: Lotus Light Publications EDITOR: Paula Horan TOPICS: Reiki TYPE: Book PRICE: $14.95

Emptiness Yoga

PUBLISHING COMPANY: Snow Lion Publications, Inc. EDITOR: J. Hopkins TOPICS: Yoga, Holistic Health TYPE: Book PRICE: $19.95

Enchanted Alphabet: A Guide To Authentic Rune Magic & Divination
PUBLISHING COMPANY: Aquarian Press EDITOR: James Peterson TOPICS: Runes TYPE: Book PRICE: $9.99

Encountering The Monster: Pathways In Children's Dreams
PUBLISHING COMPANY: Continuum Publishing Co. EDITOR: Denyse Beaudet TOPICS: Occult TYPE: Book PRICE: $15.95

Encounters In Yoga And Zen
PUBLISHING COMPANY: Routledge, Chapman & Hall, Inc. EDITOR: T. Leggett TOPICS: Yoga, Spirituality TYPE: Book PRICE: $13.95

Encounters With Eternity: Religious Views Of Death & Life After Death
PUBLISHING COMPANY: Philosophical Library, Inc. EDITOR: Christopher, et.al. Johnson TOPICS: Death TYPE: Book PRICE: $12.95

Encounters: A Psychologist Reveals Case Studies Of Contact With Extraterrestrials
PUBLISHING COMPANY: Doubleday & Co.,Inc. EDITOR: E. Flore TOPICS: UFO's, Paranormal Phenomena TYPE: Book PRICE: $17.95

Encyclopedia Of American Religions
PUBLISHING COMPANY: Gale Research Company EDITOR: Rev. J. Gordon Melton TOPICS: Psychic Phenomena TYPE: Directory

Encyclopedia Of Eastern Philosophy And Religion: Buddhism, Hinduism, Taoism & Zen
PUBLISHING COMPANY: Shambhala Publications, Inc. EDITOR: S. Bercholz TOPICS: Spirituality TYPE: Book PRICE: $39.95

Encyclopedia Of Medical Astrology
PUBLISHING COMPANY: Samuel Weiser, Inc. EDITOR: H. Cornell TOPICS: Astrology, Holistic Health TYPE: Book PRICE: $27.50

Encyclopedia Of Occultism And Parapsychology
PUBLISHING COMPANY: Gale Research Company EDITOR: Leslie A. Shepard TOPICS: Psychic Phenomena TYPE: Directory PRICE: $275.00 DESCRIPTION: Two volume reference guide to occult phenomena offering terms, definitions and descriptions in an encyclopedia format.

Encyclopedia Of Parapsychology And Psychical Research
PUBLISHING COMPANY: Paragon House EDITOR: Arthur S. Berger, J.D., Joyce Berger, M.A. TOPICS: Parapsychology, Psychic Phenomena, ESP, Yoga TYPE: Directory DATE: 1991 SIZE: 7 x 10; 554 pgs. PRICE: $45.00 DESCRIPTION: 1400 entries presented in a text/encyclopedic format providing detailed information in parapsychology & psychical research. Covers people, terms, concepts, methods,

phenomena, researchers & history on topics such as religious mysticism, channeling, healers, the New Age movement, educational centers & publications. Also offers an exhaustive bibliography & biographies giving psychic experiences of famous people.

Encyclopedia Of Pure Materia Medica
PUBLISHING COMPANY: B. Jain Publishers, Ltd. EDITOR: T. Allen TOPICS: Homeopathy TYPE: Book PRICE: $190.00

Encyclopedia Of Tarot Vol. 1
PUBLISHING COMPANY: U.S. Games Systems, Inc. EDITOR: S. Kaplan TOPICS: Tarot TYPE: Book PRICE: $25.00

Encyclopedia Of Tarot Vol. 2
PUBLISHING COMPANY: U.S. Games Systems, Inc. EDITOR: S. Kaplan TOPICS: Tarot TYPE: Book PRICE: $35.00

Encyclopedia Of Tarot Vol. 3
PUBLISHING COMPANY: U.S. Games Systems, Inc. EDITOR: S. Kaplan TOPICS: Tarot TYPE: Book PRICE: $35.00

Encyclopedia Of Unbelief
PUBLISHING COMPANY: Prometheus Books EDITOR: Gordon Stein TOPICS: Skepticism TYPE: Directory

Encyclopedia Of Unsolved Mysteries
PUBLISHING COMPANY: Contemporary Books, Inc. EDITOR: Colin Wilson TOPICS: Ghosts, Paranormal Phenomena TYPE: Book PRICE: $12.95

Encyclopedic Dictionary Of Yoga
PUBLISHING COMPANY: Paragon House EDITOR: G. Feuerstein TOPICS: Yoga TYPE: Book PRICE: $12.95

End Of Sorrow: Bhagavad Gita For Daily Living Vol 1
PUBLISHING COMPANY: Nilgiri Press EDITOR: E. Easwaran TOPICS: Spirituality TYPE: Book PRICE: $18.00

Energy: Ecstasy And Your Seven Vital Chakras
PUBLISHING COMPANY: Newcastle Publishing Co., Inc. EDITOR: Bernard Gunther TOPICS: Holistic Health TYPE: Book PRICE: $9.95

Enlightenment: Mother Of Spiritual Independence--Teachings Of Hui Neng
PUBLISHING COMPANY: Union Of Tao And Man EDITOR: M. Ni TOPICS: Spirituality TYPE: Book PRICE: $12.50

Enochian Tarot: A New System Of Divination For A New Age
PUBLISHING COMPANY: Llewellyn Publications EDITOR: G. Schueler TOPICS: Tarot, Metaphysics TYPE: Book PRICE: $12.95

Entering The Diamond Way

PUBLISHING COMPANY: Blue Dolphin Publishing, Inc. **TOPICS:** New Age **TYPE:** Book **PRICE:** $14.95

Epilogue
PUBLISHING COMPANY: Teamup **EDITOR:** Jean K. Foster **TOPICS:** New Age **TYPE:** Book

Esoteric Healing
PUBLISHING COMPANY: Lucis Publishing Company **EDITOR:** Alice Bailey **TOPICS:** Spirituality, Psychic Healing **TYPE:** Book **PRICE:** $17.00

Esoteric Orders And Their Work
PUBLISHING COMPANY: Collins, Div. of William Collins **EDITOR:** D. Fortune **TOPICS:** Occult **TYPE:** Book **PRICE:** $11.95

Esoteric Psychology 2
PUBLISHING COMPANY: Lucis Publishing Company **EDITOR:** Alice Bailey **TOPICS:** New Age, Psychology, Spirituality **TYPE:** Book **PRICE:** $17.00

Esoteric Tradition
PUBLISHING COMPANY: Theosophical University Press **EDITOR:** G. DePurucker **TOPICS:** New Age, Paranormal Phenomena **TYPE:** Book **PRICE:** $16.00

Esoterik Almanach
PUBLISHING COMPANY: L. Rossipaul Verlag GmbH **TOPICS:** Parapsychology, Occult **TYPE:** Handbook

ESP Workbook: A Practical Guide To Psychic Development
PUBLISHING COMPANY: Aquarian Press **EDITOR:** R. Davies **TOPICS:** Psychic, ESP, Psychic Phenomena **TYPE:** Book **PRICE:** $12.95

ESP, Hauntings And Poltergeists: A Parapsychologist's Handbook
PUBLISHING COMPANY: Warner Books, Inc. **EDITOR:** Loyd Auerbach **TOPICS:** New Age **TYPE:** Handbook

Essays On The Gita
PUBLISHING COMPANY: Lotus Light Publications Aurobindo **TOPICS:** New Age, Spirituality **TYPE:** Book **PRICE:** $18.95

Essence
PUBLISHING COMPANY: Samuel Weiser, Inc. **EDITOR:** A. Almaas **TOPICS:** Paranormal Phenomena, Spirituality **TYPE:** Book **PRICE:** $10.95

Essence Of Refined Gold: The Third Dalai Lama
PUBLISHING COMPANY: Snow Lion Publications, Inc. **EDITOR:** G. Mullin **TOPICS:** Spirituality **TYPE:** Book **PRICE:** $10.95

Essential Movements Of Tai Chi
PUBLISHING COMPANY: Paradigm Publications **EDITOR:** J. Kotsias **TOPICS:** Tai Chi **TYPE:** Book **PRICE:** $15.95

Essentials Of Homeopathic Therapeutics

PUBLISHING COMPANY: Boiron/Borneman **EDITOR:** Jacques Jounnay **TOPICS:** Homeopathy **TYPE:** Book **PRICE:** $49.95

Essentials Of Medical Astrology
PUBLISHING COMPANY: American Federation Of Astrologers, Inc. **EDITOR:** H. Darling **TOPICS:** Holistic Health, Astrology **TYPE:** Book **PRICE:** $14.00

Eternal Gold-Trilogy Of Truth
PUBLISHING COMPANY: Teamup **EDITOR:** Jean K. Foster **TOPICS:** New Age **TYPE:** Book

Eternal Love: Conversations With The Lord In The Heart
PUBLISHING COMPANY: Palace Publishing **EDITOR:** S. Bhaktipada **TOPICS:** Spirituality **TYPE:** Book **PRICE:** $7.95

Eternal Quest: A Mystical Story Of Love
PUBLISHING COMPANY: Treasure Publications **EDITOR:** J. Whitfield **TOPICS:** Reincarnation **TYPE:** Book **PRICE:** $14.95

Etheric Double
PUBLISHING COMPANY: Theosophical University Press **EDITOR:** Arthur E. Powell **TOPICS:** Holistic Health **TYPE:** Book **PRICE:** $6.95

Evelyn Underhill: Artist Of The Infinite Life
PUBLISHING COMPANY: Continuum Publishing Co. **EDITOR:** Dana K. Greene **TOPICS:** New Age **TYPE:** Book **PRICE:** $18.95

Even In Summer The Ice Doesn't Melt: Constructive Living Through Morita & Naikan Therapies
PUBLISHING COMPANY: William Morrow & Co. **EDITOR:** David K. Reynolds **TOPICS:** New Age **TYPE:** Book **PRICE:** $7.95

Everybody's Guide To Ayurveda Medicine
PUBLISHING COMPANY: B. Jain Publishers, Ltd. **EDITOR:** J. Dastur **TOPICS:** Holistic Health **TYPE:** Guide **PRICE:** $13.00

Everyday Health Tips: 2000 Practical Hints For Better Health And Happiness
PUBLISHING COMPANY: Rodale Press, Inc. **EDITOR:** Editors of Prevention Magazine **TOPICS:** Holistic Health **TYPE:** Book **PRICE:** $29.95

Everyone Is Psychic: The Edgar Cayce Way To Unlock Your Own Hidden Psychic Ability
PUBLISHING COMPANY: Crown Publishers, Inc. **EDITOR:** E. Fuller **TOPICS:** Psychic, Channeling **TYPE:** Book **PRICE:** $17.95

Everything Talks To Me: The True Story Of A Successful Search For Enlightenment

PUBLISHING COMPANY: Paragon House **EDITOR:** Grace Speare **TOPICS:** Psychic **TYPE:** Book **PRICE:** $9.95

Evil: The Shadow Side Of Reality
PUBLISHING COMPANY: Continuum Publishing Co. **EDITOR:** John A. Sanford **TOPICS:** Occult **TYPE:** Book **PRICE:** $10.95

Evoking The Primal Goddess: Discovery Of The Eternal Feminine Within
PUBLISHING COMPANY: Llewellyn Publications **EDITOR:** William G. Gray **TOPICS:** Occult, Witchcraft **TYPE:** Book **PRICE:** $9.95

Excalibur Briefing
PUBLISHING COMPANY: Strawberry Hill Press **EDITOR:** T. Bearden **TOPICS:** UFO's, Paranormal Phenomena **TYPE:** Book **PRICE:** $12.95

Exorcism: How To Clear A Spirit-Possessed Person
PUBLISHING COMPANY: Whitford Press/Schiffer Publishing Limited **EDITOR:** Eugene Maurey **TOPICS:** Occult, Spirituality **TYPE:** Book **PRICE:** $12.95

Expand Your Psychic Skills
PUBLISHING COMPANY: Whitford Press/Schiffer Publishing Limited **EDITOR:** Enid Hoffman **TOPICS:** Psychic **TYPE:** Book **PRICE:** $9.95

Expanded Reference Manual Of The Radiance Technique
PUBLISHING COMPANY: Radiance Technique Association International, Inc. **EDITOR:** Dr. Barbara Ray **TOPICS:** Holistic Health, Reiki **TYPE:** Book **PRICE:** $22.00

Expedition: Being An Account In Words And Artwork Of The 2358 A.D. Voyage To Darwin Iv
PUBLISHING COMPANY: Workman Publishing **EDITOR:** Waynes Douglas Barlowe **TOPICS:** UFO's, Paranormal Phenomena **TYPE:** Book **PRICE:** $18.95

Experience Of No-Self: A Contemplative Journey
PUBLISHING COMPANY: Shambhala Publications, Inc. **EDITOR:** Bernadette Roberts **TOPICS:** Meditation, Spirituality **TYPE:** Book **PRICE:** $12.95

Explore Your Psychic World
PUBLISHING COMPANY: Ariel Press **EDITOR:** A. Worrall, O. Worrall **TOPICS:** Psychic, Parapsychology **TYPE:** Book **PRICE:** $7.95

Exploring Atlantis
PUBLISHING COMPANY: Arizona Metaphysical Society **EDITOR:** Frank Alper **TOPICS:** Astrology, Metaphysics, Channeling, New Age, Crystals **TYPE:** Book; 82 pgs. **PRICE:** $9.95 **DESCRIPTION:** Three volume set.

Exploring Inner And Outer Space: A Scientists Perspective On Personal & Planetary Transformation

PUBLISHING COMPANY: North Atlantic Books EDITOR: B. O'Leary TOPICS: ESP, Psychic Phenomena, Psychic TYPE: Book PRICE: $12.95

Exploring Nature's Uncultivated Garden
PUBLISHING COMPANY: Havelin Communications PUBLISHER: Michael F. Havelin EDITOR: Deborah Lee TOPICS: Nutrition, Health Food TYPE: Book DESCRIPTION: Remarkable guide to tapping into the energies of wild food plants that abound everywhere in North America.

Exploring The Power Within: A Resource Book For Transcending The Ordinary
PUBLISHING COMPANY: Whitford Press/Schiffer Publishing Limited EDITOR: Brad Steiger TOPICS: Psychic TYPE: Book PRICE: $14.95

Exploring The World Of Lucid Dreaming
PUBLISHING COMPANY: Ballantine Books, Inc. EDITOR: S. LaBerge, H. Rheingold TOPICS: Dreams TYPE: Book PRICE: $18.95

Extraterrestrials In Biblical Prophecy: And The New Age Great Experiment
PUBLISHING COMPANY: Inner Light Publications EDITOR: G.C. Schellhorn TOPICS: UFO's, Paranormal Phenomena TYPE: Book PRICE: $12.95

Eye Of The Centaur: A Visionary Guide Into Past Lives
PUBLISHING COMPANY: Llewellyn Publications EDITOR: B. Clow TOPICS: Past Life Regression, New Age TYPE: Book DATE: 1989 PRICE: $10.95

Eye To Eye: The Quest For A New Paradigm
PUBLISHING COMPANY: Shambhala Publications, Inc. EDITOR: Ken Wilber TOPICS: New Age, Psychology TYPE: Book PRICE: $14.95

Face On Mars: Evidence For A Lost Civilization?
PUBLISHING COMPANY: Chicago Review Press, Inc. EDITOR: R. Pozos TOPICS: UFO's, Paranormal Phenomena TYPE: Book PRICE: $12.95

Faces: Reading The Divine Analogy
PUBLISHING COMPANY: Marcus Books Hilarion TOPICS: Parapsychology TYPE: Book PRICE: $7.95

Family Guide To Homeopathy
PUBLISHING COMPANY: Boiron/Borneman EDITOR: A. Horvilleur TOPICS: Homeopathy TYPE: Guide PRICE: $14.95

Far Journey's
PUBLISHING COMPANY: Doubleday & Co.,Inc. EDITOR: R. Monroe TOPICS: Astral Projection TYPE: Book PRICE: $9.95

Fatima Prophecy: Days Of Darkness, Promise Of Light

PUBLISHING COMPANY: Inner Vision Publishing Co. EDITOR: R. Stanford TOPICS: Metaphysics, Psychic TYPE: Book PRICE: $9.95

Feel Better Now, 30 Ways To Handle Frustration In 3 Minutes Or Less
PUBLISHING COMPANY: B.L. Winch & Associates/Jalmar Press EDITOR: Dr. Christan Schriner TOPICS: New Age TYPE: Book SIZE: 6x9; 180 pgs. PRICE: $9.95

Feel Better! Live Longer! Relax
PUBLISHING COMPANY: Dimi Press EDITOR: Dick Lutz TOPICS: New Age, Meditation TYPE: Book; 144 pgs. PRICE: $9.95

Feeling Good Handbook: Using The New Mood Therapy In Everyday Life
PUBLISHING COMPANY: William Morrow & Co. EDITOR: David Burns TOPICS: New Age, Psychology TYPE: Book PRICE: $19.95

Feet First: A Guide To Foot Reflexology
PUBLISHING COMPANY: Simon & Schuster, Inc. EDITOR: Laura Norman TOPICS: Acupuncture TYPE: Guide PRICE: $12.95

Feminist Hypnosis: Holistic Self-Help For Men And Women
PUBLISHING COMPANY: Grace And Goddess Unlimited EDITOR: Cindee Grace TOPICS: Hypnotism TYPE: Book PRICE: $25.00

Field Guide To Medicinal Plants: Eastern & Central North America
PUBLISHING COMPANY: Houghton Mifflin Company EDITOR: Steven Foster, James Duke TOPICS: Holistic Health, Herbalogy TYPE: Guide PRICE: $15.95

Field Of Transformations: Evolution Of Awareness According To Sacred Books Of Ancient Egypt
PUBLISHING COMPANY: Inner Traditions International, Ltd. EDITOR: Bika Reed TOPICS: New Age, Paranormal Phenomena TYPE: Book PRICE: $12.95

Fifth Dimension
PUBLISHING COMPANY: Samuel Weiser, Inc. EDITOR: V. Alder TOPICS: Occult TYPE: Book PRICE: $9.95

Fighting Disease: The Complete Guide To Natural Immune Power
PUBLISHING COMPANY: Rodale Press, Inc. EDITOR: E. Michaud, A. Feinstein TOPICS: Holistic Health TYPE: Guide PRICE: $27.95

Final Prophecies Of Nostradamus
PUBLISHING COMPANY: Putnam Publishing Group EDITOR: Erika Cheetham TOPICS: Psychic, Spirituality TYPE: Book PRICE: $9.95

Finding The Fountain Of Youth Inside Yourself: Powerful Trusth About Inner Youth

PUBLISHING COMPANY: Pocket Books EDITOR: S. Helmstetter TOPICS: New Age, Psychology TYPE: Book PRICE: $18.95

Finding Your Life's Purpose Through Astrology Workbook
PUBLISHING COMPANY: Reincarnation Books & Tapes EDITOR: Bette B. Binder, Mark Vito TOPICS: Astrology TYPE: Book PRICE: $13.00

Fine Arts Of Relaxation, Concentration And Meditation: Ancient Skills For Modern Minds
PUBLISHING COMPANY: Wisdom Publications EDITOR: J. Levey TOPICS: Meditation, Spirituality TYPE: Book PRICE: $14.95

Fine Tune Your Brain: When Everything's Going Right And What To Do When It Isn't
PUBLISHING COMPANY: Syntony Publishing, Inc. EDITOR: G. Laborde TOPICS: New Age, Psychology TYPE: Book PRICE: $13.95

Fire In The Heart: Healers, Sages & Mystics
PUBLISHING COMPANY: Paragon House EDITOR: K. Markides TOPICS: Yoga, Psychic Healing, Spirituality TYPE: Book PRICE: $18.95

Fire Without Fuel: Aphorisms Of Baba Hari Dass
PUBLISHING COMPANY: Sri Rama Publishing EDITOR: Hari Dass TOPICS: Spirituality TYPE: Book PRICE: $15.95

Fireside Treasury Of Light: An Anthology Of The Best In New Age Literature
PUBLISHING COMPANY: Simon & Schuster, Inc. EDITOR: Mary Olsen Kelly TOPICS: New Age TYPE: Book PRICE: $10.95

First Steps In Ritual: Safe, Effective Techniques For Experiencing The Inner Worlds
PUBLISHING COMPANY: Aquarian Press EDITOR: D. Ashcroft-Nowicki TOPICS: Occult TYPE: Book PRICE: $9.95

Five Keys To Inner Wisdom
PUBLISHING COMPANY: Astro-Psychology Institute TOPICS: Astrology, Psychology TYPE: Book

Fixed Stars
PUBLISHING COMPANY: Arthur Publications, Inc. EDITOR: Debra Sapp TOPICS: Astrology TYPE: Book DATE: 1978

Flight Of The Feathered Serpent: A Guide To The Maya Tarot Deck
PUBLISHING COMPANY: Lotus Light Publications EDITOR: P. Balin TOPICS: Tarot, Metaphysics TYPE: Book PRICE: $13.95

Flow: The Psychology Of Optimal Experience - A Guide To Enhancing The Quality Of Life

PUBLISHING COMPANY: Harper & Row Publishers, Inc. **EDITOR:** Mihaly Csikszentmihalyi **TOPICS:** Psychology **TYPE:** Book **PRICE:** $19.95

Flower Essences And Vibrational Healing
PUBLISHING COMPANY: Cassandra Press **EDITOR:** Gurudas **TOPICS:** Herbalogy, Holistic Healing **TYPE:** Book; 320 pgs. **PRICE:** $13.95

Flower Essences: Reordering Our Understanding And Approach To Illness & Health
PUBLISHING COMPANY: Perelandra **EDITOR:** M. Wright **TOPICS:** Homeopathy, Holistic Health **TYPE:** Book **PRICE:** $10.95

Folding The Universe: Origami From Angelfish To Zen
PUBLISHING COMPANY: Random House, Inc. **EDITOR:** P. Engel **TOPICS:** New Age **TYPE:** Book **PRICE:** $16.95

Food Combining And Digestion
PUBLISHING COMPANY: Sprout House **PUBLISHER:** Steve Meyerowitz **TOPICS:** Nutrition, Holistic Health, Health Food **TYPE:** Book

Food Governs Your Destiny: The Teachings Of Namboku Mizuno
PUBLISHING COMPANY: Japan Publications, Inc. **EDITOR:** M. & A. Kushi, Alex Jack **TOPICS:** Holistic Health, Vegetarianism, Health Food **TYPE:** Book **PRICE:** $12.95

Footprints On The Path
PUBLISHING COMPANY: Findhorn Foundation & Press **EDITOR:** Eileen Caddy **TOPICS:** Spirituality **TYPE:** Book

For The Love Of God
PUBLISHING COMPANY: New World Library **EDITOR:** Benjamin Shield **TOPICS:** Spirituality **TYPE:** Book; 220 pgs. **PRICE:** $10.95

For The Vegetarian In You
PUBLISHING COMPANY: C. Olson And Company **EDITOR:** B.R. Boyd **TOPICS:** Holistic Health **TYPE:** Book; 64 pgs. **PRICE:** $7.45 **DESCRIPTION:** The history, reasons & kinds of vegetarianism. Questions & answers section.

Forces Of The Zodiac
PUBLISHING COMPANY: Ariel Press **EDITOR:** R. Leichtman, C. Japikse **TOPICS:** Astrology **TYPE:** Book **PRICE:** $21.50

Forgiveness: How To Make Peace With Your Past And Get On With Your Life
PUBLISHING COMPANY: Warner Books, Inc. **EDITOR:** Sidney Simon, Suzanne Simon **TOPICS:** New Age, Psychology **TYPE:** Book **PRICE:** $19.95

Fortune-Teller's Workbook: A Practical Introduction To The World Of Divination
PUBLISHING COMPANY: Aquarian Press **EDITOR:** S. Fenton **TOPICS:** Metaphysics, Psychic **TYPE:** Book **PRICE:** $14.50

Fortune-Telling By Tea Leaves: Practical Guide To The Ancient Art Of Tasseography
PUBLISHING COMPANY: Aquarian Press **EDITOR:** S. Fenton **TOPICS:** Psychic, Tea Leaves **TYPE:** Book **PRICE:** $7.95

Found: A Place For Me
PUBLISHING COMPANY: Treehouse Enterprises **PUBLISHER:** Dr. Sandra G. Landsman **TOPICS:** New Age, Psychology, Holistic Health **TYPE:** Book **DESCRIPTION:** Concerns the diagnosis & treatment of Manic-Depressive illness.

Foundation For A New Consciousness
PUBLISHING COMPANY: Westgate House **TOPICS:** New Age, Meditation **TYPE:** Book **DATE:** 1981 **DESCRIPTION:** An essay on art, science & meditation with illustrations.

Fountain - Source Of Occultism
PUBLISHING COMPANY: Theosophical University Press **EDITOR:** G. DePurucker **TOPICS:** Occult, Paranormal Phenomena **TYPE:** Book **PRICE:** $10.00

Fourth Book Of Occult Philosophy, With The Heptameron Of Peter De Abano
PUBLISHING COMPANY: Heptangle Books **EDITOR:** C. Agrippa **TOPICS:** Alchemy **TYPE:** Book **PRICE:** $20.00

Fourth World Of The Hopis: The Epic Story Of The Hopi Indians As Preserved In Their Legends
PUBLISHING COMPANY: University Of New Mexico Press **EDITOR:** H. Courlander **TOPICS:** Metaphysics, Psychic **TYPE:** Book **PRICE:** $11.95

Free Flight, Celebrating Your Right Brain
PUBLISHING COMPANY: B.L. Winch & Associates/Jalmar Press **EDITOR:** Barbara Meister-Vitale **TOPICS:** New Age **TYPE:** Book **SIZE:** 6 x 9; 128 pgs. **PRICE:** $9.95

Free Spirit
PUBLISHING COMPANY: Free Spirit **TOPICS:** New Age, Channeling **TYPE:** Directory **FREQ:** bi-monthly **CIRC:** 50,000 **PRICE:** $18.00 **DESCRIPTION:** A directory of resources in New York City and surrounding areas including features, articles, book reviews and columns. Accepts ads.

Freedom From Stress
PUBLISHING COMPANY: Himalayan International Institute Of Yoga Science and Philosophy **EDITOR:** P. Nuernberger **TOPICS:** Holistic Health **TYPE:** Book **PRICE:** $10.95

Freedom In Exile: The Autobiography Of The Dalai Lama
PUBLISHING COMPANY: Harper & Row Publishers, Inc. **EDITOR:** Dalai Lama **TOPICS:** Spirituality **TYPE:** Book **PRICE:** $22.95

Freemasonry Of The Ancient Egyptians

PUBLISHING COMPANY: Philosophical Research Society, Inc. **EDITOR:** M.P. Hall **TOPICS:** New Age, Paranormal Phenomena **TYPE:** Book **PRICE:** $10.50

Fresh Life Guide
PUBLISHING COMPANY: Fresh Life Guide **TOPICS:** Holistic Healing **TYPE:** Guide

From Conflict To Caring: The Process Of Learning Loving Behavior
PUBLISHING COMPANY: CompCare Publications, Div. of Comprehensive Care Corp. **EDITOR:** J. Paul, M. Paul **TOPICS:** New Age, Psychology **TYPE:** Book **PRICE:** $12.95

From Here To Freedom: Unraveling Our Legacy Of Fear
PUBLISHING COMPANY: Creighton, Maydell & Pennington **EDITOR:** Y. Huntington-Leland **TOPICS:** Psychology **TYPE:** Book **PRICE:** $14.95

From The Heart Of A Gentle Brother
PUBLISHING COMPANY: High Mesa Press **EDITOR:** Joy Franklin **TOPICS:** New Age, Channeling **TYPE:** Book **PRICE:** $10.95

Frontiers Of The Hidden Mind
PUBLISHING COMPANY: Hunter House Publishers, Inc. **EDITOR:** S. Grof **TOPICS:** New Age, Psychology **TYPE:** Book **PRICE:** $19.95

Full Catastrophe Living: Using The Wisdom Of Your Body & Mind To Face Stress, Pain/Illness
PUBLISHING COMPANY: Delacorte Press **EDITOR:** John Kabat-Zinn **TOPICS:** Holistic Health, New Age **TYPE:** Book **PRICE:** $19.95

Full Cycle: The Human Love Story - A Novel
PUBLISHING COMPANY: Marcus Books **EDITOR:** Ripley Webb **TOPICS:** Reincarnation **TYPE:** Book **PRICE:** $10.95

Fully Alive Resource Guide
PUBLISHING COMPANY: Fully Alive Resource Guide **EDITOR:** Kaila J. Rork **TOPICS:** New Age, Metaphysics **TYPE:** Directory **DATE:** 1988 **FREQ:** 3 issues/yr **CIRC:** 10,000 **PRICE:** $6.00 **DESCRIPTION:** Lists products and services that encourage effective living. Also prints non-fiction and poetry pertinent to the Santa Barbara area it serves.

Fundamentals Of Yoga: A Handbook Of Theory, Practice & Application
PUBLISHING COMPANY: Crown Publishers, Inc. **EDITOR:** R.S. Mishra **TOPICS:** Yoga, Holistic Health **TYPE:** Book **PRICE:** $13.95

Further Dimensions Of Healing Addictions
PUBLISHING COMPANY: Cassandra Press **EDITOR:** Donna Cunningham **TOPICS:** Holistic Healing **TYPE:** Book; 168 pgs. **PRICE:** $9.95

Fusion Of The Five Elements I: Basic & Advanced Meditation For Transforming Negative Emotions

PUBLISHING COMPANY: Healing Tao Center **EDITOR:** M. Chia, M. Chia **TOPICS:** Tai Chi, Holistic Health, Meditation **TYPE:** Book **PRICE:** $12.95

Future Is Now: Last Talks In India
PUBLISHING COMPANY: Harper & Row Publishers, Inc. **EDITOR:** J. Krishnamurti **TOPICS:** Spirituality **TYPE:** Book **PRICE:** $14.95

Future Lives: A Fearless Guide To Our Transition Times
PUBLISHING COMPANY: Bear & Company, Inc. **EDITOR:** J.L. Simmons **TOPICS:** New Age **TYPE:** Book **PRICE:** $9.95

Future Now: How To Use All Methods Of Prediction From Astrology To Tarot To Discover Your Future
PUBLISHING COMPANY: Prentice-Hall, Inc. **EDITOR:** Derek Parker, Julia Parker **TOPICS:** Metaphysics, Psychic **TYPE:** Book **PRICE:** $14.95

Future Poetry
PUBLISHING COMPANY: Lotus Light Publications Aurobindo **TOPICS:** Spirituality **TYPE:** Book **PRICE:** $18.00

Future Research Directory: Individuals
PUBLISHING COMPANY: World Future Society **TOPICS:** New Age **TYPE:** Directory

Games Of The Gods: The Origin Of Board Games In Magic & Divination
PUBLISHING COMPANY: Samuel Weiser, Inc. **EDITOR:** N. Pennick **TOPICS:** Occult **TYPE:** Book **PRICE:** $12.50

Gandhi The Man
PUBLISHING COMPANY: Random House, Inc. **EDITOR:** E. Easwaran **TOPICS:** Spirituality **TYPE:** Book **PRICE:** $12.00

Gandhi: An Autobiography
PUBLISHING COMPANY: Beacon Press, Inc. **EDITOR:** M. Gandhi **TOPICS:** Spirituality **TYPE:** Book **PRICE:** $11.95

Gandhian Theology Of Liberation
PUBLISHING COMPANY: Orbis Books **EDITOR:** Ignatius Jesudasan **TOPICS:** Spirituality **TYPE:** Book **PRICE:** $14.95

Garden Of The Prophet
PUBLISHING COMPANY: Random House, Inc. **EDITOR:** K. Gilbran **TOPICS:** Channeling **TYPE:** Book **PRICE:** $14.95

Garland Of Letters
PUBLISHING COMPANY: Auromere Books & Imports **EDITOR:** J. Woodroffe **TOPICS:** Spirituality **TYPE:** Book **PRICE:** $24.00

Gary Null's Complete Guide To Healing Your Body Naturally: When Traditional Medicine Fails
PUBLISHING COMPANY: McGraw Hill Book Co., Div. of McGraw Hill, Inc. **EDITOR:** G. Null

TOPICS: Holistic Health **TYPE:** Guide **PRICE:** $17.95

Gateway To Patriarchal Son: Venerable Master Hya-Am's Dharma Talks
PUBLISHING COMPANY: Western Son (Zen) Academy Myo-Bong **TOPICS:** Spirituality **TYPE:** Book **PRICE:** $14.95

Gateway To Son
PUBLISHING COMPANY: Western Son (Zen) Academy Hye-Am **TOPICS:** Spirituality **TYPE:** Book **PRICE:** $21.95

Gem And Precious Stones Of North America
PUBLISHING COMPANY: Dover Publications, Inc. **EDITOR:** G. Kunz **TOPICS:** Crystals **TYPE:** Book **PRICE:** $11.95

Gem Elixirs And Vibrational Healing, Vol. 1
PUBLISHING COMPANY: Cassandra Press Gurudas **TOPICS:** New Age, Crystals, Holistic Health **TYPE:** Book; 304 pgs. **PRICE:** $13.95

Gem Elixirs And Vibrational Healing, Vol. 2
PUBLISHING COMPANY: Cassandra Press Gurudas **TOPICS:** New Age, Crystals, Holistic Health **TYPE:** Book; 216 pgs. **PRICE:** $11.95

Gemstone And Crystal Energies
PUBLISHING COMPANY: Lorien House **EDITOR:** T. Isaacs **TOPICS:** Crystals **TYPE:** Book **PRICE:** $10.00

Gemstones Of The World
PUBLISHING COMPANY: Sterling Publishing Company, Inc. **EDITOR:** W. Schumann **TOPICS:** Crystals **TYPE:** Book **PRICE:** $19.95

Genmai: Brown Rice For Better Health
PUBLISHING COMPANY: Japan Publications, Inc. **EDITOR:** E. Ishida **TOPICS:** Holistic Health, Vegetarianism, Health Food **TYPE:** Book **PRICE:** $16.95

Gentle Path Of Spiritual Progress
PUBLISHING COMPANY: Union Of Tao And Man **EDITOR:** M. Ni **TOPICS:** Spirituality **TYPE:** Book **PRICE:** $14.50

Gerard's Herbal
PUBLISHING COMPANY: Dover Publications, Inc. **EDITOR:** J. Gerard **TOPICS:** Holistic Health, Herbalogy **TYPE:** Book **PRICE:** $75.00

Getting Well Again
PUBLISHING COMPANY: St. Martin's Press, Inc. **EDITOR:** Carl Simonton **TOPICS:** Holistic Health, Body-Mind Connection, Psychology **TYPE:** Book **PRICE:** $14.95

Ghosts Of The Trianon: The Complete An Adventure By C.A.E. Moberly & E.F. Jourdain
PUBLISHING COMPANY: Aquarian Press **EDITOR:** M. Coleman **TOPICS:** Psychic Phenomena, ESP, Spirituality **TYPE:** Book **PRICE:** $12.95

Ghostwatch: Institute For Psychical Research-Unpublished Accounts From Their Files
PUBLISHING COMPANY: W. Foulsham & Co., Ltd. **EDITOR:** Colin Gardner **TOPICS:** ESP, Spirituality, Psychic Phenomena **TYPE:** Book **PRICE:** $18.95

Giant Steps
PUBLISHING COMPANY: Option Institute & Fellowship- A Place For Miracles **TOPICS:** Holistic Healing **TYPE:** Book

Gift For God
PUBLISHING COMPANY: Harper & Row Publishers, Inc. Mother Teresa **TOPICS:** Spirituality **TYPE:** Book **PRICE:** $10.95

Gift Of Healing: How To Receive And Use Your Natural Healing Energies
PUBLISHING COMPANY: Top Of The Mountain Publishing **EDITOR:** Gerald M. Loe **TOPICS:** Spirituality, Psychic Healing **TYPE:** Book **PRICE:** $12.95

Gift Of Healing: Selections From A Course In Miracles
PUBLISHING COMPANY: Jeremy P. Tarcher, Inc. **EDITOR:** Frances Vaughan **TOPICS:** Spirituality **TYPE:** Book **PRICE:** $10.95

Gifts Of God
PUBLISHING COMPANY: Celestial Arts Publishing Co./Sub. of Ten Speed Press **EDITOR:** H. Schucman **TOPICS:** Spirituality **TYPE:** Book **PRICE:** $19.95

Gita As It Was: Rediscovering The Original Bhagavadgita
PUBLISHING COMPANY: Open Court Publishing Co. **EDITOR:** Phulgenda Sinha **TOPICS:** Spirituality **TYPE:** Book **PRICE:** $16.95

Glands: Mirror Of The Self
PUBLISHING COMPANY: Supreme Grand Lodge of AMORC, Inc. **EDITOR:** O. Wilson **TOPICS:** Parapsychology, Holistic Health **TYPE:** Book **PRICE:** $12.50

Glimpses Of Abhidharma
PUBLISHING COMPANY: Shambhala Publications, Inc. **EDITOR:** C. Trungpa **TOPICS:** Spirituality **TYPE:** Book **PRICE:** $10.95

Glossary Index For Course In Miracles
PUBLISHING COMPANY: Foundation For A Course In Miracles Conference/Retreat Center **EDITOR:** K. Wapnick **TOPICS:** Spirituality **TYPE:** Book **PRICE:** $16.00

Glossary Of Occult Terms
PUBLISHING COMPANY: Ghost Research Society **EDITOR:** Dale Kaczmarek **TOPICS:** Occult **TYPE:** Directory **PRICE:** $6.50 **DESCRIPTION:** Lists the most frequently used terms, references & words pertaining to the Occult.

Go See The Movie In Your Head: Imagery, The Key To Awareness
PUBLISHING COMPANY: Ross Erikson, Inc. EDITOR: J. Shorr TOPICS: Meditation, Psychology TYPE: Book PRICE: $9.95

God As Mother: A Feminine Theology In India
PUBLISHING COMPANY: Branden Publishing Co. EDITOR: Cheever Brown TOPICS: Spirituality TYPE: Book PRICE: $25.00

God Spoke To Me
PUBLISHING COMPANY: Findhorn Foundation & Press EDITOR: Eileen Caddy TOPICS: Spirituality, Paranormal Phenomena TYPE: Book PRICE: $10.95

God Ultimate Unlimited Mind Speaks
PUBLISHING COMPANY: Starmast Publication TYPE: Book DESCRIPTION: Channeled by Allen Michael from ETI Space Being.

God's Arms Around Us
PUBLISHING COMPANY: Blue Dolphin Publishing, Inc. TOPICS: New Age TYPE: Book PRICE: $19.95

Goddesses
PUBLISHING COMPANY: Volcano/Kazan Press EDITOR: M. Oda TOPICS: Spirituality TYPE: Book PRICE: $14.95

Godel, Escher, Bach: An Eternal Golden Braid
PUBLISHING COMPANY: Random House, Inc. EDITOR: Douglas Hofstadter TOPICS: New Age TYPE: Book PRICE: $14.95

Gods Of Eden
PUBLISHING COMPANY: Dahlin Family Press EDITOR: William Bramley TOPICS: UFO's, Paranormal Phenomena TYPE: Book PRICE: $23.95

Gods Of The Egyptians Vol.1
PUBLISHING COMPANY: Dover Publications, Inc. EDITOR: W. Budge TOPICS: Occult TYPE: Book PRICE: $10.95

Gods Of The Egyptians Vol.2
PUBLISHING COMPANY: Dover Publications, Inc. EDITOR: W. Budge TOPICS: Occult TYPE: Book PRICE: $10.95

Gods, Spirits, Cosmic Guardians
PUBLISHING COMPANY: Aquarian Press EDITOR: Hilary Evans TOPICS: Psychic, Spirituality, UFO's, Paranormal Phenomena TYPE: Book PRICE: $12.95

Going Nowhere Fast: Step Off Life's Treadmills & Find Peace Of Mind
PUBLISHING COMPANY: Prentice-Hall, Inc. EDITOR: Melvyn Kinder TOPICS: New Age, Psychology TYPE: Book PRICE: $19.95

Gold Rush Ghosts: Strange & Unexplained Phenomena In The Mother Lode

PUBLISHING COMPANY: Borderland Science And Research Foundation EDITOR: Nancy Bradley, V. Gaddis TOPICS: Occult TYPE: Book PRICE: $9.95

Golden Age Of Chartres: Teachings Of A Mystery School & The Eternal Feminine
PUBLISHING COMPANY: Anthroposophic Press, Inc. EDITOR: R. Querido TOPICS: Spirituality, Paranormal Phenomena TYPE: Book PRICE: $20.00

Good For You: The Science Of Mind Approach To Successful Living
PUBLISHING COMPANY: Science of Mind Publications, Div. of United Church of Religious Science EDITOR: E. Holmes TOPICS: Spirituality, Psychology TYPE: Book PRICE: $12.95

Gospel Of Sri Ramakrishna: Abridged Version
PUBLISHING COMPANY: Ramakrishna-Vivekananda Center Of New York EDITOR: S. Nikhilananda TOPICS: Spirituality TYPE: Book PRICE: $24.50

Grail Legend
PUBLISHING COMPANY: Sigo Press EDITOR: E. Jung, M.L. Von Franz TOPICS: Psychology, Alchemy TYPE: Book PRICE: $16.95

Grail Seeker's Companion
PUBLISHING COMPANY: Aquarian Press EDITOR: J. Matthews, M. Green TOPICS: Paganism, Spirituality TYPE: Book PRICE: $12.95

Grandmother Of Time: A Women's Book Of Celebrations, Spells & Sacred Objects For Every Month
PUBLISHING COMPANY: Harper & Row Publishers, Inc. EDITOR: Z. Budapest TOPICS: Occult, Witchcraft TYPE: Book PRICE: $13.95

Graphology Handbook
PUBLISHING COMPANY: Whitford Press/Schiffer Publishing Limited EDITOR: C. Casewit TOPICS: Graphology TYPE: Book PRICE: $11.95

Graphology Workbook: A Complete Guide To Interpreting Handwriting
PUBLISHING COMPANY: Aquarian Press EDITOR: M. Gullan-Whur TOPICS: Graphology TYPE: Book PRICE: $12.95

Great Book Of Catalogs
PUBLISHING COMPANY: Great Book Of Catalogs, The EDITOR: Steve Pinkerton TOPICS: New Age, Metaphysics TYPE: Directory DESCRIPTION: Lists almost 3,000 of the best mail-order catalogs nationwide. Many related to the New Age & Metaphysical fields.

Great Cosmic Mother: Rediscovering The Religion Of The Earth
PUBLISHING COMPANY: Harper & Row Publishers, Inc. EDITOR: M. Sjoo, B. Mor TOPICS: Paganism, Spirituality TYPE: Book PRICE: $17.95

Great Mother

PUBLISHING COMPANY: Princeton University Press EDITOR: E. Neumann TOPICS: New Age, Psychology, Spirituality TYPE: Book PRICE: $16.95

Great Vision: Francis Bacon
PUBLISHING COMPANY: Supreme Grand Lodge of AMORC, Inc. EDITOR: P. Dalkins TOPICS: New Age TYPE: Book PRICE: $30.00

Greater Chicagoland Psychic Directory
PUBLISHING COMPANY: Ghost Research Society EDITOR: Dale Kaczmarek TOPICS: Ghosts, Psychic Phenomena, Parapsychology, Reincarnation, Past Life Regression TYPE: Directory PRICE: $7.00

Greening Of Psychology: The Vegetable World In Myth, Dream & Healing
PUBLISHING COMPANY: Spring Publications, Inc. EDITOR: Peter Bishop TOPICS: Spirituality TYPE: Book PRICE: $17.50

Growing Up Creative: Nurturing A Lifetime Of Creativity
PUBLISHING COMPANY: Crown Publishers, Inc. EDITOR: Teresa Amabile TOPICS: New Age TYPE: Book

Growing Without Schooling
PUBLISHING COMPANY: Holt Associates/Growing Without Schooling TOPICS: New Age TYPE: Book

Guide & Index To G.J. Gurdjieffs All & Everything: Beelzebub's Tales To His Grandson
PUBLISHING COMPANY: Traditional Studies Press Traditional Studies TOPICS: Spirituality TYPE: Book PRICE: $32.00

Guide Astrologique
PUBLISHING COMPANY: F.G. Gourdon TOPICS: Astrology TYPE: Guide DATE: 1970 CIRC: 120,000 DESCRIPTION: Supplement to Astre.

Guide Resources
PUBLISHING COMPANY: Guide Resources EDITOR: Christian Lamontage, Paule Lebrun TOPICS: Holistic Healing TYPE: Guide

Guide To Health-Oriented Periodicals
PUBLISHING COMPANY: Sprouting Publications EDITOR: Michael Linden TOPICS: Holistic Healing TYPE: Guide

Guide To Medicinal Plants
PUBLISHING COMPANY: Keats Publishing, Inc. EDITOR: P. Schauenberg, F. Paris TOPICS: Holistic Health, Herbalogy TYPE: Guide PRICE: $15.95

Guide To The American Occult: Directory And Bibliography
PUBLISHING COMPANY: Laird Wilcox, Editorial Research Service EDITOR: Laird Wilcox TOPICS: Psychic Phenomena, Parapsychology, Occult TYPE: Directory DATE: 1990; 104 pgs. FREQ: annually CIRC: 700 PRICE: $24.95 DESCRIPTION: Covers over 2,000 sources related to mystical & occult topics such as metaphysics, parapsychology, psychic, ESP, spiritual, faith-healing, astrology, pagan,

witchcraft, new & unconventional religions & occult organizations & serials. Includes a 1,000- item annotated bibliography, a list of counter-cult groups & skeptical organizations. Arranged alphabetically with geographical indexes.

Guide To The I Ching
PUBLISHING COMPANY: Anthony Publishing Co. **EDITOR:** Carol Anthony **TOPICS:** Parapsychology, Psychic **TYPE:** Book **DATE:** 1980 **PRICE:** $12.50

Guidebook To Ecoconsciousness
PUBLISHING COMPANY: Maui EcoPark/Center For Ecological Living **TYPE:** Book **PRICE:** $12.95 **TERM:** yearly **DESCRIPTION:** Five billion ways to create a paradise planet & harmonious human civilizations.

Guided Tour Of The Collected Works Of C.G. Jung
PUBLISHING COMPANY: Shambhala Publications, Inc. **EDITOR:** R. Hopcke **TOPICS:** Spirituality **TYPE:** Book **PRICE:** $18.95

Guiding Symptoms Of Our Materia Medica
PUBLISHING COMPANY: Thorsens Publishing House **EDITOR:** G. Kohler **TOPICS:** Homeopathy **TYPE:** Book **PRICE:** $12.95

Guilt Is The Teacher, Love Is The Lesson: A Book To Heal You, Heart And Soul
PUBLISHING COMPANY: Warner Books, Inc. **EDITOR:** J. Borysenko **TOPICS:** New Age, Spirituality, Psychology **TYPE:** Book **PRICE:** $18.95

Gulf Breeze Sightings: The Most Astounding Multiple Sightings Of Ufos In U.S. History
PUBLISHING COMPANY: William Morrow & Co. **EDITOR:** Ed Walters, Frances Walters **TOPICS:** UFO's, Paranormal Phenomena **TYPE:** Book **PRICE:** $21.95

Gypsy Sorcery And Fortune Telling
PUBLISHING COMPANY: Citadel Press **EDITOR:** Charles Lelans **TOPICS:** Metaphysics, New Age **TYPE:** Book **PRICE:** $12.95

Hags And Heroes: A Feminist Approach To Jungian Psychotherapy With Couples
PUBLISHING COMPANY: Inner City Books **EDITOR:** P. Young-Eisendrath **TOPICS:** Spirituality **TYPE:** Book **PRICE:** $15.00

Hallow-Quest: Tarot Magic & The Arthurian Mysteries
PUBLISHING COMPANY: Aquarian Press **EDITOR:** C. Matthews, J. Matthews **TOPICS:** Psychic, Tarot **TYPE:** Book **PRICE:** $12.95

Handbook Of Astral Power
PUBLISHING COMPANY: Next Step Publications **EDITOR:** R. Greene **TOPICS:** Psychic, Astral Projection **TYPE:** Book **PRICE:** $14.95

Handbook Of Ayurveda
PUBLISHING COMPANY: B. Jain Publishers, Ltd. **EDITOR:** B. Dash **TOPICS:** Holistic Health **TYPE:** Handbook **PRICE:** $22.50

Handbook Of Christian Mysticism
PUBLISHING COMPANY: Crucible Books, Inner Traditions International, Ltd. **EDITOR:** M. Cox **TOPICS:** Spirituality, Meditation **TYPE:** Book **PRICE:** $12.95

Handbook Of Materia Medica And Homeopathic Therapeutics
PUBLISHING COMPANY: B. Jain Publishers, Ltd. **EDITOR:** T. Allen **TOPICS:** Homeopathy **TYPE:** Handbook **PRICE:** $45.00

Handbook To Higher Consciousness
PUBLISHING COMPANY: Ken Keyes College **TOPICS:** New Age **TYPE:** Handbook

Handbooks For Spiritual Growth (Boxed Set: Meditation & Mantram Handbook)
PUBLISHING COMPANY: Nilgiri Press **EDITOR:** E. Easwaran **TOPICS:** Meditation, Spirituality **TYPE:** Book **PRICE:** $24.00

Handology: How To Unlock The Hidden Secrets Of Your Life
PUBLISHING COMPANY: Beyond Words Publishing **EDITOR:** Gerald E. Biccum **TOPICS:** Palmistry, Parapsychology **TYPE:** Book **PRICE:** $12.95

Hands Of Light: A Guide To Healing Through The Human Energy Field
PUBLISHING COMPANY: Bantam New Age Books **EDITOR:** B. Brennan **TOPICS:** Spirituality, Psychic Healing, Holistic Health, New Age **TYPE:** Book **PRICE:** $19.95

Hands-On Healing: Massage Remedies For Hundreds Of Health Problems
PUBLISHING COMPANY: Rodale Press, Inc. **EDITOR:** Editors of Prevention Magazine **TOPICS:** Massage **TYPE:** Book **PRICE:** $29.95

Hands: A Complete Book Of Palmistry
PUBLISHING COMPANY: Harper & Row Publishers, Inc. **EDITOR:** H. Asano **TOPICS:** Palmistry, Parapsychology **TYPE:** Book **PRICE:** $13.95

Hands: A Complete Guide To Palmistry
PUBLISHING COMPANY: Whitford Press/Schiffer Publishing Limited **EDITOR:** Enid Hoffman **TOPICS:** Palmistry **TYPE:** Book **PRICE:** $13.95

Handwriting Analysis: The Complete Basic Book
PUBLISHING COMPANY: Newcastle Publishing Co., Inc. **EDITOR:** K. Amend, M. Ruiz **TOPICS:** Graphology **TYPE:** Book **PRICE:** $9.95

Handwriting And Personality: How Graphology Reveals What Makes People Tick
PUBLISHING COMPANY: Henry Holt & Co. **EDITOR:** A. Mahony **TOPICS:** Graphology **TYPE:** Book **PRICE:** $18.95

Hanuman Chalisa
PUBLISHING COMPANY: Ma Yoga Shakti International Mission **PUBLISHER:** Ma Yoga Shakti **TOPICS:** Yoga, Meditation, Spirituality **TYPE:** Book

Happier! Healthier! Younger! Mahareshi Ayur-Ved Guide To Perfect Health & Rejuvenation
PUBLISHING COMPANY: E.P. Dutton, Inc. **EDITOR:** Roger Chalmers **TOPICS:** Holistic Health **TYPE:** Guide **PRICE:** $13.95

Happiness Principle
PUBLISHING COMPANY: Paradise Publications **EDITOR:** N. McGrath **TOPICS:** Meditation, Psychology **TYPE:** Book **PRICE:** $8.95

Harmonic Orb Information Packet (HIP)
PUBLISHING COMPANY: NALTA Foundation, Inc. **TOPICS:** New Age, Holistic Healing **TYPE:** Booklet

Harmonics Of Sound, Color And Vibration
PUBLISHING COMPANY: DeVorss & Company **EDITOR:** W. David **TOPICS:** Color Therapy **TYPE:** Book **PRICE:** $8.95

Harmonious Circle: Lives & Work Of G.I.Gurdjieff, P.D. Ouspensky & Their Followers
PUBLISHING COMPANY: Shambhala Publications, Inc. **EDITOR:** James Webb **TOPICS:** Spirituality **TYPE:** Book **PRICE:** $19.95

Hatha Yoga Manual Vol. 1
PUBLISHING COMPANY: Himalayan International Institute Of Yoga Science and Philosophy **EDITOR:** Samskrti, Veda **TOPICS:** Yoga, Holistic Health **TYPE:** Book **PRICE:** $12.95

Hatha Yoga Manual Vol. 2
PUBLISHING COMPANY: Himalayan International Institute Of Yoga Science and Philosophy **EDITOR:** S. Franks, J. Franks **TOPICS:** Yoga, Holistic Health **TYPE:** Book **PRICE:** $12.95

Hatha Yoga Workbook: A Personal Reflecting Tool For Yoga Students Of All Levels
PUBLISHING COMPANY: Timeless Books **EDITOR:** S. Radha **TOPICS:** Yoga, Holistic Health **TYPE:** Book **PRICE:** $11.95

Hatha Yoga Workbook: The Hidden Language
PUBLISHING COMPANY: Shambhala Publications, Inc. **EDITOR:** S. Radha **TOPICS:** Yoga, Holistic Health **TYPE:** Book **PRICE:** $18.95

Haunted England: Royal Spirits, Castle Ghosts, Phantom Castles AndWailing Ghouls

PUBLISHING COMPANY: Contemporary Books, Inc. EDITOR: Terence Whitaker TOPICS: Ghosts TYPE: Directory

He Hit Me Back First!, Self-Esteem Through Self-Discipline

PUBLISHING COMPANY: B.L. Winch & Associates/Jalmar Press EDITOR: Eva Fugitt TOPICS: New Age TYPE: Book SIZE: 8 1/2x 11; 116 pgs. PRICE: $12.95

Head First: The Biology Of Hope

PUBLISHING COMPANY: E.P. Dutton, Inc. EDITOR: N. Cousins TOPICS: Holistic Health, Body-Mind Connection, Psychology TYPE: Book PRICE: $19.95

Heal Yourself: A Practical Self-Help Manual Of Natural Healing

PUBLISHING COMPANY: Metamorphous Press EDITOR: W. Last TOPICS: Homeopathy, Holistic Healing, Body-Mind Connection TYPE: Handbook PRICE: $14.95

Healers On Healing

PUBLISHING COMPANY: Jeremy P. Tarcher, Inc. EDITOR: Christina Grof, Benjamin Shield TOPICS: New Age, Spirituality, Holistic Health TYPE: Book; 256 pgs. PRICE: $12.95

Healing Drum: African Wisdom Teachings

PUBLISHING COMPANY: Destiny Books, Inner Traditions International, Ltd. EDITOR: Yaya Diallo, M. Hall TOPICS: Spirituality, Psychic Healing TYPE: Book PRICE: $12.95

Healing Gathering/Healing Guide

PUBLISHING COMPANY: Healing Gathering/Healing Guide Directory TYPE: Directory PRICE: $3.00 DESCRIPTION: Publisher of Okanogan Highlands Healing Gathering Directory, offering herb information.

Healing Image The Great Black One

PUBLISHING COMPANY: Snow Lion Graphics TOPICS: New Age TYPE: Book PRICE: $14.95

Healing Love Through The Tao: Cultivating Female Sexuality

PUBLISHING COMPANY: Healing Tao Center EDITOR: M. Chia, M. Chia TOPICS: Holistic Healing, Spirituality TYPE: Book PRICE: $14.95

Healing Magnetism: The Transference Of Vital Force

PUBLISHING COMPANY: Samuel Weiser, Inc. EDITOR: H. Schiegl TOPICS: Parapsychology, Holistic Health TYPE: Book PRICE: $10.95

Healing Massage Techniques: A Study Of Eastern And Western Methods

PUBLISHING COMPANY: Prentice-Hall, Inc. EDITOR: Frances M. Tappan TOPICS: Massage TYPE: Book PRICE: $19.95

Healing Mind Of Man: Arise & Shine

PUBLISHING COMPANY: Bernard Jensen Publishing Co. EDITOR: Bernard Jensen TOPICS:

Holistic Health, Body-Mind Connection, Psychology TYPE: Book PRICE: $19.95

Healing Power Of Gemstones: In Tantra, Ayurveda & Astrology

PUBLISHING COMPANY: Destiny Books, Inner Traditions International, Ltd. EDITOR: H. Johari TOPICS: Crystals, Spirituality TYPE: Book PRICE: $12.95

Healing Power Of Love

PUBLISHING COMPANY: Whitford Press/Schiffer Publishing Limited EDITOR: Brad Steiger TOPICS: Spirituality, Psychic Healing TYPE: Book PRICE: $12.95

Healing Rainbow

PUBLISHING COMPANY: New Awareness, Inc. EDITOR: William E. Woods, J.L. Denchfield TOPICS: New Age, Holistic Healing, Occult, Crystals, Spirituality, Astrology TYPE: Book

Healing The Whole Person, The Whole Planet

PUBLISHING COMPANY: Beyond Words Publishing EDITOR: M. Nickell TOPICS: Spirituality, Psychic Healing TYPE: Book PRICE: $12.95

Healing Through Gems: A Simple Treatise On Gem Therapy

PUBLISHING COMPANY: B. Jain Publishers, Ltd. EDITOR: N. Saha TOPICS: Crystals TYPE: Book PRICE: $10.00

Healing Touch: An Introduction To Organismic Psychotherapy

PUBLISHING COMPANY: LifeRhythm EDITOR: Malcolm Brown TOPICS: Holistic Health TYPE: Book PRICE: $16.95

Healing Waters: How Bathing & Breating Can End Your Stress Addiction

PUBLISHING COMPANY: North Atlantic Books EDITOR: Marcus Laux, Kevin Michael TOPICS: Holistic Health, New Age TYPE: Book PRICE: $14.95

Healing Wise

PUBLISHING COMPANY: Ash Tree Publishing EDITOR: Susun Weed TOPICS: Spirituality, Herbalogy, Holistic Health TYPE: Book; 312 pgs. PRICE: $11.95 DESCRIPTION: Medicine for body/mind/spirit.

Healing With The Horoscope

PUBLISHING COMPANY: A.C.S. Publications, Inc./Astro Computing Services EDITOR: Maritha Pottenger TOPICS: Holistic Health, Astrology TYPE: Book PRICE: $9.95

Healing With The Mind's Eye: A Guide For Using Imagery & Visions For Personal Growth

PUBLISHING COMPANY: Simon & Schuster, Inc. EDITOR: Mike Samuels TOPICS: New Age, Spirituality, Psychic Healing, Meditation, Body-Mind Connection TYPE: Book PRICE: $19.95

Healing Your Habits: Introducing Directed Imagination, A Successful Technique For Overcoming..

PUBLISHING COMPANY: LuraMedia EDITOR: Joseph J. Luciani TOPICS: Meditation, Psychology TYPE: Book PRICE: $11.95

Health & Medicine In The Hindu Tradition

PUBLISHING COMPANY: Continuum Publishing Co. EDITOR: P. Desai TOPICS: Holistic Health TYPE: Book PRICE: $19.95

Health and Learning Quarterly

PUBLISHING COMPANY: HLQ Associates PUBLISHER: Allen Goodman EDITOR: Margaret Laske, Steve Guidas TOPICS: Holistic Health TYPE: Directory; 16 pgs. FREQ: 4 x per year PRICE PER COPY: $3.50 DESCRIPTION: Serves Pittsburgh and surrounding areas with listings of products and services.

Health Food Store List

PUBLISHING COMPANY: Haynes Business Directories TOPICS: Holistic Healing TYPE: Directory

Health From God's Garden

PUBLISHING COMPANY: Thorsens Publishing House EDITOR: M. Treban TOPICS: Holistic Health, Herbalogy TYPE: Book PRICE: $12.95

Health In The New Age: A Study In California Holistic Practices

PUBLISHING COMPANY: University Of New Mexico Press EDITOR: J.A. English-Lueck TOPICS: Holistic Health, New Age TYPE: Book PRICE: $19.95

Health Through Balance: An Introduction To Tibetan Medicine

PUBLISHING COMPANY: Snow Lion Publications, Inc. EDITOR: Y. Dhonden TOPICS: Holistic Health TYPE: Book PRICE: $12.95

Health Values: Achieving High Level Wellness

PUBLISHING COMPANY: Slack, Inc. EDITOR: Armin Weinberg TOPICS: Holistic Healing TYPE: Book

Health, Astrology And Spirituality

PUBLISHING COMPANY: American Federation Of Astrologers, Inc. EDITOR: Miss Dee TOPICS: Holistic Health, Astrology TYPE: Book PRICE: $11.00

Health, Hope And Healing

PUBLISHING COMPANY: M. Evans & Co., Inc. EDITOR: D. Tate TOPICS: Spirituality, Psychic Healing TYPE: Book PRICE: $17.95

Health, Wealth & Balance Through Feng Shui

PUBLISHING COMPANY: New Age Concepts/Color Magic EDITOR: Elaine Jay Finster TOPICS: New Age, Crystals, Holistic Healing TYPE: Book DESCRIPTION: Addresses how to be in balance with your personal surroundings & with your work place.

Healthy Harvest II: A Directory Of Sustainable Agricultural & Horticultural Groups 1989-90
PUBLISHING COMPANY: Potomac Valley Press EDITOR: S. Sanzone TOPICS: Holistic Health TYPE: Directory PRICE: $16.95

Healthy Harvest III: A Directory Of Sustainable Agriculture And Horticulture Organizations
PUBLISHING COMPANY: Potomac Valley Press TOPICS: Health Food TYPE: Directory

Heart Dance
PUBLISHING COMPANY: Heart Dance EDITOR: Donna Waago TOPICS: Spirituality, Holistic Health, New Age TYPE: Directory FREQ: monthly CIRC: 40,000 PRICE: $0.00 DESCRIPTION: A calendar of wholistic and spiritual events published for the Bay area.

Heart Of Healing, The
PUBLISHING COMPANY: Poco Press EDITOR: Bruce Davis, Ph. D., Genny Wright Davis TOPICS: New Age, Holistic Healing, Spirituality TYPE: Book PRICE: $8.95

Heart Of The Christos: Starseeding From The Pleiades
PUBLISHING COMPANY: Bear & Company, Inc. EDITOR: B. Clow TOPICS: Reincarnation TYPE: Book PRICE: $10.95

Heart Of The Goddess: Visions, Myths And Meditations Of The Sacred Feminine
PUBLISHING COMPANY: Wingbow Press EDITOR: Hallie Iglehart Austen TOPICS: Spirituality TYPE: Book PRICE: $24.95

Heart Of The Healer: W/Prince Charles, Norman Cousins, Richard Moss, Bernie Siegel &.....
PUBLISHING COMPANY: Aslan Publishing EDITOR: D. Church, A. Sherr TOPICS: Spirituality, Psychic Healing TYPE: Book PRICE: $14.95

Heart Thoughts: A Personal Treasury Of Inner Wisdom
PUBLISHING COMPANY: Hay House EDITOR: Louise Hay TOPICS: New Age, Psychology TYPE: Book PRICE: $13.00

Heartsearch: Uncovering The Roots Of An Auto-Immune Illness
PUBLISHING COMPANY: North Atlantic Books EDITOR: D. Talman TOPICS: Holistic Health, Body-Mind Connection, Psychology TYPE: Book PRICE: $12.95

Heaven On Your Head: Esoteric Stories From The Holy Land
PUBLISHING COMPANY: Research Centre Of Kabbalah EDITOR: S. Kahana TOPICS: Paranormal Phenomena, Spirituality TYPE: Book PRICE: $10.95

Helping Young Children Flourish

Helping Your Health Through Handwriting
PUBLISHING COMPANY: Aware Parenting Institute/Shining Star Press EDITOR: Aletha Solter, Ph. D. TOPICS: New Age TYPE: Book

PUBLISHING COMPANY: Strawberry Hill Press EDITOR: P. Harrison TOPICS: Parapsychology, Graphology TYPE: Book PRICE: $9.95

Henry Holt Guide To Minerals, Rocks And Fossils
PUBLISHING COMPANY: Henry Holt & Co. EDITOR: W.R. Hamilton TOPICS: Crystals TYPE: Book PRICE: $12.95

Her-Bak: Egyptian Initiate
PUBLISHING COMPANY: Inner Traditions International, Ltd. EDITOR: I. Schwaller de Lubicz TOPICS: New Age, Paranormal Phenomena TYPE: Book PRICE: $12.95

Her-Bak: Living Face Of Ancient Egypt
PUBLISHING COMPANY: Inner Traditions International, Ltd. EDITOR: I. Schwaller de Lubicz TOPICS: New Age, Paranormal Phenomena TYPE: Book PRICE: $10.95

Herbalism Through The Ages
PUBLISHING COMPANY: Supreme Grand Lodge of AMORC, Inc. EDITOR: R. Kerr TOPICS: Herbalogy, Spirituality, Alchemy TYPE: Book PRICE: $12.50

Herbs Of The Earth: A Self-Teaching Guide To Healing Remedies
PUBLISHING COMPANY: Upper Access Publishers EDITOR: M. Carse TOPICS: Holistic Health, Herbalogy TYPE: Guide PRICE: $10.95

Herbs: The Magic Healers
PUBLISHING COMPANY: Illuminated Way Publishing EDITOR: P. Twitchell TOPICS: Herbalogy, Spirituality, Alchemy TYPE: Book PRICE: $9.95

Hermes The Thief: The Evolution Of A Myth
PUBLISHING COMPANY: Lindisfarne Press EDITOR: Norman O. Brown TOPICS: Paganism, Spirituality TYPE: Book PRICE: $10.95

Hermes: Guide Of Souls
PUBLISHING COMPANY: Spring Publications, Inc. EDITOR: K. Kerenyi TOPICS: Paganism, Spirituality TYPE: Book PRICE: $10.00

Hermetic Museum: Containing 22 Most Celebrated Chemical Tracts
PUBLISHING COMPANY: Samuel Weiser, Inc. EDITOR: A.E Waite TOPICS: Alchemy TYPE: Book PRICE: $40.00

Hero Journey In Dreams
PUBLISHING COMPANY: Continuum Publishing Co. EDITOR: J. Clift, W. Clift TOPICS: Dreams TYPE: Book PRICE: $16.95

Hero's Journey: The World Of Joseph Campbell-An Oral Biography

PUBLISHING COMPANY: Harper & Row Publishers, Inc. EDITOR: Phil Cousineau TOPICS: New Age TYPE: Book PRICE: $24.95

Hero's Way: Attitudes Make The Difference
PUBLISHING COMPANY: Humanics New Age, Ltd. EDITOR: D. Boling TOPICS: New Age, Psychology TYPE: Book PRICE: $12.95

High Mysticism
PUBLISHING COMPANY: DeVorss & Company EDITOR: E.C. Hopkins TOPICS: Paranormal Phenomena, Spirituality TYPE: Book PRICE: $10.95

High Weirdness By Mail: A Directory Of The Fringe-Mad Prophets,Crackpots, Kooks, And True Visionaries
PUBLISHING COMPANY: Fireside Books EDITOR: Ian Stang TOPICS: Psychic Phenomena TYPE: Directory

Higher-Self: Altered State Explorations
PUBLISHING COMPANY: Valley Of The Sun Publishing Co., Sutphen Corporation EDITOR: Dick Sutphen TOPICS: Metaphysics TYPE: Book DESCRIPTION: Enables one to explore their higher self.

Highways Of The Mind: The Art And History Of Pathworking
PUBLISHING COMPANY: Aquarian Press EDITOR: D. Ashcroft-Nowicki TOPICS: Occult TYPE: Book PRICE: $12.95

Hildegard Of Bingen's Scivias
PUBLISHING COMPANY: Bear & Company, Inc. EDITOR: B. Hozeski TOPICS: Spirituality TYPE: Book PRICE: $14.95

Hildegard Of Bingen, 1098-1179: A Visionary Life
PUBLISHING COMPANY: Routledge, Chapman & Hall, Inc. EDITOR: Sabina Flanagan TOPICS: Paranormal Phenomena TYPE: Book PRICE: $14.95

History Of Cheirology
PUBLISHING COMPANY: Cheirological Society EDITOR: C.L. Jones TOPICS: Palmistry, Holistic Health TYPE: Book DATE: 1990

History Of Magic
PUBLISHING COMPANY: Samuel Weiser, Inc. EDITOR: E. Levi TOPICS: Occult TYPE: Book PRICE: $14.95

History Of Religious Ideas Vol 1: From The Stone Age To The Eleusinian Mysteries
PUBLISHING COMPANY: Univerity of Chicago Press, Div. of Univ. of Chicago EDITOR: M. Eliade TOPICS: Spirituality TYPE: Book PRICE: $16.95

History Of Religious Ideas Vol 2: From Guatama Buddha To The Triumph Of Christianity

PUBLISHING COMPANY: Univerity of Chicago Press, Div. of Univ. of Chicago **EDITOR:** M. Eliade **TOPICS:** Spirituality **TYPE:** Book **PRICE:** $16.95

History Of Religious Ideas Vol 3: From Muhammad To The Age Of Reforms

PUBLISHING COMPANY: Univerity of Chicago Press, Div. of Univ. of Chicago **EDITOR:** M. Eliade **TOPICS:** Spirituality **TYPE:** Book **PRICE:** $16.95

History Of Spectro-Chrome

PUBLISHING COMPANY: Dinshah Health Society **EDITOR:** Dinshah P. Ghadiali **TOPICS:** Holistic Healing, Color Therapy **TYPE:** Book; 6,000 pgs. **PRICE:** $220.00

History Of The Future: A Chronology

PUBLISHING COMPANY: Doubleday & Co.,Inc. **EDITOR:** P. Ryde, P. Lorie **TOPICS:** Metaphysics, Psychic **TYPE:** Book **PRICE:** $18.95

History Of Witchcraft: Sorcerers, Heretics And Pagans

PUBLISHING COMPANY: Thames & Hudson **EDITOR:** J. Russelll **TOPICS:** Witchcraft, Occult **TYPE:** Book **PRICE:** $11.95

Holistic Cook

PUBLISHING COMPANY: Collins, Div. of William Collins **EDITOR:** Janet Hunt **TOPICS:** Vegetarianism **TYPE:** Book **PRICE:** $15.95

Holistic Health Careers

PUBLISHING COMPANY: Grace And Goddess Unlimited **EDITOR:** Cindee Grace **TOPICS:** Holistic Health **TYPE:** Book **PRICE:** $40.00

Holistic Health Lifebook

PUBLISHING COMPANY: Stephen Greene Press, Div. of Viking Penguin, Inc. **EDITOR:** Berkeley Holistic Health Center **TOPICS:** Holistic Health **TYPE:** Book **PRICE:** $12.95

Holistic Health Resource Directory

PUBLISHING COMPANY: Holistic Health Association Of The Princeton Area **EDITOR:** Pat Hite **TOPICS:** Holistic Healing **TYPE:** Directory **DESCRIPTION:** Serves Central Jersey, Philadelphia and Bucks County areas with listings of practitioners and organizations. Published by the Holistic Health Association of Princeton Area, contains articles, reviews, ads & a calendar.

Holistic Herbal: An Herbal Celebrating The Wholeness Of Life

PUBLISHING COMPANY: Findhorn Foundation & Press **EDITOR:** David Hoffman **TOPICS:** Holistic Health, Herbalogy **TYPE:** Book **PRICE:** $16.95

Holistic Massages: The Holistic Way To Physical And Mental Health

PUBLISHING COMPANY: Sterling Publishing Company, Inc. **EDITOR:** Richard Jackson **TOPICS:** Massage **TYPE:** Book **PRICE:** $12.95

Holistic Protocol For The Immune System: Aids/Arc/HIV, Candidiasis, Epstein-Barr, Herpes

PUBLISHING COMPANY: Tree Of Life Seminars **EDITOR:** Scott Gregory **TOPICS:** Acupuncture **TYPE:** Book **PRICE:** $14.95

Holistic Reflexology: Teaching Manual & Practitioner's Guide To Diagnosis & Treatment

PUBLISHING COMPANY: Collins, Div. of William Collins **EDITOR:** A. Grinberg **TOPICS:** Acupuncture **TYPE:** Guide **PRICE:** $39.95

Holistic Resource Directory

PUBLISHING COMPANY: Insight Northwest **EDITOR:** Susan James **TOPICS:** Holistic Health **TYPE:** Directory **PRICE:** $25.00 **DESCRIPTION:** Lists holistic practitioners & suppliers located throughout the U.S. & Canada.

Holistic Resource Directory

PUBLISHING COMPANY: Holistic Resource Association **EDITOR:** Alan Green, Marc Grossman **TOPICS:** Holistic Health **TYPE:** Directory **SIZE:** 4 x 10 1/2; 40 pgs. **PRICE:** $0.00 **PRICE PER COPY:** $0.00 **DESCRIPTION:** Directory compiled by the Holistic Resource Association.Lists practitioners, health related services and products for Westchester, Fairfield County & the Hudson Valley area.

Holistic Resources Directory

PUBLISHING COMPANY: Holistic Resources **EDITOR:** Susan James **TOPICS:** Holistic Health **TYPE:** Directory **DATE:** 1988 **PRICE:** $16.95

Holy Grail: Cosmos Of The Bible

PUBLISHING COMPANY: Philosophical Library, Inc. **EDITOR:** L. Perry **TOPICS:** New Age **TYPE:** Book **PRICE:** $39.95

Holy Mother: Being The Life Of Sri Sarada Devi, Wife Of Ramakrishna & Helpmate In His Mission

PUBLISHING COMPANY: Vedanta Press, Div. of Vedanta Society **EDITOR:** S. Nikhilananda **TOPICS:** Spirituality **TYPE:** Book **PRICE:** $9.50

Home School Primer

PUBLISHING COMPANY: Home Education Press **TOPICS:** New Age **TYPE:** Book

Home School Reader

PUBLISHING COMPANY: Home Education Press **TOPICS:** New Age **TYPE:** Book

Home School Researcher

PUBLISHING COMPANY: Seattle Pacific University **TOPICS:** New Age **TYPE:** Book

Homeopathic Family Practice

PUBLISHING COMPANY: B. Jain Publishers, Ltd. **EDITOR:** M. Bhattacharya **TOPICS:** Homeopathy **TYPE:** Book **PRICE:** $12.00

Homeopathic Medicine In The Home: A Correspondence Study Course

PUBLISHING COMPANY: Ashwins Publications **EDITOR:** Jonathan Breslow **TOPICS:** Homeopathy **TYPE:** Handbook **PRICE:** $24.95 **DESCRIPTION:** Correspondence course for the study of homeopathic medicine for laypersons & health professionals. Certificate offered. Course syllabus available. Course recommended by the Council On

Homeopathic Education, the International Foundation For Homeopathy & the National Center For Homeopathy.

Homeopathic Practice In Childhood Disorders

PUBLISHING COMPANY: Boiron/Borneman **EDITOR:** M. Aubin, et.al **TOPICS:** Homeopathy **TYPE:** Book **PRICE:** $14.95

Homeopathic Therapeutics

PUBLISHING COMPANY: B. Jain Publishers, Ltd. **EDITOR:** S. Lilienthal **TOPICS:** Homeopathy **TYPE:** Book **PRICE:** $22.00

Homeopathic Treatment Of Children: Pediatric Constitutional Types

PUBLISHING COMPANY: North Atlantic Books **EDITOR:** Paul Herscu **TOPICS:** Homcopathy **TYPE:** Book **PRICE:** $18.95

Homeopathy: Medicine For The Twentyfirst Century

PUBLISHING COMPANY: North Atlantic Books **EDITOR:** D. Ullman **TOPICS:** Homeopathy **TYPE:** Book **PRICE:** $12.95

Horoscope Guide

PUBLISHING COMPANY: J.B.H. Publishing Co./ Photo Publishing Co. **EDITOR:** Barbara Robbins **TOPICS:** Astrology **TYPE:** Guide **DATE:** 1968 **FREQ:** Monthly **CIRC:** 75,000 **PRICE:** $21.00

Horoscope Symbols

PUBLISHING COMPANY: Whitford Press/Schiffer Publishing Limited **EDITOR:** R. Hand **TOPICS:** Astrology **TYPE:** Book **PRICE:** $19.95

Horoscope Yearbook

PUBLISHING COMPANY: Dell Publishing Co., Inc. **TOPICS:** Astrology **TYPE:** Yearbook **FREQ:** Semi-Annual **PRICE PER COPY:** $1.75

Horoscopes Of The Western Hemisphere

PUBLISHING COMPANY: A.C.S. Publications, Inc./Astro Computing Services **EDITOR:** M. Penfield **TOPICS:** Astrology **TYPE:** Book **PRICE:** $19.95

Hostage To The Devil: The Possession & Exorcism Of Five Living Americans

PUBLISHING COMPANY: Harper & Row Publishers, Inc. **EDITOR:** Malchi Martin **TOPICS:** Occult **TYPE:** Book **PRICE:** $9.95

Hot Numbers: Using Numerology To Discover What Makes You & Others Really Tick

PUBLISHING COMPANY: Crown Publishers, Inc. **EDITOR:** Jean Simpson **TOPICS:** Numerology, Parapsychology **TYPE:** Book **PRICE:** $15.95

How I Learned To Soul Travel

PUBLISHING COMPANY: Illuminated Way Publishing **EDITOR:** T. Willson **TOPICS:** Astral Projection **TYPE:** Book **PRICE:** $9.95

How To Change Your Life

PUBLISHING COMPANY: Science of Mind Publications, Div. of United Church of Religious Science **EDITOR:** E. Holmes **TOPICS:** Spirituality, Psychology **TYPE:** Book **PRICE:** $12.95

How To Get Well
PUBLISHING COMPANY: Health Plus Publishers **EDITOR:** P. Airola **TOPICS:** Homeopathy, Holistic Health **TYPE:** Book **PRICE:** $12.95

How To Give An Astrological Health Reading
PUBLISHING COMPANY: American Federation Of Astrologers, Inc. **EDITOR:** D. Cramer **TOPICS:** Holistic Health, Astrology **TYPE:** Book **PRICE:** $12.95

How To Grow Vegetables Indoors
PUBLISHING COMPANY: Sprout House **PUBLISHER:** Steve Meyerowitz **TOPICS:** Nutrition, Holistic Health, Health Food **TYPE:** Book

How To Have More In A Have-Not World
PUBLISHING COMPANY: Adventures In Enlightenment, A Foundation **EDITOR:** Terry Cole-Whittaker **TOPICS:** New Age **TYPE:** Book **DATE:** 1983

How To Make And Use Talismans
PUBLISHING COMPANY: Aquarian Press **EDITOR:** I. Regardie **TOPICS:** Occult, Witchcraft **TYPE:** Book **PRICE:** $7.95

How To Raise A Child Of God
PUBLISHING COMPANY: Life Action Press, Div. of Foundation for Life Action **EDITOR:** T. Singh **TOPICS:** Spirituality **TYPE:** Book **PRICE:** $14.95

How To See Your Health: Book Of Oriental Diagnosis
PUBLISHING COMPANY: Japan Publications, Inc. **EDITOR:** M. Kushi **TOPICS:** Holistic Health **TYPE:** Book **PRICE:** $12.95

How To Stay Healthy A Lifetime Without Medicines
PUBLISHING COMPANY: Juvenescent Research Corp. **EDITOR:** Betty Yulin Ho **TOPICS:** Holistic Health **TYPE:** Book **DATE:** 1979; 140 pgs. **PRICE:** $14.00 **DESCRIPTION:** Covers every facet of the living body to control life from first cell divison through adolescence, adulthood & delay death in terminal states.

How To Study Homeopathy
PUBLISHING COMPANY: Boiron/Borneman **EDITOR:** D. Demarque, P. Joly **TOPICS:** Homeopathy **TYPE:** Book **PRICE:** $14.95

How To Use The Science Of Mind
PUBLISHING COMPANY: Putnam Publishing Group **EDITOR:** E. Holmes **TOPICS:** Spirituality, Psychology **TYPE:** Book **PRICE:** $12.95

Hugh Lynn Cayce: About My Father's Business
PUBLISHING COMPANY: Donning Company Publishers **EDITOR:** Robert A. Smith **TOPICS:** New Age **TYPE:** Book **PRICE:** $19.95

Human Aura
PUBLISHING COMPANY: Summit University Press **EDITOR:** Elizabeth Clare Prophet **TOPICS:** Holistic Health **TYPE:** Book **PRICE:** $4.95

Human Encounters And Karma
PUBLISHING COMPANY: Anthroposophic Press, Inc. **EDITOR:** Athys Floride **TOPICS:** Reincarnation **TYPE:** Book **PRICE:** $9.95

Human Energy Systems
PUBLISHING COMPANY: E.P. Dutton, Inc. **EDITOR:** Jack Schwartz **TOPICS:** Holistic Health **TYPE:** Book **PRICE:** $9.95

Hymns To Mystic Fire
PUBLISHING COMPANY: Lotus Light Publications Aurobindo **TOPICS:** Spirituality **TYPE:** Book **PRICE:** $22.50

Hypnagogia: The Unique State Of Consciousness Between Wakefulness And Sleep
PUBLISHING COMPANY: Routledge, Chapman & Hall, Inc. **EDITOR:** Andreas Mavromatis **TOPICS:** Body-Mind Connection, Psychology **TYPE:** Book **PRICE:** $25.00

Hypnotizing Yourself For Success
PUBLISHING COMPANY: R & E Publishers **EDITOR:** L.O. Hook **TOPICS:** Hypnotism **TYPE:** Book **PRICE:** $11.95

I Am Ramtha
PUBLISHING COMPANY: Beyond Words Publishing **EDITOR:** J.Z. Knight **TOPICS:** Channeling **TYPE:** Book **PRICE:** $29.95

I Ching And Its Associations
PUBLISHING COMPANY: Routledge, Chapman & Hall, Inc. **EDITOR:** D. Hook **TOPICS:** Parapsychology, Psychic **TYPE:** Book **PRICE:** $13.95

I Ching Cards
PUBLISHING COMPANY: U.S. Games Systems, Inc. **TOPICS:** Holistic Health **TYPE:** Book **PRICE:** $13.00

I Ching Mandalas: A Program Of Study For The Book Of Changes
PUBLISHING COMPANY: Shambhala Publications, Inc. **EDITOR:** T. Cleary **TOPICS:** Holistic Health **TYPE:** Book **PRICE:** $12.95

I Ching Of The Goddess
PUBLISHING COMPANY: Harper & Row Publishers, Inc. **EDITOR:** Barbara Walker **TOPICS:** Holistic Health, Occult, Spirituality **TYPE:** Book **PRICE:** $12.95

I Ching On Love
PUBLISHING COMPANY: Aquarian Press **EDITOR:** G. Damian-Knight **TOPICS:** Holistic Health **TYPE:** Book **PRICE:** $12.95

I Ching Or Book Of Changes
PUBLISHING COMPANY: Princeton University Press **EDITOR:** R. Wilhelm, W. Baynes **TOPICS:** Holistic Health **TYPE:** Book **PRICE:** $17.50

I Ching: Hexagrams Revealed
PUBLISHING COMPANY: Charles E. Tuttle Company, Inc. **EDITOR:** Gary Melyan, Wen-Kuang Chu **TOPICS:** Holistic Health **TYPE:** Book **PRICE:** $11.95

I Ching: New Systems, Methods & Revelations
PUBLISHING COMPANY: Lotus Light Publications **EDITOR:** A. Hoefler **TOPICS:** Holistic Health **TYPE:** Book **PRICE:** $12.95

I Ching: Tao Of Organization
PUBLISHING COMPANY: Shambhala Publications, Inc. **EDITOR:** T. Cleary **TOPICS:** Holistic Health **TYPE:** Book **PRICE:** $14.95

I Come As A Brother
PUBLISHING COMPANY: High Mesa Press **EDITOR:** Joy Franklin **TOPICS:** New Age, Channeling **TYPE:** Book **PRICE:** $10.95

I Have Become Alive: Secrets Of The Inner Journey
PUBLISHING COMPANY: S.Y.D.A. Foundation/Siddha Yoga Meditation Ashram Muktananda **TOPICS:** Spirituality **TYPE:** Book **PRICE:** $8.95

I Was Robot
PUBLISHING COMPANY: Little Free Press **EDITOR:** Ernest Mann **TOPICS:** New Age **TYPE:** Book **DATE:** 1990 **SIZE:** 4 x 7; 320 pgs. **PRICE:** $7.95 **DESCRIPTION:** Offers information about how to live cheaper & change the world wide economic system to one that works for individuals.

I'm Special: An Experiential Workbook For The Child In Us All
PUBLISHING COMPANY: Treehouse Enterprises **PUBLISHER:** Dr. Sandra G. Landsman **TOPICS:** New Age, Psychology **TYPE:** Book

If You Want To Write: A Book About Art, Independence And Spirit
PUBLISHING COMPANY: Graywolf Press **EDITOR:** B. Ueland **TOPICS:** New Age **TYPE:** Book **PRICE:** $8.95

Illuminated Mind: A Step-By-Step Guide To Spiritual Discovery
PUBLISHING COMPANY: Alohem Publishing Co. **EDITOR:** June D'Estelle **TOPICS:** Psychic **TYPE:** Book **PRICE:** $9.95

Illuminations Of Hildegard Of Bingen
PUBLISHING COMPANY: Bear & Company, Inc. **EDITOR:** Matthew Fox **TOPICS:** Spirituality **TYPE:** Book **PRICE:** $16.95

Illuminations: The Healing Image - Finding & Learning From, The Inner Artist
PUBLISHING COMPANY: Wingbow Press **EDITOR:** M. McMurray **TOPICS:** Psychic **TYPE:** Book **PRICE:** $12.95

Illustrated Biography Of C.G. Jung

PUBLISHING COMPANY: Shambhala Publications, Inc. EDITOR: G. Wehr TOPICS: New Age, Psychology TYPE: Book PRICE: $39.95

Illustrated Dictionary Of Natural Health

PUBLISHING COMPANY: Sterling Publishing Company, Inc. EDITOR: Nevill Drury, Susan Drury TOPICS: Holistic Health TYPE: Book PRICE: $12.95

Illustrated I Ching

PUBLISHING COMPANY: Doubleday & Co.,Inc. EDITOR: R.L. Wing TOPICS: Parapsychology, Psychic TYPE: Book PRICE: $16.95

Illustrated Ramayana

PUBLISHING COMPANY: Palace Publishing EDITOR: S. Bhaktipada TOPICS: Spirituality TYPE: Book PRICE: $65.00

Imagery For Healing, Knowledge And Power; Harnessing Your Personal Energy To Create..

PUBLISHING COMPANY: Simon & Schuster, Inc. EDITOR: W. Fezler TOPICS: New Age, Meditation, Psychology TYPE: Book PRICE: $9.95

Imagery In Healing: Shamanism & Modern Medicine

PUBLISHING COMPANY: Shambhala Publications, Inc. EDITOR: J. Achterberg TOPICS: New Age, Spirituality, Psychic Healing, Body-Mind Connection TYPE: Book PRICE: $12.95

Images Of The Self: The Sandplay Therapy Process

PUBLISHING COMPANY: Sigo Press EDITOR: E. Weinrib TOPICS: New Age, Psychology TYPE: Book PRICE: $14.95

Imaginary Crimes: Why We Punish Ourselves & How To Stop

PUBLISHING COMPANY: Houghton Mifflin Company EDITOR: L. Engel, T. Ferguson TOPICS: New Age, Psychology TYPE: Book PRICE: $19.95

Immediate Hints To Health Problems

PUBLISHING COMPANY: Juvenescent Research Corp. EDITOR: Betty Yulin Ho TOPICS: Holistic Health TYPE: Book DATE: 1991; 264 pgs. PRICE: $25.00 DESCRIPTION: Immediate cures to multifarious health problems.

Immune-System Activation: Practical Programs For Maximizing Your Recovery Potential

PUBLISHING COMPANY: E.P. Dutton, Inc. EDITOR: John Selby TOPICS: Holistic Health, Body-Mind Connection, Psychology TYPE: Book PRICE: $17.95

In Praise Of Tara

PUBLISHING COMPANY: Wisdom Publications EDITOR: Martin Willson TOPICS: Spirituality TYPE: Book PRICE: $26.95

In The Company Of A Siddha

PUBLISHING COMPANY: S.Y.D.A. Foundation/Siddha Yoga Meditation Ashram

Muktananda TOPICS: Spirituality TYPE: Book PRICE: $8.95

In Touch For Health

PUBLISHING COMPANY: Touch For Health Foundation EDITOR: Barry Greenberg TOPICS: Holistic Healing TYPE: Book

Incarnation

PUBLISHING COMPANY: Truth TOPICS: New Age, Spirituality TYPE: Book DATE: 1990; 120 pgs.

Increase Your Power Of Creative Thinking In 8 Days

PUBLISHING COMPANY: Celestial Gifts Publishing EDITOR: Dr. Ron Dalrymple TOPICS: New Age TYPE: Book DATE: 1985

Index To The Psychological Commentaries On The Teaching Of Gurdjieff & Ouspensky, Vol.1-5

PUBLISHING COMPANY: Shambhala Publications, Inc. EDITOR: M. Nicoll TOPICS: Spirituality TYPE: Book PRICE: $19.95

Inevitable Grace: Finding The Right Path For Your Spiritual Journey

PUBLISHING COMPANY: Jeremy P. Tarcher, Inc. EDITOR: P. Ferrucci TOPICS: Spirituality TYPE: Book PRICE: $19.95

Initiation

PUBLISHING COMPANY: Seed Center EDITOR: E. Halch TOPICS: Paranormal Phenomena TYPE: Book PRICE: $12.00

Initiation In The Great Pyramid

PUBLISHING COMPANY: Astara Foundation, Inc. EDITOR: E. Chaney TOPICS: Metaphysics, Spirituality TYPE: Book PRICE: $14.95

Initiation Of The World

PUBLISHING COMPANY: Samuel Weiser, Inc. EDITOR: V. Alder TOPICS: New Age, Paranormal Phenomena TYPE: Book PRICE: $9.95

Initiation, Eternity And The Passing Moment

PUBLISHING COMPANY: Anthroposophic Press, Inc. EDITOR: R. Steiner TOPICS: Spirituality, Paranormal Phenomena TYPE: Book PRICE: $14.00

Inner Bridges: A Guide To Body Energy

PUBLISHING COMPANY: Humanics New Age, Ltd. EDITOR: F. R. Smith TOPICS: Holistic Health TYPE: Guide PRICE: $10.95

Inner Game Of Music

PUBLISHING COMPANY: Doubleday & Co.,Inc. EDITOR: T.W. Gallwey, B. Green TOPICS: New Age TYPE: Book PRICE: $17.95

Inner Group Teachings Of H.P. Blavatsky: To Her Personal Pupils

PUBLISHING COMPANY: Point Loma Publications, Inc. EDITOR: H. J. Spierenburg TOPICS: Occult, Spirituality TYPE: Book PRICE: $9.50

Inner Guide Meditation: A Spiritual Technology For The 21st Century

PUBLISHING COMPANY: Newcastle Publishing Co., Inc. EDITOR: E. Steinbrecher TOPICS: Psychic TYPE: Book PRICE: $10.95

Inner Impulses Of Evolution: The Mexican Mysteries And The Knights Templar

PUBLISHING COMPANY: Anthroposophic Press, Inc. EDITOR: R. Steiner TOPICS: Paranormal Phenomena TYPE: Book PRICE: $9.95

Inner Journeys: A Guide To Personal & Social Transformation

PUBLISHING COMPANY: Samuel Weiser, Inc. EDITOR: J. Early TOPICS: New Age, Spirituality, Psychology TYPE: Book PRICE: $14.95

Inner Natures: Brain, Self And Personality

PUBLISHING COMPANY: St. Martin's Press, Inc. EDITOR: Laurence Miller TOPICS: Body-Mind Connection, Psychology TYPE: Book PRICE: $19.95

Inner Power: Secrets From Tibet And The Orient

PUBLISHING COMPANY: Japan Publications, Inc. EDITOR: Christopher Kilham TOPICS: Spirituality TYPE: Book PRICE: $14.95

Inner Spiritual Attunement Pamphlet

PUBLISHING COMPANY: Floating Healing Meditation Circle TYPE: Booklet

Insights Into Open Education

PUBLISHING COMPANY: Center For Teaching And Learning TOPICS: New Age TYPE: Book

Instant Handwriting Analysis: A Key To Personal Success

PUBLISHING COMPANY: Llewellyn Publications EDITOR: R. Gardner TOPICS: Graphology TYPE: Book PRICE: $9.95

Instant Memory

PUBLISHING COMPANY: Institute Of Advanced Thinking TOPICS: New Age, Psychology TYPE: Book PRICE: $12.00 DESCRIPTION: The world's first & only instruction in Natural Memory.

Intangible Evidence: Explore The World Of Psychic Phenonmena & Learn To Develop Psychic Skill

PUBLISHING COMPANY: Simon & Schuster, Inc. EDITOR: Bernard Gittelson TOPICS: Psychic TYPE: Book PRICE: $14.95

Integral Hatha Yoga

PUBLISHING COMPANY: Henry Holt & Co. EDITOR: Satchidananda TOPICS: Yoga, Holistic Health TYPE: Book PRICE: $13.95

Interdimensional Physics: The Mind And The Universe

PUBLISHING COMPANY: Unarius Academy Of Science & Education Foundation EDITOR: Ruth

Norman, Charles Spaegel **TOPICS:** Reincarnation **TYPE:** Book **DATE:** 1954; 342 pgs. **PRICE:** $24.95

Intermediate Studies Of The Human Aura
PUBLISHING COMPANY: Summit University Press **EDITOR:** Elizabeth Clare Prophet **TOPICS:** Holistic Health **TYPE:** Book **PRICE:** $9.95

International Atlas
PUBLISHING COMPANY: A.C.S. Publications, Inc./Astro Computing Services **EDITOR:** Thomas Shanks **TOPICS:** Astrology **TYPE:** Book **PRICE:** $29.95

International Directory Of Persons Granted Degrees For Work In Parapsychology
PUBLISHING COMPANY: Parapsychology Sources Of Information Center-PSI Center **EDITOR:** Rhea A. White **TOPICS:** Parapsychology **TYPE:** Directory

International Directory of Psychic Sciences
PUBLISHING COMPANY: Ghost Research Society **EDITOR:** Dale Kaczmarek **TOPICS:** Ghosts, Psychic Phenomena, Parapsychology, Reincarnation, Past Life Regression **TYPE:** Directory **PRICE:** $7.00

International Rebirthers Directory
PUBLISHING COMPANY: Conscious Breathing Association **EDITOR:** Leonard Orr, Jane Hartley **TOPICS:** Past Life Regression, Death **TYPE:** Directory; 50 pgs. **FREQ:** annual **PRICE:** $15.00 **DESCRIPTION:** Offers listing of professional Rebirthers.

Interpret Your Rays Through The Planets
PUBLISHING COMPANY: American Federation Of Astrologers, Inc. **EDITOR:** M. Wilson-Ludlam **TOPICS:** Astrology **TYPE:** Book **PRICE:** $21.50

Interpreting The Revelation With Edgar Cayce
PUBLISHING COMPANY: Association For Research And Enlightenment, Inc. **EDITOR:** J. Everett Irion **TOPICS:** Channeling, Metaphysics **TYPE:** Book **PRICE:** $19.95

Interpreting Your Child's Handwriting And Drawings: Toddler To Teen
PUBLISHING COMPANY: Paragon House **EDITOR:** Claude Santoy **TOPICS:** Graphology **TYPE:** Book **PRICE:** $12.95

Intimates Through Time: Life Stores Of Edgar Cayce & His Companions Through The Ages
PUBLISHING COMPANY: Harper & Row Publishers, Inc. **EDITOR:** Jess Stearn **TOPICS:** Channeling, Reincarnation, Past Life Regression **TYPE:** Book **PRICE:** $17.95

Into The Unknown
PUBLISHING COMPANY: Reader's Digest **EDITOR:** W. Bradbury **TOPICS:** New Age, ESP, Psychic Phenomena, Paranormal Phenomena **TYPE:** Book **PRICE:** $21.95

Introduction To Holistic Medical Astrology
PUBLISHING COMPANY: American Federation Of Astrologers, Inc. **EDITOR:** R. Jansky **TOPICS:** Holistic Health, Astrology **TYPE:** Book **PRICE:** $11.00

Introduction To Seashell Divination
PUBLISHING COMPANY: Original Publications, Subs. of Jamil Products Corp. **EDITOR:** M. Gonzalez-Wippler **TOPICS:** Voudoun, Metaphysics **TYPE:** Book **PRICE:** $11.95

Introduction To The Musical Brain
PUBLISHING COMPANY: MMB Music, Inc. **EDITOR:** Don G. Campbell **TOPICS:** New Age **TYPE:** Book **PRICE:** $14.00

Intuiting The Future: The New Age Vision Of The 1990s
PUBLISHING COMPANY: Harper & Row Publishers, Inc. **EDITOR:** W. Kautz, M. Branon **TOPICS:** New Age, Metaphysics, Psychic **TYPE:** Book **PRICE:** $9.95

Intuition Workout: A Practical Guide To Discovering & Developing Your Intuition
PUBLISHING COMPANY: Aslan Publishing **EDITOR:** N. Rosanoff **TOPICS:** Psychic **TYPE:** Book **PRICE:** $9.95

Invisibility: The Theory And Practice Of An Occult Technique
PUBLISHING COMPANY: Aquarian Press **EDITOR:** S. Richards **TOPICS:** Occult **TYPE:** Book **PRICE:** $8.95

Invisible Guests: The Development Of Imaginal Dialogues
PUBLISHING COMPANY: Sigo Press **EDITOR:** Mary Watkins **TOPICS:** Psychic Phenomena, Channeling **TYPE:** Book **PRICE:** $16.95

Invisible Temple
PUBLISHING COMPANY: Llewellyn Publications **EDITOR:** P. DeCoppens **TOPICS:** Occult, Witchcraft **TYPE:** Book **PRICE:** $9.95

Inward Journey
PUBLISHING COMPANY: Sigo Press **EDITOR:** Esther Harding **TOPICS:** Psychology **TYPE:** Book **PRICE:** $16.95

Iron Flute: 100 Zen Koan With Commentary
PUBLISHING COMPANY: Charles E. Tuttle Company, Inc. **EDITOR:** N. Senzaki, R. McCandless **TOPICS:** Spirituality **TYPE:** Book **PRICE:** $20.95

Iron Shirt Chi Kung
PUBLISHING COMPANY: Healing Tao Center **EDITOR:** M. Chia **TOPICS:** Tai Chi **TYPE:** Book **PRICE:** $14.95

Isiac Tablet Or Bembine Tablet Of Isis
PUBLISHING COMPANY: Philosophical Research Society, Inc. **EDITOR:** W. Wynn Westcott **TOPICS:** Tarot **TYPE:** Book **PRICE:** $14.95

Isis Unveiled
PUBLISHING COMPANY: Theosophical University Press **EDITOR:** H. Blavatsky **TOPICS:** Occult, Spirituality **TYPE:** Book **PRICE:** $24.00

Iyengar: His Life And Work
PUBLISHING COMPANY: Timeless Books, Div. of Assoc. of the Development of Human Potential **EDITOR:** B. Iyengar **TOPICS:** Yoga, Holistic Health **TYPE:** Book **PRICE:** $17.95

Jacob Boehme: Essential Readings
PUBLISHING COMPANY: Crucible Books, Inner Traditions International, Ltd. **EDITOR:** Robin Waterfield **TOPICS:** Spirituality **TYPE:** Book **PRICE:** $14.95

Jaguar And The Moon
PUBLISHING COMPANY: Unicorn Press, Inc. **EDITOR:** T. Merton **TOPICS:** New Age **TYPE:** Book **PRICE:** $17.50

Jambalaya: The Natural Woman's Book Of Personal Charms & Practical Rituals
PUBLISHING COMPANY: Harper & Row Publishers, Inc. **EDITOR:** L. Teish **TOPICS:** Voudoun **TYPE:** Book **PRICE:** $9.95

Jellyfish Bones
PUBLISHING COMPANY: Blue Dolphin Publishing, Inc. **TOPICS:** New Age **TYPE:** Book **PRICE:** $9.95

Jesus Was A Leo
PUBLISHING COMPANY: Jesus Books **EDITOR:** Frank Jakubowsky **TOPICS:** New Age, Spirituality, Astrology **TYPE:** Book **PRICE:** $6.95

Jesus Was A Vegetarian
PUBLISHING COMPANY: Vegetarian Society **TOPICS:** Health Food, Nutrition, Vegetarianism **TYPE:** Book

Jesus' Church Of Truth & Light
PUBLISHING COMPANY: Truth **TOPICS:** New Age, Spirituality **TYPE:** Book **DATE:** 1990; 120 pgs. **DESCRIPTION:** Discusses truth concerning the Light & Jesus' teachings of Eternal Life in the Light. Free.

Jesus, The Son Of Man
PUBLISHING COMPANY: Random House, Inc. **EDITOR:** K. Gilbran **TOPICS:** Channeling **TYPE:** Book **PRICE:** $18.95

Jewel In The Lotus
PUBLISHING COMPANY: Concord Grove Press, Subs. of Institute of World Culture **EDITOR:** R. Iyer **TOPICS:** Spirituality **TYPE:** Book **PRICE:** $19.75

Jewish Vegetarians
PUBLISHING COMPANY: North American Vegetarian Society **TOPICS:** Health Food **TYPE:** Book

Joel Goldsmith's Gift Of Love
PUBLISHING COMPANY: Harper & Row Publishers, Inc. **EDITOR:** Joel Goldsmith **TOPICS:** New Age **TYPE:** Book **PRICE:** $10.95

John Dee: The World Of An Elizabethan Magus

PUBLISHING COMPANY: Routledge, Chapman & Hall, Inc. EDITOR: P. French TOPICS: Occult, Witchcraft TYPE: Book PRICE: $10.95

John Lilly, So Far...Pioneer Of Human Dolphin Communication & Altered States/Consciousness

PUBLISHING COMPANY: Jeremy P. Tarcher, Inc. EDITOR: John Lilly, F. Jeffrey TOPICS: New Age TYPE: Book PRICE: $19.95

JOTS

PUBLISHING COMPANY: Elysium Growth Press EDITOR: Arthur Kunkin, Ed Lange TOPICS: New Age TYPE: Book

Journey Into Consciousness: The Chakras, Jungian Psychology & Tantra

PUBLISHING COMPANY: Nicolas-Hays, Inc. EDITOR: G. Breaux TOPICS: Holistic Health TYPE: Book PRICE: $12.95

Journey Into Nature: A Spiritual Adventure Into Oneness

PUBLISHING COMPANY: H.J. Kramer, Inc. EDITOR: Michael J. Roads TOPICS: Paganism, Spirituality TYPE: Book PRICE: $10.95

Journey Of A Master: Swami Chinmayananda-The Man, The Path, The Teaching

PUBLISHING COMPANY: Asian Humanities Press EDITOR: Nancy Patchen TOPICS: Spirituality TYPE: Book PRICE: $15.95

Journey To High Places...A Spiritual Evolution

PUBLISHING COMPANY: Shastar Press EDITOR: S. Ruiz TOPICS: Death TYPE: Book PRICE: $12.95

Journey Within: Past-Life Regression And Channeling

PUBLISHING COMPANY: Inner Vision Publishing Co. EDITOR: Henry Bolduc TOPICS: Past Life Regression, Channeling, Hypnotism TYPE: Book PRICE: $10.95

Journey Without Distance

PUBLISHING COMPANY: Poco Press EDITOR: Robert Skutch TOPICS: New Age, Spirituality TYPE: Book PRICE: $7.95

Journeys Out Of The Body

PUBLISHING COMPANY: Doubleday & Co.,Inc. EDITOR: R. Monroe TOPICS: Astral Projection TYPE: Book PRICE: $10.95

Juice Fasting And Detoxification

PUBLISHING COMPANY: Sprout House PUBLISHER: Steve Meyerowitz TOPICS: Nutrition, Holistic Health, Health Food TYPE: Book

Julian Of Norwich: Showings

PUBLISHING COMPANY: Paulist Press EDITOR: E. Colledge TOPICS: Spirituality TYPE: Book PRICE: $11.95

Jung And Rorschach: A Study In The Archetype Of Perception

PUBLISHING COMPANY: Spring Publications, Inc. EDITOR: R. McCully TOPICS: Spirituality TYPE: Book PRICE: $16.50

Jung And Tarot: An Archetypal Journal

PUBLISHING COMPANY: Samuel Weiser, Inc. EDITOR: S. Nichols TOPICS: Tarot TYPE: Book PRICE: $14.95

Jungian Literary Criticism 1920-1980: An Annotated Critical Bibliography Of Works In English

PUBLISHING COMPANY: Sigo Press EDITOR: Jos Van Meurs TOPICS: Psychology TYPE: Book PRICE: $16.95

Jungian Psychology: A Comprehensive Guide

PUBLISHING COMPANY: Yes! Inc. EDITOR: Cris Popenoe TOPICS: New Age, Psychology TYPE: Guide

Kabbalah And Jewish Mysticism

PUBLISHING COMPANY: Philosophical Library, Inc. EDITOR: I. Gutwirth TOPICS: Kabbalah TYPE: Book PRICE: $17.95

Kalachakra Tantra: Rite Of Initiation

PUBLISHING COMPANY: Wisdom Publications EDITOR: Lama Dalai, J. Hopkins TOPICS: Spirituality TYPE: Book PRICE: $22.95

Karma Of Materialism

PUBLISHING COMPANY: Anthroposophic Press, Inc. EDITOR: R. Steiner TOPICS: Reincarnation TYPE: Book PRICE: $9.95

Karma Of Untruthfulness Vol. 1

PUBLISHING COMPANY: Anthroposophic Press, Inc. EDITOR: R. Steiner TOPICS: Reincarnation, Spirituality TYPE: Book PRICE: $20.00

Karma Without Stress: A Guidebook For The Soul's Journey

PUBLISHING COMPANY: Newcastle Publishing Co., Inc. EDITOR: E. Connolly TOPICS: New Age, Psychic, Reincarnation TYPE: Book PRICE: $12.95

Karma: Rhythmic Return To Harmony

PUBLISHING COMPANY: Theosophical University Press EDITOR: V. Hanson TOPICS: Reincarnation TYPE: Book PRICE: $11.50

Karmic Astrology Of Relationship

PUBLISHING COMPANY: Golden Phoenix Healing And Light Center EDITOR: Jane Greven, Rev. Mona Fore TOPICS: Holistic Healing TYPE: Book

Keys To Self-Realization: A Self-Counseling Manual

PUBLISHING COMPANY: Whitford Press/Schiffer Publishing Limited EDITOR: M. Enners TOPICS: New Age, Psychic, Spirituality TYPE: Book PRICE: $17.95

Ki In Daily Life

PUBLISHING COMPANY: Harper & Row Publishers, Inc. EDITOR: K. Tohei TOPICS: Tai Chi, Holistic Health TYPE: Book PRICE: $15.95

Ki: A Practical Guide For Westerners

PUBLISHING COMPANY: Japan Publications, Inc. EDITOR: W. Reed TOPICS: Tai Chi TYPE: Book PRICE: $15.95

Ki: Energy For Everybody

PUBLISHING COMPANY: Japan Publications, Inc. EDITOR: L. Taylor, B. Bryant TOPICS: Tai Chi TYPE: Book PRICE: $15.95

Kindness, Clarity And Insight

PUBLISHING COMPANY: Snow Lion Publications, Inc. EDITOR: Lama Dalai TOPICS: Spirituality TYPE: Book PRICE: $10.95

King Solomon's Temple In The Masonic Tradition

PUBLISHING COMPANY: Aquarian Press EDITOR: A. Horne TOPICS: Spirituality TYPE: Book PRICE: $14.95

Knights Templar And Their Myth

PUBLISHING COMPANY: Crucible Books, Inner Traditions International, Ltd. EDITOR: P. Partner TOPICS: Occult TYPE: Book PRICE: $10.95

Knowing Body: Elements Of Contemporary Performances

PUBLISHING COMPANY: Shambhala Publications, Inc. EDITOR: L. Steinman TOPICS: New Age TYPE: Book PRICE: $14.95

Knowledge Of Time And Space

PUBLISHING COMPANY: Dharma Publishing EDITOR: Tarthang Tulku TOPICS: Spirituality TYPE: Book PRICE: $14.95

Kosher Yoga: Cabalistic Roots Of Western Mysticism

PUBLISHING COMPANY: Quantal Publishing EDITOR: A. Schutz, H. de Schaps TOPICS: Psychic TYPE: Book PRICE: $9.95

Krishnamurti To Himself: His Last Journal

PUBLISHING COMPANY: Harper & Row Publishers, Inc. EDITOR: J. Krishnamurti TOPICS: Spirituality TYPE: Book PRICE: $13.95

Krishnamurti: A Biography

PUBLISHING COMPANY: Harper & Row Publishers, Inc. EDITOR: Pupul Jayakar TOPICS: Spirituality TYPE: Book PRICE: $14.95

Krishnamurti: The Reluctant Messiah

PUBLISHING COMPANY: Paragon House EDITOR: Sidney Field, P. Hay TOPICS: Spirituality TYPE: Book PRICE: $16.95

Kundalini And The Third Eye

PUBLISHING COMPANY: Astara Foundation, Inc. EDITOR: E. Chaney, W. Messick TOPICS: Spirituality TYPE: Book PRICE: $12.95

Kundalini For The New Age

PUBLISHING COMPANY: Kundalini Research Foundation, Ltd. EDITOR: Gene Kieffer TOPICS: New Age, Spirituality TYPE: Book

Kundalini Yoga

PUBLISHING COMPANY: B. Jain Publishers, Ltd. EDITOR: S. Sivananda TOPICS: Yoga, Holistic Health TYPE: Book PRICE: $15.00

Kundalini Yoga For The West

PUBLISHING COMPANY: Shambhala Publications, Inc. EDITOR: S. Radha TOPICS: New Age, Yoga, Spirituality TYPE: Book PRICE: $18.95

Kundalini Yoga: For Body, Mind And Beyond

PUBLISHING COMPANY: White Lion Press EDITOR: Ravi Singh TOPICS: Yoga, Spirituality TYPE: Book PRICE: $15.95

Kundalini, The Evolutionary Energy In Man

PUBLISHING COMPANY: Kundalini Research Foundation, Ltd. EDITOR: Gopi Krishna TOPICS: New Age, Spirituality TYPE: Book DATE: 1970

Kundalini: The Arousal Of The Inner Energy

PUBLISHING COMPANY: Inner Traditions International, Ltd. EDITOR: A. Mookerjee TOPICS: Spirituality TYPE: Book PRICE: $12.95

Lady Of The Beasts: Ancient Images Of The Great Goddess & Her Sacred Animals

PUBLISHING COMPANY: Harper & Row Publishers, Inc. EDITOR: Buffie Johnson TOPICS: Spirituality TYPE: Book PRICE: $34.95

Lakhovsky Multiple Wave Oscillator Handbook

PUBLISHING COMPANY: Borderland Science And Research Foundation EDITOR: Thomas J. Brown TOPICS: Holistic Health TYPE: Handbook PRICE: $16.95

Land Of The Living

PUBLISHING COMPANY: Blue Dolphin Publishing, Inc. TOPICS: New Age TYPE: Book PRICE: $27.95

Lands Of The Thunderbolt

PUBLISHING COMPANY: Snow Lion Graphics TOPICS: New Age TYPE: Book PRICE: $12.95

Language Of Color

PUBLISHING COMPANY: Warner Books, Inc. EDITOR: D. Mella TOPICS: Color Therapy TYPE: Book PRICE: $8.95

Language Of The Goddess: Unearthing The Hidden Symbols Of Western Civilization

PUBLISHING COMPANY: Harper & Row Publishers, Inc. EDITOR: M. Gimbutas TOPICS: Spirituality TYPE: Book PRICE: $49.95

Last Talks At Saanen 1985

PUBLISHING COMPANY: Harper & Row Publishers, Inc. EDITOR: J. Krishnamurti TOPICS: Spirituality TYPE: Book PRICE: $16.95

Law Of Mind In Action

PUBLISHING COMPANY: IBS Press EDITOR: E.L Holmes TOPICS: New Age, Psychology TYPE: Book PRICE: $10.95

Laws Of Wealth

PUBLISHING COMPANY: IBS Press EDITOR: E.L. Holmes TOPICS: Spirituality, Psychology TYPE: Book PRICE: $10.95

Leaning On The Moment: Interviews From Parabola Magazine

PUBLISHING COMPANY: Parabola Books EDITOR: J. Kulin TOPICS: Spirituality TYPE: Book PRICE: $13.95

Learning To Live, Learning To Love

PUBLISHING COMPANY: B.L. Winch & Associates/Jalmar Press EDITOR: Joanne Haynes-Klassen TOPICS: New Age TYPE: Book SIZE: 6x9; 160 pgs. PRICE: $7.95

Learning To See And Interpret Auras

PUBLISHING COMPANY: Pathways EDITOR: Patricia K. Sawyer TOPICS: Metaphysics, Spirituality TYPE: Booklet

Learning To Use A Pendulum

PUBLISHING COMPANY: Pathways EDITOR: Patricia K. Sawyer TOPICS: Metaphysics, Spirituality TYPE: Booklet

Leaves Of Yggdrasil: A Synthesis Of Rune Gods, Magic, Feminine Mysteries, Folklore

PUBLISHING COMPANY: Llewellyn Publications EDITOR: Freya Aswynn TOPICS: Spirituality, Runes TYPE: Book PRICE: $12.95

Leaving The Body: A Complete Guide To Astral Projection

PUBLISHING COMPANY: Prentice-Hall, Inc. EDITOR: D. Scott Rogo TOPICS: Astral Projection TYPE: Book PRICE: $8.95

Lectures On Ancient Philosophy

PUBLISHING COMPANY: Philosophical Research Society, Inc. EDITOR: M.P. Hall TOPICS: Occult TYPE: Book PRICE: $12.50

Lectures On Materia Medica With New Remedies

PUBLISHING COMPANY: B. Jain Publishers, Ltd. EDITOR: J. Kent TOPICS: Homeopathy TYPE: Book PRICE: $20.00

Legends Of Atlantis And Lost Lemuria

PUBLISHING COMPANY: Theosophical University Press EDITOR: W. Scott-Elliot TOPICS: New Age TYPE: Book PRICE: $12.95

Lemuria: Lost Continent Of The Pacific

PUBLISHING COMPANY: Supreme Grand Lodge of AMORC, Inc. EDITOR: W. Cerve TOPICS: New Age TYPE: Book PRICE: $12.50

Lesson Of Love: The Revelations Of Julian Of Norwich

PUBLISHING COMPANY: Walker & Co., Div. of Walker Publishing Co., Inc. EDITOR: F. John-Julian TOPICS: Spirituality TYPE: Book PRICE: $9.95

Let Go Of The Struggle

PUBLISHING COMPANY: Winning Edge, The EDITOR: Joan Fericy TYPE: Booklet DATE: 1989; 42 pgs. PRICE: $3.95 DESCRIPTION: Inspirational messages that teach one to build on your own strengths & lead a happier life. Simplifed reminder of how to reclaim your peace of mind.

Let It Rot! The Home Gardener's Guide To Composting

PUBLISHING COMPANY: Storey Communications EDITOR: Stu Campbell TOPICS: Health Food TYPE: Guide

Let There Be Light

PUBLISHING COMPANY: Dinshah Health Society EDITOR: Darius Dinshah TOPICS: Holistic Healing, Color Therapy TYPE: Book; 164 pgs. PRICE: $15.00

Let Your Body Interpret Your Dreams

PUBLISHING COMPANY: Chiron Publications EDITOR: E. Gendlin TOPICS: Dreams TYPE: Book PRICE: $14.95

Letters From The Other Side: With Love, Harry & Helen

PUBLISHING COMPANY: Upper Access Publishers EDITOR: Mary B. White TOPICS: New Age, Channeling, Paranormal Phenomena, Metaphysics TYPE: Book PRICE: $10.95

Letters Of Evelyn Underhill

PUBLISHING COMPANY: Christian Classics, Inc. EDITOR: Charles Williams TOPICS: New Age, Paranormal Phenomena, Spirituality TYPE: Book PRICE: $14.95

Letters Of The Scattered Brotherhood

PUBLISHING COMPANY: Harper & Row Publishers, Inc. EDITOR: Mary Strong TOPICS: Spirituality TYPE: Book PRICE: $15.95

Letters On Yoga

PUBLISHING COMPANY: Lotus Light Publications Aurobindo TOPICS: Spirituality TYPE: Book PRICE: $44.00

Levitation: What It Is, How It Works, How To Do It

PUBLISHING COMPANY: Aquarian Press EDITOR: S. Richards TOPICS: Occult TYPE: Book PRICE: $8.95

Liberation In The Palm Of Your Hand: A Buddhist Meditation Course By Pabongka Rinpoche

PUBLISHING COMPANY: Wisdom Publications EDITOR: Michael Richards TOPICS: Meditation, Spirituality TYPE: Book PRICE: $34.95

Life And Teaching Of The Masters Of The Far East, Vols. 1-5

PUBLISHING COMPANY: DeVorss & Company EDITOR: B. Spalding TOPICS: New Age, Spirituality TYPE: Book PRICE: $25.95

Life As Carola
PUBLISHING COMPANY: Ariel Press EDITOR: Joan Grant TOPICS: Reincarnation TYPE: Book PRICE: $9.95

Life Between Death And Rebirth
PUBLISHING COMPANY: Anthroposophic Press, Inc. EDITOR: R. Steiner TOPICS: Reincarnation TYPE: Book PRICE: $9.95

Life Divine
PUBLISHING COMPANY: Sri Aurobindo Ashram Aurobindo TOPICS: Spirituality TYPE: Book PRICE: $25.00

Life Graph: The Record Of Our Past
PUBLISHING COMPANY: Metamorphous Press EDITOR: R. Konzack TOPICS: New Age, Psychology TYPE: Book PRICE: $14.95

Life In The Twenty-First Century
PUBLISHING COMPANY: 21st Century Publications EDITOR: V. Kulvinskas TOPICS: Holistic Health, Health Food, Vegetarianism TYPE: Book PRICE: $9.95

Life Is Real Only When I Am
PUBLISHING COMPANY: E.P. Dutton, Inc. EDITOR: G. Gurdjieff TOPICS: Spirituality TYPE: Book PRICE: $17.95

Life Is Uncertain...Eat Dessert First! Finding The Joy You Deserve
PUBLISHING COMPANY: Delacorte Press EDITOR: Sol Gordon, Harold Brecher TOPICS: Holistic Healing, New Age, Psychology TYPE: Book PRICE: $12.95

Life Of Marpa The Translator
PUBLISHING COMPANY: Shambhala Publications, Inc. EDITOR: C. Trungpa TOPICS: Spirituality TYPE: Book PRICE: $12.95

Lifecycles: Reincarnation And The Web Of Life
PUBLISHING COMPANY: Paragon House EDITOR: Christopher Bache TOPICS: Reincarnation, Spirituality TYPE: Book PRICE: $18.95

Lifespring: Getting Yourself From Where You Are To Where You Want
PUBLISHING COMPANY: Simon & Schuster, Inc. EDITOR: J. Hanley TOPICS: Spirituality TYPE: Book PRICE: $17.95

Light From Light: An Anthology Of Christian Mysticism
PUBLISHING COMPANY: Paulist Press EDITOR: L. Dupre, J. Wiseman TOPICS: Spirituality TYPE: Book PRICE: $14.95

Light Of Egypt Or The Science Of The Soul And The Stars
PUBLISHING COMPANY: Sun Publishing Company EDITOR: T. Burgoyne TOPICS: Astrology TYPE: Book PRICE: $28.00

Light Of The Soul: The Yoga Sutras Of Patanjali, With Commentary
PUBLISHING COMPANY: Lucis Publishing Company EDITOR: Alice Bailey TOPICS: Yoga, Holistic Health TYPE: Book PRICE: $12.00

Light on Monterey
PUBLISHING COMPANY: Light on Monterey EDITOR: Sara Bernstein TOPICS: New Age TYPE: Directory FREQ: quarterly CIRC: 10,000 DESCRIPTION: Directory including logos and resource listing.

Light On Pranayama: The Yogic Art Of Breathing
PUBLISHING COMPANY: Newmarket Press, Div. of Newmarket Publishing & Communications EDITOR: B. Iyengar TOPICS: Yoga, Holistic Health TYPE: Book PRICE: $15.95

Light On Yoga
PUBLISHING COMPANY: Schocken Books EDITOR: B. Iyengar TOPICS: Yoga, Holistic Health TYPE: Book PRICE: $13.95

Light: Medicine Of The Future--How We Can Use It To Heal Ourselves Now
PUBLISHING COMPANY: Bear & Company, Inc. EDITOR: O.D. Liberman TOPICS: Color Therapy, Holistic Healing TYPE: Book PRICE: $22.95

Lighten Up Your Body, Lighten Up Your Life: Beyond Diet & Exercise-- Inner Path To Change
PUBLISHING COMPANY: Newcastle Publishing Co., Inc. EDITOR: L. Capacchione TOPICS: New Age, Psychology TYPE: Book PRICE: $12.95

Like A Thousand Suns: Bhagavad Gita For Daily Living Vol.2
PUBLISHING COMPANY: Nilgiri Press EDITOR: E. Easwaran TOPICS: Spirituality TYPE: Book PRICE: $18.00

Lilias, Yoga And Your Life
PUBLISHING COMPANY: Macmillan Publishing Co., Inc. EDITOR: Lilias Folan TOPICS: Yoga, Holistic Health TYPE: Book PRICE: $14.95

Lines To The Mountain Gods: Nazca & The Mysteries Of Peru
PUBLISHING COMPANY: University Of Oklahoma Press EDITOR: E. Hadingham TOPICS: Paranormal Phenomena TYPE: Book PRICE: $15.95

Lipid Nutrition
PUBLISHING COMPANY: Inquiry Press EDITOR: R.L. Wysong TOPICS: New Age, Holistic Health, Nutrition TYPE: Book DATE: 1990; 170 pgs.

Listen To Your Body: A Head-To-Toe Guide To 400 Symptoms, Their Causes & Best Treatment
PUBLISHING COMPANY: Rodale Press, Inc. EDITOR: E. Michaud TOPICS: Holistic Health TYPE: Guide PRICE: $27.95

Little Moule History

PUBLISHING COMPANY: Blue Dolphin Publishing, Inc. TOPICS: New Age TYPE: Book PRICE: $24.95

Live In The Moment
PUBLISHING COMPANY: And Books EDITOR: M. Watts TOPICS: New Age TYPE: Book PRICE: $8.95

Lives Of The Master: The Rest Of The Jesus Story
PUBLISHING COMPANY: Association For Research And Enlightenment, Inc. EDITOR: G. Sanderfur TOPICS: Reincarnation TYPE: Book PRICE: $12.95

Lives You Live
PUBLISHING COMPANY: Arthur Publications, Inc. EDITOR: Debra Sapp TOPICS: Astrology TYPE: Book DATE: 1978

Living Aikido: Form, Training, Essence
PUBLISHING COMPANY: North Atlantic Books EDITOR: B. Klickstein TOPICS: Aikido TYPE: Book PRICE: $16.95

Living Free
PUBLISHING COMPANY: Jim Stumm EDITOR: Jim Stumm TOPICS: New Age TYPE: Book

Living From The Heart
PUBLISHING COMPANY: C. Olson And Company EDITOR: Mohandas Gandhi TOPICS: New Age TYPE: Book; 128 pgs. PRICE: $9.95 DESCRIPTION: How to build into one's life strength, honesty, perseverance & inner peace.

Living Magical Arts: Imagination And Magic For The 21st Century
PUBLISHING COMPANY: Sterling Publishing Company, Inc. EDITOR: R.J. Stewart TOPICS: Witchcraft, Occult TYPE: Book PRICE: $19.95

Living Palmistry: A Unique Guide To Modern Hand Analysis
PUBLISHING COMPANY: Aquarian Press EDITOR: S. Fenton, M. Wright TOPICS: Palmistry TYPE: Book PRICE: $9.95

Living Psyche: A Jungian Analysis In Pictures
PUBLISHING COMPANY: Chiron Publications EDITOR: E. Edinger TOPICS: Psychology TYPE: Book PRICE: $19.95

Living The Good Life
PUBLISHING COMPANY: Traditional Tours EDITOR: Helen Nearing TOPICS: New Age TYPE: Book

Living The Infinite Way
PUBLISHING COMPANY: Harper & Row Publishers, Inc. EDITOR: Joel Goldsmith TOPICS: New Age TYPE: Book PRICE: $14.95

Living Together, Feeling Alone: Healing Your Hidden Loneliness
PUBLISHING COMPANY: Prentice-Hall, Inc. EDITOR: D. Kiley TOPICS: New Age, Psychology TYPE: Book PRICE: $18.95

Living With The Himalayan Masters

PUBLISHING COMPANY: Himalayan International Institute Of Yoga Science and Philosophy **EDITOR:** S. Rama **TOPICS:** Spirituality, Yoga **TYPE:** Book **PRICE:** $15.95

Llewellyn's Moon Sign Book And Daily Planetary Guide

PUBLISHING COMPANY: Llewellyn Publications **EDITOR:** Terry Buske **TOPICS:** Astrology **TYPE:** Guide

Looking Into Mind: How To Recognize Who You Are & How You Know

PUBLISHING COMPANY: Larson Publications **EDITOR:** Anthony Damiani **TOPICS:** New Age, Meditation, Spirituality **TYPE:** Book; 320 pgs. **PRICE:** $14.95

Lost Cities And Ancient Mysteries Of South America

PUBLISHING COMPANY: Adventures-Unlimited Press **EDITOR:** D. Childress **TOPICS:** New Age **TYPE:** Book **PRICE:** $12.95

Lost Cities Of Africa And Arabia

PUBLISHING COMPANY: Adventures-Unlimited Press **EDITOR:** D. Childress **TOPICS:** New Age **TYPE:** Book **PRICE:** $12.95

Lost Cities Of Ancient Lemuria And The Pacific

PUBLISHING COMPANY: Adventures-Unlimited Press **EDITOR:** D. Childress **TOPICS:** New Age **TYPE:** Book **PRICE:** $12.95

Lost Cities Of China, Central Asia, And India: A Traveler's Guide

PUBLISHING COMPANY: Adventures-Unlimited Press **EDITOR:** D. Childress **TOPICS:** New Age **TYPE:** Book **PRICE:** $12.95

Lost Years Of Jesus

PUBLISHING COMPANY: Summit University Press **EDITOR:** Elizabeth Clare Prophet **TOPICS:** Spirituality **TYPE:** Book **PRICE:** $5.95

Love And Power In A World Without Limits: A Woman's Guide To The Goddess Within

PUBLISHING COMPANY: Harper & Row Publishers, Inc. **EDITOR:** T. Cole-Whittaker **TOPICS:** Spirituality **TYPE:** Book **PRICE:** $15.95

Love Does Not Condemn: The World, The Flesh & Devil According To Gnosticism & Acim

PUBLISHING COMPANY: Foundation For A Course In Miracles Conference/Retreat Center **EDITOR:** K. Wapnick **TOPICS:** Occult, New Age, Spirituality **TYPE:** Book **PRICE:** $25.00

Love Is A Secret: The Mystic Quest For Divine Love

PUBLISHING COMPANY: Aslan Publishing **EDITOR:** Andrew Vidich **TOPICS:** New Age **TYPE:** Book

Love Of Knowledge: An Inquiry Into Knowledge, Self & Reality

PUBLISHING COMPANY: Dharma Publishing **EDITOR:** Tarthang Tulku **TOPICS:** Spirituality **TYPE:** Book **PRICE:** $14.95

Love Without Limits

PUBLISHING COMPANY: IntiNet Resource Center **EDITOR:** Dr. Deborah Anapol **TOPICS:** New Age **TYPE:** Book **DATE:** 1992 **PRICE:** $16.00

Love Your Disease

PUBLISHING COMPANY: Hay House **EDITOR:** J. Harrison **TOPICS:** Holistic Healing, Body-Mind Connection **TYPE:** Book **PRICE:** $12.95

Love Yourself Into Life

PUBLISHING COMPANY: Sovereignty, Inc. **EDITOR:** J.Z. Knight **TOPICS:** Channeling **TYPE:** Book **PRICE:** $33.00

Love Yourself, Heal Your Life Workbook

PUBLISHING COMPANY: Hay House **EDITOR:** Louise Hay **TOPICS:** Holistic Healing, Spirituality, Psychic Healing, New Age, Psychology **TYPE:** Book **PRICE:** $12.00

Love, Medicine & Miracles

PUBLISHING COMPANY: Harper & Row Publishers, Inc. **EDITOR:** Bernie S. Siegel, M.D. **TOPICS:** Holistic Health, Spirituality, Psychic Healing, Meditation, Body-Mind Connection **TYPE:** Book

Love, Medicine And Miracles Gift Set - Bernie Siegel's Personal Reflections

PUBLISHING COMPANY: Harper & Row Publishers, Inc. **EDITOR:** Bernie S. Siegel, M.D. **TOPICS:** Holistic Health, Spirituality, Psychic Healing, Meditation, Body-Mind Connection **TYPE:** Book **PRICE:** $14.95

Loving Hands Are Healing Hands: A Spiritual Approach To Transformational Bodywork/Polarity

PUBLISHING COMPANY: North Atlantic Books **EDITOR:** Bruce Burger **TOPICS:** Holistic Health, Spirituality **TYPE:** Book **PRICE:** $12.95

Loving Hands: The Traditional Indian Art Of Baby Massage

PUBLISHING COMPANY: Random House, Inc. **EDITOR:** F. Leboyer **TOPICS:** Massage **TYPE:** Book **PRICE:** $24.95

Macrobiotic Child Care And Family Health

PUBLISHING COMPANY: Japan Publications, Inc. **EDITOR:** M. Kushi, A. Kushi **TOPICS:** Holistic Health, Vegetarianism, Health Food **TYPE:** Book **PRICE:** $15.95

Macrobiotic Diet

PUBLISHING COMPANY: Japan Publications, Inc. **EDITOR:** M. Kushi, A. Kushi **TOPICS:** Holistic Health, Vegetarianism, Health Food **TYPE:** Book **PRICE:** $15.95

Macrobiotic Home Remedies

PUBLISHING COMPANY: Japan Publications, Inc. **EDITOR:** M. Kushi **TOPICS:** Holistic Health, Vegetarianism, Health Food **TYPE:** Book **PRICE:** $14.95

Macrobiotic Palm Healing: Energy At Your Fingertips

PUBLISHING COMPANY: Japan Publications, Inc. **EDITOR:** M. Kushi, O. Oredson **TOPICS:** Holistic Health, Health Food, Palmistry **TYPE:** Book **PRICE:** $15.95

Macrobiotic Way Of Zen Shiatsu

PUBLISHING COMPANY: Japan Publications, Inc. **EDITOR:** D. Sergel **TOPICS:** Holistic Health, Vegetarianism, Health Food **TYPE:** Book **PRICE:** $19.95

Macrobiotics And Human Behavior

PUBLISHING COMPANY: Harper & Row Publishers, Inc. **EDITOR:** W. Tara **TOPICS:** Holistic Health, Vegetarianism, Health Food **TYPE:** Book **PRICE:** $12.95

Macrobiotics And Oriental Medicine: An Introduction

PUBLISHING COMPANY: Japan Publications, Inc. **EDITOR:** M. Kushi **TOPICS:** Health Food, Holistic Health **TYPE:** Book **PRICE:** $17.95

Macrobiotics Beyond Food: Guide To Health & Well-Being

PUBLISHING COMPANY: Harper & Row Publishers, Inc. **EDITOR:** R. Kotzsch **TOPICS:** Spirituality, Psychic Healing **TYPE:** Book **PRICE:** $19.95

Macrobiotics In Motion: Yin And Yang In Moving Spirals

PUBLISHING COMPANY: Japan Publications, Inc. **EDITOR:** B. Polatin **TOPICS:** Health Food, New Age, Holistic Health **TYPE:** Book **PRICE:** $15.95

Macrobiotics Palm Healing: Energy At Your Fingertips

PUBLISHING COMPANY: Japan Publications, Inc. **EDITOR:** M. Kushi, O. Oredson **TOPICS:** Spirituality, Psychic Healing **TYPE:** Book **PRICE:** $15.95

Macrobiotics: Yesterday And Today

PUBLISHING COMPANY: Harper & Row Publishers, Inc. **EDITOR:** R. Kotzsch **TOPICS:** Holistic Health, Vegetarianism, Health Food **TYPE:** Book **PRICE:** $15.95

Magic And Medicine Of Plants

PUBLISHING COMPANY: Reader's Digest **TOPICS:** Holistic Health, Herbalogy **TYPE:** Book **PRICE:** $26.95

Magic And The Tarot: Using Tarot To Manipulate The Unseen Powers Of The Universe

PUBLISHING COMPANY: Aquarian Press **EDITOR:** T. Willis **TOPICS:** Psychic, Tarot **TYPE:** Book **PRICE:** $12.95

Magic In Stones

PUBLISHING COMPANY: Llewellyn Publications **EDITOR:** Pattalee Glass-Koentop **TOPICS:** Psychic, Metaphysics **TYPE:** Book **PRICE:** $9.95

Magic Island
PUBLISHING COMPANY: Paragon House EDITOR: W. Seabrook TOPICS: Voudoun TYPE: Book PRICE: $10.95

Magic Tarot
PUBLISHING COMPANY: Routledge, Chapman & Hall, Inc. EDITOR: Frederic Lionel TOPICS: Tarot, Metaphysics TYPE: Book PRICE: $17.50

Magic: An Occult Primer - The Complete Do-It-Yourself Guide
PUBLISHING COMPANY: Aquarian Press EDITOR: Deanna Conway TOPICS: Occult TYPE: Book PRICE: $12.95

Magic: The Western Tradition
PUBLISHING COMPANY: Thames & Hudson EDITOR: Francis King TOPICS: Occult TYPE: Book PRICE: $11.95

Magical Language Of Runes
PUBLISHING COMPANY: Bear & Company, Inc. EDITOR: P.M.H. Atwater TOPICS: Runes, Metaphysics TYPE: Book PRICE: $9.95

Magical Rites From The Crystal Well
PUBLISHING COMPANY: Llewellyn Publications EDITOR: E. Fitch TOPICS: Paganism, Spirituality TYPE: Book PRICE: $9.95

Magical States Of Consciousness
PUBLISHING COMPANY: Llewellyn Publications EDITOR: M. Denning, O. Phillips TOPICS: Occult, Witchcraft TYPE: Book PRICE: $12.95

Magick Circle Directory Of Occult Goods & Services
PUBLISHING COMPANY: Magick Circle EDITOR: Rev. Nelson White TOPICS: Parapsychology, Occult TYPE: Directory DATE: 1984 SIZE: 5 x 8.5; 36 pgs. FREQ: Semi-Annual CIRC: 1,000 PRICE PER COPY: $6.00 DESCRIPTION: Publication listing sources pertaining to the occult & offering related goods & services including practitioners, shops & suppliers.

Magickal Qaballah
PUBLISHING COMPANY: Technology Group, The EDITOR: Frater Zarathustra TYPE: Book SIZE: 8 1/2 x 11

Magnet Therapy In Theory And Practice
PUBLISHING COMPANY: B. Jain Publishers, Ltd. EDITOR: N. Bengali TOPICS: Parapsychology, Holistic Health TYPE: Book PRICE: $12.00

Magnet Therapy: Balancing Your Body's Energy Flow For Self-Healing
PUBLISHING COMPANY: Sterling Publishing Company, Inc. EDITOR: Holger Hannemann TOPICS: Parapsychology, Holistic Health TYPE: Book PRICE: $9.95

Magnetotherapy: Art Of Healing Through Magnets
PUBLISHING COMPANY: B. Jain Publishers, Ltd. EDITOR: H. L. Bansal TOPICS: Parapsychology, Holistic Health TYPE: Book PRICE: $12.00

Magnificent Quest: Six Paths To The Inner Grail
PUBLISHING COMPANY: Whitford Press/Schiffer Publishing Limited Kelynda TOPICS: Spirituality TYPE: Book PRICE: $14.95

Magus
PUBLISHING COMPANY: Citadel Press EDITOR: F. Barrett TOPICS: Occult, Witchcraft TYPE: Book PRICE: $14.95

Mahabarata: Peter Brook's Epic In The Making-A Documentary
PUBLISHING COMPANY: Mercury House, Inc. EDITOR: Garry O'Connor TOPICS: Spirituality TYPE: Book PRICE: $24.95

Mahamudra
PUBLISHING COMPANY: Blue Dolphin Publishing, Inc. TOPICS: New Age TYPE: Book PRICE: $9.95

Mahamudra: Quintessence Of Mind And Meditation Vol.2
PUBLISHING COMPANY: Shambhala Publications, Inc. EDITOR: L. Lhalungpa TOPICS: Meditation, Spirituality TYPE: Book PRICE: $25.00

Mahamudra: Quintessence Of Mind And Meditation Vol.1
PUBLISHING COMPANY: Shambhala Publications, Inc. EDITOR: L. Lhalungpa TOPICS: Meditation, Spirituality TYPE: Book PRICE: $18.95

Making Miracles: An Exploration Into The Dynamics Of Self-Healing
PUBLISHING COMPANY: Warner Books, Inc. EDITOR: P. Roud TOPICS: Holistic Healing, Psychic Healing, Spirituality, Body-Mind Connection TYPE: Book PRICE: $19.95

Making Miracles: Inspiring Mind-Methods To Supercharge Your Emotions & Rejuventate Health
PUBLISHING COMPANY: Rodale Press, Inc. EDITOR: Barry Fox TOPICS: Holistic Healing, Spirituality, Psychic Healing, Body-Mind Connection TYPE: Book PRICE: $19.95

Making Sprout Bread
PUBLISHING COMPANY: Sprout House PUBLISHER: Steve Meyerowitz TOPICS: Nutrition, Holistic Health, Health Food TYPE: Book

Man And Woman And Child
PUBLISHING COMPANY: Word Foundation, Inc., The TOPICS: Metaphysics TYPE: Book

Man, Minerals And Masters
PUBLISHING COMPANY: Sun Publishing Company EDITOR: C. Littlefield TOPICS: Occult TYPE: Book PRICE: $9.50

Man, The Regenerative Evolutionary Spirit
PUBLISHING COMPANY: Unarius Academy Of Science & Education Foundation EDITOR: Ruth Norman, Charles Spaegel TOPICS: Reincarnation TYPE: Book; 347 pgs. PRICE: $12.95

Man, Visible And Invisible

PUBLISHING COMPANY: Theosophical University Press EDITOR: C. Leadbeater TOPICS: Holistic Health TYPE: Book PRICE: $8.95

Mansions Of The Soul: Reincarnation, The Soul's Rebirth On Earth
PUBLISHING COMPANY: Supreme Grand Lodge of AMORC, Inc. EDITOR: H. Lewis TOPICS: Reincarnation, Spirituality TYPE: Book PRICE: $9.00

Mantram Handbook
PUBLISHING COMPANY: Nilgiri Press EDITOR: E. Easwaran TOPICS: Meditation TYPE: Book PRICE: $12.00

Manual Of Computer Programming
PUBLISHING COMPANY: Matrix Software EDITOR: Michael Erlewine TOPICS: Astrology TYPE: Handbook

Manual Of Natural Therapy: A Practical Guide To Alternative Medicine
PUBLISHING COMPANY: Citadel Press EDITOR: Moshe Olshevsky TOPICS: Homeopathy, Holistic Health TYPE: Guide PRICE: $12.95

Manual Of The Harmonic Orb (MHO)
PUBLISHING COMPANY: NALTA Foundation, Inc. TOPICS: New Age, Holistic Healing TYPE: Booklet

Many Happy Returns
PUBLISHING COMPANY: Harper & Row Publishers, Inc. EDITOR: W.H. Church TOPICS: Channeling TYPE: Book PRICE: $8.95

Map Dowsing Handbook
PUBLISHING COMPANY: Fine Median International TOPICS: Dowsing TYPE: Handbook

Maps Of The Mind: Charts & Concepts Of The Mind & Its Labyrinths
PUBLISHING COMPANY: Macmillan Publishing Co., Inc. EDITOR: Charles Hampden-Turner TOPICS: New Age, Psychology TYPE: Book PRICE: $14.95

Margins Of Reality: The Role Of Consciousness In The Physical World
PUBLISHING COMPANY: Harcourt Brace Jovanovich EDITOR: R. Jahn, B. Dunne TOPICS: New Age, Psychology TYPE: Book PRICE: $19.95

Marilyn Ferguson's Book Of Pragmagic: Pragmatic Magic For Everyday Living
PUBLISHING COMPANY: Pocket Books EDITOR: M. Ferguson TOPICS: New Age TYPE: Book PRICE: $9.95

Mars Connection
PUBLISHING COMPANY: Marcus Books EDITOR: Maurice B. Cooke TOPICS: Astrology TYPE: Book PRICE: $9.95

Martian Enigmas: A Photographic Album On The Investigation Of The Face & Other Objects/On Mars
PUBLISHING COMPANY: North Atlantic Books EDITOR: Mark Carlotto TOPICS: UFO's, Paranormal Phenomena TYPE: Book PRICE: $18.95

Mary Magdalene
PUBLISHING COMPANY: Blue Dolphin Publishing, Inc. TOPICS: New Age TYPE: Book PRICE: $8.95

Mary's Message To The World
PUBLISHING COMPANY: Blue Dolphin Publishing, Inc. TOPICS: New Age TYPE: Book PRICE: $12.95

Masonic Facts And Fictions
PUBLISHING COMPANY: Aquarian Press EDITOR: H. Sadler, J. Hamill TOPICS: Spirituality TYPE: Book PRICE: $13.50

Masonry And Its Symbols
PUBLISHING COMPANY: Word Foundation, Inc., The TOPICS: Metaphysics TYPE: Book

Masonry And Medieval Mysticism: Traces Of A Hidden Tradition
PUBLISHING COMPANY: Theosophical University Press EDITOR: I. Cooper-Oakley TOPICS: Spirituality TYPE: Book PRICE: $13.95

Mass Dreams Of The Future: What 1000s Of People Under The Future Life Progression Have Revealed
PUBLISHING COMPANY: McGraw Hill Book Co., Div. of McGraw Hill, Inc. EDITOR: Chet Snow, H. Wambach TOPICS: Metaphysics, New Age, Past Life Regression TYPE: Book PRICE: $19.95

Master Numbers: Cycles Of Devine Order
PUBLISHING COMPANY: Whitford Press/Schiffer Publishing Limited EDITOR: F. Javane TOPICS: Numerology TYPE: Book PRICE: $14.95

Master, The Monks And I: A Woman's Experience Of Zen
PUBLISHING COMPANY: Crucible Books, Inner Traditions International, Ltd. EDITOR: G. Ital TOPICS: Spirituality TYPE: Book PRICE: $14.95

Masters And Mahatmas
PUBLISHING COMPANY: Word Foundation, Inc., The TOPICS: Metaphysics TYPE: Book

Masters And The Path
PUBLISHING COMPANY: Theosophical University Press EDITOR: C. Leadbeater TOPICS: Spirituality TYPE: Book PRICE: $27.95

Masters Of Greatness
PUBLISHING COMPANY: Teamup EDITOR: Jean K. Foster TOPICS: New Age TYPE: Book

Materia Medica Of Ayurveda
PUBLISHING COMPANY: B. Jain Publishers, Ltd. EDITOR: B. Dash, L. Kashyap TOPICS: Holistic Health TYPE: Book PRICE: $36.00

Materia Medica Pura
PUBLISHING COMPANY: B. Jain Publishers, Ltd. EDITOR: S. Hahnemann TOPICS: Homeopathy TYPE: Book PRICE: $24.00

Materia Medica With Repertory
PUBLISHING COMPANY: B. Jain Publishers, Ltd. EDITOR: W. Boericke, O. Boericke TOPICS: Homeopathy TYPE: Book PRICE: $18.00

Mayan Factor: Path Beyond Technology
PUBLISHING COMPANY: Bear & Company, Inc. EDITOR: J. Arguelles TOPICS: New Age TYPE: Book PRICE: $12.95

Meaning And Significance Of Dreams
PUBLISHING COMPANY: Sigo Press EDITOR: D. Roscoe TOPICS: Dreams, Psychology TYPE: Book PRICE: $16.95

Mechanics Of Free Will: The Astrology Of Perception, Reality And Will
PUBLISHING COMPANY: Treehouse Mountain EDITOR: M. Lang-Wescott TOPICS: Astrology TYPE: Book PRICE: $22.95

Mechanics Of The Future: Asteroids
PUBLISHING COMPANY: Treehouse Mountain EDITOR: M. Lang-Wescott TOPICS: Astrology TYPE: Book PRICE: $19.95

Medical Cheirology
PUBLISHING COMPANY: Cheirological Society EDITOR: C.L. Jones TOPICS: Palmistry, Holistic Health TYPE: Book DATE: 1991

Medical Graphology
PUBLISHING COMPANY: Samuel Weiser, Inc. EDITOR: M. De Surany TOPICS: Graphology TYPE: Book PRICE: $12.95

Medical Tests And Diagnostic Procedures: A Patient's Guide
PUBLISHING COMPANY: Harper & Row Publishers, Inc. EDITOR: Phillip Shtasel TOPICS: Holistic Health TYPE: Guide PRICE: $22.50

Medicinal Plants: An Authentic Guide To Natural Remedies
PUBLISHING COMPANY: W. Foulsham & Co., Ltd. EDITOR: H. Fluck TOPICS: Holistic Health, Herbalogy TYPE: Guide PRICE: $12.95

Medicine Woman Trilogy (boxed set-Medicine Woman, Flight Of Seventh Moon & Jaguar Woman)
PUBLISHING COMPANY: Harper & Row Publishers, Inc. EDITOR: Lynn Andrews TOPICS: Holistic Health TYPE: Book PRICE: $26.85

Meditating In A Changing World
PUBLISHING COMPANY: Gothic Image Publications EDITOR: William Bloom TOPICS: Meditation TYPE: Book PRICE: $12.50

Meditation
PUBLISHING COMPANY: Ma Yoga Shakti International Mission PUBLISHER: Ma Yoga Shakti

TOPICS: Yoga, Meditation, Spirituality TYPE: Book

Meditation And Mantras
PUBLISHING COMPANY: Sivananda Yoga Vedanta Centers TYPE: Book

Meditation And Mantras
PUBLISHING COMPANY: Sivananda Ashram Yoga Retreat EDITOR: Swami Vishnu-Devananda TYPE: Book

Meditation At The United Nations
PUBLISHING COMPANY: AUM Publications TOPICS: New Age TYPE: Book

Meditation: An Eight Point Program
PUBLISHING COMPANY: Nilgiri Press EDITOR: E. Easwaran TOPICS: Meditation TYPE: Book PRICE: $12.00

Meditation: And The Creative Imperative
PUBLISHING COMPANY: Dryad Press EDITOR: Lucy Oliver TOPICS: Meditation TYPE: Book PRICE: $12.95

Meditation: First And Last Freedom
PUBLISHING COMPANY: Chidvilas, Inc. EDITOR: Osho Rajneesh TOPICS: Meditation, Body-Mind Connection, Spirituality TYPE: Book PRICE: $14.95

Meditations Through The Quran: Tonal Images In An Oral Culture
PUBLISHING COMPANY: Samuel Weiser, Inc. EDITOR: E. McClain TOPICS: New Age TYPE: Book PRICE: $12.95

Meditative And Past Life Journal
PUBLISHING COMPANY: Reincarnation Books & Tapes EDITOR: Bettye B. Binder TOPICS: Past Life Regression, Meditation TYPE: Book PRICE: $10.00

Meeting Of Science And Spirit: Guidelines For A New Age
PUBLISHING COMPANY: Paragon House EDITOR: John White TOPICS: Yoga, New Age TYPE: Book PRICE: $18.95

Menus For Impulsive Living: A Program For Self-Realization
PUBLISHING COMPANY: Doubleday & Co.,Inc. EDITOR: K. Leland, Charles Leland TOPICS: Spirituality TYPE: Book PRICE: $18.95

Merlin Awakes: Revelations And Truths For A New Age
PUBLISHING COMPANY: Sterling Publishing Company, Inc. EDITOR: Peter Qiller, C. Davis TOPICS: Occult TYPE: Book PRICE: $9.95

MetaBusiness: Creating A New Global Culture
PUBLISHING COMPANY: MetaBusiness Institute/ Conscious Books EDITOR: Greg Nielsen TOPICS: New Age TYPE: Book PRICE: $9.95

Metaphysical Handbook
PUBLISHING COMPANY: Reflecting Pond Publications EDITOR: David Pond, Luey Pond

TOPICS: Metaphysics, Occult TYPE: Book PRICE: $9.95

Mexico Mystique: The Coming Sixth World Consciousness

PUBLISHING COMPANY: Swallow Press/Ohio U Press EDITOR: F. Waters TOPICS: Metaphysics, Psychic TYPE: Book PRICE: $11.95

Middle Path Of Life

PUBLISHING COMPANY: Blue Dolphin Publishing, Inc. TOPICS: New Age TYPE: Book PRICE: $9.95

Mime And Beyond

PUBLISHING COMPANY: Hohm Press EDITOR: S. Avital TOPICS: New Age TYPE: Book PRICE: $14.95

Mind

PUBLISHING COMPANY: Project Mentifex TOPICS: New Age TYPE: Book DATE: 1991 DESCRIPTION: AI design on CD-ROM for CDTV/Amiga Library Disk #411.

Mind Jogger

PUBLISHING COMPANY: Poco Press EDITOR: Hal Zina Bennett TOPICS: Psychic TYPE: Book PRICE: $7.95

Mind Magic: The Ecstasy Of Freeing Creative Power

PUBLISHING COMPANY: Unlimited Publishing, Inc. EDITOR: Bill Harvey TOPICS: Body-Mind Connection, Psychology TYPE: Book PRICE: $20.00

Mind Of My Own: The Woman Known As Eve Tells The Story Of Her Triumph Over Mpd

PUBLISHING COMPANY: William Morrow & Co. EDITOR: Chris C. Sizemore TOPICS: Occult TYPE: Book PRICE: $19.95

Mind Sense: Fine Tuning Your Intellect And Intuition - A Practical Workbook

PUBLISHING COMPANY: Celestial Arts Publishing Co./Sub. of Ten Speed Press EDITOR: K. Rhea TOPICS: Psychic TYPE: Book PRICE: $12.95

Mind's I: Fantasies And Reflections On Self And Soul

PUBLISHING COMPANY: Bantam New Age Books EDITOR: Douglas Hofstadter TOPICS: Psychology TYPE: Book PRICE: $13.95

Mind, Body & Soul: The Self-Awareness & Health Care Guide For Northeastern Ohio

PUBLISHING COMPANY: Mind, Body & Soul: The Self-Awareness & Health Care Guide PUBLISHER: George F. Kroto TOPICS: Holistic Health, New Age, Metaphysics TYPE: Guide

Mind, Fantasy & Healing: One Woman's Journey From Conflict & Illness To Wholeness & Health

PUBLISHING COMPANY: Delacorte Press EDITOR: A. Epstein TOPICS: Holistic Healing, Body-Mind Connection, Spirituality, Psychic Healing TYPE: Book PRICE: $16.95

Mind/Body Deceptions: The Psychosomatics Of Everyday Life

PUBLISHING COMPANY: W. W. Norton & Co., Inc. EDITOR: Steven L. Dubowsky TOPICS: Body-Mind Connection, Holistic Health TYPE: Book PRICE: $22.95

Mind/Body Purification Plan

PUBLISHING COMPANY: Simon & Schuster, Inc. EDITOR: L. Chaitow TOPICS: Body-Mind Connection TYPE: Book PRICE: $13.95

Mipam

PUBLISHING COMPANY: Snow Lion Graphics TOPICS: New Age TYPE: Book PRICE: $12.95

Miracle Of Colour Healing: Aura-Soma Therapy As The Mirror Of The Soul

PUBLISHING COMPANY: Aquarian Press EDITOR: Vicky Wall TOPICS: Color Therapy TYPE: Book PRICE: $12.95

Miracle Of Love: Stories About Neem Karola Baba

PUBLISHING COMPANY: E.P. Dutton, Inc. EDITOR: Ram Dass TOPICS: Spirituality TYPE: Book PRICE: $14.95

Miracle Of Universal Psychic Power

PUBLISHING COMPANY: Pan/Ishtar Unlimited EDITOR: A. Manning TOPICS: Paganism, Spirituality, Psychic Healing TYPE: Book PRICE: $14.95

Miracle Spiritology

PUBLISHING COMPANY: Pan/Ishtar Unlimited EDITOR: A. Manning TOPICS: Occult TYPE: Book PRICE: $9.95

Mirrors: Affirmations & Actions For Daily Reflection

PUBLISHING COMPANY: Yes International EDITOR: Cheryl Wall TOPICS: New Age, Holistic Health, Psychology TYPE: Book PRICE: $11.95

Modern Magick

PUBLISHING COMPANY: Llewellyn Publications EDITOR: D. Kraig TOPICS: Occult, Witchcraft TYPE: Book PRICE: $14.95

Modern Techniques Of Acupuncture Vol. 3

PUBLISHING COMPANY: Thorsens Publishing House EDITOR: J. Kenyon TOPICS: Holistic Health, Acupuncture TYPE: Book PRICE: $39.95

Monuments Of Mars: A City On The Edge Of Forever

PUBLISHING COMPANY: North Atlantic Books EDITOR: R.C. Hoagland TOPICS: UFO's, Paranormal Phenomena TYPE: Book PRICE: $14.95

Moon Lore And Moon Magic

PUBLISHING COMPANY: Pan/Ishtar Unlimited EDITOR: A. Manning TOPICS: Occult TYPE: Book PRICE: $14.95

Moon Tides

PUBLISHING COMPANY: Kathexis Coven TOPICS: Witchcraft, Occult, Paganism TYPE: Book

Most Holy Trinosophia

PUBLISHING COMPANY: Philosophical Research Society, Inc. EDITOR: M.P. Hall TOPICS: Spirituality TYPE: Book PRICE: $15.00

Mother Of Knowledge

PUBLISHING COMPANY: Dharma Publishing EDITOR: Tarthang Tulku TOPICS: New Age, Spirituality TYPE: Book PRICE: $16.95

Mother: With Letters On The Mother

PUBLISHING COMPANY: Lotus Light Publications Aurobindo TOPICS: Spirituality TYPE: Book PRICE: $15.00

Motherpeace Tarot Playbook

PUBLISHING COMPANY: Wingbow Press EDITOR: V. Noble, J. Tenney TOPICS: New Age, Tarot, Witchcraft, Metaphysics TYPE: Book PRICE: $12.95

Motherpeace: Way To The Goddess Through Myth, Art, And Tarot

PUBLISHING COMPANY: Harper & Row Publishers, Inc. EDITOR: V. Noble TOPICS: Spirituality, Tarot TYPE: Book PRICE: $14.95

Multiple States Of Being

PUBLISHING COMPANY: Larson Publications EDITOR: R. Guenon TOPICS: New Age, Psychology TYPE: Book PRICE: $13.95

Mummies, Myth And Magic In Ancient Egypt

PUBLISHING COMPANY: Thames & Hudson EDITOR: C. El Mahdy TOPICS: Occult TYPE: Book PRICE: $19.95

Muscle/Tendon Changing And Marrow/Brain Washing Chi Kung: The Secret Of Youth

PUBLISHING COMPANY: Yang Martial Arts Assoc. EDITOR: Y. Jwing-Ming TOPICS: Holistic Health TYPE: Book PRICE: $18.00

Music, Mysticism And Magic: A Source Book

PUBLISHING COMPANY: Penguin Books EDITOR: J. Godwin TOPICS: Occult TYPE: Book PRICE: $9.95

My Baba And I

PUBLISHING COMPANY: Birth Day Publishing Company EDITOR: J. Hislop TOPICS: Spirituality TYPE: Book PRICE: $9.00

My God - The Power & Wisdom Of The Universe

PUBLISHING COMPANY: New Age World Religious & Scientific Research Foundation PUBLISHER: Victoria E. Vandertuin TOPICS: Parapsychology, New Age, Spirituality TYPE: Book

My Guide, Myself: The Psychic Odyssey Of Sylvia Brown

PUBLISHING COMPANY: New American Library EDITOR: Sylvia Brown, A. May TOPICS: Tarot, Occult, Psychic TYPE: Book PRICE: $18.95

My Journey With A Mystic

PUBLISHING COMPANY: Tale Weaver Publishing EDITOR: F. Peters TOPICS: Spirituality TYPE: Book PRICE: $22.50

My Search For Radionic Truths: With Possibilities Of Acceptance By Science & Medicine

PUBLISHING COMPANY: Borderland Science And Research Foundation EDITOR: R.M. Denning TOPICS: Metaphysics, Holistic Health TYPE: Book PRICE: $9.95

Mysteria Magica

PUBLISHING COMPANY: Llewellyn Publications EDITOR: M. Denning, O. Phillips TOPICS: Occult TYPE: Book PRICE: $15.00

Mysteries Of Atlantis Revisited

PUBLISHING COMPANY: Harper & Row Publishers, Inc. EDITOR: C.T. Cayce TOPICS: Channeling TYPE: Book PRICE: $8.95

Mysteries Of The Crystal Skulls Revealed

PUBLISHING COMPANY: J & S Aquarian Networking EDITOR: S. Bowen TOPICS: Crystals, New Age, UFO's, Paranormal Phenomena TYPE: Book DATE: 1988 PRICE: $17.95

Mysteries Of The Mexican Pyramids

PUBLISHING COMPANY: Harper & Row Publishers, Inc. EDITOR: Peter Tompkins TOPICS: Paranormal Phenomena TYPE: Book PRICE: $16.95

Mysteries Of The Unexplained: How Ordinary Men & Women Have Experienced The Uncanny

PUBLISHING COMPANY: Reader's Digest EDITOR: Colin Editors of Reader's TOPICS: Paranormal Phenomena TYPE: Book PRICE: $22.95

Mysteries Of The Unknown

PUBLISHING COMPANY: Time-Life Books TOPICS: New Age TYPE: Book DESCRIPTION: A series of books: Mystic Places, Dream & Dreaming, Psychic Voyages, Cosmic Connections, Powers Of Healing, Visions & Prophecies, Psychic Powers, Mind Over Matter, & Transformations.

Mysteries Of Time And Space

PUBLISHING COMPANY: Whitford Press/Schiffer Publishing Limited EDITOR: Brad Steiger TOPICS: New Age, UFO's, Paranormal Phenomena TYPE: Book PRICE: $12.95

Mysteries: An Investigation Into The Occult, The Paranormal And The Supernatural

PUBLISHING COMPANY: Putnam Publishing Group EDITOR: Colin Wilson TOPICS: Paranormal Phenomena TYPE: Book PRICE: $12.95

Mysteries: Papers From The Eranos Yearbooks

PUBLISHING COMPANY: Princeton University Press EDITOR: Joseph Campbell TOPICS: New Age, Paranormal Phenomena TYPE: Book PRICE: $14.95

Mysterious America

PUBLISHING COMPANY: Faber & Faber, Affil. of Faber & Faber, Ltd., London EDITOR: L. Coleman TOPICS: Paranormal Phenomena TYPE: Book PRICE: $11.95

Mystery Of The Mandalas

PUBLISHING COMPANY: Theosophical University Press EDITOR: H. Copony TOPICS: Color Therapy TYPE: Book PRICE: $18.95

Mystic Spiral: Journey Of The Soul

PUBLISHING COMPANY: Thames & Hudson EDITOR: J. Purce TOPICS: New Age TYPE: Book PRICE: $11.95

Mystic Test Book

PUBLISHING COMPANY: Newcastle Publishing Co., Inc. EDITOR: O. Richmond TOPICS: New Age, Occult, Psychic TYPE: Book PRICE: $9.95

Mystical I

PUBLISHING COMPANY: Harper & Row Publishers, Inc. EDITOR: Joel Goldsmith TOPICS: New Age TYPE: Book PRICE: $12.95

Mystical Key To The English Alphabet

PUBLISHING COMPANY: Destiny Books, Inner Traditions International, Ltd. EDITOR: Robert M. Hoffstein TOPICS: Occult TYPE: Book PRICE: $12.95

Mystical Lore Of Precious Stones Vol.1: Superstitions, Talismans And Amulets, Crystal-Gazing

PUBLISHING COMPANY: Newcastle Publishing Co., Inc. EDITOR: G. Kunz TOPICS: Metaphysics TYPE: Book PRICE: $9.95

Mystical Lore Of Precious Stones Vol.2: Birthstones, Astrology, Therapeutic & Religious Uses

PUBLISHING COMPANY: Newcastle Publishing Co., Inc. EDITOR: G. Kunz TOPICS: Metaphysics TYPE: Book PRICE: $9.95

Mystical, Magical, Marvelous World Of Dreams

PUBLISHING COMPANY: Sparrow Hawk Press EDITOR: Wilda Tanner TOPICS: Dreams TYPE: Book PRICE: $14.95

Mysticism

PUBLISHING COMPANY: New American Library EDITOR: E. Underhill TOPICS: Paranormal Phenomena, Spirituality TYPE: Book PRICE: $12.95

Mysticism And Philosophy

PUBLISHING COMPANY: St. Martin's Press, Inc. EDITOR: W.T. Stace TOPICS: Paranormal Phenomena, Spirituality TYPE: Book PRICE: $11.95

Mysticism And The Occult: A Concise Encyclopedia

PUBLISHING COMPANY: Philosophical Library, Inc. EDITOR: F. Levine TOPICS: Occult, Paranormal Phenomena TYPE: Book PRICE: $24.95

Mysticism: Journey Within

PUBLISHING COMPANY: Astara Foundation, Inc. EDITOR: E. Chaney TOPICS: Metaphysics, Spirituality, Psychic TYPE: Book PRICE: $13.95

Mysticism: The Ultimate Experience

PUBLISHING COMPANY: Supreme Grand Lodge of AMORC, Inc. EDITOR: C. Poole TOPICS: Paranormal Phenomena, Spirituality TYPE: Book PRICE: $12.50

Mystics, Magicians And Medicine People: Tales Of A Wanderer

PUBLISHING COMPANY: Paragon House EDITOR: D. Boyd TOPICS: Yoga, Spirituality TYPE: Book PRICE: $17.95

Myth Of Freedom

PUBLISHING COMPANY: Shambhala Publications, Inc. EDITOR: C. Trungpa TOPICS: Spirituality TYPE: Book PRICE: $12.95

Mythic Imagination: Your Quest For Meaning Through Personal Mythology

PUBLISHING COMPANY: Bantam New Age Books EDITOR: Stephen Larsen TOPICS: New Age, Psychology TYPE: Book PRICE: $12.95

Nada Brahma: The World Is Sound-Music & The Landscape Of Consciousness

PUBLISHING COMPANY: Destiny Books, Inner Traditions International, Ltd. EDITOR: J. Berendt TOPICS: Psychology TYPE: Book PRICE: $16.95

NALTA Exchange

PUBLISHING COMPANY: NALTA Foundation, Inc. TOPICS: New Age, Holistic Healing TYPE: Booklet

Naming God

PUBLISHING COMPANY: Paragon House EDITOR: R. Scharlemann TOPICS: Paranormal Phenomena, Spirituality TYPE: Book PRICE: $12.95

NAPSAC Directory Of Alternative Birth Services And Consumer Guide

PUBLISHING COMPANY: National Association Of Parents & Professionals For Safe Alternatives In Childbirth TOPICS: Holistic Healing, Birth TYPE: Directory

NASO International Astrological Directory

PUBLISHING COMPANY: National Astrological Society EDITOR: Barbara Somerfield TOPICS: Astrology TYPE: Directory DATE: 1984; 78 pgs. FREQ: bi-annual PRICE: $6.00

National Catalog Of Occult Bookstores

PUBLISHING COMPANY: Ghost Research Society EDITOR: Dale Kaczmarek TOPICS: Occult TYPE: Directory PRICE: $6.50 DESCRIPTION: Cross-country list of Occult Bookstores, hours of operation & their specialties.

National Directory Of Alternative Schools

PUBLISHING COMPANY: National Coalition Of Alternative Community Schools TOPICS: New Age TYPE: Directory

National Directory Of Holistic Health Professionals

PUBLISHING COMPANY: Association For Holistic Health EDITOR: Margaret Marshik TOPICS: Holistic Healing TYPE: Directory

National New Age Yellow Pages: United States Guide To Conscoiusness-Raising Services, Products & Organizations

PUBLISHING COMPANY: Highgate House Publishers EDITOR: Marcia Gervase Ingenito TOPICS: New Age, Channeling, Occult, Parapsychology TYPE: Directory DATE: 1988 PRICE: $12.95 DESCRIPTION: Comprehensive directory includes 150 national, New Age categories such as acupuncture, A Course In Miracle Studies, associations, astrologers, tapes, bodywork, music, spiritual centers, yoga, channeling, crystals, herbs, metaphysical counselors, etc. Also prints articles & ads. Advertises products & services to the New Age market. Published periodically.

National Psychic Directory

PUBLISHING COMPANY: National Psychic Directory TOPICS: New Age, Psychic, Channeling TYPE: Directory

National Register Of Haunted Locations

PUBLISHING COMPANY: Ghost Research Society EDITOR: Dale Kaczmarek TOPICS: Ghosts, Parapsychology TYPE: Directory PRICE: $6.50 DESCRIPTION: Lists haunted locations, houses & landmarks in the U.S. Gives hours of operations, tours & reference books.

National Spiritualist Association Of Churches-Yearbook

PUBLISHING COMPANY: National Spiritualist Association Of Churches EDITOR: Rev. Elizabeth R. Edgar TOPICS: Psychic Phenomena TYPE: Yearbook

Native American Prophecies: History, Wisdom & Startling Predictions Of Visionary Native American

PUBLISHING COMPANY: Paragon House EDITOR: Scott Peterson TOPICS: Metaphysics, Psychic TYPE: Book PRICE: $12.95

Natural Family Doctor: Comprehensive Self-Help Guide To Health & Natural Medicine

PUBLISHING COMPANY: Simon & Schuster, Inc. EDITOR: Andrew Stanway TOPICS: Holistic Health TYPE: Guide PRICE: $12.95

Natural Healing Through Macrobiotics

PUBLISHING COMPANY: Japan Publications, Inc. EDITOR: M. Kushi TOPICS: Health Food, Holistic Health, Homeopathy TYPE: Book PRICE: $13.95

Natural Healing With Herbs

PUBLISHING COMPANY: Hohm Press EDITOR: H. Santillo TOPICS: Holistic Health, Herbalogy TYPE: Book PRICE: $12.95

Natural Health, Natural Medicine: A Comprehensive Guide To Wellness & Self-Care

PUBLISHING COMPANY: Houghton Mifflin Company EDITOR: A. Weil TOPICS: Holistic Health TYPE: Guide PRICE: $19.95

Natural Yellow Pages

PUBLISHING COMPANY: Natural Yellow Pages EDITOR: Marie Russell TOPICS: Holistic Healing, New Age TYPE: Directory; 48 pgs. FREQ: annually CIRC: 21,000 PRICE: $2.00 DESCRIPTION: A New Age resource directory for Floridians. Features many categories including business, counseling, food, holistic health, and much more.

Nature Of Personal Reality: A Seth Book

PUBLISHING COMPANY: Prentice-Hall, Inc. EDITOR: Jane Roberts TOPICS: Channeling TYPE: Book PRICE: $10.95

Nature Of Reality: A Book Of Explanations From Hilarion

PUBLISHING COMPANY: Marcus Books Hilarion TOPICS: New Age TYPE: Book PRICE: $7.95

Nature's Big Beautiful Bountiful Feel-Good Book

PUBLISHING COMPANY: Keats Publishing, Inc. TOPICS: Holistic Healing TYPE: Book

Nature's Pharmacy: A History Of Plants & Healing

PUBLISHING COMPANY: Trafalgar Square, Inc., Div. of David & Charles, Inc. EDITOR: C. Stockwell TOPICS: Holistic Health, Herbalogy TYPE: Book PRICE: $24.95

NCGR Membership Directory

PUBLISHING COMPANY: National Council For Geocosmic Research, Inc. EDITOR: Mary Downing TOPICS: Astrology TYPE: Directory DATE: 1984 SIZE: 5.5 x 8.5; 48 pgs. CIRC: 3,000

Nectar Of Chanting

PUBLISHING COMPANY: S.Y.D.A. Foundation/Siddha Yoga Meditation Ashram Muktananda TOPICS: Spirituality TYPE: Book PRICE: $9.95

Nectar Of Devotion

PUBLISHING COMPANY: Bhaktivedanta Book Trust EDITOR: S. Prabhupada TOPICS: Spirituality TYPE: Book PRICE: $14.95

Needles Of Stone Revisited

PUBLISHING COMPANY: Gothic Image Publications EDITOR: Tom Graves TOPICS: Paranormal Phenomena TYPE: Book

Neoplationic Writings Of Numenius

PUBLISHING COMPANY: Selene Books EDITOR: K. Guthrie TOPICS: Paranormal Phenomena TYPE: Book PRICE: $15.00

New Age Astrology Annual Yearbook

PUBLISHING COMPANY: Astro-Psychology Institute TOPICS: Astrology TYPE: Yearbook FREQ: annually

New Age Astrology Guide

PUBLISHING COMPANY: Milo Kovar TOPICS: Astrology TYPE: Guide DATE: 1972 FREQ: Annual CIRC: 25,000 PRICE: $3.00 DESCRIPTION: Explains the changes in planetary patterns and their effect on the twelve zodiacal signs during the timespan of a year.

New Age Catalogue, The

PUBLISHING COMPANY: Island Publishing Co. EDITOR: Paul Zuromski, Carol Kramer TOPICS: Metaphysics, New Age TYPE: Directory DATE: 1988 SIZE: 8 1/2x 11 PRICE: $14.95 DESCRIPTION: New Age directory/catalog covering ideas, concepts & resources related to the New Age movement & metaphysics. Deals with numerous New Age topics from channeling to Zen. Gives the basic concepts behind each topic & the finest quality resources including books, tapes, organizations, magazines & manufacturers.

New Age Community Guidebook

PUBLISHING COMPANY: Community Referral Service TOPICS: New Age TYPE: Directory DATE: 1985 DESCRIPTION: Contains articles & resources on 210 communities in the U.S. & around the world.

New Age Dictionary

PUBLISHING COMPANY: Japan Publications, Inc. EDITOR: Alex Jack TOPICS: New Age TYPE: Book PRICE: $14.95

New Age Directory

PUBLISHING COMPANY: New Age Directory TOPICS: Metaphysics, Spirituality, New Age TYPE: Directory

New Age Directory

PUBLISHING COMPANY: New Age Directory TOPICS: New Age TYPE: Directory

New Age Encyclopedia

PUBLISHING COMPANY: Gale Research Company EDITOR: J. Gordon Melton TOPICS: Psychic Phenomena TYPE: Directory DATE: 1990 SIZE: 6 x 9; 586 pgs. DESCRIPTION: Provides descriptions and definitions of terms, people, organizations, etc. related to the New Age movement in an encyclopedia format. Also contains a listing of educational institutions offering courses and degree-bearing programs.

New Age Herbalist: How To Use Herbs For Healing, Nutrition, Body Care & Relaxation

PUBLISHING COMPANY: Macmillan Publishing Co., Inc. EDITOR: R. Mabey, M. McIntyre TOPICS:

Holistic Health, Herbalogy **TYPE**: Book **PRICE**: $16.95

New Age Tantra Yoga
PUBLISHING COMPANY: World University Press **EDITOR**: Howard John Zitko **TYPE**: Book **DATE**: 1974 **SIZE**: 5 1/2 x 8; 172 pgs. **PRICE**: $8.50 **DESCRIPTION**: The Tantra philosophy as the marriage standard for the New Age.

New Book Of Runes: A Handbook For Use Of An Ancient Oracle
PUBLISHING COMPANY: St. Martin's Press, Inc. **EDITOR**: R. Blum **TOPICS**: Runes **TYPE**: Book **PRICE**: $24.95

New Cells, New Bodies, New Life
PUBLISHING COMPANY: Spiritual Education Endeavours **EDITOR**: Virginia Essene **TOPICS**: New Age, Spirituality **TYPE**: Book

New Earth-New Truth
PUBLISHING COMPANY: Teamup **EDITOR**: Jean K. Foster **TOPICS**: New Age **TYPE**: Book

New Healing Yourself: Natural Remedies For Adults & Children
PUBLISHING COMPANY: Crossing Press **EDITOR**: Joy Gardner **TOPICS**: Holistic Healing, Homeopathy **TYPE**: Book **PRICE**: $12.95

New Heaven, New Earth
PUBLISHING COMPANY: Marcus Books Hilarion **TOPICS**: New Age **TYPE**: Book **PRICE**: $7.95

New Horizons: Explorations In Science
PUBLISHING COMPANY: Globe Press Books **EDITOR**: P.D. Ouspensky **TOPICS**: Spirituality **TYPE**: Book **PRICE**: $14.95

New Jersey Naturally
PUBLISHING COMPANY: City Spirit Publications **EDITOR**: Jerome Rubin **TOPICS**: New Age **TYPE**: Directory

New Magus
PUBLISHING COMPANY: Llewellyn Publications **EDITOR**: D. Tyson **TOPICS**: Occult, Witchcraft **TYPE**: Book **PRICE**: $12.95

New Marketing Opportunities
PUBLISHING COMPANY: First Editions **EDITOR**: Sophia Tarila, Ph.D., Harry Truner **TOPICS**: New Age, Metaphysics, Holistic Health **TYPE**: Directory **DATE**: 1990 **SIZE**: 8 1/2x11; 450 pgs. **FREQ**: yearly **PRICE**: $89.95 **TERM**: 2 Vols. **PRICE PER COPY**: $59.95 **DESCRIPTION**: A two volume directory geared toward the individual or company wishing to market a product or service to the New Age, Metaphysical or Holistic Health related field. Vol. 1 provides lists of bookstores. Vol. 2 offers lists of publishers, publication, mailing lists, services, co-op marketing programs, etc.

New Model Of Health And Disease
PUBLISHING COMPANY: North Atlantic Books **EDITOR**: G. Vithoulkas **TOPICS**: Homeopathy **TYPE**: Book **PRICE**: $12.95

New Tarot: Modern Variations Of Ancient Images
PUBLISHING COMPANY: Overlook Press **EDITOR**: Rachel Pollack **TOPICS**: Tarot, Metaphysics **TYPE**: Book **PRICE**: $22.50

New Teachings For An Awakening Humanity
PUBLISHING COMPANY: Spiritual Education Endeavours **EDITOR**: Eileen Caddy, John Randolph **TOPICS**: New Age, Spirituality **TYPE**: Book

New Thoughts On Tarot: Transcripts From The First Newcastle International Tarot Symposium
PUBLISHING COMPANY: Newcastle Publishing Co., Inc. **EDITOR**: K. Younger **TOPICS**: Tarot **TYPE**: Book **PRICE**: $12.95

New View Over Atlantis
PUBLISHING COMPANY: Harper & Row Publishers, Inc. **EDITOR**: J. Mitchell **TOPICS**: New Age **TYPE**: Book **PRICE**: $12.95

New World-New Age Directory
PUBLISHING COMPANY: New World-New Age Directory **TOPICS**: Holistic Healing **TYPE**: Directory

New York Naturally
PUBLISHING COMPANY: City Spirit Publications **EDITOR**: Jerome Rubin **TOPICS**: New Age, Holistic Health **TYPE**: Directory **DATE**: 1987 **CIRC**: 200,000 **PRICE PER COPY**: $5.95 **DESCRIPTION**: Serving New York, New Jersey and Connecticut with resource guidesfor each area featuring health-oriented services, products & ads.

Newcastle Guide To Healing With Gemstones: How To Use Over 70 Different Gemstone Energies
PUBLISHING COMPANY: Newcastle Publishing Co., Inc. **EDITOR**: P. Chase, J. Pawlik **TOPICS**: New Age, Crystals **TYPE**: Book **PRICE**: $12.95

Next Step...Re-Unification With The Presence Of God Within Our Hearts
PUBLISHING COMPANY: New Age Study Of Humanity's Purpose **EDITOR**: Patricia Cota-Robles **TOPICS**: Spirituality **TYPE**: Book **PRICE**: $14.98

Ngondro
PUBLISHING COMPANY: Blue Dolphin Publishing, Inc. **TOPICS**: New Age **TYPE**: Book **PRICE**: $9.95

Nicholas Roerich: The Life And Art Of A Russian Master
PUBLISHING COMPANY: Inner Traditions International, Ltd. **EDITOR**: J. Decter **TOPICS**: New Age **TYPE**: Book **PRICE**: $39.95

Night-Side Of Nature: Or, Ghosts And Ghost-Seers
PUBLISHING COMPANY: Aquarian Press **EDITOR**: C. Crowe **TOPICS**: Psychic, Paranormal Phenomena **TYPE**: Book **PRICE**: $14.95

Nine-Headed Dragon River
PUBLISHING COMPANY: Shambhala Publications, Inc. **EDITOR**: P. Matthiessen **TOPICS**: Spirituality **TYPE**: Book **PRICE**: $12.50

Nirvana-Tao: The Secret Meditation Techniques Of The Taoist And Buddhist Masters
PUBLISHING COMPANY: Inner Traditions International, Ltd. **EDITOR**: D. Odler **TOPICS**: Spirituality, Meditation **TYPE**: Book **PRICE**: $12.95

No More Secondhand Art: Awakening The Artist Within
PUBLISHING COMPANY: Shambhala Publications, Inc. **EDITOR**: P. London **TOPICS**: New Age **TYPE**: Book **PRICE**: $10.95

No Nonsense Hand Reading
PUBLISHING COMPANY: Cheirological Society **EDITOR**: Shifu T. Dukes **TOPICS**: Palmistry, Holistic Health **TYPE**: Book **DATE**: 1987

Nobody Special
PUBLISHING COMPANY: KemCo **EDITOR**: Keith McNeal, Jr. **TOPICS**: New Age **TYPE**: Book

Non-Meridial Points Of Acupuncture: A Guide To Their Location & Therapeutic Use
PUBLISHING COMPANY: Collins, Div. of William Collins **EDITOR**: Royston Low **TOPICS**: Holistic Health, Acupuncture **TYPE**: Guide **PRICE**: $29.95

North & South Nodes
PUBLISHING COMPANY: Arthur Publications, Inc. **EDITOR**: Debra Sapp **TOPICS**: Astrology **TYPE**: Book **DATE**: 1978

North American Holistic Resources Directory
PUBLISHING COMPANY: Holistic Resources **TOPICS**: New Age, Holistic Health **TYPE**: Directory

Northwest Indiana Psychic Directory
PUBLISHING COMPANY: Ghost Research Society **EDITOR**: Dale Kaczmarek **TOPICS**: Ghosts, Psychic Phenomena, Parapsychology, Reincarnation, Past Life Regression **TYPE**: Directory **PRICE**: $7.00

Nostradamus And His Prophecies
PUBLISHING COMPANY: Outlet Book Co., Affil. of Crowns Pubs., Inc. **EDITOR**: E. Leoni **TOPICS**: Psychic, Spirituality **TYPE**: Book **PRICE**: $9.95

Nostradamus And The Millennium: Predictions Of The Future
PUBLISHING COMPANY: Doubleday & Co.,Inc. **EDITOR**: J. Hogue **TOPICS**: Psychic, Spirituality **TYPE**: Book **PRICE**: $17.95

Nostradamus: Countdown To Apocalypse
PUBLISHING COMPANY: Henry Holt & Co. **EDITOR**: J-C DeFontbrune **TOPICS**: Psychic, Spirituality **TYPE**: Book **PRICE**: $12.95

Nostradamus: Prophecies Of Present Times?
PUBLISHING COMPANY: Aquarian Press **EDITOR**: D. Frances **TOPICS**: Psychic, Spirituality **TYPE**: Book **PRICE**: $9.95

Not Necessarily The New Age: Critical Essays

PUBLISHING COMPANY: Prometheus Books EDITOR: Robert Basil TOPICS: Skepticism, New Age TYPE: Book PRICE: $19.95

Notebooks Of Paul Brunton Vol. 1: Perspectives

PUBLISHING COMPANY: Larson Publications EDITOR: Paul Brunton TOPICS: New Age, Paranormal Phenomena, Spirituality TYPE: Book PRICE: $14.95

Notebooks Of Paul Brunton Vol. 2: The Quest

PUBLISHING COMPANY: Larson Publications EDITOR: Paul Brunton TOPICS: New Age, Paranormal Phenomena, Spirituality TYPE: Book PRICE: $14.95

Notebooks Of Paul Brunton Vol. 3: Part 1 - Practices For The Quest; Part 2 - Relax & Retreat

PUBLISHING COMPANY: Larson Publications EDITOR: Paul Brunton TOPICS: New Age, Paranormal Phenomena, Spirituality, Meditation TYPE: Book PRICE: $14.95

Notebooks Of Paul Brunton Vol. 4: Part 1 - Meditation

PUBLISHING COMPANY: Larson Publications EDITOR: Paul Brunton TOPICS: New Age, Paranormal Phenomena, Spirituality, Meditation TYPE: Book PRICE: $12.50

Notebooks Of Paul Brunton Vol. 4: Part 2: The Body

PUBLISHING COMPANY: Larson Publications EDITOR: Paul Brunton TOPICS: New Age, Paranormal Phenomena, Spirituality TYPE: Book PRICE: $9.95

Notebooks Of Paul Brunton Vol. 5: Part 1 - Emotions & Ethics; Part 2 - The Intellect

PUBLISHING COMPANY: Larson Publications EDITOR: Paul Brunton TOPICS: New Age, Paranormal Phenomena, Spirituality TYPE: Book PRICE: $14.95

Notebooks Of Paul Brunton Vol. 6: Ego, From Birth To Rebirth

PUBLISHING COMPANY: Larson Publications EDITOR: Paul Brunton TOPICS: New Age, Paranormal Phenomena, Spirituality, Birth, Reincarnation TYPE: Book PRICE: $14.95

Notebooks Of Paul Brunton Vol. 7: Part 1 - Healing Of The Self; Part 2 - Negatives

PUBLISHING COMPANY: Larson Publications EDITOR: Paul Brunton TOPICS: New Age, Paranormal Phenomena, Spirituality, Holistic Healing TYPE: Book PRICE: $14.95

Notebooks Of Paul Brunton Vol. 8: Reflections

PUBLISHING COMPANY: Larson Publications EDITOR: Paul Brunton TOPICS: New Age, Paranormal Phenomena, Spirituality TYPE: Book PRICE: $12.50

Notebooks Of Paul Brunton Vol. 9: Human Experience/The Artist In Culture

PUBLISHING COMPANY: Larson Publications EDITOR: Paul Brunton TOPICS: New Age, Paranormal Phenomena, Spirituality TYPE: Book PRICE: $14.95

Notebooks Of Paul Brunton Vol. 10: Orient - Its Legacy To The West

PUBLISHING COMPANY: Larson Publications EDITOR: Paul Brunton TOPICS: New Age, Paranormal Phenomena, Spirituality TYPE: Book PRICE: $12.50

Notebooks Of Paul Brunton Vol. 11: Sensitives - Dynamics & Dangers Of Mysticism

PUBLISHING COMPANY: Larson Publications EDITOR: Paul Brunton TOPICS: New Age, Paranormal Phenomena, Spirituality TYPE: Book PRICE: $14.95

Notebooks Of Paul Brunton Vol. 12: The Religious Urge & Reverential Life

PUBLISHING COMPANY: Larson Publications EDITOR: Paul Brunton TOPICS: New Age, Spirituality, Paranormal Phenomena TYPE: Book PRICE: $14.95

Notebooks Of Paul Brunton Vol. 13: Relativity, Philosophy & Mind - Through Knowledge To Wisdom

PUBLISHING COMPANY: Larson Publications EDITOR: Paul Brunton TOPICS: New Age, Paranormal Phenomena, Spirituality TYPE: Book PRICE: $14.95

Notebooks Of Paul Brunton Vol. 14: Inspiration And The Overself

PUBLISHING COMPANY: Larson Publications EDITOR: P. Brunton TOPICS: Paranormal Phenomena, Spirituality TYPE: Book PRICE: $12.50

Notebooks Of Paul Brunton Vol. 15: Advanced Contemplation - The Peace Within You

PUBLISHING COMPANY: Larson Publications EDITOR: Paul Brunton TOPICS: New Age, Paranormal Phenomena, Spirituality TYPE: Book PRICE: $14.95

Notebooks Of Paul Brunton Vol. 16: Enlightened Mind, Devine Mind

PUBLISHING COMPANY: Larson Publications EDITOR: Paul Brunton TOPICS: New Age, Paranormal Phenomena, Spirituality TYPE: Book PRICE: $14.95

Nothing Real Can Be Threatened

PUBLISHING COMPANY: Life Action Press, Div. of Foundation for Life Action EDITOR: T. Singh TOPICS: Spirituality TYPE: Book PRICE: $12.95

Nothingness Beyond God: An Introduction To The Philosohy Of Nishida Kitaro

PUBLISHING COMPANY: Paragon House EDITOR: Robert Carter TOPICS: Yoga, Spirituality TYPE: Book PRICE: $22.95

Nuclear Evolution

PUBLISHING COMPANY: University Of The Trees EDITOR: C. Hills TOPICS: New Age, Psychology TYPE: Book PRICE: $29.95

Numeric Personality: The 45 Unique Personality Patterns In Ourselves & In Our Relationships

PUBLISHING COMPANY: Doubleday & Co.,Inc. EDITOR: R. Poole TOPICS: Numerology, Parapsychology TYPE: Book PRICE: $12.95

Numerology

PUBLISHING COMPANY: Inner Traditions International, Ltd. EDITOR: Harish Johari TOPICS: Numerology TYPE: Book PRICE: $12.95

Numerology And The Divine Triangle

PUBLISHING COMPANY: Whitford Press/Schiffer Publishing Limited EDITOR: F. Javane, D. Bunker TOPICS: Numerology TYPE: Book PRICE: $14.95

Numerology And Your Future

PUBLISHING COMPANY: Whitford Press/Schiffer Publishing Limited EDITOR: D. Bunker TOPICS: Numerology TYPE: Book PRICE: $12.95

Numerology In Tantra, Ayurveda And Astrology: A Key To Human Behavior

PUBLISHING COMPANY: Destiny Books, Inner Traditions International, Ltd. EDITOR: H. Johari TOPICS: Numerology, Parapsychology TYPE: Book PRICE: $12.95

Numerology Kit

PUBLISHING COMPANY: New American Library EDITOR: C. Andrienne TOPICS: Numerology TYPE: Book PRICE: $12.95

Numerology Vol. 1: The Personality Reading

PUBLISHING COMPANY: Newcastle Publishing Co., Inc. EDITOR: M. Goodwin TOPICS: Numerology TYPE: Book PRICE: $12.95

Numerology Vol. 2: Advanced Personality Analysis, And Reading The Past, Present And Future

PUBLISHING COMPANY: Newcastle Publishing Co., Inc. EDITOR: M. Goodwin TOPICS: Numerology TYPE: Book PRICE: $14.95

Numerology Workbook: Understanding And Using The Power Of Numbers

PUBLISHING COMPANY: Aquarian Press EDITOR: J. Line TOPICS: Numerology TYPE: Book PRICE: $12.95

Numerology, Astrology And Dreams

PUBLISHING COMPANY: Whitford Press/Schiffer Publishing Limited EDITOR: D. Bunker TOPICS: Numerology TYPE: Book PRICE: $13.95

Numerology: Key To The Tarot

PUBLISHING COMPANY: Whitford Press/Schiffer Publishing Limited EDITOR: S. Konraad TOPICS: Numerology, Tarot, Metaphysics TYPE: Book PRICE: $13.95

Numerology: The Language Of Life

PUBLISHING COMPANY: Skidmore-Roth Publishers EDITOR: Ruth Dayer TOPICS: Numerology, Parapsychology TYPE: Book PRICE: $11.95

Numerology: The Romance In Your Name

PUBLISHING COMPANY: DeVorss & Company EDITOR: Juno Jordan TOPICS: Numerology TYPE: Book PRICE: $12.95

Nutrition Almanac

PUBLISHING COMPANY: McGraw Hill Book Co., Div. of McGraw Hill, Inc. EDITOR: J. Kirschmann TOPICS: Holistic Health TYPE: Book PRICE: $15.95

Nutritional Desk Reference Book

PUBLISHING COMPANY: Keats Publishing, Inc. EDITOR: R. Garrison, E. Somer TOPICS: Nutrition, Holistic Health TYPE: Book PRICE: $15.95

Nutritional Influences On Illness: A Sourcebook Of Clinical Research

PUBLISHING COMPANY: Keats Publishing, Inc. EDITOR: M. Werbach TOPICS: Nutrition, Holistic Health TYPE: Book PRICE: $17.95

Obstacles To Peace

PUBLISHING COMPANY: Foundation For A Course In Miracles Conference/Retreat Center EDITOR: K. Wapnick TOPICS: Spirituality TYPE: Book PRICE: $12.00

Occult Conspiracy: Secret Societies - Their Influence & Power In World History

PUBLISHING COMPANY: Destiny Books, Inner Traditions International, Ltd. EDITOR: Michael Howard TOPICS: Occult TYPE: Book PRICE: $10.95

Occult Establishment

PUBLISHING COMPANY: Open Court Publishing Co. EDITOR: James Webb TOPICS: Occult TYPE: Book PRICE: $11.95

Occult Experience

PUBLISHING COMPANY: Avery Publishing Group, Inc. EDITOR: Nevill Drury TOPICS: Occult, Psychic Phenomena TYPE: Book PRICE: $9.95

Occult Japan

PUBLISHING COMPANY: Inner Traditions International, Ltd. EDITOR: Percival Lowell TOPICS: Occult TYPE: Book PRICE: $12.95

Occult Principles Of Health And Healing

PUBLISHING COMPANY: Rosicrucian Fellowship EDITOR: M. Heindel TOPICS: Spirituality, Psychic Healing, Occult TYPE: Book PRICE: $12.95

Occult Publications

PUBLISHING COMPANY: Ghost Research Society EDITOR: Dale Kaczmarek TOPICS: Ghosts, Psychic Phenomena, Parapsychology, Reincarnation, Past Life Regression, Metaphysics, Holistic Health TYPE: Directory PRICE: $6.50 DESCRIPTION: Lists newsletters, tabloids, directories, encyclopedias, etc. dealing with the occult. Includes Parapsychology, Metaphysics, Demonology, Holistic Health.

Occult Underground

PUBLISHING COMPANY: Open Court Publishing Co. EDITOR: James Webb TOPICS: Occult TYPE: Book PRICE: $9.95

Occult World

PUBLISHING COMPANY: Theosophical University Press EDITOR: A.P. Sinnett TOPICS: Occult, Paranormal Phenomena TYPE: Book PRICE: $12.95

Occultism Update

PUBLISHING COMPANY: Gale Research Company EDITOR: Leslie Shepard TOPICS: Parapsychology TYPE: Directory DATE: 1978; 150 pgs. FREQ: Irregular PRICE PER COPY: $74.00 DESCRIPTION: Supplement that updates the Encyclopedia of Occultism & Parasychology & reports on new events & discoveries in the field of occultism & parapsychology.

Ocean Of Wisdom: Guidelines For Living

PUBLISHING COMPANY: Connecting Link EDITOR: Lama Dalai TOPICS: Spirituality TYPE: Book PRICE: $13.95

Off The Beaten Path: Guide To Unusual How-To Sources

PUBLISHING COMPANY: Light Living Library TOPICS: Psychic Phenomena TYPE: Directory

Official Handbook Of The Radiance Technique, The

PUBLISHING COMPANY: Radiance Technique Association International, Inc. EDITOR: Dr. Barbara Ray TOPICS: New Age TYPE: Handbook PRICE: $17.75

Old Path, White Clouds: Walking In The Footsteps Of The Buddha

PUBLISHING COMPANY: Parallax Press-Buddhism EDITOR: T. Hanh TOPICS: New Age, Spirituality TYPE: Book PRICE: $25.00

Omega New Age Directory

PUBLISHING COMPANY: Valley Newspapers EDITOR: Joy Rodgers, John Rodgers TOPICS: Holistic Healing, New Age, Metaphysics, Spirituality, Psychology, UFO's, Astrology TYPE: Directory DATE: 1972; 32 pgs. FREQ: monthly CIRC: 25,000 PRICE: $15.00 TERM: yearly PRICE PER COPY: $1.00 DESCRIPTION: Features reviews and articles on health, food, metaphysics, psychology, religions, women's issues and the environment. Offers book, music & video reviews, UFO data, Astrology & Self-Help columns, lists of ethical psychics & wholistic practitioners. Newspaper format. Accepts advertising.

On Being Mindless: Buddhist Meditation And The Mind-Body Problem

PUBLISHING COMPANY: Open Court Publishing Co. EDITOR: P. Griffiths TOPICS: Meditation, Spirituality TYPE: Book PRICE: $12.95

On Dreams And Death: A Jungian Interpretation

PUBLISHING COMPANY: Shambhala Publications, Inc. EDITOR: M.L. Von Franz TOPICS: Death TYPE: Book PRICE: $12.95

On The Air

PUBLISHING COMPANY: On The Air TOPICS: New Age TYPE: Directory DESCRIPTION: Lists radio stations that play New Age music recorded by independent musicians.

On The Mysteries: Iamblichus

PUBLISHING COMPANY: Wizards Bookshelf EDITOR: Thomas Taylor TOPICS: Paranormal Phenomena TYPE: Book PRICE: $20.00

On The Mystical Shape Of The Godhead: Basic Concepts In Kabbalah

PUBLISHING COMPANY: Schocken Books EDITOR: G. Scholem TOPICS: Kabbalah TYPE: Book PRICE: $24.95

Once And Future Goddess: A Symbol For Our Time

PUBLISHING COMPANY: Harper & Row Publishers, Inc. EDITOR: E. Gadon TOPICS: Spirituality TYPE: Book PRICE: $22.50

Open Exchange

PUBLISHING COMPANY: Open Exchange EDITOR: Bart Brodsky TOPICS: New Age, Metaphysics, Spirituality TYPE: Directory DATE: 1974; 64 pgs. FREQ: 4 issues/yr CIRC: 100,000 PRICE: $5.00 DESCRIPTION: Directory of services and classes in the Bay area.

Open Mind, Discriminating Mind: Reflections In Human Possibilities

PUBLISHING COMPANY: Harper & Row Publishers, Inc. EDITOR: C. Tart TOPICS: Spirituality, New Age, Psychology TYPE: Book PRICE: $18.95

Opening Doors Within

PUBLISHING COMPANY: Findhorn Foundation & Press EDITOR: Eileen Caddy TOPICS: Spirituality TYPE: Book PRICE: $16.95

Opening Of The Way: Practical Guide To The Wisdom Of Ancient Egypt

PUBLISHING COMPANY: Inner Traditions International, Ltd. EDITOR: I. Schwaller de Lubicz TOPICS: New Age, Paranormal Phenomena TYPE: Book PRICE: $10.95

Opening The Eye Of New Awareness
PUBLISHING COMPANY: Wisdom Publications **EDITOR:** Lama Dalai **TOPICS:** Spirituality **TYPE:** Book **PRICE:** $10.95

Opening To Channel: How To Connect With Your Inner Guide
PUBLISHING COMPANY: H.J. Kramer, Inc. **EDITOR:** S. Roman, D. Packer **TOPICS:** Psychic, Channeling **TYPE:** Book **PRICE:** $12.95

Opening Up To Your Psychic Self
PUBLISHING COMPANY: Nevertheless Press **EDITOR:** P. Stevens **TOPICS:** Psychic **TYPE:** Book **PRICE:** $9.95

Opening Up: The Healing Power Of Confiding In Others
PUBLISHING COMPANY: William Morrow & Co. **EDITOR:** James Pennebaker **TOPICS:** Holistic Health, Body-Mind Connection, Psychology **TYPE:** Book **PRICE:** $18.95

Openmind/Wholemind, Parenting And Teaching Tomorrows Children Today
PUBLISHING COMPANY: B.L. Winch & Associates/Jalmar Press **EDITOR:** Bob Samples **TOPICS:** New Age **TYPE:** Book **SIZE:** 7x9; 272 pgs. **PRICE:** $14.95

Opus 50
PUBLISHING COMPANY: Technology Group, The **EDITOR:** Nelson White, Anne White **TYPE:** Book; 75 pgs. **PRICE:** $18.00

Or Chadash
PUBLISHING COMPANY: P'Nai Or Religious Fellowship **TOPICS:** Spirituality **TYPE:** Book **PRICE:** $20.00

Oracle Of Geomancy: Techniques Of Earth Divination
PUBLISHING COMPANY: Avery Publishing Group, Inc. **EDITOR:** Stephen Skinner **TOPICS:** Psychic, Metaphysics **TYPE:** Book **PRICE:** $12.95

Order In Space: A Design Sourcebook
PUBLISHING COMPANY: Thames & Hudson **EDITOR:** K. Critchlow **TOPICS:** New Age **TYPE:** Book **PRICE:** $14.95

Organic Agriculture: What The States Are Doing
PUBLISHING COMPANY: Americans For Safe Food/Center For Science In The Public Interest **TOPICS:** Health Food **TYPE:** Book

Organization Of Psychic Research Associates-Membership Directory
PUBLISHING COMPANY: Organization Of Psychic Research Associates **EDITOR:** Wilma Arnold **TOPICS:** Psychic Phenomena **TYPE:** Directory

Origin Of The Egyptians
PUBLISHING COMPANY: Philosophical Research Society, Inc. **EDITOR:** A. LePlongeon **TOPICS:** New Age **TYPE:** Book **PRICE:** $17.50

Original American Book Of The Dead
PUBLISHING COMPANY: Gateways Books And Tapes **EDITOR:** E.J. Gold **TOPICS:** Death **TYPE:** Book **PRICE:** $12.50

Origins And History Of Consciousness
PUBLISHING COMPANY: Princeton University Press **EDITOR:** E. Neumann **TOPICS:** New Age, Psychology **TYPE:** Book **PRICE:** $12.95

Origins Of The Kabbalah
PUBLISHING COMPANY: Princeton University Press **EDITOR:** G. Scholem, A. Arkush **TOPICS:** Kabbalah **TYPE:** Book **PRICE:** $47.50

Other Dimensions: Exploring The Unexplained
PUBLISHING COMPANY: Avery Publishing Group, Inc. **EDITOR:** M. Kushi **TOPICS:** Occult **TYPE:** Book **PRICE:** $9.95

Other Kingdoms
PUBLISHING COMPANY: Marcus Books Hilarion **TOPICS:** New Age **TYPE:** Book **PRICE:** $9.95

Other Lives, Other Selves: A Jungian Psychotherapist Discovers Past Lives
PUBLISHING COMPANY: Bantam New Age Books **EDITOR:** R. Woolger **TOPICS:** Past Life Regression **TYPE:** Book **PRICE:** $9.95

Other Tongues, Other Flesh
PUBLISHING COMPANY: Brotherhood Of Life **EDITOR:** George H. Williamson **TOPICS:** Paranormal Phenomena, UFO's **TYPE:** Book **PRICE:** $15.95

Other Way: A Book Of Meditative Experiences Based On The I Ching
PUBLISHING COMPANY: Anthony Publishing Co. **EDITOR:** Carol Anthony **TOPICS:** Meditation, Spirituality **TYPE:** Book **DATE:** 1990 **PRICE:** $12.50

Otherworld Journeys: Accounts Of Near-Death Experience In Medieval & Modern Times
PUBLISHING COMPANY: Oxford University Press, Inc. **EDITOR:** C. Zaleski **TOPICS:** Death **TYPE:** Book **PRICE:** $8.95

Ouija: The Most Dangerous Game
PUBLISHING COMPANY: Harper & Row Publishers, Inc. **EDITOR:** S. Hunt **TOPICS:** Occult **TYPE:** Book **PRICE:** $8.95

Our Fascinating Earth: Strange, True Stories Of Nature's Oddities, Unexplained Phenomena
PUBLISHING COMPANY: Contemporary Books, Inc. **EDITOR:** Phillip Seff, Nancy Seff **TOPICS:** Ghosts, Paranormal Phenomena **TYPE:** Book **PRICE:** $12.95

Our Inner World Of Rage: Understanding & Transforming The Power Of Anger
PUBLISHING COMPANY: Continuum Publishing Co. **EDITOR:** Lucy Freeman **TOPICS:** New Age, Psychology **TYPE:** Book **PRICE:** $15.95

Out Of The Trap: Selected Lectures Of Alan W. Watts
PUBLISHING COMPANY: And Books **EDITOR:** M. Watts **TOPICS:** New Age **TYPE:** Book **PRICE:** $8.95

Out There
PUBLISHING COMPANY: Simon & Schuster, Inc. **EDITOR:** Howard Blum **TOPICS:** UFO's, Paranormal Phenomena **TYPE:** Book **PRICE:** $19.95

Out-Of-Body Adventures: 30 Days To The Most Exciting Experience Of Your Life
PUBLISHING COMPANY: Contemporary Books, Inc. **EDITOR:** Rick Stack **TOPICS:** Astral Projection **TYPE:** Book **PRICE:** $7.95

Outer Limits Of Edgar Cayce's Power
PUBLISHING COMPANY: Association For Research And Enlightenment, Inc. **EDITOR:** Edgar Evans Cayce, Hugh Lynn Cayce **TOPICS:** Channeling **TYPE:** Book **PRICE:** $14.95

Outline Of Occult Science
PUBLISHING COMPANY: Anthroposophic Press, Inc. **EDITOR:** R. Steiner **TOPICS:** Occult **TYPE:** Book **PRICE:** $9.95

Overlords Of Atlantis And The Great Pyramid
PUBLISHING COMPANY: Inner Light Publications **EDITOR:** B. Steiger **TOPICS:** New Age, Metaphysics **TYPE:** Book **PRICE:** $10.95

Ovid's Metamorphoses
PUBLISHING COMPANY: Spring Publications, Inc. **EDITOR:** C. Boer **TOPICS:** Spirituality **TYPE:** Book **PRICE:** $17.00

Pagan Grace: Dionysos, Hermes & Goddess Memory In Daily Life
PUBLISHING COMPANY: Spring Publications, Inc. **EDITOR:** G. Paris **TOPICS:** Paganism, Spirituality **TYPE:** Book **PRICE:** $15.00

Pagan Meditations: The Worlds Of Aphrodite, Artemis And Hestia
PUBLISHING COMPANY: Spring Publications, Inc. **EDITOR:** G. Paris **TOPICS:** Spirituality, Paganism, Meditation **TYPE:** Book **PRICE:** $14.00

Pagan Rituals III: Outer Court Training Coven
PUBLISHING COMPANY: Magickal Childe Occult Supplies, Inc. **EDITOR:** H. Slater Frnds Craft **TOPICS:** Paganism, Spirituality **TYPE:** Book **PRICE:** $9.95

Palm: A Guide To Your Hidden Potential
PUBLISHING COMPANY: New Chapter Press, Inc. **EDITOR:** Rita Robinson **TOPICS:** Palmistry, Parapsychology **TYPE:** Book **PRICE:** $9.95

Palmascope: The Instant Palm Reader
PUBLISHING COMPANY: Llewellyn Publications **EDITOR:** L. Domin **TOPICS:** Palmistry, Parapsychology **TYPE:** Book **PRICE:** $12.95

Palmistry Workbook: Art Of Psychological Hand Analysis

PUBLISHING COMPANY: Aquarian Press EDITOR: Nathaniel Altman TOPICS: Palmistry TYPE: Book PRICE: $12.95

Palmistry: Your Career In Your Hands

PUBLISHING COMPANY: Aquarian Press EDITOR: Nathaniel Altman TOPICS: Palmistry TYPE: Book PRICE: $9.95

Parapsychology Abstracts International

PUBLISHING COMPANY: Parapsychology Sources Of Information Center-PSI Center TOPICS: Parapsychology TYPE: Book

Parapsychology And The Unconscious

PUBLISHING COMPANY: North Atlantic Books EDITOR: J. Eisenblud TOPICS: ESP, Psychic Phenomena TYPE: Book PRICE: $25.00

Pardon My Dust...I'm Remodeling

PUBLISHING COMPANY: Mocha Publishing Company EDITOR: Casey Chaney TOPICS: New Age TYPE: Book

Parenthesis In Eternity

PUBLISHING COMPANY: Harper & Row Publishers, Inc. EDITOR: Joel Goldsmith TOPICS: New Age TYPE: Book PRICE: $13.95

Parzival: Chalice Of Ecstasy - A Magical & Qabbalistic Interpretation Of Drama Of Parzival

PUBLISHING COMPANY: Yoga Publications Society EDITOR: F. Achad TOPICS: Metaphysics TYPE: Book PRICE: $7.00

Passing The Torch, The Way Of The Avatar

PUBLISHING COMPANY: Forum, The TOPICS: Body-Mind Connection, Spirituality, Metaphysics TYPE: Book PRICE: $8.00

Passion For This Earth: Exploring A New Partnership Of Man, Woman & Nature

PUBLISHING COMPANY: Harper & Row Publishers, Inc. EDITOR: Valerie Andrews TOPICS: Psychology TYPE: Book PRICE: $19.95

Past Life Regression Guidebook: How Our Past Lives Influence Us Now

PUBLISHING COMPANY: Reincarnation Books & Tapes EDITOR: Bettye B. Binder TOPICS: Hypnotism, Past Life Regression, Reincarnation TYPE: Book DATE: 1992 PRICE: $10.00

Past Life Visions

PUBLISHING COMPANY: Harper & Row Publishers, Inc. EDITOR: W. DeArteaga TOPICS: Past Life Regression TYPE: Book PRICE: $9.95

Past Lives, Future Growth

PUBLISHING COMPANY: A.C.S. Publications, Inc./Astro Computing Services EDITOR: A. Druffel,

A. Marcotte TOPICS: Past Life Regression TYPE: Book PRICE: $12.95

Past Lives, Present Karma Workbook

PUBLISHING COMPANY: Reincarnation Books & Tapes EDITOR: Bettye B. Binder TOPICS: Past Life Regression, Reincarnation TYPE: Book PRICE: $13.00

Pastoral Medicine

PUBLISHING COMPANY: Anthroposophic Press, Inc. EDITOR: R. Steiner TOPICS: Spirituality, Holistic Health, Body-Mind Connection TYPE: Book PRICE: $20.00

Path Of Action

PUBLISHING COMPANY: E.P. Dutton, Inc. EDITOR: Jack Schwartz TOPICS: Holistic Health TYPE: Book PRICE: $9.95

Path Of Light

PUBLISHING COMPANY: Essence Light Center/Twelve Rays Of The Great Central Sun TOPICS: Channeling TYPE: Directory

Patterns Of The Whole Vol. 1: Healing And Quartz Crystals

PUBLISHING COMPANY: Two Trees Publishing EDITOR: J. Rea TOPICS: Crystals TYPE: Book PRICE: $12.95

Patterns Of The Whole Vol. 2: Our Subtle Selves

PUBLISHING COMPANY: Two Trees Publishing EDITOR: J. Rea TOPICS: Crystals TYPE: Book PRICE: $12.95

Paul Brunton: Essential Readings

PUBLISHING COMPANY: Crucible Books, Inner Traditions International, Ltd. EDITOR: Joscelyn Godwyn TOPICS: Paranormal Phenomena TYPE: Book PRICE: $12.95

Peeling The Sweet Onion

PUBLISHING COMPANY: New Age Publishing Company EDITOR: Martin E. Segal TOPICS: New Age TYPE: Book

Pendulum Kit

PUBLISHING COMPANY: Simon & Schuster, Inc. EDITOR: S. Loncgren TOPICS: Dowsing TYPE: Book PRICE: $19.95

People In Space

PUBLISHING COMPANY: Cassandra Press EDITOR: John Heinerman, Ph. D. TOPICS: UFO's TYPE: Book DATE: 1990; 144 pgs. PRICE: $9.95

People's Book Of Medical Tests

PUBLISHING COMPANY: Simon & Schuster, Inc. EDITOR: David S. Sobel, T. Ferguson TOPICS: Holistic Health TYPE: Book PRICE: $12.95

Perennial Dictionary Of World Religions

PUBLISHING COMPANY: Harper & Row Publishers, Inc. EDITOR: K. Crim TOPICS: Spirituality TYPE: Book PRICE: $19.95

Perennial Psychology Of The Bhagavad Gita

PUBLISHING COMPANY: Himalayan International Institute Of Yoga Science and Philosophy EDITOR: S. Rama TOPICS: Spirituality TYPE: Book PRICE: $14.95

Perfect Health: Maharishi Ayurveda, The Mind/Body Program For Total Well-Being

PUBLISHING COMPANY: Crown Publishers, Inc. EDITOR: D. Chopra TOPICS: Holistic Health, Body-Mind Connection TYPE: Book PRICE: $19.95

Personal Change Through Self-Hypnosis

PUBLISHING COMPANY: Whitford Press/Schiffer Publishing Limited EDITOR: Pam Young TOPICS: Hypnotism TYPE: Book PRICE: $12.95

Personal Karmic Astrology Workbook

PUBLISHING COMPANY: Golden Phoenix Healing And Light Center TOPICS: Holistic Healing TYPE: Book

Personal Peace: Macrobiotic Reflections On Mental And Emotional Recovery

PUBLISHING COMPANY: Japan Publications, Inc. EDITOR: D. Briscoe TOPICS: Holistic Health, Vegetarianism, Health Food TYPE: Book PRICE: $18.95

Personal Totem Pole: Animal Imagery, The Chakras And Psychotherapy

PUBLISHING COMPANY: Moon Bear Press EDITOR: S. Gallegos TOPICS: Psychic Healing, Body-Mind Connection, New Age, Psychology TYPE: Book PRICE: $12.00

Personality In Handwriting: A Step-By-Step Guide To Unlocking Hidden Talents & Desires

PUBLISHING COMPANY: Newcastle Publishing Co., Inc. EDITOR: Alfred Mendel TOPICS: Graphology TYPE: Book PRICE: $12.95

Personality: The Individuation Process In The Light Of C.G.Jungs Typology

PUBLISHING COMPANY: Sigo Press EDITOR: C.A. Meler TOPICS: Psychology TYPE: Book PRICE: $16.95

Pet Allergies: Remedies For An Epidemic

PUBLISHING COMPANY: Dr. Goodpet Laboratories TOPICS: Holistic Healing TYPE: Book

Philosophy Of Consciousness Without An Object

PUBLISHING COMPANY: Crown Publishers, Inc. EDITOR: F. Merrell-Wolff TOPICS: Paranormal Phenomena, New Age, Psychology TYPE: Book PRICE: $14.95

Philosophy Of The I Ching

PUBLISHING COMPANY: Anthony Publishing Co. **EDITOR:** Carol Anthony **TOPICS:** Parapsychology, Psychic **TYPE:** Book **DATE:** 1981

Phoenix

PUBLISHING COMPANY: Philosophical Research Society, Inc. **EDITOR:** M.P. Hall **TOPICS:** New Age, Paranormal Phenomena, Alchemy **TYPE:** Book **PRICE:** $19.95

Phoenix Cards: Reading & Interpreting Past-Life Influences

PUBLISHING COMPANY: Destiny Books, Inner Traditions International, Ltd. **EDITOR:** Susan Sheppard **TOPICS:** Past Life Regression **TYPE:** Book **PRICE:** $24.95

Photographing The Spirit World

PUBLISHING COMPANY: Aquarian Press **EDITOR:** C. Permutt **TOPICS:** Occult **TYPE:** Book **PRICE:** $12.95

Physics And Psychics

PUBLISHING COMPANY: Prometheus Books **EDITOR:** Victor J. Stenger **TOPICS:** Skepticism, Psychic **TYPE:** Book

Picture Of Health: Healing Your Life With Art

PUBLISHING COMPANY: Hay House **EDITOR:** L. Capacchione **TOPICS:** Holistic Healing, Spirituality, Psychic Healing **TYPE:** Book **PRICE:** $12.00

Planet Medicine: From Stone Age Shamanism To Post-Industrial Healing

PUBLISHING COMPANY: North Atlantic Books **EDITOR:** Richard Grossinger **TOPICS:** Spirituality, Psychic Healing **TYPE:** Book **PRICE:** $14.95

Planetary Herbalogy

PUBLISHING COMPANY: Lotus Light Publications **EDITOR:** M. Tierra **TOPICS:** Holistic Health, Herbalogy **TYPE:** Book **PRICE:** $16.95

Planetary Magick: The Heart Of Western Magic

PUBLISHING COMPANY: Llewellyn Publications **EDITOR:** M. Denning, O. Phillips **TOPICS:** Occult, Astrology, Witchcraft **TYPE:** Book **PRICE:** $19.95

Planetary Mysteries: Megaliths, Glaciers, The Face On Mars, And Aboriginal Dreamtime

PUBLISHING COMPANY: North Atlantic Books **EDITOR:** Richard Grossinger **TOPICS:** Paranormal Phenomena **TYPE:** Book **PRICE:** $12.95

Planets In Aspect: Understanding Your Inner Dynamics

PUBLISHING COMPANY: Whitford Press/Schiffer Publishing Limited **EDITOR:** R. Pelletier **TOPICS:** Astrology **TYPE:** Book **PRICE:** $19.95

Planets In Composite: Analyzing Human Relationships

PUBLISHING COMPANY: Whitford Press/Schiffer Publishing Limited **EDITOR:** R. Hand **TOPICS:** Astrology **TYPE:** Book **PRICE:** $19.95

Planets In Houses: Experiencing Your Environment

PUBLISHING COMPANY: Whitford Press/Schiffer Publishing Limited **EDITOR:** R. Pelletier **TOPICS:** Astrology **TYPE:** Book **PRICE:** $19.95

Planets In Love: Exploring Your Emotional And Sexual Needs

PUBLISHING COMPANY: Whitford Press/Schiffer Publishing Limited **EDITOR:** J. Townley **TOPICS:** Astrology **TYPE:** Book **PRICE:** $18.95

Planets In Signs

PUBLISHING COMPANY: Whitford Press/Schiffer Publishing Limited **EDITOR:** S. Alexander **TOPICS:** Astrology **TYPE:** Book **PRICE:** $18.95

Planets In Transit: Life Cycles For Living

PUBLISHING COMPANY: Whitford Press/Schiffer Publishing Limited **EDITOR:** R. Hand **TOPICS:** Astrology **TYPE:** Book **PRICE:** $22.95

Planets In Work: A Complete Guide To Vocational Astrology

PUBLISHING COMPANY: A.C.S. Publications, Inc./Astro Computing Services **EDITOR:** J. Binder **TOPICS:** Astrology **TYPE:** Book **PRICE:** $19.95

Planning The Ideal Family

PUBLISHING COMPANY: Zero Population Growth **TYPE:** Book

Platonic Quest

PUBLISHING COMPANY: Concord Grove Press, Subs. of Institute of World Culture **EDITOR:** E. Urwick **TOPICS:** New Age **TYPE:** Book **PRICE:** $15.50

Play Of Consciousness: A Spiritual Autobiography

PUBLISHING COMPANY: S.Y.D.A. Foundation/Siddha Yoga Meditation Ashram Muktananda **TOPICS:** Spirituality **TYPE:** Book **PRICE:** $9.95

Play To Live: Selected Seminars By Alan W. Watts

PUBLISHING COMPANY: And Books **EDITOR:** M. Watts **TOPICS:** New Age **TYPE:** Book **PRICE:** $8.95

Playing Ball On Running Water: The Japanese Way To Building A Better Life

PUBLISHING COMPANY: William Morrow & Co. **EDITOR:** David K. Reynolds **TOPICS:** New Age **TYPE:** Book **PRICE:** $7.95

Playing Card Workbook: A Contemporary Manual Of Cartomancy

PUBLISHING COMPANY: Aquarian Press **EDITOR:** J. Leslie **TOPICS:** Psychic, Metaphysics **TYPE:** Book **PRICE:** $10.95

Polarity Therapy: The Power That Heals

PUBLISHING COMPANY: Avery Publishing Group, Inc. **EDITOR:** A. Siegel **TOPICS:** Parapsychology, Holistic Health **TYPE:** Book **PRICE:** $12.95

Politics Of Women's Spirituality: Essays On The Rise Of Spiritual Power In The Feminist Movement

PUBLISHING COMPANY: Doubleday & Co.,Inc. **EDITOR:** Charlene Spretnak **TOPICS:** Spirituality **TYPE:** Book **PRICE:** $14.95

Poltergeist Experience: Investigations Into Ghostly Phenomena

PUBLISHING COMPANY: Aquarian Press **EDITOR:** D. Scott Rogo **TOPICS:** Occult **TYPE:** Book **PRICE:** $12.95

Pools Of Lodging For The Moon: Strategy For A Positive Life Style

PUBLISHING COMPANY: William Morrow & Co. **EDITOR:** David K. Reynolds **TOPICS:** New Age **TYPE:** Book **PRICE:** $12.95

Popul Vuh: The Mayan Book Of The Dawn Of Life

PUBLISHING COMPANY: Simon & Schuster, Inc. **EDITOR:** D. Tedlock **TOPICS:** Paranormal Phenomena, Spirituality **TYPE:** Book **PRICE:** $10.95

Porphyry: Selected Works

PUBLISHING COMPANY: Selene Books **EDITOR:** Thomas Taylor **TOPICS:** Spirituality, Paranormal Phenomena **TYPE:** Book **PRICE:** $22.50

Portrait Of A Dalai Lama: The Life And Times Of The Great Thirteenth

PUBLISHING COMPANY: Wisdom Publications **EDITOR:** C. Bell **TOPICS:** New Age **TYPE:** Book **PRICE:** $22.95

Portraits Of Homeopathic Medicines Vol. 2: Psychophysical Analyses Of Selected Types

PUBLISHING COMPANY: North Atlantic Books **EDITOR:** C. R. Coulter **TOPICS:** Homeopathy, Holistic Health, Body-Mind Connection **TYPE:** Book **PRICE:** $25.00

Portraits Of Homeopathic Medicines: Psychophysical Analyses Of Select Constitutional Types

PUBLISHING COMPANY: North Atlantic Books **EDITOR:** C. R. Coulter **TOPICS:** Homeopathy, Holistic Health, Body-Mind Connection **TYPE:** Book **PRICE:** $25.00

Positive Living And Health: Complete Guide To Brain/Body Healing & Mental Empowerment

PUBLISHING COMPANY: Rodale Press, Inc. **EDITOR:** Editors of Prevention Magazine **TOPICS:** Body-Mind Connection, Holistic Health **TYPE:** Guide **PRICE:** $26.95

Power Of Color: The Art & Science Of Making Colors Work For You

Power Of Fantasy: Where Our Daydreams Come From & How They Can Help Or Harm Us
PUBLISHING COMPANY: Continuum Publishing Co. EDITOR: Lucy Freeman, K. Kupfermann TOPICS: New Age, Psychology TYPE: Book PRICE: $16.95

Power Of Gems And Charms
PUBLISHING COMPANY: Newcastle Publishing Co., Inc. EDITOR: G. Bratley TOPICS: Occult, Witchcraft TYPE: Book PRICE: $9.95

Power Of Optimism: Your Action Plan To Bring Out The Best In Yourself
PUBLISHING COMPANY: Harper & Row Publishers, Inc. EDITOR: Alan Loy McGinnis TOPICS: New Age, Psychology TYPE: Book PRICE: $16.95

Power Of The Pendulum
PUBLISHING COMPANY: Routledge, Chapman & Hall, Inc. EDITOR: T.C. Lethbridge TOPICS: Dowsing TYPE: Book PRICE: $6.95

Power Of The Runes Kit
PUBLISHING COMPANY: Llewellyn Publications EDITOR: D. Tyson TOPICS: Runes, Metaphysics TYPE: Book PRICE: $24.95

Power Of The Witch: The Earth, The Moon & The Magical Path To Enlightenment
PUBLISHING COMPANY: Delacorte Press EDITOR: Laurie Cabot, T. Cowan TOPICS: Paganism, Spirituality, Witchcraft, Occult TYPE: Book; 320 pgs. PRICE: $17.95

Power Of Your Other Hand: A Course In Channeling The Inner Wisdom Of The Right Brain
PUBLISHING COMPANY: Newcastle Publishing Co., Inc. EDITOR: L. Capacchione TOPICS: Channeling, Psychic, New Age TYPE: Book PRICE: $10.95

Power Within: The True Stores Of Exceptional Patients Who Fought Back With Hope
PUBLISHING COMPANY: Harper & Row Publishers, Inc. EDITOR: Wendy Williams TOPICS: Holistic Health, Body-Mind Connection, Psychology TYPE: Book PRICE: $19.95

Practical Buddhism
PUBLISHING COMPANY: Blue Dolphin Publishing, Inc. TOPICS: New Age TYPE: Book PRICE: $5.00

Practical Celtic Magic
PUBLISHING COMPANY: Aquarian Press EDITOR: M. Hope TOPICS: Occult TYPE: Book PRICE: $9.95

Practical Cheirology
PUBLISHING COMPANY: Cheirological Society EDITOR: Dr. R. Cigman TOPICS: Palmistry, Holistic Health TYPE: Book DATE: 1983

Practical Encyclopedia Of Natural Healing
PUBLISHING COMPANY: Penguin Books EDITOR: M. Bricklin TOPICS: Homeopathy, Holistic Health TYPE: Book PRICE: $12.95

Practical Guide To Qabalistic Symbolism
PUBLISHING COMPANY: Samuel Weiser, Inc. EDITOR: G. Knight TOPICS: Kabbalah TYPE: Book PRICE: $29.50

Practical Handbook Of Plant Alchemy: How To Prepare Medicinal Essences, Tinctures & Elixirs
PUBLISHING COMPANY: Inner Traditions EDITOR: M. Junius TOPICS: Holistic Health, Astrology, Alchemy, Herbalogy TYPE: Handbook PRICE: $12.95

Practical Jung: Nuts & Bolts Of Jungian Psychotherapy
PUBLISHING COMPANY: Chiron Publications EDITOR: H. Wilmer TOPICS: Psychology TYPE: Book PRICE: $18.95

Practical Magic And The Western Mystery Tradition
PUBLISHING COMPANY: Aquarian Press EDITOR: W.E. Butler TOPICS: Occult, Witchcraft TYPE: Book PRICE: $11.95

Practical Magic In The Northern Tradition
PUBLISHING COMPANY: Aquarian Press EDITOR: N. Pennick TOPICS: Spirituality, Paganism TYPE: Book PRICE: $12.95

Practical Sigil Magick
PUBLISHING COMPANY: Llewellyn Publications EDITOR: U.D. Frater TOPICS: Occult, Witchcraft TYPE: Book PRICE: $9.95

Practical Work On Self
PUBLISHING COMPANY: Gateways Books And Tapes EDITOR: E.J. Gold TOPICS: Psychology TYPE: Book PRICE: $12.50

Practice Of Aromatherapy: A Classic Compendium Of Plant Medicines & Their Healing Properties
PUBLISHING COMPANY: Inner Traditions EDITOR: J. Valnet TOPICS: Holistic Health TYPE: Book PRICE: $10.95

Practice Of Classical Palmistry
PUBLISHING COMPANY: Samuel Weiser, Inc. EDITOR: Jan LaRoux TOPICS: Palmistry TYPE: Book PRICE: $13.50

Practice Of Process Meditation: Intensive Journal Way To Spiritual Experience
PUBLISHING COMPANY: Dialogue House EDITOR: I. Progoff TOPICS: Meditation, Spirituality TYPE: Book PRICE: $15.95

Practicing The Presence: A Guide To Practical Mysticism
PUBLISHING COMPANY: Harper & Row Publishers, Inc. EDITOR: Joel Goldsmith TOPICS: New Age TYPE: Book PRICE: $13.95

Pranic Healing
PUBLISHING COMPANY: Samuel Weiser, Inc. EDITOR: Choa Kok Sui TOPICS: New Age, Color Therapy, Holistic Healing TYPE: Book PRICE: $14.95

Prayers And Meditations Of The Mother
PUBLISHING COMPANY: Sri Aurobindo Ashram EDITOR: The Mother TOPICS: Spirituality TYPE: Book PRICE: $14.50

Precious Present
PUBLISHING COMPANY: Doubleday & Co.,Inc. EDITOR: Spencer Johnson TOPICS: Spirituality TYPE: Book PRICE: $15.00

Predicting Your Future
PUBLISHING COMPANY: Ballantine Books, Inc. Diagram Group TOPICS: Psychic, Metaphysics TYPE: Book PRICE: $7.95

Prediction Book Of Amulets And Talismans
PUBLISHING COMPANY: Sterling Publishing Company, Inc. EDITOR: J. Logan TOPICS: Occult, Witchcraft TYPE: Book PRICE: $5.95

Pregnant Universe
PUBLISHING COMPANY: Astrologik/Vigilantero Press EDITOR: Antero Alli TOPICS: New Age TYPE: Book DESCRIPTION: Updates archaic mystical systems in modern terms.

Prescription For Nutritional Health: A-Z Reference Using Vitamins, Minerals, Herbs
PUBLISHING COMPANY: Avery Publishing Group, Inc. EDITOR: J. Balch, P. Balch TOPICS: Holistic Health TYPE: Book PRICE: $16.95

Presence Of The Dead On The Path To Spiritual Understanding
PUBLISHING COMPANY: Anthroposophic Press, Inc. EDITOR: R. Steiner TOPICS: Occult TYPE: Book PRICE: $12.95

Present Yourself, Captivate Your Audience With Great Presentation Skills
PUBLISHING COMPANY: B.L. Winch & Associates/Jalmar Press EDITOR: Michael Gelb TOPICS: New Age TYPE: Book SIZE: 6x9; 128 pgs. PRICE: $9.95

Pretty Good Person: What It Takes To Live With Courage, Gratitude & Integrity Or Pretty Good
PUBLISHING COMPANY: Harper & Row Publishers, Inc. EDITOR: Lewis Smedes TOPICS: New Age, Psychology TYPE: Book PRICE: $14.95

Prevention's Giant Book Of Health Facts: The Ultimate Reference For Personal Health

PUBLISHING COMPANY: Avery Publishing Group, Inc. EDITOR: Morton Walker TOPICS: Color Therapy TYPE: Book

PUBLISHING COMPANY: Rodale Press, Inc. **EDITOR:** Editors of Prevention Magazine **TOPICS:** Holistic Health **TYPE:** Book **PRICE:** $26.95

Prevention's Medical Care Yearbook 1990

PUBLISHING COMPANY: Rodale Press, Inc. **EDITOR:** M. Bricklin **TOPICS:** Holistic Health **TYPE:** Yearbook **PRICE:** $19.95

Priest And Freemason: The Life Of George Oliver

PUBLISHING COMPANY: Aquarian Press **EDITOR:** R. Sandbach **TOPICS:** Psychic, Spirituality **TYPE:** Book **PRICE:** $23.95

Primordial Breath: An Ancient Chinese Way Of Prolonging Life Through Breath Control Vol.1

PUBLISHING COMPANY: Original Books, Inc. **EDITOR:** J. Huang, M. Wurmbrand **TOPICS:** Spirituality, New Age **TYPE:** Book **PRICE:** $22.50

Prince Wen Hui's Cook: Chinese Dietary Therapy

PUBLISHING COMPANY: Paradigm Publications **EDITOR:** B. Flaws, H. Wolfe **TOPICS:** Holistic Health **TYPE:** Book **PRICE:** $12.95

Principles Of Aikido

PUBLISHING COMPANY: Shambhala Publications, Inc. **EDITOR:** M. Saotome **TOPICS:** Aikido **TYPE:** Book **PRICE:** $24.95

Priority Parenting

PUBLISHING COMPANY: Tamra B. Orr **EDITOR:** Tamra B. Orr **TOPICS:** New Age **TYPE:** Book

Private Moments, Secret Selves: Enriching Our Time Alone

PUBLISHING COMPANY: Jeremy P. Tarcher, Inc. **EDITOR:** Jeffrey Kottler **TOPICS:** New Age, Psychology **TYPE:** Book **PRICE:** $17.95

Pro-Biotics: How To Boost Your Body's Natural Healing Power

PUBLISHING COMPANY: Collins, Div. of William Collins **EDITOR:** N. Trenev, L. Chaltow **TOPICS:** Holistic Healing **TYPE:** Book **PRICE:** $14.95

Proclus: The Platonic Theology Vol.1

PUBLISHING COMPANY: Selene Books **EDITOR:** Thomas Taylor **TOPICS:** Paranormal Phenomena **TYPE:** Book **PRICE:** $22.50

Proclus: The Platonic Theology Vol.2

PUBLISHING COMPANY: Selene Books **EDITOR:** Thomas Taylor **TOPICS:** Paranormal Phenomena **TYPE:** Book **PRICE:** $22.50

Projection Of The Astral Body

PUBLISHING COMPANY: Samuel Weiser, Inc. **EDITOR:** S. Muldoon, H. Carrington **TOPICS:** Astral Projection **TYPE:** Book **PRICE:** $9.95

Promenade Home: Macrobiotics And Women's Health

PUBLISHING COMPANY: Japan Publications, Inc. **EDITOR:** G. Jack, A. Jack **TOPICS:** Holistic Health,

Vegetarianism, Health Food **TYPE:** Book **PRICE:** $18.95

Prophet

PUBLISHING COMPANY: Random House, Inc. **EDITOR:** K. Gilbran **TOPICS:** Channeling **TYPE:** Book **PRICE:** $22.50

Prophey On Trial

PUBLISHING COMPANY: Lucis Publishing Company **EDITOR:** Alice Bailey **TOPICS:** Metaphysics, Psychic **TYPE:** Book **PRICE:** $10.50

Pseudo Dionysus: The Complete Works

PUBLISHING COMPANY: Paulist Press **EDITOR:** C. Luibheid **TOPICS:** Spirituality **TYPE:** Book **PRICE:** $12.95

Psionic Power: The High Technology Of Psychic Power

PUBLISHING COMPANY: Llewellyn Publications **EDITOR:** C. Cosimano **TOPICS:** Occult, Witchcraft **TYPE:** Book **PRICE:** $3.95

Psyche And Substance: Essays On Homeopathy In The Light Of Jungian Psychology

PUBLISHING COMPANY: North Atlantic Books **EDITOR:** E. Whitmont **TOPICS:** Homeopathy, Psychology **TYPE:** Book **PRICE:** $12.95

Psychic And UFO Revelations In The Last Days

PUBLISHING COMPANY: Inner Light Publications **EDITOR:** Thomas Beckley **TOPICS:** Mctaphysics, UFO's, Psychic **TYPE:** Book **PRICE:** $9.95

Psychic Breakthroughs Today: Fascinating Encounters With Parapsychology's Latest Discoveries

PUBLISHING COMPANY: Aquarian Press **EDITOR:** D. Scott Rogo. **TOPICS:** Psychic Phenomena, ESP **TYPE:** Book **PRICE:** $12.95

Psychic Dimensions

PUBLISHING COMPANY: Psychic Foundation Of Knowledge, Inc. **TOPICS:** Metaphysics, Spirituality **TYPE:** Book

Psychic Energy Workbook: An Illustrated Course In Practical Psychic Skills

PUBLISHING COMPANY: Aquarian Press **EDITOR:** R. Michael Miller **TOPICS:** Psychic **TYPE:** Book **PRICE:** $12.95

Psychic Explorer: A Practical Guide To The Magical Arts

PUBLISHING COMPANY: Simon & Schuster, Inc. **EDITOR:** J. Cainer, C. Rider **TOPICS:** Psychic **TYPE:** Book **PRICE:** $12.95

Psychic Lotus-Pictorial

PUBLISHING COMPANY: Ma Yoga Shakti International Mission **PUBLISHER:** Ma Yoga Shakti **TOPICS:** Yoga, Meditation, Spirituality **TYPE:** Book

Psychic Power And Soul Consciousness

PUBLISHING COMPANY: Hunter House Publishers, Inc. **EDITOR:** Korra Deaver **TOPICS:** Psychic **TYPE:** Book **PRICE:** $14.95

Psychic Powers

PUBLISHING COMPANY: Valley Of The Sun Publishing Co., Sutphen Corporation **EDITOR:** Dick Sutphen **TOPICS:** Metaphysics **TYPE:** Book **DESCRIPTION:** Includes programs on Aura Reading, Developing the Ability of Psychometry, Developing Clairvoyance & Developing Telepathic Ability.

Psychic Self-Defense

PUBLISHING COMPANY: Aquarian Press **EDITOR:** D. Fortune **TOPICS:** Psychic, Occult, Witchcraft **TYPE:** Book **PRICE:** $10.95

Psychic Sense: Training & Developing Psychic Sensitivity

PUBLISHING COMPANY: W. Foulsham & Co., Ltd. **EDITOR:** Mary Swainson, L. Bennett **TOPICS:** Psychic **TYPE:** Book **PRICE:** $13.95

Psychic Warfare: Fact Or Fiction?

PUBLISHING COMPANY: Aquarian Press **EDITOR:** John White **TOPICS:** Psychic Phenomena, ESP **TYPE:** Book **PRICE:** $12.95

Psychic: Awakening The Power Within

PUBLISHING COMPANY: Contemporary Books, Inc. **EDITOR:** Carole Kennedy **TOPICS:** Psychic **TYPE:** Book **PRICE:** $17.95

Psychobiology Of Mind-Body Healing: New Concepts Of Therapeutic Hypnosis

PUBLISHING COMPANY: W. W. Norton & Co., Inc. **EDITOR:** E. Rossi **TOPICS:** Hypnotism **TYPE:** Book **PRICE:** $9.95

Psychoenergetics: A Breath Of Life

PUBLISHING COMPANY: Cosmoenergetics Publications **EDITOR:** Jan Kennedy **TOPICS:** Holistic Health **TYPE:** Book **PRICE:** $14.95

Psychological Astrology

PUBLISHING COMPANY: Samuel Weiser, Inc. **EDITOR:** Karen Hamaker-Zondag **TOPICS:** Astrology **TYPE:** Book **PRICE:** $10.95

Psychological Commentaries On The Teaching Of Gurdjieff And Ouspensky Vol.1

PUBLISHING COMPANY: Shambhala Publications, Inc. **EDITOR:** M. Nicoll **TOPICS:** Spirituality **TYPE:** Book **PRICE:** $24.95

Psychological Commentaries On The Teaching Of Gurdjieff And Ouspensky Vol.2

PUBLISHING COMPANY: Shambhala Publications, Inc. **EDITOR:** M. Nicoll **TOPICS:** Spirituality **TYPE:** Book **PRICE:** $24.95

Psychological Commentaries On The Teaching Of Gurdjieff And Ouspensky Vol.3
PUBLISHING COMPANY: Shambhala Publications, Inc. EDITOR: M. Nicoll TOPICS: Spirituality TYPE: Book PRICE: $24.95

Psychological Commentaries On The Teaching Of Gurdjieff And Ouspensky Vol.4
PUBLISHING COMPANY: Shambhala Publications, Inc. EDITOR: M. Nicoll TOPICS: Spirituality TYPE: Book PRICE: $22.95

Psychological Commentaries On The Teaching Of Gurdjieff And Ouspensky Vol.5
PUBLISHING COMPANY: Shambhala Publications, Inc. EDITOR: M. Nicoll TOPICS: Spirituality TYPE: Book PRICE: $22.95

Psychology And Alchemy
PUBLISHING COMPANY: Princeton University Press EDITOR: C. Jung TOPICS: Alchemy TYPE: Book PRICE: $14.95

Psychology Of Treasure Dowsing
PUBLISHING COMPANY: Fine Median International TOPICS: Dowsing TYPE: Book

Psychology, Psychoanalysis And Medicine: An Approach To Curing The Whole Person
PUBLISHING COMPANY: Hunter House Publishers, Inc. EDITOR: P. Diel TOPICS: Body-Mind Connection TYPE: Book PRICE: $24.95

Psychonavigation: Techniques For Travel Beyond Time
PUBLISHING COMPANY: Destiny Books, Inner Traditions International, Ltd. EDITOR: John Perkins TOPICS: Occult TYPE: Book PRICE: $10.95

Psychotherapy Grounded In The Feminine Principle
PUBLISHING COMPANY: Chiron Publications EDITOR: B. Sullivan TOPICS: Spirituality TYPE: Book PRICE: $14.95

Pulse In Occident And Orient: Its Philosophy And Practice In Holistic Diagnosis And Treatment
PUBLISHING COMPANY: Aurora Press, Inc. EDITOR: R. Ambert, A. Babey-Brooke TOPICS: Holistic Health TYPE: Book PRICE: $12.50

Pulses And Impulses: A Practitioner's Guide To A Unique New Pulse Diagnosis Technique
PUBLISHING COMPANY: Collins, Div. of William Collins EDITOR: Graham Townsend, D. Ysha TOPICS: Holistic Health TYPE: Guide PRICE: $39.95

Pursuit Of Wisdom And Other Works: By The Author Of The Cloud Of Unknowing
PUBLISHING COMPANY: Paulist Press EDITOR: J. Walsh TOPICS: Spirituality TYPE: Book PRICE: $14.95

Pyramid Odyssey: Dramatic New Evidence Reveals The Ancient Secret
PUBLISHING COMPANY: Mercury Media EDITOR: William Fix TOPICS: Spirituality, New Age TYPE: Book PRICE: $12.95

Pyramid Power: A New Reality
PUBLISHING COMPANY: Stillpoint Publishing EDITOR: Bill Schul, E. Pettit TOPICS: New Age TYPE: Book PRICE: $9.95

Pythagoras: His Life And Teachings
PUBLISHING COMPANY: Philosophical Research Society, Inc. EDITOR: T. Stanley TOPICS: Spirituality TYPE: Book PRICE: $16.95

Pythagorean Sourcebook And Library
PUBLISHING COMPANY: Phanes Press EDITOR: K. Guthrie TOPICS: Paranormal Phenomena TYPE: Book PRICE: $17.00

Pythagorean Writings
PUBLISHING COMPANY: Selene Books EDITOR: K. Guthrie, T. Taylor TOPICS: Paranormal Phenomena TYPE: Book PRICE: $16.50

Qabalistic Tarot
PUBLISHING COMPANY: Samuel Weiser, Inc. EDITOR: R. Wang TOPICS: Kabbalah, Tarot TYPE: Book PRICE: $17.95

Qabbalah: The Philosophy Of Ibn Geberol, The Qabbalah & The Zohar
PUBLISHING COMPANY: Wizards Bookshelf EDITOR: I. Myer TOPICS: Kabbalah TYPE: Book PRICE: $27.00

Qigong For Arthritis
PUBLISHING COMPANY: Yang Martial Arts Assoc. EDITOR: Dr. Yang Jwing-Ming TOPICS: Holistic Health, Tai Chi TYPE: Book PRICE: $14.00

Qigong For Health: Chinese Traditional Exercises For Cure And Prevention
PUBLISHING COMPANY: Japan Publications, Inc. EDITOR: M. Takahaski TOPICS: Tai Chi TYPE: Book PRICE: $14.95

Quantum Soup: Fortune Cookies In Crisis
PUBLISHING COMPANY: Celestial Arts Publishing Co./Sub. of Ten Speed Press EDITOR: A. Huang TOPICS: Psychology TYPE: Book PRICE: $17.95

Quest: A Search For The Grail Of Immortality
PUBLISHING COMPANY: Camelot Press Limited EDITOR: R. Gawr, M. Edwards TOPICS: Occult, Witchcraft TYPE: Book PRICE: $12.95

Questions Of King Milinda
PUBLISHING COMPANY: South Asia Books EDITOR: T.W. Rhys Davids TOPICS: Spirituality TYPE: Book PRICE: $28.00

Quick & Natural Rice Dishes

PUBLISHING COMPANY: East West Health Books EDITOR: Leonard Jacobs, Mark Mayell TOPICS: Holistic Health TYPE: Book

Quiet Mind: Techniques For Transforming Stress
PUBLISHING COMPANY: Himalayan International Institute Of Yoga Science and Philosophy EDITOR: J. Harvey TOPICS: Holistic Health, New Age TYPE: Book PRICE: $12.95

Radiance Technique On The Job, The
PUBLISHING COMPANY: Radiance Technique Association International, Inc. EDITOR: Fred W. Wright, Jr. TOPICS: New Age TYPE: Book PRICE: $9.90

Radical Spirits: Spiritualism & Women's Rights In Nineteenth-Century America
PUBLISHING COMPANY: Beacon Press, Inc. EDITOR: A. Braude TOPICS: Channeling TYPE: Book PRICE: $22.95

Raiment Of Light: A Study Of The Human Aura
PUBLISHING COMPANY: Penguin Books EDITOR: D. Tansley TOPICS: Holistic Health TYPE: Book PRICE: $8.95

Rainbow Elf
PUBLISHING COMPANY: Sun-Mt. Medicine Ways TYPE: Book SIZE: 8 1/2 x 11; 100 pgs. PRICE: $15.00 DESCRIPTION: Shamanic visions for our Monday mornings.

Rainbow In Your Life
PUBLISHING COMPANY: Star Visions EDITOR: Maryanne Hoffman TOPICS: Color Therapy TYPE: Book PRICE: $14.95

Rainbow Nation Cooperative Community Guide, The
PUBLISHING COMPANY: Rainbow Family Of Living Light TOPICS: New Age TYPE: Directory FREQ: Irregular DESCRIPTION: Lists several thousand members.

Rainbow Oracle: The Divination Of Color
PUBLISHING COMPANY: Ballantine Books, Inc. EDITOR: T. Grosso, R. MacGregor TOPICS: Color Therapy, Metaphysics TYPE: Book PRICE: $18.95

Rainbow Pages
PUBLISHING COMPANY: Rainbow Pages TOPICS: New Age TYPE: Directory DESCRIPTION: Lists alternative organizations.

Raise Your Vibration
PUBLISHING COMPANY: Blue Dolphin Publishing, Inc. TOPICS: New Age TYPE: Book PRICE: $8.95

Ramakrishna And His Disciples
PUBLISHING COMPANY: Vedanta Press, Div. of Vedanta Society EDITOR: C. Isherwood TOPICS: Spirituality TYPE: Book PRICE: $9.95

Ramakrishna As We Saw Him

PUBLISHING COMPANY: Vedanta Press, Div. of Vedanta Society EDITOR: Swami Chetanananda TOPICS: Spirituality TYPE: Book PRICE: $12.95

Ramana Maharshi And The Path Of Self-Knowledge

PUBLISHING COMPANY: Samuel Weiser, Inc. EDITOR: Arthur Osborne TOPICS: Spirituality TYPE: Book PRICE: $9.95

Ramtha

PUBLISHING COMPANY: Sovereignty, Inc. EDITOR: J.Z. Knight TOPICS: Channeling TYPE: Book PRICE: $19.95

Ransoming The Mind: An Integration Of Yoga And Modern Therapy

PUBLISHING COMPANY: Yes International EDITOR: C. Bates TOPICS: Yoga, Holistic Health TYPE: Book PRICE: $11.95

Real Magic: An Introductory Treatise On The Basic Principles Of Yellow Magic

PUBLISHING COMPANY: Samuel Weiser, Inc. EDITOR: P.E.I. Bonewits TOPICS: Occult TYPE: Book PRICE: $9.95

Rebel In The Soul: A Sacred Text Of Ancient Egypt

PUBLISHING COMPANY: Inner Traditions International, Ltd. EDITOR: Bika Reed TOPICS: Occult TYPE: Book PRICE: $10.95

Rebellious Spirit

PUBLISHING COMPANY: Chidvilas, Inc. EDITOR: B. Rajneesh TOPICS: New Age, Meditation, Spirituality, Body-Mind Connection TYPE: Book PRICE: $14.95

Rebirthing In The New Age

PUBLISHING COMPANY: Celestial Arts Publishing Co./Sub. of Ten Speed Press EDITOR: L. Orr, S. Ray TOPICS: Birth, Reincarnation TYPE: Book PRICE: $9.95

Recipes From The Sproutman

PUBLISHING COMPANY: Sprout House PUBLISHER: Steve Meyerowitz TOPICS: Nutrition, Holistic Health, Health Food TYPE: Book

Recognizing, Confronting & Conquering Negative Emotions

PUBLISHING COMPANY: Pathways EDITOR: Patricia K. Sawyer TOPICS: Metaphysics, Spirituality TYPE: Booklet

Recovery Resource Book: The Best Available Information On Addictions And Co-Dependence

PUBLISHING COMPANY: Simon & Schuster, Inc. EDITOR: Barbara Yoder TOPICS: Holistic Health TYPE: Book PRICE: $12.95

Recreating The Self: Self-Hypnotic Strategies For Adult Children Of Dysfunctional Families

PUBLISHING COMPANY: W. W. Norton & Co., Inc. EDITOR: Nancy J. Napler TOPICS: Hypnotism TYPE: Book PRICE: $19.95

Rediscovering The I Ching: First Translation Reflecting Contemporary Scholarship

PUBLISHING COMPANY: Doubleday & Co.,Inc. EDITOR: G. Whincup TOPICS: Parapsychology, Psychic TYPE: Book PRICE: $18.95

Reflections Directory

PUBLISHING COMPANY: Reflections Directory TOPICS: New Age, Metaphysics TYPE: Directory DESCRIPTION: Covers the Southwest Washington & Oregon areas.

Reflections In The Light: Daily Thoughts And Affirmations

PUBLISHING COMPANY: New World Library Publishing Co. EDITOR: S. Gawain TOPICS: Meditation, Psychology TYPE: Book PRICE: $7.95

Reflections Of An Elder Brother And Planetary Brother

PUBLISHING COMPANY: High Mesa Press EDITOR: Joy Franklin TOPICS: New Age, Channeling TYPE: Book PRICE: $10.95

Reflowering Of The Goddess

PUBLISHING COMPANY: Pergamon Press, Inc. EDITOR: Gloria Orenstein TOPICS: Spirituality TYPE: Book PRICE: $17.95

Reiki Factor

PUBLISHING COMPANY: Radiance Technique Association International, Inc. EDITOR: Dr. Barbara Ray TOPICS: Reiki, Body-Mind Connection, Massage TYPE: Book PRICE: $15.00

Reiki Handbook

PUBLISHING COMPANY: PSI Press TOPICS: Reiki TYPE: Book DATE: 1980; 150 pgs. PRICE: $14.75 DESCRIPTION: World's first book about the Reiki healing system. Special section on treatment of pets & wildlife. 46 illustrations.

Reiki: Universal Life Energy - A Holistic Method Of Treatment

PUBLISHING COMPANY: LifeRhythm EDITOR: B. Baginski, S. Sharamon TOPICS: Reiki, Spirituality, Holistic Healing TYPE: Book PRICE: $12.95

Reincarnation And The Law Of Karma

PUBLISHING COMPANY: Yoga Publications Society EDITOR: William W. Atkinson TOPICS: Reincarnation TYPE: Book PRICE: $9.00

Reincarnation Explained

PUBLISHING COMPANY: Science Of Identity Foundation EDITOR: Chris Butler TOPICS: Reincarnation, Spirituality TYPE: Book PRICE: $12.95

Reincarnation Workbook: A Complete Course In Recalling Past Lives

PUBLISHING COMPANY: Aquarian Press EDITOR: J. Brennan TOPICS: Past Life Regression TYPE: Book PRICE: $12.95

Reincarnation: A New Horizon In Science, Religion And Society

PUBLISHING COMPANY: Crown Publishers, Inc. EDITOR: S. Cranston, C. Williams TOPICS: Reincarnation TYPE: Book PRICE: $16.95

Reincarnation: The Phoenix Fire Mystery

PUBLISHING COMPANY: Crown Publishers, Inc. EDITOR: J. Head, S. Cranston TOPICS: Reincarnation TYPE: Book PRICE: $12.95

Relating Psychically: Psychic Influences On Relationships

PUBLISHING COMPANY: Cassandra Press EDITOR: Sandra Stevens TOPICS: Psychic TYPE: Book; 160 pgs. PRICE: $9.95

Relaxation And Stress Reduction Workbook

PUBLISHING COMPANY: New Harbinger Publications EDITOR: M. McKay TOPICS: Holistic Health, New Age TYPE: Book PRICE: $13.95

Release

PUBLISHING COMPANY: Sedona Institute EDITOR: Virginia Lloyd, Janet Bechtel TOPICS: Holistic Healing TYPE: Book

Releasing Arthritis

PUBLISHING COMPANY: LF Pubishing EDITOR: Linda Frazer Fleming TOPICS: Holistic Health TYPE: Book PRICE: $11.00

Remembering And Forgetting: Inquiries Into The Nature Of Memory

PUBLISHING COMPANY: Walker & Co., Div. of Walker Publishing Co., Inc. EDITOR: E. Bolles TOPICS: Body-Mind Connection, Psychology TYPE: Book PRICE: $22.95

Repertory Of The Homeopathic Materia Medica With Word And Thumb Index

PUBLISHING COMPANY: B. Jain Publishers, Ltd. EDITOR: J. Kent TOPICS: Homeopathy, Holistic Health TYPE: Book PRICE: $50.00

Resolving Conflict: With Others And Within Yourself

PUBLISHING COMPANY: New Harbinger Publications EDITOR: Gini Scott TOPICS: New Age, Psychology TYPE: Book PRICE: $11.95

Resource Directory

PUBLISHING COMPANY: New Age Guild Of Connecticut TYPE: Booklet DATE: 1989 DESCRIPTION: A booklet of members' areas of interest or profession for distribution to the public. Members may be included at their option.

Resource Guide For The Responsible Non-Monogamist

PUBLISHING COMPANY: IntiNet Resource Center TOPICS: New Age TYPE: Book DATE: 1984 PRICE: $12.95

Resources For Health, Fitness And Learning

PUBLISHING COMPANY: Resources For Health, Fitness And Learning EDITOR: David I. Weiss TOPICS: Holistic Health, New Age TYPE: Directory

DESCRIPTION: Lists sources & information related to holistic health & self improvement in the New England area.

Return From Death: An Exploration Of The Near-Death Experience
PUBLISHING COMPANY: Penguin Books **EDITOR:** M. Grey **TOPICS:** Death **TYPE:** Book **PRICE:** $9.95

Return From Silence: A Study Of Near-Death Experience
PUBLISHING COMPANY: Aquarian Press **EDITOR:** D. Scott Rogo **TOPICS:** Death, Reincarnation **TYPE:** Book **PRICE:** $9.95

Return To Atlantis Vol I
PUBLISHING COMPANY: Unarius Academy Of Science & Education Foundation **EDITOR:** Ruth Norman **TOPICS:** Reincarnation **TYPE:** Book; 340 pgs. **PRICE:** $11.95

Returning To Silence: Zen Practice In Daily Life
PUBLISHING COMPANY: Shambhala Publications, Inc. **EDITOR:** D. Katagiri **TOPICS:** Spirituality **TYPE:** Book **PRICE:** $12.95

Revelation For A New Age
PUBLISHING COMPANY: DeVorss & Company **EDITOR:** Dorothy Elder **TOPICS:** New Age **TYPE:** Book **PRICE:** $11.50

Revelation: A Commentary Based On The Study Of Twenty-Four Psychic Discourses By Edgar Cayce
PUBLISHING COMPANY: Association For Research And Enlightenment, Inc. **EDITOR:** Edgar Cayce **TOPICS:** Channeling **TYPE:** Book **PRICE:** $8.95

Revelations Of Things To Come
PUBLISHING COMPANY: Astara Foundation, Inc. **EDITOR:** E. Chaney **TOPICS:** Metaphysics, Psychic **TYPE:** Book **PRICE:** $13.95

Rhythmic Integration: Wholeness And The Cycle Of Change
PUBLISHING COMPANY: Station Hill Press **EDITOR:** Ronald Robbins **TOPICS:** Holistic Healing, Spirituality **TYPE:** Book **PRICE:** $13.95

Riddle Of The Pryamids
PUBLISHING COMPANY: Thames & Hudson **EDITOR:** K. Mendelssohn **TOPICS:** New Age **TYPE:** Book **PRICE:** $12.95

Riding The Tiger
PUBLISHING COMPANY: Blue Dolphin Publishing, Inc. **TOPICS:** New Age **TYPE:** Book **PRICE:** $16.95

Right Brain Sex: Using Creative Visualization To Enhance Sexual Pleasure
PUBLISHING COMPANY: Prentice-Hall, Inc. **EDITOR:** Carol G. Wells **TOPICS:** New Age, Meditation, Psychology **TYPE:** Book **PRICE:** $18.95

Rising To The Challenge: Celebrities & Their Very Personal Health Stories
PUBLISHING COMPANY: Avery Publishing Group, Inc. **EDITOR:** Robert Phillips **TOPICS:** Acupuncture **TYPE:** Book **PRICE:** $10.95

Rites Of Odin: A Norse Book Of Shadows
PUBLISHING COMPANY: Llewellyn Publications **EDITOR:** E. Fitch **TOPICS:** Occult, Witchcraft **TYPE:** Book **PRICE:** $12.95

Rituals For The Living And Dying: How We Can Turn Loss & The Fear Of Death Into An Affirmation
PUBLISHING COMPANY: Harper & Row Publishers, Inc. **EDITOR:** D. Feinstein, Peg Mayo **TOPICS:** Death **TYPE:** Book **PRICE:** $16.95

River's Way: The Process Science Of The Dreambody
PUBLISHING COMPANY: Routledge, Chapman & Hall, Inc. **EDITOR:** A. Mindell **TOPICS:** Body-Mind Connection **TYPE:** Book **PRICE:** $10.95

Rock Crystal: The Magic Stone
PUBLISHING COMPANY: Parapsychology Education Center **EDITOR:** Korra Deaver, Ph. D. **TOPICS:** Crystals, Meditation, Holistic Healing **TYPE:** Book **PRICE:** $5.00 **DESCRIPTION:** Deal with how to choose & care for your crystal, exercises in meditation, healing, crystal gazing, programming a crystal pendulum.

Rolf Institute International Directory
PUBLISHING COMPANY: Rolf Institute For Structural Integration **EDITOR:** Marcia Richardson **TOPICS:** New Age **TYPE:** Directory

Rolfing: The Integration Of Human Structures
PUBLISHING COMPANY: Rolf Institute For Structural Integration **EDITOR:** Ida P. Rolf **TOPICS:** Massage, Holistic Health **TYPE:** Book **DATE:** 1977

Rolling Thunder: The Coming Earth Changes
PUBLISHING COMPANY: Sun Publishing Company **EDITOR:** J.R. Jochmans **TOPICS:** Metaphysics, Psychic **TYPE:** Book **PRICE:** $15.00

Root Of Chinese Chi Kung
PUBLISHING COMPANY: Yang Martial Arts Assoc. **EDITOR:** Y. Jwing-Ming **TOPICS:** Tai Chi **TYPE:** Book **PRICE:** $18.00

Rose And The Pickle
PUBLISHING COMPANY: Wisdom Book Publishers, Inc. **EDITOR:** Adrienne Golday **TOPICS:** Psychology **TYPE:** Book **PRICE:** $13.50

Rose Window
PUBLISHING COMPANY: Healing Through Arts **EDITOR:** Kay Gardner **TOPICS:** Holistic Healing **TYPE:** Book

Rosicrucian Christianity Lectures
PUBLISHING COMPANY: Rosicrucian Fellowship **EDITOR:** M. Heindel **TOPICS:** Spirituality, New Age, Astrology **TYPE:** Book **PRICE:** $16.95

Rosicrucian Esotericism

PUBLISHING COMPANY: Anthroposophic Press, Inc. **EDITOR:** R. Steiner **TOPICS:** Spirituality **TYPE:** Book **PRICE:** $14.00

Rosicrucian Seer: The Magical Works Of Frederick Hockley
PUBLISHING COMPANY: Aquarian Press **EDITOR:** J. Hamill **TOPICS:** Spirituality **TYPE:** Book **PRICE:** $13.95

Rosicrucians: The History, Mythology And Rituals Of An Occult Order
PUBLISHING COMPANY: Crucible Books, Inner Traditions International, Ltd. **EDITOR:** C. McIntosh **TOPICS:** Spirituality **TYPE:** Book **PRICE:** $12.95

Rosie Crucian Secrets: Their Excellent Method Of Making Medicines Of Metals
PUBLISHING COMPANY: Aquarian Press **EDITOR:** John Dee **TOPICS:** Spirituality, Alchemy, Holistic Health **TYPE:** Book **PRICE:** $15.00

Royal Masonic Cyclopaedia
PUBLISHING COMPANY: Aquarian Press **EDITOR:** K. Mackenzie **TOPICS:** Spirituality **TYPE:** Book **PRICE:** $19.95

Rumi And Sufism
PUBLISHING COMPANY: Post-Apollo Press **EDITOR:** E. De Vitray-Meyerovitc **TOPICS:** Spirituality **TYPE:** Book **PRICE:** $12.95

Rune Games
PUBLISHING COMPANY: Penguin Books **EDITOR:** M. Osborn, S. Longland **TOPICS:** Runes **TYPE:** Book **PRICE:** $12.95

Rune Magic
PUBLISHING COMPANY: Llewellyn Publications **EDITOR:** D. Tyson **TOPICS:** Runes, Metaphysics **TYPE:** Book **PRICE:** $9.95

Rune Magic Cards
PUBLISHING COMPANY: Llewellyn Publications **EDITOR:** D. Tyson **TOPICS:** Runes, Metaphysics **TYPE:** Book **PRICE:** $9.95

Rune Magic: The Celtic Runes As A Tool For Personal Transformation
PUBLISHING COMPANY: Newcastle Publishing Co., Inc. **EDITOR:** D. Dolphin **TOPICS:** Runes **TYPE:** Book **PRICE:** $9.95

Rune Play: A Method Of Self-Counseling With A Year-Round Runecasting Recordbook
PUBLISHING COMPANY: St. Martin's Press, Inc. **EDITOR:** R. Blum **TOPICS:** Runes **TYPE:** Book **PRICE:** $14.95

Runelore: A Handbook Of Esoteric Runology
PUBLISHING COMPANY: Samuel Weiser, Inc. **EDITOR:** E. Thorsson **TOPICS:** Runes **TYPE:** Book **PRICE:** $10.95

Runic Astrology: Starcraft & Timekeeping In The Northern Tradition

PUBLISHING COMPANY: Aquarian Press EDITOR: N. Pennick TOPICS: Occult, Witchcraft, Runes, Astrology TYPE: Book PRICE: $12.95

Runic Workbook: Understanding And Using The Power Of Runes

PUBLISHING COMPANY: Aquarian Press EDITOR: T. Willis TOPICS: Runes TYPE: Book PRICE: $10.95

S.H.A.R.E. Guide, The

PUBLISHING COMPANY: S.H.A.R.E. Guide, The EDITOR: Dennis Hughes TOPICS: New Age, Metaphysics TYPE: Directory DATE: 1989; 24 pgs. FREQ: quarterly CIRC: 10,000 PRICE: $6.00 DESCRIPTION: Serves Sonoma County readers interested in personal and global healing.

Sacred Geometry: Philosophy & Practice

PUBLISHING COMPANY: W. W. Norton & Co., Inc. EDITOR: J. Lawlor TOPICS: New Age TYPE: Book PRICE: $11.95

Sacred Power In Your Name

PUBLISHING COMPANY: Llewellyn Publications EDITOR: T. Andrews TOPICS: New Age, Occult, Witchcraft TYPE: Book PRICE: $12.95

Sacred Prostitute: Eternal Aspect Of The Feminine

PUBLISHING COMPANY: Inner City Books EDITOR: N. Qualis-Corbett TOPICS: Spirituality TYPE: Book PRICE: $15.00

Sacred Science: The King Of Pharaonic Theocracy

PUBLISHING COMPANY: Inner Traditions International, Ltd. EDITOR: R.A. Schwaller de Lubicz TOPICS: New Age, Paranormal Phenomena, Occult, Witchcraft, Spirituality TYPE: Book PRICE: $12.95

Sacred Theory Of The Earth

PUBLISHING COMPANY: North Atlantic Books EDITOR: T. Frick TOPICS: Paranormal Phenomena, Spirituality TYPE: Book PRICE: $12.95

Sad But O.K...My Daddy Died Today

PUBLISHING COMPANY: Blue Dolphin Publishing, Inc. TOPICS: New Age TYPE: Book PRICE: $9.95

Safe Eating: A Practical 4-Point Program To Reduce Your Intake & Reduce Tolerance Of Toxins

PUBLISHING COMPANY: M. Evans & Co., Inc. EDITOR: P. Quillin TOPICS: Holistic Health TYPE: Book PRICE: $18.95

Sai Baba: Holy Man And The Psychiatrist

PUBLISHING COMPANY: Birth Day Publishing Company EDITOR: S. Sandweiss TOPICS: Spirituality TYPE: Book PRICE: $9.00

Sanctified Body: An Expert On 19th & 20th Centruy Holiness Looks At Levitation

PUBLISHING COMPANY: Doubleday & Co.,Inc. EDITOR: P. Treece TOPICS: Paranormal Phenomena TYPE: Book PRICE: $17.95

Sand And Foam

PUBLISHING COMPANY: Random House, Inc. EDITOR: K. Gilbran TOPICS: Channeling TYPE: Book PRICE: $14.95

Sane & Intelligent Living

PUBLISHING COMPANY: Atrium Society TYPE: Book DESCRIPTION: A series.

Sangreal Ceremonies And Rituals

PUBLISHING COMPANY: Samuel Weiser, Inc. EDITOR: William G. Gray TOPICS: Witchcraft, Occult TYPE: Book PRICE: $12.95

Sangreal Tarot System

PUBLISHING COMPANY: Samuel Weiser, Inc. EDITOR: William G. Gray TOPICS: Occult TYPE: Book PRICE: $14.95

Santeria: An African Religion In America

PUBLISHING COMPANY: Beacon Press, Inc. EDITOR: Joseph Murphy TOPICS: Voudoun TYPE: Book PRICE: $10.95

Santeria: The Religion--A Legacy Of Faith, Rites & Magic

PUBLISHING COMPANY: Crown Publishers, Inc. EDITOR: M. Gonzalez-Wippler TOPICS: Voudoun TYPE: Book PRICE: $19.95

Satya Narayan Kathaa

PUBLISHING COMPANY: Ma Yoga Shakti International Mission PUBLISHER: Ma Yoga Shakti TOPICS: Yoga, Meditation, Spirituality TYPE: Book

Saving Your Skin

PUBLISHING COMPANY: Association For Research And Enlightenment, Inc. EDITOR: Eric Mein, M.D., Anne Hunt TOPICS: Homeopathy TYPE: Book; 64 pgs. PRICE: $4.95

Savitri

PUBLISHING COMPANY: Sri Aurobindo Ashram Aurobindo TOPICS: Spirituality TYPE: Book PRICE: $21.95

Scapegoat Complex: Toward A Mythology Of Shadow And Guilt

PUBLISHING COMPANY: Inner City Books EDITOR: S. Perera TOPICS: Occult TYPE: Book PRICE: $13.00

Scholar Warrior: An Introduction To The Tao In Everyday Life

PUBLISHING COMPANY: Harper & Row Publishers, Inc. EDITOR: Deng Ming-Dao TOPICS: Spirituality, New Age TYPE: Book PRICE: $17.95

School Of Natural Healing

PUBLISHING COMPANY: Christopher Publishing House EDITOR: John R. Christopher TOPICS: Holistic Health, Herbalogy TYPE: Book PRICE: $39.95

Science And Art Of The Pendulum: A Complete Course In Radiesthesia

PUBLISHING COMPANY: Idylwild Books EDITOR: Gabriele Blackburn TOPICS: Dowsing TYPE: Book PRICE: $10.00

Science And Health: With Key To Scriptures

PUBLISHING COMPANY: Bookmark, The EDITOR: M.B. Eddy TOPICS: Spirituality TYPE: Book DESCRIPTION: M.B. Eddy discoverer & founder of the Christian Science Movement, 1866-1910. Born 7/1821 in Bow, NH. died in 1910.

Science Of Mind

PUBLISHING COMPANY: Putnam Publishing Group EDITOR: E. Holmes TOPICS: Spirituality, Psychology TYPE: Book PRICE: $21.95

Science Of The Paranormal: Last Frontier

PUBLISHING COMPANY: Sterling Publishing Company, Inc. EDITOR: L. LeShan TOPICS: Psychic TYPE: Book PRICE: $12.95

Sea Gods After Atlantis: The Biography Of A Race Of Man

PUBLISHING COMPANY: Intaglio Publishing EDITOR: V. Bonwick, J. Bigras TOPICS: New Age TYPE: Book PRICE: $14.95

Search

PUBLISHING COMPANY: Crystal Clarity Publishers EDITOR: Donald Walters TOPICS: New Age TYPE: Book PRICE: $9.95

Search For Meaning

PUBLISHING COMPANY: Gentle Beginning, Inc. TOPICS: New Age, Spirituality, Psychic TYPE: Book; 176 pgs. PRICE: $7.95 DESCRIPTION: Analyzes the great religions & shows a common core or message at the heart of their teachings.

Search For Om Sety: A True Story Of Eternal Love & One Woman's Voyage Through The Ages

PUBLISHING COMPANY: Warner Books, Inc. EDITOR: J. Cott TOPICS: Past Life Regression TYPE: Book PRICE: $9.95

Second Coming Of Christ Vol. 1

PUBLISHING COMPANY: Amrita Foundation Yogananda TOPICS: Yoga, Spirituality TYPE: Book PRICE: $18.95

Second Coming Of Christ Vol. II

PUBLISHING COMPANY: Amrita Foundation Yogananda TOPICS: Yoga, Spirituality TYPE: Book PRICE: $18.95

Second Coming Of Christ Vol. III

PUBLISHING COMPANY: Amrita Foundation Yogananda TOPICS: Yoga, Spirituality TYPE: Book PRICE: $18.95

Second Medical Revolution: From Biomedicine To Infomedicine

PUBLISHING COMPANY: Shambhala Publications, Inc. EDITOR: L. Foss, K. Rothenberg TOPICS:

Body-Mind Connection, Holistic Health **TYPE:** Book **PRICE:** $15.95

Secondary Vessels Of Acupuncture

PUBLISHING COMPANY: Thorsens Publishing House **EDITOR:** Royston Low **TOPICS:** Holistic Health, Acupuncture **TYPE:** Book **PRICE:** $29.95

Secret Chief: The Rosicrucian & Occult Writings Of Kenneth Mackenzie

PUBLISHING COMPANY: Aquarian Press **EDITOR:** J. Hamill **TOPICS:** Spirituality **TYPE:** Book **PRICE:** $16.25

Secret Doctrine

PUBLISHING COMPANY: Theosophical University Press **EDITOR:** H. Blavatsky **TOPICS:** New Age, Spirituality **TYPE:** Book **PRICE:** $57.50

Secret Is In The Rainbow

PUBLISHING COMPANY: Samuel Weiser, Inc. **EDITOR:** R. Berger **TOPICS:** Holistic Health **TYPE:** Book **PRICE:** $6.95

Secret Magick Revealed

PUBLISHING COMPANY: Technology Group, The **EDITOR:** Nelson White, Anne White **TYPE:** Book **SIZE:** 8 1/2 x 11

Secret Of Secrets: The Unwritten Mysteries Of Esoteric Qabbalah

PUBLISHING COMPANY: Heptangle Books **EDITOR:** M.A. Macdonald **TOPICS:** Kabbalah **TYPE:** Book **PRICE:** $20.00

Secret Of The Black Chrysanthemum: Poetic Cosmology Of Charls Olson & His Use Of C.G.Jung

PUBLISHING COMPANY: Talman Company **EDITOR:** Charles Stein **TOPICS:** Spirituality **TYPE:** Book **PRICE:** $27.50

Secret Of The Siddhas

PUBLISHING COMPANY: S.Y.D.A. Foundation/Siddha Yoga Meditation Ashram Muktananda **TOPICS:** Spirituality **TYPE:** Book **PRICE:** $9.95

Secret Of The Target

PUBLISHING COMPANY: Routledge, Chapman & Hall, Inc. **EDITOR:** J. Morisawa **TOPICS:** Spirituality **TYPE:** Book **PRICE:** $14.95

Secret Of The Veda

PUBLISHING COMPANY: Sri Aurobindo Ashram Aurobindo **TOPICS:** Spirituality **TYPE:** Book **PRICE:** $18.00

Secret Places Of The Lion

PUBLISHING COMPANY: Inner Traditions International, Ltd. **EDITOR:** George H. Williamson **TOPICS:** New Age **TYPE:** Book **PRICE:** $8.95

Secret Symbols Of The Rosicrucians

PUBLISHING COMPANY: Supreme Grand Lodge of AMORC, Inc. Rosicrucian Order **TOPICS:** Spirituality **TYPE:** Book **PRICE:** $20.00

Secret Teachings Of All Ages: An Encyclopedic Outline Of Masonic, Hermetic, Qabbalistic

PUBLISHING COMPANY: Philosophical Research Society, Inc. **EDITOR:** M.P. Hall **TOPICS:** Kabbalah **TYPE:** Book **PRICE:** $35.00

Secret Teachings Of The Temple Of Isis

PUBLISHING COMPANY: Llewellyn Publications Ishbel **TOPICS:** Occult, Witchcraft **TYPE:** Book **PRICE:** $12.95

Secret Tradition In Arthurian Legend: An Examination Of The Magical And Mystical Power

PUBLISHING COMPANY: Aquarian Press **EDITOR:** G. Knight **TOPICS:** Occult **TYPE:** Book **PRICE:** $12.95

Secret Truths: A Young Adult's Guide For Creating Peace

PUBLISHING COMPANY: Spiritual Education Endeavours **EDITOR:** Virginia Essene **TOPICS:** New Age, Spirituality **TYPE:** Book

Secret World Of Drawings: Healing Through Art

PUBLISHING COMPANY: Sigo Press **EDITOR:** G. Furth **TOPICS:** Psychology **TYPE:** Book **PRICE:** $16.95

Secrets In Their Signatures

PUBLISHING COMPANY: W. Foulsham & Co., Ltd. **EDITOR:** P. Marne **TOPICS:** Parapsychology, Graphology **TYPE:** Book **PRICE:** $10.95

Secrets Of A Witch's Coven

PUBLISHING COMPANY: Whitford Press/Schiffer Publishing Limited Morwyn **TOPICS:** Witchcraft, Occult **TYPE:** Book **PRICE:** $19.95

Secrets Of Precious Stones: A Guide To The Activation Of The 7 Human Energy Centers

PUBLISHING COMPANY: Lotus Light Publications **EDITOR:** U. Raatz **TOPICS:** Holistic Health **TYPE:** Book **PRICE:** $9.95

Secrets Of The Great Pyramid

PUBLISHING COMPANY: Harper & Row Publishers, Inc. **EDITOR:** Peter Tompkins **TOPICS:** New Age, Paranormal Phenomena **TYPE:** Book **PRICE:** $15.95

Secrets Of The Palm

PUBLISHING COMPANY: A.C.S. Publications, Inc./Astro Computing Services **EDITOR:** D. Hansen **TOPICS:** Palmistry **TYPE:** Book **PRICE:** $9.95

Secrets Of The Runes

PUBLISHING COMPANY: Inner Traditions International, Ltd. **EDITOR:** S. Flowers **TOPICS:** Runes **TYPE:** Book **PRICE:** $9.95

Secrets Of The Stones: New Revelations Of Astro-Archeology & The Mystical Sciences/Antiquity

PUBLISHING COMPANY: Destiny Books, Inner Traditions International, Ltd. **EDITOR:** J. Mitchell **TOPICS:** New Age **TYPE:** Book **PRICE:** $10.95

Secrets Of The Tarot: Origins, History, And Symbolism

PUBLISHING COMPANY: Harper & Row Publishers, Inc. **EDITOR:** Barbara Walker **TOPICS:** Spirituality, Tarot **TYPE:** Book **PRICE:** $14.95

Secrets Of Voodoo

PUBLISHING COMPANY: City Lights Books **EDITOR:** R. Cross **TOPICS:** Voudoun **TYPE:** Book **PRICE:** $9.95

Sedona: Are The Vortexes Real?

PUBLISHING COMPANY: Pathways **EDITOR:** Patricia K. Sawyer **TOPICS:** Metaphysics, Spirituality **TYPE:** Booklet

Seeds Of Tomorrow: New Age Communities That Work

PUBLISHING COMPANY: Harper & Row Publishers, Inc. **EDITOR:** C. Pepone, O. Pepone **TOPICS:** New Age **TYPE:** Book **PRICE:** $10.95

Seeing Through The Visible World: Jung, Gnosis & Chaos

PUBLISHING COMPANY: Harper & Row Publishers, Inc. **EDITOR:** June Singer **TOPICS:** Psychology **TYPE:** Book **PRICE:** $18.95

Seeing Your Future: A Modern Look At Prophecy & Prediction

PUBLISHING COMPANY: Mamre Press, Inc. **EDITOR:** John Ronner **TOPICS:** Metaphysics, Psychic **TYPE:** Book **PRICE:** $10.95

Sefer Yetzirah

PUBLISHING COMPANY: Heptangle Books **EDITOR:** I. Kalish **TOPICS:** Kabbalah **TYPE:** Book **PRICE:** $20.00

Sefer Yetzirah (The Book Of Creation): In Theory And Practice

PUBLISHING COMPANY: Samuel Weiser, Inc. **EDITOR:** Aryeh Kaplan **TOPICS:** Spirituality, Kabbalah **TYPE:** Book **PRICE:** $29.95

Seizing Life's Second Change: Activating Your Inner Survival Mechanisms For Conquering Fear

PUBLISHING COMPANY: Stillpoint Publishing **EDITOR:** Paul Vigyikan **TOPICS:** Channeling, New Age, Psychology **TYPE:** Book **PRICE:** $12.95

Self Analysis, Dianetics

PUBLISHING COMPANY: Bridge Publications, Inc. **EDITOR:** L. Ron Hubbard **TYPE:** Book

Self-Esteem: A Family Affair

PUBLISHING COMPANY: Henry Holt & Co. **EDITOR:** J. Illsley **TOPICS:** New Age, Psychology **TYPE:** Book **PRICE:** $11.95

Self-Esteem: A Proven Program Of Cognitive Techniques For Assessing, Improving & Maintaining

PUBLISHING COMPANY: New Harbinger Publications **EDITOR:** M. McKay, P. Fanning

TOPICS: New Age, Psychology TYPE: Book PRICE: $11.95

Self-Mastery Through Conscious Auto-Suggestion
PUBLISHING COMPANY: Sun Publishing Company EDITOR: E. Coue TOPICS: New Age, Psychology TYPE: Book PRICE: $8.00

Self-Unfoldment By Disciples Of Realization
PUBLISHING COMPANY: Philosophical Research Society, Inc. EDITOR: M.P. Hall TOPICS: Psychic TYPE: Book PRICE: $10.95

Sengreal Tarot System
PUBLISHING COMPANY: Samuel Weiser, Inc. EDITOR: William G. Gray TOPICS: Tarot TYPE: Book PRICE: $14.95

Sensory Awareness: Rediscovery Of Experiencing Through The Workshops Of Charlotte Selver
PUBLISHING COMPANY: Felix Morrow EDITOR: Charles V.W. Brooks TOPICS: Psychology TYPE: Book PRICE: $12.95

Senya
PUBLISHING COMPANY: Mar Crafts PUBLISHER: Marty Campbell EDITOR: Senya Darklight TOPICS: Spirituality TYPE: Book PRICE: $9.00 DESCRIPTION: Spiritual poetry. Reproduced in the authors own handwriting. Illustrated.

Sepharial's Book Of Charms And Talismans
PUBLISHING COMPANY: W. Foulsham & Co., Ltd. Sepharial TOPICS: Occult, Witchcraft TYPE: Book PRICE: $7.50

Serenity Prayer Book
PUBLISHING COMPANY: Harper & Row Publishers, Inc. EDITOR: William Pietsch TOPICS: Meditation TYPE: Book PRICE: $15.95

Sermon On The Mount
PUBLISHING COMPANY: Amrita Foundation Yogananda TOPICS: Yoga, Spirituality TYPE: Book PRICE: $12.95

Serpent In The Sky: The High Wisdom Of Ancient Egypt
PUBLISHING COMPANY: Crown Publishers, Inc. EDITOR: John A. West TOPICS: New Age TYPE: Book PRICE: $13.95

Seth Material
PUBLISHING COMPANY: Prentice-Hall, Inc. EDITOR: Jane Roberts TOPICS: Channeling, Reincarnation TYPE: Book PRICE: $9.95

Seth Speaks: The Eternal Validity Of The Soul
PUBLISHING COMPANY: Prentice-Hall, Inc. EDITOR: Jane Roberts TOPICS: Channeling, Reincarnation TYPE: Book PRICE: $10.95

Seth: Dreams And The Projection Of Consciousness
PUBLISHING COMPANY: New American Library EDITOR: Jane Roberts TOPICS: Channeling TYPE: Book PRICE: $9.95

Seti Factor: How The Search For Extraterrestrial Intelligence Is Changing Our View
PUBLISHING COMPANY: Walker & Co., Div. of Walker Publishing Co., Inc. EDITOR: Frank White TOPICS: UFO's, Paranormal Phenomena TYPE: Book PRICE: $18.95

Seven Mountains Of Thomas Merton
PUBLISHING COMPANY: Houghton Mifflin Company EDITOR: M. Mott TOPICS: New Age TYPE: Book PRICE: $12.95

Seven Mysteries Of Life: An Exploration In Science And Philosophy
PUBLISHING COMPANY: Houghton Mifflin Company EDITOR: Guy Murchie TOPICS: Paranormal Phenomena, Spirituality TYPE: Book DATE: 1978 PRICE: $12.95

Seven Paths To Understanding
PUBLISHING COMPANY: A.C.S. Publications, Inc./Astro Computing Services EDITOR: Z. Dobyns, B. Wrobel TOPICS: New Age, Metaphysics, Occult TYPE: Book PRICE: $12.95

Seven Rays Made Visual: Illustrated Intro To Teachings On The 7 Rays Of D. Khul & Alice Bailey
PUBLISHING COMPANY: DeVorss & Company EDITOR: H. Burmester TOPICS: Spirituality TYPE: Book PRICE: $12.00

Seven Rays Of The Q.B.L.
PUBLISHING COMPANY: Samuel Weiser, Inc. EDITOR: Fr. Albertus TOPICS: New Age, Kabbalah, Alchemy TYPE: Book PRICE: $39.95

Seven Steps To Better Vision
PUBLISHING COMPANY: East West Health Books EDITOR: Leonard Jacobs, Mark Mayell TOPICS: Holistic Health TYPE: Book

Sevenfold Peace
PUBLISHING COMPANY: H.J. Kramer, Inc. EDITOR: Gabriel Cousens, M.D. TOPICS: New Age TYPE: Book PRICE: $4.95

Sexual Energy Ecstasy
PUBLISHING COMPANY: Peak Skill Publishing TOPICS: New Age TYPE: Book DESCRIPTION: A practical guide to lovemaking secrets of the East & West.

Sexual Politics Of Meat: A Feminist Vegetarian Critical Theory
PUBLISHING COMPANY: Continuum Publishing Co. EDITOR: Carol J. Adams TOPICS: Vegetarianism, Health Food, Holistic Health TYPE: Book PRICE: $22.95

Shadow And Self: Selected Papers In Analytical Psychology
PUBLISHING COMPANY: Chiron Publications EDITOR: Joseph L. Henderson TOPICS: Psychology, Occult TYPE: Book PRICE: $19.95

Shakti And Shakta
PUBLISHING COMPANY: Dover Publications, Inc. EDITOR: A. Avalon TOPICS: New Age, Spirituality TYPE: Book PRICE: $14.95

Shakti Gawain Collection
PUBLISHING COMPANY: New World Library Publishing Co. EDITOR: S. Gawain TOPICS: Spirituality TYPE: Book PRICE: $16.95

Shamanism For The New Age: A Guide To Radionics And Radiethesia
PUBLISHING COMPANY: Aquarian Systems, Inc. EDITOR: Jane Hartman TOPICS: Holistic Health, Metaphysics TYPE: Book PRICE: $12.95

Shamanism: The Spirit World Of Korea
PUBLISHING COMPANY: Asian Humanities Press EDITOR: C.S. Yu, R. Guisso TOPICS: Occult TYPE: Book PRICE: $12.95

Shambhala
PUBLISHING COMPANY: Inner Traditions International, Ltd. EDITOR: Nicholas Roerich TOPICS: New Age TYPE: Book PRICE: $10.95

Shining Paths: An Experience In Vision Of The 32 Paths Of The Tree Of Life
PUBLISHING COMPANY: Collins, Div. of William Collins EDITOR: D. Ashcroft-Nowicki TOPICS: Occult, Witchcraft TYPE: Book PRICE: $9.95

Shouting At The Wolf: A Guide Identifying & Warding Off Evil In Everyday Life
PUBLISHING COMPANY: Citadel Press EDITOR: Anderson Reed TOPICS: Occult, Witchcraft TYPE: Book PRICE: $11.95

Silver Bird: A Tale For Those Who Dream
PUBLISHING COMPANY: Celestial Arts Publishing Co./Sub. of Ten Speed Press EDITOR: J. Petshek TOPICS: Psychic TYPE: Book PRICE: $9.95

Simon & Schuster's Guide To Gems And Precious Stones
PUBLISHING COMPANY: Simon & Schuster, Inc. EDITOR: C. Cipriani, A. Borelli TOPICS: Crystals TYPE: Book PRICE: $11.95

Simon & Schuster's Guide To Rocks And Minerals
PUBLISHING COMPANY: Simon & Schuster, Inc. EDITOR: M. Prinz TOPICS: Crystals TYPE: Book PRICE: $13.95

Sirius Mystery
PUBLISHING COMPANY: Inner Traditions International, Ltd. EDITOR: Robert K.G. Temple TOPICS: New Age, UFO's, Paranormal Phenomena TYPE: Book PRICE: $12.95

Siva Sutras: The Yoga Of Supreme Identity
PUBLISHING COMPANY: South Asia Books EDITOR: Jaideva Singh TOPICS: Spirituality TYPE: Book PRICE: $18.50

Sivananda Companion To Yoga
PUBLISHING COMPANY: Simon & Schuster, Inc. EDITOR: Sivananda Yoga Centre TOPICS: Yoga, Holistic Health TYPE: Book PRICE: $12.95

Sixth Sense: Whole-Brain Book Of Intuition, Hunches...And Their Place In Everyday Life
PUBLISHING COMPANY: Prentice-Hall, Inc. EDITOR: Laurie Nadel TOPICS: Body-Mind Connection, Psychology TYPE: Book PRICE: $18.95

Sixty Upanishads Of The Vedas Volume 2
PUBLISHING COMPANY: South Asia Books EDITOR: P. Deussen TOPICS: Spirituality TYPE: Book PRICE: $28.50

Software For The Mind: How To Program Your Own Mind For Optimum Health & Performance
PUBLISHING COMPANY: Celestial Arts Publishing Co./Sub. of Ten Speed Press EDITOR: E. Miller TOPICS: Hypnotism TYPE: Book PRICE: $9.95

Solstice Evergreen: History, Forklore And Origins Of The Christmas Tree
PUBLISHING COMPANY: Aslan Publishing EDITOR: Sheryl Ann Karas TOPICS: Paganism, Spirituality TYPE: Book PRICE: $9.95

Son Rise
PUBLISHING COMPANY: Option Institute & Fellowship- A Place For Miracles EDITOR: Carol Wertz, Barry Neil Kaufman TOPICS: Holistic Healing TYPE: Book

Song Of Eve: An Illustrated Journey Into Myths, Symbols & Rituals Of The Goddess
PUBLISHING COMPANY: Simon & Schuster, Inc. EDITOR: Manuela Mascetti TOPICS: Spirituality TYPE: Book PRICE: $16.95

Song Of God: A Summary Study Of Bhagavad-Gita As It Is
PUBLISHING COMPANY: Palace Publishing EDITOR: S. Bhaktipada TOPICS: Spirituality TYPE: Book PRICE: $7.95

Sophia: The Future Of Feminist Spirituality
PUBLISHING COMPANY: Harper & Row Publishers, Inc. EDITOR: S. Cady TOPICS: Spirituality TYPE: Book PRICE: $14.95

Sotai: Balance And Health Through Natural Movement
PUBLISHING COMPANY: Japan Publications, Inc. EDITOR: K. Hashimoto TOPICS: Tai Chi TYPE: Book PRICE: $12.95

Soul Economy And Waldorf Education
PUBLISHING COMPANY: Anthroposophic Press, Inc. EDITOR: R. Steiner TOPICS: Spirituality TYPE: Book PRICE: $20.00

Soul Of Things
PUBLISHING COMPANY: Aquarian Press EDITOR: W. Denton TOPICS: Psychic, Occult, Psychic Phenomena TYPE: Book PRICE: $14.95

Soul Return: Integrating Body, Psyche And Spirit
PUBLISHING COMPANY: Aslan Publishing EDITOR: Aminah Raheem, Ph. D. TOPICS: Body-Mind Connection TYPE: Book PRICE: $12.95

Soul Searcher
PUBLISHING COMPANY: Foundation For Christian Psychic Research, Inc. TOPICS: Parapsychology, Occult TYPE: Book DATE: 1977 PRICE: $0.00 TERM: Members PRICE PER COPY: $6.00

Soul-Purpose: Discovering And Fulfilling Your Destiny
PUBLISHING COMPANY: Harper & Row Publishers, Inc. EDITOR: M. Thurston TOPICS: Channeling TYPE: Book PRICE: $8.95

Source Imagery: Releasing The Power Of Your Creativity
PUBLISHING COMPANY: Doubleday & Co.,Inc. EDITOR: S. Shuman TOPICS: New Age TYPE: Book PRICE: $14.95

Southern California's New Age Telephone Book
PUBLISHING COMPANY: Southern California's New Age Telephone Book EDITOR: Caryn Goldberg TOPICS: Holistic Healing, New Age TYPE: Directory; 112 pgs. FREQ: annual CIRC: 50,000 DESCRIPTION: A directory with listings in 150 categories. Serves Southern California area. Accepts ads.

Southern Cassadaga Spiritualist Camp Meeting Handbook
PUBLISHING COMPANY: Southern Cassadaga Spiritualist Camp Meeting Association TOPICS: Spirituality, Holistic Healing, Channeling, Psychic Phenomena, Psychic TYPE: Handbook; 40 pgs. FREQ: annual PRICE: $1.00 DESCRIPTION: 40 page annual informational booklet describing Cassadaga, principals of spiritualism, camp activities and the yearly calendar.

Space, Time And Medicine
PUBLISHING COMPANY: Shambhala Publications, Inc. EDITOR: Larry Dossey TOPICS: Body-Mind Connection TYPE: Book PRICE: $14.95

Speaking Of Silence: Christians & Buddhists On The Contemplative Way
PUBLISHING COMPANY: Paulist Press EDITOR: S. Walker TOPICS: Meditation, Spirituality TYPE: Book PRICE: $12.95

Special Interest Directory

Special Reports
PUBLISHING COMPANY: Ghost Research Society EDITOR: Dale Kaczmarek TOPICS: Ghosts, Psychic Phenomena, Parapsychology, Reincarnation, Past Life Regression TYPE: Directory

PUBLISHING COMPANY: Institute Of Noetic Sciences TOPICS: Body-Mind Connection, Holistic Health, Spirituality, Past Life Regression, Death, Meditation, Hypnotism TYPE: Booklet DESCRIPTION: Offers in-depth reports of specific issues such as healing, remission and miracle cures, altered states of consciousness and the possibility of survival of bodily death.

Spectrum - Unity-And-Diversity World Directory Issue
PUBLISHING COMPANY: Unity-And-Diversity World Organization EDITOR: Louis K. Acheson TOPICS: New Age TYPE: Directory

Spiral Dance: A Rebirth Of The Ancient Religion Of The Great Goddess
PUBLISHING COMPANY: Harper & Row Publishers, Inc. Starhawk TOPICS: Occult, Witchcraft, Paganism, Spirituality TYPE: Book PRICE: $12.95

Spiral Path: Essays And Interviews On Women's Spirituality
PUBLISHING COMPANY: Yes International EDITOR: T. O'Brien TOPICS: Spirituality TYPE: Book PRICE: $15.95

Spirit Communication: The Soul's Path
PUBLISHING COMPANY: Bantam New Age Books EDITOR: K. Ryerson, S. Harolde TOPICS: Channeling TYPE: Book PRICE: $18.95

Spirit Guides
PUBLISHING COMPANY: A.C.S. Publications, Inc./Astro Computing Services EDITOR: I. Belhayes TOPICS: Occult TYPE: Book PRICE: $12.95

Spirit Of Masonry
PUBLISHING COMPANY: Aquarian Press EDITOR: W. Hutchinson TOPICS: Spirituality TYPE: Book PRICE: $14.95

Spiritual Community Guide
PUBLISHING COMPANY: Spiritual Community Guide TOPICS: Holistic Healing TYPE: Guide

Spiritual Dowsing
PUBLISHING COMPANY: Gothic Image Publications EDITOR: S. Lonegren TOPICS: Dowsing TYPE: Book PRICE: $9.50

Spiritual Emergency
PUBLISHING COMPANY: Jeremy P. Tarcher, Inc. EDITOR: Stanislav Grof, M.D. TOPICS: Spirituality TYPE: Book; 256 pgs. PRICE: $12.95

Spiritual Healing
PUBLISHING COMPANY: Technology Group, The EDITOR: Nelson White, Anne White TYPE: Book PRICE: $12.00

Spiritual Intimacy

PUBLISHING COMPANY: P'Nai Or Religious Fellowship **EDITOR:** Zalmon Schachter-Shalomi **TOPICS:** Spirituality, Kabbalah **TYPE:** Book **PRICE:** $30.00

Spiritual Intimidation
PUBLISHING COMPANY: Technology Group, The **EDITOR:** Nelson White, Anne White **TYPE:** Book **PRICE:** $15.00

Spiritual Message
PUBLISHING COMPANY: Ma Yoga Shakti International Mission **PUBLISHER:** Ma Yoga Shakti **TOPICS:** Yoga, Meditation, Spirituality **TYPE:** Book

Spiritual Nutrition And The Rainbow Diet
PUBLISHING COMPANY: Cassandra Press **EDITOR:** Gabriel Cousens, M.D. **TOPICS:** Nutrition, Holistic Health **TYPE:** Book; 240 pgs. **PRICE:** $11.95

Spiritual Properties Of Herbs
PUBLISHING COMPANY: Cassandra Press **EDITOR:** Gurudas **TOPICS:** Herbalogy, Spirituality, Alchemy **TYPE:** Book; 288 pgs. **PRICE:** $11.95

Spiritual Science Of Kriya Yoga
PUBLISHING COMPANY: Temple Of Kriya Yoga Kriyananda **TOPICS:** Yoga, Holistic Health **TYPE:** Book **PRICE:** $16.95

Spiritual Teachings Of Ramana Maharshi
PUBLISHING COMPANY: Shambhala Publications, Inc. **EDITOR:** R. Maharshi **TOPICS:** Spirituality **TYPE:** Book **PRICE:** $9.95

Splendor Solis: Alchemical Treatises Of Solomon Trismosin, Adept & Teacher Of Paracelsus
PUBLISHING COMPANY: Yoga Publications Society **EDITOR:** S. Trismosin **TOPICS:** Paranormal Phenomena **TYPE:** Book **PRICE:** $12.50

Sportsmassage: Increasing Performance & Endurance In 15 Popular Sports
PUBLISHING COMPANY: Station Hill Press **EDITOR:** Jack Meagher **TOPICS:** Massage **TYPE:** Book **PRICE:** $14.95

Springs Of Creativity: The Bible & Creative Process Of The Psyche
PUBLISHING COMPANY: Chiron Publications **EDITOR:** H. Westman **TOPICS:** Psychology **TYPE:** Book **PRICE:** $17.95

Sri Aurobindo On Himself
PUBLISHING COMPANY: Lotus Light Publications Aurobindo **TOPICS:** Spirituality **TYPE:** Book **PRICE:** $17.50

Sri Caitanya-Caritamrta
PUBLISHING COMPANY: Palace Publishing **EDITOR:** S. Prabhupada **TOPICS:** Spirituality **TYPE:** Book **PRICE:** $39.95

Sri Chakra

PUBLISHING COMPANY: Lotus Light Publications **EDITOR:** S. Shankaranarayanan **TOPICS:** Spirituality **TYPE:** Book **PRICE:** $14.95

Sri Ramakrishna: A Prophet For The New Age
PUBLISHING COMPANY: Paragon House **EDITOR:** R. Schiffman **TOPICS:** Yoga, Spirituality **TYPE:** Book **PRICE:** $10.95

Starmakers, All
PUBLISHING COMPANY: Poco Press **EDITOR:** Alan Cohen **TOPICS:** New Age **TYPE:** Book **PRICE:** $7.95 **DESCRIPTION:** How to find & use your personal power.

Stars In Your Bones: Emerging Signposts On Our Spiritual Journey
PUBLISHING COMPANY: North Star Press/ St. Cloud, Inc. **EDITOR:** A. Bozarth **TOPICS:** Spirituality **TYPE:** Book **PRICE:** $19.95

Stations Of Solitude
PUBLISHING COMPANY: William Morrow & Co. **EDITOR:** Alice Koller **TOPICS:** New Age, Spirituality **TYPE:** Book **PRICE:** $19.95

Staying Healthy With The Seasons
PUBLISHING COMPANY: Celestial Arts Publishing Co./Sub. of Ten Speed Press **EDITOR:** Elson M. Haas **TOPICS:** Holistic Health, Astrology **TYPE:** Book **PRICE:** $10.95

Stigmata: The Extraordinary Story Of Christ's Wounds
PUBLISHING COMPANY: Harper & Row Publishers, Inc. **EDITOR:** Ian Wilson **TOPICS:** Paranormal Phenomena **TYPE:** Book **PRICE:** $17.95

Still Good Hand Of God: The Magic & Mystery Of The Unconscious Mind
PUBLISHING COMPANY: Nicolas-Hays, Inc. **EDITOR:** Michael Gellert **TOPICS:** Paranormal Phenomena, Spirituality **TYPE:** Book **PRICE:** $12.95

Stonehenge: An Ancient Masonic Temple
PUBLISHING COMPANY: Macoy Publishing Co. **EDITOR:** R. Herner **TOPICS:** New Age, Spirituality **TYPE:** Book **PRICE:** $15.95

Stormy Search For The Self: Understanding & Coping With Spiritual Emergency
PUBLISHING COMPANY: Jeremy P. Tarcher, Inc. **EDITOR:** S. Grof, C. Grof **TOPICS:** New Age, Spirituality **TYPE:** Book **PRICE:** $19.95

Story Of Crystal Hermitage
PUBLISHING COMPANY: Crystal Clarity Publishers **EDITOR:** Donald Walters **TOPICS:** New Age **TYPE:** Book **PRICE:** $9.95

Strange Trial Of Mr. Hyde: A New Look At The Nature Of Human Evil
PUBLISHING COMPANY: Harper & Row Publishers, Inc. **EDITOR:** M. Alexander **TOPICS:** Occult **TYPE:** Book **PRICE:** $14.95

Stranger In Tibet: The Adventures Of A Wandering Zen Monk
PUBLISHING COMPANY: Kodansha International U.S.A., Ltd., Subs. of Kodansha, Ltd., c/o Harper & Row Pubs. **EDITOR:** S. Berry **TOPICS:** Spirituality **TYPE:** Book **PRICE:** $19.95

Strategic Self-Hypnosis: How To Overcome Stress, Improve Performance & Live Your Potential
PUBLISHING COMPANY: Prentice-Hall, Inc. **EDITOR:** Roger A. Straus **TOPICS:** Hypnotism **TYPE:** Book **PRICE:** $9.95

Strategy Of The Dolphin: Scoring A Win In A Chaotic World
PUBLISHING COMPANY: William Morrow & Co. **EDITOR:** D. Lynch, P. Kordis **TOPICS:** Body-Mind Connection, Psychology **TYPE:** Book **PRICE:** $19.95

Stress: A New Positive Approach
PUBLISHING COMPANY: Trafalgar Square, Inc., Div. of David & Charles, Inc. **EDITOR:** Jenni Adams **TOPICS:** Holistic Health, New Age **TYPE:** Book **PRICE:** $12.95

Stroking The Python: Women's Psychic Lives
PUBLISHING COMPANY: Llewellyn Publications **EDITOR:** D. Stein **TOPICS:** ESP, Psychic Phenomena **TYPE:** Book **PRICE:** $12.95

Structures Of Consciousness: The Genius Of Jean Gebser, An Introduction And Critique
PUBLISHING COMPANY: Integral Publishing **EDITOR:** G. Feuerstein **TOPICS:** New Age, Psychology **TYPE:** Book **PRICE:** $14.95

Studies In Occult Philosophy
PUBLISHING COMPANY: Theosophical University Press **EDITOR:** G. DePurucker **TOPICS:** Occult **TYPE:** Book **PRICE:** $9.00

Studies In The Medicine Of Ancient India
PUBLISHING COMPANY: B. Jain Publishers, Ltd. **EDITOR:** A. Hoemle **TOPICS:** Holistic Health **TYPE:** Book **PRICE:** $24.00

Studies Of The Human Aura
PUBLISHING COMPANY: Summit University Press **EDITOR:** Mark L. Prophet **TOPICS:** Holistic Health **TYPE:** Book **PRICE:** $8.95

Subliminal Learning: An Eclectic Approach
PUBLISHING COMPANY: Progressive Awareness Research **EDITOR:** Eldon Taylor **TOPICS:** Hypnotism **TYPE:** Book **PRICE:** $12.95

Success, Riches, And Self Realization: The Thousand-Fold Path
PUBLISHING COMPANY: Open Horizons **EDITOR:** John Kremer **TYPE:** Book; 320 pgs. **PRICE:** $14.95

Sun At Midnight: The Rudolph Steiner Movement And The Western Esoteric Tradition
PUBLISHING COMPANY: Aquarian Press EDITOR: G. Ahern TOPICS: Psychic, Spirituality TYPE: Book PRICE: $18.50

Sunyata: The Recollections Of A Rare-Born Mystic
PUBLISHING COMPANY: North Atlantic Books EDITOR: Layena Camhi, E. Isenberg TOPICS: Spirituality TYPE: Book PRICE: $9.95

Surfers Of The Zuvuya: Tales Of Interdimensional Travel
PUBLISHING COMPANY: Bear & Company, Inc. EDITOR: J. Arguelles TOPICS: Occult TYPE: Book PRICE: $9.95

Survival After Death: A Scientific View
PUBLISHING COMPANY: International Foundation For Survival Research TOPICS: Death TYPE: Book

Survival Into The Twenty-First Century: Planetary Healers Manual
PUBLISHING COMPANY: 21st Century Publications EDITOR: V. Kulvinskas TOPICS: Holistic Health, Acupuncture, Health Food, Vegetarianism TYPE: Handbook PRICE: $14.95

Survival Of The Pagan Gods: The Mythological Tradition & Its Place In Renaissance Humanism
PUBLISHING COMPANY: Princeton University Press EDITOR: D. Seznec TOPICS: Paganism, Spirituality TYPE: Book PRICE: $10.95

Survive This Day: A Doctor's Guide To These Critical Times
PUBLISHING COMPANY: Bernard Jensen Publishing Co. EDITOR: Bernard Jensen TOPICS: Health Food, Holistic Health, Vegetarianism TYPE: Guide PRICE: $9.95

Sword And The Serpent: The Structure & Psychology Of Magick
PUBLISHING COMPANY: Llewellyn Publications EDITOR: M. Denning, O. Phillips TOPICS: Occult, Witchcraft, Psychology TYPE: Book PRICE: $15.00

Sword Of No-Sword: Life Of The Master Warrior Tesshu
PUBLISHING COMPANY: Shambhala Publications, Inc. EDITOR: John Stevens TOPICS: Spirituality TYPE: Book PRICE: $14.95

Symbolic Prophcy Of The Great Pyramid
PUBLISHING COMPANY: Supreme Grand Lodge of AMORC, Inc. EDITOR: H. Lewis TOPICS: New Age TYPE: Book PRICE: $8.95

Synthesis Of Yoga
PUBLISHING COMPANY: Lotus Light Publications Aurobindo TOPICS: New Age, Yoga, Spirituality TYPE: Book PRICE: $18.00

Synthesis Party

PUBLISHING COMPANY: Starmast Publication TYPE: Book

T M Technique
PUBLISHING COMPANY: Routledge, Chapman & Hall, Inc. EDITOR: Peter Russell TOPICS: Meditation TYPE: Book PRICE: $12.95

T'ai Chi Ch'uan And Meditation
PUBLISHING COMPANY: Schocken Books EDITOR: D. Liu TOPICS: Tai Chi TYPE: Book PRICE: $15.95

T'ai Chi Ch'uan: The Basic Exercises
PUBLISHING COMPANY: Japan Publications, Inc. EDITOR: Xing Van-Ling TOPICS: Tai Chi TYPE: Book PRICE: $24.95

T'ai Chi Combat
PUBLISHING COMPANY: Shambhala Publications, Inc. EDITOR: P. Crompton TOPICS: Tai Chi TYPE: Book PRICE: $14.95

T'ai Chi For Two: The Practice Of Push Hands
PUBLISHING COMPANY: Shambhala Publications, Inc. EDITOR: P. Crompton TOPICS: Tai Chi TYPE: Book PRICE: $14.95

T'ai Chi Workbook
PUBLISHING COMPANY: Shambhala Publications, Inc. EDITOR: P. Crompton TOPICS: Tai Chi TYPE: Book PRICE: $17.95

T'ai Chi Workbook
PUBLISHING COMPANY: Doubleday & Co.,Inc. EDITOR: H. Kauz TOPICS: Tai Chi TYPE: Book PRICE: $12.95

T'ai Chi: Supreme Ultimate
PUBLISHING COMPANY: Charles E. Tuttle Company, Inc. EDITOR: Man-Ghing Cheng, R. Smith TOPICS: Tai Chi TYPE: Book PRICE: $24.95

T'ai Ji: Beginner's Taiji Book
PUBLISHING COMPANY: Celestial Arts Publishing Co./Sub. of Ten Speed Press EDITOR: A. Huang TOPICS: Tai Chi TYPE: Book PRICE: $12.95

Tai Chi Ch'uan And Meditation
PUBLISHING COMPANY: Schocken Books EDITOR: D. Liu TOPICS: New Age, Tai Chi, Meditation TYPE: Book PRICE: $15.95

Tai Chi Classics: New Translations Of The 3 Essential Texts Of Tai Chi Ch'uan
PUBLISHING COMPANY: Shambhala Publications, Inc. EDITOR: Waysun Liao TOPICS: New Age, Tai Chi TYPE: Book PRICE: $14.95

Tai Chi Ruler: Chinese Yoga For Health & Longevity
PUBLISHING COMPANY: North Atlantic Books EDITOR: T. Dunn TOPICS: Tai Chi TYPE: Book PRICE: $14.95

Take Charge Of Your Health: Healing With Yogatherapy & Nutrition

PUBLISHING COMPANY: Japan Publications, Inc. EDITOR: C. Kilham TOPICS: Yoga, Holistic Health TYPE: Book PRICE: $13.95

Tales Of The Uncanny: True Stories Of The Unexplained
PUBLISHING COMPANY: Reader's Digest Editors of Reader's TOPICS: Psychic Phenomena, Paranormal Phenomena TYPE: Book PRICE: $19.95

Taming The Menagerie, Unmasking Mind Games
PUBLISHING COMPANY: Celestial Gifts Publishing EDITOR: Dr. Ron Dalrymple TOPICS: New Age TYPE: Book

Tantra In Tibet
PUBLISHING COMPANY: Snow Lion Publications, Inc. EDITOR: J. Hopkins TOPICS: Spirituality TYPE: Book PRICE: $12.95

Tantraraia Tantra
PUBLISHING COMPANY: South Asia Books EDITOR: L. Sastri, A. Avalon TOPICS: Spirituality TYPE: Book PRICE: $20.00

Tantric Sex
PUBLISHING COMPANY: Peak Skill Publishing TOPICS: New Age TYPE: Book

Tantric Yoga Techniques
PUBLISHING COMPANY: B. Jain Publishers, Ltd. EDITOR: R. Chandra TOPICS: Yoga, Holistic Health TYPE: Book PRICE: $14.00

Tao And T'ai Chi Kung
PUBLISHING COMPANY: Destiny Books, Inner Traditions International, Ltd. EDITOR: Robert Sohn TOPICS: Tai Chi TYPE: Book PRICE: $12.95

Tao Of Biotech: The Mind Code And The Life Code
PUBLISHING COMPANY: North Atlantic Books EDITOR: Johnson F. Yan TOPICS: Holistic Health TYPE: Book PRICE: $12.95

Tao Of Health, Sex And Longevity: A Modern Practical Guide To The Ancient Way
PUBLISHING COMPANY: Simon & Schuster, Inc. EDITOR: D. Reid TOPICS: Holistic Health TYPE: Book PRICE: $12.95

Tao Of I Ching: Way To Divination
PUBLISHING COMPANY: Charles E. Tuttle Company, Inc. EDITOR: Jou Tsung Hwa TOPICS: New Age, Spirituality TYPE: Book PRICE: $20.00

Tao Of Meditation: Way To Enlightenment
PUBLISHING COMPANY: Charles E. Tuttle Company, Inc. EDITOR: Jou Tsung Hwa TOPICS: Meditation, Spirituality TYPE: Book PRICE: $15.00

Tao Of Power
PUBLISHING COMPANY: Doubleday & Co.,Inc. EDITOR: R.L. Wing TOPICS: Spirituality, New Age TYPE: Book PRICE: $14.95

Tao Of T'ai Chi Chuan: Way To Rejuvenation

PUBLISHING COMPANY: Charles E. Tuttle Company, Inc. EDITOR: Jou Tsung Hwa TOPICS: Tai Chi TYPE: Book PRICE: $17.00

Tao Of Time: How To Regain Control Of Time From Within Yourself Through New Age Theory

PUBLISHING COMPANY: Henry Holt & Co. EDITOR: Diane Hunt, P. Hait TOPICS: New Age, Spirituality TYPE: Book PRICE: $18.95

Tao Te Ching

PUBLISHING COMPANY: Random House, Inc. EDITOR: G. Feng, J. English TOPICS: Channeling, Spirituality TYPE: Book PRICE: $14.95

Tao Te Ching: A New English Version

PUBLISHING COMPANY: Harper & Row Publishers, Inc. EDITOR: Stephen Mitchell TOPICS: Spirituality, New Age TYPE: Book PRICE: $15.95

Taoism: The Road To Immortality

PUBLISHING COMPANY: Shambhala Publications, Inc. EDITOR: J. Blofeld TOPICS: Spirituality TYPE: Book PRICE: $13.95

Taoist Classic: Chaung-Tzu

PUBLISHING COMPANY: China Books & Periodicals, Inc. EDITOR: Fung Yu-lan TOPICS: Spirituality, New Age TYPE: Book PRICE: $16.95

Taoist Guide To Longevity: Qigong, Movement & Massage

PUBLISHING COMPANY: China Books & Periodicals, Inc. EDITOR: B. Zhizhong TOPICS: Tai Chi, Holistic Health, Spirituality TYPE: Book PRICE: $12.95

Taoist I Ching

PUBLISHING COMPANY: Shambhala Publications, Inc. EDITOR: T. Cleary TOPICS: New Age, Spirituality TYPE: Book PRICE: $14.95

Tarot Constellations: Patterns Of Personal Destiny

PUBLISHING COMPANY: Newcastle Publishing Co., Inc. EDITOR: M. Greer TOPICS: Tarot TYPE: Book PRICE: $12.95

Tarot For Lovers

PUBLISHING COMPANY: Whitford Press/Schiffer Publishing Limited EDITOR: F.W. Neville TOPICS: Tarot TYPE: Book PRICE: $14.95

Tarot For Tomorrow

PUBLISHING COMPANY: Aquarian Press EDITOR: E. Peach, T. Willis TOPICS: Psychic, Tarot TYPE: Book PRICE: $12.95

Tarot For Your Self: A Handbook For Personal Transformation

PUBLISHING COMPANY: Newcastle Publishing Co., Inc. EDITOR: M. Greer TOPICS: Tarot TYPE: Book PRICE: $12.95

Tarot Handbook: Practical Applications Of Ancient Visual Symbols

PUBLISHING COMPANY: Arcus Publishing Co. EDITOR: A. Arrien TOPICS: Tarot TYPE: Book PRICE: $25.00

Tarot In Art, Mysticism And Divination

PUBLISHING COMPANY: Inner Traditions International, Ltd. EDITOR: Sylvie Simon TOPICS: Tarot TYPE: Book PRICE: $24.95

Tarot Made Easy

PUBLISHING COMPANY: Simon & Schuster, Inc. EDITOR: N. Garen TOPICS: Tarot TYPE: Book PRICE: $12.95

Tarot Mirrors: Reflections Of Personal Meaning

PUBLISHING COMPANY: Newcastle Publishing Co., Inc. EDITOR: M. Greer TOPICS: Tarot TYPE: Book PRICE: $14.95

Tarot Of The Magicians

PUBLISHING COMPANY: Samuel Weiser, Inc. EDITOR: O. Wirth TOPICS: Tarot TYPE: Book PRICE: $14.95

Tarot Spells

PUBLISHING COMPANY: Llewellyn Publications EDITOR: Janina Renee TOPICS: Tarot, Metaphysics TYPE: Book PRICE: $12.95

Tarot Trumps: Cosmos In Miniature

PUBLISHING COMPANY: Aquarian Press EDITOR: J. Shepherd TOPICS: Psychic, Tarot TYPE: Book PRICE: $16.50

Tarot Unveiled: The Method To Its Magic

PUBLISHING COMPANY: Visionary Enterprises, Inc. EDITOR: L. Clarson TOPICS: Tarot, Metaphysics TYPE: Book PRICE: $11.95

Tarot Workbook: Understanding And Using Tarot Symbolism

PUBLISHING COMPANY: Aquarian Press EDITOR: E. Peach TOPICS: Psychic, Tarot TYPE: Book PRICE: $12.95

Tarot: Handbook For The Journeyman

PUBLISHING COMPANY: Newcastle Publishing Co., Inc. EDITOR: E. Connolly TOPICS: Tarot TYPE: Book PRICE: $12.95

Tarot: Handbook For The Master

PUBLISHING COMPANY: Newcastle Publishing Co., Inc. EDITOR: E. Connolly TOPICS: Tarot TYPE: Book PRICE: $12.95

Tarot: Key To The Wisdom Of The Ages

PUBLISHING COMPANY: Builders Of The Adytum EDITOR: P.F. Case TOPICS: Tarot TYPE: Book PRICE: $14.50

Tastes Of Tuscany

PUBLISHING COMPANY: Blue Dolphin Publishing, Inc. TOPICS: New Age TYPE: Book PRICE: $17.95

Te-Tao Ching: A New Translation Based On The Recently Discovered Ma-Wang-Tui Texts

PUBLISHING COMPANY: Ballantine Books, Inc. EDITOR: Robert G. Hendricks TOPICS: Spirituality, New Age TYPE: Book PRICE: $19.95

Tea Cup Fortune Telling Nsa

PUBLISHING COMPANY: W. Foulsham & Co., Ltd. TOPICS: Tea Leaves, Metaphysics TYPE: Book PRICE: $3.50

Tea Cup Tales: Tales Of Tea And How To Read Tea Leaves

PUBLISHING COMPANY: Ransom Hill Press EDITOR: M.L. McWhorter TOPICS: Tea Leaves, Metaphysics TYPE: Book PRICE: $5.95

Tea Leaf Reading

PUBLISHING COMPANY: Llewellyn Publications EDITOR: William W. Hewitt TOPICS: Tea Leaves, Metaphysics TYPE: Book PRICE: $3.95

Tea With George Ohsawa: Selected Writings By The Father Of Modern Macrobiotics

PUBLISHING COMPANY: Japan Publications, Inc. EDITOR: G. Oshsawa TOPICS: Holistic Health, Vegetarianism, Health Food TYPE: Book PRICE: $19.95

Teach Yourself Fortune Telling: Palmistry, The Crystal Ball, Tea Leaves, The Tarot

PUBLISHING COMPANY: Henry Holt & Co. EDITOR: Rachel Pollack TOPICS: New Age, Palmistry, Tea Leaves, Tarot TYPE: Book PRICE: $10.95

Teaching Of Queen Kunti

PUBLISHING COMPANY: Bhaktivedanta Book Trust EDITOR: S. Prabhupada TOPICS: Spirituality TYPE: Book PRICE: $14.95

Teaching Power Of Dreams: Using Your Dreams To Change Your Life

PUBLISHING COMPANY: Whitford Press/Schiffer Publishing Limited EDITOR: Sherry Steiger, Brad Steiger TOPICS: Dreams TYPE: Book PRICE: $14.95

Teachings Of Lord Caitanya

PUBLISHING COMPANY: Bhaktivedanta Book Trust EDITOR: S. Prabhupada TOPICS: Spirituality TYPE: Book PRICE: $24.95

Teachings Of Lord Kapila: The Son Of Devahuti

PUBLISHING COMPANY: Bhaktivedanta Book Trust EDITOR: S. Prabhupada TOPICS: Spirituality TYPE: Book PRICE: $19.95

Teachings Of Ramana Mahareshi

PUBLISHING COMPANY: Samuel Weiser, Inc. EDITOR: Arthur Osborne TOPICS: Spirituality TYPE: Book PRICE: $9.95

Tear And A Smile

PUBLISHING COMPANY: Random House, Inc. EDITOR: K. Gilbran TOPICS: Channeling TYPE: Book PRICE: $15.95

Teardrops and Silicon

PUBLISHING COMPANY: Vongrutnorv Og Press, Inc. EDITOR: Steve Erickson TOPICS: Metaphysics TYPE: Book DATE: 1978

Techniques Of Pendulum & Swing-Rod Dowsing

PUBLISHING COMPANY: Fine Median International TOPICS: Dowsing TYPE: Book

Templars: Knights Of God

PUBLISHING COMPANY: Aquarian Press EDITOR: E. Burman TOPICS: Occult TYPE: Book PRICE: $9.95

Temple And The Lodge

PUBLISHING COMPANY: Arcade Publishing EDITOR: M. Baigent, R. Leigh TOPICS: Spirituality TYPE: Book PRICE: $22.95

Temple Legend

PUBLISHING COMPANY: Anthroposophic Press, Inc. EDITOR: R. Steiner TOPICS: Spirituality TYPE: Book PRICE: $18.00

Tension Turnaround: The 30-Day Program For Inner Calm, Confidence & Control

PUBLISHING COMPANY: Rodale Press, Inc. EDITOR: S. Fenton TOPICS: Holistic Health, New Age TYPE: Book PRICE: $12.95

Teutonic Magic: A Guide To Germanic Divination, Lore & Magic

PUBLISHING COMPANY: Llewellyn Publications EDITOR: Kveldulf Gundarson TOPICS: Spirituality, Occult, Runes TYPE: Book PRICE: $12.95

The Ages And The Truth

PUBLISHING COMPANY: Arthur Publications, Inc. EDITOR: Debra Sapp TOPICS: Astrology TYPE: Book DATE: 1978

The American Theosophist

PUBLISHING COMPANY: Theosophical Publishing House TOPICS: Metaphysics TYPE: Book

The Astrology Of Genius

PUBLISHING COMPANY: Evolutionary Publications EDITOR: Roy Tate TOPICS: Astrology TYPE: Book DESCRIPTION: Researches the Astrological nature of Nobel Prize winners.

The Aware Baby: A New Approach To Parenting

PUBLISHING COMPANY: Aware Parenting Institute/Shining Star Press EDITOR: Aletha Solter, Ph. D. TOPICS: New Age TYPE: Book

The Bermuda Triangle

PUBLISHING COMPANY: Avon Books EDITOR: Charles Berlitz TYPE: Book

The Bhagavad Gita

PUBLISHING COMPANY: Samuel Weiser, Inc. EDITOR: Antonio de Nicolas TOPICS: Spirituality TYPE: Book PRICE: $12.50

The Birth Partner

PUBLISHING COMPANY: Harvard Common Press EDITOR: Penny Simkin TOPICS: Birth TYPE: Book

The Book Of Kudzu

PUBLISHING COMPANY: Soyfoods Center TOPICS: Health Food TYPE: Book

The Book Of Miso

PUBLISHING COMPANY: Soyfoods Center TOPICS: Health Food TYPE: Book

The Book Of Tempeh

PUBLISHING COMPANY: Soyfoods Center TOPICS: Health Food TYPE: Book

The Book Of Tofu

PUBLISHING COMPANY: Soyfoods Center TOPICS: Health Food TYPE: Book

The Bottom Line: On Alcohol In Society

PUBLISHING COMPANY: Alcohol Research Information Service EDITOR: Robert Hammond TOPICS: Holistic Healing TYPE: Book

The Branches Directory

PUBLISHING COMPANY: Three Sisters, Ltd. EDITOR: Kyril Oakwind TOPICS: Witchcraft, Occult, Paganism TYPE: Directory DESCRIPTION: A pagan guide to professional services.

The Calendrix

PUBLISHING COMPANY: Kat Duff EDITOR: Kat Duff TOPICS: Astrology TYPE: Book

The Cloven Hoof

PUBLISHING COMPANY: Church Of Satan, Inc. EDITOR: Anton Szandor La Vey TOPICS: Occult TYPE: Book

The Complete Illustrated Book Of Yoga

PUBLISHING COMPANY: Sivananda Ashram Yoga Retreat EDITOR: Swami Vishnu-Devananda TYPE: Book

The Divining Mind

PUBLISHING COMPANY: Inner Traditions International, Ltd. EDITOR: T.E. Ross TOPICS: Dowsing TYPE: Book PRICE: $9.95

The Dream Book

PUBLISHING COMPANY: Inner Light Foundation TOPICS: Holistic Healing TYPE: Book

The Elegant Taste Of Thailand

PUBLISHING COMPANY: Snow Lion Graphics TOPICS: New Age TYPE: Book PRICE: $19.95

The Enchanted Tarot

PUBLISHING COMPANY: St. Martin's Press, Inc. EDITOR: Amy Zerner TOPICS: Psychic, Tarot TYPE: Book; 192 pgs. PRICE: $24.95

The Enchanting News

PUBLISHING COMPANY: Fanscifiaroan Church Wicca EDITOR: Frank Hedgecock TOPICS: Spirituality, Witchcraft, New Age TYPE: Booklet DATE: 1990 SIZE: 8 1/2 x 11; 70 pgs. FREQ: 6 x per year PRICE: $24.00 PRICE PER COPY: $6.00

DESCRIPTION: In search of lost traditions. Deals with witchcraft, the love of the earth, the unknown, philosophy & traditions of the craft. Free to all who contribute articles or ads.

The Facts On Astrology

PUBLISHING COMPANY: John Ankerberg Show, The EDITOR: John Ankerberg, John Weldon TOPICS: Occult TYPE: Booklet DATE: 1989

The Facts On Spirit Guides

PUBLISHING COMPANY: John Ankerberg Show, The EDITOR: John Ankerberg, John Weldon TOPICS: Occult TYPE: Booklet DATE: 1989

The Facts On The New Age Medicine & Holistic Health Treatments

PUBLISHING COMPANY: John Ankerberg Show, The EDITOR: John Ankerberg, John Weldon TOPICS: Occult TYPE: Booklet DATE: 1992

The Facts On The New Age Movement

PUBLISHING COMPANY: John Ankerberg Show, The EDITOR: John Ankerberg, John Weldon TOPICS: Occult TYPE: Booklet DATE: 1989

The Facts On The Occult

PUBLISHING COMPANY: John Ankerberg Show, The EDITOR: John Ankerberg, John Weldon TOPICS: Occult TYPE: Booklet DATE: 1991

The Facts On UFO's

PUBLISHING COMPANY: John Ankerberg Show, The EDITOR: John Ankerberg, John Weldon TOPICS: Occult TYPE: Booklet DATE: 1992

The Findhorn Community

PUBLISHING COMPANY: Findhorn Foundation & Press EDITOR: Carol Riddell TOPICS: Spirituality TYPE: Book DESCRIPTION: Traces the development of this 30 year old international spiritual community.

The First Step: A Guide For The New Jewish Spirit

PUBLISHING COMPANY: P'Nai Or Religious Fellowship EDITOR: Zalmon Schachter-Shalomi, Donald Gropman TOPICS: Spirituality, Kabbalah TYPE: Book PRICE: $5.95

The Ghostly Register

PUBLISHING COMPANY: Contemporary Books, Inc. EDITOR: Arthur Myers TOPICS: Ghosts TYPE: Directory

The God-Mind Connection

PUBLISHING COMPANY: Teamup EDITOR: Jean K. Foster TOPICS: New Age TYPE: Book

The Harmonic Orb: Reflections Of The Heart

PUBLISHING COMPANY: NALTA Foundation, Inc. EDITOR: Edward P. Gardner TOPICS: New Age, Holistic Healing TYPE: Book DATE: 1992; 288 pgs. PRICE: $12.95

The Inner Manager, Mastering Business, Home & Self

PUBLISHING COMPANY: Celestial Gifts Publishing EDITOR: Dr. Ron Dalrymple TOPICS: New Age TYPE: Book DATE: 1989

The Inner Path From Where You Are To Where You Want To Be

PUBLISHING COMPANY: Adventures In Enlightenment, A Foundation EDITOR: Terry Cole-Whittaker TOPICS: New Age, Metaphysics TYPE: Book DATE: 1986

The Inner Side Of World Events

PUBLISHING COMPANY: Gordon Davidson EDITOR: Gordon Davidson, Corinne McLaughlin TOPICS: New Age, Spirituality, Meditation, Metaphysics TYPE: Book DESCRIPTION: A Metaphysical approach to politics.

The Interpretation Of Dreams

PUBLISHING COMPANY: Original Books, Inc. TOPICS: Dreams TYPE: Book PRICE: $36.50

The Joining Of Science And Spirit

PUBLISHING COMPANY: Unarius Academy Of Science & Education Foundation EDITOR: Ruth Norman, Charles Spaegel TOPICS: Reincarnation TYPE: Book DATE: 1954; 336 pgs. PRICE: $15.95

The Light Of The Universe

PUBLISHING COMPANY: Light Of The Universe EDITOR: Helen Spitler TOPICS: Channeling TYPE: Book DATE: 1976

The Living Function Of Sleep, Life & Aging

PUBLISHING COMPANY: Juvenescent Research Corp. EDITOR: Betty Yulin Ho TOPICS: Holistic Health TYPE: Book DATE: 1967; 56 pgs. PRICE: $6.00 DESCRIPTION: A development of 3 hypotheses on the physiology of sleep, life & aging.

The Magic And Science Of Jewels And Stones, Vol. I

PUBLISHING COMPANY: Cassandra Press Kozminsky TOPICS: Crystals TYPE: Book; 176 pgs. PRICE: $9.95

The Magic And Science Of Jewels And Stones, Vol. II

PUBLISHING COMPANY: Cassandra Press Kozminsky TOPICS: Crystals TYPE: Book; 168 pgs. PRICE: $9.95

The Magical And Ritual Use Of Perfumes

PUBLISHING COMPANY: Inner Traditions International, Ltd. EDITOR: Richard Miller, Iona Miller TOPICS: Witchcraft, Occult TYPE: Book PRICE: $10.95

The Meaning Of Death

PUBLISHING COMPANY: Technology Group, The EDITOR: Frater Zarathustra TYPE: Book

The Messiah In India

PUBLISHING COMPANY: Cassandra Press EDITOR: Alan Fensin TOPICS: Metaphysics TYPE: Book; 96 pgs. PRICE: $9.95

The Mindual Of Philosopher G.

PUBLISHING COMPANY: Philosopher Press TOPICS: New Age TYPE: Book PRICE: $7.95

The Natural Yellow Pages

PUBLISHING COMPANY: Mighty Natural Distributors EDITOR: Anne I. Couceiro, Barbara Felder TOPICS: Holistic Healing TYPE: Directory

The Networker

PUBLISHING COMPANY: Networker, The EDITOR: Pamela Vipond TOPICS: Holistic Health TYPE: Directory FREQ: bi-monthly CIRC: 25,000 PRICE PER COPY: $1.95 DESCRIPTION: Prints resource directory, articles and guide to wholistic practitioners. Also publishes calendar and articles that explore alternative educational and artistic paths to self-development. Accepts ads.

The New Handbook Of Health And Preventive Medicine

PUBLISHING COMPANY: Prometheus Books EDITOR: Kurt Butler TOPICS: Holistic Health TYPE: Book

The Origin Of Variation Of Races Of Mankind & The Cause Of Evolution

PUBLISHING COMPANY: Juvenescent Research Corp. EDITOR: Betty Yulin Ho TOPICS: Holistic Health TYPE: Book DATE: 1969; 109 pgs. PRICE: $9.00 DESCRIPTION: A development of hypotheses on evolution. Principles derived for daily living.

The Parent Educator And Family Report

PUBLISHING COMPANY: Hewitt Research Foundation TOPICS: New Age TYPE: Book

The Remey Letter

PUBLISHING COMPANY: Charles Mason Remey Society TYPE: Booklet DESCRIPTION: Offered free.

The Revised Book Of Baal

PUBLISHING COMPANY: Technology Group, The EDITOR: Frater Osiris TYPE: Book SIZE: 5 x 8

The Rowan Exchange

PUBLISHING COMPANY: Rowan Exchange, The EDITOR: Kyril Oakwind TOPICS: Occult, Witchcraft, Paganism TYPE: Booklet PRICE: $3.00 DESCRIPTION: Promotes networking between Wiccans. Offers personal profiles & interests of Wiccans.

The Secret Doctrine

PUBLISHING COMPANY: Wizards Bookshelf EDITOR: H.P. Blavatsky TOPICS: Spirituality, New Age TYPE: Book PRICE: $57.50 DESCRIPTION: Consists of 2 volumes plus index.

The Sivananda Companion To Yoga

PUBLISHING COMPANY: Sivananda Yoga Vedanta Centers TYPE: Book

The Spiritual Dimensions Of Healing Addictions

PUBLISHING COMPANY: Cassandra Press EDITOR: Donna Cunningham TOPICS: Holistic Healing TYPE: Book; 176 pgs. PRICE: $9.95

The Survival Of Civilization

PUBLISHING COMPANY: C. Olson And Company Weaver Hamaker TOPICS: New Age TYPE: Book; 208 pgs. PRICE: $12.00 DESCRIPTION: Asks the question: Is an Ice Age close at hand, following past events & hastened by the carbon dioxide build-up?

The Synorgon Diet

PUBLISHING COMPANY: Inquiry Press EDITOR: R.L. Wysong TOPICS: New Age, Holistic Health, Nutrition TYPE: Book DATE: 1991; 170 pgs.

The Truth That Goes Unclaimed

PUBLISHING COMPANY: Teamup EDITOR: Jean K. Foster TOPICS: New Age TYPE: Book

The Unmanifest Self: Transcending The Limits Of Ordinary Consciousness

PUBLISHING COMPANY: Aslan Publishing EDITOR: Ligia Dantes TOPICS: New Age TYPE: Book

The Unveiling Of Lhasa

PUBLISHING COMPANY: Snow Lion Graphics TOPICS: New Age TYPE: Book PRICE: $12.95

The Vegetarian Handbook

PUBLISHING COMPANY: Vegetarian Society, The TOPICS: Health Food, Vegetarianism TYPE: Handbook FREQ: annual DESCRIPTION: Contains information about the vegetarian diet, covers developing nations, factory farming & environmental issues. New ideas for getting involved with the movement.

The Voudoun Gnostic Workbook

PUBLISHING COMPANY: Technicians Of The Sacred EDITOR: Michael Bertiaux TOPICS: Voudoun TYPE: Book PRICE: $29.95

The Way Of Hope

PUBLISHING COMPANY: Warner Books, Inc. EDITOR: Tom Monte TOPICS: Holistic Health TYPE: Book PRICE: $9.95

The Way, The Truth, The Light

PUBLISHING COMPANY: Truth TOPICS: New Age, Spirituality TYPE: Book DATE: 1990; 120 pgs. DESCRIPTION: Discusses truth concerning the Light & Jesus' teachings of Eternal Life in the Light. Free.

The Wizard's Apprentice

PUBLISHING COMPANY: Technology Group, The EDITOR: Nelson White, Anne White TYPE: Book SIZE: 8 1/2 x 11

Theology Of Arithmetic

PUBLISHING COMPANY: Phanes Press EDITOR: Robin Waterfield TOPICS: Numerology, Parapsychology TYPE: Book PRICE: $13.95

Theoretical Parapsychology

PUBLISHING COMPANY: Gordon And Breach Science Publishers, Inc. EDITOR: Richard Eageti, John Lewis TOPICS: New Age, Parapsychology TYPE: Book

There Is A River: The Story Of Edgar Cayce

PUBLISHING COMPANY: Association For Research And Enlightenment, Inc. EDITOR: T. Sugrue TOPICS: Channeling TYPE: Book PRICE: $19.95

They Call It Hypnosis
PUBLISHING COMPANY: Prometheus Books **EDITOR:** Robert A. Baker **TOPICS:** Hypnotism **TYPE:** Book

They Lived With God: Life Stories Of Some Devotees Of Sri Ramakrishna
PUBLISHING COMPANY: Vedanta Press, Div. of Vedanta Society **EDITOR:** Swami Chetanananda **TOPICS:** Spirituality **TYPE:** Book **PRICE:** $17.95

Things Of The Mind: Dialogues With J. Krishnamurti
PUBLISHING COMPANY: Philosophical Library, Inc. **EDITOR:** B. Khare **TOPICS:** Spirituality **TYPE:** Book **PRICE:** $14.95

Thinking And Destiny
PUBLISHING COMPANY: Word Foundation, Inc., The **EDITOR:** Harold Waldwin Percival **TOPICS:** Spirituality, Metaphysics **TYPE:** Book **PRICE:** $24.95 **DESCRIPTION:** Describes the unseen workings of destiny. Explains many of the mysterious occult forces operating in man & through the universe. Discusses the nature of Consciousness, how to find your greater Self & full spiritual illumination.

Thirty Years Among The Dead
PUBLISHING COMPANY: Newcastle Publishing Co., Inc. **EDITOR:** C. Wickland **TOPICS:** Parapsychology, Psychic **TYPE:** Book **PRICE:** $7.95

This New Age Business: Story Of The Ancient & Continuing Quest To Bring Down Heaven On Earth
PUBLISHING COMPANY: Findhorn Foundation & Press **EDITOR:** P. Lemesurier **TOPICS:** New Age **TYPE:** Book **PRICE:** $13.95

This Thing Called Life
PUBLISHING COMPANY: Putnam Publishing Group **EDITOR:** E. Holmes **TOPICS:** Spirituality, Psychology **TYPE:** Book **PRICE:** $12.95

This Thing Called You
PUBLISHING COMPANY: Putnam Publishing Group **EDITOR:** E. Holmes **TOPICS:** Spirituality, Psychology **TYPE:** Book **PRICE:** $12.95

Those Women
PUBLISHING COMPANY: Spring Publications, Inc. **EDITOR:** Nor Hall **TOPICS:** New Age, Paranormal Phenomena, Paganism, Spirituality **TYPE:** Book **PRICE:** $12.50

Thought Forms
PUBLISHING COMPANY: Theosophical University Press **EDITOR:** A. Besant, C. Leadbeater **TOPICS:** Psychic, Parapsychology **TYPE:** Book **PRICE:** $7.50

Thoughtline
PUBLISHING COMPANY: Arcana Workshops **EDITOR:** Marguerite Rompage **TOPICS:** Meditation **TYPE:** Book

Thoughts And Feelings: The Art Of Cognitive Stress Intervention
PUBLISHING COMPANY: New Harbinger Publications **EDITOR:** M. McKay **TOPICS:** New Age, Psychology **TYPE:** Book **PRICE:** $12.50

Thoughts Through Space
PUBLISHING COMPANY: Palmer Publications/Amherst Press, Inc. **EDITOR:** H. Sherman **TOPICS:** ESP, Psychic Phenomena **TYPE:** Book **PRICE:** $14.50

Thousand Peaks: Korean Zen - Tradition & Teachers
PUBLISHING COMPANY: Parallax Press-Buddhism **EDITOR:** M. Sunim **TOPICS:** Spirituality **TYPE:** Book **PRICE:** $14.00

Thousand Waves: A Sensible Life-Style For Sensitive People
PUBLISHING COMPANY: William Morrow & Co. **EDITOR:** David K. Reynolds **TOPICS:** New Age **TYPE:** Book **PRICE:** $6.95

Three Candles Of Little Veronica, The
PUBLISHING COMPANY: Poco Press **EDITOR:** Manfred Kyber **TOPICS:** New Age, Spirituality **TYPE:** Book **PRICE:** $6.95

Thunder Of Silence
PUBLISHING COMPANY: Harper & Row Publishers, Inc. **EDITOR:** Joel Goldsmith **TOPICS:** New Age **TYPE:** Book **PRICE:** $14.95

Thursday Night Tarot: The Weekly Talks On The Wisdom Of The Major Arcana
PUBLISHING COMPANY: Newcastle Publishing Co., Inc. **EDITOR:** J. Lotterhand **TOPICS:** Tarot **TYPE:** Book **PRICE:** $12.95

Tibetan Buddhist Medicine And Psychiatry: The Diamond Healing
PUBLISHING COMPANY: Samuel Weiser, Inc. **EDITOR:** T. Clifford **TOPICS:** Holistic Health **TYPE:** Book **PRICE:** $12.95

Tibetan Medicine And Other Holistic Health-Care Systems
PUBLISHING COMPANY: Routledge, Chapman & Hall, Inc. **EDITOR:** T. Drummer **TOPICS:** Holistic Health, Homeopathy **TYPE:** Book **PRICE:** $13.95

Tibetan Medicine With Special Reference To Yogi Sataka
PUBLISHING COMPANY: B. Jain Publishers, Ltd. **EDITOR:** B. Dash **TOPICS:** Holistic Health **TYPE:** Book **PRICE:** $15.00

Tiger's Fang
PUBLISHING COMPANY: Illuminated Way Publishing **EDITOR:** P. Twitchell **TOPICS:** Astral Projection **TYPE:** Book **PRICE:** $9.95

Time, Space And Knowledge
PUBLISHING COMPANY: Dharma Publishing **EDITOR:** Tarthang Tulku **TOPICS:** Spirituality **TYPE:** Book **PRICE:** $14.95

Titanic: Psychic Forewarnings Of A Tragedy
PUBLISHING COMPANY: Sterling Publishing Company, Inc. **EDITOR:** G. Behe **TOPICS:** New Age, Psychic **TYPE:** Book **PRICE:** $9.99

To Be One's Own Physician
PUBLISHING COMPANY: Juvenescent Research Corp. **EDITOR:** Betty Yulin Ho **TOPICS:** Holistic Health **TYPE:** Book **DATE:** 1991 **DESCRIPTION:** A holistic understanding of the living body.

To Catch The Uncatchable: Baul Songs Of Love And Ecstasy
PUBLISHING COMPANY: Destiny Books, Inner Traditions International, Ltd. **EDITOR:** B. Bhattacharya **TOPICS:** Paranormal Phenomena **TYPE:** Book **PRICE:** $16.95

To Dance With Angels: An Amaging Journey To The Heart With The Phenomenal Thomas Jacobson
PUBLISHING COMPANY: Zebra Books **EDITOR:** Don Pendleton, Linda Pendleton **TOPICS:** Channeling **TYPE:** Book **PRICE:** $18.95

To Love Is To Be Happy
PUBLISHING COMPANY: Option Institute & Fellowship- A Place For Miracles **TOPICS:** Holistic Healing **TYPE:** Book

To Love Is To Know Me: The Bhagavad Gita For Daily Living Vol.3
PUBLISHING COMPANY: Nilgiri Press **EDITOR:** E. Easwaran **TOPICS:** Spirituality **TYPE:** Book **PRICE:** $18.00

To The One I Love
PUBLISHING COMPANY: University Of The Trees **EDITOR:** C. Hills **TOPICS:** Paranormal Phenomena, Spirituality **TYPE:** Book **PRICE:** $14.95

Tom Slick And The Search For The Yeti
PUBLISHING COMPANY: Faber & Faber, Affil. of Faber & Faber, Ltd., London **EDITOR:** L. Coleman **TOPICS:** Paranormal Phenomena **TYPE:** Book **PRICE:** $11.95

Total Liberation: Zen Spirituality & The Social Dimension
PUBLISHING COMPANY: Orbis Books **EDITOR:** Ruben Habito **TOPICS:** Spirituality **TYPE:** Book **PRICE:** $12.95

Touch For Health
PUBLISHING COMPANY: DeVorss & Company **EDITOR:** John F. Thie **TOPICS:** Holistic Health **TYPE:** Book **PRICE:** $17.95

Touch For Health Workbook
PUBLISHING COMPANY: DeVorss & Company **EDITOR:** M. Marks **TOPICS:** Holistic Health **TYPE:** Book **PRICE:** $9.95

Towards Superconsciousness: Meditational Theory & Practice
PUBLISHING COMPANY: South Asia Books **EDITOR:** S. Nagatomo, C. Ames **TOPICS:** New Age, Meditation, Yoga **TYPE:** Book **PRICE:** $12.95

Traitmatch: Discovering The Occupational Personality Through Handwriting Analysis

PUBLISHING COMPANY: Newcastle Publishing Co., Inc. EDITOR: Eldene Whiting TOPICS: Graphology TYPE: Book PRICE: $9.95

Transcendental Magic

PUBLISHING COMPANY: Samuel Weiser, Inc. EDITOR: A.E. Waite TOPICS: Occult TYPE: Book PRICE: $15.95

Transformation Of Consciousness: Conventional & Contemplative Perspectives On Development

PUBLISHING COMPANY: Shambhala Publications, Inc. EDITOR: Ken Wilber TOPICS: New Age, Psychology TYPE: Book PRICE: $22.95

Transformation Of The Heart: Stories By Devotees Of Sathya Sai Baba

PUBLISHING COMPANY: Samuel Weiser, Inc. EDITOR: Judy Warner TOPICS: Spirituality TYPE: Book PRICE: $9.95

Transformations: Growth And Change In Adult Life

PUBLISHING COMPANY: Simon & Schuster, Inc. EDITOR: R. Gould TOPICS: New Age, Psychology TYPE: Book PRICE: $12.95

Transforming Stress Into Power

PUBLISHING COMPANY: Jeremy P. Tarcher, Inc. EDITOR: Mark Tager, S. Willard TOPICS: Holistic Health, New Age TYPE: Book PRICE: $12.95

Transition To Vegetarianism: An Evolutionary Step

PUBLISHING COMPANY: Himalayan International Institute Of Yoga Science and Philosophy EDITOR: R. Ballentine TOPICS: Vegetarianism, Health Food, Holistic Health TYPE: Book PRICE: $12.95

Traveler's Guide To Healing Centers & Retreats In North America

PUBLISHING COMPANY: John Muir Publications EDITOR: Martine Rudee, Jonathan Blease TOPICS: Holistic Health, Spirituality TYPE: Book PRICE: $11.95 DESCRIPTION: Detailed listing of retreats & healing centers in North America.

Traveler's Guide To The Astral Plane

PUBLISHING COMPANY: Aquarian Press EDITOR: S. Richards TOPICS: Astral Projection TYPE: Book PRICE: $7.95

Traveller's Joy

PUBLISHING COMPANY: Traditional Tours EDITOR: Juliette DeBairalli Levy TOPICS: New Age TYPE: Book

Treasures Of El Dorado

PUBLISHING COMPANY: Treasure Publications EDITOR: J. Whitefield TOPICS: Paranormal Phenomena TYPE: Book PRICE: $14.95

Treatise On Angel Magic

PUBLISHING COMPANY: Phanes Press EDITOR: A. McLean TOPICS: Kabbalah, Occult, Witchcraft TYPE: Book PRICE: $18.00

Treatise On White Magic

PUBLISHING COMPANY: Lucis Publishing Company EDITOR: Alice Bailey TOPICS: Occult TYPE: Book PRICE: $17.00

Triangles

PUBLISHING COMPANY: Lucis Publishing Company TOPICS: New Age TYPE: Book

True And Invisible Rosicrucian Order: An Interpretation Of The Rosicrucian Allegory

PUBLISHING COMPANY: Samuel Weiser, Inc. EDITOR: P.F. Case TOPICS: Spirituality TYPE: Book PRICE: $17.95

Trusting Ourselves: A Crash Course In The Psychology Of Women

PUBLISHING COMPANY: Atlantic Monthly Press, Affil. of Navarre Atlantic Co. EDITOR: Karen Johnson, Tom Ferguson TOPICS: New Age, Psychology TYPE: Book PRICE: $22.95

Truth Or Dare: Encounters With Power, Authority & Mystery

PUBLISHING COMPANY: Harper & Row Publishers, Inc. Starhawk TOPICS: Occult, Witchcraft TYPE: Book PRICE: $12.95

Turning East: New Lives In India - 20 Westerners & Their Spiritual Quests

PUBLISHING COMPANY: Paragon House EDITOR: M. Tillis, C. Giles TOPICS: Yoga, Spirituality TYPE: Book PRICE: $17.95

Turning To The Source

PUBLISHING COMPANY: Blue Dolphin Publishing, Inc. Dhiravamsa TOPICS: Meditation, Spirituality TYPE: Book PRICE: $16.95

Two Minute Lover, Building Successful Relationships In A Fast Paced World

PUBLISHING COMPANY: B.L. Winch & Associates/Jalmar Press EDITOR: Asa Sparks, Ph. D. TOPICS: New Age TYPE: Book SIZE: 6x9; 112 pgs. PRICE: $9.95

Tyranny Of Malice: Exploring The Dark Side Of Character & Culture

PUBLISHING COMPANY: Simon & Schuster, Inc. EDITOR: J. Berke TOPICS: Occult TYPE: Book PRICE: $14.95

UFO Conspiracy: The First Forty Years

PUBLISHING COMPANY: Sterling Publishing Company, Inc. EDITOR: J. Randles TOPICS: UFO's, Paranormal Phenomena TYPE: Book PRICE: $12.95

UFO's, Space Brothers And The Aquarian Age

PUBLISHING COMPANY: J & S Aquarian Networking TOPICS: UFO's TYPE: Book DATE: 1985

UFOlogy Directory

PUBLISHING COMPANY: Ghost Research Society EDITOR: Dale Kaczmarek TOPICS: Astrology TYPE: Directory PRICE: $6.50 DESCRIPTION:

Contains names of individuals, groups, organizations, magazines & newsletters on the topic.

Ultimate Asteroid Book

PUBLISHING COMPANY: Whitford Press/Schiffer Publishing Limited EDITOR: L. Lehman TOPICS: Astrology TYPE: Book PRICE: $18.95

Unarius Light

PUBLISHING COMPANY: Unarius Academy Of Science & Education Foundation EDITOR: Ruth Norman, Crystal Hampton TOPICS: Reincarnation TYPE: Book

Uncommon Sense: How To Discover The Psychic Within You

PUBLISHING COMPANY: Villard Books, Random House, Inc. EDITOR: P. Einstein TOPICS: Psychic TYPE: Book PRICE: $17.95

Unconscious And Its Empirical Manifestations

PUBLISHING COMPANY: Sigo Press EDITOR: E. Rolfe TOPICS: Psychology TYPE: Book PRICE: $16.95

Understanding Dreams

PUBLISHING COMPANY: Spring Publications, Inc. EDITOR: M. Mattoon TOPICS: Dreams TYPE: Book PRICE: $16.00

Underworld Initiation: A Journey Towards Psychic Transformation

PUBLISHING COMPANY: Aquarian Press EDITOR: R.J. Stewart TOPICS: Witchcraft, Occult TYPE: Book PRICE: $12.95

Unearthing Atlantis: An Archeological Odyssey

PUBLISHING COMPANY: Random House, Inc. EDITOR: Charles R. Pellegrino TOPICS: New Age TYPE: Book PRICE: $19.95

Unexplained Mysteries Of The Twentieth Century

PUBLISHING COMPANY: Contemporary Books, Inc. EDITOR: J. Bond, C. Bond TOPICS: Ghosts, Paranormal Phenomena TYPE: Book PRICE: $12.95

Uninvited Guests: A Documented History Of Ufo Sightings, Alien Encounters And Coverups

PUBLISHING COMPANY: Aurora Press, Inc. EDITOR: Richard Hall TOPICS: UFO's, Paranormal Phenomena TYPE: Book PRICE: $14.00

Union Of Bliss And Emptiness

PUBLISHING COMPANY: Snow Lion Publications, Inc. EDITOR: Lama Dalai TOPICS: Spirituality TYPE: Book PRICE: $10.95

Universal Language Of Cabalah: The Master Key To The God Consciousness

PUBLISHING COMPANY: DeVorss & Company EDITOR: W. Eisen TOPICS: Kabbalah TYPE: Book PRICE: $24.95

Universe, Earth And Man

PUBLISHING COMPANY: Anthroposophic Press, Inc. EDITOR: R. Steiner TOPICS: Spirituality TYPE: Book PRICE: $15.95

Unknown Man: The Mysterious Birth Of A New Species

PUBLISHING COMPANY: Simon & Schuster, Inc. Yatri TOPICS: New Age TYPE: Book PRICE: $14.95

Unknown Reality Vol 1: A Seth Book

PUBLISHING COMPANY: Prentice-Hall, Inc. EDITOR: Janes Roberts TOPICS: Channeling TYPE: Book PRICE: $9.95

Unknown Reality Vol 2: A Seth Book

PUBLISHING COMPANY: Prentice-Hall, Inc. EDITOR: Janes Roberts TOPICS: Channeling TYPE: Book PRICE: $10.95

Untouched Key: Unnoticed Childhood Traumas In Creative People

PUBLISHING COMPANY: Doubleday & Co.,Inc. EDITOR: Alice Miller TOPICS: New Age TYPE: Book PRICE: $17.95

Upside Down Circle: Zen Laughter

PUBLISHING COMPANY: Blue Dolphin Publishing, Inc. Zen Master Gilbert TOPICS: Spirituality TYPE: Book PRICE: $12.95

Uranus-Neptune-Pluto

PUBLISHING COMPANY: Arthur Publications, Inc. EDITOR: Debra Sapp TOPICS: Astrology TYPE: Book DATE: 1978

Variety Of Dream Experience: Expanding Our Ways Of Working With Dreams

PUBLISHING COMPANY: Continuum Publishing Co. EDITOR: M. Ullman, C. Limmer TOPICS: Dreams TYPE: Book PRICE: $14.95

Vegetarian Connection

PUBLISHING COMPANY: Facts On File Publications EDITOR: Joel Rose TOPICS: Vegetarianism, Holistic Health, Health Food TYPE: Directory DATE: 1985; 182 pgs. PRICE PER COPY: $14.95

Vegetarian Health Directory

PUBLISHING COMPANY: 21st Century Publications EDITOR: Viktoras Kulvinskas TOPICS: New Age TYPE: Directory DESCRIPTION: Books for health and happiness.

Venture Inward: Edgar Cayce's Story

PUBLISHING COMPANY: Harper & Row Publishers, Inc. EDITOR: Hugh Lynn Cayce TOPICS: Channeling TYPE: Book PRICE: $8.95

Vibrational Medicine: New Choices For Healing Ourselves

PUBLISHING COMPANY: Bear & Company, Inc. EDITOR: R. Gerber TOPICS: Holistic Healing TYPE: Book PRICE: $16.95

Vimalakirti Nirdesa Sutra

PUBLISHING COMPANY: Shambhala Publications, Inc. EDITOR: C. Luk TOPICS: Spirituality TYPE: Book PRICE: $12.95

Vimana Aircraft From Ancient India & Atlantis

PUBLISHING COMPANY: Adventures-Unlimited Press EDITOR: D. Childress TOPICS: New Age TYPE: Book PRICE: $15.95

Virginia Samdahl: Reiki Master Healer

PUBLISHING COMPANY: Grunwald & Radcliffe Pub. EDITOR: B. Lugenbeel TOPICS: Holistic Health, Reiki TYPE: Book PRICE: $11.95

Vision Quest

PUBLISHING COMPANY: Valley Of The Sun Publishing Co., Sutphen Corporation EDITOR: Tara Sutphen TOPICS: Metaphysics, Meditation TYPE: Book DESCRIPTION: A guided meditation to explore Psychic solutions & visit your sacred place.

Visionary Arts Council

PUBLISHING COMPANY: Visionary Arts Council Astara TOPICS: New Age, Metaphysics TYPE: Directory DATE: 1988 CIRC: 4,000 DESCRIPTION: Serves Northwest, particularly Puget Sound, with listings that include art establishments, recording studios, radio/tv stations, designers and holistic practitioners.

Visionary Video Guide

PUBLISHING COMPANY: Visionary Video Guide TOPICS: New Age TYPE: Directory PRICE: $10.00 DESCRIPTION: Provides over 1200 listings of New Age videos and purchasing information.

Visions In The Stone: Journey To The Source Of Hidden Knowledge

PUBLISHING COMPANY: Gateways Books And Tapes EDITOR: E.J. Gold TOPICS: Tarot, Occult TYPE: Book PRICE: $14.50

Visions, Apparitions, Alien Visitors: A Comparative Study Of The Entity Enigma

PUBLISHING COMPANY: Aquarian Press EDITOR: Hillary Evans TOPICS: Occult TYPE: Book PRICE: $10.95

Visitors From Other Planets: A University Of Life Answer Book

PUBLISHING COMPANY: Mark-Age, Inc./Healing Haven/Centers Of Light/University Of Life/Meditations/Inform-Nations Mark-Age TOPICS: Paranormal Phenomena, UFO's TYPE: Book PRICE: $14.00

Visualization For Change: A Step-By-Step Guide To Using Your Powers Of Imagination

PUBLISHING COMPANY: New Harbinger Publications EDITOR: P. Fanning TOPICS: New Age, Meditation, Psychology TYPE: Book PRICE: $11.95

Visualization: The Key To Fulfillment

PUBLISHING COMPANY: Aquarian Press EDITOR: Michael Page TOPICS: Psychic, Meditation, New Age, Psychology TYPE: Book PRICE: $9.95

Vivekanada: The Yogas And Other Works

PUBLISHING COMPANY: Ramakrishna-Vivekananda Center Of New York EDITOR: S. Nikhilananda TOPICS: Yoga, Holistic Health TYPE: Book PRICE: $24.50

Voices From The Circle: The Heritage Of Western Paganism

PUBLISHING COMPANY: Aquarian Press EDITOR: Prudence Jones TOPICS: Paganism, Spirituality, Occult, Witchcraft TYPE: Book PRICE: $12.95

Voluntary Controls: Exercises For Creative Meditation & Activating The Potential Of/Chakras

PUBLISHING COMPANY: E.P. Dutton, Inc. EDITOR: Jack Schwartz TOPICS: New Age, Meditation TYPE: Book PRICE: $9.95

Voodoo & Hoodoo: The Craft As Revealed By Traditional Practitioners

PUBLISHING COMPANY: Scarborough House EDITOR: Jim Haskins TOPICS: Voudoun TYPE: Book PRICE: $8.95

Voodoo In Haiti

PUBLISHING COMPANY: Schocken Books EDITOR: A. Metraux TOPICS: Voudoun TYPE: Book PRICE: $12.95

Voudon Gnostic Workbook

PUBLISHING COMPANY: Magickal Childe Occult Supplies, Inc. EDITOR: M. Bertiaux TOPICS: Voudoun TYPE: Book PRICE: $29.95

Voyage To Atlantis

PUBLISHING COMPANY: Inner Traditions International, Ltd. EDITOR: James W. Mavor, Jr. TOPICS: New Age TYPE: Book; 260 pgs. PRICE: $24.95

Voyager Tarot: Way Of The Great Oracle

PUBLISHING COMPANY: Merrill-West Publishing EDITOR: J. Wanless TOPICS: Tarot TYPE: Book PRICE: $14.95

Waking Up: Overcoming The Obstacles To Human Potential

PUBLISHING COMPANY: Shambhala Publications, Inc. EDITOR: C. Tart TOPICS: New Age, Spirituality TYPE: Book PRICE: $14.95

Walk In The Light

PUBLISHING COMPANY: Blue Dolphin Publishing, Inc. TOPICS: New Age TYPE: Book PRICE: $9.95

Walking Through Stress: Meditation In Motion

PUBLISHING COMPANY: Cassandra Press EDITOR: Dick Harding TOPICS: Holistic Health TYPE: Book DATE: 1990; 208 pgs. PRICE: $11.95

War, Progress And The End Of History: Three Conversations, Including A Tale Of The Antichrist

PUBLISHING COMPANY: Lindisfarne Press EDITOR: V. Solovyov TOPICS: Metaphysics, Psychic TYPE: Book PRICE: $12.95

Warm Logic: The Art Of Intuitive Lifestyles
PUBLISHING COMPANY: Skidmore-Roth Publishers EDITOR: Louis Wynne, C. Klintworth TOPICS: New Age, Psychology TYPE: Book PRICE: $12.95

Watchers: The Secret Design Behind Ufo Abduction
PUBLISHING COMPANY: Bantam New Age Books EDITOR: Raymond Fowler TOPICS: UFO's, Paranormal Phenomena TYPE: Book PRICE: $18.95

Water Baby Information Book
PUBLISHING COMPANY: Point Of View Productions TOPICS: Birth TYPE: Book

Water Bears No Scars: Japanese Lifeways For Personal Growth
PUBLISHING COMPANY: William Morrow & Co. EDITOR: David K. Reynolds TOPICS: New Age TYPE: Book PRICE: $6.95

Water Pollution And Purification
PUBLISHING COMPANY: Sprout House PUBLISHER: Steve Meyerowitz TOPICS: Nutrition, Holistic Health, Health Food TYPE: Book

Way Of Cartouche: An Oracle Of Ancient Egyptian Magic
PUBLISHING COMPANY: St. Martin's Press, Inc. EDITOR: M. Hope TOPICS: Occult TYPE: Book PRICE: $22.95

Way Of Harmony: Guide To Self-Knowledge Through T'ai Chi Chuan, Hsing I, Pa Kua & Chi Kung
PUBLISHING COMPANY: Simon & Schuster, Inc. EDITOR: H. Reid TOPICS: Tai Chi TYPE: Guide PRICE: $12.95

Way Of Integral Life
PUBLISHING COMPANY: Union Of Tao And Man EDITOR: M. Ni TOPICS: Spirituality, New Age TYPE: Book PRICE: $14.00

Way Of The Physician
PUBLISHING COMPANY: Harper & Row Publishers, Inc. EDITOR: Jacob Needleman TOPICS: Acupuncture TYPE: Book PRICE: $15.95

Way To Locate Acu-Points
PUBLISHING COMPANY: China Books & Periodicals, Inc. EDITOR: J. Yang TOPICS: Holistic Health, Acupuncture TYPE: Book PRICE: $13.95

Way: A Book Of Welsh Witchcraft And The Religion Of Druidism
PUBLISHING COMPANY: Camelot Press Limited EDITOR: R. Gawr TOPICS: Occult, Witchcraft, Paganism TYPE: Book PRICE: $15.95

Ways Of Life: Macrobiotics & The Spirit Of Christianity
PUBLISHING COMPANY: Kodansha InternationalU.S.A., Ltd., Subs. of Kodansha, Ltd., c/o Harper & Row Pubs. EDITOR: J. Ineson TOPICS: Holistic Health, Vegetarianism, Health Food TYPE: Book PRICE: $15.95

Ways Of Work: Dynamic Action-Nyingma In The West
PUBLISHING COMPANY: Dharma Publishing EDITOR: Tarthang Tulku TOPICS: Spirituality TYPE: Book PRICE: $14.95

We All Live Downstream
PUBLISHING COMPANY: Water Center, The TOPICS: Holistic Healing TYPE: Guide PRICE: $9.95 DESCRIPTION: A guide to waste treatment.

We Want To Help
PUBLISHING COMPANY: Mind & Miracles EDITOR: Saul Steinberg TOPICS: New Age, Parapsychology, Holistic Health TYPE: Book DATE: 1984 SIZE: 4 x 8 1/2; 32 pgs. DESCRIPTION: Also available in video.

Weaving Woman
PUBLISHING COMPANY: Samuel Weiser, Inc. EDITOR: Barbara Black Koltuv TOPICS: New Age TYPE: Book PRICE: $9.95

Web That Has No Weaver: Understanding Chinese Medicine
PUBLISHING COMPANY: Contemporary Books, Inc. EDITOR: T. Kaptchuk TOPICS: Holistic Health TYPE: Book PRICE: $12.95

Weight No More
PUBLISHING COMPANY: Association For Research And Enlightenment, Inc. EDITOR: Eric Mein, M.D., Anne Hunt TOPICS: Homeopathy TYPE: Book; 64 pgs. PRICE: $4.95

Well Adult: How To Stay Well--What To Do If You Arc Ill
PUBLISHING COMPANY: Simon & Schuster, Inc. EDITOR: Mike Samuels, Nancy Samuels TOPICS: Acupuncture TYPE: Book PRICE: $14.95

Well Being Directory, The
PUBLISHING COMPANY: Well Being Directory, The TOPICS: New Age TYPE: Directory DESCRIPTION: Published by the Healing Arts Network.

Wellness Medicine: Dr. Anderson's Comprehensive Guide
PUBLISHING COMPANY: Keats Publishing, Inc. EDITOR: Robert Anderson TOPICS: Acupuncture TYPE: Guide PRICE: $17.95

Wellness Tree: Energizing Yourself In Body, Mind And Spirit
PUBLISHING COMPANY: Yes International EDITOR: Justin O'Brien TOPICS: Holistic Health, Acupuncture, Body-Mind Connection TYPE: Book PRICE: $15.95

Western Astrology And Chinese Medicine
PUBLISHING COMPANY: Aquarian Press EDITOR: J. Willmott TOPICS: Holistic Health, Astrology TYPE: Book PRICE: $9.95

Western Mystery Tradition: Esoteric Heritage Of The West
PUBLISHING COMPANY: Aquarian Press EDITOR: C. Hartley TOPICS: Occult TYPE: Book PRICE: $11.95

Western Way V.2: A Practical Guide To The Western Mystery Tradition
PUBLISHING COMPANY: Penguin Books EDITOR: C. Matthews, J. Matthews TOPICS: Occult TYPE: Book PRICE: $9.95

What Are Paganism And Witchcraft?
PUBLISHING COMPANY: Pagan/Occult/Witchcraft Special Interest Group TOPICS: Occult, Witchcraft, Paganism, Kabbalah, Alchemy, Voudoun TYPE: Booklet FREQ: every 3 yrs.

What Color Is Your Aura? Spectrums Of Personality For Understanding And Growth
PUBLISHING COMPANY: Pocket Books EDITOR: B. Bowers TOPICS: Holistic Health TYPE: Book PRICE: $9.95

What Is Your Psi-Q? Opening Up To Your Psychic Self
PUBLISHING COMPANY: H.J. Kramer, Inc. EDITOR: P. Stevens TOPICS: Psychic TYPE: Book PRICE: $12.95

What Survives? Contemporary Explorations Of Life After Death
PUBLISHING COMPANY: Jeremy P. Tarcher, Inc. EDITOR: G. Doore TOPICS: New Age, Occult, Reincarnation TYPE: Book PRICE: $12.95

What You Think Of Me Is None Of My Business
PUBLISHING COMPANY: Adventures In Enlightenment, A Foundation EDITOR: Terry Cole-Whittaker TOPICS: New Age, Metaphysics TYPE: Book DATE: 1983

Wheatgrass: Nature's Finest Medicine
PUBLISHING COMPANY: Sprout House PUBLISHER: Steve Meyerowitz TOPICS: Nutrition, Holistic Health, Health Food TYPE: Book

Wheel Of Fortune: How To Control Your Future
PUBLISHING COMPANY: Aquarian Press EDITOR: D. Line, J. Line TOPICS: Psychic, Metaphysics TYPE: Book PRICE: $16.95

Wheel Of The Year: Living The Magical Life
PUBLISHING COMPANY: Llewellyn Publications EDITOR: P. Campanelli TOPICS: Paganism, Spirituality TYPE: Book PRICE: $9.95

Wheels Of A Soul: Reincarnation, Your Life Today And Tomorrow
PUBLISHING COMPANY: Research Centre Of Kabbalah EDITOR: P. Berg TOPICS: Spirituality, Reincarnation TYPE: Book PRICE: $10.95

Wheels Of Life: A User's Guide To The Chakra System
PUBLISHING COMPANY: Llewellyn Publications EDITOR: A. Judith TOPICS: Holistic Health TYPE: Book PRICE: $12.95

When Anger Hurts: Quieting The Storm Within

PUBLISHING COMPANY: New Harbinger Publications EDITOR: M. McKay TOPICS: New Age, Psychology TYPE: Book PRICE: $11.95

When Daylight Comes: Biography Of H.P. Blavatsky

PUBLISHING COMPANY: Theosophical University Press EDITOR: H. Murphet TOPICS: Occult, Spirituality TYPE: Book PRICE: $7.50

When The Spirits Come Back

PUBLISHING COMPANY: Inner City Books EDITOR: J. Dallett TOPICS: Spirituality, Psychic Healing TYPE: Book PRICE: $14.00

Where Are The Psychics? Psychic, Metaphysical, Holistic Healing International Directory

PUBLISHING COMPANY: Larsen Publishing EDITOR: Miriam C. Larsen TOPICS: Psychic Phenomena TYPE: Directory DATE: 1985; 530 pgs. PRICE: $14.95 DESCRIPTION: An international directory of psychic, metaphysical & holistic healing practitioners, institutions, services & products. Arranged alphabetically & geographically. Contains almost 2000 listings & has no advertising.

Where Are You Going? A Guide To The Spiritual Journey

PUBLISHING COMPANY: S.Y.D.A. Foundation/Siddha Yoga Meditation Ashram Muktananda TOPICS: Spirituality TYPE: Book PRICE: $12.95

Where Healing Waters Meet: Touching The Mind & Emotions Through The Body

PUBLISHING COMPANY: Station Hill Press EDITOR: C. Ford TOPICS: Body-Mind Connection TYPE: Book PRICE: $19.95

Where Will You Be At The Battle Of Armeggedon?

PUBLISHING COMPANY: Parapsychology Education Center EDITOR: Korra Deaver, Ph. D. TOPICS: New Age TYPE: Book PRICE: $2.00 DESCRIPTION: New thoughts concerning the end of the Piscean Age.

Whispers From Eternity

PUBLISHING COMPANY: Amrita Foundation Yogananda TOPICS: Yoga, Spirituality TYPE: Book PRICE: $12.95

White Light, The

PUBLISHING COMPANY: Technology Group, The EDITOR: Rev. Nelson H. White, Anne White TOPICS: Occult, Metaphysics TYPE: Book

Who Are You? Discovering Your Real Identity

PUBLISHING COMPANY: Identity Institute EDITOR: Chris Butler TOPICS: New Age, Psychology TYPE: Book PRICE: $12.95

Who Gets Sick: How Beliefs, Moods And Thought Can Affect Your Health

PUBLISHING COMPANY: Jeremy P. Tarcher, Inc. EDITOR: B. Justice TOPICS: Holistic Health, Body-Mind Connection, Psychology TYPE: Book PRICE: $12.95

Who's Who In The Healing Arts

PUBLISHING COMPANY: Referral Service For Health Care Information EDITOR: Julie Von Erffa TOPICS: Holistic Healing TYPE: Directory

Whole Again Resource Guide

PUBLISHING COMPANY: Source Net EDITOR: Tim Ryan, Patricia J. Case TOPICS: Holistic Health, New Age, Metaphysics, Occult, Parapsychology TYPE: Directory DATE: 1980; 350 pgs. PRICE: $24.95 DESCRIPTION: Resource guide provides indexed, annotated listings of over 3000 New Age publications. Some reviews of books and periodicals.

Whole Ozarks Resource Directory

PUBLISHING COMPANY: Whole Ozarks Resource Directory TOPICS: Occult, Parapsychology TYPE: Directory

Why Do We Dream?

PUBLISHING COMPANY: Association For Research And Enlightenment, Inc. EDITOR: J. Everett Irion TOPICS: Dreams, Channeling TYPE: Book PRICE: $15.95

Why Mediumship Has No Value

PUBLISHING COMPANY: Truth TOPICS: New Age, Spirituality TYPE: Book DATE: 1990; 120 pgs. DESCRIPTION: Free.

Why Women Worry: And How To Stop

PUBLISHING COMPANY: Prentice-Hall, Inc. EDITOR: J. Handly, P. Neff TOPICS: New Age, Psychology TYPE: Book PRICE: $18.95

Wiccan Candle, The

PUBLISHING COMPANY: Wiccan Church Of Canada TOPICS: Witchcraft, Occult, Paganism TYPE: Book

Wind Between The Worlds

PUBLISHING COMPANY: Snow Lion Graphics TOPICS: New Age TYPE: Book PRICE: $12.95

Windows Of The Mind: Consciousness Beyond The Body

PUBLISHING COMPANY: Avery Publishing Group, Inc. EDITOR: G.M. Glaskin TOPICS: Psychic Phenomena, Astral Projection TYPE: Book PRICE: $10.95

Winning The Cold War

PUBLISHING COMPANY: Association For Research And Enlightenment, Inc. EDITOR: Anne Hunt TOPICS: Homeopathy TYPE: Book; 64 pgs. PRICE: $4.95

Wisdom And The Senses: The Way Of Creativity

PUBLISHING COMPANY: W. W. Norton & Co., Inc. EDITOR: J. Erikson TOPICS: New Age TYPE: Book PRICE: $19.95

Wisdom Of The Dream: The World Of C.G. Jung

PUBLISHING COMPANY: Shambhala Publications, Inc. EDITOR: S. Segaller, M. Berger TOPICS: New Age, Dreams, Psychology TYPE: Book PRICE: $18.95

Wisdom Of The Tarot

PUBLISHING COMPANY: Aurora Press, Inc. EDITOR: E. Haich TOPICS: Tarot, Metaphysics TYPE: Book PRICE: $12.50

Wise Woman Herbal For The Childbearing Year

PUBLISHING COMPANY: Ash Tree Publishing EDITOR: Susun Weed TOPICS: Spirituality, Herbalogy, Holistic Health TYPE: Book PRICE: $8.95

Wise Woman Herbal For The Menopausal Years

PUBLISHING COMPANY: Ash Tree Publishing EDITOR: Susun Weed TOPICS: Spirituality, Herbalogy, Holistic Health TYPE: Book

Witchcraft/Paganism Directory

PUBLISHING COMPANY: Ghost Research Society EDITOR: Dale Kaczmarek TOPICS: Astrology TYPE: Directory PRICE: $6.50 DESCRIPTION: Contains names of individuals, groups, organizations, magazines & newsletters on the topic.

Witches Bible Compleat

PUBLISHING COMPANY: Magickal Childe Occult Supplies, Inc. EDITOR: Janet Farrar, S. Farrar TOPICS: Witchcraft, Occult TYPE: Book PRICE: $19.95

With The Grain: The Essentially Vegetarian Way

PUBLISHING COMPANY: Carroll & Graf Publishers EDITOR: Ellen Brown TOPICS: Vegetarianism, Health Food, Holistic Health TYPE: Book PRICE: $21.95

With The Swamis In American And India

PUBLISHING COMPANY: Vedanta Press, Div. of Vedanta Society EDITOR: S. Atulananda TOPICS: Spirituality TYPE: Book PRICE: $9.95

Witness To The Fire: Creativity And The Veil Of Addiction

PUBLISHING COMPANY: Shambhala Publications, Inc. EDITOR: Linda Leonard TOPICS: New Age TYPE: Book PRICE: $19.95

Wolf Messing: The True Story Of Russia's Greatest Psychic

PUBLISHING COMPANY: Paragon House EDITOR: T. Lungin, D. Rogo TOPICS: Psychic TYPE: Book PRICE: $18.95

Woman As Healer: A Panoramic Survey Of The Healing Activities Of Women From Prehistoric..

PUBLISHING COMPANY: Shambhala Publications, Inc. EDITOR: J. Achterberg TOPICS: Holistic Healing TYPE: Book PRICE: $19.95

Woman's Book Of Healing

PUBLISHING COMPANY: Llewellyn Publications **EDITOR:** D. Stein **TOPICS:** Spirituality, Psychic Healing **TYPE:** Book **PRICE:** $12.95

Woman's Dictionary Of Symbols And Sacred Objects

PUBLISHING COMPANY: Harper & Row Publishers, Inc. **EDITOR:** Barbara Walker **TOPICS:** Spirituality **TYPE:** Book **PRICE:** $19.95

Woman's Encyclopedia Of Myths And Secrets

PUBLISHING COMPANY: Harper & Row Publishers, Inc. **EDITOR:** Barbara Walker **TOPICS:** Spirituality **TYPE:** Book **PRICE:** $22.95

Woman's Guide To Alternative Medicine

PUBLISHING COMPANY: Contemporary Books, Inc. **EDITOR:** L. Grist **TOPICS:** Holistic Health **TYPE:** Guide **PRICE:** $13.95

Woman's Hospital Trustees' Minutes

PUBLISHING COMPANY: Dinshah Health Society **EDITOR:** Dr. Kate W. Baldwin **TOPICS:** Holistic Healing, Color Therapy **TYPE:** Booklet

Womanspirit Sourcebook

PUBLISHING COMPANY: Harper & Row Publishers, Inc. **EDITOR:** P. Wynne **TOPICS:** Spirituality, New Age **TYPE:** Book **PRICE:** $16.95

Womanspirit Sourcebook

PUBLISHING COMPANY: Womanspirit Sourcebook **TOPICS:** New Age **TYPE:** Directory **DESCRIPTION:** Directory focusing on women and their spirituality.

Women Dreaming-Into-Art

PUBLISHING COMPANY: Sigo Press **EDITOR:** Patricia Ann Ariadne **TOPICS:** Spirituality, Psychology, New Age **TYPE:** Book **PRICE:** $18.95

Women Mystics In Medieval Europeindia

PUBLISHING COMPANY: Paragon House **EDITOR:** S. Hughes **TOPICS:** Spirituality **TYPE:** Book **PRICE:** $12.95

Women's Dionysian Initiation: The Villa Of Mysteries In Pompeii

PUBLISHING COMPANY: Spring Publications, Inc. **EDITOR:** L. Fierz-David **TOPICS:** New Age, Psychology, Paranormal Phenomena **TYPE:** Book **PRICE:** $17.50

Women's Encyclopedia Of Myths And Secrets

PUBLISHING COMPANY: Harper & Row Publishers, Inc. **EDITOR:** Barbara Walker **TOPICS:** Spirituality **TYPE:** Book **PRICE:** $22.95

Wonder Crops

PUBLISHING COMPANY: Natural Food Institute **TOPICS:** Health Food **TYPE:** Book

Word And Image (Bollinger Series XCVII: 2)

PUBLISHING COMPANY: Princeton University Press **EDITOR:** A. Jaffe **TOPICS:** New Age, Psychology **TYPE:** Book **PRICE:** $19.95

Words Of Gandhi

PUBLISHING COMPANY: Newmarket Press, Div. of Newmarket Publishing & Communications **EDITOR:** M. Gandhi **TOPICS:** Spirituality **TYPE:** Book **PRICE:** $12.95

Words That Heal: Affirmations And Meditations For Daily Living

PUBLISHING COMPANY: Pallas Communications **EDITOR:** D. Bloch **TOPICS:** Meditation, Psychology **TYPE:** Book **PRICE:** $7.95

Working High Magick

PUBLISHING COMPANY: Technology Group, The **EDITOR:** Nelson White, Anne White **TYPE:** Book **SIZE:** 8 1/2 x 11

Working Inside Out: Tools For Change-Applied Meditation For Intuitive Problem Solving

PUBLISHING COMPANY: Wingbow Press **EDITOR:** M. Adair **TOPICS:** Meditation, Spirituality **TYPE:** Book **PRICE:** $11.95

Working It Through: An Elisabeth Kubler-Ross Workshop On Life, Death & Transition

PUBLISHING COMPANY: Macmillan Publishing Co., Inc. **EDITOR:** E. Kubler-Ross **TOPICS:** Death **TYPE:** Book **PRICE:** $5.95

Working With The Dreaming Body

PUBLISHING COMPANY: Penguin Books **EDITOR:** S. Mindell **TOPICS:** Body-Mind Connection **TYPE:** Book **PRICE:** $10.95

World Of The Mystic

PUBLISHING COMPANY: Philosophical Library, Inc. **EDITOR:** S. Umen **TOPICS:** Paranormal Phenomena, Spirituality **TYPE:** Book **PRICE:** $12.00

World Of The Tarot: The Gypsy Method Of Reading The Tarot

PUBLISHING COMPANY: Samuel Weiser, Inc. **EDITOR:** S. Golowin **TOPICS:** Tarot **TYPE:** Book **PRICE:** $14.95

World Wide Messenger, The

PUBLISHING COMPANY: Universal Life **TOPICS:** Channeling **TYPE:** Booklet **DESCRIPTION:** Contains information on the channeled material of the Universal Life-The Inner Religion

Worldwide Macrobiotic Directory

PUBLISHING COMPANY: Kushi Institute-East West Foundation **EDITOR:** Elaine Altman **TOPICS:** Health Food, Holistic Health, Vegetarianism, Nutrition, Spirituality **TYPE:** Directory **DATE:** 1984; 42 pgs. **PRICE PER COPY:** $3.95

Worst Pills, Best Pills: The Older Adult's Guide To Avoiding Drug-Induced Death Or Illness

PUBLISHING COMPANY: Random House, Inc. **EDITOR:** Public Citizen Health Research **TOPICS:** Holistic Health **TYPE:** Guide **PRICE:** $12.00

Woulda, Coulda, Shoulda: Overcoming Regrets, Mistakes & Missed Opportunities

PUBLISHING COMPANY: William Morrow & Co. **EDITOR:** A. Freeman, R. DeWolf **TOPICS:** New Age, Psychology **TYPE:** Book **PRICE:** $15.95

Writing The Natural Way

PUBLISHING COMPANY: Jeremy P. Tarcher, Inc. **EDITOR:** G. Rico **TOPICS:** New Age **TYPE:** Book **PRICE:** $12.95

Wrong Way Home: Uncovering The Patterns Of Cult Behavior In American Society

PUBLISHING COMPANY: Beacon Press, Inc. **EDITOR:** A. Deikman **TOPICS:** Occult **TYPE:** Book **PRICE:** $19.95

Wylundt's Book Of Incense: A Magical Primer

PUBLISHING COMPANY: Samuel Weiser, Inc. **EDITOR:** Steven R. Smith **TOPICS:** New Age, Occult, Witchcraft **TYPE:** Book **PRICE:** $12.95

Ye Olde Dream Book

PUBLISHING COMPANY: Technology Group, The **EDITOR:** Frater Zarathustra **TYPE:** Book **SIZE:** 8 1/2 x 11

Yoga And Psychotherapy

PUBLISHING COMPANY: Himalayan International Institute Of Yoga Science and Philosophy **EDITOR:** S. Rama **TOPICS:** Yoga, Holistic Health **TYPE:** Book **PRICE:** $12.95

Yoga Of Herbs: An Ayurbedic Guide To Herbal Medicine

PUBLISHING COMPANY: Lotus Light Publications **EDITOR:** V. Lad, D. Frawley **TOPICS:** Holistic Health **TYPE:** Guide **PRICE:** $11.95

Yoga Step By Step

PUBLISHING COMPANY: Narayana Press/America **EDITOR:** E. Peterson **TOPICS:** Yoga, Holistic Health **TYPE:** Book **PRICE:** $19.95

Yoga Syzygy

PUBLISHING COMPANY: Ma Yoga Shakti International Mission **PUBLISHER:** Ma Yoga Shakti **TOPICS:** Yoga, Meditation, Spirituality **TYPE:** Book

Yoga Vashishttha-Part I

PUBLISHING COMPANY: Ma Yoga Shakti International Mission **PUBLISHER:** Ma Yoga Shakti **TOPICS:** Yoga, Meditation, Spirituality **TYPE:** Book

Yoga Vashishttha-Part II

PUBLISHING COMPANY: Ma Yoga Shakti International Mission **PUBLISHER:** Ma Yoga Shakti **TOPICS:** Yoga, Meditation, Spirituality **TYPE:** Book

Yoga, Immortality And Freedom

PUBLISHING COMPANY: Princeton University Press **EDITOR:** M. Eliade **TOPICS:** Yoga **TYPE:** Book **PRICE:** $14.50

Yoga-Sutra Of Patanjali: A New Translation & Commentary

PUBLISHING COMPANY: Inner Traditions International, Ltd. EDITOR: G. Feuerstein TOPICS: Yoga, Holistic Health TYPE: Book PRICE: $12.95

Yoga: Mastering The Secrets Of Matter And The Universe

PUBLISHING COMPANY: Inner Traditions International, Ltd. EDITOR: Alain Danielou TOPICS: Yoga, Holistic Health TYPE: Book PRICE: $10.95

Yoga: Technology Of Ecstasy

PUBLISHING COMPANY: Jeremy P. Tarcher, Inc. EDITOR: G. Feuerstein TOPICS: Yoga, Holistic Health TYPE: Book PRICE: $14.95

Yoga: The Iyengar Way - The New Definitive Illustrated Guide

PUBLISHING COMPANY: Random House, Inc. EDITOR: Mira Mehta, Silva Mehta TOPICS: Yoga TYPE: Book PRICE: $18.95

You And Your Aura

PUBLISHING COMPANY: Sterling Publishing Company, Inc. EDITOR: J. Ostrom TOPICS: Holistic Health TYPE: Book PRICE: $9.95

You Can Heal Your Life

PUBLISHING COMPANY: Hay House EDITOR: Louise Hay TOPICS: Holistic Health, Body-Mind Connection, Psychology TYPE: Book PRICE: $12.00

You Can If You Think You Can

PUBLISHING COMPANY: Prentice-Hall, Inc. EDITOR: N.V. Pcalc TOPICS: New Age, Psychology TYPE: Book PRICE: $8.95

You Can Relieve Pain: How To Use Guided Imagery To Reduce Pain Or Eliminate It Completely!

PUBLISHING COMPANY: Harper & Row Publishers, Inc. EDITOR: K. Dachman, J. Lyons TOPICS: Meditation, Psychology TYPE: Book PRICE: $18.95

You Forever

PUBLISHING COMPANY: Samuel Weiser, Inc. EDITOR: T. Lobsang Rampa TOPICS: Metaphysics, Psychic TYPE: Book PRICE: $9.95

You The Healer: Do-It-Yourself 40-Day Course On How To Heal Yourself And Others

PUBLISHING COMPANY: H.J. Kramer, Inc. EDITOR: J. Silva, R. Stone TOPICS: Holistic Healing TYPE: Book PRICE: $10.95

You'll See It When You Believe It: The Way To Your Personal Transformation

PUBLISHING COMPANY: William Morrow & Co. EDITOR: W. Dyer TOPICS: New Age, Psychology TYPE: Book PRICE: $17.95

Your Astrological Guide To Fitness

PUBLISHING COMPANY: Mills & Sanderson Publishing EDITOR: Eva Shaw TOPICS: Holistic Health, Astrology TYPE: Guide PRICE: $9.95

Your Balancing Act: Discovering New Life Through Five Dimensions Of Wellness

PUBLISHING COMPANY: Metamorphous Press EDITOR: C. Taylor TOPICS: New Age, Psychology, Holistic Health TYPE: Book PRICE: $12.95

Your Body Believes Every Word You Say: The Language Of The Body/Mind Connection

PUBLISHING COMPANY: Aslan Publishing EDITOR: Barbara Hoberman Levine TOPICS: Holistic Health, Body-Mind Connection TYPE: Book PRICE: $11.95

Your Future Lives

PUBLISHING COMPANY: Whitford Press/Schiffer Publishing Limited EDITOR: Brad Steiger TOPICS: Reincarnation, Spirituality TYPE: Book PRICE: $12.95

Your Golden Shadow: Discovering And Fulfillng Your Undeveloped Self

PUBLISHING COMPANY: Harper & Row Publishers, Inc. EDITOR: W. Miller TOPICS: New Age, Psychology TYPE: Book PRICE: $15.95

Your Healing Hands: The Polarity Experience

PUBLISHING COMPANY: Wingbow Press EDITOR: Richard Gordon TOPICS: Parapsychology, Holistic Health TYPE: Book PRICE: $10.95

Your Heart, Your Planet: How You Can Make A Difference

PUBLISHING COMPANY: Hay House EDITOR: H. Diamond TOPICS: Vegetarianism, Health Food, Holistic Health TYPE: Book PRICE: $16.95

Your Horoscope Guide

PUBLISHING COMPANY: Petulengro Publications EDITOR: Eva Petulengro TOPICS: Astrology TYPE: Guide DATE: 1964 FREQ: Quartlery CIRC: 35,000

Your Name And Colors: Secret Keys To Your Beauty, Personality And Success!

PUBLISHING COMPANY: Spectra Publishing Co. EDITOR: D.G. Rolliet TOPICS: Color Therapy TYPE: Book PRICE: $12.95

Zen And The Art Of The Macintosh: Discoveries On The Path To Complete Enlightenment

PUBLISHING COMPANY: Running Press EDITOR: Michael Green TOPICS: New Age TYPE: Book PRICE: $16.95

Zen And The Psychology Of Transformation: The Supreme Doctrine

PUBLISHING COMPANY: Inner Traditions International, Ltd. EDITOR: H. Benoit TOPICS: Spirituality TYPE: Book PRICE: $12.95

Zen Buddhism And Psychoanalysis

PUBLISHING COMPANY: Harper & Row Publishers, Inc. EDITOR: E. Fromm TOPICS: Spirituality TYPE: Book PRICE: $7.95

Zen Buddhism: A History - India & China

PUBLISHING COMPANY: Macmillan Publishing Co., Inc. EDITOR: H. Dumoulin TOPICS: Spirituality TYPE: Book PRICE: $14.95

Zen Buddhism: A History--Japan

PUBLISHING COMPANY: Macmillan Publishing Co., Inc. EDITOR: H. Dumoulin TOPICS: Spirituality TYPE: Book PRICE: $14.95

Zen Imagery Exercises: Meridian Exercises For Wholesome Living

PUBLISHING COMPANY: Japan Publications, Inc. EDITOR: S. Masunaga TOPICS: Holistic Health TYPE: Book PRICE: $15.95

Zen Meditation And Psychotherapy

PUBLISHING COMPANY: Japan Publications, Inc. EDITOR: T. Hirai TOPICS: Spirituality, Meditation, Psychology TYPE: Book PRICE: $15.95

Zen To Go: Bite-Sized Bits Of Wisdom From The East & The West - From Buddha To Yogi Berra

PUBLISHING COMPANY: New American Library EDITOR: J. Winokur TOPICS: Spirituality TYPE: Book PRICE: $14.95

Zen: The Quantum Leap From Mind To No-Mind

PUBLISHING COMPANY: Chidvilas, Inc. EDITOR: B. Rajneesh TOPICS: New Age, Meditation, Spirituality, Body-Mind Connection TYPE: Book PRICE: $12.95

Zibo: Last Great Zen Master Of China

PUBLISHING COMPANY: Asian Humanities Press EDITOR: J.C. Cleary TOPICS: Spirituality TYPE: Book PRICE: $12.95

Zodiac And The Salts Of Salvation

PUBLISHING COMPANY: Samuel Weiser, Inc. EDITOR: G. Carey, I. Perry TOPICS: Holistic Health, Astrology TYPE: Book PRICE: $14.95

Zolar's Book Of The Spirits

PUBLISHING COMPANY: Prentice-Hall, Inc. Zolar TOPICS: Occult, Psychic Phenomena TYPE: Book PRICE: $9.95

Zolar's Compendium Of Occult Theories And Practices

PUBLISHING COMPANY: Prentice-Hall, Inc. Zolar TOPICS: Occult TYPE: Book PRICE: $9.95

Zolar's Encyclopedia Of Ancient And Forbidden Knowledge

PUBLISHING COMPANY: Prentice-Hall, Inc. Zolar TOPICS: Occult TYPE: Book PRICE: $10.95

Zolar's Encyclopedia Of Omens, Signs And Superstitions

PUBLISHING COMPANY: Prentice-Hall, Inc. Zolar
TOPICS: Occult **TYPE:** Book **PRICE:** $11.95

Periodicals

Included in this chapter are Magazines, Newsletters, Bulletins, Journals, Brochures, Catalogs, Newspapers, and Calendars. The terms Editors and Author are used interchangeably. For further information concerning any of these publications, contact the individual publishers listed in the Publishers Index.

12 Step Times, The

PUBLISHING COMPANY: 12 Step Times, The PUBLISHER: H.P. EDITOR: Carol Ann F. TOPICS: Holistic Health TYPE: Newspaper DATE: 1988; 16 pgs. FREQ: monthly DESCRIPTION: Deals with addiction, recovery, personal growth & healing through articles, events calendar and directory. Free, printed every 6th Thurs.

A-P Newsletter

PUBLISHING COMPANY: A-P Newsletter TOPICS: UFO's TYPE: Newsletter

A.I.P.R. News

PUBLISHING COMPANY: Australian Institute Of Parapsychological Research EDITOR: Michael Hough TOPICS: Parapsychology, Occult TYPE: Newspaper FREQ: Bi-Monthly CIRC: 140 DESCRIPTION: Covers news & various aspects of parapsychology in Australia.

AA Grapevine

PUBLISHING COMPANY: AA Grapevine, Inc. TOPICS: Holistic Healing TYPE: Magazine

AASC Newsletter

PUBLISHING COMPANY: Association For The Anthropological Study Of Consciousness EDITOR: Jeffery MacDonald TOPICS: Metaphysics TYPE: Newsletter

Abrasax

PUBLISHING COMPANY: Abrasax PUBLISHER: James M. Martin TOPICS: Metaphysics, Spirituality, Occult TYPE: Magazine DATE: 1988; 60 pgs. FREQ: quarterly PRICE: $20.00 TERM: annually PRICE PER COPY: $5.00 DESCRIPTION: Occult quarterly with emphasis on ceremonial magick.

Abstracts On Health Effects Of Environmental Pollutants

PUBLISHING COMPANY: Biosis EDITOR: Anne Marie Stefany TOPICS: Holistic Healing TYPE: Magazine

Acupuncture Newsletter

PUBLISHING COMPANY: Acupuncture Center TOPICS: Holistic Healing TYPE: Newsletter

Adamha News

PUBLISHING COMPANY: Office Of Communications EDITOR: Bernardine Moore TOPICS: Holistic Healing TYPE: Newspaper

Addiction Letter

PUBLISHING COMPANY: Manisses Communications Group, Inc. TOPICS: Holistic Healing TYPE: Newsletter

Addiction Program Management

PUBLISHING COMPANY: American Health Consultants, Inc. EDITOR: Leslie Norins, Betsy Riley TOPICS: Holistic Healing TYPE: Magazine

Addictions Alert

PUBLISHING COMPANY: American Health Consultants, Inc. TOPICS: Holistic Healing TYPE: Magazine

Addictive Behaviors

PUBLISHING COMPANY: Pergamon Press, Inc. EDITOR: R.N. Miranda, Peter Miller TOPICS: Holistic Healing TYPE: Magazine

ADPA Professional

PUBLISHING COMPANY: Alcohol And Drug Problems Association Of North America EDITOR: K. Besteman TOPICS: Holistic Healing TYPE: Magazine

Advance

PUBLISHING COMPANY: Foundation For Chiropractic Education And Research EDITOR: Kathleen Ngandu TOPICS: Holistic Healing TYPE: Magazine

Advanced Sciences Advisory

PUBLISHING COMPANY: Sarah and T. Galen Hieronymus TOPICS: Metaphysics TYPE: Magazine

Advances In Alcohol & Substance Abuse

PUBLISHING COMPANY: Haworth Press, Inc. EDITOR: William Cohen, Barry Stimmel TOPICS: Holistic Healing TYPE: Magazine

Advances In Health Economics & Health Services Research

PUBLISHING COMPANY: JAI Press, Inc. EDITOR: Richard Scheffler TOPICS: Holistic Healing TYPE: Magazine

Advances In Health Education & Promotion

PUBLISHING COMPANY: JAI Press, Inc. EDITOR: William Ward TOPICS: Holistic Healing TYPE: Magazine

Advances In Motor Development Research

PUBLISHING COMPANY: AMS Press, Inc. EDITOR: Jane Clark TOPICS: Holistic Healing TYPE: Magazine

Advances In Parapsychological Research

PUBLISHING COMPANY: Plenum Publishing Corporation TOPICS: New Age TYPE: Newsletter

Advances In Sports Medicine & Fitness

PUBLISHING COMPANY: Year Book Medical Publishers, Inc. EDITOR: William Grana TOPICS: Holistic Healing TYPE: Magazine

Aetherius Society Books & Cassettes Catalogue

PUBLISHING COMPANY: Aetherius Society TOPICS: Parapsychology TYPE: Catalog DATE: 1980; 36 pgs.

AFA Headquarters

PUBLISHING COMPANY: American Federation Of Astrologers, Inc. EDITOR: Robert W. Cooper TOPICS: Astrology TYPE: Newsletter

AFSCA Information Sheets

PUBLISHING COMPANY: Amalgamated Flying Saucer Clubs Of America EDITOR: Gabriel Green TOPICS: UFO's TYPE: Newsletter; 10 pgs. FREQ: Irregular

Agada

PUBLISHING COMPANY: Agada EDITOR: Reuven Goldfarb TOPICS: New Age TYPE: Magazine

Agape

PUBLISHING COMPANY: Truth Center EDITOR: Val Schorre TOPICS: New Age, Spirituality TYPE: Magazine DATE: 1971 FREQ: Bi-Monthly CIRC: 2,500 DESCRIPTION: Features articles dealing with the discovery of the divine Self within & the living of selfless love expressed to others.

Ahimsa

PUBLISHING COMPANY: American Vegan Society TOPICS: Vegetarianism, Health Food, Holistic Health TYPE: Magazine FREQ: quarterly PRICE: $18.00 TERM: yearly DESCRIPTION: Teaches, encourages & supports people in the compassionate lifestyle free of the use of animal products. Features in depth articles on all aspects of veganism.

AHP Perspective

PUBLISHING COMPANY: Association For Humanistic Psychology EDITOR: Deborah J. Breed, Edith Gladstone TOPICS: Holistic Health TYPE: Newsletter DATE: 1961 FREQ: monthly DESCRIPTION: Offers information & news about the Association For Humanistic Psychology such as meetings, conferences, board elections, members. Articles to explore and expand human potential and growth such as holistic health, psychotherapy, etc. Does book reviews.

Aikido Today Magazine

PUBLISHING COMPANY: Aikido Today Magazine PUBLISHER: Susan Perry EDITOR: Ronald Rubin

TOPICS: New Age, Aikido **TYPE:** Magazine **DATE:** 1987 **FREQ:** quarterly **PRICE PER COPY:** $4.00

Akhaden: The Atlantean News Journal

PUBLISHING COMPANY: Atlantean Antiquities Co. **EDITOR:** Michael Morgan **TOPICS:** Parapsychology, Occult **TYPE:** Journal **DATE:** 1987 **FREQ:** Monthly **PRICE:** $18.00

Alcyone Journal

PUBLISHING COMPANY: Alcyone Light Centre **EDITOR:** Diane Rasmussen, Sylvia Schechter **TOPICS:** New Age **TYPE:** Journal

Alive

PUBLISHING COMPANY: Alive **EDITOR:** Hilda Ward, Siegfried Gursche **TOPICS:** Health Food **TYPE:** Magazine

All My Relations

PUBLISHING COMPANY: All My Relations **TOPICS:** Witchcraft, Occult, Paganism **TYPE:** Magazine

Alternative Health Therapies

PUBLISHING COMPANY: Science Of Mind Church Counseling And Healing Center **TOPICS:** Holistic Healing **TYPE:** Magazine

Alternative Press Annual

PUBLISHING COMPANY: Temple University Press **TOPICS:** New Age **TYPE:** Journal

Alternatives

PUBLISHING COMPANY: Alternatives **EDITOR:** Lorraine Bruck **TOPICS:** New Age, Metaphysics **TYPE:** Journal **DATE:** 1989 **FREQ:** monthly **CIRC:** 50,000 **PRICE:** $10.00 **DESCRIPTION:** Aimed at encouraging personal development. Distributed in the Dallas/Fort Worth Texas area. Prints non-fiction, news, poetry, illustrations, interviews, & reviews of books & audio/video tapes.

Alternatives For The Health Conscious Individual

PUBLISHING COMPANY: Mountain Home Publishing **EDITOR:** David Williams, Deborah Kaufman **TOPICS:** Holistic Healing **TYPE:** Magazine

Alternatives Newspaper

PUBLISHING COMPANY: Alternatives **PUBLISHER:** Rochel Haigh Blehr **EDITOR:** Meghan Burke **TOPICS:** New Age, Metaphysics **TYPE:** Newspaper **DATE:** 1988; 16 pgs. **FREQ:** monthly **CIRC:** 30,000 **DESCRIPTION:** Free monthly newspaper dealing with environmental, health & social issues. Purpose is to educate the public about what's going on in our environment & what we can do to ensure survival. New Age/Metaphysical subjects. Features a calendar, non-fiction, interviews, letters & reviews.

Alternatives: An Alternate Lifestyle Newsletter

PUBLISHING COMPANY: Alternatives Resource Center **EDITOR:** Milo Thomberry, Rachel Gill **TOPICS:** New Age **TYPE:** Newsletter

American Acupuncturist

PUBLISHING COMPANY: American Association Of Acupuncture & Oriental Medicine **EDITOR:** Robert

Sohn **TOPICS:** Holistic Health **TYPE:** Journal **FREQ:** Quarterly

American Association-Electronic Voice Phenomena-Quarterly Newsletter

PUBLISHING COMPANY: American Association-Electronic Voice Phenomena **EDITOR:** Sarah Estep **TOPICS:** Metaphysics, Death, Parapsychology **TYPE:** Newsletter **FREQ:** quarterly **CIRC:** 230 **DESCRIPTION:** Newsletter included with membership. No advertising accepted.

American Astrology

PUBLISHING COMPANY: Starlog Press, Inc. **EDITOR:** Kenneth Irving, Lee Chapman **TOPICS:** Astrology **TYPE:** Magazine

American Astrology Presents Money & Success

PUBLISHING COMPANY: O'Quinn Studios **PUBLISHER:** Norman Jacobs **EDITOR:** Lee Chapman **TOPICS:** Astrology **TYPE:** Magazine **DATE:** 1986 **FREQ:** Quarterly **PRICE PER COPY:** $2.50

American Buddhist

PUBLISHING COMPANY: Association Of American Buddhists **EDITOR:** Dr. Kevin O'Neil **TOPICS:** Yoga **TYPE:** Magazine

American Demographics

PUBLISHING COMPANY: American Demographics **EDITOR:** Cheryl Russell **TOPICS:** New Age **TYPE:** Magazine **DESCRIPTION:** Offers articles related to marketing & other New Age topics.

American Dowser

PUBLISHING COMPANY: American Society Of Dowsers, Inc. **TOPICS:** Parapsychology, Psychic Phenomena **TYPE:** Journal **DATE:** 1961 **SIZE:** 5.5 x 8.5; 56 pgs. **FREQ:** Quarterly **CIRC:** 3,500 **PRICE:** $20.00 **PRICE PER COPY:** $1.00 **DESCRIPTION:** Covers all aspects of dowsing. Presents information pertaining to study & evaluation such as theories, ideas, techniques & applications.

American Federation Of Astrologers Bulletin

PUBLISHING COMPANY: American Federation Of Astrologers, Inc. **EDITOR:** Robert W. Cooper **TOPICS:** Astrology **TYPE:** Bulletin **DATE:** 1938 **SIZE:** 6 x 9; 32 pgs. **FREQ:** Monthly **CIRC:** 5,000 **PRICE:** $20.00 **DESCRIPTION:** Purpose is to promote interest in the field of Astrology. Reports & conducts research, lecturing, teaching & practice on all aspects of the science.

American Homeopathy

PUBLISHING COMPANY: United States Homeopathic Association **TOPICS:** Homeopathy **TYPE:** Magazine

American Journal Of Clinical Hypnosis

PUBLISHING COMPANY: American Society Of Clinical Hypnosis **EDITOR:** Thurman Mott, Jr. **TOPICS:** Hypnotism **TYPE:** Journal

American Journal Of Health Promotion

PUBLISHING COMPANY: American Journal Of Health Promotion **TOPICS:** Holistic Healing **TYPE:** Journal

American Journal Of Preventive Medicine

PUBLISHING COMPANY: Oxford University Press, Inc. **EDITOR:** Joseph Stokes III, M.D., Donald Pfarr **TOPICS:** Holistic Healing **TYPE:** Journal

American Natural Hygiene Society Newsletter

PUBLISHING COMPANY: New Jersey Chapter **EDITOR:** Bob Lucia **TOPICS:** Holistic Healing **TYPE:** Newsletter

American Yoga Newsletter

PUBLISHING COMPANY: California Yoga Teachers Association **EDITOR:** Linda Cogozzo **TOPICS:** Yoga **TYPE:** Newsletter

Amerrikua

PUBLISHING COMPANY: Amerrikua **TOPICS:** Spirituality, New Age **TYPE:** Magazine **FREQ:** quarterly **PRICE:** $15.00 **DESCRIPTION:** Reports on The Movement for the American Indian Solar Cultures' commitment to peace and cultural oneness of the Americas. Prints articles, illustrations, book reviews and poems.

Amis De La Radiesthesie

PUBLISHING COMPANY: Association des Amis de la Radiesthesie **EDITOR:** H. de France **TOPICS:** Parapsychology, Occult **TYPE:** Magazine **DATE:** 1930 **FREQ:** Quarterly **CIRC:** 500

Ancient Truth

PUBLISHING COMPANY: Ancient Truth Research Foundation **EDITOR:** Albert Rainey **TOPICS:** Spirituality, New Age, Metaphysics **TYPE:** Magazine **FREQ:** monthly **DESCRIPTION:** National publication dedicated to New Age/Metaphysical subjects. Prints non-fiction articles, news, reviews, poetry, interviews and photography.

Ancient Ways Newsletter

PUBLISHING COMPANY: Ancient Ways Newsletter **TOPICS:** Witchcraft, Occult, Paganism **TYPE:** Newsletter

And So It Is

PUBLISHING COMPANY: Forum, The **TOPICS:** Body-Mind Connection, Spirituality, Metaphysics **TYPE:** Newsletter **PRICE:** $12.00 **TERM:** yearly

Anima: The Journal Of Human Experience

PUBLISHING COMPANY: Anima Publications **EDITOR:** Barbara D. Rotz, Harry M. Buck **TOPICS:** New Age, Metaphysics **TYPE:** Journal **DATE:** 1974 **FREQ:** bi-annual **CIRC:** 1,000 **PRICE:** $9.95 **DESCRIPTION:** Devoted to addressing multi-cultural women and human issues especially relating to myth, history and beyond. Also available on microform.

Animal Voice Magazine, The

PUBLISHING COMPANY: Compassion For Animals Foundation, Inc. **EDITOR:** Art Cordt, Laura A. Moretti **TOPICS:** New Age, Metaphysics **TYPE:** Magazine **DATE:** 1987 **FREQ:** bi-monthly **CIRC:** 2,000 **PRICE:** $18.00 **PRICE PER COPY:** $4.00

DESCRIPTION: A publication devoted to animal rights.

Animals' Agenda
PUBLISHING COMPANY: Animal Rights Network, Inc. EDITOR: Kim Barlett TOPICS: New Age TYPE: Magazine

Anomalistics: The Csar Bulletin
PUBLISHING COMPANY: Center For Scientific Anomalies Research EDITOR: Marcello Truzzi, Ph. D. TOPICS: Ghosts, Psychic Phenomena TYPE: Bulletin

Aperture
PUBLISHING COMPANY: Aperture EDITOR: Daniel Power TOPICS: New Age, Metaphysics TYPE: Journal DATE: 1952 PRICE: $9.95 DESCRIPTION: A photography journal publishing some New Age/Metaphysical material.

Appropriate Living Media
PUBLISHING COMPANY: New Age Enterprises EDITOR: Eddie Romano TOPICS: New Age TYPE: Newsletter DESCRIPTION: A New Age newsletter offering poetry, resource guide, essays, and editorials.

Aquarian Alchemist
PUBLISHING COMPANY: Academy Research Associates EDITOR: Daniel Fritz TOPICS: Parapsychology, Occult TYPE: Magazine DATE: 1980 FREQ: Quarterly CIRC: 10,000

Aquarian Arrow
PUBLISHING COMPANY: Neopantheist Society EDITOR: Zachary Cox TOPICS: Parapsychology, Occult TYPE: Magazine DATE: 1977 FREQ: Irregular CIRC: 300 PRICE: $10.00 DESCRIPTION: Contains articles, essays, creative writing, and reader correspondence on the relationship between pantheistic, spiritual philosophies and cultural, psychological & civic developments.

Aquarian Fellowship
PUBLISHING COMPANY: Aquarian Fellowship EDITOR: Joseph November TOPICS: New Age TYPE: Magazine

Aquarian Messenger
PUBLISHING COMPANY: Aquarian Messenger TOPICS: Witchcraft, Occult, Paganism TYPE: Magazine

Aquarian Voices
PUBLISHING COMPANY: Aquarian Voices EDITOR: Kathleen Johnson TOPICS: Metaphysics, New Age, Crystals, Tarot, Astrology, Holistic Health, Holistic Healing TYPE: Magazine FREQ: monthly DESCRIPTION: Covers topics on health, metaphysics and New Age. Offers advice on harmonious living. Features articles & book reviews on various subjects including astrology, health & healing, crystal & tarot. Accepts ads.

Aquarius Ranch Communications
PUBLISHING COMPANY: Aquarius Ranch Communications TOPICS: Channeling TYPE: Magazine

Aquarius Rising
PUBLISHING COMPANY: Aquarius Rising EDITOR: Pamela Leigh Powers TOPICS: Astrology, New Age, Metaphysics TYPE: Newspaper DATE: 1988 FREQ: monthly CIRC: 10,000 PRICE: $12.95 PRICE PER COPY: $1.75 DESCRIPTION: Deals with modern-day issues pertaining to metaphysics, astrology, personal development & psychology. Publishes feature articles, non fiction, book reviews, events, poetry, cartoons, interviews, illustrations and photography.

Archaeus
PUBLISHING COMPANY: Archaeus Project EDITOR: Dennis Stillings, Gail Duke TOPICS: Parapsychology TYPE: Journal DATE: 1983; 200 pgs. FREQ: Annual CIRC: 500 PRICE: $20.00 PRICE PER COPY: $5.00 DESCRIPTION: Covers topics such as alternative medicine, body-mind connection, parapsychology & paranormal phenomena.

Archives Of Environmental Health: An International Journal
PUBLISHING COMPANY: Heldref Publications, Inc. EDITOR: Patricia McCready TOPICS: Metaphysics TYPE: Journal

Areopagus
PUBLISHING COMPANY: Dialog Center International EDITOR: Johannes Aagaard TOPICS: New Age TYPE: Journal DATE: 1977 FREQ: Quarterly CIRC: 1,000 PRICE: $15.00 DESCRIPTION: Offers current information & news on new religious movements.

Arizona Light, The
PUBLISHING COMPANY: Arizona Light, The EDITOR: Jacqueline J. Pieters TOPICS: New Age, Holistic Health TYPE: Newspaper FREQ: monthly CIRC: 30,000 PRICE: $14.00 DESCRIPTION: Holistic newspaper presenting New Thought ideas, natural health, well-being, the environment, ecology, alternative & conventional philosophy through news articles that encourage well-being and personal growth for the individual. Guide to the Mind, Body & Soul.

Arizona Networking News
PUBLISHING COMPANY: Tri Pyramids, Inc. EDITOR: Joanne Henning Tedesco TOPICS: New Age, Metaphysics, Holistic Health TYPE: Newspaper DATE: 1981; 24 pgs. FREQ: quarterly PRICE: $10.00 PRICE PER COPY: $3.00 DESCRIPTION: Holistic, New-Age, Metaphysical newspaper featuring articles & ads on various topics all dealing with health & wellness. Publishes feature articles, reviews & calendars. Accepts ads.

Artifex
PUBLISHING COMPANY: Archaeus Project EDITOR: Dennis Stillings, Gail Duke TOPICS: Parapsychology TYPE: Journal DATE: 1981 SIZE: 8.5 x 11; 26 pgs. FREQ: Bi-Monthly CIRC: 500 PRICE: $20.00 DESCRIPTION: Publishes papers on paranormal phenomena, the mind-body relationship & psi.

As-You-Like-It Library
PUBLISHING COMPANY: As-You-Like-It Library EDITOR: Phil Lipson TOPICS: Holistic Health, New Age, Metaphysics TYPE: Newsletter DATE: 1961 PRICE: $10.00 DESCRIPTION: New Age/Metaphysics newsletter devoted to book & video/audio tape reviews.

ASD Journal Of Dreaming
PUBLISHING COMPANY: Association For The Study Of Dreams TOPICS: Dreams TYPE: Journal FREQ: quarterly DESCRIPTION: New quarterly international journal of multidisciplinary scope. Features scholarly articles on every aspect of dreams & dreaming.

ASD Newsletter
PUBLISHING COMPANY: Association For The Study Of Dreams TOPICS: Dreams TYPE: Newsletter FREQ: quarterly DESCRIPTION: Features articles, research reports, book reviews, interviews with noted dream authorities, letters to the editor, an open forum for discourse & dialogue on dreams & news of the association.

ASH Smoking & Health Review
PUBLISHING COMPANY: Action On Smoking And Health TOPICS: Holistic Healing TYPE: Newsletter

Aspects
PUBLISHING COMPANY: Aquarius Workshops EDITOR: Angel Thompson TOPICS: Astrology TYPE: Journal; 40 pgs. FREQ: Quarterly CIRC: 2,500 PRICE: $20.00 PRICE PER COPY: $4.00

Association For Past-Life Research And Therapy Newsletter
PUBLISHING COMPANY: Association For Past-Life Research And Therapies, Inc. EDITOR: Terry Nash, M.A. TOPICS: Reincarnation, Past Life Regression, Hypnotism, Death, Parapsychology TYPE: Newsletter FREQ: quarterly PRICE: $10.00

Association For Past-Life Research And Therapies Journal
PUBLISHING COMPANY: Association For Past-Life Research And Therapies, Inc. EDITOR: Russell Davis, Ph. D. TOPICS: Reincarnation, Past Life Regression, Hypnotism, Death, Parapsychology TYPE: Journal FREQ: bi-annually PRICE: $15.00

Association of Body, Mind, Spirit
PUBLISHING COMPANY: Association of Body, Mind, Spirit TOPICS: New Age TYPE: Newsletter DESCRIPTION: An all-inclusive manual & New Age newsletter service.

Astara Voice
PUBLISHING COMPANY: Astara Foundation, Inc. EDITOR: Annette Shape TOPICS: Metaphysics TYPE: Newsletter DATE: 1951

Astra
PUBLISHING COMPANY: Rizzoli-Corriere della Sera EDITOR: L. Brazzoli TOPICS: Astrology TYPE: Magazine FREQ: Monthly

Astral
PUBLISHING COMPANY: F.G. Gourdon TOPICS: Astrology TYPE: Magazine DATE: 1949 FREQ: Monthly CIRC: 55,000

Astral Publications
PUBLISHING COMPANY: Astral Publications EDITOR: Frank Carson TOPICS: Holistic Health, New Age, Channeling TYPE: Newsletter FREQ: irregular DESCRIPTION: A New Age newsmagazine.

Astres

PUBLISHING COMPANY: Arcades Jaulim **TOPICS:** Parapsychology, Occult **TYPE:** Magazine **FREQ:** Monthly

Astres

PUBLISHING COMPANY: F.G. Gourdon **TOPICS:** Astrology **TYPE:** Magazine **DATE:** 1948 **CIRC:** 110,000

Astro Signs

PUBLISHING COMPANY: T-Square Pubs., Inc. **PUBLISHER:** Jack Tabatch **EDITOR:** Nancy Sussan **TOPICS:** Astrology **TYPE:** Magazine **DATE:** 1986; 32 pgs. **FREQ:** Monthly **CIRC:** 1,250,000 **PRICE PER COPY:** $0.69 **DESCRIPTION:** Sun Sign astrology booklets published each month & sold in a point-of-purchase display.

Astro-Analytics

PUBLISHING COMPANY: Astrology Book Club **EDITOR:** Robert Jansky **TOPICS:** Astrology **TYPE:** Newsletter; 10 pgs. **FREQ:** Monthly **PRICE:** $5.00

Astro-Annual

PUBLISHING COMPANY: Astro-Annual **EDITOR:** Jim Hendryx **TOPICS:** Astrology **TYPE:** Magazine **DATE:** 1984 **SIZE:** 7 x 9; 130 pgs. **PRICE:** $1.50

Astro-Carto-Graphy

PUBLISHING COMPANY: Astro-Carto-Graphy **TOPICS:** Astrology **TYPE:** Magazine

Astro-News

PUBLISHING COMPANY: Astro News **EDITOR:** Edna Lewis Rowland **TOPICS:** Astrology **TYPE:** Newspaper

Astro-Psychic Monthly Mini-Magazine

PUBLISHING COMPANY: SASE **TOPICS:** Parapsychology **TYPE:** Magazine **FREQ:** Monthly

Astro-Revue

PUBLISHING COMPANY: Astrologie und Parapscholoieschei Verlag **TOPICS:** Astrology **TYPE:** Newsletter **DATE:** 1981 **FREQ:** Annual

Astro-Talk

PUBLISHING COMPANY: Matrix Software **EDITOR:** Michael Erlewine **TOPICS:** Astrology **TYPE:** Bulletin

Astroflash

PUBLISHING COMPANY: A.C.S. Publications, Inc./Astro Computing Services **PUBLISHER:** Maria Kay Simms **EDITOR:** Maritha Pottenger **TOPICS:** Astrology, New Age **TYPE:** Newsletter **DATE:** 1973 **FREQ:** quarterly **DESCRIPTION:** Astrological newsletter. Free.

Astrologer's Almanac

PUBLISHING COMPANY: Astrologer's Almanac **TOPICS:** Astrology **TYPE:** Journal

Astrologia

PUBLISHING COMPANY: Linear **TOPICS:** Astrology **TYPE:** Journal **DATE:** 1974 **FREQ:** Semi-Annual **PRICE:** $8.00 **DESCRIPTION:** Publication concerned with state of consciousness, freedom & time.

Astrological Journal

PUBLISHING COMPANY: Astrological Association Of Great Britain **TOPICS:** Astrology **TYPE:** Journal

Astrological Magazine

PUBLISHING COMPANY: Raman Publications **PUBLISHER:** B. Niranjan Babu **EDITOR:** Dr. B.V. Raman **TOPICS:** Astrology **TYPE:** Magazine **DATE:** 1936; 72 pgs. **FREQ:** monthly **CIRC:** 25,000 **PRICE:** $35.00 **PRICE PER COPY:** $4.00 **DESCRIPTION:** Dedicated to the studies of Astrology & Indian Culture. Text in English.

Astrological Review

PUBLISHING COMPANY: Astrologers' Guild of America **TOPICS:** Astrology **TYPE:** Journal **FREQ:** quarterly **CIRC:** 450 **PRICE:** $35.00 **TERM:** year

Astrologischer Auskunftsbogen

PUBLISHING COMPANY: Baumgartner-Verlag **EDITOR:** Hermi Baumgartner **TOPICS:** Astrology **TYPE:** Magazine **DATE:** 1945 **FREQ:** Monthly

Astrology

PUBLISHING COMPANY: Diamandis Communication, Inc. **TOPICS:** Astrology **TYPE:** Magazine

Astrology

PUBLISHING COMPANY: California Astrology Association **PUBLISHER:** Skip Usen **TOPICS:** Astrology **TYPE:** Newspaper **DATE:** 1970 **SIZE:** 11.5 x 15; 16 pgs. **FREQ:** Quarterly **PRICE:** $6.00 **PRICE PER COPY:** $1.50 **DESCRIPTION:** Offers descriptions & illustrations about news, services & products pertaining to metaphysics.

Astrology And Athrishta

PUBLISHING COMPANY: K.S. Krishnamurti **EDITOR:** K. Subramaniam **TOPICS:** Astrology **TYPE:** Newsletter **DATE:** 1963 **CIRC:** 4,000 **PRICE:** $8.00

Astrology And Parapsychology

PUBLISHING COMPANY: Astrology And Parapsychology **TOPICS:** Astrology **TYPE:** Magazine

Astrology And Psychic News

PUBLISHING COMPANY: California Astrology Association **TOPICS:** Astrology **TYPE:** Newspaper **PRICE:** $20.00 **PRICE PER COPY:** $2.00 **DESCRIPTION:** Provides articles and ads on Astrology, Witchcraft, Wicca, Psychic Phenomena, Voodoo, Psychic Healing, Divination, Past Life Regression, etc. The newspaper's articles and ads are all offered on behalf of the California Astrology Association.

Astrology For The 80's

PUBLISHING COMPANY: CBS Publications **EDITOR:** Ann Keffer **TOPICS:** Astrology **TYPE:** Magazine; 100 pgs. **FREQ:** Monthly **PRICE:** $15.94

Astrology Magazine

PUBLISHING COMPANY: Walton Press Ltd. **EDITOR:** Pat Sheridan **TOPICS:** Astrology **TYPE:** Magazine **DATE:** 1977; 50 pgs. **FREQ:** Monthly

Astrology Now

PUBLISHING COMPANY: Astrology Now **TOPICS:** Astrology **TYPE:** Magazine **FREQ:** bi-monthly

Astrology Quarterly

PUBLISHING COMPANY: Astrological Lodge Of London **EDITOR:** Michael Edwards **TOPICS:** Astrology **TYPE:** Magazine **DATE:** 1926 **FREQ:** Quarterly **CIRC:** 700

Astrology Writers Newsletter

PUBLISHING COMPANY: Ninth Sign Publications **EDITOR:** C. J. Puotinen **TOPICS:** Astrology **TYPE:** Newsletter; 8 pgs.

Astrology Your Daily Horoscope

PUBLISHING COMPANY: Diamandis Communication, Inc. **PUBLISHER:** Carol Klapper **EDITOR:** Anne Kaffer **TOPICS:** Astrology **TYPE:** Magazine **DATE:** 1937 **SIZE:** 6 x 8-5/8; 100 pgs. **FREQ:** Monthly **PRICE:** $17.95 **PRICE PER COPY:** $1.50

Astrology: A Comprehensive Bibliograpy

PUBLISHING COMPANY: Yes! Inc. **EDITOR:** Cris Popenoe **TOPICS:** Astrology **TYPE:** Magazine **DATE:** 1982; 32 pgs. **PRICE:** $1.50

Astronews

PUBLISHING COMPANY: Cardinal Star Corp. **PUBLISHER:** D. Goele **EDITOR:** Zoa Goele **TOPICS:** Astrology **TYPE:** Magazine **DATE:** 1976 **SIZE:** 8 1/2 x 11; 24 pgs. **FREQ:** Monthly **CIRC:** 15,000 **PRICE:** $10.00 **PRICE PER COPY:** $0.75 **DESCRIPTION:** Publication pertaining to Astrology & concerned with self-help & positive thinking.

Astronews

PUBLISHING COMPANY: Goele Products Inc. Ostaro **TOPICS:** Astrology **TYPE:** Newspaper **CIRC:** 25,000

Asynjur

PUBLISHING COMPANY: Asynjur **TOPICS:** Metaphysics, Spirituality **TYPE:** Magazine

Atlanta Astrologer

PUBLISHING COMPANY: Metropolitan Astrological Society of Atlanta **EDITOR:** Lil Huber **TOPICS:** Astrology **TYPE:** Newsletter

Attain

PUBLISHING COMPANY: St. John's University-Congregational Church Of Practical Theology **TOPICS:** Spirituality, New Age **TYPE:** Magazine **CIRC:** 24,000 **DESCRIPTION:** Produced by the faculty of St. John's University for its students, alumni and friends. Publishes inspirational articles to help people achieve holistic wellness for success & happiness.

AUM U.S.A. Co. Ltd.

PUBLISHING COMPANY: AUM U.S.A. Co., Ltd. **EDITOR:** Joyu Fumihiro **TOPICS:** New Age **TYPE:** Magazine

Australian Journal Of Clinical And Experimental Hypnosis

PUBLISHING COMPANY: Australian Society For Clinical & Experimental Hypnosis **EDITOR:** Wendy-Louise Walker **TOPICS:** Hypnotism **TYPE:** Journal

Australian Well Being

PUBLISHING COMPANY: Australian Well Being **EDITOR:** Mandy Geddes, Jeni Edgley **TOPICS:** Nutrition, Spirituality, New Age, Metaphysics

TYPE: Magazine **DATE:** 1984; 124 pgs. **FREQ:** bi-monthly **CIRC:** 56,000 **PRICE:** $7.00 **DESCRIPTION:** Dedicated to bettering life by focusing on awareness of one's self and natural surroundings. Publishes articles, resource directory and photography.

Autre Monde

PUBLISHING COMPANY: F.G. Gourdon **TOPICS:** Parapsychology, Occult **TYPE:** Magazine **DATE:** 1978 **FREQ:** Monthly **CIRC:** 60,000

Avaloka

PUBLISHING COMPANY: Avaloka: A Journal **TOPICS:** Metaphysics, Spirituality **TYPE:** Journal

Avatar Journal, The

PUBLISHING COMPANY: Star's Edge International **TOPICS:** Metaphysics, Spirituality **TYPE:** Journal

Awakening

PUBLISHING COMPANY: Awakening **EDITOR:** Anthony Volpe, Lynn Volpe **TOPICS:** UFO's **TYPE:** Magazine **DESCRIPTION:** Promotes peace, harmony & love throughout the universe.

B.U.G.S. Flyer Newsletter

PUBLISHING COMPANY: Biological Urban Gardening Services **TOPICS:** Health Food **TYPE:** Newsletter

Balance Magazine

PUBLISHING COMPANY: Balance Publications **EDITOR:** Donna Sommers **TOPICS:** Holistic Health **TYPE:** Magazine **FREQ:** bi-monthly **PRICE:** $15.00 **DESCRIPTION:** Covers topics on new age, metaphysics, health, environment and psychology. Edited by a registered nurse & focusing on holistic health. Features articles, book & video reviews, letters, photography, artwork & poetry.

Baltimore Vegetarians-Newsletter

PUBLISHING COMPANY: Baltimore Vegetarians **TOPICS:** Health Food **TYPE:** Newsletter

Barbizon Magazine

PUBLISHING COMPANY: Barbizon Foundation **EDITOR:** Don Elzer, Steven Dafoe **TOPICS:** New Age **TYPE:** Magazine

Beacon

PUBLISHING COMPANY: Roundtable Of The Light Centers, Inc. **EDITOR:** Lorraine Cuttler **TOPICS:** Parapsychology, Occult **TYPE:** Newspaper **DATE:** 1974 **FREQ:** Monthly **CIRC:** 450 **PRICE:** $5.00

Bentwood

PUBLISHING COMPANY: Bentwood **TOPICS:** Witchcraft, Occult, Paganism **TYPE:** Magazine

Berkeley Wellness Letter

PUBLISHING COMPANY: Health Letter Associates **EDITOR:** Rodney M. Friedman **TOPICS:** Holistic Healing **TYPE:** Newsletter **DATE:** 1984 **FREQ:** monthly **CIRC:** 700,000 **PRICE:** $20.00 **DESCRIPTION:** Promotes wellness through proper fitness, nutrition & stress management.

Berkshire Alternatives

PUBLISHING COMPANY: Berkshire Alternatives **TOPICS:** New Age **TYPE:** Newspaper **DESCRIPTION:** Publishes articles on New Age subjects.

Best Of Health

PUBLISHING COMPANY: Wista Jeanne Johnson Publishers **EDITOR:** Wista Johnson **TOPICS:** Holistic Healing **TYPE:** Newsletter **DATE:** 1987 **SIZE:** 8 1/2x 11; 12 pgs. **FREQ:** quarterly **CIRC:** 1,000 **PRICE:** $14.00 **TERM:** yearly **PRICE PER COPY:** $3.50 **DESCRIPTION:** Features health articles, news, fitness, nutrition & book reviews directed toward black women.

Bestways

PUBLISHING COMPANY: Bestways **EDITOR:** Barbara Bassett **TOPICS:** Holistic Healing **TYPE:** Magazine

Better Health

PUBLISHING COMPANY: Nebraska State Department Of Health **EDITOR:** Marla Augustine **TOPICS:** Holistic Healing **TYPE:** Magazine

Better Nutrition

PUBLISHING COMPANY: Michael Kelman **EDITOR:** Michael Kelman **TOPICS:** Holistic Health **TYPE:** Magazine

Better Nutrition

PUBLISHING COMPANY: Communications Channels, Inc. **EDITOR:** William B. Manning, Robert Rawls **TOPICS:** Holistic Healing **TYPE:** Magazine

Better World

PUBLISHING COMPANY: Freedom Life Publishing **EDITOR:** Jon Stevens **TOPICS:** New Age **TYPE:** Magazine

Better World Magazine

PUBLISHING COMPANY: Intergroup For Planetary Oneness **EDITOR:** Patrick Harbula, Tricia A. Harbula **TOPICS:** Spirituality, Meditation, New Age **TYPE:** Magazine **DATE:** 1985 **SIZE:** 8 1/2x11; 96 pgs. **FREQ:** bi-monthly **CIRC:** 30,000 **PRICE:** $17.95 **TERM:** yearly **PRICE PER COPY:** $4.00 **DESCRIPTION:** Articles and reviews on various New Age topics. Offers readers exposure to diverse spiritual philosophies and practical methods of integrating spiritual principles with daily living. Prints articles, interviews, reviews and calendar.

Beyond Avalon

PUBLISHING COMPANY: Beyond Avalon **EDITOR:** John Chambers **TOPICS:** Psychic, New Age **TYPE:** Magazine **FREQ:** quarterly **PRICE:** $9.00 **PRICE PER COPY:** $2.50

Beyond Reality

PUBLISHING COMPANY: Beyond Reality Magazine, Inc. **EDITOR:** Harry Belil **TOPICS:** Parapsychology, Channeling, UFO's, Paranormal Phenomena, Psychic Phenomena **TYPE:** Magazine **DATE:** 1972 **FREQ:** Bi-Monthly **CIRC:** 10,000 **PRICE:** $8.00 **DESCRIPTION:** Reveals current research & findings in the study of UFO's, psychic phenomenon, & ESP. Available on film.

Beyond Words Newsletter

PUBLISHING COMPANY: Chidvilas, Inc. **TOPICS:** New Age, Meditation, Spirituality, Body-Mind Connection **TYPE:** Newsletter **DATE:** 1986; 8 pgs. **DESCRIPTION:** Produces newsletter, prints cartoons, artwork and reviews.

Billboard

PUBLISHING COMPANY: Billboard **EDITOR:** Ed Ochs, Dave DiMartino **TOPICS:** New Age **TYPE:** Magazine **FREQ:** weekly **DESCRIPTION:** The music industry's bible spotlights New Age music in an annual issue as well as a weekly column. Prints reviews.

Biofeedback & Self Regulation

PUBLISHING COMPANY: Plenum Publishing Corporation **TOPICS:** Holistic Health **TYPE:** Journal **DATE:** 1975 **FREQ:** quarterly **PRICE:** $36.00 **PRICE PER COPY:** $44.00 **DESCRIPTION:** Deals with various aspects of psychology, psychiatry, psychosomatic & physical medicine.

Birth Gazette

PUBLISHING COMPANY: R & E Fund **EDITOR:** Ina Gaskin **TOPICS:** Holistic Healing **TYPE:** Magazine

Black Flame, The

PUBLISHING COMPANY: Hell's Kitchen Productions, Inc. **EDITOR:** Peter H. Gilmore **TOPICS:** Occult **TYPE:** Newsletter **DATE:** 1989; 24 pgs. **FREQ:** quarterly **PRICE:** $12.00 **TERM:** yearly **PRICE PER COPY:** $3.00 **DESCRIPTION:** The international forum for the Church of Satan. Explores the implications & applications of the philosophy of Satanism as expounded in the writings of Church of Satan founder & High Priest, Anton Szandor LaVey. Includes articles, reviews, poetry & artwork that exemplifies the Satanic approach to contemporary life.

Blitz

PUBLISHING COMPANY: Alternative Research **EDITOR:** Kenneth Guse **TOPICS:** New Age **TYPE:** Newsletter **DATE:** 1977; 20 pgs. **FREQ:** Irregular **PRICE PER COPY:** $2.50 **DESCRIPTION:** Features alternative & New Age information, resources & reviews, news & notes, etc.

Bodhi Times

PUBLISHING COMPANY: Bodhi Times **PUBLISHER:** Willis Denome **TOPICS:** New Age, Metaphysics **TYPE:** Newspaper **FREQ:** bi-monthly **CIRC:** 10,000 **PRICE:** $6.00 **DESCRIPTION:** A San Francisco Bay area alternative newspaper covering health, environment and New Age topics. Prints non-fiction, news & reviews, criticisms, artwork and photography.

Body Bulletin

PUBLISHING COMPANY: Rodale Press, Inc. **TOPICS:** Holistic Healing **TYPE:** Bulletin

Body Talk

PUBLISHING COMPANY: Professional Newsletter Program **EDITOR:** Kirk Thomas, Don Rosen **TOPICS:** Holistic Healing **TYPE:** Magazine

Body, Mind & Spirit Magazine

PUBLISHING COMPANY: Island Publishing Co. **EDITOR:** Paul Zuromski, Carol Kramer **TOPICS:** Metaphysics, New Age, Holistic Health, Spirituality, Herbalogy, Channeling **TYPE:** Magazine **DATE:** 1982 **SIZE:** 8 1/2x 11 **FREQ:** bi-monthly **CIRC:** 150,000 **PRICE:** $18.00 **TERM:** yearly **PRICE PER COPY:** $2.95 **DESCRIPTION:** New Age publication covering wide range of fields from metaphysics to self-help to better nutrition. Features articles on holistic health, spirituality, natural living, healing,

herbalogy, channeling as well as reviews on books, audio & video. Prints news, interviews, artwork, photography & ads.

Bodywork Entrepreneur

PUBLISHING COMPANY: Bodywork Entrepreneur PUBLISHER: David Palmer TOPICS: Massage TYPE: Newsletter DATE: 1988 FREQ: monthly PRICE: $12.00 DESCRIPTION: Informative, monthly newsletter offering in-depth look at the business of bodywork.

Book Reader, The

PUBLISHING COMPANY: Book Reader, The EDITOR: Jay Bail TOPICS: New Age TYPE: Magazine FREQ: 6 issues/yr PRICE: $0.00 DESCRIPTION: Distributed through over 500 bookstores to customers, as a guide to new releases.

Boomstick

PUBLISHING COMPANY: Boomstick TOPICS: Witchcraft, Occult, Paganism TYPE: Magazine

Both Sides Now

PUBLISHING COMPANY: Free People Press EDITOR: Elihu Edelson TOPICS: New Age TYPE: Journal DATE: 1969; 10 pgs. FREQ: Irregular PRICE: $9.00 TERM: 10 issues PRICE PER COPY: $1.00 DESCRIPTION: A forum of New Age information, ideas, opinions & creativity. A unique spiritual, political synthesis.

Boulder Teachers' Catalog

PUBLISHING COMPANY: Boulder Teachers' Catalog EDITOR: Duane Fry TOPICS: New Age, Metaphysics TYPE: Catalog DATE: 1983 CIRC: 35,000 PRICE: $8.00 PRICE PER COPY: $1.00 DESCRIPTION: A scholarly catalog publishing fiction, non-fiction, poetry, criticisms, reviews, artwork, and satire.

Bountiful Gardens Catalogue

PUBLISHING COMPANY: Ecology Action TOPICS: Health Food TYPE: Catalog DESCRIPTION: Growing and Gathering Your Own Fertilizer, The Self-Sufficient Gardener, & Companion Plants and How To Use Them.

Brain/Mind Bulletin Newsletter

PUBLISHING COMPANY: Brain/Mind Bulletin Newsletter EDITOR: Marilyn Ferguson TOPICS: New Age, Occult, Parapsychology TYPE: Newsletter FREQ: monthly DESCRIPTION: Features articles on holistic health, new age and the occult. Prints non-fiction and news relating to self-awareness, health, fitness and inner well-being.

Break-Through

PUBLISHING COMPANY: Institute For Human Development EDITOR: Jonathan Parker TOPICS: Parapsychology TYPE: Newsletter DATE: 1985; 8 pgs. PRICE: $0.00 PRICE PER COPY: $0.00

Breathconnection

PUBLISHING COMPANY: Breathconnection TOPICS: Meditation, Yoga, Reincarnation, Holistic Healing, Channeling TYPE: Newsletter FREQ: quarterly DESCRIPTION: Newsletter covering various New Age topic such as Yoga, meditation & rebirthing.

Brimstone

PUBLISHING COMPANY: Brimstone TOPICS: Metaphysics, Spirituality TYPE: Magazine

British Homoeopathic Journal

PUBLISHING COMPANY: Royal London Homeopathic Hospital EDITOR: P. Fisher TOPICS: Homeopathy TYPE: Journal DATE: 1911 FREQ: Quarterly CIRC: 1,400 PRICE: $45.00 DESCRIPTION: Covers all aspects of homoepathy with emphasis on scientific research, clinical homeopathy, confirmation of theories & historical articles.

British Homoeopathy Research Group Communications

PUBLISHING COMPANY: British Homoeopathy Research Group EDITOR: Dr. Anita E. Davies TOPICS: Homeopathy TYPE: Magazine DATE: 1979 FREQ: Semi-Annual CIRC: 300 DESCRIPTION: Promotes the principles and practice of homeopathic medicine. Reports on research & scientific meetings in this field.

British Society Of Dowsers Journal

PUBLISHING COMPANY: British Society of Dowsers PUBLISHER: Deidre N. Rust TOPICS: Dowsing TYPE: Journal DATE: 1933 FREQ: Quarterly CIRC: 1,250 PRICE: $21.00

Bulletin Of The Society For Professional Well Being

PUBLISHING COMPANY: Center For The Well-Being Of Health Professionals EDITOR: Debra Lang, Bernard Virshop TOPICS: Holistic Healing TYPE: Bulletin

Business Ethics

PUBLISHING COMPANY: Business Ethics EDITOR: Miriam Kniaz TOPICS: New Age, Metaphysics TYPE: Magazine DATE: 1987; 32 pgs. FREQ: bimonthly CIRC: 5,000 PRICE: $49.00 DESCRIPTION: Focuses on the business executive with responsible life and work ethics. Prints feature articles, illustrations, non-fiction and reviews.

Business in Transformation

PUBLISHING COMPANY: Business in Transformation TOPICS: New Age TYPE: Journal FREQ: quarterly CIRC: 3,500 PRICE: $24.00 DESCRIPTION: Focuses on business and management topics for the New Age professional. Prints reviews, articles, news and resources.

Buzzworm-The Environmental Journal

PUBLISHING COMPANY: Buzzworm-The Environmental Journal TOPICS: New Age TYPE: Magazine FREQ: bi-monthly PRICE: $15.00 TERM: yearly DESCRIPTION: The thinking person's source for clear, unbiased information on environmental conservation, urban ecology, organic living & eco-travel.

C.E.R.E.S. Newsletter

PUBLISHING COMPANY: C.E.R.E.S. Newsletter TOPICS: Witchcraft, Occult, Paganism TYPE: Newsletter

Cahiers Astrologiques

PUBLISHING COMPANY: Editions des Cahiers Astrologiques EDITOR: Paul Rogel TOPICS: Astrology TYPE: Magazine DATE: 1938 FREQ: Bi-Monthly CIRC: 1,200

California Naturalist

PUBLISHING COMPANY: Lupin Naturalist Club EDITOR: Mollie Moore-Sullivan TOPICS: New Age TYPE: Magazine

California UFO

PUBLISHING COMPANY: California UFO TOPICS: UFO's TYPE: Magazine

Cambridge UFO Research Group Newsletter

PUBLISHING COMPANY: Cambridge UFO Research Group EDITOR: Bonnie Wheeler TOPICS: UFO's TYPE: Newsletter DATE: 1976; 60 pgs. FREQ: quarterly CIRC: 50 PRICE: $22.00 TERM: annually PRICE PER COPY: $5.00 DESCRIPTION: A potpourri of UFO data.

Canadian Holistic Healing Association Newsletter

PUBLISHING COMPANY: Vancouver Health Enhancement Center EDITOR: Batgah Fremes TOPICS: Holistic Healing TYPE: Newsletter

Canadian Journal Of Health and Nutrition

PUBLISHING COMPANY: Alive EDITOR: Hilda Ward, Siegfried Gursche TOPICS: Health Food TYPE: Journal

Canadian UFO Report

PUBLISHING COMPANY: Canadian UFO Report TOPICS: UFO's TYPE: Magazine

CAO Times

PUBLISHING COMPANY: Congress Of Astrological Organization EDITOR: Al H. Morrison TOPICS: New Age TYPE: Magazine CIRC: 1,100 DESCRIPTION: Features articles, news & information on nature & natural events.

Catalyst

PUBLISHING COMPANY: Catalyst EDITOR: Greta Belanger TOPICS: New Age TYPE: Newspaper

Causes Newsletter

PUBLISHING COMPANY: Causes Newsletter TOPICS: Metaphysics, Spirituality TYPE: Newsletter

Caveat Emptor

PUBLISHING COMPANY: Caveat Emptor TOPICS: UFO's TYPE: Magazine

Celebrations

PUBLISHING COMPANY: Celebrations New Age Store TOPICS: Holistic Healing, New Age, Metaphysics TYPE: Newspaper DATE: 1980 FREQ: quarterly CIRC: 3,500 DESCRIPTION: A quarterly which serves the Pikes Peak area with news and events relating to New Age and wholistic subjects. Accepts ads.

Celestial Visions

PUBLISHING COMPANY: Celestial Visions TOPICS: Metaphysics, Spirituality TYPE: Magazine

Celetic Dawn

PUBLISHING COMPANY: Celetic Dawn TOPICS: Metaphysics, Spirituality TYPE: Magazine

Center For Icarian Studies Newsletter

PUBLISHING COMPANY: Center For Icarian Studies EDITOR: Dr. Robert P. Sutton TOPICS: New Age TYPE: Newsletter

Center Light

PUBLISHING COMPANY: Center Light Publishing EDITOR: Andy Schneider, Jeanne Hanse TOPICS: New Age, Metaphysics TYPE: Newspaper DATE: 1976; 32 pgs. FREQ: quarterly PRICE: $10.00 DESCRIPTION: Thirty-two-page newspaper offering non-fiction articles relating to harmonious existence of all people.

Centerlines

PUBLISHING COMPANY: Center For Human Development TOPICS: New Age TYPE: Newsletter

Centro Studi Parapsicologici Bollettino

PUBLISHING COMPANY: Centro Studi Parapsicologici EDITOR: Piero Cassoli TOPICS: Parapsychology, Occult TYPE: Magazine DATE: 1980 FREQ: Semi-Annual PRICE: $30.00

Chakra

PUBLISHING COMPANY: Freelance Press EDITOR: Liz Camps, Richard Behrens TOPICS: Occult TYPE: Magazine DATE: 1988 SIZE: 8 1/2 x 11; 28 pgs. FREQ: bi-annually CIRC: 250 PRICE: $5.56 TERM: yearly PRICE PER COPY: $2.00 DESCRIPTION: Seeks Cyberotic Art for a Magickal World: non-fiction, short stories, illustrations, photos, poetry, plays, essays, reviews, interviews, etc. Deals with mysticism, eroticism, psychedelia, cybershamanism, philosophy for a new aeon & esoteric sociopolitics.

Challenge

PUBLISHING COMPANY: King's Bridge EDITOR: Kai King, Diane Akers TOPICS: New Age, Metaphysics, Channeling TYPE: Magazine FREQ: quarterly CIRC: 20,000 DESCRIPTION: New age magazine featuring articles on health, metaphysics, channeling, and the environment. Publishes articles, features, interviews & fine artwork. Books are reviewed.

Changes

PUBLISHING COMPANY: Macrobiotic Center Of Baltimore EDITOR: Murray Snyder TOPICS: Health Food TYPE: Magazine

Changes

PUBLISHING COMPANY: Changes EDITOR: Kathy Morency TOPICS: New Age, Metaphysics TYPE: Magazine DATE: 1986 FREQ: bi-monthly CIRC: 60,000 PRICE: $18.00 PRICE PER COPY: $3.75 DESCRIPTION: Publishes feature articles, fiction for adults and children, newsand reviews, poetry, cartoons and artwork aimed at helping adults who grew up in dysfunctional families.

Changes Journal

PUBLISHING COMPANY: Changes Journal TOPICS: Metaphysics, Spirituality TYPE: Journal

Changing Schools

PUBLISHING COMPANY: Changing Schools TOPICS: New Age TYPE: Magazine

Channels

PUBLISHING COMPANY: Center For Transformation EDITOR: Anne Cataldo, Arthur Cataldo TOPICS: Channeling, New Age TYPE: Newsletter; 16 pgs. DESCRIPTION: Published by The Center of Transformation and includes articles, letters and a calendar. Accepts ads.

Chaos

PUBLISHING COMPANY: Chaos TOPICS: Metaphysics, Spirituality TYPE: Magazine

Chicago's Inner Quest

PUBLISHING COMPANY: Chicago's Inner Quest EDITOR: William Sawicki TOPICS: Holistic Healing, New Age TYPE: Magazine FREQ: monthly DESCRIPTION: A holistic health publication for the Chicago area.

Chiron Review

PUBLISHING COMPANY: Chiron Press EDITOR: Michael Hathaway TOPICS: New Age TYPE: Magazine

Chiropractic

PUBLISHING COMPANY: Busch Publishing Company EDITOR: Paul A. Jaskoviak TOPICS: Holistic Healing TYPE: Magazine

Chiropractic Sports Medicine

PUBLISHING COMPANY: Williams & Wilkins EDITOR: Robert H. Hazel, Jr., Don Pfarr TOPICS: Holistic Healing TYPE: Magazine

Choices for Health! Vitality!

PUBLISHING COMPANY: Choices for Health! Vitality! EDITOR: John Meluso TOPICS: New Age, Metaphysics TYPE: Calendar DATE: 1982; 8 pgs. FREQ: monthly CIRC: 20,000 DESCRIPTION: A Portland, OR tabloid emphasizing harmonious living and offering news, reviews, interviews, illustrations and photographs.

Christian New Age Quarterly

PUBLISHING COMPANY: Christian New Age Quarterly EDITOR: Catherine Groves TOPICS: New Age, Spirituality TYPE: Journal DATE: 1989 SIZE: 7 x 8 1/2; 24 pgs. FREQ: quarterly CIRC: 200 PRICE: $12.50 TERM: yearly PRICE PER COPY: $3.50 DESCRIPTION: Mixture of Spiritualism, Christian Philosophy and the New Age Movement. Bridge supporting dialogue between New Agers & Christians. In a cooperative spirit of mutual appreciation, it clarifies both the differences & common ground of Christianity & the New Age Movement. Offers columns, features, high quality writing, sound scholarship & plain good fun. For free information send #10 SASE. Publishes non-fiction, reviews, and cartoons relating to the Christian faith and New Age.

Christian Parapsychologist

PUBLISHING COMPANY: Churches' Fellowship for Psychical & Spiritual Studies TOPICS: Parapsychology, Occult TYPE: Magazine DATE: 1975 FREQ: Quarterly CIRC: 1,500 PRICE: $8.00

Christian Research Of Aerial Phonomena Newsletter

PUBLISHING COMPANY: Christian Research Of Aerial Phenomena EDITOR: Art Leman TOPICS: UFO's TYPE: Newsletter DATE: 1968; 3 pgs. FREQ: Bi-Monthly

Church Of Light Quarterly

PUBLISHING COMPANY: Church Of Light/Brotherhood Of Life, Inc. EDITOR: Lea Riffle TOPICS: New Age TYPE: Newsletter DATE: 1925 FREQ: Quarterly CIRC: 1,000 PRICE: $8.00

Cincinnati Journal Of Ceremonial Magick

PUBLISHING COMPANY: Black Moon Publishing EDITOR: Louis Martinie, Joe Bounds TOPICS: Occult, Witchcraft, Voudoun TYPE: Journal DATE: 1976 SIZE: 5.5 x 8.2; 64 pgs. FREQ: Annual CIRC: 1,000 PRICE: $5.50 PRICE PER COPY: $5.50 DESCRIPTION: Deals in various aspects of the occult such as Western ceremonial magick, wiccan, thelemic & voodoo.

Circle Network News

PUBLISHING COMPANY: Circle Sanctuary/Church Of Circle Wicca EDITOR: Dennis Carpenter TOPICS: New Age, Metaphysics, Parapsychology, Spirituality, Occult, Paganism, Witchcraft TYPE: Newspaper DESCRIPTION: Newspaper explores nature, metaphysics and spirituality through articles and book reviews.

Circle of Light

PUBLISHING COMPANY: Circle of Light EDITOR: Ron Kendricks TOPICS: New Age, Metaphysics TYPE: Magazine DATE: 1982 FREQ: monthly CIRC: 7,000 PRICE: $15.00 DESCRIPTION: New Age/Metaphysical magazine serving the Dallas/Ft. Worth area. Publishes poetry, reviews, artwork & photography.

City Connections

PUBLISHING COMPANY: City Connections EDITOR: Darlene Sironen TOPICS: Metaphysics, Holistic Health, New Age TYPE: Magazine DATE: 1990 FREQ: monthly DESCRIPTION: A monthly serving the Las Vegas area with progressive articles covering New Age, holistic and metaphysical issues.

Clairvoyant

PUBLISHING COMPANY: Spiritual Rights Foundation, Inc. EDITOR: Debi Livingston TOPICS: Parapsychology, Channeling TYPE: Magazine DATE: 1986 SIZE: 8 1/2 x 11; 60 pgs. FREQ: Bi-Monthly CIRC: 2,000 PRICE: $15.00 PRICE PER COPY: $3.00

Clarion Call

PUBLISHING COMPANY: Gaudiya Vaishnava Society EDITOR: Thomas Beaudry, Jack Hebner TOPICS: New Age, Holistic Health, Astrology, Paranormal Phenomena TYPE: Magazine DATE: 1988; 64 pgs. FREQ: quarterly CIRC: 30,000 PRICE: $15.00 TERM: yearly DESCRIPTION: Covers different topics in each issue pertaining to New Age, health, Astrology, paranormal occurences, lost civilizations, etc. Also offers editorials, reviews & advertising. Publishes book reviews and articles.

Clarity

PUBLISHING COMPANY: Ananda Cooperative Village/Family Fellowship Of Inner

Communion/Expanding Light **EDITOR:** Sonia Wiberg **TOPICS:** New Age **TYPE:** Newsletter

Clothed With The Sun

PUBLISHING COMPANY: Naturist Society, Inc. **EDITOR:** Lee Baxandall **TOPICS:** New Age **TYPE:** Magazine

CMA Newsletter

PUBLISHING COMPANY: Council Of The Magikal Arts **EDITOR:** Lillith **TOPICS:** New Age, Paganism, Occult, Witchcraft **TYPE:** Newsletter **DATE:** 1980; 30 pgs. **FREQ:** quarterly **PRICE:** $7.00 **TERM:** annually **PRICE PER COPY:** $2.00 **DESCRIPTION:** Publication for Wiccans, Pagans, NeoPagans & New Age Philosophers. Focuses on tradition sharing, all types of positive magick, poetry, rituals & items of interest to the craft community. Magazine format. Published at Solstices & Equinoxes only.

Coming Changes

PUBLISHING COMPANY: Coming Changes **TOPICS:** Channeling **TYPE:** Magazine

Common Boundary Magazine

PUBLISHING COMPANY: Common Boundary, Inc. **EDITOR:** Anne A. Simpkinson, Charles Simpkinson **TOPICS:** Spirituality, Dreams, Meditation, Holistic Health, Metaphysics, New Age **TYPE:** Magazine **FREQ:** bi-monthly **CIRC:** 18,000 **PRICE:** $19.00 **PRICE PER COPY:** $3.75 **DESCRIPTION:** Feature articles and reviews on topics such as Shamanism, expressive arts, meditation, contemplation, ecofeminism, co-dependency, bodywork and dreams. Accepts ads.

Common Ground

PUBLISHING COMPANY: Common Ground **EDITOR:** Michael Bertrand, Joseph Roberts **TOPICS:** Homeopathy, New Age **TYPE:** Magazine **FREQ:** quarterly **CIRC:** 71,500 **DESCRIPTION:** A guide listing various resources as well as featuring articles, book reviews, interviews & ads.

Common Ground

PUBLISHING COMPANY: Common Ground **TOPICS:** Channeling **TYPE:** Magazine

Common Ground

PUBLISHING COMPANY: Common Ground **PUBLISHER:** Sara Riely **TOPICS:** New Age **TYPE:** Magazine **DATE:** 1990 **FREQ:** Quarterly

Common Ground Hawaii

PUBLISHING COMPANY: Common Ground Hawaii **EDITOR:** Ester Fein **TOPICS:** New Age **TYPE:** Magazine

Common Ground of Puget Sound

PUBLISHING COMPANY: Common Ground of Puget Sound **PUBLISHER:** John Crutcher **EDITOR:** Kathy DeHerrera **TOPICS:** Acupuncture, Dreams, Yoga, Parapsychology, New Age, Holistic Health **TYPE:** Journal; 50 pgs. **FREQ:** quarterly **CIRC:** 82,500 **DESCRIPTION:** Journal/Directory committed to exploring leading edge ideas, services & practices that help foster a more liveable world. Distributed in over 300 locations near and around Puget Sound. Prints articles concerning health and a variety of New Age topics. Free.

Common Sense Pest Control Quarterly

PUBLISHING COMPANY: Bio-Integral Resource Center **TOPICS:** Health Food **TYPE:** Magazine

Communion Letter, The

PUBLISHING COMPANY: Communion Letter, The **TOPICS:** UFO's **TYPE:** Magazine

Communities

PUBLISHING COMPANY: Fellowship For Intentional Community **TOPICS:** New Age **TYPE:** Magazine; 64 pgs. **FREQ:** quarterly **PRICE:** $18.00 **TERM:** yearly **PRICE PER COPY:** $4.00 **DESCRIPTION:** Offers current information about intentional communities & serves as a forum for issues of interest to the movement. Open to all communities wishing to air their views & concerns. Not limited to any particular style of community philosophy.

Community Jobs

PUBLISHING COMPANY: Community Careers Resource Center **EDITOR:** Barry Sims **TOPICS:** New Age **TYPE:** Newsletter

Community Spirit Magazine

PUBLISHING COMPANY: Community Spirit Magazine **EDITOR:** Jonathan Drake **TOPICS:** New Age **TYPE:** Magazine **DATE:** 1980; 88 pgs. **FREQ:** month **CIRC:** 30,000 **PRICE:** $15.00 **DESCRIPTION:** Serving Central California. Prints fiction & non-fiction articles, news & reviews, artwork, photography, cartoons and interviews.

Connecting Link

PUBLISHING COMPANY: Connecting Link **EDITOR:** Susie Konicov, Tera Thomas **TOPICS:** New Age, Metaphysics **TYPE:** Magazine **PRICE:** $15.00 **PRICE PER COPY:** $2.95 **DESCRIPTION:** Prints artwork, cartoons, book & music reviews & ads. Also offers tapes on channeling, hypnosis, music, health, etc.

Connexions

PUBLISHING COMPANY: Prana - Philadelphia Resource And Networking Association **EDITOR:** Ruth Hoskins **TOPICS:** Holistic Healing **TYPE:** Newsletter

Conocimiento De La Nueva Era

PUBLISHING COMPANY: Conocimiento De La Nueva Era **EDITOR:** Adolfo Bruziks **TOPICS:** Parapsychology, Occult **TYPE:** Magazine **DATE:** 1938 **FREQ:** Monthly **CIRC:** 8,000

Conscious Choice

PUBLISHING COMPANY: Conscious Choice **EDITOR:** Jim Slama **TOPICS:** Holistic Health, Spirituality, Parapsychology, New Age **TYPE:** Magazine **DATE:** 1988 **FREQ:** quarterly **CIRC:** 30,000 **PRICE:** $15.00 **DESCRIPTION:** Articles and resources relating to holistic health lifestyle. Serves Chicago metro and surrounding areas.

Conscious Connection

PUBLISHING COMPANY: Consciousness Village **EDITOR:** Leonard Orr **TOPICS:** Holistic Healing **TYPE:** Newsletter **DESCRIPTION:** Produced by the Center. Deals with topics such as Rebirthing, Physical Immortality & Spiritual Purification.

Conscious Living Foundation

PUBLISHING COMPANY: Conscious Living Foundation, Inc. **EDITOR:** Dr. Tim Lowenstein **TOPICS:** New Age **TYPE:** Magazine **DATE:** 1976;

16 pgs. **DESCRIPTION:** Offers products and resources available through mail order, including books, audio/video cassettes, music and health aids.

Consciousness Connection, The

PUBLISHING COMPANY: Consciousness Connection, The **EDITOR:** Susan Levin **TOPICS:** Channeling, New Age **TYPE:** Magazine **FREQ:** bi-monthly **CIRC:** 35,000

Consciousness Research And Training Project Newsletter

PUBLISHING COMPANY: Consciousness Research And Training Project, Inc. **TOPICS:** Holistic Healing, Meditation, Spirituality, Body-Mind Connection **TYPE:** Newsletter **DESCRIPTION:** Newsletter for persons who have studied with the organization.

Considerations

PUBLISHING COMPANY: Considerations **EDITOR:** Ken Gillman **TOPICS:** Astrology **TYPE:** Journal **SIZE:** 7 x 8 1/2; 80 pgs. **FREQ:** Quarterly **CIRC:** 1,200 **PRICE:** $20.00 **PRICE PER COPY:** $7.00

Constellation

PUBLISHING COMPANY: Middle Atlantic Planetarium Society **EDITOR:** Tom Cargy **TOPICS:** Astrology **TYPE:** Newsletter **DATE:** 1965; 8 pgs. **FREQ:** Quarterly

Constellations

PUBLISHING COMPANY: Constellations **EDITOR:** Karen Wilerson **TOPICS:** Astrology **TYPE:** Journal

Constructive Action Newsletter

PUBLISHING COMPANY: Act-Action **EDITOR:** Shirley Burghard **TOPICS:** Holistic Healing **TYPE:** Newsletter

Contact Quarterly-Dance Journal

PUBLISHING COMPANY: Contact Collaborations **PUBLISHER:** Nancy Stark Smith **EDITOR:** Lisa Nelson **TOPICS:** Holistic Healing **TYPE:** Journal **DATE:** 1975; 72 pgs. **FREQ:** Tri-annual **CIRC:** 2,200 **PRICE:** $17.00 **TERM:** yearly **PRICE PER COPY:** $5.00 **DESCRIPTION:** Considered to be a vehicle for moving ideas. Reports on the contemporary movement arts. Covers new developments in dance & performance, movement education, & the body-mind disciplines through a unique blend of writings & graphics.

Contemporary Astrological Observation Times-CAO

PUBLISHING COMPANY: Al H. Morrison **PUBLISHER:** Al H. Morrison **TOPICS:** Astrology **TYPE:** Magazine **DATE:** 1975 **SIZE:** 8 1/2 x 11; 48 pgs. **FREQ:** Irregular **CIRC:** 1,000 **PRICE:** $26.00 **PRICE PER COPY:** $7.00 **DESCRIPTION:** Advanced, serious approach to astrology directed towards practicing astrologers and serious students.

Convergence Magazine

PUBLISHING COMPANY: Riverside Communications Publishers **EDITOR:** Virginia Kirmayer Slayton **TOPICS:** New Age, Spirituality, Holistic Health, Metaphysics **TYPE:** Magazine **DATE:** 1987; 40 pgs. **FREQ:** 5 issues/yr **CIRC:** 3,500 **PRICE:** $12.50 **TERM:** annually **PRICE PER COPY:** $2.50 **DESCRIPTION:** A Northern New England magazine featuring articles, reviews,

interviews, cartoons and illustrations relating to personal & spiritual growth & holistic health.

Converging Paths
PUBLISHING COMPANY: Three Sisters, Ltd. **EDITOR:** Kyril Oakwind **TOPICS:** Witchcraft, Occult, Paganism **TYPE:** Magazine **DATE:** 1986; 36 pgs. **FREQ:** quarterly **PRICE:** $14.00 **DESCRIPTION:** Purpose is to promote neopagan/wiccan inter/intra communication. The communication channel of Branches, focusing on traditional wicca, its roots, its current directions, & future prospects.

Coordinate Point
PUBLISHING COMPANY: Coordinate Point **PUBLISHER:** Tom Sweeney **EDITOR:** Jan Sweeney **TOPICS:** Parapsychology **TYPE:** Journal **DATE:** 1984 **SIZE:** 8 1/2 x 11; 28 pgs. **FREQ:** Bi-Monthly **CIRC:** 500 **PRICE:** $12.00 **PRICE PER COPY:** $2.50 **DESCRIPTION:** Features letters, articles, & news pertaining to the Seth material.

Correlation
PUBLISHING COMPANY: Astrological Association Of Great Britain **EDITOR:** Simon Best, F. Griffiths **TOPICS:** Astrology **TYPE:** Journal **DATE:** 1981 **FREQ:** Semi-Annual **CIRC:** 700 **DESCRIPTION:** An astrological research journal featuring articles on research, philosophy & procedures.

Cosmic Awareness News
PUBLISHING COMPANY: Cosmic Awareness Communications **TOPICS:** Channeling **TYPE:** Newspaper

Cosmic Channelings
PUBLISHING COMPANY: Church Of Universal Love **EDITOR:** Linda Forman **TOPICS:** Astrology **TYPE:** Newsletter; 10 pgs. **FREQ:** Bi-Monthly **PRICE:** $6.00

Cosmic Clockwatch
PUBLISHING COMPANY: Cosmic Clockwatch **TOPICS:** Astrology **TYPE:** Magazine

Cosmic Connection
PUBLISHING COMPANY: American Mensa **EDITOR:** Frederick Nietert **TOPICS:** Astrology **TYPE:** Newsletter; 8 pgs. **FREQ:** Quarterly **DESCRIPTION:** Astrology for beginners as well as advanced practitioners.

Cosmic Current News
PUBLISHING COMPANY: Ancient Truth Research Foundation **EDITOR:** Albert Rainey **TOPICS:** New Age, Metaphysics, UFO's, Spirituality, Psychic Phenomena **TYPE:** Newsletter **DATE:** 1983; 12 pgs. **FREQ:** quarterly **PRICE:** $11.00 **TERM:** annually **PRICE PER COPY:** $3.00 **DESCRIPTION:** Regional monthly reporting on current New Age trends. An information & research service of the Ancient Truth Research Foundation. Publishes information on Religion, Metaphysics, Psychic Phenomena & Ufology. Prints non-fiction articles, reviews, interviews , news & poetry.

Cosmic People Magazine
PUBLISHING COMPANY: Cosmic People Magazine **TOPICS:** Metaphysics, Spirituality **TYPE:** Magazine

Cosmic Search

PUBLISHING COMPANY: Cosmic Quest, Inc. **EDITOR:** Dr. John Kraus **TOPICS:** UFO's **TYPE:** Magazine **DATE:** 1978 **SIZE:** 8 1/2 x 11; 52 pgs. **FREQ:** Quarterly **CIRC:** 10,000 **PRICE:** $10.00 **PRICE PER COPY:** $2.50 **DESCRIPTION:** Reports on outerspace, UFO's, the search for intelligent life in space and predictions of the future.

Cosmic Voice
PUBLISHING COMPANY: Aetherius Society **TOPICS:** Psychic Phenomena **TYPE:** Newsletter

Cosmic Voyage
PUBLISHING COMPANY: Cosmic Voyage **TOPICS:** Channeling **TYPE:** Magazine

Cosmiculture
PUBLISHING COMPANY: Sarah and T. Galen Hieronymus **EDITOR:** Dr. Sarah Hieronymus **TOPICS:** Metaphysics **TYPE:** Magazine

Cosmos
PUBLISHING COMPANY: Cosmos **EDITOR:** Yvonne Malykke **TOPICS:** New Age **TYPE:** Newspaper **FREQ:** monthly **DESCRIPTION:** Prominent Australian, New Age publication prints articles on a variety of topics, including book reviews.

Country Health
PUBLISHING COMPANY: Country Health **TOPICS:** Holistic Health **TYPE:** Magazine **DESCRIPTION:** Publishes articles on health issues including liver disease, arthritis and stress.

Covenant Of The Goddess News
PUBLISHING COMPANY: Covenant Of The Goddess **TOPICS:** Witchcraft, Occult, Paganism **TYPE:** Newsletter **DESCRIPTION:** Published at every Sabbat. Covers Craft & Pagan news, original articles, poetry, humor, rituals & announcements.

Creation Magazine
PUBLISHING COMPANY: Friends Of Creation Spirituality **EDITOR:** Matthew Fox **TOPICS:** New Age **TYPE:** Magazine **SIZE:** 8 x 11; 40 pgs. **FREQ:** bi-monthly **PRICE:** $17.00 **PRICE PER COPY:** $4.50 **DESCRIPTION:** Covers topics on spirituality, child development, metaphysics, and the occult. National magazine publishes reviews, interviews, resource listings, articles, letters & ads.

Creation/Evolution Journal
PUBLISHING COMPANY: Creation/Evolution Journal **EDITOR:** Frederick Edwords **TOPICS:** New Age **TYPE:** Journal

Creations
PUBLISHING COMPANY: Creations Magazine **EDITOR:** Zed J. Director **TOPICS:** New Age **TYPE:** Magazine **DATE:** 1988 **FREQ:** Quarterly **DESCRIPTION:** Acts as a showcase for Long Island's creative spirit.

Creative Alternatives Newsletter
PUBLISHING COMPANY: Pyramid Research Center **EDITOR:** M.D. Saunders **TOPICS:** New Age, Holistic Health **TYPE:** Newsletter **DATE:** 1987; 8 pgs. **FREQ:** quarterly **PRICE:** $12.00 **TERM:** annually **DESCRIPTION:** Offers articles on accelerated learning techniques, unusual health & agricultural advances & non-conventional energy discussions.

Creative Health Newsletter
PUBLISHING COMPANY: Biokinesiology Institute **EDITOR:** John Barton **TOPICS:** Holistic Healing **TYPE:** Newsletter

Crone Papers, The
PUBLISHING COMPANY: Crone Papers, The **TOPICS:** Witchcraft, Occult, Paganism **TYPE:** Magazine

Crosswinds
PUBLISHING COMPANY: Crosswinds **TOPICS:** Holistic Healing **TYPE:** Magazine

Crow Speaks
PUBLISHING COMPANY: Crow Speaks **TOPICS:** Metaphysics, Spirituality **TYPE:** Magazine

Crux Newsletter
PUBLISHING COMPANY: Project Stigma **TOPICS:** Psychic Phenomena **TYPE:** Newsletter

Crystal Age News
PUBLISHING COMPANY: Crystal Age News **TOPICS:** Metaphysics, Spirituality **TYPE:** Newspaper

Crystal Ball, The
PUBLISHING COMPANY: Crystal Ball, The **TOPICS:** UFO's **TYPE:** Magazine

Crystal Connection Newsletter
PUBLISHING COMPANY: Interdimensional Temple Of Light **TOPICS:** Channeling **TYPE:** Newsletter

Crystal Pathways
PUBLISHING COMPANY: Crystal Pathways **EDITOR:** Frank M. MacMillan **TOPICS:** New Age, Crystals, Holistic Health **TYPE:** Magazine **FREQ:** quarterly **PRICE:** $12.00 **PRICE PER COPY:** $3.00 **DESCRIPTION:** Serves the international crystal community. Features articles, excerpts and reviews relating to the awakening of the consciousness.

Cultwatch Response
PUBLISHING COMPANY: Cultwatch Response, Inc. **EDITOR:** Vicki Copeland **TOPICS:** Occult, Paganism, Witchcraft **TYPE:** Newsletter **DATE:** 1988; 24 pgs. **FREQ:** 6 per year **PRICE:** $12.00 **TERM:** annually **PRICE PER COPY:** $2.00 **DESCRIPTION:** Purpose is to educate the readers on the beliefs & practices of Wicca & other Pagan beliefs & disseminate accurate documented information on occult related crime.

Current Health 1
PUBLISHING COMPANY: General Learning Corporation **EDITOR:** Laura Ruekberg **TOPICS:** Holistic Healing **TYPE:** Magazine

Current Health 2
PUBLISHING COMPANY: General Learning Corporation **TOPICS:** Holistic Healing **TYPE:** Magazine

Cypress: The Psychic Digest
PUBLISHING COMPANY: Cypress: The Psychic Digest **EDITOR:** Dale Mann **TOPICS:** Channeling, New Age **TYPE:** Magazine **DATE:** 1988 **FREQ:** 6 issues/yr **PRICE:** $18.00 **DESCRIPTION:** Publishes articles, non-fiction, fiction, poetry, reviews & interviews, artwork & photography.

Dawn Magazine

PUBLISHING COMPANY: Himalayan International Institute Of Yoga Science and Philosophy **TOPICS:** New Age, Meditation, Holistic Health, Yoga **TYPE:** Magazine **FREQ:** quarterly **DESCRIPTION:** Published by the Himalayan Institute. Prints articles on philosophy and psychology of natural living. Accepts ads.

Day And Night

PUBLISHING COMPANY: Association For Research And Enlightenment **TOPICS:** Astrology **TYPE:** Newsletter; 10 pgs.

Daybreak

PUBLISHING COMPANY: Daybreak **EDITOR:** Oren Lyens **TOPICS:** New Age **TYPE:** Calendar **FREQ:** quarterly **PRICE:** $12.00 **PRICE PER COPY:** $3.00 **DESCRIPTION:** A celebration of our world's multiculturalism. Prints articles ,and artwork, as well as listings of resources of indigenous people.

De Kaarsvlam

PUBLISHING COMPANY: Mellie Uyldert **TOPICS:** Astrology **TYPE:** Magazine **DATE:** 1947 **FREQ:** Monthly **CIRC:** 4,000

Dead Of Night Magazine

PUBLISHING COMPANY: Dead Of Night Publications **EDITOR:** Lin Stein **TOPICS:** Vampires **TYPE:** Magazine **DATE:** 1989 **FREQ:** quarterly **PRICE:** $15.00 **TERM:** annually **DESCRIPTION:** Deals with horror/vampire related fiction. Features book & film reviews & contests.

Death Rattle

PUBLISHING COMPANY: Kitchen Sink Press **EDITOR:** Denis Kitchen, David Schreiner **TOPICS:** Parapsychology, Occult **TYPE:** Magazine **DATE:** 1972 **FREQ:** Bi-Monthly **CIRC:** 9,500 **PRICE:** $15.00

Defenders

PUBLISHING COMPANY: Defenders Of Wildlife **TOPICS:** Holistic Healing **TYPE:** Magazine

Design Spirit

PUBLISHING COMPANY: Design Spirit **EDITOR:** Suzanne Koblenz-Goodman **TOPICS:** New Age **TYPE:** Magazine **DATE:** 1989 **FREQ:** quarterly **CIRC:** 15,000 **PRICE:** $16.00 **PRICE PER COPY:** $5.50 **DESCRIPTION:** Prints non-fiction articles, news & reviews, criticisms, interviews, artwork and photography relating to the art, nature and human well being.

Destin International

PUBLISHING COMPANY: Editions Astres **EDITOR:** Michel Helmer **TOPICS:** Astrology **TYPE:** Magazine

Destiny

PUBLISHING COMPANY: Sovereign International **EDITOR:** Ruth McArthur **TOPICS:** Astrology **TYPE:** Magazine **DATE:** 1984 **FREQ:** Monthly **CIRC:** 11,000

Dharma Combat

PUBLISHING COMPANY: Dharma Combat **PUBLISHER:** James Keith, Jerry E. Smith **TOPICS:** Metaphysics **TYPE:** Magazine **DATE:** 1987 **SIZE:** 11 x 17; 64 pgs. **FREQ:** quarterly **CIRC:** 6,000 **PRICE:** $10.00 **TERM:** 4 issues **PRICE PER COPY:** $3.00 **DESCRIPTION:** A magazine concerned with spirituality, metaphysics, reality and other conspiracies. Provides interactive columns, letters, articles, some fiction but no poetry. All philosophies and persuasions welcome.

Dialogue House

PUBLISHING COMPANY: Dialogue House **TOPICS:** New Age **TYPE:** Magazine

Dimensione Psi

PUBLISHING COMPANY: Associazione Italiana Studi del Paranormale **TOPICS:** Parapsychology, Occult **TYPE:** Magazine **DATE:** 1946 **FREQ:** Semi-Annual **CIRC:** 3,000 **PRICE:** $6.00

Dimensions

PUBLISHING COMPANY: Delphi Publications **EDITOR:** Jay Harris **TOPICS:** Parapsychology, Channeling **TYPE:** Magazine

Dimensions New Age Magazine

PUBLISHING COMPANY: Fifth Sun Media, Inc. **PUBLISHER:** Alexander Blair-Ewart **TOPICS:** New Age **TYPE:** Magazine **DATE:** 1986 **SIZE:** 8 1/2 x 11; 64 pgs. **FREQ:** monthly **PRICE:** $25.00 **TERM:** annual **PRICE PER COPY:** $2.25 **DESCRIPTION:** Explores & illuminates all areas of the new consciousness, including transpersonal paradigms, esoteric movements & ideas, ecology, holistic health & fitness. Serves Toronto with articles, interviews, poetry, book reviews and a calendar.

Directions

PUBLISHING COMPANY: Fraternity For Canadian Astrologers **EDITOR:** Marilyn F. Waram, Susan Kelly **TOPICS:** Astrology **TYPE:** Newsletter

Dolphin Dreams Newsletter

PUBLISHING COMPANY: Dolphin Dreams **PUBLISHER:** Joan A. Bishop **TOPICS:** New Age **TYPE:** Newsletter; 8 pgs. **FREQ:** quarterly **PRICE:** $12.00 **TERM:** yearly **DESCRIPTION:** Explores & celebrates the Cetacean Connection, the relationship between mankind & the whales & dolphins, the intelligent marine mammals of our world. Contains stories of personal interactions, articles, poems, artwork, photos & dreams.

Dovestar Newsletter

PUBLISHING COMPANY: DoveStar Alchemian Institute **TYPE:** Newsletter **FREQ:** 3 x per year **DESCRIPTION:** Journal of articles, advertisements, news & course offerings for each trimester.

Dream International Quarterly

PUBLISHING COMPANY: Dream International Quarterly **EDITOR:** Leslie H. Jones, Charles Jones **TOPICS:** Dreams **TYPE:** Magazine

Dream Journal

PUBLISHING COMPANY: Plenum Publishing Corporation **TOPICS:** New Age **TYPE:** Journal

Dream Network

PUBLISHING COMPANY: By Design **PUBLISHER:** Helen Roberta Ossana **TYPE:** Journal **DATE:** 1982 **SIZE:** 8 1/2 x 11 **FREQ:** quarterly **PRICE:** $20.00 **TERM:** yearly **PRICE PER COPY:** $5.50 **DESCRIPTION:** Serves as a vehicle for the growing Dream Movement in the U.S., Canada, Mexico & Europe. Intent is to reach those interested in educating themselves as to the purpose, meaning & symbolic language of dreams, their relationship to myth, & their relevance to contemporary individual & cultural healing. Offers readers the opportunity to network with other dreamers internationally.

Dreamworks

PUBLISHING COMPANY: Plenum Publishing Corporation **EDITOR:** Sheldon Ruen, Kennith Atchity **TOPICS:** New Age **TYPE:** Magazine

Drug Abuse Report

PUBLISHING COMPANY: Manisses Communications Group, Inc. **EDITOR:** Fraser Lang, Jay Lewis **TOPICS:** Holistic Healing **TYPE:** Newsletter

Drug Educator

PUBLISHING COMPANY: American Council For Drug Education **EDITOR:** Lee Dogoloff **TOPICS:** Holistic Healing **TYPE:** Magazine

Druid Henge

PUBLISHING COMPANY: Craeftgemot Witancoveyne, Inc. **EDITOR:** Janice Scot-Reeder **TOPICS:** Parapsychology, Occult **TYPE:** Magazine **FREQ:** Monthly **PRICE:** $12.00

Druid Missal

PUBLISHING COMPANY: Druid Missal **TOPICS:** Witchcraft, Occult, Paganism **TYPE:** Magazine

Druid's Progress, The

PUBLISHING COMPANY: Druid's Progress, The **TOPICS:** Witchcraft, Occult, Paganism **TYPE:** Magazine

Dynamic Life Times

PUBLISHING COMPANY: Dynamic Life Times **EDITOR:** David Findlay **TOPICS:** Holistic Health **TYPE:** Journal **FREQ:** quarterly **CIRC:** 15,000 **DESCRIPTION:** Prints articles, calendar and resources relating to self-discovery.

E Magazine

PUBLISHING COMPANY: Earth Action Network **EDITOR:** Doug Moss **TOPICS:** New Age **TYPE:** Magazine **DATE:** 1988 **FREQ:** bi-monthly **CIRC:** 80,000 **DESCRIPTION:** Politically correct, non-profit environmental magazine for purists. Covers all aspects & topics of the environment for the lay person. Offers news, events & advertising.

Eagle's Cry, The

PUBLISHING COMPANY: Eagle's Cry, The **EDITOR:** David **TOPICS:** Spirituality **TYPE:** Journal; 16 pgs. **FREQ:** quarterly **PRICE:** $5.00 **DESCRIPTION:** Relates ideas and experiences of spiritualism and understanding.

Ear Magazine

PUBLISHING COMPANY: Ear Magazine **EDITOR:** Carol Tuynman **TOPICS:** New Age, Metaphysics **TYPE:** Magazine **DATE:** 1975 **FREQ:** 10 issues/yr **CIRC:** 20,000 **PRICE:** $20.00 **PRICE PER COPY:** $2.50 **DESCRIPTION:** A music magazine specializing in New Age, rock, jazz and classical. Prints articles, interviews, artwork, illustrations and criticisms.

Earth Circles News

PUBLISHING COMPANY: Great Round, Inc. **EDITOR:** Alexander Hart **TOPICS:** Spirituality, New Age **TYPE:** Magazine **DATE:** 1990; 16 pgs. **FREQ:**

quarterly **PRICE:** $15.00 **TERM:** annually **DESCRIPTION:** Networks ceremonial circles.

Earth First!
PUBLISHING COMPANY: Earth First! **TOPICS:** Holistic Healing, Occult **TYPE:** Magazine

Earth Magic Times
PUBLISHING COMPANY: Earth Magic Times **TOPICS:** Witchcraft, Occult, Paganism **TYPE:** Magazine

Earth Nation Sunrise
PUBLISHING COMPANY: Earth Nation Sunrise **TOPICS:** New Age, Metaphysics, Spirituality **TYPE:** Newspaper **DESCRIPTION:** Publishes uplifting articles, interviews and activities.

Earth Spirit Community Newsletter
PUBLISHING COMPANY: Earth Spirit Community **TOPICS:** Witchcraft, Occult, Paganism **TYPE:** Newsletter

Earth Spirit Journal
PUBLISHING COMPANY: Earth Spirit Journal **TOPICS:** Channeling **TYPE:** Magazine **FREQ:** 5 issues/yr **PRICE:** $18.00 **DESCRIPTION:** Publishes articles on the mysteries of the world around and inside all of us.

Earth Star Journal
PUBLISHING COMPANY: Earth Star Press **TOPICS:** Channeling **TYPE:** Journal

Earth Star-Whole Life New England
PUBLISHING COMPANY: Earth Star Press **PUBLISHER:** Lane Masterson **TOPICS:** Holistic Health, New Age **TYPE:** Magazine **FREQ:** 6 x year **CIRC:** 180,000 **DESCRIPTION:** Features articles on the environment, art, food, music, books, and health. Conducts reviews on products, books and music. Offers advertising & a directory of products, services, etc. dealing with health & wellness in the New England region. Accepts ads.

Earth Tones Music Review
PUBLISHING COMPANY: Earth Tones Music Review **EDITOR:** Andrew Means **TOPICS:** New Age **TYPE:** Magazine **DATE:** 1990 **DESCRIPTION:** Publishes news and reviews of New Age and contemporary music.

Earth-Light Network Newsletter
PUBLISHING COMPANY: Earth-Light Network, Inc. **PUBLISHER:** Beverley L. Brenner, M.S. **TOPICS:** New Age, Metaphysics, Spirituality **TYPE:** Newsletter; 6 pgs. **DESCRIPTION:** Reports on the occurrences & philosophies of the Earth-Light Network organization. Offers a Calendar of Events, articles & commentaries on timely issues.

Earth-Star Pathways
PUBLISHING COMPANY: Earth-Star Pathways **TOPICS:** New Age, Holistic Health, Metaphysics **TYPE:** Magazine **DESCRIPTION:** New Age magazine dealing with holistic health & metaphysics.

Earthquake Lady News
PUBLISHING COMPANY: Earthquake Lady News **TOPICS:** Metaphysics, Spirituality **TYPE:** Newspaper

East West

PUBLISHING COMPANY: East West **TOPICS:** Holistic Health, Health Food, Nutrition, Homeopathy, Vegetarianism **TYPE:** Magazine

East West Journal
PUBLISHING COMPANY: Kushi Institute-East West Foundation **EDITOR:** Michio Kushi **TOPICS:** Health Food, Holistic Health, Vegetarianism, New Age, Spirituality, Nutrition **TYPE:** Journal **DATE:** 1970 **DESCRIPTION:** Covers New Age information & macrobiotics.

East West News
PUBLISHING COMPANY: East West Books **TOPICS:** Witchcraft, Occult, Paganism **TYPE:** Newspaper **DATE:** 1980

Ecliptic
PUBLISHING COMPANY: British Columbia Astrological Society **TOPICS:** Astrology **TYPE:** Journal **SIZE:** 8 1/2 x 11; 30 pgs. **FREQ:** Quarterly **PRICE:** $15.00

Ecosense
PUBLISHING COMPANY: Maui EcoPark/Center For Ecological Living **TYPE:** Newsletter **FREQ:** quarterly **PRICE:** $20.00 **TERM:** yearly **DESCRIPTION:** Devoted to applied ecology offering practical ideas for living into the 21st century.

Eden Bulletin
PUBLISHING COMPANY: Eden Bulletin **TOPICS:** Metaphysics, Spirituality **TYPE:** Bulletin

Edges
PUBLISHING COMPANY: Canadian Institute Of Cultural Affairs **EDITOR:** Brian Stanfield, Ronnie Seagren **TOPICS:** New Age, Metaphysics **TYPE:** Magazine **DATE:** 1976; 48 pgs. **FREQ:** quarterly **CIRC:** 3,500 **DESCRIPTION:** Members of the Institute of Cultural Affairs, serves an up-scale, educated Canadian & U.S. reader, who seeks to break down the walls that separate people. Prints non-fiction, news, reviews, interviews, cartoons, and artwork. Accepts ads.

Editor's Digest
PUBLISHING COMPANY: Rio Grande Press **EDITOR:** Rosalie Avara **TOPICS:** Psychic Phenomena **TYPE:** Magazine **PRICE:** $15.00 **TERM:** yearly

El Rosacruz
PUBLISHING COMPANY: Supreme Grand Lodge of AMORC, Inc. **EDITOR:** Laura Torres **TOPICS:** Parapsychology **TYPE:** Magazine **DATE:** 1945 **SIZE:** 7.5 x 10.5; 24 pgs. **FREQ:** Bi-Monthly **CIRC:** 17,000 **PRICE:** $9.00 **PRICE PER COPY:** $1.50 **DESCRIPTION:** Covers topics such as philosophy, mysticism & science. Text in Spanish.

Elven Glen
PUBLISHING COMPANY: Elven Glen **TOPICS:** Witchcraft, Occult, Paganism **TYPE:** Magazine

Elysium: Journal Of The Senses
PUBLISHING COMPANY: Elysium Growth Press **EDITOR:** Art Kunkin **TOPICS:** New Age **TYPE:** Journal **DATE:** 1961 **FREQ:** Quarterly **CIRC:** 15,000 **PRICE:** $4.00

Emergence

PUBLISHING COMPANY: Emergence **TOPICS:** Metaphysics, Spirituality **TYPE:** Magazine

Emergence! A Journal For The Golden Age
PUBLISHING COMPANY: Light Technology Communication Services **EDITOR:** O'Ryin Swanson, Margaret Pinyan **TOPICS:** New Age **TYPE:** Journal

Emerging
PUBLISHING COMPANY: LP Publications **EDITOR:** Diane K. Pike **TOPICS:** New Age **TYPE:** Magazine **DESCRIPTION:** Has been referred to as the Love Project.

Enchanted Forest News
PUBLISHING COMPANY: Enchanted Forest News **TOPICS:** Witchcraft, Occult, Paganism **TYPE:** Newspaper

Energy Investment Research
PUBLISHING COMPANY: Energy Investment Research **TOPICS:** New Age **TYPE:** Magazine

Enlightenments
PUBLISHING COMPANY: Enlightenments **EDITOR:** Greg Helmers **TOPICS:** New Age **TYPE:** Newspaper **DATE:** 1990 **FREQ:** monthly

Environmental Action
PUBLISHING COMPANY: Environmental Action, Inc. **TOPICS:** Holistic Healing **TYPE:** Magazine

Environmental Health Perspectives
PUBLISHING COMPANY: U.S. Government Printing Office **TOPICS:** Holistic Healing **TYPE:** Newsletter

Equinox, The
PUBLISHING COMPANY: Ordo Templi Orientis **TOPICS:** Metaphysics, Spirituality **TYPE:** Newsletter **FREQ:** quarterly **DESCRIPTION:** Serial anthology of documents, essays, poetry & dramatic works of interest to current & prospective members of OTO, Thelemites in general & all others who follow Western mystical/magical paths. Available to the public. Limited advertising accepted.

Esotera
PUBLISHING COMPANY: Verlag Hermann Bauer KG **EDITOR:** Gert Geisler **TOPICS:** New Age **TYPE:** Magazine **DATE:** 1949 **FREQ:** Monthly **CIRC:** 48,000

Esoteric Encounters
PUBLISHING COMPANY: Vincent Palazzolo **EDITOR:** Vincent Palazzolo **TOPICS:** Parapsychology **TYPE:** Newsletter **DATE:** 1987; 12 pgs. **FREQ:** Monthly **CIRC:** 1,000 **PRICE PER COPY:** $1.00 **DESCRIPTION:** Information pertaining to paranormal phenomena & the supernatural.

Esoteric Review
PUBLISHING COMPANY: Support of Nature **PUBLISHER:** Timothy Bost **TOPICS:** Parapsychology **TYPE:** Newsletter **DATE:** 1983 **FREQ:** Bi-Monthly **CIRC:** 200 **PRICE:** $20.00 **PRICE PER COPY:** $4.00 **DESCRIPTION:** Provides a contemporary approach to the occult. Offers information on the New Age Movement, spirituality & astrology.

Esoteric World News Magazine

PUBLISHING COMPANY: Esoteric World News Magazine **EDITOR:** Lorraine A. DiFelice **TOPICS:** New Age, Metaphysics **TYPE:** Magazine **DATE:** 1980; 32 pgs. **FREQ:** monthly **CIRC:** 5,000 **PRICE:** $25.00 **PRICE PER COPY:** $2.50 **DESCRIPTION:** Prints articles, product reviews and literary works relating to metaphysics.

Esoterik Und Wissenschaft

PUBLISHING COMPANY: OARCA **TOPICS:** Parapsychology, Occult **TYPE:** Magazine **DATE:** 1966 **FREQ:** Semi-Annual **CIRC:** 1,100

ESP Research Associates Foundation Newsletter

PUBLISHING COMPANY: ESP Research Associates Foundation Newsletter **EDITOR:** Harold Sherman **TOPICS:** Parapsychology **TYPE:** Newsletter **DATE:** 1964 **FREQ:** Bi-Monthly **CIRC:** 500

Essays

PUBLISHING COMPANY: Maitreyans, The **EDITOR:** Jerry C. Welch (Khiron) **TOPICS:** Astrology, Holistic Health, Parapsychology, New Age, Yoga, Kabbalah **TYPE:** Newsletter **FREQ:** monthly **PRICE:** $6.00 **TERM:** annually **DESCRIPTION:** Network newsletter.

Essentia

PUBLISHING COMPANY: Paracelsus College **EDITOR:** Mary Adams **TOPICS:** Parapsychology, Occult **TYPE:** Magazine **FREQ:** Quarterly **PRICE:** $8.00

Essential Whole Earth Catalog

PUBLISHING COMPANY: Essential Whole Earth Catalog **TOPICS:** New Age **TYPE:** Catalog

Evergreens

PUBLISHING COMPANY: Evergreens **TOPICS:** Spirituality **TYPE:** Newsletter

Evolving Times Magazine

PUBLISHING COMPANY: Evolving Times Magazine **TOPICS:** New Age **TYPE:** Magazine **DESCRIPTION:** Prints feature articles and calendar.

Exceptional Human Experience

PUBLISHING COMPANY: Parapsychology Sources Of Information Center-PSI Center **EDITOR:** Rhea A. White **TOPICS:** Parapsychology **TYPE:** Journal

Executive Fitness Newsletter

PUBLISHING COMPANY: Rodale Press, Inc. **EDITOR:** Sid Kirchheimer, Robert Rodale, C.E.O. **TOPICS:** Holistic Healing **TYPE:** Newsletter

Executive Health's Good Health Report

PUBLISHING COMPANY: Executive Health Publications **EDITOR:** Ann Buzenberg **TOPICS:** Holistic Health **TYPE:** Newsletter **DATE:** 1963; 8 pgs. **FREQ:** monthly **PRICE:** $34.00 **TERM:** annually **DESCRIPTION:** Articles written by nationally known physicians or research scientists on specific health topics. Also personal health features, exercise & nutrition columns & health information for adults all written by a practitioner with university ties. No advertising accepted.

Exorcism International

PUBLISHING COMPANY: Exorcism International **TOPICS:** Metaphysics, Spirituality **TYPE:** Magazine

Expanding Light Program Guide

PUBLISHING COMPANY: Ananda Cooperative Village/Family Fellowship Of Inner Communion/Expanding Light **EDITOR:** Richard McCord **TOPICS:** New Age **TYPE:** Calendar **DATE:** 1981 **FREQ:** 3 x/yr. **CIRC:** 16,000 **PRICE:** $0.00 **DESCRIPTION:** Describes retreat programs promoting spiritual growth offered by the Fellowship.

Exploring Other Dimensions

PUBLISHING COMPANY: David Graham Associates **EDITOR:** David D. Graham **TOPICS:** Psychic Phenomena **TYPE:** Magazine

Exum

PUBLISHING COMPANY: Exum Corporation, Publishing Division **EDITOR:** David Exum **TOPICS:** New Age **TYPE:** Magazine

Eye of Gaza

PUBLISHING COMPANY: Eye of Gaza **EDITOR:** Greg Branson **TOPICS:** New Age **TYPE:** Newsletter **DATE:** 1981 **DESCRIPTION:** Explores psychic phenomenon.

F.A.A. Journal

PUBLISHING COMPANY: Federation Of Australian Astrologers Co-Operative, Ltd. **EDITOR:** Maurice Silver **TOPICS:** Astrology **TYPE:** Journal **DATE:** 1971 **FREQ:** Quarterly **CIRC:** 300 **PRICE:** $7.50

F.U.T.U.R.E. Newsletter-Calendar Of Events Section

PUBLISHING COMPANY: F.U.T.U.R.E. **TOPICS:** New Age, Metaphysics **TYPE:** Newsletter **DATE:** 1984 **FREQ:** monthly **CIRC:** 125 **PRICE:** $15.00 **PRICE PER COPY:** $2.00 **DESCRIPTION:** Supports organic grain business with news, ads, articles and illustrations.

Fact Sheets

PUBLISHING COMPANY: Zero Population Growth **TYPE:** Newsletter

Factsheet Five

PUBLISHING COMPANY: Factsheet Five **TOPICS:** Occult, Parapsychology **TYPE:** Magazine

Faerie Folk, The

PUBLISHING COMPANY: Faerie Folk, The **TOPICS:** Witchcraft, Occult, Paganism **TYPE:** Magazine

Faithist Journal

PUBLISHING COMPANY: Kosmon Publishing, Inc. **EDITOR:** Charles Benfield, Kasandra Kares **TOPICS:** New Age, Spirituality, Metaphysics **TYPE:** Journal **DATE:** 1970; 56 pgs. **FREQ:** Bi-Monthly **CIRC:** 275 **PRICE:** $12.00 **DESCRIPTION:** New Age bi-monthly magazine promoting spiritual growth & scientific information. Covers various New Age topics such as UFO's, spiritualism, life after death, vegetarianism, astral travel, crystal power and I-Ching.

Fangoria

PUBLISHING COMPANY: Starlog Press, Inc. **EDITOR:** Anthony Timpone, J. Peter Orr **TOPICS:** Astrology **TYPE:** Magazine **FREQ:** monthly **PRICE:** $18.98

Fantasy Mongers Quarterly

PUBLISHING COMPANY: W. Paul Ganley Publisher **EDITOR:** W. Paul Ganley **TOPICS:** Psychic Phenomena **TYPE:** Magazine

Fate Magazine

PUBLISHING COMPANY: Fate Magazine **EDITOR:** Mary Fuller, Jerry Clark **TOPICS:** New Age, Paranormal Phenomena, Psychic Phenomena, Metaphysics **TYPE:** Magazine **FREQ:** monthly **PRICE:** $15.00 **DESCRIPTION:** True stories of unexplained phenomena and psychic mysteries.

Fate Magazine

PUBLISHING COMPANY: Llewellyn Publications **PUBLISHER:** Patty Hohn **EDITOR:** Donald Michael Kraig, Steve Deger **TOPICS:** New Age, Metaphysics, Paranormal Phenomena **TYPE:** Magazine **DATE:** 1948; 130 pgs. **FREQ:** monthly **CIRC:** 125,000 **PRICE:** $15.95 **PRICE PER COPY:** $2.50 **DESCRIPTION:** True reports of unexplained phenomena such as UFO's, vampires, witches, and ESP. Provides leading edge science. Exposes fraud by fake psychics & overenthusiastic debunkers. Offers book reviews. Publishes news, reviews, interviews and artwork.

Feeling Better Whole Health Newsletter

PUBLISHING COMPANY: Feeling Better Whole Health Newsletter **TOPICS:** Holistic Healing **TYPE:** Newsletter

Feeling Great

PUBLISHING COMPANY: Feeling Great **EDITOR:** Tim Moriarty, Michael Schneider **TOPICS:** Holistic Healing **TYPE:** Magazine

Feminist Bookstore News

PUBLISHING COMPANY: Feminist Bookstore News **EDITOR:** Carol Seajay **TOPICS:** New Age, Metaphysics **TYPE:** Magazine **DATE:** 1976; 100 pgs. **FREQ:** bi-monthly **CIRC:** 800 **PRICE:** $60.00 **TERM:** annually **PRICE PER COPY:** $5.00 **DESCRIPTION:** For feminist bookstores, publishers, writers, readers, women's studies teachers, librarians & craftswomen. Includes over 250 book reviews per issue, announcements of new books, feminist book world news, articles on the practical & political aspects of bookselling & publishing. Rents mailing lists of feminist oriented bookstores. Ad information available.

Fessenden Review

PUBLISHING COMPANY: Fessenden Review **EDITOR:** Monte Rosen **TOPICS:** New Age, Metaphysics **TYPE:** Magazine **DATE:** 1984 **FREQ:** 4 issues/yr **PRICE:** $12.00 **DESCRIPTION:** Thought-provoking articles on New Age and Metaphysical subjects.

Festivals

PUBLISHING COMPANY: Resource Publications, Inc. **PUBLISHER:** Cheryl Lynn Porter **EDITOR:** Ken Guentert **TOPICS:** New Age, Metaphysics **TYPE:** Magazine **DATE:** 1972; 52 pgs. **FREQ:** Bi-Monthly **CIRC:** 15,000 **PRICE:** $18.00 **DESCRIPTION:** Covers various New Age topics such as personal growth, management of transition & change, & resources for celebration & rites of passage. Prints

news & reviews, fiction & non-fiction stories, & literary works such as poetry, satire, plays & criticisms.

Fifty Millesimal News Letter

PUBLISHING COMPANY: Hahnemann Homoeopathic Pharmacy EDITOR: Dr. R.P. Patel TOPICS: Homeopathy TYPE: Newsletter DATE: 1969 FREQ: quarterly CIRC: 1,600 PRICE: $2.00 DESCRIPTION: Devoted to the study of pure homoeopathy.

Fine Homebuilding

PUBLISHING COMPANY: Taunton Press, Inc. EDITOR: Mark Feirer TOPICS: New Age TYPE: Magazine

Fine Woodworking

PUBLISHING COMPANY: Taunton Press, Inc. EDITOR: Dick Burrows TOPICS: New Age TYPE: Magazine

Fire Heart

PUBLISHING COMPANY: Earth Spirit Community EDITOR: Myrriah Lavin, Ernest Walters TOPICS: New Age TYPE: Magazine DATE: 1988 FREQ: Semi-Annual CIRC: 500 PRICE: $12.00 DESCRIPTION: Deals with magic & spiritual growth & transformation in an atmosphere of undertaing and support.

FireHeart

PUBLISHING COMPANY: FireHeart EDITOR: Myrriah Lavin, Walter Wright TOPICS: New Age, Metaphysics, Witchcraft, Occult, Paganism TYPE: Journal DATE: 1980 FREQ: bi-yearly PRICE: $7.00 PRICE PER COPY: $3.95 DESCRIPTION: Publishes fiction, non-fiction, poetry, artwork, reviews and photography on world peace and harmonious level, under various subject headings.

Fitfax Journal

PUBLISHING COMPANY: Fitness Motivation Institute Of America EDITOR: Ron Useldiaga TOPICS: Holistic Healing TYPE: Journal

Fitness Bulletin

PUBLISHING COMPANY: Fitness Institute EDITOR: David Steen, William Gairdner TOPICS: Holistic Healing TYPE: Bulletin

Fitness In Business

PUBLISHING COMPANY: Williams & Wilkins, Allan Ryan, M.D. TOPICS: Holistic Healing TYPE: Magazine

Fitness Management

PUBLISHING COMPANY: Leisure Publishers EDITOR: Nancy Field, Edward Pitts TOPICS: Holistic Healing TYPE: Magazine

Flat Earth News

PUBLISHING COMPANY: Flat Earth Research Society International EDITOR: Charles K. Johnson TOPICS: New Age TYPE: Newsletter FREQ: quarterly PRICE: $10.00 TERM: yearly PRICE PER COPY: $5.00 DESCRIPTION: Each issue contains further proof of the fact- Earth is flat. Aim is to promote facts, logic, reason & sanity.

Flower Essence Society Newsletter

PUBLISHING COMPANY: Flower Essence Society/Earth-Spirit, Inc. TOPICS: Holistic Healing TYPE: Newsletter

Flying Saucers International

PUBLISHING COMPANY: Amalgamated Flying Saucer Clubs Of America EDITOR: Gabriel Green TOPICS: UFO's TYPE: Journal DESCRIPTION: Reports on UFO's, alien encounters & the study of other planets & the universe.

Focus

PUBLISHING COMPANY: Fair-Witness Project, Inc. EDITOR: William L. Moore, Jimmy Ward TOPICS: Psychic Phenomena, UFO's, Occult TYPE: Journal DATE: 1985 SIZE: 8 1/2 x 11; 32 pgs. FREQ: quarterly CIRC: 800 PRICE: $25.00 TERM: yearly PRICE PER COPY: $6.00 DESCRIPTION: Features in-depth, fact-filled articles that have been thoroughly researched on paranormal phenomena & UFOs. Reports on progress & results of investigations & research projects undertaken by the Fair-Witness Project. Heavily evidence oriented. Avoids speculation, rumor & conjecture. Distributed in 48 states & 20 foreign countries.

Focus-Educating Professionals In Family Recovery

PUBLISHING COMPANY: U.S. Journal, Inc. EDITOR: Gary Seidler, Peter Vegso TOPICS: Holistic Healing TYPE: Journal

Focus: Social And Preventive Medicine

PUBLISHING COMPANY: Community Health Services Association EDITOR: Sheila Ragush TOPICS: Holistic Healing TYPE: Magazine

Focusing Connection

PUBLISHING COMPANY: Focusing Connection EDITOR: Ann Weiser TOPICS: New Age TYPE: Magazine

Fogli Gnosis

PUBLISHING COMPANY: Instituto Gnosis Per La Ricerca Sulla Sopravvivenza EDITOR: Giorgio di Simone TOPICS: Parapsychology, Occult TYPE: Magazine FREQ: Semi-Annual

Footsteps

PUBLISHING COMPANY: Footsteps Press EDITOR: Bill Munster TOPICS: Psychic Phenomena TYPE: Magazine

Footsteps

PUBLISHING COMPANY: Pathways EDITOR: Patricia K. Sawyer TOPICS: New Age TYPE: Newsletter

Foresight Magazine

PUBLISHING COMPANY: Foresight Publications EDITOR: John W.B. Barklam, Judy Barklam TOPICS: Metaphysics, UFO's, Occult, Psychic Phenomena, New Age TYPE: Magazine DATE: 1970 SIZE: 8 x 6; 20 pgs. FREQ: quarterly CIRC: 800 DESCRIPTION: Dealing in UFO's, psychic phenomena, occult, mysticism, spiritualism, conspiracies, controversy & varied New Age topics.

Forgiveness Newsletter

PUBLISHING COMPANY: San Francisco Miracles Foundation EDITOR: Jo-Anne Hahn TOPICS: New Age TYPE: Newsletter FREQ: Irregular

Fortean Times

PUBLISHING COMPANY: John Brown Publishing LTD. EDITOR: Robert J.M. Rickard, Paul Sieveking TOPICS: Parapsychology, Occult, Psychic Phenomena TYPE: Journal DATE: 1973; 64 pgs. FREQ: bi-monthly CIRC: 3,000 PRICE: $16.96 PRICE PER COPY: $6.00 DESCRIPTION: Reports on all types of strange phenomena & anomalies worldwide & advances new explanatory theories. Covers all aspects of paranormal phenomena.

Fortune-Teller

PUBLISHING COMPANY: Carson City Pubs., Inc. EDITOR: Les Fox TOPICS: Parapsychology TYPE: Newsletter DATE: 1979 FREQ: Monthly PRICE: $34.00

Foulsham's Original Old Moore's Almanack

PUBLISHING COMPANY: W. Foulsham & Co., Ltd. TOPICS: Astrology TYPE: Magazine DATE: 1697 DESCRIPTION: Offers monthly astrological predictions on an annual basis.

Four Elements

PUBLISHING COMPANY: Madison Astrological Society EDITOR: Dennis Murray TOPICS: Astrology TYPE: Newsletter; 3 pgs. FREQ: Monthly PRICE: $3.00

Fourth Quadrant

PUBLISHING COMPANY: Digicomp Research Corp. EDITOR: Jeffrey Cox TOPICS: Astrology TYPE: Journal DATE: 1979 FREQ: Irregular CIRC: 400

Franklin's Insight

PUBLISHING COMPANY: Franklin's Insight TOPICS: New Age TYPE: Magazine

Fraternity News

PUBLISHING COMPANY: Fraternity For Canadian Astrologers EDITOR: Donna Van Toen TOPICS: Astrology TYPE: Journal DATE: 1977 SIZE: 3 1/2 x 5; 60 pgs. FREQ: Quarterly CIRC: 500 PRICE: $20.00 PRICE PER COPY: $5.00 DESCRIPTION: Journal promoting astrological education & techniques for intermediate & advanced/professional astrologers.

Free Mind

PUBLISHING COMPANY: American Humanist Association EDITOR: Bette Chambers TOPICS: New Age TYPE: Magazine

Friend's Review

PUBLISHING COMPANY: Friend's Review EDITOR: Marie Friend, Aaron Friend TOPICS: New Age TYPE: Newspaper DATE: 1989 FREQ: quarterly CIRC: 40,000 PRICE: $5.00 DESCRIPTION: A guide to metaphyscial & spiritual knowledge. Specializes in articles, ads, book and video reviews.

Fringes Of Reason: Whole Earth Catalog-New Age Frontiers, Unusual Beliefs & Eccentric Science

PUBLISHING COMPANY: Crown Publishers, Inc. EDITOR: T. Schultz TOPICS: New Age, Paranormal Phenomena TYPE: Catalog PRICE: $14.95

Full Moon, The

PUBLISHING COMPANY: Full Moon, The **TOPICS:** Witchcraft, Occult, Paganism **TYPE:** Magazine

Fusion

PUBLISHING COMPANY: Dream Psychology Northwest **PUBLISHER:** Christopher Matthews **EDITOR:** Douglas Cohen **TOPICS:** Parapsychology **TYPE:** Calendar **SIZE:** 11.5x17.5; 8 pgs. **FREQ:** Quarterly

Future Possibilities

PUBLISHING COMPANY: Evergreens **TOPICS:** Astrology **TYPE:** Newsletter; 4 pgs. **FREQ:** Quarterly **PRICE:** $15.00

Future Star Horoscope

PUBLISHING COMPANY: Future Star Horoscope **TOPICS:** Astrology **TYPE:** Magazine

Gandhi Today

PUBLISHING COMPANY: Gandhi Today **EDITOR:** Steven Krulick **TOPICS:** New Age **TYPE:** Magazine; 72 pgs. **PRICE PER COPY:** $3.00 **DESCRIPTION:** Prints non-fiction, news, children's stories, reviews and interviews, artwork, and cartoon illustrations.

Garbage Magazine

PUBLISHING COMPANY: Garbage Magazine **EDITOR:** Julie Stocker **TOPICS:** New Age **TYPE:** Magazine **DATE:** 1989; 90 pgs. **FREQ:** bi-monthly **CIRC:** 150,000 **PRICE:** $21.00 **PRICE PER COPY:** $3.95 **DESCRIPTION:** Covers-Garbage-in the environmental sense with important, technical information relayed to the common person. Publishes non-fiction, satire, cartoons, illustrations and photography. Mailing list available.

Garden Of Thoughts

PUBLISHING COMPANY: Hay House **EDITOR:** Louise Hay **TOPICS:** New Age, Psychology **TYPE:** Journal **PRICE:** $10.00

Gardom Lake International Earth Friendship Newsletter

PUBLISHING COMPANY: Gardom Lake International Earth Friendship Center **EDITOR:** Sarah Kipp **TOPICS:** Holistic Healing **TYPE:** Newsletter

Geminian

PUBLISHING COMPANY: Geminian **EDITOR:** Maxine Taylor **TOPICS:** Astrology **TYPE:** Journal

Genesis 2

PUBLISHING COMPANY: Genesis 2, Inc. **EDITOR:** Larry Bush **TOPICS:** New Age **TYPE:** Magazine

Gentle Places & Quiet Spaces

PUBLISHING COMPANY: Conscious Living Foundation, Inc. **EDITOR:** Tim Lowenstein **TOPICS:** New Age **TYPE:** Magazine **DATE:** 1983 **FREQ:** Semi-Annual **CIRC:** 240,000 **PRICE:** $1.00

Geocosmic News

PUBLISHING COMPANY: National Council For Geocosmic Research, Inc. **PUBLISHER:** Maria Simms **EDITOR:** Fran MacEvoy **TOPICS:** Astrology **TYPE:** Magazine **DATE:** 1972 **SIZE:** 8 1/2 x 11; 48 pgs. **CIRC:** 3,000 **DESCRIPTION:** Features geocosmic studies from a sociological & psychological viewpoint.

Georgian Newsletter

PUBLISHING COMPANY: Georgian Church, The **EDITOR:** Dean Fauna, Lady Fauna **TOPICS:** Occult **TYPE:** Newsletter **DATE:** 1976 **SIZE:** 8 1/2x 11; 15 pgs. **FREQ:** monthly **DESCRIPTION:** Reports on occult, witchcraft & related subjects.

German Journal Of Homeopathy

PUBLISHING COMPANY: Barthel & Barthel Publishing **EDITOR:** Dr. Michael Barthel **TOPICS:** Homeopathy **TYPE:** Journal **DATE:** 1987 **FREQ:** Quarterly **CIRC:** 1,000 **PRICE:** $29.00

Ghost Town Quarterly

PUBLISHING COMPANY: McLean Enterprises **EDITOR:** Donna B. McLean **TOPICS:** Ghosts **TYPE:** Magazine

Ghost Trackers Newsletter

PUBLISHING COMPANY: Ghost Research Society **EDITOR:** Dale Kaczmarek **TOPICS:** Ghosts, Psychic Phenomena, Parapsychology, Reincarnation, Past Life Regression, New Age **TYPE:** Newsletter **DATE:** 1982; 24 pgs. **FREQ:** tri-annually **CIRC:** 200 **PRICE:** $10.00 **PRICE PER COPY:** $4.00 **DESCRIPTION:** Publishes articles, news, criticisms, reviews, cartoons, photography, ads and illustrations that deal with ghosts and life after death.

GIST

PUBLISHING COMPANY: University Of Healing/God Unlimited **EDITOR:** Herbert Beierle, Ingeborg Puchert **TOPICS:** Holistic Healing, Metaphysics **TYPE:** Magazine **FREQ:** monthly **PRICE:** $20.00 **TERM:** yearly **DESCRIPTION:** Discusses positive philosophy.

Gnosis

PUBLISHING COMPANY: Gnosis **PUBLISHER:** Jay Kinney **EDITOR:** Richard Smoley **TOPICS:** Metaphysics, Spirituality, Occult, New Age, Kabbalah, Alchemy, Psychology **TYPE:** Magazine **DATE:** 1985; 88 pgs. **FREQ:** quarterly **CIRC:** 10,000 **PRICE PER COPY:** $4.95 **DESCRIPTION:** Deals with religion, spirituality & the occult. Publishes non-fiction articles on astrology, New Age and spirituality. Also book reviews, ads, interviews & illustrations that relate to Western spiritualism. Each issue focuses on a single theme such as Gnosticism, Magic, Kabbalah, Heresies & Heretics, Secret Societies, Alchemy, Jung & the Uncouscious, Ritual, Sects, the Goddess, Sex, the Dark Side & Ancient Civilizations.

Gnosis: A Journal Of Philosophical Interest

PUBLISHING COMPANY: Gnosis: A Journal Of Philosophical Interest **TOPICS:** New Age **TYPE:** Journal

Gnostic Times

PUBLISHING COMPANY: Gnostic Times **TOPICS:** Metaphysics, Spirituality **TYPE:** Magazine

Gnostica

PUBLISHING COMPANY: Llewellyn Publications **TOPICS:** New Age **TYPE:** Magazine **FREQ:** bi-monthly **PRICE:** $10.00

Golden Dawn

PUBLISHING COMPANY: City Of The Sun Foundation **TOPICS:** Astrology **TYPE:** Newsletter; 12 pgs. **FREQ:** Bi-Monthly

Golden Isis

PUBLISHING COMPANY: Golden Isis Press **EDITOR:** Gerina Dunwich **TOPICS:** Metaphysics **TYPE:** Magazine **DATE:** 1980; 25 pgs. **FREQ:** quarterly **CIRC:** 3,600 **PRICE:** $10.00 **PRICE PER COPY:** $3.00 **DESCRIPTION:** Salem's Neo-Pagan journal of white magick, mystical poetry, Wiccan news, art, ads, book reviews, contacts & much more. Artwork & poetry submissions welcome. Free writer's guidelines, Occult book catalog & ad rates available upon request. Include S.A.S.E. Published at the 4 Major Sabbats.

Good Health

PUBLISHING COMPANY: Good Health **EDITOR:** Ed Mounsey **TOPICS:** Holistic Healing **TYPE:** Magazine

Good Health Digest

PUBLISHING COMPANY: Dartnell's Cambridge Associates **TOPICS:** Holistic Healing **TYPE:** Magazine

Good Health Magazine

PUBLISHING COMPANY: Davis Communications Company **TOPICS:** Holistic Healing **TYPE:** Magazine

Good Life Times

PUBLISHING COMPANY: Good Life Times **EDITOR:** Patricia Miller **TOPICS:** Holistic Health **TYPE:** Magazine **FREQ:** monthly **CIRC:** 77,000 **PRICE:** $15.00 **DESCRIPTION:** Concerned with environmental and spiritual issues, this publication advocates wholistic health lifestyle and ideas. Formerly called Wholistic Living News.

Good Money Publications

PUBLISHING COMPANY: Good Money Publications **TOPICS:** New Age **TYPE:** Magazine

Grass Roots

PUBLISHING COMPANY: Night Owl Publishers **EDITOR:** Megg Miller, Kath Harper **TOPICS:** Holistic Healing **TYPE:** Magazine

Greater Cincinnati Resource Directory

PUBLISHING COMPANY: Greater Cincinnati Resource Directory **TOPICS:** New Age **TYPE:** Newspaper

Green Action

PUBLISHING COMPANY: Green Action **EDITOR:** Lare Clark **TOPICS:** New Age **TYPE:** Newspaper

Green Egg

PUBLISHING COMPANY: Green Egg **TOPICS:** Paganism, Occult, Witchcraft **TYPE:** Journal **FREQ:** quarterly **PRICE:** $13.00 **PRICE PER COPY:** $3.75 **DESCRIPTION:** Serves the early Neo-Pagan community with articles, fiction, cartoons and letters relating to gods/goddesses, ritualism, naturism, shamanism, archaelogy and mythism.

Greener Pastures Gazette

PUBLISHING COMPANY: Greener Pastures Institute/Relocation Research **EDITOR:** William

Seavey TOPICS: New Age TYPE: Newsletter DATE: 1985; 6 pgs. FREQ: quarterly CIRC: 1,000 PRICE: $22.00 TERM: annually PRICE PER COPY: $6.00 DESCRIPTION: Explores and reviews various countryside Edens where the good life still exists for people wishing to exit metropolitan centers to natural havens throughout the U.S. Prints articles, news and reviews.

Greenscene
PUBLISHING COMPANY: Vegetarian Society, The EDITOR: Fiona McPhall, Bronwen Humphreys TOPICS: Health Food, Vegetarianism TYPE: Magazine DESCRIPTION: Covers all aspects of vegetarianism. Youth, under 18 years old, oriented.

Ground Saucer Watch Newsletter
PUBLISHING COMPANY: Civilian Aerial Phenomena Research Organization EDITOR: William Spaulding TOPICS: UFO's TYPE: Newsletter; 20 pgs.

Growing And Using The Healing Herbs
PUBLISHING COMPANY: Rodale Press, Inc. EDITOR: G. Weiss, S. Weiss TOPICS: Holistic Health, Herbalogy TYPE: Magazine PRICE: $21.95

Guild News
PUBLISHING COMPANY: New Age Guild Of Connecticut TYPE: Newsletter DATE: 1989 FREQ: monthly CIRC: 150 DESCRIPTION: Keeps members informed on Guild activities & other interesting topics & happenings.

Gupta Gavesana
PUBLISHING COMPANY: Henry Munasinghe EDITOR: B.M.C. Mohatti TOPICS: Astrology TYPE: Magazine DATE: 1978 FREQ: Monthly CIRC: 10,000

Hahnemannian Homoeopathic Sandesh
PUBLISHING COMPANY: Delhi Homocopathic Medical Association TOPICS: Homeopathy TYPE: Magazine DATE: 1977 FREQ: Monthly CIRC: 1,500 PRICE: $10.00

Hallows
PUBLISHING COMPANY: Hallows TOPICS: Witchcraft, Occult, Paganism TYPE: Magazine

Halo Magazine
PUBLISHING COMPANY: Halo Magazine EDITOR: Robert Rose, Jr. TOPICS: New Age TYPE: Magazine DESCRIPTION: New age magazine. Reviews books.

Harmonies
PUBLISHING COMPANY: Harmonies EDITOR: Lydia de Fretos TOPICS: New Age TYPE: Magazine FREQ: weekly DESCRIPTION: Covers New Age music with articles, news, reviews and interviews.

Harmony Magazine
PUBLISHING COMPANY: Harmony Magazine TOPICS: New Age TYPE: Magazine FREQ: quarterly PRICE: $14.00 DESCRIPTION: Prints articles relating to personal and social transformation, relationships, and their growth.

Harvest
PUBLISHING COMPANY: Harvest Morven TOPICS: Paganism, Occult TYPE: Journal DATE: 1980 SIZE: 8 1/2 x 11; 34 pgs. FREQ: 8 x per yr CIRC: 1,000 PRICE: $10.00 PRICE PER COPY: $2.00 DESCRIPTION: Covers topics such as parapsychology & paganism. Promotes positive living for the neo-paganism community. Prints fiction, non-fiction, news, satire, reviews, interviews, cartoons and illustrations.

Hat Magazine
PUBLISHING COMPANY: Idad Press EDITOR: Ian Hogg TOPICS: Occult TYPE: Magazine

Haunts
PUBLISHING COMPANY: Nightshade Publications EDITOR: Joseph K. Cherkes TOPICS: Psychic Phenomena TYPE: Magazine

HDIREC/Newsletter
PUBLISHING COMPANY: HDIREC/Newsletter TOPICS: UFO's TYPE: Newsletter

Healing Currents
PUBLISHING COMPANY: Whole Health Institute EDITOR: Larry Krantz, Janet Lang TOPICS: Holistic Healing TYPE: Magazine

Healing Energy Forum
PUBLISHING COMPANY: Community Church By The Bay TOPICS: Holistic Healing TYPE: Magazine

Healing Newsletter
PUBLISHING COMPANY: Gerson Institute EDITOR: Gar Hildenbrand TOPICS: Holistic Healing TYPE: Newsletter

Healing Today
PUBLISHING COMPANY: Healing Research, Inc. EDITOR: Kathleen Frazier TOPICS: Holistic Healing TYPE: Magazine

Health
PUBLISHING COMPANY: HLQ Associates, Holistic Health TYPE: Newsletter

Health & Healing
PUBLISHING COMPANY: Health & Healing EDITOR: Maurice Finkel TOPICS: Holistic Health TYPE: Journal FREQ: Quarterly DESCRIPTION: Publishes articles relating to alternative health.

Health Affairs
PUBLISHING COMPANY: Project Hope EDITOR: John K. Iglehart, William B. Walsh, M.D. TOPICS: Holistic Healing TYPE: Magazine

Health And Healing
PUBLISHING COMPANY: Churches' Council For Health And Healing EDITOR: David Goodacre TOPICS: Holistic Health TYPE: Newsletter DATE: 1982 FREQ: 3 x/yr. CIRC: 3,000 DESCRIPTION: Explores ideas, information & the churches theological and spiritual role in health and healing. Dedicated to serving those who care & heal.

Health And Nutrition Update
PUBLISHING COMPANY: Canadian Schizophrenia Foundation TOPICS: Holistic Healing TYPE: Newsletter

Health Consciousness
PUBLISHING COMPANY: Lost Horizon Health Awareness Center EDITOR: Roy Kupsinel, M.D., Carl Thomason TOPICS: Holistic Healing TYPE: Newsletter

Health Education
PUBLISHING COMPANY: American Alliance For Health, Physical Education, Recreation And Dance EDITOR: Patricia Steffan, Pamela Nelson TOPICS: Holistic Healing TYPE: Magazine

Health Express
PUBLISHING COMPANY: Davis Communications Company EDITOR: Michael Cohen, Suzanne Pelisson TOPICS: Holistic Healing TYPE: Magazine

Health Foods Business
PUBLISHING COMPANY: Howmark Publishing Corporation EDITOR: Howard I. Wasserman TOPICS: Health Food TYPE: Magazine

Health Foods Retailing
PUBLISHING COMPANY: D.J. Caulfield EDITOR: D.J. Caulfield TYPE: Magazine

Health For Life
PUBLISHING COMPANY: Si-Nel Publishing EDITOR: Mirmiam Butler TOPICS: Homeopathy TYPE: Newspaper DATE: 1967 FREQ: Quarterly CIRC: 1,000,000

Health Freedom News
PUBLISHING COMPANY: National Health Federation EDITOR: Maureen Kennedy Salaman, Dan Ray TOPICS: Holistic Healing TYPE: Newspaper

Health Highlights
PUBLISHING COMPANY: American Osteopathic Hospital Association TOPICS: Homcopathy TYPE: Newsletter DATE: 1986

Health News
PUBLISHING COMPANY: University Of Toronto TOPICS: Holistic Healing TYPE: Newspaper

Health News And Reviews
PUBLISHING COMPANY: Keats Publishing, Inc. EDITOR: D.R. Bensen, Nathan Keats TOPICS: Holistic Healing, New Age, Holistic Health TYPE: Magazine FREQ: bi-monthly DESCRIPTION: Features reviews and articles on health, New Age, nutrition, fitness, products, services and food.

Health Perspective
PUBLISHING COMPANY: American Chiropractic Association EDITOR: Ruth Sirko, Mary Brown TOPICS: Holistic Healing TYPE: Magazine

Health Shopper
PUBLISHING COMPANY: Health Shopper EDITOR: Carter Sandvik TOPICS: New Age TYPE: Magazine FREQ: Monthly DESCRIPTION: Published by Swanson Health Products.

Health World Magazine
PUBLISHING COMPANY: Health World, Inc. PUBLISHER: Lois Chapman EDITOR: Kumar Pati, Laurence Badgley TOPICS: Holistic Healing TYPE: Magazine DATE: 1984 SIZE: 8 1/2 x 11; 64 pgs. FREQ: bi-monthly CIRC: 50,000 PRICE: $10.50

TERM: yearly **PRICE PER COPY:** $2.00 **DESCRIPTION:** Deals with nutrition, vitamins, alternative health therapies & all aspects of holistic health. Publishes research, product information, ads and reviews. Articles pertain to specific health issues including herbs, and sports injuries.

Health/Action

PUBLISHING COMPANY: Strang Clinic **TOPICS:** Holistic Healing **TYPE:** Newsletter

HealthAction

PUBLISHING COMPANY: Kelly Communications **EDITOR:** Joseph Kelly, Debbie Blaylock **TOPICS:** Holistic Healing **TYPE:** Magazine

Healthline

PUBLISHING COMPANY: C.V. Mosby Co. **EDITOR:** Paul M. Insel **TOPICS:** Holistic Healing **TYPE:** Magazine

Healthsharing

PUBLISHING COMPANY: Women Healthsharing, Inc. **EDITOR:** Amy Gottlieb, Susan Elliott **TOPICS:** Holistic Healing **TYPE:** Magazine

Healthways

PUBLISHING COMPANY: International Macrobiotic Shiatsu Society **EDITOR:** Patrick McCarty **TOPICS:** Holistic Healing **TYPE:** Magazine

Heart And Wings Journal

PUBLISHING COMPANY: Heart And Wings Journal **TOPICS:** Holistic Healing **TYPE:** Journal

Heart's Journey

PUBLISHING COMPANY: Heart's Journey **TOPICS:** New Age **TYPE:** Magazinc

Heartland

PUBLISHING COMPANY: Heartland **TOPICS:** Holistic Health **TYPE:** Newspaper **DESCRIPTION:** Publishes articles and book reviews relating to health, sports and change.

Hearts and Wings Journal

PUBLISHING COMPANY: Hearts and Wings Journal **TOPICS:** New Age **TYPE:** Magazine **FREQ:** bi-monthly **PRICE:** $12.00 **DESCRIPTION:** Publishes articles focusing on the Sufi perspective.

Heartsong Review

PUBLISHING COMPANY: Wahaba Heartsun Publishers **EDITOR:** Wahaba Heartsun **TOPICS:** New Age **TYPE:** Magazine **DATE:** 1986 **SIZE:** 8 1/2 x 11; 60 pgs. **FREQ:** bi-annual **CIRC:** 9,000 **PRICE:** $8.00 **TERM:** yearly **PRICE PER COPY:** $4.00 **DESCRIPTION:** Consumer's directory & resource guide for New Age socially & spiritually conscious music which connects hundreds of New Age musicians, organizations, catalogs, bookstores, radio stations, magazines & healing centers. Provides hundreds of detailed reviews, ordering addresses, vocal & instrumental music. Catagories include chanting, children, electronic, folk, etc. Promotes personal & spiritual growth, healing, meditation, ritual, music & movement. Features independently published, hard to find music.

Heaven & Earth Network News

PUBLISHING COMPANY: Heaven & Earth Network News **TOPICS:** Crystals, Alchemy, Metaphysics **TYPE:** Newsletter **DATE:** 1990 **PRICE:** $15.00

DESCRIPTION: Features articles, news and reviews relating to gemstones, crystals and their metaphysical use.

Heaven Bone Magazine

PUBLISHING COMPANY: Heaven Bone Press **EDITOR:** Kirpal Gordon, Steven Hirsch **TOPICS:** New Age, Metaphysics **TYPE:** Magazine **DATE:** 1986 **SIZE:** 8 1/2 x 11; 56 pgs. **FREQ:** quarterly **CIRC:** 1,200 **PRICE:** $14.95 **TERM:** 2 years **PRICE PER COPY:** $5.00 **DESCRIPTION:** Offers essays, poetry, fiction & reviews with an esoteric & spiritual focus. Prints fiction and non-fiction articles, interviews, plays, criticisms, ads and artwork including collages.

Hecate's Loom

PUBLISHING COMPANY: Hecate's Loom Collective **TOPICS:** Witchcraft, Spirituality, Paganism, Occult **TYPE:** Journal **DATE:** 1986; 32 pgs. **FREQ:** quarterly **PRICE PER COPY:** $2.95 **DESCRIPTION:** Provides a forum for discussion of Pagan, Wiccan & Women's Spirituality topics & to provide an opportunity for greater understanding amongst all religions. News & current events also featured.

Hefley Psychic Report

PUBLISHING COMPANY: U.S. Research, Inc. **EDITOR:** Carl Hefley **TOPICS:** Parapsychology **TYPE:** Newsletter **FREQ:** Bi-Monthly **PRICE PER COPY:** $1.00

Heilkunst

PUBLISHING COMPANY: Heilkunst Verlag GmbH **EDITOR:** Dr. Victor Harth **TOPICS:** Homeopathy **TYPE:** Magazine **FREQ:** Bi-Monthly

Herald Of Holistic Health

PUBLISHING COMPANY: American Holistic Health Sciences Association **EDITOR:** John M. Barry **TOPICS:** Holistic Healing **TYPE:** Magazine

Herb Companion

PUBLISHING COMPANY: Interweave Press, Inc. **EDITOR:** Linda Ligon **TOPICS:** Herbalogy, Health Food, Holistic Health **TYPE:** Magazine **FREQ:** bi-monthly **PRICE:** $21.00 **PRICE PER COPY:** $4.00 **DESCRIPTION:** Publishes features, articles, recipes, reviews and product listings relating to all useful plants.

Herbal Gram

PUBLISHING COMPANY: Herb Research Foundation **TOPICS:** Herbalogy, Holistic Health **TYPE:** Journal; 50 pgs. **FREQ:** quarterly **DESCRIPTION:** Summaries of the most recent scientific research on herbs, news about government regulations of herbs, international botanicals market report & book reviews. Free to members.

Herbalgram

PUBLISHING COMPANY: Herb Research Foundation **EDITOR:** Mark Blumenthal **TOPICS:** Herbalogy **TYPE:** Magazine

Herbs!

PUBLISHING COMPANY: Herbs! **EDITOR:** Leonard Hendrickx **TOPICS:** Herbalogy, Nutrition, Holistic Health **TYPE:** Journal **FREQ:** bi-monthly **PRICE:** $12.00 **PRICE PER COPY:** $2.00 **DESCRIPTION:** Publishes articles and reviews pertaining to healthy living through herbs and good nutrition.

Hidden Path

PUBLISHING COMPANY: Hidden Path **TOPICS:** Witchcraft, Occult, Paganism **TYPE:** Magazine

High Frontiers

PUBLISHING COMPANY: High Frontiers **TOPICS:** Occult, Parapsychology **TYPE:** Magazine

High Times

PUBLISHING COMPANY: High Times **EDITOR:** Steve Hager, Robert Aronson **TOPICS:** New Age **TYPE:** Magazine

Hilberg-Easley Report

PUBLISHING COMPANY: Hilberg-Easley Report **EDITOR:** Rick Hilberg **TOPICS:** UFO's **TYPE:** Newsletter; 6 pgs. **FREQ:** Irregular

Himalayan Institute Quarterly

PUBLISHING COMPANY: Himalayan International Institute Of Yoga Science and Philosophy **EDITOR:** Larry Clark **TOPICS:** New Age **TYPE:** Magazine

Hinduism Today

PUBLISHING COMPANY: Hinduism Today **EDITOR:** Swami Sivasiva Palani, Dasa Vinayaga **TOPICS:** New Age, Spirituality, Holistic Health **TYPE:** Newspaper **SIZE:** 11 x 17; 28 pgs. **FREQ:** monthly **CIRC:** 25,000 **PRICE:** $20.00 **TERM:** yearly **PRICE PER COPY:** $2.00 **DESCRIPTION:** Features articles and interviews on Hinduism. Reports on current events & issues in the Hindu religion. Each issue features a 2-page center section on a religious subject & pages for women & youths. Books are reviewed. Published in U.S.A., Malaysia, Mauritius, South Africa, Holland & Fiji.

Hippocrates Health Institute Newsletter

PUBLISHING COMPANY: Hippocrates Health Institute **EDITOR:** Alix Weill **TOPICS:** Holistic Healing **TYPE:** Newsletter

Hippocrates News

PUBLISHING COMPANY: Hippocrates Health Institute **PUBLISHER:** Brian Clement **EDITOR:** Alix Weill **TOPICS:** Holistic Health **TYPE:** Newsletter **DATE:** 1969 **SIZE:** 8 1/2 x 11; 8 pgs. **FREQ:** Semi-Annual **CIRC:** 17,000 **PRICE:** $25.00 **TERM:** yearly **DESCRIPTION:** Devoted to wellness & holistic health. Features media-covered health news. Promotes the benefits of a raw vegetarian diet as well as other health practices such as fasting, exercise, mind, body & aging.

HLQ Wellness Calendar

PUBLISHING COMPANY: HLQ Associates **TOPICS:** Holistic Healing **TYPE:** Calendar

Holistic

PUBLISHING COMPANY: Holistic Health/Academy **TOPICS:** Holistic Healing **TYPE:** Newsletter

Holistic & Preventive Update

PUBLISHING COMPANY: International Academy Holistic Health/Medicine **TOPICS:** Holistic Healing **TYPE:** Newsletter

Holistic Animal News

PUBLISHING COMPANY: Holistic Animal News **EDITOR:** Georgina Bezenar **TOPICS:** Holistic Healing **TYPE:** Newspaper

Holistic Dental Digest
PUBLISHING COMPANY: Once Daily, Inc.
EDITOR: Jerry Mittelman, DDS TOPICS: Holistic
Healing TYPE: Magazine

Holistic Education Review
PUBLISHING COMPANY: Holistic Education
Review PUBLISHER: Jeffrey Kane, Ph. D. EDITOR:
Diana M. Feige, Ed. D., Ron Miller TOPICS:
Holistic Healing TYPE: Magazine DATE: 1988
FREQ: quarterly PRICE: $16.00 PRICE PER COPY:
$7.00 DESCRIPTION: Publishes articles, reviews,
interviews and photography pertaining to non-
standard methods of education, including
Montessori, Waldorf and home schooling.

Holistic Health Focus
PUBLISHING COMPANY: Association For Holistic
Health EDITOR: John Meyer TOPICS: Holistic
Healing TYPE: Newsletter

Holistic Health Forum
PUBLISHING COMPANY: Eastern Holistic Health
Association EDITOR: Scott Wilson TOPICS: Holistic
Healing TYPE: Newsletter

Holistic Health Review
PUBLISHING COMPANY: Plenum Publishing
Corporation EDITOR: Norma Fox, Charlain Apsel
TOPICS: New Age TYPE: Magazine

Holistic Living
PUBLISHING COMPANY: Holistic Health
Association Of The Princeton Area EDITOR: Jackie
Schilder-McLaughlin TOPICS: Holistic Healing
TYPE: Magazine DESCRIPTION: Published by the
Holistic Health Association of the Princeton Area,
contains articles, reviews and a calendar.

Holistic Medicine
PUBLISHING COMPANY: American Holistic
Medical Association EDITOR: Marcia Meyer,
Tracey Weller TOPICS: Holistic Healing TYPE:
Newsletter DATE: 1980 FREQ: bi-monthly

Holistic Medicine
PUBLISHING COMPANY: John Wiley & Sons, Ltd.
EDITOR: Dr. Clive Wood TOPICS: Homeopathy
TYPE: Magazine DATE: 1986 FREQ: Quarterly

Holistic Nursing Practice
PUBLISHING COMPANY: Aspen Publishing, Inc.
EDITOR: John Marozsan, Gloria Donnelly TOPICS:
Holistic Healing TYPE: Magazine

Holistic Optometrist
PUBLISHING COMPANY: Russell Pittman EDITOR:
Russell Pittman TOPICS: Holistic Healing TYPE:
Magazine

Holyearth Network News
PUBLISHING COMPANY: Holyearth Network News
TOPICS: Occult TYPE: Newspaper

Home Business Advisor
PUBLISHING COMPANY: Home Business Advisor
EDITOR: Jan Fletcher TOPICS: New Age TYPE:
Newsletter DATE: 1987 FREQ: bi-monthly
DESCRIPTION: Reports and advises on alternative
work options, including home businesses,
telecommuting and job-sharing. Prints articles,
news, interviews and satire.

Home Education Magazine
PUBLISHING COMPANY: Home Education Press
EDITOR: Mark Hegener, Helen Hegener TOPICS:
New Age, Metaphysics TYPE: Magazine DATE:
1983 FREQ: bi-monthly PRICE: $24.00
DESCRIPTION: Publishes non-fiction, news, reviews,
interviews, satire, artwork, and photography
pertaining to home schooling.

Home Health Management Advisor
PUBLISHING COMPANY: Aspen Publishers, Inc.
TOPICS: Homeopathy TYPE: Magazine DATE:
1986 FREQ: Monthly PRICE: $95.00

Homebringing Mission Of Jesus Christ
PUBLISHING COMPANY: Christ State EDITOR:
Charlotte Surprenant TOPICS: Astrology TYPE:
Journal; 8 pgs. FREQ: Irregular

Homeopathic Educational Services
PUBLISHING COMPANY: Homeopathic Educational
Services TOPICS: Homeopathy TYPE: Magazine

Homeopathic Herald
PUBLISHING COMPANY: Homeopathic Herald
TOPICS: Homeopathy TYPE: Magazine DATE:
1940 FREQ: monthly

Homeopathic Medicine Today
PUBLISHING COMPANY: Keats Publishing, Inc.
EDITOR: T. Cook TOPICS: Homeopathy TYPE:
Magazine PRICE: $29.95

Homeopathie Francaise
PUBLISHING COMPANY: Centre Homeopathique de
France TOPICS: Homeopathy TYPE: Magazine
DATE: 1912 FREQ: Bi-Monthly

Homeopathy Today
PUBLISHING COMPANY: National Center For
Homeopathy EDITOR: Julian Winston TOPICS:
Holistic Healing TYPE: Magazine

Homoeopathic Heritage
PUBLISHING COMPANY: B. Jain Publishers, Ltd.
EDITOR: Dr. S.P. Koppikar TOPICS: Homeopathy
TYPE: Journal DATE: 1976 FREQ: Monthly CIRC:
5,000

Homocopathic World
PUBLISHING COMPANY: Sundar Homoeo Sadan
EDITOR: Sri Abinash Das TOPICS: Homeopathy
TYPE: Magazine DATE: 1964 FREQ: monthly
CIRC: 1,500

Homoeopathie Caracteristique
PUBLISHING COMPANY: Association Patients pour
l'Homoeopathie Uniciste EDITOR: Ph. Luyten
TOPICS: Homeopathy TYPE: Magazine DATE:
1988 FREQ: Quarterly CIRC: 600 DESCRIPTION:
Offers advice on current issues in pharmacology as it
relates to homeopathy.

Homoeopathisch Tijdschrift
PUBLISHING COMPANY: Vereniging tot
Bevordering der Homoeopathie in Nederland
EDITOR: J.W. Puttenstein TOPICS: Homeopathy
TYPE: Magazine DATE: 1889 FREQ: Bi-Monthly
CIRC: 7,900

Homoeopathy

PUBLISHING COMPANY: Indian Institute Of
Homoeopaths EDITOR: Dr. R.J. Murty, Sri R.
Srinivasan TOPICS: Homeopathy TYPE: Magazine
DATE: 1948 FREQ: Monthly CIRC: 2,000 PRICE:
$3.00

Homoeopathy
PUBLISHING COMPANY: British Homeopathic
Association EDITOR: Mrs. M.J. Munday TOPICS:
Homeopathy TYPE: Magazine DATE: 1932 FREQ:
Bi-Monthly CIRC: 5,500

Horizons
PUBLISHING COMPANY: Horizons EDITOR: Lois
A. Grasso TOPICS: Holistic Health, New Age
TYPE: Magazine DESCRIPTION: Publishes non-
fiction, health, music reviews, resource guide and
interviews.

Horizons Beyond
PUBLISHING COMPANY: Baker Street Publications
EDITOR: Sharida Rizzuto, Sidney J. Dragon
TOPICS: New Age TYPE: Magazine

Horizons Resource Directory
PUBLISHING COMPANY: Horizons Resource
Directory TOPICS: New Age, Holistic Health TYPE:
Newspaper FREQ: quarterly DESCRIPTION:
Tabloid offering information on seminars & products
in holistic health.

Horoscope
PUBLISHING COMPANY: Dell Horoscope
Magazines EDITOR: Ronnie Grishman, Barry R.
Mark TOPICS: Astrology TYPE: Magazine DATE:
1935 FREQ: Monthly CIRC: 240,000 PRICE:
$12.50

Horoscope
PUBLISHING COMPANY: Atlas Publishing Co., Ltd.
EDITOR: Geoff Ward TOPICS: Astrology TYPE:
Magazine DATE: 1954 FREQ: Monthly
DESCRIPTION: Features articles on each zodiac
sign, daily horoscopes, & various topics related to
astrology.

Horoscope Quotidien Eclair
PUBLISHING COMPANY: Super Magazine, Inc.
EDITOR: Paul-Henri Goulet, Roger Chabot
TOPICS: Astrology TYPE: Magazine

Horoscopo Capricho
PUBLISHING COMPANY: Abril Images EDITOR:
Victor Civita TOPICS: Astrology TYPE: Magazine
DATE: 1972 FREQ: Monthly CIRC: 100,000

Horror Show
PUBLISHING COMPANY: Phantasm Press EDITOR:
David B. Silva TOPICS: New Age TYPE: Magazine

HSA News
PUBLISHING COMPANY: Heartland Spiritual
Alliance TYPE: Newsletter FREQ: 8 x per year

Hug News
PUBLISHING COMPANY: Hugs Unlimited EDITOR:
Heather Lynne TOPICS: Holistic Healing TYPE:
Catalog DESCRIPTION: Catalog of 300 self-esteem
items.

Human Ecologist
PUBLISHING COMPANY: Human Ecology Action
League TOPICS: New Age TYPE: Newsletter

Human Stress

PUBLISHING COMPANY: AMS Press, Inc. **EDITOR:** James Humphrey **TOPICS:** Holistic Healing **TYPE:** Magazine

Hygienic Community Network News

PUBLISHING COMPANY: River Farm **EDITOR:** Helen Jean Story **TOPICS:** New Age **TYPE:** Newspaper

Hypnotherapy

PUBLISHING COMPANY: Westwood Publishing Company **EDITOR:** Dave Elman **TOPICS:** Hypnotism **TYPE:** Magazine **PRICE:** $27.50

Hypnotherapy In Review

PUBLISHING COMPANY: Academy Of Scientific Hypnotherapy **EDITOR:** Sandy Pasqua **TOPICS:** Hypnotism **TYPE:** Magazine

Hypnotherapy Today

PUBLISHING COMPANY: American Association Of Professional Hypnotherapists **EDITOR:** William Brink **TOPICS:** Hypnotism **TYPE:** Magazine

Hypnotism & Meditation

PUBLISHING COMPANY: Westwood Publishing Company **EDITOR:** Ormond McGill **TOPICS:** Hypnotism, Meditation **TYPE:** Magazine **PRICE:** $6.95

I Am News

PUBLISHING COMPANY: ICSA - Ananda Ashram **TOPICS:** New Age **TYPE:** Newspaper **DESCRIPTION:** Features news & articles on yoga methods & philosophy.

Imagine Magazine

PUBLISHING COMPANY: Imagine Magazine **EDITOR:** Adam Pryor **TOPICS:** New Age **TYPE:** Magazine **DESCRIPTION:** Prints articles, book reviews and buying guide.

In Business

PUBLISHING COMPANY: In Business **TOPICS:** New Age, Metaphysics **TYPE:** Magazine **DATE:** 1979 **FREQ:** bi-monthly **CIRC:** 70,000 **PRICE:** $21.00 **PRICE PER COPY:** $3.50 **DESCRIPTION:** Publishes articles dealing with environmental entrepreneuring, and how to run a successful, small business.

In Context: A Quarterly Of Humane Sustainable Culture

PUBLISHING COMPANY: In Context **EDITOR:** Robert Gilman **TOPICS:** New Age **TYPE:** Magazine **DATE:** 1982 **SIZE:** 8 x 11; 65 pgs. **FREQ:** quarterly **PRICE:** $14.00 **DESCRIPTION:** Publishes fiction articles, essays, interviews, and poetry dealing with the rapid changes and mounting environmental problems in our world.

In Health

PUBLISHING COMPANY: Hippocrates Partners **EDITOR:** James Martay, Eric Schrier **TOPICS:** Holistic Healing **TYPE:** Magazine **DATE:** 1987; 100 pgs. **FREQ:** Bi-monthly **CIRC:** 800,000 **PRICE:** $18.00 **TERM:** yearly **PRICE PER COPY:** $3.00 **DESCRIPTION:** National consumer magazine providing information on health & medicine.

Inconnu

PUBLISHING COMPANY: Editions Amelie **EDITOR:** Marc Tripier **TOPICS:** Parapsychology, Occult **TYPE:** Magazine **DATE:** 1975 **FREQ:** Monthly **CIRC:** 75,000

Incredible Inquiry

PUBLISHING COMPANY: Fry's Incredible Inquiry's **EDITOR:** A. Fry **TOPICS:** Parapsychology **TYPE:** Catalog **DESCRIPTION:** Catalog of unexplained phenomena.

Indian Homoeopathic Gazette

PUBLISHING COMPANY: Indian Homoeopathic Gazette **EDITOR:** Dr. Mathews **TOPICS:** Homeopathy **TYPE:** Magazine **DATE:** 1961 **FREQ:** Quarterly **CIRC:** 3,000 **PRICE:** $1.50

Indian Journal Of Homoeopathic Medicine

PUBLISHING COMPANY: Homoeopathic Education Society **EDITOR:** Dr. Vishpala R. Parthasarathy **TOPICS:** Homeopathy **TYPE:** Journal **DATE:** 1967 **FREQ:** Quarterly **CIRC:** 1,500 **PRICE:** $20.00

Infinite Light Beacon Keys

PUBLISHING COMPANY: Infinite Light Fellowship **TOPICS:** Metaphysics, Spirituality, Meditation, Dreams **TYPE:** Newsletter; 2 pgs. **FREQ:** weekly **PRICE:** $13.00 **TERM:** 13 weeks **PRICE PER COPY:** $1.00 **DESCRIPTION:** Offers weekly home practice exercises to explore energies leading to greater self-awareness, inner guidance & self-mastery. The Keys explore the nature of dreams, meditation, spiritual growth, chakras & auras, astral projection, spiritual healing & metaphysical practices.

INFO Journal

PUBLISHING COMPANY: International Fortean Organization **EDITOR:** James Theisen **TOPICS:** Psychic Phenomena **TYPE:** Journal **DATE:** 1966; 40 pgs. **FREQ:** quarterly **PRICE:** $12.00 **DESCRIPTION:** Reports research results of unexplained events as conducted by the International Fortean Organization, which studies phenomena not explained by conventional scientific theories.

Informazioni Di Parapsicologia

PUBLISHING COMPANY: Instituto Gnosis Per La Ricerca Sulla Sopravvivenza **EDITOR:** Giorgio di Simone **TOPICS:** Parapsychology, Occult **TYPE:** Magazine **DATE:** 1963 **FREQ:** Semi-Annual **CIRC:** 600

Initiator

PUBLISHING COMPANY: Planetary Citizens/Planetary Initiative For The World We Choose **EDITOR:** Mary Ann Klimek **TOPICS:** Astrology **TYPE:** Calendar **SIZE:** 11.5 x 16; 8 pgs.

Inland Sun

PUBLISHING COMPANY: Inland Sun **PUBLISHER:** Shirley **EDITOR:** Jodi **TOPICS:** New Age **TYPE:** Newspaper **FREQ:** Bi-Monthly

Inner Development

PUBLISHING COMPANY: Yes! Inc. **TOPICS:** Parapsychology **TYPE:** Magazine **DATE:** 1979; 654 pgs. **PRICE:** $9.95

Inner Life

PUBLISHING COMPANY: Inner Life **TOPICS:** Metaphysics, Spirituality **TYPE:** Magazine

Inner Light

PUBLISHING COMPANY: Inner Light Publications **EDITOR:** Timothy Beckley **TOPICS:** UFO's, Psychic Phenomena, Spirituality **TYPE:** Magazine **DATE:** 1984 **SIZE:** 8 1/2 x 11; 32 pgs. **FREQ:** Bi-Monthly **CIRC:** 60,000 **PRICE PER COPY:** $1.00 **DESCRIPTION:** Features articles on psychic phenomena, UFO's & spiritual topics.

Inner Light Beacon

PUBLISHING COMPANY: Infinite Light Fellowship, Inc. **TOPICS:** Parapsychology **TYPE:** Newsletter **DATE:** 1989 **SIZE:** 8 1/2 x 11; 4 pgs. **FREQ:** Monthly **CIRC:** 30 **PRICE:** $16.00 **DESCRIPTION:** Presents information about & for the Infinite Light Fellowship.

Inner Light Foundation Newsletter

PUBLISHING COMPANY: Inner Light Foundation **EDITOR:** Marynell Tipton, Betty Bethards **TOPICS:** Holistic Healing **TYPE:** Newsletter

Inner Mind Speaks, The

PUBLISHING COMPANY: Inner Mind Speaks, The **TOPICS:** Metaphysics, Spirituality **TYPE:** Magazine

Inner Paths

PUBLISHING COMPANY: Inner Paths Publications, Inc. **EDITOR:** Louis Rogers **TOPICS:** New Age **TYPE:** Magazine **DATE:** 1977 **FREQ:** Monthly **CIRC:** 33,500 **PRICE:** $15.00

Inner Quest Journal

PUBLISHING COMPANY: Inner Quest Journal **TOPICS:** Metaphysics, Spirituality **TYPE:** Journal

Inner Quest Newsletter

PUBLISHING COMPANY: Inner Quest Newsletter **TOPICS:** Spirituality **TYPE:** Newsletter **DESCRIPTION:** Contains articles and practical information regarding inner peace and spirituality in everyday living.

Inner Sense News

PUBLISHING COMPANY: Patricia Hayes School Of Inner Sense Development **EDITOR:** Kelly Powers **TOPICS:** Astrology **TYPE:** Newsletter; 6 pgs. **FREQ:** Quarterly **PRICE:** $0.00

Inner Vision

PUBLISHING COMPANY: Inner Vision **EDITOR:** Judith Elder **TOPICS:** Dreams, Meditation, New Age **TYPE:** Newsletter **DESCRIPTION:** Publishes articles regarding personal growth through various mediums.

Inner Voice

PUBLISHING COMPANY: Inner Voice **TOPICS:** Metaphysics, Spirituality **TYPE:** Magazine

Inner Woman

PUBLISHING COMPANY: Silver Owl Publications, Inc. **EDITOR:** Krysta Gibson **TOPICS:** New Age **TYPE:** Newspaper **DATE:** 1987 **SIZE:** 17 x 11; 16 pgs. **FREQ:** quarterly **CIRC:** 30,000 **PRICE:** $7.50 **TERM:** yearly **PRICE PER COPY:** $1.00 **DESCRIPTION:** Publication dedicated to women's spirituality, healing & evolution.

Innerconnexion

PUBLISHING COMPANY: Innerconnexion **TOPICS:** Witchcraft, Occult, Paganism, Metaphysics, Spirituality **TYPE:** Magazine

Innergy News

PUBLISHING COMPANY: Source of Innergy, Ltd. **EDITOR:** Patrick Flanagan **TOPICS:** Parapsychology, Occult **TYPE:** Newspaper **FREQ:** Quarterly **PRICE:** $0.00

Innerworld

PUBLISHING COMPANY: Innerworld **TOPICS:** Holistic Healing **TYPE:** Magazine

Inside Magazine

PUBLISHING COMPANY: Inside Magazine **EDITOR:** Kudra Maske **TOPICS:** New Age **TYPE:** Magazine **SIZE:** 8x11; 32 pgs. **FREQ:** 2 issues/yr **PRICE:** $7.00 **DESCRIPTION:** Prints fiction articles, book reviews and recipes with Arica orientation.

Insight Magazine

PUBLISHING COMPANY: OAL Research Publications, Ltd. **PUBLISHER:** Dr. O.A. Lawal **EDITOR:** Tajudeen A. Amusa **TOPICS:** New Age, Spirituality **TYPE:** Magazine **DATE:** 1987; 46 pgs. **FREQ:** Monthly **CIRC:** 25,000 **PRICE:** $2.00 **DESCRIPTION:** Promotes spiritual development. Text in English.

Insight Northwest

PUBLISHING COMPANY: Insight Northwest **TOPICS:** Holistic Health, Metaphysics, Spirituality, Channeling **TYPE:** Magazine

Insights

PUBLISHING COMPANY: Jersey Society Of Parapsychology, Inc. **EDITOR:** Phyllis Kimec-Wilhelm, B.J. McKay **TOPICS:** Parapsychology **TYPE:** Newsletter **DATE:** 1969; 6 pgs. **FREQ:** Monthly **CIRC:** 700 **PRICE:** $10.00

Insights

PUBLISHING COMPANY: Insights **TOPICS:** Metaphysics, Spirituality **TYPE:** Magazine

Insights Positive Living

PUBLISHING COMPANY: Insights Positive Living **TOPICS:** Metaphysics, Spirituality **TYPE:** Magazine

Integral Yoga Magazine

PUBLISHING COMPANY: Integral Yoga Publications **EDITOR:** Swami Prakashananda **TOPICS:** Holistic Healing **TYPE:** Magazine

Integrity International

PUBLISHING COMPANY: Integrity International **EDITOR:** Chris Foster **TOPICS:** New Age **TYPE:** Magazine **DATE:** 1972 **FREQ:** Quarterly **CIRC:** 1,000 **DESCRIPTION:** Promotes practical spirituality.

Interface Catalog

PUBLISHING COMPANY: Interface **TYPE:** Catalog **FREQ:** 3 x per year **PRICE:** $8.00 **TERM:** yearly

Internal Arts

PUBLISHING COMPANY: Internal Arts **EDITOR:** John Painter, Pierce Watters **TOPICS:** New Age **TYPE:** Magazine **FREQ:** bi-monthly **PRICE:** $21.00 **DESCRIPTION:** Prints articles on mind/body/spirit development through meditation and yoga. Accepts ads.

International Journal Of Biosocial & Medical Research

PUBLISHING COMPANY: Biosocial Publications, International **EDITOR:** Alexander Schauss, Laura Babin **TOPICS:** Holistic Healing **TYPE:** Journal

International Journal Of Childbirth Education

PUBLISHING COMPANY: International Childbirth Education Association **TOPICS:** Birth **TYPE:** Journal

International Journal Of Clinical & Experimental Hypnosis

PUBLISHING COMPANY: Society For Clinical & Experimental Hypnosis **TOPICS:** Hypnotism **TYPE:** Journal

International Journal Of Clinical And Experimental Hypnosis

PUBLISHING COMPANY: Society For Clinical & Experimental Hypnosis **EDITOR:** Martin T. Orne **TOPICS:** Hypnotism **TYPE:** Journal

International New Age Music Magazine

PUBLISHING COMPANY: International New Age Music Network, Inc. **EDITOR:** Suzanee Doucet, James Bell **TOPICS:** New Age **TYPE:** Magazine **DATE:** 1989 **CIRC:** 1,000 **DESCRIPTION:** Includes interviews, news, articles, and listings of bestselling music titles. Adopted by the International New Age Music Network as its official newsletter.

International Review Of Chiropractic

PUBLISHING COMPANY: International Chiropractors Association **TOPICS:** Holistic Healing **TYPE:** Newsletter

International Society Of Hypnosis Newsletter

PUBLISHING COMPANY: Society For Clinical & Experimental Hypnosis **TOPICS:** Hypnotism **TYPE:** Newsletter

International UFO Reporter

PUBLISHING COMPANY: J. Allen Hynek Center For UFO Studies **PUBLISHER:** Mark Rodeghier **EDITOR:** Jerome Clark **TOPICS:** UFO's **TYPE:** Magazine **DATE:** 1976 **SIZE:** 8 1/2 x 11; 20 pgs. **FREQ:** Bi-Monthly **CIRC:** 1,250 **PRICE:** $25.00 **PRICE PER COPY:** $4.00 **DESCRIPTION:** Features articles on UFO sitings & reports, book reviews, photos & correspondence.

International Yoga Guide

PUBLISHING COMPANY: Yoga Research Foundation **EDITOR:** Swami Jyotirmayananda, Swami Lalitananda **TOPICS:** Yoga **TYPE:** Magazine **SIZE:** 8 1/2 x 11; 120 pgs. **FREQ:** monthly **PRICE:** $15.00 **TERM:** yearly **DESCRIPTION:** Monthly magazine offering the finest in Yoga teachings. Features articles on meditation, classic literature, exercise & spiritual instructions.

Interspacelink Confidential Letter

PUBLISHING COMPANY: National Investigations Committee On Unidentified Flying Objects **EDITOR:** Dr. Frank E. Stranges **TOPICS:** UFO's **TYPE:** Newsletter **FREQ:** monthly **CIRC:** 1,000 **DESCRIPTION:** Reports on all aspects of UFO phenomenon including advice & confidential information.

Introduction To Homeopathic Medicine

PUBLISHING COMPANY: Keats Publishing, Inc. **EDITOR:** H. Boyd **TOPICS:** Homeopathy **TYPE:** Magazine **PRICE:** $14.95

Intuitive Explorations

PUBLISHING COMPANY: Intuitive Explorations **EDITOR:** Gloria Reiser **TOPICS:** Metaphysics, New Age, Psychic, Channeling, Spirituality **TYPE:** Newsletter **DATE:** 1987 **FREQ:** monthly **CIRC:** 1,200 **PRICE:** $20.00 **DESCRIPTION:** Publishes articles, news, interviews, artwork and photography. Also provides book/video/audio and general product reviews.

Inward Path

PUBLISHING COMPANY: Inward Path **PUBLISHER:** Evgeny Shestinsky **EDITOR:** Alexandra Yakovleva **TOPICS:** New Age **TYPE:** Magazine **PRICE:** $20.00 **TERM:** yearly **PRICE PER COPY:** $3.00 **DESCRIPTION:** Russian New Age for human development.

Iridis

PUBLISHING COMPANY: California Society For Psychical Study **EDITOR:** Donald McQuilling **TOPICS:** Parapsychology **TYPE:** Newsletter; 4 pgs. **FREQ:** Monthly **PRICE:** $2.50

Island Calendar

PUBLISHING COMPANY: Alaya Unlimited **EDITOR:** Suzi Osborn **TOPICS:** New Age, Metaphysics **TYPE:** Magazine **DATE:** 1986; 32 pgs. **FREQ:** monthly **CIRC:** 6,000 **PRICE:** $10.00 **TERM:** annually **DESCRIPTION:** An event & networking magazine connecting the Hawaiian Islands to each other & the world. Provides information and inspiration to health practitioners and businesspeople. Prints fiction and non-fiction articles, news, poetry, interviews, artwork, satire, reviews & photography.

Janmabhoomi Panchang

PUBLISHING COMPANY: Janmabhoomi Group of Newspapers **EDITOR:** Jyoti Bhatt **TOPICS:** Astrology **TYPE:** Magazine **DATE:** 1945 **FREQ:** Annual **CIRC:** 46,000

Jewish Vegetarians Of North America Newsletter

PUBLISHING COMPANY: Jewish Vegetarians Of North America **TOPICS:** Health Food, Vegetarianism **TYPE:** Newsletter **FREQ:** quarterly

Jin Shin Do Foundation Newsletter

PUBLISHING COMPANY: Jin Shin Do Foundation **EDITOR:** Iona Teeguarden **TOPICS:** Massage, Spirituality **TYPE:** Newsletter

Journal For Anthroposophy

PUBLISHING COMPANY: Journal For Anthroposophy/Anthroposophical Society In America **EDITOR:** Hilmar Moore **TOPICS:** Metaphysics, New Age, Spirituality **TYPE:** Journal **DATE:** 1965 **SIZE:** 6 x 9; 104 pgs. **FREQ:** semi-annual **CIRC:** 1,400 **PRICE:** $12.00 **TERM:** annually **PRICE PER COPY:** $6.00 **DESCRIPTION:** Publishes articles, book reviews, poetry & artwork. General subject matter is the spiritual science or anthroposophy of Rudolf Steiner, & the many endeavors that have arisen from this work in such

fields as philosophy, medicine, education, work with the handicapped & agriculture. Articles cover eurythmy, biodynamics, Waldorf education, contemporary issues & spiritual heritage. Published by the Anthroposophical Society In America.

Journal Of Astrological Studies

PUBLISHING COMPANY: International Society For Astrological Research, Inc. EDITOR: Julienne P. Mullette TOPICS: Astrology TYPE: Journal DATE: 1970 CIRC: 2,000

Journal Of Borderland Research

PUBLISHING COMPANY: Borderland Science And Research Foundation TOPICS: Metaphysics TYPE: Journal FREQ: 6xbi-monthly DESCRIPTION: Catalog of books & video tapes for sale on subjects such as homeopathy, dowsing, energy fields, alchemy, hypnosis, UFO's & fortean phenomena. Subscription free to members.

Journal Of Chiropractic

PUBLISHING COMPANY: American Chiropractic Association EDITOR: Harry Weiner, Mary Ryan TOPICS: Holistic Healing TYPE: Journal

Journal Of Geocosmic Research

PUBLISHING COMPANY: National Council For Geocosmic Research, Inc. EDITOR: Marsha Kaplan TOPICS: Astrology TYPE: Journal SIZE: 6 x 9; 84 pgs.

Journal Of Graphoanalysis

PUBLISHING COMPANY: International Graphoanalysis Society EDITOR: Kathleen Kusta, Bill Harms TOPICS: New Age TYPE: Journal

Journal Of Holistic Health

PUBLISHING COMPANY: Slawsch Communications EDITOR: Michael Gosney TOPICS: Holistic Healing TYPE: Journal

Journal Of Humanistic Psychology

PUBLISHING COMPANY: Association For Humanistic Psychology EDITOR: Thomas Greening, Ph. D. TOPICS: Holistic Health TYPE: Journal DATE: 1961 FREQ: quarterly PRICE: $34.00 TERM: yearly DESCRIPTION: Fosters a vision of human possibilites through articles on world peace, humanistic psychotherapy, holistic healing, personal growth and spiritual development which integrates theory, research and application.

Journal Of Hypnotherapy

PUBLISHING COMPANY: American Guild Of Hypnotherapists EDITOR: Reg Sheldrick TOPICS: Hypnotism TYPE: Journal

Journal Of Music Therapy

PUBLISHING COMPANY: National Association For Music Therapy TYPE: Journal DESCRIPTION: Concerned with music therapy.

Journal Of Naturopathic Medicine

PUBLISHING COMPANY: American Association Of Naturopathic Physicians TOPICS: Holistic Health, Homeopathy, Health Food, Nutrition TYPE: Journal FREQ: quarterly

Journal Of Near-Death Studies

PUBLISHING COMPANY: Plenum Publishing Corporation EDITOR: Bruce Greyson, Myrtle Bannis TOPICS: New Age TYPE: Journal

Journal Of Nutrition

PUBLISHING COMPANY: American Institute Of Nutrition EDITOR: Willard Visek, John Rice TOPICS: Holistic Healing TYPE: Journal

Journal Of Nutrition Education

PUBLISHING COMPANY: Williams & Wilkins EDITOR: Laura S. Simms TOPICS: Holistic Healing TYPE: Journal

Journal Of Parapsychology

PUBLISHING COMPANY: Foundation For Research On The Nature Of Man, Institute For Parapsychology TOPICS: Parapsychology TYPE: Journal FREQ: quarterly PRICE: $30.00 DESCRIPTION: Quarterly scientific journal covering all aspects of Parapsychology.

Journal Of Psychoactive Drugs

PUBLISHING COMPANY: Journal of Psychoactive Drugs EDITOR: Leif Zerkin TOPICS: New Age, Metaphysics TYPE: Magazine DATE: 1967 FREQ: Quarterly CIRC: 1,000 PRICE: $60.00 DESCRIPTION: Publishes non-fiction articles, reviews and photography relating to substance abuse.

Journal Of Religion And Psychical Research

PUBLISHING COMPANY: Academy Of Religion And Psychical Research EDITOR: Mary Carmen Rose TOPICS: Parapsychology, Occult, Psychic Phenomena TYPE: Journal DATE: 1981 FREQ: quarterly CIRC: 301 PRICE: $8.00 DESCRIPTION: A scholarly approach to the interaction of religion & psychical research.

Journal Of Research In PSI Phenomena

PUBLISHING COMPANY: Queen's University TOPICS: Parapsychology, Occult TYPE: Journal DATE: 1976

Journal Of Research Of The American Federation of Astrologers

PUBLISHING COMPANY: American Federation Of Astrologers, Inc. EDITOR: Richard Nolle TOPICS: Astrology TYPE: Journal

Journal Of Scientifc Exploration

PUBLISHING COMPANY: Society For Scientific Exploration EDITOR: Peter Sturrock TOPICS: Parapsychology, Psychic Phenomena TYPE: Journal

Journal Of The AAVSO

PUBLISHING COMPANY: American Association Of Variable Star Observers EDITOR: Charles Whitney TOPICS: Astrology TYPE: Journal DATE: 1972 SIZE: 5.5 x 8.5; 50 pgs. FREQ: Semi-Annual CIRC: 2,000 PRICE: $25.00 PRICE PER COPY: $10.00 DESCRIPTION: Presentation of scientific papers on variable stars.

Journal Of The American Institute Of Homeopathy

PUBLISHING COMPANY: American Institute Of Homeopathy EDITOR: Karl Robinson TOPICS: Homeopathy TYPE: Journal

Journal Of The American Society For Psychical Research

PUBLISHING COMPANY: American Society For Psychical Research, Inc. EDITOR: Rhea White TOPICS: Parapsychology TYPE: Journal DATE: 1885 SIZE: 6 x 9; 99 pgs. FREQ: Quarterly CIRC: 1,500 PRICE PER COPY: $6.25 DESCRIPTION: Scientific publication providing research reports, theoretical papers & book reviews. Available on film.

Journal Of The Canadian Chiropractic Association

PUBLISHING COMPANY: Canadian Chiropractic Association EDITOR: Dr. Allan Gotlib TOPICS: Holistic Healing TYPE: Journal

Journal Of The Canadian Dietetic Association

PUBLISHING COMPANY: Canadian Dietetic Association EDITOR: Kathleen Harrison TOPICS: Holistic Healing TYPE: Journal FREQ: quarterly PRICE: $45.00 TERM: annually PRICE PER COPY: $10.00 DESCRIPTION: Professional research journal.

Journal Of The Order of Buddhist Contemplatives

PUBLISHING COMPANY: Journal of the Order of Buddhist Contemplatives EDITOR: Rev. Kinzan Learman TOPICS: New Age, Metaphysics TYPE: Journal DATE: 1970 FREQ: quarterly CIRC: 560 PRICE: $15.00 PRICE PER COPY: $3.75 DESCRIPTION: Publishes articles on Buddhism.

Journal Of The Senses

PUBLISHING COMPANY: Journal Of The Senses EDITOR: Ed Lange TOPICS: New Age, Metaphysics TYPE: Magazine DATE: 1961 FREQ: quarterly CIRC: 14,000 PRICE: $4.00 PRICE PER COPY: $1.00 DESCRIPTION: Covers travel and books relating to nudism and alterntive lifestyles. Prints reviews.

Journal Of The Society For Psychical Research

PUBLISHING COMPANY: Society For Psychical Research EDITOR: John Beloff TOPICS: Parapsychology, Occult TYPE: Journal DATE: 1884 FREQ: Quarterly CIRC: 1,000 PRICE: $36.00 DESCRIPTION: Scientifically explores man's psychic abilities & attempts to explain the inexplicable.

Journal Of The Southern California Society For Psychical Research

PUBLISHING COMPANY: Southern California Society For Psychical Research TOPICS: Parapsychology TYPE: Journal SIZE: 6 x 8 1/2; 30 pgs. FREQ: Irregular

Journal Of Traditional Acupuncture

PUBLISHING COMPANY: Traditional Acupuncture Foundation EDITOR: Mary Ellen Zorbaugh TOPICS: Acupuncture TYPE: Journal

Journal Of Transpersonal Psychology

PUBLISHING COMPANY: Transpersonal Institute EDITOR: Miles A. Vich, Kathleen Richard TOPICS: New Age TYPE: Journal

Journal Of UFO Studies

PUBLISHING COMPANY: J. Allen Hynek Center For UFO Studies EDITOR: Michael Swords TOPICS:

UFO's **TYPE:** Journal **DATE:** 1979 **SIZE:** 6 x 9; 100 pgs. **FREQ:** Annually **CIRC:** 500 **PRICE:** $15.00 **PRICE PER COPY:** $15.00 **DESCRIPTION:** Reports on the UFO phenomenon by experts in the field.

Journal Of USPA
PUBLISHING COMPANY: United States Psychotronics Association **EDITOR:** Robert Beutlich **TOPICS:** Psychic Phenomena, Holistic Health, Homeopathy, Acupuncture, Crystals, Color Therapy, Herbalogy **TYPE:** Journal **DATE:** 1975; 30 pgs. **FREQ:** 3xyr **CIRC:** 1,500 **PRICE PER COPY:** $5.00 **DESCRIPTION:** Features articles, news and reviews of music, videos and audio tapes. Sponsors conference.

Journal Of Vampirology
PUBLISHING COMPANY: Journal Of Vampirology **TOPICS:** Occult **TYPE:** Journal

Joy of Life
PUBLISHING COMPANY: Joy of Life **TOPICS:** New Age **TYPE:** Magazine **FREQ:** quarterly **DESCRIPTION:** Covers Florida.

Jung At Heart
PUBLISHING COMPANY: Inner City Books **EDITOR:** Daryl Sharp **TOPICS:** New Age **TYPE:** Newsletter

Jyotisha-Kalpa
PUBLISHING COMPANY: Bharatiga Jyotir Vijyan Parishad **TOPICS:** Astrology **TYPE:** Magazine

K.A.M.
PUBLISHING COMPANY: Keepers Of The Ancient Mysteries **EDITOR:** Robin Culain, Tana Culain **TOPICS:** Parapsychology, Occult **TYPE:** Magazine **DATE:** 1976 **FREQ:** Semi-Annual **CIRC:** 150 **PRICE:** $5.00 **DESCRIPTION:** Covers all aspects of traditional Wicca.

Kabalarian Courier
PUBLISHING COMPANY: Kabalarian Courier **TOPICS:** Parapsychology, Occult **TYPE:** Magazine **DATE:** 1969 **FREQ:** Bi-Monthly

Kabbalah: A Newsletter Of Current Research In Jewish Mysticism
PUBLISHING COMPANY: Kabbalah: A Newsletter Of Current Research In Jewish Mysticism **EDITOR:** Hananya Goodman **TOPICS:** Psychic Phenomena **TYPE:** Newsletter

Kalnirnay
PUBLISHING COMPANY: Sumangal Publishing Co. **EDITOR:** Jayant Salgaonkar **TOPICS:** Astrology **TYPE:** Magazine **DATE:** 1973 **FREQ:** Annual **CIRC:** 2,500

Katuah Journal
PUBLISHING COMPANY: Katuah Journal **EDITOR:** Will Ashe Bason, Rob Messick **TOPICS:** New Age **TYPE:** Newspaper **DESCRIPTION:** Deals with ecology and the American Indian.

Keep Your Pet Healthy The Natural Way
PUBLISHING COMPANY: Keats Publishing, Inc. **EDITOR:** Pat Lazarus, Richard Kearns, D.V.M. **TOPICS:** Holistic Healing **TYPE:** Magazine

Keltria: Journal Of Druidism And Keltic Magick
PUBLISHING COMPANY: Keltria **EDITOR:** Tony Taylor **TOPICS:** Spirituality, Herbalogy, New Age, Metaphysics, Witchcraft, Occult, Paganism **TYPE:** Journal **DATE:** 1984; 20 pgs. **FREQ:** quarterly **CIRC:** 200 **PRICE:** $8.00 **TERM:** annual **PRICE PER COPY:** $2.00 **DESCRIPTION:** Promotes Druidic education & fellowship through articles on theology, herbalogy, ritual, art, music & philosophy. Prints reviews, non-fiction articles, interviews, illustrations and poetry.

Ken Keyes College-Cornucopia
PUBLISHING COMPANY: Ken Keyes College **PUBLISHER:** Ken Keyes, Jr. **TOPICS:** Parapsychology **TYPE:** Magazine **DATE:** 1975; 30 pgs. **FREQ:** Quarterly **CIRC:** 50,000 **DESCRIPTION:** Provides information about books, articles & training at Ken Keyes College.

KidsArt
PUBLISHING COMPANY: KidsArt **TOPICS:** New Age **TYPE:** Magazine

Kooks Magazine
PUBLISHING COMPANY: False Positive/Out-Of-Kontrol Data Korporation **EDITOR:** Donna Kossy **TOPICS:** Occult, New Age, Metaphysics **TYPE:** Magazine **DATE:** 1988 **SIZE:** 8 1/2 x 11; 40 pgs. **FREQ:** 3x per year **CIRC:** 750 **PRICE:** $15.00 **TERM:** 4 issues **PRICE PER COPY:** $4.00 **DESCRIPTION:** Deals with extremism: conspiracy theories; UFO religions; hate-mongers; eccentrics; public philosophers & leafleteers; weird science; paranoid schizophrenic rants; visionaries; New Age religions; cults of all ages; flat earth; hollow earth; Biblical twisting; and more. Focuses on educational and entertainment topics through kooks, extremists and fanatics.

Korythalia
PUBLISHING COMPANY: Korythalia **TOPICS:** Witchcraft, Occult, Paganism **TYPE:** Magazine

Kosmon Voice
PUBLISHING COMPANY: Universal Faithists Of Kosmon, Inc. **EDITOR:** Erma Jean Lee **TOPICS:** New Age, Metaphysics, Channeling **TYPE:** Magazine

Kosmos
PUBLISHING COMPANY: International Society For Astrological Research, Inc. **EDITOR:** Kenneth Gillman, Claire-France Perez **TOPICS:** Astrology **TYPE:** Newsletter **DATE:** 1968 **FREQ:** Quarterly **CIRC:** 1,000 **PRICE:** $20.00

Kosmos Tis Psychis/World Of Soul
PUBLISHING COMPANY: Psychic Society Of Athens **EDITOR:** Georgos Sakellaropoulos **TOPICS:** Parapsychology, Occult **TYPE:** Magazine **DATE:** 1947 **FREQ:** Monthly **CIRC:** 1,000 **PRICE:** $3.50

Kripalu Experience
PUBLISHING COMPANY: Kripalu Center For Yoga And Health **EDITOR:** Lisa Sarasohn **TOPICS:** Holistic Healing **TYPE:** Newsletter

Krishnamurti Foundation Bulletin
PUBLISHING COMPANY: Krishnamurti Foundation Of America **TOPICS:** New Age **TYPE:** Bulletin

Krishnamurti Foundation Of America Newsletter
PUBLISHING COMPANY: Krishnamurti Foundation Of America **EDITOR:** R.E. Mark Lee **TOPICS:** New Age **TYPE:** Newsletter

L'Ere Atlanteenne
PUBLISHING COMPANY: L'Ere Atlanteenne **TOPICS:** Parapsychology, Occult **TYPE:** Magazine **DATE:** 1979 **FREQ:** Weekly

L.A./Orange County Resources
PUBLISHING COMPANY: Community Resource Publications **EDITOR:** Brian Enright **TOPICS:** New Age, Metaphysics, Holistic Health **TYPE:** Calendar **DATE:** 1981 **CIRC:** 120,000 **DESCRIPTION:** A guide listing products and services, covering the LA. and Orange County area. Prints non-fiction and fiction articles, news, reviews, illustrations and photos.

Lakewood's Astrology Annuals
PUBLISHING COMPANY: Lakewood Books **PUBLISHER:** Thomas Stephens **EDITOR:** Don Wigal, Ph.D. **TOPICS:** Astrology **TYPE:** Journal **DATE:** 1978 **SIZE:** 3 x 5; 64 pgs. **FREQ:** Annually **CIRC:** 150,000 **PRICE:** $1.10 **PRICE PER COPY:** $0.79 **DESCRIPTION:** 12 book series on astrology by Adrian Warren published on an annual basis.

Lamp Of Learning Bookstore Books & Services Catalog
PUBLISHING COMPANY: International Church Of Ageless Wisdom Esoteric Seminary **EDITOR:** Roberta Herzog **TOPICS:** Parapsychology **TYPE:** Catalog **DATE:** 1985 **PRICE PER COPY:** $0.00

Lancaster Independent Press
PUBLISHING COMPANY: Lancaster Independent Press **TOPICS:** New Age, Metaphysics **TYPE:** Newspaper; 12 pgs. **PRICE PER COPY:** $0.50 **DESCRIPTION:** Prints news, interviews and cartoons.

Larsen File-Crystal Ball
PUBLISHING COMPANY: Larsen File **TOPICS:** Parapsychology **TYPE:** Newsletter **DATE:** 1979 **SIZE:** 8 1/2 x 11; 20 pgs. **FREQ:** Bi-Monthly **CIRC:** 400 **PRICE:** $15.00 **PRICE PER COPY:** $3.00 **DESCRIPTION:** Deals with controversial topics both past & current.

Le Bulletin Psilog
PUBLISHING COMPANY: Le Bulletin Psilog **TOPICS:** Parapsychology, Occult **TYPE:** Bulletin **DATE:** 1981

Leading Edge Bulletin
PUBLISHING COMPANY: Leading Edge Bulletin **TYPE:** Bulletin **PRICE:** $20.00 **TERM:** yearly

Leading Edge Review
PUBLISHING COMPANY: Leading Edge Review **PUBLISHER:** Sheila Grams **TOPICS:** New Age, Metaphysics **TYPE:** Newsletter **DATE:** 1988; 16 pgs. **FREQ:** quarterly **CIRC:** 80,000 **DESCRIPTION:** Free New Age bookstore newsletter. Serves New Age bookstores with New Age book & tape reviews and advertising.

Leaves Of Twin Oaks

PUBLISHING COMPANY: Twin Oaks Community **EDITOR:** Kat Kinkade **TOPICS:** New Age **TYPE:** Magazine

Les Editions Communiqu'elles

PUBLISHING COMPANY: Les Editions Communiqu'elles **TOPICS:** Holistic Healing **TYPE:** Magazine

Let's Live

PUBLISHING COMPANY: Oxford Industries, Inc. **EDITOR:** T.K. Vodrey, Keith Stepro **TOPICS:** Holistic Healing **TYPE:** Magazine

Lien Hypnotique

PUBLISHING COMPANY: Union Magnetique de Tersas **EDITOR:** Andre Cossette **TOPICS:** Parapsychology **TYPE:** Magazine **SIZE:** 5 x 8; 36 pgs. **FREQ:** Quarterly **PRICE:** $6.00

Life Affiliates

PUBLISHING COMPANY: Life Affiliates **TOPICS:** Metaphysics, Spirituality **TYPE:** Magazine

Life Scribes: The Collective Journal

PUBLISHING COMPANY: Life Scribes: The Collective Journal **TOPICS:** New Age **TYPE:** Newspaper **DESCRIPTION:** Publishes articles to promote personal exploration.

Life Times

PUBLISHING COMPANY: Life Times **TOPICS:** Holistic Healing, Occult, Parapsychology, Channeling **TYPE:** Magazine

Liftoff

PUBLISHING COMPANY: World University Roundtable **EDITOR:** Howard John Zitko **TOPICS:** Parapsychology **TYPE:** Newsletter **DATE:** 1947 **SIZE:** 8 1/2 x 11; 4 pgs. **FREQ:** bi-monthly **CIRC:** 1,000 **PRICE:** $25.00 **TERM:** yearly **DESCRIPTION:** International newsletter of current happenings in the World University development, now in 80 nations.

Ligate West

PUBLISHING COMPANY: Ligate West Publishers **EDITOR:** Audrey Bochnovich **TOPICS:** New Age, Metaphysics **TYPE:** Newsletter **DATE:** 1989 **FREQ:** bi-monthly **PRICE:** $0.00 **DESCRIPTION:** Prints articles relating to body-mind-spirit development.

Light

PUBLISHING COMPANY: College Of Psychic Studies **EDITOR:** Brenda Marshall **TOPICS:** Parapsychology, Occult **TYPE:** Journal **DATE:** 1881 **FREQ:** 3 x/yr. **CIRC:** 2,600 **PRICE:** $12.00 **DESCRIPTION:** A journal of psychic studies.

Light Bearer

PUBLISHING COMPANY: Healing Light Center Church **EDITOR:** Rev. Rosalyn Bruyere **TOPICS:** Numerology **TYPE:** Newsletter

Light Connection, The

PUBLISHING COMPANY: Light Connection, The **EDITOR:** Steve Hays, Marlene Hays **TOPICS:** New Age, Metaphysics **TYPE:** Newspaper **DATE:** 1985 **FREQ:** monthly **CIRC:** 55,000 **PRICE:** $15.00 **DESCRIPTION:** Covers topics such as New Age, health, the environment, and world peace. Reviews books. Targets San Diegans with articles, news, ads and interviews relating to cooperation and understanding.

Light Forum

PUBLISHING COMPANY: Unlimited Thought Bookstore **EDITOR:** Bill Utterback **TOPICS:** New Age, Metaphysics **TYPE:** Newsletter **DATE:** 1987 **FREQ:** monthly **CIRC:** 400 **PRICE:** $35.00 **PRICE PER COPY:** $2.95 **DESCRIPTION:** Published with the Unlimited Thought Foundation.

Light Lines

PUBLISHING COMPANY: L/L Research **EDITOR:** Jim McCarty, Carla Rueckert **TOPICS:** Metaphysics, Spirituality, Channeling **TYPE:** Newsletter **DATE:** 1981; 4 pgs. **FREQ:** quarterly **CIRC:** 5,000 **DESCRIPTION:** Free newsletter sharing spiritual insights & dealing with channeling, messages from spiritual entities & metaphysics.

Light of Consciousness

PUBLISHING COMPANY: Light of Consciousness **EDITOR:** Robert Conrow **TOPICS:** New Age, Metaphysics **TYPE:** Magazine **DATE:** 1977 **FREQ:** 3/year **CIRC:** 650 **PRICE:** $7.00 **PRICE PER COPY:** $3.00 **DESCRIPTION:** Relays the teachings of Swami Amar Jyoti through fiction, non-fiction, poetry, reviews, illustrations and photography.

Light Of Mind

PUBLISHING COMPANY: Light Of Mind Publishing **EDITOR:** David Gordon, Steve Gordon **TOPICS:** New Age **TYPE:** Catalog **SIZE:** 8x10 1/2; 30 pgs. **PRICE PER COPY:** $2.00 **DESCRIPTION:** Catalog of New Age Music, spiritual and motivational audio tapes produced primarily by the pubishers themselves.

Light Of The Egret

PUBLISHING COMPANY: Light Of The Egret **TOPICS:** Metaphysics, Spirituality **TYPE:** Magazine

Light-Net Newsletter

PUBLISHING COMPANY: Light-Net Newsletter **TOPICS:** Metaphysics, Spirituality **TYPE:** Newsletter

Light-Net Prosperity Newsletter

PUBLISHING COMPANY: Patrick O'Connell **EDITOR:** Patrick O'Connell **TOPICS:** Metaphysics **TYPE:** Newsletter

Lightworker

PUBLISHING COMPANY: Lightworker **EDITOR:** Cheri Nichols, Pam Peach **TOPICS:** New Age **TYPE:** Newsletter **DESCRIPTION:** Published by a store, includes Brevard's network.

Linguaggio Astrale

PUBLISHING COMPANY: Centro Italiana di Astrologia **TOPICS:** Astrology **TYPE:** Magazine **DATE:** 1970 **FREQ:** Quarterly **CIRC:** 1,000

Link-Age

PUBLISHING COMPANY: Link-Age· **TOPICS:** New Age **TYPE:** Newspaper **FREQ:** monthly **DESCRIPTION:** Publishes articles that promote personal growth.

Links to the New Age

PUBLISHING COMPANY: Isabelle Smith Enterprises, Ltd. **EDITOR:** Isabelle B. Smith **TOPICS:** New Age, Metaphysics **TYPE:** Newsletter **DATE:** 1988; 6 pgs. **FREQ:** quarterly **CIRC:** 1,000 **PRICE PER COPY:** $2.00 **DESCRIPTION:** Purpose is

to offer discussion of New Age topics for spiritual growth. Serving Central Virginia. Prints non-fiction and fiction articles, news and book/video/audio reviews. Free.

Little Free Press

PUBLISHING COMPANY: Little Free Press **EDITOR:** Ernest Mann **TOPICS:** New Age **TYPE:** Newsletter **DATE:** 1969 **SIZE:** 8 1/2 x 11; 8 pgs. **FREQ:** bi-monthly **CIRC:** 1,000 **DESCRIPTION:** Offers editor's opinions & information about how to live cheaper & change the world wide economic system to one that works for individuals. Subscription free except for postage.

Living Among Nature Daringly!

PUBLISHING COMPANY: Living Among Nature Daringly! **EDITOR:** Bill Anderson **TOPICS:** New Age **TYPE:** Magazine

Living Love

PUBLISHING COMPANY: Port Centauri-Communities Of Light **TOPICS:** New Age **TYPE:** Newsletter; 6 pgs. **FREQ:** quarterly **DESCRIPTION:** News articles written by the residents about their community.

Living Off The Land

PUBLISHING COMPANY: Living Off The Land **EDITOR:** Marvin VanAtta **TOPICS:** Health Food **TYPE:** Magazine

Llewellyn New Times

PUBLISHING COMPANY: Llewellyn Publications **EDITOR:** Steve Degar **TOPICS:** New Age, Metaphysics **TYPE:** Magazine **DATE:** 1987 **FREQ:** bi-monthly **CIRC:** 51,000 **DESCRIPTION:** Publishes articles relating to astrology, the occult and women's spirituality.

Llewellyn's Astrological Calendar

PUBLISHING COMPANY: Llewellyn Publications **EDITOR:** Terry Buske **TOPICS:** Astrology **TYPE:** Calendar **DATE:** 1931 **FREQ:** Annual **CIRC:** 60,000 **PRICE:** $6.95

Longevity

PUBLISHING COMPANY: Longevity **EDITOR:** Rona Cherry, George Ryan **TOPICS:** New Age **TYPE:** Magazine **FREQ:** monthly **DESCRIPTION:** Covers medicine, health, new age, psychology and fitness. Books are reviewed.

Lose Weight Naturally Newsletter

PUBLISHING COMPANY: Rodale Press, Inc. **TOPICS:** Holistic Healing **TYPE:** Newsletter

Lotus Mind

PUBLISHING COMPANY: Universal Entity **TOPICS:** New Age, Spirituality **TYPE:** Newspaper **FREQ:** monthly **DESCRIPTION:** Devoted to the teachings of Zanzoona.

Love

PUBLISHING COMPANY: Love **EDITOR:** Bob Love, Pat Warren **TOPICS:** New Age **TYPE:** Magazine **DATE:** 1978 **FREQ:** Irregular **CIRC:** 100 **PRICE:** $0.00

Love Corps Newsletter

PUBLISHING COMPANY: Spiritual Education Endeavours **TOPICS:** New Age, Spirituality **TYPE:** Newsletter

Loving Brotherhood Newsletter

PUBLISHING COMPANY: Loving Brotherhood, Inc. **EDITOR:** Ralph H. Walker **TOPICS:** New Age **TYPE:** Newsletter

LuminEssence

PUBLISHING COMPANY: LuminEssence Productions **TOPICS:** Channeling **TYPE:** Magazine

Luna Noir: New Orleans Magicks

PUBLISHING COMPANY: Black Moon Publishing **EDITOR:** Louis Martinie, Joe Bounds **TOPICS:** Witchcraft, Voudoun, Occult **TYPE:** Journal **DATE:** 1993

Lung Tsai Tien

PUBLISHING COMPANY: Lung Tsai Tien Tsa Chih She **TOPICS:** Parapsychology, Occult **TYPE:** Magazine **DATE:** 1980 **FREQ:** Bi-Monthly **PRICE:** $20.00

Macoy Astrological Digest

PUBLISHING COMPANY: Macoy Astrological Digest **TOPICS:** Astrology **TYPE:** Magazine

Macrobiotics Today

PUBLISHING COMPANY: George Ohsawa Macrobiotic Foundation **EDITOR:** Sandy Rothman, Carl Ferre **TOPICS:** Holistic Healing **TYPE:** Magazine **DATE:** 1961 **SIZE:** 8 x 10; 40 pgs. **FREQ:** bi-monthly **CIRC:** 3,000 **PRICE:** $15.00 **TERM:** yearly **PRICE PER COPY:** $3.00 **DESCRIPTION:** Timely news & articles about the macrobiotic movement & health.

Mad Scientist

PUBLISHING COMPANY: Heritage Institute of Psychic Science **TOPICS:** Psychic Phenomena, Psychic, New Age **TYPE:** Magazine **FREQ:** monthly **PRICE:** $25.00 **DESCRIPTION:** Features information on self improvement for those interested in the New Age movement.

Maggies Farm

PUBLISHING COMPANY: Maggies Farm **TOPICS:** New Age **TYPE:** Magazine **FREQ:** quarterly **DESCRIPTION:** Serves as a network platform for New Age followers.

Magic Confluence

PUBLISHING COMPANY: Magic Confluence **TOPICS:** Witchcraft, Occult, Paganism **TYPE:** Magazine

Magical Blend Magazine: A Transformative Journey

PUBLISHING COMPANY: Magical Blend Publishers **EDITOR:** Jerry Snider, Michael Peter Langevin **TOPICS:** Psychic Phenomena, Metaphysics, New Age, Astrology, Spirituality **TYPE:** Magazine **DATE:** 1980 **SIZE:** 8 1/2x 11; 98 pgs. **FREQ:** quarterly **CIRC:** 47,000 **PRICE:** $14.00 **PRICE PER COPY:** $4.95 **DESCRIPTION:** Features reviews and articles on art, New Age, astrology, photography and prominent people. Publishes articles, fiction and interviews relating to spirituality and photography. Accepts ads.

Magical Link, The

PUBLISHING COMPANY: Ordo Templi Orientis **TOPICS:** Metaphysics, Spirituality **TYPE:** Newsletter **DATE:** 1982 **FREQ:** quarterly

DESCRIPTION: Published for members only. Limited advertising accepted. Free.

Magickal Unicorn Messenger

PUBLISHING COMPANY: Temple Of Wicca **EDITOR:** Samantha Pugh **TOPICS:** Parapsychology, Occult **TYPE:** Newspaper **DATE:** 1980 **FREQ:** Quarterly **CIRC:** 200 **PRICE:** $9.00 **DESCRIPTION:** Features news, events, articles & reviews concerning the practice of paganism & wicca.

Mail Order Catalog

PUBLISHING COMPANY: Macrobiotic Book Shop **TOPICS:** Holistic Healing **TYPE:** Catalog

Main

PUBLISHING COMPANY: Mark-Age, Inc./Healing Haven/Centers Of Light/University Of Life/Meditations/Inform-Nations **EDITOR:** Pauline Sharpe **TOPICS:** New Age, UFO's, Channeling, Holistic Healing, Metaphysics **TYPE:** Magazine **DATE:** 1960 **FREQ:** quarterly **PRICE:** $20.00 **DESCRIPTION:** Publishes news, information, education & guidelines for linking of lightworkers & groups as a preparation for the Second Coming & New Age Of Aquarius around the year 2000 A.D.

Main Konnection

PUBLISHING COMPANY: Main Konnection **EDITOR:** Darlene Sironen **TOPICS:** New Age **TYPE:** Magazine **DATE:** 1990 **FREQ:** monthly **CIRC:** 25,000 **PRICE:** $12.00 **DESCRIPTION:** Formerly called New Dimensions, this publication serves Las Vegas readers with progressive articles on health and alternate lifestyles.

Main-Ly Sunshine

PUBLISHING COMPANY: Maine-Ly Sunshine **TOPICS:** New Age **TYPE:** Magazine

Many Hands

PUBLISHING COMPANY: Jeff & Diana Krauth Publishers **PUBLISHER:** Jeff Krauth **EDITOR:** Diana Krauth, Polly S. Baumer **TOPICS:** Holistic Healing, New Age, Metaphysics, Channeling **TYPE:** Newspaper **DATE:** 1979 **SIZE:** 10 1/2x 14; 40 pgs. **FREQ:** quarterly **CIRC:** 30,000 **PRICE:** $10.00 **TERM:** yearly **PRICE PER COPY:** $2.50 **DESCRIPTION:** Newsprint magazine. Helpful articles, book, video and audio tape reviews on personal growth and social development.

Massage

PUBLISHING COMPANY: Orenda/Unity Press **EDITOR:** Craig Caughlan, Shane Watson **TOPICS:** Massage **TYPE:** Magazine

Massage Magazine

PUBLISHING COMPANY: Massage Magazine **TOPICS:** Holistic Healing **TYPE:** Magazine

Massage Therapy Journal

PUBLISHING COMPANY: American Massage Therapy Association **EDITOR:** Rafael Tuburan **TOPICS:** Massage **TYPE:** Journal

Master Of Life

PUBLISHING COMPANY: Valley Of The Sun Publishing Co., Sutphen Corporation **EDITOR:** Dick Sutphen, Sharon Boyd **TOPICS:** Metaphysics **TYPE:** Newspaper **DESCRIPTION:** Tabloid newspaper.

Matrix Journal

PUBLISHING COMPANY: Matrix Software **EDITOR:** Michael Erlewine **TOPICS:** Astrology **TYPE:** Journal

Medical Self-Care

PUBLISHING COMPANY: Medical Self-Care **EDITOR:** Carole Pisarczuk, Michael Castleman **TOPICS:** Holistic Healing **TYPE:** Magazine

Medicine Ways

PUBLISHING COMPANY: Church Of Loving Hands, Inc. **EDITOR:** Skyhawk **TOPICS:** Holistic Health, Spirituality **TYPE:** Newspaper **FREQ:** 2 x per year **PRICE:** $5.00 **TERM:** yearly **DESCRIPTION:** Journal of holistic health & natural healing arts. Deals with spiritual issues, massage techniques, homeopathy & numerous holistic health topics. Contains letters, editorials, classifed, display ads & a calendar of events.

Meditate

PUBLISHING COMPANY: S.Y.D.A. Foundation/Siddha Yoga Meditation Ashram **TOPICS:** Meditation **TYPE:** Magazine

Meditation

PUBLISHING COMPANY: Meditation **TOPICS:** Psychic Phenomena **TYPE:** Magazine

Meet The Lords

PUBLISHING COMPANY: Awareness Research Foundation **EDITOR:** Helen Hoag **TOPICS:** Astrology **TYPE:** Newsletter; 4 pgs. **FREQ:** Monthly **PRICE:** $15.00

Mensch Guten Willens

PUBLISHING COMPANY: Cosmopsychologischer Verlag **EDITOR:** Gerhard Ernst Matzke **TOPICS:** New Age **TYPE:** Magazine **DATE:** 1979 **FREQ:** Quarterly **DESCRIPTION:** Covers topics such as New Age, Holistic Lifestyles & Health, New Psychology & Astromed.

Mentifex Communicat

PUBLISHING COMPANY: Project Mentifex **TOPICS:** New Age **TYPE:** Journal **FREQ:** Irregular **DESCRIPTION:** Archival journal. Free.

Mercury Hour

PUBLISHING COMPANY: Mercury Hour **EDITOR:** Edith Custer **TOPICS:** Astrology **TYPE:** Magazine **DATE:** 1974 **SIZE:** 8 1/2 x 11; 68 pgs. **FREQ:** Quarterly **PRICE:** $27.00 **PRICE PER COPY:** $6.75 **DESCRIPTION:** Magazine on astrology through which astrologers communicate with one another.

Meridian

PUBLISHING COMPANY: Ebertin-Verlag **TOPICS:** New Age **TYPE:** Magazine **DATE:** 1979 **FREQ:** Bi-Monthly

Meridian Newsletter

PUBLISHING COMPANY: Meridian Holistic Health Centre, Inc. **EDITOR:** June Cable **TOPICS:** New Age **TYPE:** Newsletter **DESCRIPTION:** Features articles on health, calendar of events, new books & Meridian programs, workshops & classes.

Mescalito - Sprung In Die Unmoeglichkeit

PUBLISHING COMPANY: Indianisches Netzwerk BRD **EDITOR:** Berthold Roeth **TOPICS:**

Parapsychology, Occult **TYPE:** Magazine **DATE:** 1979 **FREQ:** Quarterly

Messages From Michael

PUBLISHING COMPANY: Messages From Michael **TOPICS:** Channeling **TYPE:** Magazine **DESCRIPTION:** The only Michael material authorized by Chelsa Quinn Yarbro.

Messenger, The

PUBLISHING COMPANY: Messenger, The **PUBLISHER:** Robert Ownby **EDITOR:** Patricia Maldonado **TOPICS:** Spirituality, New Age, Psychic **TYPE:** Magazine **DATE:** 1992 **FREQ:** bi-monthly **PRICE:** $36.00 **TERM:** yearly **PRICE PER COPY:** $6.00 **DESCRIPTION:** A spiritualist magazine offering a forum for free expression & the exchange of ideas about spiritual growth. Encourages people to write in & share ideas & psychic experiences.

Meta Science Annual

PUBLISHING COMPANY: MetaScience Foundation **PUBLISHER:** Marc J. Siefer **TOPICS:** Parapsychology, Occult **TYPE:** Journal **DATE:** 1976 **SIZE:** 4 x 8; 160 pgs. **FREQ:** Annual **CIRC:** 2,500 **PRICE:** $25.00 **DESCRIPTION:** Objectively explores & provides information on a wide variety of parapsychological topics such as telepathy, psychokinesis, precognition, synchronicity & UFO's. Also features articles about noted experts such as Wilhelm Reich, Gurdjieff, Uri Geller, The Delai Lama, Sigmund Freud & Carl Jung.

MetaBusiness Monthly Journal

PUBLISHING COMPANY: MetaBusiness Institute/ Conscious Books **EDITOR:** Greg Nielsen **TOPICS:** New Age **TYPE:** Newsletter **FREQ:** monthly

Metamorphic Association Programme

PUBLISHING COMPANY: Metamorphic Association **EDITOR:** Gaston St. Pierre **TOPICS:** Parapsychology, Occult **TYPE:** Magazine **DATE:** 1981 **FREQ:** 3 x/yr. **CIRC:** 1,200 **DESCRIPTION:** Features articles & information on the theory and principles behind metamorphosis & on the practice of self-healing & creative growth through environmental energy.

Metaphysical Digest

PUBLISHING COMPANY: Metaphysical Digest **TOPICS:** Metaphysics, Spirituality **TYPE:** Magazine

Metaphysical Fellowship Church Newsletter

PUBLISHING COMPANY: Metaphysical Fellowship Church **EDITOR:** Yvonne Goodale **TOPICS:** Metaphysics, Parapsychology **TYPE:** Newsletter; 6 pgs. **FREQ:** monthly

Metaphysical Review

PUBLISHING COMPANY: Metaphysical Review **EDITOR:** Bruce Gillespie **TOPICS:** Metaphysics **TYPE:** Magazine

Metapsichica

PUBLISHING COMPANY: Associazione Italiana Scientifica di Metapsichica **EDITOR:** Pertangelo Garzia **TOPICS:** Parapsychology, Occult **TYPE:** Magazine **DATE:** 1946 **CIRC:** 1,000 **DESCRIPTION:** Features information from world wide conferences & articles by Italian authors in the field of parapsychological research.

Metapsychology: The Journal Of Discarnate Intelligence

PUBLISHING COMPANY: Tam Mossman Publishers **EDITOR:** Tam Mossman **TOPICS:** Metaphysics, Channeling **TYPE:** Magazine **DATE:** 1985 **SIZE:** 8 1/2x 11; 96 pgs. **FREQ:** quarterly **CIRC:** 3,500 **PRICE:** $12.00 **TERM:** 4 issues **PRICE PER COPY:** $4.50 **DESCRIPTION:** 96-page ad-free magazine devoted to exploring consciousness outside the body. No longer publishing but all 12 back issue still available. Out-of-print since 1987, this quarterly emphasized channeled material.

Metta

PUBLISHING COMPANY: Maha Guru Metta **PUBLISHER:** Maha Guru Metta **TOPICS:** Occult, Spirituality **TYPE:** Magazine **FREQ:** quarterly **DESCRIPTION:** Spiritual quarterly from Indonesia containing information from the Eastern occult world as well as esoteric articles.

Mezlim

PUBLISHING COMPANY: N'Chi **EDITOR:** Kenneth Deigh **TOPICS:** Witchcraft, Occult, Paganism **TYPE:** Magazine **DATE:** 1989 **SIZE:** 8 x 11; 54 pgs. **FREQ:** quarterly **PRICE:** $20.00 **TERM:** annually **PRICE PER COPY:** $6.00 **DESCRIPTION:** Independent journal for the working Magus. Articles on Ritual, Wicca, Shamanism, Sheya, Tuelema, Golden Dawn, Goddess Worship, Tantra, etc. Purpose is to promote understanding of New Aeonic Magick.

Midnight Horoscope

PUBLISHING COMPANY: Globe Communications Corp. **EDITOR:** Carlson Wade **TOPICS:** Astrology **TYPE:** Magazine **DATE:** 1980 **SIZE:** 6 x 9; 98 pgs. **FREQ:** quarterly **CIRC:** 50,000 **PRICE:** $15.00

Midwifery

PUBLISHING COMPANY: Churchill Livingstone **TOPICS:** Holistic Healing **TYPE:** Magazine

Midwifery Today

PUBLISHING COMPANY: Midwifery Today **EDITOR:** Elizabeth Redditt-Lyon **TOPICS:** Holistic Healing **TYPE:** Magazine

Mighty Natural Magazine

PUBLISHING COMPANY: Mighty Natural Distributors **EDITOR:** Marie Russell **TOPICS:** Holistic Healing, New Age, Metaphysics **TYPE:** Magazine **DATE:** 1985 **FREQ:** monthly **CIRC:** 3,000 **DESCRIPTION:** Resource guide with articles on holistic health, psychology, philosophy, education, events, New Age and metaphysics. Reviews books and music. Accepts ads. Serves most of Florida.

Mind Science Foundation News Bulletin

PUBLISHING COMPANY: Mind Science Foundation **TOPICS:** New Age, Parapsychology **TYPE:** Bulletin; 4 pgs. **FREQ:** quarterly

Mind Tools-Green Light News

PUBLISHING COMPANY: Kryolux, Inc. **PUBLISHER:** Steven Krulick **TOPICS:** Parapsychology **TYPE:** Magazine **DATE:** 1984 **SIZE:** 8 1/2 x 11; 32 pgs. **FREQ:** Bi-Monthly **PRICE:** $15.00 **PRICE PER COPY:** $3.00 **DESCRIPTION:** Reveals practical ways to attain wellness in body, mind & spirit.

Ming Hsiang

PUBLISHING COMPANY: Li Yuan Shu Pao She **TOPICS:** Parapsychology, Occult **TYPE:** Magazine **FREQ:** Monthly

Mini Examiner

PUBLISHING COMPANY: Irene Hamien Stephenson **TOPICS:** Astrology **TYPE:** Newsletter **DATE:** 1979; 4 pgs. **FREQ:** Bi-Weekly **CIRC:** 1,051 **PRICE:** $17.00 **PRICE PER COPY:** $1.00 **DESCRIPTION:** A character analysis of ordinary & famous people showing what they are like in their hearts through Biorhythm Character & Compatibility Analysis.

Mini-Manual For Light-Bearers

PUBLISHING COMPANY: Light Of The Universe **EDITOR:** Helen Spitler **TOPICS:** Channeling **TYPE:** Journal **DATE:** 1987 **FREQ:** quarterly

Minnesota Skeptics Newsletter

PUBLISHING COMPANY: Minnesota Skeptics-Committee For The Scientific Investigation Of Claims Of The Paranormal **EDITOR:** Robert W. McCoy **TOPICS:** Psychic Phenomena **TYPE:** Newsletter

Mito & I.E. E Magia Homem

PUBLISHING COMPANY: Editoria Tres **TOPICS:** Parapsychology, Occult **TYPE:** Magazine

Moksha Journal

PUBLISHING COMPANY: Moksha Journal **EDITOR:** Yogi Ananda Viraj, Yogi Ananda Satyam **TOPICS:** Yoga **TYPE:** Journal

Monk Magazine

PUBLISHING COMPANY: Monk Magazine **EDITOR:** Jim Crotty, Michael Lane **TOPICS:** New Age **TYPE:** Magazine; 96 pgs. **FREQ:** 4 issues/yr **CIRC:** 100,000 **PRICE:** $10.00 **PRICE PER COPY:** $2.50 **DESCRIPTION:** Publishes articles, interviews, updates, cartoons, humor and satire.

Montessori News

PUBLISHING COMPANY: International Montessori Society **TOPICS:** New Age **TYPE:** Newspaper

Monthly Aspectarian

PUBLISHING COMPANY: Monthly Aspectarian **EDITOR:** Guy Spiro **TOPICS:** New Age, Metaphysics, Spirituality, Channeling **TYPE:** Magazine **FREQ:** monthly **CIRC:** 15,000 **PRICE:** $18.00 **DESCRIPTION:** Serves Chicago with articles, calendar and interviews relating to New Age issues.

Monthly Planet

PUBLISHING COMPANY: Monthly Planet **EDITOR:** John Govsky **TOPICS:** New Age **TYPE:** Newspaper **FREQ:** monthly **DESCRIPTION:** Published by the Nuclear Weapons Freeze of Santa Cruz County, prints legislative news, a calendar, and a resource index.

Moon Sign Book

PUBLISHING COMPANY: Llewellyn Publications **PUBLISHER:** Carl Weschcke **EDITOR:** Terry Buske **TOPICS:** Astrology **TYPE:** Calendar **DATE:** 1906 **SIZE:** 4.25 x 5.7; 500 pgs. **FREQ:** Annual **CIRC:** 50,000 **PRICE:** $3.75 **PRICE PER COPY:** $3.95 **DESCRIPTION:** An astrological almanac giving Sun Signs, forecasting news, weather & the stockmarket.

Offers instruction for gardening by the Moon using the cycles of nature.

Mooncircles

PUBLISHING COMPANY: Mooncircles **TOPICS:** Witchcraft, Occult, Paganism **TYPE:** Magazine

Moonrise

PUBLISHING COMPANY: Moonrise **TOPICS:** Witchcraft, Occult, Paganism **TYPE:** Magazine

Moonstone Blue & Night Roses

PUBLISHING COMPANY: Moonstone Blue & Night Roses **EDITOR:** Allen T. Billy, Sandra Wegner **TOPICS:** New Age **TYPE:** Magazine

Morningland Spiritual Journal

PUBLISHING COMPANY: Morningland Publications, Inc. **EDITOR:** Gopi Morningstar **TOPICS:** Astrology **TYPE:** Magazine **FREQ:** Monthly **PRICE:** $7.00

Mother Jones

PUBLISHING COMPANY: Mother Jones **EDITOR:** Douglas Foster **TOPICS:** New Age **TYPE:** Magazine **DATE:** 1976 **FREQ:** monthly **CIRC:** 180,000 **DESCRIPTION:** Prints informative features of national, environmental interest.

Mothering Magazine

PUBLISHING COMPANY: Mothering Publishers, Inc. **EDITOR:** Peggy O'Mara McMahon, John McMahon **TOPICS:** Birth **TYPE:** Magazine

Mountain Astrologer

PUBLISHING COMPANY: Mountain Astrologer **EDITOR:** Tem Tarrktar **TOPICS:** Astrology **TYPE:** Magazine; 48 pgs. **FREQ:** bi-monthly **CIRC:** 3,500 **PRICE:** $14.00 **PRICE PER COPY:** $2.75 **DESCRIPTION:** Provides astrological-related articles that encourage personal growth.

Mountain Luminary

PUBLISHING COMPANY: Mountain Luminary **EDITOR:** Anne M. Thiel **TOPICS:** Metaphysics **TYPE:** Journal **DATE:** 1986; 16 pgs. **FREQ:** quarterly **CIRC:** 3,000 **PRICE:** $10.00 **DESCRIPTION:** International New Age forum. Christian oriented articles on healing, philosophy, environmental issues, poetry and reviews that aid the individual to experience personal wholeness and collective oneness.

Mountain Spirit

PUBLISHING COMPANY: Mountain Spirit **EDITOR:** Lynne Rhoads **TOPICS:** New Age, Holistic Health **TYPE:** Newspaper **DATE:** 1989 **FREQ:** monthly **CIRC:** 18,000 **DESCRIPTION:** Celebrates the spirit of the West with features, interviews, columns & business articles. Serves Sacramento & surrounding areas.

Mountain Voice

PUBLISHING COMPANY: Mountain Voice **EDITOR:** Giorgina Liguori **TOPICS:** New Age **TYPE:** Magazine

Movement Newspaper

PUBLISHING COMPANY: Movement Newspaper **TOPICS:** New Age **TYPE:** Newspaper **FREQ:** Monthly **PRICE:** $15.00

Moxie

PUBLISHING COMPANY: Weider Health & Fitness Group **EDITOR:** Joe Weider **TOPICS:** Holistic Healing **TYPE:** Newsletter

Mufon International UFO Symposium Proceedings

PUBLISHING COMPANY: Mutual UFO Network, Inc. **TOPICS:** UFO's **TYPE:** Magazine **FREQ:** annual **PRICE:** $16.50 **DESCRIPTION:** Speeches given at annual meeting.

Mufon UFO Journal

PUBLISHING COMPANY: Mutual UFO Network, Inc. **TOPICS:** UFO's **TYPE:** Magazine; 24 pgs. **FREQ:** monthly **PRICE:** $25.00 **DESCRIPTION:** Conducts investigations, research & studies to uncover the facts & truth about UFO's.

Muscular Development

PUBLISHING COMPANY: Strength & Health Publishing **EDITOR:** John Terpak, Jan Dellinger **TOPICS:** Holistic Healing **TYPE:** Magazine

Music Connection

PUBLISHING COMPANY: Music Connection **EDITOR:** Eric Patella **TOPICS:** New Age **TYPE:** Magazine **DESCRIPTION:** Targets New Age musicians. Offers music reviews and the official program for the International New Age Music Conference.

Music Of The Spheres

PUBLISHING COMPANY: Paloma Blanca Press **EDITOR:** John Patrick Lamkin **TOPICS:** New Age **TYPE:** Newsletter

Music Paper

PUBLISHING COMPANY: Music Paper **EDITOR:** Karen Wettingfeld **TOPICS:** New Age **TYPE:** Magazine **DESCRIPTION:** Targets New Age musicians and recording artists.

Mutable Dilemma

PUBLISHING COMPANY: Los Angeles Community Church Of Religious Science **EDITOR:** Mark Pottenger **TOPICS:** Astrology, Parapsychology, Occult **TYPE:** Journal **DATE:** 1977 **SIZE:** 5.5 x 8.5; 64 pgs. **FREQ:** Quarterly **CIRC:** 250 **PRICE:** $16.00 **PRICE PER COPY:** $3.00 **DESCRIPTION:** Astrology journal.

MYSIM Newsletter

PUBLISHING COMPANY: Ma Yoga Shakti International Mission **PUBLISHER:** Ma Yoga Shakti **TOPICS:** Yoga, Meditation, Spirituality **TYPE:** Newsletter

Mystic Muse

PUBLISHING COMPANY: Mystic Muse **EDITOR:** John Waltz **TOPICS:** New Age **TYPE:** Magazine **DATE:** 1987; 140 pgs. **FREQ:** 4 issues/yr **CIRC:** 400 **DESCRIPTION:** Prints fiction articles, poetry, illustrations and cartoons.

Mystic Trader, The

PUBLISHING COMPANY: Mystic Trader, The **TOPICS:** Metaphysics, Spirituality **TYPE:** Magazine

Mythos

PUBLISHING COMPANY: Mythos **TOPICS:** Metaphysics, Spirituality **TYPE:** Magazine

N-Nude & Natural

PUBLISHING COMPANY: Naturist Society, Inc. **TOPICS:** New Age **TYPE:** Magazine

Naked Truth

PUBLISHING COMPANY: Naked Truth **TOPICS:** Witchcraft, Occult, Paganism **TYPE:** Magazine

NAPRA Trade Journal

PUBLISHING COMPANY: New Age Publishing and Retailing Alliance **TOPICS:** New Age **TYPE:** Journal **DESCRIPTION:** Distributed to bookstores, publishers, libraries and NAPRA members, this journal reports about and to the publishing and bookselling trade all aspects of New Age information which supports positive individual and social change.

NASO Journal

PUBLISHING COMPANY: National Astrological Society **EDITOR:** Barbara Somerfield **TOPICS:** Astrology **TYPE:** Journal

National Council For Geocosmic Research Memberletter

PUBLISHING COMPANY: National Council For Geocosmic Research, Inc. **PUBLISHER:** Mary B. Downing **EDITOR:** Madalyn Hillis, Van Tuney **TOPICS:** Astrology **TYPE:** Newsletter **DATE:** 1984 **SIZE:** 8.5 x 11; 6 pgs. **FREQ:** Monthly **CIRC:** 3,000 **DESCRIPTION:** Reports on current news of association.

National Fitness Trade Journal

PUBLISHING COMPANY: Wally Boyko Productions, Inc. **PUBLISHER:** Wally Boyko **EDITOR:** Nancy Wager **TOPICS:** Holistic Healing **TYPE:** Magazine **DATE:** 1980; 56 pgs. **FREQ:** quarterly **CIRC:** 20,000 **PRICE:** $20.00 **TERM:** yearly **PRICE PER COPY:** $4.00 **DESCRIPTION:** Geared exclusively to the management & maintenance of health clubs & fitness facilities. Information on the latest in fitness equipment, services & products.

National Nutritional Foods Association Monitor

PUBLISHING COMPANY: National Nutritional Foods Association **TOPICS:** Holistic Healing **TYPE:** Newsletter

National Spiritualist Summit

PUBLISHING COMPANY: National Spiritualist Summit **TOPICS:** New Age **TYPE:** Magazine

National Women's Health Report

PUBLISHING COMPANY: National Women's Health Report, Inc. **EDITOR:** John T. Queenan **TOPICS:** Holistic Healing **TYPE:** Magazine

Natural Fitness Newsletter

PUBLISHING COMPANY: Natural Fitness Newsletter **EDITOR:** Bruce West **TOPICS:** Holistic Healing **TYPE:** Newsletter

Natural Food And Farming

PUBLISHING COMPANY: Natural Food Association **EDITOR:** Bill Francis **TOPICS:** Health Food **TYPE:** Magazine

Natural Food News

PUBLISHING COMPANY: Natural Food Association **TOPICS:** Health Food **TYPE:** Newspaper

Natural Foods Merchandiser

PUBLISHING COMPANY: New Hope Communications EDITOR: Steve Hoffman TOPICS: Health Food TYPE: Magazine; 75 pgs. FREQ: monthly CIRC: 15,000 DESCRIPTION: NFM is a trade tabloid for natural, organic food distributors featuring interviews, news, ads, reviews and articles on health, metaphysics, New Age, nutrition and the environment.

Natural Healing And Nutrition Annual

PUBLISHING COMPANY: Rodale Press, Inc. EDITOR: M. Bricklin TOPICS: Holistic Health, Nutrition TYPE: Magazine PRICE: $19.95

Natural Health Bulletin

PUBLISHING COMPANY: Princeton Educational Publishers EDITOR: Carlson Wade TOPICS: Holistic Healing TYPE: Bulletin

Natural Health Magazine

PUBLISHING COMPANY: East West Health Books EDITOR: Leonard Jacobs, Mark Mayell TOPICS: Holistic Health TYPE: Magazine FREQ: bi-monthly CIRC: 100,000 PRICE: $24.00 PRICE PER COPY: $3.00 DESCRIPTION: Publishes titles on natural foods, cooking, holistic health & alternative, leading edge thinking. Prints reviews of news. Approximately 4 books per year. Also known as The Journal of Natural Health and Living. Accepts ads.

Natural Health World

PUBLISHING COMPANY: Naturopath Publishing Co. EDITOR: J.W. Noble, Robert Noble TOPICS: Holistic Healing TYPE: Magazine

Natural Health World And The Naturopath

PUBLISHING COMPANY: Natural Health World And The Naturopath EDITOR: Robert W. Noble, Mrs. John W. Noble TOPICS: Holistic Healing TYPE: Magazine

Natural Health: The Guide To Well-Being

PUBLISHING COMPANY: East West TOPICS: Holistic Health, Health Food, Nutrition, Vegetarianism, Homeopathy TYPE: Magazine FREQ: bi-monthly PRICE: $15.00 TERM: yearly

Natural Physique

PUBLISHING COMPANY: Chelo Publishing EDITOR: Bob Birmingham TOPICS: Holistic Healing TYPE: Magazine

Naturally Yours

PUBLISHING COMPANY: Backwoods Books EDITOR: Marci Cunningham TOPICS: New Age TYPE: Magazine

NCGR Journal

PUBLISHING COMPANY: National Council Of Geocosmic Research PUBLISHER: Maria Kay Simms EDITOR: Maritha Pottenger TOPICS: Astrology TYPE: Journal DATE: 1971

Neometaphysical Digest

PUBLISHING COMPANY: Society of Metaphysicians Ltd. EDITOR: J.J. Williamson TOPICS: Parapsychology, Occult TYPE: Magazine DATE: 1952 FREQ: Biennial CIRC: 60,000 PRICE: $20.00 DESCRIPTION: A digest offering information on metaphysics.

Net

PUBLISHING COMPANY: Net EDITOR: Kevin Langdon TOPICS: New Age, Metaphysics TYPE: Magazine DATE: 1978; 40 pgs. FREQ: 6 issues/yr DESCRIPTION: Prints non-fiction, reviews & interviews, criticisms and essays on insights in psychology, religion, science and philosophy.

Network

PUBLISHING COMPANY: Network EDITOR: Dennis Kazmierczak TOPICS: New Age, Metaphysics TYPE: Newspaper DATE: 1986; 32 pgs. FREQ: bi-monthly CIRC: 10,000 PRICE: $15.00 PRICE PER COPY: $3.00 DESCRIPTION: Prints reviews, non-fiction articles, news, poetry and interviews, relating to promoting community and personal harmony.

Network

PUBLISHING COMPANY: Whole Life Network EDITOR: Sara Elana, Hassan Ghandchi TOPICS: New Age TYPE: Magazine FREQ: bi-monthly CIRC: 50,000 PRICE: $18.00 DESCRIPTION: Serves Santa Clara, Santa Cruz and Monterey California counties. Prints logos listings, events calendar, articles and product reviews.

Network News

PUBLISHING COMPANY: Network News TOPICS: New Age TYPE: Newspaper DESCRIPTION: Prints news, interviews and articles relating to personal growth, healing and the arts. Also lists resources.

Network Of Light

PUBLISHING COMPANY: Network Of Light TOPICS: Occult, Parapsychology TYPE: Magazine

Networker Magazine

PUBLISHING COMPANY: Networker Magazine EDITOR: Diane M. Cooper, Steve Jester TOPICS: New Age, Metaphysics, Holistic Health TYPE: Magazine DATE: 1986 SIZE: 8 x 10 1/2; 48 pgs. FREQ: 6 issues/yr. CIRC: 15,000 DESCRIPTION: Guide that promotes living a balanced life. Features articles on homeopathy, holistic health, Astrology, etc. Serves the Gold Coast & Southern Florida. Free.

New Age

PUBLISHING COMPANY: Supreme Council 33rd Degree A EDITOR: Henry C. Clausen TOPICS: New Age TYPE: Magazine

New Age - Calendar Section

PUBLISHING COMPANY: Rising Star Associates EDITOR: Karen Sosnoski TOPICS: New Age TYPE: Calendar

New Age Digest

PUBLISHING COMPANY: New Age Press EDITOR: Jim Butler TOPICS: New Age TYPE: Magazine

New Age Events

PUBLISHING COMPANY: New Age Events TOPICS: Occult, Parapsychology TYPE: Magazine

New Age Exchange

PUBLISHING COMPANY: Zoan Publishing Co., Inc. EDITOR: S. Jasinski TOPICS: New Age, Channeling, Metaphysics TYPE: Magazine DATE: 1986 FREQ: Bi-Monthly CIRC: 1,000 PRICE: $18.00 DESCRIPTION: Features current metaphysical ideas.

New Age Herald

PUBLISHING COMPANY: New Age Herald TOPICS: New Age TYPE: Magazine

New Age Journal

PUBLISHING COMPANY: Rising Star Associates EDITOR: David Thorne, Florence Graves TOPICS: New Age, Spirituality, Channeling TYPE: Magazine FREQ: monthly CIRC: 180,000 PRICE PER COPY: $2.95 DESCRIPTION: Features articles on health, metaphysics, psychology, travel and the environment. Reviews books, videos and music. Prints non-fiction, news, ads and reviews relating to self-help, science and creativity.

New Age Link

PUBLISHING COMPANY: New Age Link EDITOR: Randall Thorne TOPICS: New Age TYPE: Newsletter DATE: 1988; 12 pgs. FREQ: 3 x per year CIRC: 500 PRICE: $9.00 PRICE PER COPY: $4.00 DESCRIPTION: Reports on activities, meetings, news, announcements, etc. related to the New Age Link Association.

New Age Living

PUBLISHING COMPANY: New Age Living EDITOR: Les Bruusema TOPICS: New Age, Metaphysics, Spirituality TYPE: Magazine DATE: 1988 FREQ: quarterly CIRC: 80,000 PRICE: $11.96 PRICE PER COPY: $2.50 DESCRIPTION: Prints feature articles, news, interviews, entertainment reviews, cartoons and artwork. Offered at $11.96 per 6 issues.

New Age Marketing Newsletter

PUBLISHING COMPANY: First Editions EDITOR: Sophia Tarila, Ph.D., Harry Truner TOPICS: New Age TYPE: Newsletter DATE: 1989 FREQ: bi-monthly PRICE: $20.00 DESCRIPTION: Provides up-to-the-minute information on New Age marketing opportunities. Useful to anyone interested in promoting a product or service to the New Age, Metaphysical or Holistic Health field. Reviews books, products, services, videos and tapes. Also prints articles relating to business & marketing strategies.

New Age Network Of Colorado Springs

PUBLISHING COMPANY: New Age Network Of Colorado Springs TOPICS: Holistic Healing TYPE: Magazine

New Age News

PUBLISHING COMPANY: New Age News TOPICS: Holistic Healing TYPE: Newspaper

New Age Professional

PUBLISHING COMPANY: New Age Professional EDITOR: Glen W. Knape TOPICS: New Age, Metaphysics TYPE: Newsletter DATE: 1988; 12 pgs. FREQ: quarterly CIRC: 500 PRICE: $19.95 PRICE PER COPY: $5.50 DESCRIPTION: A source & information guide which prints non-fiction articles, satire, product reviews and news for those training to become New Age healers, teachers and practitioners.

New Age Reports

PUBLISHING COMPANY: Ancient Truth Research Foundation **TOPICS:** New Age **TYPE:** Magazine

New Age Retailer
PUBLISHING COMPANY: Continuity Publishing **EDITOR:** Duane Sweeney, Pat Freeman Brown **TOPICS:** New Age **TYPE:** Magazine **DATE:** 1987 **FREQ:** monthly **PRICE PER COPY:** $3.00 **DESCRIPTION:** New Age trade publication featuring articles, ads and reviews on books, music and specialty products.

New Age Source
PUBLISHING COMPANY: New Age Source **EDITOR:** Gene Pearcy, Dorothy Nasatir **TOPICS:** New Age **TYPE:** Magazine

New Age Teachings Newsletter
PUBLISHING COMPANY: New Age Teachings **EDITOR:** Anita Afton **TOPICS:** New Age **TYPE:** Newsletter

New Age World Polaris Newsletter
PUBLISHING COMPANY: New Age World Religious & Scientific Research Foundation **PUBLISHER:** Victoria Vandertuin **EDITOR:** David K. Roy **TOPICS:** Parapsychology **TYPE:** Newsletter **DATE:** 1978 **SIZE:** 8 1/2 x 11; 25 pgs. **FREQ:** Annual **CIRC:** 500 **PRICE PER COPY:** $5.00 **DESCRIPTION:** Features non-fiction, fiction & poetry by new authors on topics such as the New Age Movement, occult and metaphysics.

New Age-Examiner
PUBLISHING COMPANY: Scranton Times **EDITOR:** James Dillon **TOPICS:** New Age **TYPE:** Newspaper

New Alberta
PUBLISHING COMPANY: New Alberta **TOPICS:** Metaphysics, Spirituality, Holistic Healing **TYPE:** Magazine

New Atlantean Journal
PUBLISHING COMPANY: Oconnell **TOPICS:** Parapsychology, Occult **TYPE:** Journal **FREQ:** Quarterly

New Atlantean, The
PUBLISHING COMPANY: New Atlantean, The **TOPICS:** Metaphysics, Spirituality **TYPE:** Magazine

New Awareness Magazine
PUBLISHING COMPANY: New Awareness, Inc. **EDITOR:** William E. Woods, J.L. Denchfield **TOPICS:** New Age, Holistic Healing, Occult, Crystals, Spirituality, Astrology **TYPE:** Magazine **DATE:** 1987; 56 pgs. **FREQ:** monthly **PRICE:** $12.00 **DESCRIPTION:** New Age magazine featuring topics such as self-healing, occult, crystals. Also book reviews. Prints articles, reviews, columns, ads, resource guide and a local events' calendar. Deals primarily with Florida area.

New Colorado
PUBLISHING COMPANY: New Colorado **EDITOR:** Hans Schmidt **TOPICS:** New Age **TYPE:** Magazine **FREQ:** monthly **PRICE:** $15.00 **DESCRIPTION:** A calendar-format forum on natural living. Prints articles, news, reviews, and resources.

New Dimensions

PUBLISHING COMPANY: Foundation Of Human Understanding **EDITOR:** David Kupelian, David Masters **TOPICS:** Holistic Healing **TYPE:** Magazine

New Dimensions
PUBLISHING COMPANY: New Dimensions **TOPICS:** New Age, Holistic Health, Metaphysics **TYPE:** Magazine

New Dimensions Newsletter
PUBLISHING COMPANY: New Dimensions Radio **EDITOR:** Michael Toms, Justin Toms **TOPICS:** New Age **TYPE:** Newsletter; 8 pgs. **CIRC:** 35,000 **DESCRIPTION:** Accepts ads.

New Dimensions Radio Network
PUBLISHING COMPANY: New Dimensions Radio **TOPICS:** New Age **TYPE:** Newsletter

New Directions in Music/A.R.E.
PUBLISHING COMPANY: New Directions in Music/A.R.E. **EDITOR:** Keith Vonder-Ohe **TOPICS:** New Age **TYPE:** Magazine **DESCRIPTION:** Prints news and reviews on music.

New England Journal Of Parapsychology
PUBLISHING COMPANY: Franklin Pierce College **EDITOR:** W. H. Jack **TOPICS:** Parapsychology, Occult **TYPE:** Journal **DATE:** 1977 **FREQ:** Quarterly

New Environment Bulletin
PUBLISHING COMPANY: New Environment Association **EDITOR:** Harry Schwarzlander **TOPICS:** New Age **TYPE:** Bulletin **DATE:** 1974 **FREQ:** Monthly **CIRC:** 200 **PRICE:** $6.50 **DESCRIPTION:** Contains articles, reviews & announcements pertaining to the creation of a peaceful & environmentally conscious society. Also reports on activities of the New Environmental Association.

New Farm
PUBLISHING COMPANY: Regenerative Agriculture Association **EDITOR:** George DeVault **TOPICS:** Health Food **TYPE:** Magazine

New Florida
PUBLISHING COMPANY: Hibiscus Enterprises **EDITOR:** Arjuna da Silva **TOPICS:** New Age **TYPE:** Newspaper **DATE:** 1986 **FREQ:** bi-monthly **CIRC:** 15,000 **PRICE:** $18.00 **DESCRIPTION:** Serves Florida and surrounding area. Prints articles, fiction & non-fiction, children's information, literary works such as poetry, satire, plays, artwork, illustrations, cartoons, photography, multi-media reviews & ads.

New Frontier Magazine
PUBLISHING COMPANY: NRW Frontier Education Society **EDITOR:** Swami Nostradamus Virato, Michael Diamond **TOPICS:** New Age, Metaphysics, Holistic Healing, Channeling **TYPE:** Magazine **DATE:** 1980 **SIZE:** 8 x 10; 84 pgs. **FREQ:** monthly **CIRC:** 60,000 **PRICE:** $18.00 **TERM:** yearly **PRICE PER COPY:** $1.95 **DESCRIPTION:** Subtitled: Magazine of Transformation. Deals with emerging concepts in holistic health, energy medicine, natural foods & New Age general subjects. Includes news items from around the world & columns by known leaders in the field of consciousness. Offers articles, ads, illustrations, photography & reviews on music, books, holistic health & the environment. Regional editions in Florida & Rocky Mountains.

New Frontiers
PUBLISHING COMPANY: New Frontiers Center/Fellowship Farm **EDITOR:** Mary Jo Uphoff, Prof. Walter H. Uphoff **TOPICS:** Parapsychology, Holistic Health **TYPE:** Newsletter **DATE:** 1982 **SIZE:** 8 1/2 x 11; 24 pgs. **FREQ:** semi-annual **CIRC:** 1,100 **PRICE:** $5.00 **DESCRIPTION:** Supplies information, education & research on unusual events, alternative healing methods & psychic phenomena.

New Frontiers
PUBLISHING COMPANY: New Frontiers **TOPICS:** Metaphysics, Spirituality **TYPE:** Magazine

New Horizons
PUBLISHING COMPANY: New Horizons Research Foundation **TOPICS:** Parapsychology, Occult **TYPE:** Magazine **DATE:** 1972 **FREQ:** Annual

New Menorah
PUBLISHING COMPANY: P'Nai Or Religious Fellowship **EDITOR:** Arthur Waskow, Ph. D., Rabbi Shana Margolin **TOPICS:** Spirituality, Kabbalah **TYPE:** Journal; 20 pgs. **FREQ:** quarterly **PRICE:** $18.00

New Millenium-Practical Guidance For Personal Growth
PUBLISHING COMPANY: Love & Light Enterprises **EDITOR:** Ann Buzenberg, Carol A. Strickland **TOPICS:** Channeling, Spirituality, New Age **TYPE:** Newsletter **DATE:** 1990; 8 pgs. **FREQ:** monthly **PRICE:** $39.90 **TERM:** annually **PRICE PER COPY:** $3.00 **DESCRIPTION:** Articles by well known authors & practitioners. Includes personal guidance by channeled entities, Native American wisdom & daily guidance. The information given offers various ways of attuning to changing personal & cosmic energies-mentally, emotionally, physically & spiritually. Covers all aspects of the New Age movement. Illustrations, cartoons, drawings, photographs & how-to articles. Newsletter with magazine format. Ads accepted.

New Options Newsletter
PUBLISHING COMPANY: New Options **TOPICS:** Occult, New Age **TYPE:** Newsletter **DESCRIPTION:** Provides a responsible approach to news, events, politics & social change organizations.

New Options Newsletter
PUBLISHING COMPANY: Shambala Publications **TOPICS:** New Age **TYPE:** Newsletter

New Realities
PUBLISHING COMPANY: Heldref Publications, Inc. **EDITOR:** Neal Vahle **TOPICS:** Metaphysics, New Age, Holistic Health **TYPE:** Magazine **FREQ:** bi-monthly **CIRC:** 17,000 **PRICE:** $18.00 **DESCRIPTION:** Covers new age, metaphysics, health, fitness and the environment. Also does book reviews. Articles focus on personal growth and changing lifestyles. Accepts ads.

New Texas Magazine
PUBLISHING COMPANY: New Texas Magazine **EDITOR:** Steve Dodds **TOPICS:** Holistic Healing, New Age **TYPE:** Magazine **FREQ:** monthly **CIRC:** 30,000 **DESCRIPTION:** Prints articles, ads, events calendar and directory.

New Thought

PUBLISHING COMPANY: International New Thought Alliance EDITOR: Dr. Blaine C. Mays TOPICS: Metaphysics, New Age TYPE: Magazine DATE: 1913; 48 pgs. FREQ: quarterly CIRC: 5,000 PRICE: $8.00 PRICE PER COPY: $2.25 DESCRIPTION: Deals with New Age, metaphysical & spiritual issues. Offers non-fiction articles, reviews books & audio tapes, & produces tapes of speakers on spiritual topics. Accepts ads.

New Thunderbird Chronicle

PUBLISHING COMPANY: New Thunderbird Chronicle EDITOR: Ed Voynow TOPICS: New Age TYPE: Magazine CIRC: 20,000 PRICE: $0.00 DESCRIPTION: Covers L.A., Orange, Santa Barbara and San Diego counties. Prints articles focusing on health, awareness, and space age.

New Times

PUBLISHING COMPANY: Silver Owl Publications, Inc. EDITOR: Krysta Gibson TOPICS: New Age, Metaphysics TYPE: Newspaper DATE: 1985 SIZE: 22 x 14; 24 pgs. FREQ: monthly CIRC: 30,000 PRICE: $10.50 TERM: yearly PRICE PER COPY: $1.50 DESCRIPTION: Publication for people interested in personal & planetary growth, alternative spirituality & peace. Publishes articles, ads, book and music reviews relating to peace, personal and global awareness.

New Visions

PUBLISHING COMPANY: New Visions EDITOR: Edwin Treitler TOPICS: Holistic Healing, New Age, Nutrition, Spirituality, Metaphysics TYPE: Newspaper; 36 pgs. FREQ: quarterly DESCRIPTION: Wholistic publication promoting new ideas in health, metaphysics & spirituality. Prints articles on health and well-being, as well as resources such as events, conferences and products. Free.

New World

PUBLISHING COMPANY: New World TOPICS: New Age TYPE: Newspaper DESCRIPTION: New Age, holistic newspaper featuring news, events, calendar, interviews, articles & ads. Deals primarily with CA but also international issues.

Newaeon Newsletter, The

PUBLISHING COMPANY: Newaeon Newsletter, The EDITOR: G.M. Kelly TOPICS: Metaphysics, Spirituality, Skepticism TYPE: Newsletter FREQ: bi-monthly PRICE: $6.66 PRICE PER COPY: $1.31 DESCRIPTION: Exposes charlatans using Thelema & explains both Crowley & Thelema in several ways.

Newlife

PUBLISHING COMPANY: Newlife EDITOR: Mark Beck TOPICS: Nutrition, Herbalogy, Holistic Health TYPE: Magazine FREQ: bi-monthly PRICE: $10.00 PRICE PER COPY: $2.00 DESCRIPTION: Prints articles, news, restaurant and health food store guide, and a calendar.

News From Mother Grove

PUBLISHING COMPANY: News From Mother Grove TOPICS: Witchcraft, Occult, Paganism TYPE: Newspaper

News Novel

PUBLISHING COMPANY: News Novel EDITOR: Darlene Wheeler TOPICS: Parapsychology, Occult TYPE: Magazine DATE: 1969 FREQ: Irregular

Newsenfests

PUBLISHING COMPANY: Newsenfests TOPICS: Witchcraft, Occult, Paganism TYPE: Newspaper

Newsletter Of The American Association Of Music Therapy

PUBLISHING COMPANY: Newsletter Of The American Association Of Music Therapy TYPE: Newsletter

Newsletter Of The American Society For Psychical Research-ASPR Newsletter

PUBLISHING COMPANY: American Society For Psychical Research, Inc. EDITOR: Donna L. McCormick TOPICS: Parapsychology, Psychic Phenomena TYPE: Newsletter DATE: 1968 SIZE: 8 1/2 x 11; 10 pgs. FREQ: quarterly CIRC: 2,000 PRICE: $35.00 DESCRIPTION: Features articles & information about news, research & current developments in parapsychology. Discusses organizations, publications, educational opportunities and lectures about scientific parapsychology.

Newslogue

PUBLISHING COMPANY: Sohnen-Moe Associates EDITOR: Cherie Sohnen-Moe TOPICS: New Age, Holistic Health TYPE: Newsletter FREQ: 3 x per year DESCRIPTION: A newsletter & catalogue geared to healing arts practitioners.

Nexus

PUBLISHING COMPANY: Nexus: A Means Of Connection EDITOR: Ravi Dykema TOPICS: Holistic Health TYPE: Newspaper DATE: 1980; 40 pgs. FREQ: 6 x per year CIRC: 45,000 PRICE: $12.00 TERM: annually DESCRIPTION: Healthy living for Denver & Boulder. Catalog-format publication. Prints books, music & video reviews, features, ads, news and calendar.

Nexus New Times

PUBLISHING COMPANY: Nexus New Times TOPICS: New Age TYPE: Magazine FREQ: quarterly CIRC: 50,000 DESCRIPTION: Published in Australia. Prints news & articles on today's changing lifestyles and environment.

Night Owl Press

PUBLISHING COMPANY: Night Owl Press TOPICS: Metaphysics, Spirituality TYPE: Magazine

Night Vision-A Dream Journal

PUBLISHING COMPANY: Night Vision-A Dream Journal EDITOR: Steve Racicot, Anna Racicot TOPICS: Dreams TYPE: Magazine DATE: 1990; 40 pgs. FREQ: quarterly PRICE: $10.00 PRICE PER COPY: $2.50 DESCRIPTION: Explores the fascinating world of dreams, precognitive dreams, the meaning of symbols & lucid dreaming. Invites reader's participation in our travels through the suprising frontier of human consciousness. Delves behind the images of dreams to seek the reality which they represent, their meanings & the consciousness which that meaning invokes. Free brochure.

Ninth Wave Newsletter

PUBLISHING COMPANY: Ninth Wave Newsletter EDITOR: Lee LaRay TOPICS: New Age, Metaphysics TYPE: Newsletter DATE: 1987 DESCRIPTION: Informative resource for psychic fairs & related events. Prints non-fiction, fiction, news, reviews and artwork.

Nocturnal News

PUBLISHING COMPANY: Baker Street Publications TOPICS: New Age TYPE: Newspaper

Noetic Sciences Bulletin

PUBLISHING COMPANY: Institute Of Noetic Sciences TOPICS: Body-Mind Connection, Holistic Health, Spirituality, Past Life Regression, Death, Meditation, Hypnotism TYPE: Bulletin FREQ: quarterly DESCRIPTION: Reports on Institute projects, member activites, and upcoming conferences and lectures.

Noetic Sciences Catalog

PUBLISHING COMPANY: Institute Of Noetic Sciences TOPICS: Body-Mind Connection, Holistic Health, Spirituality, Past Life Regression, Death, Meditation, Hypnotism TYPE: Catalog DESCRIPTION: Resource guide to books and audio and video tapes in related fields of study.

Noetic Sciences Review

PUBLISHING COMPANY: Institute Of Noetic Sciences TOPICS: Body-Mind Connection, Holistic Health, Spirituality, Past Life Regression, Death, Meditation, Hypnotism TYPE: Journal FREQ: quarterly DESCRIPTION: Offers discussion of emerging concepts in consciousness research, the mind-body connection and healing, and our changing global reality. Free to members.

NOHA News

PUBLISHING COMPANY: Nutrition For Optimal Health Association EDITOR: Marjorie Fisher TOPICS: Holistic Healing TYPE: Newspaper

North Florida Astrology Association Newsletter

PUBLISHING COMPANY: North Florida Astrology Association EDITOR: Joan Johns TOPICS: Astrology TYPE: Newsletter DATE: 1973; 4 pgs. FREQ: Monthly CIRC: 100 PRICE: $15.00 DESCRIPTION: Covers many astrological topics & offers current news information.

North Wind Network

PUBLISHING COMPANY: North Wind Network TOPICS: Witchcraft, Occult, Paganism TYPE: Magazine

Notes From Taychopera

PUBLISHING COMPANY: Notes From Taychopera TOPICS: Witchcraft, Occult, Paganism TYPE: Magazine

Nous Letter

PUBLISHING COMPANY: Linear EDITOR: Peter Crane TOPICS: Astrology TYPE: Newsletter DATE: 1974 FREQ: Semi-Annual PRICE: $3.00 DESCRIPTION: Reports on noetics which is the study of the nature of consciousness & altering states.

Nucleus Publications-Mail Order Catalog

PUBLISHING COMPANY: Nucleus Publications EDITOR: Vimala McClure, Michael McClure TOPICS: New Age TYPE: Catalog SIZE: 8 1/2 x 11; 30 pgs. DESCRIPTION: Catalog promoting own books as well as other authors in the fields of holistic health, creativity, spirituality, relationships & community. Featuring works of P.R. Sarkar.

Nuovo Mondo Occulto

PUBLISHING COMPANY: Centro Studi Rosacrux TOPICS: Parapsychology, Occult TYPE: Magazine DATE: 1971 FREQ: Monthly

Nutrition

PUBLISHING COMPANY: Dimon, Inc. EDITOR: Michael Meguid, M.D., Clint Dimon TOPICS: Holistic Healing TYPE: Magazine

Nutrition Action Health Letter

PUBLISHING COMPANY: Nutrition Action Health Letter EDITOR: Stephen B. Schmidt TOPICS: Holistic Healing TYPE: Newsletter

Nutrition Health Review

PUBLISHING COMPANY: Nutrition Health Review EDITOR: Frank R. Rifkin, Andrew Rifkin TOPICS: Holistic Healing TYPE: Magazine

Nutrition In Clinical Practice

PUBLISHING COMPANY: Williams & Wilkins EDITOR: Alma Wills, Philip Schneider TOPICS: Holistic Healing TYPE: Magazine

Nutrition Review

PUBLISHING COMPANY: MPI Medical Publishing, Inc. EDITOR: John Stephenson TOPICS: Holistic Healing TYPE: Newsletter

Nutrition Reviews

PUBLISHING COMPANY: International Life Sciences Institute-Nutrition Foundation EDITOR: Dr. Irwin H. Rosenberg TOPICS: Holistic Healing TYPE: Newsletter

Nutrition Today

PUBLISHING COMPANY: Williams & Wilkins EDITOR: Helen Guthrie, Ph.D. TOPICS: Holistic Healing TYPE: Magazine

O.H.A.I. Bulletin

PUBLISHING COMPANY: Oriental Healing Arts Institute EDITOR: Pi-Kwang Tsung TOPICS: Homeopathy TYPE: Bulletin DATE: 1976 FREQ: Quarterly CIRC: 500 PRICE: $30.00

Occultation Newsletter

PUBLISHING COMPANY: International Occultation Timing Association TOPICS: Parapsychology TYPE: Newsletter

Odinist, The

PUBLISHING COMPANY: Odinist, The TOPICS: Witchcraft, Occult, Paganism TYPE: Magazine

Odyssey-Moving Toward Personal & Planetary Wellbeing

PUBLISHING COMPANY: Odyssey EDITOR: Ernest A. Rose TOPICS: New Age, Metaphysics TYPE: Newspaper DATE: 1990; 8 pgs. FREQ: monthly

CIRC: 10,000 PRICE: $15.00 TERM: yearly DESCRIPTION: Serves Northern New England, Maine, NH, VT, with news on wholistic living. Contains professional health practices, environmental issues, personal experiences, calendar of events, product reviews, fiction, non-fiction & news. Editorial intent is to share positive, enlightening information which will benefit the reader. Free.

Of A Like Mind

PUBLISHING COMPANY: Of A Like Mind EDITOR: Lynnie Levy TOPICS: New Age, Metaphysics, Spirituality, Occult TYPE: Newspaper DATE: 1983; 22 pgs. FREQ: quarterly CIRC: 10,000 PRICE: $13.00 PRICE PER COPY: $3.00 DESCRIPTION: A woman's spiritual publication & network serving as forum for women seeking spiritual growth. Focus is on women's spirituality, Goddess religions, paganism & our earth connections from a feminist perspective. Offers a broad variety of articles on women's spirituality, wellness, Astrology, Tarot, Psychic Development, dreams, herbs, ethics, politics, & other cultures while focusing on the Wiccan tradition.

Off Our Backs

PUBLISHING COMPANY: Off Our Backs TOPICS: New Age TYPE: Magazine

Offshoots Of Orgonomy

PUBLISHING COMPANY: Offshoots Publications TOPICS: Parapsychology TYPE: Magazine SIZE: 8 1/2 x 11; 72 pgs. FREQ: Semi-Annual CIRC: 1,000 PRICE: $15.00 PRICE PER COPY: $7.50 DESCRIPTION: Pertains to the varied forms of energy in the universe including life energy.

Old Religion, The

PUBLISHING COMPANY: Old Religion, The TOPICS: Witchcraft, Occult, Paganism TYPE: Magazine

Omega News

PUBLISHING COMPANY: Omega News EDITOR: Eileen Duveen TOPICS: New Age TYPE: Newsletter DESCRIPTION: Articles, excerpts and book reviews.

Omni

PUBLISHING COMPANY: Omni EDITOR: Marcia Schultz TOPICS: New Age TYPE: Magazine DATE: 1978 FREQ: monthly CIRC: 950,000 PRICE: $24.00 TERM: yearly DESCRIPTION: Leading consumer magazine dealing with what will happen in the future. Covers science, health, technology, space, science fiction & the mind. Prints articles both fiction & non-fiction, news, interviews and brilliant photographs.

On The Edge

PUBLISHING COMPANY: On The Edge EDITOR: Cathryn McIntyre TOPICS: New Age, Metaphysics TYPE: Magazine DATE: 1983; 40 pgs. FREQ: 3 issues/yr PRICE: $9.00 PRICE PER COPY: $3.50 DESCRIPTION: Uses literary interpretation of New Age topics. Prints fiction, non-fiction, poetry, reviews and more.

One Earth

PUBLISHING COMPANY: Findhorn Foundation & Press EDITOR: Andrew Murray, Eve Ward TOPICS: Metaphysics, New Age, Spirituality TYPE: Magazine DATE: 1976; 48 pgs. FREQ: quarterly

PRICE: $20.00 TERM: annually PRICE PER COPY: $5.00 DESCRIPTION: Offers spiritual inspiration to help create social & ecological harmony. Promotes the unity of all life, the planet & the universe. Features articles, display ads pertaining to New Age topics.

Ontario's Common Ground Magazine

PUBLISHING COMPANY: Ontario's Common Ground Magazine PUBLISHER: Julia Woodford TOPICS: Holistic Healing, New Age, Spirituality, Metaphysics TYPE: Magazine FREQ: quarterly CIRC: 39,000 PRICE: $17.00 DESCRIPTION: Serving Ontario. Explores the transformational journey of consciousness, the healing of our environment & the well being of all. Features departments, columns, articles, news, reviews & resource listings of information relating to wellness & personal growth. Accepts ads.

Open Channels

PUBLISHING COMPANY: Open Channels TOPICS: Metaphysics, Spirituality TYPE: Magazine

Open Line

PUBLISHING COMPANY: Open Line EDITOR: LuAnn Stallcop TOPICS: Metaphysics, Holistic Health TYPE: Newspaper FREQ: monthly CIRC: 2,000 DESCRIPTION: Prints articles, calendar, letter and interviews relating to metaphysical and holistic health issues.

Open Mind

PUBLISHING COMPANY: Open Mind EDITOR: Debra Trojan, Ruby Bickford TOPICS: New Age TYPE: Magazine DATE: 1988 FREQ: quarterly CIRC: 17,000 PRICE: $6.00 DESCRIPTION: Resource guide lists events, retailers, products and services that promotes personal growth in the North Bay area.

Operation Showman

PUBLISHING COMPANY: Operation Showman PUBLISHER: Rev. June Spencer TOPICS: Channeling TYPE: Magazine PRICE PER COPY: $0.50 DESCRIPTION: Channels, I Am That I Am Prophecy. Operates in the Gifts Of The Holy Spirit. Channels the word of Jehovah/God Prophecy for the New Agers. Send $.50 plus 2 first class postage stamps.

OPI Newsletter

PUBLISHING COMPANY: Office Of Paranormal Investigations TOPICS: Parapsychology, Psychic Phenomena, Ghosts TYPE: Newsletter FREQ: quarterly

Opossum Holler Tarot

PUBLISHING COMPANY: Opossum EDITOR: Larry Blazek TOPICS: Psychic Phenomena TYPE: Magazine

OPRA Newsletter

PUBLISHING COMPANY: Organization Of Psychic Research Associates TOPICS: Parapsychology TYPE: Newsletter DATE: 1975 FREQ: Monthly PRICE: $10.00 PRICE PER COPY: $1.00 DESCRIPTION: The study of holistic health & the relation of mind, emotion, body & spirit.

Order Of The Universe

PUBLISHING COMPANY: Kushi Institute-East West Foundation EDITOR: Michio Kushi TOPICS: Health

Food, Holistic Health, Vegetarianism, Nutrition, Spirituality **TYPE:** Magazine **DATE:** 1968

Organic Gardening

PUBLISHING COMPANY: Rodale Press, Inc. **EDITOR:** Bennett Zucker **TOPICS:** Holistic Healing **TYPE:** Magazine

Organica

PUBLISHING COMPANY: Aubrey Hampton Publishers **EDITOR:** Susan Hussey **TOPICS:** Holistic Health, New Age, Metaphysics **TYPE:** Newspaper **FREQ:** quarterly **DESCRIPTION:** Covers health metaphysics, New Age & the environment. Distributed through food stores. Features book reviews, music, art, ads & articles.

Oriflamme, The

PUBLISHING COMPANY: Ordo Templi Orientis **TOPICS:** Metaphysics, Spirituality **TYPE:** Journal **DESCRIPTION:** Literary journal of shorter length & more focused content than The Equinox. Available to the public. Limited advertising accepted.

Orion

PUBLISHING COMPANY: Orion **EDITOR:** Rosemary Clark **TOPICS:** Astrology **TYPE:** Journal

Orissa Homoeopathic Bulletin

PUBLISHING COMPANY: Tilottama Homoeo House **PUBLISHER:** Dr. Natabar Naik **TOPICS:** Homeopathy **TYPE:** Bulletin **DATE:** 1969; 30 pgs. **FREQ:** Monthly **CIRC:** 500 **PRICE PER COPY:** $2.00 **DESCRIPTION:** Purpose is the spread of Homeopathy.

Osho Times

PUBLISHING COMPANY: Osho Times **TOPICS:** Spirituality **TYPE:** Newspaper **CIRC:** 30,000 **DESCRIPTION:** Conveys works of Osho.

OSMA Beacon

PUBLISHING COMPANY: Occidental Society of Metempiric Analysis **EDITOR:** Bob Rondell **TOPICS:** Parapsychology **TYPE:** Newsletter **SIZE:** 8 1/2 x 14; 8 pgs. **FREQ:** Bi-Monthly

Outpost Exchange

PUBLISHING COMPANY: Outpost Exchange **EDITOR:** Art Blair **TOPICS:** Holistic Health **TYPE:** Magazine **DATE:** 1970; 40 pgs. **CIRC:** 15,000 **PRICE:** $8.00 **DESCRIPTION:** Serves Milwaukee with articles and news on health and well-being.

Over and Beyond

PUBLISHING COMPANY: Over and Beyond **EDITOR:** Judith Statezny **TOPICS:** New Age, Metaphysics **TYPE:** Magazine **DATE:** 1982 **FREQ:** 12 issues/yr **CIRC:** 1,200 **PRICE:** $14.00 **PRICE PER COPY:** $2.95 **DESCRIPTION:** Prints book reviews, poetry, interviews and photos.

Pagan Free Press

PUBLISHING COMPANY: Pagan Free Press **TOPICS:** Witchcraft, Occult, Paganism **TYPE:** Magazine

Pagana

PUBLISHING COMPANY: Pagan/Occult/Witchcraft Special Interest Group **TOPICS:** Occult, Witchcraft, Paganism, Kabbalah, Alchemy, Voudoun **TYPE:** Newsletter **FREQ:** 6xyr. **DESCRIPTION:** Available to members only. Ads accepted.

Pagans For Peace Newsletter

PUBLISHING COMPANY: Pagans For Peace **EDITOR:** Samuel Wagar **TOPICS:** Paganism, Witchcraft, Occult **TYPE:** Newsletter **DATE:** 1983 **SIZE:** 8 1/2 x 11; 10 pgs. **FREQ:** bi-monthly **PRICE:** $10.00 **TERM:** yearly **DESCRIPTION:** Purpose is the networking of politically active left-wing Pagans & Witches, their projects & reviews of various resources. Also offers thealogical discussion & exploration.

Pallas Society News

PUBLISHING COMPANY: Pallas Society **TOPICS:** Witchcraft, Occult, Paganism **TYPE:** Newspaper

Panegyria Journal

PUBLISHING COMPANY: Panegyria Journal **TOPICS:** Witchcraft, Occult, Paganism **TYPE:** Journal; 10 pgs. **FREQ:** 8 x yearly **PRICE:** $12.00 **TERM:** annually **DESCRIPTION:** Neo-Pagan/Wiccan Journal published 8 times yearly on traditional pagan Holy Days. Free sample.

Parabola Magazine: The Magazine of Myth and Tradition

PUBLISHING COMPANY: Parabola Books **EDITOR:** Rob Baker, Joe Kulin **TOPICS:** New Age, Metaphysics **TYPE:** Magazine **FREQ:** quarterly **CIRC:** 40,000 **PRICE PER COPY:** $5.50 **DESCRIPTION:** Covers topic on metaphysics and New Age. Reviews books. Focuses on mythology, story-telling and Jungian psychology. Prints fiction, non-fiction, news, ads, reviews and interviews.

ParaPhrase

PUBLISHING COMPANY: Cosmic Trend **EDITOR:** George LeGrand **TOPICS:** New Age **TYPE:** Newsletter **DATE:** 1985 **PRICE:** $2.00

Parapsychological Monographs Of The Parapsychology Foundation

PUBLISHING COMPANY: Parapsychology Foundation, Inc. **TOPICS:** Parapsychology, Psychic Phenomena **TYPE:** Journal

Parapsychology

PUBLISHING COMPANY: Canadian Institute Of Parapsychology **TOPICS:** Parapsychology, Occult **TYPE:** Magazine **DATE:** 1975 **FREQ:** Quarterly

Parapsychology Foundation, Proceedings Of International Conferences

PUBLISHING COMPANY: Parapsychology Foundation, Inc. **TOPICS:** Parapsychology, Occult **TYPE:** Magazine **DATE:** 1953 **FREQ:** Annual

Parapsychology Review

PUBLISHING COMPANY: Parapsychology Foundation, Inc. **EDITOR:** Betty Shapin **TOPICS:** Parapsychology **TYPE:** Magazine **DATE:** 1970 **SIZE:** 8 1/2 x 11; 16 pgs. **FREQ:** Bi-Monthly **CIRC:** 2,000 **PRICE:** $12.00 **PRICE PER COPY:** $2.00 **DESCRIPTION:** Offers information pertaining to current research & education in the field of parapsychology & psychic phenomena. Features articles, news & book reviews.

Parapsychology-Psychic Science Reports

PUBLISHING COMPANY: Gibbs Publishing Co. **PUBLISHER:** James Calvin Gibbs **TOPICS:** Parapsychology **TYPE:** Journal **DATE:** 1973 **FREQ:** Monthly **CIRC:** 10,000 **PRICE:** $26.00 **TERM:** yearly **DESCRIPTION:** Covers topics such as psychic phenomena & parapsychology. Offers up-dates on news & research.

Parinfo

PUBLISHING COMPANY: Parapsychology Association Of Riverside **EDITOR:** Mary Bates **TOPICS:** Parapsychology, Occult **TYPE:** Magazine **DATE:** 1972 **FREQ:** Monthly **PRICE:** $10.00

Path To The Stars

PUBLISHING COMPANY: Austin Seth Center **EDITOR:** Maude Cardwell **TOPICS:** Channeling, New Age, Metaphysics **TYPE:** Catalog **FREQ:** Annual

Pathways

PUBLISHING COMPANY: Yes! Educational Society **EDITOR:** Ollie Popenoe **TOPICS:** Holistic Healing **TYPE:** Magazine

Pathways Profiles

PUBLISHING COMPANY: Pathways **EDITOR:** Patricia K. Sawyer **TOPICS:** Metaphysics, Spirituality **TYPE:** Bulletin

Pathways To Health

PUBLISHING COMPANY: A.R.E. Medical Clinic/Energy Medicine **EDITOR:** Ann Graham, Anna Blackstone **TOPICS:** Holistic Healing **TYPE:** Magazine

Peace Resource Center

PUBLISHING COMPANY: Peace Resource Center **TOPICS:** New Age **TYPE:** Newsletter **DESCRIPTION:** Prints peace-related resource listings, calendar and articles.

Peace Studies Magazine

PUBLISHING COMPANY: Peace Studies Magazine **TOPICS:** New Age **TYPE:** Magazine

Pegasus

PUBLISHING COMPANY: Pegasus **EDITOR:** Gail Walton **TOPICS:** Body-Mind Connection **TYPE:** Newsletter **PRICE:** $10.00 **DESCRIPTION:** Informative publication devoted to issues relating to mind, body, emotions and spirit.

Pegasus Express

PUBLISHING COMPANY: Pegasus Express **TOPICS:** Witchcraft, Occult, Paganism **TYPE:** Magazine

Pend Oreille Awareness Network

PUBLISHING COMPANY: Pend Oreille Awareness Network **TOPICS:** New Age **TYPE:** Newsletter **DESCRIPTION:** Prints articles and calendar.

Permanent Central Vortex Newsletter

PUBLISHING COMPANY: Permanent Central Vortex **TOPICS:** Astrology **TYPE:** Newsletter; 8 pgs. **FREQ:** Monthly **PRICE:** $15.00

Personal Fitness

PUBLISHING COMPANY: Cromwell-Sloan Publishing Company **EDITOR:** Paul Sloan, Marlene Cromwell **TOPICS:** Holistic Healing **TYPE:** Magazine

Personal Health Advisory
PUBLISHING COMPANY: Biological Educational Products **EDITOR:** Dr. John McDonald **TOPICS:** Holistic Healing **TYPE:** Magazine

Perspective On Consciousness & PSI Research
PUBLISHING COMPANY: Association For Research And Enlightenment, Inc. **EDITOR:** Scott Sparrow, Henry Reed **TOPICS:** Parapsychology **TYPE:** Newsletter **DATE:** 1979; 4 pgs. **FREQ:** Monthly **CIRC:** 70,000 **PRICE:** $10.00

Phenomena
PUBLISHING COMPANY: Phenomena Publications **EDITOR:** Malcolm Dean **TOPICS:** Parapsychology, Occult, Astrology **TYPE:** Journal **DATE:** 1977 **FREQ:** Monthly

PhenomeNews
PUBLISHING COMPANY: Cindy Saul Publishers **EDITOR:** Cindy Saul, Gerri Magee **TOPICS:** Holistic Healing, New Age, Metaphysics, Channeling **TYPE:** Newspaper **DATE:** 1978; 32 pgs. **FREQ:** monthly **CIRC:** 36,000 **PRICE:** $14.00 **TERM:** yearly **PRICE PER COPY:** $1.00 **DESCRIPTION:** Michigan's #1 alternative resource newspaper since 1978. Produces a weekly cable show PhenomeViews-The Show With A Vision & a live call-in radio show every Friday morning. Sponsors Michigan's largest Expo-the Body/Mind/Spirit Festival, Spring & Fall each year. Part of a multi-media network for the Michigan New Age community. Explores human potential, holistic health & lifestyles. Prints book/video/audio reviews, news, ads, interviews with New Age leaders, and more.

Phoenix UFO & Metaphysics Newsletter
PUBLISHING COMPANY: Phoenix UFO & Metaphysics Newsletter **TOPICS:** UFO's **TYPE:** Newsletter

Plane Edge, The
PUBLISHING COMPANY: Plane Edge, The **TOPICS:** New Age **TYPE:** Newsletter **DESCRIPTION:** Offers a forum for New Age ideas.

Planet Watch
PUBLISHING COMPANY: Planet Watch **EDITOR:** Eleanor Bach **TOPICS:** Astrology **TYPE:** Newsletter

Planetary Citizen
PUBLISHING COMPANY: Stillpoint Publishing **PUBLISHER:** Meredith Young-Sowers **EDITOR:** Errol G. Sowers **TOPICS:** Channeling, Spirituality, New Age **TYPE:** Magazine; 40 pgs. **FREQ:** quarterly **PRICE:** $15.00 **TERM:** annually **DESCRIPTION:** Dedicated to building a society that honors the Earth, Humanity & the Sacred in all life.

Portland Reflections Quarterly Resource Directory
PUBLISHING COMPANY: Portland Reflections **EDITOR:** Beth Howell, John Ivy **TOPICS:** Metaphysics, New Age **TYPE:** Magazine **DATE:** 1978; 64 pgs. **FREQ:** quarterly **CIRC:** 35,000 **DESCRIPTION:** Resource guide featuring products, services & practitioners. Specializes in holistic health and self-improvement. Serves Portland, Oregon & surrounding cities as well as Southwest Washington. Accepts ads.

Positive Times
PUBLISHING COMPANY: Positive Times **TOPICS:** Metaphysics, Spirituality **TYPE:** Magazine

Powerline
PUBLISHING COMPANY: Environmental Action, Inc. **TOPICS:** Holistic Healing **TYPE:** Magazine

POWSIG
PUBLISHING COMPANY: Pagan/Occult/Witchcraft Special Interest Group **TOPICS:** Occult, Witchcraft, Paganism, Kabbalah, Alchemy, Voudoun **TYPE:** Brochure

Poyyamozhi
PUBLISHING COMPANY: P. Adimoolam **TOPICS:** Astrology **TYPE:** Magazine **DATE:** 1972 **FREQ:** Monthly **CIRC:** 4,500 **DESCRIPTION:** Monthly astrological guide with text given in Tamil.

PPCC Bulletin
PUBLISHING COMPANY: Planetary Professional Citizens Committee **EDITOR:** Jerome Eden **TOPICS:** UFO's **TYPE:** Bulletin; 32 pgs. **FREQ:** Quarterly **PRICE:** $16.00 **PRICE PER COPY:** $16.00

Practical Homeowner
PUBLISHING COMPANY: Practical Homeowner Publishing **EDITOR:** Sanford Beldon, Ed-Chuck McCullagh **TOPICS:** New Age **TYPE:** Magazine

Prana Yoga Leaves
PUBLISHING COMPANY: Prana Yoga Ashram - Yogalayam **EDITOR:** Saraswathi Devi, Yoganathan Devi **TOPICS:** Yoga **TYPE:** Newsletter

Prana Yoga Life Magazine
PUBLISHING COMPANY: Prana Yoga Ashram - Yogalayam **EDITOR:** Saraswathi Devi, Yoganathan Devi **TOPICS:** Yoga **TYPE:** Magazine

Prediction
PUBLISHING COMPANY: Link House Magazines, Ltd. **EDITOR:** Jo Logan **TOPICS:** Parapsychology, Occult **TYPE:** Magazine **DATE:** 1936 **FREQ:** Monthly **CIRC:** 29,796 **DESCRIPTION:** Features news, articles, ads & inquiries on astrology, palmistry, tarot, graphology & dreams. Offers tarot predictions & astrological forecasts for each sign of the Zodiac.

Present Moment
PUBLISHING COMPANY: Present Moment **EDITOR:** Michael Koucky **TOPICS:** New Age, Metaphysics **TYPE:** Magazine **FREQ:** quarterly **CIRC:** 50,000 **DESCRIPTION:** Serves midwest with health-related articles, columns and events calendar.

Presse-Inter
PUBLISHING COMPANY: Centre International d'Action Culturelle **EDITOR:** Pierre Hoaurt **TOPICS:** New Age **TYPE:** Magazine **FREQ:** Quarterly

Prevention Magazine
PUBLISHING COMPANY: Rodale Press, Inc. **EDITOR:** Marshall Ackerman **TOPICS:** Holistic Healing **TYPE:** Magazine

Prevention's New Encyclopedia Of Common Diseases
PUBLISHING COMPANY: Rodale Press, Inc. **EDITOR:** Editors of Prevention Magazine **TOPICS:** Holistic Health **TYPE:** Magazine **PRICE:** $21.95

Preventive Medicine
PUBLISHING COMPANY: Academic Press, Inc. **TOPICS:** Holistic Healing **TYPE:** Magazine

Prism
PUBLISHING COMPANY: Prism **TOPICS:** New Age **TYPE:** Newspaper **FREQ:** 6 issues/yr **CIRC:** 18,000

Probe Report
PUBLISHING COMPANY: Probe **EDITOR:** Ian Mrzglod **TOPICS:** Parapsychology, Occult **TYPE:** Magazine **DATE:** 1980 **FREQ:** Quarterly **CIRC:** 500 **PRICE:** $6.60

Probe The Unknown
PUBLISHING COMPANY: Probe The Unknown **EDITOR:** Richard De Amorelli **TOPICS:** Astrology **TYPE:** Journal

Proceedings
PUBLISHING COMPANY: Academy Of Religion And Psychical Research **TYPE:** Bulletin **FREQ:** annually **DESCRIPTION:** Annual publication reporting on the Academy's Annual Conference.

Proceedings Of The American Society For Psychical Research
PUBLISHING COMPANY: American Society For Psychical Research, Inc. **EDITOR:** Rhea White **TOPICS:** Parapsychology, Psychic Phenomena **TYPE:** Journal

Proceedings Of The Parapsychological Association
PUBLISHING COMPANY: Parapsychological Association **EDITOR:** W. G. Roll **TOPICS:** Parapsychology **TYPE:** Newsletter **DATE:** 1957 **SIZE:** 5.5 x 8.5; 120 pgs. **FREQ:** Annual **CIRC:** 1,000 **PRICE PER COPY:** $3.50 **DESCRIPTION:** Provides research reports & information presented at the annual conventions of the Parapsychological Association.

Process: Psychoanalysis & Creativity
PUBLISHING COMPANY: Process: Psychoanalysis & Creativity **EDITOR:** Helen Borel **TOPICS:** New Age **TYPE:** Magazine

Profile Of An Alien Spacecraft
PUBLISHING COMPANY: World UFO Data, Inc. **PUBLISHER:** John Frick **TOPICS:** UFO's **TYPE:** Magazine **DATE:** 1981 **PRICE PER COPY:** $5.00 **DESCRIPTION:** A unique, fascinating publication reporting on UFO's.

Projection
PUBLISHING COMPANY: Addiction Research Foundation **EDITOR:** R.J. Hall **TOPICS:** Holistic Healing **TYPE:** Newsletter

Promethian Network
PUBLISHING COMPANY: Promethian Network **TOPICS:** New Age, Occult **TYPE:** Magazine

Proteus
PUBLISHING COMPANY: Proteus **TOPICS:** UFO's **TYPE:** Magazine

Prout Journal

PUBLISHING COMPANY: Prout Journal **EDITOR:** Mike Ellison **TOPICS:** New Age, Metaphysics **TYPE:** Journal **DATE:** 1988; 32 pgs. **FREQ:** quarterly **CIRC:** 10,000 **PRICE:** $8.00 **PRICE PER COPY:** $2.00 **DESCRIPTION:** A resource tool for the Prout Institute, prints non-fiction, news, book and audio news.

PRS Journal

PUBLISHING COMPANY: Philosophical Research Society, Inc. **EDITOR:** M.P. Hall **TOPICS:** Spirituality **TYPE:** Journal **FREQ:** quarterly

PSI News

PUBLISHING COMPANY: Parapsychological Association **TOPICS:** Parapsychology **TYPE:** Newsletter

Psi Research Journal

PUBLISHING COMPANY: PSI Research **PUBLISHER:** Larissa Vilenskaya **TOPICS:** Parapsychology **TYPE:** Journal **DATE:** 1982 **SIZE:** 5.5 x 8.5; 130 pgs. **FREQ:** Quarterly **CIRC:** 450 **PRICE:** $28.00 **PRICE PER COPY:** $8.00 **DESCRIPTION:** Articles & reports covering the field of parapsychology on an international level. Discusses research, findings, events from the USSR, China & Eastern Europe.

Psi-M

PUBLISHING COMPANY: Mensa Psychic Science Special Interest Group **EDITOR:** Rich Strong **TOPICS:** Parapsychology **TYPE:** Magazine; 20 pgs. **FREQ:** 10 x/yr. **DESCRIPTION:** Non-profit research & educational organization seeking to give credibility & recognition to the psychic sciences & thereby improve humanity.

Psionics

PUBLISHING COMPANY: T & A Publications **TOPICS:** Parapsychology **TYPE:** Newsletter; 8 pgs. **FREQ:** 10 x/yr **PRICE:** $48.50

Psych It

PUBLISHING COMPANY: Psych It **EDITOR:** Charlotte L. Babicky **TOPICS:** New Age **TYPE:** Magazine **DATE:** 1988 **FREQ:** Quarterly **CIRC:** 100 **PRICE:** $8.00 **DESCRIPTION:** Psychologically based publication promoting creativity & self awareness.

Psychic Astrology Predictions

PUBLISHING COMPANY: Jalart House, Inc. **TOPICS:** Astrology **TYPE:** Magazine **FREQ:** Quarterly **PRICE PER COPY:** $1.95

Psychic Connections

PUBLISHING COMPANY: Psychic Connections **TOPICS:** Metaphysics, Spirituality **TYPE:** Magazine

Psychic Design: A Newsletter For Psychic Professionals

PUBLISHING COMPANY: Carma Press **PUBLISHER:** Elizabeth Nelson **TOPICS:** Parapsychology **TYPE:** Newsletter **DATE:** 1986; 8 pgs. **FREQ:** Bi-Monthly **PRICE PER COPY:** $5.50 **DESCRIPTION:** Purpose to improve psychic profession through research, the use of resources, interviews & printed material.

Psychic Fair Network News

PUBLISHING COMPANY: Psychic Network Directory **PUBLISHER:** Vincent Tabatneck **EDITOR:**

Shirley Tabatneck **TOPICS:** Astrology, Metaphysics, Psychic Phenomena, Parapsychology **TYPE:** Journal **DATE:** 1978 **SIZE:** 10 x 13; 20 pgs. **FREQ:** Quarterly **CIRC:** 47,669 **PRICE:** $12.00 **TERM:** annually **PRICE PER COPY:** $3.00 **DESCRIPTION:** Metaphysical forum serving the U.S. & Canada. Purpose is to educate the public. Covers Astrology, Psychic & Paranormal Phenomena. Offers articles, ads, book reviews & predictions. Geared to the individual with particular interest in these fields.

Psychic Forecaster, The

PUBLISHING COMPANY: WMP Enterprises, Inc. **PUBLISHER:** Roberto E. Veitia **TOPICS:** Psychic, New Age, Astrology **TYPE:** Newsletter **PRICE:** $29.00 **TERM:** yearly **DESCRIPTION:** Offer psychic predictions specializing in the investment-related area.

Psychic Journal

PUBLISHING COMPANY: Charlton Publications, Inc. **TOPICS:** Parapsychology, Channeling **TYPE:** Journal **DATE:** 1987 **SIZE:** 8 x 11 **FREQ:** Bi-Monthly **CIRC:** 100,000 **PRICE:** $15.00 **PRICE PER COPY:** $2.50

Psychic Life Magazine

PUBLISHING COMPANY: Deja Vu Publishing Co. **PUBLISHER:** Lewis Bostwick **EDITOR:** Susan Hull Bostwick **TOPICS:** Parapsychology, Psychic **TYPE:** Magazine **DATE:** 1979 **SIZE:** 8 1/2 x 11; 54 pgs. **FREQ:** Bi-Monthly **CIRC:** 4,000 **PRICE:** $15.00 **PRICE PER COPY:** $1.50 **DESCRIPTION:** Offers opinions & educational information about psychic skills.

Psychic Messenger

PUBLISHING COMPANY: Shafenberg Research Foundation **EDITOR:** Alice Shiver **TOPICS:** Parapsychology, Occult **TYPE:** Magazine **FREQ:** Quarterly

Psychic News

PUBLISHING COMPANY: Psychic Press, Ltd. **EDITOR:** Tony Ortzen **TOPICS:** New Age, Psychic, Occult, Metaphysics, Spirituality, ESP, Reincarnation **TYPE:** Newspaper; 8 pgs. **FREQ:** weekly **DESCRIPTION:** Contains reports on people & events as well as in-depth articles covering all aspects of the psychic & spiritualist scene. Offers ads, letters, events, book reviews, classifed & Church activites. Provides a monthly supplement, New Age Review, which covers a wide range of New Age topics.

Psychic Newsletter

PUBLISHING COMPANY: Psychic Newsletter **TOPICS:** Metaphysics, Spirituality **TYPE:** Newsletter

Psychic Pathways

PUBLISHING COMPANY: Psychic Pathways **EDITOR:** Alicia M. Sipos **TOPICS:** Psychic, New Age, Parapsychology, Metaphysics, Spirituality **TYPE:** Newsletter **CIRC:** 16,000 **DESCRIPTION:** Offers news & reviews on parapsychology. Interested in disseminating information regarding psychic phenomenon. Distributed through fairs, retailers & organizations.

Psychic Press Newspaper

PUBLISHING COMPANY: Psychic Press Newspaper **TOPICS:** Metaphysics, Spirituality **TYPE:** Newspaper

Psychic Reader

PUBLISHING COMPANY: Deja Vu Publishing Co. **EDITOR:** Sandra Kovacs **TOPICS:** Parapsychology, Psychic **TYPE:** Newspaper **DATE:** 1975 **SIZE:** 11 X 17; 24 pgs. **FREQ:** Monthly **CIRC:** 195,000 **PRICE:** $18.00 **DESCRIPTION:** Written by psychics for psychics. Offers information, news & feature articles on psychic skills. Serves Bay area.

Psychic Registry

PUBLISHING COMPANY: Unicorn Systems **TOPICS:** Psychic, Occult, Metaphysics, New Age **TYPE:** Magazine **FREQ:** quarterly **PRICE:** $9.00 **PRICE PER COPY:** $2.00

Psychic Research Newsletter

PUBLISHING COMPANY: Psychic Research Institute **PUBLISHER:** Marcel Vogel **EDITOR:** Jennet Grover **TOPICS:** Parapsychology **TYPE:** Newsletter **DATE:** 1984; 16 pgs. **FREQ:** Bi-Monthly **CIRC:** 2,000 **PRICE:** $12.50 **PRICE PER COPY:** $4.00 **DESCRIPTION:** Non-profit corporation attempting to help people through scientific research & eduction.

Psychic Research Report

PUBLISHING COMPANY: Eaton Publishing **PUBLISHER:** Frederick Willis **EDITOR:** Richard Bear **TOPICS:** Parapsychology **TYPE:** Newsletter **FREQ:** Monthly **PRICE:** $39.00

Psychic Seminar

PUBLISHING COMPANY: American Psychic Association **TOPICS:** Parapsychology **TYPE:** Newspaper **SIZE:** 11 x 15; 8 pgs. **FREQ:** Bi-Monthly

Psychic Studies

PUBLISHING COMPANY: Gordon And Breach Science Publishers, Inc. **EDITOR:** Stanley Krippner, Irene Hall **TOPICS:** Parapsychology, Occult, Psychic **TYPE:** Magazine **DATE:** 1982 **FREQ:** Irregular

Psychological Perspectives

PUBLISHING COMPANY: C.G. Jung Institute Of Los Angeles **EDITOR:** Ernest L. Rossi, Ph.D. **TOPICS:** New Age **TYPE:** Magazine **FREQ:** semi-quarter **PRICE:** $16.00

Psychology Of Addictive Behavior

PUBLISHING COMPANY: Society Of Psychologists In Addictive Behaviors **EDITOR:** W. Miles Cox, Ph.D. **TOPICS:** New Age **TYPE:** Magazine

Pu Shih Hsing Hsiang

PUBLISHING COMPANY: Wai Chi Lee Chien-Li **TOPICS:** Parapsychology, Occult **TYPE:** Magazine **PRICE:** $24.00

Publicity Circuit Monthly

PUBLISHING COMPANY: Publicity Circuit Monthly **TOPICS:** New Age, Metaphysics **TYPE:** Magazine **FREQ:** monthly **DESCRIPTION:** Reports on writers publicity tours for their publications.

Publisher's Report

PUBLISHING COMPANY: National Association Of Independent Publishers **EDITOR:** Betty Wright, Betsy Lampe **TOPICS:** New Age **TYPE:** Newsletter **DATE:** 1985; 8 pgs. **FREQ:** bi-monthly **PRICE:**

$75.00 **TERM:** annual **PRICE PER COPY:** $15.00 **DESCRIPTION:** Reports on the field of publishing. Subscription free with membership to organization. Annual dues $75.

Purple Pages

PUBLISHING COMPANY: Purple Pages Of Texas **EDITOR:** Mollie Strickland **TOPICS:** New Age, Metaphysics **TYPE:** Magazine **DATE:** 1987; 144 pgs. **FREQ:** quarterly **CIRC:** 25,000 **PRICE PER COPY:** $5.95 **DESCRIPTION:** A New Age directory that's dedicated to examining the holistic & human potential movement. Covers food, health, science, new technologies, fashion, beauty & music. Serves Houston & surrounding areas.

Pursuit - S.I.T.U.

PUBLISHING COMPANY: Society For The Investigation Of The Unexplained **EDITOR:** Robert C. Warth **TOPICS:** Parapsychology, Occult, Paranormal Phenomena **TYPE:** Magazine **DATE:** 1969 **FREQ:** Quarterly **CIRC:** 1,500 **PRICE:** $12.00

Quaderni Di Parapsicologia

PUBLISHING COMPANY: Centro Studi Parapsicologici **EDITOR:** Piero Cassoli **TOPICS:** Parapsychology, Occult **TYPE:** Magazine **FREQ:** Annual **CIRC:** 450 **PRICE:** $30.00

Quaderni Gnosis

PUBLISHING COMPANY: Instituto Gnosis Per La Ricerca Sulla Sopravvivenza **EDITOR:** Giorgio di Simone **TOPICS:** Parapsychology, Occult **TYPE:** Magazine **FREQ:** Semi-Annual

Quality Living Publication

PUBLISHING COMPANY: Quality Living Publication **EDITOR:** Rick Herrick **TOPICS:** New Age **TYPE:** Magazine **FREQ:** quarterly **PRICE:** $20.00 **TERM:** yearly

Quantis Report, The

PUBLISHING COMPANY: Quantis Report, The **TOPICS:** Channeling **TYPE:** Magazine

Que Natural!

PUBLISHING COMPANY: Que Natural! **EDITOR:** Marie Russell **TOPICS:** New Age **TYPE:** Magazine **DATE:** 1989 **FREQ:** monthly **DESCRIPTION:** The Spanish edition of Mighty Natural magazine. Prints resources and articles.

Quest, The

PUBLISHING COMPANY: Quest Enterprises Of Excelsior **EDITOR:** D. Craig **TOPICS:** New Age, Metaphysics **TYPE:** Magazine **DATE:** 1984 **FREQ:** quarterly **PRICE PER COPY:** $2.95 **DESCRIPTION:** Features thought-provoking pieces on philosophy, religion, science and the arts. Offers catalog of books, audio tapes and crystals product.

Quest, The

PUBLISHING COMPANY: Theosophical Publishing House **PUBLISHER:** H.P. Blavatsky **EDITOR:** William Metzger, Annie Besant **TOPICS:** New Age, Metaphysics **TYPE:** Journal **DATE:** 1988 **FREQ:** quarterly **PRICE:** $14.00 **PRICE PER COPY:** $3.95 **DESCRIPTION:** Examines philosophy, science, religion and the arts. Includes book reviews, interviews.

Quest-The Journal Of UFO Investigation

PUBLISHING COMPANY: Quest-The Journal Of UFO Investigation **TOPICS:** UFO's **TYPE:** Journal

Quester

PUBLISHING COMPANY: Canadian Society Of Questers **EDITOR:** Roberta Britt **TOPICS:** Parapsychology **TYPE:** Journal **DATE:** 1979 **SIZE:** 5.5 x 8.5; 40 pgs. **FREQ:** Quarterly **CIRC:** 175 **PRICE:** $18.00 **PRICE PER COPY:** $2.75 **DESCRIPTION:** Promoting dowsing & parasychology methods through education.

Question De Racines, Pensees, Sciences Eclairees

PUBLISHING COMPANY: Edition Question de **TOPICS:** Parapsychology, Occult **TYPE:** Magazine **DATE:** 1973 **FREQ:** Quarterly **CIRC:** 12,000

Quill And Sword, The

PUBLISHING COMPANY: Quill And Sword, The **TOPICS:** Witchcraft, Occult, Paganism **TYPE:** Magazine

Quill And Unicorn

PUBLISHING COMPANY: Quill And Unicorn **TOPICS:** Witchcraft, Occult, Paganism **TYPE:** Magazine

R.K.M. Publishing Tape & Book Club Bulletin

PUBLISHING COMPANY: RKM Publishing Company **EDITOR:** Eric C. Bloom **TOPICS:** Parapsychology, Occult **TYPE:** Bulletin **DATE:** 1981 **FREQ:** Quarterly **CIRC:** 5,000

Radiaesthesie

PUBLISHING COMPANY: Verlag RGS **EDITOR:** E. A. Minikus **TOPICS:** Parapsychology, Occult **TYPE:** Magazine **DATE:** 1950 **FREQ:** Quarterly **PRICE:** $6.00

Radiance Technique Journal, The

PUBLISHING COMPANY: Radiance Technique Association International, Inc. **EDITOR:** Marilyn Alvey, Fred Wright **TOPICS:** Reiki, Body-Mind Connection, Massage, Holistic Health **TYPE:** Journal **DATE:** 1980; 20 pgs. **FREQ:** quarterly **CIRC:** 5,000 **PRICE:** $20.00 **PRICE PER COPY:** $4.00 **DESCRIPTION:** Journal for members of the association. Includes a variety of features such as non-fiction, children's stories, poetry, reviews, ads, interviews, and more. Features current information & alumni sharing of the Radiance Technique.

Radio & Records

PUBLISHING COMPANY: Radio & Records **EDITOR:** Jeff Gelb **TOPICS:** New Age **TYPE:** Magazine **DESCRIPTION:** Publishes a trade publication for radio stations & audio producers specializing in New Age music.

Rainbow City Express

PUBLISHING COMPANY: Rainbow City Express **EDITOR:** Helen B. Harvey **TOPICS:** Metaphysics, Spirituality **TYPE:** Journal; 80 pgs. **FREQ:** quarterly **PRICE:** $6.00 **DESCRIPTION:** Deals with spiritual awakening & creative self-expression.

Rainbow Pages

PUBLISHING COMPANY: Rainbow Pages **TOPICS:** New Age **TYPE:** Newspaper **FREQ:** quarterly **CIRC:** 5,000

Rainbow Pages

PUBLISHING COMPANY: Theosophical Publishing House **EDITOR:** William Metzger **TOPICS:** New Age, Spirituality **TYPE:** Journal; 96 pgs. **FREQ:** quarterly **CIRC:** 40,000 **DESCRIPTION:** Dedicated to publishing thoughts on religion, philosophy, science and the arts. Prints book/video/audio reviews.

Rainbow Ray Focus

PUBLISHING COMPANY: Magnificent Consummation **EDITOR:** Angel Violet **TOPICS:** Astrology **TYPE:** Journal; 20 pgs. **FREQ:** Bi-Monthly **PRICE:** $12.00

Rainbows

PUBLISHING COMPANY: Life Spectrums/Rainbow Experience **EDITOR:** Charlotte Abell **TOPICS:** New Age **TYPE:** Newsletter; 16 pgs. **FREQ:** semi-annual **PRICE:** $5.00 **TERM:** annually **DESCRIPTION:** Prints articles and calendar.

Raj Talks

PUBLISHING COMPANY: Riverrun Press **TOPICS:** Channeling, Metaphysics, Spirituality **TYPE:** Magazine

Raphael's Astrological Almanac

PUBLISHING COMPANY: W. Foulsham & Co., Ltd. **TOPICS:** Astrology **TYPE:** Magazine **FREQ:** annual **DESCRIPTION:** Provides information sources for astrologers & gives predictions for the coming year.

Rassegna Italiana Di Ricerca Psichica

PUBLISHING COMPANY: Societa Italiana di Parapsicologia **TOPICS:** Parapsychology, Occult **TYPE:** Magazine **DATE:** 1963 **FREQ:** Quarterly **CIRC:** 600

Raven Press

PUBLISHING COMPANY: Raven Press **EDITOR:** Jean Azzato **TOPICS:** Dreams **TYPE:** Magazine

Rays From The Rose Cross

PUBLISHING COMPANY: Rosicrucian Fellowship **TOPICS:** Parapsychology, Occult **TYPE:** Magazine **DATE:** 1974 **FREQ:** Bi-Monthly

Reality Change

PUBLISHING COMPANY: Austin Seth Center **EDITOR:** Maude Cardwell, Ph. D. **TOPICS:** Channeling, New Age, Metaphysics **TYPE:** Magazine **DATE:** 1980; 68 pgs. **FREQ:** quarterly **PRICE:** $18.00 **PRICE PER COPY:** $5.95 **DESCRIPTION:** Purpose is to enhance human dignity by teaching a philosophy that empowers people to achieve positive life changes with love, fun & awareness. Prints articles, both fiction & non-fiction, news & reviews, poetry, interviews and various art materials. Accepts ads.

Reclaiming Newsletter

PUBLISHING COMPANY: Reclaiming Collective **TOPICS:** Occult, Witchcraft **TYPE:** Newsletter **FREQ:** quarterly **PRICE PER COPY:** $2.00 **DESCRIPTION:** Subscriptions available on a sliding fee basis.

Redneck Review of Literature, The

PUBLISHING COMPANY: Redneck Review of Literature, The **EDITOR:** Penelope Reedy **TOPICS:** New Age, Metaphysics **TYPE:** Magazine **DATE:**

1975; 80 pgs. **FREQ:** 2 issues/yr **PRICE:** $14.00 **DESCRIPTION:** A literary review that includes works of new and well-known writers.

Reflect
PUBLISHING COMPANY: Reflect **PUBLISHER:** William S. Kennedy **TOPICS:** New Age, Spirituality **TYPE:** Magazine **DATE:** 1979; 48 pgs. **FREQ:** quarterly **PRICE:** $8.00 **TERM:** yearly **PRICE PER COPY:** $2.00 **DESCRIPTION:** A vehicle for presenting & advancing the Spiral Mode of modern literature. Having to do with beauty & things spiritual.

Reflections
PUBLISHING COMPANY: Mafu Seminars **TOPICS:** Channeling **TYPE:** Journal **FREQ:** bi-monthly

Reflections Of Light
PUBLISHING COMPANY: Spiritual Growth Foundation **EDITOR:** Barbara Morales **TOPICS:** Metaphysics **TYPE:** Magazine

Reiki Journal, The
PUBLISHING COMPANY: American-International Reiki Association, Inc. **TOPICS:** Holistic Healing, Reiki **TYPE:** Journal

Reincarnationists
PUBLISHING COMPANY: Reincarnationists **TOPICS:** Reincarnation **TYPE:** Newspaper

Religious Research Journal
PUBLISHING COMPANY: Church Of Religious Research, Inc. **EDITOR:** Rev. Isabel Pinkston **TOPICS:** New Age, Death, Past Life Regression **TYPE:** Journal; 12 pgs. **DESCRIPTION:** Subscription included with a $45 membership contribution per year.

Renaissance Universal Journal
PUBLISHING COMPANY: Scholarly Press **EDITOR:** Dhanjoo N. Ghista **TOPICS:** Holistic Health **TYPE:** Journal **DATE:** 1979 **FREQ:** Quarterly **CIRC:** 1,000 **PRICE:** $30.00

Renaitre 2000
PUBLISHING COMPANY: Andre Dumas **TOPICS:** Parapsychology, Occult, Spirituality **TYPE:** Magazine **DATE:** 1977 **FREQ:** 5 x/yr. **CIRC:** 2,000 **DESCRIPTION:** Covers parapsychology & spiritualism.

Renewable Resource And Conservation Report
PUBLISHING COMPANY: Renewable Resource And Conservation Report **TOPICS:** New Age **TYPE:** Newsletter

Renewal
PUBLISHING COMPANY: Renewal **TOPICS:** New Age **TYPE:** Magazine

Reports Of Variable Star Observations
PUBLISHING COMPANY: American Association Of Variable Star Observers **EDITOR:** Janet Mattei **TOPICS:** Astrology **TYPE:** Magazine **DATE:** 1961; 100 pgs. **FREQ:** Irregular **CIRC:** 1,000 **DESCRIPTION:** Reports on computer-generated light curves of variables in the AAVSO observing program.

Research Bulletin
PUBLISHING COMPANY: Himalayan International Institute Of Yoga Science and Philosophy **TOPICS:** New Age **TYPE:** Bulletin

Research For Religion & Parapsychology
PUBLISHING COMPANY: International Association For Religion & Parapsychology **TOPICS:** Parapsychology, Occult **TYPE:** Magazine **DATE:** 1975 **FREQ:** Irregular **CIRC:** 8 **PRICE:** $8.00

Research In Parapsychology
PUBLISHING COMPANY: Scarecrow Press, Inc. **EDITOR:** Rhea White **TOPICS:** Parapsychology **TYPE:** Magazine

Research In Parapsychology
PUBLISHING COMPANY: Parapsychological Association **TOPICS:** Parapsychology, Psychic Phenomena **TYPE:** Newsletter

Researcher
PUBLISHING COMPANY: Astrological Research Guild, Inc. **EDITOR:** Ruth Smith **TOPICS:** Astrology **TYPE:** Magazine **DATE:** 1970 **SIZE:** 8 1/2 x 11; 30 pgs. **FREQ:** Bi-Monthly **PRICE:** $10.00 **PRICE PER COPY:** $2.00 **DESCRIPTION:** Reports on astrology, related topics & research in the field.

Resonance
PUBLISHING COMPANY: Evan T. Pritchard Publishers **EDITOR:** Evan T. Pritchard **TOPICS:** New Age, Metaphysics, Holistic Health **TYPE:** Magazine **DATE:** 1985 **FREQ:** 3 x per year **CIRC:** 2,000 **PRICE:** $12.00 **PRICE PER COPY:** $3.00 **DESCRIPTION:** A forum for uplifting & insightful art & thought. Features articles on spirituality, dreams, New Age music as an alternative health method & environmental issues such as the greenhouse effect. Offers New Age thought, ideas and living. Prints many types of literary, non-fiction and artistic works. Accepts ads.

Resonance
PUBLISHING COMPANY: International Foundation For Homeopathy **EDITOR:** Dean Crothers **TOPICS:** Holistic Health **TYPE:** Magazine

Resource Guide
PUBLISHING COMPANY: Resource Guide **EDITOR:** Frances Rosenthal **TOPICS:** New Age **TYPE:** Magazine **FREQ:** quarterly **DESCRIPTION:** A resource guide/directory serving Westchester County & Connecticut. Also, prints feature articles.

Resource Magazine For Publishing
PUBLISHING COMPANY: Resource Magazine For Publishing **EDITOR:** Lyn McFadgen **TOPICS:** New Age **TYPE:** Magazine **DESCRIPTION:** Offers information for special-interest magazine publishers.

Resurgence
PUBLISHING COMPANY: Resurgence Limited **EDITOR:** Satish Kumar **TOPICS:** New Age, Spirituality **TYPE:** Magazine **DATE:** 1966; 64 pgs. **FREQ:** bi-monthly **DESCRIPTION:** Explores environmental, spiritual & artistic values. Includes articles and reviews.

Revelation

PUBLISHING COMPANY: Revelation **EDITOR:** Peter Carman **TOPICS:** Parapsychology, Occult **TYPE:** Magazine **DATE:** 1972 **FREQ:** Irregular **CIRC:** 300 **PRICE:** $4.00

Revelations Of Awareness
PUBLISHING COMPANY: Cosmic Awareness Communications Avaton **TOPICS:** Channeling, Parapsychology **TYPE:** Newsletter **DATE:** 1972 **SIZE:** 8 1/2 x 11; 20 pgs. **FREQ:** Bi-Weekly **CIRC:** 5,000 **PRICE:** $52.00 **TERM:** yearly **PRICE PER COPY:** $3.00 **DESCRIPTION:** Information from the Universal Mind on all subjects such as religion, philosophy, mysteries, relationships, UFO's & the alien presence threat. Promotes spiritual, economic & humanitarian growth as influenced by the teachings of Edgar Cayce.

Review Of Indian Spiritualism
PUBLISHING COMPANY: Sinha Publishing House **EDITOR:** Amiya Kumar Sinha **TOPICS:** Parapsychology, Occult **TYPE:** Magazine **DATE:** 1974 **FREQ:** Monthly **CIRC:** 1,000 **PRICE:** $3.00

Review Of Metaphysics
PUBLISHING COMPANY: Philosophy Education Society **EDITOR:** Jude P. Dougherty, Mark Hurley **TOPICS:** Metaphysics **TYPE:** Newsletter

ReVision
PUBLISHING COMPANY: Heldref Publications, Inc. **EDITOR:** Cornelius W. Vahle, Jr., Sheila Donoghue **TOPICS:** Metaphysics, New Age **TYPE:** Journal **FREQ:** quarterly **CIRC:** 5,233 **PRICE:** $22.00 **DESCRIPTION:** Provides international forum for exchange of ideas on philosophy, religion, psychology, physics and the arts.

Revue Belge D'Homoeopathie
PUBLISHING COMPANY: Societe Royale Belge d'Homoeopathie **EDITOR:** J.C.L. Gregoire **TOPICS:** Homeopathy **TYPE:** Magazine **DATE:** 1949 **FREQ:** Quarterly **CIRC:** 2,000

Revue De Parapsychologie
PUBLISHING COMPANY: Groupe d'Etude et de Recherche en Parapsychologie **EDITOR:** Gisele Titeux **TOPICS:** Parapsychology, Occult **TYPE:** Magazine **DATE:** 1975 **FREQ:** Irregular **CIRC:** 1,000

Revue Du Magnetisme-Etude Du Psychisme Experimental
PUBLISHING COMPANY: Revue Du Magnetisme-Etude Du Psychisme Experimental **EDITOR:** Jean Magnes **TOPICS:** Parapsychology, Occult, Hypnotism, Meditation, Psychic Phenomena **TYPE:** Magazine **DATE:** 1975 **FREQ:** Bi-Monthly **DESCRIPTION:** Conducts research in psychic phenomena, magnetism, hypnotism, suggestion, and mediums.

Revue Metapsychique
PUBLISHING COMPANY: Institut Metapsychique international **EDITOR:** Hubert Larcher **TOPICS:** Parapsychology, Occult **TYPE:** Magazine **DATE:** 1920 **FREQ:** Irregular **CIRC:** 500

RFD
PUBLISHING COMPANY: Short Mountain Collective **TOPICS:** New Age **TYPE:** Magazine **DESCRIPTION:** Magazine by and for gay men.

Rim Institute

PUBLISHING COMPANY: Rim Institute **TOPICS:** New Age **TYPE:** Magazine **CIRC:** 60,000 **DESCRIPTION:** Publicizes events held at the Rim Institute.

Rising Star Quarterly

PUBLISHING COMPANY: Rising Star Quarterly **PUBLISHER:** Mildred Schuler **TOPICS:** Astrology **TYPE:** Magazine **DATE:** 1938 **FREQ:** Quarterly **CIRC:** 400 **PRICE:** $2.00 **PRICE PER COPY:** $0.50 **DESCRIPTION:** Features astrological information such as new moon & planetary cycle charts & natal charts of famous people & events.

Rising Sun, The

PUBLISHING COMPANY: Rising Sun, The **TOPICS:** New Age, Holistic Health **TYPE:** Newspaper **FREQ:** monthly **PRICE:** $10.00 **TERM:** yearly **DESCRIPTION:** Tabloid dealing with holistic health & personal transformation.

Robert Anton Wilson's Trajectories Newsletter

PUBLISHING COMPANY: Permanent Press **PUBLISHER:** Robert Anton Wilson **EDITOR:** Arlen R. Wilson, D. Scott Apel **TOPICS:** Metaphysics, Spirituality, New Age **TYPE:** Newsletter **DATE:** 1988; 20 pgs. **FREQ:** quarterly **PRICE:** $20.00 **TERM:** annually **PRICE PER COPY:** $5.00 **DESCRIPTION:** Journal of futurism & heresy, devoted to the writings of author/philosopher Robert Anton Wilson.

Rockhead

PUBLISHING COMPANY: Utopian Technology **EDITOR:** Eve Furchgott **TOPICS:** New Age **TYPE:** Magazine

Rocky Mountain Spiritual Emergence Network

PUBLISHING COMPANY: Rocky Mountain Spiritual Emergence Network **EDITOR:** Rebecca Browning **TOPICS:** Spirituality **TYPE:** Newsletter **DATE:** 1989 **FREQ:** monthly **CIRC:** 4,000 **DESCRIPTION:** Serves Rocky Mountain area readers seeking spiritual growth. Covers local events and services of interest.

Roebuck Journal, The

PUBLISHING COMPANY: Roebuck Journal, The **TOPICS:** Witchcraft, Occult, Paganism **TYPE:** Journal

Ron Warmouth's Prediction

PUBLISHING COMPANY: Ron Warmouth's Prediction **TOPICS:** Metaphysics, Spirituality **TYPE:** Magazine

Rose And Quill

PUBLISHING COMPANY: Rose And Quill **TOPICS:** Witchcraft, Occult, Paganism **TYPE:** Magazine

Rosicrucian Digest

PUBLISHING COMPANY: Supreme Grand Lodge of AMORC, Inc. **EDITOR:** Robin M. Thompson **TOPICS:** New Age **TYPE:** Magazine

Roxanna's Guide

PUBLISHING COMPANY: Guidera Publishing Corp. **PUBLISHER:** Rosanne Oakley **TOPICS:** Astrology **TYPE:** Newsletter **DATE:** 1987 **SIZE:** 8 1/2 x 11; 8 pgs. **FREQ:** Monthly **PRICE:** $39.00 **DESCRIPTION:** Predicts best time to fall in love, to gamble or invest money, change careers or begin any new venture.

Runestaff, The

PUBLISHING COMPANY: Runestaff, The **TOPICS:** Metaphysics, Spirituality **TYPE:** Magazine

Runner's World

PUBLISHING COMPANY: Rodale Press, Inc. **EDITOR:** Michael Perlis, Rich Benyo **TOPICS:** Holistic Healing **TYPE:** Magazine

Sacred Cycles Newsletter

PUBLISHING COMPANY: Sacred Cycles Newsletter **EDITOR:** Faith Barr-Glover **TOPICS:** New Age, Metaphysics **TYPE:** Newsletter **DATE:** 1985 **FREQ:** quarterly **CIRC:** 300 **PRICE:** $26.00 **DESCRIPTION:** Targets teachers and students practicing, and seeking sacred living and feminine spirituality.

Sacred Fire

PUBLISHING COMPANY: Sacred Fire **EDITOR:** Bob Banner **TOPICS:** Metaphysics, New Age **TYPE:** Magazine **FREQ:** quarterly **CIRC:** 20,000 **DESCRIPTION:** Formerly called, Critique: A Journal Exposing Consensus Reality. Examines Truth with thought-provoking articles and poetry. Accepts ads.

Sacred Grove News

PUBLISHING COMPANY: Sacred Grove News **TOPICS:** Witchcraft, Occult, Paganism **TYPE:** Newspaper

SageWoman Magazine

PUBLISHING COMPANY: SageWoman Magazine **EDITOR:** Lunaea Weatherstone **TOPICS:** Metaphysics, Spirituality, New Age **TYPE:** Magazine **DATE:** 1986 **FREQ:** quarterly **CIRC:** 1,400 **DESCRIPTION:** A quarterly journal of women's spirituality. Features fiction, non-fiction, poetry & collages.

Samuel Weiser Catalogue

PUBLISHING COMPANY: Samuel Weiser, Inc. **TOPICS:** Parapsychology **TYPE:** Catalog **DATE:** 1984 **SIZE:** 6 x 9; 64 pgs. **PRICE:** $0.00

San Diego Pagan Newsletter

PUBLISHING COMPANY: San Diego Pagan Newsletter **TOPICS:** Witchcraft, Occult, Paganism **TYPE:** Newsletter

Sanctuary Of Light

PUBLISHING COMPANY: Sanctuary Of Light **EDITOR:** Pat O'Connell **TOPICS:** New Age **TYPE:** Newsletter

Santa Fe Spirit

PUBLISHING COMPANY: Santa Fe Spirit **EDITOR:** Apryl Freeman **TOPICS:** New Age, Metaphysics, Spirituality **TYPE:** Magazine **DATE:** 1988 **FREQ:** monthly **PRICE:** $18.00 **PRICE PER COPY:** $2.00 **DESCRIPTION:** Prints articles, poetry, reviews, interviews, recipes and calendarrelated to its area.

Santa Fe Sun

PUBLISHING COMPANY: Santa Fe Sun Publishing Company **PUBLISHER:** James Tomarelli **TOPICS:** New Age, Metaphysics **TYPE:** Newspaper **DATE:** 1988; 16 pgs. **FREQ:** monthly **CIRC:** 17,000 **PRICE:** $0.00 **PRICE PER COPY:** $0.00 **DESCRIPTION:** Alternative newspaper. Includes directory, articles, news and reviews.

Sat Sandesh: The Message Of The Masters

PUBLISHING COMPANY: Sat Sandesh: The Message Of The Masters **EDITOR:** Art Stein **TOPICS:** New Age, Spirituality **TYPE:** Magazine **FREQ:** monthly **PRICE:** $14.00 **TERM:** yearly **DESCRIPTION:** Magazine dealing with various aspects of spiritual life by spiritual masters.

Saucer Smear

PUBLISHING COMPANY: Saucer Smear **TOPICS:** UFO's **TYPE:** Magazine

SCEH Newsletter

PUBLISHING COMPANY: Society For Clinical & Experimental Hypnosis **EDITOR:** Marion Kenn **TOPICS:** Hypnotism **TYPE:** Newsletter

Science For The People

PUBLISHING COMPANY: Science Resource Center, Inc. **TOPICS:** New Age **TYPE:** Magazine

Science Of Mind Magazine

PUBLISHING COMPANY: United Church Of Religious Science **PUBLISHER:** John S. Niendorff **EDITOR:** Sheri Cady, Kathy Juline **TOPICS:** New Age, Metaphysics **TYPE:** Magazine **DATE:** 1956 **FREQ:** monthly **CIRC:** 105,000 **PRICE:** $15.00 **PRICE PER COPY:** $1.95 **DESCRIPTION:** Concerned with New Age & Metaphysical topics. Offers interviews, illustrations, children's articles, poetry, fiction & non-fiction, critiques & reviews on audios, ads, literary articles, videos & books. Distributed internationally.

Science Quest

PUBLISHING COMPANY: Science Frontiers **EDITOR:** Gerald Baker **TOPICS:** Psychic Phenomena **TYPE:** Magazine **FREQ:** quarterly **PRICE:** $5.00

Science/Health Abstracts

PUBLISHING COMPANY: Science/Health Abstracts **EDITOR:** Phylis Austin **TOPICS:** Holistic Healing **TYPE:** Magazine

Scienza E Ignoto

PUBLISHING COMPANY: I'Talamonti Faenza Editrice **TOPICS:** Parapsychology, Occult **TYPE:** Magazine **DATE:** 1972

SCP Newsletter

PUBLISHING COMPANY: SCP Newsletter **EDITOR:** Robert J.L. Burrows **TOPICS:** Metaphysics **TYPE:** Newsletter

Scroll Of Oplontis

PUBLISHING COMPANY: Scroll Of Oplontis **TOPICS:** Witchcraft, Occult, Paganism **TYPE:** Magazine

Scuola Di Astrologia

PUBLISHING COMPANY: Curcio Periodice S.p.A. **EDITOR:** Rosanna Falconi **TOPICS:** Astrology **TYPE:** Magazine **FREQ:** Monthly **CIRC:** 95,000

Se La Vie Writer's Journal

PUBLISHING COMPANY: Rio Grande Press **EDITOR:** Rosalie Avara **TOPICS:** Psychic

Phenomena **TYPE:** Journal **PRICE:** $14.00 **TERM:** yearly **DESCRIPTION:** Publishes original poems, stories, essays. Conducts writing contests.

Search Magazine

PUBLISHING COMPANY: Palmer Publications/Amherst Press, Inc. **PUBLISHER:** Charles Spanbauer **EDITOR:** Judith Statezny **TOPICS:** Parapsychology, Psychic Phenomena, Occult, New Age, Metaphysics, Paranormal Phenomena **TYPE:** Magazine **DATE:** 1953 **SIZE:** 8 1/2 x 11; 64 pgs. **FREQ:** Quarterly **CIRC:** 2,000 **PRICE:** $14.00 **PRICE PER COPY:** $3.50 **DESCRIPTION:** Explores the supernatural, paranormal experiences & psychic phenomenon. Prints news, reviews, poetry, interviews & non-fiction relating to New Age subjects.

Secrets

PUBLISHING COMPANY: Secrets **PUBLISHER:** Norma Cox **TOPICS:** UFO's **TYPE:** Newsletter; 24 pgs. **FREQ:** Irregular **DESCRIPTION:** Reports on conspiracies regarding UFO's.

Sedona-Journal Of Emergence

PUBLISHING COMPANY: Love-Light Communications, Inc. **PUBLISHER:** O'Ryin Swanson **EDITOR:** Margaret Pinyan **TOPICS:** New Age **TYPE:** Journal **FREQ:** monthly **PRICE PER COPY:** $3.95

Seeker's Peril

PUBLISHING COMPANY: Alternative Research **TOPICS:** New Age **TYPE:** Newsletter **DATE:** 1986; 16 pgs. **FREQ:** Irregular **PRICE PER COPY:** $2.00 **DESCRIPTION:** Unmasks New Age movements. Offers a non-sectarian approach & critical reviews.

Self Hypnosis And Other Mind Expanding Techniques

PUBLISHING COMPANY: Westwood Publishing Company **EDITOR:** Charles Tebbetts **TOPICS:** Hypnotism, Psychology **TYPE:** Magazine **PRICE:** $7.95

SELF Magazine

PUBLISHING COMPANY: Conde Nast Publications, Inc. **EDITOR:** Anthea Disney, Marianne Howatson **TOPICS:** Holistic Healing **TYPE:** Magazine

Self-Publishing In The New Age: A Quarterly Newsletter For New Age/Self-Help Authors

PUBLISHING COMPANY: Paloma Blanca Press **EDITOR:** John Patrick Lamkin **TOPICS:** New Age **TYPE:** Newsletter **FREQ:** quarterly **DESCRIPTION:** News, tips & reviews for New Age & self-help authors who are considering publishing their own books or who are already doing so.

Self-Realization

PUBLISHING COMPANY: Self-Realization Fellowship **EDITOR:** Jane Brush **TOPICS:** New Age **TYPE:** Newsletter

Serenity's New Life

PUBLISHING COMPANY: Serenity Health Organization, Inc. **EDITOR:** Mark Becker **TOPICS:** Holistic Health **TYPE:** Magazine **FREQ:** Bi-Monthly **PRICE:** $10.00 **DESCRIPTION:** Provides information on wholistic health and human potential.

Offers a calendar of events, current news on products & services, techniques, research & consciousness.

Seventh Seal

PUBLISHING COMPANY: San Diego State University Press **PUBLISHER:** S. John **TOPICS:** Parapsychology **TYPE:** Newsletter **DATE:** 1980; 2 pgs. **FREQ:** Irregular **DESCRIPTION:** Explores various topics through spiritual influence such as magic, meditation, numerology, sex, incest, vampirism, dancing, perfumes, wine, astrology & saviors.

Shaman's Drum

PUBLISHING COMPANY: Cross-Cultural Shaman's Network **EDITOR:** Gregory Stafford, Timothy White **TOPICS:** Holistic Healing, Spirituality **TYPE:** Magazine; 80 pgs. **FREQ:** quarterly **CIRC:** 20,000 **PRICE PER COPY:** $4.75

Shamanic Journey

PUBLISHING COMPANY: Shamanic Journey **TOPICS:** Metaphysics, Spirituality **TYPE:** Magazine

Shanti Yoga Newsletter

PUBLISHING COMPANY: Shanti Yoga-Center For Harmony **PUBLISHER:** Victor Landa (Vyasa) **TOPICS:** Yoga **TYPE:** Newsletter **DESCRIPTION:** Covers various aspects of Yoga.

Shape

PUBLISHING COMPANY: Weider Health & Fitness Group **EDITOR:** Barbara Harris **TOPICS:** Holistic Health **TYPE:** Magazine **DATE:** 1981 **FREQ:** Monthly **CIRC:** 678,349 **PRICE:** $20.00 **DESCRIPTION:** Intergrating the body & mind for fitness.

Shapers, The

PUBLISHING COMPANY: Shapers, The **EDITOR:** Ade Y. Aro **TOPICS:** New Age, Metaphysics **TYPE:** Newspaper **DATE:** 1989 **FREQ:** monthly **CIRC:** 5,000 **DESCRIPTION:** Serves Greater Bay Area with articles focusing on African-Americans.

Share It

PUBLISHING COMPANY: Share It **EDITOR:** Anne Seward **TOPICS:** Holistic Health **TYPE:** Magazine **DATE:** 1979 **FREQ:** Irregular **CIRC:** 500 **DESCRIPTION:** Emphasizes & promotes awareness of our inner self & our true identity.

Sharings

PUBLISHING COMPANY: Universal Kingdom **EDITOR:** Brother Lou **TOPICS:** Astrology **TYPE:** Journal; 10 pgs. **FREQ:** Irregular **PRICE:** $9.60

Shavertron

PUBLISHING COMPANY: Shavertron **PUBLISHER:** Richard Toronto **TYPE:** Magazine **DATE:** 1979; 40 pgs. **PRICE:** $5.00 **DESCRIPTION:** The only fanzine in the 1990's dealing with the Shaver Mystery, the hollow earth, mind control, Fortean fantasmagoria & other mind-boggling ideas. No subscriptions. Sold by request only.

Siderealist

PUBLISHING COMPANY: Sidereal Registry & Exchange **EDITOR:** Norman Bones **TOPICS:** Astrology **TYPE:** Journal **FREQ:** Quarterly **PRICE:** $14.50

Sierra

PUBLISHING COMPANY: Sierra Club **EDITOR:** Michael L. Fischer, Jonathan F. King **TOPICS:** Holistic Healing **TYPE:** Newsletter

Simply Living Magazine

PUBLISHING COMPANY: Simply Living Magazine **TOPICS:** New Age **TYPE:** Magazine **FREQ:** quarterly **PRICE:** $25.00 **DESCRIPTION:** Full-color, sometimes radical, publication with focus on healthy living.

Sinsemilla Tips

PUBLISHING COMPANY: New Moon Publishing, Inc. **EDITOR:** Tom Alexander **TOPICS:** Holistic Healing **TYPE:** Magazine

Sirius

PUBLISHING COMPANY: Sirius **EDITOR:** David Cochrane **TOPICS:** Astrology **TYPE:** Journal

Skeptical Inquirer

PUBLISHING COMPANY: Skeptical Inquirer **EDITOR:** Mary Hays **TOPICS:** New Age **TYPE:** Magazine **FREQ:** quarterly **DESCRIPTION:** Examines the paranormal through inquisitive and thought-provoken features.

Skole

PUBLISHING COMPANY: National Coalition Of Alternative Community Schools **TOPICS:** New Age **TYPE:** Newsletter

Small Press

PUBLISHING COMPANY: Small Press **EDITOR:** Brenda Mitchell-Powell **TOPICS:** New Age, Metaphysics **TYPE:** Journal **DATE:** 1983 **DESCRIPTION:** Trade journal for New Age publishes, features book and magazine reviews.

Smoking & Health Reporter

PUBLISHING COMPANY: Center For Health & Safety Studies Indiana University **EDITOR:** William Bailey **TOPICS:** Holistic Healing **TYPE:** Newsletter

Smoking And Health Bulletin

PUBLISHING COMPANY: Technical Information Center Office On Smoking & Health **EDITOR:** Susan Hawk **TOPICS:** Holistic Healing **TYPE:** Bulletin

Smoking And Health Newsletter

PUBLISHING COMPANY: National Interagency Council On Smoking **EDITOR:** Robert Wallace **TOPICS:** Holistic Healing **TYPE:** Newsletter

Snake Power

PUBLISHING COMPANY: Snake Power **PUBLISHER:** Vicki Noble **TOPICS:** Spirituality, Witchcraft, Occult, Paganism **TYPE:** Magazine **DATE:** 1989 **FREQ:** quarterly **PRICE:** $23.00 **PRICE PER COPY:** $6.50 **DESCRIPTION:** Prints articles relating to today's female shamanism.

Social Alternatives

PUBLISHING COMPANY: Social Alternatives **TOPICS:** New Age **TYPE:** Magazine **FREQ:** 4 issues/yr **PRICE:** $18.00 **DESCRIPTION:** Analyzes social, cultural and economic issues.

Societe Journal

PUBLISHING COMPANY: Technicians Of The Sacred **EDITOR:** Courtney Willis **TOPICS:** Voudoun **TYPE:** Journal **FREQ:** bi-annually **PRICE:** $10.00

DESCRIPTION: Promotes the preservation and practice of Voudoun and other Neo-African religious systems, its magic, art and culture.

Society For Clinical & Experimental Hypnosis

PUBLISHING COMPANY: Society For Clinical & Experimental Hypnosis **EDITOR:** Marion Kenn **TOPICS:** Hypnotism **TYPE:** Newsletter

Society For Psychical Research Proceedings

PUBLISHING COMPANY: Society For Psychical Research **EDITOR:** John Beloff **TOPICS:** Parapsychology, Occult **TYPE:** Magazine **DATE:** 1882 **FREQ:** Irregular

Society For The Right To Die-Newsletter

PUBLISHING COMPANY: Society For The Right To Die, Inc. **EDITOR:** Shirley Neitlich **TOPICS:** Death **TYPE:** Newsletter

Soekaren

PUBLISHING COMPANY: Sven Magnusson **EDITOR:** Sven Magnusson **TOPICS:** Parapsychology, Occult **TYPE:** Magazine **DATE:** 1964 **FREQ:** 8 x/yr. **CIRC:** 3,000

SOLAR (SOL Association For Research)

PUBLISHING COMPANY: SOL Association For Research - The Council Speaks **TOPICS:** Channeling, Spirituality **TYPE:** Newsletter **FREQ:** quarterly

Solar Space-Letter

PUBLISHING COMPANY: Blue Rose Ministry **PUBLISHER:** Rev. Robert Short **TOPICS:** UFO's, New Age **TYPE:** Newsletter **DATE:** 1959 **FREQ:** bi-monthly **PRICE:** $12.00 **TERM:** annually **PRICE PER COPY:** $0.50 **DESCRIPTION:** Purpose is to inform & notify the public about UFO's, New Age, Archeology, Extraterrestrial subjects.

Solstice Magazine

PUBLISHING COMPANY: Solstice Magazine, Inc. **EDITOR:** Randolph Byrd, John David Mann **TOPICS:** New Age, Holistic Health **TYPE:** Magazine **FREQ:** bi-monthly **CIRC:** 56,000 **PRICE:** $36.00 **DESCRIPTION:** New Age magazine covers food, health, fitness, the environment and book reviews. Published for environmentally-concerned readers seeking natural health living. Prints articles and directory. Accepts ads.

Somatics

PUBLISHING COMPANY: Novato Institute For Somatic Research & Training **EDITOR:** Thomas Hanna **TOPICS:** Holistic Health **TYPE:** Magazine **DATE:** 1976 **FREQ:** Semi-Annual **CIRC:** 1,300 **PRICE:** $15.00 **DESCRIPTION:** Explores the interaction between body and mind for the professional & layperson.

Sound Choice

PUBLISHING COMPANY: Sound Choice **EDITOR:** Venus Louviere **TOPICS:** New Age, Metaphysics **TYPE:** Magazine **DATE:** 1984 **CIRC:** 7,500 **PRICE:** $10.00 **PRICE PER COPY:** $3.00 **DESCRIPTION:** A publication for the music and audio industry. Prints product reviews, feature articles, news and interviews.

Sounds True Catalog

PUBLISHING COMPANY: Sounds True **PUBLISHER:** Tami Simon **TOPICS:** New Age, Spirituality, Psychology, Holistic Healing **TYPE:** Catalog; 50 pgs. **DESCRIPTION:** Offers a selection of more than 150 enlightening tapes of words & music. Spoken tapes express the ideas of outstanding men & women, in their own words & voices, covering various New Age related fields of interest.

Sourcefinder II

PUBLISHING COMPANY: Boyd's **PUBLISHER:** Margaret Boyd **TOPICS:** Parapsychology **TYPE:** Newsletter **DATE:** 1981 **SIZE:** 8 1/2 x 11; 10 pgs. **FREQ:** Quarterly **CIRC:** 2,000 **PRICE:** $6.75 **PRICE PER COPY:** $2.00 **DESCRIPTION:** Provides listings of resources & New Age events happening throughout the South.

Sourcefinder Newsletter

PUBLISHING COMPANY: Sourcefinder Newsletter **TOPICS:** Holistic Healing **TYPE:** Newsletter

Sources

PUBLISHING COMPANY: Sources **EDITOR:** Kate Burton **TOPICS:** Holistic Healing, New Age, Metaphysics **TYPE:** Magazine **DATE:** 1987 **FREQ:** bi-monthly **CIRC:** 26,000 **DESCRIPTION:** Encourages personal growth and positive global changes. Provides calendar for Maryland and surrounding areas, including PA, VA & D.C. Accepts ads.

Sources Southwest

PUBLISHING COMPANY: Sources Southwest **EDITOR:** Tom Goelitz, Carrie Goelitz **TOPICS:** New Age **TYPE:** Magazine **DATE:** 1990 **FREQ:** bi-monthly **DESCRIPTION:** Serves southwestern AZ, NM, CO & El Paso, TX areas. Lists logos, products and services. Prints articles and reviews. Supports self-awareness and global changes.

Southern Crossings

PUBLISHING COMPANY: Southern Crossings **EDITOR:** Cherly Meyer **TOPICS:** New Age **TYPE:** Magazine **SIZE:** 8x12; 46 pgs. **FREQ:** 6 issues/yr **PRICE:** $5.00 **DESCRIPTION:** Articles focus on health, environment. Information on workshops and classes provided.

Spa Finder

PUBLISHING COMPANY: Spa-Finders **TOPICS:** Holistic Healing **TYPE:** Magazine

Sparrow Hawk Villager

PUBLISHING COMPANY: Sparrow Hawk Press **EDITOR:** Carol Parrish-Harra **TOPICS:** Spirituality **TYPE:** Newsletter **FREQ:** bi-monthly **DESCRIPTION:** Newsletter pertaining to the operation & events of the Sparrow Hawk Village.

Speakout

PUBLISHING COMPANY: Harmonial Philosophy Association **EDITOR:** Marilyn Awtry-Smith **TOPICS:** Metaphysics **TYPE:** Magazine

Special Delivery

PUBLISHING COMPANY: Informed Homebirth/Informed Birth & Parenting **EDITOR:** Rahima Baldwin **TOPICS:** Birth, Holistic Health

TYPE: Newsletter **FREQ:** quarterly **PRICE:** $15.00 **DESCRIPTION:** Annual, Magical Years, conference on the young child, April, Ann Arbor, MI.

Specialty Travel Index Directory/Magazine

PUBLISHING COMPANY: Alpine Hansen Publisher **PUBLISHER:** C. Steen Hansen **TOPICS:** New Age **TYPE:** Magazine **DATE:** 1980 **SIZE:** 8 1/2 x 11; 156 pgs. **FREQ:** bi-annual **DESCRIPTION:** Directory/magazine of special interest & adventure travel. Published twice a year in January & August.

Spectra Newsletter

PUBLISHING COMPANY: Spectra, Inc. **EDITOR:** Don Preister **TOPICS:** New Age, Metaphysics **TYPE:** Newsletter **DATE:** 1980; 14 pgs. **FREQ:** bi-monthly **CIRC:** 1,200 **PRICE:** $15.00 **TERM:** annually **DESCRIPTION:** Purpose is to provide Metaphysical information. Published by this non-profit organization, features articles and events calendar. Accepts ads.

Spectrum

PUBLISHING COMPANY: Spectrum **TOPICS:** Metaphysics, Spirituality, Holistic Healing **TYPE:** Magazine

Spectrum Review

PUBLISHING COMPANY: Integral Publishing **EDITOR:** Georg Feuerstein, Patricia Lamb **TOPICS:** Metaphysics, New Age **TYPE:** Newsletter **DATE:** 1986; 8 pgs. **FREQ:** quarterly **CIRC:** 2,000 **PRICE:** $14.00 **DESCRIPTION:** Includes book reviews.

Spectrum/The Wholistic News Magazine

PUBLISHING COMPANY: Spectrum/The Wholistic News Magazine **EDITOR:** Roger G. Windsor, Denise Guerringue **TOPICS:** Holistic Health, Nutrition **TYPE:** Magazine **DATE:** 1988; 36 pgs. **FREQ:** 6 x per year **PRICE:** $10.00 **PRICE PER COPY:** $3.00 **DESCRIPTION:** Newsmagazine reporting New Age news. Searches out & reports 90 concise articles in each issue on health, nutrition, mind & spirit, environment, lifestyle & society. Accepts ads.

Specular Journal - inactive

PUBLISHING COMPANY: American Association Of Meta-Science **TOPICS:** Psychic Phenomena **TYPE:** Journal

Sphaera Imagination

PUBLISHING COMPANY: Sphaera Imagination **TOPICS:** Metaphysics, Spirituality **TYPE:** Magazine

Sphere

PUBLISHING COMPANY: Sphere **TOPICS:** New Age **TYPE:** Magazine; 28 pgs. **FREQ:** bi-annual **DESCRIPTION:** Scottish magazine dealing with various New Age topics, includes mystery schools and astrology.

Sphinx

PUBLISHING COMPANY: Coven Of Isis **TOPICS:** Parapsychology, Occult **TYPE:** Magazine **FREQ:** Quarterly **PRICE:** $6.00

Spica

PUBLISHING COMPANY: R.O.S.A. **TOPICS:** Astrology **TYPE:** Magazine

Spirit Magazine

PUBLISHING COMPANY: Cosmic Circus Productions EDITOR: Rey King, Usha Muliyil TOPICS: UFO's, Metaphysics, New Age TYPE: Magazine DATE: 1974; 60 pgs. CIRC: 2,000 DESCRIPTION: Concentrates on rare audio-video music and comics. Prints news, reviews, ads and interviews.

Spirit Speaks Magazine

PUBLISHING COMPANY: Spirit Speaks, Inc. EDITOR: Molli Nickell, Glenn Mitchell TOPICS: New Age, Channeling TYPE: Magazine DATE: 1985 SIZE: 8 1/2 x 11; 75 pgs. FREQ: bi-monthly CIRC: 30,000 PRICE: $20.00 TERM: yearly PRICE PER COPY: $3.95 DESCRIPTION: Purpose is to share guidance & wisdom from the wise & loving teachers of the spirit plane through the process known as channeling. Each issue focuses on one topic as addressed by many different spirit teachers. Distributed throughout U.S. & 11 foreign countries. Shares spiritual psychology, addressing the pressing issues of life as seen from the perspective of spirit. Attempts to help people recognize their divinity & to learn to live with allowance, communication & self-responsibility.

Spiritual Advisory Council Newsletter-Outreach

PUBLISHING COMPANY: Spiritual Advisory Council EDITOR: Rev. Paul V. Johnson TOPICS: Parapsychology, Occult, Psychic, Spirituality, Metaphysics TYPE: Newsletter FREQ: 10 x yearly CIRC: 1,000 DESCRIPTION: Newsletter included with membership.

Spiritual Astrology Newsletter

PUBLISHING COMPANY: Spiritual Astrology Newsletter EDITOR: Jim Buss TOPICS: New Age TYPE: Newsletter FREQ: Bi-Weekly PRICE: $25.00

Spiritual Emergence Network Newsletter

PUBLISHING COMPANY: Spiritual Emergence Network EDITOR: Emma Bragdon, Ph. D. TOPICS: Holistic Healing, Psychic Phenomena, Death TYPE: Newsletter FREQ: bi-annual DESCRIPTION: Free with membership.

Spiritual Frontiers

PUBLISHING COMPANY: Spiritual Frontiers Fellowship EDITOR: Frank C. Tribbe TOPICS: Psychic Phenomena TYPE: Journal FREQ: quarterly DESCRIPTION: Contains articles on the relationships between religion, psychical research & parapsychology as well as on spiritual growth, reincarnation, healing, psychic phenomena & the Spiritual Frontiers Fellowship. Offers book reviews & research reports.

Spiritual Healer

PUBLISHING COMPANY: Harry Edwards Spiritual Healing Santuary Trust EDITOR: Ramus Branch, Joan Branch TOPICS: Holistic Health TYPE: Magazine DATE: 1953 FREQ: Bi-Monthly CIRC: 6,500 DESCRIPTION: Explores philosophy & spiritual healing. Free.

Spiritual Healing Bulletin

PUBLISHING COMPANY: Aetherius Society EDITOR: Dr. George King TOPICS: Psychic Phenomena TYPE: Bulletin

Spiritual Women's Times

PUBLISHING COMPANY: Spiritual Women's Times EDITOR: Krysta Gibson TOPICS: New Age, Metaphysics TYPE: Newspaper DATE: 1987 FREQ: quarterly CIRC: 15,000 DESCRIPTION: Aimed at women interested in spirituality and personal growth.

Spiritualist Gazette

PUBLISHING COMPANY: SAGB EDITOR: Thomas Johanson TOPICS: Parapsychology, Occult TYPE: Magazine DATE: 1972 FREQ: Monthly CIRC: 5,000

SPR Newsletter

PUBLISHING COMPANY: Society For Psychical Research EDITOR: Susan Balckmore TOPICS: Parapsychology, Occult TYPE: Newsletter DATE: 1981 FREQ: Quarterly CIRC: 900

Sprout House Newsletter, The

PUBLISHING COMPANY: Sprout House PUBLISHER: Steve Meyerowitz TOPICS: Nutrition, Holistic Health, Health Food TYPE: Newsletter FREQ: quarterly DESCRIPTION: Provides information to the increasing number of home growers of sprouted vegetables.

Sproutletter

PUBLISHING COMPANY: Sprouting Publications, Kit Larke TOPICS: Holistic Healing TYPE: Newsletter

SSC Booknews

PUBLISHING COMPANY: Spiritual Studies Center EDITOR: Millard Nachtwey TOPICS: New Age, Metaphysics TYPE: Newsletter DESCRIPTION: Provides book review service for the Spiritual Studies Center.

Star Charter, The

PUBLISHING COMPANY: Star Charter, The TOPICS: Astrology TYPE: Magazine

Star Lighter Newsletter

PUBLISHING COMPANY: Rev. Cylvia Archer-Lowe PUBLISHER: Cylvia Lowe TOPICS: New Age, Metaphysics TYPE: Newsletter DATE: 1990; 6 pgs. FREQ: monthly PRICE: $7.95 TERM: 6 months DESCRIPTION: Purpose is to enlighten, inform, guide & educate people on New Age & Metaphysical issues. Advertising accepted. Writers & articles welcome.

Star Reviews

PUBLISHING COMPANY: Star Reviews EDITOR: Susan Star TOPICS: New Age, Metaphysics TYPE: Magazine DATE: 1945 DESCRIPTION: Provides book/audio/video reviews of New Age publications in several categories from psychology to self-help to past lvies.

Starcraft Horoscope

PUBLISHING COMPANY: Starcraft Press EDITOR: Geoffrey Gray-Cobb TOPICS: Astrology TYPE: Journal

Starfire Journal

PUBLISHING COMPANY: Starfire Journal TOPICS: Witchcraft, Occult, Paganism TYPE: Journal

Stargazer

PUBLISHING COMPANY: Stargazer TOPICS: Channeling TYPE: Magazine

Star*Tech

PUBLISHING COMPANY: Star Tech Services PUBLISHER: Richard Nolle TOPICS: Astrology TYPE: Magazine DATE: 1987; 22 pgs. FREQ: Monthly PRICE: $16.50 PRICE PER COPY: $2.50 DESCRIPTION: Focuses on present-day ideas on astrology.

Starlight Connections

PUBLISHING COMPANY: Starlight Connections EDITOR: Goldie Hoppe TOPICS: New Age TYPE: Magazine FREQ: bi-yearly

Starscrolls

PUBLISHING COMPANY: Twelve Signs, Inc. PUBLISHER: Richard Housman TOPICS: Astrology TYPE: Magazine FREQ: Monthly PRICE PER COPY: $0.59

Staying Well Newsletter

PUBLISHING COMPANY: Foundation For Chiropractic Education And Research EDITOR: Tom Wolff TOPICS: Holistic Healing TYPE: Newsletter

Stellium Quarterly

PUBLISHING COMPANY: Stellium, Inc. EDITOR: Katherine Boehrer TOPICS: Astrology TYPE: Magazine DATE: 1975 FREQ: quarterly PRICE: $6.50 DESCRIPTION: Covers all aspects of astrology.

Stigmata

PUBLISHING COMPANY: Project Stigma EDITOR: Thomas R. Adams TOPICS: Psychic Phenomena TYPE: Magazine

Strange Magazine

PUBLISHING COMPANY: Strange Magazine EDITOR: Mark Chorvinsky, Douglas Chapman TOPICS: Psychic Phenomena, Parapsychology TYPE: Magazine FREQ: quarterly PRICE: $14.95 DESCRIPTION: Deals with the paranormal & strange phenomena. Accepts ads.

Subconsciously Speaking

PUBLISHING COMPANY: Infinity Institute International, Inc. TOPICS: Hypnotism TYPE: Newsletter SIZE: 8 1/2x11; 12 pgs. FREQ: bi-monthly DESCRIPTION: Bi-monthly newsletter reporting on the activities of the International Medical and Dental Hypnotherapy Association as well as varied articles by numerous authors on hypnosis, meditation, visualization, healing and other mind/body relationships. Book reviews and ads printed.

Substance Abuse

PUBLISHING COMPANY: Manisses Communications Group, Inc. EDITOR: Marc Galanter TOPICS: Holistic Healing TYPE: Magazine

Substance Abuse Report

PUBLISHING COMPANY: Business Research Publications, Inc. EDITOR: John Roche, Allison Knopf TOPICS: Holistic Healing TYPE: Newsletter

Success Through Mind Power

PUBLISHING COMPANY: Westwood Publishing Company EDITOR: Roy Hunter, M.H. TOPICS: Psychology, Body-Mind Connection TYPE: Magazine PRICE: $6.95

Sun Sign Book

PUBLISHING COMPANY: Llewellyn Publications PUBLISHER: Carl Weschcke EDITOR: Terry Buske TOPICS: Astrology TYPE: Calendar DATE: 1906 SIZE: 4 1/4 x 5; 500 pgs. CIRC: 25,000 PRICE: $3.75 PRICE PER COPY: $3.95 DESCRIPTION: An astrological almanac giving yearly Sun Signs & predicting stockmarket activity, weather & the news.

Sundance: The Community Dream Journal

PUBLISHING COMPANY: Sundance Community Newsletter EDITOR: Henry Reed TOPICS: Dreams TYPE: Journal

Sunrise

PUBLISHING COMPANY: Sunrise TOPICS: Metaphysics, Spirituality, Channeling TYPE: Magazine

Sunrise-Theosophic Perspectives

PUBLISHING COMPANY: Theosophical University Press EDITOR: Grace F. Knoche, W.T.S. Thackara TOPICS: New Age, Spirituality TYPE: Magazine DATE: 1951 SIZE: 6 x 9; 32 pgs. FREQ: bi-monthly PRICE: $9.00 TERM: yearly PRICE PER COPY: $2.00 DESCRIPTION: Presents a wide spectrum of thought-provoking articles on scientific, religious, & philosophical themes in the light of ancient & modern theosophy & its relationship to daily living. Includes interviews, reports on significant trends, reviews of worthwhile books, commentary on the spiritual principles at the core of the world's sacred traditions & insights into the nature of man & the universe.

Supermente

PUBLISHING COMPANY: Editorial Posada TOPICS: Psychic Phenomena TYPE: Magazine FREQ: Semi-Monthly

Supportive Lifestyles News

PUBLISHING COMPANY: Fellowship Of The Inner Light EDITOR: Myrrh Keton TOPICS: Holistic Health TYPE: Newspaper DATE: 1972 FREQ: Monthly PRICE: $25.00

Sut Anubis

PUBLISHING COMPANY: Sut Anubis EDITOR: M. John Lovett TOPICS: Parapsychology, Occult, Metaphysics TYPE: Magazine DATE: 1973 FREQ: quarterly CIRC: 500 PRICE: $10.00 DESCRIPTION: Devoted to the occult. Containing original articles on topics such as witchcraft, crowleyanity, ceremonial magic & paganism.

Swamp Gas Journal

PUBLISHING COMPANY: Ufology Research Of Manitoba PUBLISHER: Chris Rutkowski TOPICS: UFO's TYPE: Journal DATE: 1978 SIZE: 8 1/2 x 11; 10 pgs. FREQ: Irregular CIRC: 250 PRICE PER COPY: $2.00 DESCRIPTION: Articles & reviews on UFO's & paranormal phenomenon.

Sword of Drynwyn

PUBLISHING COMPANY: Association Of Cymmry Wicca EDITOR: Vickie L. Wheeler TOPICS: New Age, Occult, Witchcraft, Spirituality, Metaphysics TYPE: Journal DATE: 1969; 30 pgs. FREQ: 8 x per year PRICE: $15.95 TERM: yearly DESCRIPTION: Journal of Welsh Witchcraft in America. Prints fiction, non-fiction, news, poetry, satire, reviews, and various forms of artwork.

Symphony

PUBLISHING COMPANY: Panic Press EDITOR: Aline H. Simon TOPICS: Crystals, Occult, Tarot, Paganism, New Age, Herbalogy, Metaphysics TYPE: Newsletter DATE: 1984 FREQ: quarterly CIRC: 250 PRICE: $10.00 DESCRIPTION: Dedicated to exploring all avenues of Neo-Pagen life, New Age sciences, philosophy, magick, rituals, the environment, tarot, mythology, the occult, metaphysics, self improvement, wicca, herbs & crystals. Offers commentaries, articles, artwork, poetry & ads. Philosophy is that all living beings create a symphony when they live in harmony with themselves & their world. Published at the Solstices & Equinoxes.

T'ai Chi

PUBLISHING COMPANY: Wayfarer Publications EDITOR: Marvin Smalheiser TOPICS: Body-Mind Connection, Tai Chi TYPE: Journal FREQ: bi-monthly CIRC: 15,000 PRICE: $15.00 DESCRIPTION: An international, well-known T'ai Chi Ch'uan publication with articles, ads and catalog.

T.A.R.O.T. Newsletter

PUBLISHING COMPANY: T.A.R.O.T. PUBLISHER: Mary K. Greer EDITOR: Ed Buryn TOPICS: Tarot, Metaphysics TYPE: Newsletter

Take In Good Part

PUBLISHING COMPANY: Take In Good Part TOPICS: Metaphysics, Spirituality TYPE: Magazine

Talk Of The Month

PUBLISHING COMPANY: Institute For The Development Of The Harmonious Human Being, Inc. PUBLISHER: Nancy Christie EDITOR: Iven Lourie TOPICS: Parapsychology, Holistic Health TYPE: Journal DATE: 1983 SIZE: 8 1/2 x 11; 16 pgs. FREQ: Monthly CIRC: 150 PRICE: $120.00 PRICE PER COPY: $15.00 DESCRIPTION: Provides edited reports of recent metaphysical teachings. Explores metaphysical & transformational ideas.

Tantric Times

PUBLISHING COMPANY: Paloma Blanca Press EDITOR: John Patrick Lamkin TOPICS: New Age, Spirituality TYPE: Newsletter DATE: 1991; 24 pgs. FREQ: quarterly CIRC: 5,000 PRICE: $49.00 TERM: yearly DESCRIPTION: Dedicated to the exploration of spiritual sexuality. Offers articles, news, reviews of books, videos, audio tapes, products, workshops & seminars. Also has resource section. No advertising accepted.

Taplight

PUBLISHING COMPANY: Taplight Studio PUBLISHER: Ann Croft Strong EDITOR: Ginny Flander TOPICS: New Age, Metaphysics, Dreams TYPE: Newsletter DATE: 1987; 8 pgs. FREQ: monthly CIRC: 1,000 PRICE: $17.00 TERM: yearly PRICE PER COPY: $2.00 DESCRIPTION: A forum for emotional and spiritual healing through the sharing of personal stories. Each issue has a central theme. Purpose is to inspire self-awareness, self-love & self-responsibility. Supports self expression. Encourages healing of inner pain & the celebrating of the spirit.

Tara

PUBLISHING COMPANY: Tara TOPICS: New Age TYPE: Journal DESCRIPTION: Publication of the Women's Prout Movement with emphasis on women's spirituality.

Tarot Interpreter

PUBLISHING COMPANY: Tarot Interpreter Publications EDITOR: Judith L. Welpman TOPICS: Tarot TYPE: Magazine DATE: 1988; 24 pgs. FREQ: monthly PRICE: $18.00 TERM: 6 months DESCRIPTION: Devoted exclusively to the art of Tarot. Features interpretations, readings on issues affecting our lives today, interesting facts about Tarot, how-to features & information regarding Tarot decks & Tarot-related products.

Tarot Network News

PUBLISHING COMPANY: Taroco EDITOR: Gary Ross TOPICS: Tarot TYPE: Magazine DATE: 1981 SIZE: 7 x 8 1/2; 50 pgs. FREQ: bi-annually CIRC: 300 PRICE: $10.00 TERM: yearly PRICE PER COPY: $5.00 DESCRIPTION: An international journal of Tarot events, products, artwork, research & interpretation. The emphasis is on philosophy, psychology, ontology, Theology & comparative religion.

TAT Journal

PUBLISHING COMPANY: TAT Book Service EDITOR: Mark Jaqua TOPICS: Parapsychology, Psychology TYPE: Journal DATE: 1978 SIZE: 5.5 x 8.5; 128 pgs. FREQ: Semi-Monthly CIRC: 5,000 PRICE PER COPY: $3.75 DESCRIPTION: Reports new ideas in the fields of philosophy, parapsychology & psychology. Includes book reviews.

TAT Journal

PUBLISHING COMPANY: TAT EDITOR: Louis Khourey TOPICS: Parapsychology, Psychology, Spirituality TYPE: Journal DATE: 1978; 128 pgs. FREQ: Annual CIRC: 5,000 PRICE PER COPY: $3.00 DESCRIPTION: Explores the fields of science, psychology & religion with a liberal approach.

Tattoo Advocate Journal

PUBLISHING COMPANY: Tattoo Advocate Journal EDITOR: Shotsie Gorman TOPICS: New Age TYPE: Journal

Tea & Coffee Association Of Canada Bulletin

PUBLISHING COMPANY: Tea & Coffee Association Of Canada TOPICS: Astrology TYPE: Bulletin FREQ: 10 x/yr. PRICE: $0.00

Teaching And Learning: The Journal Of Natural Inquiry And Pathways

PUBLISHING COMPANY: Center For Teaching And Learning TOPICS: New Age TYPE: Journal

Telewoman

PUBLISHING COMPANY: Telewoman TOPICS: Witchcraft, Occult, Paganism TYPE: Magazine

Temos

PUBLISHING COMPANY: Temos EDITOR: Christopher Bamford TOPICS: New Age, Metaphysics TYPE: Magazine DATE: 1979 FREQ: bi-monthly DESCRIPTION: Prints fiction and non-fiction articles relating to the science of consciousness.

Temple Doors

PUBLISHING COMPANY: Star Of Isis Foundation EDITOR: Christine Hayes TYPE: Magazine DATE: 1980 SIZE: 8 1/2 x 11; 25 pgs. FREQ: quarterly CIRC: 100 PRICE: $25.00 TERM: yearly PRICE PER COPY: $5.00 DESCRIPTION: Channelled insights into planetary transformation, inner earth tribes, meta-sciences, ancient cultures & angelic mandates.

Tertium Quid

PUBLISHING COMPANY: Tertium Quid TOPICS: Metaphysics, Spirituality TYPE: Magazine

Tetrahedron, Inc.

PUBLISHING COMPANY: Tetrahedron, Inc. EDITOR: Leonard Horowitz TOPICS: New Age, Metaphysics TYPE: Newsletter DATE: 1978 FREQ: 2-4issues/yr PRICE PER COPY: $8.95 DESCRIPTION: Focuses on health in the workplace and in general.

Texas Journal Of Chiropractic

PUBLISHING COMPANY: Texas Chiropractic Association EDITOR: Dr. Michael Van DeWalle TOPICS: Holistic Healing TYPE: Journal

The 13th Illuminated Stratum

PUBLISHING COMPANY: Triskaidekaphobia Illuminatus Society TOPICS: Numerology TYPE: Magazine

The Alliance

PUBLISHING COMPANY: Alliance, The TOPICS: New Age TYPE: Newspaper

The American Chiropractor

PUBLISHING COMPANY: Busch Publishing Company EDITOR: Jennifer Maxfield, Elaine Fortmeyer TOPICS: Holistic Healing TYPE: Magazine

The Beacon

PUBLISHING COMPANY: Beacon, The EDITOR: Perry Coles TOPICS: New Age, Metaphysics TYPE: Magazine DATE: 1922 FREQ: bi-monthly CIRC: 2,700 PRICE: $14.00 PRICE PER COPY: $2.50 DESCRIPTION: Publishes articles that show the benefits of Ageless Wisdom in modern-day living. Concerned with spirituality for the person and the world. Prints reviews.

The Beltane Papers Octava

PUBLISHING COMPANY: Juno's Peacock Press-Northwest Graphics EDITOR: Helen Farias TOPICS: New Age TYPE: Newsletter

The Branches Wiccan Calendar

PUBLISHING COMPANY: Three Sisters, Ltd. EDITOR: Kyril Oakwind TOPICS: Witchcraft, Occult, Paganism, Astrology TYPE: Calendar

The Buddhist Review

PUBLISHING COMPANY: Buddhist Ray, Inc. EDITOR: Helen Tworkov TOPICS: New Age,

Spirituality TYPE: Magazine FREQ: quarterly PRICE PER COPY: $6.00

The Center Of The Light Newsletter

PUBLISHING COMPANY: Center Of The Light EDITOR: Eugene Graf, Eva Graf TOPICS: Holistic Healing TYPE: Newsletter

The Cheirological Society Journal

PUBLISHING COMPANY: Cheirological Society TOPICS: Palmistry, Holistic Health TYPE: Journal FREQ: quarterly DESCRIPTION: Issued free to society members.

The Count Dracula Fan Club News-Journal

PUBLISHING COMPANY: Jeanne Youngson Publishers PUBLISHER: Dr. Jeanne Keyes Youngson EDITOR: James Martin, Betsy Dukas TOPICS: Vampires TYPE: Journal DATE: 1980 SIZE: 5 1/2 x 8 FREQ: quarterly CIRC: 1,500 PRICE PER COPY: $4.50 DESCRIPTION: All about vampires, serious & comic.

The Digest Of Chiropractic Economics

PUBLISHING COMPANY: Chiropractic News Publishing Company EDITOR: Keith A. Tosolt, Mrs. Helen L. Luckey TOPICS: Holistic Healing TYPE: Magazine

The Door Opener

PUBLISHING COMPANY: New Age Guild Of Connecticut EDITOR: Jon Roe TOPICS: Holistic Health, Metaphysics, New Age TYPE: Magazine DATE: 1986 SIZE: 8 1/2 x11; 80 pgs. FREQ: quarterly CIRC: 2,000 PRICE: $8.00 TERM: yearly PRICE PER COPY: $2.50 DESCRIPTION: Holistic health & metaphysical networking magazine for Connecticut's New Age community. Keeps members informed on New Age classes, workshops, fairs & other events.

The Elisabeth Kubler-Ross Newsletter

PUBLISHING COMPANY: Elisabeth Kubler-Ross Center/Shanti Nilaya TOPICS: Holistic Healing TYPE: Newsletter

The Emshock Letter

PUBLISHING COMPANY: Vongrutnorv Og Press, Inc. EDITOR: Steven E. Erickson TOPICS: Metaphysics, New Age TYPE: Newsletter DATE: 1977 SIZE: 8 1/2 x 11; 30 pgs. FREQ: Irregular CIRC: 25 PRICE: $25.00 TERM: yearly DESCRIPTION: Concerned with the human potential movement and explores all aspects of consciousness.

The Family Travel Guides Catalogue

PUBLISHING COMPANY: Carousel Press EDITOR: Carole T. Meyers TOPICS: New Age, Holistic Health TYPE: Catalog DATE: 1984; 32 pgs. FREQ: annual PRICE PER COPY: $1.00 DESCRIPTION: Aids parents in planning family vacations.

The Free Daist

PUBLISHING COMPANY: Free Daist Communion EDITOR: Carolyn Lee, Paul Augspurger TOPICS: New Age TYPE: Magazine PRICE: $48.00

The Fun Club Nudist Newsletter

PUBLISHING COMPANY: Fun Club EDITOR: Roger Hart TOPICS: New Age TYPE: Newsletter

The Futurist

PUBLISHING COMPANY: Futurist, The EDITOR: Edward Cornish TOPICS: Metaphysics, Psychic TYPE: Journal FREQ: bi-monthly CIRC: 25,475 PRICE: $25.00 DESCRIPTION: Published by the World Future Society, this journal deals with ideas and forecasts about the future.

The Gate

PUBLISHING COMPANY: Gate, The EDITOR: Beth Robbins TOPICS: Occult TYPE: Magazine DATE: 1984 SIZE: 8 1/2 x 11; 16 pgs. FREQ: quarterly CIRC: 200 PRICE: $7.00 TERM: yearly PRICE PER COPY: $1.75 DESCRIPTION: Deals with all aspects of the paranormal. Contains factual articles as well as newsclippings from around the world.

The Good News

PUBLISHING COMPANY: Nos Amis/Our Friends, Inc. TOPICS: New Age, Psychology, Metaphysics, Spirituality TYPE: Newsletter FREQ: bi-monthly

The Haunted Journal

PUBLISHING COMPANY: Baker Street Publications TOPICS: New Age TYPE: Journal

The Himalayan News

PUBLISHING COMPANY: Himalayan International Institute Of Yoga Science and Philosophy EDITOR: Katherine Avlonitis, Dale Colton TOPICS: New Age TYPE: Newspaper

The Impossible Human Newsletter

PUBLISHING COMPANY: Pyramid Research Center TOPICS: New Age TYPE: Newsletter

The Institute For Earth Education

PUBLISHING COMPANY: Institute For Earth Education TOPICS: Holistic Healing TYPE: Newsletter

The Journal Of Mind And Behavior

PUBLISHING COMPANY: Institute Of Mind And Behavior EDITOR: Raymond Russ, Ph.D. TOPICS: Meditation, New Age, Metaphysics TYPE: Journal DATE: 1980 FREQ: quarterly PRICE: $35.00 DESCRIPTION: A scholarly approach to mind/body interrelations. Accepts ads.

The Journal Of Near Death Studies

PUBLISHING COMPANY: International Association For Near-Death Studies TOPICS: Death TYPE: Journal FREQ: quarterly DESCRIPTION: Scientific journal on the Near Death Experience.

The Journal Of The Fortean Research Center

PUBLISHING COMPANY: Fortean Research Center EDITOR: Frank Dreier TOPICS: Big Foot, Psychic Phenomena, Paranormal Phenomena, UFO's TYPE: Journal DATE: 1982 FREQ: quarterly PRICE PER COPY: $3.50 DESCRIPTION: Reports on the work of the Fortean Research Center & various aspects of paranormal phenomena. Free with membership.

The Journal Of The Order Of Buddhist Contemplatives

PUBLISHING COMPANY: M.O.B.C. EDITOR: Rev. Kinzan Learman TOPICS: Meditation TYPE: Journal

The Kabbalist

PUBLISHING COMPANY: International Order Of Kabbalists **EDITOR:** J. Sturzaker **TOPICS:** Parapsychology, Occult, Kabbalah **TYPE:** Magazine **DATE:** 1974; 22 pgs. **FREQ:** Quarterly **CIRC:** 3,000 **DESCRIPTION:** An Occult Magazine.

The Light

PUBLISHING COMPANY: Light, The **EDITOR:** William Koopman **TOPICS:** New Age **TYPE:** Magazine **DESCRIPTION:** Prints interviews and articles. Dubbed, A Magazine Of The Heart.

The Lotus

PUBLISHING COMPANY: Light Of The Universe **EDITOR:** Helen Spitler **TOPICS:** Channeling **TYPE:** Journal **DATE:** 1966 **FREQ:** quarterly

The Meridian

PUBLISHING COMPANY: Acupuncture Research Institute **EDITOR:** Louis Gasper, Ph.D. **TOPICS:** Acupuncture **TYPE:** Magazine

The Messenger

PUBLISHING COMPANY: Messenger, The **EDITOR:** Lily O'Donnell **TOPICS:** New Age **TYPE:** Magazine **DATE:** 1980 **SIZE:** 8 1/2 x 14; 24 pgs. **FREQ:** monthly **CIRC:** 500 **PRICE:** $10.00 **TERM:** yearly **PRICE PER COPY:** $0.50 **DESCRIPTION:** A magazine about, by, and for Spiritualists. Offers lists of mediums, healers, teachers as well as articles, prayers, cartoons and ads. A magazine for the Golden Age. Low advertising rates. Distributed to 100 cities in the U.S., Alaska, Hawaii, Puerto Rico & Europe.

The Michael Connection

PUBLISHING COMPANY: Michael Connection, The **EDITOR:** M.C. Clark **TOPICS:** Channeling **TYPE:** Magazine

The Montessori Observer

PUBLISHING COMPANY: International Montessori Society **PUBLISHER:** Lee Havis **EDITOR:** Elizabeth Hainstock **TOPICS:** New Age **TYPE:** Newsletter **DESCRIPTION:** Free to members with $20 annual membership fee.

The Mystic Muse

PUBLISHING COMPANY: Samadhi Dreams Press **EDITOR:** Waltz J. Alashar, Radha Mohini **TOPICS:** New Age **TYPE:** Magazine

The National Spiritualist Summit

PUBLISHING COMPANY: National Spiritual Association Of Churches **EDITOR:** Rev. Sandra Pfortmiller **TOPICS:** Spirituality **TYPE:** Magazine **DATE:** 1919; 36 pgs. **FREQ:** monthly **PRICE PER COPY:** $1.00 **DESCRIPTION:** Purpose is to educate, unify, inform & uplift the readers.

The New Age Connection

PUBLISHING COMPANY: New Age Connection **PUBLISHER:** Randy Gray **EDITOR:** Syd Baumel **TOPICS:** Holistic Health, New Age, Metaphysics **TYPE:** Magazine **DATE:** 1987 **SIZE:** 11 x 17; 16 pgs. **FREQ:** quarterly **CIRC:** 18,000 **PRICE:** $12.00 **TERM:** yearly **DESCRIPTION:** Features topics on metaphysics, wholistic health & environmental issues. Offers interviews, book reviews, articles, letters & ads. Provides reviews of metaphysical/holistic health products. Tabloid newspaper format. Free.

The New Catalyst

PUBLISHING COMPANY: New Catalyst, The **TOPICS:** Holistic Healing **TYPE:** Magazine

The Nutrition And Dietary Consultant

PUBLISHING COMPANY: American Association Of Nutritional Consultants **EDITOR:** Myra E. Holcomb, Henry C. Holcomb **TOPICS:** Holistic Healing **TYPE:** Magazine

The Rat Race Record

PUBLISHING COMPANY: Rat Race Record **EDITOR:** Conny Jasper **TOPICS:** Holistic Healing **TYPE:** Magazine

The Remey Journal

PUBLISHING COMPANY: Charles Mason Remey Society **TYPE:** Journal **PRICE:** $3.50

The Ridge

PUBLISHING COMPANY: Ridge Publishers **PUBLISHER:** George Banat **TOPICS:** New Age **TYPE:** Magazine **DATE:** 1989; 64 pgs. **FREQ:** monthly **PRICE:** $42.00 **PRICE PER COPY:** $4.50 **DESCRIPTION:** Magazine for Spiritual Enlightenment through alternative lifestyles. Purpose is to promote consciousness raising through alternative sexual practices including polygamy, swinging, bondage & discipline, fetishes & sexual role playing.

The Seeker Newsletter

PUBLISHING COMPANY: Love Project **TOPICS:** New Age **TYPE:** Newsletter

The Shaman Papers

PUBLISHING COMPANY: Denali Center For Holistic Health & Personal Growth **PUBLISHER:** Wade Greyfox **EDITOR:** Kathy Lynn Douglass **TOPICS:** Spirituality, Psychic, Tarot, Runes, Channeling **TYPE:** Newsletter **DATE:** 1989 **FREQ:** quarterly **PRICE:** $9.00 **TERM:** yearly **PRICE PER COPY:** $3.00 **DESCRIPTION:** Purpose is to spread Shamanic knowledge. Offers articles, humor & reviews.

The Skeptical Inquirer

PUBLISHING COMPANY: Committee For The Scientific Investigations Of Claims Of The Paranormal **EDITOR:** Kendrick Frazier **TOPICS:** Psychic Phenomena, Skepticism, Parapsychology, Occult **TYPE:** Magazine **DATE:** 1976 **FREQ:** quarterly **CIRC:** 38,000 **PRICE:** $25.00 **TERM:** yearly **DESCRIPTION:** Offers scientific evidence to disprove claims of paranormal phenomena.

The Source

PUBLISHING COMPANY: Rainbow Earth Dwelling Society **EDITOR:** Christine Hayes **TOPICS:** Metaphysics, New Age, Channeling, UFO's **TYPE:** Newsletter **FREQ:** quarterly **DESCRIPTION:** Focuses on channelings, UFO's, and prophecies.

The Source

PUBLISHING COMPANY: Kalani Honua By The Sea International Conference And Retreat Center **TYPE:** Newspaper **FREQ:** quarterly **PRICE:** $5.50 **PRICE PER COPY:** $1.00 **DESCRIPTION:** Produced by & for Kalani Honua. Offering articles on topics such as addiction, astrology, psychology, world affairs & poetry. Provides a calendar of events, happenings & ads pertaining to the region.

The Star Beacon

PUBLISHING COMPANY: Earth Star Publications **EDITOR:** Ann Ulrich **TOPICS:** UFO's, Metaphysics, New Age, Psychic Phenomena **TYPE:** Newsletter **DATE:** 1987 **SIZE:** 8 1/2x11; 8 pgs. **FREQ:** monthly **CIRC:** 500 **PRICE:** $14.00 **TERM:** annually **PRICE PER COPY:** $1.00 **DESCRIPTION:** Reports on UFO's, metaphysics, psychic phenomena & New Age health & living. Also contains monthly Astrology Column, book reviews & letters from readers.

The Subversive: A Journal of Dangerous Thoughts, Ignored Information and Equal Opportunity Humor

PUBLISHING COMPANY: Socratic Press **EDITOR:** John Bryant **TOPICS:** New Age **TYPE:** Journal **DATE:** 1986 **FREQ:** Irregular **PRICE:** $20.00 **TERM:** 4 issues **DESCRIPTION:** Publishes works of John Bryant and his colleagues.

The Sun

PUBLISHING COMPANY: Sun, The **EDITOR:** Sy Safransky **TOPICS:** New Age, Metaphysics, Spirituality **TYPE:** Magazine **DATE:** 1974 **FREQ:** monthly **CIRC:** 7,000 **PRICE:** $30.00 **DESCRIPTION:** Features articles and interviews on New Age issues.

The Tamulet

PUBLISHING COMPANY: Mensa **EDITOR:** Carole Jeanne Rockwell **TOPICS:** Psychic Phenomena **TYPE:** Magazine

The Truth Seeker

PUBLISHING COMPANY: Truth Seeker **EDITOR:** James Prescott **TOPICS:** Metaphysics, New Age **TYPE:** Magazine **FREQ:** bi-monthly **DESCRIPTION:** Articles on metaphysics, health, spirituality and psychology.

The Unexplained Magazine

PUBLISHING COMPANY: Krastman Productions, Inc. **EDITOR:** Dr. Hank Krastman, Ph. D. **TOPICS:** Metaphysics **TYPE:** Magazine **DATE:** 1961 **FREQ:** quarterly **PRICE:** $10.00 **PRICE PER COPY:** $2.00 **DESCRIPTION:** Official publication of Metaphysical Union. Includes feature articles, ads & video catalog supplement.

The Universalian

PUBLISHING COMPANY: Universalia, Inc. **PUBLISHER:** Sandra J. Radhoff **EDITOR:** Mary Brinkopf **TOPICS:** New Age, Channeling, Metaphysics **TYPE:** Newsletter **DATE:** 1985 **SIZE:** 7 x 8 1/2; 16 pgs. **FREQ:** bi-monthly **CIRC:** 1,500 **DESCRIPTION:** A newsletter containing New Age channeled material from members of the Universalia groups. Offered on the economics of free exchange & operates solely on voluntary contributions. Focus is to expand consciousness. Motto on newsletter & for Corporation is: God is the center; Christ is the example; Love is the motive.

The Vampire Information Exchange

PUBLISHING COMPANY: Vampire Information Exchange **EDITOR:** Eric S. Held **TOPICS:** Vampires **TYPE:** Newsletter **DATE:** 1978 **FREQ:** 6 x per year **PRICE PER COPY:** $4.00 **DESCRIPTION:** Informs paying members of association on all aspects of vampirism, fact & fiction.

The Vampire Journal
PUBLISHING COMPANY: Baker Street Publications TOPICS: New Age TYPE: Journal

The Vegetarian Travel Guide
PUBLISHING COMPANY: Vegetarian Society, The TOPICS: Health Food, Vegetarianism TYPE: Magazine FREQ: annual DESCRIPTION: Information on establishments which cater to vegetarian travelers, including hotels & guest houses, restaurants & cafes. Ideas for holidays & advice about travelling longer distances.

The Wall Street Astrologer
PUBLISHING COMPANY: Mull Publications EDITOR: Carol S. Mull TOPICS: Astrology TYPE: Magazine

The Way Fourth-A Journal Of The Fourth Way
PUBLISHING COMPANY: Tayu Center TOPICS: Spirituality, Meditation TYPE: Journal

The Wise Woman
PUBLISHING COMPANY: Wise Woman EDITOR: Ann Forfreedom TOPICS: New Age, Metaphysics, Witchcraft, Occult, Paganism TYPE: Journal DATE: 1980 SIZE: 8 1/2 x 11; 52 pgs. FREQ: quarterly PRICE: $15.00 TERM: yearly PRICE PER COPY: $4.00 DESCRIPTION: Focuses on feminist issues, Goddess lore, feminist spirituality & feminist witchcraft. Includes: women's history/herstory, news, analysis, critical reviews, art, poetry, cartoons by Bulbul, exclusive interviews & original research about witch-hunts & women. Accepts ads.

The Womanspirit Catalogue
PUBLISHING COMPANY: GAIA Bookstore & Catalogue Company EDITOR: Patrice Wynne TOPICS: New Age TYPE: Catalog

The Woodrew Update
PUBLISHING COMPANY: Space Technology And Research Foundation, Inc. EDITOR: Greta Woodrew, Richard Smolowe TOPICS: New Age TYPE: Newsletter

The Word
PUBLISHING COMPANY: Word Foundation, Inc., The PUBLISHER: A.E. Menze EDITOR: N.F. Avery TOPICS: Metaphysics TYPE: Magazine DATE: 1986 SIZE: 8 1/2 x 11; 20 pgs. FREQ: Quarterly PRICE: $15.00 PRICE PER COPY: $3.75 DESCRIPTION: Produced for the members of the Word Foundation whose purpose is to improve mankind. Geared to people interested in self-knowledge, self-help & self-improvement.

The Zetetic Scholar
PUBLISHING COMPANY: Zetetic Scholar EDITOR: Marcello Trvzzi TOPICS: Parapsychology, Channeling TYPE: Magazine PRICE: $18.00 DESCRIPTION: Acts as a scientific forum for both skeptics & believers on paranormal phenomena. Presents reviews & bibliographies.

Theologia 21
PUBLISHING COMPANY: Dominion Press EDITOR: A. Stuart Otto TOPICS: Metaphysics TYPE: Magazine DATE: 1966

Therapeutic Value Of Light And Color
PUBLISHING COMPANY: Dinshah Health Society EDITOR: Dr. Kate W. Baldwin TOPICS: Holistic Healing, Color Therapy TYPE: Brochure

These Psychic Times
PUBLISHING COMPANY: These Psychic Times EDITOR: Jimmy Finns, Jennifer Sweete TOPICS: New Age TYPE: Newspaper DATE: 1989 FREQ: bi-monthly PRICE PER COPY: $2.25 DESCRIPTION: Provides a variety of information on local and world news, UFO's,and the psychic. Offers directory and product reviews.

Thesmophoria
PUBLISHING COMPANY: Thesmophoria TOPICS: Witchcraft, Occult, Paganism TYPE: Magazine

Theta: The Journal Of The Psychical Research Foundation
PUBLISHING COMPANY: Psychical Research Foundation EDITOR: Prof. William G. Roll TOPICS: Parapsychology, Psychic Phenomena, Channeling, Psychic TYPE: Journal

Thought Trends
PUBLISHING COMPANY: Thought Trends EDITOR: Mary Pratt TOPICS: New Age TYPE: Newspaper FREQ: monthly CIRC: 30,000 DESCRIPTION: Serves southeast with news, reviews, articles, calendar and resource listings.

Thoughts From The Heart
PUBLISHING COMPANY: Thoughts From The Heart TOPICS: New Age TYPE: Magazine FREQ: Quarterly PRICE: $12.00

Thresholds Magazine
PUBLISHING COMPANY: S.O.M. Publishing & Production EDITOR: Gayle Matthes TOPICS: Metaphysics, Holistic Health, Past Life Regression, Parapsychology TYPE: Magazine DATE: 1976 SIZE: 7 1/2x 10; 36 pgs. FREQ: bi-monthly CIRC: 2,500 PRICE: $13.40 PRICE PER COPY: $2.60 DESCRIPTION: Offers interviews & educational articles in the fields of health, science, philosophy, business & mind mastery. Regular features include counsel for your whole self in, What's On Your Mind?, insight on health & past lives in, The Book Of Life & the metaphysical interpretation of Genesis. Promotes self-help & holistic health through education. Topics covered are astrology, dreams, religion, psychic abilities & alternative healing methods.

Tibetan Express
PUBLISHING COMPANY: Tibetan Express TOPICS: Channeling, New Age TYPE: Newsletter DESCRIPTION: Published by the Tibetan Foundation, includes channeled material.

Tijdschrift Voor Parapsychologie
PUBLISHING COMPANY: Studienvereniging Voor Pyschical Research TOPICS: Occult, Parapsychology TYPE: Magazine FREQ: quarterly DESCRIPTION: Features research, case studies & book reviews in the fields of psychology, philosophy & anthropology as they relate to parapsychology.

Times Ahead
PUBLISHING COMPANY: Times Ahead EDITOR: Dianne Lancaster TOPICS: New Age TYPE: Newsletter DESCRIPTION: Concerned with the environment and economic issues.

TMI Bulletin
PUBLISHING COMPANY: Monroe Institute PUBLISHER: Leslie Franch EDITOR: John Dumais TOPICS: Parapsychology TYPE: Bulletin; 2 pgs. FREQ: Quarterly CIRC: 2,000

To Life
PUBLISHING COMPANY: Sinai Hospital Of Detroit EDITOR: Kay LeMon, Dick DeRonne TOPICS: Holistic Healing TYPE: Magazine

To Your Health
PUBLISHING COMPANY: International Chiropractors Association EDITOR: Heidi Freerks, Molly Rangnath TOPICS: Holistic Healing TYPE: Magazine

Today's Astrologer
PUBLISHING COMPANY: American Federation of Astrologers, Inc. PUBLISHER: Robert Cooper EDITOR: Robbie Leckie TOPICS: Astrology TYPE: Journal DATE: 1938 SIZE: 6 x 9; 32 pgs. FREQ: Monthly CIRC: 4,500 PRICE: $20.00 DESCRIPTION: Provides information & articles on the association as well as on education & astrology.

Today's Chiropractic
PUBLISHING COMPANY: Today's Chiropractic, Inc. EDITOR: Paul Gillette, Sid Williams TOPICS: Holistic Healing TYPE: Magazine

Today's Health
PUBLISHING COMPANY: Trimel Publishing Group EDITOR: Heather Howie, A. Paul Savage TOPICS: Holistic Healing TYPE: Magazine

Today's Living
PUBLISHING COMPANY: Communications Channels, Inc. EDITOR: Patti Seikus TOPICS: Holistic Healing TYPE: Magazine

Tone Magazine
PUBLISHING COMPANY: Tone Magazine TOPICS: Holistic Healing TYPE: Magazine

TOPS News
PUBLISHING COMPANY: TOPS Club, Inc. EDITOR: Gail Schemberger, Gilbert Manz, Jr. TOPICS: Holistic Healing TYPE: Newspaper

Toronto Dimensions
PUBLISHING COMPANY: Toronto Dimensions EDITOR: Ero Talvila TOPICS: Holistic Healing, New Age TYPE: Newspaper DESCRIPTION: Examines such New Age topics as reincarnation, holistic health, karma, keltic spirit, and metahistory through fiction and interviews. Accepts ads.

Total Eclipse
PUBLISHING COMPANY: Total Eclipse TOPICS: Metaphysics, Spirituality TYPE: Magazine

Total Health
PUBLISHING COMPANY: Total Health EDITOR: Robert L. Smith, Alfred McCrary TOPICS: Holistic Health TYPE: Magazine CIRC: 70,000 DESCRIPTION: Provides news and features on

preventitive health and natural living. Circulated through women's conventions. Accepts ads.

Touchpoint Newsletter

PUBLISHING COMPANY: Suneidesis Consociation TOPICS: New Age TYPE: Newsletter

Touchstone: A Journal of Crystals & Consciousness

PUBLISHING COMPANY: Touchstone: A Journal of Crystals & Consciousness EDITOR: Garnett Arledge TOPICS: Crystals TYPE: Journal CIRC: 5,000 DESCRIPTION: Focuses all aspects of crystals and their therapy. Includes articles, reviews, poetry and a calendar.

Tranet

PUBLISHING COMPANY: Tranet EDITOR: Wiliam N. Ellis TOPICS: New Age, Metaphysics, Occult, Parapsychology TYPE: Newsletter DATE: 1976

Transformation Times

PUBLISHING COMPANY: Life Resources Unlimited EDITOR: Connie Faubel, Jim Faubel TOPICS: Holistic Healing, New Age, Metaphysics TYPE: Magazine DATE: 1983; 28 pgs. FREQ: 10 per year CIRC: 8,000 PRICE: $8.00 DESCRIPTION: New Age magazine featuring reviews and articles on holistic health, occult, spirituality, women's issues & product reviews. Dedicated to expanding awareness of physical, mental & spiritual resources.

Transformations Magazine

PUBLISHING COMPANY: Transformations Magazine EDITOR: Diane Luppi TOPICS: New Age TYPE: Magazine FREQ: 4 issues/yr DESCRIPTION: Published as a subsidiary of Santa Fe Reporter.

Transformations Santa Fe Reporter

PUBLISHING COMPANY: Transformations Santa Fe Reporter TOPICS: Holistic Healing TYPE: Magazine

Transforming Art

PUBLISHING COMPANY: Transforming Art TOPICS: New Age TYPE: Magazine FREQ: 3 issues/yr DESCRIPTION: Examines transformation in the arts.

Travel Companions

PUBLISHING COMPANY: Travel Companion Exchange EDITOR: Jens Jurgen TYPE: Newsletter FREQ: bi-monthly PRICE PER COPY: $4.00 DESCRIPTION: Offers computerized listings of members travel plans attached to each newsletter. Subscription alone starts at $24 for 6 months. Membership starts at $36 for 6 months.

Travelers Network Magazine

PUBLISHING COMPANY: Travelers Network Magazine TOPICS: Holistic Healing TYPE: Magazine

Tribune Psychique

PUBLISHING COMPANY: Societe Francaise d'Etude des Pheomenes Psychiques EDITOR: M. Lemoine TOPICS: Parapsychology, Occult TYPE: Magazine DATE: 1972 FREQ: Quarterly

Trigon

PUBLISHING COMPANY: Forlaget Stjernerne, Irene Christensen Instituttet TOPICS: Astrology TYPE: Magazine DATE: 1981 FREQ: 3 x/yr. CIRC: 1,000 DESCRIPTION: Magazine for the professional astrologer.

Trobble From River City

PUBLISHING COMPANY: Trobble From River City TOPICS: Witchcraft, Occult, Paganism TYPE: Magazine

True Astrology Forecast

PUBLISHING COMPANY: Jalart House, Inc. EDITOR: Peter Damian TOPICS: Astrology TYPE: Magazine DATE: 1978 FREQ: Quarterly CIRC: 60,000 PRICE PER COPY: $1.95

True Astrology Forecasts Annual

PUBLISHING COMPANY: Jalart House, Inc. TOPICS: Astrology TYPE: Magazine DATE: 1978 FREQ: Annual PRICE PER COPY: $1.50 DESCRIPTION: Geared to those actively involved with astrology.

True Psychic Inquirer

PUBLISHING COMPANY: Jalart House, Inc. TOPICS: Parapsychology TYPE: Magazine FREQ: Quarterly PRICE PER COPY: $2.95

Truth

PUBLISHING COMPANY: Truth EDITOR: Irene Stephenson TOPICS: Parapsychology TYPE: Journal; 4 pgs. FREQ: Monthly PRICE: $9.00

Truth Journal

PUBLISHING COMPANY: Center For Spiritual Awareness EDITOR: Roy E. Davis TOPICS: Holistic Health TYPE: Journal DATE: 1968 FREQ: 10 x/yr. CIRC: 7,500 PRICE: $6.00

Truths

PUBLISHING COMPANY: Truths EDITOR: Michael Null TOPICS: Metaphysics TYPE: Magazine

Tucson Lifeline

PUBLISHING COMPANY: Tucson Lifeline TOPICS: Holistic Healing TYPE: Magazine

Tucson Open University

PUBLISHING COMPANY: Tucson Open University TOPICS: New Age TYPE: Newspaper CIRC: 30,000 DESCRIPTION: Wide circulation, serves Tucson.

Two Worlds

PUBLISHING COMPANY: Headquarters Publishing Co., Ltd. EDITOR: Kay Hunter TOPICS: Parapsychology, Occult TYPE: Magazine DATE: 1887 FREQ: Monthly CIRC: 5,000 PRICE: $13.50

UFO Book Catalog

PUBLISHING COMPANY: S,S And S Publications EDITOR: Gene Duplantier TOPICS: UFO's TYPE: Catalog DATE: 1985; 15 pgs. PRICE: $1.00 PRICE PER COPY: $0.00 DESCRIPTION: Lists booklets on UFO subjects.

UFO Encounter

PUBLISHING COMPANY: U.F.O. Research EDITOR: Martin Gotschall TOPICS: UFO's TYPE: Magazine DATE: 1966 FREQ: Bi-Monthly CIRC: 100 DESCRIPTION: Explores the cultural & scientific aspects of UFO's & reports on sightiings investigated by UFO Research in Queensland.

UFO Forskning

PUBLISHING COMPANY: Skandinavisk UFO Information EDITOR: Lars K. Lassen TOPICS: UFO's TYPE: Newsletter DATE: 1983 FREQ: Irregular CIRC: 200

UFO Journal

PUBLISHING COMPANY: National Investigations Committee On Unidentified Flying Objects TOPICS: UFO's TYPE: Journal DESCRIPTION: Features photos, updates & information on UFO phenomena.

UFO Journal

PUBLISHING COMPANY: United Aerial Phenomena Agency EDITOR: Robert Easley TOPICS: UFO's TYPE: Journal FREQ: Monthly PRICE: $6.00

UFO Magazine

PUBLISHING COMPANY: California UFO PUBLISHER: Vicki Cooper EDITOR: Sherie Stark TOPICS: UFO's, Paranormal Phenomena, New Age, Metaphysics TYPE: Magazine DATE: 1986 SIZE: 8 1/2 x 11; 48 pgs. FREQ: Bi-Monthly CIRC: 10,000 PRICE: $18.00 PRICE PER COPY: $3.00 DESCRIPTION: International publication reporting on paranormal phenomena & philosophy. Offers an open-minded approach to research, ideas & theories. Focuses & reports on UFO occurrences. Offers a journalistic & cultural viewpoint with a broad range of approaches. Prints non-fiction, news & reviews.

UFO Newsclipping Service

PUBLISHING COMPANY: UFO Newsclipping Service PUBLISHER: Lucius Farish, Rod B. Dyke TOPICS: UFO's TYPE: Newsletter DATE: 1969 SIZE: 8 1/2 x 14; 20 pgs. FREQ: monthly CIRC: 450 PRICE: $55.00 TERM: yearly PRICE PER COPY: $5.00 DESCRIPTION: Compilations of newspaper clippings from all parts of the world obtained from National Press Clipping Bureau & from individual UFO researchers. Includes 2-4 page section of Forteana News such as Bigfoot, Loch Ness Monster, cattle mutilations, falls from the sky, etc.

UFO Ohio Newsletter

PUBLISHING COMPANY: UFO Information Network EDITOR: Dennis Pilchis TOPICS: UFO's TYPE: Newsletter SIZE: 5 x 8; 20 pgs. FREQ: Bi-Monthly PRICE: $9.00

UFO Review

PUBLISHING COMPANY: Inner Light Publications EDITOR: Tim Beckley TOPICS: UFO's TYPE: Magazine DATE: 1978 SIZE: 8 1/2 x 11; 32 pgs. FREQ: Bi-Monthly CIRC: 100,000 PRICE: $8.00 PRICE PER COPY: $1.50 DESCRIPTION: Offers research & reports on true occurrences of UFO & alien encounters.

UFO Review

PUBLISHING COMPANY: Global Communications TOPICS: UFO's, New Age TYPE: Magazine DESCRIPTION: Focuses on news & articles relating to UFO's.

UFO Service

PUBLISHING COMPANY: Mutual UFO Network Of North Carolina, Inc. PUBLISHER: George D. Fawcett TOPICS: UFO's, Paranormal Phenomena TYPE: Newsletter; 10 pgs. DESCRIPTION: Lists 162 Resources related to the worldwide phenomenon of UFO, their occupants & paranormal phenomena. Covers the U.S., England, Canada & Australia.

UFO Times

PUBLISHING COMPANY: British Unidentifed Flying Objects Research Association, Ltd. **TOPICS:** UFO's **TYPE:** Magazine **DATE:** 1989 **FREQ:** Bi-Monthly

UFO Universe

PUBLISHING COMPANY: UFO Universe **TOPICS:** UFO's **TYPE:** Magazine

UFO Update

PUBLISHING COMPANY: UFO Update **TOPICS:** UFO's **TYPE:** Magazine

UFO Vision

PUBLISHING COMPANY: Skandinavisk UFO Information **EDITOR:** Kim Moeller Hansen, Flemming Rasmussen **TOPICS:** UFO's **TYPE:** Magazine **DATE:** 1987 **FREQ:** Annual **CIRC:** 100

UFO-Nachrichten

PUBLISHING COMPANY: Ventla-Verlag **EDITOR:** Karl L. Veit **TOPICS:** UFO's **TYPE:** Newspaper **DATE:** 1956 **FREQ:** Bi-Monthly **CIRC:** 5,000

UFO-NYT

PUBLISHING COMPANY: Skandinavisk UFO Information **EDITOR:** Kim Moeller Hansen **TOPICS:** UFO's **TYPE:** Magazine **DATE:** 1958; 24 pgs. **FREQ:** Quarterly **CIRC:** 2,000 **DESCRIPTION:** Deals with all aspects of UFO's.

UFOIC Newsletter

PUBLISHING COMPANY: Unidentified Flying Objects Investigation Centre **TOPICS:** UFO's **TYPE:** Newsletter **DATE:** 1952 **FREQ:** Bi-Monthly

UFOPI News

PUBLISHING COMPANY: UFOPI News **TOPICS:** UFO's **TYPE:** Newspaper

Ultimate Energies

PUBLISHING COMPANY: Aries Productions, Inc. **PUBLISHER:** R. G. Jaegers **EDITOR:** Beverly Jaegers **TOPICS:** Parapsychology **TYPE:** Magazine **DATE:** 1973 **SIZE:** 8 1/2 x 11; 8 pgs. **FREQ:** Quarterly **CIRC:** 200 **PRICE:** $12.00 **PRICE PER COPY:** $3.00 **DESCRIPTION:** Covers topics such as ESP, PSI, dowsing, dreams, & mind development.

Ultimate Frontier

PUBLISHING COMPANY: Ultimate Frontier **TOPICS:** Occult **TYPE:** Magazine

Understanding Magazine

PUBLISHING COMPANY: Understanding Magazine **TOPICS:** Metaphysics, Spirituality **TYPE:** Magazine

Unicorn

PUBLISHING COMPANY: Rowan Tree Church **EDITOR:** Rev. Paul Beyerl **TOPICS:** Occult, Witchcraft, Paganism **TYPE:** Magazine **DATE:** 1977 **FREQ:** 8 x/yr. **CIRC:** 150 **PRICE:** $10.00 **DESCRIPTION:** Features modern Neo-Pagan Revival literature.

Univercolian

PUBLISHING COMPANY: Mark DeMaranvik **EDITOR:** Mark DeMaranvik **TOPICS:** Parapsychology, Paranormal Phenomena, Dowsing, Psychic Phenomena, Metaphysics, Spirituality **TYPE:** Newsletter **DATE:** 1982 **SIZE:** 8 1/2 x 11; 24 pgs. **FREQ:** Quarterly **CIRC:** 500 **PRICE:** $8.00

PRICE PER COPY: $2.00 **DESCRIPTION:** Investigates unusual phenomena, dowsing & psychic occurrences.

Universal Entity

PUBLISHING COMPANY: Universal Entity **EDITOR:** Ginny Huseland **TOPICS:** New Age **TYPE:** Newspaper **FREQ:** monthly

University of CA, Berkeley Wellness Letter

PUBLISHING COMPANY: University Of CA, Berkeley Wellness Letter **TOPICS:** Nutrition, Holistic Health **TYPE:** Newsletter **FREQ:** 12 issues/yr **PRICE:** $20.00 **DESCRIPTION:** Well-respected publication targeting readers interested in nutrition, fitness, stress reduction through healthy living.

Unknown Newsletter

PUBLISHING COMPANY: Luna Ventures **EDITOR:** Paul Doerr **TOPICS:** UFO's **TYPE:** Newsletter **DATE:** 1969 **SIZE:** 8 1/2 x 11; 12 pgs. **FREQ:** Monthly **PRICE:** $22.00 **PRICE PER COPY:** $2.00 **DESCRIPTION:** Features articles on topics such as witchcraft, ESP, UFO, Bigfoot, psychic phenomena, mutilations, ghosts, monsters, appearances & disappearences.

Unlimited Horizons

PUBLISHING COMPANY: Metascience Foundation **EDITOR:** George Meek **TOPICS:** Holistic Healing **TYPE:** Newsletter

Unusual

PUBLISHING COMPANY: T & A Publications **EDITOR:** Wayne Davis **TOPICS:** Parapsychology **TYPE:** Magazine; 70 pgs. **FREQ:** Bi-Monthly **PRICE:** $9.95

Upper Triad, The

PUBLISHING COMPANY: Upper Triad, The **TOPICS:** Metaphysics, Spirituality **TYPE:** Magazine

Uptown Express

PUBLISHING COMPANY: Uptown Express **EDITOR:** Greg Seu **TOPICS:** New Age, Metaphysics **TYPE:** Calendar **DATE:** 1985; 28 pgs. **CIRC:** 30,000 **PRICE:** $9.00 **PRICE PER COPY:** $0.00 **DESCRIPTION:** This publication seeks to inspire responsibility in people to create a better personal lifestyle and community. Serves the greater Houston area.

Upward Search

PUBLISHING COMPANY: Upward Search **TOPICS:** Metaphysics, Spirituality, Channeling **TYPE:** Magazine

USPA Newsletter Quarterly

PUBLISHING COMPANY: United States Psychotronics Association **EDITOR:** Henry J. Nagorka **TOPICS:** Psychic Phenomena, Holistic Health, Homeopathy, Acupuncture, Crystals, Color Therapy, Herbalogy **TYPE:** Newsletter

Utne Reader

PUBLISHING COMPANY: Lens Publishing Company **EDITOR:** Eric Utne, Jay Walljasper **TOPICS:** New Age **TYPE:** Newspaper **FREQ:** 6 x per year **CIRC:** 125,000 **PRICE:** $18.00 **DESCRIPTION:** A theme-

oriented publication which focuses on environmental, contemporary and activist ideas.

Utopia 2

PUBLISHING COMPANY: Kerista Consciousness Church **TOPICS:** Holistic Health **TYPE:** Magazine **DATE:** 1985 **FREQ:** Quarterly **CIRC:** 500 **PRICE:** $24.00

Vampire Quarterly

PUBLISHING COMPANY: Vampire Quarterly **TOPICS:** Metaphysics, Spirituality **TYPE:** Magazine

Vegetarian

PUBLISHING COMPANY: Vegetarian Society, The **EDITOR:** Fiona McPhall, Bronwen Humphreys **TOPICS:** Health Food, Vegetarianism **TYPE:** Magazine **DESCRIPTION:** Covers all aspects of vegetarianism. Adult oriented.

Vegetarian Astrologer

PUBLISHING COMPANY: Vegetarian Astrologer **EDITOR:** Ted PanDeva **TOPICS:** Astrology **TYPE:** Newsletter; 20 pgs. **FREQ:** Irregular

Vegetarian Journal

PUBLISHING COMPANY: Vegetarian Resource Group **EDITOR:** Debra Wasserman **TOPICS:** Health Food, Holistic Health, Vegetarianism **TYPE:** Journal **DATE:** 1982; 36 pgs. **FREQ:** bi-monthly **PRICE:** $12.00 **PRICE PER COPY:** $1.50 **DESCRIPTION:** Promotes vegetarianism with book reviews and articles on holistic health, food-vegetarian cooking and animal rights. Does not accept advertising. Includes catalog.

Vegetarian Living News

PUBLISHING COMPANY: Vegetarian Society **TOPICS:** Health Food, Nutrition, Vegetarianism **TYPE:** Newspaper

Vegetarian Newsletter

PUBLISHING COMPANY: University Of Florida **EDITOR:** Mark Sherman **TOPICS:** Health Food **TYPE:** Newsletter

Vegetarian Times

PUBLISHING COMPANY: Vegetarian Times **EDITOR:** Paul Obis, Sally Hayhow **TOPICS:** Health Food, Vegetarianism, Holistic Health, Herbalogy **TYPE:** Magazine **FREQ:** monthly **CIRC:** 150,000 **PRICE:** $25.00 **TERM:** yearly **DESCRIPTION:** Features books and articles on holistic health, food and herbalogy. Dedicated to natural foods, vegetarian cooking and animal rights issues. Features new holistic products, book reviews & ads.

Vegetarian Voice

PUBLISHING COMPANY: North American Vegetarian Society **EDITOR:** Jennie Collura **TOPICS:** Health Food, New Age **TYPE:** Magazine **FREQ:** quarterly **DESCRIPTION:** Covers topics on New Age, nutrition, cooking, food and health.

Vegetarianism For The Working Person

PUBLISHING COMPANY: Baltimore Vegetarians **EDITOR:** Charles Stahler, Debra Wassserman **TOPICS:** Health Food **TYPE:** Newsletter

Vegetarisk Tidsskrift

PUBLISHING COMPANY: Dansk Vegetar-og Raakostforening Ny **TOPICS:** Vegetarianism, Health Food, Holistic Health **TYPE:** Newsletter **DATE:** 1983 **FREQ:** Irregular

Venture Inward
PUBLISHING COMPANY: Association For Research And Enlightenment, Inc. **EDITOR:** A. Robert Smith **TOPICS:** Holistic Health **TYPE:** Magazine **DATE:** 1984 **FREQ:** Bi-Monthly **CIRC:** 80,000

Vestigan Newsletter
PUBLISHING COMPANY: Vestigan Newsletter **TOPICS:** UFO's **TYPE:** Newsletter

Vibrant Life
PUBLISHING COMPANY: Review And Herald Publishing Association **EDITOR:** Raymond H. Woolsey, Mark Thomas **TOPICS:** Holistic Healing **TYPE:** Magazine

Viewpoint Aquarius
PUBLISHING COMPANY: Viewpoint Aquarius **EDITOR:** Rex Dutta, Jean Coulsting **TOPICS:** Parapsychology, Occult, Meditation, UFO's, Yoga **TYPE:** Magazine **DATE:** 1972 **FREQ:** Monthly **PRICE:** $40.00 **DESCRIPTION:** Explores the occult, yoga, meditation & UFO's.

Vim & Vigor Magazine
PUBLISHING COMPANY: Vim & Vigor, Inc. **EDITOR:** Leo Calderella, Preston V. McMurray, Jr. **TOPICS:** Holistic Healing **TYPE:** Magazine

Vision
PUBLISHING COMPANY: Teaching Of The Inner Christ, Inc. **TOPICS:** New Age **TYPE:** Magazine

Vision One
PUBLISHING COMPANY: Vision One **TOPICS:** New Age **TYPE:** Newsletter **DATE:** 1988 **FREQ:** Quarterly **DESCRIPTION:** Published by Stillpoint International, provides an exchange of information and ideas for seekers of a higher quality of personal and global life through individual creative intiatives. Prints interviews and stories also.

Vital Force
PUBLISHING COMPANY: Vital Force **TOPICS:** New Age, Tai Chi **TYPE:** Journal **FREQ:** quarterly **PRICE:** $4.00 **TERM:** yearly **DESCRIPTION:** Journal dealing with T'ai Chi Chih.

Vital Signs
PUBLISHING COMPANY: Preventics, Inc. **EDITOR:** Dr. J. David Beaulieu, Lisa Beaulieu **TOPICS:** Holistic Health **TYPE:** Newsletter **PRICE:** $10.00 **DESCRIPTION:** Bi-monthly publication answering questions about health and nutrition. Promotes vitamin supplements sold by their company, Preventics. Free to their customers.

Vital Signs
PUBLISHING COMPANY: International Association For Near-Death Studies **TOPICS:** Death **TYPE:** Newsletter **FREQ:** quarterly **DESCRIPTION:** Provides information on related subjects such as new books, films or TV programs or research projects being conducted by individuals on the subject of Near Death Experiences.

Vitality

PUBLISHING COMPANY: Review And Herald Publishing Association **EDITOR:** Ralph Blodgett **TOPICS:** Holistic Healing **TYPE:** Magazine

Vitality Magazine
PUBLISHING COMPANY: Vitality, Inc. **EDITOR:** Barbara Floria, Randall L. Case **TOPICS:** Holistic Healing **TYPE:** Magazine

Vitality Magazine
PUBLISHING COMPANY: Vitality Magazine **PUBLISHER:** Julia Woodford **TOPICS:** New Age, Holistic Health **TYPE:** Magazine **FREQ:** monthly **CIRC:** 24,500 **PRICE:** $30.00 **DESCRIPTION:** Toronto's monthly wellness journal. Spotlights creative solutions for an empowered lifestyle. Offers information & newsworthy articles on personal growth, ecological living, nutrition, people, events & places. Free or sent by subscription.

Voice From Spirit
PUBLISHING COMPANY: Spiritist Publications By The Polleys **TOPICS:** Metaphysics, Channeling, New Age **TYPE:** Magazine **DATE:** 1987; 8 pgs. **FREQ:** bi-monthly **PRICE:** $4.00 **TERM:** yearly **DESCRIPTION:** Metaphysical & New Age articles on positive path. Main feature is a channeled interview with famous spirits from the past. Free subscriptions to prisoners.

Voice Of Naprapathy
PUBLISHING COMPANY: American Naprapathic Association **EDITOR:** Ray Webster **TOPICS:** Homeopathy **TYPE:** Magazine **DATE:** 1988 **FREQ:** Irregular **CIRC:** 5,000 **DESCRIPTION:** A forum for practitioners of naprapathy which is a system of hand manipulation of the body.

Voice Of The Inner Mind
PUBLISHING COMPANY: Inner Mind Spiritual Church **EDITOR:** Don Daugherty **TOPICS:** Holistic Health **TYPE:** Magazine **FREQ:** Quarterly **PRICE:** $22.00

Voice Of The New Age
PUBLISHING COMPANY: Voice Of The New Age **TOPICS:** Metaphysics, Spirituality **TYPE:** Magazine

Voz Informativa
PUBLISHING COMPANY: Voz Informativa **EDITOR:** Jose Castol Gonzalez **TOPICS:** Parapsychology, Occult **TYPE:** Magazine **DATE:** 1952 **FREQ:** Bi-Monthly **CIRC:** 1,000 **PRICE:** $6.00

VTF-Post
PUBLISHING COMPANY: Verein fuer Tonbandstimmenforschung eV. **EDITOR:** Fidelio Koeberle **TOPICS:** Parapsychology, Occult **TYPE:** Magazine **DATE:** 1975 **FREQ:** Quarterly **CIRC:** 2,000

Walking Magazine
PUBLISHING COMPANY: Raben Publishing Co. **EDITOR:** Norman Raben, Craig Woods **TOPICS:** Holistic Healing **TYPE:** Magazine

Wall Street Astrologer
PUBLISHING COMPANY: Mull Publications **EDITOR:** Carol S. Mull **TOPICS:** Astrology **TYPE:** Newsletter **DATE:** 1986 **FREQ:** Monthly **CIRC:** 350 **PRICE:** $36.00 **DESCRIPTION:** Features Wall Street predictions via financial astrology. Researches &

predicts the Dow Jones Industrial Average & reviews a different industry each month.

Warm Fuzzy Newsletter
PUBLISHING COMPANY: B.L. Winch & Associates/Jalmar Press **EDITOR:** Bradley L. Winch, Suzanne Mikesell **TOPICS:** New Age **TYPE:** Newsletter

Warrior Information Network
PUBLISHING COMPANY: Warrior Information Network **EDITOR:** Mundy Sassman **TOPICS:** New Age, Metaphysics **TYPE:** Newspaper **DATE:** 1986 **DESCRIPTION:** Provides information about products, services and events relating to martial arts, holistic health and personal growth.

Washington Living
PUBLISHING COMPANY: Washington Living **TOPICS:** Holistic Healing **TYPE:** Magazine

Wasteline
PUBLISHING COMPANY: Environmental Action, Inc. **TOPICS:** Holistic Healing **TYPE:** Magazine

Water Center News
PUBLISHING COMPANY: Water Center, The **TOPICS:** Holistic Healing **TYPE:** Newspaper

Way Of The Herbs
PUBLISHING COMPANY: Washington Square Press **EDITOR:** Michael Tierra **TOPICS:** Herbalogy **TYPE:** Magazine **DATE:** 1980 **SIZE:** 6 x 9; 216 pgs. **PRICE PER COPY:** $4.95

Way, The
PUBLISHING COMPANY: Way, The **TOPICS:** Occult, Parapsychology **TYPE:** Magazine

Welcome To Planet Earth
PUBLISHING COMPANY: Wholistic Resource Center **EDITOR:** Mark Lerner, Percy Franklin **TOPICS:** Astrology **TYPE:** Journal **FREQ:** monthly **CIRC:** 12,000 **PRICE:** $25.00 **DESCRIPTION:** Features articles, news & ads relating to astrology.

Wellness
PUBLISHING COMPANY: Yes! Inc. **TOPICS:** New Age **TYPE:** Magazine

Wellness Associates Newsletter
PUBLISHING COMPANY: Wellness Associates **EDITOR:** John W. Travis, M.D., Meryn Callander-Travis **TOPICS:** Holistic Healing **TYPE:** Newsletter

Wellness Directory For Three Rivers Area
PUBLISHING COMPANY: HLQ Associates **PUBLISHER:** Linda Klapak **EDITOR:** Allen Goodman, Dawn Richards **TOPICS:** Holistic Healing **TYPE:** Magazine **DATE:** 1980 **SIZE:** 8 1/2x 11; 56 pgs. **FREQ:** annually **CIRC:** 10,000 **PRICE PER COPY:** $3.50 **DESCRIPTION:** Primary focus is on alternative health care, global responsibility & self-sufficiency. Subscription included free with membership.

Wellness Media
PUBLISHING COMPANY: Access Innovations, Inc. **TOPICS:** Holistic Healing **TYPE:** Magazine

Wellness News

PUBLISHING COMPANY: Wellness News EDITOR: Allen Goodman TOPICS: New Age, Metaphysics TYPE: Newsletter DATE: 1980 FREQ: 8 issues/yr PRICE: $35.00 DESCRIPTION: Features news and reviews on New Age topics.

Wellness Newsletter

PUBLISHING COMPANY: Wellness Institute EDITOR: Carolyn Chambers Clark TOPICS: Holistic Healing TYPE: Newsletter

Wellness Notes

PUBLISHING COMPANY: Lifecircle Publications EDITOR: Jonathon Miller TOPICS: Holistic Health TYPE: Newsletter DATE: 1981 FREQ: Quarterly CIRC: 2,000 PRICE: $4.00

Wellness Perspectives: Research, Theory And Practice

PUBLISHING COMPANY: Penn State Universty TOPICS: Holistic Health TYPE: Magazine DATE: 1984 FREQ: Quarterly CIRC: 12 PRICE: $12.00 DESCRIPTION: Geared to the educator & professional holistic health practitioner & researcher. Promotes the idea that wellness is achieved through multiple factors such as environment & social intervention.

Westgate News

PUBLISHING COMPANY: Westgate Gallery/Press PUBLISHER: Leilah Wendell EDITOR: Lorraine Chandler, Daniel Kemp TOPICS: Parapsychology TYPE: Newsletter DATE: 1981 SIZE: 8 1/2 x 11; 10 pgs. FREQ: Irregular CIRC: 3,000 PRICE PER COPY: $2.50 DESCRIPTION: Deals with the interaction of metaphysics & spiritual entities such as THE ANGEL OF DEATH..

Where The Vegetarians Eat

PUBLISHING COMPANY: Keats Publishing, Inc. EDITOR: Nathaniel Altmann TYPE: Magazine DATE: 1982 SIZE: 4 x 7; 208 pgs. PRICE PER COPY: $4.95

White Sun Journal

PUBLISHING COMPANY: D.O.M.E. Inner Guide Meditation Center EDITOR: Edwin C. Steinbrecher TOPICS: Metaphysics, Spirituality TYPE: Journal DATE: 1973; 32 pgs. FREQ: Quarterly CIRC: 5,000 PRICE: $15.00 TERM: annually

Whole Earth Review

PUBLISHING COMPANY: Point Foundation EDITOR: David Burnor, Kevin Kelly TOPICS: New Age, Metaphysics TYPE: Magazine DATE: 1968 FREQ: bi-monthly CIRC: 50,000 DESCRIPTION: Features different themes such as the environment, self-help, health. Reviews books, videos, audio tapes and products.

Whole Life Magazine

PUBLISHING COMPANY: Whole Life Enterprises, Inc. EDITOR: Marc Medoff TOPICS: New Age, Metaphysics, Holistic Healing TYPE: Magazine DATE: 1979 SIZE: 10 x 13; 116 pgs. FREQ: 6 x per year CIRC: 250,000 PRICE: $20.00 TERM: yearly DESCRIPTION: Deals with personal & enviornmental well being. Provides information on natural foods, products, events, practitioners & health institutions. Prints non-fiction articles, reviews, interviews, news information, cartoons, photography & illustrations.

Whole Life Times

PUBLISHING COMPANY: Whole World Communications, Inc. EDITOR: Abigail Lewis TOPICS: Holistic Health, New Age TYPE: Magazine DATE: 1979 FREQ: monthly CIRC: 45,000 DESCRIPTION: Free magazine, oldest & largest in So. California. Provides articles on art, herbs and alternative medicine. Offers leading-edge information & interviews with innovative thinkers & practitioners.

Whole Network Journal

PUBLISHING COMPANY: Whole Network, The EDITOR: Joe Landwehr TOPICS: New Age, Metaphysics, Spirituality TYPE: Journal FREQ: quarterly PRICE: $20.00 DESCRIPTION: Publication for people interested in poetry, artwork and information regarding self-improvement.

Whole Person Calendar

PUBLISHING COMPANY: Whole Person Calendar EDITOR: Leslie Snyder TOPICS: New Age TYPE: Calendar CIRC: 15,000 PRICE PER COPY: $1.50 DESCRIPTION: Lists Los Angeles events. Circulated through bookstores, health food stores and restaurants, colleges and conferences.

Whole Person Health Care

PUBLISHING COMPANY: Victoria House Publishers TOPICS: Holistic Healing TYPE: Magazine

Whole Person's Health Letter

PUBLISHING COMPANY: SMB Whole Health EDITOR: S.N. Zahorian TOPICS: Holistic Healing TYPE: Newsletter

Whole Self

PUBLISHING COMPANY: Mirdad Center, The TOPICS: New Age TYPE: Magazine

Wholeperson Communications

PUBLISHING COMPANY: Wholistic Resource Center EDITOR: Ellyn Cowels TOPICS: Holistic Healing TYPE: Newsletter

Wiccan Advertiser, The

PUBLISHING COMPANY: Wiccan Advertiser, The TOPICS: Witchcraft, Occult, Paganism TYPE: Magazine

Wiccan Rede

PUBLISHING COMPANY: Silver Circle EDITOR: Merlin, Morgana TOPICS: Occult, Paganism, Witchcraft, Herbalogy TYPE: Magazine DATE: 1980; 48 pgs. FREQ: Quarterly CIRC: 250 PRICE: $12.00 DESCRIPTION: Explores all aspects of witchcraft & the occult such as heritage, paganism, wicca, herbalogy, mythology, symbolism, archetypes & natural magic. Text in Dutch & English.

Wide Open Magazine

PUBLISHING COMPANY: Wide Open Press EDITOR: Clif Simms, Lynn L. Simms TOPICS: New Age, Metaphysics, Spirituality TYPE: Magazine

Wiggansnatch Magazine

PUBLISHING COMPANY: Wiggansnatch Magazine TOPICS: Witchcraft, Occult, Paganism TYPE: Magazine

Wildfire Magazine: A Networking Magazine

PUBLISHING COMPANY: Bear Tribe Medicine Society TOPICS: Holistic Healing, New Age TYPE: Magazine CIRC: 39,000 PRICE PER COPY: $2.95 DESCRIPTION: The magazine of Bear Tribe Medicine Society Network. Prints fiction, non-fiction, news, poetry, ads, reviews and more.

Will Loy's News Bulletin

PUBLISHING COMPANY: Burchette Brothers EDITOR: Will Loy TOPICS: Psychic, Psychic Phenomena TYPE: Bulletin DATE: 1980 FREQ: monthly PRICE: $38.00 TERM: annually DESCRIPTION: Psychic prophecies by Will Loy, sharing his predictions, visions & revealtion on the future.

WIN Intelligence Summary

PUBLISHING COMPANY: Wiccan Information Network TOPICS: Witchcraft, Occult, Paganism TYPE: Newsletter FREQ: monthly PRICE: $20.00 TERM: yearly DESCRIPTION: Reports on anti-defamation topics of concern to Wiccans.

Winded Mercury Missive

PUBLISHING COMPANY: Winded Mercury Missive TOPICS: Occult TYPE: Magazine

Windstar Journal

PUBLISHING COMPANY: Windstar Foundation, Thomas Crum TOPICS: New Age TYPE: Journal FREQ: quarterly DESCRIPTION: Concerned with positive environmental & planetary transformation. Contains articles & photographs to inspire, educate & raise consciousness.

Windstar Newsletter/Products Catalog

PUBLISHING COMPANY: Windstar Foundation EDITOR: John Denver TOPICS: New Age TYPE: Newsletter

Windwords

PUBLISHING COMPANY: Windwords EDITOR: Beverly Dittrich TOPICS: Spirituality TYPE: Newspaper FREQ: monthly DESCRIPTION: Features reviews of Ramtha intensives, articles, a calendar and resource guide.

Winged Chariot

PUBLISHING COMPANY: Moon Star Enterprises EDITOR: Tracey A. Hoover TOPICS: Astrology TYPE: Newsletter DATE: 1981; 14 pgs. FREQ: Irreg. CIRC: 100 PRICE: $10.00 PRICE PER COPY: $2.00 DESCRIPTION: Covers all aspects of Tarot.

Wings Of Light

PUBLISHING COMPANY: Quest Enterprises Of Excelsior EDITOR: D.L. Craig, M.E. Thiel TOPICS: New Age, Metaphysics, Channeling TYPE: Journal DESCRIPTION: Features inspirational, thought-provoking articles from Quest Enterprises of Excelsior.

Wingspand

PUBLISHING COMPANY: Wingspand EDITOR: Bob Frenier TOPICS: Spirituality TYPE: Newspaper FREQ: quarterly CIRC: 50,000 DESCRIPTION: Features articles, calendar, interviews, poetry and letters examining male spirituality.

Wise Woman Center

PUBLISHING COMPANY: Ash Tree Publishing **EDITOR:** Susun Weed **TOPICS:** New Age, Metaphysics **TYPE:** Magazine **DATE:** 1986 **DESCRIPTION:** Reviews books and audio tapes of interest to women readers.

Witch-Press
PUBLISHING COMPANY: Witch-Press **TOPICS:** Witchcraft, Occult, Paganism **TYPE:** Magazine

Witchcraft Digest Magazine
PUBLISHING COMPANY: Hero Press **TOPICS:** Occult **TYPE:** Magazine

Witches All
PUBLISHING COMPANY: Witches All **TOPICS:** Witchcraft, Occult, Paganism **TYPE:** Magazine

Witches Almanac, The
PUBLISHING COMPANY: Witches Almanac, The **TOPICS:** Witchcraft, Occult, Paganism **TYPE:** Magazine

Witches International Craft Associates WICA Newsletter
PUBLISHING COMPANY: Hero Press **EDITOR:** Leo Louis Martello **TOPICS:** Occult **TYPE:** Newsletter

Within & Beyond
PUBLISHING COMPANY: National Alliance For Spiritual Growth **EDITOR:** Dan Latour, Melissa Latour **TOPICS:** Metaphysics, Spirituality **TYPE:** Journal **DATE:** 1984 **SIZE:** 8 1/2 x 5; 14 pgs. **FREQ:** quarterly **CIRC:** 800 **PRICE:** $10.00 **TERM:** yearly **PRICE PER COPY:** $2.50 **DESCRIPTION:** Responsible guide to teachings, services & journal for transpersonal counselors. Purpose is to uplift consciousness by instilling spiritual principles in daily life. Offers articles, teachings, events, advertising, services, discounts, health, news, programs, etc.

Wodenwood
PUBLISHING COMPANY: Keltria **TOPICS:** Paganism **TYPE:** Journal **FREQ:** 4 issues/yr **PRICE:** $5.00 **PRICE PER COPY:** $1.50 **DESCRIPTION:** Prints articles, reviews, recipes and stories relating to neo-paganism.

Woman Of Power
PUBLISHING COMPANY: Woman Of Power, Inc. **EDITOR:** Char McKee **TOPICS:** Spirituality, New Age, Metaphysics **TYPE:** Magazine **DATE:** 1983; 88 pgs. **FREQ:** quarterly **CIRC:** 15,000 **PRICE:** $26.00 **TERM:** annually **PRICE PER COPY:** $7.00 **DESCRIPTION:** Magazine of feminism, spirituality & politics. Deals with woman's spirituality, politics & encourages assertiveness. Features articles, art, sources, events, poetry & ads.

Womanspirit
PUBLISHING COMPANY: Womanspirit **TOPICS:** Witchcraft, Occult, Paganism **TYPE:** Magazine

Women's History Network News
PUBLISHING COMPANY: National Women's History Project **TOPICS:** New Age **TYPE:** Newspaper

Word To The Wise
PUBLISHING COMPANY: Word To The Wise **TOPICS:** Occult, Parapsychology **TYPE:** Magazine

Worksite Wellness Works
PUBLISHING COMPANY: Wellness Councils Of America **EDITOR:** H. Cranston Lawton, Harold Kahler **TOPICS:** Holistic Healing **TYPE:** Magazine

World Goodwill Newsletter
PUBLISHING COMPANY: World Goodwill Newsletter **EDITOR:** Josette Allan **TOPICS:** New Age, Metaphysics **TYPE:** Newsletter **DATE:** 1922 **FREQ:** quarterly **CIRC:** 6,000 **DESCRIPTION:** Published by Lucis Trust.

World Of Books
PUBLISHING COMPANY: Para Research **EDITOR:** Carol Coles **TOPICS:** Parapsychology **TYPE:** Magazine **DATE:** 1984; 18 pgs. **PRICE:** $0.00

Xcaliber Communik
PUBLISHING COMPANY: Xcaliber Communik Krystiahn **TOPICS:** New Age **TYPE:** Magazine **DESCRIPTION:** Published for truth seekers interested in all aspects of New Age.

Year Of The Goddess: A Perpetual Calendar Celebrating The Feminine Principle
PUBLISHING COMPANY: Aquarian Press **EDITOR:** L. Durdin-Robertson **TOPICS:** Spirituality **TYPE:** Calendar **PRICE:** $12.95

Yes! Books & Videos
PUBLISHING COMPANY: Yes! Inc. **EDITOR:** Chris Popenoe **TOPICS:** New Age **TYPE:** Catalog **DATE:** 1975 **SIZE:** 8 x 10 1/2; 52 pgs. **FREQ:** quarterly **CIRC:** 250,000 **PRICE:** $2.00 **DESCRIPTION:** Catalog of carefully selected books & videos on inner work, creativity, philosophy, religion & fine arts. Reviews over 800 books and 1,000 videos yearly. Distributed internationally.

Yggdrasil
PUBLISHING COMPANY: Yggdrasil **TOPICS:** Witchcraft, Occult, Paganism **TYPE:** Magazine

Yoga
PUBLISHING COMPANY: Narayanananda Universal Yoga Trust, Ashrama & Narayana Press **EDITOR:** Swami Sagunananda **TOPICS:** Yoga, Holistic Health **TYPE:** Magazine **DATE:** 1958 **FREQ:** Quarterly **CIRC:** 1,000 **PRICE:** $10.00 **DESCRIPTION:** Devoted to all aspects of Yoga which is considered to be the universal religion.

Yoga - Mimamsa
PUBLISHING COMPANY: Kaivalyadhama Institution **EDITOR:** Swami Digambarji **TOPICS:** Yoga, Holistic Health **TYPE:** Magazine **DATE:** 1924 **FREQ:** Quarterly **CIRC:** 1,500 **PRICE:** $10.00

Yoga And Total Health
PUBLISHING COMPANY: Yoga Institute **EDITOR:** Dr. Jayadeva Yogendra **TOPICS:** Yoga, Holistic Health **TYPE:** Magazine **DATE:** 1933 **FREQ:** Monthly **CIRC:** 1,500 **PRICE:** $15.00

Yoga Journal
PUBLISHING COMPANY: California Yoga Teachers Association **EDITOR:** Michael Gliksohn, Stephan Bodian **TOPICS:** Yoga, Meditation, New Age **TYPE:** Journal **FREQ:** bi-monthly **CIRC:** 58,000 **DESCRIPTION:** Primarily source for information on Yoga. Prints articles, ads and reviews relating to meditation and yoga.

Yoga Life
PUBLISHING COMPANY: International Sivananda Yoga Vedanta Centers **EDITOR:** Swami Soudanand **TOPICS:** Yoga **TYPE:** Magazine

Yoga Today
PUBLISHING COMPANY: Yoga Today, Ltd. **EDITOR:** Brian Netscher **TOPICS:** Yoga, Holistic Health **TYPE:** Magazine **CIRC:** 12,000 **PRICE:** $28.00 **DESCRIPTION:** Covers all aspects of Yoga.

Yoga Vision
PUBLISHING COMPANY: Prana Yoga Ashram - Yogalayam **PUBLISHER:** Swami Vignanananda **EDITOR:** Saraswathi Devi, Ramesh Wallen **TOPICS:** Yoga **TYPE:** Newsletter **DATE:** 1975; 30 pgs. **FREQ:** irregular **DESCRIPTION:** Spiritual articles & Yoga news.

Your Future
PUBLISHING COMPANY: Dell Publishing Co., Inc. **EDITOR:** Edward Wagner **TOPICS:** Astrology **TYPE:** Magazine **DATE:** 1931 **FREQ:** Annual **PRICE PER COPY:** $0.50 **DESCRIPTION:** Offers annual predictions relating to world prophecies, business & all the signs.

Your Health
PUBLISHING COMPANY: Summit Publishing Company **EDITOR:** Susan Gregg, Tony Miles **TOPICS:** Holistic Healing **TYPE:** Newspaper **DESCRIPTION:** Tabloid-newspaper.

Your Health
PUBLISHING COMPANY: International Academy Of Nutrition And Preventive Medicine **EDITOR:** Carroll Thompson **TOPICS:** Holistic Health **TYPE:** Calendar **FREQ:** Bi-Monthly **CIRC:** 500 **DESCRIPTION:** Informs readers of developments in preventive medicine.

Your Personal Astrology Magazine
PUBLISHING COMPANY: Sterlings Magazines, Inc. **EDITOR:** H. Howard, Marsha Kaplan **TOPICS:** Astrology **TYPE:** Magazine **DATE:** 1939 **FREQ:** quarterly **PRICE:** $5.00

Z Source
PUBLISHING COMPANY: Z Source **EDITOR:** Laura Wyche **TOPICS:** New Age **TYPE:** Magazine **DATE:** 1989 **FREQ:** quarterly **CIRC:** 40,000 **DESCRIPTION:** Distributed throughout Puget Sound area. Features artists, authors, businesses and practitioners leading alternative lifestyles and seeking personal growth.

Zeitschrift Fuer Parapsychologie Und Grenzgebiete Der Psychologie
PUBLISHING COMPANY: Aurum Verlag GmbH **EDITOR:** Prof. Dr. H. Bender **TOPICS:** Parapsychology, Occult **TYPE:** Magazine **DATE:** 1970 **FREQ:** Quarterly **CIRC:** 1,600

Zeitschrift Fuer Radiaesthesie
PUBLISHING COMPANY: Herold-Verlag, Franz Wetzel und Co. KG **EDITOR:** Claus Wetzel **TOPICS:** Holistic Health **TYPE:** Magazine **DATE:** 1949 **FREQ:** Quarterly **CIRC:** 2,000

Zero Hour

PUBLISHING COMPANY: Zero Hour **EDITOR:** Jim Jones **TOPICS:** Occult **TYPE:** Magazine

Zetetic Scholar
PUBLISHING COMPANY: Center For Scientific Anomalies Research **EDITOR:** Marcello Truzzi, Ph. D. **TOPICS:** Ghosts **TYPE:** Journal **SIZE:** 4 x 6; 100 pgs. **FREQ:** irregular **CIRC:** 600 **PRICE:** $15.00 **PRICE PER COPY:** $8.00 **DESCRIPTION:** Reports research & findings of CSAR which investigates & evaluates claims of anomalies & paranormal phenomena. While most people are looking for answers & certainties to these happenings, ZS seeks to ask the right questions. Looks for readers who've not yet made up their minds & who can tolerate uncertainty.

Zhuangzi Speaks
PUBLISHING COMPANY: Princeton University Press **EDITOR:** Brian Bruya **TOPICS:** New Age, Spirituality **TYPE:** Newsletter

ZPG Activist
PUBLISHING COMPANY: Zero Population Growth **TYPE:** Newsletter

ZPG Reporter
PUBLISHING COMPANY: Zero Population Growth **TYPE:** Newsletter

Publishers Index

This chapter is an alphabetical list of Publishers who publish materials in the New Age, Metaphysical and related fields. Publications shown in this directory can be ordered from the individual publisher, your local New Age Bookstore or by contacting Reference Press International, P.O. Box 4126, Greenwich, CT 06830, 203-629-4900.

100th Monkey Books
66 Wellesley Street, E.
Toronto, ON, M4Y1G2
Canada

12 Step Times, The
CONTACT: H.P., Pub.
P.O. Box 12115
Denver, CO 80212
(303)-836-6099

21st Century Publications
401 N. Fourth Street
P.O. Box 702
Fairfield, IA 52556
(515)-472-5105

2AM Publications
CONTACT: G. Anderson
P.O. Box 6754
Rockford, IL 61125
(312)-652-0013

A-P Newsletter
P.O. Box 273208
Tampa, FL 33688

A.C.S. Publications, Inc./Astro Computing Services
P.O. Box 16430
San Diego, CA 92116-0430
(619)-297-9203 (800)-888-9983

A.S.S.K.
2675 W. Hwy. 89A, Ste. 454
Suite 454
Sedona, AZ 86336
(602)-282-3421

AA Grapevine, Inc.
468 Park Avenue South
New York, NY 10016
(212)-686-1100

AAPE Academy Papers
Box 5076
Champaign, IL 61820
(217)-351-5076

Ablex Publishing Corp.
355 Chestnut Street
Norwood, NJ 07648
(201)-767-8450

ABNOSTICORUAF
86 Whispering Hills Drive
Chester, NY

Abrasax
CONTACT: James M. Martin
P.O. Box 1219
Corpus Christi, TX 78403-1219

Abril Images
Av. Otaviano Alves De Lima 4,400
Sao Paulo,
Brazil

Academic Press, Inc.
1250 Sixth Avenue
San Diego, CA 92101
(619)-699-6825 FAX (619)-699-6859

Academy Chicago Publishers, Ltd.
213 West Institute Place
Chicago, IL 60610
(312)-751-7302 (800)-248-7323

Academy Of Future Science
CONTACT: James Hurtack
P.O. Box FE
Los Gatos, CA 95031

Academy Of Scientific Hypnotherapy
Box 12041
San Diego, CA 92112
(619)-427-6225

Academy Research Associates
Box 1867
Santa Monica, CA 90406-1867

Acadiana Press
P.O. Box 42290
USL
Lafayette, LA 70504
(318)-662-3468

Access Innovations, Inc.
Box 40130
Albuquerque, NM 87196
(505)-265-3591

Ace Books
200 Madison Avenue
New York, NY 10016
(212)-951-8800

Act-Action
CONTACT: S. Burghard
B110 Ross Towers
710 Lodi Street, B-1104
Syracuse, NY 13203
(315)-471-4644

Action and Life Publications
CONTACT: Francis Elmo
504 E. Palace Avenue
Santa Fe, NM 87501
(505)-983-1960

Action On Smoking And Health
2013 H Street, NW
Washington, DC 20006
(202)-659-4310

Addison Wesley Publishers
Jacob Way
Reading, MA 01867

Adventures-Unlimited Press
P.O. Box 22
Stelle, IL 60919
(815)-253-6390 FAX (815)-256-2299

Advocacy Press, Div. of Girls Club of Santa Barbara
P.O. Box 236
Santa Barbara, CA 93102
(805)-962-2728

Adweek Agency Directory
49 East 21st Street
New York, NY 10160

Affinity Press
CONTACT: Judithann H. David
P.O. Box 877
Orinda, CA 94563
(415)-253-1889

Agada
CONTACT: R. Goldfarb
2020 Essex Street
Berkeley, CA 94703
(415)-848-0965

Aha! Experiences
CONTACT: Laura Rosetree
P.O. Box 13046
Silver Springs, MD 20911-3046
(301)-565-2528

Aikido Federation Of California
P.O. Box 10962
Costa Mesa, CA 92627

Aikido Today Magazine
CONTACT: Susan Perry, Editor-In-Chief
1420 North Claremont Boulevard, #111B
Claremont, CA 91711
(714)-624-7770

Akwenasa Publications
General Delivery, Department Y
Howardsville, VA 24562
(804)-286-2746

Alan R. Liss, Inc.
41 East 11th Street
New York, NY 10003
(212)-475-7700

Alaya Unlimited
52 Central Avenue
Wailuku, Maui, HI 96793
(808)-244-7400

Alcohol And Drug Problems Association Of North America
444 North Capitol Street, NW
Washington, DC 20001
(202)-737-4340

Alcohol Research Information Service
1120 East Oakland Avenue
Lansing, MI 48906

Alex Holland
210 Polk Street, No.3
Port Townsend, WA 98368
(206)-385-4383

Alive
4728 Byrne Road
Burnaby, British Columbia V5J 3H7
Canada
(604)-438-1919

Alive Publications Ltd.
32 E. 57th Street #1800
New York, NY 10022
(212)-421-5600

Alivening Publications
P.O. Box 1368
Land O Lakes, FL 34639
(813)-996-3659

All My Relations
P.O. Box 532
Hazelton, BC, V0J1Y0,
Canada

Alliance, The
2807 S.E. Stark
Portland, OR 97214
(503)-239-4991

Ally Capital Corporation
591 Redwood Highway #4000
Mill Valley, CA 94941
(415)-331-5500

Alohem Publishing Co.
8462 Larch Ave.
Cotati, CA 94928
(717)-795-0357

Alpenglow Press
CONTACT: Alec B. Combs
P.O. Box 1841
Santa Maria, CA 93456
(805)-928-4904

Alpha Publications
CONTACT: Ruth Peterman
3220 33rd Avenue
Minneapolis, MN 55406-2025
(612)-721-7856

Alphalight Publishing
CONTACT: Ann Nunley
P.O. Box 1086
Lawrence, KS 66044-8086
(913)-843-5483

Alpine Hansen Publisher
CONTACT: C. Steen Hansen
305 San Anselmo Avenue, #313
San Anselmo, CA 94960-6002
(415)-459-4900 FAX (415)-459-4974

Alta Napa Press

1969 Mora Avenue
Calistoga, CA 94515
(707)-942-4444

Altarfire Publishers
CONTACT: Margie Wileman
P.O. Box 240
Moss Landing, CA 95039
(408)-633-4170

Alternative Access Directory
P.O. Box 462
Kentfield, CA 94904

Alternative Press Center
P.O. Box 7229
Baltimore, MD 21218
(301)-243-2471

Alternative Press: Children's Books
P.O. Box 5288
Madison, WI 53705

Alternative Research
P.O. Box 1294
Kitchener, ON N2G 4G8
Canada

Alternatives
15505 Wright Brothers Drive
Dallas, TX 75244
(214)-386-6397

Alternatives
P.O. Box 566822
Atlanta, GA 30356
(404)-973-1994

Alternatives Resource Center
5263 Bouldercrest Road
P.O. Box 429
Ellenwood, GA 30049
(404)-961-0102

Amador Publishers
CONTACT: Harry Wilson
P.O. Box 12335
Albuquerque, NM 87195
(505)-877-4395

Amaryllis Press
220 West 80th Street
New York, NY 10024
(212)-496-6460

Amber Lotus
CONTACT: Jerry Horovitz
1241 21st Street
Oakland, CA 94607
(415)-839-3931

American Alliance For Health, Physical Education, Recreation And Dance
1900 Association Drive
Reston, VA 22091
(703)-476-3400

American Association Of Acupuncture & Oriental Medicine
50 Maple Place
Manhasset, NY 11030
(516)-627-0048

American Association Of Nutritional Consultants
1641 East Sunset Road
B 117
Las Vegas, NV 89119
(702)-361-1132 FAX (702)-739-7225

American Association Of Variable Star Observers
25 Birch Street
Cambridge, MA 02138
(617)-354-0484

American Chiropractic Association
8229 Maryland Avenue
St. Louis, MO 63105
(314)-862-7800 FAX (314)-721-5171

American Classical College Press
P.O. Box 4526
Albuquerque, NM 87196
(505)-843-7749

American Council For Drug Education
204 Monroe Street, #110
Rockville, MD 20850
(301)-294-0600

American Demographics
CONTACT: Cheryl Russell
P.O. Box 68
Ithaca, NY 14850
(607)-273-6343

American Federation of Astrologers, Inc.
6535 S. Rural Road
Box 22040
Tempe, AZ 85285-2040
(602)-838-1751

American Health Consultants, Inc.
67 Peachtree Park Drive, NE, #220
Atlanta, GA 30309
(404)-351-4523

American Institute For Psychological Research
P.O. Box 27040
Albuquerque, NM 87125
(505)-843-7749

American Institute Of Nutrition
9650 Rockville Pike
Bethesda, MD 20814
(301)-530-7100 FAX (301)-571-1892

American Journal Of Health Promotion
1812 South Rochester Road
Rochester, MI 48063-4816
(313)-258-3754

American Mensa
Box 1132
Douglas, AZ 85607
(602)-364-3471

American Naprapathic Association
5321 N. Central Avenue
Chicago, IL 60630
(312)-685-6020

American Osteopathic Hospital Association
1454 Duke Street
Alexandria, VA 22314-3403
(703)-684-7700

American Psychic Association
177 Madison Ave., #5B
New York, NY 10016
(212)-696-9379

American West Publishers
CONTACT: Desiree Stevens
P.O. Box 6451
Tehachapi, CA 93561
(805)-822-9655

Amerrikua
P.O. Box 35
Schuyler Falls, NY 12985
(518)-643-9254

Amethyst Books
CONTACT: Nick Bamforth
P.O. Box 895
Woodstock, NY 12498
(914)-679-5831

Amity House
1 Boston Place, #3225
Boston, MA 02108-4401
(508)-546-1600

Amrita Foundation
P.O. Box 8080
Dallas, TX 75205
(214)-521-1072

AMS Press, Inc.
56 East 13th Street
New York, NY 10003
(212)-777-4700

Ancient Truth Research Foundation
CONTACT: Albert Rainey
P.O. Box 38037
Hollywood, CA 90038-0037
(213)-464-5948

Ancient Ways Newsletter
4075 Telegraph Avenue
Oakland, CA 94609

And Books
702 S. Michigan
Suite 836
South Bend, IN 46618
(219)-232-3134

Anderson's Publications
P.O. Box 11338
Santa Rosa, CA 95406
(707)-575-1280

Andre Dumas
29 Av. des Sablons
Dammartin-en-Goele, 77230
France

Angel Press Publications
P.O. Box 1072
Mt. Angel, OR 97362
(503)-845-2569

Anima Publications
CONTACT: B.D. Rotz

1053 Wilson Avenue
Chambersburg, PA 17201
(717)-263-8303 (717)-267-0087

Animal Rights Network, Inc.
456 Monroe Turnpike
Monroe, CT 06468
(203)-452-0446

Anthony Publishing Co.
CONTACT: Carol K. Anthony
206 Gleasondale Road
Stow, MA 01775
(508)-897-7191

Anthroposophic Press, Inc.
R.R. 4, Star Route
Bell's Pond
Hudson, NY 12534
(518)-851-2054

Anubisiven Books
Box 2098, Station M
Calgary, AT, T2P2M4,
Canada

Aperture
CONTACT: Daniel Power
20 East 23rd Street
New York, NY 10010
(212)-505-5555

Apothecary Books, The
P.O. Box 331
Tomball, TX 77377

Apt Books, Inc.
141 East 44th Street
Suite 511
New York, NY 10017
(212)-697-0887

Aquarian Book Publishing
7011 Hammond Avenue
Dallas, TX 75223
(214)-328-5144

Aquarian Book Service
P.O. Box 57
Birmingham, MI 48012

Aquarian Fellowship
1328 West Newport
Chicago, IL 60657
(312)-528-7254

Aquarian Messenger
2716 Northeast 30th Place, 1
Ft. Lauderdale, FL 33306

Aquarian Press
Sterling Publishers
2 Park Avenue
New York, NY 10016

Aquarian Press
P.O. Box 625
Stockbridge, MA 01262
(413)-921-4471

Aquarian Systems, Inc.
P.O. Box 575
Placitas, NM 87043
(505)-867-3530

Aquarian Voices
Arnold Hollow Road

Box 2070
Brandon, VT 05733
(802)-247-8087

Aquarius Rising
CONTACT: Pamela Leigh
P.O. Box 21251
Concord, CA 94521
(415)-827-9633

Aquarius Workshops
Box 556
Encino, CA 91426
(213)-823-5534

Arcade Publishing
Box 5365
Berkeley, CA 94705

Arcades Jaulim
Route Royale, Rose-Hill
Ile, Maurice
Mauritius

Arcana Publishing, Div. of Lotus Light Publications
CONTACT: Santosh Krinsky
P.O. Box 2
Wilmot, WI 53192
(414)-862-2395

Arcane Cyan Planes
59 Greet Street, #109
Malden, MA 02148
(617)-324-4591

Arcanum Metaphysical Book
331 Mainstreet, West
Hamilton, ON, L8P1K1,
Canada

Arcline/KRI Publications
1800 South Robertson Boulevard, Suite 182
Los Angeles, CA 90035
(213)-551-0484

Arco Publishing Inc.
1 Gulf & Western Plaza
New York, NY 10023
(212)-373-8931 (800)-223-2336

Arcus Publishing Co.
P.O. Box 228
Sonoma, CA 95476
(707)-996-9529

Ares Publications, Inc.
7020 North Western Avenue
Chicago, IL 60645
(312)-743-1405

Ariane Publishing Company
CONTACT: Marc Vallee
5427 Avenue du Parc
Montreal, Quebec H2V 4G9
Canada
(514)-273-6467 FAX (514)-273-7682

Ariel Books
820 Miramar Avenue
Berkeley, CA 94707
(415)-525-2098

Ariel Books For Women
2766 West 4th Avenue
Vancouver, BC, V6K1R1,

Canada

Ariel Communications
P.O. Box 203550
Austin, TX 78720
(512)-250-1700

Ariel Press
3854 Mason Road
P.O. Box 249
Canal Winchester, OH 43110
(614)-837-8263 (800)-336-7769

Ariel Press
1541 Parkway Loop, Ste.9D
P. O. Box 3723
Tustin, CA 92680
(714)-259-4800

Aries Rising Press
2132 Alcyona Drive
Los Angeles, CA 90068
(213)-957-8751

Arizona Light, The
CONTACT: Jacqueline J. Pieters
P.O. Box 54488
Phoenix, AZ 85078
(602)-443-1964

Arkania
CONTACT: M. Mellow
29 W. 35th Street
New York, NY 10001
(212)-244-3336

Arthur Publications, Inc.
CONTACT: Debra Sapp
P.O. Box 23101
Jacksonville, FL 32241-3101
(904)-737-8732

Arthur Publishing
Box 6141
Scottsdale, AZ 85261
(602)-951-3964

Arthur Publishing
P.O. Box 33213
San Diego, CA 92103
(619)-295-4146

As-Siddiquyah Publications
482 Franklin Street
Buffalo, NY 14202
(716)-884-2606

**Ascended Master Teaching
Foundation (AMTF)**
CONTACT: Werner Schroeder
P.O. Box 466
Mount Shasta, CA 96067
(916)-926-4913

Ascendent Books
10991 124th Street
Edmonton, AT, T5M0H9,
Canada

Ash Tree Publishing
CONTACT: Susun Weed
P.O. Box 64
Woodstock, NY 12498
(914)-246-8081

Ashley Publishing Co., Inc.

CONTACT: Gwen Costa
4600 West Commercial Boulevard, Ste. 8
Ft. Lauderdale, Fl 33319-3140
(305)-739-2221

Ashwins Publications
P.O. Box 1686
Ojai, CA 93023
(805)-646-6622

ASI Publishers, Inc.
CONTACT: Gerard Young
545 Eighth Avenue, 10th Fl.
New York, NY 10018-4307
(212)-947-3628

Asia Book Corporation Of America
136-56 39th Avenue
Suite 100
Flushing, NY 11354
(718)-565-1342

Asian Humanities Press
P.O. Box 3523
Fremont, CA 94539-0352
(408)-727-3151

Askin Publishers, Ltd.
16 Ennismore Avenue
London, W4 1SF
England
01-994-1314

Aslan Publishing
CONTACT: Dawson Church, Pub.
P.O. Box 108
Lower Lake, CA 95457
(707)-995-1861

Aspen Publishers, Inc.
1600 Research Boulevard
Rockville, MD 20850
(301)-251-5000

Aspen Publishing, Inc.
7201 McKinney Circle
Frederick, MD 21701
(800)-638-8437

**Association des Amis de la
Radiesthesie**
70 rue du General de Gaulle
B.P. 3
95620 Parmain,
France

**Association For Applied
Psychophysiology & Biofeedback**
10200 West 44th Avenue, #304
Wheat Ridge, CO 80033
(303)-422-8436

**Association For Research And
Enlightenment**
Box 1846
Des Plaines, IL 60018

Association of Body, Mind, Spirit
1278 Glenneyre #167
Laguna Beach, CA 92651
(714)-499-4716

Association of Integrative Studies
185 Peabody Hall
Oxford, OH 45056

(513)-529-6992

**Association Patients pour
l'Homoeopathie Uniciste**
45, rue A De Boeck
Brussels, 1140
Belgium
02-735-35-25

**Associazione Italiana Scientifica di
Metapsichica**
Via S. Vittore 19
20123 Milan,
Italy

**Associazione Italiana Studi del
Paranormale**
Via Puggia 47
Genoa, 16131
Italy

Astor Publications
P.O. Box 840
Astor, FL 32002
(904)-759-3369

Astral Publications
428 Coronado Avenue, #7
Long Beach, CA 90814
(213)-438-3381

Astro News
5821 Cyrus Street
Baton Rouge, LA 70805
(504)-355-7282

Astro-Annual
350 Madison Ave.
Cresskill, NJ 07626
(201)-568-0500

Astro-Carto-Graphy
Box 959
El Cerrito, CA 94530

Astrologer's Almanac
Box 420, Midwood Station
Brooklyn, NY 11230

**Astrological Association Of Great
Britain**
Bramshot Court West
Bramshott
Nr. Liphook, Hants GU30 7RG
England

Astrological Lodge Of London
BM Astrolodge
London, WC1N 3XX
England

Astrological Research Guild, Inc.
1530 Genie Street
Orlando, FL 32826
(305)-568-5373

**Astrologie und Parapsycholoieschei
Verlag**
Landsberger Str. 429-IV
D-8000 Munich 60,
West Germany

Astrologik/Vigilantero Press
CONTACT: Antero Alli
P.O. Box 45758

Seattle, WA 98145-0758
(206)-440-0713

Astrology And Parapsychology
75 Alto Drive
Oak View, CA 93022

Astrology Book Club
16440 Haynes Street
Van Nuys, CA 91406
(818)-997-8684

Astrology Now
Box 3383
St. Paul, MN 55165

Astronomical Society Of The Pacific
390 Ashton Avenue
San Francisco, CA 94112
(415)-337-1100

Asynjur
P.O. Box 567
Granville, OH 43023

Atlantic Monthly Press, Affil. of Navarre Atlantic Co.
19 Union Sq. W., 11th Fl.
New York, NY 10003
(212)-645-4462

Atlas Publishing Co., Ltd.
Windsor House, 2nd Fl.
London SW16 4DH, Norbury SW16 4DH
England
01-679-1899 **FAX** (010)-679-8907

Atma Books
CONTACT: Sam Trout
P.O. Box 2993
Naples, FL 33939-2993
(813)-642-0799

Atma, Soul Publications
CONTACT: R. Thorne
6140 Cleveland Avenue
Columbus, OH 43229
(614)-891-9322

Atrium Society
CONTACT: T. Webster-Doyle
P.O. Box 816
Middlebury, VT 05753
(800)-848-6021

Aubrey Hampton Publishers
4419 North Manhattan Avenue
Tampa, FL 33614
(813)-876-4879

Audio Literature
CONTACT: John Hunt
3800 Palos Verdes Way
South San Francisco, CA 94080
(415)-878-8758

AUM Publications
86-24 Parsons Boulevard
Jamaica, NY 11432
(718)-291-9757

AUM U.S.A. Co., Ltd.
8 E 48th Street #2E
New York, NY 10017-1005
(212)-226-5030

Aura Enterprises
3250 Olympic Boulevard
P.O. Box 101
Santa Monica, CA 90404

Aurora Association,Inc.
1015 18th Street N.W., Suite 400
Washington, DC 20036
(202)-463-0950

Aurora News Register Publishing Co.
1320 K
Aurora, NE 68818
(402)-694-3988

Aurora Press, Inc.
P.O. Box 573
Santa Fe, NM 87504
(505)-989-9804

Aurora Publications
6214 Meridian Avenue
San Jose, CA 95120
(408)-997-0437

Aurora Publishing
P.O. Box 15324
Washington, DC 20003
(202)-544-3066

Aurora Publishing Co.
P.O. Box 2537
Garden City, KS 67846
(316)-275-7488 (800)-535-5111

Aurum Verlag GmbH
Franziskanerstr 9
Postfach 5204D-7800
Freiburg 1 Br,
West Germany
0761-36409

Australian Well Being
1/187 A Avenue Road
Mosman
Sydney, 2088
Australia
02/969-7122

Authors Unlimited
3330 Barham Blvd., Ste.204
Los Angeles, CA 90068
(213)-874-0902

Avaloka: A Journal
CONTACT: A. Versluis
249 Maynard, Northwest
Grand Rapids, MI 49504

Avery Color Studios
Star Route
Box 275
Au Train, MI 49806
(906)-892-8251

Avery Publishing Group, Inc.
CONTACT: Antoinette Benton
120 Old Broadway
New Hyde Park, NY 11040-5015
(516)-741-2155 (800)-548-5757

Avon Books
959 Eighth Avenue
New York, NY 10019
(212)-481-5600 (800)-223-0690

Awakening
948 Almshouse Road
Ivyland, PA 18974
(215)-357-2909

Ayer Co. Publishers, Inc.
P.O. Box 958
Salem, NH 03079

B. Jain Publishers, Ltd.
1921 Chuna Mandi, St. 10th
P.O. Box 5775
New Delhi, 110055
India
770430

B. Klein Publications
CONTACT: Bernard Klein, Pres.
P.O. Box 8503
Coral Springs, FL 33065
(305)-752-1708

B. Rugged Books
CONTACT: S. Cuyle
11 South Adelaide Avenue
Highland Park, NJ 08904
(201)-828-6098

B.L. Winch & Associates/Jalmar Press
CONTACT: S. Mikesell
45 Hitching Post Drive, Bldg 2
Rolling Hills Estates, CA 90274-4297
(213)-547-1240 (800)-662-9662 **FAX** (213)-547-1644 **TELEX** (209)-039-9462

Back To Eden Books
Box 1439
Loma Linda, CA 92354

Backwoods Books
McClellan Lane
P.O. Box 9
Gibbon Glade, PA 15440
(412)-329-4581

Baha'i Publishing Trust
415 Linden Avenue
Wilmette, IL 60091
(312)-251-1854

Baker Street Publications
CONTACT: Sharida Rizzuto
P.O. Box 994
Metairie, LA 70004
(504)-733-9138

Balance Beam Press, Inc.
CONTACT: M. Peterson
12711 Stoneridge Road
Dayton, MN 55327
(612)-427-3168

Balance Publications
359 Walden Green
Branford, CT 06405
(203)-481-6331

Baltimore Resources
Box 284
Stevenson, MD 21153
(301)-486-1510 (301)-337-5525

Bandanna Books
CONTACT: S. Newborn

319 Anacapa Street
Santa Barbara, CA 93101
(805)-969-2885

Bantam Books
Direct Response Department
414 East Golf Road
Des Plaines, IL 60016

Bantam New Age Books
CONTACT: c/o Bantam Direct Response, Dept. DR 70
666 Fifth Avenue
New York, NY 10103
(212)-765-6500 (800)-223-6834

Banyan Books
2715 4th Avenue
Vancouver, BC, V6K1P9,
Canada

Banyan Tree Books
CONTACT: Ernest Callenbach
1963 El Dorado Avenue
Berkeley, CA 94707
(415)-549-2690

Barbizon Foundation
Rural Route One
Lumby, British Columbia V0E 2G0
Canada
(604)-547-6621

Barn Owl Books
CONTACT: G. Covina
P.O. Box 226
Vallectios, NM 87581
(415)-528-8245

Barrington Sky Publishing
CONTACT: Paige Reynolds
P.O. Box 49428
Los Angeles, CA 90049
(213)-472-2811

Barthel & Barthel Publishing
Schatzlgasse 31
D-8137 Berg 1,
West Germany
08151-51085

Bartholomew Books
CONTACT: Barbara Dewey
1 Drake Way
Box 634
Inverness, CA 94937
(415)-669-1664

Baumgartner-Verlag
3135 Warpke
West Germany

Beacon Books
P.O. Box 555
Litchfield Park, AZ 85340
(602)-977-2380

Beacon Hill Press Of Kansas City
P.O. Box 419527
Kansas City, MO 64141
(816)-931-1900

Beacon House, Inc.
Welsh Road & Butler Park
Ambler, PA 19002
(215)-643-7800

Beacon Press, Inc.
25 Beacon Street
Boston, MA 02108
(617)-742-2110

Beacon, The
P.O. Box 722
Cooper Station
New York, NY 10276
(212)-982-8770

Bear
CONTACT: Allen Ross
P.O. Box 346
Kyle, SD 57752-0346

Bear & Company, Inc.
CONTACT: Anne Wright, Sales Mgr.
P.O. Drawer 2860
Santa Fe, NM 87504-2860
(505)-983-5968 (505)-988-5090 (800)-932-3277
FAX (505)-989-8386

Bear Publications
R.D. Box 16
Turnpike Road
Cambridge, NY 12816
(518)-677-2766

Beekman Publishers, Inc.
P.O. Box 888
Woodstock, NY 12498
(914)-679-2300

Bell Springs Publishing
CONTACT: Cathy Stevenson
Box 640
Laytonville, CA 95454
(707)-578-1135

Ben Abraham Books
97 Donnamora Crescent
Thornhill, ON, L3T4K6,
Canada

Bennett Books
P.O. Box 1553
Santa Fe, NM 87504

Bentwood
P.O. Box 021926
Juneau, AK 99802

Berg Publishing Group
1902 Valley View Road
Shakopee, MN 55379
(612)-445-4425

Berkeley Art Center
1275 Walnut Street
Berkeley, CA 94709
(415)-644-6893

Berkeley Publishing Group
200 Madison Avenue
New York, NY 10016
(212)-951-8857 (800)-631-8571

Berkeley-Cambridge Press
P.O. Box 947
Carmichael, CA 95609
(916)-485-5019

Berkshire Alternatives
10 Taconic Street
Pittsfield, MA 01201

Bernard Jensen Publishing Co.
CONTACT: Dr. Bernard Jensen
Route 1, Box 52
Escondido, CA 92025
(714)-749-2727

Bestways
P.O. Box 570
Oak Park, IL 60303-0570
(702)-883-7311

Beverly Hawkins Studio & Gallery
20104 Halloway Avenue
Matoaca, VA 23803
(804)-861-9403

Beyond Avalon
CONTACT: John Chambers
93 Jackson Avenue
Bridgeport, CT 06606
(203)-336-4994

Beyond Reality Magazine, Inc.
30 Amarillo Drive
Nanuet, NY 10954

Beyond Words Publishing
CONTACT: Richard and Cindy Cohr
Pumpkin Ridge Rd.
Rte. 3, Box 492B
Hillsboro, OR 97123
(503)-647-5109

Bhaktivedanta Book Trust
3764 Watseka Ave.
Los Angeles, CA 90034
(213)-559-4455

Bharatiga Jyotir Vijyan Parishad
78 Ashta Bhuji Durga Marg Aminabad Road
4 Lucknow,
India

Bibli O'Phile Publishing Company
156 East 61st Street
New York, NY 10021
(212)-888-1008 (800)-255-1660

Billboard
9107 Wilshire Boulevard
Suite 700
Beverly Hills, CA 90210
(213)-273-7040

Bio-Dynamic Farming
P.O. Box 253
Wyoming, RI 02898
(401)-539-2320

Biocomp Research
6399 Wilshire Boulevard, Suite 1010
Los Angeles, CA 90048
(213)-933-9451

Bioenergetics Press
CONTACT: R. Schenk
P.O. Box 9141
Madison, WI 53715
(608)-255-4028

Biofeedback Therapy Institute
5979 West Third Street, Suite 205
Los Angeles, CA 90036-0276
(213)-938-0478

Biokinesiology Institute

5432 Highway 227
Trail, OR 97541
(503)-876-2080

Biological Educational Products
P.O. Box 2677
Santa Rosa, CA 95405

Biosis
2100 Arch Street
Philadelphia, PA 19103
(215)-587-4800 **FAX** (215)-587-2016

Biosocial Publications, International
Box 1174
Tacoma, WA 98401
(206)-272-0530

Birth Day Publishing Company
P.O. Box 7722
San Diego, CA 92107
(619)-296-3194

Black Moon Publishing
P.O. Box 19469
Cincinnati, OH 45219-0469

Blagrove Publications
P.O. Box 584
Manchester, CT 06040

Blotter
CONTACT: C. Kennedy
233 Woodbine Avenue
Toronto, ON, M4L 3P3
Canada

Blue Dolphin Publishing, Inc.
CONTACT: Paul Clemens
P.O. Box 1908
Nevada City, CA 95959
(916)-265-6925 (800)-643-0765 **FAX** (916)-265-0787

Blue Eagle Publishing
CONTACT: Phil And Diane Dunn
P.O. Box 250
Hicksville, NY 11801-0250
(718)-698-6114

Blue Light Red Light
CONTACT: Joy Parker
4496A Hudson Street, Suite F42
New York, NY 10014
(718)-499-1055

Blue Rose Ministry
CONTACT: Rev. Robert Short
P.O. Box 332
Cornville, AZ 86325

Blue Unicorn
CONTACT: R. Iodice
22 Avon Road
Kensington, CA 94707
(415)-526-8439

Bluestocking Press
CONTACT: Jane A. Williams
P.O. Box 1014
Placerville, CA 95667-1014
(916)-621-1123

Bluewood House
CONTACT: Bill Yenne
111 Pine Street, Ste. 1410

San Francisco, CA 94111
(415)-989-2450

Bob Jones University Press
Bob Jones University
Greenville, SC 29614
(803)-242-5100 (800)-845-5731

Bodhi Times
P.O. Box 9094
San Rafael, CA 94912
(415)-383-5011

Body Mind Directory
CONTACT: Joy Ackerman
4050 Sorrento Valley Boulevard, Ste. 1
San Diego, CA 92121
(619)-453-3295

Bodymind Books
CONTACT: Humberto Altieri
450 Hillside Avenue
Mill Valley, CA 94941
(415)-383-4017

Bodywork Directory of North America
3150 East Presidio Road
Tucson, AZ 85716
(602)-881-4582

Bodywork Entrepreneur
584 Castro Street #373
San Francisco, CA 94114

Book Publishing Company
CONTACT: Robert Holzapfel
P.O. Box 99
Summertown, TN 38483
(615)-964-3571

Book Reader, The
831 Bay Avenue #2-E
Capitola, CA 95010-2168
(415)-982-7619

Bookleger Publishing
CONTACT: C. West
555 29th Street
San Francisco, CA 94131

Bookmark, The
P.O. Box 801143
Santa Clarita, CA 91380

Books Of Harmony
CONTACT: Joan Stover
231 Broad Street
Nevada City, CA 95959
(916)-265-9564

Bookwrights
Route 1
Box 3445
Neshkoro, WI 54960
(414)-293-8355

Boomstick
3543 18th Street, 3
San Francisco, CA 94110

Bottom Dog Press
CONTACT: Larry Smith
Firelands College
Huron, OH 44839
(419)-433-5560

Boulder Teachers' Catalog
P.O. Box 13001
Boulder, CO 80308

Boyd's
Box 6232
Augusta, GA 30906
(404)-798-3157

Brain/Mind Bulletin Newsletter
CONTACT: Randall Hough
P.O. Box 42211
4717 North Figueroa Street
Los Angeles, CA 90042
(213)-223-2500 (800)-553-6463

Brainwave
CONTACT: Mike Considine
BCM Raft
London, WC1N 3XX
England
(071) 733 7883

Branden Publishing Co.
17 Station Street
Box 843
Brookline Village, MA 02147
(617)-734-2045

Brason-Sargar Publications
CONTACT: Cheryl Blaze
P.O. Box 872
Reseda, CA 91335
(818)-700-1109

Bridge Publications, Inc.
Dept. SAF-3
1414 North Catalina Street
Los Angeles, CA 90027
(213)-382-0382 (800)-722-1733

Bridgework
CONTACT: Joan Best/Brian McKee
218 Polk Street, #218
Port Townsend, WA 98368
(206)-385-6497

Bright Mountain Books
138 Springside Road
Asheville, NC 28803
(704)-684-8840

Brimstone
P.O. Box 660
Marstons Mills, MA 02648-0006

Bristol Publishing Enterprises
CONTACT: Pat Hall
14692 Wicks Boulevard
San Leandro, CA 94577
(415)-895-4461

British Columbia Astrological Society
P.O. Box 246
Vancouver, British Columbia
Canada

British Homeopathic Association
27a Devonshire Street
London, W1N 1RJ
England

British Homoeopathy Research Group
101 Harley Street
London, W1

England

British Society of Dowsers
Sycamore Cottage
Hastingleigh
Ashford, Kent TN25 5HW
England
0233-75-253

British Unidentifed Flying Objects Research Association, Ltd.
16 Southway
Burgess Hill, Sussex RH15 9ST
England

Broadman Press
127 Ninth Avenue N.
Nashville, TN 37234
(615)-251-2433 (800)-251-3225

Brotherhood Press
CONTACT: Charlie Swanson
279 South Beverly Drive, Suite 185
Beverly Hills, CA 90212
(213)-395-5667

Buddhist Association Of United States
CONTACT: Shen
131 Tekening Drive
Tenafly, NJ 07670

Buddhist Ray, Inc.
CONTACT: Helen Tworkov, Editor
TRI Box 3000
Denville, NJ 07834

Builders Publishing Company
P.O. Box 2278
Salt Lake City, UT 84110
(801)-364-7396

Bull Publishing Company
CONTACT: Patricia Anderson
101 Gilbert Avenue
Menlo Park, CA 94025
(415)-322-2855

Burchette Brothers
P.O. Box 363
Lakeside, CA 92040-0363

Burning Books
CONTACT: M. Sumner
Route 7, Box 116 EK
Santa Fe, NM 87505

Burning Books
690 Market Street, Ste. 1501
San Francisco, CA 94104
(415)-788-7480

Burton Books
Box 370-M
Burton, OH 44021

Busch Publishing Company
5005 Rivera Court
Ft. Wayne, IN 46825
(219)-484-9600 FAX (219)-484-9604

Business Ethics
CONTACT: Miriam Kniaz
1107 Hazeltine Boulevard, Ste. 530
Chaska, MN 55318-1035
(612)-448-8864

Business in Transformation
Box 1110
Dyersburg, TN 38025

Business Research Publications, Inc.
817 Broadway
New York, NY 10003
(212)-673-4700

Butterfly Publishing Company
CONTACT: Pat Burke
2210 Wilshire Boulevard, Suite 845
Santa Monica, CA 90403
(213)-829-2002

Butterworth Publishing
80 Montvale Avenue
Stoneham, MA 02180
(617)-438-8464 (800)-366-2665

Buzzworm-The Environmental Journal
P.O. Box 6853
Syracuse, NY 13217-7930

By Design
CONTACT: Helen Roberta Ossana
1337 Powerhouse Lane, Ste. 22
Moab, UT 84532-3031
(801)-259-5936

C And R Anthony Publishers, Incorporated
CONTACT: George-Mann Associates
1710 Highway 35
Ocean, NJ 07712
(908)-531-7838

C. Olson And Company
CONTACT: Clayton L. Olson
P.O. Box 5100
Santa Cruz, CA 95063-5100
(408)-458-3365

C. W. Daniel Company, Limited
CONTACT: Ian Miller
1 Church Path, Saffron Walden
Essex CB10 1JP,
England
0799 21909

C.A.S., Inc.
2525Murworth Drive
No. 202
Houston, TX 77054
(713)-661-0346

C.E.R.E.S. Newsletter
Rural Route 1, Kispiox Road, L-21
Hazelton, BC, V0J1Y0,
Canada

C.G. Jung Institute Of Los Angeles
10349 West Pico Boulevard
Los Angeles, CA 90064
(213)-556-1193

C.V. Mosby Co.
11830 Westline Industrial Drive
St. Louis, MO 63146
(314)-872-8370

Cabala Press
2421 West Pratt Avenue
Chicago, IL 60645

(312)-761-0682

Caitlin Press
P.O. Box 2385
Pittsfield, MA 01202
(413)-442-6270

California Publications
P.O. Box 8014
Calabasas, CA 91302
(213)-880-4181

California Society For Psychical Study
Box 844
Berkeley, CA 94701

California UFO
1800 South Robertson Boulevard
Box 355
Los Angeles, CA 90035
(213)-273-9409 (818)-951-1250

Camaro Publishing Company
90430 World Way Center
Los Angeles, CA 90009
(213)-837-7500

Cambridge UFO Research Group
CONTACT: Bonnie Wheeler
170 Strathcona Street
Cambridge, Ontario N3C 1R4
Canada
(519)-658-6775

Cambridge University Press
40 West 20th Street
New York, NY 10011
(212)-924-3900 (800)-227-0247

Camelot Press Limited
CONTACT: Bill Wheeler
8 Fairway Drive
Kennesaw, GA 30144
(404)-423-9585

Canadian Chiropractic Association
1396 Eglinton Avenue, West
Toronto, Ontario M6C 2E4
Canada
(416)-781-7344

Canadian Dietetic Association
480 University Avenue, Stc. 601
Toronto, Ontario M5G 1V2
Canada
(416)-596-0857 FAX (416)-596-0603

Canadian Institute Of Parapsychology
P.O. Box 6147, Station J
Ottawa, Ontario K2A 1T2
Canada

Canadian Schizophrenia Foundation
7375 Kingsway
Burnaby, B.C. V3N 3B5
Canada
(604)-521-1728

Canadian Society Of Questers
8566 Fraser Street, #200
Vancouver, British Columbia V5X 3Y3
Canada
(604)-946-4576

Canadian UFO Report

P.O. Box 758
Duncan, BC, V9I3Y1,
Canada

Candle Publishing Company
CONTACT: Carol Estes
101 Southwestern Boulevard, #210
Sugarland, TX 77478
(713)-242-6161

Capra Press
CONTACT: Sangati Magginnis
P.O. Box 2068
Santa Barbara, CA 93120
(805)-966-4590

Capstone Press Inc.
1715 Hodgson Road
North Mankato, MN 56001
(507)-345-3438

Caravan Press
CONTACT: O. S. Lewis
343 South Broadway
Los Angeles, CA 90013
(213)-628-2563

Cardinal Star Corp.
Box A76
New York, NY 10163
(212)-535-1074

Carlton Press
11 West 32nd Street
New York, NY 10001
(212)-714-0300

Carma Press
Box 12633
St. Paul, MN 55112
(612)-631-9417

Carol Publishing Group
120 Enterprise Avenue
Secaucus, NJ 07094
(201)-866-0490

Carolina Biological Supply Company
2700 York Road
Burlington, NC 27215
(919)-584-0381 (800)-334-5551

Carousel Press
CONTACT: Carole Meyers
P.O. Box 6061
Albany, CA 94706-0061
(510)-527-5849

Carroll & Graf Publishers
260 Fifth Ave.
New York, NY 10001
(212)-889-8772

Carson City Pubs., Inc.
Box 36
Midland Park, NJ 07432

Casa Bautista de Publicaciones
P.O. Box 4255
7000 Alabama Street
El Paso, TX 79914
(915)-566-9656

Cassandra Press
CONTACT: Gurudas
P.O. Box 868

San Rafael, CA 94915
(415)-382-8507 (415)-457-2423 **FAX** (415)-382-7758

Catalyst
140 South McClelland
Salt Lake City, UT 84102
(801)-363-1505

Cauldron Publications
P.O. Box 282
San Geronimo, CA 94963
(415)-488-9641

Causes Newsletter
P.O. Box 3110
Laredo, TX 78044

Caveat Emptor
8 Gate House Lane
Edison, NJ 08820

CBS Publications
Box 5348
Boulder, CO 80322

Celebrate One
5818 Southwest Orchid Drive
Portland, OR 97219
(503)-246-1591

Celestial Arts Publishing Co./Sub. of Ten Speed Press
P.O. Box 7327
Berkeley, CA 94707
(415)-524-1801 (800)-841-2665

Celestial Communications
CONTACT: Aurora
P.O. Box 7084
Santa Cruz, CA 95061-7084
(408)-479-8126

Celestial Gems
404 State Boulevard
Centralia, WA 98531
(206)-736-5083

Celestial Gifts Publishing
CONTACT: Dr. Ron Dalrymple
P.O. Box 414
Chester, MD 21619
(410)-643-4466

Celestial Visions
2961 Industrial Road, 454
Las Vegas, NV 89109

Celetic Dawn
P.O. Box 402527
Miami Beach, FL 33140

Celtic Heritage Press, Incorporated
CONTACT: Grace E. Cameron
59-10 Queens Boulevard, #9B
Woodside, NY 11377
(718)-478-8162

Center For Chinese Medicine
230 South Garfield Avenue, #202
Montgomery Park, CA 91754
(818)-572-0424

Center For Health & Safety Studies Indiana University
H P E R Building

Rm 116
Bloomington, IN 47405
(812)-335-7975

Center For Human Development
P.O. Box 4557
Washington, DC 20017
(202)-529-7724

Center For Icarian Studies
Western Illinois University Center For Icarian Studies
University Libraries
Macomb, IL 61455
(309)-298-2411

Center For Thanatology
CONTACT: Roberta Halporn
391 Atlantic Avenue
Brooklyn, NY 11217-1701
(718)-858-3026

Center For The Well-Being Of Health Professionals
321 West Colony Place, #150
Durham, NC 27705-5569
(919)-489-9167

Center Light Publishing
CONTACT: Andy Schneider
Box 2269
Salmon Arm, BC V1E 4R3
Canada
(604)-832-8483

Centerline Press
2005 Palo Verde, Suite 325
Long Beach, CA 90815
(213)-421-0220

Centre For Traditional Acupuncture, Inc.
American City Building
Suite 100
Columbia, MD 21044
(301)-997-3770

Centre Homeopathique de France
228, blvd. Raspail
Paris, 75014
France

Centre International d'Action Culturelle
52 Av. du Hockey
1150 Brussels,
Belgium
02-771-78-92

Centro Italiana di Astrologia
Via Giacinto Collegno 12 bis.
Turin, 10143
Italy

Centro Studi Parapsicologici
Via L. Valeriani, 39
Bologna, I-40134
Italy
051-411885

Centro Studi Rosacrux
Casella Postale 2229
Naples, 80100
Italy

Ceres Press
CONTACT: David Goldbeck
Box 87
Woodstock, NY 12498
(914)-674-8561

Champagne Press
313 Walnuthaven Drive
West Covina, CA 91790
(818)-814-2052

Chan's Corp.
230 So. Garfield Avenue
Monterey Park, CA 91754
(213)-572-0425

Chandler And Sharp Publishers
CONTACT: Jon Sharp
11A Commercial Boulevard
Novato, CA 94949
(415)-883-2353

Chandler-Smith Publishing House, Inc.
P.O. Box 469
Peabody, MA 01960
(508)-741-8980

Changes
3201 Southwest 15th Street
Deerfield Beach, FL 33442
(305)-360-0909 (800)-851-9100

Changes Journal
P.O. Box 734
State College, PA 16804

Changing Schools
Teachers College, Room 1008
Ball State University
Muncie, IN 47306
(317)-285-5453

Chaos
P.O. Box 1598
Kingson, ON, K7L5C8,
Canada

Charles & Randy Elder Publications
2115 Elliston Place
Nashville, TN 37203
(615)-327-1867

Charles Franklin Press, The
CONTACT: Linda Meyer
7821 175th Street, South West
Edmonds, WA 98020-1835
(206)-774-6979

Charles T. Branford, Co.
P.O. Box 41
Newton Centre, MA 02159
(617)-964-2441

Charlton Publications, Inc.
Charlton Building
Derby, CT 06418
(203)-735-3381

Charter Oak Press
CONTACT: T. Horn
P.O. Box 7783
Lancaster, PA 17604
(717)-898-7711

Chatsworth Press

CONTACT: Scott Brastow
9135-B Alabama Avenue
Chatsworth, CA 91311
(818)-341-3156

Chela Publications
P.O. Box 40299
Memphis, TN 38174-0299
(901)-272-2750

Chelo Publishing
350 5th Avenue, #6204
New York, NY 10118
(212)-947-4322

Chelsea House Publishing
95 Madison Avenue
New York, NY 10016
(212)-683-4400

Chicago & MW Psychic Guide
2517 West 71st Street
Chicago, IL 60629

Chicago Review Press, Inc.
814 N. Franklin St.
Chicago, IL 60610
(312)-337-0747

Chicago's Inner Quest
1424 West Farragut
Chicago, IL 60604
(312)-728-8953

Child's World, Inc.
123 South Broad Street
Mankato, MN 56001-3612

Children's Press
5440 No. Cumberland Avenue
Chicago, IL 60656
(312)-693-0800 (800)-621-1115

Chiltern Yoga Foundation
1029 Hyde Street, Suite 6
San Francisco, CA 94109
(415)-776-1158

China Books & Periodicals, Inc.
2929 24th St.
San Francisco, CA 94110
(415)-282-2994

Chiron Press
Route 2
Box 111
Saint John, KS 67576
(316)-549-3933

Chiron Publications
400 Linden Avenue
Wilmette, IL 60091
(312)-256-7551

Chiropractic News Publishing Company
29229 Six Mile Road
Livonia, MI 48152
(313)-427-5720

CHL Publishing Company
CONTACT: Stanley Weinberger
P.O. Box 1013
Larkspur, CA 94939
(415)-924-6106

Choices for Health! Vitality!
2705 Southwest 221st Avenue
Hillsboro, OR 97123-6615

Christ For The Nations, Inc.
P.O. Box 769000
Dallas, TX 75376
(214)-376-1711

Christ State
Box 3549
New Haven, CT 06525

Christian Classics, Inc.
P.O. Box 30
Westminster, MD 21157
(301)-848-3065 (800)-888-3065

Christian New Age Quarterly
CONTACT: Catherine Groves
P.O. Box 276
Clifton, NJ 07011-0276

Christopher Publications
CONTACT: David Christopher
P.O. Box 412
Springville, UT 84663
(801)-489-4254

Christopher Publishing House
24 Rockland Street
Commerce Green
Hanover, MA 02339
(617)-826-7474

Chrysalis Publications
P.O. Box 3937
Grand Junction, CO 81502

Churches' Council For Health And Healing
St. Marylebone Parish Church
Marylebone Road
London, NW1 5LT
England

Churches' Fellowship for Psychical & Spiritual Studies
Warehorne Rd., Hamstreet
Ashford, Kent
England

Cin Publications
CONTACT: C. Cin
P.O. Box 11277
San Francisco, CA 94101

Cindy Saul Publishers
18444 West 10 Mile Road #105
Southfield, MI 48075-2626
(313)-569-3888 FAX (313)-559-0075

Circle of Light
P.O. Box 180732
Dallas, TX 75218
(214)-279-1126

Citadel Press
CONTACT: Lyle Stuart
120 Enterprise Ave.
Secaucus, NJ 07094
(201)-866-0490

City Connections
5040 Reno Court

Las Vegas, NV 89119
(702)-795-7122

City Lights Books
261 Columbus Ave.
San Francisco, CA 94133
(415)-362-8193

City Spirit Publications
CONTACT: Jerome Rubin
590 Pacific Street
Brooklyn, NY 11217
(718)-857-1545

Civilized Pubications
CONTACT: Sara Ollie
2019 South Seventh Street
Philadelphia, PA 19148
(215)-339-0062

Clean Yield Publications
CONTACT: Ryan Freed
P.O. Box 1800
Greenboro, VT 05842
(802)-535-7178

Clear Light Publishers
CONTACT: Marcia Keegan
823 Don Diego
Santa Fe, NM 87501
(505)-989-9590

Cliff Robertson Foundation
CONTACT: Dr. Cliff Robertson
11407 Herbert Road
Whitesville, KY 42378
(502)-233-4895

Clubhouse
P.O. Box 15
Berrien Springs, MI 49103
(616)-471-9009

Coastline Publishing
Box 223062
Carmel, CA 93922

Cold Spring Harbor Laboratory
P.O. Box 100
Cold Spring Harbor, NY 11724
(516)-367-8325 (800)-843-4388

Coleman Publishing
1147 Elmwood
Stockton, CA 95204
(209)-464-9503

Collaboration
P.O. Box 372
High Falls, NY 12440
(914)-687-9222 (914)-667-9222

College Of Psychic Studies
16 Queensberry Place
London, SW7 2EB
England

College Press Publishing Co., Inc.
Box 1132
205 N. Main
Joplin, MO 64802
(417)-623-6280 (800)-289-3300

Collier Books
MacMillan Publishing Co.-MacMillan Distribution
Center

Front and Brown Streets
Riverside, NJ 08075

Collings Books
P.O. Box 168
Appalachia, VA 24216

Collins, Div. of William Collins
50 Osgood Pl., Ste. 400
San Francisco, CA 94133
(415)-788-3651

Collinsport Record, The
CONTACT: S. Rizzuto
P.O. Box 994
Metairie, LA 70004
(504)-733-9138

Color Dynamics
CONTACT: Judith L. Powell
11701 Belcher Road South, Ste. 123
Largo, FL 34643
(813)-531-1670 (813)-530-0110

Coming Changes
937 St. Mary's Street
De Pere, WI 54115

Common Ground
CONTACT: Andy
305 San Anselmo Avenue, #313
San Anselmo, CA 94960
(415)-459-4900 FAX (415)-459-4974

Common Ground
CONTACT: Michael Bertrand
P.O. Box 34090, Station D
Vancouver, British Columbia V6J 4M1
Canada
(604)-733-2215

Common Ground
47-155 Okana Road
Kaneohe, HI 69744

Common Ground
4545 North 36th, Suite 120
Phoenix, AZ 85018
(602)-956-4996

Common Ground Hawaii
571 Kaimalind Street
Kailua, HI 96734-1611
(808)-239-7190

Common Ground of Puget Sound
CONTACT: John Crutcher
P.O. Box 30046
Seattle, WA 98103-0046
(206)-443-9504 (206)-367-2666 FAX (206)-362-6988

Communications Channels, Inc.
390 Fifth Avenue
New York, NY 10018
(212)-613-9700

Communications Unlimited
CONTACT: Gordon Burgett
P.O. Box 6405
Santa Maria, CA 93456
(805)-937-8711

Communion Letter, The
2151 Greencrest Drive
San Antonio, TX 78213-4440

Community Resource Publications
228 20th Street
Huntington Beach, CA 92648
(714)-963-7697 (714)-969-1371

Community Careers Resource Center
1601 Connecticut Avenue, NW, 6th FL.
Washington, DC 20009-1035
(202)-667-0661

Community Church By The Bay
148 East 22nd Street
Costa Mesa, CA 92626
(714)-645-0971

Community For Conscious Evolution
171 Jackson Street
Newton, MA 02159
(617)-964-7448

Community Health Services Association
455 2nd Avenue, North
Saskatoon SK S7K 2C2,
Canada
(306)-664-4243

Community Spirit Magazine
P.O. Box 4628
Carmel, CA 93921
(408)-625-1557

Compassion For Animals Foundation, Inc.
CONTACT: Art Cordts
3961 Landmark Street
Culver City, CA 90232
(213)-204-2929 (213)-204-2323

CompCare Publications, Div. of Comprehensive Care Corp.
401 South Tustin Street
Orange, CA 92666-2503
(714)-851-2273

Concept Publishers
CONTACT: B. M. Tyrka DC
303 16th Street
Watervliet, NY 12189

Concord Grove Press, Subs. of Institute of World Culture
Concord House
1407 Chapala St.
Santa Barbara, CA 93101
(805)-966-3941

Conde Nast Publications, Inc.
350 Madison Avenue
New York, NY 10017
(212)-880-8800

Connecting Arizona
4545 North 36th Street, Suite 120
Phoenix, AZ 85018
(602)-956-4996

Connecting Link
CONTACT: Susie Konicov
9392 Whitneyville Road
Alto, MI 49302-9694
(616)-698-2690 (616)-949-7894

Connecting Link
24 Blazing Ridge Way

Lawrenceville, GA 30245
(404)-822-0360

Conocimiento De La Nueva Era
Viamonte 1716
Buenos Aires, 1055
Argentina

Conscious Choice
P.O. Box 14431
Chicago, IL 60614
(312)-281-1177

Conscious Living Foundation, Inc.
CONTACT: Dr. Lowenstein
P.O. Box 9
Drain, OR 97435
(503)-836-2358

Consciousness Connection, The
CONTACT: Felicia Mahood Center
432 Altair Place
Venice, CA 90291
(213)-372-7894

Considerations
Box 655
Mt. Kisco, NY 10549
(914)-232-4452

Constellations
1317 Monterey Avenue
Monrovia, CA 91016

Contact Collaborations
P.O. Box 603
Northampton, MA 01061
(413)-586-1181

Contemporary Books, Inc.
180 North Michigan Avenue
Chicago, IL 60601
(312)-782-9181

Continuity Publishing
CONTACT: Duane Sweeney
Box 224
Greenbank, WA 98253-0224
(206)-678-7772

Continuum Publishing Co.
370 Lexington Ave.
New York, NY 10017
(212)-532-3650

Coordinate Point
P.O. Box 520
Oviedo, FL 32765
(305)-365-4087

Cornell University Press
124 Roberts Place
P.O. Box 250
Ithaca, NY 14850
(607)-257-7000

Cosmic Circus Productions
414 South 41st Street
Richmond, CA 94804
(415)-451-5818 (415)-653-9899

Cosmic Clockwatch
CONTACT: Kat Duff
P.O. Box 1178
Taos, NM 87571

Cosmic People Magazine

P.O. Box 1425
New York, NY 10163

Cosmic Quest, Inc.
Box 293
Delaware, OH 43015
(614)-486-6587

Cosmic Trend
CONTACT: Tedy Asponsen
Clarkson Road
P.O. Box 323
Mississauga, ON L5J 3Y2
Canada

Cosmic Voyage
P.O. Box 1116B
McMinnville, OR 97128

Cosmoenergetics Publications
P.O. Box 86353
San Diego, CA 92138
(619)-295-1664

Cosmopsychologischer Verlag
CONTACT: Dr. Gerhard Ernst Matzke
Pommernstr. 4a
7890 Waldshut-Tiengen 2,
West Germany
07741-61481

Cosmos
P.O. Box 322
Lane Cove, NSW 2066
Australia

Cougar Books
P.O. Box 22246
Sacramento, CA 95822
(916)-428-3271

Council Of The Magikal Arts (CMA)
CONTACT: Lillith
P.O. Box 33274
Austin, TX 78764-3274

Country Health
P.O. Box 80525
Burnaby, BC V5H 3X9
Canada
(604)-438-1054

Coven Of Isis
Box 231
Winnisquam, NH 03289
(603)-722-5668

Craeftgemot Witancoveyne, Inc.
RR 1, Box 601-C
Pompano Beach, FL 33073
(305)-428-9713

Crazy Wisdom Books
206 North Fourth Avenue
Ann Arbor, MI 48104

CRCS Publications
Box 1460
Sebastopol, CA 95473
(707)-829-0735

Creation/Evolution Journal
P.O. Box 146
7 Harwood Drive
Buffalo, NY 14226
(716)-839-5080

Creations Magazine
Box 295
Roslyn, NY 11576
(516)-484-5384

Creative Media Works
CONTACT: David Zaslow
682 Elkader Street
Ashland, OR 97520
(503)-482-0088

Creighton, Maydell & Pennington
1237 Camino del Mar
Del Mar, CA 92014
(619)-792-1473

Crestwood House, Inc.
c/o Macmillan Publishing Co., Inc.
Front & Brown Streets
Riverside, NJ 08075
(609)-461-6500 (800)-257-8247

Cromwell-Sloan Publishing Company
63 Vine Road
Stamford, CT 06905
(203)-323-6839

Crone Papers, The
P.O. Box 181
Crossville, TN 38557

Crone's Own Press
5047 49th Avenue, South
Seattle, WA 98118

Cross-Cultural Shaman's Network
Box 2636
Berkeley, CA 94702
(415)-525-5122

Crossing Press
22D Roache Road
P.O. Box 1048
Freedom, CA 95019
(408)-722-0711 (800)-777-1048

Crosswinds
P.O. Box 39
Santa Fe, NM 87504

Crow Speaks
P.O. Box 57
Wendell Depot, MA 01380

Crown Publications, Inc.
P.O. Box 688
Southbridge, MA 01550
(508)-248-3994

Crown Publications, Inc.
P.O. Box 4397
Glendale, CA 91222
(818)-244-5007 (800)-726-0600

Crown Publishers, Inc.
34 Englehard Avenue
Avenel, NJ 07001

Crown Publishers, Inc.
225 Park Avenue, South
New York, NY 10003
(212)-254-1600

Crucible Books, Inner Traditions International, Ltd.
1 Park Street

Rochester, VT 05767
(802)-767-3174 (800)-242-7737

Crystal Age News
P.O. Box 688
West Yarmouth, MA 02673

Crystal Ball, The
P.O. Box 4080
Torrance, CA 90510

Crystal Clarity Publishers
CONTACT: Paul Kelly
14618 Tyler Foote Road
Nevada City, CA 95959
(916)-292-3225 (800)-424-1055

Crystal Company, The
Box 348
Sunol, CA 94586
(415)-862-2332

Crystal Heart
CONTACT: Miriam Kaplan
Box 508
Fallsburg, NY 12733
(914)-434-7923

Crystal Network Foundation
CONTACT: Alice And Rudy Wyrsch
2425B Channing Way, #452
Berkeley, CA 94704
(415)-548-4688

Crystal Pathways
P.O. Box 37450
Denver, CO 80237
(303)-595-5758

Crystal Vogage
1713 Monroe Avenue
Rochester, NY 14618-1432
(716)-461-2137

CSA Press, Publishers
Lake Ravun Road
Lakemont, GA 30552
(404)-782-4723

Cultwatch Response, Inc.
P.O. Box 1842
Colorado Springs, CO 80901

Curcio Periodice S.p.A.
Via Corsica 4
Rome, 00198
Italy

Cypress: The Psychic Digest
5433 Glorianne Circle North
Jacksonville, FL 32207

Dahlin Family Press
5339 Prospect Rd. No. 300
San Jose, CA 95129

Daniel Publishing Company
7752 Marshall Heights Court
Fall Church, VA 22043
(703)-442-8025

Dansk Vegetar-og Raakostforening Ny
Vestergaardsvej 6
Vaerloese, 3500
Denmark

Dao Publications
CONTACT: Khigh Dheigh
P.O. Box 27806
Tempe, AZ 85285
(602)-839-5832

Dartnell's Cambridge Associates
164 Canal
Boston, MA 02114
(617)-423-5878

David Graham Associates
309 East Main Street
Decorah, IA 52101
(319)-382-5939

David Hatcher Childress
405 Kemp Street
Kempton, IL 60946
(815)-253-6390 FAX (815)-256-2299

David McKay Co., Inc.
201 East 50th Street
New York, NY 10022
(212)-751-2600

Davis Communications Company
11426 Cedar Avenue #D-3
Cleveland, OH 44106-2611
(216)-662-6969

Dawn Horse Press, The
CONTACT: R. Schorske
P.O. Box 3680
Clear Lake, CA 95422

Dawn Publications
CONTACT: Helen Purcell
14618 Tyler Foote Road
Nevada City, CA 95959
(916)-292-3484

Dawnwood Press
387 Park Avenue South
New York, NY 10016-8810
(212)-531-7160

Day'seye Press
CONTACT: D. Moomey
Box 709
La Honda, CA 94020-8810
(415)-747-0502

Daybreak
P.O. Box 315
Williamsville, NY 14231-0315

Dayton Laboratories
3235 Dayton Avenue
Lorain, OH 44055
(216)-246-1397

Dead Of Night Publications
916 Shaker Road, #143
Longmeadow, MA 01106-2416

Deja Vu Publishing Co.
95 Belvedere
San Rafael, CA 94901
(415)-459-3551

Delacorte Press
Dept. Z64
P.O. Box 5071
Des Plaines, IL 60017

Delacorte Press
1 Dag Hammarskjold Plaza
New York, NY 10017-8810
(212)-605-3000

Delhi Homoeopathic Medical Association
4457 Pahari Dhiraj
Delhi, 11006
India

Dell Horoscope Magazines
245 Park Avenue
New York, NY 10167
(212)-984-7135

Dell Publishing Co., Inc.
666 Fifth Avenue
New York, NY 10103
(212)-765-6500 (800)-255-4133

Dell Reader Services-Dell Publishing
P.O. Box 5057
Des Plaines, IL 60017

Delphi Press
CONTACT: Karen Jackson
P.O. Box 1538
Oak Park, IL 60304-8810
(708)-524-7900

Delphi Publications
P.O. Box 211
Rimrock, AZ 86335
(602)-634-2390

Design Spirit
CONTACT: Suzanne Koblentz-Goodman
438 Third Street
Brooklyn, NY 11238
(718)-636-3962 (718)-768-5796

Destiny Books, Inner Traditions International, Ltd.
1 Park Street
Rochester, VT 05767
(802)-767-3174 (800)-242-7737

Destiny Image Publishers
351 North Queen Street
P.O. Box 351
Shippensburg, PA 17257
(717)-532-3040

Destiny Publishers
43 Grove Street
Merrimac, MA 01860
(508)-346-9311

Devida Publication
6 Darby Road
East Brunswick, NJ 08816-3407
(201)-257-7257

Devin-Adair Publishers
CONTACT: Roger H. Lourie
6 North Water Street
Greenwich, CT 06830
(203)-531-7755

Devonshire Publishing Company
CONTACT: R. Reynolds
P.O. Box 85
Elgin, IL 60121-0085
(312)-242-3846

Dharma Combat
CONTACT: Jerry E. Smith
P.O. Box 20593
Sun Valley, NV 89433

Dharma Drum Publishing
90-31 Corona Avenue
Elmhurst, NY 11373
(718)-592-6593

Dharma Publishing
2425 Hillside Avenue
Berkeley, CA 94704
(415)-548-5407

Dharma Realm Buddhist Association
CONTACT: (Bhikshu) Heng Jau
P.O. Box 217
Talmage, CA 95481-0217
(707)-462-0939

Dharma Seed Tape Library
P.O. Box 66
Wendall Depot, MA 01380

Dialectic Publications
3805 NE 167th Street
North Miami Beach, FL 33160
(305)-945-5359

Dialog Center International
Katrinebjergvej 46
DK-8200 Aarhus N.,
Denmark

Diamandis Communication, Inc.
1515 Broadway
New York, NY 10036

Diamond Books
P.O. Box 10114
Berkeley, CA 94709
(415)-235-0627

Diamond Stockton
520 East Benjamin Holt Drive
Stockton, CA 95207
(209)-478-6334 (800)-835-2246

Digicomp Research Corp.
Terrace Hill
Ithaca, NY 14850
(607)-273-5900

Dilmum Press
CONTACT: Finnie
773 Cole, #8
San Francisco, CA 94117
(415)-668-5720

Dimon, Inc.
3001 North San Fernando Boulevard
P.O. Box 6489
Burbank, CA 91510
(818)-845-3748 FAX (818)-954-8916

Directors Guild Publishers
CONTACT: Constance Franklin
P.O. Box 369
Renaissance, CA 95962-0369
(916)-692-1355 (800)-383-0677

Directory Canadian Pagan Research
P.O. Box 86134
N. Vancouver, BC, V7L2L9,
Canada

Directory Of Alternative Travel Resources
CONTACT: Dianne G. Brause
81868 Lost Valley Lane
Dexter, OR 97431
(503)-937-3351

Directory of Holistic Health Practitioners
Route 1, Box 12A
Esmont, VA 22937
(804)-286-4652

Directory Of Holistic Medicine
CONTACT: Shirley Linde
P.O. Box 22001
Phoenix, AZ 85028

Directory Of Holistic Practitioners
Box 1705
Brookline, MA 02146

Dogwood Press
CONTACT: Peggy Scribner
P.O. Box 2023
Stone Mountain, GA 30089
(404)-296-1073

Dolphin Dreams
P.O. Box 1573
Ferndale, WA 98248

Dolphin-Doubleday
666 Fifth Avenue
New York, NY 10103
(212)-765-6500 (800)-223-6834

Dominion Press
P.O. Box 4608
Salem, OR 97302-8608

Dong Nam P&C Inc.
2946 N. Lincoln Avenue
Chicago, IL 60657
(312)-549-4660

Donning Company Publishers
184 Business Park Drive, #106
Virginia Beach, VA 23462-6533
(804)-461-8090 (800)-446-8572

Dophin Communications
CONTACT: John Seymore
P.O. Box 98509
Des Moines, WA 98198
(206)-878-9377

Dorchester Publishing Co., Inc.
276 Fifth Avenue
New York, NY 10001
(212)-725-8811

Dorset House Publishing Co., Inc.
353 West 12th Street
New York, NY 10014
(212)-620-4053 (800)-342-6657

Dorset Press
120 Fifth Avenue
New York, NY 10011
(212)-924-8395

Dorsett
5710 Dorsett Drive
Madison, WI 53711

(608)-263-1587

Double Helix Press
CONTACT: Dr. Jean Sanville
1300 Tigertail Road
Los Angeles, CA 90049
(213)-472-6452

Double M Press
CONTACT: C. Stein
16455 Tuba Street
Sepulveda, CA 91343
(818)-360-3166

Double Star Productions
CONTACT: Connie Ray/Mimmie Louis
P.O. Box 1861
Kahului, HI 96732
(808)-371-7737

Doubleday & Co.
501 Franklin Avenue
Garden City, NY 11530
(516)-873-4774

Doubleday & Co.,Inc.
666 Fifth Avenue
New York, NY 10103
(212)-765-6500 (800)-255-4133 (800)-323-9872

Dover Publications, Inc.
180 Varick Street
New York, NY 10014
(212)-255-3755 (800)-223-3131

Down East Books
P.O. Box 679
Camden, ME 04843
(207)-594-9544 (800)-432-1670

Down There Press
CONTACT: Joni Blank
P.O. Box 2086
Burlingame, CA 94011
(415)-342-2536

Down To Earth Publications
873 Lincoln
St. Paul, MN 55105
(612)-222-6576

Dream International Quarterly
121 North Ramona Street, #25
Ramona, CA 92065
(619)-789-3258

Dream Psychology Northwest
Box 419
Mendham, NJ 07943
(201)-325-6148

Dreams At Dawn Publishing
CONTACT: Susan Schuster
4 Wellington Road
Merrick, NY 11566
(516)-868-6343

Druid Missal
616 Miner Road
Orinda, CA 94563

Druid's Progress, The
P.O. Box 1022
Nyack, NY 10960

Dryad Press
15 Sherman Ave.

Takoma Park, MD 20912
(301)-891-3729

Dynamic Life Times
P.O. Box 6143
Clearwater, FL 34618-6143
(813)-536-8964

E.P. Dutton, Inc.
2 Park Avenue, 17th Fl.
New York, NY 10016
(212)-725-1818

Eagle's Cry, The
440 Tennyson Street
Denver, CO 80212-2310
(303)-979-7797

Eagles View Publishing
168 West 12th
Ogden, UT 84404
(801)-393-3991

Eakin Press
P.O. Drawer 90159
Austin, TX 78709
(512)-288-1771 (800)-284-0173

Ear Magazine
131 Varick Street, #905
New York, NY 10013
(212)-807-7944

Earth Action Network
28 Knight Street
Norwalk, CT 06851
(203)-226-9265 **FAX** (203)-866-0602

Earth Books
CONTACT: Dorothy Lane
P.O. Box 740
Redwood Valley, CA 95470
(707)-459-1845

Earth Heart
CONTACT: Jane English
P.O. Box 7
Mt. Shasta, CA 96067
(916)-926-3612

Earth Magic Times
2170 Broadway, 16
New York, NY 10024

Earth Nation Sunrise
RR 3 Box 507
Nashville, IN 47448

Earth Rider
CONTACT: Arline Curtiss
P.O. Box 27 - 1284
Escondido, CA 92025
(619)-489-0336

Earth Spirit Journal
Box 391, Dept. C118
Westmoreland, NH 03467

Earth Star Press
CONTACT: Lane Masterson
P.O. Box 110
Temple, NH 03084
(603)-878-4090 (617)-628-1719

Earth Star Publications
CONTACT: Ann Carol Ulrich

P.O. Box 117
Paonia, CO 81428-0117
(303)-872-4678 (303)-527-3257

Earth Tones Music Review
P.O. Box 50597
Phoenix, AZ 85076-0597
(602)-893-1911

Earth Z
CONTACT: Herbert Zobel
1575 South Lincoln Street
Kent, OH 44240-0174
(216)-678-6108

Earth-Song Press
CONTACT: M. Gillies
202 Hartnell Place
Sacramento, CA 95825-0174
(916)-927-6863

Earth-Star Pathways
1442 Lincoln Avenue, Suite 329
Orange, CA 92665

Earthquake Lady News
P.O. Box 1695
Los Gatos, CA 95030

Earthspirit, Incorporated
CONTACT: Paula Rochlis
6114 LaSalle Avenue, Suie 362
Oakland, CA 94611-0174
(415)-339-2759

East West
Box 57320
Boulder, CO 80321-0001

East West Health Books
CONTACT: Mark Mayell
17 Station Street
Box 1200
Brookline Village, MA 02147
(303)-232-1000 **FAX** (303)-232-1572

East/West Arts People
P.O. Box 1941
Bloomington, IN 47402
(812)-334-0381

Eastland Press
611 Post Avenue, Suite 3
Seattle, WA 98104
(206)-587-6013

Eastview Editions
P.O. Box 783
Westfield, NJ 07091
(201)-964-9485

Eaton Publishing
Box 3369
Boulder, CO 80307
(303)-441-9689

Ebertin-Verlag
Kronenstr 2
Postfach 167
7800 Freiberg,
West Germany

Ecotope, Incorporated
CONTACT: Waverly Fitzgerald
2812 East Madison
Seattle, WA 98112-0174

(206)-322-3753

EDC Publishing
10302 East 55th Place
Tulsa, OK 74146
(918)-622-4522 (800)-331-4418

Eden Bulletin
P.O. Box 34
Carywood, ID 83809

Edition Question de
10 rue de la Vacquerie
Paris, 75011
France

Editions Amelie
18-20 rue Claude Tillier
Paris, 75012
France

Editions Astres
10 rue de Grussol
Paris, 75011
France

Editions des Cahiers Astrologiques
7 rue Condorcet
Paris, 75009
France

Editoria Tres
Avenue Paulista 2,006
15 E 16 Andares Caixa Postal 1481
Sao Paulo,
Brazil

Editorial Posada
S.A., Oculistas No. 43
Col. El Sifon 09400
Mexico, D.F.,
Mexico

Editorial Research Service
4420 Roanoke Parkway, #105
Kansas City, MO 64111

Editorial Unilit
1360 NW 88th Avenue
Miami, FL 33172
(305)-592-6136 (800)-327-4067

Educating Hands Bookstore
261 S.W. Eighth Street
Miami, FL 33130
(305)-285-6991

Edwin Mellen Press
P.O. Box 450
Lewiston, NY 14092
(716)-754-8566

El Montecito Oaks Press, Incorporated
CONTACT: Nell C. Taylor
P.O. Box 5381
Montecito, CA 93150-5381
(805)-969-5698

Eleanor Friede Books, Incorporated
CONTACT: Eleanor Friede
45 West 12th Street
New York, NY 10011
(212)-741-2900

Element Books, Limited

CONTACT: Michael Mann
Old School House, Courtyard
Shaftsbury
Dorset SP7 BP,
United Kingdom
0747 51448

Elmer Eugene Edwards
P.O. Box 584
Miami, FL 33161

Elven Glen
P.O. Box 247
Fields Landing, CA 95537

Elysium Growth Press
CONTACT: Ed Lange
814 Robinson Road
Topanga, CA 90290
(213)-455-1000 **FAX** (213)-455-3404

Emerald Publishing
P.O. Box 11830
Reno, NV 89510

Emergence
P.O. Box 348
Arroyo Seco, NM 87514-0348

Empyreal Press
P.O. Box 49
Portland, CT 06480

Enchanted Forest News
201 West Moneta Avenue
Bakersfield, CA 93308

Energy Investment Research
Box 73
Greenwich, CT 06831
(914)-937-6939

Enlightenments
1230 Pemberton Drive
Fort Wayne, IN 46805
(219)-424-2172

Entwhistle Books
P.O. Box 611
Glen Ellen, CA 95442

Esoteric World News Magazine
CONTACT: Lorraine DiFelice
P.O. Box 931658
Hollywood, CA 90093
(213)-662-7662

ESP Research Associates Foundation
Newsletter
Hwy. 5 S.
Mountain View, AR 72560
(501)-375-5377

Essential Whole Earth Catalog
27 Gate Five Road
Sausalito, CA 94965

Eternal Enterprises
P.O. Box 1558
Fair Oaks, CA 95628-1558

Evan T. Pritchard Publishers
CONTACT: Evan T. Pritchard
P.O. Box 215
Beacon, NY 12508
(914)-838-1217

Evergreens
Box 130
Blackstock, Ontario L0B 1B0
Canada
(416)-986-5369

Evolutionary Publications
CONTACT: Roy Tate
P.O. Box 380516
Miami, FL 33238

Evolving Times Magazine
112 Fulton Avenue #G
Sacramento, CA 95825-4209
(916)-863-0409

Executive Health Publications
CONTACT: Ann Buzenberg
Box 8880
Chapel Hill, NC 27515-8880
(919)-929-7519 **FAX** (919)-929-2458

Exeter House Books
CONTACT: Charles J. Adams III
14 East 34th Street
Reading, PA 19606
(215)-779-8173

Exorcism International
3340 West Highway 89-A, 16
Sedona, AZ 86336

Exum Corporation, Publishing
Division
5705 Cochiti Drive NW
Albuquerque, NM 87120
(505)-881-4413

Eye of Gaza
New Age Center
BCM-New Age
London, WC1V 6XX
England

F.G. Gourdon
10 rue de Crussol
Paris, 75011
France

Faber & Faber, Affil. of Faber &
Faber, Ltd., London
50 Cross St.
Winchester, MA 01890
(617)-721-1427

Facts On File Publications
460 Park Avenue S.
New York, NY 10016
(212)-683-2244

Factsheet Five
41 Lawrence Street
Medford, MA 02155

Faerie Folk, The
P.O. Box 100585
Ft. Lauderdale, FL 33310

Faith Messenger Publications
P.O. Box 641
Upland, CA 91785
(714)-946-3134

Falcon Press
1209 South Casino Central, 147

Las Vegas, NV 89104
(702)-385-5749

Falcon Press
CONTACT: Alan R. Miller
2210 Wilshire #295
Santa Monica, CA 90403
(213)-821-3540

False Positive/Out-Of-Kontrol Data
Korporation
CONTACT: Donna Kossoy
P.O. Box 953
Allston, MA 02134
(617)-782-5602

Fantasy Workshop
CONTACT: Fran Kirschner
1400 West Cross Street
Lakewood, NJ 08701
(201)-363-3988

Faro House, Limited
CONTACT: Sandra Pulaski
404 Court Street
Binghamton, NY 13904-1606
(607)-729-3988 (800)-729-3988

Farrar, Straus And Giroux
19 Union Square West
New York, NY 10003
(212)-741-6900

Fate Magazine
170 Future Way
Marion, OH 43302
(419)-433-8100

Fawcett Book Group
201 East 50th Street
New York, NY 10022
(212)-751-2600 (800)-733-3000

Federation Of Australian Astrologers
Co-Operative, Ltd.
5 Gawler Court
Mont Albert, Vic. 3127,
Australia

Feeling Better Whole Health
Newsletter
152 1st Avenue North
Tierra Verde, FL 33715

Feeling Good Associates
P.O. Box S
Keala Kehua, HI 96750
(808)-383-5439

Feeling Great
45 West 34th Street
Room 407
New York, NY 10001
(212)-239-0855

Felix Morrow
13 Welwyn Rd.
Great Neck, NY 11021
(516)-482-1044

Fellowship For Intentional
Community
CONTACT: Laird Schaub, Business Manager
Sandhill Farm
Rt. 1, Box 155

Rutledge, MO 63563
(816)-883-5543

Fellowship Of The Inner Light
620 14th Street
Virginia Beach, VA 23451

Fellowship Press
P.O. Box 192
Noblesville, IN 46060

Feminist Bookstore News
CONTACT: Carol Seajay
456 14th Street, #6
P.O. Box 882554
San Francisco, CA 94188-2554
(415)-626-1556 FAX (415)-626-8970

Fenton Valley Press
657 Chaffeeville Road
Storrs, CT 06268
(203)-429-0710

Fertility Awareness Service
CONTACT: Suzannah Cooper Doyle
P.O. Box 986
Corvallis, OR 97339
(503)-753-8530

Fessenden Review
Box 7272
San Diego, CA 92107
(619)-488-4991

Fifth Sun Media, Inc.
CONTACT: Alexander Blair-Ewart
3 Charles Street West, Ste. 300
Toronto, ON M4Y 1R4
Canada
(416)-926-1483 (416)-928-6730 FAX (416)-928-1446

Fine Line Books
43 Mechanic Street
Orange, MA 01364-1208

FireHeart
P.O. Box 462
Maynard, MA 01754
(617)-395-1023

Fireside Books
Simon and Schuster, Inc.
1230 Avenue of the Americas
New York, NY 10020
(212)-373-8500

Fireside Press
Box 5293
Hamden, CT 06518
(203)-248-1023

First Editions
CONTACT: Sophia Tarila, Ph. D.
P.O. Box 2578
Sedona, AZ 86336
(602)-282-9574 (602)-282-1989 (800)-777-4751
FAX (602)-282-9730

Fitness Information Network
P.O. Box 906
Greenfield, MA 01302
(413)-773-8769

Fitness Institute
255 Yorkland Boulevard

Willowdale, Ontario M2J 1S3
Canada
(416)-491-5830

Fitness Motivation Institute Of America
36 Harold Street
San Jose, CA 95117
(408)-246-9191

Focus Practice Management Publications
Century Center, Suite 3585
1750 Kalakaua Avenue
Honolulu, HI 96826
(808)-599-2790

Focusing Connection
5825 Telegraph Avenue, # 45
Oakland, CA 94609
(415)-654-4819

Footsteps Press
Box 75
Round Top, NY 12473

Foresight Publications
CONTACT: John Barklam
44 Brockhurst Road
Hodge Hill, Birmingham B36 8JB
England
(021)-783-0587

Forest Books
CONTACT: B. Walker
20 Forest View, Chingford
London, E4 7AY
England
01 529 8470

Forest Books
61 Lincoln Road
Wayland, MA 01778
(617)-358-4043

Forlaget Stjernerne, Irene Christensen Instituttet
Nr. Farimagsgade 63-1
1364 Copenhagen K,
Denmark

Foundation For Chiropractic Education And Research
1701 Clarendon Boulevard
Arlington, VA 22209
(703)-276-7445

Foundation Of Human Understanding
P.O. Box 1009
Grants Pass, OR 97526
(503)-479-0549 FAX (503)-479-8632

Fourth Way Books
P.O. Box 2045
New York, NY 10159

Franklin's Insight
711 Atlantic Avenue
Boston, MA 02111
(617)-423-6655

Fraternity For Canadian Astrologers
13155 24th Avenue
Surrey, British Columbia V4A 2G2
Canada

(416)-466-2258

Fred B. Foster
CONTACT: L. Foster
5200 Stockston Boulevard, Stuie 155-21
Sacramento, CA 95820
(916)-383-8579

Free Assocation Books
25 Freegrove Road
London, N7 9RQ
England
01-609-5646

Free Daist Communion
12040 Seigler Canyon Road North
Middletown, CA 95461-9531

Free People Press
CONTACT: Elihu Edelson
Route 6
Box 28
Tyler, TX 75704-9712
(214)-592-4263

Free Spirit
CONTACT: Paul English
137 6th Avenue
Brooklyn, NY 11217
(718)-638-6990 (718)-638-3733

Free Spirit Publishing Company
CONTACT: Judy Galbraith
400 Fist Avenue North #616
Minneapolis, MN 55401-1724
(612)-338-2068

Freedom Life Publishing
13624 Sherman Way
Van Nuys, CA 91405
(818)-905-6826

Freelance Press
CONTACT: Elizabeth Camps
P.O. Box 8551, Dept. 9240
FDR Station
New York, NY 10022-9998

French & European Publications, Inc.
115 Fifth Avenue
New York, NY 10003
(212)-673-7400

Fresh Life Guide
2705 Southwest 221st Avenue
Hillsboro, OR 97123-6615

Fresh Press
CONTACT: Sharon Elliot
3712 Ortega Court
Palo Alto, CA 94303
(415)-493-3596

Friend's Review
Rt. 3
Box 292-L
Hillsboro, OR 97124
(503)-647-5921 (800)-767-3466

Friends Of Creation Spirituality
CONTACT: David Gentry-Akin
Box 19216
Oakland, CA 94619
(415)-253-1192 (415)-482-4984

Friends Of Dark Shadows

CONTACT: S. Rizzuto
P.O. Box 994
Metarie, LA 70004
(504)-733-9138

Friends Of The U. N.
CONTACT: Kathleen Gildred
725 Arizona Avenue
Santa Monica, CA 90401
(213)-451-1810

Friends' Press
P.O. Box 1006
Weston, CT 06883
(203)-227-6643

Frontier Co-op Herbs
Box 299
Norway, IA 52318
(319)-227-7996

Frozen Waffles Press
CONTACT: D. Wade
P.O. Box 1941
Bloomington, IN 47402
(812)-336-4887

Fry's Incredible Inquiry's
HC76, Box 2207
Garden Valley, ID 83622

Full Moon, The
78 Cottage Place
East Rutherford, NJ 07073

Full Potential
6001 Strickland Avenue
Suite 105
Brooklyn, NY 11234
(718)-531-7025

Fully Alive Resource Guide
CONTACT: Kalia J. Rork
P.O. Box 30145
Santa Barbara, CA 93130
(805)-569-0129

Fun Club
P.O. Box 428
Bellflower, CA 90706

Future Science Research Publishers
P.O. Box 06392
Portland, OR 97206

Future Star Horoscope
313 West 53d Street
New York, NY 10019

Futurist, The
4916 St. Elmo Avenue
Bethesda, MD 20814-5089
(301)-656-8274

Futurum Forlag
Hjelmsgt 3, 0355
Oslo 3,
Norway
(02) 69,12,84

G.K. Hall & Co.
70 Lincoln Street
Boston, MA 02111
(617)-423-3990 (800)-343-2806

Gale Research Company
Book Tower

Detroit, MI 48226-1822
(313)-961-2242 (800)-223-4253 TELEX (810)-221-7086

Gallopade Publishing Group
CONTACT: R.D. Longmeyer
114 Main Street
Historic Bath, NC 27808
(919)-923-4291

Gandhi Today
27 Hickory Street
Ellenville, NY 12428
(914)-647-8809

Garbage Magazine
CONTACT: Julie Stocker
435 Ninth Street
Brooklyn, NY 11215
(718)-274-9909 (718)-788-1700

Garber Communications, Incorporated
5 Garber Hill Road
Blauvelt, NY 10913
(914)-359-9292

Gardner Press, Inc.
19 Union Square West
New York, NY 10003
(212)-924-8293

Gate, The
CONTACT: Beth Robbins
P.O. Box 43518
Richmond Heights, OH 44143-0777

Gateway Books
CONTACT: Judith Merwin
13 Bedford Court
San Rafael, CA 94901-4472
(415)-821-1928

Gathering, The
CONTACT: Cheryl Jacobson
H.C. 30, Box 140
Prescott, AZ 86301
(602)-776-1832

Geminian
4 Independence Place, N.W.
Atlanta, GA 30318

General Learning Corporation
60 Revere Drive
Northbrook, IL 60062
(708)-564-4070

Genesis 2, Inc.
CONTACT: Larry Bush
30 Old Whitfield Road
Accord, NY 12404
(617)-576-1801

Genesis III Publishing, Inc.
CONTACT: Mary Guerra
P.O. Drawer JJ
Munds Park, AZ 86017
(602)-955-8034

Gentle World, Incorporated
Rural Route 4, Box 585
Alachua, FL 33615-7541
(904)-669-2822

George Braziller, Inc..

60 Madison Avenue
Suite 1001
New York, NY 10010
(212)-889-0909

George Ohsawa Macrobiotic Foundation
1511 Robinson Street
Oroville, CA 95965
(916)-533-7702

Georgian Church, The
CONTACT: Dean Fauna
1908 Verde
P.O. Box 41718
Bakersfield, CA 93384
(805)-323-3309

Gestalt Journal
CONTACT: Joe Wysong
P.O. Box 990
Highland, NY 12528
(914)-691-7192

Ghost Town Publications
P.O. Drawer 5998
Carmel, CA 93921
(408)-373-2885

Gibbs Publishing Co.
CONTACT: James Calvin Gibbs
P.O. Box 600927
North Miami Beach, FL 33160

Gifts And Decorative Accessory
51 Madison Avenue
New York, NY 10010

Global Communications
GPO Box 1994
New York, NY 10001
(212)-685-4080

Globe Communications Corp.
Box 674
Rouses Point, NY 12979
(514)-866-7744

Globe Pequot Press
138 West Main Street
Chester, CT 06412
(203)-526-9571 (800)-243-0495

Globe Press Books
P.O. Box 2045
Madison Square Station
New York, NY 10159
(914)-962-4614

Gnosis
CONTACT: Jay Kinney, Pub.
P.O. Box 14217
San Francisco, CA 94114-0217
(415)-255-0400

Gnosis: A Journal Of Philosophical Interest
CONTACT: Philosophy Department
Concordia University
1455 deMaisonneuve Blvd.W
Montreal, H3G 1M8
Canada

Gnostic Times
Rural Route 1, Box 75-C
Port Crane, NY 13833

Goele Products Inc.
402 E. 74th Street, Ste. 4c
New York, NY 10021

Gold Eagle Publications
P.O. Box 5310
Sherman Oaks, CA 91413-5310
(818)-509-3807

Gold Hill
Salina Star Route
Boulder, CO 80302

Golden Dolphin Publishing
CONTACT: Faith Barr-Glover
4118 212th Street Southwest #C104
Mountlake Terrace, WA 98043-3544
(206)-432-7045

Golden Dragon Publishers
CONTACT: Alan Goodman
P.O. Box 1529
Princeton, NJ 08540-6114
(609)-896-1332

Golden Isis Press
CONTACT: Gerina Dunwich, Editor
23233-105 Saticoy Street, Ste. 137
West Hills, CA 91304-5300
(818)-347-7399

Golden Key Publications
CONTACT: John W. Adams
P.O. Box 1463
Mesa, AZ 85211-1463
(602)-834-7000

Golden Quest
CONTACT: David Pomerantz
32 Oriole Drive
Woodstock, NY 12498
(914)-679-6461

Golden Quill Publications, Incorporated
P.O. Box 1278
Colton, CA 92324
(714)-783-0119

Golden Sceptre Publishing
CONTACT: C. Muses
1442 Walnut Street, Suite 61
Berkeley, CA 94709
(415)-525-1481

Golden Unicorn Books
15600 Northeast 8th Street #A3161
Bellevue, WA 98008-3917

Good Health
801 York Mills Road
Suite 201
Don Mills, Ontario M3B 1X7
Canada
(416)-444-4952

Good Life Times
3505 Camino del Rio South #350
San Diego, CA 92108
(619)-280-0317

Good Living Catalogue
P.O. Box 13257
North Gate Station
San Rafael, CA 94913
(800)-632-2122 (800)-227-3900

Good Money Publications
Box 363
Worcester, VT 05612
(802)-223-3911

Good News Publishing
9825 West Roosevelt Road
Westchester, IL 60154
(312)-345-7474 (800)-323-3890

Gopher Graphics
Rural Delivery 2, Box 323
Greene, NY 13778
(607)-656-4531

Gordon And Breach Science Publishers, Inc.
270 Eighth Avenue
New York, NY 10011
(212)-206-8900

Gordon Press Publishing
CONTACT: R. Gordon
P.O. Box 459, Bowling Green Station
New York, NY 10004
(718)-624-8419

Gothic Image Publications
CONTACT: Frances Howard-Gordon, Dir.
7 High Street
Glastonbury, Somerset BA6 9DP
England
0458-31453

Grace And Goddess Unlimited
P.O. Box 4367
Boulder, CO 80306-4367

Grass Roots
CONTACT: D. Miller
Box 764
Shepparton,
Australia

Graywolf Press
P.O. Box 75006
Saint Paul, MN 55175
(612)-222-8342

Great Barrington
CONTACT: Christopher Bamford
195 Main Street
Great Barrington, MA 01230
(413)-528-5245

Great Book Of Catalogs, The
CONTACT: Steve Pinkerton
209 Change Street
New Bern, NC 28560
(919)-633-6144

Great Path Publishing
CONTACT: Victory Schouten
P.O. Box 882
Freeland, WA 98249
(206)-221-7099

Greater Cincinnati Resource Directory
3514 Burch Street
Cincinnati, OH 45208
(513)-871-4950

Green Action
P.O. Box 37

Tempe, AZ 85281
(602)-968-3647

Green Egg
P.O. Box 1542
Ukiah, CA 95482
(707)-485-7787

Greener Pastures Institute/Relocation Research
CONTACT: William Seavey
P.O. Box 1122
Sierra Madre, CA 91025
(818)-355-1670

Greenwood Press
88 Post Road West
Box 5007
Westport, CT 06881
(203)-226-3571

Grinnen-Barrett Publishing
CONTACT: Miriam Erick
P.O. Box 779
Brookline, MA 02146
(617)-232-1993

Groupe d'Etude et de Recherche en Parapsychologie
8 rue Octave Dubois
Taverny, 95150
France

Grove Press
400 Hahn Road
Westminster, MD 21157
(301)-848-1900 (800)-638-6460

Grove Press
841 Broadway
New York, NY 10003
(212)-614-7850

Grove, The
Naturist Headquarters
Sheepcote
Orpington, BR5 4ET
England

Grunwald & Radcliffe Pub.
P.O. Box 64755
Virginia Beach, VA 23464
(804)-490-1132

Guadalupe Press
CONTACT: Walter Starke
P.O. Box 865
Boerne, TX 78006
(512)-537-4655

Guarionex Press, Limited
CONTACT: William Zimmerman
201 West 77th Street
New York, NY 10027
(212)-724-5259

Guide Resources
4388 St. Denis, Bureau 305
Montreal, Que H2J 2L1
Canada
(514)-847-0080 FAX (514)-277-5385

Guidera Publishing Corp.
3 Myrtle Bank Road
Hilton Head Island, SC 29926
(803)-681-3399

Guilford Press
72 Spring Street
New York, NY 10012
(212)-431-9800 (800)-365-7006

H.J. Kramer, Inc.
P.O. Box 1082
Tiburon, CA 94920
(415)-435-5367

H.U.G.S. Publishing Group, The
CONTACT: Em James
4426 Alcott Street
Denver, CO 80211
(303)-369-4850

Hahnemann Homoeopathic Pharmacy
Hahnemann House
College Road
Kottayam,
India

Haight-Ashbury Publications
CONTACT: Leif Zerkin
409 Clayton Street
San Francisco, CA 94117
(415)-626-2810

Hallows
P.O. Box 1108
Glen Allen, VA 23060

Halo Magazine
217 Kenmore
Elmhurst, IL 60126
(708)-834-5683

Hambledon Press
P.O. Box 162
Rio Grande, OH 45674-0162

Hampton Publishing Company
135 Grasshopper Drive
Ivyland, PA 18974
(215)-357-4558

Hampton Roads Publishing Company, Incorporated
CONTACT: Robert Friedman
891 Norfolk Square
Norfolk, VA 23502-3209
(804)-456-2453

Hanuman Books
CONTACT: Raymond Foye
P.O. Box 1070 Old Chelsea Station
New York, NY 10113
(212)-645-1840

Happiness Press
14351 Wycliff
Postal Drawer DD
Magalia, CA 95954
(916)-873-0294

Harbin Springs Publishing
P.O. Box 82
Middletown, CA 95461
(707)-987-2477

Harbinger House
CONTACT: Cassandra Austin
2802 North Alvernon Way
Tucson, AZ 85712-1502
(602)-326-9595

Harbor Press
CONTACT: Harry Lynn
1601 Lucille Parkway North West
Gig Harbor, WA 98335
(206)-851-9598

Harcourt Brace Jovanovich
1250 Sixth Avenue
San Diego, CA 92101
(619)-699-6716 (800)-543-1918

Harmonial Philosophy Association
P.O. Box 284
Cassadega, FL 32706
(904)-228-3798

Harmonies
7 Oak Place
Montclair, NJ 07042
(201)-783-4346

Harmony
P.O. Box 10298
Sedona, AZ 86336

Harmony Books Of Crown Publishing
225 Park Avenue, South, 7th Floor
New York, NY 10003
(212)-254-1600

Harmony Magazine
P.O. Box 431
Paddington, Q. 0644
Australia

Harper & Row Publishers, Inc.
10 East 53rd Street
New York, NY 10022
(212)-207-7000 (800)-242-7737

Harper & Row Publishers, Inc.
2350 Virginia Avenue
Hagerstown, MD 21740

Harper San Francisco
CONTACT: Ani Chamichian
Icehouse I - 151 Union Street, #401
San Francisco, CA 94111-1299
(415)-477-4400

Harrison House, Inc.
P.O. Box 35035
Tulsa, OK 74153
(918)-582-2126 (800)-331-3647

Harry Edwards Spiritual Healing Santuary Trust
Burrows Lea
Shere
Guildford, Surrey GU5 9QG
England

Harry N. Abrams, Inc.
100 Fifth Avenue
New York, NY 10011
(212)-206-7715 (800)-345-1359

Harvard Common Press
535 Albany Street
Boston, MA 02118

Harvard University Press
79 Garden Street
Cambridge, MA 02138
(617)-495-2600

Harvest
P.O. Box 228
South Framingham, MA 01701

Harvest House Publishing, Inc.
1075 Arrowsmith
Eugene, OR 97402
(503)-343-0123 (800)-547-8979

Havelin Communications
CONTACT: Michael F. Havelin
P.O. Box 8509
Asheville, NC 28814
(704)-254-6700 (704)-254-7800

Having Writ
3161 Columbus Street
Grove City, OH 43123-2309
(614)-262-0471

Haworth Press, Inc.
12 West 32nd Street
New York, NY 10001
(800)-342-9678

Hay House
CONTACT: Steven Askew
501 Santa Monica Boulevard
Suite 602
Santa Monica, CA 90401
(213)-394-7445 (800)-654-5126

Haynes Business Directories
4229 Birch Street
Newport Beach, CA 92660
(714)-540-8470

Hays Publishing Company
6304 Hamilton Avenue
Cincinnati, OH 45224
(513)-681-7559

HB Publications
P.O. Box 2806
Mobile, AL 36652-2806
(205)-432-6606

HDIREC/Newsletter
496 Hudson Street, G28
New York, NY 10014

Headquarters Publishing Co., Ltd.
203a Uxbridge Road
West Ealing
London, W13 9AA
England

Healing Gathering/Healing Guide Directory
P.O. Box 1466
Chelan, WA 98816

Healing Light Center Church
204 East Wilson
Glendale, CA 91206
(818)-244-8607

Healing Research, Inc.
257 Hyde Park Estates
Santa Fe, NM 87501
(505)-262-0541

Healing Waters Foundation
CONTACT: Larry Fontana
500 Dufossat Street
New Orleans, LA 70115

(504)-897-6600

Health & Healing
29 Terrace Street
Kingscliff, 2487
Australia
006-742-407

Health & Safety Publications
CONTACT: George Sevelius
2265 Westwood Boulevard #6
Los Angeles, CA 90064
(213)-837-2003

Health Action Press
6439 Taggart Road
Delaware, OH 43015
(614)-548-4458

Health Alert Press
CONTACT: Chris Jennings
P.O. Box 2060
Cambridge, MA 02238-0411
(617)-497-4190

Health Communications
3201 S.W. 15th Street
Deerfield Beach, FL 33442
(305)-360-0909

Health Letter Associates
University Of California
632 Broadway
New York, NY 10012
(212)-505-2255

Health Plus Publishers
Box 22001
Phoenix, AZ 85028
(602)-992-0589

Health Research
CONTACT: George Eversaul
Box 19420
Las Vegas, NV 89132
(702)-733-8476

Health Science Press
CONTACT: P. Bragg
7340 Hollister Avnue
Suite A
Goleta, CA 93117
(805)-968-1028

Health Shopper
Box 2803
1319 39th Street, Northwest
Fargo, ND 58102

Health World, Inc.
CONTACT: Dr. Kumar Pati
1477 Rollins Road
Burlingame, CA 94010
(415)-343-1637 FAX (415)-343-0503

Healthwise
CONTACT: Cindy Miller
P.O. Box 1989
Boise, ID 83701-1989
(208)-345-1161

Heart And Wings Journal
Box 574
Lebanon Springs, NY 12114
(518)-766-5344

Heart Dance
P.O. Box 5539
Berkeley, CA 94705
(415)-841-1340

Heart's Journey
279 Hookie
Kihei, HI 96753

Heartland
CONTACT: Michael Jones
7000 North Glenwood
Chicago, IL 60626
(312)-338-5247

Heartland Publications
CONTACT: Les Bruursema
1928 South Parkwood Drive
Olathe, KS 66052-2806
(913)-722-1194

Hearts and Wings Journal
P.O. Box 85569
Seattle, WA 98145

Heaven & Earth Network News
P.O. Box 1641
Gloucester, MA 01930
(508)-281-3536

Heaven Bone Press
CONTACT: Steve Hirsch
86 Whispering Hills Drive
P.O. Box 486
Chester, NY 10918
(914)-469-9018

Hecate's Loom Collective
P.O. Box 5206, Station B
Victoria, British Columbia V8R 6N4
Canada

Heian International, Inc.
P.O. Box 1013
Union City, CA 94587
(415)-471-8440

Heilkunst Verlag GmbH
Angererstr 4
D-8000 Munich 40,
West Germany
089-3004061

Heldref Publications, Inc.
CONTACT: Dawn McGrath
4000 Albemarle Street, N.W.
Washington, DC 20016
(202)-362-6445 (800)-365-9753 FAX (202)-537-0287

Helios House
CONTACT: Ariel Tomioka
P.O. Box 864
Carmichael, CA 95609
(916)-485-9588

Hell's Kitchen Productions, Inc.
CONTACT: Peter H. Gilmore
P.O. Box 499
Radio City Station
New York, NY 10101-0499

Hemisphere Publishing Corp.
79 Madison Avenue
Suite 1110
New York, NY 10016

(212)-725-1999 (800)-821-8312

Henry Holt & Co.
115 West 18th Street, 6th Fl.
New York, NY 10011
(212)-886-9200 (212)-599-7600 (800)-247-3912

Henry Munasinghe
105 2-2 Jayantha
Weerasekera Mawatha, Colombo 10
Sri Lanka

Heptangle Books
P.O. Box 283
Berkeley Heights, NJ 07922
(201)-647-4449

Herb Society of America
9019 Kirtland Chardon Road
Mentor, OH 44060
(216)-371-1486

Herbs!
P.O. Box 3524
Spokane, WA 99220-3524
(509)-535-1158

Hercules Press
13265 Grove Way
Broomfield, CO 80020

Heritage Institute of Psychic Science
Box 114
Plainfield, WI 54966

Hermes Publishing Company
P.O. Box 100819
Fort Lauderdale, FL 33310-0819

Hermetician Press
P.O. Box 611381
North Miami, FL 33261-1381
(305)-891-7312

Hermetician Press
P.O. Box 1542
Fairfield, IA 52556

Hero Press
153 West 80th Street
Suite 1B
New York, NY 10024

Herold-Verlag, Franz Wetzel und Co. KG
Kirchbachweg 16
8000
Munich 71,
West Germany

Heron Press
CONTACT: C. Stockton
P.O. Box 31539
San Francisco, CA 94131
(415)-695-0323

Hibiscus Enterprises
710 Northwest 14th Avenue
Gainesville, FL 32601-4017
(904)-332-2771

Hickman Systems: New Age
CONTACT: J. Hickman
44 Woodland Lane
Kirksville, MO 63501
(816)-665-1836

Hidden Path
P.O. Box 934
Kenosha, WI 53141

High Frontiers
P.O. Box 40271
Berkeley, CA 94704

High Mesa Press
CONTACT: Joy Franklin
P.O. Box 2267
Taos, NM 87571
(505)-758-8769

High Street Art Testube
CONTACT: T. Hunker
P.O. Box 8421
Columbus, OH 43201

High Times
211 East 43rd Street
New York, NY 10017
(212)-972-8484

High/Coo Press
CONTACT: R. Brooks
4634 Hale Drive
Decatur, IL 62526-1117
(317)-567-2596

Highgate House Publishers
CONTACT: Marcia G. Ingenito
6 Surfside Drive
Ormond Beach, FL 32176-2325
(407)-671-5663 (800)-541-0900

Hilberg-Easley Report
377 Race Street
Berea, OH 44017

Hill & Wang Inc.
19 Union Square West
New York, NY 10003
(212)-741-6900 (800)-638-3030

Himalayan Academy
107 Kaholahele Road
Kapaa, HI 96746
(808)-822-7032 (808)-822-3152 FAX (808)-822-4351

Hinduism Today
1819 Second Street
Concord, CA 94519

Hippocrates Partners
475 Gate Five Road, Ste 225
Sausalito, CA 94965
(415)-332-5866 FAX (415)-332-1606

Hippocrene Books, Inc.
171 Madison Avenue
New York, NY 10016
(212)-685-4371

Hohm Press
P.O. Box 2501
Prescott, AZ 83602
(602)-778-9189

Hohokam Press Inc.
1713 E. Broadway, Ste. 280
Tempe, AZ 85282

Holistic Animal News
c/o Georgina Bezenar

1245 S.W. Othello
Seattle, WA 98106
(206)-767-4374

Holistic Education Review
CONTACT: Jeffrey Kane, Ph. D.
39 Pearl Street
Brandon, VT 05733-1007

Holistic Resources
c/o Quality Books, Inc.
918 Sherwood Drive
Lake Bluff, IL 60044
(312)-295-2010

Holistic Resources
Box 3653
Seattle, WA 98124-3653

Holy Trinity Monastery
Jordanville, NY 13361
(315)-858-0940

Holyearth Network News
720 Lovell Avenue, North
Bainbridge Island, WA 98110

Home Business Advisor
1485 3rd Street
Astoria, OR 97103-5305

Homeopathic Herald
73 Netaji Subhas Road
Calcutta, 700001
India

Homoeopathic Education Society
Gadkari Marg, Vile Parle
Bombay, 400056
India

Hong Kong Publishing Co., Ltd.
CONTACT: D. Barrett
1801 World Trade Centre
Causeway Bay,
Hong Kong
5-8903067

Horizons
The Ecos Center
P.O. Box 331
Farmington, CT 06032
(203)-676-1717 (203)-677-1588

Horizons Beyond
CONTACT: S. Rizzuto
P.O. Box 994
Metairie, LA 70004
(504)-733-9138

Horizons Resource Directory
P.O. Box 570296
Houston, TX 77257
(713)-225-6366

Houghton Mifflin Company
1 Beacon Street
Boston, MA 02108
(617)-725-5000

Hour Press
CONTACT: J. Wallace
P.O. Box 12743
Northgate Stn.
San Rafael, CA 94913-2743
(415)-883-1539

Howmark Publishing Corporation
567 Morris Avenue
Elizabeth, NJ 07208
(201)-353-7373 FAX (201)-353-8221

Hughes Henshaw Publications
CONTACT: Robert Williams
3333 South Wadsworth Boulevard, Ste. B-104
Lakewood, CO 80227
(303)-987-8545

Hugs Unlimited
Box 4041
Huntington Beach, CA 92605
(714)-530-9918

Human Ecology Balancing Sciences, Inc.
CONTACT: Steven Rochlitz
P.O. Box 737
Mahopac, NY 10541-0737
(516)-751-3105

Human Energy Press
CONTACT: Lawrence Badgley, M.D.
1020 Foster City Boulevard
Foster City, CA 94404
(415)-349-0718

Human Growth & Development Associates
CONTACT: Mary K. Kouri, Ph. D.
1675 Fillmore Street
Denver, CO 80206
(303)-320-0991

Human Kindness Foundation
Route 1
Box 201-N
Durham, NC 27705

Human Networks Inc.
3517 Terhune
Ann Arbor, MI 48104
(313)-971-8342

Humanics New Age, Ltd.
CONTACT: Robert Hall
1389 Peachtree Street, N.E., Ste. 370
P.O. Box 7447
Atlanta, GA 30309
(404)-874-2176 (800)-874-8844 FAX (404)-874-1976

Hunter House
c/o Publishers Services
P.O. Box 2510
Novato, CA 94948
(415)-883-3530

Hunter House Publishers, Inc.
CONTACT: Kiran Rana
2200 Central Avenue J #202
Alameda, CA 94501-4451
(714)-624-2277

I'Talamonti Faenza Editrice
Via Conte di Vetry 6 Ca Post 68
Faenza Roma, 48018
Italy

I.S.C. Press
P.O. Box 779
Fortuna, CA 95540
(707)-768-3284

IBS Press
744 Pier Avenue
Santa Monica, CA 90405
(213)-450-6485

Idad Press
1A Church Lane
Croft, Lincs PE24 4RR
United Kingdom

Idea House Publishing Co.
CONTACT: Denise Breton
2019 Delaware Avenue
Wilmington, DE 19806-2207
(302)-571-9570

Identity Institute
P.O. Box 11039
Honolulu, HI 96828
(808)-487-8745

Idylwild Books
P.O. Box 246
Ojai, CA 93023
(805)-646-2646

Illuminated Way Publishing
P.O. Box 27068
Golden Valley, MN 55427-0088

Illumination Arts
CONTACT: Marisa Lovesong
70 E. Sunset Way, Ste. 292
Issaquah, WA 98027
(206)-733-4703

Imagine Magazine
P.O. Box 151
Lawson, NSW 2783
Australia
047/51-4846

Imagine, Inc.
P.O. Box 9674
Pittsburgh, PA 15226
(412)-571-1430

Impact Publishers
P.O. Box 1094
San Luis Obispo, CA 93406
(805)-543-5911

Impact Publishing Company
12 Crow Canyon Ct. #200
San Ramon, CA 94583-0506
(415)-831-1655

In Business
Box 323
Emmaus, PA 18049
(215)-967-4135

In Context
CONTACT: Robert Gilman
Box 11470
Bainbridge Island, WA 98110
(206)-842-0216

Ind-US Inc.
Box 56
East Glastonbury, CT 06025
(203)-633-0045

Indian Homoeopathic Gazette
Med-House
Chowghat S.,

India

Indian Institute Of Homoeopaths
Dr. R.J. Murty, Murty Gardens
Srinagar Colony
Kumbakonam,
India

Indianisches Netzwerk BRD
Zornstr. 11A
D-6520 Worms 1,
West Germany
06241-56099

Infinite Light Fellowship
18412 148th Avenue
Spring Lake, MI 49456

Infinite Light Fellowship, Inc.
Box 326
Sylva, NC 28779

Ingham Publishing, Inc.
P.O. Box 12642
St. Petersburg, FL 33733
(813)-343-4811

Inkblot
CONTACT: T. Green
439 49th Street, #11
Oakland, CA 94607

Inland Sun
West 1704 11th
Spokane, WA 99204

Inner City Books
Box 1271, Station Q
Toronto, Ontario M4T 2P4
Canada
(416)-927-0355

Inner Growth Books
CONTACT: T. Arraj
P.O. Box 520
Chiloquin, OR 97624
(503)-783-3126

Inner Harmony
P.O. Box 1087
Capitola, CA 95010-1087

Inner Life
214 Glengarry Avenue
Toronto, Ont. M5M 1E4
Canada

Inner Light Publications
CONTACT: Tim Beckley
Box 573
New Brunswick, NJ 08401
(212)-685-4080

Inner Mind Speaks, The
P.O. Box 3
Millburn, NJ 07041

Inner Mind Spiritual Church
9710 Dudley Street
Taylor, MI 48180
(313)-291-3273

Inner Paths Publications, Inc.
26 Reichert Circle
Westport, CT 06880

Inner Peace Prosperity Network

12628 Black Saddle Lane
Germantown, MD 20874-5001
(301)-972-1980

Inner Quest Books
42 Amherst Street
Nashua, NH 03061

Inner Quest Journal
P.O. Box 1720
Dubuque, IA 52004-1720
(414)-444-5683

Inner Quest Newsletter
P.O. Box 1162
Milwaukee, WI 52301
(414)-444-5683

Inner Traditions
64 Depot Road
Colchester, VT 15446-1103

Inner Traditions International, Ltd.
CONTACT: Mary Catherine Jones
1 Park Street
Rochester, VT 05767
(802)-767-3174 (800)-445-6638

Inner Vision
495 Ridgecrest
Los Alamos, NM 87544

Inner Vision Publishing Co.
P.O. Box 1117, Seapines Station
Virginia Beach, VA 23451
(804)-425-2245

Inner Voice
701 Pheasant
McHenry, IL 60050

Innerconnexion
P.O. Box 7731
Albuquerque, NM 87194

Innervisions
CONTACT: Marilyn Pearson
2009 Rolando Avenue
Garland, TX 75041
(214)-840-1964

Innerworld
Box 30054
St. Louis, MO 63119
(314)-822-7134

Inquiry Press
1880 North Eastman
Midland, MI 48640
(517)-631-0009

Inside Magazine
P.O. Box 3162
Eugene, OR 97403

Insight Northwest
CONTACT: Susan James
Box 25450
Seattle, WA 98125
(206)-527-3324 (206)-784-5014

Insights
1401 Johnson Ferry Road
Marietta, GA 30062

Insights And Sources
201 West Main Street

Plainfield, IN 46168

Insights Positive Living
22414 Lakeway Drive
Spring, TX 77373

Instant Improvement, Inc.
CONTACT: Mary Barclay
210 East 86th Street, Ste. 501
New York, NY 10028
(212)-439-6904

Institut Metapsychique international
1 Place de Wagram
Paris, 75017
France
47-63-65-48

Institute For Advanced Studies
131 Tenkening Drive
Tenafly, NJ 07670

Institute For Economic & Financial Research
P.O. Box 4526
Albuquerque, NM 87106
(505)-843-7749

Institute Of Advanced Thinking
845 Via De La Paz
Pacific Palisades, CA 90272

Institute Of Geomantic Research
142 Pheasant Rise
Bar Hill, Cambridge CB3 8SD
England

Institute Of Mind And Behavior
CONTACT: Ray Russ
P.O. Box 522
Village Station
New York, NY 10014
(212)-595-4853

Institute Of Universal Faith
P.O. Box 3732 Rd. 3
Grove City, PA 16127
(814)-786-9085

Institute Of Visual Thinking
CONTACT: Win Werger
P.O. Box 332
Gaitherburg, MD 20877-0332
(301)-948-1122

Institute: Study Of Man
CONTACT: Dr. Roger Pearson
1133 13th Street, NW, Ste. Comm. 2
Washington, D.C. 20005
(202)-789-0231

Instituto Gnosis Per La Ricerca Sulla Sopravvivenza
CONTACT: Prof. Giorgio di Simone
Via A-Belvedere 87
Naples, 80127
Italy

Intaglio Publishing
Box 2369
Ferndale, WA 98248
(206)-688-8795

Integral Publishing
P.O. Box 1030
Lower Lake, CA 95457

(707)-928-5751

Integral Yoga Publications
RR 1, Box 172
Buckingham, VA 23921
(804)-969-3121 (804)-969-4801 (800)-262-1008

Integrity International
P.O. Box 9
100 Mile House, British Columbia V0K 2E0
Canada
(416)-395-2026

Intergroup For Planetary Oneness
17211 Orozco Street
Granada Hills, CA 91344-1132
(818)-366-5441 (800)-266-6624 FAX (818)-360-2059

Internal Arts
Box 1777
Arlington, TX 76004
(817)-860-0129

International Academy Of Nutrition And Preventive Medicine
P.O. Box 18433
Asheville, NC 28814-0433
FAX (402)-467-2716

International Association For Religion & Parapsychology
4-11-7 Inokashira, Mitaka
Tokyo 181,
Japan

International Directory Of Psychics
P.O. Box 7078
Myrtle Beach, SC 29577

International Foundation For Survival Research
450 North Rossmore Avenue
Los Angeles, CA 90004
(213)-463-5984

International Graphoanalysis Society
111 North Canal Street, 10th Fl.
Chicago, IL 60606
(312)-930-9446

International Life Sciences Institute-Nutrition Foundation
1126 16th Street, N.W.
Washington, DC 20036
(202)-659-0074 FAX (202)-659-3859

International Macrobiotic Shiatsu Society
1122 M Street
Eureka, CA 95501
(707)-445-2290

International New Thought Alliance
5003 East Broadway Road
Mesa, AZ 85206
(602)-945-0744 (602)-830-2461

International Occultation Timing Association
6N106 White Oak Lane
St. Charles, IL 60174
(312)-584-1162

International Preventive Medicine

3325 W. New Haven Avenue
Melbourne, FL 32904
(305)-723-5640

International Publishers Alliance
CONTACT: April Shiverdecker
11701 South Belcher Road, Ste. 123
Largo, FL 34643-5117
(813)-530-0110 FAX (813)-536-3681

International Sivananda Yoga Vedanta Centers
8th Avenue
Val Morin, Quebec V0T 2R0
Canada
(819)-322-3226

International Society For Astrological Research, Inc.
70 Melrose Place
Montclair, NJ 07042

International Tae Kwon-Do
P.O. Box 281
Grand Blanc, MI 48439
(313)-655-6434

Interweave Press, Inc.
306 North Washington Avenue
Loveland, CO 80537
(303)-669-7672 FAX (303)-667-8317

Intuitive Explorations
P.O. Box 561
Quincy, IL 62306-0561
(217)-222-9082

Inward Path
CONTACT: Evgeny Shcstinsky
101 Cuthbert Street
Philadelphia, PA 19106
(215)-627-5683 FAX (215)-440-9945

Irene Hamien Stephenson
Box 3893-OX
Chatsworth, CA 91313
(818)-347-6949

Irene Serra Publishing
CONTACT: Irene Serra
P.O. Box 670022
Marietta, GA 30066
(404)-973-5259

Is Works
CONTACT: Rodger Stevens
P.O. Box 9401
Moscow, ID 83843
(208)-882-9471

Isabelle Smith Enterprises, Ltd.
P.O. Box 5039
Charlottesville, VA 22905
(804)-296-7534

Island Publishing Co.
CONTACT: Paul Zuromski
P.O. Box 701
Providence, RI 02901-9818
(401)-351-4320 (800)-338-5216 FAX (401)-272-5767

Ivory Publishing
P.O. Box 4595
Denver, CO 80204

(303)-572-8286

Ivystone Publications
937 Ogden Avenue SE
Grand Rapids, MI 49506

J.B. Lippincott Company
E. Washington Square
Philadelphia, PA 19105
(215)-238-4200 (800)-242-7737

**J.B.H. Publishing Co./ Photo
Publishing Co.**
201 East 57th Street
New York, NY 10022

JAI Press, Inc.
55 Old Post Road, #2
Greenwich, CT 06836

Jalart House, Inc.
P.O. Box 642
Scottsdale, AZ 85252
(602)-947-4169

Janmabhoomi Group of Newspapers
Janmabhoomi Bhavan, Ghoga St.
Fort, Box 62
Bombay, 400 001
India

Japan Publications, Inc.
45 Hawthorn Place
Briarcliff Manor, NY 10510

Jasmine Texts
1641 Third Avenue
Suite 8BE
New York, NY 10128
(212)-348-8487

Jay Publications
P.O. Box 1141
San Andreas, CA 95249
(209)-754-4520

Jay Publishing Company
P.O. Box 454
Lakewood, CA 90714
(714)-893-0326

Jean Day Publications
P.O. Box 524, Station Q
Toronto, ON, M4T2M5,
Canada

Jeanne Youngson Publishers
29 Washington Square West
New York, NY 10011
(212)-982-6754

Jeff & Diana Krauth Publishers
CONTACT: W. Keith Setterlund
Beyond Words Bookshop
Thorne's Market, 150 Main Street, fl. 3
Northampton, MA 01060
(413)-584-1089 (413)-586-5037

Jeremy P. Tarcher, Inc.
5858 Wilshire Boulevard
Suite 200
Los Angeles, CA 90036
(213)-935-9980 (800)-225-3362 FAX (213)-935-9986

Jesus Books

1565 Madison Street
Oakland, CA 94612
(510)-763-4324

Jesusonian Foundation
1790 30th Street, Ste. 400
Boulder, CO 80301
(303)-447-2418

Joelle Publishing Inc.
CONTACT: Janet Benner
P.O. Box 91229
Santa Barbara, CA 93190-1229
(805)-962-9887

John Brown Publishing LTD.
CONTACT: Robert J.M. Rickard
Box 2409
London, NW5 4NP
England

John Muir Publications
CONTACT: Ken Luboft
P.O. Box 613
Santa Fe, NM 87504-0613
(505)-982-4078

John Wiley & Sons, Inc.
605 Third Avenue
New York, NY 10158
(212)-850-6418

John Wiley & Sons, Ltd.
Baffins Lane
Chichester, Sussex P019 1UD
England
0243-779777

Johnny Reads, Inc.
CONTACT: E. Rodgers
2221 Calexico Way S.
St. Petersburg, FL 33712-4115
(813)-867-7647

Johnson Books
1880 S. 57th Ct.
Boulder, CO 80301
(303)-443-1576

**Journal For
Anthroposophy/Anthroposophical
Society In America**
CONTACT: Clare Moore
3700 South Ranch Road 12
Dripping Spings, TX 78620
(512)-858-1669 FAX (512)-858-4080

Journal of Psychoactive Drugs
409 Clayton Street, 2nd Floor
San Francisco, CA 94117
(415)-626-2810

**Journal of the Order of Buddhist
Contemplatives**
P.O. Box 199
Mt. Shasta, CA 96067
(916)-926-4208

Journal Of The Senses
700 Robinson Road
Topanga, CA 90290
(213)-455-2007

Journal Of Vampirology
P.O. Box 881631

San Francisco, CA 94188

Journey Publications
CONTACT: K. Babcock
P.O. Box 423
Woodstock, NY 12498
(914)-657-8434

Journeys
CONTACT: Eileen Maddocks
80 Rising Trail Drive
Middletown, CT 06457
(203)-632-1005

Jove Publications, Inc.
200 Madison Avenue
New York, NY 10016
(212)-951-8822 (800)-631-8571

Joy Meadows, Inc.
CONTACT: Valencia Chan
270 Magels Street
San Francisco, CA 94131

Joy of Life
3291 Franklin Avenue
Coconut Grove, FL 33133

**Juno's Peacock Press-Northwest
Graphics**
P.O. Box 8
Clear Lake, WA 98235
(206)-856-5494

Jupiter Publications
548 High Street
Petersburg, VA 23803
(804)-733-3777

K.M. Associates
CONTACT: M. Shivanandan
4711 Overbrook Road
Bethesda, MD 20816
(301)-652-4536

K.S. Krishnamurti
18 Brahmin Street
Saidapet
Madras, 600015
India

Kabalarian Courier
908 West 7th Ave.
Vancouver, British Columbia V5Z 1C3
Canada

**Kabbalah: A Newsletter Of Current
Research In Jewish Mysticism**
41 Palyam Street
Jerusalem, 97 890
Israel

Kaivalyadhama Institution
Lonavla
District Poona,
India

Karuna Foundation
CONTACT: Shahan Jon
P.O. Box 11422
Berkeley, CA 94701-2422
(415)-586-8895

Katuah Journal
Box 638
Leicester, NC 28748

(704)-683-1414

Keats Publishing, Inc.
27 Pine Street
P.O. Box 876
New Canaan, CT 06840
(203)-966-8721

Keepers Of The Ancient Mysteries
Box 2513
Kensington, MD 20895

Kelly Communications
410 East Water Street
Charlottesville, VA 22901
(804)-296-5676

Keltria
P.O. Box 33284
Minneapolis, MN 55433

KemCo
8928 South Florence Place
Tulsa, OK 74136
(918)-299-0480

Kenneth Hagin Ministries, Inc.
P.O. Box 50126
Tulsa, OK 74150
(918)-258-1588

Kerista Consciousness Church
547 Frederick Street
San Francisco, CA 94117
(415)-759-9508

Khaniqahi-Nimatullahi Publications
306 W. 11th Street
New York, NY 10014
(212)-924-7739

Kids Lib, Oness Press/Universing Center
CONTACT: M. Sunanda
2441 Madison
Eugene, OR 95418
(503)-942-8221

Kids Want Answers Too!
CONTACT: Kathleen J. Forti
P.O. Box 297
Virginia Beach, VA 23458
(804)-422-2925

KidsArt
P.O. Box 274
Mt. Shasta, CA 96067
(916)-926-5076

King's Bridge
1102 Aviation Boulevard
Suite A
Hermosa Beach, CA 90254
(213)-376-2980 FAX (213)-376-7397

Kioma, Inc.
CONTACT: Annette Svetlik
2611 Kingsridge Drive
Dallas, TX 75252
(214)-307-1177

Kirsten Gallery/Oracle Arts, Inc.
CONTACT: Nicholas Kirsten
5320 Roosevelt Way, North East
Seattle, WA 98105
(206)-522-2011

Kitchen Sink Press
2 Swamp Road
Princeton, WI 54968
(414)-295-6922

Kluwer Academic Publishing
101 Philip Drive
Assinippi Park
Norwell, MA 02061
(617)-871-6600

Knowledge Systems
7777 West Morris Street
Indianapolis, IN 46231
(317)-241-0749

Knowledge Unlimited
P.O. Box 52
Madison, WI 53701

Knowledge Unlimited
P.O. Box 12755
Ogden, UT 84412-2755

Kodansha InternationalU.S.A., Ltd., Subs. of Kodansha, Ltd., c/o Harper & Row Pubs.
CONTACT: Anne Cheng
10 E. 53rd St.
New York,, NY 10022
(212)-207-7050

Korythalia
P.O. Box 41363
Eagle Rock, CA 90041

Kosmon Publishing, Inc.
CONTACT: Kasandra Kares
P.O. Box 4670
Hualapai, AZ 86412
(602)-757-4569

Kregel Publications
P.O. Box 2607
Grand Rapids, MI 49501
(616)-451-4775 (800)-733-2607

Kryolux, Inc.
CONTACT: Steven Krulick
27 Hickory Street
Box 467
Ellenville, NY 12428
(914)-647-3111 (914)-647-8809

Ktav Publishing House, Inc.
Box 6249
Hoboken, NJ 07030

L'Ere Atlanteenne
CP 1223
Belleville, Ontario K8N 5E9
Canada

L. Rossipaul Verlag GmbH
Postfach 15 01 08
8000 Munchen 15,
West Germany

L/L Research
P.O. Box 5195
Louisville, KY 40205
(502)-245-6495

La Mariposa Press
CONTACT: Nancy O'Connor

P.O. Box 6117
Mesa, AZ 85216
(602)-981-8747

Lagoon Publications
CONTACT: Karen Misuraca
783 Magellan Way
Napa, CA 23451-0117
(714)-772-1880

Laird Wilcox, Editorial Research Service
CONTACT: Laird Wilcox
Box 2047
Olathe, KS 66061
(913)-829-0609

Lakewood Books
Box 857
Shelter Island, NY 11964-0019
(516)-749-1122 (813)-461-1585

Lampus Press
CONTACT: Arthur Graham
19611 Antioch Road
White City, OR 97503

Lancaster Independent Press
CONTACT: C. Bagel
P.O. Box 275
Lancaster, PA 17604

Lapis Educational Association Inc.
2621 Turtle Creek Drive
Hazel Crest, IL 60429-1827

Larsen File
Box 4080
Torrance, CA 90510
(213)-214-3494

Larsen Publishing
Box 473008
Garland, TX 75047-3008
(214)-270-0786

Larson Publications
CONTACT: Amy Opperman Cash
4936 Route 414
Burdett, NY 14818
(607)-546-9342

Las Brisas Publishing
CONTACT: Lee Coit
P.O. Box 500
Wildmar, CA 92395
(714)-229-6161

Laura Books
Box 918
Davenport, FL 33837
(813)-422-9135

Lawton-Teague Publishing
CONTACT: Dr. Terri Teague
P.O. Box 12353
Oakland, CA 94604

LBT Publisher
CONTACT: L. Tabuteau
P.O. Box 964
New York, NY 10150
(212)-249-6095

LDS Publications
2901 Wilshire Boulevard

Suite 435
Santa Monica, CA 90403
(213)-828-4480

Le Bulletin Psilog
St-Francois-du-Lac
Quebec, J0G 1M0
Canada

Leadership Dynamics
875 Poplar Avenue
Boulder, CO 80304
(303)-440-0909

Leading Edge Bulletin
P.O. Box 42247
Los Angeles, CA 90042

Leading Edge Review
CONTACT: Sheila Grams
P.O. Box 24068
Minneapolis, MN 55424
(612)-929-9534

Leah Dearen Publishing
CONTACT: H. Wolfe, Jr.
619 Green Mountain Road
Mossyrock, WA 98564
(206)-445-9611

Leisure Publishers
3923 West 6th Street
Los Angeles, CA 90020
(213)-385-3926

Lens Publishing Company
CONTACT: Helen Cordes
1624 Harmon Place
Fawkes Bldg.
Minneapolis, MN 55403
(612)-338-5040

Leon Amiel Publishers
225 Secaucus Road
Secaucus, NJ 07096
(201)-865-9200

Leonard Wiley
2927 S.E. 75th Avenue
Portland, OR 97206
(503)-777-3645

Les Editions Communiqu'elles
3585 St. Urbain
Montreal, Quebec H2X 2N6
Canada

Leslie Howard Publications
CONTACT: P. Schoon
140 Duboce Avenue, #204
San Francisco, CA 94103
(415)-863-1238

LF Pubishing
P.O. Box 3175
Falls Church, VA 22043
(703)-734-7927

Li Yuan Shu Pao She
Chiu-Lung
Hong Kong

Liar's Corner Almanac
CONTACT: G. Chorba
1836 31st Street
San Diego, CA 92102

(614)-592-2543

Liberty Tree Network
134 98th Avenue
Oakland, CA 95020
(415)-981-1326

Libra Press
CONTACT: Michael J. Kurban, Dir.
4328 N. Lincoln Avenue
Chicago, IL 60618-1712
(312)-478-2410

Libra Publishing, Inc.
3089C Clairemont Drive
Suite 383
San Diego, CA 92117
(619)-581-9449

Life Action Press, Div. of Foundation for Life Action
902 S. Burnside Ave.
Los Angeles, CA 90036
(213)-933-5591

Life Affiliates
P.O. Box 80868
S. Burnaby, BC, V5H3X6,
Canada

Life Press
P.O. Box 17142
Portland, OR 97217
(503)-485-3906

Life Resources Unlimited
P.O. Box 425
Beavercreek, OR 97004
(503)-632-7141

Life Scribes: The Collective Journal
P.O. Box 848
Livingston, MT 59047

Life Tapestry Press
CONTACT: Brenda Hoffman, Editor
1624 Harmon Place, Ste. 318
Minneapolis, MN 55403
(612)-333-0614 (800)-733-8887

Life Times
750 E Bennett Ave
Glendora, CA 91740
(818)-962-9949

Lifecircle Publications
72 North Thomas Road A #8-B
Tallmadge, OH 44278-1720

LifeRhythm
P.O. Box 806
Mendocino, CA 95460

Lifesigns: Words & Images
7102 Lockraven Road
Temple Hills, MD 20748-5308

Ligate West Publishers
CONTACT: Audrey Bochnovich
P.O. Box 1087
Virginia Beach, VA 23541
(804)-496-0834

Light Connection, The
Box 578
Cardiff-By-The-Sea, CA 92007

(619)-944-1005

Light Living Library
Box 190
Philomath, OR 97370

Light of Consciousness
10668 Gold Hill Road
Boulder, CO 80302-9716
(303)-447-1637

Light Of Mind Publishing
CONTACT: David Gordon
Box 280
Topanga, CA 90290
(818)-343-0231 (800)-824-4000

Light Of The Egret
P.O. Box 7303
Virginia Beach, VA 23458

Light on Monterey
P.O. Box 2915
Carmel, CA 93921
(408)-624-0919

Light Technology Communication Services
P.O. Box 1495
Sedona, AZ 86336-1495
(602)-282-6523

Light Unlimited Publishing
CONTACT: Jon Shore
4747 East Thomas Road
Phoenix, AZ 85018-7711

Light, The
P.O. Box 7534
Olympia, WA 98507
(206)-456-3078

Light-Net Newsletter
12628 Black Saddle Lane
Germantown, MD 20874-5001

Lightening Up Press
CONTACT: Emma Bragdon
5805 Soquel Drive, Ste. 500
Soquel, CA 95073
(408)-688-4745

Lightworker
615 Palmetto Avenue
Melbourne, FL 32901

Lindisfarne Press
P.O. Box 778
Great Barrington, MA 01230
(413)-528-5245

Linear
1817 De La Vina Street
Santa Barbara, CA 93101

Link House Magazines, Ltd.
Link House, Dingwall Avenue
Croydon, CR9 2TA
England
01-686-2599

Link-Age
6482 Jessamine Court
Westerville, OH 43081

Lisa Ekus Public Relations

CONTACT: Jennifer Trainer
57 North Street
Hatfield, MA 01038
(413)-247-9325

Little Free Press
CONTACT: Ernest Mann
Rt. 1
Box 102
Cushing, MN 56443
(218)-575-2007

Little, Brown & Company
34 Beacon Street
Boston, MA 02108
(617)-227-0730 (800)-343-9204

Littlefield Adams Quality Paperbacks
4720 Boston Way
Lanham, MD 20706
(301)-459-3366

Living Among Nature Daringly!
4466 Ike Mooney Road
Silverton, OR 97381
(503)-873-8829

Living Books - Tyndale House Publishers, Inc.
P.O. Box 80
Wheaton, IL 60189

Living Off The Land
Box 2131
Melbourne, FL 32902

Living Wellness, Inc.
CONTACT: Grady Deal, Ph. D., D.C.
P.O. Box 1147
Kapaa, Kauai, HI 96746
(808)-332-9244 (800)-338-6977

Llewellyn Publications
CONTACT: Patricia Hohn
84 South Wabasha
P.O. Box 64383
St. Paul, MN 55164-0383
(612)-291-1970 (800)-843-6666 FAX (612)-291-1908

Loizeaux Brothers, Inc.
P.O. Box 277
Neptune, NJ 07754
(800)-526-2796

Longevity
1965 Broadway
New York, NY 10023-5965
(212)-496-8100

Longwood Publishing Group, Inc.
P.O. Box 2669
Wolfeboro, NH 03894
(603)-522-6303

Lorien House
P.O. Box 1112
Black Mountain, NC 28711-1112

Los Angeles Community Church Of Religious Science
838 5th Avenue
Los Angeles, CA 90005
(213)-487-1000

Los Arboles Publications

CONTACT: J. Beckman
P.O. Box 7000-54
Redondo Beach, CA 90277
(213)-375-0759

Lotus Light Publications
CONTACT: Santosh Krinsky
P.O. Box 2
Wilmot, WI 53192
(414)-862-2395

Lotus Press
P.O. Box 6265
Santa Fe, NM 87502

Love
Box 9
Prospect Hill, NC 27314

Love & Light Enterprises
CONTACT: Ann Buzcnberg
P.O. Box 5236
Durham, NC 27717
(919)-967-1950 FAX (919)-929-2458

Love-Light Communications, Inc.
CONTACT: O'Ryin Swanson
P.O. Box 1495
Sedona, AZ 86336
(602)-282-6523

Loveshine, Inc.
CONTACT: Wilma Frederick
2921 Langford Road
Norcross, GA 30071
(404)-242-9999

Loving Brotherhood, Inc.
P.O. Box 556
Sussex, NJ 07461
(201)-875-4710

LP Publications
CONTACT: Arleen Lorrance, Exec. Dir.
P.O. Box 7601
San Diego, CA 92107-0601
(619)-225-0133

Lucis Publishing Company
113 University Place, 11th Fl.
New York, NY 10003

LuminEssence Productions
P.O. Box 19117
Oakland, CA 94619

Luna Press
Box 511
Kenmore Station
Boston, MA 02215

Luna Ventures
Box 398
Suisun, CA 94585

Lung Tsai Tien Tsa Chih She
34 Lane 66 Tung Ming Chieh
Chung-Li Shih,
Taiwan

LuraMedia
CONTACT: Adam Geiger
P.O. Box 261668
San Diego, CA 92126
(800)-367-5872

Lynx House Press
1326 West Street
Emporia, KS 66801
(316)-342-0755

Lynx Publications
P.O. Box 902
Provincetown, MA 02657

M. Evans & Co., Inc.
216 E. 49th St.
New York, NY 10017
(212)-688-2810

M.H. Macy & Co.
CONTACT: Mark Macy
845 West Linden Street
Louisville, CO 80027
(303)-666-8130

M.O.B.C.
P.O. Box 199
Mt. Shasta, CA 96067
(916)-926-4208

Macmillan Publishing Co., Inc.
866 Third Avenue
New York, NY 10022
(212)-702-2000 (800)-257-5755

MacMurray & Beck
CONTACT: Heidi Benson
P.O. Box 4257
Aspen, CO 81612
(303)-925-5284

Macoy Astrological Digest
3011 Dumbarton Road
Richmond, VA 23228

Madison Astrological Society
115 W. Main Street
Madison, WI 53703
(608)-251-6738

Maggies Farm
Media Centre
P.O. Faulconbridge 2776
Blue Mountains,
Australia

Magian Press
CONTACT: Charles C. Wing, Jr.
P.O. Box 117
Penn Laird, VA 22846
(703)-289-5596

Magic Circle Press
10 Hyde Ridge Road
Weston, CT 06883
(203)-226-1903

Magic Confluence
P.O. Box 230111
St. Louis, MO 63123

Magical Blend Books
1650 Union Avenue
Hazlet, NJ 07730

Magical Blend Publishers
CONTACT: Richard Daab
P.O. Box 421130
San Francisco, CA 94142-1130
(415)-673-1001 FAX (415)-673-0323

Magick Circle
956 N. Lake Avenue
Pasadena, CA 91104
(818)-794-6013

Magickal Childe Occult Supplies, Inc.
CONTACT: Herman Slater
35 West 19th Street
New York, NY 10011
(212)-242-7182

Magnificent Consummation
Box 1188
Sedona, AZ 86336

Main Konnection
5040 Reno Court
Las Vegas, NV 89119
(702)-795-7122

Maine-Ly Sunshine
P.O. Box 335
Bar Mills, ME 04004

Maji Books
CONTACT: Malinda Mayer
18 Ivest Drive
East Falmouth, MA 02536
(508)-564-5242

Makan Ka Koloe Publishers
2337 N. 57th
Seattle, WA 98103
(206)-775-6848

Mamre Press, Inc.
107 South Second Avenue
Murfreesboro, TN 37130-4409

Manas Systems
P.O. Box 5153
Fullerton, CA 92635
(714)-870-1064

Manchurch
CONTACT: Thomas Kearns
P.O. Box 4114
Albany, NY 12204
(518)-434-8727

Manifest Press
CONTACT: Jacqueline Whyte
P.O. Box 2103
South Hamilton, MA 01982

Manisses Communications Group, Inc.
3 Governor Street
Providence, RI 02906
(401)-831-6020 FAX (401)-861-6370

Mar Crafts
CONTACT: Marty Campbell
Box 2565A
Frederiksted, V.I. 00841-2565
U.S. Virgin Islands

Marcel Dekker, Inc.
270 Madison Avenue
New York, NY 10016
(212)-696-9000 (800)-228-1160

Marcus Books
CONTACT: Tom Rieder
P.O. Box 327
Queensville, ON L0G 1R0

Canada
(416)-478-2201 FAX (416)-478-8338

Marilyn Avery
P.O. Box 572
Trenton, NC 28585
(919)-448-7881

Mark DeMaranvik
Box 133
Cummington, MA 01026
(413)-634-5400

Marlar Publishing Co.
P.O. Box 17038
Minneapolis, MN 55417

Massage Magazine
P.O. Box 1500
Davis, CA 95617-1500
(808)-329-2433

Master Thoughts
CONTACT: F. Stuart
P.O. Box 4608
Salem, OR 97302-8608

Masterpeace Productions
CONTACT: Ken Thomas
3184 Waialae Avenue
Honolulu, HI 96816-1510
(808)-735-0077

Masterwork Press
P.O. Box 302
Pottersville, NJ 07979
(201)-439-3816

Masterworks Art Publications
932 Larson Drive
Altamonte Springs, FL 32714
(407)-682-5166

Masterworks Publishing, Inc.
P.O. Box 1677
Norman, OK 73070
(405)-799-6306

Mayflower Associates
2 Plane Tree Lane
Dix Hills, NY 11746
(516)-423-7388

McBooks Press
CONTACT: Alex Skutt
908 Steammill Road
Ithaca, NY 14850-9423
(607)-272-2114

McFarland & Co., Inc.
Box 611
Jefferson, NC 28640
(919)-246-4460

McGraw Hill Book Co., Div. of McGraw Hill, Inc.
1221 Ave. of the Americas
New York, NY 10020
(212)-512-2000

McLean Enterprises
Box 714
Philipsburg, MT 59858
(406)-859-3365

McPherson & Company

P.O. Box 1126
Kingston, NY 12401

MCS Publications
P.O. Box 486
Murray, KY 42076
(502)-753-7750

Media Spotlight
CONTACT: A. Dager
Dept. SW3
Box 1288
Costa Mesa, CA 92628
(714)-953-2900

Medicina Biologica
2937 Northeast Flanders Street
Portland, OR 97232-3258
(503)-287-6775

Meditation
17211 Orozco Street
Granada Hills, CA 91344-1132

Meeker Publishing Company
2605 Virginia Street, NE
Albuquerque, NM 87110
(505)-299-6406

Mellie Uyldert
Lomanlaan 7
Bussum,
Netherlands

Mellnnium Press
P.O. Box 7885
Santa Cruz, CA 95061

Mensa
2626 East 14th Street
Brooklyn, NY 11235

Mensa Psychic Science Special Interest Group
7514 Belleplaine Drive
Dayton, OH 45424-3229
(513)-236-0361

Mercury Hour
3509 Waterlick Road, C-7
Lynchburg, VA 24502
(804)-237-4011

Mercury House, Inc.
201 Filbert Street #400
San Francisco, CA 94133
(415)-433-7042

Mercury Media
CONTACT: William Fix
P.O. Box 54
Wake, VA 23176
(804)-776-7717

Messenger, The
CONTACT: Lily O'Donnell
1936 S.W. 63rd Terrace
Pompano Beach, FL 33068
(305)-972-8951

Messenger, The
CONTACT: Robert Ownby, Pres.
1355 East Cypress Avenue, #C
Redding, CA 96002
(916)-221-0770

Metamorphic Association
67 Ritherdon Road
London, SW17 8QE
England
01-672 5951

Metamorphous Press
CONTACT: David Balding
P.O. Box 10616
Portland, OR 97210-0616
(503)-228-4972 (800)-937-7771

Metamorphus Books
3418 Park Avenue
Montreal, QB, H2X2H5,
Canada

Metaphysical Digest
5721 182nd Place, Southwest
Lynnwood, WA 98037

Metaphysical Review
G.P.O. Box 5195AA
Melbourne, Vic. 3001
Australia

Metheun, Inc.
29 West 35th Street
New York, NY 10001

Metropolitan Astrological Society of Atlanta
Box 28336
Atlanta, GA 30358
(404)-634-2677

Meyerbooks Publisher
CONTACT: D. Meyer
P.O. Box 427
Glenwood, IL 60425
(312)-757-4950

Mho & Mho Works
CONTACT: M. Dunseath
Box 33135
San Diego, CA 92103
(619)-284-6675

Micah Publications
225 Humphrey Street
Marblehead, MA 01945

Michael Connection, The
P.O. Box 1873
Orinda, CA 94563
(415)-256-7639

Michael Kesend Publishing, Ltd.
CONTACT: Mike Kesend
1025 Fifth Avenue
New York, NY 10028
(212)-249-5150

Middle Atlantic Planetarium Society
Vanderbilt Planetarium
Centerport, NY 11721
(516)-757-7502

Middle Atlantic Press
P.O. Box 945
Wilmington, DE 19899

Midwifery Today
Box 2672
Eugene, OR 97402
(503)-345-5536 (503)-345-1979

Mighty Natural Distributors
CONTACT: Marie Russell
668 N.E. 128th Street
North Miami, FL 33161
(305)-893-8829

Milkweed Press
P.O. Box 4672
Regina, SK, S4P3Y3,
Canada

Mills & Sanderson Publishing
41 North Road #201
Bedford, MA 01730-1021
(617)-861-0992 (800)-441-6224

Milo Kovar
2640 Greenwich, #403
San Francisco, CA 94123
(415)-921-1192

Mind's I Press
Rural Route 3, Box 3400
Middlesex, VT 05602

Mind, Body & Soul: The Self-Awareness & Health Care Guide
Box 23042
Euclid, OH 44123
(216)-261-2610

Mindbody Communications
3339 Kipling Street
Palo Alto, CA 94306

Minnesota Skeptics-Committee For The Scientific Investigation Of Claims Of The Paranormal
549 Turnpike Road
Golden Valley, MN 55416
(612)-545-1113

Miracle Publishing Company, Incorporated
CONTACT: Margo Skains
P.O. Box 32070
Lafayette, LA 70593
(318)-232-3020

MMB Music, Inc.
10370 Page Industrial Blvd.
St. Louis, MO 63132
(314)-427-5660

Mocha Publishing Company
CONTACT: Berdell Moffett
8475 SW Morgan Drive
Beaverton, OR 97005
(503)-643-7591

Mockingbird Books
Box 624
Saint Simons Island, GA 31522
(912)-638-7212

Mockingbird Press
CONTACT: J. Stallings
P.O. Box 776
Needham Hts., MA 02194

Moe-Tavation Unlimited
CONTACT: David Moe
12900 246th Southeast
Issaquah, WA 98027
(206)-782-2427

Moksha Journal
49 Forrest Place
Amityville, NY 11701
(516)-691-8475

Molysdatur Publications
CONTACT: Scott O'Keefe
Box 203 Star Route
Muir Beach, CA 94965
(415)-824-9317

Monk Magazine
175 5th Avenue
Suite 2322
New York, NY 10010
(212)-465-3231

Monroe Press
CONTACT: Dorothy Towvim
16107 Gledhill Street
Sepulveda, CA 91343
(818)-891-6464

Monthly Aspectarian
P.O. Box 1342
Morton Grove, IL 60053
(708)-966-1110

Monthly Planet
P.O. Box 8463
Santa Cruz, CA 95061
(408)-458-9975

Moody Press
820 N. LaSalle Drive
Chicago, IL 60610
(312)-329-2108 (800)-621-5111

Moon Bear Press
709 Lopita Ln.
Santa Fe, NM 87505
(505)-989-8408

Moon Publications
CONTACT: Donna Galassi
722 Wall Street
Chico, CA 95928
(916)-345-5473

Moon Star Enterprises
Box 1718
Milwaukee, WI 53201-1718
(414)-327-6592

Mooncircle Books
235 Lexington Avenue
Buffalo, NY 14222

Mooncircles
4807 50th Avenue, South
Seattle, WA 98118

Moonflower Birthing Supply Catalog
P.O. Box 128
Louisville, CO 80027

Moonowl Creations
P.O. Box 488
Pagosa Springs, CO 81147
(303)-264-5655

Moonrise
P.O. Box 606
Hadley, MA 01035

Moonstone Blue & Night Roses

P.O. Box 393
Prospect Heights, IL 60070
(312)-392-2435

Morgan & Morgan Inc.
145 Palisade Street
Dobbs Ferry, NY 10522
(914)-693-0023

Morning Glory Press, Inc.
CONTACT: Jeanie Lindsey
6595 San Haroldo Way
Buena Park, CA 90620
(714)-828-1998

Morningland Publications, Inc.
2600 East Seventh Street
Long Beach, CA 90804
(213)-433-9906

Mother Courage Press
CONTACT: Barbara Lindquist
1533 Illinois Street
Racine, WI 53405
(414)-634-1047

Mother Jones
1663 Mission Street
San Francisco, CA 94103
(415)-558-8881

Mothering Publishers, Inc.
515 Don Gaspar
P.O. Box 1690
Santa Fe, NM 87504
(505)-984-8116

Mountain Astrologer
P.O. Box 11292
Berkeley, CA 94701-2272
(415)-267-3274

Mountain Home Publishing
Box 829
Ingram, TX 78025
(512)-367-4492

Mountain Luminary
CONTACT: Anne M. Thiel
P.O. Box 1187
Mountain View, AR 72560-1187
(501)-585-2260

Mountain Spirit
P.O. Box 127
Twain Harte, CA 95383
(209)-586-7090 (209)-586-6250

Mountain Voice
22 Battery Park
Suite 211
Asheville, NC 28801
(704)-251-2211

Movement Newspaper
P.O. Box 3935
Los Angeles, CA 90051-1935
(213)-737-1134

MPI Medical Publishing, Inc.
14 Roman Avenue
Toronto, Ontario M4N 2X9
Canada
(416)-481-6384

Mull Publications

P.O. Box 11133
Indianapolis, IN 46201-0133
(217)-357-6855

Music Connection
6640 Sunset Boulevard #201
Los Angeles, CA 90028
(213)-462-5772

Music Paper
P.O. Box 304
Manhasset, NY 11030
(212)-614-0300

MY Las Vegas
5035 Celebrity Circle
Las Vegas, NV 89119
(702)-739-7899

Mystic Crystal Publications
CONTACT: John V. Milewski
P.O. Box 8029
Santa Fe, NM 87504
(505)-984-1048

Mystic Garden Press
CONTACT: Daniel (Shahid) Johnson
Box 51
Crestone, CO 81131-0051
(719)-256-4137

Mystic Muse
1319 Dennis Court
Kalamazoo, MI 49007
(616)-381-7273

Mystic Trader, The
P.O. Box 1000
Taos, NM 87571

Mythos
P.O. Box 21768
Seattle, WA 98111

N'Chi
P.O. Box 19566
Cincinnati, OH 45219

Naked Truth
P.O. Box 1728
Richmond, IN 47374

NAMAC Publishing
P.O. Box 963
Ingleside, TX 78362
(512)-776-2305

Narayana Press/America
2937 North Southwest Avenue
Chicago, IL 60657
(312)-327-3650

National Consumers League
815 15th Street NW
Suite 516
Washington, DC 20005
(202)-639-8140

National Health Federation
212 West Foothill Boulevard
P.O. Box 688
Monrovia, CA 91016
(818)-357-2181 FAX (818)-303-0642

National Interagency Council On Smoking

7320 Greenville Avenue
Dallas, TX 75231

National Lilac Publishing Company
CONTACT: R. Perkins
295 Sharpe Road
Anacortes, WA 98221-9729

National Psychic Directory
P.O. 47300
Garland, TX 75047-3008

National Spiritual Association Of Churches
CONTACT: Rev. Sandra Pfortmiller, N.S.T.
Stow Memorial Foundation
P.O. Box 56039
Phoenix, AZ 85079

National Spiritualist Summit
Box 128
Cassadaga, FL 32706-0128

National Women's Health Report, Inc.
P.O. Box 25307
Georgetown Station
Washington, DC 20007

Native American Publishing Co.
P.O. Box 6338
Incline Village, NV 89450
(702)-831-7726

Natural Fitness Newsletter
Box 222797
Carmel, CA 93922
(408)-372-3370

Natural Health World And The Naturopath
3912 North East 44th Avenue
Vancouver, WA 98661-3547
(206)-695-0213

Natural Hygiene Press
Box 30630
Tampa, FL 33630
(813)-855-6607

Natural Yellow Pages
P.O. Box 61-1554
North Miami, FL 33261
(305)-893-8829

Naturally Yours
CONTACT: M. Lane
P.O. Box 9
Gibbon Glade, PA 15440
(412)-329-4581

Naturist Society, Inc.
P.O. Box 132
Oshkosh, WI 54902
(414)-231-9950 FAX (414)-231-9977

Naturopath Publishing Co.
3912 NE 44th Avenue
Vancouver, WA 98661
(206)-695-0213

Nebraska State Department Of Health
301 Centennial Mall South
Box 95007

Lincoln, NE 68509
(402)-471-2101

Neitzke Enterprises
P.O. Box 1725
Dept. 189
Laredo, TX 78044

Neopantheist Society
BCM-OPAL
London, WC1N 3XX
England

Net
CONTACT: K. Langdon
P.O. Box 795
Berkeley, CA 94701
(415)-524-0345 (415)-492-0875

Network
P.O. Box 687
Washington Station
Buffalo, NY 14205
(716)-882-1205

Network Communications, Inc.
P.O. Box 26398
San Diego, CA 92126
(619)-549-3333

Network News
P.O. Box C603
Clarence Street
New South Wales, 2000
Australia
02-29-7601

Network Of Light
P.O. Box 729
Buffalo, NY 14205

Networker Magazine
CONTACT: Diane M. Cooper
P.O. Box 2053
Jupiter, FL 33468-2053
(407)-479-3197

Networker, The
P.O. Box 6769
Station D
Calgary, Alberta T2P 2E6
Canada
(403)-253-1310

Nevertheless Press
Box 9779
Berkeley, CA 94709
(415)-527-4833

New Age Books And Crystals
140 10th Street, Northwest
Calgary, AT T2N 1V3
Canada

New Age Connection
CONTACT: Randy Gray
932 Carter Avenue
Winnipeg, Manitoba R3M 2E3
Canada
(204)-284-2856

New Age Directory
P.O. Box 255
Wethersfield, CT 06109

New Age Directory

29 Mountjoy Road
Edgerton, Huddersfield HD1 5QB
England

New Age Enterprises
P.O. Box 476
Broadbeach, Q. 4217
Australia
503 558

New Age Events
1245 Palm Street, North
Clearwater, FL 34615

New Age Herald
P.O. Box 3935
Los Angeles, CA 90051

New Age Journal
P.O. Box 51163
Boulder, CO 80321-1163

New Age Living
1928 South Parkwood Drive
Olathe, KS 66052-2806
(913)-722-1194

**New Age Network Of Colorado
Springs**
P.O. Box 6647
Colorado Springs, CO 80934
(303)-634-1855

New Age News
P.O. Box 566714
Atlanta, GA 30356
(404)-255-1369

New Age Press
P.O. Box 1373
Keala Kekua, HI 96750
(808)-328-8013

New Age Press
4636 Vineta Avenue
La Canada, CA 91011

New Age Press, Inc.
Route 2
Box 184
Waynesville, NC 28786
(704)-926-9355

New Age Professional
16222 Landmark
Whittier, CA 90604
(213)-868-7717 (213)-943-9856

New Age Publishing Company
P.O. Box 01-1549
Miami, FL 33101
(305)-534-8437

New Age Source
7538 Royer Avenue
Canoga Park, CA 91307
(213)-992-4526

New Age Teachings
37 Maple Street
Brookfield, MA 01506
(617)-867-3754

New Alberta
2127 Broadview Road
P.O. Box 6769, Station D

Calgary, Alberta T2N 3J1
Canada

New American Library
P.O. Box 999
Bergenfield, NJ 07621

New Atlantean, The
P.O. Box 9638
Santa Fe, NM 87504

New Catalyst, The
P.O. Box 99
Lilloet, British Columbia V0K 1V0
Canada

New Chapter Press, Inc.
Old Pound Road
Pound Ridge, NY 10576
(212)-683-4090

New Colorado
P.O. Box 7918
Boulder, CO 80306
(303)-444-7064

New Dawn Publications
CONTACT: Sam or Barbara Rowley
1605 Edith Lane
Colorado Springs, CO 80909
(719)-591-9556

New Dimensions
5040 Reno Court
Las Vegas, NV 89119
(702)-795-7122

New Directions in Music/A.R.E.
P.O. Box 595
Virginia Beach, VA 23451
(804)-428-3588

New Environment Association
270 Fenway Drive
Syracuse, NY 13224
(315)-446-8009

New Era Press
196 Valley Road
Katonah, NY 10536

New Era Press
CONTACT: John Edwards
P.O. Box 124
Weaverville, CA 96093
(916)-623-5966

New Frontiers
P.O. Box 2000 S.U.N.Y.
Binghamton, NY 13901

New Harbinger Publications
CONTACT: Patrick Fanning
5674 Shattuck Avenue
Oakland, CA 94609
(415)-652-0215

New Hope Communications
CONTACT: Steve Hoffman
1301 Spruce
Boulder, CO 80302
(303)-939-8440

New Horizons Research Foundation
P.O. Box 427, Station F
Toronto, Ontario M4Y 2L8
Canada

New Idea Press
CONTACT: Martha Gorman
532 West Lois Way
Louisville, CO 80027
(303)-666-5242

New Jersey Chapter
Box 57
Passaic, NJ 07055
(201)-777-8372

New London Press
Box 7458
Dallas, TX 75209
(214)-742-9037

New Moon Publishing, Inc.
P.O. Box 2046
Corvallis, OR 97339
(503)-757-2532

New Options
P.O. Box 19324
Washington, DC 20036
(202)-822-0929

New Outlook
6373 Riverside Boulevard
Box 114
Sacramento, CA 95831

New Society Publishers
4722 Baltimore Avenue
Philadelphia, PA 19143
(215)-382-6543 (800)-333-9093

New Texas Magazine
1512 1/2 South Congress Avenue
Austin, TX 78704-2437
(512)-453-0515

New Thought
CONTACT: B. Mays
5003 East Broadway
Mesa, AZ 85251
(602)-945-0744

New Thought Music Connection
CONTACT: Fran Baxter
1660 South Balsamay
P.O. Box 501
Wheat Ridge, CO 80031-0501
(303)-238-9610

New Thunderbird Chronicle
15237 Sunset Boulevard
Suite 29
Pacific Palisades, CA 90272
(213)-471-0756

New Visions
10 Taconic Street
Pittsfield, MA 01201
(413)-443-4817

New World
1043 Alamos Avenue
Sacramento, CA 95815-1207
(209)-867-4653

New World Books
336 Ludlow Avenue
Cincinnati, OH 45220
(513)-861-6100

New World Library

CONTACT: Marc Allen
58 Paul Drive
San Rafael, CA 94903
(415)-472-2100 (800)-227-3900

New World Library Publishing Co.
637 Benvenue Ave.
Los Altos, CA 94022
(415)-941-2238

New World Publishing
1401 Johnson Ferry Road
Suite 328-M7
Marietta, GA 30062

New World Publishing
CONTACT: Michael & Melodee
580 Fir Lane
Los Altos, CA 94024

New World-New Age Directory
P.O. Box 17029
Fountain Hills, AZ 85268
(602)-230-3600

Newaeon Newsletter, The
CONTACT: G.M. Kelly
P.O. Box 19210
Pittsburgh, PA 15213

Newcastle Publishing Co., Inc.
13419 Saticoy Street
North Hollywood, CA 91605
(213)-873-3191

Newlife
40 West 72nd Street
Suite 35
New York, NY 10023
(212)-496-0354

Newmarket Press, Div. of Newmarket Publishing & Communications
18 East 48th Street
New York, NY 10017
(212)-832-3575

News From Mother Grove
P.O. Box 1022
Nyack, NY 10960

News Novel
Box 3232
Riverside, CA 92519

Newsenfests
P.O. Box 5967
Providence, RI 02903

Newsletter Of The American Association Of Music Therapy
777 Education Building
New York University, Washington Square
New York, NY 10003

Next Step Publications
P.O. Box 1403
Nashua, NH 03061
(603)-883-4903

Nexus New Times
P.O. Box 51
Bowraville, NSW 2000
Australia
02-399-5043

Nexus: A Means Of Connection
CONTACT: Ravi Dykema
1680 6th Street, Ste. 6
Boulder, CO 80302
(303)-442-6662

Nicolas-Hays, Inc.
CONTACT: Betty Lundsted
P.O. Box 612
York Beach, ME 03910
(207)-363-4393 (800)-423-7087

Night Owl Press
P.O. Box 321
Meredosia, IL 62665

Night Owl Publishers
Box 764
Shepparton, Victoria 3630
Australia

Night Rose
CONTACT: A. Billy
P.O. Box 393
Prospect Heights, IL 60070
(312)-392-2435

Night Vision-A Dream Journal
CONTACT: Steve Racicot, Pres.
P.O. Box 402
Questa, NM 87556
(505)-586-0863

Nightshade Publications
P.O. Box 3342
Providence, RI 02906
(401)-781-9438

Nilgiri Press
P.O. Box 477
Petaluma, CA 94953
(707)-878-2369

Ninth Sign Publications
M-525
Hoboken, NJ 07030

Ninth Wave Newsletter
1146 Cleveland Road
Sandusky, OH 44870
(419)-627-8022

No Secrets Press
1827 Haight Street
P.O. Box 21
San Francisco, CA 94117
(415)-681-1558

Noble Press
CONTACT: David Driver
213 West Institute Place #508
Chicago, IL 60610
(312)-642-1168

Nocturnal News
CONTACT: S. Rizzuto
P.O. Box 994
Metairie, LA 70004
(504)-733-9138

Nolo Press
950 Parker Street
Berkeley, CA 94710
(415)-549-1976

North Atlantic Books

2320 Blake Street
Berkeley, CA 94704
(415)-653-9177

North Atlantic Books
2800 Woolsey Street
Berkeley, CA 94705
(415)-652-5309

North Florida Astrology Association
Box 1741
Jacksonville, FL 32201
(904)-387-2064

North Light Book Club
1507 Dana Avenue
P.O. Box 12411
Cincinnati, OH 45207
(513)-984-0717

North Point Press
CONTACT: Barbara Stevenson
850 Talbot Avenue
Berkeley, CA 94706
(415)-527-6260

North Scale Institute Publishing Company
P.O. Box 27555
San Francisco, CA 94127
(415)-759-9491

North Star Press/ St. Cloud, Inc.
P.O. Box 451
St. Cloud, MN 56302-0451
(612)-253-1636

North Wind Network
P.O. Box 14902
Columbus, OH 43214

Northwoods Press
CONTACT: Bob Olmsted
P.O. Box 88
Thomaston, ME 04861
(207)-364-6550

Notes From Taychopera
P.O. Box 8212
Madison, WI 53708

Nova Publications
P.O. Box 5187
Santa Fe, NM 87502

Novato Institute For Somatic Research & Training
1516 Grant Avenue, Ste. #220
Novato, CA 94945
(415)-897-0336

Nucleus Publications
Rte. 2
Box 49
Willow Springs, MO 65793
(417)-469-4130

Nutri-Kinetic Dynamics Inc.
850 Kam Highway
Pearl City, HI 96782
(808)-456-1022

Nutrition Action Health Letter
1501 16th Street N.W.
Washington, DC 20036
(202)-332-9110

Nutrition For Optimal Health Association
Box 380
Winnetka, IL 60093
(312)-835-5030

Nutrition Health Review
171 Madison Avenue
New York, NY 10016
(212)-679-3590

O'Quinn Studios
475 Park Avenue S.
New York, NY 10016
(212)-689-2830

OAL Research Publications, Ltd.
CONTACT: Dr. O.A. Lawal, Publisher
Cleanjohn House, 90, Ladipo Street, Matori
P.O. Box 9802
Lagos,
Nigeria
01-523-420 TELEX (000)-002-7358

OARCA
Donnersbergerstr. 11-1
8000 Munich 19,
West Germany

Oblates
15 South 59th Street
Belleville, IL 62222
(618)-233-2238

Occult Directory
814 14th
Saskatoon, SK, S7N0P8,
Canada

Ocean Tree Books
CONTACT: Richard Polese
P.O. Box 1295
Santa Fe, NM 87504
(505)-983-1412

Ocean View Books
CONTACT: Lee Ballentine
P.O. Box 4148
Mountain View, CA 94040
(415)-965-3721

Oconnell
12628 Black Saddle Lane
Germantown, MD 20874-5001
(301)-347-1213

Odinist, The
P.O. Box 1647
Crystal River, FL 32629

Odyssey
CONTACT: Ernest A. Rose
33 High Road
Box 316
Cornish, ME 04020
(207)-625-7447

Of A Like Mind (OALM)
P.O. Box 6021
Madison, WI 53716
(608)-838-8629

Off Our Backs
2423 18th Street, N.W., 2nd Fl.
Washington, DC 20009
(202)-234-8072

Office Of Communications
5600 Fishers Lane
12C-15
Rockville, MD 20857
(301)-443-3783

Offshoots Publications
Box 987
Valley Forge, PA 19481

Ohio University Press
Scott Quadrangle
Athens, OH 45701
(614)-593-1155

Old Religion, The
P.O. Box 24
Sinks Grove, WI 24976

Omdega Press
CONTACT: Bob Gebelein
P.O. Box 1546
Provincetown, MA 02657
(508)-487-1117

Omega News
Kent Hourse, Camden Park
Turnbridge Wells, Kent TN2 5AD
England
0892-36709

Omega Press
P.O. Box 574
Lebanon Springs, NY 12114

Omni
CONTACT: Kathy Keeton, Pres.
P.O. Box 3026
Harlan, IA 51593-4087

On Da Bayou Press
P.O. Box 52467
New Orleans, LA 70152
(504)-943-7041

On The Air
P.O. Box 485
Sharon, PA 16146

On The Edge
CONTACT: C. McIntyr
29 Concord Avenue, #603
Cambridge, MA 02138
(617)-354-0947

One-Eight, Inc.
P.O. Box 2075
Forks, WA 98331-0822
(206)-374-6500

Ontario's Common Ground Magazine
CONTACT: Julia Woodford
320 Danforth Avenue, Ste. 204
Toronto, Ontario M4K 1P3
Canada
(416)-463-6677

Open Channels
P.O. Box 4677
Hollywood, FL 33083

Open Connections, Inc.
CONTACT: Peter Bergson
312 Bryn Mawr Avenue
Bryn Mawr, PA 19010
(215)-527-1504

Open Court Publishing Co.
315 Fifth Street
Peru, IL 61354
(815)-223-2520 (800)-435-6850

Open Door Foundation
CONTACT: Will Bullock
P.O. Box 3703
Carmel, CA 93921
(408)-625-3307

Open Door, Inc.
CONTACT: Marie Norrisey
P.O. Box 855
Charlotteville, VA 22902
(804)-293-5068

Open Exchange
P.O. Box 7880
Berkeley, CA 94707-0880
(415)-526-7190 FAX (415)-540-1057

Open Horizons
CONTACT: John Kremer
P.O. Box 205
Fairfield, IA 52556-0205
(515)-472-6130 FAX (515)-472-3186

Open Line
P.O. Box 4061
Spokane, WA 99202
(509)-838-8155

Open Mind
P.O. Box 11006
Napa, CA 94581
(707)-255-5022

Open Path
703 North 18th Street
Boise, ID 83703
(208)-342-0208

Operation Showman
CONTACT: Rev. June Spencer
3118 North 13th Street
Milwaukee, WI 53206
(414)-372-5046

Opossum
RR 3 Box 109
Orleans, IN 47452
(812)-755-4788

Optimus Books
Waldorf Astoria Hotel
301 Park Avenue
New York, NY 10022
(212)-753-7680

Oracle Press
P.O. Box 160
Oracle, AZ 85623
(602)-896-2446

Orbis Books
Fathers & Brothers of
Maryknoll
Maryknoll, NY 10545
(914)-941-7590

Orenda/Unity Press
Box 2215
Leucadia, CA 92024
(619)-753-9331

Organization Of Psychic Research Associates
Box 60901
Oklahoma City, OK 73146
(405)-557-8048

Orient-Occipent
1728 Sunny Avenue
Eureka, CA 95501
(707)-443-2135

Oriental Healing Arts Institute
1945 Palo Verde Avenue, Ste. #208
Long Beach, CA 90815
(213)-431-3544

Original Books, Inc.
944 Indian Peak Road, #110
Rolling Hills Estates, CA 90274
(213)-544-2090

Original Publications, Subs. of Jamil Products Corp.
2486 Webster Ave.
Bronx, NY 10458
(212)-367-9589

Orion
534 Spruce Road
Bolingbrook, IL 60439

Osage Publishing
CONTACT: Kochmann
Rafter Eleven Mobile Home/ Park
Sp. 43, HC 36
Dewey, AZ 86327
(602)-573-3463

Osho Times
P.O. Box 318
Mill Valley, CA 94942
(415)-381-9861

Our Natural World
CONTACT: Edwin R. Rodgers
2221 Calexico Way South
St. Petersburg, FL 33712
(813)-867-7647

Outcomes Unlimited Press, Inc.
CONTACT: Donald Dossey
1015 Gayley Avenue #1165
Los Angeles, CA 90024
(213)-208-2952

Outlet Book Co., Affil. of Crowns Pubs., Inc.
225 Park Ave., S.
New York, NY 10003
(212)-254-1600

Outpost Exchange
CONTACT: Art Blair
102 East Capitol Drive
Milwaukee, WI 53212
(414)-964-7789

Over and Beyond
P.O. Box 81
Rosholt, WI 54473
(715)-677-3420

Overlook Press
149 Wooster Street, 4th Floor
New York, NY 10012-3179

(212)-337-5472

Owl Press, Inc.
CONTACT: Judith Statezny
P.O. Box 81
Rosholt, WI 54473
(715)-677-3420

Ox Head Press
CONTACT: Don Olsen
Route 3, Box 136
Browerville, MN 56438
(612)-594-2454

Oxford Industries, Inc.
444 North Larchmont Boulevard
Box 74908
Los Angeles, CA 90004
(213)-469-3901 (213)-469-8379 FAX (213)-469-9597

Oxford University Press, Inc.
200 Madison Avenue
New York, NY 10016
(212)-679-7300 (800)-334-4249

P. Adimoolam
64 Gaudiamath Road
Madras, 600 014
India

Pachart Publishing House
P.O. Box 35549
Tucson, AZ 85740
(602)-297-4797

Pagan Free Press
P.O. Box 55223
Tulsa, OK 74155

Page One Books By And For Women
966 North Lake Avenue
Pasadena, CA 91104
(818)-798-8694

Palace Publishing
CONTACT: Philip James, Pres.
RD 1
Box 320
Moundsville, WV 26041
(304)-845-0495 (304)-845-3890 (800)-322-7262
FAX (304)-845-9819

Pallas Communications
CONTACT: Douglas Bloch
4226 NE 23rd Avenue
Portland, OR 97211
(503)-284-2848

Palmer Publications/Amherst Press, Inc.
2001 Main Street
Amherst, WI 54406
(715)-824-3214

Paloma Blanca Press
P.O. Box 1751
Taos, NM 87571
(505)-751-2169

Pan/Ishtar Unlimited
P.O. Box 216
Edgewood, TX 75117
(214)-896-1700

Panegyria Journal

CONTACT: Rev. Peter Pathfinder
P.O. Box 85507
Seattle, WA 98145
(206)-793-1945

Panic Press
CONTACT: Aline H. Simon
Box 27465
San Antonio, TX 78227-0465

Pantheon Books
400 Hahn Road
Westminister, MD 21157

Pantheon Books/Random House
201 East 50th Street
New York, NY 10022
(212)-751-2600

Para Publishing
CONTACT: Dan Poynter
P.O. Box 4232-878
Santa Barbara, CA 93140-4232
(805)-968-7277

Para Research
1469 Morstein Road
West Chester, PA 19380

Parabola Books
CONTACT: Joe Kulin
656 Broadway
New York, NY 10012
(212)-505-6200

Paracelsus College
3555 S. 700 East
Salt Lake City, UT 84106
(801)-486-6730

Paradigm Publications
44 Linden Street
Brookline, MA 02146
(617)-738-1235 (617)-738-4664

Paradise Publications
8110 SW Wareham Cir.
Portland, OR 97223
(503)-246-1555

Paragon House
CONTACT: John Maniatis
90 Fifth Avenue
New York, NY 10011
(212)-620-2820 (212)-640-2820 (800)-727-2466

Parallax Press-Buddhism
P.O. Box 7355
Berkeley, CA 94707
(415)-525-0101

Parapsychology Association Of Riverside
Box 20151
Riverside, CA 92516-0151
(714)-784-1565

Parnell Publishing
P.O. Box 16432
Phoenix, AZ 85011
(800)-545-2778

Pasadena Press, Inc.
P.O. Box 60184
Pasadena, CA 91106
(818)-796-3840

Path Books
CONTACT: John Schmidt
Rural Route 5
Box 751
Amarillo, TX 79118-9707
(806)-622-1230

Pathfinder Publishing
458 Dorothy Avenue
Ventura, CA 93003
(805)-642-9278

Patrick Walsh Press
CONTACT: B. Nall
2017 S. Ventur
Tempe, AZ 85282-9707
(602)-894-1230

Paulist Press
997 MacArthur Boulevard
Mahwah, NJ 07430
(201)-825-7300

Peace Resource Center
5717 Lindo Paseo
San Diego, CA 92115
(619)-265-0730

Peace Studies Magazine
GPO Box 1274L
Melbourne, VIC 3001
Australia

Peaceful Living Publications
CONTACT: Geoff W. Tibbotts
61 Kulim Avenue
P.O. Box 300
Tauranga B.O.P.,
New Zcaland
075-67-250

Peak Skill Publishing
CONTACT: David Ramsdale
16118 Elza Drive
Hacienda Heights, CA 91745

Pegasus
1507 Alder Avenue
Lewiston, ID 83501
(208)-746-5322

Pegasus Express
Rural Route 3, Box 962
La Belle, FL 33935

Pend Oreille Awareness Network
P.O. Box 579
Sagle, ID 83860

Pendragon Books
5560 College Avenue, North
Oakland, CA 94618

Penguin Books
Direct Mail Order
120 Woodbine Street
Bergenfield, NJ 07021-3524

Penguin Books
40 W. 23rd Street
New York, NY 10010
(212)-337-5200 (800)-631-3577

Penguin Communications Group
P.O. Box 984
336 N.23rd Avenue

Yakima, WA 98907
(509)-575-8386

Penichet Publishing Company
2514 South Grand Avenue
Los Angeles, CA 90007

Penn State Universty
College of Health and Human Development
1 White Bldg.
University Park, PA 16802
(814)-862-0435

Penny Price Productions, Complete Guide To Channeling
7270 Hillside Street
Los Angeles, CA 90046

Pennypress
CONTACT: Jane Hatfield/Wanda Boe
1100 23rd Avenue East
Seattle, WA 98112
(206)-325-1419

Penquin USA
CONTACT: Marty Mint
375 Hudson Street
New York, NY 10014
(212)-366-2000

People for Open Space
116 New Montgomery #640
San Francisco, CA 94105

Perelandra
Box 126
Jeffersonton, VA 22724

Pergamon Press, Inc.
Maxwell House
Fairview Park
Elmsford, NY 10523
(914)-592-7700

Permanent Central Vortex
Box 1648
Sedona, AZ 86336
(602)-282-2574

Permanent Press
CONTACT: Robert Anton Wilson
P.O. Box 700305
San Jose, CA 95170

Personal Insight Data Services
P.O. Box 425
Eureka Springs, AR 72632
(501)-253-9450

Personal Pathways Press
CONTACT: Jack Clarke
2272 Powers Ferry Drive
Marietta, GA 30067
(404)-977-2272

Personal Power Potential
425 North Martingale Rd. #800
Schaumburg, IL 60173
(312)-426-6979

Petroglyph Press Ltd.
201 Kinoole Street
Hilo, HI 96720
(808)-935-6006

Petulengro Publications

11 Ship Street Gardens
Brighton, Sussex BN1 1AJ
England

Phanes Press
CONTACT: David Fideler
P.O. Box 6114
Grand Rapids, MI 49516
(616)-235-2130

Phantasm Press
14848 Misty Springs Lane
Oak Run, CA 96069
(916)-472-3540

Phenomena Publications
Box 6228
Toronto, Ontario
Canada
(416)-961-9679

Phillips Publishing Company
P.O. Box 439
Agawam, MA 01001
(413)-789-2420

Philosopher Press
CONTACT: Gary Haugen
P.O. Box 8282
Green Bay, WI 54308
(414)-468-4098

Philosophical Library, Inc.
31 West 21st Street, 11th Fl.
New York, NY 10010
(212)-727-7870 (800)-336-2650

Philosophy Education Society
Catholic University Of America
School Of Philosophy
Washington, DC 20064
(202)-635-8778

Phoenix Books
6 West 39th Street
Kansas City, KS 64111

Phoenix Books
519 Santa Monica Boulevard
Santa Monica, CA 90401

Phoenix Metaphysical Book
10202 152nd Street
Surrey, BC, V3R6N7,
Canada

**Phoenix Metaphysical Book
Publishers, Inc.**
CONTACT: D. Brown
P.O. Box 10
Custer, WA 98240
(206)-467-8219

Phoenix Rising Inc.
CONTACT: Joann Wolf
P.O. Box 3088
Glen Ellyn, IL 60138
(312)-653-0883

Phoenix Rising Publications
705 Alfred Street
Fort Erie, ON, L2A6A4,
Canada

**Phoenix UFO & Metaphysics
Newsletter**

P.O. Box 75
Buford, GA 30518

Pilgrim House
CONTACT: Elvin (Cy) Eberhart
P.O. Box 5205
Salem, OR 97304
(503)-362-4030

Pilgrim Publications
CONTACT: Bob Ross
1609 Preston
Pasadena, TX 77503
(713)-477-2329

Pilot Books
103 Cooper Street
Babylon, NY 11702
(516)-422-2225

Pittenbruach Press
CONTACT: T. Milne
P.O. Box 553
Northhampton, MA 01601

Pittsburgh Peace Institute
116 South Highland Avenue
Pittsburgh, PA 15206-3911
(412)-422-1227

Plane Edge, The
45 Vale Avenue
Cranston, RI 02910

Planet Drum Foundation
CONTACT: Judy Goldhaft
P.O. Box 31251
San Francisco, CA 94131
(415)-285-6556

Planet Watch
CONTACT: Eleanor Bach
319 W. 18th
New York, NY 10011
(212)-242-1958

**Planetary Professional Citizens
Committee**
Box 34
Careywood, ID 83809

Plenum Publishing Corporation
233 Spring Street
New York, NY 10013
(212)-620-8000 (212)-620-8468 (800)-221-9369

Pocahontas Press
CONTACT: M. C. Holliman
2805 Wellesley Ct.
Blacksburg, VA 24060
(703)-951-0467

Pocket Books
1230 Avenue Of The Americas, 13th Fl.
New York, NY 10020
(212)-698-7406 (800)-223-2336

Poco Press
CONTACT: Melody Gibson
P.O. Box 1388
Chandler, AZ 85244-1388
(602)-963-8248

Point Loma Publications, Inc.
P.O. Box 6507
San Diego, CA 92106

(619)-222-3291

Polestar Publications
CONTACT: T. Chitwood
620 South Minnesota Avenue
Sioux Falls, SD 57104
(605)-338-2888

Polymath Systems
CONTACT: Kevin Langdon
P.O. Box 795
Berkeley, CA 94701
(415)-524-0345

Pop Voice Publications
CONTACT: J. Morton
109 Minna Street
Suite 583
San Francisco, CA 94105
(415)-362-1157

Popular Medicine Press
CONTACT: John Bliss
P.O. Box 1212
San Carlos, CA 94070
(415)-594-1855

Portland Reflections
P.O. Box 13070
Portland, OR 97213
(503)-281-4486

Positive Times
P.O. Box 244
West Stockbridge, MA 02166

Post-Apollo Press
35 Marie St.
Sausalio, CA 94965
(415)-332-1458

Potomac Valley Press
1424 16th Street NW
Suite 105
Washington, DC 20036
(202)-462-8800

Powell Production
CONTACT: April Shiverdecker
11701 Belcher Road South, Ste. 123
Largo, FL 34643
(813)-530-0110

Practical Homeowner Publishing
27 Unquowa Road
Fairfield, CT 06430
(203)-259-9877

Praeger Publishing
1 Madison Avenue, 11th Fl.
New York, NY 10010
(212)-685-5300

Prairie Sky Books
871 Westminster Avenue
Winnipeg, MN, R3G1B3,
Canada

Prelude Press
CONTACT: Peter McWilliams
8165 Mannix Drive
Los Angeles, CA 90046
(213)-650-9571

Prema Publications
CONTACT: Norman Green

435 Buckland Road
South Windsor, CT 06074
(203)-644-6811

Prentice-Hall
Route 9W
Englewood Cliffs, NJ 07632
(201)-592-2000 (800)-634-2863

Prentice-Hall Media
90 S. Bedford Road
Mount Kisco, NY 10549
(914)-631-8300

Prentice-Hall, Inc.
CONTACT: Tom Martin
1 Gulf & Western Plaza
New York, NY 10023
(212)-373-8242 (800)-223-2348

Present Moment
3548 Grand Avenue South
Minneapolis, MN 55408
(612)-832-5385 (612)-824-3157

Price/Stern/Sloan Publishing
360 North LaCienega Boulevard
Los Angeles, CA 90048

Prima Materia Books
CONTACT: Nancy Shavick
P.O. Box 162
Hampton Bays, NY 11946
(516)-728-7655

Prima Publishing
CONTACT: Laura Glasover
P.O. Box 1260
Rocklin, CA 95677-1260
(916)-624-5718

Princeton Book Company
P.O. Box 57
Pennington, NJ 08534
(609)-737-8177 (800)-326-7149

Princeton Educational Publishers
117 Cuttermill Road
Great Neck, NY 11021
(516)-466-9300

Princeton University Library
P.O. Box 190
Princeton, NJ 08544
(609)-452-3184

Princeton University Press
41 William Street
Princeton, NJ 08540
(609)-452-4900

Prism
30100 Town Center Drive, Suite 0251
Laguna Niguel, CA 92677
(714)-364-0196

Prism Press
CONTACT: Oliva Orfield
11706 Longleaf Lane
Houston, TX 77024
(713)-782-5189

Pro Lingua Associates, Inc.
15 Elm Street
Brattleboro, VT 05301
(802)-257-7779 (800)-345-6665

Probe
16 Marigold Walk
Ashton, Bristol BS3 2PD
England

Probe The Unknown
1845 W. Empire Street
Burbank, CA 91504

Process Press
CONTACT: T. Kierstead
2322 Haste, No. 31
Berkeley, CA 94704
(415)-548-6510

Process: Psychoanalysis & Creativity
200 West 79th Street #9L
New York, NY 10024
(212)-362-7119

Professional Books
CONTACT: K. Keim
681 Skyline Drive
Jackson, TN 38301
(901)-423-5400

Professional Newsletter Program
Route 1
Box 632
Balsam Lake, WI 54810
(612)-279-1255

Progressive Awareness Research
CONTACT: R.K. Bey
P.O. Box 12419
Las Vegas, NV 89112
(702)-795-7940

Project Hope
Carter Hall
Millwood, VA 22646
(703)-837-2100 FAX (703)-837-1813

Prometheus Books
CONTACT: Lorraine Baranski
700 East Amherst Street
Buffalo, NY 14215
(716)-837-1475 (716)-837-2475 (800)-421-0351

Prosveta Editions, USA
P.O. Box 49614
Los Angeles, CA 90049
(213)-474-7477

Prosveta, Inc.
CONTACT: Ives Guillot, Marketing Manager
1565, Montee Masson
Duvernay est
Laval, QC H7E 4P2
Canada
(416)-889-4725 (604)-224-1299

Proteus
274 Second Street
Elizabeth, NJ 07206

Prout Journal
101 1st Street #339
Los Altos, CA 94022-2706
(408)-475-5055

PSI Press
CONTACT: Larry E. Arnold
1025 Miller Lane
Harrisburg, PA 17110-2899
(717)-236-0080

PSI Research
300 N. Valley Drive
Grants Pass, OR 97526

Psych It
2315 E. Fowler Avenue
Fowler Plaza S.
Tampa, FL 33612

Psychic Network Directory
CONTACT: Vincent Tabatneck
1259 Route 46, Bldg 1
Parsippany, NJ 07054
(201)-316-9511

Psychic Newsletter
P.O. Box 558
Estero, FL 33907

Psychic Pathways
P.O. Box 418
Woodmere, NY 11598

Psychic Press Newspaper
1044 Northwest Federal Highway
Stuart, FL 34994-1021

Psychic Press, Ltd.
CONTACT: Tony Ortzen
2 Tavistock Chambers
Bloomsbury Way
London, WC1A 2SE
England
071-405-3340

Psychic Society Of Athens
32 Tsiller Street
Athens, 905
Greece

Publicity Circuit Monthly
P.O. Box 299
Haverford, PA 19041
(215)-896-6146

Publitec Editions
CONTACT: Maggie Rowe
P.O. Box 4342
271 A. Lower Cliff
Laguna Beach, CA 92652
(714)-497-6100

Purple Pages Of Texas
CONTACT: Mollie Sticklin
4212 San Felipe #386
Houston, TX 77027
(713)-623-0419

Putnam Publishing Group
200 Madison Ave.
New York, NY 10016
(212)-576-8900 (212)-951-8400 (800)-631-8571

Pyramid Press
CONTACT: Sue Thoele
P.O. Box 1480
10398 Ridge Road
Nevada City, CA 95959
(916)-265-6683

Pyramid Research Center
CONTACT: M.D. Saunders
P.O. Box 478
Odenton, MD 21113-0478

Pyramid Systems

4486 Glen Cannon Drive
Suisun, CA 94585
(916)-756-2242

Quality Life Publishing Co.
11727 Invierno Drive
San Diego, CA 92124

Quality Living Publication
CONTACT: Rick Herrick
P.O. Box 1
Valle Crucis, NC 28691

Quantal Publishing
P.O. Box 1598
Goleta, CA 93116
(805)-964-7293

Quantis Report, The
P.O. Box 2730
Austin, TX 78755

Que Natural!
P.O. Box 611554
North Miami, FL 33261
(305)-893-8829

Queen's University
J. Bigu
Kingston, Ontario K7L 3N6
Canada

Quest Enterprises Of Excelsior
464 2nd Street, Ste. A
Excelsior, MN 55331
(612)-474-5132

Quest International, Inc.
P.O. Box 566
Granville, OH 43023
(800)-288-6401

Quest Northwest Publishing Co.
CONTACT: D. Marshall
P.O. Box 240
Salkum, WA 98582
(206)-985-2990

Quest Publishing Company
1351 Titan Way
Brea, CA 92621
(714)-738-6400

Quest Publishing Inc.
P.O. Box 27317
Salt Lake City, UT 84127
(501)-278-9460

Quest-The Journal Of UFO Investigation
106 Lady Ann Road
Soothill, Batley
England

Questpress
215 Elm Street
Barnesville, GA 30204

Quicksilver Productions
CONTACT: Jim Maynard
559 South Mountain Avenue
P.O. Box 340
Ashland, OR 97520
(503)-482-5343

Quill And Sword, The

P.O. Box 8376
Salem, MA 01971

Quill And Unicorn
Rural Route 3, Box 113
Magee, MS 39111

Quinn Publishing
7722 Eichler Drive
Houston, TX 77036
(713)-777-6854

R & E Fund
42 The Farm
Summertown, TN 38483
(615)-964-2519

R & E Publishers
P.O. Box 2008
Saratoga, CA 95070-2008
(408)-866-6303

R & E Publishers
P.O. Box 627
Plymouth Meeting, PA 19462
(215)-828-4674

R.O.S.A.
1317 Monterey Avenue
Monrovia, CA 91016

R.R. Bowker Company
245 West 17th Street
New York, NY 10011
(212)-645-9700

R.T. Coleman & Associates
CONTACT: R.T. Coleman
933 North Alvernon Way, #216
Tucson, AZ 85711
(602)-356-1332 (602)-323-6941

Raben Publishing Co.
711 Boylston Street
Boston, MA 02116
(617)-236-1885

Radiance Associates
CONTACT: M. Carter
P.O. Box 86425
St. Petersburg, FL 33738

Radiance Productions
CONTACT: Patricia Daniels
3315 Sacramento Street, Ste. #515
San Francisco, CA 94118
(415)-668-3667

Radio & Records
CONTACT: Jeff Gelb
1930 Century Park West
Los Angeles, CA 90067
(213)-553-4330

Rainbow Bridge Publishing
CONTACT: Lana Miller
P.O. Box 19730-616
Portland, OR 97219
(503)-796-1709

Rainbow City Express
P.O. Box 8447
Berkeley, CA 94707-8447

Rainbow Earth Dwelling Society
330 Laddie Place
San Antonio, TX 78201

(512)-737-1733

Rainbow Pages
1st Floor, 302 Pacific Highway
Lindfield, 2070
Australia
02/46-3938

Rainbow Pages
P.O. Box 1171
Freeland, WA 98249-1171

Rajneesh Publications, Inc.
P.O. Box 1510
Boulder, CO 80306
(303)-665-6611

Ram Metaphysical Books
7 South Main Street
Medford, NJ 08055

Rama Publishing Corporation
CONTACT: Russ McCaw
P.O. Box 520337
Salt Lake City, UT 84105
(801)-485-4958

Raman Publications
Sri Rajeswari
28, Nehru Circle
Bangalore, 560 020
India
369382

Ramana Maharashi Publishers
P.O. Box 1326
Sarasota, FL 34230

Ramifications, Unlimited
P.O. Box 2380
Julian, CA 92036
(619)-765-2525

Ramira Publishing
CONTACT: Beth Holland
P.O. Box 1707
Aptos, CA 95001
(408)-429-9311

Ramparts Press
P.O. Box 338
Forestville, CA 95436
(707)-325-7861

Random House, Inc.
400 Hahn Road
Westminister, MD 21157
(301)-848-1900

Ransom Hill Press
CONTACT: Margaret L. McWhorter
3601 Main St.
Ramona, CA 92065
(619)-789-0620

Rat Race Record
P.O. Box 10 B Kent Streeet
Somerset, NJ 08873-2186

Raven Press
1185 Avenue Of The Americas
New York, NY 10036
(212)-930-9500

Rawson Associates
866 3rd Avenue
New York, NY 10022

Re/Search Publications
CONTACT: A. Juno
20 Romolo, #B
San Francisco, CA 94133
(415)-362-1465

Reader's Digest
Pleasantville, NY 10570

Reader's Digest Association, Inc.
260 Madison Avenue
New York, NY 10016
(212)-850-7007

Rebecca House
CONTACT: David K. Waldman
1550 California Street
San Francisco, CA 94121
(415)-752-1453

Red Dragon Press, Div. of Lotus Light Publications
CONTACT: Santosh Krinsky
P.O. Box 2
Wilmot, WI 53192
(414)-862-2395

Redneck Review of Literature, The
CONTACT: Penelope Reedy
P.O. Box 730
Twin Falls, ID 83327
(208)-734-6653

Reed Books
CONTACT: Paul Reed
P.O. Box 14793
San Francisco, CA 94114

Reel Directory
CONTACT: Bonnie Carroll
P.O. Box 866
Cotati, CA 94298
(707)-795-9367

Referral Service For Health Care Information
CONTACT: Julie Van Erffa
Rt. 10
Box 133
Santa Fe, NM 87501
(505)-473-7654

Reflect
CONTACT: William S. Kennedy, Pub./Editor
3306 Argonne Avenue
Norfolk, VA 23509
(804)-857-1097

Reflecting Pond Publications
509 Orchard Lane
Port Angeles, WA 98362
(206)-437-2681

Reflections Directory
CONTACT: Beth Howell
P.O. Box 13070
Portland, OR 97123
(503)-281-4486

Regenerative Agriculture Association
222 Main Street
Emmaus, PA 18098
(215)-967-5171

Reincarnation Books & Tapes

CONTACT: Bettye B. Binder
P.O. Box 7781
Culver City, CA 90233-7781
(310)-397-5757

Reincarnationists
P.O. Box 6068
Malibu, CA 90264

Rekalla Company
P.O. Box 45941
Los Angeles, CA 90045-9998

Reliant Publishing
CONTACT: Harold Reynolds
826 North East Portland Boulevard
Portland, OR 97211
(503)-281-3586

Renewable Resource And Conservation Report
311 Miramar Road
Rochester, NY 14624
(716)-247-8197

Renewal
505 Siskiyou Boulevard
Ashland, OR 97520

Research Centre Of Kabbalah
83-84 115th Street
Jamaica, NY 11418
(718)-805-9122

Resource Applications Inc.
P.O. Box 0159
Hanover, MD 21076
(301)-962-0250

Resource Directory
3361 Executive Parkway, #302
Toledo, OH 43606-1337
(419)-536-5353

Resource Guide
P.O. Box 451
Scarsdale, NY 10583
(914)-723-8470

Resource Magazine For Publishing
CONTACT: Lyn McFadgen
18 Van Dusen Boulevard
Toronto, ON
Canada
(416)-231-7796

Resource Publications, Inc.
CONTACT: Cheryl Lynn Porter
160 East Virginia Street, Ste. #290
San Jose, CA 95112
(408)-286-8505

Resources
P.O. Box 1067
Harvard Square Station
Cambridge, MA 02138
(617)-876-2789

Resources For Health, Fitness And Learning
CONTACT: David I. Weiss
P.O. Box 1705
Brookline, MA 02146-9861
(617)-277-7546

Resurgence Limited

CONTACT: Vicky Matthews
Ford House
Hartland
Bideford, Devon EX39 6EE
England

Reunion Press, Inc.
Box 1738
Twain Harte, CA 95383

Revelation
2 Rose Cottage, Farm Road
Ruardean Woodside
Ruardean, Gloucestershire GL17 9XL
England

Review And Herald Publishing Association
55 West Oak Ridge Drive
Hagerstown, MD 21740
(301)-791-7000 FAX (301)-791-2012

Revue Du Magnetisme-Etude Du Psychisme Experimental
1 rue des Moulins de Garance
Lille, 59800
France

RFD
CONTACT: Ron Lambe
104 Trotter Place
Asheville, NC 28806
(704)-688-2447

Rice University Institute For The Arts Catalogues
Menil Foundation
1511 Branard
Houston, TX 77006
(713)-525-9400

Ridge Publishers
CONTACT: George Banat
7812 3rd Avenue
Brooklyn, NY 11209
(718)-238-8800

Right Brain Unlimited Publications
P.O. Box 160484
Cupertino, CA 95015

Rio Grande Press
P.O. Box 371371
El Paso, TX 79937
(915)-595-2625

Rising Star Associates
CONTACT: Jonathan Adolph
342 Western Avenue
Brighton, MA 02135-1011
(617)-787-2005

Rising Star Quarterly
650 N. Dellrose
Wichita, KS 67208

Rising Sun Publishing
P.O. Box 10124
Sedona, AZ 86336

Rising Sun, The
P.O. Box 570296
Houston, TX 77257
(713)-225-6366

Riverrun Press
CONTACT: Steven Schwartz
Piermont Avenue
P.O. Box 367
Piermont, NY 10968
(914)-353-1677

Riverside Communications Publishers
CONTACT: Virginia Slayton
One Sanborn Road
Concord, NH 03301
(603)-225-3720

Rizzoli-Corriere della Sera
Via A. Rizzoli 2
Milan, 20132
Italy

RKM Publishing Company
CONTACT: Stephanie
P.O. Box 23042
Euclid, OH 44123-0208
(216)-261-2610

Robert E. Krieger Publishing Company
P.O. Box 9542
Melbourne, FL 32902
(407)-724-9542

Rocky Mountain Spiritual Emergence Network
4301 North Broadway
Boulder, CO 80304
(303)-444-9537

Rodale Press, Inc.
CONTACT: Lisa Zver
33 East Minor Street
Emmaus, PA 18049
(215)-967-5171 (800)-322-6333

Roebuck Journal, The
P.O. Box 663
Tujunga, CA 91043

Ron Warmouth's Prediction
P.O. Box 4037
Los Angeles, CA 90078

Ronin Publishing, Inc., Affil. of And/Or Pr., Inc.
P.O. Box 1035
Main P.O.
Berkeley, CA 94701
(415)-540-6278

Rose And Quill
8818 Troy Street
Spring Valley, CA 92077

Ross Books
CONTACT: Elizabeth Yerkes
Box 4340
Berkeley, CA 94704
(415)-841-2474

Ross Erikson, Inc.
223 Via Sevilla
Santa Barbara, CA 93105
(805)-965-5367

Rossi
CONTACT: S. Rossi
P.O. Box 2001

Beverly Hills, CA 90213
(213)-556-0337

Roundtable Of The Light Centers, Inc.
1801 S.W. 82 Pl.
Miami, FL 33155
(305)-264-4118

Routledge, Chapman & Hall, Inc.
29 W. 35th St.
New York, NY 10001-2291
(212)-244-3336

Rowan Tree Church
Box 8814
Minneapolis, MN 55408
(612)-871-7287

Rowman & Littlefield Publishers, Inc.
4720 Boston Way
Lanham, MD 20706
(301)-459-3366

Royal London Homeopathic Hospital
Faculty of Homeopathy
Great Ormond Street
London, WC1N 3HR
England
01-837-8833

Rudolf Steiner Books
P.O. Box 472, Station Z
Toronto, ON, M5N2Z6,
Canada

Runestaff, The
P.O. Box 161
Harbor City, CA 90710

Running Press
125 S. 22nd St.
Philadelphia, PA 19103
(215)-567-5080

Russell Pittman
1703 West Christine Ave.
Peoria, IL 61614
(313)-851-8411

S,S And S Publications
CONTACT: Gene Duplantier
17 Shetland Street
Willowdale, Ontario M2M 1X5
Canada

S. Karger Publishing
26 W. Avon Road
Box 529
Farmington, CT 06085
(203)-675-7834

S.H.A.R.E. Guide, The
11191 Terrace Drive
Forestville, CA 95436
(707)-887-9483

S.O.M. Publishing & Production
CONTACT: Dr. Barbara O'Guinn
HCR 1
Box 15
Windyville, MO 65783
(417)-345-8411

Sacred Cycles Newsletter
21835 Southeast 248th Street

Maple Valley, WA 98038
(206)-432-7045

Sacred Fire
P.O. Box 91980
West Vancouver, British Columbia V7V 4S4
Canada
(604)-925-0069

Sacred Grove News
P.O. Box 1737
Fontana, CA 92334

Sacred Mountain Ashran
3305 Country Road 96
Ward, CO 80481-9606
(303)-447-1637

SAGB
33 Belgrave Square
London, SW1 8QV
England

SageWoman Magazine
P.O. Box 5130
Santa Cruz, CA 95063
(408)-798-8694 (408)-429-8637

Sagittarius Rising
Box 30
Natick, MA 01760

Salem Kirban, Inc.
P.O. Box 44
Huntingdon Valley, PA 19006
(215)-947-4894

Samadhi Dreams Press
1319 Dennis Court
Kalamazoo, MI 49007
(616)-381-7273

Samuel Weiser, Inc.
CONTACT: B. Lundsled, Vic. Pres.
P.O. Box 612
York Beach, ME 03910
(207)-363-4393 (800)-423-7087

San Diego Pagan Newsletter
P.O. Box 1255
Imperial Beach, CA 92032

San Diego State University Press
San Diego State University
San Diego, CA 92182
(619)-470-8206

San Francisco Miracles Foundation
CONTACT: Jo-Anne Hahn
1827 Haight Street, #201
San Francisco, CA 94117
(415)-995-2354

Sanctuary Of Light
CONTACT: Oconnell
12628 Black Saddle Lane
Germantown, MD 20874-5001

Sand Dollar Publishing Company
P.O. Box 11053
Springfield, IL 62791

Sandpiper Press
CONTACT: Marilyn Riddle
P.O. Box 286
Brookings, OR 97415
(503)-469-5588

Sanguinaria Publishing
CONTACT: Selma Miriam
85 Ferris Street
Bridgeport, CT 06605
(203)-576-9168

Santa Barbara Press
CONTACT: G. Erickson
223 Via Sevilla
Santa Barbara, CA 93109-1835
(805)-966-2060

Santa Fe Spirit
430 West San Francisco Street
Santa Fe, NM 87501
(505)-988-3494

Santa Fe Sun Publishing Company
CONTACT: James Tomarelli
P.O. Box 1553
Santa Fe, NM 87504-1553
(505)-988-2033 (505)-989-8381

Sarah and T. Galen Hieronymus
P.O. Box 109
Lakemont, GA 30552
(404)-782-5437

SASE
2745 W. 38 Place
Chicago, IL 60632

Sat Sandesh: The Message Of The Masters
680 Curtis Corner Road
R.D. #3
Wakefield, RI 02879
(401)-783-0662

Sat Sandesh: The Message Of The Masters
Route 1, P.O. Box 24
Bowling Green, VA 22427

Satori Resources
CONTACT: Corinn Codyce
4034 Ischia Drive
Oxnard, CA 93035-2914
(805)-687-8737

Saucer Smear
P.O. Box 1709
Key West, FL 33041

Saucerian Press
28 Morris Avenue
Richwood, WV 26261

Sawan Kirpal Publications
Route 1, P.O. Box 24
Bowling Green, VA

Scarborough House
P.O. Box 370
Chelsea, MI 48118
(313)-475-9145

Scarecrow Press, Inc.
52 Liberty Street
P.O. Box 656
Metuchen, NJ 08840

Schocken Books
201 East 50th Street
New York, NY 10022

(212)-572-2588

Scholarly Press
904 Sanford Drive
Burlington, Ontario L7T 3G6
Canada
(416)-632-5602

Science & Behavior Books, Inc.
CONTACT: Robert S. Spitzer
P.O. Box 60519
Palo Alto, CA 94306
(415)-965-0954

Science of Mind Publications, Div. of United Church of Religious Science
P.O. Box 75127
Los Angeles, CA 90075
(213)-388-2181

Science Resource Center, Inc.
1151 Massachusetts Avenue
Cambridge, MA 02138-5201
(617)-547-0370

Science/Health Abstracts
P.O. Box 319
Ft. Mitchell, AL 36856
(404)-288-5495

SCP Newsletter
P.O. Box 4308
Berkeley, CA 94704

Scranton Times
Box 59
Tunkhannock, PA 18657
(717)-836-2123 FAX (717)-836-3378

Scriptorium Press
71 S. Main Street
Alfred, NY 14802
(607)-587-9371

Scroll Of Oplontis
P.O. Box 1036
Beloit, WI 53511

Seattle Pacific University
School Of Education
3307 Third Avenue W
Seattle, WA 98119
(206)-281-2360

Second Coming Press
CONTACT: A. D. Winans
P.O. Box 31249
San Francisco, CA 94131
(415)-647-3679

Second Thoughts Publishing
CONTACT: Trudy Miller
153 Halsted
Chicago Heights, IL 60411
(312)-756-7500

Seed Center
Box 1700
Redway, CA 95560
(707)-923-2524

Seek-It Publications
P.O. Box 250012
West Bloomfield, MI 48325-0012
(313)-642-9262

Selene Books
P.O. Box 81702
Albuquerque, NM 87198

Self-Improvement Journal
CONTACT: W. Specht
Box 564
Mableton, GA 30059
(404)-944-0917

Serenity Health Organization, Inc.
Box 1408
Ansonia Sta.
New York, NY 10023
(212)-496-0354

Seven Rays Books
508 Westcott Street
Syracuse, NY 13210

Seventh Wing Publications
CONTACT: Joan Logan
515 East Washington Street
Colorado Springs, CO 80907
(303)-471-2932

Shafenberg Research Foundation
3411 Regatta Place
Oxnard, CA 93030-6416

Shamanic Journey
P.O. Box 13375
Minneapolis, MN 55414

Shambhala Publications, Inc.
314 Dartmouth Street
P.O. Box 308
Boston, MA 02117
(617)-424-0030

Shapers, The
P.O. Box 32386
Oakland, CA 94604
(415)-843-3088

Share It
Roots Church Lane
Playford, Ipswich IP6 9DS
England
0473-624556

Shastar Press
1207 Arroyo Way
Walnut Creek, CA 94596
(415)-932-7943

Shaun Tar Enterprises
P.O. Box 11784
Santa Rosa, CA 95406
(707)-544-1478

Shavertron
CONTACT: Richard Toronto
P.O. Box 5237
Napa, CA 94581

Shelter Publications Inc.
P.O. Box 279
Bolinas, CA 94924
(415)-868-0280

Sheridan House/Medical Books, Inc.
145 Palisade Street
Dobbs Ferry, NY 10522
(914)-693-2410

Shoe String Press, Inc.
P.O. Box 4327
Hamden, CT 06514
(203)-248-6307

Short Mountain Collective
P.O. Box 68
Liberty, TN 37095
(615)-536-5176

Si-Nel Publishing
1377 Barclay Circle
Marietta, GA 30068
(404)-422-8836

Sidereal Registry & Exchange
11 Valley Street
Endwell, NY 13760

Silver Circle
P.O. Box 473
AL Zeist, 3700
Netherlands

Silver Lining Consortium
5721 Fleming Avenue
Oakland, CA 94605
(415)-673-1744

Silver Owl Publications, Inc.
CONTACT: Krysta Gibson
P.O. Box 51186
Seattle, WA 98115-1186
(206)-524-9071

Silvercat Publications
CONTACT: Robert Goodman
4070 Goldfinch Street
Suite C
San Diego, CA 92103
(619)-299-6774

Simon & Schuster, Inc.
1230 Avenue Of The Americas
New York, NY 10020
(212)-698-7406 (800)-223-2336

Simon & Schuster, Inc.
CONTACT: Mail Order Dept.
200 Old Tappan Road
Old Tappan, NJ 07675

Simply Living Magazine
P.O. Box 704
Manly, NSW 2095
Australia
02-977-8566

Sinai Hospital Of Detroit
6767 West Outer Drive
Detroit, MI 48235
(313)-493-5500

Sinha Publishing House
39 S. R Das Rd.
Calcutta, 700026
India

Sipapu/Konocti Books
CONTACT: Noel Peattie
200 Old Tappian Roadt
Old Tappian, NJ 07675
(916)-662-3364

Sirius
Rte. 3

Box 88
Alachua, FL 32615
(904)-462-5741

Sirius Books
4745 Anderson Lane
Eureka, CA 95501
(707)-442-8481

Skeptical Inquirer
P.O. Box 229
Buffalo, NY 14215-0229
(716)-834-3222

Skidmore-Roth Publishers
CONTACT: Patricia Guthrie
207 Cincinnati Avenue
El Paso, TX 79902
(915)-544-3150

Slack, Inc.
6900 Grove Road
Thorofare, NJ 08086
(609)-848-1000 FAX (609)-853-5991

Slawsch Communications
165 Vallecitos de Oro
San Marcos, CA 92069
(619)-744-2299

Small Press
11 Ferry Lane West
Westport, CT 06680
(203)-226-6967

SMB Whole Health
Box 263
Little Falls, NJ 07424
(201)-256-4261

Snake Power
5856 College Avenue, #138
Oakland, CA 94618
(415)-658-7033

SNB Publishing
8607 Hinckley Circle
Cleveland, OH 44141
(216)-526-6552

Snow Lion Graphics (SLG)
CONTACT: Roger Williams, Dir.
P.O. Box 9465
Berkeley, CA 94709
(510)-841-5525 FAX (510)-841-5537

Snow Lion Publications, Inc.
CONTACT: Jeff Cox
P.O. Box 6483
Ithaca, NY 14851
(607)-273-8506 (800)-950-0313

Social Alternatives
Dept. of External Studies
University of Queenland
4067
Australia

Societa Italiana di Parapsicologia
Via dei Monteverdi, 7
00186 Rome,
Italy

Societe Francaise d'Etude des Pheomenes Psychiques
1 rue des Gatines

Paris, 75020
France

Societe Royale Belge d'Homoeopathie
91 Bld. Louis Schmidt
Brussels, 1040
Belgium
02-735-35-25

Society of Metaphysicians Ltd.
Archers' Court, Stonestile Lane
The Ridge, Hastings, E. Sussex TN35 4PG
England

Society Of Psychologists In Addictive Behaviors
Psychology Service
VA Medical Center
Indianapolis, IN 46202
(317)-635-7401

Socratic Press
CONTACT: John Bryant
P.O. Box 66683
St. Petersburg, FL 33736
(813)-367-6177

Solar Studio, The
CONTACT: Jane L. Choate
178 Cowles Road
Woodbury, CT 06798
(203)-263-3147

Solarium Analytika
CONTACT: Ann Fairbrother
P.O. Box 3594
West Sedona, AZ 86340

Solstice
136 Elmora Avenue
Elizabeth, NJ 07202
(800)-765-7842

Solstice Magazine, Inc.
310 East Main Street
Suite 105
Charlottesville, VA 22901
(804)-979-4427 FAX (804)-979-1602

Sophia Books
P.O. Box 590096
San Francisco, CA 94159

Sophia Institute Press
CONTACT: J. Barger
P.O. Box 5284
Manchester, NH 03108
(603)-641-9344

Sophia Press
P.O. Box 533
Durham, NH 03824
(603)-868-2318

Sound Choice
P.O. Box 1251
Ojai, CA 93023
(805)-646-6814

Sound Editions
P.O. Box 1162
Graham, NC 27253

Source Books
CONTACT: Denis Clarke
20341 Sycamore

P.O. Box 794
Trabuco Canyon, CA 92678
(714)-858-1420

Source Net
CONTACT: Tim Ryan
P.O. Box 6767
Santa Barbara, CA 93160
(805)-494-7123

Source of Innergy, Ltd.
Box 2285
Sedona, AZ 86336

Source Productions
11726 La Maida
North Hollywood, CA 91607
(818)-506-0236

Sourcefinder Newsletter
Box 6232B
Augusta, GA 30906

Sources
CONTACT: Kate Burton
P.O. Box 1076-RS
Columbia, MD 21044
(301)-995-1605

Sources Southwest
P.O. Box 35754
Phoenix, AZ 85069
(602)-264-1131

South Asia Books
P.O. Box 502
Columbia, MO 65205
(314)-474-0116

Southern California's New Age Telephone Book
2305 Canyon Drive
Los Angeles, CA 90068
(213)-469-4454

Southern Crossings
302-304 Pacific Highway
1st Floor Lindfield
Sydney, NSW 2070
Australia
02-46-2576

Sovereign International
Soverign House
Brentwood, Essex CM14 4SE
England

Sovereign Press
CONTACT: Kirk Damman
326 Harris Road
Rochester, WA 98579
(206)-273-5109

Sovereignty, Inc.
CONTACT: J.Z. Knight
Box 909
Eastsound, WA 98245

Sparrow Hawk Press
CONTACT: Carol E. Parrish-Harra
22 Summit Ridge Drive
Tahlequah, OK 74464
(918)-456-3421

Spectra Publishing Co.
P.O. Box 1403

Dillon, CO 80435
(303)-468-6439

Spectra, Inc.
CONTACT: Don Preister
P.O. Box 241013
Omaha, NE 68124

Spectrum
P.O. Box 50605
Jacksonville, FL 32250

Spectrum Resource Center
CONTACT: Phyliss And Nancy Martin
P.O. Box 1817
Ann Arbor, MI 48106
(313)-747-9585

Spectrum/The Wholistic News Magazine
61 Dutile Road
Laconia, NH 03246
(603)-528-4710

Spellbound Books
455 Broad Street
Bloomfield, NJ 07003

Sphaera Imagination
P.O. Box 7293
Linch Acres, GA 92047

Sphere
33B Castlegate
Jedburgh, Roxburghshire
Scotland

Spiraling Books
CONTACT: Jack Call
12431 Camilla Street
Whittier, CA 90601
(213)-692-2198

Spirit Art
CONTACT: Colleen Corah
8000 Pennsylvania Road
Bloomington, MN 55438
(612)-942-8644

Spirit Song
CONTACT: Josnnr Lattiak
P.O. Box 2941
Naperville, Il 60567-2941
(312)-369-3661

Spirit Speaks, Inc.
CONTACT: Molli Nickell
11757 Kiowa Street, Ste 3
Los Angeles, CA 90049
(213)-826-9197 (800)-356-9104

Spiritist Publications By The Polleys
P.O. Box 533065
Orlando, FL 32853-3065

Spiritual Astrology Newsletter
Box 31526
Seattle, WA 98103
(206)-547-6861

Spiritual Community Guide
Box 970
Santa Cruz, NM 87567
(415)-863-4788

Spiritual Education Endeavours

CONTACT: Josephine Denny
1556 Halford Avenue, #288
Santa Clara, CA 95051
(408)-248-8244

Spiritual Growth Foundation
891 Haywood Road
Asheville, NC 28806
(704)-252-3408

Spiritual Rights Foundation, Inc.
2550 Shattuck Ave.
Box 39
Berkeley, CA 94704
(415)-549-1991

Spiritual Warrior Press
CONTACT: Richard Oddo
P.O. Box 7012
Halcyon, CA 93421-7012
(805)-489-6445

Spiritual Women's Times
P.O. Box 51186
Seattle, WA 98115-1186
(206)-524-9071

Sport Aviation Publications & Black Mountain Books
CONTACT: Dennis Pagen
P.O. Box 101
Mingoville, PA 03/27/91
(814)-383-2569

Spring Publications, Inc.
P.O. Box 222069
Dallas, TX 75222

Springer-Verlag New York, Inc.
175 Fifth Avenue
New York, NY 10010
(212)-460-1500 (800)-777-4643

Sprouting Publications
Box 62
Ashland, OR 97520
(503)-488-2326

Sri Aurobindo Ashram
331 E. 14th St.
Apt. 6C
New York, NY 10003
(212)-254-3321

Sri Rama Publishing
161 Robles Drive
Santa Cruz, CA 95060
(408)-426-8468

St. Andrew Press
Route 1, Box 283
Big Island, VA 24526
(804)-299-5956

St. John's Publishing, Inc.
CONTACT: Lee Francis
6824 Oaklawn Avenue
Edina, MN 55435
(612)-920-9044

Star Charter, The
P.O. Box 12
Salcha, AK 99714

Star City Publications
CONTACT: Kim Wheeler

P.O. Box 2914
Lincoln, NE 68502
(402)-477-5025

Star Reviews
9346 Farewell Road
Columbia, MD 21045
(301)-730-5661

Star Visions Gallery
CONTACT: Maryanne Hoffman
173 Maple Lane
Jamestown, PA 16134
(412)-932-5019

Star-Borne Unlimited
CONTACT: Solara
Star Route, Box 82
Portal, AZ 85632
(602)-558-2311

Starcraft Press
627 Greenwich Avenue
New York, NY 10014

Starfire Journal
P.O. Box 1082
Bloomington, IN 47402

Stargazer
P.O. Box 43465
Austin, TX 78745

Starlight Connections
4985 North Chieftain Street
Las Vegas, NV 89129
(702)-798-1532

Starlog Press, Inc.
475 Park Avenue, South
New York, NY 10016
(212) 689-2830 FAX (212) 889-7933 TELEX
(910)-240-2934

Starmast Publication
CONTACT: William Schoenleber
P.O. Box 3
Stockton, CA 95201

Starseed Books
P.O. Box 486
Whitmore Lake, MI 48189

State Mutual Book
521 Fifth Avenue, 17th Fl.
New York, NY 10175
(212)-682-5844

Steeleworks
CONTACT: Sara Steele
P.O. Box 18889
Philadelphia, PA 19119
(215)-242-4107

Steinerbooks, Garber Communications, Inc.
5 Garber Hill Rd.
Blauvelt, NY 10913
(914)-359-9292

Stellar Communications
3 Sanborn Drive
Nashua, NH 03063
(603)-880-6078

Stelle Group

187 Sun Street
Stelle, IL 60919
(815)-864-0799

Stellium, Inc.
257 Vista Rio Circle
El Paso, TX 79912-2125

Stephen Greene Press, Div. of Viking Penguin, Inc.
Penguin USA
New York, NY 10014

Sterling Publishing Company, Inc.
CONTACT: Charles N. Nurnburg
387 Park Avenue South
New York, NY 10016
(212)-532-7160 (800)-367-9692

Sterlings Magazines, Inc.
355 Lexington Avenue
New York, NY 10017
(212)-391-1400

Stewart, Tabori & Chang, Inc.
575 Broadway, 5 Floor
New York, NY 10012-3230
(212)-460-5000

Stillpoint Publishing
CONTACT: Meredith Young-Sowers
P.O. Box 640
Meetinghouse Road
Walpole, NH 03608
(603)-756-9281 FAX (603)-756-9282

Storey Communications
CONTACT: J. Evraro
Pownal, VT 05261
(802)-823-5811

Strang Clinic
55 East 34th Street
New York, NY 10016
(212)-683-1000

Strange Magazine
P.O. Box 2246
Rockville, MD 20852
(301)-881-3530

Strawberry Hill Press
CONTACT: D. Osgood
3848 SE Division Street
Portland, OR 97202-1642
(503)-235-5989

Strength & Health Publishing
Box 1707
York, PA 17405
(717)-767-6481

Studienvereniging Voor Pyschical Research
Postbus 786
NL-35 AT
Utrecht,
Netherlands
(020)255469

Stugallz
339 N. Virgil Avenue
Los Angeles, CA 90004
(213)-661-8968

Sufi Islamia/Prophecy Press

CONTACT: Saadi Klotz
65 Norwich Street
San Francisco, CA 94110
(415)-285-0562

Sumangal Publishing Co.
172 M.M.G.S. Marg
Box 5547, Dadar
Bombay, 400014
India

Summit Publishing Company
5401 N.W. Broken Sound Boulevard
Boca Raton, FL 33431
(407)-997-7733

Summit University Press
CONTACT: Elizabeth Clare Prophet
Box A
Livingston, MT 59047-1390
(406)-222-8300 (800)-323-5228

Sun
CONTACT: Page Bryant
P.O. Box 4384
Albuquerque, NM 87196

Sun Eagle Publishing
CONTACT: Dr. James Dorobiala
P.O. Box 33545
Granada HIlls, CA 91344
(818)-360-2224

Sun Publishing
P.O. Box 5784
Bend, OR 97708
(503)-382-0127

Sun Publishing Company
CONTACT: Skip Whitson, Editor
P.O. Box 5588
Santa Fe, NM 87502-5588
(505)-471-5177

Sun Scape Publications
CONTACT: D. Randle
P.O. Box 42725
Tucson, AZ 85733
(602)-297-3424

Sun, The
107 North Robertson Street
Chapel Hill, NC 27516
(919)-942-5282

Sunburst Publisher/Div. of ISBE
CONTACT: Michele Meyer
520 South Pierce
Mason City, IA 50401
(515)-332-1757

Sundance Community Newsletter
503 Lake Drive
Virginia Beach, VA 23451
(804)-422-0371

Sundar Homoeo Sadan
113 Netaji Subhas Road
Calcutta 1,
India
387632

Suneidesis Consociation
P.O. Box 628
Buras, LA 70041

Sunlight Publishing
CONTACT: Verna Kragnes
Route 1, Box 180
Osceola, WI 54020
(715)-294-3136

Sunrise
P.O. Box 113
Warrenville, IL 60035

Sunstar Press
Box 1901
Prescott, AZ 86302

Sunstone Publications
CONTACT: Lori Solensten
RD 3, Box 100A
Cooperstown, NY 13326
(607)-547-8207

Super Magazine, Inc.
8050, boul, Metropolitain, est
Montreal, Quebec H1K 1A1
Canada
(514)-353-7660

Superlove
CONTACT: Tom
4245 Ladoga Avenue
Lakewood, CA 90713
(213)-429-6447

Support of Nature
Box 601
Lenoir, NC 28645
(704)-728-5431

Supreme Council 33rd Degree A
1733 16th Street, N.W.
Washington, DC 20009
(202)-232-3579

Surrey Park Press
CONTACT: John Tiddey
P.O. Box 2887
La Jolla, CA 92038-2887
(619)-454-9333

Sut Anubis
73 Kettering Road
Northampton, NN1 4AW
England
0604-27727

Sutton Publications, Inc.
14252 Culver Drive
Suite A-644
Irvine, CA 92714
(714)-786-8054

Sven Magnusson
Oestra Kanalgatan 18
S-652 20 Karlstad,
Sweden
054-111689

Swallow Press/Ohio U Press
Scott Quadrangle
Rm. 144
Athens, OH 45701
(614)-594-5852

Sweet Forever Publishing/ Island Pacific Northwest
CONTACT: Denise Shumway
P.O. Box 1000

Eastsound, WA 98245
(206)-376-2809 (206)-376-5005

Synchronity Press
CONTACT: Elisabeth Fitzhugh
P.O. Box 5420
Takoma Park, MD 20912
(301)-231-3817

Synergetic Press
CONTACT: B. Johns
3965 Sacramento Street
San Francisco, CA 94118
(415)-387-8180

Synergetic Press
CONTACT: A. Coulter
1825 North Lake Shore Road
Chapel Hill, NC 27514
(919)-942-2994

Synergetic Press, Inc.
P.O. Box 689
Oracle, AZ 85623
(602)-622-0641

Synesis Press
CONTACT: Doug York
P.O. Box 1843
Bend, OR 97709
(503)-382-6517

Synethesis Press
165 South Bent Avenue
Suite 334
San Marcos, CA 92069
(619)-744-1097

Syntony Publishing, Inc.
700 East El Camino Real, #110
Mountain View, CA 94040-2800
(415)-326-5615

Syracuse University Press
1600 Jamesville Avenue
Syracuse, NY 13244-5160
(315)-443-5534

T & A Publications
Box 195
Hancock, WI 54943
(715)-249-5611

T Byron G. Publishing
Box 26
Angels Camp, CA 95222
(209)-736-0718

T-Square Pubs., Inc.
566 Westchester Ave.
Rye Brook, NY 10573
(914)-939-2111 FAX (914)-939-5138

T.A.O. Books
CONTACT: M. Bolton
P.O. Box 40 S
Toronto,
Canada
(416)-423-4226

T.S.G. Publishing Foundation, Inc.
CONTACT: Gita Saraydarian, Pres.
P.O. Box 4273
West Hills, CA 91308
(818)-888-7850 FAX (818)-346-6457

Tai Chi Chuan Center of NY
1117 Avenue of the Americas
New York, NY 10036
(212)-221-6110

Tai Chi, Wayfarer Publications
P.O. Box 26156
Los Angeles, CA 90026
(213)-665-7773

Tail Feather
CONTACT: c/o Card Lake Services
3600 S. Harbor Boulevard
No. 178
Oxnard, CA 93030
(805)-483-0689

Take In Good Part
P.O. Box 14696
Atlanta, GA 30324

Tale Weaver Publishing
32395 Outrigger Way
Laguna Niguel, CA 92677
(714)-661-6276

Tam Mossman Publishers
CONTACT: Tam Mossman
P.O. Box 681
Clinton, WA 98236
(206)-221-8371

Tamiris Publishing House
P.O. Box 2445
Santa Clara, CA 95050-2445

Tao Of Books
174 Main Street
Medway, MA 02053

Tao Publishing
2700 Ocean Avenue
San Francisco, CA 94132
(415)-771-7181

Taplight Studio
CONTACT: Ann Croft Strong
1827 East Mississippi Avenue
Denver, CO 80210
(303)-744-2677 (800)-745-2617 FAX (303)-733-7135

Tara
P.O. Box 1055
Northampton, MA 01061
(413)-584-8291

Taroco
CONTACT: Gary Ross
P.O. Box 104
Sausalito, CA 94966
(415)-332-9254

TAT
Box 236
Bellaire, OH 43906

TAT Book Service
1686 Marshall Street
Benwood, WV 26031

Tattoo Advocate Journal
P.O. Box 8390
Haledon, NJ 07538
(201)-790-0429

Tatwa Deck
P.O. Box 27384
Omaha, NE 68127

Taunton Press, Inc.
63 South Main Street
Box 355
Newtown, CT 06470
(203)-426-8171 **FAX** (203)-426-3434

Tea & Coffee Association Of Canada
1185 Eglinton Avenue, E. #101
Don Mills, Ontario M3C 3C6
Canada

Teamup
CONTACT: Carl B. Foster
Box 1115
Warrensburg, MO 64093
(816)-747-3569

TEC Publications
P.O. Box 189601
Sacramento, CA 95818

Technical Information Center Office On Smoking & Health
5600 Fishers Lane
Park Building, Rm. 116
Rockville, MD 20857
(301)-443-1690

Technology Group, The
P.O. Box 1132
Fremont, CA 94538
(510)-796-9195

Teitan Press, Incorporated, The
CONTACT: Martin Starr
339 West Barry, Suite 16B
Chicago, IL 60657
(312)-929-7892

Telewoman
P.O. Box 2306
Pleasant Hill, CA 94523

Temos
195 Main Street
Great Barrington, MA 01230
(413)-528-5245

Temple University Press
Broad and Oxford Streets
Philadelphia, PA 19122
(215)-787-8787

Ten Speed & Celestial Arts
CONTACT: Editorial Department
P.O. Box 7123
Berkeley, CA 94707
(415)-845-8414

Tenth House Enterprises
CONTACT: Hannelore Hahn
P.O. Box 810
Gracie Station
New York, NY 10028
(212)-737-7536

Tertium Quid
551 Roosevelt Road, 312
Glen Ellyn, IL 60137

Tetrahedron, Inc.
CONTACT: Leonard Horowitz

10 B Drumlin Road
P.O. Box 402
Rockport, MA 01966
(508)-546-6586

Texas Chiropractic Association
1704 Timberwood Drive
Austin, TX 78741-5547
(512)-454-4551

Thames & Hudson
500 Fifth Avenue
New York, NY 10110
(212)-354-3763 (800)-223-4830

Theosophical Books & Library
2416 North Lake
Altedena, CA 91001

Theosophical Publishing House
CONTACT: Von Brashchler
306 West Geneva Road
P.O. Box 270
Wheaton, IL 60189-0270
(312)-668-1571 (312)-665-0123

Theosophical University Press
CONTACT: Grace F. Knoche
P.O. Bin C
Pasadena, CA 91109
(818)-798-3378 **FAX** (818)-798-4749

These Psychic Times
P.O. Box 621024
Conifer, CO 80162

Thesmophoria
5856 College Avenue
Oakland, CA 94618

Thorsens Publishing House
64 Depot Road
Colchester, VT 05446-1103

Thorson Guides
P.O. Box 470886
Tulsa, OK 74147-0886
(918)-622-2811

Thought Trends
CONTACT: Mary Pratt
P.O. Box 566714
Atlanta, GA 30356
(404)-255-1369

Thoughts From The Heart
Box 665
LaCrosse, WI 54601

Three Sisters, Ltd.
CONTACT: Kyril Oakwind
P.O. Box 63
Mt. Horeb, WI 53572

Threshold Books
Rural Route 4, Box 600
Box 600
Putney, VT 05346
(802)-254-8300

Tibetan Express
P.O. Box 252
Youngtown, AZ 85363

Tide-Mark Press Ltd.
CONTACT: Susan Poole

P.O. Box 8311
East Hartford, CT 06108
(203)-289-0363

Tilottama Homoeo House
CONTACT: Dr. Natabar Naik
P.O. Jagatsinghpur
Cuttack 4
Orissa, 754103
India

Time-Life Books
777 Duke Street
Alexandria, VA 70383
(703)-838-7000 (800)-621-7026

Timeless Books
CONTACT: Linda Seville
P.O. Box 50905
Palo Alto, CA 94303
(415)-321-8311

Timeless Books, Div. of Assoc. of the Development of Human Potential
CONTACT: Linda Seville
P.O. Box 160
Porthill, ID 83853
(604)-227-9224

Times Ahead
P.O. Box 9108
Naples, FL 33941-9108

Times Change Press
CONTACT: Lamar Hoover
P.O. Box 1380
Ojai, CA 93023
(805)-646-8595

Timewalker Productions
CONTACT: Brad Steiger
3104 East Camelback Road
Phoenix, AZ 85016
(602)-951-4466

Timewindow Publications, Subs. of Charles Bensinger Co.
P.O. Box 2685
Santa Fe, NM 87504
(505)-988-3735

Tina Lucia
586 Rimrock Trail
Stone Mountain, GA 30083
(404)-292-6720

Tissa, Inc.
CONTACT: J. Disbrow
Rt. 8, Box 90
Culpepper, VA 22701
(703)-547-2989

Today's Chiropractic, Inc.
1269 Barclay Circle
Marietta, GA 30060
(404)-424-0554

Tone Magazine
101B Third Avenue
Ottawa, Ontario K1S 2J7
Canada
(613)-235-9510

Top Of The Mountain Publishing
CONTACT: Dr. Tag Powell, Dir.
11701 South Belcher Road, Ste. 123

Largo, FL 34643-5117
(813)-530-0110 Fax (813)-536-3681

Topping International Institute
Contact: W. Topping
1419 North State
Bellingham, WA 98225
(206)-647-2703

TOPS Club, Inc.
4575 South Fifth Street
P.O. Box 07360
Milwaukee, WI 53207
(414)-482-4620

Toronto Dimensions
214 Glengarry Avenue
Toronto, Ontario M5M 1E4
Canada

Total Eclipse
P.O. Box 1055
Suisun, CA 94585

Total Health
6001 Topanga Canyon Boulevard
Suite 300
Woodland Hills, CA 91367
(818)-887-6484

Touch The Heart Press
Contact: Kathy Hand
Box 210, Main Street
Eastsound, WA 98245
(206)-376-2250

Touchstone: A Journal of Crystals & Consciousness
P.O. Box 492
Delhi, NY 13753
(607)-538-1005

Tough Dove Books
Contact: Denise Sheffield
P.O. Box 1999
Redway, CA 95560-1999

Tower Enterprises
3380 South Fourth Avenue, #18
Yuma, AZ 85365
(602)-726-0471

Tower Hill Press
P.O. Box 1132
Doylestown, PA 18901
(215)-345-1338

Tower Press
Rural Route 2, Box 411
Duncansville, PA 16635-9512
(814)-696-1131

Tower Publishing Company
34 Diamond Street
P.O. Box 7220
Portland, ME 04112
(207)-774-9813 (800)-431-2665

Traditional Studies Press
423 E. 84th St.
New York, NY 10028

Traditional Tours
P.O. Box 564
Creswell, OR 97426
(503)-895-2957

Trafalgar Square, Inc., Div. of David & Charles, Inc.
P.O. Box 257
North Pomfret, VT 05053
(802)-457-1911 (800)-423-4525

Tranet
Contact: William N. Ellis
Pond Street
P.O. Box 567
Rangeley, ME 04970
(207)-864-2252

Trans Light Publications
Contact: T. Jarno
P.O. Box 67916
Century City Station
Los Angeles, CA 90067
(213)-277-2613

Trans-Atlantic Publications
311 Bainbridge Street
Philadelphia, PA 19147
(215)-925-5083

Transformations Magazine
P.O. Box 2306
Santa Fe, NM 87504
(505)-988-5541

Transformations Santa Fe Reporter
322 Montezuma Avenue
Santa Fe, NM 87501

Transformations, Inc.
Contact: Jim Moringstar
4200 West Good Hope Road
Milwaukee, WI 53209
(414)-351-5770

Transforming Art
59 Paterson Road
Springwood, NSW 2777
Australia

Transpersonal Institute
Box 3049
Stanford, CA 94309
(415)-327-2066

Travelers Network Magazine
7501 Sebago Road
Bethesda, MD 20034
(301)-229-2802

Treasure Chest Publications
Contact: O. Branson
P.O. Box 5250
Tucson, AZ 85703
(602)-623-9558

Treasure Publications
P.O. Box 3300
Roanoke, VA 24015-1300

Treehouse Mountain
Contact: Martha Lang-Wescott
Reeds Bridge Road
Conway, MA 01341
(413)-369-4680

Tri Pyramids, Inc.
P.O. Box 5477
Scottsdale, AZ 85261-5477
(602)-951-1275

Triad Publishing Company
P.O. Box 7-966
West Hartford, CT 06107
(203)-521-3390

Trimel Publishing Group
5915 Airport Road
Suite 700
Mississauga, Ontario L4V 1T1
Canada
(416)-673-2500 Fax (416)-673-7873

Trinity Publications
Box 15608
Cincinnati, OH 45215

Triskaidekaphobia Illuminatus Society
c/o Malcolm Riviera
3637 Warren Street, N.W.
Washington, DC 20007
(202)-342-7340

Trobble From River City
3451 Elliot Avenue, South
Minneapolis, MN 55407

Truth
Box 3893
Chatsworth, CA 91313
(818)-347-6949

Truth
Contact: Christopher Huff
P.O. Box 580
Belleville, Ontario K8N 5B2
Canada
(613)-962-6692 (613)-394-4817

Truth Center
6940 Oporto Drive
Los Angeles, CA 90068-2639
(213)-876-6295

Truth Consciousness
Gold Hill
Salina Star Route
Boulder, CO 80302

Truth Seeker
P.O. Box 2832
San Diego, CA 92112-2832
(619)-239-9043

Truths
Contact: Michael Null
155 North Michigan Avenue
Sixth Floor
Chicago, IL 60601

Tucson Lifeline
Contact: Julie Noterman
Box 44028
Tucson, AZ 95733
(602)-798-1195

Tucson Open University
1041 East 6th Street
Tucson, AZ 85719

Twelve Signs, Inc.
3369 S. Robertson Boulevard
Los Angeles, CA 90034
(213)-553-8000

Twin Peaks Press

CONTACT: Helen Hecker
P.O. Box 129
Vancouver, WA 98666
(206)-694-2462

Two Trees Publishing
1272 Bear Mountain Ct.
Boulder, CO 80303
(303)-494-5192

U.F.O. Research
P.O. Box 111
North Quay, Queensland 4001
Australia

U.S. Government Printing Office
Superintendent Of Documents
Washington, DC 20402
(202)-783-3238

U.S. Journal, Inc.
3201 SW 15th Street
Deerfield Beach, FL 33442
(800)-851-9100 **FAX** (305)-360-0034

U.S. Research, Inc.
P.O. Box 7242
Burbank, CA 91510
(213)-841-2733

UFO Newsclipping Service
CONTACT: Lucius Faris
Rt. 1
Box 220
Plumerville, AR 72127
(501)-354-2558

UFO Universe
351 West 54th Street
New York, NY 10019

UFO Update
P.O. Box 428
Nanuet, NY 10954

Ufology Research Of Manitoba
Box 1918 GPO
Winipeg, MB R3C 3R2
Canada

UFOPI News
111 Neal Drive
Atlantic, NC 28511

Ultimate Frontier
P.O. Box 2381
Garland, TX 75047

Understanding Magazine
HC OZ Box 588-F
Tonapah, AZ 85354

Unicorn Press, Inc.
200 East Bessemer Avenue
Greensboro, NC 27401-1416
(919)-288-0822

Unicorn Systems
3906 Chesswood Drive
Downsview, ONT M3J 2W6
Canada

Unidentified Flying Objects Investigation Centre
P.O. Box 6
Lane Cove, N.S.W. 2066

Australia

Union Magnetique de Tersas
C P 482
Quebec, PQ G1K 6W8
Canada

Unique Publications
CONTACT: Beatrice Wong
4201 Vanowen Place
Burbank, CA 91505
(818)-845-2656

United Aerial Phenomena Agency
Box 347032
Cleveland, OH 44134-7032

United Church Of Religious Science
CONTACT: Sheri Cady
3251 West 6th Street
Los Angeles, CA 90020
(213)-388-2181

United Press, Inc.
CONTACT: Bill Partee
P.O. Box 4064
Sarasota, FL 33578
(813)-346-2823

Univerity of Chicago Press, Div. of Univ. of Chicago
5801 Ellis Ave., 4th Fl.
Chicago, IL 60637
(312)-702-7700

Universal Entity
CONTACT: Robert Draper, Pres.
P.O. Box 728
Milton, WA 98354
(206)-952-4202 (206)-848-2052

Universal Force Dynamics
CONTACT: Robert K. Spear
410 Delaware
Leavenworth, KS 66048
(913)-682-6518

Universal Kingdom
Box 938
Roseburg, OR 97490

Universal Science Press
CONTACT: Sam Sonders
P.O. Box 575
Cape Coral, FL 33910-0575
(813)-549-2518

Universalia, Inc.
CONTACT: Sandra J. Radhoff
P.O. Box 6243
Denver, CO 80206
(303)-989-8727

University Of Arizona Press
1230 N. Park No. 102
Tucson, AZ 85719
(602)-621-1441

University Of CA, Berkeley Wellness Letter
P.O. Box 359162
Palm Coast, FL 32035

University Of California Press
CONTACT: Editorial
2120 Berkeley Way

Berkeley, CA 94720
(415)-642-6683

University Of Florida
Vegetable Crop Department
1255 HSPP Building
Gainesville, FL 32611
(904)-392-2134

University Of New Mexico Press
Journalism Bldg., Rm. 220
Albuquerque, NM 87131
(505)-277-2346

University Of Oklahoma Press
1005 Asp Ave.
Norman, OK 73019
(405)-325-5111

University Of Science & Philosophy
CONTACT: Dr. Tomothy Binder
P.O. Box 520, Swannanoa
Waynesboro, VA 22980
(703)-942-5161

University Of Toronto
Faculty Of Medicine
Medical Sciences Building
Toronto, Ontario M5S 1A8
Canada
(416)-978-5411 **FAX** (416)-978-7552

Unlimited Publishing, Inc.
Rte. 17K
Box 240
Bullville, NY 10915
(914)-361-1299

Upper Access Publishers
P.O. Box 457
Hinesburg, VT 05461
(802)-482-2988 (800)-356-9315

Upper Triad, The
P.O. Box 1370
Manassas, VA 22110

Uptown Express
2990 Richmond #316
Houston, TX 77098
(713)-520-7237

Upward Search
4620 Wiecula Road, 39
Atlanta, GA 30342

Uranus Publishing Company
221 Evans Road
Sequim, WA 98382

Utopian Technology
547 Frederick Street
San Francisco, CA 94117
(415)-759-9508 **FAX** (415)-665-0637

Valkyrie Publishing House
CONTACT: M. Schuck
8245 26th Avenue North Street
Petersburg, FL 33710
(813)-345-8864

Valley Newspapers
CONTACT: John Rodgers
6418 South 39th Avenue
Phoenix, AZ 85041
(602)-237-3213 (800)-888-6634

Valley Of The Sun Publishing Co., Sutphen Corporation
CONTACT: Jan Wright Hale
P.O. Box 38
Malibu, CA 90265
(818)-889-1575 (800)-421-6603 (800)-225-4717
FAX (818)-706-3606

Valley Publishing
CONTACT: R. Allinson
333 Michigan Drive
Lower Burrell, PA 15068

Vampire Quarterly
142 Sun Valley Drive
Toms River, NJ 08753

Vancouver Health Enhancement Center
1965 West Broadway
Vancouver, British Columbia V6T 1Z3
Canada
(604)-736-6727

Vancouver Womens Books
315 Cambie Street
Vancouver, BC, V6B2N4,
Canada

VanMeer Publishing Co.
CONTACT: Mary VanMeer
P.O. Box 3431
Palm Beach, FL 33480-1631
(813)-441-8952

Vantage Press, Inc.
516 West 34th Street
New York, NY 10001
(212)-736-1767 (800)-882-3273

Vedanta Press, Div. of Vedanta Society
CONTACT: Bob Adjemian
1946 Vedanta Place
Los Angeles, CA 90068-3996
(213)-465-7114

Vedanta Society of St. Louis
205 S. Skinker Blvd.
St. Louis, MO 63105
(314)-721-5118

Vegetarian Astrologer
4216 Tod Avenue
East Chicago, IL 46312
(219)-397-9297

Vegetarian Press
P.O. Box 61273
Denver, CO 80206
(303)-753-6964

Vegetarian Times
CONTACT: Sharon Bloyd-Peshkin
P.O. Box 570
141 South Oak Park Avenue
Oak Park, IL 60303-2901
(312)-848-8100 (708)-848-8100

Ventana Press
P.O. Box 2468
Chapel Hill, NC 27515

Ventla-Verlag
Postfach 130185

6200 Wiesbaden 13,
West Germany

Verein fuer Tonbandstimmenforschung eV.
Hoehscheider Str. 2
D-4000 Duesseldorf 13,
West Germany
0211-786439

Vereniging tot Bevordering der Homoeopathie in Nederland
Nieuwe Gracht 46
3512 LT Utrecht,
Netherlands

Veritat Foundation, Inc.
3910 Los Feliz Boulevard
Los Angeles, CA 90027
(213)-663-2167

Verlag Hermann Bauer KG
Kronenstr. 2-4 Postfach 167
Freiburg, 7800
West Germany
761-7082109

Verlag RGS
Postfach
CH-9001 St. Gallen,
Switzerland
071-22 66 21

Vestigan Newsletter
Rural Delivery 2, Brookwood Road
Stanhope, NJ 07874

Victoria House Publishers
916 Northeast 66th Avenue
Portland, OR 97213-4936

Viewpoint Aquarius
Box 97, Camberley
Camberley, Surrey GU15 2LH
England
0276-21312

Viking Penguin
40 West 23rd Street
New York, NY 10010

Villard Books, Random House, Inc.
201 E. 50th St.
New York, NY 10022
(212)-751-2600

Vim & Vigor, Inc.
8805 North 23rd Avenue
Suite 11
Phoenix, AZ 85021
(602)-395-5850 FAX (602)-395-5853

Vincent Palazzolo
Box 261, Dept. E
Staten Island, NY 10302
(718)-720-8714

Vintage Books
400 Hahn Road
Westminster, MD 21157

Vinton Publishing Company
P.O. Box 35
Mound, MN 55364
(800)-221-4331

Vision One
P.O. Box 640
Walpole, NH 03068

Vision USA
CONTACT: Nashwa And Essam
10511 Tenneco Drive
Houston, TX 77099
(713)-933-8905

Visionaries' Ink Corporation
CONTACT: Victoria Blazejewski
106 Hunter Ridge Court
Inman, SC 29349
(803)-578-6379

Visionary Enterprises, Inc.
9836 Parkford Dr.
Dallas, TX 75238
(214)-349-8783

Visionary Video Guide
P.O. Box 250
Emmaus, PA 18049

Vital Force
732 Hamlin Way
San Leandro, CA 94578
(415)-895-8614

Vitality Magazine
CONTACT: Julia Woodford
320 Danforth Avenue, Ste. 204
Toronto, Ontario M4K 1P3
Canada
(416)-463-6677

Vitality, Inc.
8080 North Central, LB 78
Dallas, TX 75206
(214)-691-1480

Vivation Publishing Company
CONTACT: Phil Laut
P.O. Box 8269
Cincinnati, OH 45208
(513)-321-4405

Vivekananda Foundation
CONTACT: Ann Myren
P.O. Box 1351
Alameda, CA 94501
(415)-521-4745 (510)-521-4745

Voice Of The New Age
P.O. Box 202
Holmesville, OH 44633

Volcano/Kazan Press
P.O. Box 270
Volcano, CA 95689
(209)-296-3445

Vongrutnorv Og Press, Inc.
CONTACT: Steven E. Erickson
Randall Flat Road
P.O. Box 411
Troy, ID 83871-0411
(208)-835-4902

Vortex Communications
CONTACT: Cynthia Riddle
P.O. Box 1008
Topanga, CA 90290
(213)-455-0097

Voz Informativa
Pino 129
Mexico 4, D.F.,
Mexico

W. Foulsham & Co., Ltd.
Yeovil Road
Slough, SL1 4JH
England
0753-26769

W. Paul Ganley Publisher
P.O. Box 149
Amherst Branch
Buffalo, NY 14226
(716)-839-2415

W. W. Norton & Co., Inc.
CONTACT: William Rusin
500 Fifth Avenue
New York, NY 10110
(212)-354-5500 (800)-223-2584

W.H. Freeman & Co.
41 Madison Avenue, 37th Fl.
New York, NY 10010
(212)-576-9400

W.H. Smith Publishing, Inc.
112 Madison Avenue
New York, NY 10016
(212)-532-6600 (800)-932-0070

Wahaba Heartsun Publishers
CONTACT: Wahaba Heartsun
P.O. Box 1084
Cottage Grove, OR 97424
(503)-942-4726

Wai Chi Lee
294 King's Road, 6th Floor
Hsiang-Kang
Hong Kong

Walker & Co., Div. of Walker Publishing Co., Inc.
720 Fifth Ave.
New York, NY 10019
(212)-265-3632

Wally Boyko Productions, Inc.
P.O. Box 2378
Corona, CA 91718-2378
(714)-371-0606 FAX (714)-371-0608

Walter de Gruyter, Inc.
200 Saw Mill River Road
Hawthorne, NY 10532
(914)-747-0110

Walter J. Johnson, Inc.
355 Chestnut Street
Norwood, NJ 07648
(201)-767-1303

Walton Press Ltd.
174 Culford Road
London, N1 4DS
England

Warner Books, Inc.
666 Fifth Avenue
New York, NY 10103
(212)-484-2900 (800)-638-6460

Warner Press Publishers

1200 East Fifth Street
Anderson, IN 46012
(317)-644-7721 (800)-428-6427

Warren H. Green, Inc.
8356 Olive Boulevard
St. Louis, MO 63132
(314)-991-1335 (800)-537-0655

Washington Living
4141 California Avenue S.W.
Seattle, WA 98116

Washington Square Press
1230 Avenue Of The Americas
New York, NY 10020
(212)-246-2121

Waterfront Books
CONTACT: Sherill N. Musty
98 Brookes Avenue
Burlington, VT 05401
(802)-658-7477

Wave
95 Tussel Lane
Scotch Plains, NJ 07006
(201)-382-8450

Way, The
16222 Landmark
Whittier, CA 90604

Wayfarer Publications
Box 26156
Los Angeles, CA 90026
(213)-665-7773

Weider Health & Fitness Group
21100 Erwin Street
Woodland Hills, CA 91367
(818)-884-6800

Well Being Directory, The
P.O. Box 432
Arcata, CA 95521
(707)-839-1760

Wellbeing Books
CONTACT: Jeremiah Libermann
P.O. Box 396
Newtonville, MA 02160
(617)-969-9711

Wellness Associates
P.O. Box 5433-G
Mill Valley, CA 94942
(415)-383-3806

Wellness Councils Of America
1823 Harney Street, # 201
Omaha, NE 68102
(402)-444-1711

Wellness Institute
3451 Central Avenue
St. Petersburg, FL 33713
(813)-321-0641 (813)-321-0841

Wellness News
Box 86054
Pittsburgh, PA 15221
(412)-731-5533

West Anglia Publications
CONTACT: W. Lusk
P.O. Box 2683

La Jolla, CA 92038
(619)-453-0706

Western Son (Zen) Academy
2 Hopkins Street
Irvine, CA 92715-2125
(714)-786-9585

Westgate House
CONTACT: John Caris
56 Westgate Drive
San Francisco, CA 94127
(415)-584-8338

Westwood Publishing Company
CONTACT: Gil Boyne
312 Riverdale Drive
Glendale, CA 91204
(818)-242-3497

Whale Publishing Company
CONTACT: Gus Theodore
P.O. Box 21696
St. Louis, MO 63109
(314)-832-5734

What-Is Press
P.O. Box 37
Woodstock, NY 12498

Whatever Publishing, Inc.
Box 13257
Northgate Station
San Rafael, CA 94913

Wheelwright Press
CONTACT: Michael Wenger
300 Page Street
San Francisco, CA 94102
(415)-863-3136

White Lion Press
440 Lafayette, 3rd fl.
New York, NY 10003
(212)-475-0212

White Pine Press
CONTACT: Dennis Maloney
76 Center Street
Fredonia, NY 14063
(716)-672-5743

White Rabbit Books
1833 Spring Garden Street
Greensboro, NC 27401

Whitford Press/Schiffer Publishing Limited
1469 Morstein Road
West Chester, PA 19380
(215)-696-1001

Whole Earth Review
CONTACT: K. Kelly
27 Gate Five Road
Sausalito, CA 94965
(415)-332-1716

Whole Life Enterprises, Inc.
CONTACT: Marc Medoff
P.O. Box 2058, Madison Sq. Stn.
New York, NY 10159
(212)-353-3395 (212)-642-5354

Whole Life Network
314 Keystone Avenue

Santa Cruz, CA 95062-1106
(408)-462-5810 (408)-688-8091

Whole Life Times
P.O. Box 789
Fremantle, 6160
Australia

Whole Network, The
P.O. Box 2775
Santa Fe, NM 87504
(505)-982-1037

Whole Ozarks Resource Directory
P.O. Box 4917
Springfield, MO 65808

Whole Person Calendar
3909 Via Dolce
Marina Del Ray, CA 90291
(213)-306-3363

Whole World Communications, Inc.
726 Santa Monica Boulevard, Ste. 202
Santa Monica, CA 90401
(310)-394-3070

Wiccan Advertiser, The
P.O. Box 4034
Hamden, CT 06514

Wide Open Press
116 Lincoln Street
Santa Rosa, CA 95401
(707)-545-3821

Wiggansnatch Magazine
P.O. Box 20061
Seattle, WA 98102

William Morrow & Co.
Wilmor Warehouse
39 Plymouth Street
Fairfield, NJ 07007

Williams & Wilkins
428 East Preston Street
Baltimore, MD 21202
(301)-528-4000 **FAX** (301)-528-8550

Willow Publishing Inc.
CONTACT: W. Rossner
P.O. Box 6636-AH Station
Alamo Heights, TX 78209

Wilshire Book Company
CONTACT: Melvin Powers
12015 Sherman Road
North Hollywood, CA 91605-3781
(213)-875-1711

Wind Communications
CONTACT: Reverend Marlise Wabun/James Wind
1166 Neshaming Valley Drive
Bensalem, PA 19020

Winded Mercury Missive
6020 Piedmont Place
Lynchburg, VA 24502

Windwords
P.O. Box 576
Rainier, WA 98576
(206)-446-7799

Wingbow Press
CONTACT: Randy Fingland, Editor

7900 Edgewater Drive
Oakland, CA 94621-2004
(510)-632-4700

Wingspand
P.O. Box 1491
Manchester, MA 01944
(617)-282-3379

Winning Edge, The
CONTACT: Joan Fericy
20-E Franklin Greens
Somerset, NJ 08873
(201)-247-3685

Winston-Derek Publishers
CONTACT: J. Peebles
P.O. Box 90883
Nashville, TN 37209
(615)-329-1319

Wisconsin Books
2769 Marshall Parkway
Madison, WI 53713
(608)-257-4126

Wisdom Book Publishers
CONTACT: S. Goldfarb
8484 Wilshire Boulevard
Suite 220
Beverly Hills, CA 90211
(213)-655-5340

Wisdom Book Publishers, Inc.
5606 Highpeak Pl.
Agoura Hills, CA 91301-4013
(213)-271-1380

Wisdom Publications
CONTACT: Tim McNeill
361 Newbury Street
Boston, MA 02115-2710
(617)-536-3358

Wise Woman
CONTACT: Ann Forfreedom
2441 Cordova Street
Oakland, CA 94602
(415)-536-3174

Wista Jeanne Johnson Publishers
P.O. Box 40-1232
Brooklyn, NY 11240-1232
(718)-756-2245 (800)-649-4325

Witch-Press
P.O. Box 1392
Mechanicsburg, PA 17055

Witches All
P.O. Box 348
Cambridge, MA 02238

Witches Almanac, The
P.O. Box 348
Cambridge, MA 02238

Witkower Press, Inc.
P.O. Box 2296
Bishop's Corner, CT 06117
(203)-232-1127

Wizards Bookshelf
CONTACT: Richard Robb
P.O. Box 6600
San Diego, CA 92166

(619)-297-9879

WMP Enterprises, Inc.
CONTACT: Roberto E. Veitia, Publisher
P.O. Box 2289
Winter Park, FL 32790-9969
(800)-333-5697

Wolfgang A. Schocken
18 Trail Street
Cambridge, MA 02138
(617)-354-6192

Woman Of Power, Inc.
CONTACT: Char McKee
P.O. Box 2785
Orleans, MA 02653
(508)-240-7877

Womanspirit
2000 King Mountain Trail
Wolf Creek, OR 97497

Womanspirit Sourcebook
1400 Shattuck Avenue
Shattuck Commons
North Berkeley, CA 94709
(415)-548-4172

Women Healthsharing, Inc.
14 Skey Lane
Toronto, Ontario M6J 3S4
Canada
(416)-532-0812

Women Wise
CONTACT: Lois Shea
38 South Main Street
Concord, NH 03301
(603)-225-2739

Woodbridge Press Publishing Co.
P.O. Box 6189
Santa Barbara, CA 93160
(805)-965-7039

Woodside Publications
P.O. Box 19
Wenham, MA 01984

Word Dynamics Concept
CONTACT: W. Carlyle
6115 Center Mall Way
Sacramento, CA 95823-2717
(916)-427-6836

Word Foundation, Inc., The
P.O. Box 180340
Dallas, TX 75218
(214)-348-5006

Word To The Wise
529 Concession Street, C
Hamilton, ON, L8V1A7,
Canada

Working Assets
230 California Street
San Francisco, CA 94111
(415)-788-0777

Workman Publishing
708 Broadway
New York, NY 10003
(212)-254-5900

World Future Society

4916 St. Elmo Avenue
Bethesda, MD 20814
(301)-656-8274

World Goodwill Newsletter
P.O. Box 722
Cooper Station
New York, NY 10276
(212)-982-8770

World UFO Data, Inc.
Box 0705
Melbourne, FL 32902
(305)-777-4721

World University Press
CONTACT: Dr. Howard John Zitko, Pres.
Desert Sanctuary Campus
P.O. Box 2470
Benson, AZ 85602
(602)-586-2985

XAT Medicine Society
CONTACT: Andy Hewitt
1404 Gale Lane
Nashville, TN 37204
(605)-298-9932

Xcaliber Communik
3600 Harbor Boulevard
Channel Island, CA 93035
(805)-985-2560

Yang Martial Arts Assoc.
CONTACT: Dr. Yang Jwing-Ming
38 Hyde Park Avenue
Jamaica Plain, MA 02130
(617)-524-8892 (800)-669-8892

Yankee Books
CONTACT: Joanne Cookson
P.O. Box 1248
Camden, ME 04843
(207)-236-0933

Yara Press
CONTACT: Cil Friedman

P.O. Box 1063
Arcata, CA 95521
(707)-444-8474

Year Book Medical Publishers, Inc.
200 North LaSalle Street
Chicago, IL 60601
(312)-726-9733

Yellow Moon Press
CONTACT: Lyda Kuth
P.O. Box 1316
Cambridge, MA 02238
(617)-628-7894

Yes International
CONTACT: Theresa O'Brien
P.O. Box 75032
Saint Paul, MN 55175-0032
(612)-293-8094

Yes! Educational Society
P.O. Box 5719
Tacoma Park, MD 20912
(202)-829-3289

Yggdrasil
537 Jones Street, 165
San Francisco, CA 94102

Yoga Institute
Santa Cruz East
Bombay 400055,
India
6122185

Yoga Publications Society
P.O. Box 1268
Homewood, IL 60430

Yoga Today, Ltd.
32-34 Preston Road
Brighton, Sussex
England

Your Center for Truth Press
CONTACT: Jeanne And Ted Morris

475 Waldo Avenue, S.E.
Salem, OR 93702
(503)-370-7295

Z Source
16212 Bothell Way, Southeast
Suite F270
Mill Creek, WA 98012
(206)-742-0567

Zebra Books
475 Park Ave. S.
New York, NY 10016
(212)-889-2299

Zen Center, The
7 Arnold Park
Rochester, NY 14607
(716)-473-9180

Zephyr Press
CONTACT: Joey Tanner
P.O. Box 13448
Tucson, AZ 85732-3448
(602)-745-9199

Zero Hour
P.O. Box 766
Seattle, WA 98111
(206)-323-3648

Zetetic Scholar
Eastern Michigan University
Department Of Sociology
Ypsilanti, MI 48197
(313)-663-8823

Zivah Publishers
CONTACT: Nancy Dye
P.O. Box 13192
Albuquerque, NM 87192-3142

Zoan Publishing Co., Inc.
88 Shefield Street
Old Saybrook, CT 06475

Topic Index

The following Topic Index is comprised of 62 topics arranged alphabetically. The sources are then categorized by the same chapter headings that appear in the main body of the directory - Association, Centers, Schools, Museums, etc. Once a particular source is located in the Topic Index, the reader may refer to the corresponding chapter heading in the directory to examine the main listing.

Gateway To The Astral World: Astral
  Projection Kit
Journeys Out Of The Body
Mastering The Art Of Astral Projection
Out Of Body Adventures
Out Of Body Experiences

Astrology

Associations & Organizations

Alchemical Medicine Research And Teaching
  Association
American Federation Of Astrologers
American Federation Of Astrologers, Inc.
Aquarius Organization Of Astrologers
Arizona Metaphysical Society
Astro-Psychology Institute
Astrologers' Guild of America
Astrological Bureau
Astrological Methaphysical
Astrological Society Of Connecticut
Astrology Guild For Educaton
Astroview
Awareness Research Foundation
Aztec-Mayan Astrology
California Astrology Association
Canadian Independent Astrology
Church Of Universal Love
City Of The Sun Foundation
Cosmic Council
Cosmobiology Research
Federation Of Astrologers
Federation Of Scientific Astrologers
Financial Astrology Forecast
Foundation For Astrological Sciences
Fraternity For Canadian Astrologers
Gaudiya Vaishnava Society
Institute For Astrological Studies
International Society For Astrological
  Research
Keepers Of Holy Chalice
National Academy Of Astrology
National Alliance For Spiritual Growth
National Astrological Society
National Council For Geocosmic Research,
  Inc.
National Council Of Geocosmic Research
New Age World Religious & Scientific
  Research Foundation
New Awareness, Inc.
Para Research
Registry Of Sidereal Astrology
Rocky Mountain Research Institute
Rosicrucian Fellowship
S.T.A.R.
Sagittarius Rising
Scientific Astrol Research
Star Magic
Starborn
Transpersonal Astrology
Washington Astrology Service
Western States Astrology
Yogalayam/Prana Yoga Ashram

Centers, Spas, Retreats & Communities

Astrology And Spiritual Science Center
Astrology Et Al Metaphysical Center
D.O.M.E. Inner Guide Meditation Center
Feathered Pipe Foundation
Hawaiian Fitness Holiday
Life And Light Center
Maitreyans, The
New Age Psychic Center
New York Open Center, Inc.
Omega Institute For Holistic Studies
Planetary Citizens/Planetary Initiative For The
  World We Choose
Prana Yoga Ashram - Yogalayam
Programs For Human Development
Wainwright House-Center For Development
  Of Human Potential
Wholistic Resource Center

Schools

Academy Of Astrologers
Academy Of Astrology
American School Of Astrology
Aquilla School Of Astrology
Astrology School
Galaxie School Of Astrology
Institute For Astrology And Metaphysics
Institute Of Astro-Psychology
Institute/New Age
International College Of Astrology
Life Research Institute
Meridian School Of Astrology
Moore School Of Astrology
Navarro School Of Horary Astrology
New York School Of Astrology
Patricia Hayes School Of Inner Sense
  Development
Wright Institute Of Astrol Study

Museums

Spiritual Museum

Events

Cycles Research Conferences & Seminars
South Western Astrology Conference

Biographies

Allen, Gloria
Allen, Michael R.
Alper, Frank
Archer, Helen
Arenz, Kenneth Charles
Atwater, P.M.H.
Binder, Bettye B.
Blank, Denise
Bunker, Dusty
Buske, Terry
Byes, Connie
Calia, Stephen Paulo
Carroll, Wilma
Chabot, Roger
Chapman, Lee
Cooper, Robert W.
Davis, Judith Hope
Deal, Grady, Ph. D., D.C.
Deal, Roberleigh C.
Devlin, Mary
Duff, Kat
Dunwich, Gerina
Emery, Marcia Becker, Ph. D.
Erlewine, Michael
Ferguson, Marilyn
Franklin, Percy
Gerking, Laura N.
Goulet, Paul-Henri
Griffiths, F.
Grishman, Ronnie
Gusic, Diane Brook, M.A.
Hand, Robert S.
Hardy, Pat Esclavon
Hartly, Harriette, Ph. D.
Hayes, Patricia
Hill, Linda, M.A.
Hilsher-Kurban, Dr. Loretta
Hoffman, Maryanne
Howard, H.
Irving, Kenneth
Jeanne
Jerome, Lawrence
Kabir-Bey, Alim Haakam
Kelly, Susan
Kelynda
Kinsman, Warren
Kurban, Michael J.
Lang-Wescott, Martha
Latour, Dan
Leiva, Margaux A.
Lerner, Mark
Levy, Rev. Elizabeth Ann, M.S.C., M.S.TH
Lusher, Dr. Leah
Mark, Barry R.
McCoy, Karen P.
Minney, Gloria

Morrison, Al H.
Mull, Carol S.
Neville, F.W.
Nolle, Richard
Pond, David
Pottenger, Maritha
Quigley, Joan
Rakela, Christine
Raman, Dr. B.V.
Richter, Cynthia
Ronner, John
Rowland, Edna Lewis
Shanks, Thomas
Skinner, Stephen
Tabatneck, Shirley Ann
Tanner, Wilda
Waram, Marilyn F.
White, Larry
Willoughby, Ken

Stores

Avalon Metaphysical Center, Ltd.
Celebrations New Age Store
Enchantments, Inc.
Middle Earth Book Shop
New York School Of Astrology

Distributors/Wholesalers

A.C.S. Publications-Astro Communications
  Services
Health Research
Moving Books, Inc.

Products & Services

Asian Astrology Company
Astro Intelligence U.S.A.
Astrol-Items
Astrolabe, Inc.
Augury Press
Celestial Dynamics
Energies, Trends, Cycles, Inc.
Free Spirit Communications
Grafic Health
Greater Love Ministries
H And H Productions Light Enhancers
Mark Sebastian Astrological Counseling
Matrix Software
Maya D, Incorporated
Pacific Astrology Service
Psychic Solutions
RKM Tape and Book Club
Star Tech Services
Time Data Research
U.S. Reps & Magick Marketing

Radio/Television

Aquarius Rising
John Ankerberg Show, The
Psychic Psychology

Audio & Video Producers

Astromusic

Bibliography

American Atlas
American Book Of Nutrition And Medical
  Astrology
American Ephemeris '31-'80 (Midnight-
  includes American Table Of Houses &
  Calculations)
American Heliocentric Ephemeris For 1901-
  2000
American Sidereal Ephemeris 1976-2000
Ancient Hindu Astrology For The Modern
  Western Astrologer
Astro Essentials: Planets In Signs, Houses
  And Aspects
Astro-Data II (formerly American Book Of
  Charts)
Astrological Healing: The History & Practice
  Of Astromedicine
Astrologik: The Interpretive Art Of Astrology
Astrology Alive: Experiential Astrology,
  Astrodrama & The Healing Arts
Astrology And Past Lives
Astrology And Spiritual Development

Astrology And The Spiritual Path
Astrology And The Stock Market
Astrology And Vibrational Healing
Astrology Directory
Astrology Guide
Astrology Inside Out
Astrology Kit (2 books, note-pad & zodiac
  chart; consultant-Liz Greene)
Astrology Of The Four Horsemen
Astrology Plus
Astrology The Star Science From A To Z
Astrology, Nutrition And Health
Astrology: Do The Heavens Rule Our
  Destiny?
Astrology: Key To Holistic Health
Astrophysical Directions
Complete Horoscope Interpretation: Putting
  Together Your Planetary Profile
Cosmic Cuisine: The Astrological Cookbook
Cosmo-Biological Birth Control
Daily Planetary Guide
Dark Asteroids
Dell Horoscope Purse Book
Dictionary Of Astrology
Directory Of New England Astrologers
Encyclopedia Of Medical Astrology
Essentials Of Medical Astrology
Exploring Atlantis
Finding Your Life's Purpose Through
  Astrology Workbook
Five Keys To Inner Wisdom
Fixed Stars
Forces Of The Zodiac
Guide Astrologique
Healing Rainbow
Healing With The Horoscope
Health, Astrology And Spirituality
Horoscope Guide
Horoscope Symbols
Horoscope Yearbook
Horoscopes Of The Western Hemisphere
How To Give An Astrological Health Reading
International Atlas
Interpret Your Rays Through The Planets
Introduction To Holistic Medical Astrology
Jesus Was A Leo
Light Of Egypt Or The Science Of The Soul
  And The Stars
Lives You Live
Llewellyn's Moon Sign Book And Daily
  Planetary Guide
Manual Of Computer Programming
Mars Connection
Mechanics Of Free Will: The Astrology Of
  Perception, Reality And Will
Mechanics Of The Future: Asteroids
NASO International Astrological Directory
NCGR Membership Directory
New Age Astrology Annual Yearbook
New Age Astrology Guide
North & South Nodes
Omega New Age Directory
Planetary Magick: The Heart Of Western
  Magic
Planets In Aspect: Understanding Your Inner
  Dynamics
Planets In Composite: Analyzing Human
  Relationships
Planets In Houses: Experiencing Your
  Environment
Planets In Love: Exploring Your Emotional
  And Sexual Needs
Planets In Signs
Planets In Transit: Life Cycles For Living
Planets In Work: A Complete Guide To
  Vocational Astrology
Practical Handbook Of Plant Alchemy: How
  To Prepare Medicinal Essences, Tinctures
  & Elixirs
Psychological Astrology
Rosicrucian Christianity Lectures
Runic Astrology: Starcraft & Timekeeping In
  The Northern Tradition

Staying Healthy With The Seasons
The Ages And The Truth
The Astrology Of Genius
The Calendrix
UFOlogy Directory
Ultimate Asteroid Book
Uranus-Neptune-Pluto
Western Astrology And Chinese Medicine
Witchcraft/Paganism Directory
Your Astrological Guide To Fitness
Your Horoscope Guide
Zodiac And The Salts Of Salvation

Periodicals

AFA Headquarters
American Astrology
American Astrology Presents Money &
  Success
American Federation Of Astrologers Bulletin
Aquarian Voices
Aquarius Rising
Aspects
Astra
Astral
Astres
Astro Signs
Astro-Analytics
Astro-Annual
Astro-Carto-Graphy
Astro-News
Astro-Revue
Astro-Talk
Astroflash
Astrologer's Almanac
Astrologia
Astrological Journal
Astrological Magazine
Astrological Review
Astrologischer Auskunftsbogen
Astrology
Astrology And Athrishta
Astrology And Parapsychology
Astrology And Psychic News
Astrology For The 80's
Astrology Magazine
Astrology Now
Astrology Quarterly
Astrology Writers Newsletter
Astrology Your Daily Horoscope
Astrology: A Comprehensive Bibliograpy
Astronews
Atlanta Astrologer
Cahiers Astrologiques
Clarion Call
Considerations
Constellation
Constellations
Contemporary Astrological Observation
  Times-CAO
Correlation
Cosmic Channelings
Cosmic Clockwatch
Cosmic Connection
Day And Night
De Kaarsvlam
Destin International
Destiny
Directions
Ecliptic
Essays
F.A.A. Journal
Fangoria
Foulsham's Original Old Moore's Almanack
Four Elements
Fourth Quadrant
Fraternity News
Future Possibilities
Future Star Horoscope
Geminian
Geocosmic News
Golden Dawn
Gupta Gavesana
Homebringing Mission Of Jesus Christ
Horoscope

Horoscope Quotidien Eclair
Horoscopo Capricho
Initiator
Inner Sense News
Janmabhoomi Panchang
Journal Of Astrological Studies
Journal Of Geocosmic Research
Journal Of Research Of The American
  Federation of Astrologers
Journal Of The AAVSO
Jyotisha-Kalpa
Kalnirnay
Kosmos
Lakewood's Astrology Annuals
Linguaggio Astrale
Llewellyn's Astrological Calendar
Macoy Astrological Digest
Magical Blend Magazine: A Transformative
  Journey
Matrix Journal
Meet The Lords
Mercury Hour
Midnight Horoscope
Mini Examiner
Moon Sign Book
Morningland Spiritual Journal
Mountain Astrologer
Mutable Dilemma
NASO Journal
National Council For Geocosmic Research
  Memberletter
NCGR Journal
New Awareness Magazine
North Florida Astrology Association
  Newsletter
Nous Letter
Orion
Permanent Central Vortex Newsletter
Phenomena
Planet Watch
Poyyamozhi
Probe The Unknown
Psychic Astrology Predictions
Psychic Fair Network News
Psychic Forecaster, The
Rainbow Ray Focus
Raphael's Astrological Almanac
Reports Of Variable Star Observations
Researcher
Rising Star Quarterly
Roxanna's Guide
Scuola Di Astrologia
Sharings
Siderealist
Sirius
Spica
Star Charter, The
Star*Tech
Starscrolls
Stellium Quarterly
Sun Sign Book
Tea & Coffee Association Of Canada Bulletin
The Branches Wiccan Calendar
The Wall Street Astrologer
Today's Astrologer
Trigon
True Astrology Forecast
True Astrology Forecasts Annual
Vegetarian Astrologer
Wall Street Astrologer
Welcome To Planet Earth
Winged Chariot
Your Future
Your Personal Astrology Magazine

Music

Aspects/Shaping Charts: Planetary Patterns
Astrology
Astrology Of Genius: A Study Of The Nobel
  Prize Winners
Astrology Of Romance
Astronomy, 1 & 2
Basics Of House Interpretation 1 & 2
Descendant And Your Alter Ego

Elementary Chart Synthesis 1 And 2
Elements, Modalities, Rulerships And
  Dignitaries
Evolutionary Astrology: A Comprehensive
  Course
Jungian Concepts And The Horoscope
Nodes/Introduction To Interpretation: Twelve
  Letter Alphabet
Outer Planets And Their Cycles: The
  Astrology Of The Collective
Panel: Various Systems Of Astrology, 1 & 2
Planetary Energies
Planets, 1 & 2
Predictions '89: Journey To Inspiration
Predictions '90: The Path Within
Reading The Horoscope
Reincarnation And The Astrological Chart
Saturn/Uranus Conjunction
Spiritual Astrology
Transits As Triggers Of Meaning
What Astrology Can And Cannot Do/Signs Of
  The Zodiac
Workshop: Practical Synthesis With Examples
  1 & 2

Bermuda Triangle

Bibliography

The Bermuda Triangle

Big Foot

Associations & Organizations

Fortean Research Center
Michigan/Canadian Bigfoot Information
  Center
UFO Bureau

Biographies

Coleman, Loren

Periodicals

The Journal Of The Fortean Research Center

Birth

Associations & Organizations

American College Of Nurse-Midwives
Cunningham/Copia Foundation
Farm Midwifery Center
Informed Homebirth/Informed Birth &
  Parenting
International Childbirth Education Association
Maternal And Child Health Center
Maternity Center Association
Midwest Parentcraft Center
Midwives Alliance Of North America
National Association Of Childbearing Centers
National Association Of Parents &
  Professionals For Safe Alternatives In
  Childbirth
Zero Population Growth

Centers, Spas, Retreats & Communities

Farm, The

Schools

Sage Femme Midwifery School
Seattle Midwifery School

Biographies

Baldwin, Rahima
Brunton, Paul
Church, Dawson
Daniels, Karil
Hart, Mickey
McMahon, John
McMahon, Peggy O'Mara
Odent, Michel, M.D.
Orr, Leonard
Simkin, Penny
Walker, Dr. Morton

Audio & Video Producers

Injoy Productions
Point Of View Productions
Rykodisc USA

Bibliography

Birth Reborn
Communing With The Spirit Of Your Unborn
  Child Combo
Drinking The Divine
NAPSAC Directory Of Alternative Birth
  Services And Consumer Guide
Notebooks Of Paul Brunton Vol. 6: Ego,
  From Birth To Rebirth
Rebirthing In The New Age
The Birth Partner
Water Baby Information Book

Periodicals

International Journal Of Childbirth Education
Mothering Magazine
Special Delivery

Body-Mind Connection

Associations & Organizations

Alliance For Alternatives In Healthcare
Association For Humanistic Psychology
Borderland Science And Research Foundation
Chidvilas, Inc.
Consciousness Research And Training Project,
  Inc.
Divine Science Of Light And Sound, The
Focusing Institute
Forum, The
Haelix Plus, Inc.
Institute Of Noetic Sciences
International Association For New Science
Jin Shin Do Foundation
National Alliance For Spiritual Growth
New England Sound Healers, Inc.
NRW Frontier Education Society
Ohashi Institute
Pathways
Radiance Technique Association International,
  Inc.
Sound Healers Association, Inc.
Sundoor-Foundation For Transpersonal
  Education
Whole Health, Inc.

Centers, Spas, Retreats & Communities

Abode Of The Message
Acharya Sushil Jain Ashram-Siddhachalam
Acupressure Workshop
Ajapa Yoga Foundation
Alcyone Light Centre
Aletheia Psycho-Physical Foundation &
  Center
Alive Polarity At Murrieta Hot Springs
American Anopson Institute
Ananda Cooperative Village/Family
  Fellowship Of Inner
  Communion/Expanding Light
Centrepoint
Dream House
Enrichment Center
Esalen Institute
Fare-Thee-Well Center
Golden Phoenix Healing And Light Center
Hakomi Therapy
Hippocrates Health Institute
Insight Meditation Center
Interface
Omega Institute For Holistic Studies
Programs For Human Development
Rocky Mountain Dharma Center
Seven Oaks Pathwork Center
Strong, Stretched And Centered Body/Mind
  Institute
Synthesis Center
University Of The Trees

Zen Studies Society

Schools

Alive & Well! Institute of Conscious Bodywork
American College of Traditional Chinese Medicine
Consciousness Research And Training Project, Inc.
Great School Of Natural Science
Infinity Institute International, Inc.
Institute For Advanced Hypnosis
Institute For Holistic Healing Studies
Institute of Mentalphysics
Institute Of Postural Restructuring
International School Of Shiatsu
Jin Shin Do Foundation For Bodymind Acupressure
Le Centre Du Silence Mime School
Nine Gates, Inc.
Pansophic Institute
Rubenfeld Synergy Association
School For Esoteric Studies
Spiritual Development Guild
Trager Institute For Psychophysical Integration And Mentastics

Biographies

Arenz, Kenneth Charles
Avital, Samuel
Baker, Dr. Robert A.
Boyne, Gil
Breaux, Charles
Bromberg, Dr. Paula N.
Brooks, Svevo
Canby, Henry
Church, Dawson
Drury, Nevill
Dylan, Peggy
Earley, Jay, Ph. D.
Ferguson, Marilyn
Fleming, Linda Frazer
Gardner, Joy
Glaskin, G.M.
Haddon, Genia Pauli, Ph. D.
Harbula, Patrick
Haule, John R.
Jwing-Ming, Dr. Yang
Kargere, Audrey
Kemery, W.E., Ph. D.
Koltuv, Barbara Black, Ph. D.
Latour, Dan
Leavy, Hannelore R.
London, Peter
Metrick, S.B.
Mitchess, Edgar D.
Murchie, Guy
O'Leary, Brian
Ohashi, Wataru
Olsen, Fred C., M. Div.
Roberts, Bernadette
Sawyer, Patricia Kirven
Schechter, Sylvia
Schwarz, Jack
Siegel, Bernie S., M.D.
Sinor, Barbara
Smalheiser, Marvin
Stevens, John
Tate, D.
Teeguarden, Iona Marsag
Vandertuin, Rev. Victoria E.
Wagner, Lindsay J.
Walters (Kriyananda), J. Donald
Windsor, Roger G.

Stores

Time To Live

Products & Services

ISHK Book Service
New Age World Services & Books
Silva Mind Control Method .
Spa-Finders
Yes! Inc.
Zygon International

Audio & Video Producers

Cinergy Entertainment
Spirit Music

Bibliography

Apprentices Of Wonder: Reinventing The Mind
Beliefs: Pathways To Health And Well-Being
Beyond Illness: Discovering The Experience Of Health
Body, Self And Soul: Sustaining Integration
Body-Centered Psychotherapy: The Hakomi Method
Bodymind Energetics: Toward A Dynamic Model Of Health
Brain Building: Exercising Yourself Smarter
Brain, Symbol And Experience: Toward A Neurophenomenology Of Human Consciousness
Breaking The Mind Barrier: The Artscience Of Neurocosmology
Cerebral Symphony: Seashore Reflections On The Structure Of Consciousness
Complete Guide To Your Emotions And Your Health: New Dimensions In Mind-Body Healing
Dancing With The Fire
Don't Bite My Finger, Look Where I Am Pointing
Dreambody Toolkit: Intro To The Philosophy, Goals & Practice Of Process-Oriented Psychotherapy
Dreambody: The Body's Role In Revealing The Self
Ecstasy: The MDMA Story
Getting Well Again
Head First: The Biology Of Hope
Heal Yourself: A Practical Self-Help Manual Of Natural Healing
Healing Mind Of Man: Arise & Shine
Healing With The Mind's Eye: A Guide For Using Imagery & Visions For Personal Growth
Heartsearch: Uncovering The Roots Of An Auto-Immune Illness
Hypnagogia: The Unique State Of Consciousness Between Wakefulness And Sleep
Imagery In Healing: Shamanism & Modern Medicine
Immune-System Activation: Practical Programs For Maximizing Your Recovery Potential
Inner Natures: Brain, Self And Personality
Love Your Disease
Love, Medicine & Miracles
Love, Medicine And Miracles Gift Set - Bernie Siegel's Personal Reflections
Making Miracles: An Exploration Into The Dynamics Of Self-Healing
Making Miracles: Inspiring Mind-Methods To Supercharge Your Emotions & Rejuventate Health
Meditation: First And Last Freedom
Mind Magic: The Ecstasy Of Freeing Creative Power
Mind, Fantasy & Healing: One Woman's Journey From Conflict & Illness To Wholeness & Health
Mind/Body Deceptions: The Psychosomatics Of Everyday Life
Mind/Body Purification Plan
Opening Up: The Healing Power Of Confiding In Others
Passing The Torch, The Way Of The Avatar
Pastoral Medicine
Perfect Health: Maharishi Ayurveda, The Mind/Body Program For Total Well-Being
Personal Totem Pole: Animal Imagery, The Chakras And Psychotherapy
Portraits Of Homeopathic Medicines Vol. 2: Psychophysical Analyses Of Selected Types

Portraits Of Homeopathic Medicines: Psychophysical Analyses Of Select Constitutional Types
Positive Living And Health: Complete Guide To Brain/Body Healing & Mental Empowerment
Power Within: The True Stores Of Exceptional Patients Who Fought Back With Hope
Psychology, Psychoanalysis And Medicine: An Approach To Curing The Whole Person
Rebellious Spirit
Reiki Factor
Remembering And Forgetting: Inquiries Into The Nature Of Memory
River's Way: The Process Science Of The Dreambody
Second Medical Revolution: From Biomedicine To Infomedicine
Sixth Sense: Whole-Brain Book Of Intuition, Hunches...And Their Place In Everyday Life
Soul Return: Integrating Body, Psyche And Spirit
Space, Time And Medicine
Special Reports
Strategy Of The Dolphin: Scoring A Win In A Chaotic World
Wellness Tree: Energizing Yourself In Body, Mind And Spirit
Where Healing Waters Meet: Touching The Mind & Emotions Through The Body
Who Gets Sick: How Beliefs, Moods And Thought Can Affect Your Health
Working With The Dreaming Body
You Can Heal Your Life
You Can't Afford The Luxury Of A Negative Thought: For People With Life-Threatening Illness
Your Body Believes Every Word You Say: The Language Of The Body/Mind Connection
Zen: The Quantum Leap From Mind To No-Mind

Periodicals

And So It Is
Beyond Words Newsletter
Consciousness Research And Training Project Newsletter
Noetic Sciences Bulletin
Noetic Sciences Catalog
Noetic Sciences Review
Pegasus
Radiance Technique Journal, The
Success Through Mind Power
T'ai Chi

Music

Acoustic Supported Learning
Anatomy Of An Illness: A Guide To Healing & Regeneration
As You Think
Aura: Its Color & Their Meanings (Plus Mysterious Powers Of Mind And Serpent Fire)
Autogenics And Meditation
Awakening The Healer Within
Awakening Your Body's Energies
Be (Happy) Attitudes: Eight Positive Attitudes That Can Transform Your Life
Believe And Achieve
Beyond The Subconscious: The Ultimate Mind Game
Breaking Through Illness: Igniting The Healing Power Within
Conversations On Living: Your Thoughts Create Your Life
Creating Miracles In Your Life
Dancing With The Fire: Firewalking
Dissolving Barriers: Discover Your Subconscious Blocks To Love, Health & Self-Image
Evening With Dr. Bernie Siegal

Getting Money Right: The Psychology Of Wealth
Head First: The Biology Of Hope
Healer Within: Healing Chronic Illness
Healing Heart: Antidotes To Panic & Helplessness
Healing With Yoga, Visualization And Affirmation
Hope And A Prayer
How Shall I Live? Transforming Surgery Or Health Crisis Into Greater Aliveness
Hypertension: The Mind/Body Connection
Introduction To Universal Principles
Love, Medicine And Miracles
Love, Medicine And Miracles Gift Set (Bernie Siegel's Personal Reflections)
Mastery Of Money
Meta Fitness: Your Thoughts Taking Shape
Peace, Love And Healing: The Bodymind & The Path To Self-Healing--An Exploration
Peak Performance: Winner's Guide For Making That Quantum Leap To The Top
Positive Thinking Programming
Power Of Positive Thinking Plus Believe And Succeed
Psycho-Cybernetics
Psychoimmunity
Quick Thinking
Right-Brain Experience
Selling You! A Practical Guide To Achieving The Most By Becoming Your Best
Success Is Not An Accident
Super Joy: In Love With Living
Superimmunity: Master Your Emotions & Improve Your Health
Think And Get Well
Think And Grow Rich
Transformation And The Body
Unlocking Your Body: Regaining Youth Through Somatic Awareness
Why Is This Happening To Me...Again?
Working With Creative Imagery
Working With The Unconscious
You Can Heal Your Life
You Can't Afford The Luxury Of A Negative Thought
You'll See It When You Believe It
Your World Is A Direct Result Of Your Thoughts

Channeling

Associations & Organizations

A Course In Miracles
Alexandrian Temple Of Light And Institute
Amalgamated Flying Saucer Clubs Of America
American Parapsychology Research Foundaton
Aquarius Ranch Communications
Arizona Metaphysical Society
Association For Love And Light
Association For Research And Enlightenment, Inc.
Australian Institute Of Parapsychological Research
Awareness Research Foundation
Central PSI Research Institute
Church Of Religious Research, Inc.
Church Universal And Triumphant
Clear Light At Klara Simpla
Cosmic Awareness Communications
Cosmic Contact Channel Reference/ Psychic Services
Creative Energy Options
Dolphin Perspective
Essene Teachings, Inc.
Foundation Church Of Divine Truth
Foundation For Inner Peace-Course In Miracles
Fountain Of Light
Four Directions Foundation
Gather Of Affinity And Light
Genesis II
Golden Word

Crystals

Associations & Organizations

Centers, Spas, Retreats & Communities

Schools

Museums

Events

Biographies

Stores

Distributors/Wholesalers

Products & Services

Radio/Television

Bibliography

Periodicals

Music

American Dietetic Association
American Herb Association
American Holistic Health Sciences Association
American Holistic Veterinary Medical Assocation
American Institute For Preventive Medicine
American Natural Hygiene Society
American Oriental Bodywork Therapy Association
American Rivers
American-International Reiki Association, Inc.
Americans For The Environment
Association For Holistic Health
British Columbia Chiropractic Association
California Holistic Veterinary Medical Association
Cancer Support Community
Churchill Livingstone
Citizen's Clearinghouse For Hazardous Wastes
Clamshell Alliance
Clean Water Action Project
Coalition For Alternatives In Nutrition And Healthcare
Concerned Educators Allied For A Safe Environment
Consciousness Research And Training Project, Inc.
Cosmic Council
Council For Responsible Nutrition
Creative Energy Options
Defenders Of Wildlife
Dinshah Health Society
Dr. Edward Bach Healing Society
Earth First!
Eastern Holistic Health Association
Environmental Action, Inc.
Environmental Defense Fund
Environmental Policy Institute/Friends Of The Earth
Essene Teachings, Inc.
Foundation For Advancement In Cancer Therapy
Foundation For Homeopathic Education And Research
Global Tomorrow Coalition
Green Committees Of Correspondence
Healing Through Arts
Health Resource
Healthy Back, Healthy Mind Institute
Holistic Dental Association
Holistic Health/Academy
Inner Light Foundation
International Academy Holistic Health/Medicine
International Association of Holistic Health Practitioners
International Chiropractors Association
International Foundation For Homeopathy
International Medical And Dental Hypnotherapy Association
International Rolf Institute
International Veterinary Acupuncture Society
Islands Holistic Association
Johrei Fellowship
Maharishi Ayurveda Association Of America
Mandala Holistic Health Society
Metaphysical Church In America
Metascience Foundation
Mind Development And Control Association
NALTA Foundation, Inc.
National Center For Homeopathy
National Federation Of Spiritual Healers Of America, Inc.
National Iridology Research Association
National Nutritional Foods Association
Natural Food Association
Nature Conservancy
New Awareness, Inc.
New England Sound Healers, Inc.
North Coast Body Workers Association
Northern Lights Alternatives
Nos Amis/Our Friends, Inc.

Once Daily, Inc.
Pathways
Rockville Health Association
Rocky Mountain Research Institute
Sea Shepherd Conservation Society
Sedona Institute
Sierra Club
Sound Healers Association, Inc.
Southern Cassadaga Spiritualist Camp Meeting Association
Therapeutic Touch Network
Tools For Change
Touch For Health Foundation
Wright/Gaby Nutrition Institute

Centers, Spas, Retreats & Communities

3HO Center For Holistic Living
3HO Superhealth
A Hero's Journey
A Private Place
A.R.E. Medical Clinic/Energy Medicine
Actualism Wholistic Center
Acupuncture Center
Advancement Of Natural Teachings
Aesculapia
Akala Point
Akashic Services Network/Center & Bookstore
Albintra Wellness Center/Natural Medicine Works
Amiya Institute
Amron Metaphysical Center
Ananda Cooperative Village/Family Fellowship Of Inner Communion/Expanding Light
Ananda Healing Arts Center
Another Place
Aqua Retreat Center
Aquarian Institute
Artemisia Institute For Botanical, Medical and Preventive Health Care Education
Ashram Healthort
Aslan House-Jacksonville Center For Attitudinal Healing
Association Of Holistic Health Practitioners
Atlanta Center For Attitudinal Awareness
Atlantis Rising Health Education
Attitudinal Healing Center
Attitudinal Healing Center Of San Diego
Attitudinal Healing Center Of Southern California
Auroville Association
Avery Ranch
Awosting Retreat
Ayurvedic Wellness Center And Institute
Bald Mountain Hot Springs
Banff National Park
Bay 'N Gulf Health Resort
Beacon Hill Health Association
Bear Tribe Medicine Society
Belknap Hot Springs
Berkeley Massage Associates
Berkeley Springs State Park
Berkeley Women's Health Collective
Biba Hot Springs
Biofeedback & Family Therapy Institute
Bluegrass Retreat
Boulder Hot Springs
Brandlen Institute
Breitenbush Hot Springs Retreat And Conference Center
Bright Farm
Brockway Springs Resort
Buena Vista Women's Center
By-The-Sea
Calgary Esoteric Philosophy Centre
Camas Hot Springs
Cambridge Holistic Health Center
Camp Lenox For Adults
Camp Sunburst
Campbell Hot Springs
Canadian Attitudinal Healing Center

Canyon Ranch Spa
Casa de Marie Research Center And Bookstore
Cedar Hill Retreat
Center For Attitudinal Healing
Center for Creative Consciousness
Center For Creative Learning
Center For Effective Living
Center For Esoteric Studies
Center For Feeling People
Center For Health And Well-Being
Center For Health Promotion
Center For Holistic Healing
Center For Holistic Health
Center For Holistic Medicine
Center For Hope, Inc.
Center For Reiki Training
Center For Release & Integration
Center For Self Healing
Center For The Dances Of Universal Peace
Center For Well Being, Inc.
Center For Well-Being
Center Of Light
Center Of The Light
Centering Institute
Centre For Human Growth
Charan Springs Farm
Charles Motel & Bathhouse
Cheerhope, Inc.
Chinook Learning Center
Chrysalis Center
Church Of Loving Hands, Inc.
Claggett Retreat Center
Clam Bay Farm
Clearlake Medical Center
Cloud Mountain
Cloud Nine Flotation
Colorado's Psychic Center
Common Ground, Inc., And Inner City Hot Springs
Commonweal
Consciousness Village
Cooper Hill Inn
Cosmosis Radio
Creative Aging, Inc.
Daybreak Star Center
Desert Inn Resort And Spa
Dispensable Healing Center
Dolphin Holistic Center
Double D Ranch
Dr. Wilkinson's Hot Springs
Dream Center
Dream Of The Forest
Durham Yoga & Meditation Center
EarthStar
East Bay Center For Attitudinal Healing
El Reposo Spa
Eldorado Springs Resort
Elisabeth Kubler-Ross Center/Shanti Nilaya
Ella's Hide-A-Way Hot Springs
Emandel-A Farm On A River
Emissaries Of Divine Light
Emissaries Of Divine Light/Glen Ivy Community
Esalen Institute
Esoteric Philosopy Center
Essence Light Center/Twelve Rays Of The Great Central Sun
Essex Retreat Center
Evolutionary Education Foundation
Fannie Shaffer's Vegetarian Hotel
Farm, The
Feather Mountain Conference Center
Flower Essence Society/Earth-Spirit, Inc.
Fort Help Counseling Center
Foundation For A Course In Miracles Conference/Retreat Center
Foundation For Inner Peace
Foundation For Well-Being
Foundation Of Light
Fountain Of Health
Fox Valley Gestalt Center
Free Enterprise Health Mine

French Lick Springs Golf & Tennis Resort
Friends Of EKR
Gardom Lake International Earth Friendship Center
Gerson Institute
Gila Hot Springs Vacation Center
Glenwood Springs
Golden Door, The
Golden Phoenix Healing And Light Center
Grand Hotel Des Thermes
GRD Health Clinic
Greenbrie, The
Guadalupe River Ranch
Hailos Wholistic Living Society
Hale Akua
Harbin Hot Springs Retreat And Conference Center
Hartland Health Center
Hay Institute
Healers' Resource Center, Inc.
Healing & Spiritual Center
Healing Arts Center
Healing Arts Of Santa Fe
Healing Center of Arizona
Healing Center Of San Francisco
Healing Heart Center
Healing Light Center
Healing Pines
Health Research Institute
Health Training Group
Healthworks
Heart's Bend
Heartspring Health Center
Heartwood Institute, Ltd.
Heaven, The
Heavensong
Heights Holistic Health Associates
Hidden Blessings
Hidden Valley Health Ranch
Hideaway Hot Springs Resort
Hill Of The Hawk
Hippocrates Health Institute Of San Diego
Holistic Health Center
Holistic Health Centre
Hollyhock
Holy Spirit Retreat Center
Homestead, The
Hot Sulphur Springs Baths
Human Relations Center
Hunter's Lodge
Hunuman Temple
Image In Motion
Indian Valley Retreat
Indianapolis Center For Attitudinal Healing
Inner Garden Activity Centre/ Reflexology Centre Of Vancouver
Inner Visions
Institute For The Development Of The Harmonious Human Being, Inc.
Integral Health Services
Integral Yoga Institute/Satchidananda Ashram
Interface
International Holistic Center
Isis Oasis Lodge And Cultural Center
Iyengar Yoga In Ojai Valley/Ojai Yoga Center
Journeys Into The Known
Julian Preventive Medicine Clinic
K.C. & Company
Kai Mana
Kalamazoo Attitudinal Healing Center
Kalani Honua By The Sea International Conference And Retreat Center
Kauai Attitudinal Healing Center
Ken Keyes College
Kerr House
Kontiki Spa
Kotaka Center
Kripalu Center For Yoga And Health
Kripalu Yoga Ashram
L.I.F.E. Project
La Reginella
Lama Foundation
Las Brisas Retreat Center

Periodicals

Music

Peace, Love And Healing: The Bodymind &
The Path To Self-Healing -- An Exploration
Perspectives On Healing
Say Goodbye To Back Pain
Therapeutic Alternatives
Therapeutic Touch
Think & Get Well
Tibetan Medicine: A Buddhist Approach To
Healing
Touching The Heart Of Healing, Part 1:
Opening To Acceptance
Unlocking Your Body: Regaining Youth
Through Somatic Awareness
Visualizations For Physical Healing
What Your Doctor Didn't Learn In Medical
School...And What You Can Do About It!
You Are The Healer: A Journey To Your
Heart
You Can Heal Your Life
Your Healing Hands And Beyond:
Discovering Your Untapped Energy, Course
In Life Force
Your Healing Path

Holistic Health

Associations & Organizations

Alliance For Alternatives In Healthcare
Alternative Medical Association
American Acupuncture Association
American Dental Institute
American Holistic Medical Association
American Holistic Medical Foundation
American Vegan Society
Association For Humanistic Psychology
Association For Research And Enlightenment,
Inc.
Association Of Professional Massage
Therapists
Blue Star Healing
Body Balance Systems
C.A.F.H. Foundation
Cancer Support Community
Cheirological Society
Common Boundary, Inc.
Conscious Breathing Association
Crystal Therapeutics
Emissary Foundation International
Exceptional Cancer Patient
First Christians' Essene Church
G-JO Institute
Gaudiya Vaishnava Society
Greenpeace USA
Health Foundation
Healthy Lifestyle
Herb Research Foundation
Holistic Health Association Of The Princeton
Area
Holistic Health Works, Div. of Spiritual
Awareness Dynamics
Holistic Resource Association
Informed Homebirth/Informed Birth &
Parenting
Institute For Development Of Inner
Communications Alternatives
Institute Of Behavioral Kinesiology
Institute Of Noetic Sciences
International Foundation For Homeopathy
International Foundation Of Oriental Medicine
Jewish Meditation Network
Jin Shin Do Foundation
Magick Garden
Mark-Age, Inc./Healing Haven/Centers Of
Light/University Of
Life/Meditations/Inform-Nations
Nada Productions
National Association Of Parents &
Professionals For Safe Alternatives In
Childbirth
National Iridology Research Association
Natural Hygiene, Inc.
Near Death Experience Research Institute
New Age Guild Of Connecticut

New Marketing Resources And Services
Consortium
North American Vegetarian Society
NRW Frontier Education Society
Ohashi Institute
Pans Forest Herb Company
Rolf Institute For Structural Integration
Sound Healers Association, Inc.
Sufi Order In The West
Tree Of Life Seminars
United States Psychotronics Association
Unity In Yoga
Vegetarian Resource Group
Vegetarian Society Of San Francisco
Vegetarian Society, The
Western Research Institute
Whole Health, Inc.
Yogalayam/Prana Yoga Ashram
Zero Population Growth

Centers, Spas, Retreats & Communities

3HO Foundation
Abode Of The Message
Acharya Sushil Jain Ashram-Siddhachalam
Acupressure Workshop
Ajapa Yoga Foundation
Akahi Farm Retreat & Conference Center
Alcyone
Alcyone Light Centre
Aletheia Psycho-Physical Foundation &
Center
Alive Polarity At Murrieta Hot Springs
Aloe
Alpha Farm
American Anopson Institute
Ann Wigmore Foundation
Appletree
Arlin J. Brown Information Center
Arnel Chiropractic Center
Aurobindo Center
Auroville Cooperative
Avanta Network
Berkeley Psychic Institute-Church of Divine
Man
Biofeedback Institute Of San Francisco
Bircher-Benner Clinic
BodiFerier
Breitenbush Hot Springs Retreat And
Conference Center
Camphill Village
Center For Conscious Living
Center For Health Sciences
Center For Spiritual Awareness
Center For Taoist Arts
Church Of The Tree Of Life
Discovery Center
Dream Center
Earth Rising, Inc.
Earthsong Institute
Eternal Spring Campground
Experiences In Awareness
Farallones Institute Rural Centre
Fare-Thee-Well Center
Farm, The
Feathered Pipe Foundation
Golden Phoenix Healing And Light Center
Grand Hotel Des Thermes
Green Pastures
Hahnemann Medical Clinic
Harbin Hot Springs Retreat And Conference
Center
Hawaiian Fitness Holiday
High Wind
Himalayan International Institute Of Yoga
Science and Philosophy
Hippocrates Health Institute
HLQ Associates
Institute For Creative Solutions
Institute For Religious Development
Interface
Joy Lake Mountain Community
Judith Jackson Aromatherapy

Kripalu Center For Yoga And Health
Kushi Institute-East West Foundation
La Reginella
Looking Glass Foundation
Ma Yoga Shakti International Mission
Maitreyans, The
Manhattan Plaza Health Club
Maui EcoPark/Center For Ecological Living
Mendocino Woodlands Camp Association,
Incorporated
Mount Shasta Meditation Retreats
New Age Health Spa
New Age Psychic Center
New Frontiers Center/Fellowship Farm
New Life Health Center
New York Center For Art And Awareness
New York Open Center, Inc.
Northern Pines Health Resort
Omega Institute For Holistic Studies
Option Institute & Fellowship- A Place For
Miracles
Ortho-Bionomy
Peacehaven-Center For The Unity Of Man
Polarity Therapy Center Of San Francisco
Prana Yoga Ashram - Yogalayam
River Farm
Rocky Mountain Dharma Center
Seven Oaks Pathwork Center
Shambhala Healing Centre
Sivananda Ashram Yoga Retreat
Solstice Center For Transformational
Medicine
Spiritual Center
Spring Valley
Stelle
Summit University
Swan Center
Swiss Self Healing Retreat
Synthesis Center
Tanana Sun Chiropractic Center
Terre Nouvelle
Twin Oaks Community
Wainwright House-Center For Development
Of Human Potential
Well Being Center
White Dove Farm
Wholistic Center
Yo San University Clinic
Yoga Shakti Mission

Schools

American Institute Of Hypnotherapy
Ananda School
Anglo-American Institute of Drugless Therapy
Bastyr College
California Institute For Integral Studies
Clayton School Of Natural Healing
Dayspring Resources
Desert Institute Of The Healing Arts
East-West College
Hahnemann College Of Homeopathy
Holistic Life University
Infinity Institute International, Inc.
International Institute Of Hypnotherapy
International School Of Massage Therapy
International School Of Shiatsu
Jin Shin Do Foundation For Bodymind
Acupressure
John Fitzgerald Kennedy University
Medium Is Massage, The
Meiji College of Oriental Medicine
Millennium Institute
National College Of Naturopathic Medicine
New England Institute For Neuro-Linguistic
Programming
New Mexico Academy Of Massage And
Advanced Healing Arts
Pacific Institute Of Aromatherapy
Pansophic Institute
Royal University-School of Acupuncture and
Oriental Medicine
SAGE: Earth Awareness & Herbs
School Of Metaphysics-National Headquarters
School Of Natural Medicine

Southwest School of the Healing Arts
Thought Therapy Institute
Twin Lakes College Of The Healing Arts
Yo San University Of Traditional Chinese
Medicine

Museums

Spiritual Museum

Events

10th Annual Health And Harmony Festival
Unity Christ Church
Virginia Beach Holistic Health Expo
Whole Health Expo
Whole Life Expo San Francisco

Biographies

Altman, Nathaniel
Arenz, Kenneth Charles
Arnel, Dr. Marc D.
Beaulieu, Dr. J. David
Bedford, Tania, MsT
Berlitz, Charles
Blank, Mary of Carmel
Blumenthal, Mark
Boddie, Caroline
Brooks, Svevo
Butler, Kurt
Butler, William, M.A. M.Div.
Cayce, Charles Thomas Taylor
Choo, Joni
Ciancola, Dr. Anthony
Cousens, Gabriel, M.D.
Daniels, Karil
Deal, Grady, Ph. D., D.C.
Deal, Roberleigh C.
Der Marderosian, Ara, Ph. D.
Devi, Saraswathi
Devlin, Mary
Dorobiala, Dr. Jim
Drury, Nevill
Dukes, Dr. T.
Epstein, Gerald, M.D.
Erickson, Steven E.
Fleming, Linda Frazer
Ghyssaert, Ivan U., Ph. D.
Green, Jerry
Gregory, Dick
Guyer, Evelyn A., RN, BSN
Halpern, Steven
Hansen-Steiger, Sherry
Harbula, Patrick
Hilsher-Kurban, Dr. Loretta
Hirsch, Roger C.
Hoag, Gail Joy
Hoag, Gregory
Hopman, Ellen Evert, M. Ed.
Hopper-Butler, Deborah
Hung, Dr. David P.J.
Husch, Ann R.
Jackson, Judith
Joy, Elizabeth
Joy, W. Brugh, M.D.
Jwing-Ming, Dr. Yang
Kapuler, Alan M., Ph. D.
Kargere, Audrey
Khan, Pir Vilayat Inayat
Kok Sui, Choa
Kulvinskas, Viktoras
Kurban, Michael J.
Kushi, Michio
Latham, Rev. May Lou
Lauck, M.
Leachman, Cloris
Leavy, Hannelore R.
Levy, Rev. Elizabeth Ann, M.S.C., M.S.TH
Livngstone, Tara
Luce, Gay, Ph.D.
Macy, Mark H.
Margolin, Dr. Shoshana, M.A., N.D., P.M.D.
Mass, Elizabeth, M.A.
Masters, Roy
Matthew, Sister Paula, C.S.J.
McCready, Patricia
McGarey, Gladys Taylor, M.D.

Homeopathy

Kabbalah

Associations & Organizations

Centers, Spas, Retreats & Communities

Biographies

Products & Services

Bibliography

Periodicals

Music

Loch Ness Monster

Biographies

Massage

Associations & Organizations

Centers, Spas, Retreats & Communities

Schools

Biographies

Stores

Products & Services

Audio & Video Producers

Bibliography

Periodicals

Music

Basic Baby Massage
Classic Art Of Sensual Massage
Crystal Massage
Feeling Good Through Massage The Edgar
  Cayce Way
Massage For Health
Massage For Relaxation
Massage: Instructions For Beginners
No-Body Can Do Without Massage
Personal Massage For Health And Relaxation
Sensual Massage For Couples
Tender Touch: A Guide To Infant Massage

Meditation

Associations & Organizations

Academy Of Religion And Psychical Research
Arcana Workshops
Association For Humanistic Psychology
Association For Past-Life Research And
  Therapies, Inc.
Association Of American Buddhists
Bawa Muhaiyaddeen Fellowship
California Yoga Teachers Association
Chidvilas, Inc.
Common Boundary, Inc.
Consciousness Research And Training Project,
  Inc.
Cosmic Awareness Communications
Floating Healing Meditation Circle
Inner Circle Kethra E'Da Foundation, Inc.
Inner Light Foundation
Institute Of Noetic Sciences
Jewish Meditation Network
Light Of The Universe
National Alliance For Spiritual Growth
New England Sound Healers, Inc.
NRW Frontier Education Society
Philosophical Research Society, Inc.-
S.Y.D.A. Foundation/Siddha Yoga Meditation
  Ashram
Sound Healers Association, Inc.
Sundoor-Foundation For Transpersonal
  Education
Sylvan Society
Universal Life
Universal Life-The Inner Religion
Yogalayam/Prana Yoga Ashram

Centers, Spas, Retreats & Communities

3HO Foundation
Abode Of The Message
Acharya Sushil Jain Ashram-Siddhachalam
Acupressure Workshop
Ajapa Yoga Foundation
Akahi Farm Retreat & Conference Center
Alcyone
Aletheia Psycho-Physical Foundation &
  Center
Ananda Cooperative Village/Family
  Fellowship Of Inner
  Communion/Expanding Light
Aquarian Age Church
Aurobindo Ashram
Aurobindo Center
Avadhut Ashram, The
Badarikashrama
Berkeley Buddhist Priory
Bluegrass Retreat
Breathconnection
Breitenbush Hot Springs Retreat And
  Conference Center
Center For Reiki Training
Center For Yoga
Community Meditation Center
D.O.M.E. Inner Guide Meditation Center
Earthsong Institute
Golden Phoenix Healing And Light Center
Guru Ram Das Ashram
Healing Center of Arizona

Himalayan International Institute Of Yoga
  Science and Philosophy
Insight Meditation Center
Integral Yoga Institute/Satchidananda Ashram
Interface
Kalani Honua By The Sea International
  Conference And Retreat Center
Kripalu Center For Yoga And Health
Light Of The Mountains
Matagiri Sri Aurobindo Center
Mount Shasta Meditation Retreats
New Age Health Spa
New Frontiers Center/Fellowship Farm
New Life Health Center
New York Center For Art And Awareness
Nityananda Institute
Northern Pines Health Resort
Oasis Center: New Horizons For Mind, Body,
  And Spirit
Ojai Foundation
P'Nai Or Religious Fellowship
Prana Yoga Ashram - Yogalayam
Providence Zen Center
Sancta Sophia Seminary
Self-Actualization And Enlightenment Center
Shantivanam - Saccidananda Ashram
Sirius Community
Sivananda Ashram Yoga Retreat
Sivananda Yoga Vedanta Ashram
Sivananda Yoga Vedanta Centers
Summit University
Swaha Meditation & Yoga Center
Tayu Center
Terre Nouvelle
Unity Woods Yoga Center
Universal Great Brotherhood
University Of The Trees
White Lotus Foundation

Schools

A-On'O Center Of Light
Academy Of Chinese Culture & Health
  Sciences
College Of Buddhist Studies (International
  Buddhist Meditation Center)
College Of Oriental Medicine (Chapori-Ling
  Foundation Sangha)
Consciousness Research And Training Project,
  Inc.
Holistic Life University
Hypnotherapy Training Institute
Infinity Institute International, Inc.
Institute For Holistic Healing Studies
New Canaan Academy
Palo Alto School Of Hypnotherapy
Reevis Mountain School Of Self-Reliance
School Of Metaphysics-National Headquarters
School Of Natural Medicine
Sirius School Of Spiritual Science
Thien-An Institute of Buddhist Studies
  (International Buddhist Meditation Centers)
Trager Institute For Psychophysical Integration
  And Mentastics

Biographies

Archer-Lowe, Cylvia, Rev.
Arenz, Kenneth Charles
Binder, Bettye B.
Breaux, Charles
Brooks, Svevo
Brunton, Paul
Cayce, Charles Thomas Taylor
Chinmoy, Sri
Davidson, Gordon
Devi, Saraswathi
Douglas, Apryl
Dylan, Peggy
Gardner, Joy
Harbula, Patrick
Haule, John R.
Kabir-Bey, Alim Haakam
Kok Sui, Choa
Koob, Richard
Langevin, Michael Peter

Latour, Dan
Learman, Rev. Kinzan
Leavy, Hannelore R.
Long, Joseph K., Ph. D.
Mass, Elizabeth, M.A.
McCoy-Keyes, Viki
McLaughlin, Corinne
Mendel, Werner
Mitchess, Edgar D.
Parrish-Harra, Carol E.
Perry, Lee
Rand, William L.
Rich, Tracey
Roberts, Bernadette
Rompage, Marguerite
Ronner, John
Rozman, Deborah
Russ, Raymond, Ph. D.
Satchindananda, Sri Swami
Sharan, Farida
Singh, Ravi
Snider, Jerry
Steiger, Francie Pascal
Stuart-Patton, Susan, Ph. D.
Turner, Marlee
Vignanananda, Swami
Wagner, C.
Wagner, Lindsay J.
Walters (Kriyananda), J. Donald
White, Ganga
Windsor, Roger G.
Zuromski, Paul

Stores

Rainbow Store/Earth Products Company

Distributors/Wholesalers

Rainbow Store/Earth Products Company

Products & Services

Ananda Pilgrimages
Lightworks
MegaMind
Perchik's/The Judaic Book Service
Spa-Finders
Star-Lite Shadows Visitor Planning Service

Radio/Television

Being There Now
Mike Kurban Variety Psychic Show
WXPN 88.9

Audio & Video Producers

Dimi Press
Hartley Film Foundation
Neurosonics-The Sound/Mind Connection
Panoramic Sound
Rudra Press
Serenity
Spirit Music
Wisdom Films

Bibliography

A.R.E. Meditation Course
Active Meditation: The Western Tradition
Alchemical Mandala: A Survey Of The
  Mandala In The Western Esoteric
  Traditions
Art Of Meditation
Changing Your Destiny: Dynamic New
  Astrological & Visualization Tools To
  Shape Your Future
Complete Meditation
Conquest Of Mind
Creative Imagery: How To Visualize In All
  Five Senses
Creative Meditation And Multi-Dimensional
  Consciousness
Creative Visualization Workbook
Crystal Therapeutics: Practitioner's Guide To
  Healing & Meditation W/Crystals &
  Gemstones
Directory Of Graduate Degree Programs In
  Psychospiritual Psychotherapy
Don't Bite My Finger, Look Where I Am
  Pointing

Dynamic Stillness Vol. 1: The Practice Of
  Trika Yoga
Experience Of No-Self: A Contemplative
  Journey
Feel Better! Live Longer! Relax
Fine Arts Of Relaxation, Concentration And
  Meditation: Ancient Skills For Modern
  Minds
Foundation For A New Consciousness
Fusion Of The Five Elements I: Basic &
  Advanced Meditation For Transforming
  Negative Emotions
Go See The Movie In Your Head: Imagery,
  The Key To Awareness
Handbook Of Christian Mysticism
Handbooks For Spiritual Growth (Boxed Set:
  Meditation & Mantram Handbook)
Hanuman Chalisa
Happiness Principle
Healing With The Mind's Eye: A Guide For
  Using Imagery & Visions For Personal
  Growth
Healing Your Habits: Introducing Directed
  Imagination, A Successful Technique For
  Overcoming..
Imagery For Healing, Knowledge And Power;
  Harnessing Your Personal Energy To
  Create..
Liberation In The Palm Of Your Hand: A
  Buddhist Meditation Course By Pabongka
  Rinpoche
Looking Into Mind: How To Recognize Who
  You Are & How You Know
Love, Medicine & Miracles
Love, Medicine And Miracles Gift Set -
  Bernie Siegel's Personal Reflections
Mahamudra: Quintessence Of Mind And
  Meditation Vol.1
Mahamudra: Quintessence Of Mind And
  Meditation Vol.2
Mantram Handbook
Meditating In A Changing World
Meditation
Meditation: An Eight Point Program
Meditation: And The Creative Imperative
Meditation: First And Last Freedom
Meditative And Past Life Journal
Nirvana-Tao: The Secret Meditation
  Techniques Of The Taoist And Buddhist
  Masters
Notebooks Of Paul Brunton Vol. 3: Part 1 -
  Practices For The Quest; Part 2 - Relax &
  Retreat
Notebooks Of Paul Brunton Vol. 4: Part 1 -
  Meditation
On Being Mindless: Buddhist Meditation And
  The Mind-Body Problem
Other Way: A Book Of Meditative
  Experiences Based On The I Ching
Pagan Meditations: The Worlds Of Aphrodite,
  Artemis And Hestia
Practice Of Process Meditation: Intensive
  Journal Way To Spiritual Experience
Psychic Lotus-Pictorial
Rebellious Spirit
Reflections In The Light: Daily Thoughts And
  Affirmations
Right Brain Sex: Using Creative Visualization
  To Enhance Sexual Pleasure
Rock Crystal: The Magic Stone
Satya Narayan Katha
Serenity Prayer Book
Speaking Of Silence: Christians & Buddhists
  On The Contemplative Way
Special Reports
Spiritual Message
T M Technique
Tai Chi Ch'uan And Meditation
Tao Of Meditation: Way To Enlightenment
The Inner Side Of World Events
Thoughtline
Towards Superconsciousness: Meditational
  Theory & Practice

Metaphysics

Associations & Organizations

Technicians Of The Sacred
Telstar
Temple Of Aton
Temple Of Cosmic Religion
Temple Of Kriya Yoga
Temple Of Man
Temple Of The Masters
Teramanto
Theosophical Movement
Theosophical Society
Theosophical Society Of America
Tibetan Foundation
Transeekers
United Lodge Of Theosophis
United Sensitives Of America
Universal Aquarian Church
Universal Awareness Research
Universal Church Of Spirit Science
Universal Church Of The Master
Universal Egyptian Arts
Universal Entity
Universal Faithists Of Kosmon, Inc.
Universal Mind Adventures
Universal Mind Science
Universal Mind Science Church
Universal Perspectives
University Of Life
Unusual And Unique Esoteric
Urantia Foundation
Valaam Society Of America
Valley Of The Sun
Vedanta Society Of Southern California
Visionary Arts Council
Visionlink
Washington Astrology Service
Way Of Peaceful Warrior
Winged Mercury Networking
Womangathering
World Association Vision Experiences
World Investigations Of Strange Phenomena
World Messianity
World Prophetic Ministry
World University Roundtable
Y.C.C. Communities
Zanthyros Foundation
Zen Mission Society

Centers, Spas, Retreats & Communities

3HO Canadian Headquarters
A.T.O.M. Center, The
Akasha Metaphysical Center
Akashic Services Network/Center & Bookstore
Alcyone Light Centre
Amron Metaphysical Center
Ananda Meditation Retreat
Aquarian Center, The
Aquarian Fellowship Foundation
Arunachala Ashrama
Astara Foundation, Inc.
Astrology And Spiritual Science Center
Astrology Et Al Metaphysical Center
Austin Seth Center
Avadhut Ashram, The
Avatar Meher Baba Center
Awareness Ashram
Ayurvedic Wellness Center And Institute
Baltimore Spiritual Science Center
Brahma Kumaris Center
Builders, The
Center For Arcane Wisdom
Center For Religious Experience
Center For Shamanic Studies
Center For Spiritual Awareness
Center For Zoroastrian Research
Center Of Eagles
Center Of Light And Truth
Channeling Center
Chapel Of Prayer, Inc.
Church Of Light/Brotherhood Of Life, Inc.
Church Of Loving Hands, Inc.
Church Of Mercavah

Creative Innovations For New Age Growth
Crystal Light Center
Crystal Vision Retreats
D.O.M.E. Inner Guide Meditation Center
E. K. Learning Center
East Wind Community
Essence Light Center/Twelve Rays Of The Great Central Sun
Estar Human Awareness Center
Female Principle
Findhorn Foundation & Press
Florida LRT
Foundation For A Course In Miracles Conference/Retreat Center
Foundation Of Universal Unity
Genesis, Spiritual Life Center
Golden Leaves Book Mart & Metaphysical Centre
Gurdjieff Foundation Of California
Guru Ram Dass Ashram
Hawaiian Fitness Holiday
Heavensong
House Of The Dawn
International Church Of Ageless Wisdom Esoteric Seminary
Intuitive Development Institute
Isis Educational Center
Isis-Osiris Temple, Order Of The Golden Dawn
Keshavashram International Spiritual Center
Lama Foundation
Life And Light Center
Lily Dale Assembly
Living Awareness Foundation
Magi Center, Incorporated
Maitreyans, The
Matagiri Sri Aurobindo Center
Meditation Group For The New Age
Mendocino Sufi Camp
Metaphysical Center Of New Jersey
Miracle Distribution Center
Moonspell
Munedowk Retreat
Mystic Journey Retreat
Mystic Life Center
New Age Community Center
New Age Learning Center
New Dawn Center
New York Open Center, Inc.
Novato Center For Dreams
Olcott Library
Open Door Spirit Center
Other Dimensions Services
Parapsychology Education Center
Programs For Human Development
Psychic Learning Center
Qumrah Desert Center
Ramakrishna-Vivekananda Center Of New York
Research Center Of Kaballah
Rocky Mountain Truth Center
Ruh Inayat Sufi Center
Sakya TeGchen Choling Center
Sambodhi Rajneesh Neo-Sannyas Commune
Sandhill Farm
Science Of Mind Center
Science Of Mind Church Counseling And Healing Center
Self-Actualization And Enlightenment Center
Shanti Anatam Ashram
Shirley MacLaine's Center-Higher Life Seminars
Shri Janardan Ajapa Ashram
Sirius Community
Sivananda Yoga Vedanta Center
Spiritual Healing Center
Spiritual Life Institute
Spiritual Studies Center
Sri Aurobindo Action Center
Sri Chinmoy Center
Sunset Spiritualist Camp
SYDA Foundation & Meditation Center
T.A.R.O.T.

Taoist Center, The
Taoist Institute
Tara Center
Tayu Center
Temple Of The Eternal Light
Torralvoma Research Center
Truth Of Life Center
United Federation Of Humankind
Universal Great Brotherhood
University Of Melchizedek
Vedanta Centre
Vedanta Society Of Northern California
Vedic Research Center
Wainwright House-Center For Development Of Human Potential
Washington Center For Atitudinal Healing
Washington Psychic Institute/Church Of Divine Man
Winning Edge, The
Zen Studies Society

Schools

A-On'O Center Of Light
Academy For Intuitive Arts
Academy Of Psychic Arts And Science
Arthur Ford Academy
Arthur Ford Academy Of Medium
Beshara School Of Esoteric Training
Bhatkhande University
Bio Psiences Institute
Blazing Star Herbal School
College Of Divine Metaphysics, Incorporated
College Of Egyptian Mysteries
College Of Metaphysical Studies
Crystal Academy
Elysium Institute, Inc.
Four Winds Institute
Gateways Institute
Great School Of Natural Science
Great Western University, The Metaphysical University
Hayes School Inner Sense
Hendricks Institute
Heritage Institute Of Psychological Research
Home Education Press
Institute for Metaphysics (Universal Church of Scientific Truth)
Institute Of Diskenetics
Institute Of Life
Institute Of Mentalphysics
Institute Of Metaphysics
Institute Of Spiritual Sciences
International Association For Near-Death Studies
International University of Theology and Parapsychology/Church Of The Antiochean Rite
John Bastyr College
Kahua Institute
Logos World University
Maharishi International University
Mental Science Institute
Metaphysical Theological Seminary
Minnesota Institute For Shamanic Studies
National Metaphysics Institute
Nine Gates Mystery School
Nyigma Institute Of Arizona
Rudolf Steiner College-Waldorf Teacher Training
Rudolf Steiner Institute
School For Esoteric Studies
School Of Ageless Wisdom
School Of Creative Thought
School Of Metaphysics
School Of Metaphysics-National Headquarters
School Of Spiritual Healing And Prophecy
Shasta Abbey (Order of Buddhist Contemplatives)
Sirius School Of Spiritual Science
Sophia Divinity School
St. John's University-Congregational Church Of Practical Theology
University Of Healing/God Unlimited
Waldorf Institute

World University Of America-Ecumenical Ministry Of The Unity Of All Religions

Museums

Westgate Gallery/Press

Events

Ad-Com, Inc.
Creative Resource Systems
Intercontinental Seth And Metaphysical Conference
Magnificent You Expo
Turning Point
Unity Christ Church

Biographies

Allen, Michael R.
Alper, Frank
Altman, Nathaniel
Andrea, Miss
Archer-Lowe, Cylvia, Rev.
Arrien, A.
Astounding Velma
Awtry-Smith, Marilyn
Barklam, John W.B.
Barklam, Judy
Bartole, Reverend Barbara
Bassett, Anthony John
Beebe, Walter
Beierle, Dr. Herbert L.
Besant, Annie
Biccum, Gerald E.
Blanchard, Rick
Blank, Shyla Fern
Boddie, Caroline
Boyd, Sharon
Brown, Louise (Pat)
Bunker, Dusty
Burnett, Ruth
Burrows, Robert J.L.
Buske, Terry
Butler, William, M.A. M.Div.
Capodieci, Gregor
Cardwell, Maude
Chaney, Dr. Robert
Christeaan, Aaron
D'Andrea, Maria
Damiani, Anthony
Davidson, Gordon
Davis, Courtney
Deal, Grady, Ph. D., D.C.
Deal, Roberleigh C.
Deaver, Korra, Ph. D.
Devlin, Mary
Dotlo, Jill
Dougherty, Jude P.
Douglas, Apryl
Dunwich, Gerina
Erickson, Steven E.
Erlewine, Michael
Estep, Sarah Wilson
Ferguson, Marilyn
Feuerstein, Georg
Fry, A.
Gerking, Laura N.
Gillespie, Bruce
Gips, Elizabeth
Golowin, Sergius
Gordon, Kirpal
Gusic, Diane Brook, M.A.
Hand, Robert S.
Harbula, Patrick
Hayes, Christine
Hieronymus, Dr. Sarah
Hirsch, Donna
Hirsch, Steven
Hoffman, Enid
Hoffman, Maryanne
Holecek, Richard W.
Houston, Jean
Howell, Beth
Huff, Bert
Hurley, Mark
Ivy, John
Jermini, Dr. Ellen

Jerome, Lawrence
Johnson, Daniel (Shahid)
Johnson, Dr. Paul V.
Jones, C.B. Scott, Ph. D.
Joyce, Julian J.
Kaplan, Stuart R.
Kargere, Audrey
Keith, Jim
Kelynda
Kinsman, Warren
Krastman, Dr. Hank, Ph. D.
Laing, Betty
Lang-Wescott, Martha
Langevin, Michael Peter
Latour, Dan
Latour, Missy
MacDonald, Jeffery
MachStorm, Thadaeus A.
MacLaine, Shirley
Maurey, Eugene
Mays, Dr. Blaine C.
McCoy-Keyes, Viki
McCready, Patricia
McLaughlin, Corinne
McWhorter, Margaret L.
Medoff, Marc
Metzger, William
Minney, Gloria
Morales, Barbara
Morwyn
Murchie, Guy
Murray, Andrew
Neville, F.W.
Null, Michael
O'Connell, Patrick
O'Donnell, Lily
O'Leary, Brian
Otto, A. Stuart, Jr.
Perasso, Joy
Pollack, Rachel
Pond, David
Prophet, Elizabeth Clare
Puchert, Ingeborg
Radhoff, Sandra J.
Raja
Ramirez, Rev. Jack
Rau, Pam
Reiss, Andrew
Revels-Bey, Brother Frank
Ruhnau, Helena Elizabeth
Sawyer, Patricia Kirven
Schechter, Sylvia
Scott, Theodora
Serra, Irene
Shape, Annette
Skinner, Stephen
Smith, Fred
Smith, Jerry E.
Smith, Kimber
Snider, Jerry
Stack, Rick
Stuart-Patton, Susan, Ph. D.
Sutphen, Dick
Tabatneck, Shirley Ann
Tabatneck, Vincent
Tanner, Wilda
Tarila, Sophia, Ph. D.
Tiers, Sophia
Toca, Archbishop Dr. Sar Mar R.
Van Hulle, JP
Vandertuin, Rev. Victoria E.
Wapnick, Kenneth
Warren, Mary Alice
Waterfield, Robin
White, April
White, Larry
White, Stephen
Willoughby, Ken
Zaslow, Bob
Zitko, Dr. Howard John
Zuromski, Paul

Stores

Alchemist Shop

Bodhi Tree Bookstore
BroHuff Enterprises
Celebrations New Age Store
Conjuring Shop
Enchantments
Enchantments, Inc.
Excalibur Books
Hand Of Aries
I Am Books And Things
Metaphysical Motivation Institute
Middle Earth Book Shop
New Age Books & Things, Inc.
Northeast Metaphysics
Occultique
Planet Earth Book Center
Purple Rose Trading Company
Pyramid Treasures
Rowan Tree
Siddha International/Blue Pearl
Under The Stars
Wild Wood Fragrances

Distributors/Wholesalers

American West Distributors
Angelic Mercantile
Aquarian Specialties
Auromere Books & Imports
Bear Family Distributors
Book Tech Distributing, Incorporated
Brotherhood Of Life
Carolina Cassette Distributors
Casa De Horus, S.A.
Charles E. Tuttle Company, Inc.
Comstock Creations
Contemplations, Inc.
Creative Source, The
Deerhawk Enterprises
DeVorss & Company
Distributors, The
Don Olson Distribution
East West Books
Entrepreneur Network Int.
Excelsior Incense Works, The
Feldenkrais Resources
G.T. International
Global Peace Foundation
Golden Lee Book Distributors
Golden Spiral
Goldenrod Distribution
Great Tradition, The
Happiness Unlimited
Hare Krisna
Health Research
IPD International
Jonathan Parker's Gateways Institute
King Tut Trading
Ladyslipper
Levity
Life Unlimited
Mind & Miracles
Mountain Spirit
Moving Books, Inc.
Multi-Focus, Incorporated
Nagan Corporation
Naturegraph Publications, Inc.
New Concepts Book, Tape And Video
    Distributors
New Leaf Distributing
Omega Press
Omni Orion, Inc.
Os Brasileiros, Incorporated
Pacific Pipeline, Incorporated
Pacific Spirit Corp.
Pacific Trade Group
Pacifica Radio Archive
Paradigm Distribution
Pathway Book Service
Portland News Company
Prisma Products
Quartus Society
Quest Bookshops
Rainbow Collective
Rainbow Innerprizes

Redwing Book Company/Paradigm
    Publications
Runeworks, The
Saul Borak, Incorporated
Serendipity Couriers
Shabda
Sigo Press
Sirius Books And Crafts
Small Changes
Software For Serenity
Station Hill Press
Synektix
Ubiquity Distributors
Vision Works Distribution
Wishing Well Distributing
Worldwide Media Service, Inc.

Products & Services

2 M Communications Limited
Abracadabra Productions
Altara
Aries Productions, Inc.
As-You-Like-It Library
Astro Intelligence U.S.A.
Astrolabe, Inc.
Augury Press
Authentic Marketing
Bridge Of Beauty
Business Plans Plus
Canby's Camera
Caryn M. Carangelo
Celebration Of Life
Cerro Gordo Town Forum
Charles G. Possick
Church Of Religious Science
Comp-Type, Incorporated
Connections, Incorporated
Council Oak Books
Creative Basics
Creative Change Consultants
Crystal Congress, The
Crystal Moon
Diane Loffmin Marketing
Discovery Center
Eartheart
Ecopeace Media Network
Ed Sloan
Ellen D. Steinberg
Ethnic Market
Expo Accessories, Inc.
Fantasy Enterprises
Fell Publishers, Inc.
FMA International, Incorporated
Foresight
Freestone Innerprizes
Future Source
Future Studios
Granary Market
Greater Horizons, Incorporated
H And H Productions-Light Enhancers
Hawkwind Earth Renewal Cooperative
Healing Exchange Association
Health And Vitality Book Guild
Hygieia
Image Tech
Inner Light Resources
International Learning Institute
J & S Aquarian Networking
J.D. Holmes Bookseller & Publishing Group
Journey Into Consciousness
Kathryn Hall
Kelsey Literary Agency
Kendall Enterprises
Knoll Publishing Co., Inc.
Krastman Productions, Inc.
Krystal Haven
Linda Bruce
Linda Jones Public Relations
List Counsellors, Inc.
Literary Connection, The
Lodestar Books
M.H. Beeman
Magic Marketing
Magick Marketing

Marah
Marjosa Star
Matrix Software
Maya D, Incorporated
Metaphysical Booksellers
Metaphysically Speaking
Mind's Eye, The
Moon Stone Limited
Mountain Sunshine Books
Mystic Arts Book Society
Mystic Crone
Mystic Moon
Mystic Systems Books
NAM-New Age Mailing Lists
Network Marketing
New Age Marketing
New Age Shop, The
New Age World Services & Books
New Oracle Catalog
No. 1 Electronics
Nova Dawn: New Age Service
Oceanview Wellness Center
Open Door, The
P.J. Birosik
Pamela J. Willits Photographic Services
PR Flash Database
Pro Mark
Professional Management Associates
Professional Metaphysical Services
Professional Retail Services
Psychic And Astrological Cruise, The
Psychic Fair Network
Publishers Book & Audio Mailing Service
Publishers Exchange Network
Pyramid Books And The New-Age Collection
Pyramid Products
Rainbow Blossom
Reed Literary Agency
Renaissance Books
RKM Tape and Book Club
Rosen Agency, The
Royal Publishing, Inc.
S.R. Reps And Company
Sacred Earth News
Sacred Earth Tours
Saint Elmo's Books
Sedona Marketing Limited
Shabda/Tibetan Bells
Shyla's Mystic Gems
Singer Media Corporation
Small Press
South American Craft Imports
Southern Traveller, The
Star's Edge International
Star-Lite Shadows Visitor Planning Service
Starlight
Sun Spiritual Library
Sunburst Crystals
Synaptica
T.H. Enterprises
Teamwork Promotions
Terrie Brill And Associates
Theodora Scott & Association
Thunderbird Gems, Incorporated
Time Data Research
Tolodumare Bookstores
U.S. Reps & Magick Marketing
Unicorn Books
Universe & Other Toys
Vision Works Distribution
Visions Travel And Tours
Warrior Information Network
Writers Publishing Service Company
Zumpfe Studio

Radio/Television

ABC Radio Network News
Aquarius Rising
Celestial Dialogs
Changes
Cultural Media Services
Hearts Of Space
KEST AM
KING 1090 AM

Inner Links
Institute For Biogenetics And Gestalt
Institute For Individual And World Peace
Institute Of Behavioral Kinesiology
Institute Of Cultural Affairs
Institutes For The Enhancement Of Life
　Energy And Creativity
International Association For Near Death
　Studies
International Association Of Clinical Laser
　Acupuncturists
International Association Of Professional
　Natural Hygienists
International Communes Network
International Federation Of Festival
　Organizations
International Imports
International Institute Of Integral Human
　Sciences
International Society Of Divine Love
Japanese Commune Movement
Jersey Society Of Parapsychology, Inc.
Kibbutz-Federation International Communes
　Desk
Krishnamurti Foundation Of America
Kriya Jyoti Tantra Society
Kundalini Research Foundation, Ltd.
Legacy International
Life Spectrums/Rainbow Experience
Lifestyles Travel
Light Ages Foundation
Little Synagogue
Love Project
Loving Relationships Training, International
Lupin Naturalist Club
Lutheran General Health Care System
Magazine And Paperback Marketing Institute
Mandala Holistic Health Society
Mankind Research Foundation
Mark-Age, Inc./Healing Haven/Centers Of
　Light/University Of
　Life/Meditations/Inform-Nations
Massachusetts State Spiritualist Association
Melia Foundation
Milton Erickson Foundation
Mind Science Foundation
Mobius Society
NALTA Foundation, Inc.
National Academy Of Songwriters
National Alliance For Spiritual Growth
National Association For Music Therapy
National Association Of Independent
　Publishers
National Association Of Spiritual Churches Of
　Science & Revelation
National Campaign For Peace Tax Fund
National Commission For The Certification Of
　Acupuncturists
National Iridology Research Association
Natural Marketing Association
Near Death Experience Research Institute
Near-Death Experience Project
Network 2012
New Age Church Of Truth
New Age Guild Of Connecticut
New Age Link
New Age Publishing and Retailing Alliance
New Age World Religious & Scientific
　Research Foundation
New Awareness, Inc.
New England Network Of Light
New England Sound Healers, Inc.
New Marketing Resources And Services
　Consortium
North American Vegetarian Society
NRW Frontier Education Society
Ohashi Institute
Order Of Uriel, The
Ordo Templi Orientis
Overseas Development Network
Parapsychological Services Institute
Pathways
Peacevision

Personal Development Institue
Philosophical Research Society, Inc.
Point Foundation
Poster Market Research
Project Mentifex
Promethian Network
Publishers Marketing Association
Radiance Technique Association International,
　Inc.
Rainbow Family Of Living Light
Rocky Mountian Book Publishers Association
Rosicrucian Fellowship
Self-Awareness Association
Seva Foundation, The
Share Foundation
Shepherdsfield Community
Sisterhood Of St. Clare
Society For The Application Of Free Energy
Society of Pragmatic Mysticism
Somatics Society
Sound Healers Association, Inc.
Southwestern Booksellers Association
Space Technology And Research Foundation,
　Inc.
Spirit Of The Warrior International
Spiritual Frontiers Fellowship
Spiritual Science Fellowship
Spiritualist Association Of America
Star Of Isis Foundation
Stelle Group, The
Still Waters Foundation
Sufi Order In The West
Sun Spiritualist Camp Association
Sundoor-Foundation For Transpersonal
　Education
Supreme Grand Lodge of AMORC, Inc.
Sylvan Society
Teaching Of The Inner Christ, Inc.
Temple Of Kriya Yoga
Theosophical Society
Theosophical Society Of America
Tibetan Foundation, The
Tree Of Life Seminars
Unarius Academy Of Science & Education
　Foundation
United New Age Network
Unity-And-Diversity World Organization
Universal Aquarian Church
Universal Faithists Of Kosmon, Inc.
Universal Spiritualist Association
Urantia Foundation
Vedanta Society Of Southern California
Vegetarian Society
Vegetarian Society Of San Francisco
Visionary Arts Council
Volunteers For Peace, Inc.
Water Center, The
Windstar Foundation
Women's Spirituality Forum
World Government Of The Age Of
　Enlightenment - U.S.
World University Roundtable
Zero Population Growth

Centers, Spas, Retreats & Communities

3HO Canadian Headquarters
3HO Foundation
Abode Of The Message
Acharya Sushil Jain Ashram-Siddhachalam
ACIM Workshop
Actualizations
Akahi Farm Retreat & Conference Center
Alcyone
Alcyone Light Centre
Aletheia Psycho-Physical Foundation &
　Center
Alive Polarity At Murrieta Hot Springs
Aloe
Alpha Farm
American Anopson Institute
Ananda Cooperative Village AT Ocean Song

Ananda Cooperative Village/Family
　Fellowship Of Inner
　Communion/Expanding Light
Ananda Marga
Appletree
Aquarian Age Church
Aquarian Minyan
Arcosanti
Arlin J. Brown Information Center
Artists For Planetary Renewal - Martin
　Steinberg Center
Association Of Metaphysical And
　Philosophical Societies
Astrology And Spiritual Science Center
Atmaniketan Ashram
Aurobindo Ashram
Auroville
Auroville Cooperative
Austin Seth Center
Avadhut Ashram, The
Avanta Network
Badarikashrama
Baha'i Faith
Bear Tribe Medicine Society
Berkeley Buddhist Priory
Berkshire Village, Incorporated
Beth Or - A New Paradigm Jewish
　Community
Birchwood Hall
Breitenbush Hot Springs Retreat And
　Conference Center
Bruderhof, The
Bryn Gweled Homesteads
Builders, The
Camp Lenox
Camp Sunburst
Camphill Village
Center For Alternate Realities
Center For American Archeology
Center For Classical Homeopathy
Center For Shamanic Studies
Center For The Behavioral Sciences
Center For The Dances Of Universal Peace
Center For Transformation
Center Of Artistic Counseling
Center Of The Light
Centrepoint
Chabad House
Chinook Learning Center
Choices International
Christ Of The Hills Monastery - Orthodox
　Monks Of St. Benedict
Christiana
Chrysalis
Church Of Light/Brotherhood Of Life, Inc.
Church Of Mercavah
Church Of New World Religion
Church Of The Most High Goddess
Church Of The Tree Of Life
Collegians International Church
Community for Creative Non-Violence
Community Meditation Center
Coptic Fellowship International
Cosmic Studies Center
Course In Mastery, Inc.
Creative Innovations For New Age Growth
Dandelion
DeLano Training Systems
Dialogue House
Earthwalk
East Wind Community
Esalen Institute
Essence Light Center/Twelve Rays Of The
　Great Central Sun
Experiences In Awareness
Farallones Institute Rural Centre
Fare-Thee-Well Center
Farm, The
Federation Of Christian Ministries
Findhorn Foundation & Press
Foundation For Life Action
Foundation Of Universal Unity
Franciscan Renewal Center

Gita-Nigari Community, Iskcon Farm
God's Valley (Pandamarama)
Goodlife
Graduate Theological Union Library New
　Religous Movements Research Collection
Green Pastures
Gurdjieff Foundation Of California
Guru Ram Das Ashram
Hahnemann Medical Clinic
Harbin Hot Springs Retreat And Conference
　Center
Hardscrabble Hill
Heathcote Center
Heavensong
Herb-Pharm
High Wind
Himalayan Institute Of New York
Himalayan International Institute Of Yoga
　Science and Philosophy
HLQ Associates
I.C.S.A.
ICSA - Ananda Ashram
Insight Meditation Center
Insight Seminars
Institute For Creative Solutions
Institute For Cultural Affairs
Institute For Religious Development
Institute For The Development Of The
　Harmonious Human Being, Inc.
Institute For The Study Of Natural Systems
Institute Self Improvement
Integral Yoga Institute/Satchidananda Ashram
Integral Yoga International
Interface
Intergroup Committee
International Center For Release And
　Integration
International Church Of Ageless Wisdom
　Esoteric Seminary
IntiNet Resource Center
Isis-Osiris Temple, Order Of The Golden
　Dawn
Jemez Bodhi Mandala
Joy Lake Mountain Community
Ken Keyes College
Kerista Village
Keristan Islands Intentional Community
Keshavashram International Spiritual Center
Kinesionics Institute
Kirpal Ashram
Koinonia Partners
Krotona Institute
Kushi Institute-East West Foundation
La Sabranenque Centre International
Lama Foundation
Laurieston Hall
Life And Light Center
Life Center
Life Integration Trainings
Lifespan
Light Of The Mountains
Linnaea Farm/Wilshire House
Ma Yoga Shakti International Mission
Magna and Walt Baptiste Center
Maitreyans, The
Manhattan Plaza Health Club
Mariposa Group Community
Matagiri Sri Aurobindo Center
Matri Satsang
Maui EcoPark/Center For Ecological Living
Meditation Group For The New Age
Mele Mauka Center
Merriam Hill
Meta Tantay
Mettanokit
Miracle Distribution Center
Monroe Institute
Mount Madonna Center
Movement For A New Society-Philadelphia
　Life Center
Movement Of Spiritual Inner Awareness
Moving Center
Myers Institute For Creative Studies

Bibliography

A Coming Of Wizards
A Tibetan On Tibet
ABC's Of Crystals
Absolute Power
Acrobats Of The Gods: Dance And Transformation
Affirmations
Affordable Spas & Fitness Resorts
Akashic Record Player
All Rites Reversed
Alternative America
Alternative Press: Children's Books
Alternatives In Education
Ancient Atlantic
Ancient Legends Of Gems & Jewels
Ancient Mysteries
Angel Tech: A Modern Shaman's Guide To Reality Selection
Anthropic Cosmological Principle
Apocalypse Now: The Coming Of A New Age
Aqua Terra
Aquarian Alternatives
Aquarian Conspiracy: Personal And Social Transformation In Our Time
Aquarian Guide To The New Age
Are You Really Too Sensitive?
ArtNetwork
Astrology: Do The Heavens Rule Our Destiny?
At A Journal Workshop: The Basic Text & Guide For Using The Intensive Journal Process
At The Edge Of History And Passages About Earth
Attaining Unlimited Life: Teachings Of Chuang Tzu
Basic Dharma
Beckett And Zen
Being Human: The Art Of Feeling Alive
Between Time And Eternity
Beyond Words: Terms For Transforming Consciousness
Birthstone Coloring Book
Bodywork Directory of North America
Book Of Stress Survival: Identifying & Reducing The Stress In Your Life
Business Mastery: A Business Planning Guide For Creating A Fulfilling, Thriving Business and Keeping It Successful

Butterfly Rises
Campus-Free College Degrees
Can You Trust Your Doctor? The Complete Guide To New Age Medicine And Its Threat To Your Family
Chakras: Roots Of Power
Challenges: A Young Man's Journal For Self-Awareness & Peronal Planning
Channeling: Investigations On Receiving Information From Paranormal Sources
Chicago's New Spirit
Choices: A Teen Woman's Journal For Self-Awareness & Personal Planning
Choose Once Again
Circular Evidence: An Investigation Of The Flattened Swirled Crops Phenomenon
Cities Of Light: A Plan For A New Age
Clean Yield Publications
Color Synergy: How To Use The Power Of Color, Affirmations & Creative Visualizations
Coming To Life
Common Ground: Resources For Personal Transformation
Common Sense Diet And Health
Communing With The Spirit Of Your Unborn Child Combo
Complete Relaxation
Connecticut Naturally
Connecting Arizona
Cosmic Revelation
Cosmic Shocks
Cosmos In Man
Creation-The Evolution Controversy
Creative Imagery: How To Visualize In All Five Senses
Creative Senility
Crisis In Modern Thought: Solutions To The Problem Of Meaninglessness
Crystal Clear: Use The Earth's Magic Energy To Vitalize Your Mind, Body & Spirit
Crystal Tree
Crystals, Gems And Radionics
Cultwatch: What You Need To Know About Spiritual Deception
Cycles Of Time
Daydreaming: Your Hidden Resource For Self-Knowledge & Creativity
Descent Of The Dove
Destruction Of Atlantis: Ragnarok - The Age Of Fire And Gravel
Dimensions Of Paradise: Proportions Of Symbolic Numbers Of Ancient Cosmology
Directory Of Intentional Communities
Discovering The Lost Pyramid
Divine Partnership-Truth For The New Age
Do Less & Be Loved More
Don't Bite My Finger, Look Where I Am Pointing
Don't You Want Somebody To Love
Drawing The Light From Within: Keys To Awakening Your Creative Power
Dream Story
Dynamic Stillness Vol. 1: The Practice Of Trika Yoga
Dzog Chen & Zen
Early Writings Of Alan Watts
Earthway: A Native American Visionary's Path To Total Mind, Body & Spirit Health
Edgar Cayce Predicts: Your Role In Creating A New Age
Edinburgh And Dore Lectures On Mental Science
Egyptian Miracle: The Wisdom Of The Temple
Egyptian Mysteries: Account Of An Initiation
Emerging New Age
Entering The Diamond Way
Epilogue
Esoteric Psychology 2
Esoteric Tradition
ESP, Hauntings And Poltergeists: A Parapsychologist's Handbook

Periodicals

Music

Numerology

Associations & Organizations

Centers, Spas, Retreats & Communities

Museums

Biographies

Stores

Products & Services

Bibliography

Periodicals

Music

Nutrition

Associations & Organizations

Centers, Spas, Retreats & Communities

Music

Paganism

Associations & Organizations

Centers, Spas, Retreats & Communities

Schools

Events

Biographies

Stores

Products & Services

Radio/Television

Bibliography

Crux Newsletter
Editor's Digest
Exploring Other Dimensions
Fantasy Mongers Quarterly
Fate Magazine
Focus
Footsteps
Foresight Magazine
Fortean Times
Ghost Trackers Newsletter
Haunts
INFO Journal
Inner Light
Journal Of Religion And Psychical Research
Journal Of Scientifc Exploration
Journal Of USPA
Kabbalah: A Newsletter Of Current Research In Jewish Mysticism
Mad Scientist
Magical Blend Magazine: A Transformative Journey
Meditation
Minnesota Skeptics Newsletter
Newsletter Of The American Society For Psychical Research-ASPR Newsletter
OPI Newsletter
Opossum Holler Tarot
Parapsychological Monographs Of The Parapsychology Foundation
Proceedings Of The American Society For Psychical Research
Psychic Fair Network News
Research In Parapsychology
Revue Du Magnetisme-Etude Du Psychisme Experimental
Science Quest
Se La Vie Writer's Journal
Search Magazine
Specular Journal - inactive
Spiritual Emergence Network Newsletter
Spiritual Frontiers
Spiritual Healing Bulletin
Stigmata
Strange Magazine
Supermente
The Journal Of The Fortean Research Center
The Skeptical Inquirer
The Star Beacon
The Tamulet
Theta: The Journal Of The Psychical Research Foundation
Univercolian
USPA Newsletter Quarterly
Will Loy's News Bulletin

Psychology

Associations & Organizations

Astro-Psychology Institute
Church Of Tzaddi
Foundation For Mind Research
Inner Light Foundation
Institute For Development Of Inner Communications Alternatives
Nos Amis/Our Friends, Inc.
Rocky Mountain Research Institute
Swedenborg Foundation, Inc.
Swedenborgian Church

Centers, Spas, Retreats & Communities

Beth Or - A New Paradigm Jewish Community
Biofeedback & Family Therapy Institute
Center For Conscious Living
Centrepoint
Esalen Institute
Foundation For Well-Being
Hardscrabble Hill
Himalayan International Institute Of Yoga Science and Philosophy
Institut Fur Grenzgebiete Der Psychologie Und Psychohygiene

Ken Keyes College
Kerista Village
Looking Glass Foundation
Oasis Center: New Horizons For Mind, Body, And Spirit
Omega Institute For Holistic Studies
Phoenicia Pathwork-Center For The Living Force
Programs For Human Development
Renaissance
Seven Oaks Pathwork Center
Solstice Center For Transformational Medicine
Synthesis Center
Wainwright House-Center For Development Of Human Potential

Schools

California Institute For Transpersonal Psychology
Institute For Advanced Study of Human Sexuality
Institute For Effective Psychotherapy
Institute OF Transpersonal Psychology
Jin Shin Do Foundation For Bodymind Acupressure
John Fitzgerald Kennedy University
Le Centre Du Silence Mime School
Sonoma State University
State University Of New York At Oswego
Swedenborg School of Religion (General Convention of the New Jerusalem in the U.S.A.)
Trager Institute For Psychophysical Integration And Mentastics
University Of Colorado
Western Institute For Social Research

Biographies

Arrien, A.
Avital, Samuel
Boyne, Gil
Breaux, Charles
Bromberg, Dr. Paula N.
Butler, William, M.A. M.Div.
Canby, Henry
Devlin, Mary
Dylan, Peggy
Earley, Jay, Ph. D.
Eisner, B.
Emery, Marcia Becker, Ph. D.
Ferrier, Dr. Loretta
Hastings, Arthur, Ph. D.
Haule, John R.
Heckler, Richard Strozzi
Henry, Patricia
Hirschfield, Jerry
Hopman, Ellen Evert, M. Ed.
Houston, Jean
Jayvanti
Jones, C.B. Scott, Ph. D.
Joy, W. Brugh, M.D.
Kemery, W.E., Ph. D.
Klinger, Eric
Kok Sui, Choa
Koltuv, Barbara Black, Ph. D.
Landsman, Dr. Sandra G.
Levy, Joan, LCSW
London, Peter
Metrick, S.B.
Rozman, Deborah
Sarantos, DeLacy
Siegel, Bernie S., M.D.
Simmons, J.L., Ph. D.
Sinor, Barbara
Smith, Jerry E.
Steiger, Francie Pascal
Stranges, Dr. Frank E.
Tate, D.
Teeguarden, Iona Marsag
Uphoff, Prof. Walter H.
Van de Castle, Robert L., Ph. D.
Wagner, Prof. Dr. Mahlon W.

Distributors/Wholesalers

Great Tradition, The
Sigo Press

Products & Services

Astro Intelligence U.S.A.
ISHK Book Service
Star's Edge International
Yes! Inc.

Radio/Television

Thinking Allowed Productions

Audio & Video Producers

Achieve, Inc.
Gateways Institute
Nightingale-Conant Corporation
One To Grow On!/Trenna Productions
Thinking Allowed Productions
Treehouse Enterprises

Bibliography

Active Imagination: Encounters With The Soul-Active Imagination As Developed By C.G. Jung
Affirmations
Alchemical Studies
Alchemy: An Introduction To The Symbolism And The Psychology
Altered States Of Consciousness
Apprentices Of Wonder: Reinventing The Mind
At A Journal Workshop: The Basic Text & Guide For Using The Intensive Journal Process
Awareness Through Movement
Being Human: The Art Of Feeling Alive
Beliefs: Pathways To Health And Well-Being
Brain Building: Exercising Yourself Smarter
Brain, Symbol And Experience: Toward A Neurophenomenology Of Human Consciousness
Breaking The Mind Barrier: The Artscience Of Neurocosmology
Cerebral Symphony: Seashore Reflections On The Structure Of Consciousness
Challenges: A Young Man's Journal For Self-Awareness & Peronal Planning
Changing Your Destiny: Dynamic New Astrological & Visualization Tools To Shape Your Future
Character And Health: The Relationship Of Acupuncture And Psychology
Choices: A Teen Woman's Journal For Self-Awareness & Personal Planning
Concordance To The Science Of Mind
Cosmic Shocks
Cosmos In Man
Creating Well-Being: The Healing Path To Love, Peace, Self-Esteem & Happiness
Creative Imagery: How To Visualize In All Five Senses
Creative Mind And Success
Creative Power Of Mind
Creative Visualization Workbook
Daydreaming: Your Hidden Resource For Self-Knowledge & Creativity
Dragon Rises, Red Bird Flies: Psychology & Chinese Medicine
Dream Story
Dreams: A Portal To The Source - A Guide To Dream Interpretation
Ecstasy: The MDMA Story
Esoteric Psychology 2
Eye To Eye: The Quest For A New Paradigm
Feeling Good Handbook: Using The New Mood Therapy In Everyday Life
Finding The Fountain Of Youth Inside Yourself: Powerful Trusth About Inner Youth
Fine Tune Your Brain: When Everything's Going Right And What To Do When It Isn't
Five Keys To Inner Wisdom
Flow: The Psychology Of Optimal Experience - A Guide To Enhancing The Quality Of Life

Forgiveness: How To Make Peace With Your Past And Get On With Your Life
Found: A Place For Me
From Conflict To Caring: The Process Of Learning Loving Behavior
From Here To Freedom: Unraveling Our Legacy Of Fear
Frontiers Of The Hidden Mind
Getting Well Again
Go See The Movie In Your Head: Imagery, The Key To Awareness
Going Nowhere Fast: Step Off Life's Treadmills & Find Peace Of Mind
Good For You: The Science Of Mind Approach To Successful Living
Grail Legend
Great Mother
Guilt Is The Teacher, Love Is The Lesson: A Book To Heal You, Heart And Soul
Happiness Principle
Head First: The Biology Of Hope
Healing Dream And Ritual: Ancient Incubation & Modern Psychotherapy
Healing Mind Of Man: Arise & Shine
Healing Your Habits: Introducing Directed Imagination, A Successful Technique For Overcoming..
Heart Thoughts: A Personal Treasury Of Inner Wisdom
Heartsearch: Uncovering The Roots Of An Auto-Immune Illness
Hero's Way: Attitudes Make The Difference
How To Change Your Life
How To Use The Science Of Mind
Hypnagogia: The Unique State Of Consciousness Between Wakefulness And Sleep
I'm Special: An Experiential Workbook For The Child In Us All
Illustrated Biography Of C.G. Jung
Imagery For Healing, Knowledge And Power; Harnessing Your Personal Energy To Create..
Images Of The Self: The Sandplay Therapy Process
Imaginary Crimes: Why We Punish Ourselves & How To Stop
Immune-System Activation: Practical Programs For Maximizing Your Recovery Potential
Inner Journeys: A Guide To Personal & Social Transformation
Inner Natures: Brain, Self And Personality
Instant Memory
Inward Journey
Jungian Literary Criticism 1920-1980: An Annotated Critical Bibliography Of Works In English
Jungian Psychology: A Comprehensive Guide
Law Of Mind In Action
Laws Of Wealth
Life Graph: The Record Of Our Past
Life Is Uncertain...Eat Dessert First! Finding The Joy You Deserve
Lighten Up Your Body, Lighten Up Your Life: Beyond Diet & Exercise--Inner Path To Change
Living Psyche: A Jungian Analysis In Pictures
Living Together, Feeling Alone: Healing Your Hidden Loneliness
Love Yourself, Heal Your Life Workbook
Maps Of The Mind: Charts & Concepts Of The Mind & Its Labyrinths
Margins Of Reality: The Role Of Consciousness In The Physical World
Meaning And Significance Of Dreams
Mind Magic: The Ecstasy Of Freeing Creative Power
Mind's I: Fantasies And Reflections On Self And Soul
Mirrors: Affirmations & Actions For Daily Reflection
Multiple States Of Being

Mythic Imagination: Your Quest For Meaning Through Personal Mythology
Nada Brahma: The World Is Sound-Music & The Landscape Of Consciousness
Nuclear Evolution
Omega New Age Directory
Open Mind, Discriminating Mind: Reflections In Human Possibilities
Opening Up: The Healing Power Of Confiding In Others
Origins And History Of Consciousness
Our Inner World Of Rage: Understanding & Transforming The Power Of Anger
Passion For This Earth: Exploring A New Partnership Of Man, Woman & Nature
Personal Totem Pole: Animal Imagery, The Chakras And Psychotherapy
Personality: The Individuation Process In The Light Of C.G.Jungs Typology
Philosophy Of Consciousness Without An Object
Power Of Fantasy: Where Our Daydreams Come From & How They Can Help Or Harm Us
Power Of Optimism: Your Action Plan To Bring Out The Best In Yourself
Power Within: The True Stores Of Exceptional Patients Who Fought Back With Hope
Practical Jung: Nuts & Bolts Of Jungian Psychotherapy
Practical Work On Self
Pretty Good Person: What It Takes To Live With Courage, Gratitude & Integrity Or Pretty Good
Private Moments, Secret Selves: Enriching Our Time Alone
Psyche And Substance: Essays On Homeopathy In The Light Of Jungian Psychology
Quantum Soup: Fortune Cookies In Crisis
Reflections In The Light: Daily Thoughts And Affirmations
Remembering And Forgetting: Inquiries Into The Nature Of Memory
Resolving Conflict: With Others And Within Yourself
Right Brain Sex: Using Creative Visualization To Enhance Sexual Pleasure
Rose And The Pickle
Science Of Mind
Secret World Of Drawings: Healing Through Art
Seeing Through The Visible World: Jung, Gnosis & Chaos
Seizing Life's Second Change: Activating Your Inner Survival Mechanisms For Conquering Fear
Self-Esteem: A Family Affair
Self-Esteem: A Proven Program Of Cognitive Techniques For Assessing, Improving & Maintaining
Self-Mastery Through Conscious Auto-Suggestion
Sensory Awareness: Rediscovery Of Experiencing Through The Workshops Of Charlotte Selver
Shadow And Self: Selected Papers In Analytical Psychology
Sixth Sense: Whole-Brain Book Of Intuition, Hunches...And Their Place In Everyday Life
Springs Of Creativity: The Bible & Creative Process Of The Psyche
Strategy Of The Dolphin: Scoring A Win In A Chaotic World
Structures Of Consciousness: The Genius Of Jean Gebser, An Introduction And Critique
Sword And The Serpent: The Structure & Psychology Of Magick
This Thing Called Life
This Thing Called You

Thoughts And Feelings: The Art Of Cognitive Stress Intervention
Transformation Of Consciousness: Conventional & Contemplative Perspectives On Development
Transformations: Growth And Change In Adult Life
Trusting Ourselves: A Crash Course In The Psychology Of Women
Unconscious And Its Empirical Manifestations
Visualization For Change: A Step-By-Step Guide To Using Your Powers Of Imagination
Visualization: The Key To Fulfillment
Warm Logic: The Art Of Intuitive Lifestyles
When Anger Hurts: Quieting The Storm Within
Who Are You? Discovering Your Real Identity
Who Gets Sick: How Beliefs, Moods And Thought Can Affect Your Health
Why Women Worry: And How To Stop
Wisdom Of The Dream: The World Of C.G. Jung
Women Dreaming-Into-Art
Women's Dionysian Initiation: The Villa Of Mysteries In Pompeii
Word And Image (Bollinger Series XCVII: 2)
Words That Heal: Affirmations And Meditations For Daily Living
Woulda, Coulda, Shoulda: Overcoming Regrets, Mistakes & Missed Opportunities
You Can Heal Your Life
You Can If You Think You Can
You Can Relieve Pain: How To Use Guided Imagery To Reduce Pain Or Eliminate It Completely!
You'll See It When You Believe It: The Way To Your Personal Transformation
Your Balancing Act: Discovering New Life Through Five Dimensions Of Wellness
Your Golden Shadow: Discovering And Fulfillng Your Undeveloped Self
Zen Meditation And Psychotherapy

Periodicals
Garden Of Thoughts
Gnosis
Self Hypnosis And Other Mind Expanding Techniques
Sounds True Catalog
Success Through Mind Power
TAT Journal
The Good News

Music
Adventure Of Self-Discovery
Andromeda: Journey Through Inner Space
Art Of Loving
Awaken Your Intuition
Beyond The Brain I & II: Birth, Death & Transcendence
Boundaries Of The Soul: Explorations In Jungian Analysis
Cogitate Tape
Communication As Healing
Computers And The Mind
Cosmic Game
Covert Modeling & Covert Reinforcement
Critical Self-Awareness
Dance Of The Hi-Tech Shaman
Different Drum: Community Making And Peace
Evolution Of The Magical Child 1
Evolution Of The Magical Child 2
Evolution Of The Magical Child 3
Expanding The Limits Of Consciousness
Experiences Of Awakening
Exploring Parapsychology
Finding The Child Within
Greek Mysteries: Experiencing Your Male And Female Archetypes
Guide To Rational Living
Handbook To Higher Consciousness

He: Understanding Masculine Psychology
High And The Low
Human Dilemma: Explorations Existential Psychotherapy
Invisible Partners: How The Male & Female In Each Of Us Affects Our Relationships
Journey Into Manhood: Myths & Stories About Male Individuation
Jung: Interpreting Your Dreams
Listening I: An Introduction
Listening II: An Workshop
Living In The Light
Loving Self Meditations
Memories, Dreams, Reflectionsms
Mind Expansion/Cosmic Awareness
Musical Body: A Vitalizing Spiritua Exercise
Non-Analytic Ways Of Growth
Other Lives, Other Selves: A Jungian Psychotherapist Discovers Past Lives
Psychodynamics Of Liberation
Psychological And Spiritual Blindspots
Road Less Traveled Tape Set
Roots Of Consciousness
Self-Observation
She: Understanding Feminine Psychology
Sound Of Rippling Water: Constructive Living Through Morita & Naikan Therapies
Spiritual Psychology
Thirty-Three Steps Beyond The Earth Plane
Total Self
Touching The Heart Of Healing, Part 2: Path Of The Mindful Heart
Transforming Awareness
Transpersonal Psychology I & II
Unquiet Dead: An Introduction To Spirit Depossession Therapy
Waking Dream And Living Myth In The Creative Work Of Ingmar Bergman
Waking Up
Way Of The Dream
Women Who Run With The Wolves I & II: Myths & Stores About The Wild Woman Archetype
Working With The Unconscious

Reflexology
Associations & Organizations
G-JO Institute
Centers, Spas, Retreats & Communities
Bluegrass Retreat
Reflexology Centre Of Vancouver
Biographies
Deal, Grady, Ph. D., D.C.
Deal, Roberlcigh C.
Shirley, Christopher
Products & Services
Inner Light Resources

Reiki
Associations & Organizations
American-International Reiki Association, Inc.
Healing Seminars
North Coast Body Workers Association
Radiance Technique Association International, Inc.
Tree Of Life Seminars
Centers, Spas, Retreats & Communities
Center For Reiki Training
Center For Well Being, Inc.
Hawaiian Fitness Holiday
Jean's Place
Schools
Dayspring Resources
DoveStar Alchemian Institute
Biographies

Aurora, Barbara
Boddie, Caroline
Carter, Marvelle
Cousens, Gabriel, M.D.
Frank, Rev. Ojela
Gifford, Joseph
Gosse, Jean D.
Koury, George
Lenel, Katherine
Long, Gary
Nicholson, Darca
Niemi, Beatrice N.
Rand, William L.
St. Claire, Ginny
Stein, Diane
Tersigni, Patrick
Bibliography
Empowerment Through Reiki: The Path To Personal And Global Transformation - A Handbook
Expanded Reference Manual Of The Radiance Technique
Reiki Factor
Reiki Handbook
Reiki: Universal Life Energy - A Holistic Method Of Treatment
Virginia Samdahl: Reiki Master Healer
Periodicals
Radiance Technique Journal, The
Reiki Journal, The

Reincarnation
Associations & Organizations
Academy Of Religion And Psychical Research
Association For Past-Life Research And Therapies, Inc.
Eckankar
Ghost Research Society
International Association For New Science
Light Of The Universe
Loving Relationships Training, International
Spiritual Frontiers Fellowship
Unarius Academy Of Science & Education Foundation
Centers, Spas, Retreats & Communities
Breathconnection
Self-Actualization And Enlightenment Center
Schools
Academy Of Chinese Culture & Health Sciences
University Of Oriental Studies
Biographies
Ellis, N.
Gagnon, Leo, Ph.D.
Hampton, Crystal
Henning, Hazel M., Ph. D.
Holecek, Richard W.
Kaczmarek, Dale
Kelynda
Matlock, James G.
Norman, Ruth
O'Leary, Brian
Orr, Leonard
Parrish-Harra, Carol E.
Ray, Sondra
Sutphen, Dick
Stores
Excalibur Books
Products & Services
Excursions Into The Unknown
Bibliography
Afterlife: An Investigation
Association For Past-Life Research And Therapies Directory
Biography Of An Archangel
Born Again And Again
Boy Lama

Periodicals

Consciousness Research And Training Project
    Newsletter
Convergence Magazine
Cosmic Current News
Cosmic People Magazine
Crow Speaks
Crystal Age News
Eagle's Cry, The
Earth Circles News
Earth Nation Sunrise
Earth-Light Network Newsletter
Earthquake Lady News
East West Journal
Eden Bulletin
Emergence
Equinox, The
Evergreens
Exorcism International
Faithist Journal
Gnosis
Gnostic Times
Hecate's Loom
Hinduism Today
Infinite Light Beacon Keys
Inner Life
Inner Light
Inner Mind Speaks, The
Inner Quest Journal
Inner Quest Newsletter
Inner Voice
Innerconnexion
Insight Magazine
Insight Northwest
Insights
Insights Positive Living
Intuitive Explorations
Jin Shin Do Foundation Newsletter
Journal For Anthroposophy
Keltria: Journal Of Druidism And Keltic
    Magick
Life Affiliates
Light Lines
Light Of The Egret
Light-Net Newsletter
Lotus Mind
Love Corps Newsletter
Magical Blend Magazine: A Transformative
    Journey
Magical Link, The
Medicine Ways
Messenger, The
Metaphysical Digest
Metta
Monthly Aspectarian
MYSIM Newsletter
Mystic Trader, The
Mythos
New Age Journal
New Age Living
New Alberta
New Atlantean, The
New Awareness Magazine
New Frontiers
New Menorah
New Millenium-Practical Guidance For
    Personal Growth
New Visions
Newaeon Newsletter, The
Night Owl Press
Noetic Sciences Bulletin
Noetic Sciences Catalog
Noetic Sciences Review
Of A Like Mind
One Earth
Ontario's Common Ground Magazine
Open Channels
Order Of The Universe
Oriflamme, The
Osho Times
Pathways Profiles
Planetary Citizen
Positive Times
PRS Journal

Psychic Connections
Psychic News
Psychic Newsletter
Psychic Pathways
Psychic Press Newspaper
Rainbow City Express
Rainbow Pages
Raj Talks
Reflect
Renaitre 2000
Resurgence
Robert Anton Wilson's Trajectories Newsletter
Rocky Mountain Spiritual Emergence
    Network
Ron Warmouth's Prediction
Runestaff, The
SageWoman Magazine
Sat Sandesh: The Message Of The Masters
Shaman's Drum
Shamanic Journey
Snake Power
SOLAR (SOL Association For Research)
Sounds True Catalog
Sparrow Hawk Villager
Spectrum
Sphaera Imagination
Spiritual Advisory Council Newsletter-
    Outreach
Sunrise
Sunrise-Theosophic Perspectives
Sword of Drynwyn
Take In Good Part
Tantric Times
TAT Journal
Tertium Quid
The Buddhist Review
The Good News
The National Spiritualist Summit
The Shaman Papers
The Sun
The Way Fourth-A Journal Of The Fourth
    Way
Total Eclipse
Understanding Magazine
Univercolian
Upper Triad, The
Upward Search
Vampire Quarterly
Voice Of The New Age
White Sun Journal
Whole Network Journal
Wide Open Magazine
Windwords
Wingspand
Within & Beyond
Woman Of Power
Year Of The Goddess: A Perpetual Calendar
    Celebrating The Feminine Principle
Zhuangzi Speaks

Music

Achievement
Active Methods Of Spiritual Growth
Adona! Eloheinu Adonai Ehad (Jewish
    Tradition)
Aleluia
Attunement: A Full Spectrum Experience For
    Personal & Planetary Transformation
Ave Maria Mater Dei (Christian Tradition)
Awake In The Cosmic Dream
Awakening Bell: Thich Nhat Hanh And Cao
    Ngoc Phuong
Awakening Bell: Thich Nhat Nanh And Cao
    Ngoc Phuong
Awakening To Self Knowledge Pt. 4 Of
    Nothing Real Can Be Threatened Cim
    Video Workshop
Basic Ideas Of Science Of Mind
Beauty, Pleasure, Sorrow And Love
Beholding The One In All
Being Born, Growing Up
Being Peace
Bhagwan: The Way Of The Heart

Breaking The Chains Of Illusion
Bringing A Course In Miracles Into
    Application
Brother Sun, Sister Moon
Buddhism: Path To Enlightenment
Chakra Breathing: Meditations Of Bhagwan
    Shree Rajneesh
Chakra Sounds: Rajneesh Discourse
Chants And Mantras
Circle The Earth With Song
Commentaries On A Course In Miracles
Commentaries On The Heart Sutra
Compassion In Action
Conditioning The Child Of Light
Conversations II
Coping With Spiritual And Sexual Stress
Course In Miracles
Course In Miracles And The Destiny Of
    America
Course In Miracles And The Limitation Of
    Learning
Course In Miracles Explorations, Series I
Course In Miracles Video
Creating A World That Works
Creative Mind And Success
Creative Self
Creative Visualization Workshop
Cultivating The Heart Of Compassion I & II
Cycles Of Truth: Singing Awake The Dream
Dances Of Relationship
Dances Of Universal Peace, Vol. 1
Dances Of Universal Peace, Vol. 2
Dances Of Universal Peace, Vol. 3
Dancing Beyond The Shadow
Dawning: Chants Of The Medicine Wheel
Death And Samadhi
Deception Of Learning: Pt. 2 Of Nothing Real
    Can Be Threatened, Cim Video Workshop
Developing Intuition
Developing The Sixth Sense
Discovering Your Life's Work
Discovering Your Own Holiness
Discovering Your Soul's Purpose
Discussions On A Course In Miracles
Divine Songs
Do Only That: A Course In Miracles &
    Working With Children
Does Mind Matter
Dreamwood
Dynamic/Kundalini
Evening With Ram Dass
Evolution Of A Yogi
Feminine Ancient Vision, Modern Wisdom
Finding Peace Within
Finding Your Inner Calling
Five Steps To Personal Freedom
Flowing With The Tao
For My People
Forgotten Song: The Poetry Of A Course In
    Miracles
Freedom From Belief
Freedome Chants From The Roof Of The
    World
Function Of A Teacher Is To End Deception
Future Of Mankind: The Branching Of The
    Road
Gift Of Song
Gifts To Each Other: Native American Chants
    And Drum
Give Me Your Blessings, Holy Son Of God
God And Money
God Does Not Judge/Healing Relationships
Goddess In My Shoes: Seven Steps To Peace
Going With The Flow
Going Within: A Guide For Inner
    Transformation
Golden Triad
Guide To Walking Meditation
Guided Meditations: Basic Techniques
Gyuto Monks
Hara Hara
Healing Meditations
Healing Your Perception Of The World

Heart Of Understanding: Commentaries On
    The Prajnaparamita Heart Sutra
Heavensong Celebration Live!
Hero, The Wildman, And The Goddess: The
    Story Of Gilcamesh, Enkidu And Ishtar
Higher Self: Breakthrough To Illumination
How Miracles Happen
How Then Shall We Live #1: Opening To
    Grief/Purification By Fire
How Then Shall We Live #2: From Tradgedy
    To Grace - Stages In Process Of
    Dying/Meditation
How Then Shall We Live #3: Awakening
    Through Truthful Relationship/Work To
    Relieve Suffer
How Then Shall We Live #4: Finding A Path
    To An Open Heart/Wisdom Has No Fear Of
    Dying
How Then Shall We Live #5: Caring For An
    Endangered Planet
How Then Shall We Live #6: America's Secret
    Nuclear Policy
How Then Shall We Live #7: Dialogue For
    Human Survival
How Then Shall We Live #8: No Other
    Generation
How Then Shall We Live #9: Social Action &
    The Compassionate Heart
How To Be A True Student Of A Course In
    Miracles
How To Learn From A Course In Miracles
How To Raise A Child Of God
How To Use The Science Of Mind
I Am A Monk
I Am Spirit
I Have A Function God Would Have Me Fill
If I Defend Myself I Am Attacked
In The Cosmic Flow
Initiation Of Fire
Inner Blance/Outer Expression I
Inner Blance/Outer Expression II
Inner Dance V.1: Inner Dance Talk
Inner Dance V.2: Healing The Hurt Child
Inner Dance V.3: Lovers And Warriors Talk
Inner Dance V.4: Body Movement Exercises
Inner Palace I & II
Integral Yoga: Youga Sutras Of Patanjali
Introduction To A Course In Miracles
Is There Something Beyond Thought?
Jai Shiva! Kirtan For Shivaratri
Jambalaya: The Natural Woman's Book Of
    Personal Charms & Practical Rituals
Jay Jay Muktananda
Journey Into Dreamtime
Journey Into The Fourth Dimension: The 60-
    Day Non-Human Program
Journey Into Time: Egypt
Journey Of Awakening: A Meditator's Guide
Karma, Love And Detachment
Keepers Of The Mysteries
Knowings
Knowledge Of Light
Kuan Yin's Crystal Rosary: Devotions To The
    Divine Mother East & West
Kyrie
La Illaha Il Allah (Islamic Tradition)
Life Of Non-Compromise
Lifesong
Lifespring: Getting Yourself From Where You
    Are To Where You Want To Be
Living As A Peaceful Warrior
Living In The Light
Living Philosophically
Living Traditions
Looking Deeply
Lost Years Of Jesus
Love Without An Agenda/Becoming Deep:
    Lectures Based On A Course In Miracles
Magnum Mysterium II
Making Relationships Holy
Male And Female Energies
Man And Nature
Master Does Not Speak

Tai Chi

Associations & Organizations

Centers, Spas, Retreats & Communities

Schools

Biographies

Wagner, C.

Stores

Bibliography

Periodicals

Music

Tarot

Associations & Organizations

Centers, Spas, Retreats & Communities

T.A.R.O.T.

Biographies

Stores

Distributors/Wholesalers

Products & Services

Radio/Television

Bibliography

Wiccan Rede
Wiggansnatch Magazine
WIN Intelligence Summary
Witch-Press
Witches All
Witches Almanac, The
Womanspirit
Yggdrasil

Music

Dreamer's Web: A Journey Through The Four
  Directions
Fairy Queen
Grandmother Of Time
I Dance To Be The Woman I Can Be
Introduction To Witchcraft
Magickal Journeys
Moon Hooves In The Sand
Rebirth Of The Goddess
Spiral Dance: A Rebirth Of The Ancient
  Religion Of The Great Godess
Witchcraft Yesterday And Today
Witches And Halloween

Yoga

Associations & Organizations

Association Of American Buddhists
California Yoga Teachers Association
Inner Circle Kethra E'Da Foundation, Inc.
Kriya Jyoti Tantra Society
Little Synagogue
New Age World Religious & Scientific
  Research Foundation
NRW Frontier Education Society
Teaching Of The Inner Christ, Inc.
Yoga Research Foundation
Yogalayam/Prana Yoga Ashram

Centers, Spas, Retreats & Communities

3HO Foundation
Abode Of The Message
Acharya Sushil Jain Ashram-Siddhachalam
Acupressure Workshop
Ajapa Yoga Foundation
Akahi Farm Retreat & Conference Center
Atmaniketan Ashram
Aurobindo Ashram
Aurobindo Center
Badarikashrama
Bluegrass Retreat
Breathconnection
Center For Conscious Living
Center For Yoga
Family Spiritual Camp
Feathered Pipe Foundation
Golden Phoenix Healing And Light Center
Guru Ram Das Ashram
Hawaiian Fitness Holiday
Himalayan International Institute Of Yoga
  Science and Philosophy
Hippocrates Health Institute
Integral Yoga Institute/Satchidananda Ashram
Interface
Kalani Honua By The Sea International
  Conference And Retreat Center
Lotus Yoga Center
Ma Yoga Shakti International Mission
Maitreyans, The
Matagiri Sri Aurobindo Center
Mele Mauka Center
Mount Madonna Center
Narayanananda Universal Yoga Center
Narayanananda Universal Yoga Trust,
  Ashrama & Narayana Press
New Age Health Spa
New Life Health Center
New York Center For Art And Awareness

Nityananda Institute
Northern Pines Health Resort
Omega Institute For Holistic Studies
Piedmont Yoga Center
Prana Yoga Ashram - Yogalayam
Pyramid Center For Bhakti Yoga
Sancta Sophia Seminary
Shanti Yoga Institute
Shanti Yoga-Center For Harmony
Sivananda Ashram Vrindavan Yoga Farm
Sivananda Ashram Yoga Retreat
Sivananda Yoga Vedanta Ashram
Sivananda Yoga Vedanta Centers
Strong, Stretched And Centered Body/Mind
  Institute
Sunflower Yoga Company
Swaha Meditation & Yoga Center
Temple Of The Eternal Light
Unity Woods Yoga Center
Universal Great Brotherhood
Westchester Kripalu Yoga Center
White Lotus Foundation
Woodbury Yoga Center
Yoga Anand Ashram, Incorporated
Yoga Shakti Mission
Yoga Society Of San Francisco
Yoga Therapy Center
Yoga Works

Schools

Academy Of Chinese Culture & Health
  Sciences
American College of Traditional Chinese
  Medicine
College Of Oriental Medicine (Chapori-Ling
  Foundation Sangha)
Holistic Life University
Infinity Institute International, Inc.
Raj-Yoga Math
TSI-Yoga

Biographies

Bodian, Stephan
Breaux, Charles
Chinmayananda, Swami
Chinmoy, Sri
Choo, Joni
Cogozzo, Linda
Dass, Hari
Deal, Grady, Ph. D., D.C.
Deal, Roberleigh C.
Devi, Saraswathi
Devi, Yoganathan
Forster, Sarabess
Friedberg, Dr. Brajesh
Geiger, Esther
Gliksohn, Michael
Jyotirmayananda, Swami
Koob, Richard
Lalitananda, Swami
Mendel, Werner
Middleton, Riki
O'Neil, Dr. Kevin
Parrish-Harra, Carol E.
Pievson, Janaki
Rich, Tracey
Rozman, Deborah
Satchindananda, Sri Swami
Satyam, Yogi Ananda
Schumacher, John
Sheedy, Ally
Singh, Ravi
Soudanand, Swami
Stiles, Tara
Supera, India
Thompson, Tom
Turner, Marlee
Vignanananda, Swami
Viraj, Yogi Ananda

White, Ganga
Windsor, Roger G.
Zaslow, Bob
Zeroth, Wendy
Zuromski, Paul

Stores

Heritage Store/Center

Products & Services

Ananda Pilgrimages
Figaro Cruises
Yoga In Bali

Audio & Video Producers

Clear Lake Productions
Rudra Press
Spectrum Video

Bibliography

Acupressure Yoga And You
American Yoga Association Beginner's
  Manual
Bikram's Beginning Yoga Class
Complete Illustrated Book Of Yoga
Complete Yoga Book
Devotees' Collection: 3 Books By Yogananda
Dictionary Of Religion And Philosophy
Dynamic Stillness Vol. 1: The Practice Of
  Trika Yoga
Easy Does It Yoga: Yoga For People Over 60
Emptiness Yoga
Encounters In Yoga And Zen
Encyclopedia Of Parapsychology And
  Psychical Research
Encyclopedic Dictionary Of Yoga
Fire In The Heart: Healers, Sages & Mystics
Fundamentals Of Yoga: A Handbook Of
  Theory, Practice & Application
Hanuman Chalisa
Hatha Yoga Manual Vol. 1
Hatha Yoga Manual Vol. 2
Hatha Yoga Workbook: A Personal Reflecting
  Tool For Yoga Students Of All Levels
Hatha Yoga Workbook: The Hidden Language
Integral Hatha Yoga
Iyengar: His Life And Work
Kundalini Yoga
Kundalini Yoga For The West
Kundalini Yoga: For Body, Mind And Beyond
Light Of The Soul: The Yoga Sutras Of
  Patanjali, With Commentary
Light On Pranayama: The Yogic Art Of
  Breathing
Light On Yoga
Lilias, Yoga And Your Life
Living With The Himalayan Masters
Meditation
Meeting Of Science And Spirit: Guidelines
  For A New Age
Mystics, Magicians And Medicine People:
  Tales Of A Wanderer
Nothingness Beyond God: An Introduction To
  The Philosohy Of Nishida Kitaro
Psychic Lotus-Pictorial
Ransoming The Mind: An Integration Of Yoga
  And Modern Therapy
Satya Narayan Kathaa
Second Coming Of Christ Vol. 1
Second Coming Of Christ Vol. II
Second Coming Of Christ Vol. III
Sermon On The Mount
Sivananda Companion To Yoga
Spiritual Message
Spiritual Science Of Kriya Yoga
Sri Ramakrishna: A Prophet For The New Age
Synthesis Of Yoga
Take Charge Of Your Health: Healing With
  Yogatherapy & Nutrition
Tantric Yoga Techniques

Towards Superconsciousness: Meditational
  Theory & Practice
Turning East: New Lives In India - 20
  Westerners & Their Spiritual Quests
Vivekanada: The Yogas And Other Works
Whispers From Eternity
Yoga And Psychotherapy
Yoga Step By Step
Yoga Syzygy
Yoga Vashishttha-Part I
Yoga Vashishttha-Part II
Yoga, Immortality And Freedom
Yoga-Sutra Of Patanjali: A New Translation &
  Commentary
Yoga: Mastering The Secrets Of Matter And
  The Universe
Yoga: Technology Of Ecstasy
Yoga: The Iyengar Way - The New Definitive
  Illustrated Guide

Periodicals

American Buddhist
American Yoga Newsletter
Breathconnection
Common Ground of Puget Sound
Dawn Magazine
Essays
International Yoga Guide
Moksha Journal
MYSIM Newsletter
Prana Yoga Leaves
Prana Yoga Life Magazine
Shanti Yoga Newsletter
Viewpoint Aquarius
Yoga
Yoga - Mimamsa
Yoga And Total Health
Yoga Journal
Yoga Life
Yoga Today
Yoga Vision

Music

Easy Yoga
Experience Yoga
Hatha Yoga In Motion Vol. 1
Hatha Yoga In Motion Vol. 2
Hatha Yoga In Motion: Levels One And Two
Hatha Yoga With Don Discenza
Hatha Yoga: The Hidden Language Of The
  Body--Your Personal Tool For Expanded
  Awareness
Healing With Yoga, Visualization And
  Affirmation
Health, Yoga, Anatomy
Integral Yoga Hatha: Beginners 1
Integral Yoga Hatha: Beginners II
Kundalini Yoga Workout
Lillias Alive With Yoga
Lillias Alive With Yoga Vol. 2: Intermediate
  Yoga
Lillias Yoga For Beginning Students
Lillias Yoga For Experienced Students
New Christian Yoga: A Cowley Retreat Tape
Positively Yoga
Relax With Yoga During Pregnancy
Richard Hittleman's Yoga Video 1
Richard Hittleman's Yoga Video 2
To Body And Soul With Love
Tuning The Mind, Tuning The Body
Yoga For Beginners
Yoga For Children
Yoga For Senior Citizens
Yoga Of Love
Yoga Postures For Self Awareness
Yoga With Rita 1 & 2
Yoga, Meditation And Self Realization
Yogaworks: Complete Hatha Yoga Workout